问:哪里去查 A level
　　和 A1, A-one?

答:查 A, a.

问:哪里去查
　　computer crime,
　　computer-literate
　　和　computer
　　virus 等?

答:查 computer。

A, a [ei] ([复]A's, a's 或 Aes, aes[eiz])
英语字母表第一个字母… ‖ **A level**
(英)(中学生的)高等程度;高级考试/
A1, 'A-'one adj. 第一流的,极好的

computer [kəm'pju:tə] n. … ‖ … ‖ **~**
crime (利用计算机转移银行账户资金
等的)计算机犯罪/…/…/ ' ~ 'literate
adj. 有计算机理解和应用能力的/…/
~ virus 计算机病毒

> 复合词(含写
> 的和分写的)
> 一般收在作
> 为开首部分
> 的词条内

问:哪里去查习语
　　from A to Z?

答:查 A, a。

问:哪里去查 on
　　behalf of 和 on
　　sb.'s behalf 等
　　习语?

答:查 behalf。

问:哪里去查 as of
　　和 as if 等习语?

答:查 as。

问:哪里去查习语
　　aside from?

答:查 aside。

A, a [ei] ([复]A's, a's 或 Aes, aes[eiz])
英语字母表第一个字母… ‖ **from A to**
Z 从头至尾;彻底 ‖ …

behalf [bi'ha:f] n. ‖ **on**(或〈美〉**in**)**~ of**
代表…;为了…的利益 / **on sb.'s ~**
代表某人;为了某人的利益

> 介词短语结构
> 的习语收在作
> 介词宾语的名
> 词词条内

as [强 æz;弱 əz] adv. … — conj. …
pron. … — prep. … ‖ **~ for** 至于,就
…方面说/ **~ from** 从…时起/ **~ if**
好像,仿佛/ **~ of** 从…时起/…

> 以复合词形式
> 出现的习语收
> 在习语第一个
> 词的词条内

aside [ə'said] adv. … — n. … ‖ **~**
from 〈美〉除了…以外

A NEW POCKET ENGLISH-CHINESE DICTIONARY

REVISED EDITION

新英汉小词典

修 订 版

原编者　何永康　雷烈江　蒋照仁

修订者　张福基　俞步凡　蒋照仁

上海译文出版社

目　　录

前　言

　　修订版《新英汉小词典》终于与读者见面了。修订版增收了新词、基本词汇和习语 5,000 余条，对初版作了包括词条、释义、注音和体例在内的全面修改、更新和补充，现将从内容到形式焕然一新的词典奉献给读者。

　　《新英汉小词典》以其"着重释义，义项普遍比同类词典多"的特色自 1986 年问世以来一直深受读者的厚爱。修订后的《新英汉小词典》保持了这一特色，但也在原来的基础上作了大幅度的增、删、改，这是为了使词典更加完美，并不断适应社会的发展、语言的演变和读者的需要。目前银行中广为使用的 ATM，其标准的中文名称是什么(自动柜员机)、它在英文中代表什么(automated/ automatic teller machine)，《新英汉小词典》修订版在有关条目下一一作了回答；computer virus(计算机病毒)的出现既赋予 vaccinate 以新义，又导致 vaccine program 等新词的产生；……凡此种种，《新英汉小词典》修订版都作了较全面的反映。除新词和新义外，修订版还增收了我们认为初版本应收而未收的基本词汇和习语 4,000 余条。与此同时，修订版删去了那些以汉语拼音为根据的中国地名以及过于偏僻或专门化的词条及释义；修改了那些不甚确切、过于烦琐，在词义、用法或发音上需要改动或补充的词条。

　　修订后的《新英汉小词典》共收词 35,000 余条（包括词条内部的派生词、复合词），比初版本增加了 5,000 余条。词典的正文前增设了《音标及发音例词表》，以供读者随时查阅；正文后仍保留初版本所设的附录。

　　参加本词典校对工作的同志有彭瑞仑、姚玉燕、严有敏，在此表示深切的感谢。

　　书成之际，我们仍感到《新英汉小词典》有进一步改进的必要，错误和缺点在所难免。对此，我们期待着爱护这本词典的广大读者的批评指正。

编　者

一九九七年九月

体例说明

(一)词 条

一个词条的主要部分是词目和释义,有的词条还收有习语、派生词、复合词等。

(二)词 目

1. 词目用黑正体印刷,有些习惯上斜写的外来词语用黑斜体印刷。拼法相同、词源及词义不同的词,分立词条,在右上角标以 1、2 等数码。一个词有不同拼法时,若拼法接近,排在同一词条内,中间用逗号隔开;若拼法相差较大,分立词条,但释义只出现于一处,另一处注明等于某词。

2. 词目后用国际音标注明发音。词缀、构词成分及缩写词一般不注发音。

3. 音标后注明词性。一个词若有几种不同词性,从第二词性起前面加有破折号(即一),但派生词除外。词性用英语缩写形式注出,共分十类:名词(*n*.)、动词(包括及物动词 *vt*.、不及物动词 *vi*.、助动词 *v. aux*. 等)、代词(*pron*.)、数词(*num*.)、形容词(*adj*.)、副词(*adv*.)、前置词(*prep*.)、连接词(*conj*.)、感叹词(*int*.)、冠词(*art*.)。分写的复合词不注明发音。如:

> **pace** [peis] *n*. ...—*vi*. ...—*vt*. ...

4. 不规则动词的变化形式、名词复数的不规则变化形式、形容词及副词各比较级的不规则变化形式,均加以注明。规则变化中需重复词尾辅音字母或拼法、发音等有较大变动的,也加以注明。各变化形式一般注在词性前。如:

> **go** [gəu](went [went], gone [gɔn]) *vi*. ...
> **bind** [baind](bound [baund]) *vt*. ...
> (只注一个变化形式的,表示过去式和过去分词同形)
> **life** [laif]([复]lives [laivz]) *n*. ...
> **good** [gud](better[ˈbetə], best[best]) *adj*. ...
> **shrug** [ʃrʌg](shrugged;shrugging) *vt*. & *vi*. ...

5. 名词是复数形式或单复同形的,在词性前加以注明(放在方括号内)。如:

> **earnings** [ˈəːniŋz][复] *n*. ...
> **species** [ˈspiːʃiːz][单复同] *n*. ...

（三）释　义

1. 一个词（包括派生词、复合词）或一个习语有多条不同的释义时,各条释义分别列出,前面标以 1.、2.、3. 等数码。大体相同的若干释义则在同一条内,词义较近的用逗号分隔,精远的用分号分隔。

2. 名词释义前所注的〔~s〕、〔常~s〕、〔只用单〕等表示对该名词的数的要求;〔用作复〕、〔用作单〕等表示对后接谓语词的数的要求。如:

feature ... *n*. ...2. 脸型;〔~s〕面貌,相貌 ...

letter ... *n*. ... 3. 信;〔常~s〕证书,许可证 ...
（表示该名词释作"证书","许可证"时常用复数形式 letters）

physics ... *n*.〔用作单或复〕1. 物理学 ...
（表示该名词作主语时,后面的谓语动词可用单数或复数形式）

3. 释义后根据需要收入少量词组或句子作为例证,例证后附汉语译文。

（四）习　语

所收的常用习语用黑斜体印刷。

（五）派生词及复合词

1. 派生词及复合词大部分列在词条内部;少数由于较常用或释义、用法较复杂等原因,单独列为词条。

2. 列在词条内部的派生词及复合词用黑正体印刷,按首字母次序排列,其词目部分用代字号代表。但有些派生词的词目部分的拼法起了变化,其词目部分仍全部拼出。如:

bright 词条内的 brightness 印成 ~ness

assassinate 词条内的 assassination 印成 as.sassi'nation

3. 列在词条内部的派生词及复合词的注音问题,见（注音说明）。

4. 列在词条内部的派生词均注明词性;复合词除分写的以外,也均注明词性。某些带后缀 -ly、-ness、-tion、-al、-y 等的派生词,若释义相当于词目的释义,不再注出释义。

（六）若干符号的用法

1. 破折号（—）用于表示多词性的第二、第三个词性等部分的开始。
2. 平行号（‖）用于表示词条内习语、派生词、复合词等部分的开始。
3. 斜线号（/）用于分隔例证与例证、习语与习语、派生词与派生词、复合词与复合词。
4. 代字号（~）表示该复合词条的词目。
5. 连字号（-）用于连接复合词或表示移行。
6. 圆括号（(　)）用于:

(1)注明词形变化。如:

　　cut 词条内的(cut;cutting)

(2)加注内容或意义等方面的补充性说明。如:

　　毫米(千分之一米,略作 mm.)

　　(文章、讲话、乐曲等的)一段,一节

　　(目光等)洞察的,锐利的

　　元素氧(oxygen)的符号

　　(楼房的)底层(＝[美]first floor)

(3)括去可以省略的部分。如:

　　prolog(ue)

　　渗(透)压(力)

　　电话(号码)簿

(4)括出代换的部分。如:

　　≠ new (an old, a green) hand 新(老,生)手

　　(表示可分为"a new hand 新手"、"an old hand 老手"、"a green hand 生手"三条)

(5)在某些及物动词或不及物动词的释义中注明宾语或主语。如:

　　pass … vt. … . **2.** 通过(考试、检查等)…

　　fall … vi. … . **2.**(温度、价格等)下降…

(6)在某些动词、形容词、名词等的释义中注明常用的后接副词或前置词,如:

　　kick … vt. … **4.** …驱逐(out)…

　　dependent … adj. **1.** 依靠的,依赖的(on, upon)…

(7)归并某些词的相近的释义。

　　rich … adj. … **8.**(近乎)纯的 .**2**.

　　(表示释义为"近乎纯的"和"纯的")

7. 方括号([ ])用于:

(1)注明音标。

(2)注明地名的有关说明。如:

　　坦桑尼亚[非洲] 巴黎[法国首都]

(3)加注语法或使用等方面的补充性说明。如:

　　[总称]

　　[常用被动语态]

　　[P.]

　　(表示第一个字母 P 要大写)

　　[the ~]

　　(表示该词前要加定冠词)

　　[~ oneself]

　　(表示该词后接反身代词)

8. 尖括号(〈 〉)用于注明词源或修饰色彩。如:

　　〈法〉〈主英〉〈俚〉〈口〉〈粗〉

9. 鱼尾号(【 】)用于注明学科。

音标及发音例词表

元音和双元音

i:	*see*, *evil*	i	*it*, *pin*	ei	*age*, *face*
ɑ:	*farm*, *farther*	e	*best*, *let*	ai	*ice*, *five*
ɔ:	*all*, *order*	æ	*cap*, *hat*	ɔi	*boy*, *oil*
u:	*moon*, *rule*	ʌ	*cup*, *butter*	əu	*go*, *open*
ə:	*learn*, *term*	ɔ	*hot*, *rock*	au	*house*, *now*
		u	*full*, *put*	iə	*ear*, *hear*
		ə	*about*, *taken*	ɛə	*care*, *air*
				uə	*poor*, *sure*

辅　音

p	*up*, *pen*	f	*fat*, *if*	h	*he*, *how*
b	*bad*, *rob*	v	*very*, *save*	m	*me*, *am*
t	*tell*, *it*	θ	*thin*, *both*	n	*no*, *on*
d	*do*, *red*	ð	*then*, *smooth*	ŋ	*bring*, *long*
k	*cat*, *book*	s	*say*, *yes*	l	*land*, *coal*
g	*good*, *bag*	z	*zero*, *size*	r	*run*, *try*
tʃ	*child*, *much*	ʃ	*she*, *rush*	j	*young*, *yet*
dʒ	*jam*, *enjoy*	ʒ	*pleasure*, *seizure*	w	*want*, *will*

略语表

(一)

〈日〉	日语	〈苏格兰〉	苏格兰方言	〈美〉	美国特有用语
〈汉〉	汉语	〈英〉	英国特有用语	〈意〉	意大利语
〈加拿大〉	加拿大英语	〈拉〉	拉丁语	〈德〉	德语
〈西〉	西班牙语	〈法〉	法语	〈澳〉	澳大利亚特有用语

(二)

〈口〉	口语	〈罕〉	罕用	〈俚〉	俚语
〈方〉	方言	〈贬〉	贬义	〈粗〉	粗俗
〈书〉	书面语	〈废〉	废词，废义	〈谑〉	戏谑
〈古〉	古语	〈诗〉	诗歌用语	〈谚〉	谚语
〈讽〉	讽刺	〈昵〉	亲昵	〈喻〉	比喻

(三)

【心】	心理学	【罗神】	罗马神话	【哲】	哲学
【史】	历史	【宗】	宗教	【逻】	逻辑学
【军】	军语	【经】	经济	【商】	商业
【戏】	戏剧	【律】	法律	【摄】	摄影
【体】	体育	【音】	音乐		
【希神】	希腊神话	【语】	语言学		

(四)

【无】	无线电技术	【生理】	生理学	【矿】	矿物；矿物学
【天】	天文学	【讯】	电信	【昆】	昆虫
【化】	化学	【鸟】	鸟类	【物】	物理学
【计】	计算机科学	【动】	动物；动物学	【鱼】	鱼类
【气】	气象学	【地】	地质学；地理学	【空】	航空、航天
【电】	电学	【机】	机械	【建】	建筑，土木工程
【电子】	电子学	【农】	农业	【药】	药物；药物学
【印】	印刷	【医】	医学	【核】	核物理学
【生】	生物学	【冶】	冶金	【海】	航海
【生化】	生物化学	【纺】	纺织工业	【船】	船舶；造船

【植】　　植物:植物学　　【解】　　解剖学　　　　【数】　　数学
【微】　　微生物学

说明:1. 有些以本表略语为基础构成的略语,不再收入本表。如:〈美俚〉(指美国俚
　　　语);〈主方〉(指主要用于方言);【英史】(指英国历史)等。
　　　2. 未经缩略、意义自明的,也不收入本表。如:〈委婉语〉;【会计】;【基督教】等。

A

A, a [ei]([复]A's, a's 或 Aes, aes[eiz])英语字母第一个字母 **1.** 表示"第一"的符号 **2.**【数】第一已知量 **3.**[A]A字形 **4.**[A]【化】元素氩(argon)的符号 **5.**【音】A音, A调 **6.** 甲(指学业成绩最优)(7.(供成人观看的)A类电影 **8.**[A](英)表示"干线道路"的符号 ‖ *from A to Z* 从头至尾; 彻底 ‖ **A level** (英)(中学生的)高等程度; 高级考试/ A1, A'-one *adj.* 第一流的, 极好的

a [强读; 弱 ə], **an** [强读; 弱 ən, n] [a 用于以辅音音素开始的词前; an 用于以元音音素开始的词前] *art.* [不定冠词] **1.**(非特指的)一(个): a foreign guest 一位外宾 **2.**(一类事物)任何一个: A bicycle has two wheels. 自行车有两个轮子。**3.** 每一(个): six miles an hour 每小时六英里 **4.** 同一(个): things of a kind 同类的东西 **5.** [用于两件通常配对成套的东西前] 一副, 一套: a knife and fork 一副刀叉 **6.** [用于某些复数名词前, 表示一个单位]: spend an additional two weeks 再花两星期 **7.** [用于不可抽象名词前, 表示一种, 某种]: a deep love for one's country 对祖国的热爱 **8.** [用于某些物质名词前, 表示一种, 一客等]: a green tea 一种绿茶/ an ice cream 一客冰淇淋 **9.** [用于专有名词前, 表示某人一家的, 某一个]: a Lei Feng 一个雷锋式人物

a. *abbr.* adjective

a- *pref.* **1.** 加强语气: arise **2.** 表示"on", "in", "to", "into": afoot, asleep **3.** 表示"of", "from": abridge **5.** 表示"out": amend **6.** 表示"not": asexual

AAM *abbr.* air-to-air missile 空对空导弹

aardvark ['ɑːdvɑːk] *n.*【动】土豚, 非洲食蚁兽

ab- *pref.* 表示"脱离": abdicate, abduct

abaci ['æbəsai] abacus 的复数

aback [ə'bæk] *adv.* **1.** 向后 **2.**【海】逆帆 ‖ *be taken* ～ 吃一惊

abacus ['æbəkəs]([复]abaci ['æbəsai] 或 abacuses) *n.* **1.** 算盘 **2.**【建】(圆柱)顶板

abaft [ə'bɑːft] *adv.* 在船尾; 向船尾 — *prep.* **1.** 在…的近船尾处 **2.** 在…后面

abalone [ˌæbə'ləuni] *n.*【动】鲍(俗称鲍鱼, 古称石决明)

abandon [ə'bændən] *vt.* **1.** 放弃; 抛弃 **2.** 离弃(家园, 船只, 飞机等) **3.** 叛离, 丢弃(信仰等) **4.** 遗弃(妻、女等) — *n.* 放任, 放纵; 无拘无束 ‖ ～**ed** *adj.* 被抛弃的; 被遗弃的 **2.** 自我放任的; 无耻的 **3.** 无约束的, 无度的 / ～**ment** *n.* **1.** 放弃; 抛弃; 遗弃 **2.** 放任, 放纵

abase [ə'beis] *vt.* 使谦卑, 使降低地位(或身分等) ‖ ～**ment** *n.*

abash [ə'bæʃ] *vt.* 使羞愧, 使窘迫 ‖ ～ment *n.*

abate [ə'beit] *vt.* **1.** 减少, 减轻, 减退; 降

(价) 2. 废除，撤销(法令等)；除去(妨
碍等) — vi. 1.(洪水、风暴、病痛等)
减少，减轻，减退 2.(法令等)被废除，
成为无效 ‖ ~ment n.

abattoir ['æbətwɑ:] n. 屠宰场

abbé ['æbei]《法》n. 男修道院院长

abbess ['æbis] n. 女修道院院长

abbey ['æbi] n. 大修道院；大寺院；大教
堂；全院修士(或修女)

abbot ['æbət] n. 男修道院院长；大寺院
男住持

abbr. abbr. abbreviation

abbreviate [ə'bri:vieit] vt. 1. 缩写；简缩
2. 缩短(访问等)；节略(读物等) ‖
ab,brevi'ation n. 1. 缩写；缩略；节略 2.
缩写式；缩写词

ABC ['ei'bi:'si:](又[复] ABC's 或 ABCs) n.
1.[~s]字母表 2. 基础知识，入门 3.
〈英〉(按字母顺序排列的)全国火车车
站及客运时刻一览表

abdicate ['æbdikeit] vt. 退(位)；放弃(职
位、权力等) — vi.(国王)退位 ‖
,abdi'cation n.

abdomen ['æbdəmən, æb'dəumən] n. 腹
(部)

abdominal [æb'dɔminəl] adj. 1. 腹的，腹
部的 2.(鱼)有腹鳍的

abduct [æb'dʌkt] vt. 诱拐；劫持 ‖ ~ion
n./~or n.

abeam [ə'bi:m] adv. & adj. 正横着(的)，
与船的龙骨(或飞机机身)成直角的(的)

abed [ə'bed] adv. 在床上

aberration [æbə'reiʃən] n. 1. 离开正路，
脱离常轨，偏离 2.【医】心理失常 3.
【物】像差 4.【天】光行差 5.【生】畸变；
变型

abet [ə'bet] (abetted; abetting) vt. 1. 唆
使，嗾使；煽动 2. 帮助，支持 ‖ abetter

n. 唆使者；煽动者/**abettor** n.【律】教
唆犯

abeyance [ə'beiəns] n. 中止，暂搁；(所有
权等的)归属待定

abhor [əb'hɔ:] (abhorred; abhorring) vt. 憎
恶，厌恶

abhorrence [əb'hɔrəns] n. 憎恶；可憎恶
的事物(或人)

abhorrent [əb'hɔrənt] adj. 1.(在…看来)
可恶的，讨厌的(to) 2.(对…)感到憎
恶的，厌恶的(of) 3.(和…)不一致的，
相反的(to)

abide [ə'baid] (abode [ə'bəud] 或 abided)
vi. 1. 遵守(法律、诺言、决定等)；坚持
(意见等)(by) 2. 持续 3.〈古〉逗留，住
(at, in) — vt. 1.[常用于否定句和疑
问句]忍受，容忍 2. 等候 ‖ **abiding**
adj. 持久不变的，永久的

Abidjan [æbi'dʒɑ:n] n. 阿比让[科特迪瓦
首都]

ability [ə'biliti] n. 1. 能力 2. 才能，才
智；[abilities]技能

-ability suf. 表示"能力"，"可能性"：cur-
ability

abject ['æbdʒekt] adj. 1.(情况等)可怜
的，凄惨的 2.(人或行为)卑下的；卑鄙
的 ‖ ~ly adv./~ness n.

abjection [æb'dʒekʃən] n. 1. 落魄；屈辱
2. 羞辱；抛弃；驱逐

abjure [əb'dʒuə] vt. 发誓断绝；公开放弃
(意见等) ‖ ,abju'ration n.

ablative ['æblətiv] n. & adj.【语】(拉丁
语的)夺格(的)，离格(的)

ablaze [ə'bleiz] adj.[常作表语] & adv.
1. 着火 2. 闪耀 3. 兴奋，激昂

able ['eibl] adj. 1. 有能力的；有才干的，
能干的 2. 显示出才智的 3.【律】有法
定资格的 ‖ '~-,bodied adj. 体格健全

的,强壮的

-able *suf.* 1.[附在动词后构成形容词]表示"可…的","能…的":bear*able*, eat*able*
2.[附在名词后构成形容词]表示"可…的":sale*able*

abloom [ə'bluːm] *adj.* [常作表语] & *adv.* 开着花

ablution [ə'bluːʃən] *n.* [常～s]沐浴,洗澡;洗礼

ably ['eibli] *adv.* 能干地

-ably *suf.* [构成与 -able 结尾的形容词相应的副词]:notably

ABM *abbr.* antiballistic missile 反弹道导弹

abnegate ['æbnigeit] *vt.* 1. 克制(私心等);不容自己享受… 2. 放弃(权利等);交出(权力等)‖ abne'gation *n.*

abnormal [æb'nɔːməl] *adj.* 反常的;变态的 ‖～ity [æbnɔː'mæliti] *n.* 1. 反常;变态;畸形 2. 反常情况(或事物);变态特征 /～ly *adv.*

aboard [ə'bɔːd] *adv.* 1. 在船(或飞机,车)上;上船(或飞机,车);登机;上车;靠船边 — *prep.* 在(船、飞机、车)上;上(船、飞机、车)

abode[1] [ə'bəud] *n.* 住所;(在某地的)暂居,逗留

abode[2] [ə'bəud] abide 的过去式和过去分词

abolish [ə'bɔliʃ] *vt.* 废除(法律、习惯等);取消

abolition [æbə'liʃən] *n.* 1.(法律、习惯等的)废除;取消 2.(美国的)废除黑奴制度 ‖～ist *n.*

A-bomb ['eibɔm] *n.* 原子弹(= atom-bomb)— *vt.* 用原子弹轰炸(= atom-bomb)

abominable [ə'bɔminəbl] *adj.* 1. 可恶的,讨厌的 2.〈口〉(天气、食物等)极坏的 ‖ abominably *adv.*

abominate [ə'bɔmineit] *vt.* 厌恶,憎恨;〈口〉不喜欢 ‖ a,bomi'nation *n.* 1. 厌恶,憎恨 2. 令人讨厌的事物

aboriginal [æbə'ridʒənəl] *adj.* 土著的 — *n.* 土著居民;土生动物(或植物)

aborigine [æbə'ridʒini] *n.* 1. 土著居民 2.[～s]土生动物(或植物)群

abort [ə'bɔːt] *vi.* & *vt.* (使)流产;(使)夭折;(使)中止 — *n.* 中止;中途失败;夭折

abortion [ə'bɔːʃən] *n.* 1. 流产,小产,堕胎 2.(计划等)的失败,夭折 3. 流产胎(儿);畸形人(或动物)4.【生】(动植物器官的)败育;败育器官 ‖～ism *n.* 有权流产主义 /～ist *n.* 为人堕胎者;流产权支持者

abortion-on-demand [ə'bɔːʃənɔndi'mɑːnd] *n.* 要求流产权

abortive [ə'bɔːtiv] *adj.* 1.(药)有堕胎作用的 2.【医】起顿挫作用的;(病)顿挫的 2. 流产的;(计划等)失败的,夭折的 3.【生】败育的 ‖～ly *adv.* /～ness *n.*

abound [ə'baund] *vi.* 1.(物产)丰富,盛产,富于 2. 多,充满(*with, in*)

about [ə'baut] *prep.* 1. 在…周围;在…附近;在…身边 2. 在…各处;去…各处 3. 关于;对于 4.(时刻、大小、数量等)在…左右 5. 从事于…事 — *adv.* 1. 周围;附近;到处 2. 大约;差不多 3.(转到)相反方向 4. 在活动中;在流行(或传播)中 5. 即将(*to*)

above [ə'bʌv] *prep.* 1.[表示位置、职位等]在…上面 2. 在…的上游 3.[表示数量、年龄等]…以上 4.…高于;胜过 5.[表示品质、行为、能力等]超出…之外 — *adv.* 1. 在上面;以上 2. 在上游 3. 上述 4. 在天上 — *adj.* 上面出现(或提到)过的;上述的 — *n.* 1. 上文提到的事情(或人);上文 2. 上

级 3. 老天 ‖ ~-board [əˌbʌv'bɔːd] *adj.*
[常作表语] & *adv.* 公开的(地)，光明
正大的(地)

abracadabra [ˌæbrəkə'dæbrə] *n.* 符咒

abrade [ə'breid] *vt.* 磨损，磨蚀；擦伤(皮
肤等) ‖ **abrasion** *n.* 磨损(处)；擦伤
(处)

abrasive [ə'breisiv] *adj.* 有研磨(或磨蚀)
作用的 — *n.* (研)磨料(如金刚砂、砂
纸等)

abreast [ə'brest] *adv.* 相并，并肩 ‖ *keep*
~ *of* (或 *with*)与…保持并列；(使)
不落后于

abridge [ə'bridʒ] *vt.* 节略；缩短
‖ **abridg(e)ment** *n.* 节略；节本

abroad [ə'brɔːd] *adv.* 1. 到国外；在国外；
go — 出国 2. 到处

abrogate ['æbrəgeit] *vt.* 废除(法令等) ‖
ˌabro'gation *n.*

abrupt [ə'brʌpt] *adj.* 1. 突然的，出其不
意的 2. 陡峭的，险峻的 3. 粗鲁的，无
礼的 4.(讲话、文章等)不连贯的，支离
的 ‖ ~ly *adv.* / ~ness *n.*

abscess ['æbsis] *n.* 脓肿 — *vi.* 形成脓肿

abscond [əb'skɔnd] *vi.* 潜逃

absence ['æbsəns] *n.* 1. 不在，缺席；~
from school 缺课 2. 缺乏

absent ['æbsənt] *adj.* 1. 不在的，缺席的；
be — *from* work 不上班 2. 缺乏的 3.
不在意的，漫不经心的 — [æb'sent]
vt. [~ oneself]缺席；不到 ‖ ~ly *adv.*
不在场地

absentee [ˌæbsən'tiː] *n.* 不在者，缺席者
在外地主 ‖ ~ism *n.* 旷工；旷课

absent-minded [ˌæbsənt'maindid] *adj.* 心
不在焉的 ‖ ~ly *adv.* / ~ness *n.*

absolute ['æbsəluːt] *adj.* 1. 绝对的 2. 不
受任何限制(或约束)的，专制独裁的

3. 纯粹的，完全的 4.【语】独立的 5. 确
实的，不容置疑的 — *n.* 绝对 ‖ ~ly
adv. / ~ness *n.*

absolution [ˌæbsə'luːʃən] *n.*(罪、惩罚、责
任的)解除，免除；赦免 2.【宗】赦罪

absolve [əb'zɔlv] *vt.* 1. 解除；赦免，宽恕
2. 免除，开脱

absorb [əb'sɔːb] *vt.* 吸收(水、热、光等)；
(无反应地)承受(震动等)；忍受；缓冲
2. 吸引(注意力等)；吸引…的注意，
使专心，使全神贯注 3. 把…并入，同
化 4. 承担(费用等) ‖ ~ing *adj.* 非常
吸引人的，引人入胜的 / ~er *n.* 吸收
器；减震器

absorbent [əb'sɔːbənt] *adj.* 能吸收的，有
吸收能力的；~ cotton 脱脂棉 — *n.*
【化】吸收剂；吸收物；(动植物用以吸
收营养的)吸收体

absorption [əb'sɔːpʃən] *n.* 1. 吸收(作用)
2. 专注(*in*)

absorptive [əb'sɔːptiv] *adj.* 有吸收力的；
吸收(性)的

abstain [əb'stein] *vi.* 1. 戒绝；有意回避
(*from*) 2. 弃权(*from*) ‖ ~er *n.*

abstemious [æb'stiːmiəs] *adj.* 饮食有度
的；有节制的 ‖ ~ness *n.*

abstention [æb'stenʃən] *n.* 1. 戒绝；回避
(*from*) 2. 弃权(*from*)

abstinence ['æbstinəns] *n.* 节制；禁欲；戒
酒 ‖ **abstinent** *adj.*

abstract ['æbstrækt] *adj.* 1. 抽象的 2. 理
论上的，无实际意义的 3. 难解的，深
奥的 4.(艺术上)抽象(派)的 — *n.* 1.
摘要；梗概 2. 抽象派艺术作品(抽象
名称)；抽象概念 3.【化】提取物 —
[əb'strækt] *vt.* 1. 提取，抽取 2.(口)窃
取 3. 使抽象(化) 4. 做……的摘要(或
梗概) 5. 转移(注意力等) ‖ ~ly *adv.*
/ ~ness *n.*

abstracted [æb'stræktid] *adj*. 1. 分心的；出神的 2. 分离出来的 ‖ ~ly *adv*. / ~ness *n*.

abstraction [æb'strækʃən] *n*. 1. 抽象（化）；抽象作用 2. 抽象概念；抽象名称 3. 提神，心不在焉 4. 抽象派艺术作品 5. 提取，抽取

abstruse [æb'struːs] *adj*. 难解的，深奥的 ‖ ~ly *adv*. / ~ness *n*.

absurd [əb'səːd] *adj*. 1. 不合理的，荒谬可笑的；愚蠢的 2. 荒诞派的 —*n*. [the —或 the A-] (从存在主义出发的文学或哲学观点的)荒诞 ‖ ~ism *n*. 荒诞主义；荒诞描写／~ist *n*. 荒诞派作家；荒诞主义鼓吹者／~ity *n*. 荒诞；谬论；荒唐(或愚蠢)行为／~ly *adv*. / ~ness *n*.

Abu Dhabi [ˌɑːbuː'dɑːbi] 1. 阿布扎比(酋长国)[组成阿拉伯联合酋长国的酋长国之一] 2. 阿布扎比(市)[阿拉伯联合酋长国首都]

Abuja [ə'buːdʒə] *n*. 阿布贾[尼日利亚首都]

abundance [ə'bʌndəns] *n*. 丰富，充裕

abundant [ə'bʌndənt] *adj*. 1. 丰富的，充裕的 2. 充足的 ‖ ~ly *adv*.

abuse [ə'bjuːz] *vt*. 1. 滥用，妄用 2. 虐待；凌辱 3. 辱骂 4. ⟨古⟩欺骗 —[ə'bjuːs] *n*. 1. 滥用，妄用 2. 虐待，凌辱 3. 辱骂 4. 陋习，弊病

abusive [ə'bjuːsiv] *adj*. 1. 辱骂性的；骂人的 2. (被)滥用的 3. 陋习性的 ‖ ~ly *adv*. / ~ness *n*.

abut [ə'bʌt] (abutted; abutting) *vi*. & *vt*. 邻接，毗连，紧靠 (on, upon, against) ‖ ~ment *n*. 【建】桥台，拱座

abysmal [ə'bizməl] *adj*. 无底的，深不可测的

abyss [ə'bis] *n*. 1. 深渊 2. 阴间，地狱

Abyssinia [ˌæbi'sinjə] *n*. 阿比西尼亚(Ethiopia 埃塞俄比亚的旧称)[东非国家]

AC *abbr*. 1. alternating current【电】交流电 2. ⟨拉⟩ *ante Christum* 公元前(= before Christ)

Ac 【化】元素锕(actinium)的符号

a/c, A/C 1. account 2. account current 往来账户；活期存款账户

acacia [ə'keiʃə] *n*. 1. 金合欢(尤指阿拉伯胶树)；刺槐，洋槐 2. 金合欢胶，阿拉伯树胶

academese [əˌkædə'miːz] *n*. 学术行话；学术体，学术文章风格

academic [ˌækə'demik] *adj*. 1. (高等)专科院校的；研究院的；学会的 2. 学术的 3. 学究式的,书生气的,空谈的 —*n*. 大学生；大学教师；学究式人物

academical [ˌækə'demikəl] *adj*. = academic —*n*. [~s] 大学服装；学士(或硕士，博士)服 ‖ ~ly *adv*.

academician [əˌkædə'miʃən] *n*. 院士；学会会员

academy [ə'kædəmi] *n*. 1. (高等)专科院校；中等学校 2. 研究院；学会 3. [A-] 学园(柏拉图讲哲学的地方)；柏拉图哲学(或学派)

acanthus [ə'kænθəs] *n*. [复] acanthuses 或 a-canthi]爵床属植物 1. 【植】老鼠簕 2. 【建】莨苕叶饰

acarology [ˌækə'rɔlədʒi] *n*. 蜱螨学，螨学 ‖ acarologist *n*. 蜱螨学家

accede [æk'siːd] *vi*. 1. 答应，同意 (to) 2. 就任 (to) 3. 加入 (to)

accelerate [æk'seləreit] *vt*. 加速，加快；促进 —*vi*. 增速 ‖ ac,cele'ration *n*. / ac'celerator *n*. 加速器；油门；加速剂；促进剂

accent ['æksənt] *n.* 1. 重音 2. 重音符号 3. 音调;腔调;口音 4. 特征,特点 5. 着重(on) — ['æksent] *vt.* 1. 重读 2. 在 ... 上加重音符 3. 使显著

accentuate [æk'sentjueit] *vt.* 1. 重读 2. 在 ... 上加重音符 3. 强调,着重指出 ‖ ac,centu'ation *n.*

accept [ək'sept] *vt.* 1. 接受,领受 2. 承认,认可 3. [商] 承兑(票据等) 4. 忍受,容忍 — *vi.* 接受(of)

acceptable [ək'septəbl] *adj.* 1. 可接受的,合意的,受欢迎的 2. 可忍受的;承受得往的 3. 差强人意的,仅仅够格的 ‖ ac,cepta'bility *n.* / ~ ness *n.* / acceptably *adv.*

acceptance [ək'septəns] *n.* 1. 接受,领受;接收;验收 2. 承认,认可 3. [商] (票据等的)承兑 ‖ ~ speech [美]总统候选人接受政党提名时所作的演说

access ['ækses] *n.* 1. 接近;进入;通路;have easy ~ to sth. 容易得到某物;be easy of ~ 容易到达(或见到) 2. (疾病等的)侵袭,发作 — *vt.* 接近;使用;[计]存取,访问(信息);[讯]接入 ‖ ~ road (干道的)支路 / ~ speed [计]存取速度 / ~ time[计]存取时间

accessary [æk'sesəri] *n.* & *adj.* = accessory

accessible [æk'sesibl] *adj.* 1. 易接近的;易使用的;易得到的;易相处的;能进入的(to) 2. 易受影响的(to) 3. 可以理解的(to) ‖ ac,cessi'bility *n.* / accessibly *adv.*

accession [æk'seʃən] *n.* 1. 到达(to);接近 2. 就职,就任(to) 3. 添加;添加物(to);[律]财产自然增益 4. 同意 — *vt.* 把(新书等)登记入册

accessory [æk'sesəri] *n.* 1. 附件,附属品 2. 同谋,帮凶,从犯 3. [accessories] (妇女的)装饰品(指提包,手套等) — *adj.* 1. 附属的,附加的 2. 同谋的

accidence ['æksidəns] *n.* [语]词形变化;词法

accident ['æksidənt] *n.* 意外事件,偶然事件 2. 事故 3. [地]褶皱,不平 ‖ ~ -prone *adj.* 易遭遇意外的;易惹事故的

accidental [,æksi'dentl] *adj.* 偶然的,意外的 2. 附属的 — *n.* 1. 非本质的属性 2.[音]临时记号 ‖ ~ ly *adv.* 偶然地

acclaim [ə'kleim] *vt.* 1. 向 ... 欢呼,向 ... 喝彩 2. 以欢呼声拥戴(或推举,承认) — *vi.* 欢呼,喝彩 — *n.* 欢呼,喝彩

acclamation [,æklə'meiʃən] *n.* 1. 欢呼,喝彩 2. (以鼓掌,欢呼等表示的)拥护,赞成

acclimate [ə'klaimit] *vt.* [美] = acclimatize ‖ **acclimation** [,æklai'meiʃən] *n.* [美] = acclimatization

acclimatize [ə'klaimətaiz] *vt.* & *vi.* (使)服水土,(使)适应气候 ‖ ac,climati'zation *n.*

acclivity [ə'kliviti] *n.* [地]上行坡

accolade ['ækəleid] *n.* 1. 骑士称号授予礼(指用剑加肩,拥抱或赐予等) 2. 授奖表彰;见面时向好的接吻(或拥抱) 3.【音】连谱号

accommodate [ə'kɔmədeit] *vt.* 1. 容纳,接纳 2. 向 ... 提供;向 ... 提供住宿(或膳宿) 3. 使适应,使迁就;调节 4. 调停(争端等) — *vi.* 适应 ‖ **accommodating** *adj.* 与人方便的;随和的

accommodation [ə,kɔmə'deiʃən] *n.* 1. [美常用 ~ s]住处;膳宿;居住舱室 2. 方便设施 3. 适应,调节 4. (争端等)的和解,调停 5. 贷款 ‖ ~ collar [美俚] (为凑数或向上司作交代的)迁就性逮捕

accompaniment [ə'kʌmpənimənt] *n.* **1.** 伴随物；附属物 **2.** 伴奏；伴唱；(声乐)伴随

accompanist [ə'kʌmpənist] *n.* 伴奏者；伴唱者

accompany [ə'kʌmpəni] *vt.* **1.** 伴随；陪同 **2.** 为...伴奏 — *vi.* 伴奏

accomplice [ə'kɔmplis] *n.* 共犯，共同犯罪者

accomplish [ə'kɔmpliʃ] *vt.* 完成(任务等) ‖ ~ed *adj.* 有才艺的，有造诣的 / ~ment *n.* **1.** 完成 **2.** 成就 **3.** [~ments] 才艺，造诣，技能

accord [ə'kɔːd] *vt.* 给予(欢迎、称颂等) — *vi.* **1.** 符合，调和，一致(*with*) — *n.* 符合，调和，一致 **2.** (国家之间的)协议 **3.** 【音】和弦 **4.** 自愿，主动

accordance [ə'kɔːdəns] *n.* **1.** 一致；in ~ with 与...一致；按照，根据 **2.** 给予 ‖ **accordant** *adj.* **1.** 和谐的，一致的；相符的(*with*, *to*) 【地】平齐的

according [ə'kɔːdiŋ] *adv.* [用于下列语中] ‖ ~ as [后接从句] 根据；取决于；如果，倘若 / ~ to 按照；据...所说

accordingly [ə'kɔːdiŋli] *adv.* **1.** 照着(办、做等)，相应地 **2.** 因此；从而

accordion [ə'kɔːdiən] *n.* 手风琴 — *adj.* (似手风琴般)可折叠的

accost [ə'kɔst] *vt.* **1.** 走上前去跟(某人)讲话 **2.** (妓女等)勾引

account [ə'kaunt] *n.* **1.** 账，账目；账户 **2.** 算账 **3.** [关于事件、人物等的]报道，叙述，描写 **4.** 原因，理由 **5.** 重要性；价值 **6.** 考虑；leave out of ~ 不考虑 — *vi.* [与 for 连用] **1.** 说出(缘故等)的用途 **2.** 说明(原因等) **3.** [指数量等]占 **4.** 捕捉；杀死；击落；解决【体】得(分) — *vt.* 认为 ‖ by all ~s 大家都说 / call to ~ 要求...作出解释 / on ~

(货物)赊账 /(钱)部分支付 / on ~ of 因为 / on no ~ 决不 / on one's own ~ 为自身利益 ‖ ~ancy *n.* 会计(学)；会计职业 / ~ant *n.* 会计人员 ‖ ~ing *n.* 会计(学)；结账，结算；账单

accountable [ə'kauntəbl] *adj.* **1.** 有说明义务的；负有责任的 **2.** 可说明的 ‖ **ac'counta'bility** *n.* / **accountably** *adv.*

accouterment [ə'kuːtəmənt] *n.* 〈美〉= accoutrement

accoutrement [ə'kuːtəmənt] *n.* [常 ~ s] 装备；(除武器、军服外的)士兵装备

Accra [ə'krɑː] *n.* 阿克拉[加纳首都]

accredit [ə'kredit] *vt.* **1.** 相信；以下 任，任命(大使等) **3.** 把...归于(*to*) **4.** 鉴定...为合格 ‖ **ac,credi'tation** *n.*

accrete [ə'kriːt] *vi.* **1.** 外着生长，添加生长 **2.** 连生，合生；依附(*to*) — *vt.* 使依附；吸引(*to*) — *adj.* 【植】合生的 ‖ **accretion** *n.* **1.** 增大，添加生长 **2.** 连生，合生 **3.** 附生物 **4.** 冲积层

accrue [ə'kruː] *vi.* (利息等)自然增长 ‖ **accrual** *n.*

accumulate [ə'kjuːmjuleit] *vt. & vi.* 积累，积聚 ‖ **ac,cumu'lation** *n.* **1.** 积累 **2.** 堆积物，积聚物 ‖ **accumulator** *n.* 累加器(英)蓄电池

accumulative [ə'kjuːmjulətiv] *adj.* **1.** 积累的，堆积的 **2.** 喜欢积聚的，贪得的 ‖ ~ly *adv.*

accuracy [ˈækjurəsi] *n.* 准确(性)；精确(性)

accurate [ˈækjurit] *adj.* 准确的；精确的 ‖ ~ly *adv.*

accursed [ə'kɜːsid], **accurst** [ə'kɜːst] *adj.* **1.** 〈应〉受诅咒的；注定完蛋的 **2.** 〈口〉可恶的；糟透的

accusation [ˌækjuˈzeiʃən] *n.* **1.** 指责，谴责 **2.** 控告，指控 **3.** (被告发的)罪名

accusative [ə'kju:zətiv] *adj. & n.* 【语】宾格 (的)

accusatory [ə'kju:zətəri] *adj.* 指责的; 指控的; 控告的

accuse [ə'kju:z] *vt.* 1. 指责, 谴责 2. 指控, 控告 ‖ ~ **d** *n.* 被告 / ~ **r** *n.* 指责者; 控告者

accustom [ə'kʌstəm] *vt.* 使习惯于 (*to*) ‖ ~ **ed** *adj.* 惯常的, 习惯的, 适应了的

ace [eis] *n.* 1. (纸牌、骰子的) 一点; 一点的纸牌, A牌 2. (开赛车或飞机的) 王牌驾驶员; (任何一行的) 能手, 佼佼者 3. 少许, 毫厘 4. (网球等运动中的) 发球得分; 得一分的发球 5. 《美俚》(饭店等处的) 单人主顾; 单人座 — *vt.* 在 ... 中得好成绩

acerbity [ə'sə:biti] *n.* 尖刻; 酸, 苦涩

acetate ['æsiteit] *n.* 醋酸纤维(素); 【化】醋酸盐

acetic [ə'si:tik] *adj.* 醋(酸)的

acetone ['æsitəun] *n.* 【化】丙酮

acetylene [ə'setili:n] *n.* 【化】乙炔

ache [eik] *vi.* 1. 痛 2. 《口》想念; 渴望 — *n.* (连续固定的) 疼痛

achieve [ə'tʃi:v] *vt.* 1. 完成 2. 达到(目的); 得到(胜利)

achievement [ə'tʃi:vmənt] *n.* 1. 完成; 达到 2. 成就, 成绩

Achilles' [ə'kili:z] **heel** 致命弱点

achromatic [ˌækrəu'mætik] *adj.* 1. 【物】无色的; 消色差的 2. 【生】不受光的

acid ['æsid] *adj.* 1. 酸的, 酸味的 2. 【化】酸性的; 酸性的 3. 尖刻的 — *n.* 1. 酸味物质 2. 【化】酸 3. 《美俚》迷幻药(尤指麦角酸二乙基酰胺) ‖ ~-**head** *n.* 嗜用迷幻药的人 / ~ **rain** 酸雨

acidity [ə'siditi] *n.* 1. 【化】酸性; 酸度 2. 【医】胃酸过多 3. (言词等的) 尖刻

acidosis [ˌæsi'dəusis] *n.* 酸中毒

acidulous [ə'sidjuləs] *adj.* 1. 带酸味的 2. 尖刻的; 苛苦的

ackack ['æk'æk] *n. & adj.* 《口》高射炮火(的); 高射炮(的)

acknowledge [ək'nɔlidʒ] *vt.* 1. 承认 2. 告知收到(信件、礼物等) 3. 对(某人所做的事) 表示感谢 4. 对(人)打招呼(表示认识) ‖ ~ **d** *adj.* 公认的

acknowledg(e)ment [ək'nɔlidʒmənt] *n.* 1. 承认 2. (对收到来信等的)确认通知 3. 志谢, 鸣谢

acme ['ækmi] *n.* 顶点; 极度

acne ['ækni] *n.* 【医】痤疮; 粉刺

acolyte ['ækəlait] *n.* 【宗】侍僧; (行弥撒 等仪式时的)教士助手

aconite ['ækənait] *n.* 【植】乌头

acorn ['eikɔ:n] *n.* 橡树果实

acoustic(al) [ə'ku:stik(əl)] *adj.* 听觉的; 音响的; 受声波控制的; 声学的; 吸声的 ‖ **acoustically** *adv.*

acoustics [ə'ku:stiks] [复] *n.* 1. [用作单] 声学 2. (礼堂、剧院等的)音响效果; 音质

acquaint [ə'kweint] *vt.* 使认识; 使了解; 通知

acquaintance [ə'kweintəns] *n.* 1. 相识; 了解 2. 相识的人; 熟人

acquiesce [ˌækwi'es] *vi.* 默认, 默许(*in*)

acquiescence [ˌækwi'esns] *n.* 默认, 默许

acquiescent [ˌækwi'esnt] *adj.* 默认的, 默许的 ‖ ~**ly** *adv.*

acquire [ə'kwaiə] *vt.* 1. 取得, 获得, 得到 2. (利用探测仪器)捕获(目标) ‖ ~**ment** *n.* 1. 获得 2. 学得的东西

acquired [ə'kwaiəd] *adj.* 1. (尤指通过努力)获得的 2. 【医】后天的 ‖ ~ **immune deficiency syndrome**, ~ **immunodefi-**

ciency syndrome 【医】获得性免疫缺损综合征(略作 AIDS, 即艾滋病)

acquisition [ˌækwiˈziʃən] *n*. 1. 获得 2. (有价值的)获得物 3. 探求

acquisitive [əˈkwizitiv] *adj*. (对知识、财富等)渴望得到的;能够获得的 ‖ ～ly *adv*. / ～ness *n*.

acquit [əˈkwit] (acquitted; acquitting) *vt*. 1. 宣告 ... 无罪 2. [～ oneself] 表现;履行,完成 *acquittal n*. 1. 宣告无罪 2. (职责的)履行 3. (债务的清偿)

acre [ˈeikə] *n*. 英亩(等于 40.47 公亩或 6.07 亩) 2. [～s] 土地,地产 3. 〈口〉[～s] 大量 ‖ ～age *n*. 英亩数;以英亩计算的土地面积

acrid [ˈækrid] *adj*. 1. (气味等)辛辣的;刺激的 2. (语言等)刻毒的 ‖ ～ity [æˈkriditi] *n*. / ～ness *n*.

acrimonious [ˌækriˈməuniəs] *adj*. (语言、态度、脾气等)刻毒的,讥刺的,苛刻的 ‖ ～ly *adv*. / ～ness *n*.

acrimony [ˈækriməni] *n*. (语言、态度、脾气等)尖刻;严厉

acrobat [ˈækrəbæt] *n*. 1. 杂技演员(尤指走钢丝演员) 2. 立场政治善变的人 ‖ ～ic [ˌækrəˈbætik] *adj*. 杂技的 / ～ics [ˌækrəˈbætiks] *n*. [用作单或复] 1. 杂技;(喻)巧妙手法,技巧 2. 特技飞行

acronym [ˈækrənim] *n*. 首字母拼读词(如 USA) ‖ ～ *vt*. 把 ... 缩合成首字母缩拼词;用首字母拼读词

acropolis [əˈkrɔpəlis] *n*. (古希腊城市的)卫城

across [əˈkrɔs] *prep*. 1. 横过,穿过 2. 在 ... 的另一边 3. 交叉 4. 经过(一整段时间) — *adv*. 1. 横过,穿过;从一边向另一边 2. 交叉 3. 横,阔

acrostic [əˈkrɔstik] *n*. 离合诗(各行诗句

中的第一个词的首字母或最后一个词的尾字母或其它特定处的字母能组合成词或词组等的一种诗体) — *adj*. 离合诗的;似离合诗的

acrylic [əˈkrilik] *adj*. 丙烯酸的;丙烯酸衍生物的 — *n*. 丙烯酸树脂;丙烯酸纤维

act [ækt] *n*. 1. 行为;行动 2. 法令;条例 3. 【戏】幕;(马戏、杂耍中的)短节目 — *vi*. 1. 行动;做事 2. 【戏】表演;(剧本等)适于上演 3. [与 as 连用]担当 4. 起作用,见效 5. 假装 — *vt*. 1. 扮演(角色);演出(戏) 2. 表现出 ... 的样子;装作

acting [ˈæktiŋ] *adj*. 1. 代理的 2. 适于演出的,演出用的 — *n*. 1. 演戏 2. 表演;演技 3. 假装

actinism [ˈæktinizəm] *n*. 【化】射线化学变化,光化作用 ‖ **ac'tinic** *adj*.

action [ˈækʃən] *n*. 1. 行动;行为;活动 2. 【军】战斗 3. 作用 4. (机器等)机械装置 5. (小说等的)情节 6. (运动员等的)姿势 7. 诉讼 8. (美耍)刺激活动;赌博

actionable [ˈækʃənəbl] *adj*. 【律】可提起诉讼的 ‖ **actionably** *adv*.

activate [ˈæktiveit] *vt*. 1. 使活动 2. 正式建成(部队等) 3. 【化】使活化,激活 4. 【核】使产生放射性 ‖ **acti'vation** *n*.

active [ˈæktiv] *adj*. 1. 有活动力的,灵敏的;积极的;能动的 2. 活动中的,现行的;现役的 3. 【语】主动的 4. 【核】放射性的 ‖ ～ly *adv*. / **activist** *n*. 积极分子 ‖ ～ **service** 现役

activity [ækˈtiviti] *n*. 1. 活动性;能动性;活泼,敏捷;【化】活度 2. [常 activities] 活动,所做的事情

actor [ˈæktə] *n*. 1. 男演员 2. 行动者;参与者

actress ['æktris] *n.* 女演员

actual ['æktʃuəl] *adj.* 实际的，现实的，事实上的 ‖ ~ity [ˌæktʃuˈæliti] *n.*/~ly *adv.* 1. 实际上 2. 竟然 3. 当今；如今

actuary ['æktjuəri] *n.* (保险)精算师；保险(业务)计算员 ‖ **actuarial** *adj.*

actuate ['æktjueit, ˈæktʃueit] *vt.* 开动(机器等)；激励，驱使 ‖ **actu'ation** *n.*

acumen [əˈkjuːmen] *n.* 敏锐，聪明

acupuncture ['ækjupʌŋktʃə] *n.* 针刺；针刺疗法，针灸 ‖ ~ [ˌækjuˈpʌŋktʃə] *vt.* 对...施行针灸

acute [əˈkjuːt] *adj.* 1. 尖锐的，锐利的；【植】急尖的 2. 敏锐的 3. 剧烈的；严重的；【医】急性的 4. 高音的；尖声的 ‖ ~ly *adv.*/~ness *n.* ‖ ~ **angle** 锐角

ACV *abbr.* air-cushion vehicle 气垫船；气垫车

AD *abbr.* 〈拉〉*Anno Domini* 公元

ad [æd] *n.* 广告

ad. *abbr.* adverb

adage ['ædidʒ] *n.* 谚语；格言

adagio [əˈdɑːdʒiəu] *adj. & adv.* 【音】缓慢的(地)，宁静的(地)

Adam ['ædəm] *n.* 亚当(基督教《圣经》中所说"人类的始祖") ‖ ~'s **apple** 喉结

adamant ['ædəmənt] *n.* 坚硬的物质；【地】硬石(指金刚石、刚玉等) ‖ *adj.* 1. 坚硬的 2. 不动摇的，坚强不屈的

adapt [əˈdæpt] *vt.* 1. 使适应，使适合 2. 改制，改编；改作(for) —*vi.* 适应(to) ‖ ~er, ~or *n.* 1. 改编者 2. 接合器，接头 3. 转接器；附加器

adaptable [əˈdæptəbl] *adj.* 1. 能适应的，适应性强的 2. 可改制的，可作它用的；可改编的 ‖ a**dapta'bility** *n.*

adaptation [ˌædæpˈteiʃən] *n.* 1. 适应，适

合 2. 改制；改编，改写；改编本 3.【生理】适应性变化

adaptive [əˈdæptiv] *adj.* 适应(性)的

add [æd] *vt.* 1. 加，increase 加 —*vi.* 增添(to)；做加法 ‖ ~ **up** 把...加起来

addend ['ædend] *n.*【数】加数

addendum [əˈdendəm] ([复] addenda [əˈdendə]) *n.* 1. 补遗；附录 2. 附加物 3.【机】(齿轮的)齿顶(高)

adder ['ædə] *n.* 蝰蛇(一种小毒蛇)

addict [əˈdikt] *vt.* 1. 使沉溺(于)，使醉心(于)(to) 2. 使吸毒成瘾 ‖ ['ædikt] *n.* 有瘾的人 ‖ ~**ion** *n.* 1. 沉溺 2. 吸毒成瘾／~**ive** *adj.* 1. 使成瘾的 2. 上瘾的

Addis Ababa ['ædisˈæbəbə] 亚的斯亚贝巴[埃塞俄比亚首都]

addition [əˈdiʃən] *n.* 1. 加；【数】加法 2. 增加；增加的人(或物)；(建筑物等的)扩建部分 3.【律】(加在姓名后的)头衔，称号

additional [əˈdiʃənəl] *adj.* 附加的，追加的；另外的 ‖ ~**ly** *adv.*

additive ['æditiv] *adj.* 1. 添加的，附加的 2.【化】加成的 3.【数】加法的，加性的 —*n.* 添加物；添加剂

addle ['ædl] *adj.* 1. 变质腐坏的 2. (思想等)混乱的，糊涂的 —*vt.* 1. 使腐坏 2. 使混乱，使糊涂 —*vi.* 1. (蛋等)腐坏 2. 变混乱，变糊涂

address [əˈdres] *vt.* 1. 向...讲话；写信给 2. 讲(话等)；提出(抗议、请愿等)(to) 3. 在(信封、包裹等)上写姓名地址(函等) 4.【计】编(址)；寻(址) 5. 称呼 6. 向(女子)求爱 ‖ *n.* 1. 演说 2. 地址 ‖ ~ **book** 通讯录 3. 谈吐，风度 4. 灵巧，熟练 5. [~es] 求爱；殷勤 ‖ ~**ee** [ˌædreˈsiː] *n.* 收信人，收件人

／～er，～or *n*. 发音人；发信人；寄信人

adduce [ə'djuːs] *vt*. 引证；提出（理由等）

adduction [ə'dʌkʃən] *n*. 1. 引证，举例 2. 【生理】内收（作用）

Aden ['eidn] *n*. 亚丁〔也门南部港市〕

adenoids ['ædinɔidz] [复] *n*. 【解】腺样增殖体，增殖腺

adept ['ædept，ə'dept] *adj*. 熟练的，内行的（*at，in*）— *n*. 内行，能手 ‖ ～ly *adv*. ‖ ～ness *n*.

adequacy ['ædikwəsi] *n*. 1. 适合，恰当 2. 充分，足够

adequate ['ædikwit] *adj*. 1. 适当的；充分的，足够的 2. 可以胜任的 ‖ ～ly *adv*. ‖ ～ness *n*.

adhere [əd'hiə] *vi*. 1. 粘住，附着（*to*）2. 追随，依附（*to*）3. 坚持（*to*）

adherence [əd'hiərəns] *n*. 1. 信奉，依附 2. 坚持；固执

adherent [əd'hiərənt] *adj*. 粘着的；附着的 — *n*. 信徒，追随者；拥护者

adhesion [əd'hiʒən] *n*. 1. 粘着；附着 2. 【医】粘连 3. 【物】粘附力，附着力 3. 支持；依附；追随

adhesive [əd'hiːsiv] *adj*. 1. 粘着的 2. 带粘性的；涂有粘性物质的 — *n*. 粘合剂；胶水 ‖ ～ plaster 护创胶布，橡皮膏 ‖ ～ tape 胶布

ad hoc [æd'hɔk] *adj*. 特别的，专门的：an *ad hoc group* 专门小组

adieu [ə'djuː] *int*. 再见！— [复]adieus 或 adieux[ə'djuːz] *n*. 告别

adios [ɑːdi'ɔs] *int*. 再见！

adipose ['ædipəus] *adj*. 1. 动物脂肪的 2. 肥胖的

adj. *abbr*. adjective

adjacent [ə'dʒeisənt] *adj*. 1. 邻近的；毗连的 2. 紧接着的

adjectival [.ædʒek'taivəl] *adj*. 形容词的 ‖ ～ly *adv*.

adjective ['ædʒiktiv] *n*. 【语】形容词 — *adj*. (用作)形容词的 2. 从属的 3. 【律】程序的 ‖ ～ly *adv*.

adjoin [ə'dʒɔin] *vt. & vi*. 贴近，毗连

adjourn [ə'dʒəːn] *vt*. 使中止；休（会）— *vi*. 1. 休会 2.（口）换地方；（与会者）转移会址 ‖ ～ment *n*. 休会

adjudge [ə'dʒʌdʒ] *vt*. 1. 依法判决；裁决 2. 把 ... 判给 3. 认为 ‖ **adjudg(e)ment** *n*.

adjudicate [ə'dʒuːdikeit] *vt. & vi*. 判决，裁定 ‖ **adjudi'cation** *n*. ‖ **adjudicator** *n*.

adjunct ['ædʒʌŋkt] *n*. 1. 附属品，附属物（*to*）2. 助手，副手 3.【语】修饰成分 4. 【逻】偶有属性(指非本质属性) — *adj*. 附属的 ‖ ～ion[ə'dʒʌŋk]ʃən] *n*. 1. 添加，附加 2.【数】附益，附加

adjure [ə'dʒuə] *vt*. 恳求 2. 命令；嘱咐

adjust [ə'dʒʌst] *vt*. 1. 调整；调节；整顿 2. 校准；对准 3. 解决；调解 4.（保险业中）理算(保险索赔等)的金额 — *vi*. 1. 调整；校准 2. 适应于（*to*）‖ ～able *adj*. 可调整的；可校准的／～er，～or *n*. 1. 调整者；调停者 2. 调节器 ‖ ～ment *n*. 调整，调节

adjutant ['ædʒutənt] *n*. 1.【军】副官；人事行政参谋 2. 助手 — *adj*. 辅助的

ad-lib [æd'lib] [ad-libbed；ad-libbing] *vt. & vi*. 1. 即兴演出；即兴插入 2. 临时凑合 — *vi*. 当场作出；随手使用（口）随口说出 ‖ **ad-libber** *n*.

admass ['ædmæs] *n*. 1. 易受广告影响的社会大众 2.(旨在吸引社会大众的)大众广告

administer [əd'ministə] *vt*. 1. 管理，支配 2. 执行，施行，实施 3. 给予；投(药) 4. 操纵(物价等) 5. 主持 ... 的仪式

vi. 1. 管理(*upon*) 2. 给予帮助(*to*)

administration [ədˌminis'treiʃən] *n.* 1. 管理,经营;【律】遗产管理 2. 行政;行政机关;管理部门;[A-](总统制国家的)政府 3.(行政官员或机关的)任期期 4. 执行,施行;(药的)服法,用法;给予

administrative [əd'ministrətiv] *adj.* 行政的;管理的;政府的;后方勤务的 ‖ ~ly *adv.*

administrator [əd'ministreitə] *n.* 1. 管理人;【律】遗产管理人 2. 行政官员 3. 提供者 4. 代管教区的牧师

admirable ['ædmərəbl] *adj.* 1. 令人钦佩的,令人赞美的 2. 极妙的,极好的 ‖ **admirably** *adv.*

admiral ['ædmərəl] *n.* 1. 海军将军;海军上将 2. 舰队司令 3.〈英〉渔船队长;商船队长 4.【动】花蝶,彩蝶

admiralty ['ædmərəlti] *n.* 1. 海军上将的职位;[A-]英国海军部 3. 海事法;海事法庭

admiration [ˌædmə'reiʃən] *n.* 1. 钦佩,赞美羡慕 2. 引人赞美的人(或物)

admire [əd'maiə] *vt.* 1. 钦佩;赞美,羡慕 2.〈美口〉想要,喜欢 ‖ ~r *n.* 赞赏者;(女人的)爱慕者

admiring [əd'maiəriŋ] *adj.* 赞美的;羡慕的 ‖ ~ly *adv.*

admissible [əd'misibl] *adj.* 1. 可允许的,可采纳的;【律】(证据)容许提出的 2. 可进入的;有资格加入的 ‖ admissi'bility *n.*

admission [əd'miʃən] *n.* 1. 允许进入;No ~! 请勿入内! 2. 入场费;入场券 3. 承认

admit [əd'mit] (admitted;admitting) *vt.* 1. 让…进入;让…享有(*to*) 2. 接纳;招收 3. 容纳 4. 承认(事实、错误等) — *vi.* 1. 容许有(*of*) 2.(门等)通(向)

(*to*) 3. 承认(*to*)

admittance [əd'mitəns] *n.* 1. 进入;允许进入(尤指非公共场所) 2. 通道 3.【物】导纳

admittedly [əd'mitidli] *adv.* 公认地

admix [əd'miks] *vt. & vi.* 掺和;混合 ‖ ~ture [əd'mikstʃə] *n.* 1. 搀和;混合 2. 掺和剂;混合物

admonish [əd'mɔniʃ] *vt.* 1. 警告;告诫 2. 劝告,忠告 ‖ ~ment *n.*

admonition [ˌædmə'niʃən] *n.* 1. 警告;告诫;劝告 2. 温和的责备

admonitory [əd'mɔnitəri] *adj.* 警告的;轻责的;告诫的;劝告的

ado [ə'du:] *n.*([复] ados) *n.* 忙乱;费力,艰难;much ~ about nothing 无事忙;无事生非

adobe [ə'dəubi] *n.* 1. 砖坯 2. 制土砖的土 3. 土砖建筑物

adolescence [ˌædəu'lesns] **adolescency** [ˌædəu'lesni] *n.* 青春期;青春

adolescent [ˌædəu'lesnt] *adj.* 青春期的;青少年的 — *n.* 青少年

adopt [ə'dɔpt] *vt.* 1. 采用,采纳;采取(态度等) 2. 选定(道路、职业等) 3. 收养 4. 正式通过 ‖ ~ion *n.* / ~ive *adj.*

adorable [ə'dɔːrəbl] *adj.* 1. 值得崇拜的;值得敬慕的 2.〈口〉极可爱的 ‖ ~ness *n.* / adorably *adv.*

adoration [ˌædɔː'reiʃən] *n.* 崇拜;敬慕

adore [ə'dɔː] *vt.* 1. 崇拜(上帝);敬慕,2.〈口〉很喜欢 ‖ ~r *n.* 崇拜者;敬慕者

adorn [ə'dɔːn] *vt.* 装饰;装点;使生色 ‖ ~ment *n.* 装饰;装饰品

ADP *abbr.* automatic data processing 自动数据处理

adrenalin [ə'drenəlin] *n.* 肾上腺素

Adriatic [ˌeidri'ætik] *adj.* 亚得里亚海的;

the ~ (Sea) 亚得里亚海[欧洲南部]

adrift [ə'drɪft] *adj.* [常作表语] & *adv.* 1. 漂浮着(的);漂流着(的) 2.(喻)漂泊着(的)

adroit [ə'drɔɪt] *adj.* 灵巧的;机敏的(*in, at*) ‖ ~ly *adv.* / ~ness *n.*

adulate ['ædjuleɪt] *vt.* 谄媚,奉承 ‖ ¸adu'lation *n.*/adulator *n.* 谄媚者,拍马屁的人 /adulatory *adj.* 谄媚的,奉承的

adult ['ædʌlt] *adj.* 成年的;成年人的;成熟的 — *n.* 1. 成年人 2. 长成的动物(或植物)【生】成体;成虫 ‖ ~hood *n.* 成年

adulterate [ə'dʌltəreɪt] *vt.* 掺杂,掺假 — *adj.* 1. 掺假的 2. 通奸的 ‖ adulterant [ə'dʌltərənt] *adj.* & *n.* /a¸dulte'ration *n.* 掺杂,掺假 2. 劣等货;掺假货 / adulterator *n.* 掺假的人,造假货的人

adulterer [ə'dʌltərə] *n.* 奸夫

adulteress [ə'dʌltərɪs] *n.* 奸妇

adultery [ə'dʌltəri] *n.* 通奸(行为) ‖ adulterous *adj.*

adv. *abbr.* 1.adverb; adverbial 2. advertisement 3.advisory

advance [əd'vɑːns] *vt.* 1. 推进;促进 2. 提出(建议、看法、理论等) 3. 提前 4. 提高(价格等);提升 5. 预付;贷(款) — *vi.* 1. 前进;进展 2.(物价)上涨,在质量、地位等方面提高,提升 — *n.* 1. 前进,进展 2.(价格、工资、年龄等的)增长,提高 3. 预付;预付款;贷款 4.[~s]友好表示;挑逗,勾引 — *adj.* [只做定语] 1. 先行的;先头的 2. 出版(或发行)前的 3. 预先的 ‖ ~ment *n.*

advanced [əd'vɑːnst] *adj.* 1. 在前面的 2. 年迈的;后阶段的 3. 高级的;先进的

advantage [əd'vɑːntɪdʒ] *n.* 1. 有利条件;优点,优势;好处,利益 2.(网球中)

势分(打成平手后一方赢得的第一分) — *vt.* 使有利;有助于 ‖ *take* ~ *of* 利用;欺骗 / *to* ~ 有利地;有效地;突出优点地

advantageous [¸ædvən'teɪdʒəs] *adj.* 有利的;有助的 ‖ ~ly *adv.* / ~ness *n.*

advent ['ædvənt] *n.* 1.(事件、时期等的)出现,到来 2.[A-]【宗】基督降临(节)

adventitious [¸ædven'tɪʃəs] *adj.* 1. 外来的;偶然的 2.【生】偶生的,不定的 ‖ ~ly *adv.*/ ~ness *n.*

adventure [əd'ventʃə] *n.* 1. 冒险;冒险活动 2.(人性格上的)冒险性 3. 惊险活动;奇遇 4. 投机活动 ‖ ~r *n.* 冒险家,投机家 / ~some *adj.* 爱冒险的 / adventurism *n.* 冒险主义 / adventurist *n.* 冒险主义者

adventurous [əd'ventʃərəs] *adj.* 1. 喜欢冒险的 2. 冒险的,有危险性的 ‖ ~ly *adv.* / ~ness *n.*

adverb ['ædvɜːb] *n.* 【语】副词

adverbial [əd'vɜːbɪəl] *adj.* 副词的;状语的 — *n.* 【语】状语 ‖ ~ ly *adv.*/ ~ clause 状语从句

adversary ['ædvəsəri] *n.* 对手;敌手

adverse ['ædvɜːs] *adj.* 1.(在位置或方向上)逆的,相反的;敌对的 2. 不利的,有害的 3.【植】(叶子等)朝着茎的,对生的 ‖ ~ly *adv.* / ~ness *n.*

adversity [əd'vɜːsɪti] *n.* 1. 逆境,不幸 2. 苦难,灾难

advert [əd'vɜːt] *vi.* 提及,谈到(*to*)

advertise, advertize ['ædvətaɪz] *vt.* 1. 通知 2. 为…做广告;大肆宣扬 — *vi.* 做广告,登广告 ‖ ~ment [əd'vɜːtɪsmənt, ¸ædvə'taɪzmənt] *n.* 做广告,登广告;公告 / ~r *n.* 登广告的人

advertising, advertizing ['ædvətaɪzɪŋ] *n.* 1.[总称]广告,登广告 2. 广告业 — *adj.* 广告的;~ agency 广告商

advice [əd'vais] n. 1. 劝告,忠告;(医师、顾问等的)意见,指点 2. 通知;[常～s]报道,消息

advisable [əd'vaizəbl] adj. 可取的,适当的;贤明的 ‖ ad.visa'bility n. /～ness n. /advisably adv.

advise [əd'vaiz] vt. 1. 劝告;向 ... 提供意见 2. 建议 3. 通知,告知 — vi. 1. 提供意见,作顾问 ‖ ～dly adv. 深思熟虑地 /～ment n. 深思熟虑 2. 劝告;意见;提供劝告(或)意见 /～r, advisor n. 劝告者;顾问

advisory [əd'vaizəri] adj. 1. 劝告的,忠告的 2. 顾问的,咨询的 — n.(尤指气象方面的)报告

advocacy ['ædvəkəsi] n. 辩护;提倡

advocate ['ædvəkit] n. 1. 辩护者(法国、苏格兰等的)律师 2. 鼓吹者,拥护者,提倡者 — ['ædvəkeit] vt. 拥护;提倡

adz(e) [ædz] n. 扁斧,锛子 — vt. 用扁斧削

Aegean [i:'dʒi:ən] adj. 爱琴海的:the ～ (Sea)爱琴海[欧洲南部]

aegis ['i:dʒis] n. 庇护,保护;under the ～ of在...的庇护下

-aemia comb. form [构成名词]表示"血液":anaemia

aeon ['i:ən] n. 1. 极长的时期;永世,万古 2. [地]极长时期

aerate ['eiəreit] vt. 1. 使暴露于空气中;使通气 2. 充气于;(尤指用二氧化碳)使泡腾 3. 通过吸气供氧气给(血液) ‖ ae'ration n. /aerator n. 充气器

aerial ['eiəriəl] adj. 1. 空气的;大气的 2. 航空的 3. 高耸空中的,架空的 4. 生存在空气中的 5. 无形的,虚无的,空想中的 — n. 天线 ‖ ~ly adv.

aerie ['eiəri] n. 1. 猛禽巢穴(尤指鹰巢) 2.

猛禽(巢中)的雏 3. 高山上的房屋(或城堡)

aero- ['eiərəu] comb. form 表示"空气","气体";"飞机";"空中";"航空":aeroplane

aerobics [eiə'rəubiks] [复] n.[用作单或复](加强心肺等循环功能的)增强健身法

aerodrome ['eiərədrəum] n. 飞机场

aerodynamics [ˌeiərəudai'næmiks] [复] n.[用作单]空气动力学

aeronaut ['eiərənɔ:t] n. 飞机(或气球、飞船)驾驶员

aeronautic(al) [ˌeiərə'nɔ:tik(əl)] adj. 航空的;航空学的

aeronautics [ˌeiərə'nɔ:tiks] [复] n.[用作单]航空学;航空术

aeroplane ['eiərəplein] n.〈英〉飞机

aeroplankton [ˌeiərəu'plæŋktən] n. 气浮生物,空气浮游生物(如飞虫等)

aerosol ['eiərəsɔl] n.(气体中的烟、雾等)浮质,[化]气溶胶;喷雾剂

aerospace ['eiərəuspeis] n. 航空与航天空间(指地球大气层及其外面的空间)

Aesop ['i:sɔp] n. ‖ ～'s Fables[伊索寓言]

aesthete ['i:sθi:t] n.1. 审美家 2. 唯美主义者

aesthetic(al) [is'θetik(əl)] adj. 1. 美学的 2. 审美的 3. 美的;艺术的 ‖ aestheti- cally adv.

aesthetics [is'θetiks] [复] n.[用作单]美学

AEW abbr. airborne early warning 【军】空中预警

afar [ə'fɑ:] adv. 在远处;从远处;遥远地

affable ['æfəbl] adj. 1. 和蔼可亲的 2. 慈祥的,使人愉快的 ‖ affa'bility n. /af- fably adv.

affair [ə'feə] n. 1. 事,事情,事件 2.[～s]事务;态度 3. 恋爱事件;风流韵事;私

通 4.〈口〉东西,物

affect[1] [ə'fekt] *vt.* 1. 影响 2. 感动 3.(疾病)侵袭

affect[2] [ə'fekt] *vt.* 1. 假装 2. 喜爱,老是爱用(或穿)

affectation [,æfek'teiʃən] *n.* 假装;做作,装模作样(的言行)

affected [ə'fektid] *adj.* 假装的;做作的,不自然的 ‖ ~ly *adv.* / ~ness *n.*

affecting [ə'fektiŋ] *adj.* 令人感动的,动人的 ‖ ~ly *adv.*

affection[1] [ə'fekʃən] *n.* 1. 影响 2. 疾患,病

affection[2] [ə'fekʃən] *n.* 1. 慈爱,爱 2. [~s]爱慕,钟爱之情;感情

affectionate [ə'fekʃənit] *adj.* 充满深情的;出于柔情的 ‖ ~ly *adv.*

affiance [ə'faiəns] *n.* 1. 信赖,信用 2. 信约;婚约 —*vt.* [常用被动语态]使订婚,使定亲

affidavit [,æfi'deivit] *n.* [律]宣誓书

affiliate [ə'filieit] *vt.* 1. 接纳 . . . 为成员(或分支机构) 2. [常接 oneself 或用被动语态]使隶属(或附属) 3. 追溯. . .的来源;[律]判定(非婚生子女)的父亲 —*vi.* 发生联系,参加(with) — [ə'filiit] *n.* [美]成员;附属机构 ‖ af,fili'ation *n.*

affinity [ə'finiti] *n.* 1. 姻亲关系;密切关系 2. 吸引;有吸引力的人 3.(语言等)类似,近似 4. [化]亲合性,亲和力

affirm [ə'fəːm] *vt.* 1. 断言,肯定地说(*that*) 2. 批准 3. [律]证实;证实;确证 — *vi.* 1. 断言 2. (上级法院)确认并维持下级法院的判决 3. [律]不经宣誓而确认

affirmation [,æfəː'meiʃən] *n.* 1. 断言,肯定 2. 证实;批准 3. [律]不经宣誓而作

出的证词

affirmative [ə'fəːmətiv] *adj.* 肯定的 — *n.* 肯定词(如英语中的"yes");肯定语(如英语中的"that's so") 2. 赞成的一方 ‖ ~ly *adv.* ‖ ~ **action**(鼓励雇用少数民族成员及妇女等的)赞助性行动

affix [ə'fiks] *vt.* 1. 粘上,贴上 2. 签署;盖(印章) 3. 附加物,附件 2. [语]词缀 ‖ ~a-tion [,æfik'seiʃən] *n.* 附加 2. [语]加词缀法,附加法

afflict [ə'flikt] *vt.* 使苦恼,折磨 ‖ ~ion *n.* 1. 苦恼,折磨 2. 苦事

affluence ['æfluəns] *n.* 1. 流注,汇聚 2. 丰富,富裕

affluent ['æfluənt] *adj.* 丰富的,富饶的;富裕的 — *n.* 支流 ‖ ~ly *adv.*

afford [ə'fɔːd] *vt.* 1. [常接中 can, be able to 后]买得起;担负得起(费用、损失、后果等);抽得出(时间) 2. 提供,给予

afforest [æ'fɔrist] *vt.* 造林于 ‖ ~ation [æ,fɔris'teiʃən] *n.* 造林

affray [ə'frei] *n.* 吵架;打架;闹事(尤指在公共场所)

affront [ə'frʌnt] *vt.* 1. 当众侮辱;有意冒犯 2. 勇敢地面对 — *n.* 当众侮辱;有意冒犯

Afghan ['æfgæn] *adj.* 阿富汗的;阿富汗人的;阿富汗语的 — *n.* 1. 阿富汗人;阿富汗语 2. [a-](呈几何花纹的针织)阿富汗毛毯;阿富汗披肩;土库曼地毯

Afghanistan [æf'gænistæn] *n.* 阿富汗[西南亚国家]

afield [ə'fiːld] *adv.* 1. 在野外;在田里;下地 2. 在战场上;上战场 3. 远离着;远离着家(或家乡)

afire [ə'faiə] *adj.* [常作表语] & *adv.* 燃烧着(的)

aflame [ə'fleim] *adj.* [常作表语] & *adv.*
1. 燃烧着(的) 2. 发着火光(的);发亮
(的);发红(的)

afloat [ə'fləut] *adj.* [常作表语] & *adv.* 1.
浮着;漂浮不定 2. 在水上;在船上 3.
(甲板等)浸满着水 4. (经济上)应付自
如 5. 活动起来;在进行中 6. (消息、谣
言等)在流传中

aflutter [ə'flʌtə] *adj.* [常作表语] 1. (旗等)飘动着(的);(翅膀)鼓动着
(的)

afoot [ə'fut] *adj.* [常作表语] & *adv.* 1. 徒
步 2. 活动着;在进行中

afore [ə'fɔː] *adv.* & *prep.* 1. 在(…)前 2.
〈古〉以前,早先 ‖ a'fore,mentioned *adj.*
前面提到的 / a'foresaid *adj.* 上述的(人、
事) / a'forethought *adj.* [常放在所修饰的名
词之后] 故意的;预谋的

afoul [ə'faul] *adv.* 〈美〉冲撞着;纠缠着

Afr. *abbr.* 1. Africa 2. African

afraid [ə'freid] *adj.* [常作表语] 1. 怕,害
怕:He is ~ of snakes (the dark). 他怕蛇
(黑暗)。2.〈口〉恐怕:You are wrong,
I'm ~. 恐怕你错了。

afresh [ə'freʃ] *adv.* 重新

Africa ['æfrikə] *n.* 非洲

African ['æfrikən] *adj.* 非洲的;非洲人
的 — *n.* 非洲人

Afro ['æfrəu] ([复] Afros) *n.* & *adj.* 埃弗
罗发式的(的)(一种黑人非洲黑人自然
发式的呈圆形蓬松鬈发)

Afro- ['æfrəu] *comb. form* 表示"非洲";
"非洲的"

aft [ɑːft] *adv.* & *adj.* 在船尾;近船尾;向
船尾

after ['ɑːftə] *prep.* 1. (时间)在…以后;
(位置)在…后面 2. (顺序)跟在…
后面,次于:After you. 您先请。3. (一

个)接着(一个);(一
天)接着(一天):day ~ day 一天又一
天 4. 由于,因为:是管…;(但) 5. [与
某些动词连用] 追;探求:What are you
~? 你追求什么? / run ~ sb. 追踪某
人 6. [后接 ~ conj. 在…之后] — *adv.* 1. (一段时间) 以后,后来 2. 在
后面 — *adj.* 1. 以后的 2. 近后部的 (尤
指船的后部) ‖ '~ birth *n.* 胞衣(胎
盘及羊膜) / '~ burner *n.* (喷气发动机)
的加力燃烧室;(内燃机的)排气后燃器 / '~ care *n.* 病后(或产后)护理 / '~
ef.fect *n.* 后效;事后影响;后
果 / '~ glow *n.* 余辉,夕照 / '~ life *n.*
1. (迷信所说的)来世 2. 下半生 / '~
math *n.* 再生草 2. 灾祸 (尤指灾
祸) / '~ sales service (英) 售后服务 / '~
shave *adj.* & *n.* 剃须后搽的(润肤香
水) / '~ shock *n.* (地震的)余震 / '~
taste *n.* 回味,余味 / '~ thought *n.* 事后
的思考(或想法) / '~ wit *n.* 事后聪明
/ '~ word *n.* 跋;编后记

afternoon ['ɑːftə'nuːn] *n.* 1. 下午,午后 2.
后半期 ‖ ~s *adv.* 〈美〉每天下午;在任
何一个下午

afters ['ɑːftəz] [复] *n.* 〈英口〉正餐后的甜
食

afterward(s) ['ɑːftəwəd(z)] *adv.* 后来,以
后

Ag 【化】元素银(silver)的符号

again [ə'gein] *adv.* 1. 又一次,再一次 2.
倍:as much ~ as it …多一倍 3. [常
接在 then 等后] 而且,其次,还有 4. 另
一方面

against [ə'geinst] *prep.* 1. 逆;反对 2. 撞
击,碰着 3. 倚在;紧靠 4. 防备 5. 以
…为背景;与…对比,与…对照
6. 用…交换 7. 抵付

agape [ə'geip] *adj.* [常作表语] & *adv.* 1.
(惊奇、害怕得)张大着嘴,目瞪口呆 2.

洞开着,张开着

agaric ['ægərik] n.【植】伞菌

agate ['ægət] n. 玛瑙

agave [ə'geivi] n.【植】龙舌兰

age [eidʒ] n. 1. 年龄 2. 寿命 3. 成年 4. 老年 5. 时期,时代 6. [常~s] 〈口〉很长一段时间 — (ag(e)ing) vt. & vi. 1. (使)变老 2.(使)变陈;(使)成熟;【化】(使)老化 ‖ ~ group年龄组(指同一年龄或年龄相近的人形成的群体)/ ~-long adj. 长久的,久远的 / ~-old adj. 古老的;久远的

-age suf.[附在动词或名词后构成名词] 1. 表示"活动","动作": marriage a. 表示"身分","境遇","状态"等: bondage 3. 表示"费用": postage 4. 表示"集合": acreage

aged [eidʒd] adj. 1. ...岁的 2.(酒等)陈的 3. ['eidʒid]年老的: the ~ 老年人

ageism ['eidʒizəm] n. 对老年人(或某种人群的人们)的歧视 ‖ ageist adj. / n.

ageless ['eidʒlis] adj. 1. 长生不老的;永不显老的;永恒的 ‖ ~ly adv./~ness n.

agency ['eidʒənsi] n. 1. 力量;(能动)作用 2. 媒介;经办;代理;代理业务(或关系) 3. 代理行 4. 机构

agenda [ə'dʒendə] n. 1. 议事日程 2. 待议事项一览表

agent ['eidʒənt] n. 1.(发生作用或影响的)动因,力量 2. 代理商;代理人 3.【化】剂

agglomerate [ə'glɔməreit] vt. & vi. (使)成团(或团状);(使)结块;(使)聚结在一起 — adj. 成团的;结块的;聚结的 — n. 大团;大块;聚结物 ‖ ag.glome'ration n.

aggrandize [ə'grændaiz] vt. 1. 扩大...的权势;提高...的地位;增加...的财富 2. 夸大;吹捧 ‖ ~ment [ə'grændizmənt] n.

aggravate ['ægrəveit] vt. 1. 加重(病情、负担、罪行等),使恶化 2. 使激怒,使恼火 ‖ aggravating adj. / aggra'vation n.

aggregate ['ægrigit] adj. 聚集的;合计的;【植】聚生的 — n. 1. 合计 2. 聚集;集体;【地】集合体 3.【建】(混凝土的)集料,粒料;骨料 — ['ægrigeit] vt. & vi. 1.(使)聚集,总计 2. 总计 ‖ in the ~ 总共 ‖ aggre'gation n. 1. 聚集;聚集物,聚集体

aggression [ə'greʃən] n. 1. 侵略 2. 侵略行为;侵犯行为

aggressive [ə'gresiv] adj. 1. 侵略的 2. 爱寻衅的;(行为等)过分的,放肆的 3. 敢作敢为的,有进取心的 ‖ ~ly adv. / ~ness n.

aggressor [ə'gresə] n. 侵略者

aggrieve [ə'gri:v] vt. [常用被动语态态] 1. 使悲痛 2. 使委屈;侵害

aggro ['ægrəu] n.〈英俚〉(青少年)结帮闹事

aghast [ə'gɑ:st] adj. [常作表语] 吓呆的,惊呆的

agile ['ædʒail] adj. 敏捷的,灵活的 ‖ ~ly adv. / agility [ə'dʒiliti] n.

agitate ['ædʒiteit] vt. 1. 鼓动,煽动 2. 搅动;摇动(液体等) 3. 使不安,使焦虑 4. 热烈讨论;激到辩论(问题、计划等) — vi. 鼓动

agitated ['ædʒiteitid] adj. 1. 表现出不安(或焦虑)的 2. 颤抖的 3.(问题)被热烈讨论的;被激到辩论的 ‖ ~ly adv.

agitation [ˌædʒi'teiʃən] n. 1. 鼓动;煽动 2.(液体等的)搅动;摇动 3. 激动,不安,焦虑

agitator ['ædʒiteitə] n. 1. 鼓动者 2. 搅拌器

agleam [əˈgliːm] *adj.* [常作表语] & *adv.* 闪烁着微光的(地)

aglitter [əˈglitə] *adj.* [常作表语] & *adv.* 闪闪发光的(地)

aglow [əˈgləu] *adj.* [常作表语] & *adv.* 发亮;发红 2. 发热

agnostic [ægˈnɔstik] *n.* 不可知论者 — *adj.* 不可知论的

agnosticism [ægˈnɔstisizəm] *n.* 不可知论

ago [əˈgəu] *adv.* [常和一般过去时的动词连用]以前:two centuries — 两百年前

agog [əˈgɔg] *adj.* [常作表语] & *adv.* 1. 渴望着(的):be ~ for news 急切等待消息 2. 兴奋着(的)

agonize [ˈægənaiz] *vt.* 使极度痛苦,折磨 — *vi.* 1. 感到极度痛苦 2. 拼命挣扎 ‖ ~d *adj.* 感到(或表示)极度痛苦的 /agonizing *adj.* 使人极度痛苦的

agony [ˈægəni] *n.* 1. 极度痛苦 2. 痛苦的挣扎 3.(感情上)突然和强烈的爆发

agoraphobia [ˌægərəˈfəubiə] *n.* [心]广场恐怖

agrarian [əˈgrɛəriən] *adj.* 1. 耕地的;土地的;土地所有制的 2. 农民的;促进农民利益的 — *n.* 主张平均地权的人

agree [əˈgriː] *vi.* 1. 同意,赞同 2. 应允 3. 商定,约定 4.(性情等)投合;(意见等)一致;【语】(人称、数、性、动词时态等)呼应,一致 5.(气候、食物等)适合(*with*) — *vt.* 同意;认定(账目)正确无误

agreeable [əˈgriəbl] *adj.* 1. 惬意的,令人愉快的 2.(欣然)同意的 3. 一致的;符合的(*to*) ‖ ~ness *n.* /agreeably *adv.*

agreement [əˈgriːmənt] *n.* 1. 同意,一致;【语】呼应 2.(口头或书面)协定,协议

agricultural [ˌægriˈkʌltʃərəl] *adj.* 农业的

农艺的;农学的

agriculture [ˈægrikʌltʃə] *n.* 1. 农业;农艺 2. 农学

aground [əˈgraund] *adj.* [常作表语] & *adv.* 1. 在地上的(的) 2. 搁浅的(的)

ague [ˈeigiu] *n.* 疟疾;寒颤

ah [ɑː] [表示悲求、懊悔、蔑视、威胁、欢乐等]啊! ‖ — **reaction** [心]"啊哈"反应

a. h. *abbr.* ampere-hour 安培小时,安时

aha [ɑːˈhɑː] *int.* [表示得意、嘲弄、惊奇等]啊哈!

ahead [əˈhed] *adj.* [常作表语] & *adv.* 1. 在前 2. 向前 3. 提前 ‖ — *of time* (或 *schedule*)提前

ahoy [əˈhɔi] *int.* 喂! 啊嗬!(海员招呼船只或人的喊声)

aid [eid] *vt.* 援助,帮助 — *n.* 1. 援助,帮助;教护 2.【军】助手;助力,辅助物

aide [eid], **aide-de-camp** [ˌeiddə'kɔŋ] *n.* 副官;侍从武官;助手

AIDS [eidz] *abbr.* acquired immune deficiency syndrome 艾滋病,获得性免疫缺损综合征 ‖ — **virus** 艾滋病病毒

aikido [ai'kiːdəu] (日) *n.* 合气道

ail [eil] *vt.* 使受病痛;使苦恼 — *vi.* 有病,生病 ‖ — ing *adj.* 生病的,有病痛的;失调的(/~ ment *n.* 病痛;微恙;精神不安

aileron [ˈeilərɔn] *n.*(飞机的)副翼

aim [eim] *vi.* 1. 瞄准;对准(*at*) 2. 目的在于(*at*) — *vt.* 1. 把 ... 瞄准;把 ... 对准 2. 使计划;使目的在于(*at*) — *n.* 1. 瞄准 2. 目标;目的

aimless [ˈeimlis] *adj.* 无目标的;无目的的 ‖ ~ly *adv.* /~ness *n.*

ain't [eint] 1.〈口〉= am not 2.〈粗〉= is not; are not 3.〈粗〉= has not; have not

air [ɛə] *n.* 1. 空气;大气 2. 空中,天空 3.

微风 4. 歌曲;曲调 5. 外观,神态 6. [常～]做作的姿态,架子 — vt. 1. 晾(衣服、被褥等);烘干 2. 使(房间等)通气 3. 发表(意见,理论等);炫耀 4. (用无线电、电视)播送 5. [～oneself] 到户外呼吸新鲜空气 ‖ ～ bag 〖汽车碰撞时能自动充气使车上的人不致撞伤的)(保险)气袋/～ base 航空基地,空军基地 /~-borne adj. 1. 空气载的 2. 空中的;在飞行中的 3. 空气传播的 /～ brake n. 【机】气闸,风闸 2. (飞机的)减速板 /~-conditioned adj. 有空调的 /~ conditioner 空气调节器 /~ conditioning 空调 /~-cooled adj. 气冷的 /～ craft n. 航空器,飞机,飞艇 /～ craft carrier 航空母舰 /~-craft(s)man n. (英国)空军士兵 /~ craft(s)woman n. (英国)空军女兵 /~ cushion 气垫 /~ cushion(ed) adj. 气垫式的 /~-cushion(ed) vehicle 气垫船;气垫车 /~-drome n. 〖美〗飞机场 /~-drop vt. & n. 空投 /~ field n. 飞机场 /~-force 空军 /~ gun n. 气枪 /~ hostess 客机女服务员,空姐 /~-letter 航空便笺 /~ lane 航空路线 /~-line n. 1. 航线 2. 航空公司 /~ liner n. 大型客机,班机 /~ lock 1. 气闸(指阻挠管道中液体流动的气囊或气泡) 2. 【矿】风闸 /~ mail n. 航空邮件,航空邮政 vt. 航空邮寄 /~-man n. 1. 空军兵 2. 飞行员 /~ mattress 充气床垫 /~ miss 险些发生的撞机事故 /~ plane n. 〖美〗飞机 /~-pocket 气阱 /~-port n. 机场,航空站 /~-pump n. 气泵,抽气机 /~ raid 空袭 /~ ship n. 飞艇,飞船 /~-sick adj. 晕机的 /~ sickness n. 晕机 /~-strip n. 简易机场 /~ taxi 出租飞机,短程小客机 /~ terminal 航空终点站,机场大楼 /~ tight adj. 不漏气的,

气密的,密封的 2. (防守等)严密的;(论点等)无懈可击的 /~ traffic 空中交通 /~-wave n. 1. [~s]电波 2. 波道 /~-way n. 1. [~s]风波 2. 航线 3. [~s]航空公司 4. [~s]电波 /~-worthy adj. 飞行性能良好的,适航的

airless ['εəlis] adj. 1. 无空气的 2. 缺少新鲜空气的,闷气的 3. 无风的

airy ['εəri] adj. 1. 空气的 2. 空中的 3. 通风的 4. 空想的,不实际的;虚无飘渺的 5. 轻盈的 6. 快活的 7. 轻率的 8. 〈口〉做作的 ‖ airily adv. / airiness n. ‖ ~-fairy adj. 1. 轻盈如仙的 2. 空想的,不切实际的

aisle [ail] n. (教堂、戏院等)纵向通道,走道;侧廊,耳堂

ajar [ə'dʒɑː] adj. [常作表语] & adv. (门等)微开着(的);半开着(的)

akimbo [ə'kimbəu] adj. [常作表语] & adv. 双手叉着腰(的)

akin [ə'kin] adj. [常作表语] 1. 同族的,有血缘关系的 2. 同类的;相近似的 (to)

Al 【化】元素铝(aluminium)的符号

-al suf. 1. [构成形容词]表示"...的","具有...特性的":nautical, comical 2. [构成名词]表示"动作","过程":arrival

Alabama [.ælə'bæmə] n. 亚拉巴马[美国州名]

alabaster ['æləbɑːstə] n. 雪花石膏

à la carte [.ɑːlɑː'kɑːt] 〖法〗按菜单(点菜)

alacrity [ə'lækriti] n. 1. 乐意 2. 敏捷

à la mode [.ɑːlɑː'məud] 〖法〗 1. 按流行款式,按时尚 2. 上浇冰淇淋的

alarm [ə'lɑːm] n. 1. 警报 2. 报警器 3. 惊恐 — vi. 1. 向...报警,使警觉 2. 使惊骇 ‖ ~-ist n. 轻事重报者,危言耸听

者 ‖ ~ **clock** 闹钟

alas [ə'læs, ə'lɑːs] *int.* [表示悲痛、遗憾等] 哎咳呀!

Alaska [ə'læskə] *n.* 阿拉斯加[美国州名]

Albania [æl'beinjə] *n.* 阿尔巴尼亚[欧洲巴尔干半岛西南部国家]

albatross ['ælbətrɔs] *n.* 1.【动】信天翁 2. 沉重负担,无法摆脱的苦恼

albeit [ɔːl'biːit] *conj.* 尽管,虽然

albino [æl'biːnəu]([复] albinos) *n.* 1. 白化病患者 2.【植】白化体

ALBM *abbr.* air-launched ballistic missile 空中发射的弹道导弹

album ['ælbəm] *n.* 1. 相册;集邮簿;唱片套;一套唱片 2. 集子

albumen ['ælbjumin] *n.* 蛋白 = albumin

albumin ['ælbjumin] *n.*【生化】清蛋白,白蛋白

alchemy ['ælkimi] *n.* 炼金术,炼丹术 ‖ **alchemist** *n.* 炼金术士,炼丹术士

alcohol ['ælkəhɔl] *n.* 1.【酒】酒精,乙醇;醇 2. 酒精的;含酒精的 3. 嗜酒如命的;嗜酒者 / ~ ism *n.* 醺酒;酒精中毒

alcove ['ælkəuv] *n.* 1. 凹室;壁龛 2. (花园的)凉亭

alder ['ɔːldə] *n.*【植】桤木

alderman ['ɔːldəmən]([复] aldermen) *n.* 1. (美国和澳大利亚的)市政委员会委员 2. (英格兰和爱尔兰的)高级市政官

ale [eil] *n.* 麦芽酒

alert [ə'ləːt] *adj.* 1. 警惕的,警觉的 2. 活跃的;机灵的 — *n.* 1. 警报(期间)2. 警戒状态 3.【军】待命行动 — *vt.* 使警觉;使处于待命状态 ‖ ~ **ly** *adv.* / ~ **ness** *n.*

Alexandria [ælig'zɑːndriə] *n.* 亚历山大

[埃及北部港市]

alfalfa [æl'fælfə] *n.*【植】苜蓿

alfresco [æl'freskəu] *adv. & adj.* 在户外(的),在露天(的)

alga ['ælgə]([复] algae ['ældʒiː]) *n.* [常 algae]水藻,海藻

algebra ['ældʒibrə] *n.* 代数学 ‖ ~ **ic** [ældʒi'breiik] *adj.*

Algeria [æl'dʒiəriə] *n.* 阿尔及利亚[北非国家]

Algiers [æl'dʒiəz] *n.* 阿尔及尔[阿尔及利亚首都]

ALGOL, Algol ['ælgɔl] *n.*(计算机的)算法语言

alias ['eiliæs] *n.* 别名;化名 — *adv.* 别名叫;化名为

alibi ['ælibai] *n.* 1.【律】不在犯罪现场2.〈口〉借口,托词

alien ['eiljən] *adj.* 1. 外国的;外国人的 2. 异己的;不相容的 — *n.* 1. 外国人;外侨 2. 外人 3. 外星人

alienable ['eiljənəbl] *adj.* 可让渡的,可转让的 ‖ **aliena'bility** *n.* 可让渡性

alienate ['eiljəneit] *vt.* 1. 使疏远 2. 转让,让渡(财产等)‖ **alie'nation** *n.*

alienist ['eiljənist] *n.* (尤指在法庭上作证的)精神病学家,精神病医生

alight¹ [ə'lait] (alighted 或 alit[ə'lit]) *vi.* 1. (从马背上、车、飞机等处下来)下来(*from*)2. (鸟等)飞下,栖息;(飞机等)降落(on)3. 偶然发现;偶然碰见(*upon, on*)

alight² [ə'lait] *adj.* 常作表语点亮着的,烧着的

align [ə'lain] *vt.* 1. 使成一线,使成一行 2. 使组织;使密切协作 3. 校正;调准;校直 — *vi.* 1. 成一线,排成一行;被校正;被调准 2. 结盟(*with*)

alignment [ə'lainmənt] *n.* 1. 列队;成一直

线 2. 结盟;联合,组合 3.【测】定线;准
线 4. 调准,校正

alike [ə'laik] *adj.* [常作表语] 相同的,相
象的 — *adv.* 一样地;相似地

alimentary [͵æli'mentəri] *adj.* [关于]营养
的 ‖ ~ **canal** 消化道

alimony ['æliməni] *n.* 1.【律】(离婚后或
诉讼期间一方给另一方的)赡养费 2.
生活费,扶养费

alit [ə'lit] alight 的过去式和过去分词

alive [ə'laiv] *adj.* [常作表语] 1. 活着的,
在世的 2. 有活力的,有生气的 3. 热闹
的;充满者 ... 的(*with*) 4. 敏感的;意
识到的,注意到的(*to*) 5.【电】有电的,
通电的

alkali ['ælkəlai] ([复] alkali(e)s) *n.*【化】
碱,碱金属

alkaline ['ælkəlain] *adj.*【化】(强)碱的;含
碱的,碱性的 ‖ **alkalinity** [͵ælkə'liniti] *n.*
【化】碱度;碱性

all [ɔːl] *adj.* 1. 一切的,所有的;整个的,
全部的 2. 尽量的;极度的;with ~
speed 以最高的速度 3. 任何的;beyond
~ doubt 毫无疑问 — *adv.* 1. [加强语
气]完全,十分 2. [接牵甲比较级]更
加 3. (球赛等)双方得分相等,打平 —
pron. 一切;全部;大家,全体 ‖ ~ *at*
once 突然 / ~ *of a sudden* 突然 / ~ *in*
1.(口)筋疲力尽的 2. 一切包括在内
的 / ~ *right* 好,行 / ~ *there* 头脑清醒
的 / ~ *together* 一共 ‖ ~ '~-
im'portant *adj.* 至关重要的,首要
的 / '~-'in *adj.* 1.(主英)包括一切(费
用)的 2. 不遗余力的 / '~-in'clusive
adj. 包括一切的 / '~-'night *adj.* 通宵
(服务)的 / '~-'out *adj.* 全力的;没有
保留的 / '~-'purpose *adj.*适于各种用
途的 / '~-'round *adj.* 1. 全面的 2. 全
能的,多面的 3. 适于各种用途的;多

能的 / '~-'rounder *n.* 多面手;全能运
动员 / '~-'sided *adj.* 全面的 / '~-
'sidedly *adv.* 全面地 / '~-'sidedness *n.*
全面性 / '~-time *adj.* 1. 空前的 2. 全
部时间的;专职的 / '~-'weather *adj.*
适应各种气候的;全天候的

Allah ['ælə] *n.* 安拉,真主(伊斯兰教信奉
的神)

allay [ə'lei] *vt.* 减轻(痛苦、疼痛、忧虑等)

allegation [͵æli'geiʃən] *n.* 断言;指控

allege [ə'ledʒ] *vt.* 1. 断言,声称 2.(作为
理由、借口、辩解)提出

alleged [ə'ledʒd] *adj.* 被说成的,所谓的
‖ ~**ly** [ə'ledʒidli] *adv.*

allegiance [ə'liːdʒəns] *n.* 对国家、政府、事
业、个人等的忠诚,忠贞,拥戴

allegoric(al) [͵æli'gɔrik(əl)] *adj.* 1. 比喻
的;寓言的 ‖ ~**ally** *adv.* allegorically 地

allegory ['æligəri] *n.* 讽喻,比方;寓言

allegro [ə'leigrəu] [音] *adv. & adj.* 轻快地
(的) — ([复] allegros) *n.* 快板

alleluia [͵æli'luːjə] *n. & int.* 阿利路亚(犹
太教和基督教的欢呼语,意为“赞美
神”; = hallelujah)

allergy ['ælədʒi] *n.* 1.【医】变(态反)应性;
变态反应;过敏性 2. 反感,憎恶 ‖ **al-
lergic** [ə'ləːdʒik] *adj.* 1.【医】变应性的;
过敏性的 2.(口)对 ... 厌恶的(*to*)

alleviate [ə'liːvieit] *vt.* 减轻(痛苦等);缓
和 ‖ **alleviation** [ə͵liːvi'eiʃən] *n.*

alley ['æli] *n.* 胡同,小巷,(园中)小径

alliance [ə'laiəns] *n.* 1. 结盟;联盟,同盟
2. 联姻 3. 盟约 4.【植】群落属

allied ['ælaid, ə'laid] *adj.* 1. 结盟的 2.
[A-](一次大战中)协约国的(二次大
战中)同盟国的 3. 联姻的 4. 有关联的

alligator ['æligeitə] *n.* 1. 短吻鳄;鳄鱼 2.
短吻鳄皮 3. 水陆平底军车 4. 鳄口式

碎石机；鳄口式压轧机

alliterate [ə'litəreit] *vt.* & *vi.* 【语】(使)押头韵 ‖ **al͵lite'ration** *n.* 头韵；头韵法

allocate ['æləkeit] *vt.* 1. 分配，分派；配给 2. 把(物资、资金等)划归 ‖ **͵allo'cation** *n.* 1. 分配，分派；配给 2. 配给协作

allot [ə'lɔt] (allotted; allotting) *vt.* 1. (按份额)分配；配给(*to*) 2. (为特定用途而)拨出 3. 分派，指派 ‖ ~ment *n.*

allow [ə'lau] *vt.* 1. 允许，准许；听任，容许 2. 允给予 3. 承认 4. 酌加；酌减 — *vi.* 1. 考虑到，估及；体谅(*for*) 2. 容许，容得(*of*)

allowable [ə'lauəbl] *adj.* 容许的 ‖ **allow-ably** *adv.*

allowance [ə'lauəns] *n.* 1. 允许，准许；允给额；限额，定量 2. 津贴，补助 3. (体育比赛中)给对方的让步 4. 【商】折扣 5. 【机】(配合)容差 — *vt.* (对 ...) 定量供应(物品) 2. 发津贴给

alloy ['æli] *n.* 1. 合金 2. (金属的)成色，纯度 3. 与金(或银)熔合的贱金属；(喻)搀杂物 — [ə'lɔi] *vt.* 1. 合铸(金属)；用其他金属熔合(贵金属) 2. 减低(金属)的成色；减低(乐趣等) — *vi.* 合铸；(易于)熔合

allspice ['ɔːlspais] *n.* 1. 【植】多香果 2. (用作香料的)多香果粉

allude [ə'ljuːd] *vi.* 暗指；(间接)提到(*to*)

allure [ə'ljuə] *vt.* 1. 诱惑，引诱；吸引 — *n.* 诱惑力，魅力；吸引力 ‖ ~ment *n.* 诱惑；魅力；诱惑物 / **alluring** *adj.* 诱惑的，迷人的，引人向往的

allusion [ə'ljuːʒən] *n.* 1. 暗指；(间接)提到(*to*) 2. 典故

alluvial [ə'luːviəl] *adj.* 冲积的：~ soil 冲积土

alluvium [ə'luːviəm] *n.* 【地】冲积层

ally ['ælai] *n.* 1. 同盟国；同盟者 2. 伙伴；助手 3. 近亲动物(或植物) — [ə'lai, 'ælai] *vt.* 1. 使结盟；使联姻 2. 与 ... 关联 — *vi.* 结盟

Alma-Ata [͵ælmɑː'tɑː] *n.* 阿拉木图[哈萨克斯坦首都]

alma mater [͵ælmə'mɑːtə, ͵ælmə'meitə] (拉) 1. 母校 2. 〈美〉校歌

almanac ['ɔːlmənæk] *n.* 历书，历本；年历；年鉴

almighty [ɔːl'maiti] *adj.* 1. 全能的，万能的：the *Almighty* 上帝 2. 〈俚〉极度的 — *adv.* 〈俚〉极，非常

almond ['ɑːmənd] *n.* 杏仁；扁桃，巴旦杏

almost ['ɔːlməust, ͵ɔːl'məust] *adv.* 几乎，差不多

alms [ɑːmz] [单复] *n.* 施舍物，救济金 ‖ ~ house *n.* 救济院

aloe ['æləu] *n.* 【植】芦荟

aloft [ə'lɔft] *adv.* 1. 高高地；向上 2. 【海】在桅杆(或帆索)高处

alone [ə'ləun] *adv.* 1. 单独地；独自 2. [用在名词或代词后]只，仅仅 — *adj.* 单独的；独一无二的 ‖ *let* ~ 更不用说

along [ə'lɔŋ] *prep.* 沿着，顺着 — *adv.* 1. 向前 2. 一道，一起(*with*) 3. 〈美〉(时间)晚

alongside [ə'lɔŋ'said] *prep.* 在 ... 旁边，横靠；与 ... 并肩 — *adv.* 在旁边；并排

aloof [ə'luːf] *adv.* 离开；避开；远离 — *adj.* (常作表语) 1. 远离的；孤零的 2. 冷淡的 ‖ ~ness *n.*

aloud [ə'laud] *adv.* 出声地；大声地

alp [ælp] *n.* 1. 高山 2. (瑞士的)高山草场

alpaca [æl'pækə] *n.* 【动】(南美的)羊驼 2. 羊驼毛；羊驼毛织品

alpha ['ælfə] *n.* 1. 希腊语的第一个字母(A, α) 2. 最初，开始 3. 第一位的东西

【天】主星, α 星(星座中最亮的星) — *adj.*【化】第一位的, α 位的 ‖ ~ **decay**【物】α 衰变 / ~ **particle**【物】α 粒子 / ~ **ray**【物】α 射线

alphabet ['ælfəbit] *n.* 1. 字母表 2. 初步, 入门 ‖ ~**ize** ['ælfəbətaiz] *vi.* 1. 用字母标示 2. 依字母顺序排列

alphabetic(al) [,ælfə'betik(əl)] *adj.* 字母(表)的;依字母顺序的 ‖ **alphabetically** *adv.* 依字母顺序

alpine ['ælpain] *adj.* & *n.* 高山的(植物)

Alps [ælps] *n.* [the ~] 阿尔卑斯山脉(欧洲中南部)

already [ɔːl'redi] *adv.* 已经

alright [ɔːl'rait] *adv.* & *adj.* 行, 好

Alsace [æl'sæs] *n.* 阿尔萨斯[法国东北部一地区] ‖ **Alsatian** [æl'seiʃən] *adj.* 阿尔萨斯(人)的 — *n.* 德国牧羊狗

also ['ɔːlsəu] *adv.* 1. 也, 同样 2. 而且;(除此之外)还 — *conj.*〈口〉而且又 ‖ ~-**ran** *n.* (赛马中)落选的马;失败者;落选者

altar ['ɔːltə] *n.* 祭坛;圣坛

alter ['ɔːltə] *vt.* & *vi.* 改变, 改动 ‖ ,**alte'ration** *n.*

alterable ['ɔːltərəbl] *adj.* 可改变的, 可改动的 ‖ **altera'bility** *n.* 可变性 / **alterably** *adv.*

altercate ['ɔːltəkeit] *vi.* 争辩;争吵 ‖ ,**alter'cation** *n.*

alternate ['ɔːltəneit] *adj.* 1. 交替的, 轮流的 2. 供替换的;交替产生的 3.【植】互生的 — *n.* 1. 替补;代理人 2. 比较方案 — ['ɔːltəneit] *vt.* & *vi.* (使)交替, (使)轮流 ‖ ~**ly** *adv.* / ,**alter'nation** *n.* / **alternator** *n.* 交流发电

机 ‖ **alternating current**【电】交流电(略作 AC)

alternative [ɔːl'tɜːnətiv] *adj.* 1. 两者(或两者以上)挑一的 2. 选择的 — *n.* 1. 两者挑一;取舍 2. 替换物;供选择的东西 ‖ ~**ly** *adv.* — *adj.* 两者挑一的

although [ɔːl'ðəu] *conj.* 尽管, 虽然

altimeter ['æltimiːtə] *n.* 测高仪

altitude ['æltitjuːd] *n.* 1. 高;高度;海拔 2. [常~s] 高处, 高地 3. 高位;高级 4.【数】顶垂线, 高线

alto ['æltəu] 【音】([复] altos) *n.* 1. 女低音;男声最高音;中音部 2. 中音乐器;中音萨克号 — *adj.* 中音部的;高音的

altruism ['æltruːizəm] *n.* 利他主义 ‖ **altruist** *n.* 利他主义者

altruistic [,æltruː'istik] *adj.* 利他的;利他主义的 ‖ ~**ally** *adv.*

alum[1] ['æləm] *n.* 明矾

alum[2] [ə'lʌm] *n.*〈口〉校友, 毕业生(可指男女)

aluminium [,æljuː'miniəm] *n.*【化】铝

aluminum [ə'ljuːminəm] *n.*〈美〉= aluminium

alumna [ə'lʌmnə] ([复] alumnae [ə'lʌmniː])〈拉〉*n.* 女校友, 女毕业生

alumnus [ə'lʌmnəs] ([复] alumni [ə'lʌmnai])〈拉〉*n.* 男校友, 男毕业生

always ['ɔːlweiz] *adv.* 1. 永远, 始终 2. 一直, 总是, 老是

Am【化】元素镅(americium)的符号

am [强 æm;弱 əm] 见 **be**

AM *abbr.* 1.〈拉〉*ante meridiem* 午前, 上午 (= before noon) 2.〈拉〉*Artium Magister* 文科硕士 (= Master of Arts) 3. amplitude modulation【无】调幅

a.m. *abbr.*〈拉〉*ante meridiem* 午前,上午（= before noon）

amah ['ɑːmɑ] *n.*（某些东方国家的）保姆,女佣,阿妈

amain [ə'mein] *adv.*〈古〉〈诗〉**1.** 猛烈地 **2.** 急速 **3.** 突然

amalgam [ə'mælgəm] *n.* **1.**【冶】汞齐,汞合金 **2.** 混合物

amalgamate [ə'mælgəmeit] *vt. & vi.* **1.**【冶】(使)(金属)汞齐化 **2.** (使)混合;(使)合并 **3. a.malga**mation *n.* 汞齐化(作用);混合,合并;混合物

amanuensis [ə,mænju'ensis] ([复] amanu-enses [ə,mænju'ensiz]) *n.* **1.** 誊写员;听写员;文书助手 **2.** 〈谑〉秘书

amaryllis [,æmə'rilis] *n.*【植】孤挺花

amass [ə'mæs] *vt.* 积累,积聚

amateur ['æmətə] *n.* 业余爱好者;非专业人员 — *adj.* 业余的

amateurish ['æmətəriʃ] *adj.* 业余的;不熟练的 ‖ ~ly *adv.* / ~ness *n.*

amatory ['æmətəri] *adj.* (表示)爱情的;(表示)性爱的;恋人的

amaze [ə'meiz] *vt.* 使惊奇,使惊愕 ‖ ~dly *adv.* 惊奇地,愕然

amazement [ə'meizmənt] *n.* 惊奇,诧异

amazing [ə'meiziŋ] *adj.* 令人惊异的,惊人的 ‖ ~ly *adv.*

Amazon ['æməzən] *n.* **1.**【希神】亚马孙族女战士 **2.** [a-] 女战士 **3.** 魁梧而有男子气概的女子 **4.** [the ~] 亚马孙河[南美洲北部] **5.**【动】悍蚁 **6.** (中南美产的)绿色小鹦鹉

ambassador [æm'bæsədə] *n.* 大使;使节 ‖ ~ial [,æm,bæsə'dɔːriəl] *adj.* 大使的;大使一级的

amber ['æmbə] *n. & adj.* **1.** 琥珀(制的) **2.** 琥珀色(的)

ambergris ['æmbəgriːs] *n.* 龙涎香(抹香鲸肠道分泌物,可制香料)

ambi- *pref.* 表示"二","二者": *ambidext(e)rous*

ambiance ['æmbiəns] *n.* = ambience

ambidext(e)rous ['æmbi'dekstrəs] *adj.* **1.** 左右手都善用的 **2.** 灵巧的,非常熟练的 **3.** 两面讨好的 ‖ ~ly *adv.* / ~ness *n.*

ambience ['æmbiəns] *n.* 周围;环境;气氛

ambient ['æmbiənt] *adj.* 周围的;围绕的;环抱的 — *n.* 周围环境,氛围

ambiguity [,æmbi'gjuːiti] *n.* **1.** 意义不明确;可作多种解释 **2.** 模棱两可的话;意义不明确的话

ambiguous [æm'bigjuəs] *adj.* 模棱两可的;意义不明确的 ‖ ~ly *adv.* / ~ness *n.*

ambition [æm'biʃən] *n.* **1.** 志向,抱负 **2.** 野心 **3.** 追求的目标

ambitious [æm'biʃəs] *adj.* 有雄心的,野心勃勃的 ‖ ~ly *adv.*

ambivalent [æm'bivələnt] *adj.* 矛盾心理(或态度)矛盾的 ‖ **ambivalence** *n.*

amble ['æmbl] *vi.* **1.** (马)溜花蹄,缓行 **2.** 从容漫步 **3.** 骑马缓行 — *n.* **1.** 溜蹄 **2.** 轻松的步伐

ambrosia [æm'brəuziə] *n.* **1.**【希神】【罗神】仙果 **2.** 珍馐美味

ambulance ['æmbjuləns] *n.* 救护车;救护船;救护飞机

ambulatory ['æmbjulətəri] *adj.* **1.** 走动的;流动的:an ~ tribe 游牧部落 **2.** (病人,病人)能走动的,不需卧床的 **3.** 【律】可变更的 可撤消的:a ~ will 可变更遗嘱 ‖ **ambulatorily** *adv.*

ambush ['æmbuʃ] *n.* 伏击;设伏地点;伏兵 — *vt.* 把...埋伏好 **2.** 伏击 — *vi.* 埋伏下来

ameba [ə'mi:bə] n. = amoeba

ameliorate [ə'mi:liəreit] vt. 改善,改进,改良 — vi. 变好 ‖ a,melio'ration n.

amen [ɑ:'men, ei'men] int. (祈祷结束语) 阿们! (="So be it!" "诚心所愿!") ‖ say ~ to that 完全同意

amenable [ə'mi:nəbl] adj. 1. 有义务(或责任)的 2. 顺从的,服理的 3. 经得起检验的 ‖ a,mena'bility n. /amenably adv.

amend [ə'mend] vt. 1. 修正(议案等) 2. 改正;改进 — vi. 改过自新 ‖ ~able adj. 可修正的;可改进的

amendment [ə'mendmənt] n. 1. 修正,改善 2.(议案等的)修正案 3. 改良剂(指石灰、石膏等)

amends [ə'mendz] [复] n. 赔偿;赔罪: make ~ to sb. for sth. 因某事向某人赔罪(或赔偿)

amenity [ə'mi:niti, ə'meniti] n. 1. 舒适,宜人 2. [amenities]令人愉快的事物;生活福利设施;(社交)礼节

Amer. abbr. 1. America 2. American

Amerasian [æmə'reiʒən] adj. & n. (尤指父为美国人、母为亚洲人的)美亚混血儿(的)

America [ə'merikə] n. 1. 美洲 2. 美国

American [ə'merikən] adj. 美洲的;美国的 — n. 1. 美洲人;美国人 2. 美国式英语 ‖ ~ ism n. 1. 崇美主义 2. 美国式英语的特点 3. 美国(或美洲)文化的特点 ‖ ~ Indian (美洲)印第安人

amethyst ['æmiθist] n. [矿]紫晶,水晶,紫水晶 ‖ ~ ine [,æmi'θistain] adj. 紫晶(色)的

amiable ['eimiəbl] adj. 和蔼可亲的 ‖ ,ami'bility n. / ~ness n. /amiably adv.

amicable ['æmikəbl] adj. 友好的,温和的 ‖ ,amica'bility n. /amicably adv.

amid [ə'mid] prep. 在…之中

amidship(s) [ə'midʃip(s)] adv. 在船体中部

amidst [ə'midst] prep. = amid

amigo [æ'mi:gəu] n. ([复]amigos) n. 朋友

amino [ə'mi:nəu] adj. [化]氨基的 ‖ ~ acid 氨基酸,胺酸

amiss [ə'mis] adv. 错误地;出偏差;不恰当地 — adj. [常作表语]出差错的;有缺陷的;不恰当的

amity ['æmiti] n. 和好,和睦(尤指国与国之间)

AMM abbr. antimissile missile 反导弹导弹

Amman [ə'mɑ:n] n. 安曼[约旦首都]

ammeter ['æmitə] n. [电]安培计

ammo ['æməu] n. (口)军火,弹药

ammonia [ə'məuniə] n. [化]氨,阿摩尼亚,氨水

ammunition [,æmju'niʃən] n. 弹药,军火

amnesia [æm'ni:ziə] n. [医]记忆缺失,遗忘(症)

amnesty ['æmnesti] n. 大赦 — vt. 敕免

amoeba [ə'mi:bə] n. ([复]amoebae [ə'mi:bi:] 或 amoebas) n. 变形虫,阿米巴 ‖ amoebic adj.

amok [ə'mɔk] adv. = amuck

among [ə'mʌŋ] prep. 在…中间,在…之中[注意:between 一般指"在两者之中"; among 一般指"在三者(或三者以上)之中"]

amongst [ə'mʌŋst] prep. = among

amoral [ei'mɔrəl] adj. 不属于道德范畴的 ‖ ~ ity [,eimɔ'ræliti] n.

amorous ['æmərəs] adj. 1. 色情的 2. 多情的 3. 求爱的;表示爱情的 ‖ ~ ly adv. / ~ness n.

amorphous [ə'mɔ:fəs] adj. 1. 无定形的;非结晶的 2. 难以归类的;不规则的 ‖

~**ly** adv.

amortize [ə'mɔːtaiz, 'æmətaiz] vt. 1. 分期偿还（债务等）2.【经】摊销，摊还 ‖ a‚morti'zation n.

amount [ə'maunt] vi. 1. 合计，总共达（to）2. 等于，就是（to）— n. 1. 总数 2. 数量，总量 3. 总的意思；全部价值

amour [ə'muə] n. 1. 不正当男女关系；偷情；桃色事件 2. 性爱 3. 恋人（尤指情妇）

Amoy [ə'mɔi] n. 厦门。

amp. abbr. ampere(s)

ampere ['æmpeə] n.【电】安培 ‖ '~-hour n. 安培小时，安时 / '~‚meter n. 安培计

ampersand ['æmpəsænd] n. "&"号（表示"and"的符号）

amphetamine [æm'fetəmiːn] n. 安非他明，苯丙胺（中枢兴奋药）

amphibian [æm'fibiən] adj. 两栖的；水陆（或水空）两用的 — n. 1. 两栖动物（或植物）2. 水陆（两用）飞机（或车）

amphibious [æm'fibiəs] adj. 1. 两栖的；水陆（或水空）两用的 2. 具有双重性的 ‖ ~**ly** adv. / ~**ness** n.

amphitheatre, amphitheater ['æmfiθiətə] n. 1. 圆形剧场（或竞技场）；大会堂 2. 倾斜看台，梯形楼座 3. 圆形凹地 4.（供观看外科手术场的）梯形示教室

ample ['æmpl] adj. 1. 充裕的，足够的 2. 宽敞的 ‖ ~**ness** n. / **amply** adv.

amplification [‚æmplifi'keiʃən] n. 1. 扩大，放大；加强 2. 扩充；详述

amplifier ['æmplifaiə] n. 放大器；扩音机

amplify ['æmplifai] vt. 1. 放大；增强 2. 扩大；详述 — vi. 引伸，进一步阐述（on, upon）

amplitude ['æmplitjuːd] n. 1. 广大，广阔

2. 充足，丰富 3.【物】【电】振幅；【数】辐角

amp(o)ule ['æmpuːl] n.【医】安瓿

amputate ['æmpjuteit] vt. 1.【医】切断，截（肢）2. 砍掉；删除 ‖ ampu'tation n. 截肢；砍除 / amputator n. 施行截肢手术者 / amputee [‚æmpju'tiː] n. 截肢者

Amsterdam [‚æmstə'dæm] n. 阿姆斯特丹 [荷兰首都]

Amtrak ['æmtræk] n.〈美〉"美铁"，美国全国铁路客运公司

amuck [ə'mʌk] adv. 杀气腾腾地；疯狂地，狂暴地；run ~ 乱砍乱杀；肆无忌惮

amulet ['æmjulit] n. 护身符

Amur [ə'muə] n. 阿穆尔河（即黑龙江）

amuse [ə'mjuːz] vt. 1. 给 ... 娱乐（或消遣）2. 逗 ... 乐，逗

amusement [ə'mjuːzmənt] n. 1. 娱乐，消遣；取乐 2. 娱乐场所 ‖ ~ **arcade**（英）娱乐场 / ~ **park**（美）游乐场

amusing [ə'mjuːziŋ] adj. 1. 引起乐趣的，有趣的 2. 逗人发笑的人（或事物）‖ ~**ly** adv.

an [强 æn; 弱 ən, n] art. 见 a

-an suf. 1.［构成名词］表示"... 地方的人"；"精通 ... 的人"；"信奉 ... 的人"：American 2.；［构成形容词］表示"属于 ... 的"；"带有 ... 性质的"：European

anachronism [ə'nækrənizəm] n. 1. 时代错误（指与时代不合的错误）；年代误植 2. 与时代不合的人（或事物）‖ a‚nachro'nistic adj. 时代错误的；落伍过时的

anaconda [‚ænə'kɔndə] n. 森蚺（南美等地产的大蛇）；蟒蛇，蚺蛇

anaemia [ə'niːmiə] n. = anemia

anaemic [ə'niːmik] adj. = anemic

anaesthesia [‚ænis'θiːziə] n.【医】1. 感觉缺失，麻木 2. 麻醉（法）

anaesthetic [ˌænisˈθetik] *adj.* 麻木的;麻醉的 — *n.* 麻醉剂

anaesthetist [æˈniːsθitist] *n.* 麻醉师

anaesthetize [æˈniːsθitaiz] *vt.* 使麻醉;使麻木

anagram [ˈænəgræm] *n.* 1. (变换字母顺序而成另一词的)换音造词法,回文构词法 2. 变换字母顺序而成的词;换音词,回文词(如由 north 构成的 thorn, lived 构成的 devil)

anal [ˈeinəl] *adj.* 肛门的;【心】肛欲的

analgesic [ˌænælˈdʒiːsik] *adj.* 止痛的 — *n.* 止痛药

analog [ˈænələg] *n. & adj.* 〈美〉= analogue

analogue [ˈænələg] *n.* 1. 相似物;类似情况 2. 对等的人,对方人 3. 对应词 4.【生】同功异质体 — *n.* 1. 模拟计算机(或数据) 2.(电子手表等)模拟指针式的 3. 类似的 ‖ ~ computer 模拟计算机

analogy [əˈnælədʒi] *n.* 1. 类似,相似 2. 比拟;类推 ‖ analogous [əˈnæləgəs] *adj.*

analyse [ˈænəlaiz] *vt.* 分析;分解;解析 ‖ analysable *adj.* 可分析的;可分解的;可解析的 / ~ *r n.* 分析者

analysis [əˈnælisis] ([复] analyses [əˈnælisiːz]) *n.* 分析;分解;解析

analyst [ˈænəlist] *n.* 分析者;精神(或心理)分析学家;系统分析学家

analytic(al) [ˌænəˈlitik(əl)] *adj.* 分析的;解析的 ‖ analytically *adv.*

analyze [ˈænəlaiz] *vt.* = analyse

anarchy [ˈænəki] *n.* 无政府状态;混乱,无秩序 ‖ anarchic(al) æˈnɑːkik(əl) *adj.* 无政府主义的;混乱无序的 /anarchism *n.* 无政府主义 /anarchist *n.* 无政府主义者

anathema [əˈnæθəmə] *n.* 1.【宗】诅咒;革出教门 2. 咒骂,强烈的谴责;被诅咒的人(或物) 3. 十分讨厌的人(或物) ‖ ~ tize, ~ tise *vt. & vi.* 诅咒,强烈谴责

anatomic(al) [ˌænəˈtɒmik(əl)] *adj.* 解剖的;解剖学的;结构上的 ‖ anatomically *adv.*

anatomy [əˈnætəmi] *n.* 1. 解剖;剖析 2. 解剖学 3. 解剖学论著 4.(动植物)的结构 ‖ anatomist *n.* 解剖学家;剖析者 /anatomize, anatomise [əˈnætəmaiz] *vt.* 1. 解剖 2. 剖析

ANC *abbr.* African National Congress (南非政党)非洲人国民大会(简称非国大)

-ance *suf.* 表示"性质";"状况";"行动";"过程";"总量";"程度": perseverance, vigilance, attendance

ancestor [ˈænsestə] *n.* 1. 祖宗,祖先 2. 原型【生】原种 3.【律】被继承人

ancestral [ænˈsestrəl] *adj.* 祖先的;祖传的

ancestress [ˈænsestris] *n.* 女祖先;【律】女性被继承人

ancestry [ˈænsestri] *n.* 1.[总称]祖先,列祖 2. 家世,世系 3. 名门出身

anchor [ˈæŋkə] *n.* 1. 锚;锚状物 2.【军】(防线的)要害阵地 3. 固定桩;精神支柱,靠山 4.(俚)(汽车的)煞车 5. 新闻节目汇总主持人 — *vt.* 抛锚泊(船);把…固定[广播节目] — *vi.* 抛锚,固定 ‖ ~ gear【海】起锚装置/~ ground【海】锚地

anchorage [ˈæŋkəridʒ] *n.* 1. 抛锚停泊;锚地 2. 停泊税 3. 精神支柱;寄托

anchovy [ˈæntʃəvi] ([复] anchovy 或 anchovies) *n.*【鱼】鳀;long tailed ~ 凤尾鱼

ancient [ˈeinʃənt] *adj.* 1. 古代的;古老的;

老式的 2. 年高德劭的 一 *n.* 1. 古时的人 2. 老年人 3.［the ~s］古代民族；古人（尤指希腊、罗马时代的人）；古典作家；古典艺术家

ancillary [æn'siləri] *adj.* 辅助的；附属的 (*to*) 一 *n.* 〈英〉助手；附属物

-ancy *suf.* 表示"性质"、"状态"：buoyancy

and [强 ænd; 弱 ənd, əd] *conj.* 1.［表示并列或对称关系，用来连接词、短语或句子］和，与 2.［表示连续、反复］接连：for hours ~ hours 很久很久 3.［用来连接数词］加：Five ~ six is（或 are）eleven. 五加六是十一。 4. 那末：Come early ~ you will see him. 早些来，那末你就会见到他。 5.［位于句首，用来承上启下］于是；而且：And you may now say that things are all right. 因此你现在可以说一切都好了。 6.〈口〉［用来表示目的］：Go ~ tell him. 去告诉他。

andante [æn'dænti] [音] *adv. & adj.* 徐缓地(的)；用行板的 一 *n.* 行板；行板乐曲(或乐段)

Andes ['ændi:z] *n.*［the ~］安第斯山脉［南美洲西部］(= the ~ Mountains)

andiron ['ændaiən] *n.* (壁炉内的)柴架，炭架

anecdote ['ænikdəut] *n.* 轶事；趣闻；秘闻

anemia [ə'ni:miə] *n.* 贫血(症)

anemic [ə'ni:mik] *adj.* 贫血的

anemometer [,æni'mɔmitə] *n.* 风速表

anemone [ə'neməni] *n.* 1.［植］银莲花 2.［动］海葵

anesthesia [,ænis'θi:zjə] *n.* = anaesthesia

anesthetic [,ænis'θetik] *adj. & n.* = anaesthetic

anesthetist [æ'ni:sθətist] *n.* = anaesthetist

anesthetize [æ'ni:sθətaiz] *vt.* = anaesthetize

anew [ə'nju:] *adv.* 再；重新

angel ['eindʒəl] *n.* 1. 天使；神差 2. 守护神 3. 安琪儿，可爱的人 4.〈俚〉后台老板

angelic(al) [æn'dʒelik(əl)] *adj.* 天使的；天使般的 ‖ **angelically** *adv.*

anger ['æŋgə] *n.* 怒，愤怒 一 *vt.* 使发怒，激怒 一 *vi.* 发怒

angina [æn'dʒainə] *n.*［医］咽峡炎，咽痛；绞痛；心绞痛 ‖ **~ pectoris** ['pektəris] 心绞痛

angle¹ ['æŋgl] *n.* 1. 角；角度 2.〈喻〉角度，方面 3.〈美口〉诡计，手段；自私的动机 一 *vt.* 1. 使转一角度：~ a camera (摄影时)对角度 2. 从某一角度报道(新闻等)；使(报道等)带上色彩 一 *vi.* 转变角度 ‖ ~ **iron** 角铁

angle² ['æŋgl] *n.* 1. 钓鱼 2.(用不正当手段)攫取；追逐 (*for*) ‖ 一 *r n.* 1. 钓鱼者；追逐 ... 的人 (*for*) 2.［鱼］鮟鱇 / **angling** *n.* 钓鱼(术)

angled ['æŋgld] *adj.* 有角的；成角度的

angleworm ['æŋglwɜ:m] *n.* 蚯蚓

Anglican ['æŋglikən] *adj.* 1. 英国国教的，英国圣公会的 2.〈美〉英国圣公会的 一 *n.* 英国圣公会教徒

Anglo- *comb. form* 表示"英国(的)"：Anglo-American

Anglo-American ['æŋgləu ə'merikən] *adj.* 1. 英美的 2. 英裔美国人的 一 *n.* 英裔美国人

Anglo-Saxon ['æŋgləu'sæksən] *n.* 1. 盎格鲁撒克逊人 2. 古英语 3. 英国人(尤指祖籍是盎格鲁撒克逊族的英国人) 4. 平易的英语 一 *adj.* 盎格鲁撒克逊的

Angola [æŋ'gəulə] *n.* 1. 安哥拉［非洲西南部国家］2.［a-］= angora

angora [æŋ'gɔ:rə] *n.* 1. 安哥拉山羊毛(或

兔毛）**2.** 安哥拉山羊毛（或兔毛）纱
（或织物）‖ **Angora goat** 安哥拉山羊 /
Angora rabbit 安哥拉兔

angry ['æŋgri] *adj.* **1.** 发怒的，愤怒的 **2.**
（风雨等）狂暴的 **3.**（患处）肿痛发炎的
‖ **angrily** *adv.*

anguish ['æŋgwiʃ] *n.* 极度的痛苦；苦恼
— *vt. & vi.*（使）感到极度痛苦；（使）
苦恼 ‖ ~ **ed** *adj.*

angular ['æŋgjulə] *adj.* **1.** 有角的；角形的；
尖的 **2.** 用角度量的 **3.** 骨瘦如柴的 **4.**
不灵活的；生硬的 ‖ ~**ity** [ˌæŋgju'læriti]
n. **1.** 成角度；棱角 **2.**（样子、衣着等）
的难看；生硬 ‖ ~ **ly** *adv.*

aniline ['ænili(ː)n] *n.* 【化】苯胺

animadvert [ˌænimæd'vəːt] *vi.* 批评，谴
责；责备 ‖ **animadversion** *n.*

animal ['æniməl] *n.* **1.** 动物；兽；牲畜 **2.**
畜生般的人 — *adj.* 动物的；野兽的；
肉体的

animate ['ænimeit] *vt.* **1.** 使有生命 **2.** 使
活泼，鼓舞生气 **3.** 激励 — ['ænimit]
adj. **1.** 有生命的 **2.** 有生气的，生气勃
勃的

animated ['ænimeitid] *adj.* **1.** 栩栩如生的
2. 生气勃勃的；活跃的 ‖ ~ **ly** *adv.* ‖
~ **cartoon.** ~ **drawing** 动画片，卡通

animation [ˌæni'meiʃən] *n.* **1.** 生气；活跃；
兴奋；激励 **2.** 动画片制作 **3.** 动画影片

animosity [ˌæni'mɔsiti] *n.* 仇恨，憎恶，敌
意

animus ['æniməs] *n.* **1.** 意向 **2.** 敌意，恶
意

anise ['ænis] *n.* 【植】**1.** 茴芹 **2.** 洋茴香
（茴芹种子）

Ankara ['æŋkərə] *n.* 安卡拉（土耳其首
都）

ankle ['æŋkl] *n.* 踝；踝关节 ‖ ~ **bone** *n.*

踝骨

anklet ['æŋklit] *n.* **1.** 脚镯，踝环 **2.** 脚镣
3.（妇女和儿童穿的）踝部有扣带的鞋
4. 略高于踝的短袜

annals ['ænlz] *n.* **1.** 编年史 **2.** 历史记载
3.（学会或学科等的）年刊

anneal [ə'niːl] *vt.* **1.**【冶】使退火 **2.**〈喻〉锻
练（意志等）**3.**【生化】使（酸碱）退火

annex [ə'neks] *vt.* **1.** 附加，添加；附带 **2.**
并吞，兼并（领土等）— ['æneks] *n.*
附加物；附件；附录 **2.**【建】附属建筑
物，边房

annexation [ˌænek'seiʃən] *n.* **1.** 附加；并
吞 **2.** 附加物；并吞物（尤指领土）

annihilate [ə'naiəleit] *vt.* **1.** 歼灭，消灭 **2.**
【物】使湮灭，使湮没 ‖ **annihilator** *n.*
1. 歼灭者 **2.**【数】零化子

annihilation [əˌnaiə'leiʃən] *n.* **1.** 歼灭，消
灭 **2.**【物】湮灭，湮没

anniversary [ˌæni'vəːsəri] *n.* **1.** 周年纪念
日；周年纪念 **2.** 结婚周年（日）

Anno Domini [ˈænəu'dɔminai]〈拉〉公元
（略作 AD）—〈口〉【用作名词】老年

annotate ['ænəuteit] *vt.* 给 … 作注解（或
评注）‖ **annotator** *n.*

annotation [ˌænəu'teiʃən] *n.* 注解，注释

announce [ə'nauns] *vt.* **1.** 宣布，宣告；发
表 **2.** 报告 … 的，来到 **3.** 预告 **4.** 当
（节目、比赛等）的报幕员（或播音员
等）— *vi.* **1.** 当报幕员（或播音员等）
2. 宣布参加竞选（*for*）（在竞选中）宣
布支持某人（*for*）‖ ~ **ment** *n.* 宣布，
宣告；通告，布告 ‖ ~ **r** *n.* **1.** 宣布者；
告示者 **2.**（电台）播音员；（戏剧等的）报
幕员；（比赛等的）讲解员

annoy [ə'nɔi] *vt.* 使烦恼；使生气；打搅

annoyance [ə'nɔiəns] *n.* **1.** 烦恼，烦扰 **2.**
烦恼的事情

annoying [ə'nɔiiŋ] *adj.* 讨厌的, 恼人的 ‖ ~ly *adv.*

annual ['ænjuəl] *adj.* **1.** 每年的, 年度的 **2.** 年生的; 季生的 一 *n.* **1.** 年报; 年刊; 年鉴 **2.** 年生(或季生)的植物(或其他生物) ‖ ~ly *adv.* ‖ ~ ring【植】年轮

annuity [ə'njuiti] *n.* **1.** 年金; 年金享受权 **2.** (为养老等进行的)年金保险; 年金保险投资

annul [ə'nʌl] (annulled; annulling) *vt.* 废除, 取消(法令、合同等), 宣告...无效 ‖ ~ment *n.*

annunciate [ə'nʌnʃieit] *vt.* 宣告, 宣布; 通报

annunciation [ə,nʌnsi'eiʃən] *n.* **1.** 宣告, 宣布; 通告, 布告 **2.** [the A-]【宗】(《圣经·新约》中的)天使传报; 圣母领报节(3月25日)

anode ['ænəud] *n.*【电】阳极

anodyne ['ænəudain] *n.* **1.** 止痛药 **2.** 起安慰作用的事物

anoint [ə'nɔint] *vt.* **1.** 涂油于(尤指一种宗教仪式) **2.** 用油擦; 用油涂

anomalous [ə'nɔmələs] *adj.* 不规则的; 异常的; 破格的 ‖ ~ly *adv.* / ~ness *n.*

anomaly [ə'nɔməli] *n.* **1.** 破格, 不按常规; 异常; 反常 **2.** 畸形物 **3.**【天】近点角; 近点距离

anonymity [,ænə'nimiti] *n.* 匿名, 无名; 作者不明

anonymous [ə'nɔniməs] *adj.* 匿名的, 无名的, 不知名的 ‖ ~ly *adv.* / ~ness *n.*

another [ə'nʌðə] *adj.* **1.** 再一, 另一: Have ~ try. 再试一次。 **2.** 别的, 不同的: That's quite ~ matter. 那完全是另一回事。 **3.** 类似的: ~ Lei Feng 又一个雷锋式人物 — *pron.* 另一个; 类似的一

个: risk one's life for ~ 舍己为人

anovulant [æ'nɔvjulənt] *n.* 抑制排卵药 — *adj.* 抑制排卵(药)的

answer ['ɑːnsə] *n.* **1.** 回答, 答复; 应答 **2.** 答案 **3.** 答辩; 抗辩 — *vt.* **1.** 回答, 答复; 应答 **2.** 以...作答: She ~ed that... 她回答说...答辩 **3.** 响应(号召) **4.** 适应, 适合; 与...相符, 符合 **5.** 答辩 — *vi.* **1.** 回答 **2.** 负责, 保证: ~ for sb.'s safety 对某人的安全负责 **3.** 成功, 奏效: Our experiment has ~ed. 我们的实验成功了。 **4.** 适应; 符合: ~ to a description 与描述相符

answerable ['ɑːnsərəbl] *adj.* **1.** 可答复的; 可反斥的 **2.** 应负责任的

ant [ænt] *n.* 蚁 ‖ ~-eater *n.* 食蚁动物 / ~-hill *n.* 蚁冢; 拥挤奔忙的一群(人); 拥挤的住处

-ant *suf.* **1.** [构成形容词] 表示"...的的": defiant *n.* **2.** [构成名词] 表示"...者": accountant

antagonism [æn'tægənizəm] *n.* 对抗; 对抗性; 对抗作用

antagonist [æn'tægənist] *n.* **1.** 对抗者, 对手, 敌手 **2.**【解】对抗肌; 对合牙 **3.**【生化】拮抗物;【药】拮抗药

antagonistic(al) [æn,tægə'nistik(əl)] *adj.* 对抗(性)的; 敌对(性)的; 有反作用的 ‖ antagonistically *adv.*

antagonize, antagonise [æn'tægənaiz] *vt.* **1.** 对...起反作用; 中和; 抵消 **2.** (无意识地)引起...的对抗, 使起...的怨 **3.** (美)对抗, 反抗 — *vi.* 引起反抗(或反感等); 招怨

antarctic [ænt'ɑːktik] *adj.* 南极的: the *Antarctic* Circle 南极圈 / the *Anatarctic* Continent 南极洲 — *n.* 南极区; 南极圈

Antarctica [æn'tɑːktikə] *n.* 南极洲

ante- *pref.* 表示"前","在前": antecedent, anteroom

antecedent [ˌæntiˈsiːdənt] *adj.* 1. 先行的,先时的；先前的 2.【地】先成的 2.【逻】前件的 — *n.* 1. 前例,前事 2.【语】先行词；【数】前项 3.【逻】前件 3. [~s]经历,履历；学历；祖先 ‖ ~**ly** *adv.*

antechamber [ˈæntiˌtʃeimbə] *n.* 前厅；候见室

antedate [ˈæntiˈdeit] *vi.* 1. 在(信、文件等)上写上比实际书写日期早的日期 2. 把(事件)发生的日期说成比实际早 3. 先于,前于

antediluvian [ˌæntidiˈluːvjən] *adj.* (《圣经》所载的)大洪水以前的

antelope [ˈæntiləup] *n.* [复] antelope(s) 1. 羚羊 2. 羚羊皮

ante meridiem [ˈænti məˈridiəm] [拉] 午前,上午 (= before noon) (略作 AM 或 a.m.)

antenna [ænˈtenə] *n.* [复] antennae [ænˈteniː] 或 antennas 1.【生】触角,触须 2.【无】天线(英国一般用 aerial)

antennule [ænˈtenjuːl] *n.*【生】小触角

anterior [ænˈtiəriə] *adj.* 1. (位于)前的,前面的；头部(附近)的 2. 早前的,先前的

anteroom [ˈæntirum] *n.* 1. 前厅,候见室 2.(英)军官餐厅中的休息室

anthem [ˈænθəm] *n.* 1.【宗】赞美诗；圣歌 2. 颂歌,赞歌 3. 国歌 4. 校歌

anther [ˈænθə] *n.* 花药(花的带花粉部分) ‖ ~**al** *adj.*

anthology [ænˈθɔlədʒi] *n.* (诗、文、曲、画等的)选集 ‖ **anthologist** *n.* 选集的编者

anthracite [ˈænθrəsait] *n.* 无烟煤

anthrax [ˈænθræks] [复] anthraces [ˈænθrəsiːz] *n.*【医】炭疽(病)

anthropoid [ˈænθrəpɔid] *adj.* 1.(猿等)似人的,类人的 2. 似猿的 — *n.* 类人猿

anthropology [ˌænθrəˈpɔlədʒi] *n.* 人类学 ‖ **anthropologic(al)** [ˌænθrəpəˈlɔdʒik(əl)] *adj.* / **anthropologist** *n.* 人类学者

anti- *pref.* 表示"反","抗","阻","排斥": antiaircraft

antiaircraft [ˈæntiˈɛəkrɑːft] *adj.* 防空的 — *n.* 防空兵器

antibiotic [ˈæntibaiˈɔtik] *n.*【微】抗菌素,抗生素 — *adj.* 抗菌的,抗生的,‖ ~**ally** *adv.*

antibody [ˈæntiˌbɔdi] *n.*【生】抗体

antic [ˈæntik] *n.* 1.[常~s]滑稽动作(或姿态) 2.(古)丑角,小丑 — *adj.* 1.(古)古怪的,丑角般的 2. 嬉戏的；狂欢的 —(anticked; anticking) *vi.* 做滑稽动作

anticipate [ænˈtisipeit] *vt.* 1. 预期,期望 2. 抢 … 之先；占 … 之先 3. 行动在(请求、吩咐等)之前 4. 提前使用(工资等) 5. 使提前发生 ‖ **anticipator** *n.* 1. 期望者 2. 抢先者；占先者

anticipation [ænˌtisiˈpeiʃən] *n.* 预期,期望,预料 2. 预知,预觉

anticlimax [ˈæntiˈklaimæks] *n.* 1.【语】突降法 2.(在重要性等方面的)突降，由盛而衰；虎头蛇尾

anticonvulsant [ˈæntikənˈvʌlsənt] *adj.* & *n.* 抗惊厥的(药物),抗痉挛的(药物)

anticyclone [ˈæntiˈsaikləun] *n.*【气】反气旋；高(气)压

antidote [ˈæntidəut] *n.* 1. 解毒药 (for, against, to) 2. 矫正方法；对策 ‖ **antidotal** *adj.* 解毒的,有解毒功效的

antiestablishment [ˌæntiisˈtæblɪʃmənt] *adj.* 反正统(派)的；反现存社会体制(或现有权力结构)的 — *n.* 反正统派；反现

存社会体制(或现有权力结构)集团

antifreeze ['ænti,fri:z] *n*. 防冻剂,防冻液,抗凝剂(用于内燃机和散热器中)

Antigua and Barbuda [æn'ti:gwə ənd bɑ:'buːdə]安提瓜和巴布达[拉丁美洲岛国]

antihistamine [,ænti'histəmiːn] *n*. 抗组(织)胺药

antimagnetic [,æntimæg'netik] *adj*.(手表等)防磁的

antimatter ['ænti,mætə] *n*.【核】反物质

antimissile ['ænti'misail] *adj*. 反导弹的 — *n*. 反导弹

antimony ['æntiməni] *n*.【化】锑

antipathy [æn'tipəθi] *n*. 1. 不相容 2. 反感,厌恶 3. 被人厌恶的事物

antipollution [,æntipə'luːʃən] *adj*. 防止(或减轻)污染的

antipoverty [,ænti'pɔvəti] *adj*. 反贫困的

antiquary ['æntikwəri] *n*. 文物收藏家;文物工作者

antiquate ['æntikwit] *vt*. 1. 废弃;使变得过时 2. 使具有古旧形式 ‖ ～d *adj*. 陈旧的;老式的;过时的

antique [æn'tiːk] *adj*. 1. 古时的;自古就有的 2. 古希腊的;古罗马的 3. 古风的,古式的 — *n*. 1. 古器,古董;古玩 2. [the ～]古式(尤指古希腊、古罗马的雕塑、建筑等) 3.【印】粗体,拉丁正体 ‖ ～ly *adv*. / ～ness *n*.

antiquity [æn'tikwiti] *n*. 1. 古代(尤指中世纪前)古 2. 古人们 3. [antiquities]古迹;古物;古代的风俗习惯

antirejection [,æntiri'dʒekʃən] *adj*.(尤指移植外科中)抗(免疫)排斥的

antiseptic [,ænti'septik] *adj*. 1. 防腐的,用防腐剂的 2. 不受传染的 3.(房间等)异常整洁的 4. 冷静的;客观的,不

掺杂个人情感的 — *n*. 防腐剂;抗菌剂

antismog [,ænti'smɔg] *adj*. 防止(或消除)烟雾(污染)的

antisocial [,ænti'səuʃəl] *adj*. 1. 厌恶社交的,孤僻的 2. 反对社会组织的,反社会的

antistatic [,ænti'stætik] *adj*. 抗静电的 — *n*. 抗静电剂

antithesis [æn'tiθisis] ([复] antitheses [æn'tiθisiːz]) *n*. 1.(修辞学中的)对偶(例如 You are going; I am staying.) 2. 对偶结构的后项,对语中的后半部分 3. 对照;对立;对立面 ‖ **antithetic**(al) [,ænti'θetik(əl)] *adj*.

antitoxic [,ænti'tɔksik] *adj*. 抗毒素的,抗毒的

antitoxin [,ænti'tɔksin] *n*.【生】抗毒素

antler ['æntlə] *n*. 鹿角

antonym ['æntənim] *n*. 反义词

anus ['einəs] *n*. ([复] anus(es)) *n*.【解】肛门

anvil ['ænvil] *n*. 1. 铁砧 2.【解】砧骨

anxiety [æg'zaiəti] *n*. 1. 忧虑,担心 2. 忧虑的事 3. 渴望,热望

anxious ['æŋkʃəs] *adj*. 1. 忧虑的,担心的,焦急的 2. 令人忧虑的;在焦急中度过的 3. 渴望的,急要的 ‖ ～ly *adv*. / ～ness *n*.

any ['eni] *adj*. 1. [常用于疑问句、否定句、条件从句中或与含有否定意义的词连用]什么;一些: Any suggestions? 有什么建议吗? 2. 任何的;(三个或三个以上的人或物中)任何一个: You may take ～ one of these. 这些当中你可随便拿一个。[试比较: You may take *either* (one) of the two. 这两者之中你可以随便拿一个。— *pron*. [无论]哪一个;(无论)那些;一个;一些: Do(es) ～ of you know his address? 你们中间有谁知道他的地址吗? — *adv*. [常与比较级

连用)稍,丝毫: Is he ~ *better* today? 他
(的健康状况)今天好些吗?

anybody ['eni,bɔdi] *pron.* 无论什么人,任
何人 — *n.* 重要人物

anyhow ['enihau] *adv.* 1. 不管怎样,无论
如何 2. 不论用何种方法 3. 随随便便,
马马虎虎

anymore ['eni'mɔː] *adv.* [一般只用于否定
句中,或与含有否定意义的词连用]而
今再也: He rarely comes here ~. 现在他
难得来这儿。

anyone ['eniwʌn] *pron.* = anybody

anyplace ['enipleis] *adv.* 在任何地方,无
论那里

anything ['eniθiŋ] *pron.* 无论什么东西(或
事情);任何事(物)

anyway ['eniwei] *adv.* = anyhow

anywhere ['eniwɛə] *adv.* 无论那里 — *n.*
任何地方

anywise ['eniwaiz] *adv.* 不管怎么说;无论
以何种方式,任凭从什么角度

a/o, A/O *abbr.* account of … 账上

aorta [ei'ɔːtə] ([复] aortas 或 aortae
[ei'ɔːtiː]) *n.* 【解】主动脉

apace [ə'peis] *adv.* 飞快地,迅速地

apache [ə'pæʃ] *n.* (巴黎、布鲁塞尔等大
城市中的)流氓,强盗

apart [ə'pɑːt] *adv.* 1. 相隔,相距 2. 除去,
撇开(*from*) 3. 成零碎: take a machine
~ 把机器拆开 4. 区别,分别: tell two
things ~ 对两件东西加以区别

apartheid [ə'pɑːtheit] *n.* 种族隔离;种族
隔离法(尤指南非当局对南非的有色
人,特别是黑人,实行的一种种族歧视
政策)

apartment [ə'pɑːtmənt] *n.* 1. 房间 2. [~s]
〈英〉(特指置有家具,供人短期租用
的)套房 3. 〈美〉一套公寓房间(英国称

flat);公寓

apathetic [,æpə'θetik] *adj.* 1. 无感情的;
无感觉的 2. 冷淡的,漠然的 ‖ ~ally
adv.

apathy ['æpəθi] *n.* 1. 无感情;无感觉 2.
冷淡,漠然

APC *abbr.* aspirin, phenacetin, and caffeine
[药]复方阿司匹林

ape [eip] *n.* 1. 无尾猿;类人猿 2. 模仿
者,学样的人 3. 粗野的大汉 — *vt.* 模
仿;学…的样 — *r n.* 模仿者,学样
的人 ‖ ~ **man** 猿人

aperitif [ə,peri'tiːf] *n.* (饭前饮用的)开胃
酒

aperture ['æpətjuə] *n.* 1. 孔;隙缝;缺口
2.(照相机等镜头的)孔径 ‖ ~ **card**
(镶有缩微胶片的)窗孔卡片;穿孔卡
(片)

apex ['eipeks] ([复] apices ['eipisiːz] 或
apexes) *n.* 1. 顶,顶点 2.【天】奔赴点
(= the ~ of the sun's motion) 3.【无】反
射点 4.【矿】脉尖,脉顶

aphid ['eifid] *n.* 蚜虫

aphorism ['æfərizəm] *n.* 格言,警句

aphrodisiac [,æfrəu'diziæk] *adj.* 激发性
欲的,催欲的 — *n.* 催欲剂

Apia [ə'piːə] *n.* 阿皮亚[西萨摩亚首都]

apiary ['eipiəri] *n.* 养蜂场

apiece [ə'piːs] *adv.* 每个;每人;各

aplomb [ə'plɔm] *n.* 1. 直立 2. 镇静,
沉着;自信,自持

apocalypse [ə'pɔkəlips] *n.* 1. [the A-](基
督教《圣经》中的)〈启示录〉2. 天启,
启示

Apocrypha [ə'pɔkrifə] [复] *n.* [用作单或
复](基督教的)次经

apocryphal [ə'pɔkrifəl] *adj.* 1. [宗]次经
的 2. 作者身份不明的;真实性可疑

的;伪的;杜撰的

apogee ['æpədʒi] *n.* 1. 【天】【字】远地点 2. 最远点;最高点

apologetic [ə,pɔlə'dʒetik] *adj.* 1. 辩护的,辩解的 2. 道歉的 — *n.* 【常 ~s】(尤指对基督教教义的)辩护 ‖ -ally *adv.*

apologist [ə'pɔlədʒist] *n.* 辩护士

apologize [ə'pɔlədʒaiz] *vi.* 1. 道歉,谢罪 2. 辩解,辩护

apology [ə'pɔlədʒi] *n.* 1. 道歉,认错,谢罪 2. 辩护 3. 勉强代用的东西,哪以充数的东西

apoplexy ['æpəpleksi] *n.* 【医】卒中,中风 ‖ apo'plectic *adj.*

apostate [ə'pɔsteit] *n.* 叛教者;变节者;脱党者;背信者 — *adj.* 叛教的;变节的;脱党的;背信的 ‖ apostasy [ə'pɔstəsi] *n.*

apostle [ə'pɔsl] *n.* 1. 常用 [A-] 【基督教】使徒;传教士 2. 热心的倡导者,鼓吹者;改革家 ‖ apostolic [,æpəs'tɔlik] *adj.* 1. 使徒的 2. 使徒教义(或行为)的 3. 罗马教皇的

apostrophe [ə'pɔstrəfi] *n.* [表示所有格和复数]撇号;所有格符号(即');[如 the people's 人民的 / don't (do not 的省略形式) / five a's 五个 a 字/ the 1970's (读作 the nineteen seventies) 二十世纪七十年代]

apostrophize [ə'pɔstrəfaiz] *vt. & vi.* 用撇号标记;加撇号(于)

apothecary [ə'pɔθəkəri] *n.* 药剂师;药店,药房

apothegm ['æpəθem] *n.* 格言,箴言

Appalachians [,æpə'leitʃiənz] [复] *n.* [the ~] 阿巴拉契亚山脉[北美洲东部]

appal(l) [ə'pɔl] (appalled; appalling) *vt.* 使吃惊;使丧胆

appalling [ə'pɔliŋ] *adj.* 令人震惊的;骇人

听闻的 ‖ -ly *adv.*

apparatus [,æpə'reitəs] ([复] apparatus(es)) *n.* 1. 器械;仪器;设备;装置 2. 器官 3. 机构;(尤指政党或地下活动的)组织 4.(学术著作中的)注解(或索引等)

apparel [ə'pærəl] *n.* 1. 衣服,衣着;服装 2. 装饰物;外表,外观 3. 船具(袋具、锚等) — (apparel(l)ed; apparel(l)ing) *vt.* 给 ... 穿衣;给 ... 修饰

apparent [ə'pærənt] *adj.* 1. 明显的,显而易见的 2. 表面上的,貌似的,外观上的 ‖ -ly *adv.*

apparition [,æpə'riʃən] *n.* 1. 幻象(或怪影,鬼怪等)的出现;神奇现象 2. 鬼怪,幽灵 3.(行星、慧星等隐没后的)初现

appeal [ə'pi:l] *vi.* 1. 呼吁 2. 诉(诸);求助(于)(to) 3.【律】上诉 4.(作品等对 ...)有感染力和吸引力(to) — *vt.* 控诉;把(案件)上诉 — *n.* 1. 呼吁;恳求 2.【律】上诉 3. 感染力;号召力

appealing [ə'pi:liŋ] *adj.* 1. 有感染力的,吸引人的 2. 哀诉乞怜的,恳求似的 ‖ -ly *adv.* / -ness *n.*

appear [ə'piə] *vi.* 1. 出现,显露 2. 来到;(在公开或正式场合)露面;出庭;到案 3. 出版;发表 4. 看来(好似)

appearance [ə'piərəns] *n.* 1. 出现,显露;来到;露面 2. 出版;发表 3. 出庭;到案 4. 外貌,外观;外表 5. 出现物;(古)幽灵;幻象 6.【哲】现象

appease [ə'pi:z] *vt.* 1. 平息,抚慰,使息怒 2. 缓靖;姑息,对 ... 让步 3. 充(饥);解(渴);满足(好奇心) ‖ **appeasable** *adj.* 可平息的,可满足的 / -ment *n.*

appellant [ə'pelənt] *adj.*【律】(有关)上诉的 — *n.* 上诉人

appellate [ə'pelət] *adj.*【律】上诉的;有

权受理上诉的

appellation [æpəˈleiʃən] *n.* 名称,称号

append [əˈpend] *vt.* 附加上;贴上;挂上

appendage [əˈpendidʒ] *n.* 1. 附属物;附加物 2. 【生】附器,附属物

appendicitis [əˌpendiˈsaitis] *n.* 【医】阑尾炎

appendix [əˈpendiks] ([复] appendices [əˈpendisiz] 或 appendixes) *n.* 1. 附录;附属物,附加物 2. 【解】阑尾

appertain [ˌæpəˈtein] *vi.* 1. 属于;关于 (*to*) 2. 适合于 (*to*)

appetite [ˈæpitait] *n.* 1. 食欲,胃口 2. 欲望;爱好

appetizer, appetiser [ˈæpitaizə] *adj.* 1. (餐前的)开胃品(减少量的饮料等)2. 促进食欲的活动 2. 刺激欲望的事物

appetizing, appetising [ˈæpitaiziŋ] *adj.* 1. 促进食欲的,开胃的;鲜美的 2. 刺激欲望的,诱人的 ‖ ~**ly** *adv.*

applaud [əˈplɔːd] *vt.* 1. 鼓掌欢迎;欢呼向...喝彩;称赞;赞成 — *vi.* 鼓掌欢迎;欢呼

applause [əˈplɔːz] *n.* 鼓掌欢迎;欢呼;喝彩;称赞;赞成

apple [ˈæpl] *n.* 1. 苹果;苹果树;苹果状果实 3. (美国)炸弹;手榴弹;棒球 4. 《美俚》人,家伙

apple-pie [ˈæplˈpai] *adj.* 1. 〈口〉整齐的,井井有条的,完美的 2. (具有)美国传统优点(或价值观念的)

appliance [əˈplaiəns] *n.* 1. 应用,适用 2. 用具,器具;器械,装置

applicable [ˈæplikəbl] *adj.* 1. 能应用的,可适用的 2. 适合的,合适的 ‖ **applica'bility** *n.* (可)应用性,适用性 / ~ **ness** *n.* / **applicably** *adv.*

applicant [ˈæplikənt] *n.* 申请人

application [ˌæpliˈkeiʃən] *n.* 1. 应用,适

用;运用 2. 施用,敷用;搽剂 3. 请求,申请;申请表 4. 用功,专心

applied [əˈplaid] *adj.* 应用的,实用的

apply [əˈplai] *vt.* 1. 应用,实施;运用,使用 2. 把...应用于 (*to*) — *vi.* 1. 适用 2. 申请;请求

appoint [əˈpɔint] *vt.* 1. 任命,委任 2. 约定,指定(时间、地点)3. 命令 4.【律】处置(财产)5. [常用被动语态]装设,布置 ‖ ~**ee** *n.* 被任命人,被委派者 2.【律】被指定的财产受益人;被授权指定财产受益者的人/ ~**ive** *adj.* 任命的,委派的

appointment [əˈpɔintmənt] *n.* 1. 任命,委派 2. 职位 3. 约会,约定 4.[~s]家具;设备(尤指旅馆和船的)

apportion [əˈpɔːʃən] *vt.* 分派;分摊;按比例分配 ‖ ~**ment** *n.*

apposite [ˈæpəzit] *adj.* 适合的,适当的,恰当的 (*to*) ‖ ~**ly** *adv.* / ~**ness** *n.*

apposition [ˌæpəˈziʃən] *n.* 并置,并列 2.【语】同位,同位语 3.【植】敷着,附着

appositive [æˈpɔzitiv] 【语】*adj.* 同位(语)的 — *n.* 同位语;同位成分

appraise [əˈpreiz] *vt.* 1. 估价;评价;评价 ‖ **appraisal** *n.* / ~**r** *n.* 估价人;评价人;鉴定人

appreciable [əˈpriːʃiəbl] *adj.* 可估计的;(大得)可以看到(或感觉)的 ‖ **appreciably** *adv.*

appreciate [əˈpriːʃieit] *vt.* 1. 欣赏,鉴赏;赏识 2. 正确评价;赏识 3. 感谢,感激 4. 意识到,懂得 5. 抬高...的价格 — *vi.* 涨价;增值;增多

appreciation [əˌpriːʃiˈeiʃən] *n.* 1. 欣赏,鉴赏;赏识 2. 正确评价;赏识 3. 感谢,感激 4. 涨价;增值

appreciative [əˈpriːʃiətiv] *adj.* 1. 有眼力的,有欣赏力的;欣赏的 2. 感激的

~ly adv.

apprehend [ˌæpri'hend] vt. 1. 理解, 领悟 2. 逮捕 3. 畏惧; 忧虑 — vi. 理解, 领会

apprehension [ˌæpri'henʃən] n. 1. 理解, 领悟 2. 逮捕; 拘押 3. 恐惧; 忧虑, 担心, 挂念

apprehensive [ˌæpri'hensiv] adj. 1. 有理解力的, 善于领会的 2. 担心的; 忧虑的 ‖ ~ly adv. / ~ness n.

apprentice [ə'prentis] n. 艺徒, 学徒, 学弟; 初学者, 生手 — vt. 使当学徒 ‖ ~ship n. 1. 学徒身份; 学徒期 2. 训练(期), 见习(期)

apprise, apprize [ə'praiz] vt. (正式)通知, 告知(of)

approach [ə'prəutʃ] vt. 1. 向...靠近; 接近, 近似 2. 接近; 近乎, 同...联系 3. 探讨; 看待; 处理(问题等) 4.〈美〉企图贿赂 — vi. 靠近, 临近, 近似, 近似 — n. 1. 靠近, 临近; 接近, 近似 2. 进路; 入门 3. [常 ~es] 亲近的表示 4. 探讨; 处理; 态度; 方法 5.〔围城者修筑的〕接近敌人要塞的工事;〔装炸机的〕接敌 6.〔空〕进场, 进近(指飞机进入机场时的飞行)

approachable [ə'prəutʃəbl] adj. 1. 可接近的, 可到达的 2. 可亲近的 ‖ ap,proacha'bility n.

approbation [ˌæprə'beiʃən] n. 1. 认可; 批准 2. 赞许

appropriate [ə'prəupriət] adj. 适当的, 恰如其分的 — [ə'prəuprieit] vt. 1. 拨出(款项等) 2. 占用; 盗用; 挪用 ‖ ~ly adv. / ~ness n.

appropriation [ə,prəupri'eiʃən] n. 1. 拨付;(一笔)拨款 2. 占用; 盗用; 挪用 3.〔宗〕圣俸转拨

approval [ə'pruːvəl] n. 1. 批准; 认可 2. 赞成, 同意

approve [ə'pruːv] vt. 1. 批准; 通过 2. 赞成, 称许, 同意 — vi. 赞成, 称许, 同意(of) ‖ approvingly adv. 赞成地, 称许地

approximate [ə'prɔksimət] adj. 近似的, 大约的 — [ə'prɔksimeit] vt. 1. 使近似, 使接近 2. 使接近(to) — vi. 近似, 接近(to) ‖ ~ly adv.

approximation [ə,prɔksi'meiʃən] n. 1. 近似 2. 近似值; 粗略估计

appurtenance [ə'pəːtinəns] n. 1. 附属物, 从属物 2. 附带权利 3. [~s] 装置; 配件

appurtenant [ə'pəːtinənt] adj. 附属的, 从属的; 有关的(to) — n. 附属物

Apr. abbr. April

apricot ['eiprikɔt] n. 1. 杏子 2. [植] 杏, 杏树 3. 杏黄色

April ['eiprəl] n. 四月(略作 Apr.) ‖ ~ Fools' Day 愚人节(四月一日)

apron ['eiprən] n. 1. 围裙, 工作裙 2. [机] 挡板;(车床的)拖板箱(或溜板箱); 链板传送带 3. 停机坪 4. [地] 石裙裙, 冰川前前砂碎层 5.〔船〕(木船)副舱材, 艏舷墙 6.〔军〕(枪)的口罩 7. [电] 菱形铁丝网面; 伪装天幕 8. 台口(戏台的幕前部分) — vt. 给...结上围裙; 用围裙围住

apropos ['æprəpəu, ˌæprəpəu] adv. 1. 恰当地; 及时地 2. 附带地, 顺便 — adj. 恰当的; 适时的 — prep. 关于, 就... 而言 ‖ ~ of 关于, 就...而言

apt [æpt] adj. 1. 恰当的, 贴切的 2. 聪明的, 灵巧的 3. 易于...的, 倾向的 ‖ ~ly adv. / ~ness n.

aptitude [ˈæptitjuːd] *n.* **1.** 倾向，习性 (*for*) **2.** 能力，才能(*for*) **3.** 敏悟，颖悟

aquacade [ˈækwəˌkeid] *n.* 水上运动表演

aqualung [ˈækwəlʌŋ] *n.* 水肺，水中呼吸器(指潜水员背的氧气瓶连同戴的面罩) ‖ ～er *n.* 使用水中呼吸器的人

aquamarine [ˌækwəməˈriːn] *n.* **1.** 【矿】海蓝宝石，水蓝宝石 **2.** 浅绿色，水绿色

aquaplane [ˈækwəplein] *n.* (由小汽艇拖行的)滑水板 — *vi.* **1.** 乘滑水板滑行 **2.** (车)在积水的路面上打滑

aquarium [əˈkwɛəriəm]([复] aquariums 或 aquaria[əˈkwɛəriə]) *n.* **1.** 养鱼缸；(饲养观赏水生动植物的)水族池，水族槽 **2.** 水族馆

aquatic [əˈkwætik] *adj.* **1.** 水产的；水生的；水栖的 **2.** 水上的；水中的 — *n.* 水生植物(或动物) **2.** [～s]水上运动

aqueduct [ˈækwidʌkt] *n.* **1.** 沟渠；导水管；高架渠；桥管 **2.**【解】导管

aqueous [ˈeikwiəs] *adj.* **1.** 水的，水状的；含水的 **2.** 【岩石】水成的

aquiline [ˈækwilain] *adj.* **1.** 鹰的；似鹰的 **2.** 钩状的

Ar [化] 元素氩(argon)的符号

-ar *suf.* **1.** [构成形容词]表示"…特性的"，"…形状的": regular, triangular **2.** [构成名词]表示"…的人"；"…的物": liar, collar

Arab [ˈærəb] *n.* **1.** 阿拉伯人 **2.** 阿拉伯马 **3.** 街头流浪儿 — *adj.* 阿拉伯的；阿拉伯人的

Arabia [əˈreibiə] *n.* 阿拉伯半岛 [亚洲西南部]

Arabian [əˈreibiən] *adj.* 阿拉伯的；阿拉伯人的 — *n.* 阿拉伯人

Arabic [ˈærəbik] *adj.* 阿拉伯的；阿拉伯人

的；阿拉伯语言(或文学、文化等)的 — *n.* 阿拉伯语 ‖ ～ **numeral** 阿拉伯数字

arable [ˈærəbl] *adj.* 适于耕作的，可耕的 — *n.* 耕地；可耕地

arbiter [ˈɑːbitə] *n.* **1.** 仲裁人，公断人 **2.** 主宰者，独断者

arbitrament [ɑːˈbitrəmənt] *n.* 仲裁，公断；仲裁结论，公断决定

arbitrary [ˈɑːbitrəri] *adj.* 任意的，专断的，专横的 ‖ **arbitrarily** *adv.* / **arbitrariness** *n.*

arbitrate [ˈɑːbitreit] *vt.* **1.** 仲裁，公断 **2.** 把(争端等)交付仲裁，使听任公断 — *vi.* 进行仲裁，进行公断 ‖ **arbi'tration** *n.* / **arbitrator** *n.*

arbor [ˈɑːbə] *n.* (美) = arbour

arboreal [ɑːˈbɔːriəl] *adj.* **1.** 树木的 **2.** 树状的 **3.** 栖息在树上的，生活在树上的

arboretum [ˌɑːbəˈriːtəm]([复] arboretums 或 arboreta[ˌɑːbəˈriːtə]) *n.* 植物园；树木园

arborvitae [ˌɑːbəˈvaiti] *n.* 【植】金钟柏 **2.**【解】(小脑)活树

arbour [ˈɑːbə] *n.* (树枝等形成的)棚架；凉亭

arbutus [ɑːˈbjuːtəs] *n.* 【植】野草莓树，藤地莓

arc [ɑːk] *n.* **1.** 弧，弓形(物)；拱(洞) **2.**【电】弧光

arcade [ɑːˈkeid] *n.* **1.**【建】拱廊，连拱柱廊 **2.** 有拱廊的街道(两旁常设商店) ‖ ～d *adj.* 有拱廊的

arcane [ɑːˈkein] *adj.* 秘密的；神秘的

arch[1] [ɑːtʃ] *n.* **1.** 拱门；拱门；拱门 **2.** 拱形，半圆形；拱形门；牌楼；拱状物 — *vt.* **1.** 用拱连接；用拱覆盖 **2.** 使成弓形 — *vi.* 拱起；成为弓形

arch[2] [ɑːtʃ] *adj.* 狡黠的；调皮的 ‖ ～ly

adv.

arch- *pref.* 表示"为首的"、"主要的"、"总的"：*arch* bishop

archaeology [ˌɑːkiˈɔlədʒi] *n.* 考古学 ‖ **ar-chaeological** [ˌɑːkiəˈlɔdʒikəl] *adj.* 考古学的 / **archaeologist** *n.* 考古学家

archaic [ɑːˈkeiik] *adj.* 1. 古代的；古风的 2.(语言上)古体的；陈旧的

archaism [ˈɑːkeiizəm] *n.* 1. 古词；古语；古风 2.(语言文学上的)拟古主义

archangel [ˈɑːkˌeindʒəl] *n.* 1.(基督教《圣经》中的)天使长；(罗马天主教九级天使中的)第八级天使 2.[植]圆当归

archbishop [ɑːtʃˈbiʃəp] *n.* [宗]大主教

archduke [ˈɑːtʃˈdjuːk] *n.* 大公(昔时奥匈帝国皇太子的称号)

archer [ˈɑːtʃə] *n.* 1. 弓箭手；射箭运动员 2.[A-][天]人马座

archery [ˈɑːtʃəri] *n.* 射箭(术)

archipelago [ˌɑːkiˈpeləgəu] *n.* ([复] archipela-go(e)s) *n.* 1. 群岛 2. 多岛屿的海 3.[the A-]爱琴海[欧洲南部]

architect [ˈɑːkitekt] *n.* 1. 建筑师；设计师 2.〈喻〉缔造者

architectural [ˌɑːkiˈtektʃərəl] *adj.* 关于建筑的；建筑上的，建筑学的

architecture [ˈɑːkitektʃə] *n.* 1. 建筑学 2.[总称]建筑物；建筑式样，建筑风格 3. 结构；建筑工程

archive [ˈɑːkaiv] *n.* (常~s) 1. 档案馆，档案室 2. 档案

archway [ˈɑːtʃwei] *n.* [建]拱道；拱门；牌楼

arctic [ˈɑːktik] *adj.* 1. 北极的；北极区的：the *Arctic* Circle 北极圈 / the *Arctic* O-cean 北冰洋 2. 极冷的 — *n.* 1. 北极；北极圈；北极区 2.〈美〉[常~s]保暖防水套鞋

ardent [ˈɑːdənt] *adj.* 1. 热情的，热烈的 2. 炽热的 3. 强烈的，烈性的 ‖ **~ly** *adv.*

ardo(u)r [ˈɑːdə] *n.* 热情，热心

arduous [ˈɑːdjuəs] *adj.* 1. 艰巨的，艰难的 2. 努力的，勤奋的 3. 陡峭的，险峻的 ‖ **~ly** *adv.* / **~ness** *n.*

are [强 ɑː，弱 ə，ə]见 be

area [ˈɛəriə] *n.* 1. 空地；地面 2. 面积 3. 地区；区域 4. 范围，领域 5.(地下室窗外的)采光井 ‖ **~ code** (美国、加拿大等长途电话的)区域码，地区码 区号

arena [əˈriːnə] *n.* 1.(古罗马圆形剧场中央的)角斗场，表演场地；(一般的)竞技场 2. 活动场所；竞争场所

aren't [ɑːnt] 1. = are not 2.〈口〉= am not(用于疑问句)

areocentric [ˌɛəriəuˈsentrik] *adj.* [天]火心的，以火星为中心的

Argentina [ˌɑːdʒənˈtiːnə] *n.* 阿根廷[南美洲中南部国家]

Argentine [ˈɑːdʒəntain] *adj.* 阿根廷的；阿根廷人的 — *n.* 1. 阿根廷人 2.[the ~]阿根廷

argon [ˈɑːgɔn] *n.* [化]氩

argosy [ˈɑːgəsi] *n.* (诗)大商船(队)

argue [ˈɑːgjuː] *vi.* 争辩，争论，辩论 — *vt.* 1. 争论，辩论 2. 说服 3. 用辩论证明；表明

argument [ˈɑːgjumənt] *n.* 1. 争论，争论；论据；论点；理由 3.(文学作品等的)情节；内容提要 4. 说理；论证 5.【数】幅角；自变数

argumentation [ˌɑːgjumenˈteiʃən] *n.* 1. 推论，论证 2. 争论，辩论 3. 论据

argumentative [ˌɑːgjuˈmentətiv] *adj.* 1.(很可能)引起争论的；好争辩的 ‖ **~ly** *adv.*

aria [ˈɑːriə] *n.* 1. 曲调，调子 2.[音]咏叹调；(电影

等中的)独唱特写镜头

arid ['ærid] *adj.* 1. 干旱的；(土地)贫瘠的 2. 枯燥无味的，无生气的 ‖ ～ity [ə'riditi] *n.* / ～ly *adv.* / ～ness *n.*

aright [ə'rait] *adv.* 正确地

arise [ə'raiz] [arose[ə'rəuz], arisen[ə'rizn]] *vi.* 1. 起来 2. 出现，呈现 3. (由...而)引起，(由...而)产生 (*from*)

aristocracy [.æris'tɔkrəsi] *n.* 1. 贵族统治；贵族统治集团(特权阶级)；上层社会 2. 贵族统治的国家 3. [总称]贵族 4. (知识界等的)一批杰出代表，一批优秀分子

aristocrat ['æristəkræt] *n.* 1. 贵族中的一员，有贵族头衔的人 2. 贵族政治论者

aristocratic [.æristə'krætik] *adj.* 1. 贵族的；(主张)贵族政治的 2. 贵族式的 ‖ ～ally *adv.*

arithmetic [ə'riθmətik] *n.* 1. 算术；计算 2. 算术教科书；算术论著

arithmetic(al) [.æriθ'metik (əl)] *adj.* 算术的

Arizona [.æri'zəunə] *n.* 亚利桑那[美国州名]

ark [ɑːk] *n.* 1. (基督教《圣经》中的)方舟；(喻)避难所 2. (基督教《圣经》中的)约柜 3. [美]大而笨重的船(或车辆)

Arkansas ['ɑːkənsɔː] *n.* 1. 阿肯色[美国州名] 2. [the ～]阿肯色河[美国中部]

arm [ɑːm] *n.* 1. 臂，胳膊，上肢 2. 臂状物(如树枝、机器的曲柄、海湾等) 3. [机](轮)辐；臂；杆 4. 袖子 5. (椅子的)扶手，靠手 6. (喻)权力 ‖ ～ful *n.* 一抱 ‖ ～band *n.* 袖章 / ～chair *n.* 扶手椅 *adj.* 坐在椅子里空想的 / ～pit *n.* 腋窝 / ～rest *n.* 靠手 / ～wrestling 扳腕子(比手劲)

arm² [ɑːm] *n.* 1. [常～s]武器(尤指枪支) 2. 兵种 3. [～s]盾形纹章 — *vt.* 武装；装备 — *vi.* 武装起来

armada [ɑː'mɑːdə] *n.* 1. 舰队 2. (飞机)机群

armadillo [.ɑːmə'diləu] ([复] armadillos) *n.* [动]犰狳

Armageddon [.ɑːmə'gedən] *n.* 1. (基督教《圣经》中的)哈米吉多顿(世界末日善恶的决战场)；善恶大决战；(喻)大决战

armament ['ɑːməmənt] *n.* 1. 军队 2. [～s](一国的)军备，军事力量 3. (一个作战单位所有的)军械，武器，火力装备 4. 武装；战备 5. (动植物的)防护器官 6. [军]战斗部，弹头

armature ['ɑːmətjuə] *n.* 1. 盔甲(动植物的)防护器官 2. [电]电枢，转子；衔铁 3. [建]加强料，钢筋

armed [ɑːmd] *adj.* 1. 武装的 2. (动植物)有防护器官的

Armenia [ɑː'miːniə] *n.* 1. 亚美尼亚[外高加索中南部国家] 2. [史]亚美尼亚(亚洲古国)

armistice ['ɑːmistis] *n.* 停战，休战

armlet ['ɑːmlit] *n.* 1. (戴在上臂作装饰或标志用的)臂钏，臂章 2. 小(海)湾

armor ['ɑːmə] *n.* & *vt.* [美] = armour

armo(u)r ['ɑːmə] *n.* 1. 盔甲 2. [总称](军舰、车辆的)装甲(钢板) 3. [总称]军械；装甲兵(部队) 4. 甲壳，甲胄；鱼鳞；潜水服 5. (覆盖在电缆外的)铠装 — *vt.* 为...穿盔甲；为...装甲

armo(u)red ['ɑːməd] *adj.* 1. 穿戴盔甲的 2. 装甲的 ‖ ～ car 装甲车 / ～ division 装甲师

armo(u)ry ['ɑːməri] *n.* 1. 军械库 2. 兵工厂

army ['ɑːmi] *n.* 1. 军队;陆军 2. 野战军;集团军;兵团 3. 大群

A-road ['eiˌrəud] *n.* (高级)主干公路

aroma [ə'rəumə] *n.* 1. 芳香;香味 2. (艺术品的)风味,韵味

aromatic [ˌærəu'mætik] *adj.* 1. 芳香的;有香味的 2.【化】芳香族的;芳香植物 2. [常~s]芳香族化合物;芳香剂

arose [ə'rəuz] arise 的过去式

around [ə'raund] [around 和 round 作前置词和副词的意义基本相同, around 多用于美国, round 多用于英国] *prep.* 1. 在...周围 2. 绕过;steer a ship ~ reefs 使船绕过暗礁 3. 在...各处;在附近 大约 大约;~ two o'clock 两点钟左右 —*adv.* 1. 在周围;在附近;存在着,活着 2. 各处;The good news soon got ~ 好消息很快就传开了。 3. 整整一圈;回转;迂回;The track is 400 metres ~. 跑道一圈有四百米长。/ Another autumn harvest season has come ~. 又一个秋收季节来到了。/ pass the note ~ 传阅字条 4. 到(彼此知道的)某一地点;Come ~ this evening if you have time. 今晚有空到我那儿去。

arouse [ə'rauz] *vt.* 1. 唤醒 2. 唤起,激起,引起

arpeggio [ɑː'pedʒiəu] ([复] arpeggios) *n.*【音】琶音

arraign [ə'rein] *vt.* 1. 传讯;提讯 2. 控告 指责,责难 ‖ ~**ment** *n.*

arrange [ə'reindʒ] *vt.* 1. 整理;分类;排列 2. 筹备;安排 3. 调解,调停(纠纷,分歧等) 4. 改编(乐曲等) — *vi.* 1. 安排;准备 2. 商定

arrangement [ə'reindʒmənt] *n.* 1. 整理;排列;布置 2. [常~s]安排;准备 3. 商定;调解 4. (乐曲等的)改编;改编的乐曲

arrant ['ærənt] *adj.* 1. 彻头彻尾的;臭名昭著的 ‖ ~**ly** *adv.*

array [ə'rei] *vt.* 1. 使...排列成阵势 2. 装扮,打扮 3. (为审理某一案件)选任(陪审员),召集(陪审团) — *n.* 1. (军队等的)列阵 2. 衣服;盛装 3. (排列整齐的)一批;大量 4. 陪审员名单

arrear [ə'riə] *n.* [~s]应付欠款,逾期债款;待完成的事 ‖ ~(s)拖欠;拖延;落后

arrest [ə'rest] *vt.* 1. 逮捕;拘留;扣留(船只、货物等) 2. 阻止,抑制 3. 吸引,吸住(某人的注意力) —*n.* 1. 逮捕;拘留 2. 阻止;制动装置 ‖ ~**ing** *adj.* 引人注意的

arrival [ə'raivəl] *n.* 1. 到来;到达 2. 到达者;到达物 3. 达到,得出

arrive [ə'raiv] *vi.* 1. 来;到来 2. (时间)到来 3. 达到;得出(at) 4. 成功,成名

arrogance ['ærəgəns] *n.* 骄傲自大,傲慢

arrogant ['ærəgənt] *adj.* 骄傲自大的,傲慢的 ‖ ~**ly** *adv.*

arrogate ['ærəugeit] *vt.* 1. 冒称具有(权利等);僭取 2. 没来由地把...归于(to) ‖ **arro'gation** *n.*

arrow ['ærəu] *n.* 1. 箭 2. 箭状物;箭号(即→) ‖ ~**-root** *n.*【植】竹芋 2. 竹芋粉;(类似竹芋粉的)食用淀粉

arrowhead ['ærəuhed] *n.* 1. 箭头;楔形符号(即<) 2.【植】慈姑 ‖ ~**ed** *adj.* 箭头形的

arroyo [ə'ɔiəu] ([复] arroyos) *n.* 〈美〉旱谷;小河,溪

arsenal ['ɑːsənəl] *n.* 军火库;兵工厂;〈喻〉武库

arsenic ['ɑːsnik] *n.*【化】1. 砷 2. 三氧化二砷 (俗称 砒霜, = white ~) — [ɑː'senik] *adj.* 砷的;含砷的;五价砷的

arson ['ɑːsn] *n*. 放火(罪)，纵火(罪) ‖ ～ist *n*. 放火犯,纵火犯

art [ɑːt] *n*. 1. 艺术；美术 2. 技术,技艺: the healing ～ 医术 3. [～s] 文科: Bachelor of *Arts* 文学士/ Master of *Arts* 文学硕士 4. 人工（指与自然相对而言）5. 奸计,诡计

arteriosclerosis [ɑːˌtɪəriəuskliə'rəusis] *n*. [医]动脉硬化

artery ['ɑːtəri] *n*. 1.【解】动脉 2. 交通干线；要道；渠道 ‖ **arterial** [ɑː'tiəriəl] *adj*.

artesian [ɑː'tiːzjən] *adj*. 自流的 ‖ ～ well 自流井

artful ['ɑːtful] *adj*. 1. 狡猾的,欺诈的 2. 精明的, 机灵的 3. 人工的 ‖ ～ly *adv*. / ～ness *n*.

arthritis [ɑː'θraitis] *n*. [医]关节炎

arthropod ['ɑːθrəpɔd] *n*. & *adj*. [动]节肢动物(的)

artichoke ['ɑːtitʃəuk] *n*. 【植】洋蓟,朝鲜蓟；菊芋,洋姜

article ['ɑːtikl] *n*. 1. 文章；论文 2. 物品,物件,商品 3. 项目；条款 4.【语】冠词: the definite ～ 定冠词(指 the)/ the indefinite ～ 不定冠词(指 a, an) 5.〈俚〉人,家伙(尤指精明的、善于钻营的人) ‖ ～ *vt*. 约束；订约，约束；订约→以学徒为师徒

articulate [ɑː'tikjulət] *adj*. 1. 接合起来的；[生]有(关)节的 2.(讲话等)发音清晰的 3.(人)表达力强的；(论据等)表达得清楚有力的 4. 能说话的 5.[动]有体节的无脊椎动物；有关节的腕足动物 ‖ [ɑː'tikjuleit] *vt*. 1.(用关节)连接；使接合 2. 把(字句等)清晰地发出声来；明确 表达 3. 发(音) ‖ *vi*. 1. 连接起来；接合起来 2. 清楚地讲话；清晰地发音 3.【语】发音 ‖ ～ly *adv*. / ～ness *n*.

articulation [ɑːˌtikjuˈleiʃən] *n*. 1. 连接；接

合；连接(或接合)方式 2.(清楚的)发音；【语】发音；发出的音(尤指辅音) 3.(骨头等)的关节；【植】节 4.(传声的)清晰度

artifice ['ɑːtifis] *n*. 1. 技巧,技能；机智 2. 诡计,计谋；诡计 ‖ ～r *n*. 1. 工匠；[陆海军中的]技术兵 2. 发明者；创造者

artificial [ˌɑːti'fiʃəl] *adj*. 1. 人工的,人造的 2. 矫揉造作的,不自然的 3. 假的 ‖ ～ity [ˌɑːtifiʃi'æliti] *n*. / ～ly *adv*. / ～ness *n*. ‖ ～ intelligence[计]人工智能[计] / ～ language 人工语言；人造语言(如世界语)

artillery [ɑː'tiləri] *n*. 1.[总称]火炮;大炮 2.[the ～][总称]炮兵(部队) 3. 炮术 4.〈俚〉防身武器(尤指大小枪等) 5.〈俚〉(吸毒成瘾者用语)皮下注射器 6.〈喻〉武器 ‖ ar'tilleryman *n*. 炮手

artisan [ˌɑːti'zæn] *n*. 手艺人,工匠

artist ['ɑːtist] *n*. 1. 艺术家；美术家(尤指画家)2.(某方面的)能手 3. 玩弄诈术的人

artistic(al) [ɑː'tistik(əl)] *adj*. 1. 艺术的；美术的 2. 艺术家的；美术家的 3. 艺术性强的 4. 爱好艺术的 ‖ **artistically** *adv*.

artistry ['ɑːtistri] *n*. 1. 艺术性；艺术效果 2. 艺术才能；艺术技巧

artless ['ɑːtlis] *adj*. 1. 朴实的；天真的；不矫揉造作的,自然的 2. 粗笨的；拙劣的 ‖ ～ly *adv*. / ～ness *n*.

arty ['ɑːti] *adj*. 〈口〉冒充有艺术价值的；装作爱好艺术的；附庸风雅的 ‖ **artily** *adv*. / **artiness** *n*.

-ary *suf*. 1.[作形容词词尾]表示"与...有关的": elementary, secondary 2.[作名词词尾]表示"从事...的人"；"与...有关的物": functionary, dictionary

As【化】元素砷(arsenic)的符号

as [强 æz;弱 əz] *adv.* [表示程度]同样地; ~ **firm as a rock** 坚如磐石[注意:在 "as...as..." 结构中,第一个 as 是副词,第二个 as 是连接词或关系代词] — *conj.* 1.[表示比较]像...一样:The work is *not* so easy ~ you imagine. 这工作决不像你想象的那么简单。2.[表示方式]按照;如同:state the facts ~ they are 如实地陈述事实 3.[表示时间]当...的时候:As a young man, he lived in Japan. 他青年时代住在日本。4.[表示原因]由于,鉴于:As he was not well, I decided to go without him. 因为他身体不好,我决定独自去了。5.[表示结果或目的]以至于:Be so good ~ to come and join us. 务请来参加我们的活动。6.[表示让步]虽然,尽管:Much ~ I like it, I will not buy it. 虽然我很喜欢这东西,但不想要它。— *pron.* 1.[用在"such as"、"the same as"等结构中]像...样的人(或物);凡是...的人(或物):My hometown is no longer the *same* ~ it was. 我的家乡现在已不一样了。2.这一点:~ is well known 众所周知 — *prep.* 作为,如同:unite ~ one man 团结得像个一个人一样 ‖ ~ **for** 至于,就...方面说 / ~ **from** 从...时起 / ~ **if** 好像,仿佛 / ~ **of** 从...时起 / ~ **though** = ~ if / ~ **to** 1.至于 2.关于

asbestos [æz'bestəs], **asbestus** [æz'bestəs] *n.* 石棉

ascend [ə'send] *vi.* 1.登高,上升,升高 2.追溯(到某一时间)(*to*) 3.[天]向天顶上升 — *vt.* 攀登;登上 ‖ ~ **ing** *adj.* 上升的,向上的;[植]上升的

ascendance, ascendence [ə'sendəns] *n.* = ascendancy

ascendancy, ascendency [ə'sendənsi] *n.* 优势;支配地位

ascendant, ascendent [ə'sendənt] *adj.* 1.上升的;向上的 2.占优势的;占支配地位的 3.[天]向天顶上升的 — *n.* 优势

ascension [ə'senʃən] *n.* 1.上升,升高 2.[the A-][基督教]耶稣升天 ‖ **Ascension Day** 耶稣升天节(复活节四十天后的第一个星期四)

ascent [ə'sent] *n.* 1.上升,升高 2.登高,爬坡 3.(声望或社会地位的)提高 4.斜坡;(一段)阶梯,坡度,斜度 5.上溯,追溯

ascertain [æsə'tein] *vt.* 查明,弄清,确定 ‖ ~**able** *adj.* 可查明的,可弄清的/ ~**ment** *n.*

ascetic [ə'setik] *adj.* 苦行的;禁欲(主义)的 — *n.* 苦行者;禁欲主义者 ‖ ~**ism** [ə'setisizəm] *n.* 苦行;禁欲主义

ascorbic [ə'skɔːbik] *adj.* 抗坏血病的 ‖ ~ **acid** 【生化】抗坏血酸,维生素 C

ascribe [æ'skraib] *vt.* 把...归于(*to*) ‖ **ascribable** *adj.* 可归于的;起因于...的(*to*)

ascription [əs'kripʃən] *n.* 1.(功过等的)归于;(牧师等在布道完毕时)赞美上帝的话

ASEAN ['æsiæn] *abbr.* Association of South East Asian Nations 东南亚国家联盟(简称东盟)

asepsis [æ'sepsis] *n.* [医]1.无菌;无感染 2.无菌(疗)法

aseptic [æ'septik] *adj.* 无菌的;防腐的 ‖ ~**ally** *adv.*

asexual [ei'seksjuəl] *adj.* 无性的;[生]无性生殖的;无性行为(或性欲)的 ‖ ~**ity** [ei.seksju'æliti] *n.* / ~**ly** *adv.*

ash[1] [æʃ] *n.* 1.灰,灰末;灰烬 2.[~es]骨灰;遗骸 3.[~es]废墟 4.[~es]死灰色

‖～ bin 1.[英]垃圾箱／～ can 1.(美)垃圾箱 2.(俚)深水炸弹／'～ tray n. 烟灰缸／Ash Wednesday[基督教]圣灰星期三(四旬节的第一天)

ash² [æʃ] n.[植] 1. 梣，白蜡树 2. 梣木 3. 梣字符

ashamed [ə'feimd] adj.[常作表语] 羞耻的，惭愧的，害臊的

ashen¹ [æʃn] adj. 灰白色的；苍白的

ashen² [æʃn] adj. 梣的；梣木(制成)的

Ashkhabad ['æʃkæbæd] n. 阿什哈巴德[土库曼斯坦首都]

ashore [ə'ʃɔː] adv. 在岸上，在陆上；上岸，登陆 — adj. 在岸上的，在陆上的

ashy ['æʃi] adj. 灰的；覆盖着灰的 2. 灰色的；苍白的

Asia ['eiʃə] n. 亚洲：～ Minor 小亚细亚／Southeast ～ 东南亚

Asian ['eiʃən] adj. 亚洲的；亚洲人的 — n. 亚洲人

Asiatic [ˌeiʃi'ætik] adj. & n. = Asian

aside [ə'said] adv. 在旁边，在一边(或向)旁边，到(或向)一边 2.[常用于句首独立语中(暂且)撇开不谈：Joking ～,...不开玩笑(正经地说)...— n. 1.(戏剧等中的)旁白 2. 离题的话 ‖～ from[美]除了...以外

asinine ['æsinain] adj. 驴的；像驴的 2. 愚蠢的

ask [ɑːsk] vt. 1. 问，询问 2. 要求，请求 3. 邀请 4. 讨(价等) 5. 需要 — vi. 1. 要求，请求 2. 问(about)

askance [əs'kæns], **askant** [əs'kænt] adv. 斜着眼睛；怀疑地；不以为然地

askew [əs'kjuː] adv. & adj.[常作表语] 斜着的；歪着的

aslant [ə'slɑːnt] adv. & adj.[常作表语] 倾斜地(的) — prep. 倾斜地横在...上

asleep [ə'sliːp] adv. & adj.[常作表语] 1. 睡着的，睡熟 2.(四肢)发麻，麻木 3. 静止(状态) 4. 长眠，已死

ASM abbr. air-to-surface missile 空对面导弹

Asmara [æz'mɑːrə] n. 阿斯马拉[埃塞俄比亚北部城市]

asp [æsp] n.[动]角蝰(一种小毒蛇)

asparagus [əs'pærəgəs] n.[植] 1. 天门冬 2. 石刁柏，芦笋，龙须菜

aspect ['æspekt] n. 1. 样子，外表，面貌 2.(问题、事物等)方面 3.(建筑物等的)方向，方位 4.[语](动词的)体

aspen ['æspən] n. 1.(欧洲)山杨，(北美洲)颤杨 — adj. 1.(欧洲)山杨的，(北美洲)颤杨的 2. 颤抖的

asperity [æs'periti] n. 1. 粗糙；2.(气候等)严酷；艰苦的条件 3.(性格、语言等的)粗暴 4.[asperities]粗鲁的言语

aspersion [əs'pɜːʃən] n. 1. 泼水；诽谤；中伤 2.[宗]洒圣水

asphalt ['æsfælt] n. 沥青，柏油，(铺路用)沥青混合料 — vt. 铺沥青于

asphyxiate [æs'fiksieit] vt. & vi.(使)窒息 ‖ asphyxi'ation n.

aspirant [əs'paiərənt] n. 1. 有上进心的人 2.(名誉、地位等的)追求者(after, for, to) 3. 候补者 — adj. 1. 有上进心的 2. 有野心的，向上爬的 3. 候补的

aspiration [ˌæspə'reiʃən] n. 1. 志气，抱负；渴望(after, for) 2. 发送气音；送气音 3. 吸出

aspire [əs'paiə] vi. 渴望，追求(知识、名誉等)(to, after, at) ‖～r n. 渴望者，追求者

aspirin ['æspərin] n. 阿司匹林，乙酰水杨酸；阿司匹林药片

ass [æs] n. 1. 驴 2. 傻瓜，蠢人 3.(俗)屁

股;屁眼;阴户

assail [ə'seil] *vt.* 1. 攻击,袭击 2. 毅然应付,着手解决(任务、难题等) ‖ ~ant *n.* 攻击者

assassin [ə'sæsin] *n.* 暗杀者,行刺者,刺客

assassinate [ə'sæsineit] *vt.* 暗杀,行刺 ‖ as,sassi'nation *n.*

assault [ə'sɔːlt] *n.* 1. (武力或口头上的)攻击,袭击 2. 【军】冲击,突击,强击 3. 【律】侵犯人身 4. (委婉语)强奸 — *vt.* 1. 突击,攻击,袭击 2. 困扰,围攻 3. (委婉语)强奸 — *vi.* 发动攻击,进行攻击

assay [ə'sei] *n.* 1. 试金(指分析矿石和合金的成份),化验 2. (药物等的)分析,测定 2. 试样,试金 3. 化验报告,分析报告 4.〈古〉企图,尝试 — *vt.* 1. 化验;分析,检定 2. 企图,尝试 — *vi.* 被验明成分 ‖ ~ er *n.* 化验者;分析者;尝试者

assemblage [ə'semblidʒ] *n.* 1. 集合;装配;装配成的大件 2. 一群人,会众;集合物 3. 装配艺术(品)

assemble [ə'sembl] *vt.* 1. 集合 2. 调集 3. 装配 — *vi.* 集合

assembly [ə'sembli] *n.* 1. 集合 2. 集会;[总称]与会者 3. [A-]议会 4. (美国某些州的)州众议院 4. 装配;总成,组合体;(供装配的)部件 5.【军】集合号 6.【计】汇编 ‖ ～ line 装配线 / as'semblyman *n.* 1. 议员(尤指美国某些州中的)州众议院议员 2. 装配工

assent [ə'sent] *n. & vi.* 同意,赞成(*to*)

assert [ə'səːt] *vt.* 1. 宣称;断言 2. 维护,坚持(权利等)

assertion [ə'səːʃən] *n.* 1. 主张;断言 2. 维护,坚持

assertive [ə'səːtiv] *adj.* 1. 断言的,肯定的 2. 过分自信的,武断的 ‖ ~ly *adv.* /

~ness *n.*

assess [ə'ses] *vt.* 1. 估定(财产等)的价值(作为征税根据) 2. 确定(税款、罚款等)的金额 3. 征收(税款、罚款等)(*on, upon*) 4. 对(人物、工作等)估计,评价 ‖ ~ment *n.* 1. 估价;评价 2. 估定 3. 被估定的金额

asset [ə'æset] *n.* 1. (单项)财产 2. 宝贵的人(或物) 3. [～s]资产

assiduity [,æsi'djuiti] *n.* 1. 刻苦,勤奋 2. [常 assiduities]殷勤(*to*)

assiduous [ə'sidjuəs] *adj.* 1. 刻苦的、勤奋的(*in, at*) 2. 殷勤的(*over.*) ‖ ～ly *adv.* / ～ness *n.*

assign [ə'sain] *vt.* 1. 分配;把...分配给(*to*) 2. 委派,指派 3. 指定(时间、地点) 4. 把...归因于(*to, for*) 5.【律】把...让与(*to*) — *vi.*【律】让与财产 ‖ [常～s]受让人 ‖ ～able *adj.* 可分配的;可指派的;可指定的;(原因等)可指出的;可让与的 / ～ee [,æsi'niː, ə,sai'niː] *n.*【律】1. 受让人 2. 代理人,受托者 / ～or *n.* 分配者;委派者;【律】让与者

assignation [,æsig'neiʃən] *n.* 1. 分配 2. (时间、地点等的)指定;约会 3. 约会 4. 归属;归因(*to*) 5.【律】(财产、权利等的)转让,让与

assignment [ə'sainmənt] *n.* 1. 分配;委派 2. (分配的)任务;(指定的)课外作业 3.【律】(财产、权利的)转让;转让证书 4. (理由的)提出,陈述

assimilate [ə'simileit] *vt.* 1. 吸收(食物、思想、文化等) 2. 同化(民族、语言成分等) 3. 使相似;使相同(*to, with*) 4. 把...比作(*to, with*) — *vi.* 1. 被吸收 2. 被同化及 3. 成为相似(或相同)

assimilation [ə,simi'leiʃən] *n.* 1. 吸收(食

用) 2. 同化(作用)

assist [ə'sist] vt. 1. 协助,帮助 2. 搀扶 — vi. 1. 帮助,帮忙 2. 列席,在场(at)

assistance [ə'sistəns] n. 援助,帮助

assistant [ə'sistənt] adj. 辅助的;助理的 — n. 1. 助手,助理 2. 助教 3. 辅助物(;染色的)助剂

associate [ə'səuʃieit] vt. 1. 使发生联系;使联合(with) 2. 联…联想起来 — vi. 1. 交往,结交(with) — [ə'səuʃiit] n. 1. 合伙人;同事,朋友 2.(协会等的)准会员;准学士学会 3. 相关物 — [ə'səuʃiit] adj. 1. 联合的;有联系的,有关的 2. 副的 ‖ ~ **professor** 副教授

association [ə,səusi'eiʃən] n. 1. 联合;结合,关联;交往 2. 联想 3. 协会;社团;联盟 4.【化】缔合 5. 英式足球(= ~ football)

associative [ə'səuʃjətiv] adj. 1.(倾向于)联合的;引起联合的 2. 联想的 3.【数】结合的

assort [ə'sɔːt] vt. 1. 把…分类(或归类) 2. 为…配备花色品种 — vi. 1. 属于同类;相称,协调(with) 2. 交往(with)

assorted [ə'sɔːtid] adj. 1. 各式各样的,混杂的 2. 相配的,相称的 3. 分了类的;分类排列的

assortment [ə'sɔːtmənt] n. 1. 分类 2. 各种各样

assuage [ə'sweidʒ] vt. 1. 缓和,减轻(病痛等) 2. 使平静;平息(愤怒等) 3. 充(饥);解(渴) ‖ ~ment n.

assume [ə'sjuːm] vt. 1. 假定,设想 2. 担任;接受 3. 采取;呈现(某种形式,面貌) 4. 装出 5. 僭取;夺取;篡夺

assumed [ə'sjuːmd] adj. 1. 假定的,设想的 2. 假装的,虚构的 3. 篡夺的;夺得的 ‖ ~ly [ə'sjuːmidli] adv.

assuming [ə'sjuːmiŋ] adj. 僭越的;自负的

assumption [ə'sʌmpʃən] n. 1. 假定,设想 2. 担任(;承担;采取;假装 3. 自负,傲慢;僭越 4.[the A-](基督教)圣母升天节;圣母升天节(8月15日)

assurance [ə'ʃuərəns] n. 1. 把握,信念 2. 自信 3. 自大,狂妄 4. 保证,断言 5.(英)(人寿)保险:life ~ 人寿保险

assure [ə'ʃuə] vt. 1. 使确信;使放心 2. 向…保证;担保 3. 保证获得;保障 4. 给…保险(主要用于人寿保险)

assured [ə'ʃuəd] adj. 1. 确定的;有保证的 2. 自信的;自大的,自满的 3.(感到有把握的,感到放心的 — n.[复] assured(s)) n.〈英〉被保险人 ‖ ~ly [ə'ʃuəridli] adv. 1. 确定地,无疑问地 2. 自信地,有把握地 ‖ ~ness n.

assuring [ə'ʃuəriŋ] adj. 使人有信心的;使人放心的 ‖ ~ly adv.

astatine ['æstətiːn] n.【化】砹

aster ['æstə] n. 1.【植】紫苑 2.【植】翠菊(= China ~) 3.【生】星(状)体

asterisk ['æstərisk] n. 星标,星号(即*) — vt. 加星号于

astern [ə'stəːn] adv. 1. 在船(或飞机)的尾部;向船(或飞机)的尾部 2. 在后;向后

asteroid ['æstərɔid] adj. 星状的 — n. 1.【天】小行星 2.【动】海盘车,海星

asthma ['æsmə] n. 气喘,哮喘

astigmatism [ə'stiɡmətizəm] n. 1.【医】散光 2.【物】象散性;象散现象 3. 曲率不正确判断

astir [ə'stəː] adv. & adj.[常作表语] 1. 动起来;骚动起来;骚动起来 2. 已起床

astonish [ə'stɔniʃ] vt. 使惊讶

astonishing [ə'stɔniʃiŋ] adj. 令人惊讶的;

惊人的 ‖ ~ly adv.

astonishment [əˈstɔniʃmənt] n. 1. 惊讶 2. 使人惊讶的事物(或人)

astound [əˈstaund] vt. 使震惊,使大吃一惊

astounding [əˈstaundiŋ] adj. 使人震惊的 ‖ ~ly adv.

astray [əˈstrei] adv. & adj. [常作表语]迷路;入歧途,离开正道;犯错误 ◇ go ~ 1. 迷路;走失 2. 搞错 3. 走上邪路,堕落 4. 被遗失;被误投

astride [əˈstraid] adj. [常作表语] & adv. 两腿分开着一 prep. 跨越;跨在…上

astringency [əˈstrindʒənsi] n. 1. 收敛性 2. 严厉,严峻

astringent [əˈstrindʒənt] adj. 1. 收敛性的;味涩的 2. 严厉的;辛辣的 — n. [药]收敛剂 ‖ ~ly adv.

astro - comb. form 表示"星","天体"字宙:astronomy, astrology

astrogeology [ˌæstrəudʒiˈɔlədʒi] n. [天]天体地质学

astrologer [əˈstrɔlədʒə] n. 占星家

astrology [əˈstrɔlədʒi] n. 星占学,占星术

astronaut [ˈæstrənɔːt] n. 宇(宙)航(行)员

astronautics [ˌæstrəˈnɔːtiks] n. [用作单或复]宇宙航行学,航天学

astronomer [əˈstrɔnəmə] n. 天文学家

astronomical [ˌæstrəˈnɔmikəl] adj. 1. 天文(学)的;天体的 2. (喻)极巨大的 ‖ ~ly adv.

astronomy [əˈstrɔnəmi] n. 天文学

astute [əˈstjuːt] adj. 1. 敏锐的,精明的,聪明的 2. 狡猾的,诡计多端的 ‖ ~ly adv. / ~ness n.

Asuncion [əˌsunsiˈun] n. 亚松森[巴拉圭首都]

asunder [əˈsʌndə] adj. [常作表语] & adv. 1.(向不同方向)分开 2. 散;碎

asylum [əˈsailəm] n. 1. 收容所,救济院 2. 避难所,庇护所 3. 避难;政治避难权,庇护权

At [化]元素砹(astatine)的符号

at [强 æt; 弱 ət] prep. 1. [表示空间]在…,在…上 2. [表示时间]在…时(刻),一经…,一…就…; ~ the mere mention (thought) of …一提(想)到…3. [表示状态]在…; ~ war (peace)在交战(和平)状态中 4. 在…方面: good ~ learning 善于学习的 5. 针对着,向 6. [表示速度,价格等]以…; a low cost 以低成本大规模生产某种产品 7. 从事于: What is he ~? 他正在干什么? 8. 因为,由于: rejoice ~ others' achievements 为别人的成就感到高兴

atavism [ˈætəvizəm] n. [生]1. 隔代遗传;返祖现象 2. 呈现返祖现象的动物(或植物) ‖ atavistic [ˌætəˈvistik] adj.

ate [et, eit] eat 的过去式

-ate suf. [构成名词]1. 表示"…职务":consulate 2. 表示"牵涉及的对象等":precipitate 3. [化]表示"…酸盐":sulphate — [构成形容词]1. 表示"具有…特征的":collegiate 2. 表示"充满…的":affectionate — [构成动词]1. 表示"成为":evaporate 2. 表示"处理":vaccinate

atheism [ˈeiθiizəm] n. 无神论 ‖ **atheist** n. 无神论者

Athens [ˈæθənz] n. 1. 雅典[希腊首都] 2. [史]雅典(古希腊雅典城邦的首府)

athirst [əˈθəːst] adj. [只作表语]1.(诗)渴的 2. 渴望的

athlete [ˈæθliːt] n. 1. 运动员;体育家;(英)田径运动员 2. 身强力壮的人 ‖ ~'s foot [医]足癣

athletic [æθ'letik] *adj.* 1. 运动的, 体育的 2. 运动员的; 体育家的; 体格健壮的; 行动敏捷的; 活泼的 ‖ ~ally *adv.*

athletics [æθ'letiks] [复] *n.* 1. [用作单或复]体育运动, 竞技; 〈英〉田径运动 2. [用作单]体育(课)

athwart [ə'θwɔːt] *adv.* 1. 横跨着; 斜穿过 2. 逆, 相反 ─ *prep.* 1. 横跨 2. 逆, 相反

-ation *suf.* [构成名词] 1. 表示 "动作": agit*ation* 2. 表示 "状态": occup*ation* 3. 表示 "结果": realiz*ation*

-ative *suf.* [构成形容词]表示 "有...性质的", "有...倾向的", "有...关系的": demonstr*ative*, talk*ative*, authorit*ative*

Atlantic [ət'læntik] *adj.* 大西洋的: the ~ Ocean 大西洋 ─ *n.* [the ~]大西洋

atlas ['ætləs] *n.* 1. 地图册; 图表集 2. 大张绘图纸 3. 【解】寰椎, 第一颈椎 4. [A-]〈希神〉阿特拉斯(顶天的巨神); 〈喻〉身负重担的人 5. [A-]阿特拉斯山脉[非洲] (= the Atlas Mountains)

ATM *abbr.* automated teller machine

atmosphere ['ætməsfiə] *n.* 1. 大气; 大气层 2. 空气 3. 【物】(标准)大气压 4. 【理】雾(包围物体的介质) 5. 气氛; 环境, 气(艺术品品的)基调

atmospheric [ˌætməs'ferik] *adj.* 1. 大气的; 空气的; 大气层的 2. 大气所引起的; 产生某种气氛的; 有艺术气质的 3. ~s [复] *n.* [用复]天电; 自然产生的离散电磁波

atmospherical [ˌætməs'ferikəl] *adj.* = atmospheric ‖ ~ly *adv.*

atoll ['ætɔl] *n.* [地]环礁, 环状珊瑚岛

atom ['ætəm] *n.* 1. 原子 2. 微粒 3. 微量 ‖ ~ bomb 原子弹 / ~-bomb *vt.* 用原子弹轰炸 / ~ bomber 核动力(或载有原子弹的)轰炸机

atomic [ə'tɔmik] *adj.* 1. 原子的 2. 原子能的 3. 原子武器的 4. 以原子形式存在的; 分裂为原子的 5. 极微的 6. 强大的 ‖ ~ bomb 原子弹 / ~ energy 原子能

atomical [ə'tɔmikəl] *adj.* = atomic ‖ ~ly *adv.*

atomize ['ætəmaiz] *vt.* 1. 使分裂; 使分化; 使碎裂 2. 把...喷成雾状, 使雾化 3. 用原子弹轰炸 ‖ **atomization** *n.* 1. 原子化 2. [化]雾化 / ~ r *n.* 雾化器

atone [ə'təun] *vi.* 赎回; 偿还 (for) ‖ ~ ment *n.* 补偿; 赎罪

atop [ə'tɔp] *adv. & prep.* 在 (...的)顶上

atrocious [ə'trəuʃəs] *adj.* 1. 凶恶的, 残暴的 2. 〈口〉糟透的, 恶劣的 ‖ ~ly *adv.* / ~ness *n.*

atrocity [ə'trɔsiti] *n.* 1. 凶恶, 残暴; 暴行 2. 〈口〉庸俗不堪的东西; 令人不愉快的事物

atrophy ['ætrəfi] *n.* 1. [医]萎缩 2. (器官等的)衰退, 退化 〈喻〉萎缩, 衰退, 减退 ─ *vi. & vt.* (使)萎缩; (使)衰退

attach [ə'tætʃ] *vt.* 1. 缚上; 系, 贴上; 附加; 隶属 3. 把(重点等)放在 (to) 4. 使爱恋, 使依恋(to) 5. 任命 6. 逮捕; 扣押; 查封 7. [军]把...配属 ─ *vi.* 系, 缚; 附; 归属 ‖ ~ment *n.* 1. 附上; 系住 2. 连接(物); 附属物; 附件; 附加装置 3. 情感, 爱慕; 忠诚 3. 扣押; 扣押令

attaché [ə'tæʃei] *n.* (外交使团的)专员; (使馆、公使馆的)随员: a military ~ 武官 / a commercial ~ 商务专员 ‖ ~ case 公文包

attack [ə'tæk] *vt.* 1. 攻击, 进攻 2. 非难, 抨击 3. (干劲十足地)投入, 着手 4. (疾病)侵袭 ─ *vi.* 攻击 ─ *n.* 1. 攻击, 进攻 2. 非难, 抨击 3. (疾病等的)侵袭, 发作 4. (工作、任务等的)开始 ‖ ~er *n.* 攻击者

attain [ə'tein] *vt.* 1. 达到；完成；获得 2. 到达 — *vi.* 到达(*to*) ‖ ~**able** *adj.* 可达到的

attainment [ə'teinmənt] *n.* 1. 达到；到达 2.[常~s]成就，造诣

attar ['ætə] *n.* 香精油：玫瑰油

attempt [ə'tempt] *vt.* 1. 尝试，试图 2. 试图夺得(要塞等) 3.〈古〉企图杀害 — *n.* 1. 尝试，努力，企图，试图 2. 攻击，进攻

attend [ə'tend] *vt.* 1. 出席，参加 2. 照顾；护理；侍候 3. 陪伴；伴随 — *vi.* 1. 专心；注意(*to*) 2. 照顾；护理(*to*) 3. 伴随；侍候(*upon*)

attendance [ə'tendəns] *n.* 1. 参加；出席 2. 出席人数；出席率 3. 护理，侍候，照料

attendant [ə'tendənt] *n.* 1. 侍从；服务员 2. 出席者 3. 随从 4. 伴随物 — *adj.* 1. 在场的 2. 护理的 3. 伴随的；附随的

attention [ə'tenʃən] *n.* 1. 注意，留心；关心 2. 注意力 3.[~s]殷勤 4.[军]立正姿势；(口令)立正

attentive [ə'tentiv] *adj.* 1. 注意的，当心的 2. 有礼貌的；关心的；殷勤的(*to*) ‖ ~**ly** *adv.* / ~**ness** *n.*

attenuate [ə'tenjueit] *vt. & vi.* 1.(使)减弱；(使)减少 2.(使)变小；(使)变纤细 3.(使)变稀薄，(使)稀释 4.(使)衰减 ‖ **at,tenu'ation** *n.*

attest [ə'test] *vt.* 1. 证实，证明 2. 作为...的证明；表明 3. 使宣誓 — *vi.* 证实，证明(*to*) ‖ ~**ation** [ætes'teiʃən] *n.*

attic ['ætik] *n.* 顶楼：屋顶室

attire [ə'taiə] *vt.* 使穿衣；使穿上盛装(*in*) — *n.* 服装，衣着；盛装

attitude ['ætitjuːd] *n.* 1. 姿势，态度；看

法(*to, towards*) 3.[空]飞行姿态(= ~ of flight) 4.(芭蕾舞中的)鹤立式

attorney [ə'tɜːni] *n.* 1.(业务或法律事务中的)代理人 2.〈美〉律师(英国称 solicitor) ‖ ~**ship** *n.* 代理人(或律师)的职务；代理权 ‖ **at'torney-at-'law** *n.*〈美〉律师 / **Attorney General**〈英〉检察总长，首席检查官；〈美〉司法部长

attract [ə'trækt] *vt.* 1. 吸引 2. 引起(注意，兴趣，赞赏等)；诱惑 — *vi.* 有吸引力

attraction [ə'trækʃən] *n.* 1. 吸引 2. 吸引力；诱惑力 3. 吸引物；喜闻乐见的事物 4.[物]引力 5.[语]形态同化

attractive [ə'træktiv] *adj.* 有吸引力的，引起注意的，引起兴趣的，有迷惑力的 ‖ ~**ly** *adv.* / ~**ness** *n.*

attribute [ə'tribjut] *vt.* 1. 把...归因于；把...归咎于(*to*) 2. 认为...是某人所有；认为...是某人创造的 — ['ætribjuːt] *n.* 1. 属性；品质；特征 2.(人，物，职务等的)标志，象征 3.[语]定语

attribution [ætri'bjuːʃən] *n.* 1. 归因，归属 2. 归属物；属性

attributive [ə'tribjutiv] *adj.* 1. 归属的；属性的 2. 定语的 — *n.*[语]定语 ‖ ~**ly** *adv.*

attrit [ə'trit] *vt.* 消耗，削弱 — *n.* 消耗战；(军事上)消耗敌人的行为

attrition [ə'triʃən] *n.* 1. 摩擦 2. 磨损；消耗(死亡、退休等引起的)人员的自然缩减

attune [ə'tjuːn] *vt.* 1.[音]为(乐器)调音 2. 使协调，使合拍

atypical [,ei'tipikəl] *adj.* 非典型的，不合定型的；不规则的；不正常的 ‖ ~**ly** *adv.*

Au[化]元素金(gold)的符号

auburn ['ɔːbən] *n. & adj.* 褐色(的),赤褐色(的)

auction ['ɔːkʃən] *n. & vt.* 拍卖

auctioneer [ˌɔːkʃə'nɪə] *n.* 拍卖商 — *vt.* 拍卖

audacious [ɔː'deɪʃəs] *adj.* 1. 大胆的,有冒险精神的 2. 鲁莽的,放肆的;蛮横无礼的;厚颜无耻的 ‖ ~**ly** *adv.* / ~**ness** *n.*

audacity [ɔː'dæsiti] *n.* 1. 大胆,冒险性 2. 鲁莽,放肆;蛮横无礼;厚颜无耻 3. 鲁莽行为;放肆的话

audible ['ɔːdibl] *adj.* 听得见的 ‖ ˌaudi'bility *n.*(声音的)可闻度 / ~**ness** *n.* / **audibly** *adv.*

audience ['ɔːdiəns] *n.* 1. 听众;观众;读者 2. 倾听;被听取意见的机会 3. 正式接见;晋见

audio ['ɔːdiəu] *adj.* 1. 放音的;播音的;收音的;录音的 2. 声音的 2.(可闻)音频的,声频的

audiotape ['ɔːdiəteip] *n.* 录音磁带

audiotyping ['ɔːdiəutaipiŋ] *n.* 直接根据录音打字,听录音打字

audiotypist ['ɔːdiəuˌtaipist] *n.* 直接根据录音打字的打字员

audiovisual [ˌɔːdiəu'vizjuəl] *adj.* 利用视觉和听觉的;视听教学的 — *n.* [~s] 视听教具,直观教具

audit ['ɔːdit] *n.* 1. 审计,查账 2. 查账(或审计)报告书 — *vt.* 1. 查(账) 2.(美)旁听(大学课程) — *vi.* 审计,查账

audition [ɔː'diʃən] *n.* 1. 听;听觉,听能 2.(演员等发声的)试听,试音 3.(对演员等)进行面试,让…试唱(或试奏等) — *vi.* 试演(或试奏等)

auditor ['ɔːditə] *n.* 1. 审计员,查账人 2.

听者;听众之一 3.〈美〉(大学)旁听生

auditorium [ˌɔːdi'tɔːriəm] *n.* 1. 听众席;观众席 2.〈美〉会堂,礼堂

auditory ['ɔːditəri] *adj.* 听觉的

Aug. *abbr.* August

auger ['ɔːgə] *n.*〈机〉(钻木用的)木螺钻;(钻地用的)地螺钻

aught [ɔːt] *n.* 1. 任何事情;任何一部分 2. 零(naught 的转讹) — *adv.* 在任何方面,在任何程度上,根本

augment [ɔːg'ment] *vt.* 1. 扩大;增加;增长 2.【语】在…上增音 3.【音】在…上增半音;延长(主旋律)的音 — *vi.* 扩大;增加 — ['ɔːgmənt] *n.* 1. 增加 2.【语】增音

augmentation [ˌɔːgmen'teiʃən] *n.* 1. 扩大;增加;增长 2. 增加物 3.【音】(主旋律的)延长

augur ['ɔːgə] *n.* 1.(古罗马用观察飞鸟等方法的)占卜官 2. 预言者;占卜者 — *vt.* 1. 预言 2. 预示,成为…的预兆 — *vi.* 1. 占卜 2. 成为预兆

augury ['ɔːgjuri] *n.* 1.(古罗马的)占卜(术);占卜仪式 2. 预兆,征兆

August ['ɔːgəst] *n.* 八月(略作 Aug.)

august [ɔː'gʌst] *adj.* 尊严的,可敬的;庄严的,威严的

auk [ɔːk] *n.*〈动〉海雀(短翅、蹼足的北极海鸟)

aunt [ɑːnt] *n.* 1. 姨母;姑母;伯母;婶母;舅母 2. 大姨,大妈,阿姨(对年长妇女的尊称) ‖ **Aunt Jane**〈美俚〉珍妮大婶(指惯于逆迎讨好逆来顺受的黑人妇女)/**Aunt Sally**〈英〉1. 萨利大婶(游戏中口含烟斗的女模拟偶像,游戏者用棒或球投掷烟斗) 2. 靶子,众矢之的

auntie ['ɑːnti] *n.*〈呢〉= aunt

aunty ['ɑːnti] *n.* = auntie

aura ['ɔːrə] ([复] aurae ['ɔːriː] 或 auras) *n.*
1. (人或物发出的) 气味(或香味); 气氛, 氛围 2. 【电】电风; 辉光 3. 【医】先兆, 预感

aural ['ɔːrəl] *adj.* 1. 气味的; 香味的; 气氛的 2. 【电】电风的; 辉光的 3. 先兆的, 预感的 4. 耳的; 听觉的; 听力的

aureole ['ɔːriəul] *n.* 1. (圣像头部或身体周围的) 光环, 光轮 2. (日、月的) 晕 3. 光辉

Aureomycin [ˌɔːriəuˈmaisin] *n.* 【微】金霉素

au revoir [ˌəu rəˈvwɑː] 〈法〉再见

auricle ['ɔːrikl] *n.* 1. 【解】耳廓; 心房(心脏的) 心耳 2. 【生】耳状部, 耳状器官; 【动】耳形突; 耳状骨; 【植】(叶) 耳 ‖ -d *adj.*

auricular [ɔːˈrikjulə] *adj.* 1. (近) 耳的 2. 听觉的; 通过听觉获得的 3. 私下对人说的, 耳语的 4. 耳状的 5. 【解】心耳的

auriferous [ɔːˈrifərəs] *adj.* 含金的; 产金的

aurora [ɔːˈrɔːrə] *n.* 1. 曙光, 朝霞, 晨曦 2. 【天】极光 3. [A-] 【罗神】奥罗拉(即曙光女神) ‖ ~ **australis** [ɔːsˈtreilis] 南极光 / ~ **borealis** [ˌbɔːriˈeilis] 北极光

auspice ['ɔːspis] *n.* 1. 预兆, 前兆; 吉兆 2. (根据飞鸟行动的) 占卜 3. [~s] 支持; 赞助; under the ~s of the ... 支持下

auspicious [ɔːsˈpiʃəs] *adj.* 1. 吉利的, 吉祥的 2. 顺利的; 繁荣昌盛的 ‖ ~**ly** *adv.* / ~**ness** *n.*

austere [ɔːsˈtiə] *adj.* 1. 严峻的; 严厉的; 严正的, 严肃的 3. 简朴的, 朴素的 4. 紧缩的, 节制的 5. 酸苦的, 涩味的 ‖ ~**ly** *adv.* / ~**ness** *n.*

austerity [ɔːsˈteriti] *n.* 1. 严峻, 严厉 2. 严

正, 严肃 3. 简朴, 朴素 4. 紧缩, 节制 5. 酸苦, 涩味 6. [常 austerities] 苦行, 禁欲生活

Australia [ɔsˈtreiljə] *n.* 澳大利亚 [大洋洲国家] ‖ ~**n** *adj.* 澳大利亚的; 澳大利亚人的 *n.* 澳大利亚人

Austria ['ɔstriə] *n.* 奥地利 [欧洲中部国家] ‖ ~**n** *adj.* 奥地利的; 奥地利人的 *n.* 奥地利人 ‖ ~**-'Hungary** *n.* 【史】奥匈帝国

authentic [ɔːˈθentik] *adj.* 1. 可靠的, 可信的; 权威性的; 有根据的 2. 真的, 真正的 3. 【律】手续完备的; 依法有效的 ‖ ~**ally** *adv.*

authenticate [ɔːˈθentikeit] *vt.* 1. 证明... 是确实(或可信、真)的 2. 使具有法律效力 ‖ au,thenti'cation *n.*

authenticity [ˌɔːθenˈtisiti] *n.* 可靠性, 确实性; 真实性

author ['ɔːθə] *n.* 1. 著者; 作家 2. 创造者; 创始人, 发起人 3. 作家的著作 — *vt.* 1. 著(书), 写作 2. 创造, 创始 ‖ ~**ship** *n.* 1. 著作活动 2. 原作者之原创造(或创作)策划者

authoritarian [ɔːˌθɔriˈtɛəriən] *adj.* 权力主义的, 独裁主义的 — *n.* 权力主义者, 独裁主义者 ‖ ~**ism** *n.* 权力主义, 独裁主义

authoritative [ɔːˈθɔritətiv] *adj.* 1. 有权威的, 可相信的 2. 倚仗权势的; 命令式的 3. 官方的, 当局的 ‖ ~**ly** *adv.* / ~**ness** *n.*

authority [ɔːˈθɔriti] *n.* 1. 权, 权力 2. 职权, 权限; 许可 3. [authorities] 当局, 官方 4. 根据; 理由 5. 权威; 有权威性的典籍

authorize ['ɔːθəraiz] *vt.* 1. 授权, 委任; 委托 2. 批准, 允许, 认可 ‖ authori'zation *n.* 1. 授权; 委任 2. 核准, 认可 ‖ ~'

adj. 委任的；核准的，许可的；公认的

auto [ˈɔːtəu]([复] autos) *n.* 〈口〉汽车（automobile 的略语）

autobiography [ˌɔːtəubaiˈɔgrəfi] *n.* 自传；自传的写作

autochanger [ˈɔːtəuˌtʃeindʒə] *n.* 自动换片（电）唱机

autocracy [ɔːˈtɔkrəsi] *n.* 1. 独裁；专制 2. 独裁统治；独裁政体；独裁统治的国家

autocrat [ˈɔːtəkræt] *n.* 1. 独裁者；专制君主 2. 独断独行的人

autocratic [ˌɔːtəˈkrætik] *adj.* 独裁的；专制的；独断独行的 ‖ ~al *adj.* / ~cally *adv.*

autograph [ˈɔːtəgrɑːf] *n.* 1. 亲笔；亲笔签名 2. 手稿 3. 真迹复制品 — *vt.* 1. 亲笔书写 2. 在...上亲笔签名

autoimmunization [ˌɔːtəuimjunaiˈzeiʃən] *n.* 自身免疫（法）；自身免疫作用

automat [ˈɔːtəmæt] *n.* 1. 自动售货（或售票）机；〈主美〉用自动售货机供应食品的餐馆

automate [ˈɔːtəmeit] *vt.* 使自动化 ‖ ~d teller machine（银行的）自动柜员机

automatic [ˌɔːtəˈmætik] *adj.* 1. 自动的 2. 无意识的；机械的 — *n.* 1. 自动枪（或工具）；自动变速装置 2. 自动手枪（或步枪）‖ ~ally *adv.* ‖ ~ teller (machine) = automated teller machine

automation [ˌɔːtəˈmeiʃən] *n.* 自动化 2. 自动操作

automaton [ɔːˈtɔmətən] ([复] automata [ɔːˈtɔmətə] 或 automatons) *n.* 1. 自动机；自动玩具；自动装置；自动控制装置；机器人 2. 机械般动作的人（或动物）

automobile [ˈɔːtəməubiːl, ˌɔːtəməuˈbiːl] *n.* 〈美〉汽车 — *vi.* 乘汽车（旅行）；驾驶汽车

automotive [ˌɔːtəˈməutiv] *adj.* 1. 自动推进的 2. 汽车的

autonomous [ɔːˈtɔnəməs] *adj.* 1. 自治的；自治权的 2. 自主的

autonomy [ɔːˈtɔnəmi] *n.* 1. 自治；自治权 2. 自主

autopsy [ˈɔːtɔpsi] *n.* 1.【医】尸体剖检，尸体解剖 2. 分析，剖析 3. 亲自实地勘察 — *vt.* 解剖，剖检（尸体）‖ autopsist *n.*

autotimer [ˈɔːtəuˌtaimə] *n.*（电灶等的）自动定时器

autumn [ˈɔːtəm] *n.* 1. 秋，秋季（美国一般用 fall）2. 成熟期；渐衰期

autumnal [ɔːˈtʌmnəl] *adj.* 1. 秋，秋天的 2. 已过壮年的；已过旺盛期的

auxiliary [ɔːgˈziljəri] *adj.* 1. 辅助的 2. 附属的，从属的 — *n.* 1. 辅助者；辅助物 2.【语】助动词 3. [auxiliaries] 外国援军；辅助舰艇 4. 附属组织（或机构）

avail [əˈveil] *vi.* 有用，有益，有助 — *vt.* 对...有用，有益于，有助于 — *n.* 效用；帮助 ‖ — (*oneself*) *of* 利用

availability [əˌveiləˈbiliti] *n.* 利用（或获得）的可能；有效性；可利用（或获得）的人（或物）

available [əˈveiləbl] *adj.* 1. 可用的，合用的 2. 可得到的 3. 不太忙的，能接待的 4.（入场券等）通用的，有效的 5.（因政治背景等原因）有当选希望的；愿接受提名（或参加竞选）的 ‖ ~ness *n.* / availably *adv.*

avalanche [ˈævəlɑːntʃ] *n.* 1. 雪崩；山崩 2. 大量，突然来到的一大批 3.【物】（电子或离子）雪崩 — *vi.* 崩塌；雪崩般塌落 — *vt.*（信件等大量涌至）把...淹没，使无法应付

avant-garde [ˌævɑː̃ˈɡɑːd] *n.* 〈文学、艺术中敢于创新的〉先锋派；先锋派支持者们 — *adj.*（属于）先锋派的；大胆的

激进的

avarice ['ævəris] *n.* 贪婪

avaricious [ˌævə'riʃəs] *adj.* 贪婪的，贪得无厌的 ‖ ~ly *adv.* / ~ness *n.*

Ave. *abbr.* Avenue

avenge [ə'vendʒ] *vt.* 替……报仇；为……雪耻 ‖ ~r *n.* 报仇者

avenue ['ævinju:] *n.* 1. 林荫道 2.(英)(通往乡村住宅，两旁栽树的)小路 3. 城市中的)大街 4. 通道；路线；[喻]途径、渠道

aver [ə'və:] (averred; averring) *vt.* 1. 断言；坚称(that) 2.[律]证明……属实 ‖ ~ment *n.*

average ['ævəridʒ] *n.* 1. 平均；平均数 2. 一般水平，中等水平 3.[商]海损 — *adj.* 1. 平均的 2. 普通的；中等的；平常的 3.[商]按海损法规估价的 — *vt.* 1.(为得到更有利的平均价格而)买进；卖出 — *vi.* 1. 从……得出平均数；均分 2. 平均为 3. 使趋向平衡 4. 按比例分配

averse [ə'və:s] *adj.* 1. 反对的；不乐意的，不情愿的(to, from) 2.[植](叶子等)与茎方向相反的 ‖ ~ly *adv.* / ~ness *n.*

aversion [ə'və:ʃən] *n.* 1. 厌恶，反感 2. 讨厌的人(或东西)

avert [ə'və:t] *vt.* 1. 转移(目光、思想等)(from) 2. 挡开(灾难等)；防止(危险等) ‖ ~ible *adj.* 可避免的，可防止的

aviary ['eivjəri] *n.* 鸟舍，鸟类饲养场 ‖ aviarist *n.* 鸟类饲养者

aviation [ˌeivi'eiʃən] *n.* 1. 航空；航空学；飞行术 2. 飞机制造业 3.[总称](军用)飞机

aviator ['eivieitə] *n.* 飞行员，飞机驾驶员

aviatress ['eivieitris] *n.* = aviatrix

aviatrix ['eivi'eitriks] ([复] aviatrixes 或 aviatrices[ˌeivi'eitrisiz]) *n.* 女飞行员，女飞行驾驶员

avid ['ævid] *adj.* 1. 渴望的；急切的(for, of) 2. 劲头十足的：an ~ reader 读起书来废寝忘食的人 ‖ ~ly *adv.*

avidity [ə'viditi] *n.* 1. 渴望；急切；贪婪 2.[化]亲合力；活动性

avocado [ˌævə'ka:dəu] ([复] avocado(e)s) *n.*[植]鳄梨；鳄梨树

avocation [ˌævəu'keiʃən] *n.*(个人)副业，业余爱好

avoid [ə'vɔid] *vt.* 1. 避免；防止；避开 2.[律]使无效；撤销，废止 ‖ ~able *adj.*

avoidance [ə'vɔidəns] *n.* 1. 回避；躲避 2.[律]使无效；废止

avoirdupois [ˌævədə'pɔiz] *n.* 1. 常衡(为一磅:亦作~ weight) 2.(美口)体重；肥胖 ‖ ~ pound 常衡磅

avouch [ə'vautʃ] *vt.* 1. 保证，担保 2. 断言 3. 承认；供认 — *vi.* 作出保证(for)

avow [ə'vau] *vt.* 公开表示；坦率承认 ‖ ~al *n.*

avowed [ə'vaud] *adj.* 公开承认(或宣布)的 ‖ ~ly[ə'vauidli] *adv.*

await [ə'weit] *vt.* 1. 等候，期待 2.(事件等)等待(处理)；将降临到……身上

awake [ə'weik] (过去式 awoke[ə'wəuk]，过去分词 awoke 或 awaked) *vt.* 1. 唤醒，使醒 2. 唤起；使觉悟；使奋发 — *vi.* 1. 醒 2. 觉醒(希望等)被激起，被唤起 3. 意识到；认识到(to) — *adj.* [用作表语] 1. 醒着的 2. 警觉的，意识到的

awaken [ə'weikən] *vt.* 使觉醒；唤醒 — *vi.* 醒，醒悟(to)

award [ə'wɔ:d] *vt.* 授予；给予；判给 — *n.* 1. 裁定；判决；裁定书 2. 奖，奖品

aware [ə'wɛə] *adj.* [用作表语]意识到的；知道的(*of, that*) ‖ ~ness *n.*

awash [ə'wɔʃ] *adj.* [常作表语] 1. 被浪潮冲打的 2. 被水覆盖的

away [ə'wei] *adv.* 1. (远)离：The place is two miles ~ from here. 那个地方离这儿有两英里路。/ The sports are two weeks ~. 离运动会还有两个星期。2. ...去，...掉：wash the dirt ~ 洗掉污垢 3. [用于无动词感叹句的句首]去掉；走开：Away with you！（口）滚开！4. 继续不断地：work ~ 连续干下去 5. 立刻：right ~ 立刻 ‖ ~ match *adj.* (球赛等)客场的，在对方场地进行的

awe [ɔ] *n.* 畏惧；敬畏；怕 — *vt.* 威吓；使敬畏 ‖ ~ some *adj.* 1. 使人敬畏的；可畏的 2. 感到畏惧(或敬畏)的 ‖ '~-in,spiring *adj.* 使人畏惧的；使人敬畏的 / '~-stricken, '~-struck *adj.* 充满敬畏(或畏惧)之心的

awful ['ɔːful] *adj.* 1. 令人畏惧的，可怕的；令人敬畏的 2. 威严的；令人崇敬的 3.〈口〉极度的；非常的；极坏的 ‖ ~ly *adv.* 1.〈口〉恶劣地；令人嫌恶地 2.〈口〉非常地；极度地；十分 / ~ness *n.*

awhile [ə'hwail] *adv.* 片刻

awkward ['ɔːkwəd] *adj.* 1. 笨拙的；不熟练的 2. 使用不便的 3. 尴尬的 4. 难应付的；难处理的；棘手的 ‖ ~ly *adv.* / ~ness *n.*

awl [ɔl] *n.* 钻子，鞋钻

awn [ɔːn] *n.* [植]芒 ‖ ~ed *adj.* 有芒的 /

~less *adj.* 无芒的

awning ['ɔːniŋ] *n.* 1. 雨篷,凉篷,遮篷 2. [船]天篷

awoke [ə'wəuk]awake 的过去式和过去分词

awry [ə'rai] *adj.* [常作表语] & *adv.* 1. 曲(的)；歪(的)；斜(的) 2. 错(的)

ax(e) [æks] ([复]axes['æksiz]) *n.* 1. 斧 2. (经费、人员等的)削减 — *vt.* 1. 用斧砍 2. 大刀阔斧地削减(经费、人员等)

axes 1. ['æksiz]ax(e)的复数 2. ['æksiz]axis 的复数

axiom ['æksiəm] *n.* 1. 公理；自明之理 2. 原理；原则 3. 格言

axis ['æksis] ([复]axes['æksiz]) *n.* 1. 轴；轴线 2. 中心线；中枢 3.〈喻〉轴心(指国家间的联盟)；the Aris 轴心国(指二战中德、意、日三国联盟) 4.[解]框椎，第二颈椎 5.[植]主茎；茎轴 6.[化]晶轴

axle ['æksl] *n.* 轴；车轴

axon ['æksɔn] *n.*[解]轴突

ay(e)[ai] *adv.* & *int.* 是；当然 — *n.* 赞成票；投赞成票者

ay[ei] *adv.*〈古〉常常；永远

azalea [ə'zeiljə] *n.*[植]杜鹃花

Azerbaijan [æzəbai'dʒɑːn] *n.* 1. 阿塞拜疆[外高加索东南部国家] 2. 阿塞拜疆[伊朗一地区]

Azov ['æzɔv] *n.* ‖ the Sea of ~ 亚速海[黑海的一个支海]

azure ['æʒə] *n.* & *adj.* 1. 天蓝色(的) 2. 无云的(天空)

B

B, b [bi:]([复]B's, b's 或 Bs, bs[biz])①英语字母表第二十字母 1.[数]第二已知量 2.[化]B B字母形 3.[B][化]元素硼(boron)的符号 4.[B][物]磁感应强度(magnetic induction)的符号 5.[B][音]B音,B调 6.[B] = black(表示铅笔芯软硬度的符号) 7.乙(指学业成绩良好)

Ba [化]元素钡(barium)的符号

BA *abbr.* Bachelor of Arts 文学士

baa [bɑ:] *n.* 咩(羊叫声) — *vi.* 发咩声

babble [ˈbæbl] *vi.* 1.(婴孩)咿呀学语 2.喋喋不休,唠叨 3.吐露秘密 4.(流水)潺潺作声 — *vt.* 1.唠叨地说 2.吐露(秘密等)(*out*)— *n.* 1.咿呀学语声 2.胡言乱语 3.潺潺声 ‖ ~**r** *n.* 1.说话不清楚的人 2.胡言乱语的人 3.吐露秘密的人

babe [beib] *n.* 1.婴儿 2.天真幼稚的人 3.〖美俚〗宝贝儿,小亲亲(常用于称呼女人)

baboon [bəˈbuːn] *n.* [动]狒狒

babushka [bəˈbuːʃkə] *n.* 1.(妇女包头用的三角形)婆婆头巾 2.老太婆

baby [ˈbeibi] *n.* 1.婴儿,幼畜 2.孩子气的人;胆怯的人 3.[常作定语]小型物:a ~ car 小型汽车 4.(美俚)娃娃 5.(家庭或团体中)年龄最小的人 — *vt.* 把……当作婴孩对待;娇纵 ‖ ~**hood** *n.* 婴孩期 / ~**ish** *adj.* 孩子气的 ‖ ~**-sit** *vi. & vt.* 代人临时照看(小孩) / ~-

sitter *n.* 代人临时照看小孩者

baccalaureate [ˌbækəˈlɔːriət] *n.* 1.学士学位 2.毕业典礼上对毕业生的讲道(= ~ sermon)

bachelor [ˈbætʃələ] *n.* 1.单身男子,单身汉 2.学士:a *Bachelor* of Arts (Science)文(理)学士 3.尚未交配的雄兽(尤指海豹) 4.[史]青年侍从骑士,最低级骑士 ‖ ~**hood** *n.* / ~**ship** *n.* ‖ ~ **mother** (美俚) 1.未婚母亲 2.(离异、丧偶后独自抚养子女的)单身母亲 / ~'s **button** [植] 1.矢车菊 2.千日红 / ~'s **hall** 单身汉住处

bacillus [bəˈsiləs] *n.* [复]bacilli [bəˈsilai] *n.* [微]芽孢杆菌,杆菌

back [bæk] *n.* 1.背,背部;背脊 2.背面;(纺织品等的)反面 3.后部 4.(足球等的)[指球员或其位置]后卫 — *adj.* [无比较级;最高级用backmost] 1.[表示位置]后面的;背后的 2.边远的 3.倒的,反向的;过去回去的 4.[语]舌后的,舌根的 5.过期的;拖欠的 — *adv.* 1.在后;向后;后仰着 2.回;回原处(或原状) 3.以前 — *vt.* 1.使后退;倒(车)2.位于……后;以……为背景 3.支持(论点、行动、企业等) 4.给……装上背衬;裱(画)5.在……背面签字 6.下赌注在……上 — *vi.* 1.后退;倒退 2.(风)逆转 3.(房屋等)背向(*on, onto*)‖ ~**less** *adj.*

无(靠)背的/～most adj. 最后面的 ‖ ～ne n. 背脊酸痛/～bite vt. & vi. 背后说(...的)坏话,背后中伤/背后中伤/～,breaking adj. 断人腰背的,使人劳累之极的 / ～burner n.(多煤煤气灶的)后灶眼 2. 次要地位,从属地位/～,burner adj. 一时非优先的,暂处次要地位的 vt. 把...置于暂时不优先地位;把...搁置 ‖～'fire n. 1. 迎火(把草原或森林中的一块地带先纵火烧光,以阻止野火或林火蔓延)2.(内燃机等的)逆火;回火 vi. 放迎火;发生逆火;发生回火2.〈喻〉发生意外;产生事与愿违的恶果/～hand n. 1. 左向书法,向左倾斜的手写体 2. 反手拍球;反手击球 vt. 反手击(球)反手接(球)adj. & adv. = ～handed /～'handed adj. 1. 反手的;用手背的;a ～handed stroke反手击球 2. 间接的,转弯抹角的 3. 讽刺挖苦的 adv. 反手地;用手背/～lash n.(政治等方面的)强烈反应;强烈反对/～pack n. 背包 vt.(尤指徒步旅行时)背负(食物、装备等);把...放在背包内 vi. 背着背包徒步旅行/～scratcher n. 1. 自己搔背用的抓,"不求人" 2.(为了与己方便的)与人方便者;奉承拍马者/～side n. 1. 后侧;背面 2.[亦作～sides]〈口〉臀部/～slapper n. 亲切友好的人/～slapping adj. 亲切友好的/～'stabber n.〈口〉暗箭伤人者/～'street adj. 1. 偏僻街道的 2. 偷偷摸摸的,幕后的,秘密的/～ talk〈美口〉回嘴,顶嘴/～,water n. 1. 回水,壅水 2. 死水;死气沉沉的状态(或地方)/～'woods [复]n.[用作单或复]边远蛮荒林区(落后的边远地区)/～woodsman n. 边远蛮荒林区居民/～'yard n. 后院

backbone ['bækbəun] n. 1. 脊骨,脊柱 2. 主脉,干脉 3. 支柱;基础;重要部分 4. 骨气,勇气;坚定的性格 5. 脊

骨状物;书脊

backer ['bækə] n. 1. 支持者;赞助人 2. 粘贴衬衬的工人;做书脊的工人

backgammon ['bæk,gæmən, ,bæk'gæmən] n. 十五子棋戏(一种双方各有 15 枚棋子,掷骰子决定走棋格数的棋戏)

background ['bækgraund] n. 1. 背景;后景;经历 2. 背景情况 3. 隐蔽的地位,幕后 4.(织品组成的)底子 5.(广播、电影等的)背景音乐 6.(干扰收听电子信号的外来)杂音 ‖～er n. 背景情况介绍会:背景情况简报;(散发给记者的)背景材料

backing ['bækiŋ] n. 1. 后退;倒退 2. 后盾,支持;(一群)支持者 3. 衬衬;(镜背)水银镀层 4.(尤指录在磁带上的)伴奏;伴唱

backlog ['bæklɒg] n. 1.〈主美〉可依靠的东西 2. 备用物;贮存物 3. 积压;a ～ of work (mail, criminal cases)积压的工作(邮件、刑事案件) — (backlogged; backlogging) vt. & vi. (使)形成积压

backslide ['bæk'slaid] ([bæk'slaid] 过去式 backslid 或 back-slidden [bæk'slidən]) vi. & n. 退缩回去;退步,倒退;故态复萌;堕落 ‖～ r n.

backtrack ['bæktræk] vi.〈主美〉由原路返回;退缩回去;出尔反尔

backward[1] ['bækwəd], **backwards** ['bækwədz] adv. 1. 向后 2. 倒,逆,反 3. 往回,向原处

backward[2] ['bækwəd] adj. 1. 向后的 2. 倒的,相反的 3. 落后的,进步慢的;迟钝的,不开窍的 4. 来迟的,晚的 5. 迟疑的,畏缩的 ‖～ly adv. /～ness n.

bacon ['beikən] n.(猪肋条腌制的)熏咸肉;腊肉

bacteria [bæk'tiəriə] [复] n. [bacterium 的

复数]细菌 ‖ ~1 adj. 细菌(引起)的/~ly adv.

bacteriological [bækˌtiəriˈɔdʒikəl] adj. 1. 细菌学的 2. 使用细菌的：a ~ weapon 细菌武器

bacteriology [bækˌtiəriˈɔlədʒi] n. 细菌学 ‖ **bacteriologist** n. 细菌学家

bacterium [bækˈtiəriəm] bacteria 的单数

bad [bæd] (worse [wəs], worst [wəst]) adj. 1. 邪恶的，不道德的 2. 坏的；质量低劣的；有缺陷的；拙劣的 3. 有害的，不利的 4. (错误、疾病等)严重的，厉害的 5. 病的痛的，不舒服的 6. (食物等)腐败的；(气味等)臭的 7. 错误的；不适当的 8. 使人不愉快的，讨厌的 9. [口]懊恼的 10. [律]不成立的，无效的 ‖ n. 坏；恶；不幸 ‖ adv. [美口] = badly ‖ ~ness n. ‖ ~mouth [美俚]流言蜚语，恶意攻击 /'~-mouth vt. 说…坏话，恶意攻击 ‖ ~ news 1. 坏消息 2. 讨厌的人 3. 倒霉的局面 4. [美俚]账单

bade [beid, bæd] bid 的过去式

badge [bædʒ] n. 1. 徽章；证章；奖章 2. 标记，标识；象征

badger[1] [ˈbædʒə] n. 1. [动]獾 2. 獾皮；獾毛 3. [美][B-] 獾州人(威斯康星州人的别称)

badger[2] [ˈbædʒə] vt. 纠缠，使困恼

badly [ˈbædli] (worse [wəs], worst [wəst]) adv. 1. 坏，恶劣地 2. 有害地 3. 有缺点地；拙劣地 4. 严重地，[口]非常

badminton [ˈbædmintən] n. 1. 羽毛球运动 2. 巴德明顿饮酒，葡萄酒汽水(一种夏季饮料)

baffle [ˈbæfl] vt. 1. 使挫折，阻碍 2. 使困惑 3. 用挡板控制(气流等)；用反射板控制(声波) ‖ vi. 徒作挣扎 ‖ n. 1. 迷惑 2. 挡板；折流板；缓冲板；反射

板；遮护物；障板 ‖ **baffling** adj. 令人迷惑的，莫名其妙的；起阻碍作用的

bag [bæg] n. 1. 袋，包；钱包；手提皮包(尤指妇女用的) 2. (英口)[~s]大量，许多 3. 猎袋；(猎袋中的)猎获物；(空战中)被击落的敌机总数 4. 垒袋(棒球的)垒,全垒,垒囊；松垂的眼袋皮；衣服的鼓陷处；(母牛等的)乳房(英口)[~s]裤子 6. (俚)爱好；特长 7. (俚)无吸引力的女子；丑姑娘；妓女 8. (个人的)心情；(个人的)环境,处境；(个人的)生活方式 9. 障碍；难题 10. [俚]放一服海洛因的纸袋) — 一服海洛因或其它毒品) — (bagged; bagging) vt. 1. 把…装进袋里；[口]把…占为己有，偷窃 2. 猎获；捕杀(鸟,兽等)；击落(敌机等) 3. 使成袋状,使鼓胀 — vi. 1. (衣、裤等呈布袋那样地)膨大(或垂挂) 2. (乳牛等)长出乳房 ‖ ~ful n. 满满一袋；一袋

Bagdad [ˈbægdæd] n. = Baghdad

bagel [ˈbeigəl] n. (美)硬面包圈

baggage [ˈbægidʒ] n. 1. (美)行李(英国一般用 luggage) 2. [军]辎重 3. 精神包袱 4. 多余的东西；过时货 5. 坏女人；荡女 6. 女子；姑娘 ‖ ~ office 行李房

baggy [ˈbægi] adj. 膨松如袋的；宽松下垂的 ‖ **baggily** adv. / **bagginess** n.

Baghdad [ˈbægdæd] n. 巴格达(伊拉克首都]

bagpipe [ˈbægpaip] n. (苏格兰等地的)风笛 — vi. 奏风笛 ‖ ~ n. 吹风笛的人

bah [bɑː] int. [表示轻蔑]呸！

bail[1] [beil] n. [律]保释金；保释人；保释 — vt. 1. 将(亦犯)交保释放；保释(out) 2. 托付(财物) 3. 帮助…摆脱困境 ‖ ~able adj. / ~ee n. (财物的)受托人 / ~er n. 或 ~or n. (财物的)寄托人 / ~ment n. 1. (财物的)寄托

释

bait² [beit] *n.* 戽斗;桶(用来戽出船舱中的水) — *vt.* 戽(水);从(船)中戽出水(out) — *vi.*(从飞机上)跳伞(out) ‖ ~ er *n.* 戽斗

bailiff ['beilif] *n.* 1. 法警;郡副司法长官;市政官副手;看守人 2.(地主的)管家

bailiwick ['beiliwik] *n.* 1. 郡副司法长官(或市政官副手)的辖区(或职权范围) 2. 活动(或兴趣、知识、权力)范围

bait [beit] *n.* 1. 饵 2. 引诱物 3.(古)中途休息(或吃东西) — *vt.* 1. 装饵于;引诱(古)(在中途)喂(马或牲口)3. 欺负;折磨(人) — *vi.*(古)中途休息(或吃东西)

bake [beik] *vt.* 1. 烤,烘,焙 2. 烧硬,焙干(砖瓦等) — *vi.* 1. 烘面包(或饼等) 2.(面包等)在烘焙中;(砖瓦等)在焙干中 — *n.* 1. 烤,烘,焙 2. 吃烤面包(或其他烘焙食物)的聚餐会

baker ['beikə] *n.* 面包师傅 ‖ ~ 's dozen 十三,一打加一

bakery ['beikəri] *n.* 1. 面包烘房 2. 面包店

baking ['beikiŋ] *n.* 烤,烘,焙 ‖ ~ powder 焙粉,发(酵)粉

Baku [bɑː'kuː] *n.* 巴库[阿塞拜疆首都]

balalaika [ˌbælə'laikə] *n.*(类似吉他的)巴拉莱卡琴,俄罗斯三角琴

balance ['bæləns] *n.* 1. 秤;天平 2.(物体、收支等的)平衡;均衡;均势 3. 收付差额,余额 4. 结余;结欠;找头;尾数 5.(钟、表等的)摆轮 6. 平衡块,平衡力 7.[B]【天】天平座 8.(艺术作品中布局和比例的)协调 9.(情绪的)稳定 10. [the ~ 一]【口】剩余部分 — *vi.* 1. 使平衡;使均衡 2. 权衡,斟酌;对比,比较(计划等) 3. 使平衡

(力量等)均等 4. 结算,清(账) 5. 清消,跟……相抵;(在重量、数目或比重上)跟……相等 — *vi.* 1. 平衡 2.(价值、重量、力量方面)相等,相称 3. 收支平衡 4. 摇摆;踌躇 ‖ ~ 起平衡作用的人(或物);平衡装置;稳定器;平衡器;走钢丝者 / ~ beam【体】平衡木 / ~ sheet【会计】决算表;资产负债表 / ~ wheel(钟、表等的)平衡轮,摆轮

balcony ['bælkəni] *n.* 1. 阳台 2.(戏院的)楼厅

bald [bɔːld] *adj.* 1. 秃头的;(头)光的 2. 无毛的;无叶的;无树的;光秃的 3.(文章体裁等)单调的;不加虚饰的 4. 毫不掩饰的,赤裸裸的 ‖ ~ly *adv.* 不加虚饰地 / ~ness *n.*

bale¹ [beil] *n.* 大包,大捆 — *vt.* 把……打包 ‖ ~r *n.*

bale² [beil] *n.*, *vt.* & *vi.* = bail¹

baleful ['beilful] *adj.* 1. 邪恶的;有害的;致命的 2. 悲惨的;不幸的 ‖ ~ly *adv.* / ~ness *n.*

balk [bɔːk] *n.* 1. 阻碍,障碍 2. 错误;挫折 3.(畦间或犁沟间的)埂 4. 大木;【建】系梁 5.(尤指临时性军用桥梁的)主梁梁 — *vt.* 阻止;使受挫折 — *vi.* 1.(马等)逡巡不前;畏缩不前;回避

Balkan ['bɔːlkən] *adj.* 巴尔干半岛的;巴尔干山脉的;巴尔干半岛各国的;巴尔干人的 — *n.* 1. 巴尔干半岛;巴尔干山脉 2. [the ~s] 巴尔干半岛各国;巴尔干山脉

balky ['bɔːki] *adj.*(马等)执拗的;逡巡不前的

ball¹ [bɔːl] *n.* 1. 球,球状物 2. 星球(特指地球) 3.(人体上的)球状部位,圆形突出部位 4. 弹丸 5.(美)球类运动(尤指棒球) 6. 眼球 7.(棒球投手投出的)坏球 8. [the ~]职权 9.(俚)人,家伙 10.

[~s]胡说八道 11. [~s]〈粗〉睾丸 12. [~s]〈粗〉胆量;力气,劲儿 — **vt. &** **vi.**(把...)捏(或裹)成球形;(与...)交媾 ‖ ~ **bearing** 滚珠轴承/'~park — **n. 1.** 球场;棒球场 **2.** 活动领域;(价格、观点等的)可变通范围 — / ~ **pen,** '~ **point,** '~ **point pen** 圆珠笔

ball² [bɔːl] **n. 1.** 舞会 **2.** 〈俚〉愉快经历,赏心乐事 — **vi.** 〈美俚〉狂欢,尽情作乐 ‖ '~room **n.** 舞厅

ballad ['bæləd] **n. 1.** 叙事诗歌(的曲调) **2.** 民歌,民谣

ballast ['bæləst] **n. 1.** 压载物,压舱物;〈空〉镇重物,镇重沙袋 **2.** 使(性格等)沉着的因素,稳定因素,镇定物;〈喻〉安定;沉着 **3.** 〈交〉道渣;石渣 **4.** 〈电〉镇流器 — **vt.** 在...装压舱物(或镇重物);用压舱物(或镇重物)稳定;使稳定;使坚定 **2.** 为(铁路等)铺道碴

ballerina [ˌbæləˈriːnə] **n. 1.** (尤指演主角或独舞的)芭蕾舞女演员 **2.** 软底低跟女便鞋

ballet ['bælei, bæˈlei] **n. 1.** 芭蕾舞;芭蕾舞剧 **2.** 芭蕾舞曲;芭蕾舞剧团

ballistic [bəˈlistik] **adj.** 弹道(学)的;射弹(运动)的;发射的 ‖ ~s [复] **n.** [用作单或复] **1.** 弹道学;发射学 **2.**(兵器、弹药等)的发射特性 ‖ ~ **missile** 弹道导弹

balloon [bəˈluːn] **n. 1.** 气球;玩具气球 **2.**(蒸馏时用的)球形玻璃容器 **3.**(漫画中圈出人物讲话的)气球形圆圈 — **vi.** **1.** 膨胀如气球 **2.** 坐气球上升(或旅行) **3.** 急增 — **vt.** 使影肠成气球状 — **adj. 1.** 气球状的 **2.**(一批货物)分量轻而体积大的 **3.**(分期付款中)最后一笔款目特大的 ‖ ~**ist n.** 气球驾驶员;乘气球升空者

ballot ['bælət] **n. 1.** 选票;投票用纸 **2.** 投票总数 **3.** 投票权 **4.** 抽签决定 **5.** 候选人名单 — **vi. 1.** 投票 **2.** 抽签决定 — **vt. 1.** 向...拉票 **2.** 通过投票(或抽签)选出

ballyhoo [ˌbæliˈhuː] **n.** 〈口〉大吹大擂;夸大的宣传 — **vt. & vi.** 大吹大擂地宣扬

balm [bɑːm] **n. 1.** 香油;香脂;香膏 **2.** 止痛药膏 **3.** 〈喻〉安慰物 **4.** 香味;芳香 **5.** 【植】滇荆芥

balmy ['bɑːmi] **adj. 1.** 有香气的;出香油的;香脂的 **2.** 止痛的;安慰的 **3.**(气候)温和的 ‖ **balmily adv.** / **balminess n.**

baloney [bəˈləuni] **n.** 〈美口〉大腊肠 **2.** 〈美俚〉(尤指骗人的)鬼话,胡扯

balsa ['bɔlsə] **n.** 【植】西印度轻木

balsam ['bɔːlsəm] **n. 1.** 香脂;香膏 **2.** 安慰(物) **3.** 凤仙花 **4.** 产香脂的树

Baltic ['bɔːltik] **adj.** 波罗的海的;the ~ Sea 波罗的海[欧洲北部]

Baltimore ['bɔːltimɔː] **n.** 巴尔的摩[美国马里兰州中北部港市]

baluster ['bæləstə] **n.** 【建】栏杆柱

balustrade [ˌbæləsˈtreid] **n.** 栏杆

bamboo [bæmˈbuː] ([复] bamboos) **n.** 竹

bamboozle [bæmˈbuːzl] **vt.** 〈俚〉骗,哄骗

ban [bæn] **n. 1.** 禁止;禁令 **2.** 〈宗〉诅咒,革出教门 **3.**(封建时代的)出征诏令 **4.** 谴责(尤指舆论方面的) — **vt.**(banned; banning) **vt.** 禁止,取缔 — **vi.** 诅咒

banal [bəˈnɑːl] **adj.** 平庸的;陈腐的 ‖ ~-ity [bəˈnæliti] **n. 1.** 平庸;陈腐 **2.** 陈词滥调

banana [bəˈnɑːnə] **n. 1.** 香蕉;芭蕉 **2.** 〈美俚〉喜剧演员 **3.** 〈美俚〉大鼻子 ‖ ~ **seat**(自行车的)香蕉座

band [bænd] **n. 1.** 带;带形物;箍 **2.** 镶

边;嵌条 3.【建】扁带饰 4.【地】夹层 5.（收音机）波段,频带(wave ~ 的简称) 6.一帮,一伙(人) 7.乐队(尤指管乐队)— *vt.* 1.用带绑扎;给...装上籍 2.加条带把...绑起来 3.[后接复数反身代词,或用被动语态]把...联合起来 — *vi.* 联合起来(*with*) ‖ ~ **master** *n.* 管乐队(或军乐队)指挥 / ~ **razor** (使用安插式刀片推进的)带状保安刮刀 / ~ **sman** *n.* 管乐队(或军乐队)成员 / ~ **stand** *n.* (室外)音乐台

bandage ['bændidʒ] *n.* 绷带 — *vt. & vi.* 用绷带包扎

bandanna [bæn'dænə] *n.* 扎染印花大手帕

Bandar Seri Begawan ['bʌndəseri bə'ɡɑːwɑːn] 斯里巴加湾港(旧称 Brunei 文莱市)[文莱苏丹国首都]

bandit ['bændit] ([复] banditti [bæn'diti] 或 bandits) *n.* 1.土匪;盗匪 2.歹徒 3.〈军俚〉敌机 ‖ ~ **ry** *n.* 盗匪活动

Bandung ['bɑːnduŋ] *n.* 万隆[印度尼西亚城市]

bandy ['bændi] *vt.* 1.来回投掷(或拍击、传递) 2.来回说(话);议论;散布 — *vi.* 争斗,打架 — *adj.* 向外弯的;罗圈(腿)的 ‖ ~-**legged** *adj.* 罗圈腿的

bane [bein] *n.* 灾星,祸根

baneful ['beinful] *adj.* 1.引起灾祸(或毁灭)的;有害的 2.致死的,致命的 ‖ ~ **ly** *adv.* / ~ **ness** *n.*

bang¹ [bæŋ] *vt.* 1.使发出砰的一声,砰砰地响 2.猛撞;猛撞;撞伤 3.(粗手粗脚地)把...扔来扔去 — *vi.* 1.发出砰的一声,砰砰地响 2.猛撞;撞击 — *n.* 1.砰砰的声音 2.猛击;猛撞 3.〈口〉精力;动力 4.〈美口〉乐趣;快感 5.〈俚〉吗啡(或其它毒品)的注射 — *adv.* 1.砰地 2.蓦地,突然

bang² [bæŋ] *vt.* 把(前额头发)剪成刘海式 — *n.* 前刘海

Bangkok [bæŋ'kɔk] *n.* 曼谷[泰国首都]

Bangladesh [ˌbɑːŋɡlə'deʃ] 孟加拉国[南亚国家]

bangle ['bæŋɡl] *n.* 1.悬在手镯(或项圈等)上的小饰物 2.手镯;脚镯;臂镯

Bangui [bɑːŋ'ɡiː] *n.* 班吉[中非共和国首都]

banian ['bænien] *n.* = banyan

banish ['bæniʃ] *vt.* 1.流放,放逐 2.消除,排除(顾虑、恐惧等) ‖ ~ **ment** *n.* 流放

banister ['bænistə] *n.* 1.栏杆小柱 2.[~s]楼梯的扶手;栏杆

banjo ['bændʒəu] ([复] banjo(e)s) *n.* 班卓琴(一种类似吉他的弦乐器)

Banjul ['bændʒuːl] *n.* 班珠尔(旧称 Bathurst 巴瑟斯特)[冈比亚首都]

bank¹ [bæŋk] *n.* 1.(河、海或湖的)岸;堤;(隧道、壕沟等)堤、埂、堆 3.向上斜坡;坡级 4.(海中水面下的)浅滩,沙洲 5.(飞机、车辆等转弯时的)倾斜状态;倾斜 6.【矿】井口区;(煤矿的)工作面 — *vt.* 1.为...旁边筑堤 2.堆积 3.封(炉、炉火) 4.使倾斜 5.使(路面的弯曲部分)外侧比内侧超高 — *vi.* 1.堆积起来(*up*) 2.(飞机)倾斜着飞行;(汽车等)倾斜行驶

bank² [bæŋk] *n.* 1.银行 2.库(指血液、数据等的贮藏所) 3.储蓄箱 4.(赌博的)庄家;庄家的赌本 — *vt.* 把钱存入银行(与银行开立往来账户)(*at, with*) 2.开办银行 3.(赌博中)做庄家 — *vi.* (钱)存入银行 ‖ ~ **account** 银行往来账 / ~ **book** *n.* 银行存折 / ~ **card** 银行信用卡 / ~ **note** 钞票 / ~ **roll** *n.* 一卷钞票;〈口〉手头的钱;资金

bank³ [bæŋk] *n.* 1.(坐位等的)一排(一)组;(电梯的)一套 2.(风琴或钢

字机等的)键排 3. 报纸副标题 — *vt.* 把...排成一排(或一组)

banker ['bæŋkə] *n.* 1. 银行家 2. (赌博的)庄家 3. (某些游戏中的)发牌人

banking ['bæŋkiŋ] *n.* 银行业;银行业务

bankrupt ['bæŋkrʌpt] *n.* 1. 破产者;无力还债的人 2. 丧失了(名誉、智力等)的人 — *adj.* 1. 破产的,无力还债的 2. 亏了的;枯竭的 3. 丧失了...的(*of*, *in*) — *vt.* 使破产

bankruptcy ['bæŋkrʌptsi] *n.* 1. 破产;破产案件 2. 彻底失败 3. (名誉、智力等)的完全丧失(*in*, *of*)

banner ['bænə] *n.* 1. 旗;旗帜;(写有标语等的)横幅[注意:与 flag 比,banner 常作"旗帜"解,带有抽象的意味,而 flag 则指具体的"旗子"] 2. (美)(报纸的)通栏大字标题(= ~ headline) 3. (满族、蒙古族的)旗 — *adj.* 1. (美)杰出的,极好的 2. (美)突出地支持某一政党的

banns [bænz] [复] *n.* 结婚公告

banquet ['bæŋkwit] *n.* 宴会;盛宴 — *vt.* 宴请,设宴招待 — *vi.* 赴宴,出席宴会;痛饮,欢宴 ‖ ~**er** *n.*

bantam ['bæntəm] *n.* 1. [B-](动)矮脚鸡 2. 矮小而好斗的人 — *adj.* 矮小而好斗的 ‖ ~**weight** *n. & adj.* 最轻量级拳击运动员(的);次轻量级摔跤运动员(的)

banter ['bæntə] *n.* 善意的取笑,逗弄 — *vt.* 善意地取笑,逗弄 — *vi.* 开玩笑 ‖ ~**er** *n.*

bantering ['bæntəriŋ] *adj.* 开玩笑的 ‖ ~**ly** *adv.*

banyan ['bænjən] *n.* (植)印度榕树

baptism ['bæptizəm] *n.* 1. (基督教)洗礼,浸礼 2. (喻)洗礼,考验 3. (轮船等的)命名仪式 ‖ **baptist** *n.* 施洗礼者

baptize, baptise [bæp'taiz] *vt.* 1. 给...施洗礼,给...行洗礼,使经受考验 2. 洗礼时给...命名 ‖ ~**r** *n.*

bar [bɑ:] *n.* 1. (铁、木等)条,杆,棒;栅,栏;障碍;[~s]限制性规定 3. (光、颜色等的)线条,带;(音)小节,节线(纵)线 4. 港口、河口的)沙洲 5. (物)巴(压强单位) 6. 法庭围栏;法庭;(法庭上的)律师席(或被告席) 7. [常 the B-]律师职业;律师界 8. (喻)法庭,审判台 9. (肩章或领章上)表示军阶的横(或条);彩色勋章 10. (旅馆、饭店的)酒吧间;酒柜;(专售某一商品的)柜台 12. (美)蚊帐 = (barred; barring) *vt.* 1. 闩上 2. 阻挡,拦住 3. 妨碍;排除,排斥;(口)禁止,不准[常用被动语态]饰...以条纹 5. (英俚)讨厌,反对(人、习惯等) — *prep.* (口)除...外(= barring) ‖ ~**red** *adj.* 1. 上了门的,闩住的;装有栅栏的 2. 有条纹的 3. 被禁止的 4. 被阻塞的;被封闭的 ‖ ~**bell** *n.* (一副)杠铃 / ~ **girl** (美口)酒吧间女招待 / ~ **goddess** (指出没于酒吧间的私娼) / ~ **iron** 形铁,型铁 / ~**keeper** *n.* (美)酒吧间老板(或招待) / ~ **magnet** [电]条形磁铁 / ~ **maid** *n.* 酒吧间女招待 / ~ **man** *n.* 酒吧间男招待 / ~**room** *n.* 酒吧间 / ~**tender** *n.* 酒吧间侍者,酒保

barb [bɑ:b] *n.* 1. (箭头等上的)倒钩 2. (喻)剌人的话 3. (动)羽支;倒剌;触须 4. (美俚)(不加入大学生联谊会的)"野蛮"学生 — *vt.* 装倒剌于 ‖ ~**ed** *adj.* 1. 有倒钩的,有倒剌的 2. 尖刻讽刺的;锋利的

barbarian [bɑ:'bɛəriən] *adj.* 野蛮人的;不文明的;未开化的 — *n.* 野蛮人;原始人 2. 粗鲁无礼的人 3. 残暴的人 ‖ ~**ism** *n.*

barbaric [bɑː'bærik] *adj*. 野蛮(人)的;粗野的;肆无忌惮的 ‖ ~**ally** *adv*.

barbarism ['bɑːbərizəm] *n*. 1.(语言、文体等)不规范的,不纯;不规范的语句(或文字) 2. 野蛮状态(或行为) 3. 原始风尚

barbarity [bɑː'bæriti] *n*. 1. 残暴;暴行 2. = barbarism

barbarous ['bɑːbərəs] *adj*. 1. 野蛮的;粗俗的 2. 残暴的 3.(语言等)不规范的 ‖ ~**ly** *adv*. / ~**ness** *n*.

barbecue ['bɑːbikjuː] *n*. 1.(在篝火或地灶上烤炙的)烤全猪(或牛等);烤肉,烤鸡;烤肉 2. 户外烤肉餐;烤全性野宴 3.(可携带的)烤肉架 4.〈美俚〉(社交性的)碰头会 — *vt*. 1. 整烤(猪、牛等)2.(尤指在野外)烤(肉等)

barber ['bɑːbə] *n*. 1. 理发师 2. 话多的人 — *vt*. 为……理发刮须 ‖ '~**-shop** *n*. 理发店 *adj*.〈美口〉(尤指伤感歌曲)理发店男声无伴奏重唱的 / ('s) **pole** *n*. 理发店旋转标志彩柱 / ~**'s shop**〈英〉理发店

barbiturate [bɑː'bitjurət] *n*. 1.【化】巴比土酸盐 2.(镇静等用的)巴比妥类药物

bard [bɑːd] *n*. 1.(古代的)吟游诗人 2.(史诗等的)作者;吟唱(或朗诵)者 ‖ ~**ic** *adj*.

bare [beə] *adj*. 1. 赤裸的,光秃的 2. 无遮蔽的,无掩护的 3.(几乎)空的;缺乏……的(of);无装饰的 4. 勉强的,仅有的,勉强的 5. 不加掩饰的,直率的 6.(织物)磨损了的,穿得已无毛头的 — *vt*. 1. 露出;暴露 2. 拔出(刀、剑等) ‖ ~**ness** *n*. ‖ ~**-back** *adv*. & *adj*. 无马鞍的 / ~**-backed** *adj*. 祖骑的;无马鞍的 / ~**-bones** 梗概 ‖ '~**-faced** *adj*. 1. 不戴面具的,无鬚的 / '~**facedly** *adv*. 露骨地,无耻地 / '~-

facedness *n*. 露骨,无耻 ‖ '~**-foot** *adv*. & *adj*. 赤脚的 2.〈美俚〉(火车或引擎)没有刹车的 / '~**'footed** *adj*. 赤脚的 / '~**-handed** *adv*. & *adj*. 1. 不戴手套的 2. 赤手空拳的,手无寸铁的 ‖ '~**-headed** *adv*. & *adj*. 光着头的,不戴帽的

barely ['beəli] *adv*. 1. 赤裸裸地;无遮蔽地 2. 公开地;露骨地 3. 仅仅,勉强,几乎没有

bargain ['bɑːgin] *n*. 1.(买卖等的)协定,协议;协议的条件;交易 2. 廉价货 — *vi*. 1. 议价;讨价还价 2. 成交,商定 (on) — *vt*. 1. 通过讨价还价出售 2. 通过讨价还价促使;谈判条件后解决 3. 以……换取(for) 4.[后接 that 引导的从句]提出……的条件 ‖ ~**er** *n*.

barge [bɑːdʒ] *n*. 1. 驳船 2. 大型游艇 3.(美海军旗舰上将官用的)专用汽艇 4.〈俚〉笨重的船 — *vt*. 用驳船运载 — *vi*. 1. 蹒跚 2.〈口〉闯入(in, into) 3.〈口〉相撞(against) ‖ ~ [bɑː'dʒiː]. ~**man** *n*. 驳船船员(或船长、船主)

baritone ['bæritəun] *n*. 1. 男中音;男中音歌手 2. 上低音部;上低音乐器 — *adj*. 男中音的;上低音部的

barium ['beəriəm] *n*.【化】钡

bark¹ [bɑːk] *n*. 茎皮;树皮 — *vt*. 1. 用某种树皮鞣(革) 2. 剥去(树等)的皮 3. 擦破(指节、膝盖等处)的皮

bark² [bɑːk] *n*. 1.(狗、狐等)吠,叫;(枪、引擎等)发出声响 2.(人)叫骂,咆哮 3.〈口〉咳嗽 — *vt*. 1. 大声喊出;怒气冲冲地说出(out) 2. 大叫大骂地推销—— *n*. 1. 吠叫声;狗状似的声响(如枪击声、咳嗽声等)2. 厉声;厉声说出的话

bark³ [bɑːk] *n*. 1. 三桅帆船 2.〈诗〉轻舟;小帆船

barker ['bɑːkə] *n*. 1. 剥树皮的人(或机

器 2. 吠叫的狗(或狐等) 3. 大叫大喊的人(尤指在戏院等门口叫喊招揽观众的人) 4.〈俚〉手枪

barley ['bɑːli] n. 大麦

barm [bɑːm] n. (泡沫状)酵母

barn [bɑːn] n. 1. 谷仓 2.〈美〉牲口棚；电车(或公共汽车)车库 3.〈蔑〉没有装饰的大房子 4.【核】(恩)(核截面单位,等于10⁻²⁴厘米²) ‖ ~-yard n. 谷仓旁的场地

barnacle ['bɑːnəkl] n. 1.【动】(欧洲)黑雁 2.【动】藤壶(附在岩石,船底等处的甲壳动物) 3.〈口〉纠缠不休难以摆脱的人

barnstorm ['bɑːnstɔːm] 〈口〉 vi. 1. 在小城镇(或乡间)作巡回演出 2.(竞选等为活动中)四处游说 3. 作飞行观光,作特技飞行表演 — vt. 在…作巡回表演(或游说,飞行观光) ‖ ~er n.

barometer [bə'rɔmitə] n. 1. 气压表,气压计;晴雨表 2.(喻)晴雨表,变化的标志 ‖ **barometrical** [ˌbærəu'metrik(ə)l] adj. 气压(表)的;气压表表示的

baron ['bærən] n. 1. 男爵 2. 贵族 3.〈美〉巨商 ‖ ~age n.【总称】男爵;贵族 / ~ess n. 男爵夫人;女男爵 / ~ial [bə'rəunjəl] adj. 1. 男爵的;适合男爵身份的(可指生活等) 2. 豪华的 / ~y n. 男爵领地;男爵爵位

baronet ['bærənit] n. 准男爵 ‖ ~cy n

baroque [bə'rɔk] n. (十七至十八世纪流行于欧洲的)巴罗克风格 — adj. (建筑、文学、艺术等领域的)巴罗克风格作品

baroreceptor [ˌbærəri'septə] n.【生理】压力感受器

barque [bɑːk] n. = bark³

barrack ['bærək] n. 1. [~s]用作单或复]兵营,营房 2.(工地等的)棚屋,临时工房 3. 简陋划一的房子 — vt.

使驻兵营内;使住棚屋内 2.〈澳〉嘲弄,辱骂 — vi.〈澳〉1. 嘲笑(at);喝倒彩 2. 声援,助威 ‖ ~ bag(用以存放装备和个人物品的)士兵行李袋

barracuda [ˌbærə'kjuːdə] ([复] barracuda(s)) n.【鱼】鲟

barrage ['bærɑːʒ, bə'rɑːʒ] n. 1. 火力网;掩护射火;弹幕;齐射 2. 一连串的问题或诘辩等)(of) 3. ['bɑːridʒ]堤,拦河坝 — vt. 1. 以猛烈炮火力进攻(或阻击) 2. 向…连珠炮似地发出(问题等) ‖ ~ balloon 阻御敌机空袭用的阻塞气球

barrel ['bærəl] n. 1. 桶;琵琶桶 2.(一)桶(液量单位,美桶为31.5 美加仑,英桶为36 英加仑) 3.【机】滚转桶,滚净筒 4.【军】枪管;炮筒 5.(照相机的)镜头筒(在或水笔、铅笔、圆珠笔的)笔杆 6.〈口〉许多:a ~ of fun 很有趣 7.(马或牛的)躯干 — (barrel(l)ed; barrel(l)ing) vt. 把…装桶 — vi.〈俚〉(汽车等)高速行进

barren ['bærən] adj. 1.(土地等)贫瘠的,荒芜的,不毛的 2.(植物等)不结果实的 3.不生育的,不结子的 4.(思想等)贫乏的,无聊的(计划等)无结果的 5. 没有…的(of) — n. 瘠地 ‖ ~ness n.

barrette [bə'ret] n.(妇女用的)条状发夹

barricade [ˌbæri'keid] n. 路障,街垒;挡墙 — vt. 阻塞;设路障于

barrier ['bæriə] n. 1. 栅栏;屏障 2. 海关关卡 3. 障碍;妨碍因素 4.(思想等的)壁;限界 ‖ ~ reef【地】(扩伸到海洋中的)南极洲冰岳

barring ['bɑːriŋ] prep. 除…外,不包括…

barrister ['bæristə] n.〈英〉国有资格在任何法庭作辩护的)专门律师,出庭律师(= ~-at-law)

barrow¹ ['bærəu] n. 1.(独轮或两轮)手推车 2. 抬物架

barrow^2 ['bærəu] *n.* 阉猪

barter ['bɑːtə] *vi.* 进行易货贸易,作物物交换(*away*) *vt.* 1. 以...作易货贸易,拿...作物物交换 2.〈喻〉出卖(权利、荣誉等)(*away*) — *n.* 1. 物物交换,易货 2. 进行易货贸易的商品

baryon ['bæriən] *n.*〔核〕重子 ‖ **~ number** 重子数

barytone ['bæritəun] *n. & adj.* = baritone

basalt ['bæsɔːlt] *n.*〔地〕玄武岩 ‖ **~ic** [bə'sɔːltik] *adj.*

base^1 [beis] *n.* 1. 基础,底部;(油漆等的)底涂层 2. 根据地〔军〕基地 3.〔化〕碱;(染色)固定剂 4.〔数〕(对数的)底;(数系的)基(数) 5.〔地〕(混合物的)基本成分〔药〕赋形剂 6.〔语〕词根;词基 7.〔体〕(棒球场)垒;起点;决胜线 8.(步款到不再续降的)证券基价 — *vt.* 把...基于;把(飞机等)的基地设在(*on, upon*) ‖ **~board** *n.*〔建〕护壁板,隔脚板 / **~ line** base n.〔网球场场地〕的底线 / **~ pay** (津贴等除外的)基本工资

base^2 [beis] *adj.* 1. 卑鄙的 2. 低级的,劣等的;a ~ metal 贱金属(指铁、铅等) 3.〔语〕(语言)不纯的,谎误的 4.〔音〕低音的 — *n.*〔音〕低音,低音部 ‖ **~ly** *adv.* / **~ness** *n.*

baseball ['beisbɔːl] *n.* 1.〔体〕棒球运动 2. 棒球

baseless ['beislis] *adj.* 无根据的 ‖ **~ness** *n.*

basement ['beismənt] *n.* 1.(建筑物的)墙根,墙脚 2. 地下室

bases^1 ['beisiz] base 的复数

bases^2 ['beisiz] basis 的复数

bash [bæʃ] *vt.*〈口〉1. 猛击 2. 打坏(*in*) — *vi.* 猛地撞毁(*in*) — *n.* 1. 猛击

bashful ['bæʃful] *adj.* 害羞的,忸怩的 ‖ **~ly** *adv.* / **~ness** *n.*

BASIC, Basic ['beisik] *n.*〔计〕初学者通用符号指令码,BASIC 语言

basic ['beisik] *adj.* 1. 基本的,基础的,主要的 2.〔化〕碱的;碱性的;碱式的 3.〔地〕基性的;含氧化硅较少的 — *n.* 1.[常~s]基础,基本 2. 基础训练 ‖ **~ally** *adv.* / **~ness** *n.*

basil ['bæzl] *n.*〔植〕罗勒;小绿樵

basilica [bə'zilikə] *n.* 长方形廊柱大厅(式基督教堂);梵蒂冈大教堂;天主教大教室

basin ['beisn] *n.* 1. 盆,水盆;浴盆(或洗手)盆 2. 一盆的量 3.(带水闸的)船坞;水洼;内湾,内港 4. 盆地;流域 5.〔矿〕煤田 ‖ **~ful** *n.* 一满盆

basis ['beisis] ([复] bases ['beisiz]) *n.* 1. 基础;根据 2. 主要成分 3.〔数〕基

bask [bɑːsk] *vi.* 1.(舒适地)取暖 2.〈喻〉感到舒适;感到乐趣(*in*)

basket ['bɑːskit] *n.* 1. 篮;篓;筐 2. 一篮(或一篓、一筐)的量 3.(气球的)吊篮 4.(篮球运动)篮圈;投篮得分 — *vt.* 把...装入(或投入)篮(或篓、筐)内 ‖ **~ful** *n.* 一满篮;一满篓;一满筐 / **~ry** *n.* 1.(篮、篓、筐等的)编织术 2.[总称](篮子等编制品)

basketball ['bɑːskitbɔːl] *n.* 1. 篮球运动 2. 篮球 ‖ **~er** *n.* 篮球运动员

bas-relief ['bæsrilif] *n.* 浅浮雕;浅浮雕像

bass^1 [beis] *n.* 1. 男低音 2. 男低音歌手 3. 男低音部 4. 低音乐器(尤指低音提琴) — *adj.* 低音的;a ~ drum 大鼓 / a ~ horn 低音管,低音号 / a ~ viol 低音提琴

bass^2 [bæs] ([复] bass(es)) *n.* 鲈鱼

bass³ [bæs] n. 1.【植】椴树；椴木；〈树木的〉韧皮纤维 2. 韧皮纤维制品（如席、篮等）‖ ~ **wood** n. 椴树；椴木

bassinet [ˌbæsiˈnet] n. 1.（一端有篷的）婴儿摇篮 2. 摇篮式童车

bassoon [bəˈsuːn] n.【音】巴松管，大管 ‖ ~ **ist** n. 巴松管吹奏者

bastard [ˈbɑːstəd] n. 1. 私生子 2. 杂种；假冒品；劣等货 3.〈俚〉坏种；讨厌鬼 4.〈俚〉家伙（用于亲昵的开玩笑场合）— adj. 1. 私生的；杂交的 2. 奇形怪状的；尺码异常的 3. 不合标准的；劣质的 4. 假的；非权威的

baste¹ [beist] vt. 用长针脚疏缝，粗缝

baste² [beist] vt.（为防止烤焦）把油脂涂在（烤肉）上

bastion [ˈbæstiən, ˈbæstʃən] n. 1. 棱堡 2. 堡垒；设防地区；防御工事 3.〈喻〉堡垒

bat¹ [bæt] n. 1. 短棍 2.（棒球、板球等的）球棒；〈网球、乒乓球等的〉球拍 3.〈赛马师的〉短鞭 4.〈棒球等的〉击球手〈板球等的〉击球手 5.〈粘土等〉一块，一团 6.〈美俚〉酷胎；狂热 7.〈英俚〉步速，速度 8.〈美俚〉狂饮；狂欢 9.〈美俚〉一元 — (batted; batting) vt. 1. 用棒（或拍）打；拍打（球等）2. 挥打 3. 详细讨论；反复考虑 — vi. 1. 用球棒（或球拍）打球；轮到击球

bat² [bæt] n. 1. 蝙蝠 2. 蝙蝠式导弹 3.〈俚〉妓女；丑妇

bat³ [bæt] (batted; batting) vt.〈口〉眨（眼睛）（尤指因惊奇等而眨眼）

batch [bætʃ] n. 1.（面包等的）一炉 2. 一批投料量；一批生产量 3. 一批

bath [bɑːθ] n. 1.〈复〉baths [bɑːðz] 1. 浴，（洗）澡 2. 浴水 3. 浴缸；澡盆 4. 浴室；（公共）澡堂 5.〈常 ~s〉浴场；温泉浴场 6. 湿淋淋状态：His head was all over

in a ~ of sweat. 他满头大汗。7.【化】浴；浴器；浴锅 8.【摄】药液，冲洗液 — vi. & vt.〈给……〉洗澡 ‖ ~ **house** n. 1. 公共浴室，澡堂 2. 海滨更衣处 ‖ ~ **robe** n.〈美〉浴衣；睡衣 ‖ ~ **room** n. 浴室；盥洗室 ‖ ~ **tub** n. 1. 浴缸；澡盆 2.〈美俚〉（摩托车的）边斗

bathe [beið] vt. 1. 使蒙淋浴；给……洗澡 2.（用药水等）冲洗（伤口等）3.（日光等）沐浴，笼罩 — vi. 1. 洗澡 2.〈英〉（为取乐或凉快而）游泳 3.〈喻〉沉浸，沐浴（in）— n.〈英〉游泳；洗澡 ‖ ~ **r** n. 1. 洗澡的人 2.〈英〉游泳的人

bathing [ˈbeiðiŋ] n. 游泳，洗海水澡 ‖ ~ **cap** 游泳帽 / ~ **costume**, ~ **suit** 游泳衣

batik [ˈbætik, bəˈtiːk] n. 巴蒂克印花法，蜡防印花法；蜡防印花布

baton [ˈbætən] n. 1. 短棍，短棒；警棍 2.（用以表示官职和权力的）官杖，权杖，节杖 3.（乐队的）指挥棒 4.（接力赛用的）接力棒 — vt. 用短棍打 ‖ ~ **ist** n. 指挥者

battalion [bəˈtæliən] n. 1.【军】营；营部 2.〈~s〉部队，军队 3. 大队（的人）

batten [ˈbætən] n. 板条，压条 — vt. 用板条（或压条）固定

batter¹ [ˈbætə] vt. 1. 连续猛击；炮击；打烂 2. 捣毁（家具等）3. 用……乱打，作连续猛击 ‖ ~ **ing ram** 攻城槌（一种古代兵器）

batter² [ˈbætə] n. 1.（用面粉、鸡蛋、牛奶等调成的面糊）糊 2.【印】（活字或铅版的）字面磨损处

batter³ [ˈbætə] n.（棒球队的）击球员

battery [ˈbætəri] n. 1.【律】殴打 2. 炮兵连；兵器群 3.（舰艇上的）炮组 4.（炮的）待发射状态 5.【电】电池（组）6.（器具等的）一套，一组 6.（乐队的）一组打击乐器 7.（棒球队的）投手和捕手

8. 层架式鸡笼

batting ['bætiŋ] *n*. 1.(棒球等的)击球;击球术 2.【总称】(被褥的)棉花(或羊毛)胎

battle ['bætl] *n*. 1. 战役,会战;战斗 2. 斗争 3. 较量,竞赛 — *vi*. 1. 战斗与...斗争;奋斗 — *vt*. (美)与...作战;与...斗争与...较量 ‖ ～-ax(e) *n*. 1. (中世纪的)战斧 2.〈口〉悍妇 / ～ cruiser 战列巡洋舰 / ～ cry 1. (作战时的)呐喊 2. 战斗口号 / ～ field *n*. = ～ ground / ～ front *n*. 作战正面;前线 / ～ ground *n*. 1. 战场 2. 斗争的领域 / ～ royal 1. 混战;殊死战 2. 激烈的争论 / ～ ship *n*. 战列舰

battlement ['bætlmənt] *n*. (常～s)城垛,城堞;雉堞式装饰墙

bauble ['bɔːbl] *n*. 1. 小玩意,小摆设 2. 华而不实的东西

bauxite ['bɔːksait] *n*. 铝土矿,铝土矿,铝矾土

bawd [bɔːd] *n*. 鸨母,妓院女老板

bawdy ['bɔːdi] *adj*. 淫秽的;(言谈等)猥亵的,低级下流的 — *n*. 猥亵的语言 ‖ **bawdily** *adv*. 淫秽地

bawl [bɔːl] *vi*. 1. 大声叫嚷;吆喝(at, against, out) 2.〈口〉大哭 — *vt*. 1. 大声叫出(或宣布) 2. 叫喊得使...1. 大声卖—n. 1. 大声喊(或嚷) 2.〈口〉大哭

bay[1] [bei] *n*. 1. 海湾,湾 2. 山间平地,岙

bay[2] [bei] *n*. 1. (猎犬等的)吠声(尤指追捕猎物时的连续吠声) 2. 走投无路的处境,绝境 — *vi*. 1. (猎犬追捕猎物时连续地)吠;吠叫;吠叫;吠叫着追赶 2. 使陷入绝境,使走投无路 3. 用深沉拖长的声调说出

bay[3] [bei] *n*. 1. 月桂(树) 2. (常～s)(古时给诗人,英雄等戴的)桂冠 3.〈喻〉荣誉

‖ ～-.berry *n*. 1. 香叶多香果树 2. 宾州杨梅(指树或果实)

bay[4] [bei] *n*. 1.【建】开间;排架间距;窗柱间距 2. 浮桥桥节;(装置的)房间突出部分;侧厅;耳房 2.【军】(飞机的)舱 3. (谷仓中)堆放干草(或粮食)的处 4. 底板,机架,底座 ‖ ～ window 凸窗

bay[5] [bei] *adj*. 枣红色的 — *n*. 枣红马

bayonet ['beiənit] *n*. (枪上的)刺刀 — *vt*. 用刺刀刺;用武力(或压力)追使(into)

bayou ['baiuː] *n*. (美国南部的)牛轭湖;长沼

baza(a)r [bə'zɑː] *n*. 1. (东方国家的)市场,集市 2. 义卖市场

bazooka [bə'zuːkə] *n*.【军】(反坦克)火箭筒

BBC *abbr*. British Broadcasting Corporation 英国广播公司

BC *abbr*. Before Christ 公元前

Be 【化】元素铍(beryllium)的符号

be [强 biː;弱 bi](现在式 am, are, is;过去式 was, were;过去分词 been;现在分词 being) *vi*. 1. 是 2. 值;等于:This spade *is* five yuan. 这把铲子售价五元。/ Two and two *are* four. 二加二等于四。3.【常用命令语气或不定式】应做到;成为:*Be* quiet! 安静些! / He wants to *be* a doctor. 他要当医生。4. 在;存在:Is your mother in? 你妈妈在(家)吗? / He is no more. 他已死了。5. 逗留(继续)呆:He'll ～ in the countryside till next month. 他要在乡下呆到下个月。6.【用于完成时】去;来:We have *been* to Paris. 我们去过巴黎。/ Has any one *been* here? 有人到这儿来过吗? 7. 发生:When will the meeting ～? 会什么时候开? — *v. aux*. 1.【与动词的现在分词连用,构成各种进行时态】:The children *are* singing. 孩子们在

唱歌。**2.** [与及物动词的过去分词连用,构成被动语态] The letter *was* written yesterday. 这封信是昨天写的。**3.** [与动词不定式连用,表示职责、义务、意图、约定、可能性等] We *are* to meet at the school gate. 我们约定在校门口碰头。

beach [biːtʃ] *n*. **1.** 海滩;潮滩;河滩 **2.** [总称]海滩砂砾(或卵石) — *vt*. 使(船)冲上岸滩 ‖ ~**boy** *n*. 海滨男侍者(或男服务员);常在海滨胜地浪荡的纨绔子弟 / ~ **buggy**〈俚〉[与冲浪者为伍时本人并不下水的]海滨姑娘 / ~ **head** *n*. **1.** 滩头堡;登陆场 **2.** 立足点,据点 / ~ **wear** *n*. [总称]海滨服装

beacon [ˈbiːkən] *n*. **1.** 灯塔;信标(指示或引导飞机或舰船航行方向的火光、灯塔或无线电发射机等);灯标 **2.** (旧时作信号用的)烽火,篝火 **3.**〈英〉(标示行人可以穿越马路的)贝形灯;人行横道指示灯 **4.**〈美〉(定向无线电波等) — *vt*. 照亮;在…设置灯塔(或信号浮标等) — *vi*. 像灯塔般照耀

bead [biːd] *n*. **1.** (装饰用有孔的)小珠;念珠 **2.** 水珠;汗珠;小滴 **3.** (枪的)圆柱准星 **4.** [建]凸圆线脚,墙角圆线条 **5.** (汽车轮胎的)胎圈 — *vt*. 用珠子装饰,把…像串珠子一样连起来 — *vi*. 形成珠状;结珠 ‖ ~**y** *adj*. **1.** 珠子般的(的)(眼睛小而亮的) **2.** 饰以珠子(或珠状物)的 **3.** 有泡沫的;多泡沫的

beadle [ˈbiːdl] *n*. **1.**〈英国负责教堂秩序、侍奉教士等的)教区执事;执事 **2.**〈英国大学举行典礼时的)贝勺官员,礼仪前导官 **3.** (法院等处的)差役

beagle [ˈbiːgl] *n*. **1.** 〈英国种的)小猎兔犬 **2.** 密探;告密者 **3.** 警官

beak [biːk] *n*. **1.** (猛禽、甲鱼等的)喙;喙状嘴 **2.** (茶壶等器皿的)喙状倾出口

(古代战舰的)冲撞角 **3.** 钩形鼻 **4.** [建]鸟嘴形 **5.**〈英俚〉治安官;男数师;男校长 ‖ ~**ed** *adj*. 有钩形喙的;钩形的

beaker [ˈbiːkə] *n*. **1.** 大口酒杯;一大口酒杯的量 **2.** (实验室、药房等处用的)烧杯

beam [biːm] *n*. **1.** 梁,桁 **2.** [船]横梁;(舰船船身等的)船宽,船幅 **3.** (秤)杆;犁柄;织轴;锚柄;辘轳;杠杆 **4.** (鹿角的)主干 **5.** (灯光、日光、X光等的)光线,光柱 **6.** (喻)笑容,喜色 **7.** 射束;波束;束;[电]束指示的航道 — *vi*. **1.** 照耀 **2.** (面)露喜色;满脸堆笑;感到欣喜 — *vt*. **1.** 用梁支承 **2.** 用…照射;射出(光线或光束);流露出(感情等) **3.** 定向发出(无线电信号等);对有针对性地广播 **4.** 使定向发射;把…对准;把…对准目标

beaming [ˈbiːmɪŋ] *adj*. **1.** 发光的,耀眼的 **2.** 笑容满面的;欣喜的 ‖ ~**ly** *adv*.

bean [biːn] *n*. **1.** 豆;蚕豆;菜豆 **2.** 豆形种子(如咖啡豆);产豆形种子的植物 **3.** 无价值的东西;[~s]少量 **4.** (俚)(一文)钱 **5.**〈美俚〉脑袋一个人;〈美俚〉击…的头部 ‖ ~ **cake** 豆饼 / ~ **curd** 豆腐

bear[beə] [ˈbiːmɪŋ] (过去式 bore [bɔː],过去分词 borne 或 born [bɔːn]) *vt*. **1.** 负担,负荷;承担 **2.** 佩,带;带有,具有 **3.** 忍受,容忍 **4.** 承受;经得起,耐(得)住 **5.** 生育,养(孩子);结(果实);产生;She has *borne* two children. 她已生了两个孩子。[比较:born in Beijing 在北京出生;born (in) 1950 一九五〇年出生;"生育""生产"用 borne;讲"出生"或"出身"用 born] **6.** 怀有,抱有,心怀(感情、爱憎等) **7.** [~ oneself]举止;表现 **8.** 运动;挤压 **9.** 提供;~ witness 作证

vi. 1. 忍受,忍耐;承受 2. 结果实 3. 开动,运动;指向;转向:The ship *bore* south. 船向南开。4. 压;压迫(*on*,*upon*)

bear²[bεə] *n.* 1. 熊 2. 粗鲁的人;笨拙的人 3.【机】打孔器;小型冲孔机 4.〈证券或商品投机买卖中的〉卖空者,做空头者 — *vt.* 通过卖空使〈证券或商品〉行情下跌 — *vi.* 卖空,做空头 ‖ ~ -hug *n.* 1. 熊用前腿对猎物的紧抱 2.〈摔跤动作〉熊抱 3. 紧紧的(或粗鲁的)拥抱

bearable ['bεərəbl] *adj.* 承受得住的;可忍受的;经得起的

beard [biəd] *n.* 1.〈下巴上的〉胡须;络腮胡子 2.〈动物的〉颔毛 3.〈植物的〉芒;髯毛 4.〈牡蛎的〉鳃 5. 倒刺,钩刺;〈颜废)暂时的人 — *vt.* 抓住……的胡须;〈喻〉公开反对,公然蔑视 ‖ ~ed *adj.* 1. 有胡须的 2.〈植物〉有芒的 3.〈鱼钩等〉有倒刺的 / ~less *adj.* 1. 无胡须的 2. 年轻无知的;没有经验的〈植物〉无芒的

bearer ['bεərə] *n.* 1. 负荷者 2. 带信人,持信人;执票人〈指支票、票据等〉人 3. 结果实的植物 4. 抬棺人;抬轿人 5.【机】托架;支座;承垫

bearing ['bεəriŋ] *n.* 1. 支承 2.【机】轴承 3. 忍耐,容忍 4. 关系;联系;方面;意义 4.〈常~s〉方位,方向 5. 生育;结果实 6. 举止,姿态

bearish ['bεəriʃ] *adj.* 1. 像熊一样的;粗暴的;粗鲁的;笨手笨脚的 2. 行情下跌的 3. 缺乏信心的 ‖ ~ly *adv.* / ~ness *n.*

beast [bi:st] *n.* 1.〈四足〉兽;动物 2. 牲畜;〈英〉菜牛 3. 凶残的人;举止粗鲁的人 4.[the ~]兽性 5.[the B-]【基督教】反对基督的人

beastily ['bi:stli] *adj.* 1. 野兽(般)的 2. 残

忍的;卑鄙下流的 3.〈口〉令人厌恶的;糟透的 — *adv.*〈英俚〉非常地;极糟地 ‖ **beastliness** *n.*

beat [bi:t](beat,beaten ['bi:tn]) *vt.* 1.〈接连地〉打,敲;冲击 2. 打败,战胜;超越;设法通过 3. 踏出,走出(道路);打开(一条路)4. 在……里搜索 5. 锤捣,捣平(out)6. 打,搅拌(蛋、奶油、面粉等)使成泡沫状(或糊状)7. 振(翼),扑打(翅膀)8.[音]打(拍子)9.〈口〉难住,使惑困难 10.〈口〉欺骗 — *vi.* 1.〈接连地〉打,敲;(日)晒;(雨)打;(风)吹打 2.(心脏等)跳动 3. 在树林中(或灌木等)中搜索(for)4.(蛋、奶油等)打出泡沫 5.〈口〉获胜,赢 6.【海】(帆船)以"之"字形抢风航行 — *n.* 1.(接连的)敲打,敲击声 2.(心脏等)跳动(声)3. 节拍,拍子;[用手、指挥棒]打拍子 4.[电]拍差 4. 常走的道路;经常巡逻的路线 5. 新闻的抢先报道;抢先发表的新闻 6.〈俚〉欺骗 7. = beatnik — *adj.* 1.〈俚〉疲劳的 2. 颓废的;属于"垮掉的一代"(或类似其思想、行动)的 ‖ ~ generation[美国]"垮掉的一代"(二十世纪五十年代末出现于美国的一批年轻人,以蓄长发、穿奇装异服、对现实不满、强调"个性自我表达"等为特征)/ ~ up[美口]破旧的

beaten ['bi:tn]beat的过去分词 — *adj.* 1.(接连地)被打击的;被槌敲的;被击败的 2. 锤薄的,敲平的 3. 踏出的,走出来的(喻)陈旧的 4. 筋疲力尽的;精神沮丧的

beater ['bi:tə] *n.* 1. 敲打者 2. 拍打器;搅拌器;(造纸等用的)打浆机 3. 拍打树丛以惊起猎物的人 4.[纺]箱

beatific [,biə'tifik] *adj.* 1. 至福的,极乐的 2. 赐福的,使极乐的 ‖ ~ally *adv.*

beatitude [bi:'ætitju:d] *n.* 1. 福,至福 2.

[the Beatitudes]【基督教】八福词(耶稣登山训众论福所讲的福音)

beatnik ['bi:tnik] n.(美国)"垮掉的一代"成员(参见 **beat generation**)

beau [bəu]({复}beaus 或 beaux [bəuz]) n. 1. 花花公子 2.(女子的)情人;向女子献殷勤的男子

beauteous ['bju:tiəs] adj.(诗)美的 ‖ ~ly adv. / ~ness n.

beautiful ['bju:təful] adj. 1. 美的,美丽的;美好的 2.(口)极好的,绝妙的 ‖ ~ly adv. / ~ness n. / ~ people [亦作 B~ P~] 1.(上流社会的)时髦阶层;(文艺界的)标新立异阶层 2. 国际上层社会;(乘坐喷气机周游世界的)阔老阶层 3. 嬉皮派,颓废派

beautify ['bju:tifai] vt. 使美丽,美化;装饰 — vi. 变美 ‖ **beautification** n. / ˌbju:tifi'keiʃən] 美化;装饰 / **beautifier** n. 美化者;装饰者

beauty ['bju:ti] n. 1. 美,美丽 2. 美人;美的东西;美好的事物 3. 妙处,美点 ‖ ~ parlour / ~ shop 美容院 / ~ sleep〈口〉午夜前的酣睡 / ~ spot 1. 痣;疵瑕 2.(妇女抹布在脸部等处的)美人斑 3. 风景区

beaver ['bi:və] n. 1.【动】河狸,海狸;山狸;河狸状啮齿动物 2. 海狸毛皮;海狸皮绒 3.〈纺〉海狸呢,水獭呢;(双面斜纹)海狸绒布(=~ cloth) 4.(美团)(下巴上的)大胡子;蓄大胡子的人 5. 工作勤奋而认真的人 ‖ ~ board 硬建筑纸板

becalm [bi'kɑ:m] vt. 1. 使平静(或安静) 2.[常用被动语态]因无风而使(帆船)停止不动

became [bi'keim] become 的过去式

because [bi'kɔz] conj. 因为 — adv. 因为 (of)

beck [bek] n. 召唤的表示(如点头、招手等)

beckon ['bekən] vt.(用点头、招手等方式)召唤 — vi. 表示召唤

become [bi'kʌm](became [bi'keim], become) vi. 成为;变得 — vt. 适合;同...相称

becoming [bi'kʌmiŋ] adj. 合适的;相称的 ‖ ~ly adv.

bed [bed] n. 1. 床,床铺;垫褥;床位 2. 床座;底盘;路基,路床 3.(河)床;(湖、海的)底 4. 一层;一堆(常指树叶,木屑等)【地层】5.(苗)圃;圃;(花)坛 6. 坟墓 7. 夫妻关系;房事,性交 — (bedded; bedding) vt. 1. 使睡;〈美〉供...住宿 2. 栽,种 (out) 3. 安葬,固定 4. 把...分层;铺平;给(牲畜)铺草 (down) 5. 和...性交 — vi. 1. 上床;铺床睡下 (down) 2. 分层 3. 性交 (with) ‖ ~bug n. 臭虫 / ~clothes [复] 床上用品(指被、褥等) ~cover n. 床罩 / ~fellow n. 同床人;伙伴,同伙;同事;同盟者 / ~gown n.(妇女的)睡衣 / ~pan n.(尤指病人在床上用的)便盆 / ~post n. 床柱 / ~rock n. 1. 基岩 2.(作为理论等根据的)基本事实(或原则)3. 最低点,最少量 / ~roll n. 铺盖 / ~room n. 卧室 / ~side n. 床边(尤指病床边)临床(用的);临床的 a good ~side manner(尤指医生)对病人关心体贴的态度 / ~sitter n. [~sitting room](英)卧室兼起居室 ~ space n.(旅馆、医院等的)床位 / ~spread n. 床罩 / ~stead n. 床架(不包括床垫) / ~time n. 就寝时间 / ~wetting n. 尿床,遗尿,溺屎

bedding ['bediŋ] n. 1. 被褥;床上用品 2.(家畜的)垫草 3. 基础;底层 4.【建】基

床 5. [地] 层理

bedeck [bi'dek] *vt.* 装饰

bedew [bi'dju:] *vt.* 以露水沾湿(汗、泪等)沾湿

bedfast ['bedfɑ:st] *adj.* = bedrid

bedlam ['bedləm] *n.* 1.(古)精神病院,疯人院 2. 喧闹,混乱;喧闹混乱的场面(或场所)

Bedouin ['beduin] ([复]Bedouin(s)) *n.* 1. 贝都因人(在阿拉伯半岛或沙漠中游牧的阿拉伯人) 2. 游牧人;流浪的人

bedraggle [bi'drægl] *vt.*(在泥水中)拖湿,拖脏(衣服等) ‖ ~ d *adj.* 湿邋遢的;在泥水中拖脏的;破烂的,破旧的

bedrid ['bedrid], **bedridden** ['bedridn] *adj.*(因病或衰老等)卧床不起的

bee [bi:] *n.* 1. 蜂;蜜蜂 2. 忙碌的人 3.(为娱乐或一起工作而举行的)聚会 4. 奇思怪想,怪念头 ‖ ~ bread *n.* 蜂粮(蜜蜂的食料) / ~hive *n.* 蜂箱 2.〈口〉熙熙攘攘的地方,(女子的)蜂窝式发型 / ~keeper *n.* 养蜂人 / ~line *n.*(两点之间的)直线;(两地之间的)直路

beech [bi:tʃ] *n.* 【植】山毛榉(或其木材) ‖ ~en *adj.* ‖ ~nut *n.* 山毛榉实(可食用)

beef [bi:f] ([复]beeves[bi:vz]或 beefs) *n.* 1. 牛肉 2. 菜牛 3.(男子的)肌肉;力量 4.([复]beefs)〈美俚〉抱怨,牢骚;吵架 — *vt.*〈美俚〉加强,充实(*up*) — *vi.*〈美俚〉1. 抱怨,诉怨子 2. 告发,密告 3. 争吵 ‖ ~cattle[总称]菜牛 / ~ 'steak *n.* 牛排 / ~ tea *n.* 牛肉茶,牛肉汁

beefy ['bi:fi] *adj.* 结实的;肌肉发达的,粗壮的 ‖ beefiness *n.*

been [bi:n, bin] be 的过去分词

beep [bi:p] *n.* 嘟嘟声(如汽车喇叭声、收音机报时信号声等) — *vt.* 1. 使(汽车

喇叭等)嘟嘟响 2. 用嘟嘟声发出(信号等) — *vi.* 1.(汽车喇叭等)发嘟嘟声 2. 按喇叭 ‖ ~er *n.* 1. 寻呼机,BP机 2.(无人驾驶飞机等的)遥控员

beer [biə] *n.* 1. 啤酒 2.(由植物根酿造的)汽水;汽酒;淡酒

beeswax ['bizwæks] *n.* 蜂蜡;黄蜡 — *vt.* & *vi.* 用蜡擦(或上光,处理)

beet [bi:t] *n.* 1. 甜菜 2. = ~root ‖ ~root *n.* 甜菜根

beetle[1] ['bi:tl] *n.* 1. 甲虫 2. 近视的人 — *vi.*(像蚊虫等那样)近视,瞎撞,瞎冲撞

beetle[2] ['bi:tl] *n.* 棰;木夯;杵;捣布机

beetle[3] ['bi:tl] *vi.* 突出;高悬 — *adj.* 突出的;外伸的 ‖ ~-browed *adj.* 1. 眉毛浓而突出的 2. 皱眉的;怒目而视的

beeves [bi:vz]beef 的复数

befall [bi'fɔ:l] (befell [bi'fel], befallen [bi'fɔ:lən]) *vt.* 临到…头上,发生于 — *vi.* 发生

befit [bi'fit] (befitted; befitting) *vt.* 适合于,对…适当

befitting [bi'fitiŋ] *adj.* 适宜的,恰当的 ‖ ~ly *adv.*

befog [bi'fɔɡ] (befogged; befogging) *vt.* 1. 把…笼罩在雾中 2. 把…弄模糊,使堕五里雾中

befool [bi'fu:l] *vt.* 1. 欺骗;愚弄 2. 把…看作笨蛋

before [bi'fɔ:] *prep.* 1. [表示时间]在…以前 the day ~ yesterday 前天 2. [表示位置]在…前面;在…前面 ~ one's eyes 在眼前 /put a proposal ~ the meeting 向会议提出建议 3. [表示次序]在…之前,先于:Those with babies got into the bus ~ (the) others. 带小孩的人比别人先上公共汽车。4.(宁可…而)不愿…:He would die ~

yielding. 他宁死不屈。— adv. 1.［表示时间］以前 2.［表示位置、方向］在前面；向前 — conj. 1.［表示时间］在…前：I'll do it now ~ I forget it. 我趁着还没有忘记的时候就做吧。2.（宁可…而）不愿…：I'd die ~ I'd tell. 我宁死也决不泄密。‖ ~ Christ 公元前（略作 B.C.）/ be'fore'tax adj. 在扣除（所得）税款之前的，税前的

beforehand [bi'fɔːhænd] adv. 1. 预先，事先 2. 提前地；超前地：be ~ with the enemy 先发制（敌）人

befoul [bi'faul] vt. 1. 弄脏，弄污 2. 污蔑，诽谤

befriend [bi'frend] vt. 以朋友态度对待，亲近；帮助

befuddle [bi'fʌdl] vt. 1. 使迷醉 2. 使烂醉

beg [beg]（begged; begging）vt. 1. 乞求 2. 请求，恳求 3.（正式场合的礼貌用语）请（原谅）；请（允许）：~ leave to …请允许… — vi. 1. 乞求（for）2. 请求，恳求 3. 乞讨／靠乞讨为生

began [bi'gæn] begin 的过去式

beget [bi'get]（过去式 begot [bi'gɔt]，过去分词 begotten [bi'gɔtn] 或 begot；现在分词 begetting）vt. 1.（通常指父亲）生（子女）；为…之生父 2. 产生，引起

beggar ['begə] n. 1. 乞丐；穷人 2. 募捐者 3.〈口〉家伙 — vt. 1. 使沦为乞丐；使贫穷 2. 难以（置信，想象等）‖~-my-'neighbour，~-the-'neighbour n. & adj. 损人利己（的），利用他人亏损而自肥（的）

beggarly ['begəli] adj. 1. 乞丐般的，赤贫的 2. 少得可怜的 ‖ beggarliness n.

beggary ['begəri] n. 赤贫

begin [bi'gin]（began [bi'gæn]，begun [bi'gʌn]；beginning）vi. 开始 — vt. 1.

开始，着手 2. 创建

beginner [bi'ginə] n. 1. 初学者，生手 2. 创始人

beginning [bi'giniŋ] n. 1. 开始，开端：at the ~ of the month 在月初 2. 起源：have its ~(s) in … 起源于… 3.（书等的）开头部分 ‖ from ~s 早期阶段

begone [bi'gɔn] vi.（诗）走开！滚开！

begonia [bi'gəunjə] n.［植］秋海棠

begrudge [bi'grʌdʒ] vt. 1. 勉强给予；吝惜，妒忌；羡慕 3. 为…发牢骚；对…不感兴趣 ‖ ~r n. / begrudgingly adv.

beguile [bi'gail] vt. 1. 欺骗，欺诈（into，out of）2. 消磨（时间）3. 使高兴，娱（人）‖ ~ ment n.

beguiling [bi'gailiŋ] adj. 消遣性的 ‖ ~ly adv.

begun [bi'gʌn] begin 的过去分词

behalf [bi'hɑːf] n. ‖ on（或〈美〉in）~ of 代表…；为了…的利益 / on sb.'s ~ 代表某人；为了某人的利益

behave [bi'heiv] vi. 1. 举动，举止，表现 2. 开动，运转 3. 举止端正，循规蹈矩 — vt.（~ oneself）1. 使举动良好，使举止规矩 2. 使运转正常

behavior [bi'heivjə] n.（美）= behaviour

behaviour [bi'heivjə] n. 1. 举止，行为；表现（待人的）态度 2.（机器等的）运行情况 ‖ ~al adj. 行为的；行为方面的；行为科学的 ／ ~al science 行为科学 ／ ~ therapy［心］（对精神病患者的）行为治疗；行为疗法

behead [bi'hed] vt. 砍…的头，斩…的首

beheld [bi'held] behold 的过去式和过去分词

behest [bi'hest] n. 1. 命令；吩咐 2. 请求，邀请

behind [bi'haind] *prep.* **1.** 在…后面，在…背后 **2.** 落后于；不如 **3.** 迟于（规定时间等） **4.** 作…的后盾，支持 — *adv.* **1.** 在后；向后 **2.** 在背后（幕后） **3.** 迟 ~ in one's payment 逾期付款 — *n.* 〈口〉屁股 ‖ be'hind-the-'scene(s) *adj.* 幕后的

behold [bi'hould] [beheld bi'held]) *vt.* **1.** 见到 **2.** 注视，看 — *vi.* 看，瞧 ‖ ~ er *n.* 观看者

beholden [bi'houldən] *adj.* 〔常作表语，与 to 连用〕**1.** 负有义务的；受惠的，感恩的 **2.** 依赖的

behoove [bi'huːv] *vt.* & *vi.* 〈美〉= behove

behove [bi'houv] 〈主英〉〔主语用 it〕 *vt.* 对（某人）来说有必要，是（某人）职责所系；对…有益处于否定句适合 — *vi.* 有必要，有责任；适合

beige [beiʒ] *n.* **1.** 原色哔叽；混色线呢；薄斜纹呢 **2.** 米色 — *adj.* 米色的

being [biːiŋ] be的现在分词 — *n.* **1.** 存在，生存 **2.** 生命 **3.** 存在物；生物；人 a human ~ 人 **4.** 本质，特质 **5.** [the B-] 宗神：the Supreme *Being* 上帝

Beirut [bei'ruːt] *n.* 贝鲁特〔黎巴嫩首都〕

belabor [bi'leibə] *vt.* 〈美〉= belabour

belabour [bi'leibə] *vt.* **1.** 痛打；痛斥 **2.** 对…作过多的说明

Belarus [,bielə'rus] *n.* 白俄罗斯〔中欧国家〕

belated [bi'leitid] *adj.* **1.** 延误的，来迟的 **2.** 迟延未去的，遗留下来的 **3.** 〔旅客等〕天色已晚还在行路的 ‖ ~ly *adv.*

belch [beltʃ] *vi.* **1.** 打嗝 **2.** 〔炮、火山等〕猛烈地喷射出 — *vt.* **1.** 〔炮、火山等〕猛烈地喷射，爆发出（烟、焰等）**2.** 房间说出 — *n.* 打嗝 **2.**（烟、焰等的）爆发；〔炮、火山等的〕爆发声

beleaguer [bi'liːɡə] *vt.* **1.** 围困 **2.** 困扰，使烦恼

belfry ['belfri] *n.* 钟楼；钟塔 ‖ **belfried** *adj.* 有钟楼的

Belgian ['beldʒən] *n.* 比利时人 — *adj.* 比利时的；比利时人的

Belgium ['beldʒəm] *n.* 比利时〔西欧国家〕

Belgrade [bel'greid] *n.* 贝尔格莱德〔南斯拉夫首都〕

belie [bi'lai] *vt.* **1.** 掩饰；使人对…误解 **2.** 证明（或显示）…为虚假；与…抵触；违背 **3.** 辜负，使失望；失落空 **4.** 就…批谎 ‖ ~r *n.*

belief [bi'liːf] *n.* **1.** 相信；信心；信念 **2.** 信仰；信条

believe [bi'liːv] *vt.* **1.** 相信 **2.** 认为 — *vi.* **1.** 相信(in) **2.** 信任(in) **3.** 信奉，信仰(in) ‖ **believable** *adj.* 可相信的，可信任的 / ~r *n.* 信仰者；信徒

belittle [bi'litl] *vt.* **1.** 轻视，小看，贬低 **2.** 使相形见小

Belize [be'liːz] *n.* **1.** 伯利兹〔拉丁美洲国家〕**2.** 伯利兹(市)〔伯利兹东部港市〕

bell [bel] *n.* **1.** 钟，铃；门铃 **2.** 钟声；〔海〕车钟；八击钟声 **3.** 钟状物 **4.** [~s]（上缀下腰的）喇叭裤 — *vt.* **1.** 系铃于 **2.** 使成铃状 ‖ ~,bottom trousers（上缀下肥的）喇叭裤 / '~-boy *n.* 〈美〉(旅馆等处为客人搬运行李兼听差跑腿的)青年侍者 / ~ hop *n.* = ~boy / ~ jar 钟形玻璃罩 / '~,wether *n.* **1.** (系铃)带头羊 **2.** (一群人的)首领

belle [bel] *n.* 美女；最美的美人

bellicose ['belikəus] *adj.* **1.** 好战的；好斗的 ‖ **bellicosity** [,beli'kɔsiti] *n.*

belligerent [bi'lidʒərənt] *adj.* **1.** 交战中的 **2.** 好战的；挑起战争的 — *n.* 交战国；交战国公民（或军人）‖ **belligerence**

belligerency *n.* / **～ly** *adv.*

bellow ['beləu] *vi.* 1.(公牛、象等)吼叫 2.(人、海等)怒吼;咆哮 3.吼叫;(雷、炮等)轰鸣 — *vt.* 大声喊出(out, forth) — *n.* 1.(公牛、象等的)吼声 2.怒吼声

bellows ['beləuz][单复同] *n.* 1.风箱,手用吹风器(俗称皮老虎) 2.波纹管;膜盒 3.(照相机的)皮腔

belly ['beli] *n.* 1.(人或动物的)肚,腹部;腹腔;胃 2.胃口,食欲 3.(物件的)凸部(或凹部、内部) — *vt.* 使胀满,使鼓起(out) — *vi.* 1.张满,鼓起(out) 2.以腹贴地而前行 ‖ **～ful** *n.* 1.饱腹;满足;厌足 2.(俚)满腹;过量:We have had a ～ful of it. 我们已受够了。‖ '～ache *n.* 腹痛 *vi.* (俚)无端抱怨

Belmopan ['belmэu'pæn] *n.* 贝尔莫潘(伯利兹首都)

belong [bi'lɔŋ] *vi.* 1. 属,属于(to) 2.是…的成员(to) 3.(在分类上)应归入 4.住;于…中;任。我住在这里 5.如鱼得水地处于某一环境中

belonging [bi'lɔŋiŋ] *n.* 1.[～s]所有物;动产;2.[复]亲密关系;团体或成员间的亲密关系

Belorussia ['beləu'rʌʃə] *n.* 白俄罗斯[中欧国家]

beloved [bi'lʌvid, bi'lʌvd] *adj.* 1.[bi'lʌvd][用作表语时]为…所爱的(by, of) 2.受爱戴的;被热爱的 — *n.* 心爱的人;情人

below [bi'ləu] *prep.* 1.[表示位置、职位等]在…下面 2.[表示数量、程度、年龄等]在…以下 3.在…的下方 4.[表示能力等]低于 5. 有失…的身份,不值得(通常用 beneath) — *adv.* 1.在下面;向下 2.在下方 3.在(书的)一页的下端;在下文 — *adj.* 1.下列的;下文的 2.(摄氏度)零下的

belt [belt] *n.* 1. 带;腰带;肩带;带状物 2.

【机】皮带 3.地带;地区 4.【军】子弹带,弹链;武装带;(舰船)沿吃水线的装甲带 5.(美)环形路(线);环形铁路 6.(俚)打击 7.(美俚)大口一饮(尤指饮酒);快感,刺激 — *vt.* 1.在…上系腰带 2.用带绑住某人 3.用皮带打(…);鞭打 4.(美俚)饮(酒)(down);狂饮 — *vi.* 快速行进 ‖ **～ing** *n.* 带料;[总称]带

bemoan [bi'məun] *vt.* 1.悲叹;哀泣;痛哭 2.惋惜,不满于

bemused [bi'mjuːzd] *adj.* 困惑不解的;茫然的,发呆的 ‖ **～ly** *adv.*

bench [bentʃ] *n.* 1.长凳;(横在船中的)坐板 2.(工匠等的)工作台 3.法官席;[总称]法官;法官的职位;法院:the King's(或 Queen's) Bench 英国高等法院 4.(英国议会的)议员席 5.【地】阶地;【矿】(煤矿等的)台阶,阶段,阶梯 6.(美)替补队员席;替补队员(们) — *vt.* 1.在…放木凳 2.给…设座位 3.(美)使退出比赛 — *vi.*【地】形成阶地 ‖ '～mark *n.*【计】基准程序/～ seat (横跨汽车车厢的)长椅座

bend [bend] (过去式 bent[bent],过去分词 bent 或(罕)bended) *vt.* 1.使弯曲 2.使屈从 3.把(目光、精力等)集中于(on, to) 4.转移(脚步等)的方向 5.【海】系,缚 — *vi.* 1.变曲;屈身 2.屈从 — *n.* 1.弯曲;弯曲处 2.【海】绑结;[～s](木船的)舷侧厚板

beneath [bi'niːθ] *prep.* 1.在…(正)下方;在(或紧挨着)…底下;低于 2.有失…的身份,有损于(尊严等);不值得 — *adv.* 在下,在下方

benediction [ˌbeni'dikʃən] *n.* 1.[基督教]赐福祈祷;祝福;感谢 2.[B-][天主教]祈求上帝赐福的仪式;修道院院长任职仪式 3.(饭前或饭后的)感恩祷告

benefaction [ˌbeniˈfækʃən] *n.* 1. 善行 2. 捐助，捐赠；捐款；捐助物

benefactor [ˈbenifæktə] *n.* 捐助人；恩人 ‖ **benefactress** [ˈbenifæktris] *n.* 女捐助人；女恩人

beneficent [biˈnefisənt] *adj.* 行善的，乐善好施的；效果好的，有益的 ‖ **beneficence** *n.* / ~ly *adv.*

beneficial [ˌbeniˈfiʃəl] *adj.* 1. 有利的，有益的 2.【律】有权益的，有使用权的 ‖ ~ly *adv.*

beneficiary [ˌbeniˈfiʃəri] *n.* 1.【律】(遗嘱、保险等的)受益人 2. 受俸牧师

benefit [ˈbenifit] *n.* 1. 利益，好处 2. 恩惠 3. 津贴；救济金；保险赔偿费 4. 义演；义赛：a ~ concert 义演音乐会 — *vt.* 有益于 — *vi.* 得益(by, from)

benevolence [biˈnevələns] *n.* 1. 仁慈 2. 善行 3. 捐助物；捐款

benevolent [biˈnevələnt] *adj.* 1. 仁慈的，慈善的 2. 乐善好施的；良性的 ‖ ~ly *adv.*

Bengal [beŋˈgɔːl] *n.* 孟加拉[南亚一地区] ‖ the Bay of ~ 孟加拉湾[亚洲]

Bengali [beŋˈgɔːli] *n.* 1. 孟加拉人 2. 孟加拉语 — *adj.* 孟加拉的；孟加拉人的；孟加拉语的

benign [biˈnain] *adj.* 1. 慈祥的；宽厚的 2.(气候等)温和的；有益于健康的 3.【医】(肿瘤等)良性的 ‖ ~ly *adv.*

benignant [biˈnignənt] *adj.* 1. 善良的，温厚的；慈祥的 2. 有利的，有益的 3.【医】(肿瘤等)良性的 ‖ **benignancy** *n.* / ~ly *adv.* / **benignity** *n.*

Benin [beˈnin] *n.* 贝宁[西非国家]

bent¹ [bent] bend 的过去式和过去分词

bent² [bent] *adj.* 1. 弯的 2. 有决心的，一心的(on) 3. 爱好，癖好 2.【建】排架；横向构架

benumb [biˈnʌm] *vt.* 使麻木，使失去感觉

benzene [ˈbenzin] *n.*【化】苯

benzine [ˈbenzin] *n.*【化】轻质汽油；石油挥发油

bequeath [biˈkwiːð] *vt.* 1.(按遗嘱)把…遗赠给(to) 2. 留下；传下 ‖ ~ al *n.* 遗赠；遗赠物；遗产

bequest [biˈkwest] *n.* 1. 遗赠 2. 遗产；遗赠物

berate [biˈreit] *vt.* 严责，训斥

bereave [biˈriːv] (bereaved 或 bereft [biˈreft]) *vt.* 1.[过去式和过去分词一般用 bereft]使失去(of) 2.[过去式和过去分词一般用 bereaved](死亡等)使丧失(亲人等)(of) ‖ ~ ment *n.* 丧亲；丧友

beret [ˈberei] *n.* 贝雷帽(一种扁圆的无沿帽)：the Green *Berets* 绿色贝雷帽(指美国的"特种部队")

berg [bəːg] *n.* 冰山

beriberi [ˈberiˈberi] *n.*【医】脚气病

Bering [ˈberiŋ] *n.* ~ Sea 白令海[太平洋北端] / ~ Strait 白令海峡

berkelium [ˈbəːkliəm] *n.*【化】锫

Berlin [bəːˈlin] *n.* 柏林[德国首都]

Bern(e) [bəːn] *n.* 伯尔尼[瑞士首都]

berry [ˈberi] *n.* 1. 浆果(如草莓、葡萄、西红柿等) 2.(某些植物的)干果仁，干种子(如咖啡豆等) 3.(龙虾等)卵 4.《美俚》一元钱 — *vi.* 1. 结出浆果 2. 采集浆果 ‖ **berried** *adj.* 1. 结浆果的 2.(龙虾等)有卵的

berserk [bəˈsəːk] *adj.* 狂暴的

berth [bəːθ] *n.* 1.(船与灯塔、沙滩等之间留出的)回旋(或操作)余地，安全距离 2. 泊位，锚地 3.【船】船台 4.(船、车、飞机等的)座位；铺位 5.(轮船上的)舱 6. 职位；(球赛中的)球队位置

vt. 1. 使停泊 2. 为(旅客等)提供铺位 — 1. 停泊 2. 占铺位

beryl ['beril] *n.* 1. 绿柱石;绿玉 2. 浅蓝(色)

beryllium [bə'riliəm] *n.* 【化】铍

beseech [bi'si:tʃ] (besought [bi'sɔ:t] 或 beseeched) *vt.* & *vi.* 恳求,哀求

beseeching [bi'si:tʃiŋ] *adj.* 恳求的,哀求的 ‖ ~ly *adv.*

beset [bi'set] (beset;besetting) *vt.* 1. 镶,嵌(珠宝饰物等) 2. 困扰,围攻 3. 包围住 ‖ besetting *adj.* 1. 不断侵袭的 2. (念头等)老是缠着人的

beside [bi'said] *prep.* 1. 在...旁边;在...附近 2. 与...相比;比得上 3. 与...无关 ‖ ~ oneself 若狂,发狂

besides [bi'saidz] *prep.* 1. 除...之外(还) 2. 除...之外(不再) — *adv.* 而且;再说;此外(还)

besiege [bi'si:dʒ] *vt.* 1. 包围,围困;围攻 2. 困扰 3. 使烦扰

besmirch [bi'smə:tʃ] *vt.* 1. 弄脏;使退色 2. 玷污,污损

besought [bi'sɔ:t] beseech 的过去式和过去分词

bespeak [bi'spi:k] (过去式 bespoke [bi'spəuk],过去分词 bespoken [bi'spəukən] 或 bespoke) *vt.* 1. 订(票、货等);预定;预约 2. 暗指;预示

best [best] *adj.* [good, well 的最高级] 1. 最好的 2. 最合适的 3. 大半的:the ~ part of an hour 大半个钟头 — *adv.* 1. [well 的最高级]最好地 2. [常用来构成复合词]最:the ~-hated man in the village 村里最可恨的人;最好的人;最好的东西(指状态、结果、服装等) ‖ ~ man 男傧相 / ~ seller 1. 畅销书;畅销商品 2. 畅销书作者;畅销唱片制作者 / ~'selling *adj.* 畅销(作

品)的

bestial ['bestiəl] *adj.* 1. 野兽的;野兽般的 2. 兽性的;残忍的;无理性的 ‖ ~ly *adv.*

bestiality [ˌbesti'æliti] *n.* 兽性;兽欲;兽行

bestir [bi'stə:] (bestirred;bestirring) *vt.* [常 ~ oneself] 使(自己)发奋;激励

bestow [bi'stəu] *vt.* 1. 把...赠与,把...给予(on, upon) 2. 使用;花费(时间、精力等)

bestrew [bi'stru:] (过去式 bestrewed,过去分词 bestrewn [bi'stru:n] 或 bestrewed) *vt.* 撒满...的表面;撒,使遍布;散布于

bet [bet] (bet 或 betted;betting) *vt.* 1. 用(钱或物)打赌;与(某人)打赌 2. 敢说;确信 — *vi.* 打赌 — *n.* 1. 打赌 2. 赌金;赌注 3. 被打赌的对象

beta ['bi:tə, 'beitə] *n.* 1. 希腊语的第二个字母(B,β) 2. 第二位的东西;【天】β星(星座中第二亮的星) — *adj.* 【化】第二位的,β位的 ‖ ~ particle 【物】β粒子/ ~ ray 【物】β射线

betake [bi'teik] (betook [bi'tuk], betaken [bi'teikən]) *vt.* [~ oneself] 1. 使致力于(to) 2. 使前往;使离去(to)

bête noire ['bet'nwɑ:(r)] [法]令人厌恶(或畏惧)的人(或事物);祸根

betide [bi'taid] *vi.* 发生 — *vt.* (祸)降临于

betimes [bi'taimz] *adv.* 1. 早;及时 2. 有时,偶尔 3. 〈古〉不久;迅速地

betoken [bi'təukən] *vt.* 1. 预示 2. 表示;证明

betray [bi'trei] *vt.* 1. 背叛,出卖 2. 辜负 3. 泄漏(秘密等) 4. 暴露 5. 把...引入歧途;诱奸后抛弃(女人) ‖ ~al *n.* / ~er *n.* 背叛者;背信者;告密者;诱奸者

betroth [bi'trəuð] *vt.* 把（女儿）许配给（to）；[常用被动语态](女子)同……订婚（to）；使（男女双方）订婚 ‖ ~**al** *n.* 订婚；许婚 / ~**ed** *adj.* 订了婚的. *n.* 已订婚者；未婚夫(或妻)

better¹ ['betə] *adj.* [good, well 的比较级] 1. 较好的, 更好的 2. (健康状况)有所好转的 3. 大半的: the ~ part of a month 大半个月 — *adv.* [well 的比较级] 1. 更好地 2. 更; 更多: This pair of shoes fit(s) you ～. 这双鞋子对你更合适. / ～ than ten miles 十英里多 — *vt.* 改善; 超过: ～ a record 刷新纪录 — *vi.* 改善 — *n.* 1. 较好的事物（或条件、行为等）2. 较优者: [常见 ~s]上司

better² ['betə] *n.* 打赌者(= bettor)

betterment ['betəmənt] *n.* 改善; 改进; 提高

bettermost ['betəməust] *adj.* 〈口〉1. 最好的；高级的 2. 较大的: the ~ part of the time 大部分时间

bettor ['betə] *n.* 打赌者

between [bi'twi:n] *prep.* 1. 在（两者）之间；在……中间 2. 为……所共有 3. 由于……的共同影响: Between astonishment and joy, she could hardly say a word. 她惊喜交集, 一句话也说不出来. — *adv.* 当中, 中间: a meeting with a short break ～ 中间有短暂休息的会议

bevel ['bevl] *n.* 1. [数]斜边; 斜角; 斜面 2. [建]斜角规 — (bevel(l)ed; bevel(l)ing) *vt.* 使成斜角(或斜面) — *vi.* 成斜角(或斜面), 下斜 ‖ ~ **gear** [机]锥(形)齿轮 / ~ **wheel** [机]锥齿轮

beverage ['bevəridʒ] *n.* 饮料(如汽水、茶、酒等)

bevy ['bevi] *n.* 1. (女孩、妇女的)一群 2. (鸟等的)一群, 尤指鹌鹑的)一群

bewail [bi'weil] *vt. & vi.* (为……而)痛哭;(为……而)悲伤

beware [bi'weə] *vt. & vi.* [用于祈使句中, 或与 must, should 等连用]谨防, 当心; *Beware(of)* dangers! 提防危险!

bewilder [bi'wildə] *vt.* 迷惑; 使为难, 把……弄糊涂 ‖ ~**ment** *n.*

bewilderingly [bi'wildəriŋli] *adv.* 迷惑人地;使人手足无措地

bewitch [bi'witʃ] *vt.* 1. 施魔力于; 蛊惑 2. 使着迷, 使心醉 ‖ ~**ing** *adj.* / ~**ingly** *adv.* / ~**ment** *n.* 蛊惑; 陶醉; 销魂; 着魔; 魔力

beyond [bi'jɔnd] *prep.* 1. [表示位置]在(或向)……的那边, 远于; go ～ the mountains 到山的那边去 / from ～ the seas 从海外 2. [表示时间]迟于 ～ midnight 半夜以后 3. [表示范围、限度]超出: ～ sb.'s power 某人力所不及的 4. [常用于否定句和疑问句]除……以外: I know nothing of it ～ what he told me. 除了他告诉我的以外, 别的我都不知道. — *adv.* 在远处; 向远处; 更远地: look ～ 往远处看 — *n.* 远处: the back of ～ 极远的地方; 天涯海角 / the (great) ～ 来世

Bhutan [bu:'tæn] *n.* 不丹[南亚国家]

Bi [化]元素铋(bismuth)的符号

bi [bai] *n. & adj.* 两性(的); 雌雄同体(的)

bi- *pref.* 表示"二(倍)", "两", "双", "重", "复": biannual, biceps, bicycle

biannual [bai'ænjuəl] *adj.* 一年两次的; 半年一次的;〈罕〉两年一次的 ‖ ~**ly** *adv.*

bias ['baiəs] *n.* 1. (织物的)斜纹路; 斜折, 斜裁; cut on the ～ 斜裁 2. 偏见; 倾向性; 癖好 3. [电]偏压 — *adj. & adv.* 偏斜 — (bias(s)ed; bias(s)ing) *vt.* [常用被动语态] 1. 使有偏见; 使有倾向性 2.

【无】加偏压于 ‖ **bias(s)ed** *adj.* 有偏见的 **2.**【统】有偏的;(织物)有斜纹织的

bib [bib] *n.* (小孩的)围涎;(大人的)围裙上部

Bible ['baibl] *n.* [the ~] **1.** 基督教的《圣经》**2.** 圣经 ‖ **Biblical, biblical** ['biblikəl] *adj.*《圣经》的;出于(或符合)《圣经》的

bibliographer [ˌbibli'ɔgrəfə] *n.* **1.** 书目编制者 **2.** 目录学家;书志学家

bibliography [ˌbibli'ɔgrəfi] *n.* **1.** 参考书目;文献目录 **2.** 目录学;文献学 ‖ **bibliographic(al)** [ˌbibliə'græfik(əl)] *adj.*

bicameral [bai'kæmərəl] *adj.* **1.** 有两个议院的;两院制的 **2.**【生】二室的,两室的

bicarbonate [bai'kɑːbənit] *n.*【化】碳酸氢盐;~ of soda 小苏打;碳酸氢钠

bicentennial [ˌbaisen'tenjəl] *adj.* 二百年的;二百周年纪念的 — *n.* 二百周年纪念(或庆典)‖ ~**ly** *adv.*

biceps ['baiseps] *n.*【解】二头肌

bicker ['bikə] *vi.* 口角,争吵

bicultural [bai'kʌltʃərəl] *adj.* 二元文化的,有两种文化的,两种文化结合的

bicuspid [bai'kʌspid] *n.*【解】双尖牙,前磨牙 — *adj.* 双尖的

bicycle ['baisikl] *n.* 自行车,脚踏车 — *vi.* 骑自行车 ‖ ~**r, bicyclist** *n.* 骑自行车的人

bid [bid] (过去式 **bade** [beid, bæd] 或 **bid**,过去分词 **bidden** ['bidn] 或 **bid**;现在分词 **bidding**) *vt.* **1.** [过去式一般用 **bade**] 祝;表示 **2.** [过去式一般用 **bade**] 命令;吩咐 **3.** [过去式和过去分词一般用 **bid**] (拍卖中)喊(价),出(价) **5.** [过去式一般用 **bid**] (打桥牌时)叫(牌) **6.** [过去式和过去分词一般用 **bid**] 【美口】接纳...为成员 — *vi.* **1.** [过去式一般用 **bid**;bidding) *vi.* 出

价;叫牌;投标 — *n.* **1.** 出价,喊价;投标;出价(或投标)金额 **2.** 出价(或投标)机会 **3.** 邀请 **4.**【牌】(桥牌中的)叫牌;够叫牌资格的一手牌 **5.** 企图 ‖ **bidder** *n./bidding* *n.* **1.** 命令;请求 **2.** 召唤;邀请 **3.** 出价 **4.** 叫牌

biddable ['bidəbl] *adj.* **1.** 顺从的,听话的,易管教的 **2.** 有资格叫牌的,可叫牌的

bide [baid] (过去式 **bode** [bəud] 或 **bided**,过去分词 **bided**) *vi.* 〈古〉〈诗〉持续;住;等候 — *vt.* **1.** 忍耐 **2.** [只用于习语 ~ one's time 中]等待 ‖ ~ **one's time** 等待时机

bidet ['biːdei] *n.* (洗下身的)坐浴盆

biennial [bai'eniəl] *adj.* **1.** 两年一次的 **2.** 持续两年的 **3.**【植】二年生的 — *n.* **1.** 两年发生一次的事物 **2.**【植】二年生植物 ‖ ~**ly** *adv.*

bier [biə] *n.* **1.** 棺材架;停尸架 **2.** 棺材

bifocal [bai'fəukəl] *adj.* 双焦的;双光的 — *n.* 双焦透镜;[~s] 双光眼镜

big [big] (**bigger, biggest**) *adj.* **1.** 大的,巨大的;长大了的 **2.** 怀孕的...怀...胎着...的(with);be ~ with child (或 young)怀孕 / be ~ with rage 怒气填膺 **3.** 重要的,重大的;著名的人;(演出等)获成功的,极受欢迎的 **4.** 自大的,傲慢的;~ talk (或 words)大话 **5.** 宽宏的,大度的 — *adv.* **1.** 大量地,大大地 **2.** (口)自大地 **3.** 宽宏地,大量地 ‖ ~**ness** *n.* 大,巨大 ‖ ~ **bang** [亦作 Big Bang] 创世大爆炸/**Big Ben** 大本钟(伦敦英国议会大厦的大钟)/~**hearted** *adj.* 宽宏大量的/~**horn** *n.*【动】加拿大盘羊/~ **shot** 大人物,大亨,有权势的人/~**wig** *n.* 要人,大人物

bigamy ['bigəmi] *n.* 重婚(罪) ‖ **bigamist** *n.* 重婚的人;犯重婚罪的人/**bigamous**

adj. 重婚的；犯重婚罪的

bight [bait] *n.* **1.**【地】大湾，开展海湾；海岸（或山脉等）的弯曲部分 **2.** 绳环；绳子放松时的中间弯曲部分

bigot ['bigət] *n.* 执拗的人；抱偏见的人 ‖ ~ed *adj.* 偏执的；顽固的

bigotry ['bigətri] *n.* 偏执；顽固；执拗行为（或态度等）

bike [baik] *n. & vi.* **1.**（口）（骑）自行车 **2.**（骑）摩托车 ‖ ~r *n.* 骑自行车（或摩托车）的人

bikini [bi'ki:ni] *n.* **1.** [B-] 比基尼岛（马绍尔群岛中最北端的一个珊瑚岛）**2.**（一种分上下两部分的女式）比基尼式游泳服，三点式泳装

bilateral [bai'lætərəl] *adj.* **1.** 两边的；在两边的 **2.** 有两边的；有两边的 **3.** 存在于双方向的，双边的 ‖ ~ly *adv.*

bile [bail] *n.* **1.** 胆汁 **2.** 坏脾气；暴躁

bilge [bildʒ] *n.* **1.**【船】底舱 **2.** 舱底污水 **3.** 桶腹；鼓出部分 — *vt.* 使（船底）漏水

bilingual [bai'liŋgwəl] *adj.* **1.** 两种语言的；用两种语言写（或印）的，双语的 **2.**（能）使用两种语言的 — *n.* 能使用两种语言的人 ‖ ~ly *adv.*

bilious ['biljəs] *adj.* **1.** 胆汁的；胆汁过多的；肝气不和的 **2.** 暴躁的，易怒的

bill[1] [bil] *n.* **1.** 账单 **2.** 单子；清单 **3.**（人员、职称等的）表；a ~ of fare 菜单 **4.**（影剧等的）招帖；传单；海报 **5.** 议案，法案 **6.** 票据；汇票；凭单 **6.**（美）钞票，纸币 — *vt.* **1.** 给⋯开账单 **2.**（用招贴、传单等）通告；宣布 **3.** 把⋯列成表 ‖ ~-board *n.* 告示牌，广告牌，招贴板 ‖ ~-fold *n.* 票夹

bill[2] [bil] *n.* **1.**（细长而扁平的）鸟嘴，喙 **2.**（狭窄的）岬；【锚】爪尖；形似鸟嘴的东西 — *vi.* **1.**（鸽）接嘴 **2.** 抚爱

billet[1] ['bilit] *n.* **1.**【军】膳宿提供令（军事当局发出的招待军人住宿的书面命令）**2.**（军营以外的）士兵住宿处，宿营地 **3.** 职位，工作 **4.**（古）短简 — *vt.* **1.** 分配（士兵等）宿舍；安顿 **2.** 把膳宿提供令送交 **3.** 委派，任命 — *vi.* 投宿，驻扎

billet[2] ['bilit] *n.* **1.** 木柴块 **2.**（金属的）短锭；钢坯 **3.**【建】错齿饰

billet-doux [ˌbili'du:]（[复] **billets-doux** [ˌbili'du:z]）*n.*〈谑〉情书

billiard ['biljəd] *n.* [只作定语] 台球球的，弹子戏的 — *n.* **1.** 连撞两球的得分 **2.** [~s]【用作单】台球戏，弹子戏 ‖ ~-ist *n.*

billion ['biljən] *num.* **1.**（英国、德国）万亿 **2.**（美国、法国）十亿 ‖ ~th *num.* **1.**（英、德）第一万亿（个）；一万亿分之一 **2.**（美、法）第十亿（个）；十亿分之一

billionaire [ˌbiljə'nɛə] *n.* 亿万富翁

billow ['biləu] *n.* **1.** 巨浪；波涛 **2.** 波浪翻滚滚向前的东西（如烟火、声音、军队等）— *vi.*（波浪似地）翻腾 — *vt.* 使翻腾 ‖ ~y *adj.* 巨浪的；巨浪般的；波涛汹涌的 / billowiness *n.*

billy ['bili] *n.* **1.** 棍棒；警棍 **2.**（野营烹任或作水壶用的）铁罐 ‖ ~ goat 公山羊

bimonthly [ˌbai'mʌnθli] *adj.* **1.** 两月一次的 **2.** 一月两次的 — *adv.* 两月一次地 — *n.* 双月刊

bin [bin] *n.* **1.**（贮藏食物、煤等的）箱子 **2.** 垃圾箱 **3.**（俚）疯人院

binary ['bainəri] *adj.* 由两部分（事物）组成的【化】二元的；【数】二进制的

bind [baind]（bound[bound] bound）*vt.* **1.** 捆，绑 **2.** 包扎；裹围 **3.** 装订（书）；缝纫时）给⋯滚边 **4.** 使凝固；使结合：an ice-

bound lake 封冻的湖泊 5. 使便秘：~ the bowels 引起便秘 6. 使受法律(或合同、道义等)约束 7. 使(协议等)确定不变 — *vi.* 1. 变硬；凝固 2. (紧身衣裤等)使人活动不方便；(门窗等)开不灵便 3. 具有约束力 — *n.* 1. 捆绑物；捆紧 2. [矿](煤系中的)页岩(或泥岩) 3. [音]括线，连线(即 ⌣)

binder ['baində] *n.* 1. 包扎者；装订工 2. 包扎工具；绳索；带子 3. [建]粘结料；系梁；粘合剂 4. [医]结合剂；(产妇的)腹带；绷带 5. 捆束机；(缝纫机)卷边压脚 6. 活页夹 7. 临时契约；(购买不动产时的)定金；定金收据 8. 装订机

binding ['baindiŋ] *adj.* 1. 捆绑的 2. 粘合的；(食物)引起便秘的 3. 有约束力的；附有义务的 — *n.* 1. 捆绑 2. 绷带；滚条 3. (书的)装订；装帧；封皮 4. 粘合剂

bingo ['biŋgəu] *n.* 宾戈(一种赌博游戏)

binnacle ['binəkl] *n.* [海]罗经柜，罗经座

binocular [bi'nɔkjulə, bai'nɔkjulə] *adj.* 双目的，双筒的 — *n.* 双目镜；[~s](双筒)望远镜

bio- *comb. form* 表示"生命"，"生物"：*biography*, *biochemistry*

bioastronautics ['baiəuˌæstrəu'nɔ:tiks] [复] *n.* [用作单或复]生物航天学

biochemistry [ˌbaiəu'kemistri] *n.* 生物化学 ‖ **biochemical** *adj.* / **biochemically** *adv.*

biochip ['baiəutʃip] *n.* [电子]生物芯片

biodegradable [ˌbaiəudi'greidəbl] *adj.* 能进行生物降解的

bioelectronics ['baiəuˌilek'trɔniks] [复] *n.* [用作单]生物电子学

bioengineering [ˌbaiəuˌendʒi'niəriŋ] *n.* 生物工程

bioethics [ˌbaiəu'eθiks] [复] *n.* [用作单]生物伦理学

biofeedback [ˌbaiəu'fi:dbæk] *n.* 生物反馈

biographer [bai'ɔgrəfə] *n.* 传记作者

biographic(al) [ˌbaiəu'græfik(əl)] *adj.* 传记的；传记体的 ‖ **biographically** *adv.*

biography [bai'ɔgrəfi] *n.* 1. 传记 2. 事物发展过程的记述

biological [ˌbaiə'lɔdʒikəl] *adj.* 生物学(上)的 ‖ ~**ly** *adv.* ‖ ~ **clock** 生物钟 / ~ **control** 生物控制(指利用天敌对害虫类进行的控制) / ~ **engineering** 生物工程

biology [bai'ɔlədʒi] *n.* 1. 生物学 2. [总称](一个地区的)生物 ‖ **biologist** *n.* 生物学家

bionics [bai'ɔniks] [复] *n.* [用作单或复]仿生学 ‖ **bionic** *adj.*

biophysics [ˌbaiəu'fiziks] [复] *n.* [用作单或复]生物物理学

biopsy ['baiɔpsi] *n.* [医]活组织检查

bioremediation [ˌbaiəuriˌmi:di'eiʃən] *n.* 生物治理(指利用微生物对有毒废物场及受污染水域进行的净化处理)

bipartisan [ˌbaipɑ:ti'zæn] *adj.* 两党的；代表两党的；得到两党支持的

biped ['baiped] *n.* 二足动物 — *adj.* 有二足的

biplane ['baiplein] *n.* 双翼飞机

birch [bə:tʃ] *n.* 1. 桦，白桦 2. 桦木 3. (鞭打用的)桦条(或桦条束) — *vt.* 用桦条打

bird [bə:d] *n.* 1. 鸟，禽；a ~ of prey 猛禽(尤指鹰类) 2. [美口]火箭(或火箭、航天火箭)3. 羽毛球 4. [俚]人，家伙；少女 5. [俚](轰赶某人时的)嘘声 — *vi.* 1. 观察研究野鸟 2. 打鸟；捕鸟 ‖ ~ **cage** 鸟笼；类似鸟笼的场

(如牢房等)/`~ call` n. 鸟叫声；摹仿的鸟叫声/`~ dog` n. 捕鸟猎犬 2. 挖掘人才(如球员等)的人；兜揽生意的人 3.〈美〉〈军俚〉战斗机，歼击机/`~ farm`〈美俚〉航空母舰/`~ house` n. 鸟舍 /`~ seed` n. 鸟食/`~'s-eye` n. 开鲜艳小花的植物(如报春花等) 2.〈纺〉鸟眼花纹(织物) 3.(木材上的)椭圆形鸟眼纹理 *adj.* 1. 俯视的，鸟瞰的；概略的：a `~'s-eye view` 鸟瞰图；概观 2. 有鸟眼纹的：`~` 糙粒木(制)的/`~'s nest` 1. 鸟巢；燕窝 2. 胡萝卜 3.〈船〉瞭望台/`~'s-nest` vi. 掏鸟巢，摸鸟蛋/`~ strike` 飞机与鸟群相撞(事故)

Birmingham n. 1.[`'bə:miŋəm`]伯明翰[英国英格兰中部城市] 2.[`'bə:miŋhæm`]伯明翰[美国亚拉巴马州中部城市]

birth [bə:θ] n. 1. 分娩；出生，诞生 2. 出身，血统 3. 起源，开始/`~ control` 节育/`~ day` n. 生日；诞生的日期/`~ mark` n. 胎记，胎痣/`~ place` n. 出生地，故乡/(事物的)发源地/`~ rate` n. 出生率/`~ right` n. 生来就有的权利；长子继承权

biscuit [`'biskit`] n. 1.〈英〉饼干[美国称 cracker] 2.〈美〉软饼 3. 淡褐色 4. 陶瓷素烧坏

bisect [bai`'sekt`] vt. 把…分为二；把…二等分 ‖ `~ion` n. 1. 平分，二等分，分叉处 3. 平分的部分，均分的二分之一/`~or` n. 1. 二等分物 2.【数】平分线

bisexual [bai`'seksjuəl`] adj. 1. 两性的 2. 性欲错乱的，受两性吸引的 ‖ `bisexuality` [`baiseksju'æliti`] n.

Bishkek [bi`ʃ'kek`] 比什凯克(曾称 Frunze 伏龙芝)[吉尔吉斯斯坦首都]

bishop [`'biʃəp`] n. 1.(基督教的)主教 2.(国际象棋中的)象 3. 加有香料的果子酒

bishopric [`'biʃəprik`] n. 主教管辖区；主教职权;主教住所

bismuth [`'bizməθ`] n.【化】铋

bison [`'baisn`][单复同] n.【动】(北美洲的)犎牛,野牛

bisque [bisk] n. 海味(或野味、蔬菜)浓汤

Bissau, Bissão [bi`'sau`] n. 比绍[几内亚比绍共和国首都]

bit[bit] n. 1. 一点,一些,一些[常~s]吃剩的食物;小片 2.〈口〉一会儿 3. 辅币[美口]一角二分半 4.(戏中的)只有三四句旁白的小角色 5.〈口〉常规,老一套

bit[bit] n. 1.〈马〉嚼子 2.(工具上的)箝头,钻头;刀片;刀头;钻牙;钥匙齿 — (bitted; bitting) vt. 1. 给(马)上嚼子 2. 训练(马)使受嚼子 3. 控制;抑制 4. 给(钥匙)锉齿

bit[bit] bite 的过去式和过去分词

bitch [bitʃ] n. 1. 母狗(或母狼、母狐等) 2.〈贬〉脾气坏的妇女;坏女人;淫妇,荡妇 3.〈口〉难事;使人不愉快的事 [俚] vt. 1. 弄脏,弄污 2. 对…埋怨 3. 搞坏 — vi. 埋怨 ‖ `~y` adj.

bite [bait] (过去式 bit[bit],过去分词 bitten[`'bitn`]或 bit) vt. 1. 咬;叮,螫 2.(利器)刺穿(寒风等)刺 3.(锚等)咬住,吃住;(螺丝等)擢住 4.(酸等)腐蚀 5. 涫骗,使吃亏 — vi. 1. 咬;(狗等)爱咬人 2.(武器、工具等)穿透,弄穿(through) 3. 刺痛 4. 被蚀;(鱼)上钩(人)上当 5. 咬住住;钉牢 — n. 1. 咬;叮;(鱼的)上钩 2. 一口(食物);一顿饭 3. 被咬的伤口;伤痛 4. 蜇咬;穿透力 5.(锯、锉等)的齿 6.[医]咬合(上下齿的啮合情况) 7. 腐蚀 8.(一次收取的)一笔数目[如抽税] 9.(语言等的)尖刻;辛辣 ‖ `~ r` n.

biting ['baitiŋ] *adj.* 1. 尖利刺人的；刺痛的 2. 刻毒的；辛辣的 ‖ ~ly *adv.*

bitten ['bitn]bite 的过去分词

bitter ['bitə] *adj.* 1. 有苦味的，苦的 2. 辛酸的，痛苦的；厉害的，剧烈的 3. 严寒的，刺骨的 4. 怀恨的，抱怨的 ‖ ~ n. 1. 苦；苦味；苦味物 2. 苦啤酒；[~s]苦味药酒 — *adv.* 苦苦地；悲痛地；厉害地 — *vt.* 使变苦辛 — *vi.* 变苦 ‖ ~ish *adj.*/~ly *adv.* 苦苦地；悲痛地；厉害地/~ness n. 苦味；辛酸；苦难 ‖ ~ sweet *adj.* 又苦又甜的；又苦又乐的 — n. 1.【植】美洲南蛇藤 2.【植】千年不烂心,蜀羊泉 3. 又苦又甜，又苦又乐

bittern ['bitən] n.【动】(麻)鸻

bitumen ['bitjumin] n. 沥青

bituminous [bi'tjuminəs] *adj.* 沥青的；含沥青的 ‖ ~ coal 烟煤

bivalve ['baivælv] n.【动】双壳类动物；[植]双瓣壳 ‖ ~d, bi'valvular *adj.*

bivouac ['bivuæk] n. 露营，野营，露宿；临时宿营地 — (bivouacked; bivouacking) *vi.* 露营

biweekly [bai'wi:kli] *adj.* 1. 两周一次的，一周二次的 — *adv.* 1. 两周一次地 2. 一周两次地 — n. 1. 双周刊 2. 半周刊

bizarre [bi'zɑ:] *adj.* 奇奇古怪的，异乎寻常的

blab [blæb] (blabbed; blabbing) *vi.* 瞎说，乱谈 — *vt.* 泄漏(秘密) — n. 瞎说的人；泄漏秘密的人

blabber ['blæbə] n. 喋喋不休的人；泄漏秘密的人 ‖ ~-mouth n. 喋喋不休的人

black [blæk] *adj.* 1. 黑的；漆黑的 2. 黑肤色的；黑人的；有关黑人的 3. 暗淡的；阴郁的；怒气冲冲的 4. 邪恶的；不吉利的；the ~ art 妖术 5. 极度的；

despair 绝望 6. 弄脏的；丢脸的 7.(教士等)穿黑衣的 8. 黑市的，非法交易的；the ~ market 黑市，非法市场 9.(英)被(罢工工人)抵制卸的；a ~ ship 被抵制装卸的船 — n. 1. 黑色；黑漆；黑颜料；黑墨水；be written in ~ 用黑墨水写的 2. 黑人 3. 黑斑；污点；煤灰 4. 黑衣；wear ~ 穿黑服 5.(少数的黑墨粉,黑糖糊毒菌 — *vt.* 1. 弄黑；弄脏 2. 用黑鞋油擦 — *vi.* 变黑 ‖ ~ish *adj.*/~ly *adv.* / ~ness n. ‖ ~'ball n. 反对票 *vt.* 投票反对；排斥，开除/'~berry n. 黑刺莓 *vi.* 采黑刺莓 /'~bird n.【动】黑鸟；乌鸫；紫色鹂哥 /'~board n. 黑板/~ book 记有黑名单的册子；记人罪过的书；记过册/~browed *adj.* 满怒怒容的；蹙着脸的/~ Black English (尤指美国的)黑人英语/~ hoie[天]黑洞/'~jack n. 1. 皮酒樽 2. 二十一点(一种作庄牌戏) *vt.* 用皮棍棒打；胁迫/'~list n. 黑名单 *vt.* 把...列入黑名单/~ money(美俚)"黑钱",贿赂的非法收益/'~out n. 1.(幕间或剧终时的)灯光熄灭 2. 灯火管制(期)3. 断电,停电 4. 暂时的眩晕(或失明,记忆缺失)5. 删除;(新闻)封锁/ Black Panther《美》黑豹党人/~power(尤指美国黑人企求的)黑人权力/~ sheep 害群之马；败类/'~smith n. 铁匠；锻工/~ tea 红茶/'~thorn n.【植】黑刺李；梨山楂/~ widow(吃掉雄蜘蛛的)黑寡妇球蜘蛛

blacken ['blækən] *vt.* 1. 使变黑 2. 诽谤 — *vi.* 变黑

blackguard ['blægɑ:d] n. 恶棍,无赖 — *vt.* 谩骂 — *vi.* 耍无赖,骂人 — *adj.* 无赖的 ‖ ~ly *adv.* & *adj.*

blackmail ['blækmeil] n. 敲诈；勒索 — *vt.* 敲诈;向...勒索 ‖ ~er n. 敲诈者;勒索者

bladder ['blædə] *n.* 1.【解】膀胱；囊 2. 气泡 3. 囊状物；球胆 4. 空话连篇的人

blade [bleid] *n.* 1. 刀身；刀片 2. 草片（禾谷类等的）叶片；桨片（舌；骨等的）扁平部分；肩胛骨 3. 剑 4. 击剑人 5. 浮荡少年 6.【语】舌面 ‖ ~d *adj.* / ~ like *adj.* ‖ ~ bone *n.*【解】肩胛骨

blame [bleim] *vt.* 1. 责备，谴责；找...的差错 2.〈口〉把...归咎，推诿 (on, upon) 3. 责备，责怪 2.（过错，失败等的）责任 ‖ blamable *adj.* / ~ful *adj.*

blameless ['bleimlis] *adj.* 无可责难的；无过错的 ‖ ~ly *adv.* / ~ness *n.*

blameworthy ['bleim,wə:ði] *adj.* 该受责备的

blanch [blɑ:ntʃ] *vt.* 1. 使变白 2. 使（脸等）变苍白 3. 使（植物）不见日光而变白 4.【冶】酸洗（金属）使有光泽；在...上镀锡 5. 用沸水去（杏仁等）的皮 ‖ *vi.* 发白；变苍白

bland [blænd] *adj.* 1. 和蔼的 2. （药、食品、饮料、气候等）刺激性少的，温和的 ‖ ~ly *adv.* / ~ness *n.*

blandish ['blændiʃ] *vt.* & *vi.* 奉承，讨好 ‖ ~ment *n.* [~ments]奉承，讨好

blank [blæŋk] *adj.* 1. 空白的，空虚的 2. 没有表情的，呆板的 3. 完全的，十足的 4. 茫然的，直发表情的 5. 没有韵的 6.（墙）无门（或窗）的 ‖ *n.* 1. 空白；空白表格 2. 靶心；瞄准的对象 3.（抽中奖的）彩票 4.【机】坯件 5.【军】空包弹 ‖ *vt.* 1. 涂掉 (out) 2.〈美〉（在游戏、比赛中）使（对方）得零分 3. 使不能通行，封锁 (off) ‖ *vi.* 成为空白 ‖ ~ly *adv.* / ~ness *n.* ‖ ~ cartridge *n.*【军】空包弹

blanket ['blæŋkit] *n.* 1. 羊毛毯，毯子；毛毯 2. 一片（迷雾、白雪等）(of) ‖ *vt.* 1.（用毯子）盖，覆 2. 掩盖（丑事等）扑

blare [blɛə] *n.* 1.（像喇叭般）发嘟嘟声；吼叫 ‖ *vi.* 高声发出（或奏出）；大声宣布 ‖ *n.* 1.（喇叭的）嘟嘟声；高声 2.（颜色等的）光泽

blarney ['blɑ:ni] *n.* 1. 花言巧语；奉承话 2. 胡扯；欺人之谈 ‖ *vt.* & *vi.* 奉承；哄骗

blasé ['blɑ:zei] *adj.* 过度享乐而感到厌倦的，玩腻了的；厌世的

blaspheme [blæs'fi:m] *vt.* & *vi.* 亵渎 ‖ ~r *n.* 渎神者

blasphemous ['blæsfəməs] *adj.* 渎神的 ‖ ~ly *adv.*

blasphemy ['blæsfəmi] *n.* 亵渎；亵渎神明的言词（或行为）

blast [blɑ:st] *n.* 1. 一阵（风）一股（强而突然的气流）；疾风，狂风 2. 鼓风；送风 3. 爆炸，爆破；爆炸气浪，冲击波 4.（管乐器等的）吹奏（声）；（汽笛等的）吼鸣（声）5. 一次用的炸药量 6.〈口〉严厉的训斥 7. 喧嚣的聚会，狂欢会 8.（棒球的）安打；本垒打 ‖ *vt.* 1.（用炸药）炸裂 2. 摧毁；炸毁 3. 吹奏；斥责 ‖ *vi.* 1. 吼鸣 2. 炸，爆炸 3. 猛烈攻击 4. 枯萎 5.（火箭、导弹）发火起飞，发射 (off) ‖ ~ed *adj.* 1. 被摧毁的；枯萎的；该死的/ ~er *n.* ‖ ~ furnace *n.*【冶】鼓风炉，高炉 / ~-off *n.* （火箭、导弹的）发射

blatant ['bleitənt] *adj.* 1. 吵嚷的；喧哗的；大喊大叫的 2. 炫耀的；刺眼的 ‖ blatancy *n.* / ~ly *adv.*

blaze¹ [bleiz] *n.* 1. 火，火焰；熊熊燃烧 2. 直射的强光；光辉；闪耀 3.（感情等的）迸发；爆发 4. [~s] 地狱 ‖ *vi.* 1. 燃烧；冒火焰 2. 发（强）光；放光彩；闪耀 3. 激动；连续发射 (away) ‖ ~r *n.* 1. 燃烧体；发光物 2. 运动衫

blaze² [bleiz] *n.* 1. (牛、马等脸上的白色) 星斑 2. (割去树皮后树身上留下的) 砍痕,砍树标志 — *vt.* 1. 在(树)上刮皮留下砍号 2. 在树皮上刻砍号指示(道路等)

blazon [ˈbleizən] *vt.* 宣布;宣传

bldg. *abbr.* building

bleach [bliːtʃ] *vt.* 漂白;晒白;使脱色 — *vi.* 变白;脱色 — *n.* 1. 漂白;漂白法 2. 漂白剂 3. 漂白液

bleacher [ˈbliːtʃə] *n.* 1. 漂白工人 2. 漂白器;漂白剂 3. [~s] (美) (运动场的) 露天看台

bleaching [ˈbliːtʃiŋ] *n. & adj.* 漂白(的) ‖ ~ powder 漂白粉

bleak [bliːk] *adj.* 1. 苍白的;惨淡的,暗淡的 2. 凄凉的,萧瑟的 3. 无遮蔽的;风吹雨打的;荒凉的,光秃秃的 4. 阴冷的 ‖ ~ly *adv.* / ~ness *n.*

blear [bliə] *vt.* 使模糊 — *n.* 模糊;朦胧 — *adj.* (眼睛)视线模糊的

bleat [bliːt] *vi.* 1. (羊、小牛等)叫 2. 咩咩地叫 3. 讲蠢话;哀声哭诉 — *vt.* 轻声颤抖地说 — *n.* 羊(或小牛)叫声;咩咩声 ‖ ~er *n.*

bleed [bliːd] (bled [bled]) *vi.* 1. 出血,流血 2. (在战斗中)流血战死 3. (心)悲痛,同情 4. 渗出,流出 5. (植物)伤流,流出液汁 5. (印染、浓淡等)渗开 — *vt.* 1. 使出血 2. [医] 给……放血 3. 榨取(某人)的血汗 3. 榨取(树木)的液汁 4. 从……抽(或抽平)水;从……抽气减压 5. 放(气)放出(液、浆等)

blemish [ˈblemiʃ] *vt.* 有损……的完美;玷污 — *n.* 瑕疵,缺点 ‖ ~er *n.*

blench [blentʃ] *vi.* 退缩,畏缩

blend [blend] (blended 或 blent [blent]) *vt.* 1. 混和,把……混成一体 2. 把(不同种茶叶或酒类或烟丝等)掺在一起 3. 染(毛皮) — *vi.* 1. 混和,交融,混成一体 2. (声音、颜色等)调和,协调 — *n.* 1. 混合,融合 2. 混合物,混成品(指掺了酒精的威士忌酒等) 3. 缩合词 (= ~word);系由一词的首部分接合另一词的尾部分构成的新词,如英语中由 smoke 的首部分及 fog 的尾部分构成的新词 smog) ‖ ~er *n.* 掺和者;搅和器

blent [blent] blend 的过去式和过去分词

bless [bles] (blessed 或 blest [blest]) *vt.* 1. (用宗教仪式等)使神圣;使圣洁 2. [~oneself] (在自己)胸前划十字 3. 为……祈神赐福;为……祝福 4. 赞美(上帝),对(上帝)感恩 5. (上帝)保佑,赐福于;使幸福 6. 使有幸得到,使具有(with) 7. [过去式和过去分词一般用 blest] (口)诅咒,使倒霉

blessed [ˈblesid] *adj.* 1. 神圣的 2. [宗] 在天国享福的,有福的;使人有福的;给人愉快(或满足)的 4. 该死的 5. [作加强语气用] Not a ~ drop of rain throughout the month. 整整一个月没下一滴雨。‖ ~ly *adv.* / ~ness *n.*

blessing [ˈblesiŋ] *n.* 1. (上帝的)赐福;祈神赐福;祝福 2. (教徒在饭前后的)感恩祷告 3. 同意,允准 4. 幸事

blest [blest] bless 的过去式和过去分词 — *adj.* = blessed

blew [bluː] blow 的过去式

blight [blait] *n.* 1. (植物的)疫病,凋萎病;导致凋萎病的细菌(或真菌、病毒等) 2. (希望、计划等的)破坏因素,毁灭因素 3. 受挫;遭受损状态 — *vt.* 1. 使(植物)染上凋萎病;使凋萎 2. 挫折;毁损;摧残 — *vi.* 凋萎;患凋萎病

blimp [blimp] *n.* 1. 软式飞艇 2. [B-] 高傲自大的极端保守分子

blind [blaind] *adj.* 1. 眼睛失明的,瞎的；盲人的 2. 视而不见的；盲目的；无识别能力的 (*to*) 3. 【空】单凭仪表操纵的：～ landing 盲目着陆 4. 轻率的,鲁莽的；无目的的 5.(俚)醉的 6.(墙)无窗的;(胡同)一端不通的 7.(信件)地址写得不全的,地址难以辨认的 — *vt.* 1. 使失明；把...的眼睛弄花 2. 蒙蔽；使失去判断力：be ～ *ed* by hatred for gain 利令智昏 — *n.* 1. 遮光物；遮窗；百叶窗 2. 障眼物；挡箭牌；诱饵 — *adv.* 1. 盲目地；胡乱地 2.【空】单凭仪表操纵地：fly ～ 盲目飞行 ‖ ～**ly** *adv.* / ～**ness** *n.*

blindfold ['blaindfəuld] *vt.* 1. 蒙住...的眼睛；蒙住(眼睛) 2. 蒙蔽；使不理解 — *adj.* 1. 被蒙住眼的；看不清的 2. 盲目的 — *adv.* 盲目地；胡乱地 — *n.* 1. 蒙眼的布(或绷带) 2. 障眼物；蒙蔽人的事物(或言行等)

blinding ['blaindiŋ] *adj.* 1. 使盲的；把人弄糊涂的 2. 眩目的,使眼花缭乱的

blindman ['blaindmæn]([复]blindmen) *n.* (英)(邮局的)辨字员 ‖ ～'**s buff** 捉迷藏

blink [bliŋk] *vi.* 1. 眨眼睛 2. 闪亮;闪烁;微微闪光 3. 眼半睁闭,睡眼惺忪 — *vt.* 1. 眨(眼睛) 2.眨着眼挤掉(眼泪等) (*away*);使闪烁;使闪亮 3. 闭眼不看;不睬,不顾(事实等) 4. 以闪光信号表示 — *n.* 1. 眨眼睛;一瞥 2. 一瞬间 3. 闪光

blinker ['bliŋkə] *n.* 1. [～s](马的)眼罩 2. [～s]护目镜 3.(信号的)闪光灯 — *vt.* 给(马等)上眼罩;蒙蔽

bliss [blis] *n.* 极大的幸福;极乐

blissful ['blisful] *adj.* 极幸福的;极乐的 ‖ ～**ly** *adv.* / ～**ness** *n.*

blister ['blistə] *n.* 1. 水疱,疱 2.(植物的)

疱病 3.【药】发疱药 4.(金属上的)砂眼,泡疱;(漆器等上的)气泡 — *vt.* 1. 使(手、脚等)起疱;使(漆器等)起泡 2. 狠揍;狠责责骂;辱骂 — *vi.* 起水疱;起泡

blithe [blaið] *adj.* 1. 欢乐的,愉快的 2. 轻率的,冒失的 ‖ ～**ly** *adv.* / ～**some** *adj.*

B Lit(t) *abbr.* Bachelor of Literature 文学学士 (= Bachelor of Letters)

blitz [blits] *n.* 闪电战;(喻)突击,闪电式行动 — *vt.* 用闪电战攻击 — *vi.* 进行闪击

blitzkrieg ['blitskri:g] *n.* & *vt.* = blitz

blizzard ['blizəd] *n.* 暴风雪

bloat[1] [bləut] *vt.* & *vi.* 1. (使)肿起;(使)膨胀;(喻)得意忘形 — *vi.* 成胀病人 2.(俚)醉鬼 3.(家畜的)胃气胀 ‖ ～**ed** *adj.* 1. 肿胀的 2. 得意忘形的 3.(因多食而)病态地发胖的 4.(俚)喝醉的

bloat[2] [bləut] *vt.* 腌熏(鲱鱼等) ‖ ～**er** *n.* 腌熏的鲱鱼(或鲭鱼)

blob [blɔb] *n.* 1.(粘稠的)一滴,一团(颜色形成的)一抹,一点 2. 难以名状的一团;黑糊糊的一堆 — *vt.* (blobbed 或 blobbing) *vt.* 涂抹,弄污

bloc [blɔk] *n.* 集团

block [blɔk] *n.* 1. 大块;大块木料(或石料,金属);【建】砌砖,空心砖 2. 砧板;铁砧 3. 木(或金属)印版 4.(俚)头,脑 5. 滑轮;滑轮组,滑车 6. 一排房屋;街区(四条街道当中的地区);街段(两条平行街道之间的街的距离) 7. 大厦,大楼 8.(戏院等的)坐位划区 9. 集团 10. 障碍;障碍物;[体]阻挡 11. [无]障碍;[医](心传导)阻滞 — *vt.* 1. 阻塞;拦阻,堵塞(*up*) 2. 封锁 3. 垫高(*up*) 4. 限制使用(货币、财产等等) ‖ ～**er** *n.*

‖ '~ ˌbuster n.〈俚〉巨型炸弹 / '~ head n. 傻瓜 / '~ house n. 碉堡；掩体

blockade [blɔ'keid] n. & vt. 封锁 ‖ '~ er n. 封锁者；执行封锁的船 ‖ block'ade-runner n. 偷越封锁线的人(或船)

blockage ['blɔkidʒ] n. 1. 封锁状态 2. 障碍

bloke [bləuk] n.〈英口〉人，家伙(指男子)

blond(e [blɔnd] adj. 1.(头发)亚麻色的，淡黄色的 2.(皮肤)白晰的；白里透红的 3.(人)白肤金发碧眼的 — n. 白肤金发碧眼的人(指女人时一般拼作 blonde)

blood [blʌd] n. 1. 血，血液 2. 杀人；流血；a man of ~ 杀人成性的人 3. 血气；气质；脾气 4. 血统；世系；种族；家族关系；门第；贵族门第 5. 有血性的人，血气方刚的人，达绔子弟；浪子 6.〔总称〕人员 — vt. 1. 使出血，从…抽血 2. 使(猎狗)先尝(或先看、先闻)猎物的血；让(新手等)取得经验 ‖ ~ ed adj. 1.(牛等)纯种的 2.〔用以构成复合词〕…血的；warm-~ed 热血的，热情的；易激动的 / ~ less adj. ‖ ~ bank n. 血库 / ~ bath n. 大屠杀 / '~ hound n. 1. 大猎犬，大警犬 2. 机警凶猛的追捕者；侦探 / '~ mobile n. 流动收血车 / ~ poisoning n. 血中毒 / ~ pressure 血压 / ~ relation 有血缘关系的亲属，血亲 / '~ shed n. 流血，杀戮 / '~ shot adj.(眼)充血的 / '~ stream n. 血流 / '~ sucker n. 1. 吸血动物(尤指水蛭) 2. 吸血鬼；敲诈勒索者 / ~ thirsty adj. 嗜血的，残忍好杀戮的 / ~ transfusion [医] 输血；输血法 / ~ type 血型 / ~ vessel 血管

bloody ['blʌdi] adj. 1.(鼻子等)滴血的；有血污的 2.(战斗等)流血的，血流成渠的；残酷的 3. 好杀戮的，残忍的 4.

血红的 — vt. 1. 使流血 2. 血染 ‖ **bloodiness** n.

bloom [blu:m] n. 1.(尤指观赏植物的)花；(一棵树或一季内开出的)全部花朵 2. 开花；开花期；come into ~ 开花；pass out of ~ 过了开花期；花谢 3.〔只用单〕青春；兴旺时期；完美；the ~ of life 青春时代；兴旺时期 4.(面颊的)红润 5.(水果包皮、植物叶面等的)粉衣，粉霜 6.(过强反射在电视上引起的)刺目闪光 — vi. 1. 开花，(变得)草木繁盛 2. 进入青春时代；(尤指妇女)容光焕发 3. 发展；繁盛，突然激增 ‖ ~ ing adj.

bloomers ['blu:məz] [复] n. 女式灯笼裤

blossom ['blɔsəm] n. 1.(尤指果树的)花；(一棵树或一季内开出的)全部花朵 2. 开花；开花期 3. 兴旺时期 — vi. 1. 开花，(降落伞)展开 2. 繁盛，兴旺 3. 发展，长成(into)

blot [blɔt] n. 1. 墨水渍；污渍 2. 有损整体美的东西 3.(道德等上的)污点 — (blotted, blotting) vt. 1. 涂污(信笺等) 2.(雾等)遮住；消灭(out) 3.(古)污损(名誉等)；使蒙羞 4.(用吸墨纸等)吸干；吸去 — vi. 弄上墨渍；弄上污渍 ‖ **blotting paper** 吸墨纸

blotch [blɔtʃ] n. 1.(皮肤上的)红斑，疹块 2.墨水、颜料等的大滴污渍，大片污渍 — vt. 弄脏；涂污 ‖ ~ y adj.

blotter ['blɔtə] n. 1.(一张)吸墨纸，吸墨用具 2.〈美〉(记入正式档案前的)临时记录册(如警察分局的)逮捕人犯记录簿(= police ~)

blouse [blauz] n. 1.(工人、水手、妇女等穿的)宽大短上衣，罩衫 2. 军上装，制服上衣

blouson ['blu:zɔn] n. 束腰女服

blow¹ [bləu] (blew [blu:], blown [bləun]) vi.

1.(风)吹 2.(喇叭、口哨等)吹响 3.吹气;呼吸困难急促,喘气 4.喷水;吹 5.(保险丝)烧断;(车胎等)爆炸(*up*) 6.〈口〉吹牛 7.(苍蝇)产卵 8.〈美俚〉跑掉(*away*) — *vt.* 1.吹;吹动;使(成功的希望等)告吹 2.吹响(乐器、号角等) 3.吹(火等);使通气:~ one's nose 擤鼻子 4.使充气;使爆炸 5.吹制(玻璃器皿)6.使吹气 7.〈口〉吹嘘 8.〔常用被动语态〕使(马)喘息 10.(昆虫)产卵于 11.〔口〕挥霍 12.〈美俚〉离开 13.放大(照片等)— *n.* 1.吹风;呼吸新鲜空气 2.疾风 3.吹(指吹笛等)4.擤 5.吹牛;吹牛者 6.保险丝的烧断 7.〔口〕吹嘘 ∥ ~ *out* 1.(突然)爆裂;喷气 2.车胎爆裂 3.保险丝烧断 4.〈口〉盛宴;丰富的一餐;宴会;聚会 5.熄灭;停炉 / ~ *pipe n.* 吹管、喷焊器 / ~ *torch n.* 喷灯 / ~ *up n.* 1.充气;(轮胎等充气)2.放大的照片;扩充本 3.崩溃;破裂

blow² [bləu] *n.* 1.打,一击;打击 2.(精神上的)打击;灾祸

blown [bləun]**blow** 的过去分词 — *adj.* 1.吹胀的;(玻璃器皿)吹制的 2.喘气的 3.被炸毁的 4.(食物等)有蝇卵或蝇蛆)损害的

blubber¹ [ˈblʌbə] *vi.* 哭闹 — *vt.* 1.哭着说,哭诉 2.哭肿(脸)— *n.* 哭泣;哭泣声

blubber² [ˈblʌbə] *n.* 1.鲸脂;海兽脂 2.赘肉

bludgeon [ˈblʌdʒən]*n.*(用作武器的)大头棒 — *vt.* 1.用大头棒猛击 2.强迫

blue [blu:] *adj.* 1.蓝色的,天蓝色的 2.(人的脸色等)发青(或紫)的 3.(动物等毛皮)青灰色的 3.沮丧的,忧郁的;使沮丧的 4.穿蓝色服装的;以蓝色为标志的 5.〈英国〉保守党的 5.(女人)有学问的 6.清教徒的;禁律严的 7.下流的,淫猥的 — *n.* 1.蓝色 2.蓝颜料(或染料);〔pl〕上蓝剂 3.蓝色服装;[~s]海军蓝制服 4.女学者 5.[the ~]蓝天;海洋 6.[~s]忧郁,烦闷 7.[~s]蓝调音乐(一种伤感忧闷的美国黑人民歌);蓝调乐曲;蓝调爵士乐 — *vt.* 1.把...染成蓝色;上蓝于 2.〈美俚〉乱花(钱)— *vi.* 变蓝,呈蓝色 ∥ ~ *ness n.* ∥ ~ *bell n.* 1.蓝铃花 2.开蓝色铃状花的植物(如风信子等)/ ~ *berry n.*〔植〕乌饭树;乌饭树的蓝色浆果 / ~ *bird n.* 〔美产的〕蓝鸲;鸟 / ~ *black adj.* 深蓝色的、蓝黑色的 / ~ *bottle n.* 1.〔植〕矢车菊;风铃草 2.〔口〕反吐丽蝇 3.〈澳〉〔口〕(蓝翅帽水母)/ ~ *collar.* 穿蓝领工作服的,从事体力劳动的,蓝领的 / ~ *fish n.* 1.(北美大西洋沿岸的)蓝鱼,跳鱼 2.浅蓝色食用小鱼 3.蓝鱼 / ~ *funk*(英)不能控制的恐惧 / ~ *jay*(北美产的)有冠蓝背樫鸟 / ~ *murder* 恐怖的叫喊 / ~ *print n.* 蓝图(印出设计图样),复制蓝图;制订行动计划;为...制订计划 / ~ *s... *定详细规划 /~ *sman n.* 演唱(或演奏)蓝调歌曲(或乐曲)的人

bluff¹ [blʌf] *adj.* 1.(船头等)宽而垂直的(河岸等)壁立的;陡的 2.坦率的;粗率的 — *n.* 陡岸;悬崖;峭壁 ∥ ~ *ly adv.* / ~ *ness n.*

bluff² [blʌf] *vt.* 1.吓唬;吓住 2.以假象欺骗;愚弄 — *vi.* 吓唬人 — *n.* 1.吓唬 2.吓唬人的人 ∥ ~ *er n.*

bluing [ˈbluːiŋ] *n.*(洗染时防止白色织物变黄用的)上蓝剂(亦作 blueing)

bluish [ˈbluːiʃ] *adj.* 带蓝色的

blunder ['blʌndə] vi. 1. 跌跌撞撞,绊跌;慌乱地走(或跑) 2.(因无知、慌乱或疏忽)犯错误;犯大错 — vt. 1.(在慌乱中愚蠢地)说出,漏出(out) 2. 做错,办错(事情等) — n. 大错 ‖ ~er n. 犯大错的人

blunderbuss ['blʌndəbʌs] n. 1. 老式大口径短枪 2. 老犯错误的人

blunt [blʌnt] adj. 1.(刀子等)不锋利的,钝的 2.(感觉、理解力等)迟钝的 3.(人、人的言谈举止等)生硬的;率直的 — vt. 把…弄钝;把…弄迟钝 — vi. 变钝;变迟钝 ‖ ~ly adv. 直截了当地 /~ness n.

blur [blə] (blurred; blurring) vt. 1. 涂污,弄脏;污损(名声等) 2. 把(界线、视线等)弄得模糊不清 — vi. 1. 出上污迹 2. 变得模糊起来 — n. 1. 污迹;(道德等方面的)污点 2. 模糊不清的东西;模糊一片 ‖ blurry adj.

blurt [blət] vt. 突然说出;脱口说出(秘密等)(out)

blush [blʌʃ] vi. 1. 脸红;羞愧上(花等)呈现红色 — vt. 把…弄成红色 — n. 1. 脸红;红色;红光 3.〈古〉一瞥 ‖ ~ n. 1. 脸红的人 2. 能使脸色红润的化妆品/~ful adj.(使人)脸红的;(使人)惭愧的;易脸红的,红色的,红润的

blushing ['blʌʃiŋ] adj. 脸红的;羞愧的 — n. 脸红 ‖ ~ly adv.

bluster ['blʌstə] vi. 1.(风)呼啸狂吹;(浪等)汹涌 2.(人)咆哮;恐吓 — vt. 怒气冲冲地说出;蛮横地威入 2. 恐吓,胁迫 — n. 1. 狂风声;巨浪声 2. 大吵大嚷 3. 空洞的大话,大声的威吓 ‖ ~ n. 1. 咆哮的人;吓唬人的人

blustering ['blʌstəriŋ] adj. 狂暴的;恐吓的 ‖ ~ly adv.

blvd. abbr. boulevard

BMDS abbr. ballistic missile defence system 弹道导弹防御系统

BMEWS abbr. ballistic missile early warning system 弹道导弹预警系统

boa ['bəuə] n. 1. 蟒蛇,蟒 2.(毛皮或羽毛制的)女用长围巾(或披肩) 3. 蟒形联合浮动汇率

boar [bɔ:] n. 1.(未阉的)公猪 2. 野猪

board [bɔ:d] n. 1. 木板,板;纸板;a bulletin — 布告栏 2. 船舱;on — 在船(或车、飞机)上 3. 餐桌;伙食;— and lodging 膳宿 4. 会议桌;全体委员;委员会;(政府机关的)部门;a — of directors 董事会/the Board of Trade(英国)贸易委员会 5.[~s]舞台 6.(篮球架的)篮板 7.[~s](冰球场四周的)护板 8. 跳水板;冲浪板 — vt. 1. 用板铺;用板隔(up) 2.(收费)供…膳食 3. 上(船、车、飞机) 4.(为攻击等而)靠拢(船);强行登(船) — vi. 搭伙 ‖ ~room n.(董事会等的)会议室/~walk n.〈美〉(尤指海滨的)木板路

boarder ['bɔ:də] n. 1. 搭伙者 2. 寄宿生;a day~ 2. 寄膳不寄宿的学生 3. 乘船(或车、飞机)的人 4. 被派到强登敌船者

boarding ['bɔ:diŋ] n. 1.[总称]木板 2. 上船(或车、飞机);强行登船 ‖ ~ house n. 供膳的寄宿舍/~school 寄宿学校

boarish ['bɔ:riʃ] adj. 野猪般的;肉欲的;残忍的

boast [bəust] n. 1. 自吹自擂;自夸的话 2. 可以夸耀(或自豪)的事物 — vi. 自吹自擂;自夸(of, about) — vt. 夸口说;以有…而自豪;自恃有 ‖ ~ n. 1. 自吹自擂的人,大言不惭的人

boastful ['bəustful] adj. 1.(人)好夸口的,自负的 2.(言语等)自夸的 ‖ ~ly adv. /~ness n.

boat [bəut] n. 1.(用桨、帆或引擎的)小

船,艇 2. 大船 3. 船形器皿Ⅲ — *vi.* 乘船(游玩);划船(游玩) ‖ ~**ful** *n.* 一船所载的量 ‖ ~**ing** *n.* (尤指以娱乐为目的的)划船 ‖ ~**drill** 救生演习 / ~**hook** *n.* 有钩的篙子 / ~**house** *n.* 水边停放游艇的场所(常附设俱乐部) / ~**man** *n.* 1. 船工 2. 出租(或出售)小艇的人 / ~**race** 划船比赛 / ~**train** 配合船期接送乘客的火车

boatswain ['bəusn, 'bautswein] *n.* 水手长

bob¹ [bɔb] *n.* 1. (孩童或女子的)短发;(妇女或女孩的)短发发式 2. 剪短的马尾 — (bobbed; bobbing) *vt.* 剪短(发、尾等) ‖ bobbed *adj.* 剪短的

bob² [bɔb] *n.* 1. 〈口〉一束(或一串)叶子(或花、葡萄等) 2. 悬挂的装饰品(如耳环) 3. 浮勿 4. (钓鱼线上的)浮子 5. 【物】摆锤;测锤 6. 屈膝礼(扎) 7. 轻敲,轻打 — (bobbed; bobbing) *vi.* 1. 上下跳动 2. 突然出现(*up*) 3. (游戏中)试图咬住悬挂物体(*for, at*) 4. 行屈膝礼 — *vt.* 1. 敲;轻敲;使敲(或撞) 2. 使急速上下起伏

bobbin ['bɔbin] *n.* 1. (纺织等用的)筒管,筲子 2. 线轴 3. (电器上的)绕线管

bobby ['bɔbi] *n.* 〈俚〉警察

bobby-pin ['bɔbipin] *n.* 〈美〉〈澳新〉扁平发夹

bobolink ['bɔbəliŋk] *n.* 【动】(北美洲的)长刺歌雀

bobsled ['bɔbsled], **bobsleigh** ['bɔbslei] *n.* 大雪橇;连橇 — *vi.* 乘大雪橇

bobtail ['bɔbteil] *n.* 截短的尾;截短了尾的马(或狗) — *adj.* 截尾的;截短的 — *vt.* 截……的尾;截短

bobwhite ['bɔb'hwait] *n.* 【动】山齿鹑

bode¹ [bəud] *vt. & vi.* 预示

bode² [bəud] bide 的过去式

bodice ['bɔdis] *n.* 1. (妇女的)紧身胸衣 2. (妇女罩在衬衫等外面的)紧身马甲 3. 女连衣裙的上身

bodily ['bɔdili] *adj.* 身体的;肉体的 — *adv.* 全部地,整体地

body ['bɔdi] *n.* 1. 身体,躯体;(植物等的)躯干;车身;船身 2. 尸体,尸首 3. 主体,主要部分;正文 4. 团体;机关 5. [常用以构成复合词]人(如 anybody, everybody 等) 6. 物体;a heavenly ~ 天体 7. 质地;(液体的)稠度;(酒等的)强度 8. (一)群;(一)大批;大量(事实、知识)(*of*) 9. 核心(*of*) 10. 【数】立体 11. 【印】铅字身 — *vt.* 赋……以形体 ‖ ~**building** *n. & adj.* 增强体质的;健美运动(的) / ~**builder** 健美运动者;参加健美运动者 / ~**corporate**[律]法人团体 / ~**count** (尤指估计的)死亡人数统计;人数统计 / ~**guard** *n.* 1. 警卫员 2. 保镖 / ~**language** 身势语 / ~**stocking** (女子的)衣裤相连的紧身内衣

bog [bɔg] *n.* 泥潭,沼泽 — (bogged; bogging) *vt. & vi.* 1. [常用被动语态](使)陷入泥沼,(使)沉入泥沼(*down*) 2. (使)陷于困境;(使)停顿(*down*)

bogey ['bəugi] *n.* 1. 鬼怪,妖怪;可怕(或可憎)的人(或物) 2.〈俚〉来历不明的飞行物 ‖ ~**man** *n.* (用以恐吓孩子而实际并不存在的)怪物;可怕的人(或物)

boggle ['bɔgl] *vi.* 1. 迟疑,犹豫;退缩 2. 推诿;踌躇 3. 惊恐;困惑 — *vt.* 1. 弄坏,搞糟 2. 使惊奇;吓倒;使困惑;使为难

boggy ['bɔgi] *adj.* 沼泽的;似沼泽的;多沼泽的

bogie ['bəugi] *n.* = bogey

bogus ['bəʊgəs] *adj.* 伪造的, 伪的

bogy ['bəʊgi] *n.* = bogey

bohea [bəʊ'hi:] *n.* 武夷红茶(产于福建武夷山)

Bohemia [bəʊ'hi:miə] *n.* 1. 波希米亚(捷克一地区) 2. 放荡不羁的文化界

Bohemian [bəʊ'hi:miən] *adj.* 1. 波希米亚的 2. 波希米亚人的 3. 波希米亚语的 4. 放荡不羁的(尤指艺术家等) — *n.* 1. 波希米亚人 2. 波希米亚语 3. 放荡不羁的文化人

boil [bɔil] *vi.* 1. 达到沸点 2. 汽化 3. 像沸水一样翻滚 4.(人、感情)激动;(海)翻腾 — *vt.* 1. 煮沸 2. 在沸水中煮 3. 用煮沸方法制造(或分出)(盐、糖等) 4. 熬浓 (*down*) — *n.* 1. 煮沸;沸点;沸腾 2.【医】疖

boiler ['bɔilə] *n.* 1. 煮器(壶、锅、釜的泛称) 2. 锅炉 3. 热水贮槽 4. 熬煮东西的人

boiling ['bɔiliŋ] *adj.* 1. 沸腾的 2. 极热的 3. 激昂的;汹涌的 — *adv.* 达到沸腾程度 ‖ ~ point 1. 沸点 2. 极度兴奋;激昂

boisterous ['bɔistərəs] *adj.* 1.(风、海水、行动、言词等)狂暴的;汹涌的 2.(人或行动)吵吵嚷嚷的;兴高采烈的 ‖ ~ly *adv.* / ~ness *n.*

bold [bəʊld] *adj.* 1. 大胆的, 勇敢的 2. 冒失的, 鲁莽的;无耻的;无礼的 3.(字体、线条等)粗壮的, 粗大的 4.(山崖)陡峭的 ‖ ~ly *adv.* 1. 大胆地 2. 冒失地 / ~ ness *n.* ‖ ~-face *n.* 【印】黑体, 粗体 / ~faced *adj.* 1. 冒失的, 鲁莽的 2.【印】黑体的, 粗体的

bolero (['复]boleros) *n.* 1. [bə'lɛərəʊ]波列罗舞(曲) 2. ['bɔlərəʊ](前胸敞开抵及腰部的)西班牙男短上衣;前胸敞开的女短外套

Bolivia [bə'liviə] *n.* 玻利维亚[南美洲西部国家]

boll [bəʊl] *n.* 【植】(棉、亚麻等的)圆荚、铃 ‖ ~-worm *n.* 【动】棉红铃虫;棉铃虫

bologna [bə'ləʊnjə] *n.* 大红肠

boloney [bə'ləʊni] *n.* 〈俚〉废话, 瞎扯

Bolshevik ['bɔlʃivik] ([复] Bolsheviki [bɔlʃi'viki] 或 Bolsheviks) *n.* 布尔什维克 — *adj.* 布尔什维克的

Bolshevism ['bɔlʃivizəm] *n.* 布尔什维主义 ‖ **Bolshevist** *n.* 布尔什维主义者, 布尔什维克一分子 — *adj.* 布尔什维主义的, 布尔什维克的

bolster ['bəʊlstə] *n.* 1. 长枕;垫枕, 靠枕 2. 垫枕状的支撑物;【机】软垫, 垫木;车架承梁;【建】托木, 雀替 — *vt.* 1.(用支撑物)支撑;垫, 加固 2. 支持;提高 ‖ ~ er *n.*

bolt [bəʊlt] *n.* 1.〈古〉弩箭 2. 意外(或不幸)事件 3. 闪电;雷电 4.(门、窗的)插销, 闩;螺栓 5. 螺栓;栓 6.(棉布的)匹;(纸等的)卷 7. 枪栓;枪机 8. 突发;猛冲;逃走 — *vt.* 1. 发射(箭等) 2. 脱口说出 (*out*) 3. 囫囵吞下 4. 闩(门);闩上(门使不能出或进)(*in, out*) ~ sb. in (out) 把某人关在室内(室外) 5.〈美〉拒绝支持(自己党派的政策、提名等);退出(党派或团体) — *vi.* 1. 射;窜 2.(马)脱缰;逃跑 3. 囫囵吞下 4.〈美〉拒绝支持自己党派的政策(或提名等);退出党派(或团体) — *adv.* [后接 upright] 笔直地(坐) ‖ ~ er *n.* 脱缰马;脱党者;拒绝支持本党(或其候选人)的人 ‖ ~-'on *adj.*(汽车部件等)可用螺栓结合的

bomb [bɔm] *n.* 1. 炸弹 2. 气溶胶弹式容器;高压气体贮罐 3.【地】火山弹(指火山喷出的球状溶岩) 4.(体内照射用的)放射性物质容器, 弹, 炮 5.〈英〉惊

人的大成功;轰动一时的事物 6.【体】长传;远投 7.〈美俚〉(演出等的)大失败 — vt. 1. 投弹区,轰炸 2. 把(人)炸得无家可归(out) — vi. 1. 投弹 2.〈美俚〉大败,惨败 ‖ ~ bay(飞机上的)炸弹舱/'~ proof adj. 防炸的,防弹的/'~ shell n. 1. 炸弹 2. 出人意料的人(或事) 3. 引起轰动的人(或事)

bombard [bɔmˈbɑ:d] vt. 1. 炮击;轰炸 2.〈喻〉攻击;痛斥;向(某人)发出连珠炮似的问题 3.【核】轰击 ‖ ~ier [ˌbɔmbəˈdiə] n. / ~ment n.

bombastic [bɔmˈbæstik] adj. 夸张的 ‖ ~ally adv.

Bombay [bɔmˈbei] n. 孟买[印度西部港市]

bombed [bɔmd] adj.〈美俚〉烂醉的;因吸毒而晕晕乎乎的

bomber [ˈbɔmə] n. 1. 轰炸机 2. 投弹手

bonbon [ˈbɔnbɔn] n. 夹心软糖;糖果

bond [bɔnd] n. 1. 契约;契约所规定的义务 2. 公债;债券 3. 付款保证书;保证人 4. 结合物;粘结剂;结合力;联结 5. [~s]镣铐;羁绊 6.【化】键;键合 7.【建】砌合 8.【商】关栈保留 — vt. 1. 因未完税把(进口货物)存入关栈 2. 使结合在一起 3.【建】砌合(砖);粘着(水泥等) — vi. 1. 结合在一起 ‖ ~ed adj. 1.[木板等]由两(或多)层胶合的 2.[货物]存放关栈以待完税的/'~ man n. 奴隶;奴仆/~ paper证券纸/'~ slave n. 奴隶/'~sman n. — man 2 保证人

bondage [ˈbɔndidʒ] n. 奴役;束缚

bone [bɔun] n. 1. 骨;骨质(物) 2.[~s]骨骼;死尸;身体 3. 骨状物(如象牙等);骨制品 4. [~s]音)响板 5.〈口〉[~s]骰子 — vt. 1. 去掉...的骨 2. 施骨肥于 3:用鲸骨撑大(妇女衣服

4.〈俚〉偷 — vi.〈美俚〉专心致志(up) ‖ ~ less adj. 无骨的/~ china 骨灰瓷(一种含有骨灰或磷酸钙的瓷器)/'~ dry adj. 十分干燥的/'~ head n.〈俚〉笨蛋,傻瓜/'~idle adj. 懒极的/~ meal 骨粉(作肥料用)/'~ setter n.【医】正骨者/'~shaker n. 破旧摇晃的车辆

bonfire [ˈbɔnfaiə] n. 篝火;营火

bongo [ˈbɔŋɡəu] n. [复]bongo(e)s n.〈拉〉拉丁美洲和非洲音乐中用的小手鼓

Bonn [bɔn] n. 波恩[德国临时首都]

bonnet [ˈbɔnit] n. 1.(无边有带的)女帽;童帽 2. 烟囱帽;机器罩;阀门帽 — vt. 1. 给...戴帽子 2. 拉下(某人)的帽子(使遮住其眼睛)

bonny, bonnie [ˈbɔni] adj. 1. 美丽的 2. 健康的;强壮的 3. 快活的;好的 ‖ bonnily adv.

bonus [ˈbəunəs] n. 1. 额外给予的东西 2. 奖金 3. 红利 4.〈退伍军人〉补助金 5.〈职业运动员〉的津贴 6.〈英俚〉赒赐

bony [ˈbəuni] adj. 1. 像骨的 2.(鱼等)多骨的 3. 骨骼大的 4. 瘦的;憔悴的

boo [bu:] int.[表示嫌恶或轻蔑]呸! — n. 呸的一声 — vi. 发出呸的声音 — vt. 讥笑

booby [ˈbu:bi] n. 1. 笨蛋,呆子 2.【动】鲣鸟 3.(球队等)得分最少者 ‖ ~ prize 末名奖 /~ trap【军】饵雷;陷阱/'~ trap vt. 设...饵雷;设陷阱...设陷阱

book [buk] n. 1. 书,书籍 2.[the B-]基督教《圣经》3.(书的)卷;篇 4.(装订成册)簿册;账簿 5.登记簿;名册 6.(歌剧的)唱词;(戏剧的)剧本 7.(赛马赌博等)登记簿;赌账 — vt. 1. 把...记载入册 2. 预定,定(戏票、车位等) 3.〈英〉(在旅馆

为...预订房间(*in*) — *vi.* 1. 预定 2.
(英)(旅客在旅馆、机场等)办理登记
手续(*in*) ‖ ~ **let** *n.* 小册子 / ~
binder *n.* 装订工人；装订机 / ~ **case**
n. 书橱；书架 / ~ **end** *n.* 书立，书挡 / ~
keeper *n.* 簿记员，管记账人 / ~
keeping *n.* 簿记 / ~ **maker** *n.* 1. (赛马
等的)赌注登记经纪人 2. 作家；编辑；
编著者 3. 出版者；书商 / ~ **mark** *n.*
书签 / ~ **mobile** *n.* (设在汽车上的)流
动图书馆 / ~ **review** 书评 / ~ **seller** *n.*
书商，书店老板，书店经理 / ~ **shelf** *n.*
书架 / ~ **shop**，~ **store** *n.* 书店 / ~ **stall**
n. 书摊，书亭 / ~ **worm** *n.* 书蛀虫；书
呆子

bookie ['buki] *n.* 〈口〉(赛马等的)赌注
登记经纪人

bookish ['bukiʃ] *adj.* 好读书的；只有书
本知识的，学究式的 ‖ ~**ly** *adv.* / ~
ness *n.*

boom[1] [buːm] *n.* 1. (炮、雷、风、风琴等)
隆隆(或轰轰、嗡嗡等)声，有回响的声
音 2. (大蛙等的)叫声 — *vi.* 发出隆隆
声 — *vt.* 用隆隆声表达(*out*)

boom[2] [buːm] *n.* 1. (商业等)迅速发展；
兴隆，兴旺；(商品等)需求量激增 2.
出名 — *vt.* 1. 使迅速发展；使兴隆，使
兴旺 2. 热烈支持；支持 — *vi.* 1. (商业
的)景气，繁荣 2. (政治形势等)突
然好转 ‖ ~**ing** *n.* & *adj.* ‖ ~**town**
n. 新兴城市

boom[3] [buːm] *n.* 1. 吊杆；帆的下桁；张帆
杆 2. 水栅，拦障

boomerang ['buːmæræŋ] *n.* 1. 回飞镖(澳
大利亚土著的武器，用曲形坚木制成，
投出后可飞回原处) 2. 自食其果的言
行 — *vi.* 使人自食其果

boon [buːn] *n.* 1. 恩惠；及时的恩赐；裨
益，非常有用的东西 2.〈古〉请求 —

adj. 快活的，欢乐的；爱吃喝交际的
‖ ~ **companion** 酒友；一起寻欢作乐的
人

boondoggle ['buːndɔgl] 〈口〉*vi.* 干琐细
无用的事 — *n.* 琐细无价值的工作；
无事忙；浪费的开支 ‖ ~ **r** *n.*

boor [buə] *n.* 态度粗鲁的人 ‖ ~**ish** *adj.*
粗鲁的

boost [buːst] *vt.* 1. 升，提；推 2. 提高；促
进；支援 3. (用广告等)吹捧 4. 【电】(升
压)；给(电流)升压 — *vi.* 1. 升，提；提
高，增加 3. 帮助 4. 宣传；吹捧 ‖ ~
n. 1. 提(或推)的人 2. 支援者 3. 【电】
增压机，升压器 2. 帮助；助推火箭 5. (收音
机、电视机的)辅助(或升压)放大器 6.
【军】助爆剂 7.【药】(尤指增强免疫力
的)辅助药剂

boot[1] [buːt] *n.* 1. (美)(皮或橡胶制的)
靴 2. 筒状刑具(夹足、腿用) 3. (英)(汽车
的)行李箱 4. 罩，防护罩 5. 踢 6. 解雇
7. 〈海〉海军(或海军陆战队)新兵 —
vt. 1. 给...穿靴 2. 用刑具夹(足、腿)
3. 踢 4. 〈俚〉解雇 5.〈口〉把...揣走
(*out*) ‖ ~**black** *n.* 以擦皮靴为生的
人 / ~**lace** *n.* 靴带 / ~**lick** *vt.* & *vi.*〈美俚〉巴结，奉承 / ~**licker**
n.〈美俚〉拍马者，奉承者

bootee ['buːti] *n.* 1. 幼儿毛线鞋 2. 女用
轻便短统靴

booth [buːð, buːθ] *n.* 1. (有篷的)货摊 2.
〈美〉公用电话亭 3.(隔开的)小间(餐
厅中的)火车座 4.(选举时的)投票站
(= polling)

bootleg ['buːtleg] *n.* 1. 靴筒 2.(尤指私
酒等)非法制品 (过去式：bootlegged；现在
分词：bootlegging) *vt.* 非法携带(或制造、运输、贩卖)(酒
等)；非法获得 — *vi.* 非法制造(或运
输、贩卖)酒 — *adj.* 非法制造(或运输、
贩卖)的；非法的；违禁的 ‖ **bootlegger**

n.

booty ['bu:ti] *n.* 1. 战利品 2. 掠夺物; 赃物

border ['bɔ:də] *n.* 1. 边, 缘, 边沿; (女服的)滚边 2. 边界, 国界, 国境; 边境地区 3. (花园里沿边沿或走道两边的)花坛 — *vt.* 1. 接界(*on*, *upon*) 2. 近似(*on*, *upon*) — *vt.* 1. 在(衣服等)上镶边 2. 接近

bore[1] [bɔ:] *vt. & vi.* 钻(孔); 挖(一机)镗(孔) 2. (在人群等中)打开(一条路)(*through*) — *n.* 1. 孔, 洞; 枪膛; 炮膛(机)膛 2. 内径(枪、炮等的)口径 3. 钻孔器 ‖ ~ *r n.* 1. (机)镗床; 镗孔刀具 2.[动]蛀船虫; 钻蛀虫

bore[2] [bɔ:] *vt.* 使厌烦 — *n.* 惹人厌烦的人(或物)‖ ~ **some** *adj.* 令人厌烦的; 无聊的; 乏味的

bore[3] [bɔ:] *n.* 激潮, 涌潮, 涛

bore[4] [bɔ:] **bear**[1] 的过去式

boredom ['bɔ:dəm] *n.* 厌烦; 无趣

boric ['bɔ:rik] *adj.*[化]硼的; 含硼的 ‖ ~ **acid** 硼酸

boring[1] ['bɔ:riŋ] *n.* 1.[机]镗(孔), 钻(孔), 扩孔 2.[~s]镗屑 — *adj.* 镗孔的, 钻孔的 ‖ ~ **machine**[机]镗床

boring[2] ['bɔ:riŋ] *adj.* 令人厌烦的

born [bɔ:n] **bear**[1] 的过去分词 — *adj.* 1. 出身于...的 2. 天生的, 生来的

borne [bɔ:n] **bear**[1] 的过去分词

boron ['bɔ:rɔn] *n.*[化]硼

borough ['bʌrə] *n.* 1. (英)享有自治特权的市镇; 议会中有代表的市镇 2. (美)自治村镇 3.(美)纽约市的行政区

borrow ['bɔrəu] *vt.* 1. 借, 借用(词语等)(*from*) 3.(演算减法时)从某数借(一位)— *vi.* 借; 借东西, 借钱 ‖ ~ **er** *n.* / ~ **ing** *n.* 借; 借用的东西(或词)

向其他民族仿效的风俗习惯

bo's'n ['bəusn] *n.* = boatswain

Bosnia and Herzegovina ['bɔzniə ənd hɜ:tsəgəu'vi:nə] 波斯尼亚 - 黑塞哥维那(简称波黑)[欧洲巴尔干半岛西部国家]

bosom ['buzəm] *n.* 1. 胸; 怀; (衣服的)胸部 2.〈喻〉(家庭等的)怀抱(*of*)— *adj.* 亲密的, 知心的(朋友、伙伴)‖ ~ **friend** 隆起的;(女子)乳房发达的

boss[1] [bɔs] *n.* 1.〈口〉工头, 领班; 老板; 上司 2. (政治机构中的)头子, 首领 — *vt.* 1. 当...的首领 2. 指挥, 把...差来遣去(*about*)

bossy ['bɔsi] *adj.*〈口〉专横的, 霸道的

Boston ['bɔstən] *n.* 波士顿[美国马萨诸塞州首府]

botanical [bə'tænikəl] *adj.* 植物(学)的 — *n.* 植物性药材

botanist ['bɔtənist] *n.* 植物学家

botany ['bɔtəni] *n.* 1. 植物学 2. (某地区的)植物生态 3. 植物学书; 植物学论著

botch [bɔtʃ] *vt. & vi.* 1. 拙劣地修补 2. 笨手笨脚地弄坏 — *n.* 1. 拙劣的补钉(或修补部分) 2. 粗劣的工作 ‖ *n.* / ~ **y** *adj.*

both [bəuθ] *adj.* 两...(都), 两个...(都): *Both* his brothers are doctors. 他的两个兄弟都是医生。— *pron.* 二者; 两人, 双方: *Both* (of them) are doctors. 他们两个都是医生。— *conj.* [与 and 连用]两个都; 既...又..., 不但...而且...: *Both* industry and agriculture are making great strides. 工农业都在大踏步前进。

bother ['bɔðə] *vt.* 1. 烦扰, 打扰 2. [后接 oneself 或 one's head](为...)操心, 费脑筋(*about*) 3. [表示不耐烦的感叹]

Bother it! 讨厌! — *vi.* 1. 烦恼;操心 2. [表示不耐烦的感叹] 讨厌 — *n.* 1. 麻烦 2. 纠纷;殴斗 3. 讨厌的人;麻烦 的事物 ‖ ~some *adj.* 麻烦的;讨厌的; 令人烦恼的

Botswana [bɔt'swɑːnə] *n.* 博茨瓦纳(旧称 Bechuanaland 贝专纳) [非洲中南部国家]

bottle ['bɔtl] *n.* 1. 瓶;酒瓶 2. [盛放酒类的]皮袋 2. 一瓶(的量) 3. [the ~]酒; 喝酒 4. [the ~]奶瓶;奶瓶里的奶 — *vt.* 1. 把(酒等)装瓶;把(水果等)装瓶 贮藏 2. 抑制(怒气,感气等) 3. 把……逼入不能逃脱(或不能自由活动)的境地(*up*) ‖ ~r *n.* 装瓶工人;装瓶机 ‖ ~feed → 给婴儿用奶瓶喂(婴儿,幼小动物等) / '~neck *n.* 瓶颈 (口);交通阻塞点;窄路,狭窄的街道;妨碍生产流程的一环 *vt.* 梗塞;阻塞 *adj.* 瓶颈口似的,狭窄的

bottom ['bɔtəm] *n.* 1. 底部,底;(山)脚 2. (道路等的)尽头;(裤脚、书页等的)下端 3. (会议桌等的)末席;(名单等的)末尾 4. 船底;舱底;货船 5. [纺](织物的)底色 6. 根源;原因 7. 椅面 8. (口)屁股 9. [常~s]河边低地 — *adj.* 1. 最底下的;最低的 2. 根本的;根本的 (事实等)的 ‖ ~less *adj.* 无底的;没有根据的;深不可测的;无限的 ‖ '~land *n.* 河边低地 / '~line *n.* 账本底线,盈亏一览结算线 2. 基本意思或情况,概要 3. 底细;结果

botulism ['bɔtjulizəm] *n.* [医]肉毒中毒

bough [bau] *n.* 树枝(尤指大树枝)

bought [bɔːt] buy 的过去式和过去分词 — *adj.* 买来的;现成的(指非定制的)

bouillon ['buːjɔ̃] *n.* (牛肉或鸡肉等的)清汤

boulder ['bəuldə] *n.* 巨砾;漂砾;卵石

boulevard ['buːləvɑːd] *n.* 1. 林荫大道 2. (美)干道,大街

bounce [bauns] *vi.* 1. (球)反跳,弹起 2. (人)跳(起) 3. 上下跳动地进行;噔噔噔(或怒气冲冲)地走(*in*, *out*) 4. (俚)(支票)被拒付而退还给持票人 5. (英)吹牛 — *vt.* 1. 拍(球),使弹回 2. 使撞击;使上下跳动 3. (口)骂(人) 4. (英)强迫;诈骗 5.(俚)撑走;把……解雇 — *n.* 1. 弹,反弹;弹力 2. 跳,跳跃 3.(俚)活力 4.(英)吹牛 5.(俚)驱逐;解雇 6. 猛击 ‖ '~back *n.* 弹回;反冲;反射

bound[1] [baund] bind 的过去式和过去分词 — *adj.* 1. 被束缚的 2. 捆扎的,扎成一定的,必定的,必定的 4. (道德上或法律上)受约束的,有义务的 5. (口)下了决心的 6. 装订的 7. 便秘的 8. [化][物]结合中的

bound[2] [baund] *adj.* 准备(或正在)到……去的;(船等)前往……的(*for*)

bound[3] [baund] *n.* [常~s]边界;界限;范围 — *vt.* 1. 限止 2. 形成……的边界;邻接 3. 指明……的疆界

bound[4] [baund] *n.* (向上或向前的)跳跃 — *vi.* 跳跃;(球等)弹起;跳跃着前进 — *vt.* 使跳;使弹回

boundary ['baundəri] *n.* 分界线;边界;界限

boundless ['baundlis] *adj.* 无边际的;无限的 ‖ ~ly *adv.* / ~ness *n.*

bounteous ['bauntiəs] *adj.* 1. 慷慨的,大方的 2. 丰富的,充足的 ‖ ~ly *adv.* / ~ness *n.*

bountiful ['bauntiful] *adj.* 1. 慷慨的,大方的 2. 丰裕的,充足的 ‖ ~ly *adv.* / ~ness *n.*

bounty ['baunti] *n.* 1. 慷慨,大方 2. 赠礼物;赠礼 3. 奖金;补助金

bouquet ['buːkeɪ] *n*. 1. 花束;大串烟火 2. 恭维话 3.(酒等的)香味;(文艺作品等的)韵味,特色

bourbon ['buəbən] *n*. 亦作 B-](美)波旁威士忌酒

bourgeois ['buəʒwɑː][单复同] *n*. 1.(中世纪城镇中的)自由民 2. 资产者 3. 资产阶级分子;具有中产阶级特性的人 4. 资产(或中产)阶级 — *adj*. 资产阶级的;中产阶级的;平庸的

bourgeoisie [,buəʒwɑː'ziː] *n*. 资产阶级;中产阶级

bourgeon ['bəːdʒən] *n*. & *vi*. = burgeon

bout [baut] *n*. 1.一次,一场,一回 2. ~ of inflation 一场通货膨胀 2. 回合;较量;比赛

bovine ['bəuvaɪn] *adj*. 1. 牛的 2. 牛一般的;迟钝的

bow[1] [bəu] *n*. 1. 弓 2. 弓手 3. 琴弓 3. 弓形(部分);弓形物;虹 4. 蝴蝶结;蝶形领结 5. 凸肚窗(= ~ window) 6. 【军】7. 眼镜框;眼镜脚 — *vt*. 1. 用弓拉(琴) 2. 把……弯成弓形 — *vi*. 1. 用弓拉琴 2. 弯成弓形 ‖ ~ed *adj*. 弯曲的;弓形的 / ~ing *n*.【音】弓法 ‖ ~-leg *n*. 弓形腿 / ~ line ['bəulin, 'bəulain] *n*. 1. 张帆索 2. 单套结(= ~ line knot) / ~ man *n*. ~ string *n*. 1. 弓弦 2. 绞索 vt. 绞死 / ~ tie 蝶形领结 / ~ window *n*. 1.【建】凸肚窗 2.(俚)罗汉肚,大肚皮

bow[2] [bau] *vi*. 1. 鞠躬;点头(以示招呼、感谢、同意等) 2. 屈服,服从 — *vt*. 1. 点(头);弯(身等)(以示尊敬或屈从) 2. 点头(或鞠躬)表示(感谢、同意等) 3. 使鞠躬(down) — *n*. 1. 点头;屈从,低头

bow[3] [bau] *n*. 1.[常~s]船,船头,舰首 2. 飞艇的前缘部分 2. 前桨手 ‖ ~ sprit *n*. 船首斜桁

bowel ['bauəl] *n*. 1.[常~s]肠(特指人肠) 2.[~s]同情心 3.[~s](地球等的)内部

bower ['bauə] *n*. 1. 凉亭;树荫处 2.(诗)村舍;精致的居处 3.(诗)卧室;闺房

bowl[1] [bəul] *n*. 1. 碗[林;一碗(或一杯)的量 2. 碗状物;碗状物;(匙)的盛物部分;(烟斗的)斗;一匙(或一烟斗)的量 3. 碗形建筑;圆形剧场;(四周有看台的)椭圆形运动场 ‖ ~ful *n*. 一满碗(或钵、匙等)

bowl[2] [baul] *n*. 1.(草地滚木球戏中用的)木球;(保龄球戏中用的)圆球;[~s][用作单]草地滚木球戏 2.(草地滚木球戏中的)投球 3.【机】滚筒,滚杆 — *vi*. 1. 玩草地滚木球戏;(在草地滚木球戏中)投球 2. 翻滚地行驶 3.(在板球戏中)投球给击球员 — *vt*. 1. 滚(球,铁环等);使快而稳地行驶 2.(在草地滚木球戏中)完成(规定的回数);得到……分 3.(在板球戏中)困击中三柱门(或击落柱上横木)而迫使(击球员)退场(out) ‖ ~ing *n*. 保龄球戏

bowler ['bəulə] *n*. 1. 玩保龄球者者;(板球)投球手 2.(通常为黑色的)常礼帽,圆顶高帽(= ~ hat)

bowwow ['bau'wau] *int*. 汪! (模仿狗叫的声音) *n*. 作狗吠声;(狗)吠 — *n*. 1. 狗吠声 2.(儿语)狗

box[1] [bɔks] *n*. 1. 箱,盒;箱(或盒)状物 2.一箱(或一盒);一盒(或一盒)的内容(英)一盒礼物 3. 专席;证人席(马车等的)驾驶台座位 4. 岗亭;信号所 5.(美)邮箱,信箱 6.[报刊上的]花边文字 7.[the ~](口)电视机 8.(口)冰箱 9.(美俚)话匣子,留声机;收音机;便携式立体声收录机 — *vt*. 1.

把…装箱(或盒) 2. 给…装上罩壳箱 3. 使(帆船)抢风转向 ‖ **~ ful** *n.* 一满箱,一满盒 / **~like** *adj.* 箱形的,盒式的 ‖ '**~car** *n.* (美)棚车(英国称 box waggon) / **~ office** (戏院等的)票房,售票处 2. 卖座力,卖座力强的东西 / '**~office** *adj.* 票房的;卖座的,受欢迎的 / **~ seat** 1.(马车上的)驭者座 2.(戏院中)包厢座位 3.(运动场等)正面看台的座位 4. 利于观看的地位

box² [bɔks] *vt.* 1. 用手打(某人的耳光) 2. 和…拳击 — *vi.* 拳击;打拳 — *n.* 一罄拳;一拳

box³ [bɔks] *n.* 1. 黄杨 2. 黄杨木(= ~ wood)

boxer ['bɔksə] *n.* 1. 拳击运动员;拳师 2. [B-]义和团团员;拳师(the Boxers)义和团员 3. 斗拳狗(一种短毛德国狗)

boxing ['bɔksiŋ] *n.* 拳击;拳术 ‖ **~ weight** 拳击等级

boy [bɔi] *n.* 1. 男孩;少年 2. 〈昵〉家伙: Cheer up, old ~! 振作起来,好朋友! / Oh, ~! 〈俚〉好家伙! (表示欢欣或惊奇的感叹语) 3. 儿子 4. 勤杂人员,练习生(旅馆、饭店等的)侍者,服务员;男仆 ‖ **~hood** *n.* 1. 男孩时代;少年时代 2.[总称]男孩们;少年们 ‖ '**~friend** *n.* 〈口〉男朋友 / **~ scout** 1. 童子军队员 2.〈俚〉天真(或不切实际)的男子

boycott ['bɔikɔt] *vt.* 1.(联合)抵制;(联合)拒绝购买(或经营、使用);(联合起来)拒绝来往 — *n.* (联合)抵制;拒绝参加

boyish ['bɔiiʃ] *adj.* 男孩所特有的;男孩般的;孩子气的 ‖ **~ly** *adv.* / **~ness** *n.*

Br [化] 元素溴(bromine)的符号

bra [brɑː] *n.* 〈口〉奶罩,胸罩 ‖ '**~less** *adj.* (女子)不戴胸罩的

brace [breis] *n.* 1. 托架,支架;扣件;拉条;牵索 2.[医]牿具;[~s]牿齿矫正钢丝架 2. 一双,一对 3.[机]手摇曲柄钻 4. 大括弧(即 ‖) 5.[海]操桁索 6.(英)[~s](裤子)的背带(美国称 suspenders) 7.〈口〉(新兵等)立正偏直的立正姿势 — *vt.* 1. 拉紧,系紧 2. 支住,撑牢 3. 激励,振奋 4.〈俚〉向…借钱 5.[海]用操桁索转(帆) — *vi.* 1.〈口〉打起精神;下定决心 2. 迅速作好(进攻的)准备 ‖ **~r** *n.* 支撑(或加固)者;用来支撑(或加固)的东西

bracelet ['breislit] *n.* 1. 手镯 2.[常~s]〈俚〉手铐

bracing ['breisiŋ] *adj.* 振奋精神的;爽快的,凉爽的 — *n.* 1.[建]支撑;拉结条 2. 背带 3. 支柱;支撑物

bracken ['brækən] *n.* [植] 欧洲蕨

bracket ['brækit] *n.* 1. 托架;[建] 隅撑;托座 2.[~s]括号(指[],〈〉,(),‖) 3.(收入等的)等级;阶层,类 4.[军]夹叉射击 — *vt.* 1. 给…装上托架 2. 把…括在括号内 3. 把…分类 4.[军]夹叉射击

brackish ['brækiʃ] *adj.* 1.(水)含盐的;稍咸的 2. 味道不好的;引起恶心的 ‖ **~ness** *n.*

brad [bræd] *n.* 角钉;无头钉 ‖ '**~awl** *n.* 锥钻,打眼钻

brag [bræg] (bragged; bragging) *vi.* 吹牛,自夸(of, about) — *vt.* 夸说(that) — *n.* 自大;大话;自夸的人

braggart ['brægət] *adj. & n.* 吹牛的(人)

braid [breid] *n.* 1. 编带;缏;辫子 2.(衣服上的)镶边 — *vt.* 1. 把(草等)编成缏;把(头发)编成辫子 2. 给(衣服等)镶边

braille [breil] *n.* 布莱叶盲字;布莱叶点字法(法国人 Louis Braille 创制的用凸点

符号供盲人书写、摸读的文字符号体系 — **vt.** 用盲字印(或写)

brain [brein] **n. 1.** 脑(子); [~s]脑髓 **2.** [常~s]智力; 智慧; 智囊 **3.** 电脑, 计算机 — **vt. 1.** 打碎...的脑袋 **2.** 打...的头部 ‖ ~**less** adj. 没有头脑的、愚蠢的 ‖ '~**child** n.〈口〉脑力劳动的产物(如计划、作品等)/ ~ **death** 脑死亡 / ~ **drain** 人才外流(指有些国家的科技人员等流向国外的情况)/ '~**storm** n. 【医】脑(病)暴发 **2.**〈美〉〈谑〉妙主意 / ~ **trust** 1. 智囊团; 顾问班子 **2.**〈英〉[B·T-],在广播电台即席答听众问题的专家小组 / ~ **wave 1.** 脑波 **2.**〈口〉灵机, 妙想 / '~**work** n. 脑力劳动 / '~**worker** n. 脑力劳动者

brainwash ['breinwɔʃ] **vt. 1.** 对(人)实行洗脑; 把思想强加于(人) **2.** 通过宣传(或推销)说服 — **n.** 洗脑; 强行灌输思想 ‖ ~**ing** n.

brainy ['breini] **adj.** 多智的, 聪明的

braise [breiz] **vt.** (用文火)炖(肉等)

brake [breik] **n. 1.** 制动器, 刹车; 闸 **2.**〈喻〉阻碍力量 **3.** 大耙; 捣麻机 ‖ 大器 **4.** 【植】欧洲蕨; 丛林; 矮树林 **5.** 〈金属板的〉压弯成形机 — **vt. 1.** 制动; 刹(车) **2.** 捣碎(麻等)— **vi.** 制动, 刹车 ‖ ~**man** n. 司闸员, 制动手

bramble ['bræmbl] **n.**【植】悬钩子; 荆棘 ‖ **brambly** adj. **1.** 长满悬钩子属植物的; 多荆棘的 **2.** 像荆棘的; 多刺的

bran [bræn] **n.** 麸; 糠

branch [bræntʃ] **n. 1.** 枝, 分枝 **2.** 支流; 支脉; 支线 **3.**〈学科〉分科; 部门 **4.** 支部; 分部; 分店; 分行... **5.** 分支 **6.** 分支; 分岔; 派生, 衍生(**from**)— **vt. 1.** 使分支; 分割 **2.** 用枝叶装饰

brand [brænd] **n. 1.** 燃烧的木头 **2.** 打印用的烙铁; 烙印, 火印 **3.** 古时烙在犯人

身上的)印记; 犯罪(或耻辱)的标记; (标示所有权的)标记 **3.** 商标, 牌子 **4.**〈诗〉火炬; 剑 — **vt. 1.** 打上烙印...在...上打标记 **2.** 铭刻; 铭记 **3.** 污辱; 给...抹黑 ‖ '~-**new** adj. 崭新的, 新制的

brandish ['brændiʃ] **vt. & n.** 挥舞

brandy ['brændi] **n.** 白兰地酒 — **vt.** 在...中加白兰地酒; 把...浸泡在白兰地酒中

Brasilia [brə'zilja] **n.** 巴西利亚[巴西首都]

brass [brɑːs] **n. 1.** 黄铜 **2.** 黄铜器; 黄铜制品 [总称]铜管乐器 **3.**〈俚〉钱 **4.** 〈俚〉厚脸皮 **5.**〈美俚〉[总称]高级军官; 高级官员 **6.**【机】黄铜轴衬 — **adj. 1.** 黄铜制的; 含黄铜的 **2.**(天空等)黄铜色的 **3.**(声音)洪亮回响的 **4.** 铜管乐器的 — **vt. & vi.**〈俚〉缴纳, 支付(**up**)— ‖ ~ **band** 铜管乐队; 军乐队

brassiere [bræ'ziə] **n.** 胸罩, 奶罩

brat [bræt] **n.**〈贬〉顽童

Bratislava [ˌbræti'slɑːvə] **n.** 布拉迪斯拉发[斯洛伐克首都]

bravado [brə'vɑːdəu] ([复]**bravado(e)s**) **n.** 虚张声势的(举动); 蛮干心理

brave [breiv] **adj. 1.** 勇敢的 **2.** 很好的 — **n.** 北美印第安战士 — **vt.** 冒(风险、危险); 敢于做(某事)‖ ~**ly** adv. / ~**ness** n. / ~**ry** n. 勇敢

bravo ['brɑː'vəu] **n.** 喝彩声, 叫好声 — **int.** 好啊! 妙啊! — **vt.** 向...喝彩叫好

brawl [brɔːl] **n. 1.** 吵架; 喧闹 **2.**〈俚〉喧闹的聚会 — **vi. 1.** 吵架; 对骂 **2.**(水)哗哗地流 ‖ ~**er** n. 争吵者; 喧闹者

brawn [brɔːn] **n. 1.** 肌肉 **2.** 臂力; 体力 **3.** 腌猪肉

brawny ['brɔːni] **adj. 1.** 强壮的, 肌肉结实

的 2. 强大的 3. 严重肿胀的 ‖ **brawni-
ness** *n*.

bray [brei] *n*. 驴叫声；似驴叫声；喇叭
的嘟嘟声 — *vi*. (驴)叫；喇叭发出
嘟嘟声 — *vt*. 粗声粗气地说；刺耳地发
出

braze [breiz] *vt*. 用黄铜铸(或制作、包)；
用铜焊接 ‖ ~ **r** *n*.

brazen ['breizn] *adj*. 1. 黄铜制的；黄铜色
的；坚如黄铜的 2. 声音响而刺耳的 3.
厚颜无耻的 — *vi*. 厚颜无耻地做(或
对待)(*out*, *through*) ‖ ~**ly** *adv*. 厚颜
无耻地 ~**ness** *n*. 厚颜无耻；猖狂
‖ ~-**faced** *adj*. 厚颜无耻的，无耻的

brazier ['breiziə] *n*. 火盆，火钵

Brazil [brə'zil] *n*. 巴西[南美洲国家] ‖
~**ian** *adj*. 巴西的；巴西人的 *n*. 巴西
人

Brazzaville ['bræzəvil, 'brɑːzəvil] *n*. 布拉柴
维尔[刚果首都]

breach [briːtʃ] *n*. 1. 破坏的；违反；不履行
的 2. (尤指炮火轰开的)缺口，裂
口(*friend*关系中的)破裂(或中断)；不
和 5. (海浪的)冲击；激浪，碎浪 6. 鲸
跃 — *vt*. 攻破，突破；使有缺口 — *vi*.
(鲸)跃出水面

bread [bred] *n*. 1. 面包 2. 食物；粮食
(喻)生计 3. (俚)钱 — *vt*. 在……上涂
面包屑 ‖ ~-**and-butter** *adj*. 1.(英)
年轻的；不成熟的；女学生派头的 2.
关于生计的；日常生活的 3. 像固定收
入一样可靠的 4. 用以报谢所受款待
表示感谢的 / ~-**basket** *n*. 1.(俚)胃 2.
盛产谷物的地区 / ~-**crumb** *n*. 面包屑
/ ~-**fruit**~ **tree** *n*. 【植】生长在南太
平洋诸岛的面包果树 / ~-**line** *n*. 等
候领取救济(或施舍)食物的穷人队伍
/ ~-**stuff** *n*. 做面包的原料；面包 / ~-
winner *n*. 养家活口的人(或手艺，工

具等)

breadth [bredθ] *n*. 1. 宽度；幅度 2.(布
的)幅面(船)幅 3.(胸襟等的)宽宏，
宽容，广度 4.(艺术品等的)雄浑

break [breik] (broke [brəuk], broken
['brəukən]) *vt*. 1. 打破；折断；冲破 2.
损坏 3. 打开；破(土)；开；~ a fresh
path 开创新路 4. 破坏；违反；破除 5.
使中止，使中断 6. 越出；~ surface (潜
水艇)浮出水面 7. 弄坏；制服，使屈服
8. 超过，打破(纪录) 9. 削弱，减弱(风
力等) 10. 透露(坏消息等) 11. 驯(马
等) 12. 破(案)；破译(密码) 13. 兑开
(大额钞票等) 14. 解开(链条等) 15.
使破产；耗尽；使前途无望 16. 证明
……不实 17. 使骤崩(或剧跌) 18. 拆
散；~ a dinner set 把一套餐具拆开 19.
使放弃习惯(*of*) 20. 打开
(枪)的枪栓 — *vi*. 1. 破，破碎；断裂；
坏掉 2. 决裂(*from*, *with*) 3. 突破破
4.(噪音、天气等)突变 5.(在健康等方
面)垮掉，变弱 6.(暴风雨、事件等)突
然发生，爆发(*out*) 7.(消息等)传开 8.
(浪)冲击(*over*, *on*, *against*) 9.(军队
等)溃散 10. 破产；(银行等)倒闭 11.
(鱼等)突然冒出水面 12. 急冲，猛闯；
突袭(逃脱 13.(在壁球等运动中)自
内部破裂 14.(天气)转晴 15.(证券等)
暴跌 16. 突然转向(*away*) 17. 中断；
发展 20. 跳露舞蹈舞 ~ 破裂；破裂
处 2. 决裂；绝交 3. 破晓 4. 中止，停
顿；(电路的)断路[路]等 5.(课间)休
息 6.(天气等的)突变 7.(物价等的)暴
跌，骤跌 8.(口)机缘，机会 9.(口)失当
举止；失言 10.(俚)运气 11. 突破；急
冲；逃跑；a jail ~ 越狱/The deer made a
~ for the woods. 鹿奔向树林。‖ ~-
able *adj*. 会破的，易碎的 / ~-**age** *n*. 破
损；破损数量；破损处，破损物；破损

费;【海】亏舱 ‖ ~ dancer 跳霹雳舞者 /~ dancing 霹雳舞 /'~down *n*. 1.(机械等的)损坏,故障;倒塌 2.(身体、精神等的)垮,衰竭 3.【化】分解(作用);【电】击穿 4.(谈判等的)失败,破裂 5. 分析;分类 /'~neck *adj*.(尤指速度)可能造成事故的;危险的 /'~through *n*. 1. 突破;突破点;【军】突围,突破 2. 突破性进展;关键问题的解决 /'~ˌwater *n*. 防波堤 /'~wind *n*.〈英〉防风篱;防风林

breaker [ˈbreikə] *n*. 1. 碎浪;激浪 2. 破碎装置;轧碎机 3. 打破者;开拓者;破坏者 4.(动物的)驯服者 5.【电】断路器 6.(汽车轮胎的)缓冲层 7. 跳霹雳舞者

breakfast [ˈbrekfəst] *n*. 早餐 — *vi*. 进早餐 — *vt*. 给(或请)(某人)吃早餐

breast [brest] *n*. 1. 乳房 2. 胸(脯),胸膛;(衣服的)胸部 3. 胸怀;心绪 — *vt*. 1. 把胸部对着 2. 对付;毅然对抗;逆...而进 ‖ '~bone *n*. 胸骨 /ˌ~-ˈdeep *adj*. 齐胸深的 /'~-ˈhigh *adj*. 齐胸高的 /'~pin *n*. 领带夹针;胸口饰针 /'~plate *n*. 1. 胸铠;(胸压工具上的)胸板(或胸前护垫) 2.(乌龟等的)肚甲 /'~stroke *n*.【体】蛙泳 /'~work *n*. 1. 矮防护墙;胸墙 2. [~ works]〈美俚〉(女人的)一对奶子

breast-feed [ˈbrestfiːd] (breast-fed [ˈbrestfed]) *vt*. 母乳喂养(婴孩);给...哺乳 ‖ breast-fed *adj*. 用母乳喂养的 /~ing *n*. 用母乳喂养

breath [breθ] *n*. 1. 气息;呼吸;呼吸能力 2.(空气的)轻微流动:There isn't a ~ of air (或 wind). 一点风也没有。3. 声息;低语 4. 一瞬间;短暂休息 5. 生命 6. 示意;迹象:not a ~ of suspicion 毫无可疑之处 ‖ '~-test〈英〉*n*.(通常用呼气测醉器进行的)呼气测醉试验 *vt*. 对...作呼气测醉试验

breathe [briːð] *vi*. 1. 呼吸 2. 生存:be still *breathing* 还活着 3. 歇口气;停一下 4. 低语;(风等)发出轻微的声音 — *vt*. 1. 呼吸(空气等) 2. 使喘息 3. 发散(香气等);表示出(感情等);吐露 4. 使歇口气 5. 低声说;低声唱;【语】发(清音),发(气息音) 6. 注入;灌输:~ new life *into* 向...注入新生命

breather [ˈbriːðə] *n*. 1. 呼吸者 2.〈口〉使呼吸趋于正常的休息;短暂的休息 3. 使人轻松一下的事(或活动) 4. 通气孔;通气装置

breathless [ˈbreθlis] *adj*. 1. 屏息的,不出声的 2. 气喘吁吁的 3. 无风的;闷热的 4. 气绝的,死了的 ‖ ~ly *adv*. /~ness *n*.

breathtaking [ˈbreθˌteikiŋ] *adj*. 1. 惊人的;激动人心的 2. 惊险的 ‖ ~ly *adv*.

bred [bred] breed 的过去式和过去分词

breeches [ˈbritʃiz] [复] *n*. 马裤;〈口〉裤子

breed [briːd] (bred [bred]) *vi*. 1.(动物)生产;孕育 2. 繁殖;育种 3. 滋生,产生 — *vt*. 1.(动物)产(仔);孵(卵) 2. 使繁殖;饲养 3. 养育;培育;教养 4. 引起(疾病等);产生(偏见等) 5.【核】再生,增殖 — *n*. 品种,种类 ‖ ~er *n*. 1. 繁殖(过多)的动物(或植物);用来配种的动物 2. 饲养员;育种工作者 3. 起因;来源 4.【核】增殖反应堆 /~ing *n*. 1.(动物的)生育,繁殖 2. 饲养 3. 育种;配种 4. 教养

breeze [briːz] *n*. 1. 微风 2.〈口〉发脾气;小争吵:kick up a ~ 引起小风波 3.〈美口〉容易的事情 — *vi*. 1.〈口〉一阵风似地走(*in*, *out*, *along*) 2.〈美俚〉(快速)离去;逃走;逃出监狱 ‖ ~less *adj*. 无风的,平静的

breezy [ˈbriːzi] *adj*. 1. 有微风的;通风的

2. 活泼轻快的；快活的；爱谈笑的 ‖
breezily adv. 轻快地 /**breeziness** n. 活泼，轻快

brethren ['breðrən] [复] n. (古) = brothers

brevet ['brevit, brə'vet] [军] n. (升级而不付薪的)名誉晋级(令) — vt. 予以名誉晋级，加衔

breviary ['bri:vjəri] n. 1. (天主教的)每日折祷书 2. 每日祷告文 3. 摘要；节略

brevity ['breviti] n. 1. (陈述等的)简短，简洁 2. (生命等的)短暂，短促

brew [bru:] vt. 1. 酿造(啤酒等) 2. 泡(茶)；煮(咖啡) 3. 图谋，策划(叛乱、恶作剧等) — vi. 1. 酿酒 2. (茶)被泡(咖啡)被煮：The tea will soon be ~ing. 茶快要泡好了。 3. (风暴等)酝酿 — n. 1. 酿造；(一次)酿量 2. 酿造出来的饮料；泡(或煎煮)出的液汁

brewery ['bruəri], **brewhouse** ['bru:haus] n. 啤酒厂，酿酒厂

briar¹ ['braiə] n. = brier

briar² ['braiə] n. = brier

bribe [braib] n. 贿赂；行贿物 — vt. 向...行贿 — vi. 行贿 ‖ **bribee** [brai'bi:] n. 受贿者 /~r n. 行贿者

bribery ['braibəri] n. 行贿；受贿

bric-a-brac ['brikəbræk] n. 古玩；小摆设(如瓷器、花瓶、扇子等)

brick [brik] n. 1. 砖；砖块 2. 砖状物(如茶砖、砖形面包等) 3. 积木 4. (俗) 心肠好的人 — adj. 1. 砖砌(或铺)的 2. 砖似的 — tea 茶砖 vt. 1. 用砖砌；用砖铺 2. 用砖堵塞(洞等)(in, up) ‖ ~-kiln n. 砖窑 /~-layer n. 砌砖工人

brickbat ['brikbæt] n. 1. (尤指用作投掷的)碎砖 2. 侮辱；谴责；尖锐的批评；口头攻击 — (brickbatted; brickbat-

ting) vt. 向...掷砖块；侮辱；激烈地批评；攻击

bridal ['braidl] adj. 1. 新娘的 2. 婚礼的

bride [braid] n. 新娘 ‖ ~-cake n. 喜饼，礼饼 /~-price n. (成婚前男方给女方的)聘礼，彩礼

bridegroom ['braidgrum] n. 新郎

bridesmaid ['braidzmeid] n. 女傧相

bridesman ['braidzmən] ([复] bridesmen) n. 男傧相

bridge [bridʒ] n. 1. 桥；(喻)桥梁 2. (船上的)驾驶台，桥楼 3. (提琴等的)琴马 4. 鼻梁(眼镜上的)鼻梁；(假牙上的)齿桥 5. [电]电桥 6. 桥牌 — vt. 1. 架桥于；用桥连接 2. 把...连结(或弥合)起来；使渡过；跨越：~ over the difficulties 渡过难关 ‖ ~-builder n. 1. 造桥者 2. (纠纷等的)调停人，调解人 /~-head n. 桥头堡；立足点，据点 /~-work n. 1. 桥梁工事(或工程) 2. (假牙的)齿桥

Bridgetown ['bridʒtaun] n. 布里奇顿 [巴巴多斯首都]

bridle ['braidl] n. 1. 马勒(缰、衔、口衔等的总称) 2. 约束(物) 3. [机]限动器，限动物 4. [海]系船索 5. [解]系带 — vt. 1. 给马(上)套头 2. 抑制，约束 — vi. 昂首表示轻蔑，发怒(up)

brief [bri:f] adj. 1. 短暂的 2. 简短的；简洁的 — n. 1. (罗马教皇的)教书 2. 概要，摘要；短文 3. [律]诉讼要点；(律师的)案情摘要；辩护状 4. [~s]三角裤 5. = briefing — vt. 1. 为...作简要的介绍；向...作简要的指示，向...交代任务 2. [英]聘请(律师) 3. 向(飞行员等)作出发前的最后指示 — vt. 向...作简要指示，向...作简要指点 ‖ ~ly adv. /~-ness n.

briefcase ['bri:fkeis] n. 公事(皮)包，公文(皮)包

briefing ['bri:fiŋ] n. 1. 下达简令；情况的

简要介绍(或汇报);简况介绍(或汇报)会 : a (news) ~ officer〖美〗新闻发布官 2. 简令;简况介绍〖美〗simple 任务(或情况)简要讲解图 / ~ room(飞行员出发前的)受命室

brier[1] ['braiə] *n.* 多刺木质茎植物(如蔷薇属植物等);多刺木质茎植物丛 ‖~y *adj.* 荆棘丛生的;多刺的

brier[2] ['braiə] *n.* 〖植〗欧石南 ‖~-root *n.* 欧石南根(用欧石南根制成的)烟斗

brig[brig] *n.* 双桅横帆船

brigade[bri'geid] *n.* 1.〖军〗旅 2.(执行一定任务的)队 : a fire ~ 消防队

brigadier[,brigə'diə] *n.* 1. 旅长 2.(英国)陆军(或海军陆战队)准将 3. general〖美〗陆军(或空军、海军陆战队)准将

brigand['brigənd] *n.* 土匪;强盗 ‖~age, ~ism *n.* 土匪行为;掠夺

bright[brait] *adj.* 1. 明亮的,辉煌的;〈喻〉光辉灿烂的 2.(颜色)鲜明的 2.(酒等)晶莹的 3.(脸)欢快的;生气勃勃的 4. 聪明的,伶俐的 — *adv.* 光亮地;鲜明地;欢快地 / ~'ness *n.* ‖~-eyed *adj.* 眼睛晶莹的

brighten['braitn] *vt.* 1. 使发光,使发亮 2. 使快活,使活跃(*up*) — *vi.* 1. 发光,生辉 2. 活跃起来,活跃(*up*)

brilliance['briljəns] *n.* 1. 光辉;辉煌 2.(色彩)鲜明 3.(才华等放出的)异彩

brilliant['briljənt] *adj.* 1. 光辉的;辉煌的 2. 卓越的;英明的;杰出的 3.(色彩)鲜明的 — *n.* 宝石(尤指多角形的钻石) ‖~ly *adv.* / ~'ness *n.*

brim[brim] *n.* 1.(杯、碗、漏斗等的)边,缘 2. 帽边 — (brimming;brimming) *vt.* 注满(容器等) — *vi.* 满溢 ‖~ful *adj.* 满到边的;洋溢着...的(*of*) / ~-less *adj.* 无边缘的

brindle['brindl] *n.* 1. 带深色斑纹的灰(或棕)色 2. 有深色斑纹的灰(或棕)色动物 — *adj.* = brindled ‖~d *adj.* 灰(或棕)色底子上有深色斑纹的

brine[brain] *n.* 1. 盐水;咸水;近乎饱和的盐水 2. 海水;海 3.〈诗〉泪水 — *vt.* 用盐水浸(或泡);用盐水处理 ‖~-pan 蒸发盐的浅锅;盐田,盐场

bring[briŋ] (brought[brɔ:t]) *vt.* 1. 拿来;带来 : *Bring* the basket to me , please . (或 *Bring* me the basket , please .)请把篮子带给我。 2. 使(人)来到 : What ~s you here today? 今天是什么风把你吹来了? 3. 产生,引起,导致(某种结果) : ~ about a war 引起战争 4. 促使;劝使 : She couldn't ~ herself to believe the news. 她不能(使自己)相信这个消息。 5. 使...处于某种状态 : ~ the car to a stop 使车子停下来 6.(货品)卖得(多少钱) 7. 提出(诉讼、论据等) 8. 使恢复知觉(*to*)

brink[briŋk] *n.* 边;(河流等的)边沿;〈喻〉边缘

briny['braini] *adj.* 1. 盐水的;很咸的 2. 海水的 3.〈诗〉泪水的 — *n.* [the ~]〈俚〉大海

brisk[brisk] *adj.* 1. 活泼的,活跃的;轻快的 2.(天气等)令人爽快的,清新的 3.(生意等)兴旺的 — *vt.* 使活泼,使活跃;使兴旺 — *vi.* 活泼起来;兴旺起来(*up*) ‖~ly *adv.* / ~'ness *n.*

brisket['briskit] *n.*(动物的)胸部(或胸肉)

bristle['brisl] *n.* 1.(动、植物的)短而硬的毛(猪等的)鬃毛 2.(刷子等的)毛 3.(人的)须茬毛 — *vi.* 1.(毛发等)直立 2. 发怒;准备格斗 3. 密密地覆盖;充满(*with*) : a harbour *bristling* with masts 船桅林立的港口 — *vt.* 1. 使(毛

发等)直立 2. 给(刷子等)安鬃毛 ‖
bristly *adj*. 1.(硬而短的)毛发丛生的；
粗糙的 2.(毛发等)短而硬的

Britain ['britən] *n*. 不列颠(英格兰、威尔士和苏格兰的总称)；英国

Briticism ['britisizəm] *n*.〈美〉英国人特用的词(或短语等)

British ['britiʃ] *adj*. 1. 不列颠的，英国的；不列颠人的，英国人的 2. 英联邦的；英联邦人的 — *n*. 1. 古不列颠人的语言 2. 英国英语；[the ~][总称]英国人；英联邦人 ‖ ～**er** *n*.〈美〉英国人 / ～**ism** *n*. = Briticism

Briton ['britən] *n*. 1. 布立吞人(古代不列颠岛南部的凯尔特居民)2. 不列颠人；英国人

brittle ['britl] *adj*. 1. 易碎的，脆弱的 2. 易损失的；不永久的 → a ～ promise 靠不住的诺言 3. 容易生气的人 4. 冷淡的；专为自己打算的 — *n*. 果仁薄脆糖；peanut ～ 花生薄脆糖 ‖ ～**ness** *n*.

broach [brəutʃ] *n*. 1. 凿子；钻；铰刀；扩孔器 2.(烤肉用的)炙叉 3.(教堂的)八面锥形尖顶 4.(女服)饰针 — *vt*. 1. 在(桶)上钻孔 2. 开(矿等)3. 用凿子扩大(或锥孔)4. 提出；引入；提出；把(题目等)提出讨论(或辩论)— *vi*.(鲸等)冒出水面 ‖ ～**er** *n*. 1.[机]钻床，拉床(= broaching machine) 2. 剥床(或拉床)的操作工人

broad [brɔːd] *adj*. 1. 宽的，广阔的；辽阔的 2. 广大的；广泛的 3. 完全的；明白清楚的 → in ～ daylight 在光天化日之下 / a ～ hint 明白的暗示 4. 主要的；概括性的：achieve ～ agreement on an issue 就一问题的主要方面达成一致 5.(态度上)宽宏的 6. 粗俗的，下流的 7.(在发音等方面)有显著方言特点的；(方言)有显著地方特点的 8.(元音)开

(放)的；(注音法)宽式的 — *adv*. 完全地；be ～ awake 完全醒着 — *n*. 1.(身体的)宽阔部分；(俚)屁股 2.〈英〉[～s]开阔河段 3.〈美俚〉女人；放荡女人 ‖ ～**ly** *adv*. / ～**ness** *n*. ‖ '～**ax(e)** *n*. 钺；战斧 / '~**band** *n*. & *adj*.[无]宽频带(的)，宽带 / '~**bean** 蚕豆 / '~**cloth** *n*. 细平布；绒面呢 / ～**ga(u)ge** 宽轨距(指四英尺八英寸半以上的轨距)/ ～**ga(u)ge** *adj*. 1. 宽轨距的 2.(口)气量大的 / '~**jump**〈美〉跳远(比赛)/ '~**minded** *adj*. 容得下不同意见的；宽宏大量的 / '~**side** *n*. 1.(水面以上的)舷侧 2.(全部)舷侧炮火；舷炮齐射 3. 猛烈抨击；肆意谩骂 *adv*. 1. 以一侧对着(*to*)2. 齐射地 3. 无目标地，胡乱地 / '~**sword** *n*. 大刀，大刀

broadcast ['brɔːdkɑːst] (broadcast 或 broadcasted) *vt*. 1.(用无线电或电视)广播 2. 乱传(消息等)3. 撒播(种子)— *vi*. 1. 广播 2. 在广播节目中讲话(或演出)— *adj*. 1.(经由无线电或电视)广播的 2. 被撒播的；散布在四处的 — *n*. 1. 广播，播音 2. 广播节目 3. 散播播种 — *adv*. 1. 经过广播；四散地；sow seed ～ 撒种 ‖ ～**er** 1. 播种机 2. 广播员；广播电台；广播网 3. 广播装置 4. 广播员

broaden ['brɔːdn] *vt*. 使宽，使阔；使扩大 — *vi*. 变宽，变阔；扩大

brocade [brə'keid] *n*.(织有金银丝浮花的)锦缎，织锦 — *vt*. 在(织物)上织出花纹；把(花纹)织入织物

broccoli ['brɔkəli] *n*. 茎椰菜，嫩茎花椰菜

brochure ['brəuʃə] *n*. 小册子

brogue [brəug] *n*.(尤指爱尔兰人说英语时的)土腔，土音 — *vt*. 带有土腔音

broil[1] [brɔil] *n*. 争吵；对骂 — *vi*. 大声争吵 ‖ ～**er** *n*. 老爱吵架的人

broil[2] [brɔil] *vt*. 1. 烤，焙，炙(肉等)2. 使

受灼热 — *vi.* **1.** 烤,焙,炙 **2.** 受灼热 — *n.* **1.** 烤;灼热 **2.** 被烤焙的东西 ‖ ~ **er** *n.* **1.** 烤焙厨师 **2.** 烤焙用具 **3.** 适于烤焙的小鸡 **4.** 大热天

broke [brəuk] break 的过去式 — *adj.* 〈口〉不名一文的;破产的

broken [ˈbrəukən] break 的过去分词 — *adj.* **1.** 被打碎的,破碎的 **2.** 骨折的 **3.** 零碎的,不完整的 ‖ ~ tea 茶叶末子 **4.** (地面等)起伏不平的;崎岖的 ‖ ~ 〈天气〉阴晴不定的;a ~ sleep 时睡时醒 **5.** 被破坏的;遭违背的:a ~ home 破裂的家庭／a ~ promise 背弃的诺言 **6.** 【植】(花)有不规则斑纹的,有病斑的 **7.** 衰弱的;沮丧的;伤心的:a ~ man 潦倒的人 **8.** 破了产的,倒闭了的 **9.**〈口〉降了级的 **10.** 蹩脚的:~ English 不标准的英语 **11.** 驯养了的 ‖ ~ **ly** *adv.* ／~ **ness** *n.* ‖ ~ **-hearted** *adj.* 心碎的,悲伤过度的／~ **home** (父母已离婚或分居的)破裂家庭／~ **line** *n.* 虚线(即"---") **2.** 【数】折线／~ **reed** 难以依靠的人(或物)／~ **-winded** [ˈbrəukənˈwindid] *adj.* (马)喘息的,呼吸急促的

broker [ˈbrəukə] *n.* **1.** 经纪人;掮客;中间人;代理人.〈英〉(对债务人财物的估价或出售)人 **3.** 〈英〉旧货商 ‖ ~ **age** *n.* 经纪业;(付给中间人的)手续费,佣金,回扣

broking [ˈbrəukiŋ] *n.* & *adj.* 经纪业(的)

bromide [ˈbrəumaid] *n.* 【化】溴化物

bromine [ˈbrəumiːn] *n.* 【化】溴

bronchial [ˈbrɔŋkiəl] *adj.* 支气管的;细支气管的

bronchitic [brɔŋˈkitik] *adj.* (患)支气管炎的

bronchitis [brɔŋˈkaitis] *n.* 支气管炎

bronco [ˈbrɔŋkəu] ([复] broncos) *n.* (北美西部草原的)野马;难驯的马 ‖ ~

buster *n.* 驯马师;骑马牧者,牛仔

bronze [brɔnz] *n.* **1.** 青铜;古铜 **2.** 青铜制(艺术)品 **3.** 青铜色 — *vt.* 使青铜于;上青铜色于 — *vi.* 变成青铜色(被)晒黑

brooch [brəutʃ] *n.* 胸针,饰针

brood [bruːd] *n.* **1.** (鸡等的)一窝;同窝幼鸟;(昆虫等)一次产的卵;一次孵化的幼虫 **2.**(同种或同类的)一伙(人);一组(事物)〈贬〉(同父母的)孩子们:a ~ of ideas 一类想法 — *vt.* **1.** 孵(卵);孵出(母鸡等)用翅膀掩护(小鸡等) **3.** 盘算,细想 — *vi.* **1.** 孵蛋;伏窝似地静坐 **2.**(云等)笼罩,黑压压地笼罩(over) **3.** 郁闷地沉思;沮丧 ‖ ~ **er** *n.* **1.** 孵卵的动物 **2.**(鸡等的)孵房;孵卵器 **3.** 沉思的人／~ **y** *adj.* **1.**(母鸡等)要孵卵的;沉思的 **2.** 郁闷沉思的

brook[1] [bruk] *vt.* [通常用于否定句](不)容(拖延等)

brook[2] [bruk] *n.* 小河,溪

broom [bruːm] *n.* **1.** 【植】金雀花 **2.** 扫帚 — *vt.* 用扫帚扫,扫除 ‖ ~ **corn** *n.* 高梁,蜀黍(可制扫帚)／~ **stick** *n.* 扫帚柄

broth [brɔθ] *n.* 肉汤;清汤

brothel [ˈbrɔθəl] *n.* 妓院,窑子

brother [ˈbrʌðə] *n.* **1.** 兄;弟 **2.** 同胞;同事 **3.**(复数常作 brethren)同行业(或教会、社团)的人 — *vt.* 称…为兄弟;以兄般地对待 ‖ ~ **hood** *n.* **1.** 兄弟(般的)关系 **2.** 兄弟会 ‖ ~ **-in-law**[复] ~ **s-in-law**) *n.* **1.** 姐夫;妹夫 **2.** 内兄;内弟 **3.** 内兄;内弟

brotherly [ˈbrʌðəli] *adj.* 弟兄的;兄弟般的 ‖ **brotherliness** *n.* 兄弟情谊,友爱,友爱

brought [brɔːt] bring 的过去式和过去分词

brow [brau] *n.* **1.**[常~s]眉;眉毛 **2.**额 **3.**悬崖;山顶,坡顶,陡坡 **4.**面容,表情:an angry ~ 怒容 ‖ **~ed** *adj.*(常用以构成复合词)眉毛...的;dark- ~ed 眉毛浓的

browbeat ['braubiːt](browbeat, browbeaten) *vt.* 对...怒目而瞪眼睛,吓唬;欺侮

brown [braun] *adj.* 褐色的,棕色的;皮肤黝黑的 — *n.* **1.**褐色,棕色,褐(或棕)色颜料 **2.**《英俚》铜币 — *vt.* & *vi.*(使)变成褐色(或棕色)(尤指由于日晒或烘烤)‖ **~ bagger 1.**自带瓶装酒上餐馆(或俱乐部)者;自带午饭上班者 — **bagging 1.**自带瓶酒上餐馆(或俱乐部)2.自带午饭上班

brownie ['brauni] *n.* **1.**棕仙(传说中夜间替人做家务的善良小精灵)**2.**[B-](七八岁左右穿棕色制服的)幼年女童子军 **3.**果仁巧克力小方块蛋糕 ‖ **Brownie point 1.**(因成绩或善行而记的)幼年女童子军积分 **2.**品行良好而获的称赞;讨好上级所得的信任

browse [brauz] *n.* **1.**(牲畜吃的)嫩芽(或嫩叶等)**2.**放牧;吃草 **3.**浏览 — *vt.* **1.**(牲畜)吃;吃(on)**2.**浏览(书刊)...的;(尤指为了挑书而)随便翻阅 — *vi.* **1.**(牲畜)吃草;吃(on)**2.**浏览

bruin ['bruːin] *n.* **1.**[B-](童话中的拟人语)布伦熊 **2.**熊

bruise [bruːz] *n.* **1.**(人体或水果、植物等碰撞后)青肿,伤痕 **2.**擦伤,(感情等方面的)挫伤 — *vt.* **1.**使青肿,碰伤(水果、植物等)**2.**使(木料、金属)产生凹痕 **3.**研碎,捣烂(水果等)**4.**挫伤(感情等)— *vi.* 变成青肿;产生伤痕 ‖ **~r** *n.* **1.**职业拳击家 **2.**彪形大汉;好斗的人

Brunei ['bruːnai] *n.* **1.**文莱《东南亚苏丹

国》**2.**文莱(市)(Bandar Seri Begawan斯里巴加湾港的旧称)[文莱苏丹国首都]

brunet [bruː'net] *adj.* & *n.*(白种人中)浅黑型肤色的(男人)

brunette [bruː'net] *adj.* & *n.*(白种人中)浅黑型肤色的(女人)

brunt [brʌnt] *n.* 正面冲击;主要压力

brush [brʌʃ] *n.* **1.**刷子;毛刷;[电]电刷;《美俚》络腮胡子 **2.**画笔;a writing ~ 毛笔 **3.**粗大的尾巴(尤指狐狸尾巴)**4.**《美》灌丛;灌丛地带;柴 **5.**(一)刷 **6.**遭战战;激烈的小接触;争吵 — *vt.* 刷;擦;拂 — *vi.* 擦过,掠过(against, by, past, through)‖ **~ up 1.**擦亮;刷新;打扮整洁 **2.**温习,复习 **3.**(技巧等的)提高,改进 / ~ **wheel**【机】刷轮 / ~ **wood** *n.* **1.**灌丛 **2.**柴

brusque, brusk [brusk] *adj.* 粗暴的;鲁莽的;唐突的 ‖ **~ly** *adv.* / **~ness** *n.*

Brussels ['brʌsəlz] *n.* 布鲁塞尔[比利时首都]

brutal ['bruːtəl] *adj.* **1.**兽性的,残忍的;蛮横的 **2.**(天气等)令人难受的 ‖ **~ism** *n.*野兽主义(指一种绘画、建筑或雕塑风格)**2.** 兽性,残忍 ‖ **~ity** [bruː'tæliti] *n.* 残忍;暴行;兽行 / **~ly** *adv.* 残忍地;蛮横地

brute [bruːt] *n.* **1.**兽;畜生 **2.**人面兽心的人;残忍的人 **3.**[the ~]兽性 — *adj.* **1.**畜生的;畜生般的 **2.**残忍的;蛮横的 **3.**没有理性的:by ~ force 凭着蛮力

brutish ['bruːtiʃ] *adj.* **1.**兽的;畜生般的 **2.**野蛮的,残忍的 **3.**粗野的;愚钝的 ‖ **~ly** *adv.* / **~ness** *n.*

B.Sc. *abbr.* Bachelor of Science 理学士

bubble ['bʌbl] *n.* **1.**泡;水泡;气泡 **2.**泡影;妄想:a ~ company (为行骗而)组

设的公司 3. 冒泡(声)；沸腾(声)—
vi. 1. 冒泡；沸腾；(水等)往上冒(up)
2. 冒着泡溢出(over) 3. 抑制不住；极
为兴奋(over) 4.(水)汩汩地流；发噗
噗声；~ with laughter 格格地笑 ‖ **bub-
bly** adj. 1. 有透明圆圈的微型汽车；微型三
轮汽车 /~ **gum** 1. 泡泡糖 2.(以爱吃
泡泡糖的儿童为主要听众的)"泡泡
糖"摇滚乐

buccaneer [ˌbʌkəˈniə] n. 1. 海盗(尤指十
七、八世纪出没于中美洲、南美洲沿
海一带的海盗) 2. 冒险家 — vt. 当海
盗；掠夺 ‖ ~**ish** adj. 海盗似的

Bucharest [ˈbjuːkərest] n. 布加勒斯特[罗
马尼亚首都]

buck [bʌk] n. 1.([复]buck(s))雄鹿；公
羊；壮兔 2. 纨绔子弟、花花公子(美)
男人(尤指黑人或印第安人) 3.(美)锯
木架[体] 鞍马 4.(美俚)(一)元 5.
(英)捕鲑鱼的竹笼 — vi. 1.(马等)猛
然弓背跃起 2.(美)(山羊等)低头撞头
3.(美口)强烈反抗；反对(at、against)
4.(美)强烈反抗；反对(at、against)
— vt. 1.(马等)猛然弓背跃起把(骑
者)摔下(off) 2.(美)低着头冲…(美式
橄榄球运动中)持球冲入(对方阵地)
— adj. 雄的(美俚)男的 ‖ ~**eye** n.
1.[植]七叶树(或其种子)(口)[B-]
七叶树州人(美国俄亥俄州人的别称)
/~**shot** n. 大号铅弹 /~**skin** n. 鹿
皮 2.[~skins]鹿皮马裤 /~**wheat** n.
荞麦

buckboard [ˈbʌkbɔːd] n. 装有弹簧座椅的
四轮平板马车

bucket [ˈbʌkit] n. 1. 水桶，吊桶，提桶 2.
(挖土机等的)铲斗；勺斗；(往复泵的)
活塞；(水轮、汽轮机等的)叶片 3.(一

桶，满桶；大量 — vt. 1. 用桶打(水)；
用桶装运 2. 利用(顾客资金)买空卖
空；冒险倒卖出去 — vi.(down) ‖ ~
n.(一)桶，满桶 ‖ ~ **seat**(汽车、飞机
上的)凹背单人坐椅 /~ **shop**(利用顾
客资金买空卖空的)投机商号

bucket² [ˈbʌkit] vt.(口)催(马)拼命跑；
(横冲直撞地)驾驶(汽车等)— vi. 1.
(口)催马拼命跑 2.(口)急速行进；急
行；拼命划桨 3. 颠簸着行进
4. 游荡，溜达

Buckingham [ˈbʌkiŋəm] n. ‖ ~ **Palace** 白
金汉宫(英国王宫，在伦敦)

buckle [ˈbʌkl] n. 扣子；带扣；(鞋子、服装
的)扣形物件 — vt. 1. 把…扣住
(或扣紧)(on、up) 2. 使弯曲；使翘棱；
使起伏不平 3. 使倾注全力；使倾注全
力 — vi. 1. 扣住；扣紧 2.(由于压力
或热力)变成弯曲；翘棱；变成起伏不
平；变形；塌曲(up) 3. 屈服；屈从
‖ ~**d** adj. 1.(鞋等)扣紧的 2. 弯曲
的；翘棱的

buckler [ˈbʌklə] n. 1. 圆盾 2. 防御物；庇
护者 3.[船]锚链孔盖

buckram [ˈbʌkrəm] n. 1.(上过浆的)硬
棉布；硬麻布(用以装订书籍或作衣服
硬衬等) 2.(态度的)生硬，拘谨，刻板

bucktooth [ˈbʌktuːθ] n.([复] buckteeth
[ˈbʌktiːθ])n. [医]龋牙

bucolic [bjuːˈkɔlik] adj. 1. 牧民的 2. 农
村风味的；田园的；乡村的 ‖ ~**ally**
adv.

bud [bʌd] n. 1. 芽；萌芽；[动]芽体 2. 蓓
蕾 3. 未成熟的人(或东西)— (bud-
ded; budding) vi. 1. 使发芽 2. 蓓蕾
为…；出现芽接 — vi. 1. 发芽，萌芽
2. 开始生长(或发育、发展) 3.[植]芽
接 4. 未成闭

Budapest [ˈbjuːdəpest] n. 布达佩斯[匈牙

利首都]

Buddha ['budə] *n.* 佛;佛像;佛陀(佛教徒对释迦牟尼的尊称)

Buddhism ['budizəm] *n.* 佛教;佛教教义 ‖ **Buddhist** *n.* 佛教徒 *adj.* 佛教的;佛的

budding ['bʌdiŋ] *adj.* 1. 正发芽的;开始发育(或发展)的 2. 初露头角的 — *n.* 1. 发芽 2.【植】芽接;芽植

buddy ['bʌdi] *n.* (美male) 伙伴、弟兄(尤指男士间称呼);好朋友;小孩子(主要在称呼时用) — *vi.* 做好朋友,交朋友

budge [bʌdʒ] [用于否定句] *vi.* 微微移动 — *vt.* 推动,移动

budget ['bʌdʒit] *n.* 预算;预算案 — *vt.* 1. 把...编入预算;使按预算 2. 规划,安排(时间或费用) — *vi.* 编制预算 — *ary adj.* 预算上的 — *er n.* 编预算的人

Buenos Aires ['bwenəs 'aiəriz]布宜诺斯艾利斯[阿根廷首都]

buff [bʌf] *n.* 1.(水牛或黄牛皮制的坚韧而柔软的)暗黄皮革 2. 黄皮制服(或军外衣)3.(人的)皮肤;in the ~ 裸着身子 4. 暗黄色,米色 5.〈美〉爱好者,迷;热心者 — *vt.* 1. 用软皮擦亮(或擦净)(使皮革柔软)2.(使)皮革柔软 — *adj.* 1. 暗黄皮革制的 2. 暗黄色的

buffalo ['bʌfələu] ([复] buffalo(es)) *n.* 1. 水牛 2.(北美)野牛 3. 水陆两用坦克

buffer ['bʌfə] *n.* 1. 缓冲器;缓冲垫,减震器 2. 起缓冲作用的人(或物)— *state* 缓冲国 3.【化】缓冲(溶)液 — *vt.* 1. 缓冲为...2. 用缓冲液处理

buffet¹ ['bʌfit] *n.* 1. 殴打 2.(命运等)打击 — *vt.* 1. 殴打 2.(风、雨、波浪等)连续猛击,冲击 3. 与(波浪等)搏斗 — *vi.*(与波浪等)搏斗(with)

buffet² ['bufei, bu'fei] *n.* 1. 碗橱;餐具架

2.(车站等处的)方便食堂 3. 快餐部,点心柜;设有快餐部的餐馆 4. 自助餐 ‖ ~['bufei] *car* 餐车

buffoon [bʌ'fuːn] *n.* 滑稽戏演员;小丑 ‖ ~ery *n.* 打诨,滑稽

bug [bʌg] *n.* 1. 臭虫 2.〈美口〉虫子(尤指蟑螂等害虫)3.(口)病菌;由病菌引起的疾病 4.(机器等的)缺陷,毛病 5. 防盗报警器 6. 窃听器 7.(口)癖好,狂热;有癖好者,迷 8.(美俚)双座小型汽车 9. 要人,名人 — (bugged; bugging) *vt.* 1. 在...设防盗报警器 2. 在...装窃听器;通过窃听器窃听 3.〈美〉烦扰,激怒 4.(眼)(眼球)暴突 — *vi.* 1. 捉臭虫 2.(眼)(眼球)暴突(out)

bugaboo ['bʌgəbuː], **bugbear** ['bʌgbɛə] *n.* 1. 吓唬人的东西;鬼怪 2. 无端的恐惧 3. 令人头痛的事

bugger ['bʌgə] *n.* 1. 鸡奸者;兽奸者可卑的人,下贱的人 3.[用来表示亲昵]小伙子、家伙,坏蛋 4.(英)麻烦(或讨厌)的事(或人)5.〈粗〉微一丁点儿:not care(或 give)a ~ 毫不在乎,满不在乎 — *vt.* 1.(粗)与...鸡奸 2.(粗)鸡奸 3.(俚)骂,与...鸡(或兽)奸 3.(俚)诅咒 3.(俚)使极度疲乏 — *vi.* 1. 犯鸡(或兽)奸罪,鸡(或兽)奸 2.(粗)[用于诅咒语死]‖ ~ *about*(或 around)(粗)干无聊(或愚蠢)事;难为(某人)/ ~ *off up*(粗)使混乱;弄糟;搞坏

buggy ['bʌgi] *n.* 1.(一匹马拉的)轻便马车 2.婴儿手推车 3.[短途运输重物的]小运货车 4.(俚)旧汽车

bugle ['bjuːgl] *n.* 军号,喇叭 — *a* ~ *call* 号声;进军信号 — *vi.* 吹号 — *vt.* 吹号召集;吹号表示(冲锋、撤退等)‖ ~ *r n.* 号手,司号兵

build [bild] (built[bilt]) *vt.* 1. 建筑,造 2. 建设,建立 3. 构成,形成,使成为 — *a* ~

fire 生火 4. 抬高…的身分,把(演员)捧出去扩大(*up*) 5. 发展;集结;增长;增强(*up*) — *vi.* 1. 建造;从事营造业 2.(比赛等)到达最高峰;向最高峰发展;增长,加强,扩大 — *n.* 1. 构造;造型 2. 体格 ‖ '~**up** *n.* 1. 发展;增长;增强;积累;集结:a military ~ *up* 军事集结 2. 制造舆论

builder ['bildə] *n.* 1. 建筑工人;施工人员 2. 营造商 3. 创建者;建设者;建造者 4. 促净剂(增加洗涤剂清洁作用的物质)

building ['bildiŋ] *n.* 1. 建筑物;房屋 2. 建筑,建造;建筑术 ‖ ~ **society**(英)建屋互助会(接受会员存款并贷款给拟建屋或购屋的会员)

built [bilt] **build** 的过去式和过去分词 — *adj.* 构造(或体形)…的 ‖ '~-'in *adj.* 1. 嵌入式的,装入式的,内装的:~-*in* furniture 镶壁家具 2. 固有的,内在的

Bujumbura [,budʒəm'buərə] *n.* 布琼布拉〔布隆迪首都〕

bulb [bʌlb] *n.* 1.【植】鳞茎;球茎;球茎植物 2. 球状物;电灯泡;(温度计的)球部 3.【解】延髓 — *vi.* 1. 生球茎 2. 膨胀成球状 ‖ '~**ed** *adj.* 有球茎的;球茎状的/'~**ar** *adj.* 1.【植】球(或鳞)茎的 2.【解】延髓的

bulbous ['bʌlbəs] *adj.*【植】1. 鳞茎状的 2. 由鳞茎长出的

Bulgaria [bʌl'gɛəriə] *n.* 保加利亚〔欧洲巴尔干半岛东南部国家〕‖ ~**n** *adj.* 保加利亚的;保加利亚人的 — *n.* 保加利亚人;保加利亚语

bulge [bʌldʒ] *n.* 1. 鼓出,凸出;凸出部分 2.(体积、数字等的)暂时增大;暴增 3.(船)舱腹 4. 优势:have (or get) the ~ on 胜过 — *vi.* 鼓出,凸出(*out*) — *vt.* 使鼓出,使凸出

bulgur ['bulguə] *n.* 焦干碎麦

bulgy ['bʌldʒi] *adj.* 鼓出的,凸出的

bulk [bʌlk] *n.* 1. 容积,体积 2. 大批,大量 3. 货舱;船货;散装货物 4. 大部分,大多数 5. 肥胖的人;肥大的身体 — *vi.* 1. 显得大(或重要):~ large 显得大;显得重要 2. 膨胀,膨胀(*up*) — *vt.* 1. 使扩大,使膨胀;填,塞(*out*) 2. 使成堆 — *adj.*(货物)散装的 ‖ '~-**head** *n.* 1.(船)的舱壁 2.(飞机的)隔板;(车厢的)间壁;(矿井的)隔墙 3. 堤岸;防浪堤

bulky ['bʌlki] *adj.* 1. 体积大的;肥胖的 2.(衣服)肥大的;笨大的 ‖ **bulkiness** *n.*

bull[1] [bul] *n.* 1. 公牛;雄兽 2. 买空的证券投机商,多头 3. 体壮如牛的人,彪形大汉〔美俚〕工头(尤指大农场监工) 4.[B]【天】金牛座;(占星术)金牛宫 5.〔美俚〕警察;侦探 6.〔美俚〕火车头 7.〔俚〕空话;胡说八道 — *adj.* 1. 公牛般的;大型的 2. 雄的 3. 哄抬证券价格的 4.〔俚〕夸口,吹牛;闲谈 — *vt.* 1. 企图抬高(证券、市场等)的价格 2. 强行实现;强行打开(一条路) 3.〔俚〕以说大话来欺骗;说大话 ‖ '~-**dog** *n.* 1. 叭喇狗,斗牛狗(一种粗矮性烈的狗) 2. 刚毅的人 3. 大口径短筒左轮手枪 4.【冶】(搅炼炉的)打炉底衬料 5.(英国大学的)总监随从 6.(供运郊售售的)最早版日报 *vt.* 抓住牛角掷倒(小公牛) / '~-**doze** *vt.* 1. 强迫,威胁;压倒 2. 用推土机清除(或挖出,削平) / '~-**dozer** *n.* 1. 恐吓者,威胁者 2. 推土机 / '~-**fight** *n.* 斗牛(戏) / '~-**fighter** *n.* 斗牛士 / '~-**finch** *n.*【动】红腹灰雀 / '~-**frog** *n.*【动】牛蛙,喧蛙 / '~-**head** *n.* 1. 大头鱼(尤指杜父鱼、美洲鲇鱼) 2. 顽固的人 / '~-**necked** *adj.* 有短而粗的颈项的 / '~-**pen** *n.* 1. 牛栏 2.〔美俚〕(法庭等的)

犯人候审大房间 3.〈美俚〉拳击比赛场 /～ point(英)〈赢〉得的(一)分;优势,有利条件 /～ ring n. 斗牛场 /～ session〈美俚〉自由讨论;闲谈 /～'s-eye n. 1. 靶心,鹄的 2. 打中靶心的一击 3.【海】(舷侧)圆窗;单眼滑车 4. 厚透镜 5. 牛眼灯;厚圆透镜 6. 特硬球形薄荷糖 /～ shit n. 胡说,废话 /～ terrier 器㹴,叭喇狗,斗牛㹴

bull² ['bul] n. 教皇诏书;训令

bull³ [bul] n. 自相矛盾的话;荒诞可笑的错误(= Irish ～)

bullet ['bulit] n. 1. 枪弹,子弹,弹丸 2. 投(或踢)得快而稳的球 ‖～'s name n. 圆头的(人);〈俚〉顽固的人;傻瓜/～ 'headed adj. 圆头的;固执的;愚笨的 /～-proof adj. 防弹的,枪弹射不穿的 /～ train 高速火车,高速客车

bulletin ['bulitin] n. 1. 公报,公告 2.(医生发表的知名人士的)病情报告书 3. 新闻简报

bullion ['buljən] n. 1.(造货币等用的)条金;条银;块金;块银;锭形金属 2. 金银丝花边(或穗带)

bullish ['buliʃ] adj. 1. 公牛的;公牛般的 2. 股票行情看涨的 3. 乐观的

bullock ['buːlək] n. 1. 小公牛 2. 阉牛

bully ['buli] n. 恶霸;暴徒;恃强欺弱者 — vt. 1. 威吓 2. 欺侮 — vi. 充当恶霸(或持强欺弱者等) — adj. 好的,第一流的 — int. 好! 妙! ‖～boy n.(受人雇用的)打手,流氓

bulrush ['bulraʃ]n.【植】1. 藨草 2.〈英〉宽叶香蒲;水烛 3.(美洲)灯心草 4.〈圣经〉纸莎草的纤维;纸莎草

bulwark ['bulwək] n. 1. 堡垒;防御物;保障 2. 防波堤 3.[～s]【船】舷墙 — vt. 用堡垒防护;防御,保护

bum [bʌm]〈美口〉n. 1. 游民;叫化子 2.

闲饮 3. 不称职的人 4. 沉溺于玩乐的人 — (bummer, bummest) adj. 1. 劣质的,无价值的 2. 丧失劳动力的;伤残的 3. 假的;谬误的 — (bummed) vi. 1. 流浪;游荡 2. 纵酒 — vt. 乞讨,乞求

bumblebee ['bʌmblbiː] n.【动】熊蜂,大黄蜂

bummer ['bʌmə] n.〈俚〉1. 游手好闲的人 2. 失望;大失败;不愉快事件(或经历、局面等)

bump [bʌmp] vt. 1. 撞伤(头等);撞击 2. 把…从职位上排挤掉 3.〈美俚〉杀死;谋杀(off) 4.〈口〉增加,提高(汇价、价格等)(up) — vi. 1. 碰,撞(against) 2.(笨重车辆)颠簸地行驶(along) 3. 偶然遇到(into) — adv. 突然地;猛烈地 — n. 1. 碰,撞,撞击 2. 因碰撞而起的肿块 3.头盖骨上的隆起部分(颅相家认为是才能的象征);〈口〉能力,才能 4.(车的)颠簸 5.【空】(飞机因气流突变而感受的)空中颠簸

bumper¹ ['bʌmpə] n.【机】减震物;缓冲器;(汽车)保险杠 ‖～ sticker(或 strip) 粘贴在汽车保险杠上的小标语(宣传、广告用)

bumper² ['bʌmpə] n. 1.(干杯时的)满杯 2. 同类中特大者 3.〈俚〉丰收;满场,满座 — adj.(收成)丰足的;丰收的

bumpkin ['bʌmpkin] n.〈贬〉乡下人,土佬儿

bumpy ['bʌmpi] adj. 1. 高低不平的 2. 颠簸的 3. 困难重重的 ‖ bumpiness n.

bun [bʌn] n. 1. 小圆(果子)面包;小圆糕点 2.(盘在后脑的)圆发髻 3. [～s]〈美俚〉〈忌〉屁股

bunch [bʌntʃ] n. 1.(一)束,串 2.〈俚〉一群;一帮,一伙 3.【矿】小矿巢;管状矿脉膨大部分 — vi. 1. 捆成一束;穿成

一串 2. 凸出, 隆起 3. 打褶 — *vt.* 1. 使成一束(或一捆等) 2. 打(褶) ‖ ~ y *adj.* 成束的;隆起的

bund [bʌnd] *n.*(东方国家的)堤岸;江边道路;码头

bundle [ˈbʌndl] *n.* 1. 包袱, 包裹 2. 束;包 3.(相当大的)一堆 4.〈俚〉(数目可观的)一笔款项 4.【植】维管束;【解】(神经、肌肉的)束 *n.* 5.【纺】小包(纱线的计量单位, 一小包等于 20 亨克) — *vt.* 1. 包;捆;扎 2. 把…乱七八糟地塞进(*in*, *into*) 3. 把…匆匆撵走(*away*, *off*, *out*) — *vi.* 匆匆离开(*off*, *out*, *away*)

bung [bʌŋ] *n.* 1.(桶等的)塞子 2. 桶孔 3.(家畜的)盲肠或肛门) — *vt.* 1. 用塞子塞(桶孔) 2. 塞住 3.〈俚〉扔(石子等), 丢 ‖ ~-hole *n.* 桶孔, 桶口

bungalow [ˈbʌŋɡələu] *n.*(屋前或周围有平台的印度)孟加拉式平房;平房

bungle [ˈbʌŋɡl] *vt.* 粗制滥造;搞坏, 贻误 — *vi.* 拙劣地工作 — *n.* 拙劣的工作 ‖ ~r *n.* 工作笨拙的人 / **bungling** *adj.* 笨拙的;粗劣的

bunion [ˈbʌnjən] *n.*【医】拇囊(炎)肿

bunk[bʌŋk] *n.* 1.(车、船等舱壁内设的)床铺, 铺位 2.〈口〉睡觉处, 床 3. ~(性口的)食槽 — *vi.* 1. 在 ~ 铺位上睡 2. 同睡一个铺位(*with*) 3.〈口〉过夜 — *vt.* 为…提供睡处 ‖ ~ bed(有上下铺的)双层床

bunker [ˈbʌŋkə] *n.* 1. 煤箱(船上的)油舱;煤舱 2.(高尔夫球场上的)障碍 3.【军】掩体, 地堡 — *vt.* 1. 把(煤)堆进煤舱;把(煤)装进煤箱 2. 把(高尔夫球)击入障碍区 3. 使陷入困境

bunkum [ˈbʌŋkəm] *n.* 假话, 骗人的鬼话;胡说;夸夸其谈的演说

bunny [ˈbʌni] *n.* 小兔子(儿童对兔的爱

称) ‖ ~ **girl** 兔状打扮的夜总会女招待

Bunraku [bunˈrɑːkuː]〈日〉*n.*(传统的日本)文乐木偶戏

Bunsen [ˈbunsən] *n.* ‖ ~ **burner** 本生灯(一种实验室用的煤气灯)

bunt [bʌnt] *n.* 1. 抵;撞 2.(棒球赛中的)触击, 轻打 — *vt.* 1.(用头、角等)抵, 撞 2.(棒球赛中)触击, 轻打

bunting [ˈbʌntiŋ] *n.* 1. 旗布;(节日装饰街道、房屋等的)旗帜, 彩旗 2.【鸟】鹀(雀科鹀属鸣鸟)

buoy [bɔi] *n.* 1. 浮标, 航标 2. 发生圈 — *vt.* 1. 使浮起;使飘起(*up*) 2. 用浮标指示…的位置(*out*) 3. 鼓舞(*up*)

buoyance [ˈbɔiəns], **buoyancy** [ˈbɔiənsi] *n.* 1. 浮力 2. 轻松愉快的心情 3.(股票市场的)价格回升;保持高价

buoyant [ˈbɔiənt] *adj.* 1. 有浮力的 2. 轻松愉快的 3.(物价等)上涨的;保持高价的 ‖ ~ly *adv.*

bur[1] [bə:] *n.*【植】刺果(生刺果的植物);刺球状花序 2. 粘附物, 钩着物;难以摆脱的人

bur[2] [bə:] *n.* = burr

burden [ˈbə:dn] *n.* 1. 担子;负担;艰难;负重:a beast of ~ 驮兽 2.(船的)载重量;吨位 3.(诗歌、发言等的)重点, 要点 4.(歌曲收尾的)合唱叠句(或副歌) 5. 责任, 义务 — *vt.* 1. 装货上(船)负担 2. 使负重担(如债务、捐税等);烦扰(*with*) ‖ ~**some** *adj.* 难于负担的;(约束等)使人难以忍受的;累赘的

burdock [ˈbə:dɔk] *n.*【植】牛蒡

bureau [ˈbjuərəu] *n.*[复] **bureaux** [ˈbjuərəuz] 或 **bureaus**) *n.* 1. 局;司;处;署 2. 社;所 3.〈英〉书桌, 写字台 4.〈美〉(有镜或无镜)衣柜, 镜台

bureaucracy [bjuə'rɔkrəsi] n. 1. 官僚政治;官僚主义 2.[总称]官僚

bureaucrat ['bjuərəukræt] n. 官僚

bureaucratese ['bjuərəu,kræ'tiːz] n. 官场行话,公文术语;官僚语言,官腔

bureaucratic [,bjuərəu'krætik] adj. 官僚政治的;官僚主义的 ‖ ~ally adv.

bureaucratism [bjuə'rɔkrətizəm] n. 官僚主义 ‖ **bureaucratist** n. 官僚主义者

bureaux ['bjuərəuz] bureau 的复数

burgeon ['bəːdʒən] n. 嫩芽;蓓蕾 — vi. 1. 发芽;生出蓓蕾 2. 开花 3. 发展

burglar ['bəːglə] n. 夜盗;窃贼;破门盗窃者 ‖ ~ize vt. 破门盗窃(某处);撬窃(某人)的家;破门盗窃

burglary ['bəːgləri] n. 1. 夜盗行为 2. 破门盗窃

Burgundy ['bəːgəndi] n. (法国的)勃艮第红(或白)葡萄酒

burial ['beriəl] n. 葬;掩埋;葬礼

Burkina Faso [bu'kiːnə 'fɑːsəu]布基纳法索(旧称 Upper Volta 上沃尔特)[西非国家]

burlap ['bəːlæp] n. (做麻袋等用的)粗麻布

burlesque [bəː'lesk] n. 1. 滑稽讽刺作品(可指诗、文等);(讽刺性的)诙谐模仿;嘲弄,讽刺 2. 滑稽歌舞杂剧(包括滑稽短剧、脱衣舞等) — adj. 滑稽的;讽刺的,嘲弄的 — vt. & vi. (通过模仿取笑的)嘲弄(或)模仿

burly ['bəːli] adj. 1. 雄伟的;魁梧的;高大结实的 2. 粗鲁的;率直的 ‖ **burliness** n.

Burma ['bəːmə] n. 缅甸[东南亚国家]

Burmese [bəː'miːz] n. 1.[单复同]缅甸人 2. 缅甸语 — adj. 缅甸的;缅甸人的;缅甸语的

burn [bəːn] (burnt [bəːnt] 或 burned) vt. 1. 烧;烧毁;烧焦;烧伤 2. 烧毁;烧焦;烧伤 3. 透烧;烫痛 3. 烧灼洞 5. 晒:a sun — t face 晒黑了的脸 6. 使(喉咙等)辣得难受 7. 激起...的愤怒或欲望等 8.(俚)使遭电刑处死 9.[化]使氧化;利用(铀等)的核能 10.[用于不定式]挥霍:money to — 供挥霍的钱 11.(俚)使恼怒 12.(俚)欺骗 — vi. 1. 燃烧;(灯)点着 2. 发热;放光:The patient was ~ ing with fever. 病人在发烧。— vi. — blue 烧得发蓝光 3. 烧毁;烧焦;烫伤;烫痛 4. 烧焦 5. 激动;发怒;渴望 6.(俚)被电刑处死 — n. 1. 烧伤,灼伤;烧(或灼)伤处 2. 烙印 3.(美)(森林中用火)烧出的空地 4.(火箭发动机的)飞行途中点火 ‖ ~ bag 焚烧袋(一种存放待焚秘密文件的口袋)/ ~out n. 1. 烧尽;大火灾 2.(火箭等)停止燃烧,熄火;燃尽时刻,熄火时刻;熄火点 3. 烧坏

burner ['bəːnə] n. 1. 烧制者:a brick ~ 烧砖工人 2. 灯头;煤气头;炉膛 3. 燃烧器;炉子

burnish ['bəːniʃ] vt. 擦亮(金属等) — vi. 被擦亮 — n. 光泽,光亮 ‖ ~er n. 把东西磨光(或擦亮)的人;磨光器,抛光器

burnt [bəːnt] burn 的过去式和过去分词 — adj. 烧焦的,烧坏的;烧糊的

burp [bəːp] (口) n. 饱嗝;打嗝;饱嗝似的声音 — vi. & vt. (使)打嗝

burr [bəː] n. 1.[机]毛口,毛边 2. 磨石 3.(树瘤等上的)不规则的隆起块 4. 三角凿刀;牙钻;骨钻 5.[植]刺果

burro ['bəːrəu] ([复] burros) n. 小驴

burrow ['bʌrəu] n. 1.(狐、兔等的)地洞;地道 2. 地下躲避处 — vt. 1. 掘出(洞、通道等) 2. 在...掘洞 3. 使躲进

地洞(或隐藏处);使舒适地钻入 — *vi.*
1. 钻进(或钻入)某处;打入某组织;潜
伏 **2.** 打地洞 **3.** 搜寻 **4.** 依偎(*against*)
‖ **~ er** *n.*

burst [bəst] (burst) *vi.* **1.** 爆裂,炸破;胀
破;冲裂;溃决 **2.** 突然发生,突然发作 / ～ *into* thunderous cheers 发出雷鸣
般的欢呼 / ～ *with* laughing 捧腹大笑
3. 忽然出现/～ *into* the room 闯入房
间 **4.**(芽、蕾等)绽开 **5.** 充满(*with*) —
vt. **1.** 使破裂;突破,冲破 **2.** 致使…
破裂:He almost ～ a blood vessel. 他差
点爆了眼血血管。**2.**(谷物等)充满(粮仓
等) — *n.* **1.** 突然破裂;爆炸 **2.** 突发;
进发;[军]连发射击:a ～ of gunfire 一
阵炮火/a ～ of speed 速度的突然增加

Burundi [bu'rʌndi] *n.* 布隆迪[东非国家]

bury ['beri] *vt.* **1.** 埋葬,葬 **2.** 埋藏;遮盖;
掩蔽:be buried in thought 出神深思/～
oneself in study 埋头研究 **3.** 死去(亲
属):He has buried both parents. 他父母
都死了。**4.** 为…举行葬礼 **5.** 把(友谊
等)从记忆中除去 ‖ **burier** *n.* 埋葬者;
掩埋物

bus [bʌs] *n.* **1.** 公共汽车 **2.**〈俚〉飞机;
汽车;机器脚踏车 **3.**[电]汇流条,母线
—(bussed;bussing) *vi.* **1.** 乘公共汽车
(去) **2.** 当餐厅侍者的助手 — *vt.* 用
公共汽车运送 ‖ **bus's'ing** *n.* 公共汽车
接送(美)用校车接送学生(指为调整
学生中的种族比例把非本区学生送来
读书) ‖ **~ boy** *n.*〈美〉餐厅侍者助手
/ ～ **girl**〈美〉餐厅侍者女助手/～ -**man**
n. 公共汽车驾驶员(或售票员)/～ -
man's holiday 照常工作的例假日/～
stop 公共汽车(停车)站

bush [buʃ] *n.* **1.** 灌木;灌木丛 **2.**[the ～]
(澳大利亚等地的)未开垦灌木(或森
林)地带 **3.** 蓬头,浓密的毛发;蓬松的

尾巴 **4.**(从前用作酒店标记的)长春藤
枝 **5.**[机]衬套;轴衬;轴瓦;[电]套管
— *vi.* **1.** 丛生,浓密地生长 — *vt.*
1. 用灌木支撑(或标志,保护、装饰) **2.**
[机]加衬套(或套管)于 — *adj.* **1.**(豆
科植物等)长得低矮如灌木的 **2.** 粗野
的;粗糙但实用的;外行的;次等的;第
二流的 ‖ **~ing** *n.* 衬套;轴衬;轴瓦;
[电](绝缘)套管 ‖ **~ buck** *n.* 南非林
羚 ～ **cat**[动]薮猫/～ **fighter** *n.* 丛
林游击队员/～ **fighting** *n.* 灌木战,
丛林游击战/～ **hat**(澳大利亚森林
地带居民或士兵戴的)阔边呢帽/～(澳
大利亚陆军的)阔边军帽/～ -**man** *n.*
1.[B-]布须曼人(非洲纳米比亚和博茨
瓦纳等地的居民) **2.**〈澳〉丛林或灌木
居民(或农民、旅行者)/～ **pilot** 飞行
于人烟稀少地区的飞行员/～ **ranger**
n. **1.**(旧时澳洲的)丛林土匪 **2.** 丛林
居民;边疆居民

bushel ['buʃl] *n.* **1.** 蒲式耳(计量谷物等
的容量单位,在英国等于 3 6.368 升,
在美国等于 3 5.238 升) **2.** 一蒲式耳
的容器 **3.** 一蒲式耳东西的重量 **4.** 大
量

bushido ['bu:ʃidəu]〈日〉*n.* 武士道

bushy ['buʃi] *adj.* **1.** 灌木茂盛的 **2.** 灌木
似的 **3.**(眉毛等)浓密的 ‖ **bushily** *adv.*
/ **bushiness** *n.*

busily ['bizili] *adv.* 忙碌地

business ['biznis] *n.* **1.** 商业;生意;营业
(额) **2.** 商店;商行;工商企业 **3.** 职责;
事务,事 **4.** 权利:have no ～ to do (or
no ～ doing) 没有权利做某事或做…某
事 **5.**(需注意的)事;所关心的事 **6.**[戏](演
员)的动作(区别于"对白")‖ **~ like**
adj. 事务式的,有条理的 ‖ **~ man** *n.*
商人,实业家

bust[^1] [bʌst] *n.* **1.** 胸像,半身像 **2.**(尤指

妇女的)胸部;(妇女的)胸围

bust[2] [bʌst]〈口〉(bust(ed)) *vt*. 1. 使爆裂;使爆发;击破;打碎,使破损 2. 使破产;使失败 3. 使降级 4. 驯服(野马等) 5. 殴打 6. 逮捕 7. 搜查;抄(家) — *vi*. 1. 爆裂;爆发;破裂 2. 破产;失败(*up*) 3. 被降级 — *n*. 1. 失败;不景气;经济崩溃 2. 殴打 3. 欢闹(尤指闹饮) 4. 逮捕 5. 搜查;抄家 — *adj*. 1. 爆裂的;炸破的;胀破的 2. 破产的 ‖ ~**ed** *adj*. 破产了的;失败了的;被降级的;被逮捕的 /ˈ~-**up** *n*. 1. 失败;破产 2. 争吵;〈美〉(婚姻等的)破裂

bustle [ˈbʌsl] *vi*. 1. 奔忙(*about*) 2. 赶快行动(*up*) 3. 充满(*with*):The work site ~*d with* activity. 工地上一片繁忙景象。— *vt*. 催促,使赶快行动 — *n*. 熙攘;奔忙;忙乱 ‖ **bustling** *adj*. 忙忙碌碌的,熙攘的;活跃的

busy [ˈbizi] *adj*. 1. 忙的;繁忙的;热闹的 2.(电话线)正被占用的,没空的 3. 爱管闲事的 4.(图案等)复杂的,使人眼花缭乱的 — *vt*. 使忙 — *vi*. 忙碌,奔忙(*about*, *around*) ‖ ~**ness** *n*. 忙碌 ‖ ˈ~ˌ**body** *n*. 爱管闲事的人

but [强 bʌt;弱 bət] *conj*. 1. 但是,可是;而(是) 2. 而不;若不;除非:It never rains ~ it pours.〈谚〉不雨则已,一雨倾盆。(指事情不发生则已,一旦发生便接踵而来) 3.[用于否定词或疑问词之后,表示否定意义,相当于 that not]:No task is so difficult ~ (或 ~ *that*, ~ *what*) we can accomplish it. 不管任务怎样困难,我们都能完成。4.[用于否定词加 doubt, deny, question 等词之后,无实义,相当于连接词 that]:There is no question ~(或~ *that*) he will succeed. 他会成功,这是没有问题的。— *pron*.[关系代词,意义相当于 who not, that not]:There is no one of us ~ wishes to go. 我们人人都想去。— *prep*. 除了:Nobody knew it ~ me. 除了我以外,没有人知道这件事。/ last ~ one (two) 倒数第二(三) — *adv*. 只,仅仅:He left ~ an hour ago. 他一小时前刚走。

butcher [ˈbutʃə] *n*. 1. 屠夫;卖肉者 2. 屠杀者,残杀者 3. 拙劣的工作者 4.〈美〉(火车或剧场里兜售糖果、报纸等的)小贩 5.〈美俚〉〈贬〉军医 — *vt*. 1. 屠宰,宰割 2. 屠杀,残杀 3.(因注释、编辑不好或粗暴批评而)弄糟,搞坏 ‖ ~ **knife** 屠刀 /~'**s meat**(猪、牛、羊等的)鲜肉

butchery [ˈbutʃəri] *n*. 1. 屠宰场 2. 屠宰 3. 屠杀,残杀

butler [ˈbʌtlə] *n*. 男管家;司膳总管;专管酒类的男仆

butt[1] [bʌt] *n*. 大桶

butt[2] [bʌt] *n*. 1. 粗端;(工具的)柄;枪托 2.(树木的)残株;根端;残余(部分) 3. 烟蒂;香烟 4.〈美俚〉屁股 5.【动】比目鱼(如鲽、鲆、鲽、鳎等)

butt[3] [bʌt] *n*. 1. 靶垛 2.[~s]射击场 3. 靶;射击目标 4. 目的,目标 5. 笑柄;抨击的对象

butt[4] [bʌt] *vt*. 1. 顶撞 2. 碰撞 — *vi*. 1. 顶撞,冲撞 2. 伸出,突出 3. 邻接,毗连(*on*, *against*) 4. 用头把...顶入;插手,干涉;插嘴(*in*) — *n*. 1. 顶撞,冲撞;碰撞 2.(击剑中的)突刺 3.【建】平接,对头(连)接,对接:~ welding 对(头)焊接 4. 铰链

butte [bjuːt] *n*.〈美〉(美国西部的)地垛,孤峰,孤山

butter [ˈbʌtə] *n*. 1. 黄油(音译白脱油) 2. 似黄油的食品;(植物)脂;脂样物质:peanut ~ 花生酱 3.〈口〉奉承话,巴结话 — *vt*. 1. 涂黄油于;用黄油烹调;把

黄油放入 2.〈口〉巴结,讨好(*up*) ‖ ~**y**
adj. ‖ ~ **bean** 菜豆;利马豆;棉豆
/ '~**boat** *n.*(船形)黄油碟 / '~**cup**
n.【植】毛茛 / '~**fat** *n.* 乳脂 / '~,**fingered**
adj.〈口〉拿不稳东西的;不当心的 /
'~,**fingers** *n.*[用作单]拿不稳东
西的人;常失球的人;粗心大意的
人;笨手笨脚的人 / ~**milk** *n.* 脱脂乳;
酪乳 / '~**nut** *n.*【植】灰胡桃(树);灰胡
桃木 / '~**scotch** *n.* 黄油硬糖 / '~**wort**
n.【植】捕虫堇

butterfly ['bʌtəflai] *n.* 1. 蝴蝶 2. 轻浮的
人(尤指妇女);追求享乐的人 3.【体】
蝶泳

buttock ['bʌtək] *n.* 1. 半边屁股 2.[~s]
屁股,臀部 3.【船】船舶凸面,船尾突出
部 4.(摔角中的)过背摔 — *vt.*(摔角
中)用过背摔摔出(对手)

button ['bʌtn] *n.* 1. 纽扣 2.(电铃等的)
按钮(开关) 3.(门等的)球形把手 4. 纽
扣似的东西;圆形小徽章 4. 没有价值
的小东西: not care a ~ 毫不介意 5.
[~s][用作单]〈英口〉(旅馆等处)穿制
服的侍者 6.[口]强留(某人)长谈 / '~**hole**
n. 纽扣眼,纽眼 *vt.* 1. 在…上开纽眼 2. 抓
住(某人)的衣纽,强留(客人)长谈
/ '~**wood** *n.*【植】1.(北美)梧桐;梧桐
木 2. 锥果木

buttress ['bʌtris] *n.* 1.【建】扶垛,扶壁 2.
山边扶壁状凸出部(马蹄后腿的)骨
质隆起,(树干基部的)根肿 3. 支柱;
支持力量 — *vt.* 1. 用扶壁支持(或加

固) 2. 支撑;支持(*up*)

buxom ['bʌksəm] *adj.*(妇女)胸部丰满
的;健美的 ‖ ~**ly** *adv.* ~ **uess** *n.*

buy [bai](bought [bɔːt]) *vt.* 1. 买;买得 2.
(出一定代价)获得,换得,赢得(和平
等) 3.(用赂赂等)收买 4.〈俚〉同意;接
受;相信 — *vi.* 买 — *n.* 1. 购买 2. 买
得上算的货物: a good (bad) ~ 买得合
算(不合算)的东西 ‖ ~ **able** *adj.* 可以
可收买的 / ~**er** *n.* 1. 买者 2. 进货
员 ‖ '~-**in** *n.*〈美〉(股票的)买进;补
买,补进/'~-**out** *n.* 全部收买;全部买
下市上产品

buzz [bʌz] *vi.* 1.(蜂等)嗡嗡叫;(机器等)
营营响 2. 用蜂鸣器发出信号 3.〈口〉
匆忙行走(*about, along, off*) 4. 唧唧喳
喳 5.(谣言等)流传 — *vt.* 1. 使嗡嗡
叫;使营营响 2. 用蜂鸣器对…发出
信号 3. 异口同声地说 4. 散布(谣言
等) 5. 猛扑(石子等) 6.(飞机)低飞掠
掠;飞近(另一飞机)进行骚扰 7.
〈口〉打电话给 8.(英方)喝完(一瓶酒)
— *n.* 1. 嗡嗡声,蜂音 2. 营营声,嘈
杂声 3. 流言,谣言 4. 蜂鸣器发出的信
号 5.〈俚〉打电话 6.〈美〉圆锯(= ~
saw) — *int.*(指消息)早过时了! ‖ ~
er *n.* 蜂鸣器;汽笛 / ~**ing** *adj.* 嗡嗡响
的;营营响的 ‖ 1. 嗡嗡声 / ~ **bomb**
〈口〉【军】"V"型飞弹,嗡嗡弹,飞机型
飞弹/~ **session**〈美〉(非正式)小组讨论
会/'~-**word** *n.*(内容空洞,主要用以在
外行面前显示自己高明的)玄妙的术
语;时髦词语;口号

buzzard ['bʌzəd] *n.*【鸟】鵟;红头美洲
鹫 2. 卑鄙小人;贪婪的小人 3. 作营营
声的小虫

by [bai] *prep.* 1. 在…旁,靠近 2. 在…
身边;在…手头 3.(方向)偏于: The
ship sailed north ~ east. 船向北偏东的

方向驶去。**4.** 沿；经；由：come ~ the highway 由公路来 **5.** 经过...旁边 **6.** 在(白天、夜晚等)的情况下 **7.** 不迟于；到...时：~ the end of the month 到月底前 **8.** [表示方法、手段]靠，用，通过：travel ~ air (land, sea) 航空(陆路，航海)旅行 **9.** 由于：~ mistake 由于差错 **10.** 根据，按：~ Article 3 of the Treaty 根据条约第三条/sell ~ the kilo 论公斤出售 **11.** 被，由：essays (written) ~ Lu Xun 鲁迅(写)的杂文 **12.** 相差：miss the train ~ ten minutes 晚十分钟没赶上火车 **13.** [表示面积]：a room 5m. ~ 4m. 一间长五米宽四米的房间 **14.** 逐一：one ~ one 一个一个地 **15.** [表示关系]就...来说；...来说：a doctor ~ profession 职业医生 **16.** 对，对待：He did well ~ me. 他待我好。**17.** 对着...(发誓) — **adv. 1.** 在近旁：live close ~ 住在很近的地方 **2.** 经过：The parade has passed ~. 游行队伍已走过去了。**3.** (搁)在一边；存放：lay sth. ~ 把某物搁在一边；把某物贮存起来 ‖ `~-and-` n. 将来

by- pref. **1.** 表示"附近"，"邻近"：by-stander **2.** 表示"边"，"侧"：bypass **3.** 表示"副"，"次要的"：by-product

bye-bye [ˈbaiˈbai] *int.* 再会! 回头见!

by-effect [ˈbaiiˌfekt] *n.* 副作用

byelaw [ˈbailɔː] *n.* = bylaw

by-election [ˈbaiiˌlekʃən] *n.* 补缺选举

Byelorussia [ˌbjelərˈʌʃə] *n.* = Belorussia

bygone [ˈbaiɡɔn] *adj.* 过去的，以往的：过去的一 — *n.* [~s]过去的事情，往事

bylaw [ˈbailɔː] *n.* (地方或社团所订的)地方法规；内部章程；附则；细则

BYOB *abbr.* bring your own booze (或 bottle) (用于宴会请柬上等)请自带酒来

bypass [ˈbaipɑːs] *n.* (绕过为绕过市镇等而筑的)旁道，旁路；【机】旁通管；【电】分路器，分流器 — *vt.* **1.** 绕过，绕...走 **2.** 为...加设旁道，使(液体、气体)通过旁通管 **3.** 忽视；回避；超越

bypath [ˈbaipɑːθ] *n.* 小道；僻径

by-product [ˈbaiˌprɔdʌkt] *n.* 副产品

bystander [ˈbaiˌstændə] *n.* 旁观者

byte [bait] *n.* 【计】(二进制)字节，(二进)位组

byway [ˈbaiwei] *n.* **1.** 偏僻小路 **2.** (研究等的)次要方面，冷悔领域

byword [ˈbaiwəːd] *n.* **1.** 谚语；俗语 **2.** 笑柄；(...的)代名词(for) **3.** 绰号 **4.** 口头禅

C

C, c [si:] ([复]C's, c's 或 Cs, cs [siz]) 英语字母表第三个字母 **1.**【数】第三已知量 **2.**[C] C 字形 **3.** 罗马数字 100 **4.**[C]【化】元素碳(carbon)的符号 **5.**[C]【电】库仑(coulomb)的符号 **6.**【音】C音, C 调 ‖ **C three, C 3**(英)**.**(征兵中)体格为第三级的一类; 丙等三级 **2.** 不合格的; 蹩脚的

Ca【化】元素钙(calcium)的符号

C/A *abbr.* **1.** current account 往来账户; 活期存款户 **2.** capital account 资本账户; 股本账户; (资产减去负债后的)净值

cab [kæb] *n.* **1.** 出租马车; 出租汽车(= taxicab) **2.** (机车、卡车等的)司机室 = (cabbed; cabbing) *vi.* 乘出租马车(或汽车) ‖ ～ **man** 出租汽车司机; 出租马车车夫 / ～ **rank**(英)= cabstand /'～**stand** *n.* (候租的)出租汽车(或汽车)停车场

cabal [kə'bæl] *n.* **1.** 阴谋集团, 秘密集团 **2.** 阴谋, 密谋 ‖ **caballer** *n.*

cabana [kə'bɑ:nə] *n.* (海滩等处的)帐篷屋; 简易浴室 **2.** 小屋 ‖ ～ **set**(短袖衫及短裤成套的)男式海滨服

cabaret ['kæbərei] *n.* **1.** 有歌舞表演的餐馆(或酒吧间)(有时音译作"卡巴莱") **2.** "卡巴莱"餐馆(或酒吧间)中的歌舞表演(也称～show)

cabbage ['kæbidʒ] *n.* **1.**【植】甘蓝, 卷心菜, 洋白菜 **2.** (美俚)纸币; 钱 **3.** (英口)

对什么都不感兴趣的人 **4.**(英)(裁缝据为己有的)零星布料 — *vt. & vi.* 偷(小东西)

cabbie, cabby ['kæbi] *n.* 出租汽车司机; 出租马车车夫

cabin ['kæbin] *n.* **1.** (简陋的)小屋 **2.** 房舱; 统舱; 座舱; 货舱 **3.** (铁路的)信号所 — *vt.* 把...关在小屋里; 使拘束 ‖ ～ **boy** 船上男服务员 / ～ **class**(客轮)二等舱 /～ **cruiser**(有住宿设备的)游艇, 摩托艇 / ～ **passenger** 二等舱旅客

cabinet ['kæbinit] *n.* **1.** (存放或陈列用的)橱, 柜 **2.** 内阁; 全体阁员; (英)内阁会议; (美)(州长或市长)顾问团 ‖ ～**maker** *n.* 家具木工, 细木工

cable ['keibl] *n.* **1.** (周长十英寸或十英寸以上的)缆, 索; 钢丝绳 **2.**【电】电缆; 海底电缆 **3.** = ～('s) length **4.**【船】锚链 **5.** = ～gram **6.** = ～ TV — *vt.* **1.** 通过海底电缆发(电报等); 给...发海底电报 **2.** 用缆索缚住 — *vi.* 打海底电报 ‖ ～**gram** 海底电报 / ～ **address** 电报挂号 / ～ **car** 缆车 /～**cast** (～cast 或 ～casted) *vt.* 用电缆(或有线电视)播送 — *vi.* 用电缆(或有线电视)播送 / ～ **railway** 缆索铁路 / ～('s) **length** 链长(海上测距单位, 相当于 1/10 海里) / ～ **TV** 电缆电视, 有线电视

cablese ['keibə'li:z] *n.* (尽量节约用词的)电报体裁, 电报体文字

caboodle [kə'buːdl] *n.*〈俚〉群,伙;堆:the whole ~ 全部

caboose [kə'buːs] *n.* 1.（轮船的）舱面厨房 2.（美）货车守车（货物列车末尾供车长执行任务用的车厢）

cabriolet [,kæbriəu'lei] *n.* 1. 单马双轮轻便车 2. 四轮双座马车 3. 篷式汽车

cacao [kə'kɑːəu, kə'keiəu]（[复] cacaos）*n.* 1.【植】美洲可可树,巧克力树 2. 可可豆

cache [kæʃ] *n.* 1.（贮藏粮食、器材等的）地窖;藏物处 2.（地窖等处的）贮藏物 — *vt.* 贮藏;窖藏

cackle ['kækl] *vi.* 1.（鸡等下蛋后）咯咯叫 2. 咯咯地笑;嘁嘁咕咕地讲话 — *n.* 1. 咯咯的叫 2. 咯咯的笑;嘁嘁咕咕的讲话);废话

cacophonous [kæ'kɔfənəs] *adj.* 声音不和谐的

cacophony [kæ'kɔfəni] *n.* 不和谐的声音

cactus ['kæktəs]（[复] cacti ['kæktai] 或 cactuses）*n.*【植】仙人掌

cad [kæd] *n.* 粗俗的人,下等人;无赖

cadaver [kə'deivə] *n.* 尸体（尤指解剖用的尸体）‖ ~ic [kə'dævərik] *adj.* 尸体的 / ~ous *adj.* 尸体似的;苍白的;死灰色的

caddice, caddis ['kædis] *n.*【动】石蚕

caddie ['kædi] *n.* 1.（受雇为打高尔夫球的人背球杆等的）球童 2.（苏格兰）杂役 3.（放杂货或玻璃器皿等的）小手推车 — *vi.* 当球童

caddy[1] ['kædi] *n.* 1. 茶叶盒,茶叶罐 2.（美）（存放常用物品的）盒（或箱等）

caddy[2] ['kædi] *n.* & *vi.* = caddie

cadence ['keidəns] *n.* 1. 调子 2.（声音的）抑扬顿挫 3. 节奏,拍子 4.【音】终止式,终止 ‖ ~d *adj.* 有节奏的,抑扬顿挫的

cadenza [kə'denzə]〈意〉*n.*【音】华彩段,华彩句;华彩段风格的乐曲;自由装饰乐段

cadet [kə'det] *n.* 1. 军校学员;军官候补生 2. 练习生 2. 少子,幼子;弟弟

cadge [kædʒ] *vt.*〈口〉乞得,乞讨到 — *vi.*〈口〉以乞讨为生 ‖ ~r *n.* 乞丐;游手好闲的人

cadmium ['kædmiəm] *n.*【化】镉

cadre ['kɑːdə, 'kædri] *n.* 干部

cafe ['kæfei, 'kæfi] *n.* 咖啡;咖啡馆;小餐馆;饮食摊;茶室,茶室;酒吧

cafeteria [,kæfi'tiəriə] *n.* 自助餐馆;自助食堂

caffeine ['kæfiːn] *n.*【化】咖啡碱,咖啡因

cage [keidʒ] *n.* 1. 笼子;囚笼;牢房 2.【矿】罐笼;电梯梯箱 3. 骨架构造 4.（球类的）篮球场 4.（冰球等的）球门;练球馆 5. 薄纱（或花边）直披罩衣 — *vt.* 把...关入笼中;把（冰球等）击入球门

cagey, cagy ['keidʒi] *adj.*〈口〉1. 狡猾的;机警的;有戒心的 2. 谨小慎微的,不敢表态的 ‖ **cagily** *adv.* / **caginess** *n.*

CAI *abbr.* computer-assisted instruction 计算机辅助教学

Cairo ['kaiərəu] *n.* 开罗〔埃及首都〕

caisson [kə'suːn, 'keisən] *n.* 1.【建】沉箱 2. 浮箱闸门 3.【军】弹药箱;双轮弹药车;地雷箱 4.（打捞沉船用的）充气浮筒 5.【建】藻井 ‖ ~ **disease**【医】潜水病病病

cajole [kə'dʒəul] *vt.* 哄骗 ‖ **cajolingly** *adv.*

cajolery [kə'dʒəuləri] *n.* 哄骗

Cajun ['keidʒən] *n.* 阿卡迪亚人（法裔路易斯安那州人,祖先从阿卡迪亚迁移而来）

cake [keik] *n.* 1. 饼;糕;蛋糕 2.（苏格兰）

燕麦饼 2. 块;饼状物：a ~ of soap 一块
肥皂 3.(硬或脆的)块状物 4.〈美俚〉妖
娆女子 — vt. 1. 加块结物于 ... 上：
shoes ~d with mud 粘着泥块的鞋 2. 使
结块；使胶凝 — vi. 结块,胶凝

calabash ['kæləˌbæʃ] n.【植】葫芦

calamitous [kə'læmitəs] adj. 造成灾难的;
灾难性的 ‖ ~ly adv.

calamity [kə'læmiti] n. 灾难,灾祸;不
幸,苦难 ‖ ~ howler〈美〉预言祸事者;
杞人忧天者

calcimine ['kælsimain] n. (刷墙用的)石
灰浆,墙粉 — vt. 刷墙粉于

calcium ['kælsiəm] n.【化】钙

calculable ['kælkjuləbl] adj. 1. 能计算
的;能预测的 2. 可依赖的,可靠的 ‖
ˌcalcula'bility n.

calculate ['kælkjuleit] vt. 1. 计算,核算
估计 2. 预测,推测 3.[常用被动语态]
计划,打算 4.〈美口〉以为,认为 5.〈美〉
想要 — vi. 1. 计算,核算 2. 计划,打
算 2. 指望(on, upon)

calculated ['kælkjuleitid] adj. 1. 被计算
出来的;被估计出来的 2. 经过谋划
的;故意的 2.[后接不定式]打算作 ...
用的;适宜于 ...

calculating ['kælkjuleitiŋ] adj. 1. 计算
的;a ~ machine 计算器 2. 专为自己打
算的;精明的;狡猾的

calculation [ˌkælkju'leiʃən] n. 1. 计算;计
算出来的结果 2. 仔细的分析(或打
算);谋算熟虑 3. 预测 4. 自私的打算;
算计

calculator ['kælkjuleitə] n. 1. 计算者 2.
计算表 3. 计算器

calculus ['kælkjuləs] n. ([复] calculuses 或 calcu-
li ['kælkjulai]) n. 1.【数】微积分(学)
2.【医】结石,石;牙石,牙垢

Calcutta [kæl'kʌtə] n. 加尔各答[印度东

北部港市]

caldron ['kɔːldrən] = cauldron

calendar ['kælində] n. 1. 历法;日法：the lunar
(solar) ~ 阴(阳)历 2. 历书;日历;月历
3. 日程表;一览表 4.【律】案案日程表

calender ['kælində] n.【机】轧辊机;压
延机;(造纸的)压光机,轧光机
— vt. 把(布、纸等)轧光,压光

calf [kɑːf] ([复] calves [kɑːvz]) n. 1. 小
牛;(鲸、象等大哺乳动物的)仔 2. 小
牛皮 3. 腓,小腿 ‖ ~ love (少男或少女)
对异性的短暂爱情;早年初恋 /'~skin
n. 小牛皮

caliber ['kælibə] n.〈美〉= calibre

calibrate ['kælibreit] vt. 1. 标定;校准 2.
测量 ... 的口径 3. 使标准化 4. 调整;
调节;使和谐,使一致 ‖ ˌcali'bration n.
1. 标定;校准;调整;口径测定 2. [常
calibrations] 刻度

calibre ['kælibə] n. 1. (筒、管等的)内径;
(枪、炮的)口径;(子弹、炮弹的)直径
2. 圆柱径 3. 能力;品格;质量 ‖ ~d
adj. [常用以构成复合词]口径 ... 的;
直径 ... 的

calico ['kælikəu] n. ([复] calico(e)s) n. 1.
〈英〉白布;〈美〉印花布 2. 有斑点的动
物(例如猫) 3.〈美俚〉女人,姑娘;
— adj.〈英〉白布做的;〈美〉花布做的;
(似印花布般)有斑点的

calif ['kælif] n. = caliph

California [ˌkæli'fɔːnjə] n. 加利福尼亚
[美国州名] ‖ ~ poppy【植】花菱草

caliper ['kælipə] n. 1.[常~s]卡钳;卡尺;
弯脚圆规;测径规 2. (纸或纸板等的)
厚度 — vt. 用卡钳(或卡尺、测径规
等)测量

caliph ['keilif] n. 哈里发(伊斯兰教国家
政教合一的领袖称号)

calisthenic [ˌkælis'θenik] *adj.* = callisthenic ‖ ~s [复] *n.* [用作单或复] = callisthenics

calk¹ [kɔːk] *n.* (马蹄铁或皮靴底的)尖铁, 铁刺 — *vt.* 1. ...上装尖铁 2. 以尖铁伤害

calk² [kɔːk] *vt.* = caulk

call [kɔːl] *vt.* 1. 大声读(或说)出; 叫唤; 叫醒 2. 把...叫做, 称呼 3. 认为; 把(距离等)估计为 4. (宣布)召开; 召集 5. 下令举行(罢工等) 6. 召, 征; 传讯 7. 打电话给(在广播、电讯中)呼叫 8. 要求偿还(贷款等); 收兑(债券等) 9.(因天雨等)停止(棒球赛等) 10.(桥牌中)叫牌(某一花色的牌); 吊(对方)摊牌 — *vi.* 1. 叫, 喊; (动物)鸣, 叫 2.(任务等)召唤 3. 访问, 拜访 (on, at) 4.(车、船等)停靠(at) 5. 打电话;(在广播、电讯中)呼叫 6.(在纸牌戏中)叫牌; 吊牌; 叫对方摊牌 — *n.* 1. 叫喊, 叫声; 号召, 号令 2.(动物)叫声 3. 号声 4. 访问, 拜访;(车、船等)的停靠 5.(一次)电话, 通话; 呼叫; ~ letters (或 a ~ sign, a ~ signal)(广播、电讯中)呼叫信号, 呼号 7. 付款要求(或通知); 要求; 邀请; 请求; He has many ~s on his time. 他有许多事要办。/ respond to three curtain ~s 谢幕三次 8. [美] 用于否定句或疑问句]必要, 需要, 理由 9.(神等的)感召; (自然界等的)吸引(力) 10.(鸟兽的)叫声; 鸟声; (引诱鸟兽的)仿鸟兽叫声; 模仿鸟兽叫声的 a duck ...(用来呼鸭的)鸭声哨子 11. (在特定期内)规定入伍人数的命令 12. 点名 13.(纸牌戏中)叫花色; 吊牌; 叫对方摊牌 ‖ ~-back n.(美) 产品返修通知 2.(对暂时停歇职工的)招回 ~ box n. 1.(英)公用电话亭 2.(由用户启用领取邮件的)邮政信箱 / ~-

boy *n.* 侍者, 服务员 2.(戏院中招呼演员准备上台的)催场员 / ' ~-in *n.* (美)(电台或电视台的)听众、观众来电直播节目 / ~ loan 根据要求随时须归还的通知贷款, 活期贷款 / ~ number 图书登记号码 / ~ n. 点名 / '~-up *n.*(服兵役的)征召(令), 征集(令); the ~ -up age 征集年龄

caller ['kɔːlə] *n.* 1. 呼唤者 2. 召集者 3. 访问者 4. 打电话者

calligraphy [kə'liɡrəfi] *n.* 1. 书法 2. 笔迹 ‖ **calligrapher**, **calligraphist** *n.* 书法家

calling ['kɔːliŋ] *n.* 1.(神的)感召;(从事某种工作的)强烈冲动 2. 职业、行业 3. 雌猫的叫春(期)‖ ~ card 名片

calliper ['kælipə] *n. & vt.* = caliper

callisthenic [ˌkælis'θenik] *adj.* 健身操的; 健美体操的 ‖ ~s [复] *n.* [用作单或复]健身操; 健美体操

callous ['kæləs] *adj.* 1. 硬结的; 起老茧的 2. 无情的; 冷淡的 — 无感觉的(to); 无同情心的(to) ‖ ~ 1. 使硬结 2. 使无感觉; 使麻木不仁 ‖ ~ly *adv.* ~ness *n.*

callow ['kæləu] *adj.* 1.(鸟)羽毛未丰的 2. 无经验的

callus ['kæləs] *n.* 1. 硬皮, 老茧; [医]胼胝; 骨痂 2.[植]愈伤组织; 胼胝

calm [kɑːm] *adj.* 1.(天气、海洋等)静的, 平静的 2.(人)镇静的, 沉着的 3. 厚颜无耻的 — *n.* 1. 平静;(儿)无风 2. 镇定 — *vt.* 使平静; 使镇定 — *vi.* 平静下来; 镇定下来(down) ‖ ~ly *adv.* / ~ness *n.* ‖ ~ belt 无风带

calomel ['kæləmel] *n.* [化]甘汞, 氯化亚汞

caloric [kə'lɔrik] *adj.* 1. 热(量)的 2. 卡(路里)的

calorie ['kæləri] *n.* 1. 卡(热量单位)

[C -]大卡,千卡 **2.** 可产生一大卡热量的食物

calory ['kæləri] *n.* = calorie

calumniate [kə'lʌmnieit] *vt.* 恶言中伤,诽谤 ‖ ca**,lumni'ation** *n.* / **calumniator** *n.*

calumny ['kæləmni] *n.* 诬蔑,诽谤;中伤(的话)

calve [ka:v] *vi.* 生小牛(或小鹿等)

calves [ka:vz] calf 的复数

calypso [kə'lipsəu] ([复] calypso(e)s) *n.* 即兴讽刺歌(起源于西印度群岛)

calyx ['keiliks] ([复] calyces ['keilisiz] 或 calyxes) *n.* 【植】花萼 **2.**【解】杯状结构(或器官),盏,盂

cam [kæm] *n.*【机】凸轮

cambium ['kæmbiəm] ([复] cambia ['kæmbiə] 或 cambiums) *n.*【植】形成层

Cambodia [kæm'bəudiə] *n.* 柬埔寨[东南亚国家]

cambric ['keimbrik] *n.* **1.** 麻纱 **2.** 细薄布,细纺(棉织物)

Cambridge ['keimbridʒ] *n.* **1.** 剑桥[英国英格兰东南部城市,剑桥大学所在地] **2.** 坎布里奇(旧译剑桥)[美国马萨诸塞州东部城市,哈佛大学所在地]

came [keim] come 的过去式

camel ['kæməl] *n.* **1.** 骆驼:an Arabian (Bactrian['bæktriən]) ~ 单(双)峰驼 **2.**【船】起重浮箱,打捞浮筒 ‖ ~ ('s) hair 驼毛;驼绒

cameo ['kæmiəu] ([复] cameos) *n.* 浮雕玉石

camera ['kæmərə] *n.* **1.** 照相机;摄影机;(电视)摄像机,暗箱 **2.** 审判员密谈室 **3.** 罗马教廷的财政部 ‖ '~-man *n.* 摄影师,照相师;摄影记者 / '~-shy *adj.* 不愿照相的

Cameroon ['kæmərun] *n.* 喀麦隆[非洲

西部国家]

camouflage ['kæmuflɑːʒ] *n.* **1.** 伪装;伪装物 **2.** 幌子 — *vt.* 伪装;掩饰

camp [kæmp] *n.* **1.** 野营;临时(或半永久性)兵营;营地,设营地;帐篷 **2.** 采木区(或矿区)的新兴市镇 **3.** 扎营同一阵营 **5.** 军队生活 **6.** 露营同性恋的人 **7.**(搞同性恋者的)女性气;装模作样,扭捏作态 **8.** 矫揉造作(或古怪)同令人发笑的东西 — *adj.* **1.** 搞同性恋的 **2.**(男子)女性气的,像女子的;扭捏作态的 — *vi.* **1.** 设营;宿营;露宿(*out*) **2.** 住宿 **3.** 搞同性恋 **4.** 装模作样,扭捏作态 — *vt.* **1.** 使扎营住宿 **2.** 临时安顿 **3.** 装腔作势地做;使装模作样 ‖ ~er *n.* **1.** 野营者,露营者 **2.** 野营旅行的车辆 ‖ ~ bed 行军床,折叠床 / ~ chair 轻便折椅 / ~ fire *n.* **1.** 营火 **2.** 营火会 ‖ /~ fire girl (美国)营火女团团员(从七岁到十八岁) / ~ follower **1.** 随军杂役;随军商贩;营妓 **2.** 依附于某一集团(或派别)者 / ~-stool *n.* 轻便折凳

campaign [kæm'pein] *n.* **1.** 战役 **2.** 运动,竞选运动 — *vi.* **1.** 参加运动;搞运动(*against*) **2.** 作战;出征 **3.** 竞选 ‖ ~ er *n.*

campanile [ˌkæmpə'niːli] *n.* (独立的)钟楼

camphor ['kæmfə] *n.*【化】樟脑,茨脑:a ~ ball 樟脑丸 ‖ ~ ice 樟脑冰(樟脑、白蜡、鲸蜡和蓖麻油制成的油膏) / ~ tree【植】樟树/'~wood *n.* 樟木

camporee [ˌkæmpə'riː] *n.* (美)(地区性的)童子军野营会

campus ['kæmpəs] *n.* 校园,大学,学院

can[1] [强 kæn; 弱 kən](过去式 could [强 kud; 弱 kəd];否定式 cannot[强 'kænɔt; 弱 'kænət],can not,can't [kɑːnt]) *v. aux.* **1.** [表示能力]能,会:*Can* you drive a tractor? 你会开拖拉机吗? **2.** [表示可能性] 可能, 会得: *Can the news be true?* 这消息会是真的吗? **3.** [句首有疑问词而 * 又重读, 表示惊异、迷惑、不解等] 究竟, 到底: *What ~ he mean?* 他究竟是什么意思? **4.** 〈口〉[表示许可或请求, 代替 may, might] 可以: *Can* (或 *Could*) *I borrow two books at a time?* 我可以一次借两本书吗? **5.** [和感觉动词连用, 代替现在或过去时态]: I ~ smell (= I smell) something burning. 我闻到有东西烧焦的气味。**6.** [表示偶尔发生的事情] 有时会: *The writer ~ be* (= is sometimes) *quite sarcastic.* 这个作家有时也很会挖苦的。

can² [kæn] *n.* **1.** (盛液体等的) 容器 (如罐、壶、桶等) **2.** 〈美〉(保存食物的) 罐头 (中又重读, 亦指其内的食品) **3.** 〈俚〉监牢; 厕所 **4.** 〔军俚〕深水炸弹; 驱逐舰 **5.** 臀部 — (canned; canning) *vt.* **1.** 把 (食品等) 装罐头; 给 (机件) 装上罩子 **2.** 〈俚〉把…灌制唱片; 把…录音 **3.** 〈美俚〉开除 (学生); 解雇 (职工); 停用 ∥ ~·**ful** *n.* 一罐, 满罐

Canada ['kænədə] *n.* 加拿大 [北美洲北部国家]

Canadian [kə'neidiən] *adj.* 加拿大的; 加拿大人的 — *n.* 加拿大人

canal [kə'næl] *n.* **1.** 运河: the Grand *Canal* (中国的) 大运河 **2.** 沟渠, 水道 **3.** 〔解〕管, 道 (如耳道, 消化道等) — (canal(l)ed; canal(l)ing) *vt.* 在…开运河; 在…开凿渠 ∥ **canaller** *n.* 运河船; 运河船水手

canapé ['kænəpei] *n.* 开胃薄饼 (或面包、土司)

canard [kæ'nɑːd] *n.* 谣言, 误传, 虚假报道

canary [kə'neəri] *n.* **1.** 〔动〕金丝雀 **2.** 加

那利白葡萄酒 **3.** 〈俚〉告密者 **4.** 淡黄色 **5.** 〔美俚〕姑娘; 女歌手 ∥ ~ **bird** 金丝雀 / ~ **grass** 〔植〕卡内里草芦; 草芦

canasta [kə'næstə] *n.* (由 2 至 6 人玩的) 卡纳斯塔牌戏

Canberra ['kænbərə] *n.* 堪培拉 [澳大利亚首都]

cancel ['kænsəl] (cancel(l)ed; cancel(l)ing) *vt.* **1.** 删去, 划掉 **2.** 取消, 把…作废 **3.** (用邮戳等) 盖销 (邮票等) **4.** 抵消 **5.** 〔数〕约去 (约数); 消去 (方程式或账目上两面的相等部分) — *vi.* 相互抵消力量 (或消去) ∥ **cancel'lation** *n.* / **cancel-(l)er** *n.* **1.** 〔无〕消除器, 补偿设备 **2.** (邮票) 盖戳器, 盖销器

cancer ['kænsə] *n.* **1.** 癌, 恶性肿瘤; 癌症 **2.** 弊端; 社会恶习 **3.** [C-] 〔天〕巨蟹座 (占星中) 巨蟹宫; 出生于巨蟹宫时段的人: the Tropic of *Cancer* 北回归线, 夏至线 ∥ ~ **stick** 〔俚〕香烟

candelabrum [ˌkændi'lɑːbrəm] *n.* [复] candelabra [ˌkændi'lɑːbrə] 或 candelabrums) **1.** 大枝形烛台; 大枝形吊灯 **2.** 〔建〕烛架

candid ['kændid] *n.* **1.** 公正的, 无偏见的 **2.** 坦直的; 坦率的; 直言相告的 **3.** 趁人不备时拍摄的个人形象的 ∥ ~**ly** *adv.* / ~**ness** *n.* ∥ ~ **camera** 快拍照相机; 微型照相机

candidacy ['kændidəsi] *n.* 候选人的地位 (或资格)

candidate ['kændidət, 'kændideit] *n.* **1.** 候选人; 候补者 **2.** 投考者; 攻读学位者

candidature ['kændidətʃə] *n.* 〈英〉= candidacy

candied ['kændid] *adj.* **1.** 糖煮的; 糖腌的, 蜜饯的: ~ **fruits** 果脯 **2.** 结晶成糖的 **3.** (话等) 甜蜜的

candle ['kændl] *n.* 1. 蜡烛;烛形物 2.
【物】烛光(光强度单位) — *vt.* 对着光
检查(蛋等) ‖ '~light *n.* 1. 烛光;柔
和的人工光 2. 上灯时间,黄昏 / '~
.power *n.* 1.(用烛光表示的)光
强度 2. 旧烛光;标准烛光(发光强
度单位) / '~stick *n.* 蜡杆 / '~wick *n.*
蜡烛芯

candou**r** ['kændə] *n.* 1. 坦率,爽直 2.
公正,正直

candy ['kændi] *n.* 1.〈美〉糖果(= 〈英〉
sweets) 2. 冰糖 3.〈美俚〉可卡因 — *vt.*
1. 用糖煮;把……制成蜜饯 2. 使成冰
糖 — *vi.* 凝结成冰,成为结晶;在外层
包糖 ‖ '~floss *n.*〈英〉棉花糖 2.
浮夸(或脆薄)的东西 / ~ striper(穿条
纹工作服的)志愿做护士助手的小姑娘

cane [kein] *n.* 1.(藤、竹等的)茎 2. 藤
料;竹料 3. 手杖;笞杖 4. 甘蔗,糖.棒 4.
甘蔗 — *vt.* 1. 用藤制作(椅子或篮)2.
用笞杖打 ‖ ~ chair 藤椅 / ~ sugar 蔗糖

canine ['keinain] *adj.* 1. 犬的;似犬的 2.
犬科的 3. 犬齿的 — *n.* 1. 犬 2. 犬
齿,犬牙 ‖ ~ tooth 犬齿,犬牙

canister ['kænistə] *n.* 1.(茶叶、咖啡等
的)罐 2.【军】(榴)霰弹 3.(榴)霰弹筒 3.
【军】滤毒罐(防毒面具内用)

canker ['kæŋkə] *n.*【医】(坏疽性)溃疡 ‖
~ous *adj.*(似)溃疡的

canned [kænd] *n.* 1.〈美〉罐装的(= 〈英〉
tinned)2.〈俚〉灌制唱片的;录音的:~
music 唱片音乐 3.〈美〉(新闻稿等)同
时供几家报刊发表的,一稿数用的;刻
板的,千篇一律的 4.〈俚〉喝醉了的 5.
〈俚〉被囚禁的

canery ['kænəri] *n.* 1. 罐头食品厂 2.
〈俚〉监狱

cannibal ['kænibəl] *n. & adj.* 1. 吃人肉

的人(的) 2. 吃同类的动物(的)

cannibalism ['kænibəlizəm] *n.* 吃人肉的
习性;同类相食

cannibalistic [.kænibə'listik] *adj.* 吃人肉
的;同类的;有吃人肉(或同类的肉)
的习性的

cannibalize ['kænibəlaiz] *vt.* 1. 拆取(机
器等)的可用部件;为装配而拆用部
件;用拆下的旧部件修配 2.〈美〉将某
单位的人员(或设备)以充实另一单
位 3. 采用(其他作者或作品)中的资
料 4. 吃(同类)的肉;残杀 — *vi.* 1. 拆
取利用的部件;利用拆取零件进行
修配 2. 在同类单位间调拨人员(或设
备)3. 同类相食,自相残杀 ‖
.cannibali'zation *n.*

cannister ['kænistə] *n.* = canister

cannon ['kænən] *n.* [复] cannon(s) *n.* 1.
大炮,火炮,加农炮(现通常叫 gun)2.
榴弹炮;(飞机上的)机关炮 3.【机】空
心轴;[动]炮骨 — *vi.* 1. 开炮 2. 撞
(*against, into*) — *vt.* 炮轰 ‖ '~ball *n.*
1. 炮弹(现通常叫 shell)2. 快车 3.(网
球赛中的)炮弹式发球 *vi.*(炮弹般地)
疾驶 / ~ fodder 炮灰 / '~-shot *n.* 炮弹
(旧称);射程

cannonade [.kænə'neid] *n.* 炮轰

cannot ['kænɔt, kæ'nɔt] = can not

canny ['kæni] *adj.* 1. 精明的;机警的 2.
谨慎的 3. 节俭的 4.〈苏格兰〉幸运的
‖ canniness *n.*

canoe [kə'nu:] *n.* 独木舟;皮舟;划子 —
vi. 1. 划独木舟 2. 乘独木舟 — *vt.* 用
独木舟载运

canon ['kænən] *n.* 1. 教规,宗教法规 2.
准则,标准,原则 3. 基督教(圣经)的
正经篇各卷;公认的某作家著作集
(或书目)4.〈天主教的〉圣徒名单 5.
【音】卡农;卡农曲 6.【印】48 点西文旧

体活字 7. 天主教弥撒的祭献经文部分 8. 大教堂教士 ‖ **canonical** [kə'nɒnikəl] *adj.* ‖ ～ law 教会法规

cañon ['kænjən] (西) *n.* = canyon

canonize ['kænənaiz] *vt.* 册封(死者)为圣者 ‖ **canoni'zation** *n.*

canopy ['kænəpi] *n.* 1. 华盖;【建】天篷 2. 天穹 3.【空】(飞机的)座舱盖;(降落伞的)伞衣 4. 汽车(或马车)顶篷 ‖【植】树冠层 — *vt.* 用天篷遮盖 ‖ **canopied** *adj.* 遮有天篷的

cant [kænt] *n.* 1. 假话;伪善的话 2. 行业术语,行话 3.(小偷等的)黑话,切口 — *vi.* 1. 说伪善的话,伪谈 2. 讲行话;说黑话 ‖ ～**ing** *adj.* 伪善的

can't [kɑːnt, kænt] = cannot

cantaloup(e) ['kæntəluːp] *n.* 1.【植】罗马甜瓜 2.【美俚】棒球

cantankerous [kæn'tæŋkərəs] *adj.* 脾气不好的;爱争吵的 ‖ ～**ly** *adv.* / ～**ness** *n.*

cantata [kæn'tɑːtə] 〈意〉 *n.* 【音】康塔塔;大合唱

canteen [kæn'tiːn] *n.* 1.(兵营,工厂等的)小卖部 2.(尤指陆军兵营或海军基地附近的)军人俱乐部 3. 临时(流动)餐室 4. 水壶;饭盒 5. 炊具盒;家用分层餐具柜;(放银餐具的)银器柜

canter ['kæntə] *n.* (马的)慢跑 — *vt.* 使(马)慢跑 — *vi.* (马)慢跑,骑马慢跑

canticle ['kæntikl] *n.* 1. 赞美诗,圣歌 2. 颂歌,颂诗

cantilever ['kæntiliːvə, ,kænti'liːvə] *n.*【建】悬臂,悬臂梁 ‖ ～ **bridge** 悬臂桥

canto ['kæntəu] *n.* 〔复〕cantos 1. 诗章(长诗的篇章,相当于书的"章") 2.【音】曲调;女高音声部

canton ['kænton] *n.* 小行政区;(瑞士的)州;(法国的)县;(县以下的)村镇

cantor ['kæntɔː] *n.* (教堂歌咏班的)领唱者

canvas, canvass ['kænvəs] *n.* 1. 帆布 2.(一套)船帆 3.(一顶或一组)帐篷;指马戏团的帐篷 4. 一块油画布;一幅油画 ‖ ～ **back** *n.* 【动】(背羽呈飞鸭色的北美产)帆布背潜鸭 / ～ **shoe** 帆布鞋;网球鞋

canvass, canvas ['kænvəs] *vt.* 1. 详细检查(选票) 2. 详细讨论 3. 在(或向)...游说(或运动)投票,征求意见、订户等) — *vi.* 游说 — *n.* 游说 ‖ **canvasser** *n.* 1. 检票员 2. 游说者 3. 兜揽生意的人,推销员

canyon ['kænjən] *n.* 峡谷

cap [kæp] *n.* 1. 便帽;制服帽;军帽;(天主教红衣主教的)法冠;大学方帽 2. 盖,罩,套 3.【建】柱头,柱帽;(船)帽帽;【植】根冠;(蘑菇的)菌盖 4.【军】火帽,雷管 5. 覆盖岩,冠岩 6.【解】(膝盖骨的)子宫帽 7.【美俚】海洛因丸,迷幻药丸 8. 最高部分,顶部;(经济等的)最高限度 ~(capped; capping) *vt.* 1. 给...戴帽;覆盖 2.(苏格兰大学中)授学位给... 3. 装雷管于 4. 向...脱帽致意 5. 胜过;凌驾 6. 接引(诗句等)(除第一人外,每人引句的首字母必须跟前一人引句的首或末字母相同) — *vi.* 脱帽致意(to)

capability [,keipə'biliti] *n.* 1. 能力,才能 2. 性能;耐受力 — the ～ of a metal to be fused 金属的可熔性 3.[capabilities]潜在能力

capable ['keipəbl] *adj.* 1. 有能力的,有才能的,能干的 2. 有...能力的;(事物)可以...的;做得出(坏事)的(of) ‖ **capably** *adv.*

capacious [kə'peiʃəs] *adj.* 宽敞的,容积大的 ‖ ～**ness** *n.*

capacity [kə'pæsiti] *n.* 1. 容量, 容积 2. 生产量;生产力 3. 接受力;智能 4. 职位;资格:in the ~ of 以……的资格 5. [电]电容;负载量 6. [律]能力

caparison [kə'pærisn] *n.* (装饰性的)马衣;马饰 2. 华丽的衣饰 — *vt.* 给(马)披马衣;把……华丽地打扮起来

cape¹ [keip] *n.* 披肩, 斗篷 — *d adj.* 披斗篷的

cape² [keip] *n.* 海角, 岬; [the C-] 好望角 (= the Cape of Good Hope)

caper ['keipə] *vi.* 跳跃, 雀跃 — *n.* 1. 跳跃, 雀跃 2. 恶作剧;玩笑 3. 〈美俚〉不法行为, 犯罪行为

capillary [kə'piləri] *cdj.* 1. 毛状的 2. 毛细作用的;毛细现象的 3. 表面张力的 — *n.* [解] 毛细管

capital ['kæpitl] *n.* 1. 资本;资产 2. 首都;首府;省会 3. 大写字母 4. [建] 柱头, 柱顶 — *adj.* 1. 资本的:~ goods 资本货物(生产工业品用的生产资料) 2. 首位的;重要的;基本的:a ~ city 首都;首府;省会 3. 可处死刑的;处死的:~ punishment 死刑 4. (口)极好的, 第一流的 — *-ly adv.* 极好, 极妙 ‖ ~ account 资本账户;股本账户 / ~ assets 资本资产(包括资产和专利权等) / ~ expenditure 资本支出 / '~-in,tensive *adj.* 资本密集的, 需投入大量资本的 / ~ letter 大写字母 / ~ stock 股本 / ~ structure 资本结构

capitalism ['kæpitəlizəm] *n.* 资本主义;资本主义制度

capitalist ['kæpitəlist] *n.* 1. 资本家;富豪 2. 资本主义者 — *adj.* 1. 有资本的 2. 资本主义的

capitalistic [,kæpitə'listik] *adj.* 1. 在资本主义中存在的(或经营的) = 有资本主义特征的 2. 赞成(或推行)资本主义的

‖ ~ally *adv.*

capitalize ['kæpitəlaiz] *vt.* 1. 用大写字母写(或印);用大写字母作为开头写(或印) 2. 投资于;提供资本给 3. 使变为资本;使作为资本使用 4. 估计(某一时期内收益率等)的价值 — *vi.* 利用 (on, upon) ‖ ca,pitali'zation *n.*

Capitol ['kæpitl] *n.* 1. [the ~](美国)国会大厦 2. (美国)州议会大厦 ‖ ~ Hill (美国国会大厦所在地)国会山;(美国)国会

capitulate [kə'pitjuleit] *vi.* (有条件)投降

capitulation [kə,pitju'leiʃən] *n.* 1. (有条件的)投降 2. (文件、声明等的)摘要

capon ['keipən] *n.* 1. 阉鸡 2. 〈美俚〉女人气的男人;搞同性恋的男人 — *vt.* 阉(鸡)

caprice [kə'pri:s] *n.* 1. 思想(或行为)的突然变化;奇想、怪念头 2. 反复无常;任性;变化 3. 有丰富幻想力的艺术(尤指音乐)作品;随想曲

capricious [kə'priʃəs] *adj.* 反复无常的, 任性的,无定见的;变幻莫测的 ‖ ~ly *adv.* / ~ness *n.*

capsicum ['kæpsikəm] *n.* [植] 辣椒

capsize [kæp'saiz] *vi.* (船等)倾覆, 翻转 — *vt.* 使(船等)倾覆

capstan ['kæpstən] *n.* 绞盘, 起锚机

capsule ['kæpsju:l] *n.* 1. [医] 囊, 被膜;胶囊 2. [植] 荚膜;蒴果;孢蒴(苔藓) 3. (化)小皿, 小盖皿 4. [空] 航天舱;密封舱;弹射座舱(可与主体分离的)密封小容器;小封袋 5. (覆盖在软木塞外的金属瓶盖)帽 6. 摘要 — *adj.* 1. 简略的 2. 小而结实的 ‖ capsular *adj.*

Capt. *abbr.* Captain

captain ['kæptin] *n.* 1. (足球队等的)队长;首领 2. 船长 3. (英)陆军(或海军陆战队)上尉 4. (美)陆军(或空军、海军

陆战队)上尉 4.(英、美)海军上校 5. 名将;战略家 6.【军】舰长;(飞机)机长 — vt. 做...的首领,指挥 ‖ ~cy, ~ ship 1. 舰长(或上尉等)的职位(或衔头等) 2. 大将的才略

caption ['kæpʃən] n. 1.(章、节、文章、文件等)标题 2.(图片等的)解说词 3.(电影)的字幕 4.【律】法律文件开端部分 5.(英)依法逮捕 — vt. 在...上加标题;在(电影)上加字幕

captious ['kæpʃəs] adj. 吹毛求疵的 ‖ ~ly adv. / ~ness n.

captivate ['kæptiveit] vt. 迷住,强烈感染 ‖ cæpt'vation n. 魅力,吸引力 / captivator n. 有吸引力的人(或物)

captive ['kæptiv] n. 1. 俘虏;被监禁的人 2. 着迷的人 — adj. 1. 被俘获的;被监禁的;被控制的;(气球等)被拴住的 2. 附属于母公司的,由母公司控制的;受羁绊的 3. 被迷住的

captivity [kæp'tiviti] n. 监禁;被俘;束缚

captor ['kæptə] n. 捕捉者;夺得者

capture ['kæptʃə] n. 1. 捕获,夺得;【核】俘获 2. 俘虏;战利品,被猎品 — vt. 1. 捕获,俘获 2. 夺得,占领 3. 赢得,引起(注意)

car [kɑ:] n. 1. 车,车辆 2. 汽车,小汽车,电车 3.(火车)车厢 4. 电梯 5.(飞艇、气球等)吊舱 6.(诗)战车 ‖ ~fare n.(公共汽车、电车等的)车费 / ~load n. 车载的货物,一车的载量 / ~ park (英)停车场 / ~pool(汽车)合伙用车(指一群有汽车的人轮流合用他们汽车中的一辆的安排)/ ~port n.(屋侧的)汽车棚 / ~sick adj. 晕车的 / ~sickness n. 晕车

Caracas [kə'rækəs] n. 加拉加斯〔委内瑞拉首都〕

carafe [kə'rɑ:f] n.(餐桌上的)玻璃水瓶,饮料瓶

caramel ['kærəmel] n. 1. 焦糖;酱色(用牛奶、焦糖等制成的)卡拉梅尔糖 2. ~ize vt. 使成焦糖

carat ['kærət] n. 克拉(宝石的重量单位;等于200毫克);开(黄金成色的单位;纯金的标准为24开)

caravan ['kærəvæn] n. 1.(往返于沙漠等地带的)商队;旅行队 2. 旅行队的牲口;车队 3.(大)篷车 4.(英)(可用马或汽车拖拽的)活动房屋

caraway ['kærəwei] n.【植】葛缕子

carbide ['kɑ:baid] n.【化】碳化物 2. 碳化钙

carbine ['kɑ:bain] n. 卡宾枪

carbohydrate ['kɑ:bəu'haidreit] n.【化】碳水化合物,糖类

carbolic [kɑ:'bɔlik] adj. ‖ ~ acid【化】石炭酸,(苯)酚

carbon ['kɑ:bən] n. 1.【化】碳;~ dioxide 二氧化碳 / ~ monoxide 一氧化碳 2. 电刷碳棒;碳精片;碳精粉;碳精电极 3.(一张)复写纸 4. 复写本,副本 ‖ ~ copy 复写本,副本;(口)极相像的人(或物)/ ~-date vt. 以碳-14 年代测定法测定...的年代 / ~ dating 碳-14年代测定(法),碳定年(法)/ ~ fibre 碳素纤维 / ~ paper 复写纸

carbonic [kɑ:'bɔnik] adj.(含)碳的 ‖ ~ acid 碳酸

carboniferous [,kɑ:bə'nifərəs] adj. 1. 含碳的 2.[C-]【地】石炭纪的

Carborundum [,kɑ:bə'rʌndəm] n. 1. 金刚砂(商标名)2.[c-]金刚砂,碳化硅

carbuncle ['kɑ:bʌŋkl] n. 1.【医】痈 2.【矿】红榴石,红(宝)玉

carburet(t)er, carburet(t)or ['kɑ:bjuretə] n. 1.【机】汽化器,化油器 2.【化】增碳

器

carcass, carcase ['kɑːkəs] *n.* 1. (动物的)尸体 2. (蔑)(人的)死尸;身躯 3. (牲畜屠宰后的)躯体 4. (船舶、房屋等的)架子,骨架 5. (废船等的)遗骸

carcinogen [kɑː'sinədʒən] *n.* [医]致癌物(质) ‖ **~ic** [ˌkɑːsinəu'dʒenik] *adj.* 1. 致癌的 2. 由癌引起的

card[1] [kɑːd] *n.* 1. 卡,卡片;名片;请帖;入场券 2. 明信片 3. 纸牌;办法,手段,妙计;[~s]牌戏 4. (赛马场上、运动会等的)节目单 5. (口)引人发笑的人,怪人 6. 梦卡称废板 7. (美僵)(供吸毒者一次服用的)一服麻醉剂 — *vt.* 1. 在…上附加卡片 2. 把…制成卡片;把(得分等)记入卡片 3. 把…列入时间表 ‖ **~board** *n.* 卡纸板,薄卡纸 / **~carrying** *adj.* 1. 持会员(或党员)证的 2.〈口〉彻底的,真正的 / **~ shark** = **~ sharp(er)** / **~ sharp(er)** *n.* (玩纸牌的)作弊老手,以赌牌行骗为生者

card[2] [kɑːd] *n.* [纺] 1. 梳棉(或梳毛,梳麻)机;钢丝刷 2. 纹板 — *vt.* (用棉机等)梳理;a **~ing machine** 梳棉(或毛,麻)机

cardiac ['kɑːdiæk] *adj.* 心脏的;心脏病的

cardigan ['kɑːdigən] *n.* 卡迪根式茄克衫;卡迪根开襟毛线衣

cardinal[1] ['kɑːdinl] *adj.* 1. 主要的;基本的:~ numbers 基数 / ~ points of the compass 罗盘上的方位基点(东、南、西、北) 2. 深红的 — *n.* 1. 深红色 2. 基数 ‖ **~ flower**[植]红花半边莲

cardinal[2] ['kɑːdinl] *n.* [天主教]红衣主教

cardio- *comb. form* 表示"心脏":cardiogram

cardiogram ['kɑːdiəgræm] *n.* 心电图,心动电流图

cardiograph ['kɑːdiəgrɑːf] *n.* 心动描记器

care [kɛə] *n.* 1. 小心,谨慎,注意 2. 关怀,爱护 3. 照管,管理;负责照管(或办理)的事情 4. 忧虑,烦恼;[常~s]心事,牵累 — *vi.* 1. 关心;注意;介意 2. 计较(*for*, *about*) 3. 喜欢,愿意,想望(*for* 或接不定式) — *vt.* 介意,计较 ‖ **~free** *adj.* 无忧无虑的 / **~-laden** *adj.* 充满忧虑的 / **~taker** *n.* (空屋等的)看管人;暂时行使职权者:a **~ taker** government 看守政府 / **~-worn** *adj.* 受忧虑折磨的,忧心忡忡的

careen [kə'riːn] *vi.* 1. (为修理等)将船倾侧,(船等)倾侧 2. (车辆等)歪歪斜斜地行进 — *vt.* 1. 将(船)倾侧并进行清扫、油漆或修理) 2. 使倾斜,使歪歪斜斜 — *n.* 倾侧;倾斜;歪斜

career [kə'riə] *n.* 1. 生涯,经历 2. (政等的)历程,发展 3. 职业,专业 4. 全速 — *vi.* 猛冲,飞跑(*about*) — *adj.* 职业性的:a **~** soldier 职业军人 ‖ **~ woman** (口)职业妇女(常指长期从事某种职业而不结婚者)

careful ['kɛəful] *adj.* 1. 仔细的;小心的;细心的 2.〈口〉小气的,吝啬的 ‖ **~ly** *adv.* / **~ness** *n.*

careless ['kɛəlis] *adj.* 1. 粗心的,疏忽的;粗枝大叶的 2. 粗心引起的 3. 漫不经心的,不经意的(*about*, *of*) 4. 无忧无虑的 5. (仪态等)不做作的,自然的 ‖ **~ly** *adv.* / **~ness** *n.*

caress [kə'res] *n.* 抚爱;拥抱 — *vt.* 1. 抚爱,抚摸 2. 奉承;哄骗

caret ['kærit] *n.* [印]脱字号,补注号(即"∧")

cargo ['kɑːgəu] ([复]cargo(e)s) *n.* 船货;货物

Caribbean [ˌkæri'biːən] *adj.* 加勒比海的

加勒比人的:the ~ Sea 加勒比海[拉丁美洲] — *n.* 1.[the ~]加勒比海 2. 加勒比人

caribou ['kæribu:]([复]caribou(s)) *n.*(北美)驯鹿

caricature ['kærikətjuə] *n.* 1. 漫画,讽刺画;讽刺文 2.(对别人声音、姿态等的)夸张性模仿;笨拙的模仿 3. 漫画艺术;漫画手法 — *vt.* 用漫画(或讽刺画)表现;使滑稽化

caricaturist ['kærikətjuərist] *n.* 漫画家

caries ['kɛəri:z][单复同] *n.* [医]龋

carillon [kə'riljən] *n.* 1. 钟琴;电子钟琴 2. 钟乐

carmine ['kɑ:main] *n. & adj.* 胭脂红色(的)

carnage ['kɑ:nidʒ] *n.* 残杀,大屠杀

carnal ['kɑ:nl] *adj.* 1. 肉体的,物质的 2. 性欲的;好色的 3. 世俗的 ‖ ~ly *adv.*

carnation [kɑ:'neiʃən] *n.*[植]康乃馨,麝香石竹 2. 肉红色的,肉色

carnelian [kɑ:'ni:ljən] *n.*[矿]光玉髓,红玉髓

carnival ['kɑ:nivəl] *n.*[宗](四旬节前持续半周或一周的)嘉年华会,狂欢节 2. 狂欢;庆祝;欢宴 3. 流动游艺园;(定期的文艺或体育等)表演会;博览会

carnivore ['kɑ:nivɔ:] *n.* 1. 食肉动物 2. 食虫植物

carnivorous [kɑ:'nivərəs] *adj.* 食肉(动物)的

carol ['kærəl] *n.* 颂歌;欢乐之歌;鸟啼声 — (carol(l)ed;carol(l)ing) *vi.* 1. 愉快地唱歌 2. 唱圣诞颂歌 — *vt.* 1.(愉快地)唱歌 2. 歌颂 ‖ ~er *n.*

Carolina [kærə'lainə] *n.*[the ~s]南卡罗来纳和北卡罗来纳 ‖ **North ~**=北卡罗

来纳[美国州名]/**South ~**=南卡罗来纳[美国州名]

carom ['kærəm] *n.* 1.(台球戏中的)连中两球的一击 2. 撞击弹开,撞击弹回 — *vi.* 击中两球

carousal [kə'rauzəl] *n.* 狂欢宴会;闹饮

carouse [kə'rauz] *vi.* 痛饮;狂饮欢宴 — *n.* 闹饮

carp¹ [kɑ:p]([复]carp(s)) *n.* 鲤鱼;鲤科鱼

carp² [kɑ:p] *vi.* 找岔子,挑剔,吹毛求疵

Carpathians [kɑ:'peiθiənz][复][the ~]喀尔巴阡山脉[欧洲中部]

carpel ['kɑ:pəl] *n.*[植]心皮;分离心皮

carpenter ['kɑ:pintə] *n.* 木工,木匠 — *vi.* 做木工活 — *vt.* 以木工活制作(房屋、器物等)‖ ~'s square(木工用的)矩尺,曲尺

carpentry ['kɑ:pintri] *n.* 木工业

carpet ['kɑ:pit] *n.* 1. 地毯;地毯状物 2.[建]磨耗层 3.= ~ bombing — *vt.* 1. 在...上铺地毯;把花草铺在...上;(花草等)覆盖于 2.[英][口]叫人室内训斥 ‖ ~ing *n.* 地毯料;[总称]地毯 ‖ ~bag *n.* 毡制旅行提包(或旅行袋)/ ~bagger *n.* 1.[美](南北战争后)提毡制手提包去南方投机谋利的北方人 2.(英)不属本选区但想参加竞选的人;外来政客/~ bombing[军]地毯式轰炸

carriage ['kæridʒ] *n.* 1. 四轮马车 2.(火车)客车厢 3.(站立时等的)姿势,仪态 4. 运输;运费 5. 车架;炮架(汽车)底盘 6.[机](机床的)滑动承载部分;(打字机等的)滑动架;(电传打字机的)打架 7.(议会中提案的)通过 ‖ ~ clock(正挺放置都会走动的)旅行钟/~ drive(公园等中的)行车道/~way *n.* 车行道

carrier ['kæriə] *n.* 1. 搬运人；递送人；邮递员；送报人 2. 运输业者；运输公司 3.(自行车等的)载重架；4. 航空母舰 5.【化】载体 6.【物】载流子；载波 7.【医】带菌者；病媒 ‖ ~ **pigeon** 信鸽 / ~ **rocket** 运载火箭 / ~ **wave** [无] 载波

carrion ['kæriən] *n.* 1. 尸体的腐肉 2. 腐朽污秽的东西 ‖ ~ **crow**(欧洲产)小嘴乌鸦;(美国南部产)黑兀鹫

carrot ['kærət] *n.* 1. 胡萝卜 2.〈俚〉[~s]红头发的人 3."胡萝卜",诱人而难以得到的酬报(或好处);许诺而不兑现的酬报(或好处) ‖ ~-**top** *n.*〈俚〉红头发的人

carrousel [,kærə'sel] *n.* (游乐场中的)旋转木马

carry ['kæri] *vt.* 1. 运送;运载;手提;肩挑;担负 2. 把...带(到)(*to*) 3. 携带;佩带;怀有 4. 传送;传播 5. 刊登 6. 带有,具有 7. 支撑(柱子等);支撑(屋顶等) 8. 推进;使延伸;把(帐目等)转到下页(或下栏等) 9. 攻占,攻克 10. 使获得赞同(或通过);获得...的赞同(或通过) 11. 使(自己、自己的头部或身体)保持一定的姿势 12. 有(某种商品)出售 13.(土地等)出产 14. 饲养(牲畜) 15.(音调拖得很长地)唱;发音 16. 把...留在账册上;把...作为负债人记入账册 — *vi.* 1. 被携带 2.(枪炮、火箭、声音等)能达到,能传到 3.(议案等)获得通过 4.(文学、戏剧等)有了感染力 — *n.* 1.(枪、炮等的)射程 2. 运载;携带;运载(或携带)方法 3.(船只或货物从一河道到另一河道)水陆联运;陆运 4. 旗手持旗行进的姿势 5. 持枪(或剑)礼 6.〈美国〉需用教护车(或担架)运送的病人 ‖ ~ **out** 贯彻,执行;完成,实现 ‖ ~-**all** *n.* 1. 单马有篷轻便马车 2. 大型载客汽车;(客货两用)旅行汽车 3. 大手提包(或袋) ‖ ~-**ing** **charge** 1. 财产使用费;置存资产费用 2. 分期付款所附加的利息支出 / '~-**ings** **on**[复] *n.* 愚蠢的行为;轻率的行为 / ~-**ing** **trade** 运输业 / ~-**out** *adj.* 〈酒菜〉供顾客带出去吃的;送食上门的 / '~-**over** *n.* 留存物资;剩余物

cart [kɑ:t] *n.* 1.(马、驴、牛等拉的)大车 2.(马、狗等拉的)轻型二轮车 3. 手推车 — *vt.* 用大车运送 — *vi.* 用大车运送;赶大车 ‖ ~-**age** *n.* 运货;运费 / ~-**er** *n.* 赶大车的人 ‖ ~-**ladder** 在大车上为增加容量装的货架 / '~-**load** *n.* 一大车的装载量 / '~-**wheel** *n.* 1. 大硬币(尤指英美金元元银币) 2.(体操动作)侧手翻;(像车轮似的)旋转运动

cartel [kɑː'tel] *n.*【经】卡特尔,联合企业

cartilage ['kɑːtilidʒ] *n.*【解】软骨

cartilaginous [,kɑːti'lædʒinəs] *adj.*【解】软骨的;软骨性的

carton ['kɑːtən] *n.* 纸板箱(或盒);纸盒

cartoon [kɑː'tuːn] *n.* 1. 草图,底图 2.(尤指政治性)漫画;连环漫画 3. 卡通,动画片 ‖ ~-**ist** *n.* 漫画家;动画片画家

cartridge ['kɑːtridʒ] *n.* 1. 弹药筒;子弹筒 2. 暗盒;插入式片盒;胶卷 3.【无】(拾音器)心座 ‖ ~ **bag** 弹药包 / ~ **belt** 子弹带 / ~ **box**(串在皮带上的)子弹盒 / ~ **case** 药筒,弹壳 / ~ **chamber** 1. 药室 2. 弹膛 / ~ **clip** 弹夹 / ~ **paper** 1. 弹壳纸;弹药纸 2. 厚纸,粗面纸

carve [kɑːv] *vt.* 1. 刻,雕刻 2. 切开;切(熟肉、鸡等) — *vi.* 1. 做雕刻工作 2. 切切肉 ‖ ~-**in** *adj.* 〈古〉(诗)镌刻的 / ~-**r** *n.* 1. 雕刻师;雕刻工 2. 切肉人;切肉刀;[carvers] 切肉用具 / **carving** *n.* 雕刻;雕刻术;雕刻品

cascade [kæs'keid] *n.* 1. 小瀑布(尤指大瀑布的一支) 2. 瀑布状物 3.【化】阶式

蒸发器 4.【物】级;串联,级联 5. 一连串;连续大量涌出(或落下)的东西 6.【空】叶栅 — vi. & vt. 1.(使)瀑布似地落下 2.(使)阶式地连接

cascara [kæs'kɑːrə] n. 1.【植】药鼠李 2.【药】鼠李皮(作缓泻剂用) ‖ ~ buck-thorn【植】药鼠李

case¹ [keis] n. 1. 情况,状况 2. 事实,实情 3. 事例,实例 4. 病况,病例;患者 5. 案件;判例;有说服力的论点;情况和理由 6.【美俚】怪僻的人 7.【语】格:the nominative (possessive, objective) ~ 主(所有,宾)格 ‖ in ~ 假使;免得;以防万一 / in ~ of 假使;万一 ‖ ~ history 1. 病历 2. 个案史 / law【律】判例法(以实例为根据的法律) / ~ load (法庭等的)工作量 / ~ work n. 社会工作

case² [keis] n. 1. 箱(子),盒(子);套(子),壳(子);容器 2.(窗等的)框子,架子【印】字盘,活字分格盘 — vt. 1. 把……装入箱(或盒等)内 2. 包,包围(with, up, over) 3.【美俚】探察,查看(尤指企图盗窃时) ‖ ~ harden vt. 1.【冶】使(铁合金)表面硬化 2. 使无情;使麻木不仁 / ~harden ed adj. 1.【冶】表面硬化的 2.(思想等方面)已定形的;无感觉的;无情的

casein ['keisiin] n.【生化】酪蛋白

casement ['keismənt] n. 1.【建】窗扉 2.〈诗〉窗

cash [kæʃ] n. 现金,现款 — vt. 把……兑现 ‖ ~ account 现金账户 / ~-and-carry n. & adj.【商】付现自运(的) / ~-book n. 现金账簿 / ~ crop 商品作物 / ~ register 现金进出记录机,现金出纳机

cashew [kæ'ʃuː] n. 1. 腰果树 2. 腰果(= nut)

cashier¹ [kæ'ʃiə] n. 出纳主任;出纳员;收支员 ‖ ~'s check 出纳(银行)本票

cashier² [kə'ʃiə] vt. 1. 撤职 2. 把……处理掉,抛弃

cashmere [kæʃ'miə] n. 1. 开士米,(山)羊绒 2. 开士米织物;(山)羊绒织物

casing ['keisiŋ] n. 1. 包装;箱;套,罩 2.(油井等的)套管 3.(汽车)外胎 4.(门窗的)框 5.(做香肠用的)肠衣

casino [kə'siːnəu]([复] casinos) n. 卡西诺牌戏;卡西诺赌场

cask [kɑːsk] n. 桶;酒桶;一桶东西

casket ['kɑːskit] n. 1.(精美的)小匣子;首饰盒 2.(美)棺材

Caspian ['kæspiən] adj. 里海的;里海附近的:the ~ Sea 里海[欧亚之间]

casque [kæsk] n. 1.(有面甲的)头盔 2.【动】盔状突起

cassava [kə'sɑːvə] n. 木薯;木薯粉

casserole ['kæsərəul] n. 1.【化】勺皿 2.(烧菜和上菜用的)焙盘;砂锅

cassette [kæ'set] n. 1.(放珠宝、文件等的)盒子【摄】(照相软片的)暗盒 3. 磁带盒;盒式磁带;录像磁带盒;盒式录像磁带 5. 打字带盒 ‖ ~ tape 盒式磁带 / ~ (tape) recorder 盒式磁带录音机

cassia ['kæsiə] n. 桂皮,肉桂 ‖ ~ bark 桂皮,肉桂

cassock ['kæsək] n.(教士穿的)长袍,法衣

cassowary ['kæsəwɛəri] n.【动】鹤鸵,食火鸡

cast [kɑːst, kæst] (cast) vt. 1. 投,扔,抛,撒,掷 2. 投射(光、影、视线等);加……于(on, at);把……的 blame on sb. 归咎于某人 3. 脱落;早产(果实等):Snakes ~ their skins. 蛇蜕皮。4. 铸

(造) 5. 计算; 把(数字)加起来(*up*) 6. 选派...出演角色; 为(戏剧、角色)选派演员 7. 使乐曲; 使套 8. 解雇, 辞退; 删除(牲畜等) 9. [律]使败诉 10. 安排; 分类整理 — *vi.* 1. 投、抛钓钩(或钓丝) 2. 把几个数字加起来; 计算 3. 图谋, 筹划, 打算; 思索 4. (船)改变航向、转向 — *n.* 1. 一掷、一撒、一举; 撒网; 投掷的鱼钩[海] 锤测, (弓)的投(射)程 2. 铸型; 铸件; 模子、模型; 模压品 3. 演员表; 演员表; 派角色; 班底 5. 型、性质; 色调, 特色; 倾向; 歪斜 ‖ ～ er *n.* 1. 投掷的人 2. 翻砂工人, 铸工 ‖ ～ away *n.* 1. 被抛弃的人(或物) *adj.* 1. (人)乘船遇难的 2. 被人搀弃的; 无依无靠的 /～-iron *adj.* 1. 铸铁制的 2. 铁一般的, 刚强不屈的; 坚强的; 强壮的 /～ iron 铸铁 /'～-off *adj.* 被抛弃的; (衣服)穿旧的; 无用的 *n.* 被抛弃的物品

castanets ['kæstə'nets] [复] *n.* [音] 响板(木制或象牙制的圆形凹板, 用手指合击, 作为音乐或舞蹈的伴奏器)

caste [kɑːst] *n.* 1. (印度的)种姓; 种姓制度 种姓地位 2. 等级; (排外性的)社会集团; 等级制度(或地位) 3. [动]级

caster ['kɑːstə, 'kæstə] *n.* = castor

castigate ['kæstigeit] *vt.* 1. 惩罚; 鞭打 2. 申斥, 严厉批评 3. 修订(文章) ‖ ,casti'gation *n.* / castigator *n.*

casting ['kɑːstiŋ] *n.* 1. 投、掷, 扔 2. [机] 浇铸物; 铸件 2. [动] 脱落物(如毛、皮等) ‖ ～ vote (赞成票和反对票相等时主持会议者所投的)决定票

castle ['kɑːsl] *n.* 1. 城堡 2. 巨大建筑物 3. 船楼 4. (国际象棋的)车 5. 藏身处, 隐蔽处 — *vt.* 1. 置...于城堡中; 筑城堡防御 2. (国际象棋中)使(王)与车易位

‖ '～-,builder *n.* 空想家

castor[1] ['kɑːstə] *n.* 1. 海狸, 河狸 2. 海狸香(海狸的性腺分泌物) 3. 海狸皮; 海狸皮帽

castor[2] ['kɑːstə] *n.* 1. (瓶盖上有小孔的)调味品瓶; 调味品瓶架 2. (家具, 机器等的)小脚轮 ‖ ～ sugar 精白砂糖

castor[3] ['kɑːstə] *n.* 1. ～ bean 蓖麻子 [植]蓖麻/～ oil 蓖麻油/～-'oil plant [植]蓖麻

castrate [kæs'treit] *vt.* 1. 阉割, 使丧失精力 2. 删改(书籍) 3. 将(花)去掉雄蕊 ‖ cas'tration *n.*

casual ['kæʒjuəl] *adj.* 1. 偶然的, 碰巧的 2. (工人等)临时的, 不定期的 3. 漫不经心的, 随便的 4. 不拘礼的, 非正式的 — *n.* 1. 临时工 2. [军]待命官兵; 所属部队未定的士兵 3. [～s]便服; 便鞋 ‖ ～ly *adv.* /～ness *n.* /～ ward (英)(济贫院的)临时收容所

casualty ['kæʒjuəlti] *n.* 1. 严重伤亡事故 2. [常 casualties] [军]伤亡人员(包括被俘、失踪、患病等人员); 伤亡 2. (事故中)伤亡者(或损失的物品); 受害者

casuist ['kæʒjuist] *n.* 诡辩家

casuistry ['kæʒjuistri] *n.* 诡辩术

cat [kæt] *n.* 1. 猫; 猫科动物(包括狮、虎、山猫等); 猫皮 2. 心地恶毒的女人; 爱(用指甲)抓人的孩子 3. [船]起锚滑车; 锚架 4. [船]单柄锚钩5. 九尾鞭(旧时海军中的体罚刑具) 6. 履带式拖拉机 7. (爵士音乐演奏者或爱好者)家伙 ‖ ～like *adj.* 像猫一样的, 偷偷摸摸的 ‖ '～-bird *n.* 北美猫鸟(鸣声如猫叫) /'～-boat *n.* [船]单桅帆船 /'～- burglar 翻墙入室的窃贼, 梁上君子 /'～- call *n.* (表示反对或嘲弄的)嘘声 *vt.* 用嘘声反对 *vi.* 发出嘘声 /'～-eyed *adj.* 能在黑暗中窥物的; 有猫一样的

睛的;有旁眼的 /'～fish n. 鮎(科)鱼,鲶(科)鱼 /'～gut n. 羊肠线 /'～head n. 【船】锚架 /'～nap n. 瞌睡 /'～nip n. 【植】假荆芥 /'～-o '-nine-tails ['kætə'nainteilz][单复同] n. 九尾鞭 /～'s eye 1.【地】猫眼石 2. "猫眼",反光镜 /'～'s-paw n. 被人利用的人 2.[气]猫掌风(一种小区域微风) /'～tail n.【植】香蒲 /'～walk n. 狭窄过道

cataclysm ['kætəklizəm] n. 1. 洪水 2.【地】灾变 3. (政治和社会的)大变动 ‖～al[,kætə'klizməl],～ic[,kætə'klizmik] adj.

catacomb ['kætəkəum] n.[常 ～s]地下墓地

catalog(ue) ['kætələg] n. 1. (图书或商品等的)目录;目录册 2. (美)大学情况一览表 — vt. 为……编目录;把……编入目录;按目录分类 ‖ **catalog(u)er** n. 编目人

catalpa [kə'tælpə] n.【植】梓,梓树

catalyst ['kætəlist] n.【化】催化剂;(喻)刺激(或促进)因素

catalyze ['kætəlaiz] vt.【化】催化 ‖～r n. 催化剂

catamaran [,kætəmə'ræn] n. 双体船,双连舟

catamount ['kætəmaunt], **catamountain** [,kætə'mauntin] n. (豹、美洲狮等)猫科野兽

catapult ['kætəpʌlt] n. 1. 弹弓,弹皮弓 2. (古代发射箭、石等的)弩炮 3. (舰或飞机的)弹射器 — vt. 用弹弓射;用弹射器发射;一下子把……抛到高处 — vi. 1. 被弹射 2. 行动迅猛(指好象有发射器推动着)

cataract ['kætərækt] n. 1. 大瀑布 2. 奔流,大水;大雨 3.【医】白内障

catarrh [kə'tɑ:] n.【医】卡他,粘膜炎

catastrophe [kə'tæstrəfi] n. 1. (悲剧等戏剧的)结局 2. 大灾难,大祸;大败 3. 大变动 4.【地】灾变 5.[数]突变 ‖ **catastrophic** [,kætə'strɔfik] adj.

catch [kætʃ] (caught [kɔ:t]) vt. 1. 捉住,抓住,逮住,捕获;钩住;截住;接住;【机】挡住;接牢 2. 赶上(车等);够得上(或突然)撞见,发觉 4. 感染到;着(火) 5. 打(中) 6. 听到;听清楚;领会,理解 7. 引起(注意等) 8. 突然制住(或中止)；～ one's breath 屏息 — vi. 1. 接着,抓住;锁住;结(薄)冰 2. 被抓牢,被钩住:His foot caught on the stub. 他的脚被树根绊了一下。 3. (火柴等)燃着 4. (庄稼)发芽抽苗 5. (棒球中)当接手 — n. 1. 抓;接球 2.【化】(接)受器 3. 捕获物(或量);值得获得的物(或人) 4. 窗钩;门扣;圈套,诡计 5. 难人的问题(或办法) 6. (声息等的)梗塞,噎 7. 轮唱 8. (歌曲等中的)一段 9. 捕捉者;捕捉器;(棒球)接手 ‖～-all n. 放杂物的容器(或地方);包涵甚广的话(或法律术语) /～basin 进水口的滤污器 /～-crop[农]填闲作物 /～-drain 截水沟,泄水沟 /～fly n.【植】捕蝇植物 /～，penny adj. 1. (商品)只求便于推销的;廉价的 2. 起招徕作用的 n. 不值钱的商品 /～phrase n. 引人注意的话(或字句);时髦话;口号 /Catch-22，～-22['kætʃ'twenti'tu:] n. 1. 叫人左右为难的规定(或情况) 2. 不合理的处境 3. 难以逾越的障碍,无法摆脱的困境 4. 圈套 /'～-word n. 醒目字,导字,渡字(印在一页右下角和下页第一个词相同的词) 2. (词典等的)首词 3. 口号,标语(= gabe word) 3. (戏剧说白的)接头语 4. 口头禅;标语;字 **catching** ['kætʃiŋ] adj. 1. (疾病)传染性的 2. 动人的,有感染力的

catchup ['kætʃəp] n. 调味蕃茄酱

catchy [ˈkætʃi] *adj.* 1. 吸引人的 2.(曲调等) 易记的 3.(问题) 使人上当的，难人的 4. 时断时续的

catechism [ˈkætikizəm] *n.* 1. 问答式教学 2.[宗](基督教的)《教理问答》3.(常写成小册子的)一套问答

catechize [ˈkætikaiz] *vt.* 1.用(基督教的)问答法向…传授教义 2. 用问答法系统地教(或指导) 3. 盘问，诘问 — *vi.* 进行问答式教义传授；教授《教理问答》

categorical [ˌkætiˈɡɔrikəl] *adj.* 1. 无条件的，绝对的 2. 明白的，明确的，断言的 3. 范畴的 ‖ **~ly** *adv.*

categorize [ˈkætiɡəraiz] *vt.* 将…分类(或归入) ‖ **categoriˈzation** *n.* / **~ r** *n.*

category [ˈkætiɡəri] *n.* 1. 种类，类，类别 2.[语][哲]范畴

cater [ˈkeitə] *vi.* 1. 供应伙食；提供娱乐节目(*for, to*) 2. 迎合，投合(*for, to*) — *vt.* 为(宴会等)供应酒菜 ‖ **~ er** *n.* 包办伙食的人；筹备文娱节目的人

caterpillar [ˈkætəpilə] *n.* 1.[动]毛虫，蝎 (一般指鳞翅目幼虫) 2. 履带式拖拉机

cathartic [kəˈθɑːtik] *n.* 泻药 — *adj.* 导泻的

Cathay [kæˈθei] *n.*〈古〉〈诗〉中国

cathedral [kəˈθiːdrəl] *n.* 教区总教堂，主教座堂

cathode [ˈkæθəud] *n.*[电]阴极 ‖ **~ ray** [物] 1.(阴极发射出的)高速电子 2. 阴极射线

Catholic [ˈkæθəlik] *adj.* 天主教的 ‖ 天主教徒 ‖ **~ism** [kəˈθɔlisizəm] / **~ity** [ˌkæθəˈlisiti] *n.* 天主教义(或信仰、组织等)

catholic [ˈkæθəlik] *adj.* 1. 一般的，普遍

的，广泛的 2. 宽容的，气量大的 ‖ **~ally** *adv.* / **~ity** [ˌkæθəˈlisiti] *n.*

catkin [ˈkætkin] *n.*[植]柔荑花序

catsuit [ˈkætsjuːt] *n.* 女式紧身连衣裤

catsup [ˈkætsəp] *n.* 调味番茄酱

cattle [ˈkætl] *n.*〈总称〉1. 牛 2. 牲口 3.(贬)大众 ‖ **~ leader**(牛)鼻环 / **~man** *n.* 牧牛人，养牛人 / **~ plague** 牛瘟

catty¹ [ˈkæti] *adj.* 1. 恶毒的，刁钻刻薄的；爱散布流言蜚语的 2. 像猫的；偷偷的；警觉的 ‖ **cattily** *adv.* / **cattiness** *n.*

catty² [ˈkæti] *n.* 斤(中国和东南亚国家重量单位)

CATV *abbr.* 1. cable TV 2. community antenna television 共用天线电视接收系统

Caucasian [kɔːˈkeiziən] *n. & adj.* 高加索人(的)；白种人(的)

Caucasus [ˈkɔːkəsəs] *n.* 高加索山脉(横贯黑海和里海之间) = the ~ Mountains

caucus [ˈkɔːkəs] *n.* 1.(英国政党的)竞选指导委员会 2.(美国政党选举候选人或决定政策的)领导人小组(会)秘密预备会议；核心组织，核心小组 — *vi.* 召开核心会议(或)召开秘密预备会议

caudal [ˈkɔːdəl] *adj.* 尾的；尾部的，近尾的；似尾的 ‖ **~ly** *adv.*

caught [kɔt] catch 的过去式和过去分词

cauldron [ˈkɔːldrən] *n.* 大锅 ；(喻)煮开的一大锅

cauliflower [ˈkɔliflauə] *n.* 1.[植]花椰菜，菜花 2. 花椰菜的花(可供食用)

caulk [kɔːk] *vt.* 1. 填嵌 2.[船]捻(船)的缝；[机]敛(铆钉) ‖ **~ er** *n.* 填嵌工人；[船]捻缝锤 / **~ ing** *n.* 填嵌；捻缝；敛缝

causal [ˈkɔːzəl] *adj.* 原因的；由某种原因引起的；因果关系的

causation [kɔː'zeiʃən] *n.* (某种结果的)引起,导致;因果关系

cause [kɔːz] *n.* 1. 原因,起因 2. 理由,缘故;动机 3. 事业;(奋斗的)目标 4.【律】(诉讼)理由;案件 — *vt.* 1. 使产生,使发生,引起 2. 使遭受,给...带来 2. 使,促使

causeway ['kɔːzwei], **causey** ['kɔːzi] *n.* 1. (穿越湿地或浅水的)堤道 2. (高于路面的)人行道

caustic ['kɔːstik] *adj.* 1.【化】苛性的,腐蚀性的 2.【物】焦散的 3. 刻薄的,挖苦的,讽刺的 — *n.* 1.【医】腐蚀剂;【化】苛性硷,碱性,氢氧化合物 2.【物】焦散面;焦散曲线;焦散面 ‖ ~ally *adv.* 刻薄地,挖苦地 / ~ity[kɔː'tisiti] *n.* 1.【化】苛性;腐蚀性 2. 刻薄,挖苦 ‖ ~ potash 苛性钾,氢氧化钾 / ~ soda 苛性钠,氢氧化钠

cauterize ['kɔːtəraiz] *vt.* 1. 烙,烧灼 2. 使失去...的感觉;使麻木不仁 ‖ ,cauteri'zation *n.*

cautery ['kɔːtəri] *n.*【医】1. 烙器,烧灼器 2. 烧灼剂 3. 烧灼术,烙术

caution ['kɔːʃən] *n.* 1. 小心,谨慎 2. 告诫,警告 3. (口)令人好笑的人(或事) — *vt.* 警告,告诫(*against, to, not to*)

cautious ['kɔːʃəs] *adj.* 细心的,谨慎的 ‖ ~ly *adv.* / ~ness *n.*

cavalcade [,kævəl'keid] *n.* 1. 马队;车队,船队 2. 行列

cavalier [,kævə'liə] *n.* 1. 骑士 2. 对女人献殷勤的男子 3. [C](英国查理一世时代的)保王党党员 — *adj.* 1. 自由自在的;豪强的 2. 献殷勤的 3. 傲慢的

cavalry ['kævəlri] *n.* 1. [总称]骑兵(部队) 2.【军】高度机动的地面部队(包括骑兵部队、机械化部队和摩托化部队) ‖ ~-man *n.* 骑兵

cave [keiv] *n.* 1. 洞穴;山洞;窑洞 2. 地窖 — *vt.* 1. (流水等)使在...中(或下面)形成洞穴 2. 使塌下,使坍下(*in*) — *vi.* 1. 陷下,坍下(*in*) 2. 屈服;垮掉(*in*) ‖ ~ **dweller** 史前的穴居野人 / '~-**in** *n.* 塌落(矿井、地道等的坍陷) / '~-**man** *n.* (石器时代的)穴居野人 2. (尤指对女人)行为粗野的人

cavern ['kævən] *n.* 大洞穴;大山洞

cavernous ['kævənəs] *adj.* 1. 多洞穴的;洞穴状的 2. 多孔的;海绵状的 3. 凹背的 4. (眼睛)深陷的

caviar ['kæviɑː] *n.* 鱼子酱

cavil ['kævil] (cavil(l)ed; cavil(l)ing) *vi.* 挑剔,吹毛求疵,找岔子(*at, about*) — *vt.* 对...挑剔,找...的岔子 — *n.* 吹毛求疵

cavity ['kæviti] *n.* 1. 洞,穴,凹处 2.【解】腔,盂,窝

cavort [kə'vɔːt] *vi.* 腾跃;欢跃

cavy ['keivi] *n.*【动】豚鼠,天竺鼠

caw [kɔː] *vi.* (乌鸦等)呱呱地叫;作鸦叫声(*out*) — *n.* 鸦叫声

cayenne [kei'en] *n.* 红辣椒;红辣椒粉

cayuse [kai'juːs] *n.* 1. 马;[美国西部产的]卡尤塞马,印第安小种马 2. [C]卡尤塞人[美国华盛顿州和俄勒冈州地区的印第安人];卡尤塞语

CB *abbr.* citizens band

cc *abbr.* cubic centimetre 立方厘米

CBD *abbr.* central business district 中央商务区

CCTV *abbr.* closed-circuit television 闭路电视

CD [,siː'diː] *n.* 1. 激光唱片,CD唱片;光盘

Cd [化] 元素镉(cadmium)的符号

CD-ROM [,siːdiː'rɔm] *n.*【计】大容量只读存储器

Ce【化】元素铈(cerium)的符号

cease [sis] vi., vt. & n. 停止,停止 ‖ '~·fire n. 停火命令;停火(期)

ceaseless ['sislis] adj. 不停的,不绝的 ‖ ~·ly adv. / ~ness n.

cedar ['sixdə] n. 1.【植】雪松 2. 雪松木 ‖ '~·wood n. 雪松木

cede [sixd] vt. 割让;转让

ceiling ['sixliŋ] n. 1. 天花板;平顶 2.(价格,工资等的)最高限度 3.【空】绝对升限,使用升限,(飞行员在无氧气供应情况下的最大)升高高度;云幕,云高;云幕底部高度;垂直能见度 4.【船】舱底铺板

celebrate ['selibreit] vt. 1. 庆祝 2. 歌颂,赞美 3. 举行(仪式) — vi. 1. 庆祝 2. 举行宗教仪式〈口〉欢宴作乐 ‖ ~d adj. 著名的,驰名的 ‖ celebrator n.

celebration [ˌseli'breiʃən] n. 1. 庆祝;庆祝会;典礼 2. 宗教仪式的举行

celebrity [si'lebriti] n. 1. 著名;声名,名望 2. 著名人士,名人,名流

celerity [si'leriti] n. 迅速,敏捷

celery ['seləri] n.【植】芹菜;芹菜的茎

celestial [si'lestiəl, si'lestʃəl] adj. 1. 天的;天空的;天上的; a ~ body 天体;神圣的 3.[C-](指封建时代的)天朝的;中国的 — n. 1. 天上的人,神仙 2.[C-](指封建时代的)中国人

celibacy ['selibəsi] n. 1. 独身生活;独身 2. 禁欲

celibate ['selibit] n. 独身生活的人 — adj. 独身的

cell [sel] n. 1. 小房间;单人牢房;〈诗〉村舍;隐居者的小屋;(大修道院的)附属修道院(修道院中的)密室 2.【生】细胞 3. 盒;槽;蜂房巢室。(昆虫的)翅室 4.【植】子房小室;花粉囊 5. 电池 6. 光

电元件;单元 7.【空】机翼构架(气球等的)气囊 8.【气】云泡 9.(政治运动和党派的)基层组织 ‖ '~·block n.(若干监房组成的)监狱分区

cellar ['selə] n. 1. 地窖,地下室 2. 酒窖;藏酒量 — vt. 把...藏入地窖(或酒窖)

cello ['tʃeləu] n.([复] cellos) n. 大提琴 ‖ **cellist** ['tʃelist] n. 大提琴手

cellophane ['seləfein] n. 玻璃纸,赛璐玢

cellular ['seljulə] adj. 1. 细胞的;由细胞组成的 2. 多孔的;蜂窝状的;~ rubber 泡沫橡胶 3.【建】分格式的 ‖ ~·ity [ˌselju'læriti] n. 细胞性‖细胞结构 ~·(tele)phone 蜂窝状(无线)电话,移动电话(= tissue)蜂窝组织

celluloid ['seljuloid] n.【化】赛璐珞;假象牙;硝纤维片

cellulose ['seljuləus] n. 纤维素

Celsius ['selsiəs] adj.(温度)摄氏的

cement [si'ment] n. 1. 水泥 2. 胶结材料;胶粘剂;(牙科等用的)粘固粉 3.【解】牙骨质 — vt. 1. 用水泥结合 2. 用水泥涂 2. 粘接;胶合 3.【治】对...渗碳 4. 巩固,加强;凝成,把...结合在一起 — vi. 粘聚,粘牢

cementation [ˌsiːmen'teiʃən] n.【化】粘结(作用) 2.【治】渗碳处理

cemetery ['semitri] n. 公墓;墓地

cenotaph ['senətɑːf] n.(为葬于别处的死者而立的)纪念碑;衣冠冢

Cenozoic [ˌsiːnə'zəuik] n. & adj.【地】新生代(的),新生界(的)

censer ['sensə] n. 香炉

censor ['sensə] n. 1.(古罗马调查户口、检查社会风纪等的)监察官 2.【新闻、电影、书刊等的】审查员;(信件、电报等的)检查官;【军】保密检查员 3.(英)

大学学监 4.【心】潜意识压抑力 — **vt.**
1. 审查(新闻、书刊、电影等);检查(信件、电报等) **2.** 删改

censorious [sen'sɔːriəs] **adj.** 爱挑剔的,吹毛求疵的;苛评的 ‖ **~ly adv.** / **~ness n.**

censorship ['sensəʃip] **n. 1.** 审查(制度);检查(制度);【军】保密检查 **2.** 检查员(或审查员)的职位

censure ['senʃə] **vt.** 指责,非难;苛评 — **n. 1.** 指责,非难 **2.** 训斥

census ['sensəs] **n.** 人口调查;人口普查

cent [sent] **n. 1.** 分(货币单位) **2.** 分币 **3.** 百:five per ~ 百分之五(5%)

centaur ['sentɔː] **n. 1.**【希神】半人半马的怪物 **2.** 名骑手 **3.** [C]半人马座

centenarian [ˌsentiˈneəriən] **n.** 百岁(或百岁以上)老人 — **adj.** 百岁(或百岁以上)的;一百周年的

centenary [senˈtiːnəri] **adj.** 一百年的;一世纪的;一百周年的 — **n. 1.** 一百年;一世纪 **2.** 一百周年纪念

centennial [senˈteniəl] **adj. 1.** (每)一百年的 **2.** 一百周年纪念的 **2.** 一百岁的;继续了一百年的 — **n. 1.** 一百(周)年 **2.** 一百周年纪念

center ['sentə] **n.**, **vt. & vi.** (美) = centre

centigrade ['sentigreid] **adj. 1.** 百分度的 **2.** 摄氏度的;摄氏温度计的 ‖ ~ thermometer 摄氏温度计

centigram(me) ['sentigræm] **n.** 厘克(= 1/100 克,略作 cg.)

centilitre, centiliter ['sentiˌliːtə] **n.** 厘升(= 1/100 升,略作 cL.)

centimetre, centimeter ['sentiˌmiːtə] **n.** 厘米(= 1/100 米,略作 cm.)

centimillimetre, centimillimeter ['sentiˈmiliˌmiːtə] **n.** 忽米(= 1/1,000 厘米,略作 cmm.)

centipede ['sentipiːd] **n.**【动】百脚

central ['sentrəl] **adj. 1.** 中心的,中央的 **2.** 主要的:an argument ~ to a question 对某一问题极为重要的论据 **3.** 中枢神经系统的 **4.** 走中间道路的 **5.**【语】(中)央的:a ~ vowel(中)央元音 — **n.** (美)电话总机;电话接线员 ‖ **~ly adv.** / **~ness n.** ‖ ~ angle【数】圆心角 / ~ casting(美)电影制片厂演员选派部 / ~ city(大都市的)中心城市 / ~ force【物】辏力,有心力 / ~ processing unit【计】中央处理机

centralism ['sentrəlizəm] **n.** 中央集权制;集中制 ‖ **centralist n.** 中央集权制拥护者 **adj.** 集中制的;拥护集中制的

centralize ['sentrəlaiz] **vi.** 形成中心;集中 — **vt. 1.** 成为...的中心;把...集中起来 **2.** 把(权力等)集中在中央组织,使(国家等)实行中央集权制 ‖ ˌcentraliˈzation n.

centre ['sentə] **n. 1.** 中心,中央 **2.** 中央区 **3.** 中枢;核心;神经中枢 **4.** 中心站:a health ~ 医疗中心 **5.** [有时作 C](政党等的)中间派;中间派的意见 **6.** (球队的)中锋;(军队或舞台的)中央 **7.** 【建】框架,拱架;中心点 **8.**【机】顶针;顶尖 — **vt. 1.** 集中,使聚集在一点:~ attention(efforts)on 把注意力(精力)集中在... **2.** 把...放在中间 **3.** 定...的中心;矫正(透镜等)的中心 **4.** 传(球)给中锋 — **vi.** 居中;有中心;被置于中心:The discussion ~s on(或 round)the most important question. 讨论集中在最重要的问题上。‖ **~less adj.** 无中心的 — **most adj.** 在最中心的 ‖ ~ bit, ~ drill【机】中心钻 / ~ fold n. **1.** (报纸、杂志等中间一张折页的)跨页版面;跨页版面上的图画 **2.** (插在书刊中的)特大折叠插页 / ~ forward(足球

等的)中锋 /'~piece n. 占中心地位的东西(或人物);放在餐桌中央的装饰品

centrifugal [sen'trifjugəl] *adj.* **1.** 离心的;利用离心力的;~ force 离心力 **2.**【医】传出的,离中的 ‖ ~ly *adv.*

centripetal [sen'tripitəl] *adj.* **1.** 向心的;利用向心力的;~ force 向心力 **2.**【医】传入的,求中的 ‖ ~ly *adv.*

centrism ['sentrizəm] *n.* 中间路线;中间派的政策;温和主义 ‖ centrist *n.* & *adj.*

century ['sentʃuri] *n.* **1.** 世纪;百年 **2.** (板球赛中的)百分 **3.**〈俚〉百元 **4.** (古罗马军团中的)百人队

CEO *abbr.* chief executive officer 总经理

cephaloridine [ˌsefə'lɔ:ridi:n] *n.*【药】先锋霉素 I,头孢菌素 I

cephalothin ['sefələθin] *n.*【药】先锋霉素 I,头孢菌素 I

ceramic [si'ræmik] *adj.* 陶器的;陶瓷的;制陶的 — *n.* **1.** 一件陶瓷制品;[~s][总称]陶瓷制品 **2.**[~s][用作单]制陶术;制陶学

cereal ['siəriəl] *n.* 谷物的;谷类植物;谷物制成的 — *n.* **1.**[常~s]谷物;谷类植物 **2.** (加工而成的)谷类食物(如麦片粥) ‖ ~ **leaf beetle** 橙足负泥虫,黑角负泥虫(一种食禾草的害虫)

cerebellum [ˌseri'beləm] ([复] cerebellums 或 cerebella [ˌseri'belə]) *n.*【解】小脑

cerebral ['seribrəl] *adj.* **1.** 脑的;大脑的 **2.** (文学、音乐等)触动理智的;理智方面的(指非感情的) ‖ ~ **palsy**【医】大脑性麻痹

cerebrum ['seribrəm] ([复] cerebra ['seribrə]或 cerebrums) *n.*【解】大脑

ceremonial [ˌseri'məuniəl] *n.* & *adj.* 礼仪(的);仪式(的) ‖ ~ly *adv.*

ceremonious [ˌseri'məuniəs] *adj.* **1.** 仪式隆重的 **2.** (过分)讲究礼节的 **3.** 按照礼节的;客套的 ‖ ~ly *adv.* / ~ness *n.*

ceremony ['seriməni] *n.* **1.** 典礼,仪式 **2.** 礼节,仪仗 **3.** 虚礼,客套

cerise [sə'ri:z] *n.* & *adj.* 樱桃色(的),鲜红色(的)

cerium ['siəriəm] *n.*【化】铈

certain ['sə:tən] *adj.* **1.** 确凿的,无疑的 **2.** 可靠的;a ~ remedy for... 治疗...有效的药;纠正...的可靠方法 **3.**[只作表语]一定的,必然的;some ~ 把握的 **4.**[只作定语]某:a ~ Smith 一个姓史密斯的人/for ~ reasons 由于某些原因 **5.**[只作定语]一些:have a ~ hesitation 有点儿犹豫不决 — *pron.* 某几个;某些;~ of his friends 他的某些朋友

certainly ['sə:tənli] *adv.* **1.** 一定,必定 **2.** (口)当然,当然可以

certainty ['sə:tənti] *n.* 必然的事,毫无疑问的事;必然,确实,肯定

certificate [sə'tifikit] *n.* **1.** 证(明)书;执照 **2.** 证券;单据 ‖ ~**d** [sə'tifikeitid] *adj.* 有证书的

certification [ˌsə:tifi'keiʃən] *n.* **1.** 证明;保证 **2.** 证书

certified ['sə:tifaid] *adj.* **1.** 被证明了的,有保证的:a ~ check 保付支票 / ~ mail 保证邮件(只保证递送,不负责赔偿的一类邮件) **2.** 持有证明书的

certify ['sə:tifai] *vt.* **1.** (用保证书或许可证等)证明 **2.** (医生)证明(某人)为精神病患者 **3.** (银行)担保(支票)的可靠性 — *vi.* 用书面形式证明(to)

certitude ['sə:titju:d] *n.* **1.** 确信,自信 **2.** 准确性;必然性;确实性

cerulean [si'ru:liən] *adj.* 天蓝色的

cessation [se'seiʃən] *n.* 停止,休止

cession ['seʃən] *n.* (领土的)割让;(财产等的)转让;割让地;转让的(或权利等)

cesspit ['sespit] *n.* 污土坑;粪坑;污水坑般的地方

cesspool ['sespuːl] *n.* 1. 化粪池;污水池 2. 污秽场所,藏垢纳污之地

Ceylon [si'lɒn] *n.* 锡兰(Sri Lanka 斯里兰卡的旧称)[南亚岛国]

Chablis ['ʃæbliː] *n.* (原产法国的)夏布利酒

chafe [tʃeif] *vt.* 1. 擦热(双手或皮肤);擦破;擦伤;擦痛 2. 惹怒;使急躁 — *vi.* 1. 磨损;擦伤 2. 磨擦(against, on) 3. 着恼;不满;焦躁 4.(波浪等)翻滚,冲击 — *n.* 1. 擦痛(处) 2. 焦躁;着恼

chaff [tʃɑːf] *n.* 1. 谷壳 2. 秣,草料,切细的稻草(作饲料用) 3. 无价值的东西 4. 诙谐,打趣 — *vt.* 取笑,逗弄 — *vi.* 打趣,开玩笑

chaffer ['tʃæfə] *n.* 讲价钱,讨价还价 — *vi.* 1. 讲价钱,讨价还价 2. 讲条件;做买卖 3. 喋喋不休;闲聊 — *vt.* 1. 做买卖;以…作易货贸易 2. 对…讨价还价 3. 虚耗(时间) ‖ ~ er *n.*

chafing-dish ['tʃeifɪŋdiʃ] *n.* 1. 火锅,暖锅 2.(供桌上烹调用的)轻便炉

chagrin ['ʃæɡrin] *n.* 懊恼,悔恨;委屈 — *vt.* 使懊恼,使悔恨

chain [tʃein] *n.* 1. 链,链条;项链;表链 2. [常~s]枷锁,镣铐;囚禁;束缚 3. 一连串,一系列 4.[测]测链(= 20.1168 米) 5.[纺]经纱 6.[电]电路(= circuit) 7.[化][生]链 8.(公司下属的)联号,一连串 ~ 用链条拴住;拘禁;束缚 2.[测]用测链测量 ‖ in ~s 坐牢的,束缚着的 / ~ bridge 链索吊桥 / ~ gang 用铁链拴在一起的犯罪队

~ **letter** 连锁信(要求收信人看过信后复写成一定份数,再分寄给其他人,如此不断持续以扩大收信人范围)/ ~ **printer**[计]链式打印机 / ~ **reaction** 链式反应;(喻)连锁反应 / ~ **smoker** 一支接一支抽烟的人 / ~ **store** [美]连锁商店

chair [tʃeə] *n.* 1. 椅子;(单人)靠背椅;(单人)扶手椅 2.(会议的)主席;议长;会长;主席席位(或职位);address the ~ (开会时)向主席讲话(表示要求发言) 3. 大学教授的职位(或讲座);[铁路]轨座 5.[美]电椅 6. 轿子 7.[美]证人席 8. 单马轻便马车 — *vt.* 1. 使入座 2. 使就任要职(或会议主席 3. 任(会议的)主席(英把(比赛、选举等中的)得胜者)用椅子高抬着走 ‖ ~ **bed** *n.* 坐卧两用折叠椅 / ~ **borne** *adj.* 坐办公室的(尤指不参加战斗的军官);不搞实际工作专讲理论的 / ~ **lift** 运送滑雪者或游客上、下山的)升降椅

chairman ['tʃeəmən] ([复] chairmen) *n.* 1. 主席 2. 会长;议长;委员长 3. 轿夫 ‖ ~**ship** *n.* 主席(或议长等)的职位(或身分)

chairperson ['tʃeəpɜːsn] *n.* (美) 1. 主席;议长;委员长;董事长;会长 2.(大学的)系主任(此词不分性别,但大多用以取代 chairwoman,一般不作直接称呼用)

chairwoman ['tʃeəwumən] ([复] chair-women ['tʃeəwimin]) *n.* 女主席;女议长;女委员长

chaise [ʃeiz] *n.* 两轮(或四轮)轻便马车 ‖ ~ **lounge** 躺椅,睡椅

chalet ['ʃælei] *n.* 1.(木造的)瑞士农舍(阿尔卑斯山区的)牧人小屋 2. 农舍式房屋;(休假地)小屋

chalice ['tʃælis] *n.* 1.(高脚)酒杯 2. 圣

餐杯中;圣餐杯中的酒 3. 杯状花

chalk [tʃɔːk] *n.* 1. 白垩 2. 粉笔;彩色粉笔:a piece of ~ 一支粉笔 3. 用粉笔画的记号 4. (英)比赛的得分 — *vt.* 1. 用粉笔写(或画) 2. 用粉笔擦 3. 打...的图样 用粉笔记下(货账等) 5.(英)往(田里)施白垩 ‖ ~-**board** *n.* (美)黑板/ ~-**stone** *n.* [医]痛风石/ ~-**talk** *n.* 用粉笔在黑板上作图说明的讲话

chalky [ˈtʃɔːki] *adj.* 1. 白垩的 2. 像白垩的 ‖ **chalkiness** *n.*

challenge [ˈtʃælɪndʒ] *n.* 1. 挑战;要求决斗;邀请比赛 2. 要求;需要;艰巨 3. (对某一表决票或某人投票资格表示的)异议;怀疑 4. (哨兵的)查问 5.【律】(对某陪审员出庭等表示的)反对 6. 激发(指注入抗原以激发免疫应答) — *vt.* 1. 向...挑战;挑动 2. 要求;需要;引起(兴趣等) ~ attention 引起注意 3. 对...表示异议;非难;怀疑 4. 向...发出查问口令 5. 【律】宣布反对(对某陪审员) — *vi.* 1. 提出挑战 2. 表示异议;反对 3.(猎犬在嗅到兽迹时)吠 ‖ ~**r** *n.* 挑战者;反对者;提出争论者 / **challenging** *adj.* 挑战的,引起争论的;使人感到极大兴趣的,诱人的 ‖ ~ **cup** 优胜杯

chamber [ˈtʃeɪmbə] *n.* 1. 室;寝室;(英)[~s]单人套间 2. 议院(或司法机关的)会议室;会议厅;会所 4.[~s]法官议事室;高级官员的接待室 5.(枪的)弹膛,药室 6. (动植物体内的)腔,室 7. 便壶,夜壶 — *vt.* 1. (音乐)室内的 2. (乐队,乐器)小型的 3. 私人的;秘密的:a ruler's ~ council 统治者的私人顾问团 ‖ ~'**maid** *n.* (旅馆或寝室的)女服务员 / (美)家庭女仆 / ~ **of commerce** 商会 / ~ **pot** 便盆,夜壶

chamberlain [ˈtʃeɪmbəlɪn] *n.* 1. 国王的内侍;贵族的管家:Lord *Chamberlain* (of the Household) (英国的)宫廷大臣/ Lord Great *Chamberlain* (of England) (英国的)掌礼大臣 2. 财务管理人

chameleon [kəˈmiːliən] *n.* 1.【动】避役(变色蜥,美洲变色蜥蜴) 2. 反复无常的人 3.[天]蝘蜓座 ‖ ~-**like** [kəˌmiːliˈlaɪk] *adj.* 像变色蜥蜴般善变的;反复无常的

chamois [ˈʃæmi] *n.* [复] chamois [ˈʃæmiz] *n.* 1.【动】(欧洲和西亚山区所产的)岩羚羊 2. 羚羊皮,麂皮,油鞣革

champ¹ [tʃæmp] *vt.* 1. (马等)大声地嚼(或咬) 2. 揿烂 — *vi.* 1. (马等)大声咀嚼;发出吃牙响声 2. 不耐烦,焦急 — *n.* 嚼;嚼声

champ² [tʃæmp] *n.* 〈口〉冠军 (= champion)

champagne [ʃæmˈpeɪn] *n.* 1. 香槟酒 2. 香槟酒色(指淡橙黄色、浅灰褐色)

champion [ˈtʃæmpiən] *n.* 1. 战士,斗士;(主义等)的拥护者 2. 得胜者;冠军;(博览会中的)得奖者 3. 提倡者 — *adj.* 冠军的;优胜的;第一流的 — *vt.* 拥护,支持

championship [ˈtʃæmpiənʃɪp] *n.* 1. 冠军身份;冠军称号 2. 锦标赛 3. 拥护,支持;提倡 4. 冠军称号保持期

chance [tʃɑːns] *n.* 1. 机会 2.[常~s]可能性;或然性 3. 偶然性,运气 — *adj.* 偶然的 — *vi.* 碰巧;偶然发生 — *vt.* 冒...的险;冒险干;使遭受危险 — *vi.* 〈口〉碰碰运气看

chancel [ˈtʃɑːnsəl] *n.* (教堂内圣坛周围供牧师和唱诗班用的)高坛

chancellery [ˈtʃɑːnsələri] *n.* 大臣(或大法官、总理等)的官职(或官署、办公处)

chancellor ['tʃɑːnsələ] *n.* 1.〈英〉大臣;大法官;the *Chancellor* of the Exchequer 财政大臣 2.〈英〉大使馆(或领事馆)的一等秘书 3.〈英〉大学名誉校长;〈美国某些大学的〉校长 4.〈某奥地利等国的〉总理 5.〈美国某些州衡平法院的〉首席法官 ‖ ～ship *n.* 大臣(或大法官、总理等)的职位

chancery ['tʃɑːnsəri] *n.* 1.[C]〈英〉(高等法院的)大法官法庭 2.〈美〉衡平法院 ‖ in ～ 陷于困境的(地),进退两难的(地)

chancre ['ʃæŋkə] *n.*【医】下疳

chandelier [ˌʃændə'liə] *n.* 枝形吊灯

chandler ['tʃɑːndlə] *n.* 1. 蜡烛(制造)商 2. 杂货(零售)商

change [tʃeindʒ] *vt.* 1. 改变;变革;改造 2. 换去;交换;以…换;兑换 — *vi.* 1. 变,改变,变化 2. 换衣;换车(或船等)中的)更动;更换,调换(尤指把旧者换的衣服等) 3. 找头;零钱;辅币 4. 交易所(常作 'change)5.【音】转调,换调 — *n.* 换, 变化 ‖ ～ over *n.* (电唱机的)自动换片装置 ‖ ～ gear【机】变速器;换档齿轮 / ～ over *n.* 改变,转变;变更 / ～ wheel【机】变速齿轮 / 'changing-room *n.* 更衣室

changeable ['tʃeindʒəbl] *adj.* 可变的,易变的;不定的 ‖ ～ability,～ness *n.* / changeably *adv.*

changeful ['tʃeindʒful] *adj.* 多变的,易变的 ‖ ～ly *adv.* / ～ness *n.*

changeless ['tʃeindʒlis] *adj.* 不变的;无变化的 ‖ ～ly *adv.* / ～ness *n.*

Changjiang River 长江 (旧译 Yangtse River 或 Yangtze River)

channel ['tʃænl] *n.* 1. 海峡,水道;航道;the (English) *Channel* 英吉利海峡 2.

河床,河底 3. 沟渠 4. 槽;【机】槽铁,凹形铁 5.〈外交等的〉途径;(情报等的)渠道;系统 6.【电】电路;(电缆的)通道;【讯】频道,信道,波道;【计】通道 — (channel(l)ed; channel(l)ing) *vt.* 1. 在(某地)开辟(或形成)水道 2. 在…上开槽 3. 开辟(道路)3. 为…开辟途径;引导 ‖ ～ize *vt.* = channel

chant [tʃɑːnt] *n.* 1. 歌;单调的歌 2.【宗】赞美诗,圣歌 3. 单调的语调 — *vi.* 1. 唱 2. 单调重复地唱歌(或说话) — *vt.* 1. 唱;单调地唱(或说) 2. 歌颂,颂扬;～ the praises of 对…赞记备至 ‖ ～er *n.* 唱者;吟诵者;唱诗班成员

chantey, chanty ['tʃɑːnti] *n.* 水手的劳动号子(或歌)

chanticleer [ˌtʃænti'kliə] *n.* 雄鸡(源自法国古叙事诗 *Reynard the Fox* 中的拟人化了的雄鸡的名字)

Chanukah ['hɑːnəkə] *n.* (犹太教的)献殿节

chaos ['keiɔs] *n.* 1. [常用 C-] 浑沌 2. 混乱,无秩序

chaotic [kei'ɔtik] *adj.* 1. 浑沌的 2. 混乱的,无秩序的 ‖ ～ally *adv.*

chap¹ [tʃæp] *n.* (口)家伙;小伙子

chap² [tʃæp] (chapped; chapping) *vt.* & *vi.* (使皮肤等)皲裂,皲裂(会粗糙) — *n.* 皲裂(处),皲裂(处)

chaparajos, chaparejos [ˌtʃæpə'reihəus] [复] *n.*〈美〉(牛仔穿的)皮护腿套裤

chapel ['tʃæpəl] *n.* 1. 小教堂;(医院、学校等的)附属教堂 2.〈英〉(学校内的)私人祈祷处 3.(学校等的)礼拜仪式 4. 非国教徒的教堂 5. 印刷职工会 6. 殡仪馆;殡仪馆内的礼堂

chaperon(e) ['ʃæpərəun] *n.* (在社交场所陪伴未婚少女的)年长女伴;(行为)监

护人 — vi. 1. 陪伴,伴随(未婚少女) 2. 护送

chaplain ['tʃæplin] n. (学校、医院、军队、监狱等的)牧师

chaplet ['tʃæplit] n. 花冠;项圈;串珠

chaps [tʃæps][复] n. =chaparajos

chapter ['tʃæptə] n. 1. (书的)章、回 2. (历史或人生的)重要篇章 3.【宗】牧师会;牧师会的例行会议 4.(俱乐部、社团等的)支部、分会 || ~ **house** 1. 牧师会礼堂 2.(俱乐部、会社等的)分会会所

char[1] [tʃɑː] n. 1.[常~s]家庭杂务 2.〈英口〉勤杂女工 — v. (charred; charring) vi. 打杂;做家庭杂务 || ~**woman** n. 〈英〉勤杂女工

char[2] [tʃɑː] (charred; charring) vt. & vi. (把...)烧成炭,(把...)烧焦 — n. 炭,木炭 || **charring** n.【化】炭化

character ['kærəktə] n. 1. (事物的)特性,性质,特征 2. (人的)性格;品质;骨气,名声,声望 3. (小说、戏剧等的)人物,角色;知名人物;〈口〉怪人 4. 书写符号;印刷符号(如"A"、"a"、"4"、"+"、"£"等);(汉)字;字体 5. 身分,资格 6. 品德评语,鉴定;(雇主给雇员的)品德证明书 7. 人物素描 8. (计算机的)字符 || ~**-less** adj. 无特征的,平凡的 || ~ **actor** 性格演员 / ~ **assassination** (对知名人士等的)破坏性,诽谤

characteristic [,kærəktə'ristik] adj. 特有的,独特的;表示特性的 — n. 1. 特性,特征,特色 2.【数】(对数的)首数(环或域的)特征数 || ~**-ally** adv. || ~ **equation**【数】特征方程 / ~ **polynomial**【数】特征多项式 / ~ **root**【数】特征根 / ~ **vector**【数】特征向量

characterize ['kærəktəraiz] vt. 表示...的特性;刻划...的性质;成为...的特征

— vi. (在文艺作品中)塑造人物;描绘性格 || **characteri'zation** n.

charade [ʃə'rɑːd, ʃə'reid] n. 1. (用诗、动作等凑成一个词的)字谜(游戏) 2. 容易识破的伪装

charcoal ['tʃɑːkəul] n. 1. 炭,木炭 2. 炭笔 3. 木炭画 || ~ **burner** 烧炭人;炭炉;炭盆

chare [tʃeə] n. & vi. = char[1]

charge [tʃɑːdʒ] vt. 1. 装,装满;使充满;使饱和;~ a blast furnace with ore 为高炉装料 / The air is ~d with vapour (odours). 空气中每空水汽(各种气味)。2. 使承担(任务、责任)(with) 3. 责令;告诫;指示 4. 控告,指控(with);把...归因于(to, on, upon) 5. 要(价);收(费);要人支付(钱);把...记在账(上);在(账)上记入:~ the purchases to sb's account (或~ sb's account with the purchases) 把所购物品记在某账上 7. 袭击;冲向 — vi. 1. 冲锋,向前冲 2. 收费;要价 — n. 1. 负荷;电荷;(容器的)定量装载物;(炸子弹中所装的)炸药 2. 充电;充气;装料 3. 主管,掌管;看管,看守 4. 被托管的人(或事物);掌人瞻养的人(on) 5. 费用;索取价目;借款;任务(如命令)项目 6. 控告;指控,指责 7. 训令;指示;嘱咐 8. 突然猛攻;冲锋 9. 冲锋号 || ~**-able** adj. 1. 应(或可)支付的应入账的 2. 可能该应指控的 / ~d adj. 1. 充满强烈感情的;(气氛等)紧张的 / ~r n. 装料人;装料机 2. 充电器 3. 充电器 4. 冲锋马;战马 5. 委托者 6. 控诉者 || ~ **account**〈美〉(客户购货的)赊购制;赊欠户(= credit account) / ~ **plate**, **plate** n. 赊货牌(顾客购货时用的一种金属小牌) / ~ **nurse**〈英〉护士长 —

sheet(警察局中的)案情记录

chargé d 'affaires [ˌʃɑːʒeidə'fɛə] ([复] **chargés d 'affaires** [ˌʃɑːʒei(z)də'fɛə]) *n.* (使馆中的)代办

chariot ['tʃæriət] *n.* **1.** (古代的马拉)双轮战车；战车 **2.** 轻便四轮马车 **3.** (旧)漂亮的彩车；凯旋车 ‖ ~**eer** [ˌtʃæriə'tiə] *n.* 驾驶马车(或战车)者

charisma [kə'rizmə] ([复] charismata [kə'rizmətə] 或 charism ['kærizəm]) *n.* **1.** (一般认为领袖人物才具有的)领袖气质, 个人魅力 **2.** 魅力；性感 **3.** 神授的超凡能力 ‖ **charismatic** [ˌkæriz'mætik] *adj.*

charitable ['tʃæritəbl] *adj.* **1.** 大慈大悲的；慈善的 **2.** 宽厚的 ‖ ~**ness** *n.* / **charitably** *adv.*

charity ['tʃæriti] *n.* **1.** [宗]上帝对人类之爱, (基督教徒间的)兄弟之爱；博爱 **2.** 施舍(行为)；慈善事业；慈善团体；赈济(物) **4.**(对别人的)宽大, 宽容, 宽厚 ‖ ~ **school** 慈善学校

charlatan ['ʃɑːlətən] *n.* **1.** 庸医；骗子；冒充内行的人

charm [tʃɑːm] *n.* **1.** 魅力, 魔力 **2.** [常~s] 妩媚；诱人之处 **3.** 咒文；咒语；咒符；随身护符 **4.** 表链(或手镯等)上的小饰物 — *vt.* **1.** 对...行魔法；用魔法(或符咒)保护；(用魔法)控制；耍(蛇等)**2.** 迷住；陶醉；使...具有神力 **4.** (用魔法、魅力等)治愈(疾病、悲伤等)(*away, off*);诱出 — *vi.* **1.** 行魔法 **2.** 有魔力, 令人陶醉 ‖ ~**er** *n.* **1.** 魔术师 **2.** 要蛇的人 **3.** 使人着迷的人(或物)

charming ['tʃɑːmiŋ] *adj.* **1.** 媚人的；可爱的, 极好的 **2.** 施展魔力的；使魔法的 ‖ ~**ly** *adv.*

charnel ['tʃɑːnl] *n. & adj.* 藏骸所(的) ‖ ~ **house** 藏骸所

charrette [ʃə'ret] *n.*(邀请专家参加的)问题讨论会

chart [tʃɑːt] *n.* **1.** 海图, 航海图 **2.** 图；图表；曲线(标绘)图 **3.**(仪器带有刻度的)记录纸 — *vt.* **1.** 制...的海(或地)图；把(航线等)绘入海图；(喻)指引(航向) **2.** 用图表表示(或说明) **3.** 制订...的计划 ‖ ~**ist** *n.* 地图(或图表)绘制员；预测证券市场行情的图表制作和研究者 / ~**less** *adj.* **1.** 未绘入海图的 **2.** 无图(表)的；无向导的 ‖ ~ **house**, ~ **room**(船上的)海图室

charter ['tʃɑːtə] *n.* **1.**(政府对成立自治市、公司等的)特许状, 凭照；(社团对成立分会等的)许可证 **2.** 宪章 **3.** 特权；豁免权 **4.** 契据；证书 **5.**(船只、飞机、公共汽车等的)租用 **6.** 租船契约(= ~ party) — *vt.* **1.** 特许(成立公司等);发执照给 : a ~ed accountant (英国皇家)特许会计师(持有皇家特许状, 为会计师协会会员) **2.** 租, 包(船、飞机、车辆等) ‖ ~**er** *n.* 租船人；租用者 / ~ **member**(社团等的)创始成员 / ~ **party** 租船契约, 租船合同

chary ['tʃɛəri] *adj.*(对...)谨慎小心的(*of*)

chartreuse [ʃɑː'trɜːz] *n. & adj.* 淡黄绿色(的), 苹果绿色的)

chase [tʃeis] *vt.* **1.** 追逐, 追赶；追击；追猎 **2.** 驱逐 **3.** 寻觅, 找寻出(*down*) — *vi.* **1.** 追逐, 追赶；跟踪(*after*) **2.** 匆忙地走；奔跑 — *n.* **1.** 追逐, 追赶；追击；追猎；追求 **2.** [the ~]打猎 **3.** 被追猎的动物；被追逐的人(或物)(如船等) **4.** [总称]追猎者 **5.**(英)狩猎地；(允许在一定区域打猎或饲养猎物的)狩猎

权 6.〈美俚〉紧张而忙乱的活动

chasm ['kæzəm] **n.** 1.【地】(地壳的)陷窟，裂隙；裂口；峡谷，深渊 2.〈意见、感情、兴趣等的〉大分歧 3.〈一连串事件的〉中断

chassis ['ʃæsi]〈复 chassis ['ʃæsiz]〉 **n.** 1. 机壳；底架〈汽车等的〉底盘 2.〈飞机的〉机架；炮底架 3.〈俚〉身躯，体格

chaste [tʃeist] **adj.** 1. 贞洁的 2. 纯洁的；高雅的 2.〈文风等〉简洁朴实的 ‖ ~ly **adv.** / ~ness **n.**

chasten ['tʃeisn] **vt.** 1. 惩戒，责罚 2. 遏制；使缓和 3. 磨练；纯洁（思想等）；锤炼（文章）‖ ~er **n.** 惩戒者，责罚者

chastise [tʃæs'taiz] **vt.** 惩罚；严惩；责打 ‖ ~ment **n.** / ~er **n.** 惩罚者，责打者

chastity ['tʃæstiti] **n.** 1. 贞洁 2. 纯洁；高雅 3.〈文风等的〉简洁朴实

chat [tʃæt] **n. & vi.** 闲谈，聊天 ‖ ~show〈电视、无线电广播的〉访谈节目（= talk show）

château ['ʃætəu]〈复 châteaux 或 châteaux ['ʃætəu(z)]〉 **n.** 1. 法国城堡 2.〈法国或欧洲国家的〉别墅，庄园 3. 葡萄种植园

chattel ['tʃætl] **n.** 1.〈一件〉动产 2. 准不动产 3. 奴隶

chatter ['tʃætə] **vi.** 1. 喋喋不休；饶舌 2.（鸟）啁啾，（松鼠等）吱吱叫；（溪流）潺潺作声；（机器）震颤，震动 3.（牙齿）打战 — **vt.** 喋喋地说出 — **n.** 喋喋不休；啁啾，震颤声 ‖ ~er **n.** 1. 喋喋不休的人 2.【动】鹩莺；太平鸟，十二黄 ‖ ~box **n.** 唠唠叨叨的人，话匣子

chatty ['tʃæti] **adj.** 1. 爱闲聊的 2.（谈话等）非正式的，亲切的，聊天式的 ‖ chattily **adv.** / chattiness **n.**

chauffeur ['ʃəufə] **n.**（受雇于私人或公司等的）汽车司机 — **vi.** 做汽车司机工

作 — **vt.** 1. 为…开车，开汽车送 2. 开（汽车等）

chauvinism ['ʃəuvinizəm] **n.** 1. 沙文主义 2. 本民族第一主义；本性别第一主义 ‖ **chauvinist** n.

cheap [tʃi:p] **adj.** 1. 便宜的，廉价的 2. 低劣的，劣质的；可鄙的 3. 虚伪的；低级的 4. 轻于费的 5.（商店等）收费低廉的；〈英〉特别减价的 6.（胜利等）容易赢得的 — **adv.** 便宜地，廉价地 ‖ ~ly **adv.** / ~ness **n.** ‖ ~-jack **n.** 贩卖劣质商品的人；质量低劣的

cheapen ['tʃi:pən] **vt.** 1. 降低…的价格 2. 降低…的威信；降低…的地位 3. 使变得粗俗，使变得低级 — **vi.** 减价，跌价

cheat [tʃi:t] **n.** 1. 欺诈；欺骗行为；骗局 2. 骗子 3. 雀麦 — **vt.** 1. 骗取，诈取（某人）（out, of）2. 哄，骗（某人）（into）3. 消磨（时间）；消除（疲劳等）4. 用智谋挫败（对方）；逃脱（死亡等）— **vi.** 欺诈；作弊 ‖ ~er **n.** 1. 骗子 2.〈俚〉[cheaters] 眼镜

check [tʃek] **n.** 1. 制止；控制；制止者（或物）；挫败；制服 2. 突然停止 3. 检查，检验，核对；钩形符号，"√"号 4. 寄存物的凭证；号牌；行李票 5.〈美〉支票（=〈英〉cheque）；（餐馆的）账单；（赌博的）筹码 6.（象棋中）被"将军"的局面 7.（木材或钢铁等的）裂缝，裂口；（玻璃的）一裂小方格；格子织物；格纹 — **vt.** 1. 制止；控制；妨碍；停止 2. 检查；核对（账）；上打上"√"号，用钩形符号标出 3.〈美〉寄存；托运 4.（象棋中）将（对方的）"王"一军 5. 使产生裂缝 6. 在…上画（或印）方格图案 7.〈美〉把（田地）划成方格进行栽植；纵横成行地栽植（作物）— **vi.** 1. 逐项相符

2.〈美〉开支票 3. 开裂, 龟裂 4.(象棋中)将一军 — *int.* 1.〈口〉行! 对! 2.(象棋用语)将! ‖ ~ed *adj.* 有格子花的 ‖ ~book *n.* 〈美〉支票簿（=〈英〉chequebook）/ ~-in *n.* 住进旅馆; 签到; 报到; 抵达(出借物的)登记收回 / ~-list *n.* 1.(核对用的)清单, 选民花名册(上的"王") 3. 打败; 使受挫折 *n.* (象棋中"王"的)将死 2. 大败; 垮台 / ~nut【机】防松螺母 / ~-out *n.* 1.(从旅馆等的)结账离开(从工厂等的)下班离开(客人等的)离去; (书等的)出借 2. 查查, 检验; 〈美〉熟悉机械性能 3.(超级市场等的)付款台 / ~-over *n.* 1.(旅馆等处)旅客必须结账离开的时间 / ~post *n.* 边防(或公路)检查站 / ~-room *n.* 〈美〉衣帽间; 行李寄存处(=〈英〉cloakroom)/ ~ taker 收票员 / ~-up *n.* 1. 检查, 查对 2.〈美〉体格检查

checker ['tʃekə] *n.* 1. 制止者, 阻止者; 查对者 2. = chequer — *vt.* = chequer

checkerboard ['tʃekəbɔːd] 〈美〉 *n.* 棋盘; 方格图案 — *vt.* 在……上面纵横交错地排列(或图案)

checkered ['tʃekəd] *adj.* 〈美〉= chequered

cheddar ['tʃedə] *n.* 1.(原产英国切达的)切达干酪 2. 美国干酪

cheek [tʃiːk] *n.* 1. 面颊, 脸蛋 2. 厚脸皮; 没礼貌(或冒失)的话(或行为) 3.[~s] 机械(或器具)上两侧成对的部件; 【机】颊板; 中型箱 / ~-bone *n.* 颧骨

cheeky ['tʃiːki] *adj.* 不要脸的, 厚颜无耻的 ‖ cheekily *adv.* /cheekiness *n.*

cheep [tʃiːp] *vt. & vi.* (小鸟等)吱吱地叫 — *n.* 吱吱的叫声

cheer [tʃiə] *vt.* 1. 使振奋, 使高兴, 使安慰 2.……而欢呼; 为……而高呼 3.以

欢呼声激励 4. 为……喝彩; 向……欢呼 — *vi.* 1. 感到振奋, 感到高兴(up) 2. 欢呼; 喝彩 — *n.* 1. 振奋, 高兴 2. 欢呼; 喝彩 3. 心情; What ~? 你感到怎样? 4. 款待; 欢迎 5. 菜肴; 酒菜 ‖ ~-ing *n.* 欢呼; 喝彩 *adj.* 令人振奋的, 令人高兴的 / ~-less *adj.* 缺乏欢乐的, 阴暗的, 惨淡的 ‖ ~-leader *n.* 啦啦队队长

cheerful ['tʃiəful] *adj.* 1. 快乐的; 高兴的 2. 乐意的, 心甘情愿的 3. 使人感到愉快的; 使人振奋的 ‖ ~-ly *adv.* / ~-ness *n.*

cheery ['tʃiəri] *adj.* 1. 喜气洋洋的, 兴高采烈的; 活泼的 2.(天气等)爽快的

cheese [tʃiːz] *n.* 1. 干酪, 奶酪 2.(形状、质地或口味)像干酪的东西 / ~-burger ['tʃiːzbəːgə] *n.* 干酪汉堡包 / ~-cake *n.* 1. 干酪饼 2.(照片、广告等中的)富于性感的裸体(或半裸体)女人像; 女子的性魅力 / ~-cloth *n.* 干酪包布 / ~-paring *n. & adj.* 吝啬(的), 小气(的)

cheetah ['tʃiːtə] *n.*【动】(经训练可用于狩猎的)猎豹

chef [ʃef] *n.* 厨师; 厨师长

chemical ['kemikəl] *adj.* 化学的; 化学上用的; 用化学方法得到的 — *n.* [常~s]化学制品; 化学药品 ‖ ~-ly *adv.*

chemise [ʃə'miːz] *n.* 女式无袖衬衫

chemist ['kemist] *n.* 1. 化学家; 化学师 2.〈英〉药剂师; 药品商;a ~'s shop 〈英〉药房

chemistry ['kemistri] *n.* 1. 化学 2. 物质的化学组成(或特性) 3. 化学过程(或现象) 4. 神秘的变化; 不可思议的作用

chemotherapy [ˌkeməˈθerəpi] *n.*【医】化学疗法

chemurgy [ˈkeməːdʒi] *n.* 农业化学加工

cheque [tʃek] *n.* 支票(= 〈美〉check) ‖ '~-book *n.* 支票簿(= 〈美〉checkbook)

chequer [ˈtʃekə] *n.* 1. 西洋跳棋子;西洋跳棋 2. 方格图案;格子花 3.[植]花楸果 — *vt.* 1. 把……画(或制)成方格图案形 2.[常用被动语态]使变化无常

chequered [ˈtʃekəd] *adj.* 1. 有格子花(或方格图案)的 2. 盛衰无常的;多波折的

cherish [ˈtʃeriʃ] *vt.* 1. 爱护;抚育;珍爱 3. 抱有(希望);怀有(感情等)

cherry [ˈtʃeri] *n.* 1. 樱桃 2. 樱桃树;樱桃木 3. 樱桃色,鲜红色 4.〈俚〉处女膜;处女(状态) — *adj.* 1. 樱桃色的,鲜红色的 2. 樱桃木制的 3. 樱桃制的 ‖ 有樱桃味的

cherub [ˈtʃerəb] *n.* 1. 小天使(绘画或雕塑中可爱的孩子) 2. 天真可爱的人(尤指孩子);胖娃娃 3.([复]cherubim [ˈtʃerəbim])【宗】(九级天使中第二级可知识的)二级天使 ‖ ~ic [tʃeˈruːbik] *adj.* 小天使(似)的;天真可爱的;(脸)胖胖的

chess [tʃes] *n.* 国际象棋 ‖ '~-board *n.* 国际象棋棋盘 / '~-man *n.* 国际象棋棋子

chest [tʃest] *n.* 1. 箱子,柜子,盒子 2. 金库,钱库;公款;资金 3. 胸腔;胸膛 ‖ ~ed *adj.* [用以构成复合词]有……胸腔的:pigeon-~ed [医]鸡胸闷

chestnut [ˈtʃesnʌt] *n.* 1. 栗子 2. 栗树;栗木 3. 栗色,栗色马 4.〈口〉陈腐的笑话(或故事等) 5. 马腿内侧的胼胝 — *adj.* 栗子(似)的;栗色的

cheviot [ˈtʃeviət] *n.* [纺]啥咪呢,粗纺厚呢

chevron [ˈʃevrən] *n.* 1.(纹章)人字形标识 2.[军]V形臂章 3.[建]波浪饰,锯

齿形花饰

chew [tʃuː] *vt.* 嚼;咀嚼;嚼碎 — *vi.* 1. 咀嚼 2. 嚼烟草 3. 深思,细想(over, upon) — *n.* 1. 咀嚼 2. 咀嚼物(例如烟)

Chianti [kiˈænti] *n.*(意大利)基安蒂红葡萄酒

chic [ʃik] *n. & adj.*〈法〉漂亮(的);时式(的);潇洒(的)

Chicago [ʃiˈkɑːgəu] *n.* 芝加哥[美国伊利诺斯州东北部港市]

Chicana [tʃiˈkɑːnə] *n.* 奇卡诺女人(参见Chicano)

Chicano [tʃiˈkɑːnəu] ([复]Chicanos) *n.* 奇卡诺人(指墨西哥裔美国人)

chick [tʃik] *n.* 1. 小鸡;小鸟 2. 小孩 3.〈俚〉少妇 ‖ '~-pea *n.* [植]鹰嘴豆 / '~-weed *n.* [植]卷耳;繁缕

chickadee [ˈtʃikədiː] *n.* 〈美〉山雀

chicken [ˈtʃikin] *n.* 1. 小鸡;小鸟;〈美〉鸡;家禽 2. 鸡肉 3. 年轻人;没有经验的人;〈俚〉年轻女子 4. 胆怯的人,懦夫 5.〈美俚〉(军队中)军毛蓝皮的规定,琐规 — *adj.* 1. 鸡肉制的 2.(海虾等)小而嫩的 3.〈美俚〉胆怯的;软弱的 4.〈美俚〉严守琐规的 — *vi.*〈美俚〉害怕,畏缩;逃跑(out) ‖ '~-and-'egg *adj.* 鸡与蛋孰先难定的;因果(或先后次序)难定的 / ~ breast [医]鸡胸 / '~-breasted *adj.* [医](有)鸡胸的 / ~ cholera 鸡霍乱 / ~ feed 1. 鸡食 2.〈俚〉小额钱币;零钱;为数甚微的款项 / '~-hearted *adj.* 胆怯的;软弱的 / ~ pox [医]水痘

chicle [ˈtʃikl] *n.*[化]糖胶树胶(用于制口香糖)

chicory [ˈtʃikəri] *n.*[植]菊苣;(用作咖啡代用品的)菊苣根

chide [tʃaid](过去式 chid[tʃid]或 chided,

过去分词 chid 或 chidden ['tʃidn]或 chided) *vt. & vi.* 责骂,责备 ‖ ~ **r** *n.*

chief ['tʃiːf] *n.* **1.** 首领,领袖 **2.** 主任;首
长(称呼用)**3.** 长官 **4.** 主体,头子 **4.**
(人生等的)主要部分;最有价值的部
分 — *adj.* **1.** 主要的,首要的 **2.** 首席
的;主任的:a ~ engineer 总工程师;
【海】轮机长上士 / ~ justice 首席法官/a ~
executive 主管人;总经理(美国常指总
统、州长等)/a ~ mate(或 officer)【海】
大副/a ~ petty officer(美)海军军士
长/(英)海军上士 /a ~ warrant officer
(美)陆军(或空军)一级准尉

chiefly ['tʃiːfli] *adv.* 主要地;首要地;尤
其

chieftain ['tʃiːftən] *n.* **1.**(强盗、土匪等
的)首领,头子 **2.**(苏格兰高地的)族
长;酋长 **3.**(诗)指挥官;队长 ‖ ~**cy,**
~**ship** *n.* 首领(或头子、族长等)的地
位

chiffon [ʃiːfɔn] *n.* 【纺】雪纺绸,薄绸

chiffonier [ˌʃifəˈniə] *n.* 碗橱;五斗橱

chigger ['tʃiɡə] *n.* 【动】恙螨

chilblain ['tʃilblein] *n.* [常 ~]冻疮 ‖
~**ed** *adj.* 生冻疮的

child [tʃaild] *n.* [复] **children** ['tʃildrən]]
1. 胎儿,婴儿 **2.** 小孩子(可指男孩或女
孩) Children's Day 儿童节 **3.** 儿子;
女儿 **4.** 子孙,后裔 **5.** 有孩子气的人;
幼稚的人 **6.** 作为某种行为的产物 **7.**
产物,追随者,依附者 ‖ ~**hood** *n.* 幼
年(时代);童年;早期/~**less** *adj.* 无子
女的/~**like** *adj.* 孩子般天真的,单纯;
诚实的 ‖/~**bearing** *n.* 分娩;生产/~
bed *n.* 产褥;分娩(状态)/~**birth** *n.*
分娩;生产/~**bride** *n.* 少新娘 **2.** 童养
媳/~ **labour** 童工,童工的雇用 /
~**mind** *vi.*(代人)照看孩子,照看儿童
/~**minder** *n.*(代人)照看孩子者;保

育员/~ **proof** *adj.* 能防止孩童瞎摸弄
的;对孩童安全的、不会被孩童弄坏的
/~ **wife** 少妻

childish ['tʃaildiʃ] *adj.* **1.** 孩子的;孩子特
有的 **2.** 幼稚的;傻气的 ‖ ~**ly** *adv.*
/~**ness** *n.*

children ['tʃildrən] child 的复数

childrenese [ˌtʃildrəˈniːz] *n.*(美)儿语;儿
童的说话方式

Chile ['tʃili] *n.* 智利[南美洲西南部国
家]

Chilean, Chilian [ˈtʃiliən] *n.* 智利人 —
adj. 智利的;智利人的;智利文化的

chili ['tʃili] *n.* = chilli

chill [tʃil] *n.* **1.** 寒冷,寒气 **2.** 寒战;风寒
3. 扫兴;寒心 **4.**(态度的)冷淡 **5.**【冶】
冷铁;激冷层 **6.** 凉飕飕的(冷铁)— *adj.*
寒冷的;激冷的 — *vt.* **1.** 使
变冷;使感到寒冷 **2.**(轻度)冷冻 **3.** 使
扫兴;使寒心;使沮丧 **4.**【冶】给 ... 作
激冷处理 — *vi.* **1.** 变冷;感到寒冷,发
冷 **2.**[口]激冷 — *n.* **1.** 惊险小说
2.(冰箱内的)食品冷冻格 **3.** 脱糖冷冻
结晶器 **4.** 冷却器 **5.** 冷冻工人 ‖ ~**ness**
n. ‖ ~ **factor**[气]风寒指数

chilli ['tʃili] *n.*(干)辣椒

chilly ['tʃili] *adj.* **1.** 寒冷的 **2.** 感到寒冷
的 **3.** 冷淡的,不友好的 **4.** 使人寒心
(或恐惧)的

chime [tʃaim] *n.* **1.** 排钟,编钟,管钟
2. [常 ~s](排钟等的)钟声,钟
乐 **3.** 类似钟声的声音;悦耳的音调 **4.**
协调;和谐;一致 — *vi.* **1.**(排钟等)奏
出谐和的乐声 **2.** 协调,一致 — *vt.* **1.**
在(排钟等)上敲击出谐和的乐声;和
谐悦耳地奏出(音乐等) **2.** 用钟声报
(时);打钟召集(人) **3.** 单调而重复地
讲(话等)

chimera [kaiˈmiərə] *n.* **1.** [C]【希神】客

迈拉(狮头、羊身、蛇尾的吐火女怪) 2. 怪物 3. 幻想,妄想 4.【生】嵌合体

chimerical [kai'merikal] *adj.* 空想的;虚构的

chimney ['tʃimni] *n.* 1. 烟囱,烟道 2. (煤油灯、蜡烛等的)玻璃罩 3. (登山时仅容一人攀登的)管状裂口 4. 烟囱状的东西(火山等的喷烟口 5. (英俚)烟瘾极大的人 ‖ ~ stack(多烟道的)烟囱体 / ~ swallow 家燕,烟囱刺尾雨燕 / ~ sweep(er) 扫烟囱工人 / ~ swift 烟囱刺尾雨燕

chimpanzee [ˌtʃimpæn'zi:] *n.* 黑猩猩

chin [tʃin] *n.* 颏,下巴 1. (拉单杠的)引体向上动作 — (chinned/chinning) *vt.* 1. 用下巴夹住(提琴等) 2. [~ oneself] 在(单杠上)引体向上 — *vi.* [俚]聊天,唠叨 ‖ ~ wag *n.* & *vi.* 闲谈,聊天

China ['tʃainə] *n.* 中国 — *adj.* 1. 中国的 2. 中国产的 ‖ ~ aster【植】翠菊 / ~ town *n.* 唐人街,中国城 / ~ watcher 中国问题专家

china ['tʃainə] *n.* 瓷器;瓷料 ‖ ~ clay 瓷土,粘土 / ~ closet 瓷器(陈列)橱 / ~ ware *n.* [总称]瓷器

chinchilla [tʃin'tʃilə] *n.* 1. 绒鼠,毛丝鼠 2. 绒鼠毛皮 3. 珠皮呢(羊毛粗大衣呢)

Chinese [ˌtʃai'ni:z] [单复同] *n.* 1. 中国人 2. 中文;中国话,汉语 — *adj.* 1. 中国的(中国人的 2. 中文的,汉语的 ‖ ~ puzzle(七巧板、九连环等)中国智力玩具;复杂难懂的事物

chink¹ [tʃiŋk] *n.* 裂缝,裂口 3. 漏洞;弱点;空子 — *vt.* 堵塞…的缝隙

chink² [tʃiŋk] *n.* 1. (金属、玻璃器等的)丁当声 2. (俚)现钱 — *vi.* & *vt.* (使)丁当响

chip [tʃip] *n.* 1. (削木或凿石所留下的)

屑片;(金属等的)切屑片;(玻璃、瓷器等的)碎片 2.(土豆、水果等的)薄片;[~s]油炸土豆条 3.(器皿等的)凹口,缺口 4.(编帽或篮子等用的)木片条;棕榈叶片 5. [Chips](船上的)木匠 6.(作赌注用的)筹码 7.(喻)琐碎的、无价值的东西 8.(作燃料用的)干粪块 9.【计】芯片 — (chipped; chipping) *vt.* 1. 削;凿;铲 2. 在(瓷器等)上造成缺口;把…切成薄片 3. 削成;凿成(某种形状);刻(题词等) 4.(用话语)逗弄;挖苦 5.(小鸡)啄碎(蛋壳) — *vi.* 形成缺口 ‖ in 1. 插话,插嘴 ‖ **chippings** [复] 1. 削下或凿下的屑片

chipmuck ['tʃipmʌk], **chipmunk** ['tʃipmʌŋk] *n.*【动】花鼠,金花鼠(北美产)

chipper ['tʃipə] *adj.* 1. 兴高采烈的;活泼的 2. 精力充沛的 — *vt.* & *vi.* (使)高兴起来(*up*)

chiropody [ki'rɔpədi] *n.*【医】手足医术 ‖ **chiropodist** *n.* 治脚眼者;手足(病)医(生)

chiropractor ['kaiərəpræktə] *n.*【医】按摩技士,手治疗者 ‖ **chiro'practic** *n.* 按摩疗法

chirp [tʃə:p] *n.* 鸟叫声;虫鸣声 — *vi.* 1.(鸟等)吱吱地叫;(草虫等)唧唧地叫 2.(人)喊喳喳喳 — *vt.* 喊喳喳喳地讲出(或说出)

chirrup ['tʃirəp] *n.* & *vi.* (发出)反复不断的吱吱唧唧叫声

chisel ['tʃizl] *n.* 1. 凿子,錾子 2. (俚)欺骗,诈骗 — (chisel(l)ed; chisel(l)ing) *vt.* & *vi.* 1. 凿,镌,雕 2. (口)欺骗,诈骗 ‖ **chisel(l)er** *n.* 凿工;骗子

chitchat ['tʃitʃæt] *n.* 聊天,闲谈

chivalrous ['ʃivəlrəs] *adj.* 1. 勇武的 2.

骑士时代的 3. 有骑士气概(或品质)的 4. 对女人献殷勤的;对女人尊敬的

chivalry ['ʃivəlri] n. 1. (中世纪的)骑士制度;骑士气概(或品质) 2. 骑士团 3. 对女子献殷勤的绅士们 ‖ **chivalric** adj.

chive [tʃaiv] n. 【植】细香葱

chloric ['klɔːrik] adj. (含)氯的

chloride ['klɔːraid] n. 【化】氯化物

chlorinate ['klɔːrineit] vt. 1. 使氯化 2. 给(水)加氯消毒 3. 【冶】用氯处理 ‖ ˌchlori'nation n.

chlorine ['klɔːriːn] n. 【化】氯

chloroform ['klɔːrəfɔːm] n. 1. 【化】氯仿,三氯甲烷 — vt. 用氯仿处理;用氯仿麻醉;用氯仿杀死

chlorophyl(l) ['klɔːrəfil] n. 1. 【植】【生化】叶绿素 2. (从绿色植物提取的)蜡状叶绿素物质

chock [tʃɔk] n. 1. (防滑等用的)塞块,垫块 2. 【海】导缆钳,导缆器 — vt. 用塞块塞住,用垫块塞住 ‖ '~a'block adj. & adv. 塞满的(地),挤满的(地) / '~'full adj. 塞满的,满满的(of)

chocolate ['tʃɔkəlit] n. 1. 巧克力,朱古力 2. 巧克力糖 3. 巧克力饮料 4. 褐色 — adj. 巧克力制的;含有巧克力的;褐色的

choice [tʃɔis] n. 1. 选择,抉择 2. 选择机会;选择权;选择能力 3. 被选中的东西;入选者;精华 4. 供选择的东西 5. 审慎 — adj. 1. 精选的 2. 精选的;上等的 3. (对⋯的)挑三拣四的(of) ‖ -ly adv. / -ness n.

choir [kwaiə] n. 1. (教堂的)歌唱队,唱诗班 2. (教堂内的)高坛(即歌唱队或教士的席位) 3. 鸟群 4. 一组同类乐器

choke [tʃouk] vt. 1. 闷塞;闷死;掐死;喧塞 2. 阻塞;堵塞;塞满 3. 抑制,压住

(怒火等)(down) 4. 阻住;阻止;扑灭(火等);干死(植物) 5.【机】阻塞⋯的气门(以得到更浓缩的燃料混合物) 6. (棒球赛中)握着(球棒)的中段 — vi. 1. 窒息;喧住;说不出话来 2.(管子,渠道等)塞住 — n. 1. 窒息;喧 2.【机】阻塞门,阻气门;阻气门【电】扼流圈 ‖ ~damp n. (煤矿、深井中的)窒息性空气 / ~ pear 味涩的梨;使人哑口无言的事物

choking ['tʃoukiŋ] adj. 1. 令人窒息的 2. (声音)哽住的

cholera ['kɔlərə] n. 【医】霍乱 ‖ ~ic [ˌkɔlə'reiik] adj.

cholesterol [kə'lestərɔl] n. 【生化】胆固醇

choose [tʃuːz] (chose [tʃouz], chosen ['tʃouzn]) vt. 1. 选择,挑选 2. 决定;情愿;〈口〉愿意,想要 — vi. 作出选择

choos(e)y ['tʃuːzi] adj. 〈口〉喜欢挑剔的;难讨好的

chop [tʃɔp] (chopped;chopping) vt. 1. 砍,劈,斩 2. 切细,剁碎(up) 3. 劈(路) 4. (喻)割断(历史等)(up) — vi. 砍;猛击(at) — n. 1. 砍,劈;剁 2. (一块)排骨 3. 砍(或劈)的痕迹 4. 短风吹戗的水面 5. 【常 ~s】颌;口颊部 ‖ '~house n. 排骨餐馆;餐馆 / '~sticks【复】n. 筷子 / ~ suey['suːi]〈中国菜〉炒杂碎

chopper ['tʃɔpə] n. 1. 伐木者 2. 斧头;屠刀;大砍刀 3.【电】断路器;断续器【无】振动变流器;斩波器【核】中子选择器 4.〈美俚〉直升(飞)机 5.〈美俚〉驾驶员 6.〈美俚〉机关枪;机枪手;带机枪的匪徒 7.(定制的)前轮伸出式摩托车 8.[~s]〈俚〉一副假牙;一副牙齿 — vi. 乘直升飞机飞行 — vt. 用直升飞机运送

choppy¹ ['tʃɔpi] adj. 1. 波浪滔滔的 2. 裂缝多的;有皲纹的 3. 不连贯的

choppy[2] ['tʃɔpi] *adj.*(风)方向常变的

choral ['kɔːrəl] *adj.* 合唱队的;合唱的 ‖ ~ly *adv.*

chorale(e)[kɔˈrɑːl] *n.* 众赞歌(即合唱的赞美诗)

chord [kɔːd] *n.* 1.(乐器的)弦,琴弦,(喻)心弦 2.[音]和弦,和音 3.[解]索,带:vocal ~s 声带 4.[空]翼弦,翼梁 5.[数]弦 6.[建]弦杆,桁弦 ‖ ~ **organ** (按钮式)和弦电风琴

chore [tʃɔː] *n.*(美).[~s]家庭杂务 2.日常零星工作 3.困难(或不合意)的工作

choreography [ˌkɔriˈɒɡrəfi] *n.* 编舞术(指舞蹈动作的编排设计)‖ **choreographer** *n.*

chorister ['kɔristə] *n.* 1.(教堂内的)唱诗班歌手(尤指男孩)2.唱诗班领唱人

chortle ['tʃɔːtl] *vi.* 1. 哈哈大笑 2. 高兴地唱歌 — *n.* 哈哈大笑(声)

chorus ['kɔːrəs] *n.* 1.合唱,合唱队;歌舞队 2.合唱曲;(歌舞剧中的)合唱台词 3.齐声;(喻)(纷纷的)一致呼声 4.合唱队 5.(英国古代剧中)宣读开场白和收场白的角色 — *vt.* & *vi.* 齐声背诵;合唱;异口同声地说 3.~ **girl** 歌舞队女演员 / ~ **master** 合唱队指挥

chose [tʃəuz] choose 的过去式

chosen ['tʃəuzn] choose 的过去分词 — *adj.* 1. 挑选出来的;精选的 2.[宗]上帝选定的:the ~ **people** 上帝的特选子民(指犹太人)

chow [tʃau] *n.* 1.(一种棕色或黑色,体短,头大,舌黑色的)中国家犬 2.〈俚〉食物 3.〈澳〉〈贬〉中国佬 ‖ ~ **mein** [mein] 炒面

chowder ['tʃaudə] *n.* 海鲜杂烩浓汤(鲜鱼或蛤与咸肉、洋葱等煨成的食品)

Christ [kraist] *n.*[基督教]救世主(特指耶稣基督):before ~ 公元前(略作 B.C.)

christen ['krisn] *vt.* 1.[宗]为…施洗礼,洗礼时给…命名 2.(举行仪式)命名(船舶等)3.隆重地)首次使用(汽车、船舶等) ‖ ~**ing** *n.* 洗礼仪式;命名仪式

Christendom ['krisndəm] *n.* 基督教世界;[总称]基督教徒

Christian ['kristjən] *n.* 基督(教)徒 — *adj.* 1. 基督教的;信基督教的:the ~ era 公元,基督纪元/ a ~ **name** 教名 2. 基督的 3.〈口〉文明的,正派的 ‖ ~**ize** *vt.* 使成为基督教徒;使基督教化

Christianity [ˌkristiˈæniti] *n.* 1.[总称]基督教徒 2.基督教教义信仰 3.基督教徒的身分;基督教精神

Christmas ['krisməs] *n.* 1.[基督教]圣诞节 2.圣诞节节期(= ~**tide**) ‖ ~**-box** *n.*〈英〉(给邮递员等的)圣诞赏钱 / ~ **card** 圣诞(贺)卡 / ~ **carol** 圣诞颂歌 / ~**tide** *n.* 圣诞节节期(12 月 24 日至 1 月 6 日) / ~ **tree** 圣诞树

chromatic [krəuˈmætik] *adj.* 1.(有)颜色的;多色彩的 2.[生]易染的 3.[音]半音的;变音的

chrome [krəum] *n.* 1.[化]铬;铬黄 2.铬铬物 — *vt.* 将…镀铬;使受涔铬处理;使受铬媒处理;对…进行铬鞣

chromium ['krəumiəm] *n.*[化]铬

chromosome ['krəuməsəum] *n.*[生]染色体

chronic ['krɒnik] *adj.* 1.(疾病等)慢性的 2. 患慢性病的 2. 惯常的,经常的 3.〈英口〉极坏的,很糟的;使人不愉快的 — *n.* 患慢性病的人 ‖ ~**ally** *adv.*

chronicle ['krɒnikl] *n.* 1. 年代记,编年史

2. 历史;记事 — *vt.* 把…载入编年史;记述 ‖~*r n.* 年代史编者;记录者

chronobiology [ˌkrɔnəbaiˈɔlədʒi] *n.* (研究生物节律的)生物钟学 ‖ **chronobiologist** *n.*

chronologic(al) [ˌkrɔnəˈlɔdʒik(əl)] *adj.* 年代学的;按照年月顺序排列的; a *chronological table* 年表 ‖ **chronologically** *adv.*

chronology [krəˈnɔlədʒi] *n.* 1. 年代学 2. 年表 3.(事件等)按发生年月顺序的排列

chronometer [krəˈnɔmitə] *n.* 时计;精确计时计;天文钟

chronotherapy [ˌkrɔnəˈθerəpi] *n.* (通过调整患者睡眠和醒着的节律治疗失眠症的)生物钟疗法

chrysalis [ˈkrisəlis] ([复] chrysalides [kriˈsælidiːz]或 chrysalises) *n.* 1.(动)蝶蛹 2. 处于形成(或转化)阶段的东西

chrysanthemum [kriˈsænθəməm] *n.* (植)菊(花)

chub [tʃʌb] ([复]chub(s)) *n.* (动) 1. 圆鳍雅罗鱼 2. 裸首鲑鱼 3. 小口食鲥海鱼

chubby [ˈtʃʌbi] *adj.* 圆脸的;丰满的 ‖ **chubbiness** *n.*

chuck¹ [tʃʌk] *vi.* 1.(母鸡等)咯咯地叫 2. 咯咯地唤鸡;喔喔地催马前进 — *n.* 1. 咯咯声;喔喔声 2. 宝贝儿(表示亲热的用语)

chuck² [tʃʌk] *vt.* 1. 轻拍;抚弄 2. 扔,抛 打发走,撵走 3. 辞掉(工作)等;放弃(*up*) — *n.* 1. 轻拍;扔,抛;撵弃 3.[the ~] 辞退,解雇

chuck³ [tʃʌk] *n.* 1.(牛等的)颈肉 2.(俚)食物 ‖ ~ **wagon**(美)(拓荒、伐木等时用的)流动炊事车

chuckle [ˈtʃʌkl] *vi.* 1. 抿着嘴轻声地笑,暗笑 2.(母鸡)咯咯地叫 — *n.* 轻声笑;暗笑 ‖ ~**-head** *n.* (口)傻瓜,笨蛋 / ~**-headed** *adj.* (口)愚蠢的,呆笨的

chug [tʃʌg] *n.* (机器等的)嚓嚓声 (chugged;chugging) *vi.* 嚓嚓嚓嚓地响

chum [tʃʌm] *n.* 好朋友,密友 (chummed;chumming) *vi.* 1. 同室居住 2. 成为好朋友(*up*)

chummy [ˈtʃʌmi] *adj.* (口)亲密的;友好的

chunk [tʃʌŋk] *n.* 1. 厚片,大块 2. 相当大的数量(或部分) 3. 结实的马;矮胖的(男)人

chunky [ˈtʃʌŋki] *adj.* 矮胖的;结实的

church [tʃəːtʃ] *n.* 1. 教堂,礼拜堂 2. 教会;教派;教会全体成员 3.(宗)礼拜 4. [the ~]神职;牧师的职位 5. 全体基督教徒:*Church militant*(宗)战斗教会(存在人间与邪恶作战的基督徒的教会) — *vt.* 把(某人)带到教堂接受宗教仪式 — *adj.* 教堂的;(英)国教的 ‖ ~**-goer** *n.* 按时去教堂做礼拜的人 / ~**-key**(美俚)(前有三角形尖头的)开罐器 / ~**-man** *n.* 教士;教徒;教会成员 / ~**-warden** *n.* (英国国教会)堂区俗人委员;(美国圣公会)堂区俗人执事 / (英)陶土制的长烟斗 / ~**-yard** *n.* 教堂庭院;教堂墓地

churl [tʃəːl] *n.* 1. 粗鲁的人 2. 农民,乡下佬;出身低微的人 3. 吝啬鬼,守财奴 4.(英史)最下层自由民 ‖ ~**-ish** *adj.*

churn [tʃəːn] *n.* 1.(炼制黄油用的)搅乳器;(英)运奶大桶 2. 钻料搅拌杆 — *vt.* 1. 用搅乳器搅拌(牛奶等);用搅乳器炼制(黄油) 2. 剧烈搅拌 3.(为多赚佣金代股民)过度买卖,翻进翻出(证券)4. 粗制滥造出;费力地作出(*out*) — *vi.*

1. 用搅乳器搅拌 2. 剧烈搅动 3.(波浪)翻腾

chute [ʃuːt] *n.* 1. 急流;瀑布 2. 斜道,滑运道; 3.(机)斜槽 3.(口)降落伞(parachute 的缩略)

chutney ['tʃʌtni] *n.* 印度酸辣酱

CIA *abbr.* Central Intelligence Agency (美国)中央情报局

cicada [si'kɑːdə, si'keidə] ([复] cicadae [si'kɑːdiː, si'keidi]或 cicadas) *n.*【动】蝉,知了

cider ['saidə] *n.* 苹果汁;苹果酒

CIF, c. i. f. *abbr.* cost, insurance and freight 【商】到岸价格(成本、保险费加运费)

cigar [si'gɑː] *n.* 雪茄烟

cigaret(te) [,sigə'ret] *n.* 纸烟,香烟,卷烟

cinch [sintʃ] *n.* 1.(马鞍等的)肚带 2. 紧握手 3.〈俚〉容易的事;必然(发生)的事 — *vt.* 1. 给(马)系肚带 2. 确保

cinchona [siŋ'kəunə] *n.* 1.【植】金鸡纳树 2. 金鸡纳树皮

Cincinnati [,sinsi'næti] *n.* 辛辛那提(美国俄亥俄州西南部城市)

cinder ['sində] *n.* 1. 炉渣;矿渣;煤渣;未燃尽的煤(或木炭等) 2.[~s] 灰烬 3.【地】火山渣

cinema ['sinimə] *n.* 1. 电影院 2. 电影,影片 3. 电影工业;电影制片(技术)

cinematography [,sinimə'tɔɡrəfi] *n.* 电影制作(或摄影)术 ‖ **cinematographer** *n.*

cinephile ['sinifail] *n.*〈主英〉电影爱好者,影迷

cinnabar ['sinəbɑː] *n.*【矿】朱砂,辰砂;人造朱砂 — *adj.* 朱红的

cinnamon ['sinəmən] *n.* 1. 樟树;肉桂,桂皮;桂皮(香料) 2. 黄棕色

cipher ['saifə] *n.* 1. 零(即 0) 2. 不重要的人(或事物);无价值的东西 3. 密码;暗号,

码电报 4. 阿拉伯数字 5.(尤指姓名首字母等的)拼合字;花押字 6.【音】(风琴音管故障引起的)连响 — *vt.* 将...译成密码

circa ['səːkə]〈拉〉*prep.*[用在日期、数字等前面]大约在,接近于

circle ['səːkl] *n.* 1. 圆;圆周;圈;环状物 2. 天体运行轨道 3.(具有共同兴趣、利益的人们所形成的)圈子;集团 4. 周期,循环;完整的一系列 5.【逻】循环论证(一种逻辑错误;以乙来论证甲,而乙的真实性又是以甲来论证的) 6.(活动、势力、影响等的)范围,领域 7.(剧场的)楼厅;座位 8. 铁路的环形交叉口;圆形场地 — *vt.* 环绕;移动(圆圈) — *vi.* 1. 盘旋;旋转;环行(round, around, over) 2. 流传(round, around)

circuit ['səːkit] *n.* 1. 周线;周线;范围 2. 运行;巡回审判(或诉道);巡回区 3. 同业性的联合组织;(轮回上演或上映的)联号剧场(或电影院) 4. 事物变化的顺序 5.【电】电路,线路 — *vt. & vi.*(绕...)环行

circuitous [səː'kjuːitəs] *adj.* 1. 迂回的,绕行的 2. 间接进行的 ‖ ~ly *adv.* / ~ness *n.*

circular ['səːkjulə] *adj.* 1. 圆形的,环形的 2. 循环的;环绕一圈的 3. 迂回的 4.【逻】循环论证的 5. 供传阅的:a letter 供传阅的函件 — *n.* 供传阅的函件(或通知等);传单 ‖ ~ly *adv.*

circularize ['səːkjuləraiz] *vt.* 1. 将函件(或通知等)分发给…;传阅(函件,通知等);发征询意见表给 2. 公布 3. 使成圆形

circulate ['səːkjuleit] *vi.* 1.(血液等)循环,环流 2.(货币、报刊等)流通;通用 3.(消息、名声等)流传,传播 4.【数】(小数)循环 — *vt.* 1. 使(血液等)循环,使环流 2. 使(货币等)流通 3. 使用

转 3. 散布, 传播(消息等)

circulation [ˌsɔːkjuˈleiʃən] *n.* 1. 循环、环流 2.(货币、消息等的)传播;(报刊等的)发行 3. 发行额;流通额;销路

circulatory [ˈsɔːkjuleitəri] *adj.*(血液)循环的

circum- *pref.* 表示"绕"、"周": *circumscribe*, *circum centre*

circumcentre, circumcenter [ˌsɔːkəmˈsentə] *n.* 【数】外心

circumcise [ˈsɔːkəmsaiz] *vt.* 割到...的包皮(或阴蒂) ‖ **circumcision** [ˌsɔːkəmˈsiʒən] *n.* 割包皮;割礼

circumference [səˈkʌmfərəns] *n.* 圆周;圆周长

circumflex [ˈsɔːkəmfleks] *n.*【语】(加在元音字母上的)音调符号(亦作 ~ accent)

circumlocution [ˌsɔːkəmləˈkjuːʃən] *n.* 累赘的说法(或话语);迂回的说法(或话语);遁词

circumnavigate [ˌsɔːkəmˈnævigeit] *vt.* 1. 环绕(地球、岛屿等)航行(或飞行) 2. 绕过、绕...而行 ‖ **circum.navi'gation** *n.* 环球航行 / **circumnavigator** *n.* 环球航行者

circumpolar [ˌsɔːkəmˈpəulə] *adj.*【天】拱极的;天极附近的;【地】环极的;地极附近的

circumscribe [ˈsɔːkəmskraib] *vt.* 1. 在...周围画线;标出...的界界 2. 限制、约束 3.【数】使外接;使外切

circumspect [ˈsɔːkəmspekt] *adj.* 谨慎小心的;周到的,慎重的 ‖ **~ion** [ˌsɔːkəmˈspekʃən] *n.* / **~ly** *adv.* / **~ness** *n.*

circumstance [ˈsɔːkəmstəns] *n.* 1. [~s]情况;形势;环境 2.(事情的)详情;细节 3. 事件;事实;(有关)事项 4. [~s]境况,境遇 5. 仪式;形式: pomp and ~ 排场 ‖ ~**d** *adj.* 处于某种境况的;dif-

ferently ~**d** 处境不同的

circumstantial [ˌsɔːkəmˈstænʃəl] *adj.* 1. 与环境(或条件)有关的;依环境(或条件)而定的 2. 非常详尽的,包含所有细节的 3. 非本质的;非主要的 ‖ ~ *adv.* / ~**ness** *n.*

circumvent [ˌsɔːkəmˈvent] *vt.* 1. 围绕、包围 2. 对...用计取胜,智胜 3. 用陷阱捉住 4. 防止...发生 ‖ ~**ion** *n.*

circus [ˈsɔːkəs] *n.* 1.(圆形的)马戏场;(古罗马的)竞技场 2. 马戏,杂耍 3. 马戏团 4.(第一次世界大战时的)环形飞行队伍;表演特技的飞行小组 5. 环形广场

cirrus [ˈsirəs] ([复] cirri [ˈsirai]) *n.* 1.【动】触毛,触须;蔓足 2.【植】卷须 3.([复] cirri 或 cirrus)【气】卷云

cistern [ˈsistən] *n.* 1. 蓄水箱;水箱;贮水器;(餐桌凉酒等用的)银制大瓶(或罐) 2. 水塘,水池 3.【解】(尤指脑中的)池

citadel [ˈsitədl] *n.* 1. 城堡;堡垒;要塞 2. 避难所

citation [saiˈteiʃən] *n.* 1. 引证,引用;引文;引句 2.【律】传讯;传票;(对于法律、先例的)援引 3.【军】传令嘉奖;嘉奖;表扬;表扬词(或信) 4.(词典等中的)例证

cite [sait] *vt.* 1. 引证,引用;举(例) 2.【律】传讯 3.【军】传令嘉奖

citizen [ˈsitizn] *n.* 1. 公民 2. 市民,城镇居民 3.(美)平民,老百姓(区别于军人、警察等) ‖ ~**hood** *n.* 1. 公民(或市民)身分;公民权 2. 国籍 / ~**ry** *n.* [总称](美)平民(区别于军人等) / ~**ship** *n.* 1. 公民(或市民)身分;公民的权利和义务 2. 国籍 3. 公民应有的品行 ‖ ~'**s arrest**(根据不成文法)公民对现行犯的逮捕 / ~**s' band** 民用电台

顿带,民用波段

citron ['sitrən] *n*. 【植】枸橼;香橼

citrus ['sitrəs] (复 citrus(es)) *n*. 【植】 1. 柑橘属果树 2. 柑橘果

city ['siti] *n*. 1. 城市,都市,市 2. 全市居民 3. 城邦 (~ -state) ‖ City editor 1. 〈英〉商业金融栏编辑 2. 〈美〉[c e·]本地新闻编辑(主任) / ~ father 城市元老(如市参议员等) / ~ hall 1. 市政府 2. 市政府 / '~-state *n*. 〈古代希腊的〉城邦

civic ['sivik] *adj*. 1. 城市的 2. 市民的;公民的

civics ['siviks] [复] *n*. [用作单或复]公民学

civil ['sivl, 'sivil] *adj*. 1. 公民的;市民的;国民的;市民的 / ~ defence 民防 / ~ rights 公民权 / ~ engineering 土木工程(学) 2. 国内的;国民间的:a ~ war 内战 3. 文明的;有礼貌的,客气的 4. 【律】民事的,根据民法的,法律规定的 5. 非军职的,文职的,文官的:the ~ service[总称]文职人员,(军队外的全部)行政部门,文官 / ~ list 王室年俸,非宗教的:a ~ marriage〈西方国家中不采用宗教仪式的〉公证结婚 7. 【天】历法的:a ~ year 民用年(区别于天文年) ‖ ~ly *adv*. 1. 彬彬有礼地 2. 从公民权利角度说;根据民法

civilian [si'viliən] *n*. 1. 平民,老百姓(与军,警相对而言) 2. 非军事法律专家 — *adj*. 平民的;民间的;民众的:~ clothes 便服(区别于军警制服)

civility [si'viliti] *n*. 1. 礼貌,客气 2. 礼仪;客套

civilization [,sivilai'zeiʃən] *n*. 1. 文明 2. 开化,教化 3. 文明世界

civilize ['sivilaiz] *vt*. 1. 使文明;使开化 2. 教导;熏陶;使文雅 — *vi*. 变得文明

(或文雅)

Cl 【化】元素氯(chlorine)的符号

clack [klæk] *vi*. 1. 作噼啪声;作咯嗒声 2. 喋喋不休,唠叨 3. 〈家禽〉咯咯地叫 — *vt*. 1. 使作噼啪声;使作咯嗒声 2. 喋喋地唠叨地说 — *n*. 1. 噼啪声;咯嗒声 2. 唠叨,喋喋不休 3. 【机】瓣阀

clad [klæd] clothe 的过去式和过去分词 — *adj*. 穿...衣服的;被...覆盖的 — (clad/cladding) *vt*. 给...加包层(或镀层) ‖ **cladding** *n*. 〈金属〉包层

claim [kleim] *vt*. 1. (根据权利)要求;认领(失物等) 2. 自称,声称;主张 3. 值得,需要(注意等) 4. (根据权利而提出的)要求 2.(对某事物的)权利;要求权;所有权 3. 声称;主张;断言 4. (对矿者,移民等)申请产权的土地 ‖ — **ant** *n*. 要求权利(或所有权)者;【律】原告 ‖ — **jumper** 〈美〉强夺他人采矿权(或土地等)的矿工

clairvoyant [klɛə'vɔiənt] *adj*. 1. 有超人的视力的 2.(有)洞察力的 — *n*. 视力超人的人;明察秋毫的人 ‖ **clairvoyance** *n*. 超人的视力;洞察力 / ~ *n*.

clam [klæm] *n*. 【动】 1. 蛤肉 2. 夹钳;夹子 3.〈俚〉嘴紧的人;沉默寡言者 4. 〈美俚〉美元 5. 〈美俚〉错误 — (clammed/clamming) *vi*. 捞蛤 ‖ ~ **bake** *n*. 〈美〉 1. 海滨烤蛤野餐会 2. 喧嚣的社交集会(尤指政治集会) 3. 〈俚〉乱糟糟的广播(或电视)节目 / ~ **shell** *n*. 1. 蛤壳 2. 蛤壳状挖泥器

clamber ['klæmbə] *vi*. & *vt*. & *n*. 攀登,爬

clammy ['klæmi] *adj*. 1. 冷湿的;湿腻的粘糊糊的 2. 造成冷湿的 3. 冷淡的 ‖ **clammily** *adv*. / **clamminess** *n*.

clamorous ['klæmərəs] *adj*. 喧闹的,吵吵嚷嚷的 ‖ ~ly *adv*. / ~ness *n*.

clamo(u)r ['klæmə] *n*. 吵闹,喧嚷;(表示

支持或抗议的)叫喊；war ～s 战争叫嚣 — vi. 吵闹,喧嚷；叫喊 — vt. 1. 用喧嚷迫使 2. 用喧嚷发出(或表示)

clamp [klæmp] n. 夹钳；夹子 — vt. 1. (用夹钳)夹住；夹紧 2. 强加(任务等) — vi. (对…)施加压力；箝制；取缔 (*down, on*)

clan [klæn] n. 1.(苏格兰高地人的)宗族 2. 氏族,部族,克兰 3. 宗派,小集团,帮派 4.〈口〉家族 ‖ **clannish** adj.

clandestine [klæn'destin] adj. 秘密的,暗中的,私下的 ‖ ～**ly** adv. / ～**ness** n.

clang [klæŋ] vi. 1. 发铿锵声 2.(鹤等)鸣、叫 — vt. 使发铿锵声 — n. 铿锵声；(鹤等的)鸣叫声

clank [klæŋk] vi. & vt. (使)发当啷声,(使)发铿锵声 — n. 当啷声,铿锵声

clansman ['klænzmən] n.〔复〕**clansmen** 宗族(或氏族、集团等)的成员

clap [klæp] n. (clapped; clapping) vt. 1. 拍；轻拍 2. 振(翼),拍(翼) 3. 使砰然相击 4. 急速(或用力)地放；急忙处理；～ **up a bargain** 匆忙成交 — vi. 1. 拍手 2. 砰然出声 — n. 1. 拍手喝彩(声) 2. 霹雳声；破裂声 3. 轻拍 4. 发出碰撞声的装置 ‖ ～**board** n. 护墙模形板/护墙板

clapper ['klæpə] n. 1. 拍手者 2. 钟舌；铃舌 3. 拍板；〈英〉(用来吓鸟的)鸣器 4.〈俚〉(饶舌者的)舌头

claque [klæk] n. 1.(剧场等雇用的)一伙捧场者 2. 奉承拍马的一批人

claret ['klærət] n. 1. 干红葡萄酒,红酒(尤指法国波尔多产的) 2. 紫红色 3.〈俚〉血 — adj. 紫红色的

clarify ['klærifai] vt. 1. 澄清,讲清楚,阐明 2.【化】澄清(液体等) 3. 使(头脑等)清楚 — vi. 1.(液体等)变清 2. 变得易懂 ‖ **clarification**[ˌklærifi'keiʃən] n.

clarinet [ˌklæri'net], **clarionet** [ˌklæriə'net] n.【音】单簧管,黑管,竖笛

clarion ['klæriən] n. 1. 号角 2. 号角声 — adj. 响亮清晰的,嘹亮的

clarity ['klæriti] n. 清澈；透明；明晰

clash [klæʃ] vi. 1.(铃铛、刀剑等)碰撞作声 2. 猛撞；冲突(*into*) 3.(意见、兴趣、颜色等)抵触;不调和(*with*) — vt. 使(铃铛、刀剑等)碰撞作声 — n. 1.(刀剑等的)金属碰撞声 2. 抵触；冲突；不调和

clasp [klɑ:sp] n. 1. 扣子；钩子；扣紧物(如书夹子等) 2.(挂奖章等用的)银质横杠状别针 3. 拥抱；紧握；握手 — vt. 1. 扣住；扣紧；钩住 2. 拥抱；抱紧 3. 紧握 4.(藤等)紧紧缠绕 — vi. 扣住；钩紧 ‖ ～ **er** n. 1. 扣子；钩子 2.【植】抱茎卷须(如藤须等) 3.【动】抱(握)器；交合突,鳍脚 ‖ ～ **knife** 折刀

class [klɑ:s] n. 1. 阶级；社会等级：the upper (middle, lower) ～s 上层(中产,下层)阶级 2. 班,班级,年级；〈美〉(某年)毕业班 3.(一节)课 4.(高低、优劣的)等级；种类 5.【生】(动植物分类的)纲；【数】类,组,集；【语】类,类别 7.〈口〉优越,出众；风度 8.〈英〉(大学考试)优等 9. 同年应征士兵 — vt. 把…分类(或分级等)(与 as 或 with 连用) — vi. 分类(或分级)(与 as 或 with 连用) ‖ ～ **action**【律】共同起诉 / ～ **book** n.〈美〉1.(教师的)点名记分册 2.〈美〉毕业班纪念册 / ～ **mate** n. 同班同学 / ～ **room** n. 教室,课室

classic ['klæsik] adj. 1.(文学、艺术等)最优秀的,第一流的 2. 传统的,不朽的 3. 古典的(指古罗马、古希腊文学等)；古典派的 4. 历史上值得纪念的；与著名文学作品(或作家)有关的 5. 确实的,可靠的；典型的 — n. 1. 大艺术家；杰作；名著 2.〔～s〕经典

作);(古罗马或古希腊的)古典著作 3. 古典(指古罗马或古希腊)作家;古典学者 4. 传统事件;典型事例(可靠的出典 5.〈俚〉传统服装 ‖ ~ism *n*. 古典主义(或风格)

lassical ['klæsikəl] *adj*. 1.(文学、艺术等)标准的;第一流的;经典的 2. 古典(派)的;古典(指古希腊、古罗马)文学的;古典派作家的 3. 精通古典的 4. 传统的;权威的 5.人文科学的,文科的 ‖ ~ly *adv*. 古典派地

lassification [ˌklæsifi'keiʃən] *n*. 1. 分类;分级 2. 分类法 3. 类别;等级(文件等)的密级

lassify ['klæsifai] *vt*. 1. 把...分类;把(货物等)分等级 2. 把...归入一类(或同一等级) ‖ classified *adj*. 1. 分成类的;被归入一类的 2. 机密的,保密的 / classifier *n*. 1. 分类者 2.【矿】分级机 3.【化】粒度分级器 4.(汉语等中的)量词

lassy ['klɑːsi] *adj*.〈俚〉高级的,有气派的;时髦的,漂亮的 ‖ classily *adv*. / classiness *n*.

latter ['klætə] *n*. [只用单数] 1.(马蹄等的)得得声;(刀叉、碗碟等的)镗镗声;(机器等的)卡嗒声 2. 喧嚷,骚动 — *vi*. 得得(或卡嗒)响;喧闹嘈杂地谈笑声 3. 喧嚷;骚动 — *vi*. 得得(或卡嗒)响;喧闹嘈杂地谈笑 — *vt*. 使得得(或卡嗒卡嗒)地响 ‖ ~er *n*. 发得得声的东西或人

latteringly ['klætəriŋli] *adv*. 卡嗒卡嗒地;咭咭呱呱地

lause [klɔːz] *n*. 1. 条款,条,项 2.【语】分句

laustrophobia [ˌklɔːstrə'fəubiə] *n*.【医】【心】幽闭恐怖(症)

law [klɔː] *n*. 1.(动物的)爪,脚爪;(蟹、虾等的)钳,螯 2.〈贬〉手;魔爪 3. 爪形

器具(如拔钉锤等) 4. 被抓的伤口 — *vt*. 1. 用爪子抓(或撬、搔、撕);〈苏格兰〉搔 2. 抓住或(路)入 3.〈美俚〉逮捕,抓 — *vi*. 用爪子抓(或挖)‖ ~ed *adj*. 有爪(或螯)的 ‖ ~-and-'ball *adj*.(家具)有抓球爪式脚的;有抓球爪式脚的家具的 / '~back *n*.〈英〉弥补性收入(政府以相应增收的税款来抵偿增加的年金、补贴等开支) / ~ hammer 拔钉锤,羊角榔头

clay [klei] *n*. 1. 粘土;泥土 2. 肉体,人体：a man of common ~ 平常人 3. 似粘土的物质 4. 粘土烟斗 ‖ clayey ['kleii] *adj*. ‖ ~ pigeon 泥鸽 / ~ pipe 粘土烟斗

clean [kliːn] *adj*. 1. 清洁的,干净的;整洁的 2. 纯洁的;清白的,不淫秽的 3. 未沾染(疾病)的;不吸毒的,无毒瘾的 4. 彻底的,完全的 5. 干净利落的;巧妙的,匀称的;光洁的 7. 构造完好的：a ship with ~ lines 造型优美的船 8. 爱清洁的,有洁癖的 9. 不长杂草及其他野生植物的 10.〈原子弹、氢弹等〉爆炸时无(或很少)放射性尘埃的 11.(船舱等)出空了的;〈美俚〉分文没有的;〈美俚〉没私带枪支(或走私品、毒物等)的 12.(肉类等)可供食用的 — *adv*. 1. 干净地;纯洁地 2. 彻底地,完全地 — *vt*. 1. 把...弄干净,为...去除污垢;使净化 2. 开膛取出(鸡等)的内脏(以备烹饪)3.〈俚〉使输得精光;使一无所有 — *vi*. 1. 被弄干净 2. 做清洁工作 — *n*. 去垢;刷净 ‖ ~ *n*. 1. 打扫清洁的人;清洁工人;干洗商清洁器;除垢剂：a vacuum ~er 吸尘器 / ~ness *n*. ‖ '~ 'cut *adj*. 1. 轮廓分明的 2. 形态优美的 3. 清楚的,明确的,明晰的 4. 整洁好看的 / '~'handed *adj*. 清白的,没有做过坏事的 / '~'living *adj*. 生活严谨的,安分守己的 / '~out *n.* 清除,清洗 / ~ **room** 清洁室,清净室;无菌室 / ~ˈ**shaven** *adj.* 胡子刮得光光的 / ˈ~**up** *n.* 1. 清除;扫除;清洗 2.〈口〉暴利

cleaning [ˈkliːniŋ] *n.* 1. 去污;打扫;扫除 2. [~s] (扫除出来的)垃圾 ‖ ~ **woman** 清洁女工

cleanly [ˈklenli] *adj.* 1. 爱清洁的 2. (东西等)弄得干干净净的 ‖ [ˈkliːnli] *adv.* 干净地;利索地 ‖ **cleanlily** *adv.* / **cleanliness** *n.*

cleanse [klenz] *vt.* 1. 使清洁,清洗 2. 使纯洁,净化 ‖ 做清洁工作的人 2. 清洁剂(如去污粉等)

clear [kliə] *adj.* 1. 清澈的,光亮的,无污垢的 2. 晴朗的 3. 清晰的;分明的;条理清楚的 4. (理解)清楚的;明白的 5. (声音)嘹亮的 6. 畅通的,无阻的,清除了…的(*of*) 7. (木材)无节疤的,没有缺陷的 8. (账目)纯收益的 9. 净得的;十足的;整整的:win a ~ victory over one's opponent 彻底胜过对方 ‖ *adv.* 1. 清楚地,清晰地 2. [加重语气用]完全;一直,整整 3. 离开,不接触 (*of*): Stand ~ of the rails. 站得离轨道远些。 ‖ *vt.* 1. 使清澈;使清楚 2. 扫清,清除;结清;使(计算器)归零 3. 开拓,开垦 4. 越过 5. 为(船或船货)结关(或船只)结关后离开 6. 宣布…无罪 7. 净得 8. 交换(单据);把(支票)兑现;结清(商品) 9. (议案)在(众院等)通过;批准,准许… *vi.* 1. 变清澈;变清楚;变明朗 2. (船只)结关;结关离去 (*from*) 3. 交换票据 4. 消失;(俚)溜走 5. (文件等)送交审批:The plan must ~ through a higher body. 这项计划必须送交上一级机关审批。 ‖ *n.* 空隙;空隙 ‖ ˈ~**ly** *adv.* 1. 明白地;清晰地 2. 显然 / ~

ness *n.* ‖ ~-**air gust.** ~-**air turbulence** 【气】(造成飞机剧烈颠簸的)晴空湍流 / ˈ~ˈ**cut** *adj.* 轮廓清楚的;明确的,明晰的 / ˈ~ˈ**eyed** *adj.* 目光锐利的;能明辨是非的 / ˈ~ˈ**headed** *adj.* 头脑清楚的 / ˈ~ˈ**sighted** *adj.* 目光锐利的 / ˈ~ˈ**way** *n.* 超高速公路

clearance [ˈkliərəns] *n.* 1. 清除;清理;出空;出空;排除障碍 2. ~ **sale** 清仓削价销售 2. [建]净空;余隙,间隙 3. (船只的)结关证(= ~ papers);结关 4. (机场指挥塔发出的)起飞(或降落)许可 5. 票据交换;清算 6. [医]清除率 7. 参与机密工作的许可

clearing [ˈkliəriŋ] *n.* 1. (森林中的)空地 2. (林业用语)皆伐;皆伐区 3. 票据交换 4. (银行之间的)票据交换结算 5. [~s] 票据交换结算总额 ‖ ~ **bank** *n.* 票据交换银行;清算银行 / ˈ~**house** *n.* 1. 票据交换所;结算所 2. (技术情报)交换中心,交流中心

cleat [kliːt] *n.* 1. 固着楔 2. [海]系索具,羊角;系缆索;系绳铁角 3. 防滑(或加固)术(或铁)条 4. 加强角片

cleavage [ˈkliːvidʒ] *n.* 1. 劈开,分裂;劈开处 2. [矿]解理;[地]劈理 3. [生]卵裂

cleave[1] [kliːv] (过去式 cleaved 或 cleft [kleft]或 clove [kləuv],过去分词 cleaved 或 cleft 或 cloven [ˈkləuvn]) *vt.* 1. 劈开,劈开 2. 把…分成几个小部分(或小派别等) 3. 开(路);穿过(波浪等) — *vi.* 1. (木头等)顺着纹路) 被劈开;裂开 2. (船等)破浪前进 3. (鸟等)掠过空中;穿过 — ˈ~r *n.* 劈东西的人(或器具);[屠夫的]切肉刀;[地]劈石器

cleave[2] [kliːv] (过去式 cleaved 或 clave [kleiv],过去分词 cleaved) *vi.* 1. 粘着,粘住(*to*) 2. 依恋;坚持(*to*)

clef [klef] *n.* [音]谱号:F − 低音谱号/G

~ 高音谱号

cleft [kleft] *cleave*[1] 的过去式和过去分词 — *adj.* 1. 劈开的;裂开的 2.【植】半裂的;~ grafting【植】劈接,割接 — *n.* 1. 裂缝;裂口 2. "V"字形凹陷

clematis ['klemətis] *n.*【植】铁线莲

clemency ['klemənsi] *n.* 1. (气候等的)温暖,温和 2. 仁慈,宽厚

clement ['klemənt] *adj.* 1. (天气、性情等)温和的 2. 仁慈的,宽厚的 ‖ ~ly *adv.*

clench [klentʃ] *vt.* 1. 敲弯;敲平(钉子等);敲弯(钉头)以钉牢 2. 握紧(拳头等);咬紧(牙关) 3. 捏紧,抓牢 4. 确定,决定(论辩,交易等) — *vi.* 1. (钉、铆钉等)钉牢 2. 握紧;咬紧 — *n.* 1. 敲弯的钉头,钉牢 2. 握紧;咬紧

clergy ['klɜːdʒi] *n.* [总称]【基督教】牧师;(其他宗教的)教士(可指总体或一群教士)

clergyman ['klɜːdʒimən] ([复] clergymen) *n.* (英国国教会的)牧师;教士

clerical ['klerikəl] *adj.* 1. 牧师的;教士的 2. 办事员(式)的;办公室工作的;a ~ error(誊抄工作中的)笔误/~ work 文书工作 ‖ ~ly *adv.*

clerk [klɑːk, klɜːk] *n.* 1. 职员,办事员 2. 文书3.【美】店员 — *vi.* 当职员(或店员,文书)

Cleveland ['kliːvlənd] *n.* 克利夫兰[美国俄亥俄州东北部港市]

clever ['klevə] *adj.* 聪明的,伶俐的;灵巧的,巧妙的 ‖ ~ly *adv.* 聪明地;巧妙地 / ~ness *n.*

clew [kluː] *n.* 1. 线索(常用 clue) 2. 线团,纱团

cliché ['kliːʃei](法) *n.* 陈词滥调

click [klik] *n.* 1. 卡嗒一声(常指上锁,扣

扳机等时发出的声音) 2.【机】棘爪 — *vi.* 1. 发出卡嗒一声 2. 恰好吻合,配对;(两人)一见如故,一拍即合 3. 进行顺利;成功,受观众欢迎 — *vt.* 使发出卡嗒声;卡嗒卡嗒地敲

client ['klaiənt] *n.* 1. 委托人;(律师的)当事人;(私人医生的)病人,病家 2. (商店等的)顾客 3. = ~ state ‖ ~ state(在经济或政治方面依赖某一大国的)附属国

clientele [,kliːɑːn'tel] *n.* [总称] 1. 委托人;当事人 2. (商店等的)顾客;常客

cliff [klif] *n.* 悬崖,峭壁(尤指海边的) ‖ ~ dweller 1. 住高楼大厦的人 2. [常作 C·D·]居住在美国西南部崖洞中的史前印第安人 3. 悬崖居民 / ~ hang *vi.* 1. 以扣人心弦的未果场景结束连载故事的一个章节(或连本戏的一场电视等);采用"且听下回分解"的延宕手法 2. 等待紧张情节的启示揭晓 3. 写连载惊险故事;制作扣人心弦的电影(或戏剧等) 4. 处于危险边缘 / ~ hanger *n.* 1. (分期连载的)惊险故事;(有续集的)惊险电影(或戏剧) 2. 扣人心弦的紧张比赛

climate ['klaimit] *n.* 1. 气候;气候区 2. 一般(社会)趋势,(社会)风气;a change in mental ~ 思潮的转变 ‖ ~ic(al) [klai'mætik(əl)] *adj.*

climax ['klaimæks] *n.* 1.【语】层进法(指一种修辞手法) 2.(兴趣等的)顶点,高潮;(小说、戏剧等的)高潮;(性交时的)性高潮 3.【生】演替顶极 — *vi.* & *vt.* (使)达到顶点;(使)达到高潮 ‖ ~less *adj.*

climb [klaim] *vi.* 1. (攀)登,爬 2.(太阳、炊烟等)徐徐上升;(物价等)逐渐上涨;(飞机)爬升,爬高 3.(植物)攀缘向上;(道路、楼梯等)倾斜向上 4.(在社

会地位等方面)向上爬,钻营 — *vt*. 1. 攀登,爬;登上 2. 使(飞机)爬升(或爬高) 3.(植物)沿...攀缘而上 — *n*. 1. 攀登;【空】爬升,爬高 2. 需攀登的地方;山坡 ‖ ~ *down* 1. 往下爬,爬下 2. 退让,屈服,认错 ‖ '~**down** *n*. 1. 往下爬行 2. 退让,屈服,认错

climber ['klaimə] *n*. 1. 爬山的人 2. 攀缘植物 3. 拼命向上爬的人,野心家 4.(架线工等用的)上杆脚扣;(登山靴上的)铁钉助爬器

clinch [klintʃ] *vt*. 1. 敲弯,钉住 2. 确定,决定(论据、交易等) 3.〈俚〉拥抱 — *vi*. 1. 敲弯,钉牢 2.(摔跤等时)扭住对手 3.〈俚〉拥抱 — *n*. 1.【海】半结;用半结系绳;半结系绳法 2.(钉、铆钉等的)敲弯部分;敲弯的钉;钉牢 3. 扭住对手 4.〈俚〉拥抱 ‖ ~**er** *n*.

cling [kliŋ](clung [klʌŋ]) *vi*. 1. 粘着;缠着;紧紧握着 2. 依附,依靠;依恋(*to*) 3. 坚持;墨守(*to*)

clinic ['klinik] *n*. 1. 诊所;门诊部;医务室 2. 临床讲解;临床教学(班) 3. 会诊

clinical ['klinikəl] *adj*. 1. 临床的,临诊的:a ~ thermometer 体温表 2.(感情、态度、判断等)冷静的;不偏不倚的;分析的 ‖ ~**ly** *adv*.

clink [kliŋk] *vt*. & *vi*.(使)丁当作响 — *n*. 1. 丁当声 2.〈英俚〉钱;硬币 3.〈英方〉猛烈的一击 4.〈方〉瞬间 5.〈俚〉监狱,牢房

clinker ['kliŋkə] *n*. 1.【冶】熔渣;炉渣 2.【地】熔岩(块)

clip[1] [klip] *n*. 1. 夹,钳;回形针;别针 2.【军】弹夹 3.【无】接线柱 — (clipped; clipping) *vt*. 1. 夹住,钳牢 2. 捏紧;束紧 3.(美式足球中)背后绊(人)犯规 ‖ '~**board** *n*. 带弹簧夹的写字板,写字夹板 / '~-'**on** *adj*. 用夹子夹牢的

clip[2] [klip](clipped; clipping) *vt*. 1. 剪;剪短 2. 剪取(羊等)的毛;修剪 3. 剪(或削)取...的边端 4. 剪辑(报纸、杂志等);(从报刊上)剪取 5.(在拼法、发音方面)省略:a *clipped* word 缩略词,截短词(如 ad 就是 advertisement 的缩略词) 6. 轧(车票等) 7. 删去;削减(权力、影响等) 8.〈俚〉痛打,猛击 9.〈俚〉骗取...的钱财,敲...的竹杠 — *vi*. 1. 剪;剪辑报刊 2. 疾飞而过 — *n*. 1. 剪;剪短;修剪 2. 羊毛的一次(或一季)剪下量;剪下来的东西(如胶片的一段) 3. 猛击 4. 快步 5. 指甲刀;[~s]〈苏格兰〉大剪刀 ‖ ~ **joint**〈美俚〉索价特别高昂的咖啡馆(或夜总会等);专敲顾客竹杠的场所

clipper ['klipə] *n*. 1. 剪削者;剪取者(如剪羊毛工人等) 2.[常~s](理发、修指甲等用的)轧刀;(剪树枝或羊毛用的)大剪刀;钳子 3. 快速帆船;快速飞机(尤指巨型远程民航班机);快马 4.【无】削波器,限幅器 5.〈英俚〉出色的人(或物)

clipping ['klipiŋ] *n*. 剪下物;〈美〉(报纸、杂志等的)剪辑,剪报

clique [kliːk] *n*. 派系,小集团

cloak [kləuk] *n*. 1. 斗篷,披风;大氅 2. 覆盖(物) 3. 伪装,借口 — *vt*. 1. 给...披斗篷 2. 覆盖;包藏,掩盖 ‖ '~-**and**-'**dagger** *adj*. 1.(作品、作家等)描写间谍密探的 2. 阴谋的;间谍的,搞特务活动的 / '~**room** *n*. 1. 衣帽间;行李寄存处 2. 议院休息室 3.〈英〉〈委婉语〉厕所

clobber ['klɔbə] *vt*.〈口〉1. 痛打,狠揍 2. 抨击 3. 压倒,打垮

clock [klɔk] *n*. 1.(时)钟 2. 钟式记录(或记量)仪表;计程器 3. 上下班记时钟,考勤钟(= time ~) 4.〈口〉跑表,秒表 5.

（英俚）（人的）面孔 — vt. 1. 为（比赛等）记时 vi. 为（运动员）撕秒表（运动员等）花… 跑（或游）完 2.（用机械装置）记录（速度、距离、次数等）— vi.（用自动记时钟）记录上（下）班时间（in, on, out, off）‖ ~ er n. 1.（比赛、交通情况等的）计时员；车流量统计员 ‖ '~wise adj. & adv. 顺时针方向的（地）‖ '~work n. 钟表机械；发条装置

clod [klɒd] n. 1. 泥块 2. 呆子；乡下佬

clog [klɒg] n. 1.（绑在人或动物腿等上以阻碍其行动的）脚（或颈、手）坠 2.〈古〉障碍物 3. 木屐 — (clogged; clogging) vt. 1. 阻碍，妨碍 2. 塞满；阻塞，堵塞 — vi. 1. 阻塞，堵塞 2. 粘成（或凝成）一块 3. 跳木屐舞 ‖ ~ dance 木屐舞

cloisonné [ˌklwɑːzɒˈnei]（法）n. 景泰蓝 — adj. 用制景泰蓝方法制的；~ enamel 景泰蓝

cloister [ˈklɔistə] n. 1. 修道院；修道院的生活；隐居处 2.（修道院、教堂、学院等处的）回廊 — vt. 1. 使居于修道院中；使与尘世隔绝 2. 设回廊于 ‖ ~ed adj. 1. 居于修道院内的；隐居的 2. 有回廊的

clone [kləun] n. 1.〔生〕无性（繁殖）系，纯系，克隆；无性系个体 2. 无性系植物 3. 复制品，复本；翻版；（儿子）一模一样的人 4. 没有头脑机械行事的人，机器人 — vt. 使无性繁殖；克隆；复制 — vi. 无性繁殖，克隆

close¹ [kləus] adj. 1. 近的，接近的；紧密的，紧贴的：a ~ combat 近战 2.（衣服等）紧身的；齐整的：cut the hair — 把头发剪得极短 3. 亲密的，（关系）密切的 4. 严密的，周密的；仔细的；准确的 5. 势均力敌的；几乎相等的：a ~ match 一场不相上下的比赛 6. 关闭的，封闭的；（弄堂等）狭窄的；有限制的；

vowel〔语〕闭元音 7. 只限于少数特权人物的；a ~ corporation（由少数人控制、其股票不上市的）封闭式公司 8. 闷人的，不通风的；闷热的；潮湿的 9. 秘密的，隐藏的；嘴紧的，沉默的；keep sth. ~ 保守某事的秘密 10. 吝啬的，小气的 11.（钱等）难得到的 — adv. 接近；紧：紧密：秘密地 ‖ '~·ly adv. / ~·ness n. ‖ ~·cropped, '~·cut adj.（头发、草等）剪得短短的：头发（或毛发）剪短了的 / '~·fisted adj. 吝啬的，小气的 /（衣服）紧身的 / '~·grained adj. 1.（木头等）纹理细密的 2. 有条不紊的 / '~·knit adj. 1. 紧密结合在一起的 2.（论据等）严谨的 / '~·mouthed, '~·lipped adj. 嘴紧的 / ~·quarters 近距离：fight at ~ quarters 肉搏 / ~ season 禁猎期（=〈美〉closed season）/ '~·set adj.（眼睛或牙齿等）长得紧挨在一起的 / ~ shot（电影等的）近景 / '~·stool n.（病房等用的）有盖便桶 / '~·up n.（电影等）特写镜头 2. 仔细的观察 3. 小传

close² [kləuz] vt. 1. 关，闭；封闭 2. 终止，结束；结清（帐目）商定（交易）3. 使聚拢，使靠近；靠拢（从船到岸）；接通（电流）— vi. 1. 关闭，结束，停 2. 靠拢，接近；会合 3. 扭打，搏斗 4. 同意（on, upon, with）— n. 1. 结束，终止，尾声 2.〈古〉扭打，搏斗 3. [kləus]（四周围住的）场地，院子（英）从街道通入院子的通道）‖ ~ n. 关闭者 ‖ ~·r n. 关闭者；关闭器〔电〕闭合器 ‖ ~·down n. 1.（工厂等的）关闭，停工 2.（夜的）降临 3.（电台的）停播

closed [kləuzd] adj. 1. 关闭的，闭合的；封闭的；排外的：a ~ syllable〔语〕闭音节 / a ~ economy 闭关自守的经济 2. 保密的：a ~ ballot 秘密投票 3. 已定了的：a ~ issue 已议决的事情 / ~

chain [化]闭链 /～ **circuit** [电]闭路;闭路电视 /～'**circuit** adj. 闭合的的 /'～'**door** adj. 关着门的;秘密的 /～ **primary** 关门预选(仅由某一政党成员参加的预选) /～ **shop**(根据工会与资方协议)只雇用某一工会会员的商店(或工厂);只雇用某一工会会员的制度

closet ['klɔzit] n. 1. 私室;小房间 2.(国王、官吏等的)议事室;密室 3. 壁橱;碗橱;衣橱 4. 盥洗室;厕所;抽水马桶 — adj. 1. 关起门来的、私下的 / 闭门造车的、空谈的 — vt. 把...关在小室中,使... 引进密室会谈 / ～ **drama**(只能作为阅读用而不适合演出的)案头剧,书斋剧 /～ **queen** 暗地里搞同性关系的男子

closure ['kləuʒə] n. 1. 关闭;闭合 2. 结束;结尾;闭幕 3. 关闭物;可闭合的东西;[数]闭包,闭合 /[语]闭塞;[地]闭合度 4.(议会中的)终止辩论;提付表决 — vt.(辩论)终止(以进行投票);使(发言者)终止辩论

clot [klɔt] n. 1.(血等的)凝块 2. 粘土等的)块 2.(人、动物等的)一堆 /〈俚〉呆子,蠢人 — (clotted; clotting) vi.(血等)凝块;(人等)群集 — vt. 使凝块;使结凝块;使拥塞

cloth [klɔ:θ] ([复] cloths [klɔ:θs, klɔ:ðz]) n. 1. 布;(棉、毛、丝、麻、合成纤维等)织物;衣料 2. 布块;桌布 3.(某一职业的标志性)专门服装,制服(尤指教士服装);[the ～][总称]教士 4.[海]帆 /'～-**binding** n.(书的)布面装订 /'～-**cap** adj.〈英〉戴布帽子的,劳工阶级的 /'～-**eared** adj. 有点聋的,听觉不灵的

clothe [kləuð] (clothed 或 clad [klæd]) vt. 1. 给...穿衣;为...提供衣服 2. 覆盖;使披上 3. 表达 — an idea in unmistakable language 用明白无误的语言表达

一个想法

clothes [kləuðz] [复] n. 1. 衣服 2.[总称]床上用品 ‖～-**bag** n. 放待洗(或洗净)衣物的袋 /～ **basket** 放待洗(或洗净)衣物的篮 /～-**horse** n. 晒衣架 /～-**line** n. 1. 晒衣绳 2.〈美俚〉私人伴情 家丑 /～ **moth**(蛀蚀衣物的)衣蛾 /～-**peg** n.(英)(晒衣用的)衣夹 /～-**pin** n. = ～-**peg** /～ **prop**(英)晒衣绳支架 /～-**tree** 柱式衣架,衣帽架

clothing ['kləuðiŋ] n.[总称]衣服;[海]帆装

cloud [klaud] n. 1. 云 2. 云;云状物(如尘雾等);a mushroom ～(核爆炸形成的)蘑菇云 3.(鸟、虫、飞机等飞掠而过的)一大群 4. 遮暗物;阴影;模糊;under the ～ of night 夜色朦胧中/with a ～ on one's brow 双眉紧锁地 5. 污斑;(大理石的)云纹 — vt. 1. 使布满着云 2. 把...弄得朦胧不清;把...弄暗 3. 使黯然 4. 诽谤(名誉等);毁损(友谊等) — vi. 1. 云层密布(over);(镜面等)布满模糊斑点 2.(脸色等)阴沉下来(over) ‖～ed adj. 1. 布满着云的 2. 模糊的,含糊的;(人)头脑糊涂的 3. 斑驳的 /'～-**burst** n. 大暴雨 /'～-**hopping** n.(尤指当代飞机的)云中飞行 /'～ **seeding** [气](人工降雨用)云的催化

cloudy ['klaudi] adj. 1. 云的;云一般的 2. 多云的;被云遮住的;阴天的 3.(情绪等)阴郁的,烦恼的 4.(在意义等方面)模糊的,不明了的 5.(液体、水晶等)浑浊的;(大理石等)有云纹的 ‖ **cloudily** adv. / **cloudiness** n.

clout [klaut] n. 1.〈方〉(作补钉用的)碎布;碎皮 2.(尤指擦碗等用的)抹布,揩布 3.(婴孩等的)衣服 4. 敲击;掌击 5. 箭靶;中靶的一箭 6. 神通,门路,势力

响 7. 大平头钉 — **vt.** 1. 给…打补钉 2.〈口〉敲击;掌击

clove[kləuv]**cleave**[1]的过去式

clove[2][kləuv] **n.** 1.【植】丁香;丁香树 2.【植】小鳞茎

cloven['kləuvn]**cleave**[1]的过去分词 — **adj.** 劈开的;分成两瓣的

clover['kləuvə] **n.**【植】红花草;苜蓿 ‖'~-leaf **n.**(道路的)苜蓿叶式(或四叶式)立体交叉

clown[klaun] **n.** 1.(马戏、喜剧等的)小丑;丑角 2. 乡下佬;粗人 — **vi.** 扮小丑

cloy[klɔi] **vt.**(因过量而)倒(胃口);使腻烦,使厌倦(with) — **vi.** 倒胃口;使人感到腻烦

cloze[kləuz] **adj.**(对阅读理解能力的)填充测验法的

club[klʌb] **n.** 1. 棍棒;大头棒 2.(高尔夫球等的)球棒 3. 俱乐部;夜总会;会,社 4.(纸牌中的)梅花(一张)梅花纸牌 5.【植】(末端粗大如瘤的)球棒状结构(或器官)(clubbed;clubbing) — **vt.** 1. 用棍棒打 2. 把…当棍棒用;把…像棍棒似地施暴 3.(头发)束成棍棒状 4. 使联合,使合成一体;凑集;募集(together,with) ‖ ~ ideas and exertions 群策群力 5.〈主英〉使乱作一团 — **vi.** 1. 组成俱乐部;联合起来(together,with) 2. 分担费用 ‖'~'foot **n.** 畸形足;(先天性)足畸形 / '~'footed **adj.** 畸形足的 / '~'house **n.** 1. 俱乐部会所 2. 运动队更衣室 / '~-man **n.** 俱乐部会员 / '~ moss【植】石松

cluck[klʌk] **vi. & vt.** 1. 咯咯地叫唤 2.(用舌)发略略声 — **n.** 1.(母鸡唤小鸡时的)咯咯声 2. 略略声 3.〈俚〉笨蛋

clue[klu:] **n.** 1.(为调查、猜谜等提供的)线索,提示 2.(故事的)线索;思路 — **vt.** 为…提供线索,提示

clump[klʌmp] **n.** 1.(树、灌木等的)丛,簇 2.(人、建筑物等的)群 3.(密密的)一团;一块 3. 沉重的脚步声 4. 加厚鞋底 5.(血球等的)凝块 — **vi.** 1. 用沉重的脚步行走 2. 丛生;成群;结块,结团 — **vt.** 1. 把…栽成一丛;使成群;使结块(或结团) 2. 给(靴子)上厚皮底

clumsy['klʌmzi] **adj.** 1. 笨拙的;手脚不灵活的;姿势不雅观的 2. 愚笨的;不圆滑的 3. 制作粗陋的;(文体等)臃肿的 ‖ **clumsily adv. /clumsiness n.**

clung[klʌŋ]**cling**的过去式和过去分词

cluster['klʌstə] **n.** 1.(同类事物或人的)一串、一束、一簇、一群、一组 2.【语】辅音丛 3. 音簇 — **vi.** 1. 使成群,丛集;集成一束(或一簇、一组) 2. 群集;集中 — **vi.** 群集;丛生

clutch[klʌtʃ] **vt.** 抓住,攫住 — **vi.** 抓住,攫(at) — **n.** 1.[常 ~s]爪子;手;掌握,控制(一把)抓住,攫住 3.【机】离合器;离合器踏板;离合器杆(起重机的)抓斗 4. 紧要关头

clutter['klʌtə] **n.** 1. 杂乱,零乱 2.(房屋、商店等)拥挤而杂乱的一群 — **vt.** 乱糟糟地堆满,把…弄得杂乱(up)

cm. **abbr.** centimetre(s)

Co【化】元素钴(cobalt)的符号

co- **pref.** 1. 表示"共同"、"一起"、"相互":cooperate 2.【数】表示"角的余、补":cosine

c/o, c.o. **abbr.** 1.care of 由…转交 2.carried over(簿记用语)转入

coach[kəutʃ] **n.** 1.(旧时的)四轮大马车,公共马车 2. 长途公共汽车 3.(铁路上的)客车 4.(汽车拖着的)活动房子 5. 汽车车身(尤指轿车车身) 6.(客机的)二等座 7.(船)(军舰后甲板上

的)舰尾室(通常供舰长用) 8. 私人教师;指导员;(体育运动的)教练 — vt. 1. 训练,指导,辅导 2. 当……的指导(或教练) — vi. 1. 乘马车旅行 2. 作指导(或辅导),作基点;接受辅导 ‖ **house** 马车房/~**man** n. 赶马车人/'~**work** n. 汽车车身的设计、制造和装配

coagulate ['kəu'ægjuleit] vt. & vi. (使)凝结;(使)合成一体 — adj. 凝结成的 ‖ **co．agu'lation** n. 凝结

coal [kəul] n. 煤;煤块 — vt. & vi. (给……)上煤,(给……)加煤 ‖ '~**black** adj. 漆黑的,墨黑的/~**bunker** 煤舱/~**face** 正在开采的煤层截面/'~**field** n. 煤田/~**gas** 煤气/'~**ing station** 煤站;加煤站

coalesce [,kəuə'les] vi. 接合;结合;联合 ‖ **coalescence** n.

coalition [,kəuə'liʃən] n. 结合;联合;结合体;(政党、个人或国家间临时性的)联盟

coarse [kɔːs] adj. 1. 粗的;粗糙的;粗劣的 2. (工具等)做粗活用的;粗线条的;约略的 3. 粗鲁的,粗暴的;粗俗的 4.(言语等)猥亵的 5. 粗声粗气的;沙声的 ‖ '~**ly** adv. /'~**ness** n.

coarsen ['kɔːsn] vt. & vi. (使)变粗(或粗糙、粗俗,粗鲁)

coast [kəust] n. 1. 海岸;海滨(地区) ‖ [the C-] (美国或加拿大的)太平洋沿岸地区 2. (美)适宜滑雪的山坡;骑自行车或乘橇的)向下滑行 — vt. 沿……的沿岸航行 — vi. 1. 沿岸航行;沿岸经商 2. 作惯性滑行 3. (人)随波逐流;毫不费力地做(along) ‖ '~**wise** adv. & adj. 沿着海岸(的) ‖ '~**guard** 1. 海岸警卫队 2. 海岸警卫队队员/'~**line** n. 海岸线

coastal ['kəustl] adj. 海岸的;沿海岸的

coaster ['kəustə] n. 1. 在沿海港口间航行(或经商)的船(或人);沿海居民 2. 滑坡的车(或橇)3.(杯子、酒瓶等的)垫子;杯托

coat [kəut] n. 1. 外套,上衣;女式上装 2.(动物的)皮毛;(植物的)表皮 3. 层,膜;(漆等的)涂层 — vt. 给……穿上外套;在……上涂(或盖、包); Your tongue is ~ed. 你舌苔发厚。‖ '~**ing** n. 涂层;上衣衣料 ‖ ~ **of arms** (盾形)纹章;(政府、公司等用作标志的)盾形徽号/'~**tail** n. 1.(男外衣的)后下襟;(燕尾服的)燕尾 2. [coattails](美)提携能力 adj. 以(政治上的)提携能力为基础(或根据)的

coauthor [kəu'ɔːθə] n.(书的)合著者

coax [kəuks] vt. 1. 用好话劝;哄骗;靠哄骗获得 2. 耐心地处理;慢慢把……弄好;~ a fire to light 把火慢慢弄旺 — vi. 哄骗 ‖ '~**ingly** adv.

coaxial [,kəu'æksiəl] adj. 共轴的;同轴的 ‖ ~ **cable** 同轴电缆

cob [kɔb] n. 1.(煤、石头、矿石等的)圆块;圆石 2. 圆面包 2. 玉米穗轴;玉米穗子芯 3. [动]大黑背鸥 4. 结实的矮脚马 5. = ~ **nut** 6. 堆鸥 ‖ ~ **coal** 圆煤块/'~**nut** n. [植]欧洲榛(或其果实)

cobalt ['kəubɔːlt] n. [化]钴;钴蓝颜料

cobble[1] ['kɔbl] n. 1.(铺路等用的)大卵石,圆石 2. [地]中砾 3.(英)[~s]圆煤块 — vt. 用圆石铺(路) ‖ '~**stone** n. 圆石子,大卵石

cobble[2] ['kɔbl] vt. 1. 修,补(鞋等);粗略地补(破洞等)2. 粗制滥造(up)

cobbler ['kɔblə] n. 1. 皮匠,补鞋匠 2.(古)手艺笨拙的工匠 3. [~s](英俚)睾丸;屁话

cobra ['kəubrə] *n.* 【动】眼镜蛇

cobweb ['kɔbweb] *n.* 1. 蜘蛛网;蜘蛛丝 2. 蜘蛛网似的东西;clear away the ~s from the mind 克服思想上的紊乱状态 — (cobwebbed; cobwebbing) *vt.* 结网 (或蛛网状的东西)布满于

Coca-Cola ['kəukə'kəulə] *n.*〖美〗可口可乐(一种饮料;商标名)

cocaine [kə'kein] *n.*【药】可卡因,古柯碱

cock [kɔk] *n.* 1. 公鸡 2. 雄鸟(专指与其他动物连用指雄性);a ~ lobster 雄龙虾 3. 山鹬 4.〈古〉鸡叫;黎明 (= ~ crow) 5. 风信鸡,风标 6.(水管、煤气管等的)旋塞,龙头,开关 7.(枪的)击铁;击铁待发位置,准备击发姿势 8.(天平的)指针 9. 首领,头目;神气十足的人 10.(帽边、眼睑等的)翘起,向上翘;歪戴,歪斜 11.〖俚〗鸡巴 — *vt.* 1. 使翘起,使竖起;歪戴(帽子) 2. 扳起(枪枝)的击铁 — *vi.* 1. 大摇大摆地走 2. 翘起,竖起 3.(扳起击铁)准备击发 ‖ ~-a-doodle-doo ['kɔkədu:dl'du:] *n.* 1. 喔喔啼(鸡叫声) 2.〈儿语〉公鸡 / ~-and-'bull story 荒诞的故事,无稽之谈 / '~-crow *n.* 黎明 / '~-fight(ing) *n.* 斗鸡 / '~-pit *n.* 1. 斗鸡场;多次发生过战争的地方 2. 船尾舱,后甲板;下级军官及伤员用的伤兵室;低级军官卧室 4.(飞行员)座舱;(汽车、赛车的)驾驶座 / ~-'scomb ['kɔkskəum] *n.* 1. 鸡冠花 2.(小丑的)鸡冠状帽子 / ~-'sparrow *n.* 公麻雀;矮小而强悍的人 / '~-spur *n.* 1. 公鸡的距 2.【植】鸡距山楂

cockade [kə'keid] *n.* 帽章,帽上的花结

cockatoo [,kɔkə'tu:] *n.*【动】凤头鹦鹉,葵花鹦鹉

cockeyed ['kɔkaid] *adj.* 1. 斜视的,斗鸡眼的;斜的,歪的 2. 疯疯癫癫的;荒诞

的 3. 喝醉的

cocker ['kɔkə] *n.* 1. 西班牙小猎狗 2. 主办(或参加)斗鸡的人

cockle ['kɔkl] *n.*【动】鸟蛤 2. 轻舟 ‖ '~-boat *n.* 轻舟 / '~-shell *n.* 1. 鸟蛤壳 2. 轻舟 / ~ stairs 盘旋楼梯

cocklebur ['kɔklbə:] *n.*【植】1. 苍耳 2. 苍耳的刺果 3. 牛蒡

cockney ['kɔkni] *n.* 1. 伦敦佬(尤指住东区的人) 2. 伦敦方言

cockroach ['kɔkrəutʃ] *n.* 蟑螂

cocksure [,kɔk'ʃuə] *adj.* 绝对肯定的,坚信不疑的;过于自信的,自以为是的 (of, about) ‖ ~ly *adv.* / ~ness *n.*

cocktail ['kɔkteil] *n.* 1. 鸡尾酒 2.(西餐中头道进食的)开胃品(如果汁等)

cocky ['kɔki] *adj.* 骄傲自大的;趾高气扬的 ‖ **cockily** *adv.* / **cockiness** *n.*

coco ['kəukəu] ([复] cocos) *n.*【植】椰子树;椰子

cocoa ['kəukəu] *n.* 1. 可可粉;可可茶 2. 可可树 3. 可可色 ‖ ~ bean 可可豆,可可子

coco(a) nut ['kəukənʌt] *n.* 椰子;椰子肉 ‖ ~ butter、~ oil 椰子油 / ~ palm、~ tree 椰子树

cocoon [kə'ku:n] *n.* 1. 茧;(昆虫的)卵袋 2. 茧状物;(军用物品等的)塑料披盖;防护物 — *vt.* 把……紧紧包住;把……密封起来 — *vi.* 作茧;成茧状

COD *abbr.* cash on delivery【商】货到付款

cod [kɔd] ([复] cod(s)) *n.*【动】鳕(鱼) ‖ '~-fish *n.* 鳕(鱼) / '~-liver oil 鱼肝油

coddle ['kɔdl] *vt.* 1. 煮(蛋等) 2. 悉心照料;娇养,溺爱

code [kəud] *n.* 1. 法典,法规 2. 规则,准则;礼教习俗 3. 代号;代码;电码;密码 4.【生】遗传密码 — *vt.* 把……编成

密码(或电码、代号等);为…编码(或编号) — *vi.*(为蛋白质的合成等)指定遗传密码(*for*) ‖ ~ book 电码本 / ~ flag 信号旗

codeine ['kəudi:n] *n.*【药】可待因(用以镇痛、镇咳、催眠等)

codger ['kɔdʒə] *n.*〈口〉怪僻的人(尤指老头);名声不好的家伙

codicil ['kɔdisil] *n.* 1. 遗嘱附件 2. 附录,补遗 3. 附加物 ‖ codi'cillary *adj.*

codify ['kɔdifai] *vt.* 1. 把(法律)编集成典 2. 编纂;整理 ‖ **codification** [ˌkɔdifi'keiʃən] *n.*

co-ed ['kəu'ed] *n.*〈口〉(男女同校)女学生 — *adj.* 男女同校的;(男女同校)的女学生的

coeducation ['kəuˌedju:'keiʃən] *n.* 男女同学(制) ‖ ~al *adj.*

coefficient [ˌkəui'fiʃənt] *n.* 1. 协同因素 2.【物】【数】系数 — *adj.* 协作的

coerce [kəu'əs] *vt.* 1. 强制,胁迫,迫使 2. 强制地取得(一致等)

coercion [kəu'əʃən] *n.* 1. 强迫;压制 2. 高压统治

coercive [kəu'əsiv] *adj.* 强迫的,强制的 ‖ ~ly *adv.* / ~ness *n.*

coeval [kəu'i:vəl] *adj. & n.* 同年龄的(人);同时代的(人或东西)

coexist ['kəuig'zist] *vi.* 1. 同时(或同地)存在,共存 2. 和平共处

coexistence ['kəuig'zistəns] *n.* 1. 共存,并存 2. 和平共处

coffee ['kɔfi] *n.* 1. 咖啡;咖啡茶;咖啡粉;咖啡色 2. 咖啡色的 ‖ ~ bean, ~ berry 咖啡豆 / ~ break(工间)喝咖啡休息时间 / ~ cake(用面粉、牛奶、蛋、奶油、糖等做的)咖啡糕 ‖ ~ pot *n.* 1. 咖啡壶 2. 快餐店 / ~ shop

咖啡店;小吃部

coffer ['kɔfə] *n.* 1. 保险箱 2. [~s]资产;财源;金库 3. = dam 4.【建】花格平顶,花格镶板 — *vt.* 1. 把…装入箱中;把…放存金库内;珍藏 2. 用花格镶板装饰 ‖ ~dam *n.* 围堰;潜水箱;【船】隔离舱

coffin ['kɔfin] *n.* 棺材,棺木;灵柩 — *vt.* 把…装入棺材,收殓

cog [kɔg] *n.* 1.(齿轮的)轮齿;嵌齿,齿;(木工的)雄榫 2.〈口〉不重要但不可缺少的人(或物) — (cogged; cogging) *vt.* 在…上装轮齿(或榫) ‖ ~wheel *n.* 嵌齿轮

cogent ['kəudʒənt] *adj.* 有说服力的 ‖ cogency *n.* / ~ly *adv.*

cogitate ['kɔdʒiteit] *vi. & vt.*(慎重)考虑 ‖ cogi'tation *n.* / cogitator *n.*

cognac ['kɔnjæk] *n.*(法国)科涅克上等白兰地;(法国)白兰地,上等白兰地

cognate ['kɔgneit] *adj.* 1. 同族的;同宗的 2.【语】同源的;同根的;a ~ object 同根宾语(如"live a life"中的"life") 3. 同性质的;同类的 — *n.* 1. 亲属 2. 同源词;同根词 3. 同性质的东西;同类物

cognition [kɔg'niʃən] *n.* 1. 认识;认识能力 2. 知识

cognizance ['kɔgnizəns] *n.* 1. 察知;认识 2. 注意;承认 3.【律】审判权;审理 4. 管辖权;职责 ‖ cognizant *adj.*

cognomen [kɔg'nəumen] *n.* 1. 姓氏 2. 名字;绰号

cohabit [kəu'hæbit] *vi.*(男女)同居 ‖ ~ation [kəuˌhæbi'teiʃən] *n.*

cohere [kəu'hiə] *vi.* 1. 粘着;粘合;可粘合 2.(论据等)紧凑;连贯;符合 3. 协调,一致

coherence [kəu'hiərəns, coherency

coherent [kəu'hiərənsi] *n.* 1. 粘着；粘合性 2.〈逻辑上的〉紧凑；连贯，一致性 3.【物】相干性 4.【化】内聚现象（或作用）

coherent [kəu'hiərənt] *adj.* 1. 粘着的，粘附的 2. 紧凑的，连贯的；首尾一致的；表达清楚的 3.【物】相干的，相参的 ‖ ~ **ly** *adv.*

cohesion [kəu'hi:ʒən] *n.* 1.【物】内聚力 2. 粘着；粘合；结合 3.【植】连着

cohesive [kəu'hi:siv] *adj.* 1. 粘着的，粘合的；紧密结合在一起的 2. 内聚（力）的 ‖ ~ **ly** *adv.* / ~ **ness** *n.*

cohort ['kəuhɔ:t] *n.* 1. 一队士兵；一群（人），一帮（人），一批（伙伴）2.〈口〉同事；追随者；支持者

coiffure [kwɑ:'fjuə] 1. 发式，发型 2. 头饰；头巾

coil [kɔil] *vt.* 卷，盘绕；把……卷成圈 — *vi.* 成圈状；盘绕 — *n.* 1.〈一〉卷；〈一〉圈；（河流等的）弯绕，环绕 2.【无】线圈 3. 盘簧 4.〈头发的〉一个结 5. 子宫节育环

coin [kɔin] *n.* 1. 硬币 2.〈俚〉金钱 — *vt.* 1. 铸造硬币；把〈金属〉铸成硬币 2. 创造；杜撰〈新词、新语等〉‖ ~ **er** *n.* 1. 造币者；（英）伪造货币者 2.〈新词等的〉创造者；杜撰者 ‖ ~ **-op** ['kɔinɔp] *n.*（投入硬币后洗衣机即自行操作的）自助洗衣店

coinage ['kɔinidʒ] *n.* 1. 造币，铸币；造币权 2. 货币制度 3. 新词语的创造；新造的词语

coincide [,kəuin'said] *vi.* 1.（在空间、时间方面）恰好相合，恰好重合 2. 一致，相符

coincidence [kəu'insidəns] *n.* 符合，一致；巧合；巧合的事物

coincident [kəu'insidənt] *adj.* 1. 同时发生的 2. 相叠的 3. 相符的，一致的 ‖

coincidental [kəu,insi'dentəl] *adj.* 1. 巧合的；碰巧的 2. = coincident ‖ ~ **ly** *adv.*

coke[1] [kəuk] *n.* 焦，焦炭 — *vt.* & *vi.*（使）成焦炭

coke[2] [kəuk] *n.* = cocaine

cola ['kəulə] *n.* 可乐的复数

colander ['kʌləndə] *n.* 滤器；罗；漏斗

cold [kəuld] *adj.* 1. 冷的，寒冷的 2. 冷淡的，不热情的 3. 使人战栗的，使人寒心的；使人扫兴的；无趣味的 4. 冷静的，客观的；经过周密考虑的；冷酷的，无情的 5. 已死的；失去知觉的 6. 勉强忍住的；未到爆发程度的 ‖ with ~ fury in one's heart 心中怀着一股怒火 7.〈土壤〉粘而湿的 8.（肥料）腐烂得慢的 9.（颜色）使人生冷感的，冷的（指青、绿、灰等）9. 没有准备的，贸然的 10.（分数）确定无疑的，十足的 11.（猎物的遗臭等）已变淡的 — *adv.* 完全地；The actor had his lines down ~. 这演员把台词背得滚瓜烂熟了。 ‖ ~ **ly** *adv.* 冷淡地 / ~ **ness** *n.* ‖ ~ **-blooded** *adj.* 冷血的；无情的；残酷的 / ~ **-'bloodedly** *adv.* 无情地；残酷地 / ~ **'bloodedness** *n.* 无情；残酷 / ~ **-cock** *vt.* 把……打昏 / ~ **colour** 冷色 / ~ **-draw** *vt.* 冷拉（金属丝等）/ ~ **frame**（保护植物抗寒的）冷床，阳畦 / ~ **front**【气】冷锋 / ~ **hammer** *vt.* 冷锤（金属等）/ ~ **hearted** *adj.* 冷酷无情的，铁石心肠的 / ~ **'heartedly** *adv.* 冷酷地；无情地 / ~ **'heartedness** *n.* 冷酷；冷心肠 / ~ **-roll** *vt.* 冷轧（钢材等）/ ~ **shoulder** 冷淡 / ~ **snap** 寒汛（期），冷汛（期）/ ~ **sore**（伤风发热时）嘴边疱疹、唇疱疹 / ~ **steel** 利器（指刀、剑等）/ ~ **storage** 1. 冷

藏 **2.** 〈美俚〉坟墓 / ~ **turkey 1.** 令人不快的话;直截了当的话(或方式) **2.** 冷漠孤高的人 **3.** 突然完全停止服用毒品 **4.** 〔作状语用〕无准备地;单刀直入地 / ~ **war** 冷战 / ~ **wave** 寒潮;冷烫(指化学烫发)

coleslaw [ˈkəulslɔ:] *n.* 凉拌卷心菜丝

colic [ˈkɔlik] *n.* 绞痛,急腹痛 — *adj.* **1.** 绞痛的 **2.** 结肠的

coliseum [ˌkɔliˈsiəm] *n.* 大体育场;大剧场;大型公共娱乐场所

collaborate [kəˈlæbəreit] *vi.* **1.** 合作,协作(尤指在文艺、科学等方面) **2.** 勾结(*with*) ‖ **collaborator** *n.* 合作者,协作者;勾结者

collaboration [kəˌlæbəˈreiʃən] *n.* **1.** 合作,协作 **2.** 勾结 ‖ ~**ism** *n.* 鼓吹与敌人合作;通敌(行为) ‖ ~**ist** *n.* 通敌者

collapse [kəˈlæps] *vi.* **1.** 倒塌 **2.** 崩溃,瓦解;(价格等)暴跌 **3.** (健康、精神等方面的)衰退;垮下 **4.** (椅子等)折叠起来 — *vt.* **1.** 使倒塌;使崩溃;使衰萎 **2.** 使折叠 — *n.* **1.** 倒塌;崩溃;衰弱 **2.** (价格等的)暴跌 **3.** 〔医〕虚脱;萎陷

collapsible, collapsable [kəˈlæpsəbl] *adj.* (椅子等)可折叠的

collar [ˈkɔlə] *n.* **1.** 衣领;硬领 **2.** 项圈;护颈 **3.** 马轭,颈圈;(为驯服的)脖围,颈圈 **4.** 环状物;箍;卡圈;束套;接头;套管 — *vt.* **1.** 扭住…的领口(或头颈) **2.** 给(衣服)装上领子 **3.** 加马轭(或颈圈) **4.** 〈俚〉未经许可拿走;抓住 **5.** 〈口〉硬拉住…说话 ‖ ~**ed** *adj.* 有领圈的;上了马轭(或颈圈)的 / ~**less** *adj.* 无领的;无马轭(或颈圈)的 ‖ ~'-**bone** *n.* 〔解〕锁骨

collateral [kəˈlætərəl] *adj.* **1.** 附属的,附带的 **2.** 旁系的 **3.** 间接的 — *n.* **1.** 旁系亲属 **2.** 担保品

colleague [ˈkɔli:g] *n.* 同事,同僚

collect [kəˈlekt] *vt.* **1.** 收集,搜集,采集;收(租、税等);募集(捐款) **2.** 集中(思想等);使镇定 **3.** 领取(信件等)取走 — *vi.* **1.** 集聚;堆积 **2.** 收款,收账;搜集 — *adj.* (电话、电报等)受话人(或收报人等)付费的 ‖ a ~ **telephone call** 受话人付费电话 — *adv.* (打电话、电报等时)由受话人(或收报人)付费 ‖ ~**able,** ~**ible** *adj.* **1.** 可收集(或采集)的 **2.** 适于收藏的 **3.** 可收取的 — *n.* 收藏品

collected [kəˈlektid] *adj.* **1.** 收集成的 **2.** 泰然自若的,镇定的 ‖ ~**ly** *adv.* 镇定地 / ~**ness** *n.* 镇定

collection [kəˈlekʃən] *n.* **1.** 收集,搜集,采集;收款 **2.** 收集物;收集物 **3.** 征收;收款;募捐;捐来的数子

collective [kəˈlektiv] *adj.* **1.** 集合的;集合性的;~ **fruit** 〔植〕聚花果/a ~ **noun** 〔语〕集合名词 **2.** 共同的,集体的;集团的;集体主义的 ‖ ~ **bargaining** (由工会代表劳方与资方进行的)集体谈判 / ~ **farm** 集体农庄 / ~ **noun** 〔语〕集合名词 — *n.* **1.** 集体;集体企业;集体企业人员 **2.** 〔语〕集合名词 ‖ ~**ly** *adv.*

collectivism [kəˈlektivizəm] *n.* 集体主义(制度) ‖ **collectivist** *n.*

collector [kəˈlektə] *n.* **1.** 收集人;收藏家;采集者 **2.** 收税员;收款员;募捐人 **3.** 收集物;收集器;a **dust** ~ 招积灰尘的东西 **4.** 〔电〕收集极,集电极;〔机〕集电器,收集器

college [ˈkɔlidʒ] *n.* **1.** (综合大学中的)学院 **2.** (独立的)学院;高等专科学校;〈美〉大学 **3.** 大学预科;(英)公学(专指若干中学程度的公立学校) **4.** 职业学校;技术学校 **5.** 学院(或学校)的建筑物 **6.** 学会;社团:the **College** of **Cardinals** 〔天主教〕红衣主教团(罗马教皇的枢

密院）7.〈俚〉监狱;感化院 ‖ '～-'bred
adj. 受过大学教育的 / ～ pudding(供
一人吃的)小葡萄干布丁

collegiate [kə'liːdʒiət] adj. 1. 学院的;大
学的;大学生的 2. 社团的 ‖ ～ly adv.
‖ ～ church 1. (天主教,英国国教的)
大圣堂(苏格兰)有两个以上牧师共
同主持的教会 2. (美)联合教会;联合
教会的教堂

collide [kə'laid] vi. 1.(车、船等)碰撞,互
撞 2.冲突,抵触(with) — vt. 使碰撞

collie ['kɔli] n.(长毛)柯利牧羊犬

collier ['kɔliə] n. 1.(煤矿)矿工 2. 运煤
船;煤船船员

colliery ['kɔliəri] n. 煤矿

collision [kə'liʒən] n. 1.(车、船等的)碰
撞 2.(利益、意见等的)冲突

collocation [,kɔlə'keiʃən] n. 1. 并置;排
列;配置,布置 2.【语】(习惯上的)搭配

colloid ['kɔlɔid] n. 1. 胶体;胶质 2. 胶态

colloquial [kə'ləukwiəl] adj. 口语的,会
话的;用通俗口语的 ‖ ～ly adv.

colloquialism [kə'ləukwiəlizəm] n. 1. 口
语;口语词;口语用法 2. 口语体

colloquy ['kɔləkwi] n. 会谈;谈话,对话;
讨论

collusion [kə'luːʒən] n. 共谋,勾结,串通

collude [kə'luːd] vi. 共谋,勾结,串通 ‖
col'lusion n.

colluvial [kə'luːviəl] adj.【地】崩积的

Cologne [kə'ləun] n. 1. 科隆[德国西部
城市] 2.[c-]科隆香水

Colombia [kə'ləmbiə] n. 哥伦比亚[南美
洲西北部国家]

Colombo [kə'lʌmbəu] n. 科伦坡[斯里兰
卡首都]

colon[1] ['kəulən] n.([复] cola ['kəulə] 或
colons) n.【解】结肠 ‖ ～ic [kə'lɔnik] adj.

colon[2] ['kəulən] n. 冒号(即:)

colonel ['kəːnl] n. 1.(英)陆军(或海军陆
战队)上校;(美)陆军(或空军、海军陆
战队)上校 2. 中校(= lieutenant ～) ‖
～cy n. ‖ Colonel Blimp[blimp] 布林普
上校(漫画人物);老顽固;反动家伙

colonial [kə'ləunjəl] adj. 1. 殖民地的 2.
[C-](美国独立前)十三州殖民地时代
的;美国初期的 3. 拥有殖民地的;由
殖民地构成的 4.【地】集群的;群体的
— n. 殖民地居民

colonialism [kə'ləunjəlizəm] n. 1. 殖民主
义 2. 殖民地的地位(或持征) 3. 殖民
政策 ‖ colonjalist n. & adj. 殖民主义
者(的)

colonist ['kɔlənist] n. 1. 殖民地开拓者;
移民 2. 殖民地居民

colonize ['kɔlənaiz] vt. 1. 开拓殖民地于
(某地区) 2. 移(民)于殖民地 3.〈美〉
(为打败一党的势力)非法迁居选民非
法移入(某地区) 4.(为政治企图派人)
打入,混进(部门等) — vi. 1. 开拓殖
民地 2. 移居于殖民地 ‖ coloni'zation
n. /～r n. 殖民地开拓者;殖民者

colonnade [,kɔlə'neid] n. 1.【建】柱廊 2.
成行的树 ‖ ～d adj. 设有柱廊的

colony ['kɔləni] n. 1. 殖民地 2. 移民队,
殖民团 3.(住在外国大都市一区域的)
侨民;聚居地 4.(艺术家、外交家等的)
一群;同类人的聚居地 5.【集】集群;群
体;菌落

color ['kʌlə] n., vt. & vi. (美) = colour

Colorado [,kɔlə'rɑːdəu] n. 科罗拉多[美国
州名]

coloratura [,kɔlərə'tuərə] n.【音】(声乐
的)花腔;花腔音乐;花腔歌手;花腔女
高音

colossal [kə'lɔsl] adj. 1. 巨像的;巨像似

的;庞大的 2.〈口〉异常的,非常的

Colosseum [ˌkɔlə'siəm] *n.* 1. 古罗马圆形剧场(建于公元七五年) 2. [c-] = coliseum

colossus [kə'lɔsəs] ([复] colossi [kə'lɔsai] 或 colossuses) *n.* 巨像;巨人;巨物

colour ['kʌlə] *n.* 1. 颜色;色彩;彩色;脸色,血色;红晕 3. 肤色;肤色人种的肤色: a person of ~ 有色人种的人,非白种人 4. 颜料;染料 5. [常~s]旗帜;[~s](作为所属团体色彩标志的)绶带;徽章;衣帽;[~s]立场,观点 6. 外貌;(表面的)真实性;幌子: His story has some ~ of truth. 他的一番叙述听来似乎是真的。7. 生动,多彩: add ~ to an article 润色文章 8. [音]音色(= tone ~) — *vt.* 给…着色;染;改变...的颜色 2. 使带上色彩;渲染;伪装;曲解 — *vi.* 获得颜色 (果实成熟时等)变色;脸红(*up*): The leaves have begun to ~. 叶子已经开始发黄(或红等)。‖ ~ bar 种族障碍,肤色障碍(尤指白人对黑人的歧视) / `~ blind *adj.* 色盲的;不承认种族差异的 / ~ blindness 色盲 / `~ fast *adj.* 不退色的 / `~ film 1. 彩色胶片 2. 彩色影片 / ~ filter 彩色滤光片 / ~ guard 护旗队 / ~ line(种族歧视制度下的)种族界限 / ~ television 彩色电视

colouration [ˌkʌlə'reiʃən] *n.* 1. 着色(法);(生物等的)天然颜色;色彩,特色

coloured ['kʌləd] *n.* 有色的;[常用以构成复合词]有...色的: cream-~ 奶油色的 2. 经过渲染的;有色彩的;伪装的 3. 有色人种的(尤指黑人的) 4. 混血种的(尤指非纯白色的) — *n.* 有色人种的(尤指黑人) ;混血人

colourful ['kʌləful] *adj.* 1. 颜色丰富的;多色的;艳丽的 2. 丰富多彩的;吸引

人的 ‖ ~ly *adv.* / ~ness *n.*

colouring ['kʌləriŋ] *n.* 1. 着色(法) 2. 色彩;色调 3. 面色;外貌;伪装 4. 颜料 5.(新闻报道等)的倾向性 6. 特质 ‖ ~ matter(食物等)着色剂;染料;色素

colourless ['kʌləlis] *adj.* 1. 无色的 2. 苍白的,无血色的;色彩暗淡的 3. 无趣味的,不生动的;无特色的 4.(新闻报道等)不偏不倚的,没有倾向性的 ‖ ~ly *adv.* / ~ness *n.*

colt [kəult] *n.* 1.(4,5岁以下的)公驹;马驹 2. 生手,新手 3. 答绳

Columbia [kə'lʌmbiə] 哥伦比亚[美国南卡罗来纳州首府] 2. 哥伦比亚[美国密苏里州中部城市] 3.(诗)美国 ‖ ~n *adj.* ‖ **District of** ~ 哥伦比亚特区[美国首都华盛顿所在的行政区域]; 略作 D.C.)

columbine ['kɔləmbain] *n.* [植]耧斗菜;美洲耧斗菜;蓝花耧斗菜 — *adj.*(似)鸽的

columbium [kə'lʌmbiəm] *n.* [化]铌(niobium 铌的旧名)

column ['kɔləm] *n.* 1. 柱,支柱,圆柱;柱状物 2. [军]纵队 3.(报刊中的)栏;专栏 4. [数]列 5. [植]柱,茎柱 ‖ ~ar [kə'lʌmnə] *adj.* / ~ed *adj.* 有圆柱的;圆柱形的 / ~ist ['kɔləmnist] *n.*(报刊)专栏作家

com- *pref.* 表示"与","合","共","全"(用在 b, p, m 前;很少用在元音前): *com*bine, *com*pany, *com*mon

coma ['kəumə] *n.* 1. [医]昏迷 2. 惛怠;麻木

comb [kəum] *n.* 1. 梳;马梳 2. [纺]精梳机 3. [动]蜂巢(= honeycomb) 4. [动]肉冠;鸡冠状物 5. 梳理 6. 浪尖,浪峰 — *vt.* 1. 梳(发);用马梳梳(马)

【纺】精梳 3. 彻底搜查(某处) — vi.
(浪)涌起,卷起 ‖ ~ er n. 1. 梳刷者
2.【纺】精梳机,卷毛器 ‖ '~-out n. 1.
梳理头发 2. 彻底检查;扫荡;清除 3.
(在一个机构中)全部适龄壮丁的搜罗

combat ['kɔmbæt] n. 1. 战斗;斗争;反对
2. 竞争;争论 — (combat(t)ed;combat-
(t)ing) vt. 跟(疾病等)战斗;反对 — vi.
战斗;搏斗(with,against,for) ‖
~ car 轻型装甲车;轻型坦克 / ~ fa-
tigue 战斗疲劳症

Combatant ['kɔmbætənt] adj. 战斗的 —
n. 1. 战斗员 2. 格斗者

combative ['kɔmbətiv] adj. 好斗的 ‖ ~ly
adv. / ~ness n.

combination [,kɔmbi'neiʃən] n. 1. 结合,
联合,合并;结合体,联合体 2. 配有拖
车的摩托车 3. [~s]连衫裤 4.【化】化
合 5.【数】组合 6. = ~ lock 7. 两用(或
多用)的工具 ‖ ~ lock 暗码锁,转字锁

combine¹ [kəm'bain] vt. 1. 使结合;使联
合 2. 兼有,兼备(各种性质等);a ~d
bridge 铁路公路两用桥 3. 使化合 —
vi. 1. 结合 2. 化合

combine² ['kɔmbain] n. 1.(企业等)联
合,(以操纵物价为目的的)联合
企业 2. 联合收割机,康拜因(= ~ har-
vester) — vt. 用联合收割机收割

combustible [kəm'bʌstibl] adj. 1. 易燃
的;可燃的 2. 易于激动的 — n. [常~s]
易燃物;可燃物 ‖ com.busti'bility n. 易
燃性;可燃性

combustion [kəm'bʌstʃən] n. 1. 燃烧 2.
极度的愤怒(或激动);骚动;混乱

come [kʌm] (came [keim],come) vi. 1.
来(节日等)来临 2.(事物)到来,落
到;产生;What has ~ of his scheme? 他
的计划结果怎样? 3. 来(自);出生
(于)(from,of);No harm ~ to him.

他不会遭到伤害。4. 出现(于),位
(于);This quotation ~s on p.104. 这段
引文在一○四页上。5./Iron ~s between
manganese and cobalt in atomic weight. 铁
的原子量在锰与钴之间。5.(路线等)
达(到),伸展(到)(to) 6. 达(某一
点),谈到;Now we ~ to Chapter III. 现
在我们讲第三章。7. [后接不定式]终
于,竟能;You will ~ to realize that someday. 你总有一天会认识到那一点的。
8. [与 how 连用,构成问句;时常不用助
动词 do,而将主谓语颠倒](怎么)会
达;How did you ~ (或 How came you)
to know him so well? 你怎么会跟他那
么熟的? 9. 变成,成为;The screw has
~ loose. 螺丝钉松了。[口]变出;The
butter will not ~. 黄油做不成。(指不
能凝结成形) 11. 需要(某种)代价;~
high(商品等)售价高 12. [口]装出;~
the bully (the virtuous) over sb. 某人
装出盛气凌人(道貌岸然)的样子 13.
(货物等)被供应;This sweater ~s in
six sizes. 这种运动衫有六种尺码供应。
14. 满…足岁;My sister is coming seventeen. 我妹妹即将满十七足岁。15.
(性交时)达到高潮 — int. [表示要引起
注意、鼓励、不耐烦、责备等]喂! 嗨!
得啦! Come, we must hurry. 喂,我们
得赶紧啦。‖ ~-at-able [,kʌm'ætəbl]
adj. [口]可接近的,易得手的 / '~-back
n. 1. 复原;复辟;stage a ~back 搞复
辟,卷土重来 2. 尖刻的回答 3. 赔偿
/ '~-down n. 1. 败落 2. 屈辱,倒霉
/ '~-'hither n. & adj. 勾引(的) / '~-on
n. 1. 吸引;引诱;诱惑(物) 2. 骗子
3. 受骗的人 adj. 勾引的;引诱的
/ '~-'outer n. 〈美〉退会分子;要求取代
现有组织(例如政党)的分子;激进分
子

comedian [kə'mi:diən] n. 1. 喜剧演员 2.

喜剧作家 3. 丑角式人物

comedienne [kə,miːdi'en] *n.* 女喜剧演员

comedy ['kɔmidi] *n.* 1. 喜剧;喜剧因素 2. 喜剧场面;喜剧性事件 3. 喜剧作品

comely ['kʌmli] *adj.* 1. 标致的,秀丽的 2. (举止等)合宜的,恰当的 ‖ **comeliness** *n.*

comer ['kʌmə] *n.* 1. 来者;前来(申请、参加等)的人 2. 〈俚〉有成功希望的人(或事物)

comet ['kɔmit] *n.* 〈天〉彗星

comfort ['kʌmfət] *n.* 1. 安慰;舒适,安逸 2. 安慰者;给予安慰的东西 4. [常～s]使生活舒适的事物 5. 〈英〉盖被 — *vt.* 安慰;使舒适 ‖ ~ **er** *n.* 1. 安慰者;[the C-]〈宗〉圣灵 2. 羊毛围巾 3. 〈英〉橡皮奶头 4. 〈美〉盖被,鸭绒被 / ~ **less** *adj.* 1. 无安慰的 2. 不舒适的 ‖ ~ **station** 〈美〉公共厕所

comfortable ['kʌmfətəbl] *adj.* 1. 安慰的 2. 舒适的,惬意的;轻松自在的:Please make yourself ~. 别客气!(招待客人用语) 3. 〈美理〉喝醉了的 — *n.* 〈美〉盖被 ‖ ~ **ness** *n.* / **comfortably** *adv.*

comforting ['kʌmfətiŋ] *adj.* 安慰的;令人鼓舞的 ‖ ~ **ly** *adv.*

comic ['kɔmik] *adj.* 1. 喜剧的:a ~ strip (报刊上的)连环漫画 2. 滑稽的,可笑的 — *n.* 1. 喜剧演员 2. 喜剧成分,喜剧因素 3. 连环漫画:连环漫画杂志;[~s](报刊上的)连环漫画页

comical ['kɔmikəl] *adj.* 好笑的;滑稽的;怪里怪气的 ‖ ~ **ly** *adv.*

coming ['kʌmiŋ] *adj.* 1. 正在来到的,即将来到的:the ~ Friday 即将来到的星期五 2. (人或事物)有指望成功的,应得的:have it ~ (受奖或受罚等)应得的 — *n.* 来到,到达

Comintern ['kɔmintən] *n.* 〈史〉共产国际,第三国际(= Communist International)

comma ['kɔmə] *n.* 1. 逗号(即,); inverted ～ 引号(即''或"") 2. 小停顿 ‖ ~ **bacillus** [微] 霍乱弧菌,逗点形菌

command [kə'mɑːnd] *vt.* 1. 指挥;命令 2. 控制;对……有支配权;拥有,掌握 3. 俯临,俯瞰 4. 应得;博得,～ respect 使人不得不肃然起敬 — *vi.* 指挥;控制;命令;口令 [计] 指令 3. 司令部,指挥部 4. 在一个指挥官管辖下的部队;军区;防御区 5. 控制(权);掌握(语言等)能力 6. 〈英〉国王的邀请 — *adj.* (演出、研究等)应国王邀请的;奉命的

commandant [,kɔmən'dænt] *n.* 1. 指挥官;司令(尤指要塞或防区司令) 2. 军事学校校长

commandeer [,kɔmən'diə] *vt.* 1. 征用(粮食,马匹、房屋等);强征……入伍 2. 〈美口〉强占

commander [kə'mɑːndə] *n.* 1. 指挥员;司令员;指挥官;司令官:a company ～ 连长 2. 海军中校:a lieutenant ～ 海军少校 ‖ ～ **in chief** 总司令

commandment [kə'mɑːndmənt] *n.* 戒律;[宗] 诫:the ten ～s 〈基督教〉十诫

commando [kə'mɑːndəu] *n.* ([复] command-o(e)s) 1. 突击队;突击队员

commemorate [kə'meməreit] *vt.* 1. 纪念 2. 庆祝 3. 作…的纪念 ‖ **commemorator** *n.*

commemoration [kə,memə'reiʃən] *n.* 1. 纪念 2. 纪念会;纪念仪式;纪念物

commemorative [kə'memərətiv] *adj.* 〈集会、邮票等〉纪念性的

commence [kə'mens] *vt.* 使开始;着手 — *vi.* 1. 开始 2. 〈英〉修学位:～ doctor 得博士学位 ‖ ～ **ment** *n.* 1. 开始;开

始时间 2. 学位授予典礼(日）: 毕业典礼(日)

commend [kə'mend] *vt.* 1. 把...交托给(*to*) 2. 称赞，表扬，嘉奖

commendable [kə'mendəbl] *adj.* 值得表扬的，值得称赞的 ‖ ~**ness** *n.* / **commendably** *adv.*

commendation [ˌkɔmen'deiʃən] *n.* 1. 表扬，称赞 2. 嘉奖奖状 3. 付托，委托 4. 推荐

commensurable [kə'menʃərəbl] *adj.* 1. 可用同一标准衡量的(*with*, *to*) 2.〖数〗可公度的，有公度的 2. 相应的，相称的(*to*) ‖ **commensura'bility** *n.*

commensurate [kə'menʃərət] *adj.* 1. 同量的，同大的(*with*) 2. 相称的，相当的(*to*, *with*) ‖ ~**ly** *adv.*

comment [kɔment] *n. & vi.* 1. 注释; 评注 2. 评论

commentary ['kɔmentəri] *n.* 1. 评论 2. 注解; 评注 3. 评介文章 4. 解说词

commentate ['kɔmenteit] *vt.* 1. 注释(文章等) 2. 实况报道(比赛等) — *vi.* 当评论员(或实况广播员等)

commentator ['kɔmenteitə] *n.* 1. 评论员; 时事评论员 2. 注释者 3. 实况广播员

commerce ['kɔmə:s] *n.* 1. 商业，贸易 2. 社交(意见等的)交流 3. 性交

commercial [kə'mə:ʃəl] *adj.* 1. 商业的; 商业上的，商务的: a ~ traveller(英)旅行推销员 / a ~ attaché 商务参赞 2. 商品化的 3. 由广告商付费的 — *n.* (无线电或电视中的)商业广告，广告节目 ‖ ~**ism** *n.* 1. 商业主义，商业精神; 利润第一主义 2. 商业习惯 3. 商业用语 / ~**ist** *n.* 商业家; 商业主义者; 营利主义者 / ~**ly** *adv.*

commercialize [kə'mə:ʃəlaiz] *vt.* 1. 使商

业化; 使商品化 2. 在...发展商业 ‖ **com.mercializa'tion** *n.*

commie ['kɔmi] *n.* [常作 C-]〈贬〉〈口〉共产党员: 共产主义者

commingle [kə'miŋgl] *vt. & vi.* 搀和; 混合; 合并

commiserate [kə'mizəreit] *vt. & vi.* 怜悯; 同情 ‖ **com.mise'ration** *n.*

commissar [ˌkɔmi'sɑ:] *n.* 1. 政委(= political ~) 2. 人民委员(前苏联政府部长的旧称)

commissariat [ˌkɔmi'sɛəriət] *n.* 1. (部队的)给养部门，军需处; 给养 2. 人民委员部(前苏联政府各部的旧称)

commissary [kə'misəri] *n.* 1. 代表，代理人 2.〖宗〗代理主教 3. 军需官 4.(电影制品厂等的)食堂，餐厅 5. 军营杂货店

commission [kə'miʃən] *n.* 1. 委任; 代办(权); 代理(权); 委托(或代理)事项 2. 委任状; 任职令; 授命令; 委任职权; 所受军衔 3. 委员会 4. 职(权) 5. 佣金 — *vt.* 1. 委任，任命; 委托制作(画像等) 2. 把(船舰等)编入现役 3.(军官)受命为指挥(舰只) ‖ ~**ed** *adj.*: 受委任的，受任命的: a ~ed officer(少尉以上的)军官 2. 现役的

commissioner [kə'miʃənə] *n.* 1. 专员，委员: 政府特派员 2. 地方长官 3.(政府公益部门的)长官 4. 职业运动队的行政管理人

commit [kə'mit](committed; committing) *vt.* 1. 犯(错误，罪行); 干(坏事，傻事) 2. 把...交托给: 把...提交给(*to*) 3. 把...押交(监); 判处(*to*) 4. 使承担义务; 使作出保证; 使表态: ~ sb. to do(或 *to* doing) sth. 责成某人做某事 5. 调拨...供使用 6. 把(部队)投入战斗 ‖ **committed** *adj.* 1. 受托付的; 承担义

务的 2. 忠于某一立场的，坚定的 3. (政治上)有密切关系的；结盟的 4. (作品、作家等)根据一定(政治或宗教)观点写作的

commitment [kə'mitmənt] *n.* 1. 交托(看管或保管)；提交 2. 关禁，关押；入狱执行书 3. 承担义务；所承担的义务；许诺；(商业上的)约定 4. 信奉；赞成；赞助 5. 投入(战斗)

committee [kə'miti] *n.* 委员会

commode [kə'məud] *n.* 1. 洗脸台 2. 小衣橱；五斗橱 3. 便桶

commodious [kə'məudjəs] *adj.* 1. 宽敞的；使用起来方便的 ‖ ~**ly** *adv.* / ~**ness** *n.*

commodity [kə'mɔditi] *n.* 商品

commodore ['kɔmədɔ:] *n.* 1. 海军准将；(英)分遣舰队指挥官 2. 商船队长 3. 游艇总会会长

common ['kɔmən] *adj.* 1. 公共的；共有的；共用的；共同的 2. 普通的，一般的；通常的；平常的 3. 粗俗的；低劣的 4. 【数】公共的 5. 【语】通(性)的(数、格)共同(形式)的 — *n.* 1. [~s]总称]平民百姓 2. [the Commons](英国)下议院 3. [~s]共餐食物；(英国一些大学的)定额食餐；公共食堂 4. 公地 5. 对别人土地的使用权(= right of ~) ‖ ~**ly** *adv.* / ~**ness** *n.* / ~ **carrier**【律】公共运输商(或公司)，公共承运人(或公司) / ~ **cold** 感冒 / ~ **denominator** 1.【数】公分母 2. 共同点 / ~ **divisor**【数】公约数 / ~ **factor**【数】公因子，公因数 / ~ **law** 普通法，习惯法，判例法 / **Common Market** (欧洲)共同市场 / ~ **multiple**【数】公倍数 / ~ **room** 1. 公共休息室 2. 师生公共休息室 / ~ **school** (美)公立学校 / ~ **sense** 常识

commoner ['kɔmənə] *n.* 1. 平民(指个

人) 2. (牛)英国下议院议员 3. (英)(牛津大学的)自费生 4. 对他人土地有使用权的人

commonplace ['kɔmənpleis] *adj.* 平凡的；陈腐的 — *n.* 1. 平常话 2. 平凡的事物；毫无疑义的事物

commonwealth ['kɔmənwelθ] *n.* 1. 全体国民 2. 政治实体；国家；共和国；民主国 3. 联邦：the British *Commonwealth* of Nations 英联邦 4. (美)州(只用于肯塔基、马萨诸塞、宾夕法尼亚、弗吉尼亚四州)

commotion [kə'məuʃən] *n.* 混乱；动乱；骚动

communal ['kɔmjunəl] *adj.* 1. 公有的；公共的；共同的 2. 平民的，大众的 3. 公社(制)的；共同体的 ‖ ~**ly** *adv.*

communard ['kɔmjunɑ:d] *n.* 1. [C-] 巴黎公社社员；巴黎公社支持者 2. 公社社员，村民成员

commune[1] ['kɔmju:n] *n.* 1. 公社：the (Paris) *Commune* 巴黎公社(1871 年 3 月 18 日至 5 月 28 日) 2. (法国等国家的)最小行政区 3. (美)(嬉皮士等的)群居村

commune[2] [kə'mju:n] *vi.* 1. 亲密交谈；谈心(with) 2. (美)(宗)领受圣餐

communicable [kə'mju:nikəbl] *adj.* 1. (思想等)可以传授的 2. (疾病)传染性的 ‖ ~**ness** *n.* / **communicably** *adv.*

communicant [kə'mju:nikənt] *n.* 1. 领受圣餐者；教友 2. 传达(或提供)信息者

communicate [kə'mju:nikeit] *vt.* 1. 传达，传送(热、感情、消息等)(to) 2. 传染(疾病) — *vi.* 1. 通讯；通话；交际，交往(with) 2. (房间、道路等)互通(with) 3. (宗)领受圣餐

communication [kə,mju:ni'keiʃən] *n.* 1.

communicative [kəˈmjuːnikətiv] *adj.* 爱说话的；爱传话的

communion [kəˈmjuːnjən] *n.* 1. 共享，共有 2. (思想、感情等的)交流 3. 宗教教派 4. 【宗】圣餐(= Holy Communion)

communiqué [kəˈmjuːnikei, kəˌmjuːniˈkei] *n.* 公报

communism [ˈkɔmjunizəm] *n.* 共产主义

communist [ˈkɔmjunist] *n.* 1. [也作 C-]共产主义者 [常作 C-]共产党员 2. [C-] = Communard — *adj.* 1. 共产主义的；共产党的；共产主义者的；信仰共产主义的 ‖ ~ic[ˌkɔmjuˈnistik] *adj.* 共产主义的；共产主义者的

community [kəˈmjuːniti] *n.* 1. (由同住一地区或一国的人所构成的)社区；社会；(政治)共同体；the European Community 欧洲共同体 2. 团体(界)；社会；公众；the Chinese ~ in New York 纽约的华侨(界) 3. 共有；相同 4. 【生】群落 ‖ ~ centre 社区活动中心 / ~ chest 社区福利基金 / ~ singing (在场的人一起参加的)全场大合唱

commutate [ˈkɔmjuːteit] *vt.* 变换(电流)的方向；变(交流电)为直流电 ‖ **commutator** *n.* 1. 转换开关；转换器 2. 换向器；互换者 3. 整流子，换向器

commutation [ˌkɔmjuːˈteiʃən] *n.* 1. 交换；代偿 2. 代偿的钱 3. 减刑 4. 【数】交换；转换；变换 5.【电】换向；整流 5.(持有长期车票者在两地间的)上下班交通 ‖ ~ ticket 公交车辆月季票

commutative [kəˈmjuːtətiv] *adj.* 交换的；代替的

commute [kəˈmjuːt] *vt.* 1. 用...交换；兑换；变换 2. 改变(付款)的方式 3. 减轻(刑罚等) 4. = commutate — *vi.* 1. 补偿 2. 乘公交车辆上下班；经常乘车(或船等)往返于两地 ‖ ~r *n.* 月季票使用者；乘公交车辆上下班者；a ~ train 市郊往返列车

commy [ˈkɔmi] *n.* = commie

comp [kɔmp] 〈口〉 *n.* 1. 伴奏；伴奏者 2. 竞赛 3. 排字工人；排字 — *vt. & vi.* 1. (为...)伴奏；用(和音等)伴奏 2. (为...)排字

compact¹ [ˈkɔmpækt] *n.* 约定；合同

compact² [kəmˈpækt] *adj.* 1. 紧密的；坚实的；结实的 2.(文体)简洁的，紧凑的 3. 集中的，密集的，小巧的，袖珍的，小型的 — *vt.* 1. 使紧密；使结实 2. 使简洁 3. 组成 — *vi.* 变成紧实 — [ˈkɔmpækt] *n.* 1. 有搽粉盒 2. 小型汽车 3. 小而紧凑的东西 ‖ ~ly *adv.* / ~ness *n.* ‖ ~ disk (或 disc) 1. 激光唱片 2.【计】紧致(压缩)磁盘，光盘

companion¹ [kəmˈpænjən] *n.* 1. 同伴；同事；同乐的人；志趣相同的人 2. 成对(或成副;成双等)物之一 3. 受雇陪侍病人(或老人)的人 4. [作书名用]指南；手册 5.【天】伴星(= ~ star) ‖ ~ship *n.* 伴侣关系；友谊

companion² [kəmˈpænjən] *n.* (船)升降口盖；升降口围罩 ‖ ~ hatch 舱室升降口 / ~ ladder 升降口梯 / com'panionway *n.* 升降口

companionable [kəmˈpænjənəbl] *adj.* 好交友的；可成为好伙伴的

companionate [kəmˈpænjənit] *adj.* 1. 结伴的；同伴(似)的 2. 和谐的；相配的

company ['kʌmpəni] *n*. 1. 交际；交往；陪伴 in the ~ of 在…陪同下 2. 客人；同伴；朋友 3.(一)群，(一)队；(一)伙；a theatrical ~ 剧团 4. 公司；商号 5.【军】连，连队 ‖ ~ **man** 公司人(指忠于公司资方甚于同事的雇员) / ~ **officer**【军】尉官 / ~ **union**(美)公司工会(尤指资方控制的御用工会)

comparable ['kɒmpərəbl] *adj*. 1. 可比较的(with)；比得上的(to) 2. 类似的 ‖ **comparably** adv.

comparative [kəm'pærətiv] *adj*. 1. 比较的；相比较而言的；the ~ degree【语】比较级 2. 相当的；a ~ stranger 相当陌生的人 — *n*. 1. 对手；比拟物 2.[the ~]【语】比较级 ‖ ~**ly** adv.

compare [kəm'peə] *vt*. 1. 比较，对照 2. 比喻，把…比作(to) 3. 列示(形容词或副词)的原级、比较级和最高级形式 — *vi*. 比得上；相比(with) — *n*.〈诗〉比较

comparison [kəm'pærisn] *n*. 1. 比较，对照 2. 比喻

compartment [kəm'pɑːtmənt] *n*. 1. 分隔的空间 2.(列车车厢等的)分隔间 3. 水密舱，防水舱隔(= watertight ~)

compass ['kʌmpəs] *n*. 1. 罗盘，指南针 2.[常 ~es]圆规 3. 界限，范围 4.【音】音域 — *vt*. 1. 围绕…步行；包围 2. 了解，领会 3. 图谋，计划 4. 达到(目的)；获得

compassion [kəm'pæʃən] *n*. 同情；怜悯

compassionate [kəm'pæʃənit] *adj*. 有同情心的 ‖ ~**ly** adv. / ~**ness** n.

compatible [kəm'pætəbl] *adj*. 1. 可和谐共存的；适合的，一致的(with) 2. 兼容的；【生】亲和的(植)可异花受精的；可嫁接的；【化】可配伍的 ‖ **com.pati'bility** n. / **compatibly** adv.

compatriot [kəm'pætriət] *n*. 同国人，同胞

compel [kəm'pel] (compelled; compelling) *vt*. 1. 强迫，使不得不 2. 强求；强使发生 ‖ **compelling** adj. 激发兴趣(或爱慕等)的；令人服做的

compendious [kəm'pendiəs] *adj*. 简明扼要的 ‖ ~**ly** adv. / ~**ness** n.

compendium [kəm'pendiəm] ([复] compendiums 或 compendia [kəm'pendiə]) *n*. 1. 概要；纲要 2. 手册 3. 目录；清单

compensate ['kɒmpenseit] *vt*. 1. 补偿；酬报 2.【机】补偿 — *vi*. 补偿；赔偿(for) ‖ **compensator** n. 1. 赔偿者；赔偿物 2.【机】差动装置 / **compensatory** [kəm'pensətəri] adj. 补偿的；赔偿的；代偿的

compensation [ˌkɒmpen'seiʃən] *n*. 1. 补偿；赔偿；补偿物；赔偿费 2.【机】补偿 ‖ ~**al** adj.

compete [kəm'piːt] *vi*. 1. 比赛，竞争；对抗(with, against)

competence ['kɒmpitəns] *n*. 1. 能力；胜任 2. 足以过温饱生活的收入(或财产) 3.【律】权限，管辖权 4.【地】(河流的)挟沙能力；输沙能力 5.【生】感受态，感受性 6.【语】语言能力

competent ['kɒmpitənt] *adj*. 1. 有能力的；能胜任的(for) 2.(工作等)令人满意的 3. 有法定资格的；the ~ authorities 主管当局 4.【生】活性的，适格的 ‖ ~**ly** adv.

competition [ˌkɒmpi'tiʃən] *n*. 1. 比赛；竞争 2. 比赛(或竞争)的对手

competitive [kəm'petitiv] *adj*. 竞赛的；比赛的 ‖ ~**ly** adv. / ~**ness** n.

competitor [kəm'petitə] *n*. 竞赛者；比赛者；敌手

compile [kəm'pail] *vt*. 编辑，编制(书籍

索引, 报告等);搜集;汇编(资料等);【计】编译 compilation [ˌkɔmpiˈleiʃən] n. /compilatory adj. / ~ r n.

complacence [kəmˈpleisns], **complacency** [kəmˈpleisnsi] n. 自满(情绪);自鸣得意

complacent [kəmˈpleisnt] adj. 自满的;自鸣得意的 ‖ ~ly adv.

complain [kəmˈplein] vi. 1. 抱怨;叫屈;诉苦;抗议(of, about) 2.(病人)主诉(of) 3. 申诉;控告(to) — vt. 抱怨说 ‖ ~ant n. 1. 抱怨者;抗议者 2. 控诉人;原告(=plaintiff)

complaint [kəmˈpleint] n. 1. 抱怨;叫屈;诉说;抱怨(或痛苦)的缘由 2.(刑事)控告(=民事)控诉 3. 疾病

complaisant [kəmˈpleizənt] adj. 1. 殷勤的,谦恭的,讨好的 2. 顺从的 ‖ ~ly adv. / ~ness n.

complement [ˈkɔmplimənt] n. 1. 补充物;【语】补(足)语 2.(船上的)编制全额;装备定额 3.【数】余;补;补码;补数 4.(血清中的)补体,防御素;【计】~ ['kɔmplimənt] vt. 补充;补足

complementary [ˌkɔmpliˈmentəri] adj. 补充的;补足的;互补的

complete [kəmˈpliːt] adj. 1. 完整的,完全的;圆满的;十足的 2. 完成的;结束的 — vt. 1. 完成,结束 2. 使完整;使完美 ‖ ~ly adv. / ~ness n.

completion [kəmˈpliːʃən] n. 完成,结束;完满

complex [ˈkɔmpleks] adj. 1. 合成的;复杂的;综合的 ~ a sentence[语]复合句 2.【化】配合的,络合的 — n. 1. 复杂;合成物;综合体,集合体,复合体;综合企业:an iron and steel ~ 钢铁联合企业 3.【生】(物种的)综合体 4.【心】情结,情意综;大的情绪反应:the inferiority

(superiority) ~ 自卑(优越)情结(指心理上的一种病态) 5.【化】配(位体化)合物,络合物 ‖ ~ly adv.

complexion [kəmˈplekʃən] n. 1. 肤色(尤指面部肤色) 2.(战争等的)情况,局面;样子:put a false ~ on sb.'s remarks 曲解某人的话 3.(人的)气质,脾性 ‖ ~ed adj.[常用以构成复合词](脸部)肤色...的:fair-~ed 肤色白的

complexity [kəmˈpleksiti] n. 复杂(性);复杂事物

compliance [kəmˈplaiəns] n. 1. 依从 2. 屈从

compliant [kəmˈplaiənt] adj. 1. 依从的 2. 屈从的 ‖ ~ly adv.

complicate [ˈkɔmplikeit] vt. 使复杂;使麻烦,使难弄 — vi. 变复杂 — ['kɔmplikit] adj. 1. 复杂的;麻烦的 2.【动】(昆虫翅膀)纵褶的

complicated [ˈkɔmplikeitid] adj. 结构复杂的;难懂的;难解的 ‖ ~ly adv. / ~ness n.

complication [ˌkɔmpliˈkeiʃən] n. 1. 复杂;混乱;纠纷;复杂情况 2.【医】并发病,并发症

complicity [kəmˈplisiti] n. 同谋关系,共犯关系(in)

complier [kəmˈplaiə] n. 照做者,依从者

compliment [ˈkɔmplimənt] n. 1. 赞美的话(或行为);敬意 2.[~s]问候;道贺;贺词 — [ˈkɔmplimənt] vt. 1. 赞美;向...致意;祝贺 2. 向...送礼以表敬意

complimentary [ˌkɔmpliˈmentəri] adj. 1. 赞美的;表敬意的;问候的 2. 免费赠送的 ‖ **complimentarily** adv.

comply [kəmˈplai] vi. 按照规定(或请求等)办理,照做(with)

component [kəmˈpəunənt] adj. 组成的;

合成的 — n. 组成部分,成分;【物】分力;【数】分量;【化】组分;零件;部件;电路元件

comport [kəm'pɔːt] vt. [~ oneself] 举动,举止,表现 — vi. 一致,适合,相称(with)‖ ~ ment n.

compose [kəm'pəuz] vt. 1. 组成,构成 2. 创作(乐曲、诗歌等);为(歌词等)作曲 3.【印】排(字);排...的版;排(稿) 4. 使安定,使平静;把(思想等)理出头绪 5. 调停(纠纷等) — vi. 1. 创作;作曲 2. 排字 ‖ ~r n. 作曲者;创作者

composed [kəm'pəuzd] adj. 镇静自若的 ‖ ~ly [kəm'pəuzidli] adv. / ~ness [kəm'pəuzidnis] n.

composite ['kɔmpəzit] adj. 合成的,混成的;复合的 — n. 1. 合成物;混合物;混合式 2. 菊 ‖ ~ly adv. / ~ness n.

composition [,kɔmpə'ziʃən] n. 1. 写作;作曲;作文(法);作文(大型)乐曲 2. 构成,组成;构图;成分;合成物;混合物(尤指人造的) 4. 气质,脾性 5. 妥协 6. (偿还部分欠款以了结债务的)和解偿还;和解协议 7.【印】排字

compositor [kəm'pɔzitə] n. 排字工人

compost ['kɔmpɔst] n. 堆肥;混合物 — vt. 施...做成堆肥;施堆肥于

composure [kəm'pəuʒə] n. 镇静,沉着

compote ['kɔmpəut] n. 1. 高脚果碟 2. 糖水水果

compound¹ ['kɔmpaund] n. 1. 复合物;化合物 2. 复合词 — adj. 混合的,化合的;复合的:a ~ eye【动】复眼/a ~ fracture【医】哆开骨折,有创骨折 — [kəm'paund] vt. 1. 混合;使化合;使化合物 2.(通过互让)解决(争端、债务等) 3.【电】复绕 4. 使(困难、错误等)更严重(或更复杂) — vi. 和解;妥协(with)

compound² ['kɔmpaund] n. 1. 有围墙(或篱笆等)的房群,大院 2. 用篱笆(或围墙)圈起的场地(如战俘临时集中营等)

comprador(e) [,kɔmprə'dɔː] n. 买办

comprehend [,kɔmpri'hend] vt. 1. 理解,领会 2. 包含,包括

comprehensible [,kɔmpri'hensibl] adj. 能理解的 ‖ 'compre,hensi'bility n. / comprehensibly adv.

comprehension [,kɔmpri'henʃən] n. 1. 理解;理解力 2. 包含;包含的内容

comprehensive [,kɔmpri'hensiv] adj. 1. 包含内容多的;综合的 2. 有充分理解力的 ‖ ~ly adv. / ~ness n. ‖ ~ school (英)(招收学生不分资质的)综合中学

compress [kəm'pres] vt. 压缩;浓缩;使(语言等)简练 — ['kɔmpres] n. 1.(止血、消炎用的)敷布;压布 2.(棉花等的)打包机 ‖ ~ed adj. ~ed air 压缩空气 / ~or n. 1.【医】压迫器 2.【解】压肌 3.压缩机;压气机

compressible [kəm'presibl] adj. 可压缩的 ‖ com,pressi'bility n.【物】压缩性;压缩系数

compression [kəm'preʃən] n. 1. 压缩;压缩量 2. 压紧;压抑;压制

comprise [kəm'praiz] vt. 1. 包含,包括 2. 由...组成 3. 构成:Nineteen articles ~ Book One. 十九篇文章构成了第一卷

compromise ['kɔmprəmaiz] n. 1. 妥协,和解;互让了结 2. 妥协方案;折中办法;和解契约 3. 折中物;中间物 4. 连累;危及 — vi. (用...) (with) — vt. 1. 互让解决(分歧、争端等) 2. 危及,损害:~ one's reputation (或 oneself)有损自己的名誉 3. 放弃(利益、原则等);泄露(秘密材料等)

comptroller [kən'trəulə] *n.* 主计长；总会计师

compulsion [kəm'pʌlʃən] *n.* 强制，强迫

compulsory [kəm'pʌlsəri] *adj.* 强迫的，强制的；义务的：a ~ subject 必修科目 / a ~ service system 义务兵役制 ‖ **compulsorily** *adv.*

compunction [kəm'pʌŋkʃən] *n.* 内疚，良心责备；后悔，懊悔

computation [ˌkɔmpju:'teiʃən] *n.* 1. 计算 2. 计算法 3. 计算结果；计算出来的数（或量）4. 计算机的使用（或操作）

compute [kəm'pju:t] *vt., vi. & n.* 计算；估算；用计算机计算

computer [kəm'pju:tə] *n.* 计算机，电子计算机，电脑 ‖ ~acy *n.* 计算机理解和应用能力 / ~ist *n.* 计算机行话（或术语）/ ~ist *n.* 计算机使用（或操作）者 / ~nik *n.* 计算机迷（或专家）/ ~phobe *n.* 计算机恐怖者 ‖ ~ crime 利用计算机转移银行账户资金等的计算机犯罪 / ~ language 计算机语言；机器语言 / ~ literacy 计算机理解和应用能力 / ~-'literate *adj.* 有计算机理解和应用能力的 / ~ science 计算机科学 / ~ virus 计算机病毒

computerize [kəm'pju:təraiz] *vt.* 1. 给…装备电子计算机 2. 使电子计算机化；用电子计算机计算 — *vi.*（工业、商业等）改用计算机 ‖ **com·puteri'zation** *n.*

comrade ['kɔmreid] *n.* 同志；亲密伙伴；朋友；同事 ‖ ~ly *adj.* 同志式的；同志般的 / ~ship *n.* 同志关系；友谊 ‖ ~-in-'arms *n.* 战友

con[1] [kɔn] (conned; conning) *vt.* 研究；熟读；默记（over）

con[2] [kɔn] *adv.* 从反面 — *n.* 反对的论点；反对者；投反对票者；反对票：the

pros and ~s of mixed schooling 男女同校的利弊

con[3] [kɔn] *adj.* 骗取信任的：a ~ game（或 job）骗局 / a ~ man 骗子 ‖（conned; conning）*vt.* 欺骗；哄骗

con- *pref.* [用在 c, d, f, g, j, n, q, s, t, v 前] = com-

Conakry ['kɔnəkri] *n.* 科纳克里[几内亚首都]

concave [kɔn'keiv] *adj.* 凹的，凹面的：a ~ lens 凹透镜 — *n.* 凹面；凹面物；天穹 ‖ ~ly *adv.* / ~ness *n.*

concavity [kɔn'kæviti] *n.* 1. 凹陷(性) 2. 凹面；凹曲线；凹面物；凹处

conceal [kən'si:l] *vt.* 隐藏；掩盖；隐瞒 ‖ ~ment *n.*

concede [kən'si:d] *vt.* 1.（不情愿地）承认；给予，让予 2. 承认（竞选、比赛等）失败 — *vi.* 让步(to)

conceit [kən'si:t] *n.* 1. 自负，自高自大，骄傲自满 2. 奇想；幻想；牵强附会的比喻；作品风格上的做作

conceited [kən'si:tid] *adj.* 自负的，自高自大的，骄傲自满的 ‖ ~ly *adv.* / ~ness *n.*

conceivable [kən'si:vəbl] *adj.* 可想象的，想得到的；可相信的 ‖ **con,ceiva'bility** *n.* / ~ness *n.* / **conceivably** *adv.*

conceive [kən'si:v] *vt.* 1. 构想出（主意、计划等）；想象，设想 2. 开始怀（胎儿）；抱有（想法等）3.[常用被动语态] 表达 — *vi.* 1. 怀孕 2. 设想，想象出(of)

concentrate ['kɔnsentreit] *vt.* 1. 使（注意力等）集中于一点 2. 浓缩 — *vi.* 1. 集中；全神贯注(on, upon) 2. 浓缩 — *n.* 浓缩物；精制品／精矿 ‖ ~d *adj.* 集中起来的；经浓缩的

concentration [ˌkɔnsen'treiʃən] *n.* 1. 集

中;专心 2. 浓缩;浓度 ‖ ~ camp 集中营

concentric [kən'sentrik] *adj.* 同一中心的;同轴的: ~ circles 【数】同心圆 ‖ ~ally *adv.*

concentricity [ˌkɔnsen'trisiti] *n.* 同心(性)

concept ['kɔnsept] *n.* 概念;观念;思想

conception [kən'sepʃən] *n.* 1. 概念(或观念)的形成 2. 概念;想法 3. 怀孕;胚胎;胎儿 ‖ ~al *adj.*

conceptual [kən'septjuəl] *adj.* 概念的: ~ knowledge 理性认识

concern [kən'sə:n] *vt.* 1. 涉及,对...有关系;影响 2. 使关心;使挂念;使担心 (*about, with, over*) — *n.* 1. (利害)关系;关注 2. 关心,关怀;挂心,忧虑;挂念 (*for, about, with*) 3. 公司;企业 4. 小东西,小玩意儿;〈口〉事物

concerned [kən'sə:nd] *adj.* 1. 有关的 2. 关切的;担心的 ‖ ~ly [kən'sə:nidli] *adv.*

concerning [kən'sə:niŋ] *prep.* 关于

concert [n. 'kɔnsət] *n.* 1. 音乐会;演奏会;【音】协奏曲和声 2. 一致;协作;和谐: in 一致地,一齐 — [kən'sə:t] *vt.* 商议,共同议定;安排 — *vi.* 协力 ‖ ~-master, ~meister ['kɔnsətˌmaistə] *n.* 首席小提琴演奏者;乐队首席 / ~ pitch 1. 音乐会音高;标准音高 2. 最佳状态

concerted [kən'sə:tid] *adj.* 1. 商定的;一致的 2. 【音】分声部的 ‖ ~ly *adv.*

concertina [ˌkɔnsə'ti:nə] *n.* 1. 六角形手风琴 2. 【军】蛇腹形铁丝网 (= ~ wire)

concerto [kən'tʃeətəu] *n.* [复] concerti [kən'tʃeəti] 或 concertos] *n.* 【音】协奏曲

concession [kən'seʃən] *n.* 1. 让步(退一步)承认;让予物 2. (政府对采矿权、土

地使用权等的)特许;特许权 3. 租界;租借地

concessive [kən'sesiv] *adj.* 让步的: a ~ clause 【语】让步从句(指以 although, even if 等开始的从句) ‖ ~ly *adv.*

conch [kɔŋʃ, kɔŋk] ([复] conch(e)s) *n.* 海螺壳;海螺

conciliate [kən'silieit] *vt.* 1. 安抚,劝慰;博得...的好感(或欢心等) 2. 调和;调停 3. 博得(支持、好感等) ‖ con.cili'ation *n.* / conciliator *n.*

conciliatory [kən'siliətəri] *adj.* 抚慰的;调解的;调和的

concise [kən'sais] *adj.* 简明的,简洁的,简要的 ‖ ~ly *adv.* / ~ness *n.*

conclave ['kɔnkleiv] *n.* 秘密会议;秘密集会

conclude [kən'klu:d] *vt.* 1. 结束 2. 缔结;议定 3. 推断;断定 4. 决定 — *vi.* 1. 结束,终了 2. 作出决定 3. 推断 4. 达成协议 ‖ concluding *adj.* 结束的,最后的

conclusion [kən'klu:ʒən] *n.* 1. 结束,终了;结局 2.(条约等的)缔结;(买卖等的)议定 3. 结论;推论

conclusive [kən'klu:siv] *adj.* 最后的;结论性的;确定性的 ‖ ~ly *adv.* / ~ness *n.*

concoct [kən'kɔkt] *vt.* 1. 调合,调制(汤、饮料等) 2. 编造(借口、谎话、小说情节等);策划 ‖ ~er, ~or *n.* 调制者;策划者 / ~ion *n.* 1. 调制,调制品 2. 编造;策划;阴谋

concomitant [kən'kɔmitənt] *adj.* 相伴的,伴随的 — *n.* 伴随物 ‖ concomitance. concomitancy *n.* 1. 伴随性 2. 并存;并存物(或情况);并存物(或情况)【宗】(圣餐中耶稣的)血肉同在 / ~ly *adv.*

concord ['kɔŋkɔ:d] *n.* 1. 和谐,一致,协调;(国际间的)和睦 2.(国际间的)协

定;约定 3.【语】(人称、性、数、格的)一致(关系) 4.【音】协和音程,协和和弦

concordance [kənˈkɔːdəns] n. 1. 和谐、一致,调 2.【书籍的】主要语词索引

concordant [kənˈkɔːdənt] adj. 1. 和谐的、一致的,协调的 2.【音】谐和的 3.【地】(地层)整合的 ‖ ~ly adv.

concordat [kənˈkɔːdæt] n. 〈尤指罗马教皇与各国政府订立的〉协议,协定

concourse [ˈkɒŋkɔːs] n. 1. 集合,汇合;合流 2. 群集 3. 群集场所;〈美〉(公园或车站内的)广场;大厅;街心广场

concrete [ˈkɒŋkriːt] adj. 1. 具体的、有形的 2. 固结的,混凝土(制)的 — n. 1. 具体物 2. 混凝土:凝结物:reinforced ~ 钢筋混凝土 — [ˈkɒŋkriːt] vt. 1. 使固结;使凝结 2.〈喻〉使合一 3. [ˈkɒŋkriːt] 用混凝土修筑;浇混凝土于 — vi. 1. 凝固;固结 2. 浇筑混凝土 ‖ ~ly adv. ~ness n.

concretion [kənˈkriːʃən] n. 1. 具体化的东西 2. 凝结(物);固结(物);【医】结石;【地】结核体

concubine [ˈkɒŋkjubain] n. 1. 小老婆,妾 2. 情妇,姘妇

concupiscent [kənˈkjuːpisənt] adj. 性欲的,好色的 ‖ concupiscence n.

concur [kənˈkəː] (concurred; concurring) vi. 1. 同时发生;共同起作用 2. 同意,一致;赞成 (with, in) ‖ concurrence [kənˈkərəns] n. concurrent [kənˈkʌrənt] adj.

concussion [kənˈkʌʃən] n. 1. 冲击;震动 2.【医】震荡,震伤

condemn [kənˈdem] vt. 1. 谴责 2. 宣告(某人)有罪;判(某人)刑;证明(某人)有罪 3. 宣告…不适用 4. 宣告没收(或征用)(财产等) 5. 宣告(病人)患不治之症 ‖ ~able [kənˈdemnəbl] adj.

应受谴责的;应定罪的 / ~ed adj. 被定罪的;定了罪的人用的:a ~ed cell 死囚牢房 / ~er, ~or [kənˈdemə] n. 谴责者;宣判者

condemnation [ˌkɒndemˈneiʃən] n. 1. 谴责,定罪;宣告有罪 2. 谴责(或定罪)的理由 4.〈关于某事物〉不适用的宣告 5. 征用;没收

condensation [ˌkɒndenˈseiʃən] n. 1. 使冷凝(作用);凝缩(作用) 2.【物】聚合(作用) 3.(文章等的)压缩;经节缩的作品,节本

condense [kənˈdens] vt. 1. 使冷凝;使凝结,缩合;压缩;浓缩:~d milk 炼乳 2. 缩短;精简(文章等) 3.【化】使聚合 4. 聚集(光线) — vi. 1. 冷凝 2.(气体)变成液体(或固体) ‖ ~r n. 冷凝器;空气压缩器;凝气室;聚光器(或镜);电容器

condescend [ˌkɒndiˈsend] vi. 1. 俯就,屈尊 2. 带着优越感表示关心;用恩赐态度相待(to) 3. 堕落;丢丑(to) ‖ condescension n.

condescending [ˌkɒndiˈsendiŋ] adj. 带着优越感表示关心的;用恩赐态度相待的 ‖ ~ly adv.

condiment [ˈkɒndimənt] n. 调味品,辛辣佐料(例如胡椒)

condition [kənˈdiʃən] n. 1. 条件 2. (人、事物本身的)状况,状态:[~s]环境;形势 3.(社会)地位;身分 4.【语】条件从句 5.〈美〉需要补考的成绩)(通常用 "E"标示)— vt. 1. 决定,规定:为…的条件;制约 2. 使处于正常(或良好)状态:~ the air of the workshop 调节车间空气 3. 使适应;使习惯于环境(to) 4. 检验(生丝、棉纱等) 5.〈美〉要求(学生)补考 6. 引起(人、动物)的条件反射 ‖ ~er n. 调节器:空气调节器,空调

机

conditional [kən'diʃənəl] *adj.* **1.** 附有条件的;视……而定的(*on, upon*) **2.** [语]条件的:a ~ clause 条件从句 — *n.* [语]条件状词;条件从句 ‖ -**ly** *adv.*

condo ['kɔndəu] (〔复〕condos) *n.* 〈美口〉分套购置的公寓大楼(或公寓套间)

condole [kən'dəul] *vi.* 吊唁;哀悼;慰问(*with*)

condolence [kən'dəuləns] *n.* [常 ~s]吊唁,吊慰;慰问

condominium [ˌkɔndə'miniəm] *n.* **1.** (国际)共管区 **2.** 共有(或共管)的产权

condone [kən'dəun] *vt.* 宽恕,不咎(罪过)

condor ['kɔndɔ] *n.* [动](南美)神鹰;大秃鹫

conduce [kən'djuːs] *vi.* 导(致);有助(于)(*to*)

conducive [kən'djuːsiv] *adj.* 有助于……的,有益于……的;助长的(*to*) ‖ -**ness** *n.*

conduct ['kɔndʌkt] *n.* **1.** 行为;品行;举动 **2.** 指导;引导 **3.** 实施,处理;经营,进行 **4.** 处理(或管理)的方法;经营方式 — [kən'dʌkt] *vt.* **1.** 引导;带领,陪伴(游客等);指导;指挥(乐队等) **2.** 实施,处理;进行 **3.** [~ oneself]为人,表现 **4.** 传导,传(热、电等) — *vi.* **1.** 引导;带领;指导;指挥乐队 **2.** (路)通到(*to*)

conduction [kən'dʌkʃən] *n.* **1.** [物]传导性 **2.** [生]神经感应的传导 **3.** 输送;输导

conductivity [ˌkɔndʌk'tiviti] *n.* 传导率;传导性

conductor [kən'dʌktə] *n.* **1.** 指导者;响导者;管理人 **2.**(电车等的)售票员;〈美〉列车长 **3.**(乐队,合唱队的)指挥 **4.** [电]导体 **5.** 避雷针(= lightning ~)

conduit ['kɔndit, 'kɔndjuit] *n.* **1.** 管道;导管;渠道,引水道;水管 **2.** [电]导线管;电缆沟

cone [kəun] *n.* **1.** 圆锥体;圆锥形物;[数]直立圆锥;锥面 **2.** [植]孢子叶球;球果;球花 **3.** [地]锥状地形;火山锥 **4.** 风暴信号 **5.**(盛冰淇淋用的)圆锥形华夫卷筒

confab ['kɔnfæb] *n.* 〈口〉= confabulation — (confabbed; confabbing) *vi.* 〈口〉= confabulate

confabulate [kən'fæbjuleit] *vi.* **1.** 闲谈;谈心(*with*) **2.** 讨论;会谈(*with*) ‖ con.fabu'lation *n.*

confection [kən'fekʃən] *n.* **1.** 甜食;糖果;蜜饯 **2.** 混合;调制 **3.** [医]糖膏剂 **4.** 精致工艺品;高级时髦女服 ‖ -**ary** *adj.* **1.** 甜食的;糖果的或蜜饯的 **2.** 甜食商的;甜食业的 — *n.* **1.** 甜食店 **2.** 甜食

confectioner [kən'fekʃənə] *n.* 制造(或销售)甜食的人 ‖ ~**y** *n.* **1.** 甜食甜点 **2.** 甜食店 **3.** 甜食制造(或销售)业

confederacy [kən'fedərəsi] *n.* **1.** 同盟;联盟;邦联;全体盟员 **2.** 密谋;非法结社

confederate [kən'fedərit] *adj.* **1.** 同盟的;联合的 **2.** [C-]〈美史〉南部邦联的 — *n.* **1.** 同盟者;联合者;同盟国 **2.** 共谋者,同伙;党羽 **3.** [C-]〈美史〉南部邦联的支持者 — [kən'fedəreit] *vt. & vi.* (使)结成同盟;(使)联合;(使)结党

confederation [kənˌfedə'reiʃən] *n.* 同盟;联盟;邦联

confer [kən'fəː] *vt.* (conferred; conferring) *vt.* 授予(称号、学位等) — *vi.* 交换意见;协商(*with*) ‖ -**ment** *n.* 授予

conference ['kɔnfərəns] *n.* **1.** 讨论;会谈 **2.**(正式的)会议;讨论会;协商会 **3.** 〈美〉(体育运动队、宗教团体、学校等

的)联合会 ‖ ~ **call** 会议电话呼叫

confess [kən'fes] *vt.* **1.** 供认(罪行、过失、隐私等);承认 **2.** 宣称对...信奉 **3.** 向上帝(或神父)忏悔(罪恶)等;(神父)听取...的忏悔 — *vi.* **1.** 供认;交待;承认(*to*) **2.** 向神父听取忏悔 ‖ ~ **or** *n.* **1.** 供认者;忏悔者 **2.** 听忏悔的神父 **3.** 不畏受难的基督徒

confession [kən'feʃən] *n.* **1.** 招供,供认;交待,坦白 **2.** 自供状;自白书 **3.** (表明信仰等的)声明;表白 **4.** (尤指天主教)(向神父的)忏悔,告解 **5.** (有共同信条的)宗教团体(或教派) ‖ ~**al** *adj.* **1.** 坦白的 **2.** 忏悔的 **3.** 公开声明的 *n.* **1.** (神父听忏悔的)忏悔室,告解所 **2.** (向神父所作的)忏悔

confetti [kən'feti] [复] *n.* [用作单] (婚礼等中抛撒的)五彩纸屑(或纸带);糖果

confidant [ˌkɒnfi'dænt] *n.* 知己,密友

confide [kən'faid] *vt.* **1.** 吐露(秘密等) **2.** 信托,交托,委托 — *vi.* 信任(*in*);吐露秘密

confidence ['kɒnfidəns] *n.* **1.** 信任 **2.** 信心;自信;把握 **3.** (向知心人)吐露的秘密;私房话 — *adj.* (用于)行骗的:a ~ game (或 trick) 骗局/a ~ man (或 trickster) 骗子

confident ['kɒnfidənt] *adj.* 确信的;有信心的,自信的 — *n.* 知己,密友 ‖ ~**ly** *adv.*

confidential [ˌkɒnfi'denʃəl] *adj.* **1.** 极受信任的,心腹的,参与机密的 **2.** 秘密的,机密的 **3.** (语气等)表示信任的 **4.** 易于信任别人的

confiding [kən'faidiŋ] *adj.* 深信不疑的;易于信任别人的 ‖ ~**ly** *adv.*

configuration [kənˌfiɡju'reiʃən] *n.* 构造,结构;形状,外形 **2.** 【化】构型

confine [kən'fain] *vt.* **1.** 限制 **2.** 禁闭;使闭门不出,幽禁 **3.** [用被动语态]分娩;坐月子 — ['kɒnfain] *n.* [常 ~ s]境界,边缘;区域,范围 ‖ ~**d** *adj.* **1.** 有限的,狭窄的 **2.** 在分娩中的;坐月子的 / ~**ment** *n.*

confirm [kən'fəːm] *vt.* **1.** 使(权力等)更巩固;使(意见等)更有力;使更坚定(指在信念等方面)(*in*) **2.** 确定,确认,确认 **3.** 进一步证实,进一步确定 **4.** 坚持说(*that*) **5.** (基督教中)给...行按手礼,给...行坚信礼 ‖ ~**ed** *adj.* **1.** 坚定的 **2.** 证实了的,确定的 **3.** 成习惯的,根深蒂固的:a ~**ed** criminal 惯犯

confirmation [ˌkɒnfə'meiʃən] *n.* **1.** 证实,证明 **2.** 确认;批准 **3.** (基督教中的)按手礼,坚信礼

confiscate ['kɒnfiskeit] *vt.* 没收,把...充公 — *adj.* 财产被没收的,被充公的 ‖ ˌconfis'cation *n.*

conflagration [ˌkɒnflə'ɡreiʃən] *n.* 大火,大火灾;(战争等的)爆发

conflict ['kɒnflikt] *n.* **1.** 斗争,战斗;倾轧 **2.** 抵触;冲突;争论;论战 — [kən'flikt] *vi.* **1.** 斗争,战斗;倾轧(*with*) **2.** 抵触;冲突(*with*) ‖ ~**ing** [kən'fliktiŋ] *adj.* 抵触的,冲突的

confluence ['kɒnfluəns] *n.* **1.** 合流,汇合;合流点,汇合处;汇流而成的河 **2.** 集合,集聚 **3.** 人群

conform [kən'fɔːm] *vt.* 使一致,使符合;使遵照;使适合(*to*) — *vi.* **1.** 一致,符合,适合(*to, with*) **2.** 遵照(*to, with*) **3.** 【英史】遵奉国教会惯例 ‖ ~**able** *adj.* / ~**ist** *n.* **1.** 遵奉者 **2.** 英国国教徒

conformation [ˌkɒnfɔː'meiʃən] *n.* **1.** 结构;形态;外形 **2.** 一致,符合;适应

conformity [kən'fɔːmiti] *n.* 1. 依照,遵照;遵奉;适合;一致;in ~ with (或 to)依照;和...相一致;遵奉 2. 一致点 3.【英史】遵奉国教会惯例 4.【地】(地层的)整合

confound [kən'faund] *vt.* 1. 混淆;使(思想等)混乱 2. 使惊惶(失措) 3. 挫败 4. 把...毁灭掉(用在诅咒语中): Confound it! 讨厌! (该死的)! / Confound you! 混蛋! 去你的!

confounded [kən'faundid] *adj.* 1. 惶惑的;混乱的 2. 该受诅咒的;讨厌之极的 || ~ly *adv.* 十分,非常;讨厌地

confront [kən'frʌnt] *vt.* 1. (使)面临,(使)遭遇(with) 2. (困难等)临到...头上 3. 勇敢地面对(危险等);正视;对抗;对质,使对证(with) 5. 比较;使对照 6. 同...相对(指房屋等) || ~ation [ˌkɔnfrʌn'teiʃən] *n.* (尤指敌对国家的)对抗

Confucian [kən'fjuːʃən] *adj.* 孔子(Confucius)的,孔夫子的;儒家的;儒家学说的 — *n.* 孔子的门徒;儒士 || ~ism *n.* 孔子学说,儒学,儒教

confuse [kən'fjuːz] *vt.* 1. 使混乱,混淆;把...混同 2. 把...弄糊涂;使慌乱 || ~dly [kən'fjuːzidli] *adv.* 混乱地;慌乱地 /con'fusion *n.*

confute [kən'fjuːt] *vt.* 驳斥,驳倒 || confutation [ˌkɔnfjuː'teiʃən] *n.*

congeal [kən'dʒiːl] *vt. & vi.* (使)冻结,(使)凝结 || ~ment *n.*

congenial [kən'dʒiːniəl] *adj.* 1. 同族的,同类的;性情相似的;志趣相投的(to, with) 2. (气候,水土,职位等)相宜的,惬意的(to) || ~ity [kənˌdʒiːni'æliti] *n.* / ~ly *adv.*

congenital [kən'dʒenitl] *adj.* (疾病,缺陷等)先天的,天生的 || ~ly *adv.*

congest [kən'dʒest] *vt.* 使(城市,街道等)拥挤,拥塞阻塞(血管)充血,使(身体的某部分)充满液体 — *vi.* (血管)充血;(身体的某部分)充满液体 || ~ion *n.*

conglomerate [kən'glɔmərit] *adj.* 1. 聚成球形的 2. 由不同成分组成的 3.【地】砾岩的;【植】成簇的,簇生的;【动】聚合的 — *n.* 1. 聚集物;混合体 2.【地】砾岩 3.(多种行业、企业的)联合大企业,企业集团 — [kən'glɔməreit] *vt. & vi.* (使)成球形;(使)成团 || conglomeration [kənˌglɔmə'reiʃən] *n.*

Congo ['kɔŋɡəu] *n.* 1. 刚果[非洲中西部国家] 2. 刚果河(即扎伊尔河)[非洲中部]

congou ['kɔŋɡuː] *n.* 工夫茶(一种中国红茶)

congratulate [kən'grætjuleit] *vt.* 祝贺;向...道喜(on,upon)

congratulation [kənˌgrætju'leiʃən] *n.* 1. 祝贺;庆贺 2.[常~s]贺词

congratulatory [kən'grætjulətəri] *adj.* 祝贺的

congregate ['kɔŋɡriɡeit] *vt. & vi.* (使)集合 — *adj.* 1. 集合在一起的 2. 集体的

congregation [ˌkɔŋɡri'ɡeiʃən] *n.* 1. 集合;集会;人群 2.(教堂中的)会众;宗教区的全体教徒 3.【天主教】红衣主教委员会 4.(基督教典故)(全体)以色列人 5.(英)大学住校高级教职员全体会议

congress ['kɔŋɡres] *n.* 1.(代表)大会 2.(美国等国的)国会,议会;国会(或议会)会议(期) 3. 聚会;会议 || **congressional** [kɔŋ'ɡreʃənl] *adj.*

congressman ['kɔŋɡresmən] ([复] congressmen) *n.* 国会议员(尤指美国众议员)

congresswoman ['kɔŋɡresˌwumən] ([复]

congresswomen ['kɔŋgres,wimin]) n. 国会女议员(尤指美国女众议员)

congruent ['kɔŋgruənt] *adj.* 1. 适合的;一致的;和谐的 2.【数】全等的,叠合的,同余的 ‖ **congruence, congruency** *n.*

congruous ['kɔŋgruəs] *adj.* 1. 一致的;符合的;适当的;和谐的 2.【数】全等的 ‖ **congruity** [kɔŋ'gru:iti] *n.* / ~ **ly** *adv.*

conic ['kɔnik] *adj.* 圆锥形的;圆锥的 — *n.*【数】圆锥曲线,二次曲线;[~s]用作单)锥线法,锥线论

conical ['kɔnikəl] *adj.* 圆锥形的;圆锥的 ‖ ~ **ly** *adv.* / ~ **ness** *n.*

conifer ['kɔunifə] *n.*【植】针叶树

coniferous [kɔu'nifərəs] *adj.*【植】产球果的;针叶树的

conj. *abbr.* conjunction

conjecture [kən'dʒektʃə] *n.* 1. 推测,猜测;猜测的结果 2.(校阅时的)揣摩 — *vt.* 1. 猜测;猜测出 2.(校阅时)揣摩出 — *vi.* 猜测,推测 ‖ **conjectural** *adj.*

conjoin [kən'dʒɔin] *vt. & vi.* (使)结合;(使)联合;(使)连接

conjugal ['kɔndʒugəl] *adj.* 婚姻的;夫妻关系上的;夫妻之间的 ‖ ~ **ly** *adv.*

conjugate ['kɔndʒugeit] *vt.* 1. 结合;联合;连接;使成对 2.【语】列举(动词)的变化形式 — *vi.* 1. 结合,结亲;交交,交配 2.【生】结合,接合,并合 3.【语】列举动词的变化形式;(动词)词形变化 — ['kɔndʒugit] *adj.* 1. 结合的;配合的;【植】成对的,对生的 2.【语】同根变形的 3.【物】共轭的;【数】共轭复数的 — ['kɔndʒugit] *n.*【语】同根变形词,同源词

conjugation [,kɔndʒu'geiʃən] *n.* 1. 结合;联合;配对 2.【语】(动词)的词形变化,词形变化相似的一组动词 3.【生】(两个生殖细胞的)接合

conjunction [kən'dʒʌŋkʃən] *n.* 1. 结合;联合;并合 2.(事件的)同时发生;同处发生 3.【语】连接词 4.【天】(天体的)合

conjunctive [kən'dʒʌŋktiv] *adj.* 连接的;联合的;结合用的;连接性的 — *n.*【语】连接词,起连接作用的词 ‖ ~ **ly** *adv.*

conjuncture [kən'dʒʌŋktʃə] *n.* 1. 结合;联合 2.(事件的)同时发生;事态,局面 3. 紧要关头;危机时刻

conjure ['kʌndʒə] *vt.* 1. [kən'dʒuə] 祈求,恳求 2. 召(鬼);念咒召唤,用戏法演出;用魔术作成(或驱走);用魔术影响 4. 想象;用幻想作出 — *vi.* 1. 念咒召鬼;施魔法 2. 变戏法 ‖ ~ **r, conjuror** *n.* 1. [kən'dʒuərə] 恳求者 2. 施魔术者;念咒作法的人;变戏法的人 3. (喻)非常聪明的人

connect [kə'nekt] *vt.* 1. 使连接,使联结 2. 把……联系起来;给……接通电话(with) 3. 联想:~ germs with disease 由细菌联想到疾病 — *vi.* 1. 连接;相通;衔接(with) 2.(口)击中 ‖ ~ **er, ~ or** *n.* 1. 连接者;联系者;连接物 2. 连接器;插塞和塞孔 ‖ ~ **ing rod** [机]连杆

connected [kə'nektid] *adj.* 1. 连接的,连结的 2. 关联的;有联系的;连贯的 ‖ ~ **ly** *adv.* / ~ **ness** *n.*

Connecticut [kə'netikət] *n.* 康涅狄格[美国州名]

connection [kə'nekʃən] *n.* = connexion

connective [kə'nektiv] *adj.* 连接的,联结的 — *n.* 1. 连接物 2.【语】关联词 3.【植】药隔 ‖ ~ **ly** *adv.*

connexion [kə'nekʃən] *n.*《主英》1. 连接;联系;连接关系:parallel (series) ~ [电]并(串)联/one's social ~ 社会关系 2. 连贯性:上下文关系;方面:in this (that) ～ 在这(那)一点上 3. 连接物；(通讯、交通等的)联系手段；(火车、轮船等的)联运 4. [常～s]亲戚(尤指姻亲) 5. (政治、宗教等的)团体；教派 6. [总称]顾客；(贸易上的)往来关系 7. [电报、电话]通讯线

connivance [kə'naivəns] *n.* 默许；纵容(*at, in*)

connive [kə'naiv] *vi.* 1. 默许；纵容(*at*) 2. 共谋；取得默契(*with*) ‖ ～ **r** *n.*

connoisseur [ˌkɔnə'sə:] *n.* 鉴赏家；鉴定家；行家，内行(*in, of*)

connotation [ˌkɔnəu'teiʃən] *n.* 1. 含着；(词等的)涵义 2. [逻]内涵

connote [kə'nəut] *vt.* 1. (词、词组等)含着着；意味着 2. [逻]表示…的内涵

connubial [kə'nju:biəl] *adj.* 婚姻的；夫妻的；结了婚的 ‖ ～**ly** *adv.*

conquer ['kɔŋkə] *vt.* 1. 征服，击败；攻克，攻占 2. 克服(困难等) 3. 抑制(情欲等) —*vi.* 得胜 ‖ ～**able** *adj.* 可征服的 / ～**or** *n.* 征服者；胜利者

conquest ['kɔŋkwest] *n.* 1. 征服；赢得；获得 2. 掠取物；征服地 3. (在爱情等方面)被俘虏(或魅惑)的人 4. [the C-][英史](一〇六六年威廉的)征服英国(常作 the Norman Conquest)

conquistador [kɔn'kwistədɔ:] ([复] conquistador(e)s) *n.* (十六世纪的)西班牙征服者

consanguineous [ˌkɔnsæŋ'gwiniəs] *adj.* 同宗的；血亲的，血缘的，同源的 ‖ **consanguinity** *n.*

conscience ['kɔnʃəns] *n.* 良心，道德心 ‖ ～ **money** (为求得心安而付的)追偿金，悔罪金(如补缴所透避的捐税等) / ～-ˌsmitten, '～-ˌstricken, '～-ˌstruck *adj.* 受良心责备的；于心不安的

conscientious [ˌkɔnʃi'enʃəs] *adj.* 认真的；诚心诚意的；谨慎的；凭良心做的 ‖ ～**ly** *adv.* / ～**ness** *n.* ‖ ～ **objector** (出于道德或宗教上的原因而)拒服兵役者

conscionable ['kɔnʃənəbl] *adj.* 凭良心办事的；正直的；公正的 ‖ **conscionably** *adv.*

conscious ['kɔnʃəs] *adj.* 1. 有意识的；意识到的；自觉的；被意识到的 2. 神志清醒的 3. [常用以构成复合词]有…意识的：health -～ 有健康意识的 ‖ ～**ly** *adv.*

consciousness ['kɔnʃəsnis] *n.* 意识；知觉；觉悟；自觉

conscript [kən'skript] *vt.* 征募，征(兵)；征召 —服役 — ['kɔnskript] *n.* 应征士兵 — ['kɔnskript] *adj.* 被征募入伍的

conscription [kən'skripʃən] *n.* 征兵，征募；征集

consecrate ['kɔnsikreit] *vt.* 1. 献给 2. 奉献 3. 使神圣不可侵犯 4. 使就圣职 —*adj.* 献祭的；奉献的 ‖ **conse'cration** *n.* 1. 献祭 2. 奉献 3. 任圣职的仪式

consecutive [kən'sekjutiv] *adj.* 连续的；连贯的；顺序的 ‖ ～**ly** *adv.* / ～**ness** *n.*

consensus [kən'sensəs] *n.* 1. (意见等的)一致；合意；舆论 2. [生]同感

consent [kən'sent] *vi. & n.* 同意；赞成；应答

consequence ['kɔnsikwəns] *n.* 1. 结果；后果 2. 逻辑上必然的结果，推论，推断 3. 重要(性)；重大

consequent ['kɔnsikwənt] *adj.* 1. 作为结果的；随之发生的 2. 合乎逻辑的；必然的 —*n.* 1. 当然的结果；推论 2. [语](条件从句的)结论句 3. [数]后项；[逻]后件，推断 ‖ ～**ly** *adv.* 因而，所以

consequential [ˌkɔnsi'kwenʃəl] *adj.* 1. 作

为结果的;随之发生的 **2.** 间接(发生)
的 **3.** 巨大的,神气活现的 **4.** 推论的
5. 引出重要后果的;重大的,重要的
‖ ~ ly adv.

conservancy [kən'səːvənsi] *n.* **1.**(渔场、森
林等自然资源的)管理;保护;资源保护
区;water ~ 水利 **2.**(英)(河道、港口
等的)管理局

conservation [ˌkɔnsəˈveiʃən] *n.* **1.** 保存;
(自然资源的)保护;资源保护区 **2.**
【物】守恒,不灭

conservatism [kən'səːvətizəm] *n.* **1.** 保守
主义;守旧性 **2.** [C](英)保守党的
主张和政策;(英国)保守学

conservative [kən'səːvətiv] *adj.* **1.** 保存
的;防腐的 **2.** 保守的;守旧的 **3.** [C-]
(英国)保守党的;保守主义的;进步保守
党的 **4.** 有节制的;稳健的 — *n.* **1.** 保
守主义者;因循守旧的人 **2.** [C-](英国
等的)保守党人 **3.** 稳健派 ‖ ~ ly adv.
/~ ness n.

conservatory [kən'səːvətəri] *n.* **1.**(培养植
物的)暖房,温室 **2.** 艺术学校(如音乐
学院等)

conserve [kən'səːv] *vt.* **1.** 保存,保藏;保
养 **2.** 用糖渍保存 — *n.* [常 ~s] 蜜饯;
果酱;【医】糖膏剂,药物糖果

consider [kən'sidə] *vt.* **1.** 考虑,细想 **2.**
认为,把…看作 **3.** 考虑到;照顾;体
贴 **4.** 凝视,端详 — *vi.* 考虑,细想

considerable [kən'sidərəbl] *adj.* **1.** 值得
考虑的 **2.** 值得重视的,相当 **3.** 相当
大(或多)的;很大(或多)的 ‖ ~ ness
n. /considerably adv. 相当大地;…得
多;considerable better 好得多

considerate [kən'sidərət] *adj.* **1.** 考虑周
到的 **2.** 体谅的;体贴的,关切的(of)
‖ ~ ly adv. /~ ness n.

consideration [kənˌsidə'reiʃən] *n.* **1.** 考

虑,思考 **2.** 需要考虑的事;所考虑的
事 **3.** 体谅;照顾 **4.** 尊敬 **5.** 报酬;补偿

considering [kən'sidəriŋ] *prep.* 就…来
说,考虑到

consign [kən'sain] *vt.* **1.** 把…委托给;
把…交付与(to) **2.** 寄存;寄售;托运
(货物等) ‖ ~ee [ˌkɔnsaiˈniː] *n.* 受托
人;承销人;收件人;收货人/~ or. ~ er
n. 委托人;寄件人;发货人;寄售(或寄
存)货物的货主

consignment [kən'sainmənt] *n.* 交付;托
付,托付物(尤指一次寄存或寄售的货
物)

consist [kən'sist] *vi.* **1.** 由…组成,由…
构成(of) **2.**(自由、幸福等)以…为基
础,存在(in) **3.** 并存,一致(with)

consistency [kən'sistənsi] *n.* **1.** 坚固性;
浓度;密度;稠度 **2.**(性格上的)坚韧 **3.**
一致性;连贯性;言行一致

consistent [kən'sistənt] *adj.* **1.** 坚固的,
坚实的 **2.** 一致的;连贯的;始终如一
的 ‖ ~ ly adv.

consistory [kən'sistəri] *n.* 教会法庭;教会
议会;教会法庭(或议会)的会议

consolation [ˌkɔnsə'leiʃən] *n.* **1.** 安慰,慰
问 **2.** 起安慰作用的人(或事物)

console[1] [kən'səul] *vt.* 安慰,慰问 ‖ con-
solable *adj.* /~ r n.

console[2] ['kɔnsəul] *n.* **1.**【建】支托,托臂
2.[自]控制台(仪表板 **3.**(收音机、电
视机等的)落地柜 ‖ ~ table(靠墙放
的)螺形托脚小桌

consolidate [kən'sɔlideit] *vt.* **1.** 巩固,加
强 **2.** 把…合成一体,使联合起来;a
~d school《美》(合并而成的)公立学
校(常指农村小学) /~d annuities
〈英〉无归偿期证券;英国政府债券 —
vi. **1.** 巩固,强固 **2.** 合并,联合

consolidation [kənˌsɔliˈdeiʃən] n. 1. 巩固，加强 2. 合并，联合 3.【医】实变

consols [ˈkɔnsɔlz][复] n.〈英〉无归偿期证券；英国政府债券

consommé [kənˈsɔmei] n. 清炖肉汤

consonance [ˈkɔnsənəns] n. 1. 协调，一致：in ~ with 和…一致(或协调)/out of ~ with 和…不一致(或不协调) 2. (声音的)和谐 3.【音】协和音程 4.【物】谐和 5. 辅音韵

consonant [ˈkɔnsənənt] n.【语】辅音；辅音字母 — adj. 1. 符合的，一致的(with, to) 2. 谐音的；【音】协和音程的 3. 辅音的 ‖ ~al [ˌkɔnsəˈnæntl] adj. 辅音的 / ~ly adv.

consort [ˈkɔnsɔt] n. 1. 配偶(尤指帝王的夫或妻)；伙伴 2. 协力；联合：in ~ with sb. 与某人联合着 3. 僚舰，僚船；随航船只 4. 一组乐器；一组同类乐器 — [kənˈsɔt] vi. 1. 交往(with)；厮混(together) 2. 一致；相称(with) — vt. [常接 oneself]使结合(with)

consortium [kənˈsɔːtiəm] ([复] consortia [kənˈsɔːtiə] 或 consortiums) n. 1. 合作，合伙人 2. 国际财团；银行、企业等的)国际性协议

conspicuous [kənˈspikjuəs] adj. 1. 明显的，显著的；惹人注目的 2.(服饰等)过分花哨的，触目的 ‖ ~ly adv. / ~ness n.

conspiracy [kənˈspirəsi] n. 1. 阴谋，密谋2.同谋，共谋，共谋者 3.(事态、因素等巧合的)协同作用

conspirator [kənˈspirətə] n. 共谋者；阴谋家

conspiratorial [kənˌspirəˈtɔːriəl] adj. 1. 阴谋的；阴谋家的 2.(爱)搞阴谋的 ‖ ~ly adv.

conspire [kənˈspaiə] vi. 1. 密谋策划；搞

阴谋 2.(巧合地)协力促成：All things ~d towards that result. 一切因素都导致了那种结果。

constable [ˈkʌnstəbl] n. 警察；警官

constabulary [kənˈstæbjuləri] n. 警察机构；警察部队 [总称]警察

constancy [ˈkɔnstənsi] n. 坚定，坚贞；持久不变

constant [ˈkɔnstənt] adj. 1. 坚定的，坚贞的；经久不变的 2. 经常的，不断的 — n.【数】【物】常数，常量，恒量 ‖ ~ly adv.

constellation [ˌkɔnstəˈleiʃən] n.【天】星座；(注定命运或性格的)星象；星宿 2.(如明星般)灿烂的一群；【心】情意丛

consternate [ˈkɔnstəneit] vt.[常用被动语态]使惊愕

consternation [ˌkɔnstəˈneiʃən] n.(极度的)惊愕；惊恐

constipate [ˈkɔnstipeit] vt. 使便秘；使(肠道)秘结 ‖ **consti**pation n.

constituency [kənˈstitjuənsi] n. 1. 全体选民；选区的居民 2. 选举区

constituent [kənˈstitjuənt] adj. 1. 形成的，组成的；a ~ corporation 子公司 2. 有组阁权的；有权制定(或修改)宪法的：a ~ assembly 立宪会议 — n. 1.(有权选举议员等的)选民；选举人；委托人 2. 成分，要素；【语】成分，结构成分

constitute [ˈkɔnstitjuːt] vt. 1. 构成，组成 2. 设立(机构、委员会等)；制定(法律等)；使(文件等)成为法律手续 3. 指定，任命：the ~d authorities 合法当局 3. 指定；任命；派…为

constitution [ˌkɔnstiˈtjuːʃən] n. 1. 建立，设立；制定；任命 2.(事物的)构造，组成(方式) 3.(人的)体格；体质；性格，素质 4. 章程，法规 5. 宪法

constitutional [ˌkɔnstiˈtjuːʃənəl] adj. 1. 体

质上的;气质上的 2. 保健的 3. 符合宪法的;符合宪章的;宪法(或规章)所规定的:~ rights 宪法规定的公民权利/ ~ monarchy 君主立宪制 4. 宪法(上)的;规章的 5. 拥护宪法的 — n. 保健散步(运动) ‖ ~ism n. 1. 宪政;立宪政体 2. 立宪主义者;拥护立宪政者 / ~ly adv. 1. 在体质上 2. 在构造上;在本质上 3. 按宪法

constrain [kənˈstrein] vt. 1. 强迫,强使 (to) 2. (良心、内心的力量)促使不得不(to) 3. 禁闭;压抑;约束 4. 制止(from) ‖ ~ed adj. (态度等)勉强的,不自然的

constraint [kənˈstreint] n. 1. 强逼,强制 2. (法律等)的约束;限止 3. 拘束,局促不安

constrict [kənˈstrikt] vt. 1. 使(血管、肌肉等)收缩,收紧(嘴、孔等)使变狭小 2. (紧张的情绪、环境的压力等)束缚,抑制(某种冲动等) — vi. 收缩;变狭小 ‖ ~ed adj. 1. 收缩的,变狭小的 2. (观点等)狭窄的 ‖ ~ion n. 1. 收缩;变狭小 2. (胸口等的)塞闷感 2. (航道等的)变狭小部分;收缩部分 4. 阻塞物 5. 束缚感 5. 压制

construct [kənˈstrʌkt] vt. 1. 建造 2. 对(故事等)进行构思;创立(学说等);构(词);造(句) 3. 作(几何图)— [ˈkɔnstrʌkt] n. 概念 3. 构想 或 vn. 建造者;施工者;舰艇修建监督官

construction [kənˈstrʌkʃən] n. 1. 建造;建筑;建造 2. 建筑方法,建造;结构;建筑物,建造物 3. 【语】结构(体)、(句子、短语中词的)配列 4. 【数】作图;图形 5. 解释 6. 构成派雕塑作品 ‖ ~al adj.

constructive [kənˈstrʌktiv] adj. 1. 建设

的;建设性的 2. 推定的;经过解释的:a ~ fraud【律】(无犯罪动机的)推定欺诈 ‖ ~ly adv. / ~ness n.

construe [kənˈstruː] vt. 1. 对(句子等)作语法分析;把…逐字译出 2. 解释;把…理解作(as)3.【语】(习惯)把某运用作"Depend" is ~d with "on". 动词"depend"与介词"on"连用。— vi. 1. 作句法分析 2. (句子)可作语法分析

consul [ˈkɔnsəl] n. 领事:a ~ general 总领事 ‖ ~ar [ˈkɔnsjulə] adj.

consulate [ˈkɔnsjulət] n. 1. 领事馆 2. 领事职位 3. 领事任期

consult [kənˈsʌlt] vi. 1. 商量;磋商;协商(with) 2. 会诊 3. 当顾问 — vt. 1. 与…商量;请教,咨询;找(医生)看病 2. 查阅(词典、书籍等) 3. 考虑(他人的愿望等) ‖ ~ing adj. 咨询的;顾问的:a ~ing room 咨询室;【医】诊察室

consultancy [kənˈsʌltənsi] n. 1. 顾问工作;顾问职业;顾问职位 2. 顾问服务公司 3. = consultation

consultant [kənˈsʌltənt] n. 1. 求教者;查阅者;征询意见者 2. 顾问 3. 会诊医生;顾问工程师

consultation [ˌkɔnsəlˈteiʃən] n. 1. 商量;磋商 2.【医】会诊

consultative [kənˈsʌltətiv] adj. 咨询的;磋商的;顾问的

consume [kənˈsjuːm] vt. 1. 消费;消耗;浪费 2. 毁灭 3. 消灭;毁灭 4. (常用被动语态)使满腔是,使满脑子(仇恨、好奇心等)(with)

consumer [kənˈsjuːmə] n. 消费者;用户:~ goods 消费品,生活资料

consumerism [kənˈsjuːmərizəm] n. 1. 保护消费者利益运动(二十世纪六十年代始于美国) 2. 消费主义;消费

consummate [ˈkɔnsəmeit] vt. 1. 完成;(终

于)实现 2. 使完美；使圆满 3.(初次同房而)完(婚) — vi.(终于)完成；臻于圆满 ‖ [kən'sʌmit] adj. 1. 使完美无缺的 2. 造诣极高的；高明的 ‖ **con summation** [ˌkɔnsə'meiʃən] n.

consumption [kən'sʌmpʃən] n. 1. 消费 2. [医]消耗 2.[医]肺结核；结核 ‖ **consumptive** adj.

contact ['kɔntækt] n. 1. 接触；联络，联系 2. 交往，交际 3.[电]接触；触点；接头；接触器 2.(从飞机上对地面等的)目视；fly by ~ rather than by instruments 依靠目视而不是依靠仪器来飞行 5.【数】相切 6.[医]接触者；带菌者；接触者 7. 熟人(尤指有权有势者)；门路 — [kən'tækt] vt. 使接触；与…接触；与…联系 — vi. 保持接触的；与有联系的；由接触而引起的；a ~ battle 遭遇战 — adv. 用目视方法 — [kən'tækt] int. 开动! (叫飞机发动者) ‖ ~or[电]接触器；加速器 / ~ing[电]接触器 ‖ ~ flying[空]目视飞行 / ~ lens 隐形眼镜，接触透镜

contagion [kən'teidʒən] n. 1.(接触)传染；传染病 2.(学说，思想，感情，语言等的)蔓延；感染；传播 3.毒；歪风；腐败势力

contagious [kən'teidʒəs] adj. 1.(接触的)(有)传染性的；有感染力的；~ laughter 有感染力的笑声 2. 为对付传染病用的；a ~ ward 传染病房 ‖ **~ly** adv. / ~ness n.

contain [kən'tein] vt. 1.(瓶等)装有(物质等)含有；(名单等)载有；(书等)本身有(若干页数等)；(建筑物等)包括(若干房间等)；(农场等)占有(若干面积) 2.(容器)能容纳(若干数量) 3.(计量或容积单位)相当于，折合(若干较小单位) 4.【数】可被…除尽；作…的约数

边界 5. 控制；抑制；遏制；【军】牵制 ‖ **~ed** adj. 1. 克制的，有节制的 2. 平静的，泰然的 / ~er n. 1. 容器 2. 集装箱；a ~er ship 集装箱船

containerize [kən'teinəraiz] vt. 用集装箱运(货物)；使集装箱化 ‖ **con taineri'zation** n. 集装箱化

containment [kən'teinmənt] n. 抑制；遏制；牵制

contaminate [kən'tæmineit] vt. 弄脏；沾污；污染；传染 2. 沾染 ‖ **con tami'nation** n.

contemn [kən'tem] vt. 蔑视，对…不予管理 ‖ ~er n.

contemplate ['kɔntempleit] vt. 1. 注视，凝视 2. 思忖，思量，沉思 3. 期待；望；反复打算 — vi. 冥思苦想；仔细考虑 ‖ **contemplator** n. 沉思者；冥想者

contemplation [ˌkɔntem'pleiʃən] n. 1. 注视 2. 沉思；冥想；仔细考虑 3. 期望；意图 4.[宗]敛心默祷；感到神的存在

contemporaneous [kənˌtempə'reiniəs] adj. 同时期的，同时代的；同时发生的(with) ‖ **~ly** adv. / ~ness n.

contemporary [kən'tempərəri] adj. 1. 当代的 2. 同时代的，同年龄的(with) — n. 1. 同时代(或同期)的人；同辈的人 2. 同时期的东西(如同时期发行的报刊等)

contempt [kən'tempt] n. 轻视；轻蔑；(对法庭的)蔑视；in ~ of danger 不顾危险 / ~ of court 蔑视法庭(罪)

contemptible [kən'temptəbl] adj. 卑鄙的，不齿的；使人轻视的 ‖ **contemptibly** adv.

contemptuous [kən'temptjuəs] adj. 轻视的；轻蔑的，傲慢的 ‖ **~ly** adv. / ~ness n.

contend [kən'tend] *vi.* **1.** 竞争，斗争 **2.** 争论 — *vt.* 强调地声称(*that*) ‖ ~**er** *n.* 竞争者；斗争者；争论者

content[1] ['kɔntent] *n.* **1.** 容量；含量 **2.** [~s] (袋、罐等中)所装的东西；(书刊等的)目录 **3.** (书、文章等的)内容；要旨

content[2] [kən'tent] *adj.* **1.** 满足的，满意的；甘愿的 **2.** [常作表态语]赞成的 — *vt.* 使满意；[~ oneself]使自己满足(于)(*with*) — *n.* **1.** 满足，满意 **2.** 〈英〉赞成票

contented [kən'tentid] *adj.* 满足的，满意的，心满意足的 ‖ ~**ly** *adv.* / ~**ness** *n.*

contention [kən'tenʃən] *n.* **1.** 竞争，斗争 **2.** (争论中的)论点

contentious [kən'tenʃəs] *adj.* **1.** 爱争论的；动辄争吵的 **2.** 争论的；争论所引起的；引起争议的 **3.** 【律】双方有争议的 ‖ ~**ly** *adv.* / ~**ness** *n.*

contentment [kən'tentmənt] *n.* 满足，满意

contest [kən'test] *vt.* **1.** 争夺(土地、阵地、胜利等) **2.** 辩驳；怀疑…的正确性(或真实性)；对…表示异议 — *vi.* 竞争，辩论(*with, against*) — ['kɔntest] *n.* **1.** 争夺 **2.** 竞赛，比赛

contestant [kən'testənt] *n.* 竞争者；参赛者

context ['kɔntekst] *n.* **1.** (文章的)上下文，语境，文脉 **2.** (事物的)来龙去脉

contextual [kən'tekstjuəl] *adj.* 上下文的；按照上下文的；与上下文有关的 ‖ ~**ly** *adv.*

contextualize [kən'tekstjuəlaiz] *vt.* 将(音素、单词等)置于上下文中研究；把(事件、活动等)与有关情况一并考虑

contiguous [kən'tigjuəs] *adj.* **1.** (互相)接触着的；连成一片的 **2.** 毗邻的；相邻的 **3.** (时间或顺序上)紧接的；邻近的 ‖ ~**ly** *adv.*

continent[1] ['kɔntinənt] *adj.* 自制的，克制的；节制性欲的；禁欲的 ‖ **continence** *n.*

continent[2] ['kɔntinənt] *n.* **1.** 大陆；(大)洲 **2.** [the C-]欧洲大陆

continental [,kɔnti'nentl] *adj.* **1.** 大陆的；大陆性的 **2.** [常 C-]欧洲大陆的 *n.* 欧洲大陆人 ‖ ~**ly** *adv.* ‖ ~ **code**【讯】大陆电码(即国际莫尔斯电码) / ~ **drift**【地】大陆漂移 / ~ **shelf**【地】大陆架

contingency [kən'tindʒənsi] *n.* **1.** 偶然，偶然性；可能，可能性 **2.** 偶发的事；意外事 ‖ ~ **fund** 意外开支准备金；应急基金 / ~ **reserve** 应急储备金

contingent [kən'tindʒənt] *adj.* **1.** 可能发生的；可能的；偶然的；意外的 **2.** 应急的；依条件而定的(*on, upon*)；伴随的(*to*) — *n.* **1.** 意外事情；偶然事故 **2.** 小分队；分遣部队；分遣兵队人(派遣的)代表团 **3.** 偶然事件 ‖ ~ **fee** 有酬金，成功酬金(胜诉后付给律师的酬金)

continual [kən'tinjuəl] *adj.* 不断的，连续的；频繁的 ‖ ~**ly** *adv.*

continuance [kən'tinjuəns] *n.* **1.** 继续，持续 **2.** 持续的时间 **3.** 【律】延期审理

continuation [kən,tinju'eiʃən] *n.* **1.** 继续，连续；持续 **2.** 继续部分；延长物；扩建物；增加物 ‖ ~ **school** 成人继续教育学校

continue [kən'tinju:] *vi.* **1.** 继续；连续；延伸，延长 **2.** 留，依旧；~ at one's post 留任 — *vt.* **1.** 使继续；使连续；使延伸；使延长 **2.** 使留下，挽留；be ~d in office 被挽留继续任职

continuity [ˌkɔntiˈnjuːiti] *n.* **1.** 继续(性);连续(性);持续(性) **2.** 电影分镜头剧本;剧情说明 **3.** (广播节目之间的)节目串联;节目串联词(或音乐);节目串联稿 **4.** (连环画的)故事情节和对话

continuous [kənˈtinjuəs] *adj.* (在空间、时间或顺序上)连续不断的、不间断的;the ~ tense [语]进行时 ‖ ~ly *adv.* / ~ness *n.*

contort [kənˈtɔːt] *vt. & vi.* (剧烈地)扭曲;歪曲

contortion [kənˈtɔːʃən] *n.* 扭曲;歪曲 ‖ ~ist *n.* 柔体杂技演员;歪曲者,曲解者

contour [ˈkɔntuə] *n.* **1.** 轮廓;外形;结构;特征;(女子的)身体曲线 **2.** 等高线;轮廓线 **3.** 【语】(声调等的)升降曲线 ‖ ~ chasing *n.* 超低空掠地飞行 / ~ couch (航天员的)体形躺椅 / ~ line 等高线,轮廓线 / ~ map 等高线地图

contra- *pref.* 表示"相反","反对","相对":contra dict, contra distinction

contraband [ˈkɔntrəbænd] *n.* **1.** 走私;非法买卖;非法运输 **2.** 禁运品;违禁品;走私货 — *adj.* 禁运的;非法买卖的

contrabass [ˈkɔntrəbeis] [音] *n.* 低音提琴;倍低音(乐器) — *adj.* 倍低音的(乐器的)

contraception [ˌkɔntrəˈsepʃən] *n.* 避孕;节育

contraceptive [ˌkɔntrəˈseptiv] *adj.* 避孕的;避孕用的 — *n.* 避孕药;避孕器

contract [ˈkɔntrækt] *n.* **1.** 契约,合同 **2.** 承包契约(或合同) **3.** 婚约 **4.** [律]契约(或合同) **5.** (桥牌)定约;定约所约定要打到的副数);定约桥牌(= ~ bridge) **6.** [语]缩约词,缩约形式 — [kənˈtrækt] *vt.* **1.** 缔结;订(约) **2.** 承

包;承办;把(工程等)包给(to) **3.** 把…许配给;使订婚约(to) **4.** 得(病);染病(习惯);负(债) **5.** 使缩小;使缩短6.使缩短起来;使卷起;使变狭 — *vi.* **1.** 订契约;承包,承办 **2.** 缩小;缩短;变狭 **3.** 缔约;约缩了的 [语]缩约的;a ~ word [语]缩约词 ‖ ~ or [kənˈtræktə] *n.* **1.** 订约人 **2.** 承包人;承包商;包工头 **3.** 收缩物;收缩肌 ‖ ~ bridge 定约桥牌

contraction [kənˈtrækʃən] *n.* **1.** 收缩;缩短;[医]挛缩 **2.** [语]缩约词;缩约形式 **3.** (病的)感染;(债等的)亏欠 **4.** 订约 **5.** [经]收缩(期)

contradict [ˌkɔntrəˈdikt] *vt.* **1.** 反驳,否认 **2.** 同…矛盾;同…抵触 — *vi.* 反驳

contradiction [ˌkɔntrəˈdikʃən] *n.* **1.** 矛盾 **2.** 反驳;否认;抵触 **3.** 自相矛盾的说法

contradictory [ˌkɔntrəˈdiktəri] *adj.* **1.** 矛盾的或对立的;引起(或构成)矛盾的 **2.** 爱反驳别人的 ‖ **contradictorily** *adv.* / **contradictoriness** *n.*

contradistinction [ˌkɔntrədisˈtiŋkʃən] *n.* 对比的区别;in ~ to 与…相比较,与…截然不同

contralto [kənˈtræltəu] *n.* ([复]contraltos) 女低音;女低音歌手;(歌剧中的)女低音角色 — *adj.* 女低音的;女低音歌手(或角色)的

contraption [kənˈtræpʃən] *n.* 〈口〉〈谑〉奇妙的装置;新奇的玩意儿

contrary [ˈkɔntrəri] *adj.* **1.** 相反的(to) **2.** (风等)逆行的 **3.** [kənˈtreəri]故意作对的 — *n.* [the ~]相反;对立面 **1.** [contraries]相反事物 **3.** [逻]反对命题 — *adv.* 相反地 ‖ **contrarily** *adv.* / **contrariness** *n.*

contrast [ˈkɔntrɑːst] *n.* **1.** 对比,对照;(对

照之下形成的)悬殊差别 2. 形成对照的人(或物) 3.(绘画、电视图像等中的)并置对比；反差、衬度 — [kənˈtrɑːst] vt. 使作对比,使对照(with) — vi. 形成对照(with)

contravene [ˌkɒntrəˈviːn] vt. 1. 与...相抵触；违犯(法律等) 2. 反驳；否认 ‖ ~ r n.

contravention [ˌkɒntrəˈvenʃən] n. 1. 矛盾；抵触 2. 违犯；违法(或违章、违例)行为

contribute [kənˈtrɪbjuːt] vt. 1. 贡献 2. 捐(款);捐献,捐助 3. 投稿,撰(稿)— vi. 1. 出一份力;起一份作用;作出贡献(to, towards) 2. 捐献;捐钱(to) 3. 投稿 ‖ **contributor** n. 投稿者;捐助者／**contributory** adj.

contribution [ˌkɒntrɪˈbjuːʃən] n. 1. 贡献；捐献,捐助;贡献物;捐献物 2. 投稿,投寄的来稿 3.(占领军等征收的)特别税

contrite [ˈkɒntraɪt] adj. 悔悟的；由悔悟引起的 ‖ ~ly adv. ／ ~ness n. ／**contrition** [kənˈtrɪʃən] n. 悔恨,后悔

contrivance [kənˈtraɪvəns] n. 1. 发明；设计 2. 发明(或设计)的能力 3. 发明物；机械装置 4. 人为状态；人为的修饰

contrive [kənˈtraɪv] vt. 1. 发明；设计；想出;策划 2. 设法做到；竟然弄到...的地步(to) — vi. 1. 设计;图谋 2. 设法对付过去 ‖ ~d adj. 人造的,不自然的 ／ ~r n. 发明者;设计者;制造者;持家人

control [kənˈtrəʊl] (controlled; controlling) vt. 1. 控制；支配 2. 管理 3. 抑制(感情等) 4. 核实;检验,核对 — n. 1. 控制;支配;调节;抑制;(常 ~s)控制的手段(或措施) 2.(常 ~s)操纵装置;控制器;(收音机)调节装置 3.

(实验的)对照;对照物 4.(汽车越野赛中的)制速路段;中途停车记时检修站 ‖ **controllable** adj. ／**controllably** adv.

controller [kənˈtrəʊlə] n. 1. 控制者;管理者;控制器;调节器;(飞机)调度员 2. 主计长;总会计师

controversial [ˌkɒntrəˈvɜːʃl] adj. 1. 争论的 2. 爱争论的 3. 引起争论的,有争议的 ‖ ~ly adv.

controversy [ˈkɒntrəvɜːsi] n. 争论;论战;争吵

controvert [ˈkɒntrəvɜːt, ˌkɒntrəˈvɜːt] vt. 1. 反驳；驳斥;对...提出质疑 2. 就...开展争论(或辩论) — vi. 争论;辩论

contumacious [ˌkɒntjuˈmeɪʃəs] adj. 拒不服从的；反抗的,倔强的 ‖ ~ly adv. ／**contumacy** [ˈkɒntjuməsi] n. 拒不服从；倔强;藐视法庭

contumely [ˈkɒntjuːmli] n. 1. 傲慢无礼 2. 谩骂;侮辱行为

contuse [kənˈtjuːz] vt. 打伤;撞伤;【医】挫伤 ‖ **contusion** n.

conundrum [kəˈnʌndrəm] n. 谜,猜不透的难题;难答的问题

conurbation [ˌkɒnəˈbeɪʃən] n. (包括卫星城镇和市郊在内的)大城市,集合城市

convalesce [ˌkɒnvəˈles] vi. 恢复,康复

convalescence [ˌkɒnvəˈlesns] n. 恢复(期)康复(期)

convalescent [ˌkɒnvəˈlesnt] adj. 恢复(期)的;康复(期)的;疗养的;恢复期病人的 a ~ hospital (或 home) 康复院;疗养院;(谑)"休养所" — n. 恢复期病人

convection [kənˈvekʃən] n. 1. 传送,传导 2.(空气等的)对流

convene [kənˈviːn] vt. 召集;传唤...出庭受审 — vi. 集会;开会 ‖ ~r n. 会议召集人

convenience [kənˈviːniəns] n. 1. 便利,方

便;有便的时候;适当的机会 **2.** 便利设施;厕所

convenient [kən'vi:niənt] *adj.* **1.** 便利的,方便的;合适的 **2.** 近便的,附近的 ‖ ~**ly** *adv.*

convent ['kɔnvənt] *n.* 女修道院;女修道会

convention [kən'venʃən] *n.* **1.** (政治、宗教、政党等的)会议;大会;全国性大会 **2.** 集会 **3.** 公约;(换俘、停战等的)协定 **4.** 惯例;习俗;常规 **5.** 约定(打桥牌等时叫牌的一套常规)

conventional [kən'venʃənl] *adj.* **1.** 惯例的,常规的;普通平凡的 **2.** (艺术等)因袭的;传统的 **3.** 协定的 ‖ ~**ity** [kən,venʃə'næliti] *n.* **1.** 惯例性;因袭性 **2.** 习俗;因袭的事物 ‖ ~**ize** *vt.* 使惯例化;使习俗化 ‖ ~**ly** *adv.*

converge [kən'və:dʒ] *vi.* **1.** 会聚,集中;为共同利益而结合在一起 **2.** 【数】【物】收敛 ‖ ~**nce** *n.* ‖ ~**nt** *adj.*

conversant [kən'və:sənt] *adj.* 熟悉的,精通的(*with*)

conversation [,kɔnvə'seiʃən] *n.* 会话;谈话;非正式会谈,对话 ‖ ~ **piece 1.** 人物风俗画 **2.** 话题;可作话题的东西(尤指室内的摆设等) ‖ ~**al** *adj.* **1.** 谈话的;会话的 **2.** 爱交谈的;善于辞令的

conversationalist [,kɔnvə'seiʃənəlist] *n.* 交谈者;善于谈话者;善于辞令的人

converse¹ ['kɔnvə:s] *vi.* 交谈,谈话(*with, on, about*);与计算机进行会话 — ['kɔnvə:s] *n.* 〈古〉交谈

converse² ['kɔnvə:s] *adj.* 相反的,颠倒的,逆的 — *n.* **1.** 【逻】逆命题 **2.** 【数】逆,逆命题 ‖ ~**ly** *adv.*

conversion [kən'və:ʃən] *n.* **1.** 变换,转化 **2.** (非教徒的)皈依;(宗教、党派、意见、

信仰等的)改变 **3.** 兑换 **4.** 【逻】换位(法)【数】换算 **5.**【心】转换 **6.**(橄榄球赛中)附加得分(篮球赛中)罚球得分

convert [kən'və:t] *vt.* **1.** 使转变,使转换 **2.** 使皈依;(在宗教、党派、意见、信仰等方面)使改变 **3.** 兑换 **4.** 换算 **5.**(橄榄球赛中)以…赢触地得分后的附加分 — *vi.* 皈依;改变信仰 — ['kɔnvə:t] *n.* 皈依宗教者;改变信仰者

converter, convertor [kən'və:tə] *n.* **1.** 使改变信仰的人 **2.** 酸性转炉,贝塞麦转炉 **3.**【电】整流器;变频器,【计】转换器;转换反应堆;(汽车专用的)催化式排气净化器 **4.**【军】密码机

convertible [kən'və:təbl] *adj.* **1.** 可改变的;可变换的;~ **husbandry**【农】轮作经营 / a ~ **vehicle**(可从轮胎型转变为履带型的)两用车辆 **2.** 可兑换的 **3.** 车篷可折起(或取掉)的 — *n.* 可改变的事物;折篷汽车 ‖ ~**ibility** *n.* 可改变(性);可兑换(性) ‖ ~**ibly** *adv.*

convex ['kɔnveks] *adj.* 凸的,凸面的,凸圆的;a ~ **lens** 凸透镜 ‖ ~**ity** [kɔn'veksiti] *n.* 凸面;凸状

convey [kən'vei] *vt.* **1.** 运送(旅客、货物等);搬运;转运 **2.** 转达;传达(思想、感情等) **3.** 传播(声音等) **4.**【律】转让(财产等) ‖ ~**er, ~or** *n.* **1.** 搬运者;传送者;转让财产者 **2.** 输送机;输送设备

conveyance [kən'veiəns] *n.* **1.** 运输;搬运 **2.**(思想、感情等的)传达;传播 **3.** 运输工具(尤指车辆) **4.**【律】(财产等的)转让;转让证书

convict [kən'vikt] *vt.* **1.** 证明…有罪;判…有罪 **2.** 使知罪 — ['kɔnvikt] *n.* **1.** 罪犯 **2.** 囚犯(长期被监禁者)

conviction [kən'vikʃən] *n.* **1.** 定罪;证明有罪 **2.** 深信,确信

convince [kən'vins] *vt.* **1.** 使确信;使信服(*of, that*) **2.** 使认识(错误等)(*of*)

convincing [kən'vinsiŋ] *adj.* 有说服力的;使人信服的 ‖ **~ly** *adv.* / **~ness** *n.*

convivial [kən'viviəl] *adj.* **1.** 爱交际的 **2.** 节日似的;欢宴的;欢乐的

convoke [kən'vəuk] *vt.* 召集(会议);召集…开会 ‖ **convocation** [ˌkɔnvə'keiʃən] *n.*

convolution [ˌkɔnvə'lu:ʃən] *n.* **1.** 盘绕,回旋;卷曲;盘绕状,盘旋结构 **2.** 【解】回;脑回 **3.** 错综复杂

convoy ['kɔnvɔi] *vt.* 为…护航;护送 — *n.* **1.** 护航;护送 **2.** 护航队;护送队 **3.** 被护航的船;被护送的军队

convulse [kən'vʌls] *vt.* **1.** 使剧烈震动;使痉挛,使抽搐

convulsion [kən'vʌlʃən] *n.* **1.** 震动;骚动【地】灾变 **2.**[~s] 大笑[常~s] 痉挛;惊厥

convulsive [kən'vʌlsiv] *adj.* **1.** 震动的;起痉挛的 **2.**(笑)使人前仰后合的 ‖ **~ly** *adv.*

cony ['kəuni] *n.* **1.** 兔;兔毛皮 **2.**(基督教《圣经》中的)沙番(一种红棕色兔子,被视为不洁之物)

coo [ku:] *vi.* **1.**(鸽)咕咕地叫 **2.** 谈情话 — *vt.* 温柔爱恋地说;轻轻地说 — *n.* 鸽子的叫声;鸽子叫似的轻声

cook [kuk] *vt.* **1.** 烹调,煮,烧 **2.** 窜改;伪造(账目等);编造(谎言等)(*up*) **3.**【俚】损坏;摧垮 **4.**〈俚〉上电刑 — *vi.* **1.**〈食物〉在煮着;适合烹调 **2.** 烧菜,做菜 **3.**〈口〉发生 **4.**〈俚〉失败;完蛋 — *n.* **1.** 炊事员;厨师 **2.**〈工业、技术上的〉烧煮过程 ‖ **~-book** *n.* 〈美〉烹饪书,食谱 / **~-house** *n.* 厨房;船上厨房;野营厨房 / **~-out** *n.* 露天烤肉餐;野餐 / **~-room** *n.* = **~ house** / **~ shop**

n. 小饭馆;(新西兰的)养牛场伙房

cookery ['kukəri] *n.* **1.** 烹饪术;烹饪业;烹饪 **2.** 烹饪处,厨房 ‖ **~ book** 烹饪书,食谱

cookie , cooky ['kuki] *n.* **1.** 饼干,曲奇饼,小甜饼;(苏格兰)淡面包 **2.**〈军俚〉巨型炸弹 **3.**〈口〉爱人;厨师助手 **4.**〈俚〉家伙,人 **5.**〈美俚〉美貌女子

cooking ['kukiŋ] *adj.* 烹调用的;适合于烧煮的 ‖ **~ salt** 食盐/**~ utensils** 炊具

cool [ku:l] *adj.* **1.** 凉的,凉快的 **2.** 冷静的;沉着的 **3.** 冷淡的 **4.** 厚脸皮的 **5.**(颜色)给人凉感的(如蓝、绿、灰等) **6.** 有冷藏设施的;凉爽的 **7.**〈口〉华丽、绘画等)缺乏感情的;超然冷漠的,强调理性的 **8.**(数额等)不折不扣的;整整的 **9.**〈美俚〉妙极的 **10.**(动物的嗅迹)微弱的 — *vi.* **1.** 变凉,冷却下来 **2.**(怒气等)平息;(人)平静下来;失去热情 — *vt.* **1.** 使变冷;使冷却 **2.**(怒气等)平息;使平静下来 **3.**〈美俚〉杀掉 **4.**〈美俚〉在(考试中等)失败;失去(机会) — *n.* **1.** 凉,凉爽;凉快的地方 **2.** 冷静 ‖ **~ly** *adv.* / **~ness** *n.* ‖ **~-headed** *adj.* 头脑冷静的

cooler ['ku:lə] *n.* **1.** 冷却器;冰箱 **2.**〈俚〉监狱;单人监房 **3.** 冷饮品;冷饮料 **4.**【化】冷却剂 **5.**〈口〉空气调节器;空调设备

coolie ['ku:li] *n.* 苦力

coon [ku:n] *n.* **1.**〈美〉〈动〉浣熊 **2.** 狡猾的家伙;机灵鬼 **3.**〈俚〉黑鬼(对黑人的侮辱性称呼)

coop [ku:p] *n.* **1.**(关家禽的)笼;棚;家禽养殖场 **2.**〈英〉捕鱼笼 **3.**〈口〉(俚〉监狱) — *vt.* **1.** 把(家禽)关进笼子(或棚) **2.** 把…禁闭(或禁锢)起来(*up*)

co-op ['kəu'ɔp] *n.* 〈口〉合作社

cooper ['ku:pə] *n.* 制桶工；桶匠

cooperate [kəu'ɔpəreit] *vi.* 1. 合作，协作 2. (事物)配合 ‖ **cooperator** *n.* 合作者；合作社社员；合作主义者

cooperation [kəuˌɔpə'reiʃən] *n.* 1. 合作，协作 2.【生】(有机体间的)互助

cooperative [kəu'ɔpərətiv] *adj.* 1. 合作的，协作的；合作化的 2. 抱合作态度的 — *n.* 合作团体；合作社 ‖ **~ly** *adv.* / **~ness** *n.*

coordinate [kəu'ɔːdineit] *adj.* 1. 同等的；【语】并列的；a ~ clause 并列句子 2.【数】坐标的 — *n.* 1. 同等的人(或事物)2.【数】坐标 — [kəu'ɔːdineit] *vt.* & *vi.* (使)成为同等，(使)协调 ‖ **~ly** *adv.* / **coordinative**[kəu'ɔːdinətiv] *adj.* 使同等的；使协调的 / **coordinator** [kəu'ɔːdineitə] *n.* 1. 协调人 2.【语】并列连词 3.【医】共济器

coordination [kəuˌɔːdi'neiʃən] *n.* 1. 同等，调整，配合 2.【医】共济 3. 协作；协调

coot [kuːt] *n.* 〔复〕coot(s) *n.* 【动】骨顶鸡，白骨顶

cop [kɔp] 〈口〉*n.* 1. 警察 — (copped; copping) *vt.* 1. 逮住，抓住 2. 偷 3. 获得，取得(奖品等) ‖ **~'out** *n.* 1. 逃避；退避；虎头蛇尾 2. 自首 3. 逃避者

cope [kəup] *vi.* 对付；妥善处理(with)

Copenhagen [ˌkəupən'heigən] *n.* 哥本哈根(丹麦首都)

copier ['kɔpiə] *n.* 1. 抄写者；模仿者 2. 誊抄者 3. 复印机

copilot ['kəuˌpailət] *n.* (飞机)副驾驶员

coping ['kəupiŋ] *n.*【建】墙压顶

copious ['kəupiəs] *adj.* 1. 丰富的，富饶的；(语言)词汇丰富的 2. (文字)冗长的 3. 大量的 4. (作家)作品多的 ‖ **~ly** *adv.* / **~ness** *n.*

copper ['kɔpə] *n.* 1. 铜 2. 铜币；铜容器；铜制物 3. 铜色 — *adj.* 铜的；铜制的；铜色的 *vt.* 1. 涂铜于；用铜板包(船底等)2. (美俚)下赌注于 ‖ **~ head** *n.* 【动】铜头蝮蛇 / **~smith** *n.* 铜匠

coppice ['kɔpis] *n.* 矮林，萌生林 ‖ **~-wood** *n.* 矮林，萌芽林

copra ['kɔprə] *n.* 椰肉干，干椰肉

copse [kɔps] *n.* 矮林，萌生林 ‖ **~-wood** *n.*

copula ['kɔpjulə] *n.* 1. 连接(物)；【语】系词 2.【解】联桥 3.【律】交媾

copulate ['kɔpjuleit] *vi.* 1. 连接；结合 2. 交媾；交配 ‖ **copu'lation** *n.*

copy ['kɔpi] *n.* 1. 抄本；副本；摹本，复制品；(电影)拷贝 2. (书报等的)一本，一册，一份 3. (供排字付印的)稿子 4. 范本；字帖 — *vt.* 1. 抄写，誊写；复制；摹仿；抄袭 *vi.* 1. 抄写，誊写；复制；临摹(from)2. 模仿；效法 ‖ **~ book** *n.* 习字簿，描红簿 / **~-desk** *n.* (报馆)文字编辑部 / **~ right** *n.* 版权；著作权 *vt.* 为(书籍)取得版权；保护…的版权 *adj.* 版权的；有版权保护的 / **~writer** *n.* 广告文字撰稿人

coquetry ['kɔkitri] *n.* (女人的)卖弄风情，卖俏；媚态

coquette [kɔ'ket] *n.* 卖弄风情的女人 — *vi.* 卖弄风情，卖俏(with)

coquettish [kɔ'ketiʃ] *adj.* 卖弄风情的 ‖ **~ly** *adv.* / **~ness** *n.*

coral ['kɔrəl] *n.* 1. 珊瑚 2. 珊瑚玩具；海虾卵 4. 珊瑚色，珊瑚红 5. 珊瑚虫 — *adj.* 珊瑚的；珊瑚色的；珊瑚制的 ‖ **~ reef** 珊瑚礁

cord [kɔːd] *n.* 1. 细绳；粗线；索 2.【解】带，索 3. 灯芯绒 ‖ **[~s]** 灯芯绒(牛仔)

裤 4. 考得(木材的小材层积单位,一般为 128 立方英尺) 5.【电】塞绳,电绳 6. 束缚,约束 7.(充利用的)绞索 — vt. 1. 捆,绑,绑 2. 成捆地堆码(木材等) ‖ ~ed adj. 1. 用绳索等捆绑的 2.(织品)起凸线的,起棱纹的 3.(肌肉)紧张的 ‖ ~wood n.(以考得为单位出售的)堆积材

cordial ['kɔːdiəl] adj. 1. 热诚的;衷心的;真诚的;亲切的 2. 强心的;刺激的 — n. 1. 有兴奋(或强心)作用的食物(或饮料、药物等) 2. 露酒,加香(烈性)甜酒 ‖ ~ity[,kɔːdi'æliti] n. 热诚,热诚亲切的话语(或举动) / ~ly adv. 热诚地;真诚地 / ~ness n.

cordless ['kɔːdlis] adj. 1. 无绳的 2.【电】无塞绳式的,电池式的;交直流两用式的 ‖ ~ (tele)phone 无绳电话(机)

cordon ['kɔːdn] n. 1.【军】哨兵线;警戒线;包围圈 2. 饰带;绶章 3.【建】带饰(果树的)单干形 — vt. 用警戒线围住(off)

corduroy ['kɔːdərɔi] n. 灯芯绒;[~s]灯芯绒裤子

core [kɔː] n. 1. 果心;核心;精髓 2.【电】铁心;芯(线);(机械录音的)盘心芯子 3.【矿】岩芯 4.【冶】(空心铸件上用的)型芯;(铸造用的)砂芯 5.【建】心板 6.(为各专业学生共修的)基础课程设置 7.(绵羊体内的)肝虫病 — vt. 挖去…的果心 ‖ ~ city(美)(大都市的)市中心城市

cork [kɔːk] n. 1. 软木;软木塞 2.(钓鱼用的)软木浮子 3. 木栓 — adj. 软木制的 — vt. 1. 塞住;抑制(感情等)(up) 2. 用烧焦的软木涂黑(脸) ‖ ~ oak【植】栓皮槠 / ~ opera(美俚)(白人用烧焦的软木把脸涂黑扮黑人演出的)黑脸说唱短喜剧

corkscrew ['kɔːkskruː] n. 螺丝起子,瓶塞钻 — adj. 螺旋状的: a ~ dive (飞机)螺旋式俯冲 — vt. 1. 使盘旋着前进;使成螺旋状 2.(费力地)探得(消息等) — vi.(道路等)盘旋地向前

corm [kɔːm] n.【植】球茎

cormorant ['kɔːmərənt] n. 1.【动】鸬鹚(俗称水老鸦) 2. 贪婪的人;贪吃的人

corn¹ [kɔːn] n. 1.(英)谷物 2. 谷粒;(辣椒等)子 3.(英)小麦;(美)玉米;(苏格兰)(爱尔兰)燕麦 4.(美口)玉米威士忌酒 5. 老一套,过时货;伤感的东西(如音乐) 6.(美俚)钱 — vt. 1. 使成粒状 2. 腌(肉等) 3. 在…上喂玉米(或谷物) 4. 以谷物喂(性畜) ‖ ~ed adj. 1. 呈粒状的 2. 腌的 3.(俚)喝醉的 ‖ ~ beef 咸牛肉 / Corn Belt(美国中西部的)玉米地带 / ~ borer 玉米螟 / ~ bread 玉米面包 / ~ chip 炸玉米片 / ~ cob n. 玉米棒子芯,玉米穗轴 / ~ crake n. 长脚秧鸡 / ~ dodger(美)玉米烤饼;玉米团子 / ~ flakes [复] n. 玉米片 / ~ flour 1.(美)(精磨)玉米粉 2.(英)谷粉(米粉) / ~ flower n.【植】矢车菊 / ~ meal n. 玉米粉;谷物粉 / ~ sheller 1. 玉米脱粒机 2.(美俚)连发枪 / ~ stalk n. 玉米秆 / ~ flakes [复] n. 玉米片 / ~ starch n. 玉米淀粉

corn² [kɔːn] n.【医】鸡眼,钉胼

cornea ['kɔːniə] n.【解】角膜 ‖ ~l adj. 角膜的

corner ['kɔːnə] n. 1. 角;墙角,壁角;街角 2.(书本、箱子等)的包角 3. 边远地区;角落;冷僻处 4. 困境,绝路 5. 囤积(居奇)形势 6.(足球、曲棍球的)角球 = ~ kick) — vt. 1. 使走投无路,把…难住 2. 囤积;垄断 — vi. 1. 相交成角;形成角 2.(车辆、驾驶员)转弯 3. 囤积(in)

一 *adj.* 1. 角上的;转弯处的 2.(适)用于角隅的 ‖ ～ed *adj.* 1.[用以构成复合词]有…角的:three-～ed (有)三只角的 2. 被逼入绝境的;被难住的 ‖ ～wise, ～ways *adv.* 1. 形成角状地 2. 对角地 ‖ ～ kick(足球赛的)角球 /'～stone(墙)墙角石,隅石 2.(奠基典礼上放下的)奠基石 3.(喻)柱石;基础

cornet ['kɔːnit] *n.* 1.(乐器)短号 2.(放糖果的)圆锥形纸袋;(盛冰淇淋、奶油等用的)圆锥形蛋卷

cornice ['kɔːnis] *n.* 1.[建]飞檐;檐板;上楣;檐口 2. 雪檐(冻结在石岩边缘的雪块)

cornucopia [ˌkɔːnjuːˈkəupiə] *n.* 1.[希神]丰饶角 2. 象征丰饶的(羊角)画(或雕刻)3. 丰富,丰饶 4. 圆锥形的糖果袋,三角包 ‖ ～n *adj.* 丰富的,丰饶的

corny[1] ['kɔːni] *adj.* 1. 谷物的;谷物丰富的 2.〈口〉陈词滥调的;过时的

corny[2] ['kɔːni] *adj.*(脚)有鸡眼的

corolla [kəˈrɔlə] *n.*[植]花冠

corona [kəˈrəunə] *n.*([复]coronas 或 coronae [kəˈrəuniː]) 1.[气]华 2.[天]日晕 3.(人体的)冠状部位 4.[植]冠;副(花)冠

coronary ['kɔrənəri] *adj.* 冠的;花冠的;冠状的:～ arteries (veins)(心脏的)冠状动脉(静脉)

coronation [ˌkɔrəˈneiʃən] *n.* 加冕(典礼)

coroner ['kɔrənə] *n.* 验尸官:a ～'s inquest 验尸

coronet ['kɔrənit] *n.* 1.(王子或显贵戴的)冠 2.(女子的)冠状头饰 3.[解]蹄冠[植]冠,副花冠

corp. *abbr.* 1. corporal 2. corporation

corporal[1]   ['kɔːpərəl] *adj.* 肉体的,身体

的:～ punishment 肉刑;体罚

corporal[2] ['kɔːpərəl] *n.*[军]下士

corporate ['kɔːpərit] *adj.* 1. 社团的;法人的:a ～ body 法人团体(＝a body ～) 2.(责任等)共同的;全体的 ‖ ～ly *adv.*

corporation [ˌkɔːpəˈreiʃən] *n.* 1.[律]社团;法人,公司 2.(美)股份有限公司 3. 市镇当局;(大学的)校务委员会 4.〈口〉大肚皮

corporeal [kɔːˈpɔːriəl] *adj.* 肉体的;物质的;[律]物质的,有形的(指动产等)‖ ～ity [kɔːpɔːriˈæliti] *n.* 肉体性;形体 ‖ ～ly *adv.*

corps [kɔː]([复]corps[kɔːz]) *n.* 1. 军(介于师与集团军之间的陆军单位)2.[用作复数]通信等兵种的名称];队:the Corps of Engineers(美国)陆军工兵部队 3. 队;团:a diplomatic ～ 外交使团 4.(德国大学的)学生联谊会

corpse [kɔːps] *n.* 死尸,尸体;被废弃的东西:a political ～ 政治僵尸

corpulence ['kɔːpjuləns], **corpulency** ['kɔːpjulənsi] *n.* 肥胖

corpulent ['kɔːpjulənt] *adj.* 肥胖的

corpuscle ['kɔːpʌsl], **corpuscle** [kɔːˈpʌskjul] *n.* 1.[医]血球;细胞;小体 2. 微粒的,小体的;细胞 ‖ **corpuscular** [kɔːˈpʌskjulə] *adj.* 血球的,微粒的;小体的;细胞的

corral [kɔːˈrɑːl] *n.* 1.(美)畜栏 2. 捕兽栅栏 3.(作防御用的)车阵 ‖ (corralled;corralling) *vt.* 1.(美)把…关进畜栏 2. 把(车辆)围成车阵(以抵御敌人)

correct [kəˈrekt] *vt.* 1. 改正,纠正;修改;矫正;校正 2. 惩治 — *adj.* 1. 正确的 2.(行为、态度等)恰当的;端正的;符合一般准则的 ‖ ～ive *adj.* & *n.* ‖ ～ly *adv.* / ～ness *n.* / ～or *n.*

correction [kəˈrekʃən] *n.* 1. 改正,纠正;

修改;矫正;校正;勘误;修正量;校正值 2.(对罪犯的)教养 3. 惩治,惩罚 4.(市价上涨后的)回落 ‖ ~al *adj.*

correlate ['kɔrəleit] *vt. & vi.* (使)相互关联(*with*, *to*) — *n.* 相关事物;相互依存的人 ‖ **corre'lation** *n.* / **correlative** [kə'relətiv] *adj.*

correspond [ˌkɔris'pɔnd] *vi.* 1. 符合,一致(*with*) 2. 相当,相应(*to*) 3. 通信(*with*)

correspondence [ˌkɔris'pɔndəns] *n.* 1. 符合,一致 2. 相当,相应;【数】对应 3. 通信(联系);互通的信件 ‖ ~ **school** 函授学校

correspondent [ˌkɔris'pɔndənt] *n.* 1. 对应物 2. 通信者;(新闻)通讯员;记者 3.(与国外或外地)有商业关系的人(或公司) — *adj.* 符合的,一致的;相当的 ‖ ~**ly** *adv.*

corresponding [ˌkɔris'pɔndiŋ] *adj.* 1. 符合的,一致的;相应的,对应的 2. 通讯的 ‖ ~**ly** *adv.*

corridor ['kɔridɔː] *n.* 1. 走廊;过道 2. 走廊地带 3. 空中走廊;航空走廊 ‖ ~ **train**(英)包厢通廊列车,软席列车

corroborate [kə'rɔbəreit] *vt.* 确证,实证 ‖ **cor,robo'ration** *n.* / **corroborative** [kə'rɔbərətiv] *adj.*

corrode [kə'rəud] *vt.* 腐蚀;侵蚀 — *vi.* 起腐蚀作用

corrosion [kə'rəuʒən] *n.* 1. 腐蚀;侵蚀 2. 锈;铁锈

corrosive [kə'rəusiv] *adj.* 腐蚀的;腐蚀性的 — *n.* 腐蚀剂 ‖ ~**ly** *adv.* / ~**ness** *n.*

corrugate ['kɔrugeit] *vt.* 弄皱,使起皱,使起波纹 — *vi. @ d iron* 波纹铁/~*d paper* 瓦楞纸 — *vi.* 起皱,起波纹 ‖ **,corru'gation** *n.*

corrupt [kə'rʌpt] *adj.* 1. 腐败的;贪污的

2.(语言、版本等)讹用的;多讹误的 3. 腐烂的;污浊的 — *vt.* 1. 使败坏;腐蚀 2. 贿赂,收买 3. 使腐败;使污浊 4. 讹用(语、词等);使(稿本等)搀杂讹误 — *vi.* 1. 腐坏;腐蚀 2. 腐败;堕落 ‖ ~**ible** *adj.* 经不起腐蚀的,易腐化堕落的;可收买的;易腐坏的/~**ion** *n.* / ~**ly** *adv.* / ~**ness** *n.*

corsage [kɔː'sɑːʒ] *n.* 1. 女服胸部;胸衣 2.(戴在女服胸部或腰部的)装饰花

corsair ['kɔːsɛə] *n.* 海盗;海盗船

corselet[1] ['kɔːslit] *n.* 1. 盔甲 2.【动】(鞘翅目昆虫的)前胸;(鱼类的)胸甲

corselet[2], **corselette** [ˌkɔːsə'let] *n.* (女服)紧身胸衣

corset ['kɔːsit] *n.* (女服)紧身褡,胸衣 — *vt.* 给…穿紧身褡

cortège [kɔː'teiʒ] *n.* 1.(尤指送葬的)队伍,行列 2. 一队扈从,一队随员

cortex ['kɔːteks] *n.* [复] **cortices** ['kɔːtisiːz] 或 **cortexes**) *n.* 1. 脑皮层 2. 皮层,皮质 3. 树皮,果皮

cortisone ['kɔːtizəun] *n.*【生化】脱氢皮质酮;【药】可的松,考的松

corvette [kɔː'vet] *n.* 轻型护卫舰

coryza [kə'raizə] *n.*【医】卡他性鼻炎,鼻卡他,鼻炎

cos【数】余弦(cosine)的符号

COS *abbr.* cash on shipment【商】装船付款

cosine ['kəusain] *n.*【数】余弦

cosmetic [kɔz'metik] *n.* 1. 化妆品;装饰品 — *adj.* 1. 化妆用的;整容的 2. 装饰性的;装门面的 — *vt.* 用化妆品打扮 ‖ ~**ian** [ˌkɔzme'tiʃən] *n.* 化妆品制造(或经销商);美容师,化妆师

cosmic ['kɔzmik] *adj.* 1. 宇宙的 2. 广大无边的 ‖ **cosmically** *adv.* ‖ ~ **dust** 宇宙尘/~ **noise** 宇宙噪声/~ **rays** 宇宙

射线

cosmonaut ['kɔzmənɔ:t] *n.* 宇(宙)航(行)员

cosmonette [ˌkɔzmə'net] *n.* 女宇航员

cosmopolis [kɔz'mɔpəlis] *n.* 国际性都市

cosmopolitan [ˌkɔzmə'pɔlitən] *adj.* 1. 世界性的，全球(各地)的；世界主义的 2. 【生】世界的，广布的，遍生的

cosmos ['kɔzmɔs] *n.* 1. 宇宙 2. 秩序；一统体系 3. 【植】大波斯菊

Cossack ['kɔsæk] *n.* 1. 哥萨克人 2. 哥萨克轻骑兵 3. 哥萨克旨宿

cost [kɔst] *n. (cost)* *n.* 1. 价值为；(使)花费(金钱、时间、劳力等) 2. 使失去(生命、健康等) 3. (costed 或 cost)估计…的成本 — *vi.* 需要花费；需要付出代价：How dear the lesson ~s! 这个教训的代价多么大啊! — *n.* 1. 成本；费用 2. 代价 3. [~s](尤指判处败方胜方的)诉讼费用 ‖ ~-**benefit** *adj.* 成本效益(分析)的 /~-**ef'fective** *adj.* 有成本效益的；值得花费的，合算的 /~-**ef'fectiveness** *n.* 成本效益；成本进益比率 /~-**ef'ficiency** *n.* = cost-effectiveness /~-**ef'ficient** *adj.* = cost-effective / **inflation** 成本增加引起的通货膨胀，成本推高型通货膨胀；成本推高成本合同(或契约) /~ **push** = cost inflation

Costa Rica [ˌkɔstə'ri:kə] 哥斯达黎加[拉丁美洲国家](中美洲南部)

costly ['kɔstli] *adj.* 1. 昂贵的；代价高的 2. 价值高的；豪华的 ‖ **costliness** *n.*

costume ['kɔstju:m] *n.* 1. 服装；服装式样；装束 2. 女套服；外套 3. 古装；戏装 a ~ piece(或 play)古装戏 — *vt.* 为…提供服装

cosy ['kəuzi] *adj., adv. & n.* = cozy

cot¹ [kɔt] *n.* 1. 小屋；村舍 2. = cote 3. (手指或脚趾)套，护套

cot² [kɔt] *n.* 帆布床；吊床；[英]儿童摇床；儿童病床 ‖ ~ **death** (英)婴儿猝死

cot [数]余切(cotangent)的符号

cotangent [kəu'tændʒənt] *n.* [数]余切

cote [kəut] *n.* 羊栏；鸡舍；鸽棚

Côte d' Ivoire [ˌkɔtdiːv'wɔ:] 科特迪瓦[英文意译 Ivory Coast 象牙海岸][西非国家]

coterie ['kəutəri] *n.* (文人等排外的)小圈子；小集团

cotillion [kə'tiljən] *n.* 科蒂荣舞(十八世纪末叶和十九世纪的法国宫廷舞)

cottage ['kɔtidʒ] *n.* 1. 村舍；小屋 2. (疗养院、学校等内部的)单幢住所 3. (避暑地等的)(乡间)别墅 ‖ ~ **industry** 家庭手工业 /~ **piano** 竖式小钢琴

cotter ['kɔtə] *n.* [机]制销；开尾销；扁销

cotton ['kɔtn] *n.* 1. 棉花 2. 棉线，棉纱 3. 棉布 4. (其他植物所生的)棉状物 — *vi.* 1. 和谐，一致(together, with) 2. (口)发生好感(to, on to) 3. (口)理解，懂得(on, on to) 4. (口)讨好(up to) ‖ **boll** 棉桃，棉铃 ~ **gin** 轧棉机，轧花机 /~ **padded** *adj.* 填棉絮的 /~ **print** 印花棉布 /~-**seed** *n.* 棉籽 /~-**tail** *n.* 棉尾兔(产于北美洲的一种野兔) /~ **waste** 1. 废棉，回丝 2. 回丝(擦擦机器等用) /~-**wood** *n.* 【植】三角叶杨 /~ **wool** 1. 原棉，棉花 2. (英)脱脂棉，药棉

couch [kautʃ] *n.* 1. 长沙发；长榻 2. (诗)床；寝处 3.【植】匍匐冰草；小麦草；红顶草；鼠尾看麦娘；狗牙根；羊根草 — *vt.* 1. (用前被动语态或过去时)躺下 2. (用言词)表达(in) 3. 端着(枪、矛等)准备攻击 — *vi.* 1. 躺下 2. 蹲伏；埋伏

cough [kɔf] *n.* 咳，咳嗽 — *vi.* 咳，咳嗽；

发出咳嗽似的声音。— *vt.* 咳出(*up*)
‖ ~ **drop** 止咳糖／~ **mixture** 止咳药
水

could [强 kud／弱 kəd](can 的过去式)*v.
aux.* 1.[用于虚拟语气][表示与事实
相反的设想]能，可以：If I ~ go with
you, I should feel very glad. 假使我能同
你们一起去，我会感到非常高兴。 2.
[表示可能性]有时会：The weather here
~ be very cold in autumn. 这里秋季天
气有时很冷。 3.[用于婉转语气]能：
Could you do something for me? 你能替
我做件事情吗？[注意：本句因用了
could 语气比之用 can 要婉转、客气得
多]

couldn't ['kudnt] = could not

coulomb ['kuːlɔm] *n.*【电】库仑(电量单位)

council ['kaunsl] *n.* 1. 政务会；理事会；
委员会：the State *Council* (中国) 国务
院／the *Council* of Ministers 内阁／the
U.N. Security *Council* 联合国安全理事
会。 2. 商议会；讨论会议；宗教会议
顾问班子；立法班子：the Privy *Council*
(英国)枢密院。 4. 地方自治会；地方
政会(或会议)。 5.(若干组织的)联合
体；(某一组织的)分支机构；俱乐部；
社团。 6.(地方性的)工会代表会议 7.
议事，商讨 ‖ ~ **board** 议事桌；全体议
事者／~ **chamber** 会议室／~ **estate**
(英)(市或郡等)建房群／~ **house** 1.
(英)(市或郡等)建住房／~ **house** 1.
man *n.*(美)(市或郡政务会)的委员／~ **-manager plan**(美)(由市议会推选市长的、市长负责制)／~ **school**(英)市立学校，郡立学校)／~ **woman** *n.*(美)(市或镇政务会)的女委员

council(l)or ['kaunsələ] *n.* 1. 地方议会

议员。 2. 顾问；评议员。 3. 参赞

counsel ['kaunsl] *n.* 1. 商议；评议；审议。
2. 劝告；忠告。 3. 意见；计划；(古)意
图；目的 4. 律师；辩护人。(counsel(l)ed;
counse(l)ling) *vt.* 劝告；忠告 ‖ **counsel-
(l)or** *n.* 1. 顾问。 2.(大使馆等的)法律
顾问。 3. 律师。 4. 夏令营管理员

count[1] [kaunt] *vt.* 1. 点，数；从一数到
清点。 2. 把...算入：There are fifty people present, (not) ~ing the children. 儿
童(不)计算在内，出席者五十人。 3.
认为，以为；看作 — *vi.* 1. 数，计算 2.
有价值，有重要性；算得上：Every second
~s. 每秒钟都很重要。(或：分秒必
争。) — ~ among the largest in the country
算得上是国内最大者之一 3. 共计
信赖；指望(*on, upon*) — *n.* 1. 计算；
合计数。 2.(诉讼中)(一项)事实；(一项
数。 3.【纺】支数：fine (medium) ~ yarn
细(中)支棉纱。 4.【律】(控告的一条)罪
状 5. 争论点，问题 6.(拳击赛中)(十秒
钟计时)(裁判员给予被击倒者的再起
机会) ‖ ~**able** *adj.* 可数的 *n.*[语]可
数名词／~**-down** *n.*[发射前以前
用倒数方式进行的]倒读数，逆序计数

count[2] [kaunt] *n.*(西欧除英国外的)伯爵
(英国称 earl)

countenance ['kauntinəns] *n.* 1. 面部表
情；面容；面目；脸色 2. 赞助；赞同；支
持。3. 镇定，沉着 — *vt.* 支持；允许；容
忍

counter[1] ['kauntə] *n.* 1. 计算者 2. 计算
器；计算器 3. 柜台 4. 筹码；伪造的硬
币 5.(讨价还价的)本钱，资本，有利条
件 ‖ ~**-jumper** *n.* 站柜台的人(对店员的蔑称)

counter[2] ['kauntə] *adv.* 反方向地
(与...)相反地(*to*)：run (或 go, act) ~
to 违背，与...背道而驰 — *adj.* 1. 相

反;对立的 2. 反对的;敌意的 3. 位于对面的 4. 收回成命的: a ~ order 收回成命的命令(即宣布取消前一命令的命令)— n. 1. 相反;反面 2. 起抵消作用的事物;制止 3. 马的前胸部;船尾突出部 4.(皮鞋的)主跟,后帮 5.(拳击等)受击或挡架来拳时的)还击 — vt. 1. 反对;反击 2. 抵消 3. 反驳 — vi. 反对;反击;反击

counter- *pref.* 1. 表示"反","逆": *counter*act 2. 表示"对应": *counter*part 3. 表示"重复": *counter*foil

counteract [ˌkauntəˈrækt] *vt.* 抵抗;抵制;阻碍;中和;抵消 ‖ ~**ion** *n.*

counterattack [ˈkauntərəˌtæk] *n.*, *vt.* & *vi.* 反攻;反击

counterbalance [ˈkauntəˌbæləns] *n.* 1. 平衡(力)的力 2. 抵消(力)之力 — *vt.* 使平衡;抵消;对…起平衡作用 ‖ ~ 起平衡作用

counterclockwise [ˌkauntəˈklɔkwaiz] *adj.* & *adv.* 逆时针方向的(地)

counterculture [ˈkauntəˌkʌltʃə] *n.* 反传统文化,反主流文化(指二十世纪六、七十年代美国青年中一些不满现状的思想和生活态度)

counterfeit [ˈkauntəfit] *adj.* 1. 伪造的,假冒的;仿造的 2.(悲哀等)假装的,虚伪的,虚假的 — *n.* 1. 伪造物;仿造品 — *vt.* 1. 伪造(货币、手迹等);仿造 2. 假装 3. 与…极相似 — *vi.* 1. 假装 2. 抵消(力)之力 ‖ ~**er** *n.* 伪造者(尤指造假货币的人)

counterfoil [ˈkauntəfɔil] *n.* (支票等的)存根,票根

countermand [ˌkauntəˈmɑːnd] *vt.* 取消,撤回(已发出的命令、定货单等)

counteroffensive [ˈkauntərəˌfensiv] *n.* 反攻;反击;反攻战

counterpane [ˈkauntəpein] *n.* 床罩

counterpart [ˈkauntəpɑːt] *n.* 1. 副本;复本 2. 配对物;补足物 3. 极相似的东西;(在职位、作用、作用等方面)相对应的人,对手方

counterpoint [ˈkauntəpɔint] *n.* 1.[音]对位声部;(对位法;对位曲式;复调 2.(文学、戏剧作品中)的比法 3. 补足物;对比物;相互作用物

counterproductive [ˌkauntəprəˈdʌktiv] *adj.* 产生相反结果(或效果)的

counterrevolutionary [ˈkauntəˌrevəˈluːʃənəri] *adj.* 反革命的 — *n.* 反革命分子

countersign [ˈkauntəsain] *n.* 1. 副署,会签 2.[军]回令 3. 暗号;应答信号 — *vt.* 副署,会签(文件等);确认,认可;批准

countess [ˈkauntis] *n.* 1. 伯爵夫人 2. 女伯爵

countless [ˈkauntlis] *adj.* 无数的,多得不计其数的 ‖ ~**ly** *adv.*

country [ˈkʌntri] *n.* 1. 国家;国土 2.[the ~][总称]国民;选民 3. 家乡,故乡;祖国 4.[the ~]乡下,农村 (= the countryside);(美)乡村音乐;乡村与西部音乐 5.(具有某种地理特点的)区域;地区;知识领域 6. 土地 — *adj.* 乡下的,农村的;乡村风味的;乡气的;乡村音乐的 ‖ ~ **and western** (有)乡村与西部音乐(风格的) / ~ **club** 乡村俱乐部(附有高尔夫球场等) / ~ **cousin** 乡下亲戚;乡巴佬 / ~ **-dance** *n.* (源出英国的)乡村舞(交指排成两排的对舞) / ~ **house** = ~seat / ~ **jake** (美)乡下佬 / ~ **man** *n.* 1. 同国人,同胞;同乡 2. 乡下人 3. 某地人 / ~ **-a north** 北方人 / ~ **mile** (美口)极长的一段距离 / ~ **seat** *n.* (英国贵族或乡绅的)乡间宅第 / ~ **-side** *n.* 1. 乡下,农村 2.[总称]

村居民 / '~**wide** adj. 全国性的, 全国范围的 / '~**woman** n. 1. 女同胞 2. 乡下女人

county ['kaunti] n. 1.(英国的)郡 2.〈美〉县(州以下的最大行政区)3.〈中国等国的〉县 4.(中国西藏自治区的)宗 5.[the ~]全部(或全县)居民;〈英〉全郡士绅 / ~ **seat** 县县府所在地, 县城 / ~ **town**〈英国〉县的首府

coupé ['ku:pei], **coupe** [ku:p] n. 1. 双座四轮轿式马车 2. 双门箱式小客车 3.〈英〉(铁路客车尾部的)包房

couple ['kʌpl] n.[复] couple(s) n. 1.(一)对,(一)双;夫妇;未婚夫妻 2.〈口〉几个, 三四个:in a ~ of days 在三四天内 3.[物]力偶, 电偶 — vt. 1. 连接;使结合;把...拴在一起;[电]使耦合 2. 使成夫妇;[动]使交配 — vi. 1. 结合 2.[动]交配 ‖ ~d adj. / ~ r n.

couplet ['kʌplit] n. 对句;对联

coupling ['kʌpliŋ] n. 1. 联结;结合;[动]交配 2. 连接器;联轴节;(火车的)车钩;挂钩 3.[电]耦合

coupon ['ku:pɔn] n. 1.(债券等的)息票 2.(火车等的)联票 3.(附在商品上的)赠券(连在广告上, 需凭券享用, 优待券 4.(食品、布匹等的)配给券, 票证

courage ['kʌridʒ] n. 勇气, 胆量;勇敢

courageous [kəˈreidʒəs] adj. 勇敢的, 有胆量的, 无畏的 ‖ ~**ly** adv. / ~**ness** n.

courier ['kuriə] n. 信使;[C](用于报刊名)信使报 — vt. & vi.(为...)当信使

course [kɔːs] n. 1. 过程;经过;进程 2. 道路;行动方向;行动方针;路线 3. 河流, 航线;航向;(罗盘上的)方位点 4. 做法;行为 5. 课程;学程 6. 行程 7.(一道)菜;一道菜肴 8.[建]层;一层砖石;一排 9. 跑道;跑马场;高尔夫球场 10. 追猎

(尤指用猎犬追猎野兔等)11.[船]大横帆 12.[~s]月经 — vt. 1. 追, 追逐;(用猎犬)追猎 2. 使(马等)跑;使(猎狗)追猎 — vi. 1. 跑过 — vt. 1. 跑;追;(用猎犬)追猎 2. 运行;流动;流淌 ‖ **of** ~ 当然, 自然

court [kɔːt] n. 1. 庭院;院子 2.(网球等的)球场 3. 院落;大院;〈美〉汽车旅馆 4.(展品的)陈列室 5. 法院;法庭;开庭 6. 宫廷;朝廷;(君主)受觐 7. 奉承;殷勤;求爱 — vt. 1. 招致(失败、危险等);企求 2. 讨好, 奉承;向...求爱 — vi. 求爱 ‖ ~ **ship** n. 求爱;求婚 ‖ ~ **card** 人头牌, 花牌(纸牌中的人像) / ~ **game** 场地球类运动(常指网球、手球等)/ '~ **house** n. 1. 法院大楼 2.〈美〉县政府大楼 3.〈美〉县城 / '~ **room** n. 审判室 / '~ **yard** n. 庭院;院落

courteous ['kɔːtiəs] adj. 有礼貌的;谦恭的;殷勤的 ‖ ~**ly** adv. / ~**ness** n.

courtesan ['kɔːti'zæn] n.〈依赖达官贵人的〉高级妓女;交际花

courtesy ['kɔːtisi] n. 1. 礼貌;谦恭;殷勤;谦恭有礼的言词(或举动):a ~ call(或 visit)礼节性访问 2. 好意 ‖ **by** ~ **of** the port(美国公民回国抵港时海关给予的)行李优先检查待遇 3. = curtsey, curtsy ‖ ~ **card** 优待卡 / ~ **light** 控车室照明灯, 礼貌灯 / ~ **title**(礼节上的)尊称

courtier ['kɔːtiə] n. 1. 廷臣, 朝臣 2. 奉承者;谄媚者

courtly ['kɔːtli] adj. 1. 有宫廷气派的;显贵的;威严的;优雅的;有礼貌(或教养)的 2. 奉承的 3. 赞成(或倾向)朝廷政策的 — adv. 有礼貌地 ‖ **courtliness** n.

court-martial ['kɔːt'mɑːʃəl] n.([复] courts-martial 或 court-martials) n. 1. 军事法

庭 **2.** 军事法庭审判 — (court-martial-(l)ed; court-martial(l)ing) *vt.* 对…进行军事审判

cousin ['kʌzn] *n.* **1.** 堂(或表)兄弟(或表)姐妹 **2.** 亲戚; 远亲 **3.** (在地位等方面)同等的人 **4.** 卿(国王对贵族的尊称) **5.** 同民族而国籍不同的人 **6.** 〈美俚〉老朋友

cove[1] [kəuv] *n.* **1.** 山凹 **2.** 小湾; 小海湾; (河)湾 **3.** 〈建〉凹圆线脚; 穹窿, 拱; (墙壁顶上的)光源遮蔽槽 — *vt. & vi.* (使)成穹形; (使)向内凹

cove[2] [kəuv] *n.* 〈英俚〉家伙, 汉子

covenant ['kʌvinənt] *n.* 盟约; 契约 — *vt.* 用盟约(或契约)保证 — *vi.* 缔结盟约(立契约) **2.** 立誓约的, 受契约约束的 — /~ er *n.* 订约人

cover ['kʌvə] *vt.* **1.** 盖; 铺; 覆盖; 遮盖 **2.** 掩盖, 掩饰(up) **3.** 掩护; 掩蔽 **4.** (用枪)对准(with); (枪炮等)控制(住) **5.** 包括, 包含; 适用于 **6.** 占(若干面积); 行过(若干路程) **7.** 负担支付(开支等); 弥补(损失等); 补进(卖完的商品等); 给(货物等)保险 **8.** 对…进行新闻采访; 报道 **9.** (种马等)和…交配; (鸡等)孵(蛋) **10.** 【体】(为夺球)钉住(对手); 掩护(本队球员) **11.** (出同额赌注)接受(对方打赌); 出较大的牌以压倒(对方的牌) — *vi.* **1.** 〈美〉(替某人)掩饰(for) **2.** 做替代者(for) — *n.* **1.** 盖子; 套子 **2.** (书的)封面; 封底; 封皮; 包皮; 封袋 **3.** (自行车等的)外胎 **4.** 床罩 **5.** 隐蔽处; 躲避处; 掩蔽物 **6.** 〈气〉(云)量 **7.** 全套餐具 **8.** 〈商〉保证金 **9.** 覆盖地面的东西(如草木、积雪等) || ~ all *n.* 〈常 coveralls〉(长裤相连的)工作服 / ~ charge(夜店等)服务费 / ~ crop(护田、肥田的)覆盖作物 / ~ girl(杂志的)封面女郎 / ~ note

(保险经纪人签发给被保险人的)暂保单, 承保条 / ~-up *n.* 掩盖手段, 掩盖手法

coverage ['kʌvəridʒ] *n.* **1.** 覆盖; 覆盖范围(或区域等) **2.** 承保范围; 保险险种 **3.** 新闻报道(范围) **4.** (电台或电视台的)覆盖面 **5.** 保证金

covered ['kʌvəd] *adj.* **1.** 有盖(或篷等)的; 覆盖着的 **2.** 有掩蔽的; 隐蔽着的 **3.** 戴着帽子的 || ~ wagon **1.** 有篷大马车 **2.** (铁路的)棚车 / ~ way【建】掩蔽廊道

covering ['kʌvəriŋ] *n.* **1.** 覆盖物; 套, 罩 **2.** 掩蔽物, 掩护物 **3.** (证券或商品抛空后的)补进 — *adj.* **1.** 掩护的 **2.** 含说明的: a ~ letter(随包裹等寄出的)附信

coverlet ['kʌvəlit] *n.* 床罩

covert ['kʌvət] *adj.* **1.** 隐蔽的; 偷偷摸摸的, 暗地里的 **2.**【律】受丈夫保护的 — ['kʌvə, 'kʌvət] *n.* **1.** (小兽等的)隐蔽处(指森林、树丛等); 掩蔽处; 掩蔽物 **2.**【动】覆羽(覆盖翼羽翮基部的羽毛) || ~ly *adv.* / ~ness *n.*

covet ['kʌvit] *vt.* 垂涎(别人的东西); 渴望 — *vi.* 垂涎; 渴望(after, for)

covetous ['kʌvitəs] *adj.* 贪婪的; 妄想占有的(of) || ~ly *adv.* / ~ness *n.*

covey ['kʌvi] *n.* **1.** (鹧鸪等的)一窝; 一小群 **2.** (人的)一小群, 一伙; (物的)一套

cow[1] [kau] *n.* **1.** 母牛; 奶牛 **2.** (象、鹿、鲸、海象等的)母兽 **3.** 〈美〉家牛(兼指公牛、母牛) || ~bell *n.* **1.** 牛颈铃 **2.**【植】白玉草 / ~-bird *n.*【动】牛鹂(北美产的一种黑色小鸟) / ~-boy *n.* **1.** 牧童; 〈美国西部的〉牧牛工, 牛仔 **2.** 〈美俚〉西部风味的三明治 **3.** 莽撞的人; 横冲直撞的驾驶人 / ~catcher *n.* 〈美〉牛头等前面的排障器 / ~-fish *n.*【动】海牛; 角箱鲀 / ~-girl *n.* 放牛女工 / ~-

hand n. 牧牛工 / **~heel** n. 牛蹄冻 / **~herd** n. 放牛者 / **~hide** n. 1. 牛皮 2. 牛皮鞭 vt. 用牛皮鞭鞭打 / **~lick** n. (牛颈过似的)额前翘着的一绺头发 / **~man** n. 1. 放牛者 2. 牛场主 / **~pox** n. 牛痘 / **~puncher** n. 〖美口〗牧牛工, 牛仔 / **~shed** n. 牛棚 / **~slip** n.〖植〗黄花九轮草, 药用樱草

cow² [kau] vt. 吓唬; 威胁

coward ['kauəd] n. 懦夫, 胆怯者 — adj. 懦怯的, 胆小的

cowardice ['kauədis] n. 懦弱, 胆怯

cowardly ['kauədli] adj. & adv. 懦怯的(地), 胆小的(地) ‖ **cowardliness** n.

cower ['kauə] vi. (由于恐惧或寒冷)把身体缩成一团; 退缩

cowl [kaul] n. 1. (天主教隐修士穿的)蒙头斗篷(蒙头斗篷的)风帽 2. (女服的)胸前皱领 3. 风帽状物 4. (飞机的)整流罩 5.〖机〗罩, 外壳 6. 通风盖, 烟囱帽

coxcomb ['kɔkskəum] n. 1. 纨绔子弟, 花花公子 2. 〖古时丑角所戴〗鸡冠帽 3. 〖古〗头 4.〖植〗鸡冠花

coxswain ['kɔkswein, 'kɔksn] n. (赛艇)舵手; 艇长

coy [kɔi] adj. 1. (常指女子)怕羞的 2. 装作害羞的; 扭怩的 3. 不肯表态的 ‖ **~ly** adv. / **~ness** n.

coyote ['kɔiəut, 'kaiəut] n.〖复 coyote(s)〗 (产于北美部的)丛林狼, 郊狼

cozy ['kəuzi] adj. 1. 暖和舒服的; (感觉)舒适的 2. 亲如手足的; 密切的; 默契的 3. 谨慎小心的 — adv. 谨慎小心地 — n. (茶壶等的)保暖罩 ‖ **cozily** adv. / **coziness** n.

CP abbr. Communist Party 共产党

CPU, cpu abbr. central processing unit 〖计〗中央处理机

Cr〖化〗元素铬(chromium)的符号

crab¹ [kræb] n. 1. 蟹; 蟹肉 2. [the C-]〖天〗巨蟹座 3.〖机〗蟹爪式起重机; 绞车 4.[~s](掷骰子)失利的一掷 5. = crab louse 6. [空] 侧航; 航向偏流修正 7. 书店退给出版商的书 — (crabbed; crabbing) vi. 1. 捕蟹 2. 作蟹行; 横行 3. (飞行时)作航向偏流修正 — vt. 1. 使(飞机)作航向偏流修正 2. 〖鹰行〗扯; 拆 ‖ **~like** adj. & adv. 蟹似的(地) / **~louse**〖动〗毛虱, 阴虱 / **~pot** 蟹笼 / **~.sidle** vi. (蟹似地)横爬, 横行

crab² [kræb] n. 1. = crab apple 2. 脾气乖戾的人; 爱发牢骚的人 — (crabbed; crabbing) vt. 1. 使易发脾气; 使不高兴 2.〖口〗就……发牢骚, 抱怨 3. 脾气坏 — vi.〖口〗发牢骚; 找岔子, 挑剔 (at, about) ‖ **~apple**(英)欧洲苹果

crabbed ['kræbid] adj. 1. 脾气乖戾的; 易怒的 2.(字迹等)难认的;(文章等)难懂的, 晦涩的 ‖ **~ly** adv. / **~ness** n.

crabby ['kræbi] adj. 脾气坏的; 易怒的 ‖ **crabbiness** n.

crack [kræk] vi. 1. 发出爆裂声, 劈啪地响 2. 裂开, 爆裂; 断裂 3.(人或人的健康、精神等)衰退; 垮掉(up) 4.(嗓音)变哑; 变粗(尤指用青春期的变音) 5.〖俚〗说笑话; 嘲弄; 讥刺 6.〖化〗裂化 — vt. 1. 使发出爆裂声, 使劈啪地响 2. 使破裂, 使爆裂; 使折断(坚果壳等) 3.(砰地一声)打开(酒瓶等) 4.(砰地一声)打;(用拳、掌等)击 5. 解开(难题等); 揭开(秘密等); 宣布(价格等) 6. 使变质; 闯进(旅行);(入或出)闯 7. 撞毁; 毁损 8. 使(嗓音)变粗; 使(嗓音)变哑 9. 说(笑话) 10. 使发疯, 使神经错乱 11. 突然打断 12.〖化〗使裂化 13.(美俚)兑开(钞票) — n. 1. 破裂声,

爆裂声,劈啪声 2.〈口〉(砰的一)一击 3. 裂缝;龟裂;碎裂;缝隙 4. 弱点;缺点;瑕疵 5.(嗓子的)变音;粗哑 6.〈俚〉企图尝试 7.〈英方〉大话;谎言;谈话;闲谈; [~s]新闻 8.〈俚〉挖苦话;俏皮话 9.(一瞬,一刹那) 10.〈口〉…放在…(或东西) 11. 夜盗;夜盗行为 — adj. 第一流的,顶呱呱的 — adv. 啪地一声 ‖`~-brained` adj. 发疯的,古怪的;愚蠢的 /`~-down` n. 镇压 /`~-pot`〈口〉n. 怪人;疯子;狂想的人 adj. 古怪的;疯狂的;不切实际的 /`~sman` n. 夜盗;保险箱精窃贼 /`~-up` n. 1.(飞机、汽车等的)撞坏;撞毁 2.(健康、精神等的)衰退,衰弱;失去自制 3. 崩溃,垮台

cracked [krækt] adj. 1. 有裂缝的;弄破了、碎了的 2.(噪音)粗的;哑的 3. 发疯的,癫癫的 4.【化】裂化的

cracker ['krækə] n. 1. 击破者 2. 爆竹;(内装糖果等的)彩包爆竹 3. 薄脆饼干;〈美〉饼干(= biscuit) 4.[~s]胡桃钳,轧果壳钳(= nutcrackers) 5.〈贬〉赶马车的人(指美国南方的穷苦白人) 6. 破碎机 ‖`~-barrel` adj.〈美口〉(乡间杂货铺式)无所不谈的;粗犷风趣的;朴实的,单纯的

crackle ['krækl] vi. 1. 劈劈啪啪地响 2. 龟裂 — vt. 使发劈啪爆裂;啪地压碎 — n. 1. 劈啪声,爆裂声 2.(瓷器等上的)冰裂纹,碎裂花纹;[总称]碎纹釉陶瓷器皿

cradle ['kreidl] n. 1. 摇篮 2.〈喻〉策源地,发源地 3.〈诗〉安息地,安息所 4. 婴儿时期 5.(附在镰刀上的)配禾架(带有配禾架的镰刀) 6.(雕刻用)锯齿形凿刀 7.【船】托架,垫架,座 8.【医】支架;护床;【建】(空中作业用)吊篮;吊架 9.(修理汽车用的)骑板;【军】枪架,托架

8.【矿】淘金槽;移动式摇动洗矿槽 9.(搁电话听筒的)叉簧;听筒架 — vt. 1. 把…放在摇篮里;把(婴儿)放在摇篮里摇摇;像放在摇篮里似地轻哄着 2. 抚育 3. 用附有配禾架的镰刀刈割(作物) 4. 用架支住;支撑 5. 淘选(矿砂) 6. 把…搁在支架上 ‖`~ song` n. 摇篮曲,催眠曲

craft [krɑːft] n. 1. 工艺;手艺;(需要技艺的)行业,职业 2. 技巧;技艺 3.〈贬〉手腕,诡计 3. 行会;行会成员;同行 4.[单复同]船;航空器(指飞机、飞艇等) — vt. 精心制作 ‖`~ guild`(手工业)行会 /`~ union` 行业工会,同行工会

craftsman ['krɑːftsmən]([复] craftsmen) n. 手艺人,工匠;名匠 ‖`~ship` n.

crafty ['krɑːfti] adj. 狡猾的,诡计多端的 ‖`craftily` adv. / `craftiness` n.

crag [kræg] n. 1. 陡崖 2.【地】砂质泥灰岩

cragged ['krægid] adj. = craggy ‖`~ness` n.

craggy ['krægi] adj. 多岩的;崎岖的;崎岖的 ‖`craggily` adv. / `cragginess` n.

cram [kræm] (crammed; cramming) vt. 1. 把…塞进;把…塞满 2. 贪婪地吃 3.〈口〉填鸭式地教;死记硬背(up) — vi. 1. 贪婪地吃;吃得过多 2.〈口〉临时准备应考 — vt. 3. 为…补习功课;临时准备应考 ‖`~-'full` adj. 塞满的,充满的(of)

cramp[1] [kræmp] n. 1.(肌肉)痉挛;痛性痉挛 2.(过度使用引起的)肌肉一时局部麻痹 3.[常~s]〈腹〉绞痛 — vt. 使痉挛

cramp[2] [kræmp] n. 1. 夹;钳;扣钉 2. 约束物;约束 — vt. 1. 用夹子夹紧 2. 约转向使(车轮)向左(或右)转 3. 束缚;限制 ‖`~ iron` 铁夹钳

cramped [kræmpt] adj. 1. 狭窄的 2.(字

迹)写得又挤又潦草的;难认的

cranberry ['krænbəri] *n.*【植】酸果蔓(的果实)

crane [krein] *n.* 1.【动】鹤;鹭;鹳 2. 起重机;(供摄像机用的)机动升降支架;(机车加水用的)水鹤 — *vt.* 1. 伸(颈) 2. 用起重机起吊(或搬运) — *vi.* 1. (鹤似地)伸着脖子 2. (起跳之前)退缩;(行动前)踌躇(*at*) ‖ ~ **fly**【动】大蚊

crania ['kreiniə] cranium 的复数

cranial ['kreiniəl] *adj.*【解】颅的;颅侧的

cranio- *comb. form* 表示"颅"

cranium ['kreiniəm] ([复]craniums 或 crania ['kreiniə]) *n.*【解】颅,头颅

crank [kræŋk] *n.* 1.【机】曲柄,曲轴 2.〈古〉奇谈,奇怪的说法(或想法、行为);幻想,一时的怪念头 4.〈口〉怪人;脾气坏的人;狂热者 — *vt.* 把...弯成曲柄状;给...装上曲柄;用曲柄连结;用曲柄开动(汽车等) — *vi.* 1. 转动曲柄 2. 曲折行进 — *adj.* 1.(机器等)不正常的,有毛病;摇晃的,不稳的;(船)易颠翻的,易翻的 ‖ ~ **case** *n.* 曲轴箱 / ~ **shaft** *n.* 曲轴

cranky ['kræŋki] *adj.* 1.(机器等)不正常的,有毛病的;不稳的;(船)易翻的,易倾斜的 2.〈口,方,河等〉弯弯曲曲的 3. 古怪的;胡思乱想的;脾气急躁的 ‖ **crankily** *adv.* / **crankiness** *n.*

cranny ['kræni] *n.* 1. 裂缝,裂口 2. 冷僻的角落 ‖ **crannied** *adj.* 有裂缝的;裂缝多的

crap [kræp] *n.* 1.〈俗〉屎;拉屎 2.〈俚〉胡扯,废话;大话;假话;谎骂 3. 废物,破烂东西

crape [kreip] *n.* 1. 绉丝;绉线;绉纱;绉布;绉绸;绉呢 2.(哀悼时袖上戴的)黑纱;(帽上的)黑丧章 — *vt.* 用绉纱(或

给纱似的东西)覆盖

crappie ['kræpi] *n.*【鱼】莓鲈(北美产的一种淡水鱼)

craps [kræps] [复] *n.* [用作单]克拉普斯,双骰子赌博戏

crash¹ [kræʃ] *vi.* 1.(发出猛烈声音地)碰撞;倒下;坠落;(飞机等)坠毁;撞车 2. 发出撞击声;发出爆裂声 3.(发出很响声音地)冲,闯(*into, through, down, out*) 4. 失败;垮台,崩溃 5.〈俚〉(免费)宿客 6.〈俚〉(吸毒后)感受到副作用 — *vt.* 1.(发出猛烈声音地)撞击;碰碎;使(飞机等)坠毁;使(飞机等)撞坏 2. 使...撞击声地)冲,闯 ~ one's way through brush 闯过灌木丛 4.〈口〉无票进入(会场、剧场等);入席 5.〈美〉(突然或莫动一时地)取得在(电视、报刊大字标题等)中出现的地位 — *n.* 1.(发出猛烈声音的)碰撞声下坠;(飞机等坠毁;撞坏 2. 撞击声;爆裂声 3. 失败;垮台,崩溃 — *adj.* 应急的;速成的 — *adv.* 以哗啦一声 ‖ ~ing *adj.* 彻头彻尾的;很棒的 ‖ ~ barrier(公路等上的)防撞护栏 / ~ boat(援救海上失事飞机等的)救生艇 / ~ dive *vi.*(潜水艇)紧急下潜 / ~ halt *n.*(汽车的)突然停住,急煞车 / ~ helmet(飞行员、摩托车运动员等)防撞头盔 / ~land *vi. & vt.* 使)摔机着陆 / ~ pad(装在坦克等里边保护作用的)防震垫 2.〈美俚〉临时睡觉(或居住)处 / ~ truck(飞机失事等时用的)急救车 / ~worthy *adj.*(汽车等)耐撞的

crash² [kræʃ] *n.*【纺】1. 粗布 2. 原色,本色

crasher ['kræʃə] *n.* 1. 猛力撞击的东西;猛击 2.〈俚〉无票入场者;不速之客

crass [kræs] *adj.* 1. 粗劣的;冷酷的;愚

钝的 2. 粗厚的;粗糙的 3. 完全的,非常的:～ ignorance 极度无知 ‖ ～ly *adv*. /～ness *n*.

crate [kreit] *n*. 1. 板条箱;柳条箱(或篮、篓等) 2.〈美俚〉破旧汽车;破旧飞机 — *vt*. 用板条箱(或柳条箱等)装

crater ['kreitə] *n*. 1. 火山口 2. 坑;弹坑;陨石坑 3.[the C-]【天】巨爵座 4.(月球表面的)环形山

cravat [krə'væt] *n*.(旧式)领结;领巾;领带;围巾

crave [kreiv] *vt*. 1. 恳求,请求 2. 渴望,热望 3. 迫切需要 — *vi*. 渴望,热望(*for*)

craven ['kreivən] *n*. 懦夫,胆小鬼 — *adj*. 胆小的,怯懦的 ‖ ～ly *adv*.

craving ['kreiviŋ] *n*. 渴望,热望(*for*)

craw [krɔː] *n*.【动】(鸟或昆虫的)嗉囊;(低等动物的)胃

crawfish ['krɔːfiʃ] *n*. 淡水螯虾;龙虾 — *vi*.〈美口〉退却;退出

crawl [krɔːl] *vi*. 1. 爬,爬行;蠕动;匍匐前进 2. 徐徐行进;(时间)慢慢地过去(*by*) 3.(场所)爬满,充斥着(*with*) 4.(由于恐惧、厌恶等)起鸡皮疙瘩,汗毛直竖 5.(通过谄媚)向上爬;巴结 6. 用爬式(或自由式)游泳 — *n*. 1. 爬,爬行;蠕动;匍匐前进 2. 缓慢的行进 3. 爬泳,自由泳 ‖ ～ space(屋顶、地板等下面可供工人进入维修电线、水管等的)爬行空隙

crawler ['krɔːlə] *n*. 1. 爬行者;蠕动的东西 2. 爬行动物;爬行的昆虫 3.〈澳〉马屁精,奴颜婢膝的人 4.[～s](幼儿穿的)爬行服;连衫罩裤 5.〈英〉往来兜生意的出租汽车 ‖ ～ crane 履带式起重机 /～ tractor 履带式拖拉机

crawly ['krɔːli] *adj*.〈口〉感到毛骨悚然的;令人毛骨悚然的

crayfish ['kreifiʃ] *n*. 淡水螯虾;龙虾 — *vi*.〈澳〉像淡水螯虾般行动;表现得懦怯(或狡猾) ‖ ～ing *n*. 1. 捕淡水螯虾(或龙虾)业(或消遣) 2.〈澳〉行为懦怯(或狡猾);躲躲闪闪

crayon ['kreiən] *n*. 1. 粉笔;蜡笔;颜色笔 2. 粉笔画;蜡笔画 3.(电弧灯的)碳棒 — *vt*. 用粉笔(或蜡笔等)画

craze [kreiz] *vt*. 1.[常用被动语态]使发狂 2. 使(陶器等)产生细微裂纹 — *vi*. 1. 发狂 2.(陶器等)出现细微裂纹 — *n*. 1. 狂热;疯狂;躁狂 2. 风气;风行一时的东西 3.(陶器等的)细微裂纹

crazy ['kreizi] *adj*. 1. 疯狂的;古怪的;蠢的 2.〈口〉狂热的;热中的,着迷的(*on, about, for*) 3.(船、建筑等)破烂的;摇摇晃晃的;歪斜的;(道路等)弯弯曲曲的 4. 用不规则碎块拼成的 — *n*. 疯子;怪人;狂人 ‖ crazily *adv*. /craziness *n*. ‖ ～ bone〈美〉【解】肱骨内髁部

creak [kriːk] *vi*. 吱吱嘎嘎地作响 — *n*. 吱吱嘎嘎的声音 ‖ ～y *adj*.

cream [kriːm] *n*. 1. 奶油 2. 奶油食品:ice ～冰淇淋 3. 乳霜;(药用)乳膏;奶油状物:furniture ～ 家具蜡 4. 乳状悬浮液 5. 精华;最精彩部分 6. 奶油色,米色 — *vt*. 1. 使(牛奶)结成奶油;从(牛奶中)提取奶油 2. 从...提取精华 3. 加奶油于;加奶油煮 4. 把...打成奶油状;使成奶油状 5. 用乳霜(或乳膏)搽(脸) — *vi*. 结成奶油;结成奶油状物 ‖ ～er *n*. 1. 奶油分离器;撇奶油薄盆子 2. 盛奶油的器皿 3. 做奶油的人 ‖ '～-ˌcolo(u)red *adj*. 奶油色的,米色的 /～ laid〈主英〉白条纸 /～ puff 1. 奶油泡夫 2.〈美俚〉软弱的人;女人气的男人 3.〈美俚〉保养良好的旧汽车 /'～-ware *n*.[总称]米色陶器 /～ wove〈主英〉白布纹纸

creamery ['kri:məri] *n*. **1.** 乳品厂 **2.** 乳制品商店

creamy ['kri:mi] *adj*. **1.** 含(有大量)奶油的；**2.** 奶油般的 **3.** 奶油色的，米色的 ‖ **creaminess** *n*.

crease [kri:s] *n*. **1.** (衣服、纸等的)折缝，折痕；皱纹 **2.** (板球等投球手或击球手的)区域线；限制区域；(板球)球场 — *vt*. **1.** 使起折痕；弄皱 **2.** (美)(枪弹)擦伤 — *vi*. 起折皱，起折痕

create [kri:'eit] *vt*. **1.** 创造；创作 **2.** 引起；产生；造成 **3.** 封授 — *vi*. (英)大发脾气(口)

creation [kri:'eiʃən] *n*. **1.** 创造；创作；(骚动等的)产生；(爵位、职位等的)授予 **2.** 创造物；创作；艺术作品；服装等）**3.** 天地万物；宇宙 **4.** [the C-] (基督教《圣经》)创造天地 ‖ **~al** *adj*.

creative [kri:'eitiv] *adj*. **1.** 有创造力的；创造性的；创作的 **2.** (玩具等)启发想象力的 — *n*. 有创造力的人 ‖ **~ly** *adv*. / **~ness** *n*.

creativity [,kri:ei'tiviti] *n*. 创造性；创造力

creator [kri:'eitə] *n*. **1.** 创造者；创作者 **2.** [the C-][宗]造物主，上帝

creature ['kri:tʃə] *n*. **1.** 创造物 **2.** 生物；动物；(美)家畜；牛马 **3.** 人 **4.** (受人利用的)工具；奴才；(习惯等的)奴隶 ‖ **~ comfort** (衣、食、住等)给肉体以舒适的东西，物质享受

credence ['kri:dəns] *n*. **1.** 相信；可靠，确实 **2.** 凭证；证书

credential [kri'denʃəl] *n*. **1.** 凭证 **2.** [~s]信任状；证书；(大使等的)国书

credible ['kredəbl] *adj*. 可信的，可靠的 ‖ **credi'bility** *n*. / **credibly** *adv*. ‖ **credibility gap** 信用差距；(尤指官方言行等的)不一致，不符合

credit ['kredit] *n*. **1.** 信任，相信 **2.** 信誉；声望；荣誉 **3.** 称赞 **4.** [a~](为…)增光的(人或事物)(to) **5.** 信用；信用贷款 **6.** (个人银行存款)账面应存余额；贷方余额 **7.** [会计]贷；贷方；贷方金额(debit 之对) **8.** (美国等学校中的)学分 — *vt*. **1.** 相信 **2.** 把…记入贷方 **3.** 把…归于(to)；认为…有(某种优点或成就等)(with) ‖ ~ **account** (客户购货的)赊销账户；(赊借)贷款户；~ **card** 信用卡 — **line** **1.** (电讯、文章、电影等注明记者或作者、制片人等姓名的)荣誉行 **2.** (对某客户的信用或赊购)最高限额 — **man** (客户)信用调查员 /~ **rating** 信用评价，信用等级 /~ **squeeze** 信用紧缩，信用收缩 /~ **titles** (电影或电视片的)摄制人员名单 /~ **union** 信用合作社，互助储金会 /~**~worthy** *adj*. 信誉卓著的，有资格接受信用贷款的

creditable ['kreditəbl] *adj*. **1.** 可信的 **2.** 值得赞扬的，为…带来荣誉的(to) **3.** 值得给于信用贷款的 **4.** 可归于(功)的…的(to) ‖ **~ness** *n*. / **creditably** *adv*.

creditor ['kreditə] *n*. 债权人

credulity [kri'dju:liti] *n*. 轻信；易受骗

credulous ['kredjuləs] *adj*. 轻信的，易受骗的 ‖ **~ly** *adv*. / **~ness** *n*.

creed [kri:d] *n*. **1.** 宗教信条，教义 **2.** [the C-][宗]信经 **3.** 信念；纲领

creek [kri:k] *n*. **1.** (英)小湾；小港 **2.** 小河；支流 ‖ **~y** *adj*.

creel [kri:l] *n*. **1.** 鱼篓；鱼笼 **2.** [纺]纱架；筒子架

creep [kri:p] (crept [krept]) *vi*. **1.** (身体凑近或贴着地面)爬行，匍匐而行；(植物)蔓生 **2.** 潜行，蹑手蹑脚地走动；微微地移动；(时间)悄悄地过去(by) **3.** (由于恐惧、厌恶等)起鸡皮疙瘩，汗毛

直竖 4. 巴结,奉承 5.【海】用探海钩打捞 6.(材料)蠕变 — **v.** 1. 爬;蠕动 ⟨口⟩[~s]毛骨悚然的感觉;战栗 3. 仔畜补栏栏(仅幼仔能出入) 4.(美俚)使人害怕(或厌恶)的人;无足轻重的人 5.(材料的)蠕变；(地)蠕动,徐动 ‖~-hole **n.** 1.(动物的)藏身洞穴;通道;借口

creeper ['kriːpə] **n.** 1. 爬行者；爬行动物；爬虫 2.【植】匍匐植物 3.[常~s](绑在鞋下防滑用的)钉齿板 4.[常~s](小孩穿的)爬行服,连衫罩裤 5. 探海钩(打捞用的四爪锚) 6. 定速运送器

creepy ['kriːpi] **adj.** 1. 爬行的；蠕动的 2. 感到毛骨悚然的 3. 令人毛骨悚然的 ‖~-crawly **adj.** ⟨令人⟩感到毛骨悚然的

cremate [kri'meit] **vt.** 焚烧；火化(尸体等) ‖ cremator **n.** 1. 焚尸人 2. 焚尸炉；垃圾焚化炉

cremation [kri'meiʃən] **n.** 火葬,火化

crematory ['kremətəri] **n.** 焚化炉；火葬场 — **adj.** 火葬的

Creole ['kriːəul] **n.** 1. 克里奥耳人(常指出生于美洲的欧洲人及其后裔) 2. 克里奥耳语

crêpe [kreip] **n.** 1.[纺]绉丝绸；绉线；绉布；绉绸；绉呢 2.[化]绉(橡)胶 3. 绉纸 4.(表服用的)黑纱 5. 薄烤饼

crept [krept] creep 的过去式和过去分词

crescendo [kri'fendəu] **a.**[复] crescendo(e)s **n.** 1.[音]渐强 2. 逐渐增强；高潮；顶点 — **adj. & adv.**[音]渐强的(地)

crescent ['kresnt] **n.** 1. 月牙；蛾眉月；新月 2. 新月状(物) 3. 伊斯兰教；the Cross and the *Crescent* 基督教与伊斯兰教 — **adj.** 1. 新月状的 2.(诗)(新月般)渐渐增大的

cress [kres] **n.**[植]水田芥；独行菜

crest [krest] **n.** 1.(鸟、兽的)冠；鸡冠；冠毛 2.(头盔上的)羽饰；头盔 3. 顶饰；顶端；浪峰 5.(马、狮等的)颈脊／(马等的)鬃毛 6.【解】嵴 — **vt.** 1. 在...上加顶饰；成为...的顶饰 2. 达到...达到...的顶点 — **vi.** 达到顶点；成浪峰 ‖ ~ed **adj.** 有顶饰的；有冠毛的 ‖ ~-fallen **adj.** 羽冠垂倒的；垂头丧气的

cretonne ['kreton] **n.**(做窗帘、沙发套等用的)大花哥瑰丽印花装饰布

crevasse [kri'væs] **n.**(冰河等的)裂缝,冰隙

crevice ['krevis] **n.** 裂隙,裂缝

crew[1] [kruː] **n.** 1. 全体船员；全体机务人员；(赛艇的)全体队员 2. 水手们 3. 同事们,一起工作的人们；the ground ~地勤人员 4.⟨贬⟩一帮人,一伙人 ‖ ~ cut 平头(指发式)／'~ man **n.** 船员；机务人员

crew[2] [kruː] crow[2] 的过去式

crib [krib] **n.** 1. 有围栏的童床 2. 牛栏；栏槽 3. 简陋小屋；小房间 4.【矿】(铁或木制的)井壁基环；【建】叠木框 5.⟨美⟩(谷物等的)围栏 6.⟨口⟩(文章等的)剽窃 7.⟨口⟩学生作弊用的外文对照本(或注释本等) — (cribbed; cribbing) **vt.** 1. 把...关进栅栏(或小屋等狭小的地方) 2. 限制；关闭 3.⟨口⟩剽窃,抄袭；偷窃 — **vi.**⟨口⟩剽窃；(学生)抄夹带,作弊 ‖ ~ death⟨美⟩婴儿猝死

cribbage ['kribidʒ] **n.** 克里巴奇牌戏

crick [krik] **n.**【医】(颈或背的)痛性痉挛,痛痉

cricket[1] ['krikit] **n.** 蟋蟀

cricket[2] ['krikit] **n.** 1.[体]板球 2.⟨口⟩公平行为；光明正大行为 — **vi.** 打板

球

crier ['kraiə] n. 1. 叫喊者；好哭的人(尤指婴儿) 2. 叫卖者 3. (法庭上的)传呼员，庭吏 4. (旧时受雇在街头宣读公告的)公告传报员(= town ~)

crime [kraim] n. 1. 罪，罪行；犯罪；罪恶 2. 〈口〉憾事；羞耻事

Crimea [krai'miə] n. 克里米亚(半岛)[乌克兰一地区](临黑海和亚速海) ‖ ~n adj.

criminal ['kriminəl] adj. 1. 犯罪的；刑事上的；犯了罪的：~ law 刑法 2. 可耻的，应受谴责的 — n. 罪犯，犯人 ‖ ~ly adv.

criminology [,krimi'nɔlədʒi] n. 犯罪学

crimp [krimp] vt. 使起皱；使拳曲；使成波形 — n. 呈现皱纹(或波浪形) — n. 1. 打褶；起皱；拳曲 2. 波形层；褶曲(物) 3.[常~s]曲曲的头发

crimpy ['krimpi] adj. 拳曲的，皱缩的

crimson ['krimzn] n. 深红，绯红 — adj. 1. 深红色的，绯红色的 2. 血腥的；血污的 — vt. & vi. (使)变成绯红色

cringe [krindʒ] vi. & n. 1. 畏缩 2. 卑躬屈膝，阿谀奉承

crinkle ['kriŋkl] vt. & vi. (使)皱，(使)呈波状，(使)卷曲 — n. 1. 皱，波状，卷曲 2.[植]皱叶病 ‖ **crinkly** adv.

cripple ['kripl] n. 1. 跛子；肢足动物；有缺陷的人；伤残的人(或动物) 2. 残缺(或不完美)的事物 — vt. 1. 使跛；使伤残 2. 使丧失活动能力；削弱(经济等)

crisis ['kraisis] n.([复]crises['kraisiːz]) n. 1. 危机 2. 危急关头；决定性时刻；转折点 3.[医]病情急转(点)；危象

crisp [krisp] adj. 1. 脆的，松脆的 2.(空气)清新的 3.(天气)爽快的 4. 鲜嫩的 4. 干脆的，干净利落的；活泼的，有

生气的 5.(头发等)卷缩的，卷曲的 6.(制服、纸张等)挺括的 — n. 1.[英](常~s)油炸土豆片 2. 松脆物 3.〈俚〉钞票 — vt. & vi. 1.(使)卷曲，(使)起波纹 2.(使)发脆 ‖ ~ly adv. / ~ness n.

crisscross ['kriskrɔs] n. 1. 十字押；十字形；十字形图案 2. 杂乱无章，混乱状态 — adj. 十字形的，交叉的 — n. 1. 十字状地；交叉地 2.(向)相反方向地；别扭地 — vt. 1. 画十字押子 2. 在...上交叉往来 — vi. 交叉往来

criterion [krai'tiəriən] n.([复] criteria [krai'tiəriə]或 criterions) n.(批评、判断的)标准，准则，尺度

critic ['kritik] n. 1. 批评家，评论家；爱挑剔的人，爱非议的人

critical ['kritikəl] adj. 1. 批评(性)的；批判(性)的；评论(性)的 2. 对...表示谴责的对...感到不满的(of)；苛求的 3. 紧要的，关键性的；危急的 4.(物资等)应急所必需的 5.[物][核]临界的 ‖ ~ly adv.

criticise ['kritisaiz] vt. & vi. = criticize

criticism ['kritisizəm] n. 1. 批评 2. 批判 3. 评论；评论文章 4. 非难 5. 考证

criticize ['kritisaiz] vt. & vi. 批评；批判；评论；非难

critique [kri'tiːk] n.(文艺等)的批评；批判；评论；评论文章

CRM abbr. 1. counter-radar measures 反雷达措施 2. counter-radar missile 反雷达导弹 3. cruise missile 巡航导弹

croak [krəuk] n.(蛙、鸦等的)呱呱叫声 — vi. 1. 呱呱地叫 2. 鸣冤；发牢骚 用嘶哑的声音说话 3. 预示不祥 4.〈俚〉死 — vt. 1. 用嘶哑的声音说 2.〈俚〉杀害

croaker ['krəukə] n. 1. 呱呱叫的动物 2.

【动】石首鱼(能发蛙鸣声,如大、小黄鱼等) 3. 预报凶事者;鸣冤者:发牢骚者 4.〈英俚〉临死的人;悲观者 5.〈美俚〉医生

Croatia [krəu'eiʃjə] *n.* 克罗地亚〔欧洲东南部国家〕

crochet ['krəuʃei] *n.* 钩针编织(品);a ~ hook 钩针 — *vt. & vi.* 用钩针编织

crock [krɔk] *n.* 1. 瓦罐;瓦壶;坛子 2.〈英方〉金属罐;壶 3. 碎瓦片 4. 胡说八道:荒谬行为

crockery ['krɔkəri] *n.*〔总称〕陶器,瓦器

crocodile ['krɔkədail] *n.* 1. 鳄鱼;鳄鱼皮革 2.〈古〉假慈悲的人 3.〈英口〉(两人一排)成纵列慢步行进的人(尤指学生) ‖ ~ tears 鳄鱼的眼泪;假哭;假慈悲

crocus ['krəukəs] *n.* 1.【植】番红花,藏红花 2. 桔黄色 3. 擦粉(一种红色氧化铁粉,供打磨或抛光用)

crone [krəun] *n.* 1. 干瘪的丑老太婆 2. 老母羊

crony ['krəuni] *n.*〈俚〉密友,老用友

crook [kruk] *n.* 1. (牧羊人或主教用的)曲柄杖 2. 弯曲物;钩子;S型挂锅钩:钩形物 3.(道路、河流等的)弯曲,弯曲部分 4.〈俚〉无赖;骗子;窃贼 — *vt.* 使(手指、手臂、头颈等)弯曲 成钩形,弯(俚)歌躺;偷窃 — *vi.* 弯曲,成钩形 ‖ ~ back *n.* 驼背 / ~ backed *adj.* 驼背的

crooked ['krukid] *adj.* 1. 弯的;歪的;扭曲的 2. 畸形的;(因年老而)弯腰曲背的 3. 不正当的;欺诈的;不正派的 4. [krukt](手杖)带柄的 ‖ ~ly *adv.* / ~ness *n.* ‖ ~ stick *n.* 弯榴不直的人 2.〈口〉不诚实的人;无用的人;懒散的人

croon [kru:n] *vi.* 1. 低声哼唱,轻哼;低声柔情地唱流行歌曲 3. 悲叹;劝

哭;呻吟 — *vt.* 1. 低声柔情地唱唱 2. 对...低声哼唱 — *n.* 低哼(声);哼唱(声),轻哼(声);低声柔情地唱的歌(声) ‖ ~ er *n.*〈美〉低吟歌手

crop [krɔp] *n.* 1.(谷类、水果等的)一熟,一季收获(量),收成,庄稼 2.(同时产生的)一批,一群,一系列 4.(指发式)平头;剪平头头 5.(鸟类的)嗉囊 6. 鞭柄;乘马短鞭 7. 整张鞣革 8. 耳标(尤指剪掉牲畜耳尖作为记号) 9.(钢锭等的)切头头(食用)牛脊肉 11.【建】叶尖端;【地】露头 — (cropped; cropping) *vt.* 1. 上播种(或耕种);在...经营;种植 2. 收割;收获 3. 剪去;修剪(树木);剪短(头发、尾巴、牲畜的耳尖);切掉(书边) 4.(牛羊等)啃(草等) — *vi.* 1. 收成,收获 2. 啃草 3.(问题等)突然发生;出现(*up*) ‖

cropper *n.* 1. 庄稼人 2. 割草机;收割机 3.[鸟]鸣鸽 ‖ '~-,eared *adj.* 1.(牲畜等)被剪去耳尖的;剪短头发裂露出耳朵的

croquet ['krəukei] *n.* 槌球游戏

croquette [krɔ'ket] *n.* 炸丸子

crosier ['krəuʒə] *n.* 1.【宗】(主教)权杖 2.【植】嫩叶卷头

cross [krɔs] *n.* 1. 十字形;十字形记号;十字形物如十字架、十字勋章、十字形装饰物、立有十字架的石碑等) 2. [the C-]【基督教】(耶稣被钉死在上面的)十字架;[基督教教义 3.]磨难,苦难;烦恼 4.(动、植物的)杂交;杂种,混血儿;混合物 5.〈俚〉欺诈性比赛;骗局 6. 横穿(如从舞台一边穿到另一边)7.(字母等上的)一横 7.[电]短路;交叉 8. [the C-]【天】(南、北)十字座 — *vt.* 1. 越过;穿过;渡过 2. 把...运过;带过 3. 使交叉;使相交;与...相交 4. 遇到;(信件在邮寄过程

中)错过(另一信件) 5. 画横线于;在...上打叉;划掉;勾销(*off, out*) 6. 跨过(道路、江河等) 7.【基督教】用手画十字于 8. 反对;阻挠;使受挫折 9. 使杂交(*with*) — *vi.* 1. 横车;横过;横渡;转到另一方;投诚(*over*) 2. 交叉;相交;(信件在邮寄过程中)互相错过 3. 杂交 — *adj.* 1. 交叉的;横穿的 2. 相反的;互相矛盾的 3. 脾气坏的;易怒的;发怒的 4. 相互的 5. 杂交的;杂种的;涉及许多种类的 ‖ ~ly *adv.* 易怒地;发怒地 /~ness *n.* 易怒;发怒 /~ways *adv.* 十字交叉地;横斜地 /~wise *adv.* 交叉地 1. 横斜地 3. 与目的相反地;不对头地 *adj.* 横的;交叉的 ‖ /~bar *n.* 1. 门闩,横杠 2.(球门)横木 3.(织物的)横色条 /~beam *n.* 横梁,顶梁 /~bearings[海]交叉方位法 /~belt *n.* 斜挂皮带 /~bench *n.* (英)中立议员席 *adj.* 中立的;不偏不倚的 /~bones[复] *n.* 交叉的股骨图形(画在骷髅下,表示死亡、剧毒等,过去的海盗旗上常画有此图) /~bow *n.* 弩,石弓(一种古代武器) /~bred *adj.* 杂种的;杂交的 *n.* 杂种 /~breed *vt.* & *vi.* (使)杂交繁育 *n.* 杂种 /~buttock *n.* (摔跤中的)夹颈背,勾臀背 /~-'check *vt.* & *vi.* (从多方面)反复核对;检查 /~'country *adj.* 1. 横穿全国的 2. 越野的 *adv.* 越野地 /~-dress *vi.* 穿异性服装 /~-examine['krɔsig'zæmin] *vt.* & *vi.* 盘问 /~-eye *n.*[医]内斜视;内斜视眼,斗鸡眼 /~-fire 1.[军]交叉火力 2.[讯]串扰;串扰电流 3.(言词、意见等的)激烈交锋 /~-'grained *adj.* 1.(木材)逆纹的,斜纹的 2. 脾气坏的;固执的;难相处的 /~ hairs[复](望远镜、瞄准器等上的)十字丝,叉丝 /~'head *n.* 1.[机]十字头 2.(插在文章中的)小标题

'index *vt.* 给(词典、条目等)设互见索引;设互见索引 /~-legged *adj.* 盘着腿的;蹺着二郎腿的 /~-link *n.*[化]交联键 /~over *n.* 1. 交叉;穿过 2. 转到另一方;投诚 3.【物】跨接 4.【交】渡口;人行横道 /~patch *n.* (口)脾气坏的人;爱抱怨的人 /~piece *n.* 横挡;[船]绞盘横杆 /~'purposes[复] 1. 相反的目的,自相矛盾的目的;相反的计划 2.(用意义不同的词进行的)问答游戏 /~'question *n.* 盘问时提出的问题 /~-re'action *n.*[医](免疫)交叉反应 /~-'reference *vt.* (同一书或文件中)使相互参照 *n.* 相互参照;相互参照条目,互见条目 /~road *n.* 1. 横路;交叉路 2. [~roads]十字路;十字路口;活动中心;汇集地 3. [~roads]需作抉择的重要关头 /~ section 1. 横断面;截面;断面图 2.(核反应的)有效截面 3.(有代表性的)剖面;典型 /~-stitch *n.* 十字缝;十字形刺绣针迹 /~talk 1.[讯]串话干扰;(彩色电视机中的)色度亮度干扰 2.(口)拌嘴 3. 交谈 4. 相声 /~-walk *n.* 人行横道 /~wires = ~ hairs /~word puzzle 纵横填字谜

crossing ['krɔsiŋ] *n.* 1. 横渡;横穿;横越 2. 交叉;交叉点;十字路口 3. 渡口;(穿过街道或河流的)横道 4. 杂交 5. 反对;阻挠(尤指用不正当手段)

crotch [krɔtʃ] *n.* 1. 叉架;叉柱;树丫叉 2.(人体)两腿分叉处

crotchet ['krɔtʃit] *n.* 1. 小钩;钩状物;钩状部分 2.[医]产钩,取胎钩 3. 奇想,怪念头 4. 诡计;诀窍

crotchety ['krɔtʃiti] *adj.* 充满怪念头的;想入非非的;有怪癖的;脾气坏的 ‖ **crotchetiness** *n.*

crouch [krautʃ] *vi.* 蹲伏；蜷缩；低头弯腰 (*to*) 一 *vt.* 屈(膝)；低(头) 一 *n.* 蹲伏(姿势)

croup [kruːp] *n.* 【医】哮吼(音译格鲁布，一种喉头炎)

crouton ['kruːtɒn] *n.* 油炸面包丁(常用作汤菜的饰料)

crow¹ [krəu] *n.* 1. 鸦，乌鸦 2. 铁撬；撬棍；起货钩 (= ~ -bar) 3. [the C-]【天】乌鸦座 ‖ ~ -foot *n.* 铁撬，撬棍；起货钩 /' -foot *n.* 1. ([复] crowfoots)【植】毛茛；老鹳草 2. ([复] crowfeet) = ~ 's -foot /' - 's -foot [复] crow's-feet) *n.* 1. (常 crow's-feet)眼角皱纹 2. (军用)铁蒺藜 3. [海](船缆等的)鸦足绳 /~ 's nest 1. 桅杆瞭望台；守望楼 2. 交通岗亭

crow² [krəu] (过去式 crowed 或 crew [kruː], 过去分词 crowed) *vi.* 1. (雄鸡)啼 2. (因胜利等)欢呼；(小孩)欢叫 3. 得意洋洋；幸灾乐祸(*over*) 4. 自鸣得意；夸(*about*, *over*) 一 *n.* 1. 鸡啼 2. (因胜利等发出的)欢呼声；(小孩的)欢叫声

crowd [kraud] *n.* 1. 群，人群 2. 大众，老百姓 3. (有共同兴趣或习惯等的)一伙人，一帮人 4. 一堆，许多(东西)(*of*) 一 *vt.* 1. 挤；挤满；使挤满 2. 把…塞满；装满(*with*) 3. 催促；催逼 4. 逼近 一 *vi.* 1. 挤，拥挤 2. 聚集，群集 3. 急速前进；涌，推搡

crowded ['kraudid] *adj.* 1. 拥挤的；满座的；塞满的 2. (人、树等)繁茂的，密集的 3. 多事的；经历丰富的

crown [kraun] *n.* 1. (象征荣誉、胜利的)花冠；冠冕 2. 王冠，冕；[喻]王权；[the C-]君王；王权；王国政府 3. 王冠状的东西；花冠状的东西 4. (英国)旧制五令令硬币；(欧洲某些国家的货币)克朗 5. 头顶；头 6. 顶部；拱顶；树

顶；帽顶；顶峰 7. 齿冠(牙齿露出部分)；假齿冠 8. 锚冠 9. 【植】树冠；根颈；副花冠 10. 【植】冠毛；鸡冠 11.(手柄转柄的)柄头 12. 王冠裁(一种纸张的规格，尺寸为 15×20 英寸或 15×19 英寸) 一 *vt.* 1. 为…加冕，立…为王 2. (以荣誉等)酬报(*with*) 3. 为…加顶；使圆满完成 4. 打…的头部 5. 注满(酒杯等)使表面呈冠状 6. 为(牙齿)镶假齿冠 ‖ ~ - court *n.* (英)刑事法庭

crucial ['kruːʃəl] *adj.* 决定性的；紧要关头的 ‖ ~ly *adv.*

crucible ['kruːsibl] *n.* 1. 坩埚 2. (喻)熔炉；严峻的考验

crucifer ['kruːsifə] *n.* 1.【宗】(仪仗队中)擎十字架者 2. 十字花科植物

crucifix ['kruːsifiks] *n.* 1.【宗】耶稣钉死在十字架上的苦像 2. 十字架

crucifixion [ˌkruːsi'fikʃən] *n.* 1. 钉死于十字架；[the C-]耶稣之钉死于十字架(可指其事或画、雕像等) 2. 酷刑；折磨；苦难

crucify ['kruːsifai] *vt.* 1. 把…钉死在十字架上 2. 抑制(情欲等) 3. 折磨；虐待；迫害

crude [kruːd] *adj.* 1. 天然的，未加工的；粗制的 2.(食物等)未煮熟的，生的 3. 粗鲁的；粗野的 4. 粗糙的；原始的；拙劣的；未修饰的；赤裸裸的 5.【语】构成词的不变成分的 一 *n.* 原油 ‖ ~ly *adv.* /~ ness, crudity *n.* ‖ ~ oil 原油，石油

cruel ['kruəl] *adj.* 1. 残忍的，残酷 2. 令人痛苦的 ‖ ~ly *adv.*

cruelty ['kruəlti] *n.* 1. 残忍，残酷 2. 残酷行为；刻毒伤人的言语

cruet ['kruːit] *n.* 1. (餐桌上的)调味品瓶 2.【宗】(圣餐时盛酒或水的)盛器 ‖ ~

stand 调味品瓶架

cruise [kruːz] *vi.* 1. 巡航 2. 巡游 3. 〈口〉在街上徘徊 4. (出租汽车)兜客 5. (飞机)用巡航速度飞行;以巡行速度行驶 — *vt.* 1. 巡航于;巡行于 2. (美)勘查(林区)的木材产量 — *n.* 巡航;巡游 ∥ ~ **missile** 巡航导弹

cruiser ['kruːzə] *n.* 1. 巡洋舰 2. 游艇 3. 警察巡逻车;援客汽车 4. 巡航机;巡航艇 ∥ '~**weight** *n.*〈主英〉次重量级(拳击手)

crumb [krʌm] *n.* 1. 面包屑;糕饼屑;碎屑 2. 少许;点滴 3. 面包心(crust 之对) 4.〈俚〉可鄙的人 — *vt.* 1. 捏碎;弄碎 2. 把...裹上面包屑(油煎) 3.〈美口〉抹去...上的碎屑

crumble ['krʌmbl] *vt.* 弄碎;把...弄成细屑 — *vi.* 1. 破碎 2. 碎裂;崩溃;瓦解;灭亡;(希望等)消失 — *n.* 1.〈方〉碎屑;面包屑 2. 碎屑状(或瓦屑)的东西

crumbly ['krʌmbli] *adj.* 易弄碎的;易推碎破的

crumple ['krʌmpl] *vt.* 1. 把...弄皱;扭弯;压皱;弄皱,打折 — *vi.* 1. 起皱 2. 弄弯 3. 崩溃(up) — *n.* 折皱;皱纹 ∥ ~**d** *adj.* 1. 弄皱了的;被扭弯的 2. (牛角)弯曲的

crunch [krʌntʃ] *vt. & vi.* 1. 嘎吱嘎吱地咬嚼 2. (车轮,皮靴等)嘎吱嘎吱地踏(或踏)过 — *n.* 1. 嘎吱嘎吱的声音 2. 嘎吱嘎吱的响声 3.〈美口〉困境 4. 财政困难;经济紧缩;不足,短缺 5. 关键时刻;危急关头;转折点;症结 ∥ ~**y** *adj.* 发嘎吱嘎吱声的

crusade [kruː'seid] *n.* 1.【史】十字军 2. 圣战, (改革等)运动(against) — *vi.* 参加十字军(或圣战);从事改革(或清除公害等)运动(for);为(推进某一事业而)奋斗(against, for) ∥ ~**r** *n.* 1. 十字军

战士 2. 社会改革运动的斗士

crush [krʌʃ] *vt.* 1. 压坏;压碎;榨碎 2. 弄皱;揉皱(衣服等) 3. 压服;压倒;压垮 4. 塞;使挤在一起 5. 紧抱;拥抱 — *vi.* 被压碎;被碾碎;(衣服等)起皱;揉皱 3. 涌一,一起 4. 压碎,压坏;挤压 2. 极度拥挤;拥挤的人群;人数众多的聚会 3. (水果的)汁 4. 迷恋;迷恋的对象(尤指的分群柱) 5. 饮料 ∥ ~ **barrier** (人行道边设置的)防挤栏杆 / '~**room** *n.*〈英〉(戏院的)休息室

crust [krʌst] *n.* 1. 面包皮;干面包片 2. 硬外壳;外壳 3. (酒瓶里的)酒垢 4.【地】地壳 5.【动】甲壳 6.【医】痂 — *vt.* 用硬皮(或外壳)覆盖;在...上结硬皮(或痂) — *vi.* 结成硬皮;覆有外壳(over) ∥ ~**ed** *adj.* 1. 有硬皮的;有外壳的 2. 长了酒垢的 3. 陈旧的;古色古香的

crustacean [krʌ'steiʃən] *adj. & n.* 甲壳纲(的动物)

crusty ['krʌsti] *adj.* 1. 有硬皮的;有外壳的 2. 像硬皮(或外壳)一样硬的 3. 执拗的,乘易发脾气的;粗鲁的 ∥ **crustily** *adv.* / **crustiness** *n.*

crutch [krʌtʃ] *n.* 1. T字形拐杖 2. 支柱;叉杆 3.【海】桨架;椊座叉柱;船尾肘材 3. 胯部,(人体)两腿分叉处 4.〈喻〉支持 — *vt.* 用 T 字形拐杖支持;支撑

crux [krʌks] *n.* [复] **cruxes** 或 **cruces** ['kruːsiːz] 1. (纹章上的)十字形,十字架形 2. 难事,难题;症结 3. 关键,最重要点 4. [the C-]【天】南十字座

cry [krai] *vi.* 1. 叫喊 2. (鸟兽)叫 3. 哭,流泪 — *vt.* 1. 叫喊;大声地说 2. 公开宣布;叫卖 3. 大声恳求;哀求(for) 4. 哭出;哭得使 — *n.* 1. 叫喊;喊声;(鸟兽的)叫声 2. 叫卖声 3. (一阵)哭;哭泣;哭声 4. 呼声,舆论 5. 要求,呼吁 6. 传说,谣传 7. 口号 8. 时髦风尚 9. 一群

猎狗 ‖ '~**baby** n. 爱哭(或爱抱怨)的人

crying ['kraiŋ] *adj*. 1. 哭的；叫喊的 2. 引人注意的；急需处理的 3. 臭名昭著的，极坏的

crypt [kript] *n*. 地窖,地下室

cryptic ['kriptik] *adj*. 1. 秘密的,隐蔽的；神秘的 2. 隐义的；含义模糊的；使用密码的 3. 【动】隐蔽的；有保护色的：~ coloration 保护色,隐藏色 ‖ **cryptically** *adv*.

crystal ['kristl] *n*. 1. 水晶 2. 结晶(体) 3. 水晶饰品 4. 水晶玻璃；水晶玻璃制品；〈美〉钟面(或表面)玻璃 5.【电子】晶体 6. 水晶般明澈的东西(如水、冰等) — *adj*. 1. 水晶的；水晶制的 2. 晶莹的,清澈的；透明的 3. 晶体的；用晶体的 ‖ ~ **detector** 晶体检波器 / ~ **gazing** 水晶球凝视术,水晶球占卜(凝视水晶球以期借里面所呈现的图象来占卜未来的迷信活动)

crystalline ['kristəlain] *adj*. 1. 水晶的；水晶制的 2. 水晶般的,清澈透明的；清晰的 3. 晶质的；结晶体组成的结晶状的

crystallize ['kristəlaiz] *vt*. 1. 使结晶 2. 使定形；使(计划、思想等)具体化 3. 给(水果)裹上糖屑 — *vi*. 1. 结晶 2. 具体化；明确化 ‖ **crystalli'zation** *n*.

Cs 【化】元素铯(caesium)的符号

Cu 【化】元素铜(copper)的符号

cub [kʌb] *n*. 1. 幼兽；幼鲨 2. 不懂事的小伙子,生手(尤指初出茅庐的新闻记者) 3. (八至十岁的)幼童军 — (cubbed; cubbing) *vi*. 1. 生幼兽；猎幼狐

Cuba ['kjuːbə] *n*. 古巴 [拉丁美洲岛国](在加勒比海西北)

Cuban ['kjuːbən] *adj*. 古巴的；古巴人的 — *n*. 古巴人

cubbyhole ['kʌbihəul] *n*. 1. 舒适的地方

2. 鸽笼式文件架；分类格

cube [kjuːb] *n*. 1. 立方形；立方体 2.【数】立方,三次幂 3.〈美俚〉骰子 — *vt*. 1. 使立体至三次幂；求...的(体积)(或容积) 2. 使成立方体；把(土豆等)切成小方块 3. 用上铺方石

cubic ['kjuːbik] *adj*. 1. 立方体的；立方形的 2.【数】三次的,立方的

cubicle ['kjuːbikl] *n*. (隔成的)小室,隔间；小房间；小卧室

cuckold ['kʌkəuld] *n*. 妻子有外遇的人,"乌龟" — *vt*. 与...的妻子通奸,使做"乌龟"

cuckoo ['kuku:] *n*. 1. 杜鹃；布谷鸟 2. 杜鹃叫声；学杜鹃叫的咕咕声 3.〈美俚〉疯疯癫癫的人；蠢人 — *adj*. 1. 像杜鹃的 2. 疯癫的；蠢的 — *vi*. 1. 学杜鹃叫；学布谷鸟叫 2. 单调地重复叫(或说) ‖ ~ **clock** (报时似杜鹃叫声的)布谷鸟自鸣钟 / '~**flower** *n*.【植】布谷鸟剪秋罗 / ~**pint** *n*.【植】斑叶阿若母

cucumber ['kjuːkʌmbə] *n*. 黄瓜

cud [kʌd] *n*. 1. 反刍的食物 2.〈美〉(含在嘴里嚼的)嚼烟；口香糖

cuddle ['kʌdl] *vt*. 搂抱；搂住；偎着 — *vi*. 偎依；偎依着躺在一起,搂着睡(together, up) — *n*. 拥抱,搂抱 ‖ ~**some** *adj*. 令人想搂抱的；可爱的 / **cuddly** *adj*. 令人想搂抱的2. 喜欢拥抱的

cudgel ['kʌdʒəl] *n*. (短而重的)棍棒 — (cudgel(l)ed; cudgel(l)ing) *vt*. 用棍棒打

cue[1] [kjuː] *n*. 1.【戏】提示,暗示(指演出时给同台演员或拉幕、灯光人员作暗示的说白或动作) 2. 暗示,提示 3.【音】提示音(或小节) — *vt*. 提示；给...暗示

cue[2] [kjuː] *n*. 1.(人或车辆等待者的)长队,长蛇阵 2. 发辫 3.(台球的)球杆一

vt. 1. 把...编成发辫 2. 用球杆击

cuff[1] [kʌf] *n.* 1. 袖口 2. (裤脚的)翻边 3. [~s]手铐 —*vt.* 1. 给...装上袖口(或翻边) 2. 用手铐铐 ‖ ~ **links**(衬衫袖口的)链扣

cuff[2] [kʌf] *n.* 掌击, 一巴掌 —*vt.* 用巴掌打 —*vi.* 扭打

cuirass [kwi'ræs] *n.* 1. 胸甲上半身铠甲 2. (战舰的)装甲板 3. [动]护身甲壳; 胸甲状物 —*vt.* 给...披上胸甲

cuisine [kwi'ziːn] *n.* 烹饪(术); 菜肴, 饭菜; 厨房

culinary ['kʌlinəri] *adj.* 烹饪的; 烹饪用的; 厨房的; 适于做菜的

cull [kʌl] *vt.* 1. 采集(鲜花等); 挑选, 选拔 2. 剔去...中的整期货 —*n.* 被剔出的整期货(如不生蛋的母鸡、有病的植物等)

culminate ['kʌlmineit] *vi.* 1. 达到顶点(或高潮); (以...)告终(*in*) 2. [天]达于中天, 到子午线

culmination [ˌkʌlmi'neiʃən] *n.* 1. 达到顶点, 达到极点 2. 顶点, 极点, 最高潮 3. [天]中天

culpable ['kʌlpəbl] *adj.* 应受谴责的; 应受处罚的, 有罪的 ‖ **culpa'bility**, ~**ness** *n.* / **culpably** *adv.*

culprit ['kʌlprit] *n.* 1. 刑事被告, 未决犯 2. 导致过错的人; 产生事故的原因

cult [kʌlt] *n.* 1. 膜拜, 祭礼 2. 狂热的崇拜, 迷信; 崇拜对象: the personality ~ 个人崇拜, 个人迷信 3. 派派; 派别

cultivate ['kʌltiveit] *vt.* 1. 耕, 耕作; 开垦 2. 栽培, 种植 3. 培养; 养成; 建立, 加强(友谊等); 结交(朋友等) 4. 鼓励; 发展(科学、文化等) 5. 磨练; 陶冶 6. 使受文明教育, 使教化 ‖ **cultivable** ['kʌltivəbl], **cultivatable** ['kʌltiveitəbl] *adj.* 1. 可

耕作的; 可栽培的 2. 可培养的; 可教化的

cultivated ['kʌltiveitid] *adj.* 1. 耕作的; 栽培的 2. 有教养的; 有素养的; 优雅的

cultivation [ˌkʌlti'veiʃən] *n.* 1. 耕作; 栽培; 养殖 2. 培养, 发展, 促进 3. 修养

cultivator ['kʌltiveitə] *n.* 1. 耕种者; 栽培者 2. 培养者; 发展者; 促进者 3. [农]耕耘机, 中耕机

cultural ['kʌltʃərəl] *adj.* 1. 文化上的; 文化的 2. 修养的; 修养的 3. 栽培的; 培养的 ‖ ~**ly** *adv.* / ~ **lag** 文化调适迟缓(指文化某一方面的发展相对落后于科技发展的状况) / ~ **shock** = culture shock

culture ['kʌltʃə] *n.* 1. 文化; 文明 2. 教养; 陶冶; 修养; ~ moral (intellectual, physical) ~ 德(智、体)育 3. 栽培; 培育 4. [生]培养: silk ~ 养蚕 4. 耕作 —*vt.* 1. 使有教养 2. 耕作, 栽培; 培养(细菌等) ‖ ~ **shock** 文化冲击, 文化震惊(指面临异族文化或生活方式时可能经受到的一种困惑不安的感觉)

cultured ['kʌltʃəd] *adj.* 1. 有教养的; 有修养的 2. 耕种了的; 人工培养的; 人工养殖的

culvert ['kʌlvət] *n.* 1. 涵洞; 涵洞管道; 涵洞桥 2. 电缆管道

cumbersome ['kʌmbəsəm] *adj.* 1. 拖累的; 麻烦的 2. 笨重的; 不方便的 ‖ ~**ly** *adv.* / ~**ness** *n.*

cumbrous ['kʌmbrəs] *adj.* = cumbersome

cumulative ['kjuːmjulativ] *adj.* 1. 累积的; 渐增的; 累加的; ~ **voting** 累积投票制(指投票人可投等于候选人人数的票数, 并可将票全部投给一人) 2. [律]累积的, 附加的, 追加的 ‖ ~**ly** *adv.* / ~ -

ness n.

cumulus ['kjuːmjuləs] （[复] cumuli
['kjuːmjulai]）*n.*【气】积云 ‖ **cumulous**
adj.

cuneiform ['kjuːnifɔːm] *n. & adj.* 楔形文
字(的)

cunning ['kʌniŋ] *adj.* 1. 狡猾的；狡诈的
2. 精巧的；熟练的 3. （美）（小孩、小动
物等）可爱的 — *n.* 1. 狡黠，狡诈 2.
灵巧;熟练 ‖ ~ly *adv.* / ~ness *n.*

cup [kʌp] *n.* 1. 杯子 2. (一)杯;一杯的
容量(约半品脱) 3. 优胜杯，奖杯：the
Cup Final 争锦标杯的决赛 4.【宗】圣餐杯
5.[the ~]酒;饮酒 6. 经历，遭遇：His
~ of happiness was full. 他幸福之杯已满
7.【医】火罐,吸杯 8. 杯状物【植】等 9.
(以一种饮料为主的)混合饮料 — *vt.*
(cupped; cupping) *vt.* 1. 为…拔火罐
2. 使(手等)成杯状 3. 把…置于杯
中:把…置于杯状物中 ‖ ~ one's chin
in (the hollow of) one's hand 用手掌心
托着下巴 ‖ ~ful *n.*(一)满杯;半品脱
之量 ‖ '~cake *n.* 杯形蛋糕;纸杯蛋糕

cupboard ['kʌbəd] *n.* 碗橱;食橱 2.
(英小橱)‖ ~ love 有所企图而假装的
热情;出于私利的爱

Cupid ['kjuːpid] *n.* 1.【罗神】(爱神)丘比
特 2.[c~]丘比特画像(裸体、有双翅、手
持弓箭的美男孩)；美男孩 ‖ ~'s bow
1. 爱神丘比特之弓 2. 双弧形的上唇

cupidity [kjuː'piditi] *n.* 贪财;贪心

cupola ['kjuːpələ] *n.* 1. 穹顶,圆屋顶;(屋
顶上通风等用的)小塔 2. 化铁炉,冲
天炉 3. 旋转炮塔 4. 穹形状物【地】岩
钟;井楼

cuprous ['kjuːprəs] *adj.*【化】(亚)铜的,
一价铜的;含(亚)铜的,含一价铜的

cur [kəː] *n.* 1. 杂种狗;劣种狗;恶狗 2.
坏种,卑鄙小人;胆小鬼

curable ['kjuərəbl] *adj.* 能治愈的 ‖
ˌcura'bility *n.*

curate ['kjuərit] *n.* 助理牧师

curative ['kjuərətiv] *adj.* 治疗的;有疗效
的 — *n.* 治疗法;药品

curator [ˌkjuə'reitə] *n.* 1. 管理者,掌管者
2.(博物馆、图书馆等的)馆长 3.(英)
(大学董事会主管校产等的)董事;评
议员 4.(未成年者、疯子等的)监护人,
保护人 ‖ ~ship *n.*

curb [kəːb] *n.* 1. 马嚼子;马勒 2. 马衔索
2.(马后脚上生的)飞节肿大 3. 控制;
约束,抑制 4. 路缘;井栏;壁炉槛 5.
(美)场外证券市场(= ~ market) — *vt.*
1. 给(马)装马勒;勒住(马) 2. 控制;
约束,抑制 3. 设路缘于;设井栏于 ‖
~ bit 装有马勒的马嚼子 /~ service
(送食物到人行道边汽车乘客手上的)
路边服务 /'~stone *n.*(美)侧石,路缘
石

curd [kəːd] *n.* 凝乳;凝乳状物:bean ~ 豆
腐 — *vt. & vi.*(使)凝结

curdle ['kəːdl] *vt.* 1. 使凝结;使变稠:~
sb.'s blood 吓得某人浑身冰冷 2. 使
(牛奶等)结块变坏;使变坏 — *vi.* 1.
凝结 2. 变质;变坏

cure [kjuə] *vt.* 1. 治愈 2. 纠正;矫正 3. 消
除(弊病等) 3.(用腌、熏、晒、烤等方
法)加工处理 4. 使(橡胶硫化) — *vi.*
1. 起治疗作用;受治疗 2. 被加工处理
(指腌、熏、晒、烤等) 3.(橡胶)被硫化
— *n.* 1. 治愈;痊愈 2. 疗法;(治疗某
种疾病的)药;(处理社会问题等的)对
策 3. 治疗 4.(用腌、熏、晒、烤等方法
进行的)加工处理 5.【化】硫化,熟化 6.
(基督教)宗教监护;助理牧师职务 ‖
~less *adj.* 无法治愈的 ‖ '~-all *n.* 万
应灵药

curfew ['kəːfjuː] *n.* 1.(中世纪)晚间定时

灭火熄灯睡觉的规定;灭火熄灯就寝的晚钟(声);灭火熄灯就寝时刻 2. 宵禁(时间);宵禁令

curio ['kjuəriəu] n. [复] curios) n. 古董,珍品,古玩

curiosity [,kjuəri'ɔsiti] n. 1. 好奇(心) 2. 奇特(或罕见)的事物;古玩 3. 奇特性

curious ['kjuəriəs] adj. 1. 好奇的;爱打听的 2. 稀奇古怪的;难以理解的 ‖ ~．ly adv. / ~．ness n.

curium ['kjuəriəm] n. [化] 锔

curl [kə:l] n. 1. 卷毛;卷发;[植] 卷须 2. 卷曲物;螺旋状物 — a puff of smoke 一缕烟 3. 卷曲,卷 — a ~ of the lip(s) 嘴唇的上翘(表示轻蔑) 4. (马铃薯等的) 卷叶病 — vt. 使卷曲;使成螺旋状 — vi. 1. 卷曲;(烟) 缭绕 2. 作冰上溜石游戏 ‖ ~ er n. 1. 卷发夹,卷发器 2. 作冰上溜石游戏者 ‖ ~ paper n. 卷发纸

curlew ['kə:lju:] n. [复] curlew(s) n. [动] 杓鹬

curlicue ['kə:likju:] n. (文字等的) 花体 — vi. 形成花体 — vt. 以花体修饰

curly ['kə:li] adj. 1. 卷曲的;卷缩的 2. 有卷毛(或卷发)的 3. (木材) 有皱状纹理的

currant ['kʌrənt] n. 1. 无核小葡萄干 2. 茶藨子(灌木);茶藨子(浆果)

currency ['kʌrənsi] n. 1. 通货,货币 2. 通用;流通,流传;传播 3. 流通时间

current ['kʌrənt] adj. 1. (尤指货币) 流通的;(谣言等) 流传的;(词语等) 流行的 2. 现时的,当前的,现行的 — ~ events / ~ expenses 经常开支/the ~ month (week) 本月(周) — n. 1. 流;水流;气流 2. 电流 3. 趋势,倾向,潮流 ‖ ~ly adv. 当前,现今 / ~ ness n. ‖ ~ ac- count 往来账户/ 活期存款 / ~ assets

流动资产

curricula [kə'rikjulə] curriculum 的复数

curricular [kə'rikjulə] adj. 课程的

curriculum [kə'rikjuləm] n. [复] curriculums 或 curricula[kə'rikjulə) n. 课程

curry[1] ['kʌri] n. 咖喱(粉);咖喱食品 — vt. 在…中用咖喱调味

curry[2] ['kʌri] vt. 1. 梳剔(马匹等) 2. 加脂于(皮革);鞣(皮) 3. 揍,打 ‖ ~ . comb n. 马梳 vt. 用马梳梳刷

curse [kə:s] n. 1. 诅咒,咒骂;咒语;骂人话 2. 灾祸,祸因,祸根 3. 被诅咒的人(或事物) 4.[宗] 逐出教会 5.[the ~] [口] 月经(期) — (cursed 或 curst [kə:st]) vt. 1. 诅咒,咒骂;恶骂 2. 降祸于;使苦恼(with) 3.[宗]逐(某人)出教会 — vi. 诅咒,咒骂

cursed ['kə:sid] adj. 1. 被诅咒的 2. 该死的;可恶的;万恶的 ‖ ~ ly adv. / ~ . ness n.

cursive ['kə:siv] adj. 草书的,草写体的 — n. 草体;草书的手稿;草体字(母) ‖ ~ ly adv. / ~ ness n.

cursory ['kə:səri] adj. 粗略的;草率的 ‖ cursorily adv. / cursoriness n.

curt [kə:t] adj. 简短的,三言两语的;粗率无礼的 ‖ ~ ly adv. / ~ ness n.

curtail [kə:'teil] vt. 1. 剪短;截短 2. 削减,减少(经费等) 3. 剥夺(of) ‖ ~ . ment n.

curtain ['kə:tn] n. 1. 帘;窗帘;门窗门帘 2. (舞台上的) 幕;启幕;落幕 3. 幕状物;a fire — [军] 弹幕 4. (连接两棱堡或塔楼的) 幕墙;垣墙,非承压外墙 5. [美俚] [~s] 死;完蛋 — vt. 1. 给…装上窗帘子 2. 用帘子遮挡;隔开(off) ‖ ~ call 要求谢幕的掌声(或欢呼声);谢幕 / ~ fall n. 幕落(时的场面) / ~ . fire n.

【军】弹幕射击 / ~ raiser 1. (正戏演出前的)开场小戏 2. (事件等的)序曲,引子

curtsey, curtsy ['kɜːtsi] *n.* (西洋女子的)屈膝礼 — *vi.* 行屈膝礼

curvature ['kɜːvətʃə] *n.* 1. 弯曲;弯曲部分 2.【数】曲率

curve [kɜːv] *n.* 1. 曲线 2. 弯,弯曲;弯曲物;弯曲部分;(统计中的)曲线;曲线图 — *vt.* 弄弯;使成曲线 ‖ ... vi. 弯;成曲形;(依)曲线行进

cushion ['kuʃən] *n.* 1. 垫子;坐垫;靠垫 2. 减震垫(或器);缓冲垫(或器) 3. (汽缸中的)垫;气垫 4. (台球桌四周的)弹性衬里 5. (插针的)针垫 6. (猪等的)臀肉 6. (马的)蹄楔 7. (俚)摔球运动的坐垫 8. 起缓冲作用的东西;缓解病痛的药(或治疗) 9. 【美】使人舒适的东西;be on the ~ 景况优裕 — *vt.* 1. 把...安置在垫子上;(为安逸)用垫子支撑 2. 使坐垫上 3. 缓冲;减少震动;缓和...的冲击 4. 暗中压制(抗议等);掩盖(丑事等) 5. 使(台球)停靠在台边 ‖ ~ tyre 半实心轮胎,软心轮胎,缓冲轮胎

cusp [kʌsp] *n.* 1. 尖顶,尖端,尖突 2.【数】歧点,尖点 3.【天】月角 4.【解】尖瓣;尖头 5.【建】(叶形饰的)尖头 6.【植】(叶等的)尖

cuspid ['kʌspid] *n.*【解】犬牙,犬齿

cuspidor ['kʌspidɔː] *n.* (美)痰盂

cuss [kʌs] *n.* 1.〈口〉诅咒;咒骂 2. 家伙;畜生;贱骨头 — *vt. & vi.* 〈口〉诅咒,咒骂 ‖ ~ word 诅咒语;骂人话

cussed ['kʌsid] *adj.* 〈口〉1. 该诅咒的,可恶的 2. 执拗的,别扭的 ‖ ~ ly *adv.* / ~ ness *n.*

custard ['kʌstəd] *n.* 蛋奶糕;蛋奶沙司;软质奶油冰淇淋

custodian [kʌ'təudiən] *n.* 管理人;保管人;看守人

custody ['kʌstədi] *n.* 1. 保管;保护;监护 2. 拘留,监禁

custom ['kʌstəm] *n.* 1. 习惯;风俗;惯例 2.【律】习惯法 2. [the Customs] 海关;[总称]主顾;顾客 — *adj.* (衣服等)定制的,定做的 ‖ '~-'built, '~-'made *adj.* 定制的,定做的 / ~s duties 关税 / ~(s)house *n.* 海关

customary ['kʌstəməri] *adj.* 1. 通常的,常例的,习惯的 2. 习惯法的;惯例的 ‖ customarily *adv.* / customariness *n.*

customer ['kʌstəmə] *n.* 1. 顾客,主顾 2.〈口〉家伙

cut [kʌt] (cut; cutting) *vt.* 1. 切;割;剪;截;砍 2. 刺穿;刺破;伤害(指感情方面的);~ sb. to the heart 使某人极为伤心 3. 掘成;凿出;开辟 4. 雕刻;琢磨 5. 削减;缩短;删节;剪辑(影片) 6. 与...相交;与...相切;穿过 7. 阉割(家畜) 8. 停止,打断;和...绝交;拒斥:Cut the nonsense! 别胡说了! 9. 关(机器等);切断(电路等);拍制(电影某一场景) 10. 不理睬(某人);假装不看见(某人) 11. 显出,给人...的印象:~ a smart figure 出风头 12. 逃避(上课,开会等) 13. 溶解(美)冲淡 14.【机】切削,割削 15. 灌制(唱片);刻(蜡板) 16. 摊分(利益,赃物等) 17. 急转...的方向 18. 反手击(球) 19. 削(球) 20. 签(牌)[指把洗过的牌在发前分成两叠,上下倒置];抽(牌) — *vi.* 1. 切;割;砍(指工具或承受切割动作);This knife ~s well. 这把刀切起来快。/ This metal ~s easily. 这种金属容易切削。2. (用鞭)抽;(用刀、剑等)砍:刺痛;刺痛

(在感情方面)伤害；a remark that ~s 刺人的话 3. (议论、分析等)起作用：His analysis ~s quite deep. 他的分析相当深刻。4. 相交；相切；穿(过)，斜穿，抄近路 5. 很快地离开；疾驰 6. (拍摄电影时)停拍；改换镜头 7. 剪辑影片，编辑影片 8. 摊分；分摊 9. 急转方向 10. 打削球 11. 签牌；抽牌 12. (画色)醒目 — n. 1. (刀、剑等)砍；切；割；劈；欲；击；抽；伤口；切口；切面 3. 切下来的肉；(同一批)割下的作物；割减；缩短；删节；删掉的部分 5. 伤人的话(或行为)；不理睬 6. (人工挖凿或自然侵蚀而成的)河道；沟渠 7. 近路，捷径 8. 挖土，挖方 9. (分摊到的)一份 10. (电视或电影镜头的)切换 11. 【机】切削，割削；割切 12. 【化】馏分 13. (服装、头发等的)式样；类型 14. 等级(尤指社会地位) 15. 插图；雕刻版；版画 16. 旷课 17. (乒乓、网球等的)削球；(削球的)旋转 18. 签牌 ‖ ~- and-'come-a'gain n. 1. 大量，丰富 2. 【植】一年生罗兰 ‖ ~- and-'dried adj. 1. 早已准备好的；按预定计划的 2. 呆板的，没有生气的 ‖ ~- 'try adj. 试验性的 ‖ ~- away adj. 部分被割(切)掉的；剖面的 1. 前下摆向后斜切的燕尾服 2. (切去一角露出内部结构的)剖面图 ‖ ~- back n. 1. 倒短；被截短的东西 2. 中止；剃减 3. (沥青的)稀释产物 4. (踢足球时)带球急转 5. (故事或电影的)情节倒叙 6. (电视镜头或电影的)闪回 ‖ ~- 'in n. 1. 插入；插入镜头；插入画面 2. (分享的)一份好处，一份利益 ‖ ~- off n. 1. 切除；截断；切(或割)下的东西 2. 近路；(河流弯曲处)截弯取直(水道) 3. 中止，停止；截止点 4. 【机】停汽；【电】保险装置；截断装

置 ‖ ~- out n. 1. 切下(或删掉)的东西；剪成(或刻成)的东西 2. 【电】保险装置；断流器 3. (内燃机的)排气阀 ‖ ~- over adj. 树木被采伐的 n. 采伐迹地 ‖ ~- purse n. 小偷；扒手 ‖ ~-'rate adj. 1. 减价的；有减价许可的 2. 次等的 ‖ ~- throat n. 凶手；谋杀者 adj. 1. 杀人的；残酷的；无情的 2. (桥牌等)三人入局的 ‖ ~- up n. 插科打诨的人，胡闹的人 ‖ ~- worm n. 切根虫，地老虎

cutaneous [kju:'teiniəs] adj. 皮肤(上)的；影响(或感染)皮肤的 ‖ -ly adv.

cute [kju:t] adj. (口) 1. 聪明的，伶俐的 2. 漂亮的；逗人喜爱的 ‖ -ly adv. / ~- ness n.

cuticle ['kju:tikl] n. 1. 表皮 2. 【解】护膜 3. 【植】角质层

cutlass ['kʌtləs] n. (古时水手用的) 短弯刀；大砍刀

cutlery ['kʌtləri] n. 1. 刀剪业；刀具业 2. [总称][刀剪等]；刀具 3. [总称](西餐的)刀叉餐具

cutlet ['kʌtlit] n. (羊、牛、猪等的)肉片，肉排；羊羔排；炸肉饼(或鱼饼等)

cutter ['kʌtə] n. 1. 用于切割(或剪削等)的器械(如刀具、切草机、截煤机等) 2. 从事切割(或剪削等)工作的人(如服装裁剪师、影片剪辑人员、采煤工等) 3. 刻纹头，机械录音头 4. 快艇；小汽艇 5. (善于)击旋转球的击球手；击出的旋转球 6. 轻便雪橇

cutting ['kʌtiŋ] n. 1. 切；割；剪；削；掘 2. 切(或割)、剪、削)下的东西 3. (影片的)剪辑 4. (英)剪报 5. (英)路堑 6. (用来插种的)扦插，插条 7. (唱片的)灌制，录音 — adj. 1. 供切(或割等)用的 2. 锋利的 3. 凛冽的，寒冷刺骨的 4. (话语等)尖刻的，尖锐的 5. (声音等)刺耳的；(疼痛等)剧烈的 ‖ -ly adv.

cuttlefish ['kʌtlfiʃ] *n.* 乌贼, 墨鱼

cv., **cvt.** *abbr.* convertible

c.w.o. *abbr.* cash with order【商】定货付款

cyanide ['saiənaid] *n.*【化】氰化物

cyclamate ['saikləmeit] *n.*【化】环璜酸盐 (用作人工增甜剂)

cycle ['saikl] *n.* **1.** 周期; 循环; (一)转 **2.** (一段)长时期; (一个)时代 **3.** (故事等的)始末; (表现同一主题或描写同一人物的)一组小说(或戏剧、诗歌等); a song ~ 组歌 **4.** 自行车; 三轮脚踏车, 机器脚踏车 **5.** (天体的)运行轨道, 周 **6.**【无】周; 周/秒, 赫 **7.**【数】环 **8.**【地】旋回 — *vi.* **1.** 循环 **2.** 骑自行车 (或三轮脚踏车、机器脚踏车) ‖ ~ *n.* cyclist *n.* 骑自行车(或机器脚踏车等)的人 ‖ ~ car **1.** 三轮汽车; (三轮或四轮的)小型机动车

cyclic(al) ['saiklik(əl)] *adj.* **1.** 周期的; 循环的; 轮转的 **2.**【植】轮列的 **3.**【化】环状的; 环式的; 组歌的, 系列故事的 ‖ cyclically *adv.*

cyclone ['saikləun] *n.* **1.** 气旋; 旋风; 龙卷风 ‖ cyclonic [sai'klɔnik] *adj.*

cyclop(a)edia [ˌsaiklə'pi:diə] *n.* 百科全书; (某一学科的)大全, 全书

cyclotron ['saiklətrɔn] *n.*【核】回旋加速器

cylinder ['silində] *n.* **1.** 圆筒; 圆柱体; 【工】机筒; 钢瓶; 量筒 **2.**【机】汽缸 **3.** (印刷机的)滚筒 **4.**【数】柱面 **5.** (左轮手枪的)旋转弹膛

cylindrical [si'lindrikəl] *adj.* 圆柱体的; 圆筒形的

cymbal ['simbəl] *n.* [常 ~s]【音】钹(一种打击乐器) ‖ ~ist *n.* 击钹者

cynic ['sinik] *n.* **1.** [C-]犬儒学派的人 **2.** 不信世上有好人好事的人; 看穿人世的人; 抱怀疑(或悲观)态度的人; 好挖

苦人的人; 心狠手辣的人 — *adj.* **1.** [C-]犬儒学派的 **2.** = cynical

cynical ['sinikəl] *adj.* **1.** 不信世上有好人好事的; 看穿人世的; 怀疑的; 悲观的 **2.** 挑剔挖苦的; 冷嘲热讽的 **3.** 心眼小的 ‖ ~ly *adv.*

cynicism ['sinisizəm] *n.* **1.** [C-]犬儒主义 **2.** 愤世嫉俗, 不信世间有真和善, 认为人心皆自私; 怀疑; 悲观 **3.** 冷嘲热讽; 吹毛求疵 **4.** 愤世嫉俗的言词(或行动、想法等)

cynosure ['sinəzjuə, 'sainəzjuə] *n.* **1.** [the C-]【天】小熊座 **2.** [the C-]【天】北极星(= the North Star) **3.** 指引方向的东西(如指针) **4.** 引人注目的人(或事物); 引人注意的中心

cypress ['saiprəs] *n.* **1.** 柏; 落羽杉; 白扁柏 **2.** 柏枝(作哀悼标志用)

Cyprus ['saiprəs] *n.* 塞浦路斯[西亚岛国](在地中海东部)

cyst [sist] *n.* **1.**【生】囊胞, 包囊; 孢囊 **2.**【医】囊肿 ‖ ~ic *adj.*

cyto- *comb. form* 表示"细胞(质)"

cytoecology [ˌsaitəui'kɔlədʒi] *n.* 细胞生态学

cytomorphology ['saitəmɔ:'fɔlədʒi] *n.* 细胞形态学

cytoplasm ['saitəplæzəm] *n.* [生]细胞质

czar [zɑ:] *n.* **1.** 沙皇; 皇帝 **2.** 大权独揽的人; 特权人物

Czech [tʃek] *n.* 捷克人; 捷克语 — *adj.* 捷克的; 捷克人的; 捷克语的

Czechoslovak [ˌtʃekə'sləuvæk] *n.* [史]捷克斯洛伐克人 — *adj.* 捷克斯洛伐克的; 捷克斯洛伐克人的

Czechoslovakia [ˌtʃekəsləu'vækiə] *n.* [史]捷克斯洛伐克[原欧洲中部国家, 1993年起分为捷克、斯洛伐克两个国家]

D

D, d [diː] ([复]D's 或 Ds, ds [diz]) 英语字母表第四个字母 **1.** [D]D字形 **2.** 罗马数字500 **3.** [D]【化】元素氘(deuterium)的符号 **4.** [D]【物】密度(density)的符号 **5.** [音]D音, D调 **6.** (美)学业成绩第四等"尚可"(表示"仅能及格")的符号

d' [d](口)〈口〉= do'; did

'd [d]〈口〉= had; would

dab¹ [dæb] (dabbed; dabbing) vt. & vi. **1.** 轻拍, 轻敷 **2.** 轻敷, 轻擦 **3.** (轻敷、轻擦、轻涂用的)湿而软的小块(如颜料等) **4.** [~s]〈俚〉指纹印

dab² [dæb] n. 少量

dab³ [dæb] n. 〈口〉能手, 熟手(at)

dabble ['dæbl] vt. 弄湿; 溅湿 — vi.**1.** 玩水 **2.** 涉猎; 把…作为兴趣爱好尝试一下(in, at) ‖ ~ r n. 玩水者; 涉猎者, 浅尝者

Dacca ['dækə] n. '= Dhaka.

dace [deis] [单复同] n. 【动】鲹; 鲦; 鲹; (尤指欧洲产的)雅罗鱼

dacha ['dɑːtʃə](俄)n. 夏季别墅, 乡间别宅

dachshund ['dækshund] n. 【动】达克斯猎狗(德国种的小猎狗)

Dacron ['dækrɒn] n. 【纺】涤纶, 的确良

dad [dæd] n. 〈口〉**1.** 爸爸, 爹爹 **2.** 老头, 老家伙

daddy ['dædi] n. **1.**〈口〉= dad **2.**〈美俚〉甜爹(出钱供养情妇的男子; 尤指年老的富人) **3.** (某一表演行业内的)大师 ‖ ~ longlegs [单复同] **1.** 大蚊 **2.** 盲蛛(一种长脚蜘蛛)

daffodil ['dæfədil] n. **1.**【植】黄水仙 **2.** 淡黄色

daffy ['dæfi] adj. = daft

daft [dɑːft, dæft] adj. **1.** 傻的, 愚蠢的 **2.** 疯狂的 ‖ ~ly adv.

dagger ['dægə] n. **1.** 匕首, 短剑 **2.** 剑号(即†) **3.** 剑形物 — vt. **1.** 用剑刺 **2.** 用剑号标明

dagoba ['dɑːgəbə]〈僧伽罗语〉n.【佛教】舍利塔

dahlia ['deiljə] n. **1.**【植】大丽花, 大丽菊; 大丽花的花 **2.** 紫色染料; 浓紫色

daily ['deili] adj. 每日的; 每日一次的 — adv. 每日, 天天 — n. **1.** 日报 **2.**〈口〉(不寄宿的)女佣

dainty ['deinti] adj. **1.** 轻巧的; 精致的 **2.** (食物)美味的, 可口的; 讲究的 **3.** (人)秀丽的; 优雅的 **4.** (对食物、服装等)过分讲究的; 挑剔的 — n. 美味精致的食物 ‖ daintily adv./daintiness n.

Dairen [dai'ren] n. 见 Dalian

dairy ['dɛəri] n. **1.** 乳品间; 制酪场; 乳品场 **2.** 牛奶公司; 乳品店 **3.** 牛奶及乳品业 ‖ ~ing n. 乳品业 ‖ ~ cattle 奶牛

/ '~maid *n*. 牛奶房(或乳牛场)女工 /'~man *n*. 牛奶房(或乳牛场)男工 2. 乳牛场主、牛奶及乳品商人

dais ['deiis] *n*. 1.(宴会大厅一端的)台;高台 2.(教室的)讲台;(广场上的)演奏台,演出台

daisy ['deizi] *n*. 1.【植】雏菊 2.〈俚〉上等货;第一流的人物;漂亮姑娘

Dakar ['dækə] *n*. 达喀尔[塞内加尔首都]

Dakota [də'kəutə] ([复]Dakota(s)) *n*. 1. 达科他人(北美印第安人) 2. 达科他语 3. 达科他(美国过去一地区名);North (South)～ 北(南)达科他[美国州名]

dale [deil] *n*.〈英方〉(诗)谷;溪谷

Dallas ['dæləs] *n*. 达拉斯[美国得克萨斯州东北部城市]

dally ['dæli] *vi*. 1. 嬉戏;调戏(*with*) 2. 闲荡;误误(*over*) — *vt*.(在嬉戏中)浪费(时间)(*away*) ‖ **dalliance** *n*.

Dalmatian [dæl'meiʃən] *n*.(南斯拉夫的白毛黑斑)达尔马提亚狗

dam [dæm] *n*. 1. 坝;堤 2. 拦在堤坝里的水 3.(阻止液体、气体或空气流动的)坝状物,屏障;【矿】隔墙,密封墙 4.【医】(牙科用的)橡皮障 — (dammed; damming) *vt*. 1. 筑坝拦(水)(*up, out*) 2. 抑制,控制(*in, up*)

damage ['dæmidʒ] *n*. 1. 损害;毁坏;损失 2.[~s]【律】损害赔偿(金) 3.〈口〉费用 — *vt*. 损害;毁坏 ‖ **-able** *adj*. 有破坏性的;有害的;不利的

Damascus [də'mɑːskəs] *n*. 大马士革[叙利亚首都]

damask ['dæməsk] *n*. 1. 花缎;锦缎 2. 织台台布 3.(铸剑用的)大马士革钢(= ～ steel)(大马士革钢上的)波形花纹 4. 淡红色,粉红色 — *adj*. 1. 大马士革的 2. 花缎的;锦缎的 3. 大马士革钢制

的 4. 淡红色的,粉红色的

dame [deim] *n*. 1.〈诗〉〈古〉夫人,贵妇人 2. 老妇人 3.〈俚〉女人

damn [dæm] *vt*. 1.(上帝)罚……入地狱;诅咒 2. 指责(作品等);把……骂得一钱不值 3. 毁掉(前途等) — *vi*. 咒骂,骂该死;Damn!(或 God～!)该死! — *n*. 1. 诅咒骂 2. 丝毫 — *adj*. & *adv*. = damned ‖ **-ation** [dæm'neiʃən] *n*. 1. 罚入地狱 2.(对作品等的)指责 3.(前途等的)毁掉 *int*. 该死! / ～**atory** ['dæmnətəri] *adj*. 指责的

damnable ['dæmnəbl] *adj*. 1. 该受上帝惩罚的,该死的 2.〈口〉糟透的 ‖ **damnably** *adv*.

damned [dæmd] *adj*. 1. 罚入地狱的 2. 可恶的;讨厌的 3. 凄沉,沮丧 — *adj*. 〈俚〉十足的,完全的 — *adv*. 极,非常: be ～ hot 热得要命

dampen ['dæmpən] *vt*. 1. 使潮湿 2. 抑制;挫折 3.【物】【电】使减幅,使阻尼;【音】制止(琴弦)的音 — *vi*. 1. 变潮湿 2. 丧气

damp [dæmp] *n*. 1. 湿气,潮湿 2.(矿井)瓦斯 3. 有毒气体 4. 消沉,沮丧 — *adj*. 有湿气的,潮湿的 — *vt*. 1. 使潮湿 2.(用灰等)封(火);灭(火)(*down*) 3. 阻抑,抑止 4.【物】使阻尼,使减幅;【音】制止(琴弦)的音 5. 变潮湿 2.【物】减幅,阻尼 ‖ **-ly** *adv*. / ～**ness** *n*. / ～**course**【建】防潮层 / '~**dry** *vt*. 使(洗好的衣服)半干 *adj*.(洗好的衣服)半干的,带潮的 / ～**squib**〈英俚〉未成效的事;失败;落空

damper ['dæmpə] *n*. 1. 令人扫兴的人(或事物);起抑制作用的因素 2.【机】档板,调节风门 3.【音】制音器 4.【物】阻尼器,减震器

damsel ['dæmzəl] *n*.〈古〉〈诗〉少女,姑娘

闺女‖~ **bug**【昆】蟪蛄(一种益虫) /
'~**fish** n.【鱼】雀鲷/'~**fly** n.【昆】豆
娘

dance [dɑːns] vi. 1. 跳舞,舞蹈 2. 手舞足
蹈;(旗等)飘扬;(树枝等)摇晃 一 vt.
1. 跳(舞) 2. 使摇晃,使上下摆动(小孩)
一 n.1. 跳舞;舞蹈 2. 舞会 3. 舞曲 4.
舞蹈艺术 ‖~r n. 舞蹈演员;跳舞者

dandelion ['dændilaiən] n.【植】药蒲公
英;蒲公英

dandify ['dændifai] vt. 使像花花公子‖
dandified adj.(打扮得)像花花公子的

dandle ['dændl] vt. 1.(上下摆动着)播弄
逗乐(小孩) 2. 宠,娇养

dandruff ['dændrʌf] n. 头垢,头皮屑

dandy ['dændi] n. 1. 花花公子,纨绔子弟
2.(口)第一流的东西 3.(英国的)双桅
帆船 4.(英)(送牛奶工人用的)二轮小
车(=~**cart**)— adj. 1. 服装华丽的
2.(口)极好的,第一流的

Dane [dein] n. 丹麦人

danger ['deindʒə] n. 1. 危险 2. 危险事
物;威胁‖~ **money** 危险工作津贴

dangerous ['deindʒərəs] adj. 危险的‖~**ly**
adv.

dangle ['dæŋɡl] vi. 1. 悬荡;垂垂;悬挂 2.
追求;尾随(after)— vt. 1. 使悬荡;使
悬垂 2.(作为诱惑物)炫示‖~r n. 1.
吊着摆动的东西 2. 追逐女人的男子
‖ **dangling participle**【语】垂悬分词

Danish ['deiniʃ] adj. 丹麦的;丹麦人的;
丹麦语的 — n. 1. [the ~](总称)丹麦
人 2. 丹麦语

dank [dæŋk] adj. 阴湿的‖~**ish** adj. /
~**ly** adv. /~**ness** n.

danseur [dɑ̃'sœr]〈法〉n. 芭蕾舞男演
员

danseuse [dɑ̃'søz]〈法〉n. 芭蕾舞女演
员

Danube ['dænjuːb] n. 多瑙河[欧洲]

Danzig ['dænsiɡ] n. 但泽(Gdansk 格但斯
克的旧称)[波兰北部港市]

dapper ['dæpə] adj. 1.(常指矮小的人)
干净利落的 2. 衣冠楚楚的

dapple ['dæpl] adj. 有斑点的;有花斑的
— n. 1. 斑点;花斑 2. 花斑斑动物 —
vt. & vi.(使)有斑点‖'~'**grey**, '~'
gray adj. & n. 菊花青色的(马)

Dardanelles [ˌdɑːdə'nelz] n. 达达尼尔(海
峡)[欧亚之间]

dare [dɛə] v. aux. [后接不带 to 的不定
式;主要用于疑问、否定或条件句]1.
敢: Dare he swim across? 他敢游过去
吗? 2. 竟敢: If you ~ speak to me like
that again, you will be sorry. 如果你再敢
这样同我说话,你要后悔的。— v.1.
敢: ~ (to) jump with a parachute 敢于
跳伞 2. 竟敢: Does anyone ~ to call me
a liar? 有谁敢说我是个说谎者吗? 3.
敢于面对;敢于承担(风险) 4. 激(将):
估计…没胆量: I ~ you to do it! 谅你
也不敢! — n. n. 1. 大胆;果敢
行为 2. 挑战;激将

daredevil ['dɛəˌdevl] adj. & n. 胆大妄为
的(人);蛮干的(人)‖~**ry**, ~**try** n.
胆大妄为之事

daren't [dɛənt] = dare not

Dar es Salaam ['dɑːresə'lɑːm] 达累斯萨
拉姆[坦桑尼亚首都]

daring ['dɛəriŋ] n. & adj. 大胆(的);勇
敢(的)‖~**ly** adv. / ~**ness**
n.

dark [dɑːk] adj. 1. 黑暗的,暗的 2.(头
发、皮肤等)黑色的(颜色)浅黑的;深
的 3. 隐藏的,隐秘的: a ~ secret 十分
秘密的事 4.(意义等)模糊的,隐晦的
5. 阴郁的;郁郁的: in a ~ temper 十分
不高兴的 6. 坏的,邪恶的 7. 无知的;蒙

昧的: the *Dark Ages* 欧洲中世纪的早期(被认为是愚昧黑暗时代) 8.〈美俚〉(戏院等)已打烊的 — n. 1. 黑暗;暗处 2. 黄昏 3. 暗色 4. 模糊,隐晦;隐秘 5. 无知 ‖ ~ly *adv.* / ~ness *n.*【~room *n.*【摄】暗室

darken ['dɑːkən] *vt.* 1. 使变暗;遮暗 2. 使变黑 3. 使(视力等)模糊 4. 使阴暗;使天色… 使不乐— *vi.* 1. 变黑;转暗;变得阴暗(*up*) 2.(颜色)变深 3.(表情等)变得阴沉 4.(记忆等)变得模糊

darling ['dɑːliŋ] *n.* 心爱的人;宠儿: My ~!(或 Darling!)亲爱的(夫妻之间的称呼) 宝宝,乖乖(父母对儿女的爱称)— *adj.* 1. 心爱的,宠爱的 2. 漂亮的,吸引人的

darn¹ [dɑːn] *vt. & vi.* 织补— *n.* 织补处;织补处

darn² [dɑːn]damn 的委婉语

dart [dɑːt] *n.* 1. 镖;飞镖;镖状物 2. 突进 3.【动】射器;针刺 4. [~s]用作单)投镖游戏 5. 飞快的一瞥;飞快的动作 6. 突然的刺痛 — *vt.* 投掷(标枪等);发射 — *vi.* 急冲,突进

dash [dæʃ] *vt.* 1. 使猛撞;猛掷 ‹ 摔碎 2. 洒泼,溅 3. 搀加(*with*) 4. 使 ⟨ 希望、计划等)破灭⟨使泪丧;使窘⟨ 匆忙充满⟩撞 6.〈口〉(与 it 连用)诅咒— *vi.* 1. 撞 2. 猛冲,突进— *n.* 1. 撞击;溅泼;(水的)撞击声 2. 少量,少许 3. 闯劲,锐气 4. 炫耀;虚饰;挫折 5. 破折号[即—] 6.(莫尔斯电码的)划,长划(与 dot 相对) 7. 短跑;猛冲(赛跑中的)冲刺 8. 短跑;猛冲(赛跑中的)冲刺 9. 仪表板 ‖ ~board *n.*(马车等的)挡泥板;(船只的)遮水板 2. 仪表板

dashing ['dæʃiŋ] *adj.* 1. 精神抖擞的;冲劲很足的 2. 漂亮的 ‖ ~ly *adv.*

dastard ['dæstəd] *n.* 卑怯的人;懦夫—

adj. 卑怯的 ‖ ~ly *adv.* 卑怯地

data ['deitə] datum 的复数 ‖ ~bank *n.*【计】数据库 ~ *vt.* 把…存入数据库/ ~ processing【计】数据处理

date¹ [deit] *n.* 1. 日期;日子 2.(历史上的)年代;时期 3.(尤指男女间的)约会;(美口)约会对象— *vt.* 1. 注明…的日期 2. 确定…的年代;显出…的时代(或年龄)特征 3. 使显得过时 4. 和…约会— *vi.* 1. 注明日期 2. 属于过去年代,追溯(*from, back to*) 3. 过时 4.〈美口〉与人约会 ‖ ~d *adj.* 1. 注有日期的 2. 过时的 / ~less *adj.* 1. 无日期的 2. 无限期的 3. 远古的;古老的 4. 经住时间考验的 5.〈口〉无约会的,无伴侣的/ ~r *n.* 日期戳子 / ~line *n.* 1. 书信(或文件等)上注明的书写或发出)日期和地点 2. [常作 ~ line]日界线,国际日期变更线,国际改日线 3.(标明日期和地名的)新闻电讯电头 *vt.* 在…上注明日期(或地点);在(新闻电讯)上注电头/ ~mark *n.* 日戳 / dating bar〈美〉供单身男女幽会的酒吧间

date² [deit] *n.* 1. 海枣(果) 2.【植】海枣(树),枣椰树 ‖ ~ palm 海枣(树),枣椰树

datum ['deitəm] *n.* 1.([复]data ['deitə])论据;作为论据的事实 2. 资料,材料;数据 3.([复]datums)【数】已知数— 4.([复]datums)【测】基(准)面(= ~ plane)

daub [dɔːb] *vt. & vi.* 1. 涂抹 2. 乱涂,乱画 3. 弄脏— *n.* 1. 涂料(如泥灰等),涂抹 2. 拙劣的画 ‖ ~er *n.* 1. 涂抹的人;涂抹工具 2. 拙劣的画家

daughter ['dɔːtə] *n.* 1. 女儿;养女;儿媳 2.(某国,某地的)妇女;~s of China 中华女儿 3. 产物 4.【核】子体 ‖ ~hood *n.* 女儿身份；女儿时期/~**ly** *adj.* 女儿（似）的 ‖ ~ **element**【核】子元素/~-**in-law**〔复〕~**s-in-law**〕*n.* 媳妇

daunt [dɔːnt] *vt.* 威吓；使胆怯,使气馁

dauntless ['dɔːntlis] *adj.* 无所畏惧的,吓不倒的,大胆的 ‖ ~**ly** *adv.* ~**ness** *n.*

dauphin ['dɔːfin] *n.*【法史】王太子,王储 ‖ ~**e** ['dɔːfiːn]、~**ess** *n.* 王太子的妻子,王妃

davenport ['dævənpɔːt] *n.* **1.**（活动面板的）小书桌 **2.**〈美〉坐卧两用沙发

davit ['dævit] *n.*〔船〕吊艇柱,吊艇杆;吊柱;吊锚柱

dawdle ['dɔːdl] *vi.* 游荡,闲逛;偷懒 — *vt.* 浪费（时间等）(*away*) ‖ ~**r** *n.* 游手好闲的人,二流子,懒汉

dawn [dɔːn] *n.* **1.** 破晓 **2.**（时代、局面等）开始出现,渐露端倪 **3.** 渐被理解（或感知）(*on, upon*) *n.* **1.** 黎明,拂晓 **2.**（历史等）的开端（希望等的）曙光 ‖ ~ **chorus 1.** 清晨鸟鸣声 **2.**【无】晨噪（常在清晨听到的无线电干扰）

day [dei] *n.* **1.** 白昼,白天 **2.**（一）天,（一）日,工作日: an eight-hour ~ 八小时工作日 **3.**〔常~s〕日子,时期 **5.**〔常用来加 his, their 等物主代词连用〕年轻（有为）时期,兴旺发达时期,鼎盛时期;机会:National Day 国庆节 **8.** 竞赛;战斗,胜利:win（lose）the ~ 打胜（败）‖ ~ **blindness**【医】昼盲症/~ **boarder** 寄膳走读学生/~**book** *n.* **1.** 日记簿 **2.** 日记账/~ **boy** 走读男生/'~**break** *n.* 黎明/'~-**care center**〈美〉日间托儿站/~ **coach**〈美〉〔列车的〕座席客车/'~-**dream** *vi. & n.* 日间做梦,幻想,空想/'~-**dreamer** *n.* 空想家/~ **girl** 走读女生/~ **labour 1.** 日工 **2.** 散工/~ **labourer** 散工日工/~ **letter**〈美〉（比一

般电报缓发的）日信电报/ '~**long** *adj.* & *adv.* 整天的,整日的/~**man** *n.* **1.** 零工工人 **2.** 做日班的人/~ **nursery** 日间托儿所/ '~-**room** *n.*（学校等的）休息室/（营房等的）娱乐室/~ **school** 走读学校;日间学校/~**star** *n.* 晨星;〈诗〉太阳/~ **ticket**〈英〉当天来回火车票/ '~-**time** *n.* 白天,日间/ '~-**to-**' ~' *adj.*（工作）日常的;每天的;按日的;过一天算一天的/~ **trader**（股票的）当天买卖投机者/~ **trip** 当天来回的短途旅行

daylight ['deilait] *n.* **1.** 日光;白昼 **2.** 黎明 **3.** 公开: The truth has been brought into ~. 真相大白。**4.** 空隙;间隔（如赛船时船与船间的间隔）: No ~! （敬酒时用语）斟满! **5.**〔俚〕~**s** 知觉,神志 ‖ ~ **robbery 1.**〈英口〉明目张胆的劫夺（尤指索价过高）**2.** 阳光劫夺（指建高楼而遮暗低层光线）/~ **saving (time)** 将时钟向前拨的/日光节约时间,夏令时间

daze [deiz] *vt.* **1.** 使发昏,使迷乱,使茫然 **2.** 使眼花缭乱 — *n.* 迷乱,茫然;眼花

dazzle ['dæzl] *vt. & vi.* **1.**（光等）炫耀;眩（眼）**2.** 眩惑;迷惑 — *n.* **1.** 眩惑;炫耀;眩眼 **2.** 使人眼花缭乱的事物

dazzling ['dæzliŋ] *adj.* 眩惑的;令人眼花缭乱的 ‖ ~**ly** *adv.*

DC *abbr.* **1.** direct current 直流电 **2.** District of Columbia 哥伦比亚特区〔美国首都华盛顿所在的行政区域〕: Washington, *D. C.*（美国首都）华盛顿

DDT [ˌdiːdiːˈtiː] *n.*【化】双对氯苯基三氯乙烷,（商品名）滴滴涕〔一种杀虫剂〕

de- *pref.* **1.** 表示"离开","除去": *de*train **2.** 表示"向下": *de*press **3.** 表示"否定","倒转": *de*frost **4.** 表示"减少","降低": *de*value

deacon ['diːkən] *n.* **1.**（基督教圣公会、天

主教等的)副主祭 **2.**（浸礼会、长老会等的）执事 ‖ ~ess *n.* 女执事

dead [ded] *adj.* **1.** 死的；无生命的 **2.** 无感觉的，麻木的；死一般的：in a ~ faint 昏死过去 **3.** 〈美口〉精疲力竭的 **4.**（描写等）呆板的；（聚会等）死气沉沉的 **5.** 无动静的（空气等）不流动的；（商品、资金等）呆滞的：a ~ calm 死寂 **6.** 熄灭了的（用过的）；（感情等）消失的破灭的；a ~ oil well 废油井 /The microphone has gone ~. 话筒坏了。**7.**（语言、习惯等）废弃了的；（法律等）名存实亡的；已失去重要性的 **8.**（法律等）无弹性的 **9.** 资瘠的，不毛的；非生产的 **10.**（声音）闷住的 **11.**（色彩）灰暗的；（金属）无光泽的 **12.**（饮料等）走了味的 **13.**（停止）突然的；完全的，绝对的：a ~ loss 全部亏损 **14.** 准的；丝毫不差的：a ~ shot 神枪手 **15.** 不通电的，无电流的 — *adv.* **1.** 完全地，绝对地：be ~ asleep 沉睡着 **2.** 突然地 **3.** 直接地，正对地 — *n.* **1.** 死者；最冷的时刻；最寂静的时刻：in the ~ of winter 在隆冬/ in the ~ of night 在深夜 **3.**〈俚〉无法投递的邮件，死信 ‖ ~ness *n.* ‖ ~-a'live, ~-and-a'live *adj.* 没精打采的；（职业等）单调的 /~-beat *n.*〈口〉筋疲力尽的；~-beat 懒人；穰赖的人/~-centre 正中；【机】（冲程的）死点；（车床的）死顶尖/~-duck 必然要完蛋的人（或物）/~-end（街道、管道等）闭塞不通的一头 **2.**【无】闲端，空端 **3.** 死胡同 /~-'end *adj.* **1.**（街道等）不通的 **2.** 贫民区的 /~-heat 胜负不分的赛跑 /~-letter **1.** 形同虚设的规定 **2.**（无法投递的）死信/ ~-line *n.* **1.**（监牢周围的）死线；不可逾越的界限 **2.** 最后期限（for）/~-load 静载，底载，固定负荷；静重（于）/~-lock *n.* 僵持，僵局 *vt.* & *vi.*（使）僵持，（使）陷入僵局 /~-march

表礼进行曲 /~-pan〈俚〉*n.* 无表情的脸；无表情 *adj. & adv.* 无表情的（地）；不带感情色彩的（地）~-reckoning **1.** 航位推算 **2.** 推测，猜测/~-water **1.** 死水 **2.**【军】水面对击死角/~-weight *n.* **1.** 重负 **2.** 静载，固定负荷（船）的自重 **3.**（船）（最大）载重量/~-wood *n.* **1.** 枯枝，枯木，没有用处的东西；累赘的人（或物）**3.**（船）龙骨邦木，立材，呆木

deaden ['dedn] *vt.* **1.** 闷抑（声音等）；使（痛苦、冲击力等）缓和 **2.** 使失去光泽 **3.** 使失去感觉，使麻木（痛感等）走味 **5.** 使（墙等）具有隔音性能 — *vi.* **1.** 减弱；缓和 **2.** 失去光泽 ‖ ~ing *n.* 消音材料；消光材料

deadly ['dedli] *adj.* **1.** 致命的；揭露等中要害的；（植物）毒性的 **2.**（脸色等）死一般的 **3.** 不共戴天的；殊死的 **4.**〈口〉（社交活动等）死气沉沉的；令人受不了的 **5.** 非常的，极度的 — in haste 火急地 — *adv.* **1.** 死一般地 **2.** 非常，极（紧、苍白等）‖ deadliness *n.* ‖ ~ sins〈宗〉(使灵魂死亡的)七大罪（骄傲、贪婪、淫邪、忿怒、贪食、嫉妒、懒惰）

deaf [def] *adj.* **1.** 聋的（对…）充耳不闻的（to）‖ ~ness *n.* ‖ ~-aid *n.* 助听器/~-mute *n.* 聋哑者，聋哑人 *adj.* 聋哑的

deafen ['defən] *vt.* **1.** 使聋；使听不见 **2.**【建】使隔音 — *vi.* 变聋；震聋 ‖ ~ing *adj.* 震耳欲聋的；非常吵闹的

deal¹ [di:l]（dealt [delt]）*vt.* **1.** 分配；分给（out）**2.** 给（纸牌）**3.** 给予打击 — *vi.* **1.** 做买卖（with）；经营（in）**2.** 对付，应付；处理；安排（with）**3.** 论述；涉及（with）**4.** 发牌 — *n.* **1.**〈口〉买卖，交易；（尤指秘密的）协议 **2.** 待遇 **3.**

〈美〉特定政策;实行特定政策的时期 4. 发牌;轮到发牌 ‖ *a* ~〈口〉= a great ~/ *a great*(或 *good*) ~ 1. 大量 2.[常接比较级]…得多:She is *a great* ~ better today. 她今天(身体)好多了。‖ ~-**er** *n*. 1. 商人 2. 发牌者 3. 行为者:a plain ~*er* 质朴的人/~**ing** *n*. 1. 分配;分给 2. 对待;处理 3.[常~ings]买卖,交易;交往(*with*)

deal[2] [diːl] *n*. 松木板;冷杉木板;松(或冷杉)木木材

dealt [delt] deal[1] 的过去式和过去分词

dean [diːn] *n*. 1.(大学、学院的)院长;系主任;教务长;学监 2.(基督教的)教长 3.(一个团体中的)老前辈;长者 ‖ ~-**ery** *n*. 教长的职权(或宅邸) ‖ ~'**s list** (定期公布的)成绩优秀学生名单

dear [diə] *adj*. 1.[常用于称呼中]亲爱的:*Dear* Sir 亲爱的先生(用于书信中) 2. 可爱的;被爱的;可贵的 3. 热切的:sb's ~*est* hope 某人心底的愿望 4. 昂贵的;索价高的 — *n*. 亲爱的人,可爱的人:my ~ 亲爱的 — *adv*. 1. 深爱地 2. 高价地 — *int*. [表示伤心、焦急、惊奇等]呵! 哎呀!:*Dear*, ~! (或 *Dear* me! 或 Oh, ~!)呵! 哎呀! ‖ ~**ly** *adv*. 1. 深爱地 2. 高价地 3. 热切地/~**ness** *n*. 1. 亲爱 2. 价贵:‖ **Dear John**〈美口〉(女方给男方的)绝情信;绝交信

dearie [ˈdiəri] *n*. = deary

dearth [dəːθ] *n*. 1. 缺乏,供应不足 2. 饥馑

deary [ˈdiəri] *n*.〈口〉亲爱的,宝贝儿(常含讽刺或幽默的意思)

death [deθ] *n*. 1. 死,死亡 2. 毁灭;灭亡,消灭 3. 死因 4.[D-]死神(西方常画作手持大镰刀、身穿黑袍的骷髅) 5. 屠杀;谋杀 ‖ ~**less** *adj*. 不死的,永恒的/~**like** *adj*. 死了似的/~**ly** *adj*. 1. 致死的 2. 死(一样)的 *adv*. 1. 死了似地 2. 非常地 ‖ ~ **agony** 临死时的痛苦/ˈ~-**bed** *n*. 1. 临终床 2. 临终 *adj*. 临终时做的:a ~*bed* will 临终遗嘱/ˈ~**blow** *n*. 1. 致命的一击 2.(突发的)导致事物失败的因素/~ **chamber** 1. 死者(或濒死者)卧室 2. 死囚行刑室/~ **duty**〈英〉遗产税/~ **house**(监狱的)死囚区/~ **knell** 丧钟(声)/~ **penalty** 死刑/~ **point** 致死温度,死亡温度/~ **rate** 死亡率/~ **rattle** 临终时的喉鸣/ˈ~'**s-head** *n*. 象征死亡的骷髅头/~ **tax**〈美〉= ~ duty/ˈ~**trap** *n*. 1. 危险建筑(或车辆) 2. 危险场所(或境遇)/~ **warrant** 1. 死刑执行令 2.(对幸福、希望等的)致命打击/ˈ~**watch** *n*. 1. 临终的看护;守尸,守灵;死囚看守人 2.【昆】书虱;家书虱

debacle [deiˈbɑːkl]〈法〉*n*. 1.(冰河的)解冻 2. 融冰流;泥石流 3. 溃散;垮台 4. 大灾难;大失败

debar [diˈbɑː] (debarred; debarring) *vt*. 阻拦,阻止;排除;禁止(*from*)

debark [diˈbɑːk] *vt*. 使下船(或飞机、车等);卸(客、货) — *vi*. 下船(或飞机、车等) ‖ ~**ation** [ˌdiːbɑːˈkeiʃən] *n*.

debase [diˈbeis] *vt*. 1. 降低;贬低,使低劣 2. 降低(硬币)的成色;降低(货币)的交换价值 ‖ ~**ment** *n*.

debatable [diˈbeitəbl] *adj*. 1. 可争辩的;可争论的;会产生争论的 2.(边界、土地等)争论中的、未决定的

debate [diˈbeit] *vi*. 1. 争论;辩论;讨论 2. 思考 — *vt*. 1. 争论;辩论;讨论 2. 与…辩论 3. 思考 — *n*. 争论;辩论;讨论 ‖ ~**r** *n*. 辩论家;争论者;讨论者

debauch [diˈbɔːtʃ] *vt*. 使堕落,使道德败坏;诱奸 — *vi*. 放荡,淫逸 — *n*. 1. 放荡,淫逸 2. 狂饮暴食 ‖ ~**ee** [ˌdebɔːˈtʃiː] *n*.

放荡的人,纵欲者/～er *n.*/～ery *n.* 放荡,淫逸;狂饮暴食

debilitate [di'biliteit] *vt.* 使衰弱 ‖ **debilitating** *adj.*/**debili'tation** *n.*

debility [di'biliti] *n.* 衰弱,虚弱

debit ['debit] *n.* 〈会计〉借方;借记,借入;借项;借项总额 — *vt.* 把…记入账户的借方

debonair [ˌdebə'nɛə] *adj.* 1. 殷勤的;有礼的 2. 高兴的,快活的,轻松的

debris ['debri:] *n.* 1.〈破坏物的〉残骸;瓦砾 2.〈地〉岩屑;〈矿〉尾矿,水力采矿流出的砂砾

debt [det] *n.* 1. 债;债务;欠款 2.〈宗〉罪

debtor ['detə] *n.* 债务人;借方;〈宗〉罪人

debunk [di:'bʌŋk] *vt.*〈口〉揭穿;暴露…的虚假性

debut ['deibju:] 〈法〉*n.* 1. 初进社交界 2.〈演员的〉首次演出;首次露面

debutant ['debjutɒŋt] 〈法〉*n.* 1. 初进社交界的人 2. 初次登台的演员

debutante ['debjutɒŋt] 〈法〉*n.* 1. 初进社交界的女子 2. 初次登台的女演员

Dec. *abbr.* December

deca- *comb. form* 表示"十"：deca gon

decade ['dekeid] *n.* 1. 十;十个合成的一组 2. 十年,十年期

decadent ['dekədənt] *adj.* 颓废的 — *n.* 颓废者;颓废派艺术家〈或作家〉‖ **decadence** *n.*

decagon ['dekəgən] *n.*〈数〉十角形,十边形 ‖ **-al** [de'kægən] *adj.*

decahedron [ˌdekə'hi:drən] *n.*〈数〉十面体

decal ['di:kæl] *n.* 1. 贴花法〈尤指对瓷器、玻璃等的装饰法〉 2. 贴花纸;贴花转印的图画〈或图案〉

decalcomania [ˌdi:kælkə'meiniə] *n.* = decal

Decalog(ue) ['dekələg] *n.*〈基督教〉十诫

decamp [di'kæmp] *vi.* 1. 撤营 2. 逃走,逃亡 ‖ ～ment *n.*

decant [di'kænt] *vt.* 1. 轻轻倒出〈液体〉滗;〈化〉滗析,滗去,倾析 2. 把〈水、酒等〉倾注入另一容器 3. 倒出;卸〈货〉

decanter [di'kæntə] *n.* 1.〈化〉滗析器,倾析器 2.〈有玻璃塞的〉细颈盛水瓶

decapitate [di'kæpiteit] *vt.* 1. 将…斩首,杀…的头 2.〈美〉〈因政治理由〉强行免…的职 ‖ **de.capi'tation** *n.*/**decapitator** *n.* 1. 刽子手;断头机 2.〈美〉免职人员

decathlon [di'kæθlən] *n.*〈体〉〈田径〉十项全能运动

decay [di'kei] *vi.* 1. 腐朽,腐烂 2. 衰败,衰落;〈精力等〉衰退 — *vt.* 使腐烂,使腐烂…的 *n.* 1. 腐朽,腐烂;腐烂组织;腐烂部分 2. 衰败,衰落;衰退 3.〈核〉〈放射性物质的〉衰变,衰减;〈人造卫星等〉的能量消减

decease [di'si:s] *n.* 死亡 — *vi.* 亡故

deceased [di'si:st] *adj.* 死去了的,已死的 —〈单复同〉*n.* [the ～] 死者〈指新近死去的〉

decedent [di'si:dənt] *n.*〈美〉〈律〉死者

deceit [di'si:t] *n.* 欺骗,欺诈;虚假;欺骗行为

deceitful [di'si:tful] *adj.* 欺诈的,骗人的;不老实的 ‖ ～ly *adv.*/～ness *n.*

deceive [di'si:v] *vt.* 1. 欺骗,诓骗;使弄错 2. 使失望 — *vi.* 欺诈,行骗 ‖ ～ *r n.* 欺骗者,骗子

decelerate [di:'seləreit] *vt.* 使减速,降低…的速度 — *vi.* 降低速度;减速运转〈或行驶〉‖ **de.cele'ration** *n.* 减速〈度〉/**de-celerator** *n.* 减速器/减速者

December [di'sembə] *n.* 十二月〈略见 Dec.〉

decency ['di:snsi] *n.* **1.** 正派；(言语、举止等的)合乎礼仪；体面 **2.** [decencies]礼仪 **3.** [decencies]过象维持生活所需的东西 **4.** [decencies]行为准则

decent ['di:snt] *adj.* **1.** 正派的；(言语、举止等)合乎礼仪的 **2.** 体面的；像样的；还不错的 **3.** 公平的 **4.** 和气的；不严格的 ‖ ~ly *adv.*

decentralize, decentralise [di:'sentrəlaiz] *vt.* **1.** 分散，下放(权力) **2.** 分散...的权力 **3.** 使(工业等)疏散分布；疏散(人口) ‖ de,centrali'zation *n.*

deception [di'sepʃən] *n.* **1.** 欺骗，诡骗，蒙蔽 **2.** 受骗 **3.** 诡计 **4.** 骗人的东西

deceptive [di'septiv] *adj.* **1.** 骗人的 **2.** 靠不住的，容易使人误解的 ‖ ~ly *adv.* / ~ness *n.*

deci- *comb. form* 表示"十分之一"：*decimetre*

decibel ['desibel] *n.* 〖物〗分贝(测量音强的单位)

decide [di'said] *vt.* **1.** 决定；决意 **2.** 解决；裁决；判决 **3.** 使下决心，使决断 — *vi.* **1.** 决定；下决心；判定(*in favour of, for, against, between*) ‖ ~r *n.* **1.** 决定者；裁决者 **2.** 决胜局

decided [di'saidid] *adj.* **1.** 决定了的；坚决的，果断的 **2.** (区别、优越性等)明显的，明确的 ‖ ~ly *adv.* / ~ness *n.*

deciduous [di'sidjuəs] *adj.* **1.** (在成熟期或一定季节)脱落的：~ teeth 乳齿 **2.** 每年落叶的 **3.** 非永久的，短暂的

decimal ['desiməl] *adj.* 十进位的；小数的；十进币制的 — *n.* 〖数〗小数，十进小数 ‖ ~ point 〖数〗小数点 / ~ system 十进制

decimate ['desimeit] *vt.* (瘟疫等)使大批死亡

decimetre, decimeter ['desimi:tə] *n.* 分米

(略作 dm.，= 1/10 米)

decipher [di'saifə] *vt.* **1.** 破译(密码等) **2.** 解释(难以理解的事物、古代文字等) **3.** 辨认(潦草的字迹) ‖ ~able *adj.* / ~er *n.* / ~ment *n.* **1.** 破译；解释；辨认 **2.** (密码文电复载的)译文

decision [di'siʒən] *n.* **1.** 决定；决心 **2.** 坚决；果断 **3.** 决议；结果 ‖ de'cision maker *n.* 决策者

decisive [di'saisiv] *adj.* **1.** 决定性的 **2.** 明确的；果断的 ‖ ~ly *adv.* / ~ness *n.*

deck [dek] *n.* **1.** 甲板，舱面 **2.** 桥面；层面 **3.** 〈美〉一副纸牌 **4.** 〈美俚〉小包ища品 **5.** (公共汽车的)走带机械(唱机的)转盘支托面 **6.** 〖计〗卡片叠，卡片组 — *vt.* **1.** 给(船)装甲板 **2.** 装饰；打扮(*out*) **3.** 〈美俚〉击倒 ‖ ~ed *adj.* [用以构成复合词]有…层的东西；有一层甲板的船：triple-~er sandwiches 三层夹心面包 ‖ ~ chair 甲板躺椅；折叠帆布躺椅 / ~-hand *n.* 舱面水手，普通水手 / ~ house *n.* 甲板室 / ~ officer 船舶驾驶员(指船长、大副、二副等，以别于轮机员) / 〖军〗甲板军官

declaim [di'kleim] *vi.* **1.** 慷慨陈词；激辩 **2.** 朗诵 **3.** (激烈地)公开抨击(*against*) — *vt.* 朗诵；慷慨激昂地发表(演说等) ‖ declamation [,deklə'meiʃən] *n.* / declamatory [di'klæmətəri] *adj.*

declaration [,deklə'reiʃən] *n.* **1.** 宣布，宣告；宣言，声明 **2.** 〖律〗(原告的)诉状；(证人的)陈述 **3.** (纳税品等的)申报 **4.** (桥牌)的定约叫牌

declarative [di'klærətiv], **declaratory** [di'klærətəri] *adj.* **1.** 宣言的；公告的 **2.** 说明的，陈述的；a *declarative* sentence 〖语〗陈述句 ‖ declaratively *adv.*

declare [di'klεə] *vt.* **1.** 宣布，宣告；宣言 **2.** 表明；显露 **3.** 断言，宣称 **4.** 申报(纳税

品等) 5. (桥牌赛中)叫(牌)定约 — vi. 声明;(公开)表明态度(for, against)

declassify [di:'klæsifai] vt. (美)使解低保密级级;使不再列入保密范围 ‖ **declas-sification** [di:͵klæsifi'keiʃən] n.

declension [di'klenʃən] n. (语)词形变化;(俄语的)变格

declination [͵dekli'neiʃən] n. 1. 倾斜,下倾 2. 婉辞;谢绝;拒绝 3. 磁偏差;磁偏角 4.【天】赤纬 5. 偏离,背离 6. 衰退;衰微;堕落

decline [di'klain] vi. 1. 下倾;下降;下垂 2. 偏斜 3. 衰退,衰落 4. (一天、生命等)将近结束下降;将尽;拒绝 — vt. 1. 使下倾;使下降;使下垂 2. 谢绝;拒绝 3.(语)使变格;使(静词)发生词尾变化 — n. 1. 下倾;下降;下垂 2. 衰退,衰落 3.(一天、生命等的)最后部分;结束 部分 4.《古》消耗病(如肺结核) 5. 斜面,斜坡

declivity [di'kliviti] n. 斜坡;倾斜

decoct [di'kɔkt] vt. 煎(药);熬(汁)

decoction [di'kɔkʃən] n. 1. 煎;熬 2. 煎好的药;熬出的东西

decode ['di:'kəud] vt. 1. 译(电报等);解(码)

decompose [͵di:kəm'pəuz] vt. & vi. 1.(化)分解 2.(使)腐败,(使)腐烂 ‖ **decompo-sition** [͵di:kɔmpə'ziʃən] n.

decorate ['dekəreit] vt. 1. 装饰,装潢;修饰 2. 授勋(章)给 — vi. 装饰;布置 ‖ **decorator** n. (室内)装饰家

decoration [͵dekə'reiʃən] n. 1. 装饰,装潢 2. 饰品 3. 勋章;奖章

decorative ['dekərətiv] adj. 装饰性的;作装饰用的

decorous ['dekərəs] adj. 有礼貌的;正派的;有教养的 ‖ **~ly** adv. / **~ness** n.

decorum [di'kɔrəm] n. 1. 礼貌;正派;体

面;得体 2. [~s]礼节,礼仪

decoy [di'kɔi] n. 1. 诱致野禽的水塘;诱捕处;圈套 2.(诱捕鸟兽用的)诱饵动物;囮子;诱鸟;诱惑物 3. 诱骗者;诱人入圈套的东西 4.(军)假目标 — vt. 诱骗 ‖ **~ duck** 野鸭囮子

decrease [di'kri:s] vi. & vt.(使)减少,(使)减小 — ['di:kri:s] n. 1. 减少,减小 2. 减少额,减小量 ‖ **decreasingly** adv. 渐减地

decree [di'kri:] n. 1. 法令;政令 2.【宗】令;天命,天意 3.【律】判决 — vt. 1. 颁布(法令,政令) 2. 注定 3. 判决 — vi. 发布命令;规定

decrepit [di'krepit] adj. 1. 老朽的,衰老的;老朽的 ‖ **~ly** adv./ **decrepitude** [di'krepitju:d] n.

decrescendo [͵di:kre'ʃendəu](意)(音) adj. & adv. 渐弱的(地)(略作 decresc.) — ([复]decrescendos) n. 渐弱;渐弱的经过句(或乐句、乐节)

decriminalize [di:'kriminəlaiz] vt. 使(原属非法的东西)合法化;使不受刑事诉讼;使(同性态等)非罪行化 ‖ **de͵criminali'zation** n.

decry [di'krai] vt. 1. 诋毁 2. 大声反对 3. 公开对(货币)实行贬值

dedicate ['dedikeit] vt. 1. 奉献;供奉2.(献身)把(时间、力量等)用在(to) 3. 题献(著作)(to) 4. 为(建筑物、展览会等)举行落成式 ‖ **dedicatee** [͵dedikə'ti:] n. 被献呈者/**dedicator** n. 供献者;题献者

dedication [͵dedi'keiʃən] n. 1. 供献;献身 2. 题献;献词

deduce [di'dju:s] vt. 演绎,推论,推断(from) ‖ **deducible** adj. 可推断的

deduct [di'dʌkt] vt. 1. 扣除,减去(from) 2. 演绎

deduction [dɪ'dʌkʃən] n. 1. 扣除；扣除额 2. 演绎；演绎法 3. 推演出来的结论；推论

deductive [dɪ'dʌktɪv] adj. 演绎的，推论的 ‖ ~ly adv.

deed [diːd] n. 1. 行为，行动；(做的)事情，作为 2. 功绩；事迹 3. 【律】契约，证书 — vt. (美)立契转让(私人财产)

deem [diːm] vt. 认为；相信 — vi. (对…)有某种想法(of)：~ highly of 对…给予高度的评价

deep [diːp] adj. 1. 深的 2. 纵深的：be drawn up six ~ 排成六列横队 3. 远离中心的：球场边边处的 4. (声音)深沉的、(颜色)深浓的 5. (呼吸等)深长的，奥妙的：a ~ one 叫人莫测高深的人 7. (感情)深切的，深厚的 8. 全神贯注的，专心(in)的 9. 非常的，极度的：a ~ drinker 酒量极大的人 — adv. 深，迟：read ~ into the night 读书到深夜 — n. 1. 深处，深渊：the ~ (诗)海/in the ~ of night 在深夜 2. 深的 ‖ ~ly adv. / ~-most adj. 最深的 / ~-ness n. / '~-drawn adj. (叹息、呼吸等)深长的 / '~-dyed adj. 深染的不化的 / '~-'felt adj. 深深感到的，深切的 / '~-'freeze n. 1. 深冻冰箱(= ~ freezer)；速冻，深冻冷藏 2. (活动等的)暂时中止 — vt. 深冻冷藏；~ fry 油炸；油汆 / '~-'going adj. 深入的，深刻的 / '~-'laid adj. 秘密策划的处心积虑的 / '~-read ['diːp'red] adj. 熟读的，通晓的 / '~-'rooted adj. 根深(于习惯、偏见等)根深蒂固的 / '~-'seated adj. (感情、原因、疾病等)由来已久的，根深蒂固的 / '~-'space adj. (眼睛等)深陷的 / '~ space 深空，太空

deepen ['diːpən] vt. 加深 — vi. 深化，变得更深：the ~ing crisis 日益严重的危机/The night ~s. 夜深了。

deer [dɪə] ([复]deer(s)) n. 鹿 ‖ ~ lick 盐碱地；盐沼(鹿常去舔盐分) / ~skin n. 鹿皮；鹿皮服装 / ~stalker n. 1. 猎鹿的人 2. (前后翘起的)猎鹿帽

de-escalate [diː'eskəleɪt] vt. & vi. (使)逐步降级 ‖ de,esca'lation n. (战争等的)逐步降级

deface [dɪ'feɪs] vt. 1. 损伤…的外貌；使失面子 2. 磨灭(碑文等) ‖ ~ment n. 1. 毁损 2. 毁坏物

defame [dɪ'feɪm] vt. 破坏…的名誉；诽谤 ‖ **defamation** [,defə'meɪʃən] n. / **defamatory** [dɪ'fæmətərɪ] adj.

default [dɪ'fɔːlt] n. 1. 不履行；违约；拖欠【体】弃权 2. 缺席；【律】未到庭：judgement by ~ 缺席判决 3. 欠缺 — vi. 1. 不履行义务(或债务)；缺席；违约；拖欠 2. 【体】弃权；由于弃权而输掉 — vt. 1. 不履行；拖欠 2. 宣布…未到庭 3. 使(比赛等)弃权；因弃权而输掉(比赛等)；因弃权而取消…的参赛资格 ‖ ~er n. 1. 缺席者；拖欠者；违约者 2. 盗用公款者 3. (英)违反军规者

defeat [dɪ'fiːt] vt. 1. 战胜，击败 2. 使(希望、计划等)落空；破灭 3. 使无效，废除；使败诉 — n. 1. 战胜，击败 2. 战败，失败；挫败 ‖ ~ism n. 失败主义 / ~ist n. & adj. 失败主义者(的)

defect [dɪ'fekt] n. 缺点；欠缺；不足之处 — vi. 逃跑，开小差；背叛 ‖ ~or n. 开小差者；逃兵；背叛者

defection [dɪ'fekʃən] n. 1. 背信；(义务等的)不履行 2. 背叛，变节

defective [dɪ'fektɪv] adj. 有缺点的；有缺陷的；不完全的：a ~ verb【语】不完全变化动词(如 ought 等) — n. 1. 身心有缺陷的人【语】不完全变化词 ‖ ~ly adv. / ~ness n.

defence [dɪ'fens] n. 1. 防御，保卫；防护

防务;防御物;[~s]防御工事 3.【律】辩护,答辩·被告方(包括被告及其辩护律师) 4./(比赛中的)守方

defenceless [di'fenslis] *adj.* 无防御的;无防备的;无助的;没有保护的 ‖ ~**ly** *adv.*/~**ness** *n.*

defend [di'fend] *vt.* 1. 防守,保卫 2. 为…辩护,为…答辩 ‖ ~**er** *n.* 1. 防御者;保护人;辩护人 2.【体】卫冕队(或运动员);防守队员

defendant [di'fendənt] *n.*【律】被告

defense [di'fens]〈美〉*n.* = defence — *vt.* (在比赛中)对(对方队或对方队员)进行防守

defensive [di'fensiv] *adj.* 防御的,防卫的;防守的 ‖ ~**ly** *adv.*

defer¹ [di'fə:] (deferred; deferring) *vt.* & *vi.* 推迟,(使)延期,(使)延迟 ‖ ~**ment** *n.* 延期,迟延;【军】缓役/deferred *adj.* 推迟的,迟延的:a deferred telegram 迟发电报 ‖ deferred payment 延期付款/deferred shares, deferred stock〈英〉延期付息股票

defer² [di'fə:] (deferred; deferring) *vi.* 听从,遵从 (to)

deference ['defərəns] *n.* 1. 听从,依从 2. 敬重,尊敬

deferential [,defə'renʃəl] *adj.* 恭敬的 ‖ ~**ly** *adv.*

defiance [di'faiəns] *n.* 1. 挑战;挑衅 2. 蔑视;违抗

defiant [di'faiənt] *adj.* 挑战的;对抗的 ‖ ~**ly** *adv.*

deficiency [di'fiʃənsi] *n.* 1. 缺乏,缺少,不足 2. 不足之数;不足之处,缺陷

deficient [di'fiʃənt] *adj.* 缺乏的,不足的,欠缺的 (in) ‖ ~**ly** *adv.*

deficit ['defisit] *n.* 亏空(额);赤字

defile¹ [di'fail] *vi.* 以单列(或纵队)行进 — ['di:fail] *n.* 隘路,峡道

defile² [di'fail] *vt.* 1. 污损,弄脏 2. 玷污,亵渎 3. 败坏;使腐败 ‖ ~**ment** *n.* 污损;玷污;脏东西/~**r** *n.* 弄脏者;亵渎者

definable [di'fainəbl] *adj.* 1. 可限定的;有界限的 2. 可下定义的

define [di'fain] *vt.* 1. 解释;给…下定义 2. 立(界限);限定;规定 3. 明确表示

definite ['definit] *adj.* 1. 明确的,确切的 2. 一定的,肯定的 3. 限定的 ‖【植】有定数的:the ~ article【语】定冠词 ‖ ~**ly** *adv.*/~**ness** *n.*

definition [,defi'niʃən] *n.* 1. 定义;解说 2. 定界;限界;限定 3. 明确性,鲜明性 4.【物】清晰度,分解力

deflate [di'fleit] *vt.* 1. 放掉(或抽去)…的气 ~ a tire 放掉轮胎的气 2. 降低…地位(或重要性);使泄气 3. 紧缩(通货) — *vi.* 1. 缩小;瘪掉;泄气 2. 紧缩通货

deflation [di'fleiʃən] *n.* 1. 放气,缩小;弄瘪 2. 通货紧缩 ‖ ~**ary** *adj.* 通货紧缩的

deflect [di'flekt] *vt.* & *vi.* (使)偏斜;(使)转向;(使)挠曲

deflection [di'flekʃən] *n.* = deflexion

deflector [di'flektə] *n.* 1. 致偏器 2. 导向装置 3.【海】指向力测定仪

deflexion [di'flekʃən] *n.* 1. 偏斜;转向;挠曲 2. 偏度;偏差;挠度 3.【军】横偏;提前修正量

defog [di:'fɔg] (defogged; defogging) *vt.* 清去…的雾;除去(挡风玻璃等)上面的雾 ‖ **defogger** *n.* 除雾器

defoliant [di:'fəuliənt] *n.* 脱叶剂(尤指战争中使用的)

defoliate [di:'fəuliet] *vt.* & *vi.* (使)落叶 — *adj.* 叶落的 ‖ **defoli'ation** *n.*

deforest [di:'fɔrist] *vt.* 滥伐…的森林;砍掉 (土地上)的树林 ‖ ~ **ation** [di:fɔris'teiʃən] *n.*

deform [di'fɔːm] *vt.* 1. 损坏…的形状;使变丑 2.【物】使变形 — *vi.* 变形 ‖ ~ **ed** *adj.* 1. 形状损坏的;丑的;破相的;变了形的 2. 畸形的

deformity [di'fɔːmiti] *n.* 1. 畸形;丑恶 (道德、智力等方面的)缺陷 2. 畸形的人(或物);残缺的东西

defraud [di'frɔːd] *vt.* 欺骗,骗取,诈取 ‖ ~ **er** *n.* 诈骗者;骗子

defray [di'frei] *vt.* 支付(经费、费用等)

defrost [di:'frɔst] *vt.* 1. 给…除霜,除去…的冰霜 2. 除去…上面的雾水 3. 使解冻 — *vi.* 解冻 ‖ ~ **er** *n.* 除霜器;除雾器

deft [deft] *adj.* 灵巧的;熟练的 ‖ ~ **ly** *adv.* / ~ **ness** *n.*

defunct [di'fʌŋkt] *adj.* 1. 已死的 2. 不再存在的,已消灭的 — *n.* [常 the ~]死者

defuse, defuze [di:'fjuːz] *vt.* 去掉…的信管;(喻)使失去爆炸性;使变得无害

defy [di'fai] *vt.* 1. 公然反抗;蔑视;对…满不在乎 2. 使不能;使(企图等)落空:Things like these ~ enumeration. 诸如此类,不胜枚举。3. 向…挑战;激;惹 — *n.* (口)挑战

degenerate [di'dʒenəreit] *adj.* 1. 退化的 2. 堕落的;颓废的 3.【医】变性的 — *n.* 1. 堕落者 2. 智力衰退者 3.【生】退化生物 4.【医】性欲倒错者 — [di'dʒenəreit] *vi.* 1. 堕落;蜕化;退化(*into*) 2.【医】变性 ‖ **degeneracy** *n.*

degeneration [diˌdʒenə'reiʃən] *n.* 1. 退化;衰退;堕落 2.【生】退化(作用);【医】变

性 3.【电子】负反馈

degradation [ˌdegrə'deiʃən] *n.* 1. 降级;贬黜 2. 堕落;落魄;(价值、品质等的)低落 3.【生】退化 4.【地】陵削,减削 5.【化】降解,递降分解 6.【物】(能量的)降级;(能谱的)软化

degrade [di'greid] *vt.* 1. 使降级;贬黜 2. 使堕落;使卑微;使(价值、品质等)低落 3.【生】使退化 4.【地】使陵削,使减削 5.【化】使降解 6.【物】使(能量)降级;使软化;使衰变 — *vi.* 1.(地位、身分等)下降 2. 退化;堕落;(价值、品质等)低落 ‖ ~ **d** *adj.* 1. 降了级的 2. 退化了的;堕落的;品质恶劣的 ‖ **degrading** *adj.* 降低人格的;卑劣的

degree [di'griː] *n.* 1. 度;度数 2. 程度 3.【律】(罪行的)轻重程度;(定罪、量刑的)等级:murder in the first ~ 一级谋杀 / murder in the second ~ 二级谋杀 4. 地位;身分;阶层 5. 学位,学衔 6. 亲等:a cousin in the first ~ 嫡堂(或嫡表)兄弟(或姐妹) 7.【数】次(数) 8.【语】(形容词和副词的)级:the positive (comparative, superlative) ~ 原(比较,最高)级 9.【音】音级

dehumanize [di:'hjuːmənaiz] *vt.* 使失人性,使成兽性

dehumidify [ˌdiːhjuː'midifai] *vt.* 除去…的湿气,使干燥 ‖ **dehumidification** [ˌdiːhjuːˌmidifi'keiʃən] *n.*

dehydrate [di:'haidreit] *vt.* 1. 使脱去水分;使(食物)脱水 2. 使枯燥无味 — *vi.* 脱去水份;【化】脱水 ‖ **dehy'dration** *n.*

deice [di:'ais] *vt.* 除去…的冰(如附在飞机机翼的);防止…上结冰 ‖ ~ **r** *n.*【空】去冰器,防冰装置

deify ['di:ifai] *vt.* 把…神化;把…奉若神明;崇拜 ‖ **deification** [ˌdi:ifi'keiʃən] *n.*

deign [dein] *vi.* 降低自己的身分,屈尊

垂顾 — vt. 俯准;赐予

deity ['di:iti] n. 1. 神;[the D-]【宗】上帝 2. 神性

déjà vu [,deiʒɑ:'vju:] 〈法〉【心】似曾见过,似曾相识

deject [di'dʒekt] vt. 使沮丧,使气馁 ∥ ～ed adj. 沮丧的,情绪低落的

dejection [di'dʒekʃən] n. 沮丧,情绪低落

deka- comb. form = deca-

Delaware ['deləwɛə] n. 1. 特拉华[美国州名] 2. 特拉华河[美国东部] 3.[复] Delaware(s)德拉瓦尔人(原居住在特拉华河流域的印第安部落成员)

delay [di'lei] vt., vi. & n. 耽搁,延误;推迟 ∥ ～ er n. 卩 ～ (-ed)-'action adj. 延迟的 ∥【军】定时的,延时的:a ～ed-action bomb 定时炸弹/a camera with a ～ed-action shutter 有自拍快门的照相机

delectable [di'lektəbl] adj. 1. 使人愉快的 2. 美味的 ∥ delectably adv.

delegate ['deligət] n. 1. 代表 2.(美国众议院有发言权而无投票权的州的)准州列席代表(美国 Virginia, West Virginia, Maryland 三州州众院的)州众议院议员 — ['deligeit] vt. 1. 委派…为代表 2. 授(权);把…委托给(to) 3.【律】把(自己的债务人)转给自己的债权人

delegation [,deli'geiʃən] n. 1. (代表的)委派,派遣 2. 代表团

delete [di'li:t] vt. 1. 删除(文字等) 2. 擦掉(字迹等)

deleterious [,deli'tiəriəs] adj. 有害的;造成伤害的 ∥ ～ly adv. / ～ness n.

deletion [di'li:ʃən] n. 1. 删除 2. 删除部分 3.【生】(染色体的)缺失,中间缺失

Delhi ['deli] n. 德里[印度北部城市]

deliberate [di'libərət] adj. 1. 深思熟虑的,蓄意的,故意的 2. 审慎的,不慌不忙的

— [di'libəreit] vi. & vt. 1. 仔细考虑 2. 商议 ∥ ～ly adv. 审慎地;蓄意地,故意地/～ness n. 审慎;蓄意;故意/deliberator n.

deliberation [di,libə'reiʃən] n. 1. 考虑,细想 2. 审议;评议 3. 谨慎,审慎 4. 故意

delicacy ['delikəsi] n. 1. 细软,娇嫩 2. 精美,精致;雅致 3. 娇气;病弱;脆弱 4. 微妙,棘手 5.(色、光的)柔和,微弱 6.(感觉、仪器等的)灵敏;精密 7. 体贴 8. 灵巧 9. 美味,佳肴

delicate ['delikit] adj. 1. 纤软的,娇嫩的,纤细的 2. 精美的,精致的,雅致的 3. 娇气的;奢侈的 4. 病弱的;脆弱的;碰不起的 5. 微妙的,难以处理的,棘手的 6.(色、光)柔和的,淡的,微弱的 7.(感觉、仪器等)灵敏的;精密的 8.(行动等)体贴的,顾及别人情绪的 9. 灵巧的 10. 美味的,鲜美的 ∥ ～ly adv.

delicatessen [,delikə'tesn] n. 1. [总称]现成副食品,熟食 2. 熟食店

delicious [di'liʃəs] adj. 1. 美味的,可口的;芬芳的 2. 妙的,有趣味的 — n. (美)[D-]金香苹果(树),红香苹果(树) ∥ ～ly adv. / ～ness n.

delight [di'lait] vt. 使高兴,使愉快;使快乐 — vi. 1. 感到高兴(或愉快、快乐)(in) 2. 给人愉快 — n. 1. 快乐,高兴 2. 乐事;乐趣

delighted [di'laitid] adj. 高兴的,快乐的 ∥ ～ly adv.

delightful [di'laitful] adj. 1.(事物)令人高兴的,使人快乐的 2.(人)讨人喜欢的,可爱的 ∥ ～ly adv. / ～ness n.

delimit [di'limit] vt. 定…的界;限定

delimitate [di'limiteit] vt. = delimit ∥ de,limi'tation n. 定界,划界;限定

delineate [di'linieit] vt. 1. 画出;勾划出…的轮廓 2. 刻划,描述,描写

de,line'ation n.

delinquent [di'liŋkwənt] *adj.* 1. 失职的；有过失的；犯法的 2. 违法者(特指少年犯罪者)；有过失者 ‖ **delinquency** n.

delirious [di'liriəs] *adj.* 1. 谵妄(性)的，神志昏迷的，说胡话的 2. 极度兴奋的，发狂的

delirium [di'liriəm] *n.* 1. 谵妄，神志昏迷，说胡话 2. 极度兴奋；发狂 ‖ ~ **tremens** ['tri:menz]【医】(酒精中毒引起的)震颤性谵妄

deliver [di'livə] *vt.* 放，释放；解救(*from*) 2. 交付 3. 移交；引渡 4. 投递，传送(信件、邮包、信等) 5. 提供，供给 6. 发表(演讲)；讲(道) 7. 给(产妇)接生，使分娩；帮助产下(婴儿) 8.〖美口〗拉(选票)；兑现 9. 给予(打击)；抛(球)；(棒球赛中)投(球) — *vi.* 1. 送货；投递；传送，运输 2. 分娩 3. 履行；实现(*on*) ‖ ~ **er** *n.* 救助者；递送者

deliverance [di'livərəns] *n.* 1. 解救；释放 2. 投递，传送 3. 正式意见；判决

delivery [di'livəri] *n.* 1. 交付，交货；cash on ~ 〖商〗货到付款(略作 COD) 2. 投递，传送 3. 一次交付(或投递)的货物(或邮件) 4. 转让；授予 5. 分娩 6. 陈述；讲演；演讲(或唱歌)的腔调 7. 投出；投掷；(棒球等的)投球法 8. 释放；解救 ‖ ~ **man** *n.* 送货人

dell [del] *n.* 小山谷

delphinium [del'finiəm] *n.* 1.【植】翠雀，飞燕草 2. 靛蓝色

delta ['deltə] *n.* 1. 希腊语的第四个字母(Δ，δ) 2. 三角形物；(河流的)三角洲 3.【数】(变量的)增量 — *adj.*【化】第四位的，δ位的 ‖ ~ **ray** 〖物〗δ射线 / ~ **wing** 三角形机翼

delude [di'lu:d] *vt.* 欺骗，哄骗

deluge ['delju:dʒ] *n.* 1. 洪水 2. 大雨，暴雨 3. 洪水般的泛滥 — *vt.* 使泛滥，使满溢，淹没

delusion [di'lu:ʒən] *n.* 1. 欺骗，迷惑 2. 幻想；【医】妄想 3. 错误的印象(或想法)

delusive [di'lu:siv] *adj.* 1. 骗人的 2. 虚妄的 ‖ ~ **ly** *adv.* / ~ **ness** n.

delusory [di'lu:səri] *adj.* = delusive

deluxe [də'lʌks, də'luks] *adj. & adv.* 高级的(地)，豪华的(地)

delve [delv] *vi.* 1.〈诗〉挖，掘 — *vi.* 1.〈诗〉挖，掘 2. 探究，钻研(*in, into*)

Dem. *abbr.* 1. Democrat 2. Democratic

demagogic [,demə'gɔgik] *adj.* 煽动的，蛊惑的

demagog(ue) ['deməgɔg] *n.* 煽动者，蛊惑人心的政客 ‖ **demagoguery** [,demə'gɔgəri] *n.* 煽动，蛊惑人心的宣传

demand [di'mɑ:nd] *vt.* 1. 要求；强要；强令 2.(任务等)需要(耐心、特殊知识等) 3. 询问，查问 4. 要求(某人)到场 — *n.* 1. 要求，要求的事物 2. 需求(量) ‖ ~ **ing** *adj.* 要求高的；费力的；需要熟练技术的；苛求的 ‖ ~ **pull** 需求引起的通货膨胀

demarcation [,di:mɑ:'keiʃən] *n.* 分界；界线；界限；划分；区分

demean [di'mi:n] *vt.* 使降低身分；有辱……的人格(或地位)

demeano(u)r [di'mi:nə] *n.* 行为，举止

demented [di'mentid] *adj.* 发狂的 ‖ ~ **ly** *adv.*

dementia [di'menʃiə] *n.*【医】痴呆；精神错乱，疯狂

demerit [di:'merit] *n.* 缺点；过失

demigod ['demigɔd] *n.* 半神半人(神和人所生的后代)；受人崇拜的人

demilitarize [,di:'militəraiz] *vt.* 1. 解除武

…的军事管制 2. 使非军事化；a ~d
zone 非军事区 ‖ ,de,militari'zation n.

demise [di'maiz] n. 1. (引起财产遗赠的)死
亡；(财产的)转让，让与；遗赠 — 2.
转让；遗赠(产业)；传(王位、君权等)；
禅让(王位、君权或爵位) — vi. 转让；遗
赠；死

demitasse ['demitæs] n. 小咖啡杯；一小
杯清咖啡

demo ['deməu]([复]demos) n. 1. 录音样
带；试样唱片 2. 示威游行(或集会) 3.
示威者 4. 示范；示范产品

demob [,di:'mɔb](英)(demobbed; demobbing)
vt. = demobilize — n. demobilization

demobilize [di:'məubilaiz] vt. 使复员；遣散
(部队) ‖ de,mobili'zation n.

democracy [di'mɔkrəsi] n. 1. 民主；民主
主义；民主政治 2. 民主政体；民主国家
(或政府、团体) 3. 民众 4.[D-](美国)
民主党

democrat ['deməkræt] n. 1. 民主主义者；
民主人士 2.[D-](美国)民主党人

democratic [,demə'krætik] adj. 1. 民主
的；民主主义的；民主政体的 2. 民众的
3.[D-](美国)民主党的 ‖ ~ally adv.

democratize [di'mɔkrətaiz] vt. & vi.
(使)民主化 ‖(使)大众化

demographic [,demə'græfik] adj. 人口的；
人口统计的；人口学的 ‖ ~ally adv.

demolish [di'mɔliʃ] vt. 1. 拆毁(建筑物)；
破坏(组织)；推翻(计划、制度) 2.〈口〉
吃完，吃光

demolition [,demə'liʃən] n. 拆毁；破坏；
[军]爆破

demon ['di:mən] n. 1. 精灵；守护神 2. 恶
魔 3. 恶棍 4. 精力(或技艺)过人的人

demoniac [di'məuniæk] adj. 1. 着魔的；
恶魔般的 3. 恶魔般的，凶恶的；疯狂的

— n. 着魔的人

demoniacal [,di:mə'naiəkəl] adj. = demoniac ‖ ~ly adv.

demonstrable ['demənstrəbl] adj. 可论证
的；可表明的 ‖ ,demonstra'bility n./
demonstrably adv.

demonstrate ['demənstreit] vt. 1. 论证，证
实 2.(用实例、实验等)说明；表演 3.
显示，表露 — vi. 示威 ‖ demons'tration n.

demonstrative [di'mɔnstrətiv] adj. 1. 论证
的 2. 感情外露的 3.[语]指示的；a ~
pronoun 指示代词 — n.[语]指示词
(指指示代词、指示形容词) ‖ ~ly
adv./ ~ ness n.

demonstrator ['demənstreitə] n. 1. 证明
者；示范者 2. 示威者 3. 示范产品

demoralize [di'mɔrəlaiz] vt. 1. 使士气低落
2. 使(工作、市场等)陷入混乱 ‖
de,morali'zation n.

demote [di'məut] vt. 使降级

demotion [di'məuʃən] n. 降级

demur [di'mə:](demurred; demurring) vi. 1.
表示异议，反对(to, at) 2. 迟疑，犹豫
3.[律]抗辩 — n. 异议；反对

demure [di'mjuə] adj. 1. 娴静的；拘谨的；
严肃的 2. 假正经的 ‖ ~ly adv./ ~ ness
n.

den [den] n. 1. 兽穴，兽窟 2.(动物的)
兽笼 3. 匪窟；贼窝 4. 简陋污秽的小室
5. 私室；书斋

denature [di:'neitʃə] vt. 使失去自然属
性；使变性 2.[核]使(燃料)变性，使
中毒

denial [di'naiəl] n. 1. 否认 2. 拒绝承认；
拒绝给予(或接受、相信) 3. 脱离关系；
抛弃

denigrate ['denigreit] vt. 1. 使黑 2. 抹黑

贬低,诋毁

denim ['denim] *n.* 1. 粗斜棉布,劳动布 2.[~s]劳动布工作服(或工装裤)

denizen ['denizn] *n.* 居民

Denmark ['denmɑːk] *n.* 丹麦[北欧国家]

denominate [di'nɔmineit] *vt.* 1. 给…命名,称呼…为 2. 表明;指明

denomination [dinɔmi'neiʃən] *n.* 1. 命名;名称 2.(宗教的)教派,宗派 3.(货币的)面额;(度量衡等的)单位: money of small ~s 小面额纸币(或硬币) ‖ ~al *adj.* 1. 教派的,宗派的 2.(有关)名称的

denominator [di'nɔmineitə] *n.* 【数】分母: least common ~ 最小公分母

denote [di'nəut] *vt.* 1. 表示 2.【逻】指称 3.(符号等)代表 4. 意思是 ‖ **denotation** [ˌdiːnəu'teiʃən] *n.*

denounce [di'nauns] *vt.* 1. 谴责,痛斥,斥责 2. 告发 3. 通知废止(条约、协定等) ‖ ~**ment** *n.*/~**r** *n.* 斥责者;告发者

dense [dens] *adj.* 1. 密集的;稠密的 2.(烟、雾等)浓厚的 3. 愚钝的 4.【摄】(负片)厚的;密度大的 ‖ ~**ly** *adv.*/~**ness** *n.*

density ['densiti] *n.* 1. 密集(度);稠密(度) 2.【物】【摄】密度 3. 愚钝

densometer [den'sɔmitə] *n.* 1.(纸张的)透气度测定仪 2. 密度计

dent [dent] *n.* 1. 凹部;凹痕 2.【机】(齿轮的)齿;[纺]布齿 3. 压缩,削减 — *vt.* 1. 使凹陷;使出现凹痕 2. 削弱 — *vi.* 凹进

dental ['dentl] *adj.* 1. 牙齿的;牙科的 2.[语]齿音的 — *n.*[语]齿音(如 d, t, th 等) ‖ ~**ize** *vt.* 使齿音化

dentifrice ['dentifris] *n.* 洁齿剂(指牙粉、牙膏、洗牙剂等)

dentin(e) ['dentiːn] *n.*【解】牙质

dentist ['dentist] *n.* 牙科医生 ‖ ~**ry** *n.* 牙科学;牙医职业

denture ['dentʃə] *n.* 1. 托牙;假牙 2. 一副牙齿

denude [di'njuːd] *vt.* 1. 剥光;使赤裸;滥伐…上的树木(of) 2. 剥夺,夺去(of) 3.【地】使剥蚀,使(岩石)裸露 ‖ **denu'dation** *n.*

denunciate [di'nʌnsieit] *vt.* = denounce

denunciation [diˌnʌnsi'eiʃən] *n.* 1. 斥责,痛斥;谴责 2. 告发 3. 宣告(条约等)无效

Denver ['denvə] *n.* 丹佛[美国科罗拉多州首府]

deny [di'nai] *vt.* 1. 否认 2. 拒绝相信;拒绝(给予或接受) 3. 拒绝(某人)的要求 4. 否认…是自己的;否认与…有关系;抛弃 ‖ ~ *oneself* 节制;戒绝,屏弃/~ *oneself to* 不会见(客人)

deodorant [diː'əudərənt] *adj.* 除臭的 — *n.* 除臭剂,解臭剂

deodorize [diː'əudəraiz] *vt.* 除去…的臭味;防止…的臭味 ‖ **deˌodori'zation** *n.*/**deodorizer** *n.* 除臭剂,解臭剂;防臭剂

deorbit [diː'ɔːbit] *vt.* & *vi.* (使)(航空器等)脱离轨道 — *n.* (航空器等的)脱离轨道

depart [di'pɑːt] *vi.* 1. (人)离开;启程 2. (火车)开出 3. 违反,不合(from) 4. 去世 — *vt.* 〈古〉(诗)离去;(现只用于去世)~ this life 去世 ‖ ~**ed** *adj.* 〈古〉〈诗〉过去的,以往的;去世的: the ~ *ed* 死者

department [di'pɑːtmənt] *n.* 1. (行政、企业等机构的)部;司;局;处;科;部门: the State *Department* (美国)国务院 2. (学校、学术机构的)系;学部;研究室 3. (工厂等的)车间 4. (法国等的)县;

政区 5. 知识范围;活动范围 ‖ ~al adj. ‖ ~ store 百货商店

departure [di'pɑːtʃə] n. 1. 离开;启程;出发 2. 违背,背离 (from) 3. 〈古〉去世,死 4. 〔海〕横距,东西距;始航点 5. 偏差,偏移 6.〔新行动方针、思想等的〕开始

depend [di'pend] vi. 1. 靠,依靠,依赖 (on, upon) 2. 相信,信赖 (on, upon) 3. 依…而定 (on, upon) 4. 悬而未决 5. 〈古〉悬垂 (from)

dependable [di'pendəbl] adj. 可靠的 ‖ de.penda'bility n. / dependably adv.

dependant [di'pendənt] n. 1. 受赡养者 2. 〈古〉扈从,侍从

dependence [di'pendəns] n. 1. 依靠,依赖;相依,信任,信赖 3. 从属,隶属

dependency [di'pendənsi] n. 1. 从属;依赖 2. 从属物 3. 属地;属国

dependent [di'pendənt] adj. 1. 依靠的,依赖的 (on, upon) 2. 由…决定的,随…而定的 (on, upon) 3. 从属的,隶属的;a ~ clause 〔语〕从句 4. 悬垂的 — n. = dependant

depict [di'pikt] vt. 1. 描绘;画出 2. 描写,描述 ‖ ~er, ~or n. / ~ion n. / ~ive adj.

deplete [di'pliːt] vt. 1. (部分或全部地)倒空;使空虚;耗尽…的精力(或资源等) 2.〔医〕排除(器官、血管内)的液体(或血液),使缺失液体

depletion [di'pliːʃn] n. 1. 弄空;竭尽,耗尽 2.〔医〕(液体、血液等的)排除,缺失;(由缺液而引起的)空乏

deplorable [di'plɔːrəbl] adj. 1. 可叹的,使人很遗憾的 2. 糟糕的 ‖ deplorably adv.

deplore [di'plɔː] vt. 哀叹,悲叹;对…表示遗憾 ‖ deploringly adv.

deploy [di'plɔi] vt. & vi. (使)展开;调度;部署 ‖ ~ment n.

depollute [ˌdiːpə'luːt] vt. 清除…的污染

depopulate [diː'pɔpjuleit] vt. (战争等)使人口减少 ‖ de.popu'lation n.

deport [di'pɔːt] vt. 1. [~ oneself]举止(或表现)得体;使(自己)举止(或表现)带上某种特点 2. 驱逐…出国,放逐 ‖ ~ation [ˌdiːpɔː'teiʃən] n. 驱逐出境;放逐/ ~ee [ˌdiːpɔː'tiː] n. 被驱逐出国者;被判处放逐者

deportment [di'pɔːtmənt] n. 行为,举止,风度

depose [di'pəuz] vt. 1. 废黜;免…的职,罢…的官 2.〔律〕宣誓证明 3. 置放 — vi. 宣誓作证 ‖ deposition [ˌdepə'ziʃən] n.

deposit [di'pɔzit] vt. 1. 存放,寄存 2. 储蓄;付(保证金) 3. 产(卵);下(蛋) 4. 使沉淀;使淤积 — vi. 沉淀;淤积 — n. 1. 存放;寄存物 2. 存款;保证金 3. 沉淀;沉积物;〔矿〕矿床 4. 保藏处,仓库 ‖ ~or n. 存放者;储户 2. 沉积器

depot ['depəu, 'diːpəu] n. 1. 仓库 2.〔军〕兵站;补给站;供应站 3.〔美〕车站;航空站

deprave [di'preiv] vt. 使堕落,使腐败 ‖ ~d adj. 堕落的,腐化的

depravity [di'præviti] n. 1. 堕落,腐败 2. 腐化堕落行为

deprecate ['deprikeit] vt. 对…表示不赞成,反对 ‖ deprecatingly adv./ ˌdepre'cation n./ deprecatory ['deprikətəri] adj.

depreciate [di'priːʃieit] vt. 1. 降低…的价值;降低…的价格;使(货币)贬值 2. 蔑视,贬低…vi. 跌价,贬值 ‖ depreciatingly adv. 蔑视地,贬低地

depreciation [diˌpriːʃi'eiʃən] n. 1. 减值;跌

价;贬值 2. 折旧 3. 蔑视;贬低

depredate ['deprideit] vt. & vi. 劫掠;掠夺,劫掠;蹂躏,破坏 ‖ **depre'dation** n.

depress [di'pres] vt. 1. 降低;压低;按下(键等);抑制 2. 使沮丧,使消沉 3. 使萧条,使不景气;使衰落 4. 使减值;使跌价

depression [di'preʃən] n. 1. 降低;压低;凹地,洼地;凹陷 2. 沮丧,消沉 3. 不景气,萧条(期) 5. 【气】低(气)压;(气压表水银柱下降所显示的)气压降低 6.【医】抑郁症;衰退 7.【天】【测】俯角

depressive [di'presiv] adj. 1. 令人沮丧的,令人抑郁的;压抑的;下压的 2.【心】郁郁的 — n. 抑郁症患者

deprivation [,depri'veiʃən] n. 1. 剥夺;丧失 2. 免职(尤指圣职) 3. 匮乏

deprive [di'praiv] vt. 1. 夺去,剥夺;使丧失(of) 2. 免去…的职务(尤指圣职)(of) ‖ **~d** adj. 被剥夺生活必需品的;丧失了受良好教育权利的;贫困的

dept. abbr. department

depth [depθ] n. 1. 深;深度;厚度;(色泽)浓度 2.[~s]深处,深渊 3. 深奥;深刻;深沉 ‖ **~ bomb**, **~ charge** 深水炸弹

deputation [,depju'teiʃən] n. 1. 代表的委派 2. 代表团

deputize ['depjutaiz] vt. 委派…为代表,授权…为代表 vi. 担任代表(for)

deputy ['depjuti] n. 1. 代表;代理人(法国等)下院议员 3.[用作定语]副;代理;a ~ chairman 代理主席(或议长);副主席(或议长)

derail [di'reil] vt. [常用被动语态]使(火车等)出轨;使离开原定进程 — vi. 出轨 ‖ **~ ment** n.

derange [di'reindʒ] vt. 1. 搅乱;扰乱(秩序等);打乱(计划等) 2. 使精神错乱,使

发狂 ‖ **~ ment** n. 1. 搅乱,混乱 2. 精神错乱

Derby ['da:bi, 'dɑ:bi] n. 1. (英国 Epsom Downs 地方每年举行的)德比大赛马 2. 马赛;比赛;大赛 3.[d-]〈美〉常礼帽,圆顶高帽

deregulate [di:'regjuleit] vt. 撤消对…的管制规定,解除对…的控制 ‖ **de,regu'lation** n.

derelict ['derilikt] adj. 1. 被抛弃的,被遗弃的;无主的(尤指海上弃船) 2.〈美〉玩忽职守的,不负责的 — n. 1. 被遗弃物;无主物(尤指海上弃船) 2. 被社会抛弃的人

dereliction [,deri'likʃən] n. 1. 抛弃,遗弃,放弃 2. 玩忽职守

deride [di'raid] vt. 嘲笑,嘲弄 ‖ **~r** n. 嘲笑者,嘲弄者 / **deridingly** adv.

derision [di'riʒən] n. 1. 嘲笑,嘲弄 2. 嘲笑目标,笑柄

derisive [di'raisiv] adj. 1. 嘲笑的,嘲弄的 2. 可笑的 ‖ **~ly** adv. / **~ ness** n.

derivation [,deri'veiʃən] n. 1. 引出;诱导 2. 衍生;衍生物 3. 起源,由来 4.【语】派生;派生关系;词源 5.【数】求导;导数

derivative [di'rivətiv] adj. 1. 被引申出的;被推论出的;衍生的 2. 派生的 — n. 1.【化】引伸物,派生物 2.【语】派生词 3.【数】导数,微商 4.【化】衍生物 ‖ **~ly** adv.

derive [di'raiv] vt. 1. 取得,得到 2. 派生出,导出;衍生出 3. 引申出,推知 — vi. 1. 起源,由来(from) 2. 衍生;导出(from)

derma ['də:mə] n. 【解】真皮;皮肤

dermis ['də:mis] n. = derma

derogate ['derəgeit] vi. 1. 减损;毁损(from) 2. 偏离;违背;变坏,堕落

(*from*) — *vt.* 贬低；诽谤；损害 ‖ ,dero'gation *n.*

derogatory [di'rogətəri] *adj.* 1. 毁损的，贬抑的，减损的 2. [语]贬义的

derrick ['derik] *n.* 1. [机]转臂起重机；(船上起重用的)吊杆式起货设备 2. [矿]钻塔。(油井的)井架

descend [di'send] *vi.* 1. 下来，下降 2. 下倾，下斜 3. 传下，遗传；起源(于)(*from*) 4. 袭击；突然访问(*on, upon*) 5. 屈尊，降低身分(或人格) 6. 转而谈到(具体情况)(*to*) 7. [天]下降 — *vt.* 下(山、楼梯等)

descendant, descendent [di'sendənt] *n.* 1. 子孙，后裔 2. (某一原型的)派生物 — *adj.* 1. (从一个祖先或来源)传下的；派生的 2. 下降的

descent [di'sent] *n.* 1. 下降，降下 2. 斜坡；坡道 3. 血统；遗传 4. 袭击(*on, upon*) 5. 屈尊，降格

describe [di'skraib] *vt.* 1. 描写，描述，叙述 2. 形容，把…说成(*as*) 3. 画出(图形) ‖ describable *adj.* / ~r *n.*

description [di'skripʃən] *n.* 1. 描写，描述，叙述；形容 2. 说明 3. 种类；性质 4. 作图；绘图

descriptive [di'skriptiv] *adj.* 描述的，描写的；说明的 ‖ ~ly *adv.*

descry [di'skrai] *vt.* 1. 望见，看到，辨别出 2. 发现

desecrate ['desikreit] *vt.* 把(神物)供俗用；亵渎；污辱 ‖ ,dese'cration *n.*

desegregate [di:'segrigeit] *vt. & vi.* 〈美〉(使)取消种族隔离 ‖ de,segre'gation *n.*

desert[1] ['dezət] *n.* 1. 沙漠 2. 不毛之地；荒凉的境地；枯燥无味的事物；荒凉时代 — *adj.* 1. 沙漠的 2. 荒芜的，不毛的，无人居住的

desert[2] [di'zət] *vt.* 1. 丢弃，舍弃，抛弃，遗弃 2. 擅离(职守等) — *vi.* 逃跑掉，开小差 ‖ ~ed *adj.* 1. 被舍弃的，被抛弃的，无人(居住)的 2. 被抛弃的，被遗弃的/ ~er *n.* 背离者；叛离者；逃兵

desert[3] [di'zət] *n.* 1. 功(或过) 2. [常 ~s]应得的奖赏(或惩罚)

desertion [di'zəʃən] *n.* 1. 舍弃；抛弃，遗弃；背弃 2. 逃跑，开小差；擅离职守

deserve [di'zəv] *vt.* 应受，应得，值得 — *vi.* 应受报答，值得奖赏；应受惩罚 ‖ ~ well (ill) of 应受…的奖赏(惩罚)；有功(罪)于

deserved [di'zəvd] *adj.* 应得的，该受的；理所当然的 ‖ ~ly [di'zəvidli] *adv.* / ~ness [di'zəvidnis] *n.*

deserving [di'zəviŋ] *adj.* 值得的；该得的(*of*) ‖ ~ly *adv.*

desiccate ['desikeit] *vt.* 1. 使干燥；使脱水；干藏(食物) 2. 使…的感情(或智力等)枯竭 — *vi.* 变干燥；变枯竭 ‖ ,desic'cation *n.*

design [di'zain] *vt.* 1. 策划，谋划，设计；构思；绘制 3. [常用被动语态为]指定，指定…— *vi.* 1. 计划，谋划 2. 设计；构思；制图 — *n.* 1. 计划；企图；图谋 2. 设计；图样；图案 3. (小说等的)构思 ‖ ~er *n.* 设计者；设计师/ ~ing *adj.* 有计划的，预谋的，诡诈的

designate ['dezigneit] *vt.* 1. 指明；指定；标出 2. 指定，选派(*to, as*)(*for*) 3. 把…叫做 — ['dezignət] *adj.* [用于被修饰的名词后]指派好而尚未上任的；选出而尚未上任的

designation [,dezig'neiʃən] *n.* 1. 指明；标示 2. 指定，选派，任命 3. 名称，称号；牌号

designedly [di'zainidli] *adv.* 有意地，故意地，蓄意地

desirable [di'zaiərəbl] *adj.* 1. 称心的,合意的;吸引人的 2. 值得想望的;值得弄到手的 3. 合乎需要的 ‖ de,sira'bility *n.*/～ness *n.*/desirably *adv.*

desire [di'zaiə] *n.* 1. 愿望,心愿;欲望;情欲 2. 要求,请求 3. 想望的东西;想望的对象 — *vt.* 1. 想望,期望,希望;I ～ to see you. 我很想见见你。/leave much to be ～d 还有许多有待改进之处 2. 要求,请求

desirous [di'zaiərəs] *adj.* [用作表语]想望的,想要的,渴望的

desist [di'zist] *vi.* 停止;停止;断念(*from*)

desk [desk] *n.* 1. 书桌,写字台,办公桌 2. 【宗】读经台 3. 文书(或办事员等)的工作;(美)报馆)编辑部 4. 服务台;问讯台;出纳台;工作台 5. 乐谱架 6. (政府等机构中专门负责某方面事务的)部;司;组;室 ‖ ～ man *n.* 办公室工作人员;报馆编辑人员/'～top *adj.* & *n.* 台式的(计算机)

desolate ['desələt] *n.* 1. 荒芜的,荒凉的,无人居住的 2. 孤寂的,凄凉的 — ['desəleit] *vt.* 1. 使荒芜,使荒凉;破坏 2. 使凄寂,使凄凉 ‖ ～ly *adv.*/～ness *n.*

desolation [,desə'leiʃən] *n.* 1. 荒芜,荒凉,渺无人烟 2. 孤寂,凄凉

despair [dis'pɛə] *n.* 1. 绝望 2. 令人绝望的人(或事物) 3. (使竞争者)望尘莫及的人(或事物) — *vi.* 绝望,丧失信心(*of*)

despairing [di'spɛəriŋ] *adj.* 绝望的 ‖ ～ly *adv.*

despatch [di'spætʃ] *vt.* & *n.* = dispatch

desperado [,despə'rɑːdəu] ([复] desperado(e)s) *n.* 亡命之徒;暴徒(尤指美国西部的土匪)

desperate ['despərət] *adj.* 1. 令人绝望

危急的 2. (因绝望而)不顾一切的,拼死的,铤而走险的,孤注一掷的 3. 极度渴望的(*for*) 4. 极端的;(气候)险恶的:a ～ fool 大傻瓜/a ～ night 狂风暴雨之夜 ‖ ～ly *adv.*/～ness *n.*

desperation [,despə'reiʃən] *n.* 绝望;拼命

despicable ['despikəbl] *adj.* 可鄙的,卑鄙的 ‖ ～ness *n.*/despicably *adv.*

despise [di'spaiz] *vt.* 鄙视;藐视;看不起 ‖ despisingly *adv.*

despite [di'spait] *prep.* 不管,尽管,任凭:(in)～ of 不管,尽管,任凭

despoil [di'spɔil] *vt.* 抢劫,掠夺;剥夺(*of*)

despond [di'spɔnd] *vi.* 沮丧;泄气;失望

despondency [di'spɔndənsi] *n.* 沮丧,泄气,失望

despondent [di'spɔndənt] *adj.* 沮丧的,泄气的,失望的 ‖ ～ly *adv.*

despot ['despɔt] *n.* 专制君主,暴君

despotic [de'spɔtik] *adj.* 专制暴君的;专横的,暴虐的 ‖ ～ally *adv.*

dessert [di'zəːt] *n.* (作为正餐最后一道菜的)甜食(或水果等),甜点心

destination [,desti'neiʃən] *n.* 1. 目的地,终点 2. 目标,目的

destine ['destin] *vt.* 1. [常用被动语态]命定;注定(*to*) 2. 预定,指定(去某地,作某种用途或从事某种工作)(*for*, *to*)

destiny ['destini] *n.* 命运,命运 2. [Destinies]【希神】命运三女神

destitute ['destitjuːt] *adj.* 1. 没有的,缺乏的(*of*) 2. 贫困的,赤贫的 ‖ desti'tution *n.*

destroy [di'strɔi] *vt.* 1. 破坏,摧毁,毁坏 2. 打破(希望,计划),使失败 3. 消灭,除灭,歼灭

destroyer [di'strɔiə] *n.* 1. 破坏者;消灭者;起破坏作用的东西 2. 驱逐舰

destructible [di'strʌktibl] *adj.* 可破坏的；可消灭的 ‖ de,structi'bility *n.*

destruction [di'strʌkʃən] *n.* 1. 破坏；毁灭，消灭 2. 毁灭的原因

destructive [di'strʌktiv] *adj.* 破坏(性)的；毁灭(性)的；危害的(*of*) ‖ ~ly *adv.*/~ness *n.* ‖ ~ distillation 【化】毁馏，分解蒸馏

desultory ['dezəltəri] *adj.* 1. 杂乱的；散漫的，随意的，无条理的 2. 不连贯的 3. 胡乱的 ‖ desultorily *adv.*/desultoriness *n.*

detach [di'tætʃ] *vt.* 1. 使分开，使分离，把…拆开 2. 派遣(军队、军舰)‖ ~able *adj.* 可分开的，可拆开的

detached [di'tætʃt] *adj.* 1. 分离的，孤立的；独立的 2. 超然的，公正的 3. 分遣的 ‖ ~ly *adv.*/~ness *n.*

detachment [di'tætʃmənt] *n.* 1. 分开，分离 2. 分遣；分遣队，支队；特遣舰队 3. 独立，超然，不偏不倚

detail ['di:teil, di'teil] *n.* 1. 细目，细节，详情；详细：explain in ~ 详细解释 3. = ~ drawing 4. 枝节；项事 5. (任务的)分配，委派；(人员的)选派；选派的人(或小组、小队等) 6. 【摄】细部；清晰度 — *vt.* 1. 详述，细说 2. 派遣；选派 ‖ ~ed *adj.* 详细的，明细的 ‖ ~ drawing 详图，细部图 ‖ ~ man(美)(药厂的)新药推销员

detain [di'tein] *vt.* 1. 拘留，扣押 2. 留住 ‖ ~ee [,di:tei'ni:] *n.* (因政治等原因)被拘留者

detect [di'tekt] *vt.* 1. 察觉，发觉，发现 2. 侦查；探测，检测 3.【无】对…检波 ‖ ~able *adj.* 可察觉的；易发现的/detection *n.*

detective [di'tektiv] *n.* 侦探 ‖ ~ story 侦探小说，推理小说

detector [di'tektə] *n.* 1. 察觉者，发觉者

2. 探测器；检验器 3.【无】检波器 4. (锅炉的)水量计

détente [dei'tɑ:t] 〈法〉*n.* (国际关系等的)缓和

detention [di'tenʃən] *n.* 1. 拘留，扣押；禁闭 2. 阻留，滞留 3. (处罚学生的)课后留校

deter [di'tə:] (deterred; deterring) *vt.* 使不敢，威慑，吓住；拦住，阻止(*from*)

detergent [di'tə:dʒənt] *adj.* 使洁净的，去垢的，净化的 — *n.* 洗涤剂，去垢剂

deteriorate [di'tiəriəreit] *vt.* 1. 使恶化 2. 败坏；使变坏 3. 使退化 — *vi.* 1. 恶化 2. 变质，变坏，堕落 3. 退化 ‖ de,terio'ration *n.*

determinant [di'tə:minənt] *adj.* 决定性的；限定性的 — *n.* 1. 决定因素 2.【数】行列式 3.【生】定子；决定簇；因子

determinate [di'tə:minit] *adj.* 1. 限定的，确定的；明确的 2. 决定的 3. 坚定的，坚决的

determination [di,tə:mi'neiʃən] *n.* 1. 决定；确定；测定；限定 2. 决心 3.【律】(诉讼等的)终止

determinative [di'tə:minativ] *adj.* 有决定(或限定)作用的 — *n.* 1. 有决定(或限定)作用的东西 2.【语】限定词 ‖ ~ly *adv.*/~ness *n.*

determine [di'tə:min] *vt.* 1. 决定；确定；测定；限定 2. 使下决心；使决定 3.【律】使终止 — *vi.* 1. 决定 2. 决心(*on*) 3.【律】终止 ‖ determinable *adj.*

determined [di'tə:mind] *adj.* 决意的；坚决的 ‖ ~ly *adv.*/~ness *n.*

determiner [di'tə:minə] *n.* 1. 决定者；起决定作用的人(或事物) 2.【语】限定词，限定成分 3.【生】定子，因子

deterrence [di'terəns] *n.* 1. 制止，威慑 2. 制止物，威慑物；制止因素，威慑因素

deterrent [di'terənt] *adj.* 制止的，威慑的 — *n.* 制止物，威慑物；制止因素，威慑因素

detest [di'test] *vt.* 嫌恶，憎恶；痛恨

detestable [di'testəbl] *adj.* 可恶的，可憎的 ‖ **~ness** *n.* / **detestably** *adv.*

detestation [ˌdiːtes'teiʃən] *n.* 1. 嫌恶，憎恶 2. 极可憎的东西，极讨厌的东西

dethrone [di'θrəun] *vt.* 1. 废黜 2. 罢免 ‖ **~ment** *n.*

detonate ['detəneit] *vi.* 爆炸，起爆 — *vt.* 引爆，起爆；引起，激起 ‖ **deto'nation** *n.* 引爆，起爆，爆炸；爆炸的巨响；(内燃机的)爆燃，爆鸣

detonator ['detəneitə] *n.* 1. 雷管，起爆管；起爆剂；炸药 2.(浓雾时铁道上作信号用的)响墩

detour ['diːtuə] *n.* 弯路；迂回路；迂回 — *vt. & vi.* (使)绕道

detract [di'trækt] *vt.* 1. 毁损；贬低；减损 2. 转移，分散(注意力) — *vi.* 毁损；贬低；减损(*from*) ‖ **~ion** *n.* 毁损；贬低；减损(*or* **~or** *n.* 毁损者；贬低者

detrain [di:'trein] *vi.* 下火车 — *vt.* 使下火车 ‖ **~ment** *n.*

detriment ['detrimənt] *n.* 1. 损害，伤害 2. 损害物；造成损害的根源

detrimental [ˌdetri'mentl] *adj.* 有害的，不利的(*to*) ‖ **~ly** *adv.*

Detroit [di'trɔit] *n.* 底特律[美国密歇根州东南部港市]

devaluate [di:'væljueit] *vt. & vi* = devalue

devalue [di:'væljuː] *vt.* 降低……的价值；使(货币)贬值 — *vi.* 降低价值；(货币)贬值 ‖ **devalu'ation** *n.*

devastate ['devəsteit] *vt.* 使荒芜；破坏；劫掠[蹂躏] ‖ **devastating** *adj.* 1.(风暴、批评等)破坏性极大的 2. 使人倾倒的；

(笑话等)极有趣的 / **devas'tation** *n.*

develop [di'veləp] *vt.* 1.(逐步)展开(情节、音乐主题、方程式等) 2. 发展；发扬；发挥 3. 开发(资源、矿山等)；开辟利用(土地等) 4. 使成长(或生长)；使发达 5. 使(颜色等)显；[摄](使)显影(显) 6.(逐步)显现出；产生(某种症状、倾向等) — *vi.* 1. 发展；显现 2. 产生 3.(逐步)显现出来 ‖ **~er** *n.* 1. 开发者 2.[摄]显影剂；[化]显色剂 ‖ **~ed dye**【化】显色染料 / **~ing country** 发展中国家

development [di'veləpmənt] *n.* 1. 展开；[音]展开 2. 发展；进展 3. 开发，开辟 4. 生长；成长；进化；发达 5.【摄】显影 ‖ **~ area** (鼓励投资以减轻严重失业现象的)开发地区

deviate ['diːvieit] *vi.* 背离，偏离(*from*) — ['diːviət] *n.* 不正常者(尤指性变态者)；离经叛道者 ‖ **deviant** ['diːviənt] *n.* 不正常的；离经叛道的 — *n.* 不正常者；离经叛道者 / **deviator** *n.* 1. 偏差器 2.(政党内的)路线或偏差分子

deviation [ˌdiːvi'eiʃən] *n.* 1. 背离，偏离；偏向；偏差 2.【数】离差 3.【海】绕航；罗盘偏差

device [di'vais] *n.* 1. 方法，手段 2. 谋略，策略；诡计 3.(文学、艺术等的)手法，技巧 4. 精心设计(或设计奇异)的东西器械；装置；设备 5.(装饰性)图案；纹章图案

devil ['devl] *n.* 1. 魔鬼，恶魔 2.[the D-]魔王 3. 恶棍 4. 精力旺盛的人；无所顾忌的人 5. 可怜的家伙(常与poor连用) 6. 恶鬼；猛兽 7.(贪欲等邪恶的)化身 8.(受律师、作家等雇用的)助手 9.(破布等的)扯碎机，切碎机 10. 辣味菜肴 11. 难事；难以操纵(或控制)的东西：This door is a ~ to open. 这门真难开。

12. 【气】尘埃,小旋风 13. [the ～]〈口〉究竟(同 who, how, why, where, what 等连用):Who the ～ are you? 你到底是谁 — (devil(l)ed; devil(l)ing) vt. 1. 折磨;嘲弄;激怒 2. 用辛辣调味品烤(肉等) 3.(用扯碎机)扯碎(破布) — vi. 做律师(或作家等)的助手 ‖ '～-may-'care adj. 1. 不顾一切的,无法无天的 2. 怡然自得的 3. 轻率的,漫不经心的

devilish ['devəliʃ] adj. 1. 魔鬼似的;凶暴的;穷凶极恶的 2. 精力旺盛的 3. 可恶的;该咒骂的 4. 异常的,非常的;过分的 — adv.〈口〉非常,极;过分地 ‖ ～ly adv. / ～ness n.

devilment ['devəlmənt] n. 1. 魔鬼似的行径 2. 捣蛋;恶作剧;开玩笑 3. 怪事;怪现象

devilry ['devəlri] n. 1. 魔鬼似的行径 2. 邪恶;残暴;狂放 3. 恶作剧;开玩笑 4. 魔法,妖术 5. 恶魔研究 6. 魔界

deviltry ['devəltri] n. = devilry

devious ['di:viəs] adj. 1. 远离大路的,僻远的,偏僻的 2. 迂回的,曲折的 3.(风等)不定向移动的;误入歧途的;错误的 5. 不光明正大的(指心)奸滑的 ‖ ～ly adv. / ～ness n.

devise [di'vaiz] vt. 1. 设计;发明;筹划 2.〈律〉遗赠(不动产) 3.〈古〉图谋 ‖ devisee [divai'zi:] n.〈律〉受遗赠人 / ～r n. 设计者;发明者;策划者 / devisor n. 〈律〉遗赠人

devitalize [di:'vaitəlaiz] vt. 1. 使失去生命;使失去生命力 2. 使伤元气;使衰弱 ‖ de,vitali'zation n.

devoid [di'vɔid] adj. [常作表语] 缺乏的;没有的(of)

devolve [di'vɔlv] vi. 1.(工作等)被移交,被转移(on, upon) 2.(不动产等)转让,被继承(on, upon) 3. 依...而定

(on, upon) — vt. 移交,转移(on, upon, to);下放(权力等)

devote [di'vəut] vt. 把...奉献(给);把...专用(于)(to);～ oneself to 献身于;致力于

devoted [di'vəutid] adj. 1. 献身的,专心于...的;专用于...的(to) 2. 虔诚的;热心的;忠诚的;忠实的 3. 慈爱的;恩爱的 ‖ ～ly adv. / ～ness n.

devotee [,devə'ti:] n. 1. 信徒(尤指宗教信徒) 2. 热心之士;爱好者

devotion [di'vəuʃən] n. 1. 献身;忠诚,忠实;热心;专心 2. 热爱 3.【宗】虔诚;[～s]祈祷 ‖ ～al adj.

devour [di'vauə] vt. 1. 狼吞虎咽地吃 2. 吞没;毁灭 3. 挥霍;耗尽(财产等) 4. 贪看;贪听;盯着看 5. 吞没,吸住 ‖ ～ingly adv. 吞灭似地;贪婪地

devout [di'vaut] adj. 1. 虔诚的,虔敬的 2. 诚恳的 ‖ ～ly adv. / ～ness n.

dew [dju:] n. 1. 露,露水 2. 露水一样的东西(如泪水,汗等) — vi. 结露水 ‖ ～berry n.【植】悬钩子;露莓(指悬钩子属植物的果实)/ ～ claw n.【动】(狗等脚上与下地面接触的无用)残留趾/ '～-drop n. 露珠/ '～-fall n. 结露(黄昏)起露的时候/ '～-lap n.(牛等动物颈部下垂的)垂皮;垂肉/ ～ point 【气】露点

dewy ['dju:i] adj. 1. 带露水的;露水似的;露的 2.(诗)纯洁的,清新的;～ sleep 使人头脑清醒的安睡/ '～-eyed n. 天真无邪的,易信的;易动感情的;浪漫的

dexterity [deks'teriti] n. 1. 灵巧,敏捷(指身、手) 2. 聪明 3. 惯用右手

dexterous ['dekstərəs] adj. 1.(身、手)灵巧的,敏捷的 2. 聪明的,伶俐的;机警的 3. 惯用右手的 ‖ ～ly adv. / ～ness n.

dextrose ['dekstrəus] n.【生化】右旋糖,

葡萄糖

Dhaka ['dækə] *n.* 达卡[孟加拉国首都]

diabetes [ˌdaiə'bi:ti:z] *n.* 【医】1. 糖尿病 2. 多尿症 ‖ **diabetic** [ˌdaiə'betik] *adj.* (患)糖尿病的;治疗糖尿病的;(食物)专供糖尿病患者吃的 *n.* 糖尿病患者

diabolic(al) [ˌdaiə'bɔlik(əl)] *adj.* 恶魔似的,恶魔般的,凶暴的 ‖ **diabolically** *adv.*

diacritical [ˌdaiə'kritikəl] *adj.* 区分的;【语】表示变音的:a ～ mark 变音符,附加符号

diadem ['daiədem] *n.* 1. 王冠,冕(尤指东方君主的头带) 2. 王冠状物,花冠 3. 王权;王的尊严 4. 无上的光荣;最高荣誉

diagnose ['daiəgnəuz] *vt.* 1. 诊断(疾病);对…作下诊断结论 2. 断定…的原因(或性质),断定 ～ *vi.* 诊断;判断

diagnosis [ˌdaiəg'nəusis] *n.* ([复] diagnoses [ˌdaiəg'nəusi:z]) 1. 【医】诊断(法) 2. 【生】特征简介 3. 调查分析;判断

diagonal [dai'ægənəl] *adj.* 1. 对角线的;斜的;斜纹的 — *n.* 1.【数】对角线 2. 斜线符号"/" 3. 斜行,斜列 4. 斜行物;斜纹织物 ‖ ～**ly** *adv.*

diagram ['daiəgræm] *n.* 图形,示意图;图解;图表;简图 — (diagram(m)ed; diagram(m)ing) *vt.* 用图解释法表示

diagrammatic [ˌdaiəgrə'mætik] *adj.* 图解的;图表的;图式的 ‖ **diagrammatically** *adv.*

dial ['daiəl] *n.* 1. 日晷 2.(手)表面;钟面;罗盘面板(仪表等的)标度盘,刻度盘 3. 转盘;(电话机的)拨号盘 4.(收音机的)调谐度盘;(机器的)调节控制器 5.【矿】矿用罗盘 6.【俚】脸蛋 — (dial(l)ed; dial(l)ing) *vt.* & *vi.* 1. 用日晷测量;用标度盘测量 2. 拨(电话号码);打电话(给)

dialect ['daiəlekt] *n.* 1. 地方话,方言,土语 2.【语】(属同一语系的)同源语 ‖ ～**al** ['daiəlektəl] *adj.*

dialectics [ˌdaiə'lektiks] [复] *n.* [用作单] 辩证法:materialist ～ 唯物辩证法

dialog(ue) ['daiəlɔg] *n.* 1. 对话体(作品) 2. 对话;交换意见 3. (小说、戏剧中的)对白

diameter [dai'æmitə] *n.* 1. 直径,对径;(内或外)径 2.(透镜的)放大倍数,放大率

diametric [ˌdaiə'metrik(əl)] *adj.* 1. 直径的 2. 正好相反的

diamond ['daiəmənd] *n.* 1. 金刚石;金刚钻;钻石 2. 人造金刚石;像金刚石的物质 3. 金刚石(玻璃)割刀 4. 菱形;(纸牌中)方块;一张方块牌 5.(垒球、棒球赛的)内场;棒球场 ‖ ～ **jubilee** 六十周年(有时指七十五周年)纪念／～ **wedding** 钻石婚(结婚六十年,有时指七十五年纪念)

diaper ['daiəpə] *n.* 1. 菱形花纹织物 2. 尿布 3. 菱形图案

diaphragm ['daiəfræm] *n.* 1.【解】隔(膜)膜 2.【动】隔膜,隔板 3.【植】(茎内的)隔膜 4.【物】光阑;光圈 5.(电话机等的)膜片,振动膜 ‖ ～ **atic** [ˌdaiəfræg'mætik] *adj.*

diarrh(o)ea [ˌdaiə'riə] *n.* 【医】腹泻

diary ['daiəri] *n.* 日记;日记簿 ‖ **diarist** *n.*

diathermy ['daiəθə:mi] *n.* 【医】透热疗法

diatom ['daiətəm] *n.* 【植】硅藻

diatribe ['daiətraib] *n.* 抨击,谴责;讽刺;冗长的议论

dice [dais] *n.* 1. [单复同] 骰子 2. 掷骰子;掷骰子游戏;掷骰赌博 3.([复] dice 或 dices)(骰子形)小方块 — *vt.* 1. 将(菜等)切成小方块,将…切成丁 2. 用骰子形花纹装饰 3. 掷骰子输掉

(away)；因掷骰子使(自己)处于某种境地(如负债)④ — vi. 掷骰子 ‖ ~y adj.(英口)冒险的；投机的

dichotomy [dai'kɔtəmi] n. 一分成二，对分；[逻]二分法

dicker ['dikə] vi. & vi. 〈口〉讨价还价(for, with) — n. 1. 小生意 2. 讨价还价

dicta ['diktə] dictum 的复数

dictate [dik'teit] vt. & vi. 1. 口述；口授 2. 命令；支配 — ['dikteit] n. [~s] (理智、良心等的)命令；支配(of)

dictation [dik'teiʃən] n. 1. 口述；听写 2. 命令；支配

dictator [dik'teitə] n. 1. 独裁者；专政者 2. 口述者；口授者

dictatorial [,diktə'tɔ:riəl] adj. 1. 独裁的；专政的 2. 专横傲慢的 ‖ ~ly adv.

dictatorship [dik'teitəʃip] n. 专政

diction ['dikʃən] n. 1. 措词入〔说话或歌唱中的〕发音；发音法

dictionary ['dikʃənəri] n. 词典；字典

dictum ['diktəm] ([复] dicta ['diktə] 或 ~tums) n. 1. 名言；格言 2. [律]法官意见

did [did] do¹ 的过去式

didactic [di'dæktik, dai'dæktik] adj. 1. 教训的；教导的 2. 说教的 ‖ **didactically** adv.

didn't ['didnt] = did not

didst [didst] 〈古〉〈诗〉(用在 thou 后的) did

die¹ [dai] (died/dying) vi. 1. 死 2. (草木)枯萎，凋谢 3. 消失；灭亡；停止，结束 4.(风、声音等)变弱，逐渐消失；熄灭(away, down, out) 5. 渴得要命不受影响(to) — to shame 恬不知耻 6.[常用进行时态]渴望，切望(for) — vt. [后接同源名词]死 — a glorious death 光荣死去 ‖ '~-aıway adj. 消沉的，颓丧的；

憔悴的 n. (声音等的)逐渐消逝／'~-hard n. 顽固分子，死硬分子 adj. 顽固的，死硬的

die² [dai]([复] dice [dais]) n. 骰子状物

die³ [dai] n. 1. 模具 2. 钢型；压模；冲模；阴模；下料模；拉丝模；铸模 3. 螺丝钢板 4.[建]方形柱脚，方形墩身 ‖ ~ casting 压铸(件)／'~ sinker n. 制模工；开模机

diesel ['di:zəl] n. 1. 内燃机，柴油机 2. 内燃机车；柴油船；柴油车 ‖ '~-e'lectric adj. 内燃电力传动的／~ engine 内燃机，柴油机／~ oil，~ fuel 柴油

diet¹ ['daiət] n. 饮食；食物；(适合某种疾病的)特种饮食 — vt. 给…规定饮食 — vi. 进规定的饮食 ‖ **dietetic** [,daiə'tetik] adj.

diet² ['daiət] n. (丹麦、日本等的)议会，国会

dietary ['daiətəri] n. 规定饮食；(特殊设计的)食谱；规定饮食量 — adj. 饮食的；规定饮食的

dietitian, dietician [,daiə'tiʃən] n. 饮食学家；膳食学家

differ ['difə] vi. 1. 不同，相异(from) 2. 意见不同(或不一致)(from, with)

difference ['difərəns] n. 1. 差异，差别 2. 分歧；不和；争论 3. 差，差额；差分

different ['difərənt] adj. 1.(和…)不同的(from, than, to) 2. 各别的；各种的 3.[常作表语]不平常的，与众不同的 ‖ ~ly adv.

differential [,difə'renʃəl] adj. 1. 差别的；鉴别的；级差的：~ diagnosis [医] 鉴别诊断 2.[数]微分的：~ calculus [数]微分(学) 3.[机][物]差动的；差示的：~ gear 差动齿轮／a ~ thermometer 差示温

度计 — n. 1.【数】微分 2.【机】差动齿轮;分流器箱 3.【铁路的】差异运价 4. 差别,差异 5.(同一行业中熟练工和非熟练工的)工资级差 ‖ ~ly adv.

differentiate [ˌdifəˈrenʃieit] vt. 1. 区分,区别(from) 2. 使(生物,器官等)变异(或分化) 3.【数】求…的微分 — vi. 1. 加以区分,加以区别(between) 2.(生物,器官等)变异,分化 ‖ differenti'ation n.

difficult [ˈdifikəlt] adj. 1. 难的,困难的,艰难的 2.(人)难弄的

difficulty [ˈdifikəlti] n. 1. 困难,艰难 2. 难点,难事;难题[常 difficulties]困境(尤指经济拮据)

diffidence [ˈdifidəns] n. 1. 缺乏自信 2. 羞怯,胆怯 3. 退缩 4. 谦虚谨慎

diffident [ˈdifidənt] adj. 1. 缺乏自信的 2. 羞怯的;胆怯的 3. 畏首畏尾的 4. 谦虚谨慎的 ‖ ~ly adv.

diffraction [diˈfrækʃən] n.【物】衍射

diffuse [diˈfju:z] vt. 1. 使(热,气体等)散开,使扩散;使渗出 2. 传播(知识等)散布(谣言等);普及 3.【物】使(光线)漫射 — vi. 1. 散开,扩散;渗出 2. 传播;散布 3.【物】漫射 — adj. 1.(热,气体等)弥漫的,散开的,扩散的 2.(文章等)冗长的,噜苏的 3.(光线)漫射的 ‖ ~ly adv. /~ness n. /diffusion n.

dig [dig] (dug[dʌg]或〈古〉digged; digging) vt. 1. 掘(土);挖(洞,沟等) 2. 掘取(甘薯等);采掘(矿物等) 3. 发掘,找到 4. 把(指尖等)戳进,插入;戳(into) 5.〈俚〉理解 6.〈俚〉喜欢 7.〈俚〉看;看到 — vi. 1. 挖洞;发掘 2.〈口〉苦干;苦学(at) 3.〈口〉居住,住宿 — n. 1. 挖掘 2.〈口〉考古发掘;发掘的遗迹;发掘地点 3. 刺,戳 4.〈美〉刻苦钻研的学生;苦读 5.〈美国〉走私货藏匿处 6. [~s]〈英口〉寄宿舍;住所

digest [diˈdʒest, daiˈdʒest] vt. 1. 消化(食物) 2.〈喻〉消化,吸收;领会,领悟,融会贯通(书中要点) 3. 把…分类;做…的摘要 4. 忍受(侮辱等) 5.【化】蒸煮,煮解;浸提 — vi.(食物)消化 — [ˈdaidʒest] n. 1. 摘要;概要;简编;文摘;汇编 2. 法规汇集 ‖ ~ible adj. 1. 可消化的;易消化的 2. 可做摘要的 / di.gesti'bility n.

digestion [diˈdʒestʃən, daiˈdʒestʃən] n. 1. 消化(作用);消化力 2. 领悟 3.【化】蒸煮(作用),煮解;浸提 4.【生化】消化(污水处理中利用微生物将有机物气化、液化等)

digestive [diˈdʒestiv, daiˈdʒestiv] adj. 消化的;有消化力的;助消化的 — n. 消化剂;消化饼干

digger [ˈdigə] n. 1. 挖掘者;发掘物;挖掘器;挖掘机(挖掘机上的)铲斗 2. 矿工(尤指金矿矿工) 3. [D-] 迪格尔人(以掘食树根等为生的北美印第安人一部落) 4.〈口〉澳大利亚人;新西兰人 5.〈美俚〉扒手 6.〈美俚〉以色相诱骗男人钱财的女人 7.〈俚〉(美)向票贩子提供票源的人 = wasp) 8.〈俚〉向票贩子提供票源的人

digit [ˈdidʒit] n. 1. 手指;足趾 2. 一指宽的长度单位(相当于 3/4 英寸) 3.(0 到 9 中的任何一个)数字

digital [ˈdidʒitəl] adj. 1. 手指的;足趾的 2. 数字的;数字显示的 ‖ ~ clock 数字(显示式)时钟/~ computer 数字计算机/~ disk(或 disc)(音质经数字计算机处理而提高了的)数字唱片 /~ watch 数字(显示式电子)表

dignified [ˈdignifaid] adj. 有尊严的;高贵的

dignify [ˈdignifai] vt. 1. 使有尊严;使高贵 2.(给予好听的)名称)使显得尊贵(或高贵):~ cowardice with the name of prudence 以谨慎的名义美化怯懦

dignitary ['dignitəri] *n*. 显贵,要人

dignity ['digniti] *n*. 1. 尊贵,高贵 2. (举止、态度的)庄严,尊严,端庄 3. 高位,显职

digress [dai'gres] *vi*. 离题,扯开去 (*from*)

digression [dai'greʃən] *n*. 离题;离题话

dike [daik] *n*. 1. 堤,堤防,坝 2. 沟,渠,排水道 3. 【地】岩墙,岩脉 — *vt*. 1. 筑堤防护;用堤围绕 2. 开沟泄(水) — *vi*. 筑堤(或坝等)

dilapidated [di'læpideitid] *adj*. (房屋等)倾坍的;破旧的,破烂的

dilapidation [di,læpi'deiʃən] *n*. 1. 坍毁;倾圮 2. 破烂

dilate [dai'leit] *vt*. 使膨胀;使扩大 — *vi*. 1. 膨胀;扩大 2. 详述,铺叙(*upon*)

dilation [dai'leiʃən] *n*. 1. 膨胀,扩大 2. 【医】扩张(术)

dilatory ['dilətəri] *adj*. 拖拉的 ‖ **dilatorily** *adv*./ **dilatoriness** *n*.

dilemma [di'lemə] *n*. 1. 【逻】二难推理,两刀论法 2. 窘境,困境,进退两难

dilettante [,dili'tænti] ([复] dilettantes 或 dilettanti [,dili'tænti]) *n*. 1. 艺术爱好者 2.《艺术或科学的》半瓶子,浅薄的涉猎者 — *adj*. 半瓶子的;浅薄的

diligence ['dilidʒəns] *n*. 勤勉,勤奋,用功,努力

diligent ['dilidʒənt] *adj*. 勤勉的,勤奋的,用功的,孜孜不倦的 ‖ **~ly** *adv*.

dill [dil] *n*. 1.【植】莳萝,小茴香;莳萝(指种子) ;莳萝叶 2. 加小茴香的泡菜,加莳萝的腌黄瓜(= pickle)

dillydally ['dilidæli] *vi*. (口)磨蹭,吊儿郎当地消磨时间

dilute [dai'ljut] *vt*. 1. 冲淡;稀释 2. 削弱(效果等) — *adj*. 稀释的;淡的

dilution [dai'ljuʃən] *n*. 1. 冲淡;稀释 2. 冲淡物;稀释物 3.【化】稀溶液

dim [dim] (dimmer, dimmest) *adj*. 1. 不明亮的,昏暗的;暗淡的 2. (轮廓、声音、记忆等)模糊的,朦胧的,不清楚的 3. 无光泽的 4. (口)迟钝的 5. 悲观的;怀疑的:take a ~ view of 对…抱悲观看法 — (dimmed;diming) *vt*. & *vi*. (使)变暗淡;(使)变模糊;(使)失去光泽 ‖ **~ly** *adv*./ **~ness** *n*. ‖ '**~-out** *n*. (防止敌方空袭等的)半灯火管制/'**~wit** *n*. (口)笨蛋,傻子/'**~'witted** *adj*. 笨的,傻的

dime [daim] *n*. (美国和加拿大的)十分铸币;数目极小的钱

dimension [di'menʃən] *n*. 尺寸;尺度;线度 2.【数】维,维数度,因次:of one 一维的;线性的/of two ~s 二维的,二平面的/of three ~s(长、宽、高)三维的;立体的 3.【物】量纲 4.[~s]面积;容积;大小 ‖ **~al** *adj*.

dimethoate [dai'meθəeit] *n*. 乐果(有机磷杀虫、杀螨剂)

diminish [di'miniʃ] *vt*. 1. 减少,减小,缩减 2. 削弱…的权势;降低…的声誉 3.【音】减(音程等) — *vi*. 变少,缩小 ‖ **diminution** [,dimi'njuʃən] *n*.

diminuendo [di,minju'endəu] (意)【音】 *adj*. & *adv*. 渐弱的(地)— ([复] diminuendo(e)s) *n*. 渐弱;渐弱的经过句(或乐句、乐节)

diminutive [di'minjutiv] *adj*. 1. 小的,小型的 2.【语】指小的;昵称的,爱称的;蔑称的 — *n*. 1.【语】指小词(如 booklet);指小词缀 2. 身材极小的人;微型物 3. 昵称,爱称 ‖ **~ly** *adv*.

dimity ['dimiti] *n*. 麻纱,条格麻纱;提花布

dimmer ['dimə] *n*. 1. (汽车、舞台用电灯的)减光器,调光器 2. [~s](汽车的)停

卑鄙的 4. 下流的、黄色的 5.(气候)恶劣的;暴风雨的;雾深的 6.(颜色)灰褐的;不清的 7.(原子弹、氢弹)产生大量放射性尘埃的 8. 吸毒的 — *vt.* 1. 弄脏;玷污 2. 贬低 — *vi.* 变脏 ‖ **dirtily** *adv.*/**dirtiness** *n.*

dis- *pref.* 1. 表示"否定";"相反":*disappear, dishonest, disease* 2. 表示"分离";"除去";"剥夺":*disperse, disbar*

disability [ˌdisə'biliti] *n.* 1. 无能为力;伤残.【律】无资格

disable [dis'eibl] *vt.* 1. 使无能为力;使伤残;使失去战斗力 2.【律】使无资格 ‖ ～**d** *adj.* 伤残的;失去战斗力的/～**ment** *n.*

disabuse [ˌdisə'bju:z] *vt.* 去除…的谬误;使省悟

disadvantage [ˌdisəd'vɑ:ntidʒ] *n.* 不利;不利条件;不利地位 ‖ ～**d** *adj.* 处于不利地位的;下层社会的;贫困的

disadvantageous [ˌdisædvɑ:n'teidʒəs] *adj.* 不利的(*to*) ‖ ～**ly** *adv.*

disaffect [ˌdisə'fekt] *vt.* 使不满;使不忠;使疏远 ‖ ～**ed** *adj.* 不满的;不忠的;疏远的

disagree [ˌdisə'gri:] *vi.* 1. 意见不同;不同意;争执(*with*) 2.(报道等)不一致;不符(*with*) 3.(食物、天气等)不适合;有害(*with*) ‖ ～**ment** *n.*

disagreeable [ˌdisə'griːəbl] *adj.* 1. 不合意的;不爽快的;讨厌的 2. 难相处的;脾气坏的 ‖ ～**ness** *n.*/**disagreeably** *adv.*

disappear [ˌdisə'piə] *vi.* 1. 不见,失踪 2. 消失,消散 ‖ ～**ance** *n.*

disappoint [ˌdisə'pɔint] *vt.* 使失望;使(计划等)受挫折;使(希望等)落空 ‖ ～**edly** *adv.* 失望地

disappointing [ˌdisə'pɔintiŋ] *adj.* 使人失望的;令人扫兴的;使人不痛快的 ‖ ～**ly** *adv.*

disappointment [ˌdisə'pɔintmənt] *n.* 1. 失望;失意;扫兴;沮丧 2. 使失望的人;令人扫兴的事情

disapprove [ˌdisə'pru:v] *vt.* 不赞成,不许可;不同意 — *vi.* 不赞同;不喜欢(*of*) ‖ **disapproval** *n.*/**disapprovingly** *adv.*

disarm [dis'ɑ:m] *vt.* 1. 缴…的械;解除(城市,船只等)的武装;弄去(动物、昆虫等)的防卫器官 2. 消除(怒气、敌意、怀疑等);消除…的怒气(或敌意、怀疑等) — *vi.* 1. 放下武器 2. 裁军

disarmament [dis'ɑ:məmənt] *n.* 1. 放下武器;解除武装 2. 裁军

disarming [dis'ɑ:miŋ] *adj.* 使人消除怒气(或敌意、怀疑等)的 ‖ ～**ly** *adv.*

disarrange [ˌdisə'reindʒ] *vt.* 使混乱,扰乱 ‖ ～**ment** *n.* 混乱;紊乱

disarray [ˌdisə'rei] *vt.* 1. 弄乱,扰乱 2. 脱去…的衣服 — *n.* 1. 混乱,杂乱 2.(衣冠)不整

disaster [di'zɑ:stə] *n.* 灾难,祸患;天灾

disastrous [di'zɑ:strəs] *adj.* 灾难性的;造成惨重损失的 ‖ ～**ly** *adv.*

disavow [ˌdisə'vau] *vt.* 不承认;抵赖;拒绝对…承担责任 ‖ ～**al** *n.*/～**er** *n.*

disband [dis'bænd] *vt.* & *vi.* 解散;遣散 ‖ ～**ment** *n.*

disbar [dis'bɑ:] (disbarred; disbarring) *vt.* 【律】把…驱逐出律师界;取消…的律师资格

disbelief [ˌdisbi'li:f] *n.* 不信,怀疑

disbelieve [ˌdisbi'li:v] *vt.* 不相信,怀疑 — *vi.* 不信,怀疑(*in*) ‖ ～**r** *n.* 不信(宗教)的人

disburse [dis'bə:s] *vt.* 支付,支出 ‖ ～**ment** *n.* 支付;支出;付出款;支出额

disc [disk] *n.* 1. 圆盘;圆板;盘状物;圆面 2.【解】盘,板,片;【植】花盘 3. 唱片;录

像圆盘;电视唱片 **4.**【农】圆盘耙土;圆盘农具一 vt. **1.** 用圆盘耙耙(地) **2.** 把…灌成唱片 ‖ ～ **harrow** 圆盘耙;／**jockey**〈美俚〉流行音乐唱片节目播音员

discard [dis'kɑːd] vt. **1.** (纸牌戏中)垫补(牌);打出(无用的牌) **2.** 丢弃,抛弃;遗弃 **3.** 解雇 — vi. (纸牌戏中)去牌;垫牌 — ['diskɑːd] n. **1.** 丢弃的牌;垫出的牌 **2.** 被丢弃的物(或人)

discern [di'səːn] vt. **1.** 看出,辨出 **2.** 觉察;了解 **3.** 辨别,识别 — vi. 辨明,分清 ‖ ～**ing** adj. 有眼力(或洞察力)的/ ～**ment** n.

discernible [di'səːnibl] adj. 看得清的;辨别得出的 ‖ **discernibly** adv.

discharge [dis'tʃɑːdʒ] vt. **1.** 卸(货物等);卸下(船)上的货物 **2.** 射出;开(炮等) **3.** 排出(液体、气体等);【电】放(电) **4.** 允许…离开;释放;解雇(from) **5.** 免除;卸脱(from) **6.** 履行;清偿 **7.**【律】撤销(法院命令) **8.**【纺】拔(染);为(织物)拔条 — vi. **1.** (船)卸货 **2.** 排出液体(或气体等) **3.** (江河)注注 **3.** (枪炮等)发射 **4.** (染料、墨水等)渗开一 n. **1.** 卸货 **2.** 发射 **3.** 流出;排出,放出;【电】放电 **4.** 流出物;排泄物;流量 **5.** 解除;释放;退役;解雇 **6.** 退伍(或解职,释放)证明书 **7.** 履行;清偿 **8.**【纺】拔染;拔条剂 ‖ ～ **r** n. **1.** 卸货者;卸货工具 **2.** 发射者;发射装置;排出装置 **3.** 履行者 **4.**【电】放电器;火花隙

disciple [di'saipl] n. 门徒,信徒,追随者;【宗】耶稣的信徒;耶稣的使徒

disciplinarian [ˌdisipli'nεəriən] n. 执行纪律者;严格纪律信奉者

disciplinary ['disiplinəri] adj. **1.** 纪律的;惩戒性的 **2.** 训练的

discipline ['disiplin] n. **1.** 纪律;风纪 **2.**

训练 **3.** 惩戒;惩罚 **4.**【宗】教规,戒律;苦行修炼 **5.** 学科 — vt. **1.** 训练;训导 **2.** 使有纪律 **3.** 惩戒

disclaim [dis'kleim] vt. & vi. **1.** 放弃;不认领;不索取 **2.** 否认;不承认 ‖ ～ **er** n. 放弃声明(书);不承认声明(书)

disclose [dis'kləuz] vt. **1.** 揭开;揭发 **2.** 透露;泄露(秘密等)

disclosure [dis'kləuʒə] n. **1.** 揭发;泄露 **2.** 被揭发(或泄露)出来的事物

disco ['diskəu]([复] discos) n. **1.** 迪斯科舞会;迪斯科舞厅 **2.** 迪斯科舞曲 — vi. 跳迪斯科舞

discolo(u)r [dis'kʌlə] vt. & vi. (使)变色;(使)退色;玷污 ‖ ～**ation** [disˌkʌlə'reiʃən] n.

discomfit [dis'kʌmfit] vt. **1.**〈古〉(在战场上)打败;击溃;打乱…的计划;挫败 **3.** 使困惑;使狼狈 ‖ ～**ure** n. **1.** 失败,败北;挫败 **2.** 困窘,狼狈

discomfort [dis'kʌmfət] n. **1.** 不舒适;不自在,不安 **2.** 使人不舒适(或不自在)的事物;不便 — vt. 使不舒适;使不自在

disconcert [ˌdiskən'səːt] vt. **1.** 使仓皇失措;使困窘,使为难 **2.** 挫败,破坏(计划等)‖ ～**ingly** adv. / ～**ment** n.

disconnect [ˌdiskə'nekt] vt. 拆开;分离;断开

disconnected [ˌdiskə'nektid] adj. **1.** 分离的;断开的;不连接的 **2.** (讲话、写作等)不连贯的,支离破碎的;无条理的 ‖ ～**ness** n.

disconnexion, disconnection [ˌdiskə'nekʃən] n. 分离;分开断开

disconsolate [dis'kɔnsələt] adj. **1.** 忧郁的;郁郁不乐的 **2.** 使人不快的 ‖ ～**ly** adv.

discontent [ˌdiskən'tent] n. **1.** 不满意;不满的人 — adj. 不满的(with) — vt.

使不满‖ ~ ment n.

discontented [ˌdiskən'tentid] *adj.* 不满的‖ ~ ly *adv.* / ~ ness n.

discontinue [ˌdiskən'tinjuː] *vt.* 1. 中止,中断,停止 2.【律】撤回(诉讼);中止(诉讼程序) — *vi.* 中止,中断,停止;停刊‖ **discontinuance** n.

discord ['diskɔːd] n. 1. 不和;倾轧 2. 不一致;不调和 3.【音】不协和;不协和和弦 4. 嘈杂声

discordance [dis'kɔːdəns] n. 1. 不一致,不协调;不和,冲突 2.(声音的)不和谐 3.【地】(地层的)不整合

discordant [dis'kɔːdənt] *adj.* 1. 不一致的;不(调)和的 2.【地】不整合的‖ ~ ly *adv.*

discothèque ['diskətek] n. 迪斯科舞厅;流动迪斯科(指放送舞曲的音响设备)

discount [n. 'diskaunt] n. 1. 折扣 2.【商】贴现;贴现利息;贴现率 — ['diskaunt, dis'kaunt] *vt.* 1. 打去(若干)而将折扣卖掉 2.【商】(持票人或受票人)把(票据)贴现 3. 不全信;对…持怀疑态度 4. 看轻,把…不当一回事 — *vi.* 贴现‖ ~ broker【商】贴现票据经纪人/ ~ rate【商】贴现率

discountenance [dis'kauntinəns] *vt.* 1. 不赞同,不支持;使泄气 2. 使羞愧,使难堪

discourage [dis'kʌridʒ] *vt.* 1. 使灰心,使失去信心,使沮丧 2. 阻拦,留难;(试图)劝阻‖ ~ ment n.

discouraging [dis'kʌridʒiŋ] *adj.* 令人泄气的,使人沮丧的;阻止的‖ ~ ly *adv.*

discourse [dis'kɔːs] n. 1. 演说;讲道 2. 谈话,交谈 3. 论文‖【语】语段 — *vi.* 1. 交谈;谈话 2. 讲述;著述 (on, upon)

discourteous [dis'kɔːtiəs] *adj.* 不礼貌的,失礼的‖ ~ ly *adv.* / ~ ness n.

discourtesy [dis'kɔːtisi] n. 1. 无礼,失礼 2. 粗鲁行为

discover [dis'kʌvə] *vt.* 发现;发觉;找到;把…公诸于世,使被公众知晓‖ ~ able *adj.*

discoverer [dis'kʌvərə] n. 发现者

discovery [dis'kʌvəri] n. 1. 发现 2. 被发现的事物

discredit [dis'kredit] n. 1. 丧失信用 2. 败坏名誉的事;丢脸的事;丢脸 3. 不信,怀疑:throw(或 cast)~ on 使人对…产生怀疑 — *vt.* 1. 不信,怀疑;使不可置信 2. 使丧失信誉;使丢脸

discreditable [dis'kreditəbl] *adj.* 有损信誉的;丢脸的‖ **discreditably** *adv.*

discreet [dis'kriːt] *adj.* 谨慎的,慎重的‖ ~ ly *adv.*

discrepancy [dis'krepənsi] n. 差异;不一致;不符合‖ **discrepant** *adj.*

discrete [dis'kriːt] *adj.* 分离的,各别的;不相关联的;离散的

discretion [dis'kreʃən] n. 1. 辨别(力);判断(力):the age of ~ 解事责任年龄(英、美法律规定为十四岁) 2. 谨慎 3. 斟酌作出决定的自由;处理权‖ at ~ 随意,任意 / at the ~ of 随…的意见;由…斟酌决定

discretionary [dis'kreʃənəri] *adj.* 1. 自由决定的;便宜行事的 2. 可随意使用的‖ ~ account(证券或商品交易中的)全权客户/ ~ income(个人总收入中除去基本生活开支后)可自由支配的收入

discriminate [dis'krimineit] *vt.* 区别;辨别 — *vi.* 1. 加以区别;加以辨别(between) 2. 有差别地对待:~ against 歧视…/ ~ in favour of 特别优待…

discriminating [dis'krimineitiŋ] *adj.* 1. 形成区别的;识别性的(标记等) 2. 有辨别力的,有识别力的 3. 区别对待的,有

差别的: ~ duties (或 tariffs) 差别关税 ‖ ~ly adv.

discrimination [dis,krimi'neiʃən] n. 1. 区别;辨别 2. 辨别力,识别力 3. 不公平待遇;差别待遇,歧视

discriminatory [dis'kriminətəri] adj. 差别对待的

discursive [dis'kəːsiv] adj. 1. 离题的;东拉西扯的 2. 逐题进行的 3. 推理的,论证的

discus ['diskəs] n. 【体】铁饼: the ~ throw 掷铁饼比赛 2.【动】盘;【植】花盘

discuss [dis'kʌs] vt. 1. 讨论,商议 2. 论述;评述 ‖ ~ion n.

disdain [dis'dein] vt. 1. 轻蔑,蔑视;鄙弃 2. 不屑 (to do 或 doing) — n. 轻蔑,蔑视;鄙弃

disdainful [dis'deinful] adj. 1. 轻蔑的,蔑视的,傲慢的 (of) ‖ ~ly adv.

disease [di'ziz] n. 1. 病,疾病;【植】病害 2.(精神、道德、社会制度等的)不健全状态;弊病 — vt. 使有病;使不正常;使不健全

diseased [di'zizd] adj. 有病的,害病的;不健全的;【植】有病害的

disembark [,disim'baːk] vt. & vi. (使)登上岸,(使)登陆;使下车(或飞机);(从船或飞机等上)卸下(货) ‖ ~ation [dis,embaː'keiʃən] n.

disembody [,disim'bɔdi] vt. (使〈灵魂等〉)脱离躯体;使脱离实体;使脱离现实

disenchant [,disin'tʃaːnt] vt. 使从着魔状态解脱出来,使清醒,使不再着迷;使不抱幻想 ‖ ~ment n.

disengage [,disin'geidʒ] vt. & vi. (使)脱离;(使)解脱 ‖ ~ment n.

disentangle [,disin'tæŋgl] vt. 1. 解(结)解开…的结 2. 分清(真理和谬误等)

(from) — vi. (绳、头发等)被解开 ‖ ~ment n.

disfavo(u)r [dis'feivə] n. 1. 不赞成,不喜欢;冷待,疏远 2. 受冷待,失宠 — vt. 不赞成,不喜欢;冷待;疏远

disfigure [dis'figə] vt. 毁损…的外形;使不美观,使…为减色 ‖ ~ment n.

disfranchise [dis'fræntʃaiz] vt. 剥夺…的公民权(尤指选举权);剥夺…的权利;终止…的特许权 ‖ ~ment n.

disgorge [dis'gɔːdʒ] vt. 1. 吐出,呕出 2. 被迫交出,吐出(赃物) 3. 喷吐(江河等)倾注(流水) (into) 4.(车、船、飞机等)下客 — vi. 1. 吐出赃物 2.(河水等)注入(into) 3. 吐乘客 4.(车、船、飞机等)下客;下车(或船、飞机等)

disgrace [dis'greis] n. 1. 丢脸,耻辱,不光彩;失宠;失势 2. 丢脸的事;丢脸的人 — vt. 1. 使丢脸,使受耻辱 2. 使失宠;贬斥

disgraceful [dis'greisful] adj. 不名誉的,丢脸的,不光彩的 ‖ ~ly adv. / ~ness n.

disgruntle [dis'grʌntl] vt. 使不满,使不高兴 ‖ ~d adj. 不满的,不高兴的(at, with) / ~ment n.

disguise [dis'gaiz] vt. 1. 假扮,化装;伪装 2. 掩盖;掩饰 — n. 1. 化装用具;伪装物 2. 假装;伪装

disgust [dis'gʌst] n. 1. 作呕,厌恶,憎恶;愤慨 (at, for) — vt. 1. 使作呕,使厌恶,使讨厌;使愤慨 — vi. 令人作呕;令人厌恶;令人愤慨

disgusting [dis'gʌstiŋ] adj. 令人作呕的,可憎的,讨厌的 ‖ ~ly adv.

dish [diʃ] n. 1. 盘,碟 2. 盘装菜;盘装食品 3.(一道)菜 3. 盘形物;盘形 4. 一盘的容量 5.〈口〉漂亮女子 — vt. 1. 把(食物)放在盘中 2. 使成盘形 3.〈英

偶)挫败(对手) — *vi.* 成盘形 ‖ ～ed *adj.* 盘形凹陷的 **2.**〈俚〉失败了的;完蛋了的 / ～ful *n.* (一)满盘;一盘的容量 ‖ ～ antenna [无] 蝶抛物面天线 / '～cloth, '～rag *n.* 洗碟布 ‖ '～ towel 擦碟干布 / '～ washer *n.* **1.** 洗碟工 **2.** 洗碟机 / '～water *n.* **1.** 洗(过)碗碟的水 **2.**〈美俚〉味道蹩脚的汤(或茶、咖啡)

dishearten [dis'hɑːtn] *vt.* 使失去勇气,使沮丧,使失去信心 ‖ ～ingly *adv.* / ～ment *n.*

dishevel [di'ʃevəl] (dishevel(l)ed; dishevel(l)ing) *vt.* 使(头发、衣服等)散乱 ‖ **dishevel(l)ed** *adj.* 散乱的,乱蓬蓬的

dishonest [dis'ɔnist] *adj.* 不老实的,不诚实的;不正直的,不正当的 ‖ ～ly *adv.*

dishonesty [dis'ɔnisti] *n.* **1.** 不诚实;不正直 **2.** 不正直行为;欺诈

dishono(u)r [dis'ɔnə] *n.* **1.** 不名誉,不光彩,耻辱 **2.** 丢脸的人(或事) **3.**[商](票据的)拒绝付款,拒绝承兑 — *vt.* **1.** 使表失名誉,使丢脸,玷辱 **2.** 奸污 **3.** 拒绝承兑,拒付(票据) ‖ ～able *adj.* 不名誉的,不光彩的,耻辱的;无耻的

disillusion [ˌdisi'luːʒən] *vt.* 使醒悟;使幻想破灭,使幻灭 — *n.* 醒悟;幻灭 ‖ ～ment *n.*

disinclination [ˌdisinkli'neiʃən] *n.* 不愿,厌恶(*for*, *to do*)

disincline [ˌdisin'klain] *vt.* 使不愿,使不意于(*for*, *to do*)

disinfect [ˌdisin'fekt] *vt.* 给...消毒(或杀菌);使净化 ‖ ～ion *n.*

disinfectant [ˌdisin'fektənt] *adj.* 消毒的 — *n.* 消毒剂

disinformation [ˌdisinfə'meiʃən] *n.* 假情报,假消息

disingenuous [ˌdisin'dʒenjuəs] *adj.* 不真诚的,不坦率的;诡诈的,狡猾的

disinherit [ˌdisin'herit] *vt.* 剥夺...的继承权

disintegrate [dis'intigreit] *vt.* & *vi.* **1.** (使)崩溃,(使)溃散,(使)瓦解 **2.** (使)分裂,(使)分解;(使)崩解 **3.** [核](使)衰变,(使)衰变 ‖ **dis.inte'gration** *n.*

disinter [ˌdisin'tɜː] (disinterred; disinterring) *vt.* **1.** 从坟墓中(或地下)掘出 **2.** 发现,找到 ‖ ～ment *n.*

disinterest [dis'intrist] *n.* **1.** 无兴趣;不关心;冷漠 **2.** 公正,无私 **3.** 不利

disinterested [dis'intristid] *adj.* **1.** 无私的;公平的,无偏见的 **2.**〈口〉不关心的,不感兴趣的 ‖ ～ly *adv.* / ～ness *n.*

disjoin [dis'dʒɔin] *vt.* 拆散,把...分开

disjoint [dis'dʒɔint] *vt.* **1.** 使关节脱位,使脱臼 **2.** 使脱离,使断离,拆散 **3.** 破坏...的连贯性 — *vi.* 关节脱位,脱臼 — *adj.* [数]不相交的

disjointed [dis'dʒɔintid] *adj.* **1.** 关节脱位的,脱臼的 **2.** 不连贯的,支离的 **3.** 次序混乱的,没有条理的 ‖ ～ly *adv.* / ～ness *n.*

disjunctive [dis'dʒʌŋktiv] *adj.* [语] 转折的,反意的:a ～ conjunction 转折连词(如 but, 等)/a ～ question 反意疑问句 — *n.* [语]转折连词

disk [disk] *n.* & *vt.* = disc

dislike [dis'laik] *vt.* & *n.* 不喜爱,厌恶

dislocate ['disləkeit] *vt.* **1.** 使改变位置;使(骨头)脱位,使脱臼 **2.** 扰乱,使混乱

dislocation [ˌdislə'keiʃən] *n.* **1.** 变位;脱位,脱臼 **2.** [地]断层,断错;[物]位错 **3.** 混乱,紊乱

dislodge [dis'lɔdʒ] *vt.* **1.** 把...赶出住处(或占有的地方、有利的地位等),把...

驱逐出(from) **2.** 使(石头等)离开原位 ‖ **dislodg(e)ment** *n.*

disloyal [dis'lɔiəl] *adj.* 不忠诚的(to) ‖ **~ly** *adv.* / **~ty** *n.* 不忠

dismal ['dizmɔl] *adj.* 忧郁的;凄凉的;阴沉的 ‖ **~ly** *adv.*

dismantle [dis'mæntl] *vt.* **1.** 拆除...的设备(或装备、防御工事等) **2.** 拆卸(机器等) ‖ **~ment** *n.*

dismay [dis'mei] *vt.* 使灰心,使沮丧;使惊骇 ‖ *n.* 灰心,沮丧;惊愕

dismember [dis'membə] *vt.* **1.** 割下(动物)的肢;肢解 **2.** 割裂;把...撕成碎片;拆卸 **3.** 瓜分(国家等) ‖ **~ment** *n.*

dismiss [dis'mis] *vt.* **1.** 让...离开;打发 **2.** 免...的职;解雇,开除(工人、学生等) **3.** 遣散,解散 **4.** 消除(顾虑等);不考虑 **5.**【律】驳回,不受理

dismissal [dis'misəl] *n.* **1.** 打发 **2.** 免职;解雇;开除 **3.** 遣散,解散 **4.** 不予考虑 **5.**【律】驳回

dismount [dis'maunt] *vi.* 下马;下车 ‖ *vt.* **1.** 使下马;使落马;使丧失坐骑 **2.**(从座子上)取下,卸下(from);拆开

Disneyesque [,dizni'esk] *adj.* 迪斯尼动画式的,奇异的

Disneyland ['diznilænd] *n.* **1.**(美国洛杉矶市附近的)迪斯尼乐园 **2.** 幻想世界;奇妙景象

disobedience [,disə'bi:djəns] *n.* 不服从,不顺从(to)

disobedient [,disə'bi:djənt] *adj.* 不服从的,不顺从的(to) ‖ **~ly** *adv.*

disobey [,disə'bei] *vt. & vi.* 不服从,不顺从

disorder [dis'ɔ:də] *n.* **1.** 混乱,杂乱【物】无序 **2.** 骚动 **3.**(身心、机能的)失调;紊乱;不适,病: a nervous ～ 神经错乱

disorderly [dis'ɔ:dəli] *adj.* **1.** 混乱的,杂乱的,无秩序的 **2.** 骚乱的;扰乱治安的;骚动的 **3.**【律】妨害治安的 ‖ **disorderliness** *n.* ‖ **~ house** *n.* 赌场。妓院

disorganize [dis'ɔ:gənaiz] *vt.* 瓦解;打乱 ‖ **dis,organi'zation** *n.*

disorient [dis'ɔ:riənt] *vt.* **1.** 使迷失方位(或方向) **2.** 使迷惑,把...弄得晕头转向

disorientation [dis,ɔ:riən'teiʃən] *n.* **1.** 迷失方向;迷惑 **2.**【心】定向障碍,迷向

disown [dis'əun] *vt.* 否认...是自己的;否认,同自己有关系;声明同(子女等)脱离关系

disparage [dis'pæridʒ] *vt.* 轻视,轻蔑;贬低;毁谤,说...坏话 ‖ **~ment** *n.*

disparaging [dis'pæridʒiŋ] *adj.* 轻视的;贬低的;毁谤的 ‖ **~ly** *adv.*

disparity [dis'pæriti] *n.* 不同;不等;悬殊

dispassionate [dis'pæʃənət] *adj.* 不动情感的;平心静气的;不带偏见的 ‖ **~ly** *adv.* / **~ness** *n.*

dispatch [dis'pætʃ] *vt.* **1.** 派遣;调遣;发送(信件、电报等) **2.** 调度 **3.** 迅速办理;迅速了结;匆匆吃完 **4.** 杀死;处决 ‖ *n.* **1.** 派遣;发送 **2.** 急件;公文急报;快信(新闻电讯等) **3.** 迅速(办理);敏捷 **4.** 调度 **5.** 杀死 ‖ **~er** *n.* **1.** 发送者 **2.** 调度员;交通调度员 ‖ **~ box** 公文箱 / **~ case** 公文包 / **~ rider**【军】(骑马或摩托车的)通信员

dispel [dis'pel] (dispelled; dispelling) *vt.* **1.** 驱散(迷雾等) **2.** 消除(疑虑等)

dispensary [dis'pensəri] *n.* 药房,配药处

dispense [dis'pens] *vt.* **1.** 分配,分发(

舍物品等) **2.** 施予(恩惠等) **3.** 执行：
~ justice 执法；行使审判权 **4.** 配(药)；
配(药)/发(药) **5.** 免除，豁免 — vi. 省
却，无需(with) ‖ dispensable adj./ ~r
n. **1.** 施药者 **2.** 配药者 **3.** 配药者；药剂
师 **3.** 分配器；配出器 **3.** 自动售货机

disperse [dis'pɔːs] vt. **1.** 疏散；使分散 **1.**
击溃(敌人等)；驱散(云、雾等) **3.** 散
布，传播(消息、知识等) **4.** [物]使(光
线)色散 — vi. **1.** 分散；散开；散去 **2.**
(云雾等)消散 ‖ dispersal n. / disper-
sion n.

dispirit [dis'pirit] vt. 使气馁，使沮丧

dispirited [dis'piritid] adj. 没有精神的；
垂头丧气的 ‖ ~ly adv.

displace [dis'pleis] vt. **1.** 使离开...的位置，
转移 **2.** 迫使(某人)离家(或祖国) **3.**
取代(某人)的位置；替代 [化]取代，置
换 **4.** 撤换，把...免职 **5.** 排(水) ‖ ~d
person (因战争、饥荒、政治等原因)被
迫流落异国者；失去家园者(略作 DP)

displacement [dis'pleismənt] n. **1.** 移位，
转移；取代，置换 **2.** 撤换，免职；(被)逐
出状态 **3.** [化]置换 **4.** [物]位移 [医]
移位 **5.** [海]排水量 [机]排量 **6.** [地]
断层；位移，迁移

display [dis'plei] vt. **1.** 使展现，陈列；展
出 **2.** 展示；表现；显露 **3.** 炫耀，夸耀
4. [印](用大字等)醒目地排印 **5.** 展
现；打开 — n. **1.** 陈列；展览 **2.** 显
示；表现 **3.** 炫耀，夸耀 **3.** [印]醒目排
印 [动](雄性动物在繁殖期的)炫耀
行为

displease [dis'pliz] vt. 使不愉快，使不高
兴；使生气；惹怒 — vi. 使人不快；使
人生气

displeasing [dis'pliziŋ] adj. 使人不愉快
的；令人生气的 ‖ ~ly adv.

displeasure [dis'pleʒə] n. **1.** 不愉快，不

满，生气

disport [dis'pɔːt] vt. [~ oneself]娱乐，玩
耍 — vi. 娱乐，嬉戏 — n. 娱乐，游戏

disposal [dis'pəuzal] n. **1.** 布置；配置安
署；(物件的)安排，安放 **2.** (垃圾等的)
处理 **3.** 卖掉；让予 **4.** 解决，(事情等
的)处置 ‖ 支配权：at sb.'s ~ 由某人支配；供某人
使用

dispose [dis'pəuz] vt. **1.** 布置；部署(军队
等)；安排，安放(物件) **2.** 使倾向于，使
有意于：I am ~d to agree with you. 我倾
向于你的观点。 — vi. 处置，处理；卖
掉；干掉；处理；赶出 ‖ ~ disposable adj.

disposition [ˌdispə'ziʃən] n. **1.** 安排，安
放；[~s]布置，部署 **2.** 处理，处置，支
配；控制：at sb.'s ~ 随某人支配 **3.** (财
产等的)转让，出售 **4.** 气质，性情 **5.** 倾
向，意向

dispossess [ˌdispə'zes] vt. **1.** 剥夺，夺去
(of) **2.** 撵走，赶出 ‖ ~ion n.

disproof [dis'pruːf] n. **1.** 反证；反驳 **2.**
反证物；反驳的证据

disproportion [ˌdisprə'pɔːʃən] n. 不相称；
不均衡

disproportionate [ˌdisprə'pɔːʃənet] adj. 不
相称的，不匀称的 ‖ ~ly adv.

disprove [dis'pruːv] vt. **1.** 证明...不成
立 **2.** 反驳，驳斥

disputable [dis'pjuːtəbl] adj. 可争论的；可
质疑的

dispute [dis'pjuːt] vi. 争论；辩论；争执：~
with sb. about (或 on) sth. 与某人争论
某事 — vt. 争论；辩论；争执；a ~d
area (所属权)有争议的地区 **2.** 对(正
确性等)表示怀疑 **3.** 阻止；抵抗 **4.** 争
夺(土地等) — n. 争论；辩论；争执；争
端 ‖ disputant n. / dispu'tation n.

disqualify [dis'kwɔlifai] vt. 取消...的资
格；使不合格 ‖ disqualification

[dis,kwɔlifi'keiʃən] n. 无资格；取消资格；取消资格的缘由；无资格的原因

disquiet [dis'kwaiət] vt. 打搅，使不安，使忧虑，使烦恼 — n. 不安，不平静；焦虑 ‖ ~ing adj. 使不安的，使不平静的；使焦虑的 / ~ly adv.

disquietude [dis'kwaiətjuːd] n. 不安；焦虑

disquisition [,diskwi'ziʃən] n. 专题论文；专题演讲；专题讨论(on)

disregard [,disri'gɑːd] vt. 不理，不顾，漠视，无视 — n. 漠视，忽视(of, for)

disrepair [,disri'pɛə] n. 失修；破败

disreputable [dis'repjutəbl] adj. 1. 名誉不好的，声名狼藉的；不体面的 2. 破烂不堪的；肮脏的 ‖ ~ness n. / disreputably adv.

disrepute [,disri'pjuːt] n. 坏名声，不名誉，声名狼藉

disrespect [,disri'spekt] n. 不尊敬；无礼；失礼

disrespectful [,disri'spektful] adj. 无礼的，失礼的 ‖ ~ly adv.

disrobe [dis'rəub] vt. 脱去...的衣服；〈喻〉剥去；剥夺(of) — vi. 脱衣服

disrupt [dis'rʌpt] vt. 1. 使破裂 2. 使中断；使混乱 ‖ ~ion n. / ~ive adj. 分裂的；破坏(性)的

dissatisfaction ['dis,sætis'fækʃən] n. 1. 不满；不平(with, at) 2. 令人不满的事物

dissatisfy [dis'sætisfai] vt. 使不满；使不平 ‖ dissatisfied adj. 不满的；显出不满的

dissect [di'sekt] vt. 1. 把...分成碎片(分割；解剖(动、植物等) 2. 仔细分析(问题、理论、报告等) — vi. 进行解剖；进行分析 ‖ ~ion n. / ~or n.

dissemble [di'sembl] vt. 掩饰(思想、感情等) — vi. 进行掩饰；作伪 ‖ ~r n.

disseminate [di'semineit] vt. 1. 散播(种子等) 2. 散布，传播(思想、疾病等) ‖ dis,semi'nation n. / disseminator n.

dissension [di'senʃən] n. 意见分歧；争论(尤指党派纷争)；不和；纠纷

dissent [di'sent] vi. 1. 不同意，持异议(from) 2.〈英〉(对国教等)表示不赞同 — n. 1. 不同意，异议 2.〈英〉不信奉国教 ‖ ~er n. 1. 持异议者 2.〈英〉[D-] 不信奉国教者

dissertation [,disə'teiʃən] n.(学位)论文；学术演讲

disservice [dis'səːvis] n. 危害，损害

dissident ['disidənt] adj. & n. 不同意的(人)，持异议的(人)；持不同政见的(人)

dissimilar [di'similə] adj. 不一样的，不同的(to, from) ‖ ~ly adv.

dissimilarity [,disimi'læriti] n. 不一样，不同；异点

dissimulate [di'simjuleit] vt. 掩饰(感情、动机等) — vi. 掩饰，装假 ‖ dis,simu'lation n.

dissipate ['disipeit] vt. 1. 驱散，使(云、雾、疑虑等)消散 2. 浪费，挥霍 — vi. 1. 消散；(人群)走散 2. 放荡；酗酒 ‖ ~d adj. 1. 驱散了的 2. 浪费掉的 3. 放荡的 / ~r, dissipator n. 浪荡子

dissipation [,disi'peiʃən] n. 1. 驱散，消散 2. 浪费；消耗 3. 放荡(尤指狂饮)

dissociate [di'səuʃieit] vt. 1. 使分离；使游离出(from) 2.【化】使离解 3.【心】使分裂 — vi. 1. 分离；游离 2. 离解

dissociation [di,səusi'eiʃən] n. 1. 分离；游离 2.【化】离解(作用) 3.【心】分裂 4.【生】离解，分离变异，分离变异菌株

dissolute ['disəluːt] adj. 无节制的；放荡的 ‖ ~ly adv. / ~ness n.

dissolution [ˌdisəˈljuːʃən] *n.* 1. 分解;溶解;融化;液化 2. (婚约、契约等的)解除 3. (议会、公司等的)解散 4. 死亡;终止 5. 瓦解;消失

dissolve [diˈzɔlv] *vt.* 1. 使分解 2. 使溶解;使融化;使液化 3. 使感动,软化;~ d in tears 感动得眼泪汪汪 4. 解散(议会等) 5. 驱散,使消失;毁灭(敌舰等) 6. 使(电影、电视画面)叠化,使淡入淡出 7. 弄明白,解(证) 8. 废除,使无效 — *vi.* 1. 分解,溶解;融化;液化 2. 感动,软化;~ in grief 悲痛过度不能自持 3. (议会等)解散 4. (婚约等)解除 5. 消失;(电影、电视画面)叠化,淡入淡出 — *n.* (电影、电视画面的)叠化

dissonance [ˈdisənəns] *n.* 1. 不和谐;不协调,不一致 2. 【音】不协和音;不协和(和弦) ∥ **dissonant** *adj.*

dissuade [diˈsweid] *vt.* 劝阻,劝止 ∥ **dissuasion** *n.*

distaff [ˈdiːstɑːf] *n.* 【纺】(手工)纺纱杆 2. 女红,女子做的工作;女子关心的事 3. 女子;女性 4. 母系(= ~ side) — *adj.* 1. 女子的 2. 母系的

distance [ˈdistəns] *n.* 1. 距离 2. 远,遥远 3. 远处,远方 4. 久远;(时间上的)间隔 5. 疏远;冷淡 6.【音】音程 — *vt.* 1. 使远离;使显得遥远 2. (竞赛中)把…远远甩在后面

distant [ˈdistənt] *adj.* 1. 远的;久远的;远隔的,稀疏的 2. 疏远的,冷淡的 3. 隐约的;a ~ resemblance 约略的相像 ∥ ~ **ly** *adv.*

distaste [ˈdiːsteist] *n.* 不喜欢,厌恶(for)

distasteful [ˈdiːsteistful] *adj.* 1. 令人厌恶的;不合口味的 2. 表示厌恶的 ∥ ~ **ly** *adv.* / ~ **ness** *n.*

distemper [ˈdistempə] *n.* 1. 坏情绪;坏脾

气 2.【兽医】温热(病)

distend [diˈstend] *vt. & vi.* (使)扩张;(使)膨胀;(使)肿胀 ∥ **distension, distention** *n.*

distil(l) [diˈstil] (distilled; distilling) *vt.* 1. 蒸馏;用蒸馏法提取 2. 提取…的精华 3. 使滴下 — *vi.* 1. 滴下;渗出 2. 蒸馏 ∥ ˌdistilˈlation *n.*

distillery [diˈstiləri] *n.* 1. 蒸馏室 2. 酒厂

distinct [diˈstiŋkt] *adj.* 1. 不同的,独特的;不同种类(或性质)的(from) 2. 明显的;清晰的;清楚的(from) ∥ ~ **ly** *adv.* / ~ **ness** *n.*

distinction [diˈstiŋkʃən] *n.* 1. 区分,区别;差别(between) 2. 特性 3. 卓著;盛名 4. 荣誉;荣誉称号;勋章

distinctive [diˈstiŋktiv] *adj.* 1. 区别性的;鉴别性的 2. 有特色的,与众不同的 ∥ ~ **ly** *adv.* / ~ **ness** *n.*

distinguish [diˈstiŋgwiʃ] *vt.* 1. 区别(between);识别(from) 2. 辨认出 3. 把…分类(into) 4. [~ oneself] 使杰出 — *vi.* 加以区别(或辨别、识别)(between) ∥ ~ **able** *adj.* 区别得出的;可辨别的;辨认得出的

distinguished [diˈstiŋgwiʃt] *adj.* 1. 以…著名的(for, by) 2. 卓越的,卓著的,杰出的;高贵的

distort [diˈstɔːt] *vt.* 1. 扭歪,扭曲,使变形 2. 歪曲;曲解 3. 使畸变,使失真 ∥ ~ **edly** *adv.* 被歪曲地

distortion [diˈstɔːʃən] *n.* 1. 弄歪;歪曲;曲解 2. 变形 3.【物】(透镜成像产生的)畸变;(信号等的)失真

distract [diˈstrækt] *vt.* 分散(注意、心思等);使(人)分心(from)

distracted [diˈstræktid] *adj.* 心烦意乱的;发狂的,精神错乱的 ∥ ~ **ly** *adv.*

distractingly [diˈstræktiŋli] *adv.* 使人心烦

意乱地;使人分心地

distraction [dis'trækʃən] *n.* **1.** 注意力分散,分心;分心;心神烦乱;发狂,精神错乱 **2.** 消遣,娱乐

distraught [dis'trɔːt] *adj.* 异常激动的;心神错乱的;发狂的

distress [dis'tres] *n.* **1.** 悲痛,苦恼,忧伤 **2.** 贫困,穷苦 **3.** 危难;海难;困境;不幸;a radio ～ signal 无线电呼救信号 **4.** 【律】扣押财物;被扣押的财物 — *vt.* **1.** 使悲痛,使苦恼,使忧伤 **2.** 使贫困 ‖ ～ call 遇险(呼救)信号

distressful [dis'tresful] *adj.* 使人痛苦的,令人苦恼的;多难的,悲惨的 ‖ ～ly *adv.*

distressing [dis'tresiŋ] *adj.* 使人痛苦的,令人苦恼的 ‖ ～ly *adv.*

distributary [dis'tribjutəri] *n.* (江河的)支流,分流

distribute [dis'tribjuːt] *vt.* **1.** 分发;分配 **2.** 散布,使分布 **3.** 把...归类,分类 **4.** 【印】拆(版)还字 **5.** 【电】配(电) ‖ ～r *n.* = distributor

distribution [ˌdistri'bjuːʃən] *n.* **1.** 分发;分配 **2.** 法院对无遗嘱死亡者财产的分配 **3.** 销售 **4.** 分布;分布状态;(生物的)分布范围(或地区);(频率)分布 **5.** 分配类型 **6.** 【律】分类,分配 **7.** 【印】拆版 **8.** 【电】配电 ‖ ～al *adj.*

distributive [dis'tribjutiv] *adj.* **1.** 分发的;分配的:～ law 【数】分配律 **2.** 【语】分配的;个别的 ‖ ～ly *adv.* 分配地 — **～ education** [常作 D-E-]【学校与企业主合办的课堂教学与职业训练相结合的】职业教育;市场推销教育

distributor [dis'tribjutə] *n.* **1.** 分发者;分配者;散布者;分布者 **2.** 销售者(尤指批发商) **3.** 分配器 **4.** 【电】配电盘 ‖

【印】自动拆版机;传墨辊

district ['distrikt] *n.* **1.** 区,管区,行政区:the *District* of Columbia 哥伦比亚特区(美国首都华盛顿所在的行政区域) **2.** 地区,区域 **3.** 选区 **4.** 英国教区的分区 ‖ — **attorney**(美国)地方检察官 / — **heating** 地区供暖

distrust [dis'trʌst] *n. & vt.* 不信任,怀疑

distrustful [dis'trʌstful] *adj.* (对...)不信任的,怀疑的(of) ‖ ～ly *adv.* / ～ness *n.*

disturb [dis'tɜːb] *vt.* **1.** 打扰;扰乱(人心等);妨碍(安眠、安静) **2.** 弄乱;打乱(计划等) — *vi.* 打扰;妨碍 ‖ ～er *n.* 打扰者

disturbance [dis'tɜːbəns] *n.* **1.** 骚动,动乱 **2.** 打扰,干扰;(情绪等的)纷乱;(身心等方面的)障碍,失调 **3.** 【律】(权利的)侵犯;(治安的)妨害,骚扰

disunite [ˌdisjuː'nait] *vt. & vi.* **1.** (使)分离;(使)分裂 **2.** (使)不和;(使)不和

disuse [dis'juz] *vt.* (常以过去分词的形式出现)不用,废弃:a ～d well 废井 ‖ [dis'juːs] *n.* 不用,废弃

dísyllàbic [ˌdisi'læbik] *adj.* 双音节的

disyllable [di'siləbl] *n.* 双音节音步;双音节词

ditch [ditʃ] *n.* **1.** (明)沟,沟渠 **2.** 〈英〉[the D-](军用)英吉利海峡;北海 — *vt.* **1.** 在...上开沟;...上筑垒 **2.** 用沟渠围住 **3.** 把(汽车)开入沟内;被迫把(飞机)降落在水面上;迫使(火车)出轨 **4.** 抛弃 — *vi.* **1.** 开沟;筑垒,修渠 **2.** 被迫使飞机降落在水面上

dither ['diðə] *n.* **1.** 发抖 **2.** 慌乱;兴奋 **3.** 激动 — *vi.* **1.** 发抖 **2.** 〈口〉犹豫不决 **3.** 慌乱

ditto ['ditəu] ([复]ditto(e)s) *n.* **1.** 同上;同前;上述的人(或物) **2.** 副本:复制

品;挺相似的人(或物) — *adv.* 如上所述;同样地 ‖ — **mark** 表示同上(或同前)的符号(″)

ditty ['diti] *n.* 小调,小曲

diuretic [ˌdaijuə'retik] 【医】*adj.* 利尿的一 *n.* 利尿剂

diurnal [dai'ə:nəl] *adj.* 1. 每日的,每天的 2. 白昼的,白天的 3.【动】日间活动的,昼行性的 4.【植】(花)昼开夜闭的;(花)仅开一天的;(昆虫)只能活一天的 5.【天】周日的

divan [di'væn, 'daivæn] *n.* 1. 长沙发 2. = ~ **bed** ‖ ~ **bed** (可作床用的)两用沙发

dive [daiv] (过去式 dived 或 dove [dəuv], 过去分词 dived) *vi.* 1. (头先入水地)跳水 2. (潜艇、潜水者等)潜水 3. (飞机)的俯冲;突然下降 4. 猛冲;突然从视野中消失;~ down an alley 窜入一条小巷 5. 把手伸入(into) 6. 钻研,探究;投入(into) — *vt.* 1. 使(头、手等)伸入,插进(into) 2. 使(飞机、潜艇等)突然下降 — *n.* 1. 跳水,(飞机的)俯冲;(潜艇的)下潜 2. 猛冲;突然隐去 3. 埋头钻研 4.〈英〉地下室饮食店 5.〈美〉低级酒吧;低级夜总会(或赌场) 6.〈俚〉(拳击赛中的)假装被击倒,佯倒 ‖ '~-**bomb** *vt.* & *vi.* 俯冲轰炸 / ~ **bomber** 俯冲轰炸机

diver ['daivə] *n.* 1. 跳水者,跳水运动员;潜水员;潜水采珠者 2. 潜鸟 3. 潜水艇

diverge [dai'də:dʒ] *vi.* 1. (道路、路线等)分叉;岔开 2. (意见等)分歧;背驰(from) 3. 离题 — *vt.* 使岔开;使转向

divergence [dai'və:dʒəns] *n.* 1. 分叉;岔开;歧异;背驰;离题;偏差 2.【物】发散;【数】散度,发散(性) 3.【生】趋异 ‖ **divergent, diverging** *adj.*

divers ['daivəz] *adj.* 1. 不止一个的,好几

个的;各种各样的 2.[古]不同种类的

diverse [dai'və:s] *adj.* 1. 不一样的 2. 多种多样的,形形色色的 ‖ ~**ly** *adv.* / ~**ness** *n.*

diversify [dai'və:sifai] *vt.* 1. 使多样化 2. 把资金分投在几家公司内 3. 增加(产品)的品种 — *vi.* 从事多种经营 ‖ di,versifi'cation *n.*

diversion [dai'və:ʃən] *n.* 1. 转向;(注意力等的)转移(from);a flood ~ project 分洪工程 2. 航线(或航行目的地)的改变;〈英〉绕道 3.【军】牵制;佯攻 4. 消遣,娱乐 ‖ ~ **ist** *n.* 1. (政治上的)背离既定路线者;阴谋破坏者;反党分子 2. 敌后工作者

diversionary [dai'və:ʃənəri] *adj.* 1.【军】牵制性的 2. 转移注意力的

diversity [dai'və:siti] *n.* 多样性;差异

divert [dai'və:t] *vt.* 1. 使(河流等)改道;转移;转移…的注意力(from, to) 2. 使(车辆等)绕道,使改道,使改变;使娱乐,使高兴 — *vi.* 转向;转移;Traffic was ordered to ~ to another road. 车辆被命令改道行驶。‖ ~**ing** *adj.* 有趣的

divest [dai'vest] *vt.* 脱去…的衣服;剥夺;剥夺…的权力(或地位等)(of)

divide [di'vaid] *vt.* 1. 分,划分(into) 2. 分开;隔开,隔离(from) 3. 分配;分享;分担(up) 4. 分裂;使对立;使(意见)分歧;使意见 5. 由上标标列表 6.【数】除;除尽;把…作除数 7. 使(立法机构等)分赞成和反对两组进行表决 — *vi.* 1. 分;分开(into) 2. 分裂;意见分歧 3. 分(议会等)分赞成和反对两组进行表决 — *n.* 1. 分;分配 2. 分水界;分水岭;分界线

dividend ['dividend] *n.* 1. 红利;股息;(送给顾客的)赠品;(破产清算时)债权人分得的偿金;发给参加保险投保人的盈

余比例份额 2.【数】被除数 3. 回报

divider [di'vaidə] *n.* 1. 划分者；分割者；分裂者；间隔物 2. 分配器，分隔器；【电】分压器 3.【计】除法器 4. [~s] 两脚规，分线规

dividing [di'vaidiŋ] *adj.* 起划分(或区分、分割)作用的：a ~ line 界线/a ~ ridge 分水岭

divination [ˌdivi'neiʃən] *n.* 1. 占卜 2. 预言；预见；预测

divine [di'vain] *adj.* 1. 神的；神性的 2. 神圣的 3. 神学的 4. 神授的，天赐的 5. 非凡的，天才的 6.〈口〉好透了的 一 *n.* 神学家；牧师 一 *vt.* 占卜；预言；〈凭直觉〉发现 ‖ ~ly *adv.*

diviner [di'vainə] *n.* 占卜者；预言者；推测者

diving ['daiviŋ] *adj.* 潜水的；跳水的；潜水用的；跳水用的 ‖ ~ bell 潜水钟 / ~ board 跳(水)板 / ~ dress，~ suit 潜水衣

divinity [di'viniti] *n.* 1. 神性，神力，神威，神德 2. 神 3. [the D-]【宗】上帝 4. 神学；大学神学系 5. 令人敬慕的人，值得崇拜的人

divisibility [diˌvizi'biliti] *n.* 1. 可分性 2.【数】可除性

divisible [di'vizəbl] *adj.* 1. 可分的；可除的 2.【数】可除尽的 ‖ divisibly *adv.*

division [di'viʒən] *n.* 1. 分；分开；分割 (into) 2. 分配；分派；(the) 一分配 2. 分工 3. (意见等的)分歧 4. 一致 4. 隔阂物；分界线 5. 区；(英国的)选区 6. 部分；部门；(机关的)科 7.【军】师；(海军)舰艇分队，航空兵分队 7.【军】部(动、植物分类的单位) 8.【数】除(法) 9.(议会中赞成者与反对者分别进行的)分组表决(结果) 10.〈英〉(监狱中犯人待遇的)轻型犯罪禁级别 11.

【农】分株(繁殖法) ‖ ~ bell (英国下院通知议员的)分组表决铃

divisive [di'vaisiv] *adj.* 造成不和的，制造分裂的

divisor [di'vaizə] *n.*【数】除数

divorce [di'vɔːs] *n.* 1. 使离婚 2. 分离；脱离 一 *vt.* 1. 与...离婚；判...离婚 2. 使分离；使脱离(*from*)

divorcee [divɔː'siː] *n.* 离了婚的人

divulge [dai'vʌldʒ] *vt.* 1. 泄漏(秘密等) 2.〈古〉宣布；公布 ‖

dizzy ['dizi] *adj.* 1. 头昏目眩的 2. 使人头晕的；极高(或快)的 3. 被弄糊涂的；愚蠢的，可笑的 一 *vt.* 1. 使头晕眼花 2. 使茫然；使混乱 ‖ dizzily *adv.* / dizziness *n.*

Djakarta [dʒə'kɑːtə] *n.* 雅加达[印度尼西亚首都]

Djibouti [dʒi'buːti] *n.* 1. 吉布提[非洲东北部国家] 2. 吉布提(市)[吉布提首都]

DNA *abbr.* deoxyribonucleic acid【生化】脱氧核糖核酸

Dnieper ['dniːpə] *n.* [the ~]第聂伯河(东欧平原大河,注入黑海)

do[强 duː;弱 du] (did [did], done [dʌn]; 第三人称单数现在式 does [强 dʌz;弱 dəz]) *vt.* 1. 做，干 2. 给予帮助：Will you ~ me a favour? 帮我个忙好吗? 3. 制作；产生；写(书等)；作(曲、画等)：a film 摄制影片/~ wonders 创造奇迹 4. 算出~ sums 做算术 5. 翻译；改编 6. 学习，研究 7. 整理，使整洁：~ the bed 铺床/~ the room 收拾房间 8. 料理；照看：a garden 照料花园 9. 适合，对...合用 10. 走(完)：They *did* the journey in an hour. 他们用一小时走完了全程。11. 搞坏；弄坏：Now you've *done* it. 这回可给你弄坏了。12. 演出(戏

剧);扮演(角色);充当:〈口〉做出...的样子:~ the host 做主人〈指招待客人〉/~ the polite 表现得彬彬有礼 **13.** 〈口〉游览(城市等);参观(博物馆等) **14.** 〈口〉招待,款待:They ~ you very well at that hotel. 那家旅馆服务很周到。 **15.** 〈口〉欺骗 **16.** 〈口〉服(若干年月)的徒刑 — vi. **1.** 做;行动 **2.** 〈口〉发生:What's ~ ing over there? 那边在干什么? **3.** 行;足够:That will ~ 行了(或够了)。 **4.** 〔植物〕生长;进展 — v. substitute [用来避免动词的重复]:A: Who broke the cup? 甲:谁把杯子打碎了? 乙:是我 — [强 duː;弱 du,ə, d] (did; 第三人称单数现在式 does) v. aux. **1.** [构成疑问句子]:Do you smoke? 你抽烟吗? **2.** [构成否定句]:She doesn't (didn't) bow down before difficulties. 她不(没有)向困难低头。 **3.** [用于加强语气;发强音]:Do be careful! 一定要当心! **4.** [用于倒装句] Well — I remember it. 那个我可记得清清楚楚。 — [duː] ([复]dos 或 do's [duːz]) n. **1.** 要求做到的事:the ~s and don'ts of public hygiene 公共卫生注意事项之〔理〕职〔英口〕欢庆会;宴会 **4.** 〈英口〉欺诈;骗局 **5.** [~s] 〔英口〕分配 ‖ '~-all n. 样样工作都做的人;总管;杂役 / '~-or-'die adj. 拼死的;破釜沉舟的;生死(或紧要)关头的

do² [dou] n. 固定唱法时之 C 音;首调唱法时任何大音阶之第一音(或任何小音阶之第三音)

do. abbr. ditto

docile ['dausail, 'dosəl] adj. 容易管教的,驯顺的;驯良的 ‖ -ly adv. / docility [dəu'siliti] n.

dock¹ [dɔk] n. **1.** 船坞;干船坞;[常 ~s]

港区 **2.** 码头,船埠;港池;停泊地 **3.** (检修飞机的)棚厂;飞机棚 **4.** (铁路终点站的)站台,月台 **5.** (舞台下面的)布景存放处 — vt. **1.** 把...引入船坞;把...引入码头 **2.** 在...设置船坞 **3.** 使(宇宙飞行器在外层空间)对接 — vi. **1.** 入船坞;靠码头 **2.** (宇宙飞行器在外层空间)对接 ‖ '~yard n. **1.** 船舶修造厂 **2.** 海军船坞;海军造船厂

dock² [dɔk] n. **1.** 尾巴骨肉部分(不包括尾上的毛) **2.** (羊,狗等截尾后留下的)尾巴 — vt. **1.** 剪短(尾巴);剪短...的尾巴 **2.** 把...的头发剪短 **3.** 削减(薪给,供应,津贴等) **4.** (惩罚性地)剥夺,扣去...的应得利益(of) ‖ '~-tailed adj. 截去尾巴的,断尾的

dock³ [dɔk] n. (刑事法庭的)被告席

docket ['dɔkit] n. **1.** 摘要 **2.** 判决摘要 **3.** 〈美〉备审案件表 **4.** 议事日程;待办事务备忘录 **5.** (文件等)的标签 **6.** 〈英美〉关税完税证;凭证

docking ['dɔkiŋ] n. **1.** (航天器在轨道上的)对接 **2.** (船舶的)进坞

doctor ['dɔktə] n. **1.** 博士(缩写为 D. 或 Dr.) **2.** 医生,医师,大夫;兽医 **3.** 巫医 **4.** 〈古〉学者,先生 **5.** 〈口〉修理师,修理工 — vt. **1.** 授...以博士学位 **2.** 授...博士;诊治,医治 **3.** 修理;修复(机器等) **4.** 修改;搀杂(酒等);窜改;伪造(up) **5.** 阉割(牲畜)

doctorate ['dɔktərit] n. 博士衔;博士学位

doctrinaire [,dɔktri'nɛə] n. & adj. 空谈理论的(人),教条主义的(人)

doctrinarian [,dɔktri'nɛəriən] n. & adj. = doctrinaire

doctrine ['dɔktrin] n. **1.** 教义,教条;主义 **2.** 学说 **3.** 〈口〉教海;教导 ‖ doctrinal adj.

docudrama ['dɔkju,drɑːmə] n. 文献电视

(或电影)片

document ['dɔkjumənt] *n.* 1. 公文;文件;文献 2. 证件 — ['dɔkjument] *vt.* 1. 用文件(或证书等)证明;为…提供文件(或证书等) 2. 根据大量记实材料作成(影片、小说等) ‖ ~**al** [ˌdɔkju'mentl] *adj.*

documentary [ˌdɔkju'mentəri] *adj.* 1. 公文的;文件的;证书的 ‖ ~ **bill**(或 draft)跟单汇票 2. 纪录的,记实的 ‖ ~ **film** 纪录影片 — *n.* 纪录影片;记实小说

dodge [dɔdʒ] *vi.* 1. 闪开;闪躲 2. 推托,搪塞 — *vt.* 1. 闪避,避开(打击、车辆等) 2. 躲避,回避(困难、问题等);逃避(兵役、纳税等) — *n.* 1. 躲闪 2. 托词;伎俩;妙计

dodo ['dəudəu]([复]dodo(e)s) *n.* 1.〈产于毛里求斯现已绝种的〉渡渡鸟,孤鸽;〈产于留尼汪岛近于绝种的〉类渡渡鸟,留尼汪孤鸽 2. 落后于时代的人;旧派的人;糊涂虫

doe [dəu] *n.* 1. 雌鹿;雌兔;雌羚羊;雌山羊 2.〈美俚〉(在社交场合)无男伴的女子

doer ['du:ə] *n.* 1. 做某事的人;an evil ~ 作恶的人 2. 实干家

does [强 dʌz; 弱 dəz]do¹ 的第三人称单数现在式

doesn't ['dʌznt] = does not

doff [dɔf] *vt.* 1. 脱(帽、衣等) 2. 丢弃,废除(习惯等) 3. 落(纱);落(筒) ‖ ~ **er** *n.*【纺】 1. 小滚筒,剥棉辊(曾音译作"道夫") 2. 落纱工 3. 落纱机

dog [dɔg] *n.* 1. 狗,犬;犬科动物 2. 雄狗;雄兽(尤指狐、狼等);a ~ fox 雄狐 3.[the ~ s](英)跑狗(比赛) 4. 无赖汉,坏蛋 5.〈口〉家伙:You (dirty) ~! 你这个(坏)小子! /a lucky ~ 幸运儿 6.〈美俚〉蹩脚货 — (dogged; dogging)

vt. 1. 尾随,追踪 2.(灾难等)缠住 ‖ ~**like** *adj.* 像狗的;狗一样(忠心等)的 ‖ ~ **biscuit** (喂)狗的(于)干 ‖ ~**cart** *n.* 1. 狗拉的小车 2.(设背靠背双座的)双轮轻便马车 / ~'**cheap** *adj. & adv.* 极便宜的(地) / ~ **days** 三伏天,大热天 / ~'**ear** *n.*(书页的)折角 *vt.* 把(书页)折角 / ~ -, **eared** *adj.*(书页)折角的;(书)翻旧了的 / ~'**cat-** ~' *n. & adj.* 狗咬狗(;)损人利己(的) / ~ -**fight** *n. & vi.* 狗打架;〈口〉(战斗机)近距离激战 / ~ **fish** *n.*【动】狗鲨;弓鳍鱼 / ~**hoie** *n.* 狗窝;肮脏的住所 / ~'**house** *n.* 狗窝 / ~ **leg** *n.*(道路、跑道等)的急转弯 / ~ **s-body** *n.*〈英口〉勤杂工,杂务工 / ~ **sleep** *n.* 不时惊醒的睡眠 / ~'**s life** 悲惨的生活 / Dog Star【天】狼星(大犬座主星);南河三(小犬座主星) / ~'**s tooth**(男子衣料的)犬牙格子花纹 / ~ **tag** *n.* 狗牌,狗牌照 2.(战时士兵挂在预上的)身分识别牌 / ~ -'**tired** *adj.* 累极了的 / ~'**trot** *n. & vi.* 小步跑,慢跑 / ~ **watch** *n.*【海】下午四点到六点或六点到八点的二时班,更换班 2. 夜班(尤指最后一班) / ~ **wood** *n.*【植】狗木;狗木的木材

dogged ['dɔgid] *adj.* 顽强的,坚韧不拔的 ‖ ~**ly** *adv.* ‖ ~**ness** *n.*

doggerel ['dɔgərəl] *n.* 打油诗;拙劣的诗

doggie ['dɔgi] *n.* 小狗儿

doggo ['dɔgəu] *adv.*〈俚〉隐蔽地;lie ~ 隐伏不动

dogma ['dɔgmə] *n.* 1. 教义,教理 2. 武断的意见;教条

dogmatic [dɔg'mætik] *adj.* 1. 教义的,教理的;信条的 2. 武断的;教条(主义)的 ‖ **dogmatically** *adv.*

doh [dəu] *n.* = do²

Doha ['dəuhɑ] *n.* 多哈〔卡塔尔首都〕

doily ['dɔili] *n.* (碗碟或花瓶等下铺的装饰性)小垫

doing ['du:iŋ] *n.* 1. [~s]所做(或所发生)的事情;社交活动 2. [~s](尤指不知或忘了名称的)那东西

do-it-yourself ['du:itjɔ:'self] *adj.* 万事不求人的;自己动手或自行维修的;供业余爱好者自己装配(或使用)的

do-it-yourselfer ['du:itjɔ:'selfə] *n.* 〈口〉自己动手制造并修理东西的人;手巧的人,不求人的人‖~y *n.* 自己动手;自行维修

Dolby ['dɔlbi] *n.* = ~ system ‖ ~ system (降低磁带噪声的)道尔贝降噪系统

doldrums ['dɔldrəmz] [复] *n.* 1. 忧郁,郁闷;消沉;停滞;不景气 2. [气]赤道无风带;赤道无风带的无风天气

dole [dəul] *n.* 1.〈古〉命运 2. 救济(分期或少量发放的)救济物;一份救济金(或救济食品) 3. [the ~](英口)失业救济金;be (go) on the ~ 接受(开始接受)失业救济 — *vt.* 少量地发放(救济品) (*out*)

doleful ['dəulful] *adj.* 1. 令人悲哀的;表示悲哀的 2. 感觉悲哀的 ‖ ~ly *adv.* / ~ness *n.*

doll [dɔl] *n.* 1. 玩偶,娃娃(指玩具) 2. 好看而没有头脑的女子 3.〈美俚〉姑娘,少女 4.〈俚〉[常作称呼]宝贝儿 — *vt.* & *vi.*〈口〉(把)打扮得漂漂亮亮 (*up*) ‖ ~ face *n.* 长着一张娃娃脸的人 / ~house *n.* 1. (儿童放娃娃的)玩具小屋 2. 很小的住屋

dollar ['dɔlə] *n.* 1. 元(美国、加拿大、澳大利亚、埃塞俄比亚等国的货币单位;符号为 $ 或 $) 2. 一元硬币(或纸币) ‖ ~ area 美元区

dolly ['dɔli] *n.* 1.〈儿语〉娃娃(指玩具) 2. = ~ bird 3. (搬运重物的)台车,手推车 4. [摄]移动摄影(或摄像)车,滑动台架 ‖ ~ bird〈英口〉漂亮的摩登少女

dolorous ['dɔlərəs] *adj.*〈令人〉忧伤的,(令人)悲哀的 ‖ ~ly *adv.*

dolphin ['dɔlfin] *n.* 1. 海豚 2. [the D-] [天]海豚座

dolt [dəult] *n.* 笨蛋,傻瓜

-dom *suf.* 1. 加以构成名词 1. 表示"职位"、"领域":dukedom, kingdom 2. 表示"状态"、"性质":wisdom, freedom 3. 表示"(同一职务、行业、利益的)集体":officialdom

domain [dəu'mein] *n.* 1. 领域,领土,版图;领地 2. (活动、学问、影响等的)范围,领域 3. [数]域

dome [dəum] *n.* 1. 圆屋顶 2. 圆盖;穹顶 (蒸汽锅炉等的)干汽室 3. (观察天象的)圆顶观测室 4.〈诗〉大厦 5.〈俚〉头,脑袋 6. [地]穹地,圆丘 7.〈结晶的〉坡面 ‖ ~d *adj.* 圆(屋)顶的;圆盖形的;半球形的

domestic [də'mestik] *adj.* 1. 家里的,家庭的 2. 本国的,国内的;国内生产的 3. 一心只管家务的;一心追求家庭乐趣的 — *n.* 1. 家仆,佣人 2.〈美〉[~s]国货;本地产品 ‖ ~ally *adv.* / ~ animal 家畜 / ~ fowl 家禽 / ~ science 家政学

domesticate [də'mestikeit] *vt.* 1. 使归化;采用(异族风俗等) 2. 使喜家居;使专注于家务 3. 驯养(动物);驯化(动植物) ‖ do,mesti'cation *n.*

domesticity [,dəumes'tisiti] *n.* 1. 家庭生活;个人小天地 2. 对家庭生活的爱好;爱家

domicile ['dɔmisail] *n.* 1. 住处 2. [律](正式户口所在的)原籍;(本人有意久住的)住所 — *vt.* 使定居

dominance ['dɔminəns] *n.* 1. 优势;支配(或统治)地位 2.【生】显性;优势

dominant ['dɔminənt] *adj.* 1. 支配的,统治的;占优势的 2. 居高临下的,高耸的 3.【生】显性的;优势的 4.【音】属音的 — *n.* 1. 主因;要素;主要的人(或物) 2.【生】显性性状;显性基因;优势种 3.【音】属音,音阶第五音 ‖ **~ly** *adv.*

dominate ['dɔmineit] *vt.* 1. 支配,统治,控制 2.(山、塔等)俯视 — *vi.* 1. 处于支配地位;拥有压倒势力(*over*) 2. 位于高处,高耸(*over*) ‖ **'domi'nation** *n.*

domineer [,dɔmi'niə] *vi.* 专横;跋扈(*over*) ‖ **~ing** *adj.* 专横的;飞扬跋扈的

Dominica [,dɔmi'ni:kə] *n.* 多米尼加(岛)[拉丁美洲一向风群岛北部;全称多米尼加联邦]

Dominican [də'minikən] *adj.* 多米尼加共和国的;the ~ Republic 多米尼加共和国[拉丁美洲,位在西印度群岛海地岛东部] — *n.* 多米尼加共和国人

dominion [də'minjən] *n.* 1. 统治,管辖,支配;(山、塔等)俯视,版图;(封建地主的)领地 3. [D-]【史】英联邦自治领 ‖ **Dominion Day** 自治领日(七月一日,加拿大的法定假日,纪念一八六七年加拿大获得英帝国自治领的地位)

domino ['dɔminəu]([复] domino(e)s) *n.* 1.(化装跳舞会上穿的带有面具的)连帽化装斗篷;穿连帽化装斗篷的人 2. 黑色小圆点,半截面具 ‖ 戴半截面具的人 3. 西洋骨牌,多米诺骨牌;[~(e)s] 西洋骨牌戏,多米诺骨牌戏 ‖ **~ effect** 多米诺(骨牌)效应(指一事件连锁引起一系列类似事件)/ **~ theory** 多米诺(骨牌)理论(政治用语,指"一个倒,全部倒"或"牵一发而动全身")

Don [dɔn] *n.* [the ~] 顿河(东欧平原大河,注入亚速海)

don [dɔn](donned; donning) *vt.* 披上;穿上;戴上

donate [dəu'neit, 'dəuneit] *vt.* 捐赠;~ blood 献血 — *vi.* 捐赠(*to*) ‖ **donator** *n.* 捐赠者

donation [dəu'neiʃən] *n.* 1. 捐赠 2. 捐赠物;捐款

Donbas(s) [dɔn'bɑ:s] *n.* 顿巴斯[乌克兰一地区]

done [dʌn] do¹ 的过去分词 — *adj.* 1. 完毕了的;One more question and I'm ~. 我再提一个问题就完了。 2. 注定要完蛋的 3. 煮熟了的 4. 精疲力竭的 5. 合乎礼俗的:It isn't ~ . 那样做是失礼的。‖ **~ness** *n.* 煮熟的程度

donkey ['dɔŋki] *n.* 1. 驴 2. 笨蛋,蠢驴 3. = **~ engine** ‖ **~ engine**【机】辅助发动机;辅助机车 / **~ jacket**(野外作业工人穿的)风雨衣 / **~'s years**〈口〉很久,多年 / **~work** *n.* 呆板的例行工作;恼人的苦活

donor ['dəunə] *n.* 1. 赠与人,捐赠者 2.【医】供血者(= blood ~);献皮者(组织、器官等的)供体,借者;(人工授精的)精液提供者 2.【物】施主(指能给出电子的半导体杂质)/【化】给予体,供体

don't [dəunt] = do not — *n.* 禁忌;禁止的事

don't-know ['dəunt'nəu] *n.* 未作决定的人(或投票人);未定的事(或选票)

doodle ['du:dl] *vi.*(心不在焉地)乱涂 — *n.* 乱涂出来的东西 ‖ **~-bug** *n.*(第二次世界大战中德国使用的)"V"型飞弹;飞机型导弹;嗡嗡弹

doom [du:m] *n.* 1. 厄运;毁灭;死亡 2. 判决;定罪【宗】末日审判:the day of ~【宗】最后审判日,世界末日(= doomsday)— *vt.* 注定,命定;[用于被动语

态)注定...要失败(或毁灭、灭亡等)

doomsday ['duːmzdei] *n.*〈宗〉最后审判日,世界末日

door [dɔː] *n.* **1.** 门;通道 **2.** 家;户;门面: He lives several ~s beyond (或 off). 再过去几间门面就是他住的地方。‖ / '~bell *n.* 门铃 / '~case, '~frame *n.* 门框 / '~keeper *n.* 看门人 / '~knob *n.* 球形门拉手 / '~man *n.* 看门人,门丁 / '~mat *n.* 门前擦鞋垫 **2.** 逆来顺受的可怜虫 / '~nail *n.*(装饰性)护门帽钉 / '~plate *n.* 门牌 / '~post *n.* 门柱 / '~sill *n.* 门槛 / '~step *n.* 门阶 / '~way *n.* 出入口,门口,门道;途径,门路(to) / '~yard *n.*〈美〉门前庭院

dope [dəup] *n.* **1.** 粘稠物,胶状物 **2.** 飞机翼布涂料;涂布漆浆(制炸药等的)吸收剂;添加剂;抗爆剂 **3.**(给马等服的)兴奋剂 **4.**〈俚〉麻醉品,毒品(如鸦片等) **5.**〈俚〉呆子 **6.**〈俚〉有关赛马实力的)情报;内幕;(可靠的)内部消息 — *vt.* **1.** 给(马)服兴奋剂 **2.** 给(人)服麻醉剂(或毒品);麻醉 **3.** 服用麻醉剂(或毒品)‖ '~ fiend〈俚〉有吸毒瘾的人 / '~sheet *n.* 赛马简报;近况简报

dorm [dɔːm] *n.*〈美口〉宿舍

dormant ['dɔːmənt] *adj.* **1.**〈生〉休眠的;蛰伏的 **2.** 在眠态中的;暂停活动(或作用)的: a ~ volcano 静火山 ‖ **dormancy** *n.* ‖ ~ partner 出资而不任事的股东;隐名股东

dormer ['dɔːmə] *n.*〈建〉屋顶窗,老虎窗 (= ~ window)

dormitory ['dɔːmitri] *n.* **1.**〈英〉大寝室,集体寝室;〈美〉宿舍 **2.**(在城市工作的人们的)郊外居住区

dormouse ['dɔːmaus] *n.*〈复〉dormice ['dɔːmais]) *n.*〈动〉榛睡鼠

dorsal ['dɔːsəl] *adj.*【解】背面的,背部的 ‖ ~ ly *adv.*

dory ['dɔːri] *n.* 小平底渔船

DOS *abbr.* disc. operating system【计】磁盘操作系统

dosage ['dəusidʒ] *n.* **1.** 给药 **2.**(药的)剂量;(一)剂,(一)服

dose [dəus] *n.* **1.**(药的)剂量;(一)剂,(一)服 **2.** 一次;一番 **3.**〈口〉of flattery 一番奉承 **3.**(X 射线、辐射等的)吸收剂量 — *vt.* 给...服药,(用...)治疗(人、动物)(with) — *vi.* 服药

dossier ['dɔsiei] *n.*(一宗)档案材料,卷宗,档案(尤指关于个人经历的)

dot [dɔt] *n.* **1.** 小点,圆点 **2.** 点状物;微小的东西: a mere ~ of a child 不点儿的小家伙 **3.**【音】附点;顿音记号 **4.**【数】小数点 **5.**〈口〉句号 — (dotted; dotting) *vt.* **1.** 打点于;星罗棋布于: a dotted line 虚线 **2.**〈俚〉猛击 — *vi.* 打点

dotage ['dəutidʒ] *n.* 老年昏聩,老年糊涂

dotard ['dəutəd] *n.* 年老昏聩的人,老糊涂

dote [dəut] *vi.* **1.** 昏聩;(因年老)智力衰退 **2.** 溺爱;过分喜爱(upon, on)

doting ['dəutiŋ] *adj.* **1.** 溺爱的;偏爱的 **2.** 老糊涂的 **3.**(树木)腐朽的 ‖ ~ ly *adv.*

double ['dʌbl] *adj.* **1.** 两倍的;加倍的;双的;双重的 **2.**【植】重瓣的 a railway with a ~ track 双轨铁路 **3.** 供两人用的: a ~ bed 双人床 **4.**(意义)双关的;模棱两可的 **5.** 两面派的;play the ~ game 要两面派 **6.**〈俚〉低八度的 — *adv.* **1.** 双倍地 **2.** 双重地 **3.** 双双地: ride — 两人合乘一马 — *n.* **1.** 两倍之;折叠,两重 **2.**【军】跑步前进: at (或 on) the ~ 尽快地;以跑步方式 **4.** [~s](网

球、乒乓球等的)双打 5. 替代演员,后备演员(或歌手) 6. 极相似的人(或物) 7. 幽灵 8.(桥牌中的)叫加倍 9. 急转弯,突然转向,折回 10. 诡计;回避 11. 【印】重叠印(指同一页上由于不慎印了两次) ‖ — **vt.** 1. 是…的两倍;使加倍 2. 把…对折;握紧(拳头) 3. 替代(演员);兼演(两角) 4.(在译制片中为…)配音 5.【音】(在高或低八度上)重复 5.【海】绕过(海岬等) ‖ — **vi.** 1. 变成两倍;增加一倍;(桥牌中)叫加倍 2. 跑步 3. 往回跑(back) 4. 替代演出(for);兼演(as) 5. 兼作(as) 6. 兼奏(on) ‖ **doubly** *adv.* ‖ — '~-**acting** *adj.*【机】双动的 / '~-'**barrel**('ed *adj.* 1. 双筒的 2.(姓氏)双的(如 Fowkes-Fowey) 3. 意义双关的;模棱两可的 4. 双重目的的 / '~-'**breasted** *adj.*(外套等)双排钮扣的 / '~-'**chinned** *adj.* 双下巴的 / '~-'**cross** *n. & vt.* 〈口〉欺骗;出卖 / '~-'**dealer** *n.* 两面派人物 / '~-**decker** *n.* 双层结构;双层甲板船;双层公共汽车(或火车、客机);双层桥梁;双层床 / '~-'**digit** *adj.*(通货膨胀等)两位数的 / ~ **Dutch** 莫名其妙的话(或文章) / '~-'**dyed** *adj.* 1.(印染中)两次染色的,双染的 2.(在信仰等方面)根深蒂固的;彻头彻尾的 / '~-'**edged** *adj.* 1. 双刃的 2. 双重目的的 3. 意义双关的;两可的 / ~ **entry** 复式分录;复式记录 / '~-**exposure**【摄】两次曝光 / '~-'**faced** *adj.* 1. 两面向可的 2. 口是心非的,伪善的 / '~-'**header** *n.* 1.(由两辆机车牵引的)双机牵引列车 2.(棒球赛同两个连续赛场的)一天连续两场比赛 / '~-'**jointed** *adj.* 双关节的;前后右右可自由活动的 / '~-'**lock** *vt.* 给…上双锁;特别谨慎地锁上 / '~-'**park** *vt. & vi.* 双行停(车)(指把车停在与人行道平行停靠的另一辆车旁,常

属违章停车) / '~-'**quick** *adj.* 很快的 *adv.* 跑着步 *n.* 跑步 / '~-'**space** *vt. & vi.*(在打字机上)隔行打印 / '~-**stand-dard**(对男、女等不同对象的)双重标准 / ~ **take**(对特殊情况等)过后才恍然大悟的反应(尤指喜剧中这种表演) / '~-**talk** *n.* 1. 不知所云的话 2. 模棱两可的欺人之谈 / ~ **time** 1. 行军快步;跑步 2. 双工资

doubt [daut] *vt.* 怀疑;拿不准[注意:后接宾语从句时,如主句为疑问句和否定句用连接词 that,如主句为肯定句用连接词 whether 或 if] — *n.* 1. 怀疑;疑惑,疑问 (about, of) — *n.* 1. 怀疑;疑惑,疑问 2. 疑虑 ‖ — **er** *n.* 抱怀疑态度的人;不信宗教的人 / ~ **ing** *adj.* 抱怀疑态度的:a ~ **ing** Thomas 怀疑一切的人

doubtful ['dautful] *adj.* 1.(对…)怀疑的,疑惑的(of, about) 2. 可疑的;使人产生疑问的 3. 难料的;未定局的 4. 含糊的;不确定的 5. 未必好的:a ~ taste 低级趣味 ‖ — **ly** *adv.* / ~ **ness** *n.*

doubtless ['dautlis] *adj.* 无疑地 2.〈口〉很可能地 — *adj.*〈罕〉无疑的,肯定的 ‖ — **ly** *adv.* / ~ **ness** *n.*

dough [dəu] *n.* 1.(揉和好的)生面(团) 2. 生面团状的一团(如陶土、油灰等) 3.〈俚〉钱;现钞 / '~-**boy** *n.* 1. 油炸面团;汤团 2.〈俚〉美国步兵 / '~-**nut** *n.* 炸面圈,糖饼子

doughty ['dauti] *adj.*〈古〉〈谑〉勇猛的;能干的 ‖ **doughtily** *adv.* / **doughtiness** *n.*

doughy ['dəui] *adj.* 1. 面团(似)的 2. 夹生的,半熟的 3. 苍白的;软弱无力的 ‖ **doughiness** *n.*

dour [duə] *adj.* 1. 顽强不屈的;严厉的;执拗的 2. 阴郁的,郁郁寡欢的;〈苏格兰〉(天气)阴沉的 ‖ — **ly** *adv.* / ~ **ness** *n.*

douse [daus] *vt.* **1.** 把…浸入水里 **2.** 浇（或洒、泼）液体在…上 **3.** （口）熄灭（灯、火）— *vi.* 浸；泡 — *n.* 浇，泼

dove[1] [dʌv] *n.* **1.** 鸽；野鸽；鸽雏 **2.** [D-]【宗】圣灵 **3.** 和平的象征、和平使者；招喜人物；温和派人物 **5.** 纯洁温柔（如的）的人；（常作亲热称呼）宝贝儿 ‖ ~ like *adj.* （鸽子般）纯洁可爱的；温柔的 ‖ ~cot(e) *n.* 鸽棚,鸽房

dove[2] [dəuv] dive 的过去式

Dover ['dəuvə] *n.* 多佛尔[英国英格兰东南部港市] ‖ when ~ and Calais meet 水不（可）干

dovetail ['dʌvteil] *n.* **1.** 鸠尾榫，楔形榫 **2.** 鸠尾接合（= ~ joint）— *vt.* **1.** 用鸠尾榫接合；把…制成鸠尾榫形 **2.** 和…吻合；使响合；使相呼应 — *vi.* （与…）吻合（with）

dowager ['dauədʒə] *n.* **1.** 受有亡夫遗产（或称号）的寡妇：a queen ～ 国王遗孀，孀居的王后 **2.** （口）年长有钱的贵妇人

dowdy ['daudi] *adj.* **1.** 不整洁的，邋遢的 **2.** 不漂亮的；过时的 — *n.* 邋遢女人；懒散女人 ‖ **dowdily** *adv.* / **dowdiness** *n.*

dowel ['dauəl] *n.* **1.** 木钉，暗榫 **2.** （用以切削成暗榫的）圆榫 **3.** （嵌入墙内的）受钉木

dower ['dauə] *n.* （寡妇应得的）亡夫遗产 — *vt.* 给…亡夫遗产

down[1] [daun] （最高级 downmost）*adv.* **1.** 向下，在下面：I'll come ～ in a minute. 我马上就下（楼）来。/ The food won't stay ～. 东西吃下去就呕出来。**2.**（物价等）下降 **3.**（在情绪、健康状况等方面）处于低落状态：be ～ with flu 害了流感而病倒 **4.** 减退下去；平息下去：The fire is burning ～. 火快熄灭了。**5.**（在体积方面）由大到小；（在数量方面）由多到少：be worn ～ with use 因使用过

久而磨损/boil a long article ～ to two hundred words 把一篇长文章缩写成二百字（的摘要）**6.**（从首都、城市、北方、上游、市区、下游、海边等一般被看作下方的地方）往下方；在下方：go ～ to the countryside 下乡／～ east（或 East）（美）在美国东北部沿海地区（尤指缅因州）**7.** 往市区（或市内商业区）；在市区（或市内商业区）：Does this bus go ～? 这辆公共汽车是开往市区的吗？**8.**（在时间、顺序、地位等方面）直到（to）：from the richest ～ to the poorest 从最富的到最穷的 **9.**（记）下；（抄）下 **10.**（议案、剧本稿等）（发）下：The paper was （或 went）～ at six yesterday. 昨天报纸六点钟付印。**11.** 现（付）：half ～ and half in instalments 一半付现另一半分期付款 **12.**（道）到底：run ～ a rumour 把谣言查个水落石出 **13.** 停当；认真地：settle ～ in the countryside 在农村安家／get ～ to work 认真开始工作 **14.** 彻底地；完全地：dust ～ the house 彻底打扫房子 — （最高级 downmost）*adj.* **1.** 向下的 **2.**（列车）下行的 **3.** 现（付）的：make a ～ payment of ten yuan 现付十元 — *prep.* **1.** 沿着…往下；往下进入：go ～ the shaft of a mine 下矿井 **2.**（在河流）的下游：live ～ the stream 住在小河的下游 **3.**（由市郊区、城市的住宅区往市区、市内商业区）：He works ～ town. 他在市中心工作。**4.** 沿着（街道、海岸等）**5.**（在时间方面）…以来：～ the ages 自古以来 — *vt.* （口）**1.** 击落（敌机等）打倒；打败 **2.** 喝下；吞下 **3.** 放下：～ tools 放下工具（可指开始罢工或收工）— *n.* 1.（～s）衰落 2.（广播的节目中叙事时为了区别于对话用的）低声调 3.（口）恶感；怨气 ‖ '~-and-'out *adj.* &

n. 被击垮了的(拳击家);落泊的(人);健康垮了的(人)/'~cast *adj*. 1.(人)垂头丧气的,萎靡不振的 2.(眼)向下看的/'~draught *n*.(烟囱的)倒灌风;下向通风(或气流)/'~fall *n*. 1.(雨雪等突然或大量的)下降;垮台;(城市的)陷落 3. 垮台的原因/'~fallen *adj*. 垮了台的/~grade *n*.(路等的)下坡 *adj. & adv*. 下坡的;倾斜的/'~hill *n*.(坡)降低(商品等)的等级;降低(浪剧等)的级别 2. 降低(工人或工种)的等级和工资 3. 贬低;不重视/'~hearted *adj*. 沮丧的,灰心的,郁郁不乐的/'~hill *n*. 1.〈古〉下坡 2. 衰退(阶段) *adj*. 下坡的;倾斜的 *adv*. 1. 往山脚上;趋向衰退/'~load *n*.〈无〉(天线的)引下线/~platform 下行列车月台/'~pour *n*. 1. 倾盆大雨 2.(日光的)照射/'~right *adj*. 1. 明显不过的(谎言等);彻头彻尾的(骗子等) 2. 爽直的;直截了当的 *adv*. 1. 彻底地;十分地 2. 爽直地;直截了当地/'~stair *adj*. = stairs /'~stairs *adj*. 楼下的 *adv*. 在楼下;往楼下 *n*. 楼下/'~stream *adj. & adv*. 顺流(的);在下游(的)/'~-to-earth *adj*. 务实的,实事求是的/'~town *adj*. 在(或往)城市的商业区的 *adv*. 在(或往)城市的商业区的/'~trodden *adj*. 被踩踏的/'~wind *adj. & adv*. 顺风(的)地/*n*. 顺风气

down² [daun] *n*. 有草开阔高地;[常~s](作牧场用的)有草丘陵地/‖~-land *n*. 1. 有草开阔高地 2. 丘陵地

down³ [daun] *n*. 1.(鸟的)软毛;鸭绒,羽绒;duck ~ 鸭绒 2. 软毛;绒毛;汗毛 3.【植】短茸毛;(蒲公英等的)冠毛

Downing ['dauniŋ] **Street** 1. 唐宁街(英国伦敦西区一街名,首相官邸和一些主要政府部门的所在地) 2. 英国政府

downward ['daunwad] *adj*. 1. 向下的 2. 趋向没落的 — *adv*. = downwards

downwards ['daunwadz] *adv*. 向下

downy ['dauni] *adj*. 1. 长绒毛(或茸毛)的 2. 绒毛(或茸毛)状的;绒羽般柔软的 3. 用羽绒制成的 4.〈俚〉狡猾的;机警的

dowry ['dauəri] *n*. 嫁妆

dowse [daus] *vt., vi. & n*. = douse

doxology [dɔk'sɔlədʒi] *n*.【宗】荣耀颂 2. 赞美诗,感谢辞

doyen ['dɔiən] *n*.(一个团体中的)老前辈;地位最高的人

doz. *abbr*. dozen(s)

doze [dauz] *vi*. 打瞌睡,打盹儿(off) — *vt*. 在瞌睡中度过(时间)(away) — *n*. 瞌睡,打盹

dozen ['dʌzn] ([复]dozen(s)) *n* 1.[与数词或 many, several 等连用时,复数不加 "s"](一)打,十二个:two ~ pencils 两打铅笔 2.[~s]几十;许多:for ~s of years 好几十年以来

Dr *abbr*. Doctor

drab [dræb] *n. & adj*. 1. 黄褐色(的) 2. 单调(的),乏味(的),无生气(的) ‖~ly *adv*./~ness *n*.

drachma ['drækmə] ([复]drachmas 或 drachmae ['drækmi:]) *n*. 古希腊银币;德拉克马(现代希腊货币单位)

draft [dra:ft] *n*. 1. 草稿,底稿;草案 2. 汇票;(凭汇票的)提款;汇票的支付 3. 分遣队 4.〈美〉征集,征兵 5.【商】商品重量损耗贴补 6.【机】按模斜度 7.(石工的)凿边;琢边 8.〈美〉拉,牵引,拖,曳 9.(一)网(鱼) 10.(一)饮;(一)吸;汲取;【药】剂量;顿服剂 11.〈美〉(船的)吃水(深度) 12. 通风;气流;穿堂风;通风装置 — *vt*. 1. 起草;为…

打样, 设计 2. 选派 3. 〈美〉征集: 征
(兵) 4. 在(石)上凿槽(或琢边)‖~ee
[drɔːfˈtiː] n. 〈美〉应征入伍者/~er n.
起草人 ‖ ~ board 〈美〉征兵局/
dodger〈美〉逃避服兵役的人

draftsman [ˈdrɑːftsmən] ([复] draftsmen)
n. 1. 起草人 2. 打样人: 制图员 3. 善
于描绘的美术家(别于善于着色的人)

drafty [ˈdrɑːfti] adj. 〈美〉= draughty

drag [dræg] (dragged; dragging) vt. 1. 拖,
拉, (船)拖动(原来钩住的锚) 2. 探(海
底等)用拖网捞 3. 用耙子把(地)—
vi. 1. 拖曳; (原来钩住的锚)被拖动;
缓慢费力地行进: 落在后面 2. (会议
等)拖宕, 拖长 Time seemed to ~. 时光
过得很慢。3. 用拖网等探寻(或捕捉)
(for) 4. 吸 ~ on a cigarette 抽一口 —
n. 1. 被拖物; 大耙; 橇; 大马车; 货运
慢车: 水底捞器具 2. 拖网 3. 刹车, 制动
器; 海锚 4. 障碍物; 累赘; 成为讨厌之
的人(或事物) 5. 【空】阻力 4. 拖曳; 迟缓的
行动 5. 一吸, 一抽; 一饮; 抽烟 6. (野
兽的臭迹; (训练猎犬的)人造臭迹; 利
用人工臭迹的追赶 7.〈俚〉影响 8.~
race 9.〈俚〉男子穿的女子服装 ‖'~line
n. 1. 拉索, 导索 2.【建】拉铲挖掘机
/'~net n. 1. 拖网, 捕鱼网 2. 法网, 天
罗地网/catch all in a ~net 一网打尽/~
race〈美俚〉减重短程高速汽车赛

draggle [ˈdrægl] vt. 拖脏; 拖湿 — vi. 1.
拖脏: 拖湿 2. 慢吞吞前
进, 落在后头 ‖'~tail n. 拖着又脏又湿
裙子的(邋遢)女人

dragon [ˈdrægən] n. 1. 龙 2. 凶暴的人;
严厉的人; 凶恶严格的监护人. [the
D-]【天】天龙座 ‖'~fly n. 蜻蜓 / ~'s
blood 龙血(树脂)

dragoon [drəˈguːn] n. 1. 龙骑兵; 重骑兵
2. 暴徒 — vt. (使用军队)迫害, 镇压

强迫...就范(into)

drain [drein] vt. 1. 排去(水等液体)(off,
away)排去...的水(或其它液体) 2.
喝干 3. 耗尽: be ~ed of one's energy 精
力衰竭 — vi. 1.(水等)流掉; 渐渐枯竭
(off, away) 2.(土地)排水(衣服, 碗
碟等)滴干 — n. 1. 排水; 放干 2. 排水
沟: 排水管; 阴沟 3.【医】引流管, 排液
管(尤指排除脓水的导管) 4. 耗竭(财富
等)的不断外流; 逐渐流光 5. 清杯; 负
担 6.〈口〉一口, 一点儿(指酒等液体)
‖~er n. 滤干器; 滴水板 /'~board
n. 滴水板(= ~ing board) /'~pipe n.
排水管/'~pipe trousers 瘦裤腿紧身裤

drainage [ˈdreinidʒ] n. 1. 排水, 放水; 排
水法; 逐步流出 2. 排水设备; 排水系
统; 下水道 3. 排出的水; 污水 4. 排水
区域(河流)的流域 5.【医】导液(法)
引流(法)‖~ basin【地】排水盆地

drake [dreik] n. 1. 雄鸭 2.(打水漂游戏
用的)石片

dram [dræm] n. 1. 打兰(英制重量单位:
在药衡中 1 打兰为 1/8 盎司, 合 3.88
克; 在常衡中 1 打兰为 1/16 盎司, 合
1.77 克) 2. 液打兰 3.(酒等的)少量,
少许

drama [ˈdrɑːmə] n. 1.(一出)戏; 剧本: 戏
剧 2.[the ~] 戏剧艺术; 戏剧事业 3.
(充满巧合或冲突等的)戏剧性事件; 戏
剧性场面 4. 戏剧文学

dramatic [drəˈmætik] adj. 1. 戏剧的; 剧
本的; 演剧的 2. 戏剧般的, 戏剧性的;
激动人心的: 惹人注目的 ‖~ally adv.
1. 从戏剧角度 2. 戏剧性地; 鲜明地;
显著地

dramatics [drəˈmætiks] [复] n. [用作单
或复] 1. 戏剧表演艺术; 舞台艺术 2.
(尤指夸张的感情表露)戏剧性效果; 做
作

dramatist ['dræmətist] *n.* 剧作家,剧本作者

dramatize ['dræmətaiz] *vt.* **1.** 把(小说、故事等)改编为剧本 **2.** 演戏似地表现;把…戏剧化;使惹人注目 — *vi.* **1.** 具有戏剧性;适于改编成剧本 **2.** (演戏似地)装腔 ‖ **dramati'zation** *n.*

drank [dræŋk] drink 的过去式

drape [dreip] *vt.* **1.** (松弛随便地)披上(衣服等);披盖 **2.** (成褶皱)悬挂于;装饰 **3.** 把(衣服等)制成一定的褶皱状 — *vi.* (衣服等)成褶皱状 — *n.* [常~s] 窗帘;布帘;(手术室里的)消毒被单,消毒盖布 **2.** 褶裥 **3.** 服装式样

draper ['dreipə] *n.* (英)布料和服装商(出售布匹、被单、桌布、窗帘)

drapery ['dreipəri] *n.* **1.** (英)布,布匹;织物;服装 **2.** (英)布料和服装业 **3.** [draperies]帷幕;装饰用褶裥织物 **4.** (人物画、人像雕刻时等)的衣饰

drastic ['dræstik] *adj.* **1.** 激烈的,猛烈的 **2.** (法律等)极端的,严厉的 ‖ ~**ally** *adv.*

draught [drɑːft] *n.* **1.** 拉,牵引,拖,曳;~ animal 役用动物,役畜;耕畜(指牛、马等) **2.** (一)网(鱼) **3.** (一)饮,一口;吸;浸取;[药]剂量;顿服剂 **4.** (船的)吃水(深度) **5.** 通风;气流;穿堂风;通风装置 **6.** [~s]国际跳棋(相当于美国的 checkers) ‖ ~ **beer** 散装啤酒,鲜啤酒,生啤酒/~ **board** *n.* 国际跳棋棋盘

draughtsman ['drɑːftsmən] ([复]draughtsmen) *n.* **1.** 起草人 **2.** 打样人;制图员 **3.** 国际跳棋棋子 ‖ ~**ship** *n.* 制图术;起草术

draughty ['drɑːfti] *adj.* 过道风大的,有穿堂风的 ‖ **draughtily** *adv.* / **draughtiness** *n.*

draw [drɔː] (drew [druː], drawn [drɔːn]) *vt.* **1.** 拉,拖;拉长,拖长;拉成(丝等) **2.** 拔(牙);抽签决定 **3.** 取出…的内脏;使流出;排出(脓等);汲取;领取;提取;获得(力量、教训等);得出,引出(结论等) **5.** 引起(注意等);招致(批评、灭亡等) **6.** 吸入,(一口气)(in);吸引,逗引…说话 **8.** (船)吃(水) **9.** 泡(茶) **10.** 划,画,绘制;描会 **11.** 开(支票等);草拟,制订(up) **12.** 把…打成平局 **13.** [常用被动语态](因疼痛等)扭歪(脸等)(with) **14.** 使(牌)被打出,出(牌) — *vi.* **1.** 拉,拖 **2.** 被吸或被拔出;拔刀;拔枪 **3.** 用抽签(或抽牌等)方法决定 **4.** 支取;排账 **5.** 吸引人 **6.** (船)吃水 **7.** (茶)泡开 **8.** 划线;制图;画画 **9.** 打成平局,不分胜负 **10.** (向某一方向)移动:Summer is ~ing near, 夏天快到了。 **11.** 缩;皱 **12.** (烟囱等)通风 **13.** (猎狗)道踪(或嗅寻)猎物 — *n.* **1.** 拉,拖;吸,汲取;抽签 **3.** 有吸引力的事物(或人) **4.** 平局,不分胜负 **5.** (纸牌游戏中)抽补进的牌 **6.** (吊桥的)可吊起部分 ‖ ~ **back** *v.* **1.** 退缩;退避 **2.** 欠款;弊端 **3.** 障碍(to) **4.** 撤回/~**bridge** *n.* 吊桥;活动桥

drawer [drɔː] *n.* **1.** 抽屉:a chest of ~s 五斗橱 ‖ [~s]五斗橱;内裤 **3.** ['drɔːə](酒吧的)酒保;制图员;开票人;(汇票)出票人 ‖ ~**ful** *n.* 一抽屉之量;大量

drawing ['drɔːiŋ] *n.* **1.** 抽签 **2.** 绘图 **3.** 图画;图样;素描 **4.** 提款 ‖ ~ **block** 绘图纸本/~ **board** 制图板,画图板/~ **card** 能吸引观众的人(或物)/~ **pin** 图钉/~ **room** **1.** 客厅,起居室 **2.** (美)(客车的)特等卧室

drawl [drɔːl] *vt. & vi.* 慢吞吞地说(出);拉长声音唱(出) — *n.* 慢吞吞地说话的样子;慢吞吞地说出的话(或唱出的调子) ‖ ~**ingly** *adv.*

drawn [drɔːn] draw 的过去分词 — *adj.* **1.**

拔出鞘的 2.(比赛)不分胜负的 3.内
胜已挖去的 4.（脸）扭歪的；拉长的
‖'~-'out adj. 拉长了的；在时间方面
过长的/'~work n. 抽花刺绣，抽绣

dray [drei] n.(无围边的)大车，板车；卡车
‖'~-man n. 板车(或大车)夫；卡车
司机

dread [dred] n. 1. 畏惧；恐怖；担心 2. 引
起畏惧的人(或事物)；敬畏的对象 —
vt. & vi. 惧怕；担心 — adj. 令人畏惧
的；使人敬畏的

dreadful ['dredful] adj. 1. 可怕的 2. 令人
敬畏的 3.(口)(天气、噪声等)极讨厌
的(戏等)极无趣的；糟透的 4.(混乱
等)极端的，非常的 — n. 廉价耸激作
(尤指恐怖)小说(或杂志)(= penny ～)
‖ ly adv./~ness n.

dreadnaught, dreadnought ['drednɔ:t] n.
1. 厚呢大衣;仿熊皮粗绒大衣等 2. 无
畏级战舰(源出一九〇六年建成的英国
战舰 Dreadnought 号) 3. 无畏的人

dream [dri:m] n. 1. 梦 2. 梦境，空想 3.
理想，愿望 4. 梦一般美妙的人(或事
物);美人(= dreamed girl, dri:md式)
dreamt[dremt]) vi.-i. 做梦；梦见，梦到
(of, about) 2. 梦想，空想 3. 向往，渴望
(常 for not, little, never 等连用)想到
(不)到；(不会)有……的企图(of) —
vt. 1. 做(梦);梦到(that) 2. 想象，臆
想 3.(因空想而)虚度(时间等)(away)
4. 凭空想出,捏造(up) 5.(常与 not,
little, never 等连用)想(不)到 ‖'~-er n.
1. 做梦的人；梦想家，空想家/~less
adj. 无梦的，不做梦的/~boat n. 梦
一般的人;梦幻的/'~-boat n.(俚)理想
的人(或事物);富有吸引力的异性;情
人/'~-land n. 1. 梦境;梦乡 2. 幻想世
界/'~ reader 详梦的人/'~ world n. ‖
~-land

dreamt [dremt] dream 的过去式和过去分
词

dreamy ['dri:mi] adj. 1.(人)爱空想的 2.
令人喜爱的;理想的(美俚)刮刮叫的
3.(景色等)梦一般的、朦胧的 4.(神情
等)恍惚的 4.(诗)多梦的 5.(曲调等)
柔和怡神的、轻柔的 ‖ dreamily adv./
dreaminess n.

drear [driə] adj. = dreary

dreary ['driəri] adj. 沉闷的;阴郁的;使人
意气消沉的 — n. 枯燥无味的人 —
vt. 使沉闷;使枯燥无味 ‖ drearily
adv./dreariness n.

dredge [dredʒ] n. 1. 挖掘机;挖泥船 2.
(捕鱼等用的)耙网 — vt. 疏浚(河道、
港湾等);挖掘(泥土等)(up, away,
out) — vi. 疏浚,挖掘;采捞(for)
(喻)发掘

dreg [dreg] n.[~s]残渣;糟粕;(喻)渣滓;
废物

drench [drentʃ] vt. 1. 使湿透;浸湿 2. 使
充满 3. 给(牲口)灌药 — n. 1. 湿透;
浸湿 2. 饱饮;兽用顿服药 3. 滂沱大雨

dress [dres] n. 1. 连衣裙;套裙 2. 服装
(尤指外衣) 3. 礼服 — vt. 1. 给……穿
衣;供衣着给 2. 整理;修整;装饰(商店
橱窗等) 3. 给(伤口)敷药,包扎 4. 整
(队) 5. 梳理(头发);给(马等)梳刷
(down) 6. 修剪(树木等);使(织物、石
料等)表面光洁 7. 做(菜);适当处理(
~ a salad 拌色拉 8. 耕种(土地);给土
地,庄稼)施肥 9.[矿]选(矿石) — vi.
1. 穿衣 2. 穿礼服 3.[军]看齐 4.(禽、
畜等去毛开膛后)待得净重 ‖ ~ circle
(戏院的)第一层楼厅的前排坐位/'~
coat 燕尾服/'~-maker n.(尤指女服)裁
缝/'~-making n. 裁缝女服的)职业;缝
制/~ parade (穿军礼服的)(陆、海军)
阅兵典礼;时装表演/~ rehearsal 彩排

dresser ['dresə] *n.* 1. 备餐柜;(美)梳妆台 2.(医院的)敷裹员 3.(剧团的)服装员 4. 穿着讲究的人；与形容词连用)服装…的人：a careful (careless) ~ 服装讲究(不讲究)的人 5. 整形器;整修机;(石料)打磨机

dressing ['dresiŋ] *n.* 1. 穿衣;化妆;装饰 2. 修饰;(铸件等的)修整;(石面等的)修琢 3.【军】整队 4.【医】敷药,包扎 5.(烤鸡等腹内的)填馅;调料 6.【农】施肥 7.【矿】选矿 8.【幼】整理；上浆、梳梳 9.(口)训斥;揍 ‖ ~ case 化妆用品盒 /'~-down *n.* (口)狠狠的训斥/~ gown 晨衣/~ room 化妆室/~ station【军】绷扎所/~ table 梳妆台

dressy ['dresi] *adj.* (口)1.(人)讲究穿着的,(穿了好衣服后)挺刮刮的 2.(服装)时髦的

drew [dru:] draw 的过去式

dribble ['dribl] *vt.* 1. 让(口涎、液体)点点滴滴地流出(或落下) 2. 浪费(时间等)(away) 3.(足、篮、冰球 等)运动中)运(球);击出(慢滚跳球) — *vi.* 1. 滴滴,(烟雾、人群等)慢慢流动;逐渐消失(away) 2.(婴儿、白痴等)流口水 3.运球;(因击球水平不高击出的球)短距滚球 — *n.* 1. 点滴;细流;少量 2. 流涎;濛雨 4. 运球

driblet ['driblit] *n.* 1. 一滴 2. 点滴;少量

drier ['draiə] *n.* 1. 干燥工 2. 干燥器 3. 干燥剂;催干剂;燥性粉

drift [drift] *n.* 1. 漂流;流速 2. 漂流物;吹积物;(漂流或吹积物的)一堆;[地]冰碛 3. 趋势;动向;倾向 4. 要旨 5. 坐视;放任自流 6.【海】吹流,风生流,缓流;偏航;[无]漂移,偏移,偏差;【生】遗传漂移 — *vi.* 1. 漂流,漂泊;游荡;~ apart 变得疏远 2. 吹积 3.(任事情)放任自流 4.(价格等)缓慢地变动,

渐渐趋向(towards);不知不觉地陷入(into);~ into a habit 逐渐养成一种习惯 — *vt.* 1. 使漂流 2. 把…吹积;(吹积物等)覆盖 ‖ ~ er *n.* 1. 漂流物 2. 流浪者 3. 流网渔船,飘网渔船 ‖ ~ ice 流冰/'~-net *n.* (用以捕大西洋鲱鱼的)流网/'~-wood *n.* 1. 漂流木,散流木 2. 废弃物 3. 社会寄生虫

drill[1] [dril] *n.* 1. 操练;训练 2.(英口)规定的步骤 3. 钻;钻头;钻床 — *vt.* 1. 操练;训练 2. 钻(孔);在…上钻孔 3. 用子弹打穿;枪杀 4. 使(球等)笔直行进 — *vi.* 1. 操练;训练 2. 钻孔;钻通(through) 3.(子弹等)穿过(through) ‖ ~ er *n.* 1. 操练员 2. 钻探工 3. 钻机;钻床 ‖ ~ bit 钻头/'~-master *n.*【军】教官

drill[2] [dril]【农】*n.* 1. 条播沟 2. 条播种子,条播作物 3. 条播机 — *vt.* 1. 条播(种子);在…上开条播沟 2. 用条播机播(种);用条播机撒(肥料)

drill[3] [dril] *n.* 粗斜纹布

drily ['draili] *adv.* 1. 干燥地 2. 枯燥地 3. 冷冰冰地,不加渲染地

drink [driŋk] (drank [dræŋk], drunk [drʌŋk]) *vt.* 1. 饮,喝 2.(植物、土壤等)吸收(水分等)(in, up) 3. 贪婪地听(故事等);贪婪地欣赏(美景等)(in) 3.[~ oneself]喝酒喝得(死去、失去知觉等)(to, into) 4. 举杯祝贺 5. 把(钱等)花在喝酒上;喝酒浪费(时间、金钱等);喝酒酒(愁等)(away) — *vi.* 1. 饮,喝 2. 吸收;~ deep of what is progressive 大量吸取进步的东西 3. 喝酒;酗酒 4. 为某人的健康等)干杯(to) — *n.* 1. 饮料 2. 一杯(或一份)饮料 3. 酒;喝酒;酗酒 4.[the ~](口)一片水(指海、湖、池等水体) ‖ ~ er *n.* 酒徒

drinkable ['driŋkəbl] *adj.* 可以喝的 — *n.*

[常~s]饮料

drinking ['driŋkiŋ] *n*. 喝，饮；喝酒 ‖ ~
fountain 喷泉式饮水器(供公共饮水
用)/ ~ **water** 饮用水

drip [drip] (dripped; dripping) *vt*. 使滴下
— **sweat** 大汗淋淋 — *vi*. 1. 滴下；滴
水，湿淋淋 2.(月光等)漏下；撒下 3.
充溢，充满 — *n*. 1. 流滴；滴水(声)；
点滴 2. 滴下的液体 3.【医】滴水挑curt；
外套台 4.【医】(静脉)滴注；滴注器，滴
液 5.(俚)使人厌烦的人，讨厌鬼 ‖ ~
、,'~-**drop** *n*. 不断的滴水/ ~ **mo(u)ld**
【建】滴水台脚/'~-**stone** *n*. 1.【建】滴水
石 2. 钟乳石，石笋

drip-dry ['drip'drai] *vi*. 滴干；滴干后保
持挺括 — *adj*. 用滴干衣裳做法

dripping ['dripiŋ] *n*. 1. 滴下；滴水声 2.[~s]
滴下的液体，(烤肉上滴下的)油滴 —
adj. 滴水的，湿淋淋的

drive [draiv] (drove [drəuv], driven['drivn])
vt. 1. 驱，赶 2. 驱使；迫使；逼迫 3. 驾
驶(马车，汽车等)；用车送 4. 推动、发
动(机器等) 5. 把(钉、桩等)打入(*in-
to*)；凿穿；钻透(某种思想)(*in*) 6.
挖(隧道等) 7. 努力做(生意)；使成交
8. 用力击(球)；猛力掷(球)；猛抽(球)
— *vi*. 1. 被驱赶；(云等)疾
驰 2.(尤指雨)猛扑；驱(进) — straight
in 长驱直入 3. 用力击球；猛力掷球；抽
球 — *n*. 1. 驱赶；驱使 2. 驾驶；驱车旅
行(汽车等) 3. 驾车的一段路 4.(指私室
内的)汽车道 5.(尤指有自然景色的)道
路；街道 4. 击球；掷球；抽球 5.(顺流
而下的)木排 6.(被驱赶的)畜群 7. 冲
动；欲望；推动力；干劲；魄力；积极性，
能动性 8.(美)运动；竞赛 9.[工作等]
压力；紧张状态 10. 倾向，趋势 11.
【机】传动；传动装置 12.(击球的)驱
击 13.【矿】平巷 14.(磁带或磁盘的)驱

动器 ‖ ~-**in** *n*.(顾客无须下车即可得
到服务的)"免下车"餐馆(或剧场、银
行、邮局等) *adj*.(影院、银行等)提供
"免下车"服务的；有"免下车"服务设施
的/'~-**up** *adj*.(为顾客提供)"免下车"
服务的/'~-**way** *n*.(花园内通达房屋
的)私家车道

drivel ['drivl] (drivel(l)ed; drivel(l)ing) *vi*.
1. 说傻话；喋喋不休地胡说 2. 滴口水
— *vt*. 胡乱而愚蠢地说出 — *n*. 胡言
乱语；胡扯 ‖ drivel(l)er *n*. 说说八道的人

driven ['drivn] drive 的过去分词 — *adj*.
1. 出于不得已的 2.(尤指雪)吹积起来
的 3.【机】被驱动的 ‖ ~ **gear** 从动齿轮

driver ['draivə] *n*. 1. 驾驶员，司机；赶车
工 2. 赶牲口的人 3. 监工 4. 锤；夯；打
桩机 5.【机】传动器；主动轮；驱动器 6.
[无]激励器 7.(船)后纵帆

driving ['draiviŋ] *adj*. 1.(力等)推动的，
【机】(带等)传动的；(轴等)主动的 2.
(尤指雨)猛扑的，飘泼般的 3. 有干劲
的 — *n*. 驾驶；驱车 ‖ ~ **gear** 【机】主动
齿轮/ ~ **licence** 驾驶执照/ ~ **test** 汽
车驾驶员行车执照的考试/ ~ **wheel**
【机】主动轮

drizzle ['drizl] *vi*. 下毛毛雨 — *n*. 毛毛
雨，细雨

drizzly ['drizli] *adj*. 下着蒙蒙细雨的；毛
毛雨似的

droll [drəul] *adj*. 滑稽可笑的；古怪的 ‖
~ **ness** *n*. / ~ **y** *adv*.

drollery ['drəuləri] *n*. 1.(开)玩笑；(说)笑
话 2.(逗人发笑的)噱头

dromedary ['drɔmədəri, 'drʌmədəri] *n*.【动】
(因善跑而常被训练作乘骑用的)单峰
驼，阿拉伯驼

drone [drəun] *n*. 1. 雄蜂 2. 寄生虫；懒汉
3. 无人驾驶飞机(或船舶等) 4. 嗡嗡

声;单调沉闷的讲话;【音】持续音、低音(部) **5.** 语言无味的一段 **6.** 风笛的单音管 — *vi.* **1.** 发出嗡嗡声 **2.** 用单调沉闷的声调说话 **3.** 平平淡淡地进行 — *vt.* **1.** 低沉单调地说出(out) **2.** 无所事事地打发(日子)(*away*)

drool [druːl] *vi.* **1.** 流口水;(口水等)流出嘴巴 **2.** 说傻话;胡说八道 **3.** 过分地表示高兴(*over, about*)

droop [druːp] *vi.* **1.** (头、树枝等)低垂、下垂(眼睛)朝下 **2.**(草木)凋萎;(人)衰颓;(精神)萎靡 — *vt.* 垂下(头、双眼) — *n.* 低垂;消沉 ‖ **~ly** *adj.*

drop [drɔp] *n.* **1.** 滴;[~s]滴剂 **2.** 滴状物(如粒糖果):fruit ~ s(球形)水果糖 **3.** 点滴;微量 **4.** 一杯(或一口)酒 **5.** 落下、下降:【电】电压降 **6.** 下落物 **7.** 垂物;树木的落果;(绞刑架上的)下落板;吊架;(门上的)锁孔盖;【建】吊饰;【机】落锤 **7.** 下落距离;落差;【军】弹道降落距离 **8.** 空投;空投的人(或物资)**9.**(动物的)产仔 **10.**(邮筒等的)投入口 **11.**【体】下坠球、抛踢球(= ~ kick)**12.**(赃物的)藏匿处;(情报的)秘密传送地点 — (dropped; dropping)*vt.* **1.** 使落下;使滴下;放下;投下 **3.**(失手)落下;丢失 **4.** 遗漏;省略 **5.** 降低(声音、速度等);丢失(话题等);抛弃(坏习惯等)**6.** 卸掉(拖车等);同…断绝关系 **7.**(美)开除;解雇 **8.** 击倒;射落 **9.**(不经意地)说出(信息等);~ sb. a few lines 给某人写封短信 **10.** 下(客);卸(货)**11.**(动物)产(仔)**12.** 把(鸡蛋)打入沸水中煮 **13.**(俚)在赌博、投机等中(丧失(钱财)**14.**【体】(抛球落地反弹球)踢抛球落地反弹球得(分);击(球)入穴;投(篮)入篮 **15.**(纸牌戏中)硬打吊出(王牌等)— *vi.* **1.** 滴下;落下、掉下 **2.**(价格、温度等)

下降;(风、声音等)变弱 **3.** 停止,终止:let the matter ~ 不再提这件事 **4.**(因疲劳、受伤等)倒下 **5.**(话等)无意中漏出 **6.**(美)(动物)出生 **7.**(猎犬等扑向猎物前)蹲下 **8.**(可能的赢球者)被硬打吊出 ‖ **~ let** *n.* 微滴;~ *let* infection【医】飞沫传染/**dropper** *n.* **1.** 落下的人(或物)**2.** 滴管 ‖ ~ curtain(戏院等的)垂幕 ~ hammer【机】落锤/~ in 不速之客;顺道来访者 **2.** 意外的来访,偶一的过访 **3.**(邀人顺便参加的)非正式社交聚会;顺便(或偶尔)走访的地方/~-kick *n.*【体】抛踢球/~ out *n.*〈口〉**1.** 退出;退学 **2.** 中途退出的人;退学学生 **3.** 逃避现实社会的人

droppings ['drɔpiŋz]【复】*n.* 滴下物,落下物(如烛油,落叶、鸟粪等)

dropsy ['drɔpsi] *n.*【医】水肿,积水

dross [drɔs] *n.* **1.**【冶】浮渣,废料;杂质

drought [draut] *n.* **1.**(长期)干旱;旱灾 **2.** 长期缺乏

drove [drəuv] drive 的过去式 — *n.* **1.**(被驱赶的或向前走动的)畜群 **2.**(走在一起的)人群

drover ['drəuvə] *n.* **1.** 赶牲畜(上市)的人 **2.** 牛贩子

drown [draun] *vt.* **1.** 把…淹死 **2.** 淹没(房屋、话声等)**3.** 浸湿;eyes ~ *ed* in tears 泪汪汪的眼睛 **4.** 使沉溺于(*in*)**5.** 驱散,消除(忧愁等)— *vi.* 溺死

drowse [drauz] *vi.* **1.** 打瞌睡,打盹儿(*off*)**2.** 呆滞;不活跃 — *vt.* **1.** 使呆滞;使不活跃;使昏昏欲睡 **2.** 昏昏沉沉地消磨(时间)(*away*)**3.** 瞌睡

drowsy ['drauzi] *adj.* **1.** 昏昏欲睡的;瞌睡的 **2.** 催眠的;使人懒洋洋的 **3.**(村庄、街市等)沉寂的,没有动静的 ‖ **drowsily** *adv.***/drowsiness** *n.*

drub [drʌb] (drubbed; drubbing) *vt.* **1.** 棒

打；鞭抽；痛打 2. 彻底击败 3. 强行灌输(某种思想)(*into*)

drudge [drʌdʒ] *n.* 1. 做苦工的人 2. 做单调乏味工作的人 3. 单调乏味的工作 — *vi.* 做苦工；干单调乏味的工作(*at*, *over*)‖ ~ *n.* 苦活；单调乏味的工作

drug [drʌg] *n.* 1. 药，药物；药材 2. 麻醉药品，麻醉剂；成瘾性毒品 3. 滞销货 — (*drugged*; *drugging*) *vt.* 1. 使服麻醉药；使服毒品；掺麻醉药于 2. 使麻痹，使麻木 3. 〈美俚〉恼怒 — *vi.* 吸毒 ‖ ~ **store** *n.* 〈美〉药店，杂货店(出售药物、糖果、饮料及其他杂物的店铺)

druggist [ˈdrʌgist] *n.* 1. 药商 2. 药剂师 3. 〈美〉售杂货的药店店主

drum [drʌm] *n.* 1. 鼓 2. 鼓状物；桶；【机】鼓轮；卷筒；滚筒 2. (自动武器的)鼓形弹匣 3.【解】鼓膜，鼓室；中耳；【动】共鸣器官 4. 鼓声；(打鼓时的)咚咚声，敲击声 5.【建】(建柱子用的)圆鼓石；(支撑穹顶的)鼓形座 6.【动】(发出鼓声的)石首鱼 — (*drummed*, *drumming*) *vi.* 1. 打鼓；咚咚地敲 2. (鸟、昆虫鼓翅)发出嗡嗡声 — *vt.* 1. 打鼓奏(曲调) 2. 咚咚地敲 3. 反复灌输(某种思想)(*into*)‖ ~ **beat** *n.* 击鼓(声)/~ **fire** *n.* (进攻前发射的)猛烈炮火/~ **major** 军乐队指挥/~ **stick** *n.* 1. 鼓槌 2. (煮熟的)鸡腿下段；鸡腿与腿肉身

drummer [ˈdrʌmə] *n.* 1. 鼓手 2.〈美〉旅行推销员

drunk [drʌŋk] drink 的过去分词 — *adj.* [常作表语] 1. 醉的 2. 陶醉的；兴奋的 — ~ `n.* 〈俚〉醉汉；酒鬼；酗酒狂

drunkard [ˈdrʌŋkəd] *n.* 醉汉；酒鬼

drunken [ˈdrʌŋkən] *adj.* [常作定语] 1. 喝醉的 2. 酒醉引起的：a ~ frolic 酒后胡闹 3. 喝醉酒似的；摇摇晃晃的 ‖

~ **ly** *adv.* / ~ **ness** *n.*

dry [drai] *adj.* 1. 干的；干燥的 2. 干旱的 3. 干枯的；枯萎的；(奶牛)不再产奶的 4.〈口〉口渴的；(活儿)使人口渴的 5. 不用水的；没有水汁的(如干馏、干洗剂等)；不经滑润的 6.(面包等)不涂黄油的 7.(酒等)不甜的，无果味的 8. 干巴巴的，枯燥无味的 (讽刺等)冷冰冰的；(事实等)不加渲染的，不带个人偏见(或感情)的 10.(会见等)无预期结果的，没有收获的 11.〈口〉空弹的演习中 12. 禁酒的 — *vt.* 1. 把……弄干；使干燥 2. 使(奶牛)停止产奶 — *vi.* 变干；干涸(*up*)‖ ~ **ly** *adv.* = drily/ ~ **ness** *n.* ‖ ~ **battery** 干电池(组)/~ **cell** 干电池/~ `*clean* *vt.* 干洗/~ **cleaner** 1. 干洗剂 2. 干洗商/~ `*cleanse* *vt.* 干洗/~ **dock** 干船坞/~ `*dock* **货(如谷类)使 2.〈美〉纺织品，匹头；现成衣服/~ **ice** 干冰，固态二氧化碳/~ **measure** *n.* ~ **nurse** 1. 保姆(区别于 wet nurse 奶妈) 2. 给人不必要指导的人/~ `*nurse* *vt.* 当……的保姆；给……多余的指点/~ **rot** 干腐，褐腐；【植】干腐病；(商、社会等的)腐败/~ `*shod* *adj.* & *adv.* 不弄湿鞋(或脚)的(地)

dryer [ˈdraiə] *n.* 1. 干燥工，干燥器；干燥机；烘衣架 2. 干燥剂

dual [ˈdjuəl] *adj.* 双的，二重的；二元的；二体的 ~ **nationality** 双重国籍/~ **control** 双重控制，复式操纵；双方共管；两人合управ — *n.* [语]双数 ‖ ~ **ly** *adv.* ‖ ~ **carriageway** 〈英〉(有中央分隔带的)复式车行道/~ `*purpose* *adj.* 1. 双重目的的，两用的 2.〈农〉(家畜、家禽品种)乳肉(或卵肉)兼用的：a ~ *purpose* hen 卵肉兼用鸡

dub [dʌb] (*dubbed*; *dubbing*) *vt.* 1.(以某种

称号)授予；给...起绰号 2. 用剑拍肩封... 为爵士 3. 用油脂涂(皮革等) 4. 译制(电影)；为(电影、广播节目等)配音；复制(录音、唱片等)

dub-a-dub ['dʌbədʌb] n. 冬冬(鼓声)

Dubai [du:'bai] n. 1. 迪拜[阿拉伯联合酋长国的酋长国之一] 2. 迪拜(市) [阿拉伯联合酋长国东北部港市][迪拜酋长国首府]

dubious ['dju:biəs] adj. 1. (对事物)半信半疑的；犹豫不决的 (of, about) 2. 暧昧的，含糊的 3. 引起怀疑的，可疑的 4. 未定的，不定局的；无把握的 ‖ ~ly adv. / ~ness n.

Dublin ['dʌblin] n. 都柏林[爱尔兰共和国首都]

ducal ['dju:kəl] adj. 公爵的；公爵似的；公爵领地的

ducat ['dʌkət] n. 1. 达克特(过去曾在欧洲许多国家通用的金币名) 2. [~s] (口)钱 3. (俚)入场券，门票

duchess ['dʌtʃis] n. 1. 公爵夫人；女公爵 2. 仪表威严的妇女 3. (英俚)小贩的老婆；妻子；女人

duchy ['dʌtʃi] n. 公爵领地；公国

duck¹ [dʌk] n. 1. 鸭；雌鸭(drake 雄鸭之对)；鸭肉；[总称]鸭类 2. (口)亲爱的人，宝贝儿；亲 3. 可爱的(物或人) 4. (口)家伙 5. (登陆用水陆两用车 6. [体]鸭蛋，零分 (= ~ egg or ~'s egg) ‖ ~-bill n. 1.(动)鸭嘴兽 2.(鱼)匙吻鲟，鸭嘴装载机 / ~-weed n.(植)浮萍

duck² [dʌk] vi. 1. 突然潜入水中 2. 迅速低下头(或弯下身) 3. 闪避；躲避 — vt. 1. 把(人等)猛按入水中 2. 突然低下(头或身子) 3. (口)逃避(责任等)；回避(问题等) — n. 突然的一潜；闪避

duckling ['dʌkliŋ] n. 小鸭，幼鸭

duct [dʌkt] n. 1. 导管；管道；槽，沟；an air ~ 通气管，通气道 2.[生]管，导管 3. (电线、电缆等的)管道 — vt. 通过管道输送(气体等) ‖ ~-less adj. 无管的；~-less gland[解]无管腺，内分泌腺

ductile ['dʌktail] adj. 1. (金属等)易拉长的、可延展的、可锻的 2. (粘土等)可塑的、易变形的 3. 易教的；顺从的，驯良的 ‖ ductility [dʌk'tiliti] n. 1. 延性；可延展性；可锻性；塑性 2. (人等)可塑性

dud [dʌd] n. 1. [~s](俚)衣服；破衣服；个人衣着 2. 未爆炸炮弹(或炸弹)，哑弹 3. 不中用的东西；无用的人 — adj. 不中用的；没有价值的；假的

dude [dju:d] n. (美口) 1. 纨绔子弟，花花公子；服装讲究的人 2. (从美国东部去西部牧场度假的)城里人 3.(男)人，家伙

dudgeon ['dʌdʒən] n. 愤恨，愤怒：in high ~ 非常愤怒

due [dju:] adj. 1. 适当的；应有的；应得的；正当的 2. (车、船等)预定应到的；预期的，约定的 3. (支付的)(票据等)到期的 — adv. (罗盘指针)正(南、东等) — n. 1. 应得物；应得权益 2. [~s] 应付款，应交费用 ‖ ~ to 1. 应归功(或归咎)于 2. 由于

duel ['dju:əl] n. 1. 决斗 2. (双方的)斗争；战斗：an artillery ~ 炮战 — (duel(l)ed; duel(l)ing) vi. 决斗 ‖ ~(l)ist n. 决斗者

duet [dju:'et] n. 1.[音]二重唱(曲)；二重奏(曲、二重奏) 演出小组 2. (喻)对话；双人舞；一双，一对 ‖ duettist n. 二重唱者；二重奏者

dug [dʌg] dig 的过去式和过去分词

dugout ['dʌgaut] n. 1. 独木舟 2. 挖在山坡(或地下)的洞；防空洞；地下掩蔽部

3.〈俚〉重新服役的退伍军官;退休后重新任职者

duke [djuːk] *n.* 公爵;(欧洲公国的)君主 ‖ ~**dom** *n.* 1. 公国;公爵领地 2. 公爵的爵位

dull [dʌl] *adj.* 1. 迟钝的;笨拙的 2.(疼痛)隐约(感觉到)的 3.(颜色、光线等)暗淡的 4.(天气、天空)阴沉的 5.(声音)模糊的;不清楚的 6.(刀等)钝的 7.(商品)滞销的;(市场、生意等)呆滞的,不活跃的 8. 单调的,乏味的 9. 精神不振的,没精打采的 — *vt.* 1. 弄钝,使变钝 2. 使暗淡 3. 缓和,减轻(痛苦等) — *vi.* 1. 变得迟钝 2.(兴趣、痛苦等)减少,减轻 ‖ ~**ard** *n.* 蠢人,笨蛋/**dul-**(l)**ness** *n.* / ~**y** *adv.* ‖ ~'-'**witted** *adj.* 笨的,迟钝的

duly ['djuːli] *adv.* 1. 按时地;及时地 2. 正式地 3. 充分地;适当地

Duma ['duːmə] *n.*〈国家〉杜马(俄罗斯及旧时俄国的议会)

dumb [dʌm] *adj.* 1. 哑的,不能说话的 2. 默默无言的;沉默寡言的;没有发言权的 3. 无音的,无声的 ‖ ~ **piano**(练习运指的)哑琴 4.(因惊讶、害羞等)发不出声音的,愣住的 5. 笨的,愚蠢的 ‖ ~**ly** *adv.* / ~**ness** *n.* ‖ ~ **bell** *n.* 1. 哑铃 2.〈俚〉笨蛋,蠢货/**dum**(b)'**found** *vt.* 使惊讶得说不出话来/~ **show** 哑剧/~'**struck** *adj.* 被吓得发愣的/'~'**waiter** *n.*〈美〉(用餐时使用的)圆转台;(楼层间用的)送菜升降机

dummy ['dʌmi] *n.* 1. 哑巴,沉默的人;笨蛋 2. 挂名者;傀儡 3.〈牌戏〉明手(叫牌叫定后,摊牌于桌上的人) 4. 人形靶;(橱窗中陈列的)人体模型;(伪制的)样品 5. 虚设物;模仿物;伪装物 6.(英)橡皮奶头 — *adj.* 1. 摆样子的样子的,假的 2. 挂名的;虚设的 3. 傀

偶的,不能独立行动的 — *vi.*〈口〉(足球赛中)做假传球动作

dump [dʌmp] *n.* 1. 垃圾堆场;垃圾堆 2.(材料、衣服等的)堆存处;(军需品等的)临时堆集处 3.〈俚〉邋遢地方 4.〈俚〉(或袭)的一声 5.〈计〉(计算机的)转出,倾卸,转储 — *vt.* 1. 倾卸(垃圾);抛弃(废物、候选人等) 2. 把…卸下,砰的一声抛下 — *vi.* 1. 倒垃圾 2. 倾销商品 3. 砰地落下 ‖ ~**er** *n.* 1. 自倾货车;翻斗车;倾卸车 2. 倾卸工 3. 拆箱工,拆箱工 ~ **truck** 自动倾货车

dumpling ['dʌmpliŋ] *n.* 1. 汤团;团子;饺子;水果布丁 2.〈口〉矮胖的人(或动物)

dumps [dʌmps]〈复〉*n.* 忧郁;沮丧 ‖ (**down**) **in the** ~ 神情沮丧的

dumpy ['dʌmpi] *adj.* 矮胖的;短而粗大的 ‖ **dumpiness** *n.*

dun[1] [dʌn] *n.*(dunned; dunning) *vt.* 1. 向…催讨 2. 对…纠缠不清,使烦恼 — *vi.* 催债 — *n.* 1. 催债者 2. 催讨;催债

dun[2] [dʌn] *adj.* 1. 暗褐色的 2.(马)灰褐色的 3.〈诗〉阴郁的,阴暗的 — *n.* 1. 暗褐色,灰兔褐色 2. 灰兔褐色马

dunce [dʌns] *n.* 笨伯 ‖ ~'(s) **cap**(旧时学校中给成绩差的学生戴的圆锥形)笨蛋纸帽

dune [djuːn] *n.*(风吹积成的)沙丘,土丘

dung [dʌŋ] *n.*(牲畜的)粪;粪肥 — *vt.* 施粪肥于 ‖ ~ **beetle**【动】金龟子;蜣金龟;粪甲虫

dungaree [ˌdʌŋɡə'riː] *n.* 1. 粗蓝布,劳动布 2. [~s]粗蓝布工装裤;粗蓝布工作服;(美)劳动布

dungeon ['dʌndʒən] *n.* 土牢,地牢

dunghill ['dʌŋhil] *n.* 1. 粪堆 2. 污秽场所;邋遢人;可鄙境地;令人作呕的事物

dunk [dʌŋk] vt. 1.(吃前)把(面包等)泡一泡(或浸一浸) 2. 浸,泡

Dunkirk, Dunkerque [ˈdʌnkə:k, dʌnˈkə:k] n. 敦刻尔克[法国北部港市](1940 年英军被德军打败,从这里撤回本国) ‖ ~ **spirit**(危急时拒不投降的)敦刻尔克精神

duo [ˈdju:əu]([复] duos) n. [音]二重奏;二重唱;(艺人的)一对

duodenum [ˌdju:əˈdi:nəm](duodena [ˌdju:əˈdi:nə] 或 duodenums) n. [解]十二指肠

dupe [dju:p] vt. 欺骗;诈骗;愚弄 — n. (易)受骗的人;(易)被人操纵的工具

duplex [ˈdju:pleks] adj. 1. 双的;二重的;a ~ lamp 双芯灯 2.【钮】双联的(复式的);[讯](电报)双工的,双向的 — n. 1. (跨两层楼的)套楼公寓(= ~ apartment) 2. 两户合住的房屋(= ~ house)

duplicate [ˈdju:plikət] adj. 复制的;完全相同的;副的;二重的;二倍的;a ~ copy 副本 — n. 1. 复制品;副本;抄件 2. 完全相同的对应物 3. (纸牌比赛中的)复局 — [ˈdju:plikeit] vt. 1. 使加倍;使成双 2. 复写;复印;复制 3. 使重复 ‖ **dupli′cation** n.

duplicator [ˈdju:plikeitə] n. 1. 复制者 2. 复印机

duplicity [dju:ˈplisiti] n. 口是心非;表里不一;奸诈;欺骗

durable [ˈdjuərəbl] adj. 1. 耐用的 2. (友谊,和平等)持久的 — n. [~s]耐用品(= ~ goods) ‖ **dura′bility** n./**~ness** n./**durably** adv. ‖ **~ goods** 耐用品(指电冰箱等家用电器、汽车、机器等)

durance [ˈdjuərəns] n. (尤指长期的)监禁

duration [djuˈreiʃən] n. 持续,持久;持续时间,期间

duress [djuˈres] n. 胁迫;监禁;束缚

during [ˈdjuəriŋ] prep. 在...的期间;在...的时候

Dushanbe [djuˈʃɑ:mbi] n. 杜尚别[塔吉克斯坦首都]

dusk [dʌsk] n. 1. 薄暮,黄昏 2. 幽暗

dusky [ˈdʌski] adj. 1. 微暗的,暗淡的 2. 暗黑色的,黑黝黝的 ‖ **duskily** adv./**duskiness** n.

dust [dʌst] n. 1. 灰尘,尘土 2. 粉末;[植]花粉;[矿]金末,矽金,金泥,金粉 3.(英)垃圾;灰烬 4. 土;葬身地 5. 遗骸 6. 混乱;骚动 7.(喻)粪土,不值分文的东西 — vt. 1. 去掉...上的灰尘;把...弄成粉末 3. 撒粉末于;撒...上;撒...上(with) 4.(俚)蒙骗 ‖ **~bin** (英)垃圾箱(美国称 ash can)/**~ bowl** 干旱尘暴区/**~ cart**(英)垃圾车/**col**o(u)**r** n. 灰褐色/**~ cover** 1.(家具等)防尘罩 2.(书的)护封/**~ guard**(英)(机器的)防尘板;防尘罩/**~ jacket**(书的)护封/**~ man** n.(英)1. 垃圾工 2.(神话中使小孩睡瞌的)睡魔/**~ n.** 奋箕/**~ storm**[气]尘暴/**~up** n. 1. 争吵,争论 2. 骚动

duster [ˈdʌstə] n. 1. 打扫工 2. 揩布;尘拂,掸帚;除尘器 3. 喷粉器(尤指杀虫剂的喷洒器)/撒粉瓶;撒粉器 4.(美)防尘外衣,风衣

dusting [ˈdʌstiŋ] n. 1. 掸灰 2. 农药(或肥料等)的喷撒 3.(俚)击,打;击败

dusty [ˈdʌsti] adj. 1. 满是灰尘的 2. 灰土一般的;粉末状的 3. 土灰色的 4. 干巴巴的,无聊的 5.(答复等)含糊的,不明朗的

Dutch [dʌtʃ] adj. 1. 荷兰(人)的;荷兰语的;荷兰制的;荷兰式的 2.(美俚)德国(人)的 — n. 1. [the ~][总称]荷兰人 2. 荷兰语 3. [the ~](美俚)[总称]德国人 4.(美俚)火气,怒气 ‖ ~ **auction**

(开价基高然后逐渐降低的)荷兰式拍卖/~ bargain 饮酒时做成的交易(常指不平靠或不公平)/~ courage 酒后之勇;一时的虚勇/~ door (上下两部分可各自分别开关的)两截门/~ treat 各自付费的聚餐(或娱乐活动)/~ uncle 严厉的批评者

Dutchman ['dʌtʃmən] ([复] Dutchmen) n. 1. 荷兰人;(美俚)德国人 2. 荷兰船 3. 【建】木塞块,塞孔补缺木块

dutiable ['djuːtiəbl] adj. (货物)应征税的

dutiful ['djuːtiful] adj. 尽职的;尽本分的,恭敬的;顺从的 ‖ ~ly adv. ~ness n.

duty ['djuːti] n. 1. 责任,义务 2. 职务;勤务:on (off) ~ 值班(下班) 3. 恭顺;恭敬 4. 税;(进口)关税 5. (发动机等的)能率;功率;效力 ‖ ~-'bound adj. 义不容辞的/'~-'free adj. & adv. (货物)免税的(地)/'~-'paid adj. (货物)已付税的

dwarf [dwɔːf] n. 1. 矮子;矮生动物(或植物) 2. (北欧神话中巧于金属小工艺的)丑矮人 3.【天】矮星(= ~ star,如太阳) — vt. 使矮小;阻碍...的发育;使相形见绌 — vi. 变矮小 — adj. 矮小的

dwell [dwel] (dwelt [dwelt] 或 dwelled) vi. 1. 居住 2. 生活(于);存在(于)(in):~ in proverty 生活在贫困中 3. (马踌躇障碍前)收住(或放慢)脚步 ‖ ~ on (或 upon)1. 老是想着 2. 详述;强调 3. (眼光等)停留在;凝视 4. 使(音或音节等)持续 ‖ ~er n. 居民;居住者

dwelling ['dweliŋ] n. 住处,寓所 ‖ ~-house 住宅/~ place 住处

dwelt [dwelt] dwell 的过去式和过去分词

dwindle ['dwindl] vi. & vt. (使)缩小;(使)变小;(使)减少

dye [dai] n. 1. 染色 2. 染料 — vt. 染,给...染色;染上(颜色);使带有(或沾上)颜色 — vi. 被染色;被着色(;染料等)染上颜色 ‖ ~r n. ‖ '~-d-in-the-'wool adj. 彻头彻尾的;十足的/'~-stuff n. 染色剂;染料;染液

dyeing ['daiiŋ] n. 染色 2. 染色工艺;染业 — adj. 染色的

dying ['daiiŋ] die 的现在分词 — adj. 1. 快要死的,垂死的 2. 临终的 3. 快想灭的;行将完结的:the ~ year 年终,岁暮

dyke [daik] n., vt. & vi. = dike

dynamic [dai'næmik] adj. 1. 动力的;动力学的;动态的 2. 有生气的;能动的;有力的;精悍的 3.【医】机能的,功能的,官能的(与 organic 相对)‖ ~al adj. 1. = dynamic 2.【神学用语】(灵感)赋予神力的/~ally adv. ~ism n. 有力的行动;推动力;活力

dynamics [dai'næmiks] [复] n. 1. [用作单]力学 2. 动力学 3. 动态 4.【音】力度;力度变化

dynamite ['dainəmait] n. 1. 达纳炸药;氨爆炸药 2. 轰动一时的人(或事物);具有爆炸性(或潜在危险)的人(或事物)— vt. 用炸药炸毁

dynamo ['dainəmau] ([复] dynamos) n. 1. 发电机(尤指直流发电机);电动机 2. (口)精力充沛的人

dynasty ['dinəsti, 'dainəsti] n. 王朝;朝代

dysentery ['disəntri] n. 痢疾;(口)腹泻

dysfunction [dis'fʌŋkʃən] n. 机能障碍,机能不良 — vi. 出现机能障碍

dyspepsia [dis'pepsia] n. 消化不良

dyspeptic [dis'peptik] adj. 1. 消化不良的 2. 阴郁的;暴躁的 — n. 消化不良患者 ‖ ~ally adv.

dz. abbr. dozen(s)

E

E, e [iː] (复 E's, es 或 Es, es[iz])英语字母表第五个字母 **1.** [E]E字形 **2.** [音]E音,E调 **3.** (美)学业成绩第五等"考"(表示"须补考"的符号)[注意:E 有时也作学业成绩优良(excellent)的符号] **4.** 东(east)的符号

each [iːtʃ] *adj.* 各个;各自的;每:There is a line of trees on ~ side of the river. 河的两边各有一行树。—*pron.* 各,各自:Let us had a try. 我们各人都试一下。‖ ~ other [用作宾语]相互

eager ['iːɡə] *adj.* 热切的;渴望的(*for, about, to do*)‖ ~ly *adv.* / ~ness *n.* ‖ ~ beaver 做事特别卖力的人(尤指做事为求实力以取悦上司的人)

eagle ['iːɡl] *n.* **1.** [鸟]雕 **2.** 鹰徽;鹰旗 **3.** [E-][天]天鹰座 **4.** (高尔夫球赛中)少击两杆入洞的成绩 ‖ ~-'eyed *adj.* 眼力敏锐的;目光炯炯的

eaglet ['iːɡlit] *n.* 小雕

ear[1] [iə] *n.* **1.** 耳朵;耳状物(指水壶、杯子等的耳形提把);(泛指)耳形 **2.** 听觉;听能:have an ~ for music 能欣赏音乐 **3.** 倾听;注意:give ~ to a request 倾听…请补补考 **4.** 报头左边(或右)角小栏(刊登天气预报或简短广告等)‖ ~-'ache ['iəreik] *n.* 耳痛 / ~-'cap *n.* (御寒用的)耳套 / '~-drop *n.* 耳坠;[复]耳药水 / ~ drum *n.* [解] **1.** 鼓膜,耳膜 **2.** 鼓室,中耳 / '~-flap

n.[常 ~ flaps](帽上可放下护耳御寒的)耳扇,帽瓣 / '~-lap *n.1.* = ~ flap **2.** = ~-lobe **3.** 外耳 / '~-lobe *n.* 耳垂 / '~-mark *n.* **1.**(打在牛、羊耳朵上表示所有权的)耳记 **2.** 标记;特征 *vt.* **1.** 在(家畜)耳朵上打戳记 **2.** 在…上做标记;指定(款项等)的用途 / '~-muffs *n.* [~-muffs](御寒用的)耳套 / '~-phone *n.* 头戴受话器,耳机;耳塞 / '~-pick *n.* (听诊器等的)耳承;眼镜脚 **3.**(帽等的)耳扇,帽瓣 / ~-piercing *adj.*(声音等)撕裂耳朵的,刺耳的 / '~-plug *n.* (防水或防震聋用的)耳塞;耳栓 / '~-ring *n.* 耳环;耳饰 / '~-shot *n.* 听觉所及的范围 / '~-splitting *adj.* 震耳欲聋的 / ~ trumpet(半聋人用的)号角状助听器 / ~ wax *n.* 耳垢 / '~-wig *n.1.* [动]蠼螋 **2.** [动]地蜈蚣

ear[2] [iə] *n.* 穗 —*vi.* 抽穗

earl [əːl] *n.* (英)伯爵

earldom ['əːldəm] *n.* 伯爵爵位;伯爵领地

earliness ['əːlinis] *n.* 早;早熟

early ['əːli] *adj.* **1.** 早的;早熟的:~ vegetables 时鲜蔬菜 **2.** 及早的;早日的:an ~ bird 早到(或早起等)的人 / Please reply at your *earliest* convenience. 请尽早回复。**3.** 早期的;早先的;古时的:the ~ part of the century 世纪的初期 —*adv.* 早:in the ~ next year 明

年初 ‖ **Early English style** 【建】早期英国哥特式(指从1180到1250年间的英国建筑式样) / ~ **warning system** 预警系统

earn [ə:n] vt.1. 赚得,挣得 2. 博得;赢得;使得到

earnest¹ ['ə:nist] adj. 认真的;诚挚的;热切的 —n. 认真,认真地; in ~ 认真的(地),不是开玩笑的(地) ‖ ~**ly** adv. / ~**ness** n.

earnest² ['ə:nist] n.1. 定钱;保证金 2. 预示;保证

earnings ['ə:niŋz][复]n.1. 工资;收入 2. 利润;收益

earth [ə:θ] n.1. 地球 2. 陆地,地面,地上 3. 土,泥 4. 尘世,人间 5. 地球上的人类;人的躯体 6.(狐、獾等的)洞穴 7.【电】接地;地线 8.【化】难以还原的金属氧化物(如氧化铝、氧化锆) — vt. 把…埋入土中;用土掩盖(根部等)(up) 2. 把(狐等)追赶入洞 3.【电】把…接地 —vi. 躲进洞里 ‖ ~ **art** 大地艺术 / ~-**bound** adj.1. 离不开地球的 2. 向地球移动的 3. 世俗的;缺乏想象力的;平凡的 / ~ **closet**(主英)干土覆盖粪便的厕所 / ~ **day** n. 地球日 / ~ **mover** n. 挖(或推)土机 / ~ **nut** n. 落花生 / ~ **quake** n.1. 地震 2.(喻)大震荡;大变动 / ~ **rise** n. 地出 / ~ **science** 地球科学 / ~ **shaking** adj. 极其重大的的;震撼世界的;翻天覆地的 / ~ **station** 地球站,地面站 / ~ **work** n.1. 土木工事,土方(工程) 3. 地景艺术品 / ~ **worm** n. 蚯蚓

earthen ['ə:θən] adj.1. 泥土做的;陶制的 2. 世俗的,现世的 ‖ ~-**ware** n.[总称]陶器

earthiness ['ə:θinis] n.1. 土质,土性 2. 粗陋;朴实

earthly ['ə:θli] adj.1. 地球的;尘世的,世俗的;现世的 2.(口)[用于否定句或疑问句]可能的;想得到的 —n. have not an ~ 毫无理由 ‖ **earthliness** n. 世俗;尘缘

earthy ['ə:θi] adj.1. 泥土(似)的 2. 朴实的;现实的 4.(笑话等)粗俗的

ease [i:z] n.1. 舒适;悠闲;安心;自在 2. 容易,不费力 —vt.1. 减轻(痛苦、负担等);使舒适;使安心 2. 放松,放宽(绳索、帆等) 3. 使(轧住的抽屉等)松动 3. 小心地移置 —vi.1. 缓和;减轻;放松(off, up) 2. 灵活地移动(along, over)

easel ['i:zl] n. 画架;黑板架

easily ['i:zili] adv.1. 容易地,不费力地 2. 舒适地,适意地 3. 流畅地;顺利地 4. 毫无疑问地 5. 很可能

easiness ['i:zinis] n.1. 容易,易于(性情等的)温和,不严厉 3. 舒适;安逸 4. 平易;从容,自在 5. 漫不经心;懒散

east [i:st] n.1. 东,东方 2.[the E-]东部,东部地区;the Far(Middle, Near)East 远(中,近)东 / the East 东方的东方;(美)美国东部地区 —adj.1. 东方的;东部的;朝东的;the East End(英)伦敦的东部地区,东伦敦(劳动人民聚居区) / the East Side(美)纽约市曼哈顿区的东部 2.(风)从东方来的 —adv. 在东方;向东方

eastbound ['i:stbaund] adj. 向东行的;向东驶的

Easter ['i:stə] n.[宗](耶稣)复活节(指每年过春分月圆后第一个星期日);(从复活节开始的)复活节周

easterly ['i:stəli] adj.1. 东的;向东方的 —adv.1. 向东方 2.(风)从东方来

eastern ['i:stən] adj.1. 东的,东方的;东部的 2. 朝东的 3.(风)从东方来的 ‖ ~**er** n.1. 东方人;居住在东方的人

[E-]美国的东部人

easternmost ['i:stənməust] *adj*. 最东的；极东的

eastward ['i:stwəd] *adj*. 向东的 —*n*. 东向；东部 —*adv*. 向东

eastwards ['i:stwədz] *adv*. 向东

easy ['i:zi] *adj*.1. 容易的；不费力的 2. 安逸的；安乐的；宽裕的；小康的：be in ~ circumstances 家道小康，生活安逸 3. (在心境等方面)安心的，平静的；(在身体上)适意的 4. (衣、鞋、物质条件等)宽适的，舒服的 5. 从容的，自在的；大方的 6. 宽容的，不苛求的；易忍受的 7. 易邀的；流畅的；(价格)不硬的 8. 随随便便的；易顺从的 9.(商品)供过于求的；(市价)疲软的；低落的；(银根)松的 —*adv*.1. (口)容易地；不费力地 2. 慢慢地；当心地 ‖ ~ chair 安乐椅 / ~ mark 1. (口)易受欺骗的人；糊涂虫；傻子 2. 易达到的目标 / ~ meat = ~ mark / ~ money 来得容易的钱(指非正当所得)；以低利率借入(或贷出)的钱

easygoing ['i:zi'gəuiŋ] *adj*.1. (马)步子平稳的 2.(人)懒散的；随和的 3.(品德上)放荡的，不严肃的 4. 悠闲的；轻松的；舒适的

eat [i:t] (ate [et, eit], eaten ['i:tn]) *vt*.1. 吃；喝(汤) 2. 蛀；腐蚀；销蚀 —*vi*.1. 吃；吃饭 2. 吃上去有(某种)味道 3. 腐蚀；侵蚀(*into*)

eatable ['i:təbl] *adj*. 可食用的 —*n*.[~s] 食物，食品

eaten ['i:tn] eat 的过去分词

eaves ['i:vz] *n*.[复] *n*. (屋)檐 ‖ '~-drop *vi*. & *vt*. 偷听 / '~dropper *n*. 偷听者

ebb [eb] *n*. & *vi*.1. 落潮，退潮 2.(喻)衰落，衰退 ‖ ~ tide 落潮，退潮

ebony ['ebəni] *n*. 乌木；乌木树 —*adj*.1. 乌木制的 2. 似乌木的；乌木色的，漆黑色的

ebullient [i'bʌljənt] *adj*.(思想、感情等)奔放的，洋溢的；兴高采烈的 ‖ **ebullience** *n*. / ~ly *adv*.

EC *abbr*. European Community 欧洲共同体

eccentric [ik'sentrik] *adj*.1. (人、行为等)古怪的；偏执的 2. 不同圆心的；[机]偏心的 3.【天】(轨道)不正圆的；(天体)在不正圆轨道上运行的 —*n*.1. 行为古怪的人 2. 偏心圆 3.【机】偏心轮 ‖ ~ally *adv*.

eccentricity [,eksen'trisiti] *n*.1. 古怪；怪僻 2.【数】离心率，偏心率；【机】偏心距；【天】偏心度

ecclesiastic(al) [i,kli:zi'æstik(əl)] *adj*. 基督教会的；教士的 ‖ **ecclesiastically** *adv*.

echelon ['efələn] *n*.1.【军】梯队；梯次配置 2. 组织(或指挥)系统中的等级 3.【物】阶梯光栅(亦作 ~ grating)

echo ['ekəu] (*n*.[复]echoes) *n*.1. 回声；反响 2. 重复；仿效 3. 附和者；应声虫 4. 共鸣 5.【无】回波，反射波 6.(桥牌)牌中叫出搭档报信息的回声信号 —*vi*.1. 发出回声(声音)被传回；起反响；起共鸣 2. 重复 3.(桥牌戏中)发出回声信号 —*vt*.1. 重复；模仿(别人的话、思想等) 2. 反射(声音等) ‖ ~ gram *n*. 回声 / ~graph *n*. 回声深度记录器 ‖ ~ sounder 回声测深器

echoic [e'kəuik] *adj*. 似声的，象声的

éclair ['eikleə]《法》*n*. 狭长形松饼，手指形巧克力泡夫

eclectic [ek'lektik] *adj*. 折中(主义)的 —*n*. 折中主义者 ‖ ~ally *adv*. / ~ism [ek'lektisizəm] *n*.

eclipse [i'klips] *n*.1.【天】食 2. 被遮蔽；(声名、威望等的)黯然失色 —*vt*.1.

【天】食,掩蔽(天体)的光 2. 把…遮
暗;使失色

ecliptic [i'kliptik] *n.*【天】黄道 —*adj.* 黄
道的;(日、月等)食的 ‖ ~**ally** *adv.*

ECM *abbr.* European Common Market 欧洲
共同市场

ecocide [i:kəsaid] *n.* 生态灭绝

ecologic(al) [ˌi:kə'lɔdʒik(əl)] *adj.*【生】生态
的;生态学的 ‖ **ecologically** *adv.*

ecology [i:'kɔlədʒi] *n.*【生】生态学 ‖ **ecolo-
gist** *n.*

economic [ˌi:kə'nɔmik] *adj.* 经济(上)的;
经济学的

economical [ˌi:kə'nɔmikəl] *adj.* 1. 经济的,
节俭的,节省的 2. 经济学的;经济上
的 ‖ ~**ly** *adv.*

economics [ˌi:kə'nɔmiks] [复] *n.* [用作单或
复] 1. 经济学 2.(国家的)经济情况;经
济

economist [i:'kɔnəmist] *n.* 1. 经济学家 2.
节俭的人

economize [i:'kɔnəmaiz] *vt. & vi.* 节约,
节省 ‖ **e**‚**conomi'zation** *n.*

economy [i:'kɔnəmi] *n.* 1. 经济 2. 节约,
节省;节约措施 3. 经济实惠

ecosystem [i:'kəusistəm] *n.* 生态系(统)

ecstasy ['ekstəsi] *n.* 狂喜;心醉神迷

ecstatic [eks'tætik] *adj.* 欣喜若狂的;心
醉神迷的 ‖ ~**ally** *adv.*

Ecuador ['ekwədɔ:] *n.* 厄瓜多尔[南美洲
西北部国家]

ecumenical [ˌi:kju:'menikəl, ˌekju'menikəl]
adj. 1. 世界范围的;普遍的 2.【宗】全
基督教的;促进世界基督教(不同教
派)大联合的 ‖ **ecumenism** *n.* 普世教
会主义(或运动)

eczema ['eksimə] *n.*【医】湿疹

ed. *abbr.* edited; edition; editor

-ed *suf.* 1. [加在规则动词后,构成过
去式和过去分词]: walk*ed*, want*ed* 2.
[加在名词或动词后,构成形容词]表
示"有","具有…特征": beard*ed*

eddy ['edi] *n.*(空气,水,烟,雾等的)旋
涡,涡流 — *vt. & vi.*(使)起旋涡;
(使)旋转

Eden ['i:dən] *n.* 1.(基督教《圣经》中人类
始祖亚当和夏娃最初居住的)伊甸园
2. 天堂,乐园 3. 最大幸福,快乐

edge [edʒ] *n.* 1. 刀口;利刃,锋;锐利 2.
边,棱;边界;界线(=悬崖等的)边缘 3.
优势;优越条件 — *vt.* 1. 使(刃、剑等)
锋利,使开刃 2. 给…加上边 3. 使(衣
等)一边向前缓缓地移动;使(自己)侧
着身子挤(*in, into, through*);挤簇
(*out, off*) — *vi.* 徐徐移动;侧着移动
(*along, away*) ‖ ~**less** *adj.* 没刀刃
的;钝的 / **edging** *n.*

edgeways ['edʒweiz], **edgewise** ['edʒwaiz]
adv. 以刃向外(或前);以边缘向外
(或向前);从旁边;沿边;边对边地

edgy ['edʒi] *adj.* 1. 锋利的 2.(绘画等)轮
廓十分明显的 3. 急躁的;易怒的;紧
张不安的

edible ['edibl] *adj.* 可以吃的,供食用的
—一[~s]食品 ‖ **edi'bility** *n.* 可食用
性 / ~**ness** *n.*

edict ['i:dikt] *n.* 法令;敕令;布告

edifice ['edifis] *n.* 大建筑物;大厦

edify ['edifai] *vt.* 熏陶,开导,启发 ‖
edification [ˌedifi'keiʃən] *n.*

Edinburgh ['edinbərə] *n.* 爱丁堡[英国苏
格兰东南部城市](苏格兰首府)

edit ['edit] *vt.* 1. 编辑;校订 2. 剪辑(影
片、录音磁带等) 3. 在编辑(或剪辑)
过程中删除(*out*) — *n.* 1. 编辑;校订;
剪辑;编辑工作 2. 社论

edition [i'diʃən] *n.* 1. 版;版本;版次 2.

(喻)很相似的人(或物);翻版

editor ['edita] *n.*1. 编辑;编者;校订者 2. 社论撰写人 3. 影片剪辑装置 ‖ **~ship** *n.* 编辑的职位;编辑工作

editorial [ˌedi'tɔːriəl] *adj.*1. 编辑的;编者的 2. 社论(性)的 —*n.* 社论 ‖ **~ist** *n.* 社论撰写人 ‖ 以编者身份 2. 以社论形式;作为社论

educate ['edjukeit] *vt.*1. 教育 2. 培养;训练 3. 使受学校教育;为……付学费 ‖ **~d** *adj.* 受过教育的 / **educator** *n.* 教育者;教育工作者

education [ˌedju'keiʃən] *n.*1. 教育 2. 训导;训练;培养 3. 教育学

educational [ˌedju'keiʃənl] *adj.*1. 教育的 2. 有教育意义的 ‖ **~ly** *adv.* 用教育方法;从教育的观点

education(al)ist [ˌedju'keiʃən(əl)ist] *n.* 教育学家

educe [i'djuːs] *vt.*1. 引出 2. 演绎出;(从数据,论据)推断出

-ee *suf.*1. 表示"受动者":appointer 2. 表示"处于某一情况下的人":refugee 3. 表示"与……有关的人(或物)":goatee

EEC *abbr.* European Economic Community 欧洲经济共同体

eel [iːl] *n.*1. 鳗鲡,鳗 2. 蛇形鱼类(如黄鳝,八目鳗) 3. 油滑的人

e'er [ɛə] *adv.*〈诗〉= ever

eerie, eery ['iəri] *adj.*1.〈苏格兰〉(因迷信而)胆怯的;不安的 2. 引起恐惧的;可怕的;怪异的 ‖ **eerily** *adv.* / **eeriness** *n.*

efface [i'feis] *vt.*1. 擦掉,抹去;(喻)消除(痕迹等) 2. 使(印象等)被忘却 2. 超越;使黯然失色 3. 使(自己)不被注意(或不露面);埋没 ‖ **~ment** *n.*

effect [i'fekt] *n.*1. 结果 2. 效果;效力

作用;影响 3.(在视、听觉方面引起的)印象:a three dimensional ~ 立体感 4. 要旨,意义:a statement to the following— 大意如下的声明 5. 实行,实施 6.[~s]财物;动产 —*vt.*1. 产生;引起(变化等) 2. 实现;达到(目的)等

effective [i'fektiv] *adj.*1. 有效的;生效的 2.(演说等)有力的;给人深刻印象的 3. 实在的,实际的:the number of ~ members 实际成员人数 4.(军队、士兵等)有战斗力的 —*n.*[~s]〈军〉实际可以作战的部队(或士兵);有生力量 ‖ **~ly** *adv.* / **~ness** *n.*

effectual [i'fektjuəl] *adj.*(行动等)奏效的,有效的 ‖ **~ly** *adv.* / **~ness** *n.*

effeminacy [i'feminəsi] *n.* 柔弱;娇气;女子气

effeminate [i'feminit] *adj.* 柔弱的;娇气的;女子气的 ‖ **~ly** *adv.*

effervesce [ˌefə'ves] *vi.*1. 冒泡;起沫;【化】冒泡 2. 欢腾,兴高采烈 ‖ **effervescingly** *adv.*

effervescence [ˌefə'vesns], **effervescency** [ˌefə'vesnsi] *n.*1. 冒泡,起泡(沫)【化】泡腾 2. 生气勃勃;兴高采烈

effervescent [ˌefə'vesnt] *adj.*1. 冒泡的;【化】泡腾的 2. 生气勃勃的;兴高采烈的

effete [i'fiːt] *adj.*1. 不能生产的,贫瘠的 2. 衰老的;衰弱的;无能的 3. 过时的 4. 没有男子汉气概的,女人气的 ‖ **~ly** *adv.* / **~ness** *n.*

efficacious [ˌefi'keiʃəs] *adj.*(药物、治疗等)有效验的,灵验的 ‖ **~ly** *adv.* / **~ness** *n.*

efficacy ['efikəsi] *n.* 功效;效验

efficiency [i'fiʃənsi] *n.*1. 效率 2. 功效;效能 ‖ **~ apartment**(有小厨房和卫生设备的)小套公寓房间

efficient [i'fiʃənt] *adj.* 效率高的;有能力的,能胜任的 ‖ ~ly *adv.*

effigy ['efidʒi] *n.* (被憎恨或蔑视的人的)肖像;雕像;模拟像:burn sb. *in* ~ 把某人的模拟像烧掉

effort ['efət] *n.* 1. 努力;艰难的尝试:He made no ~ to hide his disappointment. 他没有极力掩盖自己的失望情绪。/They climbed up the deck in an ~ to see what was happening. 他们爬上甲板想看看发生了什么事。/sit up slowly and with great ~ 慢慢地费力地坐起来 2. 努力的成果;成就;事:a fine literary ~ 文学上的精心杰作 3. 【机】作用力

effortless ['efətlis] *adj.* 不费力的,容易的 ‖ ~ly *adv.*

effrontery [ə'frʌntəri] *n.* 厚颜无耻(的行为)

effusion [i'fjuːʒən] *n.* 1. 流出;泻出;喷出;【医】渗出 2. (讲话或文章中思想、感情的)抒发;倾写 3. 渗出物

effusive [i'fjuːsiv] *adj.* 流出的;喷出的;溢出的 2. 溢于言表的;感情奔放的 ‖ ~ly *adv.* / ~ness *n.*

e.g. *abbr.* 〈拉〉*exempli gratia* 例如(= for example)

egalitarian [i,gæli'teəriən] *adj.* 主张人人平等的,平等主义的 —*n.* 平等主义者 ‖ ~ism *n.*

egg[1] [eg] *n.* 1. (鸟)蛋;鸡蛋;(鱼、爬行动物等的)卵;卵细胞 2. 蛋形物 3. 〈俚〉人,家伙 4. 〈俚〉炸弹;手榴弹;鱼雷 —*vt.* 1. (烹调中)把……蛋黄(或蛋白)调和(或覆盖) 2. 〈口〉向……掷鸡蛋 ‖ ~.beater *n.* 1. 打蛋器 2. 〈美俚〉直升(飞)机 / ~.cup *n.* (吃鸡蛋用的)蛋杯 / ~.head *n.* 〈贬〉知识分子,有学问的人 / ~.nog *n.* 蛋奶酒 / ~.plant *n.* 茄子 / ~.shell *n.* 蛋壳;淡黄色;易碎的东

西

egg[2] [eg] *vt.* 怂恿,煽动(*on*)

ego ['egəu] *n.* 1. 自我,自己 2. 〈口〉自我主义;利己主义;自负 ‖ ~.trip 追求个人利益(或享受)的行为

egoism ['egəuizəm] *n.* 1. 自我主义 2. 自私自利,私心 ‖ **egoist** *n.* 自我主义者;利己主义者;自私自利的人

egoistic(al) [,egəu'istik(əl)] *adj.* 1. 自私自利的,利己的 2. 利己主义(者)的

egotism ['egətizəm] *n.* 1. 自我中心(指言必称"我"的习惯);自我吹嘘;自高自大 2. 利己主义;自私自利 ‖ **egotist** *n.* 言必称"我"者;自高自大者 / **egotistic(al)** [,iːgə'tistik(əl)] *adj.*

egotize ['egətaiz] *vi.* 言必称"我",过分地强调自我

egregious [i'griːdʒəs] *adj.* (错误、蠢事、蠢人等)异乎寻常的,惊人的;极端恶劣的 ‖ ~ly *adv.* / ~ness *n.*

egress ['iːgres] *n.* 1. 外出,外出 2. 外出权 3. 出口;出路 4. 【天】终切

egret ['iːgret] *n.* 1.【动】白鹭 2. (装饰用的)白鹭羽毛

Egypt ['iːdʒipt] *n.* 埃及[东北非国家](领土包括亚洲西南端的西奈半岛)

Egyptian [i'dʒipʃən] *adj.* 1. 埃及的 2. 埃及人的 —*n.* 1. 埃及人 2. 古埃及语

eh [ei] *int.* [表示惊奇、疑问、征求同意等]啊! 喂! 是吗?

eider ['aidə] *n.* 1.【动】绒鸭(亦作 ~ duck) 2. 绒鸭绒 ‖ ~ down *n.* 绒鸭的绒毛;鸭绒被;鸭绒垫

Eiffel ['aifəl] *n.* ‖ ~ Tower (法国巴黎的)埃菲尔铁塔(在塞纳河南岸)

eight [eit] *num.* 八;八个(人或物);第八(卷、章、页等) —*n.* 1. 8 字形(图案、缠结等) 2. 八个(人或物)一组;八人的

划船队;八桨划船;[~s]八桨划船比赛
3. 八汽缸发动机;八汽缸汽车 **4.** 八岁
5. 八点钟 **6.** 八号的衣服(或鞋子、袜子等) **7.** 八点的纸牌 ‖ ～fold *adj.* & *adv.* 八倍的(地);八重的(地) /～some ['eitsəm] *adj.* 八人里尔舞(亦作～some reel)

eighteen ['ei'ti:n] *num.* 十八;十八个(人或物);第十八(卷、章、页等) — *n.* 1. 十八岁 **2.** 十八点钟(即下午六点) ‖ ～th *num.* 1. 第十八(个) **2.** 十八分之一(的) *n.* (月的)第十八日

eighth [eitθ] *num.* 1. 第八(个) **2.** 八分之一(的) — *n.* (月的)第八日 ‖ ～ly *adv.* 第八(列举各目等时用) ‖ ～ note 【音】八分音符

eightieth ['eitiiθ] *num.* 1. 第八十(个) **2.** 八十分之一(的)

eighty ['eiti] *num.* 八十;八十个(人或物);第八十(页等) — *n.* 1. [eighties](世纪的)八十年代 **2.** 八十岁;[eighties]八十到八十九岁的时期

einsteinium [ain'stainiəm] *n.* 【化】锿

either ['aiðə, 'i:ðə] *adj.* 1. (两者之中)任一 **2.** (两者之中)每一 — *pron.* (两者之中)任何一个 — *adv.* [用于否定句或否定词组后加强语气]也;而且;根本(一般只用于"～... or ..."或 "～... or ..."结构中] ‖ ～... or ... 或者...或者...,不论...还是... ‖ ～or [计]"异" **2.** 两者择一 *adj.* 非此即彼的,两者择一的

ejaculate [i'dʒækjuleit] *vt.* 1. 突然喊出(或说出) **2.** (从生物体中)射出;射(精) — *vi.* 射出液体;射精 — *n.* (一次射出的)精液(一次)射出 ‖ ejacu'lation *n.* 1. (尤指精液等的)射出;射精 **2.** 突然的喊出(或讲出)

eject [i'dʒekt] *vt.* 1. 逐出,驱逐;排斥;(通

过诉讼)排除(租户等的)占有权;免...的职(*from*) **2.** 喷射;吐出:The chimney ～s smoke. 烟囱吐烟。**3.** (从飞机或宇宙飞船)把...弹射出来(*from*) ‖ ～ment *n.* 1. 驱逐,赶走;喷吐 **2.** 【律】要求收回不当被扣产业的诉讼;收回不动产之诉

ejection [i'dʒekʃən] *n.* 1. 驱逐;排斥 **2.** 喷出,射出 **3.**【空】弹射:an ～ seat 弹射座椅 **4.** 喷出物,射出物

ejector [i'dʒektə] *n.* 【机】抛射器;喷射器;喷射泵;推出器:an ～ seat 【空】弹射椅(= an ejection seat)

eke [i:k] *vt.* 1. 弥补(工资、收入等)的不足;(节省地供应)持久(*out*) **2.** 竭力维持(*out*):～ out a living 勉强糊口

elaborate [i'læbərit] *adj.* 1. 精心制作(或计划)的;详尽的;精巧的 **2.** (煞费)苦心的,刻苦的,辛勤的 — [i'læbəreit] *vt.* 1. 精心制作(机器等);精心研究出(一种理论、一套体系等) **2.** 详尽阐述;发挥 **3.** 使(食物或简单成分)变成复杂有机物 — *vi.* 作详细说明(on, upon)的 ‖ ～ly *adv.* / ～ness *n.* / elaborator [i'læbəreitə] *n.* 精心制作者;详尽阐述者

elaboration [i,læbə'reiʃən] *n.* 1. 精心制作(或计划);精致;详尽阐述 **2.** 精心完成的作品;详尽的细节

elapse [i'læps] *vi.* (时间)过去,消逝 — *n.* (时间)过去,消逝

elastic [i'læstik] *adj.* 1. 弹性的;有弹力的 **2.** 灵活的;可伸缩的 **3.** 易顺应的;(心情)易轻快的 — *n.* 橡皮带,松紧带;橡皮圈 ‖ ～ally *adv.*

elasticity [ˌelæs'tisiti] *n.* 1. 弹性;弹力 **2.** 灵活性;伸缩性;顺应性

elate [i'leit] *vt.* [常用被动语态]使得意洋洋;使欢欣鼓舞

elated [i'leitid] *adj.* 得意洋洋的；兴高采烈的，欢欣鼓舞的（*at*）‖ ~ly *adv.* / ~ness *n.*

elation [i'leiʃən] *n.*1. 得意洋洋；兴高采烈，欢欣鼓舞 2.（病态的）安乐感；自鸣得意

Elbe [elb(ə)] *n.* [the ~]易北河 [中欧]

elbow ['elbou] *n.*1. 肘；（衣服的）肘部 2. 肘状物（如路的急弯等）3.【机】L 形弯管；L 形弯头 — *vt.* 用肘推，挤：~ one's way through the crowd 在人群中挤过去 ‖ ~ grease〈口〉费劲；苦干；重活 / ~-room *n.* 活动余地；行动上的自由；自由行动的余地

elder¹ ['eldə] *n.*1.（尤指家属中）年龄较大的：an ~ brother (sister)兄(姐) 2. 资格老的，前辈 / an ~ statesman 政界元老（一般指已退休的）— *n.*1. 年龄较大者 2.[~s]长者，前辈 3. 前人，祖先 4.（教会的）长老 ‖ ~ly *adj.* 上了年纪的；中年以上的

elder² ['eldə] *n.*【植】接骨木

eldest ['eldist] *adj.*（尤指家属中）最年长的；排行第一的

elect [i'lekt] *vt.*1. 选举；推选 2. 选择；决定（*to do*）— *adj.*[放在所修饰的名词后]1. 选定的，选中的：the bride ~ 选中的新娘 2. 当选但尚未上任的：the president-～当选（但尚未就职的）总统 — *n.*[the ～]被选定的人(们)；特权集团；[宗]蒙上帝挑选者

election [i'lekʃən] *n.*1. 选举 2. 当选 3. 选择权(利)

electioneer [i,lekʃə'niə] *vi.*1. 拉选票 2. 进行竞选活动 — *n.*= ～er ‖ ～er *n.* 搞竞选活动的人；搞拉选票活动的人

elective [i'lektiv] *adj.*1.（职位）选任的，由选举产生的 2. 有选举权的 3.（美）（学校课程）选修的，可以选择的 4. 有选

择倾向的；【化】有择的 — *n.*（美）选修课程 ‖ ～ly *adv.* / ～ness *n.*

elector [i'lektə] *n.*1. 有选举权的人 2.（美国）选举团的成员

electoral [i'lektərəl] *adj.*1. 选举的；选举人的 2. 由选举者组成的：an ～ college（美国）总统选举团（指各州选出的专门负责选举总统和副总统的一批人）

electorate [i'lektərit] *n.* 选举人，选民

electric [i'lektrik] *adj.*1. 电的；导电的；发电的；用电的；电动的 2. 令人震惊的，惊心动魄的 — *n.*1. 带电体 2. 电气车辆 ‖ ～ blanket 电热毯 / ～ blue 铁青色／～ cable 电缆／～ chair 电椅（指干处死罪犯的）／～ eye 1. 光电池 2. 电眼／～ torch 手电筒

electrical [i'lektrikəl] *adj.* 电的；电气科学的 ‖ ～ly *adv.* ‖ ～ engineering 电机工程；电工技术

electrician [i,lek'triʃən] *n.* 电工；电气专家

electricity [i,lek'trisiti] *n.*1. 电；电学 2. 电流，电力供应 3. 强烈的兴奋感；热情

electrify [i'lektrifai] *vt.*1. 使带电；使起电 2. 使电气化；向...供电 3. 使触电 4.（喻）使震惊；使兴奋，使激动 ‖ electrification [i,lektrifi'keiʃən] *n.*

electro- *comb. form* 表示"电"，"电的"，"电解"：electrostatics, electrodeposit

electrocardiogram [i,lektrə'kɑ:diəugræm] *n.*[医]心电图，心动电流图

electrocute [i'lektrəkjut] *vt.*1. 以电刑处死（罪犯）2. 使触电而死 ‖ e,lectro'cution *n.*

electrode [i'lektrəud] *n.*[电]电极

electrodeposit [i,lektrədi'pɔzit] *n.* 电解沉积物 — *vt.* 使电解沉积

electrolyse, **electrolyze** [i'lektrəlaiz] *vt.* 电解；[医]电蚀 ‖ ～ r *n.* 电解剂

electrolysis [iilek'trɔlisis] *n.*1. 电解（作用）2. 电蚀除毛（或痣等）

electrolytic [iilektrəu'litik] *adj.* 电解的；电解质的

electromagnet [iilektrəu'mægnit] *n.*【物】电磁体；电磁铁

electromagnetic [iilektrəuæg'netik] *adj.* 电磁（体）的 ‖~s [复] *n.* [用作单]电磁学

electromagnetism [iilektrəu'mægnitizəm] *n.* 电磁；电磁学

electromotive [iilektrəu'məutiv] *adj.*【电】电动的；电动势的

electron [i'lektrɔn] *n.* 电子 ‖~ tube 电子管

electronic [iilek'trɔnik] *adj.* 电子的 ‖~. ally *adv.* ‖~ computer 电子计算机 / ~ mail 电子邮件, 电子信函 / ~ media 电子传播媒介（指广播、电视）/~ publishing 电子出版（业）

electronics [iilek'trɔniks] [复] *n.* [用作单] 电子学

electroplate [i'lektrəupleit] *vt.* 电镀 *n.* 电镀物品；镀银餐具；【印】电铸版 ‖ **electroplating** *n.* 电镀（术）

electroscope [i'lektrəskəup] *n.*【物】验电器

electrostatic [iilektrəu'stætik] *adj.* 静电的；静电学的 ‖~s [复] *n.* [用作单] 静电学 ‖~ printing 静电印刷（术）

eleemosynary [ielii:'mɔsinəri] *adj.* 慈善的；救济的；捐助的；施舍的；免费的

elegance ['eligəns], **elegancy** ['eligənsi] *n.* (举止、服饰、风格等的) 雅致, 漂亮, 优美

elegant ['eligənt] *adj.*1. (举止、服饰等) 雅致的, 漂亮的, 优美的 2. 讲究的, 精致的 3. 〈口〉上品的, 第一流的 ‖~ly *adv.*

elegy ['elidʒi] *n.* 哀歌, 挽歌

element ['elimənt] *n.*1. 要素 (古希腊哲学中土、风、水、火四大要素之一) 2. 组成部分, 成分 (先进等) 分子 3. (人或物的) 自然环境; 适宜的环境 4. [~s] 自然力; 风雨 5. [~s] 原理; 基础 6. 【机】单体, 配对零件之一 7. 元素 8. 【数】素, 元素 9.【电】电热丝, 电热元件 10. 【无】元件 11. 【军】组迫；小队, 分队

elemental [ieli'mentl] *adj.*1. (古希腊哲学) 四大要素 (土、风、水、火) 的 2. 自然力的 3. 基本的 4. 初步的 5.【化】元素的 ‖~ly *adv.*

elementary [ieli'mentəri] *adj.*1. 基本的 ‖~ species 【生】基本种 2. 初级的, 基础的 3.【化】元素的 4. 自然力的

elephant ['elifənt] *n.* 象

elevate ['eliveit] *vt.*1. 抬起；使升高 2. 提高 (思想、嗓音等)；振奋 (情绪等) 3. 提升...的职位

elevated ['eliveitid] *adj.*1. 升高的; 提高的; 高的 2. 高尚的; 严肃的 3. 振奋的; 欢欣的 4. 〈口〉微醉的 — *n.* 〈口〉高架铁路 (亦作 ~ railway)

elevation [ieli'veiʃən] *n.*1. 高度 2. 标高, 仰角 3.【军】射角 4. 海拔 5. 提高; 提升; 晋级 6. 高地; 高处 6. (皮肤上的) 隆起 7. 崇高; 庄严 8. (建筑物的) 正面图, 立视图

elevator ['eliveitə] *n.*1. 起卸机 2.〈美〉电梯 (=〈英〉lift) 3. 升降机 4.【空】升降舵 5. (能吊卸、储存、有时也进行加工的) 谷物仓库 6.【医】牙挺；起子 7.【解】(上) 提肌

eleven [i'levn] *num.* 十一；十一个 (人或物)；第十一 (卷、章、页等) — *n.*1. 十一个 (人或物) 一组 (尤指十一人的足球队等) 2. 十一点钟的茶点 3. 十一岁

eleventh [i'levnθ] *num.*1. 第十一(个) 2. 十一分之一(的) —*n.*(月的)第十一日

elf [elf]([复]elves[elvz]) *n.*1.(神话中的)小精灵 2. 顽皮的小孩 3. 矮子 4. 恶作剧的人;恶人 ‖ '~ lock *n.*[常~locks]鬈结的头发

elfin ['elfin] *adj.* 小精灵的;小精灵般的 —*n.*1. 小精灵 2. 矮子 3. 小孩

elfish ['elfiʃ] *adj.* 小精灵的;小精灵般的;淘气的 ‖ ~ly *adv.*

elicit [i'lisit] *vt.* 得出,引出(真理等);使发出,引起,诱出(回答等) ‖ e‚lici'tation *n.*

eligible ['elidʒəbl] *adj.*1. 有资格(或条件)当选的,合格的(*for*) 2. 适宜的 ‖ ‚eligi'bility *n.* / eligibly *adv.*

eliminate [i'limineit] *vt.*1. 排除,消除,消灭 2.[数]消去 ‖ elimi'nation *n.*

elite, élite [ei'li:t](法) *n.*[the ~]精华;杰出人物,高贵者

elitism, élitism [ei'li:tizəm] *n.*1. 高人一等的优越感;杰出人物统治(论)

elixir [i'liksə] *n.*1.(中世纪炼金术士所幻想的)炼金药;长生不老药 2. 万应灵药 3.[药]酏剂

Elizabethan [i‚lizə'bi:θən] *adj. & n.* 伊丽莎白女王一世时代的(人或作家等)

elk [elk] *n.*1.[动]麋,驼鹿 2. 美洲赤鹿 2. 软糅粗皮 3. '~ hound *n.* 挪威猎犬

ellipse [i'lips] *n.*1.[数]椭圆 2. = ellipsis

ellipsis [i'lipsis]([复] ellipses [i'lipsi:z]) *n.*1.[语] 省略法 2. 省略号(即 …… 号)

elliptic(al) [i'liptik(əl)] *adj.*1. 椭圆的,椭圆形的 2. 省略的 ‖ elliptically *adv.*

elm [elm] *n.*1.[植]榆 2. 榆木

elocution [‚elə'kju:ʃən] *n.*1. 演说术;雄辩术 2. 朗诵法 ‖ ~ary *adj.* / ~ist *n.* 演说术教师 2. 朗诵者;演说家

E. long. *abbr.* east longitude 东经

elongate ['i:lɔŋgeit] *vt. & vi.*1.(使)伸长,(使)延长 —*adj.*1. 拉长的;(伸长的,延伸的 2.(树叶等)细长的 ‖ ‚elon'gation *n.*1. 拉长;伸长,延长;延伸率 2.(线的)延长部分 3.[天]距离

elope [i'ləup] *vi.* 私奔 ‖ ~ment *n.* / ~r *n.*

eloquence ['eləkwəns] *n.*1. 雄辩 2. 雄辩术;口才;修辞

eloquent ['eləkwənt] *adj.*1. 雄辩的,有说服力的 2. 富于表情的;意味深长的 ‖ ~ly *adv.*

El Salvador [el 'sælvədɔ:]萨尔瓦多[拉丁美洲国家]

else [els] *adj.*[常接在疑问代词、不定代词后]其他的,别的: What ～ did he say? 他还说了些什么? / Anything ～ I can do for you? 我还能为你做些别的事吗? —*adv.*1.[常接在疑问副词后]另外,其他;When ～ shall we meet again, if Friday is not convenient for you? 要是星期五对你不便,那么另外什么时候再碰头呢? 2.[前面常用 or]否则,要不然: Go quick, (or) ～ you'll miss the train. 快走,否则你要赶不上火车了。

elsewhere ['els'hwɛə] *adv.* 在别处;向别处

elucidate [i'l]u:sideit] *vt.* 阐明;解释 ‖ e‚luci'dation *n.* / elucidative, elucidatory *adj.* / elucidator *n.* 阐明者;解释者

elude [i'l]u:d] *vt.*1.(巧妙地)逃避,躲避(责任、困难、危险等) 2. 没有被…注意到;被…忽记:难倒(某人的记忆力,理解力)

elusive [i'l]u:siv] *adj.*1. 躲避的;闪避的 2. 难以捉摸的,难以理解的;容易被忘记的 ‖ ~ly *adv.* / ~ness *n.*

elusory [i'ljuːsəri] *adj.* 难以捉摸的

elves [elvz] elf 的复数

'em [əm] *pron.* 〈口〉= them

emaciate [i'meisieit] *vt.* 使衰弱, 使消瘦 ‖ ~d *adj.* 憔悴的, 消瘦的 /e'maci'ation *n.*

E-mail ['iːmeil] *n.* 电子邮件, 电子信函

emanate ['eməneit] *vi.* 1. (气体等) 散发; (光等) 放射 (from) 2. 发源 (from) ‖ ema'nation *n.* 1. 散发; 放射 2. 散发 (或放射) 的东西 3.【核】射气 /emanative *adj.* 流出的; 散发的; 放射的

emancipate [i'mænsipeit] *vt.* 1. 解放; 使不受 (政治、社会、法律的等) 的束缚 2.【律】使 (孩子、妻子) 从男性家长控制下解放出来而获得自主权利 ‖ **emancipator** *n.*

emancipation [iˌmænsi'peiʃən] *n.* 解放

emasculate [i'mæskjuleit] *vt.* 1. 阉割; 使无男子气, 使柔弱 2. 删削 (文章等) 使无力; 使 (语言等) 贫乏 —[i'mæskjulit] *adj.* 阉割了的; 柔弱的 ‖ e'mascu'lation *n.* /emasculative, emasculatory [i'mæskjulətəri] *adj.*

embalm [im'bɑːm] *vt.* 1. 以香油 (或药料等) 涂 (尸) 防腐 2. 使不朽, 使不被遗忘 3. 使充满香气 ‖ ~ment *adj.*

embank [im'bæŋk] *vt.* 筑堤围住; 筑堤防护 ‖ ~ment *n.* 1. 筑堤 2. (河、海的) 堤岸; (铁路的) 路堤

embargo [em'bɑːgəu] ([复] embargoes) *n.* 1. (战时) 封港令 (指禁止外轮进港, 禁止商船出入港口) 2. 禁止贸易令; 禁运 (全部或部分物资) 3. 禁止 (或限制) 买卖 4. 禁止; 阻止 —*vt.* 1. 禁止 (船只出入港口); 禁运 (物资) 2. 征用 (船只、物资)

embark [im'bɑːk] *vi.* 1. 上船; 上飞机 2. 从事, 开始搞 (on, upon, in) —*vt.* 1. 使上船; 使上飞机; 搭载 2. 使从事, 使着手 3. 投 (资) ‖ ~ ation, embarcation [ˌembɑː'keiʃən] *n.* 1. 乘坐; 装载 (物) 开始; 从事

embarrass [im'bærəs] *vt.* 1. 使窘迫; 使困惑; 使为难 2. 使负债; 使财政困难 3. 麻烦; 妨碍 4. 使 (问题) 复杂化 ‖ ~ment *n.* 1. 窘迫 2. 使人为难的人 (或事物)

embarrassing [im'bærəsiŋ] *adj.* 令人为难的; 麻烦的 ‖ ~ly *adv.*

embassy ['embəsi] *n.* 1. 大使的职务 2. 大使的派遣 3. 大使馆 4. 大使及其随员; 大使馆全体人员

embattle [im'bætl] *vt.* 1. 使严阵以待; 使准备战斗 2. 筑雉堞于; 筑堡垒于, 设防于 ‖ ~d *adj.* 严阵以待的; 设防的 2. 投入战斗的; 介入论战的 3. (文章) 边缘呈雉堞形的

embed [im'bed] (embedded; embedding) *vt.* 1. 栽种 (花等) 2. 埋置; 使插入【语】嵌进 3. (制备镜检样片时的) 灌埋

embellish [im'beliʃ] *vt.* 1. 装饰, 修饰 2. 给 (叙事、文章) 添加细节; 给...润色 ‖ ~ment *n.*

ember ['embə] *n.* [常 ~s] 余火, 余烬

embezzle [im'bezl] *vt.* 盗用; 贪污 ‖ ~ment *n.* / ~r *n.*

embitter [im'bitə] *vt.* 1. 加苦味于 2. 加重 (痛苦等) 3. 激怒; 使怨恨 ‖ ~ment *n.*

emblem ['embləm] *n.* 1. 象征; 标志 2. 徽章; 纹章图案

emblematic(al) [ˌembli'mætik(əl)] *adj.* 象征的 (of) ‖ **emblematically** *adv.*

embodiment [im'bɔdimənt] *n.* 体现之; 化身; 具体化

embody [im'bɔdi] *vt.* 1. 体现; 使具体化 2. 包含, 收录 3. 使 (精神等) 肉体化

embolden [im'bəuldən] *vt.* 给…壮胆,使更勇敢

emboss [im'bɔs] *vt.* 1. 使凸出;浮雕(图案);~ed paper 凹凸纸 2. 在…上浮雕图案 ‖ ~ment *n.*

embrace [im'breis] *vt.* 1. 拥抱,抱 2. 抓住(机会等) 3. 接受;信奉(主义、信仰等) 4. 着手,从事 5. 包围,围住,环绕 6. 包括,包含 7. 看到;领会 — *vi.* (相互)拥抱 — *n.* 1. 拥抱;怀抱 2. 包围;掌握 3. 接受

embroider [im'brɔidə] *vt.* 1. 在织物上绣(花样) 2. 在(织物)上刺绣 3. 给(故事等)添油加酱;对…加以渲染 — *vi.* 1. 绣花,刺绣 2. 渲染;修饰

embroidery [im'brɔidəri] *n.* 1. 绣花,刺绣法;刺绣品 2. 润饰;装饰

embroil [im'brɔil] *vt.* 1. 使(事态等)混乱;使纠缠 2. 使卷入纠纷 ‖ ~ment *n.*

embryo ['embriəu] ([复] embryos) *n.* 1. 胚;胎胎;(尤指受孕后8周内的)胎儿 2. 萌芽时期;萌芽状态的事物 — *adj.* 胚胎的(初期的);萌芽的;未成熟的

embryonic [ˌembri'ɔnik] *adj.* 1. 胚胎的开始的(初期的);未发育好的 ‖ ~ally *adv.*

emend [i'mend] *vt.* 修改,校订 ‖ **emendation** [ˌiːmen'deiʃən] *n.*

emerald ['emərəld] *n.* 1. [矿] 祖母绿,纯绿柱石 2. 翡翠,绿宝石,绿刚玉 3. 纯翠绿,翠绿色 — *adj.* 翠绿色的,纯绿宝石制的 ‖ **Emerald Isle** 绿宝石岛(爱尔兰岛的别称)

emerge [i'məːdʒ] *vi.* 1. 浮现;出现;形成 2. (问题等)冒出 3. (事实等)暴露

emergence [i'məːdʒəns] *n.* 1. 浮现;出现 2. [植] 突出体 3. [生] 层创进化,倏忽进化

emergency [i'məːdʒənsi] *n.* 紧急情况;突然事件;非常时刻

emergent [i'məːdʒənt] *adj.* 浮现的;出现的;(国家)新兴的,刚独立的

emeritus [i'meritəs] *adj.* 1. (大学教授等)荣誉退休而保留头衔的 2. 退休的;退职的 — *n.* ([复] emeriti [i'meritai]) *n.* 荣誉退休的人

emery ['eməri] *n.* 金刚砂,刚玉

emetic [i'metik] *n.* [药] 催吐剂 — *adj.* 催吐的 ‖ ~ally *adv.*

emigrant ['emigrənt] *adj.* 移居的;移民的 — *n.* 移居外国的人,移民;迁徙的动物;移植的植物

emigrate ['emigreit] *vi.* 永久移居外国(与 immigrate(从外国)移来相对) ‖ ˌemi'gration *n.*

eminence ['eminəns] *n.* 1. (地位、造诣等的)卓越,显赫;著名 2. 高地;高处 3. [E-](天主教中对红衣主教的尊称)阁下 4. [解] 隆凸,隆起

eminent ['eminənt] *adj.* 1. 出众的,卓越的,杰出的 2. (品德等)优良的 ‖ ~ly *adv.*

emissary ['emisəri] *n.* 1. 使者(尤指传递恶耗或秘密者) 2. 间谍

emission [i'miʃən] *n.* 1. (光、热、电子、气味等的)散发;发射 2. 发出物;发射物 3. [医] 泄泄;遗精

emit [i'mit] (emitted; emitting) *vt.* 1. 散发;放射(光、热、电子、气味等) 2. 发表(意见等);发布(命令等);发行(货币、书据等) ‖ ~ter *n.* [物] 发射体;(晶体管的)发射极

emolument [i'mɔljumənt] *n.* 报酬;酬金;薪水;津贴

emotion [i'məuʃən] *n.* 1. 激动 2. 感情;情绪;情感 ‖ ~less *adj.* 没有感情的;冷

漠的

emotional [i'məuʃənl] *adj*.1. 感情（上）的；情绪（上）的 2.（易）激动的，易动情感的 3. 激起情感的，激动人的 ‖ ~ly *adv*.

empathy ['empəθi] *n*. 1.【心】神入，感情移入，移情 2. 同情；同感；共鸣 ‖ **empathize** *vt*. & *vi*.

emperor ['empərə] *n*. 皇帝

emphasis ['emfəsis]（[复] emphases ['emfəsiz]）*n*.1. 强调，重点；重要性 2.【语】强调，着重 3. 显著，突出

emphasize ['emfəsaiz] *vt*.1. 强调，着重 2. 加强...的语气；重读 3. 使（事实等）显得突出（或重要）

emphatic [im'fætik] *adj*.1. 强调的；着重的 2. 加强语气的 3. 有力的；断然的，显著的 ‖ ~ally *adv*.

empire ['empaiə] *n*.1. 帝国 2. 帝权；绝对统治(over) 3.（由一个集团或个人控制的）大地区（或企业）4.［the E-］英帝国;神圣罗马帝国 ‖ **Empire City** 帝国城（美国纽约市的别称）/ **Empire Day**（英一帝国日(5 月 24 日,现称 Commonwealth Day 联邦日) / **Empire State** 帝国州（美国纽约州的别称）

empirical [em'pirikəl] *adj*. 经验主义的，以经验为根据的 ‖ ~ly *adv*.

empiricism [em'pirisizəm] *n*.1. 经验主义 2.【哲】经验论 ‖ **empiricist** *n*. 经验主义者;【哲】经验论者

emplace [im'pleis] *vt*. 安放,安置;安装;安插；使（火炮）进入阵地 ‖ ~ment *n*.1. 位置,安置 2. 安插。炮位,炮台;安置军事装备的阵地

employ [im'plɔi] *vt*.1. 用,使用 2. 雇用 3. 使忙于。使从事于;把（时间）花于(in) — *n*. = employment

employe(e) [,emplɔi'i:] *n*. 受雇者,雇工,雇员

employer [im'plɔiə] *n*.1. 雇用者,雇主 2. 使用者

employment [im'plɔimənt] *n*.1. 使用 2. 雇用;受雇 3. 职业,工作

emporium [em'pɔ:riəm]（[复] emporiums 或 emporia [em'pɔ:riə]）*n*.1. 商场;商业中心 2. 大百货商店

empower [im'pauə] *vt*.1. 授权给;准许...使能够

empress ['empris] *n*.1. 女皇;皇后 2. 有极大权力的女人

empty ['empti] *adj*.1. 空的;（房屋等）未占用的;没人居住的;无家具设备的;（车,船等）未载东西的 2. 空洞的,空虚的;无实在意义的;缺乏力量（或效果）的 3. 无聊的,愚蠢的,傻的 4. 空闲的,无用的,徒劳的 5. 言无人烟的,空寂的;缺乏温暖的 6.〔口〕空着肚子的,饥饿的 7.（家畜）未怀孕的 — *vt*.1. 使空 2. 倒,倒空 3. 使流入(into) 4. 使失去(of) — *vi*.1. 成为空的,流空 2.（江河等）流入(into) — *n*.（常 empties）空箱;空瓶;空的货车 ‖ **emptily** *adv*. / **emptiness** *n*. ‖ '~-handed **handed** *adj*. 空手的;一无所获的 / '~-**headed** *adj*. 傻而无知的;浮薄而轻率的

emu ['i:mju:] *n*.1.【动】鸸鹋 2. 高大而不会飞的鸟

emulate ['emjuleit] *vt*.1. 同...竞争;同...竞赛;努力赶（或超）2. 竭力仿效 ‖ **emu'lation** *n*. / **emulator** *n*.

emulsify [i'mʌlsifai] *vt*.【化】使乳化

emulsion [i'mʌlʃən] *n*.1. 乳胶,乳浊液 2.【医】乳剂;【摄】感光乳剂

enable [i'neibl] *vt*.1. 使能够;使成为可能,使实现 2. 授予...权力

enact [i'nækt] *vt*.1. 制定（法律）;颁布;

通过(法案等) 2. 演出；扮演 ‖ ~ment *n.*1. 制定，规定；颁布 2. 法令；法规；条例 ‖ ~ing clause 制定条款(说明法案制定经过的条文)

enamel ['i'næməl] *n.*1. 搪瓷；珐琅 2. 搪瓷制品 3.(牙齿的)珐琅质 4. 瓷漆；瓷釉 5. 指甲油 — (enamel(l)ed; enamel(l)ing) *vt.*1. 涂瓷釉于 2. 给…上彩色，彩饰 3. 使成光滑面 ‖ **enamelware** *n.*[总称]搪瓷器

enamo(u)r ['i'næmə] *vt.* 使倾心，使迷恋 ‖ ~ed *adj.* 倾心于…的，恋慕…的(*of, with*)

encamp [in'kæmp] *vi.* 扎营；野营 — *vt.* 使扎营；把…安置于营中 ‖ ~ment *n.*1. 扎营；野营 2. 营；营地

encase [in'keis] *vt.*1. 把…装入，把…放入套(或盒、壳)内 2. 包装；围 ‖ ~ment *n.*1. 装箱；包装 2. 包装物；箱；鞘

enchant [in'tʃɑ:nt] *vt.*1. 用魔法迷惑 2. 使心醉；使喜悦 ‖ ~er *n.* 巫士；妖人 / ~ment *n.*1. 迷惑 2. 着迷 3. 妖术；魅力 / ~ress *n.* 女巫士；妖妇

enchanting [in'tʃɑ:tiŋ] *adj.* 迷人的；醉人的 ‖ ~ly *adv.*

encircle [in'sə:kl] *vt.*1. 环绕；包围 2. 绕…行一周 ‖ ~ment *n.*

enclave ['enkleiv] *n.* 飞地(指在本国境内的隶属另一国的一块领土)

enclose [in'kləuz] *vt.*1. 围住；圈起；关闭住 2. 把(公文、数据等)封入

enclosure [in'kləuʒə] *n.*1. 围绕；圈地(指把公地圈作私有的) 2. 封入 3. 围场；围栏；围墙 4. 附件；包入物

encode [in'kəud] *vt.* 把(电文等)译成电码(或密码) ‖【计】把…编码

encomium [en'kəumiəm] ([复] encomiums 或 encomia [en'kəumiə]) *n.* 高度赞扬，赞颂；赞词，颂词

encompass [in'kʌmpəs] *vt.*1. 围绕；包围；环绕 2. 包含，包括

encore ['ɔ:kɔ:] *int.* 再来一个！再演奏(或演唱)一次！ — *vt.* 要求…再演奏(或演唱)一次 — *n.*1. 重演的要求 2. 重演；重奏；重唱

encounter [in'kauntə] *vt.*1. 遭遇，遇到(困难、危险等) 2. 意外地遇见(朋友等) — *vt.*1. 冲突；遭遇战 2. 偶然(或短暂)的见面

encourage [in'kʌridʒ] *vt.* 鼓励；怂恿，赞助；促进 ‖ ~ment *n.*1. 鼓励，赞助 2. 鼓励物；奖励

encouraging [in'kʌridʒiŋ] *adj.* 鼓励的，赞助的；鼓舞人心的 ‖ ~ly *adv.*

encroach [in'krəutʃ] *vi.* 侵犯；侵占；蚕食(*upon, on*) ‖ ~ment *n.*

encrust [in'krʌst] *vt.* 包外壳于；(用银、宝石等)镶饰 — *vi.* 结壳(或皮) ‖ ~ment *n.*

encumber [in'kʌmbə] *vt.*1. 妨害，阻碍 2. 塞满；阻塞 3. 拖累，牵累 4. 使负担债务(或抵押等)

encumbrance [in'kʌmbrəns] *n.*1. 妨害，阻碍；障碍物 2. 累赘 3.【律】负担(指存在于他人不动产上的一种权利或利益，如抵押权之类)

-ency *suf.* [构成名词]表示"动作"；"性质"；"状态"；fluency, dependency

encyclic(al) [en'siklik(əl)] *n.* (罗马教皇向全世界或某地区天主教会颁发的)通谕

encyclop(a)edia [en,saikləu'pi:djə] *n.* 百科全书；(某一学科的)专科全书

encyclop(a)edic(al) [en,saikləu'pi:dik(əl)] *adj.* 百科全书的；知识广博的 ‖ 百科全书式的

end [end] *n.*1. 末端；尽头；梢，尖 2. 结尾；完结，结束，终止；限度，极限 3. 死亡；丧失；下场 4. 目的；目标 5. 残片；残余 6. 结果，结局；最终情况 一*vt.*1. 结束，终止；消灭 2. 了结 3. 位于…的结尾 一*vi.*1. 完结，结束，终止 2. 死 ‖ ~ .'all *n.* 结尾，终结；最终目标 / '~ .**paper** *n.* 扉页（书籍卷首和卷尾的空白页）/ ~ **point** 终点 / ~ **product** 最后产物；最终产品（或目标）；归宿 / ~ **run**（美）1.（橄榄球赛中）端线外侧迂回进攻 2. 迂回战术；规避伎俩

endanger [in'deindʒə] *vt.* 危害，危及，使遭到危险 ‖ ~ **ed** *adj.*1.（生命等）有危险的 2. 有灭种危险的，濒于灭绝的

endear [in'diə] *vt.* 使喜爱，使受钟爱 ‖ ~ **ment** *n.* 亲爱；亲爱的表示；爱抚

endearing [in'diəriŋ] *adj.* 可亲可爱的，惹人喜爱的 ‖ ~ **ly** *adv.*

endeavo[u]r [in'devə] *n.* 努力，尽力 一 *vi.* 努力，尽力，力图

endemic [en'demik] *adj.*1. 某地（或某种人）特有的 2.（疾病等）地方性的 3.（动、植物）某地特产的 一*n.* 地方病 ‖ ~ **ally** *adv.*

ending ['endiŋ] *n.*1. 结尾；结局 2. 死亡 3.【语】词尾

endive ['endiv] *n.*【植】莒荬菜；菊苣

endless ['endlis] *adj.*1. 无止境的，无穷的 2. 长久的，没完没了的 3. 两端接连的，环状的 一 chain（自行车等的）循环链 ‖ ~ **ly** *adv.* / ~ **ness** *n.*

endmost ['endməust] *adj.* 最（近）末端的；最后的

endocrine ['endəukrain] *n.*1.【生理】内分泌（腺）2.【生化】激素 一*adj.* 内分泌（腺）的；激素的

endorse [in'dɔːs] *vt.*1.【商】在（支票等）面签字，背书；签署（姓名）；签字支付（或表示收到）（票据上的金额）2. 批注（公文等）3. 赞同；认可；担保 ‖ ~ **ment** *n.*

endow [in'dau] *vt.*1. 捐赠基金给（人、组织等）；资助 2. 赋予（*with*）

endowment [in'daumənt] *n.*1. 捐赠；捐款；捐赠的基金 2. 才能；天资

endurable [in'djuərəbl] *adj.* 可忍的；能持久的 ‖ **endurably** *adv.*

endurance [in'djuərəns] *n.*1. 忍耐；耐劳；忍耐力 2. 持久（力）；耐久（性）

endure [in'djuə] *vt.*1. 忍受，耐 2.[常与 cannot 等否定词连用] 容忍 一*vi.*1. 忍受，忍耐 2. 持久，持续

enduring [in'djuəriŋ] *adj.* 持久的；不朽的 ‖ ~ **ly** *adv.*

endways ['endweiz]，**endwise** ['endwaiz] *adv.*1. 末端向前地 2. 末端朝上地 3. 竖着 两端相接地 4. 向着两端 5. 在末端

enema ['enimə] *n.*【医】灌肠剂；灌肠（法）；灌肠器

enemy ['enimi] *n.*1. 敌人，仇敌，仇人 2.[集合名词]敌兵，敌军 2. 敌国；敌舰；敌机 3.（喻）大敌，危害物；大害 一*adj.* 敌人的；敌方的 ‖ ~ **alien**（两国交战时）居住在敌国的侨民；被拘于敌国者

energetic [.enə'dʒetik] *adj.* 有力的；精力旺盛的；精神饱满的

energy ['enədʒi] *n.*1. 活力，劲；（语言、文笔等的）生动有力 2.[energies]精力；能力 3.【物】能；能量

enfeeble [in'fiːbl] *vt.* 使衰弱 ‖ ~ **ment** *n.*

enfold [in'fəuld] *vt.*1. 包，把…包住（*in*, *with*）2. 拥抱；怀抱 3. 折叠

enforce [in'fɔːs] *vt.*1. 实施，使生效；执行 2. 强迫，迫使；强加（*on*, *upon*）3. 加

强;坚持(要求、主张等) ‖ ~able adj.
可实施的;可强制执行的 / ~ment n.

enfranchise [in'fræntʃaiz] vt. 1. 给予…
公民权(或选举权) 2. 给(城、镇)以
政治权利(在英国指派议会议员权) 3.
释放(奴隶等) ‖ ~ment n.

engage [in'geidʒ] vt. 1. [常用被动语态]使
从事(in);使忙着 2. [~ oneself 或用
被动语态]约束;约定;使订婚(to) 3.
保证(that) 4. 雇用,聘;预订(铺位等)
5. 使参加,使卷在其中(in);与…交
战 6. 吸引住(注意力等) 7. 占去(时间
等) 8. 使(齿轮等)啮合 —vi. 1. 应允;
保证(for) 2. 从事于,参加…(in) 3. 交
战(with) 4. 啮合,接合 ‖ ~ment n.

engaging [in'geidʒiŋ] adj. 有吸引力的;迷
人的;可爱的 ‖ ~ly adv.

engender [in'dʒendə] vt. 产生;造成;引起

engine ['endʒin] n. 1. 引擎,发动机 2. 机
车,火车头 3. 机械;工具;器械 a fire
~消防车,救火车 —vt. 在…上安装
发动机 ‖ ~ driver(英)火车司机 / ~
room 发动机房;轮机舱

engineer [,endʒi'niə] n. 1. 工程师;技师
2. 火车司机 3. 发动机设计与制造
(或制造)者 4. 精明的管理家 5. [军]
工兵 —vt. 1. 设计;建造;监造 2. 指
挥;管理 3. 策划

engineering [,endʒi'niəriŋ] n. 1. 工程;工
程学 2. 操纵;管理

England ['iŋglənd] n. 1. 英格兰[英国的
主要部分] 2. (泛指)英格兰和威尔士
3.(泛指)大不列颠岛 4.(泛指)英国

English ['iŋgliʃ] adj. 1. 英格兰的 2. 英国
的(英人)的 3. 英语的 — n. 1. 英语 2.
[the ~][总称]英格兰人,英国人 3. 英
语中的对应词语,英语译名(for) ‖ ~
Channel 英吉利海峡 / ~ horn(管乐器)
英国管,中音双簧管 / ~ man n. 英格

兰人,英国人;英国男子 / ~woman n.
英国女人

engrave [in'greiv] vt. 1. 雕上,刻上 2. 在
(石、木等)上雕刻 3. 把…铭刻(在脑
海或记忆中)(on, upon) 4. 镂(版)用
镂版印;照相制(版) ‖ ~r n. 雕刻师;
雕刻工人;镂版工人

engraving [in'greiviŋ] n. 1. 雕刻;雕刻术
2. 雕版;图版;版画;雕版印刷品

engross [in'grəus] vt. 1. 用大字体书写(正
式文件等) 2. 占用(时间);吸引(注
意);使全神贯注 ‖ ~ing adj. 引人入
胜的;很有趣味的;非常引人注意的 ‖
~ment n.

engulf [in'gʌlf] vt. 吞没;席卷 2. 狼吞
虎咽,吞食

enhance [in'hɑːns] vt. 提高,增加(价值、
吸引力等);增强,增进 ‖ ~ment n.

enigma [i'nigmə] n. 1. 谜;暧昧不明的话
(或文章) 2. 不可思议的人(或物)

enigmatic(al) [,enig'mætik(ə)l] adj. 1. 谜
一般的;不可思议的 2. 莫测高深的;
莫名其妙的 ‖ enigmatically adv.

enjoin [in'dʒɔin] vt. 1. 嘱咐;责成;命令
2. [律]禁止

enjoy [in'dʒɔi] vt. 1. 享受;享有(利益、权
利、声誉等) 2. 享受…的乐趣;欣赏;
喜爱 3. [~ oneself]过得快活

enjoyable [in'dʒɔiəbl] adj. 愉快的;快乐
的;有趣的 ‖ enjoyably adv.

enjoyment [in'dʒɔimənt] n. 1. 享受;享有
2. 享乐;欢乐;愉快 3. 乐趣;乐事

enlarge [in'lɑːdʒ] vt. 1. 扩大;扩展(胸襟、
思想等) 2. 放大(照片) 3.(美)释放 —
vi. 1. 扩大,扩展 2. 详述(on, upon) ‖ ~
r n. [摄]放大机

enlargement [in'lɑːdʒmənt] n. 1. 扩大;扩
展 2. 增补物;扩建部分 3.(照相的)放
大;放大的照片 4. [医]肿大,扩大

enlighten [in'laitn] vt.1. 启发,开导;教导 2. 使摆脱偏见(或迷信)‖ ~ed adj. 开明的,进步的;有知识的 / ~ing adj. 有启发性的;使人领悟的 / ~ment n. 启蒙,启发

enlist [in'list] vt.1. 征募,使入伍 2. 谋取...赞助(或支持);利用;争取(赞助,支持等) — vi.1. 入伍,应募 2. 赞助,支持,热心参加 ‖ ~ed adj. 应募入伍的;an ~ed man〈美〉士兵 / ~ment n.1. 征募;应募入伍 2. 服役期限

enliven [in'laivn] vt.1. 使有生气,使活跃 2. 使快活

enmesh [in'meʃ] vt.1. 网捕,使陷入网中 2. 缠住;使卷入 ‖ ~ment n.

enmity ['enmiti] n. 敌意;仇恨;不和;敌对

ennoble [i'nəubl] vt.1. 封...为贵族 2. 使崇高 ‖ ~ment n.

ennui ['ɔːnwiː] n. 厌倦;无聊

enormity [i'nɔːmiti] n.1. 穷凶极恶 2. 无法无天的行为 3. 巨大,庞大

enormous [i'nɔːməs] adj.1. 巨大的,庞大的 2.〈古〉极恶的;凶暴的 ‖ ~ly adv.

enough [i'nʌf] adj. 足够的,充足的 — n. 足够,充分 — adv.1. 足够地,充分地 2. 很,十分 3. 相当地;尚 — int. 够了!

enquire [in'kwaiə] vi. & vt. = inquire

enquiry [in'kwaiəri] n. = inquiry

enrage [in'reidʒ] vt. 激怒

enrapt [in'ræpt] adj. 狂喜的;神魂颠倒的

enrapture [in'ræptʃə] vt. 使狂喜

enrich [in'ritʃ] vt.1. 使富裕 2. 使丰富 3. 使(土壤)肥沃 4. 装饰;增美 5. 加料于;增进(食品)的营养价值(或滋味),强化 6. 浓缩 ‖ ~ment n.1. 发财致富;丰富;加肥;增添装饰 2. 强化;浓

缩,加浓 3.【矿】富集

enrol(l) [in'rəul] (enrolled; enrolling) vt.1. 登记;把...编入;招收 2. 使入伍;使入会;使入学 — vi. 参军;注册;成为会员 ‖ ~ment n.1. 注册人数;入学人数

en route [ˌɔn'ruːt]〈法〉在途中的(地)

ensconce [in'skɔns] vt.1. 使隐蔽 2. 安置

ensemble [ɔn'sɔmbl]〈法〉n.1. 全体,整体;总效果 2. 全体演出者;(一次)集体演出 3.【音】合奏;合唱 4. 剧团;文工团;歌舞团;演唱(或演奏)组 5.(芭蕾舞演出中的)群舞演员;全体伴唱者 6.【数】总体 7. 全套配合协调的女式服装

enshrine [in'ʃrain] vt.1. 把...置放在龛内,把...供奉;把...奉为神圣 2.(喻)铭记;珍藏

enshroud [in'ʃraud] vt. 掩蔽,遮蔽;隐蔽

ensign ['ensain] n.1. 旗;军旗;商船旗;舰旗 2.(示职位、身分、权力等的)徽章;符号;象征 3.〈美〉海军少尉

ensilage ['ensilidʒ] n.1. 饲料的青贮 2. 青贮饲料 — vt. 青贮(饲料)

enslave [in'sleiv] vt.1. 使做奴隶,奴役 2. 征服;制服;使受制(to) ‖ ~ment n. 奴役;束缚

ensnare [in'snɛə] vt.1. 诱捕;诱惑 2. 使入圈套;陷害

ensue [in'sjuː] vi. 接着发生;因而产生;接着到来;the ensuing year 下一年

entail [in'teil] vt.1.(计划、工程等)必然需要(费用、劳力等);使(某种行动)成为必要 2.(某事对...)要求承担(费用、劳力等);(对...)产生(某种后果)(on) 3.【律】限定(地产等)的继承(on)

一 n.【律】(地产等的)限嗣继承;限嗣
继承的地产;确定的继承权顺序

entangle [in'tæŋgl] vt.1. 缠住;套住;使纠
缠;使混乱 2. 使卷入(纠纷等);使陷入;连累 ‖ ~ment n.1. 纠缠;纠纷;牵连
2. 缠住物;纠缠物;障碍物

enter ['entə] vt.1. 进入 2. 把...放入 ~
a key in the door 把钥匙插进门里 3.
加入,参加 4. 使进入;使加入,使参
加;报(名)登记 5. 把...记入;登录;
(书面)提出 6. 开始从事;开始进入,
开始研讨 7.【律】正式书面提出 8. 把
(船或货)申报海关 9. 占有(土地等)
10. 使(马、狗等)进入场地(或出猎);
训练(马、狗等) — vi.1. 进去;进来;【戏】登场,上场,上 2. 参加,加入
(for) 3. 开始进去,穿进去 4. 开始,着
手;开始探讨(on, upon)

enterprise ['entəpraiz] n.1.(艰巨、复杂或
冒险性的)事业;计划;事业单位;企业
单位 2. 办企业;干事业 3. 事业心;进
取心

enterprising ['entəpraiziŋ] adj. 有事业心
的,有进取心的;有魄力的 ‖ ~ly adv.

entertain [,entə'tein] vt.1. 招待;款待 2.
使欢乐,娱乐 3. 抱着,怀着;持
有(信心、意见等) 4. 容纳,接受;准备
考虑 — vi. 款待,请客 2. 使人欢乐
快乐(或娱乐) ‖ ~er n.1. 款待者 2. 供
人娱乐者;表演者

entertaining [,entə'teiniŋ] adj. 有趣的,使
人欢乐的 ‖ ~ly adv.

entertainment [,entə'teinmənt] n.1. 招
待;款待;招待会 2. 娱乐;乐趣;欢乐
3. 表演会;文娱节目 4. 抱有,怀有(指
希望、怀疑等)

enthral(l) [in'θrɔ:l] (enthralled; enthralling)
vt.1. 迷住,吸引住 2. 使沦为奴隶,奴
役 ‖ **enthralling** adj. 迷人的;吸引人的

/ ~ment n.

enthrone [in'θrəun] vt. 使(国王、主教等)
登位,立...为王(或主教等);使占最
高地位 2.(喻)推崇;崇拜 ‖ ~ment n.

enthuse [in'θju:z] (口) vt. 使热心;使表示
热心 — vi.(表示)热心(over, about)

enthusiasm [in'θju:ziæzm] n.1. 热情;热
心;热忱;积极性 2. 激发热情的事物;
热心研究的对象 3.(古)宗教狂信;神秘
的灵感 ‖ **enthusiast** n. 热心人;热情
者;热中者

enthusiastic [in,θju:zi'æstik] adj. 热情的,
热心的;热烈的 ‖ ~ally adv.

entice [in'tais] vt. 诱使,怂恿 ‖ ~ment
n.

enticing [in'taisiŋ] adj. 引诱的;迷人的,
动人心目的 ‖ ~ly adv.

entire [in'taiə] adj.1. 完全的,整个的;全
部的,完整的 2. 纯粹的 3.【植】全缘的
4.(马)未经阉割的 ‖ ~ly adv. 完全
地;彻底地 / ~ness n.

entirety [in'taiəti] n. 整体,总体;全部;全
面

entitle [in'taitl] vt.1. 给(书、文章等)题
名;给...称号(或尊称) 2. 给...权利
(或资格) ‖ ~ment n. 权利

entity ['entiti] n.1. 存在;实体;统一体
2.(与属性等区别的)本质

entomb [in'tu:m] vt. 1. 埋葬,掩埋 2. 作
为...的坟墓 ‖ ~ment n.

entomology [,entə'mɔlədʒi] n. 昆虫学

entourage [,ɔntu'rɑ:ʒ] (法) n.(全体)随行
人员;随从;陪随者

entrails ['entreilz] [复] n.1. 内脏;肠 2.
(物体的)内部

entrain [in'trein] vt. & vi.(使)上火车

entrance[1] ['entrəns] n.1. 进入 2. 入口,
进口;门口 3. 入场;入会;入学;入港

入场权(或费) 4. 开始,着手 5. 就任 (*into*, *upon*) 6.(演员)的登场;(合唱或合奏中歌声或乐器的)开端处

entrance² ['intrɑːns] *vt.* 使出神;使神志恍惚;使狂喜;使入迷 ‖ ~ment *n.*

entrancing [in'trɑːnsiŋ] *adj.* 令人出神的;令人神志恍惚的;令人喜悦的;迷人的 ‖ ~ly *adv.*

entrant ['entrənt] *n.* 1. 进入者 2. 新加入者;新会员;新学员;刚就业者 3. 参加竞赛者(*for*)

entrap [in'træp] (entrapped; entrapping) *vt.* 1. 诱捕,使入陷阱 2. 使陷入圈套(或罗网,困难等);诱使...妥协(*into*) ‖ ~ment *n.*

entreat [in'triːt] *vt. & vi.* 恳求,请求 ‖ ~ingly *adv.* 恳求地,哀求地

entreaty [in'triːti] *n.* 恳求,请求

entree ['ontrei] *n.* 1. 入场权,入场许可;进入 2.(美)主菜 3.(英)两道正菜之间的小菜 4. 正餐前的开胃菜

entrench [in'trentʃ] *vt.* 1. 用壕沟围;用壕沟防御;置...于壕沟中 2. 牢固地树立;使(人)处于牢固地位;使盘踞 — *vi.* 1. 掘壕;当壕沟 2. 侵占;侵犯 (*on*, *upon*) ‖ ~ment *n.* 1. 掘壕沟 2. 堑壕;堡垒;防御设施

entrepreneur [ˌɔntrəprə'nɜː]〈法〉*n.* 1. 企业家;创业者 2.(活动的)主办者;提倡者;促进者 3. 中间商;承包者

entrust [in'trʌst] *vt.* 委托,信托;托管(与...)

entry ['entri] *n.* 1. 进入;入场(权);入场(或入城等)典礼;入会权 2. 入口;门口;河口 3. 登记,记载;条目,项目;账目 4. 参加比赛的资格(或权);参加比赛的人(或物)的名单 5.【律】(为达到犯罪目的)侵入房屋(或建筑物);(对被他人侵占的土地等的)

屋等的)和平进入并占有

entwine [in'twain] *vt.* 1. 使缠绕,使盘绕;(喻)使纠缠 2. 拥抱 — *vi.* 缠绕;纠缠

enumerate [i'njuːməreit] *vt.* 1. 数,点 2. 列举,枚举 ‖ enume'ration *n.*

enunciate [i'nʌnsieit] *vt.* 1. 确切地说明;阐明(理论、原则等) 2. 宣布;发表 3.(清晰地)发...音 — *vi.*(清晰地)发音 ‖ enunci'ation *n.*

envelop [in'veləp] *vt.* 1. 包,裹;封 2. 围绕;包围 ‖ ~ment *n.*

envelope ['enviləup] *n.* 1. 包裹物;封皮,封套;信封 2. 壳层,外壳 3.(气艇、气球等的)气囊;蒙皮 4.【数】包络面,包络线 5.【生】膜,被层

enviable ['enviəbl] *adj.* 引起妒忌的;值得羡慕的 ‖ ~ness *n.* / enviably *adv.*

envied ['envid] *adj.* 被妒忌的;被羡慕的

envious ['enviəs] *adj.*(对...)妒忌的;羡慕的(*of*) ‖ ~ly *adv.*

environment [in'vaiərənmənt] *n.* 1. 环境 2. 生态环境;自然环境 3. 环境艺术(作品),环境戏剧

environmental [inˌvaiərən'mentl] *adj.* 环境的;环境产生的 ‖ ~ist *n.* 1. 环境论者;环境论信奉者 2. 环境保护论者;研究环境污染问题的专家 *adj.*(者)的 / ~ly *adv.* ‖ ~ art 环境艺术 / ~ engineer(研究环境保护的)环境工程师 / ~ theatre 环境戏剧

environs [in'vaiərənz][复] *n.* 城郊;郊区;附近的地方

envisage [in'vizidʒ] *vt.* 1. 正视,面对(现实、危机等) 2. 想象,设想

envision [in'viʒən] *vt.* 想象,预想,展望

envoy ['envɔi] *n.* 1. 使者,代表;使节;特命全权公使 2.(古)(诗、散文、文集的)跋,后记(或献词)(作为结语或献词

的)结尾诗节

envy ['envi] **n.** & **vt.** 妒忌;羡慕

enwrap [in'ræp] (enwrapped; enwrapping) **vt.1.** 包,裹;卷入 **2.** 围绕 **3.** 包围;笼罩

enzyme ['enzaim] **n.** [生化]酶

eohippus [ˌiːəuˈhipəs] **n.** [动]始祖马

eon ['iːən] **n.** = aeon

epaulet(te) ['epəulet] **n.1.** [军]肩章 **2.** (妇女外衣等上的)肩饰

ephemeral [i'femərəl] **adj.1.** (昆虫等)短生的,短命的 **2.** 极短的,一时的;只生存一天的;(疾病)一日即愈的,短暂的 ‖ ~**ly** adv.

epic ['epik] **n.1.** 史诗,叙事诗 **2.** 史诗般的文艺作品 **3.** 可写成史诗的事迹(或传说等) —**adj.1.** 史诗的,叙事诗的 **2.** 英雄的;壮丽的;庄严的 **3.** 有重大历史(或传奇)意义的 **4.** 特别长的;宏大的;极大规模的

epical ['epikəl] **adj.** = epic ‖ ~**ly** adv.

epicentre, epicenter ['episentə] **n.1.** [地]震中 **2.** 中心;集中点 ‖ **epicentral** [ˌepi'sentrəl] adj.

epicure ['epikjuə] **n.1.** 讲究饮食的人,美食家 **2.** (古)享乐主义者

epidemic [ˌepi'demik] **adj.** 流行性的 —**n.1.** 流行病 **2.** (流行病的)传播 **3.** (风尚等的)流行

epidermal [ˌepiˈdɜːməl], **epidermic** [ˌepi'dɜːmik] **adj.** [生]表皮的

epidermis [ˌepi'dɜːmis] **n.** [生]表皮(层)

epigram ['epigræm] **n.1.** 机智的短诗;讽刺短诗 **2.** 警句,隽语

epigrammatic [ˌepigrə'mætik] **adj.** 警句(式)的;讽刺短诗的;简练精辟的 ‖ ~**ally** adv.

epilepsy ['epilepsi] **n.** [医]癫痫,羊癫疯

epileptic [ˌepi'leptik] **adj.** 癫痫的;患癫痫的 —**n.** 癫痫病人

epilog(ue) ['epiləɡ] **n.1.** (文艺作品的)结尾部分,尾声;跋;后记 **2.** [戏]收场诗,收场白(常用韵文)

Epiphany [i'pifəni] **n.** (纪念耶稣向世人显现的)显节节,主显节

episcopacy [i'piskəpəsi] **n.** (教会的)主教制

episcopal [i'piskəpəl] **adj.** (基督教)主教的;主教制的:the *Episcopal* Church 美国新教(或苏格兰)圣公会 / the Protestant *Episcopal* Church 美国圣公会 ‖ ~**ian** [iˌpiskəu'peiljən] **n.** & **adj.** / ~**ly** adv.

episode ['episəud] **n.1.** (文艺作品中的)插曲,片断;一节;一出(或一集、一部分) **2.** (一系列事件中的)一个事件;(人生的)一段经历 **3.** [音]插句,插段,插部 ‖ **episodic(al)** [ˌepi'sɔdik(əl)] adj.

epistle [i'pisl] **n.1.** [the Epistles](基督教《圣经·新约》中的)使徒书信 **2.** 书信(尤指写得很华丽的正式信件) **3.** 书信体诗文

epitaph ['epitɑːf] **n.1.** 墓志铭 **2.** 纪念死者(或往事)的诗文

epithet ['epiθet] **n.1.** (表示性质、特征的形容词或名词、短语等)表述词语 **2.** 别称 **3.** (动植物学名中的)种名(或变种名等)部分

epitome [i'pitəmi] **n.1.** 梗概;概括;节录 **2.** 缩影,集中体现

epitomize [i'pitəmaiz] **vt.1.** 对…作摘要,概括 **2.** 成为…的缩影;集中体现

e pluribus unum [iːˈplʊəribəsˈjuːnəm] (拉)合众为一(尤指由诸州联合组成全国政府,过去曾用作美国国训,现作为铭文用于美国国玺及部分钱币上)

epoch ['iːpɔk] **n.1.** 时期;时代新纪元,新时期;重要时期 **2.** 值得纪念的事件

epoxy ['ep'ɔksi] 【化】 **adj.** 环氧(化物)的 —**n.** 环氧树脂(epoxied 或 epoxyed) **vt.** 用环氧树脂胶合

Epsom ['epsəm] **n.** (英国伦敦南面的城市)埃普索姆;埃普索姆的赛马场 ∥ ~ salt(s)【化】泻盐,硫酸镁七水合物,七水合硫酸镁

equable ['ekwəbl] **adj.** 1.(温度等)(相当)稳定的 2.(人、性情)平静的 ∥ **equably adv.**

equal ['i:kwəl] **adj.** 1. 相等的;均等的;相同的 2. 平等的 3. 胜任的,经得起的(to);(竞赛等)势均力敌的,不相上下的 4. 合适的(to) 5.(性情等)平静的;平稳的 —**n.** 1. 相等的事物(或数量);(地位等)相等的人 2. 匹敌者;堪与比拟的东西(=equal(l)ed;equal(l)ing) **vt.** 1. 等于 2. 比得上;敌得过 3. 完全补偿(或酬报) ∥ ~ly **adv.**

equalitarian [i:kwɔli'teəriən] **adj.** 主张人人平等的;平等主义 —**n.** 平等主义者 ∥ ~ism **n.** 平等主义

equality [i:'kwɔliti] **n.** 1. 同等;平等;均等 2.【数】相等;等式

equalize ['i:kwəlaiz] **vt.** 1. 使相等;使均等;使平均;使平等 2. 补偿,补足 3.【电】使电稳一 —**vi.** 相等一;(英式)(在比赛中)打成平局,与对方拉平比分 ∥ ,equali'zation **n.**

equanimity [i:kwə'nimiti] **n.** 沉着,平静,镇定

equate [i'kweit] **vt.** 1. 使相等;使均衡(to, with) 2. 等同;显示...的密切关系 3.【数】用符号表示...的关系;用方程式列出

equation [i'kwei∫ən] **n.** 1.(对供应等的)平衡;均衡;平均;相等 2.(个别或综合的)因素 3.【数】方程(式);等式 4.【化】反应式 5. 综合体;差,均差

equator [i'kweitə] **n.** 地球赤道;(任何天体的)赤道

equatorial [ekwə'tɔːriəl] **adj.** 1. 赤道的;赤道附近的 2.(天气)极炎热的 ∥ ~ly **adv.**

Equatorial Guinea [ekwə'tɔːriəl 'gini] 赤道几内亚 [非洲西部国家]

equestrian [i'kwestriən] **adj.** 马的;骑马的;马术的;骑士的 —**n.** 骑马者;骑手;马术家

equestrienne [i,kwestri'en] **n.** 骑马女人;女骑手;女马术家

equidistant [i:kwi'distənt] **adj.** 1. 等距离的 2.(地图上所有方向的距离)同比例的 ∥ ~ly **adv.**

equilateral [i:kwi'lætərəl] **adj.** 1.【数】等边的 2. 两侧对称的

equilibrium [i:kwi'libriəm] [复 equilibria [i:kwi'libriə] 或 equilibriums] **n.** 1. 平衡,均衡;平均;相称 2. 均势 3.(心情的)平静,不偏不倚

equine ['ekwain] **adj.** 马的;马科的;似马的;马性的 —**n.** 马;马科动物

equinox ['i:kwinɔks] **n.** 【天】1. 二分时刻,昼夜平分时 2. 二分点;vernal ~春分点;春分点/autumnal ~秋分点;秋分点 ∥ ~quinoctial [i:kwi'nɔk∫əl] **adj.**

equip [i'kwip] **vt.**(equipped; equipping) **vt.** 1. 装备,配备 2.(智力上)使有准备;训练

equipment [i'kwipmənt] **n.** 1. 装备,配备;设备;器材;装置 2. 机车车辆 3. 才能;知识;禀赋;素养

equitable ['ekwitəbl] **adj.** 1. 公平的,公正的 2.【律】衡平法的;衡平法上(有效)的 ∥ ~ness **n.** /**equitably adv.**

equity ['ekwiti] **n.** 公平,公道;公平的

事物 2.【律】衡平法；衡平法上的权利

equivalent [i'kwivələnt] *adj.*1.（在力量等上与...）相等的，相当的，相同的（*to*）2.等价的；等值的；等量的；等效的 3.同意义的 4.【化】等价的 5.【数】等积的；相等的 —— *n.*1. 相等物；等价物；等值物；等量物 2. 等价；等量 3. 意义相同的词（或符号、表达法等）4.【化】当量

equivocal [i'kwivəkəl] *adj.*1. 有歧义的，模棱两可的，含糊的 2.（行为、事件等）暧昧的，可疑的 3.（结果等）不明确的，不肯定的 ‖ **~ly** *adv.* / **~ness** *n.*

equivocate [i'kwivəkeit] *vt.* 支吾，含糊其词；躲闪，推诿 ‖ **e**,**quivo**'**cation** *n.*

Er【化】元素铒（erbium）的符号

er [ə:] *int.* 表示说话迟疑！哦！

-er[1] *suf.*［附在名词、形容词、动词和动词词组构成的复合词后，构成名词］1. 表示："...的人"，"...者"，"...派"：foreigner, runner 2. 表示"...地方的人"：villager, southerner 3. 表示"参加（机构、事件等）的人"：West Pointer 4. 表示"研究...学问的人"：astronomer 5. 表示"从事...职业的人"：writer 6. 表示"...物"，"用于...的机械（或武器、工具等）"：three-decker, boiler, fighter-bomber

-er[2] *suf.*［附在单音节形容词或以 -y、-ly、-ow 等结尾的双音节形容词及少数副词之后构成比较级］表示"更..."：greater, happier, yellower, harder

era ['iərə] *n.*1. 时代；年代 2. 纪元 3.（标志着新时期开始的）重要日子；重大事件 4.【地】代

eradiate [i'reidieit] *vt.* 发出（光线等）；辐射 ‖ **e**,**radi**'**ation** *n.*

eradicable [i'rædikəbl] *adj.* 可根除的，可

消灭的

eradicate [i'rædikeit] *vt.*1. 连根拔除 2. 根除，消灭，歼灭 ‖ **e**,**radi**'**cation** *n.* / **eradicator** *n.* 根除者；根除器；去锈剂，退色灵

erase [i'reiz] *vt.*1. 擦掉，抹掉；除去；删去 2. 擦（黑板）3. 消灭；忘掉；〈美俚〉杀死

eraser [i'reizə] *n.*1. 擦除器（如黑板擦、橡皮、挖字刀等）2.【无】消磁器；抹音器 3.〈美〉（拳击用语）击倒对手的一击

erasure [i'reiʒə] *n.*1. 擦掉（去）；消除 2. 擦掉处；删去处；擦掉（或删去）的字（或记号等）

erbium ['ə:biəm] *n.*【化】铒

ere [εə]〈古〉〈诗〉 *conj.*1. 在...以前 2.（与其...）毋宁 —— *prep.* 在...之前

erect [i'rekt] *adj.*1. 直立的，垂直的，竖直的 2. 竖起的 3.〈古〉向上的 4.〈古〉不屈的，坚毅的；警惕的 5.【生理】勃起的 —— *vt.*1. 使竖立，使竖立起 2. 树立；建立，设立 3. 安装；装配 4. 把（原理等）上升为体系（*into*）5.【数】作（垂直线等）6.【生理】使勃起 —— *vi.*【生理】勃起 ‖ **~ly** *adv.* / **~ness** *n.*

erection [i'rekʃən] *n.*1. 直立，竖立，竖直 2. 建立，建造；安装；装配 3. 建设物，建筑物 4.【生理】勃起

erg [ə:g] *n.*【物】尔格（功和能量的单位）

Eritrea [,eri'triə] *n.* 厄立特里亚［非洲东北部国家］

Erivan [,eri'vɑ:n] *n.* 埃里温（即 Yerevan 耶烈万）［亚美尼亚首都］

ermine ['ə:min] *n.*1.【动】白鼬，扫雪 2. 白鼬皮 3. 法官（或国王、贵族）的地位（或职位，职责）4. 公正纯洁的标志；高贵荣誉的标志 ‖ **~d** *adj.*1. 饰有白鼬皮的 2. 穿着白鼬皮长袍的

erode [i'rəud] *vt.*1. 腐蚀；侵蚀 2. 把...腐蚀成；把...侵蚀成 —— *vi.* 受腐蚀；遭

侵蚀 ‖ **erosion**[i'rəuʒən] *n.*

erosive [i'rəusiv] *adj.* 腐蚀性的;侵蚀性的

erotic [i'rɔtik] *adj.*(引起)性爱的;(引起)性欲的;色情的 ‖ ~**ally** *adv.*

erotica [i'rɔtikə][复] *n.*[用作单或复]色情文学(作品);色情艺术(作品)

err [ə:] *vi.*1. 犯错误;弄错;(陈述、仪器等)不正确 2. 作恶

errand ['erənd] *n.*1. 差使(如送信、买东西等) 2.〈古〉使命 ‖ ~-**boy** *n.* 供差遣的童仆

errant ['erənt] *adj.*1. 周游的;漂泊的:an ~ knight 游侠 2. 走入歧途的 3.(河道、风等)无定向的

errata [e'rɑ:tə]erratum 的复数

erratic [i'rætik] *adj.*1. 飘忽不定的;不稳定的;无规律的:an ~ star 游星 2.(人或其行为、习惯、意见等)古怪的;乖癖的;反复无常的 3.〈古〉流浪的,漂泊的 4.【地】移动的,漂移性的 5.【医】游走的;移动的 ‖ ~**ally** *adv.*

erratum [e'rɑ:təm][复]**errata**[e'rɑ:tə]) *n.*(书写或印刷中的)错误

erring ['ə:riŋ] *adj.* 做错了事的;有罪过的;走入歧途的

erroneous [i'rəunjəs] *adj.* 错误的,不正确的 ‖ ~**ly** *adv.* / ~**ness** *n.*

error ['erə] *n.*1. 谬误;错误 2. 谬见;错误思想 3. 罪过;违犯(行为);邪恶;过失 4. 差错;误差 5.(棒球赛中的)失误

ersatz ['ɛəzæts]〈德〉 *adj.* 代用的;人造的;合成的 ‖ *n.* 代用品

erstwhile ['ə:stʍwail] *adv.* 以前,从前,往昔 ‖ *adj.* 以前的,从前的,原来的

erudite ['erudait] *adj.* 博学的,有学问的 ‖ ~**ly** *adv.* / **erudition**[,eru'difən] *n.* 博学,博识;学问

erupt [i'rʌpt] *vi.*1.(火山,喷泉等)喷发;喷出;爆发;迸发 2.(疹)发出;(牙齿)冒出 ‖ *vt.* 喷出;喷射出

eruption [i'rʌpʃən] *n.*1.(火山)的喷发 2.(战争、情感等的)爆发;迸发 3.【医】发疹;疹;(牙齿的)冒出 4. 喷出物

-ery *suf.*1.[构成名词]1.[加于形容词或名词后]表示"性质","行为","习性":bravery 2.[加于动词后]表示"职业","技术":fishery, surgery 3.[加于动词后]表示"场所":bakery 4.[加于动词后]表示"境遇","身份","状况":drudgery, slavery 5.[加于名词后]表示"...类的产品(或物件)":drapery

erysipelas [,eri'sipiləs] *n.*【医】丹毒

Es【化】元素镧(einsteinium)的符号

-es *suf.*1.[加于词尾为 s, z, sh, ch, o, y, f 的大多数名词后构成复数]:glasses, fuzzes bushes, peaches, heroes, ladies, loaves 2.[加于词尾为 s, z, sh, ch 等的动词后,构成陈述语气第三人称单数现在时]:buzzes, reaches

escalate ['eskəleit] *vi.*(像自动楼梯式传送带似地)逐步上升;(战争等)逐步升级 ‖ *vt.* 使逐步上升;使...逐步升级 ‖ ,esca'lation *n.* 逐步上升;逐步升级

escalator ['eskəleitə] *n.*1.【建】自动扶梯 2. 规定(工资等)定期按生活费用上下调整的条款 ‖ *adj.* 规定(价格、工资等)定期按比例作出上下调整的

escapade [,eskə'peid] *n.* 越轨行为;恶作剧;胡作非为

escape [is'keip] *vi.*1. 逃脱;逃脱;逃亡;避免(*from*) 2. 漏出;流出 ‖ *vt.*1. 逃避;逃脱;避免 2.(错误等)没有被...注意到;被...忽略 3.(话、呻吟声等)无意中由(某人或某人的嘴里)说出;发出 ‖ *n.*1. 逃跑;逃脱;逃逸;排泄;漏出 2. 逃避(现实) 3. 逃路;出口;逃跑工具;a fire ~（火警时使用的）太平梯；安全出口 **4.**【植】野化种 ‖ **escapee** [iskei'pi:] **n.** 逃脱者；逃亡者；逃犯；逃俘 ‖ ~ **artist 1.** 有脱身术的人（尤指魔术师或杂技演员）**2.** 善于越狱的罪犯 / ~ **clause**（贸易等）例外条款 / ~ **velocity**〔字〕逃逸速度，第二字宙速度，脱离速度（指克服地球引力的速度）

escapement [is'keipmənt] **n.** 擒纵机构；（钟、表等的）擒纵轮；棘轮装置（尤指打字机上控制间隔的装置）

escapism [i'skeipizəm] **n.** 逃避现实 ‖ **escapist** **n.**

eschew [is'tʃu:] **vt.** 避免（某种行为、食物等）；避开（危害、恶事等）

escort ['eskɔ:t] **n.1.** 警卫队，护送队；护航部队；护航艇；护航飞机 **2.** 护卫之者，护送者；陪同者 **3.** 护卫，护送；护航；陪同 ─ [is'kɔ:t] **vt.** 护卫，护送；陪同

escutcheon [is'kʌtʃən] **n.** 饰有纹章的盾

-ese **suf. 1.**〔加于地名后〕表示"……人（的）"；"……语（的）"；"……国（或地方）的"：*Japanese* **2.**〔加于某些名词后，常含贬义〕表示"用语"、"风格"、"文体"等：*journalese*

Eskimo ['eskiməu] **n.**（[复]Eskimo(s)）& **adj.** 爱斯基摩人（的）；爱斯基摩语（的）‖ ~ **dog**【动】北极犬，爱斯基摩狗

esophagus [i:'sɔfəgəs] **n.**【解】食管

esoteric [ˌesəu'terik] **adj.** 秘传的；机密的；奥秘的

esp. **abbr.** especially

especial [is'peʃəl] **adj.** 特别的，特殊的 ‖ ~ **ly** **adv.** 特别，尤其，格外

Esperanto [ˌespə'ræntəu] **n.** 世界语

espionage [ˌespiə'nɑ:ʒ] **n.** 谍报；间谍活动；刺探

espousal [is'pauzəl] **n.1.**〔常~s〕订婚；订婚仪式；结婚；婚礼 **2.**（对事业、主义等的）拥护；赞助

espouse [is'pauz] **vt.1.** 娶（妻）；嫁（女）；与……结婚（或订婚）**2.** 拥护；信奉；支持；采纳

espresso [e'spresəu]（[复]espressos）**n.**（用蒸汽加压煮出的）压制咖啡

espy [is'pai] **vt.** 窥探；窥见，（偶然）看见 **2.** 发现（缺点等）

Esq. **abbr.** Esquire

esquire [is'kwaiə] **n. 1.**（英）[E-]……先生（略作 Esq.）：Henry Barker, *Esq.* 亨利·巴克先生（信件中等用的尊称）**2.** 绅士

-ess **suf.**〔加于名词后表示阴性〕：actress

essay ['esei] **n.1.** 小品文；论说文；随笔，散文 **2.** 尝试；企图 ─ [e'sei] **vt.** 试做；试图 ‖ ~ **ist n.** 小品文（或随笔等）作者 ‖ ~ **question** 问答题（与填充题、是非题相对而言）

essence ['esns] **n.1.** 本质，实质；本体，实体 **2.** 精华，精髓；要素 **3.** 精醇；香精；香料；香油；香气

essential [i'senʃəl] **adj.1.** 本质的，实质的；基本的 **2.** 必要的，必不可少的（to）**3.** 提炼的；精华的 **4.**【医】特发的，自发的，原发性的 ─ **n.**〔常~s〕**1.** 本质，要素；要点；必需品：*Essentials of Physics*（物理学基础）‖ ~ **ly** **adv.** 本质上，实质上 ‖ ~ **hypertension** 原发性高血压 / ~ **oil**（香）精油

-est **suf.**〔接在大多数单音节的、某些双音节的和少数多音节的形容词和副词后，构成最高级〕表示"最"：*fattest*, *latest*, *luckiest*, *oftenest*

establish [is'tæbliʃ] **vt.1.** 建立；设立（公司等）；创办（学校、医院等）**2.** 制定（规则等）；规定 **3.** 派，委任；安置；使定居

4. 使开业,使营业;使立足于(in) **5.** 确立(信誉、信仰等) **6.** 确定(事实、真相等);证明;使人们承认(要求权等) **7.** 定;为国教 **8.** 安放;固定(大炮等)的位置

establishment [is'tæbliʃmənt] *n.* **1.** 建立;设立;确立;确定;创办,开设 **2.** 〔常设的〕机构(或组织);行政机关;企业;公司;(仆人众多的)家庭;(大)住宅 **3.** 〔常作 the E-〕(社会)现存权力机构(或体制);权势集团,统治集团 **4.** 定员;编制

estate [is'teit] *n.* **1.** (有特定政治权和义务的)等级;社会阶层;集团:the third ~ 第三等级(常指法国 1789 年大革命前的资产阶级) **2.** (大块)房地产 **3.** 〔律〕财产;产业;资产;财产权;地产权:real ~ 不动产,房地产/personal ~ 动产 **4.** 庄园,种植园 **5.** 地位;状况 **6.** (人生)阶段:reach man's ~ 达到成年男子时期 ‖ ~ car(英)客货两用轿车

esteem [is'tiːm] *vt.* **1.** 尊重,尊敬;珍重 **2.** 认为;感到 —*n.* 尊重,尊敬

ester ['estə] *n.* 〔化〕酯

esthete ['iːsθiːt] *n.* = aesthete

esthetic(al) [iːs'θetik(əl)] *adj.* = aesthetic(al)

esthetics [iːs'θetiks] [复] *n.* 〔用作单〕= aesthetics

estimable ['estiməbl] *adj.* **1.** 值得尊重的;值得称道的 **2.** 可估计的;可估量的

estimate ['estimeit] *vt.* **1.** 估计;估量 **2.** 评价;判断 —*vi.* 估计;估价 — ['estimit, 'estimeit] *n.* **1.** 估计,估计数 (承包人的)估价单,投标 **3.** 看法;评价;判断 ‖ **estimator** *n.* (对所需人力、物力等的)估计者

estimation [ˌesti'meiʃən] *n.* **1.** 估计;估价 **2.** 看法;评价;判断 **3.** 尊重,尊敬

Estonia [es'təunjə] *n.* 爱沙尼亚〔欧洲波罗的海沿岸国家〕

estrange [is'treindʒ] *vt.* 使疏远;离间 (from) ‖ ~ ment *n.* / ~ r *n.*

estuary ['estjuəri] *n.* 港湾,河口湾;河口段三角港,河口

etc. *abbr.* 〔拉〕et cetera

et cetera [it'setərə] 〔拉〕等等,以及其他等等(略作 etc. 或 & c.)

etch [etʃ] *vt.* **1.** 蚀刻(图案等);浸蚀;铭刻,深印;刻划,描述 —*vi.* 蚀刻,使用腐蚀法 ‖ ~ er *n.* 蚀刻者;蚀刻器

etching ['etʃiŋ] *n.* **1.** 蚀刻;蚀刻法 **2.** 蚀刻画;蚀刻版;蚀刻版印刷品

eternal [i'təːnl] *adj.* **1.** 永久的,永恒的;无穷的 **2.** 永存的,不朽的 **3.** 〔口〕冗谈,争吵等)不停的,无休止的 **4.** 〔the E-〕〔宗〕上帝 ‖ ~ly [i'təːnəli] *adv.* / ~ness *n.*

eternity [i'təːniti] *n.* **1.** 永恒,无穷;世世代代 **2.** 不朽,永生;来世;来生 **3.** 〔eternities〕永恒的真理;无限的时间;永远不变的事物 **4.** (似乎)无终止的一段时期

ethane ['eθein] *n.* 〔化〕乙烷

ether ['iːθə] *n.* 〔化〕醚;乙醚 **2.** 〔物〕以太,能媒 **3.** 〔诗〕〔古〕太空,苍天

ethereal, etherial [i'θiəriəl] *adj.* **1.** 轻飘的,飘渺的;稀薄的 **2.** 天上的;太空的;非人间的 **3.** 微妙的;精致的;轻雅的 **4.** 〔物〕以太的 **5.** 〔化〕(乙)醚的,似(乙)醚的(有高度挥发性的) ‖ ~ity [iˌθiəri'æliti] *n.* / ~ly *adv.*

etherize ['iːθəraiz] *vt.* 〔医〕用乙醚麻醉 **2.** 使失去知觉 ‖ **ether'zation** *n.* / ~ r *n.* 麻醉剂;麻醉师

ethical ['eθikəl] *adj.* **1.** 伦理学的;伦理的;道德的 **2.** 合乎道德的(尤指合乎

职业道德或规矩）3.（药品）凭处方
出售的 ‖ ~ly *adv*.

ethics [ˈeθiks] [复] *n*. 1. [用作单] 伦理学;
道德学 2. [用作单] 伦理学论文（或书
籍）3. 道德体系; 道德准则, 行为准
则;（某种职业的）规矩

Ethiopia [ˌiːθiˈəupjə] *n*. 埃塞俄比亚（旧
称 Abyssinia 阿比西尼亚）[东非国家]

ethnic [ˈeθnik] *adj*. = ethnical — *n*. 少数
民族集团的成员

ethnical [ˈeθnikəl] *adj*. 种族的; 种族上
的; 人种学的 ‖ ~ly *adv*. 按种族; 按
种族特征

ethnology [eθˈnɔlədʒi] *n*. 1. 人种学; 民族
学 2. 文化人类学

ethyl [ˈeθil, ˈiːθail] *n*. [化] 1. 乙基; 乙烷
基 2. 四乙铅（加于汽油中的抗爆化合
物）

ethylene [ˈeθiliːn] *n*. [化] 乙烯; 乙撑

etiquette [ˌetiˈket] *n*. 1. 礼节; 礼仪 2. [总
称]（同业间的）道德规范; 道德准则; 习
惯

Eton [ˈiːtn] *n*. 1. 伊顿（英国伦敦西面的
一个市镇）2. 伊顿公学（位于伊顿的
一所培养英国上层政界人物的中学, 本
办公=College）

-ette *suf*. [加于名词或少数形容词后] 1.
表示"小": kitchen*ette* 2. [指商品等] 表
示"假", "人造": leather*ette* 3. 表示"女
性": suffrag*ette* 4. 表示"组", "组合":
quart*ette*

étude [eiˈtjuːd] 〈法〉 *n*. [音] 练习曲

etymology [ˌetiˈmɔlədʒi] *n*. 1. 词源学 2.
词形变化 3. 阐述词源; 词源说明

EU *abbr*. European Union 欧洲联盟

Eu [化] 元素铕（europium）的符号

eucalyptus [ˌjuːkəˈliptəs] *n*. [复] eucalýpti
[ˌjuːkəˈliptai] 或 eucalýptuses] *n*. [植] 桉
（树）

Eucharist [ˈjuːkərist] *n*. [宗] 圣餐; 圣餐
面饼（及酒）‖ ~ic(al) [ˌjuːkəˈristik(əl)]
adj.

Euclidean, Euclidian [juːˈklidiən] *adj*.
[数] 欧几里得（Euclid）的

eugenic [juːˈdʒenik] *adj*. 优生（学）的 ‖
~s [复] *n*. [用作单或复] 优生学

eulogistic [ˌjuːləˈdʒistik] *adj*. 颂扬的, 称
赞的, 歌功颂德的 ‖ ~ally *adv*.

eulogize [ˈjuːlədʒaiz] *vt*. 颂扬, 赞颂

eulogy [ˈjuːlədʒi] *n*. 1. 颂扬, 赞颂 2. 颂
词; 颂文; 悼词; 悼文

eunuch [ˈjuːnək] *n*. 宦官, 太监; 阉人

euphemism [ˈjuːfimizəm] *n*. [语] 委婉说
法; 委婉语

euphemistic(al) [ˌjuːfiˈmistik(əl)] *adj*. 委
婉的; 婉言的 ‖ euphemistically *adv*.

euphony [ˈjuːfəni] *n*. 声音的悦耳; 声音的
和谐; 悦耳声音; 谐音

euphoria [juːˈfɔːriə] *n*. [心] 欣快症; 欣快
异常

euphoric [juːˈfɔrik] *adj*. 欣快症的; 欣快
异常的

Euphrates [juːˈfreitiz] *n*. 幼发拉底河 [西
南亚]

Europe [ˈjuərəp] *n*. 欧洲

European [ˌjuərəˈpiːən] *adj*. 欧洲的; 欧洲
人的 — *n*. 欧洲人; 拥护参加欧洲经济
共同体的人 ‖ ~ plan（美）欧洲式收费
制（包括宿费和服务费而不包括膳食
费的旅馆收费制）

Europeanize [ˌjuərəˈpiːənaiz] *vt*. 使欧化;
使具有欧洲风味 ‖ ˌEuroˌpeaniˈzation
n. 欧化

europium [juːˈrəupiəm] *n*. [化] 铕

euthanasia [ˌjuːθəˈneiziə] *n*. 1. 安乐死, 安
然去世 2.（为结束不治之症患者的痛
苦而施行的）安乐死术, 无痛苦致死术

evacuate [i'vækjueit] *vt.*1. 撤退,撤走;转移,疏散(居民),撤离,撤出 2. 使空,撤空(房子等) 3. 抽空 4. 排泄;排除;清除;排空(肠胃等) — *vi.*1. (有组织地)撤走;撤离,疏散 2. 排尿;排粪 ‖ **e,vacu'ation** *n.*

evacuee [i,vækju:'i:] *n.* 被わ撤的人;被疏散的人

evade [i'veid] *vt.* 逃避;躲避;回避;规避

evaluate [i'væljueit] *vt.*1. 估...定值,估...的价;评价 2.【数】求...的值;以数目表示 ‖ **e,valu'ation** *n.*

evanescent [i:və'nesnt] *adj.*(印象等)很快消失的;短暂的;瞬息的 ‖ **evanescence** *n.*

evangelic(al) [,i:væn'dʒelik(əl)]【宗】*adj.*1. 福音的;合乎福音的 2. 福音派新教的 3.[E-]英国低教会派的 4. 热衷于传道的 — *n.* 新教徒;福音会教徒 ‖ **evangelicalism** *n.* 福音派教义(的信仰) / **evangelically** *adv.* 按照福音;福音传道士般地 / **evangelist** [i'vændʒilist] *n.*1. 福音传道者 2.[E-]《福音书》作者

evaporate [i'væpəreit] *vt.*1. 使蒸发;使挥发;(通过升华)使(金属等)沉淀 2. 使脱水,去除...的水分 3. 发射(电子) 4. 使弹开,消灭 — *vi.*1. 蒸发;挥发;发散蒸气 2. 〈口〉消失;(人)失踪;死亡 ‖ **~d** *adj.* 浓缩的;脱水的;蒸发干燥的;**~d milk** 炼乳 ‖ **e,vapo'ration** *n.*

evasion [i'veiʒən] *n.*1. 逃避;躲避;回避(捐税等的)偷漏 2. 遁词,借口,推诿

evasive [i'veisiv] *adj.*1. 逃避的;规避的;偷漏(捐税等)的 2. 托词的;推诿的 3. 闪避的,难以捉摸的;含糊其词的 ‖ **~ly** *adv.* / **~ness** *n.*

Eve [i:v] *n.* 夏娃(基督教《圣经》中的人物,亚当之妻)

eve [i:v] *n.*1.(节日等的)前夜,前夕 2. (重大事件发生的)前一刻,前夕 3. 〈诗〉傍晚

even[1] [i:vən] *adv.*1.[加强语气]甚至(...也),连(...都);He doubts ~ the facts.他甚至怀疑事实。2.[后接比较级]甚至(比...)更,还;This applies ~ more to physics.这一点对物理学甚至更适用。‖ **~ if**(或 ~ **though**)即使,纵然

even[2] [i:vən] *adj.*1. 平的;平坦的;平滑的(海岸线等)不曲折的 3.(呼吸,节拍、质量等)均匀的,平稳的 4. 一致的,同样的;齐的(*with*) 5. 对等的;均等的 6. 公平的;对等的;平衡的 7.(性情等)平静的 8. 双数的;偶数的 9. 恰好的,整整的 — *vt.* 使平;使平坦;使相等(*out*, *up*) — *vi.* 变平;成为相等 ‖ **~ness** *n.* ‖ **~ handed** *adj.* 不偏不倚的,公正的 / **~ tempered** *adj.* 性情平和的

even[3] [i:vən] *n.*〈古〉〈诗〉〈方〉黄昏,傍晚(= evening)‖ **~ fall** *n.*〈诗〉黄昏,薄暮 / **~ song** *n.*(英国国教的)晚祷 / **~ tide** *n.*〈诗〉黄昏,薄暮

evening [i:vniŋ] *n.*1. 黄昏,傍晚;晚上(从日落至就寝);Good ~! 晚上好!(晚上分别时也可用,表示"再见")this (yesterday and last) ~[用作状语]今天(昨天)晚上 2.(联欢性的)晚会;晚上娱乐活动时间 3. 后期;末期;衰落期 ‖ **~s** *adv.* 〈美〉每晚;在任何晚上 ‖ **~ dress** 夜礼服 / **~ primrose** [植]月见草,夜来香 / **~ school** 夜校 / **~ star** 昏星;金星,长庚星;水星

event [i'vent] *n.*1. 事件;大事;值得注意的事物 2.(运动会等的)比赛项目;field and track ~ 田径赛项目 ‖ **~less** *adj.* 无大事的;平静无事的

eventful [i'ventful] *adj.* 多事的;充满大事的;多变故的 ‖ **~ly** *adv.* / **~ness** *n.*

eventual [i'ventjuəl] *adj.* 最后的，结局的 ‖ ~**ly** *adv.* 终于，最后

eventuality [i,ventjuˈæliti] *n.* 可能发生的事；不测事件

ever ['evə] *adv.* 1. 永远 2. 不断地，老是 3. [用于一般疑问句]否定句以及条件和比较的从句]在任何时候：This is the profoundest lesson I (have) ~ had. 这是我有生以来最深刻的一课。/ Nowadays he hardly (或 scarcely) ~ comes. 最近他简直不大来了。/He is seldom, if ~, absent from school. 他简直从不缺课。4. [与形容词的比较级、最高级连用,加强语气]比以往任何时候：the biggest crop ~ 空前的大丰收 5. [用于特殊疑问句中,加强语气]究竟,到底：Which ~ do you want? 你究竟要哪一个？6. [美口][用在动词"to be"所谓语的倒装句中,加强语气]非常,极：Was he ~ delighted! 他高兴极了！

Everest ['evərist] *n.* 埃佛勒斯峰(即珠穆朗玛峰)

evergreen ['evəgri:n] *adj.* 1. 常绿的,常青的 2. (喻)永葆青春的,永久的 — *n.* 1. 常绿树；常绿植物 2. [~s](装饰用的)常绿树树枝

everlasting [,evəˈlɑ:stiŋ] *adj.* 1. 永久的,不朽的；持续不尽的,无穷尽的 2. 持久的；耐久性的 3. 冗长的,使人厌烦的 4. [植](植物或花)干后保持原来形状和颜色的 — *n.* 1. 永久,永恒；无穷 2. 干后花的形状和颜色保持不变的植物(尤指蜡菊属植物) 3. (全毛或毛棉交织、作鞋料等用的)水固级绒织物 ‖ ~**ly** *adv.* 永久地；无穷地,持续不尽地

evermore ['evəˈmɔ:] *adv.* 1. 永远,始终 2. 将来,今后

every ['evri] *adj.* 1. 每一的,每个的 2. 每一年的 /~ person 每个人 3. 每

隔...的,每...中的：receive an injection ~ three days (或 ~ third day) 每三天打一针 /choose one out of ~ ten boys 每十个男孩中选一个 3. 一切可能的；充分的：He was given ~ chance to try the job. 他得到一切可能的机会去试试做这件事。/have ~ reason to say he有充分的理由说 ‖ ~-**way** *adv.* 用各种办法；从各个方面

everybody ['evribɔdi, 'evribədi] *pron.* 每人,人人

everyday ['evridei] *adj.* 日常的；平常的；普通的

everyone ['evriwʌn] *pron.* = everybody

everything ['evriθiŋ] *pron.* 1. 每件事,事事,凡事 2. [通常只用作表语]最重要(或优秀)的事物：be ~ to sb. 在某人看来是最重要(或宝贵)的

everywhere ['evrihwεə] *adv.* 处处,到处；无论那里：He has looked ~ for you. 他到处都找过你了。— *n.* 处处,到处：People come from ~ to celebrate the victory. 从各处来庆祝胜利。

evict [i'vikt] *vt.* 驱逐,赶出(佃户、房客等)；(依法)追回(财产等)(*from*) ‖ ~**ion** *n.*

evidence ['evidəns] *n.* 1. 明显,显而易见：He was nowhere *in* ~. 到处都看不到他。2. 形迹；迹象 3. 根据；证据 — *vt.* 表明；证明

evident ['evidənt] *adj.* 明显的 ‖ ~**ly** *adv.*

evil ['i:vl] (evil(l)er, evil(l)est) *adj.* 1.(人、思想、行为等)坏的，邪恶的；罪恶的 2. 有害的；中伤的；恶毒的：an ~ tongue 谗言；谗言者 3.(消息等)不幸的；不吉的；(征兆等)不祥的：an ~ hour 不幸的时刻 4.(气味、天气等)讨厌的；不愉快的 — *n.* 1. 邪恶；罪恶；恶行；弊病

2. 不幸;不吉;祸害;灾难;痛苦 ‖ ~ly
adv. ‖ '~·doer n. 坏人;作恶的人 ‖ '~·
'doing n. 坏事;恶劣行为 ‖ /'~·'minded
adj. 心怀邪恶的

evince [i'vins] vt. (人、行为) 表示,表明,
显示(某种感情或品质)

eviscerate [i'visəreit] vt. 取出...的内脏
(或肠) ‖ e,visce'ration n.

evocation [,evə'keiʃən] n.1. 唤起;引起 2.
【律】(下级法院向上级法院的)案卷移
送 3.【生】(胚胎学用语)启发作用

evocative [i'vɔkətiv] adj. 唤起...的;引
起...的

evoke [i'vəuk] vt.1. 唤起;博得(喝彩
等);引起;召(魂)2.【律】(下级法院)
把(案卷)移送至上级法院

evolution [,i:və'lju:ʃən, ,evə-] n.1.
进化;演进,演变 2.(气体等的)放出,
散出 3.【生】进化;进化论 4.【生】发生;
发育 5.【数】开方 6.【天】演化 7.【军】
(按计划的)队形变换;位置变换 8.(舞
蹈者等的)按计划动作的一个部分;旋
转方式 ‖ ~·al, ~·ary adj. 发展的;进
化的;进化论的 ‖ ~ism n. 进化论

evolve [i'vɔlv] vt.1. 发展;使逐渐形成;使
进化;使渐进 2. 引申出;推
论;推定(事实等)(from) 3. 放出;发出
(气体、热等) —vi.1. 进展;发展 2.
进化;渐进;演化;发达;发育 ‖ ~ment
n.

ewe [ju:] n. 母羊 ‖ ~ lamb 独生子;独生
女;最珍爱的东西

ewer ['ju:ə] n. 大口水壶;花瓶状水罐

ex- pref. 1. 表示"出(自)";"向外";"向
上";"超过";"全部";高开";"免除";
ex.pel, ex.alt, ex.ceed, ex.terminate, exempt 2. [附在名词前] 表示"前...",
"前任的": ex-president

exacerbate [eks'æsəbeit] vt.1. 使(痛苦

等)更甚(或加深);使(病等)加剧(或
恶化)2. 触怒;使气恼;使烦恼 ‖
ex,acer'bation n.

exact [ig'zækt] adj.1. 确切的;正确的 2.
精确无误的;精密的 3. 严格的;严厉
的 —vt.1. 强要;强求 2. 急需;需要 ‖
~ing adj.1. 苛求的;严格的 2.(工作
等)需付出极大努力的;艰难的 ‖ ~ness
n. / ~or, ~er n. 强征(捐税等)者

exaction [ig'zækʃən] n.1. 强求;强征;勒
索 2. 强索的费用;强征的税收;苛捐
杂税

exactitude [ig'zæktitju:d] n.1. 正确(性);
精确(性)2. 严格

exactly [ig'zæktli] adv.1. 确切地;精确地
2. 恰恰正是 3.(表示赞同地回答)确实
如此

exaggerate [ig'zædʒəreit] vt.1. 夸张;夸
大,把...言过其实 2. 使增大;使过大,
使逾常 —vi. 夸张,夸大,言过其实 ‖
~d adj. / ~dly adv. / **exaggerator** n.
夸张者,言过其实的人

exaggeration [ig,zædʒə'reiʃən] n.1. 夸张,
夸大;evt 2. 夸张的言语(或比喻)3.
(艺术等的)夸张手法

exalt [ig'zɔ:lt] vt.1. 使高,高举,升起 2.
提升,提拔;提高...的地位(或荣誉
等)3. 赞扬;吹捧 4. 使喜悦;使欢喜;
使昂扬 5. 加深(色彩等);加强(想象
力等)‖ ~ation [,egzɔ:l'teiʃən] n.1. 升
高,高举 2. 提拔;晋升;提高 3. 兴高采
烈;意气风发 4.【医】过度兴奋,异常
兴奋 ‖ ~ed adj.1. 高贵的;崇高的 2.
兴奋的;高涨的

exam [ig'zæm] n.(口)= examination

examine [ig'zæmin] vt.1. 检查;细查;诊
察 2. 对...进行审查;查问 3.(就某学
科)对...进行考试(in) —vi. 检查;细
查;调查(into) ‖ ex.ami'nation n. / ~r
n.

example 307 exchange

n. 检查人;审查人;主考人

example [ig'zɑ:mpl, ig'zæmpl] *n*.1. 例子, 实例;例题:for ~ 例如 2. 范例,样本 3. 模范,榜样 4. 儆戒:make an ~ of sb. 惩罚某人以儆他人

exasperate [ig'zɑ:spəreit, ig'zɑ:spəreit] *vt*.1. 激怒,触怒;使气愤 ‖ ~dly *adv*. / **exasperating** *adj*. 使人恼怒的;激发人的 / **exasperation** [ig,zɑ:spə'reiʃən, ig,zɑ:spə'reiʃən] *n*.

excavate ['ekskəveit] *vt*.1. 开凿;挖掘(壕沟等);在...挖掘 2. 挖出(矿砂、泥土等);发掘(古物等) — *vi*. 凿;挖掘;变成窟隆 ‖ **exca'vation** *n*.1. 开凿;挖掘;挖土;发掘 2. 洞,穴;坑道:开凿成的山路 发掘物;出土文物 / **excavator** *n*.1. 开凿者;发掘者 2. 挖掘器,挖土机;电铲

exceed [ik'si:d] *vt*.1. 超过,胜过 2. 越(权等);超(速) — *vi*.(在数量,大小或质量方面)超过其他;突出(*in*)

exceeding [ik'si:diŋ] *adj*. 超越的,胜过的;非常的;极度的 — *adv*.〈古〉= ~ly ‖ ~ly *adv*. 极端地,非常

excel [ik'sel](excelled; excelling) *vt*. 胜过,优于 — *vi*. 胜过他人;杰出(*in*, *at*)

excellence ['eksələns] *n*.1. 优秀,卓越,杰出(*in*, *at*) 2.[常 ~s]优点;美德

excellency ['eksələnsi] *n*.1. [E-]阁下(对大使、总督、主教等的尊称):Your *Excellency* 阁下(直接称呼时用) / His(或Her) *Excellency* 阁下(间接提及时用) 2.[常 excellencies]优点;美德(= excellence)

excellent ['eksələnt] *adj*. 优秀的,卓越的,杰出的,极好的 ‖ ~ly *adv*.

excelsior [ik'selsiə] *n*. 木丝,细刨花(包装易碎物品等用的填塞物)

except [ik'sept] *prep*.1. 除...之外 2.[~

for]除...之外;要不是 — *vt*. 把...除外;不计 — *vi*. 反对(*to*, *against*) — *conj*.1.〈古〉除非(= unless) 2. 只是;要不是:I would go ~ it's too late. 要不是时间太晚的话我就去。

excepting [ik'septiŋ] *prep*. 除...外

exception [ik'sepʃən] *n*.1. 例外 2. 除外反对;异议;[律]反对;除外条件;抗辩

exceptionable [ik'sepʃənəbl] *adj*. 可反对的,会引起反对的;例外的,特殊的

exceptional [ik'sepʃənl] *adj*.1. 例外的;异常的;罕见的;特殊的 2. 较优的;优越的 ‖ ~ly *adv*.

excerpt ['eksə:pt] *n*. 摘录,选录,节录 — [ek'sə:pt] *vt*. 摘,选;引用(*from*)

excess [ik'ses] *n*.1. 超越,超过:in ~ of 超过 2. 超额量 3. 过量;过剩 4.[饮食等的]过度,无节制 5.[~es]过激行为;暴行 — *adj*. 过量的;额外的;附加的:~ fare(舟、车等的)补票费 / ~ luggage 超重行李 / ~ postage 应补的欠资邮费

excessive [ik'sesiv] *adj*.1. 过度的,过分的;极度的 ‖ ~ly *adv*. / ~ness *n*.

exchange [iks'tʃeindʒ] *vt*.1. 交换;调换(*for*) 2. 互换;交流;交易(货物):~ greetings 相互问好 / ~ ambassadors 互派大使 / ~ blows 互殴 3. 兑换;把...换成(*for*) — *vi*.1.(货币)交换;兑换 2. 调换岗位;交替 3. 交易 — *n*.1. 交换;调换;互换;交流;交易 2. 汇兑;兑换;外汇;汇水;汇价;兑换手续费;汇率;兑换率;贴水;[~s]交易所所交换的)票据;汇票 3. 交易所 4.(电话)交换局;交换机 5.(美)专门经营某种货物的场所:合作商店;合作社;a post ~(美国)军人服务社,军营小卖部(略作 PX) 6. 刊物交换;从报纸翻印的文章 7. 交火,交战;争吵 ‖ ~ force 【物】交换力 / ~ rate 汇率;兑换率:汇

价 /~ **student**(两国之间)交换的留学生

exchangeable [iks'tʃeindʒəbl] *adj.* 可交换的;可兑换的(*for*) ‖ **ex.changea'bility** *n.*

exchequer [iks'tʃekə] *n.* 1. 国库;金库 2. 资金;财源;(个人的)资财 3. [E-]英国财政部: the Chancellor of the *Exchequer* (英国)财政大臣 4. [E-](英国旧时的)财务大臣法院,理财法院

excise[1] [ek'saiz] *n.* 1.(烟、酒等的)消费税,国内货物税 2. 领许可证税;执照税 —*vt.* 1. 向...征消费税 2.(英)向...索高价

excise[2] [ek'saiz] *vt.* 1. 割去,切除;删去 2. 在...上切切口,将...开槽

excision [ek'siʒən] *n.* 1. 切除;删除 2. [医]切除(术) 3.[宗]逐出教会

excitable [ik'saitəbl] *adj.* 能被激动的;易兴奋的,易激动的 2.[生理]应激的,(可)兴奋的 ‖ **ex.cita'bility** *n.* 1.[物]可激发性 2.[生理]应激性,兴奋性

excitation [ˌeksi'teiʃən] *n.* 1. 刺激,激动;激励,鼓舞 2.[物]励磁;激发 3.[植]激惹(现象)

excite [ik'sait] *vt.* 1. 刺激;使兴奋,使激动 2. 激发;激励;唤起;引起(注意、兴趣、妒忌等) 3.[物]激起(电流);使励磁;激发(原子等) 4. 使(器官、组织等)产生(或增加)应激作用 —*vi.*(口)兴奋,激动;鼓动 2. 刺激的事物 ‖ ~**ment** *n.* 1. 刺激;兴奋,激动;鼓动 2. 刺激的事物 ;兴奋剂 3.[无]激励器;主控振荡器;辐射器 4. 励磁机

excited [ik'saitid] *adj.* 1. 兴奋的;激昂的 2.[物]已激发的;受激的 ‖ ~**ly** *adv.*

exciting [ik'saitiŋ] *adj.* 令人兴奋的,使人激动的 ‖ ~**ly** *adv.*

excitonics [ˌeksi'tɔniks] [复] *n.* [用作单][物]激子学

exclaim [iks'kleim] *vi.* & *vt.* (由于惊讶、痛苦、愤怒、高兴等而)呼喊;惊叫;大声说

exclamation [ˌeksklə'meiʃən] *n.* 1. 呼喊;惊叫 2. 感叹;惊叫声 3. [语]感叹词;感叹语 ‖ ~ **mark**, ~ **point** 感叹号(即!)

exclamatory [eks'klæmətəri] *adj.* 叫喊的;感叹的;惊叫的: an ~ sentence 感叹句

exclude [iks'kluːd] *vt.* 1. 拒绝接纳(或考虑);把...排除在外(*from*) 2. 排斥(可能性等)

exclusion [iks'kluːʒən] *n.* 1. 排斥;排除在外 2. 被排除在外的事物

exclusive [iks'kluːsiv] *adj.* 1. 除外的;排外的,排他的;不包括...在内的(*of*) 2. 孤傲的;势利的 3. 专有的,独占的;唯一的 4.(注意力等)全部的 5.(美)时式的;时髦的 6.(商店、商品等)专卖高昂的;高级的;别处没有的 7.(社团、俱乐部等)不愿吸收新成员的 —*n.* 1. 独家新闻;独家经营的项目(或产品等);专有权,专营权 2. 孤傲的人 ‖ ~**ly** *adv.* / ~**ness** *n.*

excommunicate [ˌekskə'mjuːnikeit] *vt.* [宗]开除...的教籍;把...逐出教会 —[ˌekskə'mjuːnikit] *adj.* & *n.* 被开除教籍的(人),被逐出教会的(人) ‖ **'exco.mmuni'cation** *n.*

excoriate [eks'kɔːrieit] *vt.* 1. 擦伤...的皮肤 2. 严厉指责;痛骂 ‖ **ex.cori'ation** *n.* 1. 皮肤擦伤 2. 严厉指责 3.[医]表皮脱落

excrement ['ekskrimənt] *n.* [常~s]粪便;排泄物

excrescence [iks'kresns] *n.* 赘生物;赘疣;瘤 ‖ **excrescent** *adj.*

excreta [eks'kri:tə][复] *n.* 排泄物(如汗、尿、粪等)

excrete [eks'kri:t] *vt.* 排泄;分泌

excretion [eks'kri:ʃən] *n.1.* (动、植物的)排泄;分泌 *2.* 排泄物

excretory [eks'kri:təri] *adj.* 排泄的;有排泄功能的

excruciate [iks'kru:ʃieit] *vt.1.* 使受酷刑;拷打 *2.* 折磨;使苦恼

excruciating [iks'kru:ʃieitiŋ] *adj.1.* (疼痛等)剧烈的,极度的 *2.* 造成剧痛的,使苦恼的;难忍受的

exculpate ['ekskʌlpeit] *vt.* 开脱;使无罪,证明(某人)无罪 ‖ **excul'pation** *n.*

excursion [iks'kə:ʃən] *n.1.* 短途旅行;(集体)游览 *2.* 【物】偏移,偏离 ‖ ~**ist** *n.* 远足者;短途旅行者;游览者

excusable [iks'kju:zəbl] *adj.* 可原谅的 ‖ ~ **ness** *n.* ‖ **excusably** *adv.*

excuse [iks'kju:z] *vt.1.* 原谅 *2.* [~ oneself]为自己辩解;请求准予离开,说声"请原谅"离开;表示要走开 *3.* [用于否定句](不能)嫌为(某种不正当行为)的理由 *4.* 给...免去(某种义务)(*from*) —[iks'kju:s] *n.1.* 原谅;饶恕 *2.* [~s]歉意;谦辞 *3.* 借口;辩解理由

ex-directory ['eksdi'rektəri] *adj.* 〈英〉未列入电话(号码)簿的;其电话号码未列入电话簿的人的

execrable ['eksikrəbl] *adj.1.* 该死的;令人憎恶的;讨厌的 *2.* 恶劣的;坏透的 ‖ **execrably** *adv.*

execrate ['eksikreit] *vt.1.* 痛骂;咒骂(古)诅咒 *2.* 憎恶,嫌恶 —*vi.* 咒骂 ‖ **exe'cration** *n.*

execute ['eksikju:t] *vt.1.* 实行;实施;执行;履行;贯彻;完成 *2.* 将...处死 *3.* 作成,制成(艺术品等);演奏(乐曲等)

4. 【律】(履行必要手续)使(证书、契约等)生效;执行(命令、遗嘱、判决等);〈英〉让渡(财产)

execution [,eksi'kju:ʃən] *n.1.* 实行;实施;执行;履行;完成 *2.* 处死刑 *3.* 制作;演奏;技巧;手法 *4.*(武器等的)破坏效果,杀伤力 *5.*【律】(合同的)履行;(法律文件的)生效;(判决的)执行;执行令 ‖ ~ **er** *n.* 刽子手;死刑执行人

executive [ig'zekjutiv] *adj.1.* 执行的;善于执行的;实施的 *2.* 行政上的 *3.* 行政官的;总经理的 —*n.1.* [the ~]行政部门(工会、党派等的)执行委员会 *2.* 执行者;高级官吏;高级职员 *3.* the (chief) ~〈美〉最高行政官,行政长官(指总统或州长) *3.*〈美〉主管企业的人;经理

executor *n.1.* ['eksikju:tə] 执行者;实行者 *2.* [ig'zekjutə](指定的)遗嘱执行人

executrix [ig'zekjutriks] *n.1.* 女执行者 *2.* 遗嘱女执行人

exemplary [ig'zempləri] *adj.1.* 模范的,值得模仿的 *2.* 警戒性的;惩戒性的 *3.* 作样板的,示范的;作例证的;典型的

exemplify [ig'zemplifai] *vt.* 举例说明;作为...的例子(或榜样) ‖ **exemplification** [ig,zemplifi'keiʃən] *n.*

exempli gratia [ig'zemplai'greiʃiə]〈拉〉例如(缩作 e.g., = for example)

exempt [ig'zempt] *vt.* 免除;豁免(*from*) —*adj.* 被免除的;被豁免的(*from*) ‖ ~ **ion** *n.*

exercise ['eksəsaiz] *n.1.* 行使;运用;实行;履行 *2.* 训练;锻炼[常~s]体操;运动 *3.* 练习,习题;功课 *4.*【军】演习;操练 *5.*〈美〉[~s]仪式;礼式 *6.* 获取学位的考试形式)传统做法 —*vt.1.* 实行;行使(权力等);履行;运用;施加 *2.* 训练;锻炼;[~ oneself]练习 *3.* [常用被动语态]使担忧,使烦恼;使

气(*about*) — *vi*. 锻炼;练习 ‖~ r *n*.1. 行使(职权等)的人 2. 锻炼者;受训练者 3.[复]练练肌肉用的)体育器械

exert [ig'zə:t] *vt*.1. 尽(力);发挥(威力等);施加(压力等);产生(影响等);行使(职权等) 2.[~ oneself]尽力,努力 ‖ **exertion** [ig'zə:ʃən] *n*.1. 尽力,努力力;用气力 2. 行使;发挥

exeunt ['eksiʌnt](拉) *vi*.(舞台指示)(某几个角色)退场.

exhale [eks'heil] *vt*. 呼出,呼(气);发散出(蒸气、气味等) — *vi*.(气味等)蒸发;发散;呼气 ‖ **exhalation** [,ekshə'leiʃən] *n*.1.(蒸气、气味等的)散发;呼气 2. 发散物(如气体、蒸气、气味等);薄雾

exhaust [ig'zə:st] *vt*.1. 抽完,汲干;把⋯的内容抽空 2. 用完,花光,耗尽;竭尽;试尽 3.[~ oneself]或用被动语态)使筋疲力尽 4. 详尽无遗地论述(或研究) — *vi*.1. 排出气体 2.(气体等)被排出一*vt*.1. 排出;排气(或水等) 2. 排出的气 3. 排气装置;排气管 ‖ -**ing** *adj*. 使耗尽的;使人筋疲力尽的 / -**ion** *n*. ‖ ~ **gas** 废气 / ~ **pipe** 排气管

exhaustive [ig'zə:stiv] *adj*.(论述)彻底的,详尽无遗的 ‖ -**ly** *adv*. / -**ness** *n*.

exhibit [ig'zibit] *vt*.1. 展览;展出;陈列 2. 显出,显示(某种情感、品质等) 3.【律】提供出示(证据等) — *vi*. 开展览会;展出产品(或作品等) — *n*.1. 展出;展览(会) 2. 展览品;陈列品 3. 显示,显出 4.【律】(展览会的)证件,证据,物证 ‖ ~ **or**, ~ **er** *n*.(展览会的)参加者,展出者;电影放映员;电影院老板(或经理)

exhibition [,eksi'biʃən] *n*.1. 展览;(体育运动等的)表演;显示 2. 展览会;展览品;陈列品 3.(英)奖学金 ‖ -**er** *n*. 展出者;(英)获得奖学金的大学生

exhibitionism [,eksi'biʃənizəm] *n*.1. 表现癖 2.【心】裸露癖;露阴狂;裸露(或露阴)癖 ‖ **exhibitionist** *n*. 好出风头者;有裸露癖者

exhilarate [ig'ziləreit] *vt*. 使高兴;使活跃;使振奋 ‖ **ex,hila'ration** *n*.

exhilarating [ig'ziləreitiŋ] *adj*. 使人高兴的;令人振奋的 ‖ -**ly** *adv*.

exhort [ig'zə:t] *vt*.1. 规劝,激励;告诫 2. 提倡,主张(改革等) — *vi*. 规劝;告诫 ‖ **exhortation** [,egzə:'teiʃən] *n*.

exhume [eks'hju:m] *vt*.1.(从墓内等)掘出(尸体等) 2.(喻)发掘(旧剧目等) ‖ ,**exhu'mation** *n*.

exigency ['eksidʒənsi], **exigence** ['eksidʒəns] *n*.1. 紧急(状态);危急(关头);事变 2.[exigencies]急事;迫切的需要

exigent ['eksidʒənt] *adj*.1. 紧急的;危急的;迫切的

exile ['eksail] *n*.1. 流放,放逐,充军;离开本国;离乡背井 2. 被放逐者;离乡背井者;离国者 — *vt*. 流放,放逐;使离乡背井

exist [ig'zist] *vi*.1. 存在 2. 生存;生活

existence [ig'zistəns] *n*.1. 存在 2. 生存;生活(方式) 3. 存在物;实体

existent [ig'zistənt] *adj*. 存在的;现存的

existential [,egzis'tenʃəl] *adj*.1.(关于)存在的;基于存在(或经验)的 2.【哲】存在主义(者)的

existing [ig'zistiŋ] *adj*. 现存的;目前的

exit ['eksit] *n*.1.(演员的)退场;退出 2. 出口,通路;安全门,太平门 3. 去世,死亡 — *vi*. 退出,离去;去世

exit ['eksit](拉) *vi*.(舞台指示)(某一个角色)退场,下

exobiology [,eksəubai'ələdʒi] *n*. 外空生物

说明的;辩明的

expletive [eks'pli:tiv] *n.* 1. 填充词,语助词,虚词(如 "It is easy to say so." 中的 It) 2. 感叹语(如 My goodness!);脏语;咒骂语(如 Damn it!)

explicable ['eksplikəbl] *adj.* 可解释的,可说明的;可辩明的

explicit [iks'plisit] *adj.* 1.（指示、意见等）清楚的;明确的 2. 直率的;不含糊的 ‖ ~ly *adv.* / ~ness *n.* ‖ ~ **function** 【数】显函数

explode [iks'pləud] *vt.* 1. 使爆炸;使爆发;使爆破;使破裂 2. 破除（迷信等）;戳穿;驳倒（理论等）3.【语】爆发音发出（塞音）— *vi.* 1. 爆炸;爆发;突发 ~ *with anger* 勃然大怒 2.（人口等）激增 ‖ ~d *adj.* 爆炸了的;被戳穿的;被破除的;分解的;分解的;an ~d view（机器、飞机等的）分解图

exploit[1] ['eksplɔit] *n.* 功绩,功勋;辉煌的成就;英勇的行为

exploit[2] [iks'plɔit] *vt.* 1. 开拓,开发;开采 2. 利用;利用……而自肥 3. 剥削;the ~ed 遭受剥削的人们 ‖ ~ation [,eksplɔi'teiʃən] *n.*

explore [iks'plɔ:] *vt.* 1. 探究,探索;钻研;考察,勘探;探测;在……探险 2.【医】仔细检查;探察（伤处等）— *vi.* 1.（有系统地）探索;考察,勘探;探险 2.探险 ‖ **exploration** [,eksplɔ:'reiʃən] *n.* / **explorative** [iks'plɔrətiv] *adj.* / ~r *n.* 探索者;考察者 2. 勘探者,勘测器;探测器;探索线圈 3.【医】探察器;探针

explosion [iks'pləuʒən] *n.* 1. 爆炸（声）,炸裂（声）;爆发 2.（人口等的）激增 3.（怒火,笑声等的）爆发,迸发 4.【语】爆发,破裂

explosive [iks'pləusiv] *adj.* 1. 爆炸（性）

的;爆发(性)的 2.【语】爆发的,破裂的 3. 暴躁的 — *n.* 1. 炸药 2.【语】爆发音,破裂音 ‖ ~ly *adv.* / ~ness *n.*

expo ['ekspəu]（[复]expos）*n.* 展览会,博览会

exponent [eks'pəunənt] *n.* 1.（原理、方法等的）说明者,讲解者 2.（理论、观点等的）倡导者;代表者;拥护者 3.【语】（语言范畴的）成分 4. 典型;标本;例子;代表者 5.【数】指数

export [eks'pɔ:t] *vt.* 输出,输出品;思想,信仰等）— *vi.* 出口 — ['ekspɔ:t] *n.* 1. 输出品;出口物 2. 输出;出口 ‖ ~able *adj.* 可输出的 / ~ation [,ekspɔ:'teiʃən] *n.* 1. 输出;出口 2. 输出品;出口物 / ~er *n.* 输出者;出口商,出口公司

expose [iks'pəuz] *vt.* 1. 使曝光;暴露(to) ~ *sb. to danger* 使某人面临危险 2. 揭露,揭发 3. 陈列（商品等）4. 把（婴孩）遗弃在户外 5. 袒露,裸露

exposé [eks'pəuzei]〈法〉*n.* 1.（事实等的）陈述 2.（丑事、罪恶等的）暴露;揭露

exposition [,ekspə'ziʃən] *n.* 1.（理论、计划等的）说明,讲解;评注;说明性讲话（或文章等）2. 展览会,博览会,陈列 3. 暴露,显露;露光;曝光 4.（对婴儿的）遗弃户外 5.【戏】提示部分 6.【音】显示部

expostulate [iks'pɔstjuleit] *vi.* 规劝;忠告 (*with*) ‖ **ex.postu'lation** *n.* / **expostulatory** [iks'pɔstjulətəri] *adj.*

exposure [iks'pəuʒə] *n.* 1. 暴露;揭露,揭发 2. 曝光量;曝光时间;软片,底片 3.（房屋、房间的）方向,方位,a house with a southern ~ 一座朝南的房子 4.（商品等的）陈列,展出 5.（婴孩的）被遗弃户外

expound [iks'paund] *vt.* 1. 详述（理论、观点等）;陈述（意见等）2. 解释,说明

《〈圣经〉等)

express [iks'pres] *vt.* **1.** 表达;表示;表白 **2.** 特快发送,快运(包裹、钱、货物等);特快发送(邮件)**3.** 榨,榨出东西来;压出(汁水等)— *adj.* [只作定语] **1.** (命令、规定等)明确的 **2.** (形象等)酷似的 **3.** (目的)特殊的 **4.** (火车、邮递等)特快的,快速的 — *adv.* 乘快车;以快速方式 — *n.* **1.** (英)专差;由专差递送的急件 **2.** 快运之物;快运的钱 **4.** 〈美〉捷运公司 ‖ ~ly *adv.* **1.** 明显地;明确地 **2.** 持意地,特地 ‖ ~ **delivery** (英)特快专递(美国称 special delivery) / ~ **lift** (英)(不是每层都停的)直达电梯 / **expressway** *n.* 快速干道;高速公路

expression [iks'preʃən] *n.* **1.** 表达;表示 **2.** 表情;脸色;声调;腔调 **3.** 表达方式;词语;措词,措词 **4.** 榨取 **5.** 【数】式;表达式 【生】表现力;表现度;表现方式 ‖ ~less *adj.* 没有表情的,木然呆板的

expressive [iks'presiv] *adj.* **1.** 表现的;表达...的(*of*) **2.** 富于表情的,富有意味的 ‖ ~ly *adv.* / ~ness *n.*

expropriate [eks'prəuprieit] *vt.* **1.** 没收(财产等);征用(土地等);把(他人的财产)转移到自己名下 **2.** 剥夺(某人)的所有权 ‖ ex.propri'ation *n.* / **expropriator** *n.* 剥夺者;没收者;征用者

expulsion [iks'pʌlʃən] *n.* **1.** 驱逐 **2.** 开除(*from*) ‖ ~ **order** (对外国人的)驱逐出境令

expunge [eks'pʌndʒ] *vt.* **1.** (从书、名单等上)删去;划掉(字句、名字等)(*from*) **2.** 擦去,抹掉(记忆中的往事、指纹等)

expurgate ['ekspəgeit] *vt.* 删除(书籍等)中的不当处,使洁净;修订;删除(不当处) ‖ ex.pur'gation *n.*

exquisite ['ekskwizit] *adj.* **1.** 优美的;高雅的;精巧的,精致的 **2.** (痛苦、快乐、愚蠢等)极度的 **3.** (听觉等)敏锐的 — *n.* 爱修饰的人;花花公子 ‖ ~ly *adv.* / ~ness *n.*

ex-serviceman ['eks'sə:vismən] ([复] ex-servicemen ['eks'sə:vismen]) *n.* 退役军人,复员军人

extant [eks'tænt] *adj.* (书籍、文件等)现存的,尚存的;未佚失的

extemporaneous [,ekstempə'reinjəs] *adj.* = extempore ‖ ~ly *adv.* / ~ness *n.*

extempore [eks'tempəri] *adj.* (演说等)无准备的,即席的,当场的 — *adv.* 无准备地,即席地 ‖ ex,tempori'zation *n.*

extemporize [iks'tempəraiz] *vt. & vi.* 临时(或当场)做成;即席发(言);即席演奏;即兴创作 ‖ ex,tempori'zation *n.*

extend [iks'tend] *vt.* **1.** 伸,伸出;伸展(身子等) **2.** 延长;使延伸;使展期 **3.** 扩大,扩充;扩展 **4.** 使达到 **5.** (向...)致(敬礼、问候等);(向...)提供(帮助等);(向...)发出(邀请等)(*to*) **6.** 扩写出(速记等)的全文 **7.** 〈英〉【律】对(地产等)估价;占有,征用 **8.** [常用被动语态]使(比赛者或马等)竭尽全力 **9.** 把...掺杂;(掺入东西)增加(食品等)的数量(或改德程度) **10.** 【会计】把(数字)转入另一栏;算出...的总金额;写出...的金额 — *vi.* **1.** 伸展;扩大;延续 **2.** (在范围或应用上)达到,延伸

extension [iks'tenʃən] *n.* **1.** 伸长;伸展;扩大;(可)扩展的范围 **2.** 延长;延期;(可)延长的程度;延长的日期 **3.** 延长部分;附加部分;增设部分 a university ~大学的附设部分(如夜校、函授班等) **4.** 电话分机;分机号码 **5.** 【逻】外延 **6.** 【医】伸展,牵伸(术)

【物】广power(性) 8.【军】延伸 9.【会计】(从另一捐)转来的金额,转赚数;(发票上所示单价与数量相乘而得的)横栏总金额,合计数 ‖ ~ **ladder**(可拉伸加长的)伸缩梯 / ~ **spring** 【机】牵簧 / ~ **table**(可加装活动板的)伸缩桌

extensive [iks'tensiv] *adj.* **1.** 广大的,广阔的;广泛的;广博的 **2.**【农】粗放的,大面积浅耕粗作的 **3.** 处延的 **4.** 广延的 ‖ ~**ly** *adv.* / ~**ness** *n.*

extent [iks'tent] *n.* **1.** 广度;宽度;长度 **2.** 范围 **3.** 程度;限度;to some (a great, a certain) ~ 在某种(很大,一定)程度上 **4.** 一大片(地区)(of)

extenuate [eks'tenjueit] *vt.*(用偏袒的辩解或借口)减轻(罪行等)的严重性;为…提供理由或找借口 ‖ **extenuating** *adj.* 使减轻的;情有可原的:*extenuating* circumstances【律】可使罪行减轻的情况 / **ex,tenu'ation** *n.*(罪行等的)减轻;意存偏袒的辩护

exterior [eks'tiəriə] *adj.* **1.** 外面的;外部的;外表的;外来的 **2.** 对外的;外交上的 **3.**【建】(适合)外用的 — *n.* **1.** 外部;外表;表面 **2.**(戏剧的)户外场景;(电影、电视的)外景 ‖ ~**ly** *adv.* 在外部;从外表上看

exterminate [eks'tə:mineit] *vt.* 根除,灭绝;消灭,扑灭 ‖ **ex,termi'nation** *n.*

external [eks'tə:nl] *adj.* **1.** 外(面)的;外部的,在外的 **2.** 外界的;客观的,物质的 **3.**【医】外用的 **4.** 外表的,外观的 **5.** 表面的,形式(上)的;肤浅的 **6.** 对外的;外国的;外来的 — *n.* [~s]外表,外形 ‖ ~**ly** *adv.* 在(或从)外面;在(或从)外部;外表上

extinct [iks'tiŋkt] *adj.* **1.**(火、希望等)熄灭了的了的;消灭了的了 **2.** 绝种的,灭绝的 **3.**(职位等)废除了的;(贵族称号等)无

合法继承人的 **4.**(法令等)过时的,失效的

extinction [iks'tiŋkʃən] *n.* **1.** 熄灭;消灭;灭绝;废除 **2.**【物】消光

extinguish [iks'tiŋgwiʃ] *vt.* **1.** 扑灭;熄灭(火、希望、热情等) **2.** 消灭(生命等) **3.** 使(权利、要求等)无效 **4.** 偿清(债务等) ‖ ~**er** *n.* 熄灯(或抽)器;灭火器

extirpate ['eks:tə:peit] *vt.* **1.** 根除(杂草、恶习等)清除 **2.** 消灭 **3.** 破除(异端、邪说等) **3.**【医】摘除(肿瘤等) ‖ **,extir'pation** *n.*

extol(l) [iks'təl] (extolled; extolling) *vt.* 赞美,颂扬

extort [iks'tɔ:t] *vt.*(向...)敲诈;勒索(钱财);(对...)进行威逼获得(秘密、允诺等)(from)

extortion [iks'tɔ:ʃən] *n.* **1.** 敲诈;勒索;强求,逼取 **2.** 被勒索的财物 ‖ ~**ate** *adj.* **1.** 敲诈的;强求的 **2.**(要求、价格等)过高的 / ~**er** *n.* 敲诈者;勒索者;强求者

extra ['ekstrə] *adj.* **1.** 额外的,外加的;另外收费的 **2.** 特大的;(质量)特佳的 — *adv.* **1.** 特别地;格外地;非常 **2.** 另外(收取费用) — *n.* **1.** 额外人手;额外的东西 **2.** 另收费用的项目;[常 ~s]外加费用 **3.**(报纸的)号外 **4.** 质量特佳的东西 **5.**(拍摄电影群众场面时雇来的)临时演员 **6.**(板球赛中非击球所得的)额外得分

extra- *pref.* [一般加在形容词之前]表示"在...之外","越出","超出":*extra* curricular, *extra* sensory

extracorporeal [,ekstrəkɔ:'pɔriəl] *adj.*(位于或发生在)体外的:heart surgery employing ~ circulation 采用体外血液循环的心脏手术 ‖ ~**ly** *n.*

extract [iks'trækt] *vt.* **1.**(用力)取出;(使

劲;拔出;开采 2. 用强迫手段获得(钱财、诺言等) 3. 榨取;提取(蜜等);蒸馏取得 4. 得到(乐趣等) 5. 摘录;选录;选取(精华) 6.【数】开(方),求(根) 7.【军】退(弹) —['ekstrækt] *n.* 1. 摘录,选录 2. 蒸馏液 3.【化】提取物;萃取物 4.【药】浸出物;浸膏

extraction [iks'trækʃən] *n.* 1. 抽(牙等)的拔出;开采;开采 2.【化】提取(法);萃取(法) 3. 拔出物;提取物;采出物 4. 摘录;摘要;精选 5. 血统;出身 6.【数】求根(法),开方(法)

extracurricular ['ekstrəkə'rikjulə]、 **extracurriculum** ['ekstrəkə'rikjuləm] *adj.* (活动等)课外的;业余的

extradite ['ekstrədait] *vt.* 引渡(逃犯、战俘等) ‖ **extradition** [ɩekstrə'diʃən] *n.*

extramarital ['ekstrə'mærit1] *adj.* 婚外的

extraneous [eks'treinjəs] *adj.* 1. 体外的,外部的;外来的;新异的 2. 无关的;不重要的;枝节的 ‖ ~**ly** *adv.* / ~**ness** *n.*

extraordinary [iks'trɔːdnri, ˏekstrə'ɔːdinəri] *adj.* 1. 非常的;特别的;破例的;非凡的 2. 离奇的,使人惊奇的 3. [ˏekstrə'ɔːdinəri](大使等)特命的,特派的 ‖ **extraordinarily** *adv.* /extraordinariness *n.*

extrasensory ['ekstrə'sensəri] *adj.* 超感官的,超感觉的

extrasolar ['ekstrə'səulə] *adj.* (存在于)太阳系之外的

extraterrestrial [ˏekstrətə'restriəl] *adj.* 地球(或其大气圈)外的;行星际的;宇宙的 —*n.* 另一行星来的生物,天外来客

extravagance [iks'trævigəns] *n.*、 **extravagancy** [iks'trævigənsi] *n.* 1. 奢侈;铺张;浪费 2. 过分;无节制 3. 放肆;放肆的话(或行动)

extravagant [iks'trævigənt] *adj.* 1. 奢侈的;浪费的 2.(要求、夸奖等)过分的;超越情理的 3.(价钱)过高的 4.(言行等)放肆的;越轨的 ‖ ~**ly** *adv.*

extreme [iks'triːm] *adj.* 1. 末端的;在尽头的 2. 极度的;极端的;过分的 3. 急进的;激烈的 —*n.* 1. 极端;激烈手段(或步骤等) 2. 极端;极点;极其,非常 / ~**ness** *n.* ‖ ~ **term**【数】外项 / ~**unction** 终傅(天主教牧师对临终病人涂油的礼节) / ~**value**【数】极值

extremism [iks'triːmizəm] *n.* 极端主义

extremist *n.* 极端主义者;过激分子 *adj.* 极端主义的;过激论的

extremity [iks'tremiti] *n.* 1. 末端;终极;尽头 2. 极端;极度 3. 极窘困(或危险)的境地;绝境 4. 临终时刻;覆灭时刻 5.[常 extremities]非常手段;过激措施 6.(身体的)一肢;(人的)手;足: the *extremities* 四肢,手足

extricable ['ekstrikəbl] *adj.* 解脱得了的,能脱离的;脱得了身的,能脱险的

extricate ['ekstrikeit] *vt.* 使解脱,使脱出;解救(*from*) ‖ **,extri'cation** *n.*

extrinsic [eks'trinsik] *adj.* 1. 外在的;非固有的;非本质的 2. 外来的;外部的;外表的;体外的 ‖ ~**ally** *adv.*

extroversion [ˏekstrəu'vəːʃən] *n.* 1.【医】外翻 2.【心】外倾,外向性

extrovert ['ekstrəuvəːt] *n.* 性格外倾者,性格外向者

extrude [eks'truːd] *vt.* 挤压出;挤压成 ‖ **extrusion** [eks'truːʒən] *n.*

exuberant [ig'zjuːbərənt] *adj.* 1. 繁茂的,茂盛的 2.(情感、想象力等)丰富的;(精力等)充沛的;(健康)极佳的 3.(人、行动等)热情洋溢的;兴高采烈

的;充满活力的 ‖ **exuberance** *n.* /~**ly** *adv.*

exude [ig'zju:d] *vt.* **1.** 使渗出;使流出 **2.** 使(气味等)发散 —*vi.* **1.** (汗等)渗出;流出 **2.** 发散开来 ‖ **exudation** [ˌeksju:'deiʃən] *n.*

exult [ig'zʌlt] *vi.* 狂喜;欢跃

exultant [ig'zʌltənt] *adj.* 狂喜的;欢欣鼓舞的;兴高采烈的 ‖ ~**ly** *adv.*

exultation [ˌegzʌl'teiʃən] *n.* 狂喜;欢跃(*at*);高兴,得意(*over*)

ex-works ['ekswə:ks] *adv.* 〈英〉直接来自工厂地;以工厂交货方式;按出厂价

eye [ai] *n.* **1.** 眼睛;眼圈:the apple of the ~ 瞳孔,眼珠;〈喻〉珍爱物,珍爱的人 **2.** 眼光;视力;观察力 **3.** 注目,注意:be in the public ~ 公开露面;为公众所注目;著名 **4.** [常~s]见解;观点;判断:In my ~*s*, that will do. 我看那样能行。**5.** 眼子,孔;眼状物(如针眼、靶心、孔雀翎斑等);索眼;圈,环:a hook and ~(扣住衣领的)一副风纪扣;一副领钩 **6.** 风吹来的方向;【气】(台)风眼 **7.**【植】(马铃薯等的)芽眼;花心;(菊科的)花盘;【微】眼点;【物】光电池;光电管 **8.** 〈美俚〉侦探 —*vt.* **1.** 看,注视 **2.** 在...上打孔眼 ‖ ~**less** *adj.* 无眼的;瞎的 /~**let** *n.* (供穿线、挂钩等用的)圆孔眼;针眼,小孔;(镶小孔用的)金属圈,金属环 ‖ '~**ball** *n.* 眼球 /'~**brow** *n.* 眉毛,眉 /'~-ˌ**catcher** *n.* 引人注目的人(或物) /'~-ˌ**catching** *adj.* 引人注目的 /~ **chart** 视力表 /'~**cup** *n.* 洗眼杯 /'~**glass** *n.* **1.** 镜片 **2.** [~glasses]眼镜;夹鼻眼镜 **3.** 洗眼杯 **4.** (望远镜等装置中的)(接)目镜 /'~**hole** *n.* **1.** 眼窝 **2.** = ~let /'~**lash** *n.* 睫毛 /'~**lid** *n.* 眼睑 /'~ˌ**liner** *n.* (化妆用的)眼线膏;眼线笔 /'~-ˌ**opener** *n.* 使人大开眼界(或恍然大悟)的事物(尤指新闻、新发现等) /'~**piece** *n.* (望远镜等装置中的)(接)目镜 /~ **shadow** 眼睑膏 /'~**shot** *n.* 视界,视野 /'~**sight** *n.* 视力,目力 /~**s only**〈美〉(收信或收件人)亲启的;亲阅的,绝密的:an ~*s only* letter to the Minister 部长亲启信 /'~**sore** *n.* 丑东西;不顺眼的东西(或人) /'~**strain** *n.* 眼疲劳 /'~**tooth** *n.* 上尖牙,上犬齿 /'~**wall** *n.*【气】眼壁 /'~**wash** *n.* **1.** (洗)眼药水;洗眼剂 **2.** 〈俚〉胡说;吹牛;拍马;把戏,骗局;表面文章 /'~ˌ**water** *n.* **1.** 眼泪;眼分泌液 **2.** (洗)眼药水;洗眼剂 /'~'**witness** *n.* 目击者;见证人

eyed [aid] *adj.* **1.** 有眼的 **2.** [常用以构成复合词]长着...眼睛的;有着...眼光的

eyeful ['aiful] *n.* **1.** 满眼 **2.** 〈俚〉美人儿;非常悦目的东西

F

F, f [ef]([复]**F's, F's** 或 **Fs, fs** [efs]) 英语字母表第六个字母 1. [F]F字形 2. [F]【化】元素氟 (fluorine) 的符号 3. [F] 【音】F音, F调 4. [美]学业成绩不及格 (failure) 的符号

fa [fɑː] **n.** [音] 1. 固定唱法时之 F 音 2. 首调唱法时任何大音阶之第四音 (或任何小音阶之第六音)

fable ['feibl] **n.** 1. 寓言 2. 传说 3. 虚构的故事; 无稽之谈 4. 大众闲谈的题材, 话题 ‖ **~d adj.** 寓言中的; 虚构的

fabric ['fæbrik] **n.** 1. 织物, 织品; 布 2. 构造, 结构; 组织: the ~ of society 社会结构 3. 构筑, 建筑; 建筑方法; 建筑风格

fabricate ['fæbrikeit] **vt.** 1. 制作; 装配; 组合 ‖ a ~d building 装配式房屋 / a ~d ship 组合船 2. 捏造, 伪造 ‖ ,fabri'cation **n.** / **fabricator n.**

fabulous ['fæbjuləs] **adj.** 1. 寓言般的 2. 寓言中的; 传说上的 3. 惊人的; 难以置信的; 非常的; 巨大的 4. [口] 极好的 ‖ **~ly adv.** / **~ness n.**

facade, façade [fə'sɑːd] **n.** 1. [建] (房屋的) 正面, 立面, 门面 2. [掩饰真相的] 表面, 外观

face [feis] **n.** 1. 脸, 面孔; 面貌; 面容 2. 面子, 威信; 厚颜 3. 硬币, 纸币等的正面, 票面; 表面; (有文字, 图案或加工装饰的) 面 4. 外观, 外表; 局面 5. 地形; [矿] 采掘面, 工作面; (矿石等的)

晶面; [机] (刀具的) 切削面 6. [印] (铅字字模的) 字面, 模面 ‖ (版) 面 7. [军] (队伍的) 阵面 — **vt.** 1. 面向, 面对 2. 面朝, 面向 3. 正视; 对付 4. (困难, 死亡, 毁灭等) 面临 (某人) 5. (用石灰, 水泥等) 抹盖; 给 (衣服等) 镶边; 给 (饮料等) 搀色 6. 使 (石料等) 的表面光洁 (off. up) 7. [军] 命令 (队伍) 改变方向 8. 翻转 (纸牌) 的正面 — **vi.** 向, 朝 ‖ **~d adj.** 常用以构成复合词有...面容的; 有...表面的; 有...镶边的 / **~less adj.** 匿名的; 身份不明的 ‖ **~-ache n.** [医] 面部神经痛 / **~ brick** [建] 面砖 / **~ card** (纸牌中的) 人头牌 (指 K, Q, J 三种) / **'~-centred adj.** [物] (晶体) 面心的 / **'~-cream n.** 面霜; 雪花膏 / **~ 'down adv.** 面朝下地 / **~ card** (纸牌中的) 人头牌 (指 ['feisdaun] **n.** 直接对抗, 摊牌 / **~ guard** (厂矿、击剑等用的) 面具, 面罩 / **'~ harden vt.** 使...的表面硬化 / **'~ing n.** 1. (除去面部纹痕等的) 整容术; 整容 2. (建筑物, 汽车等的) 改建, 翻新 / **'~-saving n. & adj.** 保全面子 (的) / **'~-to-' ~ adj. & adv.** 面对面的; 面对面的 (地) / **'~up adv.** 面朝上地 / **~ value** 1. 票面价值 2. 表面价值; 字面意义

facet ['fæsit] **n.** 1. (宝石等的) 琢面 2. (问题等的) 一个方面

facetious [fə'siːʃəs] **adj.** 1. 滑稽的 2. 爱开玩笑的 ‖ **~ly adv.** / **~ness n.**

facial ['feiʃəl] **adj.** 面部的; 面部用的: ~

tissue 擦脸纸巾 — n.〈口〉面部按摩；美容

facile ['fæsail, 'fæsil] *adj.* 1. 易做到的；易得到的，不花力气的 2. 敏捷的；流畅的 3.（性格）柔顺的，温和 ‖ ~**ly** *adv.* / ~**ness** *n.*

facilitate [fə'siliteit] *vt.* 1. 使容易；使便利 2. 推进，促进 ‖ **fa**'**cili**'**tation** *n.*

facility [fə'siliti] *n.* 1. 容易，简易 2. 熟练；灵巧；敏捷 3.〔常 facilities〕设备，设施；工具；方便，便利 4. 温顺

facing ['feisiŋ] *n.* 1.（衣服等的）贴边，饰条 2.【建】饰面，贴面

facsimile [fæk'simili] *n.* 1. 摹本原本 2.【讯】电传真；传真通信；传真图文本

fact [fækt] *n.* 1. 事实 2. 实际，实情，真相 3.〔the ~〕(犯罪)行为；事实: before (after) the ~作案前(后) ‖ ~-**finding** *adj.* 实情调查的；进行调解的

faction ['fækʃən] *n.* 1. 派别，宗派，小集团 2. 派系斗争；内讧 ‖ -**al** *adj.*

factious ['fækʃəs] *adj.* 1. 好搞宗派活动的 2. 宗派引起的

factitious [fæk'tiʃəs] *adj.* 1. 人为的 2. 做作的，不自然的 ‖ -**ly** *adv.* / ~**ness** *n.*

factor ['fæktə] *n.* 1. 因素；要素 2.【数】因子，商数，系数 3.【化】当量换算因素 2.【生】遗传因子，基因 3.【摄】曝光系数 3. 代理商；(苏格兰)地产管理人；管家

factorize ['fæktəraiz] *vt.*【数】将…分解成因子 ‖ **factori**'**zation** *n.*

factory ['fæktəri] *n.* 制造厂，工厂 ‖ ~ **farm** 工厂化农场 / ~ **ship**(附有鱼类加工设备的)捕鲸队加工船

factotum [fæk'təutəm] *n.* 家务总管；打杂的人

factual ['fæktjuəl] *adj.* 事实的，真实的 ‖ ~**ly** *adv.* / ~**ness** *n.*

faculty ['fækəlti] *n.* 1. 能力；技能；官能 2.(高等院校或系的)全体教员及有学衔的行政人员；(美)(任何学校的)全体教员 3.(大学的)系；院

fad [fæd] *n.* 一时的风尚，一时的狂热 ‖ **faddish**, **faddy** *adj.* 1. 一时流行的 2. 喜欢赶时髦的

fade [feid] *vi.* 1. 凋谢，枯萎 2.(颜色)退去 3.(声音等)衰弱下去；消失 — *vt.* 使退色 — *n.*(电影、电视中画面的)淡入；淡出 ‖ ~ **away** *n.* 逐渐消失 / ~-**in** *n.*(电影、电视中画面的)淡入，渐显；(电影、广播中声音的)渐强 / ~-**out** *n.*(电影、电视中画面的)淡出，渐隐；(电影、广播中声音的)渐弱

fadeless ['feidlis] *adj.* 不凋谢的；不退色的；不衰落的 ‖ -**ly** *adv.*

faeces ['fisiz] 〔复〕*n.* = feces

fag [fæg] *n.* 1. 累人的活儿；苦劳 2.(英国学校中)受高年级学生使唤的低年级生；奴仆；做苦工的人 3.〈俚〉香烟 —(fagged; fagging) *vi.* 1. 辛苦地工作 2. 听高年级使唤 — *vt.* 1. 使疲劳(*out*) 2. 强迫(低年级生)干活 3. 磨损；拆散(绳索的末端)‖ ~ **end** 1. 绳索的散端；(布匹的)散口边 2. 末尾；(英口)香烟；烟蒂 3. 吃亏的一方

fag(g)ot ['fægət] *n.* 1. 柴把，柴捆；枝条捆 2.(用以捆铁条、束铁)3. 香草束，碎肉卷 4.(英)讨厌的女人 5. 搞男性同性恋的人

Fah(r) *abbr.* Fahrenheit

Fahrenheit ['færənhait] *adj.* 华氏温度计的，华氏的:the ~ scale 华氏温标

fail [feil] *vi.* 1. 失败；不及格 2.(电力、自来水供应等等)中断；(人在某方面)不足；(作物)歉收 3.(健康、体力、视力等)衰退；衰弱 4.(心脏、发动机等)停止作用 5. 破产 — *vt.* 1. 使失望；舍

弃: My memory ～s me at this moment. 我一时想不起来了. **2.**［后接不定式］不, 不能; 忘记: Don't ～ to ring me up. 不要忘记给我打电话. **3.** 评(学生等)不及格; 没有通过(考试): 没有通过(某一学科)的考试 — **n.**(考试)不及格 ‖ ~ed **adj.** 已失败的 ‖`~-safe` **adj.** 故障安全的; 装有安全保障装置的; (计划等)保证不会失败的, 万全的; (核武器)出现故障自动除缘的

failing ['feiliŋ] **n.** 缺点; 弱点; 失败 — **prep.** 如果没有 ……, 若无 …… 时

faille [feil, fail] **n.** 罗缎, 菲尔绸

failure ['feiljə] **n. 1.** 失败 **2.** 失败的人; 失败的尝试(或经验) **3.**(电力等供应的)中断; (作物的)歉收 **4.**(心脏的)停跳; 衰竭; (引擎等的)失灵, 故障 **5.**(力量等的)衰退 **6.** 破产 **7.** 疏忽: 不履行, 没做到; ～ to keep a promise 失约, 不守诺言 **8.**(美)学业成绩不及格; 不及格等级(符号"F")

faint [feint] **adj. 1.** 虚弱的, 衰弱的 **2.** 懦怯的; (行动等)软弱无力的 **3.** 微弱的, 不明显的; 不清楚的 **4.**［只作表语］眩晕的; 行将昏厥的 — **n.** 昏厥 — **vi. 1.** 昏厥, 晕倒 **2.** 变得没气力了. 变得微弱; 变得暗淡 ‖～ly **adv.** / ～ness **n.**

fainthearted ['feint'hɑːtid] **adj.** 懦怯的; 无决断的 ‖ ～ly **adv.** / ～ness **n.**

fair[1] [feə] **adj. 1.** 美丽的; 女性的 **2.**(肤色)白皙的; (头发)金色的 **3.**(誊写本等)清楚的, 干净的 **4.**(天气)晴朗的; (风向)顺的; 顺利的, 有希望的 **5.** 公平的, 合理的 **6.** 按法律可借得的 **7.**(财产等)丰富的 **8.** ……的; 尚好的; 中等的 **9.**(言论, 诺言等)说得好听的, 花言巧语的 — **adv. 1.** 公平地, 公正地 **2.** 正面地, 直接地 **3.**

清楚地(抄写) ‖ ～ness **n.** ‖`~-haired` **adj. 1.** 金发的 **2.**(口)被宠爱的 /`~-'minded` **adj.** 公正的, 无偏见的 /`~ sex ie女性` (口)女性 /`~-'spoken` **adj.**(谈吐等)有礼貌的; 温和的; 婉转的; 嘴甜的 /`~-trade` 互惠贸易 /`~-'trade agreement` 互惠贸易协定(厂商规定代理商不得低于规定价格抛售的约定) /`~-way` **n. 1.**(河流, 海港等的)航道 **2.**【空】(水上飞机升降用的)水面跑道 /`~-weather` **adj.** 只适宜于好天气的; 只能同安乐不能共患难的

fair[2] [feə] **n. 1.** 定期集市 **2.** 商品展览会; 商品交易会 **3.** 义卖会 ‖`~ ground` 集市场所

fairly ['feəli] **adv. 1.** 公正地; 正当地 **2.** 完全; 简直 **3.** 相当; 还算

fairy ['feəri] **n. 1.** 小妖精; 仙人 **2.** 众仙子, 仙界 **3.**(口)男性同性恋爱者, "相公" ‖`~like` **adj.** 小妖精似的; 仙女般的 ‖`~ godmother`(危难时提供及时帮助的)女恩人 /`~-land` **n.** 仙界 /`~-lights` 彩色小灯 /`~ tale` **1.** 神话; 童话 **2.** 谎言

fait accompli ['feit ə'kɔmpliː] (法)既成事实

faith [feiθ] **n. 1.** 信任; 信念 **2.** 信仰; 宗教信仰; 信条 **3.** 信义; 诚意; 忠诚; in good ～ 真诚地/in bad ～ 欺诈地 ‖`~-cure`, `~ healing`(靠祈祷等治病的)信仰疗法

faithful ['feiθful] **adj. 1.** 守信的; 忠实的; 忠诚的 **2.** 如实的; 正确的; 可靠的 **3.**(诺言等)切实遵守的 — (［复］faith-ful(s]) **n. 1.** [the ～]［总称］虔诚的宗教徒(尤指伊斯兰教徒) ‖ ～ly **adv.** 忠实地; 如实地; 切实遵守地; Yours ～ly(或 *Faithfully* yours)你的忠诚的(正式或商业信件等信末署名前

的客套语) / ~ness n.

faithless ['feiθlis] adj. 1. 背信弃义的；不忠的 2. 不可靠的；不老实的；奸诈的 3. (罕)无(宗教)信仰的 ‖ ~ly adv. / ~ness n.

fake [feik] vt. vi. 1. 伪造；赝造；捏造 2. 装(病等)：(在球类等比赛中)假装做(某一动作) — vi. 假装 — n. 1. 假货；赝品；捏造的报道；虚构的故事 2. 魔术用具 3. 冒充者；骗子 — adj. 假的；赝造的；冒充的 — vt. n. 1. 伪造者；捏造者 2. 骗子；卖滑头货的小贩 ‖ ~book(美)伪歌本(指未经版权所有人同意而出版的流行歌曲曲调集)

fakir ['feikiə] n. 1. (伊斯兰教或印度教的)托钵僧：苦行者

falcon ['fɔːlkən, 'fɔːlkən] n. 1.【动】隼、游隼 2. (猎鸟用的)猎鹰(术语上专指雌鹰) ‖ ~er n. 养猎鹰者；鹰猎者 / ~ry n. 猎鹰训练术；鹰猎

fall [fɔːl] (fell [fel], fallen ['fɔːlən]) vi. 1. 落下；降落；跌落；跌倒 2. (温度、价格等)减低，减弱；(情绪等)低落 3. (头发等)下垂、松垂 4. (地面等)倾斜；(河流)向下流；注入(into)；(潮汐)退去；(羊羔等)出生 5. (房屋等)坍倒；(城市、阵地等)陷落；被攻克；(政府、政权等)垮台；被推翻 7. 降临；成为；死亡 8. (地位、声音、威信等)降低 9. (脸色)变阴沉，变坏；陷入罪恶 11. (暮色等)降临；(日期、节日)来临 12. (目光、重音、责任等)落到(on) 13. (光线等)射上 — vt. 变成；成为 asleep (ill) 睡着(病倒) 15. 被说出：Not a word fell from her lips. 她一声也不吭。— vt. 1. (美、英方)击倒；砍倒(树木 —) n. 1. 落下；跌落；下垂；(房屋等)坍倒 2. (雨、雪等)降落；降落量 3. (树木等)伐倒；(木材)采伐量 4. (温度、价格等的)下降；向下倾斜；落差；(情绪等的)低落 5. 下崽；(一)胎(主要指一次所生的羊羔) 6. (城市、要塞等的)陷落；(政府、政权等的)垮台、崩溃；衰亡；失败 7. (地位、声望、威信等的)降低 8. 堕落 9. [常 ~s]瀑布 10. (主要用作 A 名 ‖ ~back n. 可依靠的东西(或人) 2. 退却 / ~off n. 下降；减少 / ~out n. 放射性坠尘；污染性坠尘；坠尘沉降 / ~pipe n. 水落管 / ~-trap n. 落体陷阱

fallacious [fə'leiʃəs] adj. 1. 谬误的 2. 靠不住的；虚妄的；令人失望的 ‖ ~ly adv. / ~ness n.

fallacy ['fæləsi] n. 1. 谬误 2. 谬论；谬见

fallen ['fɔːlən] fall 的过去分词 — adj. 1. 落下的；倒下的 2. 跌落的；减少的 3. 摧毁的；倒坍的 3. 陷落的；被攻克的；被推翻的 4. 堕落的 5. 死去的，倒毙的：the — [总称]阵亡者，战死者

fallible ['fælibl] adj. 易犯错误的；难免有错误的 ‖ falli'bility n. / fallibly adv.

Fallopian [fə'ləupiən] adj. ‖ ~ tube【解】输卵管，法鲁皮欧氏管

fallow[1] ['fæləu] adj. 休闲的 — n. 休闲地、休耕地

fallow[2] ['fæləu] adj. 淡棕色的 ‖ ~deer 黇鹿(一种欧洲小鹿，毛色淡黄)

false [fɔːls] adj. 1. 假的、虚伪的，不真实的 2. 谬误的；不正确的，无信义的；欺诈的、不老实的 4. 伪造的 5. (植物)假而似而冻饰的 — eggplant(植)茄子 6. (音)不合调的 — adv. 欺诈地；叛卖地[只用于以下短语]：play sb. — 欺骗某人；叛卖某人 ‖ ~alarm；(骗人或因虚惊而误发的)假警报；引起一场空欢喜的人(或事物) / ~arrest【律】不法逮捕；非

法逮捕 /~ **bottom**(船只、箱子、抽屉等隔夹夹层的)假底板, 活底 /~ **card** 诱张(指为迷惑对方面出的牌) /~ **hearted** adj. 心存欺诈的 /~ **imprisonment** 非法监禁 /~ **keel**(船)防擦龙骨, 保护龙骨 /~ **position** 使人看来仿佛违反原则行事的处境; 被人误解的处境 /~ **pretences** 诈欺取财(罪) /~ **start** 起跑犯规, 偷跑, 抢跑; 失败的开端 /~ **step** 失足的一步; 失策的一步 /~ **teeth**(整副的)假牙

falsehood ['fɔːlshud] n. 1. 谬误、不真实 2. 说谎; 欺骗 3. 谎言

falsetto [fɔːl'setəu] ([复] falsettos) n. 〈意〉【音】假声

falsify ['fɔːlsifai] vt. 1. 窜改(文件等); 伪造 2. 歪曲 3. 证明……是假的, 证明……是无根据的 ‖ **falsification** [ˌfɔːlsifi'keiʃən] n.

falsity ['fɔːlsiti] n. 1. 虚假, 不真实; 不正确 2. 欺诈, 不老实; 不忠实 3. 谎言

falter ['fɔːltə] vi. 1. 蹒跚, 跟跄; 摇晃 2. (声音)颤抖 3. 踌躇, 犹豫; 畏缩 — vt. 支吾地说话; 结巴地讲出 (out)

faltering ['fɔːltəriŋ] adj. 1. 踉跄的; 摇晃的 2. 颤抖的; 支吾的 ‖ **~ly** adv.

fame [feim] n. 名声; 名望 ‖ **~d** adj. 有名的, 著名的

familial [fə'miliəl] adj. 1. 家庭(或家族)的 2. 某一家庭(或家族)所特有的

familiar [fə'miljə] adj. 1. 熟悉的 (to); 通晓的 (with) 2. 亲近的 3. 无拘束的, 随便的; 放肆的; 冒昧的 ‖ an ~ essay 小品文 4. (男女间)亲昵的 — n. 1. 熟友; 伴侣 2. 常客 ‖ **~ly** adv.

familiarity [fəˌmili'æriti] n. 1. 熟悉; 通晓 2. 亲近; 亲昵; 随便; 放肆 3. [常 familiarities] 放肆的言行; 爱抚

familiarize [fə'miliəraiz] vt. 1. 使熟悉; 使

通晓 2. 使家喻户晓 ‖ **familiari'zation** n.

family ['fæmili] n. 1. 家、家庭; 家属; 亲属 2. 子女 3. 氏族; 家族; 族属, 传种; 宗教、哲学信念等方面的)派、派别 5. 门第; 名门 6. 【动】【植】科; 【化】【数】【天】族; 【语】语族 7. [时]〈黑帮党的〉家族 ‖ **~ allowance**(服役期间给付的家庭补贴) /~ **Bible** 家用(大型)〈圣经〉(附有空白页, 供记载家属生死、结婚等事项用) /~ **circle** 1. 家庭圈子 2. (剧场中廉价的)家庭座 /~ **doctor**(通看各科的)家庭医生 /~ **man** 1. 有妻子儿女的人, 有家累的人 2. 忠于家庭的人 /~ **name** 姓 /~ **planning** 计划生育 /~ **tree** 家谱; 家谱图

famine ['fæmin] n. 1. 饥荒 2. 奇缺

famish ['fæmiʃ] vt. & vi. (使)挨饿 ‖ **~ment** n.

famous ['feiməs] adj. 1. 著名的, 出名的 2. 〈口〉极好的, 非常令人满意的 ‖ **~ly** adv. 〈口〉极好地, 非常令人满意地

fan[1] [fæn] n. 1. 扇子; 风扇; 鼓风机 2. 扇形物(如孔雀尾、棕榈树叶等) — (fanned; fanning) vt. 1. 扇; 煽动; 激起 3. 扇旁(away) 4.(微风)吹拂 5.使……展成扇形(out) 6. 〈美俚〉拍打; 投打; 鞭打 — vi. 1. 飘动; 拍翅 2. 成扇形展开(out) ‖ **~-like** adj. 1. 像扇的; 风扇 扇般转动的 2. 折叠的 ‖ **~-jet** n.【空】涡轮风扇发动机; 装有涡轮风扇发动机的飞机 /~ **light** n. 扇形窗 /~ **~-tail** n. 1. 扇形尾; 扇形末端 2.【动】扇尾鸽; 扇尾金鱼; 扇尾鹧 3.【建】扇形饰

fan[2] [fæn] n. 1. (运动、电影等的)狂热爱好者, 迷 2. 狂慕者(通常指对演员等) ‖ **~ mail** [总称]影迷(或球迷等)写给明星表示崇拜的信件

fanatic [fəˈnætik] *adj.* 狂热的；盲信的；盲目热中的 — *n.* 狂热者；盲信者

fanatical [fəˈnætikəl] *adj.* = fanatic ‖ ~ly *adv.*

fanaticism [fəˈnætisizəm] *n.* 狂热；盲信

fancier [ˈfænsiə] *n.* 1. 育种者 2. 爱好者，迷

fanciful [ˈfænsiful] *adj.* 1. 爱空想的；沉湎于空想的 2. 存在于空想中的，想象出来的 3.（服装等）奇异的 ‖ ~ly *adv.* / ~ness *n.*

fancy [ˈfænsi] *n.* 1. 想象力；幻想力 2.（无充分根据的）设想，幻想，空想 3.（一时的）爱好；迷恋 (for) 4.（在艺术、穿着等方面）审美观点，时兴 5. 时兴纺织品；杂色花朵（或植物）6. 珍贵动物的培育技能 7. [the ~]（在艺术、娱乐等方面）有特殊嗜好的人们；迷（尤指拳击迷）8. 嬖好（尤指拳击）— *adj.* 1. 根据想象的，空想出来的 2.（衣着、食品等）花式的 3. 奇特的；异样的，种种类的；杂色的 4.（小鸟等）太高的；供应高价品的 5.〈美〉（商品，特指食品）特级的，最高档的 — *vt.* 1. 想象，设想；*Fancy that!* 那真想不到！2.（无根据地）相信，（自负地）认为 3. 喜爱，爱好 4. 词养，培育（品种奇特的动植物）— *vi.* 1. 想象，幻想；*Just ~!* 你想想看！；试（好？有想！）2.（对…）有自信 ‖ ~-**free** *adj.* 没有恋爱对象的；未婚的 / ~-**house**〈俚〉妓院 / ~-**man** 1. 情夫 2. 靠情妇过活的男人 / ~-**woman** 1. 情妇 2. 妓女 / ~-**work** *n.* 刺绣品；钩编织品

fanfare [ˈfænfeə] *n.* 1. 嘹亮的喇叭声 2. 夸耀；鼓吹

fang [fæŋ] *n.* 1.（犬、狼等的）尖牙；犬齿 2.（毒蛇的）毒牙 3. 牙根 4. 尖端；（工具等的）齿；爪 ‖ ~ed *adj.* 有尖牙的，有毒牙的

fanny [ˈfæni] **pack** 腰带包

fantasia [fænˈteiziə] *n.* 1.[音] 幻想曲；（多种曲调凑成的）集成曲 2. 幻想作品（如幻想诗等）；怪诞事物；怪异

fantasize [ˈfæntəsaiz] *vt.* & *vi.* 幻想；想象 ‖ **fantasizer** *n.*

fantastic [fænˈtæstik] *adj.* 1. 幻想的，异想天开的 2. 奇异的，古怪的 3. 庞大的，大得难以相信的 4.〈口〉极好的，极妙的 ‖ ~ally *adv.*

fantasy [ˈfæntəsi, ˈfæntəzi] *n.* 1. 幻想 2. 怪念头 3. 幻想曲；幻想作品 4. 想象力的产物；离奇的图案；奇妙的发明 5. 想入非非

FAO *abbr.* Food and Agriculture Organization（联合国）粮农组织

far [faː]（farther [ˈfaːðə] 或 further [ˈfəːðə], farthest [ˈfaːðist] 或 furthest [ˈfəːðist]）*adv.* 1.（在空间或时间上的距离）远，遥远地；久远地 2.（常用于比较，强调程度、性质）大大…；…得多 ~ better 好得多 / ~ different 大不相同 — (farther and further, farthest 或 furthest) *adj.* 1.（常用于书面语）遥远的；远方的；久远的 2.（对地名远近的）the *Far* East 远东 3. 较远的，那一边的；对面的；at the end of the street 在街道的那一头 — *n.* 远处，远方 ‖ ~-**away** *adj.* 1.（时间，距离，程度等）遥远的；远远的 2.（表情）心不在焉的，恍惚的；出神的 / ~-**fetched** *adj.* 牵强的；不自然的 / ~-**flung** *adj.* 1. 分布广的；覆盖面大的；广为延伸的 2. 遥远的 / ~-**off** *adj.* 遥远的 / ~-**out** *adj.* 异乎寻常的，奇特的，标新立异的 / ~-**reaching** *adj.* 深远的；广泛的 / ~-**sighted** *adj.* 远视的；有远见的 / ~-**sightedness** *n.* 远视；远见

farce [faːs] *n.* 1. 笑剧，闹剧，滑稽戏 2. 滑稽；可笑的事物

farcical ['fɑːsikəl] *adj.* 笑剧的、闹剧的；笑剧性的、闹剧性的；滑稽的 ‖ ~**ly** *adv.*

fare [feə] *vi.* 1. 过活；遭遇；进展 2. 吃，进食 3. 〈古〉行走；旅行 — *n.* 1. 车费；船费；乘客 2. 伙食 3. 伙食费 4. 精神食粮(尤指文艺、娱乐方面的)

farewell ['feə'wel] *int.* 再会，再见，祝你顺利，一路平安 — *n.* 1. 告别话；告别；欢送会；告别演出

farm [fɑːm] *n.* 1. 农场 2. 饲养场、畜牧场(水产的)养殖场 3.〈儿童常用的〉寄养所 4. 包出税收；包税区 — *vt.* 1. 耕(田)；耕种 2. 在...上经营农场(或饲养场等)；种植；养殖 3. 承包收养(小孩等)(out) 4. 承包(企业等) 5. 租出；出租(土地、企业，把(囚犯等)作为劳动力出租)(out) 6. 包出(工件、活计、税收)(out) 7. 把(土地)耕种薄、(地)耗力耗尽(out) — *vi.* 种田，务农；经营农场；从事畜牧 ‖ ~**ing** *n.* 农业 农事；耕作；畜牧 / ~**hand** *n.* 农场工人 / ~**house** *n.* 农场里的住所 / ~**labo(u)rer** *n.* = ~ **hand** / ~ **land** *n.* 农田 / ~**stead** *n.* 农场建筑物和周围场地；农庄 / ~**yard** *n.* 农场建筑物周围(或圈内)的空地(尤指仓前空地)

farmer ['fɑːmə] *n.* 1. 农民，农夫 2. 农场主 3. 牧场主；养殖场主 4. 承包者；包税人

farmost ['fɑːməust] *adj.* 最远的

farrow ['færəu] *n.* 1. 一胎小猪 2. 产小猪 — *vt.* 产(小猪) 3. 产小猪(down)

fart [fɑːt] *n.* 〈俗〉屁 — *vi.* 放屁

farther ['fɑːðə] *adv.* [far 的两种比较级形式之一，另一形式为 further；farther 常用于本义"更远"，further 常用于引申意义"进一步"] — *adv.* 1. [距离、时间上]更远地，再往前地：Can you go any ~? 你还走得动吗? 2. 进一步地；而且；此

外(现代英语多用 further) — *adj.* 较远的，那一(边或头)的：on the ~ side of the road 在路的那一边

farthermost ['fɑːðəməust] *adj.* 最远的(= farthest)

farthest ['fɑːðist] [far 的两种最高级形式之一，另一形式为 furthest] — *adj.* [距离、时间上]最远的 — *adv.* 1. [距离、时间上]最远地 2. 最大程度地；最大限度地

farthing ['fɑːðiŋ] *n.* 法寻(英国四分之一旧便士的硬币或币值)

fascinate ['fæsineit] *vt.* 1. 迷住，使神魂颠倒；强烈地吸引住 2.(蛇等)用目光使(被捕食的动物)呆住

fascinating ['fæsineitiŋ] *adj.* 迷人的，消魂夺魄的 ‖ ~**ly** *adv.*

fascination [ˌfæsi'neiʃən] *n.* 1. 迷惑力，魅力 2. 迷恋；强烈爱好

fascism ['fæʃizəm] *n.* 法西斯主义

fascist ['fæʃist] *n.* [常作 F-] 1. 法西斯主义者；法西斯党员 2. 法西斯匪徒 — *adj.* 法西斯主义的；法西斯党的

fashion ['fæʃən] *n.* 1. 样子；方式：in an expansive ~ 奢华地 2.(服饰等的)流行式样(或款式)；(言语、行为等的)风尚，风气 3.[the ~]风行一时的事物；红人；名流 4. 上流社会 — *vt.*(用手工等)制作(from, out of)；使成形；把...塑造成(into) ‖ ~ **plate** 1. 时装图样 2. 穿着时髦的人

-fashion *comb. form* 表示"...式地"：crab-fashion 蟹般地

fashionable ['fæʃənəbl] *adj.* 1. 流行的、时髦的 2. 赶时髦的 3. 上流社会的；为上流社会的人们所欢迎的 ‖ ~**ness** *n.* / **fashionably** *adv.*

-fashioned *comb. form* 表示"...式的"：old-fashioned

fast¹ [fɑːst] *adj.* 1. 紧的;牢的 2.(朋友)忠实的,可靠的 3.(色)不退的 4.(睡眠)酣畅的 5. 快的、迅速的 6.(钟表)偏快的 7. 放荡的 8.【摄】(胶片)快速的;(镜头)快的、强光的 9.(快门)快速的 — *adv.* 1. 紧紧地;牢固地 2. 酣畅地 3. 快;迅速地 ‖ /~'**food** *n.*(餐馆等)供应快餐的 /~/**lane** *n.*(道路的)快车道 /~'**talk** *vt.* 花言巧语地企图说服(或影响)

fast² [fɑːst] *vi.* 1. 禁食;斋戒;绝食 2. 节制饮食;忌食 — *n.* 禁食;斋戒;绝食;节食;禁食期;绝食期;节食期 ‖ ~ **day** 斋戒日

fastback [ˈfɑːstbæk] *n.*(美)(车顶向尾部平缓倾斜的)斜背;斜背式车身;斜背式车身小客车

fasten [ˈfɑːsn] *vt.* 1. 扎牢;扣住;闩住;钉牢 2. 把(目光、注意力、思想等)集中于(on, upon) 3. 把(绰号、罪名等)强加于(on, upon) 4.[~ oneself]纠缠(on, upon) — *vi.* 1. 扣住;抓住;钉住 2. 抓住;钉住不放地进行攻击(on, upon)

fastener [ˈfɑːsnə] *n.* 扣件;钮扣;揿钮;钩扣(钉纸张的)扣钉

fastening [ˈfɑːsniŋ] *n.* 1. 扣紧;扎牢 2. 紧固件,扣件,扣拴物(如锁、闩、钩、扣、钉等)

fastidious [fæsˈtidiəs] *adj.* 1. 爱挑剔的;难讨好的;过分讲究的 2.(微生物等)在合成培养基上不易生长的 ‖ -ly *adv.* /~ness *n.*

fastness [ˈfɑːstnis] *n.* 1. 牢固;固定(性) 2. 快速,迅速 3. 不退色(性);【纺】坚牢度 4. 放荡 5. 要塞;辟静的处所

fat [fæt] (fatter, fattest) *adj.* 1. 肥胖的;肥大的;丰满的;饱满的 2.(肉)肥的;多油脂的;多脂肪的 3.(牛、羊等)养肥了供食用(或销售、展览)的 4. 肥沃的;富的;(职务等)收益多的;(薪给等)优厚的 5. 厚的;(费用、银行存款等)巨大的 6. 丰富的;塞得满满的 — *n.* 1. 肥肉;脂肪;油脂 2. 最优美的文艺作品;最好的部分 3. 肥胖 — (fatted; fatting) *vt.* 1. 养肥(up, out) 2. 用油脂处理(皮革) ‖ -less **adj.** /~ly *adv.* 1. 富饶地;丰富地 2. 像胖子般地 /~ness *n.* ‖ ~ **cat** (美国) 1. 政治运动的出资人(尤指本人即为竞选人) 2. 有财有势的人,大亨 3. 自鸣得意的懒人 /~ **farm** (美国)减肥疗养地 /~'/**head** *n.*(口)笨蛋,呆子 /~'**headed** *adj.*(口)愚笨的

fatal [ˈfeitl] *adj.* 1. 命运的;决定命运的 2. 命中注定的 3. 致命的;毁灭性的;不幸的 ‖ ~ly *adv.*

fatalism [ˈfeitəlizəm] *n.* 宿命论 ‖ **fatalist** *n.* 宿命论者

fatalistic [ˌfeitəˈlistik] *adj.* 宿命的;宿命论的 ‖ -ally *adv.*

fatality [fəˈtæliti] *n.* 1. 命运决定的事物 2. 命运,天数;厄运;宿命论 3. 灾祸,灾难 4. 死亡(事故) 5. 致命性

fate [feit] *n.* 1. 命运,天数 2. 毁灭;灾祸 3. 死亡 — *vt.*[常用被动语态]命定,注定 ‖ -d *adj.* 1. 命运决定的 2. 注定要毁灭的

fateful [ˈfeitful] *adj.* 1. 命中注定的 2. 与命运有关的,重大的;a ~ decision 重大决定 ‖ ~ly *adv.* /~ness *n.*

father [ˈfɑːðə] *n.* 1. 父亲 2.[常~s]祖先;前辈;长辈 3. 创始人,奠基人;创造者,发明者;根源,源泉 4.[常~s](城市、团体等的)长老,长者;(议会的)元老;(古罗马)元老院议员 5.[F-]上帝;(三位一体中的)圣父[常作 F-](阐明教义的)早期基督教著作家;[用作对教士、牧师的尊称]神父 — *vt.* 1.(指

父而言)生(孩子);当... 的父亲;承认自己为... 的父亲 2. 父亲般对待;保护;治理 3. 创立;制订(计划等);创作,发明;培养 ‖ ~hood *n.* 父亲的身份(或资格);父性;父权 / ~less *adj.* 1. 没有父亲的 2. 生父不明的 / ~like *adj.* & *adv.* 父亲般的(地) ‖ Father Christmas 圣诞老人 / ~-in-law([复] ~s-in-law) *n.* 1. 岳父;公公(丈夫的父亲) 2. 继父 / ~land *n.* 祖国

fatherly ['fɑːðəli] *adj.* 1. 父亲的 2. 父亲般的;爱护的;慈祥的 ‖ **fatherliness** *n.*

fathom ['fæðəm] ([复] fathom(s)) *n.* 拓,英寻(长度单位,合6英尺或 1.829 米,主要用于测量水深) — *vt.* 1. (用测深绳)测量... 的深度 2. 推测;揣摩;了解

fathomless ['fæðəmlis] *adj.* 1. 深不可测的;无法计量的 2. 无法了解的 ‖ ~ly *adv.* / ~ness *n.*

fatigue [fə'tiːg] *n.* 1. 疲劳,劳累 2. 【物】(金属材料等的)疲劳 3. 【医】疲劳(指组织、器官等暂时失去对刺激的反应能力) 4. 累活 5.【军】杂役,劳动 5. [~s](士兵担任杂役时穿的)劳动服,工作服 — *vt.* 1. 使疲劳 2. 使(金属材料等)疲劳 — *vi.* 1. 疲劳 2. (金属材料等)疲劳 3. (士兵)干杂役 ‖ ~ clothes,~ dress【军】劳动服,工作服 / ~ duty【军】杂役,劳动(如打扫兵营) / ~ party【军】杂役队,劳动队

fatling ['fætliŋ] *n.* 养肥备宰的幼畜

fatten ['fætn] *vt.* 1. 养肥(*up*) 2. 使肥沃 3. 使充实 — *vi.* 1. 长肥 2. (靠 ...)发财,致富(*on*)

fatty ['fæti] *adj.* 1. 脂肪的;油脂的;油腻的 2. 肥胖的 3.【医】脂肪组织的 — *n.* 胖子

fatuity [fə'tjuːiti] *n.* 愚昧;昏庸;蠢

fatuous ['fætjuəs] *adj.* 1. 愚昧的;昏庸的;蠢的 2. 虚幻的,不真实的 ‖ ~ly *adv.* / ~ness *n.*

faucet ['fɔːsit] *n.* 1. (美)旋塞,开关,水龙头 2. (英)(连接管子的)承口,插口

fault [fɔːlt] *n.* 1. 缺点,毛病 2. 错误 [只用单](承担错误的)责任;过失 4.【地】断层 5. 故障 6. (网球等的)发球失误 — *vt.* 1. 找 ... 的缺点;挑剔 2. 【地】为... 产生断层 — *vi.* 1. 弄错,出差错 2.【地】产生断层 ‖ ~ finder *n.* 喜欢挑剔的人,吹毛求疵的人;故障探测器 / ~ finding *n.* 找岔子,挑剔 *adj.* 喜欢挑剔的,吹毛求疵的

faultless ['fɔːltlis] *adj.* 无错误的;无缺点的,完美无缺的;无可指责的 ‖ ~ly *adv.* / ~ness *n.*

faulty ['fɔːlti] *adj.* 有错误的;有缺点的,不完善的 ‖ **faultily** *adv.* / **faultiness** *n.*

faun [fɔːn] *n.* (古罗马传说中半人半羊的)农牧之神

fauna ['fɔːnə] ([复] faunae ['fɔːniː] 或 faunas) *n.* (某一地区或某一时期的)动物群

faux pas ['fəu 'pɑː] ([复] faux pas ['fəu 'pɑːz]) (法) 有失检点的(或 动) 行动

favo(u)r ['feivə] *n.* 1. 好感;喜爱;欢心,宠爱 2. 偏爱;偏袒 3. 赞成,赞同 4. 恩惠;善意的行为 5. 庇护 6. (古)信,函件 7. 纪念品;礼物(尤指小礼物);徽章 — *vt.* 1. 喜爱;宠爱;支持;赞成 2. 赐予,给予(*with*) 3. 有利于,有助于 4. 偏爱;偏袒

favo(u)rable ['feivərəbl] *adj.* 1. (对于...) 赞成的(*to*);称赞的 2. 有利的 ‖ ~ness *n.* / **favo(u)rably** *adv.*

favo(u)red ['feivəd] *adj.* 1. 受到优待的;有天赋的 2. 受优惠的;优惠的 3. [常用以构成复合词]有... 容貌的,有...

外貌的;ill-～容貌难看的

favo(u)rite ['feivərit] *n.* **1.** 特别喜欢的人 (或物) **2.** 受宠爱的人;亲信,心腹 **3.** 最有希望获胜者(尤指马) — *adj.* 特别喜爱的 ‖ ～ son *n.* 受宠爱的儿子 **2.** 在故乡受到尊敬和称赞的人 **3.** 《美》在政党全国代表大会上被本州代表拥护为总统候选人的人

favo(u)ritism ['feivəritizəm] *n.* **1.** 偏爱;偏袒 **2.** 得宠

fawn¹ [fɔːn] *vi.* **1.** (狗等)摇尾乞怜 **2.** 奉承;讨好 (*on, upon*)

fawn² [fɔːn] *n.* **1.** (未满一岁的)幼鹿 **2.** 小山羊;小动物 **3.** 鹿毛色;浅黄褐色 — *vt.* & *vi.* 生(小鹿,小山羊或小动物) — *adj.* 浅黄褐色的

fax [fæks] *n.* 传真;传真机 — *vt.* 用传真传输(文件)

fay [fei] *n.* 《诗》小妖精;仙女

faze [feiz] *vt.* 打扰;惊扰;使窘狼;使担忧 — *n.* 混乱;狼狈;忧虑

FBI *abbr.* Federal Bureau of Investigation(美国)联邦调查局

fc. *abbr.* franc

Fe [化] 元素铁(iron)的符号

fealty ['fiːəlti] *n.*(对封建主的)效忠;孝顺

fear [fiə] *vt.* **1.** 害怕,畏惧 **2.** 担心(about) **3.** 敬畏(神等) — *vi.* **1.** 害怕;感到顾虑 **2.** 担心;担忧,担心 — *n.* **1.** 害怕,恐惧 **2.** 担心;忧虑;值得忧虑之处 **3.** (对神等的)敬畏

fearful ['fiəful] *adj.* **1.** 可怕的,吓人的;害怕的;担心的;胆怯的 (*of, that, lest*) **2.** 《口》非常的;极坏的;很大的:in a ～ mess 非常混乱/a ～ liar 大骗子 ‖ ～ly *adv.* / ～ness *n.*

fearless ['fiəlis] *adj.* 不怕的,大胆的,无畏的 ‖ ～ly *adv.* / ～ness *n.*

fearsome ['fiəsəm] *adj.* **1.** 可怕的,吓人的 **2.** 胆小的;羞怯的 ‖ ～ly *adv.* / ～ness *n.*

feasibility [ˌfiːziˈbiliti] *n.* 可行性;可能性 ‖ ～ study 可行性研究

feasible ['fiːzibl] *adj.* **1.** (计划等)可行的,行得通的,可实行的 **2.** 《口》似真的;可能的;有理的 / **feasibly** *adv.*

feast [fiːst] *n.* **1.** 盛宴;筵席 **2.** 节日,节期(尤指宗教节日) **3.** 《感官,精神等方面的》享受,使人极感愉快的东西 — *vt.* **1.** 盛宴款待;设宴招待 **2.** 使十分愉快;使(感官等)得到享受 (*on, upon*) — *vi.* 参加宴会;享受;尽情地吃,饱餐 (*on, upon*)

feat [fiːt] *n.* **1.** 功绩;业绩 **2.** 武艺;技艺

feather ['feðə] *n.* **1.** 羽毛;翎毛 **2.** (箭、帽的)羽饰 **3.** 禽类(指猎物) **4.** 种类;本类:birds of a ～ 一丘之貉 **5.** 心情:in high ～ 情绪好 — *vt.* **1.** 为…镶上羽毛;用羽毛覆盖;用羽毛装饰 **2.** (收回划桨时)使(桨)与水面平行 — *vi.* **1.** 长羽毛 **2.** 使桨与水面平行 ‖ ～ bed **1.** 羽毛褥垫;安有羽毛褥垫的床 **2.** 安适的处境;闲职 / ～ **1.** 实施限产超额 **2.** 使实施限产超额 **2.** 以政府津贴资助 **3.** 娇养,溺爱 / ～brain. ～ **bed** *n.* 愚蠢的人;轻率的人 / ～.brained. / ～.headed *adj.* 愚蠢的;轻率的 / ～weight *n.* **1.** 体重很轻的人;轻微的东西 **2.** 《拳击》次轻量级(或羽量级)运动员;(择跃的)轻量级运动员 *adj.* **1.** 轻的 **2.** (拳击)次轻量级(或羽量级)的;(择跃的)轻量级的 **3.** 轻微的;琐细的

feathery ['feðəri] *adj.* **1.** 长着羽毛(或羽状物)的 **2.** 羽毛似的 **3.** 轻软的

feature ['fiːtʃə] *n.* **1.** 面貌的一部分(眼、口、鼻等) **2.** 脸型;[～s]面貌,相貌 **3.**

特征;特色;(地理)要素;地形地物 4. (报纸等的)特写;(电影)正片,故事片;特别吸引人的东西 — **vt. 1.** 是…的色角 **2.** 以…为特色 **3.** 特写;特载;以…作为号召物;(电影)由…主演 **vi.** 描绘…的特征 — **vi.** 起重要作用;作重要角色 ‖ ~less **adj.** 无特色的、平凡的 / '~ film 正片,故事片 / '~-length **adj.** (电影)达到正片应有长度的

featured ['fiːtʃəd] **adj.** [用以构成复合词]有…面貌特征的:sharp-~ 面部轮廓分明的

Feb. **abbr.** February

February ['februəri] **n.** 二月(略作 Feb.)

feces ['fiːsiːz] [复] **n.** 粪;排泄物;渣滓

fecund ['fiːkənd, 'fekənd] **adj.** 生殖力旺盛的;多产的;丰饶的;肥沃的 ‖ ~ity [fi'kʌnditi] **n.**

fed [fed] feed 的过去式和过去分词

federal ['fedərəl] **adj. 1.** 联盟的;联合的 **2.** 联邦的;联邦制的 **3.** [F-]美国联邦政府的 ‖ **Federal Bureau of Investigation** (美国)联邦调查局(略作 FBI) / **Federal Reserve Bank** (美国)联邦储备银行(略作 FRB)

federate ['fedərət] **adj.** 同盟的;联邦的 — ['fedəreit] **vt. & vi.** (使)结成同盟(或联邦)

federation [ˌfedə'reiʃən] **n.** 同盟,联盟;联合会;联邦;联邦政府 ‖ ~ist **n.** 联合主义者

fedora [fi'dɔːrə] **n.** 浅顶软呢男帽

fee [fiː] **n. 1.** 费(如会员费,学费,入场费,手续费等);酬金 **2.** 赏金,小费 — **vt. 1.** 付费(或小费)给…;雇;雇用;聘请

feeble ['fiːbl] **adj. 1.** 虚弱的,无力的 **2.** 微弱的;薄弱的 ‖ ~ness **n.** / **feebly** **adv.** ‖ ~'-minded **adj.** 极笨的;弱智的

feed [fiːd] (fed [fed]) **vt. 1.** 喂(养);词(养);给…吃,饲吃 **2.** 供应(饲料)给…(某物)喂(给) **3.** 向…供给(with);加进(原料等)(to) **4.** [电子]馈给,馈送;通过线路向电台传送;以供广播 **5.** 放牧(牲畜) **6.** 满足(欲望等);加深(恶感等)情绪 **7.** 为(某种情绪)提台词;传球给…(喂球) — **vi. 1.** (牛、马等)吃东西 **2.** 用餐 **3.** 以…为食物(on, upon) **4.** 流入;进入(into)【电子】馈入 — **n. 1.**(动物或婴儿的)一餐,一顿;喂食;进食 **2.** 饲料;牧草一次喂给的饲料 **3.** 【机】进给;进料;给水;进料器;进刀;【电子】馈电,供电 **4.**〈口〉一餐;丰盛的一餐 ‖ ~ **back** **n. 1.** 反馈;(信息等的)返回,反应;反馈的信息 ~ **bag** (挂在马头下的)饲料袋 / '~-in **n.** 食物赈济会 **adj.** 【机】进给的;进料的

feeder ['fiːdə] **n. 1.** 饲养员;给食的人;喂饲料工人 **2.** 奶瓶;〔英〕围涎 **3.** 进食的人(或动物等) **4.** 进料器;给水器;加油器;加煤器;(机床的)进刀装置 **5.** 【电子】馈电线,馈路 **6.** (河流的)支流;【矿】支脉 **7.** 铁路支线(= ~ line);航空支线(= ~ airline) **8.** 喜剧演员的逗哏搭档 **9.** 煽动者;刺激物

feel [fiːl] (felt [felt]) **vt. 1.** 摸,触;摸索,探索 **2.** 感到;觉得,感知 **3.** 以为,认为 **4.** 摸索…的身体(尤指生殖器等部位) — **vi. 1.** 有…的感觉 **2.** (人)有某种感觉 **3.** (东西)摸上去有某种感觉;给人某种感觉 **3.** 摸索;摸索着寻找;同情(for) **3.** [只用单] **1.** 摸,触;触觉,感觉 **2.** (事物给人的)感受(for) ‖ ~er **n. 1.** 触角;触须 **2.** 试探手段;试探者;试探器;探子 **3.** 侦察兵 ‖ [机]测微规,厚薄规 **4.**〈美〉手指(尤指中指)

feeling ['fiːliŋ] **n. 1.** 触觉;知觉;感觉 **2.**

心情,情绪 3.[~s](与理智相对而言的感情)情感,情感:hurt sb.'s ~s 伤害某人的感情/relieve one's ~s 发泄感情 4. 同情;怜悯 5. 恶感;反感;气愤:an act that arouses strong ~(s)引起强烈反感的行为 6. 看法;感想;预感 7.(对艺术等的)感受;敏感,鉴赏力 — **adj. 1.** 富于感情的;富于同情心的 **2.** 衷心的 ‖ **~·ly** *adv.*

feet [fi:t] **foot** 的复数

feign [fein] *vt.* **1.** 假装,佯作 **2.** 捏造(借口等)

feint [feint] *n.* **1.** 假象,假装 **2.** 佯攻,佯击 — *vi.* 佯攻,虚击(*against,at,upon*)

feldspar ['feldspɑ:] *n.*【矿】长石

felicitate [fi'lisiteit] *vt.* 祝贺 ‖ **fe·lici'tation** *n.*

felicitous [fi'lisitəs] *adj.*(措词等)恰当的;巧妙的

felicity [fi'lisiti] *n.* **1.** 幸福,福气 **2.**(措词等的)恰当;巧妙 **3.** 恰当(或巧妙)的语句

feline ['fi:lain] *adj.* **1.** 猫的;猫科的 **2.** 像猫一样的;疼痒的,奸诈的 — *n.* 猫;猫科动物

fell[1] [fel] **fall** 的过去式

fell[2] [fel] *vt.* **1.** 击倒,打倒;(疾病等)致…于死地 **2.** 砍倒;砍伐

fell[3] [fel] *n.*(带毛的)兽皮,生皮

fell[4] [fel] *adj.* 凶猛的;残暴的;可怕的;致命的

fellow ['feləu] *n.* **1.** 伙伴;同事;同辈;同时代人 **2.** 同伙;同谋者 **3.** 对等者;对手:pass all one's ~s 超过所有的对手 **4.** 人;家伙;小伙子;某个人 **5.** 男朋友;求婚者 **6.** 配对物,一对中之一 **7.**(大学中的)研究员 **8.**(学术团体的)会员 — *adj.* 一起(学习、工作等)的;同

类的:a ~ student 同学/a ~ countryman 同胞/~ creatures 同类的动物;(同属人类的)人 ‖ '~'man *n.*(同属人类的)人,同胞/~ trave(l)er *n.* 旅伴 **2.**(政治上的)同路人,同情者

fellowship ['feləuʃip] *n.* **1.** 伙伴关系;交情;友谊 **2.**(经历、活动、利害关系等方面的)共同参与;合伙关系 **3.**(在共同的宗旨下组成的)团体;会;联谊会 **4.**(常指学术团体的)会员资格 **5.**(大学中的)研究员职位;研究员薪金;研究员基金

felon ['felən] *n.* 重罪犯

felonious [fi'ləuniəs] *adj.* 重罪(性质)的

felony ['feləni] *n.*【律】重罪

felspar ['felspɑ:] *n.* = feldspar

felt[1] [felt] **feel** 的过去式和过去分词

felt[2] [felt] *n.* 毡;毡制品:毡状材料 — *adj.* 毡制的 ‖ '~-tip **(ped) pen** 毡制粗头笔

fem. *abbr.* **1.** female **2.** feminine

female ['fi:meil] *adj.* **1.** 女(性)的;妇女的 **2.** 雌的;【植】雌性的;雌蕊的 **3.**【机】凹的,内的:a ~ screw 阴螺旋,内螺纹 **4.** 柔弱的;(声、色)柔和的;(音调)高的 — *n.* **1.** 女子 **2.** 雌性动物 **3.**【植】雌性植物,雌株 ‖ ~ **impersonator** 扮女子的男演员/~ **suffrage** 妇女选举权(或参政权)

feminine ['feminin] *adj.* **1.** 女性的;妇女的 **2.** 娇柔的;女子气的 **3.**【语】阴性的:a ~ noun 阴性名词/the ~ gender 阴性

femininity [,femi'niniti] *n.* **1.** 女子气质 **2.** 女人气 **3.**[总称]妇女

feminism ['feminizəm] *n.* **1.** 男女平等主义 **2.** 争取妇女权运动 ‖ **feminist** *n.* 男女平等主义者

femur ['fiːmə] *n.* 1.【解】股骨 2.(昆虫的)腿节、股节

fen [fen] *n.* 1. 沼泽 2. [the Fens] (英国剑桥郡及林肯郡的)沼泽地带

fen [fʌn] (单复同) (汉) *n.* 分(中国辅币单位)

fence [fens] *n.* 1. 栅栏;围栏;篱笆 2. 击剑(术) 3. 买卖赃物的人(或场所) 4.《美》(常~s)(公职人员)争取政治支持的途径;政治利益 — *vt.* 1. 把…用栅(或篱)围起来(about. in. round. up) 2. 筑栅防护(from. against) 3. 用栅栏拦开;隔开(off. out) — *vi.* 1. 击剑 2. 搪塞;回避正面答复问题 ‖ ~ **r** *n.* 1. 击剑者 2. 修筑栅篱的人 ‖ ~ **rider**《美》牧场中检修栅栏的工人;骑墙派 / ~ **sitter** *n.* 骑墙派

fencing ['fensiŋ] *n.* 1. 栅栏;围栏;篱笆 2. 筑栅栏的材料 3. 击剑(术)

fend [fend] *vt.* 挡开(off) — *vi.* 供养;照料(for)

fender ['fendə] *n.* 1. 防御物;防护板;防撞物 2. 火炉围栏 3.(车辆的)挡泥板 4.(船只的)碰垫,护舷木

fennel ['fenl] *n.*【植】茴香

feoff [fef] *n.* 采邑,封地 — *vt.* 授封地给

ferment ['fəːment] *n.* 1. 酵素;酶 2. 发酵 3. 激动;骚动 — [fə'ment] *vt.* & *vi.* 1.(使)发酵 2.(使)激动;(使)骚动 ‖ ~ **ation** [ˌfəːmen'teiʃən] *n.* / ~ **ative** [fə'mentətiv] *adj.* 发酵的

fermium ['fəːmiəm] *n.*【化】镄

fern [fəːn] *n.*【植】蕨 ‖ ~ **y** *adj.* 蕨的;像蕨的;多蕨的

ferocious [fə'rəuʃəs] *adj.* 1. 凶恶的;凶猛的;残忍的 2.(口)(风、热等)十分强烈的;(胃口等)极大的 ‖ ~ **ly** *adv.* / ~ **ness** *n.*

ferocity [fə'rɔsiti] *n.* 1. 凶恶;凶猛;残忍 2. 暴行

ferret ['ferit] *n.* 雪貂,白鼬 — *vi.* 1. 用雪貂狩猎 2. 搜索(about. around. for) — *vt.* 搜出,查获(秘密;罪犯等)(out)

Ferris ['feris] *n.* ‖ ~ **wheel** 费里斯转轮(在垂直转动的巨轮上挂有坐位的游乐设施)

ferro- *comb. form* 1. 表示"铁": ferroconcrete 2. 表示"铁和…": ferrochrome 3. 表示"亚铁": ferrocyanide

ferrochrome ['ferəukrəum] *n.*【冶】铁铬合金

ferroconcrete ['ferəu'kɔŋkriːt] *n.*【建】钢筋混凝土

ferrocyanide [ˌferəu'saiənaid] *n.*【化】氰亚铁酸盐,亚铁氰化物

ferrous ['ferəs] *adj.* 1. 铁的;含铁的:~ and non-~ metals 黑色及有色金属 2.【化】亚铁的,二价铁的

ferrule ['ferul] *n.* 1.(棍棒顶端等的)金属箍,金属包头 2.【机】套圈;箍

ferry ['feri] *n.* 1. 摆渡;渡口;渡船场 2. 渡船 — *vt.* 1. 渡运(乘渡船)渡过 2. 运送 3.(越海)空运 — *vi.* 摆渡(船)来往行驶 ‖ ~ **boat** *n.* 渡船 / ~ **man** *n.* 渡船工人

fertile ['fəːtail] *adj.* 1. 肥沃的;富饶的 2. 丰产的,多产的 3.(创造力或想象力)丰富的 4.(在主意等方面)多的(in) 5.【植】有雌蕊的;(花药)含花粉的,产孢子的;(核)可变为易裂变物质的,增殖性的 ‖ ~ **ly** *adv.* / ~ **ness** *n.*

fertility [fəː'tiliti] *n.* 1. 肥沃;肥力;丰产,多产 2.【生】能育性;繁殖力 3.(思想等的)丰富 4. 人口出生率

fertilize ['fəːtilaiz] *vt.* 1. 使肥沃;施肥于;使多产;使丰富 2.【生】使受精

,fertili'zation *n.*

fertilizer ['fə:tilaizə] *n.* 肥料(尤指化学肥料)

fervent ['fə:vənt] *adj.* 热情的；强烈的 ‖ **~ly** *adv.*

fervid ['fə:vid] *adj.* 热情的；热烈的；激烈的 ‖ **~ly** *adv.* / **~ness** *n.*

fervo(u)r ['fə:və] *n.* 热烈；热情

festal ['festəl] *adj.* **1.** 节日的；假日的 **2.** 喜庆的；欢乐的 ‖ **~ly** *adv.*

fester ['festə] *vi.* **1.** 溃烂；化脓 **2.** (怨恨等)郁积 —*vt.* 使溃烂；使化脓

festival ['festəvəl] *n.* **1.** 节日；喜庆日：the Spring *Festival* 春节 **2.** (定期举行的)音乐节；戏剧节 **3.** 欢乐；欢庆

festive ['festiv] *adj.* **1.** 节日的；节日似的；欢宴的；欢乐的；欢庆的 ‖ **~ly** *adv.*

festivity [fes'tiviti] *n.* **1.** 欢乐；欢庆 **2.** [常 festivities] 庆祝；庆祝活动

festoon [fes'tu:n] *n.* **1.** (中间下垂两端挂住的)花彩：~ lighting (电)灯彩 **2.** 【建】垂花雕饰 —*vt.* 给 ... 饰花彩；结彩于

fetal ['fi:tl] *adj.* 胎儿的

fetch [fetʃ] *vt.* **1.** (去) 拿来；(去) 请来；(去) 接来 **2.** 吸(一口气)；发出(叹声，呻吟等) **3.** 引出(笑声、眼泪等)；吸引(观众等) **4.** 售得、卖得 **5.** 给以(一拳、一击等) **6.** 〈口〉使信服 (round) —*vi.* **1.** 取物 **2.** (猎狗)衔回猎获物 **3.** 绕道而行 (about，round) —*vt.* **1.** 拿，取；衔回猎获物 **2.** 计谋；诡计

fetching ['fetʃiŋ] *adj.* 〈口〉动人的，吸引人的，迷人的 ‖ **~ly** *adv.*

fete, fête [feit] *n.* **1.** 节日；喜庆日 **2.** 盛大的招待会；(为募捐而举行的)户外招待会 —*vt.* 款待；盛宴招待；(通过举行宴会等)纪念

fetid ['fetid] *adj.* 恶臭的 ‖ **~ly** *adv.* /

~ness *n.*

fetish ['fi:tiʃ] *n.* **1.** 原始人认为具有神力而加以崇拜的物品；物神 **2.** (喻)迷恋(物)；迷信(物) **3.** [心]恋物 ‖ **~ism** *n.* **1.** 拜物教；物神崇拜 **2.** 盲目崇拜 [心]恋物癖 ‖ **~ist** *n.* 拜物教徒；盲目崇拜者；[心]恋物癖者

fetlock ['fetlɔk] *n.* **1.** (马蹄后上部的)丛毛，距毛 **2.** 球节 (生距毛的突起部分) **3.** (生距毛的)肢关节

fetology [fi:'tɔlədʒi] *n.* 胎儿学 ‖ **fetologist** *n.* 胎儿学家

fetter ['fetə] *n.* **1.** [常~s] 脚镣 **2.** (喻) 桎梏；束缚；羁绊 —*vt.* **1.** 为 ... 上脚镣 **2.** 束缚；羁绊

fettle ['fetl] **1.** (身体)状况 **2.** 情绪；精神

fetus ['fi:təs] *n.* 胎；胎儿

feud [fju:d] *n.* 长期不和；(部落或家族间的)世仇 —*vi.* 长期争斗；世代结仇

feudal ['fju:dl] *adj.* 封建的；封建制度的

feudalism ['fju:dəlizəm] *n.* 封建主义；封建制度 ‖ **feudalist** *n.* 封建主义者

feudalistic [ˌfju:də'listik] *adj.* 封建主义(者)的

fever ['fi:və] *n.* **1.** 发热，发烧；热度 **2.** 发病 **3.** 高度兴奋，狂热 ‖ **~ed** *adj.* 发烧的；高度兴奋的 ‖ **~ blister** 【医】唇疱疹 / **~ heat 1.** 发热(指发烧时的体温) **2.** 高度兴奋，狂热 / **~ pitch** 高度兴奋，狂热

feverish ['fi:vəriʃ] *adj.* **1.** 发烧的；有热病症状的 **2.** 发烧引起的 **3.** 容易引起热病的 **4.** 狂热的；兴奋的；激动的 ‖ **~ly** *adv.* / **~ness** *n.*

few [fju:] *adj.* **1.** 少数的，不多的：every ~ weeks 每隔几星期 **2.** [表示否定] 很少的，几乎没有的：[a ~] [表示肯定] 有些，几个：*Few* people know it. 几乎没有什么人知道这一点。/ A ~ people know it. 有几个人知道这一点。— *n.* [用作复] **1.** [表示否定]很少数，几乎没有：[a～] [表示肯定]少数。几个 *Few of my friends were there.* 我的朋友中几乎没有人在那里。/A ～ of us speak French. 我们中间有几个人能讲法语。/[the ～] 少数人：the privileged ～ 少数特权阶层分子

fez [fez] *n.* 非斯帽，土耳其帽(地中海东岸各国男人戴的圆筒形无边毡帽)

fiancé [fi'ɔnsei, fiɔŋ'sei]〈法〉*n.* 未婚夫

fiancée [fi'ɔnsei, fiɔŋ'sei]〈法〉*n.* 未婚妻

fiasco [fi'æskəu]([复] fiasco(e)s) *n.* 大败，惨败；可耻的下场

fiat ['faiæt] *n.* **1.** 命令；法令 **2.** 许可；批准

fib [fib] *n.* 无伤大雅的谎言，小谎 — (fibbed; fibbing) *vi.* 撒小谎 ‖ **fibber** *n.* 惯撒小谎的人

fiber ['faibə] *n.* = fibre

fibr- *comb. form* 表示"纤维"：fibrin

fibre ['faibə] *n.* **1.** 纤维；纤维物质 **2.** 纤维制品；硬化纸板 **3.** 结构；质地；力量；性格 **4.** 【植】须根 ‖ ～ **board** *n.* 纤维板 / ～ **glass** 玻璃纤维，玻璃棉 / ～ **optics** 纤维光学；光学纤维

fibrin ['faibrin] *n.* 【生化】(血)纤维蛋白

fibro- *comb. form* = fibr-

fibroid ['faibrɔid] *adj.* 纤维性的；纤维样的；由纤维组成的 — *n.* 【医】纤维瘤；子宫肌瘤

fibrous ['faibrəs] *adj.* **1.** 含纤维的；纤维状的 **2.** 纤维构成的 **2.** 能分成纤维的 **3.** 坚韧的；有筋骨的

fibster ['fibstə] *n.*〈口〉惯撒小谎的人

fibula ['fibjulə] *n.* 【解】腓骨

-fication *suf.* 表示"形成"，"…化"：amplification, glorification

fickle ['fikl] *adj.* (在感情等方面)易变的，无常的 ‖ ～**ness** *n.*

fiction ['fikʃən] *n.* **1.** 虚构，杜撰，捏造 **2.** 小说 **3.** 虚构的事 **4.** (以可能虚构的事为事实作出的)法律上的推定

fictional ['fikʃənl] *adj.* 虚构的；小说的 ‖ ～**ize** *vt.* 把…编成小说 / ～**ly** *adv.*

fictitious [fik'tiʃəs] *adj.* **1.** 虚构的，杜撰的；非真实的 **2.** 习惯上假定的；(假设的) ‖ ～**ly** *adv.* / ～**ness** *n.*

fiddle ['fidl] *n.* **1.**〈口〉小提琴；提琴类乐器 **2.** 欺骗行为 — *vi.* **1.** 拉提琴 **2.** 无目的地用手摆弄(*with*) **3.** 触摸；乱动(指别人的东西)(*with*) **4.** 游荡；不经意地干活(*about, around*) — *vt.* **1.** 用小提琴演奏(曲调) **2.** 浪费(时间)(*away*) **3.**〈俚〉欺骗；伪造(帐目等) ‖ ～**deedee** [ˌfidldi'di:] *int.* 胡说！废话 / ～**-faddle** ['fidlˌfædl] *vi.* 忙于琐事；大惊小怪 — *n.* 琐碎小事 / ～**stick** *n.* 〈口〉提琴弓 / ～**sticks** *int.* 胡说；讨厌

fiddler ['fidlə] *n.* **1.**〈口〉小提琴手；小提琴家；胡乱拨弄者；瞎摆弄者；游荡者；(帐目等的)弄虚作假者 **2.** 【动】招潮(蟹之一大小的蟹)(= ～ crab)

fidelity [fi'deliti] *n.* **1.** 忠诚，忠实(*to*) **2.** 逼真，精确 **3.** (收音，录音设备等的)逼真度，保真度

fidget ['fidʒit] *vi.* **1.** 坐立不安，烦躁 **2.** (不安地或心不在焉地)乱弄；玩弄(*with*) — *vt.* 使坐立不安；使烦躁 — *n.* **1.** [常～s]坐立不安，不安定；烦躁 **2.** 烦躁不安的人

fidgety ['fidʒiti] *adj.* **1.** 坐立不安的，不安的 **2.** 烦躁的 **2.** 为琐事操心的；过分注意细节的 ‖ **fidgetiness** *n.*

fiducial [fi'dju:ʃjəl] *adj.* 信托的；信用的

fiduciary [fi'dju:ʃjəri] *adj.* **1.** 信托的；信用的 **2.** 受信托的；(纸币)信用发行的

— n. 受信托者

fie [fai] **int.** [表示嫌恶、震惊等]呸! 啐! *Fie* upon you! 去你的!

fief [fi:f] **n.** = feoff

field [fi:ld] **n. 1.** 原野、旷野 **2.** (一块)田;牧场 **3.** (冰、雪等的)茫茫一大片 **4.** 战场,战地;作战训练(或演习)区域 **5.** 战斗;战役:a hard-fought ~血战 **6.** 运动场;(飞行等用的)场(地);(棒球等)外场 **7.** (参加比赛的)全体运动员;上场队员(棒球、板球运动的)防守队员 **8.** (煤、天然气等的)埋藏地带,矿田:煤田;油田:an oil ~ 油田 **9.** 实地;野外 **10.** 现场,现地 **11.** 【物】场;【数】场 **12.** (望远镜等的)视场,视野 **13.** (旗、画、钱币等的)底子,底色 — **vt. 1.** 把(谷物等)留于场上 **2.** 使(球队或球员等)上场;把…投入战场 **3.** (棒球、板球运动中)接(或截)(球);守(球) **4.** 圆满地答复 — **vi.** (棒球、板球运动中)担任外场员(或守队队员) **‖ ~ day 1.** 田间(或)野外的实地的一天 **2.** 野外的、实地的 **3.** 【体】田赛的 **‖ ~er n.** (棒球、板球运动)外场员;守场员 **‖ ~ army** 野战集团军;~book 野外工作记录本 **~ day 1.** 野外演习日 **2.** 户外集会 **3.** 体育比赛日 **4.** 野外科学活动日 **5.** 特别愉快的时刻;获得意外成功的日子 **6.** 有重要意义(如辩论等)的日子 **/ ~ event** 【体】田赛项目 **/ ~ glasses** 双简望远镜 **/ ~ grade** 【军】校级 **/ ~ hand 1.** 田间农业劳动者 **2.** (美)农场黑奴 **/ ~ hospital** 野战医院 **/ ~ marshal** (英)陆军元帅 **/ ~ mouse** 田鼠 **/ ~ sports** 野外运动(打猎、赛马、射击等) **/ ~ work 1.** 野战工事 **2.** 野外测量;野外考察;实地考察工作;现场调查工作

fiend [fi:nd] **n. 1.** 魔鬼;[the F-]魔王;撒

且 **2.** 恶魔般的人,极邪恶的人 **3.** 〈口〉…迷;…狂;对…嗜好成癖者 **4.** (某方面的)能手,神手

fiendish ['fi:ndiʃ] **adj.** 恶魔似的;残忍的;极坏的 **‖ ~ly adv. / ~ness n.**

fierce [fiəs] **adj. 1.** 凶猛的;残忍的(风暴、风势等)猛烈的 **3.** (战斗、演说等)激烈的(热、怒火、仇恨等)强烈的(脾气)暴躁的 **4.** (努力等)十分积极的,十分坚决的 **5.** (美)(疼痛等)难受的(光线)刺眼的 **‖ ~ly adv. / ~-ness n.**

fiery ['faiəri] **adj. 1.** 火的;冒火焰的;燃烧着的 **2.** 火一般的,如火如荼的 **2.** 火热的;红的;火红的 **3.** 激烈的 **4.** 易怒的,暴躁的 **5.** (眼)冒火的 **6.** 易燃的,易爆炸的 **‖ fierily adv. / fieriness n.**

fiesta [fi'esta] 〈西〉 **n.** 节日(特指在西班牙和拉丁美洲以游行和舞蹈等来庆祝的宗教节日);喜庆日;假日

fife [faif] **n.** (军乐中与鼓同奏发尖音的)横笛

fifteen ['fif'ti:n] **num.** 十五;十五个(人或物);第十五(卷、章、页等) — **n. 1.** 十五个(人或物)一组;橄榄球队队 **2.** (网球赛)一局中一方获得的第一分 **3.** 十五岁 **4.** 十五点钟(即下午三点) **‖ ~th num. 1.** 第十五(个)**2.** 十五分之一(的)**n.** (月的)第十五

fifth [fifθ] **num. 1.** 第五(个)**2.** 五分之一(的)— **n. 1.** (美)五分之一加仑(瓶)**2.** (月的)第五日 **‖ ~ly adv.** 第五(列举条目等时用)**‖ ~ column** 第五纵队(泛指敌人派入本国配合敌应的内奸)**/ ~ columnist** 第五纵队队员;间谍,内奸 **/ ~ wheel 1.** 备用轮 **2.** 多余的人(或物)

fiftieth ['fiftiiθ] **num. 1.** 第五十(个)**2.**

五十分之一(的)

fifty ['fifti] *num.* 五十;五十个(人或物);第五十(卷、章、页等) — *n.* 1. 五十个(人或物)一组 2.[fifties](世纪的)五十年代 3. 五十岁;[fifties]五十到五十九岁的时期 — *adj.* 许多的 ‖ `~·'` ~ *adv.* & *adj.* 各半(的),对半(的)

fig [fig] *n.* 1.【植】无花果;无花果树 2. 少许,一点儿 ‖ ~ **leaf** 1. 无花果叶 2.(裸体塑像上遮蔽阴部的)叶形物;遮羞布 / ~ **tree** 无花果树

fight [fait] (fought [fɔːt]) *vi.* 1. 打仗;搏斗;打架;争吵 2. 奋斗;战斗 3. 斗争;当职业拳击手 — *vt.* 1. 与 ... 打仗;与 ... 战斗;与 ... 斗争;与(火,疾病等)搏斗;与 ... 争吵;打(仗) 2. 指挥(士兵,军舰)进行战斗;与风暴搏斗 3. 为(事业,诉讼等)进行战斗;对(问题)进行争辩 4. 逗引(鸡、犬等)相斗 5. 用 ... 打 — *n.* 1. 战斗;打斗 2. 战斗精神;战斗力 3. 拳击赛;争吵 ‖ ~ **back** *n.* (英)回击等

fighter ['faitə] *n.* 1. 战士;兵士;斗争者,奋斗者 2. 战斗机,歼击机 3. 好斗的人 4.(职业)拳击手 ‖ ~ **bomber** *n.* 战斗轰炸机 / ~ **interceptor** *n.* 战斗截击机 / ~ **plane** 战斗机,歼击机

fighting ['faitiŋ] *n.* & *adj.* 战斗的;搏斗的(人) ‖ ~ **chance** 经过努力奋斗才能获得成功的机会;可能但不易得到的机会 / ~ **cock** *n.* 斗鸡;好斗的人 / ~ **top** 战斗樯楼(作为射击指挥所或高射炮台)

figment ['figmənt] *n.* 臆造的事物;虚构的事

figurative ['figjurətiv] *adj.* 比喻的,借喻的 ‖ ~ **ly** *adv.*

figure ['figə] *n.* 1. 外形,轮廓;体形;隐约可见的人影(或物影) 2. 图形;图案;(书本中的)插图;插表 3. 画像;塑像 4. 形象;人物 5. 数字(指数目字0到9或统计数字等);[~s](五位、六位等)位数 6. [~s]计算;算术 7. 价格 8. [~s]行情 ‖ ~ **of speech** 【语】修辞手段,修辞格 9.(溜冰,飞行的)花式 10.(舞蹈中的)舞步 — *vt.* 1. 描绘;塑造;想象 2. 用图案(或花纹等)装饰 3. 用数字表示(或标出) 4. 计算 5. 相信;估计,揣测 — *vi.* 1. 出现;露头角;扮演角色(as) 2. 计算;做算术 3. 考虑;估计 ‖ ~ **d** *adj.* 有形状的;用图画(或图表)表现的;有图案的 / ~ **eight** 8字形(如绳结、溜冰姿式、飞行样式等)/ ~ **head** *n.* 1.【船】船饰像 2. 挂名首脑;傀儡

figurine ['figjuriːn] *n.* 小雕像;小塑像

Fiji ['fiːdʒiː] *n.* 斐济(南太平洋岛国)

filagree ['filəgriː] *n.* = filigree

filament ['filəmənt] *n.* 1. 细丝;丝状物 2.【纺】长丝;单纤维 3.【植】花丝 4.(电灯泡、电子管的)灯丝;丝极

filbert ['filbət] *n.* 1.【植】欧洲榛;欧洲榛果实;榛果果实 2.〈美俚〉狂热者 — 迷

filch [filʃ] *vt.* 偷(不贵重的东西)

file¹ [fail] *n.* 1. 文件夹 2. 汇订的文件(或卡片等);档案;案卷;套书 3. 纵列 4.(国际象棋棋盘上的)格子纵列 — *vt.* 1. 把 ... 归档 2. 提出(申请等);呈请把 ... 备案 3. 用电话(或电报)向通讯社发送(稿子) 4. 命令(士兵)排成纵队行进 — *vi.* 1. 排成纵队行进 2.(在预选中)备案作候选人

file² [fail] *n.* 锉(刀) 2. 狡猾的人 — *vt.* 锉;把 ... 锉平;把 ... 锉光

filial ['filiəl] *adj.* 1. 子女的;孝顺的 2.【生】子代的,杂交后代的 ‖ ~ **ly** *adv.* ‖ ~ **piety** 孝道

filibuster ['filibʌstə] 〈美〉n.(用冗长的演说以妨碍议事等的)使用阻挠手段;阻挠议事者的行动 — vi. 阻挠议事 — vt. 阻碍(议案)通过

filigree ['filigri:] n. 金丝(或银丝、铜丝)的细工饰品

filings ['failiŋz] [复] n. 锉屑

Filipino [ˌfili'pi:nəu] n. 菲律宾人 — adj. 菲律宾人的;菲律宾的

fill [fil] vt. 1. 装满;盛满;注满;充满全部占据;占满;坐满 3. 堵塞;填塞;补(牙);填(表格等)(in, up, out)填有(姓名、地址等)(in) 4.(以食物)供给...(with) 5. 担任(职务);补(缺) 6. 满足(需要、要求) 7. 供应(定货);配(药方) 8.[海](风)张满(帆);调整(帆)使帆背受风 — vi. 充满;(帆被风)张满(with) 2. 饱;够;eat (weep) one's ~ 吃个饱(哭个够) 2. 足以填满某物之量;装填物 3.(铁路的)路堤;填方;填土 ‖ ~ er n. 1. 装填者 2. 装填物;搀入物(如搀入肥料中的土等);(油漆前堵塞缝隙的)填料 3.(报纸等的)补白 / ~ing n. 填补物(尤指牙科医生用来补牙的材料);(糕点的)馅子 ‖ ~ in n. 1. 临时填补空缺的人,替工;临时填补的工 2.(事实等)简明摘要 adj. 临时填补性的 / ~ing station 〈美〉汽车加油站

fillet ['filit] n. 1. 头串带;束发带 2. 肉片;鱼片;(猪、牛等的)里脊(肉);去骨纯鱼肉;牛排 — vt. 把(肉、鱼)切成鱼片;去掉(肉、鱼)的骨

fillip ['filip] n. 1. 弹指;轻击 2. 刺激;刺激因素 — vt. 1. 用指弹(弹)指 2. 刺激;激起(精神、记忆)

filly ['fili] n. 1. 小雌马(通常未满四岁) 2.〈俚〉活泼的姑娘

film [film] n. 1. 薄层;膜,薄膜 2. 薄雾;

轻烟 3. 胶卷;软片 4. 影片;电影 5.[医](眼的)薄翳 — vt. 1. 在...上覆以薄膜 2. 拍摄;把...拍成电影 — vi. 1. 生薄膜;变成朦胧 2. 摄制电影 3. 适于拍照(或摄成电影) ‖ ~ pack(装亮光下装入照相机的)软片暗盒 / ~ star 电影明星 / ~ strip n.(教学用的)片带,片条;幻灯片 / ~ studio 电影制片厂

filmlet ['filmlit] n. 电影短片

filmset ['filmset] n. 电影布景 — (filmset; filmsetting) vt. 照相排版(版) ‖ **filmsetter** n. 照相排版机 / **filmsetting** n. 照相排版

filmy ['filmi] adj. 1. 薄膜似的 2. 蒙着薄雾的;朦胧的 ‖ **filminess** n.

filter ['filtə] n. 1. 滤器;滤纸;多孔过滤物质(如砂、炭、纸、布等) 3. 滤光器;滤色镜;滤波器 4.(香烟嘴上的)过滤嘴;过滤香烟 5. 去尘(或烟、菌等)器 6.〈英〉(设在路口的)绿色箭头交通信号灯(亮时表示:主信号灯红灯亮时既允许车辆左转弯又允许车辆右转弯) — vt. 1. 过滤 2. 用过滤法除去(off, out) 3.〈英〉(车流在路口遇红灯时)允许(车辆)按绿色箭头向左(或向右)行驶 — vi. 1. 透过;渗出(口)(消息等)走漏;慢慢传开(out, through) 3.〈英〉(车流在路口遇红灯时)(车辆)按绿色箭头向左(或向右)行驶 ‖ ~ paper 滤纸 / ~ tip(香烟嘴上的)过滤嘴;过滤嘴香烟 / ~-tipped adj. 有过滤嘴的

filth [filθ] n. 1. 污秽;污物 2. 淫猥;猥亵语

filthy ['filθi] adj. 不洁的,污秽的;猥亵的 ‖ **filthily** adv. / **filthiness** n.

fin [fin] n. 1. 鳍 2.[机]翅(片);(铸件的)周缘薄片;散热片 3.[空]垂直安定

面；垂直尾翅 **4.**（火箭的）舵；尾翼，尾翅 **5.**（潜水时缚在脚上的）脚蹼

finable ['faɪnəbl] *adj.* 可罚款的；该罚款的

final ['faɪnl] *adj.* **1.** 最后的；最终的 **2.** 决定等不可更改的 — *n.* **1.**（常～s）期终考试；课程终结考试；决赛 **2.**（口）（报纸在一天中的）最后一次印刷；最后版 ‖ ～ist *n.* 决赛选手 ／～ly *adv.* **1.** 最后；最终 **2.** 不可更改地

finale [fɪ'nɑːli] *n.* **1.**（戏剧的）终场；最后一幕 **2.** 结尾 **3.**[音]终曲

finality [faɪ'nælɪti] *n.* 定局，不可改变性

finalize ['faɪnəlaɪz] *vt. & vi.* 把（计划等）最后定下来 ‖ ～**finali'zation** *n.*

finance ['faɪnæns, fɪ'næns] *n.* **1.** 财政；金融；财政学 **2.**（常～s）财源；资金 — *vt.* 供资金给为...提供资金

financial [faɪ'nænʃəl, fɪ'nænʃəl] *adj.* 财政的；金融的 ‖ ～ly *adv.* ／～ **year**（英）财政年度，会计年度（美国称 fiscal year）

financier [faɪ'nænsɪə, fɪ'nænsɪə] *n.* 财政家；金融家

finch [fɪntʃ] *n.*[动] 雀科鸣鸟（如燕雀、金翅雀等）

find [faɪnd]（found [faʊnd]）*vt.* **1.** 找到 **2.** 发现，发觉；感到 **3.** 找出；查明（out）**4.** 得到，获得（满足、支持、勇气等）**5.** 裁决；作出（子弹等）击中（目标）**7.** 供给，供应；筹集（经费等）— *vi.* 作出裁决（for, against）— *n.* 发现；发现物（尤指猎物、矿藏等）；被发现有惊人能力的人

finder ['faɪndə] *n.* **1.** 发现者；探测器 **2.**（大望远镜上的）寻星镜；（照相机的）取景器

finding ['faɪndɪŋ] *n.* **1.**[律] 裁决 **2.**（常～s）调查（或研究）的结果

fine¹ [faɪn] *adj.* **1.** 美好的；优良的；优

的；杰出的 **2.**（盐、糖、茶叶等）精制的 **3.**（金银等）纯净的；含量高的 **4.** 细的；纤细的；纤巧的；（差别等）细微难察的 **5.**（刀刃等）快的，锋利的；（感觉等）敏锐的，灵敏的 **6.** 好看的，漂亮的；硕大的 **7.**（天气）晴朗的 **8.**（情况等）良好的；健康的 **9.**（讲话、写作等）假作恭维的；委婉的；过分夸饰的；炫耀的 — *adv.* **1.**（口）很好 **2.**[常用以构成复合词] 细微地；精巧地；a ～-toothed comb 细齿梳子 — *n.* 好天气；in rain or ～不管天晴下雨 — *vt.* 使纯；澄清；精炼；使精细（在线条、比例等方面）使细（小）（*away, down*）— *vi.* **1.** 变纯；（液体）澄清；变得精细；（天气）转晴 **2.**（在线条、比例等方面）变细（小）；缩小（*away, down*）— ‖ ～**ly** *adv.* ／～**ness** *n.* ‖ ～ **art 1.**[总称] 美术作品 **2.**[fine arts] 美术（指诗歌、音乐、绘画、雕塑、建筑等）／'～-'drawn *adj.* **1.**（铅丝等）拉细的 **2.**（推理、论证等）过于精细的；微妙的 ／'～-'tooth-'comb *vt.* 仔细搜查

fine² [faɪn] *n.* 罚金，罚款 — *vt.* 处......以罚金

fineable ['faɪnəbl] *adj.* = finable

finery ['faɪnəri] *n.* 华丽的服饰

finesse [fɪ'nes] *n.* **1.** 手腕，手段；策略；技巧 **2.** 飞牌，飞张（指桥牌赛中先出较小的牌保留好牌以赢牌的手法）

fine-tune ['faɪn'tjuːn] *vt.* **1.** 对（收音机、电视机等）进行微调 **2.**（用适当的调节方法）使稳定（或改进）；调整，调节

finger ['fɪŋɡə] *n.* **1.**（尤指大拇指以外的）手指 **2.** 指状物；（手套的等）套手指部分 **3.**[机] 棘爪；作手指用的东西；指针 **3.** 一指之阔（约 3/4 英寸）；一中指之长（约 4½ 英寸）— *vt.* **1.** 用指触碰；拨弄；抚摸 **2.** 用指弹奏（乐器、

调);给(乐谱)标明指法符号 ‖ ~ed
adj. 1. 有指的;[动]有指的;[植]掌状
的 2.[用以构成复合词]有...指的;手
指...的 light-~ed 手指轻巧的;善于
扒窃的 ‖ ~alpha.bet (聋哑人的)手势
语字母 / '~board *n.* 1. (提琴等的)指
板;(钢琴等的)键盘 2. = ~ post /
bowl (餐桌上供人餐后用的)洗手指的
碗 / '~language 手势语 / '~mark 指迹,
指痕 / '~nail *n.* 指甲 / ~painting 指
画法(一种用手指蘸颜料洒在湿纸上
的画法);指画法作品 / ~post *n.* 指路
牌;指向柱 / '~print *n.* 指纹印,手印
vt. 打下...的指纹印 / '~stall *n.* (皮或
橡皮制的)护指套 / '~tip *n.* 指尖

fingerling ['fiŋgəliŋ] *n.* 1. 一指长的小鱼;
仔鱼 2. 小东西;微不足道的东西

finical ['finikəl], **finicky** ['finiki], **finick-
ing** ['finikiŋ] *adj.* 过分讲究(吃、穿等)
的;过分讲究的;过分讲究细节的

finis ['fainis, 'finis] *n.* [只用单](书、电影
等的)结尾;完终;(生命等的)终止

finish ['finiʃ] *vt.* 1. 结束,完毕,完成 2.
给...抛光,给...磨光 ~,使完美;润
饰 3. 用完;耗尽;吃完;喝光(up,
off);(口)消灭;杀掉;使完蛋(off) —
vi. 结束,终止 — *n.* [只用单] 1. 结
束;最后阶段 2. 致使完蛋的原因 3. 完
美(举止、谈吐、姿态等的)优雅 4. (家
具等表面的)抛光(剂);罩面漆;末道
漆

finishing ['finiʃiŋ] *adj.* 最后的 ‖ ~ touches
(绘画等时)最后修饰的几笔 ‖ ~
school 精修学校(为已受普通教育的青
年女子作进入社交界准备的一种学
校,内授音乐等课)

finite ['fainait] *adj.* 1. 有限的 2.[数]有
穷的,有限的 3.[语]限定的;a
~ verb 限定动词 ‖ ~ly *adv.* / ~ness

n.

Finland ['finlənd] *n.* 芬兰[北欧国家]

Finn [fin] *n.* 芬兰人

finned [find] *adj.* 1. 有鳍的;有鳍状物的
2.[用以构成复合词]有...鳍的:long-
~ 长鳍的

Finnish ['finiʃ] *adj.* 芬兰的;芬兰人的;芬
兰语的 — *n.* 芬兰语

fiord [fjɔːd] *n.* 峡湾(尤指挪威海岸边的)

fir [fəː] *n.* [植]冷杉,枞;松科常绿树
(如黄杉等) 2. 冷杉木,枞木 ‖ '~.
apple, '~.**ball**, '~.**cone** 冷杉球果
/ '~.**needle** 冷杉针叶,枞叶

fire ['faiə] *n.* 1. 火 2. 炉火 3. 火灾,失火
4. 发光(或炽热)体;闪光 5. 发烧 6.
炮火;(喻)猛烈的批评 7. 热情;激情
8. 火刑;(火刑)烧死 9. 发光,苦难 —
vt. 1. 放火烧(房子等);点燃(up) 2.
烧制(砖等);烤,焙制(茶叶等) 3. 给
(炉子等)加燃料 4. 使发光;使发红;
使发亮 5. 放(枪、炮等);射出(子弹);
使爆炸 6. 激起(想象力等);使充满热
情 7.(兽医学)烧灼 8.[美口]猛力投
掷;突然提出(问题) 9.(口)解雇;开除
— *vi.* 1. 着火,烧火,司炉 2. 激动;突
然发怒(up) 3. 开火,(枪炮)射击 ‖
~ **alarm** *n.* 火警报警器;火警铃 / ~
arm *n.* 火器(在美国一般仅指步枪、手
枪等) / '~.**ball** *n.* 1. 火球(指武器爆
炸后在空中出现的圆球体) 2. 火流
星;球状闪电 3.(旧式)燃烧弹 4.[美
口]工作起来劲头十足的人 / '~.**boat**
n. 消防艇 / '~.**bomb** 火焰炸弹(燃烧弹
或汽油弹等) / '~.**box** *n.* 1.
[机]机车锅炉炉膛;燃烧室 2. 火警自
动报警匣 / '~.**brand** *n.* 1. 燃烧的木头
2. 煽动叛乱者;挑动争执者 / ~.**break**
n. 防火障(指森林等处伐去树木以防
野火蔓延的一条地带) / '~.**brick** *n.* 耐

火砖 /~ **brigde** 消防队 /~ **bug** n.〈口〉纵火者;放火狂者 /~ **clay** n. 耐火粘土 /~ **company** 1.〈美〉消防队〈英〉火灾保险公司 /~ **control** 1. 射击指挥;火力控制;(用电子仪器等进行的)射击控制 2. 消防 /~ **cracker** n. 爆竹,鞭炮 /~ **damp** n. 沼气 /~ **drill** 消防演习;(原始的)钻木取火法 /~ **eater** n. 1. 吞火魔术师;玩火发光灯的人;脾气暴躁的人 /~ **engine** 救火车 /~ **escape** 太平梯;安全出口 /~ **extinguisher** 灭火器 /~ **fighter** 消防队员 /~ **fly** n. 萤火虫 /~ **grate** 炉篦 /~ **guard** n. 1. 炉栏 2. = **break** 3. 火灾警戒员 /~ **hose** 消防水带,水龙(软管) /~ **house** n. 消防站 (= **station**) /~ **hydrant** 消防栓,消防龙头 /~ **insurance** 火灾(保)险 /~ **irons** 炉用具(如火钳、通条、火铲) /~ **lane** = ~ **break** /~ **light** n. (炉)火光 /~ **line** 1. = ~ **break** 2. [常 **fire lines**] 火灾现场的警察警戒线(或召拥线) 3. (草原、森林等的)防火线 /~ **man** n. 1. 司炉工,烧火工人 2. 消防队员 /~ **place** n. 壁炉 /~ **plug** n. 灭火塞,消防栓;消防龙头 /~ **policy** n. (火灾)险单 /~ **power** n. 【军】火力;火量 /~ **proof** adj. 防火的;耐火的 vt. 使防火;使耐火 /~ **raising** n.〈英〉放火 /~ **side** n. 1. 炉边 2. 家 adj. 炉边的;亲切的;非正式的,不拘束的 /~ **station** 消防站 /~ **storm** n.(原子弹爆炸等引起的)风暴性大火 /~ **tower** (森林等处的)火警瞭望塔 /~ **trap** n. 无太平门(或消防设施)的建筑物;易引起火灾的建筑物 /~ **water** n.〈口〉烈酒 /~ **wood** n. 木柴 /~ **work** n. 1. 爆竹;花炮;[~**works**] 烟火 2. 烟火信号弹 3. [~**works**] 激情(如暴躁、紧张、热情等)的表现

firing ['faiəriŋ] n. 1. 生火,点火 2. 烧窑;烘烤 3. 射击 /~ **line** 1. 【军】射击线;射击线上的部队 2.〈喻〉第一线 (尤用于 on the ~ line 一语中) /~ **squad**(对判处死刑的犯人执行枪决的)行刑队;(举行军人葬礼时的)鸣枪队

firm[1] [fəm] adj. 1. 结实的;坚硬的 2. 牢固的,稳固的 3. 坚定的;坚决的;强有力的;严格的 4.(行市等)坚挺的 — adv. 稳固地;坚定地 — vt. 1. 使牢固,使稳固;使稳定;使坚实 2. 使坚定 3. 确认(契约等) — vi. 1. 变牢固,变稳固;变稳定;变坚定 2. 变坚实 ‖ ~**ly** adv. 一牢固地;坚定地 ‖ ~**ness** n. ‖ ~**ware** n.(计算机的)固件

firm[2] [fəm] n.(合伙)商号,商行

firmament ['fəməmənt] n. 天空,天

first [fəst] num. 第一(个);第一 — n. 1. 开始;开端;from the (very) ~ 从开始起 2. 第一(等);[~s](商品)一等品 3.(比赛)冠军;(考试)第一名;优等生;(分数)优等 4. [... the F-](帝王称号)... 一世 5.(月的)第一日:the ~ of May(或 May (the) ~)五月一日 — adj. 1. 第一位的;首要的;第一流的:the ~ grade 头等,甲级 2. 首先的;最初的,开始的:the ~ snow 初雪 3. 基本的,概要的:the ~ principles 基本原理(或原则) — adv. 1. 首先;最初;come in ~(在赛跑等中)最先到达终点,得第一 2. 第一次,首次 3. 第一(列举各条目时) 4. 宁愿(后接 rather, sooner) ‖ ~**ly** adv. 第一,首先(列举条目时) ‖ ~ **aid**(对病人的)急救 /~**born** adj. & n. 头生的(儿子或女儿),最长的(子或女) /~**class** adj. 1.(火车、船舱等)头等的;(成绩等)第一流的 2.(邮件)第一类的,快速的 3.〈口〉极好的 adv. 乘头等客车(或

舱等)2. 作为第一类邮件 3.〔口〕极好／～ floor 1.〔英〕二〔美〕楼 2.〔美〕底层, 一楼／～ form〔英〕(中等学校)一年级／'～fruits〔复〕n. 1. 第一批果实(指谷物、瓜果等一个季节中最早的收获,常指用以供神的祭品)2.〔喻〕〔工作的〕最初成果／'～hand adj.〔资料等〕第一手的, 直接的, 原始的; 直接的 adv. 直接地／～lady, First Lady 第一夫人(指总统夫人或元首夫人等)／'～line adj. 第一线的, 头等的, 最重要的／～name 名字, 教名(如 Anna Louis Strong 中的 Anna)／～ night〔戏剧、歌剧等〕初演, 首次上演／～offender 初次犯罪者者, 初犯／'～officer〔海〕大副／'～quarter〔天〕(月的)上弦; 上弦月／'～rate adj. 第一流的, 优秀的; 〔口〕极好的 adv. 〔口〕很好地／'～'run adj. 美(电影)第一轮(或首轮)放映的; (电影院)专映第一轮(或首轮)影片的, 头轮的／'～'strike adj.〔核〕武器作第一次打击的／～water 1.(钻石、珠宝)第一水、头等(光泽最纯)2. 喻 第一流, 最优秀 3.〔贬〕极端: a fool of the ～ water 头号大傻瓜

firth [fəθ] n. 河口湾; 港湾

fiscal ['fiskəl] adj. 1. 国库的; 国家岁入的 2. 美 财政的; 会计年度的／～year〔英 financial year〕／'～ly adv. 在国库方面; 在国家岁入方面; 财政上 ‖～stamp 印花税票(= revenue stamp)

fish [fiʃ] ([复]fish(es)) n. 1. 鱼; 鱼肉[常用以构成复合词]水生动物: cuttle～墨鱼 2.〔贬〕鱼; 人物; 人 3.〔口〕捕; 钓(鱼等); 采集(珊瑚) 2. ～ 中捕鱼 3. 搜索; 掏出(out, up) 3. 用吊钩器吊起(锚)— vi. 1. 捕鱼, 用钩捕鱼; 摸索寻找; 转弯抹角地引出; 间接探问(for) ‖～-and-'chips〔复〕n. 炸鱼加

炸土豆条／～cake 煎鱼饼／～fry 1. 炸鱼 2. 吃炸鱼的野餐 3. 鱼秧／～globe 金鱼缸／'～hook n. 鱼钩, 钓钩／'～-monger n.〔主英〕鱼贩子／'～net n. 1. 鱼网 2. 网眼织物／～story 夸张的叙述; 吹牛／'～-wife, '～woman n. 1. 卖鱼妇 2. 骂街的泼妇

fisher ['fiʃə] n. 1. 捕鱼人 2. 捕鱼船 ‖～man 捕鱼人; 捕鱼者

fishery ['fiʃəri] n. 1. 渔业; 水产业 2. 渔场; 养鱼场

fishing ['fiʃiŋ] n. 1. 捕鱼; 捕鱼权 ‖～ground 渔场／～line 钓丝／～net 鱼网／～rod 钓竿／～tackle 钓具

fishy ['fiʃi] adj. 1. 鱼的, 鱼的 2.(在味道等方面)像鱼的 3.(目光等)呆滞的, 无表情的; 冷冰冰的; 无光彩的 4. 可疑的, 靠不住的 ‖ **fishiness** n.

fissi- comb. form 表示"分裂": fissile

fissile ['fisail] adj. 1. 易分裂的; 可分裂的 2.〔核〕可裂变的 ‖ **fissility** [fi'siliti] n. 〔核〕可裂变性

fission ['fiʃən] n. 1. 分裂, 裂开 2.〔生〕分裂生殖 3.〔核〕裂变 — vt. & vi.〔核〕(使)裂变 ‖～able adj.

fissure ['fiʃə] n. 裂缝, 裂隙

fist [fist] n. 1. 拳(头)(口手); 口手; 手迹; 笔迹 — vt. 拳打 ‖～ful n. 一把

fisticuff ['fistikʌf] n. 1. 拳的一击 2. [～s]用拳或拳斗殴; 互殴

fit[1] [fit] (fit ted) fitting) vt. 1.(使)适合; 使符合; (使)配合 2. 使(服装等)合身; (服装等)合身 3. 使适合; 使胜任; 训练 5. 对...提供设备; 在...安装设备 — vi. 1. 适合: 符合配合 2.(服装等)合身, 合适 3. 适应 —(fitter, fittest) adj. 1. 适合的; 恰当的, 适当的 = 合理的 2. 健康的; 健全的; 正当的 3. 称的; 合格的; 能胜任的 4.

〈口〉[常用作状语]就要 ... 的;几乎要 ... 的:laugh ~ to burst oneself 捧腹大笑 — n. 1. [常用单,前加不定冠词和形容词]适合(合身的衣服):This garment is a tight (good) ~. 这件衣服很贴(合)身。 2. 【机】配合 ‖ ~ness n. 适合;恰当;合理 / fitter n. 1. 试衣匠(指为顾客试衣并作必要修改的裁缝) 2. 装配工;钳工 3. 合适的人(或东西)

fit² [fit] n. 1. (病的)发作;阵发;昏厥;痉挛:~s of coughing 一阵阵咳嗽 2. (感情等的)突发:a ~ of fury 勃然大怒

fitful ['fitful] adj. 间歇的,一阵阵的;不定的;不规则的 ‖ ~ly adv. / ~ness n.

fitting ['fitiŋ] adj. 适合的;恰当的;相称的 — n. 1. 试穿,试衣 2.〈英〉(服装、鞋袜等的)尺寸,尺码 3. 装配;修整 ~ shop 装配车间;装配厂 4. [常~s]装置(设备)部件;附件;附件 5. [常~s]【机】(接头)配件;附件;零件 ‖ ~ly adv. / ~ness n.

five [faiv] num. 五;五个(人或物);第五(卷、章、页等) — n. 1. 五个(人或物)一组 2. 五岁;五点钟 3. 五号的衣服(或鞋袜等) ‖ ~fold adj. & adv. 五倍的;五重的 / ~r n.〈英俚〉五英镑的钞票;〈美俚〉五美元的钞票 / ~-and-'dime n.〈美口〉= ~-and-ten -cent store)/ ~-and-'ten -cent store)〈美〉五分一角商店;出售低价小商品的杂货商店 / ~-star adj. 五颗星的;五星级(美国最高军衔)的:a ~ star general 五星上将 2.〈宾馆、饭店等〉五星级的;第一流的

fix [fiks] vt. 1. 使固定;装置;安装;【军】上(刺刀) 2. 凝视;用(眼睛)盯住,把(注意力)集中于 ... 上 3. 吸引(注意力) 4. 把 ... 牢记(在脑海中)(in) 5. 决定;确定(日期、年代、价格等)6. 归(咎)于(于

(on) 6. 修理 7. 整理 8. 安排;准备(饭食等) 9.〈口〉向 ... 报仇;惩罚;收拾 10.〈口〉用不正当手段操纵(选举、陪审团等)11.【化】使凝固;使不挥发 12. 使(颜色)固着;使(颜色等)经久不退;【摄】定(影)— vi. 1.〈美口〉把目光(注视)、确定;决定;选定(on, upon) 2.〈美口〉准备,打算 5.【化】凝固,不挥发 — n. 1. 困境,窘境 2.(船只、飞机等的)方位;定位 3. 贿赂;串通;舞弊事件 ‖ ~er n.

fixation [fik'seiʃən] n. 1. 固定;【摄】(负片、相片等的)定影;定色 2.【心】固恋,固着

fixative ['fiksətiv] n.【生】【化】固定剂;定影液;定色剂

fixature ['fiksətʃə] n. (头发的)定型胶,发胶

fixed [fikst] adj. 1. 固定的 2.(日期等)确定的;(颜色等)不易褪的 3. 坚定的;固执的 4.〈美口〉(在经济上)处境 ... 的 ‖ ~ly ['fiksidli] adv. / ~ness ['fiksidnis] n. ‖ ~ capital 固定资本

fixings ['fiksiŋz] [复] n.〈美口〉1.(菜的)配料;主菜以外的配菜;调味品 2. 设备;装备;装饰;服饰品;附属品

fixture ['fikstʃə] n. 1. 固定物;[常~s]房屋内的固定装置 2. 体育活动(或庆祝活动)的预定举行日;预定的体育活动(或庆祝活动)3. 固定于某地(或某项工作)的人

fizz [fiz] vi. 1. 嘶嘶地响 2. 显示兴奋;表示高兴 — n. 1. 嘶嘶声 2. 活跃 3. 充气饮料、起泡和发嘶嘶声的饮料(如香槟酒)

fizzle ['fizl] vi. 1. 嘶嘶地响 2.〈口〉(在开始时大有成功希望的计划等)终于失败(out) — n.〈口〉失败

fizzy ['fizi] adj. 嘶嘶发声的;起泡的

fjord [fjɔːd] *n*. = fiord

flabbergast ['flæbəgɑːst] *vt*. 〈口〉使大吃一惊,使目瞪口呆

flabby ['flæbi] *adj*. **1.** (肌肉等)不结实的,松弛的 **2.** 优柔寡断的;软弱的 ‖ flabbily *adv*. / flabbiness *n*.

flaccid ['flæksid] *adj*. **1.** (肌肉等)不结实的,松弛的 **2.** 软弱的 ‖ -ity [flæk'siditi] *n*. / ~ness *n*.

flag[1] [flæg] *n*. **1.** 旗 **2.** 旗舰旗,司令旗;旗舰旗 **3.** 鹿尾;(猎狗等的)茸尾 — (flagged/flagging) *vt*. **1.** 悬旗于 **2.** 打旗号表示;打旗号(或用其他信号)使(火车等)停下(*down*) **3.** (英)公益事业基金募捐日,旗日(捐者得一小旗,故名) / **Flag Day** (美)国旗制定纪念日(六月十四日) / '~ man *n*. 信号兵;信号旗手;(铁道等的)旗工 / ~ officer (能在舰上悬挂表示职位的)海军将官 / '~ pole *n*. 旗杆 / '~ ship *n*. 旗舰 / '~ staff *n*. 旗杆 / ~ station (铁道上的)旗站,信号停车站 / ~ stop (美)(公共汽车,火车等的)招呼停车站 / ~ ,waving *n*. 沙文主义(或爱国情绪、党派意识)的强烈表现(或煽动)

flag[2] [flæg] *n*. **1.** (铺路用的)石板,扁石 **2.** [~s]石板路 — (flagged/flagging) *vt*. 用石板铺(路等) ‖ '~-stone *n*. (铺路用的)石板,扁石

flag[3] [flæg] *n*. 【植】菖蒲,鸢尾;香蒲;菖蒲叶(或花)

flag[4] [flæg] (flagged/flagging) *vi*. **1.** 无力地下垂;(草木)垂萎 **2.** (力气、兴趣、热情等)衰退,减退,低落 **3.** 失去吸引力

flagella [flə'dʒelə] flagellum 的复数

flagellate ['flædʒəleit] *vt*. **1.** 鞭打,鞭笞 **2.** 痛斥;严惩;[喻]鞭挞 — *adj*. **1.** 【动】

有鞭毛的;鞭毛形的 **2.** 鞭毛虫(所致)的 **3.** [植]有鞭状匍匐枝的 — *n*. 鞭毛虫 ‖ ~d *adj*. / flagel'lation *n*.

flagellum [flə'dʒeləm] ([复] flagella [flə'dʒelə]或 flagellums) *n*. **1.** 【动】鞭毛;鞭状体;(昆虫触角的)鞭节 **2.** 【植】状匍匐枝

flagon ['flægən] *n*. 酒瓶;大肚酒瓶

flagrancy ['fleigrənsi] *n*. 罪恶昭彰;臭名远扬;目张胆

flagrant ['fleigrənt] *adj*. 罪恶昭彰的,臭名远扬的,公然的 ‖ ~ly *adv*.

flail [fleil] *n*. **1.** 连枷 **2.** 扫雷装置 — *vt*. & *vi*. **1.** 用连枷打(谷类);鞭打 **2.** 乱打

flair [flɛə] *n*. 鉴别力,眼光;资质

flak [flæk] [单复同] *n*. **1.** 高射炮火;高射炮 ...

flake [fleik] *n*. **1.** 薄片;~s of snow 雪片 **2.** 剥落的碎片 — *vt*. **1.** 使成薄片 **2.** 像雪花般覆盖 — *vi*. **1.** 剥落(*away*, *off*) **2.** 雪片似地降落(*down*)

flaky ['fleiki] *adj*. **1.** 片状的;薄片状的 **2.** 易剥落的;易剥落的 ‖ flakiness *n*.

flamboyance [flæm'bɔiəns] flamboyancy [flæm'bɔiənsi] *n*. **1.** 艳丽 **2.** 浮夸

flamboyant [flæm'bɔiənt] *adj*. **1.** 艳丽的 **2.** 浮夸的

flame [fleim] *n*. **1.** 火焰,火舌 **2.** 光辉,光芒 **3.** 热情;激情 **4.** [谑]情人 — *vi*. **1.** 发火焰,发光 **2.** 发红光;勃然大怒(*out*, *up*) **3.** 闪耀;发光 — *vt*. **1.** 激起(情感) **2.** 用火焰烧(或加热);用火焰给…灭菌 **3.** 照亮;使成火红色 ‖ ~ out vi. (喷气发动机)燃烧终止,熄火 / '~,thrower *n*. 喷火器

flamingo [flə'miŋgəu] ([复] flamingo(e)s) *n*. 【动】红鹳,火烈鸟

flammable ['flæməbl] *adj*. 易燃的

flange [flændʒ] *n*. **1.** 【机】凸缘,法兰

(盘);凸缘(制造)机 2.(火车的)轮缘;【建】(梁)翼缘

flank [flæŋk] *n.* 1. 胁;胁腹 2. 侧面;【建】厢房 3.【军】翼侧、侧翼 — *vt.* 1. 位于…的侧面(或两侧);经过…的侧面 2. 掩护…的翼侧;攻击(或威胁、包抄)…的翼侧 — *vi.*(堡垒等)侧面与…相接(*on*, *upon*)

flannel ['flænl] *n.* 1. 法兰绒;绒布;棉法兰绒 2.[~s]法兰绒衣服(如内衣、男子长裤等) 3.〈英〉(洗、擦用)法兰绒布块 4.〈英口〉花言巧语 —(flannel(l)ed; flannel(l)ing) *vt.* 1. 用法兰绒包(或裹) 2. 给…穿上法兰绒衣服 3. 用法兰绒揩擦 4.〈英口〉奉承;吓唬 ‖ '~-'**mouthed** *adj.* 花言巧语的

flap [flæp](flapped; flapping) *vt.* 1. 拍打、拍击 2. 使(上下、前后地)拍动;摆动;飘动;(鸟)振(翅) 3. 拉下(帽)的边 4. 扔、掷 — *vi.* 1. 拍动、摆动;飘动;(鸟翼等)振动、扑动 2. 拍翅飞行 3.(帽边等)垂下(*down*) 4. 讲蠢话、空讲;乱吹(*about*) 5.〈口〉慌张起来 — *n.* 1. 拍打;拍动;(鸟翅的)振动 2.〈口〉慌张 3. 垂下物;(袋)盖;(帽)边;信封口盖 4.【空】襟翼、阻力板 5.【医】(切肢手术后遗下或供移植用的)皮瓣、皮片 6. 勒口(书的护封的内折边) 7.(折叠式桌子的)折板、铰链板;(活板门的)活板 8.(鱼的)鳃盖 ‖ '~**jack** *n.* 煎饼;烤饼

flapper ['flæpə] *n.* 1. 拍击者;拍击物;苍蝇拍;惊鸟器 2. 片状悬垂物(如连枷的打禾板等) 3. 阔鳍;鳍状肢;(潜水时缚在脚上的)鸭脚板、脚蹼 4. 刚学飞的小野鸭(或小鹧鸪等小禽鸟)

flare [flɛə] *vi.* 1.(火焰)闪耀;突然烧起来;闪亮;〈喻〉突然发怒(*out*, *up*) 2.(衣裙等)呈喇叭形展开 — *vt.* 1. 使闪闪地燃烧;使闪亮 2. 使(衣裙等)呈喇叭形展开 — *n.* 1. 摇曳的火焰;闪耀;闪烁 2.(衣裙等的)呈喇叭形展开(或展开部分) 3.(声、激情、怒气等的)爆发 4. 照明弹;照明灯 5.(美式橄榄球中的)急球、短传球 ‖ ~ **path**(使飞机在夜间安全降陆和起飞的)照明跑道 / '~-'**up** *n.* 1. 突然起燃 2.(怒气或疾病的)突然发作(或加剧) 3. 昙花一现

flash [flæʃ] *n.* 1. 闪光 2.(信号灯等的)闪亮;(信号旗的)挥动 3.(希望等的)闪现 4. 刹那、瞬间 5.(简短的)电讯 6. = ~back 7.(掺入酒中含焦糖的)酒类染色剂 8.(为帮助行船而开闸)灌注的水;堰闸 9.【军】徽章;肩章 10.(服装、外表等的)浮华、虚饰;(人、行为等的)浮夸、华而不实 11. 引人注目者(尤指优秀运动员);惹人注目的东西 12.(盗贼等的)黑话、切口 13. 手电筒;(电影的)闪景;短景 14.(注射海洛因等毒品后的)瞬间快感 — *vt.* 1. 闪烁地发出(光线、信号等);使(剑、手电筒等)发出闪光 2.(眼)闪现(怒火等);(人)闪现(笑容);使(眼色)(*at*) 3.(火速地)发出(电讯、电报等);使迅速传遍(*across*, *around*, *over*) 4. 用水突然灌注(或灌满);灌水使(船)浮过障碍 5.〈口〉炫耀、炫示 — *vi.* 1.(闪电、灯塔等)发出闪光 2.(眼光等)闪耀;(思想等)闪现 3. 飞驰;掠过(*by*, *past*) 4.(河水等)冲泻;泛滥;暴涨 5.〈美俚〉(吸毒后)感到心荡神驰 — *adj.* 1.(服装、外表等)浮华的;(人、行为等)浮夸的、华而不实的 2.(文电等)火急的 3. 带有闪光(照相)设备的 ‖ '~**back** *n.*(小说等的)倒叙;(电影的)闪回(指穿插倒叙往事的镜头);火舌回闪;(致幻药效过后的)药效幻觉重现 / ~ **bomb** 闪光炸弹 / '~**bulb** *n.*【摄】闪光泡 / ~ **burn**(原子弹等的)闪光烧伤 / '~**cube** *n.* 方

形闪光灯/~ **flood**(暴雨等造成的)暴发的洪水/~~.**forward** n.(小说、电影等中的)提前叙述法 事件/~ **gun**[摄](与闪光灯配合的)闪光枪/~·**light** n. 1.(灯塔、机场等的)闪光信号灯 2.手电筒/~ **point** 1.闪(或燃)点 2.(战斗等的)爆发点

flashy ['flæʃi] adj. 1. 闪光的;闪烁的;昙花一现的 2. 浮华的;华而不实的;俗艳的 3.(颜色等)暴烈的 ‖ **flashily** adv. /**flashiness** n.

flask [flɑːsk] n. 1. 瓶;长颈瓶;[化] 烧瓶 2.(旅行者携带的)水瓶(或酒瓶)

flat[1] [flæt] adj. 1. 平的,平坦的 2. 扁平的,平伸的,平展的;倒伏的 3.(锅、碟等)浅的 4.(车胎)瘪了的;蓄电池(电用完了的 5. 断然的;直截了当的:a ~ refusal(denial)断然拒绝(否认) 6.(人物、生活、精神状态等)无聊的;单调的;没精打采的 7.(饮料等)走了气(或味)的 8.(市场等)萧条的,不景气的(价格等)无涨落的,一律的 9.(美口)一贫如洗的,不名一文的 10.(图画等)平涂的;无立体感的(颜色等)单调的;暗淡的:~ lighting 无深浅反差的(灯光安排)无明暗的;轮廓不清的 11.[音]降音的;降半音的 — adv. 1.平直地;仰卧地 2.断然地;恰恰,正好(十秒钟等) 4.[音]以降调 — n. 1. 扁平部分(如手掌等) 2. 平地;低洼沼泽地;沙州,浅滩 3. 扁车胎 4.[音]降半音;降低半音的记号 ‖ ~**ly** adv. 断然,毅然,直截了当地/~·**ness** n. ‖ ~**boat** n.(美)平底船/~·**car** n.(美)(铁路)平(板)车,平板货车,敞车/~·**fish** n.比目鱼/~·**foot** n.([复]~ **feet**)平足;有平足缺陷的人/~·'**footed** adj. 1. 平足的 2. 果

断的/~.**iron** n. 熨斗/~·**race**(无障碍物的)平地赛跑/~ **spin**(飞机的)水平螺旋/~·**top** n. 1. 平顶(建筑)物 2.(美俚)航空母舰/~·**worm** n. 扁虫(如肝蛭、绦虫等)

flat[2] [flæt] n.(主英)(在同一层楼上的)一套房间(通常指包括起坐室、卧室、浴室、厨房等的公寓房间) ‖ ~**let** n.(英)公寓小套间

flatten ['flætn] vt. 1. 把…弄平 2. 击倒;使倒伏 — vi. 1. 变平 2. 倒伏

flatter ['flætə] vt. 1. 谄媚,阿谀,奉承 2. 使高兴,使满意:I feel greatly ~ ed by your invitation. 承蒙邀请,十分高兴 3.(画、肖像等上的形象)胜过(真人或实物) ‖ ~**er** n. 奉承者,拍马屁的人

flattery ['flætəri] n. 1. 奉承,捧场 2. 恭维话

flatulence ['flætjuləns] n.[医]肠胃气胀

flatulent ['flætjulənt] adj. 1.肠胃气胀的 2.(食物)能使肠胃气胀的

flaunt [flɔːnt] vi.(旗等炫耀地)飘扬,招展 — vt.(炫耀地)挥动;夸耀;夸示

flavo(u)r ['fleivə] n. 1. 味 2. 风味,风韵;情味 — vt. 1. 给…调味,加味于 2. 给…增添风趣 ‖ ~**less** adj. 无味的;无风味的,乏味的

flavo(u)ring ['fleivəriŋ] n. 调味品;调味香料

flaw [flɔː] n. 1. 缺点;瑕疵 2.(使证件、程序等无效的)缺陷 — vt. 使有缺陷;使无效

flawless ['flɔːlis] adj. 无缺点的;无瑕的 ‖ ~**ly** adv. /~**ness** n.

flax [flæks] n. 1.[植]亚麻 2. 亚麻纤维;亚麻布 ‖ ~**seed** n. 亚麻籽,亚麻仁

flaxen ['flæksən] adj. 1. 亚麻的;亚麻制的 2.(头发)亚麻色的,淡黄色的

flay [flei] *vt.* 1. 剥 ... 的皮 2. 掠夺 3. 严厉批评；痛责

flea [fli:] *n.* 1. 蚤；跳蚤 2. (伤害植物叶和芽的) 跳甲 (= ~ beetle) ‖ '~-bag *n.* 廉价低级旅馆 2. 生蚤的动物 /~-market跳蚤市场 /'~-pit *n.* 〈俚〉被认为有跳蚤 (或臭虫等) 的公共场所 (如电影院), 窝窝

fleabite ['fli:bait] *n.* 1. 蚤咬；蚤咬的红斑 2. 轻微的痛痒；小麻烦；少量的花费

fleck [flek] *n.* 1. (皮肤的) 斑点；雀斑 2. 色斑；光斑 3. 微粒；小片 — *vt.* 使有斑点；使斑驳

fled [fled] flee 的过去式和过去分词

fledgeling ['fledʒliŋ] *n.* 1. 刚会飞的小鸟 2. 初出茅庐的人, 无经验者

flee [fli:] (fled [fled]) *vi.* 逃跑；逃避 — *vt.* 逃离;避开

fleece [fli:s] *n.* 1. (尤指未剪下的) 羊毛 2. 一只羊身上一次剪得的羊毛 3. 羊毛状物 (如白云、白雪、头发等) — *vt.* 1. 剪下 (羊) 的毛 2. 诈取...的钱财；向...收取过高的代价

fleecy ['fli:si] *adj.* 羊毛似的

fleet[1] [fli:t] *n.* 1. 舰队 2. [the ~]海军 2. (统一指挥下或同属某种行业、单位的) 船队；机群；(汽) 车队 ‖ ~ admiral (美) 海军五星上将 /~ air arm 海军航空兵

fleet[2] [fli:t] *adj.* 快速的；敏捷的 ‖ ~ of foot 走路快的, 快腿的 ‖ ~ly *adv.* /~ness *n.* ‖ '~-'foot(ed) *adj.* 走路快的, 快腿的

fleeting ['fli:tiŋ] *adj.* 疾驰的；飞逝的；短暂的

flesh [fleʃ] *n.* 1. 肉 (指人或脊椎动物身体的肌肉组织) 2. (供食用的) 兽肉 (与鱼、禽的肉相区别) 3. 果肉 (指水果、

蔬菜的可食部分) 4. [the ~]肉体 (与灵魂、精神相对而言)；情欲 5. 亲骨肉;亲属 [主要用于短语 one's own)— and blood) 6. 人体;肌肤 ‖ '~-colo(u)red *adj.* 肉色的 /'~-pots [复] *n.* 1. 奢侈的生活 2. 满足肉欲的场所 /~ tights (杂技演员穿的) 肉色紧身衣 /~ wound 皮肉之伤；轻伤

fleshly ['fleʃli] *adj.* 1. 肉体的 2. 肉欲的 3. 多肉的;肥胖的 4. 尘世的, 世俗的 5. 心软的;易受感动的 ‖ **fleshliness** *n.*

fleshy ['fleʃi] *adj.* 1. 多肉的、肥胖的 2. 肉的；似肉的 3.〔植〕肉质的

flew [flu:]fly 的过去式

flex [fleks] *vt.* 屈曲 (四肢) — *n.* 〈主英电〉花线;皮线

flexible ['fleksibl] *adj.* 1. 柔韧的, 易弯曲的 2. 柔顺的 3. 可变通的, 灵活的 ‖ **flexi'bility** *n.* / **flexibly** *adv.*

flick [flik] *n.* 1. (鞭等的) 轻打; (手指的) 轻弹; (手帕等的) 轻拂 2. (击球时手腕的) 急速转动 3. (鞭等的) 轻击声 4. 〈俚〉电影；[~s]电影院；电影的放映；[总称]电影 — *vt.* 1. (用鞭等) 急速地轻打 (用指等轻轻) 弹去, 拂去 (away, off, from) 3. 急速地轻抽 (鞭子);轻拨 (开关) — *vi.* 1. (急速地) 轻击;轻弹, 轻拂 (at) 2. (翅) 拍动;(旗) 飘扬 3. 急速翻动书页 (through) ‖ ~ knife (一柄柄上的按钮刀刃就弹出的) 弹簧折刀 (常用作武器)

flicker ['flikə] *vi.* 1. (鸟) 扑动短膀 2. (光、火焰等的) 闪烁；摇曳;忽隐忽现;(希望等) 闪现 — *vt.* 使摇曳;使闪烁不定;使忽隐忽现 — *n.* 1. 扑动;闪烁;摇曳;忽隐忽现 2. (希望等的) 闪现

flickering ['flikəriŋ] *adj.* 扑动的;闪烁的;摇曳的;忽隐忽现的 ‖ ~ly *adv.*

flier ['flaiə] n. = flyer

flight[1] [flait] n. **1.** 飞翔；飞行 **2.** 飞翔的一群；飞行的一队；(箭等的)齐发 **3.** 飞机的航程；(有特定航线的)定期客机、班机；搭机旅行 **4.** (鸟的)能飞的距离；(箭、炮弹、导弹等的)射程 **5.** (鹰等对猎物的)追逐；(候鸟等的)迁徙 **6.** 楼梯(或阶梯)的一段；(时间的)飞逝；(才智、想象力等的)飞跃：a ～ of fancy 奇思、异想天开 ‖ ～ **deck** **1.** (航空母舰上的)飞行甲板 **2.** 驾驶舱 ／ **engineer** 随机工程师 ／ ～ **feather** (鸟翼的)拨风羽、飞羽 ／ ～ **formation** 空军小队(泛指)；飞行编队 ／ ～ **lieutenant** (英)空军上尉 ／ ～ **sergeant** (英)空军上士 ／ ～ **strip** 简易机场；应急跑道

flight[2] [flait] n. **1.** 逃跑、溃退 **2.** (资金等的)抽逃、外流

flighty ['flaiti] adj. **1.** 喜欢幻想的 **2.** 反复无常的；轻浮的 **3.** (马等)易惊的 **4.** 痴呆的，有些疯癫的 ‖ **flightily** adv. ／ **flightiness** n.

flimsy ['flimzi] adj. **1.** 轻而薄的；脆弱的；易损坏的 **2.** 没价值的；不足信的 — n. 薄纸(尤指复写用的) ‖ **flimsily** adv. ／ **flimsiness** n.

flinch [flintʃ] vi. 退缩；畏缩(from)

fling [fliŋ] (flung [flʌŋ]) vt. **1.** (用力地)扔、抛、掷、甩 **2.** 使突然陷入(into)；粗暴推入(into) **3.** [～ oneself]使投身(突然)跳入(into)；使扑(against、upon) **4.** 急伸；挥动(手臂、腿等) **5.** (向…)投(眼光)(upon) **6.** (猛烈地)推(门、窗等) **7.** (匆忙地)披上(衣服)(on)；脱下(衣服)(off) **8.** 冲、奔(into、out of) — vi. **1.** 怒气冲冲地走掉(off) **2.** (马等)乱蹦(out) — n. **1.** 扔、抛、掷、甩 **2.** 讽刺、嘲弄；攻击 **3.** (口)(随意的)尝试 **4.** (一时的)放荡；放纵

flint [flint] n. 燧石、打火石；(打火机用的)电石 ‖ ～ **lock** n. 燧发枪；明火枪

flinty ['flinti] adj. **1.** 燧石似的；坚硬的；强硬的 **2.** 冷酷的

flip [flip] (flipped、flipping) vt. **1.** 把…往上一抛使在空中翻转；掷 **2.** 用指轻弹；轻击 **3.** (用指等)挥击(蛋、糖等) **4.** 翻(纸牌等) — vi. **1.** 用指轻弹；(用鞭等)抽打(at) **2.** 一蹦一蹦地跳跃；(用鳍状肢)啪嗒啪嗒地走动 **3.** 翻动书页(through) **4.** (俚)发疯 **5.** (俚)惊喜若狂；极感兴趣 — n. **1.** 抛、弹；轻击；抽打 **2.** (跳水或体操动作的)空翻 **3.** (足球赛的)短距离传球 **4.** 加有香料(有时还加牛奶和鸡蛋)的热甜啤酒(或苹果酒等饮料) — (flipper、flippest) adj. (口)无礼的；冒失的 ‖ ～ **flap** n. 啪嗒啪嗒的响声(或动作) **2.** 后手翻 **3.** (游乐场所内的)旋转游乐器 ／ ～ **flop** n. **1.** 啪嗒啪嗒的响声(或动作) **2.** (美)后手翻 **3.** [～ flops]塑料(或橡胶的)平底人字拖鞋 ／ ～ **side** (口)唱片的反面(常录有较不出名的乐曲)

flippancy ['flipənsi] n. **1.** 无礼、轻率 **2.** 轻率(或无礼)的行动(或话)

flippant ['flipənt] adj. 无礼的、轻率的 ‖ ～ **ly** adv.

flipper ['flipə] n. **1.** 前肢、鳍足；(鲸等的)鳍状肢 **2.** (潜水员绑在脚上的)脚蹼、鸭脚板；橡皮脚掌

flirt [flə:t] vi. **1.** 调情、卖俏(with) **2.** 闹着玩地来考虑(with) — n. 调情者、卖俏者 ‖ ～ **ation**[flə:'teiʃən] n. 调情 ／ ～ **atious**[flə:'teiʃəs] adj. 轻佻的、爱调情的

flit [flit] (flitted、flitting) vi. **1.** 掠过；迅速飞过(across) **2.** 迁移；离开不久 **3.** (鸟、蝙蝠等)飞 — n. 暗中迁移、搬家(尤指引的在豢债的)

flivver ['flivə] *n.* 〈美俚〉(旧)(廉价)小汽车

float [fləut] *vi.* 1. 漂浮,浮动;飘动 2. (往事等在眼前)浮现(*before*) 3. 流遗 4. 【经】(货币)浮动 — *vt.* 1. 使漂浮(水面、水域等)负载、容纳(舰队等) 2. 使(沉船等)浮升 3. 发行(公债、债券等);筹(款) 4. (通过发行债券等方式)筹资开办(公司、商号等) 5. 实行(计划等) 6.【经】使(货币)浮动 — *n.* 1. 漂浮物;木筏;浮标;(动植物的)浮囊;(钓鱼用的)浮子;(水箱)浮球;(水上飞机的)浮筒 2.(游行时用的)彩车,装载展品模型的车辆 3.[常～s](舞台的)脚灯 4.【经】浮动

floatation [fləu'teiʃən] *n.* 1. 漂浮;(船的)下水 2.(企业等的)筹资开办,创立;(为创立企业的)筹款

floating ['fləutiŋ] *adj.* 1. 漂浮的;(货币等)浮动的;浮置的 2. (人口、资本等)流动的,不固定的;a ～ debt 流动债券,短期债务/the ～ vote 一批无党派投票人(的投票) ‖ ～ bridge 浮桥 / ～ dock 浮坞 / ～ kidney【医】浮游肾 / ～ rate【经】浮动汇率 / ～ rib【解】浮肋,浮动肋助

flock [flɔk] *n.* 1. (飞禽、牲畜等的)群;羊群 2. (某一人管理之下的)一群人;(同属一个牧师管辖的)全体教徒;一家的子女 3. 成群的人们 — *vi.* 聚集,群集;成群地去(或来)

floe [fləu] *n.* 大片浮冰;浮冰块

flog [flɔg] (flogged; flogging) *vt.* 1. (用鞭、棍等)鞭打,鞭挞,抽打 2. 驱使;迫使;～ oneself into a rage 使自己的脾气发作起来 3. 严厉批评 4.〈俚〉打败,胜过 5.〈英俚〉出售(尤指非法地) ‖ **flogging** *n.* 鞭打

flood [flʌd] *n.* 1. 洪水;水灾 2. 涨潮,涨水;潮水最高点 3. 大量(的信件、眼泪等);大批(的人等);滔滔不绝(的话)(*of*) 4.〈口〉泛光灯(＝～light) — *vt.* 1. 淹没;使泛滥 2. 涌到;涌进;充满,充斥 — *vi.* 1. 为水所淹;(江河)泛滥出;(潮水)涨 2. 大量地涌进(或入,*in*,*into*) 3.【医】患月经过多;患血崩 ‖ ～gate *n.* (泄)水闸门;防洪闸门 / ～light *n.* 泛光灯;泛光照明 — *vt.* 用泛光灯照明(～lit)/～mark *n.* 高潮(或高水位)标记,高潮痕 / ～plain *n.* 涝原,泛滥平原,漫滩 / ～tide 1. 涨潮(ebb tide"落潮"之对) 2. 高峰 / ～water *n.* 洪水

floor [flɔː] *n.* 1. (房间,门廊等的)地面;地板 2. (室内供比赛、跳舞等用的)场地;舞底地板 3. (海洋、山洞等的)底 4. (海等的)底 5. 楼房的层(常略作厅):the ground ～(英)底层,一楼(相当于美国说法the first ～)/the first (second)～(英二(三)楼;(美一(二)楼 6. 物价,工资等的最低额;底价 7. (议会)的议员席位;(证券交易所等的)交易厅(或场)8.(在会上)发言权 — *vt.* 1. 给…铺地板;给…铺地面(或基面)2. 把…打翻在地;击倒;克服 3.〈口〉难倒;使困住 4.〈美口〉踩足(汽车的油门) ‖ ～board *n.* 1.[总称]适合做地板用的木料 2. 一块地板(常指可掀起的活动地板)3. 汽车驾驶室的车底板)/～cloth *n.* 1. 铺地布 2. 擦地板布 / ～exercise 自由体操/～lamp (放在地板上可移动的)立灯,落地灯 / ～show 夜总会的系列文娱表演 / ～through *n.* 占整层楼面的公寓房间,全层公寓 / ～,walker *n.* (百货商店的)铺面巡视员

flooring ['flɔːriŋ] *n.* 1. (全部)室内地面 2. 铺室内地面的材料

flop [flɔp] (flopped; flopping) *vi.* 1. 扑动;脚步沉重地走 2. 猛然躺下(或坐下,跑下等)(*down*) 3.〈俚〉上床 4.(作品,

戏剧等)彻底失败;不受欢迎 — **vt.** 噗地一声放下;啪啪地翻动 — **n. 1.** 拍击(声);重坠(声) **2.**(书、戏剧等的)大失败 — **adv.** 噗地一声;恰巧 ‖ ~ **house** n. 廉价旅馆,寄宿舍 / ~ **over** n. 电视图象的上下跳动

floppy ['flɔpi] *adj.* 松软的

flora ['flɔːrə][复](floras 或 florae['flɔːriː]) *n.* **1.** 植物群(尤指某一地区或某一时期的植物群,与 fauna 动物群相对) **2.**[植]植物区系 **3.** 植物志

floral ['flɔːrəl] *adj.* **1.** 植物群的;植物区系的 **2.** 花的;像花的

floret ['flɔːrit] *n.* 小花(尤指菊科植物管状花冠的管状小花)

floriculture ['flɔːrikʌltʃə] *n.* 花卉栽培;花卉园艺学

florid ['flɔrid] *adj.* **1.**(文体等)华美的;过于修饰的 **2.**(脸)红润的 ‖ ~ **ity** [flɔ'riditi] n. / ~ **ly** adv. / ~ **ness** n.

Florida ['flɔridə] n. 佛罗里达[美国州名]

florin ['flɔrin] n. **1.**(金币名)弗罗林(一二五二年首先在佛罗伦萨铸造,后为英、法等国仿造) **2.**(银币名)弗罗林(初在十九世纪末叶英国的两先令银币;荷兰货币盾与匈牙利货币福林等均用此名称的)

florist ['flɔrist] n. **1.** 花商 **2.** 种花者 **3.** 花卉研究者

floss [flɔs] n. **1.**(蚕茧外的)茧衣,绪丝 **2.** 绣花丝线;低拈捻轻毛线 **3.**絮状纤维(材料);木棉 **4.**[植]绒毛;(玉米的)蚕须 **6.**[冶](浮于熔化金属表面的)浮渣 ‖ ~ **silk** 绪丝;绣花丝线

flotilla [flə'tilə] n. **1.** 小舰队 **2.**(美海军)纵队(下辖二个以上中队) **3.** 船队

flotsam ['flɔtsəm] n. **1.**(遇难船只的)漂浮残骸(或货物物) **2.**[总称]流浪贫民 **3.**[总称]零碎杂物

flounce¹ [flauns] n.(衣裙上的)荷叶边 — vt. 镶荷叶边于

flounce² [flauns] vi. 挣扎;肢体乱动 **2.** 猛然离开;悻然离开(out, off)

flounder¹ ['flaundə] vi. 挣扎;肢体乱动;跟趄 **2.** 错乱地做事(或说话)

flounder² ['flaundə] n.[动]鲆;鲽

flour ['flauə] n. **1.** 面粉;(任何谷类磨成的)粉 **2.** 粉状物质 — vt. **1.** 撒粉于 **2.** 把…做成粉 ‖ ~ **y** adj. 面粉的;粉状的;撒满粉的

flourish ['flʌriʃ] vi. **1.** 茂盛;繁荣;兴旺 **2.**(作家、哲学家等)处于活跃状态,处于旺盛时期 **3.**茂谙;身体健康 — vt. **1.** 挥舞 **2.** 炫耀,夸耀 — n. **1.**(手写花体字上的)花饰 **2.** 挥舞;戏剧性动作 **3.** 装饰乐句;嘹亮的铜管乐声 ‖ ~ **ing** adj. 茂盛的;欣欣向荣的;蓬蓬日上的

flout [flaut] vt. **1.** 藐视,轻视 **2.** 嘲弄;侮骂

flow [fləu] vi. **1.**(河水、血、眼泪等)流;(潮)涨 **2.**(河水等)泛滥(over) **3.**(财富等)来自…的结果(from) **4.**(车辆等)川流不息 **5.**(谈话、文体等)流畅 **6.**(头发、发辫等顺畅地)(披)飘扬 **7.**(国家等)富有,充满(with) — n. **1.** 流动;流量;流速;流率 **2.** 洋溢;(资源、供应等的)丰富 **4.**(潮)涨 **5.**(人、车等的)川流不息;(谈话等的)流畅 ‖ ~ **chart** 流程图;作业图;生产过程图解 / ~ **meter** n. 流量表,流量计;流速计 / ~ **sheet** = ~ **chart**

flower ['flauə] n. **1.** 花;开花植物;花卉 **2.** 精华 **3.** 开花;盛开 **4.**[~s][化]华 — vi. **1.** 开花 **2.** 充分发展 — vt. 使开花;用花(或花纹)装饰 ‖ ~ed adj. **1.** 开花的;有花的 **2.** 用花(或花纹)装饰的 / ~ **less** adj. 无花的 ‖ ~ **pot** n. 花盆

flowery ['flauəri] *adj*. 1. 多花的 2. 词藻华丽的 ‖ **floweriness** *n.*

flowing ['fləuŋ] *adj*. 1. 流动的 2.(文章等)流畅的，通顺的；(线条、轮廓等)平滑的 ‖ **~ly** *adv*.

flown [fləun] fly¹ 的过去分词

flu [flu:] *n*.〈口〉流行性感冒(= influenza)

fluctuate ['flʌktjueit] *vi*. 1. 波动，涨落，起伏 2. 动摇，不定 ‖ **fluctu'ation** *n*.

flue [flu:] *n*. 1. 烟道 2. 暖气管

fluency ['flu:ənsi] *n*. 流利；流畅

fluent ['flu:ənt] *adj*. 流利的；流畅的 ‖ **~ly** *adv*.

fluff [flʌf] *n*. 1.(织物上的)绒毛，蓬松毛；软毛 2.蓬松的一团头发，一团头发 (或毛等)无价值的东西；没有内容的娱乐剧 4. 失误；错误；误读 — *vi*. 1. 起毛；变松 2. 出错(演员)忘词；念错 — *vt*. 1. 使起毛；抖开；抖松(羽毛等) 2. 把…搞糟 3. 忘记(台词等)；念错(台词等)

fluffy ['flʌfi] *adj*. 绒毛状的；有绒毛的；蓬松的 ‖ **fluffiness** *n.*

fluid ['flu:id] *adj*. 1. 流动的；流体的；液体的 2. 不固定的；易变的 — *n*. 流体(液体与气体的总称)；溯 ‖ **~ic** [-ik] *adj*. 流体性的 / **~ity** [flu:'iditi] *n*. 流动性；流度 / **~ly** *adv*. / **~ness** *n*. ‖ **'~-ounce** *n*. 液量盎司(〈美〉= 1/16 品脱；〈英〉= 1/20 品脱)

fluidics [flu:'idiks] [复] *n*. [用作单]射流学, 流体学

fluke¹ [flu:k] *n*. 1.(球类比赛中)侥幸的击中 2. 侥幸；侥幸成功 ‖ **fluk(e)y** *adj*. 凭运气的

fluke² [flu:k] *n*.【动】1. 比目鱼；鲽鱼 2. 吸虫，蛭；羊肝蛭

flume [flu:m] *n*. 1. 峡沟 2. 引水槽；放水沟

flummox ['flʌməks] *vt*.〈英口〉使惶惑, 使慌乱

flump [flʌmp] *vi*. 砰地落下；砰地移动 — *vt*. 砰地放下 — *n*. 砰的一声；重落

flung [flʌŋ] fling 的过去式和过去分词

flunk [flʌŋk] *vi*.〈主美口〉*vi*.(在考试中)失败，不及格 — *vt*. 1. 使不及格；给…打不及格分数 2. 通不过(考试)；通不过(某一学科)的考试

flunk(e)y ['flʌŋki] *n*. 1.〈贬〉(穿号衣的)仆从；奴才；走狗 2. 奉承者；势利小人

fluoresce [fluə'res] *vi*. 发荧光

fluorescence [fluə'resns] *n*. 荧光

fluorescent [fluə'resnt] *adj*. 荧光的；发荧光的：a ~ lamp 荧光灯, 日光灯/a ~ screen 荧光屏

fluoridate ['fluərideit] *vt*. 1.(为防治龋齿)在…中加入微量氟化物 2. 用含氟药剂治疗(牙齿) — *vt*. 在饮用水中加入微量氟化物

fluoridation [,fluəri'deiʃən] *n*. 加氟作用, 氟化反应

fluoride ['fluəraid] *n*.【化】氟化物

fluorine ['fluəri:n] *n*.【化】氟

fluoroscope ['fluərəskəup] *n*. 荧光镜(或屏), 荧光检查仪 — *vt*. 用荧光镜(或屏)检查

flurry ['flʌri] *n*. 1. 阵风, 疾风 2. 小雪；小雨 3. 慌张, 仓皇 — *vt*. 使慌张

flush¹ [flʌʃ] *vi*. 1.(水等)奔泻；涌上(脸)发红；(人)脸红 3.(植物)绽出新芽 — *vt*. 1.(用水)冲洗, 使注满；淹没 2. 使(脸等)涨红；使发红 4. 使激动；使得意 5.(植物)绽出新芽 — *n*. 1. 奔流；涌 2. 冲洗 3. 萌发；茂盛；活力 4. 兴奋；激动；得意 5. 红光；红晕 6. 发烧, 升火 ‖ **~ toilet** 有抽水设备的

厕所;抽水马桶

flush² [flʌʃ] *adj.* **1.**(江河等)涨满的;泛滥的 **2.** 很有钱的;富裕的 **3.** 齐平的;贴合成一个平面的;紧接着的 **4.** 面色红润的 — *adv.* **1.** 齐平地;贴合无缝地 **2.** 直接地

flush³ [flʌʃ] *vi.* (鸟)惊起,惊飞 — *vt.* 使(鸟)惊飞

fluster ['flʌstə] *vt.* 使慌张 — *vi.* 慌张地行动,慌乱 — *n.* 慌张

flute [fluːt] *n.* **1.**【音】长笛 **2.**(柱子等上的长条形)凹槽;【纺】褶子的沟纹(或沟槽) **3.**【机】(刀具的)出屑槽 — *vi.* **1.** 吹长笛 **2.** 发出长笛般的声音唱(或说) — *vt.* **1.** 用长笛奏(乐曲);用长笛般的声音唱(或说) **2.** 在…上做出凹槽(或沟纹) ‖ **flutist** *n.* 吹长笛的人

flut·e·y ['fluːti] (flutier, flutiest) *adj.* 长笛声般柔和而清澈的

flutter ['flʌtə] *vi.* **1.**(鸟)振翼,拍翅 **2.**(旗帜等)飘扬 **3.** 飘动;(脉搏、心脏)不规则跳动;心绪不宁;发抖 **4.** 焦急地乱动,坐立不安 — *vt.* **1.** 拍动(翅)膀 **2.** 使焦急,使不安 — *n.* **1.** 振翼;飘动,飘扬 **2.** 焦急,不安;(情绪、市场等)的波动 **3.**【医】(心房等)扑动,振颤 **4.**(电视的)图像颤动;【无】音失真 **5.** 颤动

fluvial ['fluːviəl] *adj.* **1.** 河的,河流的 **2.** 生长在河中的 **3.** 河流冲刷作用形成的

flux [flʌks] *n.* **1.** 流;流出;流动 **2.** 涨潮 **3.** 不断的变动;波动 **4.**【物】通量 **5.** 助熔剂;焊剂 **6.**【医】(血液、体液的)流出

fly¹ [flai] (flew [fluː], flown [fləun]) *vi.* **1.** 飞,飞行;驾驶飞机;乘飞机旅行 **2.**(旗帜等)飘扬,飘荡 **3.** 飞舞 **4.** 飞跑,飞奔 **5.**(时间)飞逝 **6.**(门、窗等)突然打开;

(玻璃等)飞散;碎 **5.** 逃跑;逃避(= flee) **6.**(钱财等)很快用完 — *vt.* **1.** 驾驶(飞机);空运(乘客、货物等) **2.** 飞越;乘(某航空公司)的飞机旅行 **3.** 执行(飞行任务) **4.** 使(旗等)飘扬;挂(旗) **5.** 放(风筝,信鸽等);打猎时放(鹰) **6.** 逃离,逃出 — *n.* **1.** 飞;飞行;飞行距离 **2.**(衣服等)的钮扣盖布;(帐篷)的门帘(或外层帆布);帐篷的外沿;旗幅 **3.** [flies](舞台上面悬吊布景的)吊景区 **4.** 公共马车;运货马车;(主英)轻便出租马车 **5.**(棒球等)高飞球 ‖ ' ~-away *adj.* **1.**(人)轻浮的;轻率的 **2.**(衣服)过于宽大的,不合身的 / ' ~ ball(棒球赛)高飞球 / ' ~ by *n.* **1.**(一架或几架飞机)编队低空飞越;定点飞越 **2.**(宇宙飞船的)近天体探测飞行;进行近天体探测飞行的宇宙飞船 **3.** 绕月球轨道运行而不作一圈的飞行 / ' ~-by-night *n.* 喜欢夜间外出的人;〈美俚〉夜逃的负债者;无信用的借债人 *adj.* 无信用的,不可靠的 / ' ~ leaf *n.* [书籍前后的]飞页,扉页 / ' ~ over *n.* **1.**〈英〉立交桥 **2.** = ~ past / ' ~ past *n.*〈英〉(阅兵等时的)低空编队飞行 / ' ~ sheet 单张小小广告)传单;单张说明书 / ' ~-way *n.* 候鸟飞行路线 / ' ~ wheel *n.*【机】飞轮,惯性轮

fly² [flai] *n.* **1.** 蝇;苍蝇;(作伪饵用的)假蝇 **2.** 蝇类虫害 ‖ ' ~-blow *n.* 蝇卵;蛆 *vt.* **1.** 产蝇卵于 **2.** 玷污(声誉等) / ' ~-blown *adj.* **1.** 沾满蝇卵的,生蛆的;满是蝇卵的 **2.**(声誉等)玷污了的 / ' ~-catcher *n.* **1.**【动】鹟 **2.**【植】捕蝇草 / ' ~-fish *vi.* 用(假)蝇钓鱼 / ' ~ flap *n.* 蝇拍;蝇驱拍 / ' ~ paper *n.* 粘蝇纸,蝇纸 / ' ~-swat(ter) *n.* 蝇拍 / ' ~ trap *n.* **1.** 捕蝇器 **2.**【植】捕蝇草 / ' ~ weight *n.* **1.** 次最轻量级职业拳击选手 **2.** 小东西,无足轻重的东西

flyer ['flaiə] *n.* **1.** 飞鸟；飞行物；航空器 **2.** 飞行员 **3.** (火车、公共汽车等的)特快专车 **4.** 能飞跑的动物 **5.** 小(广告)传单

flying ['flaiiŋ] *adj.* **1.** 飞的，飞行(员)的 **2.** (旗帜等)飘扬的；飞舞的 **3.** 飞似的，飞速的；(特警队等)快速行动的 **4.** 匆匆的；短暂的 **5.** (谣言等)到处流传中的 — *n.* **1.** 飞行 **2.** [~s][纺]飞花；飞毛 ‖ ~ boat 水上飞机；飞艇 ~ bomb [军]飞弹(爆炸性的无人驾驶飞机、导弹和火箭的统称)/ ~ bridge **1.** 最上层船栈；(旗舰等)驾驶桥楼 **2.** 浮桥 / ~ buttress [建]拱扶垛 / ~ colo(u)rs 全胜；大成功 / ~ column [军]快速突击部队/摩托别动队 / ~ crane 飞行起重机，起重直升机 / ~ field 飞行场(常指私人飞机起落的场地) / ~ fish [动]文鳐鱼，飞鱼 / ~ fox [动]狐蝠 / ~ jib [船]飞(伸)三角帆 / ~ lemur [动]鼯猴 / ~ officer (英)空军中尉 / ~ saucer 飞碟，不明飞行物 / ~ school 飞行学校 / ~ squirrel [动]美洲飞鼠；鼯鼠

Fm [化]元素镄(fermium)的符号

foal [foul] *n.* 驹(尤指一岁以下的马、驴、骡) — *vt. & vi.* 产(驹)

foam [foum] *n.* **1.** 泡沫；(马等的)唾沫(或大汗) **2.** 泡沫材料；泡沫状态；泡沫橡胶；泡沫塑料 — *vi.* **1.** 起泡；冒汗水 **2.** 吐白沫；(发怒时)唾沫四溅；发怒 **3.** 起泡沫流动 ‖ ~ed plastics 泡沫塑料，多孔塑料 / ~ rubber 泡沫胶，海绵橡胶

foamy ['foumi] *adj.* 起泡沫的；布满泡沫的；泡沫似的

fob¹ [fɔb] (fobbed; fobbing) *vt.* (用诡计、借口等)把…对付掉，搪塞(off)

fob² [fɔb] *n.* **1.** (男裤上的)表袋 **2.** 怀表短链(或短带)

focal ['foukəl] *adj.* **1.** 焦点的；在焦点上的；有焦点的 **2.** [医]病灶的；灶的 ‖ ~ distance, ~ length 焦距 / ~ point 焦点；活动(或注意、兴趣等)的中心

foci ['fousai] focus 的复数

fo'c's'le ['fouksl] *n.* = forecastle

focus ['foukəs] (复 ~es 或 foci ['fousai]) *n.* **1.** 焦点 **2.** 焦距；调焦；聚焦 **3.** (活动、兴趣等的)中心；集中点 **4.** [医]病灶 **5.** [地] (地震的)震源 — *vt.* **1.** 使聚焦；集中 **2.** 调节…的焦距 — *vi.* **1.** 聚焦；集中 **2.** 调节焦距 ‖ ~ing screen (照相机背部的)对焦屏

fodder ['fɔdə] *n.* **1.** 饲料(尤指粗饲料)；〈谑〉(人的)食物 **2.** (创作的)素材 **3.** 〈美俚〉弹药

foe [fou] *n.* **1.** 敌人；敌军 **2.** 反对者；危害物

foetus ['fi:təs] *n.* = fetus

fog¹ [fɔg] *n.* **1.** 雾 **2.** 烟雾；尘雾 **3.** 迷惑，困惑 **4.** [摄] (底片的)灰雾；(影像的)模糊 **5.** (灭火机喷出的)泡沫；喷雾 — (fogged; fogging) *vt.* **1.** 以雾笼罩 **2.** 使困惑，使迷惘；使模糊 **3.** [摄]使(底片)产生雾翳 — *vi.* 被雾笼罩；(因蒙上雾)变得模糊(up) ‖ ~ bank 雾堤(指海上浓雾) / ~ bound *adj.* **1.** 被雾笼罩的 **2.** 受雾所阻的 / ~ broom *n.* 散雾器 / ~ horn *n.* **1.** 雾喇叭，雾号(用以警告雾中的船只) **2.** 响亮尖的声音

fogey ['fougi] *n.* = fogy

foggy ['fɔgi] *adj.* **1.** 有雾的；多雾的 **2.** 雾蒙蒙的；(玻璃窗等)不明净的 **3.** 模糊的，朦胧的 ‖ **foggily** *adv.* / **fogginess** *n.*

fogy ['fougi] *n.* (常作 old ~)守旧者；老守守

foible ['fɔibl] *n.* (性格上的)小缺点，弱点；怪癖；癖好

foil¹ [fɔil] *n.* 1. 箔，金属薄片 2.【建】叶形饰 3.(镜底的)银箔(宝石等的)衬底；食品包装箔 4. 陪衬物；陪衬者 5.(船、艇的)水翼；水翼艇

foil² [fɔil] *vt.* 挫败；使成泡影 — *n.* 花剑，轻剑

foist [fɔist] *vt.* 1. 骗售(假货、劣货) (*on, upon*) 2. 把…强加(于)；把…塞(给) (*on, upon*)

fold¹ [fəuld] *vt.* 1. 折叠；对折 2. 合拢，交叠 3. 抱住 4. 包；裹 5. 调入，拌进(食物作料) — *vi.*1. 折叠起来；对折起来 2. 彻底失败；倒闭 (*up*) — *n.* 1. 折，折叠 2. 褶；褶痕；褶页 3.(盘起来而成的)层 4.〈主英〉山脉等的起伏；【地】褶皱 5.【动】(腕足类的)盘绕 6.【解】褶 ‖ ~**er** *n.* 1. 折叠者；折叠机 2. 文件夹 3. 折叠式印刷品(如传单等) ‖ ~**away** *adj.* 可折挠藏起的；可折向一边的 / ~**out** *n.* (书册中的)褶页

fold² [fəuld] *n.* 1. 羊栏 2. 羊群 3.【集合名词】具有共同信仰的信徒(或人们)

-fold *suf.* [附于数词后]表示"倍"，"重": fivefold

folding [ˈfəuldiŋ] *adj.* 可折叠的 ‖ ~ **chair** 折叠椅 / ~ **door** 折门 / ~ **money** 纸币，大笔现款 / ~ **stair** 折梯 / ~ **stool** 折凳

foliage [ˈfəuliidʒ] *n.* 1.【总称】叶，叶子 2. 一簇叶子 3.【建】叶饰 ‖ ~ **leaf** (别于花叶等的)营养叶 / ~ **plant** 叶子供观赏的植物

folio [ˈfəuliəu] ([复] folios) *n.* 1. 对折纸；对折本；对开本 2.(手抄本或书的)一张 3.【会计】(帐簿中的)页(有时面对面的两页也作一页) — *adj.* 对开的；对折的

folk [fəuk] ([~s] folk(s)) *n.* 1. 人们(现常用 people) 2.〈口〉【复】家属；亲属 — *adj.* 民间的；~ **music** 民间音乐 ‖ ~ **dance** 民间舞蹈 / ~ **etymology** 通俗词源(指通过长期使用而使一个词变成通俗的形式，如 bridegome 变为bridegroom) / ~**lore** *n.* 1. 民间传说 2. 民俗学 / ~ˈ**lorist** 民俗学家 / ~ **song** 民歌 / ~ **story** ~ **tale** /ˈ~ **tale** *n.* 民间故事

folksy [ˈfəuksi] *adj.* 〈美口〉1. 和气的；友好的 2. 随便的，无拘束的(常指故意做作的) 3. 有民间风味的

foll. *abbr.* following

follicle [ˈfɔlikl] *n.* 1.【解】小囊，滤泡；囊状卵泡 2.【植】蓇葖 ‖ **follicular** [fəˈlikjulə] *adj.*

follow [ˈfɔləu] *vt.* 1. 跟随；(在时间、顺序上)紧接在…后面 2. 追赶；追逐；追求 3. 沿着…前进 4. 听从；追随(某人)；遵循；仿效 5. 注视；注意(运动、发展中的事物) 6. 领会；听清楚 7. 从事(职业等)；以…为业 8. 因…而起ˌ由…的结果 9. 做…的后继人 — *vi.* 1. 接着来(或去、发生) 2. 做后继人 3.(由…)所产生，所造成 (*from*) 4. [通常以 it 或 that 做主语，表示某种推论]一定合真实等理，一定正确 ‖ ~-ˈ**up** *adj.* 作为重复(或补充)的；继续的；接着的 — *n.* 1. 连续广告(或推销)法 2.(对病人的)随访 3.(对已刊登或播送的报道的)后续报道

follower [ˈfɔləuə] *n.* 1. 随着者；信徒；拥护者 2. 侍从

following [ˈfɔləuiŋ] *adj.* 1. 接着的(一天、星期等) 2. 下列的，下述的 3.(潮)顺船向前流的；(风)顺船向吹的 — *n.* 1. 一批追随者(或拥护者，部下等) 2. [the ~] 下述的人(或事物) — *prep.*

在…以后

folly ['fɔli] *n.* 1. 愚笨,愚蠢 2. 蠢事,愚蠢行为;傻念头;傻话 3. 〈古〉放荡;罪恶 4. 耗费巨大而又无益的事(或无用的建筑物)

foment [fə'ment] *vt.* 1.【医】热敷,热罨 2. 激起,煽动 ‖ ~ation [ˌfəumen'teiʃən] *n.* / ~er *n.* 激起者,煽动者

fond [fɔnd] *adj.* 1.[只作表语]喜爱的,爱好的(*of*) 2. 溺爱的;多情的 3.(愿望等)不大可能实现的 ‖ ~ly *adv.* 1. 亲爱地 2. 天真地,盲目轻信地 / ~ness *n.*

fondant ['fɔndənt] *n.* 1. 软糖料 2.(半软的)方旦糖

fondle ['fɔndl] *vt.* 爱抚;抚弄

fondu(e) ['fɔndjuː, fɔn'djuː] *n.* 1.(蘸烤面包或苏打饼干用的)热融制干酪(常加酒,蛋等作料制成) 2. 涮制菜肴会;(制涮菜用的)火锅 3. 蛋白酥 ‖ ~ **fork** *n.* 涮叉

font[1] [fɔnt] *n.* 1.【宗】洗礼盆,圣水器 2.〈诗〉泉;源;始

font[2] [fɔnt] *n.*【印】(同样大小和式样的)一副铅字

food [fuːd] *n.* 食物;食品;养料 ‖ ~ **stuff** *n.* 食品;食物中的营养成份

fool [fuːl] *n.* 1. 蠢人,傻子(白痴;莽汉 2. 受愚弄(或欺骗)的人 3.(中世纪封建宫廷内或贵族家中供人娱乐的)弄臣;小丑 4. 有癖好(或特长)的人 — *vt.* 1. 愚弄;欺骗;诈取 2. 浪费;虚度(*away*) — *vi.* 1. 干蠢事 2. 开玩笑 3. 游荡,游手好闲(*about, around*) 4. 瞎弄(*with*) — *adj.*〈美口〉愚蠢的,傻的 ‖ ~**hardy** *adj.* 莽撞的,蛮干的 / ~**proof** *adj.*(方法等)简单(或明了,可靠)得决不会出乱子的 / ~'**s errand** 白费气力的事

foolish ['fuːliʃ] *adj.* 1. 愚蠢的,傻的,笨的 2. 鲁莽的;荒谬的;可笑的 ‖ ~**ly** *adv.* / ~**ness** *n.*

foolscap ['fuːlzkæp] *n.* 1. 大裁(指13×16英寸到13¼×17英寸的大页书写纸) 2.(宫廷弄臣或丑角帽)滑稽帽;(处罚学生用的)圆锥形纸帽

foot [fut] ([复]feet[fiːt]) *n.* 1. 脚,足 2. 步;脚步;步调 3.(床等)放脚的一头;(长袜等的)脚部 4. 最下部;底,底部;底座(行列等的)末尾 5. 英尺(=12英寸,略作 ft.) 6.([复]foots)沉淀物;渣滓;油渣;糟粕 7.(缝纫机的)压脚板 8.[总称]步兵 9.〈诗〉的音步 10.(地衣的足胞;基足 11.【植】花托;发根 12.【韵】(帆的)下缘 — *vt.* 1. 跳(舞);(后接 it)步行 2. 给(袜子等)换底 3. 结算(*up*) 4.〈口〉付(帐单) — *vi.* 1. 跳舞 2. 总计(*up to*) ‖ ~**age** ['futidʒ] *n.*(以英尺表示的)英尺长度(尤指电影胶片的总长度) / ~ **ed** *adj.*[常用以构成复合词] 1. 有脚的;有…脚的 2. 脚步…的;soft-~ *ed* 脚步轻的 / ~ **er** *n.* 1.[常用以构成复合词]高…英尺的人;长…英尺的东西 2. 步行者 ‖ ~-**and-mouth disease**(牛羊等的)口蹄疫 / ~**ball** *n.* 1. 足球;足球运动;橄榄球(运动) 2. 被踢来踢去的悬案(或难题) / ~**baller** *n.* 足球(或橄榄球)运动员 / ~**bath** *n.* 1. 洗脚 2. 脚盆 / ~**board** *n.*(马车、汽车等的)踏脚板 / ~**bridge** *n.* 人行桥,步行桥 / ~**fall** *n.* 脚步;脚步声 / ~ **fault**(网球)脚步犯规;(使)脚步犯规 / ~**gear** *n.*[总称]鞋袜 / ~**hill** *n.* 山麓小丘;[~ hills]山麓丘陵 / ~**hold** *n.* 1. 立足点 2. 稳固的地位(或基础) / ~**light** *n.*[常~**lights**] 1.[戏]脚灯 2. 舞台生涯 / ~**loose** *adj.* 到处走动的;自由自在的 / ~**man** *n.* 1. 男仆 2. 步兵 / ~**mark** *n.* = ~

/'～note *n*. 脚注 *vt.* 给…作脚注 /'～pad *n*. 徒步的拦路强盗 /'～path, *n*. 人行小径 /'～pound *n.* ～pound *n.* 【物】英尺-磅(功的单位) /'pound'second *adj*. 【物】英尺-磅-秒单位制的 /'～print *n.* 1. 脚印,足迹 2. (宇宙飞船等的)预定着陆点 /'～race *n.* 竞走 /'～rest *n.* 搁脚板 /'～slog *vi.* (在泥泞中)费力地行进 /'～slogger *n.* (英俚)长途步行者；步兵 /'～soldier 步兵 /'～sore *adj*. (因走路过多而)脚痛的,脚酸的 /'～step *n.* 1. 脚步；一步的距离；脚步声 2. 足迹 /'～stool *n.* 脚凳 /'～sure *adj*. 脚步稳的 /'～way *n.* ～path /'～wear *n.* 鞋类 /'～well (汽车前座前面供驾驶员及乘客放脚的)脚坑 /'～work *n.* 1. 【体】步法 2. 要跑腿的工作

footing ['futiŋ] *n.* 1. 立足处,立足点 2. 地位；基础；【建】基脚,底脚 3. (友好或平等的)关系 4. 合计,总额 5. 站稳；脚步动作；步法 6. (跑道等的)路面情况

fop [fɔp] *n.* 纨绔子弟,花花公子

foppery ['fɔpəri] *n.* 纨绔习气

foppish ['fɔpiʃ] *adj.* 浮华的；有纨绔子弟习气的 ‖ ～ly *adv.* / ～ness *n.*

for [强 fɔ:; 弱 fə] *prep.* 1. [表示目的]为了：fight ～ national independence 为民族独立而斗争 2. [表示对象、用途等]对；供；适合于：good ～ the health 对健康有好处的 /an instrument ～ measuring speed 测量速度用的仪器 /He is the man ～ the job. 他是做此事的恰当人选。3. [表示目标、去向]往,向：the train ～ Beijing 开往北京的火车 4. 代,替；代表：teach ～ sb. 代某人代课 /the member ～ Coventry (英国)英文考文垂市的议员 5. 表示等值或比例关系]换：He sold it ～ twenty dollars. 他以二十美元把它卖掉

了。/a kilo of tomatoes ～ fifty *fen* (或 fifty *fen* ～ a kilo of tomatoes)五角钱一公斤番茄 /He answered my argument point ～ point. 他逐点答复了我的议论。6. [表示愿望、爱好、持长等]对于：a desire ～ money 金钱欲 /He has an eye ～ colour. 他有审辨色彩的目力。7. 赞成；拥护；有利于：Which candidate are you ～？你赞成哪一位候选人？8. 由于,因为：jump ～ joy 高兴得跳起来 9. 虽然,尽管 For all your explanations, I understand no better than before. 尽管你作了解释,我还是不懂。10. 当作,作为：take sb. ～ a fool 把某人看成是傻瓜 11. 至于,就…而言：So much ～ today. 今天就讲(或做)这些。/ The day is warm ～ April. 在四月份这样的天气算是暖和的了。12. [表示时间、距离、数量]达：march (～) 50 km. a day 一天行军五十公里 13. [表示约定的时间]在：an appointment ～ Monday 星期一的约会 14. [用于插入语,表示列举]：Many people want to buy it because. ～ one thing. the price is low. 许多人想买它,原因之一就是价格便宜。15. [与名词或代词连用,后接动词不定式,构成名词短语]：It is shameful ～ you to do so. 你这样做是可耻的。— *conj.* 因为 (较复杂的为正式,少用于口语中,但语气比 because 弱；回答 why 时应当用 because)

fora ['fɔ:rə] forum 的复数

forage ['fɔridʒ] *n.* 1. (牛马等的)草料,词料 2. 搜寻粮秣 3. 翻找；搜寻 — *vt.* 1. 向…征集粮秣 2. 给(牛马等)吃草料 — *vi.* 1. 搜寻粮秣；征集粮秣 2. 翻找 (*about*)；搜寻 (*for*) ‖ ～ cap 军帽缨

foray ['fɔrei] *vi.* (尤指为掠夺粮食等而)进行突袭 (*into*) — *n.* 突袭

forbade [fə'beid], **forbad** [fə'bæd] forbid 的

forbear 354 **foreclose**

过去式

forbear[1] [fɔːˈbeə](forbore[fɔːˈbɔː], forborne [fɔːˈbɔːn]) vt. 制止自己(做某事),克制 — vi. 1. 制止自己,克制(from) 2. 容忍,忍耐(with)

forbear[2] [ˈfɔːbeə] n. [常～s]祖先

forbearance [fɔːˈbeərəns] n. 1. 忍耐;克制 2.【律】(债务偿还期的)延展

forbearing [fɔːˈbeəriŋ] adj. 宽容的;能忍耐的 ‖ ~ly adv.

forbid [fəˈbid](过去式 forbade[fəˈbeid]或 forbad[fəˈbæd], 过去分词 forbidden [fəˈbidn]; 现在分词 forbidding) vt. 禁止,不许

forbidden [fəˈbidn] forbid 的过去分词 — adj. 被禁止的 ‖ Forbidden City 紫禁城 / ～ degrees 世法通婚的亲等 / ～ fruit 1.【基督教】禁果 2. 因被禁而反而更想弄到手的东西;(偷情等)非法的欢乐

forbidding [fəˈbidiŋ] adj. 可怕的,令人生畏的;险恶的 ‖ ～ly adv.

forbore [fɔːˈbɔː] forbear[1] 的过去式

forborne [fɔːˈbɔːn] forbear[1] 的过去分词

force [fɔːs] n. 1. 力,力量 2. 力气;精力;魄力 3. 势力 4. [常～s]军队,部队;队伍;兵力 5.(从事某种活动的)队;组;人员(如突击部队、推销人员等) 6. 强力;暴力;(舆论等的)压力 7. 推动力;控制力;说服力 8.【物】力 9. (法律、条约、规章等的)效力,约束力 10.(文字、言语等的)确切意义;(精神)实质;要旨 — vt. 1. 强迫,强使,逼 2. 用力打开(门、窗、一条路等);勉强作出(笑脸等);把…强加于(on, upon)3.(用暴力)夺取;夺取(通道、渡口);推动(事物)4. 竭力提高(说话声等);(拍卖时)抬高(喊价);加快(速度)6.(通过温室栽培等)促成(植物)早熟;(通过增加作业等)加速(学生

的)学业 7. 迫使(对手)出某张牌;迫出(某张牌)8. 强奸 ‖ ～d labo(u)r 强迫劳动 / ～d landing 迫降 / ～d march 急行军 / ～'feed vt. 强制进食;强制喂食

forceful [ˈfɔːsful] adj. 1. 强有力的;坚强的 2. 有说服力的 ‖ ～ly adv. / ～ness n.

forceps [ˈfɔːseps] [单复同] n. 1.(医用)镊子,钳子 2.【动】(昆虫的)尾铗 3.【解】钳状体

forcible [ˈfɔːsibl] adj. 1. 强迫的;用暴力的 2. 强有力的;有说服力的 ‖ forcibly adv.

ford [fɔːd] vt. & vi. 涉水而过 — n. 可涉水而过的地方,浅滩 ‖ ～able adj. 可涉水而过的

fore [fɔː] adv. 在前面;在船头 — adj. 在前部的 — n. 前部;船头;前桅 — int.(打高尔夫球者的叫声)前面当心!

fore- comb. form 表示"先"、"前"、"预" forecast, forearm, foresee

fore-and-aft [ˌfɔːrənd'aːft] adj. 从船头到船尾的;纵向的

forearm[1] [ˈfɔːrɑːm] n. 前臂

forearm[2] [fɔːr'ɑːm] vt. 预先武装;使预作准备

forebear [ˈfɔːbeə] n. = forbear[2]

forebode [fɔːˈbəud] vt. 1. 预示 2. 预感(灾祸等)

foreboding [fɔːˈbəudiŋ] n.(凶事的)预知;先兆

forecast [ˈfɔːkɑːst] (forecast(ed)) vt. 1. 预测,预报 2. 预示 — n. 预测,预报

forecastle [ˈfəuksl] n. [船] 1. 前楼 2. 前桅前的上甲板 — deck 艏楼甲板

foreclose [fɔːˈkləuz] vt.【律】取消(抵押人)的抵押品赎回权;取消(赎回权);对(抵押品)行使取消抵押品赎回权 —

vi. 取消抵押品赎回权

foreclosure ['fɔː'kləuʒə] *n.* [律] 取消抵押品赎回权((的法律手续)

foredoom [fɔː'duːm] *vt.* [常用被动语态] 注定

forefather ['fɔː,faːðə] *n.* [常 ~s] 祖先，祖宗；前人

forefinger ['fɔː,fiŋgə] *n.* 食指

forefoot ['fɔːfut] ([复] forefeet ['fɔːfiːt]) *n.* 1.(兽的)前足 2.[船]前踵船柱脚

forefront ['fɔːfrʌnt] *n.* 最前线，最前列

forego[1] [fɔː'gəu] (forewent [fɔː'went], foregone [fɔː'gɔn]) *vt.* 走在…之前；发生于…之前 ∥ ~**er** *n.*

forego[2] [fɔː'gəu] (forewent [fɔː'went], foregone [fɔː'gɔn]) *vt.* = forgo

foregoing [fɔː'gəuiŋ] *adj.* 前述的，前面的

foregone [fɔː'gɔn] foregu 的过去分词 — *adj.* 1.以前的，过去的 2.预先决定的；预知的；无可避免的 ∥ ~ **conclusion** 产生于调查研究前的结论；预料中的必然结局

foreground ['fɔːgraund] *n.* 1.(图画等的)前景 2.突出的地位

forehand ['fɔːhænd] *n.* 1.马身前部(在骑者前面的部分) 2.(网球赛中的)正手击球 — *adj.* 正手击的

forehead ['fɔrid, 'fɔːhed] *n.* 1.额 2.前部

foreign ['fɔrin] *adj.* 1.外国的；在外国的 2.外国来的；外国产的 3.外地的；外省的；(用的 *to*) 5.[医]外来的；异质的 ∥ ~ **aid** 外援-/ ~ **exchange** 外汇 / ~ **minister** 外交部长 / **Foreign Office**(英国等的)外交部 / **Foreign Secretary**(英国)外交大臣

foreigner ['fɔrinə] *n.* 外国人

foreknowledge [fɔː'nɔlidʒ] *n.* 预知，先见

foreleg ['fɔːleg] *n.* (兽的)前腿

forelock ['fɔːlɔk] *n.* 额发，前发；鬃毛(尤指马的)

foreman ['fɔːmən] ([复] foremen) *n.* 1.工头，领班 2.陪审团团长

foremast ['fɔːmaːst] *n.* [船]前桅 ∥ '~ **man** *n.* 普通水手

foremost ['fɔːməust] *adj.* 1.最初的；最前面的 2.第一流的；最重要的 — *adv.* 在前面；最重要地

forename ['fɔːneim] *n.* 名(在姓之前，例如 John Smith 中的 John)

forenoon ['fɔːnuːn] *n.* 午前，上午

forensic [fə'rensik] *adj.* 1.(在公众前)辩论的 2.(用于)法庭的 ∥ ~ **medicine** 法医学

foreordain [,fɔːrɔː'dein] *vt.* 预先决定；注定

foreordination [,fɔːrɔːdi'neiʃən] *n.* 命中注定；天数；预先决定

forerunner ['fɔː,rʌnə] *n.* 1.先驱者 2.(疾病等的)前征，前兆

foresee [fɔː'siː] (foresaw [fɔː'sɔː], foreseen [fɔː'siːn]) *vt.* 预见，预知 ∥ ~**able** *adj.* 可预见到的

foreshadow [fɔː'ʃædəu] *vt.* 预示，是…的预兆

foresight ['fɔːsait] *n.* 1.先见之明；预见 2.深谋远虑 3.[测]前视 4.(枪炮的)准星

foreskin ['fɔːskin] *n.* [解] 包皮

forest ['fɔrist] *n.* 1.林区；森林(森林般的)一丛 2.[英史]御猎场 — *vt.* 在…造林；使成为森林

forestall [fɔː'stɔːl] *vt.* 1.抢在…之前采取行动 2.(用先发制人的办法)预先阻止 3.(以囤积)垄断(市场)

forestation [,fɔris'teiʃən] *n.* 造林；护林

forester ['fɔristə] *n.* 1.林务员 2.森林居

民；森林动物 3.【动】虎蛾；斑蛾

forestry ['fɔristri] *n.* 1. 林地 2. 林学 3. 林业

foretaste ['fɔːteist] *n.* 1. 预示；迹象 2. 先尝；预尝到的滋味 — ['fɔː'teist] *vt.* 先尝；预尝到…的滋味

foretell [fɔː'tel] (foretold [fɔː'təuld]) *vt.* 预言；预示

forethought ['fɔːθɔːt] *n.* 1. 预谋；事先的考虑 2. 深谋远虑

foretold [fɔː'təuld] foretell 的过去式和过去分词

forever [fə'revə] *adv.* 〈美〉永远；常常（＝〈英〉for ever）

forevermore [fə,revə'mɔː] *adv.* 〈美〉永远（比 forever 语气强）

forewarn [fɔː'wɔːn] *vt.* 预先警告

forewent [fɔː'went] forego 的过去式

foreword ['fɔːwəːd] *n.* 序，序言，前言

forfeit ['fɔːfit] *n.* 1.（因犯罪、失职、违约等）丧失的东西；没收物；罚金 2.（公民权等的）丧失 — *vt.* 丧失（权利、名誉、生命等）；（作为惩罚被没收或被剥夺而）丧失 — *adj.* 丧失了的；被没收的

forfeiture ['fɔːfitʃə] *n.* 1. 丧失 2. 没收 3. 没收物；罚金

forgather [fɔː'ɡæðə] *vi.* 1. 聚会 2. 偶遇（*with*）3. 交往（*with*）

forgave [fə'ɡeiv] forgive 的过去式

forge¹ [fɔːdʒ] *n.* 1. 锻造车间；铁匠店 2. 锻铁炉 — *vt.* 1. 打（铁等）；锻造 2. 努力形成；努力促成（团结、协议等）3. 伪造 ‖ ~r *n.* 1. 锻工 2. 伪造者

forge² [fɔːdʒ] *vi.* 稳步前进；突然加速前进（*ahead*）

forgery ['fɔːdʒəri] *n.* 1.（签字、文件等的）伪造；伪造罪 2. 伪造品；赝品

forget [fə'ɡet]（过去式 forgot [fə'ɡɔt]，过去

分词 forgotten [fə'ɡɔtn] 或 forgot；现在分词 forgetting）*vt.* 1. 忘，忘记 2. 遗忘（某制）3. 不再把（争论、分歧等）放在心里 — *vi.* 忘记（*about*）

forgetful [fə'ɡetful] *adj.* 1. 健忘的 2.（对…）不注意的，疏忽的（*of*）‖ ~ly *adv.* / ~ness *n.*

forget-me-not [fə'ɡetminɔt] *n.*【植】勿忘草

forgivable [fə'ɡivəbl] *adj.* 可宽恕的

forgive [fə'ɡiv]（forgave [fə'ɡeiv]；forgiven [fə'ɡivn]）*vt.* 1. 原谅，饶恕，宽恕 2. 豁免（债务等）3. 饶恕，宽恕 ‖ ~ness *n.* 饶恕，宽恕

forgiving [fə'ɡiviŋ] *adj.* 宽大的，仁慈的 ‖ ~ly *adv.*

forgo [fɔː'ɡəu]（forwent [fɔː'went]，forgone [fɔː'ɡɔn]）*vt.* 摒弃；放弃

forgot [fə'ɡɔt] forget 的过去式和过去分词

forgotten [fə'ɡɔtn] forget 的过去分词

fork [fɔːk] *n.* 1. 叉；把（；耙等的）叉；叉架 2. 餐叉 3.（路、河、树木等的）分岔；分岔点，岔口；岔路；岔流 4. 叉状电光 5.【音】音叉（＝tuning ~）— *vi.* 分岔，分叉 — *vt.* 1. 使成叉状 2. 叉起；把 ‖ ~ed *adj.* 叉状的；有叉的；~ed lightning 叉状闪电 ‖ ~lift *n.*【机】铲车，叉式升降机

forlorn [fə'lɔːn] *adj.* 1. 被遗弃的；孤独凄凉的 2. 可怜的，悲惨的 3. 几乎无望的 ‖ ~ly *adv.* / ~ness *n.* ‖ ~ hope 渺茫的希望；成功希望很少的计划（或举动）

form [fɔːm] *n.* 1. 形；形态 2.（人、动物的）形体；体型；人体模型，模特儿 3. 形式；方式 4. 类型 5.（组织等的）体制；（文艺等的）体裁 6. 格式；表格（纸）7.【语】词形，形式 8.（运动员等的）竞技状态 10.【物】（晶）面式；【印】印版 11.（中等学校的）年级 12. 长板凳 — *vt.* 1. 形成；构成；

【语】构(词);造(句) **2.** 塑造 **3.** 使组成;建立;养成 **4.** 使排列;编(队伍) **5.** 想出(意见等);作出(结论、判断) — *vi.* **1.** 形成;产生 **2.** (士兵等)排成某种队形(*into*);排好队(*up*) ‖ **~less** *adj.* 无形状的;无定形的 ‖ **~ letter**(内容相同可分寄多人的)通函;印刷函件;打印信件

formal ['fɔːml] *adj.* **1.** 外形的;形态的;形式(上)的 **2.** 正式的;拘泥形式的;拘谨的;刻板的 **4.** 布置得很整齐的;匀称的;有条理的 **5.** 合乎格式的;正规的;有效的 **6.** 【语】规范的 ‖ **~ly** *adv.* 形式上;正式地

formaldehyde [fɔː'mældɪhaɪd] *n.* 【化】甲醛

formalin ['fɔːməlɪn] *n.* 【化】甲醛水溶液,福尔马林

formalism ['fɔːməlɪzəm] *n.* 形式主义;拘泥形式 ‖ **formalist** *n.* 形式主义者;拘泥形式的人 *adj.* 形式主义的;拘泥形式的 / **formalistic** [,fɔːmə'lɪstɪk] *adj.* 形式主义的

formality [fɔː'mælɪtɪ] *n.* **1.** 拘泥形式;拘谨 **2.** [常 formalities] 正式手续 **3.** 礼节;俗套

formalize ['fɔːməlaɪz] *vt.* **1.** 使具有形式;使定形 **2.** 使成正式 ‖ **formali'zation** *n.*

format ['fɔːmæt] *n.* **1.** (出版物的)版式;开本 **2.** 【计】(数据安排的)格式 **3.** (安排等的)样式,方式(录像带之间的)制式

formation [fɔː'meɪʃən] *n.* **1.** 形成;构成;组成;塑造 **2.** 形成物;组成物;结构 **3.** 【军】队形;编队 **4.** 【语】(词的)构成 **5.** 【地】地(岩)层

formative ['fɔːmətɪv] *adj.* **1.** 形成的;有形成性格的 **2.** 【语】构词的 **3.** 造型的

former ['fɔːmə] *adj.* **1.** 以前的,从前的 ‖ [the ~]前者(与 the latter 相对);前者

的 ‖ **~ly** *adj.* 以前,从前

formic ['fɔːmɪk] *adj.* 蚂蚁的 ‖ **~ acid** 【化】甲酸,蚁酸

formidable ['fɔːmɪdəbl] *adj.* **1.** 可怕的,令人生畏的 **2.** 难对付的;难克服的 ‖ **~ness** *n.* / **formidably** *adv.*

Formosa [fɔː'məusə] *n.* 福摩萨(某些外国人沿用的十六世纪葡萄牙殖民主义者对我国台湾省的称呼)

formula ['fɔːmjulə] *n.* [复] formulas 或 formulae ['fɔːmjuliː]) *n.* **1.** (日常礼节、法律文件或宗教仪式等的)惯用语句,俗套话(如见面时讲的 How do you do? 及信尾的 Very truly yours 等) **2.** 公式;程式;(作为讨论、协商或行动的基本原则的)准则;方案 **3.** 处方;(婴儿食物等的)配方;(用牛奶等)配制成的婴儿喂养奶 **4.** 【数】公式;【化】分子式 — *adj.* (赛车)符合规格的

formulate ['fɔːmjuleɪt] *vt.* **1.** 用公式表示;把…化成公式 **2.** 系统地阐述(或提出) **3.** 制定(肥皂、塑料等)的配方;按配方制造(或配制) ‖ **formu'lation** *n.*

fornicate ['fɔːnɪkeɪt] *vi.* 私通(常指未婚男女间或一方未婚者而言) ‖ **forni'cation** *n.*

forsake [fə'seɪk] (forsook [fə'suk], forsaken [fə'seɪkən]) *vt.* 遗弃,抛弃;摒绝

forsooth [fə'suːθ] *adv.* 的确,当然(现多用于反语或讽刺语句中)

forswear [fɔː'sweə] (forswore [fɔː'swɔː], forsworn [fɔː'swɔːn]) *vt.* **1.** 发誓抛弃;断然放弃 **2.** 发誓否认 **3.** [~ oneself] 发伪誓;作伪证

forsythia [fɔː'saɪθɪə] *n.* 【植】连翘

fort [fɔːt] *n.* **1.** 堡垒,要塞 **2.** 边界贸易站(原设有堡垒)

forte [fɔːt, 'fɔːteɪ] *n.* **1.** 长处,特长,擅长 **2.** 刀身强部(自中央至刀柄)

forte ['fɔːti]（意）【音】*adj*. 响的,强的 — *adv*. 用强音,响亮地,有力地 — *n*. 强音记号(略作f);用强音奏的一段乐曲

forth [fɔːθ] *adv*. 1. 向前方;向前 2. 向外;由隐而显

forthcoming [ˌfɔːθ'kʌmiŋ] *adj*. 1. 即将到来的;即将出现的 2.[只作表语]现有的;(需要时)唾手可得的 3.[口]愿意帮助的;乐于供给消息的

forthright ['fɔːθrait] *adj*. 直率的;直截了当的

forthwith [ˌfɔːθ'wiθ] *adv*. 即刻

fortieth ['fɔːtiiθ] *num*. 1. 第四十(个) 2. 四十分之一(的)

fortification [ˌfɔːtifi'keiʃən] *n*. 1. 筑城;城垒;防御;筑城学 2.[常～s]防御工事(如城、碉堡等) 3. 防御区;设防阵地 4.(食品的)强化;(酒)的加度

fortify ['fɔːtifai] *vt*. 1. 增强(体力、结构等) 2. 筑垒于;设防于 3. 使(论点等)坚强有力;坚定(信心等) 4. 给(酒)加度,增加(酒)的酒精含量 5. 强化(食品),在(食品中)增加(以维生素或矿物质等) — *vi*. 筑御工事

fortissimo [fɔː'tisiməu]（意）*adj. & adv*. 【音】极强的(地),特强的(地)

fortitude ['fɔːtitjuːd] *n*. 坚忍;刚毅

Fort-Lamy [ˌfɔːt'lɑːmiː] *n*. 拉密堡（Ndjamena 恩贾梅纳的旧称）[乍得首都]

fortnight ['fɔːtnait] *n*. 十四日,两星期

fortnightly ['fɔːtˌnaitli] *adj. & adv*. 每隔一次的(地);每两周的(地) — *n*. 双周刊

fortress ['fɔːtris] *n*. 堡垒,要塞

fortuitous [fɔː'tjuːitəs] *adj*. 1. 偶然的;偶然发生的 2. 幸运的 ‖ ~**ly** *adv*. / ~**ness** *n*.

fortunate ['fɔːtʃənit] *adj*. 1. 幸运的;侥幸

的 2. 带来幸运的 ‖ ~**ly** *adv*.

fortune ['fɔːtʃən] *n*. 1. 命运;运气 2.[F-]命运女神 3. 财富;大量财产 ‖ ~**-less** *adj*. 不幸的;无财产的 / ~**-hunter** 企图通过结婚发财的男子 / ~**-teller** *n*. 给人算命的人

forty ['fɔːti] *num*. 1. 四十;四十个(人或物);第四十个(卷、章、页等) — *n*. 1.[forties](世纪的)四十年代 2. 四十岁;[forties]四十到四十九岁的时期 3.(阿拉勃赛)一局中一方获得的第三分 ‖ ~**'five** *n*. 1. .45口径的手枪(常写作 .45) 2. 每分钟四十五转的密纹唱片(常写作 45) / ~**'niner** *n*.（美国)一八四九年涌往加利福尼亚州淘金的人 / ~ **winks** 午睡,盹儿

forum ['fɔːrəm] *n*.（[复] forums 或 fora ['fɔːrə]）1.（古罗马城镇）用于公开讨论的广场(或市场) 2. 论坛;讨论会;(广播、电视)专题讨论节目

forward ['fɔːwəd] *adj*. 1. 在前面的;向前的 2. 进步的;急进的;过激的 3.(庄稼、季节、儿童等)早的;早熟的 4. 热心的;易于…的;动辄就…的 5. 唐突的;冒失的;孟浪的 6.[商]期货的;预约的 7.[海](船身)前部的 — *adv*. 1. 向前,前进 2. 将来,今后 3.[与 put、bring 连用](身体)(足球、篮球等)的前锋 — *vt*. 1. 促进;促使(植物等)生长 2. 发送;寄发(货物等) 3. 转递,转交(信件等) ‖ ~**ly** *adv*. 热心地;热切地;热心地;唐突地、鲁莽地 / ~**ness** *n*. 热切;热心;早熟;唐突,鲁莽 ‖ ~ **echelon**【军】先头梯队;前进指挥所 / ~**-looking** *adj*. 向前看的;有远见的

forwards ['fɔːwədz] *adv*. = forward

forwent [fɔː'went] forgo 的过去式

fossil ['fɔsl] *n*. 1. 化石 2. 僵死的事物;

语中保持的旧词(如 to and fro 中的 fro)
3. 老顽固;守旧者 — *adj.* 1. 化石的 2. 陈旧的;顽固的

fossilize ['fɒsilaiz] *vt.* 1. 使成化石 2. 使 (思想等)僵化 — *vi.* 1. 变成化石 2. (思想等)僵化 ‖ fossili'zation *n.*

foster ['fɒstə] *vt.* 1. 养育,抚养 2. 培养; 鼓励;促进 3. 抱有(希望等) — *adj.* 收养的;收养孤儿的;所收养的孩子的 ‖ ~ **brother** 义兄弟 / ~ **child** 收养的孩子;养子女 / ~ **daughter** 养女 / ~ **father** 养父 / ~ **home** 寄养家庭 / ~ **mother** 养母 / ~'**mother** *vt.* 收养;领养 *n.* (英)带养小鸡的暖壶 / ~ **parent** 养父(或养母) / ~ **sister** 义姐妹 / ~ **son** 养子

fought [fɔ:t] fight 的过去式和过去分词

foul [faul] *adj.* 1. (味道)难闻的,恶臭的; (食物等)腐败的,腐烂发臭的 2. 肮脏的,污浊的;泥泞的 3. 罪恶的,邪恶的,可恶的 4. (言语)下流的:恶语咒骂的 5. (天气等)恶劣的,暴风雨的(风)逆的 6. 不利于航行的 7. (比赛中)犯规的;不正当的 8. (管道、通路等)塞满的,淤塞的 9. (船)污秽的(指船底粘满了海藻、贝壳) 9. (绳索等)被缠住的 10. [印]错误很多的:错误百出的 11. (口)讨厌的;令人作呕的 — *adv.* 违反规则地;不正当地 — *vt.* 1. (比赛中)对...犯规 2. 缠绕 3. 碰撞 — *vt.* 1. 弄脏;污染;玷污 2. 使壅塞;缠住 4. 碰撞 5. (船)行驶污秽 3. (风)逆 败,腐烂 5. (管道等)壅塞(*up*) 3. (绳索,链条等)缠结 4. (船)行驶碰撞 5. (比赛中)犯规 ‖ ~ **ly** *adv.* 下流地;卑鄙地 / ~ **ness** *n.* ‖ ~' **mouthed** *adj.* 讲话下流的;恶语咒骂的 / ~ **play** 1. (比赛中的)犯规动作 2. 奸诈行径;暴行 / ~' **up** *n.* 混乱;故障

found[1] [faund] find 的过去式和过去分词

found[2] [faund] *vt.* 1. 为(房屋等)打基础;建立;缔造 2. 创立(学说等);用基金创办 3. 使有根据(*on, upon*) — *vi.* ‖ ~ **father** 创建人;发起者;开国元勋

found[3] [faund] *vt.* 铸;铸造;熔;熔制(玻璃等)

foundation [faun'deiʃən] *n.* 1. 建立,创办 2. 地基,地脚;底座 3. 基础;基本原理;根据 4. 基金;基金会 5. (衣服等)的衬底;妇女胸衣(= ~ garment) ‖ ~ **cream** 粉底霜(涂敷其他化妆品前打底用) / ~ **school** 靠基金维持的学校 / ~ **stone** 1. (特指建筑物等开工典礼上放置的)基石 2. 基础;根本

founder[1] ['faundə] *n.* 奠基者;创立者;缔造者 ‖ ~'**member** *n.* (团体等)的创办人;发起人

founder[2] ['faundə] *vi.* 1. (马或骑马者因奔驰过度而)摔倒(在泥潭等中)动弹不得 2. (船)沉没 3. 垮掉;失败 — *vt.* 使(马)摔倒

foundling ['faundliŋ] *n.* 弃儿,弃婴

foundry ['faundri] *n.* 1. 铸造,翻砂 2. 铸工车间;铸工厂 3. 玻璃(制造)厂

fount[1] [faunt] *n.* 1. (诗)泉,源泉 2. (灯的)贮油器;墨水缸

fount[2] [faunt, font] *n.* = font[2]

fountain ['fauntin] *n.* 1. 泉水;喷泉 2. 人造喷泉;喷水池;喷嘴式饮水器(= drinking ~) 3. 源泉;根源 4. 液体贮藏器(如灯的贮油器,墨水缸) ‖ ~'**head** *n.* 源头;源泉;根源;本源 / ~ **pen** 自来水笔

four [fɔ:] *num.* 四;四个(人或物);第四(卷、章、页等) — *n.* 1. 四个(人或物)一组 2. [~s][机]四汽缸发动机;四汽缸汽车 3. 四人赛艇的划船队;四人赛

艇;[～s]四人赛艇划船比赛 4. 四岁 5. 四点钟,四时 ‖ ～fold adj. & adv. 四倍;四重 ‖ '～-di'mensional adj. 【数】四维的 / '～-'footed adj. 足足的 / '～-'letter word 四字母粗俗下流词 / '～-part adj. 【音】四声部的 / '～-pence n. 四便士 / '～-penny adj. 四便士的 / '～-'poster n. 有四根帐杆的床 / '～-'pounder n. 发射四磅炮弹的火炮 / '～-'score n. & adj. 八十 / '～-'square adj. 方形的; 坚定不移的;直率的;坦白的 / '～-star adj. (美) 1. 极好的(宾馆、饭店等)四星级的 2. 四星(上将)级的 / '～-'stroke cycle[机]四冲程循环 / '～-'wheeler n. 四轮(出租马)车

fourteen ['fɔː'tiːn] num. 十四;十四个(人或物);第十四(卷、章、页等) n. 1. 十四岁 2. 十四点钟(即下午两点钟) ‖ ～th num. 1. 第十四(个) 2. 十四分之一(的) n. (月的)第十四日

fourth [fɔːθ] num. 1. 第四(个个) 2. 四分之一(的) n. 1. [～s](商品)四等品 2. 【音】四度音程;四度和音;第四音级 3. (月的)第四日 ‖ ～ dimension [物]第四维(相对论中指时间) / ～ estate, Fourth Estate 第四等级(指报刊、新闻界) / Fourth Republic (法兰西)第四共和国 (1946-1958)

fowl [faul] n.[复]fowl(s) n. 1. 禽 2. 家禽(鸡、鸭、鹅,尤指长成的鸡) 3. 禽肉 ‖ ～ run 养鸡场

fowling ['fauliŋ] n. 捕猎野禽 ‖ ～ piece 鸟枪;猎枪

fox [fɔks] n. 1. 狐 2. 狐皮 3. 狡猾的人 — vt. 1. 使(啤酒等)发酵变酸 2.[常用过去分词]使(书页等)生褐色(或黄色)斑点 3. 为(皮鞋)换面 4.(口)欺骗;难住 — vi. 1.(啤酒等)变酸 2.(书

页等)生斑变色 3.(口)装假 ‖ '～-brush n. 狐尾 / ～ earth 狐穴 / ～ glove n.[植]毛地黄 / ～ hole n.[军]散兵坑(可容一、二人的小型掩体) / '～-hound n. 狐犬(用以捕捉的大猎狗) / '～-hunt vi.(用猎狗)猎狐 (用猎狗的)猎狐 / '～-hunter n. 猎狐者 / '～-tail n. 1. 狐尾 2.[植]狐尾草(尤指看麦娘、狗尾草等);石松 / '～-trot n. 1. 狐步舞 2.(骑马的)狐步、轻步 — vi. 跳狐步舞

foxy ['fɔksi] adj. 1. 似狐的;狡猾的 2. 狐色的、赤褐色的 3. 变了色的;有褐斑的 4.(美)吸引人的 ‖ foxiness n.

foyer ['fɔiei] n.(剧场、旅馆等的)门厅;剧场休息室

Fr[化]元素钫(francium)的符号

fracas ['frækɑː, 'freikɑː] ([复] fracas ['frækɑːz]或 fracases ['freikɑːsiz]) n. 喧闹的打架;大声吵架

fraction ['frækʃən] n. 1. 小部分;片断;碎片 2. 一点儿,一些 3.【数】分数 4.【化】馏分;级分

fractional ['frækʃənəl] adj. 1. 部分的;碎片的 2. 分数的;小数的;(有)零头的 3. [商]不足某单位的;(证券交易中)零股的 3. 【化】级分的;分步的

fractious ['frækʃəs] adj. 1. 倔强的;反抗的 2. 暴躁的;易怒的 ‖ ～ly adv. / ～ness n.

fracture ['fræktʃə] n. 1. 破裂;断裂;折断 2. 裂缝;裂面;裂痕 3.【医】骨折 4.【矿】断面 — vt. & vi. (使)破裂;(使)断裂;(使)折断

fragile ['frædʒail] adj. 1. 脆的;易碎的 2. 脆损坏的 2. 脆弱的;虚弱的;体质弱的 ‖ fragility[frə'dʒiliti] n.

fragment ['frægmənt] n. 1. 碎片,破片,碎块;断片 2.(文艺作品等的)残存部分 — [fræg'ment] vi. & vt. (使)成碎片

(使)分裂

fragmentary ['fræɡməntəri] *adj.* **1.** 碎片的,碎块的,断片的 **2.** 不完全的;不连续的 **3.** [地]碎屑的

fragmentation [ˌfræɡmen'teiʃən] *n.* **1.** 碎裂;分裂;破碎 **2.** (思想等的)崩溃;【心】行为错乱 ‖ ~ **bomb** 杀伤炸弹

fragrance ['freiɡrəns] *n.* 芬芳;香味;香气

fragrant ['freiɡrənt] *adv.* 芬芳的;香的 ‖ ~ **ly** *adv.*

frail [freil] *adj.* **1.** 脆弱的;易损的;虚弱的 **2.** 意志薄弱的,易被引诱的 ‖ ~ **ly** *adv.* / ~ **ness** *n.*

frailty ['freilti] *n.* **1.** 脆弱;虚弱 **2.** 意志薄弱 **3.** (因意志薄弱而犯的)过失;弱点

frame [freim] *n.* **1.** 构架;骨架;结构;【机】架;座 **2.** 框架;框子 **3.** (人或动物的)骨骼;身驱 **4.** 心情,精神状态 **5.** (社会、政府等的)机构,组织 **6.** (电影的)画面,镜头;(电视图像的)帧 **7.** (船)肋骨 **8.** 【农】(可掀动的)御寒玻璃罩,便携式温床 **9.** [印]排字架;排字台 **10.** (美俚)诬陷 — *vt.* **1.** 构造;塑造 **2.** 制定;拟出(计划等);设计;想象 **3.** 给…装框子(或框架) 4. 使适合 **5.** (俚)陷害,诬害;捏造(*up*) **6.** 说出,讲出;发出 ‖ ~ **antenna** [无]框形天线 / ~ **house** 框架房屋 / ~ **-up** *n.* (美俚)诬害;阴谋 / ~ **work** *n.* **1.** 构架(工程);框架;结构;构造 **2.** 参照标准;基准体系;准则

franc [fræŋk] *n.* 法郎(法国、比利时和瑞士等国的货币单位)

France [frɑːns] 法国,法兰西[西欧]

franchise ['fræntʃaiz] *n.* **1.** 公民权(尤指选举权) **2.** (美)(政府给于个人、公司或社团经营某种事业的)特权,特许 **3.** 保险免赔限度;保险免赔额 — *vt.*

…以特许;给予…公民权(或选举权)

francium ['frænsiəm] *n.* 【化】钫

Franco- *comb. form* 表示"法国"

frank [fræŋk] *adj.* **1.** 坦白的,直率的;真诚的 **2.**【医】症状明显的 — *vt.* **1.** 免费邮寄 **2.** 盖免费递寄邮戳于(邮件);用自动邮资盖印机盖印于…在…上盖"邮资已付"戳 — *n.* 免费邮寄戳(或签字) ‖ ~ **ly** *adv.* 坦白地,直率地 / ~ **ness** *n.* / ~ **ing-ma'chine** *n.* (加盖"邮资已付"印记的自动)邮资机

frankfurter ['fræŋkfətə] *n.* 法兰克福香肠,熏猪牛肉香肠

frankincense ['fræŋkinˌsens] *n.* 乳香(乳香属植物圣皮渗出的一种树脂)

frantic ['fræntik] *adj.* **1.** (因愤怒、痛苦、悲哀或快乐等)发狂似的 **2.** 狂暴的,狂乱的 ‖ ~ **(al)ly** *adv.*

fraternal [frə'tə:nl] *adj.* **1.** 兄弟的;兄弟般的 **2.** (美)兄弟会的,互助会的 ‖ ~ **ly** *adv.* ◇ ~ **order** · **society** (美)兄弟会,共济会

fraternity [frə'tə:niti] *n.* **1.** 兄弟关系;友爱;博爱 **2.** (美国)大学生联谊会(常以希腊字母命名,并有秘密仪式);兄弟会,互助会 **3.** 一群同职业(或同兴趣、同信仰)的人

fraternize ['frætənaiz] *vi.* **1.** 亲如兄弟;亲善;友善(*with*, *together*) **2.** (占领军)与敌人;与占领区人民友善交往;(口)与敌国女性发生性关系(*with*) ‖ ˌfraterni'zation *n.*

fratricide ['frætrisaid] *n.* **1.** 杀兄弟(或姊妹)的行为 **2.** 杀兄弟(或姊妹)的人 **3.** 【军】自残

fraud [frɔːd] *n.* **1.** 欺骗,欺诈;欺诈行为;诡计 **2.** 骗子;假货

fraudulence ['frɔːdjuləns] *n.* 欺骗性;欺诈

fraudulent ['frɔːdjulənt] adj. 1. 欺骗性的;欺诈的 2. 骗得的 ‖ **~ly** adv.

fraught [frɔːt] adj. [只作表语] 充满的 (with)

fray[1] [frei] n. 1. 吵架;打架;冲突 2. 争论;辩论

fray[2] [frei] vt. 1. 磨损(织物的边缘);磨擦(绳子的末端)以致纤维散开 2. 使(关系、神经等)紧张 — vi. 1. 被磨损;被擦碎 2.(关系、神经等)变得紧张

frazzle ['fræzl] n. & vi. 1.(把…)穿破;(使)磨损 2.(使)疲惫 — n. 1. 磨损 2. 磨损的边缘(或末端) 2. 疲惫 ‖ **~d** adj. 穿破了的;磨损了的;疲惫的

freak [friːk] n. 1. 任性举动;怪诞行为;怪念头 2. 畸形的人(或动植物)(= ~ of nature);反常现象 — adj. 反常的;奇特的 — vt. 在…上形成奇特的斑纹(或条纹) ‖ **~ed** adj. 有奇特的斑纹(或条纹) ‖ **~-out** n. 1. 吸毒引起的幻觉;逃避现实(尤指通过吸毒);通过吸毒逃避现实的人 2. 嬉皮士聚会 3. 反常行动

freakish ['friːkiʃ] adj. 1. 异想天开的;捉摸不定的 2. 畸形的;反常的;奇特的 ‖ **~ly** adv. / **~ness** n.

freckle ['frekl] n. 雀斑;小斑点 — vt. & vi.(使)生雀斑;(使)生小斑点

free [friː] adj. 1. 自由的;无约束的 2. 空闲的;(空间,房间等)空余的 3. 无…的:an ice-~ harbour 不冻港 4. 免费的;免税的 5.(用钱)大手大脚的;慷慨的;(言论、生活等)随便的,不严肃的,不检点的 6.(讲话等)直爽的,坦白的(with) 7.【化】游离的 8.(步伐等)轻快的,从容的 9.(道路等)畅通无阻的;(港口、城市等)自由开放的 — adv. 1. 自由地,无阻碍地 2. 免费地 — vt. 自由,解放;免除,解除,使摆脱(of,

from) ‖ **~board** n.(船)干舷高;干舷 / **~booter** n. 海盗;强盗 / **~born** adj. 生来自由的 / **Free Church** n.(英国国教分离出来的)自由教会 / **~drop** n. 不用降落伞的自由空投(物) vt. 自由空投 / **~fall** n.(投掷物的)自由下落;(降落伞张开前的)自由下落 2.(火箭等的)惯性运动 / **~flight** 自由飞行;(导弹等的)惯性飞行,无动力飞行 / **~-for-all** n. 可供自由参加的竞赛(或赛跑);可自由发表意见的辩论;在场者都参加的混战 adj. 可供自由参加的;在场者都参加的 / **~hand** adj.(不用器械)徒手画的 / **~handed** adj. 慷慨的;(用钱)大方的 / **~hold** n. 地产(或职位全期)的终身保有的地产 / **~house**(英)出售各种牌子酒的酒店 / **~labo(u)r** n. 自由人的劳动(与奴隶劳动相对而言) 2.[总称]不属于工会的工人(的劳动) / **~lance** n.(无固定职业,以卖文、卖艺为生的)自由作家(或演员) vi. 做自由作家(或演员) / **~list** n. 免税货物单 2. 免费入场者名单 / **~living** adj. 1. 沉溺于吃喝玩乐的 2.【生】独立生存的;非寄生的,非共生的 / **~loader** n.(口 老是被用别人慷慨占便宜的人 / **~love** 自由性爱(主义) / **~man** n. 自由民;享有市民特权的人 / **~market** 自由市场 / **Free mason** n. 共济会(Free & Accepted Masons)成员 / **Free masonry** n. 共济会的纲领;共济会仪式;[集合名词]共济会成员 / **~radical** [化] 游离基 / **~soil** [美史](南北战争前禁铅的)自由土壤区 / **~speech** 言论自由 / **~spoken** adj. 直言的;说话坦率的 / **~standing** adj.【建】独立式的 / **Free State** 1.[常 Free States] [美史](南北战争前禁铅的)自由州 2.[史] 爱尔兰自由邦(= Irish Free State) / **~stone** n. 1.

毛石、乱石、砂石；易切砂岩 **2.** 离核果实(如桃、梅等)；离核果实的核 *adj.* 离核的 /'~'thinker n. (尤指宗教上的)自由思想家；思想自由的人 /'~'thinking *adj.* 自由思想的 (尤指宗教上)/'~'thought 不受传统宗教思想束缚的自由思想 /~ trade 自由贸易 /~ trader 自由贸易主义者 /~ verse(不受格律约束的)自由诗 /'~'way *n.* (免费)高速公路、(免费)高速干道 /~ wheel(汽车的)空转轮、自由轮(自行车的)飞轮 /'~'wheel *vi.* **1.** (骑自行车或开汽车时)惯性滑行 **2.** 随心所欲(或放任自流)地行动(或生活) /'~ will 自愿；自由意志 /'~ will *adj.* 自愿的，非强迫的

freedman ['friːdmæn] ([复] freedmen ['frixdmen]) *n.* **1.** 自由民 **2.** (法律上)解除了约束的人

freedom ['friːdəm] *n.* **1.** 自由 **2.** 自主(行动、使用等的)自由权 **3.** 直率，放肆；过分亲密 **4.** 免除，解脱(from)**5.**(城市、公司等的)特权

freely ['friːli] *adv.* **1.** 自由地；无拘束地，随意地 **2.** 直率地，坦白地 **3.** 慷慨地；大量地

Freetown ['friːtaun] *n.* 弗里敦[塞拉利昂首都]

freeze [friz] (froze [frəuz], frozen ['frəuzn]) *vi.* **1.** 结冰，凝固 **2.** 大冷起来；感到极冷；冻僵 **3.** 冻牢，凝住 **4.** 愣住；变呆板；变得冷淡 **5.** 站住不动 — *vt.* **1.** 使结冰；使凝固；使冻住 **2.** 冷冻(食物)**3.** 使冻僵(或冻伤、冻死)**4.** 使呆住；用冰冷的目光打量；使害怕 **5.** 冻结(工资、物价等)— *n.* **1.** 冰冻；凝固 **2.** (工资、物价等的)冻结 **3.** 冰冻期，严寒期 ‖ ~ r *n.* **1.** 制冰淇淋者；制冷工 **2.** 致冷器；冷藏箱；冰箱 **3.** 冷藏车，

藏库 ‖ '~-'dry *vt.* 使(食品、疫苗等)冷冻干燥，使升华干燥 /~ frame(电影图像的)定格处理

freezing ['friːziŋ] *adj.* **1.** 冻结的；致冷的；凝固的 **2.** 极冷的 **3.** (态度)冷淡的 ‖ ~ mixture 冷凝剂，冷冻混合物 /~ point[物]冰点，凝固点

freight [freit] *n.* **1.** 船货；货物 **2.** 运费 **3.** 货运 **4.** 货船；货车(= ~ train)**5.** 负担；重担 — *vt.* **1.** 装货于 **2.** 运输(货物)**3.** 租(船等)运货；出租(船等)运费 ‖ ~ car〈美〉(一节)货车 /'~ liner *n.* 〈英〉集装箱定期直达列车

freighter ['freitə] *n.* **1.** 租船人 **2.** (货物的)托运人；承运人 **3.** 货船；运输机

French [frentʃ] *adj.* **1.** 法国的，法兰西的 **2.** 法国人的 **3.** 法语的 **4.** 法国式的 — *n.* **1.** [the ~]总称]法国人 **2.** 法语 ‖ ~ bean〈英〉菜豆(= kidney bean)/~ chalk 滑石 /~ horn 法国号(一种涡旋形铜管乐器)/'~'man *n.* 法国人，法兰西人 /~ window 落地窗 /'~'woman *n.* 法国妇女，法兰西女人

frenetic [frə'netik] *adj.* **1.** 极度激动的，发狂似的 **2.** 精神错乱的，疯狂的 — *n.* 疯子，狂人

frenzied ['frenzid] *adj.* 狂乱的；疯狂的；狂暴的 ‖ ~ly *adv.*

frenzy ['frenzi] *n.* 狂乱，疯狂似的激动

frequency ['friːkwənsi] *n.* **1.** 频繁，屡次 **2.** 次数，重复发生率 **3.** [物]频率，周率

frequent¹ ['friːkwənt] *adj.* **1.** 时常发生的，频繁的；屡次的 **2.** 经常的；习以为常的；常见的 **3.** (脉搏)快的，急的 ‖ ~ly *adv.*

frequent² [fri'kwent] *vt.* 常到，常去，时常出入于 ‖ ~er *n.* 常到某处的人；常客

fresco ['freskəu] ([复]fresco(e)s) *n.* **1.** 湿壁画技法 **2.** 湿壁画

fresh [freʃ] *adj.* **1.** 新的；新近的；新到的 **2.** 新鲜的；未经腌熏的 **(水)**淡的 **3.** 另外的；外加的 **(水)**淡的 无经验的；不熟练的 **5.** (空气、气候)清新的；凉爽的 **(风)**强劲的 **6.** (颜色)鲜艳的；明亮的 有生气的；气色好的 **7.** 精神饱满的 **8.** (谈话等)有创见的；生动的；有启发性的 **9.** (对异性)冒失的；放肆的(with) — *adv.* 刚，オ — *n.* **1.** (一天、一年等的)开始 **2.** 河水的暴涨；泛滥 **3.** (流入海中的)淡水流 ‖ ~ er *n.* 〈英俚〉大学一年级学生 / ~ ness *n.* ‖ ~ breeze 清劲风(五级风，风速每小时 29-38 公里) / ~ gale 强风(风速每小时 62-74 公里) / '~ man *n.* **1.** 新手，生手 **2.** 大学一年级学生；〈美〉中学一年级学生 / '~ water *adj.* **1.** (生在)淡水的 **2.** 内河航行的 **3.** 无经验的；不熟练的 **4.** 内地的；地方的；不知名的

freshen ['freʃn] *vt.* **1.** 使显得新鲜；使显得鲜艳 **2.** 使精神饱满；为(自己)梳洗一番(up) **3.** 使减少咸味；使(水)淡化 **4.** 添(饮料) — *vi.* **1.** 显得新鲜；显得鲜艳 **2.** 变得精神焕发；梳洗一番(up) **3.** (风)变暴 **4.** 减少咸味；变淡 ‖ ~ er *n.* 恢复精力的东西(如饮料等)

freshet ['freʃit] *n.* **1.** (入海的)淡水水流 **2.** (大雨或融雪引起的)山洪，洪水

freshly ['freʃli] *adv.* **1.** 精神饱满地；容光焕发地 **2.** 气味清新地 **3.** 刚，才

fret¹ [fret] (fretted; fretting) *vt.* **1.** 使烦恼；使烦躁；使心焦 **2.** 侵蚀；腐蚀；使消损；使磨损 **3.** (经侵蚀而)形成(沟槽等) **4.** 使(水面)起皱纹 — *vi.* **1.** 烦恼；烦躁；发怒 **2.** (对精神等)起折磨作用 **3.** 消损；磨损；被腐蚀 **4.** (水面)起波纹 — *n.* **1.** 烦恼；烦躁 **2.** 蚀坏；被侵蚀之处

fret² [fret] *n.* **1.** 〔建〕回纹饰，格子细工 **2.**

【音】(吉他等弦乐器指板上定音的)品 **3.** (中世纪妇女作为头饰的)饰网 — (fretted; fretting) *vt.* 用回纹装饰(天花板等) ‖ '~ saw *n.* 线锯 / '~ work *n.* 回纹细工，格子细工；浮雕细工

fretful ['fretful] *adj.* **1.** 烦恼的；烦躁的 **2.** (水面)起波纹的 **3.** (风)一阵阵的 ‖ ~ ly *adv.* / ~ ness *n.*

Freudian ['frɔidiən] *adj.* (奥地利心理学家和精神病医生)弗洛伊德(Freud)学说(或实践)的；弗洛伊德的；弗洛伊德派精神分析法的 ‖ ~ slip (说话漫不经心而漏嘴的)口误，失言

Fri. *abbr.* Friday

friable ['fraiəbl] *adj.* 脆的，易(粉)碎的 ‖ friability [.fraiə'biliti] *n.*

friar ['fraiə] *n.* 〔天主教〕托体体修会修士

fricassee [.frikə'si:] *n.* 原汁焖(或煎)鸡(或肉)块 — *vt.* 把…烹制成原汁焖(或煎)鸡(或肉)块

fricative ['frikətiv] 〔语〕 *adj.* (辅音)摩擦的，由摩擦产生的(如[f],[v],[θ]等) — *n.* 摩擦音

friction ['frikʃən] *n.* **1.** 摩擦；摩擦力 **2.** 摩擦治疗；头发按摩 **3.** 不和，摩擦，倾轧 ‖ ~ al *adj.*

Friday ['fraidi] *n.* **1.** 星期五 **2.** 忠仆(源于英国小说《鲁滨逊飘流记》中鲁滨逊逊的仆人的名字) ‖ ~ s *adv.* 〈美〉每星期五；在任何星期五

fridge [fridʒ] *n.* 〈英口〉= refrigerator

friend [frend] *n.* **1.** 朋友，友人 **2.** 赞助者；支持者；同情者 **3.** 相识者 **4.** 有帮助的事物(或品质) **5.** [F-]〔基督教〕公谊会教友

friendless ['frendlis] *adj.* 没有朋友的 ‖ ~ ness *n.*

friendly ['frendli] *adj.* **1.** 友好的 **2.** 赞助的；支持的(to) — *adv.* 友好地，朋友

般地 — n. 友谊赛 ‖ **friendlily** adv. /
friendliness n.

friendship ['frendʃip] n. 友谊;友好

frieze [friz] n. 【建】壁缘;饰带;雕带

frigate ['frigit] n. 1. (十八世纪至十九世纪)装有大炮的快速帆船 2. 驱逐领舰
3. 护卫舰;护航舰

fright [frait] n. 1. 惊吓 2. 〈口〉奇形怪状的人(或物)

frighten ['fraitn] vt. 使惊恐,吓唬 — vi. 惊恐,害怕 ‖ ~ed adj. 1. 受惊吓的 2.
〈口〉害怕…的(of)

frightful ['fraitful] adj. 1. 可怕的 2.〈口〉非常的,王的;讨厌的 ‖ ~ly adv. 可怕地;〈口〉非常地 / ~ness n.

frigid ['fridʒid] adj. 1. 寒冷的 2. 冷淡的,索然无味的 3. (妇女)性感缺失的,性寒的;性交时达不到高潮的 ‖ ~ly adv. / ~ness n.

frigidity [fri'dʒiditi] n. 1. 寒冷;冷淡;索然无味 2.【医】性感缺失,性寒(尤指妇女的)

frill [fril] n. 1. (服装的)褶边,饰边 2.【动】壳簧 3.【摄】(胶片边缘的)脱膜,脱边 4. [~s]〈口〉不必要的装饰;虚饰;臭架子 — vt. 在…上镶褶边(或饰边) — vi.(胶片边缘)脱膜,脱边 ‖ ~ed adj. 有饰边的 / ~ery n. 衣褶边

fringe [frindʒ] n. 1. 穗;缘饰;流苏;毛边,蓬边 2. 边缘;〈喻〉(学问的)初步,皮毛 3. 一群略知皮毛(或见解偏激)的人 4. (妇女头发的)前刘海 5.【理】伞;缘饰 6.【物】(光学中的)干扰条纹 7. = ~ benefit — vt. 1. 加穗于;在…上装以缘饰 2. 镶边于 ‖ ~ area 【无】条纹区,接收边缘区;散乱边缘区;干扰区域;(城市的)边缘地区 / ~ benefit (工资以外的)附加福利;附带的好处

frippery ['fripəri] n. 1. 便宜而俗艳的服装 2. 便宜的装饰品;无用的小东西;3.(衣着等的)俗艳;过分的装饰;(态度、言语等的)浮夸;低俗;(文体的)炫耀

Frisbee ['frizbi] n. (投掷游戏用的)飞碟 ‖ ~ golf (按高尔夫球打法玩的)飞碟高尔夫运动

frisk [frisk] vi. 欢跃;轻快活泼地跳跃,跳跳蹦蹦 — vt. 1. 使快地摇动(尾巴等) 2. 搜(某人)的身 3.〈俚〉扒窃 — n. 1. 欢跃 2. 搜身

frisky ['friski] adj. 好欢跃的,活泼的 ‖ **friskily** adv. /**friskiness** n.

fritter[1] ['fritə] vt. 消耗;浪费(金钱、时间、精力等)(away)

fritter[2] ['fritə] n. (果馅或肉馅)油煎饼

frivolity [fri'vɔliti] n. 轻薄,轻浮;无聊举动;轻薄话

frivolous ['frivələs] adj. 1. 轻薄的,轻浮的 2. 琐屑的,无意义的 ‖ ~ly adv. / ~ness n.

friz(z) [friz] (frizzed; frizzing) vt. 使卷曲;使(呢面)卷结 — vi.(头发)卷曲 — n. 卷曲的头发;卷结物;卷结物的头发

frizz [friz] vt. & vi. 吱吱地煎(或炸)

frizzle[1] ['frizl] vt. 使(头发等)卷曲(up) — vi. 卷曲起来(up) — n. 1. 卷发;小卷结 2. 卷曲状态

frizzle[2] ['frizl] vt. & vi. 1.(使)发吱吱声(如油煎时) 2.(使)煎(或烤)得很脆

frizzly ['frizli], **frizzy** ['frizi] adj. 满是卷结的;(头发)卷的

fro [frəu] adv.(离)开;回,向后(只用于 to and — 一语中的):to and ~ 来回地

frock [frɔk] n. 1. 女式礼服;连衣裙 2. 工装 3. 僧袍 4.(男子的)礼服大衣(= ~ coat)

frog [frɔg] *n.* 1. 蛙 2.【动】(马蹄底中部的)蹄楔 3. 盘花钮扣 4.（腰带上挂剑或武器等的）搭环 5.（铁路）辙叉 6. [F-]（贬）法国佬;法国话 ‖ ~**man** *n.* 蛙人（使用蛙式潜水设备的人）/ ~-**march** *vt.* 蛙式抬运（犯人）（由四人执犯人四肢，将其面朝下抬着走）;蛙式押送（将人双臂反拧后强推行走）

frolic ['frɔlik] *n.* 1. 嬉戏;欢乐;嬉闹 2. 欢乐的集会 — (frolicked; frolicking) *vi.* 嬉戏;闹着玩

frolicsome ['frɔliksəm] *adj.* 嬉戏的;爱闹着玩的 ‖ ~**ly** *adv.* / ~**ness** *n.*

from (弱 frəm, frm; 强 frɔm) *prep.* 1. [表示起点]从…起 — now on 从现在起,今后 2. [表示来源]从,从…来; a fact learned ~ reading 从阅读中了解到的事实/ She is ~ Scotland. 她是苏格兰人。3. [表示根据]据: I am speaking ~ a personal point of view. 我是在谈个人看法。/ paint ~ nature (绘画)写生 4. [表示原因、动机]由于,出于;act ~ necessity 不得已而采取行动 5. [表示原料]由;Steel is made ~ iron. 钢是由铁炼成的。6. [表示情况、状态的转变]recover ~ illness 病愈 7. [表示脱离、离开]: Why was he absent ~ school yesterday? 他昨天为什么缺了学?8. [表示去除、免掉、阻止等]: be free ~ arrogance and rashness 不骄不躁/protect seedlings ~ frost 保护幼苗使不受霜冻之害 9. [表示识别、区别]: know right ~ wrong 分清是非 10. [后接副词或前置词]: long ago 从很久以前起/a sound ~ behind the door 从门后传出的声音

frond [frɔnd] *n.* 1.（蕨类或棕榈类、苏铁类的）叶 2.（藻类的）藻体;植物体（指苔藓）3.（某些动物机体中的）叶状扩张

front [frʌnt] *n.* 1. 前面,正面;建筑物的(正)面;前部 2. 前线,前方;战线 3.（政治上的）阵线 4. [诗]前额;脸 5.（企业、团体等的）名誉负责人;掩护门面 6. 外表;装腔作势;厚颜无耻 7. 态度;看法 8. [the ~](海滨避暑地的)滨海人行道;海边（或湖边等）土地;临海地 9. [气]锋（冷热空气团的分界处）10.（妇女的）额前假发 11.（男子衬衫的）前胸 12.（旅馆职员呼唤侍者时用语）来人 — *vt.* 1. 面对,朝向 2. 位于…的前面 3. 对付;反对,对抗;藐视 4. 装饰…的正面 5. [建]给…加上舌前位置(音) — *vi.* 朝,朝向(on, upon, to, towards) — *adj.* 1. 前面的;前部的;(位置)在前的 2. [语]舌前的 — *adv.* 向前;向前面;在前面 ‖ ~ **bencher**（英国下议院的）前座议员 / ~ **burner** 1.（多眼炉灶的）前灶眼 2. 优先地位,主要地位 / ~ **line** 前线;第一线 / ~**line** *adj.* 前线的;第一线的 / ~ **man**（企业、团体等的）名誉负责人;（为他人）作掩护的人 / ~ **matter**（书籍的）文前事项 / ~ **office**（机关、机构中的）前办事处 / ~ **page**（报纸的）头版 / ~-**'page** *adj.* (消息、新闻等)头版的,重要的,惹动的 *vt.* 把…登在头版 / ~-**'runner** *n.* 1.（赛跑中）领先的人 2.（竞争中的）领先者

frontage ['frʌntidʒ] *n.* 1.（建筑物等的）正面,前方 2. 临街（河、湖等）土地 3.（临街的）屋前空地;临街地界

frontal ['frʌntl] *adj.* 1. 前面的,正面的 2. 前额的 — *n.* 1. 额骨 2. 额前装饰物 3.（建筑物的）前部 4. [建]（门、窗上面的）三角顶饰 ‖ ~**ly** *adv.*

frontier ['frʌntiə] *n.* 1. 国境,边境;边疆 2.（靠近未开发地带的）边远地区 3.（未经充分分析或利用的科学、文化等

方面的)知识边缘;新领域

frontiersman ['frʌntiəzmən] ([复] frontiersmen ['frʌntiəzmən]) *n*. 靠近未开发地区的)边远地区居民

frontispiece ['frʌntispi:s] *n*. 1. (书籍等的)卷首插画 2. 【建】(房屋的)主立面;(门、窗上面的)三角顶饰

frost [frɒst] *n*. 1. 冰冻,严寒;冰点以下的温度 2. 霜 3. (感情、感情等的)冷淡 4. 〈俚〉(演出、旅行、宴会等的)失败;扫兴;乏味 — *vt*. 1. 结霜于;冻坏(植物等) 2. 在(糕饼等)上加糖霜混合物 3. 使(玻璃、金属等)具有无光泽的霜状表面 4. 使(头发等)变霜白 — *vi*. 1. 受冻;起霜 2. (油漆等)干成霜状 ‖ ~ ing *n*. 1. 结冰 2. (糕饼上的)糖霜混合物 3. (玻璃、金属等的)无光泽霜状表面,毛面 4. (与清漆等混合的)装饰玻璃碎粉 5. (使用化学品的)闪色头发化妆 ‖ ~ bite *n*. 霜害;冻伤;冻疮 *vt*. 使遭霜害;冻伤/ ~ bitten *adj*. 受霜害的;冻伤的;冷淡的,冷若冰霜的/ ~ bound *adj*. (土地等)冰冻的;结霜的冻的

frosty ['frɒsti] *adj*. 1. 霜冻的,结霜的 2. 严寒的,冰冻的 3. 冷若冰霜的,冷淡的 4. (头发等)白的,灰白的;年老的 ‖ frostily *adv*. / frostiness *n*.

froth [frɒθ] *n*. 1. 泡,泡沫;(由于激动或患病而生的)口边白沫 2. 渣滓,废物 3. 空谈 — *vi*. 起泡沫 口吐白沫 — *vt*. 使(啤酒等)起泡沫

frothy ['frɒθi] *adj*. 1. 起泡沫的;多泡沫的 2. 空洞的;浅薄的 3. 质料轻薄的 ‖ frothily *adv*. / frothiness *n*.

froward ['frəʊwəd] *adj*. 难驾驭的;固执的 ‖ ~ly *adv*. / ~ness *n*.

frown [fraʊn] *vi*. 1. 皱眉,蹙额;表示不满,不赞许(*at, on, upon*) 2. (峭壁等)

令人畏而生畏 — *vt*. 1. 用不悦的表情把…压下去(*down*) 2. 用皱眉蹙额表示(不满等) — *n*. 皱眉,蹙额

frowzy, frowsy ['fraʊzi] *adj*. 1. 肮脏的,邋遢的;不整洁的 2. 被臭的;霉臭的

froze [frəʊz] freeze 的过去式

frozen ['frəʊzn] freeze 过去分词 — *adj*. 1. 冰冻的;冻结的 2. 严寒的 3. (资产等)冻结的 4. 冷淡的;呆板的

FRS *abbr*. Fellow of the Royal Society (英国)皇家学会会员

fructify ['frʌktifai] *vt*. & *vi*. (使)结果实;(使)有成果;(使)多产 ‖ fructification [ˌfrʌktifi'keiʃən] *n*. / fructifier *n*.

frugal ['fruːgəl] *adj*. 节约的,俭朴的;花钱少的 ‖ ~ity [fru:'gæliti] *n*. / ~ly *adv*.

fruit [fruːt] *n*. 1. 水果 2. [~s] 植物产物 3.【植】果实 4. 成果 5. [~s] 收入;收益;报酬 6. (人的)后代;(动物等的)仔,崽 — *vi*. 结果实 ‖ ~ ed *adj*. 结有果实的;加水果(调味)的 ‖ ~ cake *n*. 水果蛋糕 / ~ fly【动】1. 实蝇科小蝇 2. 果蝇 / ~ knife 水果刀

fruiter ['fruːtə] *n*. 1. 果树 2. 运水果船 3. (英)果农 ‖ ~ er *n*. 水果商;运水果船

fruitful ['fruːtful] *adj*. 1. 果实结得多的;多产的;收效很多的,富有成效的 2. 肥沃的;丰饶的 ‖ ~ly *adv*. / ~ness *n*.

fruition [fruː'iʃən] *n*. 1. 享用;享受 2. 结果实 3. 实现;完成

fruitless ['fruːtlis] *adj*. 1. 不结果实的,无效的;无益的 ‖ ~ly *adv*. / ~ness *n*.

fruity ['fruːti] *adj*. 1. 水果的;(酒)有水果味的 2. (声音)圆润的;洪亮的 3. 〈口〉(谈话,故事等)富有风趣的 4. 〈美俚〉古怪的;发疯的 5. 〈美俚〉(男子)带娘娘腔的(男子)同性恋的

Frunze ['frʊnzə] *n*. 伏龙芝(现称 Bishkek 比什凯克)[吉尔吉斯斯坦首都]

frustrate [frʌs'treit] *vt.* 1. 挫败;阻挠 2. 使感到灰心

frustration [frʌs'treiʃən] *n.* 1. 挫败;挫折 2. 受挫;灰心丧气

frustum ['frʌstəm] ([复]frustums 或 frusta ['frʌstə]) *n.*【数】平截头体;截头锥体

fry¹ [frai] *vt.* 1. 油煎;油炸 2.〈俚〉处以电刑 — *vi.* 1. 在油里煎(或炒、炸) 2.〈美俚〉被处电刑 — *n.* 1. 油煎食品;炒杂碎(指动物内脏) 2. 油煎品聚餐(或野餐);激动 ‖ ~ **ing pan** 煎锅,长柄平底锅 / '~ **pan** 〈美〉 = ~ **ing pan**

fry² [frai] *n.* [总称] 1. 鱼秧,鱼苗 2. 成群的小鱼 3. 群生的幼小动物(如蜂等)

ft. *abbr.* foot;feet

fuchsia ['fjuːʃə] *n.*【植】倒挂金钟

fuck [fʌk]〈俚〉*vt.* 1. (男子)与…性交;把…搞糟;使(计划等)失败(*up*) — *vi.* 1. 性交(*with*) 2. 闲混,浪荡(*about*、*around*) 3. 滚开(*off*) — *n.* 1. 性交;性交对象(尤指女子) 2. 一丁点儿,些微 — *int.* 他妈的! 混帐! 滚开! ‖ ~ **er** *n.* 混蛋 / ~ **ing** *adj.* 1. 该死的 2. 讨厌的 ‖ '~ -**up** *n.* 大笨蛋;一团糟

fuddle ['fʌdl] *vt.* 1. 使喝醉 2. 使迷糊 — *n.* 1. 醉;泥醉 2. 迷糊,糊涂

fudge [fʌdʒ] *n.* 1. 乳脂软糖 2. 欺骗 3. 胡言 — *vt.* 1. 胡乱拼凑(*up*) 2. 捏造 3. 不彻底地处理(问题等) — *vi.* 1. 行为不诚实 2. (对…)逃避责任(*on*) — *int.* 胡说!

fuel ['fjuəl] *n.* 燃料—(fuel(l)ed; fuel-(l)ing) *vt.* 1. 对…供给燃料;给…加油(或其他燃料) 2. 支持;促进 — *vi.* 得到燃料;加油(或煤等) ‖ ~ **cell** 燃料

电池

fug [fʌg] *n.* 室内的闷热空气(或气味) ‖ **fuggy** *adj.* (空气)污浊闷热的

fugitive ['fjuːdʒitiv] *n.* 1. 逃亡者;亡命者 2. 难以捉摸的东西 — *adj.* 1. 逃亡的;躲避的 2. 短暂的;变动的;易消失的 3. 流浪的,飘泊的

-ful *suf.* 1. [构成形容词] 表示"充满…", "有…性质","有…倾向(或能力)": eventful, peaceful, helpful 2. [构成名词] 表示"充满…所需的量": handful, mouthful

fulcrum ['fʌlkrəm] ([复]fulcrums 或 fulcra ['fʌlkrə]) *n.* 1. 支点;支轴 2. (杠杆的)支柱,支持物等 3.【机】支点;喙基骨;转节;舌骨;鞣状鳞

fulfil(l) [ful'fil] (fulfilled; fulfilling) *vt.* 1. 履行(诺言、责任);把…付诸实现 2. 完成(任务、计划等) 3. 达到(目的);满足(愿望、要求等);执行(命令、法律等) 4. 充分发挥(自己)的才智;实现自己的抱负 ‖ ~ **ment** *n.* 履行;实现;完成;满足

full [ful] *adj.* 1. 满的;充(或持)满…的(*of*);满到…的(*to*);吃饱的(*up*) 2. (心)充满激情的,激动的 3. (一顿饭)丰盛的;(花)盛开的;(生活等)丰富的,充实的;(感情等)丰满的,肥胖的;(衣服)肥大的 4. (工资、年、月等)十足的;(支持等)充分的;(文本等)完全的;(月亮)全圆的 5. (速度等)高得不能再高的;(风力等)大得不能再大的 6. (会员等)正式的 7. 专心思考(一问题)的;一味想到(自己、自己的困难等)的(*of*);报道等详尽的(*on*) 9. (声音)洪亮的;(颜色、滋味等)浓的 — *n.* 1. 全部;整个 2. 顶点,盛期 — *adv.* 1. 十分: We know ~ well that it's a good idea.

我们非常清楚这是个好主意。**2.** 十足地,整整地(十公里等);完全地 **3.** 恰恰,直接地(打中、照射等) ‖ '~**back** n.(足球)防守后卫 / ~'**blooded** adj. **1.** 血气旺盛的 **2.** 精力充沛的,热烈的 **2.** 情欲强烈的 **3.** 非混血的,(动物)纯种的 **4.** 内容充实的;(议论等)有力的 **5.** 真正的;十足的 / ~'**blown** adj. **1.** (花)盛开的;(帆)张满的 **2.** 成熟的;充分发展的 / ~'**bodied** adj. **1.** 体格大的;肥胖的 **2.**(酒)醇的,浓烈的,(墨水等)浓的 **3.** 意义重大的 **4.**(作品等)规模大的;内容充实的 / ~ **brother** 同胞兄弟,嫡亲兄弟 / ~ **dress** 礼服 / '~-'**dress** adj. **1.** 礼服的 **2.**(正式宴会等)须穿礼服的 **3.**(会谈、辩论等)正式的,全力以赴的 / ~-**face** n.(观者能看清楚的)正面 / '~-'**fledged** adj. **1.**(鸟)羽毛长全的 **2.**(喻)成熟的;经过充分训练或培养的 **3.** 正式的,完全合格的 / '~-'**grown** adj. 长足的,成熟的 / '~-'**hearted** adj. **1.** 满腔热情的;十分旺盛的 **2.** 充满信心的;勇敢的 / ~-**house 1.** 客满 **2.** 满堂红(扑克牌戏中三张同点和两张同点的一组牌) / ~'**length** adj. **1.**(照相)全身的;(镜)能照见全身的 **2.**(电影等)标准长度的;(作品等)未删节的 / ~ **moon** 满月(期) / '~'**mouthed** adj. **1.**(牛等)口牙长齐的 **2.**(狗等)大声叫的 **3.**(演讲等)声音响亮的 / '~-**page**(报纸等的)全页;整版 / '~-**scale** adj. **1.**(图样等)与原物一样大小的,足尺的 **2.**(战争等)全面的;竭尽全力的 **3.**(作品等)完整的,未删节的 / ~-**sister** 同胞姐妹,嫡亲姐妹 / ~ **stop 1.** 句点,句号 **2.** 完全停止 / '~-'**throated** adj. 大声的 / '~-'**time** adj. 全部(规定)工作时间(或时期)的;全日制的;专职的 / '~-'**timer** n.(英)全日制小学生;专职人员

fullness ['fulnis] n. **1.**(充)满;充分;全部,完全;胀饱 **2.**(供应、储藏、资源等的)丰富;充实 **3.**(体形等的)圆胖;丰满 **4.**(光的)强烈;(声的)洪亮;(颜色的)深度,浓度;丰满度

fully ['fuli] adv. **1.** 完全地;充分地;彻底地 **2.** 足足;至少

fulminate ['fʌlmineit] vi. **1.** 使爆炸 **2.** 大声疾呼(斥责等) — vt. **1.** 轰响喝,大声呵斥;谴责(at. against) **3.**(疾病)暴发 — n.【化】雷酸盐;烈性炸药 ‖ **fulmi'nation** n.

fulness ['fulnis] n. = fullness

fulsome ['fulsəm] adj. 令人厌恶的(恭维等)过分的;虚伪的;令人作呕的 ‖ **~-ly** adv. / **~-ness** n.

fumble ['fʌmbl] vi. **1.** 摸索;乱摸 **2.** 笨手笨脚地做事 **3.** 犯大错 **4.**(球赛中)漏接球;失球 — vt. **1.** 摸索;乱做;笨拙地处理 **2.**(球赛中)漏接(球)、失(球) — n. **1.** 摸索;乱摸;笨拙的处理 **2.**(球赛中的)漏接球,失球 ‖ ~**r** n. 摸索者;粗手笨脚的人;工作拙劣的人 / **fumbling** adj.

fume [fjum] n. **1.**(浓烈或难闻的)烟;气;汽 **2.** 愤怒 — vt.(用香)熏;熏(木材等)使表面呈深色 — vi. **1.** 冒烟;出汽;(烟)冒出;(汽)发出 **2.** 发怒;怒斥

fumigant ['fjumigənt] n.(消毒、杀虫用)熏烟剂,熏剂

fumigate ['fjumigeit] vt.(为消毒、杀虫等)熏蒸,烟熏 ‖ **fumi'gation** n. / **fumigator** n. 烟熏者;烟熏器

fun [fʌn] n. **1.** 玩笑;嬉戏;娱乐;乐趣 **2.** 有趣的人(或事物) **3.**(使人感觉有趣的)紧张场面 — adj. 好玩的,有趣的

function ['fʌŋkʃən] n. **1.** 官能;功能;作用(器官) **2.** 职务;职责 **3.** 盛大的集会(或宴会、宗教仪式) **4.**【数】函数

vi. 1.(器官等)活动;(机器等)运行;起作用 2. 行使职责 ‖ ~ **word**【语】(主要表示语法关系的)功能词

functional ['fʌŋkʃənəl] *adj.* 1. 官能的;机能的 2. 职务上的;(感官等)有功能的;(人)在起作用的 3.(建筑物等)从实用观点设计(或构成)的 4.【数】函数的 ‖ ~ly *adv.* ‖ ~ **illiterate** 半文盲/~ **shift**【语】功能转变

functionary ['fʌŋkʃənəri] *n.*(机关等的)工作人员;官员;公务员

fund [fʌnd] *n.* 1. 资金;基金;专款;基金管理机构 2. [~s](银行)存款 3. [~s]现款 4. 储备,贮备;She has a great ~ of stories. 她肚子里有许多的故事。— *vt.* 1. 把(短期债款)转为有固定年限的长期借款 2. 拨款偿付(债款)的利息(或本金);为…提供资金

fundamental [ˌfʌndə'mentl] *adj.* 1. 基础的;根本的;基本的;十分重要的 2. 原始的;主要的 3.【物】基频的;基波的 4.【音】基音的;基音的 — *n.* 1. [常~s]基本原则(或原理);基本法则(或规律);基础 2.【物】基频;基波 3.【音】根音;基音 ‖ ~ly *adv.* ‖ ~ **particle**【物】基本粒子

fundamentalist [ˌfʌndə'mentəlist] *n. & adj.* 基要主义者(的) ‖ **fundamentalism** *n.* 基要主义

funeral ['fjuːnərəl] *n.* 1. 丧礼,葬礼;出殡的行列 2.〈口〉需要操心的事 — *adj.* 丧葬的;葬礼的;出殡的 ‖ ~ **director** 丧葬承办人/~ **home**,~ **parlour**〈美〉殡仪馆/~ **pile** 火葬柴堆

funereal [fjuː'niəriəl] *adj.* 1. 丧葬(似)的 2. 悲哀而严肃的 3. 阴森的;阴郁的

fungi ['fʌŋɡai, 'fʌndʒai] fungus 的复数

fungi- *comb. form* 表示"真菌":*fungicide*

fungicide ['fʌndʒisaid] *n.* 杀真菌剂

fungous ['fʌŋɡəs] *adj.* 1. 真菌的;有真菌特征的;由真菌引起的 2. 突发而不持久的

fungus ['fʌŋɡəs] ([复] funguses 或 fungi ['fʌŋɡai, 'fʌndʒai]) *n.* 1. 真菌 2. 突然发生并迅速生长的东西 3.【医】海绵肿 4. 真菌病

funicular [fjuː'nikjulə] *adj.* 1. 索状的;与索相连的 2. 用缆索(或缆索)运转的 3.【解】索的;脐带的;精索的 — *n.* 缆索铁路

funk [fʌŋk]〈口〉*n.* 1. 恐怖;惊惶 2. 懦夫 — *vi.* 惊恐;畏缩 — *vt.* 害怕;逃避(工作、战斗等) ‖ ~ **hole** 掩蔽洞

funnel ['fʌnl] *n.* 1. 漏斗 2. 漏斗形物 3.(蒸汽机、轮船等的)烟囱 — (funnel(l)ed; funnel(l)ing) *vt. & vi.* 1.(使)成漏斗形 2.(使)经过漏斗 3.(使)汇集 ‖ **funnel(l)ed** *adj.* 1. 有漏斗的;漏斗形的 2. 有烟囱的

funny ['fʌni] *adj.* 1. 滑稽可笑的;有趣的;爱开玩笑的;不严肃的 2.〈口〉古怪的、奇妙的;不舒服的;有病的 4. 玩滑的;欺骗性的 — *n.* 1. 滑稽人物 2. [常 funnies](报纸或期刊的)滑稽连环漫画(栏) ‖ **funnily** *adv.* / **funniness** *n.* ‖ ~ **bone**(肘部尺骨的)麻癖突 / ~ **business**〈口〉不正当行为 2. 滑稽可笑的动作/~ **man** *n.* 幽默者;滑稽演员/~ **money** *n.* 膨胀的通货(尤指为了政治目的等滥发的钱)/~ **paper** 报纸滑稽连环漫画栏;连载滑稽漫画的报纸

fur [fəː] *n.* 1.(兽类的)软毛 2. 毛皮 3. [~s] 皮衣;裘;毛皮围脖(或手套等)4. [总称] 软毛兽 5. 舌苔 6.(锅、壶中生的)水垢,水碱;酒垢 — (furred; furring) *vt.* 1. 用毛皮覆盖;用毛皮村里 2. 用毛皮镶;使穿毛皮服装 2. 使(舌)生垢

3. 使(锅、壶等)生水垢,使积垢 — *vi.* 生苦苔;生水垢 ‖ ~ **seal** [动]海狗

furbelow ['fɜːbiləu] *n.* 1. 裙褶,皱襞裙饰 2. [~s]俗丽的装饰

furbish ['fɜːbiʃ] *vt.* 1. 磨光,擦亮(*up*) 2. 刷新;整修(房屋等)(*up*) 3. 温习(*up*)

furious ['fjuəriəs] *adj.* 1. 狂怒的 2. 狂暴的;猛烈的 3. (速度)极快的 ‖ ~**ly** *adv.* / ~**ness** *n.*

furl [fɜːl] *vt.* 卷起,卷紧(帆、旗等);折拢(扇子);收拢(伞);拉拢(帷)— *vi.* (帆、旗等)卷起;卷紧;(扇子)折拢;(伞)收拢

furlong ['fɜːlɒŋ] *n.* 弗隆,浪(英国长度单位,= 1/8 英里或 201.167 米)

furlough ['fɜːləu] *n.* (军人等的)休假 — *vt.* (美) 1. 准…休假 2. 暂时解雇

furnace ['fɜːnis] *n.* 1. 炉子,熔炉 2. 极热的地方

furnish ['fɜːniʃ] *vt.* 1. 供应;提供 2. 装备;为(房间)配备家具

furnishing ['fɜːniʃiŋ] *n.* [常~s] 1. (房间等里的)家具;室内陈设 2. 服饰;装饰 3. 供应;装备

furniture ['fɜːnitʃə] *n.* [总称]家具

furor ['fjuərɔː] *n.* 1. 盛怒 2. (风暴等的)咆哮 3. = furore

furore [fjuə'rɔːri] *n.* 1. 轰动;鼎沸 2. 风行一时的事物

furrier ['fʌriə] *n.* 1. 皮货商 2. 毛皮加工者 3. 缝制(或修补,改制)毛皮衣服的人

furrow ['fʌrəu] *n.* 1. 沟;犁沟;垄沟 2. 航迹;车辙 3. (前额或面部的)皱纹 — *vt.* 1. 犁(田);挖垄沟于;在…上形成沟道;在…上留下车辙痕 2. 使(前额)起皱纹

furry ['fɜːri] *adj.* 1. (有)毛皮的;像毛皮

的 2. 穿毛皮衣物的;衬有毛皮的;镶有毛皮的 3. 有水垢的 4. 有舌苔的

further ['fɜːðə] [far 的两种比较级形式之一,另一形式为 farther; farther 常用于本义"更远",further 常用于引申意义"进一步"] — *adv.* 1. (距离,时间上)更远地,再往前地 2. 进一步地;深一层 3. 而且;此外(= ~more) — *adj.* 1. 更远的,较远的 2. 更多的;进一步的;深一层的 — *vt.* 促进,推动 ‖ ~**ance** *n.* 促进,推动 ‖ ~ **education** 继续教育,进修

furthermore ['fɜːðə'mɔː] *adv.* 而且;此外

furthermost ['fɜːðəməust] *adj.* 最远的(= furthest)

furthest ['fɜːðist] [far 的两种最高级形式之一,另一形式为 farthest] — *adj.* (距离、时间上)最远的 — *adv.* 1. (距离、时间上)最远地 2. 最大程度地;最大限度地

furtive ['fɜːtiv] *adj.* 偷偷摸摸的,鬼鬼祟祟的 ‖ ~**ly** *adv.* / ~**ness** *n.*

fury ['fjuəri] *n.* 1. 大怒,狂怒 2. 猛烈,剧烈 3. 极度兴奋状态 4. 泼妇

furze [fɜːz] *n.* [植]荆豆(花) ‖ **furzy** *adj.*

fuse¹ [fjuːz] *n.* 1. 把保险丝接入(电路) 2. (因保险丝熔断而)使(电器等)中断工作 3. 熔化;熔合;熔接 — *vi.* 1. (保险丝)熔断;(电器等)因保险丝熔断而中断工作 2. 熔化;熔合 — *n.* [电]保险丝,熔丝

fuse² [fjuːz] *n.* 1. 导火线,导火索 2. (炸弹、炮弹等的)引信,信管 — *vt.* 装导火线(或引信)于

fuselage ['fjuːziləːʒ] *n.* [空]机身

fusible ['fjuːzibl] *adj.* 易熔的;可熔化的 ‖ **fusi'bility** *n.*

fusilier [ˌfjuːzi'liə] *n.* (旧时的)燧发枪手,

明火枪手

fusillade [ˌfju:zi'leid] *n.* (枪炮的)连续齐射；(批评等)齐射式的东西

fusion ['fju:ʒən] *n.* 1. 熔化，熔解 2. 熔化状态，熔解状态 3. 熔合，熔接 4. 【核】核聚变 5. (政党等的)联合；合并 ‖ ~ **bomb** 热核弹(尤指氢弹)

fuss [fʌs] *n.* 1. 忙乱；大惊小怪；紧张不安 2. 大惊小怪的人。反对；抱怨；异议 4. 争吵 — *vi.* 1. 忙乱；小题大做，大惊小怪 2. 过分体贴，过分关怀 3. 过分讲究 4. 烦恼 5. 抱怨；唠叨 — *vt.* 1. 使烦恼；烦扰 2. 使忙乱 ‖ **~pot** *n.* 口 老是大惊小怪的人

fussy ['fʌsi] *adj.* 1. 大惊小怪的；焦躁不安的；瞎忙的 2. 过分注意细节的；爱挑剔的；为琐事烦恼的 3. (服装等到)过分装饰的 ‖ **fussily** *adv.* / **fussiness** *n.*

fusty ['fʌsti] *adj.* 1. 发霉的；霉臭的 2. 守旧的，古板的 ‖ **fustily** *adv.* / **fustiness** *n.*

futile ['fju:tail] *adj.* 1. 无益的；无效的；无用的 2. (人)没出息的；轻浮的 ‖ **~ly** *adv.* / **~ness** *n.*

futility [fju:'tiliti] *n.* 1. 无益；无效；无用 2. 无益的举动(或事物)

future ['fju:tʃə] *n.* 1. 将来，未来，今后 2. 前途；远景 3. 【语】将来时；(动词的)将来式 4. [~s]【商】期货(交易) 5. (美俚)未婚夫；未婚妻 — *adj.* 将来时，未来的；the ~ **tense**【语】将来时 ‖ **~less** *adj.* 无前途的；无希望的

futurism ['fju:tʃərizəm] *n.* (摒弃传统文艺形式的)未来主义 ‖ **futurist** *n.* 1. 未来主义者；未来派文艺家 2. = futurologist *adj.* 未来主义的；未来派的

futurity [fju:'tjuəriti] *n.* 1. 将来，未来 2. 未来的事；远景

futurology [ˌfju:tʃə'rɔlədʒi] *n.* (预测社会与科学技术的发展及其相互关系的)未来学 ‖ **futurological** [ˌfju:tʃərə'lɔdʒikəl] *adj.* / **futurologist** *n.* 未来学家

fuze [fju:z] *n.* & *vt.* 〈美〉= fuse²

fuzz [fʌz] *n.* 1. (织物或果实等表面上的)细毛，绒毛，茸毛 2. [俚]警察；侦探

fuzzy ['fʌzi] *adj.* 1. 有细毛的，有绒毛的；绒毛状的 2. (照片等)模糊的：a ~ **sound** 模糊的声音 ‖ **fuzzily** *adv.* / **fuzziness** *n.*

-fy *suf.* 表示"使成为"、"使…化"：beautify, liquefy, magnify

G

G, g [dʒiː] ([复]G's, g's 或 Gs, gs[dʒiːz])
英语字母表第七个字母 1. [G]G 字形
2. [音]G 音,G 调 3. [美]学业成绩"良
好"(good)的符号 4. [G][电]电导(conductance)的符号 5. [G]〈美理〉1000 美
元 6. [g][物]重力加速度(acceleration of
gravity)的符号 7.[g]普通(或一般)智
力(general intelligence)的符号 8.[G](电
影)适合各种年龄的一般观众(general
audience)观看的

G . . g. *abbr.* gram(s)

Ga【化】元素镓(gallium)的符号

gab [gæb] *n.* 1.〈口〉空谈;闲聊;唠叨 2.
【机】凹节 一 (gabbed; gabbing) *vi.* 空
谈;闲聊;唠叨

gabardine [ˌgæbəˈdiːn, ˌgæbəˈdiːn] *n.* = gaberdine

gabble [ˈgæbl] *vi.* 急促不清地说话;喋喋;
咕噜 一 *vt.* 1. 上气不接下气地说 2.
急促朗读(over, out) 一 *n.* 急促不清的
话

gabby [ˈgæbi] *adj.*〈口〉多嘴的,饶舌的

gaberdine [ˈgæbədiːn] *n.* 1.[英](英
国工人的)工作服;衣服 2.(中世纪犹
太人穿的)粗布长袍 3. 轧别丁,华达
呢;华达呢衣服

gable [ˈgeibl] *n.*【建】1. 山墙,三角墙 2.
三角墙建筑部分;三角形饰物

Gabon [gæˈbɒŋ], **Gabun, Gaboon** [gəˈbuːn]
n. 加蓬[非洲西部国家]

Gaborone [ˌgɑːbəˈrəuni] *n.* 哈博罗内[博茨
瓦纳首都]

gad [gæd] (gadded; gadding) *vi.* 1. 游荡,闲
荡(about, abroad, out) 2. 追求刺激 3.
蔓延,蔓生 一 *n.* 游荡,闲荡‖~about
n. 游荡者,游手好闲的人;寻欢作乐的
人 *adj.* 游荡的,游手好闲的

gadfly [ˈgædflai] *n.* 1.【动】虻,牛虻 2. 惹
人讨厌的人;有意搅得别人不得安宁
者

gadget [ˈgædʒit] *n.*〈口〉1. 小发明物;小
装置 2. 小玩意儿

gadolinium [ˌgædəˈliniəm] *n.*【化】钆

gaff [gæf] *n.* 1.(弯齿)鱼叉;(把大鱼拉
上岸用的)手钩,挽钩 2.(爬电杆用的)
攀钩;(肉铺的)挂钩 3.【船】斜桁 4.〈英
理〉低级娱乐场所;杂要场 5. 欺骗;诡
计;花招;鬼把戏 6. 折磨;无休止的虐
弄;粗暴的对待 一 *vt.* 1. 用鱼叉叉
(鱼);用手钩拉(鱼) 2. 欺骗,诈骗;在
(赌具)上暗设机关进行欺骗

gaffer [ˈgæfə] *n.* 1.〈贬〉〈谑〉(乡下)老头
子 2.〈口〉工头;雇主 3.(电影、电视拍
摄的)照明电工

gag [gæg] *n.* 1. 塞口物;(牲畜的)口衔 —
【医】张口器 2. 对言论自由的压制;
(议会的)制制辩论的手段;结束辩论 3.
插科打诨;笑话 4. 哄骗;〈俚〉欺诈 一
(gagged; gagging) *vt.* 1. 塞住…的口,
使窒息 2.【医】用张口器使张开口 2. 压

制(某人)言论自由；限制(某人)发言 3. 在(表演等)中插科打诨 4. 欺骗 5. 关闭(阀门等) — vi. 1. 窒息；作哽 2. 插科打诨 3. 欺骗 ‖ ~ strip (一组)滑稽漫画

gage [geidʒ] n. & vt. = gauge

gaggle ['gægl] vi. (鹅)嘎嘎叫 — vt. 嘎嘎地说出(或发出) — n. 1. (鹅)嘎嘎叫声 2. (鹅)群；(美口)一群

Gaia ['geiə] n. 1.【希神】盖亚(大地女神) ‖ ~ hypothesis (或 theory) 盖亚假设,盖亚理论(认为地球是一个像生物体一样不断进行自我调节的统一生命系统的核心)

gaiety ['geiəti] n. 1. 快乐,高兴 2. [常 gaieties] 狂欢；娱乐；喜庆 3. (服装的)华丽

gaily ['geili] adv. = gayly

gain [gein] vt. 1. 获得；博得；使获得 2. 赢得；挣得 3. 增加；(钟,表等)走快 4. (经过努力力)到达(某地) — vi. 1. 获得利益 2. 增加；增长 3. (钟,表等)走快 — n. 1. 营利,获利 2. [~s] 收获,得益；利益 3. [~s] 收益；利润 4. 增加,增进；[无] 增值量 ‖ ~ er n. 1. 获得者；得利者；得胜者 2. (面对池)反身跳水

gainful ['geinful] adj. 1. 有利益的；有收益的 2. 唯利是图的

gainsay [gein'sei] (gainsaid [gein'seid]) vt. [主要用于否定句和疑问句] 1. 否认；否定 2. 反驳；抗拒

gait [geit] n. 1. 步态,步法 2. (走、跑、生产等的)速度 — vt. 训练(马)的步法

gaiter ['geitə] n. 1. 鞋罩；绑腿 2. 高帮松紧鞋；布面高帮皮鞋

gal. abbr. gallon(s)

gala ['gɑːlə, 'geilə] n. 1. 节日；庆祝；盛会 2. (古)盛装 — adj. 节日的；欢庆的；

欢乐的

galactic [gə'læktik] adj. 1. 乳液的；得自乳液的；催乳的 2.【天】银河的 3. 极大的；巨额的

galaxy ['gæləksi] n. 1.【天】星系；[G-] 银河系；银河 2. 一群出色的(或著名的)人物；一堆光彩夺目的东西

gale [geil] n. 1. 大风(尤指 8 级风)；〈诗〉微风 2. (突发的)一阵 3.〈口〉高兴,欢乐

galena [gə'liːnə] n.【矿】方铅矿

gall[1] [gɔːl] n. 1. 胆汁；胆液 2. 痛苦难忍的事；苦的东西 3. 怨恨；愤恨 4.〈美口〉厚颜无耻；厚脸皮 ‖ ~ bladder n.【解】胆囊/~ stone n. 【医】胆石

gall[2] [gɔːl] n. 1. 擦痛处；擦伤处；(马的)鞍伤 2. 磨损处；眼疾；弱点 3. (田野或树丛的)光秃处 4. 恼怒；烦恼；恼怒(或烦恼)的原因 — vt. 1. 擦伤；擦痛；磨损 2. 激怒；烦扰；羞辱 — vi. 1. (被)擦伤；(被)擦痛；(被)磨损 2.【机】(因摩擦过度而)咬住,卡住

gall[3] [gɔːl] n. 瘿,虫瘿(植物体上的瘤状物)；【药】五倍子,没食子,栲子

gallant ['gælənt] adj. 1. (服装)华丽的；堂皇的；雄伟的 2. 勇敢的；骑士风度的；豪侠的 3. [gə'lænt] (对女子)献殷勤的；色情的 — ['gælənt, gə'lænt] n. 1. 豪侠之士；时髦人物；对女子献殷勤的人；求爱者；情夫 — [gə'lænt] vt. 1. 向…求爱 2. 伴送(女子) — vi. 调情,求爱(with) ‖ ~ ly adv.

gallantry ['gæləntri] n. 1. 勇敢；豪侠；英勇的言行 2. (对女子的)殷勤；风流言行；淫荡

galleon ['gæliən] n. (15 至 18 世纪作军舰或商船用的)西班牙大帆船

gallery ['gæləri] n. 1. 长廊；游廊；门廊；

柱廊；走廊；晒台；阳台 **2.**（剧场中票价最低的）顶层楼座；（教堂、议院等的）边座；楼座 **3.**[the ～]顶层楼座的观众；（网球赛等的）观众 **4.** 画廊；美术陈列室；美术馆；（美术馆等展出或收藏的全部）藏品 **5.** 长长的房间；摄影室；照相馆；室内靶场 **6.** 地下通道；地道；[矿]水平巷道，平巷 **7.**[船]船尾瞭望台；炮座，……在……建筑楼座（或游廊等）；在……挖地道 ∥ *vi.* 建筑长廊（或游廊等）；挖地道

galley ['gæli] *n.* **1.**（古代用奴隶等划桨的）桨帆船；大帆船；（古希腊、罗马等的）战舰 **2.** 舰长用艇 **3.**（船上的）厨房 **4.**[印]活版盘；长条校样 ∥ ～ **slave 1.** 划桨的奴隶（或犯人）；[喻]苦工 **2.**[美俚]排字工人

gallium ['gæliəm] *n.*[化]镓

gallivant [ˌgæli'vænt] *vi.*[常用现在分词和动名词形式]游荡，闲荡；与异性游荡；寻欢作乐

gallon ['gælən] *n.* **1.** 加仑（液量单位，= 4 quarts） **2.** 加仑（干量单位，= 1/8 bushel） **3.** 一加仑的容器

gallop ['gæləp] *n.* **1.**（马等的）飞跑，疾驰 **2.** 骑马奔驰 **3.**（口）快步；敏捷动作；迅速发展 ∥ *vi.* **1.**（马等）飞跑，疾驰 **2.** 匆匆地读（或说）**3.** 急速进行，迅速发展 ∥ *vt.* **1.** 使飞跑，使疾驰 **2.** 迅速运输，迅速运送

gallows ['gæləuz] ([复]gallows(es)) *n.* **1.** 绞刑架，绞台 **2.**（类似绞刑架的）架状物；挂架；[船]支承架 **3.** 绞刑；该受绞刑的人 **4.**[方][～es]（裤子的）背带，吊带

Gallup ['gæləp] *n.* ∥ ～ **poll**（美国）盖洛普民意测验

galore [gə'lɔː] *n. & adj.* 多(的)；大量(的)

galosh [gə'lɔʃ] *n.*[常 ～es]高统橡皮套鞋

gals. *abbr.* gallons

galvanic [gæl'vænik] *adj.* **1.**【电】(伏打)电流的；产生(伏打)电流的；(伏打)电流引起的 **2.** 使人震惊（或振奋、激动）的 **3.** 触电似的 ∥ ～ally *adv.*

galvanize ['gælvənaiz] *vt.* **1.** 通电流于；对……施行电疗 **2.** 给……镀锌 **3.** 使震惊，使激动；激起；使兴奋

galvanometer [ˌgælvə'nɔmitə] *n.*【电】电流计

Gambia ['gæmbiə] *n.* 冈比亚[西非国家]

gambit ['gæmbit] *n.* **1.**（国际象棋中的）开局让棋法 **2.** 精心策划的一着；(带风险的)策略

gamble ['gæmbl] *vi.* **1.** 赌博；打赌 **2.** 投机；冒险 ∥ *vt.* **1.** 赌掉，赌光（*away*）**2.** 以……打赌；冒……的险 ∥ *n.* 赌博；投机；冒险 ∥ ～**r** *n.* 赌博者，赌徒

gambol ['gæmbl] *n.*（小孩、小羊等的）跳跃；嬉戏，玩笑 ∥（gambol(l)ed；gambol(l)ing）*vi.* 蹦跳；嬉戏

game [geim] *n.* **1.** 游戏；运动；玩要；娱乐；玩笑 **2.**（体育、棋类等的）比赛；[～s]运动会 **3.**（比赛中的）一局；一盘；一场 **4.** 比分；（获胜所需的）得分；得胜，赢 **5.**（棋、纸牌类的）游戏器具；比赛用具 **6.** 比赛规则；比赛方式（或技巧）**7.** 策略；把戏，花招 **8.**（美俚）行业；职业；（冒险的）行当 **9.**（对勇气、耐心等的）考验 **10.**[总称]猎物；野味 **11.**[总称]追求物；目的物；嘲弄（或攻击）的对象 **12.**（饲养天鹅的）一群 ∥ *vi.*（打牌等时）赌博 ∥ *vt.*（古）赌掉（*away*）∥ *adj.* **1.** 野味的；关于猎物的 **2.**（口）堆起来的；有精神准备的 ∥ ～**ly** *adv.* 堆起地；有精神准备地 / ～**ness** *n.* 勇气；兴致勃勃 ∥ '～-**cock** *n.*（雄的）斗鸡；好斗的人；

'~ˌkeeper n. 猎场看守人 / ~ preserve 禁猎区，野生动物保护区 / ~ warden (一个地区的)渔猎法执行官

gamin ['gæmin] n.(街头)流浪儿；顽童

gamine [gɑː'miːn] n.(街头)流浪女孩；男孩气的女孩，假小子

gaming ['geimiŋ] n. 赌博

gamma ['gæmə] n. 1. 希腊语的第三个字母(Γ, γ) 2. 第三位的东西【天】γ星(星座中第三最亮的星) 3.【物】伽马(磁场强度单位);γ射线 3.【摄】灰度系数，反差系数 5. 微克(百万分之一克) ‖ ~ ray【物】γ射线

gammer ['gæmə] n.〈贬〉〈谑〉(乡下)老太婆

gamut ['gæmət] n. 1.【音】音阶；音域 2.〈喻〉全范围，全部

gamy ['geimi] adj. 1.(森林等)猎物多的 2. 有臭味的，有霉气味的 3. 有强烈气味的 3. 生龙活虎的，好斗的；胆子大的(尤指妇女)，丢脸的；下流的，腐败的，声名狼藉的

Gana ['gɑːnə] n. = Ghana

gander ['gændə] n. 1. 雄鹅 2. 糊涂虫，傻瓜 3.〈俚〉一看，一眼 — vi.〈方〉漫步；闲逛

gang [gæŋ] n. 1.(劳动者的)一队，一组 2.(囚犯等的)一群，(歹徒等的)一伙 3.(口)〈贬〉(青少年等的)一伙 4.(工具等的)一套 5.(英方)路；路程 6.(美俚)大量 — vi. 1. 成群结队；合伙行动 2.(苏格兰)走；走 — vi. 1. 使分成班组 2.(美口)合伙袭击 3. 使成套排列；使成套运转 ‖ ~ bang〈俚〉轮奸；集体淫乱活动/'~-bang vi. & vi.(参与)轮奸

gangboard ['gæŋbɔːd] n.【船】步桥；跳板

Ganges ['gændʒiːz] n. 恒河[南亚]

gangling ['gæŋgliŋ] adj. 瘦长得难看的；

瘦长得动作笨拙的

ganglion ['gæŋgliən]([复] ganglions 或 ganglia ['gæŋgliə]) n. 1.【解】神经节 2.〈喻〉力量(或活动、兴趣)的中心 3.【医】腱鞘囊肿

gangplank ['gæŋplæŋk] n. = gangboard

gangrene ['gæŋgriːn] n. 1.【医】坏疽 2.〈喻〉道德败坏 — vt. & vi.(使)生坏疽

gangster ['gæŋstə] n.(一帮中的一名)匪徒，歹徒；暴徒

gangway ['gæŋwei] n. 1. 通路；(工地等处)木板铺成的走道 2.【船】舷门；舷梯；跳板 3.(剧场等)座间通道 4.〈英〉(下议院中)划分前后座的通道；划分内阁与反对派的通道 5.【矿】主运输平巷 6.(木材从水上输送到锯木厂的)斜道 — int. 避开! 让路!

gannet ['gænit] n. 1.【动】鲣鸟 2.〈俚〉贪婪的人

gantlet ['gɔːntlit, 'gæntlit] n. 〈美〉= gauntlet²

gantry ['gæntri] n. 1. 桶架【机】起重龙门架；龙门起重机，起重台架 3.(铁路上的)轨线桥 4.(火箭或导弹的)竖立和维护塔架

gaol [dʒeil] [注意:英国文件中用 gaol，一般文字中 gaol 与 jail 通用;美国用 jail] n. 监狱；监禁 — vt. 监禁,把…关进监狱

gaoler ['dʒeilə] n. 监狱看守,看守监狱者

gap [gæp] n. 1. 豁口,裂口;破口【军】突破口 2. 峡谷;山隘口3. 间隙;【机】火花隙;【摄】裂,(缺)隙【空】(双翼机的)翼隔 4. 中断;(文章等中的)空白;(知识等的)空白 5. 分歧;隔阂;差距:the generation ~ 代沟 — (gapped; gapping) vt. & vi.(使)豁开

gape [geip] vi. 1. 张口;打呵欠 2. 目瞪

口呆地凝视(*at*) 3. 张开；裂开 — *n*. 1.
张口；呵欠 2. 目瞪口呆；瞠目 4. 口
张时的阔度；〔动〕裂缝，嘴裂

gar [gɑː] (〔复〕gar(s)) *n*. 1. 雀鳝(一种
淡水硬鳞鱼) 2. 颚针鱼

garage ['gærɑːʒ] *n*. 1. 汽车间(或库)；飞
机库 2. 汽车修理厂 — *vt*. 把(汽车
等)送入汽车库(或修理厂)

garb [gɑːb] *n*. 1. 服装；装束；制服 2. 外
表；外衣 — *vt*. 〔常用被动语态或接
oneself〕穿；装扮

garbage ['gɑːbidʒ] *n*. 1. 废料；垃圾；污物
2. 食物下脚；〔美俚〕食物 3. 下流(或
无聊)的读物(或作品) 4.〔计〕无用数据

garble ['gɑːbl] *vt*. 1. 对(文章、报告等)断
章取义；篡改；歪曲 2.(非有意地)混淆
(或歪曲) 3.〈罕〉筛去…的杂质；精选；
挑拣

garden ['gɑːdn] *n*. 1.(花、菜、果)园；庭园
2.〔常~s〕公园；(动物、植物)园 3. 沃
土地区 4.〔英〕〔用于……的大都市或
房屋的命名中〕(花)园 5. 露天饮食
店 — *vi*. 从事园艺 — *vt*. 把……开垦为
花园(或菜园、果园) — *adj*. 1.(花、
菜、果)园的 2. 园中生长的 3. 普通
的；平凡的；老一套的 ‖ ~ing *n*. 园艺
(学)

gardener ['gɑːdnə] *n*. 园林工人；园丁

gardenia [gɑːˈdiːnjə] *n*.〔植〕栀子(花)

gargle ['gɑːgl] *vt*. 1. 漱(喉) 2. 从喉底发
出(咕噜声) — *vi*. 1. 漱口；含漱 2.
〔美俚〕喝酒 — *n*. 1. 漱口药 2. 含漱剂；
漱口声；喉头发出的咕噜声 3.〔美俚〕
酒

gargoyle ['gɑːgɔil] *n*. 1.〔建〕怪兽状滴水
嘴；怪兽饰 2. 面貌古怪的人

garish ['gɛəriʃ] *adj*. 1.(衣物等)鲜艳夺目
的；花花绿绿的；打扮(或装饰)得俗不
可耐的

garland ['gɑːlənd] *n*. 1. 花环；花冠(金
属制的花环形物) 2. 荣誉，锦标，奖品
3.〈古〉诗(文)集 4.〔海〕索环；食物网
袋 5.〔建〕华饰 — *vt*. 1. 把……做成花
环 2. 给……戴上花环饰；用花环装饰

garlic ['gɑːlik] *n*. 大蒜；蒜头 ‖ ~ky *adj*.
有大蒜味的(麦等)与野大蒜生长在
一起的

garment ['gɑːmənt] *n*. 1.(一件)衣服(尤
指长袍、外套) 2.〔~s〕服装，衣着 3.
外表 — *vt*. 给……穿衣服

garner ['gɑːnə] *n*. 1. 谷仓 2. 贮备物；积
蓄物；积累物 — *vt*. 1. 把……储入谷仓；
收集；贮藏 2.〔美口〕得到

garnet ['gɑːnit] *n*.〔矿〕石榴石 2. 石榴
红(色)，深红(色)

garnish ['gɑːniʃ] *vt*. 1. 装饰；修饰 2.(烹
饪)加配菜于 3.(因甲乙双方争讼)传
讯(有关的第三者) — *n*. 1. 装饰品；
(文章的)修饰；华丽的词藻 2.(为色香
味而添饰的)拼盘菜

garnishee [ˌgɑːniˈʃiː] *n*.〔律〕第三债务人
— *vt*. 1. 通知(受托人)扣押债务人的
财产(或工资)；向(第三债务人)下达
扣押令 2. 扣押(债务人的财产)；扣发
(债务人的工资) — ~ment *n*.

garret ['gærət] *n*. 1. 屋顶层，顶楼；阁楼
2.〈俚〉头

garrison ['gærisn] *n*. 驻军，卫戍部队；警
卫部队；驻地；要塞；卫戍区 — *vt*. 镇
守(城市、要塞等)；驻防(某地)；派(兵)
驻防

garrote [gəˈrɒt, gəˈrəut] *n*. 1. 铁环绞刑；
绞刑用的铁环 2. 勒杀抢劫；勒杀(用
绳或皮带等) — *vt*. 处……以铁环绞刑；
扼死，勒杀；勒杀抢劫 ‖ ~r *n*.

garrulous ['gæruləs] *adj*. 1. 饶舌的，喋喋
不休的 2.(鸟声)叽叽喳喳的；(水声)
潺潺的

garter [ˈgɑːtə] *n.* **1.** 〈吊〉袜带 **2.** 〈英〉[the G-]嘉德勋位(英国的最高勋位);获得嘉德勋位者:嘉德勋章 **3.** 〈英〉[G-]嘉德勋章院的(五个主管中的)第一主管 — *vt.* **1.** 用袜带带扣住(袜子);在(腿)上系袜带 **2.** 授给…嘉德勋位(或勋章)

gas [gæs] *n.* **1.** 气,气体 **2.** 可燃气体;煤气;天然气 **3.** 〈矿〉瓦斯 **4.** 笑气;麻醉气 **4.** 毒气 **5.** 〈美口〉汽油;(汽车等的)油门 **6.** (俚)空谈;废话;夸大的话,吹牛 **7.** 〈美俚〉成功;令人非常满意的事 — (gassed; gassing) *vt.* **1.** 向…供应气体(加煤气等);给…充气;给(汽车等)加汽油(*up*) **2.** 用气体处理;〈纺〉为(布、线等)烧毛 **3.** 向(某处)放毒气;用毒气杀伤(人) **4.** (俚)使得到极大快感 — *vi.* **1.** 放出气体 **2.** (给汽车等)加油(*up*) **3.** (口)空谈;吹牛 ∥ ~ dy'namics [复] *n.* [用作单]〈物〉气体动力学 / ~ mask 防毒面具 / ~ station 加油站

gaseous [ˈgæsiəs] *adj.* **1.** 气体的;气态的 **2.** 过热的 **3.** 空虚的,无实质的

gash [gæʃ] *n.* **1.** (深长的)切口(或伤口) **2.** (地面等的)裂缝 **3.** 划开 — *vt. & vi.* **1.** (在…上)划深长切口;划开

gasify [ˈgæsifai] *vt. & vi.* (使)成为气体,(使)气化

gasket [ˈgæskit] *n.* **1.** 〈机〉垫圈;衬垫;填密片;密封垫;填料 **2.** 〈海〉束帆带,束帆索

gasohol [ˈgæsəhɔl] *n.* 汽油-酒精混合燃料

gasoline, gasolene [ˈgæsəliːn] *n.* 〈美〉汽油(= 〈英〉petrol)

gasp [gɑːsp] *vi.* **1.** 喘气,喘息;透不过气 **2.** 热望,渴望(*for, after*) — *vt.* 气吁吁地说(*out*) — *n.* **1.** 喘气,喘息;透不过气

gastric [ˈgæstrik] *adj.* 胃的 ∥ ~ juice 胃液

gastronomic(al) [ˌgæstrəˈnɔmik(əl)] *adj.* 美食的;烹饪学(或法)的

gate [geit] *n.* **1.** 大门;篱笆门;城门 **2.** 出入口;洞口 **3.** 狭长通道;峡谷;隘口 **4.** 门扇;阀门;闸门 **5.** 锯架 **6.** 〈运动会、展览会等的〉观众(数);门票收入 **7.** 〈冶〉浇注系统,浇口 **8.** 〈计〉门;(电子)门;门电路,选通电极 **9.** (俚)解雇 — *vt.* **1.** 给…装门 **2.** 〈英〉(大学的)一种处分不准(学生)外出 **3.** 用门控制 ∥ ~ way *n.* **1.** 大门口;出入口;门道;通道;门框 **2.** 途径;方法;手段

gather [ˈgæðə] *vt.* **1.** 使聚集,使集拢 **2.** 搜集;采集;收(庄稼等) **3.** 渐增;积聚;恢复;鼓足(劲头等);(~ oneself)使操作 **5.** 得出(印象、想法等);推测 **5.** 皱拢(眉头等) **1.** 打折缝 — *vi.* **1.** 聚集,聚拢 **2.** 增长;积累 **3.** 化脓;(脓疮)出头 **4.** (眉头等)皱起来 — *n.* 褶裥;折皱

gathering [ˈgæðəriŋ] *n.* **1.** 聚集(或搜集、采集等) **2.** 集会 **3.** 捐款 **4.** 脓肿

gauche [gəuʃ] *adj.* 缺乏社交经验的;不圆滑的;笨拙的

gaucho [ˈgautʃəu] *n.* 〈南美草原上的〉牧人

gaudy [ˈgɔːdi] *adj.* 〈衣服、装饰、文风等〉华丽而俗气的;炫丽的;华而不实的

ga(u)ge [geidʒ] *n.* **1.** 标准尺寸;标准规格;(铁板等的)厚度;(枪、炮的)口径;(电线等的)直径 **2.** 规,量规,量器,量计;表 **3.** 〈交〉(铁道的)轨距;(汽车等的)轮距 **4.** 容量;范围 **5.** 〈海〉满载吃水深度;(船只对风或其他船只的)相对位置 **6.** (估计、判断等的)尺度,标准 **7.** 〈建〉铺于屋顶上的瓦、石板、木瓦等的露出部分,葺脚;(掺和用的)熟石膏用量 **8.** 〈纺〉隔距 — *vt.* **1.** (用

量具)量;测量,测定 2. 使(石块等)成为标准尺寸;使符合标准 3.【建】(按比例)掺和(石膏) 4. 估计;评定认标准

gaunt [gɔːnt] *adj.* 1. 瘦削的;憔悴的 2. 荒瘠的;荒凉的

gauntlet¹ ['gɔːntlit] *n.* 1.(中世纪武士用的)铁手套;宽口铁套 2. 长手套;防护手套 3. 挑战

gauntlet² ['gɔːntlit] *n.* 1. 夹道鞭打刑罚(执行者) 2. 夹攻;夹击;折磨;重重困难

gauze [gɔːz] *n.* 1.(棉、丝等织成的)薄纱;纱罗;纱布;(金属、塑料等的)网纱 2. 薄雾

gauzy ['gɔːzi] *adj.* 薄得透明的;纱罗似的

gave [geiv] give 的过去式

gavel ['gævl] *n.* 1. 石工大木锤 2.(拍卖人、法官或会议主席用的)小木槌 — *vt.*（会议主持人）敲槌致使;拖槌强令

gawk [gɔːk] *n.* 笨人,呆子 — *vi.* 呆呆地看着

gawky ['gɔːki] *adj.* 笨拙的;粗笨的;腼腆的 — *n.* 笨人;腼腆的人 ‖ **gawkily** *adv.*/ **gawkiness** *n.*

gay [gei] *adj.* 1. 快乐的;愉快的;轻快的 2. 鲜明的;艳丽的;装饰华丽的 3. 寻欢作乐的;淫荡的;放荡的;同性恋爱的 4.〈美俚〉股皮厚的;冒失的 — *n.* 同性恋爱者 ‖ ~**ly** *adv.* / ~**ness** *n.*

gaze [geiz] *vi.* 凝视,注视,盯(at, on, up·on, into) — *n.* 凝视,注视

gazelle [gə'zel] ([复] gazelle(s)) *n.*【动】瞪羚(产于非洲和亚洲的一种小羚羊)

gazette [gə'zet] *n.* 1. 报纸;〔G-〕(用于报刊名)……报 2.〈英〉(政府、大学等的)公报 — *vt.*〈英〉在公报上公布;在公报上刊载

gazetteer [ˌgæzə'tiə] *n.* 地名词典;地名索引

GB *abbr.* Great Britain 大不列颠,英国

Gd【化】元素钆(gadolinium) 的符号

GDR *abbr.* German Democratic Republic〔史〕德意志民主共和国

Ge【化】元素锗(germanium) 的符号

gear [giə] *n.* 1. 齿轮;传动装置 2.(汽车等的)排挡 3. 工具;用具;马具;帆具 3. 衣着,服装;〈口〉青年人的衣着;(士兵等的)装备 4. 所有物,财物 5.〈英口〉胡说 6.〈英口〉事情;事件 — *vt.* 1. 将齿轮装上(机器等);用齿轮连接;使接上齿轮;使(机器等)开动 2. 装备;给(马等)套上马具;使适合(to) — *vi.* 1.(齿轮)连接上(into);(机器)开动 2. 适合,一致(with) ‖ ~**·shift** *n.*【机】变速杆,换挡杆,齿轮变速手柄

gee¹ [dʒiː] *int.* 〔驾驭牛、马的吆喝声〕向前跑! 快跑! 向右转! — *vt. & vi.* 1.(使)向右转 2. 激动,策励(up)

gee² [dʒiː] *int.* 〔俚〕〔表示惊奇、兴奋等〕哎呀!

geese [giːs] *n.* goose 的复数

Geiger ['gaigə] *n.* ‖ ~ **counter**【核】盖革计数器

geisha ['geiʃə] ([复] geisha(s))〈日〉 *n.* 艺妓

gelatin ['dʒelətin], **gelatine** [ˌdʒelə'tiːn] *n.* 1.(白)明胶;动物胶;骨胶;胶 2. 凝胶体;植物胶 3.(舞台灯光用)彩色透明滤光板 ‖ **gelatinous** *adj.*

gelding ['geldiŋ] *n.* 1. 骟马,去势的马;阉过的动物 2.〈古〉阉人;太监

gelid ['dʒelid] *adj.* 1. 极冷的,冰冷的 2. 冷漠的,冷若冰霜的 ‖ ~ **ly** *adv.* / ~**ness** *n.*

gem [dʒem] *n.* 1. 宝石;美玉;珍宝;珍品 2. 精华 3. 被人喜爱的(或尊敬的)人 4. 粗面

松饼 — (gemmed; gemming) *vt.* 用宝石装饰(或镶嵌)

Gen. *abbr.* General

gendarme ['ʒɔ:ŋdɑ:m] *n.*(法国、比利时等的)宪兵;警察

gender ['dʒendə] *n.* **1.**【语】(名词、代词等的)性 **2.**〈口〉(生理上的)性

gene [dʒi:n] *n.*【生】基因 ‖ ~ **bank** 基因(文)库 / ~ **pool** 基因库

genealogy [,dʒi:ni'ælədʒi] *n.* **1.** 系谱(图);家谱(图) **2.** 家系;血统 **3.** 系谱学;家谱学

genera ['dʒenərə] genus 的复数

general ['dʒenərəl] *adj.* **1.** 一般的;普通的;综合的 **2.** 普遍的;全体的 **3.** 总的;全面的 **4.** 大体的;笼统的 **5.**(用于职位)总…;…长 — *n.* **1.** 普通(或一般、普遍等)的事(或物) **2.**〈古〉大众 **3.** 将军;(英美)陆军(或海军陆战队)上将;(美)空军上将;军事家 **4.**〈英口〉做杂务的仆人 **5.**【天主教】耶稣会会长;【基督教】救世军军长

generalissimo [,dʒenərə'lisiməu] ([复] generalissimos) *n.* 大元帅;总司令;最高统帅

generality [,dʒenə'ræliti] *n.* **1.** 概括性的话 **2.** 一般见解;一般原则;通则;一般规律;一般性;普遍性 **3.** 通(用)性 **4.** [the ~]主体,大多数,大部分

generalization [,dʒenərəlai'zeiʃən] *n.* **1.** 一般化;普遍化 **2.** 概括;(贬)判断

generalize ['dʒenərəlaiz] *vt.* **1.** 使一般化 **2.** 归纳出,概括出;从…引出一般性结论 **3.**(绘画中)表达出…的基本特征 **4.** 推广;使广义化 — *vi.* **1.** 形成概念 **2.** 笼统地讲(或写) **3.** 普遍化 **4.** 扩散至全身

generally ['dʒenərəli] *adv.* **1.** 一般地 **2.** 通常地 **3.** 广泛地;普遍地

generalship ['dʒenərəlʃip] *n.* **1.** 将军职位;将军任期 **2.** 将才;指挥才干;智略 **3.** 领导(能力);管理(能力)

generate ['dʒenəreit] *vt.* **1.** 生殖,生育 **2.** 发生,产生(光、热、电等) **3.** 引起;导致 **4.**【数】形成,生成(线、面、体等)

generation [,dʒenə'reiʃən] *n.* **1.** 生殖;发生,生育,产生 **2.** 代,一代(约指 20 至 30 年);世代;一代人 **3.**【数】(线、面、体的)形成 **4.**【语】生成

generative ['dʒenərətiv] *adj.* **1.** 生殖的,生育的;生产的 **2.** 有生殖力(或功能)的;有生产力的 **3.**【语】生成的

generator ['dʒenəreitə] *n.* **1.** 生殖者;发生者;创始者 **2.** 发电机;发生器

generic [dʒi'nerik] *adj.* **1.**【生】属的 **2.** 一般的,普通的;通用的 **3.** 非商标(或专利)的;不受商标注册保护的

generosity [,dʒenə'rɔsiti] *n.* **1.** 宽宏大量;慷慨,大方 **2.** 宽大的行为;慷慨的行为 **3.** 丰富,大量;充足

generous ['dʒenərəs] *adj.* **1.** 宽宏大量的;慷慨的,大方的 **2.** 丰富的;丰盛的 **3.** 肥沃的 **4.**(酒、色彩等)浓的 ‖ ~**ly** *adv.*

genesis ['dʒenisis] ([复] geneses ['dʒenisiz]) *n.* **1.** 起源;发生;创始 **2.** [G-]《创世记》(基督教《圣经》中《旧约全书》的第一卷)

genetic [dʒi'netik] *adj.* **1.** 创始的;发生的 **2.** 遗传学的 **3.** 基因的;遗传(性)的 ‖ ~ **engineering** 遗传工程

genetics [dʒi'netiks] *n.* [用作单]遗传学 ‖ **geneticist** [dʒi'netisist] *n.* 遗传学家

Geneva [dʒi'ni:və] *n.* 日内瓦[瑞士西南部城市]

genial ['dʒi:njəl] *adj.* **1.** 亲切的;和蔼的,友好的 **2.** 适宜于动植物生长的;宜人

的;温和的;温暖的 3. 显示天才的 ‖ ～ity ['dʒi:njæli'ti] n. / ～ly adv.

genie ['dʒi:ni] ([复] genies 或 genii ['dʒi:niai]) n. (阿拉伯神话中的) 魔仆,神怪,神灵

genii ['dʒi:niai] 1. genie 的复数 2. genius 的复数

genital ['dʒenitl] adj. 生殖的;生殖器的 — n. [～s] 生殖器,外阴部

genius ['dʒi:njəs] ([复] geniuses 或 genii ['dʒi:niai]) n. 1.[只用单] 天才;天资,天赋;才华;创造能力 2.([复] geniuses) 天才人物 3.(语言、制度等的) 全部特征,本质;(民族、时代等的) 精神;思潮,倾向;风气 4.([复] genii)[常 G-] 守护神 5.[复] genii 神仙;恶魔;对别人有好(或坏)影响的人

genocide ['dʒenəusaid] n. 种族灭绝;灭绝种族的屠杀

genteel [dʒen'ti:l] adj. 假斯文的;装作高贵样子的;赶时髦的

gentian ['dʒenʃiən] n. 1.[植] 龙胆;黄龙胆 2.(由黄龙胆根部浸出的) 龙胆健胃剂

gentile ['dʒentail] n. 1.[常 G-] 非犹太人;不信犹太教的人;非摩门 (Mormon) 教徒 2. 异教徒 3.【语】表明国籍 (或民族) 的词 — adj. 1.[常 G-] 非犹太人的;不信犹太教的;非摩门门教徒的 2. 异教徒的 3. 氏族的;部落的;民族的 4.[语] 表明国籍 (或民族) 的

gentility [dʒen'tiliti] n. 1. 出身高贵;上流阶层;绅士们 2. 斯文;文雅;彬彬有礼;有教养 3.(讽) 装体面;假斯文

gentle ['dʒentl] adj. 1. 出身高贵的;上流阶层的 2. 有礼貌的;文雅的;优美的 3. 慷慨的;好心的;(古) 豪侠的 4.(动物等) 驯服的 5. 从容的;耐心的;温柔的 6. 柔和的;轻度的和缓的,不猛定

的 — n. 1.[常～s] 出身高贵的人;绅士上层人 2. 蛆 — vt. 1. 使高贵 2. 使温和;使柔和 3. 驯服 (马等);抚弄;轻拍 ‖ ～ness n. ‖ ～-folk(s) [复] n. 出身高贵的人;上流人士

gentleman ['dʒentlmən] ([复] gentlemen) n. 1. 出身高贵的人;有身份的人;绅士 2. 有教养的人;彬彬有礼的人 3.[常 gentlemen] 男子 (尊称) 4.〈英〉[gentlemen] [用作单] 男厕所 5.(王室、贵族的) 侍从,男仆 6. 有收入而不从事任何职业的人 7.〈美〉(众议院的) 议员 ‖ ～ly adj. & adv. ‖ ～'s agreement 君子协定

gentlewoman ['dʒentl,wumən] ([复] gentlewomen ['dʒentl,wimin]) n. 1. 贵妇人;女士;淑女 2.(王室、贵族的) 侍女,女仆

gently ['dʒentli] adv. 1. 有礼貌地;文雅地;温柔地 2. 柔和地;轻轻地;渐渐地 3. 出身高贵地;有教养地

gentrification [,dʒentrifi'keiʃən] n. 中产阶级向日趋破败 (或新近重建) 市区的移居

gentrify ['dʒentrifai] vt. 把 (贫困的或工人阶级的住宅区) 改造为较值钱的地区

gentry ['dʒentri] n. 1. 贵族们;绅士们;〈英〉(地位,出身低于贵族的) 中上阶层 2.〈贬〉〈谑〉人们;一类人;一批人

genuflect ['dʒenjuflekt] vi. 1.(尤指宗教仪式中) 屈膝 2. 屈服,屈从

genuflection [,dʒenju'flekʃən] n. 1. 屈膝下跪 2. 卑躬屈膝;屈从

genuflexion [dʒenju'flekʃən] n. 〈英〉= genuflection

genuine ['dʒenjuin] adj. 1. 真正的;名副其实的 2. 真诚的;坦率的 3. 纯血统的 ‖ ～ly adv. / ～ness n.

genus ['dʒi:nəs] ([复] genera ['dʒenərə] 或 (罕) genuses) n. 1. 类, 种类 2. 【生】【逻】属

geo- comb. form 表示"地球", "土地": geology

geochemistry [,dʒi:u'kemistri] n. 地球化学

geodesic [,dʒi:u'desik] adj. 大地测量学的; (最) 短程线的 一 n. 【数】测地线, (最) 短程线

geographer [dʒi'ɔgrəfə] n. 地理学家

geographic(al) [,dʒiə'græfik(əl)] adj. 地理(学)的; 地区(性)的 ‖ **geographically** adv.

geography [dʒi'ɔgrəfi] n. 1. 地理; 地理学 2. 地形; 地貌 3. 地理书; 地志 4. (生产、建设等的) 布局, 配置

geologic(al) [,dʒiə'lɔdʒik(əl)] adj. 地质(学)的 ‖ **geologically** adv.

geology [dʒi'ɔlədʒi] n. 1. 地质学 2. (某地方的) 地质 3. 地质学书 (或论著) ‖ **geologist** n. 地质学字

geomagnetic [,dʒi:əumæg'netik] adj. 地磁的

geomedicine [,dʒi:u'medisin] n. (研究疾病地理分布等的) 风土医学

geometric(al) [,dʒiə'metrik(əl)] adj. 1. 几何学的 2. 几何图形的 ‖ **geometrically** adv.

geometry [dʒi'ɔmitri] n. 1. 几何学 2. 几何形状 3. 几何学书 (或论著)

geophysics ['dʒi:u'fiziks] [复] n. [用作单] 地球物理学 ‖ **geophysical** [,dʒi:u'fizikəl] adj. 地球物理学的/**geophysicist** [,dʒi:u'fizisist] n. 地球物理学家

geopolitics [,dʒi:u'pɔlitiks] [复] n. [用作单] 地缘政治学, 地理政治学

geopolitic(al) [,dʒi:əupə'litik(əl)] adj.

Georgetown ['dʒɔ:dʒtaun] n. 乔治敦 [圭亚那首都]

Georgia ['dʒɔ:dʒjə] n. 1. 佐治亚 [美国州名] 2. 格鲁吉亚 [外高加索西南部国家] 3. 乔治亚(女子名)

geostationary [,dʒi:u'steiʃənəri], **geosynchronous** [,dʒi:u'sinkrənəs] adj. (人造地球卫星) 与地球旋转同步的, 对地静止的: a ~ satellite (地球) 同步卫星 ‖ ~ orbit (同步卫星的) (地球) 同步轨道

geranium [dʒi'reinjəm] n. 【植】老鹳草; 天竺葵

geriatrics [,dʒeri'ætriks] [复] n. [用作单] 老年病学; 老人学 ‖ **geriatric** adj. / **geriatrician** [,dʒeriə'triʃən], **geriatrist** n.

germ [dʒə:m] n. 1. 微生物; 细菌; 病菌 2. [生] 芽孢; 胚; 胚芽; 幼芽; 生殖细胞; 配子 3. 萌芽; 起源 一 vi (喻) 萌芽 ‖ ~ cell 生殖细胞; 卵子; 精子 / ~ free adj. 无菌的 / ~ plasm 【生】种质

German ['dʒə:mən] adj. 1. 德意志的, 德国的; 德国人的; 德语的 一 n. 1. 德意志人, 德国人 2. 德语 3. 德国境外讲德语的人 3. 德语 4. (一种调步复杂、舞伴变换频繁的) 德国交际舞: (方) 德国交际舞舞会 ‖ ~ silver 德国银, 镍黄铜, 铜镍锌合金

germane [dʒə:'mein] adj. 有密切关系的; 恰当的, 适合的(to)

germanium [dʒə:'meinjəm] n. 【化】锗

Germany ['dʒə:məni] n. 德意志, 德国

germicide ['dʒə:misaid] n. 杀菌剂 ‖ **germi'cidal** adj. 杀菌(剂)的

germinate ['dʒə:mineit] vt. 使发芽; 使发生; 使发展 一 vi. 发芽; 开始生长 ‖ **germi'nation** n. 萌芽; 发生

gerund ['dʒerənd] n. 【语】动名词

Gestapo [ge'stɑːpəu] (〔复〕Gestapos)〔德〕 *n.* 盖世太保(纳粹德国的秘密国家警察)

gestation [dʒes'teiʃən] *n.* 1. 怀孕(期)、妊娠(期) 2. (计划等的)构思、酝酿、形成、孕育

gesticulate [dʒes'tikjuleit] *vi.* (讲话时等)做手势;用姿势(或动作)示意 — *vt.* 用手势表达;用姿势(或动作)表示 ‖ ges.tic.u'la.tion *n.*

gesture ['dʒestʃə] *n.* 1. 姿势;手势 2. (外交等方面的)姿态;表示 — *vi.* & *vt.* 做手势;用姿势(或动作)表示

get [get] (过去式 got [ɡɒt], 过去分词 got 或〈古〉〈美〉 gotten ['ɡɒtn], 现在分词 getting) *vt.* 1. 获得、得到 2. 赚得、买进、收获;捕获;赢得 4. 收到;受到(罚、打击等) 5. (电话通话时)接通、收听到 6. 搞到;拿 7.〈口〉理解;记住;学得;听到 8. 抓住;打击;击中;杀死;使受伤 9. 感染上(疾病)(毒品等)使上瘾 10.〈口〉难住 11.〈口〉吃;准备(饭) 12.〔俚〕注意到(过去完成时态)引起 13.〔用完成时态,后接不定式〕必须 15.〔后接复合宾语〕使得;把…弄得;使被弄得: *Get everything ready!* 把一切准备好! 16. 说服;使信服 17. 〈口〉使的感情;使高兴;使激动;使惹怒 18. (动物)生(仔) — *vi.* 1. 到达 2. 变得;成为 3. (用于命令句)走(逐渐)来到 4.〔加过去分词构成被动式〕被;受: *caught in the rain* 遇上雨 5.〔俚〕立即走开 6. 获得财产 7. 起床(*up*) — *n.*

gewgaw ['ɡjuːɡɔː] *adj.* & *n.* 华而不实的(东西);好看但不值钱的(装饰品或玩具)

geyser *n.* 1. ['ɡaizə] 间歇(喷)泉 2. ['ɡiːzə] 〈英·水〉的(蒸汽)加热器(浴室等的)热水锅炉

GFR *abbr.* German Federal Republic 德意志联邦共和国,德国

Ghana ['ɡɑːnə] *n.* 加纳〔西非国家〕

ghastly [ɡɑːstli] *adj.* 1. 可怕的,恐怖的 2. 死人般的,像一样的;苍白的 3.〈口〉极坏的,糟透的;令人不快的 4. 极大的 5. (微笑等)勉强的 — *adv.* 可怕地;死人般地

gherkin ['ɡəːkin] 1. 西印度黄瓜 2. (做泡菜用的)小黄瓜,嫩黄瓜;泡黄瓜

ghetto ['ɡetəu] (〔复〕ghetto(e)s)〔意〕 *n.* 1. (城市中的)犹太人区 2. (城市中)少数民族聚居区;贫民区

ghost [ɡəust] *n.* 1. 鬼;幽灵 2. 灵魂 3. 幻影;阴影;微量,一点儿 4. 〔口〕(光学和电视机)的重像 5.〈口〉受雇代他人作文(或作画)的人,捉刀人 — *vt.* 1. 像鬼似地出没于(某人)作文(或作画);给…当作刀人 — *vi.* 1. 像鬼似地游荡 2. 当捉刀人(*for*) ‖ **~ station**〈英〉被废弃的火车站 / **~ town**〈美〉被废弃的城镇

ghostly ['ɡəustli] *adj.* 1. 鬼的;幽灵的;鬼一样的 2. 灵魂的;精神的;神灵的;宗教上的 3. 代人写作的人的,捉刀人的

ghoul [ɡuːl] *n.* 1.〔东方神话中的〕食尸鬼 2. 盗尸者;盗墓者 3. 做恐怖事情的人;以恐怖事情为乐的人 ‖ **~ish** *adj.* 食尸鬼的;盗墓的;残忍的

GI ['dʒiː'ai] (〔复〕GIs 或 GI's)〈美〉 *n.* 美国兵(亦作~ Joe)

giant ['dʒaiənt] *n.* 1. (童话中的)巨人;力大无比的人,巨汉 2. 身材、能力、力量等特别大的人 2. 巨物;巨大的动(或植)物 — *adj.* 1. 巨大的 2. (用于动、植物名前)大的 ‖ **~ panda** 大熊猫

giantess ['dʒaiəntes, 'dʒaiəntis] *n.* 女巨人

gibber ['dʒibə, 'ɡibə] *vi.* 急促而不清楚地说话;东拉西扯;瞎扯 — *n.* = gibberish

‖ ~ish n. 急促而不清楚的话;莫名其妙的话;胡扯;嘈杂的声音

gibbet ['dʒibit] n. 1. 绞刑架;示众架 2. 绞刑 3. (起重机的)臂 — vt. 1. 处以绞刑;把(某人)悬在示众架上 2. 使众出丑

gibbon ['ɡibən] n. 〖动〗长臂猿

gibe [dʒaib] vt., vi. & n. 嘲笑,嘲弄

giblet ['dʒiblit] n. [常] ~ s(鸡、鸭等禽类的可食用的)内脏,杂碎

Gibraltar [dʒiˈbrɔːltə] n. 1. 直布罗陀:the Strait(s) of ~ 直布罗陀海峡[地中海与大西洋之间的通道] 2. 坚不可破的要塞

giddy ['ɡidi] adj. 1. 头晕的;眼花缭乱的 2. 使人眩晕的;使人眼花缭乱的 3. 轻率的;轻浮的,轻佻的 4. 急速旋转的 — vi. & vt. (使)眩晕;(使)急速旋转 ‖ giddiness n.

gift [ɡift] n. 1. 赠品,礼物 2. 天赋,天资;才能 3. 赠与;授予权 — vt. 1. 〈英〉赠送 2. (宗教语信用语)(天)付与权力(或才能等)授予 ‖ ~ed adj. 有天赋的;有才华的

gig [ɡiɡ] n. 1. 旋转物 2. 轻便双轮马车 3. 轻便快艇;赛艇 4. 〖纺〗起绒机 5. 怪人 — (gigged; gigging) vi. 乘轻便双轮马车 2. 乘轻便快艇

giga- ['dʒiɡə, 'dʒaiɡə] comb. form 表示"吉(咖)","千兆","十亿"

gigantic [dʒaiˈɡæntik] adj. 巨人似的;巨大的,庞大的

giggle ['ɡiɡl] vi. 咯咯地笑,傻笑 — vt. 咯咯地笑着说 — n. 咯咯笑,傻笑

gigolo ['dʒiɡələu, 'ʒiɡələu] n. [复] gigolos (~ s) 1. 舞男;(妇女的)男伴 2. 女子(或妓女)供养的情人

Gila ['hiːlə] n. (美国西南部和墨西哥中美洲产的)希拉毒蜥(亦作 ~ monster)

gild[1][ɡild] (gilded 或 gilt[ɡilt]) vt. 1. 把…镀金;给…涂上金色 2. 使有光彩 3. 装饰;虚饰 4. 使有钱;使阔绰气

gild[2][ɡild] n. = guild

gill[1][ɡil] n. 1. 鳃(鱼等水生动物的呼吸器) 2. (鸡等的)下 颚 垂肉 3. [常~s](人的)腮下肉;〈美俚〉嘴巴 4. 〖植〗(蘑菇的)菌褶 — vt. 用刺网捕(鱼);去鳃(鱼)的内脏 — vi. (鱼)被刺网捕住

gill[2][dʒil] n. 吉耳(液量单位:1/4 pint)

gilt[1][ɡilt] gild[1] 的过去式和过去分词 — adj. 1. 镀金的;金色的 — n. 1. 镀金材料;金色涂层 2. 炫目的外表 3. 〈俚〉金钱

gilt[2][ɡilt] n. 小母猪

gimcrack ['dʒimkræk] n. 华而不实的东西;小摆设,小玩意儿 — adj. 华而不实的;质量差的,粗制滥造的 ‖ ~y adj. 华而不实的

gimlet ['ɡimlit] n. 手钻 — adj. 1. 有钻孔能力的;锐利的 2. 有钻劲的 — vt. 用手钻钻;穿透

gimmick ['ɡimik] 〈口〉n. 1. (魔术师等用的)暗机关 2. 小玩意儿;小革新,小发明 3. 花招;诡计;骗局 — vt. 1. 要花招改变(或影响) 2. 给…安装小发明

gin[1][dʒin] n. 1. (捕猎用的)陷阱;网;渔网 2. 三脚起重机;起重装置 3. 轧棉机,轧花机 — (ginned; ginning) vt. 1. 轧(棉) 2. 用陷阱(或网等)捕捉

gin[2][dʒin] n. 杜松子酒;荷兰杜松子酒

ginger ['dʒindʒə] n. 1. 生姜,姜 2. 〈口〉精神,活力 3. 姜黄色 — vt. 1. 使有姜味 2. 使有活力;鼓舞 ‖ ~ ale 干姜水(一种增添味的汽水)/ ~bread n. 姜饼 2. 华而不实的东西;俗丽的装饰 adj. 华而不实的;俗丽的

gingerly ['dʒindʒəli] *adv. & adj.* 小心谨慎地(的),战战兢兢地(的)

gingham ['giŋəm] *n.* 1. 方格(条纹)布 2.〈口〉伞 — *adj.* 方格(条纹)布做的

ginseng ['dʒinseŋ] *n.* 1. 人参;西洋参 2. 人参(或西洋参)制剂

gipsy ['dʒipsi] *n., adj. & vi.* = gypsy

giraffe [dʒi'rɑːf] ([复] giraffe(s)) *n.* 1.【动】长颈鹿 2.[G-]【天】鹿豹座

gird [gəːd] (girded 或 girt [gəːt]) *vt.* 1. 束,缚;束紧(衣服等) 2. 佩带;给…佩带;赋予 3. 围绕;包围 4.[~ oneself]准备(for) — *vi.* 准备

girder ['gəːdə] *n.*【建】大梁,主梁

girdle ['gəːdl] *n.* 1. 带;腰带 2. 环形物,围绕物 3.(美)(女子)的紧身褡 4.(剥去一圈树皮而形成的)环带 5.(宝石的)腰棱翻光面,抱角 6.【解】支持四肢的肢带骨 — *vt.* 1. 束,缠,绕 2. 围绕 3. 剥去(树木)的一圈皮

girl [gəːl] *n.* 1. 女孩子,少女;未婚女子 2. 女儿 3. 女仆;保姆 4.(商店等的)女雇员 5.[用作定语]女…:a ~ scout 女童军 6.〈口〉女朋友;女人 7.(美俚)同性恋男子 ‖ ~-hood *n.* 1. 少女时期 2.[总称]少女

girlish ['gəːliʃ] *adj.* 少女的;少女似的;少女时期

girth [gəːθ] *n.* 1.(马等的)肚带 2.(树干、圆筒、腰身等的)干围;围长 3. 大小;尺寸 — *vt.* 1. 围绕;包围 2. 用肚带束(或缚) 3. 缚以肚带 4. 量…的围长 — *vi.* 量得围长

gist [dʒist] *n.* 1. 诉讼根据;依据 2. 要旨

give [giv] (gave [geiv], given ['givn]) *vt.* 1. 送给;给予 2. 授予;赐予;施舍;捐赠 3. 供给;(给病人)服用(药物);传给 4. 付出;出售 5. 献出[~ oneself,或用被动语态]使沉湎于(to) 6. 交给;托付;

嫁出 7. 产生;引起 8.[表示做一次动作]…出:a loud laugh 大笑一声 9. 作出;举出;表示出;提出(建议等) 10. 举行(音乐会、宴会等);演出 11. 让出 12. 对…施行(责罚等) — *vi.* 1. 赠送;捐助 2. 给予;陷下;塌下;弯下 3. 弯曲不住 4.(气候)转暖;(冰雪)融化 4.(用具等)有弹性 — *n.* 弹性;可让性;可弯性 ‖ ~-and-take [,givən'teik] *n.* 1. 公平交易;互谅互让 2. 交谈;交换意见 / ~ away *n.*〈口〉1.(真相等的)无意泄露;无意中泄露的事(或物) 2.(用以招揽顾客的)赠品(或廉价品);赠阅的报刊(货品等)近于赠送的价格 3.(电台或电视台举办的)有奖问答节目 4. 无偿赠与(或津贴;让予、赠予、放弃);赠予(或让予)物

given ['givn] give 的过去分词 — *adj.* 1. 给予的;赠送的 2. 特定的;一定的 3. 假设的[数]已知的 4. 癖好的;喜爱的;习惯的 5.(正式文书于某一日期)签订的 ‖ ~ name (美) 1.(不包括姓的)名字 2. 教名(受洗礼时起的名字)

gizzard ['gizəd] *n.* 1.(鸟等的)砂囊,胗 2.〈口〉(禽)胃 3. 内脏

glacial ['gleisjəl] *adj.* 1. 冰的;冰状的(结晶)的 2. 冰河(时期)的;冰川的;冰冷的 3. 冷淡的 4. 像冰河运动般缓慢的

glacier ['glæsjə] *n.* 冰河,冰川

glad [glæd] (gladder, gladdest) *adj.* 1.[用作表语]高兴的,乐意的 2. 令人高兴的;使人愉快的 3. 充满欢乐的,兴高采烈的 4.(自然景色等)明媚的 ‖ ~-ly *adv.* / ~-ness *n.*

gladden ['glædn] *vt.* 使高兴,使快乐 — *vi.*〈古〉高兴,快乐

glade [gleid] *n.* 1. 林间空地(或通道) 2. 沼泽地

gladiator ['glædieitə] *n.* 1.(古罗马的)斗

士 **2.** 论争者,辩论家 **3.** 格斗者(尤指职业拳击者)

gladiola [ˌɡlædiˈəulə] *n.* = gladiolus

gladiolus [ˌɡlædiˈəuləs] ([复] **gladioluses** 或 **gladioli** [ˌɡlædiˈəulai]) *n.* **1.**【植】唐菖蒲 **2.**【解】胸骨体

gladsome [ˈɡlædsəm] *adj.* **1.** 令人高兴的,可喜的 **2.** 喜悦的,欢乐的

glamo(u)r [ˈɡlæmə] *n.* 魔力;魅力 — *vt.* 迷惑,迷住 ‖ **~ous** *adj.* 富有迷惑力的,有魅力的

glance [ɡlɑːns] *vi.* **1.** (粗略地)看一下,一瞥;扫视 **2.** 擦过(*off, aside*);掠过 **3.** (简单地而间接地提到);影射(*at*);快而简略地谈 **4.** 闪光,闪耀 — *vt.* **1.** 瞥见;用(眼睛)扫视,使擦过表面,使掠过 — *n.* **1.** 一瞥;眼光 **2.** 闪光

gland [ɡlænd] *n.* **1.**【解】【植】腺;腺状组织

glanders [ˈɡlændəz] [复] *n.* [用作单或复](马等)的鼻疽(病)

glandular [ˈɡlændjulə] *adj.* **1.** 腺的;似腺的;起腺功能的 **2.** 天生的,固有的,肉体的

glare [ɡlɛə] *vi.* **1.** 眩目地照射,闪耀;炫耀 **2.** 瞪眼;怒目注视(*at, on*)— *vt.* 瞪着眼睛表示(敌意等)— *n.* **1.** 眩目的光;强烈的阳光 **2.** 耀眼的阴这;显耀 **3.** 瞪眼;愤怒的目光 **4.** (冰等的)光滑明亮的表面

glaring [ˈɡlɛəriŋ] *adj.* **1.** 耀眼的,闪光的 **2.** 瞪眼的;怒目而视的 **3.** 显眼的;突出的 **4.** (色彩等)粗俗的,俗丽的

Glasgow [ˈɡlɑːzɡəu] *n.* 格拉斯哥[英国苏格兰中南部港市]

glass [ɡlɑːs] *n.* **1.** 玻璃;玻璃状物 **2.** [总称]玻璃制品;玻璃器皿;玻璃暖房;玻璃窗 **3.** 玻璃杯;一玻璃杯的(容量);

酒 **4.** 镜子 **5.** 透镜;望远镜;显微镜;[~es]眼镜;双筒镜 **6.** 气压计;晴雨表;沙漏 — *vt.* **1.** 给…装上玻璃 **2.** 把…装入玻璃瓶中 **3.** 反映;(~ oneself)映照 **4.** (为了寻找猎物等)用望远镜瞭望 — *vi.* **1.** 成玻璃状;(目光)变得无神迟钝 **2.** 用望远镜瞭望(寻找)猎物 ‖ **~blower** *n.* 吹玻璃工人/ **~ fibre** 玻璃纤维/ **~ ware** *n.* [总称]玻璃制品;玻璃器皿;料器

glassful [ˈɡlɑːsful] *n.* 一玻璃杯的(容量)

glassy [ˈɡlɑːsi] *adj.* **1.** 像玻璃的 **2.** (眼睛等)没有神采的,呆滞的 **3.** (水等)明净的,平静如镜的

glaze [ɡleiz] *vt.* **1.** 配玻璃于;装玻璃于 **2.** 上釉于;上光于 **3.** 打光;擦亮 **4.** 浇糖浆于(食物)的表面 **5.** 使(眼睛)蒙上薄膜 — *vi.* **1.** 变光滑;变光亮 **2.** (眼)变呆滞;变模糊 — *n.* **1.** 釉料;釉面 **2.** 光滑面;光滑层 **3.** 糖浆的薄冰层 **4.** (熟肉表面的)冻胶层 **5.**【气】雨淞,冻雨 **6.** 薄膜;(眼睛的)翳

glazier [ˈɡleizjə] *n.* 装玻璃工人;釉工

gleam [ɡliːm] *n.* **1.** 微光;闪光 **2.** (喻望暂微弱的)显现;微量 — *vi.* **1.** 发微光;闪烁 **2.** 短暂微弱地显现;突然露出闪光 **3.** 发微光;使闪亮;显露出

glean [ɡliːn] *vt.* **1.** 拾(落穗);拾起(田)里的落穗 **2.** 搜集(新闻,资料等) **3.** 发现,找到;探明 — *vi.* **1.** 拾落穗 **2.** 搜集新闻(或资料等) ‖ **~ing** *n.* **1.** 拾穗;收集材料(或事实等) **2.** [~ings]从地里拾起的谷物;收集到的材料(或事实等)

glee [ɡliː] *n.* **1.** 高兴,快乐,欢欣 **2.**【音】(无伴奏的)三部(或三部以上)重唱歌曲(尤指男声) ‖ **~club** 合唱队

gleeful [ˈɡliːful] *adj.* 极高兴的,欢乐的

令人兴奋的

glen [glen] *n.* 峡谷;幽谷

glib [glib] (glibber, glibbest) *adj.* 1. 随便的;圆滑的;油嘴滑舌的 2. 流利的;善辩的 ‖ ~ly *adv.* / ~ness *n.*

glide [glaid] *vi.* 1. 滑动;滑行 2. 悄悄地走;(时间等)消逝;(事情)渐变 3.[空]滑翔;下滑 4.[语](从一音向另一音)滑移 — *vt.* 使滑动;使滑行 — *n.* 1. 滑动,滑行 2.[空]滑翔,下滑 3.[语]滑移;过渡音 4.[语]滑音,延音

glider ['glaidə] *n.* 1. 滑动者(或物);滑行者(或物) 2. 滑翔机,滑翔者(或物);助滑器,助滑装置 3. 摆动式长椅

glimmer ['glimə] *n.* 1. 微光;微弱的闪光 2. 模糊的感觉;少许,微量 3.[矿]云母 4. 一瞥,一看 5.(俚)[~s]眼睛 — *vi.* 1. 发出微光;发出闪烁的微光 2. 隐约出现

glimpse [glimps] *n.* 1. 一瞥,一看 2. 隐约的一见;微微的感觉 3. 微光 — *vt.* 瞥见 — *vi.* 1. 一瞥,看一眼 (at) 2.(诗)隐约出现;露出曙光

glint [glint] *vi.* 1. 发微光(光线)反射 2. 迅速移动,掠过 3. 窥视 4. 隐约地闪出 — *vt.* 使反射;使闪光;使反射 — *n.* 1. 微光;闪光;反光 2. 隐约的闪现

glisten ['glisn] *vi.* 闪耀;反光 — *n.* 闪光;反光

glitch [glitʃ] *n.* 1.(俚)[电]短时脉冲波形干扰 2.(电视图像的)低频干扰 3.(设备等的)突然不规则运转;失灵;小故障 4.(计划等的)缺点;差错;难题

glitter ['glitə] *vi.* 1. 闪闪发光,闪光 2.(服装等)华丽夺目;炫耀 — *n.* 1. 闪光;灿烂的光辉 2.[总称](装饰用的)小发光物

gloaming ['gləumiŋ] *n.* 黄昏,薄暮

gloat [gləut] *vi.* 1. 爱慕地凝视;贪婪地盯着(over, on, upon) 2. 心满意足地注视(或沉思) — *n.* 1. 爱慕的凝视;贪婪的盯视 2. 心满意足的注视(或沉思) 3. 扬扬得意;幸灾乐祸

global [gləub] *adj.* 1. 球形的;球面的 2. 全球的;全世界的 3. 总括的,综合的;完全的;普遍的 ‖ ~ly *adv.*

globe [gləub] *n.* 1. 球;球状物 2.[the ~]地球;世界 3. 天体;行星;太阳 4. 地球仪;天球仪 5. 球状玻璃器皿;球形金鱼缸;球形玻璃灯罩;灯泡 6.[军]眼球 7.(标志君主权力的)小金球 — *n.* & *vt.*(使)成球状 ‖ ~-trotter *n.* 环球旅行者

globular ['glɔbjulə] *adj.* 1. 球状的;地球状的 2. 世界范围的 3. 有小球的

globule ['glɔbjul] *n.* 1. 小球 2. 液滴;药丸;血球

glockenspiel ['glɔkənspi:l] *n.*[音]钟琴

gloom [glu:m] *n.* 1. 黑暗;阴暗;朦胧 2. 黑暗处;阴暗处 3. 阴郁;忧愁;情绪低落 — *vi.* 1.(天色等)变黑暗;变阴暗;变朦胧 2. 变郁闷;变忧伤;现愁容 — *vt.* 1. 使黑暗;使朦胧 2. 使郁闷;使忧郁 3. 忧伤地说

gloomy ['glu:mi] *adj.* 1. 黑暗的;阴暗的;朦胧的 2. 令人沮丧的 3. 郁闷的;忧郁的;悲哀的;无望的 ‖ gloomily *adv.* / gloominess *n.*

glorify ['glɔ:rifai] *vt.* 1. 颂扬,夸耀;给…以荣誉 2. 赞美(上帝);崇拜 3. 使增光,美化 4. 使辉煌,使光彩夺目 ‖ glorification *n.* 1. 颂扬;赞美 2.(口)庆祝,庆祝的事 3. 美化

glorious ['glɔ:riəs] *adj.* 1. 光荣的 2. 辉煌的,灿烂的;壮丽的 3.(口)令人愉快的;非常高兴的 4.(谑)可怕的 5.(口)

酒后狂乐的

glory ['glɔːri] *n.* 1. 光荣.荣誉 2. 荣耀的事;可赞源的事物;可夸耀的事 3. 壮丽.壮观;天上的光辉;灿烂 4. 繁荣;昌盛;全盛 5.【宗】(对上帝的)赞颂;崇拜 6.【宗】天国的荣耀(或幸福);天国;永恒 7.(神像后的)光轮 — *vi.* 自豪,得意(*in*)

gloss [glɔs] *n.* 1. 光泽,光彩 2. 虚饰,假象 — *vt.* 1. 使具有光泽;上光于 2. 掩盖,掩饰(*over*)— *vi.* 发光

glossary ['glɔsəri] *n.* (注释)词表;术语(或特殊用语)汇编

glossy ['glɔsi] *adj.* 1. 有光泽的;光滑的 2. 虚饰的;貌似有理的,似是而非的

glottis ['glɔtis] *n.*【解】声门

glove [glʌv] *n.* 1. 手套;有指手套 2. 拳击用手套 — *vt.* 1. 供给(某人)手套 2. 给(手)戴上手套

glow [gləu] *vi.* 1. 发白热光;灼热;发光;发热 2.(因运动或激动等脸庞,身体)发红;(眼睛)发光;容光焕发 3. 洋溢着感情;燃烧着;鲜艳夺目 — *n.* 1. 白热光;光辉 2. 激情;热烈;兴高采烈 3. 色彩鲜艳;红光 ‖ ~worm *n.* 萤火虫

glower¹ ['glauə] *n.* 白热体;灯光

glower² ['glauə] *vi.* & *n.* 怒视;凝视

glucose ['gluːkəus] *n.*【化】葡萄糖,葡糖

glue [gluː] *n.* 1.(由动物的皮,蹄,骨等熬制而成的)胶水;胶水 2. 胶粘物 — *vt.* 胶合,粘贴;粘牢;使与某物紧附 ‖ ~y *adj.* 胶的;胶质的;粘着物

glum [glʌm] *adj.* 闷闷不乐的;阴郁的;愁闷的 ‖ ~ly *adv.* / ~ness *n.*

glut [glʌt] (glutted; glutting) *vt.* 1. 使吃得过饱;使满足;使厌腻 2. 使(市场)充斥 — *vi.* 狼吞虎咽;暴食 — *n.* 1. 过饱;过食 2. 充斥;供过于求

gluten ['gluːtən] *n.* 1. 面筋,麸质,谷胶 2. 谷蛋白粘胶质;粘性物质

glutinous ['gluːtinəs] *adj.* 1. 粘的;胶质的 2.(美喻)感伤的,缠绵的 ‖ ~ly *adv.*

glutton ['glʌtn] *n.* 1. 贪食者,好食者;暴餐 2. 酷爱……的人,对……入迷的人 3.【动】狼獾 ‖ ~y *n.* 暴食;暴饮;贪吃

gluttonous ['glʌtənəs] *adj.* 贪吃的 ‖ ~ly *adv.*

glycerin ['glisərin], **glycerine** ['glisərin], **glycerol** ['glisərɔl] *n.*【化】甘油,丙三醇

G-man ['dʒiːmæn] *n.* (复) G-men n. (口)(美国)联邦调查局(或司法部)调查员;联邦政府警探(government man的缩略)

gnarl [nɑːl] *n.* 木节,木瘤 — *vt.* 扭曲;拗弯 2. 使有节 — *vi.* 生节 ‖ ~ed, ~y *adj.* 1. 多节的,多瘤的;扭曲的 2.(性情)粗暴的,乖戾的

gnash [næʃ] *vt.* 咬(牙);啮 — *vi.* (由于愤怒或痛苦而)咬牙;(牙)啮咬 — *n.* 咬

gnat [næt] *n.* 1.(咬或叮人的)小昆虫;(英)蚊子 2. 小烦扰;琐事

gnaw [nɔː](过去式 gnawed,过去分词 gnawed或 gnawn)*vt.* 1. 咬,啮,啃;咬断;咬成 2. 消耗;腐蚀;侵蚀 3. 折磨;使烦恼 — *vi.* 1. 啃,咬(*at, into*)2. 消耗;腐蚀;侵蚀(*at, into*)3. 折磨;烦恼

gnome [nəum] *n.* 1.(民间传说中)地下宝藏守护神;土地神 2. 矮子,侏儒

GNP *abbr.* gross national product 国民生产总值

gnu [nuː, njuː]([复] gnu(s))*n.*【动】(非洲产的)牛羚,角马

go [gəu] (went [went], gone [gɔn]) *vi.* 1.

去 2. 离去 2. 走;驶 3. 通到、达到 4. 归,
属 5. 诉诸、求助(于);查阅(to) 6.〈机
器等〉运转;行动;进行;起作用;行得
通 7. 消失;衰退 8.〈时间〉过去 9. 完结、
垮;断开;死 9. 废弃;放弃 10. 花费;售
出 11. 变为,成为 12. 处于…的状态;
处于一般的状况 13. 流传;表达;〈货
币等〉流通 14. 相配;〈诗、歌词〉有节
奏;与曲调相配(to) 15. 发出声音;
〈钟〉报时 16. 合起来构成;有助(于);
趋向(于) 17. 被容得下 18.〖数〗
〈除〉得整数 19.〖用进行时态,后接
不定式〗将要;打算 20.〖用不定式,作
定语〗将来 — n.〖美方〗想 — vt. 1.
打赌;〈桥牌赛中〉叫(牌);出(价) 2.
承担…的责任 3. 忍受;熬得起〔常用
于否定句〕享受 4. 生产、产 — n. 1.
去;进行 2. 活动,精力 3.〈口〉事情
〔尤指棘手的事〕4.〖the ~〗时髦
5.〈口〉试一下;干一下 6.〈口〉成功;
〈口〉机会 8.〈美口〉约定 9.〈口〉一杯
〈酒〉一份〈食物〉10. 拳击比赛;竞
赛。— adj.〖美口〗一切正常的,可
以开始的;好的,行的 ‖ ~-be.tween
n. 中间人;掮客;媒人/ ~'getter n.1.
能干而有进取心的人;志在必得的人

goad [gəud] n. 1.〈赶家畜用的〉刺棒、
刺棒物;刺激物 — vt. 1. 用刺棒驱赶
(家畜) 2. 刺激;驱使;煽动;唆使

goal [gəul] n. 1.〈赛跑等的〉终点;〈旅行
的〉目的地 2. 目的,目标 3.〈球赛等
的得分,赢分 4.〖足球等运动的〗球
门;守门员 — vi. 得分 ‖ ~-keeper.
'~-tender n.〖足球等运动的〗守门员

goalie ['gəuli] n.〈口〉〖足球等运动的〗守
门员

goat [gəut] n. 1. 山羊 2. 色鬼 3.〈俚〉替
罪羊,牺牲品 4.〖the G-〗〖天〗摩羯宫
‖ ~-herd n. 羊倌;牧羊人/ ~-skin n. 山

羊皮(革);山羊皮衣;〈装酒或水的〉羊
皮囊

goatee [gəu'ti:] n. 山羊胡子

gob [gɔb] n. 1.〈俗〉〈粘性物的〉一块、一
团〈如痰块〉2.〖常 ~s〗大量 3.〖美俚〗
水兵 4.〈俚〉嘴 — (gobbed;gobbing) vi.
吐;唾痰

gobbet ['gɔbit] n. 1. 一片、一块〔尤指生
肉或食物〕;一堆 2. 一口〈食物〉3.〈为
翻译或评论而摘录的〉引文、片段

gobble ['gɔbl] n. 火鸡的叫声 — vt. 1.
狼吞虎咽 2.〈美口〉急急抓住(up) —
vi 1. 贪食;狼吞虎咽 2. 发出火鸡般的
咯咯叫声 ‖ ~ r n. 公火鸡

gobbledygook, gobbledegook ['gɔbldiguk]
n.〖美俚〗浮夸、冗长而费解的语言〈或
文字〉;官样文章

goblet ['gɔblit] n.〈无柄〉酒杯;高脚杯

goblin ['gɔblin] n. 妖怪

god [gɔd] n. 1. 神〈泥塑或木雕的〉神
像;偶像 2.〖G-〗〖宗〗上帝 3. 神化的人
〈或物〉,被极度崇拜的人〈或物〉
4.〖~s〗〖剧院中〗顶层楼座〈的观众〉
— (godded;godding) vt. 使神化,崇拜
‖ ~-child n. 教子;教女/ ~-
daughter n. 教女/ ~-father n. 1. 教父
2. 名字被用以命名某人〈或物〉的人 vt.
做(某人)的教父/ ~-mother n. 教母
/ ~-parent n. 教父;教母/ ~-send n. 令
人喜出望外的事物;天赐之物/ ~-son
n. 教子

goddess ['gɔdis] n. 1. 女神 2. 美人 3. 非
常善良的女子

godless ['gɔdlis] adj. 1. 没有神的;不
信神的 2. 不虔诚的 3. 邪恶的 ‖ ~-ly
adv. / ~ ness n.

godlike ['gɔdlaik] adj. 如神的;上帝般
的;神圣的;超绝的

godly ['gɔdli] adj. 1. 神的;神圣的 2. 虔

诚的 ‖ **godliness** n.

goggle ['gɔgl] vi. 1. 瞪眼看；斜眼看(at) 2. 转动眼珠 — vt. 转动(眼珠) — n. 1. 瞪视；转眼 2. [~s]护目镜，风镜；〈俚〉(圆镜片)眼镜 — adj. (眼珠)突出的(瞪住的)眼；转动的 ‖ ~-eyed adj. 眼珠突出的；瞪视的；转动眼珠的

goitre, goiter ['gɔitə] n.[医]甲状腺肿

gold [gəuld] n. 1. 金，黄金；金币 2. 钱财；财富 3. 宝贵的东西；宝贵；优美 4. 金色，金黄色 5. 包金(或镀金)材料(如金箔，金粉、金线) 6. 金色靶心 — adj. 1. 金(制)的：含金的 2.(货币等)可以兑换成黄金的；金本位的 3. 金(黄)色的；黄金般的 ‖ ~-brick n.〈口〉假金砖；赝品；虚有其表的东西 2.〈军俚〉逃避工作的人，懒汉；逃避工作，拈轻怕重，吊儿郎当 vt. 欺骗 / ~-flinch n. 红颜金翅雀；黄雀 / ~-fish n. 金鱼 / ~-smith n. 金匠；金器商

golden ['gəuldən] adj. 1. 金(黄)色的；黄金般的 2. 贵重的；绝好的；重要的 3. 繁荣的，兴盛的 4. 朝气蓬勃的；有出息的 5.(声音)洪亮的；产金的：the *Golden State* 黄金州〔美国加利福尼亚州的别称〕 7. 金(制)的 ‖ ~-rod n. [植]一枝黄花 / ~-rule n. 人生准则；指导原则

golf [gɔlf] n. 高尔夫球运动 — vi. 打高尔夫球 ‖ ~-er n. 高尔夫球运动员 / ~-club n. 高尔夫球杆；高尔夫球俱乐部 / ~-course 高尔夫球场

gondola ['gɔndələ] n. 1.(意大利威尼斯的)凤尾船，刚朵拉 2. 大型平底船 3.〔铁路上的〕无盖货车 4.〔飞艇或气球的〕吊舱，吊篮；缆车 5.〔设在商店中央的〕商品陈列台 6.〔运输混凝土的〕有漏斗状容器的卡车(或拖车) ‖ **gondo-**

lier [,gɔndə'liə] n. 凤尾船船夫

gone [gɔn] go 的过去分词 — adj. 1. 已去的；过去的 2. 遗失了的；无可挽回的 3. 深重的 4. 怀孕的 5. 死的 6. 虚弱无力的；发晕的 7. 用光了的 8.〈美俚〉了不起的 ‖ ~-n.(事物)

gong [gɔŋ] n. (铜)锣

gonorrh(o)ea [,gɔnə'riə] n.[医]淋病 ‖ ~l adj.

good [gud] (better ['betə], best [best]) adj. 1. 好的 2. 愉快的 3. 健全的；新鲜的 4. 有益的，有效的，适合的 5. 可靠的；真的 6. 大大的；充分的；十足的 7. 好心的；乐于助人的；慈善的 8. 有教养的；懂礼的；诚实的 9.〔用于称呼或问好〕好的，平安的 —(better ['betə], best [best]) adv. = well* — n. 1. 好；好事；慷慨的行为 2. 利益；好处，用处 3. [the ~][总称]好人 **Good Friday** 【基督教】受难节〔复活节前的星期五〕/ ~-hearted adj. 好心肠的 / ~-humo(u)red adj. 心情好的；脾气好的；愉快的 / ~-'natured adj. 脾气好的 / ~-'sized adj. 大号的；相当大(或多)的 / ~-'tempered adj. 脾气好的；和气的 / ~-'will n. 1. 友好，亲善；好意 2.(商店、企业等的)信誉，商誉

good-by(e) [,gud'bai] int. 再见! — n. 告别

goodish ['gudiʃ] adj. 还好的；相当好(或长、大等)的

goodly ['gudli] adj. 1. 漂亮的；讨人喜欢的 2. 好的，不错的 3. 颇大的

goodness ['gudnis] n. 1. 优良；德性；善行；仁慈 2. 精华；真髓

goods [gudz] [复] n. 1. 商品，货物 2. 动产 3.〈美口〉[the ~]真货；符合要求的

东西；真本领；实在的事

goody ['gudi] *n.* **1.** [古][常加在姓氏前](下层社会的)妇女；老妇人 [常 goodies]口 好吃的东西；糖果；吸引人的东西 **2.** 伪善者，表面虔诚的人 — *adj. & adv.* 伪善的；跟道学的(地)；假正经的(地) — *int.* (儿语)太好啦！

goof [guf] *n.* **1.** 可笑的蠢人，呆子 **2.** 大错；疏忽 — *vi.* **1.** 出大错 **2.** [俚]闲荡，混日子(*off*) — *vt.* 把(事情)弄糟，搞坏

goose [gus] ([复]**geese** [gis]或[军 gooses]) *n.* **1.** 鹅；雌鹅；鹅肉 **2.** 呆头鹅，傻瓜 **3.** [复]**gooses**]鹅颈式熨斗 — *vt.* **1.** 俚]突然增加(汽车等)的油门 **2.** [俚]作嘘嘘声反对(某人)，嘘骂 ‖ **~ flesh.** **~ pimples** *n.* 鸡皮疙瘩

gooseberry ['guzbəri] *n.* **1.** [植]醋栗，茶藨子 **2.** 醋栗果实；醋藨酒

GOP *abbr.* Grand Old Party 老大党(美国共和党的别称)

gopher ['goufə] *n.* **1.** [动](美国东南部产的)穴居沙龟 **2.** [动]囊鼠；黄鼠 **3.** [G-]黄鼠州人[美国明尼苏达州人的别称]

gore¹ [gɔː] *n.* (流出的)血；成块的血

gore² [gɔː] *vt.* **1.** (牛、羊等)以角抵破，抵伤 **2.** 军](岩石)划破(船只)

gorge [gɔːdʒ] *n.* **1.** 咽喉 **2.** 胃 **3.** 暴食；饱食，贪吃 **4.** [书面语]的食物 **5.** 山峡，峡谷 **6.** (堡垒等后部的)通口 **7.** [阻塞通道的]障碍物；原始的鱼钩 — *vt.* **1.** 塞饱 **2.** 跟虎咽地吃 — *vi.* 狼吞虎咽

gorgeous ['gɔːdʒəs] *adj.* **1.** 灿烂的；华丽的；豪华的 **2.** [俚]美丽的；极好的；令人喜欢的 ‖ **~ly** *adv.* / **~ness** *n.*

gorilla [gə'rilə] *n.* **1.** [动]大猩猩 **2.** [美俚]貌似大猩猩的人 **3.** [美俚]暴徒，打手

gory ['gɔːri] *adj.* **1.** 沾满鲜血的；血淋淋的；血迹斑斑的 **2.** 流血的，残杀的 **3.** 骇人听闻的

gosling ['gɔzliŋ] *n.* **1.** 小鹅 **2.** 笨人，傻瓜；没有经验的人

gospel ['gɔspəl] *n.* **1.** [常 G-][基督教]福音，喜讯 **2.** (新约)四部福音书之一 **3.** (行动的)准则，信条，主义 — *adj.* 福音的；传播福音的；福音派美以诗的

gossamer ['gɔsəmə] *n.* **1.** 蛛丝，游丝 **2.** 纤细的东西 **3.** 薄纱 **4.** 薄雨衣(或织物) — *adj.* 轻薄的；薄弱的；虚无飘渺的

gossip ['gɔsip] *n.* **1.** 闲谈，聊天 **2.** 爱讲闲话的人；爱传流言蜚语的人 **3.** (报刊上有关社会新闻或个人隐私的)闲话 **4.** [英方]朋友，同伴 — *vi.* 闲聊；传播流言蜚语

got [gɔt] get 的过去式和过去分词

gotten ['gɔtn] 美 get 的过去分词

gouge [gaudʒ] *n.* **1.** 半圆凿，弧口凿，扁凿 **2.** 美口]凿槽，凿成的槽(或孔) **3.** 美口]欺骗，诈取；榨取；骗子 **4.** [地]断层(软壁)泥 — *vt.* **1.** 用半圆凿凿 **2.** 凿成(洞)；凿出洞(或孔)；用拇指挖出(某人)的眼睛(*out*)；用拇指挖出(某人)的眼睛(*out*) **3.** 口]敲诈；榨取 ‖ **~ r** *n.*

goulash ['guːlæʃ] *n.* 菜和红辣椒炖牛肉；匈牙利红烩牛肉

gourd [guəd] *n.* **1.** 葫芦科植物；葫芦(植物或其果实) **2.** 葫芦制成的容器

gourmand ['guəmənd] *adj.* 贪吃的 — *n.* 贪吃的人；美食家

gourmet ['guəmei] *n.* 美食家；美馔美食的品尝家

gout [gaut] *n.* [医]痛风 ‖ **~y** *adj.* 患痛风(病)的；(似)痛风的；痛风引起的；引起痛风的；供患痛风时用的

Gov.，gov. *abbr.* 1. government 2. governor

govern ['gʌvən] *vt.* 1. 统治；管理 2. 指导；支配 3. 决定；影响 4. 抑制；控制（感情等）4. 调节（车速）5.【语】支配（在英语中指动词或前置词与其所眼的宾格名词或代词的关系）— *vi.* 统治；管理

governable ['gʌvənəbl] *adj.* 可统治的；可控制的

governess ['gʌvənis] *n.* 1. 家庭女教师；保育员；保姆 2. 女统治者；女管理者；总督（或州长）的夫人

government ['gʌvənmənt] *n.* 1. 政府；（英）内阁 2. 政治；政体 3. 政治学 4. 行政管理；管理机构 5. 行政管理区域 6.【语】支配关系 ‖ ~al [,gʌvən'mentl] *adj.* 政府的；政治的

governor ['gʌvənə] *n.* 1. 统治者；管辖者 2. 地方长官（如省长）；（英国殖民地）总督；（美国）州长；（要塞或卫戍区的）司令官；（英）典狱长 3.（组织、机构的）主事人员（如学校董事、银行总裁等）4.【机】调速器；调节器 5.〈口〉老板；先生；爸爸 ‖ ~ship *n.* 统治者（或地方长官等）的职位（或任期）

Govt.，govt. *abbr.* government

gown [gaun] *n.* 1. 长袍；长外衣（尤指教士、法官、教授等的礼服或妇女的睡衣等）2. [集合名词]大学全体师生 — *vt.* [主要用过去分词]使穿长袍；使穿礼服

grab [græb] (grabbed; grabbing) *vt.* 1. 攫取；抓住 2. 强夺；霸占 3.（急速地）抓住；抓牢 — *vi.* 1.（急速地）抓住 2.（马）后踢踢着前蹄踏 — *n.* 1. 攫取；掠夺；（急速）抓住 2.【机】抓具（如抓斗）；抓斗挖土机

grace [greis] *n.* 1. 优美，雅致 2. [常~s]风度；魅力 3. 体面（感）；情理 4. 恩惠，

恩赐；宽厚，仁慈；赦免；[~s]恩遇 5.【宗】神的恩典；恩化；（对神的）皈依 6.（票据等到期后的）宽限（期）7.【宗】（饭前或饭后的）谢恩祷告 8.[音]装饰音 9. [the Graces]【希神】美惠三女神 10. [His（或 Her, Your）Grace]（对公爵、公爵夫人或大主教的尊称）大人 — *vt.* 1. 使优美；使增光 2.【音】级…以装饰音

graceful ['greisful] *adj.* 优美的，雅致的；得体的 ‖ ~ly *adv.* / ~ness *n.*

graceless ['greislis] *adj* 1. 不优美的，不雅致的 2. 无礼貌的；不知情理的 3. 堕落的，道德败坏的 ‖ ~ly *adv.* / ~ness *n.*

gracious ['greiʃəs] *adj.* 1. 有礼貌的；通情达理的；谦和的 2. 宽厚的，仁慈的 3. 优美的，雅致的 — *int.* [表示惊异等]：*Gracious!*（或 *Good ~!* 或 *Gracious Heaven!* 或 *Gracious me!* 或 *My ~!*）天哪！啊呀！‖ ~ly *adv.* / ~ness *n.*

grackle ['grækl] *n.*【动】1. 美洲黑羽椋鸟 2. 鹩哥

gradation [grə'deiʃən, grei'deiʃən] *n.* 逐渐的变化；分等，分级；层次 ‖ ~ al *adj.* / ~ally *adv.*

grade [greid] *n.* 1. 等级；级别；阶级 2. 程度 3.（中小学的）年级；某一年级的全体学生；[the ~](美)小学 4.（美）学校的）评分等级 5.（美）坡度；斜坡 6.【动】（与良种杂交产生的）级进杂种 7.【语】音变 ‖ 1. 给…分等级；给…分类 2.（美）给…评分 3. 把（路面等）筑平或筑成小坡度）4.【动】与纯种杂交改良（up）5. 使（颜色等）逐渐变化 — *vi.* 1. 属于某种等级 2.（颜色等）逐渐变化，从一等级逐渐地进入另一等级 3.【语】语变 4.（牛等）品种被改良（up）‖ ~ school（美）小学

gradient ['greidiənt] *n.* 1. 坡度；斜面；

gradual

【物】梯度；梯度变化曲线 3.【数】梯度；斜率 4.【生】轴性梯度；生理梯度

gradual ['grædjuəl, 'grædʒuəl] *adj.* 1. 逐渐的,逐步的 2. 渐进的,顺序变化的；逐渐上升(或下降)的 ∥ ~ly *adv.*

graduate ['grædʒuit, 'grædʒuət] *n.* 1. 大学毕业生；(美)毕业生 2.【化】量筒;量杯 — ['grædʒueit, 'grædʒuət] *vt.* 1. (主美)准于…毕业;授于…学位 2. 给(量杯等)标上刻度 3. 把…分等级 4. 蒸发浓缩(溶液等) — *vi.* 1. 大学毕业;得学位;(美)毕业 2. 取得资格 3. 渐渐变为(*into*);逐步演进(*away*) — *adj.* 1. 毕业的 2. 研究生的 3. 刻度的 4. 分等级的

graduation [,grædju'eiʃən, ,grædʒu'eiʃən] *n.* 1. (大学毕业时的)授学位;获学位;毕业 2. (美)毕业典礼;授学位典礼 3. 刻度;分度 4. 分等级 5. 蒸浓

Graeco- *comb. form* = Greco-

graffito [grə'fi:təu] (*[复]* graffiti [grə'fi:ti]) *n.* (在墙上等处的)涂写,乱涂乱写

graft [grɑ:ft] *n.* 1.【农】嫁接;嫁接用的嫩枝(或芽);嫁接法 2.【医】移植物;移植片 3.(美)贪污;受贿;不义之财 — *vt. & vi.* 1. 嫁接(*in, into, on, upon*) 2. 用嫁接法移植(水果,花卉) 3.【医】移植(皮肤,骨等) 4.(美)贪污;受贿 ∥ ~er *n.* 1. 嫁接者;移植者 2.(美)贪污者;受贿者

graham ['greiəm] *adj.* [亦作 G-]全麦(面粉)的;粗面粉的 ∥ ~ bread 全麦面包;粗面粉面包

grain [grein] *n.* 1. 谷物,谷类,谷类植物 2. 谷粒;颗粒 3. 粒子;细粒;晶粒;(喻)些微,一点儿 4. 格令(英美最小的重量单位,等于 64.8 毫克,原为小麦谷粒的平均重量) 5.(木材或大理石的)纹理;(喻)性格;本质 6. 皮革的正

面,粒面 7. 胭脂虫;胭脂;胭脂虫红(染料);红色染料;不退色染料 3. [~s]麦芽渣,(酒)糟 — *vt.* 1. 使成粒状;使粒化;使结晶 2. 把(某物)的表面漆(或画)成木纹(或大理石纹) 3. 把(皮等)去毛;对(皮革)的粒面进行处理 — *vi.* 形成粒状 ∥ ~y *adj.* ∥ ~-field *n.* 粮田

gram [græm] *n.* 克(重量单位)

-gram *suf.* 表示"书写物","描绘物";*telegram*

grammar ['græmə] *n.* 1. 语法(学),文法(学);语法规则 2. 语法书 3.(某人的)语法知识;(符合语法规则的)文理 4. 语法现象 5.(艺术,科学,技术等的)基本原理;入门书 ∥ ~ian [grə'meəriən] *n.* 语法学家

grammatical [grə'mætikəl] *adj.* 1. 语法(上)的 2. 符合语法规则的 ∥ ~ly *adv.*

gramme [græm] *n.* (英) = gram

granary ['grænəri] *n.* 谷仓,粮仓;产粮区

grand [grænd] *adj.* 1. (最)重大的,主要的;(同一官衔,爵位中)最高的 2. 堆伟的;宏大的 3. 豪华的;华丽的 4. 自负的,傲慢的 5.(口 极好的,美妙的 6. 全部的,总的 7. 庄重的,堂皇的 8.(亲属关系中)(外)祖(父),(外)孙... 9. 大钞等 2 [单复同](美理 1000 美元 ∥ ~ly *adv.* / ~ness *n.* ∥ ~ aunt *n.* 叔(或伯)祖母;舅婆;姑婆;姨婆/ ~child ['grændtʃaild] *n.* (外)孙(女);外孙(女)/ ~ daughter ['grænd,dɔ:tə] *n.* (外)孙女/ ~ nephew ['grænd,nevju:] *n.* 侄孙;(外甥孙)/ ~ niece ['grændni:s] *n.* 侄(外)孙女;(外)甥孙女/ ~ parent ['grænd,peərənt] *n.* (外)祖父;(外)祖母/ ~ son ['grændsʌn] *n.* (外)孙子/ ~ uncle *n.* 叔(或伯)祖父;舅公;姑(或姨)丈公

grandee [græn'di:] *n.* 1.(西班牙或葡萄牙的)最高爵位)大公 2. 显贵,要人,大人物

grandeur ['grændʒə] *n.* 1. 宏伟,壮观,庄严 2. 富丽堂皇,豪华 3. 伟大,崇高

grandfather ['grænd,fɑːðə] *n.* 1.(外)祖父 2. 老大爷 3. 祖先 ‖ ~ly *adj.* 老祖父(似)的;慈祥的 ‖ ~('s) clock 落地式大摆钟

grandiose ['grændiəus] *adj.* 1. 宏伟的,壮丽的 2. 过分华丽的;夸大的,做作的 ‖ ~ly *adv.* / ~ness *n.*

grandmother ['grænd,mʌðə] *n.* 1.(外)祖母 2. 老奶奶 3.(女性)祖先 — *vt.* 悉心照料;溺爱 ‖ ~ly *adj.* 老祖母(似)的;慈祥的;溺爱的;晴叨的

grandstand ['grændstænd] *n.* 1.(运动场等的)大看台 2.(大看台)观众 — *vi.* (口)(球赛等时)做花式动作(以博取观众喝彩)

grange [greindʒ] *n.* 1. 农场,田庄 2.《古》谷仓 3.[G-]格兰其(1867 年成立的美国农业保护者协会);格兰其分会

granite ['grænit] *n.* 1. 花岗岩,花岗石 2. 坚毅;冷酷无情‖ **Granite State** 花岗岩州(美国新罕布什尔州的别称)

granny, grannie ['græni] *n.*(口)1. 奶奶;外婆 2. 老婆婆,老奶奶 3. 婆婆妈妈的人,晴叨挑剔的人 4.(美)接生婆 5. 老奶奶结(反向打的方结,不牢且易成死结)(亦作 ~ knot)

granola [grə'nəulə] *n.* 格兰诺拉(燕)麦片(用作早餐或营养品)

grant [grɑːnt] *vt.* 同意,准于(补助等);授予(权利等)2. 让渡,转让(财产等)3. 假定…(正确);(姑且)承认 — *n.* 1. 同意,准许;授予;转让;容让 2. 授给物(如补助、拨款、拨地等);转让物;转让证书

granular ['grænjulə] *adj.* 颗粒状的;粒面的;有细粒的

granulate ['grænjuleit] *vt.* 1. 使形成颗粒;使成粒状;使粒化 2. 使表面粗糙 — *vi.* 1. 形成颗粒;成粒状;粒化 2. 表面变粗糙 3.(伤口等)形成肉芽 ‖ **granu'lation** *n.*

granule ['grænju:l] *n.* 细粒,颗粒,微粒

grape [greip] *n.* 1. 葡萄;葡萄藤 2. 葡萄色,深紫色 3. 葡萄酒 4.《军》霰弹,葡萄弹(亦作 ~ shot)5.[~s]马体葡萄疮;牛结核 ‖ ~ fruit *n.* 葡萄柚 / ~ vine *n.* 1. 葡萄藤 2. 谣言,传闻,小道新闻 3.(小道新闻等的)流传;消息的秘密来源

graph [græf, grɑːf] *n.* 1.(曲线)图;图表;图解 2.《数》图;图像;图(形);网络 — *vt.* 用图表显示;绘…的图(或图形);描绘

-graph *suf.* 1. 表示"书写器"、"描绘器"、"记录器":mimeograph, monograph, telegraph 2. 表示"书写(或描绘、记录)的结果":autograph, monograph, photograph

graphic ['græfik] *adj.* 1. 图的;图解的;图示的 2. 书写的;书法的;绘画的;雕刻的;印刷的 3. 生动的;(轮廓)鲜明的 — *n.* 1. 生动的图画作品 2.(说明性的)图画或地图,图表

graphical ['græfikəl] *adj.* = graphic ‖ ~ly *adv.*

graphite ['græfait] *n.*《矿》石墨

-graphy *suf.* 1. 表示"写法"、"书法"、"图示法"、"画法":calligraphy, photography 2. 表示"记"、"志":biography, geography

grapnel ['græpnəl] *n.* 1.(四爪或五爪的)多爪锚 2.(用于钩住敌船等的)爪钩

grapple ['græpl] *vt.* 1. 抓住,捉牢,握紧 2. 与…扭打,与…格斗 3. 缚紧 — *vi.*

1. 用抓钩钩住船 **2.** 抓住：抓打，格斗（*with*） — *n.* **1.** = grapnel 抓钩 **2.** 抓住：扭打，格斗 **3.** [机]抓具：抓斗

grasp [grɑːsp] *vt.* **1.** 抓住，抓紧：抱住 **2.** 掌握，领会 — *vi.* 抓 — *n.* **1.** [常用单] 抓住，紧握：抱住 **2.** 控制 **3.** (对知识等的)掌握，了解 **4.** 把手(船的)锚尔

grasping ['grɑːspiŋ] *adj.* **1.** 抓的，想抓住的 **2.** 攫取的：贪婪的

grass [grɑːs] *n.* **1.** [青]草 **2.** [植]禾草 **3.** 草地：牧场：放牧 **4.** 叶用莴苣(色拉中的)生菜 **5.** [矿]矿山地面：矿井地面 **6.** [无] (雷达接收上的)噪声细条，茅草干扰，杂乱脉冲干扰 **7.** [俚]大麻 **8.** 〈美俚〉(高加索人种典型的)直头发 — *vt.* **1.** 使吃草，放牧 **2.** 使长草：给…铺上草皮 **3.** 把(网、绳、亚麻等)摊在草上晒白 **4.** 把(鱼)弄上岸,把(鸟)打落地 **5.** 打倒：摔倒 **6.** 〈英俚〉背叛，出卖 — *vi.* **1.** 长草 **2.** 〈英〉告密，变节，出卖人 ‖ ~**y** *adj.* **1.** 盖满草的：长满草的 **2.** 像草的：青草味的 **3.** (动物)食草的 ‖ ~**hopper** *n.* **1.** 蚱蜢，蝗虫 **2.** 轻型单翼飞机/~**land** *n.* 牧场：草地：草原/~**roots** *n.* **1.** 乡村地区(与城市和工业区相对而言) **2.** 基层：基层群众 **3.** 基础，根本 **4.** 地表层的土壤

grate[1] [greit] *n.* **1.** 炉格,炉箅,炉篦 **2.** 火炉，壁炉 **3.** (门、窗等的)格栅 **4.** [矿]篦条筛,固定筛 — *vt.* 装炉格于：装格栅于

grate[2] [greit] *vt.* **1.** 摩擦：磨碎：轧 **2.** 擦响：磨(牙) **3.** 使焦急：激怒：刺激 — *vi.* **1.** 摩擦：擦响：发出嘎嘎声 **2.** 使人烦躁：触怒(常 *upon*, *upon*) ‖ ~ *r* *n.* 磨碎(或擦碎)东西的人(或工具)：(香料,蔬菜等的)磨碎机

grateful ['greitful] *adj.* **1.** 感激的，感谢的 **2.** 令人愉快的,可喜的 ‖ ~**ly** *adv.*/~-

ness *n.*

gratification [ˌgrætifiˈkeiʃən] *n.* **1.** 满足：满意：喜悦 **2.** 使人满意的事：可喜的事 **3.** 奖金：报酬

gratify ['grætifai] *vt.* **1.** 使满足 **2.** 使满意：使高兴

grating ['greitiŋ] *n.* **1.** (门、窗等的)格栅 **2.** [物]衍射光栅

gratis ['greitis] *adv.* 免费地,无偿地 — *adj.* 无需代价的：免费的,无偿的

gratitude ['grætitjuːd] *n.* 感激,感谢,感恩

gratuitous [grəˈtjuːitəs] *adj.* **1.** 免费的,无偿的 **2.** 无缘无故的,没有理由的

gratuity [grəˈtjuːiti] *n.* **1.** 赏钱,小费 **2.** (军人的)退役金：遣散费：(给被释罪犯的)安家费

grave[1] [greiv] *n.* **1.** 墓穴：坟墓：墓碑 **2.** 死亡：终结 **3.** (名誉等的)葬送处 **4.** (储藏土豆的)贮坑 ‖ ~ *digger* *n.* 掘墓人：埋葬虫/~**stone** *n.* 墓碑/~**yard** *n.* 墓地,坟场

grave[2] [greiv] (过去式 graved, 过去分词 graven 或 graved) *vt.* **1.** 雕刻 **2.** 喻铭记,牢记

grave[3] [greiv] *adj.* **1.** 严重的：重大的 **2.** 严肃的：庄重的 **3.** 沉重的：阴沉的：(颜色)黯淡的 **4.** (声音)低沉的：[语]有沉音符的 — *n.* [语]沉音符 ‖ ~**ly** *adv.*/~**ness** *n.*

gravel ['grævəl] *n.* **1.** [总称]砾,砂砾：砾石 **2.** [矿](尤指含金砂的)砂砾层 **3.** [医]尿砂症 — (gravel(l)ed 或 gravel-(l)ing) *vt.* **1.** 以砾石铺(路) **2.** 使(船)搁浅在沙滩上 **3.** 使困惑：使窘困：怒怒,刺激 ‖ ~**ly** *adj.* 充满砾石的：含有砾石的：像砾石的：用砾石铺筑的

gravimeter [grəˈvimitə] *n.* [物]重力仪：比重计

gravitate ['græviteit] *vi.* **1.** 受引力作用：受重力作用 **2.** 受吸引力；倾向 (*to, towards*) **3.** 下沉；下降 — *vt.* 使受重力吸引而移动；吸引

gravitation [,grævi'teiʃən] *n.* **1.**〔物〕(万有)引力作用 **2.** 引力作用；重力作用 **3.** 下沉；下降‖ **~al** *adj.*

gravity ['græviti] *n.* **1.** 严肃，庄重；认真 **2.** 严重性；危险性；重要性 **3.**〔物〕(万有)引力；重力 **4.** 重量 **5.**〔音〕(音调的)低沉

gravy ['greivi] *n.* **1.** 肉汁，肉卤 **2.**〔美俚〕(演员)轻易博得的笑声；轻易得来的‖‡钱；外快；赏钱；非法所得

gray [grei] *adj.*, *n.*, *vt.* & *vi.* 〔美〕= grey‖ '~-collar *adj.* 〔美〕灰领阶层的，从事维修保养的技术工人的

grayling ['greiliŋ] (〔复〕grayling(s)) *n.*〔动〕 **1.** 茴鱼 **2.** 眼蝶

graze[^1] [greiz] *vi.* **1.** 喂草；放牧；(牲畜)吃草 — *vt.* **1.** 吃(田野)里的草；在田野里吃(草等) **2.** 用牧草喂；放牧 — *vi.* **1.** 吃草；放牧 **2.** 牧草

graze[^2] [greiz] *vt.* **1.** 擦过，掠过 **2.** 擦伤；抓破 — *vi.* 擦伤 — *n.* **1.** 轻擦；擦过 **2.** 抓破；擦破处

Gr. Br., Gr. Brit. *abbr.* Great Britain 大不列颠，英国

grease [griːs] *n.* **1.** 动物脂；脂肪；润滑脂(俗称牛油)；油脂状物 **2.** 未脱脂的羊毛；生羊毛 **3.** 马粪炎 **4.**〔俚〕贿赂；小费；钱 **5.**〔美俚〕黄油 **6.**〔美俚〕射击；枪杀 — [griːz, griːs] *vt.* **1.** 涂油脂于；用油脂润滑；使油污 **2.** 使(马)患踵炎 **3.**〔美俚〕略胜 ‖ '~-paint *n.* 化妆用油彩

greasy ['griːzi, 'griːsi] *adj.* **1.** 沾有油脂的，油污的；油腻似的 **2.** (羊毛)未脱脂的 **3.** 像油脂般的，滑(腻)的 **4.** (言行‖

等)谄媚的 **3.** (马)患踵炎症的 **4.**〔天气等〕阴湿的

great [greit] *adj.* **1.** 伟大的；大的 **2.**〔极〕重大的；超乎寻常的；强烈的 **3.**〔数量〕极大的 (时间) 久的 **4.** [用在名词前的，名副其实的] 真的 **5.** 〔口〕 [用在其他形容词前面] 多么…的 **6.** 〔口〕美妙的 **7.** 崇高的；显贵的 **8.** (字母)大写的 **9.** [用在由 grand 构成的表示亲属关系的复合词前，表示更远一辈的亲属关系] 曾祖(或孙)的；外曾祖(或孙)的‖ '~-grandfather 曾祖父；外曾祖父/ a~-granddaughter 曾孙女；外曾孙女 — *adv.*〔口〕很好地，成功地 — *n.* **1.** 全部，整体 **2.** [the ～(s)] 大人物们 **3.**〔美俚〕(文艺、体育等方面的)大师；名家 **4.**〔美俚〕牛津大学文学士学位考试‖ '~ly *adv.* **1.** 大大地，非常 **2.** 崇高地/ '~ness *n.*‖‡ 'aunt *n.* = grandaunt/ '~coat *n.* 厚大衣/ '~nephew *n.* = grandnephew/ '~niece *n.* = grandniece/ '~uncle *n.* = granduncle

grebe [griːb] *n.*〔动〕鸊鷉

Grecian ['griːʃən] *adj.* 希腊的；(建筑、容貌等)希腊式的 — *n.* **1.** 希腊人 **2.** 希腊语学者

Greco- *comb. form* 表示"希腊"

Greece [griːs] *n.* 希腊 [欧洲巴尔干半岛南部国家]

greed [griːd] *n.* 贪心，贪婪 (*for*)

greedy ['griːdi] *adj.* **1.** 贪吃的，嘴馋的 **2.** 贪心的，贪婪的 **3.** 渴望的；(兴趣等)强烈的‖ greedily *adv.*/ greediness *n.*

Greek [griːk] *adj.* **1.** 希腊的；希腊风格的；希腊人的；希腊语的 **2.**〔宗〕希腊正教的 — *n.* **1.** 希腊人 **2.** 希腊语；古希腊语 **3.** 难懂的事 **4.** 玩滑的家伙；骗子 **5.**〔俚〕(以希腊字母命名的)美国大学

生联谊会会员 6.【宗】希腊正教教徒

green [griːn] *adj.* 1. 绿的 2. 青葱的；温暖的；无雪的；妩媚的 3. 新鲜的；新近的；(伤口) 未愈合的 4. 精力旺盛的；青春的；未成熟的；嫩的 6. 无经验的；没有受过训练的；幼稚的；易受欺骗的 7. 未干的；未经处理过的；尚未能用的；(酒) 不陈的；(鱼) 未到排卵期的；(鳖等) 刚刚蜕壳用的 8. (脸色等) 发青的；苍白的；(喻) 妒忌的 — *n.* 1. 绿色 2. 绿色颜料；绿色染料 3. 绿色的东西 (尤指衣、布等) 4. [~s] 青枝绿叶 5. [~s] 蔬菜；植物 6. 青春；生气 7. (公共) 草地；草坪 8. 〈美俚〉纸币 — *vt.* 1. 使变绿；把…染成绿色 2. 〈俚〉欺骗；哄骗 — *vi.* 变成绿色 ‖ ~**ly** *adv.*/~**ness** *n.* ‖ ~**back** *n.* 美钞/~ **card** 〈美〉绿卡 (指允许墨西哥等外国人进入美国工作的就业许可证)/'~**carder** *n.* 〈美〉持绿卡者/~ **fingers** [复]〈主英〉= ~ **thumb**/'~**born** *n.* 1. 生手；没有经验的人 2. 易受欺骗的人 3. 初到新到的移民/'~**house** *n.* 1. 暖房，温室 2.〈军俚〉周围有玻璃的座舱；装炸员座舱/'~**house effect** [气] 温室效应/~ **manure** 绿肥/**Green Panther** 绿豹党人 (用于称呼要求保护环境的激进分子)/**Green Paper**〈英〉绿皮书 (指供讨论的政府文件)/'~**sward** *n.* 草地；草皮 ~**tea** 绿茶/~ **thumb** 手指 (指种植花木蔬菜的高超技能)/'~**wood** *n.* 绿林；湿材，生材

greenery [ˈgriːnəri] *n.* 1. 草木；[总称] 绿叶；(装饰用的) 青枝绿叶；葱翠 2. 暖房

greenish [ˈgriːniʃ] *adj.* 略呈绿色的

Greenland [ˈgriːnlənd] *n.* 格陵兰 (岛) [北美洲东北] (属丹麦)

Greenwich [ˈgrinidʒ] *n.* 格林尼治 (旧译格林威治) [英国伦敦东南一市镇，为本初子午线所经过的地方]

greeny [ˈgriːni] *adj.* 略呈绿色的

greet [griːt] *vt.* 1. 问候，迎接，欢迎；向…致敬…致意 2. 被 (耳、鼻、眼) 所感知；呈现在 (某人) 前

greeting [ˈgriːtiŋ] *n.* 问候；致敬；祝贺；贺词；欢迎词

gregarious [greˈɡeəriəs] *adj.* 1. 群集的；群居的 2. 爱群居的；爱交际的 3.【植】聚生的 ‖ ~**ly** *adv.*/~**ness** *n.*

gremlin [ˈɡremlin] *n.* 1.〔亦作 G-〕(据认为使飞机发生原因不明故障的) 小妖精；造成麻烦的原因 2. 捣乱的人

Grenada [ɡriˈneidə] *n.* 格林纳达 [拉丁美洲岛国] (在向风群岛南部)

grenade [ɡriˈneid] *n.* 1. 手榴弹；枪榴弹 2. 燃弹

grenadier [ˌɡrenəˈdiə] *n.* 1. 掷弹兵 2. 精锐部队的士兵

grew [ɡruː] grow 的过去式

grey [ɡrei] *adj.* 1. 灰色的；灰白的 2. 灰暗的；阴暗的；阴郁的 3. 灰白头发的；老的；老练的；成熟的 4. 古代的；太古的 5. (某些教派的教士) 穿灰色衣服的 6. 半黑市的 — *n.* 1. 灰色；暗淡 (光) 2. 灰色颜料；灰色染料 3. 灰色动物 (尤指马) 3. 未经漂白的状态；坯布，本色布 — *vt. & vi.*(使) 变成灰色 ‖ ~**ish** *adj.* 淡灰色的/~**beard** *n.* 1. (白胡子) 老人 2. 石酒壶；粗陶大酒壶 3.〈英〉【植】铁线莲/'~**hound** *n.* 1. 灵狸 (一种身体细长、善跑的猎狗) 2. 快速艇 (尤指远洋班轮)/~ **market** 灰市 (以过高的价格成交短缺商品的市场)/~ **matter** 1. (中枢神经系统) 灰质 2.〈口〉头脑，智力

grid [ɡrid] *n.* 1. 铁格子，格栅 2.【电】蓄电池电极板 3.【无】栅极板 4. (地图等的)

格冈.坐标方格 5.(电力、铁路的)网络
6.棋盘式街道布局 ‖ ~lock n.(棋盘
式街道的)交通全面大堵塞

griddle ['gridl] n. 1.(烘烤糕饼等用的)铁
盘 2.[矿]筛子:大孔筛 — vt. 1. 用铁
盘烘(或烤) 2. 筛 ‖ ~ cake 薄饼:浇格
饼

gridiron ['grid,aiən] n. 1.(炙烤食物用的)
烤架 2. 格状物;格状结构(如管网、道
路网、铁路网等)【船】船台 4.(舞台
上承受升降布景装置的)布景骨架 5.
棋盘式街道布局 6.(美口)橄榄球球场

grief [gri:f] n. 1. 悲痛,悲伤 2. 不幸;灾
难;伤心事

grievance ['gri:vəns] n. 1. 不满,不平 2.
冤情;苦情

grieve [gri:v] vt. 使悲痛,使伤心 — vi. 悲
痛,伤心;哀悼(at. about. for. over)

grievous ['gri:vəs] adj. 1. 令人悲痛的,使
人伤心的 2. 表示悲痛的,显悲愁的;
剧烈的,严重的 4.(罪恶等)极大的;惨
无人道的 ‖ ~ly adv.

grill[1] [gril] n. 1.(炙烤肉等用的)烤架
2. 一盘烤菜(尤指烤肉等的)3. = room —
vt. 1. 在烤架上炙烤 2. 加酷热于 3. 以
酷热对…行刑 3. 炙烤般地折磨 4. 对
…严加盘问 — vi. 1. 在烤架上炙烤
2. 受酷热 3. 严厉盘问 ‖ ~ room n. 烤
菜餐馆(或餐室)

grill[2] [gril] n. = grille

grille [gril] n. 1.(汽车散热器的)护栅
(邮局或银行等柜台上的)格栅,铁窗

grim [grim] (grimmer, grimmest) adj. 1. 严
厉的;冷酷无情的;残忍的 2. 坚强的,
不屈的 3. 可憎的,讨厌的;可怕的 4.
不祥的;邪恶的 ‖ ~ly adv./ ~ness n.

grimace [gri'meis] n. 1.(表示痛苦,厌恶,
不以为然,自鸣得意等的)怪相,鬼脸 —
vi. 作怪相,装鬼脸

grime [graim] n. 尘垢;烟灰;污垢;(皮肤
等表面上的)积垢 — vt. 使肮脏;使积
垢

grimy ['graimi] adj. 肮脏的;积满污垢的

grin [grin] (grinned, grinning) vi. 1. 露齿
而笑 2.(因痛苦或愤怒,因愤恨)龇牙
咧嘴 — vt. 龇齿咧笑着表示 — n. 1. 露
齿的笑 2.(表示痛苦、愤怒、轻蔑等的)
咧嘴

grind [graind] (ground [graund]) vt. 1. 磨
(碎);碾(碎) 2. 碾快;磨光;磨薄;磨成
…形 3.(用手摇风琴)奏出;苦苦地奏
出 4. 推,摇(石磨等);摇奏(手摇风琴)
5. 嘎嘎出声地挤压;咬(牙) 6.折磨;
压榨(出) 7. 苦苦教授,灌输 — vi. 1.
磨;碾;磨碎;磨快;磨光 2. 摩擦得嘎
嘎响 3. 苦学;苦干 4.(某些舞剧中的)
扭摆 — n. 1. 磨;摩擦声;磨细的程度
2. 苦差使;枯燥乏味的活;专心的学习
3.(美)埋头读书的人;书呆子 4.(英)
步行锻炼;越野障碍赛马(或赛跑) 5.
(某些舞剧中的)扭摆

grinder ['graində] n. 1. 磨工,研磨机;
磨床 3.(石磨的)上磨盘 4. 臼齿,牙
齿;(美口)[~s]牙齿 5.(美方)大型三
明治

grindstone ['graindstəun] n. 1. 磨石;砂轮
2. 石磨

grip[1] [grip] n. 1. 紧握,紧咬;紧夹 2. 握
力;握法;(秘密社团人员之间的)作为暗
号的握手式 3. 掌握;支配;控制 4.(理
解(力) 5.(器物的)柄把 6.(美)手提
包;旅行包 7. 阵痛 8.(美俚)舞台工作
人员 — (gripped 或(古) gript; gripping)
vt. 1. 握(或咬,夹) 2. 掌握;支配;
控制;抓住(注意力等) 3. 把(某物)接
牢(to) 4.(秘密社团人员之间作为暗
号)与(某人)握手 — vi. 握(或咬,夹)
得牢

grip² [grip] *n.* = grippe

gripe [graip] *vt.* 1. 〔美口〕惹烦、激怒 2. 使患肠（或胃）绞痛 — *vi.* 1. 患肠（或胃）绞痛；引起肠（或胃）绞痛 2.〔口〕（不停地）抱怨，发牢骚 — *n.* 1. 怨言，牢骚 2.〔常～s〕肠（或胃）绞痛

grippe [grip] 〈法〉*n.*〔医〕流行性感冒

grisly ['grizli] *adj.* 可怖的，吓人的

grist [grist] *n.* 1. 制粉用谷物；（一次磨成的）谷粉;面粉；（酿造用的）碎麦芽 2.〔美口〕大量，许多 3. 有利的东西 ‖ '～-mill *n.* 磨坊

gristle ['grisl] *n.* 软骨 ‖ **gristly** *adj.* 软骨的；有软骨的

grit [grit] *n.* 1. 粗砂，砂砾；磨料（妨害机器运转的）砂粒，硬渣 2. 粗砂岩 3. 粒度;（砂砾的）粗细等级 4.〔黑人用语〕食物 5. 坚忍;刚毅;勇气 — (gritted/gritting) *vi.* 摩擦作声 — *vt.* 1. 在…上铺（或撒）砂粒;磨料磨光（大理石）2. 摩擦;摩擦（牙齿等）作声;愤怒（或坚决）地咬(牙)

grits [grits] 〔复〕*n.*〔用作单或复〕粗磨粉;粗面粉;粗燕麦粉;美粗玉米粉

gritty ['griti] *adj.* 1. 含砂的;砂砾般的 2. 勇敢的;坚韧不拔的 ‖ **grittiness** *n.*

grizzle ['grizl] *n.* 1. 灰白头发;灰色假发 2. 灰色;灰玉灰皮色（兽）*n.* 灰狗 3.〔建〕欠火砖;次等砖 — *vt. & vi.* （使）灰色 — *adj.* 灰色的 ‖ ～d *adj.* 1. 灰色的;有灰斑的 2. 灰白头发的

grizzly ['grizli] *adj.* 灰的;灰白的;有灰斑的 — *n.* 〔北美产〕灰熊（亦作 bear）

groan [grəun] *vi.* 1. 哼;呻吟呻吟声 2. 渴望（*for*）3. 受压迫;受虐待（*beneath, under*）4. 承受重压面作声 — *vt.* 1. 呻吟着说（*out*）2. 发哼声阻止

…讲话（*down*）— *n.* 呻吟;呻吟声;哼声

grocer ['grəusə] *n.* 食品杂货商

grocery ['grəusəri] *n.* 1.〔复〕常用作单食品杂货 2. 食品杂货店 3. 食品杂货业

grog [grog] *n.* 1. 格罗格酒(酒精和水的混和物) 2. 澳新口 烈酒;啤酒 3.〔泡〕(制坩埚等用的)陶渣 — (grogged; grogging) *vi.* 喝格罗格酒 — *vt.* 用热水从（空酒桶）中滤出一点酒 ‖ **groggy** *adj.* 1. 喝醉酒的 2. 头昏眼花的;脚步跟跄的

groin [grɔin] *n.* 1.〔解〕腹股沟 2.〔建〕（交又）穹棱;穹棱肋 — *vt.* 〔建〕使成(交又)穹棱;穹棱肋于

grommet ['grɔmit] *n.* 1.〔海〕索环、索眼 2. 扣眼;帽顶圈;绝缘垫圈

groom [grum] *n.* 1. 马夫 2. 新郎 3. 王室侍从官 4.〔古 用仆〕男人;家伙 — *vt.* 1. 照料(马等);擦洗(马等);洽料(马等)梳毛 2. 使整洁;打扮 3. 使准备参加竞选 — *vi.* 打扮

groomsman ['grumzmən]（[复] grooms-men）*n.* 男傧相

groove [gruv] *n.* 1. 槽，沟;(车)辙;(唱片的)纹(道);(管子、骨的)沟;〔印〕字沟 2. 常规、习惯 3.（适合能力和兴趣的）理想境况 4. 顶刮刮的东西;称心的东西;活泼的经历 — *vt.* 开槽于;用沟(或槽)连接

grope [grəup] *vi.* 1.（暗中）摸索 2. 探索（*for, after*）— *vt.* 摸索 — *n.* 摸索

grosbeak ['grəusbik] *n.* 〔动〕松雀;主红雀;锡嘴雀;黄昏蜡嘴雀

gross [grəus] *adj.* 1. 总的;毛的;～ weight 毛重 2. 显著的,十足的;严重的:思亏的 3.（语言、举止）粗俗的,粗野的;下流的 4.（食物）粗的;油腻的;喜欢吃粗

(或油腻)食物的 5.(感觉)迟钝的 6.(人、身体)臃肿的;粗壮的 7.世俗的;肉体的 8.(不用显微镜)肉眼能够看到的 9.剧厚的;浓密的,茂盛的 — n. 1.总额;大体 2.[单复同][商]罗(= 12 打) — vt. 获得…总收入(或毛利) ‖ ~ly adv. / ~ness n. ‖ '~-'out n. 1.(粗话或野蛮行为造成的)触犯;侮辱 2.美国 令人作呕的人(或行为)

grotesque [grəʊ'tesk] adj. 1.奇形怪状的,奇异的;怪诞的,荒唐的 2.(绘画或雕刻)风格奇异的 — n. 1.奇形怪状的人(或动物、图形等) 2.(绘画或雕刻上的)奇异风格(指将人、动物、植物的图案奇怪地凑在一起);风格奇异的作品 3.[印]哥特字体;英 粗黑体字 ‖ ~ly adv. / ~ness n.

grotto ['grɒtəʊ] n. [复]grotto(e)s n. 1.岩洞,洞穴 2.(人工开挖的)洞窟(如避暑洞室、神龛等)

grouch [graʊtʃ] vi.(口)发脾气;发脾气 — n. 口 1.一阵牢骚;坏脾气 2.怨气;常发牢骚的人;脾气坏的人 ‖ ~y adj.

ground¹ [graʊnd] n. 1.地,地面 2.土地 3.场地,场 — 场: fishing ~ 渔场 4.[~s] (附属于厂房、校舍等周围的)场地;庭园 5.(问题所涉及的)范围,领域 6.基础(绘画等的)底子,底色 7.地界 8.[常~s]根据,理由 9.原因 9.底;海底 10.[电]接地,地线 11.[~s]渣滓;沉淀物 12.(戏场的)正厅后座 13.[地]地质 — vt. 1.把…放在地上 2.[海]使搁浅;使停飞 3.把…建立在牢固的基础上;把(论点等)建立在 (on) 4.以…给(画面涂一底色 5.[电]使接地 — vi. 1.具有基础;依靠 (on, upon) 2.落地着陆 3.(船)搁浅 ‖ ~ cover 地被物;地被植物 / ~ crew [总称][空] 地勤

人员 / ~ effect machine 气垫船;气垫车 (略作 GEM) / ~ floor 1.(英 (楼房的)底层(= 美 first floor) 2.有利地位;优先机会 / ~ hog n.[动]花白旱獭;美洲旱獭 / ~ sea (飓风或地震等引起的)海涌,长涌,激涌/~ swell 1. = sea 2.(情绪、舆论等的)迅速高涨(或发展)/ '~-to-' ~ adv. & adj. 地对地的/ ~ work n. 基础;底子

ground² [graʊnd] grind 的过去式和过去分词 — adj. 嚓过的;嚓碎的

groundless ['graʊndlis] adj. 无根据的,无理由的

group [grup] n. 1.群,批,簇 2.(小)组;团体 3.[化]基;根;原子团 4.[界] 5.(英、美的)空军大队 6.群像(指雕塑) — vt. 1.把…分组(或归类);聚集 2.把…组合为艺术构图 — vi. 1.聚集,集中 (with) 2.组合为艺术构图

grouse¹ [graʊs] [单复同] n.[动] 松鸡

grouse² [graʊs] 俚 vi. 抱怨,发牢骚 — n. 1.怨言,牢骚 2.惯出怨言的人,老是发牢骚的人

grove [grəʊv] n. 小树林,树丛;园林

grovel ['grɒvl] (grovel(l)ed;grovel(l)ing) vi. 1.卧,匍匐 2.卑躬屈节,奴颜婢膝 ‖ grovel(l)er n. 1.趴着的人 2.卑躬屈节的人

grow [grəʊ] (grew [gru]; grown [grəʊn]) vi. 1.生长,成长;发育 2.成为,增长 3.渐渐变得 4.(风俗等)形成 (up) 产生 — vt. 1.种植,栽 2.[常用被动语态]使长满 3.养,养成

grower ['grəʊə] n. 1.种植者,栽培者;饲养者 2.以……方式生长的植物(或人):a fast ~ 长得快的植物

growl [graʊl] vi.(狗等)嗥叫 (at);(雷、

炮等) **轰鸣** 2.(人)**咆哮** — *vt.* **咆哮着说**(*out*) — *n.*(狗等的)**嗥叫**(声);(人的)**咆哮**;**轰鸣**(声)

grown [grəun] *grow* 的过去分词 — *adj.* 1. 长成了的;成熟的 2. 被…长满的 3. 供…栽种的 — *adj.* 1. 成人的 2. 供成年人用的

growth [grəuθ] *n.* 1. 生长,成长;发育 2. 发展;增大;增长 3. 种植,栽 4. 生长物;产物 5.[医]赘生物,肿瘤

grub [grʌb] *n.* 1.[动]蛴螬蛆;(昆虫的)幼虫 2. 苦干的人;穷苦文人 3. 邋遢人 4.(板球赛等中的)地滚球 5.[俚]食物 — *v.* (grubbed; grubbing) *vi.* 1. 掘地,刨地 2. 搜寻 3. 做苦工(*on, along, away*) 4.[俚]吃 — *vt.* 1.(把土地的)根翻起;掘出 2.(从书本等中)找出(*up, out*) 3.[俚]养活;给(住宿者等)伙食 ‖ ~-stake *n.* 1.(分享部分发现的矿物而提供给探矿者的)装备(或资金,食物等) 2. 贷款 *vt.* 给(探矿者等)提供贷款(或物品等)

grubby [ˈɡrʌbi] *adj.* 1. 生蛆的 2. 污秽的;邋遢的 3. 卑鄙的 ‖ **grubbily** *adv.*/ **grubbiness** *n.*

grudge [grʌdʒ] *vt.* 1. 妒忌 2. 吝惜,不愿给(某物) — *n.* 怨恨,恶意

gruel [ˈɡruəl] *n.* 粥,薄糊 — (gruel(l)ed; gruel(l)ing) *vt.* 使极度紧张;(用重罚或逼口供等)使筋疲力尽 ‖ **gruel**(l)ing *adj.* 折磨的;使筋疲力尽的;艰巨的;惩罚

gruesome [ˈɡruːsəm] *adj.* 可怕的;可憎的,令人厌恶的 ‖ ~**ly** *adv.*/ ~**ness** *n.*

gruff [grʌf] *adj.* 1.(说话、态度等)粗暴的,生硬的;脾气坏的 2.(声音)粗哑的 ‖ ~**ly** *adv.*/ ~**ness** *n.*

grumble [ˈɡrʌmbl] *vi.* 1. 抱怨,发牢骚(*at, about, over*) 2. 咕哝,嘟囔 3. 隆隆

响 — *vt.* 1. 抱怨地表示(*out*) 2. 嘟囔着说 — *n.* 1. 怨言,牢骚;咕哝 2. 隆隆声 ‖ ~**r** *n.* 爱抱怨的人,爱发牢骚的人

grumpy [ˈɡrʌmpi], **grumpish** [ˈɡrʌmpiʃ] *adj.* 脾气坏的;粗暴的 ‖ **grumpily** *adv.*/ **grumpiness** *n.*

grunt [grʌnt] *vi.* 1.(猪等)作呼噜声,喉鸣 2.(因愤怒、反对、疲劳、轻蔑等)发哼声,咕哝 3. 咕哝着说出(或表示) — *n.* 1.(猪等的)呼噜声 2. 哼哼声,咕哝声 3.[美俚](电气)线路工的助手 4.[美俚]猪肉 5. = ~er *n.* 1. 作呼噜声的动物(尤指猪) 2. 咕哝的人 3.[动]石鲈 4.[美俚]撑竿运动员

Gt. Br., Gt. Brit. *abbr.* Great Britain 大不列颠,英国

Guam [ɡwɑːm] *n.* 关岛[西太平洋](美国的重要海空军基地)

guarantee [ˌɡærənˈtiː] *n.* 1. 保证;保证书 2. 保证人 3. 接受保证的人 4. 起保证作用的东西;担保物;抵押品 — *vt.* 1. 保证;担保 2. 确保;保障;I ~ that he'll go. 我保险他会去。

guarantor [ˌɡærənˈtɔː] *n.* 保证人

guaranty [ˈɡærənti] *n.* 1. 保证;保证书 2. 担保物;抵押品 3. = guarantor — *vt.* = guarantee

guard [ɡɑːd] *n.* 1. 守卫了,警戒;看守 2. 卫兵(队);哨兵;警卫员;看守员 3. 护卫队;[Guards](英国的)近卫团 4.[英]列车长(= (美) conductor);[列车上的]制动员 5.[篮球队等的]后卫 6. 防护装置 7.(击剑、拳击的)防御姿势 — *vt.* 1. 保卫;守卫 2. 警卫;看守;监视 3. 谨慎使用(言词等) 4. 给…安装防护装置;对…进行拉丝绕 5.[体]防守 — *vi.* 1. 防守;警惕;防范 2. 警戒 3.(击剑、拳击中)取守势 ‖ ~-house,

'~-room *n.* 警卫室; 卫兵室; 禁闭室

guarded ['ɡɑːdid] *adj.* 1. 被保卫着的 2. 被看守着的; 被监视着的 3. 谨慎的

guardian ['ɡɑːdjən] *n.* 1. 护卫者; 保护人; 管理者 2.【律】监护人 3. [G-]〈英国的〉〈卫报〉—*adj.* 守护的 ‖ ~-ship *n.* 守护; 保护; 监护人的职责(或身份)

guardsman ['ɡɑːdzmən] ([复] guardsmen) *n.* 1. 卫兵; 卫士 2.〈英〉近卫团士兵;〈美〉国民警卫队士兵

Guatemala [ˌɡwæti'mɑːlə] *n.* 1. 危地马拉[拉丁美洲国家](位于中美洲西北部) 2. 危地马拉(城)[危地马拉首都](亦作 ~ City)

gubernatorial [ˌɡjuːbənə'tɔːriəl] *adj.* 1. 统治(或管辖)者的 2. 地方长官的; 州长的; 总督的

gudgeon ['ɡʌdʒən] *n.* 1.【动】鮈鱼 2. 易欺的人; 易受骗的人

guer(r)illa [ɡə'rilə] *n.* 1.〈古〉游击战(现通常用 ~ war) 2. 游击队员

guess [ɡes] *vt.* 1. 猜测; 推测 2. 猜中; 猜着 3.〈口〉想, 认为—*vi.* 1. 猜测; 推测—*n.* 猜测; 推测 ‖ ~work *n.* 猜测; 推测

guest [ɡest] *n.* 1. 客人, 宾客 2. 旅客; 宿客; 顾客 3. 客串演员, 特约演员 4.【动】寄虫; 寄生虫; 寄居动物; 寄生生物—*vt.* 招待, 款待—*vi.* 作客; 寄宿 ‖ ~ worker 客籍工人

guffaw [ɡʌ'fɔː] *n.* 哄笑; 狂笑—*vi.* 哄笑; 狂笑—*vt.* 大笑着说

guidance ['ɡaidəns] *n.* 1. 指引; 指导; 领导 2.【空】制导

guide [ɡaid] *n.* 1. 领路人; 向导者; 向导; 指导者 2.【军】基准兵; 基准舰; 基准车 3. 指南; 指导 4. 入门书; 手册;(旅行、游览)指南; 路标; 指引号 5.【印】指示标记; 【计】波导; 向导装置; 导杆; 导向的)职业登山向导 6.〈英〉女童子军

vt. 1. 为…领路; 带领 2. 引导; 指引; 指导 3. 管理; 操纵; 支配—*vi.* 任向导 ‖ ~-book *n.*(旅行)指南;(参考)手册 /~d missile 导弹 /~ post *n.* 路标/~ word (词典或工具书的)书眉词、眉题

guild [ɡild] *n.* 1.(中世纪的)行会; 同业公会(互助性质的)协会 2.【植】依赖植物集团

guilder ['ɡildə] *n.* = gulden

guile [ɡail] *n.* 狡诈; 诡计 ‖ ~ less *adj.* 不狡诈的; 坦率的; 正直的

guileful ['ɡailful] *adj.* 狡诈的, 诡计多端的 ‖ ~ ly *adv.*

guillotine ['ɡiləˌtiːn] *n.* 1. 断头台 2. 剪断机; 立式切纸机, 裁切机 3.【医】割除刀, 环状刀 4. 截止辩论(或对议案表决)(指议会中采用的在预定时间内对议案等进行表决的一种办法)—*vt.* 1. 在断头台上处决 2.(用剪断机等)剪断 3. 截止审议(议案等)以付表决

guilt [ɡilt] *n.* 1. 有罪; 罪; 犯罪; 过失 2. 内疚 ‖ ~ less *adj.* 1. 无罪的, 无辜的 2. 没有…经验的; 不熟悉…的; 没有…的(of)

guilty ['ɡilti] *adj.* 1. 有罪的; 犯罪的; 自觉有罪的, 内疚的 ‖ guiltily *adv.* / guiltiness *n.*

Guinea ['ɡini] *n.* 几内亚[西非国家]

guinea ['ɡini] *n.* 1. 几尼(旧英国金币的) 2.【动】珠鸡 ‖ ~ fowl【动】珠鸡/~ hen【动】雌珠鸡/~ pig 1.【动】豚鼠, 天竺鼠 2. 供进行医学(或其他科学)实验的人(或物), 实验品

Guinea-Bissau ['ɡini bi'sau] 几内亚比绍[西非国家]

guise [ɡaiz] *n.* 1. 外观; 姿态; 装束 2. 伪装; 借口—*vt. & vi.*〈英方〉伪装

guitar [ɡi'tɑː] *n.*【音】吉他, 六弦琴—*vi.* 弹吉他

gulch [gʌlʃ] *n.* 〈美〉【地】冲沟;沟壑;急流峡谷

gulden ['guldən] ([复] gulden(s)) *n.* 荷兰盾(荷兰货币单位)

gules [gju:lz] [单复同] *n. & adj.* (用于纹章上的)红色(的)

gulf [gʌlf] *n.* 1. 海湾 2. 深渊,深坑;悬隔,鸿沟 3. 旋涡;吞没一切的东西 \ 〈诗〉海 — *vt.* 吞没;使深深卷入

gull[1] [gʌl] *n.* 【动】鸥

gull[2] [gʌl] *n.* 易受骗的人;笨人 — *vt.* 欺骗;使上当

gullet ['gʌlit] *n.* 1.【解】食管;咽喉;颈 2. 沟;排水沟;峡谷 3. 锯沟,锯齿尖端间空隙

gullible ['gʌləbl] *adj.* 易受骗的,易上当的;轻信的 ‖ **gulli'bility** *n.* / **gullibly** *adv.*

gully ['gʌli] *n.* 1. 冲沟;溪谷 2. 水沟;阴沟 — *vt.* 在…上开沟(或槽);水流冲成(沟渠)

gulp [gʌlp] *vt.* 1. 吞,一口吞(下);狼吞虎咽地吃 2. 忍住,抑制 — *vi.* 1. 吞咽;狼吞虎咽 2. 喘不过气来;哽塞 — *n.* 1. 吞咽;一口吞下的量,一大口

gum[1] [gʌm] *n.* 1. 树胶;树胶制品 2. 胶姆糖,口香糖(亦作 chewing ~);橡皮擦(亦作~drop) 3. 胶树;桉树(亦作~tree) 4. 橡皮;〈美〉[~s]橡皮套鞋(亦作~boots) 5. 眼屎;(眼)睑边、信封口等处的)胶,粘合剂 — (gummed; gumming) *vt.* 1.(用树胶)粘合(down, together, up);在…上面涂树胶 2.〈美俚〉欺骗 — *vi.* 1. 分泌树胶;结胶 2. 发粘

gum[2] [gʌm] *n.* [常~s]齿龈;牙床 — (gummed; gumming) *vt.* 1. 扩大(锯子的)锯齿 2. 用牙床咀嚼 ‖ ~ boil *n.*【医】

gumbo ['gʌmbou] ([复] gumbos) *n.* 1.【植】秋葵;秋葵荚 2.(用秋葵荚调浓的)秋葵汤

gummy ['gʌmi] *adj.* 1. 胶粘的;粘性的 2. 含有树胶的;涂有树胶的;分泌树胶的;产胶的 3.(脚腕或腿)肿的 4.〈美俚〉抽劣的;讨厌的

gumption ['gʌmpʃən] *n.* 〈口〉1. 机智;精明,才智 2. 进取心,事业心;积极性;魄力;精力

gun [gʌn] *n.* 1. 炮;枪;〈美〉手枪 2.(信号枪、礼炮的)鸣放 3. 枪状物;喷射器 4.(引擎的)油门,风门 5. 猎人 6.〈美俚〉扒手;持枪歹徒 7.〈美俚〉毒品注射针 8.〈谑〉烟斗 — (gunned; gunning) *vt.* 1. 用枪射击;用枪打猎 2. 加大油门快速前进 — *vt.* 1. 向…开炮 2. 开大(引擎、汽车的)油门 ‖ ~ boat *n.* 炮艇/ ~ cotton *n.* 棉花火药/ ~ fire *n.* 炮火/ ~ lock *n.* 枪机/ ~ powder *n.* 1. 黑色火药,有烟火药 2.(中国珠茶〈亦作~powder tea〉/ ~ shot *n.* 1. 枪炮射击 2. 射程

gunner ['gʌnə] *n.* 1. 炮手;大炮瞄准手;猎枪手 2.(海军等的)枪炮军士长

gunnery ['gʌnəri] *n.* 1. [总称]重炮 2. 枪炮射击 3. 射击学;射击技术;枪炮操作

gunny ['gʌni] *n.* 1. 黄麻袋布 2. 黄麻袋(亦作~sack 或~bag)

gunwale ['gʌnl] *n.*【船】舷缘(材)

guppy ['gʌpi] *n.*【动】虹鳉(一种淡水热带鱼)

gurgle ['gə:gl] *vi.* 1.(流水)作汩汩声;(人)发咯咯声 2. 汩汩地流 — *n.* 1. 流水的汩汩声;(欢乐的)咯咯声

guru ['guru:] *n.* 1. 古鲁(印度教,锡克教的宗教教师或领袖) 2.(精神)领袖,头

师 3. 专家；权威 4.〈美俚〉精神病医生 5.〈美俚〉(服用迷幻药时的)指导者 6. 古鲁衫(一种长而宽松的罩衫)

gush [gʌʃ] *vi*. 1. 涌出，进出 2. 滔滔不绝地说或洋洋洒洒地写作；表现出过分的热情或感情 — *vt*. 涌出，喷出，进出 2. 滔滔不绝地说或洋洋洒洒地写 — *n*. 涌出，喷出，进出 2. 感情的迸发；过分的热情 3. 滔滔不绝的讲话；洋洋洒洒的文章 ‖ ~**er** *n*. 1. 喷油井；自喷井 2. 喷油井 2. 说话滔滔不绝的人；装腔作势的人 — **y** *adj*.

gusset [ˈgʌsit] *n*. 1. 三角形材料(用以填补、加固或放大衣服) 2.【建】结点板；角撑板 — *vt*. 缝三角形材料；装结点板(或角撑板)

gust [gʌst] *n*. 1. 阵风；一阵狂风 2.(雨、雹、烟、火、声音等的)突然一阵；(感情的)迸发，涌涌

gustatory [ˈgʌstətəri] *adj*. 味觉的；品尝的 ‖ **gustatorily** *adv*.

gusto [ˈgʌstəu] *n*. [复] gusto(e)s *n*. 1. 津津有味；兴致勃勃；热情；充沛的精力 2. 趣味；爱好(*for*)

gusty [ˈgʌsti] *adj*. 1. 阵风的；多阵风的；起大风的 2. 迸发的

gut [gʌt] *n*. 1.[~s]内脏 2. 下消化道，肠；胃；消化道〈口〉[常~s]肚子，腹部 3.[常~s]内容；内部；实质 4.〈俚〉[~s]勇气；毅力；力量；价值；厚颜无耻，无礼 5.(提琴、网球拍等的)羊肠线 6. 钓鱼线；肠钩线 7. 狭水道；海峡；隘路，狭道，狭巷 8.〈美俚〉香肠 9.〈美俚〉容易的课程(亦作~ course) — (gutted; gutting) *vt*. 1. 取出(鱼等)的内脏 2. 损毁(房屋等)的内部装置；抽去(书籍等)的主要内容 3.〈口〉贪婪地吃

guttapercha [ˌgʌtəˈpəːtʃə] *n*. 古塔波胶，

杜仲胶，胶木胶(一种类似橡胶的热塑性材料)

gutter [ˈgʌtə] *n*. 1. 天沟，檐槽 2.(道路的)排水边沟，街沟，明沟 3.【印】版面间的填空材料；(书籍等)左右两页间的空白，口口 4. 贫民区，贫民窟 — *vt*. 开沟于……；装天沟于……*vi*. 流，(蜡烛)淌蜡(烛光等)摇曳不定；趋于熄灭

guttural [ˈgʌtərəl] *adj*. 1.【解】喉的 2. 喉中形成(或发出)的 3.【语】颚(音)的

guy[1] [gai] *n*. 牵索，支索，拉索 — *vt*. 用牵索稳定(或加固)

guy[2] [gai] *n*. 1.〈英〉衣着古怪的人；怪模样的人〈口〉家伙，人，小伙子；朋友 3.(俚)逃走，溜走 — *vt*. 取笑，嘲弄；将……的模拟像示众 — *vi*.(俚)逃走，溜走

Guyana [gaiˈænə] *n*. 圭亚那[南美洲北部国家]

guzzle [ˈgʌzl] *vt*. 1. 狂饮；滥吃 2. 大量消耗(或花费) — *vi*. 狂饮；滥吃 ‖ ~**r** *n*.

gym [dʒim] *n*.〈口〉1. 体操馆；健身房 2. 体操；体育

gymnasium [dʒimˈneiziəm] *n*. [复] gymnasia [dʒimˈneizia] 或 gymnasiums] *n*. 1. 体操馆；健身房〈口〉2.(古希腊的)运动场 3. 德国等培养学生升入高等学校的)高级中学

gymnast [ˈdʒimnæst] *n*. 体操运动员

gymnastic [dʒimˈnæstik] *adj*. 体操的 ‖ 操训练的 — *n*. 1. 体操课 2.[~s]用作单或复]体操

gyn a) **ecology** [ˌgaiˈnɔlədʒi, ˌdʒaiˈnɔlədʒi] *n*.【医】妇科学

gyp [dʒip] (gypped; gypping) *vt*.，*vi*. & *n*.〈俚〉诈骗

gypsum [ˈdʒipsəm] *n*. 1.【矿】石膏 2.【建】

石膏灰泥板 — *vt.* 给(庄稼)施石膏；施石膏于(土地)；用石膏处理(土壤、水等)

gypsy ['dʒipsi] *n.* **1.** [常 G-]吉卜赛人 **2.** [G-]吉卜赛语 **3.** 像吉卜赛人的人；(谑)动人(或顽皮)的姑娘；黑脸妇女 **4.**【船】(锚机或绞车上的)绞车副卷筒 — *adj.* (像)吉卜赛人的 — *vi.* 吉卜赛人似地生活(或流浪) ‖ ~ **moth**【动】舞毒蛾

gyrate [ˌdʒaiə'reit] *vi.* 旋转、回旋；螺旋形地运转 — ['dʒaiəreit] *adj.* 旋转的；螺旋状的 ‖ **gy'ration** *n.*

gyrodynamics ['dʒairəudai'næmiks] [复] *n.* [用作单]【物】陀螺动力学

gyroscope ['dʒairəskəup] *n.* 陀螺仪、回转仪 ‖ **gyroscopic** [ˌdʒairə'skɔpik] *adj.*

H

H, h [eitʃ] ([复]H's, h's 或 Hs, hs [ˈeitʃiz]) 英语字母表第八个字母 1. [H]H 形 2. [H]〈化〉元素氢(hydrogen)的符号 3. 〈电〉亨利(henry)的符号 4. [H]〈物〉地磁水平分量(horizontal component of terrestrial magnetism)的符号 5. [H] = hard (表示铅笔芯软硬度的符号)

ha [bɑː] *int.* [表示惊异、愉快、怀疑、胜利等]哈! — *vi.* 发出"哈"声 — *n.* "哈"声

haberdasher [ˈhæbədæʃə] *n.* 1.〈美〉男子服饰用品商 2.〈英〉零星服饰用品商 ‖ ~y *n.* 1. [总称]男子服饰用品;零星服饰用品 2. 男子服饰用品店;零星服饰用品店

habit [ˈhæbit] *n.* 1. 习惯 2. 习性;气质;气性 3. 体型 4. 举止,行为 5. (表示宗教级别的)衣服;女骑装 6. 毒瘾 — *vt.* 1. 给 … 穿衣 2.〈古〉居住在

habitable [ˈhæbitəbl] *adj.* 可居住的;适于居住的

habitant *n.* 1. [ˈhæbitənt] 居住者 2. [ˌɑːbiˈtɔ̃] (法)(加拿大或美国路易斯安那州的)法裔农民(亦作 habitan)

habitation [ˌhæbiˈteiʃən] *n.* 1. 居住 2.〈书面语〉住处;住宅 3. 聚居地

habitual [həˈbitjuəl] *adj.* 1. 习惯(性)的;习以为常的 2. 惯常的,已成规则的 ‖ ~ly *adv.* / ~ness *n.*

habituate [həˈbitjueit] *vt.* 1. [常 ~ oneself]使习惯(*to*) 2.〈美〉常去(某地) — *vi.* 1. 致瘾 2. 成为习惯;(对刺激等)习以为常

habitué [həˈbitjuei] *n.* 1. 常客 2. 有毒瘾的人

hacienda [ˌhæsiˈendə]〈西〉*n.* 1. (西班牙及中、南美洲的)种植园,庄园;(郊外的)农场;牧场;工厂;矿山 2. [美国西南部用语]庄园住宅

hack¹ [hæk] *vt.* 1. 劈,砍;砍出 2. 耙(地),平(地),翻(地);碎土播(种) 3. (橄榄球赛中)踢(对方)的小腿(篮球赛中打(对方)的手犯规) 4.〈英方〉对付;宽容 — *vi.* 1. 劈,砍;乱劈,乱砍(*at*) 2. 断续地干咳 3. (橄榄球赛中)故意踢对方小腿(篮球赛中)打手(英方)结巴着说 5.〈俚〉游荡,闲逛(*around*) — *n.* 1. 劈(或砍)的工具,鹤嘴锄 2. 砍痕;伤疤;(橄榄球赛中的)踢人犯规;(篮球赛中的)打手犯规 3. 干咳 4.〈英方〉结巴 5. [美方]窘迫,困窘 6.(对海军军官的)营房拘禁 ‖' ~·saw. [机]弓锯;钢锯

hack² [hæk] *n.* 1. 出租的马;骑用马;役用马;驾马,老而无用的马 2. 出租马车;出租汽车;出租马车赶车人;出租汽车司机 3. 雇佣文人 4.〈美俚〉监狱看守 5.〈俚〉(运货列车后面的)管理员货车 6.〈美〉唯命是从的政党

工作人员 — **vt.** 1. 出租(马等) 2. 雇用写文章 3. 用旧、使变陈腐 — **vi.** 1. 用普通速度骑走(尤指骑者出租的马)(along) 2. (口)驾驶出租汽车(或出租马车)— **adj.** 1. 出租的；被雇作用的；雇佣文人做的 2. 陈腐的；平凡的

hackle ['hækl] **n.** 1.【纺】(梳棉机的)针排 2.(雄鸡、雉孔雀颈等的)细长预羽；[总称]预羽 3.(钓鱼用)假蝇；假蝇的蝇；制假蝇用的一簇羽毛 4. [~s](狗等受惊时会竖起的)颈背部毛；脾气；暴怒 — **vt.** 1. 梳理 2. 为(假蝇)装上预毛

hackney ['hækni] **n.** 1. 普通的乘骑马 2. 出租马车、出租汽车 3.(古)被雇用干苦活的人 — **adj.** 1. 出租的 2. 陈腐的；平凡的 — **vt.** 1. 出租 2.[常用被动语态]役使；用旧、使变陈腐 ‖ **~ed** **adj.** 陈腐的；平凡的

had [强 hæd; 弱 həd, əd] have 的过去式和过去分词

haddock ['hædək] ([复] haddock(s)) **n.**【动】(产于北大西洋的)黑线鳕, 黑斑鳕

hadn't ['hædnt] = had not

haemoglobin [ˌhiːməʊ'gləʊbin] **n.**【生化】血红蛋白

haemorrhage ['heməridʒ] **n.** (大)出血；大量流损 — **vt.** 大出血；大量流损 — **vi.** 使大量流损

haemorrhoid ['heməroid] **n.**[常~s]【医】痔(疮)

hafnium ['hæfniəm] **n.**【化】铪

haft [hɑːft] **n.**(鞭、斧、刀等的)柄, 把 — **vt.** 给...装柄

hag [hæg] **n.** 1. 女巫(尤指做坏事的)老丑妇；(古)母夜叉；妖怪 2.【动】盲鳗

haggard ['hægəd] **adj.** 1. 憔悴的, 形容枯

槁的 2. 样子凶暴的 3.(鹰)成年被捕的；不驯服的 — **n.** 不驯服的鹰, 悍鹰

haggle ['hægl] **vi.**(在价格、条件等方面)争论不休(about, over, for, with)— **vt.** 1. 乱砍, 乱劈 2.(古)(因争论)使烦恼, 使疲惫 — **n.** 争论；论价, 讨价还价

Hague [heig] **n.** [The ~]海牙[荷兰西部城市](中央政府所在地)

ha-ha [hɑː'hɑː] **int.** [表示嘲笑等]哈哈! — **n.** 哈哈的笑声

hail¹ [heil] **vt.** 1. 向...欢呼；为...欢呼 2. 招呼 — **vi.** 招呼；打信号招呼(尤指招呼过路船只)— **vt.** 欢呼；招呼 — **int.** [表示欢呼、祝贺等]好啊!

hail² [heil] **n.** 1. 雹, 冰雹；下雹；雹暴 2.(雹子般的)一阵 — **vi.** 1. 下雹 2. 雹子般地落下；像雹子般地落下 ‖ **~stone** **n.** 雹块 / **~storm** **n.** 雹暴

Haiphong ['hai'fʊŋ] **n.** 海防[越南北部港市]

hair [heə] **n.** 1. 头发；毛发；汗毛 2.(动、植物的)毛；茸毛 3. 毛状物；粗毛交织物 4. 些微, 一点儿 ‖ **~ed** **adj.** 有毛发的 [常用以构成复合词]长...头发的, 头发为...的: a short-haired dog 短毛狗 / **~less** **adj.** 秃头的；无毛的 ‖ **~breadth** **n.** 一发之差，极微小的距离 / **~brush** **n.** 发刷 / **~cloth** **n.** 马尾衬(用马毛或驼毛等与线布的织物, 室内装璜用) 2.(苦行者用的)粗硬发毛织物制品 / **~cut** **n.** 理发 / **~-do** **n.** (口)(女子)发式(女子)(新)做好的头发 / **~dresser** **n.** 1. 高级理发师(尤指为女子服务的) 2.(英)= barber / **~dressing** **n.** 理发, 做发；理发业 **adj.** (女子)理发用的 / **~pin** **n.** 1. 发夹, 发叉 2. 发夹状的东西；(道路的)U 字形急转弯 3.(美俚)女人 / **~-raiser** **n.** 使人毛发竖起的东西(或事情) / **~-raising** **adj.**

〈口〉使人毛发竖起的，恐怖的/'～spray
n.喷发定型剂/'～spring n.【机】细发
条,游丝

hairy ['hɛəri] adj. 1. 毛的；多毛的；有茸
毛的 2.毛状的 3.〈美俚〉粗鲁的；使人
不快的 4.〈俚〉(笑话等)陈腐得发了
霉的 ‖ hairiness n.

Haiti ['heiti] n. 1. 海地岛 [拉丁美洲] 2.
海地 [拉丁美洲国家] (在海地岛西部)

halcyon ['hælsiən] n. 1.【动】翡翠(鸟) 2.
神翠鸟(传说中巢居海上,冬至产卵时
能使海波平静) — adj. 1. 翡翠(鸟)
的;翡翠(鸟)产卵期的 2. 平静的 3. 愉
快的;美好的 4. 富饶的

hale¹ [heil] adj.〈尤指老人〉强壮的,矍铄
的

hale² [heil] vt. 强拉;硬拖

half [hɑːf]([复] halves [hɑːvz]) n. 1. 半,
一半 2.〈球赛的〉半场 3.〈英〉半学年,
学期 4.〈美俚〉(足球) 前卫 — adj. 1.
半的 2. 不完全的,部分的 — adv.
1. 一半地 2. 相当地 ‖'～back n.(足
球) 前卫/'～breed n. & adj. 混血
(的);(动植物)杂种(的)/'～,brother
n. 异父(或异母)兄弟/'～,hearted
adj. 半心半意的,不认真的/'～life
n. 半衰期;半排出期,半存留期(放射
性同位素从生物体内排出一半所需
的时间)/'～,sister n. 异父(或异母)
姐妹/'～way adv. 1. 半途;不彻底地
2.几乎,快要 adj. 半途中的/'～wit
n. 笨蛋/'～witted adj. 愚笨的;智力
上有缺陷的

halibut ['hælibət] n.【动】(产于大西洋、
太平洋的)庸鲽,大比目鱼

halide ['hælaid]【化】 n. 卤化物 — adj.
卤族的

halitosis [,hæli'təusis]([复] halitoses
[,hæli'təusiːz])n.【医】口臭

hall [hɔːl] n. 1. 会堂,礼堂;大厅 2. 歌舞
杂耍剧场 3. 门厅;(大厦的)过道;走
廊 4.(大学的)教学(或科研)大楼;学
生宿舍 5.〈英〉(大学中的)公共食堂;
公共食堂里的一餐 6.(协会、工会等
的)办公楼;会所 7.〈英〉府第 8.(中世
纪王公贵族的)城堡 ‖～way n.〈美〉
门厅;过道

hallelujah, halleluiah [,hæli'luːjə] n. &
int. 哈利路亚(表示赞美、欢乐或感谢
等的欢呼)

hallow ['hæləu] n. 圣徒 — vt.〔常用被动
语态〕 1. 使神圣;把…视为神圣 2. 崇
敬

Halloween ['hæləui:n] n.〈西方风俗〉诸
圣日前夕(指 10 月 31 日,是夜儿童可
以纵情玩闹)

hallucination [hə,luːsi'neiʃən] n. 幻觉,幻
觉症

halo ['heiləu]([复] halo(e)s)n. 1.(环绕
日月等的)晕 2.(绘于神像头上的)光
轮 3.(赋予理想化人物或事物的)光
辉,荣光 4.(乳头等四周的)晕 — vt.
使成晕(或晕状物);以光环围绕 — vi.
形成晕(或晕状物)

halogen ['hælədʒən] n.【化】卤(素)

halt¹ [hɔːlt] n. 1.(行进间的)暂停前进;
止步 2. 停住,停车 3.〈英〉(火车的)小
站,旗站 — vi. 1.(军队等口令)立定,
站住 2. 停止前进;停止 — vt. 使停止
前进;使停止;使终止

halt² [hɔːlt] vi. 1. 蹒跚;跛行 2. 踌躇,犹
豫 3.(论点,诗的格律等)有缺点;不合
逻辑 — n. & adj.〈古〉跛(的)

halter ['hɔːltə] n.1.(马等的)笼头;缰绳
2.绞索;绞刑 3.(女用)三角背心 —
vt. 1. 给…套上笼头(up) 2. 绞死(某
人) 3. 束缚,限制

halve [hɑːv] vt. 1. 对半分 2. 对半分享

(或分担) 3. 将...减半 4. 半嵌接, 槽舌接, 合缺接(两块木料)

halves [hɑːvz] *half* 的复数

halyard [ˈhæljəd] *n.* 〈船〉吊索, 升降索

ham [hæm] *n.* 1. 火腿 2. (兽类的)后腿; [常 ~s] 股腘部 3. 〈俚〉拙劣的表演者, 表演过火的演员 4. 业余无线电爱好者 5. 〈俚〉做作的人 — *adj.* 1. 过火的、做作的 — 〈俚〉整顿的 2. 业余无线电的 — (hammed; hamming) *vt. & vi.* (把剧中角色等)演得过火

Hamburg [ˈhæmbəːg] *n.* 1. 汉堡〈德国北部港市〉2. 汉堡鸡(欧洲种的红冠青脚鸡) 3. = ~ steak ‖ ~ steak = hamburger steak

hamburger [ˈhæmbəːgə] *n.* 1. = ~ steak 牛肉饼 2. 汉堡包 3. 〈俚〉被打得满身伤痕的拳击手 ‖ ~ steak 汉堡煎牛肉饼, 汉堡牛排

hamlet [ˈhæmlit] *n.* (尤指没有教堂的)小村庄

hammer [ˈhæmə] *n.* 1. 锤子, 榔头 2. (电铃的)小锤子; 锣锤; (钢琴等的)音锤 (会议主席或拍卖人用的)小木槌 4. 〈机〉锤; 冲击式凿岩机 5. 〈军〉(用以击动撞针或击发火帽的)击铁 6. 〈体〉链球 7. 〈解〉(中耳的)锤骨 — *vt.* 1. 锤击; 锤成; (反复)锤打 2. 〈英〉(交易所)击槌宣布(某人)无力偿债 3. 〈口〉(在战争或比赛中)使惨败 — *vi.* 接连敲击

hammock [ˈhæmək] *n.* (帆布或网状的)吊床

hammy [ˈhæmi] *adj.* 1. 有火腿香味的 2. 〈俚〉(演员)表演过火的

hamper[1] [ˈhæmpə] *vt.* 妨碍, 阻碍; 牵制 — *n.* 1. 阻碍物 2. 〈海〉障碍船具(指平时不可少但在紧急时会妨碍操作的船具)

hamper[2] [ˈhæmpə] *n.* 有盖大篮, 盖篮

hamster [ˈhæmstə] *n.* 〈动〉仓鼠

hamstring [ˈhæmstriŋ] *n.* [解]腘绳肌腱; 腘绳肌; [动] (兽类的)大腿腱, 后腿腱 — (hamstringed 或 hamstrung [ˈhæmstrʌŋ]) *vt.* 割断...的腘腱; 使瘫痪

hand [hænd] *n.* 1. 手 2. (猴子的)脚; (四足兽的)前脚 3. (钟表等的)指针 4. 人手, 雇员(指工人、船员等) 5. 作某种工作的人; 干某事的人 6. 手艺; 才能 7. 字迹, 手迹 8. 〈公文用语〉签字 9. 支配, 掌管, 照管 10. 插手; 经手; 参与 11. 帮助(尤指动手帮助) 12. 方面, 面; at (the 或 on) sb's left 在左边 13. [与序词连用, 表示来源] 第...手; material at second ~ 第二手材料 14. 答允; 许诺 15. 惯手的东西(香烟的一串(烟草、麻等的)束 16. (纸牌游戏中)手中的牌; 打牌的人; 牌戏的一盘 17. 一手之宽(约4英寸, 用来量马的高度等) 18. 〈古〉鼓掌 — *vt.* 1. 交出; 传递, 给 2. 搀扶 3. 〈海〉收卷(风帆) ‖ ~ bag *n.* 1. (女用)手提包 2. 旅行包 ‖ ~ ball *n.* 墙手球; 墙手球运动 ‖ ~ bill *n.* 传单 ‖ ~ book *n.* 手册 ‖ ~ car *n.* (铁路上所用手稟式(或以小马达开动的)四轮小车 ‖ ~ cart *n.* 手推车 ‖ ~ clasp *n.* 握手 ‖ ~ craft *n.* = handicraft *vt.* 用手工制作 ‖ ~ cuff *n.* 手铐 ‖ ~ gun *n.* 手枪 ‖ ~ made *adj.* 手工制的 *n.* 手工制品(尤指手织品、手制服装) ‖ ~ maid, ~ maiden *n.* 侍女, 女仆; (喻)起陪衬(或侍奉)作用的东西 ‖ ~ organ 手摇风琴 ‖ ~ out *n.* 1. 施舍物 2. 免费散发的印刷品 3. (送给报界刊登的)声明, 新闻, 宣传材料 ‖ ~ rail *n.* 扶手, 栏杆 ‖ ~ shake *n.* 握手 ‖ ~ spring *n.* 〈体〉

手翻;前手翻腾越 /'~-to-'~ adj. 1. 逼近的 2. 传递到对手的 /'~-to-'mouth adj. 勉强糊口的 /'~-work n. 手工 / '~'woven adj. 手织的

handed ['hændid] adj. 1. 有手的 2.[用以构成复合词]有…手的 3. 用手的;left-~ 惯用左手的 3.[用以构成复合词]…个人玩的:a three-~ game 三人玩的游戏

handful ['hændful] n. 1. 一把:a ~ of rice 一把米 2. 少数,一小撮 3.[口]难控制的人(或动物);麻烦事

handicap ['hændikæp] n. 1. 障碍,不利条件 2.(给强者不利条件,给弱者有利条件以使弱者取胜机会均等的)让步赛 3. 给强者的不利条件;给弱者的有利条件 vt. 1. 妨碍,使不利 2. 给(竞赛者)不利条件(或有利条件)

handicraft ['hændikrɑːft] n. 1. 手艺 2. 手工业;手工艺 3.[总称]手工艺品 ‖ ~sman n. 手工业者;手工艺人

handily ['hændili] adv. 便利地;灵巧地

handiness ['hændinis] n. 近便;便利;灵巧

handiwork ['hændiwɜːk] n. 1. 手工;[总称]手制品 2.(某人)亲手做的事情

handkerchief ['hæŋkətʃif](复) handkerchiefs 或 handkerchieves ['hæŋkətʃiːvz]) n. 1. 手帕 2. 围巾;头巾

handle ['hændl] n. 1. 柄,把手 2.[喻]把柄;可乘之机 3.[口]称号,头衔 4.(织物等摸上去的)手感 5.(对赛马等所投下的)赌金总额 vt. 1. 触,摸;拿;弄 2. 操纵,驾驭(马,船等) 3. 处理;对待 4. 经营;买卖 5.[美]训练(拳击选手) vi. 1.(用手)搬运 2. 易于操纵:This car ~s well. 这车很好驾驶。‖ ~r n. 1. 处理者;操纵者 2.[美]拳击

教练员 2. 操作装置;处理机 ‖ ~ bar n.(自行车等的)把手

handsome ['hænsəm] adj. 1. 相当大的,可观的 2. 慷慨的,大方的;气量大的 3.(男子)漂亮的,清秀的;(女子)端庄的,温雅的 4. 堂皇的;美观的 5. 熟练的,灵敏的;(方)操纵起来灵便的,适便的 6.(方)合适的 ‖ ~ly adv. 1. 漂亮地;美观地;慷慨地,优厚地 2.[海] 缓慢小心地;秩序井然地

handwriting ['hændˌraitiŋ] n. 1. 笔迹;笔法 2.(古)手写物;手抄文件;手稿 3. 书写;手写

handy ['hændi] adj. 1. 手边的,近便的 2. 便于使用的;方便的 3.(船等)驾驶起来灵便的 4. 手灵巧的 ‖ ~man n. 1. 干零碎杂活的人 2. 手巧的人

hang [hæŋ](hung[hʌŋ]或 hanged) vt. 1. 悬挂 2.(用悬挂的东西)装饰 3. 贴(墙纸等) 4. 垂下 5. 安装(活动的东西) 6.[过式和过去分词用 hanged]绞死;吊死 7.[用于诅咒语中] Hang it! 该死!(指事)/ Hang you! 该死!(指人) 8.(美)使(陪审团)不能作出一致决定 9. 悬挂起(油画等) — vi. 1. 悬挂,吊着 2. 垂下,挂下 3. 被绞死;被吊死 4. 悬而不决 5. 逗留;紧紧缠住 6.(陪审团)不能作出一致决定 ‖(用单]1. 悬挂方式 2.[口]做法;用法;诀窍 3.[口]大意,要点 4.(动作的)暂停 ‖ '~-dog n. 卑鄙的人 adj. 卑鄙的;惭愧的,自觉有罪的 / ~ glider 悬挂式滑翔机(运动员) / '~ man n. 执行绞刑者;刽子手 / '~-nail n.(指甲旁的)逆剥皮,逆刺 / '~-out n.[俚]常去的地方;聚集处 / '~-over n. 1. 遗留物(尤指习惯等) 2.[俚]宿醉 / '~-up n.(尤指精神方面的)烦恼,苦衷

hangar ['hæŋə] n. 飞机棚,飞机库 — vt.

把(飞机)放入机库

hanger ['hæŋə] *n.* **1.** 挂东西的人;糊墙的人 **2.** 挂物的东西;挂钩;衣架;悬挂工具 **3.** 挂着的东西(尤指挂在皮带上的短剑) **4.** 执行绞刑者 **5.** 钩状笔划 **6.**(英)陡坡林地

hank [hæŋk] *n.* **1.**(一)绞,(一)亨克(长度单位;在棉线中为 840 码,在毛线中为 560 码) **2.**[海]帆眼圈 **3.**(方)优势;控制 — *vt.* 用帆眼圈将(帆)系牢

hanker ['hæŋkə] *vi.* 渴望,追求

Hanoi [hæ'nɔi] 河内〔越南首都〕

hansom ['hænsəm] *n.*(御座高居车后的)双轮双座马车

Hanukkah ['hɑːnukə] *n.*(犹太教的)献殿节,光明节

haphazard [,hæp'hæzəd] *n.* 偶然性;随意性 — *adj.* 没有计划的;偶然的;随意的 — *adv.* 偶然地;随意地 ‖ ~·ly *adv.* /~·ness *n.*

hapless ['hæplis] *adj.* 不幸的;运气不好的

happen ['hæpən] *vi.* **1.**(偶然)发生了[后接不定式]碰巧 **2.** 巧遇;偶然发现(on, upon) ‖ ~·ing *n.* **1.**(发生的)事情;事件 **2.** 机遇剧,事件剧(一种即兴的或演出节目,常将观众卷入)自发(或生动)的表现场面

happily ['hæpili] *adv.* **1.** 幸福地;幸运地 **2.** 愉快地 **3.** 适当地

happiness ['hæpinis] *n.* **1.** 幸福;(古)幸运 **2.** 愉快 **3.** 恰当,合适

happy ['hæpi] *adj.* **1.** 幸福的;幸运的 **2.** 愉快的,快乐的 **3.** 感到幸福的,乐意的 **4.** 恰当的;巧妙的 **5.**[常用以构成复合词]陶醉于 ... 的,老是喜欢 ... 的: trigger-~ 动不动爱扳枪机的 ‖ ~·go-lucky *adj.* 逍遥自在的,无忧无虑的,乐天的

harangue [hə'ræŋ] *n.* **1.** 演讲;慷慨激昂的演说 **2.** 长篇大论的讲话(或文章) **3.** 冗长的训话;言词激烈的讲话 — *vi.* 高谈阔论;慷慨陈词 — *vt.* 向 ... 夸夸其谈地演讲;大声训斥

Harare [hə'rɑːri] *n.* 哈拉雷〔津巴布韦首都〕

harass ['hærəs] *vt.* **1.** 使烦恼;折磨 **2.** 扰乱;骚扰 ‖ ~·ment *n.* **1.** 折磨;骚扰 **2.** 折磨人的东西

harbinger ['hɑːbindʒə] *n.* **1.**(古)(军队或王室一行的)先行官 **2.** 通报器 **3.** 预言者;先驱;预兆 — *vt.* 充作 ... 的前驱;预告,预示

harbou**r** ['hɑːbə] *n.* **1.**(海)港,港口;港湾 **2.** 避难所;退避所 — *vt.* **1.** 隐匿,窝藏;包庇(罪犯等) **2.** 聚藏;怀念 **3.** 怀有,怀有 — *vi.* **1.** 入港停泊 **2.** 躲藏;(动物等)聚集

hard [hɑːd] *adj.* **1.** 硬的;坚固的 **2.**(问题、工作等)困难的 **3.**(人)难对付的;使劲费力的 **4.** 艰难的;难以忍受的 **5.** 强烈的,猛烈的,剧烈的 **6.** 冷酷无情的;严格的,不妥协的 **7.** 确凿的;不容置疑的 **8.**(在身体方面)洁实的 **9.**(钱币)金属制的,硬的 **10.**(币制)可兑换成金子的 **11.**(物价等)高而坚不下降的 **12.**(颜色等)刺目的 **13.**(声音等)刺耳的 **14.** 含无机盐的 **15.**(底片等)反差强的 **16.**(字母 c 发)[c]音的,(字母 g 发)[g]音的 **17.**(酒)烈性的,酒精成分高的 — *adv.* **1.** 硬 **2.** 努力地;艰苦地 **3.** 困难地;困苦地 **4.** 猛烈地;重重地 **5.** 牢固地;紧紧地 **6.** 接近地;立即地 — *n.* **1.**(主英)(拉着上岸的)硬料坡道 **2.**(英里)(囚犯的)苦工,苦役 **3.**(美俚)阴茎勃起 ‖ ~·ness *n.* ‖ '~·core *adj.* 最坚定的;中坚的,骨干的;顽固不化的 **2.**(性描写)赤裸裸

的/'~ hat n. (建筑工人、矿工等戴的)防护帽、安全帽；(美国)建筑工人；(美)强硬保守派/'~headed adj. 1. 冷静的；精明而讲求实际的 2. 固执的 /'~hearted adj. 心肠硬的、无同情心的、冷酷的 /'~line 强硬路线(或政策、立场) /'~palate 硬腭 /'~science 硬科学 /'~tack n. [总称](供船上食用)硬饼干，压缩饼干 /'~ware n. [总称] 1. 金属器具，五金制品 2. 重武器 3. (计算机的)硬件；(喻)硬件；机件：装备、设备 /'~wood n. 1. 硬(木)材：阔叶树 2. 阔叶树材 adj. 阔叶材的；硬材制的

harden ['hɑːdn] vt. 1. 使硬 2. 使锻炼得结实(或坚强)，使坚强 3. [常用被动语态]使变得冷酷；使麻木 4. 将(导弹发射场或导弹)设置在地下以免受到敌方空袭，使有防核攻击能力 — vi. 1. 变硬；变坚固 2. 变得冷酷(或麻木) 3. (价格等)变得坚挺：上涨

hardihood ['hɑːdihud] n. 1. 大胆；刚毅 2. 鲁莽；傲慢 3. 强壮

hardiness ['hɑːdinis] n. 1. 强壮，耐劳(性)／耐寒(性) 2. 勇气，胆子

hardly ['hɑːdli] adv. 1. 几乎不，简直不(常用作"不"的委婉语) 2. 不十分；仅，才：We ~ know him. 我们不大认识他。3. 严厉地：粗暴地 4. 艰辛地，费力地

hardship ['hɑːdʃip] n. 1. 受苦，吃苦 2. 苦难，困苦

hardy ['hɑːdi] adj. 1. 勇敢的；果断的 2. 鲁莽的；厚脸皮的 3. 强壮的、能吃苦的；强壮的 4. [植物]耐寒的

hare [heə] ([复] hare(s)) n. 1. 野兔 2. (英俚)坐车不买票的人 — vi. 飞跑 ‖ '~brained adj. 轻率的；浮躁的／'~lip n. [医]兔唇，唇裂

harem ['hɑːrim] n. 1. (伊斯兰教)女眷居住的内室，闺房 2. [总称]妻妾；女眷；女仆

hark [hɑːk] vi. [主要用于祈使句]听(to)

harken ['hɑːkən] vi. = hearken

Harlem ['hɑːləm] n. 哈莱姆(美国纽约市的一个黑人居住区)

harlot ['hɑːlət] n. 妓女，娼妓

harm [hɑːm] n. & vt. 损害，伤害；危害

harmful ['hɑːmful] adj. 有害的(to) ‖ ~ly adv. ‖ ~ness n.

harmless ['hɑːmlis] adj. 1. 无害的；无恶意的 2. 未受损害的 ‖ ~ly adv. ‖ ~ness n.

harmonic [hɑːˈmɔnik] adj. 1. 和睦的，融洽的 2. [数]调和的 3. [音]和声的；泛音的 4. [物]谐波的 — n. [音]泛音 2. [物]谐波；谐音 ‖ ~ally adv.

harmonica [hɑːˈmɔnikə] n. 口琴；玻璃钟琴；古玻璃琴

harmonious [hɑːˈməunjəs] adj. 1. 协调的，相称的，匀称的 2. 和睦的，融洽的 3. 悦耳的 ‖ ~ly adv. ‖ ~ness n.

harmonize ['hɑːmənaiz] vi. 1. 协调，相称(with) 2. 以和声唱(或演奏) — vt. 1. 使协调；使调和；使一致 2. 使(曲调)和谐 ‖ ~r n. 协调者；调和者

harmony ['hɑːməni] n. 1. 协调；调和；和谐 2. 融洽；一致 3. (内心的)平静 4. [音]和声，和声学

harness ['hɑːnis] n. 1. (古)铠甲 2. 马具，挽具 3. [纺]综(线) 4. (提花机上的)综丝 5. 降落伞吊带 6. (美俚)警察制服；(摩托车驾驶员的)全套衣帽装备 — vt. 1. 给 … 上挽具；套(马等) 2. 治理

harp [hɑːp] n. 1. 竖琴 2. 竖琴状的东西 3. [the H-][天]天琴座 4. (美俚)爱尔

兰人 — *vi.* 1. 弹竖琴 2. 唠唠叨叨地
反复讲(*on, upon*) ∥ ~**er**, ~**ist** *n.* 弹
竖琴的人;竖琴师

harpoon ['hɑ:'puːn] *n.* (捕鲸等的)鱼叉,
标枪 — *vt.* 用鱼叉叉

harpsichord ['hɑ:psikɔːd] *n.* 拨弦古钢琴,
羽管键琴

harrier ['hæriə] *n.* [动]猎兔犬

harrow ['hærəu] *n.* 耙 — *vt.* 1. 把(地)
耙 2. 弄伤;抓伤;使痛苦,折磨 — *vi.*
(地)被耙松

harry ['hæri] *vt.* 1. 掠夺,蹂躏 2. 折磨,
骚扰 3. 驱走

harsh [hɑːʃ] *adj.* 1. 粗糙的 2. (声音)刺
耳的;(味道)涩口的;(光)刺目的 3.
严厉的;苛刻的 ∥ ~**ly** *adv.* / ~**ness** *n.*

hart [hɑːt] *n.* [复]hart(s) *n.* (主英)公鹿

harum-scarum ['hɛərəm'skɛərəm] *adj. &*
adv. 轻率的(地),冒失的(地) — *n.* 冒
失鬼;轻举妄动

Harvard ['hɑːvəd] *n.* 1. (美国)哈佛大学
(亦作~ University) 2. 哈佛大学学生
(或毕业生)

harvest ['hɑːvist] *n.* 1. 收获,收割 2. 收
成,产量 3. 收获季节,收获期 4. 结果;
后果;成果 — *vt.* 1. 收割(农作物);收
获;获得(成果等) 2. 在 ... 上收割作物
的人;收获者 2. 收割机 ∥ ~**er** *n.* 1. 收割庄稼
的人;收获者 2. 收割机

has [强 hæz;弱 həz, əz, z] have 的第三人称单
数现在式

hash [hæʃ] *vt.* 1. 把(肉、蔬菜等)切细
(*up*) 2. (口)把 ... 搞糟;把 ... 弄乱
3. 反复推敲,仔细考虑(*over*) — *n.* 1.
剁碎的食物;(回锅)内末土豆泥 2. 杂
乱无章的一大堆;搞得乱七八糟的事
3. 改头换面;重新表述 4. (美俚)传闻

hasheesh, hashish ['hæʃiːʃ] *n.* (由印度大
麻的茎和叶制成的)大麻麻醉剂;印度

大麻制剂;大麻(烟)

hasn't ['hæznt] = has not

hasp [hɑːsp] *n.* (门或窗、盖等的)搭扣 —
vt. 用搭扣扣上

hassle ['hæsl] *n.* 1. 激战 2. 激烈的争
论;持久的辩论 3. 混乱 — *vi.* 争论;
辩论 — *vt.* 1. 与 ... 争辩 2. (不断)打
扰

hassock ['hæsək] *n.* 1. 草丛 2. 跪垫,膝
垫 3. (美俚)(棒球的)垒

haste [heist] *n.* 1. 急速,紧迫;仓促 2. 草
率 — *vi.* 赶紧;匆忙 — *vt.* (古)催促

hasten ['heisn] *vt.* 1. 催促 2. 加紧,加速
— *vi.* 赶紧,赶快

hasty ['heisti] *adj.* 1. 急速的 2. 仓促的;
草率的;急速赶制成的 3. 性急的;暴
躁的;动辄要发火的 ∥ **hastily** *adv.* /
hastiness *n.*

hat [hæt] *n.* 1. 帽子(注意:hat 一般指有
沿的帽子,无沿的帽子是 cap) 2. 区别
职务的帽子;职务,职位;[天主教]红
衣主教帽;红衣主教职位 — (hatted;
hatting) *vt.* 给 ... 戴上帽子

hatch[1] [hætʃ] *vt.* 1. 孵出;孵 2. 内心下
着;图谋,策划 — *vi.* (蛋)孵化;(小鸡
等)出壳 — *n.* 1. 孵化 2. (小鸡等的)
一窝,一窝 3. 结果

hatch[2] [hætʃ] *n.* 1. (飞机等的)短门,小
门;下半扇门 2. 出口;天窗;格子口;开口
2. 升降口;舱口;舱盖 3. 闸门
4. 鱼栏 ∥ ~**-back** *n.* (小客车的)仓门
式后背;仓门式后背车身小客车 / ~**-**
way *n.* 舱口;舱口盖

hatchery ['hætʃəri] *n.* 1. (尤指鱼和家禽
的)孵卵处,孵化场 2. (大型)苗猪场

hatchet ['hætʃit] *n.* 短柄小斧 ∥ ~ **man**
1. 职业刺客 2. 受雇写诽谤文章的人;
受雇诽谤文人;(专为上司执行不愉快

事情的)心腹执事,亲信

hate [heit] *vt.* **1.** 恨,憎恨 **2.** 嫌恶 **3.** 〈俗〉不愿;不喜欢 — *vi.* 仇恨 — *n.* **1.** 怨恨;憎恶;憎厌 **2.** 憎恨的东西

hateful ['heitful] *adj.* **1.** 可恨的;可恶的;讨厌的;无耻的 **2.** 有敌意的 ‖ ~**ly** *adv.* / ~**ness** *n.*

hatred ['heitrid] *n.* 憎恨;憎恶;敌意

hatter ['hætə] *n.* 制帽匠;帽商

haughty ['hɔːti] *adj.* **1.** 傲慢的,目中无人的;轻蔑的 **2.** 〈古〉崇高的,高贵的 ‖ **haughtily** *adv.* / **haughtiness** *n.*

haul [hɔːl] *vt.* **1.** 拖曳;用力拖(或拉);把(鱼等)拖网里 **2.** 运;运送 **3.** [海]〈尤指为了迎风行驶〉使(船)改变航向 **4.** 硬拖,硬拉;拘捕 — *vi.* **1.** 拖,拉 **2.** (风)改变方向 **3.** [海]改变航向,改变方向 **4.** [海]改变船的航向;(船)改变航向 — *n.* **1.** 拖,拉 **2.** 捕获物;一网捕得的鱼 **3.** 运送的距离 **4.** 运输量

haunch [hɔːntʃ] *n.* **1.** (人的)臀部 **2.** (动物的)腰腿;腰腿肉 **3.** [建]拱肢

haunt [hɔːnt] *vt.* **1.** 常去,常到(某地);缠住(某人) **2.** (鬼魂等)常出没于…;老是附在…身上 **3.** (思想、回忆等)萦绕;(疾病等)缠住 — *vi.* **1.** 经常出没;逗留 **2.** (鬼魂等)作祟 — *n.* **1.** 常去的地方 **2.** (动物的)出没场所 **3.** (罪犯等的)巢穴 **4.** 〈主方〉鬼 ‖ ~**ed** *adj.* 常出现鬼的,闹鬼的

Havana [hə'vænə] *n.* **1.** 哈瓦那[古巴首都] **2.** 哈瓦那烟草;哈瓦那雪茄

have [强 hæv;弱 hæv, əv, v](过去式和过去分词 had[强 hæd;弱 həd, əd],第三人称单数现在式 has[强 hæz;弱 həz, əz])*vt.* **1.** 有,怀有,持有 **2.** 拿;得到,取得 **3.** 吃;喝 **5.** 进行,从事(某事) **6.** 享有;经历;遭受 **7.** [用于否定句中]容忍;允许 **8.** 使,让;招致 **9.** 要;叫;使

10. [接不定式]必须,不得不 **11.** 表明;坚持住 **12.** 明白,懂得 **13.** 〈口〉击败,胜过 **14.** 〈英俚〉哄骗,欺骗 **15.** 生(子)— *v. aux.* **1.** [加过去分词,构成完成时态]已经;曾经 **2.** [用于虚拟语气]:If I had known. ...(或 Had I known. ...)如果我那时知道的话......— *n.* **1.** 〈口〉[常 ~s]有钱人;富国 **2.** 〈英俚〉诈骗,欺诈

haven ['heivn] *n.* **1.** 港;避风港;抛锚处 **2.** 避难所,(有掩护的)安全地方 — *vt.* **1.** 开(船)入港 **2.** 为...提供避难所,掩护

haven't ['hævnt] = have not

haversack ['hævəsæk] *n.* (行军或旅行时用的)帆布背包;干粮袋

havoc ['hævək] *n.* **1.** 大破坏,浩劫 **2.** 混乱,杂乱 — *vt.* (havocked; havocking) *vt.* 严重破坏

haw[1] [hɔː] *n.* **1.** [植]山楂 **2.** 山楂果

haw[2] [hɔː] (主要) *int.* **1.** (吆喝驮畜左转)嗯嗯一 **2.** "嗯"的吆喝声 — *vi.* & *vt.* (喝令)(驮畜)向左转

Hawaii [hɑː'waiiː] *n.* 夏威夷[美国州名]

hawk[1] [hɔːk] *n.* **1.** 鹰;隼 **2.** (似鹰般)贪婪的家伙;骗子 **3.** 鹰派分子,主战派成员 — *vt.* **1.** 携鹰打猎 **2.** (像鹰般)猛扑(at);(像鹰般)翱翔;(燕等)追捕昆虫 — *vt.* (像鹰般)捕捉

hawk[2] [hɔːk] *vt.* **1.** 叫卖;兜售 **2.** 散播(谣言等)

hawk[3] [hɔːk] *vi.* 清嗓;咳嗽 — *vi.* 咳出

hawker[1] ['hɔːkə] *n.* **1.** 携鹰打猎的人 **2.** 驯鹰者

hawker[2] ['hɔːkə] *n.* 叫卖的小贩

Hawkeye ['hɔːkai] *n.* "鹰眼"人[美国衣阿华州人的别称]:the ~ State 鹰眼州(衣阿华州的别称)

hawser ['hɔːzə] *n.*【海】缆索,大索;锚链,锚索

hawthorn ['hɔːθɔːn] *n.*【植】山楂

hay [hei] *n.* **1.** (作牲口饲料用的)干草 **2.** 成果;酬答 **3.** 小额款项 **4.** 〈美俚〉床 — *vi.* 割草晒干 — *vt.* **1.** 用干草喂 **2.** 将(草)晒成干草 **3.** 在…上植草供制干草用 ∥`~-cock` *n.* 圆锥形干草堆 / `~ fever`【医】枯草热,花粉病 / `'~-fork` *n.* 干草叉 / `'~ loft` *n.* (马厩等处)储藏草料的顶阁 / `'~-mow` *n.* **1.** (仓中的)干草堆 **2.** 干草棚 / `'~rick` *n.* = `~stack` *n.* 大干草堆 / `'~-wire` *n.* 捆绑干草用的铁丝 *adj.* **1.** 乱七八糟的;残旧的 **2.** 仓忙做成的;拼凑而成的;蹩脚的

Hayti ['heiti] *n.* = Haiti

hazard ['hæzəd] *n.* **1.** 掷骰子游戏 **2.** 机会;偶然的事 **3.** 危险;公害(指工业废气、废水等的危害) **4.** (网球场中)得分区 **5.** (高尔夫球)障碍物 **6.** (英方)马车停车场 — *vt.* **1.** 使遭危险 **2.** 冒险行事

hazardous ['hæzədəs] *adj.* **1.** 碰运气的 **2.** 危险的,冒险的 ∥`~ly` *adv.* / `~ness` *n.*

haze[1] [heiz] *n.* **1.** 霾;烟雾 **2.** 迷糊,糊涂 — *vt. & vi.* (使)变朦胧;(使)变糊涂

haze[2] [heiz] *vt.* **1.** 使劳累,用劳役折磨 **2.**〈美〉欺侮;戏弄;(为折服对方)让(新学生等)行恶作剧 **3.**〈美方〉骑马放牧(或驱赶)

hazel ['heizl] *n.* **1.** 榛树;榛木;榛子 **2.** (尤指眼睛的)淡褐色 — *adj.* **1.** 榛树的;榛木的;榛子的 **2.** 淡褐色的

hazelnut ['heizlnʌt] *n.* 榛子

hazy ['heizi] *adj.* **1.** 多烟雾的;雾蒙蒙的 **2.** 模糊的,不明确的;有些迷惑的 **3.** 微醉的 ∥`hazily` *adv.* / `haziness` *n.*

H-bomb ['eit∫bɔm] *n.* 氢弹(= hydrogen bomb) — *vt.* 用氢弹轰炸

He【化】元素氦(helium)符号

he [hiː;弱 iː, hi, i] *pron.* (主格) **1.** 他 **2.** 某人,任何人 — [hiː] ([复] hes [hiːz]) *n.* 男孩;男人;雄性动物 ∥`~-man` *n.*〈美〉男子汉;雄赳赳的汉子

head [hed] *n.* **1.** 头;头像 **2.** 头状物体;(植物茎梢顶端的)头状叶丛,头状花序;谷穗 **3.** 首脑,首长 **4.** 头脑,才智 **5.** 脑袋,生命 **6.** 人;个人 **7.** 猪物群;[单复同](牛羊等的)头数 **8.** (队伍、名单等)最前面的部分;(书页等的)眉头;书眉,天头;(楼梯等的)顶端;(某位的)首部;船头;弹头 **9.** (河流的)源头 **10.** (疮、疖等的)脓头 **11.** 头痛(= ~-ache) **12.** [常~s] (印有头像的硬币的)正面 **13.** 标题;项目;方面 **14.** 泡沫 **15.** 酒沫;(英)(牛奶上的)奶酪层 **16.** 顶点;危机 **17.** (水站等的)蓄水高度,水位差,扬水压力 **18.** 海角,岬 **19.** 【矿】水平巷道,(煤层中的)开拓巷道 **20.**〈俚〉(尤指舰船上的)厕所 **21.**【机】盖,帽 — *vt.* **1.** 作为…的首脑;率领;处在…前头 **2.** 用头顶(足球);碰…的头;代(或修整)…的顶枝;收割(庄稼) **4.** 对着 **5.** 绕水源而过(小溪、湖泊等) **6.** (车等)对着某处行驶 **7.** 拦截(羊群等);〈喻〉阻止;使转移方向(off) **8.** 为(葡等)装头;构成…的顶部 **9.** 在…上加标题 **10.** (在赛跑等中)先于…,超过…中 — *vi.* **1.** 成头状物(指果结实、麦成葱等) **2.** (向特定方向)出发,动身;(船)驶往 **3.** (疮、疖等)出脓头 **4.** (河流等)发源 — *adj.* **1.** 头上的;头部的 **2.** 主要的,首要的 ∥`~ed` *adj.* **1.** 有头的 **2.** 有标题的 **3.** (植物等)长成头状的 / `'~-ache` *n.* **1.** 头痛 **2.** 令人头痛的事 **3.**〈美俚〉令人头痛的人;妻 / `'~-`

band n. 1. 头带,束发带 2.【印】书眉线,顶线;章首饰 3. 书背顶带 ‖ /~dress n. 头饰 / ~ gear n. 1. 头饰;帽子;盔 2. 马首挽具 / ~ land ['hedlənd] n. 1. 旺头(或篱边)未耕地 2. 岬 / ~long adv. n. 1. 头向前地 2. 轻率地 adj. 1. 头向前的 2. 轻率的 3. 〈古〉险峻的 / ~master n. 校长 / ~mistress n. 女校长 / ~ phone 头戴式受话器,耳机 / ~ piece n. 1. 头盔;帽子;头巾 2. 头戴式受话器,耳机 3.【印】(书的)卷页;(章节开头的)页首花饰 4. 头脑,智力 / ~ rest n.(理发店等处坐椅上的)头靠;(汽车座上的)弹性头垫 / ~ stall n.【马】笼头 / ~ stone n. 1. 墓碑 2. 墙基石 / ~ strong adj. 不受管束的;任性的,刚愎自用的 / ~water n. 上游源头 / ~way n. 1. 前进;进展 2. 前进的速度 3.【建】净空高度 4.(同一路线上两车的)时间间隔 / ~work n. 1. 脑力劳动;动脑筋 2.【建】拱顶石饰

heading ['hediŋ] n. 1.【空】【海】航向 2. 标题;题名;题头;章首文字(如信笺上端所印文字) 3.(足球赛中的)顶球 4.【矿】平巷;平巷端

headline ['hedlain] n. 1.(报刊的)大字新闻标题;(书籍的)栏外标题 2. [~s](新闻广播的)内容提要 — vt. 1. 给…加标题 2. 大肆宣传

headquarters ['hed'kwɔːtəz] [复] n. [用作单或复] 1. 司令部;指挥部 2.(机构、企业等的)总部,总店

heady ['hedi] adj. 1. 鲁莽的,轻率的;任性的;暴躁的 2. 易醉的;(酒类等)易使人陶醉的;〈喻〉令人兴奋的 4. 精明的

heal [hiːl] vt. 1. 使愈合,治愈(尤指伤口);使恢复健康 2. 使和解,调停 — vi.(伤口)愈合,痊愈 ‖ ~ er n. 医治者(尤指用宗教或迷信方式治病的人);治疗物

health [helθ] n. 1. 健康;健康状况 2. 兴旺 3. 祝健康的干杯 ‖ ~ food 保健食品 / ~ spa 减肥温泉疗养地

healthful ['helθful] adj. 1. 有益于健康的 2. 健康的,健全的 ‖ ~ly adv. / ~ness n.

healthy ['helθi] adj. 1. 健康的;健壮的;有益于健康的 2. 旺盛的;相当大的 ‖ healthily adv. / healthiness n.

heap [hiːp] n. 1.(一)堆 2.〈口〉大量,许多 3.〈美俚〉(尤指破旧的)汽车 — vt. 1. 堆积,堆起(up, together) 2. 装满;大量地给;倾泻

hear [hiə] (heard [həːd]) vt. 1. 听见;听见 2. 听说;得知 3. 注意听;听取 4. 审理;听(证人)陈述 5. 同意,允准 — vi. 1. 听见;听 2. 听到(of, about) ‖ ~ er n. 听的人,旁听者

heard [həːd] hear 的过去式和过去分词

hearing ['hiəriŋ] n. 1. 听(指动作或过程) 2. 听力 3. 听力所及的距离 4. 倾听 5. 审讯 6.〈美〉意见听取会 ‖ ~ aid 助听器

hearken ['haːkən] vi. 倾听;给予注意

hearsay ['hiəsei] n. 风闻;传闻 — adj. 传闻的;道听途说得来的

hearse [həːs] n. 1. 柩车,(古)棺材 2.(饰有悼文等的)棺罩;墓架 — vt. 1. 用柩车装运 2. 埋葬

heart [haːt] n. 1. 心脏;胸 2. 内心,心地,心肠 3. 感情;爱好;爱情 4. 精神;勇气 5. 心情,心境 7.(表示亲爱的称呼)宝贝儿 8. 中心,核心 9.〈主英〉(土地的)肥沃程度 10. 心形的东西;(纸牌的)红桃,红心;[~s]一组红桃(或红心)牌 — vt. 1. 把…安

放在中心部 2.〈古〉使振作 ‖ **~ ache** *n.* 痛心；伤心 / **~ attack** 心力衰竭；心脏病发作 / **~beat** *n.* 心跳 / **~'break** *n.* 悲度伤心；令人伤悲的事情 *vt.* 使心碎 / **~'breaking** *adj.* 使心碎的 / **~'broken** *adj.* 极度伤心的 ‖ **~ felt** *adj.* 衷心的 / **~rending** *adj.* 使伤心的，使断肠的 / **~ sease** ['hɑːtsiːz] *n.* 1.内心平静 2.【植】三色堇 / **~ sick** *adj.* 沮丧的；闷闷不乐的 / **~ string** *n.* [常 ~strings]心弦；深情 / **~'wood** *n.*(树木的)心材

hearten ['hɑːtn] *vt.* 振作；鼓励，激励 — *vi.* 振作起来(*up*)

hearth [hɑːθ] *n.* 1.壁炉地面 2.炉边；〈喻〉家庭生活；家 3.【冶】炉床，炉膛，炉缸 ‖ **~ stone** *n.* 1.炉膛底石板；软磨石 2.炉边；〈喻〉家庭生活

heartily ['hɑːtili] *adv.* 1.衷心地；亲切地；热心地；尽情地 2.精神饱满地 3.胃口很大地 4.非常；完全

heartless ['hɑːtlis] *adj.* 无情的；残忍的 ‖ **~ly** *adv.* / **~ness** *n.*

hearty ['hɑːti] *adj.* 1.衷心的；亲切的；热诚的；尽情的 2.精神饱满的；健壮的 3.丰盛的；(主英)丰饶的；肥沃的 4.强烈的；猛烈的 5.胃口好的 — *n.* 1.(水手用语)好伙伴 2.水手 3.(英)大学的)运动员 ‖ **heartiness** *n.*

heat [hiːt] *n.* 1.热；暑热；热度；热辐射 2.热烈；激烈；激怒 3.(赛跑中的一次)竞赛；(预赛中的)一次 4.【冶】(一次)熔炼；(每炉)熔炼量 5.(芥末等的)辣味 6.(母畜交尾期的)发情；发情期 7.压力；强迫 8.〈美俚〉警察对罪犯的穷追；大力侦查；活动地区 9.〈美俚〉枪治 10.〈美俚〉枪 11.〈美俚〉迷醉 — *vt.* 1.把……加热 使激动；刺激 — *vi.* 变热；发热；激动；发怒 ‖ **~ed**

adj. 1.加了热的 2.热烈的；激烈的 / **~ er** *n.* 1.加热工；发热器；加热器；灯丝 2.(美俚)手枪 ‖ **~ island** *n.*指市内因街道和建筑密集而吸热和贮热较周围地区高得多的区域，或大城市上方平均温度高于周围气温的现象

heath [hiːθ] *n.* 1.【植】欧石南 2.〈英〉欧石南丛生的荒野

heathen ['hiːðən] *n.* 1.异教徒(指基督教徒、犹太教徒、伊斯兰教徒以外的人)；多神教信仰者 2.不信教的人 3.野蛮的人，未开化的人 — *adj.* 1.异教的 2.不信教的；野蛮的，未开化的

heather ['heðə] *n.*【植】杜鹃花；欧石南 — *adj.* 似欧石南的；淡石南色的

heating ['hiːtiŋ] *adj.* 加热的；供暖的 — *n.* 加热；供暖；供暖的(装置) ‖ **~ element** 电热元件 / **~ pad** 电热垫

heave [hiːv] (heaved 或 hove[həuv]) *vt.* 1.(用力地)举起 2.使胀起，使鼓起 3.(费劲地)发出(叹息、呻吟等) 4.〈口〉投掷；扔 5.【海】绞(缆绳等)；使(船)移动 6.【地】使平错，使降起 — *vi.* 1.胀起，鼓起 2.起伏 3.隆起；呕吐 4.【海】绞(*at, on*) 5.(船)行驶 — *n.* 1.举；拉；扔 2.胀起，鼓起(，有节奏的)起伏；船体在水中的升沉 3.【地】平错，降起 4.[~s]用作单或复](马的)肺气肿

heaven ['hevn] *n.* 1.[常 ~s]天，天空 2.[常 H]【宗】天国，天堂；天；上帝 3.极乐；极乐之地

heavenly ['hevnli] *adj.* 1.天的，天空的 2.天国的；超凡的；神圣的 3.〈口〉极好的；逗人喜爱的 — *adv.* 1.极，无比地 2.借天神之力

heavily ['hevili] *adv.* 1.重重地；沉重地 2.沉闷地 3.缓慢地；吃力地 4.大量地 5.暴虐地

heaviness ['hevinis] *n.* 1.重 2.沉闷 3.

忧伤;情绪低落 4. 迟钝;笨拙

heavy ['hevi] *adj.* 1. 重的;重型的;繁重的 2. 装备着重武器的 3. 沉重的;有力的 4. 大的;大量的;多的 5. 狂暴的;猛烈的 6. 令人忧郁的;(心情)沉重的 7. (眼皮等)重垂着的;昏昏欲睡的 8. 笨重的;迟钝的 9. (天空等)低压的;阴沉的 10.(作品风格等)冗长乏味的 11.(道路)泥泞难走的;(土地)难以耕作的 12.(食物等)难消化的;【面包等】没发酵好的 13.(剧中角色)严肃的;庄重的 14.〈美俚〉深沉的;含义深的 15.〈美俚〉狡好的 16.〈美俚〉老于世故的;时髦的 — *adv.* 1. 沉重地;大量地 — *n.* 1. 重型物(尤指重炮;重装炸弹等) 2. 庄重角色;演庄重角色的演员 3.〈美俚〉强盗 ‖ ~-'duty *adj.* 重型的;厚重耐穿的;关税重的 / ~-'handed *adj.* 落手重的;笨手笨脚的;粗鲁的;粗暴的;严厉的 / ~-'hearted *adj.* 心情沉重的 / ~-'water [化]重水 / ~ weight *n.* 1. 特别重的人(或物) 2. 最重级拳击(或摔跤)运动员 3.〈俚〉有影响的要人

Hebrew ['hi:bru:] *n.* 1. 希伯来人;犹太人 2. 希伯来语言 3.〈口〉不易听懂的话 — *adj.* 1. 希伯来人的;犹太人的 2. 希伯来语的

heckle ['hekl] *vt.* 1.【纺】梳梳(麻) 2. 诘问,诘难(演说者等) — *n.* [纺]针排 ‖ ~ **r** *n.* 诘问者

hectare ['hekta:] *n.* 公顷(等于100公亩或2.471英亩,合15市亩;略作 ha.)

hectic ['hektik] *adj.* 1. 有痨病症状的;患痨病的 2.(因患病)潮红的;有潮热的 3. 兴奋的;激动的;闹哄哄的 — *n.* 1. 痨病热;潮热;潮热病人 2. 痨病患者 3.(肺病患者脸上的)潮红 ‖ ~ally *adv.*

hecto- *comb. form* 表示"一百";hectometre

hectometre, hectometer ['hekta,mi:ta] *n.* (长度单位)百米(略作 hm.)

hector ['hekta] *n.* 威吓者;虚张声势的人 — *vt. & vi.* 1.(向...)说大话;吓唬 2. 折磨;愚弄

he'd [hi:d] 1. = he had 2. = he would

hedge [hedʒ] *n.* 1.(矮树)树篱 2. 障碍(物) 3.[商]套期保值,套期保值 4.(赌博中的)两面下注 5. 模棱两可的话 — *vt.* 1. 用树篱围住(或隔开) 2. 设障碍于...;妨碍;包围 3. 两面下注以避免(赌博、冒险等)的损失 — *vi.* 1. 筑树篱;修整树篱 2. 躲闪,规避;推诿 3. 两面下注以防损失 — *adj.* 1. 树篱的;树篱之下的(或旁边的) 2. 偷偷摸摸的;名声不好的 ‖ ~-**hog** *n.* [动]刺猬;美洲箭猪,豪猪 2.[军]菱形拒马;刺猬弹(一种反潜用的深水炸弹);环形筑垒阵地 3.[植]野毛莨 4. 易怒的人;难以付的人 / ~-**hop** *vi.* 掠地飞行;跳栏飞行(一种连续超越障碍的低空飞行的) / ~,**hopper** *n.* 掠地飞行的飞机(或驾驶员) / ~ **row** *n.* 灌木树篱

hedonist ['hi:dənist] *n.* 享乐主义者 ‖ **hedonism** *n.* / ~**ic** [,hi:də'nistik] *adj.*

heed [hi:d] *vt., vi. & n.* 注意,留意 ‖ ~-**ful** *adj.* 注意的,留心的(of) / ~**less** *adj.* 不注意的;掉以轻心的(of)

heel¹ [hi:l] *n.* 1.(足)跟;(马等)后肢跗蹠;跗后脚;后脚 2.(鞋、袜等)的后跟 3. 靴状物;底部;梯子的底脚(植物的)节瘤;(提琴的)弓尾部;(枪托的托踵 4.(酒瓶中剩下的)酒脚;干酪皮;面包头 5.〈美俚〉卑鄙的家伙;小偷 — *vt.* 1. 给...装后跟;(紧跟;追赶 3.(足球赛中)用脚后跟践踏 4.〈美俚〉供枪给;武装 5.(足球赛中)用脚跟向后传(球);(高

尔夫球中)用棒杆弯头击(球) — *vi.*
1. 在后紧随;快跑 2. 用脚下跟向后传
球(*out*) 3. 用脚下跟击球 3. 用脚后跟
跳舞 ‖ ~**less** *adj.* 没有后跟的

heel[hi:l] *n.*(船的)倾侧 — *vt.*(使)(船)
倾侧 — *vi.*(船)倾侧(*over*)

heft[heft] *n.* 1. 重量 2. 重要
(性);势力 3. 大半,大部分 — *vt.* 举
起;举起...以掂重量 — *vi.* 称得重
量

hefty['hefti] *adj.*〈美口〉1. 很重的 2. 有
力的;健壮的 3. 异常大的 — *n.*〈美
俚〉魁梧大汉

Hegelian[hei'gi:ljən] *adj. & n.*〈德国哲学
家〉黑格尔(Hegel)学派的(人)

hegemony[hi'geməni, hi'dʒeməni] *n.* 盟主
权;霸权 ‖ **hegemonic(al)**[,heɡi'mɔnik(əl)],
[,hedʒi'mɔnik(əl)] *adj.* 霸权的 / **hege-
monism** *n.* 霸权主义

heifer['hefə] *n.* 1.(未生过牛犊的)小母
牛 2.〈美俚〉漂亮姑娘

height[hait] *n.* 1. 高;高度;海拔 2.[常
~s]高处,高地 3. 顶点,绝顶

heighten['haitn] *vt.* 1. 加高;提高 2. 增
加;增大;加强 3. 加深(颜色等);使显
著;使出色 — *vi.* 1. 变大 2.(颜色等)变
深;变显著 3. 升高,长高,变高

heinous['heinəs] *adj.* 可恨的,可恶的,十
恶不赦的 ‖ ~**ly** *adv.* / ~**ness** *n.*

heir[εə] *n.* 继承人 2. 后继承人

heirloom['εəlu:m] *n.* 1.【律】(随不动产
转移的)动产继承物 2. 祖传遗物;传
家宝

held[held] hold 的过去式和过去分词

helicopter['helikɔptə] *n.* 直升(飞)机 —
vt. 用直升(飞)机载送 — *vi.* 乘直升
(飞)机

heliotrope['hi:liətrəup, 'heliətrəup] *n.*

【植】1. 天芥菜 2. 向阳开花的植物

heliotropic[,hi:liə'trɔpik] *adj.*(植物等)
向日的;向光的 ‖ ~**ally** *adv.*

heliport['helipɔ:t] *n.* 直升机机场

helium['hi:ljəm] *n.*【化】氦

hell[hel] *n.* 1. 地狱,阴间 2. 极大的痛
苦;苦境 3.[常用于加强语气或咒骂]:
cold as ~ 冷得要命 / Go to ~! 滚开!
见鬼去吧! 4. 大混乱;娱坊 5. 训斥;大
骂 6. 胡闹;鏖战 7.〈俚〉(印刷所的)碎
铅字箱;(裁缝作场的)碎布箩 8. 赌窟
— *vi.* 1. 放荡地饮酒;闹饮 2.(车辆)
疾驶

he'll[hi:l] 1. = he will 2. = he shall

hello[he'ləu] *int.*[表示问候、惊奇等或用
以唤起注意]喂! — ([复]hello(e)s) *n.*
表示问候(或惊奇,或唤起注意时)的
叫声 — *vi.* Say ~ to him for me. 代我向候
他。— *vi.* 发"喂"声 — *vt.* ...发
"喂"声

helm[helm] *n.* 1. 舵;舵柄;舵轮;转舵装
置;舵机 2.(组织、企业等的)领导 —
vt. 给...掌舵;指挥 ‖ ~**sman** *n.* 舵
手

helmet['helmit] *n.* 1. 头盔;钢盔 2. 软木
遮阳帽;(救火员、运动员等的)防护
帽;保护头部的盔状物 3. 盔状花冠
(或花等) 4.〈美俚〉警察 — *vt.* 给...
戴上(或配备)头盔

help[help] *n.* 1. 帮助 2. 援助;助长;促
进(成长等) 3. 治疗;补救 4. 给...夹
菜;(在餐桌旁)同候 5.[与 can, could 连用]避免;防止;忍住,
控制住 — *vi.* 1. 有帮助;有用 2.[呼
救用语]Help! Help! 救人啊! 救人
啊! 3.(宴会时)招待;伺候 — *vi.* 1. 帮
助 2. 帮手,助手 3. 治疗;补救办法 4.
〈美〉佣工 5.〈口〉(食物的)一份 ‖ ~**er**
n. 1. 帮手,助手;佣工 2. 起帮助作用的

的东西

helpful ['helpful] *adj.* 有帮助的;有用的;
有益的 ‖ ~**ly** *adv.* / ~**ness** *n.*

helping ['helpiŋ] *n.* (食物的)一份 —
adj. 1. 帮助人的 2. 辅助的

helpless ['helplis] *adj.* 1. 无助的;未受到
帮助的;无依无靠的 2. 不能自立的;
孤弱的 3. 无能的;没用的;无效的 ‖
~**ly** *adv.* / ~**ness** *n.*

Helsinki ['helsiŋki] *n.* 赫尔辛基[芬兰首
都]

helter-skelter ['heltə'skeltə] *adv.* 手忙脚
乱地,慌慌张张地,狼狈地 — *adj.* 手
忙脚乱的,慌张的,狼狈的 — *n.* 手忙脚
乱,慌乱

hem [hem] *n.* 1. (衣服等的)折边;(钢
板、塑料板等的)卷边 2. 边,缘 —
(hemmed; hemming) *vt.* 1. 给 … 缝
边,给 … 镶边 2. 包围;禁锢(*in, around,
about*) — *vi.* 做折边

hemi- 表示"半",*hemisphere*

hemisphere ['hemisfiə] *n.* 1. (地球或天
球的)半球 2. 半球地图;半球模型 3.
半球上的国家(或居民) 4. (活动、知识
等的)范围,领域 5. 大脑半球 ‖ **hemi-
spheric(al)** [,hemi'sferik(əl)] *adj.*

hemlock ['hemlok] *n.* 1. [植]芹叶钩吻;
毒芹 2. 铁杉;铁杉木

hemoglobin [,himə'gləubin] *n.* 〈美〉[生
化]血红蛋白

hemorrhage ['heməridʒ] 〈美〉*n.* (大)出
血;大量流损 — *vi.* 大出血;大量流损
— *vt.* 使大量流损

hemorrhoid ['heməroid] *n.* [常~s]〈美〉
[医]痔

hemp [hemp] *n.* 1. 大麻 2. 大麻纤维 3. 纤
维;长纤维植物 3. [the ~]用大麻制成
的麻醉剂;大麻烟卷 4. 〈谑〉绞索

hen [hen] *n.* 1. 母鸡 2. 雌禽;雌鸟(或
鱼、蟹等) 3. (鸟、虾等的)雌性 4. 〈美
俚〉女人(尤指嘴碎的或爱管闲事的中年
女人) — (henned; henning) *vi.* 〈美俚〉
(女人)聊天;传播流言蜚语(*about*) ‖ ~**like**
adj. ‖ ~**pecked** *adj.* 常受老婆责骂
的;怕老婆的

hence [hens] *adv.* 1. 从此地;从今世;
〈古〉从此以后;今后 2. 因此;由此 —
int. 〈诗〉去!

henceforth ['hens'fɔ:θ]、**henceforward**
['hens'fɔ:wəd] *adv.* 从今以后,今后

henchman ['hentʃmən] [复] henchmen)
n. 1. 亲信,心腹 2. (政治上的)支持
者,随从

henna ['henə] *n.* 1. [植]散沫花 2. 散沫
花染剂(用于染发或染指甲等) 3. 棕
红色 ‖ ~**ed** *adj.* 用棕红色散沫花染剂
染过的

hept(a)- *comb. form* 表示"七";*hepta*gon

heptagon ['heptəgən] *n.* 七角形,七边形
‖ ~**al** *adj.*

her [hə:;弱 ə,hə,ə] *pron.* 1. [she 的宾格]
她 2. (口)[用作表语]她(= she) 3.
(口)[用于 than 后面]她(= she) 4.
她自己(= herself) 5. [she 的所有
格]她的

herald ['herəld] *n.* 1. (旧时)传令官 2.
(英国的)司宪谱纹章的官 3. (常用作报
纸的名称)先驱;通报者;使者;预言
者 — *vt.* 1. 宣布;通报 2. 预示 … 的
来临 3. 欢呼

heraldic [he'rældik] *adj.* 1. 纹章的 2. 纹
章官的 3. 纹章学的

heraldry ['herəldri] *n.* 1. 纹章学 2. 纹章
3. (军人的)勋章

herb [hə:b] *n.* 1. 草本植物 2. 芳草;药草
‖ **herbaceous** [hə'beiʃəs] *adj.* (植物)草
本的;草质的 / ~**al** *adj.*

herbage ['hə:bidʒ] *n*. 1. 草;牧草;草本植物群 2.(草本植物的)绿叶软茎部分 3.〔律〕放牧权

herbivorous [hə:'bivərəs] *adj*. 1. 食草(动物)的 2. 身体粗大而肠子细长的

herd [hə:d] *n*. 1. 兽群;牧群(尤指牛群)2.〔常用以构成复合词〕牧人 3. 〔贬〕民众,百姓 *vt*. 1. 使集在一起;把 … 赶在一起 2. 放牧 *vi*. 成群(*together*, *with*) ‖ ～**er** *n*. 1. 牧人 2.〔美俚〕监狱看守

herdsman ['hə:dzmən] (〔复〕**herdsmen**) *n*. 1. 牧人 2. 牧主 3.〔the H-〕〔天〕牧夫座

here [hiə] *ad*. 1. 这里,在这(里)里;到这里 3. 在这点上;这时 4.〔用在名词后,以引起注意或加强语气〕: This book ～ is very useful. 这本书非常有用。 *n*. 1. 这里 2.〔宗〕今世 ‖ ～ **about**(**s**) ['hiərə'baut(s)] *adv*. 在这里附近 / ～ **after**['hiə'ɑ:ftə] *adv*. 从今以后,今后 *n*. 未来;死后的生活 / ～**at** ['hiə'æt] *adv*. 在这时 / ～ **by** ['hiə'bai] *adv*.(用于公文等中)以此方式,兹,特此 / ～**in** ['hiər'in] *adv*. 此中,于此 / ～**of** ['hiər'ɔv] *adv*. 此中,关于此(件)中 / ～ **on** ['hiər'ɔn] *adv*. = ～ *upon* / ～**to** ['hiə'tu:] *adv*. 1. 到这里,至此 2. 对于这点 / ～**tofore** ['hiətu'fɔ:] *adv*. 以前;直至以前 / ～**upon** ['hiərə'pɔn] *adv*. 1. 于是 2. 关于这个 / ～ **with** *adv*. 1. 与此一道 2. 用此方法

hereditary [hi'reditəri] *adv*. 1. 世袭的 2. 遗传的 3. 祖传的 4.(可)继承的 ‖ **hereditarily** *adv*.

heredity [hi'rediti] *n*. 1. 遗传(性) 2. 遗传特征 3. 继承人 传统

heresy ['herəsi] *n*. 1. 异教;异端邪说;信奉异教 2. 信奉异教;持异端邪说

heretic ['herətik] *n*. 1. 异 教 徒;持异端者 2. 信奉左道邪说的人 ‖ ～**al**

['hi'retikəl] *adj*.

heritable ['heritəbl] *adj*. 1. 可继承的;被继承人的 2. 可遗传的;被遗传的

heritage ['heritidʒ] *n*. 1. 世袭财产 2. 继承物;传统;遗产 3. 长子继承权;生来就有的权利

hermetic(al) [hə:'metik(əl)] *adj*. 1. 炼金术的;奥妙的 2. 密封的;与外界隔绝的 ‖ **hermetically** *adv*.

hermit ['hə:mit] *n*. 1. 隐士 2. 加核桃仁和葡萄干的小甜饼 3.〔动〕蜂鸟

hermitage ['hə:mitidʒ] *n*. 1. 隐士住处;寺院;修道院 2. 隐居处;僻静的住处 3. 隐士生活;隐居

hernia ['hə:niə] (〔复〕**hernias** 或 **herniae** ['hə:niː:]) *n*.〔医〕疝,突出 ‖ ～**l** *adj*.

hero ['hiərou] (〔复〕**heroes**) *n*. 1.(神话和传说中的)神人,半神 2. 英雄,伟大的人物;勇士 3.(戏剧,小说中的)男主角,男主人公 4.(某一事件或时期的)中心人物 ‖ ～**ism** *n*. 1. 英雄行为;英雄品质 2. 英雄主义

heroic [hi'rouik] *adj*. 1.(像)古代神话中英雄的;神异的 2. 英雄的;英勇的;崇高的 3. 歌颂英雄的;史诗的;(诗剧等)属于英国王政复辟时期的 4.(语言)夸大的;堂皇的;(声音等)洪大的;(塑像等)大于真人的 5.(措施等)冒险一试的;(药物)猛烈的;(剂量)大的 *n*. 1. 英雄诗;史诗;英雄诗体 2. 〔～**s**〕英勇的行为;夸大(或过火)的语言(或动作等)

heroical [hi'rouikəl] *adj*. = heroic ‖ ～**ly** *adv*.

heroin ['herouin] *n*.〔药〕海洛因,二乙酰吗啡

heroine ['herouin] *n*. 1.(神话和传说中的)女神人,女半神 2. 女英雄,女英雄人物;女勇士 3.(戏剧、小说中的)女主

角,女主人公 4.(某一事件或时期的)
女中心人物

heron ['herən]([复]heron(s)) *n.*[鸟]鹭

herring ['heriŋ]([复]herring(s)) *n.*[鱼]
鲱

hers [həz] *pron.*[物主代词]她的(东
西);她的家属(或有关的人)

herself [həˈself] *pron.* 1.[反身代词]她自
己 2.[用以加强语气]她亲自,她本人
3.[用于 be,become,come to 等之后]她的
正常情况(指健康,情绪等)

hertz [hɜːts] *n.*[电]赫,赫兹(频率单位;
周/秒)

he's [hiːz;弱 hiz,iz](口) 1. = he is 2. = he
has

hesitance ['hezitəns], **hesitancy** ['hezitənsi]
n. 踌躇,犹豫

hesitant ['hezitənt] *adj.* 踌躇的,犹豫的
‖ ~ly *adv.*

hesitate ['heziteit] *vi.* 1. 踌躇,犹豫 2. 心
存疑虑;不愿意;言语支吾 3. 稍停,停
顿 ‖,hesi'tation *n.*

hesitatingly ['heziteitiŋli] *adv.* 踌躇地,犹
豫地;含糊地

heterodox ['hetərədɔks] *adj.* 异教的;异
端的;信奉异教的;持特异见解的 ‖
~ly *adv.*

heterogeneous [ˌhetərə'dʒiːniəs] *adj.* 1.
各种各样的 2. 由不同成分组成的,混
杂的

heterosexual [ˌhetərəu'seksjuəl] *adj.* 1.
[生]异性的 2. 异性恋的 — *n.* 异性恋
恋者 ‖ ~ly *adv.*

hew [hjuː][过去式 hewed,过去分词 hewn
[hjuːn]或 hewed) *vt.* 1.(用斧子,刀等)
砍;劈 2. 砍成;开出;开辟 —
vi. 1. 砍;劈 2. 坚持;遵守(*to*)‖ ~er
n.

hide¹ [haid](过去式 hid[hid],过去分词
hidden ['hidn]或 hid) *vt.* 1. 把 ... 藏
起来,隐藏 2. 隐瞒 3. 遮掩,掩盖 —
vi. 躲藏,隐藏 — *n.*(观察野兽活动
的)埋伏处 ‖ '~-and-'seek *n.* 捉迷藏
(游戏)‖(喻)捉迷藏 ‖ '~away *n.* 1. 隐
藏处 2. 偏僻的小餐馆(或娱乐处)‖
'~out *n.*(尤指盗匪的)躲藏处

hide² [haid] *n.* 1. 兽皮;皮革 2.(口)(人
的)皮肤;(俚)厚脸皮 — *vt.* 1. 剥

hewn ['hjuːn] hew 的过去分词 — *adj.* 被
砍劈成的

hex [heks] *n.* 1.(美方)巫婆;术士 2.(美
口)巫语;妖法;不祥的东西 — *vt.* 施魔
魔法给;带坏运气给;破坏 — *vi.* 施魔
法

hex-(a)- *comb. form* 表示"六":hexagon

hexagon ['heksəgən] *n.* 六角形,六边形
‖ ~al ['hek'sægənəl] *adj.*

hey [hei] *int.*[表示惊讶、疑问、喜悦或用
以唤起注意等]嗨!

heyday ['heidei] *n.* 1. 全盛期 2.(古)高
兴

Hf[化]元素铪(hafnium)的符号

Hg[化]元素汞(mercury)的符号

hgt. *abbr.* height

hi [hai] *int.*[表示问候或用以唤起注意]
嗨!

hibernate ['haibəneit] *vi.* 1.(动物)冬眠
2.(人)避寒,过冬 ‖,hiber'nation *n.*

hiccup ['hikʌp] *n.* 打嗝,打噎儿;打嗝声
— (hiccup(p)ed;hiccup(p)ing) *vi.* 打嗝;
作出嗝声 — *vt.* 打着呃说出(*out*)

hickory ['hikəri] *n.* 1.[植]山核桃 2. 山
核桃木;山核桃木制的手杖(或鞭子)

hid [hid] hide¹ 的过去式或过去分词

hidden ['hidn] hide¹ 的过去分词 — *adj.*
隐藏的,秘密的;神秘的

的皮 2. 痛打

hideous ['hidiəs] *adj.* 丑陋的;骇人听闻的;可怕的 ‖ ~**ly** *adv.* ~**ness** *n.*

hiding[1] ['haidiŋ] *n.* 躲藏(指动作或情况);躲藏处

hiding[2] ['haidiŋ] *n.* 痛打;鞭打

hie [hai] (hieing 或 hying) *vi.* [常接 oneself] 使赶紧,催促 — *vi.* (诗)赶往(*to*)

hierarchy ['haiərɑ:ki] *n.* 等级制度;僧侣统治(集团)

hieroglyphic [ˌhaiərə'glifik] *adj.* 1. 象形文字的;用象形文字写的 2. 符号的 3. 难读难懂的 — *n.* 1. 象形字 2. [~s] 象形文字 3.[~s] 难以解读的文字,难懂的文字

hi-fi ['hai'fai] *n. & adj.* (收音,录音设备等)高保真度(的)

higgledy-piggledy ['higldi'pigldi] *adv.*, *adj. & n.* 杂乱无章(的),乱七八糟(的)

high [hai] *adj.* 1. 高的 2. 高原的 3.(指程序、数量、大小等)高度的;强烈的;很大的;非常的 4.(指等级、质量等)高级的,高等的 5. 高尚的 6. 高音调的,尖声的 7.(时间、季节)正盛的;(时机)成熟的 8. 昂贵的;奢侈的 9. 傲慢的;自负的 10.(肉类)开始变质的 11. 偏激的;严正的 12. 严重的;重大的 13. 久远的 14.(果)醉了的;被麻醉品麻醉了的 15.[地]纬度高的,离赤道较远的 16.[机](汽车等变速器的档)高的高速的 17.[语](元音)高的 — *adv.* 1. 高 2. 高价地;高额地 3. 奢侈地 — *n.* 1. 高峰;高水准 2. 高地;高处 3. 天上,天空 4.(汽车等变速器的)高档,高速挡 5. 高(气)压;高气压地带 6.(美)中学 7.(纸牌中的)王牌 ‖ '~**brow** *n.*(自以为)有高度文化修养的人 *adj.*(贬)高级趣味的,有高度文

化修养的 / '~・'energy physics 高能物理学 / ~ falutin ['haifə'lu:tin]、~**faluting** ['haifə'lu:tiŋ] *n.* 大话,夸张的言词 *adj.* 1.(言词等)夸大的 2. 自大的,傲慢的 / ~ **fashion**(女服的)最新式样(或设计) / ~ **fidelity**(收音,录音设备等的)高保真度的 / '~・'flown *adj.* 高超的;好高骛远的;夸张的,言过其实的 / '~・'handed *adj.* 高傲的;专横的 / ~・hat 高顶黑色大礼帽 / '~・'hat *n.*,*vt.* 自以为了不起的人;势利鬼 *adj.* 1. 傲慢的;势利的 2. 华贵的;时髦的 *vt.* 盛气凌人地对待;冷待 / ~・jump 跳高 / '~・land *n.* 1. 高原,高地 2. [the Highlands] 苏格兰高地 *adj.* 1. 高原的 2. [H~] 苏格兰高地的 / '~・lander *n.* 1. 住在高原的人 2. [H~] 苏格兰高地人;苏格兰高地兵团士兵 / '~・light *n.* 1.(图画,照片等)光线最强处 2. 最精彩的场面;最重要的部分 *vt.* 1. 以强烈光线照射 2. 集中注意力于,着重 3. 使显著,强调 / '~・'rise *adj.*(建筑)高层的;高耸的;高层建筑的(美)(自行车)高把手的;高把手自行车的 / '~・'road *n.* 1. 主要 大路,公路 2. 捷径;途径 / ~・school 学校 / ~・school 1. 中学 2.(英)(为大学培养新生的)公立中等学校 / ~ seas 公海 / ~・'spirited *adj.* 1. 勇敢的;高尚的 2. 兴奋的;易怒的 / '~・'strung *adj.* 十分敏感的;易激动的;紧张的 / ~・tide 高潮 / '~・way *n.* 1. 公路 2.(水陆)交通干线 3. 捷径;途径 / '~・wayman *n.* 拦路抢劫的强盗

highly ['haili] *adv.* 1.(指地位、等级等)在高水平上 2. 高度地;很,非常 3. 赞许地 4. 高贵地;庄严地 5. 高价地,按高额

highness ['hainis] *n.* 1. 高;高度 2. 高尚;高贵 3. [H~](对王室成员的尊称)殿下

high-tech ['haitek] *n.* 高技术

hijack ['haidʒæk] *vt.* 〈口〉1. 抢劫(禁卖的酒等);拦路抢劫(车、人等) 2. 劫持;绑架 3. 强逼 — *vt.* 劫持作(尤指劫持飞机)‖ **~ er** *n.* 抢劫者;劫持者

hike [haik] *vi.* 1. 作长途徒步旅行;步行 2. 飞起,扬起,飘起(*up*) 3.〈美俚〉在高空检修电线 — *vt.* 1. 拉起,升起 2. 急遽抬高(价格等)〈美俚〉涂改(支票)(指提高支票上开的金额) — *n.* 1. 徒步旅行 2. 抬高,增加‖ **~ r** *n.* 1. 徒步旅行者 2.〈美俚〉高空电线检修工

hilarious [hi'lɛəriəs] *adj.* 1. 欢闹的,狂欢的 2. 引人发笑的;滑稽的 ‖ **~ ly** *adv.*

hilarity [hi'læriti] *n.* 欢闹,狂欢

hill [hil] *n.* 1. 小山;丘陵;斜坡;高地 2.(播种用的)点播穴;培在植物根部的泥土;丘土堆;小堆 3. 经培土的植物 4.[the H-]〈美〉(美国国会所在地)国会山;美国国会 — *vt.* 1. 把...堆成土堆(*up*) 2. 给(植物)培土‖ **~ billy** *n.* 〈美〉(住在美国南部)乡下人;乡下人/**~ side** *n.*(小山)山腰,山坡/**~ top** *n.*(小山)山顶

hillock ['hilək] *n.* 小丘

hilly ['hili] *adj.* 1. 多小山的;丘陵多坡的,陡的

hilt [hilt] *n.*(刀、剑、工具等的)柄 — *vt.* 装柄于

him [him; 弱 im] *pron.* 1.[he 的宾格]他 2.〈口〉[用作表语]他(= he) 3.〈口〉[用于 than 后面]他(= he) 4.〈古〉他自己(= himself)

Himalayas [,himə'leiəz; 复] *n.* [the ~]喜马拉雅山脉[亚洲南部]

himself [him'self] *pron.* 1.[反身代词]他自己 2.[用以加强语气]他自己,他本人 3.[用于 be, become, come to 等之后]他的正常情况(指健康、情绪等)

hind [haind](比较级 hinder,最高级 hind-

most, 或 hindermost) *adj.* 后面的,后部的;在后的 ‖ **~ quarter** *n.* 1.(牛、羊、猪等的)后腿肉 2.[~ quarters](四腿动物的)后腿/**~ sight** *n.* 1.(来福枪的)表尺,后瞄准器 2. 事后的认识,事后聪明

hinder[1] ['hində] *vt.* 阻止,阻碍;妨碍 — *vi.* 起阻碍作用;成为障碍

hinder[2] [haində] *adj.* 后面的,后部的;在后的

hindrance ['hindrəns] *n.* 1. 障碍;妨碍;起妨碍作用的人(或物)

Hindu ['hindu] *n.* 印度人;印度教徒 — *adj.* 印度人的;印度教的

hinge [hindʒ] *n.* 1. 铰链;折叶 2.(蚌等的)铰合部;螺纹 3. 关键;转折点 4.(在集邮薄上粘贴邮票用的)透明胶水纸 5.〈美俚〉一瞥,一看 — *vt.* 给...装上铰链或螺纹‖ **~** *vi.* 1. 靠铰链转动(或连接)(*on*, *upon*) 2. 随...而定以 ...为转移(*on*, *upon*)

hinny ['hini] *n.* 駃騠(公马和母驴所生的杂种)

hint [hint] *n.* 1. 暗示 2. 提示;(建议或指导性的)线索 3. 点滴,微量 — *vt.* 暗示 — *vi.* 作暗示

hinterland ['hintəlænd] *n.* 1. 内地 2. 穷乡僻壤,远离城镇的地方 3.(港口、城市或文化中心的)外围地区 4.(受别国控制的)资源区

hip [hip] *n.* 1.[解]臀部;髋,髋部 2.[动](昆虫的)基节 3.[建]屋脊 4.[~ s]〈美俚〉失败的结局 — (hipped; hipping) *vt.* 给(屋顶)造屋脊

hippie ['hipi] *n.* = hippy

hippodrome ['hipədraum] *n.* 1.(古希腊、古罗马的)赛马场 2. 马戏场

hippopotamus [,hipə'potəməs]([复] hip-

popotami [,hipə'pɔtəmai] 或 hippopota-
muses) **n.** [动]河马

hippy ['hipi] **n.** 嬉皮士(指美国国内对社
会现实抱有某种不满情绪的消极颓废
派一员,其特点为蓄长发、穿奇装异
服、吸毒、主张非暴力等)

hire ['haiə] **vt. 1.** 租;雇 **2.** 出钱雇人做
(某事) — **vi.** 接受雇佣(on, out) —
n. 1. 租用;雇用 **2.** 工钱

hireling ['haiəliŋ] **n.** 〈常蔑〉雇佣工;受雇
(或受雇)后听人使唤者

Hiroshima [,hiroʃi'ʃiːmə, hi'rɔʃimə] **n.** 广岛
[日本本州岛西南岸港市]

hirsute ['həːsjuːt] **adj. 1.** 多毛的;毛发蓬
乱的 **2.**[生]有长硬毛的 **3.** 毛发的;硬
毛状的

his [hiz;弱 iz] **pron. 1.**[he 的所有格]他
的 **2.**[he 的物主代词]他的(东西);他
的家属(或与他有关的人)

Hispanic [his'pænik] **n.** 西班牙(或墨西
哥)裔美国人 — **adj.** 西班牙(人)的;
西班牙语言(或文化)的;西班牙和葡
萄牙(文化)的;拉丁美洲的

hiss [his] **vi. 1.**(蛇、沸水等)嘶嘶作声
用嘘声表示反对 — **vt. 1.** 发嘶嘶声表
示;嘶嘶地说出 **2.** 用嘘声责骂(或轰
赶) — **n.** 嘶嘶声;[语]咝音

historian [his'tɔːriən] **n. 1.** 编年史工作
者;撰史人 **2.** 历史学家

historic [his'tɔrik] **adj. 1.** 历史上有名
的;有历史意义的 **2.** 历史上重大的

historical [his'tɔrikəl] **adj. 1.** 历史的;历
史上的 **2.** 有关历史的 **3.**(时态)写过
去事件所用的 **4.** 根据历史上的发展
(或演变)叙述的 ‖ ~**ly adv.** 在历史
上

history ['histəri] **n. 1.** 历史;历史学 **2.**
过去事情的记载;沿革;来历 **3.** 过去
的事;过时了的事物

histrionics [,histri'ɔniks] [复] **n. 1.**[常
用作单]戏剧表演;演戏 **2.**[常用作复]
装腔作势;矫揉造作的举动(或言谈)

hit [hit](hit;hitting) **vt. 1.** 打;打击;击中
2. 碰撞;使碰撞 **3.** 袭击;使遭受 **4.**(精
神上的)打击;伤害 **5.** 使...的感情 **6.**(到
达)到达 **6.** 偶然碰上;找到 **7.** 猜对;说中
8. 投合 **9.**(板球赛中等)得(分) **10.**
〈美俚〉击中 **11.**〈美俚〉沉湎于(喝酒等
恶习) **12.** 给...注射麻醉剂 — **vi. 1.**
打;打击;击中 **2.** 碰撞(against) **3.** 偶
然碰上;找到 **4.**(在内燃机汽缸内)点
火 **5.** 给自己注射麻醉剂 — **n. 1.**
一击;打击 **2.** 碰撞 **3.** 讽刺;抨击;俏皮话
4. 好运气 **5.** 风行一时的作品(或电
影、戏剧、演出等) **6.**(板球赛中的)成功人
物(或事物) **6.**(板球赛中的)得分 **7.**
一次注射的麻醉剂 **8.** 谋杀;抢劫 ‖
'hitter n. 1. 打击者;打击器具 **2.**(棒
球)击球员 / ~ **man**〈美俚〉职业杀手

hitch [hitʃ] **vi. 1.** 蹒跚 **2.** 被拖住;被套
住;被套住 **3.**〈美俚〉= ~ **hike 4.**〈口〉
和谐;融洽 — **vt. 1.** 急拉;急推 **2.**(用
环、钩、结等)钩住;拴住;套住 **3.**〈美
俚〉[常用被动语态]使结婚 **4.**〈美俚〉
= ~ **hike** — **n. 1.** 急拉;急推 **2.** 蹒跚
3. 故障;障碍 **4.** 钩住;拴住;拴住;
套住 **5.**〈美军俚〉(士兵的)服役期 **7.**
〈美俚〉搭便车旅行 ‖ '~ **hike vi.** 沿途
免费搭便车旅行 / **vt.** 求得(免费搭
车);免费搭车行(路)

hither ['hiðə] **adv.** 这里;向这里;到这里
— **adj.** 这边的;附近的;邻面的

hitherto ['hiðə'tuː] **adv.** 迄今;到目前为止

HIV abbr. human immunodeficiency virus
人体免疫缺损病毒,艾滋病病毒

hive [haiv] **n. 1.** 蜂箱 **2.** 蜂群 **3.** 麇集的
人群 **4.** 喧闹而繁忙的场所 — **vt. 1.**
使(蜂)入蜂箱 **2.** 贮(蜜)于蜂箱中 **3.**

贮备 — vi. 1.(蜂)进入蜂箱 2.聚居

hives [haivz][复] n. [用作单或复][医]荨麻疹

Ho [化]元素钬(holmium)的符号

ho [həu] int. 1.(表示喜悦、嘲笑、惊讶等)嗬! 2.[用以引起注意]嗨! 嗬!

hoagie, hoagy ['həugi] n. [美]用整只长圆形面包做的)大型三明治

hoar [hɔː] adj. 1.灰白的 2.(因年老)须发灰白的 3.[方]发霉的 ‖ n. 1.灰白 2. = ~ frost ‖ ' ~' frost n. 白霜

hoard [hɔːd] n. 1.窖藏的钱财 2.秘藏的东西 — vt. 1.贮藏(积累(财宝、物品等)(up) 2.把 … 珍藏在心中;心怀 — vi. 贮藏;囤积 ‖ ~er n. 贮藏者;囤积者

hoarse [hɔːs] adj.(声音)嘶哑的;嗓门嘶哑的 ‖ ~ly adv. /~n vt. & vi.(使)变粗哑 /~ness n.

hoary ['hɔːri] adj. 1.灰白的 2.(因年老)须发灰白的 3.古老的;久远的 4.(植物)被灰白色毛的

hoax [həuks] n. 欺骗,骗局;戏弄 — vt. 欺骗;戏弄 ‖ ~er n. 欺骗者

hob[1] [hɔb] n. 1.壁炉(或火炉)搁架 2.(掷环套桩游戏中用的)掷环套桩游戏桩 ‖ [机]螺旋铣刀,滚(铣)刀 — (hobbed;hobbing) vt. 1.给 ... 钉平头钉 2.[机]滚铣

hob[2] [hɔb] n.〈英方〉1.顽皮的小妖精 2.乡下佬

hobble ['hɔbl] vi. 跛行;蹒跚 — vt. 1.使跛行 2.把(马)的脚拴住 3.阻碍 — n. 1.跛行 2.缚住马腿的绳子(或镣铐等) 3.〈古〉困境

hobby ['hɔbi] n. 癖好;业余爱好,消遣 ‖ ~ horse n. 1.(用作玩具的)竹马 2.(旋转游乐台上的)木马;弹簧摇马 2.

(乡村舞会中系于跳舞者腰间用柳条编制的)马形道具;腰系马形道具的表演者 3. 反复受讨论的话题 4. 癖好

hobgoblin ['hɔb,gɔblin] n. 1. 淘气的小妖精 2. 吓人(或令人厌恶)的东西,怪物

hobnail ['hɔbneil] n. 1.(钉在鞋底上的)平头钉 2. 穿钉有平头钉鞋子的人;乡下人 — vt. 钉平头钉于 ‖ ~ed adj. 钉有平头钉的;土里土气的

hobnob ['hɔbnɔb] (hobnobbed; hobnobbing) vi. 1. 过从甚密;亲近 2.(亲切随便地)交谈 3. 共饮 — n. 关系密切;亲密交谈;共饮

hobo ['həubəu] ([复]hobo(e)s n.[美俚] 1. 流动工人 2. 流浪汉 — vi. 过流浪生活

Ho Chi Minh City ['həu 'tʃi: 'min 'siti] 胡志明市(旧称 Saigon 西贡)[越南南部城市]

hock[1] [hɔk] n. [动](有蹄类的)跗关节

hockey ['hɔki] n.(冰上)曲棍球

hocuspocus ['həukəs'pəukəs] n. 1. 霍克斯波克思(施魔法时惯用的无意义咒语) 2. 魔法;戏法 3. 骗局;欺骗 4. 神秘动作,花招;故弄玄虚的言词

hod [hɔd] n. 1.(搬运灰泥、砖瓦等用的)砂浆桶,灰砂斗 2. 煤斗

hodgepodge ['hɔdʒpɔdʒ] n. 1.(菜肉等合煮的)杂烩菜 2. 大杂烩,混杂物

hoe [həu] n. 锄头 — vt. & vi. 锄

hog [hɔg] n. 1. 猪(尤指供食用的、重 120 磅以上者) 2. 阉公猪;猪科动物 2. 羯羊(写作 hogg)(英方)尚未剪毛的小羊;从小羊身上剪下的毛 3.[海](清扫船底用的)船底长扫帚 4.[口]自私,贪婪、贪吃、粗鄙、肮脏)的人 5. 横冲直撞的骑车者(或驾车者) 6.[美俚]火车头 7.[建]拱曲 —(hogged;hogging) vt. 1.(像猪一样)拱起(背);使(船、船底

等)中拱 2. 修剪(马鬃) 3. 用船底长扫帚清扫(船底) 4. 【美俚】贪心攫取，过多地象取 — vi. 1.(船底或龙骨)中部拱起 2.(口)横冲直撞

hoggish [ˈhɔɡiʃ] adj. 像猪的：自私的；贪婪(或贪吃)的；粗鄙的；肮脏的 ‖ ~ly adv. / ~ness n.

hogshead [ˈhɔɡzhed] n. 1.(容量为 63 - 140 美制加仑的)大桶 2. 豪格海(液量单位，等于 52 于，英制加仑或 63 美制加仑)

hoist [hɔist] vt. 升起；吊起；绞起 — vi. 被吊起或绞起 — n. 1. 升起；吊起；绞起 2.【机】起重机，吊升机械；绞车；运物电梯 3.【海】帆高；旗宽；(船上一次挂起的)信号旗

Hokkaido [hɔˈkaidəu] n. 北海道[日本的第二大岛]

hold [həuld] (held [held] held) vt. 1. 拿着，握住 2. 抓住；夹住 3. 支持，托住 4. 掌握(权力等) 5. 担任(职务) 6. 占据；占有；吸住(注意力等) 7. 抑制，止住，约束 7. 认为，认 … 为 8. 包含有；持有(见解等) 9. 拥有(财产、股票等) 10. 举行 11. 容纳，装得下；包含 12.(美) 扣留；拘留 13. 使保持某种状态 14. 使受约束；使遵守 15.【律】裁定；约束或约定；依法占有 16.【音】延长(音符或休止) — vi. 1. 顶住，支持；持续，保持有效，适用 4.【常用于命令式】停止 — n. 1. 把握，掌握，控制 2. 可掌握(或可踏脚)的东西，支撑点 3. 货舱；底层船舱 4. 监禁；监牢 5. 保留(或延迟)的通知 6.(拳击、摔跤等中)的搂拿法 7.【音】延长记号 ‖ ~ up n. 1. 停顿；阻碍 2. 拦劫；抢劫 3.(口)索高价

holder [ˈhəuldə] n. 1. 持有者；占有者；(支票、汇票等的)持票人 2. 托(或夹)的东西

holding [ˈhəuldiŋ] n. 1. 占有物；所有物；占有的土地；租入的土地 2. 占有或保有的财产(尤指股票、债券) 3. 支持物，托住物 4.(法院的)裁定 5.【体】持球：拉人(或阻挡)犯规

hole [həul] n. 1. 洞 2. 孔眼；破洞，裂开处 3.(动物的)洞穴，巢穴 4. 水流深凹处；潭 5.(常与地名连用)水湾；小(海)湾 6. 阴暗肮脏的狭小地方(或房间) 7. 牢房 8. 躲藏处 9. 漏洞；缺陷，缺点 10.(口)为难的处境，困境 11.(高尔夫球场)穴；(高尔夫球)得分 12.【物】空穴；空子 13.(铁路的)侧线 — vt. 1. 凿洞于，穿孔于 2. 把 … 放入(或打入，赶入)洞中 3. 筑，挖(矿井、隧道等) — vi. 1.(高尔夫球等)入穴 2. 凿洞；挖通矿井

holiday [ˈhɔlədi] n. 1. 假日；节日 2.(主英)(常 ~s)假期 — vi. 出外度假

holiness [ˈhəulinis] n. 1. 神圣 2.【H-】(对罗马教皇的尊称，常与 His 或 Your 连用)陛下

Holland [ˈhɔlənd] n. 1. 荷兰[西欧国家](= the Netherlands) 2.[h-]荷兰亚麻布；洁白亚麻细布；充亚麻窗帘布 3.[h-]荷兰语

hollandaise [ˌhɔlənˈdeiz] n. 荷兰酸辣酱

holler [ˈhɔlə] vi. 1.(唤起注意或在痛苦时等)叫喊 2. 诉苦，抱怨 — vt. 喊出 — n. 1. 叫喊 2. 诉苦 3.(美国黑人劳动时喊口哼的)号子

hollow [ˈhɔləu] adj. 1. 空的；中空的 2. 凹的，凹陷的 3. 空虚的；虚假的 4. 空腹的(声音)空洞的；沉重的 — adv.(俗)完全 — n. 1. 洼地；洞，穴；坑 2. 山谷 — vt. 挖空(out) — vi. 变空

holly [ˈhɔli] n.【植】冬青

hollyhock [ˈhɔlihɔk] n.【植】蜀葵

Hollywood ['hɒliwud] *n.* 1. 好莱坞(美国电影业中心地;洛杉矶市的一部分);(好莱坞所制的)美国电影 2. 美国电影业;美国电影界 — *adj.* 1. 好莱坞(式)的 2.《美俚》(衣服等)艳丽的,花哨的;(人)做作的

holmium ['həulmiəm] *n.*【化】钬

holocaust ['hɒləkɔːst] *n.* 1. 整只焚烧的燔祭品 2. 大屠杀(尤指大量残杀人畜) 3. 大破坏 4.[the H- 或 the ～](第二次世界大战期间纳粹对犹太人的)大屠杀

hologram ['hɒləɡræm] *n.*【物】全息图

holograph ['hɒləɡrɑːf] *vt.* 把 ... 制成全息图,用全息术制作

holography [hə'lɒɡrəfi] *n.* 全息(摄影)术;全息(摄影)学 — *vt.* 用全息术摄制,把 ... 制成全息图 ‖ **holographic (al)** *adj.* 全息(摄影)术的;用全息(摄影)术制作的

holster ['həulstə] *n.* 手枪皮套

holy ['həuli] *adj.* 1. 神圣的;神的;供神用的 2. 献身于宗教的 3. 圣洁的;至善的 4. 唤起敬仰的 5.《俚》非常的,极其的 — *n.* 神圣的东西;圣堂 ‖ **Holy Ghost, Holy Spirit**【宗】圣灵

homage ['hɒmidʒ] *n.* 1.(封建制度下封臣等对君主的)效忠;效忠仪式 2. 封建主与封臣的关系 3. 尊敬;敬意

home [həum] *n.* 1. 家 2.《美》住宅 3. 家乡 3. 本国 4. 疗养所;养育院;收容所 5. 产地;发源地,老家 6.(活动的)中心地,根据地 7.【体】(径赛的)终点;(棒球赛等)本垒 — *adj.* 1. 家庭的 2. 家乡的 ‖ 本地的;(球赛等)主场的,在本场地进行的 3. 本国的;国内的;总部的 4. 中要害的 — *adv.* 1. 在家;回家;到家 2. 在家乡;回家乡 3. 在本国;回本国 4. 中要害;深入地 — *vi.* 1. 回家 2. 安

家;设总部(或总公司) 3.【军】寻的,自导引 — *vt.* 1. 把 ... 送回家 2. 给 ... 住处 ‖ ～**less** *adj.* 无家可归的 / ～**like** *adj.* 1. 像家一样的;舒适的;亲切的 2.(饭菜等)简单而有益于健康的 / ～**ward** *adv. & adj.* 向家(的);向家乡(的);向本国的 / ～**wards** *adv.* 向家(乡);向本国 ‖ ～**land** *n.* 祖国 / ～**made** *adj.* 家里做的;本国制的 / ～**maker** *n.* 持家的妇女;主妇 / ～**plate** (棒球)本垒板 / ～**run** (棒球)本垒打 / ～**sick** *adj.* 想家的;患怀乡病的 / ～**sickness** *n.* 思家病;怀乡病 / ～**spun** *adj.* 1. 家里纺的;家里做的 2. 简朴的;粗陋的 3. 朴实的,不做作的 — *n.* 土布;手工纺织品;棉花呢 / ～**stead** *n.* 1. 家宅(包括房屋及周围的田地);家园;宅地 2. 在美国与某些英国领地分给定居移民耕种的)公地 / ～**steader** *n.* 1. 拥有宅地的人 2.(分得公地的)定居移民 / ～**stretch** *n.* 1.(赛马跑道的)终点直道 2.(任何工作的)最后部分,最后阶段 / ～**town** *n.* 故乡,家乡 / ～**work** *n.* 1.(学生的)家庭作业;课外作业 2. 家里做的工作 3.(讨论等之前的)准备工作

homely ['həumli] *adj.* 1. 家常的;简朴的 2. 朴实的,不做作的 3. 如在家里的,不拘束的,亲切的 4.《美》(人或其容貌)不好看的 ‖ **homeliness** *n.*

homer ['həumə] *n.* 1. 传书鸽,信鸽 2.(垒球)本垒打 3.【空】归航设备 4. 自动引导装置

Homeric [həu'merik] *adj.* 1.(古希腊诗人)荷马(Homer)的;荷马风格的;荷马史诗的 2. 英勇的;史诗般的 3. 大规模的

homey ['həumi] *adj.*《美口》家庭似的;温暖的,舒适的;亲密的

homicidal [ˌhɔmiˈsaidl] *adj.* 杀人的

homicide [ˈhɔmisaid] *n.* 杀人；杀人者

homily [ˈhɔmili] *n.* 1. 说教；讲道 2. (使人厌烦的)道德说教；陈词滥调

homing [ˈhəumiŋ] *adj.* 1. 回家的；归来的；(动物)有返回习性的 2.【空】归航的；导航的；自导引的 ∥ ~ **pigeon** 信鸽
‖ ~ **instinct** (鸽等的)返回性 2.【空】归航；导航；自导引 ∥ ~ **pigeon** 信鸽

hominy [ˈhɔmini] *n.* 玉米片；玉米片粥

homo [ˈhəuməu] ([复] homos) *n.* & *adj.* = homosexual

hom(o)- *comb. form* 表示"同"：homogeneous

homogeneous [ˌhɔməˈdʒiːniəs] *adj.* 1. 同类的；同族的；相似的 2. 均匀的；同质的；均一的 3.【数】齐性的；齐次的 ∥ **homogeneity** [ˌhɔmədʒiˈniːiti] *n.*

homogenize [hɔˈmɔdʒinaiz] *vt.* 1. 使均匀 2. 使均质(尤指使牛奶中的油脂粒均匀分布) — *vi.* 变均匀

homograph [ˈhɔməgrɑːf] *n.* 同形异义词

homonym [ˈhɔmənim] *n.* 1. 同音异义词；同形异义词；同形同音异义词 2. 同名的人(或物) 3.【生】异物同名

homophone [ˈhɔməfəun] *n.* 1. 同音字母 2. 同音异义词

homosexual [ˌhɔməuˈseksjuəl] *adj.* 同性恋爱的 — *n.* 同性恋者

Honduras [hɔnˈdjuərəs] *n.* 洪都拉斯[拉丁美洲国家](在中美洲北部)

hone [həun] *n.* (细)磨石；磨孔器 — *vt.* 把 … 放在磨石上磨

honest [ˈɔnist] *adj.* 1. 诚实的；正直的；〈古〉贞节的 2. 可敬的；有声誉的 3. 〈主英〉可信任的，可靠的 4. 用正当手段获得的 5. 真正的；纯正的 6. 简单的；普通的 ∥ ~**ly** *adv.*

honesty [ˈɔnisti] *n.* 1. 诚实，老实；正直；贞节 2.【植】一年生缎花

honey [ˈhʌni] ([复] honeys 或 honies) *n.* 1. 蜂蜜，蜜 2. 甜；甜蜜 3. 宝贝儿(常用作称呼) 4. 极出色的东西；妙品 —(honeyed 或 honied) *vt.* 1. 加蜜于 2. 对 … 说甜言蜜语；奉承 — *vi.* 说甜言蜜语；奉承 — *adj.* 1.(似)蜂蜜的 2. 〈古〉心爱的 ∥ ~ed 的；甜蜜的；多蜜的 2. 甜如蜜的 ∥ ~ -**bee** *n.* 蜜蜂 / ~**comb** *n.* 蜜蜂巢；蜂窝状的东西 *vt.* 1. 使成蜂窝状 2. 把 … 弄成千疮百孔；充斥 *vi.* 满是洞孔 / ~**dew** *n.* 1. 蜜汁；蜜露 2. 甜味烟草 / ~**moon** *n.* 蜜月 *vi.* 度蜜月 / ~**suckle** *n.*【植】忍冬

Hong Kong, Hongkong [ˈhɔŋˈkɔŋ] 香港

honied [ˈhʌnid] honey 的过去式和过去分词 — *adj.* = honeyed

honies [ˈhʌniz] honey 的复数

honk [hɔŋk] *n.* 1. 雁叫声 2. 汽车喇叭声 — *vi.* 1.(雁)叫；发雁叫声 2.(汽车喇叭)鸣喇叭 — *vt.* 1. 鸣喇叭 — … 避开(*off*) 2. 撤(喇叭) 3. 用雁叫似的声音说出

Honolulu [ˌhɔnəˈluːluː] *n.* 火奴鲁鲁(即檀香山)[美国夏威夷州首府]

honor [ˈɔnə] *n.* & *vt.* 〈美〉= honour

honorable [ˈɔnərəbl] *n.* 〈美〉= honourable

honorary [ˈɔnərəri] *adj.* 1. 荣誉的，光荣的 2. 名誉的 3. 纪念性的 4.(债务、义务等)道义上的；信用的 — *n.* 1. 名誉团体 2. 名誉学位；获名誉学位的人

honour [ˈɔnə] *n.* 1. 荣誉，光荣 2. 尊敬，敬意 3. 名誉；面子；自尊心；廉耻 4. 道义 5.(妇女的)贞操 6.(用于客套语中)荣幸 7.[H-](对法官或某些高级官员的尊称，与 Your, His 或 Her 连用)阁下；

honourable 先生 8.[与不定冠词连用]光荣的人；光荣的事 9.徽章；勋章 10.表示敬意的仪式；荣典 11.[商]信用 12.[~s](大学中的)优等成绩；给予优等生的荣誉；(英)优等成绩奖金 13.[纸牌中]大牌(指 10.J,Q,K,A)[常~s]点子 14.[高尔夫球的]先打权 — vt. 1. 尊敬；使增光；给...以荣誉 2.[商]承兑、承认并如期支付；使...兑现、兑准

honourable ['ɔnərəbl] *adj.* 1. 荣誉的、光荣的 2. 可尊敬的、高尚的 3. 正直的 4. 声誉好的；体面的 5.[H-]尊称(英国议员、侯爵以下的贵族子弟及高级官员和美国国会议员及高级官员的名字前用的尊称；略作 Hon.) ‖ **honourably** *adv.*

Honshu ['hɔnʃuː] *n.* 本州(岛)[日本的第一大岛]

hood [hud] *n.* 1. 风帽；兜帽；头巾(大学制服外以其颜色表示学位的)2.(马、猎鹰的)头罩 3.[机](发动机)罩；烟囱风帽；折式车篷 4.[建]出檐 5.[动]羽冠 — vt. 用头巾包上；给...戴头罩；加罩于 ‖ **~ed** *adj.* 1. 戴头兜的；有头巾的；头巾状的 2.(眼镜蛇等因肋骨运动而)颈部皮褶能膨胀的 3. 头部颜色与身体其他部分截然不同的 4. 顶饰羽冠状的

-hood *suf.* 1. 表示"身份"、"资格"：childhood 2. 表示"性质"、"状态"：falsehood

hoodlum ['huːdləm] *n.* 强盗；行凶的年轻无赖；小阿飞；恶棍

hoodwink ['hudwiŋk] *vt.* 1.(古)蒙住...的眼睛 2. 欺骗；蒙蔽

hoof [huːf]([复]hoofs 或 hooves [huːvz]) *n.* 1. 蹄；(马等的)足 2.[俚](人的)足 1. 走 2. 踢；踏；用蹄踏蹄 — vi. 1. 走 2. 踢；踏；跳舞 ‖ **~ed** *adj.* 有蹄

hook [huk] *n.* 1. 钩；挂钩；针钩 2. 钩状物 3. 镰刀 4.[俚]锚 5. 钩状师；河湾 6.(喻)陷阱、圈套 7.(美俚)妓女 8.[~s](美俚)手；手指 9.(美俚)麻醉药(大指海洛因)10.(拳击赛中的)钩拳；(高尔夫球赛)左曲球 11.[音]符尾 — vt. 1. 用钩连结；钩住 2. 用钩钩(鱼)3. 引(人)上钩；欺骗 4.偷；扒 5.[俚]用角尖挑刺 6. 使成钩状 7.[纺]用钩针编结 8.(拳击赛中)用钩拳击打；(高尔夫球赛)击出(左曲球)— vi. 1. 弯成钩状；弯曲 2. 钩住；钩紧 ‖ **~ worm** *n.*[动]钩虫

hooligan ['huːligən] *n.* 小流氓；街头恶棍 ‖ **~ism** *n.* 流氓行为

hoop [huːp] *n.* 1. 箍 2. 箍状物(孩子玩的铁环)(马戏团中供表演者穿过的)大圈 3.(旧时妇女撑开裙子下摆用的)圆环 4. 戒指 5.(篮球)篮圈 6.(槌球戏中的)拱门 — vt. 加箍于；用箍把...围住

hoot [huːt] *vi.* 1. 作猫头鹰叫声 2. 作汽笛响声；作汽车喇叭响声 3. 表示蔑视不满的叫喊 — vt. 1. 用呵斥声表示(轻蔑等)2. 轰赶 — n. 1. 猫头鹰叫声 2. 汽笛声；汽车喇叭响声 3. 表示蔑视不满的叫声 4. 极少量 ‖ **~er** *n.* 汽笛

hooves [huːvz] hoof 的复数

hop¹ [hɔp] (hopped; hopping) *vi.* 1.(人)单足跳；(蛙、鸟等)齐足跳 2.(口)跳舞 3.(俚)去 4. 作短途旅行(尤指飞行)— vt. 1. 跳过；(口)飞过 2. 使(球)跳跃上(火车等)3. 免费搭乘；得到(免费乘坐)的机会 — n. 1. 单足跳；弹跳 2. 跳舞会 3.(口)(长距离飞行中的)一段航程 4. 短途旅行 5. 免费搭乘 ‖ **~ scotch** *n.*(小孩独脚跳踢石子的)跳房

子"游戏

hop² [hɔp] *n.* 1.【植】忽布,啤酒花藤 2. [~s]啤酒花(用以使啤酒等带苦味) 3.〈美俚〉毒品(尤指鸦片);吸毒成瘾的人 — (hopped; hopping) *vt.* 1. 加啤酒花于;用啤酒花给 ... 加味 2. 给 ... 服毒品;用毒品刺激(*up*) 3. 超额增大(发动机)的功率;增大(车辆)的发动机额定功率(*up*) — *vi.* 长啤酒花;采啤酒花

hope [həup] *n.* 1. 希望 2. 所希望的人(或物) — *vt.* 希望;盼望;期待 — *vi.* 1. 希望;盼望;期待 2.〈古〉信任(*in*)

hopeful ['həupful] *adj.* 1. 怀有希望的 2. 有希望的 — *n.* 有希望成功的人;有希望当选的人 ‖ ~ly *adv.* 怀着希望;给人以希望地;〈口〉但愿,作为希望 /~ness *n.*

hopeless ['həuplis] *adj.* 没有希望的;绝望的;医治不好的 ‖ ~ly *adv.* /~ness *n.*

hopper¹ ['hɔpə] *n.* 1. 跳跃者;跳虫(尤指跳蚤、千酪蛆等) 2.(磨粉机等的)漏斗,送料斗,加料斗;(卸除垃圾等用的)底卸式船(或车);贮水槽 3.(投放要求立法机关讨论的)议案箱 4. 顶杆(钢琴琴键后抬举小木槌的机件)

hopper² ['hɔpə] *n.* 采摘啤酒花的人(或机械)

horde [hɔːd] *n.* 1.(亚洲等地的)游牧部落;游牧部族 2.〈贬〉人群;群 — *vi.* 形成游牧部落;成群结队

horehound ['hɔːhaund] *n.* 1.【植】欧夏至草,苦汁薄荷;薄荷 2. 欧夏至草苦汁;欧夏至草咳嗽药;苦汁薄荷糖

horizon [hə'raizn] *n.* 1. 地平,地平线;天球地平圈 2. 水平 3.〈喻〉眼界;见识 4.【地】层位

horizontal [ˌhɔri'zɔntl] *adj.* 1. 地平的,地平线的 2. 水平的;横的 3. 同一类人的 — *n.* 水平线;水平面;水平方向(或位置) ‖ ~ly *adv.*

hormone ['hɔːməun] *n.*【生化】荷尔蒙,激素

horn [hɔːn] *n.* 1.(牛、羊、鹿等动物的)角;触角;(动物头上的)角状羽毛,触须 2. 魔鬼头上的角 3. 角质;角质物;角制物;角状物;角状容器 4. 半岛;岬,海角;河流的支流;海湾的分叉 5.(新月的)钩尖;(铁砧的)尖角;(马鞍的)鞍头 6.(角制的)号角;(管乐器)喇叭;号;管 7. 角状扩声器;扬声器;警报器 8.【地】角峰 9.〈喻〉防卫手段;力量;光荣 10.〈美俚〉鼻子 11.【空】操纵摇臂 12.[the ~]〈美俚〉电话 — *vt.* 1. 装角于 2. 把 ... 做成角状 3.(动物)用角抵触(或刺挑) 4. 把(牛角)截去(或截短) 5. 使(船的框架)与其龙骨成直角 ‖ *a ~ of plenty* 丰饶角;丰饶的象征 ‖ ~less *adj.* 无角的 /~like *adj.* 似角的 ‖ '~book *n.* 角帖书(盖有透明角片的儿童识字书);初级读本,入门书 /'~pipe *n.* 1. 角笛(一种单簧管乐器) 2. 角笛舞(英国水手跳的一种活泼民间舞);角笛舞曲

horned [hɔːnd] *adj.* 1. 有角的 2. 角状的 ‖ ~ toad【动】角蟾

hornet ['hɔːnit] *n.*【动】大黄蜂

horny ['hɔːni] *adj.* 1. 角制的;角的 2. 角状的;有角的 3. 似角一样坚硬的;粗硬起老茧的 4.〈美俚〉好色的;猥亵的

horoscope ['hɔrəskəup] *n.* 1. 星象;星象算命 2.(算命用的)天宫图;黄道十二宫图

horrendous [hɔ'rendəs] *adj.* 可怕的,令人恐怖的,骇人的

horrible ['hɔrəbl] *adj.* 1. 令人毛骨悚然的,可怕的,恐怖的 2.〈口〉极讨厌的;糟透的 — *n.* 可怕的人(或事物) ‖

horribly *adv.*

horrid ['hɔrid] *adj.* 1.〈古〉粗糙的, 粗硬的 2. 可怕的, 恐怖的 3.〈口〉引起反感的, 令人厌恶的 ‖ **~ly** *adv.*

horrify ['hɔrifai] *vt.* 1. 使恐怖, 使毛骨悚然; 使〈表情等〉显出恐怖的样子 2.〈口〉使震惊, 使极度厌恶感

horror ['hɔrə] *n.* 1. 恐怖, 战栗 2. 极端厌恶 3. 引起恐怖(或厌恶)的事物

hors d'oeuvre [ɔː'dəːv] *n.* (餐前或餐间的)开胃小吃

horse [hɔːs] *n.* 1. 马(尤指成年公马); 马科动物 2.[总称]骑兵 3. 像马的东西; 有脚的木架(如锯木架、烘衣架等) 4.[体]鞍马; 鞍马 5.〈口〉(象棋等中的)马 6.[矿]夹块, 夹石 7.[海](作系帆或其他用途的)绳索; 滑竿, 踏脚索 8. 马力 9.〈美俚〉碎牛肉 10.〈美俚〉(考试作弊时用的)夹带 11.〈美俚〉1000美元 12.〈美俚〉雄性剧 — *vt.* 1. 使骑马上马; 为… 备(或套)马 2. 把…放在背上(或木马)上加以鞭挞; 鞭打 3. 背(人) 4.〈俚〉作弄; 猛推; 粗暴地拉 — *vi.* 1. 骑马 2. 作弄人; 胡闹 — *adj.* 1. 马的 2. 马拉的; 骑(或套)着马的 3.〈同类中〉大而粗硬的 ‖ **~ back** *n.* 1. 马背 2.[地]马背岭 *adv.* 在马背上 / **~ chestnut**[植]七叶树 / **~** 虹; 马绳 / **~ hair** 马毛; 马鬃 / **~ latitudes**[气]副热带无风带(约南北纬30一带) / **~ man** *n.* 1. 骑马者; 骑师 3. 马夫 / **~ manship** *n.* (骑)马术 / **~ opera**〈美俚〉西部剧 / **~ play** *n. & vi.* (作)粗鄙而喧闹的游戏; 胡闹 / **~ power** *n.*[机]马力 / **~ race** *n.* 赛马 / **~ radish** *n.*[植]辣根 / **~ shoe** *n.* 1. 马蹄铁 2. 马蹄形(即 U 形)的东西 *vt.* 给(马)钉掌 / **~ whip** *n.* 马鞭

horticulture ['hɔːtikʌltʃə] *n.* 园艺(学) ‖ **,horti'cultural** *adj.* 园艺的 / **horti'culturist** *n.* 园艺家

hosanna [həu'zænə] *n.*【宗】和散那(赞美上帝之语)

hose [həuz] (*hose*(s)) *n.* 1.([复]*hose*)长统袜; 短统袜 2.(旧时)男式紧身裤; 齐膝短裤 3.(用于救火、浇水等的)软管; 水龙带 — *vt.* 1. 用软管浇(或洗、喷) 2.〈美俚〉拍…马屁; 欺骗

hosiery ['həuʒəri] *n.*[总称] 1. 袜 2. 主英 针织品

hospitable ['hɔspitəbl] *adj.* 1. 好客的; 殷勤的; 招待周到的 2.(气候、环境等)宜人的; 适宜 3. 易接受的 ‖ **hospitably** *adv.*

hospital ['hɔspitl] *n.* 1. 医院 2.[用于机构名称中]慈善收养院 3.〈古〉旅客招待所 4.(钢笔等小东西的)修理商店

hospitality [,hɔspi'tæliti] *n.* 1. 好客; 殷勤 2.(气候、环境等)宜人; 适宜

hospitalize ['hɔspitəlaiz] *vt.* 把…送入医院治疗 ‖ **,hospitali'zation** *n.*

host[1] [həust] *n.* 1. 主人 2. 旅馆老板人 3.(广播、电视的)节目主持人 4.【生】寄主; 宿主; 受体 5.[矿]基岩 — *vt.* 作主人招待…; 当…上作东主人

host[2] [həust] *n.* 1.〈古〉军队 2. 一大群; 许多

host[3] [həust] *n.*[常 H-]【宗】圣体

hostage ['hɔstidʒ] *n.* 人质; 抵押品

hostel ['hɔstəl] *n.* 1. 旅店 2. 寄宿舍(在校外的)学生宿舍; (有关当局为徒步或骑自行车旅行的青年所设的)青年

招待所 ‖ ~ry *n.* 旅店,旅馆

hostess ['həustis] *n.* **1.** 女主人 **2.** 旅馆女老板 **3.** (客机上的)女服务员;(美)(列车、公共汽车上的)女服务员 **4.** (美)(舞厅里的)舞女

hostile ['həstail] *adj.* **1.** 敌方的;敌意的;敌对的 — *n.* 〈美〉**1.** 反对白种人的印第安人 **2.** 敌对分子 ‖ ~ly *adv.*

hostility [hɔ'tiliti] *n.* **1.** 敌意;敌视 **2.** 敌对(状态);敌对行动;[hostilities] 战争行动

hostler ['ɔslə] *n.* **1.** 旅店中料理马(或骡)的人 **2.** 机车(或机器)的维修人

hot [hɔt] (hotter, hottest) *adj.* **1.** 热的 **2.** 热情的;热切的,激动的;急躁的;发火的;激烈的,猛烈的 **3.** 刚做好的;刚到达的;(公债等)刚发行的;(消息等)最新的 **4.** 不友善的,生气的 **5.** 活跃繁忙的 **6.** (味道)辣的;辣的;(打猎时野兽留下的气味)强烈的 **7.** (颜色)鲜艳浓烈的,暖(色)的(如红、黄等) **8.** 紧随的;紧迫的 **9.** (爵士音乐)节奏急促强烈的 **10.** 通高压电的 **11.** [核]强放射性的 **12.** 杰出的,极好的 **13.** 极其走运的;极有利的(在体育比赛中)竞技状态极好的 **14.** (车辆等)快的 **16.** 违禁的,非法的 **17.** 被警察通缉的;(被窃物品)刚被偷窃的;正被警察大肆搜查中的 **18.** (俚)(被窃的珠宝等)因易于识别难以出手的 **19.** (俚)荒诞的;不可信的 **20.** 淫秽的;性欲强的 — (hotter, hottest) *adv.* **1.** 热 **2.** 热切地;紧迫地 **3.** 愤怒地 — (hotted: hotting) *vi.* + 主宾 变热;变得激动(或骚动)起来(*up*) — *vt.* **1.** 使热,烧热;使...加温 **2.** 使激动起来;使鼓动 ‖ ~ly *adv.* / ~ness *n.* ‖ '~-bed *n.* 温床 / '~-blooded *adj.* **1.** 易激动的;易怒的 **2.** 急躁的;鲁莽的 **3.** 感情强烈的;热切的 **4.** (马)温血的 / ~ dog **1.** 〈口〉熏红肠;红肠面包,热狗 **2.** (美)(表示高兴、热情、激动的感叹语) 好极了! / '~-foot *n.* ([复] ~foots) 透脚板(指暗中将火柴放在别人鞋中点燃的恶作剧) *adv.* 匆忙地 *vi.* 匆匆忙忙地走 / '~-head *n.* 急性子的人;鲁莽的人 / '~-headed *adj.* 急性子的;鲁莽的 / '~-house *n.* 温室 / ~ line **1.** 热线(指政府首脑间在发生紧急情况时互相进行即时联系的直通电话或电报线路) **2.** (美)私人问题电话咨询服务 **3.** 电话咨询广播(或电视)节目 / ~ plate 轻便电(或煤气)灶 / ~ rod 〈美〉(改装而成的)减重高速汽车 / ~ water **1.** 热水 **2.** 困境

hotel [həu'tel] *n.* 旅馆 — (hotelled: hotelling) *vt.* 使在旅馆

hound [haund] *n.* **1.** 猎狗;狗;〈英〉[~s] 猎狗,一群猎狗 **2.** (猎狗捉兔游戏中)扮演猎狗的人 **3.** 卑鄙的人 **4.** [动] 角鲨,星鲨;弓鳍鱼 **5.** [常用于构成复合词] 有...癖的人 — *vt.* **1.** 用猎狗追逐;追逐;追逼 **2.** 唆使(*on*);使追逐(*at*)

hour ['auə] *n.* **1.** 小时 **2.** 时间,时刻 **3.** 目前,现在 **4.** 一段时间 **5.** 钟点 **6.** [~s] 小时连续计时制中的)...点钟 **7.** 课时;[~s] 工作时间 **8.** (以正常速度)一小时内所完成的行程;一小时内所做的工作 **9.** [天] 赤经 15 度 **10.** [~s] [宗] (每日 7 次的)祈祷礼拜(时间) ‖ ~ glass *n.* 沙漏;水漏(古代计时器)

hourly ['auəli] *adj.* **1.** 每小时的;每小时一次的(以钟点计算的) **2.** 时时刻刻的 — *adv.* **1.** 每小时一次 **2.** 时时刻刻,随时

house [haus] ([复] houses ['hauziz]) *n.* **1.**

房子;住宅 2. 家庭;家务 3. 库;房 4.
(养动物的)棚 5. 机构;所,社;商号 6.
议院 7. (议院举行会议的)大楼,会议
厅;(议院开会时的)法定人数 7. 家族
(尤指王族或贵族);王朝 8. 剧场;戏
剧的一场;(剧场或音乐厅的)观众;听
众 9. 宗教团体;宗教团体的会所;教
堂;庙;庵 10. 供膳的寄宿舍;住在寄
宿舍里的男学生们 11. [美]旅馆 12.
[美]妓院 13. [英][the H-]下议院;上
议院 14. [口]证券交易所;贫民习艺所 ||
~ [hauz] vt. 1. 给 …… 房子住;给 ……房
子住 2. 收藏 3. 覆盖;藏有 4. 给(机
器,齿轮等)上油 5. [建]安置 …… 嵌入
6. [海]安置(桅等) — vi. 1. 住 2. 躲
藏(up) || ~ boat n. 居住船;水上住宅
/ ~ fly n. 家蝇;苍蝇 / ~ keeper n. 主妇;女
管家 / ~ keeping n. 家务管理,家政
2. (企业中)房屋的管理 / ~ mother n.
(青年寄宿舍等的)女舍监 / ~ top n.
屋顶,房顶 / ~ warming n. 乔迁宴,进宅酒
/ ~ wife n. 1. (['hauswaiz]) 家庭主妇;家庭妇女 2. (['hazif]) ([复]~wifes 或 ~ wives ['hauswaivz]) ([复] ~ hzifs 或 ~ wives ['hazivz])针线
盒 / ~ work n. 家务劳动

household ['haushəuld] n. 1. 一家人;家
庭;户 2. [the ~]王室 3. [~s]通用面
粉 — adj. 1. 家庭的 2. 家常的;普通
的 || ~ er n. 1. 屋主;住户 2. 户主;家
长

housing ['hauziŋ] n. 1. 住房供给;住房建
筑 2. [总称]房屋 3. 遮蔽物;住处;遮
盖物 4. [建]榫穴;榫眼,槽口;槽 5.
[机]外套,外壳 6. [海]帆脚,帆座;(遮
盖入坞船只的)顶棚

Houston ['hjustən] n. 休斯敦[美国得克
萨斯州东南部港市]

hove [həuv] heave 的过去式和过去分词

hovel ['hovl] n. 1. 陋屋;放杂物的小房

屋;茅舍 2. 棚;窑的圆锥形外壳

hover ['hovə] vi. 1. (鸟等)翔用,盘旋
(over, about) 2. 徘徊;逗留在附近
(near, about) 3. 彷徨,犹豫 4. (人)
窝窝化 — n. 翔用;徘徊 || ~ craft n.
气垫船/ ~ ferry n. (英)气垫渡船/
~ port n. 气垫船港/ ~ train n. 气垫
列车

how [hau] adv. 1. (指方式,方法)怎样;
怎么 2. (指数量,程度)多少;多么 3.
(指健康等情况)怎样 4. (指价值)多少
5. (指原因或目的)怎么 6. [用于间接
陈述中,意义及作用和 that 相仿] 方式;
方法

howdah ['haudə] n. 象轿(驮在象或骆驼
背上可供几人乘坐的亭子状坐位)

however [hau'evə] adv. 1. 无论如何,不
管怎样 2. 可是;仍然 — conj. 1. 不管
用什么方法 2. 〈古〉虽然

howl [haul] n. 1. (狼,狗等的)嗥叫 2. 号
叫,嚎哭 3. (表示蔑视或高兴的)狂笑;
〈美俚〉令人发笑的东西,笑话 4. [无]
啸声;啸鸣;颤啸效应 — vi. 1. 嗥叫
2. 号叫;嚎哭 3. 狂笑;狂闹,欢闹 4.
(风等)怒吼,怒号 — vt. 狂喊着表示;
喝住

hr. abbr. hour(s)

ht. abbr. 1. heat 2. height

Huanghe ['hwɑːŋhə] **River** 黄河(亦作
Yellow River)

hub [hʌb] n. 1. [机](轮)毂;(推进器、风
扇等的)旋翼叶毂 2. (兴趣、活动等的)
中心 3. (电器面板上的)电线插孔

hubbub ['hʌbʌb] n. 吵闹声,喧嚷;骚动

huckleberry ['hʌklbəri] n. 1. [植]黑果木
2. 黑果

huckster ['hʌkstə] n. 1. (叫卖)小贩;贩
子 2. 〈美〉为人写无线电广播(或电视)
商业广告者;吃广告饭的人 3. 为金钱

而工作的人;受雇佣者 — *vt.* **1.** 叫卖; 小本经营 **2.** 对…大事讨价还价 **3.** 用大吹大擂的手段推销 — *vi.* **1.** 叫卖;做小商贩 **2.** 讨价还价(*over*)

huddle ['hʌdl] *vi.* **1.** 挤作一团(*together*) **2.** 卷缩(*up*) **3.** 聚在一起商量(*up*) 开会;(暗中)碰头 — *vt.* 乱堆;乱挤 **2.** 把…卷作一团 **3.** 草率地做 **4.** 把 …隐藏起来 — *n.* **1.** (杂乱的)一堆; 一堆;一群 **2.** 混乱 **3.** 〔美〕秘密商议;(私下)碰头会;〔美式橄榄球〕队员临赛前在对阵方球线后面举行的指示听取会

Hudson ['hʌdsn] *n.* [the ~]哈得孙河[美国东北部] ‖ ~ the Bay 哈得孙湾[加拿大东北部]

hue[1] [hjuː] *n.* **1.** 形式;样子 **2.** 颜色;色彩

hue[2] [hjuː] *n.* 呼喊,呐喊

huff [hʌf] *vt.* **1.** 把…吹胀;提高(股票等)的价格 **2.** 吓唬 **3.** 激怒 — *vi.* **1.** 喷(或吹)气 **2.** 进行恫吓,发怒 — *n.* 发怒

huffy ['hʌfi] *adj.* **1.** 发怒的 **2.** 易激怒的;易生气的 **3.** 傲慢的 ‖ **huffily** *adv.* / **huffiness** *n.*

hug [hʌɡ] (hugged; hugging) *vt.* **1.** 紧抱,紧紧拥抱 **2.** (熊用前腿)紧紧搂抱 **3.** [~ oneself]使沾沾自喜;使深自庆幸 **4.** 抱有;坚持(观点、信仰、偏见等) **5.** 紧靠 — *n.* **1.** 紧紧拥抱 **2.** (摔跤中的)抓握 **3.** (熊用前腿的)搂抱

huge [hjuːdʒ] *adj.* 巨大的,庞大的,其大无比的 ‖ -**ly** *adv.* / -**ness** *n.*

hula、hula-hula ['huːlə,huːlə] *n.* (美国夏威夷的)呼拉舞,草裙舞(波利尼西亚女子跳的一种舞蹈);呼拉舞曲,草裙舞曲 ‖ **hoop** 呼拉圈

hulk [hʌlk] *n.* **1.** 巨大笨重的船 **2.** 巨

笨重的人(或物) **3.** [废船]船体;用作仓库的废船;[常~s][史]用作监狱的船,囚船 **4.** (房屋等的)残骸,空壳架 — *vi.* **1.** [英]〔方〕笨重地移动(或走动) **2.** 显得巨大(*up*) ‖ ~**ing** *adj.* 庞大的;笨重的

hull [hʌl] *n.* **1.** (果、实等的)外壳;(豆荚)荚 **2.** [海]船壳,船体 **3.** [空]机身;壳体;(船)的船身 — *vt.* 去…的壳 **2.** (用炮弹、鱼雷等)轰击(或击穿)…的船体

hullabaloo [,hʌləbə'luː] *n.* ([复] hullabaloos) *n.* 喧嚷;吵闹;吵闹声;骚乱

hullo(a) ['hʌ'ləu] *int.*、*n.*、*vi.* & *vt.* (主英) = hello

hum[1] [hʌm] (hummed; humming) *vi.* **1.** (蜜蜂等)发嗡嗡声 **2.** 发哼哼声;哼曲子 **3.** 〔口〕忙碌;活跃起来 **4.** 〔俚〕发出难闻的气味 — *vt.* **1.** 哼(歌) **2.** 哼着歌使… — *n.* **1.** 嗡嗡声;哼哼声;嘈杂声 **2.** 〔俚〕恶臭

hum[2] [hʌm] *int.* [表示不满、怀疑、轻视、惊奇、高兴等]哼! **2.** [清嗓以引人注意等时发出的声音]哼!呣!

human ['hjuːmən] *adj.* **1.** 人的;人类的 **2.** 凡人皆有的;显示人的特点的 **3.** 有人性的;通人情的 — *n.* 人(= ~ being) ‖ **by** ~ *adv.* 从人的角度 从人力所及范围 **3.** 充满人性地 ‖ ~ **being** 人/人、~ **'kind** *n.* 人类/~ ~ **rights** 人权

humane [hjuː'mein] *adj.* **1.** 仁慈的;人道的 **2.** (指学科)使人文雅的;高尚的 ‖ -**ly** *adv.* / ~ -**ness** *n.*

humanism ['hjuːmənizəm] *n.* 人文主义;人本主义;人道主义 ‖ **humanist** *n.*

humanistic [,hjuːmə'nistik] *adj.* 人文主义的;人本主义的;人道主义的)

humanitarian [hjuː,mæni'teəriən] *n.* **1.** 博

受主义者:慈善家 2. 人道主义者 — *adj.* 1. 博爱的:慈善的 2. 人道主义的

humanity [hjuːˈmæniti] *n.* 1. 人性:[humanities]人的属性(尤指美德) 2. 人类(许多)人 3. 博爱:仁慈:[humanities]仁慈的行为

humble [ˈhʌmbl] *adj.* 1. 谦逊的,谦虚的 2. 地位低下的:卑贱的 3. 恭顺的:谦虚地提出的:卑躬屈膝的 4. 低劣的:简陋的 — *vt.* 1. 降低 ... 的地位:使 ... 的威信(或权力)丧失殆尽 2. 使谦卑 ‖ ~ness *n.* / humbly *adv.*

humbug [ˈhʌmbʌɡ] *n.* 1. 欺骗:欺瞒 2. 骗子:吹牛的人 3. 空话:骗人的鬼话:用来骗人的东西:骗子之举 4.(有条纹的)薄荷硬糖 — (humbugged; humbugging) *vt.* 欺骗;哄骗 — *vi.* 行骗

humdinger [ˌhʌmˈdiŋɡə] *n.*〈美俚〉极出色的人(或事物)

humdrum [ˈhʌmdrʌm] *adj.* 单调的:平凡的:无聊的 — *n.* 1. 单调:平凡:无聊 2. 无聊的话 3. 无聊的人 — (humdrummed; humdrumming) *vi.* 单调乏味地进行

humid [ˈhjuːmid] *adj.* 潮湿的,湿润的

humidify [hjuːˈmidifai] *vt.* 使湿润 ‖ humidifier *n.* 增湿器:湿润器

humidity [hjuːˈmiditi] *n.* 1. 湿气 2. 湿度

humidor [ˈhjuːmidɔː] *n.* 保湿器:保湿罐(或盒):保湿贮藏间

humiliate [hjuːˈmilieit] *vt.* 羞辱,使丢脸 ‖ humili'ation *n.* 羞辱:丢脸:蒙耻

humility [hjuːˈmiliti] *n.* 1. 谦单 2.[humilities]谦单的行为

humming [ˈhʌmiŋ] *adj.* 1. 发嗡嗡声的:哼着唱的 2.〈口〉活跃的,热气腾腾的:精力旺盛的:(酒)起泡的 ‖ ~bird *n.*【动】蜂鸟

hummock [ˈhʌmək] *n.* 1. 小圆丘、冈 2.

(冰原上的)冰丘 3.(沼泽中的)肥沃高地

humor [ˈhjuːmə] *n.* & *vt.*〈美〉= humour

humorist [ˈhjuːmərist] *n.* 幽默家:幽默作家

humorous [ˈhjuːmərəs] *adj.*(富于)幽默的:幽默感的 ‖ ~ly *adv.*

humour [ˈhjuːmə] *n.* 1. 幽默,诙谐:幽默感 2. 幽默的东西 3. 脾性:情绪,心情 4.【生】液,体液 5. 古怪念头:想入非非 — *vt.* 1. 使满足:迁就 2. 使自己适应于 3.(针对特点)用技巧调理(或拨弄)

hump [hʌmp] *n.* 1.(驼)峰 — (一些动物背部的)驼肉 2. 驼背 3. 小圆丘:冈 4. 山脉 5. 愁闷,烦心 6. 危机 7. 努力 — *vt.* 1. 使作弓状隆起 2.[~ oneself]〈美俚〉使努力苦干 3.〈英〉把 ... 背在背上:搬运 — *vi.* 1. 努力:苦干 2. 急速移动:飞跑 3. 隆起 ‖ ~ed *adj.* 驼背的:有隆起的 / ~back *n.* 1. 驼背,弓背 2. 驼背者 3.【动】座头鲸 / ~backed *adj.* 驼背的

hunch [hʌntʃ] *vt.* 1. 使(背部等)弯成弓状:使隆起 2. 推 — *vi.* 1. 向前移动 2. 弯成弓状:隆起 — *n.* 1. 隆肉峰:隆起 2. 厚片,大块 3. 推:〈口〉预感 ‖ ~back *n.* 驼背:驼背者 / ~backed *adj.* 驼背的

hundred [ˈhʌndrəd] *num.* 百:百个(人或物) — *n.* 1. 一百个(人或物)一组 2.[~s]数以百计:许多 3.〈英〉100 镑:〈美〉100 美元:100 美元票面的钞票 4. 百户郡(旧时英国郡以下的或旧时美国几个州的州以下的行政单位) 5. 百岁一组:许多 ‖ ~fold *adj.* & *adv.* 百倍的(地) / ~th *num.* 1. 第一百(个) 2. 百分之一的(个)

hung [hʌŋ] hang 的过去式和过去分词 — *adj.*〈美俚〉堕入情网的

Hungary ['hʌŋgəri] *n.* 匈牙利[欧洲中部国家]

hunger ['hʌŋgə] *n.* 1. 饥饿 2. 饥荒 3. 渴望(*for, after*)— *vi.* 挨饿 2. 渴望(*for, after*)— *vt.* 使饥饿 ‖ ~ **strike** 绝食抗议

hungry ['hʌŋgri] *adj.* 1. 饥饿的;显出饥饿样子的 2. [可用以构成复合词]渴望的 3. 引起食欲的 4. (土壤等)贫瘠的,不毛的 ‖ **hungrily** *adv.*/**hungriness** *n.*

hunk [hʌŋk] *n.* (口)大块,大片;厚块

hunt [hʌnt] *vt.* 1. 追猎;猎取 2. 在...中搜猎 3. 用(马、猎犬)狩猎 4. 追赶;搜索;追捕 — *vi.* 1. 打猎 2. (兽类等)猎食 3. 搜寻 4. 摆动;振荡 — *n.* 1. 打猎 2. 猎队 3. 猎区 4. 搜索,搜寻

hunter ['hʌntə] *n.* 1. 猎人 2. 猎取其他动物的)猎兽 3. 猎犬 4. 猎马 5. 猎用表(= hunting watch) 6. 搜索者,搜寻者

huntress ['hʌntris] *n.* 1. 女猎人 2. 雌性猎兽

huntsman ['hʌntsmən]([复]**huntsmen**) *n.* 1. 猎人 2. 管猎犬的人

hurdle ['hə:dl] *n.* 1. (用树枝等编成的)临时篱栏 2. (赛马用)跳栏;(跨栏赛跑用)栏架;the high (low)~ 高(低)栏 3. (旧时押送犯人到刑场的)囚笼 4. 障碍 — *vt.* 1. 用篱笆围(*off*) 2. 跨过(栏)—越过 3. 克服(障碍)‖ ~ **r** *n.* 1. 跨栏运动员 2. 制篱笆者;制栏者 ‖ **race** 跨栏赛跑

hurdy-gurdy ['hə:di,gə:di] *n.* (街头艺人用的)手摇风琴

hurl [hə:l] *vt.* 1. 猛投,猛掷 2. 猛推 3. 激烈地叫出(或说出)— *vi.* 1. 猛投,猛掷 2. 猛冲,猛撞 — *n.* 猛投,猛掷

hurrah [hu'rɑ:], **hurray** [hu'rei] *int.* 好!万岁!— *n.* 1. 叫好声;喝彩声;欢呼声 2. 激动;混乱;骚动 — *vi.*

vt. & vi. (向...)叫好;(为...)喝彩

hurricane ['hʌrikən] *n.* 1. 飓风 2. 暴风雨 3. (喻)风暴

hurried ['hʌrid] *adj.* 1. 匆促的;慌忙的 2. 急速的 ‖ ~**ly** *adv.*

hurry ['hʌri] *n.* 1. 匆忙,仓促;急忙 2. [用于疑问句及否定句中]必须赶紧的理由 3. 渴望,急切 — *vt.* 1. 使赶紧;使加快;催促 2. 急派;急运 — *vi.* 赶紧;匆忙

hurt [hə:t](**hurt**) *vt.* 1. 弄痛;使受伤 2. 危害,损害 3. 伤...的感情,使痛心;使(感情)受伤害 — *vi.* 1. 痛;受伤苦 2. 致痛;带来痛苦;造成损失;(口)[用于否定句]有妨害 3.(美方)生活困难;缺乏衣食 — *n.* 伤痛;伤害;(精神、感情上的)创伤

hurtful ['hə:tful] *adj.* 造成伤痛的;有害的(*to*)

hurtle ['hə:tl] *vi.* 1. 猛烈碰撞;发出碰撞声 2. 猛飞,急飞 — *vt.* 1. 猛投,猛掷 2.(古)使猛烈冲撞 — *n.* 碰撞

husband ['hʌzbənd] *n.* 1. 丈夫 2.(英)管家 3. 节俭的人;管理人 — *vt.* 1. 节俭地使用(或经营) 2. 做...的丈夫 3.(诗)(谑)使有丈夫 4.(古)耕(地);栽培(植物)

husbandry ['hʌzbəndri] *n.* 1. 农业;饲养业(事务、资财或资源的)管理 2. 家政;节俭

hush [hʌʃ] *vt.* 1. 使静下;使不作声 2. 使平息 — *vi.* 静下来;沉默下来 — *n.* 1. 静寂;沉默 2. (对丑闻等的)禁止张扬,秘而不宣 — [ʃ, hʌʃ] *int.* 嘘! 别作声!

hush-hush ['hʌʃ'hʌʃ] *adj.* 秘密的,秘而不宣 — *n.* 秘密气氛;秘密政策 — *vt.* 1. 勒令...闭嘴不作声 2. 压下...不作张扬

husk [hʌsk] *n.* 1. 外皮;壳;荚 2.〈喻〉外壳,空壳 3. 支架 4.(牛羊等的)蠕虫性气管炎 — *vt.* 除去 ... 的外皮(或壳、荚)

husking ['hʌskɪŋ] *n.* 1. 外皮(或壳、荚)的去除 2.〈美〉剥玉米会(农村中邻居、亲友聚集在一起剥玉米苞叶,常为欢庆活动或聚会的一部分)

husky[1] ['hʌski] *adj.* 1. 壳的;像壳的;多壳的 2.(人)喉咙发干的;(嗓子)沙哑的 ‖ **huskily** *adv.* / **huskiness** *n.*

husky[2] ['hʌski] *adj.* 1. 结实的,强健的;大个子的 2. 庞大的;强大的 — *n.* 强健结实的人

hussy ['hʌsi] *n.* 1. 粗野女子;淘气姑娘 2. 轻佻女子;荡妇;贱妇

hustle ['hʌsl] *vt.* 1. 硬挤;乱推;乱搡 2. 硬逼,逼使 3.(口)使匆匆做成 4. 强卖;强夺 — *vi.* 1. 硬挤过去;奔忙 2.(口)使劲赶快做 3. 非法经营(尤指诱人赌钱,妓女拉客等) — *n.* 1. 挤;推 2.(口)努力 3. 拉生意的骗局 ‖ ~r *n.* 1. 乱挤乱推的人(尤指以扒手合作的同伙等) 2. 非法攒钱的人(尤指妓女等) 3. 精力充沛的人

hut [hʌt] *n.* 1. 小屋;棚屋 2.(用木材或金属建造的)临时营房 3.〈美军〉监房 — (hutted; hutting) *vt. & vi.*(使)住进小屋;(使)住进临时营房

hutch [hʌtʃ] *n.* 1.(盛物用的)箱;橱;碗架 2.(动物、家禽的)笼,舍;兔箱 3. 小屋;棚屋 4.〈矿〉洗矿槽;(跳汰机的)跳汰下室;(通过跳汰机筛板的)细料 5. 矿车 — *vt.* 1. 把 ... 装在箱内 2.〈矿〉在洗矿槽里洗(矿)

hyacinth ['haɪəsɪnθ] *n.* 1.〈矿〉红锆石 2.〈植〉风信子 3. 紫蓝色

hyaena [haɪ'iːnə] *n.* = hyena

hybrid ['haɪbrɪd] *n.* 1.〈生〉杂种 2. 混血儿;受两种不同文化(或传统)熏陶的人 3. 混合源物;合成物 4.(由不同民族语言中的词组成的)混合词 — *adj.* 混合的;杂种的

hydrangea [haɪ'dreɪndʒə] *n.*【植】绣球花;八仙花

hydrant ['haɪdrənt] *n.* 给水栓;消防栓;消防龙头

hydraulic [haɪ'drɔːlɪk] *adj.* 1. 水力的;液力的 2. 水力学的 3. 水压的;液压的【建】水硬的,在水中凝固的 ‖ ~ally *adv.*

hydraulics [haɪ'drɔːlɪks] [复] *n.*【用作单或复】水力学

hydr(**o**)- *comb. form* 表示"水","氢化的","氢的": hydrocarbon

hydrocarbon [,haɪdrəʊ'kɑːbən] *n.*【化】烃,碳氢化合物

hydrochloric [,haɪdrə'klɔrɪk] *adj.* ‖ ~ **acid**【化】盐酸,氢氯酸

hydrodynamic [,haɪdrəʊdaɪ'næmɪk] *adj.* 1. 水力的;水压的 2. 流体动力学的 ‖ ~s [复]【用作单或复】流体动力学

hydroelectric [,haɪdrəʊɪ'lektrɪk] *adj.* 水力发电的

hydrofoil ['haɪdrəfɔɪl] *n.*【船】1. 水翼 2. 水翼船

hydrogen ['haɪdrədʒən] *n.*【化】氢 ‖ ~ per-'oxide 过氧化水 ‖ ~ **bomb** 氢弹

hydrology [haɪ'drɒlədʒi] *n.* 水文学

hydrolysis [haɪ'drɒlɪsɪs] *n.*【化】水解(作用)

hydrolytic [,haɪdrə'lɪtɪk] *adj.*【化】水解的

hydromagnetics [,haɪdrəʊmæg'netɪks] [复]【用作单】磁流体动力学 ‖ **hydromagnetic** *adj.*

hydronautics [,haɪdrə'nɔːtɪks] [复] *n.*【用作单】水航工程学

hydrophobia [ˌhaidrə'foubiə] *n.* 1.【医】恐水、畏水、狂犬病; 2.【化】(物质的) 疏水性、憎水性

hydroplane ['haidrəplein] *n.* 1. 水上飞机 2. 水上滑行艇 3.(潜水艇的) 水平舵 4. 水翼 — *vi.* 1. 乘水上飞机 2. 掠过水面

hydroxide [hai'drɔksaid] *n.*【化】氢氧化物

hyena [hai'iːnə] *n.* 1.【动】鬣狗 2. 残酷(或阴险、贪婪) 的人

hygiene ['haidʒiːn] *n.* 卫生; 卫生学

hygienic(al) [hai'dʒiːnik(əl)] *adj.* 1. 卫生学的 2. 卫生的; 促进健康的

hygienist ['haidʒiːnist] *n.* 卫生学家

hygrograph ['haigrəɡrɑːf] *n.*(自记) 湿度计

hygrometer [hai'ɡrɔmitə] *n.* 湿度计

Hymen ['haimen] *n.* 1.【希神】【罗神】许门(婚姻之神) 2.【古】[h-] 婚姻; 婚礼之歌(或诗)

hymen ['haimen] *n.*【解】处女膜

hymn [him] *n.* 1.【宗】赞美诗、圣歌 2. 赞歌 — *vt. & vi.* 1. 唱赞美诗 2. 用赞美诗表示 ‖ ~al ['himnəl] *n.* 赞美诗集 *adj.* 赞美诗的、圣歌的 ‖ ~ book *n.* 赞美诗集

hyper- *pref.* 1. 表示"超出";"过于";"极度": *hyper*sensitive 2.【化】表示"过": *hyper*oxide

hyperactive [ˌhaipə'ræktiv] *adj.* 活动过强的、活动亢进的; 极度活跃的 ‖ **hyperac'tivity** *n.*

hyperbola [hai'pəːbələ] ([复] hyperbolas 或 hyperbolae [hai'pəːbəliː]) *n.*【数】双曲线

hyperbole [hai'pəːbəli] *n.*【语】夸张法

hypercharge ['haipətʃɑːdʒ] *vt.* 使超荷; 使充斥 — *n.*【核】超荷

hypercritical [ˌhaipə'kritikəl] *adj.* 批评苛刻的、苛求的、吹毛求疵的

hyperexcitability ['haipəik,saitə'biliti] *n.* 兴奋过度、超兴奋性

hyperfine ['haipəfain] *adj.*【物】超精细的: ~ structure 超精细结构

hyperlipidemia ['haipəlipi'diːmiə] *n.*【医】血脂过多、高脂血

hypermarket ['haipəmɑːkit] *n.*(英) 超大型自助商场(通常设在市郊)

hyperoxide [ˌhaipə'rɔksaid] *n.*【化】过氧化物

hyperphagia [ˌhaipə'feidʒiə] *n.*【医】食欲过盛

hypersensitive ['haipə'sensitiv] *adj.* 1. 过敏的 2. 高灵敏度的

hypersexual ['haipə'seksjuəl] *adj.* 性欲过度的; 纵、欲的 ‖ **hypersexuality** ['haipə,seksju'æliti] *n.* 性欲过度; 纵欲

hypertension [ˌhaipə'tenʃən] *n.* 1.【医】高血压(症) 2.(情绪等)过度紧张

hypha ['haifə] ([复] hyphae ['haifiː]) *n.*【植】菌丝

hyphen ['haifən] *n.* 连字号(即"-") — *vt.* 用连字号连接

hyphenate ['haifəneit] *vt.* 1. 用连字号连接; 把 … 用连字号移行 2. 用连字号书写(或排印) — *n.*(美) 归化的公民 ‖ **hyphe'nation** *n.* 使用连字号

hypnosis [hip'nəusis] ([复] hypnoses [hip'nəusiz]) *n.* 1. 催眠; 受催眠状态 2. 催眠状态 3. 似睡眠状态

hypnotic [hip'nɔtik] *adj.* 1. 催眠的; 有催眠性的 2. 易被催眠的; 受催眠术影响的 — *n.* 1. 催眠药 2.(易)受催眠的人

hypnotism ['hipnətizəm] *n.* 1. 催眠术 2. 催眠状态 ‖ **hypnotist** *n.* 催眠术研究 ‖ **hypnotist** *n.* 施行催眠术的人

hypnotize ['hipnətaiz] *vt.* 1. 对 … 施用催眠术; 使进入催眠状态 2. 使着迷

hypochondria [ˌhaipəˈkɔndriə] n. 1. 疑病（症）(指病态的自疑患病) 2. (无缘无故的)意气消沉, 忧郁 ‖ **hypochondriac** [ˌhaipəˈkɔndriæk] adj. & n.

hypocrisy [hiˈpɔkrəsi] n. 伪善; 虚伪

hypocrite [ˈhipəkrit] n. 伪君子, 虚伪的人

hypocritic(al) [ˌhipəˈkritik(əl)] adj. 伪善的; 虚伪的 ‖ **hypocritically** adv.

hypodermic [ˌhaipəˈdəːmik] adj. 1. 皮下的;【动】真皮的 2. 皮下注射用的 3. 刺激性的 — n. 1. 皮下注射 2. 皮下注射器

hypotenuse [haiˈpɔtinjuːz] n.【数】(直角三角形的)斜边, 弦

hypothesis [haiˈpɔθisis] ([复] hypotheses [haiˈpɔθisiːz]) n. 1. 假说, 假设; 前提 2.【逻】前件

hypothetic(al) [ˌhaipəuˈθetik(əl)] adj. 1. 假设的 2.【逻】假言的; 假说的

hysterectomy [ˌhistəˈrektəmi] n.【医】子宫切除(术)

hysteria [hisˈtiəriə] n. 1.【医】癔病, 歇斯底里 2. 病态的兴奋

hysteric [hisˈterik] adj. = hysterical — n. 1. [～s] [用作单或复] 歇斯底里发作 2. 癔病患者

hysterical [hisˈterikəl] adj. 1. 癔病的, 歇斯底里的 2. 患癔病的 ‖ ～**ly** adv.

Hz, hz abbr. hertz

I

I, i [ai]([复]I's, i's 或 Is, is[aiz])英语字母表第九个字母 **1.** 罗马数字的 1 **2.** [U]I 形 **3.** [U]【化】元素碘(iodine)的符号 **4.** [U]【物】转动惯量(moment of inertia)的符号 **5.** [U]【物】电流(electric current)的符号 **6.** 表示课程未修完(incomplete)的符号 **7.** [i]虚数单位

I [ai] *pron.* [主格] 我 —([复]I's 或 Is [aiz]) *n.* **1.** 自我 **2.** 极端自私的人;说起话来老是"我怎么怎么"的人 **3.** [the I]自我意识

-ial *suf.* 表示"具有 ... 性质的"、"属于 ... 的":judic*ial*, dictator*ial*

-ian *suf.* = -an

ib., ibid. *abbr.* (拉 *ibidem*)

ibidem [i'baidem] *adv.* (拉 出自处同上

-ibility *suf.* 表示"可能性":feasib*ility*

ibis ['aibis]([复]ibis(es)) *n.* [鸟]鹮(鹮科的涉禽)

-ible *suf.* 表示"可(被) ... 的"、"能 ... 的":permiss*ible*, divis*ible*

-ic *suf.* [构成形容词] **1.** 表示"与 ... 有关的":Asiat*ic*, volcan*ic* **2.** 表示"像 ... 的"、" ... 性质的"、"具有 ... 特征的":poet*ic* **3.** 表示"由 ... 产生的"、"由 ... 引起的":photograph*ic*, symphon*ic* **4.** 表示"由 ... 组成的"、"含有 ... 的":alcohol*ic* **5.**【化】表示"原子价较高"(指与-ous结尾的词相比):ferr*ic* —[构成名词] **1.** 表示"具有某种性质

或特征":classic, critic **2.** 表示"呈现出 ...,"、"受 ... 影响":rustic **3.** 表示"产生 ...":anaesthetic **4.** 表示"学术"、"艺术":logic, music

-ical *suf.* [构成形容词] = -ic

ICBM *abbr.* intercontinental ballistic missile 洲际弹道导弹

ice [ais] *n.* **1.** 冰;冰块 **2.** 冰制食品;冰淇淋 **3.** 冰状物;糖霜、糖衣(指撒在糕饼上的冰屑层) **4.** (态度等的)冷若冰霜 **5.** [俚] 钻石 **6.** 贿赂:为弄到好票子私下付给剧院工作人员的钱 — *vt.* **1.** 冻冻;使成冰 **2.** 用冰覆盖 **3.** 在(糕饼等)上面涂上,糖霜(或糖衣) — *vi.* 结冰(*up, over*) ‖ ~ berg *n.* **1.** 冰山;流冰 **2.** (感情上)冷冰冰的人;微露端倪的事物 /'~ boat *n.* 冰上滑艇 **2.** = ~ breaker /'~ bound *adj.* 冰封的 /'~ box *n.* **1.** 冰箱 **2.** [俚 单人牢房 **3.** [美俚] 严寒地带 **4.** [美俚 演员(或运动员)等候上场的地方 /'~ breaker *n.* 破冰船;碎冰器 / ~ cap *n.* [地]冰盖,冰冠 **2.** 冰帽,头戴式冰袋 /'~-'cold *adj.* 冰冷的 / ~ cream *n.* 冰淇淋 / ~ cream *adj.* 含冰淇淋的;奶黄色的 / '~-'cream chair *n.* (咖啡馆等处的)无靠圆垫坐椅 /'~-'cream man *n.* **1.** 卖冰人;送冰人 **2.** 善于在冰上行走的人 **3.** 制冰人 /'~-out *n.* (湖面等的)解冻 /'~-skate *vi.* 溜冰 /'~-tray *n.* (冰箱内制冰块用)冰格

Iceland ['aisland] *n.* 冰岛[欧洲岛国](在大西洋北部)

ichthyology [ˌikθiˈɔlədʒi] *n.* 鱼类学;鱼类学著作 ‖ **ichthyologic** [ˌikθiəˈlɔdʒik] *adj.* /**ichthyologist** *n.* 鱼类学家

icicle ['aisikl] *n.* 1. 冰柱 2. 冷冰冰的人

icily ['aisili] *adv.* 冰冷地;非常冷淡地

iciness ['aisinis] *n.* 冰冷;冰冷的状态

icing ['aisiŋ] *n.* 1.(糕饼表层的)糖霜,糖衣,酥皮 2.【空】结冰

icon ['aikon] *n.* 1. 塑像;画像;肖像;雕像 2.【宗】圣像 3. 偶像;崇拜对象

iconoclast [aiˈkɔnəklæst] *n.* 反对崇拜偶像者;打破传统信仰(或习俗)者 ‖ ~**ic** [aiˌkɔnəˈklæstik] *adj.*

-ics *suf.* [构成复数名词] 1. [用作单或复数]表示"...学","...术":electron*ics*, opt*ics* 2. [用作复数]表示(特定的)"实践","活动","体系","性质":acrobat*ics*, tact*ics*

icy ['aisi] *adj.* 1. 冰的;多冰的;冰覆盖着的 2. 冰似的;冰冷的 3. 冷冰冰的,冷淡的;不友好的

I'd [aid]〈口〉1. = I had. 2. = I would = I should

Idaho ['aidəhəu] *n.* 爱达荷[美国州名]

ID card 身份证

IDDD *abbr.* international direct distance dialing 国际直接长途拨号

idea [aiˈdiə] *n.* 1. 思想;概念 2. 意见 3. 主意;念头;打算;计划 4. 想象;模糊的想法 5.【哲】观念

ideal [aiˈdiəl] *adj.* 1. 理想的,称心如意的;完美的 2. 观念的;概念的 3. 空想的;虚构的;不切实际的 4. 唯心论的;理想主义的 — *n.* 1. 理想 2. 完美典型;典范 3. 设想,想象中的事物 4. 努力目标;最终目的 ‖ ~**ism** *n.* 1. 唯心

主义,唯心论;观念论;理念论 2. 理想主义 / ~**ist** *n.* 1. 唯心主义者,唯心论者;理想主义者;空想家 *adj.* 1. 唯心主义的,唯心论的 2. 理想主义的;空想家的 / ~**ly** *adv.*

idealistic [aiˌdiəˈlistik] *adj.* 1. 唯心主义者的;理想主义者的;空想家的 2. 唯心论的

idealize [aiˈdiəlaiz] *vt.* 使理想化;使观念化 — *vi.* 1. 形成理想(或观念)2. 用唯心的(或理想主义的)方式表现事物;作理想化的解释;持理想化的看法 ‖ i,deali'zation *n.*

identical [aiˈdentikəl] *adj.* 1. 同一的 2. 完全相同的;相等的 3. 有同一原因的;有同一来源的 4.【数】恒等的;【生】(双胞)同卵的 ‖ ~**ly** *adv.* 同一;同样

identification [aiˌdentifiˈkeiʃən] *n.* 1. 认出;识别;鉴定;验明 2. 身份证明 3.【心】自居作用(以理想中的某人自居的一种变态心理)‖ ~ **card** 身份证

identify [aiˈdentifai] *vt.* 1. 使等同于;认为...等同于(*with*)2. 认出;识别;鉴定;验明 3.【生】确定(生物体)的类别 — *vi.* 一致,成为一体;【心】认同,认为同一(*with*)

identity [aiˈdentiti] *n.* 1. 同一(性);一致 2. 身份;正身;本体;个性;特性 3.【数】恒等方程 ‖ ~ **card** 身份证

ideological [ˌaidiəˈlɔdʒikəl] *adj.* 思想上的;思想体系的;意识形态的;观念形态的 ‖ ~**ly** *adv.*

ideologist [ˌaidiˈɔlədʒist] *n.* 思想家;空想家

ideology [ˌaidiˈɔlədʒi] *n.* 1. 思想(体系);思想意识 2. 思想方式;意识形态;观念形态 3. 空想;空论 4. 观念学

id est [id 'est]〈拉〉那就是;即(略作 i.e., = that is)

idiocy ['idiəsi] *n.* 1. 白痴；极端愚蠢 2. 白痴样的举止；极端愚蠢的行动(或话)

idiom ['idiəm] *n.* 1. 习语；成语 2.(某一)语言的习惯用法；语言的特性 3. 土语；方言；(个人特有)用语 4.(某一作家、艺术家等的)风格；特色

idiomatic [.idiə'mætik] *adj.* 1. 符合语言习惯的；成语的 2. 用许多习语的，富于习语的 3. 富有习语性质的 4.(某一团体或个人)特有的，独特的 ‖ ~ally *adv.*

idiosyncrasy [.idiə'siŋkrəsi] *n.* 1.(个人的)气质，习性；癖好 2.(某作者特有的)表现手法，风格 3.【医】(对药物的)特异反应，过敏；特异体质

idiot ['idiət] *n.* 1. 白痴 2.(口)傻子，极端愚蠢的人 ‖ ~ **box** (口)电视机

idiotic [.idi'ɔtik] *adj.* 白痴的；愚蠢的 ‖ ~ **ally** *adv.*

idle ['aidl] *adj.* 1. 空闲的，闲着的 2.【机】空转的 3. 懒散的；无所事事的 4. 无用的；无效的；无根据的 — *vi.* 1. 虚度，空费；使空闲；使闲滞 3. 使(发动机等)空转 — *vi.* 1. 闲逛；懒散；无所事事(*about、along*) 2.【机】空转 ‖ ~**ness** *n.* / ~**r** *n.* 1. 游手好闲者；懒汉 2.【机】滚轮；惰轮；导轮；中间齿轮；空转轮 3.【铁】空车 /**idly** *adv.*

idol ['aidl] *n.* 1. 偶像 2. 崇拜的对象；宠物 3.(多种教徒崇拜的)神 4. 幻象；幽灵 5.【逻】谬论，谬见

idolatry [ai'dɔlətri] *n.* 偶像崇拜；盲目崇拜 ‖ **idolater** *n.* / **idolatrous** *adj.*

idolize ['aidəlaiz] *vt.* 把 ... 当偶像崇拜；过度崇拜 — *vi.* 崇拜偶像

idyll ['aidl, 'idil] *n.* 田园诗；【音】田园乐曲；牧歌 ‖ **i'dyllic** *adj.*

i.e. ['ai'i:] *abbr.*〈拉〉*id est*

-ie *suf.*〈构成名词〉1. 表示"小"，"小而

可爱"：bird*ie*，lass*ie* 2. 表示"属于 ... 的人(或物)"，"与 ... 有关的人(或物)"：book*ie* 3. 表示"having ... 类型的人(或物)"，"having ... 性质的人(或物)"：cut*ie*，tough*ie*

-ier *suf.* 表示"与某事物(或活动)有关的人"：bombard*ier*，coll*ier*

if [if] *conj.* 1.[表示条件]如果 2.[表示假设]要是，假如 3.[表示让步]虽然，即使 4.[表示问句]是否 5.是不是 6.[表示和事实相反的愿望]用过去时态的虚拟语气]要是 ... 多好 7.[表示惊奇或恼怒,用陈述语气的否定句,意义则是肯定的]：If I haven't repeated the mistake! 我真不该重犯这样的错误! — *n.* 条件；设想

igloo, iglu ['iglu:] *n.* 1.(爱斯基摩人的)拱形圆顶小屋 2. 拱形建筑物

igneous ['igniəs] *adj.* 1. 火的；似火的 2.【地】火成的

ignite [ig'nait] *vt.* 1. 点燃；点火于；使燃烧 2. 使灼热 3. 使兴奋；使激动 — *vi.* 着火；发火；变得灼热 ‖ ~**r**, **ignitor** *n.* 1. 点火器；点火剂；点火物；点火者；引燃装置

ignition [ig'niʃən] *n.* 1. 点火；着火 2.【机】点火(开关)；【化】灼烧【机】发火装置，点火开关

ignoble [ig'nəubl] *adj.* 1. 卑鄙的；不体面的；可耻的 2. 卑贱的，低下的；出身微贱的 ‖ **ignobly** *adv.*

ignominious [.ignə'miniəs] *adj.* 1. 耻辱的，不名誉的；丢脸的 2. 可鄙的；可耻的 ‖ **ignominy** *n.*

ignoramus [.ignə'reiməs] *n.* 浑噩无知的人；笨蛋

ignorance ['ignərəns] *n.* 1. 无知；愚昧 2. 不知

ignorant ['ignərənt] *adj.* 1. 无知的；没有

学识的；愚昧的 2. 由无知（或无经验）引起的 3. 不知道的 ‖ ~ly adv.

ignore [ig'nɔ:] vt. 1. 不顾；不理；忽视 2.【律】驳回

iguana [i'gwɑ:nə] n.【动】鬣蜥（一种产于美洲和西印度群岛的大蜥蜴）

ikon ['aikɔn] n. = icon

il- pref.（用在 l 前）表示"否定"：il limitable, illiteracy

ilk [ilk] n.（常贬）类；等级：Hitler and his ~ 希特勒之流 — adj.〈古〉同一的，相同的

ill [il]（worse[wə:s], worst[wəːst]） adj. 1.（一般用作表语）有病的，不健康的；要呕吐的 2.（用作定语）坏的；不良的；邪恶的；恶意的；粗暴的 3.（用作表语）拙劣的；不完美的；不良的；不恰当的 4. 难以处理的，麻烦的 —（worse, worst）adv. 1. 坏；不利地 2. 不完全；不充分；几乎不 3. 粗暴地，不友好地 — n. 1. 坏，恶 2. 罪恶 3.［常 ~s］病害；灾祸，不幸 ‖ ～-ad'vised adj. 欠考虑的，不明智的 /'～-'bred adj. 1. 教养不好的；粗鲁的 2.（动物等）劣种的 /'～-'fated adj. 注定要倒霉的；运气不好的；带来不幸的 /'～-'mannered adj. 举止粗鲁的 /'～-'natured adj. 怀着恶意的；脾气坏的 /'～-'tempered adj. 情绪不好的；易发火的 /'～-'treat. '～-'use vt. 虐待；不友好地对待 /'～-'treatment. '～-'usage n. 虐待；苛待 /'～will adj. 恶意；怨恨

I'll [ail]〈口〉1. = I shall 2. = I will

illegal [i'li:gəl] adj. 不合法的，非法的；违规的 ‖ ～-ity[ili:'gæləti] n. /~ly adv.

illegible [i'ledʒəbl] adj. 难以辨认的；字迹模糊的；印刷模糊的 ‖ **illegibility** [iledʒi'biləti] n. / **illegibly** adv.

illegitimate [ˌili'dʒitimit] adj. 1. 非法的，

违法的 2. 私生的 3. 不合理的；不合逻辑的 4. 不符合惯例的；【语】不合规则的；非惯用的 — n. 没有合法身份的人（尤指私生子） — [ˌili'dʒitimeit] vt. 宣布 … 为非法 ‖ **illegitimation** [ˌili'dʒiti'meiʃən] n. / ～ly adv.

illiberal [i'libərəl] adj. 1. 狭隘的；偏执的 2. 吝啬的，小气的 ‖ ~ly adv.

illicit [i'lisit] adj. 违法的；违禁的；不正当的 ‖ ~ly adv.

Illinois [ˌili'nɔi, ˌili'nɔiz] n. 伊利诺斯[美国州名]

illiteracy [i'litərəsi] n. 1. 文盲；未受教育；无知 2. 语言差错；粗糙

illiterate [i'litərit] adj. 1. 文盲的；未受教育的；无知的 2. 缺乏语言（或文学等）方面知识的 3. 语言错误的 — n. 文盲；无知的人 ‖ ~ly adv.

illness ['ilnis] n. 病，疾病

illogical [i'lɔdʒikəl] adj. 不合逻辑的；缺乏逻辑的，说不通的；无条理的；无意义的 ‖ ～ly adv.

illuminate [i'lju:mineit] vt. 1. 照亮，照明 2. 阐明，使明白；启发；教导 3. 使显扬：使光辉灿烂 4. 用灯饰物（街道、房屋等）5. 用金色（或银色、鲜明色彩、图案等）装饰（起首字母、书籍、手稿等）— vi. 照亮；用灯装饰

illumination [iˌlju:mi'neiʃən] n. 1. 照亮，照明；光亮；照（明）度 2. 阐明，解释；启发 3.［常 ~s］灯彩，灯饰 4.［~s］（书稿第一个字母等的）彩饰，图案花饰

illumine [i'lju:min] vt. 1. 照亮；启发 2. 使发亮

illusion [i'lju:ʒən] n. 1. 错觉；幻觉 2. 假象 3. 幻想；错误想法 4. 薄纱

illusive [i'lju:siv] adj. 1. 产生错觉的；因错觉产生的 2. 虚幻的；迷惑人的

illusory [i'lju:səri] adj. = illusive

illustrate ['iləstreit] vt. 1. (用图或例子等)说明, 阐用 2. 用插图等装饰(书、报等) — vi. 举例 ‖ **illustrator** n. 插图画家, 画插图者

illustration [,iləs'treiʃən] n. 1. 说明; 图解 2. 例证, 实例; 插图

illustrative ['iləstreitiv] adj. 用作说明的, 解说性的, 作为例证的

illustrious [i'lʌstriəs] adj. 1. 辉煌的; 卓越的; 著名的; 杰出的 2. 有光泽的; 明亮的

illy ['ili] adv. 〈口〉坏, 恶劣地

im- pref. (用在 b, m, p 前) 1. 表示"向...内","在...上","向...": imbed, immigrate 2. 表示"否定": impotent, immortal

I'm [aim] 〈口〉= I am

image ['imidʒ] n. 1. 像; 肖像; 偶像 2. 映像; 影像; 图像 3. 相像的人(或物); 翻版 4. 形象; 典型 5. 形象化的描绘 6. 【语】(修辞中的)比喻 7. 印象; 概念; 思想 8. 【心】意象; 表象 — vt. 1. 作...的像 2. 想像 3. 成像 2. 反映 3. 想象 4. 形象地描写; 用比喻描写 5. 象征

imagery ['imidʒri] n. 1. 〔总称〕像; 画像; 雕像; 偶像 2. 塑像术, 雕像术 3. 〔总称〕意象, 表象 4. 〔总称〕形象化描述; 比喻

imaginable ['imædʒinəbl] adj. (常与最高级形容词或 all, every, only 等连用, 放在被修饰的名词后)可以想象得到的

imaginary [i'imædʒinəri] adj. 1. 想象中的; 假想的, 虚构的; 幻想的 2. 【数】虚数的

imagination [i,mædʒi'neiʃən] n. 1. 想象; 想象力; 创造力 2. 空想, 妄想 3. 想象出来的事物

imaginative [i'imædʒinətiv] adj. 富于想象力的; 唤起想象力的; 想象的 ‖ ~**ly**

adv.

imagine [i'mædʒin] vt. 1. 想象; 设想; 料想 2. 捏造 — vi. 想象起来; 想起来; 料想起来

imam, imaum [i'mɑːm] n. 1. (伊斯兰教) [I-]伊斯兰教目(指伊斯兰教国家元首哈利发、什叶派宗教领袖或声称继承穆罕默德的任何政教领袖) 2. 伊玛目(指清真寺内率领穆斯林作礼拜的人, 或对伊斯兰著名学者的尊称)

imamate [i'mɑːmeit] n. 1. 伊玛目统治的国家(或地区); 伊玛目职位(或地位、任期)

imbalance [im'bæləns] n. 1. 不平衡, 不均衡, 失调 2. 【医】(各眼肌之间的)不平衡, 失调, 平衡缺失

imbecile ['imbisiːl] n. 1. 弱智者, 低能者 2. 笨人 — adj. 1. 弱智的, 低能的 2. 愚笨的 ‖ **imbecility** [,imbi'siləti] n. 1. 弱智, 低能 2. 蠢事; 愚蠢的行为

imbed [im'bed] (imbedded; imbedding) vt. = embed

imbibe [im'baib] vt. 1. 喝, 饮 2. 吸入(空气等) 3. 吸引(思想、知识等) — vi. 1. 喝, 饮 2. 吸引水分(或光、热等) ‖ ~ **r** n.

imbroglio [im'brəuljəu] n. 错综复杂局面; (人际等的)纠葛; 乱糟糟的一堆(东西)

imbue [im'bjuː] vt. 1. 使充沛; 灌输; 深深影响 2. 使浸透 ‖ ~**ment** n.

imitate ['imiteit] vt. 1. 模仿, 仿效, 摹拟; 学样 2. 仿制, 仿造; 伪造 ‖ **imitator** n. 模仿者; 临摹者; 仿造者; 伪造者

imitation [,imi'teiʃən] n. 1. 模仿, 仿效; 摹拟; 仿造 2. 仿制; 仿制品; 伪造物; 赝品 3. 【生】拟态 — adj. 仿造的; 伪造的

imitative ['imitətiv] adj. 1. 模仿的, 摹拟的 2. 爱模仿的 3. 仿制的, 仿造的; 伪

造的

immaculate [iˈmækjulit] *adj.* 1. 纯洁的；无瑕疵的 2. 无斑点的 3. 无过失的，清白无辜的 ‖ **～ly** *adv.*

immanent [ˈimənənt] *adj.* 内在的；【宗】(上帝)无所不在的 ‖ **immanence, immanency** *n.* / **～ly** *adv.*

immaterial [ˌiməˈtiəriəl] *adj.* 1. 非物质的；无形的 2. 不重要的

immature [ˌiməˈtjuə] *adj.* 1. 发育未全的，未成熟的 2. 未完成的；不完全的；粗糙的 3.【地】幼年的，未成年的 ‖ **～ly** *adv.* / **imma'turity** *n.*

immeasurable [iˈmeʒərəbl] *adj.* 无法计量的；无边无际的 ‖ **immeasurably** *adv.*

immediacy [iˈmiːdiəsi] *n.* 1. 即时(性)；直接(性) 2. [immediacies]迫切需要的事物 3. 直观性，直觉性

immediate [iˈmiːdjət] *adj.* 1. 直接的；最接近的 2. 紧靠着的 3. 立即的；即时的 4. 直觉的

immediately [iˈmiːdjətli] *adv.* 1. 立即，马上 2. 直接地；紧密地 — *conj.* (主英)一经 ...的(立即)

immemorial [ˌimiˈmɔːriəl] *adj.* 无法追忆的；古老的，远古的

immense [iˈmens] *adj.* 1. 广大的；巨大的 2.〔俚〕极好的 3. 伟大的；大大地；无限地 4.〔口〕非常，很 / **immensity** *n.* 1. 广大；巨大；无限；无限的空间 2. 巨物

immerse [iˈməːs] *vt.* 1. 使浸没 2.【宗】给 ... 施浸礼 3. 使沉浸于；使专心于；使深深陷入(*in*)

immersion [iˈməːʃən] *n.* 1. 浸没；沉浸 2.【宗】浸礼 3. 专心；陷入 4.【天】掩始 — *adj.* (学习外语时)沉浸式强化训练的

immigrant [ˈimigrənt] *adj.* (从外国)移来的；移民的；侨民的 — *n.* 1. 移民；侨

民 2. 从异地移入的动物(或植物)

immigrate [ˈimigreit] *vi.* (从外国)移来；移居入境 — *vt.* 使移居入境

immigration [ˌimiˈgreiʃən] *n.* 移居；外来的移民

imminence [ˈiminəns] *n.* 急迫的；迫近的危险(或祸患)；危急

imminent [ˈiminənt] *adj.* 急迫的；迫近的；危急的 ‖ **～ly** *adv.*

immobile [iˈmoubail] *adj.* 1. 不动的；固定的 2. 不可动的；稳定的 3. 不变的；静止的 ‖ **immobility** [ˌiməuˈbiliti] *n.*

immobilize [iˈməubilaiz] *vt.* 1. 使不动；使固定 2. 使(部队、车辆)不能调动；使无(或丧失)机动性 3. 收回(硬币)使不流通；变(流动资本)为固定资本 4. (用夹板等)使(肢、关节)不动 ‖ **im.mobili'zation** *n.*

immoderate [iˈmɔdərit] *adj.* 1. 不适中的；无节制的；过多的 2. 不合理的；过分的

immodest [iˈmɔdist] *adj.* 1. 不谦虚的；不礼貌的；不正派的 2. 冒失的，鲁莽的 ‖ **～ly** *adv.* / **～y** *n.*

immolate [ˈiməuleit] *vt.* 1. 宰杀 — 作祭品 2. 牺牲 3. 杀死 ‖ **immo'lation** *n.*

immoral [iˈmɔrəl] *adj.* 1. 不道德的，道德败坏的；邪恶的 2. 淫荡的；猥亵的 ‖ **～ity** [ˌiməˈræliti] *n.* 1. 不道德；道德败坏 2. 不道德的行为；伤风败俗的行为 / **～ly** *adv.*

immortal [iˈmɔːtl] *adj.* 1. 不朽的，流芳百世的 2.〔口〕永久的，不变的 3. 不死的，永生的 4. 神的 — *n.* 1. 不朽的，流芳百世的人 2. [常 Immortals](希腊、罗马神话中的)神 3. [I-](法兰西学院)院士 ‖ **～ity** [ˌimɔːˈtæliti] *n.* 不朽；永存；不灭的声誉 / **～ly** *adv.*

immortalize [iˈmɔːtəlaiz] *vt.* 使不朽，使不

灭

immovable [i'muːvəbl] *adj.* **1.** 不可移动的;固定的 **2.** 不动的;静止的 **3.** 不可改变的;不屈的;坚定不移的 **4.** 不激动的;无感觉的;冷淡的 **5.** 【律】不动的 — *n.* **1.** 不可移动的东西 **2.** [~s]【律】不动产 ‖ **immovably** *adv.*

immune [i'mjuːn] *adj.* **1.** 免除的 **2.** 不受影响的;无响应的 **3.** 有免疫力的;可避免的 **4.**【医】免疫的 — *n.* 免疫者 ‖ **immunity** *n.* **1.** 免除;豁免 **2.** 免疫(力);免疫性

immunize ['imjunaiz] *vt.* 使免除;使免疫 ‖ **immuni'zation** *n.*

immuno- *comb. form* 表示"免疫";immunodeficiency

immunoassay [ˌimjunəu'æsei] *n.*【医】免疫测定

immunocompetence [ˌimjunəu'kɔmpitəns] *n.*【生】免疫活性

immunodeficiency [ˌimjunəudi'fiʃənsi] *n.*【生】免疫缺陷 ‖ **~ disease** 免疫缺陷病

immunogenetics [ˌimjunəudʒi'netiks] [复] *n.* (用作单)免疫遗传学

immunoglobulin [ˌimjunəu'glɔbjulin] *n.*【生】免疫球蛋白

immunoh(a)ematology [ˌimjunəuˌhiːmə'tɔlədʒi] *n.* 免疫血液学

immunology [ˌimju'nɔlədʒi] *n.*【医】免疫学

immunopathology [ˌimjunəupə'θɔlədʒi] *n.* 免疫病理学

immunosuppression [ˌimjunəusə'preʃən] *n.*【生】免疫抑制

immure [i'mjuə] *vt.* **1.** 监禁;禁闭 **2.** [~ oneself]使闭门不出 ‖ **~ ment** *n.*

immutable [i'mjuːtəbl] *adj.* 不可改变的;永远不变的 ‖ **immutably** *adv.*

imp [imp] *n.* **1.** 顽童,小淘气 **2.** 魔鬼的后代;小魔鬼 **3.**〈古〉孩子;后代

impact ['impækt] *n.* **1.** 冲击,碰撞;冲击力 **2.** 效果;影响 **3.**【军】弹着,命中;(火箭)降落 — [im'pækt] *vt.* **1.** 塞紧;压紧;楔牢(into, in) **2.** 充满,挤满 **3.** 冲击,碰撞

impair [im'pɛə] *vt.* **1.** 削弱;减少 **2.** 损害;损伤 ‖ **~able** *adj.* / **~ed** *adj.* / **~er** *n.* / **~ment** *n.*

impale [im'peil] *vt.* **1.** 刺穿;刺住 **2.** 把...钉在尖桩上;对...施以刺刑 **3.** 使绝望;使尴尬 **4.** (用栅)围住 ‖ **~ment** *n.*

impalpable [im'pælpəbl] *adj.* 摸不着的;感觉不到的;难以理解的;细得不能觉察的 ‖ **impalpably** *adv.*

impanel [im'pænl] (impanel(l)ed; impanel-(l)ing) *vt.* 把(某人)列入陪审员名单;挑选(陪审团)‖ **~ment** *n.*

impart [im'pɑːt] *vt.* **1.** 把...分给;给予;传逼 **2.** 告诉;透露

impartial [im'pɑːʃəl] *adj.* 公正的,不偏袒的;无偏见的 ‖ **~ity** ['impɑːʃi'æləti] *n.* / **~ly** *adv.*

impassable [im'pɑːsəbl] *adj.* **1.** 不能通行的;不可逾越的 **2.** 不可流通的

impasse [im'pɑːs]〈法〉*n.* **1.** 死路;死胡同 **2.** 绝境;僵局

impassion [im'pæʃən] *vt.* 激起...的热情,使充满热情;激动 ‖ **~ed** *adj.* 充满热情的,热烈的;激动的

impassive [im'pæsiv] *adj.* **1.** 缺乏热情的,冷淡的;无动于表的;无表情的 **2.** 无感觉的 **3.** 不易受伤害的 **4.** 不动的 ‖ **~ly** *adv.*

impatience [im'peiʃəns] *n.* **1.** 不耐烦,急躁 **2.** 渴望,切望

impatient [im'peiʃənt] *adj.* **1.** 不耐烦的,急躁的;忍受不了的 **2.** 切望的;急切的 ‖ **~ly** *adv.*

impeach [im'piːtʃ] *vt.* **1.** 控告；检举；弹劾 **2.** 对 ... 表示怀疑，不信任；指责，非难，责问 ‖ ～ment *n.*

impeccable [im'pekəbl] *adj.* **1.** 不会做坏事的；不易做坏事的 **2.** 没有缺点的；无瑕疵的 — *n.* 不会做坏事的人；无瑕疵的人 ‖ impeccably *adv.*

impecunious [ˌimpi'kjuːnjəs] *adj.* 没钱的，贫穷的

impede [im'piːd] *vt.* 妨碍；阻碍；阻止

impediment [im'pedimənt] *n.* **1.** 妨碍；阻碍；障碍物 **2.** 口吃 **3.** 合法婚姻的障碍（如年龄不足）**4.** [～s]行李；辎重

impel [im'pel] (impelled; impelling) *vt.* **1.** 推动，推进；激励 **2.** 驱使；迫使；促成

impend [im'pend] *vi.* **1.** (罕) 悬挂 (*over*) **2.** 即将发生；逼近 (*over*)

impending [im'pendiŋ] *adj.* 即将发生的；逼近的

impenetrable [im'penitrəbl] *adj.* **1.** 刺不进的；穿不过的；透不进的 **2.** 费解的；不可测知的 **3.** 顽固的；不接受的 **4.** [物] 不可入性的 ‖ im.penetra'bility *n.*/impenetrably *adv.*

impenitence [im'penitəns], **impenitency** [im'penitənsi] *n.* 不知悔悟，无悔意

impenitent [im'penitənt] *adj. & n.* 不知悔悟的(人)；无悔意的(人)

imperative [im'perətiv] *adj.* **1.** 绝对必要的；紧急的；迫切的 **2.** 命令的；强制的；专横的 — *n.* **1.** 命令；规则；必须履行的责任 **2.** [语]祈使语气；祈使语气动词

imperceptible [ˌimpə'septəbl] *adj.* **1.** 感觉不到的；察觉不到的 **2.** 微妙的；细微的 ‖ imperceptibly *adv.*

imperfect [im'pəːfikt] *adj.* **1.** 不完美的；有缺陷的 **2.** 未完成的；不完整的 **3.** 法

律上不可实施的 **4.** 减弱的；缩小的 **5.** [语]未完成时的；未完成过去时的 — *n.* [语]未完成时；未完成过去时 ‖ ～ion [ˌimpə'fekʃən] *n.*/～ly *adv.*

imperial [im'piəriəl] *adj.* **1.** 帝国的；(英)(常 I-)英帝国的；有属地的 **2.** 皇帝(或皇后)的；最高权力的 **3.** 帝王一般的；威严的；堂皇的 **4.** 特大的，特等的 **5.** (度量衡)英制的 — *n.* **1.** 纸张尺寸((英)22×30 英寸；(美)23×31 英寸) **2.** 特大号；特等品 **3.** 帝嘴(留在下唇下面的小络胡须；因拿破仑三世留此须，故名) **4.** 帝俄时代的金币(=10 卢布) **5.** 公共马车的车顶;(放在公共马车上的)大行李箱 **6.** [I-][史]神圣罗马皇帝的拥护者(或士兵) ‖ ～ly *adv.*

imperialism [im'piəriəlizəm] *n.* 帝国主义

imperialist [im'piəriəlist] *n.* **1.** 帝国主义者 **2.** 皇帝的支持者；帝制的拥护者 **3.** [I-][史]神圣罗马皇帝的拥护者(或士兵) — *adj.* 帝国主义的

imperialistic [imˌpiəriə'listik] *adj.* **1.** 帝国主义的；帝国主义者的 **2.** 赞成帝国主义的

imperil [im'peril] (imperil(l)ed; imperil(l)ing) *vt.* 使处于危险；危害

imperious [im'piəriəs] *adj.* **1.** 专横的；老爷式的；傲慢的 **2.** 紧要的；迫切的 ‖ ～ly *adv.*

imperishable [im'periʃəbl] *adj.* 不朽的，不灭的 ‖ imperishably *adv.*

impermanent [im'pəːmənənt] *adj.* 非永久的，暂时的

impermeable [im'pəːmiəbl] *adj.* 不可渗透的，不能透过的；不能通过的 ‖ im.permea'bility, ～ness *n.*/impermeably *adv.*

impersonal [im'pəːsənəl] *adj.* **1.** 非个人的，

非特指某一个人的;不受个人情感影响的 2. 不具人格的;与人力无关的 3.【语】非人称的 — n. 非人称动词(或代词) ‖ ~ly adv.

impersonate [im'pə:səneit] vt. 1. 使人格化;体现 2. 扮演;模仿;假冒 ‖ im,perso'nation n. /impersonator n. 扮演者;模仿者;假冒者

impertinence [im'pə:tinəns], **impertinency** [im'pə:tinənsi] n. 1. 不恰当,不适合 2. 不得要领;离题 3. 不礼貌;傲慢;鲁莽 4. 无礼的举动(或言论)

impertinent [im'pə:tinənt] adj. 1. 不恰当的,不适合的 2. 不得要领的;离题的 3. 不礼貌的;傲慢的;鲁莽的 ‖ ~ly adv.

imperturbable [,impə:'tə:bəbl] adj. 沉着的,冷静的 ‖ **imperturbability** [,impə:,tə:bə'biliti] n. /imperturbably adv.

impervious [im'pə:vjəs] adj. 1. 不可渗透的,透不过的;穿不过的 2. 不受影响的;不受打扰的 3. 无动于衷的;不接受的

impetuous [im'petjuəs] adj. 1. 激烈的,猛烈的;迅疾的 2. 鲁莽的;冲动的;性急的,急躁的 ‖ **impetuosity** [im,petju'ɔsiti] n. / ~ly adv.

impetus ['impitəs] n. 1. 动力;原动力 2. 促进,推动;激励 3.【物】动量

impiety [im'paiəti] n. 1. 不虔诚,不敬神 2. 不敬;不孝 3. 不敬(或不孝)的行为(或言论)

impinge [im'pindʒ] vi. 1. 撞击;冲击(on, upon, against) 2. 紧密接触(on) 3. 侵犯;侵害(on, upon) — vt. (气体等)撞击

impious ['impiəs] adj. 1. 不虔诚的,不敬神的 2. 邪恶的 3. 不敬的;不孝的 ‖

~ly adv.

impish ['impiʃ] adj. 小鬼的;似小鬼的;顽皮的 ‖ ~ly adv.

implacable [im'plækəbl] adj. 1. 不饶恕的,不宽容的;难平息的;不能缓和的 2. 不能改变的 ‖ implacably adv.

implant [im'plɑ:nt] vt. 1. 插入;嵌入;种植 2. 牢固树立;灌输,注入 3.【医】移植 — ['implɑ:nt] n.【医】1. 植入物;植入片 2.(治疗癌症用的镭等放射性物质)植入管

implausible [im'plɔ:zəbl] adj. 难以置信的;不像真实的,似乎不合情理的 ‖ im,plausi'bility n.

implement ['implimənt] n. 1.(常~s)工具;器具 2. 家具;服装 3.〈苏格兰律〉履行 — ['impliment] vt. 1. 贯彻;完成;履行(契约,诺言等) 2. 给…提供方法为…供应器具 3. 把…填满;补充 ‖ ~ation [,implimen'teiʃən] n.

implicate ['implikeit] vt. 1. 含有…意思 2. 使(某人)牵连(于罪行等之中) 3.〔用被动语态〕影响 4.〈古〉绕住;使缠在一起 — ['implikit] n. 包含的东西 ‖ 'impli'cation n.

implicit [im'plisit] adj. 1. 含蓄的,不言明的 2. 内含的;固有的 3. 无疑的;无保留的;绝对的 ‖ ~ly adv.

implore [im'plɔ:] vt. 乞求,恳求,哀求

imply [im'plai] vt. 1. 含有…意思 2. 暗指;暗示;意指

impolite [,impə'lait] adj. 不礼貌的,失礼的;粗鲁的 ‖ ~ly adv. / ~ness n.

impolitic [im'pɔlitik] adj. 失策的;不当的;不审慎的;没见识的

imponderable [im'pɔndərəbl] adj. 不可称量的,无法正确估计的

import [im'pɔ:t] vt. 1. 进口;输入;引入 2. 意味着;表明 3.〈古〉对…重要;对

... 有关 — *vi.* 有关系;具重要性 — ['impɔ:t] *n.* 1. 进口;输入;进口物;输入品 2. 意义;含意 3. 重要(性) ‖ ~-ation [ˌimpɔː'teiʃən] *n.* 1. 进口,输入 2. 进口物;输入品 / ~er *n.* 进口商;输入者

importance [im'pɔ:təns] *n.* 1. 重要(性);重大;价值 2. 傲慢,自大

important [im'pɔ:tənt] *adj.* 1. 重要的;重大的 2. 大量的,许多的;大的 3. 有权力的;有地位的;显要的 4. 自高自大的 ‖ ~ly *adv.*

importunate [im'pɔ:tjunit] *adj.* 1. 强求的;缠扰不休的;讨厌的 2. 迫切的;坚持的 ‖ ~ly *adv.*

importune [im'pɔ:tjun] *vt.* 1. 向 ... 强求;向 ... 不断要求 2. 纠缠 3. (妓女)拉(客) — *vi.* 强求;纠缠不休 — *adj.* = importunate ‖ **importunity** [ˌimpɔː'tjuːniti] *n.*

impose [im'pəuz] *vt.* 1. 征(税等)把 ... 强加 3. (用欺骗手段)把(坏货、赝品等)硬塞给 4.【印】把 ... 拼版 — *vi.* 1. 利用(*on, upon*) 2. 欺骗(*on, upon*) 3. 施影响(*on, upon*)

imposing [im'pəuziŋ] *adj.* 1. 给人深刻印象的 2.(建筑物等)庄严的 3.(仪表)堂堂的

imposition [ˌimpə'ziʃən] *n.* 1. 征税;税款 2. 苛捐杂税;不公平的负担;过高的索价;不合理的要求 3. 欺诈;哄骗 4.〈英〉罚学生做的作业 5.〈宗〉按手礼

impossible [im'pɔsəbl] *adj.* 1. 不可能的,办不到的 2. 不可能存在;不会发生 3.〈口〉使人受不了的;非常讨厌的;很难对付的 ‖ im.possi'bility *n.* 不可能;不可能的事 / **impossibly** *adv.*

impost ['impəust] *n.* 1. 税;进口税;关税 2.【建】拱墩 3.(俚)(赛马用语)赛马负载重量(指在障碍赛或让分赛中) — *vt.* 对(进口商品)分类以估税

impostor, imposter [im'pɔstə] *n.* 冒名顶替者;江湖骗子

imposture [im'pɔstʃə] *n.* 冒名顶替;欺骗,欺诈

impotence ['impətəns]、**impotency** ['impətənsi] *n.* 1. 无力;软弱无能;虚弱 2. 无效;无法可想 3.【医】阳痿

impotent ['impətənt] *adj.* 1. 无力的;软弱无能的;虚弱的;不起作用的 2.【医】阳痿的 ‖ ~ly *adv.*

impound [im'paund] *vt.* 1. 将(牛等)关在栏中 2. 没收(物件);扣押(人) 3. 贮(水)备灌溉用

impoverish [im'pɔvəriʃ] *vt.* 1. 使穷困 2. 使力衰竭、资源等)枯竭

impracticable [im'præktikəbl] *adj.* 1. 不能实行的,行不通的 2. 不能用的;不能通行的 3. 难对付的;顽强的

impractical [im'præktikəl] *adj.* 1. 不切实际的;不能实行的;不现实的 ‖ ~ly *adv.*

imprecation [ˌimpri'keiʃən] *n.* 诅咒;咒骂;咒语

imprecise [ˌimpri'sais] *adj.* 1. 不精确的;不明确的,含糊不清的 ‖ ~ly *adv.*

impregnable [im'pregnəbl] *adj.* 1. 攻不破的;不可推的 2. 坚定不移的,毫不动摇的 3. 可以受孕的,(卵等)可以受精的

impregnate ['impregneit] *vt.* 1. 使怀孕,使妊娠;使受精 2. 使充满;灌满;灌输;使(土地)肥沃;施肥于 — [im'pregnit] *adj.* 1. 怀孕的,妊娠的 2. 充满的;浸透的(*with*) ‖ impreg'nation *n.* 1. 受孕;受精 2. 充满;饱和;浸渍 3. 注入,灌输 4. 浸渍液;充满他物的东西;灌输的影响

impresario [ˌimpre'sɑːriəu] ([复] impresa-

rios〉〈意〉n.(乐团、歌剧团等的)经理;
乐队指挥;演出人;主办者;舞台监督;
监制人

impress [im'pres] vt. 1. 印;压印;铭刻;
给…极深的印象 2. 传递,发送 4.
【电】外加(电压或电动势) — vi. 给人
印象;引人注目 —['impres] n. 1. 印
记;压痕;特征 2. 效应;效应

impression [im'preʃən] n. 1. 压印;印记;
压痕 2.【印刷】印数;印次;印刷品;
(雕版等的)印图 3.(油画的)底色;(作
装饰等用的)漆层 4. 印象;感想 5. 效
果;影响 6.【医】(牙齿的)印模 7.(绘
画、戏剧等中所用的)漫画式模仿‖
~ism n.(绘画、文艺等方面的)印象主
义;印象派 / ~ist adj. 印象主义的 n.
印象派艺术家

impressionable [im'preʃənəbl] adj. 1. 易
刻的;易印的;可塑的 2. 易受影响的;
敏感的‖ **impressionably** adv.

impressive [im'presiv] adj. 给人深刻印象
的;感人的:an ~ scene 难忘的场面‖
~ **ly** adv.

imprint [im'print] vt. 1. 印;盖(印);压
(印) 2. 在…上压出记号;使带上…
的特征(on, in) 3. 铭刻;使被牢记 —
['imprint] n. 1. 印记;痕迹;特
征;深刻的印象 3.(出版者在标题页或
版权页上关于出版时间、地点等的)出
版事项,版本说明

imprison [im'prizn] vt. 1. 关押;监禁 2.
限制;束缚‖ ~ **ment** n. 关押;监禁

improbable [im'prɔbəbl] adj. 1. 未必会
的;不大可能(发生)的;未必确实的 2.
奇异的;荒谬可笑的‖ **im.proba'bility**
n. 不大可能;不大可能的事 / **improba-
bly** adv.

impromptu [im'prɔmptju:] adj. & adv. 无
准备的(地),临时的(地),即兴的

(地),即席的(地) — n. 即兴演奏;临
时讲话;即席之作

improper [im'prɔpə] adj. 1. 不适当的,不
合适的 2. 不正确的;不正确的,错误
的 3. 不合礼仪的;不成体统的;不正
派的‖ ~ **ly** adv.‖ ~ **fraction**【数】假
分数

impropriety [,imprə'praiəti] n. 1. 不适当;
不正确;不得体的话;不合标准 2. 不
合适的举止;不正当的行为 3. 用词错
误;用词不当

improve [im'pru:v] vt. 1. 使更好,改善,改
进;增进 2. 利用(机会等) 3. 抓住(机
会等)进行开导 4. 提高(田地、地产)
的价值 — vi. 1. 变得更好 2. 增加;升
值‖ ~ **r** n. 1. 改进者;改进物 2.(英)
学徒,练习生

improvement [im'pru:vmənt] n. 1. 改进;
增值;增进 2. 经改进的东西;改进措
施 3.(为使田地、地产增值所进行的)
改良 4. 更优秀(或更进步)的人

improvidence [im'prɔvidəns] n. 无远见;不
顾将来;不节约

improvident [im'prɔvidənt] adj. 无远见
的;不顾将来的;不注意节约的

improvisation [,imprəvai'zeiʃən] n. 1. 即
席创作;即席演奏(或演唱) 2. 临时凑
合成的东西;即兴作品

improvise ['imprəvaiz] vt. vi. 1. 即席创作(诗
歌等);即席演奏(或演唱) 2. 临时准
备;临时凑成

imprudence [im'pru:dəns] n. 1. 轻率;鲁
莽 2. 轻率的行为;鲁莽的行为

imprudent [im'pru:dənt] adj. 轻率的;鲁
莽的‖ ~ **ly** adv.

impudence ['impjudəns] n. 1. 厚颜无耻;
冒失;无礼 2. 厚颜无耻(或冒失、无
礼)的行为(或言语)

impudent ['impjudənt] adj. 厚颜无耻的;

冒失的；无礼的 ‖ ~ly *adv.*

impugn [im'pju:n] *vt.* 指责，非难；对（言词等）表示怀疑；反驳

impulse ['impʌls] *n.* 1. 推动；冲力 2. 冲动；刺激 3.〔物〕冲量；脉冲；〔生理〕神经冲动 — *vt. & vi.* 推动；促进

impulsion [im'pʌlʃən] *n.* 1. 推动；推动力 2. 冲动；刺激

impulsive [im'pʌlsiv] *adj.* 1. 冲动的；由冲动所造成的 2. 冲击的 ‖ ~ly *adv.*

impunity [im'pju:niti] *n.* 不受惩罚；免罪；不受损失；不受损害

impure [im'pjuə] *adj.* 1. 不纯的；掺假的；掺杂的 2.（颜色、音调等）混合的 3. 不纯洁的；脏的；不道德的；下流的 4.（语言）不规范的 ‖ ~ly *adv.*

impurity [im'pjuərəti] *n.* 1. 不纯；不洁 2. 杂质；混杂物 3. 下流；不道德；不贞节

imputation [impju:'teiʃən] *n.* 1. 归罪；转嫁罪责 2. 诋毁；非难；污名

impute [im'pju:t] *vt.* 1. 把…归因于，把…归咎于；把（罪名、责任等）推于；把…转嫁于 (*to*)

In〔化〕元素铟(indium)的符号

in [in] *prep.* 1.〔表示地点、场所、部位〕在…里；在…上 2.〔表示时间〕在…期间；在…以后 3.〔表示过程〕在当儿，在…过程中 4.〔表示范围、领域、方面〕在…之内；在…方面 5.〔表示状态、情况〕处在…中 6.〔表示职业、活动〕从事于；参加着 7.〔表示地位、形式、方式等〕按照，以，符合于 8.〔表示述意的途径或表示所用的原料、材料〕以用，以 9.〔表示服饰〕穿着；戴着 10.〔表示数量、程度〕以，以…的；以…中 11.〔表示方向〕朝，向 12.〔表示能力、含有〕包含在…之中 13.〔表示同一性〕在…身上 14.〔表示原因〕由于，为了，作为…的表

示 15.〔表示动作的对象〕对于；在于 16.〔表示动作的方向和结果〕进入到，进…，为(= into) — *adv.* 1. 进，入 2. 朝里；道近；里头 3. 在屋里；在家 4. 在狱中 5.（季节、车、船等）已到达；已来临 6.（庄稼等）已收进已储藏；（土地）已耕好 7. 完全成功；取胜 8.（服装等）入时；（食品等）正上市 9. 当政，在朝；（候选人）当选 10.（火等）燃烧着；（灯）亮着 11.（板球等）正在攻球 12.（油井）产油中 13.（法令等）在执行中；（证据等）在手头 14. 一致 15. 处于某种关系 — *adj.* 1. 在里面的；朝里面的 2. 执政的，在朝的 3.（车、船等）到站的；抵港的 4.（美口）赚进…的 5. 时髦的，流行的 — *n.* 1.〔常～s〕在朝派，执政者；知情者 2.〔常～s〕（板球赛）攻球方 3.（美口）入口；门路 4.（美俚）（与大人物的）特殊关系；提携 ‖ '~-and-'out *adj.* 1.（短期内同一证券买进卖出的，吃进抛出的，短期证券交易的 2.（旅游者等）进进出出的；时来时去的；暂时的 3.（工作等）时断时续的；时好时坏的；不正常的；非法的 *adv.* 时进时出地 *n.*（美俚）性交，交媾

in [in] *prep.*〔拉〕= in(只接用拉丁文的名词，构成状语词组，这些词组多用于法律文件、科技文献等中) ‖ ~ *absentia* [æb'senʃiə] 缺席 /~ *memoriam* [mi'mɔ:riæm] 作为纪念 /~ *statu quo* ['steitju:'kwəu] 按原样；维持着原状 /~ *vitro* ['vaitrəu] 在试管内；在体外

in. *abbr.* inch(es)

in- *pref.* 1. 表示"在内"，"进"，"入"，"向"，"朝" : inmate, invasion 2. 附在形容词或由该形容词派生而来的词之前，构成相应的新形容词及其派生词) 表示"不"，"非"，"无" : inactive, inactively

-in *comb. form* 1. 表示"有组织的抗议（或

示威)"；teach-*in* **2.** 表示"公开的集体活动"

inability [ˌinəˈbiləti] *n.* 无能；无力；无能为力，不能

inaccessible [ˌinækˈsesəbl] *adj.* 达不到的；进不去的；难接近的；难得到的 ‖ **inaccessibility** [ˈinækˌsesəˈbiləti] *n.*

inaccuracy [inˈækjurəsi] *n.* **1.** 不精密(性)；不精确(性)；不准确(度) **2.** 不精确的东西，错误

inaccurate [inˈækjurit] *adj.* 不精密的；不准确的；错误的 ‖ **~ly** *adv.*

inactive [inˈæktiv] *adj.* **1.** 不活动的；不活跃的；迟钝的；懒散的 **2.** 暂停不用的；闲散没事做的【军】非现役的 **3.**【医】静止性的，非活动性的 **4.**【化】不旋(光)的；非放射性的 ‖ **~ly** *adv.* ，**inac-tivity** *n.*

inadequacy [inˈædikwəsi] *n.* **1.** 不充足；不适当 **2.** 不够格；无法胜任 **3.** 不足之处；弱点，缺陷

inadequate [inˈædikwit] *adj.* **1.** 不充足的；不适当的；不够格的；不能胜任的 ‖ **~ly** *adv.*

inadmissible [ˌinədˈmisəbl] *adj.* 不可接受的；不能承认的；不允许的，不许可的

inadvertence [ˌinədˈvətəns]，**inadvertency** [ˌinədˈvətənsi] *n.* **1.** 漫不经心 **2.** 粗心大意；疏漏，错误

inadvertent [ˌinədˈvətənt] *adj.* **1.** 不经心的；疏忽的 **2.** 出于无心的，非故意的 ‖ **~ly** *adv.*

inadvisable [ˌinədˈvaizəbl] *adj.* 不可取的；不妥当的；失策的；不明智的

inalienable [inˈeiljənəbl] *adj.* 不可分割的；不能让与的；不可剥夺的

inane [iˈnein] *adj.* **1.** 空洞的；空虚的 **2.** 空洞的，空虚的；无意义的；愚蠢的 — *n.* [the ~] 空洞无物；无限空间 ‖ **~ly** *adv.*

inanimate [inˈænimət] *adj.* **1.** 无生命的 **2.** 无生气的，没精打采的 ‖ **~ly** *adv.*

inanition [ˌinəˈniʃən] *n.* **1.** 空虚，空洞 **2.** (营养不足造成的)虚乏 **3.** 死气沉沉，没精打采

inanity [iˈnænəti] *n.* **1.** 空虚；虚幻 **2.** 愚昧，无知 **3.** 蠢事；蠢话

inapplicable [inˈæplikəbl] *adj.* 不适用的；不适宜的

inappreciable [ˌinəˈpriːʃəbl] *adj.* 小得难以觉察的；微不足道的

inappropriate [ˌinəˈprəupriət] *adj.* 不恰当的；不相宜的 ‖ **~ly** *adv.* ／**~ness** *n.*

inapt [inˈæpt] *adj.* **1.** 不适当的，不合适的(*for*) **2.** 不熟练的；笨拙的；拙劣的(*at*)

inaptitude [inˈæptitjuːd] *n.* **1.** 不适当，不合适 **2.** 不熟练；拙劣

inarticulate [ˌinɑːˈtikjulət] *adj.* **1.** 口齿不清的，发音不清楚的 **2.** 哑口无言的；说不出的；不能言喻的；未经表达的 **3.** 不善于表达内心思想的 **4.**【动】无关节的，无铰的

inasmuch [ˌinəzˈmʌtʃ] *adv.* [与 as 连用，起连接词的作用]因为，由于

inattention [ˌinəˈtenʃən] *n.* 不注意；漫不经心；疏忽

inattentive [ˌinəˈtentiv] *adj.* 不注意的；漫不经心的；疏忽的 ‖ **~ly** *adv.* ／**~ness** *n.*

inaudible [inˈɔːdəbl] *adj.* 听不见的 ‖ **inaudibly** *adv.*

inaugural [iˈnɔːgjurəl] *adj.* 就职的；开幕的；创立的；首次的；一 — *n.* [美] 就职演说；就职典礼；首次讲课

inaugurate [iˈnɔːgjureit] *vt.* **1.** 开始；开创 **2.** 为...举行就职典礼 **3.** 为...举行开幕式；为...举行落成(或通车等)仪

式 ‖ **i**,**naugu'ration** n.

inauspicious [ˌinɔːs'piʃəs] adj. 不祥的，凶
兆的；不利的 ‖ **~ly** adv.

inborn ['in'bɔːn] adj. 1. 生来的，天生的 2.
先天的，遗传的

inbreed ['in'briːd] (inbred['in'bred]) vt. 1.
【生】使同系交配，使近交 2. 使在内部
发生（或产生）

inc. abbr. incorporated

Incabloc ['iŋkəblɔk] n.（手表内的）因加百
录防震器

incalculable [in'kælkjuləbl] adj. 1. 数不清
的，无数的，极大的 2. 难预测的；不可
靠的，易变的

incandescence [ˌinkæn'desəns] n. 白热
光；白炽（光）

incandescent [ˌinkæn'desənt] adj. 1. 白热
的，白炽的；an ~ lamp 白炽灯 2. 极亮
的，灿烂的；闪闪发光的；炽热的；热情
的

incantation [ˌinkæn'teiʃən] n. 咒语；符咒；
妖术

incapable [in'keipəbl] adj. 1. 无能力的，
不能的；不会 2.【律】无资格的 ‖
in,**capa'bility** n.

incapacitate [ˌinkə'pæsiteit] vt. 1. 使无能
力，使伤残 3.【律】使（在法律上）无
行为能力

incapacity [ˌinkə'pæsəti] n. 1. 无能力 2.
【律】无行为能力

incarcerate [in'kɑːsəreit] vt. 监禁；禁闭，
囚于，局限于 ‖ **in**,**carce'ration** n.

incarnate [in'kɑːneit] vt. 1. 赋予…以形
体；使成化身；使实体化 2. 使具体化
化；使体现 — [in'kɑːnit] adj. 1. 化身
的；人体化的；实体化的 2. 肉色的；红
的；玫瑰红的 ‖ **in**,**car'nation** n. 化身 2.
【医】入肉

incendiary [in'sendjəri] adj. 1. 放火的，纵
火的；燃烧的 2. 煽动性的 — n. 1. 纵
火者；燃烧弹；可引起燃烧的东西 2.
煽动者

incense¹ ['insens] n. 1. 香；焚香时的烟 2.
香气 3. 奉承，恭维 — vt. 用香熏；
对…焚香 — vi. 焚香

incense² [in'sens] vt. 使发怒，激怒

incentive [in'sentiv] n. 刺激；鼓励 — adj.
刺激的；鼓励的

inception [in'sepʃən] n. 开始，发端；初期

incessant [in'sesənt] adj. 不停的，连续的，
持续不断的；频繁的 ‖ **~ly** adv.

incest ['insest] n. 乱伦（罪）；血亲相奸 ‖
in'cestuous adj.

inch [intʃ] n. 1. 英寸（略作 in.）2. [~es]
身高；身材 3.（距离、数量、程度等的）
少许，一点儿 — vt. & vi.（使）缓慢地
移动；（使）渐进

inchoate ['inkəueit, in'kəuit] adj. 1. 刚开
始的；初期的 2. 不完全的；不成熟的
‖ **~ly** adv. / **~ness** n.

incidence ['insidəns] n. 发生；影响；发生
（或影响）方式；发生率

incident ['insidənt] n. 1. 所带事件；小事
件，事情 2.（政治性）事件，事变 3.（小
说、剧本中的）插曲；枝节 4.【律】附带
条件；附属于财产的权利和义务 —
adj. 1. 易发生的；伴随而来的（to）2.
【律】附带的，附属的（to）3.【物】入射
的

incidental [ˌinsi'dentl] adj. 1. 附带的，伴
随的，非主要的 2. 偶然碰到的；偶然
发生的 — n. 1. 附带事件 2. [~s] 附
项；杂费 ‖ **~ly** adv. 附带地；偶然
地；顺便说及地

incinerate [in'sinəreit] vt. 把…烧成灰；
烧尽；火化，把…火葬 — vi. 烧成灰，

烧尽;火化,火葬 ‖ **in·cine'ration** *n.* 焚化;火化,火葬 / **incinerator** *n.* 焚化者;焚化炉;火化炉,焚尸炉

incipient [in'sipiənt] *adj.* 开始的;刚出现的;早期的

incise [in'saiz] *vt.* 1. 切入;切开 2. 雕刻

incision [in'siʒən] *n.* 1. 切入;切开;切口 2.【植】(叶的)缺刻 3. 雕刻

incisive [in'saisiv] *adj.* 1. 切入的;锋利的 2. 尖锐的;深刻的;透彻的 3.【解】切牙的,门齿的

incisor [in'saizə] *n.*【解】切牙,门齿

incite [in'sait] *vt.* 激动;刺激;煽动;促成 ‖ ~ment *n.*

incivility [,insi'viləti] *n.* 1. 无礼貌;粗暴 2. 不礼貌的言行;粗暴的言行

inclemency [in'klemənsi] *n.* 1. 险恶;严寒;狂风暴雨 2. 冷酷;无情

inclement [in'klemənt] *adj.* 1.(天气、气候)险恶的,酷烈的;寒冷的;狂风暴雨的 2.(人)严酷的,无情的

inclination [,inkli'neiʃən] *n.* 1. 倾斜;点头;弯腰 2. 斜坡;倾度;【数】倾角,斜角 3. 倾向;爱好;爱好的事物

incline [in'klain] *vi.* 1. 倾斜 2. 曲身;弯腰;点头 3. 倾向(于);赞同;喜爱 4.【军】侧转前进 — *vt.* 1. 使倾斜 (身);点(头);弯(腰) 2.[常用被动语态]使倾向于;使想要 — *n.* 斜面;斜坡 ‖ ~d *adj.*

inclose [in'klauz] *vt.* = enclose

inclosure [in'klauʒə] *n.* = enclosure

include [in'klu:d] *vt.* 1. 包住;关住 2. 包括;包含;把…算入

inclusion [in'klu:ʒən] *n.* 1. 包括;包含 2. 内含物;[生](细胞原生质的)内含物;【地】包体;【数】包含

inclusive [in'klu:siv] *adj.* 1. 首末日(或页

码)包括在内的 2. 包括的;包含的 3. 一切开支(或项目)包括在内的 ‖ ~ly *adv.* / ~ness *n.*

incognito [in'kɔgnitəu] *adj. & adv.* 隐姓埋名的(地);微行的(地) — *n.* 隐姓埋名者;微行(者)

incoherence [,inkəu'hiərəns] *n.* 1. 无凝聚性;支离破碎;松散 2. 不连贯;无条理;语无伦次

incoherent [,inkəu'hiərənt] *adj.* 1. 无凝聚力的;支离破碎的;松散的 2. 不连贯的;无条理的;语无伦次的 ‖ ~ly *adv.*

income ['inkʌm] *n.* 收入;收益;进款;所得 ‖ ~ tax 所得税

incoming ['in,kʌmiŋ] *adj.* 1. 进来的 2. 正从外国移入的 3. 新来的;继任的 4. (收益等)正在产生的;即将取得的 — *n.* 1. 进来;到来 2.[常~s]收入

incommunicable [,inkə'mju:nikəbl] *adj.* 1. 不能传达的;不能表达的;不能言传的 2. 不爱说话的;孤僻的

incomparable [in'kɔmpərəbl] *adj.* 1. 无比的,无双的 2. 不能比较的;无共同衡量基础的 (with, to) ‖ **incomparably** *adv.*

incompatible [,inkəm'pætəbl] *adj.* 1. 不相容的;不一致的;不能共存的 (with): Water is ~ with fire. 水火不相容 2. 【医】(药物)配伍禁忌的;(血型、机体组织)不能配合的 3. 不能溶合成一体的 ‖ **'incom·pati'bility** *n.* / **incompatibly** *adv.*

incompetence, [in'kɔmpitəns] **incompetency** [in'kɔmpitənsi] *n.* 1. 不胜任;不称职;不适合;不够格 2. 无能;不熟练 3.【律】无行为能力;法律上无资格

incompetent [in'kɔmpitənt] *adj.* 1. 不胜任的;不称职的;不适合的;不够格的 2. 无能的;不熟练的 3.【律】无行为能力

的,法律上无资格的 ‖ ~ly adv.

incomplete [ˌinkəmˈpliːt] adj. 不完全的;未完成的;不完善的 ‖ ~ly adv.

incomprehensible [inˌkɔmpriˈhensəbl] adj. 1. 不能理解的;难懂的;莫名其妙的 2. 〈古〉无边的;无限的 ‖ incomprehensibly adv.

inconceivable [ˌinkənˈsiːvəbl] adj. 1. 不能想象的;不可思议的;不可理解的 2. 〈口〉难以相信的;惊人的 ‖ inconceivably adv.

incongruous [inˈkɔŋɡruəs] adj. 1. 不调和的;自相矛盾的;不一致的(with) 2. 不适合的;不恰当的;不合理的

inconsequential [inˌkɔnsiˈkwenʃəl] adj. 1. 无意义的;无关紧要的;微不足道的 2. 不连贯的;不合逻辑的 — n. 无关紧要的事物 ‖ ~ly adv.

inconsiderable [ˌinkənˈsidərəbl] adj. 不值得考虑的;无足轻重的;微小的

inconsiderate [ˌinkənˈsidərət] adj. 1. 不替别人着想的,不体谅别人的 2. 考虑不周的,粗心的;轻率的

inconsistency [ˌinkənˈsistənsi] n. 1. 不一致;不协调;前后矛盾;不一贯 2. 不一致的事物;自相矛盾的行为(或言论) 3. 反复无常,易变

inconsistent [ˌinkənˈsistənt] adj. 1. 不一致的;不协调的(with) 2. 前后矛盾的,不一贯的;不合逻辑的 3. 反复无常的,易变的 ‖ ~ly adv.

inconsolable [ˌinkənˈsəuləbl] adj. 没法安慰的;极度沮丧的

inconspicuous [ˌinkənˈspikjuəs] adj. 1. 难以觉察的;不显著的;不引人注意的 2. 〔植〕(花)不显著的(指花朵小、色泽淡等) ‖ ~ly adv.

inconstancy [inˈkɔnstənsi] n. 1. 反复无常,易变;不坚定 2. 不规则;常变

inconstant [inˈkɔnstənt] adj. 1. (人)反复无常的,轻率易变的;不坚定易变的 2. (事物)无规则的;常变的

incontestable [ˌinkənˈtestəbl] adj. 无可争辩的;不可否认的

incontinent [inˈkɔntinənt] adj. 1. 不能自制的,无节制的 2. 荒淫的 3. 不能保持(或控制)的 4.〔医〕失禁的 ‖ incontinence, incontinency n.

incontrovertible [ˌinkɔntrəˈvəːtəbl] adj. 无可辩驳的;颠扑不破的;不容置疑的

inconvenience [ˌinkənˈviːnjəns] n. 1. 不方便;打扰 2. 不便之处;烦扰事 — vt. 使感不便

inconvenient [ˌinkənˈviːnjənt] adj. 不方便的;引起不方便的;烦扰的 ‖ ~ly adv.

inconvertible [ˌinkənˈvəːtəbl] adj. 1. 不能变换(或转换)的 2.(货币)不能兑换成外汇的;(纸币)不能兑换成硬币的

incorporate [inˈkɔːpəreit] vt. 1. 结合;合并;收编 2. 使混合的;使具体化;使实体化/体现 4. 使结成社团;使组成公司 3. 使加入社团团体 — vi. 1. 合并;混合(with) 2. 成为社团;组成公司 — [inˈkɔːpərət] adj. 1. 一体化的;合并在一起的 2. 紧密结合的 3.(结成)社团的;公司的 ‖ ~d adj. / inˌcorpoˈration n. 1. 结合;合并;社团;公司 2. 掺合;混合

incorporeal [ˌinkɔːˈpɔːriəl] adj. 1. 非物质的,精神的;无实体的,无形的 2.〔律〕无形体的 ‖ ~ly adv.

incorrect [ˌinkəˈrekt] adj. 不正确的,错误的;不妥当的,不合适的 ‖ ~ly adv. / ~ness n.

incorrigible [inˈkɔridʒəbl] adj. 难以纠正的;不可改造的,不可教育的;固执的;难弄的 — n. 不改悔的人,不可救药的人 ‖ incorrigibly adv.

incorruptible [ˌinkə'rʌptəbl] *adj.* **1.** (物) 不易腐蚀的；不易败坏的 **2.** (人) 收买不了的、廉洁的 — *n.* 不易腐蚀的东西 ‖ **incorruptibly** *adv.*

increase [in'kriːs] *vt.* 增加；增殖；增进 — *vi.* 增加；繁殖 — ['inkriːs] *n.* 增加；增长；增殖；增进

increasingly [in'kriːsiŋli] *adv.* 继续增加地；越来越多地；日益

incredible [in'kredəbl] *adj.* **1.** 不可信的；难以置信的 **2.** (口) 不可思议的；未必可能的；惊人的 ‖ **incredibly** *adv.*

incredulity [ˌinkri'djuːliti] *n.* 不相信；不轻信；怀疑

incredulous [in'kredjuləs] *adj.* **1.** 不相信的；不轻信的 (of) **2.** 表示怀疑的 ‖ **~ly** *adv.*

increment ['inkrimənt] *n.* **1.** 增长；增额；增值 **2.** 【数】增量

incriminate [in'krimineit] *vt.* **1.** 控告；显示...有罪 **2.** 连累 (某人)；归咎于

incrust [in'krʌst] *vt.* & *vi.* = encrust

incubate ['inkjubeit] *vt.* **1.** 孵(卵)、孵化 **2.** 使发育；酝酿 — *vi.* 孵卵；【医】潜伏；酝酿 ‖ **incu'bation** *n.* **1.** 孵卵、孵化 **2.**【医】潜伏 **3.** 酝酿 ‖ **incubator** *n.* **1.** 孵化器；孵化员 **2.** 恒温箱 (用于放置早产婴儿及需要特殊照顾的新生儿) **3.** 恒温器 (用于培养细菌等)

inculcate ['inkʌlkeit, in'kʌlkeit] *vt.* **1.** 反复灌输 **2.** 谆谆教诲

incumbency [in'kʌmbənsi] *n.* **1.** 现存职位 (或职权)；任期 **2.** 责任；义务 **3.** 上覆状态；上覆物

incumbent [in'kʌmbənt] *adj.* **1.** 成为责任的；义不容辞的 (on, upon) **2.** 压 (或覆)盖在上面的 (on) **3.** 靠着的 **4.** 现任的 **5.** (地层)上覆的 **6.**【植】(花药)内曲的；(子叶)背倚的 — *n.* **1.** 领圣

职者；教区牧师 **2.** 现任者；在职者

incumber [in'kʌmbə] *vt.* = encumber

incur [in'kɜː] (incurred; incurring[in'kɜːriŋ]) *vt.* 招致；惹起；遭受

incurable [in'kjuərəbl] *adj.* (人或病)医不好的；不可救药的；不能矫正的 — *n.* 患不治之症的病人 ‖ **incurably** *adv.*

incurious [in'kjuəriəs] *adj.* **1.** 不好奇心的；不爱穷究细问的；不感兴趣的 **2.** 不关心的 **3.** 没趣味的；不新颖的；不吸引人的

incursion [in'kɜːʃən] *n.* **1.** 进入；流入 **2.** 侵入；袭击；侵犯

indebted [in'detid] *adj.* **1.** 负债的 (to) **2.** 受惠的；蒙恩的；感激的 ‖ **~ness** *n.*

indecency [in'diːsnsi] *n.* **1.** 下流；猥亵；粗鄙；下流言行 **2.** (口) 不适当；不合适

indecent [in'diːsnt] *adj.* **1.** 下流的；猥亵的；粗鄙的 **2.** (口) 不适当的；不合适的

indecision [ˌindi'siʒən] *n.* 无决断力，优柔寡断，犹豫不决

indecisive [ˌindi'saisiv] *adj.* **1.** 非决定性的；非结论性的 **2.** 不决断的，优柔寡断的，犹豫不决的 **3.** 未清楚地标明的；不明确的；模糊的 ‖ **~ly** *adv.* ‖ **~ness** *n.*

indeed [in'diːd] *adv.* **1.** 真正地；实际上 **2.** [加强语气]确实，实在 **3.** [表示让步]当然，固然 **4.** [表示进一层的意思]甚至 **5.** [表示惊讶、讽刺、轻蔑等]真的；真是

indefatigable [ˌindi'fætigəbl] *adj.* 不倦的；不屈不挠的；坚持不懈的

indefensible [ˌindi'fensəbl] *adj.* **1.** 无法防御的，无法守卫的 **2.** (理论等)站不住脚的 **3.** 不可原谅的

indefinite [in'definət] *adj.* **1.** 无定限的；无限期的 **2.** 不明确的；模糊的 **3.**【语】

不定的：the ～ article 不定冠词 4.【植】
(雄蕊）无定数的 ‖ ～ly adv.

indelible [in'delibl] *adj.* 1. 去不掉的；洗
不掉的；擦不掉的；持久的 2. 留下下不
易除去的痕迹的 ‖ **indelibly** *adv.*

indelicacy [in'delikəsi] *n.* 1. 不雅，粗俗；
粗鲁，粗率 2. 粗俗的东西；粗鄙的言
行

indelicate [in'delikit] *adj.* 1. 不文雅的，粗
俗的 2. 粗鲁的，粗率的 ‖ ～ly *adv.*

indemnify [in'demnifai] *vt.* 1. 保障；保护
2. 使免于受罚 3. 赔偿；补偿

indemnity [in'demniti] *n.* 1. 保障；保护
2. 免罚；赦免 3. 赔偿；补偿 4. 赔偿
物（尤指战败国的）赔款

indent[1] [in'dent] *vt.* 1. 把…刻成锯齿
形，使成犬牙状；打缺刻于 2. 把（一张
抄本或一式两份或两份以上文件的纸
张）按犬牙状割开（以备将来拼接验证
文件真伪之用）3. 一式两份（或两份
以上）地起草（文件、合同等）4.（印刷
中或书写中）缩排；缩格书写 5.（英）
(用双联单）订（货）6. 用榫眼接牢 —
vi. 1. 刻成锯齿形；打缺刻 2. 订合同
3. 缩排；缩格书写 4.（英）(用双联单
订货（向…）正式申请（on）；动用
(on) — ['indent] *n.* 1. 锯齿形；(V 字
形）凹口、缺口，凹陷 2.（印刷
中的）首行缩排；书写时的）首行缩排
4.（英）国外订货单 5.（英）征用令

indent[2] [in'dent] *vt.* 1. 在…上压凹痕 2.
压凹印（图案等）— ['indent] *n.*

indentation [,inden'teiʃən] *n.* 1. 呈锯齿
形；凹口，缺口，凹陷 2.（海岸等的）湾
入，凹入 3.（印刷中的）首行缩排；(书
写时的）首行缩排 4. 压凹；凹痕

indention [in'denʃən] *n.* 1.（印刷中的）首
行缩排（书写时的）首行缩排 2.（缩排
或缩格书写留出的）空格 2. 呈锯齿

形；凹口，缺口，凹陷

indenture [in'dentʃə] *n.* 1. 契约；双联合
同 2.（常～s）师徒契约；定期服务合
同；take up one's ～s 学徒期满 3. 凭单
(如商业上的传票、清单等）4. 凹口，
缺口，凹陷 — *vt.* 以契约束缚（学徒
等）

independence [,indi'pendəns] *n.* 1. 独立；
自主；自立：Independence Day 美国独立
纪念日（7 月 4 日）2. 足以维持闲居生
活的收入（或资产）

independent [,indi'pendənt] *adj.* 1. 独立
的；自治的；有主见的 2. 不愿受约束
的（从人等）是够维持独立生活的；
富裕得无须为生计而操劳的 4. 单独
的，不接受外援的；不承担义务的 5.
无党派的 6.[I-]【宗】独立派的 7.【语】
独立的 8.【数】无关的，独立的 — *n.*
1. 独立自主的人 2. 无党派人士 3.
[I-]【宗】独立派教徒，公理会教徒 ‖
～ly *adv.*

indescribable [,indis'kraibəbl] *adj.* 1. 难以
形容的；描写不出的 2. 模糊的；不明
确的 ‖ **indescribably** *adv.*

indestructible [,indis'trʌktəbl] *adj.* 破坏不
了的，不可毁灭的 ‖ **indestructibility**
['indis,trʌktə'biləti] *n.* / **indestructibly**
adv.

indeterminate [,indi'təminit] *adj.* 1. 不确
定的，无定限的；不明确的；模糊的 2.
不会有结果的；仍有疑问的；未决定
的；未解决的 3. 无法预先知道的 4.
【语】不定的，中性的 5.【数】不（确）定
的；未定元的 6.【植】总状的；无限的

index ['indeks] ([复] indexes 或 indices
['indisiz]) *n.* 1. 索引 2. 指标；标志；标
志 3. 指数 4.（刻度盘上的）指针；【机】
(铣床）分度头；【印】指示符号；参见
号（即☞）5. 食指（亦作 ～ finger）6.

[the I-]（天主教的教廷禁书目录）— vt. 1. 为［书籍等］做索引 2. 把（资料等）编入索引 3. 指向；指明 — vi. 做索引 ‖ ~ation[ˌindek'seiʃən] n.【经】（工资等的）指数化

India ['indjə] n. 印度［南亚国家］

Indian ['indjən] adj. 1. 印度的；印度人的；印度文化的 2. 印第安人的；印第安文化的；西印度群岛的；西印度群岛文化的 3. 玉米制的 — n. 1. 印度人 2. 印第安人 3. 印第安语 4. 长期住在印度的欧洲人（尤指英国人）‖ ~ club（体操用的）瓶状木操棒 / ~ corn（英）玉蜀黍，玉米，包米 / ~ Ocean [the I- O-]（美国北部或其他国家的）晚秋的晴暖宜人气候，小阳春 2. 兴旺的晚景；愉快宁静的晚年

Indiana [ˌindi'ænə] n. 印第安纳［美国州名］

indicate ['indikeit] vt. 1. 指示；指出 2. 表明（症状、原因等）；象征；预示；暗示 3. 需要；使或为必要 4. 简要地说明

indication [ˌindi'keiʃən] n. 1. 指示；指出；表示 2. 象征；暗示；迹象 3. 【医】指征；适应症 4. 指示器读数

indicative [in'dikətiv] adj. 1. 指示的；表示的；象征的；预示的 2.【语】陈述的，直陈的 — n.【语】陈述语气；动词的陈述语气形式

indicator ['indikeitə] n. 1. 指示者；指示物 2.【机】指示器；示功器 3.【化】指示剂

indices ['indisiz] index 的复数

indict [in'dait] vt. 控告，告发；对……起诉

indictment [in'daitmənt] n. 1. 控告，告发；起诉 2. 起诉书，诉状

indifference [in'difrəns] n. 1. 不关心；冷淡；不计较 2. 无关紧要；不在乎 3. 中立；中性

indifferency [in'difrənsi] = indifference

indifferent [in'difrənt] adj. 1. 不关心的；冷淡的；不感兴趣的 2. 无关紧要的；不在乎的 3. 一般的；质量不高的；能力平常的；差得很的 4. 无偏袒的；中立的 5.【化】【物】中性的，惰性的；随遇的 6.【生】不分化的；随遇的 — n.（在政治或宗教等方面）冷淡的人 ‖ ~ly adv.

indigenous [in'didʒinəs] adj. 1. 本土的；土生土长的 2. 生来的，固有的（to）

indigent ['indidʒənt] adj. 贫困的，贫穷的 ‖ indigence, indigency n.

indigested [ˌindi'dʒestid, ˌindai'dʒestid] adj. 1. 未消化的 2. 考虑不充分的；条理不清的；杂乱的

indigestible [ˌindi'dʒestəbl, ˌindai'dʒestəbl] adj. 1. 难消化的；无法消化的 2. 难理解的，难领会的

indigestion [ˌindi'dʒestʃən, ˌindai'dʒestʃən] n. 消化不良（症）；〔喻〕难理解，难领会

indignant [in'dignənt] adj. 愤慨的，义愤的 ‖ ~ly adv.

indignation [ˌindig'neiʃən] n. 愤慨，义愤

indignity [in'digniti] n. 无礼，侮辱；侮辱的言行

indigo ['indigəu]（[复] indigo(e)s） n. 1. 靛蓝，靛青；靛蓝染料 2. 靛蓝色 3.【植】槐蓝，木蓝

indirect [ˌindi'rekt, ˌindai'rekt] adj. 1. 间接的；迂回的或曲折的；an ~ object【语】间接宾语 2. 不直截了当的；不坦率的；不诚实的 ‖ ~ly adv. / ~ness n.

indiscernible [ˌindi'sənəbl] adj. 难辨别的；觉察不出的

indiscreet [ˌindis'kri:t] adj. 不慎重的，轻率的；不得体的；不明智的 ‖ ~ly adv.

indiscretion [ˌindis'kreʃən] n. 不慎重，轻率；言行失检

indiscriminate [ˌindisˈkrimənət] *adj.* 1. 不加区别的，无选择的，不分青红皂白的 2. 杂乱的；任性的

indispensable [ˌindisˈpensəbl] *adj.* 1. 必不可少的，必需的 (to, for) 2. 不能撇开的；责无旁贷的 —— 非做不可的人(或物) ‖ **indispensability** [ˈindispensəˈbiləti] *n.* / **indispensably** *adv.*

indispose [ˌindisˈpəuz] *vt.* 1. 使不愿 2. 使不能；使不适合 3. 使疾感不适

indisposed [ˌindisˈpəuzd] *adj.* 1. 不愿，不倾向的；厌恶的 2. 不舒服的，身体不适的

indisposition [ˌindispəˈziʃən] *n.* 1. 不舒服，身体不适 2. 无意；厌恶

indisputable [ˌindisˈpjuːtəbl] *adj.* 无可争辩的；无可置疑的 ‖ **indisputably** *adv.*

indissoluble [ˌindiˈsɔljubl] *adj.* 1. 不可溶解的；不能分解的 2. 稳定的；持久的；不能撤销的 3. 【化】不溶解的

indistinct [ˌindisˈtiŋkt] *adj.* 1. 不清楚的，模糊的；微弱的 2. 难辨认的；不确定的 ‖ ～ly *adv.* / ～ness *n.*

indistinctive [ˌindisˈtiŋktiv] *adj.* 无特色的；不显著的 ‖ ～ly *adv.*

indistinguishable [ˌindisˈtiŋgwiʃəbl] *adj.* 1. 难区分的，不能辨别的；不易觉察的 2. 无特征的 ‖ **indistinguishably** *adv.*

indite [inˈdait] *vt.* 写；赋(诗)；作(文)

indium [ˈindiəm] *n.* 【化】铟

individual [ˌindiˈvidjuəl] *adj.* 1. 个人的，个体的；个别的，单独的 2. 独特的；个性的 —— *n.* 个人，个体；独立单位 ‖ ～ism *n.* 个人主义；利己主义 2. 个性；独特性 3.(国家对经济和政治的)不干涉主义，自由放任主义 / ～ist *n.* 个人主义者；利己主义者 *adj.* 个人主义(者)的 / ～ly *adv.* 1.以个人资格地；分别地，各个地；各自地 2. 独特地

individuality [ˌindividjuˈæləti] *n.* 1. 个性；个人特征 2. 个人；个体，单个实体 3.[常 individualities]个人的趣味(或爱好等)

indivisible [ˌindiˈvizəbl] *adj.* 1. 不可分的 2.【数】不能被整除的，除不尽的 —— *n.* 不可分的东西；不能被整除的数 ‖ **divisibility** [ˈindiviziˈbiləti] *n.* 不可分性 / **indivisibly** *adv.*

Indo-China [ˈindəuˈtʃainə] *n.* 印度支那半岛(即中南半岛)；印度支那(常指印度支那半岛东部的越南、老挝和柬埔寨三国)

indoctrinate [inˈdɔktrineit] *vt.* 1. 灌输 2. 教；教导 ‖ **in.doctri'nation** *n.*

indolence [ˈindələns] *n.* 1. 懒惰；不积极 2.【医】无痛；进展缓慢；顽性，愈合缓慢

indolent [ˈindələnt] *adj.* 1. 懒惰的；不积极的 2.【医】无痛的；进展缓慢的；顽性的，愈合缓慢的

indomitable [inˈdɔmitəbl] *adj.* 不可屈服的，不屈不挠的；不气馁的 ‖ **indomitably** *adv.*

Indonesia [ˌindəuˈniːzjə] *n.* 印度尼西亚[东南亚岛国]

indoor [ˈindɔː] *adj.* 1.(在)室内的，(在)屋里的 2. 室内进行的；住在室内的

indoors [ˈinˈdɔːz] *adv.* 在屋里；进入室内

indorse [inˈdɔːs] *vt.* = endorse ‖ ～ment *n.*

indubitable [inˈdjuːbitəbl] *adj.* 不容置疑的；明确的 ‖ **indubitably** *adv.*

induce [inˈdjuːs] *vt.* 1. 引诱；劝使 2. 引起；导致 3.【逻】归纳出 4. 诱导；【电】感应；感生

inducement [inˈdjuːsmənt] *n.* 1. 引诱；劝诱 2. 诱因；动机 3.【律】(诉状中释明案情的)引叙部分；(订立合同的)诱因；犯罪动机

induct [in'dʌkt] vt. **1.** (通过正式仪式)使就职(*to, into*) **2.** 使正式入会;征调...入伍(*to, into*) **3.** 介绍(知识等);使初步入门 **4.** 引入;引导 **5.** 【电】感应;感生 **6.** 【逻】归纳出

induction [in'dʌkʃən] n. **1.** 就职;入会;入伍;入伍仪式 **2.** 首次经验;入门 **3.** (古)前言;序幕 **4.** 【逻】【数】归纳法 **5.** 【机】进气,吸气,吸气 **6.** 【医】人工引导(方法);诱导;【电】(电磁)感应

inductive [in'dʌktiv] adj. **1.** 引入的;诱进的 **2.** 【逻】归纳的;归纳法的 **3.** 【电】感应的;电感的,感生的

indulge [in'dʌldʒ] vt. **1.** 使(自己)沉湎;放纵(感情、欲望);纵情享受 **2.** 使满足,使称心;迁就 **3.** 【商】容许(某人)延期付款 — vi. **1.** 沉湎,沉溺;纵情(*in*) **2.** (口)酗酒;嗜酒

indulgence [in'dʌldʒəns], **indulgency** [in'dʌldʒənsi] n. **1.** 任性,放肆;沉湎;着迷 **2.** 纵容;娇养 **3.** 嗜好,着迷的事物 **4.** 【商】延期;延期优惠 **5.** (天主教的)特赦;赦宥

indulgent [in'dʌldʒənt] adj. 纵容的;宽容的;溺爱的 ‖ ~ly adv.

industrial [in'dʌstriəl] adj. **1.** 工业的,产业的,实业的 **2.** 从事工业的 **3.** 工业高度发达的 **4.** 供工业用的 **5.** 因勤奋努力而得到的 — n. **1.** 工业工人,产业工人 **2.** 工业公司 **3.** 【商】工业股票 ‖ ~ist n. 工业主义者;实业家 / ~ly adv.

industrialize [in'dʌstriəlaiz] vt. 使工业化 — vi. 工业化 ‖ in,dustriali'zation n. 工业化

industrious [in'dʌstriəs] adj. 勤劳的,勤奋的 ‖ ~ly adv.

industry ['indəstri] n. **1.** 勤劳,勤奋 **2.** 有组织的劳动;经常的工作(或努力) **3.**

工业,产业;行业 **4.** [总称]工业企业的资方人员

-ine suf. **1.** [构成形容词或名词]表示"属于...的(事物)","具有...属性的(事物)":divine, marine **2.** [构成名词]表示"女性的名字(或称呼)":heroine **3.** [构成抽象名词]表示【化】[用于构成衍生物的名称]:caffeine

inebriate [i'ni:briət] adj. 陶醉的;醉醺醺的 — n. 酒鬼;酗酒者 — [i'ni:brieit] vt. 使醉;使陶醉

inedible [in'edibl] adj. 不可食的;不适合食用的

ineffable [in'efəbl] adj. **1.** 无法表达的;不可言喻的 **2.** 因神圣而不容称呼的;须避讳的 ‖ ineffably adv.

ineffective [ini'fektiv] adj. **1.** 无效的,不起作用的 **2.** 效率低的 **3.** 缺乏艺术性的 ‖ ~ly adv. / ~ness n.

ineffectual [ini'fektjuəl] adj. 无效的;徒劳无益的;不灵验的 ‖ ~ly adv. / ~ness n.

inefficiency [ini'fiʃənsi] n. 无效率;无能;不称职

inefficient [ini'fiʃənt] adj. **1.** 无效的;效率低的 **2.** 无能的;不熟练的;不称职的 — n. 效能低的人 ‖ ~ly adv.

inelastic [ini'læstik] adj. **1.** 无弹力的;无伸缩性的 **2.** 无适应性的,僵硬的;不能变通的

ineligible [in'elidʒəbl] adj. 无被选(或录取)资格的;不合格的;不可取的 — n. 不合格的人 ‖ ineligibility [in,elidʒə'biləti] n.

inept [i'nept] adj. **1.** 不适当的;不符要求的;不合场面的 **2.** 笨拙的;愚蠢的;无能的;不称职的 ‖ ~ly adv.

inequality [ini'kwɔləti] n. **1.** 不平等;不平均;不平衡;不等量 **2.** 不相同,互异

3.(平面等的)不平坦 4.【数】不等(式)

inert [i'nə:t] *adj.* 1. 无自动力的;无活动力的 2. 呆滞的;迟缓的;无生气的 3.【生】【化】惰性的,不活泼的,钝的 4.【医】无作用的,无效果的;中性的 ‖ ～ly *adv.* / ～ness *n.*

inertia [i'nə:ʃjə] *n.* 1.【物】惯性;惯量 2.【医】无力 3. 不活动;惰性;迟钝

inertial [i'nə:ʃ(ə)l] *adj.*【物】惯性的;惯量的

inescapable [ˌinis'keipəbl] *adj.* 逃避不了的;必然发生的 ‖ **inescapably** *adv.*

inestimable [in'estiməbl] *adj.* 1. 无法估计的 2. 极珍贵的,无价的

inevitable [in'evitəbl] *adj.* 1. 不可避免的,无法规避的;必然(发生)的 2.〈口〉照例如此的;老一套的 ‖ **in,evita'bility** *n.* / **inevitably** *adv.*

inexact [ˌinig'zækt] *adj.* 1. 不精确的;不准确的 2. 不严格的;不仔细的 ‖ ～ly *adv.* / ～ness *n.*

inexcusable [ˌiniks'kju:zəbl] *adj.* 1. 不可原谅的,不可宽恕的 2. 无法辩解的 ‖ **inexcusably** *adv.*

inexhaustible [ˌinig'zɔ:stəbl] *adj.* 1. 用不完的;无穷无尽的 2. 不会疲劳的,不倦的 ‖ **inexhaustibly** *adv.*

inexhaustive [ˌinig'zɔ:stiv] *adj.* 不详尽的;不彻底的 ‖ ～ly *adv.*

inexorable [in'eksərəbl] *adj.* 1. 不屈不挠的;坚决不变的 2. 无情的;毫不宽容的 ‖ **inexorably** *adv.*

inexpedient [ˌiniks'pi:djənt] *adj.* 不适当的;不明智的;不得计的

inexpensive [ˌiniks'pensiv] *adj.* 花费不多的;价格公道的;廉价的 ‖ ～ly *adv.* / ～ness *n.*

inexperience [ˌiniks'piəriəns] *n.* 缺乏经验,不熟练 ‖ ～d *adj.* 无经验的;不熟练

的

inexpert [ˌiniks'pə:t, in'ekspə:t] *adj.* 不熟练的;不老练的;业余的 ━ [in'ekspə:t] *n.* 生手 ‖ ～ly *adv.* / ～ness *n.*

inexplicable [in'eksplikəbl] *adj.* 不能说明的,费解的,莫名其妙的 ‖ **inexplicably** *adv.*

inexpressible [ˌiniks'presəbl] *adj.* 表现(或表达)不出的,说不出的,无法形容的 ‖ **inexpressibly** *adv.*

inexpressive [ˌiniks'presiv] *adj.* 1. 不表现的;无表情的;无表示的 ‖ ～ly *adv.* / ～ness *n.*

inextricable [in'ekstrikəbl] *adj.* 1. (困境等)无法摆脱的 2. (问题等)不能解决的 3. (疙瘩,结)解不开的 ‖ **inextricably** *adv.*

infallible [in'fæləbl] *adj.* 1. 没有错误的,无过失的;不会犯错误的;一贯正确的 2. 确实可靠的 ━ *n.* 一贯正确的人;可靠的事物 ‖ **infallibly** *adv.*

infamous ['infəməs] *adj.* 1. 声名狼藉的,臭名昭著的 2. 丢脸的;无耻的;不名誉的 3. 犯有丧失廉耻罪行的;〈律〉(因犯罪)被褫夺(全部或部分)公权的;(罪行)可招致公权褫夺的 4.〈口〉很差的,低劣的 ‖ ～ly *adv.*

infamy ['infəmi] *n.* 1. 臭名;声名狼藉,臭名昭著 2. 出丑;丑事 3.【律】(因犯罪)丧失(全部或部分)公权;丧失法律上的信任权

infancy ['infənsi] *n.* 1. 婴儿期;幼年期 2. 初期;摇篮时代 3.【律】未成年

infant ['infənt] *n.* 1. 婴儿,幼儿 2. 未成年者 ━ *adj.* 1. 婴儿的;幼儿的;初期的 2. 未成年的 3. 为婴儿(或幼儿)设置的

infantile ['infəntail], **infantine** ['infəntain] *adj.* 1. 婴儿(期)的;幼儿(期)的;～

paralysis【医】脊髓灰质炎,小儿麻痹症 2. 适合于婴儿的;幼稚的,孩子气的 3. 早期的,初期的

infantry ['infəntri] *n*. 1. [总称]步兵(队) 2. 步兵团 ‖ **~man** *n*. 步兵

infatuate [in'fætjueit] *vt*. 1. 使冲昏头脑;使糊涂 2. 使迷恋;使错爱 — *adj*. 冲昏头脑的;迷恋者的 — *n*. 变得昏头昏脑的人;迷恋者 ‖ **in,fatu'ation** *n*.

infatuated [in'fætjueitid] *adj*. 变得昏头脑的;迷恋着的

infect [in'fekt] *vt*. 1. 传染;侵染;传播病菌于 2. 使受影响;感染

infection [in'fekʃən] *n*. 1. 传染;侵染 2. 传染病 3. 影响;感染

infectious [in'fekʃəs] *adj*. 1. 传染的;传染性的 2. 感染性的,易传播的 3. 有坏影响的;有损害的

infer [in'fə:] (inferred; inferring [in'fə:riŋ]) *vt*. 1. 推论,推断 2. 猜想,臆测 3. 意味着;暗示;指出,指明 — *vi*. 作出推论

inference ['infərəns] *n*. 1. 推论,推断,推理 2. 推断的结果;(逻辑上的)结论

inferior [in'fiəriə] *adj*. 1. 下等的;下级的 2.(质量等)劣等的,差的,次的 3.(位置)在下的,下部的 4.【天】(行星)在地球轨道内侧的,在太阳和地球之间的 5.【植】下位的;在下的 6.【解】在下的;在其他器官之下的 7.【印】下标的 — *n*. 1.(地位、能力等)低于他人者;部下,下员 2. 次品 3.【印】下标(字母);下标数字;下标符号 ‖ **~ity** [in,fiəri'ɔrəti] *n*. 下等;劣等;下级;下位

infernal [in'fə:nl] *adj*. 1. 阴间的,地狱的 2. 地狱般的;恶魔似的;穷凶极恶的 3.〈口〉可恨的;坏透的;该死的 ‖ **~ly** *adv*.

inferno [in'fə:nəu]([复]infernos) *n*. 1. 地

狱 2. 像地狱的地方;恐怖的景象 3. [I-]《地狱篇》(但丁所作《神曲》的第一部)

infertile [in'fə:tail] *adj*. 1. 不肥沃的,贫瘠的;不毛的 2. 不结果实的,不生育的

infest [in'fest] *vt*. 1.(害虫、盗贼等)大批出没于;侵扰 2. 寄生于 3. 遍布于 ‖ **~ation** [,infes'teiʃən] *n*.

infidel ['infidəl] *n*. 1. 不信仰基督教者 2. [宗]异教徒;不信奉正统宗教者 — *adj*. 1. 不信宗教的 2. 异教徒的 3. 不信仰的;怀疑的 ‖ **~ity** [,infi'deləti] *n*. 1. 不信宗教;不信基督教 2. 背信;不信任;不忠诚 4.(夫妇间的)不忠实;不忠实的行为

infield ['infi:ld] *n*. 1. 农舍周围的耕地;可耕地 2.【体】(垒球或棒球场的)内野,内场;全体内野(或内场)手 3. 椭圆形跑道内的运动场地 ‖ **~er** *n*.【体】内野手,内场手

infighting ['in,faitiŋ] *n*. 1.(拳击中的)近击 2. 混战;乱打 3. 暗斗

infiltrate ['infiltreit; in'filtreit] *vt*. 1. 使(液体等)渗入,透过(through, into);使浸润 2.【军】渗透,通过;伪装 — *vi*. 渗入;混进 — *n*. 渗入物 ‖ **infil'tration** *n*. 渗透(作用);浸润物

infinite ['infinit] *adj*. 1. 无限的,无穷的,广大无边的 2.[用复数名词前]无数的,极多的 3.【语】非限定的(不受人称、数、时态的限制,如动词不定式、动名词等)4.【数】无穷(大)的,无限(大)的 — *n*. 1. 无限(的空间或时间)2.【数】无穷(大),无限(大) 3. [the I-]【宗】上帝 ‖ **~ly** *adv*.

infinitesimal [,infini'tesiməl] *adj*. 1. 无穷小的,无限小的 2. 细微末节的 — *n*.【数】无穷小,无限小

infinitive [in'finitiv] 【语】*n*. 原形(动词),

不定式 — adj. 原形的、不定式的

infinity [inˈfiniti] n. 1. 无限、无穷；无限量，无穷数；无限的范围 2.(数目、数额的)大量、大宗 3.【数】无穷大，无穷(符号为∞)

infirm [inˈfəm] adj. 1. 体弱的、虚弱的 2. 意志薄弱的；不坚定的、动摇的 3. 不牢靠的；不生效的

infirmary [inˈfəməri] n. 医院；医务室(尤指学校、教养所等附设的病房或配药处)

infirmity [inˈfəmiti] n. 1. 体弱，虚弱 2. 疾病，病症 3. 懦弱；薄弱；弱点

inflame [inˈfleim] vt. 1. 使燃烧；使炽热 2. 使极度激动；引起…的热情；使脸红耳赤；使愤怒；激怒 3. 使火上加油 4.【医】使发炎 — vi. 1. 着火 2. 激动；发怒 3. 发炎

inflammable [inˈflæməbl] adj. 1. 易燃的 2. 易激动的；易激怒的；性情暴躁的 — n. 易燃物

inflammation [ˌinfləˈmeiʃən] n. 1. 点火；燃烧 2. 激动 3.【医】炎(症)

inflammatory [inˈflæmətəri] adj. 1. 使激怒的、煽动性的 2.【医】炎性的，炎的

inflatable [inˈfleitəbl] adj. 可膨胀的

inflate [inˈfleit] vt. 1. 使充气；使膨胀、使胀大 2. 使得意；使骄傲 3. 使(通货)膨胀；抬高(物价) — vi. 进行充气；膨胀 ‖ **~ion** n. 1. 充气；膨胀 2. 夸张；自满 3. 通货膨胀；信用膨胀；物价飞涨 ‖ ~ary adj. 膨胀的、通货膨胀的；由通货膨胀引起的

inflect [inˈflekt] vt. 1. 弯曲；使向内弯曲；使屈折 2.【音】变(音)；转(调)【语】使(词)发生屈折变化 — vi.【语】发生屈折变化 ‖ ~ion n. = inflexion

inflexible [inˈfleksəbl] adj. 1. 不可弯曲的；僵硬不可变的 2. 坚定不移的；固执的(不

屈服的；不可动摇的 3. 不可改变的；固定的；不可变更的

inflexion [inˈflekʃən] n. 1. 弯曲；向内弯曲 2.【音】变音；转调 3.【语】屈折变化(形式) 4.【数】拐折；拐点，回折点 ‖ ~al adj.

inflict [inˈflikt] vt. 1. 予以(打击)；使遭受(损伤、苦痛等)；使承受 2. 处(罚)；加(刑) ‖ ~ion n.

inflorescence [ˌinfləˈresns] n. 1. 开花(期) 2.【植】花序；花簇；花朵；开花部位

inflow [ˈinfləu] n. 1. 流入 2. 流入物 — vi. 流入，涌入

influence [ˈinfluəns] n. 1. 影响；感化(upon, on) 2. 势力、权势 3. 有影响的人(或事物)；有权势的人 4.【电】感应 — vt. 影响；感化；对…起作用；左右

influential [ˌinfluˈenʃəl] adj. 1. 有影响的；施以影响的 2. 有权势的

influenza [ˌinfluˈenzə] n. 1.【医】流行性感冒 2.(马、猪等的)家畜流行性感冒

influx [ˈinflʌks] n. 1. 流入，注入；涌进；汇集(指人或物) 2. 河口；河流的汇合处

inform [inˈfəm] vt. 1. 告诉，通知；向…报告；使充满；使活跃(with) — vi. 告发(against) ‖ ~er n. 1. 通知者；通报者 2. 告密者

informal [inˈfəməl] adj. 1. 非正式的；非正规的 2. 日常使用的 ‖ ~ity [ˌinfəˈmæləti] n. 1. 非正式；不拘礼节 2. 不拘礼节的行动 ‖ ~ly adv.

informant [inˈfəmənt] n. 1. 提供消息(或情报)的人；【语言学】(调查方言等的)被调查者 2. 告密者，检举者

information [ˌinfəˈmeiʃən] n. 1. 通知；报告 2. 消息，信息 3. 知识，见闻；资料(检察官的)控告；检举，告发 5.【计】信息；数据，资料 ‖ ~ highway 信

息高速公路／～ **retrieval** 信息检索／～ **science** 信息科学／～ **theory** 信息论

informative [inˈfɔːmətiv] *adj.* 报告消息的；提供资料的；增进知识的）

infraction [inˈfrækʃən] *n.* (法规等的)违反，违背

infrared [ˌinfrəˈred] 【物】*adj.* 红外线的；红外区的；产生红外辐射的；对红外辐射敏感的 — *n.* 红外线；红外区外

infrequent [inˈfriːkwənt] *adj.* 很少发生的；稀罕的；偶有的；不寻常的 ‖ ～**ly** *adv.*

infringe [inˈfrindʒ] *vt.* 违犯；侵犯；违反 — *vi.* 侵犯；侵害(*on, upon*) ‖ ～**ment** *n.*

infuriate [inˈfjuərieit] *vt.* 使发怒，激怒 — *adj.* 狂怒的

infuse [inˈfjuːz] *vt.* 1. (向…)注入；(向…)灌输 2. 泡(茶)；浸渍；泡制(草药) 3. 使充满；鼓舞 — *vi.* 注；浸泡

infusion [inˈfjuːʒən] *n.* 1. 注入；灌输 2. 【医】输液；输注；输液用溶液 3. 泡制；浸渍 4. 浸剂

-ing *suf.* 【构成动名词或名词】1. 表示"动作(或动作的过程)"：swimm*ing* 2. 表示"动作的结果(或产物)"：engrav*ing*, build*ing* 3. 表示"与某一事物有关的材料"，"职业"：account*ing* 4. 表示"动作的对象"，"与某一动作有关的器物"：sew*ing* 5. 表示"与某一动作有关的事物"，"用于制造(或形成)某物的东西"：colour*ing* 6. 表示"与某一概念有关的事物"：off*ing* — 1. 【构成动词的现在分词】：read*ing* 2. 【构成现在分词形式的形容词】：entertain*ing*

ingenious [inˈdʒiːnjəs] *adj.* 1. 机灵的；足智多谋的；有独创性的 2. 精巧制造的；巧妙的 ‖ ～**ly** *adv.*

ingenuity [ˌindʒiˈnjuːiti] *n.* 1. 机灵；足智

多谋；独创性 2. 精巧；设计新颖；独出心裁

ingenuous [inˈdʒenjuəs] *adj.* 坦率的；天真的；单纯的 ‖ ～**ly** *adv.* ／～**ness** *n.*

inglorious [inˈɡlɔːriəs] *adj.* 1. 不光彩的；不名誉的；可耻的 2. 不出名的；湮没无闻的 ‖ ～**ly** *adv.*

ingot [ˈiŋɡət] *n.* 【冶】铸模；铸块，锭

ingrained [ˌinˈɡreind] *adj.* 1. 根深蒂固的 2. 彻头彻尾的 3.【纺】深染的 ‖ ～**ly** *adv.* ／～**ness** *n.*

ingrate [inˈɡreit] *n.* 忘恩负义的人 — *adj.* 〈古〉忘恩负义的

ingratiate [inˈɡreiʃieit] *vt.* 使讨好，使巴结，使迎合

ingratiating [inˈɡreiʃieitiŋ] *adj.* 讨好的，迎合的，奉承的 ‖ ～**ly** *adv.*

ingratitude [inˈɡrætitjuːd] *n.* 忘恩负义

ingredient [inˈɡriːdjənt] *n.* 1. (混合物的)组成部分；配料，成分 2. (构成)要素，因素

inhabit [inˈhæbit] *vt.* 居住于；(动物)栖息于 ‖ ～**able** *adj.* 可居住(或栖息)的

inhabitant [inˈhæbitənt] *n.* 1. 居民，住户；常住居民 2. 栖居的动物

inhalant [inˈheilənt] *n.* 吸入剂，吸入药；吸入器 — *adj.* 供吸入用的；吸入的

inhalation [ˌinhəˈleiʃən] *n.* 吸入，吸气；吸入物

inhale [inˈheil] *vt.* 1. 吸入 2. 〈美俚〉急切(或贪婪)地吃；猛喝 — *vi.* 吸入气体(或烟，香味)

inharmonious [ˌinhɑːˈməunjəs] *adj.* 1. 不和谐的；不合调的；嘈杂的 2. 不和睦的 ‖ ～**ly** *adv.*

inhere [inˈhiə] *vi.* 生来即存在(于)；作为不可分割的部分(或成分)(*in*)

inherent [inˈhiərənt] *adj.* 内在的；固有的，

生来的 ‖ ～ly adv.

inherit [in'herit] vt. 1. 继承(传统、遗产、权利等) 2. 经遗传而得(性格、特征等) — vi. 接受遗产; 成为继承人 ‖ ～or a. 继承人; 后继者

inheritance [in'heritəns] n. 1. 继承 2. 继承物; 遗产; 遗赠 3. 继承权 4. 遗传; 得自遗传的特征 5. 传统; 从自然界承袭的共有资产(指土地、水、空气等)

inhibit [in'hibit] vt. 1. (罕) 禁止; 阻止 2. 抑制; 约束 — vi. 起抑制作用 ‖ ～ion [,inhi'biʃən] n. 禁止; 阻止; 抑制; 抑制物; 受抑制

inhospitable [in'hɔspitəbl] adj. 1. 不好客的; 不殷勤的; 冷淡的 2. (地带、海滨等) 不适于居住的; 荒凉的 ‖ inhospitably adv.

inhuman [in'hju:mən] adj. 1. 无人性的; 非人的 2. 野蛮的; 残酷的 ‖ ～ly adv.

inhumane [,inhju:'mein] adj. 1. 不仁慈的; 不近人情的; 无人道的; 残忍的 ‖ ～ly adv.

inhumanity [,inhju:'mæniti] n. 1. 无人性; 野蛮; 残酷 2. 残酷无情的行为

inimical [i'nimikəl] adj. 1. 敌意的; 不友好的 2. 有害的; 不利的

inimitable [i'nimitəbl] adj. 1. 不能模仿的 2. 无双的; 无与伦比的 ‖ inimitably adv.

iniquitous [i'nikwitəs] adj. 1. 不公正的; 不正直的; 邪恶的; 罪恶的

iniquity [i'nikwiti] n. 1. 不公正; 不正直; 邪恶; 罪恶 2. 不义行为; 邪恶的事物

initial [i'niʃəl] adj. 1. 最初的; 开头的; 词首的 — n. 1. 首字母 2. (书刊文章中的段落、章节的) 特大的大写首字母 3. [～s] (姓名或组织名称首的) 首字母 — (initial(l)ed; initial(l)ing) vt. 1. 用姓名的首字母签名(或作标记)于 2. 草

签 ‖ ～ism n. 首字母缩略词

initiate [i'niʃieit] vt. 1. 开始; 发动 2. 使入门 3. 正式介绍; 引进 — [i'niʃiət, i'niʃieit] adj. & n. 1. 被传授了初步知识的(人) 2. 新入会的(人)

initiation [i,niʃi'eiʃən] n. 1. 开始; 创始 2. 指引; 传授 3. (会、社等的) 加入; 入会

initiative [i'niʃiətiv] n. 1. 发端; 创始; 创精神; 主动; 积极性 2. (公民的) 创制权; (立法机关对新法案的) 动议权 — adj. 起始的; 创始的; 初步的

inject [in'dʒekt] vt. 1. 注射, 注入 2. 注满 3. 插进(话); 引入 4. [机] 喷射 ‖ ～or n. 1. 注射者; 注射器, 注入器 2. (锅炉的) 注水器 3. 喷射器

injection [in'dʒekʃən] n. 1. 注射 2. 注射剂, 针剂 3. 充满; 注满 4. [机] 喷射 5. (卫星、宇宙飞船等的) 射入轨道; 射入轨道的时间

injunction [in'dʒʌŋkʃən] n. 命令; 责戒; [律] 禁制令

injure ['indʒə] vt. 损害; 伤害; 毁坏

injurious [in'dʒuəriəs] adj. 有害的; 致伤的

injury ['indʒəri] n. 1. 损害; 伤害; 毁坏 2. 伤害的行为 3. 受伤处

injustice [in'dʒʌstis] n. 1. 非正义; 不公正, 不公平; 侵犯(别人的) 权利 2. 非正义(或不公正)的行为

ink [iŋk] n. 1. 墨水; 油墨; 墨; 墨汁 2. (乌贼体内分泌的) 墨汁 3. (美俚) 咖啡; 廉价酒 4. (美俚) (贬) 黑人 — vt. 1. 涂墨水或油墨)于; 用墨水写(或画、涂) 2. 使沾上墨水(或油墨) 3. (美俚) 签(契约) ‖ ～-born n. (旧时用角制的) 墨水瓶 adj. 学究气的; 卖弄学问的 / ～-stand n. 1. 墨水台 2. ＝～well / ～-well n. (镶在桌上或墨水台上的) 墨

水池

inkling ['iŋkliŋ] *n.* **1.** 暗示;细微的迹象 **2.** 略知;模糊样的想法

inky ['iŋki] *adj.* **1.** 墨似的;漆黑的 **2.** 给墨水弄污的

inlaid ['in'leid]inlay 的过去式和过去分词 — *adj.* 镶嵌的;嵌饰的,嵌花样的

inland ['inlənd] *adj.* **1.** 内地的,内陆的 **2.** 国内的 — *n.* 内地 —['in'lænd] *adv.* 在内地;到内地 ‖ ~ **er** *n.* (生长在)内地的人

in-law ['inlɔː] *n.* 〈口〉[常 ~s]姻亲

inlay [,in'lei] (inlaid ['in'leid]) *vt.* **1.** 镶嵌,嵌入 **2.** 用镶嵌物装饰 —['inlei] *n.* **1.** 镶嵌物及所用的材料;镶嵌工艺 **2.** 牙充填

inlet ['inlet] *n.* **1.** 进口;入口 **2.** 水湾;小港 **3.** 镶嵌物;插入物 **4.** 让人,纳人 —(inlet;inletting) *vt.* 使进入;使嵌入;插入

inmate ['inmeit] *n.* **1.** (房屋等的)居住者,同住者 **2.** (监狱等的)被收容者 **3.** (医院的)住院者

inmost ['inməust] *adj.* 最内的;最深入的;内心深处的

inn [in] *n.* **1.** (尤指乡村或公路旁的)小旅馆,客栈 **2.** 小酒店;小饭店 — *vi.* 住旅馆 ‖ ~ **-keeper**,~ **-holder** *n.* 小旅馆老板

innate [,i'neit] *adj.* **1.** 天生的,生来的;固有的 **2.** 【植】底着的,内生的 **3.** 〔哲〕天赋的,(头脑)固有的

inner ['inə] *adj.* **1.** 内部的;里面的;(尤指权势)接近中心的 **2.** 心灵的;精神的;内心的;亲密的 — *n.* 内部;里面 **2.** (箭靶的)内圈 ‖ ~ **-most** *adj.* 最里面的;最深处的 *n.* 最深处 ‖ ~ **ear**[解]内耳

Inner Mongolia 内蒙古(亦作 Nei Mong-

gol)

inning ['iniŋ] *n.* **1.** (荒地,尤指水洼田、沼泽的)围垦;[~s]围垦地 **2.** [~s]用作单或复【体】(尤指棒球、板球赛中的)局;回合 **3.** [~s]用作单或复]显身手的机会;(个人或政党的)执政期;当权

innocence ['inəsns] *n.* **1.** 清白;无罪 **2.** 天真;单纯 **3.** 无知;头脑简单 **4.** 无害 **5.** 无罪的人,清白无辜者 **6.** [植]蓝眼寇林希草;二色寇林希草;贵格淑女花,蓝花杜鹃

innocent ['inəsnt] *adj.* **1.** 清白的;无罪的 **2.** 天真的;单纯的 **3.** 无知的;头脑简单的 **4.** 无害的 **5.**【医】良性的 **6.** 没有…的 — *n.* **1.** 天真无邪的人(尤指小孩)**2.** 头脑简单的人;笨蛋 ‖ ~ **ly** *adv.*

innocuous [i'nɔkjuəs] *adj.* **1.** 无害的;无毒的 **2.** 不关痛痒的;不会招怨的;乏味的

innovate ['inəuveit] *vi.* 革新,创新;变革 (*in, on, upon*) ‖ **innovator** *n.* 革新者,创新者

innovation [,inəu'veiʃən] *n.* 革新,创新,改革;新方法;新事物

innuendo [,inju'endəu] ([复]innuendo(e)s) *n.* 影射(的话);暗讽(的话) — *vi.* 影射 — *vt.* 旁敲侧击地表达;暗示

innumerable [i'njuːmərəbl] *adj.* 无数的,数不清的

inoculate [i'nɔkjuleit] *vt.* **1.**【医】给…接种;给…作预防注射(将微生物等)移入(土壤,培养基等);将(微生物)移入合适环境 **2.** 〈古〉[植]芽接 **3.** 向…灌输

inoculation [i,nɔkju'leiʃən] *n.* **1.**【医】接种;预防注射(微生物等的)移入土壤(或培养基等)**2.** [植]芽接 **3.** (思想等

的)灌输 4.【治】孕育(处理)

inoffensive [,inə'fensiv] *adj.* 1. 无害的、不伤害人的 2. 不触犯人的 3. 不令人讨厌的

inopportune [in'ɔpətju:n] *adj.* 不凑巧的；不合时宜的、不合适的

inordinate [i'nɔ:dinət] *adj.* 1. 无节制的、放纵的 2. 无规则的；紊乱的 3. 极度的；非常的 ‖ ~ly *adv.* / ~ness *n.*

inorganic [,inɔ:'gænik] *adj.* 1. 无生物的 2.【化】无机的 3. 非自然生长而成的、人造的 4. 非本质的、外界的 5.【语】无据的(指不能用词源学解释的)

input ['input] *n.* 1.【电】输入、输入量 2.【计】输入程序、输入信息【电】输入功率(或电压)、投入物；投入的资金(或物资) — (inputting 或 inputted 或 input; inputting) *vt. & vi.* 输入

inquest ['inkwest] *n.* 1.(尤指有陪审团参加的)审理、讯问、验尸 2. 调查死因的陪审团 3. 陪审团关于死亡原因的裁决 4. 查询、调查

inquire [in'kwaiə] *vi.* 1. 询问 2. 调查、查问 — *vt.* 1. 询问、打听 2. 调查 ‖ ~r *n.* 询问者、调查人

inquiring [in'kwaiəriŋ] *adj.* 1. 好询问的、爱打听的 2. 显得好奇的 ‖ ~ly *adv.*

inquiry [in'kwaiəri] *n.* 1. 询问、打听 2. 质询、质问 2. 调查 3.(真理、知识等的)探究

inquisition [,inkwi'ziʃən] *n.* 调查、查究；审讯

inquisitive [in'kwizitiv] *adj.* 1. 好询问的、好奇的 2. 爱打听别人隐私的 — *n.* 1. 好询问的人 2. 爱打听别人隐私的人 ‖ ~ly *adv.* / ~ness *n.*

inroad ['inrəud] *n.* 侵袭；侵犯；得手、进展(*into*, *on*, *upon*)

insane [in'sein] *adj.* 1. 精神错乱的、精神病的 2. 疯狂的 3. 精神病患者的、为疯

人而设的 3. 极其愚蠢的；脱离实际的 ‖ ~ly *adv.*

insanitary [in'sænitəri] *adj.* 不卫生的；有害健康的、易引起疾病的

insanity [in'sænəti] *n.* 1. 精神错乱；精神病；疯狂 2. 极其愚蠢；毫无意义 3. 愚行；蠢事

insatiable [in'seiʃjəbl] *adj.* 不能满足的；贪得无厌的

inscribe [in'skraib] *vt.* 1. 刻；雕 2. 题写；写；印 3. 把(某人)的名字登记入册；将...注册；(英)登记(公债等)持有人的名字 4. 题献(书籍、歌曲等)；题赠 5. 牢记；铭记 6.【数】使内接；使内切

inscription [in'skripʃən] *n.* 1. 题铭；铭文；碑文(碑刻或勒牌、图章等上的)刻印文字 2. 题词；献词 3. 编入名单；注册；(英)记名公债等持有人名字的)登记 4.(英)[~s]记名公债

insect ['insekt] *n.* 1. 昆虫、虫 2. 可鄙的人；渺小的人

insecticide [in'sektisaid] *n.* 杀虫剂

insecure [,insi'kjuə] *adj.* 1. 不安全的；无保障的；危险的 2. 不可靠的；不牢靠、不稳定的；动摇的 ‖ ~ly *adv.* / insecurity *n.*

inseminate [in'semineit] *vt.* 1. 播种于(种) 2. 使怀孕；使受精；对... 施人工授精 3. 灌输之(喻)为... 提供养料；哺育 ‖ insemi'nation *n.*

insensate [in'senseit] *adj.* 无感觉的、无理性的；无情的 ‖ ~ly *adv.* / ~ness *n.*

insensible [in'sensəbl] *adj.* 1. 失去知觉的；麻木的、无感觉的 2. 不知道的、没察觉到的(*of*) 3. 不被觉察的、极微的 4. 无感情的；冷淡的 5. 莫名其妙的、无意义的 6. 不敏感的 ‖ **insensibly** *adv.*

insensitive [in'sensitiv] *adj.* 感觉迟钝的、

不敏感的；不灵敏的(*to*) ‖ ~**ly** *adv*. / **insensitivity** [ˌinˌsensi'tivəti] *n*.

inseparable [in'sepərəbl] *adj*. 分不开的；不可分割的 — *n*. [~s]不可分的事物；形影不离的伙伴(或好友) ‖ **inseparably** *adv*.

insert [in'sə:t] *vt*. 1. 插入；嵌入；登载(广告等) 2.(缝纫中)镶；补 — *vi*. [医](肌肉)附着 — ['insə:t] *n*. 插入物；插页

insertion [in'sə:ʃən] *n*. 1. 插入；嵌入；(广告的)登载 2. 插入物；登载的广告 3.(服装上的)嵌饰；边饰 4.[医](肌肉的)附着

inset ['inset] *n*. 1. 水道；(潮水等的)流入 2. 插入物；插页；套印在大地图(或大图表)中的小地图(或小图表) 3. 镶料 — [in'set] (inset 或 insetted; insetting) *vt*. 插入，嵌入

inside ['in'said] *n*. 1. 里面；内部 2.(人行道、道路的)内侧；(跑道的)内圈，里道 3. 内心，内在思想 4. 期中 5. [口]肚子，肠胃 6.[俚]内幕情报，内情；能通内情的境地 — *adj*. 1. 里面的；内部的；在屋里的 2. 内幕的，秘密的 3. 干室内工作的一副的 — *prep*. 在…的里面；在…之内 ‖ ~ **r** *n*. 1.(组织、团体等)内部的人 2. 知情者，了解内幕的人

insidious [in'sidiəs] *adj*. 1. 阴险的；狡诈的；暗中为害的 2.(疾病)不知不觉之间加剧的 3. 伺机陷害的；毒而诱人的

insight ['insait] *n*. 1. 洞察(力)；洞悉；见识 2.[心]领悟

insignia [in'signiə]([复] insignia(s)) *n*. 1. 勋章；国徽 2. 认别符号；徽章 3. 标记，标志

insignificance [ˌinsig'nifikəns] *n*. 1. 无意义；不足道；无价值；不重要 2. 低微；

可鄙

insignificant [ˌinsig'nifikənt] *adj*. 1. 无意义的；无关紧要的；无足轻重的；无价值的 2. 小的；低微的；可鄙的 ‖ ~**ly** *adv*.

insincere [ˌinsin'siə] *adj*. 1. 不真诚的；不诚恳的 2. 虚假的；伪善的，不可信任的 ‖ ~**ly** *adv*. / **insincerity** [ˌinsin'serəti] *n*.

insinuate [in'sinjueit] *vt*. 1. 使逐渐而巧妙地进入；使潜入 2. 暗示；暗讽 ‖ **insinu'ation** *n*.

insinuating [in'sinjueitiŋ] *adj*. 讨好的，献媚的；暗示的

insipid [in'sipid] *adj*. 1. 无味的；淡而无味的 2. 枯燥乏味的；无吸引力的；无生气的

insist [in'sist] *vt*. & *vi*. 1. 坚持；坚决主张；坚决认为 2. 坚决要求；定要

insistence [in'sistəns] *n*. **insistency** [in'sistənsi] *n*. 坚持；坚决主张；坚决要求

insistent [in'sistənt] *adj*. 1. 坚持的 2. 逼人注意的，显眼的，显著的 ‖ ~**ly** *adv*.

insolence ['insələns] *n*. 1. 傲慢，目空一切，无礼；蛮横 2. 傲慢的态度；侮辱性的行动(或言论)

insolent ['insələnt] *adj*. 傲慢的，目空一切的；无礼的；蛮横的，侮慢的 ‖ ~**ly** *adv*.

insoluble [in'sɔljubl] *adj*. 1. 不可溶解的；难以溶解的 2.(问题等)不能解决的；不能解释的 ‖ **insolubility** [inˌsɔlju'biləti] *n*. / **insolubly** *adv*.

insomnia [in'sɔmniə] *n*. 失眠；失眠症

insomuch [ˌinsəu'mʌtʃ] *adv*. 1. 到这样的程度，如此地 2. 因为，由于(与 as 连用，= inasmuch as)

inspect [in'spekt] *vt.* 1. 检查;审查 2. 检阅;视察;参观 — *vi.* 检查

inspection [in'spekʃən] *n.* 1. 检查,检验;审查,检阅 2. 视察;参观

inspector [in'spektə] *n.* 1. 检查员;监察员;检阅者;视察者 2. 巡官

inspiration [,inspə'reiʃən] *n.* 1. 吸入;吸气 2. 鼓舞,激励;鼓舞人心的人(或事物) 3. 灵感;[宗](神的)灵感,神感,神灵感应 4.〈口〉妙计,好办法 5. 授意;指使 ‖ ~al *adj.* 1. 鼓舞人心的 2. 受灵感支配的 3.(有)神感的

inspire [in'spaiə] *vt.* 1. 吸入;吸(气)2. 鼓舞,激励;唤起 3. 引起;产生 4. 注入,灌注 5.[常用被动语态]使产生灵感,使感悟 6. 授意;唆使 — *vi.* 吸入;赋予灵感

inst. *abbr.* 1. instant 2. institute

instability [,instə'biləti] *n.* 1. 不稳定性 2. 不坚决,动摇;三心两意

instal(l) [in'stɔ:l] (installed; installing) *vt.* 1. 任命;使就职 2. 安装;设置 3. 安顿,安置

installation [,instə'leiʃən] *n.* 1. 就任,就职;委职礼 2. 安装;设置;安置 3. 装置,设备 4.(军事)设施

instal(l)ment [in'stɔ:lmənt] *n.* 1. 分期付款;偿款的分期摊还款;分期交付 2.(分期连载的)一部分;分期出版的分册;(戏剧的)分本演出或播送)

instance ['instəns] *n.* 1. 例子,事例,实例 2. 请求,建议 3. 诉讼,诉论(手续)— *vt.* 1. 举...为例;引证 2.[常用被动语态]用例子说明

instant ['instənt] *adj.* 1. 紧迫的;刻不容缓的 2. 立即的;直接的 3. 本月的(用于商业或正式函件中,常略作 inst.)4.(食品)已配制好的;速溶的 — *n.* 1.(某一)时刻 2. 瞬息,霎时 ‖ ~er *adv.*

立刻,马上 / ~ly *adv.* 立即,即刻 *conj.* 一...(就): I recognized her ~ ly I saw her. 我一看见她就把她认出来了。‖ ~ camera 一次成像照相机 / ~ photography 一步摄影,立拍立现摄影 / ~ replay (录像镜头的)即时重放;可即时重放的录像

instantaneous [,instən'teinjəs] *adj.* 瞬间的;即刻的 ‖ ~ly *adv.* / ~ness *n.*

instead [in'sted] *adv.* 代替;更换 ‖ ~ of 代替,而不是...: He will go ~ of you. 他将代你去。

instep ['instep] *n.* 1. 足背,足弓;跗 2.(鞋面的)覆盖足背部分;袜背 3.(马后蹄的)胫骭部分

instigate ['instigeit] *vt.* 1. 教唆;怂恿 2. 煽动 ‖ **insti'gation** *n.* / **instigator** *n.*

instil(l) [in'stil] (instilled; instilling) *vt.* 1. 滴注;逐渐灌输 ‖ ~ment *n.*

instinct[1] ['instiŋkt] *n.* 1. 本能,直觉 2. 生性,天性

instinct[2] [in'stiŋkt] *adj.* 充满的(with)

instinctive [in'stiŋktiv] *adj.* (出于)本能的;(出于)天性的;~ behaviour 本能行为 ‖ ~ly *adv.*

institute ['institju:t] *n.* 1. 学会;协会;学院;(大专)学校;(研究)所;院 2. 讲习会;讲座 3. 会址;院址;所址 4.(公认的)基本原理,基本原则;[~s]法理概要 — *vt.* 1. 建立,设立,制定 2. 创立;实行 3. 任命;[宗]授予...圣职(into, to)

institution [,insti'tju:ʃən] *n.* 1. 建立,设立;制定 2. 制度;惯例;风俗 3.(慈善、宗教等性质的)公共机构;协会;学校 4. 会址;院址;校址;所址 5.〈口〉(与某地或某种活动紧密相联的)为人熟悉的人(或事物)6.[宗]被授予圣职

institutional [,insti'tju:ʃənəl] *adj.* 1. 惯例

的；制度（上）的；风俗（上）的 2. 公共机构的；社会事业性质的 3.〈美〉（广告）旨在提高企业产品声誉的

instruct [in'strʌkt] *vt.* 1. 教，教育；指导 2. 通知；向…提供事实情况 3. 指示；命令

instruction [in'strʌkʃən] *n.* 1. 教育；指导；训练 2.（长辈等的）教训，教诲 3. [～s]指示；命令

instructive [in'strʌktiv] *adj.* 1. 教育的；指导性的；用于传播知识的 2. 有教益的；有启发的 ‖ ～**ly** *adv.*

instructor [in'strʌktə] *n.* 1. 指导者；教员 2.〈美〉大学讲师

instructress [in'strʌktris] *n.* 1. 女指导者；女教员 2.〈美〉大学女讲师

instrument ['instrumənt] *n.* 1. 仪器；器械；器具 2. 手段；工具 3. 乐器 4.【律】文书 — *vt.* 1. 用仪器装备 2. 给乐器谱写（乐曲）；把…改编成管弦乐 3. 向…提交文书

instrumental [ˌinstru'mentl] *adj.* 1. 仪器的；器械的；器具的 2. 作为手段（或工具）的；有帮助的；起作用的 3. 乐器（上）的；为器乐谱写的；用乐器演奏的 4.【语】工具格的 ‖ ～**ist** *n.* 乐器演奏者 / ～**ly** *adv.*

insubordinate [ˌinsə'bɔːdənit] *adj.* 1. 不顺从的，不服从的；反抗的 2. 地位不低（劣）的 — *n.* 不顺从的人；反抗者 ‖ **insubordination** ['insəˌbɔːdi'neiʃən] *n.*

insubstantial [ˌinsəb'stænʃəl] *adj.* 1. 无实质的，无实体的；非实在的；幻想的 2. 不坚固的，不牢的；薄弱的 ‖ ～**ly** *adv.*

insufferable [in'sʌfərəbl] *adj.* 难以忍受的；不可容忍的；难堪的 ‖ **insufferably** *adv.*

insufficiency [ˌinsə'fiʃənsi] *n.* 1. 不充分，不足；不适当；不胜任 2.【医】闭锁不全，机能不全

insufficient [ˌinsə'fiʃənt] *adj.* 1. 不足的，不够的 2. 不适当的；无能的 ‖ ～**ly** *adv.*

insular ['insjulə] *adj.* 1. 海岛的，岛屿的；岛形的 2. 岛民的；像岛民的；具有岛民特征的 3. 在岛上居住的；位于岛上的 4. 像岛似的；隔绝的；孤立的 5. 思想狭窄的；保守的；有偏见的 6.【医】（皮疹等）岛状的，岛屿状散开的；【解】胰岛的；脑岛的

insulate ['insjuleit] *vt.* 1. 隔离；使孤立 2.【物】使绝缘；使隔热；使隔音 ‖ ˌ**insu'lation** *n.* 1. 隔离；孤立 2.【物】绝缘；隔热；隔音；绝缘（或隔热、隔音）材料 / **insulator** *n.*【物】绝缘体；绝缘子；绝热体；隔音物

insulin ['insjulin] *n.*【生化】胰岛素

insult ['insʌlt] *n.* 1. 侮辱，凌辱 2.〈古〉攻击，袭击 3.（对身体或其一部分的）损害 — [in'sʌlt] *vt.* 侮辱；辱骂；冒犯；蔑视；损害

insuperable [in'sjuːpərəbl] *adj.* 1. 不能克服的；难以越过的 2. 不可战胜的；无敌的 ‖ **insuperably** *adv.*

insurance [in'ʃuərəns] *n.* 1. 安全保障 2. 保险；保险业 3. 保险单（通常称～ policy）4. 保险费（通常称 premium）5. 保险金额

insure [in'ʃuə] *vt.* 1. 给…保险：the ～d 被保险人 2. 保证；确保 — *vi.* 投保；承保 ‖ ～**r** *n.* 保险业者；保险公司；保证人；起保证作用的事物

insurgent [in'səːdʒənt] *adj.* 1. 起义的；暴动的；造反的；反抗的 2.（波涛等）汹涌而来的 — *n.* 起义者；暴动者；造反者；反抗者

insurmountable [ˌinsə'mauntəbl] *adj.* 难以超越的；不可克服的；难以制胜的 ‖

insurmountably adv.

insurrection [ˌinsəˈrekʃən] n. 起义;暴动;造反(指行动)

insusceptible [ˌinsəˈseptəbl] adj. 1. 不为所动的;不易受影响的 2. 不容许的

intact [inˈtækt] adj. 未经触动的;未受损的;完整的

intake [ˈinteik] n. 1. 吸入;纳入;收纳 2. 纳入量;【物】输入能量 3.【水、气体等流入沟、管的】入口 4.【矿】进风巷道 4. 被收纳的东西;被吸收(到团体或组织里)的人;新生;新兵;新加入者 5.(英方)(从沿泽等开拓的)垦地 6.【航】进气口,进气孔

intangible [inˈtændʒəbl] adj. 1. 触摸不到的;无形的 2. 不可捉摸的;难以确定的;模糊的 — n. 无形的东西;不可捉摸的事物

integer [ˈintidʒə] n. 1.【数】整数 2. 完整的东西

integral [ˈintigrəl] adj. 1. 构成整体所必需的;固有的;基本的;组成的 2. 完整的整体的 3.【数】整的;积分的 — n. 1. 整体;整数 2.【数】积分

integrate [ˈintigreit] vt. 使结合(with);使并入(into);使一体化 2.(美)取消(学校等)种族隔离;使(黑人等)享受平等待遇 3.【数】求...的积分 4. 表示(面积、温度等)的总数 — vi.(与...)结合起来(with);成一体 — [ˈintigrit] adj. 完整的;完全的;综合的 ‖ ~d circuit 集成电路

integration [ˌintiˈgreiʃən] n. 1. 结合;综合;集成 2. (美)取消种族隔离;给予(种族上的)平等待遇 3.【数】积分(法) 4. 整合(作用);同化(作用)

integrity [inˈtegriti] n. 1. 完整;完全;完善 2. 正直;诚实

integument [inˈtegjumənt] n. 1.(动、植物天生的)覆盖物;包裹物 2. 包在外面的东西;the ~ of a book 书的包皮

intellect [ˈintilekt] n. 1. 智力,才智;理解力 2. 有才智的人

intellectual [ˌintiˈlektjuəl] n. 知识分子 — adj. 1. 智力的;理智的 2. 用脑筋的;需智力的 3. 一昧凭理智行事的;旨在打动人的理智的;理性的 ‖ ~ly adv.

intelligence [inˈtelidʒəns] n. 1. 智力;才智;理解力;聪明;灵性,悟性 2. 情报;情报工作;情报机构 3.【宗】智力的人格化(指鬼神) 4.【计】智能 5. 消息,信息

intelligent [inˈtelidʒənt] adj. 理解力强的;聪明的;理智的;明智的;(计算机部件)智能的 ‖ ~ly adv.

intelligible [inˈtelidʒəbl] adj. 1. 可理解的;明白的,易懂的 2.【哲】仅能用智力了解的;纯概念性的 ‖ intelli'bility n. / intelligibly adv.

intemperance [inˈtempərəns] n. 1. 无节制;过度;放纵 2. 饮酒过度,酗酒

intemperate [inˈtempərət] adj. 1. 无节制的;过度的;放纵的 2. 饮酒过度的 ‖ ~ly adv.

intend [inˈtend] vt. 1. 想要,打算 2. 打算使...(成为) 3. 意指;意思

intense [inˈtens] adj. 1. 强烈的;剧烈的;紧张的 2. 热切的;热情的;认真的 3.【摄】(负片)厚密度的 ‖ ~ly adv.

intensification [inˌtensifiˈkeiʃən] n. 1. 增强,强化 2.【摄】(负片)加厚

intensify [inˈtensifai] vt. 1. 加强;加剧 2.【摄】加厚(部分负片) — vi. 强化;增强 ‖【摄】(部分负片)加厚

intensity [inˈtensəti] n. 1. (思想、感情等的)强烈;剧烈 2. 强度 3.【摄】密度

intensive [inˈtensiv] adj. 1. 加强的;密集的;深入细致的 2.【逻】内包的 3.【

精耕细作的,集约的 4.【语】加强词意
的 5. 采用大剂量高疗效药物的 — n.
1. 加强器;加强剂 2.【语】强调成分(指
加强词意的副词或前缀等) ‖ ~ care
重病特别护理

intent [in'tent] adj. 1. (目光等)不转移
的,集中的;急切的 2. 专心的;坚决的
‖ ~ly adv. / ~ness n.

intention [in'tenʃən] n. 1. 意图,意向;打
算;目的 2. 含义;意思 3. [~s]求婚意
图 4.【逻】意念 5.【医】愈合

intentional [in'tenʃənl] adj. 有意(识)的,
故意的 ‖ ~ly adv.

inter [in'tə:] (interred; interring) vt. 埋葬

inter- comb. form 表示"在…中","在…
间","在…内","相互": interact, in-
terpenetrate

interact[1] ['intərækt] n. 【戏】幕间表演;插
曲;幕间休息

interact[2] [,intər'ækt] vi. 互相作用;互相
影响

interaction [,intər'ækʃən] n. 相互作用;相
互影响

intercede [,intə'si:d] vi. 1. 代为请求,说情
2. 调解,调停

intercept [,intə'sept] vt. 1. 拦截;截击(敌
军等);截取(情报等) 2. 窃听,侦听 3.【数】截断;截取
— ['intəsept] n. 1. 拦截;截击 2. 窃听,侦
听 3.【数】截距;截段 ‖ ~ or, ~ er n.
1.【军】截击机;截击导弹 2. 遮断器;拦
截器;拦截机

interception [,intə'sepʃən] n. 1. 拦截;截
击;截取 2. 窃听,侦听 3.
(球类运动中的)截球,抢断球

intercession [,intə'seʃən] n. 调解;说情;
【宗】代人祈祷

intercessor [,intə'sesə] n. 调解者;说情者;
【宗】代理主教

interchange [,intə'tʃeindʒ] vt. 1. 交换,互
换 2. 交替(位置等) 3. 使更迭发生;轮
流进行 — vi. 交替发生;交换位置 —
['intətʃeindʒ] n. 1. 交换;交替 2.【建】
互通式立体交叉;道路立体枢纽;交换
道

interchangeable [,intə'tʃeindʒəbl] adj. 1.
可交换的,可互换的 2. 可交替的 ‖ in-
terchangeably adv.

intercollegiate [,intəkə'li:dʒiət] adj. 学院
(或大学)间的;学院(或大学)间进行
的

intercontinental ['intə,kɔnti'nentl] adj. 洲
际的

intercourse ['intəkɔ:s] n. 1. 交际;往来;交
往 2.(思想、感情等的)交流,交换 3.
性交,交媾

interdepend [,intədi'pend] vi. 互相依赖,
互相依存 ‖ ~ence, ~ency n.

interdependent [,intədi'pendənt] adj. 互相
依赖的,互相依存的

interdict [,intə'dikt] vt.(以禁令)禁止;制
止 — ['intədikt] n. 禁令,强制令 ‖ ~-
ion [,intə'dikʃən] n. 禁止;制止;禁令

interdisciplinary [,intə'disiplinəri] adj. 学
科间的,涉及若干学科的,跨学科的

interest ['intrist] n. 1. 兴趣;关心;注意;
趣味 2. 感兴趣的事,爱好 3. 利益;利
害关系;权利;股权 4. 利息 5. 行业 —
vt. 1. 使发生兴趣;引起…的注意(或
关心) 2. 使参与,使发生关系

interested ['intristid] adj. 1. 感兴趣的,关
心的;注意的 2. 有(利害)关系的,有
份儿的 3. 有私心的,有偏见的

interesting ['intristiŋ] adj. 有趣味的;引起
兴趣的 ‖ ~ly adv.

interface [ˈintəfeis] ***n.*** 1.(分)界面 2.(不同系统间相互衔接并影响的)接合部位,边缘区域 —***vt.*** & ***vi.***(使)联系;(使)接合;(使)互相作用(或影响);(使)互相配合工作

interfere [ˌintəˈfiə] ***vi.*** 1. 干涉,干预 2. 妨碍,打扰 3.(事物)抵触,冲突(*with*) 4.(马等在行走、奔跑时)绊脚,碰踝 5.【物】干扰 6.(橄榄球赛中)掩护阻挡;阻挡犯规 7.【律】(在专利诉讼中)对专利权提出(优先)主张

interference [ˌintəˈfiərəns] ***n.*** 1. 干涉,干预 2. 妨碍,打扰;阻碍物 3. 抵触,冲突 4.【物】(电波、光波、声波等的)干扰,干涉

interferon [ˌintəˈfiərɔn] ***n.***【生化】干扰素

interim [ˈintərim] ***n.*** 间歇;过渡期间 —***adj.*** 1. 间歇的;过渡期间的 2. 暂时的;临时的

interior [inˈtiəriə] ***adj.*** 1. 内的,内部的 2. 内地的 3. 国内的 4. 内心的;本质的;深藏的 —***n.*** 1. 内部;内景 2. 内地 3. 内心;内在性质 4. 内务,内政

interj. *abbr.* interjection

interject [ˌintəˈdʒekt] ***vt.***(突然)插入

interjection [ˌintəˈdʒekʃən] ***n.*** 1.【语】感叹词,感叹语 2. 插入;插话

interlace [ˌintəˈleis] ***vt.*** 使交织;使交错 —***vi.*** 交织;交错

interlard [ˌintəˈlɑːd] ***vt.*** 1. 将肥肉(或咸肉等)分层夹入(待煮的肉)中 2. 使混杂;使夹杂

interline [ˌintəˈlain] ***vt.*** 1. 在...的字行间书写(或做记号);在字行间写入 2. 加内衬于

interlock [ˌintəˈlɔk] ***vt.*** & ***vi.***(使)联锁;(使)连结 —[ˈintəlɔk] ***n.*** 联锁;连结;联锁装置

interlocutor [ˌintəˈlɔkjutə] ***n.*** 对话者;参加谈话者

interlocutory [ˌintəˈlɔkjutəri] ***adj.*** 1. 对话的;发生在对话中的;插话性质的 2.【律】在诉讼程序进行中(宣布)的;中间的;非最后的

interlope [ˌintəˈləup] ***vi.*** 1. 侵害他人权利(如营业权等) 2. 闯入;干涉 3. 无执照营业 ‖ ~**r** [ˈintələupə] ***n.*** 闯入者;(为图私利而)干涉他人事务者;无执照营业者

interlude [ˈintəluːd] ***n.*** 1. 幕间;幕间表演 2. 插曲 3. 间歇;插入的事物

intermarry [ˌintəˈmæri] ***vi.*** 1. 不同家族(或种族、宗教徒等)间通婚 2. 内部通婚,近亲结婚 ‖ **intermarriage** [ˌintəˈmæridʒ] ***n.***

intermeddle [ˌintəˈmedl] ***vi.*** 干涉;多管闲事(*in*,*with*)

intermediary [ˌintəˈmiːdjəri] ***adj.*** 1. 中间的;居间的 2. 中间人的;媒介的;调解人的 —***n.*** 1. 中间人;调解人 2. 中介(物),媒介(物);手段;工具 3. 中间形态;中间阶段

intermediate [ˌintəˈmiːdiət] ***adj.*** 中间的;居间的 —***n.*** 1. 中间体;媒介物 2. 中间人;调解人 —***vi.*** 起媒介作用;起调解作用(*between*) ‖ ~**ly** ***adv.*** 在中间

interment [inˈtəːmənt] ***n.*** 1. 埋葬;安葬 2. 葬送,搁置,不予考虑

intermezzo [ˌintəˈmetsəu]([复] intermezzi [ˌintəˈmetsiː]或 intermezzos) ***n.***【音】间奏曲;【戏】幕间表演,幕间剧

interminable [inˈtəːminəbl] ***adj.*** 漫无止境的;没完没了的;冗长不堪的 ‖ **interminably** ***adv.***

intermingle [ˌintəˈmiŋgl] ***vt.*** 使混合;使搀和 —***vi.*** 混合(*with*)

intermission [ˌintəˈmiʃən] ***n.*** 间歇;中断;

休息(时间);幕间休息

intermittent [ˌintəˈmitənt] adj. 间歇的;断断续续的;周期性的 ‖ ~ly adv.

intermix [ˌintəˈmiks] vt. 使混合;使混杂 — vi. 混合;混杂

intern[1] [inˈtən] vt. 拘留(俘虏等);扣留(船只等) — n. = internee

intern[2] [ˈintən] 〈美〉 vi. 做实习医生 — n. 实习医生 (= interne)

internal [inˈtənl] adj. 1. 内的、内部的 2. 内在的,固有的 3. 内心的 4. 国内的;内政的 5. 体内的;内服的 — n. [~s] 1. 内脏,内部器官 2. 本质,本性 ‖ ~ly adv.

international [ˌintəˈnæʃənl] adj. 国际的;世界的 — n. 1. 国际性的组织 2. 参加国际比赛的人;国际比赛 3. 侨居外国的人 ‖ ~ly adv.

Internationale [ˌintənæʃəˈnɑːl] 〈法〉 n. [the ~]《国际歌》

internationalism [ˌintəˈnæʃənəlizəm] n. 国际主义

internationalist [ˌintəˈnæʃənəlist] n. 1. 国际主义者 2. 国际事务专家;国际法学家 — adj. 国际主义的

internationalize [ˌintəˈnæʃənəlaiz] vt. 使国际化;把...置于国际共管之下 ‖ **inter,nationali'zation** n. 国际化;国际共管

interne [ˈintən] n. 〈美〉实习医生

internecine [ˌintəˈniːsain] adj. 1. 自相残杀的;两败俱伤的 2. (集团内部)互相冲突的

internee [ˌintəˈniː] n. 被拘留者;拘留民;拘留犯

internet [ˈintənet] n.【讯】1. 网间,网际 2. 互连网络(亦作 internetwork)

internist [inˈtənist] n. 内科医生

internment [inˈtənmənt] n. 拘留

internship [ˈintənʃip] n.〈美〉实习医生的职务;实习期

interplanetary [ˌintəˈplænitəri] adj. 行星际的;行星与太阳间的;太阳系内的

interplay [ˈintəplei] n. & vi. 相互影响;相互作用

interpolate [inˈtəpəuleit] vt. 1. 篡改 2. 插入(字句等);插(话) 3.【数】插(值);内插,内推 — vi. 1. 进行篡改 2. 插入 ‖ **in,terpo'lation** n.

interpose [ˌintəˈpəuz] vt. 插入;插(话);干预;提出(异议等) — vi. 插进来;插嘴;干预

interposition [inˌtəpəˈziʃən] n. 1. 插入;插嘴;干预,干涉;提出(异议) 2. 插入物

interpret [inˈtəprit] vt. 1. 解释,说明;阐明 2. 把...理解(为),把...看(作) 3. (根据本人的理解)表演;表现(剧中人物);演奏(乐曲) — vi. 口译,通译;当译员;解释

interpretation [inˌtəpriˈteiʃən] n. 1. 解释;阐明 2. 翻译 3. 表演;演奏

interpretative [inˈtəpritətiv] adj. 解释的;阐明的

interpreter [inˈtəpritə] n. 1. 译员,口译者;解释者 2.【军】判读员 3.【计】译印儿;解释程序

interracial [ˌintəˈreiʃəl] adj. 不同种族间的

interrelate [ˌintəriˈleit] vt. & vi. (使)相互联系

interrelation [ˌintəriˈleiʃən] n. 相互关系,相互联系(性) — ~ship n. 相互关系

interrogate [inˈterəgeit] vt. & vi. 讯问;审问;质问

interrogation [inˌterəˈgeiʃən] n. 1. 讯问;审问,质问 2.【语】疑问句;问号(亦作

~ point)

interrogative [ˌintəˈrɒgətiv] *adj.* 疑问的；讯问的；质问的 — *n.* 1.【语】疑问词 (如 who, which, what 等)；疑问句 2.问号

interrogator [inˈterəgeitə] *n.* 1. 讯问者；审问者；质询者 2.【无】询问器；问答机

interrogatory [ˌintəˈrɒgətəri] *adj.* 疑问的；讯问的；质问的 — *n.* 1. 询问；问题 2.【律】质询(书)

interrupt [ˌintəˈrʌpt] *vt.* 1. 中断；遮断；阻碍；打断(讲话、讲话人等)；打扰 — *vi.* 打断；打扰

interruption [ˌintəˈrʌpʃən] *n.* 1. 中止；遮断；打断 2. 障碍物；阻拦物 3. 间歇；休止 4. 打扰；干扰

intersect [ˌintəˈsekt] *vt.* 1. 贯穿；横穿；和 … 相交；和 … 交叉 — *vi.* (线)相交；交叉 ‖ ~ion [ˌintəˈsekʃən] *n.* 1. 横断；交叉 2. 交叉点；十字路口

intersperse [ˌintəˈspɜːs] *vt.* 1. 散布，散置 (between, among) 2. 点缀

interstate [ˌintəˈsteit] *adj.* (主美)州与州之间的，州际的 — *n.* 州际公路

interstellar [ˌintəˈstelə] *adj.*【天】星际的

interstice [inˈtɜːstis] *n.* 空隙；间隙；裂缝

intertwine [ˌintəˈtwain] *vt. & vi.* (使)缠结；(使)缠绕在一起

interval [ˈintəvəl] *n.* 1. (时间的)间隔；间歇；幕间(或工间)休息 2. (空间的)间隔；空隙 3. (在品质、地位等方面的)差别；差异 4.【音】音程 5.【数】区间

intervene [ˌintəˈviːn] *vi.* 1. 干涉；干预 2. 插进；介入；(时间和空间)介于 3. 调停 4.(与案件有利害关系的第三人)参加诉讼

intervention [ˌintəˈvenʃən] *n.* 1. 干涉；干预；妨碍 2. 插进；介入 3. 调停 ‖ ~ist *n. & adj.*

interview [ˈintəvjuː] *n.* 1. 接见；会见 2.(记者的)采访，访谈；访问记 3.(对求职者、学校考生等的)面谈，面试，口头审查 — *vt.* 1. 接见；会见；(记者等)访问，采访 2. 对 … 进行面谈(或面试) — *vi.* 面谈；面试 ‖ ~er *n.* 接见采访者；进行面试者

interweave [ˌintəˈwiːv] (过去式 interwove [ˌintəˈwəuv] 或 interweaved, 过去分词 interwoven [ˌintəˈwəuvən] 或 interweaved) *vt.* 1. 使交织，使交错编织 2. 使紧密结合；使混杂 — *vi.* 交织；混杂

intestate [inˈtesteit] *adj.* 无遗嘱的；无遗嘱嘱明处置的 — *n.* 未留遗嘱的死亡者

intestinal [inˈtestinl] *adj.* 肠的；肠内的

intestine [inˈtestin] *adj.* 内部的；国内的 — *n.*[常 ~s]肠

intimacy [ˈintiməsi] *n.* 1. 亲密；密切 2.[委婉语]行为 3.[intimacies]亲昵行为(或言语)

intimate [ˈintimit] *adj.* 1. 亲密的；密切的 2. 熟悉的；经过认真调查研究的 3. 内部的；内心深处的；本质的 4. 私人的；个人的 5.[委婉语]有性关系的 — *n.* 熟友，知己 ‖ ~ly *adv.*

intimate² [ˈintimeit] *vt.* 1. 宣布；通知；明白表示 2. 暗示；提示 ‖ intiˈmation *n.*

intimidate [inˈtimideit] *vt.* 恫吓，恐吓，威胁 ‖ inˌtimiˈdation *n.*

into [ˈintu, ˈintə] *prep.* 1.[表示动作的方向]到 … 里 2.[表示时间]进入到 3.[表示变化]成，为；转入 4.【数】除 5.into 20 is 4. 五除二十等于四。5.〈古〉【数】乘：4 into 5 is 20. 四乘五等于二十。

intolerable [inˈtɒlərəbl] *adj.* 1. 不能忍受的；无法容忍的 2. 过度的，过分的；极

端的 ‖ **intolerably** *adv*.

intolerance [in'tɔlərəns] *n*. **1**. 不容忍;不容异说;偏狭,偏执 **2**.【医】不耐性;(对药物、食物等的)过敏反应

intolerant [in'tɔlərənt] *adj*. 不容忍的;不容异说的;偏狭的 一 *n*. 不容忍的人;偏狭的人 ‖ ～**ly** *adv*.

intonation [ˌintəu'neiʃən] *n*. **1**. 语调;声调 **2**. 抑扬之声 **3**.【宗】(圣歌等的)起始短句;(圣歌等的)吟咏,吟诵 **4**.【音】音准,音调

intone [in'təun] *vt*. **1**. (以单调音吟)吟咏,吟诵(赞美诗、祷文等) **2**. 给...一种特殊音调 **3**. 唱(圣歌)的起始短句 一 *vi*. **1**. 吟咏,吟诵 **2**. 发抑扬音调

intoxicant [in'tɔksikənt] *adj*. **1**. 致醉的 **2**. 令人陶醉的 **3**. 使中毒的 一 *n*. **1**. 酒类饮料 **2**. 致醉药物

intoxicate [in'tɔksikeit] *vt*. **1**. 使喝醉 **2**. 使陶醉;使高兴欲狂 **3**. 使中毒 ‖ **in·toxi'cation** *n*.

intractable [in'træktəbl] *adj*. **1**. 难驾御的;难管付的;难处理的;倔强的 **2**. 难加工的;难操作的 **3**. 难治疗的;难消除的

intramural [ˌintrə'mjuərəl] *adj*. **1**. (国家、城市、团体等)自己范围内的、单位内部的 **2**.【解】(器官)壁内的

intransigent [in'trænsidʒənt] *adj*. 不妥协的;不让步的 一 *n*. 不妥协者 ‖ ～**ly** *adv*.

intransitive [in'trænsitiv]【语】*adj*. 不及物的 一 *n*. 不及物动词

intravenous [ˌintrə'vi:nəs] *adj*. 静脉内的;进入静脉的 ‖ ～**ly** *adv*.

intrench [in'trentʃ] *vt*. & *vi*. = entrench

intrepid [in'trepid] *adj*. 无畏的;勇猛的;坚韧不拔的 ‖ ～**ly** *adv*.

intricacy ['intrikəsi] *n*. **1**. 错综;复杂;缠结 **2**. [intricacies] 错综复杂的事物

intricate ['intrikət] *adj*. 错综的;复杂的;缠结的;难懂的 ‖ ～**ly** *adv*.

intrigue [in'tri:g] *n*. **1**. 阴谋,诡计 **2**. 私通 一 *vi*. 策划阴谋,捣鬼(*against*);私通(*with*) 一 *vt*. **1**. 用诡计取得(古) 哄骗 **2**. (新闻用语)引起...的兴趣(或好奇心) ‖ **intriguing** *adj*. 引起兴趣(或好奇心)的;有迷惑力的

intrinsic [in'trinsik] *adj*. 内在的;固有的;本质的;真正的【解】内部的、(本)体内的 ‖ ～**ally** *adv*.

introduce [ˌintrə'dju:s] *vt*. **1**. 带领;引进 **2**. 输入,采用 **3**. 介绍,引荐 **4**. 作为(文章、讲话等)的开头 **5**. 提出(议案、话题等) **6**. 把...插入(*into*) **7**. 推销(商品等) **8**. 导入,纳入,添入 ‖ ～**r** *n*. 创始人;传入者;介绍人;提出人

introduction [ˌintrə'dʌkʃən] *n*. **1**. 引进,传入;引荐 **2**. 采用;被采用的东西 **3**. 介绍 **4**. 导言,引言;序曲 **5**. 入门(书)

introductory [ˌintrə'dʌktəri] *adj*. 介绍的,导言的

introspection [ˌintrəu'spekʃən] *n*. 内省,自省,反省 ‖ ～**al** *adj*.

introvert ['intrəuvə:t] *n*. 性格内向的人 ‖ **intro'version** *n*. 内向,内省

intrude [in'tru:d] *vi*. 侵入;闯入;打扰 一 *vt*. **1**. 硬挤,强加 **2**.【地】使(岩浆等)侵入地层 ‖ ～**r** *n*. 入侵者;闯入者

intrusion [in'tru:ʒən] *n*. **1**. 侵入;闯入;打扰 **2**.【地】侵入;侵入岩浆 ‖ **intrusive** *adj*.

intrust [in'trʌst] *vt*. = entrust

intuition [ˌintju'iʃən] *n*. **1**. 直觉;直观 **2**. 直觉到的事物;直觉知识

inundate ['inʌndeit] vt. 1. 淹没 2. 使充满 ‖ **inun'dation** n. 泛滥; 洪水

inure [i'njuə] vt. [常用被动语态]使习惯(不利条件) — vi. 生效; 施行; 起作用

invade [in'veid] vt. 1. 侵略, 侵入(别国); 侵犯(权利等) 2. 拥入入, 3.(疾病, 感情, 声音等)侵袭 ‖ ~s r n. 侵略者, 侵入者; 侵扰物

invalid¹ ['invəlid] adj. 1. 有病的; 病弱的; 伤残的 2. 病人用的 — n. 病人, 病弱者; 伤病员; 伤病军人 一 ['invə'li:d] vt. 1. 使病弱; 使伤残 2. 把…作为伤病员处理 一 vi. 1. 变得病弱; 变成伤残 2. 因伤病而退伍

invalid² [in'vælid] adj.(尤指法律上)无效的; 无效果的; 无价值的

invalidate [in'vælideit] vt. 使无效; 使无价值

invalidism ['invəlidizəm] n. 久病; 伤残

invaluable [in'væljuəbl] adj. 无法估价的; 无价的; 非常宝贵的

invariable [in'vɛəriəbl] adj. 不变的; 恒定的; 一律的 ‖ **varia'bility** n. 不变; 不变性 / **invariably** adv. 不变地; 永恒地; 总是

invasion [in'veiʒən] n. 1. 侵略; 入侵; 陷入 2. 侵害, 侵犯 3.(疾病等)侵袭

invective [in'vektiv] n. 1. 痛骂; 抨击; 恶骂 2. [~s]骂人的话 — adj. 抨击的; 恶骂的

inveigh [in'vei] vi. 猛烈抨击; 痛骂; 申斥(against)

inveigle [in'vi:gl] vt.(用甜言蜜语)诱骗; 骗取

invent [in'vent] vt. 1. 发明, 创造 2. 捏造, 构构

invention [in'venʃən] n. 1. 发明, 创造; 发明物 2. 发明才能; 创造力 3. 捏造, 虚

构 4.【音】创意曲

inventive [in'ventiv] adj. 发明的, 创造的; 有发明才能的; 有创造力的

inventor [in'ventə] n. 发明者的, 创造者

inventory ['invəntri] n. 1. 财产目录; 存货清单; 存货盘存(目录); 存货, 库存 — vt. 为…编制财产目录; 列入存货清单; 把…编入目录

inverse [in'vəːs] adj. 相反的, 倒转的 一 n. 相反[in'vəːs] vt. 使倒转; 使成反面 ‖ ~ly adv. 相反地

inversion [in'vəːʃən] n. 1. 反[倒]转; 倒置; 转换 2. 倒置物; 颠倒现象 3.【化】转化 4.【数】反演 5.【医】内翻 6.【心】同性态; 性颠倒 7.【生】(染色体的)倒位 8.【语】(词序)倒装; (语音的)卷舌 9.【音】转位 10.【气】逆温, 逆增

invert [in'vəːt] vt. 1. 使颠倒; 使内翻; 反向; 使倒转; 转换 2.【化】使转化 3.【音】使转位 一 ['invəːt] n. 1. 颠倒了的事物 2. 同性态者; 性颠倒者 3.【建】仰拱 一 ['invəːt] adj.【化】转化的

invertebrate [in'vəːtibrət] adj. 1.【动】无脊椎的; 无脊椎动物的 2.(喻)无骨气的; 软弱无能的 一 n. 1. 无脊椎动物 2. 软弱的人

invest [in'vest] vt. 1. 给…披上; 覆盖; 使带有 3. 授予(with) 4.【军】包围; 围攻 5. 投(资); 投入(时间, 精力等) — vi. 1. 投资(in) 2.〈口〉买进(in)

investigate [in'vestigeit] vt. & vi. 调查; 调查研究; 审查 ‖ **investigator** n. 调查者; 调查研究者; 审查者; 侦查员

investigation [in,vesti'geiʃən] n. 调查; 调查研究

investiture [in'vestitʃə] n. 1. 授职(仪式); 授权 2. 覆盖物; 装饰 3.(封建时代的)封地仪式

investment [in'vestmənt] n. 1. 投资(额);

(时间、精力等的)投入；(可)投入资金
的东西 2.【军】围困；封锁 3.覆盖 4.
授职(仪式);授权

investor [in'vestə] n. 投资者

inveterate [in'vetərət] adj. 根深蒂固的；
顽固不化的：an ～ experimenter 锲而不
舍的实验者 ‖ **inveteracy** n.

invidious [in'vidiəs] adj. (会)引起不满
(或反感、怨恨、嫉妒)的 ‖ ～**ly** adv./
～**ness** n.

invigorate [in'vigəreit] vt. 使精力充沛；使
健壮；使活跃；鼓舞

invincible [in'vinsəbl] adj. 无敌的、战无不
胜的 ‖ **vinci`bility** n. / **invincibly** adv.

inviolable [in'vaiələbl] adj. 不可侵犯的；
不可违反的；不容亵渎的，神圣的 ‖
in,viola`bility n. / **inviolably** adv.

inviolate [in'vaiələt], **inviolated**
[in'vaiəleitid] adj. 不受侵犯的，无损的；
不受亵渎的；纯洁的

invisible [in'vizəbl] adj. 看不见的；无
形的，微小得觉察不出的；不显眼的
3. 不露面的，谢绝来客的 4. 未列在公
开账目上的；未反映在统计表上的 — n. 看
不见的物(或人) ‖ **in,visi`bility** n. / ～ **ness** n. / **invisibly**
adv.

invitation [,invi'teiʃən] n. 1. 邀请；招待；
请帖 2. 吸引；引诱；挑逗；招致

invite [in'vait] vt. 1. 邀请；招待 2. 请求；
征求 3. 引起；招致；吸引 — ['invait]
n. 〈口〉邀请

inviting [in'vaitiŋ] adj. 吸引人的，诱人的
‖ ～**ly** adv.

invocation [,invəu'keiʃən] n. 1. 祈祷，乞
灵 2. 召唤魔鬼；符咒 3. (法权的)行使
(法规的)行使 4.

invoice ['invɔis] n. 1. 发票；装货清单 2.
货物的托运 — vt. & vi.(把….)开发

票；(把….)开清单

invoke [in'vəuk] vt. 1. 祈求(神等)保佑，
乞灵于；用符咒召唤(魔鬼) 2. 恳求，
乞求 3. 行使(权力等)；实行 4. 援引
(法规、条文等) 5. 引起，产生

involuntary [in'vɔləntəri] adj. 1. 非故意
的；偶然的 2. 非自愿的；不随意的 3.
无意识的；不自觉的 ‖ **involuntarily**
adv.

involve [in'vɔlv] vt. 1. 包缠；卷绕 2. 使卷
入，使陷入；拖累 3. 使专注 4. 必须包
括；包含 有 5. 包围，困住；笼罩 6.
【数】把(某数字)乘方 — ～**d** adj. 不易
懂的；复杂的

involvement [in'vɔlvmənt] n. 1. 卷入；牵
连；包含 2. 牵连到的事物；复杂的情
况 3.(经济上的)困窘

invulnerable [in'vʌlnərəbl] adj. 1. 不会受
伤害的，刀枪不入的；不会遭到攻击
的；攻不破的 2. 无懈可击的 ‖
in,vulnera`bility n. / **invulnerably** adv.

inward ['inwəd] adj. 1. 里面的；内部的；
内在的，固有的；精神上的 2. 向内的；
进来的；进口的；输入的 3. 内地的；
〈古〉国内的 4.(声音)沉沉的；暗自说
者的 5. 亲密的；熟悉的 — n. 1. 里
面；内部；内心；实质 2.[～s]内脏；肠
胃 — adv. 1. 向内；向中心去 2. 向着内
心；进入心灵 ‖ ～**ly** adv. 1. 在内部，
内里；向内；向中心去 2. 在心灵深处；思
想上，精神上 3. 暗自地 / ～ **ness** n. 1.
本质；深意 2. 灵性，精神性 3. 思想(或
感情)的深度；诚挚

inwards ['inwədz] adv. & n. = inward

inweave [,in'wi:v] vt. (inwove [,in'wəuv],
inwoven [,in'wəuvən]或 inweaved) vt. 使织入；使交织

Io 【化】元素𬭳(ionium)的符号

iodide ['aiədaid] n. 【化】碘化物

iodine ['aiədi:n] n. 【化】碘

iodize ['aiədaiz] *vt.* 用碘(或碘化物)处理；使碘化 *n.*

ion ['aiən] *n.* 【物】【化】离子

-ion *suf.* [构成名词] 1. 表示"行为的过程"：*fusion* 2. 表示"行为(或过程)的结果"：*translation*, *correction* 3. 表示"状态(或情况)"：*inflation*

ionic [ai'ɔnik] *adj.* 【物】【化】离子的

ionium [ai'əuniəm] *n.* [核]【化】锾，钍230

ionization [,aiənai'zeiʃən] *n.* 【化】电离作用

ionize ['aiənaiz] *vt. & vi.* 【化】(使)电离；(使)离子化

ionosphere [ai'ɔnəsfiə] *n.* 【物】电离层

iota [ai'əutə] *n.* 1. 希腊语字母表中的第九个字母(I, ι) 2. 微小，小点儿

IOU [,aiəu'ju:] *n.* 1. 借据 2. 债款；债务 [由 I owe you 的读音缩略转义而成]

-ious *suf.* [构成形容词] 表示"具有...性质的"：*furious*, *anxious*

Iowa ['aiəuə, 'aiəwə] *n.* 衣阿华[美国州名]

IPA *abbr.* 1. International Phonetic Association 国际语音学协会 2. International Phonetic Alphabet 国际音标

ipecac ['ipikæk], **ipecacuanha** [,ipikækju'ænə] *n.* 1.【植】吐根 2. 吐根的根茎和根 3. 吐根制剂

IQ *abbr.* intelligence quotient 智商；智力商数

Ir 【化】元素铱(iridium)的符号

ir- *pref.* [用在以 r 开始的字面前] 1. 表示"不"，"非"：*ir*replaceable, *ir*responsible 2. 表示"进入"，"在内"：*ir*rigation

Iran [i'rɑːn] *n.* 伊朗(原称 Persia 波斯)[西南亚国家]

Iraq, Irak [i'rɑːk] *n.* 伊拉克[西南亚国家]

irascible [i'ræsəbl] *adj.* 易怒的；性情暴躁的

irate [ai'reit] *adj.* 发怒的，愤怒的，被激怒的

ire ['aiə] *n.* 〈诗〉愤火

Ireland ['aiələnd] *n.* 1. 爱尔兰岛[西欧] 2. 爱尔兰[西欧国家](在爱尔兰岛南部)

iridescence [,iri'desns] *n.* 1. 彩虹色 2. 【气】虹彩

iridescent [,iri'desnt] *adj.* 1. 彩虹色的 2.【气】虹彩的 3. 灿烂光辉的 ‖ ~ly *adv.*

iridium [ai'ridiəm, i'ridiəm] *n.* 【化】铱

iris ['aiəris]([复] irises 或 irides [ai'ridiːz]) *n.* 1. 虹；虹彩；彩虹色；虹状物；[I-]【希神】(为诸神报信的)彩虹女神 2.【解】虹膜 3.【植】鸢尾；蝴蝶花 4.【摄】虹彩光圈，可变光阑 5.【矿】彩虹宝石英

Irish ['aiəriʃ] *adj.* 爱尔兰的；爱尔兰人的；爱尔兰语的 —— *n.* 1. [the ~][总称]爱尔兰人 2. 爱尔兰语 3. 〈口〉愤火

irk [əːk] *vt.* 使厌烦，使厌倦；使恼怒

irksome ['əːksəm] *adj.* 使人厌烦的，使人厌倦的；使人恼怒的 ‖ ~ness *n.*

iron ['aiən] *n.* 1. 铁；【喻】铁一般的刚强，坚强；严酷 2. 铁制品；烙铁；熨斗 3. [~s]镣铐；马镫 4. [俚]手枪；火器 5. (俚)(半羊身上打的)烙印 6.【药】铁质；铁质补剂 7. (高尔夫球)铁头球棒 —— *vt.* 1. 用铁铸造；用铁包 2. 给(犯人等)戴上镣铐 3. 熨，烫平(衣服等) —— *vi.* 1. 烫衣服 2. (衣服等)被烫平 ‖ ~ **curtain** (为阻止思想、文化等交流而设置的)无形屏障，铁幕；无法逾越的障碍 /~ **lung** 人工呼吸器，铁肺 /~ **monger** 〈英〉金属器具商；小五金商 /~ **wood** *n.* 铁木(一种硬质坚木的木材) /~ **work** *n.* 1. 铁工，铁制部件

2. [总称]铁制品

ironic(al) [ai'rɔnik(ə)l] *adj.* 1. 冷嘲的；反话的；挖苦的 2. 令人啼笑皆非的 ‖ **~ly** *adv.*

irony ['aiərəni] *n.* 冷嘲；反话；反语；讥讽文体

irradiance ['ireidjəns] *n.* 1. 光辉，灿烂 2. 启示 3. [物]辐照度

irradiate [i'reidiieit] *vt.* 1. 照耀；使发光 2. 阐明；启发 3. 放射；扩散；送出 4. 用(紫外线、X 射线或日光等)照射；[物]辐照 — *vi.* 1. 发光 2. 变得光辉灿烂

irradiation [i,reidi'eiʃən] *n.* 1. 照耀；发光 2. 焕发才智；启迪 3. [物]光渗；辐照；辐照度 4. [医](射线)照射(法) 5. 光；光线

irrational [i'ræʃənl] *adj.* 1. 无理性的 2. 不合理的；荒谬的 3. [数]无理的 — number 无理数 — *n.* 1. 无理性的生物 2. [数]无理数 ‖ **~ly** *adv.*

irreconcilable [i'rekənsailəbl] *adj.* 1. 难和解的；势不两立的 2. 不可调和的；不相容的 — *n.* 1. 不能和解的人；政敌 2. [~s]不可调和的思想(或信仰等)

irrecoverable [,iri'kʌvərəbl] *adj.* 1. 不能恢复(或挽回)的；(创伤等)医治不好的

irredeemable [,iri'di:məbl] *adj.* 1. 不能赎回的 2. (公债、纸币等)不能偿还的；不能兑成硬币的 3. 不能改变的；不能挽回的 4. 不可救药的

irreducible [,iri'dju:səbl] *adj.* 1. 不能降低(或削减)的；不能缩小的 2. [医]难复位的；难以回复的 3. [数](公式等)不能化简的，不可约的

irrefutable [i'refjutəbl] *adj.* 无可辩驳的，无法反驳的(证据)

irregular [i'regjulə] *adj.* 1. 不规则的；无规律的 2. [语]不规则变化的 3. 不整齐

的；参差不一的 3. 非正规的；非正式的 4. 不合常规的；不正当的 5. (美)(商品)等外的，有小缺陷的 — *n.* 1. 非正规的人(或物) 2. [常 ~s]非正规兵 3. (美)[常 ~s]等外品 ‖ **~ly** *adv.*

irregularity [i,regju'læriti] *n.* 1. 不规则，无规律；[语]不规则变化 2. 参差不一 3. [常 irregularities]不规则的事物；不正当行为

irrelevance [i'relivəns], **irrelevancy** [i'relivənsi] *n.* 不相干；不中肯；离题；枝节问题

irrelevant [i'relivənt] *adj.* 不相干的；不中肯的；离题的 ‖ **~ly** *adv.*

irreligious [,iri'lidʒəs] *adj.* 1. 无宗教的；无宗教信仰的；反对宗教的；漠视(或敌视)宗教的 2. 违反宗教原则的；亵渎的；不敬神的

irreparable [i'repərəbl] *adj.* (损失、损伤等)不可弥补的，不可挽救的；不能恢复的 ‖ **irreparably** *adv.*

irreplaceable [,iri'pleisəbl] *adj.* 1. 不能恢复原状的 2. 不能替代的；失掉了无法补偿的

irrepressible [,iri'presəbl] *adj.* 压抑不住的；约束不了的；控制不住的 — *n.* 〈口〉控制不住的人 ‖ **irrepressibly** *adv.*

irreproachable [,iri'prəutʃəbl] *adj.* 无可指责的，无瑕疵的；无缺点的

irresistible [,iri'zistəbl] *adj.* 1. 无可抵抗的；不能压制的 ‖ **irresistibly** *adv.*

irresolute [i'rezəljut] *adj.* 无决断的；犹豫不决的；优柔寡断的；摇摆不定的 ‖ **~ly** *adv.*

irresolution [,irezə'lju:ʃən] *n.* 无决断；犹豫不决；优柔寡断；摇摆不定

irrespective [,iris'pektiv] *adj.* 不考虑的；不问的；不顾的(*of*)

irresponsible [,iris'pɔnsəbl] *adj.* 1. 不承担

责任的；不需负责任的 **2.** 无责任感的；不负责任的(*for*)；不可靠的 — *n.* 不称职责任的人；不负责任感的人 ‖ **irres,ponsi'bility** *n.* / **irre'sponsibly** *adv.*

irretrievable [.iri'triːvəbl] *adj.* 不能恢复的；无法挽救的；不能弥补的 ‖ **irretrievably** *adv.*

irreverence [i'revərəns] *n.* **1.** 不虔诚；不尊敬 **2.** 不敬的言语(或行动) **3.** 无礼；傲慢

irreverent [i'revərənt] *adj.* **1.** 不虔诚的；不尊敬的 **2.** 无礼的；傲慢的 ‖ **~ly** *adv.*

irreversible [.iri'vəːsəbl] *adj.* **1.** 不可逆的；不能倒置的；不能倒转的；不能翻转的 **2.** 不可改变的；不可撤销的

irrevocable [i'revəkəbl] *adj.* **1.** 不可改变的；不能挽回的 **2.** 不可取消的，不可废止的 ‖ **irrevocably** *adv.*

irrigate ['irigeit] *vt.* **1.** 灌溉 **2.** 【医】冲洗(伤口) **3.** 滋润；使清新 — *vi.* **1.** 进行灌溉 **2.** 〈美俚〉饮酒过度

irrigation [.iri'geiʃən] *n.* **1.** 灌溉；水利 **2.** 【医】冲洗液

irritable ['iritəbl] *adj.* **1.** 易怒的；急躁的 **2.** 【医】过敏的 ‖ **irritability** [.iritə'biləti] *n.* **1.** 易怒；急躁 **2.** 【医】过敏；兴奋增盛；【生】应激性、感应性 / **irritably** *adv.*

irritant ['iritənt] *adj.* 刺激(性)的；会引起发炎的 — *n.* 【医】刺激物，刺激剂

irritate ['iriteit] *vt.* **1.** 激怒，使恼怒；使烦躁 **2.** 使不舒服；使发炎；使疼痛 **3.** 刺激；使兴奋 — *vi.* 引起不愉快

irritation [.iri'teiʃən] *n.* **1.** 激怒，恼怒，生气 **2.** 刺激物 **3.** 【医】刺激；过敏；兴奋过盛；疼痛；发炎

irrupt [i'rʌpt] *n.* 侵入，闯进(*into*) — *vt.* 【地】使侵入

irruption [i'rʌpʃən] *n.* 侵入，闯进

is [强 iz；弱 z, s] 见 **be**

is- *comb. form* = **iso-**

-ish *suf.* [构成形容词] **1.** 表示"…民族的"，"…语的"：Spanish, Irish **2.** 表示"…似的"，"…一样的"：boyish, foolish **3.** 表示"趋向于…的"，"近乎…的"，"稍带…的"：bookish, tallish, bluish **4.** 〈口〉表示"大约…"，"…左右"，"…前后"：thirtyish — [构成动词]：abolish, finish, polish

isinglass ['aizinɡlɑːs] *n.* **1.** 鱼胶；牛皮胶 **2.** 【地】白云母薄片

Islam ['izlɑːm] *n.* **1.** 伊斯兰教；回教 **2.** 〔总称〕伊斯兰教徒，穆斯林 **3.** 〔总称〕伊斯兰国家；伊斯兰世界

Islamabad [is'lɑːməbɑːd] *n.* 伊斯兰堡〔巴基斯坦首都〕

Islamic [iz'læmik] *adj.* 伊斯兰教的；穆斯林的

island ['ailənd] *n.* **1.** 岛；岛屿 **2.** 岛状物；孤立体；孤立的组织 **3.** 〈美〉(航空母舰的)飞行甲板上层建筑 **4.** (道路的)安全岛，安全带 **5.** 【解】脑岛；胰岛 **6.** (两边临铁道的)双面月台，双面站台 — *vt.* **1.** 使成岛(状)；孤立 **2.** 使成岛般分布在 ‖ **~er** *n.* 岛民，岛上居民

isle [ail] *n.* 岛；小岛 — *vt.* 使成岛(状) — *vi.* 住在岛上

islet ['ailit] *n.* **1.** 小岛；岛状地带，孤立地点 **2.** 【解】胰岛

-ism *suf.* **1.** 表示"主义"，"学说"，"信仰"，"制度"：Marxism **2.** 表示"行为"，"行动"：criticism **3.** 表示"状态"：barbarism **4.** 表示"特征"，"特性"：colloquialism **5.** 表示"病态"：alcoholism

isn't ['iznt] 〈口〉= **is not**

iso- *comb. form* [构成科技性质的名词或

isobar 形容词] 1. 表示"同"、"等"、"均匀"：
isobar 2. [化] 表示"(同分)异构"：
isomer (同分)异构体

isobar ['aisəubɑː] *n.* 1. [气] 等压线 2.
[物][化] 同量异位素

isolate ['aisəleit] *vt.* 1. 隔离；孤立；使脱离
2. [微] 使(细菌)分离；使与种群隔离
3. [化] 使离析 4. [电] 使绝缘 — *n.*
[微] 分离菌；隔离种群

isolation [,aisə'leiʃən] *n.* 1. 隔离；孤立；脱
离；分离 2. [物] 隔绝；绝缘 3. [化] 离析
(作用) ‖ ~**ism** *n.* 孤立主义 / ~**ist** *n.*
孤立主义者 *adj.* 孤立主义的；孤立主
义者的

isometrics [,aisəu'metriks] [复] *n.* [用作
单或复] 静力锻炼法

isosceles [ai'sɔsiliz] *adj.* [数] 等腰的

isotope ['aisəutəup] *n.* [物][化] 同位素

Israel ['izreiəl] *n.* 1. [总称] 以色列人、犹
太人；[宗] 上帝的选民 2. 以色列[西
南亚国家]

Israeli [iz'reili] *n.* 以色列人；以色列语 —
adj. 以色列的；以色列人的

Israelite ['izriəlait] *n.* 1. 古以色列人；犹
太人 2. [宗] 上帝的选民 — *adj.* 古以
色列(人)的；犹太人的

issuance ['iʃuːəns, 'isjuəns] *n.* 1. 发行；颁
布 2. 发给

issue ['iʃuː, 'isjuː] *n.* 1. (血、水等的)流
出；放出；流出物 2. 流出物 3. 结
果、结局 4. 发行；发行物；一次发行
量；(书刊的)期、号；版次 5. 问题；争
端、争论点 6. [律] 子女；后嗣 7. (土地、
地产的)收益 — *vt.* 1. 使流出；放出
2. 发行；颁布 3. 发给、分配 — *vi.* 1.
出来；流出 (from) 2. 由……得出、
发生 (from) 3. 发行；颁布出 (from)
4. [律] 产生；生息；诞生、传代

-ist *suf.* [构成名词] 1. 表示"专业人

员：geolog*ist*、pian*ist* 2. 表示"动作的实
践者"：antagon*ist*、moral*ist* 3. 表示"……
主义者"、"信仰者"：Marx*ist*、com-
mun*ist*、athe*ist* — [构成形容词] 表示
"具有……特性的"

isthmus ['isməs] *n.* 1. 地峡 2. [解] 峡 ‖
the Isthmus 1. 巴拿马地峡 2. 苏伊士地
峡

it [it] *pron.* 1. [指心目中或上下文中的人
或事物] 这、那、它 2. [指无生命的东
西，在性别不详或性别无关紧要时，亦
可指动物、幼孩等] 它 3. [作无人称动
词的主语，表示时间、气候、距离等] It
is ten o'clock. 10点钟了。4. [作先行代
词，引导后面的短语或从句] 这一
点：It is difficult to learn written Chinese.
汉语文字很难学。5. [作先行代词，用
于表示强调的句型中]：It is Tommy
that (或 who) answered the telephone. 是
汤米来接电话的。6. [接在某些由名
词变来的动词之后，无实义，构成习惯
性动词或词组]：We'll foot ~. 我们将步
行去。7. [用于某些动词或前置词的后
面，词义含糊，构成习语]：fight ~ out
决一雌雄；go ~ 干 ‖ 绝妙的人(或
物)；最好的东西 9. ~ 口 性感；性交 ‖
\葜罂 傻瓜，笨蛋

Italian [i'tæljən] *adj.* 意大利(人)的；意大
利语(或文化)的 — *n.* 意大利人；意大
利语

italic [i'tælik] *adj.* 1. [印] 斜体的 2. [I-]
古意大利(人)的；[I-] 意大利的
语族的 — *n.* 1. [常 ~s] 斜体字 2. [I-]
(印欧语系) 意大利语族

italicize, italicise [i'tælisaiz] *vt.* 1. 用斜体
字印刷；把……排成斜体 2. 在(词语)下
划横线(表示印刷时该用斜体字) 3. 强
调；突出

Italy ['itəli] *n.* 意大利[南欧国家]

itch [itʃ] *n.* **1.** [前接定冠词或不定冠词] 痒；[the～][医] 疥疮 **2.** [前常接不定冠词或物主代词]渴望 — *vi.* **1.** 发痒 **2.** 渴望

itchy ['itʃi] *adj.* 生疥疮的；(发)痒的；渴望的

it'd ['itəd] **1.** = it had **2.** = it would

-ite *suf.* [构成名词词] **1.** 表示"...的居民"、"...的后代"的信徒"：Israelite **2.** 表示"...的产物"：ebonite **3.** 表示"化石结构"：ammonite **4.** 表示"矿物"、"岩石"：graphite **5.** 表示"身体的组成部分"、"器官"**6.** [化] 表示"亚...酸盐"：sulphite **7.** 表示"爆炸物"：dynamite

item ['aitəm] *n.* **1.** 条；项；条款；项目 **2.** (新闻等的)一条，一则 — *adv.* (用于介绍目录表或细目中这个项目之前)又，同样地｜～ize *vt.* 逐条记载；详细登录 / itemi'zation *n.*

iterate ['itəreit] *vt.* 重述；反复申说；重复 ‖ iteration *n.* / iterative *adj.*

itinerant [i'tinərənt] *adj.* 巡回的，巡游的 — *n.* 巡回者(如行商，巡回传教士)

itinerary [ai'tinərəri] *n.* **1.** 旅程；路线 **2.** 预定的行程；旅行计划 **3.** 旅行记录；行程记 **4.** 旅行指南 — *adj.* 旅行的；旅程的；路线的；道路的

-itis *suf.* **1.** 表示"...炎"、"发炎"：appendicitis **2.** 表示"由...引起的疾病(或病态)"：vacationitis 假日病 **3.** 表示"...癖"：jazzitis 爵士音乐癖 **4.** 表示"过分的...派头"：big-businessitis 过分的大企业派头

it'll ['itl] **1.** = it will **2.** = it shall

its [its] *pron.* [it 的所有格]它的

it's [its] **1.** = it is **2.** = it has

itself [it'self] *pron.* **1.** [反身代词]它自己，

它本身；正常状况；健全状态 **2.** [用以加强语气]自身，本身：The work ～ is easy. 这工作本身很容易。

-ity *suf.* [构成名词词] 表示"性质"、"状态"，"程度"：purity, alkalinity

I've [aiv] = I have

-ive *suf.* [构成形容词词] **1.** 表示"...的"，"与...有关的"，"属于...的"，"具有...性质的"：native, substantive **2.** 表示"倾向于某一活动的"：creative

IVF *abbr.* in vitro fertilization 体外受精

ivied ['aivid] *adj.* 常春藤覆盖的，爬满常春藤的

ivory ['aivəri] *n.* **1.** 象牙；(海象等的)长牙 **2.** 牙质 **3.** 象牙色，乳白色 **4.** [ivories] 象牙制品；仿象牙制品 **5.** 高级白板纸 **6.** [俚] [ivories] 琴键；牙齿；骰子；台球、弹子（球）— *adj.* 象牙制成的；似象牙的 **2.** 象牙色的，乳白色的

Ivory Coast ['aivəri 'kəust] 象牙海岸 Côte d'Ivoire 科特迪瓦的英文意译 [西非国家]

ivy ['aivi] *n.* [植] 常春藤 — *adj.* **1.** 常春藤联合会名牌大学的；常春藤联合会名牌大学(或大学生)派头的 **2.** 纯理论的；无实用意义的

-ization *suf.* [构成与-ize 相应的名词]：realization

-ize *suf.* [构成及物动词词] **1.** 表示"使成为"，"使...化"，"使形成"：revolutionize, systemize, unionize **2.** 表示"作...处理"，"使渗透"，"使与...结合"：dramatize, idolize, oxidize **3.** 表示"使变成...状"，"产生..."：crystallize **4.** 表示"像...似地从事活动"，"照...法处理"：pasteurize ｜ [构成不及物动词]表示"有...感情"，"实行..."：sympathize

izzard ['izəd] *n.* 〈古〉〈方〉字母 Z

J

J.j [dʒei]([复]J's,j's 或 Js,js[dʒeiz])英语字母表第十个字母 1.[J]]字形 2.[J][物]焦耳(joule)的符号 3.[数]与 y 轴平行的单位矢量

jab [dʒæb](jabbed;jabbing) *vt.*1. 猛刺,猛戳 2. 用(拨火棒等)插 3.(用拳)猛击 — *vi.* 猛刺,猛戳;猛击(at) — *n.* 猛刺,猛戳;猛击

jabber ['dʒæbə] *vi.*1. 急促而含糊地说话 2. 闲聊 3.(猴等)吱吱喳喳地叫 — *vt.* 急促而含糊地说出 — *n.* 急促含糊的话;莫名其妙的话

jabberwocky ['dʒæbə,wɔki] *n.* 毫无意义的话(或文章)

jack [dʒæk] *n.*1.[J-]杰克(男子名:也可用作 John 的俗称或昵称)2.[J-]普通人;男人;男孩;家伙;仆人 3.[常 J-]水手;水兵;海员 4. 伐木工人;打杂工;工人 5. 烤肉炙叉旋转器;V字形脱靴器 6.[机]起重器,千斤顶;(舞台台背景后的)木撑,木支柱 7. 公驴;公畜;狗鱼;寒鸦;长耳大野兔 8.〈美理〉钱 9.(纸牌中的)杰克;老相片 10.(滚球游戏中作靶子的)小白球;(抛接子游戏中所用的)小卵石(或小金属片)11.〈美〉(夜间打猎或捕鱼用的)篝灯 12.[电](标志圆筒的)插首嵌入 13.[电]插座;插口,塞孔 14. 苹果酒;水果白兰地 15. 屈体跳水,折刀式跳水 — *vi.* 用篝灯打猎(或捕鱼)— *vt.*1. 用起重

器举(或顶)2.(用篝灯)猎(兽);(用篝灯)捕(鱼)3. 增加:提高(水平、质量、物价,工资等)(up) 4. 责备(up);规劝...尽职(up) 5. 放弃(企图等)(up) || 〈美理〉找(枪)弹(out) — *adj.* 公驴的 ‖ ~ass *n.*1. 公驴 2. 笨蛋,傻瓜 / ~ bean [植] 刀豆 / ~ daw *n.* [动] 寒鸦;鹩哥 / ~ fish *n.* [动] 狗鱼 / Jack Frost 箱;严寒 / ~ -in-the,box [复] [~ -in-the-boxes 或 ~ s-in-the-box] *n.*1. 玩偶匣(揭起盖子即有玩偶跳起)2.[动]寄居蟹 / ~ -knife *n.*1.(可放袋内的)大折刀 2.(跳水中前弯身的)屈体跳水,折刀式跳水 *vt.* 用大折刀切(或戳) *vi.* 作屈体跳水 / Jack-of-'all-trades [[复] Jacks-of-all-trades] *n.*1. 能做各种事情的人,万能博士 2. 杂而不精的人 / ~ -o'-,lantern *n.*1. 磷火 2. 行踪不定的人 3. 使人迷惑的事物 4.(以南瓜刻成人面形的)杰克灯 / ~ -pot *n.*1.(赌者须有一对杰克或更好的牌才能赢的)赌注 2.(彩票等的)头彩;(屡次得奖而积累的)大笔收入;巨额资金;(在冒险的事情中获得的)意外大成功 3.〈美〉困境 / ~ ,rabbit *n.*(北美西部产)长耳大野兔

jackal ['dʒækɔ:l] *n.*1.[动]豺,黑背豺,亚洲胡狼 2. 走狗,爪牙,狗腿子

jacket ['dʒækit] *n.*1. 短上衣,茄克衫 2.(动物的)皮毛;马铃薯皮 3.(书籍的)护封;封面;文件套;公文夹;唱片套

弹壳 4. 外罩；保护罩；隔热罩；绝热罩 5.〔机〕套 — vt.1. 给…穿短上衣 2. 给…加护封（或封套）

jade[dʒeid] n.1.〔矿〕玉 2. 绿玉色 — adj.1. 玉制的 2. 绿玉色的

jade[dʒeid] n.1. 老马；驽马 2.〈贬〉荡妇；轻佻女子 3.〈谑〉〈贬〉女子 — vt. & vi.1.（使）疲倦 2. 精疲力竭 3. 迟钝的；厌倦的 3. 用旧了的

jag[dʒæg] n. 尖突，齿状突起 —（jagged; jagging）vt. 把…切（或撕）得参差不齐；在…上弄出锯齿状凹口

jag[dʒæg] n.1.（草、木等的）一车人 —小担；一小捆 2.（酒等引起的）醉态，昏醉 3. 狂欢，闹饮 4. 一阵

jagged[ˈdʒægid] jaggy [dʒægi] adj. 锯齿状的，有缺口的；参差不齐的；粗糙的；凹凸不平的

jagged[ˈdʒægid] adj.〈美俚〉喝醉的；昏醉的

jaguar[ˈdʒægjuə] n.〔动〕美洲虎，美洲豹

jail[dʒeil] n. & vt.〈美〉= gaol ‖ — er, ~ or = gaoler ‖ ~bird n. 囚犯；惯犯 / ~break n. 越狱

Jakarta[dʒəˈkɑːtə] n. = Djakarta

jal(l)opy[dʒəˈlɔpi] n.〈口〉破旧汽车（或飞机）

jam[dʒæm]（jammed; jamming）vt.1. 把…挤进；把…楔进；挤进；塞进 2. 轧伤；压碎 3. 使塞满；使挤满 4. 使轧住不动 5.（通道等）堵塞 6.〔无〕干扰 — vi.1. 堵塞；楔紧；轧住 2. 拥挤；挤满 3.〈美俚〉参加爵士音乐即席演奏会 — n.1. 拥挤；塞满；机器等的）轧住 2. 阻塞；堵塞；困窘 3.〈俚〉困境 4. 爵士乐即兴演奏会

jam[dʒæm] n.1. 果酱 2. 令人愉快的事物；轻松活儿

Jamaica[dʒəˈmeikə] n. 牙买加[拉丁美洲岛国]

jamb[dʒæm] n.1.〔建〕门窗边框；壁炉侧墙 2.〔矿〕矿柱 3. 胫甲

jamboree[ˌdʒæmbəˈriː] n.1. 闹饮〈欢乐的聚会 2. 大集会；童子军大会 3. 有娱乐活动的集会

Jan. abbr. January

jangle[ˈdʒæŋɡl] vi.1.（铃等）发出刺耳声 2. 吵架 — vt.1. 使发出刺耳声 2. 刺耳地发出 3. 烦扰；使极度烦躁 — n.1. 吵嚷 2. 刺耳声 3. 空谈

janitor[ˈdʒænitə] n.1. 看门人，管门人 2. 照管房屋的工友

January[ˈdʒænjuəri] n. 一月（略作 Jan.）

Japan[dʒəˈpæn] n. 日本，日本国[亚洲东部岛国]

Japanese[ˌdʒæpəˈniːz] adj. 日本的；日本人的；日语的 —[单复同] n.1. 日本人 2. 日语

jar[dʒɑː]（jarred; jarring）vi.1. 发出刺耳声；轧轧作响 2. 使人感到不快；刺激（upon, on）3. 剧烈震动 4. 不一致；不和谐；冲突；争吵（with）— vt.1. 震动；摇动 2. 使感不快；刺激（神经）3. 使发出刺耳声 — n.1. 刺耳声；轧轧声 2. 突然的震动 3. 震动，震惊 4. 不调和；不一致；口角，争执 5.（节奏等的）突然中止；失调

jar[dʒɑː] n.1. 罐子；坛子；广口瓶 2. 一罐所装的量（或物）

jargon[ˈdʒɑːɡən] n.1. 多专门术语的话；行话；黑话 2. 听不懂的话，莫名其妙的话；胡言乱语 3. 粗俗下流的言语；混杂语 5.（鸟等的）喳喳叫声 — vi.1. 喳喳喳地叫 2. 讲难懂（话）写难懂的文章

jasmin(e)[ˈdʒæsmin] n.1.〔植〕素馨，茉

莉;素方花;常绿钩吻 2. 茉莉花茶 3. 淡黄色 ‖ ~ tea 茉莉花茶

jasper ['dʒæspə] n. 1. 〖矿〗碧玉 2. 墨绿色

jaundice ['dʒɔːndis] n. 1. 〖医〗黄疸 2. 猜疑、偏见、厌恶 — vi. 1. 使患黄疸病 2. 使妒忌;使不满;使有偏见

jaundiced ['dʒɔːndist] adj. 1. 患黄疸病 (似)的 2. 妒忌的;有偏见的;厌恶的; 怀有敌意的

jaunt [dʒɔːnt] vi. 作短途旅行 — n. 短途旅行

jaunty ['dʒɔːnti] adj. 1. 漂亮的;时髦的 2. 活泼的;洋洋得意的;逍遥自在的 — n. 〈英俚〉(舰艇上的)纠察长 ‖ jauntily adv. / jauntiness n.

Java ['dʒɑːvə] n. 1. 爪哇(岛)〖印度尼西亚南部〗 2. 爪哇咖啡 3. 〖常作 j-〗〈俚〉咖啡 4. 〖黑毛或毛上有黑斑点的〗爪哇鸡 ‖ ~ man 爪哇(直立)猿人

javelin ['dʒævəlin] n. 〖体〗标枪 ‖ ~ throw 掷标枪

jaw [dʒɔː] n. 1. 颌;颚 2. 〖~s〗口部;嘴 3. 〖机〗牙;钳口 4. 〖~s〗(山谷、水道等的) 狭窄入口 5. 〖~s〗险境 6. 〈口〉饶舌;喋喋不休;说教 7. 〖俚〗闲聊 — vt. 〈俚〉训斥;对…说教 — vi. 〈俚〉唠叨;漫骂

jay [dʒei] n. 1. 〖动〗松鸦;北美蓝鸦鸟 2. 〈俚〉爱唠叨的人;饶舌者 3. 花花公子;笨伯;易受骗的人

jaywalk ['dʒeiwɔːk] vi. 〈口〉不遵守交通规则地乱穿马路 ‖ ~ er n. 乱穿马路者

jazz [dʒæz] n. 1. 爵士乐;爵士舞(曲) 2. 〈美俚〉爵士乐持征;活泼;热烈;狂欢 3. 歇人之谈;陈词滥调 — adj. 爵士乐的;色彩浓的;花哨的 — vt. 1. 把…奏成爵士乐;使有刺激性;使活泼(up) 3. 加快…的速度 — vi. 1. 游荡(around) 2. 奏爵士乐;跳爵士舞

jealous ['dʒeləs] adj. 1. 妒忌的;善嫉妒的 2. 猜疑的,留意提防的 3. 注意的;戒备的;唯恐失掉的 4. 〖基督教〗〈圣经〉中指上帝〖要求绝对忠实的;容不得抗争的〗 ‖ ~ ly adv. / ~ ness n.

jealousy ['dʒeləsi] n. 1. 妒忌;猜忌;嫉妒 2. 留意提防;谨慎戒备

jean [dʒiːn] n. 1. 〖纺〗三页细斜纹布 2. 〖~s〗(三页细纹布做的)紧身工装裤;紧身裤;牛仔裤;裤子

jeep [dʒiːp] n. 1. 吉普车,小型越野汽车 2. 〖军〗护航航空母舰 — vi. 乘吉普车旅行 — vt. 用吉普车运送

jeer [dʒiə] vi., vt. & n. 嘲笑;嘲弄

Jehovah [dʒi'həuvə] n. 〖基督教〗〈圣经〉中的)耶和华(指上帝)

jell [dʒel] vi. 1. 胶凝,结冻 2. 定形,具体化;变明确 — vt. 1. 使结冻 2. 使定形,使具体化,使明确化 — n. 果子冻,冻;胶状物

jelly ['dʒeli] n. 1. 果子冻;肉冻 2. 胶状物;糊状物,浆 3. 畏惧;犹豫不决 4. 〈美俚〉轻而易举的事;免费得来的东西 — vt. 1. 使结冻,使成胶状 2. 由…上加胶状物 — vi. 1. 结冻;凝结;成胶状 2. 〈美俚〉闲逛着聊天 ‖ ~ fish n. 1. 〖动〗水母;海蜇 2. 〈美俚〉无骨气的人;优柔寡断的人

jennet ['dʒenit] n. 1. 西班牙小马 2. 母驴

jenny ['dʒeni] n. 1. 詹尼纺沙机 2. 雌鸟;母兽,母驴幼兽 3. 移动式起重机

jeopardize ['dʒepədaiz] vt. 使处于危险境地;危及

jeopardy ['dʒepədi] n. 1. 危险,危逆 2. 〖律〗刑事案件中被告有被判罪或受处罚的〗危险处境

jerk [dʒəːk] vt. 1. 把…猛地一拉(或一推、一扭、一掷等) 2. 突然急促和断续地说出 3. 配制并端上(苏打饮料)—

vi.1. 急拉;猛推;扔;猛地一动 2. 颠簸地行进 3. 痉挛 — *n*.1. 急拉;急推;急扭;急扔;急动 2. 颠簸、震摇 3.【医】反射;[～s](因激动引起的)抽搐;舞蹈病 4.【体】(举重运动中的)上挺 5.〈俚〉愚笨(或古怪)的人

jerkin [ˈdʒəːkin] *n*.1.(旧时男子穿的)紧身皮大衣 2. 无袖紧身外套

jerky [ˈdʒəːki] *adj*.1. 急拉的;急动的;急扔的 2.(车等)不平稳的、颠簸的;(文体)多突变的 3. 痉挛性的 4. 愚蠢的 ‖ **jerkily** *adv*. /**jerkiness** *n*.

jerry-built [ˈdʒeribilt] *adj*. 1. 偷工减料建成的;用劣质材料建成的 2. 草草拼凑成的

jersey [ˈdʒəːzi] *n*.1.【纺】平针织物 2. 紧身(运动)套衫 3. 针织紧身内衣 4.[J-]泽西种乳牛

Jerusalem [dʒəˈruːsələm] *n*. 耶路撒冷(西南亚巴勒斯坦地区著名古城、伊斯兰教、犹太教和基督教的圣地)

jessamine [ˈdʒesəmin] *n*. = jasmin(e)

jest [dʒest] *n*.1. 玩笑;滑稽事 2. 笑话;俏皮话 3. 戏谑、诙谐;快活 4. 笑柄;笑料 — *vi*.1. 说笑话;嘲弄(*at*)2. 开玩笑;打趣;戏谑;做滑稽动作 — *vt*. 对...开玩笑;嘲笑 ‖ ～**er** *n*. 爱开玩笑的人;小丑;(中世纪的)弄臣

Jesus [ˈdʒiːzəs] *n*.【基督教】耶稣

jet[1] [dʒet] (jetted; jetting) *vt*.1. 喷射出(烟、水流等)2. 用喷气式飞机运送 — *vi*.1. 喷出、射出 2. 乘喷气式飞机旅行 — *n*.1. 喷射流;【天】喷流;【气】急流 2. 喷嘴、喷射口 3.【空】喷气发动机;喷气式飞机 4. 喷涌而出的东西 — *adj*. 喷气(发动机)推进的 ‖ ～ **airplane** 喷气式飞机 /～ **engine** 喷气发动机 /～ **lag** 喷气飞行时差综合征 /～ **plane** 喷气式飞机 /ˈ～-**proˈpelled** *adj*. 喷气推进的;疾驶的;马力极大的 /～ **propulsion** 喷气推进 /～ **stream** 1.【气】急流 2.【空】射流、喷流

jet[2] [dʒet] *n*.1.【矿】煤玉;黑色大理石 2. 乌黑发亮的颜色 — *adj*.1. 黑色大理石制的 2. 乌黑发亮的

jetsam [ˈdʒetsəm] *n*.1.(船舶遇险时)投弃的货物(或设备等);沉入水底(或冲到岸上)的投弃物品 2. 被抛弃的东西;无家可归的穷人

jettison [ˈdʒetisn] *n*.1.【海】【空】(在紧急情况下的)投弃货物;投弃的货物 2. 抛弃、丢弃 — *vt*.1. 投弃(货物)2. 抛弃、丢弃(累赘或无用之物)3.(飞机)在飞行中投下(辅助装备、弹药、燃料等)

jetty [ˈdʒeti] *n*.1. 防波堤;突堤 2. 登岸码头;突码头 3.(建筑物的)突出部 — *vi*. 伸出、突出

Jew [dʒuː] *n*.1. 犹太人 2. 犹太教徒 3.〈贬〉守财奴;高利贷者;奸商 — *vt*.[常作 j-]〈口〉杀(某人)的价(*down*);拼命跟(某人)讨价还价

jewel [ˈdʒuːəl] *n*.1. 宝石 2. 宝石饰物;首饰 3. 珍贵的人(或物)4.(手表内的)宝石轴承、钻 5. 睾丸 — (jewel(l)ed; jewel(l)ing) *vt*.1. 用宝石装饰 2. 把宝石轴承装进(手表) ‖ **jewel(l)er** *n*. 宝石商、珠宝商;钟表商;宝石匠;钟表匠

jewellery, jewelry [ˈdʒuːəlri] *n*.[总称]珠宝;首饰

Jewish [ˈdʒuːiʃ] *adj*. 犹太人的;犹太人似的;犹太人作风的 — *n*. = Yiddish

jib [dʒib] *n*. 艏三角帆 — (jibbed; jibbing) *vt*. 使(帆、桁等)从一舷转至另一舷;使(帆)改变方向 — *vi*.(船帆等)从一舷转至另一舷、转帆

jibe[1] [dʒaib] *vi*., *vt*. & *n*. 嘲笑、嘲弄

jibe[2] [dʒaib] *vi*.〈美口〉一致、符合(*with*)

Jibuti [dʒiˈbuːti] *n.* = Djibouti

jiff [dʒif], **jiffy** [ˈdʒifi] *n.*〈口〉一会儿，瞬间

jig [dʒig] *n.*1.（通常为三拍子的快步的）吉格舞曲；吉格舞曲 2.拟饵手钓钩，滚钩 3.〔矿〕跳汰机 4.〔机〕夹具，钻模；样板；装配架 — *v.*（jigged; jigging） *vt.*1.轻快地跳（舞）；急速上下（或前后）的急动 3.用拟饵手钓钩钓（鱼）4.〔矿〕跳汰选（矿）‖ 用夹具加工

jigger [ˈdʒigə] *n.*1.跳汰机工 2.〔矿〕跳汰机；筛 3.大滚钩；冰下张网器（用木框制的加拿大渔具）4.〔机〕辘轳车 5.容量为 1 忌 盎司的配酒用小量杯 6.伸展后桅帆，（有伸缩桅帆的）小渔船；辅桅（多桅帆船的第四帆）7.（二桅帆船的）后桅 7.〔俚〕（没有确切名称的）新发明，小玩意儿

jiggle [ˈdʒigl] *vt. & vi.*（使）轻轻摇晃（或跳动） — *n.*轻轻的摇晃（或跳动）

jigsaw [ˈdʒigsɔː] *n.*钢丝锯，镂花锯；线锯 — *vt.*1.用线锯（或钢丝锯）锯 2.使互相交错拼接 ‖ **~ puzzle** 拼图玩具；七巧板

jilt [dʒilt] *vt.*抛弃（情人） — *n.*抛弃情人者（尤指女子）‖ **~ee** [dʒilˈtiː] *n.*被抛弃者

jimmy [ˈdʒimi] *n.*〈美〉（强盗用的）撬棍 — *vt.*撬

jingle [ˈdʒiŋgl] *vi. & vt.*1.（使）丁当响 2.（使）（诗或音乐）重复同一个韵（或声音） — *n.*1.（硬币、小铃、钥匙等的）丁当声；（美俚）电话铃声；发丁当声的东西 2.反复出现同一声音的诗（或歌）；音韵铿锵的诗（或歌）；以声音而不是以意义取引人的语句 3.〈澳大利亚和澳洲的）双轮有篷马车 ‖ **jingly** *adj.*

jinrikisha, jinricksha [dʒinˈrikʃə] *n.* 人力车，黄包车

jinx [dʒiŋks] 〈口〉*n.*不祥的人（或物） — *vt.*使倒霉；使失败

jitney [ˈdʒitni] *n.*〈美俚〉1.五分的镍币 2.（收费便宜的）小公共汽车

jitterbug [ˈdʒitəbʌg] *n.*1.吉特巴舞（一种活泼欢快的双人社交舞）2.跳吉特巴舞的人 — *vi.*跳吉特巴舞

jitters [ˈdʒitəz] 〔复〕*n.*[用作单或复]〈口〉极度的紧张不安

job [dʒɔb] *n.*1.工作 2.零活 3.职责；任务；作用 4.〈口〉职位；职业 5.〈口〉费力的事情 6.假公济私的事情 7.〈俚〉犯罪行为（尤指偷窃等）8.成果；成品 — (jobbed; jobbing) *vi.*1.受雇工，做临时工 2.做批发生意；做掮客 3.假公济私；营私舞弊 — *vt.*1.批购（货物）转卖给零售商 2.把（工作、工程等）分包出去（out）3.假公济私的手段办理（或实现、作成）4.短期包租（车、马等）5.〈俚〉欺骗，欺诈 ‖ **~less** *adj.*失业的；失业者的 ‖ **~ printer** 零件印刷商 ~ **work** 1.包工；散工 2.零件印刷

jobber [ˈdʒɔbə] *n.*1.批发商 2.零工；散工

jockey [ˈdʒɔki] *n.*1.职业赛马骑师 2.驾驶员（机器等的）操作者 3.〈英〉小伙子；下属；帮手 4.马贩子；精明的生意人 — *vt.*1.骑（马）比赛；驾驶；操作 2.欺骗；诈骗；诱使 3.移动 — *vi.*1.当赛马骑师 2.运用手段图谋利益

jocose [dʒəˈkəus] *adj.*爱开玩笑的；滑稽的；逗乐的

jocular [ˈdʒɔkjulə] *adj.*1.诙谐的；滑稽的；喜开玩笑的 2.打趣的；寻乐的

jocund [ˈdʒɔkənd] *adj.*欢乐的；快活的

jodhpur [ˈdʒɔdpə] *n.*1.[~s]马裤 2.短马靴

jog[1] [dʒɔg] (jogged; jogging) *vt.*1.轻推；轻轻摇动；轻撞 2.唤起（记忆）；提醒 3.

使(马等)缓步行进 — vi.1. 颠簸地移动 2. 慢吞吞地走,缓步前进:慢跑(on, along)3. 缓慢平稳地进行(on, along) 4. 度过时间 — n.1. 轻推;轻摇;轻撞 2. 慢步;缓行:慢跑 ‖ jogger n. 慢跑(健身锻炼)者

jog² ['dʒɔg](美) **n.1.**(面或线上的)凹进;凸出 2. 突然的转向 — (jogged) jog-ging) vi.1. 凹进;凸出 2. 突然转向

joggle ['dʒɔgl] vt., vi. & n. 轻轻颠摇

johnny, johnnie ['dʒɔni] n.1.[常用 J-](口)纨绔子弟 2.(住院病人穿的)短袖无领后开罩衫 ‖ **johnnycake** n.[美]玉米烤饼(美)面粉饼

join [dʒɔin] vt.1. 连接;接合;使结合 2. 参加,加入,作...的成员和...作伴 3. 回到(岗位等)4.(口)和...毗连 — vi.1. 连接;相遇 2. 参加,加入;结合,一起(in)3. 邻接,毗连 — n.1. 连接;结合之接连处;接合点;接合线

joiner [dʒɔinə] n.1. 接合物 2. 细木工人 3.(口)爱参加各种社团组织活动的人

joint [dʒɔint] n.1. 接头,结点;接缝;接合处 2. 关节 3. 接合(方式),连接(方式)4.(牛、羊等的带骨的)大块肉 5.【植】关节 6.【地】节理 7. 书脊封面连接处,书脊槽 8.(俚)下流场所(指赌窟、烟馆、小酒店等)(任何)场所 9.(俚)大麻烟卷 — adj.1. 连接的;接合的 2. 联合的,共同的;同时的 3. 合伙的;共有的;全连带的 — vt.1. 连接;接合 2. 使有接缝;为...装上接头 3.(从关节处)切断;把...以及带骨的大块肉 — 切成小块 4. 使接合,贴合 7.【植】拔节:长节 ‖ ~ed adj. 有接缝的;有节的;有关节的 / ~ly adv. 联合地,共同地;连带地

joist [dʒɔist] n.[建]搁栅;托梁;檩 —

vt. 为...架搁栅;为...装托梁

joke [dʒəuk] n.1. 笑话;玩笑 2. 笑柄;笑料 3. 极易办妥的事情;无实在内容的东西;空话 — vi. 开玩笑,开...的玩笑,戏弄

joker ['dʒəukə] n.1. 爱开玩笑的人;诙谐者 2.(美)(为使法案等失效含糊而在条文中埋下的)伏笔,曲笔;(留着待用的)诡计 3. 没有预见到的困难,隐患 4.(纸牌中的)百搭(可作任何点数的牌或王牌)5.(俚)家伙

joking ['dʒəukiŋ] adj. 开玩笑的 ‖ ~ly adv.

jollity ['dʒɔliti] n. 欢乐(英)欢聚

jolly ['dʒɔli] adj.1. 快活的,兴高采烈的;有趣的 2.(口)令人高兴的;很愉快的,很舒畅的;好极的 3.(英口)大大的 4.(英)微醺的 — adv.(英口)很,非常 — vt.1.(口)(用捧、哄或开玩笑等)使高兴,使快活(along)2. 开...玩笑,戏弄 — vi. 开玩笑 — n.[英俚]皇家海军陆战队队员

jolt [dʒəult] vt.1. 震摇;使颠簸 2.(拳击中)给(对手)猛然一击 3.(粗暴地)突然干涉 —(车辆等)震摇;颠簸 — n.1. 震摇;颠簸 2. 猛击(尤指拳击)3. 震惊;引起震惊的事情 4. 严重挫折 5. 少量

jonquil ['dʒɔŋkwil] n.[植]长寿花

Jordan ['dʒɔdn] n.1. 约旦[西南亚国家] 2.[the ~]约旦河[西南亚]

josh [dʒɔʃ](美口)n.(无恶意地)戏弄哄骗 — vi.(无恶意地)开玩笑,戏弄开玩笑,戏弄

jostle ['dʒɔsl] vi.1. 推搡;拥挤 2. 贴近;竞争,争夺 — vt.1. 推(用肘)推搡 2. 贴近 3. 激惹,煽动,使激动 4. 与...竞争,争夺 — n. 推搡;拥挤

jot [dʒɔt] n. 一点儿;(最)小额;(最)少

量 — (jotted; jotting) vt. 草草记下 (down)

jounce [dʒauns] vt. & vi. (使)震动;(使)摇动;(使)颠簸 — n. 震动;颠簸

journal [ˈdʒɜːnl] n.1. 日志;日记;航海日志 2. (立法机构、委员会等的)议事录 3. 日报;期刊;杂志 4.【会计】日记帐 5.【机】轴颈

journalism [ˈdʒɜːnəlizəm] n.1. 新闻业;新闻工作:新闻写作;新闻报道 2.【总称】报章杂志 3. 新闻学 ‖ **journalistic** [ˌdʒɜːnəˈlistik] adj.

journalist [ˈdʒɜːnəlist] n.1. 新闻工作者,报人:报纸撰稿人 2. 记日志者

journey [ˈdʒɜːni] n.1. 旅行;旅程;路程(常指陆上的):(主方) 一天行程 2. 历程 — vi. 旅行 — vt. 在...旅行;旅行过(某地) ‖ ~ man n.1. 雇工;计日工;短工 2. 熟练工人;满师学徒工 3.【矿】斜井罐笼工

joust [dʒaust] n.1.(骑士等的)马背长矛打斗;(马上)比武 2. 格斗;竞争 — vi.1. 骑着马用长矛比武式(或策打)2. 格斗;竞争

jovial [ˈdʒəuviəl] adj.1.[J-]【罗神】(主神)朱庇特的 2.[J-]【天】木星的 3. 快活的,愉快的 ‖ ~ly adv. 快活地

jowl [dʒaul] n.1. 颔;下颚;(无脊椎动物的)下颚 2. 颊部;腮肉 3. 下颌垂肉,二下巴;(牛、羊等的)颈垂肉;(鸟的)嗉囊 4. 鱼头及头部分

joy [dʒɔi] n.1. 欢乐;乐事;乐趣 vi. 欢欣 — vt. (古) 使高兴;享受

joyful [ˈdʒɔiful] adj.1. 十分喜悦的,高兴的,快乐的 2. 使人喜悦的 ‖ ~ly adv. / ~ness n.

joyous [ˈdʒɔiəs] adj. 高兴的,快乐的 ‖ ~ly adv. / ~ness n.

Jr., jr. abbr. junior

jubilant [ˈdʒuːbilənt] adj. 欢呼的;兴高采烈的,喜气洋洋的

jubilee [ˈdʒuːbiliː] n.1.[常作 J-](犹太史)五十年节,禧年 2.【天主教】大赦年 3.(结婚)五十周年纪念(或庆祝);二十五周年纪念(或庆祝)4. 喜庆时节;欢庆 5.(美)(歌唱未来幸福时代的)黑人欢快民歌

Judaism [ˈdʒuːdeiizəm] n.1.【宗】犹太教 2. 对犹太风俗(或仪式等)的恪守 3.[总称]犹太文明;犹太生活方式 4.[总称]犹太人

judge [dʒʌdʒ] n.1. 审判员,法官 2.(比赛等的)裁判员;(纠纷等的)评判员 3. 鉴定人;鉴赏家 4.[J-]最高审判者(指上帝)5.[史](犹太诸王以前的统治者)士师;[Judges](用作单)【基督教《圣经·旧约全书》】(《士师记》)— vt.1. 审判;审理;判决 2. 裁判(比赛);评定决定(争端等)3. 判断;断定 4. 鉴别;评价 5. 认为 6.(古) 批评;指责 — vi.1. 下判断;作出裁判 2. 作评价(of)

judge ment [ˈdʒʌdʒmənt] n.1. 审判;判决,判定 2. 判决确定的债务;确定债务的判决书 3. 判断;评价 4. 判断力;识(别)力 5. 意见,看法 6. 批评;指责 7. 天罚;报应 8.[J-]上帝的最后审判 9.(基督教《圣经》用语)公正;正义

judicial [dʒuːˈdiʃəl] adj.1. 司法的;审判(上)的 2. 审判员(或法官)的;法院判决的(或规定)的 3. 法官似的;合乎法官身分的 4. 公正的;考虑周密的;慎重决择的 5. 明断的;批评的 6. 上帝审判的,天罚的

judiciary [dʒuːˈdiʃiəri] adj. 审判员的;法院的;司法的 — n.1. 司法部 2.[总称]审判员 3. 法院系统(或制度)

judicious [dʒuːˈdiʃəs] adj. 明断的;明智

的;审慎的;有见识的 ‖ ~ly *adv.*/ ~ness *n.*

judo ['dʒuːdəu] (〔复〕judos)〈日〉*n.*1. 现代柔道,现代柔术 2. = jujitsu

jug [dʒʌg] *n.*1.(有柄的小口)大壶,罐,盂 2. 壶中物,罐中物;一壶的量 3.〔美俚〕监牢 4.〔美俚〕保险箱(-jugged; jugging)*vt.*1.把 ... 放入壶(或罐)中 2. 炖,煨(兔等)3.〔俚〕监禁,关押

juggle ['dʒʌgl] *vi.*1.(用球、小刀等)玩杂要;变戏法 2. 玩把戏,耍花招;欺骗3. 歪曲;篡改 — *vt.*1. 耍(球、盘等)要弄 2. 把 ... 抓得不牢(或摆弄不稳)3. 歪曲;篡改;颠倒(事实等)4. 欺骗,诈取 — *n.*1. 玩杂要;变戏法,魔术 2. 耍花招;欺骗,欺诈 ‖ ~r *n.*1. 玩杂要的人;魔术师 2. 骗子

Jugoslavia [ˌjuːgəu'slɑːvjə] *n.* = Yugoslavia

jugular ['dʒʌgjulə] *adj.* 颈的;喉的;颈静脉的 — *n.*1. 颈静脉 2. 致命处 ‖ ~ vein 颈静脉

juice [dʒuːs] *n.*1.(水果、蔬菜等的)汁,液 2.〔常 ~s〕体液 3. 精,精髓;精力 4.〔俚〕电流;汽油;〔俚〕润滑油5.〔美俚〕酒(尤指烈士忌酒)6.[J-]〔美俚〕(舞台等的)照明员,灯光员 7.〔俚〕幽默,敲诈等所得的钱,油水;(债主索取的)高利;(从官职等所得的)薪水,收入 — *vt.*1.〈口〉从 ... 榨出汁(或液)2.〔俚〕使 ... 挤牛奶 3. 在 ... 中加汁(或液)

juicy ['dʒuːsi] *adj.*1.多液汁的 2. 多雨的;潮湿的 3.〈口〉津津有味的;有趣的;刺激性的(指可口的一部分)轶事、丑闻、笑话等)4. 活力充沛的 5. 富于色彩的;绚烂的 6. 报酬多的;油水多的 ‖ juiciness *n.*

jujitsu [dʒuː'dʒitsuː]〈日〉*n.* 柔术,柔道 —

vt. 用柔术制服(对手)

juke [dʒuːk] *n.*〔美俚〕1. = jukebox 2. 自动唱机音乐 ‖ '~box *n.*(丢进硬币按钮选唱听唱片的)自动唱机

Jul. *abbr.* July

July [dʒu(ː)'lai] *n.* 七月(略作 Jul.)

jumble ['dʒʌmbl] *vt.* 搞乱;使混乱(up, together)— *vi.* 混乱;搞乱;乱堆 — *n.*1. 混乱,杂乱;混乱的一堆 2.〔英〕废旧杂货廉价义卖(或拍卖);〔总称〕廉卖的废旧杂货

jumbo ['dʒʌmbəu] (〔复〕jumbos) *n.* 巨型喷气客机;庞然大物 — *adj.* 特大的;巨型的

jump [dʒʌmp] *vi.*1. 跳,跳跃 2.(因喜悦、吃惊、紧张等)跳起;跳动 3. 跳过,跳过去(over);越级升职 4. 暴涨;猛增 5.(对结论等)匆匆作出(对话题、主张等)突然变动转移;奔向他处 7. 猛扑(on, upon);〈口〉斥责,吐责 8. 踊跃行动;奔忙,活跃 9. 欣然接受;抢着接受(at);急切地投入(in, into)10. 符合,一致 11.〈口〉从高处上下跳动,抖动 12.(桥牌等)跳叫 — *vt.*1. 跳过;越过 2. 使跳跃;使颠动 3. 使惊起 4. 跳上,搭上(车辆);从(开动中的火车等)跳下 5.(使物价等)猛升 6. 使(人)连升几级;跳过(几级职位等)7. 突然离开(轨道、职位等);〔俚〕(因欠债等)逃离 8. 猛地扑向;〈口头上〉攻击,吐责 9.(赛跑等)抢在 ... 前出发 10. 非法侵占(采矿权等)11.(把杂志等文章的一部分)转入(他页)12.(桥牌等)跳叫呼应(搭档的叫牌)13.〔电〕跨接 14. 用长凿在(岩石)上冲击打眼 15.(在煎锅中)跳着烹煮(土豆等)— *n.*1. 跳跃;跳跃运动 2. 跳的距离;需越过的障碍 2. 惊跳;[the ~s]震颤;心神不安 3. 暴涨;猛增 4.(空航

途中的)一段短程 5.〈在起步、出发时的)占先 6.〈杂志等文章的)转入他页；转入他页的部分：页附注 7. 跳变、特变、突变；突然转移 8.【计】转移 9.【军】跳伞 10. 略去部分、跳过部分 11.〈俚〉强节奏爵士乐

jumper¹ ['dʒʌmpə] *n*. 1. 跳跃者；(送货车上)跳上跳下的送货员 2. 跳虫(如蚤等)；训练成能越障碍物的马、滑橇、拖橇 4.【机】长钻；跳动的器械 5.【电】跨接线、跳线 6.〈篮球比赛中的)跳投；跳投的球；跳投者 7.(悬吊帘杆等的)支索

jumper² ['dʒʌmpə] *n*. 1. 工作服(水手穿的)短上衣 2.〈美〉(穿在衬衫外的)无袖连衣裙、女学生裙 3.〈~s〉美 连衫裤童装 4.〈英〉(针织)女套衫

jumping ['dʒʌmpɪŋ] *adj*. 1. 跳跃的；用于跳跃的 ‖ ~ jack "蹦蹦跳跳"(玩具)

jumpy ['dʒʌmpi] *adj*. 1. 跳动的；急剧变化的 2. 神经过敏的；心惊肉跳的 ‖ jumpily *adv*. / jumpiness *n*.

Jun. *abbr*. 1. June 2. Junior

junction ['dʒʌŋkʃən] *n*. 1. 连接、接合 2. 接合点之交义点；(铁道的)联轨站、枢纽站；(河流的)合流处 3.【电】接头、接点；【电子】结

juncture ['dʒʌŋktʃə] *n*. 1. 接合、接合点；交接处 2. 情势、事态、形势 3. 时刻；关键时刻、危急关头 4.【语】音渡、连音

June [dʒuːn] *n*. 六月(略作 Jun.)

jungle ['dʒʌŋgl] *n*. 1. 丛林、密林、热带丛林 2.〈美俚〉(无业游民的)露营地；(大萧条时期的)失业工人集结地 3. 杂乱的一堆、弱肉强食的地方、生存竞争激烈残酷的地方

junior ['dʒuːnjə] *adj*. 1. 年少的、较年幼的(常作 Jr. 或 Jun.、加在姓名后) 2. 资历较浅的、等级较低的 3. 由青少年组

成的；专为青少年设计的 4.〈美国中学或四年制大学中)三年级(生)的；低年级的一 *n*. 1. 年少者 2. 等级较低者；晚辈 3.〈美国中学或四年制大学中的)三年级生 4. 瘦小的女服尺寸

juniper ['dʒuːnɪpə] *n*. 1.【植】1. 桧、杜松 2.〈美〉桧状植物(常用于装饰)

junk¹ [dʒʌŋk] *n*. 1.(作麻絮、垫料等用的)旧绳；绳屑 2.(金属、玻璃等可重新利用的)废旧杂物；破烂货；无用之物 3. 冒充古物、假货；胡说八道 4.〈英〉(木材、肉类等的)大块、厚片 5.(供船上用的)硬咸牛肉 6.〈俚〉麻醉品、毒品(尤指海洛英) 7.(抹香鲸头部)含鲸脑油的部位 — *vt*. 1.〈口〉把…(当作废物)丢弃 2. 把…分成大块(或切成厚片)

junk² [dʒʌŋk] *n*. 中国式帆船

junket ['dʒʌŋkɪt] *n*. 1. 凝乳食品、乳冻甜食 2. 野餐、宴会 3.〈美〉郊游；旅游 4.(尤指政府官员的)公费旅行 — *vi*. 1. 举行野餐 2.〈美〉郊游；作公费旅游 — *vt*. 宴请、设宴招待 ‖ ~ eer [ˌdʒʌŋkɪ'tiə] *n*. & *vi*. / ~ er *n*.

junta ['dʒʌntə] *n*. 1.(尤指政变后上台的)军人集团、军政府 2. 阴谋集团、私党 3.(西班牙等的)政务会 4. 团体

Jupiter ['dʒuːpɪtə] *n*. 1.【罗神】朱庇特(罗马神话中的主神) 2.【天】木星

jurisdiction [ˌdʒuəris'dikʃən] *n*. 1. 司法；司法权；裁判权 2. 管辖权；权限；管辖范围

jurisprudence [ˌdʒuəris'pruːdəns] *n*. 法(律)学 ‖ jurisprudent *n*. 法学家 *adj*. 精通法律的

jurist ['dʒuərist] *n*. 1. 法学家 2.〈美〉律师；法官 3. 法律系学生(或毕业生)

juror ['dʒuərə] *n*. 1. 陪审员；(竞赛时的)评奖人 2.(表示忠诚的)宣誓人

jury ['dʒuəri] *n*. 1.【律】陪审团 2. 验尸陪审

团：a grand ~（由十二至二十三人组成的）大陪审团 **2.**（竞赛时的）评奖团 ‖ *hang the ~*（美）使陪审团意见分歧而不能作出决定 ‖ ~ **box** 陪审席 /~-**man** *n.* 陪审员 /~，**woman** *n.* 女陪审员

just [dʒʌst] *adj.* **1.** 正义的；公正的，正直的；公平的 **2.** 应得的 **3.** 合理的；恰当的；正当的 **4.** 有充分根据的 **4.** 正确的；精确的 **5.** 合法的 — *adv.* **1.** 正好，恰好 **2.** 仅仅，只是 **3.** 刚才，方才 **4.** [常与 only 连用]勉勉强强地，差一点就不能，好不容易才 **5.** 直接，就 **6.**〔口〕[用于加强语气]真正，非常 **7.** [用于祈使语气中]试请，且请 ‖ ~ *ly adv.* 公正地；正当地；应得地

justice [ˈdʒʌstis] *n.* **1.** 正义；公正；公平；正当；公道原则；公正的赏罚 **2.** 正确，确实；正当的理由 **3.** 司法；审判 **4.**（英）（高等法院）法官；[J-]（美）司法部

justifiable [ˈdʒʌstifaiəbl] *adj.* **1.** 可证明为有理的；有理的；无可非议的 **2.** 惜有可原的；可辩护的 ‖ **justifiably** *adv.*

justification [ˌdʒʌstifiˈkeiʃən] *n.* **1.** 证明

为正当；辩护；正当的理由 **2.** 无过失，无咎 **3.** [印]齐行；整版

justify [ˈdʒʌstifai] *vt.* **1.** 证明···是正当的（或有理的）；为···辩护 **2.** 为···提供法律根据；证明（自己）有资格作保 **3.** [宗]使称义 **4.** [印]（填入空铅等）使齐行；整理···的版面 — *vi.* **1.** 提出充分法律根据；证明合法 **2.** 证明有资格作保证人（或保释人）**3.** [印]排整齐；把版面整理得符合要求

jut [dʒʌt]（jutted；jutting）*vi.* 突出；伸出（*out，up*）— *vt.* 使突出；使伸出 — *n.* **1.** 突出；伸出 **2.** 突出部；伸出部

jute [dʒuːt] *n.* **1.** [植]黄麻 **2.** 黄麻纤维

juvenile [ˈdʒuːvinail] *adj.* **1.** 少年的 **2.** 适合于青少年的；青少年特有的 **3.** 幼稚的 — *n.* **1.** 少年 **2.** 演少年角色的演员 **3.** 少儿读物 **4.** 雏鸟；两岁的赛马 ‖ ~ **delinquency** 少年犯罪 / ~ **delinquent** 少年罪犯

juvenility [ˌdʒuːviˈniliti] *n.* **1.** 年少，年轻 **2.** 幼稚 **3.** [常 juvenilities]幼稚的行动（或思想等）**4.** [总称]少年人

juxtapose [ˈdʒʌkstəpəuz] *vt.* 使并置（以示对比）；把···并列

K

K, k [kei]（[复]K's, ks 或 Ks, ks[keiz]）英语字母表第十一个字母 1.[K]K 字形 2.[K]【化】元素钾（potassium）的符号（由拉丁名 kalium 而来）3.[K]【数】常数（constant）的符号 4. 开（karat）的符号 5.【数】与 Z 轴平行的单位矢量

Kabul ['kɔːbul] *n*. 喀布尔[阿富汗首都]

kaiser ['kaizə] *n*. 1.（神圣罗马帝国、德国、奥国等的）皇帝 2. 独裁者

kale [keil] *n*. 1.【植】羽衣甘蓝 2.（苏格兰）蔬菜：蔬菜汤 3.〈美俚〉钞票；钱

kaleidoscope [kə'laidəskəup] *n*. 1. 万花筒 2. 千变万化，变化多端

Kampala [kɑːmˈpɑːlə] *n*. 坎帕拉[乌干达首都]

Kampuchea [ˌkæmpuˈtʃiə] *n*. = Cambodia

kangaroo [ˌkæŋgəˈruː]（[复]kangaroos）*n*.【动】袋鼠

Kansas ['kænzəs] *n*. 堪萨斯[美国州名]

Kantian ['kæntiən] *adj*.（德国哲学家）康德（Kant）的；康德哲学的 — *n*. 康德学派的人，康德主义者

kaolin ['keiəlin] *n*. 高岭土，瓷土

kapok ['keipɔk] *n*. 木棉

kaput [kæ'put] *adj*.〈口〉[只作表语]1. 完蛋了的，失败了的 2. 过时的 3. 没用的；坏了的 ‖ ~ go ~ 失败；没用

Karachi [kəˈrɑːtʃi] *n*. 卡拉奇[巴基斯坦南部港市]

karaoke [ˌkɑːrɑːˈəukei]〈日〉*n*. 卡拉 OK（一种为歌唱者提供音乐伴奏并能将歌唱与音乐一起录下的装置）

karat ['kærət] *n*. 开（黄金成色的单位.略作 K 或 k；纯金的标准为 24 开）

karate [kəˈrɑːti]〈日〉*n*. 空手道（一种徒手自卫武术）— *vt*. 用空手道猛击 ‖ **karateist** *n*.

karma ['kɑːmə] *n*. 1. 嗜噎.业（佛教名称）2. 命运；因果报应 3. 气氛，气质

Kat(h) mandu [ˌkætmænˈduː] *n*. 加德满都[尼泊尔首都]

katydid ['keitidid] *n*.【动】美洲大螽斯

kayak ['kaiæk] *n*. 爱斯基摩划子

kayo ['kei'əu]〈美俚〉[复]kayos] *n*.（拳击用语）击倒 — *vt*. 把 ... 击倒；把 ... 打昏

Kazak(h) stan [ˌkɑːzɑːkˈstɑːn] *n*. 哈萨克斯坦[亚洲中部国家]

kazoo [kəˈzuː] *n*. 卡祖笛（一种玩具小笛）

kc. *abbr*. kilocycle(s)

keel [kiːl] *n*. 1.（船、飞艇等的）龙骨 2.【动】龙骨；脊；脊棱；【植】龙骨瓣 3.〈诗〉舟 — *vt*. 1. 给（船等）装龙骨 2.（为了修理等）把（船等）翻转；使倾覆 — *vi*.（船等）翻身，倾覆

keen[1] [kiːn] *adj*. 1. 锋利的；刺人的 2. 激烈的；强烈的 3. 敏锐的；敏捷的 4. 热心的；渴望的 5.〈美俚〉极好的；漂亮的

‖ ~**ly** *adv.* / ~**ness** *n.*

keen² [kiːn] *n.*〈哀悼死者的〉挽歌,
悼诗;号哭,痛哭 — *vi.* 唱挽歌,诵悼
诗;号哭,痛哭 — *vt.*〈按民间习俗〉
为 ... 唱挽歌(或诵悼诗);哀
哭着发出 ‖ ~**er** *n.* 以哀哭唱出挽歌
的人;痛哭者

keep [kiːp] (**kept**[kept]) *vt.* 1. 保持;保
存;保留;保守〈秘密〉2. 使〈人或物〉
保持在(某一状态)3. 履行(诺言等);
遵守(惯例等)4. 庆祝;过(节日或生
日等);守(宗教节日等)5.
保护;看守 6. 整理,料理 7. 备有(商品
等);经售 8. 记(日记,帐等)9. 饲养;
雇用 10. 饲养 11. 经营;开设(商店等)
12. 拘留;留住 13. 留在(房屋等)内;
保持在(坐位等上);沿 ... 走
— *vi.* 1. 保持着某一状态 2. 继续不
断 3. (食物等)保持不坏 4. 搁,摆 5.
(学校)上课 6. (口)住,呆 7. 保持某种
路线(或方向,活动等) — *n.* 1. 生计,
保养 3. 生计,衣食;饲料 3.【史】要塞;
城堡主楼;最强固部分 4. 牢监,监狱

keeper [ˈkiːpə] *n.* 1. 看守人,守护人 2. (动
物园中的)饲养员;保管员;管理人
3. (商店,客栈等的)经营人 4.【机】夹
头;锁紧螺帽;衔铁 5. 耐藏的水果(或
蔬菜等)

keeping [ˈkiːpiŋ] *n.* 1. 保管,保存;看守
2. (诺言等的)遵守 3. 供养;饲养 4. 一
致;协调 ‖ *in* ~ *with* 与 ... 一致(或
协调)/ *out of* ~ *with* 与 ... 不一致
(或不协调)

keepsake [ˈkiːpseik] *n.* 纪念品

keg [keg] *n.* 1. 小桶(容量通常在三十加
仑以下)2. 一小桶的东西

kelp [kelp] *n.* 1. 海藻;巨藻;大型褐藻
2. 海藻灰(从中可提取碘)

ken [ken] (**kenned** 或 **kent** [kent]; **kenning**)

vt. 1.〈苏格兰〉知道 2.〈古〉看见 3.
〈方〉认出 — *vi.*〈苏格兰〉知道(*of*,
about)— *n.* 1.〈罕〉视野;景象 2. 认
识范围,知识范围

kennel [ˈkenl] *n.* 1. 狗窝;[~s] 养狗场
2. 一群(猎)狗;一群人;〈狐等的〉窝
4. 鄙陋住所(kennel bed; kennel(l)ing)
— *vt.* 1. 使进狗窝;使呆在狗窝内 2.
使住进鄙陋的住所 — *vi.* 1. 进狗窝;
呆在狗窝内 2. (人)住在鄙陋的住所中

Kentucky [kenˈtʌki] *n.* 肯塔基[美国州
名]

Kenya [ˈkiːnjə, ˈkenjə] *n.* 肯尼亚[东非国
家]

kept [kept] keep 的过去式和过去分词 —
adj.〈由于有暧昧的性关系而〉被供养
的

kerchief [ˈkɜːtʃif]〈[复] kerchiefs 或
kerchieves [ˈkɜːtʃiːvz]〉*n.* 1. 〈妇女用〉方
头巾;方揩巾 2. 〈诗〉手帕

kernel [ˈkɜːnl] *n.* 1. 〈方〉(果实的)仁 2.
(谷物的)颗粒 3. (细胞)核;(种子的)
核 4. 【数】核 4. 〈喻〉核心,中心 5.【语】核心
句

kerosene, kerosine [ˈkerəsiːn] *n.* 煤油,火
油

ketch [ketʃ] *n.* 双桅纵帆船

ketchup [ˈketʃəp] *n.* 调味蕃茄酱

kettle [ˈketl] *n.* 1. (烧水用的)水壶;锅 2.
〈地〉锅状陷落 3. 茶壶 ‖ ~ **drum** *n.*
铜鼓,定音鼓

key¹ [kiː] *n.* 1. 钥匙 2. (钢琴、打字机等
的)键 3. (辞书、地图等的)略语表、发
音表、符号表;凡例;题解;解答书(动
植物分类的)检索表;(符号或缩写的)
解释 4. (疑难事件或问题的)线索;秘
诀;答案 5. 关键;要害;要冲 6.【音】
调;(文章、演说等的)调子;基调 7.【电
信】键;关键码 8. (上钟表发条的)钥

匙;【机】栓,楔,销子;扳手 9.【建】拱顶石 10.【植】翅果 — vt. 1.(用钥匙)锁上;插上(栓、销子等);【建】用拱顶石装饰 2.向 ... 提供解决的线索(或答案) 3.【音】为 ... 调音;为(演奏等)定调 4.(使用检索表)鉴定(生物标本) — vi. 使用检索表;发挥 — adj. 主要的,关键的;基本的 ‖ '~-board n. 1.(钢琴、打字机等的)键盘 2. 挂钢匙的板 vt. 用键盘式排字机排字 vi. 用键盘式排字机排(字) /'~hole n. 锁眼,钥匙孔 adj. 透露内情的;涉及隐私的 /'~note n.【音】主音 2. 要旨;基调 — vt. 定下基调;作主题性的演讲 vi. 作定调子的发言 /'~stone n.【建】塞缝石;拱顶石 2. 基础;基本原则,主旨

key² [ki:] n. 低岛;礁;暗礁

Keynesian ['keinziən] adj.〔英国经济学家〕凯恩斯(Keynes)的;凯恩斯主义的 — n. 凯恩斯主义者 ‖ ~ism n. 凯恩斯主义

kg. abbr. kilogram(s)

KGB abbr.〔俄〕Komitet Gosudarstvennoi Bezopasnosti (前苏联)国家安全委员会 (= Committee of State Security),克格勃

khaki ['kɑ:ki] adj. 1. 土黄色的,卡其色的 2. 卡其布做的 — n. 1. 土黄色,卡其黄 2. 卡其布 3. [~s]卡其布服装 (尤指军装)

khan [kɑ:n] n. 1.【史】可汗,汗(鞑靼、蒙古、突厥等族最高统治者的称号) 2. 汗(阿富汗、伊朗、巴基斯坦等国官吏的称号)

Khart(o)um [kɑ:'tu:m] n. 喀土穆[苏丹首都]

kibbutz [ki'bu:ts] ([复] kibbutzim [ki'bu:tsim]) n.(以色列的)聚居区,基布兹(尤指合作农场)

kibitz ['kibits]〈口〉vi.(纸牌戏的旁观者等)乱出主意;多管闲事 — vt. 对(纸牌戏等)乱出主意 ‖ ~er n. 乱出主意者

kick [kik] vi. 1. 踢 2.(枪炮等)反冲,后坐 3.〈口〉发牢骚;反对;抗议(against, at) — vt. 1. 踢 2.(枪炮等)朝 ... 反冲,朝 ... 后坐 3.(足球)踢进(球门)得分 4.(用强硬手段等)赶出,驱逐(out) 5. 戒除(毒瘾) — n. 1. 踢;〈英〉球员 2.(枪炮的)反冲;后坐 3.〈口〉牢骚;反对;抗议 4.〈口〉吸引力,活力;气力 5.〈口〉(酒等)的刺激性;极度的快感(或兴奋) 6.〈俚〉开除;解雇 7.〔英俚〕六便士的硬币 8.(事态或情节等的)突然转折,意外发展(或结局) 9.〈美俚〉加薪 ‖ ~-off n.(足球赛等的)开球;〈口〉开始

kid¹ [kid] n. 1. 小山羊;小羚羊 2. 小山羊肉;小山羊皮;[~s]小山羊皮手套(或皮鞋) 3.〈俚〉小孩;〈美口〉年轻人 — adj. 1. 小山羊皮制的 2.〈口〉较年幼的 — (kidded; kidding) vt. & vi.(山羊或羚羊)产(羔)

kid² [kid]〈俚〉n. 欺骗 — (kidded; kidding) vt. & vi. 1. 欺骗,哄骗 2. 嘲笑;戏弄

kidnap ['kidnæp] (kidnap(p)ed; kidnap(p)ing) vt. 诱拐(小孩等);绑架 ‖ **kidnapee** [,kidnæ'pi:] n.〈美〉被诱拐的人,被绑架者 /kidnap(p)er n. 拐子;绑架者

kidney ['kidni] n. 1. 肾,肾脏 2. 个性,脾气 ‖ ~ bean 菜豆,四季豆,云豆

Kiev ['ki:ef] n. 基辅[乌克兰首都]

Kigali [ki'gɑ:li] n. 基加利[卢旺达首都]

kill [kil] vt. 1. 杀死,弄死;宰(猪等);(霜、酷暑等)冻死,枯死(植物);(疾病、战争等)使丧生 2. 拖杀,毁掉(希望等) 3. 中和;抵消 4. 关掉(发动机、电灯等);截断 ... 的电流;掐灭(烟头) 5.

清嗓(时间) 6.〈口〉使着迷;使绝倒;使倾倒;使折服 7. 否决(议案等) 8. 删除 9.〈网球等中的口〉扣杀 10. 喝光(酒) 11. 使非常痛苦 使精疲力竭 —— *vi.* 1. 引起死亡,致死;杀人;被杀死 2.(植物等)被冻死;被枯死 3. 杀;杀人 ‖ *n.* 1. 杀人者;嗜杀成性的人(或畜或物);凶手 2. 杀灭物;宰杀的器具 3.〈口〉迷人的人(或物) 4.[~s]〈口〉供屠宰食用的动物 5. 逆钩鲸,虎鲸 6. 牲口麻醉冒冷机 7. 邮票盖销记号;邮票盖销器 8.〈美理〉大麻烟卷 ‖ ~joy *n.* 令人扫兴的人(或事)

kiln [kiln, kil] *n.* 窑 —— *vt.* 把...放在窑内烧(或烘干)

kilo ['ki:ləu] ([复]kilos) *n.* 1. 千克,公斤 2. 千米,公里

kilo- *comb. form* 表示“千”:*kilocycle, kilogram, kilowatt*

kilocycle ['kiləˌsaikl] *n.*【无】千赫(兹);千周(略作 kc.)

kilogram(me) ['kiləgræm] *n.* 千克,公斤(略作 kg.)

kilohertz ['kiləhə:ts] *n.*【物】千赫(兹)(略作 kHz.)

kiloliter, kilolitre ['kiləˌli:tə] *n.* 千升(略作 kl.)

kilometre, kilometer ['kiləˌmi:tə] *n.* 千米,公里(略作 km.)

kilowatt ['kiləwɔt] *n.*【电】千瓦(特)(略作 kw.) ‖ ~'hour *n.* 千瓦时—一度(略作 km.)

kilt [kilt] *n.* 1.(苏格兰高地男子和苏格兰兵团士兵穿的)苏格兰褶裥短裙(通常用格子呢缝制) 2. 苏格兰褶裥短裙式的童装(或女服) —— *vt.*〈苏格兰〉

卷起(裙等)(*up*) 2. 使有直褶 —— *vi.* 动作敏捷,灵巧

kilter ['kiltə] *n.*〈口〉正常运转状态;正常状况

kimono [ki'məunəu] ([复]kimonos)(日)*n.* 1. 和服 2. 和服式女晨衣

kin [kin] *n.* 1. 家属 2.[总称]亲属;亲属 3. 亲属关系 —— *adj.* 有亲属关系的(*to*) ‖ ~ship *n.* 家属(或亲属)关系;类似家属(或亲属)的密切关系

-kin *suf.* 表示“小”:lambkin

kind[1] [kaind] *n.* 1. 种;类;特定种类的;同类的人(或事物) 2. 性质;本质 3.〈古〉家族

kind[2] [kaind] *adj.* 1. 仁慈的;和蔼的;好意的;友爱的 2. 亲切的 ‖ ~'hearted *adj.* 仁慈的,好心的

kindergarten ['kindəˌgɑ:tn] *n.* 幼儿园

kindle ['kindl] *vt.* 1. 点燃(使人、感情等)激动起来 3. 照亮,使明亮 —— *vi.* 1. 着火,燃起 2.(人、感情等)激动起来 3. 发亮 ‖ **kindling** *n.* 1. 点燃 2.[总称]引火物

kindly ['kaindli] *adj.* 1. 仁慈的;和蔼的;友好的;体贴的 2.(气候等)宜人的,温和的 3.〈古〉合法的 —— *adv.* 1. 仁慈地;和蔼地;友好地 2. 有礼貌地 3. 诚恳地,衷心地 3. 请:*Kindly tell me your address.* 请告诉我你的地址。 4. 自然地;容易地 ‖ **kindliness** *n.*

kindness ['kaindnis] *n.* 1. 仁慈;和气;好意 2. 友好行为;好事

kindred ['kindrid] *n.* 1. 宗族 2. 血缘关系 3. 亲属关系 3.[总称]家属 4. 同源;相似 —— *adj.* 1. 宗族的;亲属的 2. 同种的;同源的;同性质的;类似的

kinescope ['kiniskəup] 〈主美〉*n.* 1.(电视)显像管 2. 屏幕录像 —— *vt.* 把(电视

节目)摄制成录像

kinetic [kai'netik] *adj.* 1.【物】运动的;运动引起的 2. 活跃的;有力的;令人振奋的 ‖ ~s [复] *n.* [用作单]动力学

kinfolk ['kinfəuk] *n.*〈方〉= kinsfolk

king [kiŋ] *n.* 1. 王,国王;(部落的)首领,头子 2.(某范围内)最有势力者,大王 3.(纸牌)老K;(国际象棋)王;(西洋跳棋)王棋 4. [K-]【宗】上帝;基督 5.(水果、植物等中)最佳者 — *vt.* 立 … 为王 ‖ ~ fisher *n.* 翠鸟,鱼狗(一种食鱼鸟)/ '~-size(d) *adj.* 1. 特大的;特长的 2. 非寻常的

kingdom ['kiŋdəm] *n.* 1. 王国 2. 领域;(动、植物)界 3. [K-]【宗】天国;上帝的统治

kinglet ['kiŋlit] *n.* 1.〈贬〉小国王,小王 2. [鸟]戴菊

kingly ['kiŋli] *adj.* 1. 国王的;君主地位的 2. 国王似的;适合国王身分的 3. 君主政体的 — *adv.* 国王似地,君主似地

Kingston ['kiŋstən] *n.* 金斯敦[牙买加首都]

kink [kiŋk] *n.* 1.(绳索、头发等的)纽结,绞缠 2. 奇想,怪念头;怪癖 3.(行为的)乖僻 4.(颈、背等处的)肌肉痉挛;抽筋 5.〈美〉(结构或设计等的)缺陷 — *vt.* 使纽结,使绞缠 — *vi.* 纽结,绞缠

kinsfolk ['kinzfəuk] *n.* [总称]家属;亲属

Kinshasa [kin'ʃɑːsə] *n.* 金沙萨[扎伊尔首都]

kinsman ['kinzmən](|[复] kinsmen) *n.* 男亲属

kinswoman ['kinz,wumən]([复] kinswomen ['kinz,wimin]) *n.* 女亲属

kipper ['kipə] *n.* 腌(或熏)鲱鱼(或鲑鱼等)

Kirg(h)izia [kəːˈgiziə] *n.* 吉尔吉斯[亚洲中部国家]

Kiribati ['kiribæs] *n.* 基里巴斯[西太平洋岛国]

Kishinev ['kiʃinef] *n.* 基什尼奥夫[摩尔达维亚首都]

kismet ['kismet] *n.* [常作 K-]命运,天命

kiss [kis] *vt.* 1. 吻 2.(风、波浪等)轻拂,轻触 — *vi.* 1. 接吻 2. 轻拂,轻触 — *n.* 1. 吻 2. 轻拂,轻触 3. 糖果;蛋白甜脆饼

kit[1] [kit] *n.* 1.〈英〉小木桶 2. 成套工具;成套元件;【军】(士兵武器以外的)装备 3. 工具包;用品箱 4.〈口〉(人或事物)的全部 5.(适应特定需要的)成套用品;(士兵的)个人装具;(供学生等用的)成套资料

kit[2] [kit] *n.* 1. 小猫(= kitten) 2. 软毛小动物;软毛小动物的毛皮

kitchen ['kitʃin] *n.* 1. 厨房,灶间 2.(全体)炊事人员 3. 全套炊具 ‖ ~ garden 家庭菜园 / '~ware [总称] 厨房用具

kitchenette [,kitʃi'net] *n.* 小厨房

kite [kait] *n.* 1. [鸟] 鸢 2. 贪得无厌的人;骗子 3. 风筝 4. [~s]〈微风时用的〉帆,最高层轻帆 5.【商】空头支票;通融票据;空白支票 — *vt.* 使(物价等)迅速上升 2.【商】开(空头支票或通融票据);涂改(支票)— *vi.* 1.〈口〉(价等像鸢那样)迅速上升;迅速上升 2. 突然离去;突然起立 3. 用空头支票骗钱

kith [kiθ] *n.* [总称] 1.〈古〉朋友;邻居;亲戚;同族人

kitten ['kitn] *n.* 小猫;小动物(如小兔等)*vt. & vi.* 产(小猫)‖ '~-ish *adj.* 小猫似的;嬉耍的

kitty ['kiti] *n.* 小猫;猫咪(对猫的爱称)

kiwi ['kiːwi] *n.* 1. [鸟] 鹬鸵,几维(新西

兰产的一种不能飞行的鸟）2. [K-]〈口〉新西兰人 3. 〈俚〉【军】空军中的非飞行人员‖ — **fruit**【植】弥猴桃

KKK *abbr.* Ku Klux Klan

kleptomania [ˌkleptəʊ'meiniə] *n.* 偷窃狂，盗窃癖

kleptomaniac [ˌkleptəʊ'meiniæk] *n.* 偷窃狂者，有盗窃癖的

km. *abbr.* kilometre(s)

knack [næk] *n.* 1. 诀窍；妙法 2. 技能，本领；熟练技巧 3. (行为、言语等的)习惯、癖，玩具；小玩意儿

knapsack ['næpsæk] *n.*(军用或旅行用)背包

knave [neiv] *n.* 1. 流氓，无赖，恶棍 2. (纸牌中的)杰克(jack)

knead [niːd] *vt.* 1. 揉，捏(面粉、陶土等)；捏制(面包、陶器等) 2. 按摩(肌肉等)

knee [niː] *n.* 1. 膝；膝盖；膝关节 2. (裤子、长袜等的)膝部 3. 膝状物；(楼梯的)弯木；肘;(树的)木结，瘤;木瘤;(沼泽生树木的)根隆;【建】隅撑,角撑,斜撑;【船】肘板形,肘村 4. 用膝的撞击 — *vt.* 1. 用膝盖碰 2. 向 … 下跪 3.〈口〉使(裤子的)膝部鼓起‖ ~ **cap** 1.【解】膝盖骨 2. 护膝

kneel [niːl] [knelt[nelt] 或 kneeled] *vi.* 跪下(*down*)；跪着

knell [nel] *n.* 钟声；丧钟声；死亡(或灭亡、失败等)的凶兆 — *vi.* 1. 敲丧钟；(钟)发出丧钟声 2. 发出悲哀(或不祥)之声 3. 敲丧钟召集(或宣布)；发出丧钟声般的声音召集(或宣布)

knelt [nelt] kneel 的过去式和过去分词

knew [njuː] know 的过去式

knickers ['nikəz] [复] *n.* 1.〈口〉(膝下扎紧的)灯笼裤 2. 女用短衬裤

knickknack ['niknæk] *n.* 小装饰物(如小衣饰、小家具等) - 小摆设小玩意儿

knife [naif] ([复]knives[naivz]) *n.* 1. 刀;餐刀 2. 匕首 3. (机器上的)刀片(或刀具) 4. 外科手术刀 — *vt.* 1. 用刀切(或戳、刺) 2.〈美口〉用阴险手段背着 3. 刀切似地穿过 — *vi.* (仿佛)用刀推进(或穿刺)

knight [nait] *n.* 1. (欧洲中世纪)骑士 2. 爵士(其名前称号用 Sir) 3.【英史】御选议员(在〈古希腊〉骑士(雅典的第二等级的公民);(古罗马)骑士(奴隶主集团中一个阶级或成员) 5. (供妇人的)护卫者,侍人从 6.〈谑〉专家,从事某种专业的人 7. (国际象棋中的)马 — *vt.* 封 … 为骑士(或爵士)‖ ~ **hood** *n.* 1. 骑士(或爵士)的地位(或身分) 2. 骑士精神;侠义 3. [总称]骑士,爵士/ ~ **ly** *adj.* 1. 骑士(般)的;侠义的;英勇而文雅的 2. 由骑士(或爵士)组成的 *adv.* 骑士般地;侠义地

knit [nit] (knitted 或 knit; knitting) — *vt.* 1. 编结;针织(编织);机织 2. 结合(衣服等) 3. 蹙起;皱紧 4. 愈合(折骨等)愈合;使紧密结合;联合(指通过共同利益、婚姻等) 5. [常用过去分词]使严密,使紧凑 — *vi.* 1. 编结;针织 2. [口头]蹙起;皱紧 3. (折骨等)愈合;紧密结合 4.【英方】(植物)生长;结果实;(蜂)蜂拥,成群‖ **knitter** *n.* 1. 编结者;针织工 2. 编织机;针织机

knitting ['nitiŋ] *n.* 1. 编结(法);针织(法) 2. [总称]编织物;针织品

knives [naivz] knife 的复数

knob [nɔb] *n.* 1. 球形突出物;(树干等的)节;(棒等的)圆球 2. 节;瘤;疙瘩;(犁头 3. (门、抽屉等的)球形捏手;(旗杆等上的)顶球;【建】雕球饰 4. (

音机等的)旋钮 5. 圆形小丘;[~s]丘
陵地带 6.〈英〉小块 一 (knobbed;
knobbing) *vt.* 使有球形突出物;给(门
等)装球形把手 一 *vi.* 鼓起,突出

knock [nɔk] *vi.* 1. 敲;击,打 2. 相撞,碰
撞 3.(发动机等由于故障)发爆震声;
(机器等)发碰撞声 4.〈美俚〉找岔子;
说坏话 5.〈美〉(金罗美纸牌戏)推牌,
叫停 一 *vt.* 1. 敲;击,打;敲掉;打掉,
拍去;去除,袪除 2. 使碰撞 3.〈英俚〉
给 ... 强烈印象;使震惊 4.〈美俚〉找
...的岔子;说 ...的坏话 一 *n.* 1.
敲;(敲)击声 2. 击;打击 2. 叩击;扣
折;困难 3.(发动机等由于故障发出
的)爆震声;碰撞声 4. 敲击;叩击声
击声,敲门声 5.〈美俚〉指摘;挑剔 6.
〈英俚〉板球赛的)一局 ‖~-knee *n.*
[医]膝外翻;[~s]外翻腿 /~-kneed
adj. 膝外翻的 /~-out *n.* 1.(拳击赛
中)击昏对手的一击(略作 K.O.);判敲击(对
方)击昏对手的一击 2. 〈口〉给人留下深刻印象的人(或物);
异常动人的人 3. 联袼拍卖(互相勾结
的一伙人在拍卖时将一批货以低价买进
后同伙内转售);联袼拍卖人 4. 联袼分
子 — *adj.* 1. 击倒对手的 2. 给人深刻印象的;迷
人的;轰动的 3. 摧毁性的

knocker ['nɔkə] *n.* 1. 门环 2. 敲击者;敲
门的人 3.〈美俚〉吹毛求疵的人,挑剔
的人

knoll [nəul] *n.* 小山;圆丘;土墩;海(底)
丘

knot [nɔt] *n.* 1.(绳等的)结;(装饰用的)
花结 2. 结合(指婚姻等) 3. 一小群,一
小队 4.(树干或木板上的)节;节疤,节
瘤 5. 难题;麻烦事;疙瘩 6.〔英〕节(=
1 海里/小时);海里 7.〔英〕搬运工用
的)垫肩 一 (knotted; knotting) *vt.* 1.
把 ... 打成结;把 ... 结牢;捆扎 2. 使
密切结合(指姻缘等) 3. 使纠结,使纠

缠(指藤蔓等) 4. 皱(眉) 一 *vi.* 1. 打
结,成结;作花结(指花边等) 2. 纠结,
纠缠 ‖~-hole *n.*(树干或木板上的)节
孔

knotty ['nɔti] *adj.* 1. 有结的;多结的;有
节(疤)的;多节(疤)的 2. 难解决的;棘
手的;难解释的;使人困惑的

knout [naut] *n.* 皮鞭(旧时俄国的刑具)
— *vt.* 鞭笞

know [nəu] (knew [nju:], known [nəun])
vt. 1. 知道;了解,懂得 2. 认识;熟悉
(地方等)记牢 3. 精通(语言等) 4. 认
出;识别 5. 体验,经历 6.〈古〉与 ...
... 交媾 一 *vi.* 知道;了解,懂得 一
n.〈口〉知情 ‖~able *adj.* 可知的;可
认识的 ‖~-how *n.*〈口〉技术,本事;
实际知识;技能;诀窍

knowing ['nəuiŋ] *adj.* 1. 知道的;有知识
的;有见识的 2. 老练的;世故的;狡猾
的 3. 机警的,灵敏的 4. 会意的 一 心
意的 6.〈口〉(帽子等)时髦的 一 *n.* 知
道;认识 ‖~ly *adv.* 1. 故意地 2. 老
练地 3. 会意地

knowledge ['nɔlidʒ] *n.* 1. 知识;学识;学
问 2. 认识 3. 知道;了解;消息 4.〈古〉
学科 5.〈古〉性交 ‖~able *adj.* 知识渊
博的,有知识的;有见识的

known [nəun] know 的过去分词 — *adj.*
大家知道的;知名的;已知的

knuckle ['nʌkl] *n.* 1. 指(关)节 2.(供食
用的猪等的)肘;蹄 3.[机]关节;(火车
车轮的)钩舌;铰链连接;(屋顶等的)
肘形接合 4.[船]船体棱缝 4.[~s]指节
铜套(套在四指关节上的铜套,戴着时
铜套向外,用以打人) 5. 指节状突出物
— *vt.* 用指关节敲打(或压、摩、触)
— *vi.*(儿童在地上打弹子时)以指关节贴
地(down)

KO ['kei'əu]〈美俚〉(KO'd; KO'ing) *vt.*〈拳

koala ['kou'ɑːlə] *n.*【动】树袋熊(澳大利亚产的一种貌似小熊, 栖于树上的无尾动物)

Kobe ['kəubi] *n.* 神户[日本本州岛西南岸港市]

KO'd ['kei'əud]KO 的过去式和过去分词

kodak ['kəudæk] *n.* 1. 小型照相机 2. [K-]柯达(一种小型照相机的商标) — *vt.* & *vi.* 用小型照相机拍摄

kohl [kəul] *n.* 眼圈粉(阿拉伯妇女用来把眼圈涂黑的一种化妆品)

kohlrabi ['kəul'rɑːbi] *n.* 1.【植】撇蓝 2. 撇蓝的球茎

kook [kuːk] *n.* 怪人; 狂人; 傻瓜 — *adj.* 怪癖的; 疯狂的; 愚蠢的 ‖ ~**ly** *adj.* 怪癖的; 疯狂的; 愚蠢的

Koran [kɔ'rɑːn] *n.*(伊斯兰教)《古兰经》(也译作《可兰经》) ‖ ~**ic** [kɔ'rænik] *adj.*《古兰经》的

Korea [kɔ'riə] *n.* 朝鲜[亚洲东部]

Korean [kɔ'riən] *adj.* 朝鲜的; 朝鲜人的; 朝鲜族的; 朝鲜语的 — *n.* 朝鲜人; 朝鲜族人; 朝鲜语

kosher ['kəuʃə] *adj.* 1.(食品等)按犹太教规制成的, 洁净的, 可食的 2.[口铺]供应(符合犹太规教的)洁净食品的 3.〈口〉真的; 正确的; 合法的; 合适的 — *vt.* 按犹太教规调制(食品); 按犹太教规洗涤(厨房器皿) — *n.*(符合犹太教规的)洁净食品; 供应洁净食品的店铺

kotow ['kəu'tau] *n.* & *vi.* = kowtow

Kowloon ['kau'luːn] *n.* 九龙

kowtow ['kau'tau]〈汉〉 *n.* 叩头, 磕头 —

vi. 1. 叩头 2. 卑躬屈节(*to*)

Kr【化】元素氪(krypton)的符号

kremlin ['kremlin] *n.* 1.(俄国的)城堡 2. [the K-] 克里姆林宫; (前)苏联政府 ‖ **Kremlinologist** [,kremli'nɔlədʒist] *n.* 克里姆林专家; (前)苏联问题专家

krimmer ['krimə] *n.*(灰色或黑色的)克里米亚卷毛羔皮

krona ['krəunə] *n.* 1.([复] kronor ['krəunɔː]) 克朗(瑞典货币单位) 2. ([复]kronur ['krəunuə])冰岛克郎(冰岛货币单位)

krone ['krəunə]([复] kroner ['krəunə]) *n.* 1. 丹麦克朗(丹麦货币单位) 2. 挪威克朗(挪威货币单位)

krypton ['kriptɔn] *n.*【化】氪

Kuala Lumpur [,kwɑːlə'lumpuə] 吉隆坡(马来西亚首都)

kudos ['kjuːdɔs] *n.*[单复同] *n.* 名声; 威信

Ku Klux Klan ['kjuː klʌks 'klæn] 三K党(用私刑等迫害黑人和进步工人的美国恐怖组织)

kumquat ['kʌmkwɔt]〈汉 *n.*【植】金橘, 金柑

kung fu ['kuŋ 'fuː]〈汉〉功夫, 中国拳术

Kuomintang ['kwəumin'tæŋ] *n.*(中国)国民党

Kuwait, Kuweit [kə'weit] *n.* 1. 科威特(国)[西南亚国家] 2. 科威特(市)[科威特国首都]

kw. *abbr.* kilowatt(s)

kWh *abbr.* kilowatt-hour(s) 千瓦小时

Kyoto [ki'əutəu] *n.* 京都[日本(本州岛中西部)城市]

Kyushu ['kjuːʃuː] *n.* 九洲(岛)[日本的第三大岛]

L

L, l[el]（[复]L's,l's 或 Ls,ls[elz]）英语字母表第十二个字母 1.[L,l] 字形 2.[L] 罗马数字的 50 3.[L]【物】潜热(latent heat)的符号 4.（美口）高架铁路(elevated railroad)的符号

La【化】元素镧(lanthanum)的符号

la [lɑː] n.【音】固定唱法时之 A 音：首调唱法时任何大音阶之音阶第六音(或任何小音阶之第一音)

label ['leibl] n. 1. 标签，签条 2. 标记；标号 3. 称号；绰号 4. 说明性略语,标示词（如词典中的(古)、(美)等)5.【建】披水石 6. 带胶邮票 7.（古)布条；带子；飘带；(附于文件上带有封印的)丝带 — label(l)ed；label(l)ing) vt. 1. 贴标签于；用签条标明 2. 把…称为；把…列为 3.【核】指示踪

labial ['leibiəl] adj. 1. 唇状的；嘴唇音的 2.【语】唇音的 — n. 1.（管风琴的)唇管 2.【语】唇音(如：[b]、[p]、[m]等)

labium ['leibiəm]（[复] labia ['leibiə]) n.【解】唇；唇状部分

labor ['leibə] n., vi. & vt.（美）= labour

laboratory [lə'bɔrətəri] n. 1. 实验室；研究室 2. 化学试验；药厂 3. 实验课

laborious [lə'bɔːriəs] adj. 1. 勤劳的；2. 吃力的 3.（文体等)矫揉造作的；不流畅的 ‖ ~ly adv.

labour ['leibə] n. 1. 劳动 2. 努力 3. 工作；活计 4.［总称］工人，劳工；工会 5. 分

娩；阵痛 6.[L-]（英国或英联邦国家的)工党 (= the Labour Party） — vi. 1. 劳动 2. 苦苦地干 3. 努力争取(for)；努力4. 费力地前进；(船只)纵横摇摆，浪中挣扎 5. 分娩 — vt. 1. 在…上过分花费精力；过于详尽地阐述 2. 麻烦3. 使辛勤地工作 ‖ ~ed adj. 1. 吃力的；缓慢的 2.(文体等)不自然的，矫揉造作的 / ~er n. 劳动者；工人 ‖ Labour Day 1 五一国际劳动节 2.（美国、加拿大等国的)劳动节(九月的第一个星期一) / '~-in·tensive adj. 劳动密集型的；劳动集约的

labyrinth ['læbərinθ] n. 1. 迷宫；曲径 2.（事情等)的错综复杂，曲折；难以摆脱的处境 3.【解】(内耳)的迷路

lac [læk] n.（紫胶虫分泌的)紫胶；【化】虫胶

lace [leis] n. 1. 鞋带；系带 2. 花边,饰带，滚带 3.（有图案的)网眼织物；透孔织品 4.（加在咖啡或茶等中的)少量烈性酒 — vt. 1. 用带子束紧(up) 2. 穿带子于；使交织 3. 用花边装饰；使成彩色条纹 4. 打；鞭打 5. 加少量烈性酒于；使有风味 — vi. 束带子；用带子束紧

lacerate ['læsəreit] vt. 1. 撕碎；割碎(软组织等) 2. 伤害；使痛苦 ‖ **lacerable** adj. / **lace·ration** n. 1. 撕裂；划碎 2. 伤口；破口

lachrymal ['lækriməl] *adj.* 1. 泪的；生泪的；流泪的 2.【解】泪腺的

lachrymose ['lækrimous] *adj.* 1. 爱哭的；含泪的 2. 催人泪下的；哀痛的

lack [læk] *n.* 1. 缺乏；不足 2. 缺少的东西；需要的东西 — *vi.* 缺乏；短少；没有 — *vt.* 缺乏；短少；没有；需要

lackadaisical [,lækə'deizikəl] *adj.* 懒洋洋的；没精打采的

lackey ['læki] *n.* 1. (穿号衣的)男仆；跟班 2. 走向 — *vt.* 服侍，侍候

laconic [lə'kɔnik] *adj.* 1. (说话、文章等)简洁的，精练的 2. 说话简短的；文章写简洁的

lacquer ['lækə] *n.* 1. (涂在木材、金属等上的)漆；中国漆；日本漆；硝基漆，清喷漆 2. 漆器 — *vt.* 用漆涂；使表面光洁

lacrosse [lə'krɔs] *n.* 兜网球，长曲棍球(运动)

lactic ['læktik] *adj.* 乳(汁)的；从酸乳(或乳清)中取得的

lactose ['læktəus] *n.*【化】乳糖 (= milk sugar)

lacuna [lə'kju:nə] ([复] lacunae [lə'kju:ni:] 或 lacunas) *n.* 1. 空隙；(书籍等中的)脱漏；(知识等的)空白 2.【解】腔隙，陷窝

lacy ['leisi] *adj.* 1. (有)花边的；(有)带子的 2. 花边状的；带子状的

lad [læd] *n.* 1. 男孩，少年；青年男子，小伙子 2. (表示亲密的称呼)家伙，伙伴 3. 情侣 4. (英)马夫

ladder ['lædə] *n.* 1. 梯子；梯状物；阶梯；发迹的途径 2. (英)(长统袜等上的)抽丝 — *vi.* (长统袜等)发生抽丝现象

laddie ['lædi] *n.* 男孩

laden ['leidn] *adj.* 1. 装满了的；充满了的(*with*) 2. 负担沉重的；苦恼的

lading ['leidiŋ] *n.* 1. 装载；汲取 2. 船货；货物 ‖ **bill of ~** 提(货)单

ladle ['leidl] *n.* 长柄勺子；【冶】铸勺，铁水包 — *vt.* (用勺)舀

lady ['leidi] *n.* 1. 女士；夫人；小姐；贵妇人 3. [L-](英国拥有爵位的贵族妻女的尊称)…夫人 … 小姐；女主人(现只用于 ~ of the house 一语中) 5. 妻子；情人；情妇 6. [Ladies] [用作单] 公共厕所，女盥洗室 — *adj.* 女性的；(谑)雌的 ‖ ~'s 似贵妇人的；适合于贵妇人的身份的 2. (男子)带女人腔的 /~**ship** n. 贵妇人身分；夫人，小姐 ‖ **ladies' room** 公共女厕所，女盥洗室 / ~ **beetle**, '~**bird**, '~**bug** n. 瓢虫 / '~**finger** n. 指状小松糕 / ~'**(s) slipper** n. 杓兰；欧洲杓兰

lag [læg] (lagged; lagging) *vi.* 1. 走得慢；落后；延迟 2.【电】滞后 3. 变慢；松懈 — *vt.* 落后于；滞后于 — *n.* 1. 落后；滞后；延迟 2. (一个现象和另一个相关现象中间的)相隔时间 3. (指牛羊等的)落后者；掉队者 — *adj.* 最后的

lager ['lɑ:gə] *n.* 陈贮啤酒 — *vt.* 将(啤酒)贮藏起来使其陈化并澄清，使贮陈

laggard ['lægəd] *n.* 1. 落后者；迟钝者；懒散的人 2. 滞价证券 — *adj.* 落后的；迟缓的

lagoon, lagune [lə'gu:n] *n.* 环礁湖；咸水湖；泻湖

Lagos ['leigɔs] *n.* 拉各斯 [尼日利亚西南部港市]

laid [leid] lay¹ 的过去式和过去分词

lain [lein] lie¹ 的过去分词

lair [lεə] *n.* 1. 兽穴；兽窝；躲藏处 2. 床 3. (英)(赶牲口去市场途中)用围栏 — *vi.* 进穴；休息 — *vt.* 把…置于穴中；给…设洞穴 2. 作为…的洞穴

laissez faire [,lesei 'fεə] (法) (政府对工

商业的)自由放任(政策)

laity ['leiiti] *n.* [the ~] [总称] 1. 俗人 2. 外行, 门外汉

lake [leik] *n.* 1. 湖 2. (贮油或其他液体的)池

lama ['lɑːmə] *n.* 喇嘛(藏、蒙佛教的僧侣) ‖ **Lamaism** *n.* 喇嘛教

lamasery ['lɑːməseri] *n.* 喇嘛寺

lamb [læm] *n.* 1. 羔羊, 小羊 2. 小羚羊 3. 羔羊肉 4. 羔羊皮 5. 羔羊般柔弱的人; (对孩子等的爱称)宝贝儿; 乖乖 6. 易受骗上当者(尤指在证券交易方面) 5. [the L] [宗]耶稣 — *vi.* 生小羊 — *vt.* 1. 生(小羊) 2. 照管(产期中的母羊) ‖ '~kin *n.* 1. 羔羊 2. (对孩子等的爱称)宝贝儿; 乖乖

lambent ['læmbənt] *adj.* 1. (光等)闪烁的, 轻轻摇曳的 ‖ **lambency** *n.*

lame [leim] *adj.* 1. 跛的, 瘸的; 伤残的 2. 僵直而疼痛的 3. 站不住脚的; 有缺陷的 4. 不合诗韵的 — *vt.* 1. 使跛; 使伤残 2. 使不中用 — *vi.* 跛行 ‖ '~ly *adv.* / '~ness *n.* ‖ ~ **duck** (俚)1. (美)(任期快满但没有被重新选上的)官员(或议员) 2. 伤残的人 3. (交易所投机失败后)无力偿债的人 4. 无能的人

lament [lə'ment] *vi.* 悲痛; 哀悼; 伤心 (*for, over*) — *vt.* 1. 为…而哀悼; 哀悼; 痛惜 2. 悲叹 — *n.* 1. 悲哀的表现; 哀悼; 挽歌 2. 挽歌; 悼词

lamentable ['læməntəbl] *adj.* 1. 可悲的; 令人痛惜的 2. 表现悲哀的 3. 质量低劣的; 糟糕的

lamentation [ˌlæmen'teiʃən] *n.* 悲伤; 哀悼; 挽歌

lamina ['læminə] ([复] **laminae** ['læmini] 或 **laminas**) *n.* 薄片, 薄层; 层状体

laminate ['læmineit] *vt.* 1. 把…压成薄片

2. 把…分成薄片 3. 用薄片叠成 4. 用薄片覆盖 — *vi.* 分成薄片 — ['læminət] *adj.* 由薄片叠成(或覆盖)的 — ['læminət] *n.* 薄片制品, 层压板 ‖ ~**d** *adj.* 由薄片叠成的; 层压的

lamp [læmp] *n.* 1. 灯 2. (诗)日; 月; 星 3. 智慧的源泉; 精神力量的来源 4. (俚)眼睛 — *vt.* 1. 照亮 2. (俚)看; 看到 ‖ '~-black *n.* 灯黑

lampoon [læm'puːn] *n.* 讽刺文章(或言词) — *vt.* 冷嘲热讽; 奚落

lamprey ['læmpri] *n.* [动]七鳃鳗, 八目鳗

lance [lɑːns] *n.* 1. 长矛 2. 长矛轻骑兵 3. 矛状器具 4. [医]柳叶刀, 小刀 — *vt.* 1. 用矛刺穿 2. [医]用柳叶刀切开 3. 投, 掷 — *vi.* 急速前进

lancet ['lɑːnsit, 'lænsit] *n.* [医]柳叶刀, 小刀

land [lænd] *n.* 1. 陆地; 地面 2. 土地; 田地 3. 国土; 国家 4. 地带; 境界 5. 地皮; 地产; 田产 6. (枪炮的)阳膛线 7. [美][L-](用于惊叹句)上帝, 主(= Lord) — *vt.* 1. 使上岸; 使登陆; 使(飞机等)降落 2. 使到达, 把…送到 3. 使陷入; 使处于被动地位 4. 把(鱼)捕上岸(或船) 5. (口)弄到, 捞到 6. (口)打 — *vi.* 1. 上岸; 登陆; 降落 2. 到达; 靠脚; (船)靠岸 ‖ ~-less *adj.* 无地的 ‖ ~ **breeze** **Tobk** (指从陆地吹向海洋的)风 / '~,holder *n.* 1. 土地所有者 2. 土地租用人 / '~,lady *n.* 1. 女房东; (旅馆等的)女店主 2. 女地主 / [地]陆圈的; (鱼等)内陆水域的, 闭合水域的 / '~,lord *n.* 1. 地主 2. 房东, (旅馆等的)店主/ '~-lubber *n.* "旱鸭子"(水手用语; 指不谙航海的人或蹩脚水手) / '~-mark *n.* 1. 界标 2. 地标, 陆标 3. (历史上的)里程碑 — *vt.* 表明…地界 / '~,owner *n.* 地主; 土地所有者 / '~-slide *n.* 1. 山崩; 崩塌; 塌方 2. 压

倒的优胜(尤指竞选中选票的一面倒)
3. 呈崩溃之势的事物

landau ['lændɔː] *n.* 车顶四轮马车;活顶
小汽车

landed ['lændid] *adj.* 1. 有土地的 2. 地皮
的;不动产的

landing ['lændiŋ] *n.* 1. 上岸;登陆;着陆;
降落 2. (码头上装卸货物或旅客上下
的)登陆处;码头 3. 楼梯平台 4. 【矿】停
车平台,停车装卸台 5. (鱼)捕鱼上岸(或
上船) ‖ ~ craft 登陆艇 / ~ field(小
型)飞机场 / ~ gear 【空】起落架 / ~
stage(浮)码头 / ~ strip【空】简易跑道;
简易机场

landscape ['lændskeip] *n.* 1. (一张)风景
画;风景绘画;风景摄影 2. 风景,景色
3. 地形 4. 全景 —— *vt.* 对...作景观美
化;美化(如加铺草皮、加栽树木等)——
vi. 从事景观美化工作

lane [lein] *n.* 1. 小巷,小径,胡同;里弄
2. (狭窄的)通道,过道 3. 车道;航道 4.
【体】(跑道的)分道;泳道;(保龄球场
的)球道;(篮球场的)罚球区

language ['læŋgwidʒ] *n.* 1. 语言;语言课 2.
语言表达能力 3. 骂人话(= bad ~)4.
【计】语言

languid ['læŋgwid] *adj.* 1. 倦怠的 2. 没精
打采的 3. 慢吞吞的 ‖ ~ly *adv.* / ~
ness *n.*

languish ['læŋgwiʃ] *vi.* 1. 变得衰弱无力;
失去活力(植物等)凋萎 2. 苦思;因渴
望而苦闷(for)3. 作出楚楚可怜的倦
态(或感伤神色)‖ ~ment *n.*

languishing ['læŋgwiʃiŋ] *adj.* 1. 日趋衰弱
的;(疾病等)久拖不愈的 2. 苦思的;渴
望的 3. 感伤而惹人爱怜的;含情脉脉
的 ‖ ~ly *adv.*

languor ['læŋgə] *n.* 1. 衰弱无力;消沉 2.
(常 ~ s)郁情 3. 倦怠;沉闷 ‖ ~ous *adj.*

lank [læŋk] *adj.* 1. 细长的;瘦的;(草)稀
少的 2. (头发)平直的,不鬈的 ‖ ~ly
adv. / ~ness *n.*

lanky ['læŋki] *adj.* 过分瘦长的,瘦长得难
看的 ‖ lankily *adv.* / lankiness *n.*

lanolin ['lænəlin] *n.* 羊毛脂

lantern ['læntən] *n.* 1. 提灯;灯笼 2. 灯塔
上的灯室 3.【建】穹隆顶塔;百叶式气
窗 4. 幻灯(= magic ~)—— *vt.* 1. 给...
装上提灯 2. 把...吊在街灯柱上处死 ‖
~ jaw 突出的下巴;瘦削的下巴

lanthanum ['lænθənəm] *n.*【化】镧

lanyard ['lænjəd] *n.* 1.【海】收紧索,绞收
索 2. (水手用以系小刀或哨子等的)颈
带,项带;(军服)绶带 3.【军】(发
射火炮等用的)拉火绳,牵索

Laos [lauz] *n.* 老挝[东南亚国家]

lap¹ [læp] *n.* 1. (衣服的)下摆;裙兜,衣兜
2. (人坐着时)腰以下到膝为止的大腿
部 3. 山坳 4. 互搭;搭接 5. 重叠部分;
重叠量 6. (滚筒上绳索的)一圈;棉卷;
毛卷;纱卷 7. (跑道的)一圈;一段行
程;工作阶段 8. (磨玻璃、金属等用的)
磨盘 —— (lapped;lapping) *vt.* 1. 用...包
扎;用...裹住(around,round,over)2.
(环境等)包围 2. 把...抱在膝上;怀抱
3.【纺】绕(棉花等)成卷 4. 使形成部分
重叠;部分重叠 5. (赛跑中)比...领先整
整一圈(或几圈);(赛跑中)比(某人)领先一圈(或几圈)6. 用磨盘磨(玻璃、金属)等——
vi. 1. 被折叠;围绕 2. 部分重叠;搭接
3. 延伸;伸进 4. (跑道的)跑完一圈;领
先一圈 ‖ ~ful *n.* 一满兜 / ~ belt(汽
车或飞机座位上的)安全腰带 /
'~ dog *n.* 叭儿狗/ '~ top *adj.* & *n.* 便
携式的(电脑)

lap² [læp] (lapped;lapping) *vt.* 1. 舐;舐食
(流质食物)(up)2.〈口〉贪婪地喝(或
吃);爱听(恭维等)(up,down)3.(波

浪)拍打,泼溅 — vi.1. 舐 2.(波浪)拍
打,泼溅 — n.1. 舐;一匙之量 2.(波浪
的)拍打声 3.(俚)(淡)酒

laparoscope ['læpərəuskəup] n.【医】腹腔
镜

laparoscopy [ˌlæpə'rɔskəpi] n.【医】腹腔镜
检查

La Paz [lɑː 'pɑːz]拉巴斯[玻利维亚首都]

lapel [lə'pel] n.(西服上衣延向胸前的)翻
领

lapidary ['læpidəri, 'læpideri] n. 宝石工,
玉石工 — adj. 简洁精确的

lapin ['læpin] n. 兔

lapse [læps] n.1. 失误,小错 2.(气温、气
压等的)跌落,下降 3. 失检;偏离 4.(时
间的)流逝;间隔 5.(权利、所有权等)
的消灭,丧失 — vi.1. 失检;背离
(from) 2. 堕入,陷入(某种状态)(in-
to) 3.(时间)流逝 4.(权利、所有权等)
消灭,丧失 5.(律)(因失效而)转归他人
5. 消失;终止 — vt. 使失效

larboard ['lɑːbəd] n.(船)左舷(现用 port)
— adj. 左舷的 — adv. 朝左舷方向

larceny ['lɑːsni] n.1. 盗窃 2. 非法侵占财
产

larch [lɑːtʃ] n.1.【植】落叶松 2. 落叶松木

lard [lɑːd] n. 猪油 — vt.1. 涂油于,搽油
于2.(烹调前)嵌肥猪肉(或咸肉片)
于…中3.加装饰物于;润色(文章、谈
话等)

larder ['lɑːdə] n.1. 食物贮藏处(或柜)、食
品室 2. 贮藏的食品

large [lɑːdʒ] adj.1. 大的,巨大的 2.(见解
等)广博的;开阔的 3.(权限等)广泛的
3.(古)(心胸等)宽广的 5.(艺术风格等)奔放
的;粗犷有力的 6.【海】(风)顺的 —
adv.1. 大,大大地 2. 夸大地 3.【海】顺
风地 ‖ at ~1.(罪犯、野兽等)自由的,

未被捕获的 2. 大多数;整个 3. 全面
地;充分地 4. 笼统地;不具体地 5. 随
便地,任意地 ‖ ~ness n. / ~'hearted
adj. 慷慨的;富于同情心的

largely ['lɑːdʒli] adv.1. 大量地 2. 主要地

largess(e) [lɑː'dʒes] n. 慷慨的赠与(物)

largish ['lɑːdʒiʃ] adj. 颇大的

largo ['lɑːgəu] adj. & adv.【音】缓慢的
(地)

lariat ['læriət] n.1.(捕捉马等用的)套索
2.(拴住吃草马匹等用的)系绳 — vt.
用套索捕捉;用系绳拴住

lark[1] [lɑːk] n.【鸟】云雀

lark[2] [lɑːk] vi.1. 嬉耍;闹着玩 2. 骑马越
野 — vt.1. 愚弄;取笑 2. 骑(马)越野;
(骑着马)跳越 — n. 嬉耍;玩乐

larkspur ['lɑːkspəː] n.【植】翠雀

larva ['lɑːvə] ([复] larvae ['lɑːviː] 或 larvas)
n.【动】幼虫;幼体

larynx ['læriŋks] ([复] larynges [lə'rindʒiːz]
或 larynxes)n.【解】喉

lascivious [lə'siviəs] adj. 好色的;淫荡
的;猥亵的

laser ['leizə] [light amplification by stimulat-
ed emission of radiation 的首字母缩略词]
n. 激光;激光器 ‖ ~ beam 激光束 / ~
bomb 激光制导炸弹 / ~ card (用激光器
读出的)激光磁卡 / ~ disc 激光视盘,
镭射影碟(片) / ~ printer(计算机输出
的)激光打印机、激光印刷机 / ~
surgery 激光(外科)手术

LASH [læʃ] n. 载驳船(指装载若干装有
货物的驳船的轮船);载驳船系统(亦作
lash)[由 lighter aboard ship 缩拼而
成]

lash[1] [læʃ] n.1. 鞭打;抽打;猛击;[the
~]答刑 2. 鞭子;鞭梢 3. 责骂;讽刺;
尖锐的话;严厉的批评 4. 眼睫毛 —

vt. 1. 鞭打；打 2. 急伸(手、脚)；(动物)猛烈甩动(尾巴等) 3. (波浪等)猛烈冲击；(雨水等)猛烈扑击 4. 痛斥；讽刺；嘲笑，挖苦 5. 激起；煽动 — *vi.* 1. 猛烈地甩；(雨水、波浪等)冲洗 2. 用鞭打；猛打 3. 痛骂；严斥

lash² [læʃ] *vt.* 用绳(或链等)捆绑 ‖ ～ing *n.* 1. 捆绑 2. 捆绑用的绳子

lass [læs] *n.* 1. 少女；小姑娘 2. 情侣 3. (苏格兰)女佣

lassie [ˈlæsi] *n.* 1. 少女；小姑娘 2. 情侣

lassitude [ˈlæsitjuːd] *n.* 1. 困乏，无力 2. 厌倦，没精打采

lasso [læˈsuː] ([复] lasso(e)s) *n.* (捕捉野马等用的)套索 — *vt.* 用套索捕捉

last¹ [lɑːst] *adj.* 1. 最后的；唯一剩下的 2. 临终的 3. 最近过去的，紧接前面的 4. 极少可能的；最不可能的 5. 结论性的；权威性的 6. 极端的 7. 最新式的；最时髦的 8. 最糟糕的，最坏的 9. [加强语气用]每一的 — *adv.* 1. 最后 2. 上一次，最近一次 3. 最后(一点) — *n.* 1. 最后，末尾；临终 2. 最后的人(或东西) 3. (指动作的)最后一次 ‖ ～ly *adv.* 最后

last² [lɑːst] *vi.* 持续；维持；持久 — *vt.* 够……之用 — *n.* 够用，持久下去；经受住

last³ [lɑːst] *n.* (鞋)楦头 — *vt.* 楦(鞋)

lasting [ˈlɑːstiŋ] *adj.* 持久的；耐久的 — *n.* 厚实斜纹织物 ‖ ～ly *adv.* / ～ness *n.*

latch [lætʃ] *n.* 1. 闩；门闩；窗门 2. 碰锁，碰簧锁 — *vt.* 用门把……闩上；用碰锁把……锁上 ‖ ～ 1. 闩上；关上 2. 闩住；用碰锁锁上

late [leit] *adj.* 1. 迟的，晚的 2. 新近的 3. 已故的；去世不久的 4. 前任的；不久前卸任的 — *adv.* 1. 迟，晚 2. 在晚期 3. 最近；不久前 ‖ ～ness *n.*

lately [ˈleitli] *adv.* 最近；不久前

latent [ˈleitənt] *adj.* 潜伏的，潜在的；隐而不见的 — *n.* 隐约指纹，潜指印 ‖ ～ly *adv.*

lateral [ˈlætərəl] *adj.* 1. 侧面的；旁边的；横(向)的 2. [语] 边音的，旁流音的 — *n.* 1. 位于侧面的东西；侧向生长着的东西 2. [电] 支线 3. [矿] 走向平巷 4. [建] 横向排水沟 5. [语] (舌)边音 ‖ ～ly *adv.*

latex [ˈleiteks] ([复] latices [ˈlætisiːz] 或 latexes) *n.* [植] 乳液；胶乳；橡浆

lath [lɑːθ] ([复] lath(s)) *n.* [建] 木板条，条板；[总称] 板条，竹骨胎 — *vt.* 给……钉板条；在……上安放竹骨胎

lathe [leið] *n.* 车床 — *vt.* 用车床加工，用车床切削

lather [ˈlɑːðə] *n.* 1. (肥皂水等的)泡沫 2. (马等的)汗沫 3. 〈喻〉激动；焦躁 — *vt.* 1. 在……上涂以皂沫；以泡沫布满 2. 〈俚〉狠狠地打 — *vi.* 形成泡沫；起泡沫

Latin [ˈlætin] *adj.* 1. 拉丁的；拉丁语的；拉丁语系的 2. 天主教的(尤用以与东正教相区别) — *n.* 1. 拉丁语；拉丁字母表 2. 拉丁人(尤指拉丁美洲人)；古罗马人 3. 天主教徒 ‖ ～ America 拉丁美洲 / ～-A'merican *adj.* 拉丁美洲的 / ～ American 拉丁美洲人

latitude [ˈlætitjuːd] *n.* 1. 纬度 2. [天] 黄纬 3. [～s] 纬度地区(尤指从温度上而言) 4. 宽度；范围；幅度 5. (言论、行动等的)回旋余地，自由 6. (胶片)曝光宽容度

latrine [ləˈtriːn] *n.* (沟形或坑形的)厕所；公共厕所

latter [ˈlætə] *adj.* 1. 后面的；后半的；末了的 2. (两者中)后者的

lattice [ˈlætis] *n.* 1. 格子 2. [物] 点阵，格；栅格 3. [建] 斜条格构 — *vt.* 1.

把...制成格子状 2. 用格子(或格子花样)覆盖(或装饰) ‖ '~work *n*. 格子;格子细工

Latvia ['lætviə] ***n***. 拉脱维亚[欧洲波罗的海沿岸国家]

laud [lɔːd] ***n***.1. 赞美,称赞;赞歌,颂歌 2. [Lauds][用作单或复](天主教西派教会的)晨经 — ***vt***. 赞美,称赞

laudable ['lɔːdəbl] ***adj***. 值得称赞的

laudanum ['lɔːdənəm] ***n***.【药】鸦片酒,鸦片酊

laugh [lɑːf] ***vi***.1. (大)笑;发笑 2. (山川、草木等)呈现欢欣景象 — ***vt***.1. 以笑表示 2. 使笑得 — ***n***.1. 笑;笑声 2. 引人发笑的事情 3. 嘲笑;[~s]玩笑

laughable ['lɑːfəbl] ***adj***. 可笑的;有趣的 ‖ ~**ness** ***n***. / **laughably** ***adv***.

laughing ['lɑːfiŋ] ***adj***. 笑的;带着笑的;可笑的 — ***n***. 笑 ‖ '~**stock** ***n***. 笑柄

laughter ['lɑːftə] ***n***.1. 笑;笑声 2. (古)可笑的事物

launch[1] [lɔːntʃ] ***vt***.1. 发射;投掷 2. 使(船)下水 3. 发动(战争等);开展(运动、斗争等)4. 发出(命令等);提出(抗议等);施以(打击、漫骂等) 5. 开办;发起;使投入;使开始从事 — ***vi***.1. 起飞;(船)下水 2. 投入(*into*) 3. 着手进行,开始(*on*, *upon*) — ***n***. 发射;(船的)下水 ‖ ~**er** ***n***. 发射器;弹射器;发射装置;起动装置 ‖ ~ **pad** (导弹、火箭等的)发射坪,发射台

launch[2] [lɔːntʃ] ***n***. 汽艇;游艇

launching ['lɔːntʃiŋ] ***n***.1. 发射 2. 船的下水;下水典礼 3. 开办 ‖ ~ **pad** (弹导、火箭等的)发射坪,发射台

launder ['lɔːndə] ***n***.【矿】流槽,流水槽 — ***vt***. 洗涤;浆洗;洗熨;清洗;把(来路可疑的钱财)弄得貌似合法;掩饰(丑行) — ***vi***.(经受)洗涤;(经受)浆洗;洗熨;清洗 ‖ ~**er** ***n***. 洗衣工

laundress ['lɔːndris] ***n***. 洗烫衣物的女工

laundry ['lɔːndri] ***n***.1. 洗衣 2. 洗衣作;洗衣店 3. 付洗衣物;已洗好的衣物 ‖ '~**man** ***n***. 洗衣男工(尤指为洗衣店取送顾客衣物的人)

laureate ['lɔːriət] ***adj***.1. (桂冠)用月桂树枝编成的 2. 戴桂冠的 3. 配戴桂冠的,卓越的(尤指诗人) — ***n***.1. 戴桂冠的人;(由于艺术或科学上的成就)获得荣誉者 2. [the L-]桂冠诗人(英国王室御用诗人的称号) — ['lɔːrieit] ***vt***.1. 使戴桂冠;授...以荣誉 2. 授...以桂冠诗人的称号

laurel ['lɔrəl] ***n***.1.【植】月桂;月桂树 2. 月桂树叶(古代希腊人用以编成冠冕、授予竞赛的优胜者) 3. 桂冠;殊荣;[~s][用作单或复]冠军;胜利 — (laurel(l)ed; laurel(l)ing) ***vt***.1. 使戴桂冠 2. 给予...荣誉

lava ['lɑːvə] ***n***.【地】熔岩

lavatory ['lævətəri] ***n***.1. 洗脸盆;【宗】洗手式 2. 盥洗室;厕所;浴室

lave [leiv] ***vt***. 1. 洗濯;为...沐浴 2. (河水等)冲刷;沿...流淌

lavender ['lævində] ***n***.1.【植】熏衣草 2. 干熏衣草的花(或叶、茎) 3. 淡紫色 — ***adj***. 淡紫色的 — ***vt***. 用熏衣草熏香

lavish ['læviʃ] ***adj***.1. 过分大方的;浪费的;慷慨的,不吝惜的 2. 过分丰富的;过度的;丰富的,大量的 — ***vt***. 过多地赠送;滥花费;慷慨地给予 ‖ ~**ly** ***adv***. / ~**ness** ***n***.

law [lɔː] ***n***.1. 法律;法令;法 2. 法制 3. 法学;法律知识 4. 司法界;律师行业 5. 诉讼 6. 法律体系,法统 7. (与衡平法相对而言的)普通法,习惯法,不成文法 8. 法则;规律;定律 9. (艺术、运动、某

一生活部门中的)规则、守则 10.【基督教】(摩西)律法(= ~ of Moses) 11.〈英〉(在赛跑中给予弱手的)先跑时间(或距离);宽限期 — vi. 起诉,诉诸于法 — vt.〈主方〉对...起诉 ‖ '~a,biding adj. 守法的 的 /'~breaker n. 犯法的人 /'~maker n. 立法者 /'~,making n. 立法 adj. 立法的 的 /'~suit n. 诉讼(案件)

law-and-order ['lɔːː(ˌ)ɔnd'ɔːdə] adj. 法治的;遵纪守法的

lawful ['lɔːful] adj. 1. 合法的,法定的 2. 守法的 ‖ ~ly adv. / ~ness n.

lawless ['lɔːlis] adj. 1. (国家等)没有法律的;失去法律控制的 2. 不法的;非法的;无法无天的 ‖ ~ly adv. / ~ness n.

lawn[1] [lɔːn] n. 上等细布;上等细麻布

lawn[2] [lɔːn] n. 1. 草坪,草坪 2.〈古〉林间空地 ‖ ~ mower 割草机 ‖ ~ tennis 【体】草地网球

lawrencium [lɔːˈrensiəm] n.【化】铹

lawyer ['lɔːjə] n. 1. 律师 2. 法学家

lax [læks] adj. 1. (肠)宽松的,易通便的;腹泻的 2. 松弛的;质地松的 3. 不严格的;不精密的;马虎的 4. 不紧的 5.【植】(花簇)疏松的 5.【语】(元音)松弛)的 — n.【语】松弛音 ‖ ~ly adv. / ~ness n.

laxative ['læksətiv] adj. 1. 致轻泻的,通大便的 2. 有轻度腹泻的 3. 放松的;缓解的 — n.【药】轻泻剂

lay[1] [lei] (laid [leid]) vt. 1. 放,搁 2. 把...压平;使倒下 3. 使处于某种状态(或地位) 4. 铺设;敷设;砌(砖) 5. 铺;涂 6. 布置;安排〔常用被动语态〕7. 为(故事等)设置特定地点或场所 7. 拟订(计划等);策划 8. 提出(问题,主张,要求等) 9. 平息(风浪等);消除(疑虑等);平服,驱除(鬼怪)等 10. 下(蛋);(飞机)投

(弹);放(烟幕) 11. 归(罪)于;把...归于 12. 把(惩罚、职责、负担等)加于 13. 用上,施上 14. 押(赌注);赌钱;就...打赌;打赌 15. 调节(火炮等)至瞄准位置 16. 搓,编(绳等) — vi. 1. 下蛋 2.〈俚〉躺下(= lie) ‖【海】就位,定向 5. 全力以赴 — n. 1. 位置;地理形势 2.〈婉〉隐蔽处 3. 行动计划 4. 行业;职业 5.(买卖等)的条件;(捕鲸船上代替工资的)捕获物分红 6.(绳索的)股数及拧法;(粗纱的)圈距 7. 下蛋,产卵 8.〈俚〉交媾;性交的女方 ‖ '~of n. 1. 布局;陈设;安排;设计 2.(报纸的)版面编排 3. 一套器具(或工具,衣服等) 4.〈美口〉态势;情况 5. 地方;场所

lay[2] [lei] n. 1.(供吟唱的)短叙事诗;短抒情诗 2. 歌曲

lay[3] [lei] adj. 1. 凡俗的,世俗的(与教会中神职人员相对而言) 2. 外行的,非专业化的 ‖ '~man n. 1. 俗人(别于僧侣、牧师) 2. 门外汉,外行

lay[4] [lei]lie[8] 的过去式

layer ['leiə] n. 1. 层;阶层;层次 2. 铺设者;涂抹机 3.【军】瞄准手 4. 生蛋鸡 5.【植】压条;用压条法分出的植物 — ['leiə] vt. 用压条法培植 — vi. 1.(庄稼)倒伏 2.(植物)借助压条法生根繁殖 3. 分层堆积

layette [lei'et] n. 新生婴儿的全套用品(如衣服、被褥、洗涤用具等)

lazy ['leizi] adj. 1. 懒惰的;懒散的 2. 慢吞吞的 2.(河川)流动缓慢的 3. 令人懒散的 4. 垃坊的,下垂的 ‖ lazily adv. / laziness n.

lb. abbr.〈拉〉libra(e) 磅(= pound(s))

lbs. abbr.〈拉〉librae 磅(= pounds)

LD abbr. laser disc

lea [liː] n. 1.〈诗〉草原;草地;牧地 2.(

草的)休闲地,未耕地 — *adj.* (土地)休闲的,未耕的

leach [li:tʃ] *vt.* 沥滤(液体) 滤去(物质);滤去(物质) — *vi.* 被滤掉 — *n.* 1. 沥滤 2. 沥滤器

lead[1] [li:d] (led[led]) *vt.* 1. 领导;率领 2. 带领,引领;走在(队伍等)的最前头 3. 搀;牵(马等) 4. 致使;诱使;对(证人)进行诱供引问 5. 过(活);使过(某种生活) 6. 前置瞄准(飞鸟、飞禽等);传球至(接应队员)的前方 7. 率先出(牌) 8. (拳击赛中)对准对手猛击一(拳) 9. 在...中领先;胜过 — *vi.* 1. 领导;领先 2. 带头 3. 通向;导致 (*to*) 3. 率先出牌(或开球等) — *n.* 1. 领导;榜样;引导;带头;领先;首位 2. 领先的程度(或距离) 4. 线索 5. (戏中)主角;扮演主角的演员 6.[新闻报道等]的首段导语;头版新闻报道 7.(通向物体的)导线 8.[电]导线;引线;联络线 9.[矿]矿脉 10.(牵狗等的)绳索,皮带 11.(纸牌游戏中)先出牌(权);率先打出的一张牌(或一组牌) 12.(拳击赛中)先出拳 — *adj.* 1. 领头的,领先的;最重要的,以显著地位刊载的

lead[2] [led] *n.* 1. 铅;铅制品(铅笔中的)铅心 2. (英)[~s]铅皮屋顶 3. (印)加空铅,铅条 4. [海]测深锤 5. [总称]子弹 — *vt.* 1. 用铅包(...中衬铅);灌铅增加...的重量 2. (印)用行间插铅条 3. 加铅(或铅的化合物)于(汽油等) 4. 用铅使固住 — *vi.* 用测深锤测深水深 2. 被铅覆盖;(枪等)被铅卷住

leaden ['ledn] *adj.* 1. 铅制的 2. 铅灰色的 3. 质量差的,低劣的 4. 沉重的;缓慢的 5. 呆滞的;沉闷的;阴郁的 ‖ ~ly *adv.* / ~ness *n.*

leader ['li:də] *n.* 1. 领袖;领导者;首领;指挥者 2. 乐队指挥;领奏者;首席演奏者 3. (英)(诉讼)的首席律师,主要辩护人 4. (英)社论;重要文章 5. 居首位的事物(如最易传染的疾病、最热门的股票等) 6. 先导句;领衔;领机 7. [建]水落管 8. [海]导缆器,导缆装置 9. [~s][印]指引线(指图表上引导视线用的连续的点或短划) 9. [植]顶枝 10.[矿]矿脉 11. [解]腱 12. (起招徕作用的)廉价商品

leadership ['li:dəʃip] *n.* 1. 领导 2. [总称]领导人员 3. 领导能力

leading ['li:diŋ] *adj.* 1. 领导的;指导的 2. 第一位的,最主要的 3. (戏中)扮演主角 — *n.* 1. 领导;指挥;指导 2. 引导 ‖ ~ article 1. (报上的)重要文章(英社论 2. (起招徕作用的)廉价商品

leaf [li:f] ([复] leaves[li:vz]) *n.* 1. 叶;[总称]叶子 2. 花瓣 3. (书页等的)一张(即正反两页) 4. 薄金属片 — [总称]箔 5. (撑起来或插入即可增大桌面的)活动面板 6.(窗、门等的)翻 7. 汽车等片弹簧的)簧片 8.(英方)帽边 9. (步枪的)瞄准尺 — *vi.* 1. 生叶,长叶(*out*) 2. 翻书页 — *vt.* 翻(书页) ‖ ~less *adj.* 无叶的 / ~stalk *n.* [植] 叶柄

leaflet ['li:flit] *n.* 1. 小叶,嫩叶 2. 复叶的一片 3. 叶状器官(或部分) 4. 传单;散页印刷品 — (leafletted; leafletting) *vt.* 向...散发传单给

leafy ['li:fi] *adj.* 1. 叶子覆盖着的;叶状的 2. 叶茂的 3. 阔叶的;由叶组成的

league [li:g] *n.* 1. (政治性的)同盟,联盟;盟约 2. (运动、文艺等方面的)联合;社团 3. 种类;范畴 — *vt. & vi.* (使)结盟;(使)联合

leak [li:k] *vi.* 1. 漏;渗 2. 泄漏出去 — *vt.* 使(空气、液体等)渗漏;使(消息等)泄

漏 — *n.* 1. 漏洞;漏隙 2. 漏、漏出 3.【电】漏泄电阻;漏电 4. 漏出物 5. 〈俚〉撒尿

leakage ['liːkidʒ] *n.* 1. 漏、漏出;泄漏出物 2. 漏出物;漏出量 3.【商】渗漏;漏损

leaky ['liːki] *adj.* 1. 漏的;有漏洞的 2. 〈口〉易泄密的 ‖ **leakiness** *n.*

lean[1] [liːn] (**leaned** [lent, liːnd] 或 **leant** [lent]) *vi.* 1. 倾斜;屈身;倾向;偏向 2. 靠;依赖 — *vi.* 使倾斜 2. 把...靠在某种东西上 — *n.* 倾斜;倾向 ‖ '~-to *n.* 单披屋顶;披屋 *adj.*【建】单坡的

lean[2] [liːn] *adj.* 1. (人、家畜等)瘦的;(肉)无脂肪的,精瘦的 2. 贫乏的;贫瘠的;缺乏营养的;收益差的 3. (文体等)简洁的 — *n.* 瘦肉 — *vt.* 使变瘦 ‖ ~-ness *n.*

leant [lent] 〈主英〉**lean**[1] 的过去式和过去分词

leap [liːp] (**leapt** [lept] 或 **leaped** [lept, liːpt]) *vi.* 1. 跃、跳 2. 猛然行动;迅速行动 — *vt.* 1. 跃过 2. 使跃过 — *n.* 跳跃;飞跃;跃进 3. (必须)跃过的地方;跃过的距离 ‖ '~-frog *n.* 跳背游戏 2.【军】(两支部队的)交互跃进 3. 竞相提高 *vi.* 1. 作跳背游戏;跳跃 2. 交替前进;相互越过;相互超越 3.【军】使(两支部队)交互跃进 3. 从旁超越;避开 4. 竞相要求提高(工资等) / ~ year 闰年

leapt [lept] **leap** 的过去式和过去分词

learn [ləːn] (**learnt** [ləːnt] 或 **learned** [ləːnt, ləːnd]) *vi.* 1. 学习;学 2. 听到,获悉(*about, of*) — *vt.* 1. 学到;学会 2. 听到;认识到 3. 记住 4. 〈俗〉教;教训 ‖ ~er *n.* 学习者;初学者

learned ['ləːnid] *adj.* 1. 有学问的;博学的;精通的;〈英〉精通法律的 2. 学术性的

3. [lænd 或 lænt] 通过学习(或经验等)获得的 4. 由学者从事(或提出、写成)的

learning ['ləːniŋ] *n.* 1. 学习 2. 知识;学问

learnt [ləːnt] **learn** 的过去式和过去分词

lease [liːs] *vt.* 1. 出租(土地等) 2. 租得,租有(土地等) — *n.* 1. 租约;租赁;租赁期限 2. 租借,租赁;租赁权 4. 租赁物

leash [liːʃ] *n.* 1. (系狗等的)皮带,皮条 2. (打猎用语)(狗、狐等的)三只;成三的一组 3.〈纺〉综束、综把(指握花机上连于同一根颈线下的若干综线)4. 约束,控制 — *vt.* 1. 用皮带系住 2. 约束,控制

least [liːst] *adj.* [**little** 的最高级] 1. 最小的 2. 最不重要的;地位最低的 3.〈美方〉年纪最小的;(鸟类)很小的,极小型的 — *adv.* [**little** 的最高级] 最小;最少 — *n.* 最小物;最少量

leather ['leðə] *n.* 1. 皮革 2. 皮革制品;〈俚〉(板球,足球等运动的)球;皮夹子;〈美俚〉拳击手套;[~s](骑马用的)皮马裤;皮鞭蹬 3. 皮扶 4.〈口〉皮带(等)的下垂部分 5. [the ~]〈美俚〉拳击赛中的一击 — *adj.* 皮革的;皮革制的 — *vt.* 用皮革包遮(或擦、擦拭、擦亮) 2.〈口〉(用皮鞭)抽打

leathery ['leðəri] *adj.* 1. 似皮革的 2. 坚韧的

leave[1] [liːv] (**left** [left]) *vt.* 1. 离开;脱离 2. 把...留下;留下;剩下;把...遗留给 3. 遗忘;丢下 4. 使处于(某种状态);*Leave the door open.* 让门开着吧。 5. 把...交给;委托 6. 听任;让(= let) 7. 遗弃(妻、女等);舍弃 8.(从某个方位)经过(某物)— *vi.* 离去;动身,出发(*for*);~ *for London* 去伦敦

leave[2] [liːv] *n.* 1. 许可,同意 2. 准假;休

假;假期 3. 离去;告别

leave³ [li:v] *vi.* 生叶,长叶

leaved [li:vd] *adj.* [常用以构成复合词] 有…叶的;a broad-~ plant 阔叶植物

leaven ['levn] *n.* 1. 酵母于;面肥,老面 2. 引起渐变(或致使渐变)的因素,潜移默化的影响 3. 气味;色彩 — *vt.* 1. (加发酵剂)使发酵 2. 使渐变;使渐变;在…中掺入改变因素

leaves [li:vz] leaf 的复数

leavings ['li:viŋz] [复] *n.* 残余;残渣

Lebanon ['lebənən] *n.* 黎巴嫩[西南亚国家]

lecherous ['letʃərəs] *adj.* 好色的,淫荡的,纵欲的 ‖ **lechery** *n.*

lectern ['lektən] *n.* 1. (教堂中的)读经台 2. 讲演者及讲稿的)斜面演讲台

lecture ['lektʃə] *n.* 1. 演讲;讲课;讲稿 2. 训斥;训话 — *vi.* 讲演;讲课 — *vt.* 1. 向…讲课 2. 训斥…;给…讲课 ‖ ~**r** *n.* 1. 讲演者 2. (大学、学院中的)讲师

led [led] lead¹ 的过去式和过去分词

ledge [ledʒ] *n.* 1. 壁架;架状突出物 2. [矿]矿脉 3. 岩石突出部,岩架 4. (近海岸的)暗礁,岸边礁,岩礁

ledger ['ledʒə] *n.* 1. 分类帐;分户帐 2. [建](搭脚手架用的)横木 3. (坟墓的)盖基石板

lee [li:] *n.* 1. 庇护,保护 2. 庇护所;背风处 3. [海]下风 — *adj.* 1. 避风处的 2. 下风的;背风面的 3. 背冰川面的

leech [li:tʃ] *n.* 1. (古)(内科或外科)医生 2. [动]水蛭,蚂蟥 3. 吸血鬼,寄生虫,食客 — *vt.* 1. (为治疗疾病用)用水蛭给…放血;治疗 2. 依附并榨取(他人脂膏) — *vi.* (水蛭似)依附并榨取他人(on to)

leek [li:k] *n.* [植]韭葱

leer [liə] *n.* (表示敌意、嘲弄、会意等的)一瞥;秋波 — *vi.* 斜眼看;送秋波(at)

leery ['liəri] *adj.* (口)1. 机警的;狡猾的 2. 留神的;猜疑的(of)

lees [li:z] [复] *n.* (酒缸等中的)沉淀物;渣滓

leeward ['li:wəd] *adj.* 背风的,下风的 — 向下风的 — *adv.* 向下风 — *n.* 下风;背风面

leeway ['li:wei] *n.* 1. 偏航;偏航角 2. 余地;余时;灵活性

left¹ [left] leave¹ 的过去式和过去分词 ‖ ~-over *adj.* 剩余的 *n.* 剩余物;吃剩的食物

left² [left] *adj.* 1. 左面的,左边的,左侧的 2. 左翼的;[常作 L-]左派的 — *adv.* 在左边;向左 — *n.* 1. 左手,左手拳 3. [常作 L-]左翼;激进分子们;议长席左侧的议员们,左派议员们 4.[军]左翼 ‖ ~-**hand** *adj.* 左边的;左手的 2. = ~-handed / ~-**handed** *adj.* 1. 惯用左手不灵活的 2. 左手的;用左手做的 3. 笨拙的 4. 含恶意的 5. 反时针的;向左旋转的 6. (婚姻)门第不相当的 *adv.* 用左手

leftist ['leftist] *n.* 1. 左派;左派政党成员 2. (美口)左撇子 — *adj.* 左派的,左倾的

leg [leg] *n.* 1. 腿,(猪、羊等)供食用的腿;腿肉 2. 假腿 3. 裤腿;袜筒;靴统 4. 支撑柱条 5. 裤脚管;袜统;靴统 5.(直角三角形的)直角边 5.(三角形的)侧边 6.(帆船航所行的)一段航程;一段行程;(接力赛中的)一段赛程 7.[电]引线;支线 8. (多相系统的)一个相 8. (英俚)骗子 9.(板球)左(或右)外场 10.(桥牌)一条腿(指在双局桥牌中任

何一方得到的第一局) — (legged; legging) vi. 1. 跑 2. (撑船者仰卧)用腿蹬洞壁使船通过运河隧洞 3. (为…)奔走;卖力(for) — vt. 用腿腿洞壁使(船)通过运河隧洞 ‖ legged adj. [常用以构成复合词]有…腿的: a long-legged man 腿长的人 / legging n. [常作 leggings] (帆布或革制的)裹腿、绑腿 / ~-less adj. 无腿的 ‖ ~ room n. (坐位前)供伸腿的空间

legacy ['legəsi] n. 1. 遗赠物(一般指动产);遗产 2. 传代物

legal ['liːgəl] adj. 1. 法律(上)的 2. 合法的;正当的 3. 法定的 — n. 1. 法定权利 2. 法律公告 3. [~s](储蓄银行或信托公司等依法发行的)合法证券 ‖ ~ly adv.

legality [liːˈgæliti] n. 1. 依法,合法性 2. [legalities]法律上的义务

legalize ['liːgəlaiz] vt. 使合法化;使得到法律认可 ‖ legali'zation n.

legate[1] ['legət] n. 使者,使节(尤指罗马教皇的使节)

legate[2] [liˈgeit] vt. 把…遗留给,把…遗赠给

legatee [ˌlegəˈtiː] n. 遗产承受人;受遗赠者

legation [liˈgeiʃən] n. 1. 使节的派遣(或节的)使命 2. 公使馆;公使馆全体人员 3. 使节的职权

legend ['ledʒənd] n. 1. 传说;传奇;传奇文学 2. 传说(或传奇)中的人物 3. (奖章、硬币等上的)题铭,铭文 4. (地图的)图例;(插图的)说明

legendary ['ledʒəndəri] adj. 传说(中)的,传奇(中)的;传说(或传奇)似的

legerdemain [ˌledʒədəˈmein] n. 戏法;手法;花招

legible ['ledʒibl] adj. 易读的,字迹清楚的

legibility [ˌledʒiˈbiliti] n. / **legibly** adv.

legion ['liːdʒən] n. 1. 古罗马军团(约有三千至六千名步兵,辅以骑兵) 2. 军团;兵团 3. [L-]美国军团(系美国全国性退伍军人组织) 4. 众多,大批

legislate ['ledʒisleit] vi. 立法,制定(或通过)法律 — vt. 通过立法使产生(或实现);通过立法规定

legislation [ˌledʒisˈleiʃən] n. 1. 立法 2. 法规 3. 由立法机构审议的事项

legislative ['ledʒislətiv] adj. 1. 立法的 2. 有立法权的 3. 由立法机构组成或成立的 4. 由法律规定的,根据法律执行(或产生)的 5. 立法机构的;由立法机构产生的 ‖ ~ly adv.

legislator ['ledʒisleitə] n. 立法机构成员,议员;立法者

legislature ['ledʒisleitʃə] n. 立法机关;议会

legitimacy [liˈdʒitiməsi] n. 合法性;正统性

legitimate [liˈdʒitimət] adj. 1. 合法的,合理的 2. 正统的 3. 由合法婚姻所生的,婚生的 4. (感情等)真实的 — [liˈdʒitimeit] vt. 1. 使合法;给…以合法地位(或权力);宣布…为合法 2. 证明…有理 ‖ ~ly adv.

legitimize [liˈdʒitimaiz] vt. 使合法化;宣布…为合法 ‖ legitimi'zation n.

legume ['legjuːm] n. 1. 豆科植物 2. (豆)荚 3. 豆(豆科植物的种子) ‖ **leguminous** [liˈgjuːminəs] adj.

lei [lei] n. (夏威夷人戴的)花环,花冠

Leipzig ['laipzig] n. 莱比锡[德国东部城市]

leisure ['leʒə, 'liːʒə] n. 1. 空闲,闲暇 2. 悠闲,安逸 — n. 1. 空闲的 2. 有闲的

leisurely ['leʒəli, 'liːʒəli] adj. 从容的,慢慢的 — adv. 从容地,慢慢地

LEM, lem [lem] n. (lunar excursion module

的首字母缩拼词]登月舱

lemon ['lemən] **n.1.** 柠檬;柠檬树 **2.** = ~ yellow **3.**〈俚〉不中用的东西;次品;讨厌family的;无用的人 一 **adj.** 柠檬色的; 柠檬香的;柠檬味的;柠檬制的 ‖ ~ yellow 淡黄色的,柠檬黄

lemonade [ˌleməˈneid] **n.** 柠檬汽水

lemur ['liːmə] **n.** 狐猴

lend [lend](lent[lent])**1.** 把…借给;出借 **2.** 贷(款);出租(书籍等)**3.** 提供;给予;增添 一 **vi.** 贷款

length [leŋθ] **n.1.** 长,长度 **2.**(时间的)长短;期间 **3.**【语】音长 **4.**(一)段,(一)节 **5.** 一段(或一节)标准长度;身体全长;衣长 ‖ ~ways、~wise **adv. & adj.** 纵长地(的)

lengthen ['leŋθən] **vt.** 使延长 一 **vi.** 变长,长起来;延伸

lengthy ['leŋθi] **adj.1.** 过长的;漫长的 **2.**(演说、文章等)冗长的;(讲话人、作者等)罗罗唆唆的 **3.**〈口〉个子高的 ‖ lengthily **adv.** /lengthiness **n.**

lenient ['liːniənt] **adj.1.** 宽大的,宽厚的;怜悯的 **2.**〈古〉减轻痛苦的 ‖ lenience、leniency **n.** /~ly **adv.**

Leningrad ['leningræd] **n.** 列宁格勒(现称 Saint Petersburg 圣彼得堡)[俄罗斯西北部港市]

Leninism ['leninizəm] **n.** 列宁主义

Leninist ['leninist] **n.** 列宁主义者 一 **adj.** 列宁的;列宁主义的;列宁主义者的

lens [lenz] **n.1.** 透镜;(凹、凸)镜片 **2.**(眼球的)晶状体 **3.**(照相机的)镜头 **4.** 双凸透镜状物品;【矿】透镜状体;扁豆状矿体

Lent [lent] **n.**〈基督教〉大斋节(指复活节前的四十天);封斋期 ‖ Lenten **adj.**

lent [lent] lend 的过去式和过去分词

lentil ['lentil] **n.** 小扁豆(指植物或其种子)

leonine ['liːənain] **adj.** 狮子的;狮子似的;【医】麻面癞风的

leopard ['lepəd] **n.** 豹;美洲虎、美洲豹 ‖ ~ess ['lepədis] **n.** 母豹

leper ['lepə] **n.1.** 麻风病患者 **2.**(由于道德和社会原因)大家避之唯恐不及的人;被排斥的人

leprechaun ['leprəkɔːn] **n.**(爱尔兰民间传说中的)矮妖精

leprosy ['leprəsi] **n. 1.**【医】麻风(病) **2.** 堕落,败坏

lesbian ['lezbiən] **n.** 女性同性恋者 一 **adj.** 女性同性恋的

lesion ['liːʒən] **n.1.** 损害;损伤 **2.**【医】(因伤、病而致的)机能障碍;器官损害

Lesotho [ləˈsəutəu] **n.** 莱索托(旧称 Basu-toland 巴苏陀兰)[非洲东南部国家]

less [les] **adj.** [little 的比较级]更少(或更小)的;较少(或较小)的 一 **adv.** [little 的比较级]更少(或更小)地;较少(或较小)地 一 **n.** 更少(或更小);较少(或较小) 一 **prep.** 减去;少掉

-less **suf.** [附在名词或动词后,主要构成形容词或副词]表示"没有","无","不":fearless、careless、countless、doubtless

lessee [le'siː] **n.** 承租人,租户

lessen ['lesn] **vt.1.** 减少;减轻 **2.** 缩小;贬低 一 **vi.** 变少;变小

lesser ['lesə] **adj.** [little 的比较级]**adj.** [只作定语]较小的;更少的;次要的 一 **adv.** 较少地;较次要地

lesson ['lesn] **n.1.** 功课;课业 **2.** [常 ~s]课程 **3.** 一节课;(教科书的)一课 **4.** 教训;训诫 **5.**〈宗〉(指早、晚祷时的)圣经选读 一 **vt.1.** 教,给…上课 **2.** 训斥;教训

lessor [le'sɔ:] *n.* 出租人

lest [lest] *conj.* 1. [在被连接的状语从句里常用 should 或原形动词]唯恐；免得 2. [用于 fear, worry 一类动词后面，起连接从句的作用，相当于 that]: I was afraid ~ the kid (should) fall down the staircase. 我怕这孩子会从楼梯上掉下来。

let¹ [let] (let; letting) *vt.* 1. [用于第一或第三人称的祈使句中，表示建议、请求、命令、警告等]让: Let me try. 让我试一下。2. [用于祈使句]假设: Let AB be equal to CD. 设 AB 等于 CD。3. 允许，让: The child was ~ (to) do it. 这孩子被允许去做那件事。4. 让流出；放出 5. 让…进入(或通过) 6. 出租；租给 7. (投标后)把…承包出去: ~ a contract to sb. [经]向某人发包订约 — *vi.* 1. 被出租 2. [工程承包]被承包出去 — *n.* (英)出租；租出的房屋

let² [let] (letted 或 let; letting) *vt.* 〈古〉妨碍，阻碍 — *n.* 1. 障碍 2. (网球赛等中发球时的)触网重发

-let *suf.* 1. 表示"小"; booklet 2. 表示"在…上佩带的饰品"; armlet

lethal ['li:θəl] *adj.* 致命的 — *n.* 致死物[生]致死基因(亦作 ~ gene)

lethargy ['leθədʒi] *n.* 1. [医]昏睡，嗜眠 2. 没精打采，懒散；无生气，呆滞 ‖ **lethargic** ['le'θɑːdʒik] *adj.*

let's [lets] = let us

letter ['letə] *n.* 1. 字母 2. [印]铅字 3. 信 [常 ~s]证书；许可证 4. [~s](用作单数或复)文学；学问 5. 字面意义 6. (美)(作为奖品授予校队优秀运动员的)校名首字母标志 — *vt.* 1. 用印刷体字母写(或印) 2. 用字母标号 3. 给…(题)字 — *vi.* 用(或刻)印刷体字母 ‖ ~ing *n.* 1. 写字；印字 2. [总

称](写或刻印的)字 ‖ ~ box 信箱/ ~ head *n.* 信笺抬头(指印于信笺上端的文字，包括姓名、机构、地址等)；印有抬头的信笺

lettered ['letəd] *adj.* 有学问的；有文化的

lettuce ['letis] *n.* 1. 莴苣 2. (俚)纸币

leuk(a)emia [lu:'ki:miə] *n.* [医]白血病

levee¹ ['levi] *n.* 1. (旧时君主或显贵起床时或起床后的)早晨接见 2. 〈英〉午后接见会(由君主或其代表举行，接见对象仅限于男子) 3. (总统或其他高级官员举行的)招待会

levee² ['levi] *n.* 1. 堤；堤岸 2. 码头 3. (天然的)冲积堤 — *vt.* 给…筑堤

level ['levəl] *n.* 1. 水平面；水平线；水平状态 2. 水平；水准 3. 程度；等级 4. 水准仪；水准测量 5. 水平高度 6. 平地，(建筑物的)层 [矿]主平巷 7. [电]电平；级 8. (观察事物的)角度，层面 — *adj.* 1. 水平的；平的与同高度的；同水平的；同程度的 [物]等势的 3. 平稳的，稳定的；坚定的，不动摇的 4. 平静的，冷静的 5. 均匀的；平衡的 6. 合理的，明智的 — (level(l)ed; level(l)ing) *vt.* 1. 使成水平；把…弄平；平整 2. 夷平；毁坏；击倒 3. 使同等；把…(目的)放在或向下)拉平；消除(差别) 4. 举(枪)瞄准(at); 使(话，目光，批评等)针对 5. 使(颜色等)变淡; 使(声调)变平 6. 对(土地)作水平测量 — *vi.* 1. 变平 2. 拉平(with) 3. 用枪瞄准(at) 4. 坦诚对待 ‖ level(l)er *n.* 1. 使平等(或平均)的人(或事物) 2. 水准测量具；校平器 3. 平等主义者；[L](英国十七世纪资产阶级革命时期)平均派成员/~ly *adv.*/~ness *n.*

lever ['li:və, 'levə] *n.* 1. 杆；杠杆 2. 途径；工具；手段 — *vt.* 1. 用杠杆撬动；用杠杆移动 2. 用杠杆操纵 — *vi.* 用杠杆

leverage [ˈliːvəridʒ, ˈlevəridʒ] n. 1. 杠杆作用 2. 杠杆效率 3. 手段；力量；影响

leviathan [liˈvaiəθən] n. 海中怪兽；巨轮；庞然大物；有权势的人

levity [ˈleviti] n. 1. 轻率；轻浮 2. 不稳定；多变；无常

levy [ˈlevi] n. 1. 征收；征税；征收额 2. 征集；被征的兵员 — vt. 1. 征收(捐税、罚款、贡品等)；强索 2. 征集(兵员) 3. 【律】扣押 — vi. 1. 征税 2. 【律】扣押

lewd [luːd] adj. 淫荡的；猥亵的；下流的 ‖ ~ly adv. / ~ness n.

lexicographer [ˌleksiˈkɔɡrəfə] n. 词典编纂者

lexicography [ˌleksiˈkɔɡrəfi] n. 1. 词典编纂 (业)；词典编纂学

lexicon [ˈleksikən] n. 1. 词典；字典(尤指拉丁语等古代语言的词书) 2. (某一作家或学科的)特殊词汇，专门词汇

lexis [ˈleksis] n. [复] **lexes** [ˈleksiːz] n. 【语】(某一语言的)词汇(层)

Li 【化】元素锂(lithium)的符号

liability [ˌlaiəˈbiliti] n. 1. 责任 2. 倾向 3. [liabilities] 债务；负债 4. 不利条件

liable [ˈlaiəbl] adj. 1. 有(法律)责任的；有义务的(财产等)可受(法律)处理的 2. 应受罚的；应付(税)的；应服从的 3. 易于…的；有…倾向的(to) 4. [口]可能的，大概的

liaison [liˈeizɔn] n. 1. 【语】连音，连读 2. 联络；联系军官；联系人 3. 私通 4. (烹调中的)勾芡，加浓糊

liar [ˈlaiə] n. 说谎的人

libel [ˈlaibəl] n. 1. 【律】诽谤；诽谤罪 2. 诽谤性文字(或图画) 3. (海事法、教会法及苏格兰法中的)原告陈诉状 — (li-bel(l)ed; libel(l)ing) vt. 1. 以文字(或图画等)诽谤 2. 诬蔑；对…造谣中伤(

(教会法等中)对…提出控告 — vi. 以文字(或图画等)进行诽谤(against, on) ‖ ~(l)ous adj. 诽谤(性)的；爱诽谤的

libel(l)er [ˈlaibələ], **libel(l)ist** [ˈlaibəlist] n. 诽谤者

liberal [ˈlibərəl] adj. 1. 自由主义的；[L-](英国等)的自由党的 2. 慷慨的；大方的 3. 丰富的，丰盛的 4. 心胸宽大的；不受清规戒律约束的 5. 自由随便的；不拘泥字面的 — n. 1. 开明的人 2. 自由主义者 3. [L-]自由党党员；支持自由党的人 ‖ ~ism n. / ~ly adv.

liberality [ˌlibəˈræliti] n. 1. 慷慨；慷慨的施舍物 2. 心胸宽大；公正 3. 丰富；丰满；宽阔

liberalize [ˈlibərəlaiz] vt. 1. 使自由主义化；使自由化 2. 放宽…的范围(或限制) 3. 解除官方对…的控制 — vi. 自由主义化

liberate [ˈlibəreit] vt. 1. 解放 2. 【化】释出，放出 3. [俚]劫掠；偷盗 ‖ **liberator** n. 解放者

liberation [ˌlibəˈreiʃən] n. 1. 解放；解放运动 2. 【化】释出，放出

Liberia [laiˈbiəriə] n. 利比里亚 [西非国家]

libertine [ˈlibətin] n. 放荡的人；浪荡子；淫荡的人；不受约束的人(或物)

liberty [ˈlibəti] n. 1. 自由；自由权 2. 越轨；失礼；过分亲昵的言行；未经许可的行为 3. [常 liberties] 特典；特权 4. 许可，允准(一定范围内的)自由活动(或使用)权 5. 特权地区，特别行政区 6. (水兵水手等的)上岸短假；短假期 7. [哲]意志自由

libido [liˈbiːdəu] n. [复] **libidos** n. 性欲 ‖ **libidinous** [liˈbidinəs] adj. 性欲的；好色的

librarian [lai'brɛəriən] *n.* 1. 图书馆管理员 2. 图书馆学专家

library ['laibrəri] *n.* 1. 图书馆 2. 藏书楼；藏书室 3. 藏书；收藏的作品（指唱片、手稿等）4. 丛书；文库（指装帧相同的一套书）

libretto [li'bretəu]（[复] librettos 或 -ti [-tiː]）*n.*（歌剧等的）歌词；剧本

Libreville [ˌliːbrə'viːd] *n.* 利伯维尔 [加蓬首都]

Libya ['libiə] *n.* 利比亚 [北非国家]

lice [lais] louse 的复数

license, licence ['laisəns] *n.* 1. 许可，特许 2. 许可证；持许证；执照 3. 放纵；放肆 4.（文艺、美术、音乐等的）破格、自由 — *vt.* 发许可证给；准许；批准（书籍、戏剧等）的出版（或上演等）∥ ~ plate. ~ tag（汽车等的）牌照

licentious [lai'senʃəs] *adj.* 1. 放荡的；淫乱的 2. 放肆的

lichen ['laikən] *n.* 1. [植] 地衣 2. [医] 苔癣（病）— *vt.* 使生满地衣

licit ['lisit] *adj.* 合法的；准许的 ∥ ~ly *adv.*

lick [lik] *vt.* 1. 舔；舔吃 2.（火舌）卷过、吞没（*up*）；（波浪）轻轻拍打 3. [俚] 鞭打 4. [俚] 战胜；超越 — *vi.* 1.（火焰）伸舌头一样伸吐；（波浪）轻轻拍打 2. [俚] 高速行进 — *n.* 1. 舔；舔食 2.（舌）一击 3. [俚] 速度；步速 5. [俚]（常 ~s）轮到的机会 6.（野兽常去舔盐的）盐碱地（= salt ~）7. [美里]（即有插入的）爵士乐装饰乐句，小过门

licorice ['likəris] *n.*（欧亚）甘草

lid [lid] *n.* 1. 盖子 2. [生] 盖；萌盖 3.（软体动物的）厣 4. [俚] 眼睑（= eyelid）5. 制止；约束 4. — *vt.* 给…装盖子；给…盖盖子 ∥ **lidded** *adj.* 1. 有盖子的；盖着的 2. [常用以构

lie[1] [lai]（lay [lei], lain [lein]；lying）*vi.* 1. 躺，平躺 2.（东西）被平放 3. 展现；伸展 4. 处于某种状态 5. 位于 6.（抽象事物）存在；在于 7. 被储存 8.（船只）停泊；（猎物）不起飞 9.（部队）驻扎 10. 被埋葬 11. [律] 可立案；可受理 — *n.* 1. 位置；状态 2.（鸟、兽等的）栖息处 3.（英口）躺；躺在床上的一段时间

lie[2] [lai]（lying）*vi.* 1. 说谎 2. 造成假象；不可靠 — *vt.* 用谎骗使得 — *n.* 1. 谎话；谎言 2. 造成错觉的事物；假象 ∥ ~ detector 测谎器

Liechtenstein ['liktənstain] *n.* 列支敦士登 [中欧国家]

lief [liːf] *adv.* 乐意地，欣然

liege [liːdʒ] *adj.* 1.（封建制度下）有权受臣服的 2.（封建制度下）有臣服义务的 3. 忠诚的 — *n.* 1. 君主；受臣服的领主 2.（常 ~s）[总称] 臣民

lien [liən, 'liːən] *n.* [律] 留置权，扣押权

lieu [luː] *n.* 位置，替代 ∥ *in* ~（*of*）（以…）替代

lieutenant [lef'tenənt, luː'tenənt] *n.* 1.（英）陆军中尉；（美）陆军（或空军、海军陆战队）中尉、少尉 2.（英、美）海军上尉 3. 副职官员；代理官员 ∥ **lieutenancy** *n.* 陆军中尉（或陆军少尉、海军上尉）的军衔（或职权）∥ ~ colonel（英）陆军中校；（美）陆军（或空军、海军陆战队）中校 / ~ commander（英、美）海军少校 / ~ general 陆军（或空军、海军陆战队）中将 / ~ junior grade（美）海军中尉

life [laif] *n.*（[复] lives [laivz]）*n.* 1. 生命；性命 2. [总称] 生物 3. 寿命 [核]（亚原子粒子的）寿命 4. 一生；人生阶段 5. 传

记 6. 生活;生存 7. 事务;人生;生活方式 8. 生命力;活力;生气 9. 生命般宝贵的人(或事物);活力的源泉;活跃气氛的人(或事物) ‖ ～ like *adj.* 逼真的，栩栩如生的 ‖ ～ belt 救生带 /～-boat *n.* 救生艇 /～ buoy 救生圈 /～-guard *n.* 救生员 /～ insurance 人寿保险 /～-long *adj.* 毕生的，终身的;持久的 /～ preserver 1. 救生用具 2. 护身棒 /～ raft 救生筏 /～, saver *n.* 救命者;帮助解除困境的人(或物) /～-saving *n.* 救生(术) *adj.* 救生用的 /～ science 生命科学 /～ sentence 无期徒刑 /～-'size(d) *adj.* 与真人(或实物)一样大小的 /～-'span *n.* 寿命 2. 预期生命 /～ style *n.* 生活方式 /～-sup'port system (宇航员等的)生命维持系统 /～-time *n.* 1. 一生，终身 2. [核]寿期;(事物的)存在期,使用期,有效期

lifeless ['laiflis] *adj.* 1. 无生命的;死的 2. 没有生气的;沉闷的;单调的 3. 没有生命的

lift [lift] *vt.* 1. 提起;举起;抬;吊 2. 提高;提升;鼓舞 3. 送送;空运 4. 挖出;拔起;拔(帐、营)5. 解除;解除(封锁,包围等);撤销(命令)6. 【俚】偷;(口)剽窃 7. 清唱 8. (高尔夫、挑(球))(乒乓球)提拉(球) ~ *vi.* 1. 被提(或举)起;升起 2. (云,雾等)消散 3. 耸立 4. (船)随海浪升高 5. (地面)隆起 ～ *n.* 1. 提;举;抬;升 2. 一次提(或吊等)的量 3. 情绪激昂;鼓舞 4. 高昂姿态 5. 地面的隆起 6. (英)电梯;升降椅;上山吊椅 7. (修理汽车等用的)千斤顶;起重机 8. 空门升力;空运;运输 9. 【机】升程;提升高度 10. (皮鞋的)后跟层,插层 11. 帮助;挽扶;(给步行者的)免费搭车 ‖ ～-boy, '～-man *n.* (英)电梯司机

lift-off ['liftɔf] *n.* (火箭等的)升空,离

地;升空(或离地)时间

ligament ['ligəmənt] *n.* 1. 纽带 2. 【解】韧带

light[1] [lait] *n.* 1. 光;光线;亮光 2. 日光;白昼;黎明 3. 发光体;光源;灯;信号灯;灯塔;天体 4. 明星;名人,显赫人物 5. 窗;天窗;[律]采光权 6. 火花;活火 7. 光觉;(诗)视力;(俚)[～s]眼睛 8. 眼神 9. (绘画中的)亮部 10. 显露;众所周知 11. (启发性的)事实,知识,信息;了解;解释 12. (事物呈现的)状态;(观察人、物等的)角度,眼光 13. [～s][戏](剧场大门罩上的)演员姓名灯光牌 14.[宗]圣灵亮光 ～ *adj.* 1. 明亮的 2. 淡色的 ～(lit [lit]或 lighted) *vt.* 1. 点(火);点燃 2. 照亮;使发亮 3. 用灯光指引 ～ *vi.* 1. 点着 2. 变亮 ‖ ～ adaptation (眼的)光适应 /～ -a'dapted *adj.* (眼)适应了光的 /～ house *n.* 灯塔 /～'proof *adj.* 防光的,不透光的 /～ tracer 曳光弹 /～ wave【物】光波 /～ 'year *n.* [天]光年

light[2] [lait] *adj.* 1. 轻的 2. 容易承担(或忍受)的 3. 少量的;分量不足的 4. 轻微的,微弱的 5. (噪音)柔和的 6. 轻的;灵巧的 7. 轻便的;轻型的;轻装的 8. (船等)不装货的;轻载的 9. 不重要的;琐碎的 10. 轻率易变的;轻浮的;水性杨花的 11. 轻松愉快的 12. 易醒的 13. 清淡的;易消化的 14. 晕眩的 15. (食物)发得松软的;松的;粗的;砂质的 16. 精巧的 17. (音节)不重读的 18. 缺少人员的;人手不足的 ～ *adv.* 轻地;轻装地 ‖ '～-face *n. & adj.* [印]细体活字(的) '～' headed *adj.* 1. 眩晕的 2. 神志不清的 3. 头脑简单的,无知的,愚蠢的 4. 轻浮的 /～-'hearted *adj.* 轻松愉快的;无忧无虑的 /～-weight *n.* 1. 体重在平均重量以下的人

(或动物);轻量级运动员 2. 无足轻重的人 3. 无能的人 **adj.** 1. 轻量级(的)2. 平均重量以下的 3. 无足轻重的

light[3][lait](lighted 或 lit [lit])**vi.** 1.〈罕〉下车 2. 停落 3.(灾难、好运、打击等)突然降临(on, upon)4. 偶然碰到;偶然得到

lighten[1][laitn]**vt.** 1. 照亮,使明亮 2. 闪出;闪电般地显现出(out, forth)3. 调淡(色彩等)4.〈古〉使明白;启发一**vi.** 1. 发亮;变亮 2. 打闪

lighten[2][laitn]**vt.** 1. 减轻...的负荷;减轻 2. 使轻松;使愉快一**vi.** 1. 变轻;(船、载货等)分量减轻下来 2.(心情等)变得轻松

lighter[1][laitə]**n.** 1. 点火者 2. 引燃器;打火机

lighter[2][laitə]**n.** 驳船一**vt. & vi.** 驳运(货物)

lighterage[laitəridʒ]**n.** 1. 驳运费 2. 驳船装卸(或运送)3.〔总称〕驳运船

lighting[laitiŋ]**n.** 1. 照明;照明设备;〔总称〕舞台灯光 2. 点火;发火 3.(画面等)布光

lightly[laitli]**adv.** 1. 轻轻地;轻微地;轻盈地;轻巧地 2. 轻率地;轻浮地;轻佻地 4. 轻而易举地

lightness[1][laitnis]**n.** 1. 光亮;光亮度 2.(颜色的)浅淡

lightness[2][laitnis]**n.** 1. 轻;轻率;轻浮;轻佻 3. 轻盈;轻巧 4. 轻松 5. 精巧;优美

lightning[laitniŋ]**n.** 1. 闪电 2. 突如其来的好运 3.〈美俚〉劣等威士忌酒一**adj.** 闪电似的;神速的 ∥ ~ **bug**〈美〉萤火虫 / ~ **conductor** 避雷导线 / ~ **rod** 1. 避雷针 2.〈美俚〉喷气式战斗机

lignite[lignait]**n.** 褐煤

likable, likeable[laikəbl]**adj.** 可爱的;讨人喜欢的 ∥ ~**ness n.**

like[1][laik]**vt.** 1. 喜欢 2.〔常与 should、would 连用〕希望,想要 3.〔用于否定句〕愿意 4.〔用于否定句〕适合...的胃口一**vi.** 1. 感到喜欢;希望;愿意 2.〈方〉赞同(of, with)一**n.**〔常~s〕爱好

like[2][laik](more like, most like;〔诗〕〈罕〉liker, likest)**adj.** 1. 相像的;相同的;类似的 2.〈方〉(好像)就要;可能一**prep.** 1. 像,如;跟...一样 2. 像要;想要一(more like, most like;〔罕〕liker, likest)**adv.** 1.〈古〉一样地 2.〔常用于插入语中〕可能;多半 3.〈口〉有点儿,可以说得上一**conj.**〈口〉如同,好像一**n.** 1. 同样(或同类)的人(或事物)2. 种类;类型

likelihood[laiklihud]**n.** 1. 可能(性)2. 可能发生的事物;成功的迹象

likely[laikli](more likely, most likely;或likelier, likeliest)**adj.** 1. 很可能的 2.(像是)可靠的;可信的 3. 有希望的;很有可能实现的 4. 漂亮的,吸引人的一**adv.** 很可能

liken[laikən]**vt.** 把...比作(to)

likeness[laiknis]**n.** 1. 类似,相像 2. 相似物;肖像;画像;照片 3. 外表;伪装

likewise[laikwaiz]**adv.** 1. 同样地,照样地 2. 也;又

liking[laikiŋ]**n.** 喜欢;爱好

lilac[lailək]**n.** 1. 丁香;丁香花;丁香香料 2. 丁香紫,淡紫色一**adj.** 淡紫色的

Lilongwe[li'lɔŋwi]**n.** 利隆圭〔马拉维首都〕

lilt[lilt]**vt.** 轻快有节奏地唱(或演奏)一**vi.** 1. 轻快有节奏地唱;用抑扬的声调说 2. 轻快地跳动一**n.** 1. 轻快活泼的歌曲 2. 节奏轻快的摆动(或旋律)3.

轻快的动作

lily ['lili] **n.1.**〖植〗百合；百合花；百合(指百合的鳞茎) **2.** 纯洁的人；洁白的东西 **3.**〈美俚〉女人腔的男子 **4.**〖常 lilies〗(象征法国王室的)百合花徽 — **adj.** 百合花般纯洁的；洁白的；脆弱的

Lima ['liːmə] **n.** 利马(秘鲁首都)

lima ['laimə] **n.** = ~ bean ‖ ~ **bean 1.**〖植〗利马豆 **2.** 利马豆荚

limb [lim] **n.1.** 肢；翼、翅膀 **2.**〖植〗大枝，主枝 **3.** 分支；执行者，代理人；(建筑物的)突出部，延伸部分 **4.**〖地〗山嘴，坡尖，山鼻子 **5.** 顽童 **6.** (句子中的)从句 **7.** 给...截肢；截肢；肢解(躯体) **2.** 从(倒下的树)上砍去树枝 ‖ ~ **less adj.** 无肢的；无翼的；无大枝的

limbed [limd] **adj.** [常用以构成复合词]有...肢(或枝、翼)的；long-~ 有长肢(或枝、翼)的

limber ['limbə] **adj.1.** 可塑的；柔软的，易弯曲的 **2.** 富于弹性的；思想活泼的；风格明快的 — **vt.** 使柔软 — **vi.** 变得柔软

limbo ['limbəu] (〖复〗limbos) **n.1.**〖宗〗地狱的边境 **2.** 被忘却的人(或物件)的安置场所；被忘却，湮没无闻

Limburger ['limbəːgə] **n.** 林堡软干酪

lime[1] [laim] **n.1.** 石灰 **2.** 粘鸟胶 — **vt.1.** 用石灰处理，撒石灰于 **2.** 把(鸟)投入水中；涂粘鸟胶于；用粘鸟胶捕捉 ‖ ~ **light n.1.** (舞台照明用的)石灰光灯；石灰光 **2.** 石灰光灯所照射的舞台部分 **3.** 众人注目的中心 **v.** 把光集中在...上；使成注目中心，使着名 / ~ **stone n.** (石)灰岩 / ~ **water n.** 石灰水

lime[2] [laim] **n.** 〖植〗酸橙

limerick ['limərik] **n.** 五行打油诗

limit ['limit] **n.1.** 界线，界限 **2.** 限度；限

制；[~s] 范围，境界 **3.** 极限，极点 **4.** (渔猎等的)限额；(一次下的)赌注限额 — **vt.** 限制，限定 ‖ ~ **less adj.** 无限制的；无限的

limitation [limi'teiʃən] **n.1.** 限制 **2.** 局限；限制因素；限度；弱点 **3.**〖律〗追诉时效

limited ['limitid] **adj.1.** 有限的 **2.** (企业等)有限责任的 **3.** (火车等)限制座席和停车站的，特快的 — **n.1.** 特别快车 **2.** 股份有限公司 ‖ ~ **company**，~ **liability company** 股份有限公司

limn [lim] **vt.1.** 画；勾划 **2.** 描述；刻划

limousine ['liməziːn, limu'ziːn] **n.1.** 轿式汽车；(前后座间用玻璃隔开的)豪华高级轿车 **2.** (机场、车站等接送旅客的)中客车

limp[1] [limp] **vi.1.** 一瘸一拐地走，跛行；蹒跚 **2.** 缓慢费力地进行 — **n.** 跛行

limp[2] [limp] **adj.1.** 柔软的，易曲的 **2.** 弱的，无生气的；无精神的 ‖ ~ **ly adv.** / ~ **ness n.**

limpid ['limpid] **adj.1.** 清澈的；透明的 **2.** (文体等)清晰的，畅达的 **3.** 宁静的，无忧虑的

limy ['laimi] **adj.1.** 涂有粘鸟胶的；含有粘鸟胶的；粘鸟胶似的；粘的 **2.** 石灰质的；含石灰的；含有石灰的

linden ['lindən] **n.** 〖植〗椴

line[1] [lain] **n.1.** 线，索，绳；[常~s] 缆绳 **2.** 电话线；线路；管道 **3.**〖数〗线；直线；〖音〗谱线 **4.** 路线；züç线；航线；线；铁轨；(固定路线的)运输公司，航行公司 **5.** 生产线，流水线 **6.** 界线；边界；场界 **7.** [the ~] 赤道 **8.** 防线；前线 **9.** (政治)路线；方针 **10.** 轮廓；[~s] 设计思路，概况 **11.** (货物的)类，种 **12.** 行

业,行当;擅长 13. 排,行列;【军】(两列)横队,战斗编队 14. [~s](英军的)营房地 15. [the ~](英陆军的)战列步兵(美军的)战斗部队 16. 诗行;短简,便条;台词 17. [~s]结婚证书(= marriage ~s) 18. 一系列家系,家族 19. [~s]命运;生活遭遇 20. 迹象;消息 21.(皮肤上的)条纹;皱纹;掌纹 22.(长度单位)英分(十二分之一英寸) — vt.1. 用线标示;用线描画;划线于 2. 使有线条;使起皱纹 3. 使排成一列 4. 沿…排列;排成(队);排齐 (up) ‖ ~ man n.1.【电】线务员;架线工 2.(铁路)护路工,养路工 3.(橄榄球队的)锋、卫等)线上球员 4.[测]执线人 / ~ manager n.[经]部门经理

line² [lain] vt.1. 给(衣服,箱子等)装衬里,加衬里于 2. 用作(衣服,箱子等)的衬里 3. 填(腰包)

lineage [ˈliniidʒ] n.1. 直系,后裔 2. 家族,家族,宗 3.(某项专业技能的)嫡派

lineal [ˈliniəl] adj.1. 直系的;同宗的;世袭的 2.(直线的)直线的

lineament [ˈliniəmənt] n.1.[常 ~s]外貌;面部特征 2.[常 ~s]轮廓特征;线性特征;特征 3.[地]区域断陷线;地貌轮廓线

linear [ˈliniə] adj.1. 线的,直线的 2. 长度的 3.[数]一次的,线性的 4. 线构的;利用线的,线形的,细长的 ‖ ~ algebra 【数】线性代数

linen [ˈlinin] n.1. 亚麻布(或纱,线) 2. 亚麻织物(如台布,床单等) 3. 仿真亚麻制品(如衬衫,内衣等) 4. 亚麻布纸(= ~ paper) — adj.1. 亚麻的 2. 亚麻布制的

liner¹ [ˈlainə] n.1. 画线的人 2. 画线的工具 3. 班轮;班机 4.(棒球赛中的)平直球;(化妆用)眼线液;眼线笔;眼线刷

描唇笔

liner² [ˈlainə] n.1. 衬里;【机】衬垫;衬圈;垫片 2. 制衬里(或衬垫等)的人;装衬里(或衬垫等)的人

line-up [ˈlainʌp] n. 一排人;一组人;行列;阵容

-ling suf.1.[附在名词后构成名词]表示"小";"不重要";"低劣";duckling 2.(古)〈方〉[附在名词后构成副词]表示"方向";"状态":darkling 在黑暗中

linger [ˈliŋgə] vi.1. 逗留;徘徊;闲荡 2. 拖延;苟延 — vt.1. 拖延;慢慢地挨过(时间等)

lingerie [ˈlɔ̃ʒəri] n. 女式贴身内衣裤,女内衣;女睡衣

lingo [ˈliŋgəu] ([复]lingoes) n.〈谑〉〈贬〉奇怪而难懂的语言;外国话;行话;隐语

lingual [ˈliŋgwəl] adj.1. 舌的;舌状的 2. 舌音的;发音的 3. 语言的

linguine, linguini [liŋˈgwiːni] n.(意大利)扁面条

linguist [ˈliŋgwist] n.1. 通晓数国语言的人 2. 语言学家

linguistic [liŋˈgwistik] adj. 语言的;语言学的

linguistics [liŋˈgwistiks] [复] n.[用作单]语言学

liniment [ˈlinimənt] n.[药] 搽剂,擦剂

lining [ˈlainiŋ] n.1.(衣服,箱子等的)衬里 2.【机】内村;村层;衬料 3. 加村,砌村;搪 3.(衣袋等中)内装的东西

link [liŋk] n.1.【机】连杆 2.(链状物的)环,节;环状物,圈(香肠串的)一节香肠;香肠小香肠 3. 环节;纽带;关系,联系 4.[常 ~s](村衫袖口的)链扣(= cuff ~) 5.[无]中继线;链路;网络节点[电]熔断片,保险丝管 6. 令(长度单位 = 0.201168 米) 7.

〈方〉[~s]河川转弯处 — vt. 1. 用环连接；连接；联系 2. 挽住；勾住(in...through) — vi. 连接起来；联系起(来)(~up) n. 1. 连接；联系(部队、航天器等)的合会 2. 连接物、连接因素

links ['liŋks] n. [复]同 1. 〈苏格兰〉海边生草的沙丘 2. [用作单或复]高尔夫球场

linnet ['linit] n. [动]朱顶雀

linoleum [li'nəuljəm] n. 〈亚麻〉油地毡；漆布

linotype ['lainəutaip] n. 1. 整行铸排机 2. 整行铸排机排版；整行铸排机排版印刷品 — vt. & vi. 用整行铸排机排(版)

linseed ['linsi:d] n. 亚麻籽 ‖ ~ oil 亚麻籽油

linsey ['linzi] 〔又作 **linsey-woolsey** ['linzi'wulzi]〕n. 1. 麻(经)毛(纬)交织物 2. 乱七八糟的混杂；胡说八道

lint [lint] n. 1. 皮棉 2. 棉绒、飞花 3. (经刮绒后外科用的)软麻布、绒布

lintel ['lintl] n. [建](门窗的)过梁

lion ['laiən] n. 1. 狮子 2. (象征英国的)狮子纹章 3. 勇猛的人；慓悍的人 4. 名人、名士 5. [~s]〈英〉(参观名胜(源出游伦敦者必去参观的伦敦塔狮子) 6. [the L.]〔天〕狮子座；狮子宫

lioness ['laiənis] n. 母狮

lip [lip] n. 1. (嘴)唇 2. [嘴]唇状物(杯口、洞口等)的边缘(茶壶等的)嘴 3. [植]唇瓣 4. [管乐器的]吹口(吹奏时的唇形、运舌法) 4. 〈俚〉唐突无礼的话 5. 咧(嘴)、刀刃 6. [~s]口 唇 — adj. 1. 口头上的、不真诚的 2. 唇音的 — (lipped;lipping) vt. 1. 用嘴唇触及、吻 2. 轻轻地接(一嘴)、(美俚)吻浪等)轻轻拍打 3. 把高尔夫球打到(洞口)而未进入 — vi. 1. (在吹奏管乐器时)运唇 2.(液体)满溢(over, in)3. 用嘴唇；吻(at) ‖ ~less adj. 没有嘴唇的、(器皿等)没有嘴的 ‖ ~print(嘴唇留下的)唇印 /'~stick n. 唇膏；口红

lipped [lipt] adj. 1.(器皿等)有嘴的 2.[植]有唇的 3.(常用以构成复合词)长着...嘴唇的；嘴唇呈...状的 ‖ thick-~唇厚嘴唇的

liquefy ['likwifai] vt. & vi. (使)液化 ‖ **liquefaction** [,likwi'fækʃən] n. 液化

liqueur [li'kjuə] n. 1. 利口酒、甜酒 2. 酒心巧克力

liquid ['likwid] adj. 1. 液体的；液态的；流动的(眼睛)泪汪汪的 2. 清澈的、透明的；明亮的 3.(声音)柔和的、清晰的；(诗等)流利的、流畅的 4. 不稳定的、易变的；易变为现金的 5.[语]流音的 — n. 1. 液体 2.[语]流音(如[l],[r]等) ‖ ~ly adv. /~ness n.

liquidate ['likwideit] vt. 1. 清理、清算(破产的企业等)2. 清偿(债务等)3. 将(资产)变换为现金、变卖 4. 消灭、清洗 5. 消除(疑虑等)、杜绝(反对等) — vi. 清理债务(或资产等);(公司等)破产、停业清理

liquidation [,likwi'deiʃən] n. 1.(债务的)清偿、了结;(企业的)清理、清算;(资产的)变卖、变现 2. 杀戮、清洗 3. 消除、杜绝

liquor ['likə] n. 1. 液;汁 2.[药]溶液;液剂 3. 酒、烈性酒 — vt. 1. 用液态物质处理、把...浸于溶液中 2. 给(鞋子、皮革等)上油 — vi.〈俚〉使喝醉(up) — vi.〈俚〉酗酒(up)

lira ['liərə] n. [复]lire ['liəri]或 liras]里拉(意大利货币单位)

Lisbon ['lizbən] n. 里斯本[葡萄牙首都]

lisle [lail] n. 莱尔线;莱尔线织物

lisp [lisp] vi. 1. 咬舌(指将[s][z]音发作[θ][ð]) 2.(孩子似地)说话口齿不清 — vt. 咬着舌说;口齿不清地说(out) n.1. 咬舌；口齿不清 2. 咬舌发出的声音；(树叶等的)沙沙声

list[1] [list] n.1. 表；一览表；目录；名单 2. 〔总称〕(交易所)上市证券表 3. ~ price — vt.1. 把…编列成表；把…编入目录(或名单)；列举 2. [~ oneself]. 把…算作(as) 3. 〈古〉征召…入伍 — vi.1. 列入价目表 2. 〈古〉入伍 ‖ ~ price 价目单定价

list[2] [list] n.1. 布条，布边；织边 2. 狭条；(木板上截下的)边材木条 3. 塞，沟 4. 【建】嵌条，平缓脚 5. [~s]用作单或复]竞技场，斗技场；论战场所；竞技场栅栏 6. 颜色条纹(尤指马背中央的深色条纹)—(list(ed))vi.1. 从(木板)上截下边条 2. 翻(地)成畦 3. 给…装布边

list[3] [list] (list(ed)) vi.(船只、房屋、篱笆等)倾侧 — vt. 使倾侧 — n. 倾侧；倾侧程度

listen ['lisn] vi.1. 听；留神听 2. 听从；听信(to) 3. 听上去，听起来 — vt.1. 〈古〉听

listener ['lisnə] n. 听者；收听者，听众之一

listless ['listlis] adj. 百无聊赖的；倦怠的；没精打采的 ‖ ~ly adv. / ~ness n.

lit [lit] light[1].light[2] 的过去式和过去分词 — adj.1. 照亮的；点着的 2.〈美俚〉喝醉了的；被毒品麻醉过的

litany ['litəni] n.【宗】连祷；应答祈祷 2. 连续；系列 3. 枯燥冗长的陈述

liter ['li:tə] n.〈美〉= litre

literacy ['litərəsi] n.1. 识字；有文化；阅读写作能力 2. 精通文学；善于写作

literal ['litərəl] adj.1. 文字上的 2. 照词句本义的，字面的；逐字的；原义的 3. 字母的；用字母代表的 4. 确确实实的，不加夸张的；朴实的 5. 只讲究实际；刻板的；缺乏想象力的 — n. 误排，错字；印

刷错误 ‖ ~ly adv.1. 照字义；逐字地 2.〈口〉确实地，不加夸张地 / ~ness n. ‖ '~-minded adj.(人)只讲究实际的，缺乏想象力的

literary ['litərəri] adj.1. 文学(上)的 2. 从事写作的；精通文学的；文人的 3. 书本的；(词语等)书面的；书卷气的

literate ['litərit] adj.1. 有读写能力的 2. 精通文学的；善于写作的 — n. 识字的人；有文化的人

literature ['litəritʃə] n.1. 文学；文学作品 2.(关于某一学科或专题的)文献；〔总称〕作品 3. 写作(业) 4.〈口〉〔总称〕印刷品；宣传品(如广告、传单等) 5.【音】音乐文献 6.〈古〉学识；文学修养

lithe [laið] adj.1. 柔软的；易弯曲的 2. 轻巧自如的 ‖ ~ly adv. / ~ness n.

lithesome ['laiðsəm] adj. = lithe

lithium ['liθiəm] n.【化】锂

lithograph ['liθəgrɑːf] n. 平版印刷品，石印品 — vt. & vi. 用平版印刷术印刷 ‖ ~er [li'θɔgrəfə] n. 石印工，石印工人 / ~y [li'θɔgrəfi] n. 平版印刷术，石印术

lithosphere ['liθəsfiə] n.【地】陆界，岩石圈

Lithuania [ˌliθju'einiə] n. 立陶宛〔欧洲波罗的海沿岸国家〕

litigant ['litigənt] adj. 进行诉讼的 — n. 诉讼当事人

litigate ['litigeit] vi. 诉讼 — vt.1. 就…争论 2.〈古〉为…争论，为…争辩 ‖ .liti'gation n.1. 诉讼，诉争 2.〈古〉争论，争执

litmus ['litməs] n.【化】石蕊 ‖ ~ paper 石蕊试纸

litre ['li:tə] n. 升(容量单位略作 L.)

litter ['litə] n.1. 轿，舆 2. 担架 3.(供动物睡眠或防植物受冻等用的)褥草；厩肥 4. 枯枝落叶层 5.(猪、狗等多产动物

的)一窝(仔育)6.[总称]废弃物,被胡乱扔掉的东西;杂乱 — vt.1.为(动物)垫褥草,在...上垫褥草 2.(多产动物)产(仔) 3.使凌乱;乱扔东西于 4.乱丢 — vi.1.产仔 2.四下乱丢东西 ‖ ~er n.(在公共场所)乱扔废物的人 ‖ ~bag n.(汽车等中的)废物袋 / ~bug n.乱扔废物的人 vi.(在公共场所)乱扔废物

little ['litl] (比较级 less [les] 或 lesser,最高级 least [liːst]) **adj.1.** 小的 2.(人或动物)幼小的,小得可爱的 3.矮小的 4.短暂的 5.琐碎的;微不足道的;渺小的 6.狭小的;可鄙的 7.[表示否定]少的,不多的 [a ~]表示肯定]一些,一点点 — (比较级 less [les] 或 lesser,最高级 least [liːst]) **adv.1.** 少,一点儿;sleep ~ 睡得少 / sleep a ~ 睡一会儿 2.[用在 know, suspect, believe, care 等动词之前]毫不 — **n.1.** 少量;有多少[a ~]一点,少量: Little remains to be done about it. 在这件事上几乎没有什么可做的了。/ A ~ remains to be done. 还有一点要做的事 2. 短距离,短时间 ‖ ~ness n. ‖ Little Rhody 小罗得[美国罗得岛州的别称;因该州是美国最小的州] / Little Rock 小石城[美国阿肯色州首府]

liturgical [li'təːdʒikəl] **adj.**【宗】礼拜仪式的;圣餐仪式的

liturgy ['litədʒi] **n.**【宗】礼拜仪式;圣餐仪式

livable ['livəbl] **adj.1.**(房子、气候等)适于居住的 2.(生活)过得去的;过得有价值的 3.(人)容易相处的(with) ‖ .**liva.bility** n.1.(家禽、牲畜等)存活率 2. 适居性

live¹ [liv] **vi.1.** 活着;活,生存 2. 生活;过活 3. 居住 4. 留存在人们记忆中;流传

下去 5. 享受人生,过丰富有意义的生活 6. (度)(过),经历(过)(through) 7.(以某物为主食;(靠吃某物)维持生命(on) — vt.1. 过(生活);度过 2. 实践;经历(过) ‖ '~-in adj.(佣工)住在雇主家的(雇员、店员等);(需要)住在工作场所的 2. 关于居住的 n.1.(未结婚)同居的 n.1. 住在雇主家(或工作场所)的人 2.(未结婚)同居者 3. 住宮示威(指集体住进工作场所以示抗议) / '~-out adj.(佣工)不住在雇主家的;(雇员、店员等)不住在工作场所的

live² [laiv] **adj.1.** 活的,有生命的 2.〈谬〉[常接在 real 后且真的]活生生的 3. 精力充沛的,充满活力的,生气勃勃的 4. 燃着的,激烈的,愤怒的 5. 当前大家关心的;尚在争论中的 6. 弹性足的(球等)处于比赛状态的,有效的 7.(机器等)运转着的;传动的;驱动的 8. 装着炸药(或可裂变物质)的,未爆炸的;(火柴)未划用过的;通电的,带电的 9.[印]尚未排好的铅字]在用的,待用的;(原稿)待排字的 10.(岩石等)原生的,天然的,未经开采的 11.(空气)清新的;(颜色)鲜艳的 12. 实况转播的;现场直播的;在现场看(或听)演出的 13.(火山)活动着的 — **adv.** 在(或从)实演现场以实况 ‖ '~-stock n.[总称]家畜,牲畜 / ~ wire 1. 载电线,火线 2. 活跃分子;富有进取心的人

livelihood ['laivlihud] **n.** 生活;生计

livelong ['livlɔŋ] **adj.** 漫长的;整个的

lively ['laivli] **adj.1.** 活泼的,充满生气的;活跃的;快活的 2.(情绪等)热烈的,强烈的 3.〈谬〉紧张的,惊险的 4. 报春的,提神的 5.(色彩等)明快的;鲜明的 6. 栩栩如生的,真实的 7.(舞蹈等)轻快的;(球等)弹力足的 8.(船)行驶轻快的,驾驶灵便的 — **adv.** 活泼地;轻快

地 ‖ **liveliness** *n.*

liven ['laivn] *vt. & vi.* (使)活跃;(使)愉快(*up*)

liver ['livə] *n.*1.肝脏 2.(供食用的鸡、牛等的)肝 3.(无脊椎动物的)类似肝的器官

liveried ['livərid] *adj.* 穿特殊制服的;穿号衣的

Liverpool ['livəpuːl] *n.* 利物浦[英国英格兰西部港市]

liverwurst ['livəwəːst] *n.*〖美〗肝泥香肠

livery ['livəri] *n.*1.(封建贵族侍从、仆人等所穿的)制服;号衣 2.[总称](伦敦)同业公会会员 3.〈古〉侍从,仆从 4.(马的)代养业务 5.(马或马匹的)出租 5.(出租马、马车的)马车行,马房(= ~ stable) 6.(汽车、自行车等的)出租行 7.〖律〗财产所有权让与(证书)8.制服,工作服;(诗)(喻)服装,束装 9.〈古〉(尤指给仆人的)衣食必需品分配;分配的口量;马料配置

lives [laivz]肺的复数

livid ['livid] *adj.*1.(皮肉被打伤而呈现的)青黑色的 2.青灰色的;铅色的 ‖ **~ ly** *adv.* ‖ **~ ness** *n.*

living ['liviŋ] *adj.*1.活的;活着的;现存的 2.在活动中的;在使用者的;起作用的 3.充满生气的;活跃的;生动的 4.逼真的 5.生活的;维持生活的 6.适于居住的 7.(岩石等)原生的,天然的,未经开采的 8.[加强语气用,= very]: scare the ~ daylights out of sb. 把某人吓得半死 ‖ *n.*1.生活;生计 2.活,生存 3.(英)教士的俸金 4.〈古〉产业,地产 ‖ **~ room** 起居室 / **~ will** 活遗嘱,生前嘱咐(指一种由本人声明,表示当本人将来因不治之症等原因康复无望时,可任其自然死亡,不必用人工方法延续生命)

lizard ['lizəd] *n.*1.〖动〗蜥蜴 2.〖鸟〗蜥羽金丝雀 3.[L-]蜥蜴[美国亚拉巴马州人的别称]

Ljubljana [ljuː'bljɑːnə] *n.* 卢布尔雅那[斯洛文尼亚首都]

llama ['lɑːmə] *n.*〖动〗羊驼,美洲驼,亚美利加驼

Lloyd's [ləidz] *n.*(英国)劳埃德保险社 ‖ **~ - Register** 1.劳氏船舶年鉴(= 载明吨位、等级等)2.劳氏船级社(= ~ Register of Shipping)

lo [ləu] *int.*[表示惊讶或用于唤起注意]看哪! 瞧!

load [ləud] *n.* 1.负荷,负载;(喻)负担;重任 2.一车(或一船、一驮、一飞机)装载量;(弹药的)一次装填(量)3.(电机、机器等的)负载,负荷;(发电站的)发电量 4.工作量 5.(口)[~s]大量,许多,一大堆 6.(俚)足醉量 一 *vt.*1.装;装载 2.把弹药装入(枪、炮);把胶卷装入(照相机)3.装填;使负担重;加负担重;(用低劣物质)搀入(以增加重量等)4.(酒等)中搀假 一 *vi.*1.装货;上客 2.装弹药;装料 3.上船(或车等)‖ **~ er** *n.* 装货工人;装货设备;装弹机;装填手

loadstar ['ləudstɑː] *n.* = lodestar

loadstone ['ləudstəun] *n.* = lodestone

loaf[1] [ləuf] *n.*[复]loaves [ləuvz] *n.*1.一条面包,一只面包(通常有一定的重量,如一磅、二磅或四磅)2.圆锥形糖块(英)(糖未等的)圆锥形茶点 3.(用肉、鱼等烘制成的)面包形茶肴;面包形食品 4.〖英俚〗脑袋

loaf[2] [ləuf] *vi.*1.游荡,闲逛 2.懒散地工作 一 *vt.* 闲混,消磨(时间)(*away*)一 *n.* 游荡 ‖ **~ er** *n.* 游手好闲者,二流子;无业游民 2.懒汉鞋

loam [ləum] *n.*1.肥土,沃土;壤土 2.〖冶〗

烂砂 — *vt.* 用肥土填(或覆盖)‖ ~y *adj.* 肥土(似)的，含肥土的

loan [ləun] *n.* 1. 贷款 2. 暂借；暂借的东西 3. 借字，外来词 (= ~word) — *vt.* 借出，贷与 — *vi.* 贷款

loath [ləuθ] *adj.* [用作表语]不愿意的，厌恶的

loathe [ləuð] *vt.* 1. 厌恶，憎恨 2.〈口〉不喜欢 ‖ **loathing** *n.* 厌恶，憎恨

loathsome [ˈləuðsəm] *adj.* 讨厌的，可厌的；令人恶心的 ‖ ~ly *adv.* / ~ness *n.*

loaves [ˈləuvz]**loaf** 的复数

lob [lɔb] *n.* 1.〈英方〉笨拙迟钝的人 2.〔板球的〕缓慢的低手球 3.〔网球的〕挑出的高球 — (lobbed/lobbing) *vt.* 1.〔网球、乒乓球等〕挑高；〔板球〕缓慢地低手挥(球) 2.使〔球〕挑高；用力向(或笨拙地)掷出 3.〈古〉使垂下 — *vi.* 挑高球 1.以高弧线射出炮弹(或掷出石块等)；沉重(或笨拙地)走动

lobby [ˈlɔbi] *n.* 1.〔剧院、旅馆等的〕门廊；门厅 2.议会走廊；议会休息室；议会接待室；〔英议会下院〕选民接待厅；〔赞成及反对的两派议员在内的〕投票分组投票厅 3.〔企图说服议员支持某项行动的〕院外活动集团〔因活动在议会走廊、休息室而得名〕 — *vi.* 1.对议员进行疏通活动以影响其投票 2.游说，疏通 — *vt.* 1. 对(议员等)进行疏通活动 2.用疏通的方法使(议案、计划等)顺利通过(through) — *ist n.* 院外活动集团成员，专门受雇对议员(或政府官员)进行疏通的人；说客

lobe [ləub] *n.* 1. 耳垂 2.〔解〕(脑、肺、肝等的)叶片 3.〔植〕裂片 4.〔机〕凸角 5.〔无〕瓣，波瓣 6.〔空〕(气球的)陀囊

lobster [ˈlɔbstə] *n.* 1. 龙鳖虾；龙鳖虾肉 2. 龙虾；龙虾肉 3.〔俚〕笨拙的人；易受骗的人

local [ˈləukəl] *adj.* 1. 地方的；当地的；本地的 2.【讯】本地的，本地通话的 3. 乡土的，狭隘的 4. 局部的 5.〈美〉(公共交通工具)每站停的；(关于)位置的；占有一定空间的 — *n.* 1. 当地居民，本地人 2.(报纸上的)地方新闻 3.〈美〉地方分会(尤指工会) 4.(每站停车的)市郊列车，慢车；(每站停的)市内公共汽车(或电车等)；高层停电梯 5.〈口〉邻近小酒店 6. 局部麻醉药 ‖ ~ly *adv.* ‖ ~ examination (英)(某些大学在各地举行的)地方考试 / ~ government 地方自治；地方政府

locale [ləuˈkɑːl] *n.* (事情发生的)地点，场所

locality [ləuˈkæliti] *n.* 位置；地点；地方；发生地点

localize [ˈləukəlaiz] *vt.* 1. 使局部化 2. 使(新闻等)带有地方色彩，使具有地方性 3. 确定(传统等)的起源；确定(传统等起源)的地方 — *vi.* 局部化；积聚，集中 ‖ **locali'zation** *n.*

locate [ləuˈkeit] *vt.* 1. 确定…的地点(或范围) 2. 把…设置在…；使(常用被动语态)使坐落于 3. 探出，找出 — *vi.*〈美口〉居住下来，定居

location [ləuˈkeiʃən] *n.* 1. 定位；测位；探测，勘定 2. 位置；场所；地点 3.〔采矿等的〕指定地区 4.(电影)外景；外景拍摄地 5.(南非的)黑人(或有色人种)居住区；黑人保留地 6.〔罗马法、苏格兰法〕租赁；雇用 7.〔计〕(计算机存储器的)存储单元

lock[1] [lɔk] *n.* 1. 锁 2. 止动器；制轮楔；〔机〕闭塞，气塞；液压卡塞；〔机〕锁心 3.(运河等的)船闸 4.〈英〉(车辆的)前轮转向角 5.(交通的)阻塞 6.(摔跤中的)抱，夹 7.〈英〉性病医院 (= ~ hospital) 8.〔英式橄榄球〕第二排前锋 —

lock *vt.* 1. 锁,锁上 2. 把…锁藏起来;秘藏 3. 使固定;使紧密衔接 4. 紧抱住;挽住;(格斗时)揪住 5. 卡住;塞住 6. 为(运河等)设置船闸;使(船)通过船闸;用水闸隔开(河道)(*off*) 7. 搁死(资金)(*up*) 8. 将(铅字等)装版(*up*) — *vi.* 1. 锁住;锁得上 2. 紧闭 3. 交接;连接 4. (齿轮等)卡住;塞住 5. (船)过闸;建造船闸 ‖ ～ **jaw** *n.* 【医】牙关紧闭;破伤风 / ～ **smith** *n.* 锁匠

lock² [lɔk] *n.* 1. 一绺头发;发[～s]头发 2. 【纺】毛撮(羊毛、亚麻纤维等的一簇)

locker ['lɔkə] *n.* 1. (公共场所供个人存放衣帽等用的)锁柜 2. (船上贮藏衣服、食物或弹药等的)箱、室、库 3. 冷藏格 4. 上锁人 5. (英国海关的)仓库管理人 6. 车轮上的)锁具,锁扣装置 ‖ ～ **room** 衣物间;(运动员等的)更衣室

locket ['lɔkit] *n.* (挂在项链下珍藏亲人头发或小照等的)纪念品盒

lock-in ['lɔkin] *n.* 【美】(示威群众把自己关在建筑物或办公处的)封锁行动

lock-on ['lɔkɔn] *n.* (电子)跟踪;锁定

lockout ['lɔkaut] *n.* (资方对付罢工工人的)闭厂,停工

locomotion [,ləukə'məuʃən] *n.* 1. 运动(力);移动(力);运转(力) 2. 旅行(方式)

locomotive ['ləukəməutiv] *adj.* 1. 运动的;有运动力的 2. 机动的 3. (谑)旅行的;经常迁移的 4. 有能力促进经济增长的 — *n.* 1. 火车头,机车 2. (比赛时候啦啦队拳着火车头行驶时)节奏由慢到快的欢呼声 3. [～s](英俚)腿 4. (古)自动推进器

locust ['ləukəst] *n.* 1. 蝗虫 2. 蝉 3. 【植】洋槐;刺槐;洋槐(或刺槐)木 4. 破坏成性的人;贪吃的人 5. (美俚)警棍 ‖ ～ **years** [复]艰难的岁月

lode [ləud] *n.* 【地】矿脉

lodestar ['ləudstɑ:] *n.* 1. 【天】北极星;指示方向的星 2. 指导原则;目标

lodestone ['ləudstəun] *n.* 1. 天然磁石 2. 吸引人的东西

lodge [lɔdʒ] *n.* 1. (工厂、学校等的)门房;(花园宅第大门口或花匠等住的)小屋 2. (狩猎期间居住的)小舍;旅舍;(印第安人居住的)圆锥形棚屋;北美印第安人棚屋住户 3. (游览区的)中心楼处 4. [用以构成专有名词]大旅馆 5. (隐蔽社团或联谊会的)地方分会;分会集会处 6. (尤指水獭等的)兽穴 7. (剑桥大学院长住宅 — *vt.* 1. 供应(某人)住宿;接纳(寄宿者);租房间给(某人)住 2. 容纳 3. 把…射入(或投入,打在) 4. 寄放;存放 5. 提出(申诉、抗议等) 6. 使(庄稼)倒伏 — *vi.* 1. 暂住;借宿,投宿 2.(子弹等)射入而停留 3.(庄稼等)倒伏 ‖ ～ **r** *n.* 租住者;房客

lodg(e)ment ['lɔdʒmənt] *n.* 1. 住宿;住宿处 2. 提出 3. 沉积;沉积物;沉积处;存放;存放物;存放处 4. 【军】立足点,占领;(对争议地区的)进据

lodging ['lɔdʒiŋ] *n.* 1. 寄宿,借宿 2. 住所 3. [常～s]租借的房间(别于旅馆的房间而言) 4. 存放处 5.(庄稼等的)倒伏 ‖ ～ **house** 寄宿舍

loft [lɔft] *n.* 1. 阁楼,顶层楼;厩楼 2. (美)(仓库、工厂不分隔的)统楼面 3. (教堂等中的)楼厢 4. 鸽舍;鸽群 5. (高尔夫球赛中)(高尔夫球棒端的)倾斜角度 — *vt.* 1. 把…放在阁楼中 2. 把(鸽子)关在鸽舍内 3. (高尔夫球赛中)把(球)打高 4. (高尔夫球棒)制成倾斜 5. 给…的线形图(或轮廓线)放样 — *vi.* (高尔夫球赛中)打高球

lofty ['lɔfti] *adj.* 1. 高耸的;极高的 2. 崇高的,高尚的 3. 高傲的,傲慢的 4. 地

位高的，高级的 5. 玄虚的 ‖ **loftily** *adv.* / **loftiness** *n.*

log[log]*n.* 原木，圆材，干材；短棍木柴— (logged; logging) *vt.*1. 伐(林木)；把(某地区)的林木砍掉运走 2. 把(树木)锯成段木 ‖ **logger** *n.*

log²[log]*n.*1. 测程仪，计程仪 2. 航海日志；飞行日志 3.(机器)运转记录；(工程、试验等的)工作记录簿 — (logged; logging) *vt.*1. 把…记入航海(或飞行)日志 2. 航行；飞行(若干里或小时) 3. 以…速度航(或飞)行 ‖ '~**book** *n.* 航海日志；飞行日志

log³[log]*n.* = logarithm

loganberry['lougənbəri, 'lougən,beri] *n.* 【植】罗甘莓

logarithm['logəriðəm] *n.* 【数】对数

loge[louʒ]〈法〉*n.*1.(集市上的)篷摊 2.(戏院等)包厢；(楼厅)前座 3.(房间等)的分隔间

loggerhead['logəhed]*n.*1. 傻瓜，笨蛋 2. 【动】蠵龟(= ~ turtle) 3.(熔解柏油或加热液体用的)铁头棒

logic['lodʒik]*n.*1. 逻辑(学) 2. 逻辑学著作 3. 逻辑性，条理性 4. 推理(法) 5. 必然的联系(或结果)

logical['lodʒikəl]*adj.*1. 逻辑(上)的 2. 符合逻辑的；有逻辑的；有逻辑头脑的 3. 逻辑上必然的 ‖ ~**ly** *adv.* / ~**ness** *n.*

logician[lə'dʒiʃən]*n.* 逻辑学家

logistics[lə'dʒistiks][复]*n.*【用作单或复】【军】后勤(学)

logy['lougi]*adj.*1. 迟钝的；懒散的，缺乏生气的 2. 弹性不足的

-logy *comb. form* 1. 表示"言词"：eulogy 颂词 2. 表示"…学"，"…论"：geology

loid[loid]〈俚〉*n.*(窃贼等用的)万能开锁片 — *vt.* 用万能开锁片开(门)

loin[loin]*n.*1.[常~s]腰 2.(牛、羊等的)腰肉 3.[~s]耻骨区；生殖器官

loiter['loitə]*vi.*1. 闲逛，游荡；蹓跶 2. 消磨时光(*about*) — *vt.* 消磨(时间)；混(日子)(*away*) ‖ ~**er** *n.* 闲逛的人；混日子的人

loll[lol]*vi.*1. 懒洋洋地倚靠(或躺)；懒散地闲荡 2.(头等)垂下 3.(舌头等)伸出(*out*) — *vt.*1. 垂；伸(舌头等)(*out*) 2. 把(头、四肢等)懒洋洋地倚靠着

lollipop, lollypop['lolipop]*n.*1.[常~s]糖果 2. 棒糖 3.〈英俚〉钱

Lomé[lou'mei]*n.* 洛美[多哥首都]

London['lʌndən]*n.* 伦敦[英国首都] ‖ ~**er** *n.* 伦敦人

lone[loun]*adj.*1. 孤独的，无伴的 2. 寂寞的 3. 独身的；守寡的 4. 孤(单)的；人迹稀少的，荒僻的 ‖ ~**some** *adj.*1. 孤独的；寂寞的 2. 人迹稀少的；荒凉的 *n.* 自己 ‖ **Lone Star State** 孤星州[美国得克萨斯州的别称]

lonely['lounli]*adj.*1. 孤独的 2. 寂寞的 3. 人迹稀少的；荒凉的 ‖ **loneliness** *n.*

long¹[loŋ](longer['loŋgə], longest['loŋgist])*adj.*1. 长的，长久的；长期的 2. 超过一般长度(或数量)的；过长的，冗长的；缓慢的 4. 达到远处的；长远的 5. 高的：a ~ man 高个子的人 6. 众多的；充足的；大量的 7. 长音的；(诗的音节)重读的 8.(在股票市场)做多头的 9. 长于…的(*on*)：be ~ *on* understanding 理解力强 — (longer['loŋgə], longest['loŋgist])*adv.*1. 长久；长期地 2. 始终；遥远地 — *n.*1. 长时间；长时期 3. 长音节的音 4.[语](股票市场上)做多头的人 4.(服装的)特长号 5.(莫尔斯电码中的)长信号 6.[~s]长期公债券；购买长期公债券的人 ‖ ~-'**distance** *adj.*1. 长途的 2. 长距离的 *adv.*

通过长途电话 /~ **distance** 1. 长途电话通讯 2. 长途电话交换局(或交换机);长途话务员 /'~**hand** *n*. 普通书写(与 shorthand 速记相对而言) /'~-'**lived** *adj*. 长寿的 /~ **play**, '~-'**playing record** 慢转唱片、密纹唱片 /'~-'**range** *adj*.1. 远程的 2. 长期的;长远的 /~ **shot** 1. 获胜可能性极小的赛马(或竞选者等) 2. 冒险图利的赌博(或事业) 3.【摄】远景 4. 胡乱的猜测;牵强的解释;大胆的尝试;轻率的冒险 /'~-'**sighted** *adj*.1. 远视的 2. 有远见的 /'~-'**suffering** *n*. & *adj*. 长期忍受苦难(的) /'~-**term** *adj*. 长期的 /~ **ton** 长吨(=2,240 磅) /~ **vacation**〈英〉1.(大学的)暑假 2.(法院的)暑期休庭/'~,**winded** *adj*. (讲话或文章)冗长的

long[2] [lɔŋ] *vi*. 渴望(*for*、*to do*)

longevity [lɔn'dʒeviti] *n*.1. 长寿、长命 2. 长期供职;资深、高年资

longing ['lɔŋiŋ] *n*. 渴望(*for*) — *adj*.(显示)渴望的 ‖ ~**ly** *adv*.

longish ['lɔŋiʃ] *adj*. 稍长的、略长的

longitude ['lɔndʒitju:d] *n*.1. 经度 2.【天】黄经 3.〈谑〉长;长度

longitudinal [ˌlɔndʒi'tju:dinl] *adj*.1. 经度的 2. 纵的、纵向的 ‖ ~**ly** *adv*.

longshore ['lɔŋʃɔ:] *adj*. 沿海岸的;在海岸工作的 — *adv*. 沿海岸 ‖ '~**man** *n*.1. 码头工人 2. 从事近海渔业(或船舶装卸等)的陆地居民

look [luk] *vi*.1. 看(*at*) 2. 注意、留神;找、寻(*for*) 3. 朝向;倾向 4. 显得;看上去 — *vt*.1. 看;打量 2. 看上去与(年龄、地位等)相称;看上去与...一样 3. 用眼色(或脸色)表示出 4. 期待 5. 探明、查问清楚 — *n*.1. 看 2. 脸色、神态;外容、外表 3.[~s]容貌;美貌 ‖ ~**ing glass** 镜子 /'~**ing-glass** *adj*.〈口〉完全颠倒的,正好相反的

lookout ['luk'aut] *n*.1. 警戒;注意 2. 瞭望台;监视哨;瞭望员;监视者 3. 景色;前景

loom[1] [lu:m] *n*.1. 织机;织造(术) 2. 桨柄 3.【空】翼肋腹部

loom[2] [lu:m] *vi*.1. 隐隐呈现 2. 赫然耸现;逼近 — *n*. 隐隐呈现的形象;巨大的影子

loon[1] [lu:n] *n*.1.【鸟】(捕鱼的)潜鸟;阿比 2. 潜鸟式导弹

loon[2] [lu:n] *n*.1. 笨蛋、傻瓜 2. 游手好闲的人 3.〈苏格兰〉男孩 4.〈苏格兰〉情妇;妓女

loop [lu:p] *n*.1.(线、带等打成的)圈、环;环孔 2. 环状物;襻;拎环 3.【空】筋斗、翻筋斗 4.【电】回路;滞后回线;【物】(波)腹;腹中点;环形线路;环形天线 5. 节育环 6. 环路、环线、环道 7.[the L-]大环(指芝加哥闹市区) — *vt*.1. 打环扣住 2. 把(绳)等打成环、使成圈;【电】把(导线)连成回路 3. 使(飞机)翻筋斗 — *vi*.1. 打环、成圈 2.【空】翻筋斗 3.(似尺蠖似地)伸屈前进

loophole ['lu:phəul] *n*.1.(碉堡等墙上开的)观察孔;枪眼、窥孔;透光孔;透气孔 2.(条文等中的)漏洞、空子 — *vt*. 在(墙等)的上面开枪眼

loose [lu:s] *adj*.1. 松的、宽的;松散的 2. 没加束缚的;松开的;自由的 3. 松掉了的 4. 散放的;散装的 5. 散慢的;放荡的、荒淫的 6. 不严格的;不确切的;不明确的 7.(色、染料等)易退的 8. 咳得出痰的 9.(身材等)难看的 — *adv*. 松松地;松散地;不紧凑地;不严格地 — *vt*.1. 释放;把...放开 2. 解开(结等) 3. 放(枪);射(箭)(*off*) — *vi*.1. 变松;松开;松弛 2. 放射;开火(*at*) 3.〈主英〉放学 4. 起锚 — *n*.1.(箭的)放射 2. 放

纵 ‖ ~ly adv. / ~ness n. ‖ '~-'jointed adj. 接头松的;结构差的;行动灵便的 / '~-leaf adj. 活页的

loosen ['luːsn] vt.1. 放松、解开 2. 使(纪律等)松弛 3. 使(肠)通畅;使(咳嗽)咳得出痰 — vi. 变松;松开;松弛

loot [luːt] n.1.[总称]掠夺物;战利品 2.(官吏的)非法收入;[总称]赃物 3. 掠夺,抢劫 4.〈俚〉值钱的东西;钱 — vt.1. 洗劫(都市等)2. 强夺,掠夺,抢劫(物品等) — vi. 进行掠夺 ‖ ~er n. 掠夺者,抢劫者

lop [lɔp] (lopped; lopping) vt. & vi. 砍,剪;修剪;删除

lope [ləup] vt. & vi. (使)大步慢跑 — n. (能维持较久的)大步慢跑

lopsided ['lɔp'saidid] adj. 倾侧的;不平衡的 ‖ ~ly adv. / ~ness n.

loquacious [ləu'kweiʃəs] adj. 多话的,过于健谈的 ‖ ~ly adv. / ~ness n./lo-quacity [ləu'kwæsiti] n. 多话,话多

loquat ['ləukwɔt] n.[植] 枇杷树;枇杷

lord [lɔːd] n.1.[总称] 掌实权者;统治者 2.(官吏的)非法收入 2. 君主 3. 勋爵于(侯、伯、子、男爵等贵族或高级官员的尊称);[L-](英国)上议院议员;[the Lords](英国)上议院全体议员 4.[L-] 主人 5.(工商界的)大王,巨头;(在某方面有特殊影响的)大师,泰斗 6.[L-]〈英〉夫人,阁下〈谑〉丈夫 — vt. 称王称霸 — vt. 封(某人)为贵族;赐(某人)贵族衔

lordly ['lɔːdli] adj.1. 贵族的、贵族似的,气派十足的 2. 高傲的,傲慢无礼的 — adv. 贵族似地,气派十足地;高傲地

lordship ['lɔːdʃip] n.1. 贵族身份 2. 勋爵爵位 3. 领地

lore [lɔː] n.1. 学问;学识 2.(有关某一学科的)全部知识(或传说)3.〈古〉教导;忠告

lorgnette [lɔː'njet] n.(一副)长柄眼镜;(一副)长柄眼镜式望远镜

lorn [lɔːn] adj. 被弃的;孤寂的;毁灭了的

lorry ['lɔri] n.1. 平板四轮车 2.(在轨道上行驶的)手车,运料车,推料车 3.〈英〉运货汽车,卡车(美国通用 truck)

Los Angeles [lɔs 'ændʒələs] 洛杉矶[美国加利福尼亚州西南部港市]

lose [luːz] (lost[lɔst]) vt.1. 失去;损失;丧失 2. 使失去 3. 抓不住;听(或看)不见 4. 错过 5. 白费,浪费 6. 迷失;使迷路;使迷糊不清 7. 输掉;未赢得(奖品等)8. 使沉溺于 9.[用被动语态的]使毁灭;使死去;使降失 10. 摆脱 11.〈谚俗中〉摆脱,甩开;把…抛开一段距离 — vi.1. 受损失;赔钱 2. 失败,输掉 3.(钟、表等)走慢

loser ['luːzə] n.1. 损失者;损失物 2. 失败者,输家 3.〈俚〉坐进(若干次)牢的人 4.〈英〉(台球游戏中)主球着目标球自落(的一击)

loss [lɔs] n.1. 丧失;遗失 2. 损失;亏损;损耗 3. 失败,输 4. 损费;[~es][军]兵员损失,伤亡及被俘人员数 5. 错过;浪费 6. ~'maker n.〈英〉老是亏损的企业 / '~making adj.〈英〉老是亏损的

lost [lɔst] lose 的过去式和过去分词 — adj.1. 失去的;丧失的;丧失的 2. 错过的;浪费掉的 3. 迷途的,不知所措的 4. 输掉的;失败了的;无望的 5. 遭难的,死了的 6. 再不来的

lot [lɔt] n.1. 签,阄;抽签,拈阄 2. 份额,份儿 3. 命运,运气 4.〈俚〉(一块)地;(作特定用处的)地方 5.〈美〉电影摄制场 6.(商品、拍卖品或人)一批,一组;一类的人 7.[亦作~s][用作单]大量,许多;Thanks a ~. 多谢。8.[the ~]全部,一切 — (lotted; lotting) vt.1. 划分

把(商品等)分组 2. 分配 — **vi.** 抽签,拈阄

loth [ləuθ] **adj.** = loath

lotion ['ləuʃən] **n.** 洗液,洗剂;(化妆用的)搽液,涂剂 — **vt.** 用洗液时;搽涂剂于

lottery ['lɒtəri] **n.** 1. 抽彩给奖法;抽签法 2. 难于预测的事

lotus ['ləutəs] **n.** 1.【植】莲 2.【建】荷花饰

loud [laud] **adj.** 1.(声音)响亮的 2. 发出强声的 3. 吵闹的,喧嚷的 4. 强调的;坚持的 5.(衣服颜色等)俗艳的;过分花哨的;(举止)招摇的 6.(气味)难闻的 — **adv.** 大声地;响亮地 ‖ **～ly adv.** / **～ness n.** 1. 高声,大声 2. 喧闹 3. 俗艳 ‖'**～mouth n.** 叫里呱啦的人;爱吹牛(或攻击他人)的人;高谈阔论的人/'**～mouthed adj.** 叫里呱啦的;高谈阔论的;唠唠叨叨的/'**～speaker n.** 扬声器,喇叭

Louisiana [luːˌiziˈænə] **n.** 路易斯安那[美国州名]

lounge [laundʒ] **vi.** 1.(懒洋洋地)倚,靠;躺 2. 闲荡;闲逛 — **vt.** 吊儿郎当地混(时间)(away) — **n.** 1. 懒洋洋的姿势;懒洋洋的步子 2. 闲荡;漫步;混过的时间 3. 起居室(旅馆等处的)休息室;休息处 4. 躺椅

lour ['lauə] **vi.** 1. 皱眉头;露愠色(at, on, upon) 2.(天空等)变昏黑

louse [laus]([复]**lice** [lais]) **n.** 1. 虱 2. 吸吸动物血(或植物液汁)的昆虫;(鸟的)羽虱 3.([复]**louses**)(俚)卑鄙家伙 — **vt.** 清除…上的虱子

lousy ['lauzi] **adj.** 1. 多虱的;全是虱子的 2. 糟糕的;劣等的 3.(美俚)很多的,丰富的(with) 4.(美俚)卑鄙下流的;讨厌的 5.(铋)(丝)有茸毛的 ‖ **lousily adv.** / **lousiness n.**

lout [laut] **n.** 粗鲁的人;蠢人

louver ['luːvə] **n.** 1. 百叶窗板;百叶窗 2. 气窗;天窗;烟窗

Louvre ['luːvrə] **n.** [the ～](巴黎)罗浮宫(或译卢浮宫,卢佛尔宫;现辟作国立美术博物馆)

lovable ['lʌvəbl] **adj.** 可爱的,讨人喜欢的 ‖ **lovably adv.**

love [lʌv] **n.** 1. 爱;热爱;爱戴 2. 爱好 3. 恋爱,爱情 4. 性爱;男女关系 5. 亲爱的(夫妇,情侣间,或对孩子的爱称) 6. [L]爱的化身,爱神 7.(多指女性)情人;情妇 8.(口)讨人喜欢的人;可爱的东西 9.(网球等比赛中的)零分 — **vt.** 1. 爱;热爱;爱戴 2. 抚爱 3. 爱好,喜欢 — **vi.** 爱 ‖ **～ affair** 1. 恋爱关系;风流韵事 2. 强烈爱好 /'**～bird n.** 1.【鸟】情侣鹦鹉 2. 恋爱中的人(常指一对)/'**～in n.**(颓废派青年)举行集会的爱情聚会 /～ letter 情书/'**～sick adj.** 害相思病的;相思的

lovely ['lʌvli] **adj.** 1. 秀丽的;好看的;优美的 2.(口)令人愉快的;美好的 3. 可爱的 4.(美)高尚的;潇洒的 — **n.** 1. 美女 2. 漂亮的东西 ‖ **loveliness n.**

lover ['lʌvə] **n.** 1. 爱好者 2. [～s]情侣 3.(指男性)情人,爱人

loving ['lʌviŋ] **adj.** 爱的;表示爱的 ‖ **～ly adv.**

low[1] [ləu] **adj.** 1. 低的;浅的 2. 低声的 3.(元音,声调等)低的 3.(在量,度,价值等方面)少的,低下的 4. 贬的 5. 不足的,快枯竭的;缺货的 6. 地位低的,卑微的;低下的 7. 粗俗的;下流的;卑劣的 8. 营养差的;(体质弱的 9. 没精神的,情绪低落的 10.(衣服)领口开得低的;(鞋)浅帮的 11. [L-](英国)低教会(派)的 — **adv.** 1. 低;向下地 2. 低声地;以低音调 3. 低价地;程度低地 4. 地位低地,卑微地;下贱地 5. 营养差地

穷困地 6. 在(或至)较近的年代 —
*n.*1.[常～s]低地 2. 低水平;低点;低数
字3. 低速;低速档 4.[气]低气压区 5.
(体育比赛、纸牌游戏等中)最低的得
分;得最低分的人(或队);最小的王牌
‖ ~-brow(口)*n.* 缺乏文化修养的人,
对文化艺术不感兴趣的人 *adj.* 缺乏文
化素养的;适于文化素养低的人的 /
~-browed *adj.* 文化修养(或趣味)低级
的/~ profile 1. 低姿态,低调(或克制)
的姿态 2. 低姿态的人,有节制的人

low² [ləu] *n.* 牛叫声,哞 — *vi.*(牛等)哞
哞叫 — *vt.* 牛叫似地说

lower¹ ['ləuə] *adj.*1. 较低的 2. 地位较低
的,较低级的;下等的 3. 低年级的 4.
下游的 5. 南部的 6.(日期)较近的 7.
[L-][地]早期的 ‖ ~ **case**[印]小写
体,小写字母 /~ **case** 小写铅字;小写
铅字字盘 /~ **case** *adj.*(用小写字母的)
adj.(用小写字母的)/(字母)小写的
vt. 用小写字母排印(或书写)/~ **class**
下层阶级 /~ **house**,~
chamber 下(议)院,众议院 /~ **orders** 下
层社会

lower² ['ləuə] *vt.*1. 放下;降下;放低 2. 减
低;减弱 3. 贬低 — *vi.*1. 降落,降低;
减弱 2. 放下小艇;降下帆篷(*away*)

lowland ['ləulənd] *n.*[常～s]低地 — *adj.*
低地的

lowly ['ləuli] *adj.*1. 谦逊的,卑微的,地
位低的 2. 低级的 3. 普通的,平凡的 —
*adv.*1. 谦逊地 2. 卑微地;低贱地;低下
地 3. 声音低沉地,不响亮地 ‖ **lowliness**
n.

loyal ['lɔiəl] *adj.* 忠诚的,忠心的 — *n.*
[常～s]忠实信徒 ‖ ~ **ly** *adv.*

loyalty ['lɔiəlti] *n.* 忠诚,忠心

lozenge ['lɔzindʒ] *n.*1. 菱形 2. 菱形物 3.
【药】锭剂;糖锭

LP *abbr.* long playing 慢转唱片,密纹唱片

(= ~ record)

LPG, LP-gas *abbr.* liquefied petroleum gas
液化石油气

Lr【化】元素铹(lawrencium)的符号

Lt. *abbr.* Lieutenant

Ltd. *abbr.* Limited(常用于股份有限公司
的名称后)

Lu【化】元素镥(lutetium)的符号

Luanda [lu'ændə] *n.* 罗安达[安哥拉首都]

lubber ['lʌbə] *n.* 大而笨拙的人,傻大个
儿;(无经验的)笨拙水手 ‖ ~-**like** *adj.*
/ ~-**ly** *adv.* & *adj.*

lubricant ['lu:brikənt] *adj.* 润滑的 — *n.*1.
润滑剂;润滑油 2. 能减少磨擦(或困
难)的因素

lubricate ['lu:brikeit] *vt.*1. 使润滑 2. 加润
滑油于 3. ...上油;上润滑 4.
〈美俚〉收买 5. 使顺畅,促进 — *vi.*1.
起润滑作用 2.〈美俚〉饮酒 ‖
lubri'cation *n.* 润滑(作用);上油 /**lubri-
cator** *n.* 加油工;加油器;润滑器;润滑
剂

lubricious [lu:'briʃəs], **lubricous** ['lu:brikəs]
*adj.*1. 润滑的,光滑的 2. 难以捉摸
的,不稳定的 3.〈书〉淫荡的,好色的

lucid ['lju:sid] *adj.*1. 清楚的,易懂的 2.
神志清醒的;头脑清楚的 3. 透明的;清
澈的 4.〈诗〉光辉的,明亮的 ‖ ~ **ly**
adv. / ~ **ness** *n.*

luck [lʌk] *n.*1. 运气 2. 好运;侥幸 3. 带
来运气的东西 ‖ ~ **out**〈美俚〉走运化为
吉;靠运气(*out*);凑巧碰上;偶尔发现
(*in, into, on, onto*)

lucky ['lʌki] *adj.*1. 幸运的,侥幸的 2. 吉
祥的,吉利的 ‖ **luckily** *adv.*

lucrative ['lu:krətiv] *adj.* 生利的,赚钱
的,有利的

lucre ['lu:kə] *n.*〈贬〉金钱,财富;金钱欲

益,利润

ludicrous ['lu:dikrəs] *adj.* 荒唐得滑稽的,荒谬可笑的 ‖ ~ly *adv.* / ~ness *n.*

luff [lʌf] *n.* , *vi.* & *vt.* (使)抢风行驶

lug [lʌg] (lugged; lugging) *vt.* 1. 用力拖,使劲拉;吃力地携带 2. 硬扯 — *vi.* 1. 拖;拉(*at*) 2. 费力地(或摇摆着)移动 — *n.* 1. 拖,拉;被拖(或被拉)的东西 2. [~s]装腔作势;架子 3. 《美俚》勒索;勒索的钱财

luggage ['lʌgidʒ] *n.* [总称] 1. 行李(美国一般用 baggage) 2. 《美》(店家出售的)箱笼 3. 《英》辎重 ‖ '~-rack *n.* (火车等的)行李架 / '~ van《英》行李车(= 《美》baggage car)

lugubrious [lu:'gu:briəs] *adj.* 悲哀的;忧郁的;过分伤心的(尤指做作或假装的) ‖ ~ly *adv.* / ~ness *n.*

lukewarm ['lu:kwɔ:m] *adj.* 1. (液体)微温的 2. 不热情的;半心半意的

lull [lʌl] *vt.* 1. 使安静;哄(小孩)睡觉 2. 哄骗 3. 使平静;使缓和(斗志等) — *vi.* 变平静 — *n.* 1. 间歇;暂停 2. 催眠的东西(尤指摇篮曲)

lullaby ['lʌləbai] *n.* 1. 催眠歌;摇篮曲 2. 轻柔的声音(如溪流的水声,潺潺的流水声) — *vt.* 唱催眠曲使入睡;使安静

lumbago [lʌm'beigəu] ([复] lumbagos) *n.* 【医】腰痛

lumbar ['lʌmbə] *adj.* 腰的;(在)腰部的

lumber[1] ['lʌmbə] *n.* 1. 无用的材料;赘肉;家用废旧杂物;废旧家具 2. 成材;锯制板;木料 — *vt.* 1. (以碎旧东西)堆满;零乱地堆放 2. 伐(树);采伐…的林木 — *vi.* 伐木制材 ‖ '~jack *n.* 1. 伐木工;原木采运工 2. 短茄克衫 / '~man *n.* 伐木工;原木采运工 / '~yard *n.* 贮木场

lumber[2] ['lʌmbə] *vi.* 笨重地移动;隆隆地

行进 — *n.* 隆隆声

luminary ['lju:minəri] *n.* 1. 发光天体(指日、月等) 2. 发光体 3. (学识等方面的)杰出人物;名人;泰斗

luminescent [,lju:mi'nesnt] *adj.* 【物】发光的 ‖ luminescence *n.* 发光

luminous ['lju:minəs] *adj.* 1. 发光的,发亮的 2. 光明的,灿烂的 3. 照亮着的;被照耀发光体的 4. 明白易懂的 5. 光明的;有 启发的 ‖ luminosity [,lju:mi'nɔsiti] *n.* / ~ly *adv.*

lump[1] [lʌmp] *n.* 1. (不定形的)块;小方块(糖) 2. 大量;一大堆;多数 3. 隆起,肿块 4. 《口》粗壮的人;傻大哥 5. 《美俚》[~s]责打;指责;惩罚;报应 6. [the ~][总称]《英》(建筑业等的)转包工,临时工,个体劳动者 — *vt.* 1. 把…归并在一起;把…混为一谈 2. 使重重地坐下 3. 把…弄成七高八低 — *vi.* 1. 结块;起小疙瘩 2. 蹒跚着行进(*along*) 3. 做装卸工,做码头工

lump[2] [lʌmp] *vt.* 对…感到不高兴;勉强忍受

lunacy ['lu:nəsi] *n.* 1. 精神错乱 2.【律】心神丧失 2. 疯狂愚蠢的行为;荒谬、愚蠢

lunar ['lu:nə] *adj.* 1. 月的;太阴的;以月球公转而测度的 2. 似月的;新月形的;半月形的 3. (光等)青冷的;微弱的 4. 银的;含银的 ‖ ~ calendar 阴历 / ~ eclipse 月食 / ~ module[字]登月舱

lunatic ['lu:nətik] *adj.* 1. 精神错乱的,疯狂的 2. 为收容精神病人而设立的 3. 疯狂(的);极端愚蠢的 — *n.* 精神错乱者,疯子 2. 狂人;怪人;大傻瓜 ‖ ~ asylum 疯人院(现称 mental hospital)

lunch [lʌntʃ] *n.* 1. 午餐;便餐 2. 午餐食品 — *vi.* 吃午餐(或便餐) — *vt.* 为…供应午餐(或便餐)

luncheon ['lʌntʃən] *n.* 1. 午餐 2. 宴客便

luncheon n.餐;(工商、社交团体等的)午餐会

luncheonette [ˌlʌntʃə'net] n.《美》便餐馆,小吃店

lung [lʌŋ] n.1. 肺 2.《某些无脊椎动物的》呼吸器官 3. 单人潜水呼吸器;(人工)呼吸器,铁肺 4.《英》空气新鲜的空旷地方

lunge [lʌndʒ] n.1.(刀、剑等的)刺;戳 2. 猛冲 — vi. 冲刺;猛向前冲(at, out) — vt. 刺、刺、戳、猛刺

lupin(e) ['lju:pin] n. 羽扇豆

lurch [lə:tʃ] vi.1.(船)突然倾斜 2. 蹒跚,东倒西歪地向前 — n.(船的)突然倾斜;倾侧 2. 蹒跚,东倒西歪 3. 倾向;爱好

lure [ljuə] n.1. 诱回猎鹰的一束羽毛 2.(捕鱼用的)诱饵 3. 诱惑力;吸引力,魅力 — vt.1. 用引诱物召回(猎鹰)2. 引诱,诱惑;吸引

lurid ['ljuərid] adj.1.(脸色等)苍白的;灰黄的 2.(火焰、云霞等)火红的,血红的 3. 可怕的,惊人的,骇人听闻的 4. 过分渲染的(装腔、色彩等)俗艳的 ‖ ~ly adv. / ~ness n.

lurk [lə:k] vi.1. 潜伏;埋伏 2. 潜藏;潜在 3. 偷偷地行动,鬼鬼祟祟地活动 — n.1. 潜伏;潜行 2.《澳新俚》诡计,妙计

Lusaka [lu:'sɑ:kə] n. 卢萨卡[赞比亚首都]

luscious ['lʌʃəs] adj.1. 甘美的;芬芳的 2.《古》过分香甜的(腻味的);肉感的,诱惑的 3.(文体等)华丽的,绚烂的 ‖ ~ly adv. / ~ness n.

lush[1] [lʌʃ] adj.1.(草木)茂盛的;葱翠的 2. 多汁的;味美的;芬芳的 3. 丰富的;豪华的;繁荣的,有利的 5. 肉感的 6.(口)花哨的 ‖ ~ly adv. / ~ness n.

lush[2] [lʌʃ] n.《美俚》n.1.(烈性)酒。醉汉;酒鬼 — vt. 喝(酒) — vi. 喝酒

lust [lʌst] n.1. 不良欲望;贪欲 2. 性欲。淫欲 3. 渴望,热烈追求(of, for) — vi. 贪求;渴望(after, for) ‖ ~ er n. 贪欲的人;好色之徒 / ~ful adj.1. 贪欲的 2. 好色的

lustre, luster ['lʌstə] n.1. 光泽;光辉;光彩 2. 荣光;显赫 3. 玻璃吊灯架;玻璃架枝形吊灯 4. 光泽彩料,光泽瓷料(= ~ware)5.(主英)釉全毛纬)有光呢 — vt.1. 使有光泽;使有光彩 2. 给……上虹彩 — vi. 有光泽,发光

lustrous ['lʌstrəs] adj.1. 有光泽的;有光彩的 2.(品德,声誉等)光辉的;显赫的

lusty ['lʌsti] adj.1. 强壮的;精力充沛的;朝气蓬勃的 2. 有力的、强烈的、贪欲的;好色的 3.《古》欢乐的 ‖ lustily adv.

lute [lju:t] n.(十四至十七世纪的一种拨弦乐器)诗琴,鲁特琴 — vi. 弹诗琴 — vt. 用诗琴弹奏

lutecium [lu:'ti:ʃiəm] n.《化》镥

Lutheran ['lu:θərən] adj. 路德教的,以"因信称义"为教义的;路德宗的

Luxembour**g** ['lʌksəmbə:g] n.1. 卢森堡[西欧国家] 2. 卢森堡(市)[卢森堡首都]

luxuriant [lʌg'zjuəriənt] adj.1. 繁茂的;丰饶的 2. 丰富的 3.(文体等)华丽的,绚烂的 4. 奢华的;精美的 ‖ luxuriance n. / ~ly adv.

luxuriate [lʌg'zjuərieit] vi.1. 纵情享乐,过着侈华生活 2. 尽情享受,感到非常愉快(in)3. 茂盛地生长;迅猛地发展

luxurious [lʌg'zjuəriəs] adj.1. 爱好豪侈的;放纵的;纵欲的 2. 奢侈的;非常舒适的;精美而昂贵的;词藻华丽的 ‖ ~ly adv. / ~ness n.

luxury ['lʌkʃəri] n.1. 奢侈;奢华;华贵 2. 奢侈品;昂贵难得的东西 3. 给人以享

乐的事物;舒适的环境 — *adj.* 奢华的;
豪华的

Luzon ['lu:'zɔn] *n.* 吕宋(岛)[菲律宾北部]

-ly *suf.* [附在名词后构成形容词] **1.** 表示
"似...的","有...性质的";man*ly*,
scholar*ly* **2.** 表示"反复发生的","每一
特定时期发生一次的";week*ly*, hour*ly*
— [构成副词] **1.** 表示"方式"、"状态"、
"时间"、"地点"、"程序"、"程度"、"方
向";great*ly*, first*ly*, smiling*ly* **2.** 表示
"从...方面(或观点,角度)";economi-
cal*ly*, technical*ly*

lyceum [lai'siəm, 'laisiəm] *n.* (学术)演讲
厅;讲学(或讨论)场所

lye [lai] *n.* 【化】碱液 — *vt.* 用碱液洗涤

lying[1] ['laiŋ] lie[1] 的现在分词 — *n.* 躺;躺
的地方

lying[2] ['laiŋ] lie[2] 的现在分词 — *adj.* 欺
骗的,不诚实的;假的

lying-in ['laiŋ'in] ([复] lyings-in 或 lying-
ins) *n.* 生产,分娩 — *adj.* 与分娩有关

的,为分娩的

lymph [limf] *n.* **1.**【解】淋巴 **2.**【医】浆、苗

lymphatic [lim'fætik] *adj.* **1.**【解】淋巴的;
输送(或分泌)淋巴的 **2.** 粘液质的;苍
白无力的;委顿的 — *n.*【解】淋巴管

lynch [lintʃ] *vt.* 以私刑处死

lynx [liŋks] ([复] lynx(es)) *n.* **1.** 猞猁,林㹱
2. 猞猁毛皮 **3.** [the L-]【天】天猫座

lyre ['laiə] *n.* **1.** 里拉(古希腊的一种弦乐
器) **2.** [the L-]【天】天琴座 ‖ `~bird` *n.*
(澳洲产的)琴鸟

lyric ['lirik] *n.* **1.** 抒情诗;抒情作品 **2.**
[~s]歌词;抒情词句 — *adj.* **1.** (古希
腊乐器)里拉的 **2.** 适合用里拉伴奏的
3. 抒情的 **4.** 感情丰富的;奔放的

lyrical ['lirikəl] *adj.* = lyric ‖ `~ly` *adv.* /
`~ness` *n.*

lyricism ['lirisizəm] *n.* **1.** 抒情性;抒情风
格 **2.** 抒情体 **3.** 狂放的抒情;奔放的激
情

M

M, m [em]([复]M's, m's 或 Ms, ms
[emz])英语字母表第十三个字母 1.
[M]M形 2.[M]罗马数字的 1,000 3.
[M]【电】互感(mutual inductance)的符
号

Ma【化】元素钔(masurium)的符号

ma [mɑː] n.〈口〉妈

ma' am [mæm, mɑːm, 弱 məm] n.〈口〉
(madam 的缩略) (1). (对女王及其他王
室贵妇的称呼)夫人;女士 2. (仆佣对
女主人的称呼)太太,小姐

macabre [məˈkɑːbrə, məˈkɑːbə] adj. 1. 恐
怖的,可怕的 2. 关于死亡的;涉及死
亡问题的 ‖ ~ly adv.

macadam [məˈkædəm] n. 1. [总称](铺路
用的)碎石 2. 碎石路(= ~ road);碎石
路面 ‖ ~ize vt.用碎石筑(路);用碎
石铺路

Macao [məˈkau] n. 澳门

macaque [məˈkɑːk] n. 猕猴,恒河猴;短
尾猴

macaroni [ˌmækəˈrəuni] n. 1. 通心面,空
心面;通心粉 2.([复]macaroni(es)(十
八世纪醉心于仿效欧洲大陆派头的)
英国花花公子;浮华少年,纨绔子弟

macaroon [ˌmækəˈruːn] n. 蛋白杏仁甜饼
(干),小杏仁饼

macaw [məˈkɔː] n.【鸟】金刚鹦鹉

mace¹ [meis] n. 1. 权标,权杖 2. 持权
杖者 3. 狼牙棒,钉头锤(一种中古时

代武器) 4.(旧式击台球用的)平头杆

mace² [meis] n. 肉豆蔻衣(干皮)(用作
香料或调味品)

Macedonia [ˌmæsiˈdəuniə] n. 1. 马其顿
[欧洲巴尔干半岛中南部国家] 2. 马
其顿(区)[希腊行政区名]

Mach [mæk, mɑːk] n.【物】马赫数(亦作
~ number)

machete [məˈtʃeti] n. (中美、南美人割
甘蔗或当武器用的)大砍刀 2. 葡萄牙
四弦小吉他

Machiavellian [ˌmækiəˈveliən] adj.(意大
利政治家)马基雅弗利(式)的;诡计多
端的;不择手段的 ‖ ~ly adv.

machination [ˌmækiˈneiʃən] n.〈罕〉图
谋,策划 2. 诡计,奸计;阴谋

machine [məˈʃiːn] n. 1. 机器,机械 2. 汽
车;自行车;机动车辆 3. 身体器官 4.
机械地工作的人(或机构) 5. 机构;控
制政党的核心组织 6. 制造舞台效果
的装置;(文学作品中为取得戏剧效果
的)布局,设计(尤指安排在小说、诗中
的超自然力量) — vt. 机制;用机床加
工(如切、削、磨、铣等) ‖ ~ gun 机枪 /
ma'chine-gun vt.用机枪扫射;用机枪击
中 / ~gunner 机枪手 / ~ language 计
算机语言,机器语言 / ~ shop 金工车
间 / ~ tool 工作母机,机床 / ~ translation 机器翻译

machinery [məˈʃiːnəri] n. 1. [总称]机器,

机械 2.(机器的)运转部分 3.(政府等的)机构 4. 方法 5. 制造舞台效果的装置(文学作品中为取得戏剧效果的)布局,设计(尤指安排在小说、诗中的超自然力量)

machinist [mə'ʃiːnist] n. 1. 机工;机械师 2. 机器操作工人(尤指缝纫车工) 3. 海军机械军士长

machismo [mɑːˈtʃiːzməu, mæˈkizməu] n. 大男子气概

macho ['mɑːtʃəu] ([复]machos) n. 大丈夫,男子 —adj. 大男子气的;勇敢的

mackerel ['mækərəl] ([复]mackerel) n. [动]鲭;鲐;欧洲鲐

mackintosh ['mækintɔʃ] n. 1. 橡胶防雨布 2.(英)雨衣

macramé [mə'krɑːmi, 'mækrəmei] n. (装饰家具等用的)流苏花边

macr(o)- comb. form 表示"长";"大";"宏";macro为词缀

macrobiotic [ˌmækrəubai'ɔtik] adj. 长寿的;长寿饮食(法)的;(供应)长寿食物的

macrocosm ['mækrəukɔzəm] n. 宏观世界

macron ['mækrɔn] n.[语]长音符号"‾" (如在[a], [e], [i], [o]中等)

mad [mæd] a. 1. 发疯的,发狂的;(狗等)患狂犬病的 2. 疯狂的;狂烈的;狂热的,着迷的 3. 愚蠢的 4. 狂妄的 5.(口)狂怒的;be ~ at sb. 对某人情火 6. 狂欢的,热闹的 vt. & vi.(罕)=madden n. 狂怒 ‖ ~ly adv. / ~ness n. ‖ ~cap adj. 鲁莽的;不顾前后的 n. 鲁莽的人;狂妄的人 / ~ house n. 疯人院 2. 吵闹混乱的场所 / ~man n. 疯子,狂人 / ~woman n. 女疯子

Madagascar [ˌmædə'gæskə] n. 马达加斯加[非洲岛国](在印度洋西部)

madam ['mædəm] ([复]madams 或 mes-

dames['meidæm]) n. 1.(对妇女的尊称)夫人,女士;太太;小姐 2.(用于姓名或职称前)…夫人;…女士;…太太;…小姐 3.(家庭)主妇 4.(口)喜欢使唤他人的女子 5. 鸨母

madame [mə'dɑːm, 'mædəm] ([复]mesdames[mei'dɑːm, 'meidæm] 或 madames) (法) n. 1. ([复]mesdames)(用于非英语民族的已婚妇女及有职业的妇女,相当于 Mrs.;略作 Mme.)夫人;女士;太太 2. 鸨母

madden ['mædn] vt. 1. 使发疯,使发狂 2. 使狂怒,使恼火 —vi. 发疯,发狂

made [meid] make 的过去式和过去分词 —adj. 1. 人工制造的 2. 虚构的,捏造的 3. 保证会成功(或发达)的 ‖ ~-dish 拼盘 / '~-to-'order adj. 定制的 / '~-'up adj. 1. 制成的;编排好的 2. 虚构的,捏造的 3. 做作的 4. 坚定的;决定了的 5. 化了妆的;化了装的

mademoiselle [ˌmædəmwɑ'zel] ([复]mademoiselles [ˌmædəmwɑ'zelz] 或 mesdemoiselles[ˌmeidmwɑ'zel]) (法) n. 1. 小姐(相当于 Miss) 2. 法国女(家庭)教师

Madonna [mə'dɔnə] n. 圣母马利亚(耶稣的母亲)

madras ['mædrəs, mə'drɑːs] n. 马德拉斯狭条状衬衫布

Madrid [mə'drid] n. 马德里[西班牙首都]

madrigal ['mædrigəl] n.[音]牧歌

maelstrom ['meilstrəm] n. 1. 大漩涡 2. 大混乱,大动乱;不可抵抗的破坏力

maestro ['maistrəu] ([复]maestros 或 maestri ['maistriː]) n. 艺术大师(尤指杰出的作曲家、指挥、音乐教师)

maf(f)ia [ˈmæfiə, 'mɑːfiə] n.[常作 M-] 1. 黑手党(起源于意大利西西里岛的秘密犯罪组织) 2. 黑手党式秘密犯罪集

团；秘密组织

magazine [ˌmægə'ziːn] *n.* 1. 杂志，期刊；(报纸的)星期专刊 2. 仓库；(城堡,舰船等的)弹药库,弹药仓；库存物；库存弹药 3.(枪上的)弹仓,弹盒,弹膛 4. 胶卷暗盒

magenta [mə'dʒentə] *n.*【化】品红(色)；洋红(色)

maggot ['mægət] *n.* 1. 蛆 2. 狂想,空想；怪念头

Maghreb, Maghrib ['mʌɡreb] *n.* 马格里布(北非突尼斯、阿尔及利亚、摩洛哥三国的总称)

Magi ['meidʒai] Magus 的复数

magic ['mædʒik] *n.* 1.(迷信的)魔法,巫术 2. 魔术,戏法 3. 魔力,魅力 — *adj.* [只作定语] 1. 巫术的；魔术的 2. 有魔力的,不可思议的 ∥ ~ lantern 幻灯

magical ['mædʒikəl] *adj.* 1. 巫术的；魔术的 2. 有魔力的,不可思议的

magician [mə'dʒiʃən] *n.* 1. 魔术师 2. 术士

magisterial [ˌmædʒi'stiəriəl] *adj.* 有权威的；专横的

magistrate ['mædʒistreit] *n.* 1. 地方行政官 2. 文职官员 3. 地方法官

magma ['mægmə] ([复] magmas 或 magmata ['mægmətə]) *n.* 1.(有机物或矿物的)稀糊状混合物；【药】乳(浆)剂 2.【地】岩浆

magnanimity [ˌmægnə'nimiti] *n.* 1. 宽宏大量；高尚 2. 宽宏大量的行为；高尚行为

magnanimous [mæg'næniməs] *adj.* 宽宏大量的,高尚的 ∥ ~ly *adv.*

magnate ['mægneit] *n.* 1. 大官；权贵；阔人 2.(资本主义工商业的)巨头,大王

magnesia [mæg'niːʃə] *n.*【化】镁氧；氧化镁

magnesium [mæg'niːziəm] *n.*【化】镁

magnet ['mægnit] *n.* 1. 磁体,磁铁,磁石 2. 有吸引力的人(或物)

magnetic [mæg'netik] *adj.* 1. 磁的；有磁性的；(可)磁化的；由磁性引起的 2. 有吸引力的,有魅力的 3. 催眠术的 — *n.* 磁性物质 ∥ ~ field 磁场 / ~ needle 磁针,指南针 / ~ pole 磁极 / ~ tape 磁带

magnetism ['mægnitizəm] *n.* 1. 磁；磁力；磁学 2. 魅力,吸引力 3. 催眠术

magnetize ['mægnitaiz] *vt.* 1. 使磁化,使生磁性,使有磁力 2. 使醉迷,吸引 3.〈罕〉催眠 — *vi.* 受磁

magneto [mæg'niːtəu] *n.* ([复] magnetos) 磁电机,永磁发电机

magnificence [mæg'nifisns] *n.* 1. 壮丽,宏伟,宏大 2. 华丽,豪华

magnificent [mæg'nifisnt] *adj.* 1. 壮丽的；宏伟的,宏大的 2. 华丽的,豪华的 3. 漂亮得惊人的,极其动人的；(人、动物等体型)优美的,健壮的 4.(思想等)高尚的,高贵的 5.〈口〉极好的 ∥ ~ly *adv.*

magnifier ['mægnifaiə] *n.* 放大者；放大器,放大镜

magnify ['mægnifai] *vt.* 1. 放大,扩大 2. 赞美,推崇 3. 夸张,夸大 — *vi.* 有放大能力 ∥ ~ing glass 放大镜 / ~ing power 放大率,放大倍数

magniloquent [mæg'niləukwənt] *adj.* 1. 夸张的,过分夸语言的 2. 自夸的,自负的,大言不惭的 ∥ magniloquence *n.* / ~ly *adv.*

magnitude ['mægnitjuːd] *n.* 1. 巨大；广大；〈古〉伟大 2. 重大；重要性 3. 大小；

积;量,数量;音量 4.【天】星等(指星的亮度)5.【量】量值 6.【地】震级

magnolia [mæg'nəuljə] *n.* 1.【植】木兰;木兰花 2. 浅桃红色

magpie ['mægpai] *n.* 1.【动】(喜)鹊 2. 爱说话的人,叽叽喳喳的人3.(靶子上自外数起的)第二环;击中第二环的一枪

Magus ['meigəs] ([复] Magii ['meidʒai]) *n.*《圣经》中向东方来朝见初生耶稣的三贤人之一)东方博士

Maharajah [,mɑːhə'rɑːdʒə] *n.*(印度的)土邦主,王公

Maharanee [,mɑːhə'rɑːniː] *n.*(印度的)土邦主的妻子(或遗孀);女土邦主

mah-jong(g) ['mɑː'dʒɔŋ] (汉) *n.* 麻将牌

mahogany [mə'hɔgəni] *n.* 1. 桃花心木,红木 2.【植】桃花心木 3. 赤褐色 4. 餐桌 5.(英)杜松子酒搀蜜糖 6. 搀水白兰地

Mahomet [mə'hɔmit] *n.* 穆罕默德(即 Muhammad)

maid [meid] *n.* 1. 少女;(未婚的)青年女子 2.(老)处女 3. 侍女;女仆 ‖ ~ of honour 1. 女王(或王后、公主)的未婚侍女(通常出身贵族);(婚礼中)首席女傧相 3. 柠檬杏仁馅饼

maiden ['meidn] *n.* 1. 少女;未婚女子;处女 2.【英史】(苏格兰的)断头台 3.(赛马中)未得过奖的马 4.(板球赛中)未得分的投球 —*adj.* 1. 少女的;未婚女子的;处女的 2. 适合未婚女子的 3.(雌性动物)未交配的;未生育过的 4.(马)未得过奖的;(赛马)为未得过奖的马举行的 4.(植物)从种子长成的 5.(士兵等)无经验的,未经考验的;新的,原封未动的 6. 初次的 ‖ ~hood *n.* 处女身分;少女时期 / ~ly *adv.* ‖ ~hair *n.*【植】掌叶铁线蕨;铁线蕨 / ~hair tree【植】银杏,白果树 / ~ name

(子的)婚前姓,娘家姓

mail[1] [meil] *n.* 1. 邮件 2.〈主美〉[the ~]邮件的一次发送(或收集) 3. 邮政(一般用 post) 3.〈美〉邮递;邮政制度(英国用 post) 4. 邮递员,邮政工具(指邮车等) 5.(邮局间邮装运邮件的)邮袋 6.(苏格兰)袋;旅行包 —*vt.*〈美〉邮寄(英国用 post) ‖ '~box *n.*〈美〉邮筒;邮箱(收信人的)信箱 / ~ car(铁路)邮政车 / '~ man *n.*〈美〉邮递员(英国用 postman) / ~ order 函购,邮购

mail[2] [meil] *n.* 1. 锁子甲,铠甲 2.(龟等动物护身的)硬壳状甲片 3.(鹰的)丰满的胸羽 —*vt.* 使披上铠甲;给…装甲

maim [meim] *vt.* 残害;使伤残;使负重伤

main [mein] *n.* 1. 体力,力气;力量 2. 主要部分;要点 3.(自来水、煤气等的)总管道(电、铁路等的)干线 4.(诗)海洋,沧海 5.【船】主桅;(主桅上的)主帆 6. 大陆(对小岛和半岛而言) —*adj.* 1. 主要的;最重要的;总的 2. 尽力的,全力的 3.(与主帆或主桅)相近的;相接的 4.(英方)粗壮的,强大的;[用作状语]大体上;主要地 ‖ ~ chance 自身利益,私利 / '~land *n.* 大陆(对小岛和半岛而言) / '~mast *n.*【船】主桅 / '~sail *n.*【船】主帆 / '~ sheet *n.*【船】主帆帆脚索 / '~spring *n.* 1.(钟表的)主发条 2. 主要动机;主要动力;主要原因 / '~stay *n.* 1.【船】主桅支索 2. 主要依靠 / '~stream *n.* 1. 主流;主要倾向 —*vt.* 把(残疾儿童)纳入正规班级 把(残疾人)纳入正规工作岗位 / '~stream smoke(从烟支内直接进入抽烟者嘴里的)主流烟 / '~top *n.*【船】主桅上平台

Maine [mein] *n.* 缅因[美国州名]

maintain [men'tein] *vt.* 1. 维持,保持;继续 2. 维修,保养 3. 坚持;维护 4. 供

养，扶养 5. 〈坚决〉主张；强调

maintenance ['meintənəns] *n.* 1. 维持；保持 2. 维修，保养 3. 扶养；生活(费)；生计 4. 坚持；主张；拥护 5.【律】扶养(费)，赡养费；包摄诉讼罪

maitre d'hôtel [,metrədəu'tel]〈法〉总管；旅馆经理

maize [meiz] *n.* 1.〈主英〉玉蜀黍，玉米 2. 玉米色，黄色

Maj. *abbr.* Major

majestic [mə'dʒestik] *adj.* 雄伟的，壮丽的；庄严的，威严的；崇高的 ‖ ~ally *adv.*

majesty ['mædʒisti] *n.* 1. 雄伟，壮丽；庄严；崇高 2.〈帝王的〉威仪；尊严；威严 3. 君权；最高权力；君主 4.【M-】〈尊称〉陛下 5.【宗】〈上帝或基督的〉环以光轮的圣像

majolica [mə'jɔlikə, mə'dʒɔlikə] *n.*〈意大利〉花饰上釉陶器

major ['meidʒə] *adj.* 1. 较大的；较多的；较年长的；较重要的；较大范围的 2. 主要的 3.【专业课程中】主修的 4. 成年的 5. 严重的 6.【音】大调的，大音阶的 — *n.* 1. 成年人；长者 2.〈英〉陆军(或海军陆战队)少校；〈美〉陆空军、海军陆战队少校；【军俚】军士长 3.【逻】大项，大前提 4.【音】大调；大音阶 5.〈美〉〈大学中的〉主修科目，专业学生 — *vi.* 〈美〉主修，专攻(*in*) ‖ ~ **general**〈英〉陆军(或海军陆战队)少将；〈美〉陆军(或空军、海军陆战队)少将 / ~'**medical** *adj. & n.*〈美〉重病医疗保险(的)

majordomo [,meidʒə'dəuməu] *n.*〈复〉majordomos) *n.* 男管家；男总管；管理人

majorette [,meidʒə'ret] *n.* 军乐队女指挥(或队长)

majority [mə'dʒɔriti] *n.* 1. 多数；大多数；

半数以上 2. 得票多的党(或集团)，多数党；〈选举等中〉多得的票数 3. 成年；法定年龄 4.【军】少校级

make [meik] (made[meid]) *vt.* 1. 做，制造；建造；创造 2.〔和某些名词连用时，意义上等于相应的动词〕作出〈某种举动〉：~ a decision 作出决定 3. 写作；制定；订立 4. 造成；构成；组成；成为…的组成分子 5. 成为，变成 6. 使成为；使作为 7. 使上去或成为 8. 使得；迫使 9. 使适合；注定 9. 使成功；保证…飞黄腾达 10. 整理；布置；准备 11. 给…做；为…作成；为…提供(或准备) 12. 引起；产生 13. 认为，估计；抱有(怀疑、犹疑等) 14. 获得；挣得；赢得(比赛中)得(分) 15. 走；保持(航行等速度)；到达…；包括在行程内；赶上 16. 实行；进行 17. 总计；等于 18. 吃 19.【海】(开始)看见，发现 20.【电】使闭合；使接通 21.〈纸牌戏中〉洗(牌)；打满(叫牌数)；出(牌)胜一圈；胜(一圈) — *vi.* 1. 开始；似乎要 2. 前进；朝某方向走去；行进；指向；趋向 3.〈潮汐等〉增高；增大 4. 被制造；被处理 5.〔后接形容词，表示某种状态、方式〕~ sure 查明，弄确实〈纸牌戏中〉洗牌；〈口牌〉吃掉旁人的牌 — *n.* 1. 制造(法)；构造；样式；(产品)来源 2.〈矿井等某一期间的〉产量 3. 性情；品质；体格 4.【电】合拢；接通 5.〈口牌戏中〉(轮值)洗牌 ‖ ~-**be·lieve** *n.* 假装，假托；假装者) *adj.* 假装的；虚假的 / ~-**shift** *n.* 权宜之计；临时凑合的代用品 *adj.* 权宜的；临时凑合的 / ~-**up** *n.* 1. 组成；构造 2. 性格；特质；体格 3. 虚构，捏造 4. 补足；补充 5.〈演员的〉化装(术)；化妆用具；(妇女的)化妆(品) 6.〈学校的〉补考 7.【印】排版；拼版；(印刷品的)编排

maker ['meikə] *n.* 1. 创造者；【M-】【宗】

上帝 2. 制造者;制作者;制造商 3. 期票出票人 4. [电]接合器,接通器 5. (桥牌赛中)定王牌的人

making ['meikiŋ] *n.* 1. 制造,制作,形成;发展 2. 成功的原因(或手段) 3. [~s]素质;内在因素 4. [~s]赚头 5. 制造物;一次制造量 6. [~s]材料 7. [美俗][~s]卷纸烟用的纸和烟叶 8. [~s][矿]载槽煤粉

mal- *pref.* 1. 表示"坏","恶","不良":*mal*nutrition 2. 表示"不","非";"不当":*mal*adjusted

Malabo ['mɑːlɑːbəu] *n.* 马拉博(旧称 Santa Isabel 圣伊萨贝尔)[赤道几内亚首都]

Malacca [mə'lækə] *n.* 马六甲[马来西亚港市]:the Strait of ~ 马六甲海峡[亚洲东南部]

maladjusted [ˌmælə'dʒʌstid] *adj.* 1. 调节得不好的 2. (人)欲望与现实矛盾的;不适应环境的 3. [心]顺应不良的

maladjustment [ˌmælə'dʒʌstmənt] *n.* 1. 调节不良,失调 2. (人)不适应环境

maladminister [ˌmæləd'ministə] *vt.* 对...管理不善(或执行不公) ‖ *malad*ˌmini'stra·tion *n.*

maladroit [ˌmælə'drɔit] *adj.* 笨拙的

malady ['mælədi] *n.* 1. 病,疾病 2. 病态;堕落

malaise [mæ'leiz] *n.* 1. 不自在,不适;抑郁 2. 身体不适,心神不宁;浑身虚弱 3. 不安(或不满)意识

malaria [mə'lɛəriə] *n.* 1. [医]疟疾 2. (古)污浊(或有毒)的空气;瘴气

Malawi [mɑː'lɑːwi] *n.* 马拉维(旧称 Nyasaland 尼亚萨兰)[非洲东南部国家]

Malay [mə'lei, 'meilei] *n. & adj.* 马来人(的);马来语(的)

Malaya [mə'leiə] *n.* 1. 马来半岛[亚洲东南部] 2. 马来亚[马来西亚一地区]

Malaysia [mə'leiʃə] *n.* 1. 马来群岛[亚洲] 2. 马来西亚[东南亚国家]

malcontent ['mælkən,tent] *adj.* 心怀不满;不满现状的;反叛的 *n.* 心怀不满者;不满现状者;反叛者 ‖ ~ed *adj.* 不满(现状)的;反叛的

mal de mer [ˌmældə'mɛə] (法)晕船

Maldives ['mɔːldaivz] *n.* 马尔代夫(群岛)[亚洲岛国]

Male ['mɑːlei] *n.* 马累[马尔代夫首都]

male [meil] *adj.* 1. 男(性)的;公的,雄的 2. 由男子组成的 3. 雄壮刚劲的;有力的 4. (桶)雄的,只有堆蕊的 5. [机]阳的,凸形的,插入的 一 *n.* 男子;雄性动物;雄性植物 ‖ ~ness *n.* | ~ chauvinism 大男子主义 | ~ chauvinist 大男子主义者(的)

maledict ['mælidikt] *vt.* (书)咒骂;诽谤;憎恶 ‖ ˌmale'diction *n.*

malefactor ['mælifæktə] *n.* 罪犯;作恶者

malevolent [mə'levələnt] *adj.* 含有恶意的;恶毒的 ‖ malevolence *n.*

malfeasance [mæl'fiːzəns] *n.* 渎职;违法乱纪

malformation [ˌmælfɔː'meiʃən] *n.* 畸形(体);变形(体)

malformed [mæl'fɔːmd] *adj.* 畸形的;变形的

Mali ['mɑːliː] *n.* 马里[西非国家]

malice ['mælis] *n.* 1. 恶意;怨恨 2. 蓄意犯罪(或害人);[律]恶意,预谋

malicious [mə'liʃəs] *adj.* 1. 恶意的,恶毒的 2. 蓄意的;[律]恶意的 ‖ ~ly *adv.*

malign [mə'lain] *adj.* 1. 有害的;邪恶的 2. 恶意的,恶毒的 3. [医]恶性的,致命的;癌的 一 *vt.* 诽谤,中伤,诬蔑

malignancy [mə'lignənsi] *n.* 1. 恶意;恶毒行为 2.【医】恶性;[常作 malignancies]恶性肿瘤

malignant [mə'lignənt] *adj.* 1. 恶意的,恶毒的 2. 有害的;邪恶的 3.【医】恶性的,致命的;癌的 ‖ ～ly *adv.*

malinger [mə'liŋgə] *vi.* (尤指逃避工作)诈病,装病 ‖ ～er *n.*

mallard ['mæləd] ([复] mallard(s)) *n.* 1.【动】绿头鸭(雄);绿头鸭肉

malleable ['mæliəbl] *adj.* 1.(金属)有延展性的,可锻的,韧性的 2.(性格)柔顺的,顺从的;易适应的;可训练的 ‖ ,mallea'bility, ～ness *n.*

mallet ['mælit] *n.* 1. 大头锤 2.(槌球的)木槌;(马球的)球棍

mallow ['mæləu] *n.*【植】锦葵

malnutrition [,mælnju:'triʃən] *n.* 营养不良

malodorous [mæl'əudərəs] *adj.* 难闻的,恶臭的

malpractice [,mæl'præktis] *n.* 1. 不端行为;营私舞弊;玩忽职守,渎职 2. 治疗失当;失职行为

malt [mɔːlt] *n.* 1. 麦芽 2. 麦芽酒;啤酒 3. 麦乳精 —*vt.* 使成麦芽;用麦芽(或麦精)处理(或调制) —*vi.*(麦芽)发芽;制麦芽 ‖ ～ed milk 麦乳精(饮料)

Malta ['mɔːltə] *n.* 马耳他[欧洲岛国](在地中海中部)

maltose ['mɔːltəus] *n.* 麦芽糖

maltreat [mæl'tri:t] *vt.* 1. 粗暴地对待;虐待 2. 乱用,滥用(机器等) ‖ ～ment *n.*

mam [mæm], **mama, mamma** [mə'mɑː] *n.*〈儿语〉妈妈

mammal ['mæməl] *n.* 哺乳动物

mammary ['mæməri] *adj.*【解】乳房的;乳腺的;乳房样的

mammon ['mæmən] *n.* 1. 钱财 2. 贪欲,贪财

mammoth ['mæməθ] *n.* 1. 猛犸,毛象(已绝种的古代哺乳动物) 2. 巨物,庞然大物 —*adj.* 巨大的,庞大的

mammy ['mæmi] *n.*〈儿语〉妈妈 2.〈美〉(给白人照顾小孩的)黑人保姆;保姆

man [mæn] ([复] men [men]) *n.* 1. 人(指男人或女人);个人;(任何)人 2. [单][不用冠词]人类;[生]人科 3. 成年男子;男子汉;男子气概 4. 丈夫;〈方〉(男)情人 5.【史】封臣;佃户;侍从;部下;男仆 6. [men]雇工;雇员 7. [men]士兵;水手 8. [用在主代词后]合适的对象 9.(亲热、戏谑的称呼)老兄,伙计 10. [表示不耐烦、轻蔑等的感叹语] Nonsense!, ～ 胡扯! 11. [the M-或 the ～]〈美俚〉白人社会;白人现存统治体制;法律;执法史;警察;私人侦探;老板;乐队领队 12. 球队队员 13. 棋子 —(manned; manning) *vt.* 1. 给…配备人员 2. 在…就位;操纵 3. 使增强勇气;使振作精神 ‖ '～-day *n.* 人工作日,人工日(即一人一天完成的工作量) /'～-hole *n.*(进入人孔(指锅炉等的修理入口等)) /'～-'made *adj.* 人造的,人工的 /'～-of-'war *n.* 军舰 /'～-power *n.* 人力;劳动力;劳动力 /'～servant *n.* 男仆,男用 /'～-slaughter *n.* 杀人【律】过失杀人,非预谋的杀人罪

manacle ['mænəkl] *n.* [常～s] 1. 手铐;束缚 —*vt.* 给…上手铐;束缚

manage ['mænidʒ] *vt.* 1. 管理;处理;经营;安排 2. 运用;操纵;控制;驾驭 3. 设法;〈谑〉弄得 4.〈口〉(常与 can, could, be able to 连用)对付;吃 —*vi.* 处理,办理;设法对付 ‖ ～able *adj.*

management ['mænidʒmənt] *n.* 1. 管理；处理；经营；安排 2. 运用；操纵；驾驭 3. 手段；经营手腕；经营才能 4.〈工商企业的〉管理部门；资方

manager ['mænidʒə] *n.* 1. 经理；管理人；干事；当家人 2.〈英〉（议会中）处理两院共同事务的委员 3.〈英〉〈律〉（法院指定的）财务管理人 ‖ ~**ial** [ˌmæni'dʒiəriəl] *adj.* / ~**ship** *n.* 经理的职位（或权力）

Managua [mə'nɑːgwə] *n.* 马那瓜［尼加拉瓜首都］

Manama [mə'nɑːmə] *n.* 麦纳麦［巴林首都］

mañana [mɑː'njɑːnɑː]〈西〉*adv.* & *n.* 明天；来日；（在）将来某个不确定时刻

Manchester ['mæntʃistə] *n.* 1. 曼彻斯特［英国英格兰西北部城市］ 2.〈英〉棉织物

Manchuria [mæn'tʃuəriə] *n.* 满洲（我国东北的旧称）

mandarin[1] ['mændərin] *n.* 1.【史】（中国清朝九品及九品以上的）官员 2. 官话（旧时欧美人指的北京方言）3. 高官贵人 — *adj.* 1.（服装）中国式紧身马褂的 2.（作品风格）过分文雅的

mandarin[2] ['mændərin], **mandarine** ['mændərin] *n.* 柑橘(= ~ orange)；柑橘树(= ~ tree)

mandate ['mændeit] *n.* 1. 命令；训令 2. 委任；(前国际联盟的)委任统治权；托管地 3.（选民对选出的代表、议会等的）授权 4.【律】（上级法院给下级法院的）指令，执行令（英国法律中的）私人财产委托；（罗马法中的）委任契约）；代理契约 — *vt.* 把（某地区）置于委任统治下；托管

mandatory ['mændətəri] *adj.* 1. 命令的；

训令的 2. 强制性的；义务的 3. 受（前国际联盟）委托的；受托管理的 一 *n.* 受托管理国；受命者；受托者

mandible ['mændibl] *n.* 1.【动】（昆虫的）上颚；（鸟喙的）上（或下）部 2.【解】下颌骨

mandolin ['mændəlin], **mandoline** ['mændəliːn] *n.* 曼陀林（琴）（一种琵琶类乐器）

mandrake ['mændreik] *n.*【植】1. 曼德拉草；曼德拉草根（旧时用作药物）2. 盾叶鬼臼

mandrel ['mændril] *n.*【机】心轴

mandrill ['mændril] *n.*【动】山魈

mane [mein] *n.* 1.（马、狮等的）鬃毛 2.（人的）长而密的头发 ‖ ~**d** *adj.* 有鬃毛的；长着长而密的头发的

maneuver [mə'nuːvə] *n.*, *vi.* & *vt.*〈美〉 = manoeuvre

maneuverable [mə'nuːvərəbl] *adj.*〈美〉 = manoeuvrable

manful ['mænful] *adj.* 大丈夫气概的；勇敢的；坚定的，果敢的 ‖ ~**ly** *adv.* / ~**ness** *n.*

manganese [ˌmæŋgə'niːz, 'mæŋgəniːz] *n.*【化】锰

mange [meindʒ] *n.* 兽疥癣，家畜疥

manger ['meindʒə] *n.*（马、牛等的）食槽

mangle[1] ['mæŋgl] *vt.* 1. 乱切；乱砍；(用拳等)乱打；弄伤 2.（因大错而）损坏；弄糟；（因乱发音）使无法听懂

mangle[2] ['mæŋgl] *n.*【纺】轧液机，碾光机，轧布机 — *vt.* 把（布等）送入轧布机中轧压

mango ['mæŋgəu]（[复]mango(e)s）*n.* 1. 芒果树；芒果 2. 灯笼椒；狮头辣椒 3.（灯笼椒等制成的）泡菜

mangrove ['mæŋgrəuv] *n.*【植】红树

mangy ['meindʒi] *adj.* 1.(兽、畜)患疥癣的 2. 污秽的;褴褛的

manhandle ['mæn,hændl] *vt.* 1. 用人力搬动(或操作) 2. 粗暴地对待

Manhattan [mæn'hætən] *n.* 1. 曼哈顿(美国东部哈得孙河口的岩岛,为纽约市中心) 2.[亦作 m-]曼哈顿鸡尾酒

manhood ['mænhud] *n.* 1.(男子的)成年;成年期 2. 男子气概;勇气;刚毅 3.[总称]男子

mania ['meiniə] *n.* 1.[医]躁狂;狂 2. 狂热,癖好

maniac ['meiniæk] *adj.* 1.[医]躁狂的 2. 疯狂的 3. 狂热的;狂乱的 —*n.* 1.[医]躁狂(症)者 2. 疯子,狂人

maniacal [mə'naiəkəl] *adj.* = maniac

manic ['mænik, 'meinik] 【医】*adj.* 躁狂的 —*n.* 躁狂者

manicure ['mænikjuə] *n.* 1. 修指甲(包括修剪、洗净、涂染指甲) 2. = manicurist —*vt.* 1. 修…的指甲;为…修指甲;修剪;修平 ‖ **manicurist** *n.* 指甲修剪师

manifest ['mænifest] *n.* 1. 明显的;明显的 —*vt.* 1. 表明;证明 2. 显示,表现(人的品质、感情等) 3. 把…记在船货清单上(=~ oneself) 4.显出(= ~ oneself)(事物、现象等)出现,显露 —*vi.* (鬼等)出现,显露 —*n.* 1. 显示,表白 2. 宣言 3.(飞机或船的)旅客名单,舱单 4. 快运货车;列车编组顺序单

manifestation [,mænifes'teiʃən] *n.* 1. 表明;表现形式;现象 2.(鬼魂的)显灵 3.(政府或政党的)示威行动

manifesto [,mæni'festəu] 〔复〕 manifesto(e)s) *n.* 宣言;声明 —*vi.* 发表宣言(或声明)

manifold ['mænifəuld] *adj.* 1. 多样的;种种的;多方面的 2. 多种特征(或用途)

的;同时具有多种功能的;作成多份的;由同类的几部分组成的 3. 许许多多的 —*n.* 复写本 —*vt.* 复写

manikin ['mænikin] *n.* 1. 矮人,侏儒 2. 人体模型 3.(时装)模特儿

Manil(l)a [mə'nilə] *n.* 1. 马尼拉〔菲律宾首都〕 2. 吕宋烟(马尼拉产的雪茄烟) 3. 吕宋绳,白棕绳(= ~ rope) 4. 马尼拉麻(= ~ hemp) 5. 马尼拉纸(以马尼拉麻为原料的包装纸)(= ~ paper)

manipulate [mə'nipjuleit] *vt.* 1. 熟练地使用;操作;处理;操纵 2. 操纵;摆布 3. 应付;(巧妙地)处置 4. 窜改;伪造(账目等) ‖ **ma·nipu'lation** *n.* / **manipulator** *n.*

mankind *n.* 1. 用作单或复〕1.[mæn'kaind] 人类 2.['mænkaind] 男子,男性

manly ['mænli] *adj.* 1. 男子气概的;雄赳赳的;果断的 2. 适合男子的 3.(女子)有男子气的 —*adv.* 男子般地;雄赳赳地;果断地 ‖ **manliness** *n.*

manna ['mænə] *n.* 1. 吗哪(基督教《圣经》中所说古以色列人经过旷野时获得的神赐食物) 2. 意外收获;精神食粮 3. 甘露,木蜜

manned [mænd] *adj.* 载人的;由人操纵的

mannequin ['mænikin] *n.* 人体模型;时装模特儿

manner ['mænə] *n.* 1. 方式;样式;方法 2.[~s]礼貌;规矩 3. 态度;举止;风度 4. 习惯 5.[~s]风俗;(文艺上的)风格;手法 7. 种类 ‖ ~ly *adj. & adv.* 有礼貌的(地);谦恭的(地)

mannerism ['mænərizəm] *n.* 1.(文艺上)对独特风格的过分强调(或偏爱) 2.(说话、举止的)癖性;习气

mannish ['mænɪʃ] *adj.* (女子)男子似的;(孩子)大人似的 ‖ **~ly** *adv.* / **~ness** *n.*

manoeuvrable [mə'nu:vrəbl] *adj.* 1. 机动的;可调动的 2. 操纵灵活的 ‖ **manoeuvra'bility** *n.* 1. 机动性 2. (船只、飞机、车辆的)操纵的灵活性

manoeuvre [mə'nu:və] *n.* 1. (部队等的)调动;机动;(船只、飞机、车辆的)机动动作 2. [~s][军]对抗演习 3. 策略;花招 — *vi.* 1. (部队等)实施调动;演习 2. 用策略;耍花招 — *vt.* 1. 调动;使演习 2. 诱使 3. (敏捷地)操纵;使(飞机)作持续飞行

manor ['mænə] *n.* 1. 庄园;庄园主宅第 2. [英史]采地,采邑 ‖ **-ial** [mə'nɔ:riəl] *adj.*

mansard ['mænsɑ:d] *n.* [建]复斜屋顶

manse [mæns] *n.* 牧师住宅

mansion ['mænʃən] *n.* 1. 大厦,大楼 2. 宅第;官邸 3. [主英][常~s]公寓大厦(大楼中的)一套房间 5. [天]宿;黄道带

mantel ['mæntl] *n.* 1. 壁炉架;壁炉台 ‖ **'~piece**, **'~shelf** *n.* 壁炉台

mantilla [mæn'tilə] *n.* 1. (西班牙等妇女戴的)丝面纱;薄头罩;黑丝披巾;晚礼服斗篷

mantis ['mæntis] ([复] mantises 或 mantes ['mæntiz]) *n.* 螳螂

mantle ['mæntl] *n.* 1. 披风,斗篷 2. 覆盖物;罩幕 3. (煤气灯的)白炽罩 4. (高炉的)炉身 5. 壁炉架 6. [地]地幔 7. 【解】外套 8. (鸟等的)套膜;(鸟的)翕 — *vi.* (用披风等)盖,罩,覆盖 — *vi.* 1. (液体)表面上结皮;被盖上泡沫 2. 笼罩(windows);(血液上)脸)发红,涨红 4. (鹰)展开翅膀

mantra ['mæntrə] *n.* (印度教等的)曼特罗,祷文,符咒

manual ['mænjuəl] *adj.* 1. 手的;用手(操作)的;手工做的 ‖ **~ training**(学校等的)手工课(或手艺训练)2. 体力的 3. 【律】实际占有的 — *n.* 1. 手册,便笺,指南 2. (风琴等的)键盘 3. (兵器)教范 ‖ **~ism** *n.* (对聋哑人的)手(势)语教学 / **~ly** *adv.* 用手;用手工操作;人工地

manufactory [ˌmænju'fæktəri] *n.* 制造厂,工厂

manufacture [ˌmænju'fæktʃə] *vt.* 1. (大量)制造;加工 2. 粗制滥造 3. 捏造,虚构(证据、借口等)— *vi.* 制造 — *n.* 1. (大量)制造 2. 制造业,产品 4. (文艺作品等的)粗制滥造

manufacturer [ˌmænju'fæktʃərə] *n.* 1. 制造人;制造商,工厂主 2. 制造厂(或公司)

manure [mə'njuə] *n.* (人、畜的)粪,粪肥;肥料 — *vt.* 给(土地)施肥;施肥于

manuscript ['mænjuskript] *n.* 手稿;打字稿;底稿,原稿;手写本

many ['meni] (more [mɔ:], most [məust]) *adj.* [后接复数名词]许多的,多的 — *pron.* [用作复]许多人(或物);许多 — *n.* [用作复]多数;[the ~]许多人;群众

map [mæp] *n.* 1. 地图 2. 天体图 3. (类似地图的)图 4. [美俚]面孔 5. [美俚](存款不足的)空头支票 (mapped; mapping) *vt.* 1. 绘制…的地图;在地图上标示出 2. (为制地图而)勘测 3. (详细地)制订;筹划 (out)

maple ['meipl] *n.* 1. 【植】槭树,枫树 2. 槭木 3. 槭树汁味;槭糖味 4. 淡棕色;灰黄色 ‖ **~ sugar** 槭糖 / **~ syrup** 槭树浆,槭树汁

Maputo [məˈpuːtəu] *n.* 马普托[莫桑比克首都]

mar [mɑː] (marred; marring) *vt.* 损坏,毁坏;弄糟

Mar. *abbr.* March

maraschino [ˌmærəˈskiːnəu] ([复] maraschinos) *n.* 1. 黑樱桃酒 2. 酒浸樱桃

marathon [ˈmærəθən] *n.* [有时作 M-] 【体】马拉松赛跑(全长 42.195 公里) 2.(游泳、滑冰等的)长距离比赛;耐力比赛 3. 持久的活动(或事件) — *adj.* [有时作 M-] 马拉松式的;耐力的 — *vi.* 参加马拉松赛跑;参加马拉松式的活动(或比赛)

maraud [məˈrɔːd] *vi.*, *vt.* & *n.* 抢劫,掠夺 ‖ ~er *n.*

marble [ˈmɑːbl] *n.* 1. 大理石,大理岩,云石;大理石制品 2. 大理石状的东西 3. 大理石花纹 4.(小孩玩的用玻璃、石头等做的)弹子[~s]用作单]打弹子游戏 — *adj.* 大理石的;大理石般的 — *vt.* 常用被动语态之]把(书边、纸等)弄上大理石花纹

March [mɑːtʃ] *n.* 三月(略作 Mar.)

march [mɑːtʃ] *vi.* 1.(齐步)前进;行进;行军 2. 走过,通过 3. 进行,进展 — *vt.* 使行进;使行军;迫使前进 — *n.* 1. 行进;行军;(部队一日的)行程 2. 进展 3.[the ~]进行,进展 4. 长途跋涉 5. 进行曲

marchioness [ˈmɑːʃənis] *n.* 侯爵夫人;女侯爵

mare [meə] *n.* 牝马,母马;母驴

margarine [ˌmɑːdʒəˈriːn] *n.* 麦淇淋,人造黄油

margin [ˈmɑːdʒin] *n.* 1. 页边空白;栏外 2. 边缘 3. 界限 4.(时间、金钱上保留的)余地,余裕 5. 差数;幅度 6.【商】(成本与售价的)差额,赚头;保证金,垫头 — *vt.* 1. 加边于;成为…的边 2. 加旁注于 3.【商】为…付保证金

marginal [ˈmɑːdʒinəl] *adj.* 1. 记在页边的;在页边的 2. 边缘的;边际的;边沿地区的 3. 介乎两者之间的;(文化等)部分结合而未完全同化的 4. 临界的;勉强够格的;(土地)贫瘠的;收益仅敷支出的

marguerite [ˌmɑːɡəˈriːt] *n.* 【植】1. 木茼蒿 2. 雏菊 3. 春黄菊

Mariana [ˌmæriˈɑːnə] **Islands , Marianas** [ˌmæriˈɑːnəz] 马里亚纳群岛[西太平洋]

marigold [ˈmæriɡəuld] *n.* 【植】1. 金盏花 2. 万寿菊

marijuana [ˌmæriˈhwɑːnə] , **marihuana** [ˌmæriˈhwɑːnə] *n.* 1.【植】大麻 2. 大麻叶和花,大麻烟;大麻毒品

marimba [məˈrimbə] *n.*【音】马林巴琴,木琴

marina [məˈriːnə] *n.*(供小船停泊、补充物资和修理等的)小艇船坞(或小艇)港池

marinade [ˌmæriˈneid] *n.* 腌泡计,腌泡的鱼(或肉) — [ˈmæriˌneid] *vt.* 把…腌泡在腌泡汁中

marinate [ˈmæriˌneit] *vt.*(烹饪前)把…浸泡于盐水(或醋等腌泡汁)中;使受浸泡 — *vi.* 浸泡,腌泡

marine [məˈriːn] *adj.* 1. 海的,海产的 2. 船舶的;船用的;航海的 3. 海上的;海事的;海运的 4. 海军陆战队的 — *n.* 1.[只用单][总称]海(或船)舶 2. 海军陆战队士兵(或军官);(英)两栖突击作战专家 3.(法国等国家的)海军部 4. 春景画 5.(美俚)空酒瓶 ‖ **Marine Corps**(美国)海军陆战队

mariner [ˈmærinə] *n.* 水手;海员;航海者

marionette [ˌmæriəˈnet] *n.* 活动木偶；牵线木偶

marital [ˈmæritl] *adj.* 婚姻的；夫妻的 ‖ ～ly *adv.*

maritime [ˈmæritaim] *adj.* 1. 海(上)的；海事的；海运的 2. 沿海的；近海的 3. 海员的

marjoram [ˈmɑːdʒərəm] *n.*【植】牛至菜

mark¹ [mɑːk] *n.* 1. 痕迹；斑点；瘢疤 2. 符号；标记；唛头；商标；邮戳 3. 标识；刻度；【海】(测深线上的)测标；【船】载重线位置 4.(文件上代替签名的)花押 5.(考试等的)分数；(品行等的)等第 6. 标志；特征 7. 靶子；目标；指标 8. 标准；常态 9. 量度；名次 10.(深刻的)印象；影响 12. 起跑线 13.(拳击用语)心窝 14.【史】(中世纪日耳曼村社的)公地 15. [M-](与数字连用表示武器的)型，式 — *vt.* 1. 留痕迹于；在…作记号于，标明 2.(用记号等的)(常用主动语态的)(人、动物等身上)具有(斑纹等)3. 明显表示，表明 4. 标志；表示…的特征 5. 记下；注意；留心 6. 给(试卷等)打分数 8. 在…上贴价目(或尺寸等)标签 9. 给(比赛等)记得分 10. 使注定要；记录 11. 标明…的界限 12. [英](球赛中)钉(人)— *vi.* 1. 作记号(或符号)2. 注意 3.(比赛中)记得分

mark² [mɑːk] *n.* 1. 马克(德国、芬兰的货币单位)2. 金银重量单位(约等于 8 盎司，旧时用于欧洲大陆)

marked [mɑːkt] *adj.* 1. 打上记号的；有标记的，有唛头的 2. 显著的；清楚的 3. 被监视的；受人注目的 ‖ ～ly *adv.*

marker [ˈmɑːkə] *n.* 1. 打记号(或分数)的人 2.(比赛中)记分员，记分器；【休】得分 3. 书签 4. 纪念碑；墓碑；里程碑 5. 标识，标志【空】指点标 6.【军】

market [ˈmɑːkit] *n.* 1. 市场；商业中心 2. 集市；集市场；集市日；商品买卖 3. 食品店 4. 市面，市况；行情，市价 5. 行销地区；销路；需求 — *vt.* (在市场上)销售 — *vi.* (在市场上)买卖(或卖出) ‖ ～able *adj.* ‖ ～place *n.* 市场

marking [ˈmɑːkiŋ] *n.* 1. 打记号；作标志；记分 2. 记号；识别标志 3.(兽皮、鸟羽等的)斑纹

marksman [ˈmɑːksmən] ([复] marksmen) *n.* 1. 射手；神射手 2.〈美〉【军】二等射手 ‖ ～ship *n.* 射击术，枪法

markup [ˈmɑːkʌp] *n.* 涨价；提高标价

marlin [ˈmɑːlin] ([复] marlin(s)) *n.* 枪鱼；青枪鱼

marmalade [ˈmɑːməleid] *n.* 果酱；橘子酱；柠檬酱

marmoset [ˈmɑːməzet] *n.*【动】狨(产于美洲的小型长尾猴)

marmot [ˈmɑːmət] *n.*【动】旱獭，土拨鼠

maroon¹ [məˈruːn] *n.* 1. 栗色，紫酱色 2. 爆竹，鞭炮 — *adj.* 栗色的，紫酱色的

maroon² [məˈruːn] *n.* 1.(17-18 世纪居住在西印度群岛等地的)逃亡黑奴(或其后代)2. 被放逐到孤岛的人 — *vt.* 1. 把…放逐到孤岛(或无人烟的海滩)；使处于孤立无援(或无法逃脱)的境地 — *vi.* 1. 从奴役下逃亡 2. 闲荡 3.〈美〉去野营；去野餐

marquee [mɑːˈkiː] *n.*【建】大门罩，大帐幕

marquis, marquess [ˈmɑːkwis] *n.* 侯爵

marquise [mɑːˈkiːz] *n.* 1. 侯爵夫人；女侯爵(用于英国以外的国家，在英国用 marchioness)2. 大帐篷 3. 橄榄形宝石(或数颗宝石镶成那形座)的戒指

marquisette [ˌmɑːkiˈzet] *n.* [纺]薄罗纱

marriage [ˈmæridʒ] *n.* 1. 结婚；婚姻，婚

姻生活 2. 结婚仪式，婚礼 3. 密切结合 ‖ ~**able** *adj.*

married ['mærid] *adj.* 1. 结了婚(而未表偶或离婚)的，有配偶的；夫妇的；婚姻的 2. 密切结合的

marrow ['mærəu] *n.* 1. 髓，骨髓；脊髓 2. 精髓，精华；实质 3. 活力，生气 4.【植】西葫芦

marry ['mæri] *vt.* 1. 娶；嫁；和…结婚 2. [常用被动语态] 使成婚 3. 把(女儿等)嫁出；为… 娶亲 4.(牧师等)为…证婚 5. 使密切结合；(海)(不增加圈长)插接(绳端) —*vi.* 结婚；结合

Mars [mɑːz] *n.* 1.【天】火星 2.【罗神】马耳斯，战神 3. 战争

Marseillaise [ˌmɑːsə'leiz]〈法〉 *n.* 马赛曲(法国国歌)

Marseilles [mɑː'sei, mɑː'seilz] *n.* 马赛[法国东南部港市]

marsh [mɑːʃ] *n.* 沼泽，湿地 ‖ ~ **mallow** *n.* 1.【植】药用蜀葵 2. 果浆软糖 / ~ **marigold** *n.* 驴蹄草，西洋樱草

marshal ['mɑːʃəl] *n.* 1. 元帅；陆军元帅；相当于陆军元帅的其他军种将领；最高级指挥官；(英)空军元帅 2.(集合的)司仪；(宫廷的)典礼官 3.【史】(中古时期王室的)司令官；宫内司法官 4.【军】宪兵主任 5.(美国)联邦司法区执法官；市执法官；市警察局长；消防队长 ‖ ~(marshal(l)ed; marshal(l)ing) *vt.* 1. 排列，安排；整理 2.(讲究礼节地)引领 3. 将(列车)编组 —*vi.* 排列；集合

Marshall ['mɑːʃəl] **Islands** 马绍尔群岛[西太平洋]

marshy ['mɑːʃi] *adj.* 沼泽般的；生于沼泽的；湿软的

marsupial [mɑː'sjuːpiəl] *adj.*【动】有袋(目)的 2. 袋状的 —*n.* 有袋(目)动物

mart [mɑːt] *n.* 商业中心；市场；拍卖场

marten ['mɑːtin] ([复] marten(s)) *n.* 1.【动】貂 2. 貂(毛)皮

martial ['mɑːʃəl] *adj.* 1. 军事的；战争的 2. 军人的，英勇的；尚武的 3.[M-]【罗神】战神的 4.【天】火星的 ‖ ~ **art**(柔道、空手道、拳术等)(东方)武术 / ~ **law** 军事管制法，戒严令

Martian ['mɑːʃən] *adj.* 1.【天】火星的 2.【罗神】战神的 3.(假想的)火星人的 —*n.*(假想的)火星人

martin ['mɑːtin] *n.*【动】圣马丁鸟；紫崖燕；毛脚燕；燕科小鸟(如岩燕、雨燕等)

martinet [ˌmɑːti'net, 'mɑːtinet] *n.* 严格执行纪律的人

martini [mɑː'tiːni] *n.* 马提尼酒(一种用杜松子酒、苦艾酒等混合而成的鸡尾酒)

martyr ['mɑːtə] *n.* 1. 烈士，殉难者 2. 殉教者，殉道者 3.(因疾病等)长期受痛苦的人 —*vt.* 1. 处死(坚持信仰者)；使殉难 2. 折磨 ‖ ~**dom** *n.* 殉难；牺牲 2. 折磨；苦难

marvel ['mɑːvəl] *n.* 1. 令人惊奇的事物；(某一事物的)奇特的例子(*of*) 2.〈古〉惊异，惊奇 —(marvel(l)ed; marvel(l)ing) *vi.* 惊异，惊奇(*at*) —*vt.* 对…感到惊异

marvel(l)ous ['mɑːvələs] *adj.* 1. 奇异的，奇迹般的，惊人的，不可思议的 2.〈口〉不起的，绝妙的 ‖ ~**ly** *adv.*

Marxian ['mɑːksiən] *adj.* & *n.* = Marxist

Marxism ['mɑːksizəm] *n.* 马克思主义

Marxist ['mɑːksist] *adj.* 1. 马克思的 2. 马克思主义的 —*n.* 马克思主义者

Maryland ['meərilænd] *n.* 马里兰[美国州名]

mas(c). *abbr.* masculine

mascara [mæs'ka:rə] *n*. 染睫毛(或眉毛)膏 —*vt*. 在…上涂染睫毛(或眉毛)膏

mascot ['mæskət] *n*. (被认为能带来好运气的)吉祥物

masculine ['mæskjulin] *adj*. 1. 男性的；男子气概的 2. (女子)有男子气的 3. (组织、行业等)由男子组成(或控制)的 4. [语]阳性的 —*n*. 1. 男性的东西 2. 男子 3. [语]阳性；阳性词(或短语) ‖ ~ly *adv*. / ~ness, ,mascu'linity *n*.

Maseru ['mæzəru:] *n*. 马塞卢[莱索托首都]

mash [mæʃ] *n*. 1. 麦芽浆(啤酒原料) 2. 谷糠(或麦麸等)煮成的饲料 3. 捣成糊状的东西 4. [俚]马蛤薯泥 4. 乱糟糟的一堆 —*vt*. 1. 把(捣碎的麦芽等)制成麦芽浆 2. 捣碎；捣烂；压碎

mashie ['mæʃi] *n*. (高尔夫球的)5号铁头球棒

mask [mɑ:sk] *n*. 1. 面具，面罩；防护面具；口罩 2. 假面具；伪装；遮盖物；遮蔽物 3. (作建筑装饰等用的)假面；面部模型 4. 假面舞会；假面剧；假面剧剧本 5. 戴假面具的人 6. [印]蒙片 [摄]蔽光框 7. [军]掩蔽，掩蔽物 8. [印]头 [动]蟑螂的脸盖 —*vt*. 1. 在(脸)上戴面具 2. 掩饰(感情等)；伪装；遮蔽 3. 阻拦(敌人)行动；妨碍(某军)射击 4. 使…不被觉察 5. [摄]用蔽光框修改(照相的大小、形状等) [印](制版时)用蒙片修正(底片色调) —*vi*. 1. 戴面具；化装；参加假面舞会 2. 掩饰；伪装起来

masochism ['mæsəkizəm] *n*. (性)受虐狂 ‖ **masochist** *n*. (性)受虐狂者

mason ['meisn] *n*. 1. 石工；砖石工；泥瓦工，圬工 2. [M-]共济会会员 —*vt*. 用石料建造；用石加固 ‖ ~ry *n*. 1. 石工

(业)；圬工(业) 2. 砖石建筑 3. [M-]共济会纲领；共济会仪式；[总称]共济会成员

masque [mɑ:sk] *n*. 1. 假面舞会 2. (英国 16-17 世纪流行的)假面剧；假面剧剧本

masquerade [,mæskə'reid, ,mɑ:skə'reid] *n*. 1. 化装舞会；化装聚会 2. 化装舞会上穿的服装 3. 伪装；掩饰 —*vi*. 1. 化装；参加化装舞会(或聚会) 2. 假装；冒充 ‖ ~r *n*. 参加化装舞会(或聚会)者；伪装者

Mass, mass[1] [mæs, mɑ:s] *n*. [宗]弥撒；弥撒曲

mass[2] [mæs] *n*. 1. (聚成一体的)团，块，堆，片，群 2. 众多；大量；大宗 3. [the ~s]群众，民众 4. 主体；主要部分 5. [军]密集队形 6. [物]质量 7. [矿]体 —*adj*. 1. 群众的，民众的；群众性的 2. 大量的，大批的；大批的 3. 整个的，总的 —*vt*. 集中，聚集 —*vi*. 集聚 ‖ ~less *adj*. [物]无质量的 ‖ ~, produce *vt*. 成批生产

Massachusetts [,mæsə'tʃusits] *n*. 马萨诸塞(旧译麻省)[美国州名]；‖ Institute of Technology(美国)马萨诸塞理工学院，麻省理工学院

massacre ['mæsəkə] *n*. 1. 大屠杀；残杀 2. (牲畜的)成批屠宰 —*vt*. (大规模地)屠杀，残杀

massage ['mæsɑ:ʒ] *n*. 按摩；推拿 —*vt*. 给(某人或身体某部位)按摩(或推拿) ‖ ~r *n*. 按摩师；按摩器

masseur [mæ'sə:] *n*. 男按摩师

masseuse [mæ'sə:z] *n*. 女按摩师

massive ['mæsiv] *adj*. 1. 大而重的，厚实的(面貌五官等)粗大的 2. 魁伟的，结实的；给人深刻印象的 3. 大规模的，巨大的；大量的 4. (金银器等)实心

的 5.[地]块状的；(成层岩)以厚层出现的 6.[矿]均匀构造的，非晶质的

massy ['mæsi] *adj.* 1. 大而重的，厚实的；[物]有质量的 2. 实心的 3. 大而浓密的

mast[mɑːst] *n.* 1. 桅杆，船桅，旗杆 2. 杆，柱；天线杆 —*vt.* 在…上装桅杆

master ['mɑːstə] *n.* 1.(男)主人，主子；户主；雇主；(商船的)船长 2. 师傅；能手；优秀者；获胜者 3. 男教师；(学院的)院长 4. 大师；名家；名家作品 5.[M-]硕士 6.[M-](用在人名前作称呼)…少爷；(苏格兰)少爷；(用于对长子男爵的)长子 7.(用于职位名称)长，官 8.[the M-][宗]耶稣基督，主；[常作 M-]宗教领袖 9.[机]主导装置，母机 11. 唱片模版；(录音或录像的)原版，母(磁)带 —*adj.* 1. 主人的；支配的，统治的 2. 精通的，熟练的；优秀的 3. 主要的；总的 —*vt.* 1. 做…的主人 2. 控制；统治；制服 3. 精通，掌握 ‖ **~key** 1. 万能钥匙 2.(解决困难、争论等的)关键 / **~ piece**, '**~ piece** *n.* 杰作；名作；绝无仅有的人(或事物) / **~sergeant** (美国陆军、空军、海军陆战队的)军士长 / **~stroke** *n.* 绝招，高招；妙的表现；妙策

masterful ['mɑːstəful] *adj.* 1. 好支配人的，专横的 2. 熟练的；巧妙的；名家的 ‖ **~ly** *adv.*

masterly ['mɑːstəli] *adj.* 熟练的；高明的 —*adv.* 熟练地；巧妙地；高明地

mastermind ['mɑːstəmaind] *n.* 1. 才子，才华横溢的人 2. 出谋划策的人 —*vt.* 策划

mastery ['mɑːstəri] *n.* 1. 控制；统治；优势；优胜 3. 精通；掌握

masthead ['mɑːsthed] *n.* 1. 桅顶 2.(报刊

上载有报刊名称、发行人姓名、广告收费率、订费等的)刊头 —*vt.* 1. 派(水手)登桅顶；罚(水手)登桅顶 2. 把(帆)升至桅顶

masticate ['mæstikeit] *vt.* 1. 咀嚼 2. 塑炼(橡胶等) —*vi.* 1. 咀嚼 2.(橡胶)塑炼 ‖ **masti'cation** *n.*

mastiff ['mæstif] *n.*[动]獒，大驯犬

mastodon ['mæstədɔn] *n.* 1. 乳齿象(古哺乳动物) 2. 巨人；庞然大物

mastoid ['mæstɔid] *n.* 1.[解]乳突 2.〈口〉[医]乳突炎(手术)

masturbate ['mæstəbeit] *vt.* & *vi.* (对…)行手淫 ‖ **mastur'bation** *n.*

mat[1][mæt] *n.* 1. 地席；席子；草席；蒲席 2.(体操或摔跤用的)垫子；(放在门口处的)擦鞋垫；(花瓶、茶杯等的)垫子 3. 丛，簇 4.〈俚〉甲板 —(matted; matting) *vt.* 1. 给…铺上(或盖上)席子；给…铺上垫子；使纠结 —*vi.* 缠结

mat[2][mæt] *adj.* 1. 无光泽的，暗淡的；表面粗糙的；不光滑的 —*n.* 1. 无光表面 2.(油漆、镀金等的)无光粗糙层 3.[印]字模；纸型 4.(画或照片的)衬边，框边 —(matted; matting) *vt.* 1. 使(金属、玻璃等)无光 2. 给(画或照片)加衬边

matador ['mætədɔː] *n.* 1. 斗牛士 2.(纸牌戏中的)主要王牌

match[1][mætʃ] *n.* 1.(一根)火柴 2. 导火线，火绳 ‖ **~lock** *n.* 1. 火绳枪 2. 火绳

match[2][mætʃ] *n.* 1. 比赛，竞赛 2. 对手；敌手 3. 相配者；配对物 4. 相配的两个(或两个以上)人(或物) 5. 婚姻；婚姻对象 —*vt.* 1. 使较量，使比赛(*against*, *with*) 2. 敌得过；比得上 3. 和…相配，和…相称 4. 使成对，使相配；

使相称 5. 使比较 6. 使结婚 7. 抛掷
(硬币)后按正反面作决定;用(某人)
抛掷硬币以作决定 —*vi.* 1. 相配;相
适合 2. 结婚 ‖ —**less** *adj.* 无敌的;无
比的 ‖ —**maker** *n.* 媒人;好做媒
的人 2.(尤指拳跤比赛或职业拳击赛
的)比赛安排者

mate [meit] *n.* 1. 伙伴,同事(常用在称
呼中)老兄;老弟 2. 配偶;配偶 3.(鸟
兽的)偶 **【海】**(商船的)大副;副手 4.
(美国海军的)军士 — *vt.* 使成配
偶;使配对;使(鸟等)交配 2. 使聚密
配合 — *vi.* 1. 成配偶;成伙伴(*with*)
2. 紧密配合 3.(鸟类等)交尾

mater ['meitə] *n.*〈英口〉母亲,妈妈

material [mə'tiəriəl] *n.* 1. 材料;原料;物
质 2. 素材;题材;资料 3. 织物;料子
4. [～s]用具;设备 — *adj.* 1. 物质的;
实体的,有形的;物质性的;身体上的
肉体的 3. 物欲的,追求实利的;卑
俗的 4. 重要的,实质性的 ‖ —**ly** *adv.*
1. 物质上;实质上 2. 大大地,相当地

materialism [mə'tiəriəlizəm] *n.* 1. **【哲】**唯
物主义,唯物论 2.【艺术上的】写实主
义 3.(注重物质利益的)实利主义 ‖
materialist *n.* 唯物主义者,唯物论者
2. 唯物主义者 *adj.* 唯物主义的;唯物
主义者的

materialistic [mə,tiəriə'listik] *adj.* 1. 唯物
主义的;唯物主义者的 2. 物质第一主
义的;实利主义的;实利主义者的 ‖
～**ally** *adv.*

materiality [mə,tiəri'æliti] *n.* 1. 物质性
2. 重要性 3. [常用复]物质;实体

materialize [mə'tiəriəlaiz] *vt.* 1. 使物质
化;使具体化 2. 使追求物质利益 3. 使
(鬼魂等)显形;使突然出现 — *vi.* 1.
物质化;具体化 2. 成为事实,(希望、
计划等)实现 3.(鬼魂等)显形;突然出

现

materiel [mə,tiəri'el]〈法〉*n.* 设备;(军队
的)装备;作战物资

maternal [mə'tə:nl] *adj.* 1. 母亲的;母性
的;母亲似的 2. 母方的,母系的 ‖ ～**ly**
adv.

maternity [mə'tə:niti] *n.* 1. 母性;母道 2.
产科病房;产科医院(＝～ hospital) 3.
怀孕 — *adj.* 产妇的;孕妇的

math [mæθ] *n.*〈口〉= mathematics

mathematical [,mæθi'mætikəl] *adj.* 1. 数
学的;数学上的 2. 精确的;确定无疑
的 3. 可能性极小的 ‖ —**ly** *adv.*

mathematician [,mæθimə'tiʃən] *n.* 数学
家

mathematics [,mæθi'mætiks] [复] *n.* [用
作单]数学

maths [mæθs] *n.*〈英口〉= mathematics

matinée ['mætinei]〈法〉*n.* 1. 午后的演
出,日戏;日场,午场 2. 女式晨衣

matins ['mætinz] [复] *n.*【宗】晨正经;晨
祷

matriarch ['meitriɑ:k] *n.* 女家长;女族
长;国家的)女统治者;(组织、团体等
的)女负责人

matriarchy ['meitriɑ:ki] *n.* 母权制,母系
氏族制

matriculate [mə'trikjuleit] *vt.* 录取 — *vi.*
被录取 ‖ **ma,tricu'lation** *n.*

matrimonial [,mætri'mounial] *adj.* 婚姻
的;夫妇的;婚礼的 ‖ ～**ly** *adv.*

matrimony ['mætriməni] *n.* 1. 结婚;婚
礼;婚姻;婚姻生活 2. 觅对(一种抽对
子牌戏)

matrix ['meitriks]([复]matrices['meitrisiz]
或 matrixes) *n.* 1. 模型;阴模;型片;基
片 2. 唱片模版;[印]字模;纸型 3. 母
质;基体 4. 子宫;(牙齿等的)床,形成

层 5.【地】基质 6.【数】【计】矩阵 ‖ ~ printer 矩阵式打印机

matron ['meitrən] *n.* 1.(年长有威望的)已婚妇女；主妇 2.(学校等的)女总管；女舍监；(监狱等的)女看守；(妇女团体的)总干事；护士长 3. 母和畜 ‖ ~ly *adj.* 1. 主妇(或女总管等)的；主妇(或女总管等)似的；适合主妇(或女总管等)的身份的 2.庄重的；安详的；沉着的 *adv.* 主妇(或女总管等)似地

matter ['mætə] *n.* 1. 物质；物料 2. 物品；文件；邮件 3. 事情；问题；[~s]事态；情况 4.(文章、讲话等的)内容；素材 5. 要紧事；要紧 6.[the ~]麻烦事；毛病 7. 理由，根据 8.(表示数量)左右，上下 9.【医】脓；生命体排出物(如尿、屎等) 10.【印】原稿；排版 一 *vi.* 1.[主要用于否定句和疑问句]有关系；要紧 2.【医】化脓；出脓 ‖ ~-of-fact [ˌmætərə'fækt] *adj.* 1. 注重事实的；讲究实际的 2. 平淡无味的；干巴巴的

matting ['mætiŋ] *n.* 1.[总称]地席；席；草席；蒲席 2. 编席的材料；编席

mattock ['mætək] *n.* 鹤嘴锄

mattress ['mætris] *n.* 1. 褥垫，床垫 2.(土木工程用的)柴排，沉排，沉床

mature [mə'tjuə] *adj.* 1. 成熟的 2. 成年人的；【地】壮年的，成熟的 3.(考虑等)慎重的；周到的 4.【商】(票据等)到期的 一 *vt.* 使成熟；使长成 一 *vi.* 1. 成熟；长成 2.【商】(票据等)到期 ‖ ~ly *adv.* / ~ness *n.*

maturity [mə'tjuəriti] *n.* 1. 成熟 2.【商】(票据等的)到期；到期日 3.【地】壮年(期) 4.【生】成熟期；发身期

maudlin ['mɔːdlin] *adj.* 1. 易伤感的；感情脆弱的；爱哭的 ‖ ~ly *adv.* / ~ness *n.*

maul [mɔːl] *n.*(木制的)大槌 一 *vt.* 1. 殴

打；打伤；(用言语)挫伤 2. 粗手粗脚地弄(或做) 3. 用楔和大槌劈开

Mauritania [ˌmɔːri'teiniə] *n.* 毛里塔尼亚[西非国家]

Mauritius [mə'riʃəs] *n.* 毛里求斯[非洲岛国]

mausoleum [ˌmɔːsə'liəm] ([复] mausoleums 或 mausolea [ˌmɔːsə'liə]) *n.* 1. 陵墓 2. 大而阴森的房屋(或房间)

mauve [məuv] *n.* 1.(碱性)木槿紫，苯胺紫(一种紫色染料) 2. 紫红色 一 *adj.* 紫红色的

maw [mɔː] *n.* 1.(动物的)胃(尤指反刍动物的第四胃) 2.(鸟的)嗉囊 3. 鱼鳔，鱼泡 4.(食肉动物的)咽喉(或食道等) 5.(贪婪的)大肚(人)胃

mawkish ['mɔːkiʃ] *adj.* 1. 淡而无味的；令人作呕的 2. 多愁善感的；感情用事到幼稚可笑(或令人作呕)地步的 ‖ ~ly *adv.* / ~ness *n.*

max. *abbr.* 1. maxim 2. maximum

maxim ['mæksim] *n.* 1. 格言，箴言；准则 2. 谚语

maxima ['mæksimə] maximum 的复数

maximal ['mæksiməl] *adj.* 1. 最大的；最高的 2. 最带总括性的；最全的

maximum ['mæksiməm] ([复] maxima ['mæksimə] 或 maximums) *n.* 1. 最大量；最大数；最大限度 2. 顶点，极限 3.【数】极大(值) 一 *adj.* 最大的，最多的；最高的；顶点的

May [mei] *n.* 1. 五月 2.[常作 m-]青春；壮年 3.(英国风俗)五朔节欢庆活动 4.[m-]山楂；[英国山楂;](春天开花的)绣线菊 5.(英国剑桥大学俚语)五月考试；五月赛艇会 ‖ ~ Day 1. 五一国际劳动节 2.(英国风俗)五朔节

may [mei] (might [mait]) *v. aux.* [无人称变化，后接不带 to 的动词不定式] 1.

[表示可能性]可能,也许 2.[表示许可或用于表示请求时,相当于 can]可以 3.[用于问句中,表示不确定]会,究竟:Who ~ the man be? 这个人会是谁呢? 4.[表示希望、祝愿、祈求等]祝,愿 5.[常与 well 连用,表示(完全)能],(满)可以 6.[用于从句中表示目的](以便),(使…)可以 7.[用于从句中表示让步]不管,无论,不论:无论 8.[用于从句中表示期望]能够,会 9.[用于法令条款中,相当于 shall,must]须,应

maybe ['meibi] *adv.* 大概,或许;可能 — *n.* 可能性;不确定性

mayhem ['meihem] *n.*【律】(以暴力毁伤他人肢体的)重伤害

mayn't [meint] = may not

mayo ['meiəu] *n.* 〈口〉= mayonnaise

mayonnaise [ˌmeiə'neiz] *n.* 1.(用蛋黄、橄榄油、柠檬汁等调制的)蛋黄酱 2.用蛋黄酱调制的肉(或鱼)

mayor [meə] *n.* 市长 ‖ **mayoral** *adj.*/**mayoralty** *n.* 市长职位(或任期)

maze [meiz] *n.* 1. 迷宫,迷津;曲径 2. 混乱,迷惑 — *vt.* 1. 使如入迷津,使困惑;使为难

mazurka [mə'zə:kə] *n.*(波兰民间的)玛祖卡舞(曲)

Mbabane [əmbɑː'bɑːni] *n.* 姆巴巴纳(斯威士兰首都)

MD *abbr.* (拉) *Medicinae Doctor* 医学博士(= Doctor of Medicine)

me [mi; 弱 mi] *pron.* 1.[I 的宾格]我 2.〈口〉[用作表语]我 3.[用于 than 后而言]我(= I) 4.[用于感叹句]Ah(或 Dear)~! 哎哟! 5.〈古〉我自己(= myself)

mead [mid] *n.* 蜂蜜酒

meadow ['medəu] *n.* 1. 草地;牧草地 2. (河或湖边)肥沃的低草地,水草地 ‖ '~-lark *n.*(北美产)草地鹨

meagre, meager ['migə] *adj.* 1.(人等)瘦的;(土地)不毛的 2. 贫乏的;不足的;贫弱的;思想贫乏的

meal¹ [mid] *n.* 1. 膳食,一餐;一顿(饭);进餐(时间) 2.〈英方〉挤奶(时间);一次挤奶量 — *vi.* 进餐

meal² [mid] *n.* 1.(谷、豆类的)粗磨粉 2. 像粗磨粉的东西;粉末;玉米粉

mealy ['midi] *adj.* 1. 粉状的;含粉的;撒上粉的 2. 杂有另一种颜色的,有斑点的 3. 苍白的 4. = ~-mouthed ‖ **mealiness** *n.* / '~-'mouthed *adj.* 说话转弯抹角的;油嘴滑舌的

mean¹ [min] (meant [ment]) *vt.* 1.(词语等)表示…的意思;作…解释 2. 意指,意谓 3. 意味 4. 意欲,打算;怀着 5. 预定;指定 — *vi.* 1. 用意 2. 具有意义

mean² [min] *adj.* 1. 卑鄙的;自私的 2. 低劣的;平庸的 3. 简陋的;难看的 4. 吝啬的,小气的;刻薄的 5. 卑贱的,下贱的 6. 麻烦的,讨厌的 7. 不好意思的,惭愧的 8. 不适的;不舒服的 9.〈口等〉脾气坏的,难驯服的 10.〈美俚〉出色的;巧妙的;有效的

mean³ [min] *adj.* 1.(在位置、时间、顺序等方面)中间的;中庸的 2. 中等的;普通的 3. 平均的 4.【数】中项的 — *n.* 1. 中间;中庸 2.【数】平均(数);平均(值);中项 3.【逻】(三段论式的)中项 4.【音】中音部

meander [mi'ændə] *n.* 1.[常 ~s]曲流,河曲;绕弯曲的路 2. 漫步,散步 3.[回纹]波形饰 — *vi.* 1. 蜿蜒曲流;迂回曲折地前进 2. 漫步,闲逛;漫谈,闲谈 — *vt.* 1. 使迂回曲折 2. 循着(河流、道路等)迂回曲折地前进

meaning ['mi:niŋ] *n.* 1. 意义;意思;含意 2. 意图 3. 〔逻〕内涵;外延 — *adj.* 1. 意味深长的 2. 怀有(某种)意图的 ‖ ~less *adj.* 无意义的

meaningful ['mi:niŋful] *adj.* 意味深长的;富有意义的

means [mi:nz] [复] *n.* 1. [常用作单]方法;手段;工具 2. 财产;资力;收入

meant [ment] mean[1] 的过去式和过去分词

meantime ['mi:n,taim] *n.* 间隔时间;其时,其间 — *adv.* 在间隔时间里;当时,(与此)同时

meanwhile ['mi:n,hwail] *n. & adv.* = meantime

measles ['mi:zlz] [复] *n.* [用作单或复] 1. 〔医〕麻疹;麻疹斑;风疹 2. 家畜囊尾蚴病

measly ['mi:zli] *adj.* 1. 患麻疹的 2. (肉类中)有囊尾蚴的,有米珠的 3. 〈口〉微不足道的,小(或少)得可怜的

measurable ['meʒərəbl] *adj.* 可测量的

measure ['meʒə] *n.* 1. 量度;测量 2. 分量;尺寸 3. 计量制度;度量法 4. 计量单位;(特种商品习惯用的)容量单位(如 bushel 等) 5. 量具,量器 6. (衡量)标准,尺寸 7. 程度;限度;范围;适度,分寸 8. 本分,份儿 9. 措施,办法 10. 议案 11. (诗歌的)韵律;〔音〕拍子;小节;(慢步而庄重的)舞蹈 12. 【数】测量法 13. [~s][地]层组 14. 【印】行宽;页宽 — *vi.* 1. 量,测量;计量 2. (按尺寸)划分 (off);(按量)配给;分派 (out) 3. 打量;估量,衡量 4. 拿…作较量 5. 酌量;权衡;调节;使均衡 — *vi.* 1. 量 2. 有…长(或阔、高等)

measured ['meʒəd] *adj.* 1. 量过的;按标准的,精确的 2. (言语)有分寸的,慎重的,经过斟酌的 3. 整齐的;有节奏的

4. 韵律的

measurement ['meʒəmənt] *n.* 1. 衡量;测量 2. [~s]量得的尺寸,大小;长(或宽、深)度 3. 度量制;量法

meat [mi:t] *n.* 1. (可食用的)肉 2. (蛋、贝、果子等的)食用部分,肉 3. 内容;实质;要点 4. 〈古〉〈方〉食物 5. 〈古〉(一餐)饭 6. 〈美俚〉爱好;特长 ‖ ~y *adj.* 1. (多)肉的 2. 内容丰富的;发人深省的;耐人寻味的 3. 重要的

Mecca ['mekə] *n.* 1. 麦加(伊斯兰教徒的朝圣地,在沙特阿拉伯西部) 2. [常作 m-]圣地;胜地;策源地,诞生地;向往的目标

mechanic [mi'kænik] *n.* 1. 技工;机械工;机修工 2. 〔美俚〕玩牌时善于作假的人

mechanical [mi'kænikəl] *adj.* 1. 机械(制)的;用机械的 2. 力学的;物理上的 3. 〔哲〕机械论的 4. 机械似的,呆板的 5. 手工操作的;技工的 ‖ ~ly *adv.*

mechanics [mi'kæniks] [复] *n.* [用作单或复] 1. 力学;机械学 2. 结构;构成;技巧

mechanism ['mekənizəm] *n.* 1. 机械装置;机构;结构;〔生〕机制,机理 2. (自然现象的)作用过程;〔化〕历程 3. 手法;技巧;途径 4. 〔哲〕机械论 ‖ mechanist *n.*

mechanistic [,mekə'nistik] *adj.* 1. 〔哲〕机械论(者)的 2. 机械学的

mechanize ['mekənaiz] *vt.* 用机械做(或操作);使机械化;使机械装备 ‖ ,mechani'zation *n.* 机械化

medal ['medl] *n.* 奖章;勋章;纪念章;奖牌 —(medal[l]ed)—(medal[l]ing) *vt.* 授予…奖章(或勋章等) ‖ ~ist *n.* 奖章设计的(或制作、获得)者

medallion [mi'dæljən] *n.* 1. 大奖章;大勋

章;大引念章;大奖牌 **2.**【建】圆雕饰;【纺】团花;花边装饰纹

meddle ['medl] **vi. 1.** 干涉,干预;管闲事 **2.** 乱弄,瞎弄 ‖ **~r** *n.* 干涉者;爱管闲事的人 / **~some** *adj.* 好干涉的;爱管闲事的

media ['miːdiə] medium 的复数

mediaeval [ˌmedi'iːvəl] *adj.* = medieval

median ['miːdiən] *adj.* 中央的;当中的 — *n.* 中部;当中

mediate ['miːdieit] *vi.* 处于中间地位 **2.** 调停,调解 — *vt.* **1.** 调停,调解;作为引起…—作为引起… **2.** 间接的;介于中间的 —['miːdiit] *adj.* **1.** 居间的,介于中间的 **2.** 间接的

mediation [ˌmiːdi'eiʃən] *n.* 调停,调解

mediator ['miːdieitə] *n.* 调停者;调解国 **2.**【化】【生】介体,介质 **3.** [M-]【宗】中保(指耶稣)

medic ['medik] *n.* 〈口〉**1.** (随军或战地)卫生员 **2.** 实习医生 **3.** 医生

Medicaid ['medikeid] *n.* 〈美〉(由政府资助,以穷人和伤残人为对象的)医疗补助(制度)

medical ['medikəl] *adj.* **1.** 医学的;医术的;医疗的;医用的 **2.** 内科的;医药的 — *n.* 〈口〉**1.** 体格检查 **2.** 医科学生;医生 ‖ **~ly** *adv.*

medicament [mi'dikəmənt] *n.* 药物,药剂

Medicare ['medikeə] *n.* (美国、加拿大的)老年保健医疗(制度)

medicate ['medikeit] *vt.* **1.** 用药治疗;用药(剂)浸渍;加药于;敷药于 ‖ **~d** *adj.* 加入药品的,含药的;药制的

medication [ˌmedi'keiʃən] *n.* **1.** 药疗法 **2.** 加入药物;加药物处理 **3.** 药物,药剂

medicinal [me'disinl] *adj.* **1.** 药的;药用的;治疗的 **2.** 有益健康的;有益的一

n. 药物,药品 ‖ **~ly** *adv.*

medicine ['medsin, 'medisin] *n.* **1.** 医学;医术;内科学 **2.** 内服药(剂) **3.** 带来幸福的事物 **4.**(原始民族迷信的)符咒;巫术;〈美俚〉〈方〉情报 — *vt.* 给…用药,用药给…治病 ‖ **~man** 巫医

medieval [ˌmedi'iːvəl] *adj.* **1.** 中世纪的,中古(时代)的 **2.** 类似中世纪的 **3.** 古老的(过时的) ‖ **~ism** *n.* **1.** 中世纪性质(或特点、状态);对中世纪文化的爱好 / **~ist** *n.* 中世纪问题专家;中世纪文化艺术爱好者

Medina [me'dinə] *n.* 麦地那(伊斯兰教圣地之一,在沙特阿拉伯西部)

mediocre ['miːdiəukə] *adj.* **1.** 普普通通的;中等的 **2.** 低劣的

mediocrity [ˌmiːdi'ɔkriti] *n.* **1.** 平庸;平凡 **2.** 平庸的才能;平凡的成就 **3.** 平庸的人

meditate ['mediteit] *vt.* 考虑;策划,企图 — *vi.* 深思,沉思;反省;冥想 ‖ **meditation** *n.* **1.** 深思,沉思;反省;冥想 **2.** 沉思录

meditative ['meditətiv] *adj.* **1.** 沉思的;冥想的 **2.** 爱思考的

Mediterranean [ˌmeditə'reiniən] *n.* **1.** 地中海(亦作 ~ Sea) **2.** 地中海的居民 **3.** 地中海沿岸的高加索人 — *adj.* **1.** 地中海的;地中海地区的 **2.** 地中海沿岸的高加索人种的

medium ['miːdiəm] ([复] mediums 或 media ['miːdiə]) *n.* **1.** 中间;中庸;适中 **2.** 媒质,媒介物;传导体;(颜色的)溶剂 **3.** 手段;工具;[media] 宣传工具,新闻媒介 **4.**(喻)环境;生活条件;【生】培养基 **5.** 中号纸(通常为 18 × 23 英寸的印刷纸) **6.**(舞台上用的)灯光滤光片 **7.** 调解人;中间人;〈搞迷信活动的〉关亡人;巫师 — *adj.* 中等的;中间的;适中

的

medley ['medli] *n.* 1. 杂乱的一团；混杂的人群；混合物；杂烩 2. (诗，文等的)杂集 3.【音】集成曲(几首歌曲的片断凑成的乐曲) 4.〈古〉混战 —*adj.* 混杂的；混合的 —*vt.* 使成杂乱一堆(或一团)；使混杂

meed [mi:d] *n.* 1.〈诗〉(称赞等的)应得之份；〈古〉(应得的)报酬；工资 2. 适当的报答

meek [mi:k] *adj.* 1. 逆来顺受的；温顺的 2. 缺乏勇气和胆量的 ‖ ~ly *adv.* / ~ness *n.*

meerschaum ['miəʃəm, 'miəʃɔm] *n.* 1.【矿】海泡石 2. 海泡石烟斗

meet [mi:t] (met [met]) *vt.* 1. 遇见，与…相遇；碰上 2.〈讯〉(社交)会见，会谈 3. 迎接 4. 满足；符合 5. 对付，应付；如期偿付；践(约) 6. 和…作接触；与…接触 7. 与…对抗；与…会战 8.(路等)与…交叉；与…相合 —*vi.* 1. 相遇；相会；相识 2. 接触；会合；交谈 3. 集合；聚会；开会 4.(品质方面)兼备，共有(*in*) —*n.* 1. 集会；运动会 2.(狩猎前猎人和猎犬的)集合 3.【数】交(集)

meeting ['mi:tiŋ] *n.* 1. 会议，集会 2. 聚合；会见 3. 汇合点，交叉点 4. 会战；〈古〉决斗 5.【宗】(基督教教友会的)聚会；聚会所 ‖ ~house *n.*【宗】(基督教教友会的)聚会所 / ~place *n.* 会场；会面地点

mega *comb. form* 表示"兆"，"百万"，"巨大的"；*mega*cycle, *mega*phone

megabit ['megabit] *n.*【计】兆位

megabyte ['megabait] *n.*【计】兆字节

megacycle ['megə,saikl] *n.*【无】兆周

megadose ['megədəʊs] *n.*(药物、维生素等的)大剂量 —*vt.* 给予…大剂量

megahertz ['megəhə:ts] *n.* [单复同]【物】

兆赫(略作 MHz)

megalomania [,megələ'meiniə] *n.*【医】夸大狂；妄自尊大 ‖ ~c [,megələ'meiniæk] *n.*【医】夸大狂者；妄自尊大的人

megalopolis [,megə'lɔpəlis] ([复] mega-lopolises 或 megalopoli [,megə'lɔpəlai]) *n.* 特大城市(的生活方式)

megaphone ['megəfəun] *n.* 1. 喇叭筒；话筒；扩音器 —*vt.* 1. 用喇叭筒说出；向…用话筒喊话 2. 广泛宣传 —*vi.* 用话筒喊话

megastructure ['megə,strʌktʃə] *n.* 巨型建筑物

megatanker ['megə,tæŋkə] *n.*(吨位在 20 万以上的)巨型油轮

megaton(ne) ['megətʌn] *n.* 兆吨(级)，百万吨(级)(核武器爆炸力的计算单位，相当于一百万吨梯恩梯炸药) ‖ 'mega,tonnage *n.*

megavitamin [,megə,vaitəmin] *adj.*(用)大剂量维生素的

Mekong ['mei'kɔŋ] *n.* 湄公河[东南亚]

melancholy ['melənkəli] *n.* 1. 忧郁；意气消沉 2.【医】忧郁症 —*adj.* 1. 忧郁的；意气消沉的 2. 使人抑郁的；令人伤感的

Melanesia [,melə'ni:ziə] *n.* 美拉尼西亚[西南太平洋的岛群]

mélange ['mei'lɑ:ʒ] 〈法〉*n.* 1. 混合物；大杂烩；杂乱的一群 2.[纺]混色毛纱

Melbourne ['melbən] *n.* 墨尔本(即新金山)[澳大利亚东南部港市]

melee, mêlée ['melei, mei'lei] *n.* 混战；论战；混乱的人群

meliorate ['mi:liəreit] *vt. & vi.* 改善，改进，改良 ‖ ,melio'ration *n.* / meliorative *adj.* / meliorator *n.*

mellifluous [mi'lifluəs] *adj.* 声音甜美的；

流畅的;悦耳的 ‖ ~ly adv. / ~ness n.

mellow ['meləu] adj. 1.(水果)甘美多汁的;(酒)芳醇的 2.(声音)圆润的;(光、色等)柔和的 3.(土地)肥沃的;松软的 4.(人的戏剧的);成熟的 5.〈口〉温和的;高兴的;微醺的 6.〔美俚〕好的;极好的 —vt. 1.使丰美;使醇香 2.使圆润;使柔和 3.使成熟;使成老 —vi. 1.变得丰美;变得醇香 2.变得柔和 3.变得老成;成熟起来 ‖ ~ness n.

melodeon [mi'ləudiən] n.〔音〕1.美国式簧风琴 2.美乐器(一种小手风琴)

melodious [mi'ləudiəs] adj. 1.音调悦耳的;音调优美的 2.旋律的;有旋律的 ‖ ~ly adv. ~ness n.

melodrama ['melədrɑːmə] n. 1.〔戏〕情节剧;传奇剧(一种不着重刻划人物、一味追求情节奇异、通常有惩恶扬善结局的戏剧);音乐戏剧 2.轰动事件;耸人听闻的言行

melody ['melədi] n. 1.悦耳的声音;美妙的音乐 2.歌曲;可咏唱的诗 3.〔音〕旋律;曲调;主调 ‖ melodic [mi'lɔdik] adj.

melon ['melən] n. 1.瓜(尤指甜瓜、西瓜等) 2.瓜状圆物;隆起的肚子 3.〈俚〉红利;脏物;横财

melt [melt] (过去式 melted, 过去分词 melted 或 molten ['məultən]) vi. 1.融化;熔化;(食物)酥融 2.溶化;液解 3.〈口〉受到热恼 4.消散;消失;(空)(风雨 5.(人、人的心肠或态度等)变软,软化 6.(声音)变得柔润 6.融合 —vt. 1.使融化;使熔化;使溶解 2.使消散;使消失;软化 3.(俚)把(支票等)兑现 —n. 1.熔(或溶)解;熔化了的金属 2.熔(或溶)解量 3.〔熔炉的〕一次装料 ‖ ~down n. 1.(核反应堆活性区心的)熔毁 2.〈口〉灾难

melting ['meltiŋ] adj. 1.融化的;熔化的

2.温柔的;感伤的 ‖ ~ point 熔点 / ~ pot 1.熔化锅 2.各种族融合的国家(或地方)

melton ['meltən] n.〔纺〕麦尔登呢

member ['membə] n. 1.(团体、组织等的)成员,一分子;会员 2.[M-]议员 3.部分;〔语〕句;〔逻〕成员,分子 4.〔数〕元;〔机〕构件,部件 5.(政治团体的)部门;支部 6.(人体或动、植物的)一部分;器官 7.〔~ship n.〕1.成员资格,会员资格;会籍;党籍;团籍 2.全体成员;全体会员 3.成员人数;会员人数

membrane ['membrein] n. 1.〔解〕〔生〕膜;细胞膜 2.膜状物;薄膜 3.羊皮纸

membranous [mem'breinəs] adj. 1.膜的;膜状的 2.(指疾病)膜性的

memento [mi'mentəu] ([复] memento(e)s) n. 1.纪念品 2.引起回忆(或联想)的东西 3.(古)警告,告诫 3.回忆

memo ['miːməu, 'meməu] ([复] memos) n.〈口〉= memorandum

memoir ['memwɑː] n. 1.[~s]回忆录 2.传记;传略;报道 3.学术论文;研究报告;专题报告;[~s](学会的)讨论事项记要 4.(罕)(外交上的)备忘录

memorabilia [,memərə'biliə] n. 1.值得纪念的事;纪念品 2.大事记

memorable ['memərəbl] adj. 值得纪念的;值得注意的;难忘的 ‖ memorably adv.

memorandum [,memə'rændəm] ([复] memorandums 或 memoranda [,memə'rændə]) n. 1.备忘录;(契约等条文的)节略 2.〔商〕便笺,便函

memorial [mi'mɔːriəl] adj. 1.记忆的 2.纪念的;追悼的 —n. 1.纪念物;纪念日;纪念碑;纪念仪式 2.[~s]年代记;编年史 3.请愿书;抗议书 4.

(外交上的)备忘录;节略 ‖ **Memorial Day** 1.(美国)阵亡将士纪念日(5月份最后一个星期一) 2.(英国)南部邦联阵亡将士纪念日(日期因州而异)

memorize ['meməraiz] *vt.* 记住;熟记,背熟 —*vi.* 默记

memory ['meməri] *n.* 1. 记忆;记忆力 2. 记忆中的人(或事物);回忆 3. 记忆范围记忆所及年限 4. 纪念 5. (死后的)名声 6.【计】存储(器);(存储器的)存储量

men [men] *man* 的复数 ‖ ~'s **room**(美)男盥洗室,男厕所

menace ['menis] *n.* 1. 威胁;恐吓 2. 威胁者;危险物;引起烦扰者 —*vt.* 威胁,恐吓;危及 —*vi.* 进行威胁,进行恐吓 ‖ **menacingly** *adv.* 威胁地,恐吓地

ménage [mei'nɑːʒ] *n.* 1. 家庭 2. 家政

menagerie [mi'nædʒəri] *n.* 1. 动物园;兽栏;兽笼 2.【总称】(供展览等的)被囚野生动物

mend [mend] *vt.* 1. 修理,修补;织补,缝补 2. 改正,纠正;改善,改进 3. 加快;添(火)4. 治愈;使恢复健康 —*vi.* 1. 渐愈;好转;改善,改进 —*n.* 1. 修补;缝补;修补好的地方 2. 好转;痊愈 ‖ ~ **er** *n.* 修补者

mendacious [men'deiʃəs] *adj.* 1. (爱)撒谎的 2. 虚假的 ‖ ~ **ly** *adv.* / ~ **ness** *n.* / **mendacity** [men'dæsiti] *n.* 撒谎习惯,撒谎癖;虚假

mendelevium [ˌmendə'liːviəm] *n.*【化】钔

mendicant ['mendikənt] *adj.* 行乞的;乞讨的;托钵修道会的 —*n.* 乞丐;[常作 M-]托钵修会

menfolk(**s**)['menfəuk(s)][复] *n.*【总称】1. 男人 2.(家庭、社团中的)男成员

menhaden [men'heidn][复] **menhaden**(**s**) *n.*【动】油鲱

menial ['miːniəl] *adj.* 1. 仆人的,奴仆的 2. 奴性的;卑下的 —*n.* 1. 仆人,奴仆 2. 奴性的人;卑下的人

meningitis [ˌmenin'dʒaitis] *n.*【医】脑(脊)膜炎

menopause ['menəpɔːz] *n.* (生理上的)绝经(期)

menses ['mensiːz][复] *n.* [用作单或复]月经

menstrual ['menstruəl] *adj.* 月经的

menstruate ['menstrueit] *vi.* 行经,月经来潮

menstruation [ˌmenstru'eiʃən] *n.* 月经;行经;行经期

mensurable ['menʃuərəbl] *adj.* 可测量的;有固定范围的

menswear ['menzweə] *n.*【总称】男服

-ment *suf.* [附在动词或动词词根后构成名词]表示行为的"结果"、"手段"、"工具"、"过程"、"状态"、"程度":entertainment, development, astonishment

mental ['mentl] *adj.* 1. 精神的,思想上的 2. 内心的 2. 脑力的,智力的 3. 精神病的 —*n.* (口)精神病;精神病患者 ‖ ~ **ly** *adv.* 精神上;在内心;智力上

mentality [men'tæliti] *n.* 1. 脑力,智力 2. 精神,思想;心理

menthol ['menθɔl] *n.*【化】薄荷醇

mention ['menʃən] *n.* 1. 提及,说起 2. (战报等中对杰出事迹的)传令嘉奖,通报表扬;提名表扬 —*vt.* 1. 提到,说起 2. 传令嘉奖;提名表扬 ‖ ~ **able** *n.*

mentor ['mentə] *n.* 顾问;良师

menu ['menjuː] *n.* 1. 菜单 2. 饭菜;菜肴

meow [mi'au] *n.* 1. 咪,喵(猫叫声)2. 恶言 —*vi.* 1. 咪咪叫,喵喵叫 2. 吐恶言

mercantile ['məːkəntail] *adj.* 1. 商业的,贸易的;商人的 2. 重商主义的 ‖

marine [总称] **1.**(一个国家的)全部商船,商船队 **2.**(一个国家的)全体商船船员

mercenary ['mɜːsɪnərɪ] *adj.* **1.** 为钱的,唯利是图的,贪财的 **2.** 被雇佣在外国军队中的;雇佣的 — *n.* 外国雇佣兵;佣工

mercerize ['mɜːsəraɪz] *vt.* 【纺】将…作丝光处理

merchandise ['mɜːtʃəndaɪz] *n.* [总称] 商品,货物 — *vi.* 经商 — *vt.* 买卖;推销

merchant ['mɜːtʃənt] *n.* **1.** (批发) 商人 (尤指进出口贸易商人) **2.** 零售商 **3.** [接在所经营的商品名词之后作复合词] …商:a coal ~ 煤炭商 **4.** 〈俚〉好…的人,迷于…的人 — *vt.* 经营,买卖 — *adj.* 经营的;商业的;商船的 ‖ ~**man** *n.* 商船 — **marine**、**service** [总称] **1.**(一个国家的)全部商船,商船队 **2.**(一个国家的)全体商船船员

merciful ['mɜːsɪfʊl] *adj.* 仁慈的,宽大的 ‖ ~**ly** *adv.*

merciless ['mɜːsɪlɪs] *adj.* 冷酷无情的,残忍的 ‖ ~**ly** *adv.* / ~**ness** *n.*

mercurate ['mɜːkjʊreɪt] *vt.* 【化】使汞化;用汞(或汞盐)处理 — ['mɜːkjʊrɪt] *n.* 汞化产物;汞盐

mercurial [mɜː'kjʊərɪəl] *adj.* **1.** 汞的,含水银的;由水银引起的 **2.** 活泼的,易变的 **3.** [M-]墨丘利神(Mercury)的;水星的 **4.** 雄辩的;狡诈的;贼性的 — *n.* 汞制剂

mercuric [mɜː'kjʊərɪk] *adj.* 【化】(正)汞的,含二价汞的

mercurous ['mɜːkjʊrəs] *adj.* 【化】亚汞的,含一价汞的

mercury ['mɜːkjʊrɪ] *n.* **1.** 汞,水银 **2.**(温度计等中的)水银柱 **3.** 活泼 **4.** [the M-]【天】水星 **5.** [M-]【罗神】墨丘利(为

众神传信并掌管商业、道路等的神) **6.** [常作 M-](用于报刊名)信使;〈古〉向导 **7.** 【植】山靛;亨利藜

mercy ['mɜːsɪ] *n.* **1.** 怜悯,宽恕;仁慈;恩惠 **2.** 幸运;侥幸 — *int.* [表示惊异或假装惊恐等]哎呀!

mere [mɪə] *adj.* **1.** 仅仅的,只不过的 **2.** 纯粹的 ‖ ~**ly** *adv.* 仅仅,只不过

meretricious [ˌmerɪ'trɪʃəs] *adj.* **1.** 娼妓的 **2.** 浮华的;耀眼的;俗气的 **3.**(论据等)虚夸的;似是而非的 ‖ ~**ly** *adv.* / ~**ness** *n.*

merganser [mɜː'gænsə] *n.* 【动】秋沙鸭

merge [mɜːdʒ] *vt.* **1.** 使(企业等)合并,使并入 **2.** 使结合 **3.** 使渐渐消失;吞没 — *vi.* 合并;结合;渐渐消失 ‖ **mergence** *n.* / ~ **r** *n.* (企业等的)合并,兼并

meridian [mə'rɪdɪən] *n.* **1.** 【天】子午线,经线 **2.** 顶点,极点 **3.** 全盛时期 — *adj.* **1.** 【天】子午线的,经线的 **2.** 顶点的,极点的;全盛时期的

meringue [mə'ræŋ] 〈法〉 *n.* **1.** (糕、饼的)蛋白酥皮 **2.** (放水冰淇淋、水果等的)蛋白筒(或卷)蛋白甜饼

merino [mə'riːnəʊ] ([复] merinos) *n.* **1.** 美利奴绵羊(产细密的丝状羊毛) **2.** 美利奴羊毛;美利奴精纺毛纱;美利奴织物;棉毛混纺针织物 — *adj.* 美利奴绵羊的;美利奴羊毛(织)的

merit ['merɪt] *n.* **1.** 长处,优点;价值 **2.** 功绩,功劳,荣誉 **3.** [有时 ~s]功过,功罪 **4.** 法律意义上;法律的实情 ‖ [~s]是非曲直 — *vt.* 值得,应受 — *vi.* 应受赏(或罚)

meritorious [ˌmerɪ'tɔːrɪəs] *adj.* 有功的;值得称赞的;配受奖励的 ‖ ~**ly** *adv.*

mermaid ['mɜːmeɪd] *n.* **1.** (传说中的)美人鱼 **2.** 〈美〉女子游泳健将

merman ['mɜːmæn] ([复] mermen

['mæmen]) n. 1.（传说中的）男性人鱼 2.〈美〉男子游泳健将

merry ['meri] *adj.* 1. 欢乐的，愉快的，兴高采烈的 2. 微醉的 3. 轻快的；激烈的；[用以加强语气]很猛的 4.〈古〉令人愉快的；可爱的 ‖ **merrily** *adv.* ／ **merriment** *n.* ‖ '～-go-round *n.* （儿童玩乐用的）旋转木马 2.（美俚）[指工作、活动等]高度的繁忙；走马灯似的打转 ／ '～maker *n.* 寻欢作乐者，狂欢者 ／ '～making *n.* 作乐，欢乐，狂欢

mesa ['meisə] *n.* [地] 平顶山；阶地；岩滩

mesdames [mei'dæm] madam 和 madame 的复数

mesdemoiselles [ˌmeidmwa'zel] mademoiselle 的复数

mesh [meʃ] *n.* 1. 网眼，网孔；筛目，筛孔；每英寸长度内的网孔（或筛孔）数 2.[常～es] 网（丝）；网络；网状结构 3. 网织品；网状物 4.[常～es] 罗网，圈套；纠缠；错综复杂 5.[机]（齿轮的）啮合 —*vt.* 1. 用网捕捉；使缠住 2. 使成网状 3. 使紧密配合 [机] 使啮合 —*vi.* 1. 被网缠住；落网 2. 紧密配合 [机] 相啮合

mesmerize ['mesməraiz] *vt.* 1. 对…催眠 2. 使入迷；迷住；迷惑 ‖ **mesmerism** ['mesmərizəm] *n.* 催眠（术）；催眠力

Mesozoic [ˌmesəu'zəuik] [地] *adj.* 中生代的 —*n.* [the ～] 中生代

mesquit(e) ['meskit] *n.* [植] 牧豆树

mess [mes] *n.* 1. 伙食团（尤指军人的）；食堂；集体用膳人员；伙食 2. 一份食品（常指半流质的）；（给猎狗等吃的）杂食；〈古〉一道菜 3. 足够一顿饭的量；一次（抓、捕）所得量 4. 混乱，杂乱；大杂烩；肮脏 5. 困境 6.（美俚）笨人，傻瓜 —*vt.* 1. 使就餐，给…供膳；〈英方〉配给（食物）；分（菜）2. 弄糟，搞

乱；弄脏 3. 妨碍；干扰 4. 粗暴地处理 —*vi.* 1. 准备伙食；供膳 2. 集体用膳 3. 搞乱；搞糟；摆弄；干涉

message ['mesidʒ] *n.* 1. 文电；通讯；信息，音信；祝词 2. 差使 3.〈美〉公文 4. 启示；寓意 5. 广告词句 6. 电报；报文 7.[生] 遗传信息 —*vt.* 通知；发信号传达；同…通讯联系 —*vi.* 带信息；通信联系

messenger ['mesindʒə] *n.* 1. 送信者；报信者；信使；使者；通信员 2.[生] 信使 3.[海] 引缆，引缆

Messiah [mi'saiə] *n.* 1. 弥赛亚（犹太人期望中的复国救主）2.[基督教] 救世主，耶稣；[m-]（民族或国家的）救星

Messrs. ['mesəz] *abbr.* Mr. 的复数

messy ['mesi] *adj.* 凌乱的，混乱的；肮脏的 ‖ **messily** *adv.* / **messiness** *n.*

mestizo [mes'tiːzəu] ([复] mestizo(e)s) *n.*（尤指西班牙人与美洲印第安人的）混血儿 ‖ **mestiza** [mes'tiːzə] *n.* 女混血儿

met [met] meet 的过去式和过去分词

metabolic [ˌmetə'bɔlik] *adj.* 新陈代谢的，代谢作用的 ‖ **～ally** *adv.*

metabolism [me'tæbəlizəm] *n.* 新陈代谢，代谢作用

metal ['metl] *n.* 1. 金属；金属制品 2. 合金 3.（英）[～s]（铁路的）钢轨 4. 铸铁溶液；熔融液 5.[印] 活字合金，字铅；铅字；排好的活字版 6. 气质，本性；勇气 7.[军]（军舰的）炮火力；[总称] 坦克；装甲车 8.（英）[铺路用的] 碎石料 9.〈美俚〉[强节奏、大音量的] "重金属" 电子摇滚乐—（=metal(l)ed; metal(l)ing）—*vt.* 1. 用金属包 2. 用碎石（或矿渣）铺（路）—*vi.*〈美俚〉演奏 "重金属" 电子摇滚乐

metallic [mi'tælik] *adj.* 1. 金属的；金属制的；含金属的 2. 产金属的 3.（颜色等）像金属的（态度、声音等）是硬的；

刺耳的

metallurgical [ˌmetəˈlɜːdʒikəl] *adj.* 冶金（学）的

metallurgy [meˈtælədʒi] *n.* 冶金学；冶金术 ‖ **metallurgist** *n.*

metalware [ˈmetəlweə] *n.* 〖总称〗金属器皿（尤指炊具、餐具等）

metamorphic [ˌmetəˈmɔːfik] *adj.* 变形的；变质的；改变结构的

metamorphose [ˌmetəˈmɔːfəuz] *vt.* 使变 （*to, into*）；使变形；使变质 — *vi.* 变化；变形；变质

metamorphosis [ˌmetəˈmɔːfəsis] （〖复〗 metamorphoses[ˌmetəˈmɔːfəsiːz]）*n.* 1. 变形；变质；变状 2. 魔术引起的变形 3. 〖生〗变态；代谢（作用）

metaphor [ˈmetəfə] *n.* 〖语〗隐喻（一种修辞手段）；比喻；比喻说法

metaphysics [ˌmetəˈfiziks] 〖复〗 *n.* （用作单）形而上学，玄学 2. ‖ **metaphysical** *adj.* / **metaphy'sician** *n.*

mete [miːt] *vt.* 1. 给予；派给 2. 〈古〉计量

meteor [ˈmiːtiə] *n.* 1.〈废〉大气现象 2. 流星；陨星 3. 流星体

meteoric [ˌmiːtiˈɔrik] *adj.* 1. 大气的；气象的 2. 流星（体）的 3. 流星似的；转瞬即逝的；闪烁的

meteorite [ˈmiːtiərait] *n.* 〖天〗1. 陨星 2. 流星

meteorologic(al) [ˌmiːtiərəˈlɔdʒik(əl)] *adj.* 气象学的；气象的 ‖ **meteorologically** *adv.*

meteorology [ˌmiːtiəˈrɔlədʒi] *n.* 1. 气象学 2.（一地区的）气象 ‖ **meteorologist** *n.*

meter[1] [ˈmiːtə] *n.* 1. 计量器；计，仪表 2. 计量员；邮资机 — *vt.* 1. 用表测量（或计量）2. 计量（或按规定量）供给 3. 用邮资机在（邮件）上打戳

meter[2] [ˈmiːtə] *n.*〈美〉= **metre**[1], **metre**[2]

-meter *comb. form* 1. 表示"计量器"；"计"，"表"：thermo*meter* 2.〈美〉表示"米"：kilo*meter*, centi*meter* 3. 表示"（诗的）音步"：penta*meter* 五音步的

methane [ˈmiːθein] *n.* 〖化〗甲烷，沼气

methanol [ˈmeθənɔl] *n.* 〖化〗甲醇

method [ˈmeθəd] *n.* 1. 方法，办法；教学法 2. 条理；秩序

methodic(al) [miˈθɔdik(əl)] *adj.* 有方法的；有条理的 ‖ **methodically** *adv.*

methyl [ˈmiːθail, ˈmeθil] *n.* 〖化〗甲基

meticulous [miˈtikjuləs] *adj.* 1. 过分注意细节的，谨小慎微的 2. 过细的，细致的 ‖ ~**ly** *adv.* 过细地，细致地

metre[1] [ˈmiːtə] *n.* 1.（诗歌等的）韵律，格律 2.〖音〗拍子

metre[2] [ˈmiːtə] *n.*（公制长度单位）米

metric [ˈmetrik] *adj.* 公制的，米制的 ‖ **metricate** *vi.* 采用（或改用）公制 *vt.* 将…改为公制；使…适用于公制 / **metri'cation** *n.* 采用（或改用）公制；公制化 / **metricize** [ˈmetrisaiz] *vt.* 将…改为公制；使…适用于公制；用公制单位表示；使公制化 ‖ ~ **system** 公制，米制

metrical [ˈmetrikəl] *adj.* 1.（诗歌等的）韵律的，格律的；诗韵的；用诗体写的 2. 测量的；度量的 3.（公制长度单位）米的；公制的，米制的

metro [ˈmetrəu] *n.*（〖复〗metros）*n.*〈口〉（尤指巴黎的）地铁，地下铁道

metronome [ˈmetrənəum] *n.* 〖音〗节拍机

metropolis [miˈtrɔpəlis] *n.* 1.（一国的）首要城市；大城市，大都会 2.（某种商业活动的）中心 3.（殖民地的）宗主国（或宗主城市）4.〖宗〗都主教教省

metropolitan [ˌmetrəˈpɔlit(ə)n] *adj.* 1. 首要城市的；大城市的，大都会的 2.〖宗〗都

主教(教省)的 3. 宗主(国)的 — *n.* 1. 大城市人;大城市派头的人 2. 都主教

mettle ['metl] *n.* 气质;气概;勇气;精神

mew [mju:] *n.* 咪,喵(猫叫声) — *vi.* 咪咪叫,喵喵叫

mewl [mju:l] *vi.* (婴儿)低声地哭,呜呜地哭

Mexican ['meksikən] *n.* 1. 墨西哥人;有墨西哥血统的人 2. 有西班牙人和印第安人混合血统的人 3. (印第安语系中的)尤特 — 阿兹特克语 — *adj.* 墨西哥的;墨西哥人的

Mexico ['meksikəu] *n.* 1. 墨西哥[拉丁美洲国家] 2. 墨西哥城[墨西哥首都] (= ~ City)

mezzanine ['metsəni:n, 'mezənin] *n.* 1. (尤指一楼和二楼间的)夹层楼面 2. 〈英〉(舞台下面的)底层空间 3. 〈美〉(剧场的)楼厅包厢,楼厅前座

MFN *abbr.* most favo(u)red nation 最惠国

mg. *abbr.* milligram(me)(s)

MHz *abbr.* megahertz

mi [mi:] *n.* [音]七个唱名之一(在固定唱名法中相当于音名 E)

mi. *abbr.* mile(s)

MIA *abbr.* missing in action 战斗中失踪的(人)

Miami [mai'æmi] *n.* 迈阿密[美国佛罗里达州东南部港市]

miaow, miaou [mi:'au] *n. & vi.* = meow

miasma [mi'æzmə] *n.* ([复] miasmas 或 miasmata [mi'æzmətə]) *n.* 臭气;瘴气;不良气氛

mica ['maikə] *n.* [矿]云母

mice [mais] mouse 的复数

Michigan ['miʃigən] *n.* 1. 密歇根(或译密执安)[美国州名] 2. 密歇根湖(或译密执安湖)[美国北部](= Lake ~)

micr(o)- *comb. form* 1. 表示"小","微";"微量";"百万分之一": microlitre, microampere 微安 2. 表示"扩大","放大": microphone, microscope

microbe ['maikrəub] *n.* 微生物;细菌

microcard ['maikrəukɑ:d] *n.* 缩微卡(每张纸单印卯印刷物二百页以上,供以后放大阅读)

microclimate ['maikrəu,klaimit] *n.* 【气】小气候(指小块局部地区的气候)

microcopy ['maikrə,kɔpi] *n.* (印刷物等的)缩微复制品,缩微本 — *vt. & vi.* 缩微复制

microcosm ['maikrəukɔzəm] *n.* 小天地;小宇宙;微观世界

microfiche ['maikrəufi:ʃ] *n.* [摄]缩微平片

microfilm ['maikrəufilm] *n.* (印刷物等的)缩微胶卷 — *vt.* 把……拍摄在缩微胶卷上 — *vi.* 用缩微胶卷拍摄

microimage ['maikrəu,imidʒ] *n.* 缩微图像;缩微复制品

micrometer [mai'krɔmitə] *n.* 测微计,千分尺 ‖ = caliper 千分卡尺

micron ['maikrɔn] *n.* 微米(千分之一毫米,符号为 μ)

Micronesia [,maikrəu'ni:zjə] *n.* 1. 密克罗尼西亚[西太平洋的岛群] 2. 密克罗尼西亚联邦[西太平洋岛国]

microorganism [,maikrəu'ɔ:gənizəm] *n.* 微生物

microphone ['maikrəfəun] *n.* 传声器,扩音器,话筒麦克风

microscope ['maikrəskəup] *n.* 显微镜

microscopic(al) [,maikrə'kɔpik(əl)] *adj.* 1. 显微镜的;像显微镜的 2. 用显微镜可见的;微观的 3. 微小的,细微的 ‖ microscopically *adv.*

microwave ['maikrəweiv] *n.* 微波 — *vi.*

用微波炉烹调(或加热)(食物等) ‖ ~ **oven** 微波炉

mid [mid] *adj.* **1.** 中部的;中间的,居中的;当中的 **2.** [常用以构成复合词]中间,中间:the *Mid*-Autumn Festival 中秋节 **3.** 【语】央元音的,半开元音的 — *prep.* 〈诗〉= amid ‖ ~ **day** *n. adv.* & *n.* 正中,中间;斜内部 ‖ ~ **day** *n.* 正午,日中 /'Mideast *adj.* 【地】中东的 /'~ **night** *n.* 半夜 12 点钟中;午夜;漆黑 /'~ **rib** *n.* 【植】(叶的)中脉 /'~ **shipman** *n.* 〈美〉海军学校学员;〈英〉海军候补生 /'~ **summer** *n.* 仲夏;夏至(6 月 22 日左右) /'~ **way** *n.* **1.** 中途 **2.** 〈美〉(博览会等中的)娱乐场,游艺场 *adv.* & *adj.* 中途(的) /'Midway **Islands** 中途岛(北太平洋) /'~ **week** *n.* 一星期的中间 ‖ [M~]〈基督教贵格会教友的〉星期三 /'~ **winter** *n.* 仲冬;冬至(12 月 22 日左右) /'~ **year** *n.* 年中间;学年中期 ‖ *n.* 学年中期考试; [midyears]学年中期考试期

middle ['midl] *n.* **1.** 中部,中间,当中 **2.** 身体的中部,腰部 **3.** (中间物);中年 **4.** 中间派 **5.**〈希腊语法中的〉动词中间态 **6.** 〈英〉[报刊上常排在政论文与书评之间的]文学性短文(= ~ article) **7.**【逻】中项(中项);【数】中项(= ~ term) — *adj.* **1.** 中部的,中间的,当中的 **2.** 中等的,中级的 **3.** [M~]【语】中古的 **4.** 〈希腊语法中的〉中间态的 **5.** 中产阶级的 — *vt.* & *vi.* (把…)放在中间(把…)对折 ‖ ~ **age** 中年 /'~ 'aged *adj.* 中年的 /Middle **Ages** 中世纪 /Middle **America 1.** 美国中产阶级 **2.** 中部美洲(包括墨西哥及西印度群岛等地) **3.** 美国中西部 ~ **class** 中产阶级 /Middle **East** 中东 /'~ **man** *n.* 经纪人,中间人,中人 /'~ **weight** *n.* **1.** 中等体重的人 **2.** 中量级拳击(或摔跤)运动员 /Middle **West** 〈美国的〉中西部

middling ['midliŋ] *adj.* 中等的;二等的;普通的;一般的 — *n.* **1.** 二流人物(或事物) **2.** [常作 ~ s]中档货 **3.** [~ s]用作单或复]麦麸,粗面粉

middy ['midi] *n.* 〈美口〉海军军官学校学员;〈英〉海军候补生 **2.** 水手领上衣;水手领罩衫

midge [midʒ] *n.* **1.**【动】蠓;摇蚊 **2.** 矮人,侏儒 **3.** 极小的鱼

midget ['midʒit] *n.* **1.** 矮人,侏儒 **2.**〈同类事物中的〉极小者 — *adj.* 小型的

midland ['midlənd] *n.* (一国的)中部(地区);内陆,内地

midriff ['midrif] *n.* **1.**【解】膈 **2.** 上腹部 **3.** 〈美〉裸露上腹部的女服

midst [midst] *n.* 中部,中间,当中 — *prep.* 〈诗〉= amidst

Midwest ['mid'west] *n.*(美国的)中西部;中西部的人(或事物)

midwife ['midwaif] *n.* [复] midwives ['midwaivz] *n.* **1.** 助产士;接生婆 **2.** 催生因素,促成因素 ‖ ~ **ry** *n.* **1.** 产科学,助产学 **2.** 催生,促生

mien [miːn] *n.* **1.** 风度;神采;态度 **2.** 外表,外貌

miff [mif] *n.* **1.** 发脾气;愠怒 **2.** 无谓的争吵 — *vt.* & *vi.* **1.**(使)生气 **2.**(使)发脾气

might[1] [mait] *n.* **1.** 力量;威力;能力 **2.** 强权,势力 **3.**〈方〉大量,很多

might[2] [mait] *v. aux.* (may 的过去式)[无人称变化;后接不带 to 的动词不定式;只用于表示现在或将来的概念] **1.** [表示可能、不确定、期望、许可等,相当于 may,但更带迟疑、婉转、谦逊等色彩]可能,也许,可以 **2.** [用于表示与事实相反情况的虚拟语气中]会;能 **3.** [表示请求或婉转的责备]请;应该

mightily ['maitili] *adv.* 1. 强有力地;猛烈地 2. 非常,极

mightn't ['maitnt] = might not

mighty ['maiti] *adj.* 1. 强大的;强有力的 2. 巨大的,浩大的 3.〈口〉伟大的;非凡的;了不得的 —*adv.*〈口〉非常,很 ‖ **mightiness** *n.*

migraine ['maigrein, 'mi:grein] *n.*【医】偏头痛

migrant ['maigrənt] *adj.* = migratory —*n.* 1. 候鸟;移栖的动物 2. 移居者;移民 3. (美)农业季节工人

migrate [mai'greit] *vi.* 1. 迁移;移居(尤指移居外国) 2. (候鸟等)定期移栖;(鱼群)回游 3.【化】【物】移动,蠕动 —*vt.* 使移居;使蠕动

migration [mai'greiʃən] *n.* 1. 迁居;移居外国;移民群 2. (候鸟等的)定期移栖;(鱼群)回游;移栖群 3.【化】【物】移动,蠕动

migratory ['maigrətəri] *adj.* 1. 迁移的;移居的;移民群的 2. 流浪性的;游牧的;(应季节性劳动需求而)流动的 3.【化】【物】移动的,蠕动的

mikado [mi'kɑːdəu] *n.* 〔常作 M-〕日本天皇

mike [maik] *n.* 〈口〉话筒(= microphone)

mil [mil] *n.* 密耳(测量金属线直径的长度单位) = 0.001 英寸)

milady [mi'leidi] *n.* 夫人,太太(旧时欧洲大陆人对英国贵妇人的尊称)

milage ['mailidʒ] *n.* = mileage

Milan [mi'læn], **Milano** [miː'lɑːnɔ] *n.* 米兰〔意大利西北部城市〕

milch [miltʃ] *adj.* (家畜)有奶的,生乳的;为取乳而饲养的;适于产奶的 ‖ ~ cow 奶牛,乳牛 2. 财源;摇钱树

mild [maild] *adj.* 1. 温和的;温柔的 2. 温暖的,暖和的 3.(酒、烟等)味淡的 4.(在动作或作用方面)和缓的;适度的 5.(处罚等)轻微的;微小的 6.【冶】低碳的,软的 ‖ ~ly *adv.* 1. 温和地 2. 适度地 / ~ness *n.*

mildew ['mildju:] *n.* 1. 霉;霉菌 2.【植】霉病 —*vi.* 发霉,长霉,生霉 —*vt.* 使发霉

mile [mail] *n.* 1. 英里(略作 mi.) 2. 1 英里赛跑(或赛马) 3. 海里(= nautical ~) 4. 很大的距离(或程度) ‖ ~ post *n.* (英里)里程标 / ~stone *n.* 1. (英里)里程碑 2.〔喻〕里程碑,(个人或人类历史上的)重大事件;转折点

mileage ['mailidʒ] *n.* 1. 英里数;英里里程 2. 按英里计算的运费 3. 按英里计算的旅费(或交通补贴) 4. 汽车消耗 1 加仑汽油所行的英里里程 5. 好处;利益;用处

milieu ['miːljə] *n.* 环境;背景

militancy ['militənsi], **militance** ['militəns] *n.* 1. 战斗性,战斗精神 2. 交战状态;好战(性)

militant ['militənt] *adj.* 1. 战斗(性)的;富于战斗性的 2. 好战的 3. 交战中的,战斗中的 —*n.* 富有战斗精神的人;好斗分子;激进分子

militarism ['militərizəm] *n.* 1. 军国主义 2. 好战精神;尚武精神 ‖ **militarist** *n.* 1. 军国主义者 2. 军事家

militarize ['militəraiz] *vt.* 1. 使军事化;使带上军事性质 2. 使具有军国主义化;使好战

military ['militəri] *adj.* 1. 军事的;军用的 2. 军人的;军队的 3. 陆军的 —([复] military 或 militaries) *n.* 1. [the ~]武装部队;军方;陆军 2. [the ~][总称]军人(尤指军官) ‖ **militarily** ['militərili, mili'terili] *adv.* 在军事上,从

军事角度

militate ['militeit] *vi.* 起作用；发生影响

militia [mi'liʃə] *n.* 1. 民兵组织；〔总称〕民兵 2.（紧急情况下召集的）国民军 ‖ ~ man *n.*（男）民兵

milk [milk] *n.* 1. 乳；牛奶 2.（植物、果实的）乳液，乳状物；〔药〕乳剂 —*vt.* 1. 挤…的奶；挤（奶）2. 抽取（树等）的乳液；抽取（乳液等）；取出（蛇等）的毒液 3. 压，榨，榨取 4. 套出（消息等）；〈俚〉窃取（电话、电报线）上的消息 5. 加牛奶于 —*vi.* 1. 挤奶 2. 出奶 ‖ ~ maid *n.*（牛奶场）挤奶女工 / ~ man *n.* 卖（或送）牛奶的人 / ~ powder 奶粉 / ~ shake 泡沫牛奶（将牛奶和冰淇淋等混合后搅打至起泡的饮料）/ ~ tooth 乳齿 / ~ weed *n.*〔植〕马利筋

milkiness ['milkinis] *n.* 1. 乳状 2. 混浊不清；乳白色 3. 柔弱；温顺

milky ['milki] *adj.* 1. 牛奶的；掺奶的；多乳的；出乳的 2. 像牛奶的；乳白色的；（液体）混浊不清的；浊白的 3. 柔弱的；温顺的 ‖ Milky Way〔天〕银河；银河系

mill¹ [mil] *n.* 1. 磨坊；碾磨厂；面粉厂 2. 磨臼；磨（粉）机；碾磨机 3. 制造厂，工厂；制造机构 4. 钱币压印机；榨汁机；〔冶〕轧钢机床 5.〔机〕铣床；铣刀 6.（刻纹镀模的）铜芯子 7.〔机〕拳击 8.〈美俚〉监狱 9.〈美俚〉机车（飞机等的）马达 10.〈美俚〉打字机 —*vt.* 1. 碾磨；碾碎；磨细 2.〔机〕铣 3. 搅拌；将…打成泡沫 4.［常以过去分词形式出现］在（钱币）上压印花边 5. 使（畜群）绕圈子转 6.〔纺〕使（织物）缩绒（或缩呢）7.〈美俚〉用拳打 —*vi.* 1.（人、家畜）成群地乱转 2.〈美俚〉殴斗 3. 被研磨 ‖ ~ er *n.* 1. 磨坊主；面粉厂主 2. 碾磨工，铣工 3. 铣床；铣床用工具 4.

蛾 ‖ ~ race *n.* 1. 磨坊水车动力水流 2.（水车用）水沟 / ~ stone *n.* 1. 磨石 2. 重负；磨难；折磨 / ~ wheel（磨坊的）水车轮

mill² [mil] *n.*〈美〉密尔，厘（等于千分之一美元；只用作记账货币）

millennium [mi'leniəm]（[复] millenniums 或 millennia [mi'leniə]）*n.* 1. 一千年，千年期 2. 千年周年纪念日（或庆典）3.【基督教】千禧年（据《圣经·启示录》，基督将再来统治人间一千年）4.（未来或想象中的）太平盛世，黄金时代

millet ['milit] *n.*〔植〕黍，稷；粟，小米

milli- *comb. form* 表示"毫"，"千分之一"；*milli* gram(me)

milliard ['miliɑːd] *num.*（英）十亿（美国称 billion）

millibar ['milibɑː] *n.*〔气〕毫巴

milligram(me) ['miligræm] *n.* 毫克（千分之一克，略作 mg.）

millilitre, milliliter ['mili,liːtə] *n.* 毫升（千分之一升，略作 ml.）

millimetre, millimeter ['mili,miːtə] *n.* 毫米（千分之一米，略作 mm.）

milliner ['milinə] *n.* 女帽设计（或制造、整修、销售）者

millinery ['milinəri] *n.* 1.〔总称〕女帽；妇女头饰用品 2. 女帽制造（或整修、销售）业

million ['miljən] *num.* 百万；百万个（人或物）—*n.* 1. 百万元（或镑、法郎等）2.［~s］无数 3.［the ~］大众 ‖ ~ th *num.* 1. 第一百万（个）2. 一百万分之一（的）

million(n)aire [,miljə'nɛə] *n.* 百万富翁；巨富

millipede ['milipiːd], **milliped** ['miliped] *n.*【动】倍足（亚）纲节肢动物（如马陆、

蝾蚰等)

milt [milt] *n.* (充满精液的)雄鱼生殖腺;(雄鱼的)精液,鱼白

mime [maim] *n.* 小丑,丑角;滑稽演员;哑剧演员

mimeograph ['mimiəgra:f] *n.* 1. 油印机 2. 油印品 — *vt. & vi.* (用油印机)油印

mimic ['mimik] *adj.* 1. 模仿的;好模仿的;摹拟的;假装的 2.[生]拟态的 — *n.* 1. 好学样者;效颦者;滑稽演员;小丑 2. 仿制品 — (mimicked ['mimikt]; mimicking['mimikiŋ]) *vt.* 1. 模仿;摹拟 2. 细致地临摹 3. 酷似;以…的形象呈现 ‖ ~ly *adv.*

mimosa [mi'məuzə] *n.*[植]含羞草

min. *abbr.* 1. minimum 2. minute(s)

minaret ['minəret] *n.* (清真寺旁的)光塔

mince [mins] *vt.* 切碎,剁碎,斩细;(用绞碎机)绞碎 2. 吞吞吐吐地说,婉转地说 — *vi.* 1. 碎步走;扭担捏捏地走 2. 矫揉造作,装腔作势 — *n.* ‖~meat *n.* 1. 开采,开采 2. 在…下挖坑道;在地下挖(…),从(水、空气等)中提取;[昆虫]下钻洞 2. 在…下挖坑道;在地下挖(…) 3. 在…中(或在…下)敷雷;(用雷)炸爆 4. 暗害;破坏 — *vi.* 1. 开矿;挖坑道 2. 布雷 ‖~ *n.* 1. 矿工 2. 地雷工兵 3. 联合采矿 ‖'~field *n.* 布雷区;危险区域 ‖危险形势 /'~ layer *n.* 布雷舰艇(或飞机) /'~ sweeper *n.* 扫雷舰;扫雷器

mineral ['minərəl] *n.* 1. 矿物 2.[化]无机物 3. [~s]〈英〉= mineral water — *adj.* 1. 矿物的,矿质的 2. 无机的 ‖ ~wa-ter 矿泉水,矿泉水;软饮料(如苏打水;姜汁啤酒等)

mineralogy [,minə'rælədʒi] *n.* 矿物学 ‖ **mineralogist** *n.* 矿物学家

mince ‖~meat *n.* 1. 切碎,剁碎,斩细;(用绞碎机)绞碎 2. 吞吞吐吐地说,婉转地说 — *vi.* 1. 碎步走;扭担捏捏地走 2. 矫揉造作,装腔作势 ‖ ~meat *n.* 剁碎的肉;百果馅;肉馅 ‖ ~ pie *n.* 肉馅饼;甜馅饼 ‖[~ pies]

mind [maind] *n.* 1. 头脑;精神;心(神) 2. 意向,愿望;意见,见解 3. 记忆,心理;心情;绪 5. 理智;智能;有才智的人 6.[宗]追思弥撒;[M⁻]基督教]上帝;神道 — *vt.* 1. 注意;听从,留心,当心 2. 专心于;从事[常用于疑问,否定、条件句中] 3. 反对 4. (细心地)照看,照料,关心 5.〈方〉意欲,想要 6.〈方〉想起;记得 — *vi.* 1. 注意;听话;留心,当心 2. 介意 3. 关心,照料

minded ['maindid] *adj.* 1. [常用以构成复合词]有…心的;有…思想的;关心…的;重视…的 absent~心不在焉的 2.

[只作表语]有意于…的;心想…的

mindful ['maindful] *adj.* 留心的,注意的;记挂着的,不忘的(*of*)

mindless ['maindlis] *adj.* 1. 没头脑的;愚笨的 2. [常作表语]不注意的;粗心大意的

mine¹ [main] *pron.* 1. [物主代词]我的(东西);我的家属(或有关的人) 2.〈古〉我的(= my)

mine² [main] *n.* 1. 矿(藏);矿山;矿井;(英)铁矿砂 2. 宝库;源泉 3. 地雷;水雷 4. 坑道;地雷坑 5. (在空中爆发成多种火花的)烟火 6.[动](昆虫的)潜道 — *vt.* 1. 开采;开矿

minestrone [,mini'strəuni] *n.* (意大利式)蔬菜浓汤

mingle ['miŋgl] *vt.* 使混合,使相混 — *vi.* 混合起来,相混合(*in, with*)

mini- *comb. form* 表示"小":~ bus

miniature ['minitʃə] *n.* 1. 小画像,袖珍画(尤指刻在象牙或画在牛皮纸上的)微小绘画术 2. 雏型;缩样;小型物 — *adj.* 雏型的;小型的 — *vt.* 是…

的缩影

miniaturize ['minitʃəraiz] vt. 使小型化,使微型化 ‖ ˌminiaturi'zation n. /~d adj.

minibus ['minibʌs] n. 小型公共汽车,面包车

minicab ['minikæb] n. 微型出租汽车

minim ['minim] n. 量滴(液量容量单位,相当于一滴水的容量)

minima ['minimə] minimum 的复数

minimal ['miniml] adj. 最低限度的;最小的

minimize ['minimaiz] vt. 1. 使减到最少;使缩到最小 2. 把…估计得最低;极度轻视

minimum ['miniməm] ([复] minima ['minimə]或 minimums) n. 1. 最小量;最小数;最低限度 2.【数】极小(值)— adj. 最小的;最少的;最低的

mining ['mainiŋ] n. 1. 采矿;矿业 2.【军】布雷

minion ['minjən] n. 宠儿;奴才;部属

miniskirt ['miniskət] n. 超短裙 ‖ ~ed adj. 穿超短裙的

minister ['ministə] n. 1. 部长;大臣 2. 公使;外交使节 3.(基督教新教)牧师;(某些教派的)教长(= ~ general) 4. 代理者;执行者;工具 1. 伺候;照顾;给予帮助(to) 2. 执行牧师职务 — vt. 1.〈古〉供给 2. 举行(祭祀等)

ministerial [ˌminis'tiəriəl] adj. 1. 部长的;部的;公使的;[常作 M-]内阁的;支持内阁方面的 2. 奉命令做的;代理的;行政(性)的(与 judicial 司法的相对)3. 起作用的;作为成因的(to)4. 牧师的

ministry ['ministri] n. 1.(政府)部;部的办公楼 2.[常作 M-](全体)部长;内

阁 3.[the ~](全体)牧师 4. 部长(或公使、牧师)的职位(或任期)5. 服务

mink [mink]([复] mink(s)) n. 1.【动】貂(尤指水貂) 2. 水貂毛皮,貂皮;貂皮外衣

Minnesota [ˌmini'səutə] n. 明尼苏达[美国州名]

minnow ['minəu]([复] minnow(s)) n. 1. 米诺鱼;鲤科淡水小鱼 2. 用作钓饵的活小鱼(或假小鱼)

minor ['mainə] adj. 1. 较小的;较少的;较年幼的;次要的 2. 未成年的 3.(疾病等)不严重的,无生命危险的 4.〈美〉(大学学科)副修的 5.【音】小调的;小音阶的〈古〉少数的 n. 1. 未成年人;次要的人(或机构等);次要事物 2.【逻】小项;小前提 3.【音】小调;小音阶 4.〈美〉(大学中的)副修科目;副修科学生 5.[M-]〈天主教〉小兄弟会修士 — vi.〈美〉副修(in)

minority [mai'nɔriti] n. 1. 少数;少数党;少数派 2. 少数民族 3. 未成年;未达法定年龄

Minsk [minsk] n. 明斯克[白俄罗斯首都]

minstrel ['minstrəl] n. 1.(中世纪的)吟游诗人(或歌手);豪门艺人 2. 音乐家;诗人 3.(白人扮演黑人的)滑稽唱团演员,滑稽说唱团演员(= ~ show)

mint[1] [mint] n. 1.【植】薄荷 2. 薄荷糖

mint[2] [mint] n. 1. 造币厂;〈喻〉制造所,来源 2. 巨额的钱;大量 — adj. 崭新的;完美的;新造的一 vt. 1. 铸造(硬币);把(金属)铸成硬币(into) 2. 制造,创造(词语等)

minuend ['minjuend] n.【数】被减数

minuet [ˌminju'et] n. 1. 米奴哀舞(一种小步舞) 2. 米奴哀舞曲

minus ['mainəs] *prep.* 1. 减(去) 2.〈口〉没有；失去 — *adj.* 1. 负的；减去的 2. (通常放在被修饰的词之后)略差一些的 — *n.* 1. 〖数〗负号；减号(= ~ sign)；负数;负量 2. 不足；缺陷

minuscule ['minəskju:l] *adj.* 很小的，微小的；不重要的

minute¹ ['minit] *n.* 1. 分(一小时或一度的六十分之一)；一分钟的路程 2. 一会儿，片刻；瞬间 3. 备忘录；笔记;底稿；[~s] 会议记录 4. (角度的)分(= ~ of arc) — *vt.* 1. 记录;摘录;将…制成备忘录(*down*);将…列入会议记录 2. 测定…的精确时间 ‖ ~ly *adv.* & *adj.* 每分钟地(的)；连续不断地地(的) ‖ ~ man *n.* 1. [美国独立战争期间]召之即来的民兵 2. [M-]民兵式洲际导弹;(美国极right组织)"民兵"的成员

minute² [mai'nju:t] *adj.* 1. 微小的，微细的;不足道的 2. 详细的;细致的;精密的 ‖ ~ly *adv.*

minutia [mi'nju:ʃiə, mai'nju:ʃiə] ([复] minutiae [mi'nju:ʃii:, mai'nju:ʃii:] *n.* [常作minutiae] 细枝末节；微小细节

minx [miŋks] *n.* 冒失(或轻佻)的少女

miracle ['mirəkl] *n.* 1. 奇迹；非凡的事例;令人惊奇的人(或事物) 2.(中世纪表演基督教〈圣经〉故事的)奇迹剧;圣迹剧(= ~ play)

miraculous [mi'rækjuləs] *adj.* 1. 超自然的;非凡的 2. 像奇迹一样的;令人惊叹的;不可思议的 3. 能创造奇迹的 ‖ ~ly *adv.*

mirage ['mirɑ:ʒ, mi'rɑ:ʒ] *n.* 1. 海市蜃楼，蜃景;幻景 2. 幻想;妄想

mire ['maiə] *n.* 淤泥;泥潭;泥坑;困境 — *vt.* 使陷满污泥;使陷入泥坑;使陷入困境 — *vi.* 掉进泥坑;陷入困境 ‖ **miry** *adj.*

mirror ['mirə] *n.* 1. 镜 2.〈喻〉镜子,真实反映情况的东西;借鉴 — *vt.* 反映;反映;反射,映照 ‖ ~ image 〖物〗镜像;〈喻〉映像，翻版

mirth [mə:θ] *n.* 欢笑，高兴 ‖ ~less *adj.*

mirthful ['mə:θful] *adj.* 欢笑的，高兴的 ‖ ~ly *adv.*

MIRV *abbr.* multiple independently-targeted reentry vehicle 〖军〗多弹头分导再入飞行器(弹头)

mis- *pref.* 表示"坏"，"错"，"误": *misfortune, misunderstand*

misadventure [ˌmisəd'ventʃə] *n.* 1. 不幸的事;不幸的遭遇;灾难 2.〖律〗意外事故

misanthrope ['misənθrəup] *n.* 厌恶人类者;厌世者

misapply [ˌmisə'plai] *vt.* 1. 误用;滥用 2. 挪用；盗用 ‖ **misapplication** ['misˌæpli'keiʃən] *n.*

misapprehend [ˌmisˌæpri'hend] *vt.* 误解，误会 ‖ **misapprehension** *n.*

misappropriate [ˌmisə'prəuprieit] *vt.* 1. 挪用;盗用;侵吞;私占 2. 滥用 ‖ **'mis,appro'pri'ation** *n.*

misbegotten [ˌmisbi'gɔtən] *adj.* 私生的，非婚生的;靠非法手段获得的

misbehave [ˌmisbi'heiv] *vt.* [~ oneself] 使行为不当,使举止不端 — *vi.* 1. 行为不当，举止不端 2. 行为失常,举止出人意外

misbehavio(u)r [ˌmisbi'heivjə] *n.* 不正当的行为,不端的举止

miscalculate [ˌmis'kælkjuleit] *vt.* & *vi.* 算错;错误地估计 (或判断) ‖ **'mis,calcu'lation** *n.*

miscarry [mis'kæri] *vt.* 1.(计划等)失败 2.(信件等)被误投,被误送 3.(孕妇)

小产,流产 ‖ **miscarriage** *n.*

miscegenation [ˌmisidʒi'neiʃən] *n.* 种族间通婚;混种

miscellaneous [ˌmisi'leiniəs] *adj.* 1. 混杂的,各种各样杂在一起的 2. 有各种特点的;多方面的;兴趣杂的;多才多艺的

mischance [mis'tʃɑːns] *n.* 1. 不幸;厄运;坏运气 2. 意外的不幸事件;倒霉事

mischief ['mistʃif] *n.* 1.(尤指人为的)损害;伤害;危害;毒害 2. 造成损害的行为(或人);祸根 3. 调皮,淘气,捣蛋,恶作剧 4. 调皮的人,淘气鬼 5. [the ~]用于特殊疑问句,加强语气]究竟

mischievous ['mistʃivəs] *adj.* 1. 有害的;为害的 2. 调皮的,淘气的;恶作剧的 ‖ **~ly** *adv.* / **~ness** *n.*

misconceive [ˌmiskən'siːv] *vt. & vi.* 误解 ‖ **misconception** [ˌmiskən'sepʃən] *n.*

misconduct [ˌmiskən'dʌkt] *vt. & vi.* 1. 办错;对…处置不当 2. [~ oneself] 使行为不端 — [ˌmis'kɔndʌkt] *n.* 1. 办错;处置不当 2.(尤指官吏的)胡作非为;渎职 3. 不端行为;通奸

misconstrue [ˌmiskən'struː] *vt.* 误解;误解…的意图(或图谋)

miscreant ['miskriənt] *adj.* 1. 堕落的;恶的;无赖的 2.〈古〉异端的;异教的;不信教的 — *n.* 1. 恶棍,歹徒,无赖 2.〈古〉异端者;异教徒

misdeal [ˌmis'diːl] (misdealt [ˌmis'delt]) *vt. & vi.* 发错(牌) — *n.* 发错牌

misdeed [ˌmis'diːd] *n.* 不端行为;罪行

misdemeanor [ˌmisdi'miːnə] *n.* [律] 轻罪

miser ['maizə] *n.* 守财奴;财迷;吝啬鬼,小气鬼

miserable ['mizərəbl] *adj.* 1. 痛苦的;悲惨的;可怜的 2. 糟糕的;使人难受的

3. 蹩脚的;粗劣的 4. 可耻的;卑鄙的 ‖ **miserably** *adv.* 1. 悲惨地 2. 糟糕地 3.〈口〉极其

miserly ['maizəli] *adj.* 1. 守财奴的;吝啬鬼的 2. 爱钱如命的;吝啬的,小气的

misery ['mizəri] *n.* 1. 痛苦;悲惨;[miseries]痛苦的事,苦难 2.〈方〉疼痛 3.〈口〉老是忧愁的人

misfire [ˌmis'faiə] *vi. & n.*(火器等)不发火;(计划等)未产生预期效果,失败

misfit ['misfit] *n.* 1. 不合身的衣着 2. 不适应环境的人;不称职的人 3. 不合适;不相称 — [ˌmis'fit] (misfitted) misfitting) *vt.* 1.(衣着等)对…不合身 2. 对…不合适;对…不相称 — *vi.* 不合适;不相称

misfortune [mis'fɔːtʃən] *n.* 1. 不幸;不幸的事;灾祸 2.〈方〉生私生子;私生子

misgiving [mis'giviŋ] *n.* [常~s] 疑虑,担忧,害怕

misguide [ˌmis'gaid] *vt.* [常用被动语态]误导;使误入歧途

mishap ['mishæp, mis'hæp] *n.* 不幸的事;灾祸

mishmash ['miʃmæʃ] *n.* 杂乱的一堆;杂烩;大杂烩

misinform [ˌmisin'fɔːm] *vt.* 向…提供误消息(或情报);向…误报

misinformation [ˌmisinfə'meiʃən] *n.* 误报;错误的消息(或情报)

misinterpret [ˌmisin'təːprit] *vt.* 错误地理解(或解释、说明) ‖ **'misin,terpre'tation** *n.*

misjudge [ˌmis'dʒʌdʒ] *vt. & vi.* 判断错;估计错 ‖ **misjudg(e)ment** *n.*

mislay [mis'lei] (mislaid [mis'leid]) *vt.* 1. 把…布置错误;放错 2. 丢失 2. 丢弃

mislead [mis'liːd] (misled [mis'led]) *vt.* 1.

把…带错路；引导错 2. 把…带坏，使
入歧途 3. 给错误印象；使误解；欺骗

mismanage [ˌmisˈmænidʒ] *vt.* 对…管理
不善(或处置不当)

misnomer [ˌmisˈnəumə] *n.* 误用的名称；
误称

misogyny [miˈsɔdʒini] *n.* 厌女症，女人嫌
忌 ‖ **misogynist** *n.*

misplace [ˌmisˈpleis] *vt.* 1. 把…放错地
方，误放 2. 把(感情等)寄托于不该寄
托的对象 3. 使(言行等)不合时宜

misprint [ˌmisˈprint] *vt.* 印错，误印 —
[ˈmisprint] *n.* 印刷错误

mispronounce [ˌmisprəˈnauns] *vt.* 发错
(词等)的音；读错(词等)的音 —*vi.* 发
错音；读错音

mispronunciation [ˈmisprənʌnsiˈeiʃən] *n.*
发音错误

misquote [ˌmisˈkwəut] *vt. & vi.* 用错引
语；误引 ‖ **misquo'tation** *n.*

misread [ˌmisˈriːd] (misread [ˌmisˈred]) *vt.*
1. 读错；错看 2. 解释错，误解

misrepresent [ˈmisˌrepriˈzent] *vt.* 1. 误传，
误述；歪曲，把…颠倒黑白 2. 不适当
地代表；误制地代表

misrule [ˌmisˈruːl] *vt.* 对…施暴政；对…
治理不当 —*n.* 暴政；苛政；治理不当；
混乱，无政府状态

miss¹ [mis] *n.* 1. [M-](用于姓名或姓名之
前对未婚女子的称呼)小姐 2. (不用于
姓名前的称呼语)小姐 3. (课)姑娘；小
女孩；小女学生 4. [M-](用于地名或行
业名称前指在健美、技巧等方面具
有代表性的青年女子)…小姐；…皇
后；…女皇. Miss Volleyball 排球皇后

miss² [mis] *vt.* 1. 未击中；未得到；未达
到 2. 未看到；未听到；未觉察，未领会
3. 未履行；未出席；未赶上，错过 4. 逃

脱，免于 5. 发觉没有；发觉遗失；感到
不在，惦念 6. 遗漏；省去 —*vi.* 1. 未
击中；打偏 2. 失败 3. (内燃机等)发动
不起来 —*n.* 1. 击不中；失误；失败 2.
逃脱，幸免 3. (内燃机等的)发动不起
来 4. [口]流产，小产

missal [ˈmisəl] *n.* (天主教的)弥撒书；祈
祷书

misshapen [ˌmisˈʃeipən] *adj.* 1. 奇形怪状
的；畸形的；形态丑陋的 2. (道德或思
想上)丑恶的

missile [ˈmisail] *n.* 1. 发射物；投掷物(尤
指武器) 2. 导弹，飞弹；弹道导弹 —
adj. 可发射的；可投掷的

missing [ˈmisiŋ] *adj.* 缺掉的，失去的；失
踪的，下落不明的：the ~ [总称](战争
中的)失踪者，下落不明的人

mission [ˈmiʃən] *n.* 1. (外交)使团；代表
团；使馆 2. 传教团；传教机构；传教地
区；传教机构，布道 3. 慈善机构，救济机构 4. 使命，任务；天职；
[军]战斗任务；飞行任务 5. (使团等
的)派遣 —*vt.* 1. 派遣…为传教士 2.
向…传教

missionary [ˈmiʃənəri] *adj.* 教会的；传教
的；传教士的 —*n.* 1. 传教士 2. 削弱
罢工者斗志的人(= ~ worker)

Mississippi [ˌmisiˈsipi] *n.* 1. 密西西比
[美国州名] 2.[the ~]密西西比河[美
国中部]

missive [ˈmisiv] *n.* 信件；公文；公函 —
adj. (罕)(信件等)已发出的；将发出的

Missouri [miˈzuəri] *n.* 1. 密苏里[美国州
名] 2.[the ~]密苏里河[美国中西部]

misspell [ˌmisˈspel] (misspelled [ˌmisˈspelt,
ˌmisˈspeld] 或 misspelt [ˌmisˈspelt]) *vt.* 拼
错 ‖ **~ ing** *n.* 拼写错误

misstate [ˌmisˈsteit] *vt.* 1. 误述 2. 谎报；
伪称 ‖ **~ment** *n.*

misstep [ˌmisˈstep] *n.* 失足；失检；失策

mist [mist] n. 1. 薄雾, 霭 2. (眼睛的) 迷糊不清; 眼翳 3. (喻) 迷雾; 起模糊作用的东西; 造成理解上困难的事物 — vi. 1. 下薄雾; 被蒙上薄雾 2. 变得模糊, 迷糊 — vt. 使蒙上薄雾; 使模糊

mistake [mis'teik] ([mistook [mis'tuk], mistaken[mis'teikən]) vt. 1. 误解, 弄错 2. 把 … 错认 (for) 3. 挑选错; 估计错 — vi. 弄错, 搞错 — n. 1. 错误; 过失; 误会 2. 意外的怀孕; 不该出生的婴孩

mistaken [mis'teikən] mistake 的过去分词 — adj. 错误的, 弄错的 ‖ ~ly adv.

mister ['mistə] n. 1. [M-](常略作 Mr. 或 Mr, 复数略作 Messrs. ['mesəz]) 用于姓名或姓, 职称前) 先生 〈口〉(不用于姓名前的称呼语) 先生 3. 没有职称 (或头衔) 的人, 普通男人, 平民 4. 丈夫 5. [M-](用于地名或行业名称前指在事业、技巧等方面具有代表性的男子) … 先生; … 之王 — vt. 称呼 … 先生

mistletoe ['misltəu] n. [植] 槲寄生 (西俗用作圣诞节的装饰物)

mistook [mis'tuk] mistake 的过去式

mistreat [ˌmis'triːt] vt. 虐待 ‖ ~ment n.

mistress ['mistris] n. 1. 女主人, 主妇; 女庶主; 起支配作用的女子 2. 有专长的妇女; 女能手 3. 〈英〉(中学的) 女校长; 女教师 4. [M-]〈古〉小姐 (用于青年女子姓名前作称呼) ; … 夫人 (现只用缩写 Mrs. ['misiz], 放在已婚女子的夫性或姓名前) 5. [苏格兰][M-]子爵 (或男爵) 的长女 6. 情妇; 〈古〉情人, 恋人 (指女子) 7. 称霸的国家; 霸主

mistrial [ˌmis'traiəl] n. [律] 无效审判

mistrust [mis'trʌst] vt., vi. & n. 不信任; 不相信, 怀疑

misty ['misti] adj. 1. 有薄雾的; 薄雾笼罩的 2. 朦胧不清的, 模糊的; 糊涂的 ‖ **mistily** adv. / **mistiness** n.

misunderstand [ˌmisʌndə'stænd] (misunderstood [ˌmisʌndə'stud]) vt. 误解; 误会; 曲解 ‖ ~ing n.

misuse [ˌmis'juːz] vt. 1. 误用; 滥用 2. 苛待, 虐待 — [ˌmis'juːs] n. 误用; 滥用

MIT abbr. Massachusetts Institute of Technology (美国) 马萨诸塞理工学院, 麻省理工学院

mite [mait] n. 1. 螨 2. 小 (面值) 硬币 3. 极少的一笔钱; 力所能及的微小贡献 4. 少许, 一点儿 5. 小东西 (尤指小孩, 用时常带同情色彩)

miter[1], **mitre**[1] ['maitə] vt., vi. & n. (使) 斜接; (使) 斜拼接

miter[2], **mitre**[2] ['maitə] n. 1. [天主教或主教教] 在典礼时戴的主教冠 — vt. 给 (主教等) 加冕; 提升 … 为主教

mitigate ['mitigeit] vt. & vi. (使) 缓和; (使) 减轻 ‖ **miti'gation** n.

mitosis [mi'təusis] ([复] mitoses [mi'təusiːz]) n. [生] 有丝分裂

mit(t) [mit] n. 1. (女用) 露指长手套 2. 连指手套 3. 棒球手套 4. 拳击手套 5. (俚) 手 6. (复俚) 逮捕; [~s] 手铐 7. 〈美俚〉看手相者 (= ~ reader) — (mitted, mitting) vt. 〈美俚〉1. 与 … 握手 2. 用手铐铐住; 逮捕

mitten ['mitn] n. 1. 连指手套 2. (女用) 露指长手套 3. 拳击手套 4. [~s](俚) 手铐

mix [miks] vt. 1. 使混合, 搀和 2. 使结合; 使结交 3. 配制; 调制 4. 混淆, 搞混 5. 使杂乱 — vi. 1. 相混合; 相协调, 相容 2. 交往, 相处 3. 发生牵连; 参与 (in) 4. 杂交 — n. 1. 混合料 2. 混合物, 拌和物 3. (由几种成分组成的) 混合方便食品 4. 糊涂; 迷惑 ‖ ~er n. 1. 混合者; 搅拌器 2. [无] 混频器 3. 调酒器 4. 〈口〉交际家 5. 〈美俚〉交谊会

‖~-'up *n*. **1**. 混乱,杂乱 **2**. 混合物;
混合体 **3**. 〈口〉厮打,打架

mixed [mikst] *adj*. **1**. 混合的;混杂的 **2**. 男女混合的 **3**. 〈口〉头脑混乱的;糊涂的 **4**. 【语】混合的,中央的 ‖
~ **number**【数】带分数

mixture ['mikstʃə] *n*. **1**. 混合;混合状态;混合气 **2**. 混合物;混合料;混合气;【药】合剂

miz(z)en ['mizn] *n*. 【海】后桅;后桅纵帆 ‖~**mast** *n*. 【海】后桅

ml. *abbr.* millilitre(s)

mm. *abbr.* millimetre(s)

Mme. *abbr.* Madame

Mn【化】元素锰(manganese)的符号

mnemonic [ni:'mɔnik] *adj*. 记忆(性)的;助记(忆)的;用以助记的

Mo【化】元素钼(molybdenum)的符号

mo. *abbr.* **1**. month(s) **2**. monthly

moan [məun] *n*. **1**. 呻吟声;呜咽声,悲叹声 **2**. (风、树等)萧萧声 —*vi*. 呻吟;呜咽;悲叹;哀悼;抱怨 —*vt*. **1**. 呻吟(或呜咽等)声说出;悲叹;哀悼;抱怨

moat [məut] *n*. (城堡等的)护城河;壕;深沟 —*vt*. 以护城河(或壕等)围绕

mob [mɔb] *n*. **1**. (蔑)暴民;[the ~]下层民众,群氓 **2**. 一群暴徒;会众 **3**. 〈美俚〉(盗贼等的)一伙;一群罪犯 **4**. 一群人;〈美俚〉被雇用的一伙人 — (mobbed; mobbing) *vt*. **1**. 成群结队地袭击(某人);成群结队地涌进(或围着) **2**. 成群结队地围着…欢呼 —*vi*. 聚众生事

mobile ['məubail, 'məubil, 'məubi:l] *adj*. **1**. 运动的;活动的 **2**. 流动的;机动的;装在车上的;用车辆运输的 **3**. 易变的;多变的;(在社会地位方面)升降很大的 **4**. 具有灵活性的 **5**. 运动物

体的;活动装置的 —*n*. **1**. 运动物体;(由空气流动而转动的)活动装置 **2**. 〈美〉汽车(automobile 之略) ‖~**home**〈美〉旅游居住车,活动住房(指一种改装的由汽车拖拉的活动房屋) /~**phone** 移动电话

mobility [məu'biliti] *n*. **1**. 运动性;流动性;机动性 **2**. 变动性;灵活性 **3**. 【物】【化】迁移率,淌度 **4**.【医】可动性,动度

mobilize ['məubilaiz] *vt*. **1**. 调动 **2**. 使可动;使流通 —*vi*. 动员起来 ‖ **,mobili'zation** *n*. 动员

moccasin ['mɔkəsin] *n*. **1**. (北美印第安人穿的)鹿皮(或其他软皮)鞋 **2**. 软鞋;软拖鞋 **3**. 〈口〉食鱼蝮(一种美国南产的毒蛇) ‖~**flower** 杓兰

mocha ['mɔkə, 'məukə] *n*. 优质阿拉伯咖啡

mock [mɔk] *vt*. **1**. (尤指通过模仿进行的)嘲弄;嘲笑;模拟 **2**. 使失望;欺骗 **3**. 使无效 —*vi*. 嘲弄 —*n*. **1**. 嘲弄;嘲弄的对象 **2**. 模仿;仿造;仿造品 —*adj*. 假的;虚幻的;模拟的 —*adv*. [常用以构成复合词]虚伪地;假冒地:~-serious 假装严肃的 ‖~**orange**【植】**1**. 山梅花 **2**. 桑橙 **3**. 葡萄牙桂樱 **4**. 似橙子的葫芦

mockery ['mɔkəri] *n*. **1**. 嘲笑;愚弄 **2**. 嘲弄的对象 **3**. 拙劣的模仿 **4**. 恶劣(或可鄙)的假冒,歪曲

mockingbird ['mɔkiŋbə:d] *n*. 【动】嘲鸫(产于美国南部,善于模仿别种鸟的叫声)

mockup ['mɔkʌp] *n*. (供试验等用的)实体模型;模型

mod [mɔd] 〈口〉*adj*. 时髦的;新潮的;习俗的 —*n*. **1**. 〈英〉摩登派 **2**. 极时髦的人(或物)

modal ['məudəl] *adj*. **1**. 形式的;样式的 **2**. 【语】语气的;情态的

mode [məud] *n.* 1. 方式；方法；(服饰的)式样,时式 2. 风气,风尚,时尚 3.【语】语气(= mood) 4.【逻】式,形式,模态 5.【音】调式 6.(统计学中的)众数

model ['mɔdl] *n.* 1. 模型；雏型；原型 2. 模范；典型 3.〈英方〉极相似的人(或东西) 4. 样式 5.(供画家等作描绘对象的)模特儿；(供顾客挑选服装等用的)时装模特儿(指活人或用木、蜡等制的) — (model l)ed model l)ing) *vt.* 1. 做...的模型 2. 按模型制作；使模仿(on, upon, after) 3. 当模特儿展示(服装等) 4. 使(图画等)有立体感 — *vi.* 1. 做模型；塑像 2. 当模特儿

moderate ['mɔdərit] *adj.* 1. 中等的；适度的 2. 温和的；稳健的；有节制的 3.(价钱)公道的；花费不多的 — *n.* 温和主义者；稳健派 — ['mɔdəreit] *vt.* 1. 使和缓；使减轻；节制 2. 主持(会议等) — *vi.* 1. 变和缓 2. 主持会议 ‖ ～ly *adv.* / ～ness *n.*

moderation [,mɔdə'reiʃən] *n.* 1. 中等；适度 2. 温和；缓和；节制 3.【核】减速；慢化 4.〈英〉[～s]牛津大学文学士学位的第一次考试

moderator ['mɔdəreitə] *n.* 1. 调解人；仲裁人 2. 会议主席；议长 3.(节目)主持人

modern ['mɔdən] *adj.* 现代的；近代的；新式的 — *n.* 现代人；近代人；现代派

modernistic [,mɔdə'nistik] *adj.* 1. = modern 2. 外表现代化的；假摩登的 3. 现代主义(者)的

modernize ['mɔdənaiz] *vt.* 使现代化 — *vi.* 现代化 ‖ **moderni'zation** *n.* 1. 现代化 2. 现代化的事物 3.(剧本等的)现代版本

modest ['mɔdist] *adj.* 1. 谦逊的、谦让的；谦恭的 2.(尤指妇女)端庄的、庄重的；贞节的 3. 羞怯的 4.(希望、要求等)有节制的,不过分的 5. 朴素的；朴实的 ‖ ～ly *adv.* / ～ness *n.*

modesty ['mɔdisti] *n.* 1. 谦逊；虚心 2.(尤指妇女的)端庄,稳重 3. 羞怯 4. 节制,中肯 5. 朴素；朴实

modification [,mɔdifi'keiʃən] *n.* 1. 缓和；减轻；限制 2. 更改；修改；改变 3.【语】修饰 4.【语】(变音符引起的)元音变异

modicum ['mɔdikəm] ([复] modicums 或 modica['mɔdikə]) *n.* 少量、一点点：a ～ of cash 少量现金

modify ['mɔdifai] *vt.* 1. 缓和；减轻 2. 更改；修改 3.【语】修饰 4.【语】用变音符变异(元音) ‖ **modifier** *n.* 1. 更改者；修改者 2.【语】修饰语；修饰成分；变音符

modish ['mɔudiʃ] *adj.* 时髦的、流行的

modiste [məu'di:st] *n.* 时式女衣帽裁缝

modulate ['mɔdjuleit] *vt.* 1. 调整；调节(声音等) 2. 声调抑扬地唱(歌)等 3.【音】使转调 4.【无】调制 — *vi.* 1. 声调抑扬地歌唱(或演奏) 2.【音】转调 3.【无】调制 ‖ **modu'lation** *n.*

module ['mɔdjuːl] *n.* 1.(建筑或一般工业上应用的)模数 2.【数】模；(加法群及微型)组件；(航天器的)舱 ‖ **modular** ['mɔdjulə] *adj.*

Mogadishu [,mɔgə'diʃu], **Mogadiscio** [,mɔgə'diʃiəu] *n.* 摩加迪沙(索马里首都)

mohair ['məuhɛə] *n.* 1. 马海毛,安哥拉山羊毛 2. 马海毛织物；马海毛纱；马海毛混纺织物；马海绒 — *adj.* 马海毛制的；马海绒织成的

Mohammedan [məu'hæmidən] *adj.*(伊斯兰教创始人)穆罕默德(Mohammed)的；伊斯兰教的；伊斯兰教(徒)的 — *n.* 穆斯林,伊斯兰

教徒(= Moslem) ‖ ~ism n. 伊斯兰教

moiety ['mɔiəti] n.1. 一半 2. 部分 3. 份额

moil [mɔil] vi. 做苦工 —n. 苦工;辛劳

moist [mɔist] adj. 1. 潮湿的;微湿的;多雨的 2. 含泪的;泪汪汪的 3.【医】湿(性)的;有分泌物的 ‖ ~ly adv. / ~ness n.

moisten ['mɔisn] vt. 弄湿;沾湿;使润湿 —vi. 变(潮)湿

moisture ['mɔistʃə] n. 1. 潮湿;潮气,湿气,湿度;水分;降雨量

molar ['məulə] n.【解】白齿,磨牙(= ~ tooth) —adj. 1. 用于研磨的;能磨碎的 2. 白齿的;近白齿的

molasses [mə'læsiz] n.[单复同] 1. 糖蜜;废糖蜜

mold [məuld] n., vt. & vi.〈美〉= mould¹, mould², mould³

molder ['məuldə] n., vi. & vt.〈美〉= moulder¹, moulder²

molding ['məuldiŋ] n.〈美〉= moulding

Moldova [mɔl'dəvə] n. 摩尔多瓦[东欧国家]

moldy ['məuldi] adj.〈美〉= mouldy

mole¹ [məul] n. 1. 鼹鼠;鼹鼠毛皮 2. 在黑暗中工作的人 3. 长期潜伏的间谍 —vi. 掘地道;打地洞 ‖ ~hill n. 鼹鼠丘;鼹鼠洞

mole² [məul] n. 痣

mole³ [məul] n. 1. 防波堤;堤道 2. 有防波堤的海港

molecular [məu'lekjulə] adj.【化】1. 分子的;摩尔的

molecule ['mɔlikjul] n.【化】1. 分子 2. 微小颗粒;些微,一点儿

molest [məu'lest] vt. 骚扰;干扰;使烦恼

moll [mɔl] n. 1. 歹徒的情妇(或女帮凶);女贼 2. 女流氓 ;妓女,婊子 3. 女人;姑娘;情人

mollify ['mɔlifai] vt. 1. 使平静;平息 2. 使软 3. 缓和;减轻

molluse, mollusk ['mɔləsk] n.【动】软体动物

mollycoddle ['mɔli,kɔdl] vt. 娇养;纵容;宠坏 —n. 娇惯的人;伪善的人

molt [məult] vi., vt. & n. = moult

molten ['məultən] melt 的过去分词 —adj. 1. 熔融的,熔化的 2. 铸造的 3. 灼热的

molybdenum [mɔ'libdinəm] n.【化】钼

mom [mɔm] n.〈美〉妈妈(=〈英〉mum)

moment ['məumənt] n. 1. 片刻;霎时,刹那;时刻 2. 重大,重要;〈哲〉环节,契机 3.【物】(力)矩 4.（历史发展的)关头,转折点 5.(统计学用语)矩,动差 2.【机】时刻

momentary ['məuməntəri] adj. 1. 瞬息间的,顷刻的;短暂的 2. 随时可能发生的 3. 时时刻刻的 ‖ **momentarily** ['məuməntərili, ,məumən'terili] adv.

momentous [məu'mentəs] adj. 重大的,重要的;严重的 ‖ ~ly adv. / ~ness n.

momentum [məu'mentəm] n.([复] momentums 或 momenta [məu'mentə]) 1.【物】动量,冲量 2. 冲力;势头;动力 3.〈哲〉要素,契机

Mon. abbr. Monday

Monaco ['mɔnəkəu] n. 1. 摩纳哥[欧洲西南部国家] 2. 摩纳哥(市)/摩纳哥首都]

monad ['mɔnæd] n.【生】单孢体;单孢虫;单孢菌

monarch ['mɔnək] n. 1. 君主;最高统治者 2.〈喻〉王,大王 3.【动】黑脉金斑蝶

monarchy ['mɒnəki] *n.* 1. 君主政体；君主制 2. 君主国 ‖ **monarchism** *n.*

monastery ['mɒnəstəri] *n.* 1. 修道院，隐修院；寺院 2. 修道院全体修道士（或修女）

monastic [mə'næstik] *adj.* 1. 修道院的；寺院的 2. 修道士的；修女的；僧侣的；禁欲生活的 —*n.* 僧侣，修道士；修女

Monday ['mʌndi] *n.* 星期一 —*adv.* 在星期一

Mondays ['mʌndiz] *adv.* 在每星期一

monetary ['mʌnitəri] *adj.* 钱的；货币的；金融的

money ['mʌni] （[复]moneys 或 monies）*n.* 1. 货币(铜币和纸币) 2. 金钱；财富,财产 3.（[复]moneys 或 monies）款项 4. [总称]富翁；金融界 5.（赛马、赛狗中）前三名优胜者；优胜奖金 ‖ **~ed** *adj.* 1. 有钱的,富有的 2. 钱财方面的 ‖ **~ order** 汇票,汇兑单

monger ['mʌŋɡə] *n.*（常用以构成复合词）商人,贩子：专事…的人：a fish ~鱼贩子 /a war ~ 战争贩子 ‖ **~y** *n.* 贩卖；散布

Mongol ['mɒŋɡɒl] *n.* 1. 蒙古人；蒙古族人 2. 蒙古语 3. 蒙古人种的人 —*adj.* = Mongolian

Mongolia [mɒŋ'ɡəuliə] *n.* 1. 蒙古〔亚洲中部国家〕2. = Inner Mongolia

Mongolian [mɒŋ'ɡəuliən] *adj.* 1. 蒙古的；蒙古族的；蒙古人的；蒙古人种的 2. 蒙古语的；蒙古文化的 3. 蒙古人种的 —*n.* 1. 蒙古人；蒙古族人 2. 蒙古语 3. 蒙古人种的人

mongoose ['mɒŋɡuːs] *n.*【动】1. 獴 2. = ~ lemur ‖ **lemur**（马达加斯加岛产的）獴狐猴

mongrel ['mʌŋɡrəl] *n.* 1. 杂种狗，杂种植物（或动物）3.〔蔑〕杂种人 —*adj.* [只

作定语]杂种的，杂交的；混杂的

monitor ['mɒnitə] *n.* 1.（学校的）班长，级长；导生(指英国学校中负有某些指导学生职责的高年级学生) 2.（对外国广播等的）监听员；监听器；监视器；(放射性等的)监测器 3. 告诫物，提醒物；告诫者,提醒者 4.（旧式的）低舷铁甲舰；浅水重炮艇 5.（采矿、救火用）喷(水)枪 6.【动】巨蜥 —*vt.* 监听；监控,监视,检测 3. 监视；密切注视；监督 —*vi.* 监听,监控；监测

monitory ['mɒnitəri] *adj.* 告诫的，警告的

monk [mʌŋk] *n.* 修道士；僧侣

monkey ['mʌŋki] *n.* 1. 猴子；猿；长毛猴 2.〔谑〕猴子似的人；淘气鬼；顽童；易受欺的人 3. 打桩锤 4.（制玻璃用的）小坩埚 5.〔俚〕五百英镑；五百美元 —*vi.* 胡闹,捣蛋；瞎弄 —*vt.* 学…的样；嘲弄 ‖ **~shine** *n.*〔美俚〕[常 ~ s] 恶作剧；胡闹 / **~ wrench** 1.【机】活动扳手 2. 破坏性因素

monkshood ['mʌŋkshud] *n.*【植】舟形乌头

mon(o)- *comb. form* 表示"单"，"一"：*monoplane*

monochrome ['mɒnəkrəum] *adj.* 1. 单色的；黑白的：a ~ television set 黑白电视机 2. 单调的，乏味的

monocle ['mɒnəkl] *n.* 单片眼镜

monogamy [mɒ'nɒɡəmi] *n.* 1. 一夫一妻制 2. 一生一婚主义 3.【动】单配偶，单配性 ‖ **monogamist** *n.* / **monogamous** *adj.*

monogram ['mɒnəɡræm] *n.* 交织字母，花押字(姓名或公司名等起首字母相互交织成图案状,用作信笺或商标等的标记) ‖ (monogrammed; monogramming) *vt.* 把交织字母印(或绣,刻)于 ‖ **~med** *adj.*

monograph ['mɔnəgrɑːf] *n.* 专(题)著(作);专论 — *vt.* 写关于…的专著(或专论)

monolith ['mɔnəliθ] *n.* 独块巨石;独石柱(或碑等);庞然大物

monolithic [ˌmɔnə'liθik] *adj.* 1. 独块巨石的 2. 整体式的 3.(集成电路等)单片的 4. 坚如磐石的;庞大的;一统的 ‖ ~ally *adv.*

monolog(ue) ['mɔnəlɔg] *n.* 【戏】独白;独白场面;独演剧本;独脚戏;独白式文学作品 3.(使别人无法插嘴的)滔滔不绝的话;长篇大论 ‖ **monolog(u)ist** *n.*

monoplane ['mɔnəplein] *n.* 单翼(飞)机

monopolize [mə'nɔpəlaiz] *vt.* 垄断;独占;专卖;专利 ‖ **monopolist** [mə'nɔpəlist] *n.*

monopoly [mə'nɔpəli] *n.* 1. 垄断;独占;专利品 2. 垄断商品;专利品;专利事业 3. 垄断权;专利权 4. 垄断者;专利者;垄断集团;垄断企业

monosyllable ['mɔnəˌsiləbl] *n.* 单音节词 ‖ **monosyllabic** [ˌmɔnəsi'læbik] *adj.*

monotone ['mɔnətəun] *n.* 1. 单调,无变化 2. 单调的语调(或声音)3.【音】单音调 4. 用单音调唱歌(或说话)的人

monotonous [mə'nɔtənəs] *adj.* 1. 单音调的,无抑扬顿挫的 2. 单调的,一成不变的;使人厌倦的 ‖ ~ly *adv.* / ~ness *n.*

monotony [mə'nɔtəni] *n.* 单音;单调;无变化,千篇一律

Monrovia [mɔn'rəuviə] *n.* 蒙罗维亚[利比里亚首都]

monsieur [mə'sjə] ([复] **messieurs** [mei'sjə]) 〈法〉 *n.* 先生(相当于 Mr. 或 Sir)

Monsignor [mɔn'siːnjə] ([复] **Monsignors** 或 **Monsignori** [ˌmɔnsiː'njɔːri])〈意〉 *n.* 阁下(对天主教高级神职人员的尊称)

monsoon [mɔn'suːn] *n.*【气】季风.2.(印度等地的)西南季风季节,雨季

monster ['mɔnstə] *n.* 1. 怪物;怪兽 2. 畸形动物(或植物);【医】畸胎 3. 巨兽;异常大的东西;极可怕的东西 4. 极丑陋的人,恶人;残忍的人 — *adj.* 巨大的,庞大的

monstrous ['mɔnstrəs] *adj.* 1. 畸形的;怪异的 2. 巨大的,庞大的 3. 可怕的;极恶的;极可笑的;荒谬的 4. [用以加强语气]极大的 — *adv.*〈方〉极,非常 ‖ ~ly *adv.*

montage [mɔn'tɑːʒ]〈法〉 *n.* 1. 综合画;综合画结构 2.(文学或音乐的)综合表现手法 3.(电影等的)蒙太奇,剪辑 — *vt.* 把…混合成(或画入)综合画;把…辑成(或辑入)连贯的影片

Montana [mɔn'tænə] *n.* 蒙大拿[美国州名]

Monte Carlo ['mɔnti 'kɑːləu] 蒙特卡洛(或译蒙的卡罗)[摩纳哥城市](世界著名赌城)

Montenegro [ˌmɔnte'neɡrə] *n.* 黑山(音译门的内罗罗)[南斯拉夫成员共和国名]

Montevideo [ˌmɔntivi'deiəu] *n.* 蒙得维的亚[乌拉圭首都]

month [mʌnθ] *n.* 月;一个月的时间

monthly ['mʌnθli] *adj.* 每月的;每月一次的;按月计算的;以一个月为期的 — *adv.* 每月;每月一次 — *n.* 1. 月刊 2. [monthlies]月经

Montreal [ˌmɔntri'ɔːl] *n.* 蒙特利尔[加拿大东南部港市]

monument ['mɔnjumənt] *n.* 1. 纪念碑;纪念馆;纪念像;纪念物;纪念性作品;纪

念文 2.(常由政府加以保管的历史上的)遗迹;遗址 3. 有永久价值的作品;不朽的功业 4. 标石,界石 5. 墓碑 6.[古]记录;标记 7.[the M-](1666 年)伦敦大火纪念塔

monumental [ˌmɔnju'mentl] *adj.* 1. 纪念碑(或雕像)的;纪念碑的 2. 巨大的;雄伟的;不朽的 3.[用以加强语气]非常的,极大的

moo [muː] *n.* 哞(牛叫声) — *vi.*(牛)哞哞地叫

mooch [muːtʃ] *vi.* 1. 闲逛;漫步 2. 鬼鬼祟祟地走,溜 3. 撺掇,敲竹杠 — *vt.* 1. 偷取,揩取 2.〈美〉讨取,乞取 ‖ **~er** *n.*

mood¹ [muːd] *n.* 1. 心境,心情,情绪;(精神)状态 2. 基调 3.[~s]喜怒无常 4.〈古〉大怒

mood² [muːd] *n.* 1.[语]语气,语气 2.[逻]三段论形式 3.[音]调式

moody ['muːdi] *adj.* 1. 喜怒无常的,易怒的 2. 心情易变的 2. 忧郁的,闷闷不乐的 ‖ **moodily** *adv.* / **moodiness** *n.*

moon [muːn] *n.* 1. 月球,月亮 2. 朔望月,太阴月;[诗]月份(= month) 3. 月光 4. 月状物;新月状物 5.[美][天]月相 7.〈美俚〉酒;非法酿造的威士忌酒 — *vi.* 闲荡;出神,呆看(about, around, over) — *vt.* 虚度(时间)(away) ‖ **~ beam** *n.* 一线月光 / **~ cake**(中国的)月饼 / **~ flight** *n.* 月球飞行 / **~ ship** *n.* 月球飞船,月球航天器 / **~ stone** *n.*[矿]月长石 / **~ walk** *n. & vi.*(作)月球行走

moonlight ['muːnlait] *n.* 1. 月光 2.〈口〉夜间潜逃 — *adj.* 有月光的;夜间下的;夜间的 — *vi.* 1. 夜间活动;夜袭 2.(尤指在夜间)从事第二职业 3. 夜间潜逃

moonshine ['muːnʃain] *n.* 1. 月光 2. 大

话,废话,空话,蠢话 3.〈美口〉非法酿造的酒;走私酒(尤指威士忌酒)— *vt. & vi.* 非法酿酒(酒)‖ **~r** *n.*

moor¹ [muə] *n.* 1.〈英〉荒野 2.[地](湿泥炭)沼泽,高沼,酸沼 ‖ **~ land** *n.*[地]高沼地

moor² [muə] *vt.* 1. 使停泊,系泊(船只);系留(飞艇等) 2. 使固定,系住 — *vi.* 2. 系泊;系留 2. 固定,系住

mooring ['muəriŋ] *n.* 1. 系泊 2. 系泊用具;系留用具;系泊处 3.[~s](道德、精神上的)支柱

moose [muːs][单复同][动]北美麋,麇,驼鹿

mop [mɔp] *n.* 1. 拖把;洗碗刷 2. 拖把似的东西;蓬乱的头发 — (mopped; mopping) *vt.* 用拖把拖洗;擦,拭 ‖ **~ up** *n.*〈口〉1. 扫除;清除 2. 扫尾(或善后)工作 3.[军]扫荡;肃清残敌

mope [məup] *vi.* 1. 忧郁,意气消沉;闷荡 — *vt.* 1. 使忧郁;使闷闷不乐 2. 闷闷不乐地度过(away) — *n.* 1. 忧郁的人 2.[~s]忧郁;郁闷

moped ['məuped] *n.* 机动脚踏两用车

moppet ['mɔpit] *n.*〈口〉小孩 2. 心肝,宝贝

moraine [mɔ'rein] *n.*[地]冰碛

moral ['mɔrəl] *adj.* 1. 道德(上)的 2. 合乎道德的;有道德的;道德教育的 3. 能辨别是非的 4. 精神上的;心理上的;道义上的 5. 内心确信的 — *n.* 1.(由事件、故事等引出的)道德上的教训;寓意 2.[~s]道德;品行;道德规范;伦理学 3. 士气 ‖ **~ly** *adv.* 1. 道德上,道义上 2. 根据道德;正直地 3. 精神上,心理上 4. 确实地 ‖ **~ist** *n.*

morale [mɔ'rɑːl, mɔ'rɑ:l] *n.* 1. 士气;风纪;精神 2. 信心,信念 3. 道德;道义

morality [mə'ræliti] *n.* 1. 道德；美德；德行；品行 2. 教训；寓意，说教 3. 有道德寓意的作品；道德剧(= ~ play) 4. 道德观；道德规范

moralize ['mɔrəlaiz] *vi.* 论道德，说教 —*vt.* 1. 从道德上解释 2. 提高…的道德

morally ['mɔrəli] *adv.* 1. 道德上 2. 有道德地 3. 精神上，心理上 4. 确实地

morass ['mɔræs] *n.* 1. 沼泽；泥淖 2. 陷阱；困境 3. 乱糟糟的一堆

moratorium [,mɔrə'tɔːrjəm] *n.* 1. 【律】(债务人的)延期偿付(权)；延期履行债务(权) 2. 暂停，中止

morbid ['mɔːbid] *adj.* 1. 疾病的；生病的；致病的 2. 病态的；病理学的 (精神、思想等)不健康的，病态的 3. 可怕的，令人毛骨悚然的 ‖ **~ly** *adv.* / **~ness** *n.*

morbidity [mɔː'biditi] *n.* 1. 成病，发病 2. (国家、地区等的)发病率 3. 病态；忧郁

mordant ['mɔːdənt] *adj.* 尖锐的；尖刻的；讽刺性的 ‖ **mordancy** *n.*

more [mɔː, mɔə] *adj.* 1. [many, much 的比较级]更多的；较多的；更高程度的 2. 另外的，附加的 —*n.* 1. 更多的数量；较多的数量 2. 额外的数量；另外的一些 —*adv.* 1. [much 的比较级，常和两音节以上的形容词或副词连用]更多；更 2. 倒不如说 3. 另外 —*int.* 4. 而且

moreover [mɔː'rəuvə] *adv.* 再者，加之，此外，而且

mores ['mɔːriːz, 'mɔːreiz] *n.* 1. 民德 2. 道德观念 3. 风俗；习惯

morgue [mɔːg] (法) *n.* 1. 陈尸所；停尸室 2. (报社等的)资料室；资料；资料档案

moribund ['mɔːribʌnd] *adj.* 垂死的，临终的；即将消灭的 —*n.* 垂死的人

Mormonism ['mɔːmənizəm] *n.* 摩门教 ‖ **Mormon** *n. & adj.*

morn [mɔːn] *n.* 1. (诗)黎明；日出；早晨 2. (苏格兰)[the ~]明天 3. 东方

morning ['mɔːniŋ] *n.* 1. 早晨；上午 2. (诗)破晓，黎明 3. 初期，早期 ‖ **glory** 1.【植】牵牛花 2. 昙花一现的人(或物) / **~ star**[天]晨星(尤指启明星)

Morocco [mə'rɔkəu] *n.* 1. 摩洛哥[北非国家] 2. [m-]摩洛哥革,(植鞣山羊)搓纹革;仿摩洛哥革

moron ['mɔːrɔn] *n.* 1.【医】痴愚者(指智能程度停留在8岁至12岁的成人) 2. (口)蠢人 3. 性(欲)倒错者,性反常者

Moroni [mə'rəuni] *n.* 莫罗尼[科摩罗首都]

morose [mə'rəus] *adj.* 脾气坏的;闷闷不乐的 ‖ **~ly** *adv.* / **~ness** *n.*

morpheme ['mɔːfiːm] *n.*【语】语素,词素

Morpheus ['mɔːfjəs, 'mɔːfiəs] *n.*(希神)摩耳甫斯(睡梦之神)

morphia ['mɔːfjə], **morphine** ['mɔːfiːn] *n.* 吗啡

morphology [mɔː'fɔlədʒi] *n.*【生】【地】【语】形态学;形态;【语】词法

morrow ['mɔrəu] *n.* 1. [the ~]次日,翌日 2. (重大事件后)紧接着的时期 3. (诗)早晨

Morse [mɔːs] *n.* (讯)摩尔斯电码 ‖ **~ code**, **~ alphabet** 摩尔斯电码

morsel ['mɔːsəl] *n.* 1. (食物的)一口一小份;一小片 2. 少量,一点点;片断 3. 佳肴;乐事;使人愉快的人 4. 微不足道的人 —(morsel(l)ed; morsel(l)ing) *vt.* 使分成小块;少量地分配

mortal ['mɔːtl] *adj.* 1. 终有一死的;死的;临死的 2. 致死的,致命的 3. 你死我活的;不共戴天的 4. 世间的,凡人

的；人的，人类的 5.〈口〉极大的；极度的；冗长沉闷的 6.〔与 any, every, no 等连用〕想像得出的，可能的 7.〔天主教〕要堕入地狱的，不可饶恕的 —*n.* 1. 终有一死的人，凡人 2.〈谑〉人 —*adj.*〈口〉〈方〉极，非常 ‖ ~**ly** *adv.* 1. 致命地 2.〈口〉极，非常

mortality [mɔːˈtæliti] *n.* 1. 致命性，必死性 2. 大量死亡 3. 死亡数；死亡率；〔事业等的〕失败次数；失败率 4. 人类 5.〈古〉死

mortar [ˈmɔːtə] *n.* 1. 臼，研钵 2.〔砌砖用的〕灰浆，砂浆，胶泥 3. 迫击炮 —*vt.* 1. 用灰浆砌合 2. 用迫击炮轰击

mortgage [ˈmɔːɡidʒ] *n.* 1. 抵押借款 2. 抵押契据；〔受押人对财产留置的〕抵押权 —*vt.* 1. 抵押 2. 把…当作抵押；把…许给 ‖ ~**e** [ˌmɔːɡiˈdʒiː] *n.* 受押人，抵押人者 / **mortgagor** *n.* 抵押人，押出人

mortician [mɔːˈtiʃən] *n.*〈美〉殡葬业者

mortify [ˈmɔːtifai] *vt.* 1.〔通过苦行〕抑制，克制 2. 使屈辱；伤害引起人的感情 —*vi.* 1. 禁欲，苦行 2.〔医〕变成坏疽 ‖ **mortification** [ˌmɔːtifiˈkeiʃn] *n.*

mortise [ˈmɔːtis] *n.* 榫眼 —*vt.* 用榫接合；在…上开榫眼；使牢固相接

mortuary [ˈmɔːtjuəri] *n.* 停尸室，太平间，殡仪馆 —*adj.* 1. 丧葬的 2. 悲哀的，阴郁的；死一般的

mosaic [məˈzeiik] *n.* 1. 镶嵌细工，镶嵌〔工艺〕；镶嵌图案；〔建〕镶嵌砖，马赛克 2. 拼成的东西；航摄相片镶嵌图 3.〔电视的〕感光镶嵌屏 4.〔植〕花叶病 —*adj.* 1. 镶嵌细工的；嵌花式的 2. 拼成的 —(mosaicked; mosaicking) *vt.* 1. 用马赛克装饰 2. 把…构成镶嵌图案

Moscow [ˈmɔskəu] *n.* 莫斯科〔俄罗斯首都〕

mosey [ˈməuzi] *vi.* & *n.*〈俚〉闲逛，溜达，漫步

Moslem [ˈmɔzləm] *n.*〔复〕Moslem(s)〕 *adj.*〔宗〕穆斯林(的)，伊斯兰教徒(的)

mosque [mɔsk] *n.* 清真寺，伊斯兰教寺院

mosquito [məsˈkiːtəu] *n.*〔复 mosquito(e)s〕 *n.* 蚊(子) ‖ ~ **net** 蚊帐

moss [mɔs] *n.* 1. 苔藓；地衣 2. 泥炭沼；沼泽 —*vt.* 以苔覆盖；使长满苔藓

mossy [ˈmɔsi] *adj.* 1. 生了苔的；长满苔的，多苔的 2. 苔状的

most [məust]〔many, much 的最高级〕 *adj.* 1. 最多的；最高程度的 2. 多数的；大部分的；多半的 —*n.* 1. 最大量；最多数；最高额 2. 大多数；大部分；大多数人 —*adv.* 1.〔much 的最高级，与两音节或以上的形容词或副词连用〕最 2. 极，很，十分 3.〈英方〉〈美口〉差不多，几乎(= almost) ‖ ~**ly** *adv.* 主要地，大部分；多半；通常

-most *suf.*〔构成最高级形容词〕表示"最"：fore**most**，inner**most**

mote [məut] *n.* 1. 尘埃；微粒，屑 2. 瑕疵，小缺点

motel [məuˈtel] *n.*〔附有停车场等设施的〕汽车旅馆

moth [mɔθ] *n.* 蛾，飞蛾；衣蛾

mothball [ˈmɔθbɔːl] *n.* 1. 樟脑丸，卫生球 2.〔~s〕封存，保藏 —*vt.* 封存，保藏 —*adj.* 贮藏着的，备用的

mother [ˈmʌðə] *n.* 1. 母亲，妈妈 2.〔the ~〕母爱 3.〔M-〕(常用于姓氏前)大妈，大娘，女主管人；妇女宗教团体的女主持人 5. 根由 6.〔动，植物〕母体 —*a* bird 母鸟 7.〔小鸡等的〕人工养育器 8.〔微〕醋母 —*vt.* 1. 生；产生 2.〔母亲般地〕照管 3.〔军〕照料 4. 收养…为子女；承认自己为…的母亲；承认自己是…的作者 ‖ ~ **hood** 母性；母亲身份

分；[总称]母亲 /~·ly *adj.* 母亲的；慈母般的 *adv.* 慈母般地 ‖ ~ country 1. 祖国 2. 发源地 3. (殖民地的) 母国 / '~-in-law /[复]~s-in-law/ *n.* 岳母；婆婆/(英)继母/ ~ land *n.* = ~ country / '~-of-'pearl *n.* 珍珠母，螺钿 / ~ ship (英)[海]母舰 /~ tongue 本国语；本族语

motif [məu'ti:f, mɔ'ti:f] 〈法〉 *n.* (文艺作品的) 主题，中心思想

motion ['məuʃən] *n.* 1. (物体的) 运动，运动 2. 手势；眼色；动作；姿势 3. 动机；意向 4. (会议上的) 提议，动议 5. [律] (诉讼人向法院提出的) 请求，申请 6. (钟、表等的) 摆动 7. (音乐中) 运动机构 7. (音乐中) 几个声部的) 进行 8. 大便；[~s]粪便 —*vi.* 1. 打手势；摇 (或点) 头示意 2. (钟表等) 摆动，走 —*vt.* 1. 打手势；向···摇 (或点) 头示意 ‖ ~·less *adj.* 不动的，静止的 ‖ ~ picture 电影；影片

motivate ['məutiveit] *vt.* 使有动机；构成 (行为) 的动机；促动，激发 ‖ ,moti'vation *n.*

motive ['məutiv] *n.* 1. 动机；主旨；目的 2. (文艺作品的) 主题 —*adj.* [只作定语]发动的；运动的 —*vt.* = motivate

motley ['mɔtli] *adj.* 1. 杂色的，五颜六色的 2. 穿杂色衣的 3. 混杂的；成分杂乱的 —*n.* 1. 杂色呢；杂色布 2. (小丑穿的) 彩衣；小丑 3. 混杂物

motor ['məutə] *n.* 1. 原动力 2. 发动机；内燃机；摩托，电动机，马达 3. 机动车；汽车 4. [美]〈口〉汽车公司股票 5. [解]运动原 —*adj.* 1. 原动的；运动的 2. 汽车的 3. [解]运动的，运动神经的 —*vi.* 驾驶汽车；乘汽车 —*vt.* 用汽车运送 ‖ ~·bike *n.* 机动脚踏两用车 2. 轻型摩托车 /~ boat *n.* 汽艇 *vi.* 乘汽艇 / '~cade *n.* 一长列汽车；

(汽) 车队 / '~·car *n.* 1. 汽车 2. (铁道上的) 机动巡道车 / '~·cycle *n.* 摩托车 *vi.* 骑摩托车；坐摩托车 / (市区内附有停车场设施的) ~ hotel 汽车旅馆 / '~·lorry 〈英〉卡车，载重汽车 / ~ scooter 小型摩托车 / '~·truck *n.* 〈美〉= ~·lorry / ~ vehicle 机动车辆；汽车 / ~ vessel 内燃机船

motorist ['məutərist] *n.* (经常) 开汽车的人；(经常) 驾车旅行的人

motorize ['məutəraiz] *vt.* 1. 给···装上发动机 2. 用机动车辆装备 3. 使 (部队) 摩托化；使机动化

mottle ['mɔtl] *vt.* 使呈杂色，使成斑驳 —*n.* 1. 杂色；斑点；斑纹 2. 杂色毛纱 ‖ ~d *adj.* 杂色的；斑驳的

motto ['mɔtəu] ([复]motto(e)s) *n.* 1. 箴言；座右铭；格言 2. 题词；[书籍扉页上或章节前所引用的]警句

mould[1] [məuld] *n.* 1. 模子，模型；铸模，铸型；[印] (铸铅字的) 字模 2. 模制品，铸造物 3. 类型；性状；气质 4. [建] (装饰)线条，(凹凸) 线脚 —*vt.* 1. 用模子做；把···放在模子里做；浇铸 2. 对···产生影响；形成 3. 与···的轮廓相符合 4. [建]用线条 (或雕刻) 装饰 5. 〈古〉把 (陶土等) 捏成形

mould[2] [məuld] *n.* 1. 耕作土壤；松软沃土 2. (英方) 地面；坟场的泥土 —*vt.* 用泥土覆盖 (*up*)

mould[3] [məuld] *n.* 霉；霉菌 —*vt.* & *vi.* (使) 发霉

moulder[1] ['məuldə] *n.* 1. 制模工；铸工；造型者 2. [印] (复制用的) 电铸板

moulder[2] ['məuldə] *vi.* & *vt.* 1. (使) 崩碎；(使) 腐朽 2. (使) 衰退

moulding ['məuldiŋ] *n.* 1. 模制；浇铸；造型 (法) 2. [建] (装饰) 线条，(凹凸) 线

脚

mouldy ['məuldi] *adj.* 1. 发霉的;陈腐的;过时的 2.《俚》乏味的;令人厌烦的 3.《俚》肮脏破烂的;不像样的

moult [məult] *vi.* 换羽,脱羽,脱毛;蜕皮 — *vt.* 1. 换(羽);脱(毛、角);蜕(皮) 2. 去除(旧习惯、旧思想等) — *n.* 1. 换羽;脱毛;脱皮;蜕皮;换羽(或脱毛等)期 2. 换下的羽;脱下的毛(或角等);蜕下的皮

mound [maund] *n.* 1. 土墩;土石堆;土冈 2. 土丘 3. 坟堆 4.《城堡的》护墙 4.(物件的)堆,垛 — *vt.* 1.《古》筑堤围住;筑墙防卫 2. 堆起 — *vi.* 积成堆

mount[1] [maunt] *n.* 1.《诗》山,丘 2. [M-](用于山名前或缩写 Mt.)…山;…峰 3. 土墩;土石堆;土冈

mount[2] [maunt] *vi.* 1. 登,爬上 2. 骑上马 2. 增长,上升 — *vt.* 1. 登上,爬上(山、梯、王位等)2. 使骑上(马等);扶(某人)上马 3. 架起;装有(枪炮等)4. 安放(镜片、宝石等);镶嵌(画、邮票、照片等)5. 制作(动植物)的标本;把(动植物)固定在标本架上;把(标本等)固定在显微镜的载片上 6. 发动(攻势);进行(袭击)7. 设置(岗哨);担任(警卫)8. 把(剧本)搬上舞台,上演;展出 9.(雄性动物)与…交配 — *n.* 1. 登,爬 2.(赛马时的)坐骑;骑马机会 2. 可乘骑的东西(如马、车等)3. 坐骑底座;座架;炮架 4.(镶宝石的)底座,托板 5. 扇托,图衬

mountain ['mauntin] *n.* 1. 山,山岳;[~s]山脉 2. 巨大如山的人(或物);大堆,大量 3. [the M-]山岳派(1793年法国资产阶级革命时期占据国民议会大厅最高处坐位的革命民主派)‖ ~ lion

美洲狮 / ~ range 山脉;巨大如山脉的东西 / ~-side *n.* 山腰;山坡

mountaineer [ˌmaunti'niə] *n.* 1. 山地人,山区人 2. 爬山家;登山运动员 — *vi.* 爬山,登山 ‖ -ing *n.* 爬山,登山;登山运动

mountainous ['mauntinəs] *adj.* 1. 多山的的;有山的 2. 巨大如山的

mountebank ['mauntibæŋk] *n.* 走江湖(卖假药)的人;江湖医生,走方郎中;骗子

mounting ['mauntiŋ] *n.* 1. 登上;上马;上车;乘骑 2. 装置;安放;上驾;固定 3. 底座;座架;炮架;(镶宝石的)底板,托板 4.(书画等的)装帧;衬托纸,裱画纸 5.(显微镜的)载片 6. 舞台效果

mourn [mɔːn] *vi.* 1. 哀悼,哀悼 (for, over) 2. 痛心,遗憾 (for, over) 3.(鸽子似地)咕咕低鸣 — *vt.* 1. 为(某事)哀痛;向(某人)致哀 2. 对…感到痛心(或遗憾) 3. 悲哀地说 ‖ — er *n.* 1. 哀痛者;哀悼者;送葬者;(受雇的)职业送葬人 2.【宗】(奋兴会上的)公开忏悔者

mournful ['mɔːnful] *adj.* 悲哀的,哀痛的;令人沮丧的 ‖ -ly *adv.* / — ness *n.*

mourning ['mɔːniŋ] *n.* 1. 悲哀,哀痛 2. 举哀;居丧 3. 丧服;戴孝;表示哀悼的服饰 ‖ — dove[əv]哀鸽(北美洲产的一种鸣声凄凉的小野鸽)

mouse [maus]([复]mice[mais]) *n.* 1. 鼠,耗子 2.《俚》胆小怕羞的人 3.《俚》姑娘;女人;女朋友 4.《俚》(眼部等被击伤后起的)青肿,乌青块 5. 鼠灰色,灰褐色 6.【海】钩口系索 7.《美俚》小火箭—[mauz] *vi.* 1. 捕鼠 2. 窥探;偷偷地搜寻;蹑手蹑脚地走动 — *vt.* 仔细搜寻;揪出 (out) ‖ — trap *n.* 1. 捕鼠器 2. 陷阱 3.(橄榄球赛的)引诱战术 4. 狭小的地方,斗室 *vt.* 诱捕;引诱…入

毂

mouser ['mauzə] *n.* 1. 捕鼠动物(如猫、猫头鹰等) 2. 探头探脑地打听的人

mousse [muːs] *n.* 1. 奶油冻 2. 摩丝(做头发的定型剂) —*vt.* 用摩丝做(头发)

moustache [məs'tɑːʃ] *n.* 1. 髭;八字须 2. 须状物(哺乳动物的)触须 ‖~d *adj.*

mousy ['mausi] *adj.* 1. 似鼠的;胆小的;鬼鬼祟祟的 2. 多鼠的;鼠害成灾的

mouth [mauθ] ([复] mouths [mauðz]) *n.* 1. 口,嘴 2. 人;动物 3. 口状物;进出口;河口;容器口;枪口;管乐器的吹口 4. (表示厌恶或引人发笑的)鬼脸;苦相 5. 话声;话;代言人 —[mauð] *vt.* 1. 说出;清楚地讲出 2. 做作地说;夸大地说 3. 随和着说;有口无心地说 4. 不清楚地说;含糊地说 5. 把…放入嘴内;吃 6. 用嘴接触物 7. 训练(马)咬马嚼子 —*vi.* 1. 做作地说话;夸大地说话;咬口 2. 做怪脸 ‖~ organ 1. 口琴;排箫 2.(昆虫等的)口器 /~piece *n.* 1. 口状物;管头吹器;乐器的吹口(电话的送话口;马嚼子;(拳击手用的)护齿 2. 喉舌;代言人;(俚)(刑事案件的)辩护律师;律师

mouthful ['mauθful] *n.* 1. 满口,一口量 2. 冗长而拗口的词(或词组)3. (俚)妙语

movable ['muːvəbl] *adj.* 1. 可移动的,活动的;姿势 2.(指日期)每年变动的,不固定的 —*n.* 可移动的东西;可搬动的家具;[~s]动产(尤指家具)

move [muːv] *vt.* 1. 使移动;使改变位置(或姿势)2. 使运行,开动;使前进;摇动 3. 感动;激起 4. 鼓动,推动,促使 5.(在会议上)提议 6. 使(肠子)通便 7. 卖掉;租赁 —*vi.* 1. 移动;离开,动身;前进;(事情等)进展;(下棋)走一子 2. 运行,转动;摇动 3. 迁移;搬

家 4. 提议;请求,申请;呼吁 5. 采取行动;行动 6. 频繁活动,忙碌;活跃 7. 生存;生活;过活;生活于(某种环境);周旋于(*in*)8.(肠子)通便 —*n.* 1. 动,移动;迁移;搬家 2. 步骤;行动 3.(下棋用语)走棋,一着 ‖~ *n.* 1. 搬运家具人 2. 搬场公司 3. 原动力 2. 提议人 4. 鼓动者

moveable ['muːvəbl] *adj. & n.* = movable

movement ['muːvmənt] *n.* 1. 运动;活动;动作;姿势 2. 移动;迁移;迁徙 3.(部队及装备等的)调动;调遣;输送;行进 4.(政治、社会或思想)运动 5. 倾向;动向;动态;思想动机 6.(诗或故事等情节的)变化;曲折;(雕刻、绘画等的)动势 7.[机]动程;机构;装置 8.(市面的活动)(价格的)变动 9.[音]乐章;进行;律动;拍子;[语]节奏;韵律 10. 通便;粪便

movie ['muːvi] *n.* 1. 电影;影片 2. [the ~s]电影的放映,一场电影;电影业 3. 电影院

moving ['muːviŋ] *adj.* 1. 行进的;活动的;移动的 2. 动人的,感人的;鼓动的 3. 原动的 4. 前进的,发展的 5.(用于)搬家的 6. 行驶中的车辆的 ‖~ly *adv.* ‖~ picture 电影;影片

mow[1] [mau] 〈美方〉 *n.* 1. 干草(或麦杆、谷物)堆 2. 干草(谷物、谷物)堆贮处 —*vt.* (把干草、麦杆或谷物)堆积(或贮藏)起来(*away*)

mow[2] [məu] *n.* (过去式 mowed, 过去分词 mowed 或 mown) *vt.* 1. 刈;割 2.(似刈草一样)刈倒;扫除;扫杀;撞倒;压倒,打垮(对手等)(*down*) —*vi.* 刈草;割庄稼 ‖~er *n.* 刈割者;割草机;收割机

Mozambique [ˌməuzæm'biːk] *n.* 莫桑比克[非洲东南部国家]

mph, m.p.h. *abbr.* miles per hour 每小时英里数，英里/小时

Mr., Mr ['mistə] *abbr.* Mister 先生

Mrs., Mrs ['misiz] *abbr.* Mistress 夫人

Ms., Ms [miz] *abbr.* Miss 或 Mrs. 女士（用在婚姻状况不明的女子姓名前）

Mt. *abbr.* Mount, Mountain

mtn. *abbr.* mountain

MTV *abbr.* music TV 音乐电视

much [mʌtʃ] ([more [mɔː], most [məust]) *adj.* 许多，多；大量的；很大程度的 — *n.* 1. 许多，大量 2. 重要（或有意义）的事物 — *adv.* 1. 很；非常 2. [加强比较级或最高级]…多；更… 3. 常常；好久 4. 差不多，几乎

mucilage ['mjuːsilidʒ] *n.* 1.（海草等植物的）粘液；粘胶 2. 胶水；胶浆 ‖ **mucilaginous** [ˌmjuːsiˈlædʒinəs] *adj.*

muck [mʌk] *n.* 1. 湿粪；粪肥；腐殖土 2.〈口〉污秽；污物；讨厌的东西；腐化堕落的事物 3.〈口〉乱七八糟的状态 4. [总称] 中伤的言词（或作品）；废话；胡言乱语 5.（开挖或采矿中清出的）废料；垃圾 — *vt.* 1. 给…施粪肥；弄脏；搞糟 3. 清除…中的污物；清除（污物）— *vi.*〈口〉闲逛；鬼混（*about*）‖ '~-up *n.*〈英俚〉一团糟；混乱局面 2. 大错；惨败

muckrake ['mʌkreik] *vi., vt. & n.* 揭露（…的）丑事 ‖ ~ r *n.* /**muckraking** *n. & adj.*

mucous ['mjuːkəs] *adj.* 1.（有）粘液的；蒙上粘液的；粘液质的 2. 像（或像蒙上）粘液的 3. 分泌（或含）粘液的 ‖ ~ membrane【解】粘膜

mucus ['mjuːkəs] *n.*【生】（粘膜分泌的）粘液

mud [mʌd] *n.* 1.（软）泥；泥浆；淤泥；〈喻〉无价值的东西 2.〈口〉污蔑，毁谤 3.〈美俚〉黑糊糊的食品（如咖啡、巧克力布丁等）4.〈美俚〉黑糊糊的液体（如铁水、石油等）5.〈美俚〉不清晰的无线电（或电报）信号 — (mudded; mudding) *vt.* 使沾上污泥；弄泥

muddle ['mʌdl] *vt.* 1. 使浑浊；使多淤泥 2. 使糊涂；使泥醉 3. 使混乱；弄糟 4. 糊里糊涂地在花掉（时间等）(*away*) — *vi.* 胡乱对付；瞎混 (*on, along*) — *n.* 混乱，杂乱（头脑）糊涂

muddy ['mʌdi] *adj.* 1. 多泥的；泥泞的；泥状的 2. 泥土般的；（在光、色、声音等方面）浑浊的；模糊的 3. 糊涂的；混乱的 4.（道德上）不纯的；下流的 — *vt.* 1. 使沾上污泥；把…弄脏；使浑浊，搅浑 2. 使糊涂；使混乱 ‖ **muddily** *adv. n.* / **muddiness** *n.*

muff¹ [mʌf] *n.* 1.（妇女防寒用的）手笼，手筒 2.【机】套筒，轴套

muff² [mʌf] *n.* 1. 笨拙的运动员；笨拙的人；笨拙的行动；接球失误 — *vt.* 1. 弄糟 2. 漏接（球）；〈俚〉错过（机会）— *vi.* 1. 行为笨拙；做出笨事；〈口〉失败 2. 漏接球

muffin ['mʌfin] *n.*〈主英〉松饼；小松糕

muffle ['mʌfl] *vt.* 1. 包裹，裹住；蒙住；蒙住（某人）的头部（或脸）2. 压住；压抑（声音）；裹住（铃、鼓等）使其声音低沉 — *n.* 1. 围裹物，蒙盖物 2. 低沉的声音，闷声 3.〈动〉拳击手套（苏格兰）连指手套 4. 隔焰窑；隔焰室

muffler ['mʌflə] *n.* 1. 围巾；手套；无指手套 2. 消声物，消声器，消音器（铜琴的）消音器

mufti ['mʌfti] *n.* 便服

mug [mʌg] *n.* 1.（有柄）大杯；一大杯的容量 2. 脸 3.〈俚〉脸部照片 4.〈美俚〉

粗鲁丑陋的人;恶棍 5.〈俚〉(二流的)职业拳击手;破相的职业拳击手 6.〈英俚〉傻瓜;易受骗者;易被击败者 7.〈英俚〉用功学习的人 (mugged; mugging) *vt.* 从背后袭击并抢劫;掐住…的脖子 — *vi.*〈俚〉扮鬼脸

muggy ['mʌgi] *adj.* 闷热的;湿热的 ‖ **mugginess** *n.*

Muhammadan [mu'hæmədən] *adj. & n.* = Mohammedan

Mukden ['mukdən] *n.* 沈阳(Shenyang 的旧称)

mulberry ['mʌlbəri] *n.* 1. 桑树 2. 桑葚 3. 桑葚色;深紫红色

mulch [mʌltʃ] *n.* (为护根、遏制杂草生长等所用的)覆盖物;覆盖料 — *vt.* 用覆盖料覆盖(地面、树木根部等)

mulct [mʌlkt] *vt.* 处…以罚金 2. 敲竹杠;诈取;骗得

mule[1] [mjuːl] *n.* 1. 骡,马骡(公驴和母马所生的种间杂种) 2.(动物或植物的)杂种 3. 顽固的人 4.〈纺〉走锭精纺机 5.(拖曳船只、煤车等的)小型电动机车(在码头等处拖运货车等的)轻便牵引机 6.〈俚〉运送毒品者 ‖ ~ skinner 〈美〉赶骡人

mule[2] [mjuːl] *n.* 拖鞋;拖鞋式女鞋

muleteer [ˌmjuːli'tiə] *n.* 赶骡人

muley ['mjuːli] *n. & adj.* = mulley

mulish ['mjuːliʃ] *adj.* 1. 骡的;骡子似的 2. 执拗的、顽固的 3. 杂种的 ‖ ~ly *adv.* / ~ness *n.*

mull[1] [mʌl] *vt. & vi.*〈口〉仔细考虑,反复思考

mull[2] [mʌl] *vt.* (加糖和香料将)…制成热饮

mulla(h) ['mʌlə] *n.*【伊斯兰教】毛拉(某些地区对伊斯兰教学者的尊称)

mullein ['mʌlin] *n.*【植】毛蕊花

mullet ['mʌlit] *n.* 1. 鲻鱼 2. 鯡鲤;胭脂鱼

mulley ['mʌli] *n.* 1. 无角动物;无角牛 2. 母牛 — *adj.* 无角的;截角的

mulligan ['mʌligən] *n.*〈美口〉蔬菜烩肉(或鱼)

multi- *comb. form* 表示"多":*multi*lateral

multifarious [ˌmʌlti'fɛəriəs] *adj.* 由不同的部分(或成分)形成的;多种多样的;多方面的

multilateral [ˌmʌlti'lætərəl] *adj.* 多边的;涉及多方的;多国参加的

multinational [ˌmʌlti'næʃənl] *adj.* 多民族的;多国参加的 — *n.* 多国公司,跨国公司

multiple ['mʌltipl] *adj.* 1. 多个(或多部分、多种、多次等)的 2.由多个(或多部分、多种、多次等)组成的 2. 许多的;多种多样的 3.【电】并联的;多路的 4.【植】聚花的 5. 多人享有(或参加)的 ~ rape 轮奸 6.〈英〉(商店)连锁的 7. 倍数的 — *n.* 1.【数】倍数 2.【电】并联;多路系统 3.〈英〉联锁商店(= ~ shop 或 ~ store) 4. 成批制作的艺术品(如画、雕塑等)

multiplicand [ˌmʌltipli'kænd] *n.*【数】被乘数

multiplication [ˌmʌltipli'keiʃən] *n.* 1. 增加,增多;倍增 2. 增殖;繁殖 3.【数】乘法;乘法运算;相乘

multiplicity [ˌmʌlti'plisiti] *n.* 多样性;【物】相重性、相重数

multiplier ['mʌltiplaiə] *n.* 1. 增加者;增殖者 2.【数】乘数 3. 乘法器;【物】倍加器;【电】扩程器 4.【经】(增加投资所产生的)增殖

multiply[1] ['mʌltiplai] *vi.* 1. 增加,增多

2. 增殖;繁殖 3. 做乘法 — *vt.* 1. 使增加;使成倍地增加 2. 【数】乘;使相乘

multiply² [ˈmʌltipli] *adv.* 1. 多样地;多重地 2. 多倍地;多次地;多方面地 3. 【电】并联地;多路地

multistage [ˈmʌltisteidʒ] *adj.* 1. 多级(式)的 2. 多阶段的,分多阶段进行的

multitude [ˈmʌltitjuːd] *n.* 1. 大批,大群;[the ~]民众,大众 2. 众多,大量

multitudinous [ˌmʌltiˈtjuːdinəs] *adj.* 1. 数目众多的,极多的 2. 由许多部分组成的各种各样的 ‖ **~ly** *adv.* / **~ness** *n.*

mum¹ [mʌm] *adj.* 沉默的,缄默的 — *n.* 沉默,缄默 — *int.* 别说话! 别作声!

mum² [mʌm] *n.* (英)妈妈(= (美) mom)

mumble [ˈmʌmbl] *vi.* 含糊地说话;咕哝 — *vt.* 1. 含糊地说;咕哝 2. 抿着嘴唇;瘪着嘴嚼 — *n.* 含糊的话;咕哝

mumbo jumbo [ˈmʌmbəuˈdʒʌmbəu] 繁文缛节,无意义(或迷惑人)的活动(或事物)

mummer [ˈmʌmə] *n.* 1. (在节日)戴面具(或化装)作乐的人 2. 演员

mummery [ˈmʌməri] *n.* 化装(或戴面具)的表演;哑剧演员的表演;虚伪(或做作、可笑、愚蠢而无意义)的仪式(或表演)

mummy¹ [ˈmʌmi] *n.* 1. 木乃伊,干尸 2. 木乃伊似的人,干瘪的人;没有生气的人 3. 稀烂的一团

mummy² [ˈmʌmi] *n.* 〈英口〉妈妈

mumps [mʌmps] [复] *n.* [用作单或复] 1. 【医】流行性腮腺炎 2. 愠怒;生气

munch [mʌntʃ] *vt.* 1. 用力嚼;出声嚼 2. 使(颚)咀嚼 — *vi.* 用力嚼;出声咀嚼

mundane [ˈmʌndein] *adj.* 1. 尘世的;世俗的;庸俗的 2. 宇宙的;世界的

Munich [ˈmjuːnik] *n.* 1. 慕尼黑[德国东

南部城市] 2. (出卖别国利益、姑息侵略者的)慕尼黑事件;绥靖行为

municipal [mju(ː)ˈnisipəl] *adj.* 1. 市的;市政的;市立的,市办的 2. 自治城市的;地方自治的;地方(性)的 3. 内政的

municipality [mju(ː)ˌnisiˈpæliti] *n.* 1. 自治城市;自治地区 2. 市政府,市政当局 3. [总称]市民

munificent [mju(ː)ˈnifisənt] *adj.* 1. 慷慨的;(礼物等)丰厚的 ‖ **~ly** *adv.* / **~ness** *n.*

munition [mju(ː)ˈniʃən] *n.* [常 ~s] 1. 军需品(尤指枪、炮、弹药);军火 2. 必需品 — *vt.* 供给…军需品

mural [ˈmjuərəl] *adj.* 1. 墙壁的;墙壁上的 2. 似墙壁的 — *n.* 壁画;壁饰

murder [ˈmɜːdə] *n.* 1. 谋杀,凶杀;谋杀案;谋杀罪;(战争中的)屠杀 2. 极艰险的事 — *vt.* 1. 谋杀,凶杀;屠杀 2. 扼杀(真理、艺术等);糟蹋(语言、乐曲等) 3. 折磨(人心等) — *vi.* 杀人 ‖ **-er** *n.* 谋杀犯,凶手 / **-ess** *n.* 女谋杀犯,女凶手

murderous [ˈmɜːdərəs] *adj.* 1. 杀人的,行凶的;蓄意谋杀的 2. 凶恶的;杀气腾腾的 3. 厉害的;势不可挡的;要命的 ‖ **~ly** *adv.*

murk [mɜːk] *n.* 1. 黑暗;昏暗 2. 雾;烟雾 — *adj.* 〈古〉阴暗的;朦胧的

murky [ˈmɜːki] *adj.* 1. 昏暗的;阴暗的;漆黑的;昏暗的;雾状的;雾状的 3. 难懂的;隐晦的 ‖ **murkiness** *n.*

Murmansk [murˈmɑːnsk] *n.* 摩尔曼斯克[俄罗斯西北部港市]

murmur [ˈmɜːmə] *n.* 1. 低沉连续的细声(如微风的沙沙声、流水的潺潺声等) 2. 咕哝;怨言 3. 低语声,喊喳声 4. 【医】(心脏)杂音 — *vi.* 1. 发低沉连续的细声 2. 咕哝;低声抱怨(*against* ,

3. 低声说话 —vt. 1. 低声抱怨 2. 低声说

murrain ['mʌrin, 'mərin] n. 家畜瘟疫；牛疫

muscadine ['mʌskədin] n.[植]圆叶葡萄

Muscat ['mʌskət, 'mʌskæt] n. 马斯喀特[阿曼首都]

muscat ['mʌskət, 'mʌskæt] n. 麝香葡萄(酒)

muscatel [,mʌskə'tel] n. 麝香葡萄酒；麝香葡萄干

muscle ['mʌsl] n. 1. 肌肉；[解]肌 2. 体力，膂力 3.〈口〉力量;(酒等的)劲道 4.〈美理〉大力士；打手 —vt. 1. 强推 2. 使具有力量 3.〈方〉用体力搬运 —vi. 用劲走;用力挤着走 ‖ ~-bound adj. 1.(因过度运动)肌肉僵大的 2. 僵硬的;死板的 /~ car 大功率高速中型汽车

muscular ['mʌskjulə] adj. 1. 肌肉的;[解]肌的 2. 肌肉发达的，强健的;强有力的

muse¹ [mjuz] n. 1.[the Muses]〈希神〉缪斯(掌管文艺、音乐、天文等的九位女神) 2.[the—]诗人的灵感,诗才,诗兴 3.〈诗〉诗人

muse² [mjuz] vi. 1. 沉思, 冥想 2. 若有所思地凝望 3.〈古〉惊讶，惊异 —vt. 沉思, 冥想 —n. 沉思, 冥想

museum [mju'ziəm] n. 1. 博物馆, 博物院 2.[总称]收藏物, 展览品

mush¹ [mʌʃ] n. 1. 烂糊状东西;软块 2.〈美玉米粥〉3.〈口〉多愁善感;婉情(话);废话;无聊文字 4.〈美俚〉嘴巴;脸 —vt.〈方〉使成烂糊状 —vi.〈飞机因控制器失灵〉半失速下行;升不高

mush² [mʌʃ]〈美〉vi. 坐狗拉的雪橇旅行 —n. 坐狗拉雪橇的旅行 —int.〈赶拉雪橇的狗前进的吆喝声]快走!

mushroom ['mʌʃrum] n. 1. 蘑菇;伞菌 2. 蘑菇形物;蘑菇形女式扁帽;蘑菇云;〈俚〉伞 3.〈口〉蘑菇般迅速增长的事物;〈古〉暴发户 —adj. 蘑菇形的;蘑菇般迅速增长的;蘑菇形短命的, 短暂的 —vi. 1. 采蘑菇 2. 蘑菇般迅速增长;雨后春笋般涌现 3.(子弹等)打扁成蘑菇形;(烟云等)呈蘑菇状升腾

music ['mjuzik] n. 1. 音乐;乐曲;乐谱 2. 乐队 3. 音乐欣赏能力,乐感 4. 和谐悦耳的声音(如鸟鸣声,泉水声等)5.(猎犬见猎物时的)吠叫声;喧闹 ‖ ~ box[音]八音盒

musical ['mjuzikəl] adj. 1. 音乐的;配乐的 2. 音乐般好听的;和谐的;悦耳的 3. 爱好音乐的;精通音乐的;有音乐才能的 4. 音乐家的;音乐爱好者的 —n. 音乐喜剧(= ~ comedy);(电影的)音乐片;〈古〉音乐(晚)会 ‖ ~ly adv. ‖ ~ box[音]八音盒 /~ comedy 音乐喜剧

musician [mju'ziʃən] n. 音乐家;乐师;作曲家

musk [mʌsk] n. 1. 麝香;[动]麝、香獐、麝香植物(尤指香沟腺等) ‖ ~ deer [动]麝, 香獐 /~ melon n. 甜瓜; 香瓜 /~ ox [动]麝牛 /~ rat n.[动]麝鼠; 麝鼠的毛皮

musket ['mʌskit] n. 火枪, 滑膛枪

musketeer [,mʌski'tiə] n. 火枪手, 用火枪装备的步兵

musky ['mʌski] adj. 麝香(气味)的; 麝香的 ‖ muskiness n.

Muslim ['muzlim] n. & adj. = Moslem

muslin ['mʌzlin] n. 平纹细布;麦斯林纱

muss [mʌs]〈美口〉vt. 使混乱,把…弄乱;弄脏 —n. 1. 混乱,一团糟 2. 乱作一团的吵闹 ‖ ~y adj.

mussel ['mʌsl] *n.* 【动】 1. 贻贝,壳菜,淡菜 2. 珠蚌;河蚌

must¹ [强 mʌst;弱 məst] *v. aux.* (无时态和人称变化,后接不带 to 的动词不定式) 1. [表示义务、命令或必要]必须,应当 2. [表示不可避免性或肯定性]必然要,必定会 3. [表示主张]一定要,坚持要 4. [表示推定或指具有较大的可能性]很可能,谅必 5. [表示与说话人愿望相反及不耐烦]偏要 6. (方) [表示请求]可以 — *n.* 必须做的事;不可少的事物 — *n.* *adj.* 绝对必要的

must² [mʌst] *n.* 1. (未发酵或发酵中的)葡萄汁;果汁 2. 新酿葡萄酒 3. 葡萄渣

mustache [məs'tɑːʃ] *n.* = moustache

mustang ['mʌstæŋ] *n.* 1. (墨西哥和美国加利福尼亚州产的)野马 2. (美俚)行伍出身的军官

mustard ['mʌstəd] *n.* 1. 【植】芥菜;芥菜花 2. 芥子酱;芥子粉;芥末 3. 芥末色,暗黄色 4. 【化】芥子气(= ~ gas)

muster ['mʌstə] *n.* 1. 集合;集结;被集合在一起的人(或物) 1. 一群;一批 2. 检阅 3. 清单;花名册 4. 样品 5. 孔雀群 — *vt.* 1. 集合;召集;召集…点名 2. 搜集,收集 3. 鼓起(勇气等);奋(力);激起(感情等);唤起 5. 总数达,合计 — *vi.* 集合;聚集;集结

mustn't ['mʌsnt] = must not

musty ['mʌsti] *adj.* 1. 有霉的,发霉的;霉臭的 2. 陈腐的;老朽的 ‖ **mustiness** *n.*

mutate [mjuːˈteit] *vt. & vi.* (使)变化;【生】(使)突变 ‖ **mutable** ['mjuːtəbl] *adj.* / **mutation** *n.*

mute [mjuːt] *adj.* 1. 缄默的,不出声的;一时说不出话的;不以言语表达的 2. 哑的;(猎犬)追猎时不吠叫的 3. (矿物)敲上去不响的 3. 【律】故意不答辩的 4. 【语】不发音的 — *n.* 1. 哑子;沉默的人 2. 雇用的送丧人;(古)(没有台词讲的)无言演员 3. 【音】弱音器 — *vt.* 减弱…的声音;柔和…的色调

mutilate ['mjuːtileit] *vt.* 1. 使断肢;残害;毁伤;切去(手、足或身体的重要部分) 2. 使残缺不全;把…删改得支离破碎 ‖ **muti'lation** *n.*

mutineer [ˌmjuːtiˈniə] *n.* 反叛者,叛变者;犯叛乱罪的人 — *vi.* 反叛;参加叛变

mutinous ['mjuːtinəs] *adj.* 1. 反叛的;参与哗变之类的 2. 表示反抗的 3. 骚乱的;难控制的 ‖ ~ly *adv.*

mutiny ['mjuːtini] *n.* 反叛,叛变;反抗;兵变 — *vi.* 反叛;参加反叛 (*against*)

mutt [mʌt] *n.* 1. 笨蛋;糊涂人;庸人 2. (贬)杂种狗;小狗

mutter ['mʌtə] *vi.* 1. 轻声低语;咕哝 2. 抱怨 (*at, against*) 3. 发出低沉的轰隆声;发出轻微持续的声音 — *vt.* 1. 轻声含糊地说 2. 暗地里说;咕哝;抱怨 3. (号筒)嘟嘟地发出(信号) — *n.* 1. 轻声低语;抱怨 2. 咕哝的话;怨言

mutton ['mʌtn] *n.* 羊肉

mutual ['mjuːtjuəl, 'mjuːtʃuəl] *adj.* 1. 相互的;彼此的 2. 共同的;共有的 ‖ ~ly *adv.*

muzzle ['mʌzl] *n.* 1. (狗、狐等凸出的)口鼻部;动物的口套 3. (动物的)口套 3. 嘴口 4. 炮口;枪口 5. 禁止;抑制 — *vt.* 1. 给(动物)套口套 2. 封住…的嘴;使缄默 3. 收(帆) ‖ ~ velocity 初速(射弹离开炮口瞬间的速度)

muzzy ['mʌzi] *adj.* 迟钝的;迷惑的;醉得发呆的 ‖ **muzzily** *adv.* / **muzziness** *n.*

MV *abbr.* motor vessel 内燃机船

my [mai;弱 mi] *pron.* 1. [I 的所有格]我

的 2.[用于称呼]我的 3.[用于感叹句，表示惊奇；有时与 eye, foot 等连用，表示怀疑或不赞成] My, what a down-pour! 哎呀！好大的雨呀！

Myanmar ['mjænmɑ:] *n.* 缅甸[东南亚国家](即 Burma)

myna(h) [mainə] *n.*【动】家八哥；鹩哥，秦吉了

myopia [maiˈəupiə] *n.* 1.【医】近视 2. 目光短浅，缺乏深谋远虑 ‖ **myopic** [maiˈɔpik] *adj.*

myriad ['miriəd] *n.* 1. 无数，极大数量 2.〈诗〉万，一万 —*adj.* 1. 无数的 2. 各种各样都有的；包罗万象的 3.〈诗〉一万的

myriapod ['miriəpɔd]【动】*n.* 多足纲节肢动物(如马陆、蜈蚣) —*adj.* 多足纲节肢动物的；多足的

myrrh [mə:] *n.* 1.【药】没药 2.【植】没药树；欧洲没药

myrtle ['mə:tl] *n.*【植】1. 桃金娘；香桃木，爱神木 2. 常春花 3. 香桃梅；加州桂

myself [maiˈself] *pron.* 1.[反身代词]我自己 2.[加以加强语气]我亲自，我本人 3.[用于 be, become, come to 等之后]我的正常情况(指健康、情绪等)：I'm not quite ~ today. 今天我有点不舒服

(或不正常)。

mysterious [misˈtiəriəs] *adj.* 1. 神秘的，不可思议的；难以理解的 2. 爱故弄玄虚的；诡秘的 ‖ ~**ly** *adv.* / ~**ness** *n.*

mystery ['mistəri] *n.* 1. 神秘的事物，不可思议的事物；难以理解的事物 2. 神秘；秘密 3. 故弄玄虚 4. 推理小说，侦探小说(或故事)、戏剧) 5.[mysteries](古希腊、罗马的)秘密宗教仪式 6.【宗】奥秘；[Misteries](基督教的)圣餐礼 7.【宗】神秘剧(欧洲中世纪一种宣传宗教的戏剧)(= ~ play) 8.〈美俚〉菜肴

mystic ['mistik] *adj.* 1. 神秘的；玄妙的；不可思议的 2. 具有心灵象征意义的 —*n.* 神秘主义者 ‖ ~**ly** *adv.*

mystical ['mistikəl] *adj.* = mystic

mysticism ['mistisizəm] *n.* 神秘主义

mystify ['mistifai] *vt.* 使神秘化；蒙蔽，迷惑 ‖ **mystification** [ˌmistifiˈkeiʃən] *n.*

myth [miθ] *n.* 1. 神话 2. 神话式人物(或事物)的故事；荒诞的说法

mythic(al) ['miθik(əl)] *adj.* 1. 神话的；只存在于神话中的 2. 幻想出来的，虚构的 ‖ **mythically** *adv.*

mythology [miˈθɔlədʒi] *n.* 1.[总称]神话 2. 神话学 3. 神话集；关于神话的书 4.〈喻〉神话 ‖ **mythological** [ˌmiθəˈlɔdʒikəl] *adj.*

N

N, n [en]([复]N's 或 n's 或 Ns, ns[enz])英
语字母表第十四个字母 1.[N]N 形 2.
[N]〈化〉元素氮(nitrogen)的符号 3.
〈数〉不定使(尤指常整数)的符号 4.
[n]〈物〉中子(neutron)的符号 5.北
(north)的符号

n. *abbr.* 1. noon 2. noun 3. number

Na 〈化〉元素钠(sodium)的符号

nab [næb](nabbed; nabbing) *vt.*〈口〉1. 猛
然抓取 2. 逮捕;捉住(现行犯等)

nabob ['neibɔb] *n.* 1.(印度莫卧儿帝国
时代的)地方行政长官 2. 在印度(或
其他东方国家)发财归国的欧洲人 3.
富豪;大人物,名人

nacelle [næ'sel, nə'sel] *n.*〈空〉发动机舱;
短舱

nacre ['neikə] *n.* 1. 珠母贝,珍珠母 2. 真
珠质;真珠层

nadir ['neidiə, 'nædiə] *n.* 1.〈天〉天底 2.
最低点;情绪的最低点;最不幸时刻

NAFTA *abbr.* North American Free Trade
Agreement 北美自由贸易协定

nag¹ [næg](nagged; nagging) *vt.* 1. 唠唠
叨叨地责骂;不断地找...的岔子 2.(问
题等)困扰 — *vi.* 1. 唠叨;责骂不停;
老是催促(*at*)2. 恼人(*at*)— *n.* 1. 唠
叨;不停的责骂;不断的催促 2.〈口〉爱
唠叨的人(尤指妇女)

nag² [næg] *n.* 1.(作坐骑的)矮小马 2.
〈口〉马(尤指老马或驽马)

Nagasaki [,nægə'sɑːki] *n.* 长崎[日本九州
岛西岸港市]

Nagoya [nɑː'gɔujɑ] *n.* 名古屋[日本本州
岛中南岸港市]

naiad ['naied]([复] naiads 或 naiades
['naiədiːz]) *n.* 1.〈希神〉[罗神]那伊阿
得(住在河、湖、泉中的仙女)2.〈动〉稚
虫(尤指水生昆虫的若虫);淡水贝 3.
游泳女

nail [neil] *n.* 1.(手、脚的)指甲;爪 2. 钉
3.(软嘴鸟及鸭子等)喙上的硬甲质 4.
纳尔(英旧制量布长度单位,相当于 2
1/4 英寸)5.〈俚〉香烟 — *vt.* 1. 钉;
将...钉牢;使固定 2. 使(目光、注意力
等)集中于一点 3. 揭露;揭穿 4. 拦住;留下
5.〈口〉抓住;捕获 6. 成交(一笔生意)
7.〈美俚〉击,打 8.〈棒球赛用语〉把(跑
垒者)杀出局 ‖ ~ brush 指甲刷

nainsook ['neinsuk] *n.*〈纺〉奈恩苏克布
(一种平纹轻软棉织物)

Nairobi [nai'rəubi] *n.* 内罗毕[肯尼亚首
都]

naïve, naive [nɑː'iːv, nɑːˈiːv] *adj.* 1. 天
真的;幼稚的 2. 朴素的;朴实的 3.
(鼠、兔等)首次用于实验的 4.(艺术方
面)未受过正规训练的;缺乏技巧,
不成熟的 ‖ ~ly *adv.* / ~ness *n.*

naïveté, naivete [nɑː'iːvti] *n.* 1. 天真;
幼稚;轻信;朴素 2. 天真(或幼稚)的话
(或举动)

naïvety, naivety [nɑːˈiːvti, naiˈiːvti] *n.* = naïveté

naked [ˈneikid] *adj.* **1.** 裸体的，光身的 **2.** 无遮蔽的;无保护的;无防备的;(灯火)无罩的;(房屋等)未加隔设的;(土地等)无树木的,暴露的 **3.** 无掩饰的;坦白的;直率的;赤裸裸的 **4.** 无证据的;无保证的 **5.** 裸的;无毛的;无鳞的;无贝壳的 ‖ ~ly *adv.* / ~ness *n.* **1.** 裸;裸体 **2.** 无掩饰 **3.** 光秃,无防备状态 ‖ ~ape 人;人类

namby-pamby [ˈnæmbiˈpæmbi] *adj.* **1.** 感伤的;无生气的;浮华的 **2.** 纤弱的;无决断的人;没有决断的人

name [neim] *n.* **1.** 名字;姓;姓名;名称 **2.** 义义 **3.** [只用单数]名声;名人 **4.** 名义 **5.**(同姓的)族人;家族 **6.** [逻][语]名词 — *vt.* **1.** 给……取名 **2.** 正确叫出……的名字;列举 **3.** 任命;提名 **4.** 说出;提到;指定 **5.**(英)(下院议长因国会议员不服从裁决等而)点……的名 — *adj.* **1.** 姓名的 **2.**(作品等)据以取名的;取某人名字的 **3.**(美口)著名的;有声誉的 ‖ namable, ~able *adj.* / ~r *n.* ‖ ~plate *n.* **1.** 名牌 **2.**(印在报头上或封面上的)报刊名 ‖ ~sake *n.* 同名人(尤指以他人的名字取名的人);同名物

nameless [ˈneimlis] *adj.* **1.** 没有名字的;不知其名的 **2.** 无名的;不提名的 **3.** 不可名状的,难以形容的 **4.**(罪恶等)坏得说不出口的 **5.** 无合法名义的;私生的 ‖ ~ly *adv.* / ~ness *n.*

namely [ˈneimli] *adv.* 即,那就是

Namibia [nɑːˈmibiə] *n.* 纳米比亚(旧称 South-West Africa 西南非洲)[非洲西南部国家]

nankeen [næŋˈkiːn], **nankin** [ˈnænkin]

n. **1.** 紫花布,南京棉布 **2.**[~s]紫花布长裤 **3.** 紫花布色,淡黄色 **4.** [N-]白江布青花瓷器

nanny [ˈnæni] *n.* 〈主英〉**1.** 保姆 **2.** 雌山羊(= ~goat)

nap[¹] [næp](napped; napping) *vi.* **1.** 小睡,打盹 **2.** 疏忽,不留神 — *n.*(白天的)小睡,打盹,瞌睡

nap[²] [næp] *n.* **1.**(织物或皮革表面的)绒毛 **2.**(某些植物表面的)短茸毛 —(napped; napping) *vt.* **1.** 使起绒,使拉毛 **2.** 修整;使平滑

napalm [ˈneipɑːm] *n.* [化]凝固汽油(弹) — *vt.* 用凝固汽油弹(或喷火器)攻击(或轰炸) ‖ ~bomb 凝固汽油弹

nape [neip] *n.* [解]项,颈背,后颈

napery [ˈneipəri] *n.* 布巾;台布;餐巾

naphtha [ˈnæfθə] *n.* [化] **1.** 石脑油 **2.** 石油

naphthalene [ˈnæfθəliːn] *n.* [化]萘

napkin [ˈnæpkin] *n.* **1.** 餐巾 **2.** 小毛巾;〈英方〉手帕;〈苏格兰〉头巾;围巾 **3.** 〈英〉尿布;〈美〉月经带

Naples [ˈneiplz] *n.* 那不勒斯[意大利西南部港市]

Nara [ˈnɑːrə] *n.* 奈良[日本本州岛中西部城市]

narcissism [nɑːˈsisizəm] *n.* **1.** 自我陶醉;孤芳自赏 **2.** [心]自恋(癖) ‖ narcis'sistic *adj.*

narcissus [nɑːˈsisəs] *n.* **1.** [N-]〈希神〉那喀索斯(因爱恋自己在水中的影子而憔悴致死的美少年;死后化为水仙花) **2.**([复] narcissuses 或 narcissi [nɑːˈsisai]) [植]水仙,水仙花 **3.** 橘黄色

narcotic [nɑːˈkɔtik] *adj.* **1.** 麻醉(性)的;麻醉剂的 **2.** 起精神麻痹作用的 **3.** 吸毒成瘾者的;治疗吸毒成瘾者的 — *n.*

1. 麻醉剂;致幻毒品 **2.** 起麻痹作用的事物 **3.** 吸毒成瘾者

narrate ['næreit] *vt.* 讲;讲(故事) ;叙述 — *vi.* 讲故事;叙述 ‖ **narrator**, ~ **r** *n.* 讲述者;叙述者

narration [næ'reiʃən] *n.* **1.** 讲述 **2.** 故事;(一篇)报道 **3.** 记叙体

narrative ['nærətiv] *adj.* 叙述的;叙事体的 — *n.* **1.** 记事;叙述(可指文章或讲话);记叙文;故事 **2.** 记叙体

narrow ['nærəu] *adj.* **1.** 狭的,狭窄的;(布匹等)狭幅的(通常指 18 英寸以下) **2.** 范围狭小的 **3.** 眼光短浅的,有偏见的 **4.** 自我中心的 **5.** 气量小的,《方》吝啬的 **6.** 勉强的 **7.** 精细的;严密的 **8.**[语]窄(音)的 — *vi.* 变狭;缩窄;(眼睛)眯成一条缝 — *vt.* 弄窄;使缩小;使(观点等)变得狭隘 — *n.* **1.** (山谷、道路等的)狭窄部分 **2.**[常~s]用作单或复]海峡 ‖ ~**ness** *n.*

narrowly ['nærəuli] *adv.* **1.** 狭窄地 **2.** 勉强地 **3.** 仔细地;严密地 **4.** 严格地 **5.** 努力地

narrow-minded ['nærəu'maindid] *adj.* 眼光短浅的;有偏见的;气量狭窄的 ‖ ~**ly** *adv.* / ~**ness** *n.*

narwhal ['nɑːwəl], **narwhale** ['nɑːhweil] *n.*[动]一角鲸,独角鲸(一种齿鲸,雄性有一长牙)

NASA *abbr.* National Aeronautics and Space Administration(美国)国家航空和航天局

nasal ['neizəl] *adj.* 鼻的;带鼻音的 — *n.* **1.** 鼻音;鼻音字母 **2.**[解]鼻骨 **3.**(头盔上的)护鼻 ‖ ~**ly** *adv.* 以鼻音

Nassau ['næsɔː] *n.* 拿骚[巴哈马首都]

nasturtium [nə'stəːʃəm] *n.* **1.**[植]水田芥;旱金莲 **2.** 橙黄色 **3.**(谑)诽谤

nasty ['nɑːsti] *adj.* **1.** 龌龊的;极脏的;(气味等)令人作呕的 **2.** 淫猥的,下流的 **3.**(天气等)非常恶劣的;使人感到极不愉快的 **4.** 平庸的;俗丽的 **5.** 脾气不好的;(手段等)卑鄙的;恶意的 **6.** 险恶的;非常有害的;严重的 **7.** 棘手的;问题多的;别扭的 — *n.* 讨厌的家伙;讨厌的事物 ‖ **nastily** *adv.* / **nastiness** *n.*

natal ['neitl] *adj.* **1.** 出生的;出生时的 **2.** = native

nation ['neiʃən] *n.* **1.** 民族 **2.** 国家 **3.**[总称]国民 **4.**(北美印第安人等的)部落;部落联盟;部落(或部落联盟)的领地 **5.**(中世纪或一些苏格兰大学中的)学生同乡会 ‖ '~'**wide** *adj.* 全国性的 *adv.* 在全国范围内;全国性地

national ['næʃənəl] *adj.* **1.** 民族的;国家的;国民的 **3.** 全国性的 **4.** 国有的;国立的 **5.** 国家主义的,爱国的 **7.** 各党联合的 — *n.* **1.** 国民(尤指侨居于外国的) **2.**[常~s]全国体育比赛 ‖ ~**ly** *adv.* 在全国范围内;全国性地

nationalism ['næʃənəlizəm] *n.* **1.** 民族主义 **2.** 国家主义 **3.** 民族性;民族特征(或习惯、惯用语) **4.** 工业国有化主义

nationalist ['næʃənəlist] *adj.* **1.** 民族主义的 **2.** 国家主义的 **3.**[N-]民族主义(或国家主义)政党的 — *n.* **1.** 民族主义者 **2.** 国家主义者 **3.**[N-]民族主义(或国家主义)政党成员

nationalistic [ˌnæʃənə'listik] *adj.* **1.** 民族主义(者)的;国家主义(者)的 **2.** 民族的;国家的 ‖ ~**ally** *adv.*

nationality [ˌnæʃə'næliti] *n.* **1.** 国籍 **2.** 民族;族 **3.** 民族性 **4.** 民族主义;国家主义 **5.** 国民身分 **6.** 独立国地位

nationalize ['næʃənəlaiz] *vt.* **1.** 把 … 收归国有;使国有化 **2.** 使具有某国国

3. 使组成国家 4. 使民族化 ‖ ˌnationali'zation *n*.

native ['neitiv] *adj*. 1. 出生的；出生地的 2. 本土的；本国的；土生土长的 3. 天生的 4. 朴素的，不做作的 5.（金属等）天然的，自然的 6.〈主澳〉(动植物)似英国种的 7. 土人的，土著的；非欧美(人)的 — *n*. 1. 本地人；本国人 2. 当地人(与暂居者相对) 3.〈常贬〉土人，土著 4. 当地土生的动(或植)物 5.〈英〉当地本地的牡蛎 ‖ **Native American**〈美〉美洲印第安人(的)

nativity [nə'tiviti] *n*. 1. 出生，诞生；出生情况 2. 诞生地 3. [N-]〖宗〗耶稣诞生；耶稣诞生图；圣母马利亚诞生 4. [N-]〖宗〗圣诞节，耶稣诞生节(= Christmas)；圣母马利亚诞生节 5.（占星术的）算命天宫图

NATO ['neitəu] *abbr*. North Atlantic Treaty Organization 北大西洋公约组织(简称北约组织)

natty ['næti] *adj*. 1.（外貌、衣着）整洁的，漂亮的 2. 敏捷的；灵巧的 ‖ **nattily** *adv.* / **nattiness** *n*.

natural ['nætʃərəl] *adj*. 1. 自然界的；关于自然界的 2. 天然的 3. 自然的；不加做作的 4. 物质的；物质世界的；非精神的 5. 合乎自然规律的；正常的；惯常的 6. 天生的，生来的 7. 自然状态的；蒙昧的；野生的，未开垦的 8. 逼真的 9. 私生的；私生关系的 10.〈主方〉(父母)生身的；(子女)有血统关系的(别于领养) 11.〖数〗自然(数)的；正整数的 12.〖音〗本位音的；标有还原号的 ‖ **~ ness** *n*. **~ number**〖数〗自然数 2. [无]逼真度 ‖ **~ resources** 天然资源 / **~ scientist** 自然科学家

naturalist ['nætʃərəlist] *n*. 1. 自然主义者；自然主义作家 2. 博物学家(尤指直接观察动植物者) 3.〈英〉买卖玩赏动物的商人 4.〈英〉动物标本剥制者 — *adj*. = naturalistic

naturalistic [ˌnætʃərə'listik] *adj*. 1. 自然主义的 2. 博物学(家)的

naturalize ['nætʃərəlaiz] *vt*. 1. 授予…以国籍，使入籍 2. 使(动、植物)驯化；顺化；移植；移栽 3. 采纳(外国语词、风俗等) 4. 使自然化；使摆脱习俗 5. 用自然法则解释(发生的事)；使摆脱神秘性 — *vi*. 1. 入籍，归化 2.（动、植物)被采纳 3. 研究博物学 ‖ **naturali'zation** *n*. 1. 入籍，归化 2.（动、植物)的驯化；顺化 3.（外国语词等)的采纳

naturally ['nætʃərəli] *adv*. 1. 自然地 2. 天然地 3. 生来 4. 当然 5. 逼真地

nature ['neitʃə] *n*. 1.[拟人化时作 N-]大自然，自然界 2. 本性，天性；性情；具有某种性格的人 4. 性质；种类 5. 生命力；生命机能；生理；生理需要 6.(人的)原始状态；躯体；(动、植物)野生状态 7. 天然 8.〔艺术上的]自然，逼真 9.[宗]未受天恩的罪人状态

naught [nɔːt] *n*. 1. 无 2.〖数〗零 3. 无用的人(或物) — *adj*. 无价值的，无用的；不存在的

naughty ['nɔːti] *adj*. 1. 顽皮的，淘气的，不听话的 2. 猥亵的，下流的 ‖ **naughtily** *adv.* / **naugh-tiness** *n*.

Nauru [nɑː'uːruː] *n*. 瑙鲁[西太平洋岛国]

nausea ['nɔːsiə] *n*. 1. 恶心；晕船 2. 极端的憎恶(或厌恶)

nauseate ['nɔːsieit] *vt*. 1. 使恶心；使作呕 2. 使厌恶 — *vi*. 作呕；厌恶(*at*)

nauseating ['nɔːsieitiŋ] *adj*. 1. 令人作呕的 2. 令人厌恶的 ‖ **~ly** *adv*.

nauseous ['nɔːsiəs] *adj*. 1. 令人恶心的，

令人作呕的 2. 令人厌恶的

nautical ['nɔːtikəl] adj. 航海的；海员的；船舶的；海上的 ‖ ～ly adv. 在航海方面 ‖ ～ mile 海里（= 1,852 米）

nautilus ['nɔːtiləs] （[复] nautiluses 或 nau-tili ['nɔːtilai]） n. [动] 1. 鹦鹉螺 2. 船蛸

naval ['neivəl] adj. 海军的；军舰的；船的

nave [neiv] n. 1. (教堂的)中殿 2. (火车站等建筑物的)中间广场

navel ['neivəl] n. 1. 脐, 肚脐 2. 中心(点)

navigable ['nævigəbl] adj. 1. (河、海等)可航行的, 可通航的 2. (船舶等)适航的;可操纵航向的 ‖ naviga'bility n. (河、海或船舶等)的适航性

navigate ['nævigeit] vi. 1. 航行;飞行 2. 驾驶船舶(或飞机等) 3. (醉汉等)行走 — vt. 1. 航行于;横渡, 飞越 2. 驾驶, 操纵(船舶、飞机等) 3. 使通过 ‖ navigator n. 1. (船舶、飞机的)驾驶员;领航员 2. 航海者;航行者;(早期的)航海探险家

navigation [ˌnævi'geiʃən] n. 1. 航行;航海;航空 2. 航行术;航行学 3. 导航;领航 4. 航运;水上运输

navy ['neivi] n. 1. 海军;海军官兵 2. 〈古〉〈诗〉船队;舰队 3. 藏青色(= ～ blue)

nay [nei] adv. 1. 〈古〉否, 不 2. 不仅如此, 而且;甚至 — n. 1. 否定;否认;拒绝;否定的答复 2. 反对票;投反对票的人

Nazi ['nɑːtsi] n. 1. 德国国社党党员;纳粹分子 2. [常用 n-]法西斯分子 — adj. 德国国社党的;纳粹党的;纳粹的 ‖ ～(i)sm n. 纳粹主义

Nb 【化】元素铌(niobium)的符号

NBC abbr. National Broadcasting Company (美国)全国广播公司

N-bomb ['enbɔm] n. 中子弹 (= neutron bomb)

Nd 【化】元素钕(neodymium)的符号

Ndjamena [ˌendʒə'meinə] n. 恩贾梅纳 (旧称 Fort-Lamy 拉密堡)[乍得首都]

Ne 【化】元素氖(neon)的符号

NE, n. e. abbr. northeast;northeastern

Neandert(h)al [ni'ændətɑːl] n. ‖ ～ man 尼安德特人(旧石器时代中期的古人化石,分布在欧洲、北非、西亚一带)

neap [niːp] adj. (潮汐)升降幅度最小的;小潮的 — n. 小潮 ‖ ～ tide 小潮

near [niə] adv. 1. (空间、时间)接近, 临近 2. 差不多, 几乎 3. 亲近地;亲密地 4. 节俭地;吝啬地 — adj. 1. (空间、时间)近的 2. 接近的, 临近的;亲密的 3. 关系接近的;亲疏的 4. (车轮等)在左侧的 5. (路等)直达的;近的 6. 〈古〉吝啬的 — prep. 接近, 靠近 — vt. 接近;走近;驶近 — vi. 接近;走近;驶近 ‖ ～ness n. ‖ Near East [地] 近东 /'～-sighted adj. 1. [医] 近视的 2. 目光短浅的 /'～-sightedness n. 1. [医] 近视 2. 目光短浅

nearby ['niəbai] adj. 附近的 — adv. 在附近 — prep.〈方〉在…的附近

nearly ['niəli] adv. 1. 差不多, 几乎 2. 极其 3. 密切地;亲密地 4. 吝啬地

neat [niːt] adj. 1. 整洁的;简洁的;整齐的 2. 匀称的;样子好的 3. 熟练的;灵巧的 4. 平滑的, 光滑的 5. 纯净的;不掺水的 6. 〈俚〉好的、美妙的 ‖ ～ly adv. / ～ness n.

neb [neb] n. 1. (鸟、龟的)嘴;(人的)嘴 2. (人、兽的)鼻 3. 尖头, 尖端;笔尖

Nebraska [ni'bræskə] n. 内布拉斯加[美国州名]

nebula ['nebjulə] （[复] nebulae ['nebjuliː] 或

nebulas] *n.* 1.【天】星云 2.【医】薄翳；角膜云翳；(尿的)混浊；喷雾剂 ‖ ~ r *adj.* 星云；星云状的

nebulous ['nebjuləs] *adj.* 1. 星云的 2. 模糊不清的；朦胧的 3.〈古〉多云的 ‖ ~ly *adv.* / ~ness *n.*

NEC *abbr.* Nippon Electric Company 日本电气公司

necessary ['nesəsəri] *adj.* 1. 必要的，必需的 2. 必然的，不可避免的 3. 强制的，非做不可的；被迫的，非自愿的 — *n.* 1.[常 necessaries]必需品 2.[the ~]钱；必须做的事 3.〈英方〉厕所 ‖ **necessarily** ['nesəsərili, ,nesə'serəli] *adv.* 必定，必然

necessitate [ni'sesiteit] *vt.* 1. 需要；使成为必需品 2.[常用被动语态]迫使

necessity [ni'sesiti] *n.* 1. 需要；必要性 2. 必然(性) 3. 必需品 4. 贫穷；困难；危急

neck [nek] *n.* 1. (头)颈，脖子 2. (动物的)颈肉 3. (衣服的)领圈 4. (物的)颈状部分 5. 狭窄地带，隘口；地峡；海峡 6.【地】岩颈 7.【建】颈708体 8.〈俚〉厚脸 — *vt.* 1. 割颈杀死(家禽) 2. 缩小…的口径使变成颈状(*down*，*in*) 3.〈俚〉与…接吻；爱抚 — *vi.* 1.〈俚〉接吻；爱抚 2. 收缩，缩小 ‖ ~-lace ['neklis] *n.* 项圈，项链 / ~-line *n.* 领口；开领 / ~-piece *n.* 毛皮围巾；领饰 / ~-tie *n.* 1. 领带；围巾 2.〈美俚〉绞索

neckerchief ['nekətʃif][复]neckerchiefs 或 neckerchieves['nekətʃivz] *n.* 围巾，颈巾

necrology [ne'krɔlədʒi] *n.* 1. 亡故者名录 2. 死亡通知；讣告

necromancy ['nekrəmænsi] *n.* 召亡魂问卜的巫术；巫术，妖书 ‖ **necromancer** *n.*

necrosis [ne'krəusis] ([复] necroses

[ne'krəusi:z]) *n.* 1.【医】坏死 2.【植】枯斑

nectar ['nektə] *n.* 1.〈希神〉众神饮的酒 2. 甘美的饮料；水果原汁 3.【植】花蜜

nectarine ['nektərin] *n.*【植】蜜桃

née, nee [nei]〈法〉*adj.* 娘家姓…的(表示已婚妇女的婚前姓名)

need [ni:d] *n.* 1. 需要；必要 2. 需要的；需求 3. 贫穷；困窘 — *vt.* 需要；必需 — *vi.* 1. 缺衣少食 2. 是需要的；是必要的 v. *aux.* [无时态、人称变化；多用于疑问句和否定句]需要；必须

needful ['ni:dful] *adj.* 需要的；必要的 — *n.* 1. 必须做的事 2. 个人必需品 3.〈口〉钱 ‖ ~ly *adv.* / ~ness *n.*

needle ['ni:dl] *n.* 1. 针；缝针；编织针；唱针；注射针 2. 指针；磁针 3.【植】针叶；【矿】针状结晶体；针状物(如尖岩、方尖塔等) 4.【建】撑木 5. 放射性物质器 — *vt.* 1. 用针缝；用针穿刺；像针一样地刺 2. 用撑木支撑 3.〈口〉刺激；煽动；戏弄 4. 加强(讲话等)的效果；使更尖锐辛辣；掺酒精使(饮料)浓烈 — *vi.* 1. 缝纫；刺绣 2. 成针状结晶 ‖ ~-therapy 针刺疗法 / ~-woman *n.* 缝纫女工，女裁缝 / ~-work *n.* 1. 缝纫；刺绣；编结 2. 针线活；缝纫职业

needless ['ni:dlis] *adj.* 不需要的；不必要的 ‖ ~ly *adv.* / ~ness *n.*

needn't ['ni:dnt] = need not

needs [ni:dz] *adv.* [现只与 must 连用]一定；必须

needy ['ni:di] *adj.* 贫困的 ‖ **neediness** *n.*

ne'er [nɛə] *adv.*〈诗〉= never

ne'er-do-well ['nɛədu,wel], **ne'er-do-weel** ['nɛədu;wi:l] *n.* 无用的人；游手好闲的人 — *adj.* 无用的；游手好闲的

nefarious [ni'fɛəriəs] *adj.*〈阴谋等〉恶毒

的;极坏的 ‖ ~ly adv. / ~ness n.

negate [ni'geit] vt. 1. 否定;否认 2. 取消,使无效 — n. 反面,对立面

negation [ni'geiʃən] n. 1. 否定;否认;表示否定的话(或主张) 2. 反面,对立面 3. 虚无;不存在 4. 【逻】(命题)的否定

negative ['negativ] adj. 1. 否定的;否认的 2. 反面的;消极的 3. 【数】负的;【电】阴性的;负的;【医】阴性的;【摄】底片的 — n. 1. 否定词;否定语;否定观点 2. 否决权 3. 消极的属性 4. 【数】负数;【电】阴电;阴极板;【摄】底片 — vt. 1. 否认;驳斥 2. 否决;拒绝 3. 抵消;使中和 4. 否定 ‖ ~ly adv. 否定地;消极地 / ~ness n. 否定性;消极性

negativity [negə'tiviti] n. 否定性;消极性

neglect [ni'glekt] vt. 1. 忽视;忽略 2. 疏忽,忽视;弃置;漏做(某事) — n. 忽略;疏忽,忽视;忽置;疏漏

neglectful [ni'glektful] adj. 疏忽的,不注意的(of) ‖ ~ly adv. / ~ness n.

négligé ['negliʒei](法) n. 1. 妇女长睡衣 2. 随便的衣着;不整齐的穿戴 — adj. 穿着随便的;服饰不整的

negligee ['negliʒei] n. & adj. = négligé

negligence ['neglidʒəns] n. 1. 疏忽,玩忽;粗心大意;疏忽行为 2. 【律】过失 3. (文学作品等风格的)奔放

negligent ['neglidʒənt] adj. 疏忽的,玩忽的,粗心大意的 ‖ ~ly adv.

negligible ['neglidʒəbl] adj. 无关紧要的;微不足道的 ‖ **negligibly** adv.

negotiable [ni'gəuʃiəbl] adj. 1. 可谈判的;可协商的 2.(票据、证券等)可转让的;可流通的 3.(道路、河流等)可通行的 ‖ **ne͵gotia'bility** n.

negotiate [ni'gəuʃieit] vi. 谈判;协商,洽谈 — vt. 1. 议定,议妥;通过谈判达成(或解决) 2. 转让;兑现(票证等) 3. 处

置,处理;解决(难题等) 4. 通过,越过(障碍等) 5. 完成(旅程等) ‖ **negotiator** n. 谈判者,商谈者;洽谈者;交易者

negotiation [niɡəuʃi'eiʃən] n. 谈判;协商

Negress ['niːgris] n.(贬)女黑人

Negro ['niːɡrəu][复] Negroes) n. 1. 黑人 2. 具有黑人血统的人 — adj. 1. 黑人(似)的 2. 黑色的 ‖ ~ness n.

Negroid ['niːɡrɔid] adj. 黑人的;具有黑人特征的 — n. 黑人

neigh [nei] vi.(马)嘶;发马嘶般的声音 — n. 马嘶声

neighbo(u)r ['neibə] n. 1. 邻居;邻人;邻座;国家;邻接的东西 2. 世人 3.(对不知姓名者的称呼)朋友 — adj. 邻接的;邻近的 — vt. 邻接;邻近;与...结邻 — vi. 1. 住在邻近处;位于邻近 2. 友好往来;有睦邻关系(with) ‖ ~ing adj. 邻近的,附近的;接壤的

neighbo(u)rhood ['neibəhud] n. 1. 邻接;邻近;附近 2. 邻居关系 3. 四邻,街坊;街道,地区 4.【数】邻域

neighbo(u)rly ['neibəli] adj. 邻人似的;睦邻的;友好的 ‖ **neighbo(u)rliness** n. 睦邻;和睦;亲近

Nei Monggol ['neimɔn'ɡəul] 内蒙古(亦作 Inner Mongolia)

neither ['naiðə, 'niːðə] adj.(与单数名词或代词连用)既非此又非彼的,(两者)都不的 — pron. 两者中无一 — conj. 也不 — adv. 1. 也不 2.〈口〉也(= either)

nemesis ['nemisis] ([复] nemesises 或 nemeses ['nemisiz]) n. 1. [N-]【希神】报应女神,复仇女神 2. 天谴;报应 3. 复仇者 4. 难以取胜的对手;无法抗拒的事物;不可避免的后果

ne(o)- comb. form 表示"新":neophyte

neodymium [niːəu'dimiəm] n.【化】钕

Neolithic [ˌniːə'liθik] *adj.* 新石器时代的

neologism [niː'ɒlədʒizəm] *n.* 新词；旧词新义

neon ['niːən, 'niːɒn] *n.* 1.【化】氖 2. 氖灯，霓虹灯(＝〜 lamp 或〜 light) 3. 霓虹灯广告

neophyte ['niːəʊfait] *n.* 1. 新入教者；新入修道院的人；新受圣职的教士 2. 初学者；新手，生手

Nepal [ni'pɔːl] *n.* 尼泊尔[南亚国家]

nephew ['nevjuː, 'nefjuː] *n.* 1. 侄子；外甥 2.(教士的)私生子

nepotism ['nepətizəm] *n.* 重用亲属；偏袒亲属；任人唯亲；裙带关系

Neptune ['neptjuːn] *n.* 1.【罗神】尼普顿(海神) 2. 海洋 3.【天】海王星 4.(美国的)海王式巡逻机

neptunium [nep'tjuːniəm] *n.*【化】镎

nerd [nəːd] *n.*【俚】讨厌鬼；乏味的人；无足轻重的人；蠢人

nerve [nəːv] *n.* 1. 神经 2.〈诗〉筋，腱 3. 勇敢；沉着，果断 4.(力量、行动等的)中枢，核心 5. 力量；精力；活力 6.〈口〉厚颜；鲁莽 7.[〜s]神经质；神经紧张 8. 脑依或兴奋的事物 9.【动】翅脉；[植]脉 — *vt.* 给 …以力量；给 …以勇气 ‖〜 **agent** 神经毒气 / 〜 **cell**【解】神经细胞 / 〜 **fibre**【解】神经纤维 / 〜 **impulse**[医]神经冲动

nerveless ['nəːvlis] *adj.* 1. 神经麻木的；没有劲的；无生气的；无勇气的；虚弱的 2.(风格)松散的 3. 沉着的，镇静的 4.【动】无翅脉的；[植]无(叶)脉的 5.【解】无神经的

nervous ['nəːvəs] *adj.* 1. 神经的；神经方面的 2. 神经元的；神经元构成的 3. 易激动的；神经质的，紧张不安的 4. 胆怯的，害怕的(of) 5.〈古〉强有力的 6.(文体等)凝练的；刚劲的 7. 摇摆不定

nervy ['nəːvi] *adj.* 1. 易激动的；紧张不安的 2. 大胆的，有朝气的 3.〈俚〉厚脸皮的；粗鲁的 4.〈俚〉使人心烦的 ‖ **nerviness** *n.*

-ness *suf.*【构成抽象名词】表示"性质"，"状态"，"程度"：*goodness, sickness*

nest [nest] *n.* 1. 巢；窝；穴 2. 安逸的处所；住所，家；隐蔽处 3.(盗、贼等的)窝；(罪恶等的)渊薮，温床 4.(盗、贼等的)(一)伙 5.(同巢一窝的鸟、昆虫等的)群 6. 一组同类物件；(相互套得起来的)一套物件 7.【矿】矿巢 8.[建]蜂窝(混凝土缺陷) — *vi.* 1. 筑巢；巢居；找鸟巢；摸鸟蛋 3. 套叠 — *vt.* 1. 为 …筑巢；把 …放入巢中 2. 使套叠；安放，放置

nestle ['nesl] *vi.* 1.(舒适地)安顿下来；安卧 2. 偎依 3. 半隐半现 — *vt.* 1. 抱；使紧贴 2. 使(舒适地)安顿下来

nestling ['nestliŋ] *n.* 1.(还不会飞的)雏鸟 2. 幼儿；幼小动物

net[1] [net] *n.* 1. 网；网状物 2. 网眼织物；网眼花边 3. 罗网 4. 网状系统；通信网 5.(乒乓、网球赛等中的)落网球；擦网球 —(netted; netting) *vt.* 1. 把 …编结成网状；用网制作 2. 用网覆盖；用网拦住 3. 用网捕；抓住 5.(球)落网 — *vi.* 编网；编结网状物

net[2] [net] *adj.* 1. 净的，纯的 2. 基本的；最后的 —(netted; netting) *vt.* 1. 净得，净赚 2. 得到；使得到 — *n.* 1. 净数；净重 2. 净利；净值 3. 要点，要旨

nether ['neðə] *adj.* 1. 下面的 2. 地下的 ‖〜**world** *n.* 1. 阴间 2. 下层社会

Netherlands ['neðələndz] [复] ‖ [the 〜] [用作单或复]荷兰[西欧国家](＝ Holland)

nethermost ['neðəməust] *adj.* 最下面的

最低的

nett [net] *adj.* 〈英〉= net²

netting ['netiŋ] *n.* **1.** 网;网状(织)物 **2.** 结网;用网;网状物编织 **3.** 网鱼;网鱼权

nettle ['netl] *n.* **1.**【植】荨麻 **2.** 使人烦恼(或恼火)的事物 — *vt.* **1.** 以荨麻鞭打,以荨麻刺 **2.** 惹怒;使烦恼;使恼火

network ['netwə:k] *n.* **1.** 网眼织物 **2.** 网状物;网状系统(如道路网、运河网等) **3.** 广播网;电视网;广播(或电视)联播公司 **4.**【电】【计】网络 — *adj.* 在广播网(或电视网)联播的 — *vt.* **1.** 使成网状 **2.** (广播网、电视网)联播;使加入联播公司

neural ['njuərəl] *adj.*【解】神经的;神经系统的;神经中枢的

neuralgia [nju'rældʒə] *n.*【医】神经痛

neuritis [nju'raitis] *n.*【医】神经炎 ‖ **neuritic** [nju'ritik] *adj.* & *n.*

neurology [njuə'rɔlədʒi] *n.*【医】神经病学 ‖ **neurologist** *n.* 神经病学家;神经病科医师

neuron ['njuərɔn], **neurone** ['njuərəun] *n.*【解】神经元,神经细胞

neurosis [njuə'rəusis] ([复] **neuroses** [njuə'rəusi:z]) *n.* **1.**【医】神经官能症 **2.** 恐惧症 ‖ **neurotic** [njuə'rɔtik] *adj.* & *n.*

neuter ['nju:tə] *adj.* **1.**【语】(名词等)中性的;(动词)不及物的 **2.**【植】【动】无性的,无性生殖器的,生殖器发育不完全的 **3.** 中立的 — *n.* **1.**【语】中性;中性词;中性形式 **2.** 无性植物(或动物);生殖器发育不完全的动物(如工蜂、工蚁等) **3.** 已阉割的动物 **4.** 守中立者(或团体) — *vt.* **1.** 阉割 **2.** 抵消

neutral ['nju:trəl] *adj.* **1.** 中立的;中立国的 **2.** 非彩色的(指墨、灰或白色的,尤

指灰色的) **3.**【植】【动】无性的;被阉割过的;生殖器发育不完全的 **4.**【化】中性的;【电】不带电的 **5.**【语】(元音)松弛的,中性的 — *n.* **1.** 中立者;中立国;中立国国民 **2.** 非彩色(指墨、灰或白色,尤指灰色) **3.**【机】空档(指传动装置空转状态) ‖ ~**ly** *adv.*

neutrality [nju:'træliti] *n.* **1.** 中立;中立地位 **2.**【化】中性

neutralize ['nju:trəlaiz] *vt.* **1.** 使中立化 **2.** 使无效;抵消 **3.**【军】压制(火力) **4.**【电】使中和 — *vi.* **1.** 中立化 **2.** 成为无效 **3.** 中和 ‖ **neutrali'zation** *n.*

neutrino [nju:'tri:nəu] ([复] **neutrinos**) *n.*【核】中微子

neutron ['nju:trɔn] *n.*【物】中子 ‖ ~ **bomb** 中子弹 / ~ **star**【天】中子星

Nevada [ne'va:də]【美国州名】内华达

never ['nevə] *adv.* **1.** 永不,决不;从来没有 **2.** 不,没有(= not,但语气较强) **3.** 不要(= do not,但语气较强) **3.** 〈口〉[表示惊异或不信]不会;不可能

nevermore ['nevə'mɔ:] *adv.* 永不再;决不再

nevertheless [,nevəðə'les] *conj.* 然而,不过 — *adv.* 仍然,不过

new [nju:] *adj.* **1.** 新的 **2.** 近出现的;新制成的;新就任的 **3.** 精神恢复了健康(体力)的;改变了的,更新的 **4.** 新发现的 **5.** (土地)新开发的 **6.** 重新开始的;周而复始的 **7.** 不熟悉的;不习惯的;没经验的 **8.** 另加的,附加的 **9.** [N-](语言)中世纪以来所用的,现代的 — *adv.* [常用以构成复合词]新;最近;~-**built** 新建的 — *n.* 新的东西;新 ‖ ~**ness** *n.* 新的东西;新 **2.** 再生的 *n.* ([复] ~-**born**(s))新生儿,新生者 / '~-**comer** *n.* 新来的人;移民;新手 / '~-**fangled** *adj.* **1.** 新花样的,新

奇的 2. 爱好新奇的 /~ **moon**【天】新月；朔 /**New World** 新大陆，西半球，美洲 /**New Year** 新年：*New Year's* Day 元旦 / *New Year's* Eve 除夕

New Delhi [nju:'deli] 新德里[印度首都]

newel ['nju:əl] *n.*【建】拐弯角柱；楼梯端柱；螺旋型楼梯中柱

New England 新英格兰[美国](美国东北部 Maine, Vermont, New Hampshire, Massachusetts, Rhode Island 和 Connecticut 六州的总称)

Newfoundland ['nju:fəndlənd] *n.* 纽芬兰(岛)[加拿大东部一地区]

New Hampshire 新罕布什尔[美国州名]

New Jersey 新泽西[美国州名]

newly ['nju:li] *adv.* 1. 新近，最近 2. 重新；以新的方式 ‖ ~ **wed** *n.* 新婚的人

New Mexico 新墨西哥[美国州名]

New Orleans ['ɔ:liənz] 新奥尔良[美国路易斯安那州东南部港市]

news [nju:z] [复] *n.* [用作单] 1. 新闻，消息；新闻报道 2. [N-](作报刊名用)新闻报刊 ‖ ~ **agency** 通讯社 /~ **boy** *n.* 报童 /~ **break** *n.* 有新闻价值的事件，值得报道的新闻 /~ **cast** *n.* 新闻广播 /~ **letter** *n.* 1. (定期出版的)时事通讯；【史】新闻信札 2. (公司等刊印的)业务通讯 /~ **man** *n.* 1. 卖报人；送报人 2. 新闻记者 /~ **print** *n.* 新闻纸，白报纸 /~ **reader** 1. 报纸读者 2. (英)新闻播音员 /~ **reel** *n.* 新闻(短)片 /~ **stall** (英) = ~ **stand** /~ **stand** *n.* 报摊；报刊柜；报刊出售处

newspaper ['nju:zpeipə] *n.* 1. 报纸，报；印刷用纸 2. 报馆，报社，白报纸 ‖ ~ **man** *n.* 1. 报社从业人员(尤指编辑、记者等) 2. 报纸主办人(或出版人)

newsy ['nju:zi] (口) *adj.* 1. 新闻多的 2. 饶舌的，喜谈论的 3. 有报道价值的 — *n.* 报童；

卖报人

newt [nju:t] *n.*【动】水螈

Newtonian [nju:'təuniən] *adj.* (英国物理学家)牛顿(Newton)的；牛顿学说的；信奉牛顿学说的；经典的 — *n.* 牛顿学说的信奉者

New York ['nju:'jɔ:k] 1. 纽约[美国州名] 2. 纽约(市)[美国纽约州东南部港市] (= New York City)

New Yorker ['nju:'jɔ:kə] 纽约市(或州)人

New Zealand [nju:'zi:lənd] 新西兰[大洋洲国家]

next [nekst] *adj.* 1. 紧接(在后面)的，其次的 2. 紧邻的，隔壁的 3. 紧接着来到的；下(年、月、星期 等) 4. [the ~]任何别的 — *adv.* 1. 其次；然后 2. 贴近下一次 — *prep.* 靠近，贴近 — *n.* 下一个人(或物)

nexus ['neksəs] ([复] nexus(es)) *n.* 1. 联系，连结，关系 2. 连结的一系列，一组

Ngwane [əŋ'gwɑ:ni] *n.* 恩格瓦尼(非洲人对 Swaziland 斯威士兰之称呼)[非洲东南部国家]

NHK *abbr.* *Nippon Hoso Kyokai* 日本放送协会，日本广播协会(= Japan Broadcasting Corporation)

Ni 【化】元素镍(nickel)的符号

niacin ['naiəsin] *n.*【生化】烟酸，尼克酸，抗糙皮病维生素，维生素 PP

Niamey [njɑ:'mei] *n.* 尼亚美[尼日尔首都]

nib [nib] *n.* 1. 鹅毛管笔尖尖；钢笔尖 2. (鸟的)嘴 3. (工具等的)尖头，尖端 4. (大镰刀的)短柄 5. 咖啡豆；[~s]炒熟并碾碎的可可豆 — (nibbed) (nibbing) *vt.* 削尖(鹅毛管笔)；修(笔)尖；在(笔杆)上装笔尖

nibble ['nibl] *vt.* 啃，一点一点地咬(或

吃);一点一点地去掉 — *vi.* 1. 啃,一点一点地咬(或吃);小心谨慎地对付(或着手)(*at*) 2. 吹毛求疵;找错儿(*at*) 3.〈对交易、建议、诱惑等〉显出有意接受的样子(*at*) — *n.* 1. 啃;轻咬 2. 咬一小口的量;少量 3.〈口〉少量食物

Nicaragua [ˌnikəˈræɡjuə] *n.* 尼加拉瓜[拉丁美洲国家](在中美洲中部)

nice [nais] *adj.* 1. 美好的;合宜的;令人愉快的和蔼的;友好的亲密的 2. 有教养的;贞洁的;正派的 3. 须慎重对待的;微妙的 4. 细微的;精密的;慎重的 5. 挑剔的,难以满足的 6. 拘泥的;多考虑的 7. [用作反语]不好的;糟透的 ‖ **~ness** *n.*

nicely [ˈnaisli] *adv.* 1. 恰好地 2. 谨慎地;拘泥地 3. 令人满意地;令人愉快地;很好地 — *adj.*〈主方〉健康的

nicety [ˈnaisiti] *n.* 1. 美好,优美,优美的东西 2. 准确;精确 3. 微妙 4.〈常niceties〉细微的区别;细节 5. 拘泥;细节;挑剔

niche [nitʃ] *n.* 1. 壁龛(放置雕像、花瓶等的墙壁凹入处) 2. 合适的职务(或地位等) 3.〈生〉生态龛 — *vt.* 1. [常用被动语态]把(雕像等)放入壁龛 2.[~ oneself]〈用或被动语态〉把…安顿在适当位置

nick [nik] *n.* 1. 凹痕;伤痕;痕记;缺口 2.[印]刻痕记 3.〈英俚〉身体的情形,状况;in good (bad) ~ 情况很好(不好) 4.〈英口〉监狱 — *vt.* 1. 刻痕于;使有凹痕(或缺口) 2.〈英口〉偷;捞 3.〈英俚〉逮捕 4.〈英口〉索(高价) ‖ *in the ~ of time* 就在事情发生的当口上;在关键时刻

nickel [ˈnikl] *n.* 1.〈化〉镍 2.〈美国和加拿大的〉五分镍币;五分钱 3.〈美俚〉五

美元;五美元一袋的毒品 4.〈美口〉自己花的钱 — *vt.* 把…镀镍

nickelodeon [ˌnikəˈləudiən] *n.*〈美〉1. 入场费为五分钱的电影院(或杂耍剧场等) 2. 投币式自动唱机 3. 投币式自动钢琴

nicker [ˈnikə] *vi.* 1.〈马〉嘶 2. 闷笑 — *n.* 1. 马嘶声 2. 闷笑

nickname [ˈnikneim] *n.* 1. 绰号,浑名 2.(教)名的略称,爱称 — *vt.* 1. 给…起绰号;以绰号(或爱称)称呼 2. 误称

Nicosia [ˌnikəuˈsiə] *n.* 尼科西亚[塞浦路斯首都]

nicotine [ˈnikətiːn] *n.*〈化〉烟碱,尼古丁

nicotinic [ˌnikəˈtinik] *adj.* 1.〈化〉烟碱的 2.〈生化〉烟酸的 ‖ **~ acid**〈生化〉烟酸,尼克酸

niece [niːs] *n.* 侄女;甥女

Nietzschean [ˈniːtʃiən] *adj.*〈德国哲学家、诗人〉尼采(Nietzsche)的;尼采学说的 — *n.* 尼采学说的信奉者

nifty [ˈnifti] *adj.* 漂亮的,时髦的,有吸引力的美妙的

Niger [ˈnaidʒə] *n.* 尼日尔[西非国家]

Nigeria [naiˈdʒiəriə] *n.* 尼日利亚[西非国家]

niggard [ˈnigəd] *n.* 小气的人,吝啬鬼

niggardly [ˈnigədli] *adj.* 1. 小气的,吝啬的 2. 很少量的 — *adv.* 小气地;吝啬地 ‖ **niggardliness** *n.*

nigger [ˈnigə] *n.*〈俚〉黑人,黑鬼

niggle [ˈnigl] *vi.* 1. 为小事操心(或费时);做无聊事;找岔子 3. 啃 — *vt.* 小气地给…;少量地给 ‖ **niggling** *adj.* 1. 细小的;琐屑的;小心翼翼的;过于精细的;缺乏魄力的

nigh [nai] *adv.* 1.(地点、时间、关系等)(接)近地,靠近地(*on, onto*) 2. 几乎

— *adj*. 1.(接)近的;亲密的 2.〈主方〉直接的;短的 3. 在左侧的 4.〈主方〉吝啬的 — *prep*.(接)近 — *vi*. & *vt*.〈古〉接近,靠近

night [nait] *n*. 1. 夜晚,夜间 2. 黑夜;黑暗 3. 夜晚的活动(如晚会、游戏等) 4. 黑夜般的状况;黑暗时期;悲伤时刻;死亡 5. 黄昏 ‖ '~club *n*. 夜总会 /'~-fall *n*. 黄昏 /'~dress, '~gown *n*.(妇女或孩子穿的)睡衣 /'~hawk *n*. 1.【动】(北美产的)夜鹰 2.【动】欧夜鹰 3. 晚睡的人 4. 夜间服务的出租汽车 5. 牧场的夜工(尤指看马人) 6. 夜间行窃(或干其他坏事)的人 /~mare ['naitmεə] *n*. 1. 梦魇;恶梦 2. 无法摆脱的恐惧;可怕的事物 /'~marish *adj*. 1. 梦魇似的 2. 经常使人恐惧的;可怕的 /~ school 夜校/'~shade *n*.【植】茄(如龙葵、颠茄等) /'~ shirt *n*.(男用)衬衫式长睡衣 /~ spot〈口〉夜总会 /~ table 床头柜 /'~time *n*. 夜间

nightingale ['naitiŋgeil] *n*. 1.【动】夜莺,哥鸲 2. 夜间鸣叫的鸟 3. 音调悦耳的歌唱者(或演说者) 4.〈美俚〉告密者;坐探

nightly ['naitli] *adj*. 1. 夜晚的;夜间的 2. 每夜的 3.〈诗〉夜的;适于夜晚的 — *adv*. 在夜间;每夜

nighty, nightie ['naiti] *n*. 1.(妇女或孩子穿的)睡衣 2.(男用)衬衫式长睡衣

nihilism ['naiilizəm] *n*. 虚无主义 ‖ **nihilist** *n*. / ˌni-hi'listic *adj*.

nil [nil] *n*. 1. 无,零 2. 无价值的事物

Nile [nail] *n*. 尼罗河[非洲东北部]

nimbi ['nimbai] nimbus 的复数

nimble ['nimbl] *adj*. 1. 灵活的;灵巧的;敏捷的 2. 聪明的;机智的;敏锐的;敏感的;易起反应的 ‖ ~ness *n*. /nimbly *adv*.

nimbus ['nimbəs]([复]nimbi['nimbai]或 nimbuses) *n*. 1.【气】雨云 2.(神像等头部上方或周围的)光轮;光环;灵光;光晕

nimrod ['nimrɔd] *n*.1.[N-]宁录(《圣经》故事人物,作为英勇的猎手而闻名) 2. 猎人

nincompoop ['ninkəmpuːp] *n*. 傻子,笨蛋;易受骗者

nine [nain] *num*. 九;九个(人或物);第九(卷、章、页等) — *n*. 1. 九个(人或物)一组(尤指棒球队) 2. [the N-]【希神】缪斯九女神 3. 九岁 4. 九点钟 ‖ '~-pin *n*.【体】九柱戏的木柱;[~pins][用作单]九柱戏

nineteen ['nain'tiːn] *num*. 十九;十九个(人或物);第十九(卷、章、页等) — *n*. 1. 十九岁 2. 十九点钟(即下午七点)

nineteenth ['nain'tiːnθ] *num*. 1. 第十九(个) 2. 十九分之一(的) — *n*.(月的)第十九日

ninetieth ['naintiiθ] *num*. 1. 第九十(个) 2. 九十分之一(的)

ninety ['nainti] *num*. 九十;九十个(人或物);第九十(页等) — *n*. 九十岁

ninny['nini], **ninnyhammer** ['niniˌhæmə] *n*. 笨人,傻瓜

ninth [nainθ] *num*. 1. 第九(个) 2. 九分之一(的) — *n*. 1.【音】九度音程;第九音;九度和音 2.(月的)第九日

niobium [nai'əubiəm] *n*.【化】铌

nip[1] [nip](nipped; nipping) *vt*. 1. 夹,钳;掐;捏;咬 2. 剪断;夹断;摘取 3. 阻止,制止;使受挫折 4.(风、霜等)摧残;冻伤 5.〈俚〉攫夺;偷 — *vi*. 1. 夹,钳;掐;捏;咬 2.(寒冷等)刺骨 3.〈英口〉敏捷地走;飞快地跑(*off*, *away*, *along*);跳,跃 — *n*. 1. 夹,钳;掐;捏;咬;被掐(或咬)下的东西 2. 寒冷 3. 讥刺 4. 刺鼻

的气味 **5.** 少量

nip² [nip] *n.* 一小口(酒);一呷 —(nipped; nipping) *vt. & vi.* 一小口一小口地抿(酒)

nipper ['nipə] *n.* **1.** 夹(或捏、掐)的人(或器具) **2.** [~s]钳子,镊子 **3.** (马的)门齿(尤指复数的) **4.** [~s]夹鼻眼镜 **5.** 〈俚〉手铐;脚镣 **6.** 〈英口〉少年;小孩(尤指流浪儿或被雇为搬聩帮手的儿童)

nipple ['nipl] *n.* **1.** 乳头;橡皮奶头 **2.** (皮肤、金属、玻璃等表面的)乳头状隆起 **3.** 【机】螺纹接套;(喷灯)喷嘴 **4.** 【军】(枪炮的)火门

Nippon ['nipon]〈日〉*n.* = Japan

nippy ['nipi] *adj.* **1.** 剌人的;寒冷刺骨的 **2.** 刺鼻的;尖锐的 **3.**〈英口〉敏捷的;轻快的

nirvana [ˌniə'vɑːnə] *n.* **1.**〈宗〉(佛教)涅槃(印度教)生命之火的熄灭 **2.** 无忧无虑的境界,极乐世界,天堂 **3.** 不能实现的梦想

nit [nit] *n.* **1.** (虱等的)卵;幼虫 **2.**〈英口〉傻瓜,笨蛋;糊涂虫 ‖ ~-**pick** *vi. & vt.*〈口〉挑剔,(吹)毛求疵

niter ['naitə] *n.*〈美〉 = nitre

nitrate ['naitreit] 【化】*n.* **1.** 硝酸根 **2.** 硝酸盐(或酯);硝石 **3.** 硝酸盐类化肥 — *vt.* 使硝化

nitre ['naitə] *n.* 【化】**1.** 硝石,硝酸钾 **2.** 硝酸钠

nitric ['naitrik] *adj.* 【化】(含)氮的 ‖ ~ **acid** 硝酸

nitro ['naitrəu] *adj.* 【化】**1.** 含硝基的 **2.** = nitric — ([复] nitros) *n.*〈口〉硝化甘油(= nitroglycerin(e))

nitrogen ['naitridʒən] *n.* 【化】氮

nitroglycerin(e) [ˌnaitrəu'glisərin] *n.* 【化】

硝化甘油

nitrous ['naitrəs] *adj.* 【化】**1.** 亚硝的 **2.** 含氮的

nitty-gritty ['niti'griti]〈俚〉*n.* 基本事实;本质;实质;细节 — *adj.* 基本的,根本的;详细的

nitwit ['nitwit] *n.*〈口〉傻瓜,笨蛋;糊涂虫

nix [niks] *adv.*〈俚〉不,不是;并不;决不 **N. lat.** *abbr.* north latitude 北纬

nm *abbr.* nautical mile(s)

No 【化】元素锘(nobelium)的符号

no [nəu] *adj.* **1.** 没有 **2.** 很少;很小 **3.** 并非;决不 **4.** [用于不同省略或固定结构中]不许;没有;不要: No admittance except on business. 非公莫入。/ No thoroughfare. 此路不通。5.[用于带 is ...... ing 结构中]不可能: There is ~ knowing when he would be back. 无法知道他什么时候回来。— *adv.* **1.** [用在形容词、副词的比较级前]并不;毫不 **2.** [用以表示否定的回答]不,不是(yes 之对) **3.** [用以加强否定语气]不 **4.** [用以表示惊奇、怀疑或不信]不 **5.** [用于 or 之后]...... 与否: Pleasant or ~, the news is true. 不管是好是坏,反正消息是真的。**6.** [用于委婉的说法中]不,并非一([复] no(e)s) *n.* **1.** 不;拒绝;否定;否认 **2.** 反对票;反对的决定 **3.** 投反对票者

No., no. *abbr.* number

Nobel [nəu'bel] *n.* ‖ ~**ist** *n.* 诺贝尔奖金获得者 ‖ ~ **Prize** 诺贝尔奖金

nobelium [nəu'beliəm] *n.* 【化】锘

nobility [nəu'biliti] *n.* **1.** 高贵;崇高 **2.** 高位 **3.** [the ~][总称]贵族(阶层)

noble ['nəubl] *adj.* **1.** 贵族的;显贵的(指贵族出身、称号、头衔等) **2.** (品质、思想等)高尚的,崇高的 **3.** 壮丽的,宏伟的

的 4. 极好的,杰出的 5.(金属)贵重的;(气体)惰性的 — *n*. 1. 贵族 2.(中世纪后期的)英国金币(合英国旧币六先令与八便士) 3.〈美俚〉(破坏罢工的)工贼头目 ‖ ~ness *n*. ‖ ~man *n*. 贵族 /~,woman *n*. 女贵族

nobly ['nəubli] *adv*. 1. 高贵地;高尚地;豪侠地 2. 豁达地 2. 杰出地,极好地;壮丽地,宏伟地 3. 出身于贵族

nobody ['nəubədi] *pron*. 没有人,无人 — *n*. 无足轻重的人,小人物

nocturnal [nɔk'tə:nl] *adj*. 1. 夜的;夜间发生的;夜间开花的 2.(植)夜间活动的;夜出的 2.〔音〕夜曲的 ‖ ~ly *adv*.

nocturne ['nɔktə:n] *n*. 1.〔音〕夜曲;梦幻曲 2. 夜景画

nod [nɔd] (nodded; nodding) *vi*. 1. 点头(表示同意或打招呼等) 2. 打盹,瞌睡 3. 不当心而弄错 4.(树梢、花等)上下摆动;(建筑物等)倾斜 — *vt*. 1. 点(头) 2. 点头表示;向…点头示意 — *n*. 1. 点头 2. 打盹,瞌睡 3.(树梢等的)上下(或前后)摆动 4.(点头表示的)同意

node [nəud] *n*. 1. 节;结;瘤 2.(故事、戏剧情节等的)曲折,纠葛 3. 中心点 4.〔解〕淋巴结 5.〔天〕交点 6.〔物〕(波)节 7.〔数〕结(点),叉点 8.〔植〕节(茎上生叶处)

nodule ['nɔdju:l] *n*. 1. 小结节 2. 小瘤 2. 小块 3.〔植〕(根)瘤 4.〔菌〕瘤节 5. 小结;〔地〕〔矿〕结核 ‖ nodular *adj*.

noel [nəu'el] *n*.〔基督教〕 1.[N-] 圣诞节 2. 圣诞颂歌

no-fault ['nəu'fɔ:lt] *adj*.(汽车保险)不追究过失责任的;〔律〕(离婚案例中男女双方当事人)无责任的,无过失的

noggin ['nɔgin] *n*. 小杯子;少量饮料

noise [nɔiz] *n*. 1. 喧闹声,嘈杂声 2. 响声;声音 3. 噪声,杂音 — *vt*. 纷纷传说;谣传 — *vi*. 1. 大声(或公开)议论 2. 喧闹 ‖ ~maker *n*. 发出嘈杂声的人;噪声发生器(尤指狂欢等时用来凑热闹的汽车喇叭、铃铛等) /~ pollution 噪声污染

noiseless ['nɔizlis] *adj*. 1. 无声的;寂静的 2. 噪声小的;声音很轻的 ‖ ~ly *adv*. /~ness *n*.

noisome ['nɔisəm] *adj*. 1. 有害的;有毒的;不卫生的 2. 恶臭的;可厌的;令人不快的 ‖ ~ly *adv*. /~ness *n*.

noisy ['nɔizi] *adj*. 1. 喧闹的,嘈杂的;熙熙攘攘的 2.(颜色、服装等)过分鲜艳的;(文体)过分渲染的 ‖ **noisily** *adv*. / **noisiness** *n*.

nom [nɔm]〈法〉*n*. 名 ‖ ~ de guerre [də gɛə]假名,化名 /~ de plume [də 'plu:m]笔名

nomad ['nəumæd] *n*. 1. 游牧民 2. 游荡者 — *adj*. 1. 游牧的 2. 流浪的

nomadic [nəu'mædik] *adj*. 1. 游牧的;游牧生活的 2. 流浪的;流浪生活的

nomenclature [nəu'menklətʃə] *n*. 1. 名称;术语;专门名词 2. 命名(过程);命名法 3.(某一学科的)术语表;术语集

nominal ['nɔminl] *adj*. 1. 名义上的;有名无实的 2. 名字的;(名字)署名性的 3.〔语〕名词性的 4.(金额)微不足道的 5. 按计划进行的;令人满意的 — *n*. 名词性的词(指代词、形容词、代词) ‖ ~ly *adv*.

nominate ['nɔmineit] *vt*. 1. 提名 2. 任命;指定 3. 命名 4.(赛马中)登记(马名)

nomination [,nɔmi'neiʃən] *n*. 1. 提名;任命 2. 提名权;任命权 3.(赛马中)马名的登记

nominative ['nɔminətiv] *adj*. 1. 主格的

2. 被提名的；被任命的 3. 具有姓名的 — *n.*【语】主格；主格词 ‖ ~ **case**【语】主格

nominator ['nɔmineitə] *n.* 提名者；任命者

nominee [ˌnɔmi'ni:] *n.* 被提名者（尤指被提名为候选人）；被任命者

non- *pref.* [常用在名词、形容词或副词前] 1. 表示"非"，"无"，"不（是）"：*non*combatant 2. 表示"不重要的"，"无价值的"：*non*book 无真实价值的书 3. 表示"缺少传统（或习惯）上的特征的"：*non*hero 非正统派主角

nonagenarian [ˌnɔnədʒi'neəriən] *adj. & n.* 九十到九十九岁的（人）

nonaggression [ˌnɔnə'greʃən] *n.* 不侵略，不侵犯：a ~ pact 互不侵犯条约

nonaligned [ˌnɔnə'laind] *adj.* 不结盟的

nonalignment [ˌnɔnə'lainmənt] *n.* 不结盟

nonce [nɔns] *n.* 眼下，当前：for the ~ 目前，暂且 — *adj.* 一度发生（或使用）的 ‖ ~ **word**（为特定场合的需要而）临时造的词

nonchalance ['nɔnʃələns] *n.* 漠不关心；冷淡；若无其事；不激动，无动于衷

nonchalant ['nɔnʃələnt] *adj.* 漠不关心的；冷淡的；若无其事的；不激动的，无动于衷的 ‖ **~ly** *adv.*

noncombatant [ˌnɔn'kɔmbətənt] *n.* 1.【军】非战斗人员（非军医等）2.（战争时期的）平民 — *adj.* 非战斗（人员）的

noncommissioned [ˌnɔnkə'miʃənd] *adj.* 无委任状的；非受任命的；未受军官衔的 ‖ ~ **officer** 军士

noncommittal [ˌnɔnkə'mitl] *adj.*（态度、观点等）不明朗的；不表明意见的，不承担义务的 ‖ **~ly** *adv.*

nonconductor [ˌnɔnkən'dʌktə] *n.*【物】非

导体，绝缘体

nonconformist [ˌnɔnkən'fɔːmist] *n.* 1. [常作 N-]【宗】不信奉国教（尤指英国国教）的新教徒 2. 不（求）符合准则（或规范）的人 — *adj.* 1. [常作 N-] 不信奉国教（尤指英国国教）的 2. 违反准则（或规范）的；不落俗套的

nonconformity [ˌnɔnkən'fɔːmiti] *n.* 1. [常作 N-]【宗】不信奉国教（尤指英国国教）；[总称] 新教教徒；新教教徒的教义（或活动）2. 不墨守成规 3. 不一致；不符合 4.【地】非整合

nondairy ['nɔn'dɛəri] *adj.* 不含奶的；非乳制的

nondescript ['nɔndiˌskript] *adj.*（因无特征而）难以归类的；难以形容的 — *n.* 难以形容（或归类）的人（或物）

none [nʌn] *pron.* [用作单或复] 1. 没有人；没有任何东西 2. ...中任何一个人（或任何事物、任何部分）都不 < *of* it left. 那东西一点儿也没有剩下。— *adj.* [用于文学体裁中，被修饰的名词通常提前或省略] 没有的：Money Tom has ~. 汤姆没有钱。— *adv.* [常与 so 或 too 连用] 一点也不，毫无

nonentity [nɔ'nentiti] *n.* 1. 不存在；不存在（或虚构）的东西 2. 无足轻重的人（或物）

nonessential [ˌnɔni'senʃəl] *adj.* 非本质的，不重要的；非必需的 — *n.* 不重要的人（或物），可有可无的人（或物）

nonetheless [ˌnʌnðə'les] *adv.* = nevertheless

nonexistent ['nɔnig'zistənt] *adj.* 不存在的

nonfiction ['nɔn'fikʃən] *n.* 非小说类写实文学（如传记、随笔等）‖ **~al** *adj.*

nonflammable [ˌnɔn'flæməbl] *adj.* 不易燃的

noninterventio [ˌnɔnintə'venʃən] *n.* 不

干涉(政策)

no-no ['nəunəu] (〔复〕no-nos 或 no-no's) *n.* 〈美俚〉被禁止的东西,不准干(或说)的事,禁忌

nonpareil [ˌnɒnpəˈreil] *adj.* 无比的,无双的 一 *n.* 1. 无可匹敌的人(或物);完美无缺的人(或物) 2.〔印〕相当于六点的老式活字;六点间隔 3. 洁糖扁圆巧克力糖(装饰糕点用的)彩色糖球

nonpartisan, nonpartizan [ˌnɒnpɑːtiˈzæn] *adj.* 超党派的;不受任何党派控制(或影响)的,不支持任何党派的;无偏袒的

nonplus [ˌnɒnˈplʌs] (〔复〕nonplus(s)es) *n.* 迷惑;为难;窘境 — (nonplus(s)ed; nonplus(s)ing) — *vt.* 使迷惑,使为难,使狼狈

nonproductive [ˌnɒnprəˈdʌktiv] *adj.* 1. 不能生产的;无生产力的 2. 非生产性的;不直接用于生产的 3.〈喻〉(咳嗽)干咳

nonresident [ˌnɒnˈrezidənt] *adj.* 不在在工作地点的;不寄宿的 — *n.* 不在在工作地点的人;暂居的人;走读学生

nonscheduled [ˌnɒnˈʃedjuːld] *adj.* 〈航空〉不定期的;不定期航线的,不按计划的

nonsectarian [ˌnɒnsekˈteəriən] *adj.* 无派性的;不属于任何宗教派别的

nonsense ['nɒnsəns] *n.* 胡说,废话;胡闹;愚蠢的举动 2. 无价值的东西;无用的装饰品 — *int.* 胡说!废话!

nonsensical [nɒnˈsensikəl] *adj.* 无意义的;愚蠢的;荒谬的;可笑的 ‖ ~**ly** *adv.* ‖ ~ **school** 师范学校

non sequitur ['nɒnˈsekwitə]〈拉〉【逻】不根据前提的推理;不合逻辑的推论 2. 前后不连贯(或毫无逻辑联系)的陈述(或回答)

nonstop ['nɒnˈstɒp] *adj.* 不停的,不断的,不休息的 — *adv.* 不停地,不断地;直

noodle[1] ['nuːdl] *n.* 1. 笨蛋,傻子 2.〈俚〉脑袋瓜

noodle[2] ['nuːdl] *n.*〔常~s〕面条;鸡蛋面

nook [nuk] *n.* 凹角;偏僻隐蔽的角落;隐蔽处;隐匿处

noon [nuːn] *n.* 1. 中午,正午 2. 最高点;全盛期 — *vi.*〈主方〉1. 午休;歇手进午餐 2. 达最高点 ‖ ~ **tide** *n.* 1. 中午,正午 2. 最高点;全盛期 /~ **time** *n.* 正午,中午;午休;午餐

noonday ['nuːndei] *n.* 中午,正午

noose [nuːs] *n.* 1. 绞索;套索 2. 羁绊,束缚 3. 圈套;陷阱 — *vt.* 1. 用套索捕捉;使陷入圈套 2. 把(绳索)打成活套结 3. 把…处绞刑 4. 和…结婚;使成婚

nor [nɔː] *conj.* 1.〔常与 neither 或 not 连用,有时也与 no, never 等表示否定的词连用〕也不;也没有 2.〔用在肯定句后〕也不;不 3.〈方〉比(= than)

Nordic ['nɔːdik] *adj. & n.* 北欧人(的)

norm [nɔːm] *n.* 1. 标准;规范;准则 2. 平均数;(每一工作日的)定额

normal ['nɔːməl] *adj.* 1. 正常的;正规的;标准的 2. 智力正常的;精神健全的 3. 平常的;通常的 4. 解剖的 5.【化】规度的,当量的;6.【数】垂直的,正交的;法线的 7.【生】未经免疫的;正态的 — *n.* 1.〔只用单〕正常的状态(或数量、程度等);标准 2. 师范学校 3.【数】法线;直交 ‖ ~ **ly** *adv.* ‖ ~ **school** 师范学校

normalcy ['nɔːməlsi] *n.* 正常状态

normality [nɔːˈmæliti] *n.* 1. 正常状态 2.【化】规度,规定浓度,当量浓度

normalize ['nɔːməlaiz] *vt. & vi.* (使)正常化;(使)标准化;(使)规范化 ‖ **normali'zation** *n.*

Norman ['nɔːmən] *n.* 1. 诺曼人(10世纪

定居在法国塞纳河口，接受了法国文化的一支斯堪的纳维亚人及其后裔） 2. 诺曼语 — *adj.* 1. 诺曼人的；诺曼人的；诺曼语的 2. [建] 诺曼式的

Norse [nɔːs] [单复同] *n.* 1. [总称] 斯堪的纳维亚人；挪威人；古代斯堪的纳维亚的纳维亚方言（或语言）；斯堪的纳维亚语 — *adj.* 1. 古代斯堪的纳维亚（语）的 2. 挪威的；挪威人的；挪威语的

north [nɔːθ] *n.* 1. 北，北方 2. [N-] （一国或一地区的）北部 3. [常作 N-] 地球的北部（尤指北极地区）4. 北风 — *adj.* 1. 北的，北方的 2. [N-] （一国、一洲或一地区）北部的：*North America* 北美洲 3. 挪威的 4. （风）来自北方的；在北方；向北方 ‖ '~**land** *n.* [诗] 北国，北方 / **North Pole** 北极 / **North Star** 北极星

northbound ['nɔːθbaund] *adj.* 向北行的；向北驶的

North Carolina 北卡罗来纳 [美国州名]

North Dakota 北达科他 [美国州名]

northeast [ˌnɔːθ'iːst] *n.* 1. 东北（泛指东北方向，或指正东以北 45°；略作 NE）2. [N-] （一国或一地区的）东北部 — *adj.* 1. 位于东北的；朝东北的 2. （风）来自东北的 — *adv.* 在东北；向东北；从东北

northeastern [ˌnɔːθ'iːstən] *adj.* 1. （在）东北的 2. （风）来自东北的 3. [N-] （一国或一地区的）东北部的

northerly ['nɔːðəli] *adv. & adj.* 1. 在北方（的）；向北方（的）2. （风）来自北方的（的）— *n.* 北风

northern ['nɔːðən] *adj.* 1. [常作 N-] （一国或一地区的）北部的；北部方言的 2. （风）来自北方的 3. 朝北的 4. 有北方地区特征的 — *n.* 1. = ~**er** 2. [常作

N-] 美国北部方言 ‖ ~**er** *n.* [常作 N-] 1. 北方人；居住在北方的人 2. 美国北方人 ‖ ~ **lights** [物] 北极光

northward ['nɔːθwəd] *adv.* 向北方 — *adj.* 向北的 — *n.* 向北的方向；北方地区

northwards ['nɔːθwədz] *adv.* 向北方

northwest [ˌnɔːθ'west] *n.* 1. 西北（泛指西北方向，或指正西以北 45°；略作 NW）2. [N-] （一国或一地区的）西北部 — *adj.* 1. 位于西北的；朝西北的 2. （风）来自西北的 — *adv.* 在西北；向西北；从西北

northwestern [ˌnɔːθ'westən] *adj.* 1. （在）西北的；向西北的 2. （风）来自西北的 3. [N-] （一国或一地区的）西北部的

Norway ['nɔːwei] *n.* 挪威 [北欧国家]

Norwegian [nɔː'wiːdʒən] *adj.* 挪威的；挪威人的；挪威语的 — *n.* 1. 挪威人 2. 挪威语

Nos., nos. *abbr.* numbers

nose [nəuz] *n.* 1. 鼻子 2. （动物的）鼻口部 2. 嗅觉 3. 气味；觉察力 4. 鼻状物（如喷嘴、管口、鼻锥、机件的凸头、弹头等）5. 突出部分（如船头、飞机机首之类，突出的岩角等）6. [俚] 暗探；告密者 — *vt.* 1. 闻出；探出，侦察出 2. 用鼻子触；用鼻子擦；把鼻子塞入 3. （船、飞机等）用头部探（路）前进 4. （在赛马或比赛中）以微小差距胜过（*out*）— *vi.* 1. 嗅，闻（*at, about*）2. 探头，干涉 3. （船等）缓慢小心地前进 4. （地层）下倾（*in*）；露出（*out*）5. [俚] 做暗探；告密 ‖ ~**bleed** *n.* [医] 鼻出血，鼻衄 / ~**dive** *n.* （飞机）俯冲（如船头、飞机垂直下降，暴落）/ ~**dive** *vi.* 1. 俯冲 2. （价格等）猛跌，暴落 / '~**gay** *n.* 花束

nosed [nəuzd] *adj.* [用以构成复合词] 有...鼻子的：red~ 红鼻子的

nosey ['nəuzi] *adj.* = nosy

nostalgia [nɔs'tældʒiə] *n.* 1. 怀乡病 2. 留恋过去，怀旧 3. (小说等的)怀旧感染力

nostalgic [nɔs'tældʒik] *adj.* 1. 怀乡的 2. 留恋过去的，(引起)怀旧的 ‖ ~ally *adv.*

nostril ['nɔstril] *n.* 1. 鼻孔 2. 鼻孔内壁

nostrum ['nɔstrəm] *n.* 1. 秘方;有专利权的药品 2. 江湖郎中卖的药 3. 〈贬〉(社会或政治改革方面的)灵丹妙药;万应药

nosy ['nəuzi] *adj.* 1. 大鼻子的 2.〈俚〉好打听的,爱管闲事的 3. 发臭味的 4. (茶等)香的 — *n.* 1. 鼻子很大的人 2. 爱管闲事的人

not [nɔt] *adv.* 1. 不 2. [用在动词 think, suppose, believe, expect, fancy, trust, hope, seem, appear 等,副词 perhaps, probably, absolutely 等和词组 be afraid 等的后面,代表否定的从句]不是这样 3. [用在其他省略结构中,代替词、短语或句子] Correct or ~, the expression is unpopular. 不管正确与否,这个表达法是不通俗的。4. [与 all, both, every 等词连用,表示部分否定] All is ~ gold that glitters. (谚)发亮的东西不一定都是金子。5.[用于委婉的说法中]; ~ a few 不少

notability [,nəutə'biliti] *n.* 1. 〈主英〉名人,显要人物 2. 值得注意;显著

notable ['nəutəbl] *adj.* 1. 值得注意的;显著的 2. 著名的,重要的 3. 可察觉的;有相当分量的 4. (有时读作 ['nɔtəbl])〈方〉(主妇)会当家的;能干的;勤勉的 — *n.* 1. 名人,显要人物 2. [N-]〈史〉(法王召开紧急会议时的)应召显贵 3. 值得注意的事物(或事件) ‖ notably *adv.* 显著地;著名地

notarize ['nəutəraiz] *vt.* 以公证人资格证实;公证

notary ['nəutəri] *n.* 公证人,公证员(= ~ public)

notation [nəu'teiʃən] *n.* 1. 标志;标志法 2. 记号;记法 3.【音】乐谱;记谱法 4. 注释;批注;记录 ‖ ~al *adj.*

notch [nɔtʃ] *n.* 1. (V字形)槽口,凹口 2. 〈美〉山峡,峡谷 3. (记数等用的)刻痕 4. 〈口〉等,级 — *vt.* 1. 在...上开槽口 2. 刻痕记(数等) 3. 赢得 4. 把(箭)搭在弦上

note [nəut] *n.* 1. 笔记;记录 2. 按语;评论;注释 3. 短笺,便条 4. (学术或科技上的)短文 5. (外交上的)照会 6. 票据;借据;纸币 7. 口气;调子;特征 8. 重要;名望 9. 符号;标记 10.【音】乐音,(一个)音;音符;音键 11. (诗)曲调;歌子 12. 叫声;声音;鸟鸣声 13. 注意 14. 暗示;提示 — *vt.* 1. 记下;摘下 2. 注意,留心到 3. 特别提到 4. 指明,表明 5. 为...加注 6.【音】用音符记 ‖ ~-book *n.* 笔记簿;明票簿

noted ['nəutid] *adj.* 著名的,知名的

noteworthy ['nəut,wə:ði] *adj.* 值得注意的;显著的 ‖ noteworthiness *n.*

nothing ['nʌθiŋ] *n.* 1. 没有东西,没有什么 2. 不存在;不存在的东西 3. 微不足道的事物(或人) 4.【数】零 — *adv.* 一点也不;并不 ‖ ~ness *n.* 1. 无;虚无;不存在 2. 无价值的(事物);微不足道的(事物) 3. 死 4. 无知觉

notice ['nəutis] *n.* 1. 通告,布告;通知 2. 预先通知(尤用于雇主与雇员或房东与房客之间) 3. 注意 4. (事情发生之前的)征兆;预告 5. 关注;理会 6.(对图书,戏剧等的)短评;简介 — *vt.* 1. 注意;注意到 2. 通知 3. 简评 4. 提到;谈到 5. 关注;理会 客气对待 — *vi.*

引起注意;引人注目

noticeable ['nəutisəbl] *adj.* 1. 显而易见的;显著的 2. 值得注意的;重要的 ‖ **noticeably** *adv.*

notification [,nəutifi'keiʃən] *n.* 1. 通知;通报 2. 通告,布告 3. 通知单,通知书

notify ['nəutifai] *vt.* 1. 通知 2. 报告;宣告

notion ['nəuʃən] *n.* 1. 概念 2. 想法,看法,见解 3. 打算,意图 4. 精巧的小玩意儿 5.〈美〉[~s](针线等)小件日用品

notional ['nəuʃənl] *adj.* 1. 概念的;纯理论的 2. 想象的,空想的,不根据实际的;想法古怪的 3. 名义上的;象征性的 4.【语】意念的;实义的

notoriety [,nəutə'raiəti] *n.* 1. 臭名 2. 声名狼藉 3. 远扬的名声;名声远扬 4.〈主英〉著名人物

notorious [nəu'tɔːriəs] *adj.* 1. 臭名昭著的;声名狼藉的 2. 著名的;众所周知的 ‖ ~**ly** *adv.* / ~**ness** *n.*

notwithstanding [,nɔtwiθ'stændiŋ] *prep.* 尽管 — *adv.* 尽管;还是 — *conj.* 虽然,尽管

Nouakchott [nwɔːk'tɔt] *n.* 努瓦克肖特[毛里塔尼亚首都]

nougat ['nuːgɑː] *n.* 1. 杏仁(或胡桃、花生等)蛋白糖,牛轧糖 2.〈俚〉笨蛋

nought [nɔːt] *n. & adj.* = naught

noun [naun] *n.*【语】名词

nourish ['nʌriʃ] *vt.* 1. 养育;滋养;施肥于 2. 怀抱(希望、仇恨等) 3. 培育;供给;支持 ‖ ~**ing** *adj.* 滋养的,富于营养的 / ~**ment** *n.* 1. 食物;滋养品 2. 营养情况

Nov. *abbr.* November

novel ['nɔvəl] *adj.* 新的;新颖的;新奇的 — *n.* 1.(长篇)小说 2.〈罗马法〉新法,

新附律 ‖ ~**ist** *n.*(长篇)小说家

novelty ['nɔvəlti] *n.* 1. 新颖,新奇 2. 新奇的事物 3. [常 novelties]新颖小巧而价廉的物品(尤指装饰品、玩具等)

November [nəu'vembə] *n.* 十一月(略作Nov.)

novice ['nɔvis] *n.* 1.【宗】见习修士(或修女) 2. 新皈依的教徒(尤指新基督教徒) 3. 新手;初学者

novitiate [nəu'viʃiət] *n.* 1.【宗】修士(或修女)的见习期(或见习处) 2.(新手的)见习;见习期

Novocaine ['nəuvəkein] *n.*【药】奴佛卡因,盐酸普鲁卡因(局部麻醉剂)

now [nau] *adv.* 1. 现在,此刻,目前;直到现在 2. 立刻,马上 3.(在叙述中表示所涉及的时间)于是,然后;当时 4.(不表示时间,而用于语言者的语气,包含说明、命令、请求、警告、安慰等意):*Now* listen to me. 且听我讲。(命令口气) — *n.* 现在,此刻 — *conj.* 既然,由于 — *adj.* 现任的,现在的

nowadays ['nauədeiz] *adv.* 现今,现在(常用于将现在的风俗习惯等与过去相比时) — *n.* 现今,当今

nowhere ['nəuhweə] *adv.* 1. 任何地方都不 2. 毫不顶用;毫无结果 3. 远远地落在后面 — *n.* 1. 无处 2. 不知道的地方

nowise ['nəuwaiz] *adv.* 一点也不;决不

noxious ['nɔkʃəs] *adj.* 1. 有害的;不卫生的;有毒的 2. 使道德败坏的 3. 可憎的

nozzle ['nɔzl] *n.* 1.(茶壶等的)嘴;管嘴;喷嘴;喷管 2.〈俚〉鼻子

Np【化】元素铹(neptunium)的符号

-n't [nt]〈口〉= not;isn't,needn't

nth [enθ] *adj.* 1. 第 n 号的;第 n 位的;n 倍的;n 次的;n 阶的 2.〈口〉(经过无数次以后)又一次的 3. 极大的,极度的

nuance ['nju:ɑ:ns] *n.* (意义、感情、意见、颜色、音调变化的)细微差别

nub [nʌb] *n.* (故事等的)要点,要害;核心

nubbin ['nʌbin] *n.* 1. (玉蜀黍的)小穗(或发育不完全的穗) 2. 矮小(或发育不完全)的东西;发育不完全的果实 3. 一小块

nubile ['nju:bail] *adj.* (年轻女子在年龄或身体发育方面)适合结婚的;(年轻女子)性机能发育成熟的;有性感的 ‖ **nubility** [nju:'biliti] *n.*

nuclear ['nju:kliə] *adj.* 1. 核心的;中心的 2. 核的;(使用)核能的;(拥有)核武器的;(物)核子的 3. [生]细胞核的 ‖ ～ energy 核能 /～ family (仅由父、母以及子女组成的)核心家庭 /～ physics [复]用作单)核物理学 /～ weapon 核武器

nucleon ['nju:klion] *n.* [核]核子

nucleus ['nju:kliəs] ([复]nuclei['nju:kliai]或nucleuses) *n.* 1. 核;核心,中心 2.[生]细胞核 3.[天]核 4.[核]核 5.[化]环;(晶)核

nude [nju:d] *adj.* 1. 裸体的 2.(房间等)无点缀品的;光秃的 3.(尤指袜子)肉色的 4.[律](契约无偿的 — *n.* 1. [the ～]裸体 2. 裸体画(或雕像等) 3.裸体者 ‖ ～ly *adv.* /～ness *n.*

nudge [nʌdʒ] *vt.* 1.(用肘)轻推(以引起注意或暗示) 2. 引起...注意 3. 接近 — *n.* 轻推;推动

nudism ['nju:dizəm] *n.* 裸体主义 ‖ **nudist** *n. & adj.*

nudity ['nju:diti] *n.* 1. 赤裸;裸体处 2. 裸体画(或雕像等)

nugatory ['nju:gətəri] *adj.* 1. 琐碎的;无价值的 2. 不起作用的;没用的;无效的

nugget ['nʌgit] *n.* 1. 小块 2. 天然金块

nuisance ['nju:sns] *n.* 1. 损害;妨害 2. 讨厌(或有害)的东西(或事情、行为等);讨厌(或麻烦)的人

nuke [nju:k] (美口) *n.* 1.(热)核武器 2. 原子核 3. 核动力发电站,核电站 — *vt.* 用(热)核武器攻击(或摧毁)

Nukualofa [,nu:kuə'lɔ:fə] *n.* 努库阿洛法 [汤加首都]

null [nʌl] *adj.* 1. 无束缚力的;无效的;不存在的;等于零的 2. 无效的 3. 无价值的;无用的 4. 无(个性)特征的;没有表情的 5. 指针为零的;零(位)的 — *n.* 1. [数]零 2. [无]零位 3. [电]无意义暗码

nullification [,nʌlifi'keiʃən] *n.* 1. 无效;废弃;取消 2.(美国)州对联邦法令的拒绝执行(或承认)

nullify ['nʌlifai] *vt.* 1. 使无效;废弃;取消 2. 使无价值;使变得无用;抵消

nullity ['nʌliti] *n.* 1.(尤指法律上的)无效 2. 无效的东西(尤指无效的法案、文件等) 3. 无价值的东西;无足轻重的人 4. 无,不存在

numb [nʌm] *adj.* 1. 麻木的;失去感觉的 2. 冷淡的,无感情的 — *vt.* 使麻木;使麻痹 ‖ ～ly *adv.* /～ness *n.*

number ['nʌmbə] *n.* 1. 数;数字 2.(略作 No.,复数略作 Nos.)号码;...数 3. (报刊等的)期,期 3. 数目;[～s]大批;数量上的优势 4. 一群人,一帮人 5. [～s]算术 6.(美)人(尤指活泼而动人的姑娘);商品的某一型号(或式样) 7.[语]数 8. (一个)节目;(歌剧的)部分 9.[音]节奏;[～s]拍子,调子 10. 韵律;[～s]韵文;诗 11.[宗][the ～s]《民数记》(《旧约全书》第四篇) 12. [the ～s] [用作单或复](把赌注押在任何 3 位数上的)彩票赌博 — *vt.* 1. 给...编号 2. 达...之数,总计 3. 把...算作,认

为(among, in, with) 4. [常用被动语态]使在数目方面受到限制 5. 计算，数 6. (古)列举(up) 7. (古)活了... — vi. 1. 计：visitors ~ing in the thousands 数以千计的参观者 2. 报数 ‖ ~less adj. 1. 无号码的 2. 数不清的

numeral ['nju:mərəl] adj. 数字的；示数的 — n. 1. 数字 2. [语]数词 3. (美)[~s]（奖给在课外活动某一方面有显著成绩的班级的）荣誉年号

numerate ['nju:məreit] vt. 1. 数；计算；列举 2. 读(数) — ['nju:mərət] adj. 识数的；懂数学的；有计算能力的

numeration [,nju:mə'reiʃən] n. 1. 计算；读数 2. [数]命数法，读数法

numerator ['nju:məreitə] n. 1. [数](分数中的)分子 2. 计算者；计数器

numerical [nju:'merikəl] adj. 数字的；用数字表示的；数值的 2. 擅长计数的 ‖ ~ly adv. 在数字上

numerous ['nju:mərəs] adj. 1. [修饰单数名词]为数众多的 2. [修饰复数名词]许多的 ‖ ~ly adv. / ~ness n.

numismatics [,nju:miz'mætiks] [复] n. [用作单]钱币学，古钱学；钱币搜集

numskull ['nʌmskʌl] n. 笨蛋，傻瓜

nun [nʌn] n. 1. 修女；尼姑 2. 德国种家鸽 3. [鸟]僧冠舞毒蛾，油杉毒蛾

nuncio ['nʌnʃiəu] n. [复]nuncios) n. 罗马教皇的使节

nunnery ['nʌnəri] n. 女修道院；尼姑庵

nuptial ['nʌpʃəl] adj. 1. 婚姻的；结婚的，婚礼的 2. 动物交配季节的 — [~s] n. 婚礼

nurse [nə:s] n. 1. 保姆；奶妈；保育员；护士；看护 3. 养育者；养护者；发挥地(of) 4. (森林中起屏障作用的)保护树[动]保育虫(如保护幼蚁的工蚁等)；(为非已生幼兽哺乳的)保姆兽

代哺母兽 5. 养育；护理 — vt. 1. 给...喂奶；带乳；看顾；(孩子)吃...的奶 2. 护理，护理(病人、疾病等) 3. 培养；培育；精心料理；小心操纵；节约地使用(或消耗) 6. 紧抱；爱抚 7. 怀有(希望、仇恨等) — vi. 1. 喂奶；吃奶 2. 看护病人；照料孩童 ‖ ~ maid n. 保姆；照管人

nursery ['nə:səri] n. 1. 托儿所；保育室；(私人家里专供儿童游戏、吃饭等用的)儿童室 2. 养成所 3. 苗圃；养鱼池；动物繁殖场 ‖ ~ man n. 苗木培养工

nurture ['nə:tʃə] n. 1. 营养物；食物 2. 养育；培育；教养 3. [总称]环境因素 — vt. 1. 给...营养物 2. 养育；培育；教养

nut [nʌt] n. 1. 坚果(如胡桃、栗子等)；坚果仁 2. 难事；难题；难对付的人 3. (俚)脑袋 4. [机]螺母，螺帽 5. 小煤块 6. (美俚)疯子；傻瓜；(行为或信仰方面的)怪人；狂热者；(罕)花花公子 7. (美俚)[~s]睾丸 8. [音](弦乐器的)琴马 9. [印]开半 — (nutted; nutting) vi. 采坚果；拾坚果 ‖ ~ let n. 1. 小坚果 2. 果核 ‖ ~ cracker n. 1. [常 ~s]胡桃夹(轧碎坚果的钳子，一端有校) 2. [动]星鸦 3. 瘪嘴 / ~ hatch n. [动]鸸 / ~ s- and- bolts adj. 基本的；有关具体细节的；实际的；具体的

nutmeg ['nʌtmeg] n. [植]肉豆蔻(树) ‖ Nutmeg State 肉豆蔻州(美国康涅狄格州的别称)

nutria ['nju:triə] n. 1. [动]海狸鼠 2. 海狸鼠毛皮 3. 淡棕色

nutrient ['nju:triənt] n. 营养物；滋养物 — n. 营养品；滋养物；食物

nutriment ['nju:trimənt] n. 营养品；食物；促进生长的东西

nutrition [nju:'triʃən] n. 1. 营养；滋养 2.

营养物;滋养物;食物 3. 营养学 ‖~-al *adj.*

nutritious [nju:'triʃəs] *adj.* 有营养的;滋养的 ‖~ly *adv.* /~ness *n.*

nutritive ['nju:tritiv] *adj.* 有关营养的;有营养的;滋养的 — *n.* 营养品;滋养物

nuts [nʌts] *adj.* 〈俚〉1. 发疯的;发狂的 2. 狂热的;忙乱的

nutshell ['nʌtʃel] *n.* 1. 坚果外壳 2. 小的东西;小数量(或范围)的东西;小容器;小住所

nutter ['nʌtə] *n.* 1. 采集坚果者 2.〈英俚〉疯子,狂人;怪人

nutty ['nʌti] *adj.* 1. 多坚果的;生坚果的 2. 有坚果味的 3.〈俚〉狂热的,迷恋的 (*upon, over, about*) 4.〈俚〉古怪的;傻的;发疯的 5.〈俚〉愚蠢的

nuzzle ['nʌzl] *vi.* 1.(用鼻、口等)掘;擦;触;伸入 2. 舒服地躺着;紧挨地躺着 — *vt.* 1.(用鼻、口等)挨擦 (*against*);

把(鼻子等)伸入(*into*) 2. [~ oneself] 使舒服地躺着;使紧挨地躺着

NW, n. w. *abbr.* northwest;northwestern

NY *abbr.* New York 纽约[美国州名];纽约市

Nyasaland ['niæsəlænd] *n.* 尼亚萨兰(Malawi 马拉维的旧称)

NYC *abbr.* New York City 纽约市(市)

nylon ['nailən] *n.* 1.[纺]锦纶,尼龙,尼纶 2. 耐纶制品;[~s]耐纶长袜

nymph [nimf] *n.* 1.【希神】居于山林水泽的仙女 2.〈诗〉美女 3.(昆虫的)若虫,蛹

nymphet ['nimfit] *n.* 1. 仙女般的少女 2. 早熟女孩 3. 放荡的少妇

nymphomania [,nimfə'meiniə] *n.* 1.【心】慕男狂,女性色情狂 2.(牛等动物的)慕雄 ‖~c [,nimfə'meiniæk] *adj.* 慕男狂的 *n.* 慕男狂,女性色情狂

O

O, o [əu]([复]**O's**, **o's** 或 **Os**, **os** 或 **Oes**, **oes** [əuz])英语字母表第十五个字母 **1.** [O]O字形;圆形物 **2.**零 **3.**【物】欧姆(ohm)的符号 **4.** [O]【化】元素氧(oxygen)的符号 **5.** [O]O血型

O [əu] *int.* **1.**[用在称呼前]啊! 哦! **2.**[表示惊讶、痛苦等]哎呀! 唉!

o' [ə, əu] *prep.* **1.**〈口〉〈古〉= of: a cup ~ tea 一杯茶 **2.**〈主方〉= on

oaf [əuf]([复]**oafs** 或 **oaves** [əuvz]) *n.* **1.**畸形儿;痴儿 **2.**蠢人,笨汉 ‖ **~ish** *adj.*畸形儿(似)的;蠢人(似)的

oak [əuk] *n.* **1.**[植]栎,橡 **2.**栎木 **3.**栎树叶(常作装饰用) **4.**栎木家具;栎木器具 **5.**〈英俚〉栎木大门 **6.**〈诗〉木船 — *adj.*栎木的;栎木制的

oaken ['əukən] *adj.* **1.**栎木制的 **2.**坚实的

oakum ['əukəm] *n.*(用以填塞船缝或管子接头等的)麻絮,填絮

oar [ɔ:] *n.* **1.**桨;橹 **2.**划手;桨手 **3.**桨状器官(如鳍、蹼等) **v.** 划,划动 — *vi.*划行;划行似地前进 ‖ ~ **lock** *n.* 〈美〉[船]桨架,桨叉 /'~**sman** *n.*桨手;划桨能手

oasis [əu'eisis]([复]**oases** [əu'eisiːz]) *n.* **1.**(沙漠中的)绿洲;(不毛之地中的)沃洲 **2.**(枯燥或不愉快环境中的)令人欣慰的事物;安全的地方

oat [əut] *n.* **1.**[常~s]燕麦 **2.**[常~s][用

作单或复]燕麦田;燕麦种子;燕麦庄稼 **3.**[常~s][用作单]燕麦粥;麦片粥 **4.**〈诗〉麦笛;田园诗,牧歌 ‖ **~meal** *n.* **1.**燕麦粉;燕麦片;燕麦粥 **2.**米灰色

oath [əuθ]([复]**oaths** [əuðz]) *n.* **1.**誓言,誓约;宣誓 **2.**(发怒或加强语气时的)妄用神名;诅咒;渎神话;咒骂语

obdurate ['ɔbdjurət] *adj.* **1.**顽固(不化)的;倔强的;执拗的 **2.**冷酷无情的;坚硬的;牢固的 ‖ **obduracy** *n.*

obedience [ə'biːdiəns] *n.* **1.**服从,顺从 **2.**【宗】管辖;辖区 [总称]辖区教徒

obedient [ə'biːdiənt] *adj.*服从的;顺从的,恭顺的 ‖ **~ly** *adv.*

obeisance [əu'beisəns] *n.*敬礼;敬重;敬意 ‖ **obeisant** *adj.* / **obeisantly** *adv.*

obelisk ['ɔbəlisk] *n.* **1.**【建】方尖塔;方尖碑;方尖碑形物 **2.**[印]剑号

obese [əu'biːs] *adj.*(过分)肥胖的

obesity [əu'biːsiti] *n.* **1.**(过度)肥胖 **2.**【医】肥胖(症)

obey [ə'bei] *vt.* **1.**服从,顺从;听从 **2.**按照...行动;执行 — *vi.*服从;听话

obfuscate ['ɔbfʌskeit, ɔb'fʌskeit] *vt.* **1.**使混乱,使搞错,迷惑 **2.**使暗淡;使模糊 ‖ ~**d** *adj.* / **obfu'scation** *n.*

obituary [ə'bitjuəri] *n.*讣告 — *adj.*报告死亡的;有关死者的;讣告的

object ['ɔbdʒikt] *n.* **1.**物,物体 **2.**对象,

〈口〉外表可笑(或可鄙、可怜)的人(或物) 4. 目的 5.〈语〉宾语 6.〈哲〉客体; 客观; 对象 — [əb'dʒekt] vt. 反对; 不喜欢; 抱反感; 不赞成 (to) — vt. 提出...作为反对的理由; 反对说 (that) ‖ ~or n.

objection [əb'dʒekʃən] n. 1. 反对; 异议; 不喜欢 2. 缺点; 缺陷 3. 妨碍 4. 反对的理由

objectionable [əb'dʒekʃənəbl] adj. 1. 会引起反对的; 要不得的 2. 令人不快的, 讨厌的

objective [əb'dʒektiv] adj. 1.〈哲〉客观的; 真实的 2. 客观(上)如实的; (人)实际的 3. 目标的 4.〈语〉宾格的 5.〈医〉(症状) 客观的, 他觉的 — n. 1. 目标; 目的;〈军〉出击目标 2. (望远镜等的)物镜 3.〈语〉宾格; 用于宾格的词 ‖ ~ly adv. 客观地 ‖ ~ case〈语〉宾格

objectivity [ˌɔbdʒek'tiviti] n. 客观(性); 客观现实

objurgate ['ɔbdʒəːgeit] vt. 谴责; 痛骂; 训斥 ‖ ﹐objur'gation n. / **objurgatory** [əb'dʒəːgət(ə)ri] adj.

oblate ['ɔbleit] adj. 扁圆的, 椭圆的 ‖ ~ly adv.

oblation [ə'bleiʃən] n.〈宗〉1. 祭献 2. 供物, 祭品 3. 奉献, 捐献

obligate ['ɔbligeit] adj. 1. 有责任的; 必须的 2.〈生〉专性的; 固性的 — vt. 1. [常用被动语态, 后接不定式]使在道义上(或法律上)负有责任(或义务) 2. 使恩惠于; 使感激 3. 指定(某笔收入、款项等)作偿还债务之用

obligation [ˌɔbli'geiʃən] n. 1. (道义上或法律上的)义务; 责任 2. 合约, 契约; 债券 3. 人情债; 恩惠; 感恩 4. 债务

obligatory [ə'bligət(ə)ri] adj. 1. (道义上或法律上的)必须履行的, 应尽的; 强制性

的 2.〈生〉专性的; 固性的

oblige [ə'blaidʒ] vt. 1. 迫使; 责成 2. 以誓言(或契约等)束缚某人) 3. 施恩惠于; 答应...的请求; 使满足 4. [用被动语态]使感激 5. 使(行为等)成为必要 — vi. 施恩惠

obliging [ə'blaidʒiŋ] adj. 1. 乐于助人的, 有礼貌的; 恳切的 2.〈罕〉(道义或法律上)必须履行的, 应尽的; 强制性的 ‖ ~ly adv. / ~ness n.

oblique [ə'bliːk] adj. 1. 斜的, 倾斜的; 偏斜的 2.〈数〉非直角的; 非垂直的 3. 转弯抹角的, 不坦率的, 不直截了当的 4. 躲躲闪闪的; 闪烁的 5. 间接的 6. (照片)从空中倾斜摄制的 — vi. 1. 倾斜; 歪 2.〈军〉斜行进, 与原方向成45度角前进 — n. 1. 倾斜物 2.〈解〉斜肌 — adv. 成45度角地 ‖ ~ly adv. / ~ness n., **obliquity** [ə'blikwəti] n.

obliterate [ə'blitəreit] vt. 1. 涂抹; 擦去; 去掉...的痕迹 2. 使被忘却, 使湮没 3. 使消失; 除去 4. 盖销(邮票等) ‖ ﹐oblite'ration n.

oblivion [ə'bliviən] n. 1. 忘却; 被忘却; 健忘 2. 被忘却的状态(或事实) 3. 湮没; 漠视 4.〈律〉大赦; 敕免

oblivious [ə'bliviəs] adj. 1. 忘却的; 健忘的 2. 不在意的, 不知不觉的 3. 令人忘却的

oblong ['ɔblɔŋ] n. 长方形; 椭圆形 — adj. 长方形的; 椭圆形的; 拉长的

obloquy ['ɔbləkwi] n. 1. (公开的)指责; 辱骂; 诽谤 2. 丑名; 耻辱

obnoxious [əb'nɔkʃəs] adj. 1. 令人非常不快的, 引起反感的, 讨厌的 2. 易受...的 3.〈罕〉有责任的 4. 应受谴责的 ‖ ~ly adv.

oboe ['əubəu] n.〈音〉1. 双簧管 2. (风琴中)发出似双簧管音的音栓 ‖ **oboist** n.

obscene [əb'si:n] *adj*. **1**. 猥亵的;淫荡的 **2**. 可憎的;污秽的;令人厌恶的 ‖ ~**ly** *adv*.

obscenity [əb'si:niti] *n*. **1**. 猥亵;淫荡 **2**. [常 obscenities]猥亵的话(或行为)

obscurantism [,ɔbskju'ræntizəm] *n*. **1**. 蒙昧主义 **2**.(文艺创作的)晦涩(风格)、朦胧(风格) ‖ **obscurantist** *n*. & *adj*.

obscuration [,ɔbskju'reiʃən] *n*. **1**. 遮蔽;昏暗 **2**. 晦涩,费解 **3**.[天]掩星;食

obscure [əb'skjuə] *adj*. **1**. 暗的,昏暗的,黑暗的;朦胧的 **2**. 模糊的;含糊的,不清楚的;不分明的;晦涩的;难解的,不引人注目的;偏僻的;隐匿的 **4**. 无名的;微贱的 — *vt*. **1**. 使暗,使黑暗;遮掩 **2**. 使难理解;搞暗 **3**. 使不分明;使失色 — *n*. = obscurity ‖ ~**ly** *adv*.

obscurity [əb'skjuriti] *n*. **1**. 暗,暗淡;朦胧 **2**. 模糊;含糊,不清楚;不分明;晦涩;难解 **3**. 不引人注目;偏僻;隐匿 **4**. 无名(的人);微贱(的人) **5**. 无名的地方

obsequies [ˈɔbsikwiz] [复] *n*. 葬礼

obsequious [əb'si:kwiəs] *adj*. **1**. 巴结的,卑躬曲膝的,奉承拍马的 **2**. 服从的;顺从的 ‖ ~**ly** *adv*. / ~**ness** *n*.

observable [əb'zə:vəbl] *adj*. **1**. 可遵守的;应遵守的 **2**. 可庆祝的;应庆祝的 **3**. 看得见的,观察(或观测)得到的;可辨别的 **4**. 值得注意的;显著的 — *n*. **1**.(可直接或间接)感觉到(或看得见)的事物;现象 **2**.(古)值得注意的东西 ‖ **observably** *adv*.

observance [əb'zə:vəns] *n*. **1**. 遵守,奉行 **2**.(节日、生日等的)纪念,庆祝 **3**. 惯例,习惯 **4**. 礼仪;仪式 **5**. 注意,观察 **6**. 观礼 **7**. [O-]天主教教规 **7**.(古)敬意;恭顺

observant [əb'zə:vənt] *adj*. **1**. 严格遵守…的 **2**. 留心的,当心的 **3**. 观察力

敏锐的 — **1**. [O-]天主教严守会规的)方济各会修士 ‖ ~**ly** *adv*.

observation [,ɔbzə'veiʃən] *n*. **1**. 注意;监视;观察;观测 **2**. 观察力 **3**. 观察(或观测)资料(或报告) **4**.(观察后发表的)言论;意见 **5**.[海][空]测天

observatory [əb'zə:vətəri] *n*. **1**. 天文台 **2**. 气象台 **3**. 瞭望台;观测站

observe [əb'zə:v] *vt*. **1**. 遵守,奉行(法律、习俗、规章等) **2**.(按传统习惯)纪念,庆祝(节日、生日等) **3**. 看到;注意到;监视,观察;观测(天体、气象等) **4**. 说;评述,评论 — *vi*. **1**. 注意,观察 **2**. 说;评述,评论(*on, upon*)

observer [əb'zə:və] *n*. **1**. 遵守者,奉行者 **2**. 注视者;监视人 **3**. 观察者,观测者;测候员 **4**.[军]观察员;观测员 **5**. 评述者 **6**.(出席会议的)观察员,旁观者

observing [əb'zə:viŋ] *adj*. **1**. 注意观察的;从事观察的 **2**. 观察力敏锐的 ‖ ~**ly** *adv*.

obsess [əb'ses] *vt*. **1**.(魔鬼、妄想等)迷住,使着迷;缠住 **2**. 使窘困;使烦扰 ‖ ~**ion** *n*. 着迷;缠住;摆脱不了的思想(或情感等) / ~**ive** *adj*. **1**. 使人着迷的,缠人的;引起着迷(或困扰)的 **2**.(兴趣等)过分(到不正常程度)的

obsidian [əb'sidiən] *n*.[矿]黑曜岩

obsolescent [,ɔbsə'lesənt] *adj*. **1**. 在逐步废弃中,即将过时的 **2**.[生]正在废退的 ‖ **obsolescence** *n*. **1**. 废弃,淘汰;过时 **2**.[生]废退,废迟

obsolete [ˈɔbsəli:t] *adj*. **1**. 废弃的,淘汰的 **2**. 过时的,陈腐的;老式的 **3**.[生]废退的,退化的 — *n*. 被废弃的事物;废词

obstacle [ˈɔbstəkl] *n*. 障碍(物);妨碍

obstetrics [əb'stetriks] [复] *n*. [用作单]产科学 ‖ **obstetric** *adj*.

obstinacy [ˈɔbstinəsi] *n*. **1**. 固执,顽固 **2**.

顽强 3.（病痛等的）难治；难解除；难抑制 4. 固执行为

obstinate [ˈɔbstinit] *adj.* 1. 固执的，顽固的 2. 顽强的，不屈服的，不让步的 3.（病痛等）难治的，难解除的；难抑制的 ‖ ~**ly** *adv.*

obstreperous [əbˈstrepərəs] *adj.* 1. 喧闹的 2. 不守秩序的，不服约束的，骚乱的 ‖ ~**ly** *adv.* / ~**ness** *n.*

obstruct [əbˈstrʌkt] *vt.* 1. 阻塞，堵塞 2. 阻挡，阻止，阻碍 3. 挡住（视线）；遮住 — *vi.* 设置障碍，妨碍

obstruction [əbˈstrʌkʃən] *n.* 1. 阻塞，堵塞 2. 阻挡，阻止，阻碍 3. 障碍物 4. 阻挠；阻挠议事 ‖ ~**ism** *n.* 蓄意阻挠；阻挠议事行为 / ~**ist** *n. & adj.* 蓄意阻挠（者）的

obstructive [əbˈstrʌktiv] *adj.* 1. 引起阻塞的 2. 妨碍的，阻挡的 3. 妨碍议事的 — *n.* 1. 障碍物 2. 妨碍议事者（尤指英下议院议员）‖ ~**ly** *adv.* / ~**ness** *n.*

obtain [əbˈtein] *vt.* 获得，得到；买到 — *vi.* 1.（习惯等）流行；通行；得到公认 2. 如愿以偿 3.〈古〉得到

obtainable [əbˈteinəbl] *adj.* 可获得的，可取得的；可买到的

obtrude [əbˈtruːd] *vt.* 1. 强加，强行（*on*，*upon*）2. 伸出，突出 — *vi.* 强行进入，闯入；打扰（*on*，*upon*）‖ **obtrusion** *n.* 强加；闯入；强加（或闯入）的东西 / **obtrusive** *adj.* 1. 强加的；闯入的；冒失的 2. 伸出的，突出的

obtuse [əbˈtjuːs] *adj.* 1. 钝的，不尖的；不锐利的 2.【数】（角）钝的；钝角的 3.（感觉）迟钝的；愚笨的 4.（形状）不鲜明的；（疼痛）不剧烈的 5.【植】（叶、花瓣等）钝（形）的，圆头的 ‖ ~ **angle**【数】钝角

obverse [ˈɔbvəs, əbˈvəs] *n.* 1.（钱币等的）正面 2. 前面，正面；主要的一面 3. 对立面；对应物 — *adj.* 正面的；对应的；起对应作用的 ‖【植】倒（转）的 ‖ ~**ly** *adv.*

obviate [ˈɔbvieit] *vt.* 1. 排除，消除（困难等）2. 使成为不必要；避免

obviosity [ˌɔbviˈɔsiti] *n.* 显而易见的事物

obvious [ˈɔbviəs] *adj.* 明显的，显然的，无疑的；平浅的 ‖ ~**ly** *adv.* / ~**ness** *n.*

ocarina [ˌɔkəˈriːnə] *n.* 奥卡里那笛，小鹅笛（卵形，有 6-8 个指孔）

occasion [əˈkeiʒən] *n.* 1. 场合；（重大的）时刻；时节 2. 时机，机会 3. 偶然原因；诱因（常与 *for* 连用）；必要；需要 5.〈古〉[~s] 事务 — *vt.* 引起；惹起

occasional [əˈkeiʒənl] *adj.* 1. 偶然的，非经常的 2. 盛会（或重大活动）的；供盛会（或重大活动）使用的 3. 临时的 ‖ ~**ly** *adv.* 偶然，非经常地

Occident [ˈɔksidənt] *n.* 1. [o-]〈诗〉西；西部 2. [the ~]西方国家；欧美；西方；西半球 3. 欧洲文明

Occidental [ˌɔksiˈdentəl] *adj.* 1. 西方的 2. 西方人的；西方文化的 — *n.* 西方人；欧美人

occlude [əˈkluːd] *vt.* 1. 使闭塞，堵塞 2. 隔断；挡住 3.【医】使（上下齿）咬合 — *vi.*【医】（上下齿）咬合 ‖ **occlusion** *n.*

occult [ˈɔkʌlt, əˈklʌlt] *adj.* 难以理解的；奥秘的；神秘的；秘密的 — *n.* [the ~]神秘学；神秘仪式

occupancy [ˈɔkjupənsi] *n.* 1. 占有；占用；居住 2. 占有（或占用、居住）期间 3. 供占用的房屋 4.【律】先占

occupant [ˈɔkjupənt] *n.* 1. 占有者；占用者；居住者 2.【律】先占取得者；实际占有人

occupation [ˌɔkjuˈpeiʃən] *n.* 1.（军事）占领，占据；占领政策；占领军 2. 占有；

占用；居住 3. 占有(或占用、居住)期 4. 职业；工作 5. 日常事务；消遣

occupational [ˌɔkjuˈpeiʃənəl] *adj*. 1. 职业的；工作的；职业引起的 2. 军事占领的 ‖ ~ly *adv*.

occupy [ˈɔkjupai] *vt*. 1. 占领，占据 2. 占(时间，空间)；占用；住(房子等) 3. 处于(某种地位)；担任(职务等) 4. 使忙碌；使从事 — *vi*. 占领；占有

occur [əˈkəː] (occurred; occurring) *vi*. 1. 发生 2. 出现；被发现；存在 3. 被想到，被想起(to)

occurrence [əˈkʌrəns] *n*. 1. 发生；出现 2. (偶发)事件；事变；发生的事情 3.【矿】(矿床等的)赋存，埋藏

ocean [ˈəuʃən] *n*. 1. 海洋；(诗)大海 2. 洋 3. 一大片，广阔，无际；大量，许多 ‖ ~-going *adj*. 远洋的；适用于远洋航行的

oceanaut [ˈəuʃənɔːt] *n*. 海底(实验室)工作人员

Oceania [ˌəuʃiˈeiniə], **Oceanica** [ˌəuʃiˈænikə] *n*. 大洋洲

oceanic [ˌəuʃiˈænik] *adj*. 1. 海洋的；(气候)海洋性的；生活在海洋中的；海洋产于的 2. 似海洋的；广阔的；无边无际的 3.[O-]大洋洲的

oceanography [ˌəuʃəˈnɔgrəfi] *n*. 海洋学 ‖ **oceanographer** *n*. / **oceanographic** [ˌəuʃəˈgræfik] *adj*.

oceanology [ˌəuʃəˈnɔlədʒi] *n*. 海洋学 ‖ **oceanologist** *n*. 海洋学家

ocelot [ˈəusilɔt] [复]ocelot(s) *n*. 豹猫；豹猫毛皮

ocher, ochre [ˈəukə] *n*. 1.【矿】赭石 2. 赭色，浅暗橘黄色 3.(俚)钱

o' clock [əˈklɔk] ...点钟(of the clock 的缩略)

Oct. *abbr*. October

oct-, octa-, octo- *comb. form* 表示"八"：octagon

octagon [ˈɔktəgən] *n*. 八边形，八角形 ‖ ~al [ɔkˈtægənəl] *adj*.

octane [ˈɔktein] *n*.【化】(正)辛烷，辛(级)烷

octave [ˈɔktiv, ˈɔkteiv] *n*. 1. 八个一组的事物 2.【音】八度音阶；八度(音)；八度和音；八度音栓 3. 八行诗体；(十四行诗的)前八行 4.(击剑防守姿势的)第八姿势 5.【宗】节日起第八天；节日算起的八天 6.(英)容量为十三加仑半的酒桶 — *adj*. 八个一组的；八行的 2.【音】高八度音的

octavo [ɔkˈteivəu] [复]octavos *n*.(纸张的)八开；(书的)八开本；八开的纸；八开本的书

octet [ɔkˈtet] *n*. 1. 八个一组 2.(十四行诗的)前八行 3.【音】八重唱(曲)；八重奏(曲)；八重唱(或八重奏)演出小组

October [ɔkˈtəubə] *n*. 十月(略作 Oct.)

octogenarian [ˌɔktəudʒiˈnɛəriən] *n*. 八十至八十九岁的人

octopus [ˈɔktəpəs] *n*. 1. 章鱼 2. 章鱼状物(尤指到处伸手的势力或组织)

ocular [ˈɔkjulə] *adj*. 1. 眼(睛)的；视觉(上)的 2. 用眼的；凭视觉的 3. 目击的 4. 像眼睛的；起眼睛作用的 — *n*.(望远镜、显微镜的)目镜

oculist [ˈɔkjulist] *n*. 眼科医生；眼科专家

odd [ɔd] *adj*. 1. 奇数的；单数的 2. 单只，不成对的；零散的 3. 有零数的；带零头的 4. 临时的，不固定的；额外的 5. 奇特的，古怪的 6. 偏僻的 — *n*.[the ~](高尔夫球赛中)多于对方的一次击球 ‖ ~ly *adv*. 奇特地，古怪地 / ~ness *n*. 奇特，古怪

oddity ['ɔditi] *n.* 1. 奇特, 古怪 2. 怪人; 古怪的事物; 怪癖

odds [ɔdz] [复]*n.* [用作单或复] 1. 〈古〉不平等 2. 差异 3. 区别; 差异; 差额 4. (事物发生的) 可能性; 机会 (*on, a-gainst*) 5. (比赛或打赌时给对方的) 让步 6. 优势 7. 投注赔率 ‖ ~-'on *adj.* 大半有希望赢的

ode [əud] *n.* 颂诗; 颂歌

odious ['əudiəs] *adj.* 可憎的; 丑恶的; 令人作呕的 ‖ ~ly *adv.* / ~ness *n.*

odium ['əudiəm] *n.* 1. 憎恨; 厌恶 2. 不名誉, 臭名

odometer [ɔ'dɔmitə] *n.* (车辆等的) 里程计

odor ['əudə] *n.* 〈美〉= odour

odoriferous [əudə'rifərəs] *adj.* 1. 散发气味的; 香的 2. 发臭味的, 臭的 3. (道德上) 臭的, 令人反感的

odorous ['əudərəs] *adj.* 有气味的; 香的; 好闻的; 臭的; 难闻的

odour ['əudə] *n.* 1. 气味; 香气; 臭气 2. 味道; 迹象 3. 名誉, 声誉 4. 〈古〉[常 ~s]香水; 香料 ‖ ~less *adj.* 没有气味的

OECD *abbr.* Organization for Economic Co-operation and Development 经济合作与发展组织

o'er ['əuə] *adv.* & *prep.* 〈诗〉= over

of [强 ɔv; 弱 əv, v, f] *prep.* 1. [属于]...的 2. [关于]...的 3. [表示同位]: the month ~ May 五月 4. [表示具有某种性质、状况等]: a man ~ ability 能干的人 5. [表示...的数量或种类]: a sheet ~ paper 一张纸 6. [表示...的部分或全部]: the whole ~ China 全中国 7. [表示...中最突出的]: the hero ~ heroes 最杰出的英雄 8. [表示在...方面]: be slow ~ speech 讲话慢 9. [表示在...一方]: It's very kind ~ you to

help us. 谢谢你给了我们帮助。10. 来自...的; 从...的 11. 由于; 因为 12. 由...组成(或做成)的 13. [表示动作的对象]: love ~ one's country 爱国 14. [表示动作的主体]: the arrival ~ the dele-gation 代表团的到来 15. [表示除去、剥夺等]: cure sb. ~ a disease 医好某人的病 16. [表示方位、时间等的范围]: three minutes ~ ten 〈美〉十点缺三分 17. [表示在...时候或时刻] ~ recent years 近年来 18. 〈古〉[用在动词被动语态后]被: He is beloved ~ all. 他被大家所爱戴。

off [ɔf] *adv.* 1. 离, 距 2. (离)开; (走)开 3. (脱离)掉 4. (断)掉; (休)止 5. 完, 光 6. [表示情况]: be well ~ 生活过得好 7. [戏]不在舞台中 — *prep.* 1. 从; 从...离开(或脱离、去掉) 2. 与...相隔(离, 等)从...分岔 3. 靠...(养活、赚钱等) 4. 从...扣除 — *adj.* 1. (离人)较远的(一边); 反(面)的 2. (车轮等)在右侧的(船的)向海一边的 3. (路等)分支的; 非主要的 4. 停止的(工作); 休歇的; 空闲的 5. 低于通常水平的; 较差的; (可能性)极小的 6. (口)有点怪的, 不舒服的 — *int.* [号哩]1. 与...一块 2. 性交 3. 杀掉 — *vi.* [用于祈使句]走开, 滚开; 站开 ‖ ~'shore *adj.* 1. 离岸的 2. [近]离岸的 — *adv.* 离岸; 近海岸; 向海 / ~'stage *adv.* & *adj.* 台后) 1. 幕后(的) / '~-the-'cuff *adj.* & *adv.* 〈美口〉即席的(地); 即兴的(地) / ~-the-'job *adj.* 1. 业余的 2. 进行的 2. 失业的 / ~-the-'record *adj.* & *adv.* (谈话等)私下的(地), 不许发表(或引用)的(地)

off. *abbr.* 1. office 2. officer 3. official

offal ['ɔfəl] *n.* 1. 下水, 杂肉 2. 垃圾, 废物 3. 腐肉 4. 工业下脚(如木屑、皮革边料等) 5. [常~s]糠, 麸 6. 无用的

人;被鄙弃的人

offbeat ['ɔf'biːt] *adj.* 非常规的,非正统的,不落俗套的;异常的

offence [ə'fens] *n.* 1. 冒犯,得罪;触怒 2. 犯法(行为);罪过;过错 3. 讨厌的东西;冒犯反感的事物 4.〈罕〉失足(的原因);绊脚石 5. 进攻;攻击 6. 进攻的一方;进攻队;进攻的方法

offend [ə'fend] *vt.* 1. 冒犯,得罪;触怒;伤害……的感情 2. 违反;违犯 3. 使不舒服 — *vi.* 1. 犯过错;违犯;犯罪(*a-gainst*) 2. 冒犯,得罪;引起不舒服,引起愤怒

offender [ə'fendə] *n.* 冒犯者;罪犯;犯规者

offense [ə'fens] *n.*〈美〉= offence

offensive [ə'fensiv] *adj.* 1. 冒犯的;唐突的 2. 讨厌的;令人作呕的 3. 进攻的;进攻性的;攻势的 4.〈体〉攻击性的;进攻方的 — *n.* 进攻;攻势 ‖ **～ly** *adv.* ‖ **～ness** *n.*

offer ['ɔfə] *vt.* 1. 提供;提出 2. 奉献;贡献 3. 试图 4. 出(价);开(价);有……出售 5. 呈现出;使出现 6. 演出 — *vi.* 1. 出现 2. 献祭 3. 提议;求婚 4.〈古〉试图(*at*) — *n.* 1. 给予;提供;提议 2. 意图;愿欲 3.〔商〕报价,发价 4. 求婚

offering ['ɔfəriŋ] *n.* 1. 给予,提供;奉献,贡献 2. 礼物;捐献物(给教会的)捐款;祭品 3. 出售物 4. 课程 5. 削价出售 6. 演出

offertory ['ɔfətəri] *n.*〔宗〕1. 奉献仪式 2. 献金;献金仪式 3. 奉献经;奉献曲

offhand ['ɔf'hænd] *adv.* 立即,当下;未经准备地 — *adj.* 1. 即席的;临时的;随便的 2. 简慢的

offhanded ['ɔf'hændid] *adv. & adj.* = offhand ‖ **～ly** *adv.* ‖ **～ness** *n.*

office ['ɔfis] *n.* 1. 办公室;办事处;事务

所;营业所;〈美〉诊所 2. 处;局;社;行;公司 3.〔O-〕〈英〉部;〈美〉厅;局 4. 公职;官职 5. 职责;功能 6.〔～s〕照料;帮助 7.〈英〉〔～s〕下房(指厨房、贮藏室等) 8. 礼仪〔宗〕仪式;祷告 9.〔the ~〕暗号,暗示 10.〈俚〉(飞机驾驶员的)座舱 ‖ **～holder** *n.* 官员 / **～ hours** 办公(或营业、门诊)时间 / **～ work** 办公室工作

officer ['ɔfisə] *n.* 1. 官员;办事员 2.(团体、组织等)干事;高级职员(如主任、秘书、司库等) 3. 军官 4. 警官;法警 5.(商船的)高级船员 — *vt.* 〔常用被动语态〕1. 给……配备军官(或高级船员) 2. 指挥;统率

official [ə'fiʃəl] *adj.* 1. 官员的;公务(或职务上)的 2. 官方的;法定的;正式的 3. 官气十足的;讲究形式的 4.〔医〕药典许可的 — *n.* 1. 官员;行政人员;高级职员 2.〔宗〕宗教法庭法官 ‖ **～ly** *adv.*

officiate [ə'fiʃieit] *vi.* 1. 行使职务 2.〔宗〕司祭,司仪 — *vt.* 1. 执行(公务) 2. 司(仪) 3. 充当(比赛等)的裁判 ‖ **officiator** *n.*

officious [ə'fiʃəs] *adj.* 1. 过分殷勤的;好管闲事的 2.(外交上)非官方的,非正式的(official 之对) ‖ **～ly** *adv.* ‖ **～ness** *n.*

offing ['ɔfiŋ] *n.* 1.(在视界范围内的)远处海面;离岸不太远的位置 2.〔海〕近岸锚泊 3. 不远处;不远的将来

offset ['ɔf'set] *n.* 1. 分支,旁支;(山的)支脉;支族;后裔 2. 抵消;补偿 3. 陪衬物 4.〔建〕墙台;壁架 5.〔建〕踏步(台阶)短简茎 7.〔机〕偏置,偏距;支管 8.〔印〕胶印;胶印印张;背面釉粉 9.〔地〕水平断错 10.〔船〕型值 11.〔测〕支距 — (offset; offsetting) *vt.* 1. 抵消;补偿 2.

【建】建壁阶于；【机】偏置 3.【印】用胶印法印；蹭脏（另一印张）— vi. 1.【机】形成支管 2.【印】背面蹭脏

offshoot [ˈɔːfʃuːt] n. 1. 分枝 2. 分株 3. 支脉；支流；支线 3. 支族（的后裔）；旁系（的一员）4. 衍生事物

offspring [ˈɔːfsprɪŋ]（[复] offspring(s)）n. 1. 儿女；子孙，后代 2. 结果；产物 3. 幼苗，仔，崽

oft [ɔft] adv. 〈古〉〈诗〉经常，常常（= often）

often [ˈɔːfn, ˈɔːftn]（比较级 oftener 或 more often，最高级 oftenest 或 most often）adv. 经常，常常

ogle [ˈəʊgl] n. 媚眼，秋波 — vt. 对...送媚眼；贪婪地看 — vi. 做媚眼，送秋波（at）

ogre [ˈəʊgə] n. 1.（民间传说等中的）吃人妖魔 2. 残暴的人；可怕的东西 ‖ ~ish adj.

ogress [ˈəʊgris] n. 吃人女妖

oh [əʊ] int. [表示惊讶、恐惧、痛苦等]喔！哦！唉呀！哎哟！

Ohio [əʊˈhaiəʊ] n. 俄亥俄 [美国州名]

ohm [əʊm] n. 【物】欧（姆）（电阻单位）

-oid suf. [构成名词或形容词]表示"似"，"像"：petaloid 花瓣状的，celluloid

oil [ɔil] n. 1. 油；润滑油 2. 石油 3. [常~s]油画颜料；油画作品 4. [常~s]油布；油布雨衣 5.〈口〉奉承话；〈美俚〉废话，废话；(贿赂的)钱财 — vt. 1. 加油于；涂润滑油于 2. 使（机器）浸透油 3. 使（脂肪等）融化 4. 贿赂 — vi. 1.(轮船等)加燃料油 2.(脂肪等)融化 ‖ ~ cloth n. 油布；〈美〉field ~ 油田 / ~ painting n. 1. 画油画 2. 油画作品 / ~-skin n. 油布；油布雨衣 [~s]油布衣裤 / ~ tanker 油轮，油船 / ~ well 油井

oiler [ˈɔilə] n. 1. 加油工 2. 加油器；油壶

oily [ˈɔili] adj. 1.(含)油的；多油的；油状的 2. 涂油油的；浸透油的；油腻的 3.（言行等）圆滑的；讨好人的 ‖ oiliness n.

ointment [ˈɔintmənt] n. 【药】软膏，油膏

O.K., OK [ˈəʊˈkei]〈主口〉(美口) adj. & adv. 对；好；可以；行（= all right）— n.（[复] O.K.'s 或 OK's）n. 批准，认可 —（O.K.'d 或 OK'd；O.K.'ing 或 OK'ing）vt. 在...上签 O.K. 两字，对...表示同意；对...予以认可

okapi [əʊˈkɑːpi]（[复] okapi(s)）n. 【动】霍加狓(产于非洲，类似长颈鹿而较小，无斑，其颈也较短)

okay [əʊˈkei] adj., adv., n. & vt. = O.K.

Okinawa [ˌɔːkiˈnɑːwə] n. 冲绳(群岛)；冲绳(岛) [日本]

Oklahoma [ˌəʊkləˈhəʊmə] n. 俄克拉何马 [美国州名]

okra [ˈəʊkrə] n. 【植】黄秋葵

old [əʊld] adj. 1. 老的；年老的；年代久的；古老的；古时的 2....岁的；...久的；a baby a few months ~ 一个出生几个月的婴儿/How ~ are you? 你多大岁数? 3. 旧的；过去的 4. 旧的；陈旧的；破旧的；废弃的 5. 熟悉的 6. 老练的；老资格的 7. 暗褐色的 8.〈口〉[招呼用语，表示亲密]：Old Joe! 老乔 9.〈口〉[用在名词前，加强语气]：have a fine（或 good, high）~ time 过得极愉快 10. 古时的；旧时的〔只用于"古一"语中〕2....岁的人（或动物）：a four-year-~ 四岁的孩子（或马等）3. [the ~]从前的 ‖ of ~ 从前 1. 从前的；很久前 ‖ bachelor 坚持独身的男子 /Old Dominion 老自治领(州)(美国弗吉尼亚州的别称) /Old English 古英语(450-1150 年间通用的英语)

/′-′fashioned adj. 1. 老式的；过时的 2. 老派的，守旧的 3.〈英方〉(目光等)责备的；含义深刻的 /Old Glory〈美〉星条光荣(美国国旗的俗称) /~ lady 1. 妻子 2. 母亲 3. 老处女式的人物(可指男人) /~ maid 1. 老处女 2. 老处女式的人物(可指男人) 3. "老处女"(一种抽牌子的牌戏) /~ man〈美俚〉1. 丈夫 2. 父亲 3. 老板；工头 4. 船长；(美国兵用的称呼)长官 5. 老资格者；老前辈 6.(招呼用语)老朋友，老兄 7. 姘夫 /′-,timer n. 1. 老资格的人；老前辈；老手 2. 上了年纪的人 3. 守旧的人 4. 老式的东西 /Old World 旧世界，东半球(与美洲新大陆相对而言；尤指欧洲) /′-world adj. 1. 旧时代的 2. 旧世界的，东半球的；欧洲的 3. 旧式的；古老风味的

olden [′əuldən] adj.〈古〉〈诗〉古时的，往昔的 — vt. & vi.(使)变老；(使)见老

oldish [′əuldiʃ] adj. 上了点年纪的；有点旧的

oldster [′əuldstə] n.〈口〉上了年纪的人

oleaginous [ˌəuli′ædʒinəs] adj. 1. 油质的；含油的 2. 产油的 3. 油似的；滑腻的 4. 油嘴滑舌的；甜言蜜语的 ‖ ~ly adv. /~ness n.

oleander [ˌəuli′ændə] n.【植】夹竹桃

oleomargarin [ˌəuliəu′mɑːdʒərin] n. 麦淇淋；人造黄油

olfactory [ɔl′fæktəri] adj. 嗅觉的 — n. [常 olfactories]嗅神经；嗅觉能力；嗅觉器官

oligarch [′ɔliɡɑːk] n. 寡头统治集团成员，寡头统治者

oligarchy [′ɔliɡɑːki] n. 1. 寡头政治，寡头统治 2. 寡头统治的政府(或国家) 3. 寡头统治集团 4.(少数人垄断的)寡头组织 ‖ oli′garchic adj.

olive [′ɔliv] n. 1.【植】油橄榄；橄榄；橄榄木 2. 橄榄色；茶青色 3.(作为和平象征的)橄榄叶；橄榄枝；橄榄枝叶圈 — adj. 油橄榄的；橄榄色的 ‖ ~ branch 橄榄枝(和平的象征) /~ oil 1. 橄榄油 2.〈美俚〉再会

Olympia [ə′limpiə] n. 奥林匹亚[希腊南部一平原](古希腊人竞技的地方)

Olympian [ə′limpiən] adj. 1. 奥林匹亚的；奥林匹斯山的 2.【希神】奥林匹斯山神的；像奥林匹斯山神的；似神的；天上的 3. 威严的；崇高的；高傲的 4. 奥林匹克运动会的 — n. 1.【希神】奥林匹斯山十二神之一 2. 奥林匹亚人 3. 奥林匹克运动会选手 4. 超然冷静的人；造诣很深的人

Olympic [ə′limpik] adj. = Olympian — n. 1. 奥林匹克运动会比赛项目 2. [the ~s]奥林匹克运动会 ‖ ~ Games 1. (古希腊)奥林匹克竞赛会 2. 奥林匹克运动会(简称奥运会)

Oman [əu′mɑːn] n. 阿曼[西南亚国家]

ombudsman [′ɔmbudzmən] n. [复]ombudsmen) n.(专门调查公民对政府官员投诉的)监察员

omelet(te) [′ɔmlit] n. 煎蛋卷，炒蛋，煎蛋饼

omen [′əumen] n. 预兆，征兆，兆头；预知性 — vt. 预示；预告；预测，预言

ominous [′ɔminəs] adj. 1. 不祥的，不吉的 2. 预兆的；预示的(of) ‖ ~ly adv. /~ness n.

omission [əu′miʃən] n. 1. 省略；删节；排除 2. 遗漏；疏忽；懈怠 3. 省略(或删节、遗漏)的东西

omit [əu′mit] (omitted; omitting) vt. 1. 省略；删节；排除 2. 遗漏；忽略；忘记

omnibus [′ɔmnibəs] n. 1. 公共汽车；公共马车 2. 选集；汇编(= ~ book) — adj.

综合的;包括多项的;作多种用途的 ‖
~ bill〈美〉综合议案

omnipotent [ɔm'nipətənt] *adj.* 全能的;有无990权力(或力量)的;彻头彻尾的 — *n.* 万能者;[the O-]〈宗〉全能的上帝 ‖ **omnipotence** *n.* / ~ly *adv.*

omnipresent [ɔmni'prezənt] *adj.* 普遍存在的,无所不在的 ‖ **omnipresence** *n.* / ~ly *adv.*

omniscient [ɔm'nisiənt] *adj.* 无所不知的,全知的,博识的 — *n.* 无所不知者;[the O-]〈宗〉上帝 ‖ **omniscience** *n.* / ~ly *adv.*

omnivorous [ɔm'nivərəs] *adj.* 1.〈动〉杂食性的 2. 无所不吸收的;什么书都读的;什么都喜欢的 ‖ ~ly *adv.*

on [ɔn] *prep.* 1. 在...上 2. 在...旁;靠近...3. 向,朝...4. 在...的时候;在...后立即 5. 根据;凭...等 6. 关于7. 是...的成员;在...供职 8. 在从事...中;处于...情况中 9. 通过...;以...的方式 10. 由...支付(指费用等) 11.(一个)接(一个)...又... — *adv.* 1.〈安置〉在(身上)上去 2. 向前去;(进行)下去;(继续)下去 — *adj.* 1. 在发生(或活动着)的;起着作用的 2.〈口〉同意的,乐意参加的 3.〈俚〉醉了的 ‖ ~ coming *adj.* 1. 迎面而来的;即将到来的 2. 正在兴起的;新兴的 3. 友好的 *n.* 来临 / ~ going *adj.* 不断前进中的;不断发展中的 *n.* 1. [~ goings](常指不正常或不正当的)行为,举动;事态 2. 前进,发展 / ~ looker *n.* 旁观者 / ~ rush *n.* 1. 猛冲;直冲;冲击 2. 奔流 / ~ set *n.* 攻击,袭击 3. 开始 4.〈印〉静电印刷术 / ~ slaught *n.* 攻击;袭击;猛攻

once [wʌns] *adv.* 1. 一次 2. 曾经,一度3. [用于否定句]一次也;完全 4. [用于

条件句等]一旦 5. 乘以一 6.〈亲属关系上〉隔一亲等,隔一代 — *conj.* 一旦...的...) — *n.* 以前的,一度的 ‖ *at* ~ 1. 立刻,马上 2. 一起,同时 ‖ '~-over *n.* 〈口〉草草检查;大略一看;草草了事;毒打

one [wʌn] *num.* 一;一个(人或物);第一(卷,章,号等) — *pron.* 1. 一个(任何)人;本人 2. 一个 3. [表示与别的对照]这一个...4. 一致的;同一的 2. 完整的;一体的 3. 唯一的;单独一个的 4. 某一的 5. [表示与别的对照]这一个...2. 怪人 3. 一岁 4. 一点钟 5. 一击 6. (食品的)一客 ‖ '~-'sided *adj.* 1. 单边的;单侧的 2. 片面的,不公正的;单方面的 / '~-time *adj.* & *adv.* 从前(的);一度(的) / '~-'track *adj.* 1.〈铁路〉单线的,单轨的 2. 头脑偏狭的,思路狭窄的 / '~-'way *adj.* 单程的;单行的;单方面的;单向的

oneness ['wʌnnis] *n.* 1. 唯一(性);单一(性) 2. 同一性 3. 一体,完整,一致,协调

onerous ['ɔnərəs] *adj.* 1. 沉重的;繁重的;麻烦的 2.【律】有偿的;承担(过重)义务的 ‖ ~ly *adv.*

oneself [wʌn'self] *pron.* 1. [反身代词]自己,自身 2. [用于加强语气]亲自;本人

onion ['ʌnjən] *n.* 1.【植】圆葱,洋葱;洋葱头 2.〈俚〉头,脑袋;脸 3.〈美俚〉讨厌的家伙;笨蛋 4.〈美俚〉搞糟的事 5.〈美俚〉一元钱 ‖ ~ dome(俄罗斯东正教教堂或建筑的)洋葱头形圆顶 / '~-domed *adj.* 有洋葱头形圆顶的

only ['əunli] *adj.* 1. 唯一的,仅有的 2. 最好的,独一无二的 — *adv.* 1. 只;仅仅;才 2. 反面;结果却;不料 — *conj.* 可是,不过 ‖ *not* ~...*but* (*also*)...不

但...而且...

onto ['ɔntu] *prep.* 1. 到...之上；向...之上 2.〈俚〉对...心中有数

onus ['əunəs] *n.* 1. [只用单] 负担；责任；义务 2. [律] 举证责任

onward ['ɔnwəd] *adj.* 向前的；前进的 — *adv.* = onwards ‖ ~**ly** *adv.* / ~**ness** *n.*

onwards ['ɔnwədz] *adv.* 向前；在前面

onyx ['ɔniks] *n.* [矿] 缟玛瑙

oodles ['u:dlz] [复] *n.* [用作单或复]〈俚〉许多，大量

ooze [u:z] *n.* 1. 淤泥 2. [地] (硅藻) 软泥；沼地 3. (皮革的) 鞣液 4. 渗流；分泌 5. 渗出物；分泌物 — *vi.* 1. 渗出；分泌出；冒出 2.〈喻〉(秘密等) 泄露 (out) 3. (勇气等) 逐渐消失 (away) 4. 慢慢行进；溜 — *vt.* 1. 渗出；分泌出；冒出 2. 显示出；表现出；洋溢

opacity [əu'pæsiti] *n.* 1. 不透明，不透光；不透明性 (或度) 2. (对热、声等的) 不传导 (性) 3. 不透明体；浊质 4. 隐涩，难解 5. 愚蠢

opal ['əupəl] *n.* 1. [矿] 蛋白石 2. 乳白玻璃 (= glass)

opalescent [ˌəupə'lesənt] *adj.* 乳白色的；发乳光的 ‖ **opalescence** *n.* / ~**ly** *adv.*

opaque [əu'peik] *adj.* 1. 不透光的；不透明的 2. 不发光的；暗的 3. 不传导的 4. 难理解的；晦涩的 5. 愚钝的；迟钝的 — *n.* 1. 不透明体 2. [the ~] 黑暗 3. [摄] 不透明颜料

OPEC, Opec ['əupek] *n.* (Organization of Petroleum Exporting Countries 的缩略) 石油输出国组织，欧佩克

open ['əupən] *adj.* 1. 开 (着) 的 2. 开阔的；空旷的；敞开的 3. 开始工作的；营业着的；活动着的 4. 开放的；无管制的；(赌博等) 不受禁止的 5. 公开的；坦率的 6. 悬而未决的；空缺的 7. 散开

的；稀疏的 8. (河流、港口等) 不冰封的；(气候) 温和的 9. 无冰冻的 9. 不设防的 10. [音] 不用指按的 11. [医] (肠) 通畅的 — *vt.* 1. (打) 开；张开；展开 2. 开放；开始；开立；开设 3. 开出；开发；开具；揭开；揭开；表明 5. [医] 使 (肠) 畅通 6. 开松；疏开 (队列) 7. [海] (改变船位以避开挡住视线的障碍物而) 使呈现出能看见 8. [律] 撤回 (判决等) 9. (牌戏中) 开始 (叫牌)；开始 (出牌) — *vi.* 1. 开，打开；张开；展开 2. 开始；开放；开设 3. 开演；开讲；展现；被看见 4. (猎狗) 开始吠叫；(人) 畅谈 5. (牌戏中) 叫牌；开局下注；首攻 6. (股市) 开盘 ‖ ~**ly** *adv.* 公开地；公然地；直率地；坦率地 / ~**ness** *n.* ‖ ~-'**air** *adj.* 户外的，野外的；喜欢野外生活的 / '~-**and**-'**shut** *adj.* 1. 显而易然的 2. (天气) 时晴时阴的 / '~-'**handed** *adj.* 1. 慷慨的 2. 摊着手的 / ~ **letter** 公开信 / '~-'**minded** *adj.* 思想开通的，无先入之见的，无偏见的；虚心的 / ~ **sesame** 开门咒；秘诀；关键 (源出《一千零一夜》中一个故事) / '~**work** *n.* 透雕细工；网状细工；透孔织物

opening ['əupəniŋ] *n.* 1. 开；启 2. 穴，孔；空隙；通道 3. (林中) 空地 4. 开始；开端 5. (职位的) 空缺；机会 6. (象棋等) 的开局 — *adj.* 开的；开始的；首场演出的

opera[1] ['ɔpərə] *n.* 1. 歌剧 2. 歌剧曲谱；歌剧脚本；歌剧艺术 3. 歌剧演出 4. 歌剧院；歌剧团 ‖ ~ **glasses** 观剧镜 / ~ **house** 歌剧院；〈美〉剧场 ‖ **operatic** [ˌɔpə'rætik] *adj.*

opera[2] ['ɔpərə] opus 的复数

operable ['ɔpərəbl] *adj.* 1. 可操作的 2. 可施行手术的 3. 可实施的，可实行的

‖ **operably** adv.

operate ['ɔpəreit] vi. 1. 操作；工作；运转 2. 起作用；(药物等)奏效 3. 开动 4. 【军】作战 5. 从事证券交易 — vt. 1. 操作；开动(机器等) 2. 〈主美〉经营；管理(= manage) 3. 对…动手术 4. 引起，产生(变化等)

operation [ˌɔpə'reiʃən] n. 1. 操作；工作；运转(方式) 2. 作用；效力 3. (外科)手术 4.【军】(常～s)作战；军事行动；[～s]【军】地面(或作战)指挥部 5.〈美〉经营；业务 6. 交易，买卖 7.【数】运算

operational [ˌɔpə'reiʃənəl] adj. 1. 操作上的；用于操作的；实施中的 2. 业务上的 3.【数】运算上的 4. 作战上的；用于军事行动的 5. 可使用的(或起作用的) ‖ ~ly adv. ‖ ~ research 运筹学

operative ['ɔpərətiv] adj. 1. 操作的；工作着的 2. 起作用的 3. 有效的；施行的 4. 手术的 — n. 1. 技工；熟练工人 2. 特务；侦探

operator ['ɔpəreitə] n. 1. 操作人员；驾驶员；报务员；机务员；话务员；电话接线员 2. (外科)手术者 3.〈主美〉(工商企业的)经营者；经纪人；投机商 4. 骗子；精明圆滑的人 5.【数】(运)算子，算符

operetta [ˌɔpə'retə] n. 小歌剧，轻歌剧

ophthalmia [ɔf'θælmiə] n. 【医】眼炎

ophthalmology [ˌɔfθæl'mɔlədʒi] n. 【医】眼科学 ‖ **ophthalmologist** n.

opiate ['əupiit] n. 1. 鸦片制剂；麻醉剂；镇静剂；起镇静(或催眠)作用的东西，慰藉物

opinion [ə'pinjən] n. 1. 意见，看法；主张 2. 意见；舆论；评价 3. 专家意见；鉴定；判定

opinionated [ə'pinjəneitid] adj. 固执己见的；武断的 ‖ ~ly adv. / ~ness n.

opium ['əupiəm] n. 1. 鸦片 2.〈喻〉鸦片

— adj. 鸦片的；与鸦片有关的

opossum [ə'mɔsəm] n.【动】1. 负鼠 2. 袋貂

opponent [ə'pəunənt] adj. 对立的；对抗的；反对的；敌对的 — n. 1. 对手；敌手；反对者 2.【解】对向肌

opportune ['ɔpətjuːn, ˌɔpə'tjuːn] adj. 恰好的；适宜的；及时的，适时的 ‖ ~ly adv. / ~ness n.

opportunism ['ɔpətjuːnizəm] n. 机会主义

opportunist [ˌɔpə'tjuːnist] n. 机会主义者 — adj. 机会主义的；机会主义者的

opportunity [ˌɔpə'tjuːniti] n. 机会；良机

oppose [ə'pəuz] vt. 1. 反对；反抗；抵抗；阻挡 3. 使反对；使对抗 4. 使相对(或相反) 5. 使对向 — vi. 反对

opposite ['ɔpəzit] adj. 1. 对面的；相对的 2. 相反的；对立的 3.【植】对生的；(花部)重叠的 — n. 对立面或对立物；对立物 — prep. 在…的对面 — adv. 在对面；对过

opposition [ˌɔpə'ziʃən] n. 1. 反对；反抗 2. (位置)相对；对相对 3. 相反；对立 4. [常作 O-]反对党 5. 反对物(如反对派的政策等)；反对派 6.【天】冲 7.【逻】对当

oppress [ə'pres] vt. 1. 压迫；压制 2. 压抑；使沉重；使烦恼 ‖ ~ or n. 压迫者；压制者

oppression [ə'preʃən] n. 1. 压迫；压制 2. 压制物 3. 沉闷；压抑；苦恼

oppressive [ə'presiv] adj. 1. 压迫的；压制的；暴虐的 2. 压抑的；沉重的；令人烦恼的；难以忍受的 ‖ ~ly adv. / ~ness n.

opprobrium [ə'prəubriəm] n. 1. 轻蔑；辱骂 2. 耻辱，不光彩 ‖ **opprobrious** adj.

opt [ɔpt] vi. 选择；作出抉择(for, between) ‖ ~ in 决定参加 / ~ out 决

定退出(或不参加)

optic ['ɒptik] *adj.* 1. 眼的；视力的；视觉的 2.【物】光学的

optical ['ɒptikəl] *adj.* 1. 眼的；视力的；视觉的 2.【物】光学的；光的 3. 有助于视力的 ‖ ~ **fibre**【物】光学纤维

optician [ɒp'tiʃən] *n.* 眼镜商；眼镜制造者；眼镜配制技师

optics ['ɒptiks] [复] *n.* [用作单]光学

optimism ['ɒptimizəm] *n.* 乐观；乐观主义 ‖ **optimist** *n.* 乐观主义者

optimistic [ˌɒpti'mistik] *adj.* 乐观的；乐观主义的 ‖ ~**ally** *adv.*

optimum ['ɒptiməm] *adj.* 最适的；最优的；最佳的

option ['ɒpʃən] *n.* 1. 选择；选择权；选择自由 2.(供选择的)事物 3. 购买(或出售)权，期权(指在规定期限内按照规定价格买卖股票、货物等的权利) 4.(规定时间内的)履行契约权 5.(保险)投保人对赔偿方式的选择权

optional ['ɒpʃənəl] *adj.* 可任意选择的；非强制的 ‖ ~**ly** *adv.*

optometry [ɒp'tɒmitri] *n.* 视力测定(法)；验光配镜(法)；验光配镜业 ‖ **optometrist** *n.*

opulence ['ɒpjuləns] *n.* 富裕；丰富；大量

opulent ['ɒpjulənt] *adj.* 富裕的；丰富的；大量的

opus ['əupəs] ([复] **opera** ['ɒpərə]或 **opuses**) *n.* 作品(尤指乐曲)；杰作

or [ɔː, 弱 ə] *conj.* 1. [表示选择]或，或者；还是 2. [表示不明确]大约，或许 3. [引导同义或同义短语]即，或者说 4. [常和 else 连用]否则；要不然 5.(诗)[在 either...or 中代 either]不是...(就是)

-or *suf.* [构成名词] 1. 表示"...者"，

"...物"，"...器"：author, tractor 2.〈美〉表示"动作"；"状态"；"性质"：demeanor

oracle ['ɒrəkl] *n.* 1.【宗】(古希腊等的)神示所 2.【宗】神谕；传神谕者，神使；神的启示 3. 圣言；至理名言 4. 圣贤；哲人 5. 可靠指示器 6. [the ~ s]基督教《圣经》

oracular [ɒ'rækjulə] *adj.* 1. 神谕的；像神谕的 2. 哲人的；大智的；玄妙深奥的；隐晦的

oral ['ɔːrəl] *adj.* 1. 口头的；口述的 2. 口的；口区的 3.【动】口的，口侧的 4.【语】口腔发声的 5.(药等)口服的；口用的 6.【心】口欲的 — *n.* 〈口〉口试 ‖ ~**ly** *adv.*

orange ['ɒrindʒ] *n.* 1. 橙(树)；柑(树)；橘(树) 2.【植】柑橘(尤指甜橙、酸橙) 3. 橙黄色，橘黄色 — *adj.* 1. 柑橘的 2. 橙黄色的，橘黄色的

orangeade [ˌɒrindʒ'eid] *n.* 橙子水，鲜橘水

orangutan [ɔːˌræŋuː'tæn]，**orangoutang** [ɔːˌræŋuː'tæŋ] *n.*【动】猩猩

oration [ɔː'reiʃən] *n.* 1. 演说，演讲 2.【语】引语

orator ['ɒrətə] *n.* 1. 演说者；演说家；雄辩家 2. 在重大场合代表校方发表演说的大学演说官员 3.【律】请愿人，原告

oratorical [ˌɒrə'tɒrikəl] *adj.* 1. 演说的；演说家的 2. 演说术的；雄辩术的 3. 爱用辞藻的；高谈阔论的 ‖ ~**ly** *adv.*

oratorio [ˌɒrə'tɔːriəu] ([复] **oratorios** *n.*【音】通常以基督教《圣经》故事为主题的清唱剧，神剧

oratory ['ɒrətəri] *n.* 1. 演讲术；雄辩术 2. 慷慨激昂(或辞藻华丽)的言辞 3. 小礼拜堂；祈祷室

orb [ɔːb] *n.* 1.〈罕〉环；圆；圆面 2. 球体；天体 3.(行星等的)轨道 4.(星球

的)影响范围 5.〈诗〉眼,眼珠 6.〈象征王位的〉顶上有十字架的〉宝球 7. 集体,整体 — vt. 1. 使成球状(或圆形) 2.〈诗〉包围 — vi. 1.〈古〉沿轨道运行 2. 成球状;呈圆形

orbit ['ɔːbit] n. 1. 眼窝;眼眶;眼睛;眼球(鸟的)眼睑;(昆虫等的)眶 3.〈天体等的)运行)轨道 4. 势力范围;活动范围;生活圈子 — vt. 1. 环绕(天体等)作轨道运行 2. 使进入轨道 — vi. 1.(卫星等)沿轨道运行;环行 2. 进入轨道 ‖ ~al adj. 轨道的;(眼)眶的

orchard ['ɔːtʃəd] n. 1. 果园 2. 果树林 3.〈美俚〉棒球场

orchestra ['ɔːkistrə] n. 1. 管弦乐队;管弦乐队的乐器组 2.(古希腊剧场舞台前的)半圆形台面或场地 3.(古罗马剧场舞台前的)半圆形贵宾席 4.(剧场的)正厅前座 ‖ ~l [ɔː'kestrəl] adj. 1. 管弦乐队的;供管弦乐队演奏的 2. 管弦乐队演奏的;有管弦乐队风格的

orchestrate ['ɔːkistreit] vt. 1. 把...谱写成管弦乐曲 2.〈主美〉精心安排;把...协调起来 — vi. 谱管弦乐 ‖ ~r, orchestrator n.

orchid ['ɔːkid] n. 1.〈植〉兰,兰花 2. 淡紫色 3.〈常～s〉勋章,表扬 — adj. 1. 淡紫色的 2. 有兰花的;兰花构成的

ordain [ɔː'dein] vt. 1. 委任(某人)为牧师;授(某人)以圣职 2.(用法律等)规定;命令;注定 3.〈神,命运注定〉命令;下达命令 ‖ ~ment n.

ordeal [ɔː'diːl] n. 1. 苦难经历;折磨;煎熬 2. 神裁法(古条顿族施行的判罪法;例如将嫌疑者的手放于沸水中,受神意主宰,手无损,则定为无罪)

order ['ɔːdə] n. 1. 次序;顺序 2. 有条理;整齐;工作(或健康等)状况 3. 治安;秩序;制度;(会议等的)规程;程序 4.

【军】队形;序列 5. 种类【生】目 6. 阶层;界 7. 勋章;勋位;勋爵士团 8.【~s】牧师职;牧师授职(仪式)9.【常～s】命令 10.【律】法院决议,法院指令 11. 定购;定货(单);定货量;(点)一份菜;(叫)一客饭 12. 汇票,汇单 13. 许可证;授权证明书;参观券;免费入场券 14.【数】阶,级;序,次序 15.【建】柱式,柱型 — vt. 1. 命令;安排;命令;指令 3. 定购 4. 任命(某人)为牧师;授圣职给一 — vi. 1. 发命令;指挥 2. 定货

orderliness ['ɔːdəlinis] n. 1. 整洁;整齐;有条理 2. 有秩序;守纪律

orderly ['ɔːdəli] adj. 1. 整洁的;整齐的;有条理的 2. 有秩序的;守纪律的 3.【军】传达命令的 — n. 1.【军】传令兵;勤务兵;通讯员 2.(尤指医军医院的)护理员;勤杂工 3. 街道清洁工 — adv. 1. 依次地;顺序地 2. 有规则地;适当地 3. 条理地

ordinal ['ɔːdinəl] adj. 1. 依次的,顺序的;~ numbers 【数】序数(如 first, second, twentieth 等)2.【生】"目"的 — n. 1.【数】序数词 2.【O-】(英国国教)授圣职礼书;(天主教)礼拜式书

ordinance ['ɔːdinəns] n. 1. 法令;命令;条例 2.【宗】仪式(尤指圣餐式)3. 习俗;惯例 4. 上帝(或命运)注定的事

ordinary ['ɔːdinəri] adj. 1. 普通的;一般的,平常的;平凡的 2. 差劲的;低等的;不精致的 3.(官员等)常任的;(司法权)直接的 — n. 1.【律】常任法官 2.【史】死囚忏悔牧师;[the O-]管区长,教区长 3. 礼拜式规程书;典籍 4.〈英〉客饭;供应客饭的小旅馆 5.〈美〉[律]遗嘱验证法官 6.(纹章中的)普通图记 ‖ **ordinarily** ['ɔːdinərili, ,ɔːdi'nerili] adv. / **ordinariness** n.

ordination [,ɔːdi'neiʃən] n. 1.【宗】授圣职

(礼) 2. 被授予圣职(的状态) 3. 颁布
法令

ordnance ['ɔːdnəns] n. 1. [总称]大炮 2.
[总称]军械,军用器材 3. [the ～]军械
署

ore [ɔː] n. 矿;矿砂;矿石

oregano [ˌɔri'gɑːnəu] n. 1. [植]牛至 2. 牛
至叶粉(用作调味品)

Oregon ['ɔrigən] n. 俄勒冈 [美国州名]

organ ['ɔːgən] n. 1. 器官 2.〈婉〉阴茎 3.
机构;机关 4. 喉舌;报刊 5. 风琴:管风
琴;簧风琴;手摇风琴;电风琴;口琴

organdie, organdy ['ɔːgəndi] n. [纺]蝉翼
纱,奥甘迪

organic [ɔː'gænik] adj. 1. 器官的 2. 有机
的,有机物的;【化】有机的 3. 有机
的;有组织的;建制的 — n.
有机物 ‖ ～ally adv.

organism ['ɔːgənizəm] n. 1. 生物体,有机
体 2. 微生物 3. 机体,有机组织

organist ['ɔːgənist] n. 风琴演奏者,风琴手

organization [ˌɔːgənai'zeiʃən] n. 1. 组织
(指动作或状态) 2. 体制;编制 3.(政党、
社会、企业等的)组织,机构 4.〈罕〉生
物,有机体 ‖ ～al adj.

organize ['ɔːgənaiz] vt. 1. [常用被动语态]
使有机化;使成有机体 2. 组织(起来) 3.〈美〉
使组成工会 4.(在工厂、企业中)组织工
会 — vi. 1. 形成有机体 2.
组织起来;建立组织工会 ‖
～r n. 1. 组织者 2. 工会组织人 3.
[生]组织导体,组织元

orgasm ['ɔːgæzəm] n. 【生理】性高潮 2.
极度兴奋,(感情等的)爆发

orgiastic [ˌɔːdʒi'æstik] adj. 纵欲的;纵酒
的;狂欢的

orgy ['ɔːdʒi] n. 纵欲;纵酒;狂欢;无节制
行为

orient ['ɔːriənt] n. 1.〈诗〉东方 2. [the O.]
东方;亚洲;远东;[总称](地中海以东
的)东方国家 3. 优质珍珠;珠的光
泽 — adj. 1.〈诗〉东方的 2. 光辉夺目
的;珍贵的 3.〈诗〉(太阳等)升起的;新
生的 — [ˈɔːrient] vt. 1. 使(建筑物等)
朝东;把(教堂)建成圣坛在东 2. 调
整;给……定向(或定位);以……为方向
(或目的);使适应 3. 给……使定向 —
vi. 1. 向东 2. 面对特定方向;适应

oriental [ˌɔːri'entl] adj. 1. [O-]东方的 2.
东方国家的;东方人特有的;远东的 2.
(珍珠等)最优质的;(珍珠等)有特殊光
泽的 — n.[O-]东方人(尤指中国人和
日本人)

orientation [ˌɔːrien'teiʃən] n. 1. 向东 2. 定
位;定向;方针(或态度等)的确定 3.
方向;方位;倾向性 4.(对周围环境与
的)适应;熟悉 5.(鸟等的)归巢能力

orifice ['ɔrifis] n. 孔,口;通气口

origin ['ɔridʒin] n. 1. 起源;由来;起因 2.
出身;血统 3.【数】原点 4.【解】起(端)

original [ə'ridʒənəl] adj. 1. 最初的,最早
的;原始的;原先的 2. 新鲜的;非抄袭
的;有独创性的;有独到见解的 3. 原
版的;原作的 — n. 1.[the ～]原物;
原作;创作作品;原件;原文 2. 原型
(指文艺作品中描绘形象原件或人
物或真事) 3. 有独创性的人 4. 脾气古
怪的人 5.〈古〉来源;起因 ‖ ～ly adv. 1.
就起源而论 2. 起初;原来 3. 独创地;
新颖地

originality [əˌridʒi'næliti] n. 1. 创造力;独
创性;创见;创举 2. 新颖,别致

originate [ə'ridʒineit] vi. 发源;来自;产
生;(车、船等)起乘,起航 — vt. 1. 引
起 2. 创始;发明;创作 ‖ o.rigi'nation n.
/ originator n. 1. 创始人;发明者;创作
者 2. 起源;来源;起因

oriole [ˈɔːriəul; ˈɔːriəl] n. 【鸟】金黄鹂;拟黄鹂

orison [ˈɔrizən] n. [常~s]祈祷

Orlon [ˈɔːlɔn] n. 【纺】奥纶(奥纶纤维;奥纶织物)

ornament [ˈɔːnəmənt] n. 1. 装饰物,装饰品 2. 装饰;修饰 3. 增添光彩的人(或行动)(to) 4. [常~s]礼拜用品(如圣坛、圣杯等) 5. [常~s]【音】装饰音 — [ˈɔːnəment] vt. 装饰;美化;为…增光

ornamental [ˌɔːnəˈmentəl] adj. 装饰的;作装饰用的 — n. 1. 装饰品 2. 观赏植物

ornamentation [ˌɔːnəmenˈteiʃən] n. 1. 装饰;修饰 2. 装饰品 3. 装饰术

ornate [ɔːˈneit] adj. 1. 装饰华丽的;过分装饰的 2. (文体)华美的,绚丽的;矫揉造作的 ‖ ~ly adv. / ~ness n.

ornery [ˈɔːnəri] adj. 〈美方〉1. 脾气坏的;爱争吵的 2. 卑下的;差的 4. 一般的

ornithology [ˌɔːniˈθɔlədʒi] n. 鸟类学 ‖ **ornithological** [ˌɔːniθəˈlɔdʒikəl] adj. / **ornithologist** n.

orotund [ˈɔːroutʌnd] adj. 1. (噪音)洪亮的,圆润的 2. 浮夸的,说得天花乱坠的

orphan [ˈɔːfən] n. 1. 孤儿 2. 失去母兽的小动物 — adj. 1. 无父母的;无父(或母)的;孤儿的 2. (小动物)失去母兽的 3. 无人支持的;被遗弃的 — vt. 使成孤儿

orphanage [ˈɔːfənidʒ] n. 1. 孤儿身份;孤儿状态 2. 孤儿院 3.[罕][总称]孤儿

orris [ˈɔris] n. 1. 【植】鸢尾 2. 鸢尾根

orthodox [ˈɔːθədɔks] adj. 1. 正统的;正宗传统的;习俗的;保守的 2. [O-]【宗】东正教(会)的 — n. 1. 正统信仰;正统观念;正统做法 2. 【宗】正教

orthography [ɔːˈθɔɡrəfi] n. 1. 正字法 2.拼字法 3.【建】正射投影 4.【数】正(交)射影 ‖ **orthographic**(al)[ˌɔːθəˈɡræf-ik(əl)] adj.

orthopaedics [ˌɔːθəˈpiːdiks] n. [用作单]【医】矫形外科,整形外科 ‖ **orthop-(a)edic**(al)/ **orthop(a)edist** n.

-ory suf. [构成形容词] 1. 表示"…性质的","属于…的":preparatory 2. 表示"作…之用的":"主张…的";"产生…的":justificatory 认为正当的 — [构成名词] 1. 表示"…的处所":observatory 2. 表示"作…之用的东西":directory

Os 【化】元素锇(osmium)的符号

Osaka [əuˈsɑːkə; ɔːˈsɑːkə] n. 大阪[日本本州西部西南岸港市]

Oscar [ˈɔskə] n. 1. 奥斯卡(男子名) 2.〈美〉(电影界)奥斯卡金像(奖);(口 奖 3. [o-]〈澳〉钱;现款

oscillate [ˈɔsileit] vi. 1. 摆动;【物】振荡;振动 2. 摆动;犹豫 3.【无】发杂音 4.(银行利率等)上下波动 — vt. 1. 使摆动;使动摇;使波动 2.【物】使振荡;使振动;动摇的人;振荡器 ‖ **oscil'lation** n. / **oscillator** n. 摆动物;动摇的人;振荡器

osculate [ˈɔskjuleit] 〈谑〉 vt. 吻 — vi. 接吻 ‖ **oscu'lation** n. / **osculatory** [ˈɔskjulətəri] adj.

osier [ˈəuʒə, ˈeizə] n. 1.【植】柳;柳条;柳枝

Oslo [ˈɔzləu] n. 奥斯陆[挪威首都]

osmium [ˈɔzmiəm] n. 【化】锇

osmosis [ɔzˈməusis] n. ([复] **osmoses** [ɔzˈməusiːz]) n. 渗透;渗透作用

osprey [ˈɔspri, ˈɔsprei] n. 1.【动】鹗 2. (装饰女帽用的)鸟羽

osseous [ˈɔsiəs] adj. 【解】骨的;骨状的;由骨构成的;多骨的 ‖ ~ly adv.

ossify ['ɔsifai] *vi. & vt.* **1.** (使)骨化 **2.** (使)僵化，(使)墨守成规，(使)变得极端保守 ‖ **ossification** [ˌɔsifiˈkeiʃən] *n.*

ostensible [ɔsˈtensibl] *adj.* **1.** 可公开的；显然的 **2.** 外表的，表面的；假装的，诡称的 ‖ **ostensibly** *adv.*

ostentation [ˌɔstenˈteiʃən] *n.* 夸示；卖弄；炫耀；风头主义

ostentatious [ˌɔstenˈteiʃəs] *adj.* 夸示的；卖弄的；虚饰的；炫耀的

osteopathy [ˌɔstiˈɔpəθi] *n.* 【医】疗骨术，整骨术；骨病 ‖ **osteopath** ['ɔstiəpæθ] *n.* 整骨医生 / **osteopathic** [ˌɔstiəˈpæθik] *adj.*

ostracize ['ɔstrəsaiz] *vt.* **1.** 放逐，把……流放 **2.** 排斥 ‖ **ostracism** ['ɔstrəsizəm] *n.* 放逐，流放；排斥

ostrich ['ɔstritʃ] *n.* **1.** 鸵鸟；美洲鸵 **2.** 鸵鸟般的人，回避现实的人，自以为不正视危险便可避开危险的人

other ['ʌðə] *adj.* **1.** 另外的，其他的 **2.** (常the ~)(两个中)另一个的；其余的 **3.** 不久前的；以前的 **4.** 第二的；隔一个的 **5.** 更多的；额外的 **6.** 不同的一 *pron.* **1.** (~s)另外的人(或物)，其他的人(或物) **2.** [the ~](两个中的)另一个人(或物)；[the ~s]其余的人(或物) **3.** 不同者；对立物一 *adv.* 另外地，不同地

otherwise ['ʌðəwaiz] *adv.* **1.** 另外，别样 **2.** 在其他方面 **3.** 要不然；否则一 *adj.* **1.** 另外的；不那样的 **2.** 其他方面的

otiose ['əuʃiəus] *adj.* **1.** 倦怠的；懒惰的 **2.** 不活泼的，不起作用的 **3.** 无价值的，微不足道的；无益的，无效的 **3.** 无用的，多余的 ‖ **~ly** *adv.* / **~ness** *n.*

Ottawa ['ɔtəwə] 渥太华[加拿大首都]

otter ['ɔtə] ([复]otter(s)) *n.* **1.** 【动】水獭；加拿大水獭；海獭 **2.** 水獭毛皮

ottoman ['ɔtəmən] *n.* 软垫(搁脚)凳

Ouagadougou [ˌwɑːgəˈduːguː] *n.* 瓦加杜古[布基纳法索首都]

ouch [autʃ] *int.* **1.** [突然受痛时的叫声]哎哟！ **2.** [表示不满]哎！一 *n.* 〈美俚〉伤痛

ought [ɔːt] *v. aux.* [无时态和人称变化，后接动词不定式] **1.** [表示责任、合适性、可能性等]应当，应该；总应该 **2.** [后接动词不定式的完成式]早应该，本应，本当一一 **3.** 义务；责任

ought[2] [ɔːt] *n.* = aught

oughtn't [ɔːtnt] = ought not

ounce [auns] *n.* **1.** 盎司(常衡 = 1/16 磅；金衡及药衡 = 1/12 磅；略作 oz.) **2.** 少量 **3.** 液盎司

our ['auə] *pron.* [we 的所有格] **1.** 我们的 **2.** (报刊编者等用语)本报(或本刊、本庭)的 **3.** (帝王在正式场合中用以代替 my)朕的，寡人的 **4.** (指与交谈双方都有关的人)咱们的

ours ['auəz] *pron.* [物主代词]我们的；属于我们的

ourselves [ˌauəˈselvz] *pron.* **1.** [反身代词]我们自己 **2.** [用以加强语气]我们亲自，我们本人 **3.** [用于 be, become, feel 等之后]我们的正常情况(指健康，情绪等)

-ous *suf.* [构成形容词] **1.** 表示"具有……的"；"多……的"；"有……特性的"：dangerous, poisonous 【化】表示"亚……的"：ferrous

oust [aust] *vt.* **1.** 驱逐，把……撤职；罢黜 **2.** 【律】剥夺(of) **3.** 取代

ouster ['austə] *n.* **1.** 驱逐，撤职，罢黜 **2.** 【律】(尤指非法的)剥夺，驱逐 **3.** 剥夺者；驱逐者；取代者

out [aut] *adv.* **1.** 出；在外；向外 **2.** 出声

地 3. 出现, 显露; 问世 4. 殆尽; 至灭绝 5. 熄灭地, 熄灭 6. 从头至尾地; 彻底地 7. 有差错地; 不一致地 8. 脱漏地 9. 一份一份地; 以分类形式 10. 处于在野状态 11. 处于缺席状态; 在野党中 12. 〈棒球运动中〉出局 13.〈无线电通话用语〉"报文完, 不必回话" ― *adj.* 1. 外面的; 往外去的; 外侧的 2. 外出的; 下台的 3. 特大的 4.〈棒球等运动中〉出局的 5.〈美口〉不时髦的, 不流行的 6.〈美俚〉不谙内情的; 古板的 7.〈美俚〉最新式的 8.〈美俚〉公开宣称同性恋的 ― *n.* 1. 外面, 外部 2. 外出; 旅游 3. 在野党人; [~s] 在野党人士 4.〈英〉体面 5. 推脱之词; 脱身之计; 出路 6.〈货品等的〉缺点; 〈境遇的〉不利处 7.〈英〉[~s] 付出的钱; 税款 8.【印】〈字句的〉漏排 9. 脱销货 10.〈棒球赛等的〉界外球 ― *vt.* 1. 赶出, 驱逐 2.〈俚〉击倒; 击昏 3.〈在板球赛等中〉使出局 ― *vi.* 外出; 体面 5. 〈俚〉暴露; 成为人所共知 3. 拿出; 说出〈*with*〉― *prep.* 1. 通过...而出 2. 沿着....而去 ‖ ~-of-'door *adj.* 过时的; 废弃的 /'~-of-'door *adj.* 室外的, 露天的 /'~-of-'doors *adj.* = ~-of-door *adv.* 在室外, 在露天 *n.* [the] 室外; 露天

out- *pref.* 1.〈构成动词、名词、形容词〉表示"出","向外","在外","远"; *out*spread, *out*building, *out*lying, *out*spoken, *out*post 2. 〈构成动词〉表示 *out*smart 3. 〈加在具有某一显著特点的人名前构成动词〉表示"在某一特征上超过" *out*-Hitler 比...更奇特得

out-and-out ['autənd'aut] *adj.* 1. 完全的, 不折不扣的, 彻头彻尾的 2. 不加掩饰的, 公开的

outboard ['autbɔd] *adj.* 1. 舷外的, 在船外的 2.〈飞机〉外侧的 2. 装有舷外发动

机的 ― *adv.* 向舷外; 在〈飞机〉紧靠翼尖处 ‖ ~ motor 舷外发动机, 尾挂发动机

outbound ['autbaund] *adj.* 开往外地的; 开往外国的; 离港的

outbreak ['autbreik] *n.* 1.〈战争、火山、感情等的〉爆发;〈瘟疫、虫害等的〉突然发生; 暴乱

outbuilding ['aut,bildiŋ] *n.*【建】外屋; 附属房屋

outburst ['autbɜst] *n.* 1.〈感情等的〉爆发, 迸发 2.〈火山等的〉喷发 3. 暴动

outcast ['autkɑst] *adj.* 被遗弃的; 被放逐的; 无家可归的; 无人可吐的 ― *n.* 被遗弃者; 被逐出者; 流浪者 2.〈英方〉争吵

outclass ['aut'klɑs] *vt.* 超过; 比...高一档; 轻易击败

outcome ['autkʌm] *n.* 1. 结果; 后果; 结局 2. 出口; 出路

outcrop ['autkrɔp] *n.* 1.【地】露头; 外露 ― *vi.* 露出地表 2.〈地〉出现; 发生; 爆发

outcry ['autkrai] *n.* 1. 喊叫; 吆喝; 呐喊 2. 强烈抗议 (或反对)〈*against*〉; 强烈要求〈*for*〉3. 拍卖, 叫卖 ― *vt.* [aut'krai] *vt.* 喊叫〈*at*〉―响; 叫声压倒

outdate ['aut'deit] *vt.* 使过时; 把...废弃 ‖ ~d *adj.* 过时的; 已废弃的

outdid ['aut'did] outdo 的过去式

outdistance ['aut'distəns] *vt.* 跑在...的前面, 把...抛在后面; 大大超越

outdo [aut'du] (outdid [aut'did], outdone [aut'dʌn]) *vt.* 1. 胜过, 超过 2. 战胜

outdone [aut'dʌn] outdo 的过去分词 ― *adj.*〈美方〉激怒的; 恼火的

outdoor ['autdɔ] *adj.* 户外的, 室外的; 露天的; 野外的 ‖ ~ relief〈英〉〈教济院的〉院外救济 (指对不住在救济院的贫

民的救济)

outdoors [ˈautˈdɔːz] *adv.* 在户外;在野外 — *adj.* = outdoor — [复] *n.* [the ~] [用作单]户外,野外;野外活动

outer [ˈautə] *adj.* 1. 外部的,外面的;外侧的 2. 远离中心的 3. 客观外界的;物质的 — *n.* (靶子的)外圈;外圈命中 ‖ ~most *adj.* 最外面的;离中心最远的 ~ city〈美〉郊区

outfield [ˈautfiːld] *n.* 1. [体](棒球、板球场等的)外场;[总称]外场手 2. 离农舍较远的田地 ‖ ~er *n.* [体](棒球队的)外场手

outfight [autˈfait] (outfought [autˈfɔːt]) *vt.* 战胜,击败

outfit [ˈautfit] *n.* 1. 装备(指动作) 2. 全套工具(或全部用品) 3. 全套装备 3.(精神)素质 4.(特定场合穿的)全套服装 5.(班、组、队等的)单位(如连队);(某人手下的)全班人马 (outfitted; outfitting) *vt.* 装备,配备 — *vi.* 得到装备 ‖ **outfitter** *n.* 1.(男式)服装商店 2. 体育(或旅游、野营等)用品商店 3.[船]机器安装工

outflank [autˈflæŋk] *vt.* 1. 包抄;迂回绕过 2. 智胜

outgo [autˈgəu] (outwent[autˈwent], outgone [autˈgɔn]) *vt.* 走得比…远(或快);胜过,优于 — [ˈautgəu] *n.* 1. 外出;发支 2. 支出;消耗 3. 出口

outgoing [ˈautgəuiŋ] *adj.* 1. 往外去的;离去的 2. 即将离职的;即将终结业的 3. 对人友好的;开朗的 — *n.* 1. 外出,离去 2.[~s] 支出;开销

outgone [autˈgɔn] outgo 的过去分词

outgrow [autˈgrəu] (outgrew [autˈgruː], outgrown[autˈgrəun]) *vt.* 1. 生长速度超过,长得比…快 2. 长大(或发展)得使…不再适用 3. 成长(或发展)得不再

outgrowth [ˈautgrəuθ] *n.* 1. 长出 2. 长出物;分枝;赘疣 3. 副产品;结果

outhouse [ˈauthaus] *n.* 1. 外屋,附属建筑,副屋 2.〈美〉户外厕所

outing [ˈautiŋ] *n.* 1. 出游;户外活动;远足 2. 体育比赛;划船练习;跑马练习 — *adj.* 供户外活动用的

outlandish [autˈlændiʃ] *adj.* 1. 外国模样的,外国腔的 2. 希奇古怪的;奇特的 3. 偏僻的;边远的

outlast [autˈlɑːst] *vt.* 比…持久;比…经久;比…活得长;从…中逃脱

outlaw [ˈautlɔː] *n.* 1. 被剥夺公民权者;被放逐者 2. 被禁的组织 3. 歹徒;逃犯;亡命之徒 4. 难驯服(或未驯服)的动物(如马) — *vt.* 1. 剥夺(某人)的公民权;将(某人)放逐 2. 宣布…在法律上失效;宣告…为不合法 ‖ ~ry *n.* 1.[律]被剥夺法律保护(或公民权)宣布非法,非法化

outlay [autˈlei] (outlaid [autˈleid]) *vt.* 花(钱),花费 — [ˈautlei] *n.* 花费;支出;费用

outlet [ˈautlet] *n.* 1.(河流等的)出口路;通风口(或孔) 2. 发泄(感情或精力等)的方法(或机会) 3. 销路;商店 4.[电]电源插座;出线盒

outline [ˈautlain] *n.* 1. 轮廓,外廓 2. 略图;素描 3. 大纲;提纲;草案;概要;[~s] 要点;主要原则 4. 隔夜设下的钓鱼线 — *vt.* 1. 画出…的轮廓;打…的草图 2. 概括;提出…的纲要;略述

outlive [autˈliv] *vt.* 1. 比…死时尚未死,比(某人)活得长;比(某物)经久;渡过(风暴、危机等)而健在 2. 老到超过…的程度

outlook [ˈautluk] *n.* 1. 瞭望处;望楼;注视;瞭望 2. 景色;风光 3. 观点,看法

4. 展望；前景

outlying ['aʊt,laɪɪŋ] *adj*. 1. 远离中心（或主体）的 2. 无关的；题外的

outmoded [aʊt'məʊdɪd] *adj*. 过时的；老式的；废弃的

outmost ['aʊtməʊst] *adj*. 最外面的；离中心最远的

outnumber [aʊt'nʌmbə] *vt*. 比...多，在数量上超过

outpatient ['aʊt,peɪʃənt] *n*. 门诊病人

outplay [aʊt'pleɪ] *vt*. （在球赛等中）打得比...好，击败

outpost ['aʊtpəʊst] *n*. 1.【军】前哨；前哨基地；警戒部队 2. 边远居民点 3. 国境

output ['aʊtpʊt] *n*. 1. 产量 2. 产品；作品 3.【电】输出功率；输出油量 4.【医】排出量；排出物 5.【计】输出；输出设备

outrage ['aʊtreɪdʒ] *n*. 1. 暴行 2. 凌辱；冒犯 3. 严重的违法（或败坏道德）行为 4.（因暴行而引起的）义愤，痛恨 — *vt*. 1. 对...施暴行；伤害；违反 2. 激起...的义愤 3. 强奸

outrageous [aʊt'reɪdʒəs] *adj*. 1. 蛮横的，残暴的 2. 无耻的；使人憎厌的；令人不能容忍的 3. 毫无节制的；惊人的 4. 极好的

outran [aʊt'ræn] outrun 的过去式

outright ['aʊtraɪt] *adj*. 1. 直率的，无保留的；公开的 2. 彻底的；全部的 — [aʊt'raɪt] *adv*. 1. 直率地；无保留地；公然 2. 彻底地；全部地 3. 立即，当场

outrun [aʊt'rʌn] (outran [aʊt'ræn], outrun; outrunning) *vt*. 1. 比...跑得更快（或更远，更好）超过；胜过 2. 从...逃脱 3. 超出...所要做的；比...要做更多选择

outsell [aʊt'sel] (outsold [aʊt'səʊld]) *vt*. 1. 比（别的货品）更畅销 2. 比（别的推销员）更能推销 3.〈古〉售价比...高

outset ['aʊtset] *n*. 开端，开始

outshine [aʊt'ʃaɪn] (outshone [aʊt'ʃɒn]) *vt*. 1. 比...更亮，比...更灿烂；发光比...更久 2. 胜过，优于；使相形见绌 — *vi*. 发光

outside [aʊt'saɪd, 'aʊtsaɪd] *n*. 1. 外部，外面；外侧 2. 外表，外观 3. 外界 4.（英国旧时四马大车等车外座位的）乘客 5.[~s] 一令纸最外层的上下两张 — *adj*. 1. 外部的，外面的；表面的；外侧的 2. 外界的 3.（英国旧时四马大车等）顶上的 4. 最大限度的 5.（美俚）私生的 — *adv*. 1. 向外面；在外面；向室外 2. 在室外 3. 向海上；在海上；在露天 4. 外表上，外观上 5.[体] 出线，出界 5. 在车里坐位 — prep. 1. 向...外；在...外面 2. 超出...（的范围）3.〈口〉除了

outsider [aʊt'saɪdə] *n*. 1. 外人，局外人；非会员 2. 外行，门外汉 3.（与特定社会群体不能融洽相处的）人 4.（比赛中）不大可能获胜的选手（或赛马等）

outsize ['aʊtsaɪz] *n*. 1. 超过标准的尺寸，超大号 2. 超大号的东西（尤指服装）；特别庞大的人；特大发展 — *adj*. 超大型的；极大的；太大的

outskirt ['aʊtskɜːt] *n*. [常~s] 郊区；远离中心的部分，外围，边缘

outsmart [aʊt'smɑːt] *vt*.〈口〉比...更精明；智胜

outsold [aʊt'səʊld] outsell 的过去式和过去分词

outspoken [aʊt'spəʊkən] *adj*. 直言的；坦率的；毫无保留的 ‖ ~**ly** *adv*. / ~**ness** *n*.

outspread [aʊt'spred] (outspread) *vt. & vi*. (使) 伸开，（使）展开；（使）展开 — *n*. 伸开，展开；辽阔的区域

outstanding [aʊt'stændɪŋ] *adj*. 1. 突出的 2. 杰出的；显著的 3. 未完成的；未解

决的;未付款的 **4.**(股票、公债等)已发行的,在外的 — *n.* [~s] 未偿贷款;未清账款 ‖ ~**ly** *adv.* / ~**ness** *n.*

outstay [aut'stei] *vt.* **1.** 比...逗留得久久;逗留得超过...的时间 **2.** 在耐力上超过

outstretch [aut'stretʃ] *vt.* **1.** 伸出;展开 **2.** 伸展得超过...的范围 **3.** 扩大;发展

outstrip [aut'strip] (outstripped; outstripping) *vt.* **1.** 越过 **2.** 胜过;超过

outward ['autwəd] *adj.* **1.** 外面的;外表的 **2.** 明显的;可见的;公开的 **3.** 向外的;外出的 **4.** 肉体的;外界的 — *adv.* 向外;(船等)往海外去 — *n.* **1.** 外表;外界;外部 **2.** [~s] 外在事物;周围世界 ‖ ~**ly** *adv.* **1.** 向外 **2.** 外表上,在外

outwards ['autwədz] *adv.* = outward

outwear [aut'wɛə] (outwore [aut'wɔː], outworn [aut'wɔːn]) *vt.* **1.** 穿坏;用旧;耗尽(力气等) **2.** 比...经久(或耐用) **3.** 熬过;经受住 **4.** 长大得穿不下(衣服)

outweigh [aut'wei] *vt.* **1.** 在重量上超过 **2.** 在价值(或重要性、影响等)上超过

outwent [aut'went] outgo 的过去式

outwit [aut'wit] (outwitted; outwitting) *vt.* 智胜;骗过;使上当

outwore [aut'wɔː] outwear 的过去式

outworn [aut'wɔːn] outwear 的过去分词

ova ['əuvə] ovum 的复数

oval ['əuvəl] *adj.* 卵形的;椭圆形的 — *n.* **1.** 卵形(物);椭圆形(物) **2.** 椭圆形跑道 **3.**(美口)橄榄球

ovary ['əuvəri] *n.* **1.** [解] 卵巢 **2.** [植] 子房 **3.**(肉质果的)核心;果核 ‖ **ovarian** [əu'vɛəriən] *adj.*

ovation [əu'veiʃən] *n.* **1.**(古罗马)小凯旋式(次于凯旋式的一种欢迎仪式) **2.** 热烈鼓掌;欢呼;热烈欢迎

oven ['ʌvn] *n.* 炉;灶;烘箱;窑;火化室

over ['əuvə] *prep.* **1.** 在...上方;在...上面 **2.**[表示地位、职权、势力等]高于...;在...之上 **3.**[表示数目、程度]多于...;以上,超过 **4.** 越过;从...边缘向下下 **5.** 在(街道、边界等)的那一边 **6.**[表示时间]在...期间;直到...;过后 **7.** 遍及;从...的开头至结束 **8.** 从事...的时候 **9.** 在...方面;关于;由于 **10.** 通过...的媒介(或手段);通过 — *adv.* **1.** 翻倒;翻转过来 **2.** 从一边到另一边 **3.**(越)过;(越)出 **4.** 在另一处,在那边 **5.** 从头至尾地;全部地;通盘地 **6.** 剩下来;多一些 **7.** 过分地;太多 **8.** 结束;完了 **9.** 再 **10.**(无线电通话用语)"报文完,请回复。" — *adj.* **1.** 上面的;上级的 **2.** 外面的 **3.** 过分的 — *vt.* 跳过;越过 — *n.* **1.** 飘砾(或多余)的东西 **2.**[军]远弹(超过目标落下或爆炸的射弹)

overage ['əuvəridʒ] *n.* **1.**[商] 商品过剩;超过部分,超额 **2.** 账外财产(或物资);销售溢余款 — ['əuvər'eidʒ] *adj.* 超龄的;老朽的

overall ['əuvərɔːl] *n.* **1.**[~s] 工装裤 **2.**(英)[~s] 紧身制服裤 **3.**(英)外衣,罩衫 — *adj.* **1.** 包括一切的;全面的;综合的 **2.** 从头至尾的;终点的 — *adv.* **1.** 大体上;总的说来 **2.** 从头到尾;从船头到船尾

overate ['əuvər'et] overeat 的过去式

overawe [,əuvər'ɔː] *vt.* 吓服,吓倒,吓住

overbearing [,əuvə'bɛəriŋ] *adj.* **1.** 傲慢的;专横的 **2.** 压倒一切的;支配的

overboard ['əuvəbɔːd] *adv.* 向船外;落水

overcame [,əuvə'keim] overcome 的过去式

overcast ['əuvəkɑːst] *n.* **1.** 遮敝物(指云、雾等) **2.**[气]阴,阴天 **3.** 沮丧;忧郁 **4.**[矿]风桥 — *adj.* **1.**(被云、雾等)遮敝

的 2. 多云的；阴的 3. 沮丧的；忧郁的 4. 包边缝纫的，锁边的 — [ˌtəuəˈevəst] (overcast) vt. 1. 遮蔽，使阴 2. 使阴 3. 包(边)缝纫，拷(边)；锁(边) — vi. 1. 变多云；变阴 2. 变得沮丧(或忧郁)

overcharge [ˌəuvəˈtʃɑːdʒ;əuvər-] vt. 1. 对...要价(或收费)太高；收(费)太多 2. 使过量装填；使充电过度 3. 渲染，夸张 — vi. 要价太高 — n. 1. 过高的要价 2. 超载 3. 过量的装填

overcoat [ˈəuvəkəut] n. 1. 外套，大衣 2. 保护层，护膜

overcome[ˌəuvəˈkʌm] (overcame[ˌəuvəˈkeim], overcome) vt. 1. 战胜；征服；制伏；胜过；克服 2.[常用被动语态]压倒 — vi. 取胜

overconfident [ˌəuvəˈkɔnfidənt] adj. 过分相信的；过于自信的，自负的

overcrowd [ˌəuvəˈkraud] vt. 使过度拥挤；把...塞得过满

overdo [ˌəuvəˈduː] (overdid[ˌəuvəˈdid], overdone[ˌəuvəˈdʌn]) vt. 1. 把...做得过头，使用过度；对...作过火表演 2.[常用被动语态]把...煮得太久(或太熟) 3. 使过于劳累；耗尽 — vi. 做得过头，演得过火

overdose [ˈəuvədəus] n. (药物等的)过量用量 — [ˌəuvəˈdəus] vt. 使服药过量；过量用(药物等) 2. 使过分沉湎

overdraw [ˌəuvəˈdrɔː] (overdrew[ˌəuvəˈdruː], overdrawn[ˌəuvəˈdrɔːn]) vt. 1. 透支(银行账户) 2. 过分描述，夸张 3. 把(弓等)拉得过紧 — vi. 1. 透支 2. 夸张

overdue [ˈəuvəˈdjuː] adj. 1. 过期(未付)的 2. 迟误的；过度的 4. 期待已久的；早该来到的；早就成熟的

overeat [ˌəuvəˈiːt] (overate [ˌəuvəˈet], overeaten[ˌəuvəˈiːtn]) vi. 使吃得过多 — vi. 吃得过多

overestimate [ˌəuvəˈestimeit] vt. 过高估计；过高评价 — [ˌəuvəˈestimit] n. 过高的估计；过高的评价

overflight [ˈəuvəflait] n.(飞机的)飞越上空

overflow [ˌəuvəˈfləu] vt. 使涨满；使泛滥 — vi. 1. 泛滥；满(或多)得溢出 2. 充满；洋溢(with) — [ˈəuvəfləu] n. 1. 泛滥；溢流 2. 充溢；过剩；超出额；溢出物 3. 溢流管；溢流口；溢流受器

overfulfil(l) [ˌəuvəfulˈfil] (overfulfilled；overfulfilling) vt. 超额完成(计划、指标等)

overgrow[ˌəuvəˈgrəu] (overgrew[ˌəuvəˈgruː], overgrown[ˌəuvəˈgrəun]) vt. 1.[常用被动语态]长满在...上；在...上丛生 2. 长得越过...的范围 — vi. 1. 长得过大(或过快) 2. 长满(with)

overgrown[ˌəuvəˈgrəun] overgrow 的过去分词 — adj. 1. 簇叶丛生的 2. 长得过大的；畸形发展的

overhand [ˈəuvəhænd] adj. 1.【体】(排球、网球等中)高手的，上手的，超手的；肩上的(游泳划水)大拨手的 2. 手掌朝下的 3.(缝纫)平式缝接的 — adv. 1.【体】用上手；用上手，肩上；肩上地 2.手掌朝下地 3. 平式缝接地 — n.(网球的)高手击球；(排球的)上手球；(游泳的)大拨手划水，爬泳

overhang [ˌəuvəˈhæŋ] (overhung[ˌəuvəˈhʌŋ]) vt. 1. 悬于...之上；突出于...之上 2. 用悬挂物(如吊帘等)装饰 3.(危险、灾难等)逼近；威胁 — vt. 1. 伸出；突出于 — [ˈəuvəhæŋ] n. 1. 悬垂物；伸出物；悬垂(或突出)部分；伸出量 2.【船】(水线以上的)突出船首(或船尾) 3.【建】(屋顶、房屋等)悬挑部分 4.【空】(双翼机的)横翼量

overhaul [ˌəuvəˈhɔːl] vt. 1. 彻底检修，大修；全面检查 2. 彻底革新(或改革)

全面修订 3. 赶上;道上 4. 放松(船的缆绳)— ['əuvəhɔ:l] n. 1. 大修;全面检查 2. 彻底革新(或改革);全面修订

overhead ['əuvəhed] *adj.* 1. 在头顶上的,上面的;高架的 2. 【经】(费用)经常的,管理的 — n. 1.[常～s]经常费,管理费 2. 天花板;(船舱的)顶板 3. (网球赛等中的)过顶扣球 4. 吊灯 — ['əuvə'hed] *adv.* 1. 在头顶上;在上面;在楼上;在天空 2. 深深地

overhear ['əuvə'hiə](overheard ['əuvə'hə:d]) *vt. & vi.* 1. 无意中听到;偶然听到 2. 偷听到

overheat ['əuvə'hi:t] *vt.* 1. 使过热 2. 使十分激动 — *vi.* 变得过热

overhung ['əuvə'hʌŋ]overhang 的过去式和过去分词

overjoy [əuvə'dʒɔi] *vt.* 使狂喜;使非常高兴

overjoyed [əuvə'dʒɔid] *adj.* 非常高兴的,大喜的

overkill [əuvə'kil] *vt.* 1. 超量毁伤— ['əuvəkil] *n.* 1. 超量毁伤;(尤指核武器的)超量毁伤力 2. 过分;过分行为,过分的反应

overlaid [əuvə'leid] overlay 的过去式和过去分词

overland ['əuvəlænd] *adj.* 经由陆路的;横越大陆的 — *vt. & vi.* 转场放牧(牲口) — ['əuvə'lænd] *adv.* 经由陆路;横越大陆地

overlap [əuvə'læp] (overlapped; overlapping) *vt.* 1. 与...部分重叠 2. 与...部分一致;与...部分巧合 — *vi.* 交搭、叠盖 2. 部分一致;部分巧合 — ['əuvə'læp] *n.* 1. 交搭,重叠 2. 交搭处,重叠部 3.【地】超覆

overlay [əuvə'lei] (overlaid ['əuvə'leid]) *vt.* 1. 在...上铺(或盖、涂)(*with*) 2. 遮

掩;遮暗 3. 把(睡在身旁的婴儿或幼仔)覆闷致死 4. 使负担过重 5.【印】加上衬子 — ['əuvəlei] *n.* 1. 覆盖物;遮盖层 2.【印】上衬;上垫 3.(苏格兰)领带;床罩;小台布

overload [əuvə'ləud] *vt.* 1. 使超载,使过载 2. 装填...过满 3. 使负担过重 — ['əuvələud] *n.* 超载;过负荷;过满装填;过重负担

overlook [əuvə'luk] *vt.* 1. 眺望;俯瞰 2. 耸出;检查;监督 4. 看漏;忽略 5. 放任;宽容 6. 看得...心懐意乱;用眼光迷住 — ['əuvəluk] *n.* 1. 可眺望四周的高地 2. 俯瞰中的景色 3. 看漏

overlord ['əuvələ:d] *n.* 1. 最高领主;最高君主 2. 最高统治者;霸主;霸王;巨头

overly ['əuvəli] *adv.* 过度地

overnight [əuvə'nait] *adv.* 1. 在前一天晚上 2. 一夜(间);突然,一下子 — ['əuvənait] *adj.* 1. 前一天晚上的 2. 一夜(间)的;突然出现的 3. 持续(或使用)一夜的;只供一夜使用的

overpass [əuvə'pɑ:s] *vt.* 1. 通过;越过;历过 2. 超出;超过 3. 忽视;不注意 4. 克服(困难等)— ['əuvəpɑ:s] *n.* 1.(主要)上跨立体交叉;上跨路;跨线桥,天桥,立桥

overpower [əuvə'pauə] *vt.* 1. 制服;压倒 2. 给...安装功率过大的发动机

overproduction [əuvəprə'dʌkʃən] *n.* 生产过剩

overran [əuvə'ræn] overrun 的过去式

overrate [əuvə'reit] *vt.* 对...估计(或估价)过高

overreach [əuvə'ri:tʃ] *vt.* 智胜;[~ oneself]手伸得太长;因好高骛远而失败;弄巧成拙

overreact [əuvəri'ækt] *vi.* 反应过火(*to*) ‖ ~**ion** *n.*

override [,əuvə'raid] (overrode [,əuvə'rəud], overridden[,əuvə'ridn]) vt. 1. 奔越过 2. 践踏过 3. 制服, 压倒; 把...搁在一边; 使无效 4. 把(马等)骑得过累; 对...驱使过度 5. 使(骨折端、浮冰等)重叠 6. 根据代销额给(经理人)以佣金 — n. 1. 酬金, 佣金 2. 撤销, 推翻

overripe [,əuvə'raip] adj. 1. 过于成熟的, 熟到快要烂的 2. 衰落的; 颓废的; 失去活力的

overrule [,əuvə'ru:l] vt. 1. 否决; 驳回; 宣布...无效 2. 强使...变更 3. 统治; 支配; 对...施加影响

overrun [,əuvə'rʌn] (overran [,əuvə'ræn], overrun; overrunning) vt. 1. 溢出(杂草等)蔓延于 2. (虫害等)侵扰 3. (侵略军等)横行于; 窜犯; 蹂躏 4. (思想、风尚等)流行于 5. 超越(期限、范围等)6. (古)比...跑得快 6. 跑得过度 7. 【印】超量印刷(书刊等); 加印; 移行接排 (排版) — vi. 1. 溢出; 泛滥 2. 超过限度 3.【机】超限运动 — n. 1. 泛滥; 横行 2. 风行一时 3. 超越限度; 超出量 4.(机场跑道的)保险道

oversaw [,əuvə'sɔ:] oversee 的过去式

oversea(s) [,əuvə'si:(z)] adv. 在(或向)海外; 在(或向)国外 — adj. 1.(向或来自外国的)2.(在海外的); (在)国外的

oversee [,əuvə'si:] (oversaw [,əuvə'sɔ:], overseen [,əuvə'si:n]) vt. 1. 俯瞰; 瞭望 2. 监督; 监视 3. 检查; 检查; 偷看一无意中看到 ‖ ~ r n. 1. 监工; 监督人 2. 【英史】(属于济贫院的)教会执事济贫助理

overshadow [,əuvə'ʃædəu] vt. 1. 给...蒙上阴影; 遮暗; 使暗淡; 使模糊 2. 夺去...的光彩; 使相形见绌

overshoe [,əuvə'ʃu:] n.(套穿在皮鞋外面以防湿或御寒的)套鞋; 罩靴

oversight [,əuvə'sait] n. 1. 失察; 疏忽出错; 忽略 2. 监督; 看管; 细心照料

oversimplify [,əuvə'simplifai] vt. & vi.(使)过分简单化(以致引起误会、歪曲等)

oversize [,əuvə'saiz] adj. 1. 太大的 2. 比普通尺码大的 — [,əuvə'saiz] n. 1. 特大型 2. 过大的东西; 超大型物

oversleep [,əuvə'sli:p] (overslept [,əuvə'slept]) vi. 睡过(某时刻); 使(自己)睡过头 — vi. 睡过头; 睡过度

overspread [,əuvə'spred] (overspread) vt. 铺盖, 布满 — vi. 蔓布

overstate [,əuvə'steit] vt. 把...讲得过分; 过分强调; 夸大 ‖ ~ ment n.

overstep [,əuvə'step] (overstepped; overstepping) vt. 逾越; 违犯

overstuff [,əuvə'stʌf] vt. 1. 装填...过度 2. 给(沙发、椅子等)加厚填料 ‖ ~ ed adj. 垫得又软又厚的

oversupply [,əuvəsə'plai] n. 过多的供应(品)— [,əuvəsə'plai] vt. 过多供应

overt [əu'və:t] adj. 公开的; 明显的 ‖ ~ ly adv. / ~ ness n.

overtake [,əuvə'teik] (overtook [,əuvə'tuk], overtaken [,əuvə'teikən]) vt. 1. 追上; 赶上; 超过 2. 突然侵袭; 压倒; 代替

overthrow [,əuvə'θrəu] overthrew [,əuvə'θru:], overthrown [,əuvə'θrəun]) vt. 1. 推翻; 打倒; 废除; 背弃 2.(棒球赛等中)把球拋出(全)— vt. 把球拋得过远 — [,əuvə'θrəu] n. 1. 推翻; 打倒; 终止; 废弃 2.(棒球赛等中)拋得过远的球

overtime [,əuvə'taim] n. 1. 超过时间; 加班; 加班时间 2.(体育比赛中赛成平局后的)决胜期 3. 加班费 — adj. 超过规定时间的, 超时的; 加班的 — adv.

在规定(工作)时间之外 — ['əuvə'taim]
vt. 使超过时间

overtone ['əuvətəun] *n.* 1.【音】泛音 2. 折光的色彩 3.[常 ～s]弦外之音,含蓄之意;暗示

overtook [,əuvə'tuk] overtake 的过去式

overture ['əuvətjuə] *n.* 1.[常 ～s]主动表示;姿态;提议 2. 开端,序幕;(歌剧等的)前奏曲;序诗 3.(基督教长老会中)向最高教会法庭(或地方教会法庭)提出的(建议(或问题等) — *vt.* 1. 把…作为提议提出;向…提议 2. 为…奏前奏曲

overturn [,əuvə'tə:n] *vt.* 1. 打翻;使翻倒来 2. 推翻;颠覆;毁灭 — *vi.* 翻身;倒下 — ['əuvətə:n] *n.* 1. 打翻;翻转 2. 推翻;颠覆;毁灭;废除

overview ['əuvəvju:] *n.* (主美)概述;概观

overweening [,əuvə'wi:niŋ] *adj.* 过于自负的;过分自信的;过分傲慢的;过分的;夸大的 ‖ ～ly *adv.* / ～ness *n.*

overweight ['əuvə'weit] *vt.* 1. 给…太多的分量;使超重 2. 使超载 3. 过于着重,过于重视 — *adj.* 超重的 — ['əuvəweit] *n.* 1. 超重 2. 偏重;优势

overwhelm [,əuvə'welm] *vt.* 1. 淹没;倾覆 2. 覆盖;淹没 3. 制服,压倒;使受不了,使不知所措 ‖ ～ing *adj.* 势不可挡的;压倒(之势)的

overwork ['əuvə'wə:k] *vt.* 1. 使劳累过分;使工作过度;对…使用过度 2. 装饰满;点缀遍 3. 把…做过头;把…说过火,使…于激动(情绪,紧张) — *vi.* 1. 工作过度;劳累过分 2. 做得过分;说得过火 — *n.* 1. ['əuvəwə:k]额外工作 2. 过度工作,过分劳累 3. 过于繁重

overwrought ['əuvə'rɔ:t] *adj.* 过于劳累的;过度兴奋的

oviparous [əu'vipərəs] *adj.*【生】卵生的

ovoid ['əuvɔid] *adj.* 卵形的;梨形的 — *n.* 卵形体(或面);卵形物

ovule ['ɔuvju:l] *n.*【生】小卵;【植】胚珠

ovum ['əuvəm] ([复] ova ['əuvə]) *n.* 1.【生】卵;卵细胞 2.【建】卵形饰

owe [əu] *vt.* 1. 欠(债等);应该(或有必要)做;应给予 2. 应感激 3. 应该把…归功于(to) 4. 怀有 — *vi.* 欠债

owl [aul] *n.* 1.【鸟】鸮,猫头鹰;鸮头脑 2. 惯于夜间活动的人;夜生活者;常熬夜的人 3. 表情严肃的人;貌似聪明而肚肠的人 — *vi.*〈方〉像猫头鹰一样地叫(或凝视) — *adj.* 深夜(或通宵)活动的

owlet ['aulit] *n.* 小鸮,小猫头鹰

owlish ['auliʃ] *adj.* 1. 像鸮的,像猫头鹰的 2. 面孔严肃的;笨的

own¹ [əun] *adj.*[用在所有格后以加强语气] 1. 自己的 2. 特有的 3.[不用所有格]嫡亲的

own² [əun] *vt.* 1. 有,拥有 2. 承认 3. 承认是…的作者(或主人,父、母) 4. 顺从(指) — *vi.* 承认;供认(to)

owner ['əunə] *n.* 所有人,物主,业主 ‖ ～ship *n.* 所有(权);所有制

ox [ɔks] *n.*[复]oxen ['ɔksən]) *n.* 1. 牛 2. 去势公牛 ‖ ～cart *n.* 牛车 / ～fence 牛栏

Oxford ['ɔksfəd] *n.* 1. 牛津(英国英格兰中南部城市)(牛津大学所在地) 2. 牛津大学 ‖ ～ shoes 牛津鞋(一种系带浅帮鞋)

oxidase ['ɔksideis] *n.*【生化】氧化酶

oxidation [,ɔksi'deiʃən] *n.*【化】氧化(作用)

oxide ['ɔksaid] *n.*【化】氧化物

oxidize ['ɔksidaiz] *vt. & vi.* (使)氧化;(使)生锈 ‖ oxidi'zation *n.*

oxyacetylene [,ɔksiə'setilin] *adj.*【化】氧

乙炔的

oxygen [ˈɔksidʒən]【化】*n.* 氧;氧气

oyster [ˈɔistə] *n.* 1.【动】牡蛎,蚝 2. 蚝状鸡背肉 3. 沉默寡言的人 4. 可以从中得到好处的东西 ‖ ~ **bed**, ~ **farm** 牡蛎繁殖地;牡蛎养殖场/'~ **man** *n.* 采 (或卖、养殖等)牡蛎者;采牡蛎船

oz *abbr.* ounce(s)

ozone [ˈəuzəun] *n.* 1.【化】臭氧;〈口〉清新的空气 2. 使人愉快(或振奋)的影响

ozs *abbr.* ounces

P

P,p [pi:]([复]P's, p's 或 Ps, ps[piz])英语字母表第十六个字母 1. [P]P 字形 2.【生】亲代(parental generation)的符号 3. [P]【化】元素磷(phosphorus)的符号 4.【物】功率(power)的符号 5. [P]【物】压力,压强(pressure)的符号

P. *abbr.* 1. page 2. penny

Pa【化】元素镤(protactinium)的符号

pa [pɑ:] *n.* ⟨口⟩爸爸(papa 的缩略)

pace [peis] *n.* 1. (一)步;步伐;步(指一步跨出去的长度) 2. 步速;速度;进度 3. 步态;步调 4. 流畅 5. 侧对步(指马的同侧两蹄同时举起和放下的步法) 6.【建】梯台,楼梯转弯处的宽台 ‖ *—vi.* 1. 踱步;慢慢地走 2. (马)走侧对步 ‖ *—vt.* 1. 用步子测 2. 踱步于 3. 为…定步速(或速度) 4. 跑在…前头,为…的标兵 5. (马)以侧对步跑完;训练(马)的步法 6. 和…并进前进 ‖ ~**d** *adj.* 1. (常用以构成复合词)有…步的;步法…的;slow~**d** 慢步的 2.(赛马中)定了步速的;按规定步速奔跑的 3. 节奏(或速度)均匀的步测的的 / ~**r** *n.* 1. 训练马的步法的人;走侧对步的马;领步的人 3. = ~**setter** 2. ~**maker** ‖ ~**maker** *n.* 1. = ~**setter** 2.【医】起搏器 / '~**making** *n.* 1. 定步速 2.【医】起搏 / ~**setter** *n.* 定步速者;领跑者;带头人;标兵,先导 / ~**setting** *adj.* 定步速的;带头的,领头的

pachyderm ['pækidə:m] *n.* 1. 厚皮动物 (如象、犀、河马等) 2. 脸皮厚的人;麻木不仁的人;迟钝的人

pacific [pə'sifik] *adj.* 1. 和平的;爱好和平的;和解性的 2. 温和的;平静的 3. [P-]太平洋的 —*n.* [the P-]太平洋

pacification [,pæsifi'keiʃən] *n.* 1. 镇定;平定;绥靖(政策);媾和;安定 2. 和约

pacifism ['pæsifizəm] *n.* 1. 和平主义 2. 不抵抗主义;消极态度 ‖ **pacifist** *n.* 和平主义者;不抵抗主义者;持消极态度者 *adj.* 和平主义的;不抵抗主义的;持消极态度的 / **paci'fistic** *adj.*

pacify ['pæsifai] *vt.* 1. 使镇静;抚慰(占领区人民等) 2. 平定;绥靖 3. 使服从 4. 使(国家等)实现和平 ‖⟨美⟩使保持中立 ‖ **pacifier** *n.*

pack [pæk] *n.* 1. 包;捆;包裹 2.⟨美⟩小包,小盒 3.(猎犬、野兽、飞禽等的)一群 4.⟨常贬⟩(追求同一目的)一伙(人),一帮 5. 大堆,大量 6. 包(指包装货物的计量单位,如羊毛包为240 磅) 7.(纸牌的)一副 8.【军】背包;驮包;驮载;降落伞包 9.(作战飞机或舰艇的)一队 10.(海里成堆的)流冰群(亦作~ ice)11.【医】(包)裹(疗)法;湿(或干)裹法;冷(或热)裹法;(裹法所用的)湿布;冰袋;包 12. ⟨美⟩一年中食物的)装罐量;包装量 13. 包装;包装法;包装材料 14. 容器 15.

【摄】软片暗包；16.(依次排列的)一堆舞台背景屏 17. 护肤霜；发乳 18.(一个橄榄球队的)全体前锋 19. 部件，组件 20.【计】压缩 —vt.1. 捆扎；包装；把…打包(或装箱)；打(行李)；整(装) 2. 把(食品等)装罐 3. 挤满；塞满；装满 4. 填塞(空隙，漏缝等)；把…包(或垫)起来 5. 压紧；捣固；夯实 6. 使(牲口料)驮载 7. 背运；驮运(货物等) 8. 经常备带(装备等)；配有，备有 9. 把…裹起来 10.【医】(用裹布)包裹 11. 使(狗等)集成阱形 12. 把(全副纸牌)叠在一起 13.(俚)(拳击时)猛击…一拳 —vi.1. 包装(或捆扎)货物；收拾装备；整理行装 2. 用牲口载运着行李去旅行 3.(牲口等)驮载货物，挤入 4. 被包紧；能被挤紧 5. 增加密度，变结实 6. 匆忙离去(off) 7. 群集，集集 —adj.1.(适)用于包装(或打包)的 2. 成包的；成捆的 3. 用于驮运东西的 ‖ ~ animal 驮畜(如马、骡、驴等)/'~ horse n. 驮马

package ['pækidʒ] n.1.(中、小型的)包裹；包；捆；(商品、产品等的)(一)件，件头2.包装用物(如纸、盒、箱、封套等)3.(一并出售的)整套广播(或电视)节目4.插件，标准部件，组件【计】(软件或数据)包5.(由工会出面集体交涉得到的)一揽子利益6.一揽子交易7.(古)打包(指动作或过程)—vt.1.把…打包(或装箱)2.把(商品)打包；把…作为整体推销(或提出)—adj. 组合的；一揽子(交易)的

packed [pækt] adj.1. 挤满的，塞满的 2. 压紧的 ‖ ~ meal 盒饭

packer ['pækə] n.1. 包装工人；打包工人；食品包装工2. 打包机，打包机；装料机3.(美)(车站、旅馆等处的)行李搬运工4. 为驮畜装货者5. 包装食品

生产厂厂主；包装货物批发商

packet ['pækit] n.1. 小包(裹)；小捆；小盒；小袋2.(一次发送的)一批信件；一小批3.(定期)邮船，班轮4.(英)工资袋；(英俚)一大笔钱5.(军俚)倒霉事—vt. 把…打成小包；把…包起来

packing ['pækiŋ] n.1. 包装；打行李2. 包装法3. 驮运；背运4. 填密；密封；垫密；包装材料5.【医】(美)食品加工业(如罐头食品业等)；(美俚)食物，口粮 ‖ '~ house，~ plant n. 牲畜屠宰加工厂；食品加工冷藏厂

pact [pækt] n.1. 合同，契约；协定 2. 条约；公约；盟约

pad [pæd] n.1. 垫；衬垫；(球类运动员护身用的)护垫；(骑者用的)鞍垫2.(打)印台，印油盒3.(狗、狐狸等动物的)肉掌；脚；脚爪4.(水生植物的)浮叶5. 拍纸簿6.(简易的)降落场7.(导弹、火箭等的)发射台8.(外科敷伤口用的)纱布块9. 垫料；【船】垫板；【机】缓冲器；把手柄10.(一捆)一束(尤指送入卷烟机的烟叶束)11.(美俚)睡榻；床12.(美俚)吸毒窝；娼妓窝；安乐窝13.(美俚)房间；公寓14.(美俚)汽车牌照15.(美俚)求太平锁(指为免祸而付给治论诈犯罪的钱)—adj. padded；padding —vt.1.(用软物)填塞；衬填2.(用废话等)拉长，铺张(文章等)3.(美)虚报(账目等)…的费用—vi. 徒步行走；发出闷的声音；使(声音)沉闷5. 把(散页张纸)装订成拍纸簿 ‖ padding n.1. 垫塞；垫料2.(文章、讲话中的)冗词赘句，废话3. 虚报的费用

paddle[1] ['pædl] n.1.(短而阔的)桨2. 桨状的；(桨状)搅拌器；捣衣棒；扁形刑杖3.(船的)明轮；(明轮的)轮叶4.【动】鳍状肢5. 小闸门—vi. 依靠桨

或明轮)在水中行进;划小船;荡桨 —*vt*.1. 用桨划(船) 2. 划船运送 3.(用桨状物)搅;打;(用刑杖)鞭挞 ‖ ~steamer 明轮船 /~ wheel(船的)明轮

paddle[2] [ˈpædl] *vi*.1. 在浅水中行走,涉水;(用脚或手)玩水 2.〈古〉(用手或手指)抚弄 3.(小孩)摇摇晃晃地走

paddock [ˈpædək] *n*.1.(用来放牧、驯马等的)围场 2.(赛马场的)赛前鞍具着装场;(赛车前的)停车场 3.〈澳〉围起来的土地 4.【矿】井口临时堆场 —*vt*.1. 把…关入围场 2.〈澳〉把(土地)围起来 3. 临时堆集(矿石)

paddy [ˈpædi] *n*.1. 稻;稻谷 2. 水稻田(亦作~field)

padlock [ˈpædlɔk] *n*.1. 挂锁,扣锁 2.(官方下令的)关闭 —*vt*.1. 用挂锁锁上 2. 正式关闭(公共场所或工厂等)

paean [ˈpiːən] *n*.1.(古希腊对神尤指对太阳神的)赞歌;赞美歌 2. 凯歌;欢乐歌

paediatrics [ˌpiːdiˈætriks] [复] *n*.[用作单]【医】儿科学 ‖ **paediatric** *adj*. 儿科(学)的 / **paediatrician** [ˌpiːdiəˈtriʃən] *n*. 儿科医师;儿科学家

pagan [ˈpeigən] *n*.1. 异教徒(指非基督教徒、非犹太教徒或非伊斯兰教徒) 2. 没有宗教信仰的人 —*adj*. 异教(徒)的;不信教的

page[1] [peidʒ] *n*.1. 页(略作 p.) 2.[常~s]记录 3. 值得记载的事件(或时期) 4.(报刊的)专页 5.【印】一页版面 — *vt*. 为…编页码,给…标页码 —*vi*. 翻阅(*through*)

page[2] [peidʒ] *n*.1.(中世纪欧洲的)学习骑士 2.(有身分者的)青年侍从 3. 侍从官 4.(旅馆、办事处等处穿制服的)小听差,男侍 5.〈美〉(国会或其他立法机关中的)青年听差 6.(新娘的)男小傧相 —*vt*.1. 给…当听差;侍候 2.(在旅馆、机场等处)喊叫找寻(某人)

pageant [ˈpædʒənt] *n*.1.(当地历史事件等的)露天表演 2. 庆典;华丽的展览;壮丽的行列(或游行等) 3. 炫耀,虚饰 ‖ ~**ry** *n*.1. 壮丽的展示(或庆典) 2. 壮观 3. 夸耀,虚饰 4.[总称]露天历史剧;历史性场景

pagoda [pəˈgəudə] *n*.(东方国家的)塔,宝塔;塔式建筑物;塔式寺庙

paid [peid] pay 的过去式和过去分词 —*adj*.1. 支取薪金的;受雇的 2. 已付的;付清的

pail [peil] *n*. 桶,提桶;一桶的量 ‖ ~**ful** *n*. 满桶,一桶;一桶的量

pain [pein] *n*.1. 痛,疼痛 2. 痛苦,悲痛 3.[~s]辛苦;刻苦;努力;苦心;操心 4.[~s]分娩阵痛 5. 惩罚(现仅用于下列短语):~*s* and penalties 刑罚 / on (或 upon, under) ~ of (death)违者处(死) 6.〈美〉讨厌的人(或事物);厌恶 —*vt*. 使疼痛;使痛苦 —*vi*. 引起疼痛;感到疼痛 ‖ ˈ~-ˌ**killer** *n*.〈美口〉止痛药;解痛物

painful [ˈpeinful] *adj*.1. 使痛的;使痛苦的 2.(需要)费力的;费心的,伤脑筋的,棘手的 3. 讨厌的,麻烦的 4.〈古〉细心的;辛勤的 ‖ ~**ly** *adv*. /~**ness** *n*.

painless [ˈpeinlis] *adj*.1. 无痛(苦)的,不痛(苦)的 2.〈口〉不难的,不费力的 ‖ ~**ly** *adv*./~**ness** *n*.

painstaking [ˈpeinzˌteikiŋ] *adj*.1. 苦干的;辛勤的;费力的,艰苦的 2.(煞费)苦心的,精心的;刻苦的 —*n*. 苦干;辛勤;煞费苦心,精心 ‖ ~**ly** *adv*. /~**ness** *n*.

paint [peint] *vt*.1.(用颜料等)画,绘 2. 描写;(用语言、文字等)描绘 3. 油漆;着色于;刷(标语等) 4. 用油漆(或涂料等)修整;装饰,点缀 5. 用油漆(或涂料等)涂掉,刷掉;覆盖;〈喻〉掩盖 6.

涂,搽(伤口、药、化妆品等) — vi.1.(用颜料等)绘画 2. 搽脂粉(或化妆品) — n.1. 涂漆;绘画作品 2. 颜料;[~s](一套)颜料(包括若干管或若干块颜料) 3. 油漆;一层漆(皮);涂料 ‖ ~ brush n. 画笔;漆刷

painter ['peintə] n. 漆匠;画家

painting ['peintiŋ] n.1. 油漆;油漆业 2. 绘画;绘画艺术;绘画业 3.(一幅)画;[总称](某一画家的)绘画作品

pair [pɛə]([复]pair(s)) n.1. 一对,一双 2. 一对夫妇;已订婚的一对;一对情侣 3.(有特征或相互关联的)一对(人或物) 4.(桥牌赛中的)搭档,对子 5.(相约对某议案不投票的)对立政党的两个议员;对立政党两个议员之间的不投票协议(比赛,议会等)两人的伙伴关系 6.(动物)交配的一对;(同挽并排的)两匹马;双套马 7.(成对物的)另一只 8.(纸牌等的)同点子的一对 9.(方)(楼梯等的)一段 10.(方)一串(或一套)小东西(如念珠、项链等) — vi.1. 成对,配对 2. 交配;成对 — vt.使…分成对 3. 结婚;(动物)交配,交尾(with) — vt.1. 使成对;把(人或物)组成对;使成为配偶 2. 使(对立政党的两名议员)组成对某议案不投票的一对

paisley ['peizli] n.[亦作P-][纺](苏格兰)佩斯利涡旋纹花呢(制品)

pajamas [pəˈdʒɑːməz][复] n. = pyjamas

Pakistan ['pɑːkisˈtɑːn] n. 巴基斯坦[南亚国家] ‖ ~i [ˌpɑːkisˈtɑːni] n. 巴基斯坦人 adj. 巴基斯坦的

pal [pæl] n.(口)1. 伙伴;好友 2. 同谋;同犯 — (palled; palling) vi. 交友,结伴;成为好友(with, up)

palace ['pælis] n.1. 王宫,宫殿 2.(英)大主教(或主教)宅邸 2. 豪华住宅;大

厦;宏伟的(公共)建筑物;豪华的娱乐场所

pal(a)eolithic [ˌpæliəuˈliθik] adj.[亦作P-]旧石器时代的

Pak(a)eozoic [ˌpæliəuˈzɔuik] n. & adj.[地]古生代(的);古生代岩石(的)

palanquin [ˌpælənˈkiːn] n.(旧时在东方国家使用的由两人或多人抬的)轿子 — vi. 坐轿子

palatable ['pælətəbl] adj.1. 好吃的,可口的;配胃口的 2. 合意的,受欢迎的

palate ['pælət] n.1.[解]腭;硬腭 2. 味觉;嗜好;爱好;趣味;鉴赏力

palatial [pəˈleiʃəl] adj. 宫殿(似)的;宏伟的,壮丽的 ‖ ~ly adv.

palaver [pəˈlɑːvə] n.1.(尤指历史上非洲土人和欧洲商人间的)交涉,谈判;讨论,话谈,空谈 3. 奉承,恭维话

pale[1] [peil] adj.1. 苍白的,灰白色的 2. 暗淡的;软弱的,无力的 — vi. 变苍白;变暗淡;失色 — vt. 使变苍白;使暗淡;使失色 ‖ ~ness n.

pale[2] [peil] n.1.(做栅栏用的)尖板条,尖桩 2. 栅栏;围篱 3.(某一范围内或管辖权下的)地区 4. 界限;范围 — vt.1. 用栅栏(或篱笆)把…围起来 2. 包围,围绕

Palestine ['pæləstain] n. 巴勒斯坦[西南亚一地区] ‖ **Palestinian** [ˌpæləˈstinian] adj. 巴勒斯坦的;巴勒斯坦人的 n. 巴勒斯坦人

palette ['pælit] n.1. 调色板 2.(调色板或某画家用的)一组颜色

palfrey ['pɔːlfri] n.(古)(尤指供妇女乘骑的)驯马

paling ['peiliŋ] n.1.(做栅栏用的)尖板条,木栅栏 2. 栅栏;围篱 3. 打桩做围栏

palisade [ˌpæliˈseid] *n.*1. 栅，木栅，栅栏 2.[~s](河边的)岩壁；绝壁 —*vt.* 用栅圈护,用栅防卫

pall[¹] [pɔːl] *n.*1. 棺罩；柩衣；棺布 2.(尤指内有尸体的)棺材 2.【宗】圣杯(或祭台等)的罩布(教皇、大主教的)白羊毛披肩带 3.(阴暗的)笼罩物；幕 —*vt.* 给…盖上棺罩；使笼罩阴影；覆盖 ‖ '~bearer *n.*(丧礼中)抬棺材的人

pall[²] [pɔːl] *vi.*1.〈古〉(酒)走味，失味 2.不发生作用；丧失吸引力(on, upon) 3. 感到腻烦，厌倦 —*vt.* 使腻烦；使乏味

palladium [pəˈleidiəm] *n.*【化】钯

pallet[¹] [ˈpælit] *n.*1. 草荐；简陋小床

pallet[²] [ˈpælit] *n.*1. 托板；制模板 2.【机】棘爪；锤垫 3.【音】(管风琴等上的)调节簧 4.调色板 5.(成组装卸用的)托盘，货盘，货板

palliate [ˈpælieit] *vt.* 减轻，缓和(痛苦、疾病等)；掩饰(罪过等) ‖ **palliative** *adj./palliator* *n.*

pallid [ˈpælid] *adj.*1. 无血色的，苍白的；病状的 2. 无生气的，无趣味的

pallor [ˈpælə] *n.*(脸色等的)苍白，灰白

palm[¹] [pɑːm] *n.*1. 手掌，手心 2.(测量的)手掌宽 3.(手套等的)掌部 —*vt.*(变戏法、打牌等时)把…藏在手(掌)中

palm[²] [pɑːm] *n.*1. 棕榈(树) 2. 棕榈叶(常作为胜利的象征) 3. 胜利，优胜 4.[喻]指庆祝棕榈主日非基督教国家用以代替棕榈树枝的庆贺树枝 ‖ **Palm Sunday**【基督教】棕榈主日(即复活节前的星期日)

palmate [ˈpælmeit] *adj.*1. 掌状的 2.【动】有蹼的，蹼足的

palmetto [pælˈmetəu] *n.*(复)palmettos 或 palmettoes *n.*1.【植】美洲蒲葵 2. 蒲葵枝条 ‖

Palmetto State 蒲葵州(美国南卡罗来纳州的别称)

palmistry [ˈpɑːmistri] *n.* 手相术

palmy [ˈpɑːmi] *adj.*1. 多棕榈的 2. 棕榈(似的) 3. 茂盛的；兴旺的，繁荣的

palomino [ˌpæləˈmiːnəu] *n.*(复)palominos *n.*(美国西南部产的)帕洛米诺马，银鬃马

palpable [ˈpælpəbl] *adj.*1. 可感知的，易察觉的；明显的 2. 触摸得到的【医】(肿瘤等)可触知的 ‖ ~ness *n./palpably adv.*

palpitate [ˈpælpiteit] *vi.*1.(尤指心脏)悸动；突突跳；急速不规则地跳动 2. 颤抖

palsy [ˈpɔːlzi] *n.*1. 麻痹，瘫痪，中风 2. 痉挛；颤抖 —*vt.*1. 使瘫痪 2. 使丧失能力，使无活动力

paltry [ˈpɔːltri] *adj.*1. 没价值的；微不足道的；低劣的 2. 可鄙的

pampa [ˈpæmpə] *n.*1.[常~s]南美大草原 2.[P~]南美大草原上的印第安人

pamper [ˈpæmpə] *vt.*1. 纵容，姑息；娇养 2. 使满足 3.〈废〉使吃得过饱

pamphlet [ˈpæmflit] *n.* 小册子 ‖ ~eer [ˌpæmfliˈtiə] *n.* 小册子作者(或出版者)

Pan [pæn] *n.*【希神】潘(人身羊足、头上有角的畜牧神)

pan[¹] [pæn] *n.*1. 平底锅；盘子；一满锅；一满盆 2. 盘状器皿(天平的)秤盘；【矿】淘金盘 3.(旧式枪的)火药池 4. 盘状凹地，盆地 5. 小块浮冰 6.(不透水的)硬土层 7.〈口〉脑壳；〈俚〉脸(panned; panning)—*vt.*1.(用平底锅)烧(菜) 2.(用淘选盆)选淘(金子或含金的矿石等)(off, out) 3.〈口〉严厉批评 —*vi.*1. 淘金；出金，产金 2.〈口〉(结果)成为；成功(out)

pan² [pæn] (panned; panning) *vi.* 摇镜头；
摇摄 — *vt.* (使)摇摄 — *n.* 摇镜头；摇
摄；摇摄拍下的镜头 — *adj.* 全景的

panacea [ˌpænəˈsiːə] *n.* 治百病的灵药；
〈喻〉万应灵药

Panama [ˈpænəˌmɑː, ˌpænəˈmɑː] *n.* 1. 巴
拿马[拉丁美洲国家](在中美洲东南
部) 2. 巴拿马城[巴拿马首都](亦作
~ City) 3. 巴拿马(式)草帽(亦作~
hat) ‖ ~ Canal 巴拿马运河[中美洲巴
拿马中部]

pancake [ˈpænkeik] *n.* 1. 薄煎饼 2. 〈空〉
平降，平坠着陆(亦作~ landing) — *vi.*
(飞机)平降 — *vt.* 使(飞机)平降

pancreas [ˈpæŋkriəs] *n.* 〈解〉胰(腺)

pancreatic [ˌpæŋkriˈætik] *adj.* 〈解〉胰(腺)
的

panda [ˈpændə] *n.* 1. 小猫熊，小熊猫(=
lesser ~) 2. 大猫熊，大熊猫(= giant
~) ‖ ~-car(英)(车身涂蓝白两色的)
巡逻警车

Pandemonium [ˌpændiˈmounjəm] *n.* 1. 魔
窟，阎王殿；地狱 2.[p-]无法无天；大
吵大闹；大混乱；无法无天的混乱场面

pander [ˈpændə] *n.* 1. 拉皮条的男人；妓院
老板；迎合他人淫欲者；助恶者 —
vt. & *vi.* (给…)作淫媒(或拉皮条);
(为…)拉皮条

pane [pein] *n.* 1. 窗格玻璃；窗格；长方格
2.(门或墙上的)镶板，嵌板 3.(螺帽，
钻石等的)面 — *vt.* 嵌玻璃于；镶嵌板

panegyric [ˌpæniˈdʒirik] *n.* 颂扬的演说;
颂文；赞颂

panel [ˈpænəl] *n.* 1. 陪审员名单；全体陪
审员 2.(英)国民健康保险医师名单 3.
(选定的)专门小组(广播或电视节目
的)专题讨论小组；猜谜小组 4.(有
代表性的)一组调查对象；对一组典型

对象进行的调查 5.(箱、盒等的)面 6.
〈建〉镶板，嵌板；节间；板条 7. 配电盘；
仪表板;(控制)操纵板 8. 连环漫画(中
的一幅) 9.〈空〉(飞机的)翼段 10.〈军〉
(地面向空中飞机提供的作目视信号
用的)信号布板 11. 油画画板；油画板上
的画 12.(苏格兰法律中的)被告 13.
(女服上的)嵌料，嵌条，饰条 — (panel-
(l)ed; panel(l)ing) *vt.*1.(用镶板等)装
镶板(门、墙等);(以杂色或不同质的布
块)镶饰(女服) 2. 选定(陪审团) 3.
(苏格兰法律中)对…起诉，控告 ‖
panel(l)ing *n.* 1. 镶板细工 2.(镶板等的)镶
板 3. 镶板材料 / **panel(l)ist** *n.* 专门小
组成员

pang [pæŋ] *n.* 剧痛；一阵极度的悲痛 —
vt. 使剧痛；使极度痛苦；折磨

panhandle [ˈpænˌhændl] (美口) *vi.* (在街
上)行乞 — *vt.* (在街头)向…乞讨；乞
讨得到 ‖ ~r *n.* 街头行乞者，叫化子

panic [ˈpænik] *n.* 1. 恐慌，惊慌 2.(金融
方面的)大恐慌 3.〈俚〉非常滑稽的人
(或事、物) — *adj.* 恐慌的；起于恐慌
的；莫名其妙的 — (panicked; panicking)
*vt.*1. 使恐慌 2. 使狂热；使喝彩 — *vi.*
感到惊慌；惊慌失措 ‖ '~-stricken,
'~-struck *adj.* 恐慌，惊慌失措的

panicky [ˈpæniki] *adj.*1. 恐慌的；由恐慌
引起的 2. 易恐慌的

panicle [ˈpænikl] *n.*〈植〉圆锥花序，散穗
花序，复总状花序 ‖ ~d *adj.*

panoply [ˈpænəpli] *n.* 全副盔甲

panorama [ˌpænəˈrɑːmə] *n.*1. 全景画；回
转画；活动画景 2. 风景的全貌；全景
照片 3. 全景；概观；概论 4. 不断变化
的一连串的景象(或事件);(脑海中呈
现的)一系列形象(或景象) ‖
panoramic [ˌpænəˈræmik] *adj.* 全貌的;
全景的

panpipe, Panpipe ['pænpaip] *n.* 潘神箫；排箫(芦杆制的乐器)

pansy ['pænzi] *n.* 1.[植]圆三色堇；圆三色堇花 2.〈俚〉〈贬〉无丈夫气的男子；同性恋男子

pant [pænt] *n.* 1. 气喘 2. 心跳 3.(机车等的)喷气 —*vi.* 1. 气喘 2.(心等)悸动，剧跳 3.(机车等)喷气 4. 渴望(*for, after*) —*vt.* 气喘吁吁地讲(*out, forth*) ‖ **~ingly** *adv.*

pantalet(te)s [ˌpæntə'lets] [复] *n.* 1.(19世纪中期女子穿的露在裙外的)宽松长裤；(长衬裤上的)可卸饰边 2.(骑自行车穿的)女式灯笼裤

pantaloon [ˌpæntə'lu:n] *n.* 1.[P-](古代意大利喜剧中常见角色)傻老头子；(现代哑剧中为丑角取笑对象的)傻角式人物 2.[~s]马裤 3.〈美〉〈俚〉裤子；中裤

panther ['pænθə] *n.* 1.[动]豹；黑豹；美洲豹；美洲豹 2.[P-](美国)黑豹党人

panties ['pæntiz] [复] *n.* (口)(儿童或妇女穿的)紧身短衬裤；童短裤；女式运动短裤

pantograph ['pæntəgrɑ:f] 1. 缩放仪，比例绘图仪 2.(电气列车等顶上的)导电弓(架)

pantomime ['pæntəmaim] *n.* 1.(古罗马或现代的)哑剧；哑剧演员 2.(英口)(圣诞节演出的)童话剧 3. 手势；表意动作 —*vt.* 用手势表达 —*vi.* 演哑剧 ‖ **pantomimist** *n.* 哑剧演员(或作者)

pantry ['pæntri] *n.* 1. 餐具室；食品(储藏)室；冷菜厨房 2.〈美俚〉胃

pants [pænts] [复] *n.* 1.〈主美〉裤子 2.〈主英〉短衬裤

panty ['pænti] *n.* = panties ‖ **~ hose** 连袜裤，连裤袜

panzer ['pænzə] *n.* 1. 装甲车；坦克；[~s] 装甲部队 —*adj.* 装甲的；装甲师的

pap [pæp] *n.* 1.(婴儿或病人吃的)软食，半流质食物 2. 政治上的恩惠(或津贴等) 3. 缺乏营养的东西；幼稚的话；消遣而无实际价值的作品

papa [pə'pɑ:] *n.* 〈古〉爸爸(尤用作儿语)

papacy ['peipəsi] *n.* 教皇职位(或职权)

papal ['peipl] *adj.* 教皇的；教皇职位的；天主教(教会)的

papaw ['pɔːpɔ:] *n.* 1. = papaya 2.[植]巴婆树；巴婆果

papaya [pə'paiə] *n.*[植]番木瓜树；番木瓜果

paper ['peipə] *n.* 1. 纸；a sheet of ~ 一张纸 2. 文件；[~s] 个人(或家庭)书信文件集 3. 文章，论文；书面作业；试卷，考卷 4.(装有东西的)一纸包；一纸袋 5. 报纸；出版物；〈俚〉广告宣传单 6. 证券；票据；纸币 7.(戏院等的)免费入场券；免费入场观众 8.[~s] 身份证件 9. 糊墙纸 10. 似纸的东西(如纸草等) 11.〈美俚〉纸牌 —*adj.* 1. 纸做的；硬板纸做的；制型纸做的 2. 似纸的；薄薄的 3. 文书工作的 4. 纸上的；名义上的；仅在理论上存在的 5. 持免费入场券的名流入场的 —*vt.* 1. 用纸包裹(或覆盖)；用纸裱糊；用纸折成 2.(发免费入场券)使(剧场等)满座 3.〈古〉在纸上写下；用文字描绘 4. 弥补；掩饰 —*vi.* 贴糊墙纸 ‖ **~ back** *n.* 纸面(装订)本，平装本 *adj.* = ~ backed /'~backed *adj.* (书)纸面(装订)的，平装的 / ~ mill 造纸厂 / ~ money 纸币 / ~ tape [计] 纸带 / ~ tiger (外强中干的)纸老虎 /'~-weight *n.* 镇纸，压纸器 / ~ work 日常文书工作

papery ['peipəri] *adj.* 〈轻蔑〉如纸的

papier-mâché [ˌpæpjei'mæʃei, ˌpeipə'mæʃei] *n.* 纸型；制型纸

papilla [pə'pilə] ([复] papillae [pə'pili:]) *n.*

乳头,乳突;乳头状物 ‖ **~ry** *adj.*

papist ['peipist] 〈贬〉〈宗〉 *n.* 天主教徒;教皇至上主义者 一 *adj.* 天主教的 ‖ **papism** *n.* 天主教(教义)

papoose [pə'pus] *n.* 1. 北美印第安人的婴孩(亦作 papoose) 2.〈美俚〉与工会会员一起工作的非会员工人

paprika ['pæprikə] *n.* 红灯笼辣椒;辣椒粉

Papua New Guinea ['pæpjuə njuː 'gini] 巴布亚新几内亚[南太平洋岛国]

papyrus [pə'paiərəs] ([复] papyri [pə'paiərai] 或 papyruses) *n.* 1.【植】纸(莎)草 2.(纸(莎)草纸;草纸;古代在纸草纸上的)古代文稿;纸草纸卷轴

par [paː] *n.* 1.(两种货币间对比的)平价 2.(股票等的)票面价值 3.(= value) 等;同等 4. 常态;一般标准(或水平) 5.(高尔夫球赛中的)规定击球次数 一 *adj.* 1. 与票面价值相等的,平价的 2. 常态的;平均的;一般水平的

parable ['pærəbl] *n.*(道德说教性的)寓言;比喻

parabola [pə'ræbələ] *n.* 1.【数】抛物线 2. 碗状物(如话筒等) ‖ **parabolic** [,pærə'bɔlik] *adj.*

parachute ['pærəʃut] *n.* 1. 降落伞 2.(在形状或功用上)像降落伞的东西 3.【动】翅膜 一 *vi.* 跳伞;伞降;似用降落伞降落 一 *vt.* 伞投;似用降落伞投送 ‖ **parachutist** *n.* 跳伞者;跳伞运动员;伞兵(parachutists)伞兵部队

parade [pə'reid] *n.* 1. 游行;队列;行列 2. 阅兵分列(或行进)式 3. 阅兵场 4. 散步广场;散步的人群 5. 显示;炫耀 一 *vt.* 1. 一游行;二在…散步 2. 使列队行进 3. 使游街 4. 炫耀;展示 一 *vi.* 游行;列队行进 ‖ **~ r** *n.*

paradigm ['pærədaim, 'pærədim] *n.* 范例;

样式;【哲】范式

paradise ['pærədais] *n.* 1.[P-]【宗】伊甸园;天国 2. 乐园,福地,天堂;极乐;至福 3.(养禽兽供狩猎的)苑

paradox ['pærədɔks] *n.* 1.(与通常见解对立的)悖论 2. 似非而是的论点 3. 自相矛盾的话(或事、物、人等);谬论;怪事;妄人 ‖ **para'doxical** *adj.*

paraffin ['pærəfin], **paraffine** ['pærəfin] *n.* 1. 石蜡;硬石蜡 2.【化】链烷(属)烃 3.〈主英〉煤油,火油 一 *vt.* 用石蜡涂(或浸透);用石蜡处理

paragon ['pærəgən] *n.* 1.(尽善尽美的)模范(或典型) 2. 十分优秀的人(或物);完人;珠玉 3.(100 克拉以上的)无瑕钻石;圆形大珍珠 4.【印】20点活字(一种西文活字的旧称)

paragraph ['pærəgraf] *n.* 1.(文章的)段落,节 2. 段落号,节号;参照符号 3.(报刊的)短文;短讯 一 *vt.* 1. 写短文分段落 2. 将…分成段落 一 *vi.* 为报刊写短文(或短讯)

Paraguay ['pærəgwai] *n.* 巴拉圭[南美洲中南部国家]

parakeet ['pærəkit] *n.*【鸟】长尾小鹦鹉

parallax ['pærəlæks] *n.* 视差

parallel ['pærəlel] *adj.* 1. 平行的;并行的 2. 相似的;类似的;并联的一 *n.* 1. 平行线(或面) 2. 类似的(可相比拟的)事(或物、人、情况等) 3. 比拟 4. 纬线;纬圈 5. 相似(平行号(即"∥") 6.[复]并联 7.【军】平行堑壕 一(parallel(l)ed; parallel(l)ing) *vt.* 1. 使成平行;与…平行 2. 比拟(*with*)

parallelogram [,pærə'leləgræm] *n.* 1.【数】平行四边形 2. 平行四边形物

paralyse, paralyze ['pærəlaiz] *vt.* 1. 使麻痹;使瘫痪 2. 使无力;使无能为力;使气馁;使惊呆

paralysis [pə'rælisis]（［复］paralyses
[pə'ræləsiːz]）n.1.［医］麻痹（症）；瘫痪
（症）2.〈喻〉瘫痪 ‖ **paralytic**
[ˌpærə'litik] adj. & n.

Paramaribo [ˌpærə'mæribəu] n. 帕拉马里
博［苏里南首都］

paramecium [ˌpærə'miːsiəm]（［复］parame-
cia [ˌpærə'miːsiə]）n.［动］草履虫

paramedic [ˌpærə'medik, 'pærəˌmedik] n.
护理人员；医疗辅助人员

paramedical [ˌpærə'medikəl] adj. 医疗辅
助（人员）的

parameter [pə'ræmitə] n.1.［数］参（变）
数；参（变）量 2. 起限定作用的因素，
参数

paramilitary [ˌpærə'militəri] adj. 准军事
（部队）的

paramount ['pærəmaunt] adj. 最高的，至
上的；卓越的；首要的 — n. 最高统治
者

paramour ['pærəmuə] n. 情夫；情妇

paranoia [ˌpærə'nɔiə] n. 妄想狂，偏执狂；
多疑症 ‖ ～c [ˌpærə'nɔiæk] n. & adj.

parapet ['pærəpit] n.1.［军］胸墙 2.［建］
（阳台、桥等旁边的）栏杆；护墙；女儿
墙

paraphernalia [ˌpærəfə'neiliə]（［复］） n.1.
随身物品 2. 设备；装备；器材 3.［律］
（除嫁妆外）妻子（可自由处理）的财产

paraphrase ['pærəfreiz] n.（对一段文字
的）释义 — vt. 将 … 释义（或意
译）— vi. 释义；意译

paraplegia [ˌpærə'pliːdʒiə] n.［医］截瘫，下
身麻痹 ‖ **paraplegic** n. & adj.

paraprofessional [ˌpærəprə'feʃənəl] n. &
adj. 专业人员的助手（的）

parasite ['pærəsait] n.1. 寄生生物；攀附
植物 2.〈喻〉寄生虫 3. 食客，清客

parasitic(al) [ˌpærə'sitik(əl)] adj. 寄生的；
（疾病等）由寄生生物引起的

parasol ['pærəsɔl] n.1.（女用）阳伞 2.［航
空］伞式单翼机

paratroop ['pærətruːp] n.［～s］伞兵部队
— adj. 伞兵（部队）的 ‖ ～er n. 伞兵

parboil ['pɑːbɔil] vt.1. 把 … 煮成半熟，预
煮 2. 使过热 — vi. 变得过热

parcel ['pɑːsl] n.1. 小包；包裹 2.（货物
的）一宗 3.（土地的）一块 4.〈贬〉一批，
一群 — (parcel(l)ed; parcel(l)ing) vt.1.
分；分配 (out) 2. 把 … 包起来 (up) 3.
［海］用涂油帆布条包（绳索等）；用涂
油帆布条缠（缝）— adj. 部分的；兼职
的 — adv.〈古〉部分地；局部地 ‖ ~ blind
半盲的

parch [pɑːtʃ] vt.1. 烘，焙 2. 使焦干；使
干透 3. 使冷得皱缩 — vi. 焦干；干透；
烤干 ‖ ~ed adj.

parcheesi [pɑː'tʃiːzi] n.（似古代印度 25 点
棋戏的）帕奇齐棋戏

parchment ['pɑːtʃmənt] n.1. 羊皮纸，仿
羊皮纸 2. 羊皮纸文稿（或文件）；毕业
文凭；学位证书

pardon ['pɑːdn] n.1. 原谅，饶恕，宽恕 2.
［律］赦免(状) 3.［宗］赦罪；免罪符 —
vt.1. 原谅，饶恕 2.［律］赦免

pardonable ['pɑːdnəbl] adj. 可以原谅的；
可以宽恕的

pare [pɛə] vt.1. 削（果子等）的皮；剪，修
（指甲等）2. 修除（角、边等）(off,
away) 3.（逐渐）削减，缩减 (down,
away)

paregoric [ˌpærə'gɔrik] n.（鸦片）复方樟
脑酊；止痛剂

parent ['pɛərənt] n.1. 父亲；母亲；［～s］
双亲；祖先 2.（动、植物的）亲本，母体
3. 起源，根源；原因 — adj. 母（体）的；
作为渊源（或来源）的 ‖ ～hood n. &

母身份;家长身份

parentage ['pɛərəntidʒ] *n.*1. 出身,家系,门第 2. 来源 3. 父母的身份(或地位)

parental [pə'rentl] *adj.*1. 父母的;父的;母的(*生*)亲本的 2. 作为渊源(或来源)的

parenthesis [pə'renθisis]([复] parentheses [pə'renθisiz]) *n.*1.[常 parentheses]圆括号 2.[语]插句;插入语 3.(喻)插曲

parenthetic(al) [,pærən'θetik(əl)] *adj.*(作为插入成分的;用作附带说明的;解释性的,插曲的

paresis [pə'riːsis]([复] pareses [pə'riːsiz]) *n.*1.[医]轻瘫;麻痹性痴呆

parfait [paː'fei]〈法〉 *n.* 冻奶糊;奶油重冻糕;冷甜点

pariah [pə'raiə, 'pæriə] *n.*1.(印度南部和缅甸的)贱民 2. 爱憎观的人(或动物);被社会遗弃者

pari-mutuel [,paːriː'mjuːtjuːel] *n.*(赛马或赛狗时的)同注分彩赌博(法);同注分彩计算器

Paris ['pæris] *n.* 巴黎[法国首都] ‖ ~ Commune 巴黎公社

parish ['pæriʃ] *n.*1. 堂区(主教管区下的分区,有自己的教堂和牧师) 2. 堂区的全体居民(或教徒)

parishioner [pə'riʃənə] *n.* 堂区居民

Parisian [pə'riziən] *adj.* 巴黎的;巴黎式的;巴黎文化的;巴黎人的 一 *n.* 巴黎人

parity ['pæriti] *n.*1. 同等,平等 2.[逻]类似,相似 3. 平价(指官定货币汇兑比价);价值对等(两方势力对时,相持)均势 5.[物]字称(性);[数]奇偶性

park [paːk] *n.*1. 公园(国家)天然公园 2.[律](英国国王特许的)猎园 3.(乡村别墅四围的)园林 4.(汽车等的)停

车场 5.[军](枪炮、军需品等的)放置场;(放置场上所放置的)全部东西 一 *vt.*1. 停放(车辆、飞机等) 2. 把(某地)圈为公园 3. 把(炮车等)安排在放置场 4.(美俚)存放;放置 一 *vi.* 停放车辆 ‖ ~ oneself 坐下

parka ['paːkə] *n.* 风雪大衣,派克大衣

parking ['paːkiŋ] *n.*1. 停车;准许停车;停车场地 2. 公园场地 3. 路中(或路侧的)草坪 ‖ ~ lot 停车场,停车区/ ~ meter 汽车停放计时器 / ~ ticket 违章停车传票

parkway ['paːkwei] *n.*(两旁有草地、树木等的)园林路

parlance ['paːləns] *n.* 说法,用语: in medical ~ 用医学用语来说

parlay ['paːli] *vt. & vi.* 把(赌本和赢金)再作赌注

parley ['paːli] *n.* 会谈;谈判;(与敌方的)非正式会谈 一 *vi.* 会谈;谈判(with) 一 *vt.* 讲(外语等)

parliament ['paːləmənt] *n.*1. 议会,国会 2.[P-]英国议会;议会两院(英国等的)下议院 3.(法国大革命的)最高法院 4. 薄姜饼(= ~ cake)

parliamentary [,paːlə'mentəri] *adj.*1. 议会的,国会的 2. 议会政治的 3. 议员的 3.(合于)议会法规的

parlo(u)r ['paːlə] *n.*1. 客厅,会客室;起居室 2.(小酒馆等处的)雅座 3.〈美〉(接待顾客的)店堂 一 *adj.*1. 客厅的;适于客厅用的 2. 空谈而无行动的;崇尚空谈的

parochial [pə'rəukiəl] *adj.*1. 堂区的 2. 地方范围的,狭隘的 3.〈美〉(学校)由宗教团体兴办的

parody ['pærədi] *n.*(作为一种讽刺文学形式的)诙谐模仿诗文 一 *vt.* 通过模仿嘲弄

parole [pə'rəul] *n.*1.(俘虏)宣誓(如保证永不逃脱等) 2.(美)【军】口令,特用符号 3.有条件释放;假释 —*vt.*1.凭誓释放(俘虏) 2.假释

paroxysm ['pærəksizəm] *n.*(疾病、感情的)突然发作,阵发 ‖ ~al *adj.*

parquet ['pɑːkei, pɑː'kei] *n.*1.镶木地板 2.(美)剧场正厅(座位)

parrakeet ['pærəkiːt] *n.* = parakeet

parricide ['pærisaid] *n.*1.杀父(或母);杀尊长罪;杀父(或母)者;杀尊长者 ‖ ₁parri'cidal *adj.*

parrot ['pærət] *n.*1.鹦鹉 2.应声虫,人云亦云者,学舌者 —*vt.*1.鹦鹉学舌般地复述 2.训练(人)机械地复述

parry ['pæri] *vt.*1.挡开;避开 2.回避 —*vi.*1.挡开武器(或打击);避开 —*n.*1.挡开;避开 2.回避;遁词

parse [pɑːs] *vt. & vi.* 从语法上分析(词、句等)

parsimony ['pɑːsiməni] *n.* 极度节俭;吝啬,小气;惜暂如金

parsley ['pɑːsli] *n.*【植】欧芹,香芹菜

parsnip ['pɑːsnip] *n.*【植】欧洲防风;欧洲防风的根;类欧洲防风

parson ['pɑːsn] *n.*1.堂区牧师 2.(口)牧师 ‖ ~age *n.*(堂区)牧师住所

part [pɑːt] *n.*1.一部分,局部 2.部分,分之一;等分 3.基本构成成分,要素 4.本分,职责;份儿,作用 5.(剧中)角色;(角色的)台词 6.地区,区域 7.(争论、交易等中的)一方 8.(~s)才华 9.(文艺作品等的)篇 10.(头发的)分缝,头路 11.【语】词类;~s of speech 各种词类 12.部件,部件;配件 13.【数】整除部分;部分分数,部分分式 14.【音】声部;分谱;(曲式中的)部,段 15.(身体的)部位 —*vt.*1.分;使分开 2.断绝(关系、联系) 3.区别,辨别(学说、

论等) 4.(用化学方法)使析出,使分解出 5.【海】断断(缆索、锚链等) —*vi.*1.(河流等)分又;分道 2.断裂 3.分手,分别;中止联系;断绝关系 4.放弃 5.离开;死去 6.(口)出钱;付款 —*adj.*部分的;局部的 —*adv.*部分地 ‖ ~ly *adv.*部分地;不完全地;在一定程度上 ‖ '~'time *adj.*部分时间的,非全日的;(教师等)兼任的,兼职的 —*adv.*花部分时间;兼任地,兼职地

part. *abbr.*1.participle 2.particular

partake [pɑː'teik] (partook [pɑː'tuk], partaken [pɑː'teikən]) *vi.*1.参与,参加(in) 2.分享;吃,喝(of) 3.带有(某种性质或特征的),有几分(of) —*vt.*1.分享;参与 2.吃,喝 ‖ ~r *n.*参与者;分享者

parted ['pɑːtid] *adj.*1.分开的;分成几部分的 2.(常用以构成复合词)【植】深裂的

partial ['pɑːʃəl] *adj.*1.偏袒的,不公平的 2.癖好的,偏爱的(to) 3.部分的;不完全的 —*n.*【音】分音 ‖ ~ly *adv.*

partiality [ˌpɑːʃi'æliti] *n.*1.偏心,不公平 2.特殊爱好,偏爱;癖好

participant [pɑː'tisipənt] *n.*参加者,参与者 —*adj.*分享的,参与的(of)

participate [pɑː'tisipeit] *vi.*1.参与,参加(in) 2.分享;分担(in) 3.含有,带有(of) ‖ par₁tici'pation *n.*参与,参加;分享 / participator *n.* / participatory *adj.*

participle ['pɑːtisipl] *n.*【语】分词 ‖ ₁parti'cipial *adj.*

particle ['pɑːtikl] *n.*1.粒子,微粒 2.极小量 3.【物】粒子,质点 4.【语】小品词,语助词;词缀 ‖ ~ accelerator 粒子加速器 /~ physics[复]【用作单】粒子

理学,高能物理学

parti-colo(u)red ['pɑːtiˌkʌləd] *adj.***1.** 杂色的,斑驳的 **2.** 多样化的

particular [pə'tikjulə] *adj.***1.** 特殊的;特异的 **2.**[逻] 特称的 **2.** 特定的;各个的;(人)个别的 **3.** 特指的 **3.** 个别的;(人)个别的 **3.** 特指的 **3.** 独特的;[异常的 **4.** 分项的;列举的;细致的;详细的 **5.**(过于)讲究的;苛求的,挑剔的 — *n.***1.**(可分类或列举的)项目;(消息、情报等的)一条,一项,一点 **2.** 细节;[~s]详细情况 **3.** 特点;特色 ‖ ~**ly** *adv.***1.** 特别,尤其,格外 **2.** 详细地;细致地

parting ['pɑːtiŋ] *adj.***1.** 分开的,分离的,分隔的 **2.** 离别的,临别的 **3.** 临死的,临终的 — *n.***1.** 分裂,分离 **2.** 分手处;分界线(或点);[头发的]分缝,头路 **3.** 分开物,分离物;[冶]分金,切断 **4.** 分手;告别;离别 **5.** 死亡

partisan, partizan [ˌpɑːti'zæn, 'pɑːtizæn] *n.***1.** 党人;党徒;坚决支持者;敌后游击队员 — *adj.***1.** 党派的;派性的;偏袒的 **2.** 由一个党派组织(或控制)的 **3.** 游击队的 ‖ ~ **ship** *n.* 党派心;派性;党派行为

partition [pɑː'tiʃn] *n.***1.** 分开;分割,划分 **2.** 隔开物;隔墙;隔板;隔开部分;隔开的房间 **3.** 分部;隔开部分;隔开的房间 **4.**[律]财产分割 **5.**[逻]划分,分类 **6.**[数]划分;分拆 — *vt.***1.** 把…分成部分 **2.**(用隔板等)分隔

partner ['pɑːtnə] *n.***1.** 伙伴,合作者;合伙人,股东 **2.** 搭档;同伴;舞伴 **3.** 配偶(指夫或妻) **4.**[常~s]甲板穿孔加强结构 — *vt.***1.** 同…合作(或合伙);做…的伙伴 **2.** 使有搭档 — *vi.* 做伙伴;搭档(*with*) ‖ ~ **with** 与…伙伴关系,合伙(或合股)关系;合伙关系;全体合伙(或合股)人;合伙(或合股)契

约

partook [pɑː'tuk] partake 的过去式

partridge ['pɑːtridʒ] *n.***[动]** 山鹑;灰山鹑;鹑鸡;山齿鹑;披肩鸡

parturition [ˌpɑːtjuə'riʃn] *n.* 分娩,生产

party ['pɑːti] *n.***1.** 党,党派,政党 the Communist Party of China 中国共产党 **2.** 结党;党派活动 **3.**(条约、会议、诉讼等有关的)一方;当事人;参与者 **4.**(参加共同活动的)一批,一组,一伙人;随行人员 **5.**[军]分遣队,组 **6.**(社交性或娱乐性的)聚会 **7.**(俚)(谑)(一个)人 — *vi.* 举行(或参加)社交聚会 — *vt.* 为…举行社交聚会

paschal ['pɑːskəl, 'pæskəl] *adj.***宗** **1.**(犹太人的)逾越节的 **2.** 复活节的

pasha ['pɑːʃə, 'pæʃə] *n.* 帕夏(旧时奥斯曼帝国和北非高级文武官员的称号,置于姓名后);拥有帕夏称号的高级文武(或武)官

pass [pɑːs, pæs](过去式 passed,过去分词 passed 或 past[pɑːst]) *vt.***1.** 经过;穿过;越过,超过 **2.** 通过(考试、检查等);使…批准(议案等) **2.** 被…批准(或通过) **3.** 度过,耗过,超越(能力、范围、限度等) **5.** 传递(用具等);传达(命令、消息等);(球)传、送(货币等)流通;传播(谣言等) **7.** 使移过;使行进 **8.** 把…略过不提;忽略 **9.** 宣布(判决等);提出(批评、意见等);立(誓),保证 **10.** 排泄;(大、小便)排;分泌 — *vi.***1.** 经过;穿过;超过;(思想、眼光等)掠过 **2.** 变化,转化;(在所有权等方面)转换;(时间)推移,流逝;(货币等)流通,通用;(文件等)被传阅;(问候等)交流,来往 **5.** 及格,合格;被…批准;宣判,判决 **6.** 发生;下场 **7.** 终止;消失;离开;死亡 **8.** 被众所承认 **9.** 被看作白人 **10.**(带有黑人血统的)被看作白人 **10.**

(桥牌中)不叫牌,放弃叫牌 11. 传球 —*n.*1. 经过;通过 2. 关口;要隘;海峡;(河流)渡口 3.(常指不利的)境况,处境;及格;及格分数;及格证书 5. 出入证;通行证;护照 6. 一次完整的机械操作 7. 传球;(击剑中的一次)戳刺 8.(飞机、人造卫星等的)飞过 9.(桥牌戏中的)放弃叫牌(或补牌 10.(魔术中的)手法 11.〈俚〉勾引,调情 ‖ '～-book *n.* 银行存折 /'Pass'over *n.*〈宗〉(犹太人的)逾越节 /'～port *n.*1. 护照 2. 保障 /'～word *n.*(通过警戒线等时使用的)口令;进入(或通过)手段

passable ['pɑːsəbl] *adj.*1. 可通行的,能通过的 2. 合格的;过得去的,还好的,尚可的 3.(钱币等)可流通的,通用的 4.(建议的法律条文等)可予通过的 ‖ **passably** *adv.* 过得去地;还好;相当;稍微

passage ['pæsidʒ] *n.*1. 通过;经过;过渡 2. 迁移 3.(法案等的)通过 4.(乘船或飞机的)旅行,旅程,航程 5. 通过自由;通行权 6. 通道 7. 走廊,过道 8.[～s](两人间言辞等的)交换 9.(文章、讲话等的)一段,一节;(绘画等艺术作品的)段落,细部;[音]乐句;经过句 10.[医]排便 11.(病原体等的)传代 12.[解]道,通道 ‖ ～-way *n.* 走廊;通道

passé ['pæsei]〈法〉*adj.*1. 已过盛年的(女子)已过青春妙龄的 2. 过时的,落伍的;陈旧的

passenger ['pæsindʒə] *n.*1. 乘客;旅客 2.〈口〉(球队、船员等中)不中用的成员

passer ['pɑːsə] *n.*1. 过路人 2. 使通行(或通过)的人 ‖ '～-by([复]～s-by) *n.* 过路人

passing ['pɑːsiŋ] *adj.*1. 经过的;穿过的 2. 短暂的,一时的 3. 仓促的;粗略的

随便的 4. 及格的,通过的 5. 供通行的 —*adv.*〈古〉极其,非常 —*n.*1. 经过;通过;消逝;消失 2. 通过的手段;可以通过的地方(如渡口等) 3.〈婉〉去世

passion ['pæʃən] *n.*1. 激情,热情;[～s] 感情(与理智相对而言) 2. 酷爱,热爱;酷爱的东西 3. 恋情;情欲 4. 大怒,激怒 5.〈古〉病痛 6.[the P-]〈宗〉(十字架上)耶稣的受难 ‖ ～less *adj.*

passionate ['pæʃənət] *adj.*1. 热情的;热烈的;激昂的 2. 易动情的 3. 易怒的,性情暴躁的 4. 被情欲所支配的 ‖ ～ly *adv.*

passive ['pæsiv] *adj.*1. 被动的;消极的 2.[语]被动的;被动(语态)的 3. 顺从的;驯顺的 4.[化]惰性的(如金属);(电子原件等)无源的 4. 无利息的 —*n.*1. 被动消极的东西 2.[语]被动(语)态;被动式 ‖ ～ly *adv./*～ness *n.*

passivity [pæ'siviti] *n.*1. 被动;被动性;消极状态 2. 顺从 3. 钝性;钝态 4.[语]被动(语态的)结构

past [pɑːst, pæst] *pass* 的过去分词 —*adj.*1. 过去的;刚过去的 2.[语]过去(时)的 3. 前任的,已卸任的 —*n.*1. 过去,昔日 2. 往事;经历(尤指不为人的历史) 3.[语]过去时;(动词的)过去式 —*prep.*1.(指时间,地点、数量,程度等)过 2.(指范围、限度、能力等)越过 —*adv.* 经过;run ～ 跑过去

pasta ['pæstə, 'pɑːstə] *n.* 意大利面食

paste [peist] *n.*1.(做糕点用的)面团,油酥面团 2. 软糊 3. 糊,酱;糊状食物;浆糊 5.(制陶、瓷器用的)湿粘土 6.(做人造宝石的)铅质玻璃;人造宝石 —*vt.*1. 用浆糊粘贴 2. 在…上贴满

pasteboard ['peistbɔːd] *n.*1. 纸板 2. 名片 3. 纸牌 4. 门票;火车票 —*adj.*1. 纸板

做的 2. 不坚实的;假冒的,人造的

pastel ['pæstəl] *n.*1. 菘蓝染料;【植】菘蓝 2. 彩色粉笔;蜡笔 3. 粉(笔)画或画法;蜡笔画(或画法) 4. 随笔;散文 5. 淡而柔和的色彩

pastern ['pæstən] *n.*(马、牛等足的)骹;骹骨

pasteurize ['pæstəraiz] *vt.*【医】对…进行巴氏消毒 || **pasteuri'zation** *n.* 巴氏消毒法,低热消毒法

pastiche [pæs'ti:ʃ] *n.*(文学或艺术的)模仿作品

pastille ['pæstil] *n.*(药的)锭剂;糖锭;芳香熏剂

pastime ['pɑ:staim] *n.* 消遣;娱乐

pastor ['pɑ:stə] *n.*1.(基督教的)本堂牧师;精神生活指路人 2. 牧人;牧羊人 3.【鸟】粉红椋鸟

pastoral ['pɑ:stərəl] *adj.*1. 牧(羊)人的;关于牧人生活方式的 2. 畜牧的;以畜牧为基础的 3. 乡村的;描写牧人(或乡村)生活的;田园诗的 4. 牧师的;主教的 —*n.*1.【宗】牧函(指主教写给其教区内神职人员或教友的公开信) 2. 田园诗(或剧、画);牧歌;【音】田园曲;田园(歌)剧 3. 乡村景色 4. 主教权杖(亦作～staff) 5. 牧师职责手册

pastorale [,pɑ:stə'rɑ:l] *n.* 田园曲;田园式文学作品

pastrami [pæs'trɑːmi] *n.* 五香烟熏牛肉

pastry ['peistri] *n.* 油酥糕点;一块糕点

pasture ['pɑ:stʃə] *n.*1. 牧场 2. 牧草 3. 放牧 —*vt.*(牛、羊等)吃(草);放(牛、羊)吃草;把…用作牧场 —*vi.*(牛、羊等)吃草 || **pasturage** *n.* 牧草;牧场;放牧

pasty¹ ['peisti] *adj.*1. 面糊似的 2.(脸色)苍白的;不健康的

pasty² ['pæsti] *n.* 馅饼;肉馅饼

pat¹ [pæt] *n.*1.(用掌或扁平物)轻拍;轻打 2. 轻拍声 3.(黄油等的)小块;似小块黄油的东西 —(patted; patting) *vt.*1. 轻拍;轻拍…使平滑(或成形) 2. 轻拍…以示抚慰(或赞同) —*vi.*1. 轻拍;轻敲 2. 轻轻地走(或跑)

pat² [pæt] *adj.*1. 恰好合适的;完全适时的 2. 过于巧合的;人为的 3. 学(或记)得一点不差的 4. 准备好的 5. 坚定的,不屈服的;〈美俚〉固定不变的 —*adv.*1. 适当地;及时地;立即 2. 熟记地

pat. *abbr.* patent

patch [pætʃ] *n.*1. 补钉,补片 2.(护伤的)膏药;裹伤布;(保护病眼或伤眼的)眼罩 3. 臂章 4. 小块土地 5. 碎片;碎屑;与周围不同的部分;斑;【医】斑膜斑 6. 饰颜片,美人斑(尤指17-18世纪欧洲贵族妇女脸上的黑色圆形贴片) 7.〈主英〉时期 —*vt.*1. 补缀;暂时解决(分歧等) 2.(匆忙)拼凑(*up*) || ～work *n.*1. 缝缀起来的各色布片,拼缝物 2. 拼凑的东西;杂烩

patchy ['pætʃi] *adj.*1. 有许多补钉的;缀的;拼缀而成的 2. 零落的;局部地区的 3. 不完全的,不规则的;部分尚好的 || **patchily** *adv.* / **patchiness** *n.*

pate [peit] *n.* 头;头顶;〈谑〉头脑

patella [pə'telə] ([复] patellas 或 patellae [pə'teli:]) *n.*【解】髌(骨),膝盖骨

patent ['peitənt, 'pætənt] *adj.*1. 专利(权)的;受到专利保护的;特许的 2.〈口〉首创的;独出心裁的 3.(门)开着的;公开的;显然的 4.【植】开展的,伸展的 —*n.*1. 专利,专利权;专利证;专利品 2. 独享的权利,特权 —*vt.*1. 给予…专利权(或证) 2. 取得…的专利权(或证)

paternal [pə'tə:nəl] *adj.*1. 父亲的;像父

亲的 2. 父方的；父系的；得自(或传自)父亲的 ‖ ~**ly** adv.

paternalism [pə'tə:nəlizəm] n. 家长式统治；家长作风 ‖ **paternalist** n. / **paterna'listic** adj. 家长式(统治)的；家长作风的

paternity [pə'tə:niti] n. 父亲身份；父系；父权 ‖ ~ **test** 亲子鉴定

paternoster [ˌpætə'nɔstə] n.〈宗〉(尤指拉丁文的)主祷文

path [pɑ:θ] n. 1.(走出来的)路；小道，小径 2.(公路旁的)人行道 3.(竞走或自行车比赛用的)跑道 4.(思想、生活、行为等的)道路，途径 5.路线；路径 ‖ '~**way** n. 小道，小径

pathetic [pə'θetik] adj. 1. 哀婉动人的，可怜的 2. 悲哀的；忧郁的 3. 感情(上)的；情绪(上)的 4. 微弱的，可怜巴巴的 ‖ ~**ally** adv.

pathology [pə'θɔlədʒi] n. 1. 病理学 2. 病理，病状，病征 ‖ **pathological** [ˌpæθə'lɔdʒikəl] adj. 1. 病理(学)的 2. 病态的 / **pathologist** n. 病理学家

pathos ['peiθɔs] n.(事物、作品、言词等中)引起怜悯(或同情)的因素；伤感力

patience ['peiʃəns] n. 1. 忍耐；容忍；耐心；忍耐力；坚韧 2.〈英〉单人纸牌戏

patient ['peiʃənt] adj. 忍耐的，容忍的，有耐心的，有忍耐力的；坚韧的 — n. 1. 病人 2.(美容院等的)顾客 ‖ ~**hood** n. 患病(状态) / ~**ly** adv.

patina ['pætinə] n. 铜绿，绿锈

patio ['pætiəu, 'pɑ:tiəu]([复]patios)〈西〉n. 1. 庭院，天井 2.(连接房屋并铺有地面的)露台，平台

patriarch ['peitriɑ:k] n. 1. 家长；族长 2.(宗教、学派等的)创始者，鼻祖 3. 可尊敬的老人；(一群人中的)最年长者 4.〈宗〉牧首；教长；(天主教)教皇;(东

正教)最高级主教

patriarchal [ˌpeitri'ɑ:kəl] adj. 1.家长(或族)长的;家长的;族长的;(东正教)牧首的;教长的;最高级主教的 2.家长(或族长,元老派头的 3.家(或族)长似的;元老派头的 4.可尊敬的,德高望重的;古老的

patriarchy ['peitriɑ:ki] n. 父权制(社会)

patrician [pə'triʃən] n. 1.(古罗马的)贵族;(罗马帝国在意大利及非洲各城市共和国的)长官;(中世纪意大利各自由市的)显贵 2.贵族,有教养的人 — adj. 贵族的;贵族似的

patrimonial [ˌpætri'məuniəl] adj. 1. 祖传的;世袭的 2. 世袭财产的 3. 教会财产的

patrimony ['pætriməni] n. 1. 祖传财产;遗产 2. 教会基金(或财产) 3.(喻)继承物

patriot ['peitriət, 'pætriət] n. 爱国者,爱国主义者

patriotic [ˌpætri'ɔtik, ˌpeitri'ɔtik] adj. 爱国的;有爱国心的 ‖ ~**ally** adv.

patriotism ['pætriətizəm, 'peitriətizəm] n. 爱国主义;爱国精神,爱国心

patrol [pə'trəul] n. 1. 巡逻;巡查 2. 巡逻兵;巡逻队 3. 巡逻艇队;巡逻机队 3. 童子军小队 — (patrolled; patrolling) vt. & vi. 巡逻;巡查 ‖ **pa'trolman** n.〈美〉巡警

patron ['peitrən] n. 1. 庇护人,保护人;恩主 2. 赞助人,资助人 3. 老顾客;主顾 4.(旅店等的)老板 5.(英国教会中)有圣职授予权的人 6.(教会、城镇等的)守护神,主保圣人 7.(古罗马)(释放奴隶后保留一定控制权的)旧奴隶主

patronage ['pætrənidʒ] n. 1. 庇护人(保护人、赞助人等)的身份(或影响、作用等) 2. 庇护,保护;赞助,资助 3. 恩赐的态度;(以恩赐的态度施于的)恩惠

4. 光顾，惠顾 5. 任意授予官职(或特权)的权力;官职的恩赐;被恩赐的官职 6.[宗]圣职的授予权

patronize ['pætrənaiz] *vt.*1. 庇护，保护;赞助，资助 2. 光顾，惠顾 3. 对…以恩人自居;对…摆出屈尊俯就的样子

patter[1] ['pætə] *n.*(急促的)嗒嗒声 —*vi.*1. 发出嗒嗒声 2. 嗒嗒地跑 —*vt.*使发出嗒嗒声

patter[2] ['pætə] *n.*1. 行话;黑话,切口 2. (小贩等的)连珠炮似的话;顺口溜 3. (滑稽演员的)急口词;快板;(滑稽歌曲的)快板插词;歌词 4. 喋喋不休的废话(语) —*vt.*喋喋不休地念;念念似地说 —*vi.*1. 喋喋不休 2. 祷告;念经 3. 唱顺口溜;说快板

pattern ['pætən] *n.*1. 模范，榜样;典范 2. 型，式样;(服装)纸样;(浇铸用的)模具，模型 3. 样品 4. 图案，花样;(电视的)测试图(形) 5. 方式;形式;格局;(文艺作品的)格调 6. 复杂衣料 7. (炮弹等的)散布面;(靶上的)子弹洞图 8. (飞机的)起落航线 —*vt.*仿制，仿造 2. 以图案装饰,给…加上花样 3. 〈英方〉与…相等;与…相配 (*to, with*);模仿 —*vi.*形成图案 ‖ —*ed adj.*有图案的,组成图案的

pattie, patty ['pæti] *n.*1. 小馅饼 2.〈美〉肉饼 3. 扁形薄饼

paucity ['pɔːsiti] *n.*1. 小数目;少 2. 量少;不足;缺乏

paunch [pɔːntʃ] *n.*1. 肚子,腹;大肚皮 2. [动]瘤胃(即反刍动物的第一胃) 3. [海]防磨席(= *rubbing ~*) —*vt.*把…剖腹,剖腹取出…的内脏 ‖ —*y adj.*

pauper ['pɔːpə] *n.*1. 靠救济过活的人;乞丐 2. 穷人,贫民 3.[律](可免交诉讼费用的)贫民起诉人

pause [pɔːz] *n.*1. 中止,暂停;停顿;停留

2. 跨踌 3. 停顿符号(如句号、逗号等);(诗的)主要停顿 4.[音]延长号 —*vi.*1. 中止;暂停;停顿;停留 2. 跨踌

pave [peiv] *vt.*1. 铺,筑(路等);作铺设…之用 2. 铺满;密布

pavement ['peivmənt] *n.*1. 铺筑过的地面(或路面);铺过的道路 2.〈主英〉人行道(= 〈美〉sidewalk) 3. 铺筑材料

pavilion [pə'viljən] *n.*1.(尖顶)大帐篷 2.(公园等中的)亭子;楼阁;(博览会等的)展出馆 3. 医院、疗养院内的)分馆式病房 4.[解]耳郭 —*vt.*1. 为…搭篷(或建亭) 2. 置于篷(或亭、馆)中

paving ['peiviŋ] *n.*1. 铺路;铺面;铺砌 2. 铺筑材料

paw [pɔː] *n.*1. 脚爪,爪子 2.〈口〉(尤指笨拙的)手;笔迹 —*vt.* & *vi.*1.(用脚)扒;爪抓 2. 笨拙地搔;粗鲁地摸弄;乱抓

pawl [pɔːl] *n.*[机]棘爪;掣爪,止动爪,卡爪

pawn[1] [pɔːn] *n.*1. 典,当;押 2. 当出物;抵押品;人质 —*vt.*1. 当;抵押 2.〈喻〉用…作担保(或抵押) ‖ *~ broker n.* 当铺老板 / *~-shop n.* 当铺

pawn[2] [pɔːn] *n.*1.(国际象棋中的)兵,卒 2.〈喻〉马前卒;爪牙,工具

pawpaw ['pɔːpɔː] *n.* = papaw

pay [pei](*paid* [peid]) *vt.*1. 支付,付,缴 2. 付钱给;给…报酬;出钱雇佣 3. 偿还;抵偿;补偿 4. 对…有利;对…合算 5. 给(注意等);致以(问候等);进行(访问等) 7.[过去式和过去分词 payed]放松(绳索等)(*out, away*) —*vi.*1. 付款;交款 2. 偿还债务;偿付代价;〈喻〉受到惩罚;得到报应(*for*) 3. 有利;合算 4. 有收益(职位等)有报酬 —*n.*1. 支付;受雇报酬 2. 偿还;报答;报应 3. 酬

用;工资;薪金(尤指军饷);津贴 4. 有支付能力的人;按期付款的人;有信用的人 5. 可采矿石;产油层 —adj. 1. 含富矿的;有开采价值的 2. 需付费的,收费的;自动收费的 3. 有关支付的 ‖ ~ee [pei'i:] n. 受款人,收款人 / ~er, ~or n. 付款人 ‖ ~day n. 发薪日 / ~load n. 1.(运输工具的)营运负载 2.(火箭的)有效载荷 / ~off n. 1. 发工资;分配盈利 2. 分赃 3. 盈利;报酬;报偿;报应 3.(事件、叙述等)的高潮 4. 出乎意料(或不可思议)的事 5. 决定性的事;决定因素 adj. 得出结果的;决定的 / ~out n. 付出款项,花费,支出 / ~out ratio 股利发放率,盈利率,派息率 / ~roll n. 1. 工资表;在职人员名单 2. 发放工资额 / ~sheet n. 〈英〉= ~roll

payable ['peiəbl] adj. 1. 可支付的;(到期)应支付的 2.(矿山投资等)可获利的

payment ['peimənt] n. 1. 支付;支付的款项(或实物) 2. 报偿;报应

Pb [化] 元素铅(lead)的符号

PBS abbr. Public Broadcasting Service (美国)公共广播公司

PC abbr. personal computer 个人计算机,个人电脑

Pd [化] 元素钯(palladium)的符号

pea [pi:] n. 1. [植] 豌豆 2. 豌豆般的东西 ‖ ~jacket 〈美〉水手短外套,双排钮甲呢上装

peace [pi:s] n. 1. 和平;和平时期 2. 和约 3.(常作 the ~)治安,社会秩序 4. 和睦,和解 5. 安宁,安定 ‖ ~feeler 和平触角,和平试探 / ~maker n. 调解人,和事佬 / ~time n. 和平时期,平时

peaceable ['pi:səbl] adj. 1. 平和的;息事

宁人的;安静的 2. 和平的,太平的

peaceful ['pi:sful] adj. 1. 和平的;爱好和平的 2. 安静的,平静的;安宁的,太平的 3. 和平时期的;平时的 4. 平和的 ‖ ~ly adv. / ~ness n.

peach [pi:tʃ] n. 1. 桃子;桃树 2. 桃色,桃红色 3.〈俚〉受人喜欢的人(或物);杰出的人;极好的东西;漂亮女子

peacock ['pi:kɔk] n. 1. 雄孔雀;孔雀 2. 爱炫耀自己的人,虚荣骄傲的人 —vi. 炫耀,招摇;装模作样地行走

peafowl ['pi:faul] n. 孔雀

peahen ['pi:hen] n. 雌孔雀

peak [pi:k] n. 1. 山顶,巅,山峰 2. 最高点,顶峰,顶端 3. 尖端,尖顶 4. 帽舌 5.(船)(船首或船尾的)尖舱 —vi. 1. 达到高峰 2. 消瘦,变憔悴 3. 逐渐变小(或减少) —vt. 1. 使尖起;使成峰状 2. 使达到最高点;使达到高峰 ‖ ~ed adj. 有峰的;尖的,有帽尖的;消瘦的,苍白的,憔悴的

peal [pi:l] n. 1. 钟声;(组钟奏出的)钟乐;(奏钟乐的)编钟 2. 响亮持续的声音 —vt. 使鸣响;大声发出;大声说 —vi. 大声响,轰鸣

peanut ['pi:nʌt] n. 1.[植] 花生 2. 花生果;花生米 3.〈美俚〉小人物 4.[~s]〈俚〉(尤指与总数相比的)小数目;无甚价值之物;少许的,微不足道的 ‖ ~butter 花生酱

pear [peə] n. 梨子;梨树;梨木

pearl [pə:l] n. 1. 珍珠;珍珠母(如露珠、洁白的牙齿等) 2. 珍品;人杰;杰出典型 4. 珍珠色,蓝灰色 5.(煤、金属等的)珠状散粒 6.〈英方〉[医]白内障 7.[印] 珠体活字(即小型活字) —vt. 1. 用珍珠镶嵌(或装饰) 2. 使成珠状;使成小圆粒 3. 珠子似地散布在…上 4. 使呈珍珠色(或光

泽）— vi. 1. 成珠子状 2. 采珍珠 ‖ ~y adj. 1. 珍珠似的；珠母似的 2. 产珍珠的；产母的 2. 用珍珠（或珠母）装饰的 4. 珍贵的 ‖ **Pearl Harbor** 珍珠港 [美国夏威夷州檀香山]（重要海军基地）

peasant [ˈpezənt] n. 1. 农民，小农；雇农 2. 庄稼人；乡下人；粗野的人

peasantry [ˈpezəntri] n. 1. [总称]农民 2. 农民的地位（或身份）3. 农民行为；粗野

peat [piːt] n. 泥炭，泥煤 ‖ ~y adj. '~bog ~ moor, ~ moss [地]泥炭沼

pebble [ˈpebl] n. 1. 卵石；圆砾 2. 水晶；水晶透镜 3. (皮革、纸张等上的)粗糙表面，碎石花纹

pecan [ˈpiːkən, piˈkæn] n. [植]美洲山核桃(树)

peccadillo [ˌpekəˈdiləu] n. [复]peccadillo(e)s n. 轻罪；过失，小错误

peccary [ˈpekəri] n. [动]西貒(美洲野猪)

peck[1] [pek] n. 1. 配克(英美干量名，= 8 夸脱)(略作 pk.)；1 配克的容器 2. 许多,大量

peck[2] [pek] vt. 1. 啄；啄起；啄穿；啄成 2. (用尖头的工具)凿，琢 3. 〈口〉匆匆轻吻 — vi. 1. 啄；啄起；啄食；凿 2. 连续敲击 3. 斯文地吃，一小口一小口地吃；吃 5. 找岔子，吹毛求疵(at) — n. 1. 啄；啄起 2. 啄成(或凿、或琢)出的洞 3. 〈口〉匆忙的一吻 4. 〈俚〉食物；〈美俚〉(卡车驾驶员等用语)短暂吃饭时间

pectin [ˈpektin] n. [生化]果胶

pectoral [ˈpektərəl] adj. 1. 胸(部)的；戴在胸前的 2. 治疗胸病的 3. 出自个人感情的；主观的 — n. 1. 胸饰；胸铠 2. [医]治疗胸病的药 3. 胸肌；胸鳍；胸部器官

peculate [ˈpekjuleit] vt. & vi. 盗用，侵吞(钱财) ‖ **pecu**'**lation** n.

peculiar [piˈkjuːliə] adj. 1. (个人或团体)特有的，独具的 2. 特别的，特殊的 3. 罕见的；奇怪的，乖僻的 — n. 1. 特有财产；特权 2. (不受当地司法机关管辖的)特殊教会(或教区) ‖ ~ly adv.

peculiarity [piˌkjuːliˈæriti] n. 1. 奇特；古怪 2. 独特性；特色 3. 特质 3. 特殊的东西；怪异的东西 4. 怪癖

pecuniary [piˈkjuːniəri] adj. 1. 金钱(上)的；钱财方面的 2. 应课罚金的

pedagogic(al) [ˌpedəˈgɔdʒik(əl)] adj. (小学)教师的；适宜于(小学)教师的；教学法的；教育(学)的 ‖ **pedagogically** adv.

pedagog(ue) [ˈpedəgɔg] n. 1. (小学)教师，教员 2. 卖弄学问的教师；学究

pedagogy [ˈpedəgɔdʒi] n. 教育学；教学法；教学(工作)

pedal [ˈpedl] adj. 1. [动]足的 2. 踏板的；脚踏的 3. [数]垂足的 — n. 1. (自行车、缝纫机等机械的)踏脚，踏板，脚蹬 2. (管风琴等的脚键盘；(钢琴的)踏板 —(pedal(l)ed; pedal(l)ing) vi. 1. 踩踏板 2. 骑自行车 — vt. 踩……的踏板

pedant [ˈpednt] n. 1. 卖弄学问的人，空谈家 2. 学究，迂夫子 ‖ ~ry n.

pedantic [piˈdæntik] adj. 卖弄学问的；迂腐的，学究式的

peddle [ˈpedl] vi. 1. 沿街叫卖；兜售 2. 做无聊事；闲混；游荡 — vt. 1. (沿街)叫卖；兜售(理论等)；散播(传闻等)

peddler [ˈpedlə] n. = pedlar 2. 〈美俚〉沿途零担搞挂列车

pedestal [ˈpedistl] n. 1. [建]柱脚；基座，底座,台座；(雕像等的)垫座；[机]轴架；轴承 2. 基础；支柱 3. 显要地位 —(pedestal(l)ed; pedestal(l)ing) vt. 1. 把

…搁在垫座上;给…装上座子 2. 提高…的地位;颂扬

pedestrian [pi'destriən] *adj.*1. 徒步的,步行的 2.(作品风格等)缺乏想象力的;平淡的;沉闷的 — *n.* 步行者,行人

pediatrics [ˌpiːdi'ætriks] *n.* [用作单](美) = paediatrics ‖ **pediatric** *adj.* / **pediatrician** [ˌpiːdiə'triʃən] *n.*

pediculous [pi'dikjuləs] *adj.*(多)虱的

pedicure ['pedikjuə] *n.*1. [医] 足医;修脚师 2. 脚病治疗(如拔鸡眼等) 3. 修脚指甲 — *vt.* 修(脚);医(脚)

pedigree ['pedigriː] *n.*1. 家谱 2. [生] 谱系 2. 家系,血统;门第,出身;名门出身 3.(事物的)起源和历史;[语] 词源 4.(家畜的)种;纯种

pediment ['pedimənt] *n.* [建] 山头,人字墙;三角饰

pedlar, pedler ['pedlə] *n.*1.(挨户兜售的)小贩 2.(沿街叫卖的)商贩,货郎 2.(主意、想法等的)兜售者;(谣言、闲话等的)传播者

pedometer [pi'dɔmitə] *n.* [测] 计步器,步程计

pee [piː] *vi.* & *n.* 〈口〉撒尿,小便

peek [piːk] *vi.*1. 从缝隙(或隐蔽处)看 2. 偷看,窥视 — *n.* 偷偷的一看一瞥

peel [piːl] *n.*(水果、蔬菜等的)皮,外皮 — *vt.* 剥(皮);削(皮);剥(或剥)…的皮 — *vi.*1. 脱皮 2. 脱落,剥落 3. 脱衣服

peen [piːn] *n.*(锤的)尖头

peep[1] [piːp] *adj.*1. 偷看的,一瞥;不完全的景象 2. 初现;隐约显现 3. 露头 — *vi.*1.(从缝隙等中)偷看,窥视 2. 出现(*out*);(品质等)露出真相 ‖ ~**er** *n.*1. 窥视者 2.〈俚〉[常~s]眼睛 3.〈美俚〉私家侦探

peep[2] [piːp] *n.*1.(小鸟、鼠等的)唧唧声,啾啾声 2.(表示埋怨、抗议等的)嘀咕 — *vi.*1.(小鸟、鼠等)唧唧叫 2. 嘀咕 ‖ ~**er** *n.*1. 唧唧叫的鸟(或鼠) 2. [动] 雨蛙 3. 啾咕的人

peer[1] [piə] *vi.*1. 凝视,盯着看(*at, into*) 2. 隐约出现;出现

peer[2] [piə] *n.*1. 同等的人;同等地位的人,同事;同辈人 2. 贵族;(英)有爵位的贵族 — *vt.*1. 与…相比;与…同等 2. 封…为贵族 ‖ ~**age** *n.*[总称]贵族;贵族爵位;贵族名册 / ~**less** *adj.* 无比的,无可匹敌的

peeve [piːv] 〈口〉 *vt.* 惹恼,使恼怒 — *n.*1. 气恼,生气 2. 惹人生气的事情

peevish ['piːviʃ] *adj.*1. 易怒的,暴躁的;乖戾的 2. 刚愎扭的;倔强的 3. 带怒气的 ‖ ~**ly** *adv.* / ~**ness** *n.*

peg [peg] *n.*1. 木(或金属)钉;栓;短桩 2. [建] 标杆;(桶)塞;(弦乐器的)弦轴 2.(用以挂、撑、钩、钩的)天钉;木钉 3.(用以挂衣的)衣夹 3. 栓与栓的间隔;(喻)等级;(价物等的)限定标准 4. 主题;借口,遁词 5.〈口〉[~s]腿;裤子 6.〈口〉木腿;(美俚)装假腿的人(= ~ leg) 7.〈口〉牙齿 8.〈主英〉含酒的饮料 9.(一)扔—(pegged) pegging *vt.*1. 用木钉钉;用短桩固定(*down*, *in*, *out*)2.(用木夹把(洗的衣服)夹在晒衣绳上 3. 固定;限制;限定(价格、工资等)4. 鉴定 4. 用木桩在地上标出;用木钉记(分数)5. 扔 — *vi.*1. 坚持不懈地工作(*away*)2. 用木钉记分数 3. 急忙前行(*along*)— *vt.* 用力投;用…击中‖ ~-**top** *adj.*(裤子、裙子等)上宽下窄的

Peking ['piː'kiŋ] *n.* 北京(Beijing 的旧称)

pekoe ['piːkəu] 〈汉〉 *n.* 白毫(茶);香红茶(一种高级红茶)

pelican ['pelikən] *n.* [动] 鹈鹕,伽蓝鸟,

塘鹅,海河鸟 ‖ **Pelican State** 鹈鹕州(美国路易斯安那州的别称)

pellagra [pə'leigrə] n.【医】糙皮病,陪拉格病(即烟酸缺乏症)

pellet ['pelit] n.1. 小圆,小球;药丸 2.(中世纪作战用的)石弹;炮弹;子弹;弹丸 3.(鼠、兔等的)屎粒 4.(硬币上的)连珠形浮雕图案 —vt.1. 使形成小球(或丸子等) 2. 用子弹击

pell-mell [pel'mel] adv.1. 混乱地,乱七八糟地 2. 匆促地 —adj. 混乱的,乱七八糟的;匆促的 —n. 纷乱,混乱;杂乱

pellucid [pe'ljursid] adj. 1. 透明的,清澈的 2. 清楚明白的 ‖ ～ly adv. / ～ness n.

pelt[1] [pelt] n.1. 毛皮(;去毛待鞣的)生皮 2.(做衣服用的)兽皮;皮袄 3.(谑)(人的)皮肤 —vt. & vi. 剥(兽)皮

pelt[2] [pelt] vt.1. 连续地向…投掷;连续投掷 2. 重地拍打;不停地打击 3. 猛烈攻击;抨击 —vi.1. 连续地投掷;打出;拍打(at, on) 2. 下大雨(down) 3. 匆匆地走 —n.1. 投掷;打击 2. 抨击;质问 3.(雨等的)不停拍打 4. 快速,高速 5.(皮的)一件大怒

pelvic ['pelvik] adj.【解】骨盆(区)的

pelvis ['pelvis] ([复] pelvises 或 pelves ['pelviz]) n.【解】骨盆

pen[1] [pen] n.1. 笔;笔尖 2. 文笔,笔调 3.[the ～](文学;文章;写作 4. 笔杆子 5.【动】(枪乌贼等的)羽状壳 —(penned; penning) vt. 写 ‖ ～knife n.1. 袖珍折刀 / ～ name[作家的]笔名

pen[2] [pen] n.1.(家畜的)栏,圈 2. 小围栏(堆积货物等用的)栅棚 3.(小河中的)栏水坝 3.(修理潜艇的)掩蔽坞 4.(牙买加的)农场;种植场 —(penned 或 pent; penning) vt. 把(家畜)关入栏

圈;把…关起来(in, up)

penal ['pi:ml] adj.1.(有关)刑罚的 2. 当受刑罚的 3.(课税等)极其苛刻的

penalize ['pi:nəlaiz] vt.1. 对…处以刑罚;处罚 2. 使处于严重不利地位

penalty ['penlti] n.1. 处罚,惩罚;刑罚 2. 罚款 3.【体】犯规的处罚;(桥牌赛中的)罚分 4.(行为等造成的)困难;障碍,不利后果

penance ['penəns] n.1.(赎罪的)苦行,苦修 2.(为得到赦罪的)补赎 —vt. 使(某人)以苦行赎罪

pence [pens] penny 的复数

penchant ['pentʃənt] n.1. 强烈的倾向,偏向 2. 偏爱,爱好;have a ～ for gardening 爱好园艺

pencil ['pensl] n.1. 铅笔 2.〈古〉画笔 3.(画家的)笔调,笔法 4. 笔状物(如药笔、眉笔等) 5.〈美俚〉左轮手枪 6.【物】光线锥;(数)束 7.〈俚〉局 —(pencil(l)ed; pencil(l)ing) vt.1. 用铅笔写(或画、标);用画笔画(或描) 2. 用药笔治;用眉笔涂

pend [pend] vi. 未定,未决;待定,待决 —vt. 推迟对…的决定,使暂而不决

pendant ['pendənt] n.1. 垂饰;挂件;(怀表的)表环 2. 装饰;吊灯架 3.(成对物中的一个);补充的东西;(书的)补编 4.【海】短索;尖旗,三角旗 —adj. = pendent

pendent ['pendənt] adj.1. 下垂的;向外伸出的,突出的 2. 悬而未决的 —n. = pendant

pending ['pendiŋ] adj.1. 悬而未决的 2. 迫近的 —prep. 1. 在…期间 2. 在…以前

pendulous ['pendjuləs] adj. 悬垂的;摆动的

pendulum ['pendjuləm] n.1.(钟等的)摆

2. 摇摆不定的人(或事态、局面等)

penes ['piːniz] penis 的复数

penetrable ['penitrəbl] *adj.*1. 可穿透的;可被刺穿的; 2. 可被渗透的 2. 可进入的 3. 可被看见的 4. 可看透的;可识破的

penetrate ['penitreit] *vt.*1. 穿透;刺入;透入 2. 看穿,看透;识破 3. 渗入;弥漫;扩散于 4. (思想、感情等)深入,打动一*vi.*1. 穿入;刺入;透入(*into*, *through*) 2. 看穿,看透;识破 3. 渗入;弥漫;扩散 4. (思想、感情等)深入人心;打动人心

penetrating ['penitreitiŋ] *adj.*1. 穿透的;贯穿的;渗入的 2.(目光等)尖锐的;深刻的;透剤的 3.(声音等)响亮的;尖剤的 4.(伤口等)深的

penetration [ˌpeni'treiʃən] *n.*1. 穿入;进入;穿透能力;穿透深度 2. 渗透;浸入 3.〔军〕突破(空战中)深入敌方的飞行 4.(目光等)尖锐;洞察力;分辨(力)

penguin ['peŋgwin] *n.*1.〔动〕企鹅 2.〔美俚〕陆军(或空军)地勤人员 3.〔美俚〕(电影中的)群众演员,龙套 ‖ ~ **suit**〔俚〕企鹅服(指宇航员的太空服)

penicillin [ˌpeni'silin] *n.* 青霉素,盘尼西林

peninsula [pi'ninsjulə] *n.* 半岛;半岛状地方,突出的地方

penis ['piːnis] ([复] **penes** ['piːniz] 或 **penises**) *n.*〔解〕阳具 ‖ ~ **envy** 〔心〕阴茎妒忌(指女性想成为男性的潜在欲望)

penitence ['penitəns] *n.* 悔罪,悔过;后悔,忏悔

penitent ['penitənt] *adj.* 悔罪的;后悔的,忏悔的 —*n.* 悔罪者,悔过者;忏悔者

penitentiary [ˌpeni'tenʃəri] *n.*1.(罪犯)教养所 2.〔英〕妓女收容所 3.〔美〕州(或联

邦)监狱 2.(天主教)宗教裁判所(或官)—*adj.*1. 教养的;监禁的;引起监禁处分的 2. 后悔的,忏悔的;苦行赎罪的

penman ['penmən] ([复] **penmen**) *n.*1. 抄写员 2. 书法家 3. 作家 4.(善于)写信者 ‖ ~ **ship** *n.*1. 书法 2. 笔迹,字迹 3. 写作;文体;写作风格

pennant ['penənt] *n.*1.〔海〕短索;尖旗,三角旗 2.(体育比赛中的)奖旗,锦旗

penniless ['penilis] *adj.* 身无分文的,穷的

Pennsylvania [ˌpensil'veiniə] *n.* 宾夕法尼亚〔美国州名〕

penny ['peni] ([复] **pennies** 或 **pence** [pens]) *n.*1. 便士(英国辅币单位) 2. 分〔美国或加拿大辅币〕(= cent) 3.〔古罗马〕小银币 3. 一枚钱;一笔钱 4.〔英〕[用于数词后构成复合词,作定语,表示价格]…便士;a ten~ supper 一顿 10 便士的晚餐 ‖ ~ **weight** *n.* 本尼威特(英美金衡单位,合公制 1.555 克) /~wise *adj.* 小钱目上节约的;在处精明的;小事聪明的;蓬头小慎微的 /~worth ['penəθ, 'peniwəθ] *n.*1. 1 便士的价值;1 便士价值的东西;少量 2.(合算的)交易

pension[1] ['penʃən] *n.*1. 抚恤金;养老金,退休金 2.(艺术家等所领的)津贴,补助金;年金 —*vt.* 给予…抚恤金(或养老金等)‖ ~ **er** *n.*1. 领取抚恤金(或养老金等)者 2.(英国剑桥大学的)自费生

pension[2] ['pɔŋ'sjuŋ]〈法〉*n.*1.(欧洲大陆国家的)膳宿学校;膳宿公寓 2. 膳宿费

pensive ['pensiv] *adj.*(使人)沉思的;(令人)忧郁的 ‖ ~ **ly** *adv.* / ~ **ness** *n.*

penstock ['penstək] *n.*1.〔美〕水栗,水槽;

压力水管 2. 水闸门

pent [pent] pen² 的过去式和过去分词 — *adj.* 被囚禁的,被关押的

pentagon ['pentəgən] *n.* 1. 五边形,五角形 2. [the P-] 五角大楼 (美国国防部的五角形办公大楼) ‖ ～al [pen'tægənl] *adj.* 五边形的,五角形的

pentameter [pen'tæmitə] *n.* 五音步诗(行)

Pentateuch ['pentətjuːk] *n.* 【宗】《五经》(犹太教和基督教指《圣经》的首五卷)

pentathlon [pen'tæθlɔn] *n.* 五项全能运动(田径比赛全能运动之一)

Pentecost ['pentikɔst] *n.* 【宗】1. (基督教重大节日之一的) 五旬节,圣灵降临节

penthouse ['penthaus] *n.* 1. 屋顶房间;(豪华的) 顶层公寓 2. (靠在大楼旁边上撑的) 披屋;(建于大楼平顶上的) 楼顶房屋,小棚屋 3. (靠墙的) 单斜顶棚;庇檐 4. 遮篷,雨篷

pent-up ['pent'ʌp] *adj.* 被禁锢的;被压抑的,被抑制的

penult [pi'nʌlt, 'piːnʌlt] *n.* 1. 倒数第二个 2. 【语】(词的) 倒数第二音节

penultimate [pi'nʌltimət] *adj.* 1. 倒数第二的 2. 【语】(词的) 倒数第二音节的

penumbra [pi'nʌmbrə] ([复] penumbrae [pi'nʌmbriː] 或 penumbras) *n.* (日、月蚀的) 半影

penurious [pi'njuəriəs] *adj.* 1. 手紧的,吝惜的 2. 拮据的,贫困的 3. 不足的,缺乏的 ‖ ～ly *adv.* / ～ness *n.*

penury ['penjuri] *n.* 1. 手紧,吝啬 2. 拮据,贫穷 3. 不足,缺乏①

peon ['piːən, pjuːn] *n.* 1. (拉丁美洲的) 散工,短工;雇农 2.【史】(墨西哥) 以劳役偿债者 3. [pjuːn, piːən] (印度等地的) 土著士兵 (或警察,听差);勤杂工 ‖ ～age

---

n. 劳役偿债(制);当劳工,做苦工

peony ['piəni] *n.* 芍药;牡丹

people ['piːpl] *n.* 1. 人民 2. 民族;种族;(某国的) 国民 3. 人,人类 (区别于其他动物而言) 4. (泛指) 人,人们 5. 〈口〉家族 (家人,亲属 (尤指父母);祖先 6. (某一个阶级、地区、团体、行业的) 人;人员 7. 公民;选民 8. 平民,老百姓 9. 仆从;随员;(武装) 随从 10.【基督教】教区内的教徒 11. (某种或某一特定场合的) 小动物 — *vt.* 1. 使住着 (或住满) 人 2. 栖息在;布满 ‖ ～ mover (自动人行道、小型有轨电车等) 短程快速载客交通工具

pep [pep] 〈美俚〉 *n.* 锐气,活力,劲头 — (pepped; pepping) *vt.* 激励,给…打气,叫…加油 ‖ **'peppy** *adj.*

pepper ['pepə] *n.* 1. 胡椒;胡椒粉 2. 辛辣 (或富于刺激性、尖刻) 的事物 (如评论等) 3. 活力;精力;劲头;勇气 — *vt.* 1. 加胡椒粉于 2. 雨点般地撒 (或洒满) 3. 使 (文章等) 尖刻 (或富于刺激性) 殴打;鞭打;连续打击 (某人) 5. 重罚 ‖ ～ mint *n.* 1.【植】(胡椒) 薄荷 2. (胡椒) 薄荷油 3. (胡椒) 薄荷糖

peppery ['pepəri] *adj.* 1. 胡椒的,胡椒似的;加了很多胡椒的,辛辣的,辣的 2. (讲话、文章等) 辛辣的,尖刻的 3. 易怒的,暴躁的

pepsin ['pepsin] *n.* 胃蛋白酶 (制剂)

peptic ['peptik] *adj.* 胃蛋白酶的;消化性的;促进消化的

per [强 pə; 弱 pə] *prep.* 1. 经,由,靠 ‖ ～ rail 由铁路 2. 每,每一 ‖ ～ day 每日 3. 按照,根据 ‖ *per annum* 每年 / *per capita* ['kæpitə] 人均;按人口计算的 (地)

peradventure [ˌpərəd'ventʃə] *n.* 疑问;猜测 — *adv.* 〈古〉〈谑〉或许,可能

perambulate [pə'ræmbjuleit] *vt. & vi.* 漫

步(于);走过 ‖ **per**am**bu**'lation *n.* / per**ambulator** *n.* 1. 漫步者 2.〈主英〉手推童车,婴儿车

percale [pə'keil] *n.* 高级密织棉布

perceive [pə'siːv] *vt.* 1. 察觉;感知;看出 2. 领悟;理解 3. 认为 ‖ per'**ceivable** *adj.*

percent, per cent [pə'sent] *n.* 1. 每百中,百分之… 2.〈主英〉[~s]利率为…厘的债券 3.〈口〉百分率

percentage [pə'sentidʒ] *n.* 1. 百分比,百分率 2. 所占比例;部分 3.〈商〉手续费,佣金 4. 利润,赚头;好处;用处 5.(根据统计得出的)可能性

percept ['pəːsept] *n.* 1. 感知;认识 2.〈哲〉知觉对象

perceptible [pə'septəbl] *adj.* 1. 感觉得到的,察觉得到的;看得出的 2. 可领悟的,可理解的,可认识的

perception [pə'sepʃən] *n.* 1. 察觉;知觉 2. 感性认识;观念;概念 3. 直觉;理解力;理解力 4.〈律〉(地租、农作物、收益等的)获取,占有

perch[1] [pəːtʃ] *n.* 1.(禽鸟的)栖木;挂物木杆,挂针 2.(尤指在高处的)休息处,有利的位置;高位 3.〈机〉(联系前后车轮的)连杆,主轴;架 4. 杆(英国长度单位,= 5/12 码);石料容量单位(= 24 3/4 立方英尺) 5.〈纺〉验布架 6.〈海〉杆标志,浮筒顶标 — *vi.* 栖息,停歇;坐(或落)于高处 — *vt.* 1. 使(鸟)栖息;放置(人或物)于高处(或危险处) 2. 验(布)

perch[2] [pəːtʃ] *n.*〈鱼〉鲈;金鲈;河鲈;真骨鱼

perchance [pə'tʃɑːns] *adv.*〈古〉1. 偶然,意外地 2. 可能,或许

percolate ['pəːkəleit] *vt.* 1. 滤;使渗透;使渗透 2.(用渗滤器)煮(咖啡) — *vi.* 渗

开;滤过 — *n.* 滤过液;渗(或滤)出液 ‖ **percolator** *n.* 渗滤器

percolation [,pəːkə'leiʃən] *n.* 渗滤(过)

percussion [pə'kʌʃən] *n.* 1. 撞击,叩击;碰撞 2.(由敲、击产生的)震动,声响 3.【医】叩诊(法) 4.(枪、炮等火器的)击发 5.【音】打击,敲打;[总称]打击乐器;打击乐器演奏者,敲打手 ‖ ~ist *n.* 打击乐手;弹奏乐器弹奏者 ‖ ~ **instrument**【音】打击乐器;弹奏乐器(如钢琴)

perdition [pə'diʃən] *n.* 1.〈宗〉大劫,永劫;(恶人的)恶报 2. 万劫不复之地,地狱

peregrinate ['perigrineit] *vi.* 漫游 — *vt.* 走遍;走过 ‖ **peregri'nation** *n.*

peremptory [pə'remptəri] *adj.* 1. 紧急的 2. 最后决定的,无需说明理由的 3. 专横的,霸道的,盛气凌人的 4.【律】绝对的;强制的 ‖ **peremptorily** *adv.* / **peremptoriness** *n.*

perennial [pə'renjəl] *adj.* 1. 四季皆有的,终年的 2. 长期的,不断的;常在的,反复的;一再的 3. 多年生的 — *n.* 多年生植物 ‖ ~**ly** *adv.*

perfect ['pəːfikt] *adj.* 1. 完美的,无暇的;极好的,理想的 2. 完全的,完备的;全然的,纯然的;绝对的;毋容置疑的 3. 熟练的,精通的 4.〈主英〉忠于原文的 5. 法律上有效的 6.【语】完成的 7.【植】雌雄(蕊)同花的;具备的 8.【印】无线胶订的 — *n.*【语】完成时;完成体 — [pə'fekt, 'pəːfekt] *vt.* 1. 使完美,使完善;改善 2. 使熟练;使精通 ‖ ~**ly** *adv.* / ~**ness** *n.*

perfection [pə'fekʃən] *n.* 1. 尽善尽美,尽整无缺;登峰造极 2. 无比精确;圆满成熟 3. 完成;改善 4. 理想的人(或物);完美的典型 5. 精良,精湛;成就;造诣 ‖ **to** ~ 完美地,完善地

perfectionism [pə'fekʃənizəm] *n.* 1.【哲】至善论 2. 十全十美主义；求全思想；求全做法 ‖ **perfectionist** *n.*

perfidious [pə'fidiəs] *adj.* 背信弃义的；叛卖的，不忠的 ‖ **~ly** *adv.* / **~ness** *n.*

perfidy ['pə:fidi] *n.* 背信弃义；叛变，出卖

perforate ['pə:fəreit] *vt.* 1. 穿孔，打眼 2. 打一排孔于（邮票等）以便于撕开 — *vi.* 1. 穿孔 2. 穿过；贯穿；刺穿（*into*, *through*） — ['pə:fərit] *adj.* (邮票等)有孔的，穿孔的(尤指有一排孔的) ‖ **,perfo'ration** *n.*

perforce [pə'fɔ:s] *adv.* & *n.* 必须；必定

perform [pə'fɔ:m] *vt.* 1. 做；施行；履行；执行；完成(事业等) 2. 演出；表演 — *vi.* 1. 行动；进行 2. 演出；表演 3. (驯兽)表演游戏 ‖ **~er** *n.* 1. 履行者；执行者；完成者 2. 表演者，演出者；演奏者

performance [pə'fɔ:məns] *n.* 1. 履行；执行；完成 2. 行为；行动；动作 3. 功绩；演出；表演；演奏；把戏 4. (机械等的)工作性能，特性

perfume ['pə:fju:m] *n.* 1. 香味，芳香 2. 香料；香水 — [·] *vt.* 使发香；使充满香气；洒香水于

perfunctory [pə'fʌŋktəri] *adj.* 敷衍塞责的，草率的，马马虎虎的 ‖ **perfunctorily** *adv.* / **perfunctoriness** *n.*

perhaps [pə'hæps, præps] *adv.* 也许，可能；多半，大概 — *n.* 猜想；尚属疑问的事(或物)

perigee ['peridʒi:] *n.*【天】近地点

perihelion [,peri'hi:ljən] (【复】perihelia [peri'hi:ljə] 或 perihelions) *n.*【天】近日点

peril ['peril] *n.* 1. (严重的) 危险 2. 危险的事物 3. 冒险 — (peril(l)ed; peril(l)ing) *vt.* 置…于危险中；危及

perilous ['periləs] *adj.* 危险的；冒险的

perimeter [pə'rimitə] *n.* 1. 周；周边；周长 2.【军】环形防线 3.【医】视野计 ‖ **perimetric** [,peri'metrik] *adj.*

period ['piəriəd] *n.* 1. 时期；时代 2. [the ~]现代；当代 3. 周期；期；【地】纪；[常~s]月经期 4. 一段时间；(比赛的)一节时间 5. 句号；句点；结束，终止 6. 完整句(常指复合句) — [~s]婉饰的(或华丽的)词藻 7.【语】尾重句，圆周句(= periodic sentence) 8.【音】乐段 — *adj.* (关于)过去某一特定历史时期的；似过去某一特定历史时期的 — *int.* [强调说话过程是这话;就是这回事

periodic [,piəri'ɔdik] *adj.* 1. 定期的，周期的；间歇的，间发性的；循环的 2. 一定时期的 3.【语】(用)尾重句的，(用)圆周句的

periodical [,piəri'ɔdikəl] *adj.* 1. 定期的，周期的；间歇的 2. 定期刊行的 3. 期刊(中的)一个。期刊，杂志 ‖ **~ly** *adv.*

periphery [pə'rifəri] *n.* 1. 圆周；周边 2. (圆体的)外面 3. 边缘(地区)；外围 4.【解】体表；(神经)末梢周围 ‖ **peripheral** *adj.*

periscope ['periskəup] *n.* 潜望镜(镜头)

perish ['periʃ] *vi.* 1. 灭亡；消灭；死去；暴卒；夭折 2. 凋谢；枯萎；褪色 — *vt.* 1. 毁灭；使死去 2. 使困顿；使麻木

perishable ['periʃəbl] *adj.* 1. 易腐烂的；易凋谢的；易死的；不经久的 — *n.* [~s]易腐烂物(或凋谢)的东西

peritonitis [,peritə'naitis] *n.*【医】腹膜炎

periwinkle ['peri,wiŋkl] *n.* 1.【动】滨螺，玉黍螺，海螺；北美淡水螺 2.【植】长春花；小长春花

perjure ['pə:dʒə] *vt.*【律】1. [常作 ~ oneself]使作伪证，使发假誓 2. 为…作伪证

perjury ['pɜːdʒəri] n. 1.【律】伪证(罪),假誓(罪) 2. 背信弃义

perk [pɜːk] vi. 1. 昂首;意气风发 2. 振作,活跃起来(尤指消沉或疾病之后) —vt. 1. 竖起(耳朵等);昂(首);翘(尾) 2. 打扮,修饰 —adj. = perky

perky ['pɜːki] adj. 1. 生龙活虎的,意气风发的 2. 傲慢的,自信的 3. 打扮漂亮的 4. 鲁莽的,莽撞的

perm [pɜːm]〈口〉n. (电烫或化学烫出的)波浪发型;烫(头)发(= permanent wave) —vt. 烫(头发)

permanence ['pɜːmənəns] n. 永久(性);持久(性)

permanent ['pɜːmənənt] adj. 永久的,持久的 —n. (电烫或化学烫出的)波浪发型;烫(头)发(= ~ wave) ‖ ~ly adv. /~ness n. ‖ ~ press【纺】耐久压烫,耐久定形;耐久定形织物

permeable ['pɜːmɪəbl] adj. 可渗透的;具渗透性的

permeate ['pɜːmɪeɪt] vt. 渗入,透过;弥漫,充满 —vi. 渗透;透入(through,among)‖ ,perme'ation n.

permissible [pə'mɪsɪbl] adj. 可允许的;容许的,许可的;准许的 ‖ permissibly adv.

permission [pə'mɪʃən] n. 允许,许可,同意;准许

permissive [pə'mɪsɪv] adj. 1. 容许的,许可的 2. 随意的;放任的;放纵的;性自由的

permit [pə'mɪt](permitted;permitting) vt. & vi. 允许,许可 —n. ['pɜːmɪt] n. 1. 许可 2. 执照,许可证

permutation [ˌpɜːmjuː'teɪʃən] n. 1. 改变,更动 2. 互换,交换 3.【数】排列;置换

pernicious [pə'nɪʃəs] adj. 有害的;恶劣

的;有毒的;致命的;恶性的

peroration [ˌperə'reɪʃən] n. (演讲的)结束语,总结语

peroxide [pə'rɒksaɪd] n.【化】过氧化物;过氧化氢;双氧水

perpendicular [ˌpɜːpən'dɪkjulə] adj. 1. 垂直的,成直角的,正交的(to),陡峭的,矗立的 3. [P-]【建】垂直式的(指14-16世纪一种英国哥特式建筑风格的)(俚)站着的 —n. 1. 垂直(姿势) 2. 垂线;直垂面 3. 垂规 4. 正直,刚正

perpetrate ['pɜːpɪtreɪt] vt. 犯(罪行、错误等);作(恶);做(坏事);胡说

perpetual [pə'petjuəl,pə'petʃuəl] adj. 1. 永远的,永恒的,正交的(to)终身的 2. 四季开花的 3. 不断的;重复不停的 —n. 多年生植物;四季开花的蔷薇 ‖ ~ly aav.

perpetuate [pə'petjueɪt,pə'petʃueɪt] vt. 使永久存在;使不朽

perpetuity [ˌpɜːpɪ'tjuːɪti] n. 1. 永久,永恒;不朽 2. 终身职位;终身年金 3.【律】永久拥有;(房地产的)永久(或长期)不得转让;永久(或长期)不得转让的房地产

perplex [pə'pleks] vt. 1. 困惑;难住 2. 使复杂化;使纠缠不清

perplexed [pə'plekst] adj. 1. 困惑的,茫然不知所措的 2. 复杂的;纠缠不清的

perplexity [pə'pleksɪti] n. 1. 困惑;窘困 2. 令人困惑的事物 3. 纠缠,扭结

perquisite ['pɜːkwɪzɪt] n. 1. 额外收入,外快(如奖金、小费等) 2. 特权,特殊待遇 3. 工资,薪金

persecute ['pɜːsɪkjuːt] vt. 1. 迫害,残害 2. 困扰,为难 ‖ persecutor n. 迫害者,残害者

persecution [ˌpɜːsɪ'kjuːʃən] n. 迫害,残害;困扰

perseverance [ˌpəsi'viərəns] *n.* 坚持,坚忍不拔,不屈不挠

persevere [ˌpəsi'viə] *vi.* 1. 坚持,不屈不挠(*in*, *at*, *with*) 2. 固执己见 ‖ **persevering** *adj.*

Persia ['pəːʃə] *n.* 波斯(现称 Iran 伊朗)[西南亚国家]

Persian ['pəːʃən] *n.* 1. 波斯人;波斯语 2. 波斯猫 — *adj.* 波斯的;波斯人的;波斯语的

persimmon [pəː'simən] *n.* 【植】柿;柿树

persist [pə'sist] *vi.* 1. 坚持;执意(*in*) 2. 持续;存留 3. 坚持;追问

persistence [pə'sistəns], **persistency** [pə'sistənsi] *n.* 1. 坚持;固执 2. 持续;存留

persistent [pə'sistənt] *adj.* 1. 坚持的;固执的 2. 持续的,持久的,不断的 3. 【植】宿存的,不落的 4.【动】持续生存的;终生保留的 ‖ ~**ly** *adv.*

person ['pəːsn] *n.* 1. 人 2.（贬）家伙 3. 人身,身体 4. 本人,自身 5. 容貌,外表;风度 6.【语】人称 7.（古）（戏剧、小说中的）人物,角色 8.【宗】（三位一体的）位;（基督的）神人一位 ‖ ~**hood** *n.* 做人;人格

personable ['pəːsnəbl] *adj.* 1. 动人的,讨人喜欢的 2.【律】具有权利能力和行为能力的

personage ['pəːsənidʒ] *n.* 1. 要人,名流,显贵 2. 人,个人;（图案中的）人形 3. 人物,角色

personal ['pəːsənl] *adj.* 1. 个人的,私人的 2. 本人的,亲自的 3. 人身的;容貌的 4. 人身的;涉及个人（或隐私）的 — *n.*（报纸上的）人事要闻;私人广告 ‖ ~**ly** *adv.* 1. 亲自地 2.（引导句子）就个人而言;针对个人地 3. 就自己而言 ‖ ~**column**（报上登载的）私人广告栏;人事

要闻栏 / ~ **computer** 个人计算机,个人电脑 / ~ **pronoun**【语】人称代词 / ~ **property**【律】动产

personality [ˌpəːsə'næliti] *n.* 1. 人的存在;人 2. 个性;人格 3.（国家等）独有的特性 4.（尤指有名的）人物 5.（常 personalities）人身攻击

personalize ['pəːsənəlaiz] *vt.* 1. 使成为个人所有 2. 使针对个人;使个人化;使个性化 3. = personify ‖ **personali'zation** *n.*

personification [pəːˌsɔnifi'keiʃən] *n.* 1. 拟人化,人格化;【语】拟人法 2. 化身;体现;象征;典型

personify [pəː'sɔnifai] *vt.* 1. 拟（某物）为人,赋予…以人性,使人格化 2. 表现;体现;象征;是…的化身

personnel [ˌpəːsə'nel] *n.* 1.［总称］全体人员;工员 2. 人事部门

perspective [pə'spektiv] *n.* 1. 透视;透视画法;透视图 2. 正确观察事物相互关系的能力;观点 3. 远景,前景;展望,前途;景象 4. 观点,看法 5. 事物相互关系的外貌;整体各个部分的比例（或关系）— *adj.* 透视的;透视画的

perspicacious [ˌpəːspi'keiʃəs] *adj.* 聪颖的,敏锐的 ‖ **perspicacity** [ˌpəːspi'kæsiti] *n.*

perspicuous [pə'spikjuəs] *adj.* 表达得清楚的;易懂的;明白的 ‖ **perspicuity** [ˌpəːspi'kjuːiti] *n.*

perspiration [ˌpəːspə'reiʃən] *n.* 1. 排汗,出汗,流汗 2. 汗,汗水

perspire [pə'spaiə] *vi.* 1. 出汗,流汗 2. 分泌;渗出

persuade [pə'sweid] *vt.* 1. 说服,劝服 2. 使相信 — *vi.*（被）说服

persuasion [pə'sweiʒən] *n.* 1. 说服,劝服;劝说 2. 说服力 3. 信念;（宗教的）信仰 4.（持某一见解的）派别;教派 5.（谑）

种类，类别

persuasive [pə'sweisiv] *adj.* 有说服力的；劝导性的；劝诱的 —*n.* 引诱语 ‖ ～ly *adv.* / ～ness *n.*

pert [pət] *adj.***1.** 没有礼貌的；冒失的 **2.** 活跃的；精神抖擞的 **3.** (服装等) 雅致的；时髦的 **4.** (言语等) 辛辣的，痛快的

pertain [pə'tein] *vi.***1.** 从属，属于 (*to*) **2.** 关于，有关 (*to*) **3.** 适合；相称 (*to*)

pertinacious [ˌpəːti'neiʃəs] *adj.* 坚持不放的；顽执的；顽固的；(疾病等) 难以治好的 ‖ ～ly *adv.* / ～ness *n.*

pertinent [ˈpəːtinənt] *adj.***1.** 恰当的；贴切的；中肯的 **2.** 有关的，相干的 (*to*) ‖ pertinence, pertinency *n.* / ～ly *adv.*

perturb [pə'təːb] *vt.***1.** 使不安，烦扰 **2.** 使紊乱，扰乱 **3.** 〖天〗使摄动

Peru [pə'ruː] *n.* 秘鲁〖南美洲西部国家〗

peruse [pə'ruːz] *vt.***1.** (仔细) 阅读 **2.** 仔细察看；仔细考虑 **3.** 浏览；(随便) 翻阅 ‖ perusal *n.*

pervade [pəː'veid] *vt.* 弥漫；渗透；遍及，充满 ‖ pervasion *n.* / pervasive *adj.*

perverse [pə'vəːs] *adj.***1.** 不正当的；堕落的；邪恶的 **2.** 违反常情的，反常的 **3.** 坚持错误的；刚愎的；任性的 **4.** (情况等) 违背意愿的 **5.** 〖律〗(判决等) 不合法的 ‖ ～ly *adv.* / perversity *n.*

pervert [pə'vəːt] *vt.***1.** 使走上邪路；使变坏；使错乱，使反常 **2.** 歪曲，曲解 **3.** 误用，滥用 **4.** 唆使进…性欲倒错— [ˈpəːvəːt] *n.*；性欲倒错者 ‖ perversion *n.* / ～er *n.*

peseta [pə'seitə] *n.* 比塞塔〖西班牙货币单位〗

peso [ˈpeisəu] ([复] *pesos*) *n.* 比索〖菲律宾和某些拉丁美洲国家的货币单位〗

pessimism [ˈpesimizəm] *n.* 悲观；悲观主义，厌世主义 ‖ pessimist *n.* 悲观者；悲

观主义者，厌世者

pessimistic [ˌpesi'mistik] *adj.* 悲观的；悲观主义的，厌世的 ‖ ～ally *adv.*

pest [pest] *n.***1.** 有害生物；害虫 **2.** 讨厌的人；害人虫；有害的东西 **3.** 〈罕〉瘟疫；鼠疫

pester [ˈpestə] *vt.* 烦扰，纠缠

pesticide [ˈpestisaid] *n.* 杀虫剂；农药

pestilence [ˈpestiləns] *n.***1.** 疫，瘟疫；恶性流行病 (尤指鼠疫) **2.** 散布毒害的事物 (如学说等)；罪恶 ‖ pestilent *adj.*

pestle [ˈpesl, ˈpestl] *n.***1.** (捣研用的) 杵；碾槌 —*vt. & vi.* (用杵) 捣；研碎

pet¹ [pet] *n.***1.** 玩赏动物，宠畜，爱畜 **2.** 宠儿；宝贝儿 —*adj.***1.** 作为玩赏动物蓄养的；宠爱的 **2.** 表示亲昵的 **3.** 最得意的 **4.** 〈谑〉第一号的；特别的— (*petted*; *petting*) *vt.***1.** 把…当作宠儿 **2.** 抚弄；爱抚 **3.** 溺爱，宠爱 —*vi.* 拥抱；接吻，爱抚

pet² [pet] *n.* 生气，愠怒，不开心 — (*petted*; *petting*) *vi.* 生气，不开心

petal [ˈpetl] *n.* 花瓣

peter [ˈpiːtə] *vi.* 逐渐枯竭；渐趋清淡 (*out*)

petiole [ˈpetiəul] *n.***1.** 〖植〗(花、果等的) 柄，梗 **2.** (昆虫的) 柄，腹柄 **3.** 〖解〗(胸骨的) 柄

petiolule [ˈpetiəljuːl] *n.* 〖植〗小叶柄

petit [ˈpeti, pəˈtiː] 〈法〉*adj.* 小的；次要的

petite [pəˈtiːt] 〈法〉*adj.***1.** (妇女服装) 小号的 **2.** (女人) 小个子的，娇小的

petition [pi'tiʃən] *n.***1.** 请愿；申请，请求；祈求 **2.** 请愿书；〖律〗(向法院递交的) 申请书，诉状 —*vt.* 向…请愿；请求；祈求 ‖ ～er *n.* 请愿人；请求者；离婚诉讼的原告

petrel [ˈpetrəl] *n.* 海燕

petrify [ˈpetrifai] *vt*.1. 使石化 2. 使僵化;使丧失活力 3. 使惊呆 —*vi*.1. 石化 2. 僵化 3. 变呆;吓呆

petrodollar [ˈpetrəuˌdɔlə] *n*.[常~s](石油输出国赚取的)石油美元 —*adj*. 石油美元的

petrol [ˈpetrəl] *n*.1.〈英〉汽油(美国称 gasoline) 2.〈古〉石油 ‖ ~ **bomb**〈英〉燃烧弹,汽油弹

petroleum [piˈtrəuliəm] *n*. 石油

petrology [peˈtrɔlədʒi] *n*.【地】岩石学

petticoat [ˈpetikəut] *n*.1. 衬裙;(旧时妇女或幼儿穿的)裙子 2.〈口〉女人;少女;[~s][总称]〈贬〉女性 3. 裙状物 —*adj*.1. 女性的 2.〈贬〉女人腔的

pettily [ˈpetili] *adv*.1. 琐碎地;小规模地 2. 器量小地,偏狭地

pettiness [ˈpetinis] *n*.1. 微小,琐碎;小规模 2. 器量小,偏狭

pettish [ˈpetiʃ] *adj*.(人)任性的,易怒的;(语言、行为等)怒气冲冲的 ‖ ~**ly** *adv*. / ~**ness** *n*.

petty [ˈpeti] *adj*.1. 小的,微小的;小规模的;次要的 2. 渺小的,不足道的;器量小的,偏狭的;派头小的;卑劣的 3. 地位低微的;下级的 ‖ ~ **cash** 小额现金;小额备用金 / ~ **officer** 海军军士

petulant [ˈpetjulənt] *adj*.1. 易怒的;使性子的;脾气坏的 2.〈古〉无礼的;莽撞的;粗野的 ‖ **petulance** *n*.

petunia [piˈtjuːniə] *n*.1.【植】矮牵牛;矮牵牛花 2. 暗紫色

pew [pjuː] *n*.1. 教堂长凳 2. 教堂会众 3.〈口〉座位 —*vt*. 为(教堂)安装座位

pewee [ˈpiːwiː] *n*.【动】美洲小鹟

pewit [ˈpiːwit] *n*.【动】1. = pewee 2. 凤头麦鸡 3. 红嘴鸥

pewter [ˈpjuːtə] *n*.1.【冶】白镴,锡镴 2. 白镴器皿 3.〈英俚〉奖杯;奖金 —*adj*. 白镴制的

PG *abbr*. parental guidance (电影)宜在家长指导下观看的

pg. *abbr*. page

phaeton [ˈfeiətən] *n*. 1. 四轮敞篷轻便马车 2.〈美〉敞篷旅游车

phalanx [ˈfælæŋks, ˈfeilæŋks] ([复]phalanxes 或 phalanges[fæˈlændʒiːz]) *n*. 1. 密集队形排列;方阵 2.【解】指骨;趾骨

phallus [ˈfæləs] ([复]phalli[ˈfælai]或 phalluses) *n*.1.【解】阴茎 2.(某些宗教作为生殖力的象征加以崇拜的)阴茎图像

phantasm [ˈfæntæzəm] *n*. 幻影,幻景;幽灵,鬼魂

phantasmagoria [ˌfæntæzməˈgɔriə] *n*. 幻觉效应;变幻不定的景象

phantasy [ˈfæntəsi] *n*. = fantasy

phantom [ˈfæntəm] *n*.1. 幽灵;鬼怪;阴影;令人恐惧的东西 2.[P-]鬼怪式飞机 3. 幻象 4. 影子;有名无实的人(或物);〈美俚〉在工资单上挂假名的人 5.(脑海中的)印象 6.(抽象品性等的)化身 7. 人体模型;(机器等内部部分结构的)剖视图 —*adj*.1. 幽灵(似)的;鬼怪(似)的 2. 幻象的;幻觉的 3. 无形的 4. 虚拟的;傀儡性的

Pharaoh [ˈfɛərəu] *n*.1. 法老(古埃及君王称号) 2. 暴君

Pharisee [ˈfærisiː] *n*.1. 法利赛人(古犹太教的一派,标榜墨守传统礼仪) 2.[p-]伪善者

pharmaceutical [ˌfɑːməˈsjuːtikəl] *adj*. 药学的;药(剂)师的;药(物)的;药用的 —*n*. 药品,药剂,药物

pharmaceutist [ˌfɑːməˈsjuːtist], **pharmacist**[ˈfɑːməsist] *n*.1. 药(剂)师 2. 药商

pharmacology [ˌfɑːməˈkɔlədʒi] *n*. 药理学;

药物学 ‖ **pharmacological** [ˌfɑːməkə'lɔdʒikəl] *adj.* / **pharmacologist** *n.* 药理学家;药物学家

pharmacopoeia [ˌfɑːməkə'piə] *n.* 1. 药典 2. 一批备用药品

pharmacy ['fɑːməsi] *n.* 1. 药学 2. 制药;配药 3. 药房,药店 4. 一批备用药品

pharyngal [fə'riŋgl], **pharyngeal** [ˌfærin'dʒiəl] *adj.* 【解】咽的

pharynx ['færiŋks] ([复]pharynxes 或 pharynges[fə'rindʒiːz]) *n.*【解】咽

phase [feiz] *n.* 1. 阶段,时期 2. 方面,面 3. [天]相;[物]相,周相,位相 4.【电】突变型;期 — *vt.* 1. 使定相 2. 分阶段(或逐步)实行

phaseout ['feizaut] *n.* 分阶段(或逐步)的结束或停止、完成等

Ph. D. *abbr.* (拉) *Philosophiae Doctor* 哲学博士(= Doctor of Philosophy)

pheasant ['feznt] ([复]pheasant(s)) *n.* 雉鸡,野鸡

phenobarbital [ˌfiːnəu'bɑːbitəl], **phenobarbitone** [ˌfiːnəu'bɑːbitəun] *n.* 苯巴比妥,鲁米那(一种安眠镇静剂)

phenol ['fiːnɔl] *n.*【化】(苯)酚,石炭酸 ‖ **phenolic** *adj.* (苯)酚的

phenomena [fi'nɔminə] phenomenon 的复数

phenomenal [fi'nɔminl] *adj.* 1. (关于)现象的 2. 可知觉的 3. 不寻常的;非凡的;出众的 ‖ ~**ly** *adv.*

phenomenon [fi'nɔminən] ([复]phenomena [fi'nɔminə]) *n.* 1. 现象 2. 独特的事件;奇迹 3. 非凡的人,杰出人材

phial ['faiəl] *n.* 小瓶(尤指盛药水瓶)

-phil *comb. form* = -phile

Philadelphia [ˌfilə'delfiə] *n.* 费拉德尔菲亚(即费城)【美国宾夕法尼亚州东南部港市】

philander [fi'lændə] *n.* 1. [P-]菲兰德(古代爱情小说或诗歌中的情人名) 2. 玩弄女性;调情 3. = philanderer — *vi.* 玩弄女性;调情 2. 饶倪认真地对待(或处理);玩弄(*with*) ‖ ~ **er** *n.* 玩弄女性者;爱调情的人

philanthropic [ˌfilən'θrɔpik] *adj.* 1. 慈善的;有善心的 2. 慈善事业的 ‖ **philanthropically** *adv.*

philanthropist [fi'lænθrəpist] *n.* 慈善家

philanthropy [fi'lænθrəpi] *n.* 1. 慈善,善心;博爱 2. 善行;慈善性捐赠;慈善事业 3. 慈善性机构,慈善团体

philately [fi'lætəli] *n.* 1. 集邮 2. [总称]集邮者;集邮家 ‖ **philatelic** [ˌfilə'telik] *adj.* / **philatelist** *n.* 集邮家

-phile *comb. form* 表示"爱好","亲";"爱好者"; bibliophile 书籍爱好者

philharmonic [ˌfilhɑː'mɔnik, ˌfilɑː'mɔnik] *adj.* 1. 爱好音乐的,爱乐的 2. 交响乐团的;爱乐团体的 — *n.* [P-]交响乐团;爱乐团体

Philippine ['filipin] *adj.* 菲律宾(群岛)的;菲律宾人的

Philippines ['filipinz] *n.* [the ~] 1. 菲律宾[东南亚岛国] 2. 菲律宾群岛[东南亚]

philistine ['filistain, fi'listin] *n.* 平庸之辈,庸人;门外汉

philology [fi'lɔlədʒi] *n.* 1. 语文学 2. 文献学;文学 3. 历史比较语言学;语言学 ‖ **philologist** *n.* 语文学家;语言学家;文献学家 / **philologer** *n.* 文字学家

philosopher [fi'lɔsəfə] *n.* 1. 哲学家 2. 思想家;学者 3. 哲人;(逆境中)泰然自若的人;达观者 4. 炼金术士 5. 贤哲大道理的人 6. (古)炼金术士

philosophical [ˌfilə'sɔfikəl] *adj.* 1. 哲学的

的;哲学(上)的 2. 有哲人态度的;镇静的;达观的;泰然自若的 3. 富于哲理性的 ‖ **philosophically** *adv.*

philosophize [fi'lɔsəfaiz] *vt. & vi.* 哲学家似地思考(或对待)

philosophy [fi'lɔsəfi] *n.* **1.** 哲学;哲学体系 2. 哲理 3. 人生观;宗旨 4.(某一学科的)基本原理 5.〈古〉自然科学 6. 达观;镇静

philtre, philter ['filtə] *n.* 催情药,春药;灵丹妙药

phlebotomy [fli'bɔtəmi] *n.* 静脉切开术,放血术 ‖ **phlebotomize** [fli'bɔtəmaiz] *vt.* 给(病人)施行静脉切开手术,给(病人)放血 *vi.* 施行静脉切开手术,放血

phlegm [flem] *n.* **1.** 痰 2. 粘液(古生理学所称四种体液之一,据信此液多则人迟钝)3. 迟钝;冷淡;不动感情;镇定的 ‖ **~y** *adj.* 痰的;似痰的;含痰的

phlegmatic [fleg'mætik] *adj.* **1.** 粘液质的 2. 迟钝的;冷淡的;不动感情的;镇定的 ‖ **phlegmatically** *adv.*

phlox [flɔks] *n.* **1.**【植】福禄考 2. 福禄考花

Phnom Penh ['nɔm 'pen] 金边[柬埔寨首都]

-phobe *comb. form* [用以构成名词]表示"恐惧...的人"

phobia ['fəubiə] *n.* **1.** 恐惧症,恐怖症 2. 惧怕;憎恶 ‖ **~c** ['əubiæk] *n.*

phoebe ['fi:bi] *n.* 【鸟】东菲比霸鹟(产于北美)

Phoebus ['fi:bəs] *n.* **1.**【希神】福玻斯(太阳神)2.〈诗〉太阳

phoenix ['fi:niks] *n.* **1.** 埃及神话中阿拉伯沙漠的不死鸟,长生鸟(相传此鸟每500年自行焚死,然后由灰中再生)2.(中国古代传说中的)凤凰 3. 死而复生的人(或事物)4. 完人;殊品

phone [fəun] *n.* **1.**〈口〉电话;电话机(= telephone)2. 受话器,耳机,听筒 —〈口〉*vt.* **1.** 给...打电话 2. 打电话通知(一件事)—*vi.* 打电话(to)

phoneme ['fəuni:m] *n.* 【语】音素,音位

phonetic [fə'netik] *adj.* **1.** 语音的;语音学的 2. 表示发音的 ‖ **~ally** *adv.*

phonetics [fə'netiks] [复] *n.* [用作单] **1.** 语音学 2.(一种语言的)语音体系

phoney ['fəuni] *adj. & n.* = phony

phonics ['fɔuniks] [复] *n.* [用作单] **1.** 声学 2. 读音法 3.〈罕〉语音学

phonograph ['fəunəgrɑ:f] *n.*〈美〉留声机,唱机(=〈英〉gramophone)‖ **~ record** (留声机)唱片 —**ic** [ˌfəunə'græfik] *adj.*

phony ['fəuni]〈俚〉*adj.* 假的;伪造的;假冒的;不可信的;虚伪的 —*n.* **1.** 骗子,假冒者;假内行 2. 假货 ‖ **phoniness** *n.*

phosgene ['fɔsdʒi:n] *n.*【化】光气,碳酰氯

phosphate ['fɔsfeit] *n.*【化】**1.** 磷酸盐(或酯)2. 磷肥

phosphoresce [ˌfɔsfə'res] *vi.* 发磷光

phosphorescence [ˌfɔsfə'resns] *n.* 磷光(现象)

phosphorescent [ˌfɔsfə'resnt] *adj.* 发磷光的

phosphorus ['fɔsfərəs] *n.*【化】**1.** 磷 2. 磷光体 ‖ **phosphoric** [fɔs'fɔrik], **phosphorous** *adj.*

photo ['fəutəu]([复]photos) *n.*〈口〉照片(photograph 的缩略)—*vt.* 给...照相 —*vi.* **1.** 照相 2. 被照相

photocell ['fəutəsel] *n.*【物】光电池,光电管

photocopy ['fəutəukɔpi] *n.* 摄影复制品,复印件 —*vt. & vi.* 摄影复制,复印 ‖ **~ing** *n.*

photoelectric [,fəutəui'lektrik] *adj.*【物】光电的 ‖ — **cell** 光电池;光电管

photoengrave [,fəutəuin'greiv] *vt.*【印】制作...的照相凸版 ‖ **photoengraving** *n.* 照相凸版制版法 /— *n.*

photogenic [,fəutəu'dʒenik] *adj.* 上照的;上(电影)镜头的

photograph ['fəutəgrɑːf] *n.*1. 照片 2. 逼真的描绘;栩栩如生的形象 — *vt.*1. 为...拍照 2. 逼真地描绘;使印入脑中 — *vi.*1. 拍照 2. 被照相 ‖ — **er**['fə'tɔgrəfə] *n.* 摄影师,照相师;摄影者

photographic [,fəutə'græfik] *adj.*1. 摄影(术)的;摄影用的 2.(描写、叙述等)逼真的;生动的 3. 能原原本本地把所见事物记住的

photography [fə'tɔgrəfi] *n.* 摄影术;摄影,照相;一组照片

photoplay ['fəutəuplei] *n.* 故事影片;戏剧片;电影剧本

photosensitive [,fəutəu'sensitiv] *adj.* 对光敏感的,光敏的 ‖ **'photo,sensi'tivity** *n.* 光敏性

photostat ['fəutəustæt] *n.* 复印机,(直接)影印机 — *vt.* & *vi.* 照相复制 ‖ **photos'tatic** *adj.*

photosynthesis [,fəutəu'sinθəsis] *n.*【生化】光合作用,光能合成

photosynthetic [,fəutəusin'θetik] *adj.*【生化】光合的

phototropism [,fəutəu'trəupizəm] *n.*1.【生】向光性 2.【物】光色互变(现象);趋光性

phrase [freiz] *n.*1.【语】短语,片语,词组 2. 习惯用语 3. 措词,用语 4. 警句 5.【音】短句,乐句 6.[~s]空话;废话 — *vt.*1. 用话表示;用短语表达 2.【音】分成短句 ‖ **phrasal** *adj.* 短语的

短语的

phraseology [,freizi'ɔlədʒi] *n.*1. 说法,措辞,用语 2. 特殊用语,术语 3.[总称]短语,词组;习语,片语

phrenetic [fri'netik] *adj.*1. 精神错乱的;精神病的 2. 极度激动的;发狂似的

phrenology [fri'nɔlədʒi] *n.* 颅相学 ‖ **phrenologist** *n.*

phylum ['failəm] ([复] phyla['failə]) *n.*1.(生物分类上的)门 2.【语】语群

physic ['fizik] *n.*1.〈口〉药品;泻药 2.〈罕〉物理学 3.〈古〉医术;医学;医业 — (physicked; physicking) *vt.*1. 给...服药;给...服泻药 2. 治愈

physical ['fizikəl] *adj.*1. 物质的;有形的;确确实实的 2. 自然(界)的;自然科学的;按自然规律的 3. 物理的 4. 身体的,肉体的 5. 一味追求肉欲的 — *n.* 体格检查(=~examination)‖ —**ly** *adv.* ‖ — **science** 自然科学(指物理学、化学、天文学等);物理学

physician [fi'ziʃən] *n.*1. 医生;内科医生 2.(解除精神痛苦等的)医治者;抚慰者

physicist ['fizisist] *n.*1. 物理学家 2.〈罕〉自然科学家

physics ['fiziks] [复] *n.*1. [用作单或复]物理学 2. 物理过程;物理现象;物理成分

physiognomy [,fizi'ɔnəmi] *n.*1. 容貌,相貌 2. 观相术,相面术 3.(事物的)外貌;地貌

physiography [,fizi'ɔgrəfi] *n.*1. 自然地理学 2. 地文学 3.〈美〉地貌学 4. 自然现象志

physiologic(al) [,fiziə'lɔdʒik(əl)] *adj.* 生理学的;生理的 ‖ **physiologically** *adv.*

physiology [,fizi'ɔlədʒi] *n.*1. 生理学 2. 生理(机能)‖ **physiologist** *n.* 生理学家

physique [fi'zi:k] *n.* 体格

pi [pai] *n.*【数】圆周率(π)

pianissimo [piə'nisiməu] (意) *adj. & adv.* 非常轻的(地)

pianist ['pjænist] *n.* 钢琴家;钢琴演奏者

piano [pi'ænəu] ([复]pianos) *n.* 钢琴 ∥ ~ bar (有钢琴演奏助兴的)钢琴酒吧

pianoforte [pi'ænəu'fɔ:ti] *n.* = piano

piastre, piaster [pi'æstə] *n.* 1.(旧)比亚塔(西班牙货币) 2. 皮阿斯特(埃及等国的辅币单位)

piazza [pi'ætsə] *n.* 1.(尤指意大利城市中的)广场;市场 2.(外形)顶的长廊 3. [pi'æzə] (美)游廊,外廊

pica ['paikə] *n.* (西文)12点活字

picayune [ˌpikə'ju:n] *adj.* 微不足道的,无价值的;可鄙的;气量小的

piccalilli ['pikəlili] *n.* 酸辣泡菜

piccaninny ['pikənini] *n.* (英)(贬)黑人小孩;澳大利亚土著小孩 — *adj.* 极小的

piccolo ['pikələu] (意) *n.* 短笛;短笛吹奏者 — *adj.* (乐器)小型的;像短笛的

pick¹ [pik] *n.* 1. 鹤嘴锄,镐 2. 尖头挖掘工具;牙签 3.(弹弦乐器用的)拨子 4. 撬锁工具;撬锁贼(亦作~lock) ∥ ~ ax(e) *n.* 鹤嘴锄,镐 *vt. & vi.* 用鹤嘴锄凿

pick² [pik] *vt.* 1.(用鹤嘴锄等)凿,掘,挖;凿成(洞等) 2.(用手指等)挖(鼻子,耳朵等);剔(骨头,牙齿等);剔去3. 摘,采(花朵,果实等);拔(禽类的)羽毛 4.(鸟类等)啄食;(家畜等或挑料拣肥地)吃 5. 撕开,扯开(纤维等) 6. 挑选,选择 7. 找(碴儿);寻找机会吵(架) 8. 拨(弦乐);弹(弦乐器等) 9. 撬(锁);扒窃(口袋中的东西) — *vi.* 1.(用鹤嘴锄等)凿,掘,挖 2.(被)采摘 3. 啄食;少量地(或挑精拣肥地)

吃 4. 挑选 5. 偷窃;扒窃 — *n.* 1. 凿,掘 2. 选择;选出物;一次采摘的作物 3. [the ~] (人或物的)精华;最好的部分

pickaninny ['pikənini] *n. & adj.* = piccaninny

picker ['pikə] *n.* 1. 用鹤嘴锄挖掘者 2. 采摘者;采集者;拣选者 3. 捡拾者 4. 采摘棉机

pickerel ['pikərəl]([复]pickerel(s)) *n.*【动】(北美)狗鱼;小狗鱼

picket ['pikit] *n.* 1. 桩;尖桩;站桩刑(古时使罪犯以一只脚站在桩上的刑罚);站桩刑用的桩 2.【军】前哨;警戒哨(或队、船、飞机) 3.(罢工时工会派出的)纠察员;用鹤嘴桩围住;用篱笆(或栅栏)护围 2. 把(马等)拴在桩上 3. 派…担任警戒哨;用警戒哨保卫 4. 在(工厂等)设置(或担任)纠察;用纠察包围 — *vi.* 担任纠察;警戒哨 ∥ ~ line 1. 哨兵线,前哨线;纠察线 2. 拴马(或骡)索

pickle ['pikl] *n.* 1.(保卤、蔬菜等的)盐卤;醋渍液 2. 腌制食品;腌菜;泡菜 3.(清洁金属表面的)稀酸浴,酸洗液 4.(处理皮革用的)浸酸 5. 逆境;困境 6.(口)淘气孩子 — *vt.* 1.(以盐水或醋)腌制,腌渍 2. 酸洗

pickpocket ['pikˌpɔkit] *n.* 扒手

pickup ['pikʌp] *n.* 1. 拾起 2. 加速;(汽车等的)突然加速能力 3. 小吨位运货汽车 4. 偶然结识;偶然结识的人 5.(商业等的)好转 6.(口)兴奋剂;刺激品;刺激物 7. 拾取,捡音;唱头;唱音,拾音器;电视摄像;电视摄像管 8. 实况转播地点;连接实况转播的电路系统 — *adj.* 1. 临时拼凑成的

picnic ['piknik] *n.* 1.(自带食物的)郊游,野餐;各自自带食品的聚餐 2.(口)愉快的经历;轻松的工作 — (picnicked, picnicking) *vi.* (去)野餐；参加野餐

pictograph ['piktəgrɑːf] *n.* 1. 古代(或史前)石壁画 2. 象形文字；用象形文字所作的记载 3. 统计图表，象形图

pictorial [pik'tɔːriəl] *adj.* 1. 画家的；画的；绘画的 2. 图片的；由图片组成的；用图片表示的；有插图的 3. 图画似的；形象化的 — *n.* 画报，画刊

picture ['piktʃə] *n.* 1. 画；画像；图片；照片 2. 美景；美的事物(或人) 3. 生动描写，写照 4. 相似的形象，化身；体现 5. 心象；情景；局面，状况 6. 电影；影片；[~s]电影的放映 7. [无]图像 — *vt.* 1. 画；用图表示(抽象的东西) 2. (生动地)描写，描述 3. 想象 4. 把…摄成电影 ‖ ~ book 图画书，画册 / ~ card 1. (纸牌中的)花牌 2. 美术明信片

picturesque [ˌpiktʃə'resk] *adj.* 1. (景色)似画的 2. 别致的 3. (语言等)生动的，形象化的

piddling ['pidliŋ] *adj.* 不重要的，不足道的，微小的

pidgin ['pidʒin] *n.* 1. (不同语种的人们在商业交往中发展起来的)混杂语；混杂行话 2. = ~ English 3. [口] (关心的)事情 ‖ ~ English 洋泾浜英语

pie[1] [pai] *n.* 1. 馅饼；馅饼状物 2. [俚]轻而易举的事情

pie[2] [pai] *n.* 1. [动]喜鹊；[英]绿啄木鸟 2. 杂色动物 3. [古]爱叽叽喳喳说话的人

piebald ['paibɔːld] *adj.* 1. 杂色的；(马等)黑白斑的；花斑的 2. 混杂的；杂种的 — *n.* 有花斑的动物；花斑马

piece [piːs] *n.* 1. 碎片；断片；切片；部分；部件 2. 块；片；段 3. 项；番 4. (按固定规格格的)篇；出；首；幅；文艺作品的)篇；出；首；幅 5. (按件计算的)工作量 6. (成套中的)件↑

8. [常用以构成复合词]轻武器；枪炮 9. 钱币；标志物；筹码 10. 棋子(国际象棋)兵、士等的棋子 11. [用以构成复合词](乐器的)演奏者 — *vt.* 1. 修理；修补(*up*) 2. 拼合(*together*) 3. 增补；补充；接补 ‖ ~ together 1. 拼凑，串成 2. [纺]接(线头) ‖ ~meal *adv.* 一件一件地；逐渐地；零碎地 *adj.* 一件一件的；逐渐的；零碎的 *n.* 块；片 / ~work *n.* 计件工作 / ~worker *n.* 计件工

pied [paid] *adj.* 1. 斑驳的，杂色的 2. 穿花衣服的

pieplant ['paiplɑːnt, 'paiplænt] *n.* [植]食用大黄

pier [piə] *n.* 1. (桥)墩 2. 凸式码头，突码头；突堤 3. [建]窗间壁；户间壁；扶壁；支柱；方柱

pierce [piəs] *vt.* 1. 刺穿；刺破；突入；突破(防线等) 2. 穿(洞、孔) 3. 看穿，洞察 4. 打动，感动 — *vi.* 穿入；刺入；突破(*into*, *through*)

piercing ['piəsiŋ] *adj.* 1. 刺穿的，尖锐的；沁人心脾的 2. 尖厉的 3. 敏锐的；洞察的，洞悉的 ‖ ~ly *adv.*

piety ['paiəti] *n.* 1. 虔敬，虔诚 2. 孝顺，孝敬 3. 虔敬的行为

pig [pig] *n.* 1. 猪；小猪；野猪 2. 猪肉；宰好的小肉猪；猪皮 3. [口] 猪一般的人(指肮脏、贪吃等的人) 4. [美俚]警察；密探；荡妇；赛马用的马(尤指老弱的)；(调车场用的)火车头 5. 生铁块或锭；生铁 — (pigged; pigging) *vi.* 1. 生小猪；像猪一样地产子 2. 像着猪般地过活 — *vt.* 1. 生(小猪) 2. 贪婪地吃 ‖ ~-iron 生铁 / ~pen, ~sty *n.* 1. 猪圈 2. 肮脏的地方 / ~tail *n.* 1. 辫子 2. 辫状烟草束

pigeon[1] ['pidʒin] *n.* 1. 鸽子(泛指野鸽和家鸽) 2. [俚]傻瓜；易受骗的人；受骗↑

上当者 **3.** (抛入空中作为射击目标的)粘土制圆盘,土鸽 **4.** 特别关心的事物(或人) **5.** 少女;少妇;情人 *—vt.* (尤指赌博时)诈骗 ‖ '~-toed *adj.* 【医】足内翻的,内八字的

pigeon² ['pidʒin] *n.* = pidgin

pigeonhole ['pidʒinhəul] **I.** *n.* **1.** (鸽棚中隔开的)鸽巢;(门、墙上的)鸽子出入孔 **2.** (书橱中、书桌上的)鸽笼式分类架,文件架,信件架 **3.** 极小的房间 *—vt.* **1.** 把(文件等)插入分类架中 **2.** 把(文件等)分类(或归档) **3.** 把…搁置一边,把…束之高阁 **4.** 把…记在脑子里

piggery ['pigəri] *n.* **1.** 养猪场;猪圈 **2.** [总称]猪 **3.** 猪似的行为;贪得无厌的习性

piggish ['pigiʃ] *adj.* 猪一般的;肮脏的;贪吃的;贪婪的;顽固的;讨厌的

piggy ['pigi] *n.* 小猪 *—adj.* **1.** 猪一般的 **2.** 肮脏的;贪婪的 **3.** (母猪)看上去怀小猪的 ‖ ~ bank (猪形)储蓄罐,(猪形)扑满

pigheaded ['pig'hedid] *adj.* 顽固的;愚蠢的

pigment ['pigmənt] *n.* **1.** 颜料;涂料 **2.** 【生】色素,色质 *—ary adj.*

pigmentation [ˌpigmən'teiʃən] *n.* **1.** 【生】色素沉着,着色,染色 **2.** (动植物的)天然颜色

pigmy ['pigmi] *n. & adj.* = pygmy

pike¹ [paik] *n.* **1.** 长矛,长枪;矛头,枪刺;(行人防滑用的)尖头杖 **2.** 【动】鱼 **3.** (英方)[尤用于地名中]尖顶山 **4.** 【方】鱼嘴鲸,镰 *—vt.* 用矛刺穿(或刺伤、刺死)

pike² [paik] *n.* **1.** 收税栅;收费门;关卡 **2.** 通行税 **3.** 税道,收税路 *—vi.* 〈美俚〉走;离开(along)

piker ['paikə] *n.* 〈俚〉胆小鬼

pilaster [pi'læstə] *n.* 【建】壁柱,半露柱

pile¹ [pail] *n.* **1.** 堆 **2.** 火化堆(火化尸体等的燃料堆) **3.** 高大建筑物;建筑物群 **4.** 〈口〉大量;大数目;大笔钱财 **5.** 【电】电池组 **6.** 【核】核反应堆 *—vt.* **1.** 把…堆积(或叠聚) **2.** 把成堆物装上 *—vi.* **1.** 堆积;聚成堆 **2.** 拥,挤

pile² [pail] *n.* 桩;桥桩 *—vt.* **1.** 把桩打入 **2.** 用桩支撑;用桩加强

pile³ [pail] *n.* **1.** (动物的)软毛、细毛,茸毛 **2.** (织物的)绒毛,绒头

pile⁴ [pail] *n.* [常~s]【医】痔疮

pilfer ['pilfə] *vt. & vi.* 小偷小摸;偷窃 ‖ ~age *n.*

pilgrim ['pilgrim] *n.* **1.** (在国外)旅行者;流浪者 **2.** 香客;朝圣者 **3.** 修来生的人 **4.** 早期移民;[P-](1620 年移到美洲的英国)清教徒蒙移民 *—vi.* 去朝圣;漫游 ‖ Pilgrim Fathers 清教徒前蒙移民(指 1620 年移到美洲建立普利茅斯殖民地的一批英国清教徒)

pilgrimage ['pilgrimidʒ] *n.* **1.** 朝圣,朝觐 **2.** 漫游 **3.** 人生历程 *—vi.* 去朝圣;漫游

piling ['pailiŋ] *n.* **1.** [总称]桩;桩结构 **2.** 打桩;打桩工程

pill [pil] *n.* **1.** 药丸,丸剂;药片,片剂;[the ~](女用)口服避孕药 **2.** 讨厌而必须忍受的事;屈辱 **3.** 〈俚〉讨厌的家伙;医生 **4.** 〈俚〉苦丸子;炸弹;炮弹;子弹;手榴弹;高尔夫球;棒球;网球 **5.** (英)[~s]台球戏,弹子戏 **6.** 〈美俚〉(鸦片)烟泡;鸦静剂;香烟 *—vt.* **1.** 把…做成丸(或片)剂 **2.** 使服药丸(或药片) **3.** 投票反对 ‖ '~-head *n.* (安非他明等药物的)服药成瘾者

pillage ['pilidʒ] *n.* **1.** (尤指战争中的)掠

夺,抢劫 2. 抢得物;战利品 —*vt.*1. 对…进行掠夺;抢劫…的财物 2. 抢得 —*vi.* 掠夺,抢劫

pillar ['pilə] *n.*1. 柱,柱子 2.〈喻〉栋梁; 台柱 3. 柱形物(如水柱、火柱等)— *vt.* 用柱支持;用柱加固

pillbox ['pilbɔks] *n.*1. 药丸盒,药片盒。 永备发射点;坚固的机枪掩体 3.(平顶 无边的)筒状女帽

pillory ['piləri] *n.t.*颈手枷(用以将罪犯 示众的古代刑具) 2. 示众 —*vt.*1. 给 …上颈手枷 2. 使受公众嘲笑,将…示 众

pillow ['piləu] *n.*1. 枕头 2.【机】轴枕,垫 座 3.〈美俚〉拳击手套;(棒球中的)全 —*vt.*1. 把…搁在枕上;使靠在(on) 2. 成为…的枕头 —*vi.* 枕着头;靠(on) ‖'~case, '~slip *n.* 枕套 /~ talk 枕 边私房话

pilot ['pailət] *n.*1. 领港员;领航员;引水 员;舵手,舵工 2.(飞机、宇宙飞船等) 的驾驶员,飞行员;正驾驶;机长 3. 向导,带路人;领导人(机车中的)排 障器 5.【机】导向器 —*vt.*1. 给(船等) 领航(或领港) 2. 驾驶(飞机);掌 管;指引,引导 —*adj.*1. 引导的;指引 的 2.【机】控制的,导向的 3. 小规模 的试验性的,试点的

pimento [pi'mentəu] ([复]pimento(s)) *n.* 【植】1. 多香果 2. 灯笼椒,甜椒

pimiento [pi'mjentəu] ([复]pimientos) *n.* 灯笼椒,甜椒

pimp [pimp] *n.*1. 拉皮条的人;为妓女拉 客的人 2. 干坏事的人 3.〈美俚〉男妓 —*vi.* 拉皮条;为妓女拉客

pimpernel ['pimpənel] *n.*【植】海绿;海绿 花

pimple ['pimpl] *n.*【医】丘疹;小脓疱 ‖ ~d, pimply *adj.* 有丘疹的,有小脓疱 的

pin [pin] *n.*1. 针,别针;大头针 2. 饰针; (背面有别针的)徽章;像章;针状物 3. 钉;销;栓 4.(弦乐器上调弦用的)弦槽; 琴栓;发夹 5.(电器插头等上的)插脚 5.【海】桨栓;系索栓 6.(容量为四加仑 半的)小啤酒桶 7.(钉扣的)插入锁孔 部分 8. 小事;小东西 9.[~s]〈口〉腿 —(pinned; pinning) *vt.*1.(用别针等) 别住,(用钉等)钉住;(用针等)刺穿 2. (用栅栏等)圈住;使不能行动,牵制 3. 把…归罪于(on) —*adj.*1. 针的;钉的; 销的 2.(皮革)有针头似小粒的 ‖'~- acushin *n.* 针垫 /'~ up *adj.*1.(可钉在 墙上的) 2.(女子)其照片被倾慕者钉在 墙上的,漂亮 *n.* 钉在墙上的东西(如 壁灯、漂亮女子的照片等);漂亮的女 子

pinafore ['pinəfɔː] *n.*(小孩的)围涎;反穿 衫;围裙;无袖连衣裙

pince-nez ['pænsnei, 'pinsnei]〈法〉*n.* 夹 鼻眼镜

pincers ['pinsəz] [复] *n.*[用作单或复]1. 钳子;镊子 2.【动】螯 ‖ pincer(s) move- ment【军】钳形运动

pinch [pintʃ] *vt.*1. 捏,拧;夹痛,轧痛 2. 【农】(为控制生长)给…摘心(或打尖) (out, off, back) 3. 使不舒服;使苦恼 4. 使冻僵;使收缩 5. 使窘缩 6. 勒索; 诈取(钱财)(from, out of) 7.〈俚〉盗 窃;攫自拿取;抢…的东西 8.〈俚〉逮 捕;拘留 9.【海】使(帆船)紧抢风行驶 10.〈英〉〈赛马时〉催(马)使劲 —*vi.*1. 挤压;收缩;(鞋等)紧得使人感到痛 2. 节省;吝惜 3.(矿脉等)狭缩,变薄 — *n.*1. 捏,拧 2.(一撮)撮量 3. 掌 缺;窘迫 4. 紧急情况;紧要关头 5. 〈俚〉盗窃 6.〈俚〉逮捕;拘留 ‖~ er *n.* ‖~ hit(棒球赛中替补队员在关键时

刻的)替补击球 /'～ hit *vi.*〈棒球赛中替补队员在关键时刻时〉替补击球;〈美口〉(紧急时)充当替代者,代替(*for*)／～ hitter *n.*〈棒球赛中关键时刻上场的)替补击球员。代者者,替身

pine[1] [pain] *n.*1.松树;松木 2.〈口〉凤梨,菠萝 /'～ **cone** 松球,松果

pine[2] [pain] *vi.*1. 衰弱,憔悴;消瘦(*away*) 2. 怀念;渴望(*for, after*)

pineapple ['painˌæpl] *n.*1. 凤梨,菠萝 2.〈俚〉炸弹;手榴弹;轻型迫击炮

piney ['paini] = piny

pinfeather ['pinˌfeðə] *n.* (鸟类的)新生毛

ping-pong ['piŋpɔŋ] *n.* 乒乓球(= table tennis)

pinion[1] ['pinjən] *n.*1. 鸟翅的端部,翼尖;飞羽,翮 2.(昆虫的)翅前缘 — *vt.*1. 缚住(鸟)的飞羽;剪去(鸟)的飞羽 2. 缚住(或剪去)(翅膀) 3. 绑住的双臂;把...绑住;把...铐住

pinion[2] ['pinjən] *n.*〔机〕小齿轮;齿杆

pink[1] [piŋk] *n.*1.〔植〕石竹;石竹花 2. 桃红色,粉红色 3. 顶点;化身;典型 4. 衣着入时的人,时髦的人;〔亦作 P-〕较激进的人 5.〈英〉(猎狐家穿的)红色上衣;猎狐者 — *adj.*1. 粉红色的 2. 有点左倾的,有点激进的 3.〔面红耳赤的;激怒的 — *vt. & vi.*(使)变粉红色 /'～**collar** *adj.*〈美〉粉红领阶层的;(职业等)多由妇女从事的 /'～**eye** *n.*〔医〕传染性结膜炎 2.〈俚〉廉价威士忌酒

pink[2] [piŋk] *vt.*1. 刺,扎,戳 2.(用讽刺、嘲笑等)刺伤,刺痛 3. 在(布、皮、纸等)上打花孔 4. 把(布等)的边剪成锯齿形 5. 装饰

pinkish ['piŋkiʃ] *adj.*1. 带粉红色的 2. 带点左倾色彩的

pinna ['pinə]([复]pinnae ['pini] 或 pinnas) *n.*1. 翼;羽;翮;翼(或羽、鳍)状结构 2.【解】耳郭 3.【植】(复叶的)羽片

pinnacle ['pinəkl] *n.*1.(尤指哥特式建筑上的)小尖塔;尖顶 2. 山顶,山峰 3. 顶峰,极点,顶点 — *vt.*1. 把...置于小尖塔上;把...放在尖顶 2. 在...上造小尖塔

pinpoint ['pinpɔint] *n.*1. 针尖;尖端极少量极微的东西;琐事 — *adj.*1. 针尖的;极微小的 2. 精确的,精确定位的,详尽的 3. 需要精确定位的;定位精确的 — *vt.*1. 精确地确定...的位置;确定,确认 2. 瞄准;精确地从空中拍摄 3. 使突出,使显著

pint [paint] *n.*1. 品脱(英美干量或液量单位,略作 pt.) 2.1 品脱的量器(或容器)

pintle ['pintl] *n.*1. 枢轴;柱销;扣针 2. 牵引装置

pinto ['pintəu]〈美〉([复]pinto(e)s) *n.*1. 花马,杂色马 2. 菜豆(= ～ bean) — *adj.* 有花斑的;杂色的

pinwheel ['pinhwil] *n.*1. 玩具纸风车 2. 五彩转轮(一种烟火) 3. 快速转动的东西

piny ['paini] *adj.*1. 松树丛生的 2. 松树(似)的

pioneer [ˌpaiə'niə] *n.*1. 拓荒者,开辟者 2. 先驱者,先锋;倡导者 3.〔军〕轻工兵 4.〔生〕先锋生物 — *vt.* 开辟;倡导 — *vi.* 当先驱,当开辟者 — *adj.*1. 最早的,原先的 2. 开拓的;先驱的;首创的

pious ['paiəs] *adj.*1. 虔诚的;敬神的;虔奉宗教的 2. 本分的,孝顺的 3.〈古〉孝顺的 4. 可嘉的;有宗教虚构的;道貌岸然的 4. 可嘉的;有良意向的 5. 神圣的 ‖ ～**ness** *n.*

pip[1] [pip] *n.*1.(苹果、橘子、梨等的)籽,种子 2.〈俚〉出众的人(或物)

pip² [pip] (pipped; pipping) (英口) *vt.* 1. 投票反对; 排斥; 挫败(计划等) 2. 射击;击伤;击死 —*vi.* 死(out)

pip³ [pip] *n.* [the ~] 1. 禽鸟舌喉炎之形容不出的小毛病;无以名状的疾病; (俚)梅毒 2. 烦躁;抑郁;闷闷不乐

pip⁴ [pip] *n.* 1. (纸牌、骰子、骨牌上的)点(或符号) 2. [无](雷达显示器上的)反射点,尖头信号 3. (英国军官肩章上表示等级的)星

pip⁵ [pip] *n.* (广播中的)报时信号;电话信号

pipe [paip] *n.* 1. 管子;导管;输送管 2. (人或动物的)管状器官; [常~s]嗓子;发声器官;呼吸器官 3. 烟斗;管风琴的音管;[苏格兰等地的]风笛; [海](水手长的)长口哨;哨子声 4. 歌声;鸟叫声 5. 烟斗;旱烟筒;一斗烟丝;[美俚]雪茄 6. 量(英美液量单位 = 105 英加仑或 126 美加仑) (同上容量盛酒、油等的)大桶 7. (俚)容易干的事 8. [矿]竖井;[俚]烟斗 [地]筒状火成岩脉,火山筒 9. [美俚]短信;交谈 —*vt.* 1. 为…装管子;用管道输送(液体、气体等) 2. 用管乐器吹奏(曲调);[喻]雷笛 6. 吹 3. (俚)用长口哨召集(船员);吹奏管乐引领 4. 用尖嗓子说;尖声唱 5. 为(衣服)拷边,为…滚边;在(糕点上)裱花 5. [俚]令人喜爱的人(或物) —*vi.* 1. 吹奏管乐 2. 尖声叫喊;发出尖声 3. [美俚]雷笛 6. 吹 ‖ ~ **down** (口) 1. 白日梦;幻想 2. (吸鸦片产生的)梦幻 / ' ~ **line** *n.* 1. 管道,管线 2. (信息等传递的)途径,渠道 *vt.* 用管道输送 3. 为…装管道

piper ['paipə] *n.* 1. 管乐器吹奏者(尤指流浪艺人);风笛吹奏者 2. 管道工 3. 拷边工;(缝纫机上的)拷边装置 4.

[鱼]琴鲂鲱,笛鲂鲱 5. 气喘的马 6. 幼鸽 7.(英)(用以诱捕猎物的)跑狗,诱犬

pipet(te) [pi'pet] *n.* 移液管,吸(量)管

piping ['paipiŋ] *n.* 1. 管乐器吹奏;吹响;尖声唱 2. 管道系统;管道,管线 3. (衣服等的)拷边,滚边 4. (蛋糕上的)裱花花饰 —*adj.* 1. 吹奏的;高亢的

pippin ['pipin] *n.* 1. (适于作餐后果品的)点心苹果 2. (英方)(水果的)种子、籽 3. (俚)令人喜爱的人(或物)

piquant ['pi:kənt] *adj.* 辣味的;开胃的;刺激的;可爱的

pique [pi:k] *n.* 生气, 赌气 —*vt.* 1. 使生气,激怒 2. 激起,引起(兴趣等)

piqué [pi:kei, pi'kei] (法) *n.* 凹凸织物

piracy ['paiərəsi] *n.* 1. 海盗行为,海上掠夺 2. 侵犯版权;非法翻印;侵犯专利权

pirate ['paiərit] *n.* 1. 海盗;掠夺者 2. 海盗船 3. 侵犯版权者;非法翻印者 4. 非法广播者 5.(英)私自招揽乘客的私营公共汽车(公司) —*vt.* 1. (以海盗方式)掠夺 2. 非法翻印 3. 盗(别人所雇用的人) —*vi.* 做海盗;从事劫掠

piratic(al) [pai'rætik(əl)] *adj.* 1. 海盗的;像海盗的 2. 非法翻印的;非法仿制的

pirouette [,piru'et] *n. & vi.* (芭蕾舞中)(作)单脚(或单脚尖)着地旋转;(作)皮鲁埃特旋转;(作)快速旋转 ‖ ~ **r** *n.*

Pisa ['pi:zə] *n.* 比萨[意大利西北部城市](城内有著名的比萨斜塔)

piscatorial [,piskə'tɔ:riəl] *adj.* 鱼类的;渔民的;流盗的;从事捕鱼的

piss [pis] (俗) *n.* 尿,小便 —*vi.* 撒尿,解小便 —*vt.* 1. 排(尿);撒尿弄湿(床铺等) 2. 尿(血等)

pistachio [pis'tɑ:ʃiəu] *n.* 1. [植]阿月浑子

2. 阿月浑子的果实(可食用) **3.** 阿月浑子果仁的香味 **4.** 淡草绿色

pistil ['pistil] *n.* 【植】雌蕊

pistol ['pistl] *n.* 手枪; 信号枪 —(pistol-(l)ed; pistol(l)ing) *vt.* 用手枪射击

piston ['pistən] *n.* **1.** 【机】活塞 **2.** 【音】(铜管乐器上的)活塞阀键

pit[1] [pit] *n.* **1.** 坑, 洼 **2.** 专用坑, 工业用坑(如锯木坑、鞣革坑)**3.** 深渊; [the ~]地狱;〈方〉坟墓 **4.** 陷阱;〈喻〉圈套 **5.** 叠坑(如石灰窑、炭窑)**6.**〈英〉(剧场)正厅后座; 正厅后座观众;(舞台前的)乐池 **7.** 兽栏; 斗狗场; 斗鸡场 **8.** 躯体凹部(物体表面上的)凹陷; 天花疤痕, 痘凹, 麻点 **9.** (交易所中某种商品的)交易场地 **10.** (赛车途中的)检修加油站 —(pitted; pitting) *vt.* **1.** 把…放进坑内, 窖藏 **2.** 使凹陷, 使坑下陷; 在…坑上挖坑; 使留下麻点 **3.** 使(鸡等)放进斗场内互斗; 使相斗; 使对立; 使竞争(against)— *vi.* **1.** 起凹点; 变得坑坑洼洼 **2.** 【医】(浮肿者的皮肤被揿后)凹陷 ‖ ~ fall **1.** 陷阱; 圈套 **2.** 隐蔽的危险, 隐患; 易犯的错误; 意想不到的困难

pit[2] [pit]〈美〉*n.* (如桃、杏、梅子等)核 —(pitted; pitting) *vt.* 除去…的核

pit-a-pat [ˌpitəˈpæt] *adv.* 劈劈啪啪地, 卜卜地 — *n.* 噼啪声, 卜卜声 —(pit-a-patted; pit-a-patting) *vi.* 劈劈啪啪地跑; 卜卜地跳

pitch[1] [pitʃ] *n.* **1.** 沥青; (针叶树的)树脂; 人造沥青; 人造树脂 — *vt.* 用沥青涂; 用沥青覆盖 ‖ ~-'black, '~-'dark *adj.* 漆黑的 / ~ blende *n.* 沥青铀矿

pitch[2] [pitʃ] *vt.* **1.** 搭(帐)扎(营)**2.** 投, 掷, 抛 **3.** 把…定于特定角度(或程度、价值、标准、性质等)**4.** 【音】为…定音

高; 为…定调; 用特定风格表达 **5.** 竭力推销; 叫卖〈主英〉陈列(商品)**6.** (用石子等)铺(路)**7.**〈英俚〉讲(故事)**8.** 装腔作势地讲(或念)**9.** (棒球赛中)以…为投手; 作为投手打(一场比赛)— *vi.* **1.** 安营; 搭起帐篷; 驻足位置 **2.** 投掷 **3.** (头向下)扎倒; 摔倒; 跌入 **4.** (地面、道路等)倾斜 **5.** (船只)前后颠簸, 纵摇(区别于 roll 横摇)**6.** 吹牛, 说大话 **7.** (棒球赛中)作为投手 — *n.* **1.** 投掷; 投掷物; 投掷量; 投球 **2.** 前倾; (船只)纵摇 **3.** 坡度; 【建】屋顶的斜度 **4.** (地层或矿脉的)倾斜角 **4.** 【机】螺距; (齿轮的)齿节, 节距; 【空】螺距(指飞机螺旋桨旋转一次的前移距离)**5.** 【音】音高; 音高标准 **6.** 程度; 高度; 强度 **7.** (货物的)摊位, 设定处; 〈英〉(街头艺人的)表演场所 **8.** 一批陈列商品 **9.** 商品推销员的行话; 竭力推销的广告语 **10.** 〈美俚〉情况; 现状 ‖

pitched [pitʃt] *adj.* 对阵战的, 激战的 ‖ ~ battle **1.** 对阵战; 激战, 酣战 **2.** 激烈的争论

pitcher[1] ['pitʃə] *n.* **1.** (有嘴和柄的)罐, 壶 **2.** 一罐(或一壶)的量 **3.** 【植】瓶状叶; 瓶状体

pitcher[2] ['pitʃə] *n.* **1.** 投掷者; (棒球)投手 **2.**〈英〉摊贩 **3.**〈英〉铺路石

pitchfork ['pitʃfɔːk] *n.* **1.** 干草叉 **2.** 音叉 — (用干草叉)叉起并抛出 **2.** 强行把…塞进(或抛入)(into)

piteous ['pitiəs] *adj.* **1.** 引人哀怜的; 乞怜的; 可怜的 **2.**〈古〉慈悲的; 怜悯的 ‖ ~ ly *adv.* / ~ ness *n.*

pith [piθ] *n.* **1.** (木)髓, 树心 **2.** 骨髓(羽毛的)髓部 **3.** 核心; 精髓; 要旨 **4.** 重要性; 意义 **5.**〈古〉精力; 力气 — *vt.* **1.** 除去(茎)中的木髓 **2.** 刺毁(动物)的脊髓

pithecanthrope [ˌpiθiˈkænθrəup] *n.* 猿人

pithy [ˈpiθi] *adj.* 1. 髓的；多髓的；似髓的 2. 精辟的；简练的 ‖ **pithily** *adv.* / **pithiness** *n.*

pitiable [ˈpitiəbl] *adj.* 1. 引人怜悯的；可怜的 2. 可怜而又可鄙的 ‖ **pitiably** *adv.*

pitiful [ˈpitiful] *adj.* 1. 令人怜悯的；可怜的 2. 可鄙的 3.〈古〉慈悲的；有同情心的 ‖ ~ **ly** *adv.* / ~ **ness** *n.*

pitiless [ˈpitilis] *adj.* 没有怜悯心的；无情的 ‖ ~ **ly** *adv.* / ~ **ness** *n.*

pittance [ˈpitəns] *n.* 微薄的收入；少量，小额

pitter-patter [ˈpitəˌpætə] *adv.*, *n.* & *vi.* = pit-a-pat

Pittsburgh [ˈpitsbəːg] *n.* 匹兹堡[美国宾夕法尼亚州西南部城市][钢铁工业中心]

pituitary [piˈtjuitəri] *n.* 1.【解】垂体；垂体制剂 —*adj.* 1. 垂体的 2. 垂体分泌失调引起的 ‖ ~ **gland**（或 **body**）【解】垂体

pity [ˈpiti] *n.* 1. 怜悯；同情 2. 可惜的事，憾事 —*vt.* 怜悯，同情 ‖ **what a ~** 多么可怜又可鄙 —*vi.* 有怜悯心；觉得可怜

pivot [ˈpivət] *n.* 1. 枢，枢轴，支板，支点 2.【军】基准兵；基准部队 3.〈喻〉中枢，枢纽；要点；中心点 4. 关键（点）；人物 5. 在枢轴上的转动，旋转运动 —*adj.* 在枢轴上转动的；枢要的 —*vi.* 1. 在枢轴上转动；转过身 2. 随…转移；依…而定（*on*, *upon*） —*vt.* 1. 装枢轴于；把…放在枢轴上；使绕着枢轴转动

pivotal [ˈpivətl] *adj.* 1. 枢轴的 2. 中枢的，枢要的；关键性的 ‖ ~ **ly** *adv.*

pixie, pixy [ˈpiksi] *n.* 小精灵，小淘气 —*adj.* 淘气的，恶作剧的，调皮捣蛋的

pizza [ˈpiːtsə] *n.*（意大利）皮杂饼

pizzeria [ˌpiːtsəˈriːə] *n.* 皮杂饼店

pk. *abbr.* 1. park 2. peak 3. peck(s)

pkg., pkge. *abbr.* package

pl. *abbr.* plural

PLA *abbr.* People's Liberation Army（中国）人民解放军

placable [ˈplækəbl, ˈpleikəbl] *adj.* 易平息的，易抚慰的；易和解的；宽容的；温和的 ‖ **placably** *adv.*

placard [ˈplækɑːd] *n.* 1. 招贴；布告；标语牌 2.（钉在门上的）小牌子 —*vt.* 1. 张贴布告于；悬挂布告于 2.（用布告或招贴）公布于；替…做广告；揭示 3. 张贴；悬挂

placate [pləˈkeit] *vt.* 安抚，抚慰；使和解 ‖ **placation** *n.*

place [pleis] *n.* 1. 地方，地点；地区；位置 2. 住所，寓所 3.（有特定用途的）场所 4.（身体等表面的）部位 5. 席位，坐位 6. 名次（赛马）前几名中的任何一名（英国指前三名；美国指前二名，尤指第二名）7. 地位；处境 8. 职位；公职；职责；职权 9.【数】位 10.（书刊的）段落，页 11.［常用于专有名词］广场；街 —*vt.* 1. 放置，安置；寄托（希望等）；给予（信任等）2. 安插；任命；安置（难民等）4. 完全认定；认清（人）5. 投（资）；存（款）；发出（订单）；安排（存货等）7.（唱歌、讲话时）调整（嗓音）8.（赛跑、赛马等）定出（选手）的名次 —*vi.* 1. 名列前茅，得名次（赛马等）得第二名 ‖ ~ **ment** *n.* 放置；安插（学生的）编班 ‖ ~ **-kick** *n.*（足球等）的定位踢 *vt.* & *vi.* 踢（定位球）

placebo [pləˈsiːbəu]（［复］placebos）*n.* 1.【天主教】为死者唱的晚祷歌 2. 安慰剂（指无药效，仅产生心理作用的制剂）3. 安慰物；宽慰话 4.（用作对照试

验的)无效对照剂

placenta [plə'sentə] ([复] placentae [plə'senti] 或 placentas) *n*.1. 胎盘 2.【植】胎座

placer ['plæsə] *n*.(含金等的)砂矿;砂矿开采地

placid ['plæsid] *adj*. 平静的, 安静的;温和的 ‖ **pla'cidity** *n*. / ~ly *adv*. / ~ness *n*.

plagiarism ['pleidʒiərizəm] *n*.1. 剽窃, 抄袭 2. 剽窃物,抄袭物 ‖ **plagiarist** *n*. 剽窃者,抄袭者

plagiarize ['pleidʒiəraiz] *vt*. 剽窃,抄袭(别人的学说,著作等) — *vi*. 剽窃,抄袭 ‖ ~**r** *n*. 剽窃者,抄袭者

plague [pleig] *n*.1. 瘟疫 ‖ [the ~]鼠疫,黑死病 2. 天灾;灾害;祸患 3.〈口〉讨厌的人(或东西) — *vt*. 使染瘟疫致;使得灾祸 2. 折磨;烦扰;使苦恼

plaid [plæd] *n*.1. 彩格呢(或布)披风(苏格兰高地人穿的民族服装) 2.(苏格兰)彩格呢;彩格布 3. 格子图案

plain [plein] *adj*.1. 清楚的,明白的;平易的 2. 简单的;朴素的;单纯的;不掺杂的 3.(景色等)清晰的;无障碍的 4. 无装饰的;无花纹的(图画等)不着色的 5.〈纺〉平(纹)的;素(色)的 5. 坦白的;直率的;爽快的 6. 普通的,明显的 7. 家常的;(相貌等)平常的,不好看的 8. 十足的,彻底的 9.〈古〉平的,平坦的 — *n*. 平原;旷野 7.【纺】平针 — *adv*. 清楚地;平易地 — *vi*.〈古〉抱怨(= complain);哀悼 ‖ ~**ly** *adv*. / ~**ness** *n*.

plaint-[pleint] *n*.1.〈诗〉悲叹,哀诉 2. 抱怨,诉苦

plaintiff ['pleintif] *n*.【律】原告,起诉人

plaintive ['pleintiv] *adj*. 表示哀怨的,悲哀的;表示悲痛的,伤心的 ‖ ~**ly** *adv*. / ~**ness** *n*.

plait [plæt, pleit] *n*.1. 褶,裥 2. 辫子 3. 辫状物 — *vt*.1. 在(布)上打褶 2. 把…编成辫 3. 打辫编成

plan [plæn] *n*.1. 计划;规划;方案;打算 2. 方法,办法 3. 进度表,程序表 4. 平面图;示意图;详图 5. 轮廓;概略 — (planned; planning) *vt*.1. 计划;打算;部署 2. 设计;绘制…的图样(或图表) — *vi*. 订计划;想办法

plane[¹] [plein] *n*.1. 平面 2. 程度;水平;阶段,级 3. 飞机(aeroplane的缩写) 4.【空】翼面;机翼 — *adj*. 平的,平面的;平面的 — *vi*.1. 飞行,滑翔 2.(水上飞机等)在水面滑行;在水面掠过 3. 乘飞机旅行

plane[²] [plein] *n*.1. 木工刨,刨子 2.(泥水工的)镘 — *vt*.1. 刨;刨平 2. 刨掉(down, away) 3.〈罕〉弄平,使平滑 — *vi*.〈罕〉刨;刨平

plane[³] [plein] *n*.【植】悬铃木(= ~ tree)

planet ['plænit] *n*.【天】行星

planetarium [,plæni'tɛəriəm] ([复] planetariums 或 planetaria ['plæni'tɛəriə]) *n*.1. 天象仪;天像器;天象模型 2. 天文馆,天象放映馆

planetary ['plænitəri] *adj*.1. 行星的 2. 行星般运动的;像行星的 3. 流浪的;迁移不定的 4. 地球(上)的 5.【机】行星齿轮的

plank [plæŋk] *n*.1. 厚木板 2. 木板制品(如桌、凳、板桥等) 3. 支持物;基础 4. 政纲条目;政策要点 — *vt*.1. 在…上铺板 2.〈口〉用力放下,摔下 3.〈美口〉立即(或当场)支付(或down, out)

planking ['plæŋkiŋ] *n*.1. 铺板 2.[总称]板材 3. 船壳外板

plankton ['plæŋktən] *n*.[总称]浮游生物

plant [plɑ:nt] *n*.1. 植物 2. 苗木 3. 工厂

4.(医院、学校等的)成套设备,设施 5. 隐藏着的赃物 — *vt.*1. 种,栽,栽种;播种 2. 养殖(鱼秧等) 3. 插(旗子等);安插(间谍、奸细等) 4. 灌输;使(思想等)生根 5. 移植(植物);移殖(动物) 6. 建立;设立(城镇、教会等) 7. 殖(民),移民于(某一地点) 8.〈俚〉编造(证据等) 9.〈俚〉(对准目标)给予(打击) 10.〈俚〉窝藏(赃物等);栽(赃) 11. 埋葬;埋藏 — *vi.* 种植 ‖ ~ like *adj.* ‖ ~ louse 蚜虫;木虱

plantain ['plæntin] *n.*〖植〗1. 车前 2. 大蕉

plantation [plæn'teiʃən] *n.*1. 种植园,大农场 2. 栽植;植树造林;人造林 3. 移民;殖民;殖民地;新开垦地

planter ['plɑːntə] *n.* 1. 种植者,栽培者 2. 种植机 3. 种植园主,大农场主 4. 殖民者 5. 花盆;花架

plaque [plɑːk] *n.*1.(用金属、象牙、陶瓷等制的)圆,饰板 2. 胸襟徽物;勋章;奖章;徽章 3.〖医〗斑;血小板

plasma ['plæzmə] *n.*1.〖解〗血浆;肌浆;浆 2.〖生〗原生质,原浆 3.〖物〗等离子体;等离子区 4.〖矿〗深绿玉髓

plaster ['plɑːstə] *n.*1.〖建〗灰泥 2. 硬膏;膏药 3. 熟石膏(亦作 ~ of Paris) — *vt.*1. 在…上抹灰泥;厚厚地涂抹 2. 敷膏药于 3. 安慰;减轻 4. 使紧贴 5. 用熟石膏处理 6. 张贴于;贴满;(喻)掩盖,掩饰 7.(俚)重创(敌手等);彻底击败;鞭挞

plastic ['plæstik, 'plɑːstik] *adj.*1. 可塑的,塑性的 2. 塑料的;塑料制成的 3. 造型的;塑造的;产生立体感的 4. 能适应的;易受影响的 5. 有形成力的;创造力的 6. 不真实的;人造的;不自然的 7.〖医〗整形的,成形的;整复的 8.〖生〗有适应力的;能形成活组织的 —

*n.*1.[常 ~s]塑料;塑料制品 2.[~s][用作单或复]〖医〗整形外科 ‖ ~ity [plæs'tisiti] *n.*

plat [plæt] *n.*1. 小块地 2. 图;地图;地籍图 —(platted; platting) *vt.* 绘制…的图(或地图等)

plate [pleit] *n.*1.(金属等的)平板,薄板 2. 金属牌(尤指刻有居住人姓名等的黄铜门牌);(汽车等的)牌照 3.(制铠甲的)金属片;装甲板;铠甲 4.〖印〗版;(书的)整版插图 5.[总称]金属(或银质)餐具;镀金(或镀银)餐具 6. 盘子,盘子 7.(一)满盘;(一)盘菜;一道菜;一客版菜 8.(教堂中的)捐款盘,奉献盘 9.〖动〗骨板;鳞甲 10.〖建〗横木 11. 假牙托;一副假牙 12.(电子管的)阳极;(蓄电池的)极板,电容器板 13.〖摄〗干板,感光板 14. = ~ rail 15. 平板玻璃(亦作 ~ glass) 16.〖地〗板块 17.(棒球赛中的)投手板;本垒板 — *vt.*1. 覆镀 2. 给(船体等)装钢板;给…镶甲 3.〖印〗把(铅字等)制成印版;为(书籍等)制印版 4. 用板固定 ‖ ~ block(印有顺序号的)版号四方联邮票 /~ rail 1.(主菜)平轨(一供用的铁轨) 2.(墙上供安放盘、盆等摆设的)壁架

plateau ['plætəu]([复] plateaus 或 plateaux ['plætəuz]) *n.*1. 高原 2.〖心〗(学习曲线中的)高原;(上升后的)稳定水平(或时期、状态) — *vi.* 达到稳定水平(或时期、状态)

platform ['plætfɔːm] *n.*1. 平台;台 2.(铁路等的)站台,月台;(美)(车厢等进口处的)通道台 3. 讲台;戏台 4.〖军〗炮床;〖地〗地台;台地;(海上)钻井平台 5.(政党等的)纲领;政纲;宣言 6.[专~]演讲 — *vt.*1. 把…放在台上 2. 为…设月台 — *vi.*(在台上)演讲

plating ['pleitiŋ] *n.*1.〖冶〗覆镀 2. 覆以金

属板;外覆的金属板板;(金属)镀层 3. 装甲;(金属)制板 4.(全部)船壳板

platinum ['plætinəm] *n.*1. 铂,白金 2. 银灰色,青灰色

platitude ['plætitjuːd] *n.*1. 平凡;陈腐 2. 老生常谈,陈词滥调

Platonic [plə'tɔnik] *adj.*1.〈古希腊哲学家〉柏拉图(Plato)的;柏拉图哲学的;柏拉图式的;柏拉图学派的 2.[也作 p-] 理论上的,空谈的;不实际的;无害的 ‖ ~ love 精神恋爱

platoon [plə'tuːn] *n.*【军】排 2.(相当于一排的)一队 3.(有共同点的一群人;一组东西 4.(橄榄球队等中的)专职排球攻(或防守)队 ‖ ~ sergeant 副排长

platter ['plætə] *n.*1. 大浅盘(通常呈椭圆形) 2.〈俚〉(留声机)唱片 3.〈俚〉棒球赛中的)本垒板

platypus ['plætipəs] *n.*【动】鸭嘴兽

plaudit ['plɔːdit] *n.*[常~s]喝彩;称赞,赞扬

plausible ['plɔːzibl] *adj.*1. 似乎有理的;似可能的 2. 嘴巧的,花言巧语的 ‖ ~ ness *n.* / plausibly *adv.*

play [plei] *vi.*1. 玩耍,玩;装扮;假装 2. 戏弄;嘲弄;玩弄 3. 参加体育活动;参加比赛 4. 演奏,弹奏(或吹)奏,(乐器)奏出 5.(戏剧)演出,表演 6.(乐器)适于吹奏(或弹奏);(戏剧)适于演出 7. 赌博 8. 跳来蹦去;闪动;激动 9. 浮现 9.(机器部件等)运转 10.(唱片、录音机等)放音 11.(接连)发射;(泉水等)喷射 12.(光)照射 12. 发挥作用 13.停工;休假 —*vt.*1. 做(游戏),玩;装扮 2. 开(玩笑);嘲弄,愚弄 3. 要(花样等)玩弄 3. 玩(球戏等);打(球),赌博 4.(乐器等)奏;奏乐迎(或送)5. 扮演,演出,上演于(某地,某剧场等)6.

赌;与(某人)打赌;对(赛马等)打赌;打出(牌)7. 使跳动;使闪动;使飘动 8.(接连)发射;使(泉水等)喷射 9.(灵敏地或用劲地)挥舞(刀、剑等)10. 利用;操纵,摆布 11.(要手腕)对待,对付 12.(恶作剧地)造成,引起 13. 让上钩的(鱼)不停地拉动钓线而筋疲力竭 —*n.*1. 游戏;玩耍;消遣 2. 玩笑;玩弄;调戏;花样;把戏 3.(体育)运动;比赛作风(或进程)4.赌博;表演 5. 赌博;(美俚)一次赌局的赌注总数 6. 跳动;闪动;飘动;波动 7.(对刀剑或工具等灵巧的)使用;挥舞 8. 活动的范围(或余地);作用(于智等的)运用 9.【机】间隙,隙 9. 交易;(投机性)企业 10. 停工;休假 ‖ ~ back *n.*(录音,录像等的)放音;重放(或唱片的)放唱;回放装置;重放装置 ‖ ~ boy *n.* 花花公子;追求享乐者 / ~ fellow *n.* 玩耍伙伴 / ~ girl *n.*〈口〉寻欢作乐的女子,花花小姐 / ~ goer *n.*(经常)看戏的人;戏迷 / ~ ground *n.*(学校的)操场,运动场;(儿童)游乐场;游憩胜地 / ~ house *n.* 1. 剧场 2. 儿童游戏房;娱乐房 / ~ list *n.* 1.(电台的)录音节目播放表 2. 演出剧目表 / ~ mate *n.* = ~ fellow / ~ room *n.* 1. 儿童游戏室 2. 文娱活动室 / ~ thing *n.* 玩具;供玩耍的东西;被玩弄的人,玩物 / ~ time *n.* 游玩时间 / ~ wright *n.* 剧作家

player ['pleiə] *n.*1. 游戏(或玩耍)的人;打牌人;下棋的人 2. 比赛者;选手 3. 演员;演奏者 4.(自动钢琴等的)自动演奏装置;(电唱机)(= record)5. 赌徒;游手好闲的人

playful ['pleiful] *adj.*1. 爱玩耍的,嬉戏的;顽皮的 2. 开玩笑的,幽默的;滑稽的 ‖ ~ ly *adv.* / ~ ness *n.*

playing ['pleiiŋ] *n.* ‖ ~ card 纸牌,扑克牌 / ~ field 比赛场地;(学校的)运动

场

play-off ['pleiɔf] n.【体】(平局后的)延长赛,加时赛,平分决胜;〈美〉(赛季之间的)夺标决赛

plaza ['plɑːzə] 〈西〉 n.(城市中的)广场;购物中心

plea [pliː] n.1.【律】辩护;申诉,答辩;〈古〉诉讼 2.托词,口实 3.恳求,请求

plead [pliːd] [pleaded 或 pled [pled]] vt.1.【律】为(案件等)辩护;作为答辩提出;承认,认(罪) 2.以…为理由,以…为借口 —vi.1.辩护;答辩,申诉 2.恳求,请求 ‖ —er n. 答辩人;辩护律师;恳求者;代为求情者

pleading ['pliːdiŋ] n.1.辩护;答辩 2.调停;说项 3.[常~s](原告的)诉状;(被告的)答辩状 4.恳求 — adj. 恳求的,请求的 ‖ —ly adv.

pleasant ['pleznt] adj.1.令人愉快的;舒适的;合意的 2.举止文雅的;外貌悦人的 3.〈古〉滑稽的 ‖ —ly adv. / —ness n.

pleasantry ['plezntri] n.1.幽默;诙谐;开玩笑;打趣话;愉快的事情

please [pliːz] vt.1.使高兴,使喜欢;使中意 2.[用于祈使语气]请 —vi.1.使高兴;中意;讨人喜欢;讨好 2.欢喜;愿意

pleased [pliːzd] adj.1.高兴的,喜欢的 2.满意的

pleasing ['pliːziŋ] adj. 使人愉快的;合意的;可爱的 ‖ —ly adv.

pleasurable ['pleʒərəbl] adj. 令人愉快的;舒适的

pleasure ['pleʒə] n.1.愉快,快乐,高兴;满足 2.乐事;乐趣 3.肉体享乐;放荡(行为) 4.愿望;意向 —vt. 使高兴,给…以快乐 —vi.1.觉得高兴;感到满意(in) 2.追求享乐;游荡

pleat [pliːt] n. 褶襇;褶状皱起物 —vt.1.给…打褶子 2.把…编成辫;打辫编结

plebeian [pliˈbiːən] n.1.〈古罗马的〉平民,庶民 2.百姓,普通公民 3.平庸的人,粗俗的人 — adj.1.庶民的,平民的;百姓的 2.普通的,平庸的,粗俗的

plebiscite ['plebisit] n.1.公民投票 2.〈古罗马的〉平民表决 3.公众舆论

plectrum ['plektrəm]〈复〉[plectra 'plektrə 或 plectrums] n.(弹弦乐器用的)拨子,琴拨,拨弦片

pled [pled] plead 的过去式和过去分词

pledge [pledʒ] n.1.誓言;保证;诺言 2.信物;(象征爱情的)孩子 3.抵押(品);典当(物);保人,保证人 4.祝酒;祝愿 5.立誓入会的人 —vt.1.(使)保证;决心(做) 2.抵押;典当 3.向…祝酒;为…祝愿

plenary ['pliːnəri] adj.1.完全的;充分的;绝对的 2.全体出席的;a ~ session 全体会议

plenipotentiary [ˌplenipəˈtenʃəri] n. 全权代表 —adj. 有全权的;全权代表(或大使、大臣)的

plenitude ['plenitjuːd] n.1.完全,充分 2.充足,丰富;大量

plenteous ['plentiəs] adj.〈诗〉丰富的;丰硕的;丰产的

plentiful ['plentiful] adj. 富裕的;丰盛的;多的 ‖ —ly adv.

plenty ['plenti] n. 丰富;充足;大量;富裕;繁荣 — adj. 很多的;足够的 — adv.〈口〉充分地,十分

plethora ['pleθərə] n.1.过多;过剩 2.【医】多血(症)

pleurisy ['pluərisi] n.【医】胸膜炎,肋膜炎

Plexiglas(s) ['pleksiglɑːs, 'pleksiglæs] n. 普列克斯玻璃(常用以制造飞机座舱罩、

镜片等)

plexus ['pleksəs]([复] plexus(es)) *n.*【解】(血管、淋巴管、神经等的)丛

pliable ['plaiəbl] *adj.* 1. 易弯的,柔软的 2. 柔顺的,顺从的;圆通的 3. 能适应的 ‖ **plia'bility** *n.* 柔韧(性);柔顺(性);能适应(性) / **pliably** *adv.*

pliant ['plaiənt] *adj.* = pliable ‖ **pliancy** *n.*

pliers ['plaiəz][复] *n.*[用作单或复]钳子;镊子

plight[1] [plait] *n.* 境况;困境,苦境

plight[2] [plait] *vt.* 宣誓;保证;[~ oneself]订婚 — *n.* 誓约;婚约;盟约

PLO *abbr.* Palestine Liberation Organization 巴勒斯坦解放组织

plod [plɔd] (plodded; plodding) *vi.* 1. 沉重缓慢地走(on, along) 2. 努力从事;沉闷地苦干 — *vt.* 沉重缓慢地走(路) — *n.* 1. 沉重缓慢的脚步(或脚步声) 2. 沉闷的苦干;吃力的工作 ‖ **plodder** *n.*

plot [plɔt] *n.* 1. 小块土地,小块地皮 2. 标绘图;平面图 3. 情节 4. 秘密计划;阴谋 — (plotted; plotting) *vt.* 1. 把…划成小块地;划分 2. 标绘,绘制…的图 3. 测定(点、线)的位置;作图表示(方程式) 4. 为(文学作品)设计情节 5. 密谋,策划 — *vi.* 1. 设计情节;构思 2. 密谋,策划

plotter ['plɔtə] *n.* 1. 阴谋者;密谋者 2. 绘图员 3. 标绘器;绘图仪 4.(文学作品的)情节设计人,构思人

plough [plau] *n.* 1. 犁 2. 犁过的地;耕地 3. 犁形工具,扫雪机;开沟机;(木工的)槽刨;[印]切书边刀具 4. [the P-]【天】北斗(七星);大熊星座 5.〈英俚〉(考试的)不及格 — *vt.* 1. 犁,耕 2. 犁出;〈喻〉使起皱纹 3. 清除;奋力开(路);冲裂(水面) 4. 投(资) 5.〈英俚〉使…不及格 6. 与(女子)性交 — *vi.* 1. 犁

地;用犁 2. 可犁,耐犁 3. 奋力前进;奋力从事 4.〈英俚〉考试不及格 ‖ **~ man** *n.* 把犁人;庄稼汉 / **~ share** *n.*(犁)铧,铧头

plover ['plʌvə] *n.*[鸟]鸻

plow [plau] *n.*, *vt.* & *vi.*〈美〉= plough

pluck [plʌk] *vt.* 1. 采,摘;拔 2. 拔…的毛 3. 扯,拉 4. 拨;弹 5. 拆毁(down) 6. 杀…的威风(down) 7.〈俚〉诈骗 8.〈英〉不录取,使(军官)退伍;调动…的职务(尤指提升) 10.[俚](冰川)拔削,拖蚀(岩石)— *n.* 1. 拉,拔 2.(供食用的)动物内脏 3. 被拉扯的东西(弹拨乐器用的)弹拨器 4. 精神;勇气 5.〈古〉(考试的)不及格;不录取 6.(图画等的)鲜明,清晰

plucky ['plʌki] *adj.* 1. 有勇气的,有胆量的 2.(图画等)鲜明的,清晰的

plug [plʌg] *n.* 1. 塞子,栓;堵塞物;(龋齿的)填料 2. 插头,〈口〉插座 3.(内燃机的)火花塞 4. 消防龙头,消防栓 5.(压制的)扁形烟草块 6.【地】嚼烟草块 6.【地】岩颈 7.[俚](尤指电台等播播的)广告;捧场 8.[俚]老旧的东西,累赘;推荐 8.〈口〉无用的东西,累赘老马;驽足的马(通常体轻的)9.(马桶的)抽水装置 — (plugged; plugging) *vt.* 1. 塞,堵(up) 2.〈俚〉枪击;拳打 3.〈俚〉大肆宣传(政策等)4.〈口〉[英瓜等]切切下一小块(用以检验成熟程度)— *vi.* 1. 被塞住,被堵住(up) 2.〈口〉苦干 3.〈俚〉枪击;拳打(at) ‖ **plugger** *n.*

plum [plʌm] *n.* 1. 洋李;李;梅 2.(用于布丁、蛋糕等的)葡萄干 3. 糖果 4. 最好的东西;佳品(如书中的一段精彩文章);期望得到的东西(尤指待遇好的职位);美缺 5. 紫红色;青紫色 6.〈古〉十万英镑 7. 意外收获 8. 混凝土用石料块 ‖ **like** *adj.*

plumage ['plu:mid3] *n*.1.(鸟的)全身羽毛,羽衣 2. 漂亮精致的衣服

plumb¹ [plʌm] *n*. 铅锤,测锤,垂球 — *adj*.1. 垂直的 2.〈口〉完全的,绝对的 — *adv*.1. 垂直地 2. 恰恰;正 3.〈主方〉完全地 — *vt*.1. 用铅锤测…的深度;用铅锤测(深) 2. 用铅垂线校正(或测定);使垂直 3. 探究,探索 4. 用铅垂准…的分量;用铅密封 — *vi*. 成垂直 ‖ ~ line 铅垂线;垂规 / ~ rule 【建】垂规,垂线尺

plumb² [plʌm] *vi*. 当管子工 — *vt*. 1. 对(管道)进行作业;给(建筑物等)敷设(或检修)管道 2. 把(洗衣机等)与给排水管道接通

plumber ['plʌmə] *n*.1. 管子工;水暖工 2.〈美口〉(防止政府人员泄密的)堵漏人员

plumbing ['plʌmiŋ] *n*.1. 铅锤测深;测深 2. 管子工行业;管道工程 3. 管道设备,水暖设备 4.[the ~]抽水马桶 5. 探究,探索

plume [plu:m] *n*.1. 羽毛,大羽,长羽;羽衣 2. 羽饰 3. 羽状物;【动】【植】羽状部;(动物)多毛的尾巴 4.〈喻〉荣誉的标志;奖品 — *vt*.1.(鸟)整理(羽毛);[~ itself](鸟)整理(羽毛);[~ oneself]打扮 2. 用羽毛装饰,翎帝 3.[~ oneself]自夸,自矜,自庆 — *vi*. 形成羽毛状烟云

plummet ['plʌmit] *n*. 铅锤,垂球;铅垂线 1. 垂直落下 2. 骤然跌落

plump¹ [plʌmp] *adj*.1. 丰满的,(钱包等)饱满的,鼓起的 — *vt*. 使丰满;使鼓起(*up*) — *vi*. 变丰满;鼓起(*out*, *up*) ‖ ~ness *n*.

plump² [plʌmp] *vi*.1. 扑通地坐下;猛地触撞 2. 突然进入(*in*);蓦地冲出(*out*) 3. 投票赞成;坚决拥护(*for*)〈主英〉

(在规定选举二人或二人以上时)只投票选一人 — *vt*.1. 扑通地放落 2. 冲口说出(*out*) 3. 为…说好话;宣扬 — *n*.1.(重物的)坠落;坠下;碳撞 2. 坠落声;扑通声;冲撞声 — *adj*.1. 爽直的;老实的;直率的,直截了当的 2. 一次付清的 — *adv*.1. 扑通一声地;沉重地;突然,蓦地 3. 直截了当地;坦白地

plunder ['plʌndə] *vt*.1. 掠夺,劫掠,抢劫 2. 偷,盗窃 — *vi*. 劫掠,抢劫 — *n*.1. 掠夺,抢劫;盗窃 2. 掠夺物;赃物 3.〈方〉利润,收益 4.〈主方〉行李;货物;配备用品

plunge [plʌndʒ] *vt*.1. 使投入;使插入;刺进,插入;使陷入;使遭受 2. 把(盆栽植物)埋入土中 — *vi*.1. 投入;跳(入);跳(入)陷(入)等2. 陡峭地下倾 3.(船只)颠簸;(马等)猛烈前冲 4.〈口〉盲目投资(或投机);赌博;负债 — *n*.1. 投身入水处;游泳池;跳水;游水 3. 陷入;落下;下跌,投入(突然、猛烈)的冲击 5.〈口〉盲目投资(或投机) 6. 阵雨 7.〈主方〉水塘;窝泔 / ~

plural ['pluərəl] *adj*.1.【语】复数的 2. 由复数组成的;包含复数的 — *n*.1.【语】复数;复数形式;复数形式的词(或词组)

plurality [pluə'ræliti] *n*.1. 多数状态;诸多,众多 2.【语】复数(形式) 3.【数】大于1的数 4. 多数;〈美〉(选举中的)相对多数(票)

pluralize ['pluərəlaiz] *vt*. 使成复数;以复数形式表示 — *vi*.1. 兼职;(教会中)兼任有俸圣职 2. 成为复数

plus [plʌs] *prep*. 加,加上 — *adj*.1. 正的 2.〈口〉有利的,有好处的;外加的 3.[通常放在被修饰的词之后]略高一些的;略好一些的 — *n*.1.【数】正号;加号

(= ~ sign) 2. 外加物；外加额；【数】正数；正量 3. 好处；有利因素

plush [plʌʃ] *n.*1. 长毛绒 2. [~es](差役等穿的)毛绒裤 —*adj.*1. 长毛绒(做)的 2.〈俚〉奢侈豪华的；富裕的；优裕的

Pluto ['plu:təu] *n.*1.【希神】普路托，冥王[阴间之神] 2.【天】冥王星

plutocracy [plu:'tɔkrəsi] *n.*1. 富豪统治，财阀统治 2. 富豪(或财阀)统治集团 3. 富豪(或财阀)统治的国家(或政府)

plutocrat ['plu:təkræt] *n.*1. 富豪，财阀 2.〈口〉有钱人

plutonium [plu:'təuniəm] *n.*【化】钚

ply[1] [plai] *n.*1.(木材、布等的)厚度，层；(绳子等的)一股 2. 倾向；癖性 —*vt.*折；弯；使绞合 ‖~**wood** *n.* 胶合板

ply[2] [plai] *vt.*1. 使劲挥动，不停地使用 2. 努力从事；经营 3. 不断给，硬给；不断攻击(或打击)；不断问 4.(船等)来回于，往返于 —*vi.*1. 努力从事 2.(车、船等)定期地来回，定期地往返(*between*) 3.〈诗〉驾驶；把舵 3.【海】(帆船)抢风调向 4.(出租汽车司机、船夫等)候客，待雇

Plymouth ['plimǝθ] *n.* 普利茅斯[英国英格兰西南部港市]

Pm【化】元素钷(promethium)的符号

p. m. *abbr.*〈拉〉post meridiem 下午，午后(= afternoon)

pneumatic [nju:'mætik] *adj.*1. 空气的；气体的；风的(或)充气的 2. 压缩空气推动(或操作)的；气力的；风动的 3.【动】有气腔(腔)的 4.【宗】精神的，灵魂的；神灵的 ‖~**ally** *adv.*

pneumonia [nju:'məunjə] *n.*【医】肺炎

Pnompenh ['nɔm'pen] *n.* = Phnom Penh

PO, p. o. *abbr.* post office 邮局

Po【化】元素钋(polonium)的符号

poach[1] [pəutʃ] *vt.* 水煮(荷包蛋)

poach[2] [pəutʃ] *vi.*1.(侵入他人地界)偷猎(或偷捕) 2. 陷入烂泥；(泥土等)被踏得坑坑洼洼；变得泥泞 3.(网球、羽毛球等双打比赛中)抢打同伴的球 4. 侵犯 —*vt.*1. 侵入(他人地界)偷猎(或偷捕)；偷猎(偷捕鱼) 2. 不公平地占取(便宜或好处) 3. 在(地)上踩出坑洼(踩踏，踩烂(草地等) 4.(网球、羽毛球等双打比赛中)抢打(同伴的球) 5. 把(棒、手指等)戳入(*into*) 6. 漂洗(纸浆)等) 7. 侵犯；挖(其他公司雇员等) ‖~**er** *n.* 偷猎(或偷捕)者

pock [pɔk] *n.* 痘痕，麻点 —*vt.* 使留有痘痕，使有麻点

pocket ['pɔkit] *n.*1. 口袋；钱袋；衣袋；(英)(用作计量单位的)一袋(尤指一袋啤酒花，约168磅) 2. 钱；财力 3. 贮器，容器；囊；(台球桌四角的)球袋；(袋鼠等动物的)囊，袋 4.(口袋形)被围的地方；(战斗中部队占领的)小块地区；(长跑比赛中运动员的)受阻(或受挤)位置 5.【空】(大气中的)气阱(= air ~) 6. 死胡同 7.【矿】矿穴；小矿体；矿囊 —*adj.*1. 可放在衣袋内的，袖珍的，小型的 2. 压缩的，紧凑的 3.钱的 4. 放在袋中作零用的 —*vt.*1. 把…放入袋内；包藏；封入 2. 侵吞，盗用(款项等) 3. 忍受；隐藏；抑制，压抑 4. 阻挠；搁置(议案等)使不通过 5.(在台球戏中)击(球)落袋 ‖~**book** *n.*1. 袖珍本；笔记本 2.(放钞票等的)皮夹子 3.(美)(妇女用的)钱袋，手提包 4. 财力；进项；经济利益 /~**knife** *n.*(随身携带的)小刀，折刀 / ~ **money** 零用钱

pockmark ['pɔkmɑ:k] *n.* 痘痕，麻点 —*vt.*1. 使布满痘痕，使布满麻点 2. 使密密麻麻地布满

pod [pɔd] *n.*1. 豆荚；荚果 2. 蚕茧；(蝗

虫等的)卵囊 **3.** (海豹等的)一群 **4.** 【矿】近圆柱形矿体,扁豆形矿体,透镜形矿体 **5.** 【空】容器;吊舱;(宇宙飞船等的)分离舱 —(podded; podding) **vt.1.** 把(豆等)剥出荚 **2.** 把(海豹等)赶拢成群 —**vi.1.** 生荚果;结荚 **2.** 聚成群

podgy ['pɔdʒi] *adj.* 矮胖的;胖乎乎的

podium ['pəudiəm] ([复] podiums 或 podia ['pəudiə]) *n.* **1.** 【建】墩座;讲台;乐队(或交通)指挥台 **3.** 【动】足;管足;【植】梗,柄

poem ['pəuim] *n.* **1.** 诗;韵文;诗体文 **2.** 诗似的事物;富有诗意的东西

poet ['pəuit] *n.* **1.** 诗人 **2.** 富有想象力的人;有诗人气质的人 ‖ —**ess** *n.* 女诗人 ‖ —**laureate** 桂冠诗人;最杰出诗人

poetic [pəu'etik] *adj.* **1.** 诗的;韵文的;用诗写成的 **2.** 诗人的;爱好(或善于)写诗的;富有诗意的;具有想象力的

poetical [pəu'etikəl] *adj.***1.** = poetic **2.** 理想化的 ‖ —**ly** *adv.*

poetry ['pəuitri] *n.***1.** [总称] 诗,诗歌;诗作;诗集 **2.** 作诗;作诗法 **3.** 诗意;富有诗意的东西

pogrom ['pɔɡrəm, pəu'ɡrɔm] *n.* (尤指沙俄时代对犹太人的)集体迫害,大屠杀 —*vt.* 对...集体迫害;大肆屠杀

poignancy ['pɔinənsi] *n.***1.** 辛酸;悲痛(事) **2.** 尖锐 **3.** 强烈;深刻 **4.** 切当;尖刻

poignant ['pɔinənt] *adj.***1.** 辛酸的 **2.** 尖锐的;深刻的 **3.** 强烈的 **4.** 切中要害的;切当的 ‖ —**ly** *adv.*

poinsettia [pɔin'setiə] *n.* 【植】一品红

point [pɔint] *n.***1.** 【数】点;小数点;【语】标点(尤指句号);【音】点子;【刻度表上的)度 **2.** (表示位置的)点;(英)(警察值勤的)固定岗位;(球类运动员的)位置;(在某一位置上的)球员

3. (时间上的)一点;(特定)时刻,瞬间 **4.** 要点;中心意思;论据;观点,想法 **5.** 细目;条款 **6.** 特点;特征 **7.** 意义;目的;用处 **8.** 尖;(端);尖物;(用在专有名词中)岬;峰顶 **9.** 针绣花边(= ~lace) **10.** 【军】尖兵 **11.** (身体上突出部分的)末端;尖端(如鹿角叉等);[~s]动物的四肢(尤指马蹄等) **12.** (针炙等的)穴位 **13.** 分(数);(比赛中的)得分;学分;用作计量单位的)点,分 **14.** (证券、商品价格计算单位的)点 **15.** 【海】罗经点;两罗经点间的夹角(= 11 1/4 度) **16.** 【印】(铅字规格的)点(相当于 1/72 英寸或 0.3478 毫米) **17.** 英(常~s)(铁路的)尖轨;轨尖;道岔 **18.** (插头等的)接触点;[主英](电)插座 **19.** (猎犬发现猎物时)站住以头指向猎物的动作 —*vt.***1.** 弄尖;削尖 **2.** 使尖锐;加强;强调 **3.** 指出;指向;把...对准,使对准 **4.** 给...加标点;给...加小数点(off);【语】给...注元音符号 **5.** (泥水工用灰泥等)嵌填,勾抹(墙壁等)(up);(用锹等)把(肥料)插入土中(in);翻(土)(over) **6.** (猎犬)站住以头指向猎物 —*vi.***1.** 指,指向;面向(to, at, towards) **2.** 表明;暗示(to, at, towards) **3.** (船)迎风行驶 **4.** (猎犬)站住以头指向猎物(为参加比赛)进行强化训练(for) **6.** [英(脏窄等)]起脏头 ‖ '~-blank *adj.***1.** 【军】近距离平射的 **2.** 直截了当的;断然的 *adv.***1.** 近距离平射地;在一条直线上 **2.** 直截了当地;断然 / ~ man [美军] 先头侦察兵

pointed ['pɔintid] *adj.***1.** 尖的;尖头的 **2.** (言语等)尖锐的,犀利的;直截了当的;率直的;有所指的;中肯的 **3.** 显然的;突出的

pointer ['pɔintə] *n.***1.** 指示者;指示物;(钟表等的)指针 **2.** 教鞭 **3.** (会示指

出猎物位置的)猎犬 4.〈口〉暗示;线索;点子 5.[the Pointers]【天】(大熊星座中的)两颗指极星 6.【军】(炮兵中的)瞄准杆

poise ['poiz] vt.1. 使平衡,使保持均衡 2. 使(头部等)保持某种姿态;使悬着 3. 使作好准备 — vi.1. 平衡;悬着 2. 作好准备 3. 犹豫不决,踌躇 — n.1. 平衡,均衡 2. 沉着,泰然自若;自信 3. 静谧,安静,沉静 4.(身体或头部的)姿态 5. 悬而不决,犹豫 6. 砝码;秤锤 7.【物】泊(流体动力黏度单位)

poison ['poizn] n.1. 毒药;毒物 2. 有毒害的事物 3.〈俚〉劣酒 4. 抑制剂 — vt.1. 放毒;放毒于;使受感染(或污染) 2. 毒害;败坏;伤害;玷污 3. 阻碍,抑制 — vi. 放毒,下毒 — adj.1. 有毒的 2. 放了毒的 3. 恶毒的,刻毒的 || ~er n. 下毒者;毒化(或毒害)他人者 || ~ gas 毒气 / ~ hemlock【植】芹叶钩吻;毒芹 / ~ ivy【植】毒漆 / ~ oak【植】美国毒漆 / ~ sumac【植】太平洋漆树;栎叶漆树 / ~-pen adj. 匿名诽谤的;写匿名诽谤信的 / ~ sumac【植】美国毒漆

poisonous ['poizənəs] adj.1. 有毒的;有毒害的;有恶意的 2.〈口〉讨厌的;不愉快的

poke[1] [pəuk] vt.1.(用棍棒等)戳,刺,捅;插;拨弄 2.(用手指,肘等)捅,戳 3.〈俚〉(用拳)揍,击;打(一拳) 3. 伸(头等);放置;把…指向(或指向) 4.〈口〉使困居(up) 5.〈美俚〉挺(牛,羊等) 6.〈美俚〉激发,引起 7.〈俚〉与(女子)性交 — vi.1. 戳,刺,捅;拨弄,翻弄 2.(头等)伸出;〈喻〉探听,刺探;瞎管;干涉 3. 混日子;进展缓慢 4.(男子)与(女子)性交 — n.1. 戳,捅;拨;触;〈美俚〉一拳;(棒球等中的)一击 2. 懒汉,游手好闲的人,慢性子的人(= slow ~);

蠢得讨厌的人 3.(用来防止牛、马等越栏的)触地颈轭 4. 宽前檐女帽;(女帽的)宽前檐 5.〈美俚〉(美国西部的)骑马牧人,牛仔 7.〈俚〉性交

poke[2] [pəuk] n.1.〈方〉袋 2. 放金矿石(或金砂)的袋 3.〈俚〉票夹,皮夹子;积起的一笔钱;一叠钞票 4.(羊的)颈部袋状肿大

poker[1] ['pəukə] n.1. 戳(或拨弄)的人 2. 拨火棒,火钳 3.(在白木上)烙花的铁扦 — vt. 烙制(图案等);用烙花装饰

poker[2] ['pəukə] n. 扑克牌戏 || ~ face〈口〉没有表情的脸;一本正经的面容;面无表情的人 / ~-faced adj. 面无表情的;一本正经的;不动声色的

poky, pokey ['pəuki] adj. 慢吞吞的;迟钝的 || pokily adv. / pokiness n.

Poland ['pəulənd] n. 波兰[欧洲中部国家]

polar ['pəulə] adj.1. 南极的;北极的;地极的;近地极的 2.【物】【化】极的;极性的;【数】配极的 3. 有两种相反性质的(有两个相反方向的) 4.【地】极或北极星似地)指引的,指导的 — n.【数】极线;极面 || ~ bear【动】北极熊,白熊 / ~ circle 极圈

Polaris [pə'lɑːris] n.1.【天】北极星 2. 北极星导弹

polarity [pə'læriti] n.1.【物】极性 2. 截然不同;极端

polarization [ˌpəulərai'zeifən] n.1.【物】极化(作用) 2.【物】偏振(现象) 3. 两极分化

polarize ['pəuləraiz] vt. & vi.1.【物】(使)极化 2.【物】(使)偏振 3.(使)两极分化

Pole [pəul] n. 波兰人

pole[1] [pəul] n.1. 杆;支杆;电线杆;旗杆;(撑竿跳用的)撑竿;篙;车辕 2. 杆(长

度名,=5½码) 3. 齐胸高处直径为4至12英寸的树 —*vt.*1. 用杆支撑 2. 用杆撑;用篙撑(船) —*vi.*1. 用篙撑船 2. 用滑雪杖加速 ‖ ~ jump, ~ vault【体】撑竿跳高

pole[2] [paul] *n.* 1. 极(点);磁极;电极 the North (South) Pole 北(南)极 ‖ ~ star *n.* 1.【天】北极星 2. 指导原则;指南;(注意力等的)集中点

polecat ['pəulkæt] *n.* 1.【动】鸡貂 2.〈美〉臭鼬 2.〈美口〉可鄙的人

polemic [pə'lemik] *adj.* 争辩的;爱争辩的 —*n.* 1. 争辩,辩论 2. 辩论文章 3. 争论者;爱争论者

polemics [pə'lemiks] [复] *n.* (用作单) 1. 争辩(术);辩论(法) 2.(基督教神学课题之一的)争辩学

police [pə'li:s] [单复同] *n.* 1. [the ~] 警察当局;警方 2. 警察(= policemen) 3. 警察性组织;警察性组织的人员 4. 治安,公安 5.〈美〉(兵营中的)内务值勤;内务值勤兵 —*vt.*1. 维持…的治安;警备;守卫,保卫;为…配备警察 2. 管理;监督 3.〈美〉维持…的整洁;打扫(up) 4.〈古〉统治 ‖ ~ constable(英)警员 / ~ dog 警犬;德国牧羊犬 / po'liceman *n.* 警察 / po'lice,woman *n.* 女警察

policy[1] ['pɔlisi] *n.* 1. 政策;方针 2. 策略(性);精明;计谋 ‖ ~,maker *n.* 制订政策的人,决策者

policy[2] ['pɔlisi] *n.* 1. 保险单 2.〈美〉玻利希彩票(一种抽彩赌博) ‖ ~ ,holder *n.* 投保人,保险客户

polio ['pəuliəu] *n.* 〈口〉= poliomyelitis

poliomyelitis [,pəuliəu,maiə'laitis] *n.*【医】脊髓灰质炎,小儿麻痹症

Polish ['pəulif] *adj.* 波兰的;波兰人的;波兰语(或文化)的 —*n.* 波兰语

polish ['pɔlif] *vt.*1. 磨光;擦亮;琢磨 2. 使优美;使精练;润饰 —*vi.* 发亮;变光滑;变优美 —*n.* 1. 磨光;擦亮;琢磨 2. 光泽;光滑;优美;完善 3. 擦光剂;上光剂

Politburo ['pɔlit,bjuərəu] ([复] Politburos) *n.* (共产党的)政治局 (= political bureau)

polite [pə'lait] *adj.* 1. 有礼貌的 2. 有教养的;高雅的 ‖ ~ly *adv.* / ~ness *adv.*

politic ['pɔlitik] *adj.* 1.(人)精明的;策略的 2. 明智的 3.〈罕〉政治(上)的

political [pə'litikəl] *adj.* 1. 政治的;政治上的 2. 政党的,党派的 ‖ ~ly *adv.* ‖ ~ animal 擅长搞政治的人;热中政治的人

politician [,pɔli'tiʃən] *n.* 1. 政治家 2.〈贬〉政客;专操党派政治的人

politics ['pɔlitiks] [复] *n.* (用作单或复) 1. 政治;政治学 2. 政治活动;政治生活 3. 政纲;政见;策略;党派关系

polity ['pɔliti] *n.* 1. 政治形态;政体 2. 政治组织;国家组织

polka ['pɔlkə] *n.* 1. 波尔卡舞;波尔卡舞曲 2. 女式紧身上衣 —*vi.* 跳波尔卡舞 ‖ ~ dot (衣料上的)圆点花纹;圆点花纹衣料

poll [pəul] *n.* 1.(人)头;头顶和后脑部 2.(一群人中的)一名;人头数 3. 投票 4. 记票;点票;投票结果;投票数 5. [常 ~s]投票处 6. 民意测验;民意测验记录(或结果) 7.(锤等的)钝端 —*vt.*1. 收受(或统计)…的选票 2. 要求…的每个成员明确表态 3. 获得(若干票数);投(票);组织…进行投票 4. 对…进行民意测验 5. 剪掉(或剪短)…的头发(或羊毛);剪平(或剪齐)…头发 6. 截去(树木)的树梢;截去(牛等)的角 —*vi.* 投票

pollack ['pɔlək] *n.*【鱼】绿鳕, 青鳕

pollen ['pɔlən] *n.*1.【植】花粉 2.【动】粉面 (双翅目昆虫的易落粉)— *vt.* = pollinate

pollinate ['pɔlineit] *vt.*【植】传花粉给 ‖ ˌpolli'nation *n.* 传粉作用; 已授粉状态

polliwog ['pɔliwɔg] *n.* 蝌蚪

pollock ['pɔlək] *n.* = pollack

pollster ['pəulstə], **polltaker** ['pəulˌteikə] *n.* 民意测验经办人, 民意调查者

pollutant [pə'luːtənt] *n.* 污染物质(尤指工业废物、废气、放射性物质等); 造成污染者; 污染源

pollute [pə'luːt] *vt.*1. 弄脏, 污染 2. 玷污; 亵渎; 败坏(道德等) ‖ **pollutive** *adj.*

pollution [pə'luːʃən] *n.*1. 污染 2. 玷污; 亵渎; 败坏 3.【医】遗精 ‖ ~ **tax** 污染税

pollywog ['pɔliwɔg] *n.* = polliwog

polo ['pəuləu] *n.*【体】1. 马球(运动) 2. 水球(运动)

polonaise [ˌpɔlə'neiz] *n.*1.(18 世纪流行的)波兰式围裙, 连衫裙 2. 波洛奈兹舞(曲)

polonium [pə'ləuniəm] *n.*【化】钋

poltergeist ['pɔltəgaist] (德) *n.*(用噪声作祟的)闹鬼

poltroon [pɔl'truːn] *n.* 胆小鬼, 懦夫

poly- *comb. form* 表示"多","复","聚": polygon, polymer

polyandry ['pɔliændri, ˌpɔli'ændri] *n.*1. 一妻多夫(制) 2.【植】多雄蕊式 3.【动】一雌多雄(配合) ‖ **polyandrous** [ˌpɔli'ændrəs] *adj.*

polyester [ˌpɔli'estə] *n.*1.【化】聚酯 2. 聚酯纤维, 涤纶

polyethylene [ˌpɔli'eθiliːn] *n.*【化】聚乙烯

polygamist [pə'ligəmist] *n.* 行多配偶生活者; 多配偶的人

polygamous [pə'ligəməs] *adj.*1. 多配偶(制)的; 一夫多妻(制)的; 一妻多夫(制)的 2.【动】多配性的, 一雄多雌(配合)的;【植】杂性的

polygamy [pə'ligəmi] *n.*1. 多配偶(制); 一夫多妻(制); 一妻多夫(制) 2.【动】多偶性, 一雄多雌(配合);【植】杂性式

polyglot ['pɔliglɔt] *n.*1. 使用多种语言的人 2.【P-】(书籍的)多种文字对照本(尤指有数种文字对照的基督教《圣经》) 3. 多种语言(或术语)的混用 — *adj.*1.(使用)多种语言的 2. 多种文字对照的 3. 多种语言混用的

polygon ['pɔligən] *n.*【数】多边形, 多角形 ‖ ~**al** [pə'ligənəl] *adj.*

polyhedron [ˌpɔli'hiːdrən, ˌpɔli'hedrən] ([复] polyhedrons 或 polyhedra [ˌpɔli'hiːdrə, ˌpɔli'hedrə]) *n.*【数】多面体

polymer ['pɔlimə] *n.*【化】聚合物

polymerize ['pɔliməraiz] *vt. & vi.*【化】(使)聚合

Polynesia [ˌpɔli'niːzjə] *n.* 波利尼西亚(中太平洋的岛群)

polyp ['pɔlip] *n.*1.【医】息肉 2.【动】(水螅型)珊瑚虫, 水螅虫

polyphonic [ˌpɔli'fɔnik] *adj.*1.【语】多音的 2.【音】复调(音乐)的

polystyrene [ˌpɔli'staiəriːn] *n.*【化】聚苯乙烯

polysyllabic [ˌpɔlisi'læbik] *adj.* 多音节的; 有多音节词的

polytechnic [ˌpɔli'teknik] *adj.*(有关)多种工艺的; 工艺教育(或培训)的 — *n.*(英)工艺专科学校; 理工专科学校

polytheism ['pɔliˌθiːizəm] *n.* 多神论, 多神主义; 多神教 ‖ **polytheist** *n.* 多神论者, 多神主义者; 多神教徒

polythene ['pɒliθiːn] *n.*【化】聚乙烯(=
polyethylene)

polyvinyl [ˌpɒli'vainil] *n. & adj.*【化】聚乙
烯基的

pomade [pə'mɑːd, pə'meid] *n.* 润发脂;头
油 —*vt.* 用润发脂(或头油)搽

pomegranate ['pɒmiˌgrænit] *n.* 石榴;石榴
树;石榴状饰物

pommel ['pʌml] *n.*1.(刀剑等柄上的)圆
头 2.(马鞍的)前鞍桥 —(pommel(l)ed;
pommel(l)ing) *vt.*1.(用刀剑等柄上的圆
头)击,打;用拳头连续搂

pomp [pɒmp] *n.*1. 壮丽景象;(典礼等
的)盛况 2.(马戏或庆祝的)游行
行列 2. 浮华;炫耀的行为;浮华的举
止

pompadour ['pɒmpəˌduə] *n.*1. 高卷式(一
种女子发型);大包头(一种男子发型)
2. 方形低领口女式紧身胸衣 3.【纺】小
花卉纹(一种丝绸图案)

Pompeii [pɒm'peii] *n.* 庞培(或译庞贝)
(意大利南部古城,因附近火山爆发而
湮没)

pompon ['pɒmpɒn] *n.*1.(妇女、儿童衣帽
等上作装饰的)绒球;(军帽上的)毛球
2.【植】绒球菊花(或大丽花);淡红洋蔷
薇

pompous ['pɒmpəs] *adj.*1. 壮丽的;豪华
的 2. 浮华的;浮夸的;夸大的;自负的
‖ **pomposity** [pɒm'pɒsiti] *n.* / ～ly *adv.*
/ ～ness *n.*

poncho ['pɒntʃəu]([复]ponchos) *n.*1. 南
美披风(南美人所穿,形似毯子,中间
开有领口) 2.(尤指橡胶制的)雨披

pond [pɒnd] *n.*1. 池塘;水库 2.〈谑〉
海 —*vt.* 堵(流水)成池(back, up) —
vi. 筑成(或形成)池塘

ponder ['pɒndə] *vt.*1. 默想;深思;考虑
2. 衡量,估量 —*vi.* 默想;沉思,沉思

(on, over)

ponderous ['pɒndərəs] *adj.*1. 沉重的,笨
重的 2. 行动缓慢的;费力的 3.(文章、
谈话等)冗长的;沉闷的;生硬的

pongee [pɒn'dʒiː, 'pɒndʒiː] *n.*【纺】茧绸,山
东府绸;充茧绸

poniard ['pɒnjəd] *n.* 短剑;匕首 —*vt.* 用
短剑(或匕首)刺死(或刺伤)

pontiff ['pɒntif] *n.*1. 教皇 2. 主教 3. 大
祭司

pontificate [pɒn'tifikit, pɒn'tifikeit] *n.* 教
皇(或主教)职位(或任期) —
[pɒn'tifikeit] *vi.*1. 行使教皇(或主教)
职责 2. 自负(或武断)地说话 —*vt.* 自
负(或武断)地说

pontoon[1] [pɒn'tuːn] *n.*1. 浮桥;(架设浮
桥用的)浮舟,(装在飞机上使从水面
浮起的)浮筒,浮囊 2. 趸船;浮码头 —
vt. 架浮桥于;用浮桥渡(河等)‖ ～
bridge 浮桥

pontoon[2] [pɒn'tuːn] *n.*〈英〉21 点牌戏

pony ['pəuni] *n.*1. 矮种马;小型马 2. 赛
马用马 3.〈美口〉小酒杯 4. 一小杯酒
5.〈美俚〉(歌舞队列中的)小个子 5.〈美
俚〉(尤指赛马赌注的)25 英镑 6.〈美俚〉
(教学用外语书中的)直译本,(考试作
弊用的)逐行对照译文 —*vt. & vi.*〈美
俚〉1. 付清(up) 2. 借助逐字直译文翻
译 —*adj.*1. 小(型)的 2.(新闻)每日
摘要性的 ‖ ～ **car**(赛车型)小型汽车,
小马型汽车

poodle ['puːdl] *n.*1. 鬈毛狗 2.〈喻〉走狗
—*vt.* 把(狗)的毛剪修成拳曲状

pooh [puː] *int.*（表示轻蔑、不耐烦、不赞
成等）呸! 啐!

pool[1] [puːl] *n.*1. 池塘;水池;游泳池(=
swimming ～) 2. 小水坑,潭 3.【地】贮
油层;瓦斯层 —*vi.*1. 形成池塘(或潭

2. (血)淤积 — *vt*. **1.** (采矿或采石时)开
(楔眼) **2.** 底切,下切(煤层等) **3.** 使形
成池塘(或潭) **4.** 使(血)淤积

pool² [puːl] *n.* **1.** (赌博者所下的)全部赌
注;(某一项目上的)赌注总额;贮放赌
金的容器 **2.** (赢者独得全部赌注的)赌
注式台球;落袋台球戏(通常有6袋,
用16球) **3.** 联营;集合基金(尤指用来
操纵证券或商品市场的) **4.** 共用物(或人员) **5.** 【医】库;血库;郁血
6. (击剑中的)分组循环赛 — *vt*. **1.** 合
伙经营;把(钱等)投入集合基金 **2.** 使
成为共同利益 — *vi*. 组织……的联营 — *vi*.
成为共同利益集团;组成(或参加)联
营

poop [puːp] *n.* 艉楼;艉;船尾

poor [puə] *adj*. **1.** 穷的;贫困的 **2.** 贫
乏的;缺少的;贫瘠的 **3.** 粗劣的;蹩脚
的;不好的 **4.** 可怜的;不幸的;卑劣的
5. 乏味的,无聊的,没意思
的 **7.** 浅薄的;不重要的 **8.** 已故的(=
late, deceased) ‖ ~ness *adj.*

poorly ['puəli] *adj*. [一般作表语]〈口〉身
体不舒服的;健康不佳的 — *adv*. **1.** 贫
穷地;贫乏地;不足地 **2.** 蹩脚地,拙劣
地

pop¹ [pop] *n.* **1.** 砰的一声,啪的一声;
枪击声 **2.** (开瓶塞的声音) **3.**〈口〉含气的饮料(如汽水、
啤酒等) **4.**〈口〉迅速打上的印记,点痕 **5.**
〈英俚〉典当 **6.**〈俚〉尝试 — *vi*. **1.** (突
然)爆开 **2.** (枪)射击 **3.** 突然不防地出
现(或发生)(*up*);突然(或迅速)行动;
不意来到(或走开) **3.** (眼睛)瞪出,张
大;突出(*out*) **4.**〈美〉爆(玉米等) — *vt*. **1.** 突然放出
1. 开枪打 **2.** (突然地)伸出;拋出;提
出(问题等) **3.**〈英俚〉典当(东西) —
adv. 砰地(一声);突然地 ‖ ~corn *n.*
爆玉米花 / ~eyed *adj.* (因惊讶等)瞪
圆眼睛的,张大眼睛的;眼球突出的 /

~ wine 果子甜酒;果味甜酒

pop² [pop] *adj*. (音乐、绘画、电影等)流
行的;通俗的;(尤指通俗报纸、电台
等)普及的 — *n*. **1.**〈美口〉流行音乐;流
行歌曲;流行音乐(歌曲等)唱片 **2.**
〈口〉[~s]流行音乐会 **3.** 通俗艺术(=
~ art) **4.** 通俗文化

pop³ [pop] *n.*〈美口〉**1.** 爸爸 **2.**(常用作
对老年人的昵称)大伯

pope [pəup] *n.* **1.** [P-](天主教)教皇
2. 权威,大师;自诩一贯正确的人 **3.**(希
腊东正教的)牧首,教父

poplar ['poplə] *n.* 杨树;杨木

poplin ['poplin] *n.*〖纺〗府绸;毛葛

popover ['pop,əuvə] *n.* **1.**〈美〉膨松饼 **2.**
〈英〉约克夏布丁

poppa ['popə] *n.*〈美口〉爸爸

poppy ['popi] *n.* **1.** 罂粟;罂粟花卉(含罂
粟碱) 罂粟蒴果汁;鸦片 **3.** 红色;深橘红
色(= ~ red) ‖ ~cock *n.* 胡扯;废话

populace ['popjuləs] *n.* **1.** 平民;大众 **2.**
人口,全体居民 **3.**(蔑)群氓

popular ['popjulə] *adj*. **1.** 民众的;大众
的,人民的 **2.** 普及的;通俗的,大众化
的;(价格)低廉的 **3.** 流行的;大众(或
某种人)喜爱的;(民间)流传的 **4.** 为一
般人接受(或认为)的 **4.** 受欢迎的;
被爱戴的 — *n.*〈英〉通俗报刊 ‖ ~ly
adv. 通过民众,公选地;普遍地

popularity [,popju'læriti] *n.* **1.** 通俗性;
大众性 **2.** 普及;流行 **3.** 名望

popularize ['popjuləraiz] *vt*. **1.** 使普及;推
广 **2.** 使通俗,使大众化;使受欢迎 **3.** 使
普及化;通俗化 ‖ populari'zation
n. 普及;推广;通俗化

populate ['popjuleit] *vt*. **1.** 居住于 **2.** 构
成……的人口(或动植物的总数);移民
于 **3.** (事物等)占据,在……中占有位置

population [͵pɔpju'leiʃən] *n*.1. 人口；全体居民 2.(人或物的)全体,总数 3.(人口的)聚居 4.(统计学用语)(对象的)总体 5.【生】种群(量);群体；虫口 ‖ ~ census 人口普查／~ explosion 人口爆炸,人口激增

populous ['pɔpjuləs] *adj*.1. 人口稠密(或众多)的 2. 数量多的 3. 挤满的 4. 民众的

porcelain ['pɔːslin] *n*. 瓷；[总称]瓷器；一件瓷器 —*adj*. 瓷制的；瓷的

porch [pɔːtʃ] *n*.1.(上有顶棚的)门廊；入口廊 2.(美)走廊,游廊；阳台 3.[the P-]雅典画廊(公元前 4 世纪斯多葛派哲学家 Zeno 在雅典的讲学处)；画廊学派,斯多葛学派

porcine ['pɔːsain, 'pɔːsin] *adj*. 猪的；像猪的；肥猪似的；蠢猪似的

porcupine ['pɔːkjupain] *n*.【动】豪猪,箭猪

pore[pɔː] *vi*.1. 注视,凝视(*over*) 2. 钻研;熟读(*over*) 3. 默想;沉思(*on*, *up-on*, *over*)

porgy ['pɔːdʒi] ([复]porgies 或 porgy) *n*.【鱼】真鲷；油鲷

pork [pɔːk] *n*.1. 猪肉 2.〈美口〉政治恩惠(指政府用以笼络地方民心的拨款等) ‖ ~ barrel 〈美〉政治拨款

porker ['pɔːkə] *n*. 肉用猪;肥育猪

porn [pɔːn], **porno** ['pɔːnəu] *n*. = pornography

pornograph ['pɔːnəgrɑːf, 'pɔːnəgræf] *n*. 色情(或淫秽)作品

pornographer [pɔː'nɔgrəfə] *n*. 色情(或淫秽)作品作者(或发行人、出售商)

pornography [pɔː'nɔgrəfi] *n*. 色情描写;[总称]色情(或淫秽)作品 ‖ **pornographic** [͵pɔːnə'græfik] *adj*.

porous ['pɔːrəs] *adj*.1. 多孔的；有孔的；

(〈喻〉多漏洞的 2. 能渗透的

porpoise ['pɔːpəs] ([复] porpoise(s)) *n*.【动】鼠海豚;海豚

porridge ['pɔridʒ] *n*. 麦片粥;粥

porringer ['pɔrindʒə] *n*. 小汤碗(儿童用)有柄浅碗

port¹ [pɔːt] *n*.1. 港;〈喻〉避风港 2. 港市,口岸 3. 空港 4.(驻有海关关员的)进口港,报关港;入境港(= ~ of entry)

port² [pɔːt] *n*.1.〈主苏格兰〉门(尤指城门) 2.(船舶或飞机的)舱窗口;(装卸货物的)舱口 3.(装甲车、工事等的)炮眼,枪眼;射击孔;展望口 4.【机】口;汽门;通道 ‖ ~ hole *n*.1. 舷窗口;舱口 2. 炮眼,枪眼;射击孔

port³ [pɔːt] *n*.(船舶或飞机的)左舷 —*vt*. 向左转(舵)(使船头左转) —*vi*. 向左转舵

port⁴ [pɔːt] *n*.1. 姿势,姿态 2. 含意,意义 3.(枪筒向上,自左肩至右胯的)斜持枪姿势 —*vt*. 双手斜持枪(步枪)

port⁵ [pɔːt] *n*. 波尔图葡萄酒(原产葡萄牙的一种高酒精度葡萄酒;亦作 ~ wine)

portable ['pɔːtəbl] *adj*. 轻便的;手提(式)的;便于携带的;可随带(或转移)的 —*n*.1. 手提式打字机;手提式收音机(或电视机) 2. 活动房屋 ‖ **porta'bility** *n*./**portably** *adv*.

portage ['pɔːtidʒ] *n*.1. 搬运;运输 2. 水陆联运;(两条水路间的)陆上运输路线 3.〈古〉搬运费,运费 —*vt. & vi*.在(两条水路间)(把……)搬运越过

portal ['pɔːtl] *n*.1. 门,入口(尤指大建筑物的正门) 2. 桥门;隧道门 3.〈诗〉〈喻〉门,入门口 —*adj*.【解】肝门的;门静脉的

Port-au-Prince [͵pɔːtəu'prins] *n*. 太子港

[海地首都]

portcullis [pɔːtˈkʌlis] *n.*(城堡的)吊闸，吊门 — *vt.*给…装吊门;用吊门关闭

portend [pɔːˈtend] *vt.*1. 预示;预告 2. 表明;意味着

portent [ˈpɔːtent] *n.*1. 不祥之兆;征兆;预兆 2. 奇事;奇观;奇才

portentous [pɔːˈtentəs] *adj.*1. 预兆的;凶兆的,不祥的 2. 怪异的;奇特的;可惊的 3. 自命不凡的,自大的 ‖ **~ly** *adv.*

porter[1] [ˈpɔːtə] *n.*(主英)看门人;门房

porter[2] [ˈpɔːtə] *n.*1. 搬运工人;(火车站、旅馆等的)搬行李工人 2.(卧车或持客列车的)服务员 3.(银行、商店等的)杂务工;清洁工 4.(英)黑啤酒 ‖ **~house** *n.* 大背脊骨牛排(= ~ house steak)

portfolio [pɔːtˈfəuliəu] (〔复〕**portfolios**) *n.*1.(皮制)公事包;文件夹 2. 大臣职;部长职 3. 投资组合,有价证券清单 4.(艺术家等的)代表作选辑

portico [ˈpɔːtikəu]〔复〕**portico(e)s**) *n.*〔建〕(有圆柱的)门廊,柱廊

portion [ˈpɔːʃən] *n.*1. 一部分;一份 2.(食物的)一份,一客 3. 一份遗产(或赠与财产) 4. 嫁妆 5.〔只用单〕命运 — *vt.*1. 把…分成若干;分配(*out*) 2. 给…一份嫁妆(或遗产)

Portland [ˈpɔːtlənd] *n.* 波特兰〔美国俄勒冈州西北部港市〕 ‖ **~ cement** 波特兰水泥,普通水泥,硅酸盐水泥

Port Louis [ˈpɔːtˈluːis] 路易港〔毛里求斯首都〕

portly [ˈpɔːtli] *adj.*1. 肥胖的;粗壮的,魁梧的(常指中年长者) 2.〔主方〕举止庄重的 ‖ **portliness** *n.*

Port Moresby [ˈpɔːt ˈmɔːzbi] 莫尔斯比港(或译莫尔兹比港)〔巴布亚新几内亚首都〕

Port-of-Spain [ˈpɔːtəvˈspein] *n.* 西班牙港〔特立尼达和多巴哥首都〕

Porto -Novo [ˈpɔːtəuˈnəuvəu] *n.* 波多诺伏〔贝宁首都〕

portrait [ˈpɔːtrit] *n.*1. 肖像;画像;人像 2.(半身)雕塑像 3.(物体的)画;照片 4. 生动的描写;人物描写 5.〔喻〕型式;相似

portray [pɔːˈtrei] *vt.*1. 画(人物、风景等);描绘、描写,描述 ‖ **~al** *n.*1. 描绘,描写,描述 2. 肖像;画像;人像

Portsmouth [ˈpɔːtsməθ] *n.*1. 朴次茅斯〔英国英格兰南部港市〕 2. 朴次茅斯〔美国弗吉尼亚州东南部港市〕

Portugal [ˈpɔːtjugəl] *n.* 葡萄牙〔欧洲西南部国家〕

Portuguese [ˌpɔːtjuˈɡiːz] *adj.* 葡萄牙的;葡萄牙人的;葡萄牙语的 — *n.*1.〔单复同〕葡萄牙人 2. 葡萄牙语

portulaca [ˌpɔːtjuˈlækə, ˌpɔːtjuˈleikə] *n.*1.〔植〕马齿苋;半枝莲 2. 马齿苋花;半枝莲花

pose[1] [pəuz] *vt.*1. 使摆好姿势;把…摆正位置 2. 提出;造成,引起 — *vi.*1. 摆好姿势 2. 摆样子(做作姿态);假装 3.(西洋骨牌戏中)打出第一张牌 — *n.*1.(摄影、画像、表演时的)姿势;姿态 2. 装腔作势;伪装

pose[2] [pəuz] *vt.* 把…难住;使为难

poser[1] [ˈpəuzə] *n.*1.(为照相等)摆姿势的人 2. 故作姿态的人,装腔作势的人

poser[2] [ˈpəuzə] *n.* 难题

poseur [pəuˈzəː]〈法〉 *n.* 故作姿态的人,装腔作势的人

poseuse [pəuˈzəːz]〈法〉 *n.* 故作姿态的女人,装腔作势的女人

posh [pɔʃ] *adj.*1. 漂亮的;时髦的 2. 第一流的,高档的 — *vt.* 使变得漂亮(或

时髦) —adv. 漂亮地;时髦地

position [pəˈziʃən] n.1. 位置;方位 2. 地位;身分 3. 职位;职务 4. 形势,状况,境况 5. 姿势;姿态 6. 主张,见解;立场;态度 7.【军】阵地 8.【音】和弦位置;(演奏乐器时的)把位 9.【语】(音节中)元音位置 —vt.1. 把…放在适当的位置;给…定位 2.【军】屯（兵），驻扎(部队)

positive [ˈpɔzitiv] adj.1. 确定的;明确的;确实的 2. 确信的;有自信的 3. 过于自信的;独断的 4. 绝对的 5. 积极的;建设性的;确有助益的;肯定的 6. 实证的,实际的 7.〈口〉过度的;习惯等)规定的 8.〈口〉完全的;纯粹的 9.【语】原级的 10.【数】正的 11.【物】正的,阳性的 12.【摄】正片的;正像的 13.【生】(刺激源)向性的,趋性的 —n.1. 明确;实在;确实 2. 正面【摄】正片,正像 3.[the ~]【语】原级;原级词 4.(电池的)阳极 5.【数】正数 ‖ -ly adv. / ~ness n.

posse [ˈpɔsi] n.1.〈美〉一群武装人员 2. 地方武装团队 3.一队,一群,一批

possess [pəˈzes] vt.1. 占有,拥有(财产等);使占有,使拥有(of, with) 2. 具有(品质、才能等) 3. 掌握（思想、语言，知识、技能等） 4.(常指心情方面)保持;克制,抑制 5. 支配;控制 6.(妖魔,情欲等)迷住,缠住

possession [pəˈzeʃən] n.1. 有,所有,拥有;占有物;财产 2. 领地,属地,殖民地 5. 自制;镇定自若 6. 着魔

possessive [pəˈzesiv] adj.1. 所有的;占有的 2.〈贬〉占有欲极强的 3. 表示所有格的 —n.【语】所有格;物主代词;表示属有关系的词组 ‖ ~ case【语】所有格 / ~ pronoun【语】物主代词

possessor [pəˈzesə] n. 所有人;占有人;持有人,拥有者

possibility [ˌpɔsiˈbiliti] n.1. 可能(性) 2. 可能的事;可能发生的事

possible [ˈpɔsibl] adj.1. 可能的;可能存在(或发生、做到)的;潜在的 2. 合理的;可允许的 3.〈口〉过得去的;可以接受的;还算可以的;差强人意的;潜在性上 2. 可能的人(或物);可能出现的事物 3. 最高得分(尤指射击) 4.[~s]必需物品(尤指金钱;给养等)

possibly [ˈpɔsibli] adv.1. 可能地;合理地 2. 也许,可能 3.[用于否定句、疑问句]无论如何;不管怎样;究竟

possum [ˈpɔsəm]〈口〉n.【动】负鼠;〈澳新〉袋貂 ‖ play ~ 装睡;装病;装死,装傻

post¹ [pəust] n.1. 柱;桩;杆;标柱,界柱 2.【矿】煤柱;矿柱;厚砂岩层;厚石灰岩层 3.(枪管前方的)准星 —vt.1. 贴出(布告、通告等)(up) 2.(把布告等)贴在…上(over) 2.(用布告)宣布;公告 3. 把…登入榜(英)(大学)宣布(不及格学生的名单 4.(出布告、用布告牌等)警告;禁止进入(某地);(出布告)公开揭发;公开谴责 5. 公布(失事或失踪船只) 6.〈美〉【体】得(分)

post² [pəust] n.1. 邮政(制度);邮寄 2.〈英〉(一批)邮件(=〈美〉mail)邮件的一次投递(或收进) 3.〈英〉邮局;邮筒;〈方〉邮递员 4. 驿马;驿车;邮船 5.〈古〉邮驿站;(两驿站之间的)行程,路程 6. 邮报(用作报纸或杂志名) 7. 剖(一种信笺或抄写纸的尺寸,约 20×16 英寸) —vi.1. 乘驿马旅行 2. 快速旅行;赶紧走 —vt.1. 投寄,邮寄(=〈美〉mail)〈古〉急派(某人) 2. 过(账),誊(账)(尤指由日记账过入分类账);登入(总账) 3.[常用被动语态]使

熟悉;使了解 —adv. 1. 乘驿马 2. 快速地;加急地 ‖ '~ bag n. (主英) 1. 邮袋 2. 一天发送(或收进)的邮件 / '~ box n. 信箱;邮筒;邮政信箱 / '~ card n. 明信片 / '~ code n. (英)邮政编码 / '~ 'free adj. (主英)免付邮资的,邮费已付的 / '~ 'haste n. 尽可能快速地,急速地 / '~ man n. 邮递员 / '~ mark n. 邮戳 vt. 盖邮戳于 / '~ master n. 1. 邮政局长 2. (旧时的)驿站长 / ~ mistress n. 女邮政局长 / ~ office 邮局 / '~ office box 邮政信箱 / '~ 'paid adj. 邮费已付的

post³ [pəust] n. 1. 岗位(尤指哨兵站岗位置);哨所,站 2. (部队的)驻地;兵营;营区;守备部队 3. 职位;职守 4. (英)一天头次收进的邮件 5. (美)退役军人地方分会 6. 商埠;贸易站;租界;(证券交易所的)交易台 —vt. 1. 设置(岗哨等) 2. (英)任命,派任(尤指军职) 3. (隆重地)把(国旗)送到指定地点

post- pref. 表示"后…";"次…": posthumous, postdate.

postage ['pəustidʒ] n. 邮资,邮费;~ due 欠(邮)资 ‖ ~ stamp 1. 邮票;代邮标记 2. (口)极小区域

postal ['pəustəl] adj. 邮政的;邮局的;邮件的 —n. (美口)明信片 ‖ ~ card (主美)明信片 / ~ code (加拿大)(英)邮政编码 / ~ course 函授课程 / ~ order(英)邮政汇票

postbellum ['pəust'beləm] adj. 战后的;美国南北战争的

postdate [,pəust'deit] vt. 1. 填迟…的日期 2. 在…上填写比实际晚的日期 3. 接在…的后面 —['pəustdeit] n. (票证等上的)填迟日期,晚于实际发生的日期

poster ['pəustə] n. 1. 招帖(画),海报;布告;标语牌 2. (广告、招贴等的)张贴者

posterior [pɔs'tiəriə] adj. (时间上)以后的;(次序上)其次的;(位置上)后面的 —n. [常~s]臀部;身体后部

posteriority [pɔs,tiəri'ɔriti] n. (时间、次序、位置上的)在后

posterity [pɔs'teriti] n. 后裔,子孙;后代,后世

postgraduate [,pəust'grædjueit, ,pəust'grædʒueit] adj. 大学毕业后的;研究生的;研究生课程的 —n. 研究生

posthaste ['pəust'heist] adv. 赶紧地,急忙地;尽快地

posthumous ['pɔstjuməs] adj. 1. 父亲死后出生的,遗腹的 2. 著作者死后出版的;死后的,身后的 ‖ ~ly adv. / ~ness n.

postmeridian [,pəustmə'ridiən] adj. 午后的;下午的(发生)的

post meridiem ['pəustmə'ridiəm] (拉)午后的;下午(发生)的

postmortem ['pəust'mɔːtəm] adj. 1. 死后的;验尸的;用来验尸的 2. 事后的 —n. 1. 尸体解剖,验尸(= examination) 2. 事后检讨,事后剖析

postpone [pəust'pəun] vt. 1. 延迟,使延期,延缓 2. 把(人或事物)放在次要地位;[语]把(某种词)放在后面(或句尾)— an adjective 把形容词放在后面 —vi. (疟疾等)延缓发作(或复发) ‖ ~ment n. 延迟,延期

postscript ['pəustskript, 'pəusskript] n. 1. (信末签名后的)又及,附笔(略作 PS) 2. (书籍等正文后的)附言;补充说明;附录;跋 3. (美)(新闻广播等后的)结束语;播后白;附加消息

postulate ['pɔstjuleit] vt. 假定;以…为出发点 3. [数]公设,假设 —['pɔstjulit, 'pɔstjuleit] n. 1. 假定,假设 2. 先决条

件;必要条件 3.【数】公设 4. 基本原理 ‖ ,postu'lation n. 假定,假设

posture ['pɔstʃə] n.1. 姿势;姿态;仪态;体位 2. 状态;态势 3. 态度;心境 —vt. 使作出某种姿势(或态度) —vi. 取某种姿势(或态度);故作姿态

postwar ['pəust'wɔ:] adj. 战后的 —adv. 在战后 —n. 战后时期

posy ['pəuzi] n.1.〈古〉(刻在戒指等上的)铭文(如诗句、格言等) 2. 花束;花朵

pot [pɔt] n.1.(常用以构成复合词)罐;锅;盆:a tea 一茶壶 2. 一罐(或锅、壶)的容量 3.【冶】罐,锅,坩埚 4. 罐状物(尤指捕鱼虾等用的篓笼) 5.〈运动会等的〉奖杯;奖品 6. 大笔(款子) 7.(纸牌戏的)一局;赌注的总额;奖金的总额;(一个团体的)基金总额 8. 一壶酒;酒;饮酒 9.〈美俚〉大麻叶 10.一~-shot 11. 375 × 312mm 的纸张 12.〈俚〉大肚皮 13.(台球戏中)把球打入袋中的一击 14.(俚)电位计 — (potted; potting) vt.1. 把…放在罐里;把…装罐 2. 把…栽在花盆里 3. 删节;摘录 4.(为取得食物而)向…射击;射击杀死(动物);获得(猎物) 5. 抓住,捕获 6. 把(台球)打入袋中 —vi. 射击;乱射(at) ‖~herb n.1. 熟食叶用菜;野菜 2. 调味用香草(如薄荷) / ~hole n.1.【地】锅穴,壶穴 2.(路面上的)坑洼 / ~shot n.1. 滥辔射击 2. 近距离射击;乱射;任意射击 3. 随意的乱射 vt. & vi.1.(向…)乱射 2. 随意攻击(或批评)

potable ['pəutəbl] adj. 可饮的,适合饮用的 —n.[常作~s]饮料;烈性酒 ‖~-ness n.

potash ['pɔtæʃ] n.【化】钾碱,碳酸钾,氢氧化钾;含钾物

potassium [pə'tæsiəm] n.【化】钾

potation [pəu'teiʃən] n.1. 喝,饮;一饮的量 2. 纵酒 3. 酒;酒类饮料

potato [pə'teitəu] n.([复] potatoes) n.1. 马铃薯,土豆 2. 甘薯,山芋 3.〈澳俚〉姑娘,女人(尤指难看的脸) 4.[~es]〈美俚〉钱 5.〈口〉(袜子上的)破洞

potency ['pəutənsi] ([亦作 potance ['pəutəns]) n.1. 力量;权力;权势;(药、酒等的)效力,效能 2. 潜能;潜力;(发育)能力;(男子的)性交能力 3. 超凡(或超自然)力量

potent ['pəutənt] adj.1. 有力的;强有力的;有势力的 2.(药、酒等)有效力的;有效能的;浓烈的;(议论等)有说服力的 3.(茶等)浓的 4.(男性)有性交能力的 ‖~ly adv.

potentate ['pəutənteit] n. 君主;统治者;有权势的人

potential [pə'tenʃəl] adj.1. 潜在的;【物】势,位的 2. 有可能性的 3.〈罕〉有力量的 —n.1. 潜势;潜能;潜力 2.【语】表示可能性的 3.【语】可能性;动词可能式 ‖~ly adv. 潜在地

potentiality [pə,tenʃi'æliti] n. 潜在性;潜在的可能;可能性;[potentialities]潜力,潜能

pother ['pɔðə] n. 喧闹;忙乱;烦恼 —vt. & vi.(使)烦恼,(使)感到心神不宁

potion ['pəuʃən] n. 饮剂;饮料;一次饮用量

potpourri [,pəu'puəri, pəupu'ri:] n.1. 百花香(指放在罐内的干燥花瓣和香料混合物,能散发香味) 2.(文学作品的)集锦,杂录;(音)集锦曲 3. 混杂物;杂烩

potter[1] ['pɔtə] n. 陶工,制陶工人

potter[2] ['pɔtə]〈英方〉vi.1. 松松垮垮地做事(at, in) 2. 闲逛,闲荡(about, *around*) —*vt.* 混(日子);浪费(时间等)(*away*)

pottery ['pɔtəri] *n.* 1.〖总称〗陶器 2. 陶器制造(术)3. 陶器制造厂(或作坊)

potty¹ ['pɔti] *adj.* 1.〈英口〉琐碎的;微不足道的 2.〈英口〉傻的,有些疯狂的;迷恋的,着迷的(*about*)3. 傲慢的;势利的

potty² ['pɔti] *n.*〈小孩用的〉便盆,尿壶

pouch [pautʃ] *n.* 1.〈随身携带的〉小袋;烟草袋;〖古〗钱袋 2. 皮制弹药袋 3. 邮袋;文件袋 4.〈苏格兰〉〈衣服的〉口袋 5.〖动〗袋鼠等有袋动物雌体腹部的)育儿袋 6.〖囊肌等的〗颊袋 7.〖植〗囊,袋 7.〖解〗陷凹 —*vt.* 1. 把…放入袋中;把…占为己有 2. 把(衣服的一部分)做成袋状;使成袋状;使鼓起 3.〈古〉〈鱼·鸟等〉吞下 4.〈英俚〉付水壶给 —*vi.* 1. 成袋状;悬垂如袋 2. 用邮袋(或文件袋等)递送邮件(或文件)

poultice ['pəultis] *n.*〖医〗泥罨(敷)剂 —*vt.* 敷泥罨(敷)剂于

poultry ['pəultri] *n.*〖总称〗家禽

pounce [pauns] *n.* 1.〈猛禽等的〉猛扑;飞扑 2.〈猛禽的〉爪 —*vi.* 1. 猛扑;突然袭击(*on, upon*)2. 猛扑(*at*)3.〈喻〉攻击(*on, upon*)—*vt.* 扑过去攫住

pound¹ [paund] *n.* 1. 磅(重量单位,一般指常衡磅)2. 英镑(= ~ *sterling*)(符号为£)3. 镑(爱尔兰、马耳他、埃及、苏丹等国的货币单位)

pound² [paund] *vt.* 1. 捣碎;舂碎 2.〈连续〉猛击;〈猛烈〉敲打 3.〈不断重复地〉灌输 4.〈沉重地或持续地〉沿着…移动 —*vi.* 1.〈连续〉猛击 2.〈猛烈〉敲打 3. 脚步沉重地走(或跑);隆隆行驶(或飞行)3.〈持续地〉苦干 —*n.* 重击;重击声

pound³ [paund] *n.* 1.〈走失牲畜的〉认领栏 2.〈关禁无执照或未驯养牲畜的〉牲畜栏;〖野兽的〗拘禁栏 3.〈捕鱼或养鱼的鱼塘;养龙虾池;鲜活龙虾出售处 4.〈喻〉拘留所;拘留;围住;围紧 5.〈扣压财物的〉待赎所;待领所 —*vt.* 1.〖古〗把(走失的牲畜)关进认领栏(*up*);〈喻〉监禁;拘留 2.〖古〗筑堤拦(水)

poundcake ['paundkeik] *n.* 1. 重糖奶油蛋糕 2.〈美俚〉甜姐儿

pour [pɔ:] *vt.* 1. 倒;灌;注 2. 倾注;源源输送 3. 倾吐;诉说(*out, forth*)—*vi.* 1. 倾泻;不断流出 2. 涌出;涌来;源源而来 3. 下倾盆大雨;〈雨〉倾盆而下 4. 斟茶;〈美〉〈作为女主人〉斟茶招待客人 —*n.* 1. 倒;倾泻;浇注;一次浇注(入模)的量 2. 倾盆大雨

pout [paut] *vi.* 1. 撅嘴;板脸;不高兴 2. 撅起;凸出,鼓起 —*vt.* 1. 撅起(嘴唇等);使凸出;使(羽毛等)张开 2. 撅嘴板脸地说 —*n.* 1. 撅嘴 2.[常~s]生气,不悦

poverty ['pɔvəti] *n.* 1. 贫穷,贫困 2. 缺乏,缺少 3.〈土地等的〉贫瘠 4. 虚弱 ‖ ~ *level* = ~ *line* / ~ *line* 贫困线(维持一般生活所需收入的最低标准)/'~-,stricken *adj.* 贫穷的,贫困的;贫乏的

POW *abbr.* prisoner of war 战俘

powder ['paudə] *n.* 1. 粉;粉末 2. 化妆用粉 3.〖医〗药粉剂 4. 火药;炸药;〈喻〉推动力;爆炸力 5. 粉状雪,干细雪 6.〈美俚〉一杯酒 7.〈美俚〉逃跑;逃遁 —*vt.* 1. 酒粉于;用粉状物覆盖(*with*)2. 在…上搽粉 3. 用点状物装饰;点缀(*with*)4. 使成粉末 —*vi.* 1. 变成粉末 2. 搽粉 3.〈美俚〉离去,逃跑 ‖ ~ **flask**, ~ **horn**(牛角制的)火药筒 / ~ **puff** 1. 粉扑 2.〈俚〉性格软弱的人

/'~-puff *adj*.1.（体育运动或比赛项目）由女子参加的 2.〈口〉软弱无力的 /~ room 女盥洗室；女厕所

powdery ['paudəri] *adj*.1. 粉的；粉状的 2. 易碎成粉末的 3. 布满粉状物（或尘埃)的

power ['pauə] *n*.1. 能力 2.〈生理〉机能；体力；精力；才能 3. 力，力量；动力；电力；功率；率 4. 权；政权；权力；势力 5. 权力范围；权限 6.〈授权的〉证书 7. 强国；大国 8. 有权力的人；有影响的机构 9.〈数〉幂，乘方 10.〈光学仪器的〉放大率，〈透镜的〉焦器 11.〈口〉许多，大量 12. 神，神仙 —*vt*. 给…提供动力，使开动；促进，推动 ‖ ~ base 权力基础（尤指支持竞选人、政治家、政策等的）/'~boat *n*.1. 摩托艇，汽艇 /~ broker〈美〉(能影响有权势人物以操纵权力的）权力经纪人 /'~house *n*.1. 发电站 2.〈影响力等〉源泉 3. 权贵 4.【体】强队 5. 精力充沛的人 /~ station 发电站

powerful ['pauəful] *adj*.1. 强有力的，强大的 2. 效力大的 3. 有权力的 4.〈美方〉很多的，大量的 —*adv*.〈美方〉很，非常 ‖ ~ly *adv*.

powerless ['pauəlis] *adj*.1. 无力量的，软弱的；无资源的 2.［常接不定式］无权力的；无能力的；无能为力的 ‖ be ~ to do so 没有能力办这样做 ‖ ~ly *adv*.

powwow ['pauwau] *n*.1.（北美印第安人的）巫师；巫医 2.（北美印第安人为庆祝胜利等举行的）帕瓦瓦式 3.〈口〉会议；商谈；聚会 —*vi*.1. 举行帕瓦瓦式 2.〈口〉讨论，商议（*about*）—*vt*. 用巫术医治

pox [pɔks]（［复］pox(es)) *n*.1.【医】痘，痘疮 2.〈口〉梅毒 3.（植物的）痘病 —*vt*.

使染上痘疮（或梅毒）

pp. *abbr*. pages

p. p. *abbr*. past participle 过分去词

Pr【化】元素镨(praseodymium)的符号

pr. *abbr*. pair(s)

practicable ['præktikəbəl] *adj*.1. 能实行的；可行的 2. 适用的（舞台布景等）能实际使用的 3. 可通行的

practical ['præktikəl] *adj*.1. 实践的；实际的 2. 实际上的；事实上的；实事求是的 3. 注重实效的，讲究实际的 有实际经验的，（贬）只讲实用的 4. 可行的；有实效的；实用的 ‖ ~ joke 恶作剧

practicality [,prækti'kæliti] *n*.1. 实践性；实际性；实用性 2. 实际事物；实例；实用的东西

practically ['præktikəli] *adv*.1. 实际上；事实上；实用上 2. 通过实践；从实践出发 3.〈口〉几乎；简直

practice ['præktis] *n*.1. 实践；实际；实行 2. 练习；实习；熟练 3. 惯例，习惯做法；习俗 4.（医生、律师等的）业务；(一批）主顾 5.［律］诉讼手续，诉讼程序 —*vt*. & *vi*.〈美〉= practise ‖ ~d *adj*. = practised

practise ['præktis] *vt*.1. 实践；实行 2. 练习；使练习；训练 3. 惯常地进行 4. 开业从事 —*vi*.1. 实践；实行 2. 练习；实习 3.（医生、律师等）开业 ‖ ~d *adj*. 有经验的；熟练的；精通的

practitioner [præk'tiʃənə] *n*.1. 开业者（尤指医生、律师等）2. 实践者；从事者

pragmatic [præg'mætik] *adj*.1.〈罕〉忙碌的；爱管闲事的 2.〈罕〉独断的；固执己见的；自负的 3. 讲究实际的；重实效的 4.【哲】实用主义的 5. 国事的，国务的；团体事务的 6. 系统论述史实的一

n. 爱管闲事的人;自负的人

pragmatical [præg'mætikəl] *adj.* 1. 爱管闲事的 2. 独断的;固执己见的;自负的 3. 讲究实际的;重实效的 4. 【哲】实用主义的 ‖ ~ly *adv.* / ~ness *n.*

pragmatism ['prægmətizəm] *n.* 1. 实用性;实用观点 2.【哲】实用主义 ‖ **pragmatist** *n.* 实用主义者

Prague [prɑːɡ], **Praha** ['prɑːhɑː] *n.* 布拉格[捷克首都]

Praia ['praiə] *n.* 普拉亚[佛得角首都]

prairie ['prɛəri] *n.* 大草原〈(尤指北美的)高草原;草地〉 ‖ ~ chicken, ~ hen 北美草原松鸡 / ~ dog(北美产)草原犬鼠 / ~ schooner, ~ wagon(美)(早期移民过此草原时用的)大篷马车 / **Prairie State** 大草原州[美国伊利诺斯州的别称]

praise [preiz] *n.* 1. 赞扬,表扬;[~s]赞词,赞美的话 2.〈古〉受赞扬的人(或物);值得赞扬之处;值得赞扬的理由 3.【宗】(基督教用语)赞美;崇拜;荣耀 — *vt.* 1. 赞扬,表扬;歌颂 2. 吹捧 3.【宗】赞美(上帝) — *vi.* 赞扬,表扬 ‖ ~ r *n.*

praiseworthy ['preiz,wəːði] *adj.* 值得赞扬的,可嘉的

pram [præm] *n.* (英口)婴儿车;手推送奶车

prance [prɑːns] *vi.* 1. (马)腾跃 2. (人)跃马前进 3. 昂首阔步;神气活现地走(或骑马) 4. 欢跃(about) — *vt.* 使(马)腾跃 — *n.* 1. (马)的腾跃 2.昂首阔步 3. 欢跃,跳跃

prank¹ [præŋk] *n.* 胡闹;恶作剧;玩笑 — *vi.* 胡闹;恶作剧;开过分的玩笑 ‖ ~ster *n.* 恶作剧者

prank² [præŋk] *vt.* 装饰;打扮 — *vi.* 炫耀自己

praseodymium [,preiziəu'dimiəm] *n.*【化】镨

prate [preit] *vi.* 唠叨;空谈;吹嘘(about) — *vt.* 瞎扯 — *n.* 唠叨;空谈;瞎扯

prattle ['prætl] *vi.* 1. 闲扯;胡扯 2. 小孩般咿咿呀呀说话;发出咿咿呀呀的声音 — *vt.* 天真地说;轻率地说 — *n.* 1. 闲扯;胡扯 2. 孩子气的话;咿咿呀呀的声音(如流水声)

Pravda ['prɑːvdə](俄) *n.*《真理报》

prawn [prɔːn] *n.* 对虾,明虾;虾 — *vi.* 捕虾

pray [prei] *vt.* 1. 请求,恳求;【宗】祈祷,祈求 2. 请(= I pray you or please) — *vi.* 请求,恳求;【宗】祈祷,祈求 ‖ ~ in *n.*(教堂等处的)祈祷示威

prayer [prɛə] *n.* 1. 祈祷,祈求 2.[常~s]祈祷式;祈祷文 3. 恳求;恳求(或祈求)的事物 4.[~s]祝福;祝愿 5. ['preiə]祈祷者;恳求者 ‖ **~full** *adj.* ‖ ~ **book** 祈祷书 / ~ **rug**, ~ **mat**(穆斯林祈祷时用的)跪垫,跪毯 / ~ **wheel**(喇嘛教用的刻有祷文的)祈祷轮,地藏轮

PRC *abbr.* People's Republic of China 中华人民共和国

pre- *pref.* 表示"前";"先","预先"; prehistoric, premolar, prepay

preach [priːtʃ] *vt.* 1.【宗】布道,宣讲(道) 2. 鼓吹 — *vi.* 1. 讲道;说教 2. 宣扬,鼓吹 3.劝诫 — *vt.* 1. 宣讲(道);说教;训诫 ‖ ~er *n.* 传道士;说教者;鼓吹者

preamble [priː'æmbl] *n.* 1.(法规、条约等的)序言;绪论;开场白 2. 开端;(事件的)前奏

precarious [pri'kɛəriəs] *adj.* 1. 不稳定的;不确定的;不安全的,危险的 2. 前有问题的;根据不足的;靠不住的 3.

〈古〉由他人摆布的 ‖ **~ly** adv. / **~. ness** n.

precaution [pri'kɔːʃən] n.1. 预防;警惕;谨慎 2. 预防方法,预防措施 — vt. 预先警告,使提防 ‖ **~ary** adj. 预防的;警惕的

precede [pri'siːd] vt.1. 先于…,位于…之前;比…优先 2. (地位等)高于… 2. 在…前加上,在…前先说;为…加上引言(by, with) — vi. 在前面,居前,领先

precedence ['presidəns] n.1. (次序、时间、重要性等的)在前,领先;优先 2. (正式场合、举行仪式等时的)优先地位,上座;(按地位的)先后次序

precedent[1] ['presidənt] n.1. 先例,前例;【律】判例 2. 惯例

precedent[2] [pri'siːdənt] adj. 在前的,在先的,前面的;优先的

preceding [,pri'siːdiŋ] adj. 在前的,在先的,前面的

precept ['priːsept] n.1. 教训;戒律;格言;箴言 2. (技术上的)规则;方案 3.【律】训令;令状

preceptor [pri'septə] n.1. 导师;教师;校长 2.(青年或实习医生的)指导医师

precinct ['priːsiŋkt] n.1. (教堂等的)围地,境域 2.【美】管辖区;(选举)区 3. [~s](城镇的)周围地区 4. 分区 5. (思想等的)境界;范围;领域

precious ['preʃəs] adj.1. 宝贵的,珍贵的 2.〈口〉十足的 3. 大大的 4.(语言、工艺等)过分讲究的;矫揉造作的 — adv. 〈口〉极其,非常 ‖ **~ly** adv. / **~ness** n.

precipice ['presipis] n.1. 悬崖,峭壁 2. 危局,险境,艰难的边缘

precipitate [pri'sipiteit] vt.1. 猛掷,猛投;猛然抛下;把(某人)猛然推下 2. 使突然陷入(into) 3. 使突然发生;加速;促

使 4.【化】使沉淀;【气】使(水汽等)凝结成雨(或露) — vi.1. 猛然落下(或摔下);陡斜地落下 2. 突然冲入(指状态等) 3. 仓促行事;鲁莽地行动 4.【化】沉淀;【气】(水汽等)凝结(成雨、露等)— [pri'sipitit] n.1. 猛然落下(或摔下)的;陡斜地落下的;猛冲的,流得很快的 2. 急躁的;鲁莽的;仓促的 3. 突然的 — [pri'sipitit] n.1.【化】沉淀物;【气】凝结物(如雨、露等)

precipitation [prisipi'teiʃən] n.1. 猛然落下(或摔下);猛冲 2. 急躁;鲁莽;仓促 3. 促使;催促 4.【化】沉淀(作用) 5. (雨、雪、冰雹等的)降下;降水(性);降水量

precipitous [pri'sipitəs] adj.1. (似)悬崖峭壁的,险峻的,陡峭的 2. 急躁的;鲁莽的;仓促的;猛冲的

précis ['preisiː, prei'siː] n. ([复] **précis** ['preisiːz, prei'siːz]) n. 提要;概略,梗概 — vt. 提出…的要点;概略…的大意

precise [pri'sais] adj.1. 精确的;准确的,确切的 2. 明确的;清晰的 3. 恰好的 4. 刻板的;严谨的 ‖ **~ly** adv.1. 精确地;明确地 2. 刻板地 3. 正好,恰恰 4.[用于肯定性答复]相当于"yes",但语气更为肯定或正式]正是的;确实;的确:Precisely so. 正是这样。/ **~ness** n.1. 精确,确切 2. 拘泥

precision [pri'siʒən] n. 精确(性);精确(度);准确(性);确切(性)— adj. 精确的;精密的

preclude [pri'kluːd] vt.1. 防止;排除;杜绝 2. 阻止;妨碍(form) ‖ **preclusion** n. / **preclusive** adj.

precocious [pri'kəuʃəs] adj.1.(人)发育过早的;早熟的;早慧的;(行为、知识等)过早发展的;超前的 2.(植物)早熟的;早开花的;早结实的 ‖ **~ly** adv. / **~.**

ness *n.* /precocity [pri'kɔsiti] *n.*

preconceive [ˌpriːkən'siːv] *vt.* 事先形成（看法、想法等）

preconception [ˌpriːkən'sepʃən] *n.* 先入之见；偏见

precondition [ˌpriːkən'diʃən] *n.* 前提；先决条件；先决事物 —*vt.* 预先处理；使事先有准备；使预先适应

precursor [priˈkəːsə] *n.* 1. 先驱者；先锋 2. 前辈；前任 3. 预兆，先兆

predacious, predaceous [priˈdeiʃəs] *adj.* （动物）以捕食其他动物为生的，食肉的；食肉动物的 ‖ ~ness *n.*

predator ['predətə] *n.* 1. 食肉动物 2. 掠夺者；掠夺成性的人

predatory ['predətəri] *adj.* 1. 【动】捕食其他动物的，食肉（性）的 2. 掠夺成性的；损人利己的；故意破坏的 ‖ ~ness *n.*

predecessor ['priːdisesə] *n.* 1. 前辈；前任 2.（被取代的）原有事物，前身 3.〈古〉祖先

predestination [priːˌdestiˈneiʃən] *n.* 1. 预先指定；预先确定 2. 注定；命运 3.【宗】得救预定论

predestine [priːˈdestin] *vt.* 1. 预先指定；预先确定 2. 注定 3.【宗】（上帝）预定（某人）得救

predetermine [ˌpriːdiˈtəːmin] *vt.* 1. 预定，定决 2. 使先有一定倾向；对⋯⋯先规定方向；使先存成见

predicament [priˈdikəmənt] *n.* 1. 困境，尴尬的处境；危境 2.【逻】范畴‖ [~s]（亚里士多德的）十大范畴

predicate ['predikit] *n.* 1.【语】谓语 2.【逻】谓项 —*adj.* 【语】谓语（性）的，作表语的 — ['predikeit] *vt.* 1. 断定；断言；肯定 2. 使取决于；使基于（on, upon） 3. 意味；暗示 4.【逻】就命题主项阐述（或断言）；把⋯⋯作为命题谓项一

['predikeit] *vi.* 作出论断；断言 ‖ predication [ˌprediˈkeiʃən] *n.*

predicative [priˈdikətiv] *adj.* 1. 表示断定（或肯定）的 2.【语】表语的；用作表语的 —*n.* 表语 ‖ ~ly *adv.*

predict [priˈdikt] *vt. & vi.* 预言；预料；预计；预报 ‖ ~able *adj.* / ~or *n.*

prediction [priˈdikʃən] *n.* 1. 预言，预料；预报；预计 2. 被预言的事物；（气象等的）预报

predilection [ˌpriːdiˈlekʃən] *n.* 偏爱，偏好（for）

predispose [ˌpriːdiˈspəuz] *vt.* 1. 预先安排（或处理）2. 使预先倾向于；使易感染（或接受）‖ 'pre.dispo'sition *n.*

predominance [priˈdɔminəns] *n.* 1. 支配地位；优势 2. 突出；显著

predominant [priˈdɔminənt] *adj.* 1. 占支配地位的，占优势的（over）2. 主要的；突出的；显著的 ‖ ~ly *adv.*

predominate [priˈdɔmineit] *vi.* 居支配地位；统治；（尤指在数量上）占优势 —*vt.* 支配；统治 — [priˈdɔminit] *adj.* = predominant

preeminent [priːˈeminənt] *adj.* 卓越的，杰出的 ‖ preeminence *n.* / ~ly *adv.*

preempt [priːˈempt] *vt.* 1. 抢先占有（或得到）；抢先购买；预先占用⋯⋯的先买权 2. 抢在⋯⋯之前行动；预先制止 3. 夺取；霸占 —*vi.* 抢先占有（或取得）‖ ~ion *n.*

preen [priːn] *vt.* 1.（鸟）用嘴整理（羽毛）2. [~ oneself]（人）打扮（自己）3. [~ oneself] 赞扬（自己），夸耀（自己）—*vi.* 1. 把自己打扮得漂亮 2. 自满，自负

prefab ['priːfæb] *adj.* 预制的；用预制件装配的 —*n.* 〈口〉预制构件；预制装配式房屋（prefabricated house 的缩略）

prefabricate [ˌpriːˈfæbrikeit] *vt.* 1. 预制，

预构 2. 预先编造；预先准备 ‖
'pre·fab·ri·ca·tion n.

preface ['prefis] n.1. 序言，前言；开场
白；〈口〉开端，序幕，前奏 2. [P-]〈宗〉
(弥撒的)序诵，序祷 —vt. 给…作序
(或加开场白)；作为…的开端(或序
幕，前奏) 3. 位于…的前面 —vi. 作
序；写前言；讲开场白

prefect ['priːfekt] n.1.〈古罗马〉的长官，
高级文官(或武官) 2. 地方行政长官；
(法国等的)省长；(日本的)县长；(巴
黎的)警察局长 3.〈尤指英国公学的〉
级长，班长

prefecture ['priːfektjuə, 'priːfektʃə] n.1.
〈古罗马〉长官的职位(或任期，官邸)
2. 地方行政长官的职位(或任期，官
邸)；(法国等)省长(或县长等)的职位
(或任期，官邸) 3. 级长的职位(或任
期) 4. 府；专区；县 ‖ **pre'fectural** adj.

prefer [pri'fəː] (preferred, preferring) vt.1.
宁可，宁愿；更喜欢 2. 提出〔声明、请
求、控诉等〕3.〔常用被动语态〕提升，
提拔(to)；〈古〉推荐，介绍 4.〔律〕给
〔债权人〕优先权 —vi. 愿意，喜欢

preferable ['prefərəbl] adj. 更可取的，更
好的(to) ‖ **preferably** adv. 更可取地，
更好地，宁可

preference ['prefərəns] n.1. 偏爱 2. 偏爱
的事物(或人) 3.〔关税方面的〕优
惠权 4.〔债务等的〕优先偿还权，优
先(权)；优先选择(权)

preferential [ˌprefə'renʃəl] adj.1. 优先
的；优待的 2.〔关税等〕优惠的，特惠的

preferment [pri'fəːmənt] n.1. 提升，晋升
2.〔尤指教会中的〕美差，肥缺 3.〔购置
财产等的〕优先权 4.〔控告等的〕提出
5. 选择；偏爱

prefix ['priːfiks] n.1.〈语〉前缀 2.〔人名
前的〕称谓(如 Mr.，Dr.，Sir 等)—

[pri'fiks, 'priːfiks] vt.1. 把…作为前缀
(或前言)加于(to) 2. 把…置于前面
3.〈古〉预先确定

pregnancy ['pregnənsi] n.1. 怀孕，妊娠；
怀孕期 2. 丰富；丰硕；深长的含义

pregnant ['pregnənt] adj.1. 怀孕的，妊娠
的；(喻)孕育着的；充满的；富有的 2.
意义深长的；含蓄的 3. 富于想象力
的，有创造力的 4. 富于成果的；多产
的

prehensile [pri'hensail] adj.〈动〉(猴等的
足、尾)能握的，抓握的；能缠绕的

prehistoric [ˌpriːhis'tɔrik] adj.1. 有历史
以前的，史前的 2.〈口〉古老不堪的，陈
腐的

prejudge [ˌpriː'dʒʌdʒ] vt.(未经查明事实)
对…预先作出判断(或判决)

prejudice ['predʒudis] n.1. 偏见；成见 2.
损害，侵害；不利 3. 歧视 —vt.1. 使抱
偏见；使怀成见 2. 损害，侵害；不利于
‖ ~d adj. 有偏见的，有成见的

prejudicial [ˌpredʒu'diʃəl] adj.1. 引起偏
见的；有成见的 2. 有损害的；不利的
~ly adv.

prelate ['prelit] n. 高级教士(如主教等)

preliberation [ˌpriːlibə'reiʃən] adj. 解放
前的

prelim ['priːlim] n.〈口〉1.〔尤指大学中
的〕预考，预试 2.[~s] 正文前的书页

preliminary [pri'liminəri] adj. 预备的；初
步的；开端的 —n.1.〔对学生等的〕预
考，预试 2.〔体〕预赛；预选赛 3.〔常
preliminaries〕初步，开端；准备(指步骤、
措施等) 4.[preliminaries] (英)正文前的
书页，正文前的内容(如序言等)

prelude ['preljud] n.1. 序言；序幕；开场
戏；序曲；前奏曲；预兆 —vi. 作序
言；演开场戏；作序曲；奏序曲 —vt. 为
…作序；成为…的序曲(或序幕)；成为

…的预兆

premature [ˌpreməˈtjuə, ˌpriːməˈtjuə] *adj.*1. 早熟的；不成熟的 2. 过早的；不到期的 —*n.*1. 早产儿 2. 过早爆炸的炮弹 3. 过早发生的事物 ‖ **-ly** *adv.* / **-ness** *n.* / **prematurity** *n.*

premeditate [priːˈmediteit] *vt. & vi.* 预先思考；预先计划；预谋 ‖ **pre'medi'tation** *n.*

premier [ˈpremiə] *n.* 总理，首相 —*adj.*1. 首位的，首要的；最前的 2. 最早的

première [ˈpremiə, prɪˈmiə] (法) —*n.*1. 首次公演；首次展出 2.(戏剧，舞蹈等的)女主角 —*vi.* 首次上演 —*vi.* 首次公演；首次出现；(名演员等)首次露面 —*adj.* 首次的；首位的或首要的；扮演女主角的

premise [ˈpremis] *n.*1. 前提 2.[~s]房屋及地基 3.[~s][律](合同用语)上述各点；上列各财产；(契约等文证的)说明部分；(作为文证述及主体的)财产，房地产 —[priˈmaiz] *vt.*1. 预先提出；事先提到 2. 提出以…为前提 3. 引出，导出 —*vi.* 提出前提

premium [ˈpriːmiəm] *n.*1. 奖品；奖金 2. 优惠；酬金；额外补贴，津贴 3. 保险费 4.[商]贴水，升水；贴息 5.[商]溢价 6. 习艺费

premolar [priːˈməulə] *n. & adj.*[解]前臼齿(的)

premonition [ˌpriːməˈniʃən] *n.*1. 预先的警告(或告诫) 2. 预感；预兆 ‖ **premonitory** [priˈmɔnitəri] *adj.*

preoccupied [priːˈɔkjupaid] *adj.*1. 被先占有的 2.入神的；全神贯注的；一心想一的；心事重重的 3.[生](种或属的名称)不能再以新义使用的

preoccupy [priːˈɔkjupai] *vt.*1. 使全神贯注；使入神 2. 抢先占据；抢先占有 3.

使有偏见 ‖ **preoccupation** [priːˌɔkjuˈpeiʃən] *n.*

preordain [ˌpriːɔːˈdein] *vt.* 预先决定，预先规定；注定

prep [prep] *n.*1.〈口〉〈英〉(学生用语)准备功课；准备功课的时间 2.〈美〉预备学校(= preparatory school)；预备学校的学生；手术前准备工作 —*adj.* 预备的，准备的 —(prepped; prepping) *vi.*1.〈美〉上预备学校 2. 进行预备训练(或学习)；通过培训(或学习)作准备；作准备 —*vt.*〈美〉把…准备好，使预备好；给(病人)作手术前准备

prep. *abbr.* preposition

prepaid [ˌpriːˈpeid] *adj.*(邮资等)预先付讫的

preparation [ˌprepəˈreiʃən] *n.*1. 准备，预备；[常~s]准备工作；准备措施 2. 预习；备课；预习(或备课)时间 3. 制备；(食品等)配制(或制作)成的东西；制剂 4.(为解剖、检查等用的)动物体标本

preparatory [priˈpærətəri] *adj.* 准备性的，预备性的；引导性的，作为准备的 —*n.* 预备学校(在美国指为升入大学作准备的学校，在英国指为升入中学作准备的学校) —*adv.* 作为准备 ‖ **-school** 预备学校

prepare [priˈpeə] *vt.*1. 准备，预备；筹备 2. 使有准备；为…作准备 3. 训练；配备，装备 4. 起草；写出；制作，制造 5. 配制，调制 —*vi.* 预备，准备；作准备

preparedness [priˈpɛədnis, priˈpɛəridnis] *n.* 准备状态，预备状态；战备状态

prepay [ˌpriːˈpei] (prepaid) *vt.* 预付，先付(邮资等)

preponderant [priˈpɔndərənt] *adj.* 占优势的；多数的；主要的；突出的 ‖ **preponderance** *n.*

preposition [ˌprepəˈziʃən] n. 1. 【语】前置词,介词 2. 前面的位置;前置

prepositional [ˌprepəˈziʃənl] adj. 【语】前置词的,介词的;前置性的

prepossessing [ˌpriːpəˈzesiŋ] adj. 给人好感的,打动人的;有吸引力的

preposterous [priˈpɔstərəs] adj. 反常的,乖庚的;十分荒谬的;愚蠢的

prerequisite [priːˈrekwizit] adj. 必须预先具备的,先决条件的;必要的(to) — n. 先决条件;前提;必备条件(for)

prerogative [priˈrɔgətiv] n. 特权

pres. abbr. 1. present 2. president

presage [ˈpresidʒ] n. 1. 预示,预兆;不祥之兆 2. 预言;预先警告 3. 预知;预感 — vt. 1. 预示,预兆 2. 预言;预先警告 3. 预知;预感

presbyterian [ˌprezbiˈtiəriən] 【宗】adj. 长老(制)的 — n. [P-]长老会教友;长老制支持者

preschool [ˈpriːˈskuːl] 〈美〉adj. 学龄前的;入学前的 — n. 幼儿园

prescience [ˈpresiəns] n. 预知,先知;预知能力 ‖ **prescient** adj. 预知的;有预见的;有先见之明的

prescribe [prisˈkraib] vt. 1. 命令,指示;规定 2. 处(方);开(药);嘱咐,建议 3. 【律】(因法定期限完结)使失效 — vi. 1. 命令;指示;规定 2. 处方 3. 【律】(由于长期使用等而)取得权利(to, for) 4. 【律】(因过期限而)失效

prescription [prisˈkripʃən] n. 1. 命令;指示;规定;法规 2. 药方,处方;处方的药 3. 旧习;惯例;传统 4. 【律】(由于长期使用等而)取得的权利;(由于长期使用等而)取得的权利;时效

prescriptive [prisˈkriptiv] adj. 1. 规定的;指示的;命令的 2. 【律】(权利等)由于长期使用等而取得的;因时效而取得

的 3. 约定俗成的;惯例的

presence [ˈprezns] n. 1. 出席,到场 2. 在,存在;存在的人(或物) 3. 面前,眼前;〈英〉[the ~]御前 4. 风采;风度;(能引起观众亲切感的)表演风度 5. (某国在国外的)政治(或军事、经济)势力 6. 感觉(或信念)中的存在物;神灵,鬼魂 ‖ ~ of mind 镇定自若,遇事不慌

present¹ [ˈpreznt] adj. 1. 现在的,目前的;现存的 2. 出席的,在座的;到场的 3. 在处理(或考虑)中的;本,此;the ~ writer 本作者,笔者 4. 〈古〉即刻有用的;应急的;随时的 — n. 现在,目前 ‖ in the ~ 现在在时(态)

present² [priˈzent] vt. 1. 介绍;引见 2. 赠送;呈献;送给 3. 提出;呈递 4. 呈现;描述;出示 5. 上演;使扮演 6. 以(武器)瞄准;举(枪等)致敬 7. 【律】控告 8. 【宗】推荐(牧师)任圣职 — vi. 1. 举枪瞄准;举枪致敬 2. 【宗】推荐牧师任圣职 3. 【医】(分娩时胎儿)露出,先露 — [ˈpreznt] n. 1. 礼物,赠品 2. (举枪)瞄准(姿势);(举枪)致敬(姿势)

presentable [priˈzentəbl] adj. 1. 拿得出的;像样的;体面的 2. 可提出(或提供、递交)的 3. 〈古〉(神职)可推荐人员担任的 4. 可显示(或表现、描述)的 5. 【律】可控告的 ‖ **presentably** adv.

presentation [ˌprezenˈteiʃən] n. 1. 介绍;引见 2. 赠送;礼物;授予仪式 3. 提出;呈递 4. 呈现;展示;描述 5. 上演,演出 6. 【电子】图像;显示;扫描 7. 【宗】(圣职的)推荐 8. 表象 9. 【医】(胎儿的)先露位置,产位

presentiment [priˈzentimənt] n. (尤指不祥的)预感

presently [ˈprezntli] adv. 1. 一会儿;不久 2. 〈主美〉现在,目前 3. 〈古〉立刻

presentment [priˈzentmənt] n. 1. 陈述,叙

述;描写 2. 呈现;展示(物) 3. 描画;画像 4. 赠送(物) 5. 演出 6. 提出;呈递 7.【律】(陪审团等根据对罪行的调查提出的)呈文 8. (向上级的)呈诉,呈报 9.【哲】表象

preservation [ˌprezəˈveiʃən] *n.*1. 保存;保管;保藏 2. 防腐

preservative [priˈzɔːvətiv] *adj.* 有保存能力的;防腐性的 — *n.*1. 防腐剂;保护剂 2. 起维持作用的原则(或因素等)

preserve [priˈzɔːv] *vt.* 1. 保护;防护;维护;维持 2. 保存,保藏;防腐 3. 腌(肉等);把…做成蜜饯(或果酱);把…制成罐头 4. 使(某人的名声)流传;把(某人)铭记在心;使(诗歌等)留存 5. 禁猎;把…圈为禁地 — *vi.*1. 做蜜饯;制果酱;储藏猎食 2. 禁猎;设为禁地 — *n.*1. [常~s] 蜜饯;果酱;罐头水果 2. 禁猎地;(畜养鸟兽的)苑,林;鱼塘 3. 独占的事物(或范围);禁区 4. 防护用品;[~s] 护目镜 ‖ ~ *r n.* 1. 保护者;保存者;防腐剂;救生用具 2. 鸟兽保护者

preside [priˈzaid] *vi.*1. 作会议的主席,主持(*at, over*) 2. 统辖;控制;负责(*at, over*) 3. 领奏,主奏(*at*)

presidency [ˈprezidənsi] *n.*1. 总统(或校长、会长、行长等)的职位(或职权、任期) 2. 管辖;主宰;支配 3. (美国)总统直属机构

president [ˈprezidənt] *n.*1. 总统 2. 长官;大臣,(部门的)议长 2. [P-]院长 3.(美国大学)校长;(英国大学)院长 4. 会长;社长;(会议)主席 5.(银行等)行长;董事长;总经理 6.【史】州长;(殖民地)总督

presidential [ˌpreziˈdenʃəl] *adj.*1. 总统(或校长等)的;总统(或校长等)职务的 2. 统辖的;主宰的;支配的

presidium [priˈsidiəm] ([复] presidia [priˈsidiə] 或 presidiums) *n.* 主席团;常务委员会;执行委员会

press[1] [pres] *vt.*1. 压;揿;压;扳 2. 挤压,榨取(汁等);压缩;压制;熨平;压印(花纹等) 3. 使贴紧;紧抱;紧握;逼迫,使苦恼;使窘迫 6. 敦促;竭力劝说 7. 迫使接受;把…强加于(*upon, on*) 8. 坚持;坚决进行;贯彻 9. 用模子压制(唱片) — *vi.*1. 压;重压 2. 紧迫 3. 催,逼;迫切要求(*for*) 4. 奋力前进;挤向前(*on, ahead, forward*) 5. 拥挤;密集(*about, round*) 6. 承压,受压 — *n.*1. 压;揿;挤;压力;紧握 2. 人丛;拥挤;蜂拥向前;紧迫;繁忙 3. 压榨机;压机 4. 印刷机;印刷所;印刷(术);印刷业 5. 新闻报道;[the ~][总称]报刊(包括广播及电视新闻报道);新闻界;出版界;出版社;通讯社 6. 报刊上的评论 7. 衣橱;柜橱 8. 夹具;(网球拍等的)夹子 9.(举重中的)推举 ‖ — *er n.* ‖ — **agent**(机构或个人雇用的)新闻广告员,宣传员 / ~ **baron** 报业巨头,报业大王 / ~ **button** *n.* 按钮,电钮 / ~ **clipping**, ~ **cutting** 剪报 / ~ **conference** 记者招待会 / ~-**man** *n.*1. 印刷工人 2.(英)新闻工作者,记者 / ~-**pho'tographer** *n.* 摄影记者

press[2] [pres] *vt.*1. 强征…入伍;强迫…服务 2. 征用 — *vi.* 强征兵员,抓壮丁 — *n.* 强迫征兵(令)

pressing [ˈpresiŋ] *adj.*1. 紧迫的,迫切的 2. 恳切的;再三要求的 — *n.*1. 压;按;榨;冲压 2. 冲压件;模压制品 3. 唱片;[总称]压制的同一批唱片:the first ~ of that song 那首歌的第一批压制唱片 ‖ ~**ly** *adv.*

pressure [ˈpreʃə] *n.*1. 压;按;榨;挤 2. 压

力;强制;紧迫;艰难 3.【物】压力;压强 4. 大气压力(= atmospheric ~) 5. 血压 (= blood ~) —vt. 1. 对…加压力于;迫使 2. 使(高空飞行的飞机机舱等)增压;密封 3. 用压力锅蒸煮 ‖ ~ **cabin**【空】增压舱

prestidigitation [ˌprestiˌdidʒiˈteiʃən] n. 1. (变戏法等时的)手法敏捷 2.(变)戏法 ‖ **presti·digitator** n. 变戏法的人;魔术师

prestige [presˈtiːʒ] n. 1. 威信,威望;声望;(由于财富等而产生的)显赫 2. 吸引力

presto [ˈprestəu] (意) adv. & adj.【音】快(的),急速(的) — (【复】prestos) n.【音】急板 —int. 立刻,一转眼

presumable [priˈzjuːməbl] adj. 可假定的;可推测的;可想象的 ‖ **presumably** adv. 据推测;大概,可能

presume [priˈzjuːm] vt. 1. 擅自;敢于(用于第一人称时为客套语) 2. 假定,假设(没有证据地)相信 3. 足以推定;意味着 —vi. 1. 擅自行动;放肆 2. 设想;相信

presuming [priˈzjuːmiŋ] adj. 自行其是的;冒昧的,放肆的 ‖ ~ly adv.

presumption [priˈzʌmpʃən] n. 1. 专横,自以为是;傲慢;冒昧;放肆 2. 假定,设想;推测,推断 3. 作出推论的根据(或理由;证据) 4.【律】事实的推定(从其他的已知事实推定某事)(= ~ of fact)

presumptive [priˈzʌmptiv] adj. 1. 可据以推定的;假定的,设想的

presumptuous [priˈzʌmptjuəs] adj. 专横的,自以为是的;傲慢的;冒昧的;放肆的 ‖ ~ly adv. / ~ness n.

presuppose [ˌpriːsəˈpəuz] vt. 1. 预先假定;预料,推测 2. 以…为先决条件 ‖ **presupposition** [ˌpriːsʌpəˈziʃən] n. 预先假定

(的事);推测(的事)

pretax [ˈpriːtæks] adj. (纳)税前的

pretence [priˈtens] n. 1. 假装;矫饰;虚伪;做作 2. 借口,托词;口实 3. 自称,自称;自吹 4.(无事实根据的)要求;虚假的理由

pretend [priˈtend] vt. 1. 佯称(有);佯装,假装(演戏等中)装扮 2. 自命,自称 —vi. 1. 假装,装作 2. 自封,自称;妄求,觊觎(to) 3. 追求;求婚(to)

pretender [priˈtendə] n. 1. 妄求者,觊觎王位者 2. 佯装者,冒充者

pretense [priˈtens] n.(美) = pretence

pretension [priˈtenʃən] n. 1. 借口,托词 2. 做作,虚荣 3.〔常～s〕(权利)要求;权利;自称,自命 4. 抱负;企图

pretentious [priˈtenʃəs] adj. 1. 自负的,自命不凡的,狂妄的;矫饰的,做作的 3. 用力的,使劲的;需要技巧(或才能)的 ‖ ~ly adv. / ~ness n.

preterit(e) [ˈpreterit] 【语】 adj. 过去时的 —n. 过去时;过去式动词,动词过去式

preternatural [ˌpriːtəˈnætʃərəl] adj. 超自然的;异常的;不可思议的

pretext [ˈpriːtekst] n. 借口,托词;掩饰 —[priːˈtekst] vt. 以…为借口,假托

Pretoria [priˈtɔːriə] n. 比勒陀利亚[南非共和国首都]

prettify [ˈpritifai] vt. 1.(过分地)修饰,装饰;(过分地)润饰,雕琢(文章等) 2.(贬)美化 ‖ **prettification** [ˌpritifiˈkeiʃən] n. / **prettifier** n.

pretty [ˈpriti] adj. 1. 漂亮的,标致的,俏丽的;美丽的;秀丽的 2. 优美的;悦耳的(游戏等)有趣的;愉快的 3.〈常讽〉好的,妙的(常含反意) 4.〈口〉巧妙的;狡猾的 5. 十分恰当的;贴切的 6.〈口〉好多的;相当大的 —adv. 相当,颇 —n. 1. 漂亮的人(常指孩子

2. 漂亮的东西；[pretties]漂亮的衣服 **3.**〈英〉(玻璃杯的)槽纹部 —*vt.* 使漂亮；使可爱；美化(*up*) ‖ **prettily** *adv.* / **prettiness** *n.*

pretzel ['pretsl] *n.***1.** 椒盐卷饼；扭结状椒盐脆饼 **2.**〈美俚〉(乐器)法国号(= French horn)

prevail [pri'veil] *vi.***1.** 获胜；占优势，占上风(*over, against*)；成功；奏效 **2.** 流行，盛行

prevailing [pri'veiliŋ] *adj.***1.** 占优势的；主要的；有力的 **2.** 流行的，盛行的，通行的；普遍的

prevalence ['prevalans] *n.***1.** 流行，盛行；普遍 **2.**〈罕〉优势

prevalent ['prevalant] *adj.***1.** 流行的，盛行的；普遍的 **2.**〈罕〉优势的 —*n.* 流行的事物 ‖ **～ly** *adv.* / **～ness** *n.*

prevaricate [pri'værikeit] *vi.***1.** 支吾；搪塞；推诿 **2.** 撒谎 ‖ **prevari'cation** *n.* / **prevaricator** *n.*

prevent [pri'vent] *vt.***1.** 防止；预防 **2.** 阻止，阻挡；制止，妨碍(*from*) **3.**〈古〉先做；预先迎合(愿望等)；预先应付(问题等)；[宗]引导 —*vi.* 阻止，妨碍

preventable, preventible [pri'ventabl] *adj.* 可防止的，可预防的；可阻止的

preventative [pri'ventativ] *adj.* = preventive

prevention [pri'venʃən] *n.* 防止；预防；阻止；妨碍

preventive [pri'ventiv] *adj.* 防止的；预防的 —*n.* 预防法；预防措施；预防药；预防物 ‖ **～ detention** [律]〈美国对嫌疑犯、英国对惯犯的〉预防性拘留

preview ['pri:vju:] *vt.* 预观；预演(戏剧等)；预映，试映(电影)；预展；预习 —*n.***1.** 预观，预演；预映，试映；预展 **2.**〈美〉(电影、申视等的)预告片

previous ['pri:vjəs] *adj.***1.** 先的，前的，以前的 **2.**〈口〉过早的；过急的 —*adv.* 在前，在先，在…以前(*to*) ‖ **～ly** *adv.*

prewar ['pri:'wɔ:] *adj.* 战前的 —*adv.* 在战前

prey [prei] *n.***1.** 被捕食的动物，捕获物 **2.**〈喻〉牺牲者；牺牲品 **3.** 捕食 **4.** 掠夺品；战利品 —*vi.***1.**(猛禽等)捕食，攫食(*on, upon*) **2.** 掠夺，劫掠；诈取(*on, upon*) **3.**(疾病等)折磨；损害(*on, upon*)

price [prais] *n.***1.** 价格，价钱；〈口〉高价 **2.**(给杀死或捉拿某人者的)赏金；赎赂，赎价 **3.** 代价 **4.** 价值 **5.**(赌博中)赌注与赢款的差额 —*vt.***1.** 给…定价；给…标价 **2.** 由于抬价过高而使 **3.**〈口〉问…的价格 ‖ **～ index** 物价指数，价格指数 / **～ list** 价目表，价格表

priceless ['praislis] *adj.***1.** 无价的；贵重的；无法估价的 **2.**[俚] 极有趣的；极荒唐的

pricey ['praisi] *adj.*〈口〉价格(或物价)高的，昂贵的 ‖ **priciness** *n.*

prick [prik] *vt.***1.** 刺(穿)，扎(穿)，戳(穿)，刺痛 **2.** 用刺标出，用针扎、小圆点标出；(在名单等上)用刺痕选择，圈选 **4.** 竖起(耳朵)(*up*) **5.** 用刺棒驱赶；〈喻〉驱使(*on, off*) **6.** 道path(野兔) **7.** 缝(帆) **8.** 移植(幼苗)(*in, out, off*) **9.** 使(酒等)发酸 —*vi.***1.** 刺；感到刺痛 **2.**〈古〉用靴刺驱马；策马前进 **3.**(耳朵)竖起(*up*) **4.**(酒等)发酸 —*n.***1.** 一刺，一扎 **2.** 刺痛，刺伤 **3.** 刺痕；点刺；刺孔；野兔的足迹 **4.**(植物的)刺；(动物等的)刺状尖形器官(牙或部位) **5.** 尖器；尖头武器（往往皆用的刺棒 **6.** 靶心点 **7.**[鄙]阴点 —*adj.*(狗耳等)竖起的；听着的 ‖ **～er** *n.***1.** 刺(或扎，戳)的人 **2.** 刺(或扎、

钻)的工具(如刺孔针、锥子等) 3. 荆棘；刺 4.〈古〉轻骑兵；骑者

prickle ['prikl] *n.* 1.(动植物的)皮刺；刺棘 2. 针刺般的感觉；刺痛 —*vt.* 1. 针一般地刺 2. 使感到刺痛 —*vi.* 引起刺痛；感到刺痛

prickly ['prikli] *adj.* 1. 多刺的；满是针刺的 2. 针刺般痛的；痒的 3. 易动怒的；敏感的 ‖ ~ **ash** 【植】花椒 / ~ **heat** 痱子 / ~ **pear** 【植】仙人掌；仙人果的果实

pricy ['praisi] *adj.* = pricey

pride [praid] *n.* 1. 骄傲，傲慢，自大 2. 自满；得意 3. 自豪 4. 使自豪的人(或事物) 5. 最优秀部分，精华；全盛(期);顶点 6.〈古〉华丽；壮观；美观 7.(马的)精力，冲气 8.(鸟、兽等的)群 —*vt.* [~ oneself] 使得意；以……自豪(*on, upon*)

priest [priːst] *n.* 【基督教】教士；牧师；神父(英国国教或天主教位于执事及主教之间的)僧侣 2.【基督教以外宗教的】祭司；和尚；术士 —*vt.* 使成为教士；任命……为祭司(或教职);使做和尚 ‖ ~ **ess** *n.* (基督教以外宗教的)尼姑；女祭司；女术士 / ~ **hood** *n.* 1. 教士(或祭司等)的职位(或身份) 2.(教会的)全体教士(或牧师)

priestly ['priːstli] *adj.* 教士的；似教士的；适于教士的

prig [prig] *n.* 一本正经的人；自命不凡的人；学究式的人；令人厌恶的人

prim [prim](primmer, primmest) *adj.* 1. 整洁的；端正的 2. 一本正经的；拘谨的；古板的 —*vt.* 1. 使(脸、嘴)显出一本正经的表情 2. 整洁地打扮(或装称) —*vi.* 做出一本正经的样子 ‖ ~ **ly** *adv.* / ~ **ness** *n.*

prima ['priːmə]〈意〉*adj.* 第一的；主要的

‖ ~ **ballerina** [ˌbæləˈriːnə]芭蕾舞剧女主角演员 / ~ **donna** ['dɔnə]([复] ~ donnas) 1.(歌剧中的)女主角女演员;(音乐会的)首席女歌手 2. 极其敏感(或妄虚荣、不守纪律)的人 3.(口)(尤指女性)喜怒无常的人；自负的人；爱虚荣的人

primacy ['praiməsi] *n.* 1. 第一位，首位；卓越 2.【宗】(基督教)首主教的职责(或身份、权力);(天主教)教皇的职责(或身份、权力)

primaeval [prai'miːvəl] *adj.* = primeval

primal ['praiməl] *adj.* 1. 最初的；原始的 2. 首要的，主要的；根本的

primary ['praiməri] *adj.* 1. 最初的；原始的 2. 原有的，本来的；原著的：~ (颜色)原色的 / ~ colours 基色，原色(指红、黄、蓝三色) 3. 初级的；初等的，初等的 4. 首要的，主要的 5.【电】一次的，第一级的 6.【地】原生的 7.【植】初生的 8.【化】伯的：连上一个碳原子的，(无机盐)一代的 —*n.* 1.(次序、质量等)居首位的事物 2. 原色；原色感 3. 候选人选拔会；初选 4.【天】主星(= ~ planet) 5.【动】初级飞羽 6.【电】初级线圈，原线圈 ‖ **primarily** ['praiˈmerili, praiˈmerili] *adv.* 1. 首先；起初；原来 2. 首要地，主要地；根本上

primate ['praimit, 'praimeit] *n.* 1.【宗】主教 2.(罕)首颁 3. ['praimeit]灵长目动物

prime[^1] [praim] *adj.* 1. 最初的；原始的，基本的；原有的 2. 首要的，主要的；首位的 3. 最好的；第一流的 4.【数】质数的，素数的 —*n.* 1. 最初；初期 2. 春；青春；全盛时期 3. 精华，最好部分 4.【数】质数，素数 5. 黎明 6.【宗】晨祷 7.【音】同度 7.(击剑中八个防御姿势的)第一姿势 —*adv.* 极好地 ‖ ~ **minister**

（口）总理；首相

prime² [praim] *vt.* 1. 灌注；装填；为…装雷管（或火药）2.（给注水或油等）使起动 3. 在…上涂底漆（或底色）4. 使准备好，使完成准备工作 5. 事先给…指导；事先为…提供消息（或情报等）6.（口）使吃饱；使喝足 — *vi.* 1.（为枪等）装火药；装雷管 2.（为水泵等）注水；（蒸汽机）让水蒸与压入汽缸的蒸汽混合 3. 涂底漆（或底色）4. 作准备 5. 质量变好

primer¹ [ˈpraimə, ˈpriːmə] *n.* 1. 识字课本；初级读本 2. 入门书；入门

primer² [ˈpraimə] *n.* 1. 雷管；底火；发火药；导火线 2. 装火药者；底漆；涂底料 4.【机】预注装置；初给器 5.【生化】引物，引子

primeval [praiˈmiːvəl] *adj.* 原始的；远古的；早期的

primitive [ˈprimitiv] *adj.* 1. 原始的；远古早期的 2. 粗糙的；简单的；未开化的 3. 地球科学的；自然的 4. 原始的；非派生的 5. 自学而成的；自学的艺术家所创作的 — *n.* 1. 原（始）人；原始事物 2.（一种文化运动或艺术流派的）早期艺术家（或其作品）；模仿早期风格的艺术家；原始派艺术家 3. 文艺复兴前的艺术家（或其作品）4. 学风面成的艺术家；风格质朴的艺术家3. 纯朴的人 6.【语】原词，根词；原始（语）；原素 7.【数】本原，原始；基本式 ‖ ~ness *n.*

primp [primp] *vt. & vi.*（仔细地或过分讲究地）打扮；装饰；整理

primrose [ˈprimrouz] *n.* 1.【植】报春花；樱草；樱草属 2. 报春花色，淡黄色 3. 最佳部分，精华 — *adj.* 报春花的；报春花色的；淡黄色的

prince [prins] *n.* 1. 王子；王孙；亲王

（封邑、公国或小国的）君主；诸侯 3.（英国以外封建的）贵族；公爵；侯爵；伯爵；…公；…侯 4.（诗）帝王，君王 5.（喻）巨头；大王；名家 6.（美俚）好人 ‖ ~dom *n.* 1. 小国君主（或亲王、侯等）的权位（或尊严）2. 公国；侯国 ‖ ~ consort 女王（或女皇）的丈夫

princely [ˈprinsli] *adj.* 1. 王侯的；王子的 2. 王族般的；王子似的；似贵公子的 3. 高贵的；堂皇的；庄严的 4. 与王侯（或王子）相称的；豪华的；奢侈的；挥霍的

princess [prinˈses] *n.* 1. 公主；王妃；亲王夫人 2.（英国以外封建的）贵妇人；公爵夫人；侯爵夫人；伯爵夫人 3.（古）女王；女豪杰；女名家

principal [ˈprinsəpəl] *adj.* 1. 主要的；首要的，最重要的 2. 负责人的；首长的 3. 资本的；本金的 — *n.* 1. 负责人；长，首长；校长 2. 主要演员，主角 3.【律】主犯；主债务人 4.（经纪人或代理人所代表的）委托人；本人 5. 资本；本金；基本财产 6.【建】（主要）屋架 7.【音】主音栓（音乐会的）主奏者；独唱者独奏者 8.（艺术作品的）主题 ‖ ~ly *adv.* ‖ ~ parts【语】（动词的）主要部分

principality [ˌprinsiˈpæliti] *n.* 1. 公国；侯国；封邑 2. 公国君主的职位（或权力、领地）3. 首长（或校长）的职位（或权力）

principle [ˈprinsipl] *n.* 1. 原则；原理 2. 主义；道义；准则；正直 3. 本原，起源 4. 天性；本能；天资 5.【化】（要）素；成分

print [print] *vt.* 1. 印；铭刻；打上（印记等）2. 印刷；把…印上；用书面形式表达；印发 3.【计】打印 4. 用印刷体书写 4. 在（织物）上印花；印（花）5.【摄】印；晒印；复制（电影拷贝等）(*off*, *out*) 6.（美俚）取…的指纹 — *vi.* 1. 印刷；刊印；从事

印刷,印 2. 用印刷体写字 —*n*.1. 印痕;印记〈美俚〉[~s]指纹 2. 印刷;印刷术;印刷品 3. 印出的字;印刷字体 4. 印刷品;出版物 5. 图片;照图;版画〔摄〕正片,照片;电影拷贝 6. 印花布;印花布服装;印花布制品 7. 印章,戳子 8.〔冶〕模样芯头类型(= core ~) 9. 打着印痕的东西;印模制物 10. 版本;印次 ‖ ~able *adj*.

printer ['printə] *n*.1. 印刷工(包括排字工) 2. 印花工 3.〔摄〕印相机〔讯〕〔计〕打印机 4. 印刷商

printing ['printiŋ] *n*.1. 印刷;印刷术;印刷业 2.〔纺〕印花工艺 3.〔摄〕印相,(电影拷贝等的)复制 4.(书籍的)一次印数 5.[~s]印刷用纸 6. 印刷字体 ‖ ~press 印刷机(一般指电动的)

printout ['printaut] *n*.〔计〕打印输出;〔摄〕晒像

prior[1] ['praiə] *adj*. 1. 在先的,在前的,居先的 2. 优先的;更重要的 ‖ ~ to 在…以前;先于;优先于

prior[2] ['praiə] *n*.1. 大修道院副院长 2. 小修道院院长 ‖ ~ess *n*. 大女修道院副院长;小修道院院长

priority [prai'ɔriti] *n*.1. 先,前 2. 优先;重点;优先权;先取权 3. 优先配给;优先考虑的事

priory ['praiəri] *n*. 小修道院;小女修道院

prise [praiz] *vt*. & *n*.〈主英〉= prize[3]

prism ['prizəm] *n*.1.〔数〕棱柱(体),角柱(体) 2.〔物〕棱镜;棱柱 3. 折光物(如水滴)

prismatic [priz'mætik] *adj*.1. 棱柱的;棱镜的;棱柱形的 2.(如 = 像)棱镜的,分光颜色的 3.〈光〉呈光谱状的;射出七色光彩的;五光十色的,灿烂的,耀眼的

prison ['prizn] *n*.1. 监狱;监狱 2. 看守所;拘留所;羁押室,禁闭室 —*vt*.〈诗〉〈方〉监禁,关押

prisoner ['priznə] *n*.1. 囚犯 2. 刑事被告;拘留犯;羁押犯 3. 俘虏;战俘(= ~ of war) 4. 失去自由的人(或动物等);被控制的东西

privacy ['praivəsi, 'praivəsi] *n*.1. 隐退;隐居(不受干扰的)独处 2.〈古〉退隐处;隐居处 3. 秘密;私下 4. 私生活;私事;隐私

private ['praivit] *adj*.1. 私人的,个人的;私有的 2. 私营的;私立的;民间的 3. 不让人知道的,私下的;保密的;秘密的(信件等)亲启的 4. 非公开的 5. 非官职的;士兵的 6.(地方等)隔绝的;隐蔽的;幽僻的 7. 不宜公开谈论(或显露)的 —*n*.[~s]阴部,(外)生殖器 2. 职位低的人 3. 列兵;〈英〉陆军二等兵〈美〉陆军(或海军陆战队)二等兵;士兵 ‖ as Private First Class〈美〉陆军(或海军陆战队)一等兵 4.〈古〉退职者;隐士 ‖ ~ly *adv*.

privateer [ˌpraivə'tiə] *n*.1.〈战时特准攻击敌方商船等的〕武装民船,私掠船 2. 私掠船船长(或船员)—*vi*. 私掠巡航 ‖ ~ing *n*.

privation [prai'veiʃən] *n*.1. 丧失;缺乏 2.(生活必需品的)匮乏;贫困 3.(被)剥夺

privet ['privit] *n*.〔植〕女贞

privilege ['privilidʒ] *n*.1. 特权;优惠;特免;特殊荣幸;特别待遇 —*vt*. 给予…特权(或优惠) 2. 特免;免除(*from*)

privileged ['privilidʒd] *adj*.1. 有特权的;特许的 2.(由于特殊情况)不受一般法规节制的

privy ['privi] *adj*.1. 私人的,个人的 2.(地方、物件等)秘密的;隐蔽的;(行

为)暗中参与的 —n.1.【律】利害关系人 2. 厕所 ‖ **Privy Council**(英国等的)枢密院 /~ **counsellor**, ~ **councillor**(英)枢密院官员;枢密顾问官

prize¹ [praiz] **n.**1. 奖赏;奖金;奖品,赠品 2.〈喻〉众人争求的东西;〈值得〉竞争的作为奖品的;极好的东西 —**adj.**1. 得奖的;作为奖品的;为得奖而参加的 2.〈常谑〉该得奖的;了不起的;第一流的 —**vt.**1. 珍视;珍藏 2. 估价;评价 ‖ ~ **fighter** *n.* 职业拳击手

prize² [praiz] **n.**1. 捕获(尤指战时在海上捕获敌方的船、货等) 2. 俘获品,战利品;(战时)捕获的船只(或货物) 3. 意外的收获;横财 —**vt.** 捕获

prize³ [praiz] **vt.**(用杠杆等)撬;撬起;撬动(*up, off, out*) —**n.**1. 撬;杠杆作用 2.〈方〉杠杆;撬杠;撬棒

pro¹ [prəu] **adj. &** 〔复〕pros **n.**〈口〉= professional

pro² [prəu] **adv.** 从正面;正面地 —〔复〕pros) *n.* 赞成者;赞成的意见;赞成票

pro- **pref.**1. 表示"副","代";*pronoun* 2. 表示"亲","亲";表示"前进","向前";*proceed, progress* 4. 表示"按照";*proportion* 5. 表示"公开";*proclaim, pronounce* 6. 表示"先","前";*prologue*

probability [ˌprɔbəˈbiliti] **n.**1. 或有;可能性,或然性;【逻】盖然性(介于 *certainty* 和 *possibility* 之间的性质) 2. 或有的事;可能的结果 3.【数】概率,几率,或然率

probable [ˈprɔbəbl] **adj.**1. 有的,或然的;很可能发生的一有的;可能有似乎为事实的 2. 像真实的,似确有的;很有希望的 ‖ **probably** *adv.* 很可能,大概,或许

probate [ˈprəubeit] 【律】**n.**1. 遗嘱验证

遗嘱验证文件,经验证的遗嘱文本 —**adj.** 遗嘱验证的 —**vt.**1. 验证(遗嘱) 2. 处(犯人)以缓刑

probation [prəˈbeiʃən] **n.**1. 验证,检验;鉴定 2. 试用;见习;试读 3. 试用期;见习期;试读期;预备期 4.(以观后效的)【律】缓刑(期) ‖ ~**al**, ~**ary** **adj.**1. 试用的;见习的;(党员等)预备期的 2.【律】缓刑(中)的 /~**er** **n.**1. 试用人员;见习生;见习护士 2.【律】缓刑犯

probe [prəub] **n.**1.【医】探针,探子 2.【电子】探针,探头;探极 3.(对伤处等的)针探;探查 3. 刺探;探查,查究,调查(*into*) 4.【宇】探测器;探测飞船 5. 空中加油管 —**vt.**1. 用探针(或探测器)探查 2. 刺探;探索;查究;探测;调查 —**vi.** 探查;探索;深查,深挖(*into*)

probity [ˈprəubiti] **n.** 正直;诚实;德行

problem [ˈprɔbləm] **n.**1. 问题;疑难问题;令人困惑的事(或人、情况等) 2.(下棋时须按规定的)布局问题 3.【数】【物】习题;问题;几何作图题 —**adj.**1. 成为问题的;难于对付的 2. 论及社会问题的 3. 意图不明的

problematic(al) [ˌprɔbliˈmætik(əl)] **adj.**1. 成问题的;有疑问的;疑难的;未定的 2.【数】盖然性的;或然性的

proboscis [prəuˈbɔsis] **n.**1. 象鼻子 2.(兽的)吻;长鼻;(昆虫的)喙 3.〈谑〉(人的)大鼻子

procedure [prəˈsiːdʒə] **n.**1. 过程;步骤 2. 程序 3. 传统的做法;办事惯例;常规;(外交、军队等的)礼仪,礼节 ‖ **procedural** *adj.*

proceed [prəˈsiːd] **vi.**1. 进行 2. 继续进行;继续做(或进)下去 3. 开始;着手;出发 4. 发出;出(自)(*from*) 5.【律】起诉,进行诉讼(*against*) 6.〈英〉升迁;获

得高一级学位(*to*)

proceeding [prəˈsiːdiŋ] *n.* 1. 程序；进程；进行 2. 行动；举动；做法 3. [~s] 事项；项目；活动 4. [~s] 诉讼(程序) 5. [~s] (学会或其他团体的)会议录；活动记录；记录汇编

proceeds [ˈprəusiːdz] [复] *n.* (从事某种活动或变卖财物等的)收入，收益

process[1] [ˈprəuses] *n.* 1. 过程；进程；变化过程 2. 步骤；方法；程序；工序；制作过程 3. [印]照相制版法 4. [律](诉讼)程序；(法律)手续；传票 5. [生] [解]突，突起 — *vt.* 1. 加工 2. 处理；初步分类；分理；办理 3. [律]对…起诉；(要求)对…发出传票 4. 用照相版影印 — *adj.* 1. 经过加工的；处理过的 2. [印]照相制版法的 3. (电影镜头等)有幻觉效应的；合成的

process[2] [prəˈses] *vi.* 〈主英〉〈口〉列队行进

procession [prəˈseʃən] *n.* 1. (列队的)行进 2. (人或车辆等的)行列；队伍 3. 一(长)列；一(长)排 4. 谁也无法取胜的赛跑 — *vi.* 列队行进 ‖ **~al** *adj.* 列队行进的；行进中唱的(或唱的) *n.* 列队行进时用的(或唱的)歌

proclaim [prəˈkleim] *vt.* 1. 宣告；宣布；公布；声明 2. 称颂，赞扬 3. 表明，显示 4. 禁止(集会等)；宣布…为非法；管制(某地区等)

proclamation [ˌprɔkləˈmeiʃən] *n.* 1. 宣布；公布；声明 2. 公告；布告；宣言声明

proclivity [prəˈkliviti] *n.* 癖性；倾向

procrastinate [prəuˈkræstineit] *vi.* 拖延；耽搁；因循 ‖ **pro·crasti·nation** *n.* /**pro·crastinator** *n.*

procreate [ˈprəukrieit] *vt. & vi.* 生殖，生育 ‖ **procre·ation** *n.*

procure [prəˈkjuə] *vt.* 1. (努力)取得；(设法)获得；为…获得；采办 2. 实现；达成，完成 3. 〈古〉促使；引起 4. 介绍(娼妓) — *vi.* 作淫媒；介绍娼妓；作淫媒，拉皮条 ‖ **~ment** *n.*

procurer [prəˈkjuərə] *n.* 1. 取得者，获得者之2. (为组织机构)采办货物(或获得供应)者 3. 做淫媒者，拉皮条者

prod [prɔd] *n.* 1. 刺，戳 2. 刺(或戳)的东西；刺针；刺棒；锥 3. 刺激(物)；促使；推动 — *vt.* (prodded; prodding) 1. 刺，戳 2. 刺激；惹起；促使；激励 — *vi.* 刺，戳(*at*)

prodigal [ˈprɔdigəl] *adj.* 1. 非常浪费的，挥霍的；奢侈的 2. 不吝惜的，十分慷慨的(*of*) 3. (物产等)丰富的，大量的 — *n.* 1. 浪费者，挥霍者 2. 浪子

prodigality [ˌprɔdiˈgæliti] *n.* 1. 浪费，挥霍；奢侈 2. 丰富，大量

prodigious [prəˈdidʒəs] *adj.* 1. 巨大的，庞大的 2. 异常的，惊人的；奇妙的 3. 〈古〉预兆的，不吉利的

prodigy [ˈprɔdidʒi] *n.* 1. 奇迹，奇事；奇物；奇观 2. 奇才，天才(尤指神童) 3. 〈古〉预兆

produce [prəˈdjuːs] *vt.* 1. 生产，出产，制造；生，生育 2. 产生；引起 3. 提出；拿出；出示 4. 上演，演出；(电影)制(片)；上映；出版；创作 5. 使(线)延长；使(面)扩展 — *vi.* 生产，制造；创作 — [ˈprɔdjuːs] *n.* 1. 产量；物产 2. 产品；[总称]农产品(尤指水果、蔬菜等) 3. 结果，成果 4. (常指雌性动物的)后代

producer [prəˈdjuːsə] *n.* 1. 生产者，制造者；制造商；出产地 2. (戏剧等的)演出人 3. 剧院老板；舞台监督 ; 电影、电视制片人，监制人 3. 煤气发生炉 4. [矿]生产井

product [ˈprɔdʌkt] *n.* 1. 产品，产物，制

品;产量;出产 2. 结果;成果;〈喻〉产物 3. 作品;创作 4.【数】(乘)积

production [prə'dʌkʃən] *n.*1. 生产 2. 制作;(电影、戏剧等的)摄制;演出;(戏剧般)夸张的行动;小题大做 3. 产品;总产量;成果;(文艺)作品 4. 拿出;提供

productive [prə'dʌktiv] *adj.*1. 生产的;生产性的 2. 丰饶的;多产的 3. 出产…的;产生…的 (of) 4.【语】有构词能力的,能产的 5. 分泌黏液的;生痰的

productivity [,prɒdʌk'tivɪti] *n.* 生产率;生产(能)力

Prof. *abbr.* Professor

profane [prə'fein] *adj.*1. 渎神的;亵渎的,不敬(神)的;不圣洁的;好咒骂的 2. 世俗的,非宗教的 3. 异教的 4. 未受秘传的(尤指关于教义的);外行的 — *vt.* 亵渎;玷污 ‖ **profanation** [,prɒfə'neiʃən] *n.* / ~**ly** *adv.*

profanity [prə'fæniti] *n.*1. 渎神;亵神;使用亵渎语言 2. [profanities]亵渎的语言

profess [prə'fes] *vt.*1. 表示;声称;承认 2. 自称;冒充;假装 3. 宣称信奉(宗教等);立(誓)信条;正式接受…入教 4. 以…为业 5. 当…学科的教授;(以教授身份)教,讲授 — *vi.*1. 表白;承认 2. 正式入教 3. 当教授

professed [prə'fest] *adj.*1. 公开表示的;公开声称的 2. 自称的;假装的 3. 专业的;专门的 4. 已立誓信条的;已受戒的

profession [prə'feʃən] *n.*1. (尤指需要专门知识或特殊训练的)职业 2. [the ~][总称]同业,同行;〈俚〉演员3. 明言;声明;表白;诺许 4. 立誓信教;入教的誓言;信奉的宗教

professional [prə'feʃənl] *adj.*1. 职业的;专业的;业务的 2. 职业性的,非业余

的 3. 职业上的;同行中的 — *n.*1. 以特定职业为生的人(如自由职业者、职业运动员等) 2. 专业人员;内行 ‖ ~**ly** *adv.*

professor [prə'fesə] *n.*1. (大学)教授;(主美)教师,泛指)教师;老师 2. 公开表示信仰者(宗教的)人;声称…的 (of) 3.〈俗〉〈谑〉(跳舞、拳术、魔术等的)专家;教授;(戴眼镜的)书呆子 4.〈美俚〉(酒吧间等处的)弹钢琴者 ‖ ~**ial** [,prɒfe'sɔːriəl] *adj.* 教授的;教授似的 / ~**ship** *n.* 教授职位(或身份)

proffer ['prɒfə] *vt.* 提供;贡献;提出 — *n.* 1. 提供;贡献;提议;建议

proficiency [prə'fiʃənsi] *n.* 熟练;精通 (in)

proficient [prə'fiʃənt] *adj.* 熟练的;精通的 (at, in) — *n.* 能手;专家 ‖ ~**ly** *adv.*

profile ['prəufail] *n.*1. 侧面(像) 2. 外形,轮廓;外观,形象 3. 人物;简介;概况 4. 纵断面(图),剖面(图) 5. 〈美〉个人能力(或特征)侧面图 — *vt.*1. 描(或显出)…的轮廓 2. 给…画侧面图 3. 作…纵断面图 4. 给…铣出轮廓 5. 写(某人)的传略

profit ['prɒfit] *n.*1. 益处;得益 2. 利润;(财产中的)收益 3. 红利 — *vt.* 有益于 — *vi.*1. 有益;有利 2. 得益;获利

profitable ['prɒfitəbl] *adj.*1. 有益的;有用的 2. 有利(可图)的 ‖ **profitably** *adv.*

profiteer [,prɒfi'tiə] *n.*(进行投机倒把等)牟取暴利的人;投机商;奸商 — *vi.* 牟取暴利;获得暴利

profitless ['prɒfitlis] *adj.*1. 无益的;无用的 2. 无利的,无利可图的

profligate ['prɒfliɡət] *adj.*1. 放荡的,荒淫的 2. 恣意挥霍的,极其浪费的 — *n.*1.

放荡的人，浪子 2. 恣意挥霍的人 ‖
profligacy n.

profound [prəˈfaund] adj.1. 意味深长的；意义深远的；深奥的 2. 知识渊博的 3. 深厚的；深刻的；深切的；深深的；极度的 — n. (诗) 深渊；深海 (灵魂) ‖ ~ly adv. 深深地，深切地 / ~ ness n.

profundity [prəˈfʌnditi] n.1. 深度；深渊；深处 2. 深奥；深刻；深厚 3. [常 profundities]深奥的事物；深刻的思想；意义深刻的话

profuse [prəˈfjuːs] adj.1. 毫不吝惜的，十分慷慨的；挥霍的，浪费的(in, of) 2. 极其丰富的，充沛的；过多的 ‖ ~ly adv. / ~ness n.

profusion [prəˈfjuːʒən] n.1. 慷慨；挥霍，浪费；奢侈 2. 丰富，充沛，大量

progenitor [prouˈdʒenitə] n.1. (人或动、植物等的)祖先 2.(喻)(政治或学术上的)先驱，前辈，创始人 3.(文件的)原本，正本

progeny [ˈprɔdʒəni] n.1. 子孙，后裔；(动、植物的)后代 2.(喻)结果，成果

prognosis [prɔgˈnəusis] ([复] prognoses [prɔgˈnəusiːz]) n.1. [医] 预后 [指根据症状对疾病结果的预测] 2. 预测

prognosticate [prɔgˈnɔstikeit] vt.1. 预言；预示 2. 预兆 2. 预测(疾病的结果) — vi. 作出预言(或预测) ‖ progˌnostiˈcation n.

program(me) [ˈprəugræm] n.1. 节目单；说明书；节目，表演 2. 纲要，纲要；(教学)大纲；提纲 3. 计划，方案；程序表；计划表 4.[计]程序 5. 布告 — (program(m)ed; program(m)ing) vt.1. 为…安排节目；把…列入节目 2. 为…制订计划(或规划) 3.[计]为…编制程序；使按程序工作 4. 为(自学教科书)配

习题及题解 — vi. 安排节目；编制程序 ‖ **programmer** n.1. 排节目者；订计划者 2.[计]程序编制员；程序设计者

progress [ˈprəugres, ˈprɔgres] n.1. 前进，行进 2. 进步；上进；发展 3.(帝王等的)巡行；游历 — [prəˈgres] vi. 前进，进展；进行；进步 — vt. 使前进；使(工作等)取得进展 ‖ in ~ 在进行中

progression [prəˈgreʃən] n.1. 前进，行进 2.(行为、动作、事件等的)接续，连续，一系列 3. 进步；上升 4.[数]级数 5.[音](乐音或和弦的)相继进行；(各声部的)和谐进行

progressive [prəˈgresiv] adj.1. 进步的；先进的 2. 向前进的，逐渐的；渐进的；累进的 4. 主张进步的；[常 P-]【美史】进步党的 5.[医] 进行性的 6.【语】进行(时)的 7.(牌戏搭档或舞伴等)轮换的 — n.1. 进步分子，进步人士；革新主义者；改良主义者 2.[P-]【美史】进步党党员 ‖ ~ly adv. / ~ness n.

prohibit [prəˈhibit] vt. 禁止；阻止；妨碍

prohibition [ˌprouhiˈbiʃən] n.1. 禁止；遭禁 2. 禁令；法律 3.[律](上级法院禁止下级法院对无权受理案件审理的)诉讼中止令 4. 禁酒；[P-]【美国】禁酒时期 ‖ ~ist n. 禁酒主义者；(美国)禁酒修正案拥护者

prohibitive [prəˈhibitiv] adj.1. 禁止(性)的 2.(费用、价格或成本等)过分高昂的，高得负担不起的，令人望而却步的

project [ˈprɔdʒekt] n.1. 计划，规划 2. 工程，方案 3. 科研项目；(学校的)课题 — [prəˈdʒekt] vt.1. 设计；规划 2. 投掷；发射；喷射 3. 投射(光线、阴影等) 4. 映现；突出 5. 使…凸出 5. 描画…的特点，使…的特点呈现 6. 生动地表演 7.【心】投射；使(思想、感情

等)形象化;使(观念等)具体化;设想
一 vi. 突出;伸出

projectile [prə'dʒektail] *n*.1. 抛射体 2. 射
弹(如子弹、炮弹等) 3. 自动推进武器
(如火箭) 一 *adj*.1. 抛射的;射弹的 2.
供抛掷用的 3.【动】(触角等)能伸出的

projection [prə'dʒekʃən] *n*.1. 设计;规划
2. 投掷;发射;喷射 3. 凸出;凸出物 4.
投射;投影;投影图;投影法 5. 放映 6.
【心】投射;(观念等)具体化 7.(根据
趋势所作的)预测,推测,估计

projector [prə'dʒektə] *n*.1. 计划人;规划
人;设计人 2. 公司等的)发起人 2.(电
影)放映机;幻灯机;投影仪 3. 探照灯
4. 发射装置;发射器

proletarian [,prəuli'tɛəriən] *n*. 无产者;产
业工人;劳工 一 *adj*. 无产阶级的;(大
工业的)工人阶级的

proletariat [,prəuli'tɛəriət] *n*.1. 无产阶
级;(大工业的)工人阶级 2.【史】(古罗
马社会中的)最下层阶级

proliferate [prəu'lifəreit] *vi*.【生】增殖,
增生;多育 2. 激增;扩散 一 *vt*. 使激
增;使扩散 || **prolife'ration** *n*.

prolific [prə'lifik] *adj*.1. 多产的,多育
的 2. 丰富的,富饶的;
富于…的(*of, in*)

prolog(ue) [prəulɔg] *n*.1. 序言;序诗;(戏
剧的)开场白,开场诗,引子 2.(喻)(一
系列事件等的)开端,序幕(*to*) 3. 念开
场白的演员 一 *vt*. 为…作序;为…念开
场白

prolong [prə'lɔŋ] *vt*.1. 延长;拉长;拖延
2. 拖长(音节等)的发音

prolongation [,prəulɔŋ'geiʃən] *n*.1. 延长;
拉长;拖延 2. 延长部分;拖长的部分

promenade [,prɔmə'nɑːd, ,prɔmə'neid]
n.1.(为散心或炫耀等所作的)散步;
骑马;开车兜风 2. 散步场所(如大街、

海滨大道、剧场走廊等) 3.(正式)舞
会;(正式舞会开始时全体参加者的)
列队行进 一 *vi*.1. 散步;兜风 2.(舞会
中)列队行进 一 *vt*. 在…散步(或兜
风);(炫耀地)带着(某人)散步(或兜
风)

promethium [prə'miːθiəm] *n*.【化】钷

prominence ['prɔminəns], **prominency**
['prɔminənsi] *n*.1. 突起,凸出;凸出物
2. 显著;显著;杰出,卓越;声望 3.【天】
日珥

prominent ['prɔminənt] *adj*.1. 突起的;凸
出的 2. 突出的;显著的;显眼的;杰出
的,卓越的;重要的;著名的 || ~**ly**
adv.

promiscuity [,prɔmis'kjuːiti] *n*.1. 混杂;杂
乱 2. 简短的社交活动 3.(男女之间的)
乱交

promiscuous [prə'miskjuəs] *adj*.1. 混杂
的;杂乱的,乱七八糟的 2. 不加区别
的;不分男女的;男女乱交的 3.(口)偶
然的;随意的 || ~**ly** *adv*.

promise ['prɔmis] *n*.1. 允诺,诺言;字据
2. 允诺的东西;约定的事项 3.(有)希
望;(有)指望;(有)前途 一 *vt*.1. 允诺,
答应;给人以…的指望;有…的可能
3.(口)保证;向…断言 4.把(某
人)许配(给)(*to*) 一 *vi*.1. 允诺;作出
保证 2. 有指望,有前途

promising ['prɔmisiŋ] *adj*. 有指望的,有
希望的;有出息的;有前途的 || ~**ly**
adv.

promissory ['prɔmisəri] *adj*.1. 应允的,
承诺的;约定的 2.【商】约定支付的

promontory ['prɔməntəri] *n*.1.【地】岬
(角);海角;(伸入海中的)悬崖 2.【解】
岬

promote [prə'məut] *vt*.1. 促进;发扬;增
进;提倡 2. 提升;使(学生)升级 3. 发

起;创办(企业等) 4. 宣传;推销(商品等) 5. 促使(法律、议案等)通过 6.〈美俚〉用不正当的手段获得 7.(国际象棋赛中)使(卒)升格(为王后等) ‖ ～r *n*. 1. 促进者;助长者;提倡者 2.(企业等的)发起人,创办人;推销商 3.〈美〉(营业性体育比赛的)承办人,出资人,赞助人 4.【化】促进剂,助催化剂

promotion [prəˈməuʃən] *n*.1. 促进,增进;发扬;助长 2. 提升 3.(企业等的)发起,创立 4.〈美〉(商品等的)宣传,推销,推销运动

prompt [prɔmpt] *adj*.1. 敏捷的,迅速的;及时的 2.【商】当场交付的 3.(演剧中的)提白员的,提词员的 —*adv*. 准时地;正(指时间) —*vt*.1. 敦促;促使;激励,鼓舞;怂恿 2. 引起,激起 3. 提示;为(演员)提白,给…提词 —*n*.1. 催促;提醒;付款通知单 2. 付款期限;付款期限协定 3. 提示;(对演员的)提白,提词 ‖ ～er *n*.1. 敦促者;激励者,鼓舞者 2. 提白员,提词员;提词机 / ～ly *adv*. / ～ness, **promptitude** [ˈprɔmptitjuːd] *n*.

promulgate [ˈprɔməlgeit] *vt*.1. 颁布,公布 2. 散播,传播(信仰、知识等) ‖ ˌpromulˈgation *n*. / promulgator *n*.

pron. *abbr*. pronoun

prone [prəun] *adj*.1. 俯伏的,面向下的 2. 有…倾向的;易于…的(*to*) 3. 倾斜的;陡的 4. 卑躬屈节的 ‖ ～ly *adv*. / ～ness *n*.

prong [prɔŋ] *n*.1. 叉子;干草耙 2. 尖头;(叉、耙的)尖齿;鹿角尖 —*vt*.(用叉等)刺,戳;耙开(泥土等) ‖ ～ed *adj*. 有叉的;有叉尖(或尖齿)的

pronghorn [ˈprɔŋhɔːn]([复] pronghorn(s)) *n*.【动】叉角羚(产于墨西哥及北美)

pronoun [ˈprəunaun] *n*.【语】代(名)词 ‖ **pronominal** [prəuˈnɔminəl] *adj*. 代词(性)的 *n*. 代词

pronounce [prəˈnauns] *vt*.1. 宣布;宣判 2. 宣称;宣告;断言;表示 3. 发…的音;注…的音 —*vi*.1. 发表意见;作出判断;表态 2. 发音

pronounced [prəˈnaunst] *adj*.1. 发出音的;读(或讲)出来的 2. 显著的;明显的;明确的;断然的

pronouncement [prəˈnaunsmənt] *n*.1. 声明;公告 2. 见解,看法;决定

pronunciation [prəˌnʌnsiˈeiʃən] *n*. 发音;发音法;读法

proof [pruːf] *n*.1. 证据;证物;证言 2. 证明;论证 3. 检验;考验 4.(火器或爆炸物的)试验(或试验场所) 5. 试管 6.【印】校样;样张 7.(酒类的)标准酒精度 8.【数】证,证明;验算 9.〈古〉(盔甲等的)不穿透性,坚固性 —*adj*.1. 不能穿透的;能防...的(*against*) 2. 验证用的;检验用的 3. 规定的;(酒等)标准度数的 —*vt*.1. 检验;试验;试印;把…印成校样 2. 校对 3. 使(某物)不被穿透;使有耐力;使(布等)不透水,使防水 4. 发(面) ‖ ˈ～read *vt*. & *vi*. 校对 / ˈ～ˌreader *n*. 校对员

prop[1] [prɔp] *n*.1. 支柱;撑材;支持物 2.(机关、企业等的)支持者,拥护者;后盾;靠山 —(propped; propping) *vt*. 支撑;支持;维持 —*vi*.1. 架,搁 2.〈澳〉(马等)前腿挺直着骤停

prop[2] [prɔp] *n*.【戏】道具;道具管理员

prop[3] [prɔp] *n*.〈口〉【空】螺旋桨;推进器

propaganda [ˌprɔpəˈgændə] *n*.1. 宣传的思想(或主张等);传播的消息(或谣言等) 2. 宣传;宣传运动

propagandist [ˌprɔpəˈgændist] *n*. 宣传者;传播者 —*adj*. 宣传(者)的

propagandize [ˌprɔpə'gændaiz] *vt.* **1.** 宣传;传播 **2.** 对…进行宣传 — *vi.* 进行宣传(或传播)

propagate ['prɔpəgeit] *vt.* **1.** 繁殖,增殖 **2.** 使遗殖 **3.** 传播;宣传;普及 **4.** 使(疾病等)蔓延 **5.** 【物】传播 — *vi.* **1.** (动物、植物)繁殖,增殖 **2.** 蔓延 ‖ ,propa'gation *n.*

propel [prə'pel] (propelled; propelling) *vt.* 推进,推动

propellant, propellent [prə'pelənt] *adj.* 推进的;有推动力的 — *n.* 推进者;推动者;推进剂;发射火药

propeller, propellor [prə'pelə] *n.* **1.** (轮船、飞机等上的)螺旋桨;推进器 **2.** 推进者

propensity [prə'pensiti] *n.* **1.** (性格)倾向;习性 **2.** 癖好,偏爱

proper ['prɔpə] *adj.* **1.** 适合的,适当的,恰当的 **2.** 合乎体统的,正当的;规矩的,正经的;高尚的 **3.** 特有的;专门的 (to) **4.** 固有的,本来的;正确的 **5.** 自己的 **6.** [用在名词后]严格意义上的,本身的 **7.** (纹章)本色的 **8.** 〈主英口〉完完全全的,彻底的 **9.** 出色的,极好的;〈主方〉漂亮的,好看的 — *adv.* 〈主方〉完完全全地,好好地 **10.** 〈宗〉特定节日的礼仪(或祈祷等) ‖ ~ **fraction** 【数】真分数

properly ['prɔpəli] *adv.* 适当地;合适地 **2.** 严格地讲;正确地 **3.** 〈主英口〉完全地,彻底地;非常

property ['prɔpəti] *n.* **1.** 财产;资产;(房)地产 **2.** 财产权;所有权 **3.** 性质;性能;特性;属性 **4.** 【哲】非本质属性;固有属性 **5.** (戏剧、电影等中用的)道具

prophecy ['prɔfisi] *n.* 预言;预言能力;预示;先兆;〈宗〉预言书

prophesy ['prɔfisai] *vt. & vi.* 预言;预示

prophet ['prɔfit] *n.* **1.** 预言者,预言家;〈宗〉先知 **2.** (主义等的)宣扬者;提倡者 **3.** 〈俚〉(赛马输赢等的)预测者 ‖ ~**ess** *n.* 女预言家

prophetic(al) [prə'fetik(əl)] *adj.* 预言的;预示的(of);预言家的 ‖ **prophetically** *adv.*

prophylaxis [ˌprɔfi'læksis] ([复] prophylaxes [ˌprɔfi'læksi:z]) *n.* 【医】预防;预防法

propinquity [prə'piŋkwati] *n.* (时间等方面的)接近;(地点方面的)邻近;(血统上的)近亲关系;(性质、观念等方面的)类似,近似

propitiate [prə'piʃieit] *vt.* **1.** 劝解;抚慰;使息怒 **2.** 讨好…的好感

propitious [prə'piʃəs] *adj.* **1.** (神等)慈悲的 **2.** 吉祥的,吉利的 **3.** 顺利的;有利的;合适的(for, to)

proponent [prə'pəunənt] *n.* **1.** 建议者,提议者 **2.** 支持者;辩护者 **3.** 【律】提出认证遗嘱者;(法律文书的)提出者

proportion [prə'pɔ:ʃən] *n.* **1.** 比,比例 **2.** 相称;均衡;调和 **3.** 部分;份儿 **4.** [~s] 面积;容积;体积;大小;程度;范围 — *vt.* 使成比例;使相称;使均衡

proportional [prə'pɔ:ʃənl] *adj.* **1.** 比例的;成比例的 **2.** 相称的;均衡的 — *n.* 【数】比例项 ‖ ~**ly** *adv.*

proportionate [prə'pɔ:ʃənit] *adj.* **1.** 成比例的;相称的 **2.** 均衡的 — *vt.* [prə'pɔ:ʃəneit] 使成比例;使相称;使均衡 ‖ ~**ly** *adv.*

proposal [prə'pəuzl] *n.* **1.** (建议等的)提出;提议,建议;计划;提案 **2.** 求婚

propose [prə'pəuz] *vt.* **1.** 提议,建议;提出 **2.** 提(名);推荐 **3.** 打算;计划 **4.** 求(婚) — *vi.* **1.** 作出计划;提出建议 **2.** 求婚(to)

proposition [ˌprɔpə'ziʃən] *n.*1. 提议，建议；计划 2. 陈述；主张 3.【逻】【数】命题；【语】(讨论)题；主题；主题句 4.〔口〕事业；企业 5.〔口〕事情；目的；问题；家伙 6. 下流的建议，猥亵的要求 — *vt.*〔口〕向…提出要求(尤指猥亵下流的要求)

propound [prə'paund] *vt.*1. 提出(问题、计划等)供考虑(或讨论) 2.【英律】提出(遗嘱等)请求验证

proprietary [prə'praiətəri] *adj.*1. 所有人的，业主的 2. 拥有财产的 3. 专卖的；专利的；专用的 —*n.*1.[指个人或总称]所有人，业主 2. 所有(权)；财产 3. 专卖药品

proprietor [prə'praiətə] *n.* 所有人，业主

proprietress [prə'praiətris] *n.* 女所有人，女业主

propriety [prə'praiəti] *n.*1. 适当，妥当；正当；得体，合宜 2. 礼貌 3.[proprieties]礼仪，礼节

propulsion [prə'pʌlʃən] *n.*(被)推进；推进力

propulsive [prə'pʌlsiv] *adj.* 推进的；有推进力的

prorate [prəu'reit, 'prəureit] *vt. & vi.*(主美)按比例分配(或摊派) ‖ **proratable** *adj.* / **pro'ration** *n.*

prosage ['prəusidʒ] *n.*(以植物蛋白为原料的)素香肠

prosaic [prəu'zeiik] *adj.*1. 散文的；散文体的 2. 无诗意的；平凡的；乏味的 3. 如实的 ‖ ~ally *adv.*

proscribe [prəus'kraib] *vt.*1.(古罗马)公布(死囚)的姓名 2. 剥夺…的公权，使失去法律保护 3. 把…充军，放逐 4. 排斥；禁止

proscription [prəus'kripʃən] *n.*1. 剥夺公权；放逐 2. 排斥；禁止

prose [prəuz] *n.*1. 散文；散文体 2. 平凡；单调；无聊 3. 平凡的话；无趣的议论 — *vi.*1. 写散文 2. 平铺直叙地写；乏味地讲(*about*) — *vt.* 把(诗等)改写成散文 — *adj.*1. 散文的；用散文写的 2. 平凡的；乏味的；无趣味的

prosecute ['prɔsikju:t] *vt.*1. 彻底进行；执行 2. 从事；经营 3. 对…提起公诉；告发；起诉；依法进行 — *vi.*1. 起诉；告发 2. 作检察官

prosecution [ˌprɔsi'kju:ʃən] *n.*1. 彻底进行；执行 2. 从事；经营 3. 起诉，告发；检举；[总称](提出刑事诉讼的)原告及其律师；代表原告的律师 5. 检察当局

prosecutor ['prɔsikju:tə] *n.*1. 检察官，公诉人 2. 原告，起诉人 3.(商业等的)从事者

proselyte ['prɔsilait] *n.* 改变信仰(或意见)者 — *vt. & vi.*(使)改变信仰(或意见等)；劝诱，搜罗(运动员等) ‖ **proselytize** ['prɔsilitaiz] *vt. & vi.* 使改变信仰(或意见等)

prospect ['prɔspekt] *n.*1. 展望；视野；景色；景象 2. 指望；预期；期望中的事物 3.[常~s]前前景；前程，前途 4. 可能成为主顾(或委托者)的人；有希望的候选人 5.(有希望开采的)矿藏，矿床；(待检验的)矿石样品；(从样品中得知的)含矿率 —[præs'pekt] *vt.* 勘探(矿藏)；勘察(地区)(*for*) 2.(矿)有达到(规定产量)的可能 ‖ ~or [præs'pektə] *n.* 勘探者；探矿者

prospective [prəs'pektiv] *adj.* 预期的；盼望中的；未来的；即将发生的 ‖ ~ly *adv.*

prospectus [prəs'pektəs] *n.*1.(创办企业等的)计划书，发起书，说明书 2.(即将

出版的书等的)内容简介

prosper ['prɔspə] *vi.* 繁荣,昌盛;成功 — *vt.* 使繁荣,使昌盛;使成功

prosperity [prɔs'periti] *n.* 繁荣,昌盛;成功;富足;茂盛

prosperous ['prɔspərəs] *adj.* 1. 繁荣的,昌盛的;成功的;富裕的 2. 有利的,顺利的;幸运的 ‖ ~ly *adv.*

prostate ['prɔsteit] *n. & adj.* 【解】前列腺(的)

prosthesis ['prɔsθisis] ([复] prostheses ['prɔsθisiz]) *n.* 1. 【语】词首添音(或音节等) 2. 【医】修补术,假体

prostitute ['prɔstitjut] *n.* 1. 妓女,娼妓 2. 出卖节操者(如金钱而粗制滥造的文人等) — *vt.* 1. 使沦为娼妓 2.(喻)出卖(名誉等);滥用(才能等) — *adj.* 1. 卖淫的 2. 堕落的 ‖ prosti'tution *n.* 卖淫;滥用;糟蹋

prostrate ['prɔstreit] *adj.* 1. 俯卧的;平卧的,倒在地上的 2.(表示尊敬或顺从等)俯伏的,拜倒的 3. 被征服的;降伏的;屈服的 4. 衰竭的,疲惫的;沮丧的 — ['prɔstreit] *vt.* 1. 使俯卧;弄倒 2. [~ oneself] 使(自己)俯伏,使(自己)拜倒 3. 使屈从 ‖ pros'tration *n.* 1. 俯伏;平卧 2. 拜倒,屈服 3. 衰竭,疲惫;【医】虚脱

prosy ['prəuzi] *adj.* 1. 散文(体)的 2. 沉闷的;冗长乏味的;罗唆的

protagonist [prəu'æɡənist] *n.* 1.(故事、小说等中的)主人公 2.(戏剧等中的)主角;主角演员,主演演员 3. 领导者;重要人物

protect [prə'tekt] *vt.* 1. 保护;警戒 2.【经】(对进口物资征收保护性关税等)保护(国内工业) 3. 备款以支付(期票等) 4. 在…上装防护(或保险)装置以避免伤人

protection [prə'tekʃən] *n.* 1. 保护;警戒 2. 保护物;防护物 3. 护照;通行证 4. 保护贸易制度 5.(罪犯等通过贿赂而取得的)免予起诉;(歹徒所勒索的)"保护费"

protectionism [prə'tekʃənizəm] *n.* 保护(贸易)主义;保护(贸易)制 ‖ protectionist *n.* 1. 保护(贸易)主义者 2. 野生动、植物保护主义者

protective [prə'tektiv] *adj.* 1. 保护的;防护的 2. 保护贸易的 ‖ ~ly *adv.* / ~ness *n.*

protector [prə'tektə] *n.* 1. 保护者;防御者 2. 保护装置,保护器 3. 摄政者;[P-]【英史】护国公(= Lord Protector, 指 17 世纪英国共和国时代的摄政者克伦威尔)

protectorate [prə'tektərit] *n.* 1.(尤指 1653-1659 英国克伦威尔父子摄政时期的)护国公政体;摄政政体;摄政职位(或时期) 2.(较强国对较弱国的)保护关系;受保护国;受保护领地 3. 保护国行使的权力

protégé ['prəutəʒei, 'prɔtəʒei] *n.* 被保护人;门徒

protégée ['prəutəʒei, 'prɔtəʒei] *n.* 女被保护人;女门徒

protein ['prəutiːn] *n.* 蛋白质 — *adj.*(含)蛋白质的

protest [prə'test] *vt.* 1. 明言;断言;主张;(坚决)表示 2. 抗议;反对 3.【商】拒付(票据等) — *vi.* 1. 明言;断言;主张 2. 抗议;反对(*against*) — ['prəutest] *n.* 1. 明言;主张 2. 抗议;反对 3.【律】(对票据等的)拒付证书;(证明船的损坏系由灾难造成的)船长海事报告书;(纳税人对苛捐等的)抗议书

Protestant ['prɔtistənt] *n.* 1. 新教徒 2. 抗

议者(指 1529 年德国国会中对恢复天主教特权之决议案提出抗议的新教诸侯) 3. [p-]抗议者；持异议者 一 *adj.* 1. 新教(教徒)的 2. [p-]抗议的；持异议的 ‖ ～ism *n.* 新教；新教教义

protestation [ˌprəutes'teiʃən] *n.* 1. 明言；断言；主张 2. 抗议；异议；反对

protium ['prəutiəm] *n.* 【化】氕(氢的同位素)

protocol ['prəutəkəl] *n.* 1. (条约等的)草案，草约；(外交)议定书；会谈记录(或备忘录) 2. 礼仪；外交礼节一(protocol(l)ed; protocol(l)ing)*vt.* 把…写入议定书 一 *vt.* 把…写入议定书

proton ['prəutɔn] *n.* 【物】质子

protoplasm ['prəutəplæzəm] *n.* 【生】 1. 原生质 2. 细胞质

prototype ['prəutətaip] *n.* 1. 原型；样品；样本 2. 典型；模范 ‖ **prototypical** [ˌprəutə'tipikəl] *adj.*

protozoan [ˌprəutə'zəuən] *n. & adj.* 【动】原生动物(的)

protozoon [ˌprəutə'zəuən] ([复] protozoa [ˌprəutə'zəuə]) *n.* 【动】原生动物

protract [prə'trækt] *vt.* 1. 延长；拖延 2. (用量角尺)绘制 3. 【动物器官】伸展；突出 ‖ ～ion [prə'trækʃən] *n.*

protractor [prə'træktə] *n.* 1. 延长者；拖延者 2. 量角器，分度规 3. 【解】牵引肌 4.【医】钳取器

protrude [prə'truːd] *vt.* 使伸出；使突出 — *vi.* 伸出；突出

protrusion [prə'truːʒən] *n.* 1. 延长；突出 2. 突起部，隆起物

protrusive [prə'truːsiv] *adj.* 伸出的；突出的

protuberant [prə'tjuːbærənt] *adj.* 1. (常指呈圆形)隆起的，凸出的 2. 招人注意

的 ‖ **protuberance** *n.* / ～ly *adv.*

proud [praud] *adj.* 1. 骄傲的，妄自尊大的，自高自大的 2. 自尊的，有自尊心的 3. 自豪的；得意的；高兴的 4. 辉煌的，壮丽的；值得夸耀的 5. (马等)精力充沛的 6. (河流等)涨了水的，泛滥的 ‖ ～ly *adv.*

prove [pruːv] (过去式 proved, 过去分词 proved 或 proven['pruːvən]) *vt.* 1. 证明，证实 2. 检验；试验；考验 3. 勘探；钻探；探明(*up*) 4.【数】证，证明；验算 5. 认证(遗嘱等) 6. 发(面团) 7. 试印；把…印成校样(或试印张) — *vi.* 证明为；表明是；结果是

provender ['prɔvində] *n.* 1. (家畜的)粗饲料；草料 2. (口)(人的)食物

proverb ['prɔvəb] *n.* 1. 谚语，俗语，常言；箴言 2. 尽人皆知的人(或事) 3. [～s] (猜)谚语游戏

proverbial [prə'vəːbiəl] *adj.* 1. 谚语的；谚语式的 2. 众所周知的，出名的 ‖ ～ly *adv.*

provide [prə'vaid] *vt.* 1. 提供；供应，供给(*with*) 2. (法律、协议等)规定，订定(*that*) — *vi.* 1. 作准备(*for*)；预防(*against*) 2. 赡养，提供生计(*for*) 3. 规定，订定(*for, against*)

provided [prə'vaidid] *conj.* 以…为条件；除非；假如

providence ['prɔvidəns] *n.* 1. 远见；远虑 2.〈古〉节俭 3. 天意，天道，天命；天佑 4. [P-]上帝

provident ['prɔvidənt] *adj.* 1. 有远见的；有远虑的 2. 节俭的

providential [ˌprɔvi'denʃəl] *adj.* 上帝的；天意的；天佑的，神助(似)的；幸运的；凑巧的 ‖ ～ly *adv.*

provider [prə'vaidə] *n.* 供应者；提供者；养家活口的人

providing [prə'vaidiŋ] *conj.* = provided

province ['prɔvins] *n.*1. 省；行政区 2. [~s]京都大邑以外的省区，外地 3. 本分；职权；(学术)领域；部门；(活动)范围 4.〔史〕(古罗马在意大利以外的)行省 5.(旧时英国在北美的)殖民地 6.〔宗〕大主教辖区，教省

provincial [prə'vinʃəl] *adj.*1. 省的 2. 外省的，外地的 3. 乡气的，乡下派头的 4.(家具等的装饰风格)朴素的，平常的 — *n.*1. 外省人，外地人，地方居民 2. 兴趣(或眼界)狭窄的人；粗野的人 3.〔宗〕(管辖教省的)大主教 4.[~s]地方部队

provision [prə'viʒən] *n.*1. 供应；(一批)供应品 2. 预备；防备；措施 3. [~s]存粮；粮食，食物；口粮；给养 4. 规定；条款 — *vt.* 向…供应食物(或必需品等)

provisional [prə'viʒənl] *adj.* 临时的，暂时的，暂定的 — *n.*(正式邮票发行前的)临时邮票

proviso [prə'vaizəu] ([复] proviso(e)s) *n.* 附文，但书，(附带)条件，限制性条款

provocation [ˌprɔvə'keiʃən] *n.*1. 挑衅；挑拨；惹起；激怒；刺激 2. 挑衅性的事；激怒的原因；惹人恼火的事

provocative [prə'vɔkətiv] *adj.*1. 挑衅的；挑拨的；激起…的(*of*)；激怒的；刺激的 2. 引起争论(或议论、兴趣等)的 — *n.* 刺激物，吊胃口的东西 || ~ly *adv.*

provoke [prə'vəuk] *vt.*1. 对…挑衅；挑拨；煽动；激怒；刺激；挑逗；激起；引起

provoking [prə'vəukiŋ] *adj.* 惹人恼火的，使人烦恼的；挑动的 || ~ly *adv.*

provost ['prɔvəst, 'prəuvəst] *n.* = ~ marshal || ~ marshal 宪兵司令

prow[1] [prau] *n.*1. 船头，(飞机等)机首；突

出的前端 2.〈诗〉船

prow[2] [prau] *adj.*〈古〉英勇的，勇猛的

prowess ['prauis] *n.*1. 英勇，勇猛；无畏 2. 杰出的才能(或技巧等)；高超的本领

prowl [praul] *vi.*1.(野兽等)四处觅食；(偷)暗中来回寻食 2. 徘徊；潜行(想偷窃等) — *vt.* 徘徊于；潜行于 — *n.*1. 四处觅食；暗中来回寻食 2. 徘徊；潜行 || ~ er *n.*

proximity [prɔk'simiti] *n.* 临近；接近，邻近；亲近

proxy ['prɔksi] *n.*1. 代理权；代表权 2. 代理人；代表人 3.(给代理人等的)委托书

prude [pruːd] *n.* 过分拘谨的人；装作正经的人(尤指女人)

prudence ['pruːdəns] *n.*1. 谨慎；慎重；深谋远虑 2. 精明 3. 节俭

prudent ['pruːdənt] *adj.*1. 谨慎的；慎重的；深谋远虑的 2. 精明的 3. 节俭的 || ~ly *adv.*

prudential [pruː'denʃəl] *adj.*1. 谨慎的，慎重的；深谋远虑的 2. 备咨询的 — *n.* [~s]需慎重考虑的事项；慎重的考虑

prudery ['pruːdəri] *n.* 过分拘谨；装作正经

prudish ['pruːdiʃ] *adj.* 过分拘谨的；装作正经的

prune[1] [pruːn] *n.*1. 洋李干；李子干 2. 深紫红色 3.〔俚〕乏味的人；讨厌的人；傻瓜

prune[2] [pruːn] *vt.*1. 修剪(树枝等) 2. 删除；删节；削减(预算等) — *vi.* 整枝；删除；删节；减少

prurient ['pruəriənt] *adj.* 好色的，淫秽的；引起淫欲的；(病态地)渴望的 || prurience, pruriency *n.*

Prussia [ˈprʌʃə] *n.*【史】普鲁士

Prussian [ˈprʌʃən] *adj.* **1.** 普鲁士的；普鲁士人的 **2.** 普鲁士式的（指训练严酷、崇尚军国主义或妄自尊大的）—*n.* 普鲁士人；普鲁士语；古普鲁士语

pry¹ [prai] *vi.* 窥探；盯看看（*into*, *about*）；打听，探问（*into*）—*n.* **1.** 窥探；打听 **2.** 过于好奇（或受打听）的人

pry² [prai] *vt.* **1.**（用杠杆等）撬开，撬起，撬动 **2.** 费力地得到；使劲分开—*n.* **1.** 杠杆；撬杠 **2.** 杠杆作用

prying [ˈpraiiŋ] *adj.* 窥探的；盯看看的；爱打听的

PS *abbr.* **1.** postscript **2.** public school

psalm [sɑːm]【宗】*n.* 赞美诗，圣诗，圣歌—*vt.* 唱赞美诗祝祷

pseudo [ˈpsjuːdəu] *adj.* 伪的，假的；冒充的—*n.*〈口〉说谎者；不真诚的人，伪君子

pseud(o)- *comb. form*〈希〉表示"伪"，"拟"，"假"：*pseudonym*

pseudonym [ˈpsjuːdənim] *n.* 假名，笔名

psychedelic [ˌpsaiki'delik] *adj.* **1.** 迷幻药的，幻觉剂的 **2.** 引起幻觉的

psychiatry [saiˈkaiətri] *n.* 精神病治疗；精神病学 ‖ **psychiatric(al)** [ˌsaikiˈætrik(əl)] *adj.* 治疗精神病的 / **psychiatrist** *n.* 精神病学家，精神科医生

psychic [ˈsaikik] *adj.* **1.** 精神的；心灵的；（桥牌中叫牌）心理的；超自然的 **2.** 对超自然力量敏感的；通灵的—*n.* **1.** 对超自然力量敏感的人；通灵的人；巫师 **2.** 灵物 **3.** 心灵现象 **4.**（桥牌中的）心理叫牌

psychical [ˈsaikikəl] *adj.* = psychic

psycho- *comb. form* 表示"精神"、"灵

魂"，"心理"：*psychology, psychoanalysis*

psychoanalysis [ˌsaikəuəˈnæləsis] *n.* 精神分析（学）‖ **psychoanalyst** [ˌsaikəuˈænəlist] *n.* 精神分析学家 / **psychoanalytic(al)** [ˌsaikəuˌænəˈlitik(əl)] *adj.* 精神分析（原理）的 / **psychoanalyze** [ˌsaikəuˈænəlaiz] *vt.* 给…作精神分析；用精神分析法治疗

psychological [ˌsaikəˈlɔdʒikəl] *adj.* 心理（上）的；心理学（家）的 ‖ ~ **ly** *adv.* 心理上；从心理（学）角度

psychologist [saiˈkɔlədʒist] *n.* 心理学家

psychology [saiˈkɔlədʒi] *n.* **1.** 心理学 **2.**（人与动物的）行为科学 **3.** 心理 **4.** 心理学著作（或学派、体系）

psychoneurosis [ˌsaikəunjuəˈrəusis] *n.*（［复］psychoneuroses [ˌsaikəunjuəˈrəusiz]）【医】精神神经病 ‖ **psychoneurotic** [ˌsaikəunjuəˈrɔtik] *adj.* 精神神经病的 —*n.* 精神神经病患者

psychopath [ˈsaikəupæθ] *n.* 精神变态者，精神病患者；变态人格者

psychopathic [ˌsaikəuˈpæθik] *adj.* 精神变态（者）的；变态人格（者）的 —*n.* = psychopath

psychopathy [saiˈkɔpəθi] *n.* 精神变态；变态人格，病态人格

psychosis [saiˈkəusis] *n.*（［复］psychoses [saiˈkəusiːz]）*n.* **1.** 精神病；精神失常 **2.** 精神极度紧张 ‖ **psychotic** [saiˈkɔtik] *adj.* 精神病的 —*n.* 精神病患者

psychosomatic [ˌsaikəusəˈmætik] *adj.*【医】身心的，心身的

psychotherapy [ˌsaikəuˈθerəpi] *n.*【医】心理疗法，精神疗法 ‖ **psychotherapist** *n.*

psychotoxic [ˌsaikəuˈtɔksik] *adj.*（药等）对心理（或个性）有害的；能引起精神病的

Pt【化】元素铂（platinum）的符号

pt. *abbr.* **1.** pint(s) **2.** point **3.** port

ptarmigan ['tɑːmigən]([复] ptarmigan(s)) *n.* [鸟]雷鸟

pterodactyl [ˌterə'dæktil] *n.* 翼手龙(已绝迹的古代动物)

PTO, p.t.o. *abbr.* please turn over 请看背面,请看下页

ptomaine ['təumein] *n.* [化]尸碱,尸毒,肉毒胺

Pu [化]元素钚(plutonium)的符号

pub [pʌb] *n.*〈口〉1.〈主英〉酒店 2.〈澳〉旅馆,客栈

puberty ['pjuːbəti] *n.* 发身;青春期

pubic ['pjuːbik] *adj.*〈近〉阴部的;(近)耻骨的;~ hair 阴毛

pubis ['pjuːbis]([复] pubes [pjuːbiːz]) *n.* [解]耻骨

public ['pʌblik] *adj.* **1.** 公(有)的;公众的 **2.** 政府的,国家的;公家的;公立的 **3.** 公众事务的;社会的;为公的 **4.** 公用的;公共的 **5.** 公开的;当众的 知名的;突出的 **7.**〈牢〉国际的;全人类的 **8.**〈英〉大学的;为大学的 **9.** 可感知的;物质性的 —*n.* **1.**[the ~]用作单或复)公众,民众;众人 **2.**〈口〉酒店(=public house)|| **~ly** *adv.* **1.** 当众,公开地;公然地 **2.** 由公众;由政府(出资或经营等)|| **~ house** **1.**〈美〉旅馆,客栈 **2.**〈主英〉酒店 **opinion** 舆论,民意 /~ **prosecutor** 检察官,公诉人 /~ **relations** 公关,公共关系;公关活动;公关事业 /~ **school 1.**〈英国的〉公学 **2.**〈美国的〉公立学校 / '~-'spirited *adj.* 热心公益的,有公益精神的

publication [ˌpʌbli'keiʃən] *n.* **1.** 发表;公布 **2.** 出版;发行 **3.** 出版物

publicity [pʌb'lisiti] *n.* **1.** 公开场合 **2.** 公众的注意;名声 **3.** 宣传;宣扬;(向报

界等散发的)宣传品;广告

publicize ['pʌblisaiz] *vt.* 引起公众对...的注意;(尤指用广告等)宣传

publish ['pʌbliʃ] *vt.* **1.** 公布,发布 **2.** 发表;刊登 **3.** 出版;发行 **4.** 出版...的著作 **5.** 公开;散布 —*vi.* **1.** 出版;发行 **2.**(作者)发表著作 ||~ **vt.** **1.** 出版商;出版者;发行者 **3.**〈英〉报社业主,报刊发行人 **4.** 发表者;公布者 ||~-**ing house** 出版社

puck¹ [pʌk] *n.* **1.** [P-](莎士比亚戏剧等中的)顽皮的小妖精 **2.** 顽童

puck² [pʌk] *n.*(冰球运动中用的)冰球

pucker ['pʌkə] *vt.* 使成褶;使起皱;使缩拢 —*vi.* 折成褶;起皱;缩拢 —*n.* 皱纹;皱褶

pudding ['pudiŋ] *n.* **1.** 布丁(西餐中的一种糊状甜食);布丁状物; **2.** 血香肠,黑香肠 **3.**[英]船首碰垫 **4.**(俚)(赃给看屋狗吃的)毒饵

puddle ['pʌdl] *n.* **1.** 水坑;泥潭;洼 **2.** 胶土(由黏土和沙)炒捣制成;混合成 —*vt.* **1.** 把(湿黏土和沙)捣制成胶土;搅浑;用胶土填塞 **2.**[冶]搅炼 **3.**[农]粘闭,粘制 —*vi.* 搅泥浆;在污水中涉溅(或打滚)about

pudgy ['pʌdʒi] *adj.* 矮胖的;短而粗的;丰满的 || **pudginess** *n.*

pueblo [pu'ebləu, 'pwebləu]([复] pueblos) *n.* **1.**(美国西南部或墨西哥等地的)印第安人村落 **2.**[P-]普韦布洛人(印第安人村落的居民) **3.**(拉丁美洲的)镇;村 **4.**(西班牙语的)镇

puerile ['pjuərail] *adj.* 幼稚的,孩子气的;不成熟的;傻的 || **puerility** [pjuə'riliti] *n.*

Puerto Rican ['pwəːtəu 'riːkən] **1.** 波多黎各的;波多黎各人的 **2.** 波多黎各人

Puerto Rico ['pwætuː 'riːkəu] 波多黎各(岛)[拉丁美洲] (在大安的列斯群岛东端)

puff [pʌf] *n.*1. (一)喷；(一)吹；一阵，一股(气味、烟雾等)；噗的一声 2. 隆起的小块、小肿胀 3. 蓬松的(的)团；衣服的蓬松部分；蓬松的发卷 4. 粉扑 5. (奶油)松饼，泡夫 6. 被子；鸭绒被 7. 吹捧性的短文(或书评、广告等) —*vi.*1. 一阵阵地吹(或喷)；一口一口地抽烟(或喷烟)；喷着烟(或蒸汽)驶去(*away, out*) 2. 喘气，趾高气扬；盛气凌人 4. 肿胀，肿起(*up*) 5. 膨胀；—*vt.*1. 一阵阵地吹(烟)；喷(烟等) 3. 使气急 4. 喘着气说；使充气；使膨胀(*out*) 6. 使劲做(自大，使显耀)(*up*) 7. 吹捧(书等)；为(商品)作广告 8. 使成蓬松的一团团(或一卷卷)

puffin ['pʌfin] *n.*[动]角嘴海雀

puffy ['pʌfi] *adj.*1. 一阵阵地吹(或喷)的 2. 气喘吁吁的；容易气急的 3. 肿大的；鼓起的；肥胖的 4. 虚荣的，爱炫耀的 5. 蓬松的，松的

pug [pʌg] *n.*1. 哈巴狗(= ~ dog) 2. 狐狸 3. 狮子鼻，(翘起的)扁鼻(= ~ nose) 4. 发髻 5.〈英〉调车机车

pugilism ['pjuːdʒilizəm] *n.* 拳击(术) ‖ **pugilist** *n.* 拳击运动员

pugnacious [pʌg'neiʃəs] *adj.* 好斗的；好战的；爱吵架的 ‖ **~ly** *adv.* / **~ness**, **pugnacity** [pʌg'næsiti] *n.*

puke [pjuːk] 〈口〉*vt.* & *vi.* 呕吐 —*n.* 呕吐，(俚)令人恶心的东西

pulchritude ['pʌlkritjuːd] *n.* 美丽，标致 ‖ **pulchritudinous** *adj.*

Pulitzer ['pulitsə, 'pjuːlitsə] *n.* ‖ ~ Prize (美国)普利策奖(金) (一年一度颁发给文学、戏剧、音乐、新闻等优秀作品的奖金)

pull [pul] *vt.*1. 拉；拖；牵；扯 2. 拔；抽；采；摘 3. 撕开，扯开 4. 搬走 5. 划(桨、船)；(船)被…划动；划运 6. 运用力量而弄伤；拉伤 7. 吸引；招徕；获得 8. (赛马中为防获胜而)控(马)慢跑；(拳击中为防获胜而)控(拳)轻击 9.【印】(旧时在手动印刷机上)打(样)，印(样张等) 10.(棒球、高尔夫球赛中)从右手把(球)向左侧击去；从左手把(球)向右侧击去 11. 放肆地进行；干(勾当)；犯(罪)；犯…的过错 12.〈美俚〉逮捕；(派警察)突然袭击(赌窟等) 13. 号召进行(罢工)—罢工 —*vt.*1. 拉；拖；拔 2. 能被拉(或拖、拔) 3. 拔枪(或刀) 4. 行驶(船)划动，划船 5. 有吸引力；吸引顾客 6. (赛场同情)拉拢(*for*) 7. (赛马中为防获胜而)控马慢跑 8. 大口喝(*at*)；猛抽，深吸(*at*) 9. 费力地前进 —*n.*1. 拉，拖；拔 2. 拉力，牵引力 3. 供拉的东西，拉手，把手 4. 划船 5. 费力的前进；爬高 6. 携带；门路，有利条件 7. 吸引力 8.【印】草样，校样 9.(赛马中为防)控马慢跑(拳击中的)控拳轻击 10. 一口(酒)、(烟)的一抽，一吸 ‖ ~ **date** (盖印在易腐食品包装上的)销售截止日期 / ~**over** *n.* 套头毛衣等无领无扣的套衫 *adj.* 套穿的

pullet ['pulit] *n.*(未满一岁的)小母鸡

pulley ['puli] *n.*【机】滑轮，滑车；滑轮组；皮带轮

Pullman ['pulmən] *n.* 普尔曼式火车卧车(或客车)(= ~ car)

pulmonary ['pʌlmənəri] *adj.*1. 肺的；肺状的；发生在肺部的 2. 有肺的；有肺状器官的 3. 由肺进行的

pulp [pʌlp] *n.*1. 果肉；(植物的)髓；牙髓 2. 浆状物；纸浆 3.(主要)低级黄色书刊 —*vt.*1. 使成浆状；把…制成纸浆

2. 除去(咖啡豆等)的果肉 —vi. 成浆状 ‖ ~wood n. 木浆原料；纸浆材

pulpit ['pulpit] n.1.[宗] 布道坛，讲坛 2. [the ~] 布道；布道职业；[总称]传道士；牧师 3.(钢铁厂等的)高架操纵台

pulpous ['pʌlpəs], **pulpy** ['pʌlpi] adj. 果肉质的；(果肉状的)多汁的；软糊状的

pulsar ['pʌlsɑ:] n.[天] 脉冲星；中子星

pulsate [pʌl'seit, 'pʌlseit] vi.1.(脉等)搏动；(心脏)跳动；有节奏地鼓动 2. 震动；抖动；[物]脉动

pulsation [pʌl'seiʃən] n.1. 跳动；有节奏的鼓动；一次跳动；震动；[物]脉动

pulse[pʌls] n.1. 脉搏；脉；有节奏的跳动(或拍打) 2.[物]脉冲；(光波、声波等的)脉动；(喻)激情 3. 意向，心态；活力 —vi. 搏动；跳动 —vt.1. 使跳动；使产生脉冲 2. 用脉冲输送(血液等)(in, out) 3. 脉动地产生(或调节)

pulse[pʌls] n. 豆类植物；[用作单或复]豆子

pulverize ['pʌlvəraiz] vt.1. 使成粉末；使(液体)成雾状 2. 粉碎；彻底摧毁 —vi. 变成粉末；变成尘埃；被彻底摧毁 ‖ ,pulveri'zation n.

puma ['pju:mə] n.1. 美洲狮 2. 美洲狮毛皮

pumice ['pʌmis] n. 浮石，轻石(常用于去污和磨光)(= ~stone) —vt. 用浮石磨光

pummel ['pʌml] n. &(pummel(l)ed; pummel(l)ing) vt. = pommel

pump[pʌmp] n.1. 泵，抽水(或气)机，唧筒 2. 抽吸；抽送；泵送 —vt.1. 用泵抽吸(或抽送)；用泵从...中抽水(或气等) 2. 用打气筒打(气等)；为...打气 3. 盘问，追问(以追问(或巧妙方式)探

出(秘密等)(out) 4. 灌输；大量提供；注入 5. 使疲惫；使剧烈喘息 6. 使上下摇动(或晃动) —vi.1. 用泵抽(或送)水(或油等)；操作唧筒 2. 盘问 3.(唧筒把手如钮)上下往复运动 ‖ ~er n.1. 使用泵的人(或机器) 2. 消防车；灭火泵车

pump[pʌmp] n. 无带轻软舞鞋；〈美〉(正式场合穿的)女式无带轻便鞋

pumpernickel ['pʌmpənikl] n. 裸麦粗面包，黑面包

pumpkin ['pʌmpkin] n.1. 西葫芦；南瓜；西葫芦(或南瓜)藤 2.〈美口〉重要人物，大亨 3.〈俚〉头，脑袋瓜 4.[the ~s]〈美俚〉乡间

pun[pʌn] n.(修辞中的)双关语 —(punned; punning) vi. 谐用双关语 —vt. 用双关语说服(或促使)

punch[pʌntʃ] n.1. 冲压机，冲床；冲头 2.(纸、纸板等的)打孔器，穿孔机 3.(木工用的)钉锤 4. 压印器，凸模冲头 5.(冲出或打出的)孔；切口 —vt.1.(用冲床)冲；(用打孔器)穿孔 2.(用冲床)冲出(孔)；(用打孔器)打出(孔) 3.(用钉锤)打进(或起出)(钉子) 4.(用压印器)压印；(用凸模冲头)冲印 —vi.(用打孔机，冲床)冲印 ‖ ~er n.1.〈俚〉电报报务员；冲床工，钻床工

punch[pʌntʃ] vt.1.(用拳)猛击 2. 用力击；用力按 3.(用棒)戳，刺 4. 赶(牲口)；放牧(牲口) 5. 竭力推挤 —vi.1. 用拳猛击 2. 用力击；用力按 —n.1. 拳打 2. 力量；活力；效力

punch[pʌntʃ] n. 潘趣酒(一种用果汁、牛奶、酒等调合的饮料)

punch[pʌntʃ] n.1.[P-] 潘趣(英国木偶剧 Punch and Judy 中驼背的滑稽角色) 2.[P-]《笨拙周报》(英国幽默插画杂志) 3.〈英〉(萨福克郡产的)矮壮种马，

〈英方〉矮而结实的人;粗而短的东西

punctilious [pʌŋk'tiliəs] adj. 1. 小心谨慎的 2. 拘礼的;拘谨的

punctual ['pʌŋktjuəl, 'pʌŋktʃuəl] adj. 1. 严守时刻的;准时的;不误期的 2. (表达方式等)正确的 3. 点状的;【数】点的 4. 〈古〉= punctilious ‖ ~ity [ˌpʌŋktju'æliti, ˌpʌŋktʃu'æliti] n. 严守时刻;准时;按期 / ~ly adv. 1. 守时地;准时地;按期地 2. 正确地;精确地

punctuate ['pʌŋktjueit, 'pʌŋktʃueit] vt. 1. 加标点于;标点(文章等) 2. 强调;加强 3. 不时打断 ~vi. 加标点 ‖ **punctu'ation** n. 1. 加标点;标点法 2. 标点符号 (= punctuation mark)

puncture ['pʌŋktʃə] n. 1. 刺;刺穿 2. 刺痕;(车胎等)刺孔 3. 【生】刻点 ~vt. 1. (用针)刺;刺穿;戳破 2. 揭穿;使无用 ~vi. 被刺穿;被戳破

pundit ['pʌndit] n. 专家,学者,权威;自封的学者(或权威)

pungent ['pʌndʒənt] adj. 1. (气味等)刺激性的,刺鼻的;辣的 2. (语言等)辛辣的,尖刻的,尖锐的 3. 【生】锐利的 ‖ **pungence, pungency** n. / ~ly adv.

punish ['pʌniʃ] vt. 1. 罚,处罚,惩罚 2. 严厉(或粗暴)地对待;折磨;损害 3. 〈口〉大量消耗;耗尽 ~vi. 处罚,惩罚

punishable ['pʌniʃəbl] adj. (人、罪行等)可处罚的;该处罚的

punishment ['pʌniʃmənt] n. 1. 罚,处罚,惩罚;刑罚 2. 〈口〉严厉的对待;痛击;折磨;损害

punitive ['pjuːnitiv] adj. 给予惩罚的;惩罚性的;刑罚的

punk¹ [pʌŋk] n. 1. 〈口〉〔总称〕废物;废话;胡言乱语 2. 无用的人;小流氓;小阿飞 3. 年轻无知的人;小伙子 4.〈古〉

妓女 —adj.〈俚〉1. 无用的;不好的;低劣的 2. 身体不好的

punk² [pʌŋk] n. 1. (点火用的)干朽木 2. (干蕈等制的)火绒;(点爆竹用的)细棒状点火物 —adj. 腐朽的

punt¹ [pʌnt] n. 用篙撑的方头浅平底船 —vt. 1. 用篙撑(船) 2. 用方头浅平底船运载 ~vi. 乘方头浅平底船

punt² [pʌnt] vt. 踢(悬空球) ~vi. 踢悬空球 —n. 踢悬空球

punt³ [pʌnt] vi. 1. (打纸牌时)向庄家下赌注 2. 赌博 ~n. 向庄家下赌注者;赌博者

puny ['pjuːni] adj. 1. 小的;弱小的;软弱无力的 2. 不足道的;次要的

pup [pʌp] n. 1. 小狗,幼犬 2. 幼畜;幼兽 (尤指小海豹)—(pupped; pupping) vi. & vt. 生(小狗等)

pupa ['pjuːpə] ([复] pupae ['pjuːpiː] 或 pupas) n. 【动】蛹 ‖ ~l adj.

pupate ['pjuːpeit] vi.【动】化蛹;经历蛹期

pupil¹ ['pjuːpəl] n. 1. 小学生;学生;门生,弟子 2.【英律】(有监护人的)未成年人,受监护人

pupil² ['pjuːpəl] n.【解】瞳孔

puppet ['pʌpit] n. 1. (演木偶戏用的)木偶;玩偶 2. 受他人操纵的人(或集团),傀儡 —adj. 1. 木偶的 2. 傀儡的,受人操纵(或支配)的 ‖ ~like adj.

puppy ['pʌpi] n. 1. (常指未满一岁的)小狗,幼犬 2. 幼小动物(尤指鲨鱼) 3. 自负的青年

purchase ['pəːtʃəs] n. 1. 买,购买,购置;购置物;刚购得之物 2. (废)获得物;猎物 3. (地产的)年租,年收益 4. 〔史〕买军官职位 5.【律】(房地产等的)置得(指非继承所得的) 6. 紧握,紧抓(以拉或举某物,或防止其滑落) 7. 用来

移动(或举动等)的机械装置;【海】绳索;绞辘;起锚机 —vt.1. 买,购买,赎 2.(用牺牲物)换得 3.【律】置得(房地产等) 4. 用机械装置(或机械力)举起(或移动) ‖ ~r n. 买主,购买人;采购人

pure [pjuə] *adj.*1. 纯粹的,不搀杂的;(颜色)纯的 2. 纯净的;洁净的,无垢的 3. 无暇的;无错的;完美的;纯正的 4.(品德等)纯洁的;清白的;贞洁的 5.(马等)纯种的;纯血统的 6. 完全的,十足的 7. 纯理论的;抽象的 8.【哲】纯粹的,非经验的 9.(声音)清亮的;圆润的 10.【语】(元音)在另一元音后的;(词根)以元音结尾的;(辅音)不与其他辅音相连的 ‖ ~ly *adv.* | ~ness *n.* | ~-bred *adj. & n.* 纯种的(动物或植物)

puree ['pjuərei] 〖法〗*n.*1.(蔬菜、水果等制成的)泥;酱 2. 浓汤 —vt. 把…做成泥(或浓汤)

purgative ['pəːgətiv] *adj.*1. 净化的,清洗的;清除的;涤罪的 2. 通便的 —n. 泻药

purgatory ['pəːgətəri] *n.*1.【宗】炼狱;(在炼狱中的)涤罪 2. 暂时受苦的地方;暂时的苦难 —adj. = purgative

purge [pəːdʒ] *vt.*1. 使洁净;使净化;清除;清洗;肃清 2.【律】以认错作为…的补偿 3. 用药物使(肠)通便;使(人)通便 —vi.1. 净化;清除;清洗;肃清 2. 通便;泻药 ‖ purgation [pəːˈgeiʃən] *n.*

purification [ˌpjuərifiˈkeiʃən] *n.*1. 纯化;净化;净身 2. 提纯;精炼 3.【宗】涤罪;斋戒;洁净礼

purify ['pjuərifai] *vt.*1. 使洁净;使洁净 2. 使道德上净化 3. 精炼(金属等);提纯 —vi. 变纯净;变清净

Purim ['pjuərim, puˈriːm] *n.*(犹太教的)

普林节(阿达尔[Adar]月 14 及 15 两日,纪念犹太人免遭 Haman 的杀害)

Puritan ['pjuəritən] *n.*1. 清教徒(基督教新教的一派) 2. [p-]清教徒似的人,道学先生,宗教(或道德)上极端拘谨的人 —adj.1. 清教徒的 2. [p-]清教徒似的;道学先生的;宗教(或道德)上极端拘谨的;禁欲的,苦行的

puritanical [ˌpjuəriˈtænikəl] *adj.*1. [P-]清教徒的;清教主义的 2. 清教徒似的,道学先生的;宗教(或道德)上极端拘谨的;禁欲的,苦行的

purity ['pjuəriti] *n.*1. 纯净;洁净;纯正 2. 纯洁;清白;贞洁 3. 纯色;【化】纯度

purl [pəːl] *vi.* 用反针(或朝上针)编织 —vt. 朝上针编织 —n.(编织的)反针,朝上针

purloin [pəːˈlɔin] *vt. & vi.* 偷窃

purple ['pəːpl] *n.*1. 紫色,紫红色 2. 紫色染料(或颜料);〖古〗泰尔红紫(从海螺中浸出的紫色染料) 3. 紫色布衣;紫衣;紫袍 4. [the ~]帝位;王位;显位;红衣主教的职位 —adj.1. 紫的,紫色的;〖古〗泰尔红紫的 2. 帝王的 3. 词藻华美的;华而不实的 4. 亵渎的 —vi. & vt.(使)成紫色

purplish ['pəːpliʃ], **purply** ['pəːpli] *adj.* 略呈紫色的

purport ['pəːpɔːt, 'pəːpət] *n.*1.(文件、演说等的)意义;涵义;主旨 2. 目的,意图 —vt.1. 意味着;似乎有…的意义;大意是 2. 声称;号称 3. 意图;意欲

purpose ['pəːpəs] *n.*1. 意图;目的 2. 意志;决心 3. 效用;效果 4.(讨论中的)议题;(进行中的)行动 —vt. 决意(做);打算(做) ‖ ~ly *adv.* 特意地,故意地

purposeful ['pəːpəsful] *adj.*1. 有意图的,有目的的;有意义的;故意的 2. 坚定

的；果断的；有决心的 ‖ ~ **ly** adv. /
~ **ness** n.

purposeless ['pəːpəslis] adj. 1. 无目的的；
无意义的 2. 无决心的 ‖ ~ **ly** adv. /
~ **ness** n.

purr [pəː] n. 1. (猫等高兴时的)呼噜声，
呜呜声 2. (汽车引擎等)低沉的咕隆声
—vi. 1. (猫等)满足地呜呜叫，发呼噜
声 2. 汽车引擎等)发出咕隆声 3. (人)
发嘀嘀声；不怀好意地说话 —vt. 1. 呼噜
(或嘀嘀)作声表示(满足、愉快等)

purse [pəːs] n. 1. 钱包，小钱袋 2. 〈美〉
(手提或肩挂的)女用小包 3. 金钱；资
金，财力 4. (募集或捐赠的)一笔款子；
一笔奖金 5. 囊状物 —vt. 1. 〈古〉把…
放进钱袋 2. 使皱拢；使皱起(up) —
vi. 缩拢；皱起 ‖ ~ **string** 1. 钱袋口上
的收口绳 2. [~ strings]钱袋口上的
收口绳 2. [~ strings]金钱的支配；
财权；财源

purser ['pəːsə] n. (轮船、班机等的)事务
长

pursuance [pəˈsjuːəns] n. 1. 追赶；追随
追求 2. 遵循；进行；实行

pursuant [pəˈsjuːənt] adj. 1. 追赶的；追随
的；追求的，遵循的 2. 按照的，依据的
(to) —adv. 按照(to)

pursue [pəˈsjuː] vt. 1. 追赶；追踪；追捕；
追击 2. 追随，跟随；(疾病、灾祸等)纠
缠 3. 追求，寻求；向…求爱 4. 进行；实
行；从事；继续 —vi. 1. 追，追赶(after)
2. 继续进行 3. (苏格兰法律)起诉 ‖ ~
r n. 1. 追赶(或追踪等)者；追求者
2. 从事者；研究者 3、(英)(民法和苏格
兰法律)起诉人，原告

pursuit [pəˈsjuːt] n. 1. 追赶；追踪；追捕；
追击 2. 追求，寻求 3. 追赶(或追求等)
的对象 4. 事务；职业；消遣 5. 【军】驱
逐飞机(= ~ plane)

purulent ['pjuərulənt] adj. 脓的；化脓的

含脓的；流脓的；像脓的 ‖ **purulence,**
purulency n. —**ly** adv.

purvey [pəˈvei] vt. 1. 承办(伙食等)；供应
(货物等) 2. 传播 —vi. 承办伙食；供
应货物(for)

purveyor [pəˈveiə] n. 1. 承办伙食者(货
物、服务、消息等的)供应者；提供者 2.
【英史】(王室)征发官员

pus [pʌs] n. 脓

push [puʃ] vt. 1. 推；按；推动；推进 2. 使
突出；使伸出；使延伸 3. 大力推进；推
行 4. 逼迫，催逼；促使 5. 使引人注意；
提携(人)；推销(商品)；(俚)贩卖(毒
品) 6. 扩展；扩大；增加 2. 推进 2.
推进；努力前进 3. 伸展；扩展；增加 4.
奋力争取，力求取得(for) —n. 1. 推；
推动；推进；促进 2. 奋力；努力 3. 攻
击；攻势；运动；推销运动 4. 压力；逼
迫；紧急关头 5. 劲头；进取心；事业心
6. (英俚)解雇；断绝关系 7. 一伙人；
(主澳俚)一帮贼(或罪犯等) 8. (刀锋
或兽角等的)刺；触 ‖ ~ **er** n. 1. 推(或
按)的人(或物) 2. 推动者；推动器 3.
(口)推销者；(俚)(毒品等的)贩卖者
3. 推进式飞机(= ~ er airplane) ‖ ~
button 按钮，电钮 /'~ ,**button** adj. 按
钮式的；按钮控制的；完全自动化的；一
召之即来的 /'~ **cart** n. 手推车 /'~
over n. 1. 易被击败(或引诱、欺骗、劝
服等)的人 2. 轻易做的事(或取得的
胜利)

pushing ['puʃiŋ] adj. 1. 有进取心的；有
冲劲的 2. 莽撞的，一意孤行的

pushy ['puʃi] adj. 1. 爱出风头的 2. (尤指
为自身利益)急于求成的 ‖ **pushily**
adv. / **pushiness** n.

pusillanimous [,pjuːsiˈlæniməs] adj. 胆怯
的；优柔寡断的 ‖ ~ **ly** adv. / ~ **ness** n.

puss [pus] n. 1. [用作爱称]猫咪，小猫

小妮子，小姑娘 2.〈英〉野兔；老虎 3.〈方〉〈俚〉脸；嘴 4.〈粗〉〈俚〉女阴，尿

pussy[1] ['pusi] *n.*1.[用作爱称和儿语]猫咪 2.[植]〈绿色柳等的〉柔荑花序 3.〈粗〉〈俚〉女阴，尿；性交 ‖ ~ **willow** 【植】绿色柳

pussy[2] ['pʌsi] *adj.* 多脓的；有脓的；似脓的

pussyfoot ['pusifut] *vi.*〈口〉1.〈猫一般〉不出声地走；蹑行 2.持暧昧或骑墙态度；观望

pustule ['pʌstjul] *n.*1.脓疱 2.【动】色点，小疱 3.【植】小疱

put [put](put; putting) *vt.*1.放置，装 2.移动；推动；推进 3.使放置；使出现；使存在 4.投掷；发射 5.渡送；使航行 6.使处于〈某种状态〉7.写上；标上 8.提出 9.表达；表述；翻译 10.使从事；把…付诸 11.使受到〈*to*〉11.驱使；迫使；促使 12.估计 13.课〈税〉投〈资〉；下〈赌注〉14.赋予；给予；推诿〈*on*〉15.配乐〈或谱曲〉；使行进，使穿过 —*vi.*1.出发，走；匆忙离开 2.〈向…〉航行 —*n.*1.〈铅球等的〉投掷，推 2.〈证券交易中〉以固定价格，约期出售选择权 —*adj.*〈口〉固定不动的 ‖ ~ **out** *n.* 〔棒球等中的〕杀出局

putative ['pju:tətiv] *adj.*1.假定存在的 2.普遍被认为是推定的 3.【语】推定的 ‖ ~**ly** *adv.*

putrefaction [,pju:tri'fækʃən] *n.*1.腐烂（作用）；腐败（作用）2.坏疽；化脓 3.腐化，堕落

putrefy ['pju:trifai] *vt.* & *vi.*1.〈使〉坏死 2.〈使〉化脓；〈使〉腐败；〈使〉腐败 3.〈使〉腐化，堕落

putrescent [pju:'tresnt] *adj.*1.正在腐烂〈或坏死〉的 2.腐败〈或坏死等〉的 3.与腐败〈或坏死等〉有关的

putrid ['pju:trid] *adj.*1.腐烂的；腐败的 2.腐化的，堕落的 3.〈口〉坏透的；质量很差的；毫无用处的

putt [pʌt] *vt.* 把〈高尔夫球〉轻击入洞〈或击至洞穴附近〉—*n.* 轻击，转击入穴，短打球

putter ['pʌtə]〈美〉*vi.*1.闲荡；行动懒散〈*about*, *around*〉2.不经意地干活；工作偷懒 —*vt.* 闲混，虚度，消磨〈时日〉〈*away*〉

putty ['pʌti] *n.*1.【建】油灰，腻子；油灰状黏性材料 2.淡灰褐色；淡灰色 3.易被摆弄的人 —*vt.* 用油灰填塞〈或黏接等〉

puzzle ['pʌzl] *n.*1.难题；令人费解的人〈或事〉2.智力测验题〈或游戏，玩具〉谜 3.[只用单]迷惑；困窘 —*vt.* 使迷惑；使为难；使困窘 —*vi.*1.冥思苦想地进行〈*out*〉2.冥思苦想地进行 —*vi.*1.迷惑 2.苦思〈*over*〉‖ ~ **ment** *n.* 困惑；苦思；谜 / ~ *r n.* 使人困惑的人〈或物〉；难题

pygmy ['pigmi] *n.*1.[P-]〔分布在中非、东南亚和大洋洲一带的身体矮小的〕俾格米人 2.矮人，侏儒 3.智力低下的人；微不足道的东西〈或事〉4.小仙人，小精灵 —*adj.*1.[P-]俾格米人的 2.矮小的 3.极小的，无足轻重的；智力低下的

pyjama [pə'dʒɑ:mə] *n.*1.[~ s]〔宽大的〕睡衣裤 2.[~ s]〔印度和巴基斯坦穆斯林穿的〕宽松裤 —*adj.*〈需穿〉睡衣裤的

pylon ['pailən] *n.*1.塔式建筑物 2.〔飞机场等的〕标示塔；标杆；塔 3.〔架高压输电线的〕电缆塔 4.〔机翼下悬挂副油箱或炸弹等的〕外挂架，吊架

pylorus [pai'lɔ:rəs]〔[复] pylori [pai'lɔ:rai]〕*n.*【解】幽门

Pyongyang [ˈpjʌŋˈjɑːŋ] *n*. 平壤 [朝鲜民主主义人民共和国首都]

pyorrh(o)ea [ˌpaiəˈriə] *n*. 【医】脓溢；牙槽脓溢

pyramid [ˈpirəmid] *n*. 1. (古埃及的) 金字塔 2. 【数】棱锥 (体)，角锥 (体) 3. 角锥状物；角锥形的一堆东西；长成 (或剪成) 角锥形的树 4. 宝塔诗 5. 金字塔现象 — *vi. & vt.* 1. (使) 成尖塔形；(使) 成堆 2. (使) 步步升级，(使) 节节增加 ‖ ~**al** *adj*.

pyre [ˈpaiə] *n*. (火葬用的) 柴堆；燃料堆

Pyrenees [ˌpirəˈniːz] [复] *n*. 比利牛斯山脉 [欧洲西南部]

pyrite [ˈpaiərait] *n*. 黄铁矿

pyromania [ˌpaiərəuˈmeiniə] *n*. 放火狂，纵火狂

pyromaniac [ˌpaiərəuˈmeiniæk] *n*. 放火狂者

pyrotechnic(al) [ˌpaiərəuˈteknik(əl)] *adj*. 1. 烟火的，烟火制造 (术) 的；有关烟火施放的 2. 烟火般的，令人眼花缭乱的；出色的

pyrotechnics [ˌpaiərəuˈtekniks] [复] *n*. 1. [用作单或复] 烟火制造 (术)；烟火施放 (法) 2. 烟火；军用烟火 3. (机智或辩才等的) 出色表现，炫示

python [ˈpaiθən] *n*. 1. [P-] 【希神】皮同 [被阿波罗杀死的巨蟒] 2. 蟒蛇，蚺蛇；巨蛇 3. 鬼魂附身的预言者

Q

Q, q [kju:]([复]Q's, q's 或 Qs, qs[kju:z])
英语字母表第十七个字母 [Q]Q字形
(物)

Qatar [' kɑːtɑr] *n.* 卡塔尔[亚洲]

qt. *abbr.* 1.quantity 2.quart

quack¹ [kwæk] *vi.* 1.(鸭子)嘎嘎叫 2.咭
咭呱呱 — *n.* 鸭叫声;呱呱声

quack² [kwæk] *n.* 1. 庸医;江湖骗子;冒充
内行的人 — *adj.* 1. 庸医(用)的;冒充
内行医病的;骗子的 2. 冒牌的;骗人的;骗子
用的;胡吹的 — *vi.* 1. 用骗术行医 2.
胡吹;充内行 — *vt.* 1. 用假药(或骗术)治疗 2. 吹嘘(疗法等)

quackery ['kwækəri] *n.* 庸医骗术(或行
为);招摇撞骗

quad [kwɔd] *n.*〈口〉四方院

quadr- *comb. form* = quadri-

quadrangle ['kwɔdræŋgl] *n.* 1. 四角形,四
边形 2.(有建筑物围着的)四方院;围
住四方院的建筑物 3.〈美〉标准图幅,
梯形图幅

quadrangular [kwɔ'dræŋgjulə] *adj.* 四角
形的,四边形的 ‖ ~ly *adv.*

quadrant ['kwɔdrənt] *n.* 1. 四分之一圆
(周);九十度弧 2. 扇形体 3. 象限仪
4.【数】象限

quadraphonic [ˌkwɔdrə'fɔnik] *adj.* 四声道
(立体声)的

quadrat ['kwɔdrət] *n.* 1.【印】空铅,铅条：

em ～ 正方形空铅 / en ～ 对开空铅 2.
(进行生态或人口调查的)样方

quadrate ['kwɔdrit] *adj.* 正方形的;长方
形的;【解】方骨的：a ～ bone 方骨 — *n.*
正方形;长方形;【解】方骨;方肌 —
[kwɔ'dreit] *vt. & vi.* 1.(使)成正方形;
(使)划分正方形 2.(使)适合;(使)成
为一致 (to, with)

quadrennial [kwɔ'drenial] *adj.* 连续四年
的;每四年一次的 — *n.* 1. 四年 2. 每
四年一次的事 3. 四周年纪念

quadrennium [kwɔ'dreniəm]([复] quadren-
niums 或 quadrennia [kwɔ'dreniə]) *n.* 四年

quadri- *comb. form* 1. 表示"四";"第四"
2.【数】表示"平方","二次"

quadrilateral [ˌkwɔdri'lætərəl] *adj.* 四边
的;四边形的 — *n.* 1. 四边形 2. 四边
形的;有四座堡垒防御的四边形地区

quadrille [kwɔ'dril] *n.* 1. 方阵舞,四对
舞,夸德里尔舞;四对(或方阵)舞曲 2.
夸德里尔舞戏(十八世纪流行,四人用
四十张牌)3.(印格、图案等)有正
(或长)方形标记的

quadrillion [kwɔ'driljən] *num.* 1.(英、德)
10^{24}(百万的四次幂)2.(美、法)10^{15}
(千的五次幂)

quadroon [kwɔ'druːn] *n.* 1.(有四分之一
黑人血统的)黑白混血儿 2.(动植物)
四分之一杂交种

quadru- *comb. form* = quadri-：*quadruped*

quadruped ['kwɔdruped] *n.* 四足动物(尤指哺乳动物) — *adj.* 有四足的;四足动物的

quadruple ['kwɔdrupl] *adj.* 1. 四倍的 2. 四重的;由四部分组成的 3.【音】四拍子的 — *adv.* 四倍地 — *n.* 四倍 — *vt. & vi.* (使)成为四倍

quadruplet ['kwɔdruplit] *n.* 1. [~s] 四胞胎 2. 四胞胎之一 3. 成套的四件,四联组 4. 四人自行车

quadruplex ['kwɔdrupleks] *adj.* 1. 四倍的;四重的 2.【讯】四路多工的,四工的

quadruplicate [kwɔ'druplikət] *n.* 一式四份中的一份;一式四份 — *vt.* 把…作成一式四份 ‖ *in* ~ 一式四份地

quaff [kwɑːf] *vt. & vi.* 大口地喝(或吞);痛饮,畅饮 — *n.* 大口的喝(或吞);畅饮;一饮而尽的酒

quag [kwæg] *n.* = quagmire

quagmire ['kwægmaiə] *n.* 1. 沼泽地;泥潭,泥坑 2. (难以解脱的)困境

quahog ['kwɑːhɔg, 'kwɔːhɔg] *n.* 【动】(北美产的)圆蛤

quail[1] [kweil] *n.* [复]quail(s)) *n.* 1.【动】鹌鹑;北美鹑 2.【美俚】漂亮姑娘;青年女子

quail[2] [kweil] *vi.* 胆怯,畏缩(*at, before, to*) — *vt.* 〈古〉使胆怯;威吓

quaint [kweint] *adj.* 1. 离奇的,古怪的;富有奇趣的;古雅的 2.(工艺、设计等)灵巧的;精致的 3.(仅应等)英俊的(漂亮的);(语言等)优雅的 ‖ ~**ly** *adv.* ‖ ~**ness** *n.*

quake [kweik] *vi.* 1. 震动;颤动 2. 颤抖,发抖(*with, for*) — *n.* 1. 震动;颤抖;地震;a ~ looter 乘地震抢劫者

Quaker ['kweikə] *n.* 1.(基督教)贵格会教徒,公谊会教徒 2.[q-]发抖的人;震摇

的东西

qualification [ˌkwɔlifi'keiʃən] *n.* 1. 资格;合格;合格证明 2. 限制条件;限定 3. 称作;认作

qualified ['kwɔlifaid] *adj.* 1. 有资格的;合格的;胜任的;a ~ technician 合格的技术员 2. 有限制的;有保留的

qualifier ['kwɔlifaiə] *n.* 1. 合格的人(或物) 2.【语】限定语,修饰语

qualify ['kwɔlifai] *vt.* 1. 使具有资格;使合格 2. 限制,限定;【语】修饰,限定 3. 把…称作;形容,描述 4. 证明…合格 5. 授予…法律上的权力;准予 6. 缓和,减轻 7. 改变(液体)的浓度(或风味) — *vi.* 取得资格;具备合格条件(*as, for*)

qualitative ['kwɔlitətiv] *adj.* 质的,质量的;性质上的 ‖ ~**ly** *adv.* ‖ ~ **analysis**【化】定性分析

quality ['kwɔliti] *n.* 1. 质,质量 2. 优质 3. 品质;特性 4. 品种 5. 身分;地位 6. 才能,本领 7. 音质,音色 8.(色泽的)鲜明(性) 9.【逻】(命题的)质(指肯定的或否定的) 10.〈古〉〈俗〉社会地位;高地位;贵族 — *adj.* 1. 优质的,高级的 2. 上流社会的;贵族化的

qualm [kwɑːm] *n.* 1.(一阵)眩晕;(一阵)恶心 2. 疑虑,疑惧;不安 ‖ ~**ish** *adj.* 在点发晕的;有点疑虑不安的

quandary ['kwɔndəri] *n.* 窘境;犹豫不定

quantify ['kwɔntifai] *vt.* 1. 确定(或表示)…的数量;用数量表示 2.【逻】量化;以量词(如 all, none)限定

quantitative ['kwɔntitətiv] *adj.* 1. 量的,数量的 2.【语】音量的(尤指诗歌的音节等) ‖ ~**ly** *adv.* ‖ ~ **analysis**【化】定量分析

quantity ['kwɔntiti] *n.* 1. 量,数量;分量 2. [常 quantities]大量,大宗 3.【语】(元

音、音节等的)音量 4.【逻】(命题的)量
5.【数】量

quantum ['kwɔntəm] ([复] quanta
['kwɔntə]) *n.* 1. 量；定量；份额 2. 总量
3.【物】量子

quar. *abbr.* 1. quarter 2. quarterly

quarantine ['kwɔrəntiːn] *n.* 1.(对船舶等
的)检疫，留验；检疫处；检疫期 2.(为
防止传染病流行而对人、畜等实施的)
隔离；隔离区 3. 四十天 — *vt.* 1.
对...进行检疫 2.(在政治等方面)隔
离，使孤立

quarrel ['kwɔrəl] *n.* 1. 争吵，吵架；吵闹；
不和 2. 争吵的原因；怨言；责备 —
(quarrel(l)ed; quarrel(l)ing) *vi.* 1. 争吵，
吵架；不和 2. 责备；埋怨；挑剔(*with*)

quarrelsome ['kwɔrəlsəm] *adj.* 好争吵的；
好争论的

quarry[1] ['kwɔri] *n.* 1.(采)石场，石坑，石
矿 2. 菱形(或方形)玻璃片(或石、瓦
等) 3. 消息(或资料)的来源 — *vt.* 1.
采(石)；挖掘 2.(在古书等中)极力搜
索(证据等)；发掘 — *vi.* 费力地搜寻

quarry[2] ['kwɔri] *n.* 1. 猎物(指鸟、兽等)
2. 追求物；追求的目标

quart [kwɔːt] *n.* 1. 夸脱(英美干量或液
量单位 = 2 品脱)；略作 qt.) 2. 一夸脱
的容器 3.(纸牌戏中的)四张同花顺

quarter ['kwɔːtə] *n.* 1. 四分之一；一刻
钟 2. 季度，三个月 3.(每学年分为四
学期制度中的)学季 4.(美国、加拿大
的)两角五分钱币 5.(美国、加拿大的
两角五分硬币 6. 四分之一英担(英国为 28 磅，美国为
25 磅) 7. 四分之一码；四分之一英里
8. 四分之一英寻 9.(谷物等的容量单
位)八蒲式耳(= 1/4 吨) 10. 包括整条
腿的大块肉 11.[常～s](活的四肢动
物的)一股；臀腿部 12.(受刑者被肢解
后的)四分之一尸体 13.(罗盘针)方

位，方角 14.(罗盘)四个主要点中的一
点；(罗盘上三十二点中任何两点间距
离的)四分之一；象限 15. 方向；地区；
方面 16.(城市中的)地区，一区中的居
民 17.[～s]住处；营房 18.[常～s](船
员或水兵的)岗位；[～s]集合 19. 船
(舷)的后部 20.(鞋帮等的)后帮
部 21. 月球公转的四分之一；弦 22.
(橄榄球赛等的)四分之一场 23.(机器
零件的)相互垂直 24.(纹章中)盾的四
分之一 25.(对投降者的)生命保障；
(对敌人的)宽恕 26. 四分之一英里赛
跑 — *vt.* 1. 把...分为四等分 2.
供...住宿；使(部队)驻扎 3.(猎犬等)
到处来回搜索(某地区) 4.〈古〉把(受
刑者)分裂成四分 5. 使(曲柄等)与
机器连结部分成直角 6. 将(纹章)置
于四分之一盾面上；将(别家的纹
章)置于自家的分成四份的盾面上；纵
横划分(盾面)为四部分 — *vi.* 1. 住
宿；驻扎(at, with) 2.(猎犬)到处来回
搜索 3.(风)向船后侧吹来 — *adj.* 四
分之一的；相当于四分之一的 ‖ ～
back *n.* 1.(橄榄球赛中指挥反攻的)四
分卫 2. 四分卫位置 *vt.* 1. 担任(橄榄
球队)四分卫 2. 为...发号施令；操纵
vi. 担任四分卫 /～**deck** *n.* 1.(高级船
员使用的)上层后甲板区 2.[总称]舰
上军官；高级船员 /～**horse** *n.*(善于短距
离冲刺，原用于 1/4 英里比赛的)夸特
马 /～**master** *n.* 1. 军需官 2.【海】舵
工 /～**staff** *n.*(英国农民过去用作武
器的)铁头木棍；铁头木棍格斗(运动)
/～**wind**[海]后侧风

quarterly ['kwɔːtəli] *adj.* 1. 季度的；按季
度的 2.(每年)分为四部分的 — *adv.*
1. 季度地；按季 2.(盾面)纵横四分地
— *n.* 季刊

quartet(te) [kwɔːˈtet] *n.* 1.【音】四重唱
(曲)；四重奏(曲)；四重唱(或四重奏

演出小组 2. 四人一组；四件一套

quarto ['kwɔːtəu] ([复] quartos) n. 四开；四开本(书) — adj. 四开(本)的

quartz [kwɔːts] n. 【矿】石英‖ ~ watch 石英(手)表

quasar ['kweizɑː] n. 【天】类星体

quash [kwɔʃ] vt. 1. 【律】撤销；废止；使无效；宣布(判决等)无效 2. 镇压 3. 平息

quasi ['kwɑːzi] adj. 类似的，有几分像的；部分的，半的 — adv. 即；宛如

quasi- *pref.* 表示"类似","准","半"

quaternary [kwə'təːnəri] adj. 1. 四个一组的；四部组成的；第四的 2. 【化】四元的；四价的；季的 3. 【数】四进制的 4. [Q-]【地】第四纪的 — n. 1. 四，四个一组；第四组中的组成部分 2. 【数】四进制 3. [Q-]【地】第四纪

quatrain ['kwɔtrein] n. (通常隔句押韵的)四行诗节；四行诗

quaver ['kweivə] vi. 1. 震动；颤抖 2. 发颤声 — vt. 用颤音唱；用颤音演奏；用颤声说(out) — n. 1. 颤音 2. 【音】八分音符

quay [kiː] n. 码头

queasy, queazy ['kwiːzi] adj. 1. 不稳的；动荡不定的 2. 催人呕吐的；使人眩晕的；(人)要呕吐的 3. 易呕吐的，使人不自在的；局促不安的，不舒服的 4. 脆弱的；动辄要烦恼的 5. 谨小慎微的；过挑剔的

Quebec [kwi'bek] n. 1. 魁北克省[加拿大省名] 2. 魁北克(市)[加拿大东南部港市]

queen [kwiːn] n. 1. 王后（也称为 consort）；首长夫人 2. 女王；女首长；女首脑；Queen Victoria(英国)维多利亚女王 3. (权力、地位、相貌等)出众的女人；美女比赛的第一名 4. 女神 5. 心爱的女子(指妻子、女儿等) 6. (喻)出类

拔萃的事物；胜地 7. (蜜蜂、蚂蚁等的)后 8. (纸牌中的)王后，"Q"；(国际象棋中的)后 9. 雌猫 10. (俚)同性恋男子 — vt. 1. 立…为女王(或后) 2. 使成为电影界(或交际界等)的王后 3. (国际象棋中)使(兵)变后 — vi. 1. 做女王(或国王殷)行事 2. (国际象棋中)变后 ‖ ~ship n. 女王(或后)的地位(或身份)‖ '~-cake n. 心形葡萄干小蛋糕‖ '~-size adj. 1. 大号的；很大的；特大的 2. 供大号床用的

queenly ['kwiːnli] adj. 1. 女王(或后)的；女王般的；威严的 2. 适合于女王(或后)的 — adv. 女王(或后)般地

queer [kwiə] adj. 1. 奇怪的，古怪的，精神不很正常的 2. (口)可疑的 3. 眩晕的，不舒服的；想呕吐的 4. 对…着了迷的(for, on, about) 5. (俚)假的，伪造的；无价值的 6. (俚)搞同性恋的 7. (英俚)喝醉的 — adv. = ~ly — vt. 1. 把…弄糟；破坏 2. 使陷于不利地位(或窘境) — n. (俚) 1. [the ~](伪造的货币 2. 搞同性恋的男子 ‖ ~ly adv. 奇怪地，古怪地；可疑地；眩晕地

quell [kwel] vt. 1. 镇压；平息 2. 消除，减轻

quench [kwentʃ] vt. 1. 熄灭，扑灭 2. 压制，抑制；解(渴) 3. (俚)迫使(反对者)住嘴 4. 把…淬火;使骤冷;使淬硬;猝想 — vi. 1. 熄灭；冷却 2. 平静下来；平息

querulous ['kweruləs] adj. 爱发牢骚的；抱怨的；易怒的

query ['kwiəri] n. 1. 质问；询问；疑问；怀疑 2. 引导问句，或用作插入语；略作 qu.请问 3. 疑问号(画于校样、文件的边上，表示疑问) — vt. 1. 询问，问 2. 作为问题提出 3. 对…表示怀疑

4. 画疑问号于 — *vi.* 询问；表示怀疑

quest [kwest] *n.* 1. 寻找；追求；探索 2. 调查 3. 验尸陪审团；〈英〉〈古〉验尸 4. (中世纪骑士的)探求(过程) — *vi.* 1. (狗等)跟踪搜寻；吠叫 2. 追求；探索 (*for*) — *vt.* 寻找；探索

question ['kwestʃən] *n.* 1. 发问，询问 2. 问题；议题 3. 疑问，不确定 4. 〖语〗疑问句 5. (法庭上的)争端 (大会上的)争论点(或议题) 6. (对问题的)投票表决；付表决的问题 7. 审问；〈古〉拷问 8. 可能性；机会 — *vt.* 1. 询问；讯问；审问，怀疑，对……表示疑问 3. 争论 4. 分析；探究 — *vi.* 询问；探问 ‖ ~**er** *n.* / ~**less** *adj.* 1. 不发问的；无异议的 2. 无疑的 *adv.* 无疑地 ‖ ~ **mark** 问号(即"?")

questionable ['kwestʃənəbl] *adj.* 可疑的；(品德等)有问题的；不可靠的

questioningly ['kwestʃəniŋli] *adv.* 质问地；怀疑地

questionnaire [,kwestʃə'nɛə] *n.* 1.〈调查情况用的〉一组问题；问题单 2. 调查表；征求意见表 3. 用调查表进行的调查

quetzal [ket'sɑl] 〈复〉quetzals 或 quetzales [ket'sɑːleis] *n.* 大咬鹃(中美洲产的一种毛色鲜艳的鸟)

queue [kjuː] *n.* 1. 辫子 2. (人或车辆等的)行列；长队 — (queue(e)ing) *vt.* 把(头发)梳成辫子 — *vi.* 排(成长)队；排队等候 (*up*)

quibble ['kwibl] *n.* 1. 遁词；诡辩；支吾 2. 吹毛求疵的理由 3. 双关语 — *vi.* 1. 使用遁词，含糊其词 (*over*) 2. 吹毛求疵；找岔子；(为小事)争吵 — *vt.* 就……进行诡辩 ‖ ~**r** *n.* 诡辩者

quiche [kiːʃ] *n.* 蛋奶火腿蛋糕

quick [kwik] *adj.* 1. 快的，迅速的，急速的 2. 敏捷的；灵活的；灵敏的；伶俐的

3. 性急的；易怒的 4. 活泼的；活跃的 5. 〈古〉(溪水等)流动的 6. 急剧的 6. 〈古〉怀孕进入胎动期 7.〈古〉活的 8. 〈古〉灼热的；(火)旺的 — *adv.* [用在口语中或复合词中]快；~-**drying** 快干的 — *n.* 1. (皮肤下,尤指甲下的)活肉；伤口的嫩肉；感觉敏锐部位；感情敏感部位；痛处 2. 要害；核心 ‖ ~**ly** *adv.* / ~**ness** *n.* ‖ /~'**freeze** *vt.* 将(食品)速冻 /~'**lime** *n.* 生石灰 /~'**lunch** *n.* 快餐店 /~'**sand** *n.* 1. 流沙(区) 2. 流沙般隐伏的危险,陷阱 /~'**set** *n.* 树篱 /~'**silver** *n.* 1. 水银,汞 2. (气质或心情的)易变 *vt.* 涂水银于 *adj.* 水银似的；易变的 /~'**step** *n.* 1. 〖军〗齐步 2. 轻快舞步 3. 快步进行曲 /~'**tempered** *adj.* 性情急躁的,易怒的 /~'**witted** *adj.* 机智的,机灵的,有急智的

quicken ['kwikən] *vt.* 1. 加快 2. 刺激,鼓舞；使活跃 3. 使活；使复活 4. 使(曲线)更弯；使(斜坡)更陡 — *vi.* 1. 加快；变快 2. 变活跃；变生动 3. 活过来；生长 4. (胎)动；(孕妇)进入胎动期 5. 变明亮

quid[1] [kwid] *n.* 含在口中咀嚼的烟草块；咀嚼物

quid[2] [kwid] 〈复〉quid(s) *n.* 〈英俚〉一镑

quid pro quo ['kwid prəu 'kwəu] 〈拉〉报酬；补偿(物)；交换物；替代物

quiescence [kwai'esns] *n.* **quiescency** [kwai'esnsi] *n.* 1. 静止；沉寂 2. (昆虫等的)静止期,休眠 3. (疾病的)被遏制状态

quiescent [kwai'esnt] *adj.* 1. 静止的；沉寂的；a ~ area 沉寂的地方 2. (昆虫等)静止期中,休眠中的 3. (尤指疾病的)没有症状的

quiet ['kwaiət] *adj.* 1. 静止的；寂静的

安静的；轻声的、不出声的 3. 温和的；不易激动的，文静的 4. 朴素的；不显眼的 5. 闲适的；从容的 6.〈环境、生活方式等〉单调的；无变化的 7. 僻静的 8. 暗中的 9. 非正式的 10.〈商业〉清淡的、不活跃的 — n. 静寂，平静 2. 安静，清静〈社会、政治状况的〉安定、和平 4. 沉着的举止 — vt. 1. 使静；使平静；使（争论等）平息 2. 抚慰，安慰 — vi. 静下来（down）— adv. 平静地 — ~ly adv. — ~ness n.

quietude ['kwaiitju:d] n. 寂静，平静；宁静

quietus [kwai'i:təs] n. 1.〈债务等的〉偿清；解除 2.〈罕〉清欠收据 3. 寂灭，死 4. 平息，制止 5. 静止状态

quill [kwil] n. 1. 羽毛管；羽（毛）根，翎 2. 羽毛管制成的东西；羽毛管状物；鹅毛管；羽毛管琴拨；（钓鱼用的）浮子；羽毛管牙签 3.（芦茎制的）芦管 3.【纺】纤管；纬管 4.（刺猬或豪猪的）刺 5.【药】（桂皮或金鸡纳皮等的）刺皮 6.【机】套管轴 7.（炸药的）导火线 — vt. 1.（用羽毛管刺穿；拔掉…的羽毛管 2. 把（线或纱）绕在筒管上 3. 在（布）上打褶裥 4.〈俚〉拍…马屁

quilt [kwilt] n. 被（子）；被状物 — vt. 1. 缝（被）；用垫料填塞 2. 绗缝（衣服等）；把（钱等）缝进衣内 3. 在多层布上缝出（花样）4. 摘抄剪贴地编辑；东拼西凑地做成 5.〈主方〉痛打 — vi. 制被 4. 被子

quince [kwins] n.【植】榅桲（或其果实）

quincuncial [kwin'kʌn∫əl], **quincunxial** [kwin'kʌŋksiəl] adj. 1. 梅花形的 2.【植】双盖覆瓦式的

quinine ['kwi'ni:n; 'kwainain] n.【药】奎宁，金鸡纳碱

quinsy ['kwinzi] n.【医】扁桃体周脓肿

quintal ['kwintl] n. 1. 英担（英制重量单位，英国为 112 磅，美国等为 100 磅）2. 公担（公制重量单位，= 100 公斤；略作 q.）

quintessence [kwin'tesns] n. 1.〈古〉【哲】（空气、火、水、土之外的）第五要素，以太 2. 精华，精髓 3. 典型；典范

quintet(te) [kwin'tet] n. 1.【音】五重唱（曲）；五重奏（曲）；五重唱（或五重奏）小组 2. 五人一组；五件一套 3. 男子篮球队

quintuplet ['kwintjuplit] n. 1. 五胞胎之一；[~s]五胞胎 2. 五人一组；五件一套

quip [kwip] n. 1. 讽刺话语；嘲弄；妙语 2. 遁词 3. 奇怪行为；古怪举动 — vi.（quipped; quipping）讥讽；嘲弄；说妙语 — vt. 讥讽；嘲弄

quire [kwaiə] n. 1. 帖（四张纸对折叠成的八张）；对折的一叠纸（用来钉成书等）2.（纸的）一刀（共二十四张或二十五张）

quirk [kwə:k] n. 1. 急转、急弯；（书写等的）花体 2. 突发事件；无法逆料的变化 3. 遁词；俏皮话；含糊其辞 4. 古怪举动；怪癖 5.【建】槽口槽，深槽 6.【音】甩腔 — vt. 1. 使急速一动，抽动 2. 使有深槽 — vi. 1. 弯曲；扭曲 2. 古怪地说话（或行动）

quisling ['kwizliŋ] n. 卖国贼；内奸；傀儡政府头子（Quisling, 挪威政客，第二次世界大战德国占领期间任傀儡政府总理）

quit [kwit]（quitted 或 quit; quitting）vt. 1. 离开；辞去 2. 免除 3. 偿清（债务等）；回报 4.[~ oneself]〈古〉表现 5. 放弃；停止；中止 6. 离开；搬出，迁出 2. 停止，停下；放弃；认输 3.〈口〉辞职 — adj.〔只作表语〕摆脱了…的（of）— n. 1. 离开；退出 2. 离职；辞职

quitclaim ['kwitkleim] n.【律】n. 1.（对起诉权、财产权等的）放弃；放弃权利（或

求）**2.** 产权转让契约；放弃权利证书 — **vt.** 放弃对...的要求

quite [kwait] **adv. 1.** 完全，十分，彻底 **2.** 相当，颇；或多或少 **3.** 的确，真正

Quito ['ki:təu] **n.** 基多[厄瓜多尔首都]

quits [kwits] **adj.** [只作表语](因偿清而) 抵消的；对等的；不分胜负的

quittance ['kwitəns] **n. 1.** (债务或义务的)免除 **2.** 免除债务(或义务)的证书；收据 **3.** 酬报；赔偿

quitter ['kwitə] **n.** 轻易放弃工作(或职务等)的人；半途而废的人（尤指失败主义者）；懦夫

quiver¹ ['kwivə] **vi.** (轻微地)颤动,抖动 — **vt.** 使颤动;抖动(翅膀) — **n. 1.** 颤动,抖动;颤声 **2.** 一闪

quiver² ['kwivə] **n. 1.** 箭袋,箭筒 **2.** 箭袋的箭

Quixote ['kwiksət, ki'həuti] **n.** 堂吉诃德(西班牙作家塞万提斯所著小说 *Don Quixote*(堂吉诃德)中的主人公)式的人物,充满幻想的理想主义者,热热而侠义的人 ‖ **quixotic(al)** [kwik'sɔtik(əl)] **adj.** 堂吉诃德式的;侠义的;不切实际的,空想的

quiz [kwiz]([复] **quizzes**) **n. 1.** 恶作剧;挖苦,嘲笑,戏弄 **2.** 考查,测验;询问;(广播、电视节目等中的)智力竞赛,答问比赛 **3.** 爱嘲笑、戏弄人的人,戏弄者;嘲笑者或爱取笑的人;戏弄者;(罕)怪人,举止奇特的人;容貌古怪的人一(quizzed;quizzing) **vt. 1.** 挖苦,嘲弄 **2.** (嘲弄地或以恶作剧的方式嘲弄地)张望人 **3.** 对(学生或班级)进行测验 **4.** 盘问 ‖ ~ **game**(广播或电视节目中的)答问比赛 /~ **kid** 神童 /~ **master** **n.**(答问比赛节目中的)提问者 /~ **show**、~ **program** 答问比赛节目

quizzical ['kwizikəl] **adj. 1.** 古怪的,可笑的 **2.** 爱挖苦的;嘲弄的 **3.** 探询的;好

奇的;疑惑的 ‖ ~**ly adv.**

quod [kwɔd](英俚) **n.** 监狱 — (quodded; quodding) **vt.** 关押,监禁

quoin [kwɔin] **n. 1.**【建】(房屋的)外角;(接合墙壁用的)隅石块;(拱门的)楔形石 **2.** 楔子(用来防止圆桶滚动或夹紧印版等) — **vt.** (用楔子)夹紧,固住 **2.** 给...装嵌隅石块

quoit [kɔit] **n. 1.** (掷环游戏中用的)铁圈(或绳圈) **2.** [~s](用作单或复)掷圈(铁圈游戏) — **vt.** 掷,抛

quondam ['kwɔndæm] **adj.** 一度曾是的;以前的

Quonset ['kwɔnsit] **n.** (用预制构件搭成的)半圆拱形活动房屋(亦作 ~ hut)

quorum ['kwɔːrəm] **n. 1.**〈古〉(英国法庭开庭时必须达到的)治安法官人数 **2.**〈英〉[总称]治安法官 **3.** 挑选出的一群人 **4.** 法定人数

quot. abbr. 1. quotation **2.** quoted

quota ['kwəutə] **n.** 定额;(分)配额;限额

quotation [kwəu'teiʃən] **n. 1.** 引用;引证 **2.** 引语;引文;语录 **3.**【商】报价,牌价 **4.**【印】空铅 ‖ ~ **mark(s)** 引号(即" ")

quote [kwəut] **vt. 1.** 引证;引用;引述 **2.** 把...放在引号内,用引号把...括起来 **3.**【商】报...的价,开...的价;(开始)开(价) — **vi. 1.**〈口〉引语;引文 **2.** 引号 ‖ **quotable adj.** / ~**r n.**

quoth [kwəuθ] **vt.**〈古〉[过去式]用于第一人称和第三人称] 说(= said)

quotidian [kwɔ'tidiən] **adj. 1.** 每日的;每日发生的 **2.** 平凡的;普通的 — **n.** [医]日发疟;日发热

quotient ['kwəuʃənt] **n. 1.**【数】商 **2.** 定额,应分得的部分

Qy.、qy. abbr. query

R

R, r [ɑː]([复]R's, r's 或 Rs, rs [ɑz])英语字母表第十八个字母 1.[R]R字形 2.[R]【化】基(radical)的符号 3.【电】电阻(resistance)的符号 4.【数】半径(radius)的符号；[R]比(ratio)的符号 5. [R]物气体常数的符号(gas constant)的符号 6.[R](电影)限制观看的(restricted)(指十七岁以下青少年除有家长陪同外不得观看)

Ra【化】元素镭(radium)的符号

Rabat [rə'bɑːt] *n*. 拉巴特/摩洛哥首都]

rabbi ['ræbai], **rabbin** ['ræbin] *n*. 1. 拉比(指犹太教负责教规、律法、仪式的人员或会众领袖) 2.(犹太人的尊称)先生,老师 ‖ **rabbinic(al)** *adj*.

rabbit ['ræbit] *n*. 1. 兔;野兔 2. 兔子的毛皮 3.(英口)蹩脚运动员(尤指板球、网球等的) 4. 干酪烤面包(以融化的干酪浇在烤面包上的英国点心)(= Welsh ~) — *vi*. 猎兔 ‖ ～ears(电视机的)兔耳形(接收)天线

rabble ['ræbl] *n*. 1. 乌合之众;乱民,暴民 2.[the ~](蔑)下层民众,下等人 3.(动物或昆虫的)一群;(东西)混乱的一堆 — *vt*. 聚众攻击(或侮辱) ‖ ~rouser *n*.[暴动等]煽动者

rabid ['ræbid] *adj*. 1. 狂暴的;狂怒的 2. 偏激的;固执的;狂热的;无理性的 3.(患)狂犬病的 ‖ ~ly *adv*. / ~ness *n*.

rabidity [rə'biditi] *n*. 1. 狂暴;狂怒 2. 偏

激;固执;狂热;无理性 3. 患狂犬病

rabies ['reibiz][单复同] *n*.【医】狂犬病

raccoon [rə'kuːn] *n*. = racoon

race¹ [reis] *n*. 1.(速度上的)比赛;竞赛;竞争 2.[~s]赛跑竞赛;赛马会,跑马会 3.(江、海的)急流,水道 4.日(或月)的运行;人生的历程 5.【空】滑流 6.【机】(滚珠轴承的)座圈,滚道;(织布机的)走梭板 — *vi*. 1. 比速度;参加竞赛;参加赛马;以赛马为业 2. 疾走,全速行进;(机件因阻力或负荷减少而)猛转 — *vt*. 1. 和…比速度(或竞赛) 2. 使(马等)参加比赛 3. 使疾走,使全速行进;使(发动机)空转 4.(在速度上)试图超过 ‖ ~ course *n*. 赛马场;跑道(尤指赛马所用的);水道 / ~ horse *n*.比赛用的马 / ~ track *n*.(体育比赛用的)跑道/'~walk *n*. & *vi*.【体】竞走

race² [reis] *n*. 1. 人种;种族;民族 2. 宗族;世系 3.(动、植物)族;种;(人、生物的)宗,类 4.(有同样活动、习惯、思想等的)一批人 5.(食物、酒等)特殊的(或强烈的)风味(语言的)尖锐泼辣

raceme [rə'siːm, rei'siːm] *n*.【植】总状花序 ‖ ~d *adj*.

racer ['reisə] *n*. 1. 参加(速度)比赛者,比赛用的马(或快艇、自行车、汽车、飞机等) 2. 火炮转台 3.【动】(美洲产的)游蛇属黑蛇;糠蛇属青蛇

racial ['reiʃəl] *adj*. 种族的;人种的;由种

族引起的;种族间的 ‖ ~ism *n*. 1. 种族偏见;种族歧视 2. 种族主义 / ~ly *adv*.

racism ['reisizəm] *n*. 1. 种族主义;种族歧视 2. 种族歧视(或隔离等)的主张(或行为)

racist ['reisist] *n*. 种族主义者 — *adj*. 种族主义的;种族歧视(或隔离等)的

rack [ræk] *n*. 1. 饲草架(盛饲草喂牲畜用的架子) 2. 搁物架;挂物架;格状文件分类架 3.【军】(飞机的)炸弹架 2. 形刑架(拷问犯人时拉其四肢使关节脱离的一种刑具) 4. 极大的苦痛,折磨;痛苦的根源 5.(火车等坐位上方的)行李架 6.【机】齿条;齿轨 — *vt*. 1.(主英)在饲草架中装满草料喂(马等);把(牲畜)系在饲草架前 2. 放...放在架子上 3. 在架上制作(或处理)(皮革、矿石等) 4. 把...放在肢刑架上施刑;使苦痛;折磨 6. 使猛力摇动;扭伤 7. 压榨(尤指索取高额租金);榨取 8. 过度使用(土地)而致贫瘠 — *vi*. 1. 把饲草架装满干草;把牲畜系在饲草架前 2. 变形;变歪斜

racket[1] ['rækit] *n*. 1. (网球、羽毛球等的)球拍;乒乓球拍 2.[~s][用作单]在四周有围墙的院子里玩的)网拍式球 3. 球拍形雪鞋

racket[2] ['rækit] *n*. 1.[只用单]喧嚷;吵闹声 2. 繁忙的社交;闹饮;纷乱;骚闹 3. 放荡生活 4. 敲诈勒索;格状文化卖(或职业);易赚钱的营生 5. 严格考验;苦痛的经历 6.〈俚〉生意,行当,职业—行当 7. 忙于社交活动;过放荡生活(*about*)

racketeer [ˌrækiˈtiə] *n*. 诈骗者;敲诈勒索者 — *vi*. & *vt*. 诈骗;敲诈勒索

raconteur [ˌrækɔnˈtəː]〈法〉*n*. 讲轶事(或故事)的人

racoon [rəˈkuːn] *n*.【动】浣熊;浣熊毛皮

racy ['reisi] *adj*. 1. 保持原来的;具有特色的 2. 新鲜的;活泼的,充满活力的 3.(讲话、文章等)生动的;辛辣的 4.(美)(讲话、文章等)猥亵的,挑逗性的

radar ['reidə] (radio detecting and ranging 的首字母缩略词) *n*. 雷达,无线电探测器,无线电定位装置 ‖ ~ fence, ~ screen 雷达网,雷达防线 / ~man *n*. 雷达员 / ~ scope *n*. 雷达显示器,雷达屏 / ~ trap (警方监测车速的)雷达阱(路段)

RADCM *abbr*. radar countermeasures 反雷达措施

radial ['reidiəl] *adj*. 1. 光线的 2. 放射的;辐射状的 3. 半径的;径向(运动)的 ‖ ~ly *adv*. / ~-ply tire, ~ tire 子午线轮胎

radiance ['reidjəns], **radiancy** ['reidjənsi] *n*. 1. 发光;光辉 2. 容光焕发;喜色 3. 辐射(率) 4. 深粉红色

radiant ['reidjənt] *adj*. 1. 光芒四射的;光辉灿烂的;绚丽的 2.(人、面容等)喜悦的;容光焕发的 3. 放射的,辐射的 4. 发出辐射热的 — *n*. 1. 辐射源 2.(电炉或煤气炉的)白炽部分 3.【天】辐射点 ‖ ~ly *adv*. / ~ energy 辐射能

radiate ['reidieit] *vi*. 1. 发光线;放射热量;发射电磁波;闪闪发光 2.(光、热等)辐射,散发 3.(感情等)流露,显出 4. 辐射状地,从中心向各方伸展出 — *vt*. 1. 发射(光、热等) 2. 照亮 3. 散发;传播 4.(通过无线电或电视)广播 — *adj*. 有光的;具辐射的 2.【动】【植】辐射(状)对称的,放射形的

radiation [ˌreidiˈeiʃən] *n*. 1. 发射,放射;发光;发热;辐射 2. 放射物;[总称]辐射线;辐射能 3. 辐射状排列,放射形

4.(暖气设备等的)散热器 5.【医】放射疗法

radiator ['reidieitə] *n.* 1. 辐射体;辐射器;辐射源 2.(暖气设备等的)散热器;(汽车的)水箱;冷却器 3. 取暖电炉(或煤油炉) 4.【无】发射天线

radical ['rædikəl] *adj.* 1. 根本的;基本的 2. 激进的;激进派的 3.【数】根的;【植】根的【音】根音的,原子团的 4.【语】词根的 ‖ *n.* 1.【化】基;原子团;原子团价 2.【语】词根,词干 5.(汉字的)部首 ‖ ~ism *n.* 激进主义;激进运动 ‖ ~ly *adv.*

radicalize ['rædikəlaiz] *vt.* 使激进 — *vi.* 变得激进

radii ['reidiai] radius 的复数

radio ['reidiəu] ([复] radios) *n.* 1. 无线电,射电;无线电话;无线电传送;无线电广播 3. 无线电收发报机;收音机 4. 无线电台;无线电广播台;无线电事业 — *vt.* 1. 向…发无线电报(或无线电话) 2. 用无线电发送(或广播) — *vi.* 用无线电通讯;用无线电传送 ‖ ~ wave 无线电波

radio- *comb. form* 1. 表示"放射","辐射": radioactive, radiometer 辐射计 2. 表示"无线电": radiotelegraph 无线电报机,无线电报 3. 表示"镭","X 射线" 4. 表示"光线" 5. 表示"半径"

radioactive [ˌreidiəu'æktiv] *adj.* 【核】放射性的;放射引起的

radioactivity [ˌreidiəuæk'tiviti] *n.* 【核】放射性;放射(现象)

radiobiology [ˌreidiəubai'ɔlədʒi] *n.* 放射生物学

radiobroadcast [ˌreidiəu'brɔːdkɑːst] (radiobroadcast 或 radiobroadcasted) *vt.* 用无线电广播 — *n.* 无线电广播(节目)

radiogram ['reidiəugræm] *n.* 1. 无线电报 2. 射线照片 3.〈英〉收音电唱两用机

radish ['rædiʃ] *n.* (红或白的)小萝卜(可放在色拉中生吃)

radium ['reidiəm] *n.* 【化】镭 ‖ ~ emanation 镭(放)射气 /~ therapy 【医】镭疗法

radius ['reidiəs] ([复] radii ['reidiai] 或 radiuses) *n.* 1. 辐射光线;【无】径向射线 2. 辐射状部分;【植】(菊科的)边花 3. 半径;半径距离;半径范围(车轮的)辐条 4. 界限,范围 5.【解】桡骨;【动】径脉;(昆虫的)径脉

radon ['reidon] *n.* 【化】氡

RAF *abbr.* Royal Air Force (英国)皇家空军

raffia ['ræfiə] *n.* 【植】酒椰;酒椰叶纤维

raffish ['ræfiʃ] *adj.* 1. 俗艳的;趣味低下的 2. 好看而不值钱的;(行为、穿着等)落拓不羁的

raffle ['ræfl] *n.* (常为义卖等举行的)抽彩售货(法) — *vi.* 抽彩 — *vt.* 以抽彩法出售

raft¹ [rɑːft] *n.* 1. 木排;木筏;筏子;救生筏 2. 妨碍航行的流木(或浮冰等) 3.(昆虫的)卵筏 — *vt.* 1. 筏运(木材) 2. 把(木头等)扎成筏子 3. 用筏子渡(人、货物等) 4. 用筏子渡过(或通过) — *vi.* 乘筏行;放筏行

raft² [rɑːft] *n.*〈口〉一大堆,大量

rafter¹ ['rɑːftə] *n.*【建】椽 — *vt.* 装椽于

rafter² ['rɑːftə] *n.* 筏夫,撑筏人;木材放运人

rag [ræg] *n.* 1. 破布,碎布;抹布 2. 碎片,残片 3.[~s]破旧衣服;[谑]衣服 4.[~s]制造优质纸的破布 5. 破布似的无价值东西;〈贬〉旗子;手帕;帷幕;报

纸;微不足道的人 6.【海】小块风帆 7. 橘络 8.[the R-]〈英俚〉陆海军俱乐部 9.〈俚〉钱币;铄票 ∥~-man n. 收旧货的人/~-top n. 折叠式布制汽车顶 /~-weed n.【植】豚草

ragamuffin ['ræɡəˌmʌfin] n. 衣衫褴褛的人(尤指小孩)

rage [reidʒ] n. 1. (一阵)狂怒,盛怒 2. (风、浪等的)狂暴,凶猛 3. 风行一时的人(或物) 4. 强烈的感情;热情;士气的激昂;狂热 — vi. 1. 大怒 2. (风)狂吹;(浪等)汹涌 3. 盛行,流行;(病等)猖獗

ragged ['ræɡid] adj. 1. 穿(或撕)破的 2. 衣衫褴褛的 3. 高低不平的;外形参差不齐的 4.(毛发等)乱蓬蓬的 5. 不协调的;粗糙的,不完善的 ∥~ly adv. /~ness n.

raglan ['ræɡlən] n. 套袖大衣

ragout ['ræˌɡuː, ræˈɡuː] n. 五香菜炖肉,五香杂烩

ragtime ['ræɡtaim] n. 拉格泰姆音乐(一种源于美国黑人乐队的早期爵士音乐);拉格泰姆舞;拉格泰姆调 — adj. 滑稽的,使人发笑的

raid [reid] n. (突然)袭击 2.(警察的)突然搜查;搜捕 3.(对公款等的)侵吞,盗用;抢劫 4.(对竞争对手等的)突然行动;劫夺 5.(证券的)猛跌 — vt. & vi. 1. 袭击;侵入 2. 搜查;搜捕 ∥~er n. 1. 袭击者;侵入者;劫掠商船的武装快船 2. 袭击机 4.[R-]美国海军陆战队的近战兵

rail[1] [reil] n. 1. 横条,横木 2. 栏杆;围栏 3.(门等)的横档 4. 铁轨,钢轨,轨道;铁路 5.[~s]铁路股票;铁道网 — vt. 1. 用栏杆围起(in);用栏杆隔开(off);用栏杆围出(out) 2.〈英〉由铁路运输

rail[2] [reil] vi. 责骂;挑剔;抱怨(at, against)

rail[3] [reil] [复]rail(s))n.【动】秧鸡

railing ['reiliŋ] n. 1. 做栏杆用的材料 2.[总称]栏杆,扶手 3. 围栏

raillery ['reiləri] n. 1. 善意的嘲笑,戏弄 2. 戏弄人的行为(或话)

railroad ['reilroud] n.〈美〉 1. 铁道,铁路 2. 铁路系统;铁路部门;铁路公司 — vt. 1. 由铁路运输 2. 给(或为)...筑铁路 3.〈口〉使草率通过 4.〈俚〉凭捏造的罪名(或草率审判)而陷...有罪;使入狱 — vi. 在铁路上工作

railway ['reilwei] n. 1.〈英〉铁道,铁路 2.〈主英〉铁道部门 3.〈轻便车辆等的)轨道 — vi. 乘火车旅行

raiment ['reimənt] n.〈诗〉[总称]衣饰,服装

rain [rein] n. 1. 雨,雨水;一场雨;[~s]季节雨;一阵一阵的雨 2. 雨天;[the ~s](热带的)雨季;[the Rains](大西洋上北纬雨季至十度间的)雨区 3.(雨点般的)落下;(下雨般的)一阵 — vi. 1. 下雨;降雨 2. 雨点般地落下;雨水般地淋下 — vt. 1. 使(雨等)下 2. 大量地给...如雨而下 2. 大量地给;厚施 ∥~less adj. 缺少雨的;无雨的 ∥~-coat n. 雨衣 /~-drop n. 雨点 /~-fall n. 雨量 /~-proof adj. 防雨的;a ~proof bag 防雨布袋 n. 雨衣;雨披 vt. 使能防雨 /~-storm n.【气】雨暴 /~-worm n. 蚯蚓

rainbow ['reinbou] n. 1. 虹,彩虹 2. 彩虹似的现象 3. 虚无缥缈的东西;幻想 — adj. 五彩缤纷的 ∥~like adj.

rainy ['reini] adj. 1. 下雨的;多雨的 2.(云、风等)含雨的,带雨的

raise [reiz] vt. 1. 举起;使升高 2. 使起来;建立起 3. 唤起;引起;惹起(骚乱

等);扬起;(从巢穴中)赶起(猎物) 4. 提高或引起,提拔 5. 使出现;使复活;使苏醒 6. 筹集 7. 等(款);招(兵);召集;纠集 8. 解除(禁运、封锁等) 9. 使隆起;(皮肤上)起(水泡);(纱)起毛 10. 使(面团等)发酵 11. 种植;饲养;养育 12.【数】使自乘 13.【海】看得见(地平线上的物体) 14. 用涂改等手法)增加(支票的面值) 15.(赌牌时)下赌注超过(前面的赌注或最高的赌注) 16. 和...建立无线电联系 — vi. 1.(方)上升 2.(口)咳出восе 3.(赌牌时)加赌注 — n. 1. 举起;升起 2. 增加(尤指工资) 3. 路的高处 4.【矿】坡道

raiser ['reizə] n. 1. 举起者(或提出者、提高者等) 2. 饲养者;培育者 3.(资金等的)筹集者 4.(面包厂的)发酵工人

raisin ['reizn] n. 葡萄干(常指无核的)

raja(h) ['rɑːdʒə] n. 1.【史】拉甲、罗阇(指印度历的土邦王公,首领)

rake¹ [reik] n. 1.(长柄)耙,钉齿耙,草耙;(马或拖拉机等牵引的)耙机 2. 耙状物(赌台上用的)钱耙 — vt. 1.(用耙子)耙;耙松 2. 搜索;探索到 3. 迅速(或大量)取得(钱财等)(in) 4. 痛骂,痛斥(over) 5. 擦过,掠过 6. 扫视;(窗等)俯瞰 7. 扫射;以...扫射 — vi. 1.(用耙)耙 2. 搜索;探索 3. 擦过,掠过(across)

rake² [reik] n. 放荡的人;浪子;流氓 — vi. 放荡;过浪荡生活

rakish¹ ['reikiʃ] adj. 1.(船等)流线型的;轻捷灵巧的 2. 不拘俗套的;潇洒的

rakish² ['reikiʃ] adj. 放荡的;浪荡的;(似)浪子的

rally ['ræli] vt. 1.(重新)集合,重整(溃散的队伍等) 2. 召集;团结 3. 振作(精神等);恢复(元气) — vi. 1.(重新)集

合;重整 2. 团结 3.(在健康、精力等方面)恢复,复元 4.(网球、羽毛球等)连续对打 5.(股票市场)止跌回升,跌价后复涨,跌价回升 — n. 1.(重新)集合;团结;鼓;恢复;振作 2.(群众性的)大会 3. 汽车竞赛会 4.(网球、羽毛球等)的连续对打 5.(市场的)降后复升,跌价回升

ram [ræm] n. 1. 公羊 2. [R-]【天】白羊(星)座 3. 攻城锤(旧时军舰舰首的)装甲撞角;撞角军舰 4.【机】撞杆;锤;夯;压头;(压力泵的)柱塞 — (rammed; ramming) vt. 1. 猛撞 2. 迅速移动 3. 猛击;撞击;捣击 4. 塞;压;装(弹药) 5. 迫使别人接受;灌输(思想、知识等)

ramble ['ræmbl] vi. 1. 闲逛;漫步(about、over) 2. 漫谈,聊天 3.(草木等)蔓生,蔓延 — vt. 在...闲逛;漫步于 — n. 1. 闲逛;漫步,随意逛 ‖ ~ r n. 1. 漫步者(或漫谈者) 2. 蔓生植物;攀缘蔷薇

rambunctious [ræmˈbʌŋkʃəs] adj. 〈口〉粗暴的;蛮横的;任性的 ‖ ~ly adv. / ~ness n.

ramee, ramie ['ræmi] n.【植】苎麻

ramification [ˌræmifiˈkeiʃən] n. 1. 分枝,分叉 2.(枝的)分布 3. 支脉;支流;细节 3. 衍生物;结果

ramify ['ræmifai] vt. 1. 使分枝,使分叉 2. 使成网状 — vi. 1. 分枝,分叉 2. 成网状

ramjet ['ræmdʒet] n. 冲压式喷气发动机

ramp¹ [ræmp] n. 1. 斜面;斜坡;(弯曲的)斜道 2.【建】楼梯扶手弯曲段 3.(客机)活动舷梯;停机坪 4. 使有斜坡;有斜坡 2.【建】使弯

ramp² [ræmp] vi. 1.(狮等)用后脚立起,跃立 2. 作恫吓姿势;暴跳;乱撞;猖獗

3. (草木等)蔓生, 蔓延 — n. 1. (狮等的)跃立 2. 恫吓姿势; 猖獗

rampage ['ræm'peidʒ] n. & vi. 暴跳; 横冲直撞

rampant ['ræmpənt] adj. 1. 繁茂的; 蔓生的 2. (疾病、恶习等)猖獗的 3. (行为、态度、说话等)猛烈的; 不能控制的 4. (狮等)用后脚立起的, 跃立的 5. 【建】拱嵌有高低的 ‖ ~ly adv.

rampart ['ræmpɑːt] n. 1. 城墙; 垒垒; 壁垒 2. (喻)堡垒 — vt. 用壁垒防护; 筑垒保卫

ramrod ['ræmrɔd] n. 1. 【军】推弹杆; (枪的)通条 2. 严格执行纪律者 — adj. 笔直不弯的; 死板的; 生硬的; 严厉的

ramshackle ['ræm,ʃækl] adj. 1. 快要解体的, 摇摇欲坠的 2. 草率造成的 3. 放荡的; 任性的

ran [ræn] run 的过去式

ranch [rɑːntʃ, ræntʃ] n. (北美)大牧场; 大农场;专业性的牧场(或农场) — vi. 1. 经营牧场(或农场) 2. 在牧场(或农场)工作 — vt. 1. 在...经营牧场(或农场) 2. 在牧场饲养 ‖ ~er n. 1. 大牧场(或农场)主(或管理人) 2. 大牧场(或农场)工人

rancid ['rænsid] adj. 有陈腐脂肪臭味的; 败坏的; 恶臭的 ‖ ~ity, ~ness n.

rancorous ['ræŋkərəs] adj. 充满(或表示)仇恨的 ‖ ~ly adv.

ranco(u)r ['ræŋkə] n. 深仇; 积怨

R and D, R & D abbr. research and development 研究与发展

random ['rændəm] n. [现只用于下列短语中] : at ~ 胡乱地, 随便地, 任意地 — adj. 1. 胡乱的; 随便的, 任意的 2. (石料建筑等)石块形状不规则的; 不一律的 3. 【数】随机的, 【物】无规则的 ‖ ~ adv. 胡乱地; 随便地, 任意地 ‖ ~-ac-

cess memory 【计】随机存取存储器

R and R, R & R abbr. 1. rest and recuperation (美)【军】休整假期 2. rock and roll 摇滚舞(曲)

rang [ræŋ] ring² 的过去式

range [reindʒ] n. 1. 排, 行; 一系列 2. 山脉 : a mountain ~ (或 a ~ of mountains) 山脉 3. 范围; 区域 4. 变动范围; 视觉(或听觉)范围; 知识面; 能力范围; 有效范围 5. (动植物的)生长区, 分布区; 放牧区; 猎区 6. 射程; 有效距离; 行程 7. 射击场, 靶场 8. 方向; 位置 9. 徘徊; 漫游 10. 炉灶 11. 一类 12. 【数】值域 13. (统计学用语)极差 14. (美)(公地测量中相距 6 英里的两子午线间的)一排市镇, 行 6 英里地区 ‖ — vt. 1. 排列; 将...排成行 2. 使...列队; 使进入行列 3. 把...分类; 使系统化 4. 把(枪、炮、望远镜等)对准 5. 在...来回走动; 徘徊; 沿(海岸)巡航 6. 放牧 7. 解开(锚链)放在甲板上 — vi. 1. 平行; 列成一行 2. 绵亘, 延伸 3. 漫游; 排徊; 涉及 4. (在一定范围内)变动, 变化 5. 测距; 试射测距; 射程为 6. (动植物)生长, 分布

ranger ['reindʒə] n. 1. 徘徊者; 漫游者 2. 巡逻骑兵 3. (美)[R-]别动队员 4. (英)皇家园林(或森林)管理人 5. (美)国家森林看守官

rang(e)y ['reindʒi] adj. 1. 徘徊的; 喜欢漫游的 2. 有回旋余地的; 宽广的 3. (兽)四肢和身体细长的; (人)修长的

Rangoon [ræŋ'guːn] n. 仰光[缅甸首都]

rank¹ [ræŋk] n. 1. 排, 横列 2. 【军】行列 [注意 : rank 指"横列", file 指"纵列"] 2. [~s]队伍 3. 军队; 士兵 3. 秩序; 队形 4. 社会阶层; 军阶, 军衔 5. 等级; 地位; 身分 : 显贵 6. (棋盘的)横排, 横格 7. (主英)(待雇的)出租汽车停车处 8.

【数】秩 — vt. 1. 把…列成横列;
把…列队 2. 把…分等;把…评级
3.(美)等级(或级别)高于 1. 列
为 2. 列队;列队前进 (past, off) 3.
【律】对破产者的财产有要求权

rank² [ræŋk] adj. 1. 繁茂的;丛生的;过
于茂盛的 2. 多杂草的;易生杂草的;
过于多产的;过于肥沃的 4. 臭气难闻
的;腥臭的;(味道等)令人讨厌的 5.
粗鄙的;下流的 6. 极坏的;彻头
(贬)十足的 ‖ ~ly adv. / ~ness n.

rankle ['ræŋkl] vi. 1. 引起怨恨;使人痛
恨 2. 使激怒 3.(古)(创伤)化脓;发炎;
使人疼痛不已 — vt. 激怒;使怨恨

ransack ['rænsæk] vt. 1. 彻底搜索;在…
中仔细搜查 2. 洗劫;抢劫;掠夺

ransom ['rænsəm] n. 1. 赎金;赎身;
赎款 2.【宗】赎价 3. 敲诈, 勒索 —
vt. 1. 赎;赎回,赎出 2. 揣(人)勒赎 3. 向
(某人)勒索赎金 4. 得赎金后释放(某
人) 5.【宗】赎救

rant [rænt] vi. 1. 喧嚣夸张地说话;激昂
地说话 2. 咆哮,怒吼;大声斥骂 3.(英
方)狂欢 — vt. 把…以恶里(夸张地说
话 (out);装腔作势地朗诵 — n. 1. 喧
嚣夸张的话;激昂的长篇演说;夸夸其
谈 2.(英方)狂欢 ‖ ~er n. 喧嚣夸张
地说话的人

rap [ræp] n. 1. 叩击(声);敲击(声);急
拍(声) 2. 责备,责骂;严厉批评 3.(美
俚)坏事责任;罪犯的(罪犯的)认
定;罪名;徒刑 —(rapped; rapping) vt.
1. 叩击;敲击;急拍 2. 突然说出;厉声
敲击致使 4. 严厉批评 5.(美俚)追
究…的刑事责任;判处 — vi. 1. 敲击;
急拍急拍 2. 发出敲击声;厉声急促地说
(out) 3. 说粗野话

rapacious [rə'peiʃəs] adj. 1. 掠夺的;强取

的 2. 贪婪的;贪得无厌的;贪吃的 3.
(猛禽等)捕食生物的 ‖ ~ly adv. / ~ness n.

rape¹ [reip] vt. 1. 强奸 2. 强夺 3. 洗劫
(城市等) — n. 1. 强奸;强奸罪 2. 强
夺 3. 洗劫 ‖ rapist n. 强奸犯

rape² [reip] n. 1.(去汁后供制醋用的)葡
萄渣 2. 制醋桶

rape³ [reip] n.【植】芸苔,欧洲油菜 ‖ ~
cake [总称]菜籽饼 / ~ oil 菜油 / ~-
seed n. 油菜籽 / ~seed oil 菜油

rapid ['ræpid] adj. 1. 快的,迅速的;动作
快的 2.(斜坡)陡的,险峻的 — n.[常
~s]急流;湍滩 ‖ ~ly adv. / ~ness n.
‖ ~ deployment force 快速部署部队 / ~
fire【军】速射 / ~-'fire, ~-'firing
adj. 1.(枪炮)速射的 2.(讲话等)快而
失声的 / ~ transit 城市高速铁路交通

rapidity [rə'piditi] n. 1. 快,迅速 2. 陡,
险峻

rapier ['reipiə] n.(决斗或剑术中用的)轻
剑 ‖ ~-thrust n. 轻剑的刺戳;机智灵
敏的对答(或反驳)

rapine ['ræpain] n.(书)强夺,抢劫,劫掠

rapport [ræ'pɔː] n. 关系,和睦关系;联系

rapprochement [ræ'prɔʃmɔŋ] n.(法)n. 友
好关系的重建(或恢复);和睦,友好

rapscallion [ræp'skæljən] n. 流氓,无赖,
恶棍

rapt [ræpt] adj. 1. 着迷的;销魂的 2. 全
神贯注的 3. 欣喜若狂的

rapture ['ræptʃə] n. 1. 着迷;销魂 2. 全
神贯注 3. [~s]欢天喜地,狂喜 — vt.
使欢天喜地,使狂喜

rare¹ [rɛə] adj. 1. 稀薄的;稀疏的 2. 稀
有的, 罕见的;不常发生的 3. 杰出的;
珍贵的 4.(口)非常的,极端的 — adv.
(口)很,非常;a — fine view 极好的景

色 ‖ ~**ly** adv. **1.** 很少，难得 **2.** 极好地 **3.** 不平凡地，非常地 /~**ness** n. ‖ '~·**earth element【化】**稀土元素 /~**earth** 稀土元素

rare² [reə] adj. (肉类)半熟的，煮得嫩的

rarebit ['reəbit] n. (化开后加入调味品浇在烤面包片上的)威尔士干酪

rarefy ['reərifai] vt. **1.** 使稀薄(如气体等)稀薄 **2.** 使纯化；精练 **3.** 使(人格、思想等)纯净，使崇高 — vi. **1.** 变稀薄 **2.** 变纯净

rarity ['reəriti] n. **1.** 稀有；希罕；罕见的事物(或人)；希罕的东西 **2.** 稀薄；稀疏 **3.** 杰出；珍贵

rascal ['rɑːskəl] n. **1.** 流氓，无赖，恶棍 **2.** 〈谑〉小淘气，(小)坏蛋 — adj. 〈罕〉下贱的，卑鄙的 ‖ ~**ity** [rɑːˈskæliti] n. /~**ly** adv.

rash¹ [ræʃ] n. **1.** (皮)疹 **2.** 一下子大量出现的事物

rash² [ræʃ] adj. **1.** 急躁的，性急的，鲁莽的 **2.** 草率从事的，轻率的 ‖ ~**ly** adv. /~**ness** n.

rasher ['ræʃə] n. 咸肉(或火腿)薄片

rasp [rɑːsp] n. **1.** 粗锉(刀)，木锉 **2.** 锉磨的声音；粗哑的刺耳声 — vt. **1.** 用粗锉刀锉，锉磨锉光(away, off) **2.** 伤(感情)；刺激(神经)；使焦躁 **3.** 粗声粗气地说；生气地说 — vi. **1.** 粗锉，粗擦 **2.** 发出刺耳的声音

raspberry ['rɑːzbəri] n. **1.** 悬钩子，覆盆子，树莓 **2.** 〈俚〉(表示憎恶、嘲笑、不赞成等的)咂舌声，呸声；遣开

RAT abbr. rocket-launched antisubmarine torpedo 火箭发射式反潜鱼雷

rat [ræt] n. **1.** 老鼠，耗子 **2.** 讨厌鬼；可耻的人；叛徒，变节者；告密者；密探 **3.** 破坏罢工的工人，工贼 **4.** 〈口〉假发卷

5. 〈美俚〉新学生 **6.** 〈美俚〉下流女人 — (ratted; ratting) vi. **1.** 捕鼠 **2.** 叛变，变节；当工贼 — vt. 〈美〉使(头发)蓬松隆起

RATAN abbr. radar and television aid to navigation 雷达电视导航设备

ratchet ['rætʃit] n.【机】棘轮；棘爪；棘轮机构

rate [reit] n. **1.** 比率，率 **2.** 速度，速率 **3.** 价格；费用；等级 **4.** 〈英〉地方税 **5.** 房地产税率 **6.** (钟、表的)快慢差率 — vt. **1.** 对…估价 **2.** 认为；列为 **3.** 定(货物)的运费 **4.** 估定…的保险费 **5.** 评价 **6.** 〈英〉[常用被动态后]给…核定应缴税款 **7.**【海】定(船员)的等级 **8.** 确定(钟表)的快慢率；找出(钟表)的快慢差率 — vi. 被评价；被列入等级；有价值

rater ['reitə] n. **1.** 评估人；评定人 **2.** [用以构成复合词]…等级的人(或物)：This machine is a first~ 这部机器是第一流的。

rather ['rɑːðə] adv. **1.** 宁可，宁愿；(与其…)倒不如 **2.** 更确切地 **3.** 相当，颇；有点儿 **4.** 相反地 **5.** ['rɑːˈðə] 〈英口〉当然，的确(回答问题时用)：A: Do you like the film? B: Rather! 甲：你喜欢这部片子吗？乙：当然啦！ ‖ ~… than otherwise 不是别的而是…；It is ~ cold than otherwise. 天还是挺冷的。/~ too 稍微…一点：This one is ~ too large. 这一个稍微大了一点。/the ~ that 何况；因为…所以更加；I'll not go and the ~ that it's too late. 因为太迟了，所以我现在更不想去了。

rathskeller ['rɑːtskelə] n. (德国式)地下啤酒店(或饭馆)

ratification [,rætifi'keiʃən] n. 批准；认可

ratify ['rætifai] *vt.* 批准；认可

rating[1] ['reitiŋ] *n.* **1.** 级别，等级；军阶 **2.** 额定值；定额 **3.** 〈主英〉水兵；普通海员 **4.**(商人、商店等的)信用程度度 **5.**(电台节目)收听率；(电视节目)收视率

rating[2] ['reitiŋ] *n.* 责骂，申斥

ratio ['reiʃiəu] *n.* **1.** 比，比率 **2.**【经】(金银复本位制中的)金银比价

ratiocination [,rætiɔsi'neiʃən] *n.* 推理(过程)；推论

ration ['ræʃən] *n.* **1.**(食物等的)定量，配给量 **2.**〈常~s〉【军】给养；口粮；食物 **3.**(配给物的)一份 — *vt.* 配给，定量供应；分发

rational ['ræʃənl] *adj.* **1.** 理性的；推理的 **2.** 有理性的，有推理能力的；有理解力的 **3.** 出于理性的；合理的，适度的；明事理的 **4.**【数】有理(数)的 — *n.* 有理数(/ = ~ number) ‖ **-ity** [,ræʃə'næliti] *n.* / **~ly** *adv.* ‖ ~ number 有理数

rationale [,ræʃə'nɑːl] *n.* **1.** 基本原理；理论基础 **2.** 原理的阐述

rationalism ['ræʃənəlizəm] *n.* **1.** 理性至上，唯理主义 **2.**【哲】唯理论，理性主义 ‖ **rationalist** *n.* / **,rationa'listic** *adj.*

rationalize ['ræʃənəlaiz] *vt.* **1.** 使合理；使合理化 **2.** 合理地说明(或处理) **3.** 合理化地改革(工业、农业等)【数】使消根，使成为有理数 **5.**【心】文饰 — *vi.* **1.** 合理地思索 **2.** 文过饰非 ‖ **,rationali'zation** *n.* **1.** 合理化 **2.**【心】文饰(作用)

rato, RATO ['reitəu] (rocket-assisted takeoff 的首字母缩略词) *n.* 火箭助推起飞；火箭起飞助推器

rattan [rə'tæn] *n.* **1.**【植】省藤、白藤 **2.** 藤条；藤杖

ratter ['rætə] *n.* **1.** 捕鼠者；捕鼠动物 **3.**〈俚〉告密者；叛变者；逃兵

rattle ['rætl] *vi.* **1.** 发出嘎嘎声 **2.**(车等)嘎嘎地行进(或掉下) **3.** 喋喋不休 — *vt.* **1.** 使发出嘎嘎声 **2.** 急促地讲(或诵唱)；匆忙地做；使迅速移动(或通过) **3.**〈口〉使慌乱；扰乱。使觉醒振作(*up*) **5.** 从(草丛)中赶出猎物 — *n.* **1.** 嘎嘎声；吵闹声 **2.** 喋喋不休的话；喋喋不休的人 **3.** 泼浪鼓(一种幼儿玩具) **4.**(尤指人临死前喉间发出的)呼噜声，临终喉鸣 **5.**(响尾蛇尾部的)角质环 **6.** 果实成熟时在荚中嘎嘎作响的植物 ‖ ~**snake** *n.* 响尾蛇；'~**brained** *adj.* 破旧得嘎嘎响的东西；破旧车辆 **2.**〈俚〉饶舌的人；唠叨 **3.** 古玩；零碎东西 *adj.* 破旧得嘎嘎响的；破旧的

rattler ['rætlə] *n.* **1.** 嘎嘎响的东西 **2.**〈美〉响尾蛇 **3.** 饶舌的人 **4.**〈口〉出类拔萃的东西 **5.** 货运列车；〈美俚〉有轨电车 **6.** 磨砖机

rattling ['rætliŋ] *adj.* **1.** 发出嘎嘎声的 **2.**〈口〉非常快的；轻捷的；活跃的 **3.**〈口〉极好的；令人满意的 — *adv.* 很，非常

raucous ['rɔːkəs] *adj.* **1.** 沙哑的；粗声的 **2.** 喧闹的 ‖ ~**ly** *adv.* / ~**ness** *n.*

ravage ['rævidʒ] *vt. & vi.* 蹂躏；劫掠，(使)荒废；毁坏 — *n.* **1.** 蹂躏；劫掠；荒废；毁坏 **2.**〈~s〉破坏的痕迹 ‖ ~**r** *n.*

rave [reiv] *vi.* **1.** 胡言乱语；狂骂；激烈地说话 **2.** 醉心地说，痴心地说(*about, of*) **3.**(风等)呼啸，咆哮；汹涌前进 — *vt.* **1.** 语无伦次地说出，狂乱地说 **2.** 醉心地说，痴心地说出 **3.**〈~ oneself〉使叫嚷(或呼喊)得...... — *n.* **1.** 胡言乱语；狂骂；呼啸 **2.**〈美俚〉狂乱，狂乱 **3.**〈俚〉醉心，痴心；醉心的话

ravel ['rævəl] (ravel(l)ed; ravel(l)ing) *vt.* **1.** 使纠缠；使混乱；使错综复杂 **2.** 拆散

解开(*out*) 3. 弄清(复杂的事件)— *vi.* 1.(编织物等)散开;松散 2. 解开;得到解决(*out*)— *n.* 1. 纠缠的东西;纷乱的一堆;错综复杂的一团 2.(编织物等)的绽线部位;散纹

raven[¹] ['reivən] *n.*【动】渡鸦 — *adj.* 乌油油的,墨黑的

raven[²] ['rævn] *vi.* 1. 贪食;狼吞虎咽 2. 悄悄地捕食 3. 掠夺,抢劫 — *vt.* 狼吞虎咽地吃

ravenous ['rævinəs] *adj.* 1. 贪婪的;狼吞虎咽的 2. 饿极了的,受饥的 3. 渴望的 ‖ ~**ly** *adv.* / ~**ness** *n.*

ravine [rə'vi:n] *n.* 沟壑;深谷

ravioli [ˌrævi'əuli] [单复同] *n.* 意大利式小方饺

ravish ['rævif] *vt.* 1. 强夺;抢去 2. 使出神;使陶醉;使狂喜 3. 强奸 ‖ ~**er** *n.* / ~**ment** *n.*

raw [rɔ:] *adj.* 1. 未煮过的,生的 2. 未加工的;处于自然状态的 3.(酒精等)不掺水的,纯的 4. 生疏的;未经训练的;无经验的 5.(在艺术方面)不成熟的,半生的 6. 阴冷的;湿冷的 7.(伤口等)露肉的;擦掉皮的;刺痛的;赤裸的;(织物)毛边的 8.〈口〉粗野的;下流的 9.〈俚〉苛刻的;不公正的;粗暴的一 *n.* 擦伤处;红肿发炎处 — *vt.* 擦破(马背等) ‖ ~**ly** *adv.* ~**ness** *n.* ‖ '~**boned** *adj.* /~'**hide** *n.* 生牛皮;牛皮鞭/~'**hide** *adj.* 生生皮的/~ **material** 原料/~ **silk** 生丝/~ **water** 原水,未经净化的水

Rawalpindi [ˌrɔːwəl'pindi] *n.* 拉瓦尔品第[巴基斯坦北部城市]

rawish ['rɔːif] *adj.* 有点生的,夹生的

ray[¹] [rei] *n.* 1. 光线;射线(热、能等的)辐射线 2. 辐射状的线;辐射线束 3. 光辉;一线光芒 4. 微量;丝毫 5.【数】

半直线;半径 6.【植】伞形花序枝;星状毛分枝(动】蜍刺 一 *vt.* 放射线;(思想、希望等)闪现;向周围放出 — *vt.* 放射,射出(光线等);显出(智慧、才能等)

ray[²] [rei] *n.*【动】鳐

rayon ['reiɔn] *n.* 1. 人造丝,粘胶;嫘萦 2. 人造丝织物

raze [reiz] *vt.* 1. 夷平;拆毁 2. 擦去;抹掉,铲去 3.〈罕〉轻度擦伤;擦破

razor ['reizə] *n.* 剃刀;a safety ~ 保安刀 — *vt.*〈罕〉剃,刮 2.〈美俚〉瓜分(赃物)

razz [ræz] *n.*〈美〉(表示嘲笑、不赞成的)咂舌声 — *vi.*〈美〉嘲笑,讥笑;戏弄

razzle-dazzle ['ræzl'dæzl] *n.*〈俚〉1. 混乱;狂饮喧闹 2. 波动式旋转木马 3. 令人眼花缭乱的动作(或场面);骗局

Rb [化] 元素铷(rubidium)的符号

RBC *abbr.* red blood cell 红血球,红细胞

RCM *abbr.* radar countermeasure(s) 反雷达措施 2. radio countermeasure(s) 无线电干扰措施

Rd. *abbr.* 1. road 2. rod(s) 3. round

Re [化] 元素铼(rhenium)的符号

re[¹] [ri:, rei] *n.* 【音】1. 固定唱法时之 D 音 2. 首调唱法时任何大音阶之第二音(或任何小音阶之第四音)

re[²] [ri:, rei] *prep.* 1. 兹就…,2.〈口〉关于

re- *pref.* 1. 表示"回","答报","相互":*react, reciprocal, revenge* 2. 表示"反对":*rebel, resist, revolt* 3. 表示"在后","后的":*relic, relish, remorse* 4. 表示"退隐","秘密":*recluse, remote, reticent* 5. 表示"离开","下":*reside, relinquish, resign* 6. 表示"反复","加强":*refine, research, revolve* 7. 表示"否定"

"非": reproach, resign, reveal 8. [可自由加于动词及其派生词前]表示"再","又","重新","回复": reappear, reconstruction, reenter, reopen, retell, reunite

reach [ri:tʃ] vt. 1. 抵达，到达; 达到 2. 伸出(手、树枝等) 3. 伸手(或脚)及到 4. 把……递来 5. 影响, 对……起作用 6. 与……取得联系 — vi. 1. 达到; 延伸 2. 伸出手(或脚) 3. 竭力想得到(after) 4. 传开; 深入 5. [海]横风行驶 — n. 1. 伸, 伸出 2. 到达距离 3. (智力、影响等)能及的范围 4. 区域; [地]河段; 河流流程 5. 岬 6. [海]横风行驶 7. 一段旅程 8. (运驶马车前后轴的)连杆 ‖ ~-me-down《主英》adj. 1. 现成的(常指廉价而劣等的) 2. 用旧的; 别人用过的 3. (美哩)无个性的; 千篇一律的; 不真诚的 n. [常~es] 1. 现成(或穿旧)的衣服 2. 旧家俱

react [ri'ækt] vi. 1. 起反应(to) 2. 有影响; 起化学反应; 起作用(on, upon) 3. 反抗 4. 回复原状 5. [军]反攻 6. 受到化学反应

re-act [ri:'ækt] vt. 1. 重作, 再做 2. 重演, 再演

reaction [ri'ækʃən] n. 1. 反应; 感应 2. [化]反应; [物]反应 3. 反动; [医]反应 4. 反作用力 5. 反动; 极端保守 6. 回复原状 7. [无]反馈, 回授 8. [军]反攻, 反击 ‖ ~ism n. 反动主义; 极端保守主义 / ~ist n. 反动分子 adj. 反动的

reactionary [ri'ækʃənəri] adj. 反动的 — n. 反动分子

reactor [ri'æktə] n. 1. 引起(或经受)反应作用的人(或物) 2. [化]反应器 3. [电]电抗器; 扼流圈 4. (核)反应堆 5. [医](对外来物质)呈阳性反应的人(或动物)

read [ri:d] (read[red]) vt. 1. 读, 阅读; 默

读; 朗读 2. 看懂, 辨认; 觉察 3. 解释; 理解; 解答; 预言 4. 读, 达到; 获悉 5. 攻读, 学习 6. 记明, 标明; (由于显示上)定出(己方飞机)的位置 7. (指不同版本等中词语的)特定形式; (印)作 8. (勘误等)改作, 换用(for) 9. 演奏(音乐等) 10. 使……读得 11. 校对 12. [计]读, 阅读; 读出(out) 把……读入(in) — vi. 1. 读, 阅读; 朗读 2. 读到; 获悉(about, of) 3. 攻读, 学习 4. (文章等)内容是; 读起来 5. [计]读数据 — n. 〈英〉一段阅读时间 ‖ ~·'in n. 1. [计]读入 2. 宣读活动(如议员在国会宣读某种文件以反对某事) / ~·'only memory[计]只读存储器 / ~·out n. 1. (数字、信息、数据或图像等的)读出 2. 读出器 2. [计]读出

readable ['ri:dəbl] adj. 1. (书等)易读的; 使人爱读的; 有趣味的 2. (字迹等)可看懂的, 清楚的 ‖ **reada'bility** n. 1. 易读性; (文章的)可读性, 有趣味性 2. (字迹等)的清晰可认 / **readably** adv.

reader ['ri:də] n. 1. 读者; 朗诵者 2. 读物; 读本; 文选 3. (出版物的)审稿人; 校对人 4. (水、电等的)抄表员 5. [宗]读经师 6. 代教授阅卷的助教; (英国某些大学的)高级讲师 7. 显微阅读器; [计]阅读器 8. (美哩)营业(或演出)执照 9. (美哩)绀播通告 10. (注明售价等的)标签 ‖ ~·ship n. 1. 读者(或审稿人、讲师等)的身分 2. (某一书刊等的)读者们; 读者总数; increase the ~ship of a magazine 增加杂志的读者数量

readily ['redili] adv. 1. 乐意地 2. 很快地 3. 无困难地, 容易地

readiness ['redinis] n. 1. 准备就绪 2. 愿意 3. 迅速, 敏捷 4. (谈话等的)流畅

reading ['ri:diŋ] n. 1. 读, 阅读; 朗读 2.

朗诵会；朗读的章节 3. 读书；学识 4. 读物；阅读材料 5. 读起来...的东西 6.〈仪器〉指示数，读数 7.（不同的）文本 8. 阐释；看法 9.（对剧本人物等的）阐述表演 10.（议案在议会的）宣读；（分别代表议案提出、审议、表决等三个程序的）三读之一 — adj. 阅读的 ‖ ~ room 1. 阅览室 2.（印刷厂的）校对室／~ wand〈英〉(零售商品的)条形码读出)记(录)器

readjust [ˌriːə'dʒʌst] vt. 再整理；再调整 ‖ ~ment n.

ready ['redi] adj. 1.〔用作表语〕准备好的 2.〔用作表语〕思想有准备的；愿意的；乐意的 3.〔用作表语〕快要...的；易于...的，动辄...的 4. 快的，迅速的 5. 敏捷的，机灵的 6.〔用作表语〕用起来便利的；预先准备好的，现成的 — adv. 1. 预先准备好了〔常用比较级或最高级〕迅速 — n. 1. 射击准备姿势 2.〈口〉〔常作 the ~〕现款 — vt. 使准备好 ‖ ~-'made adj. 1. 现成的，预先制成的 2.（卖）现成物品的 3. 平凡的，因循的；毫不新鲜的

reaffirm [ˌriːə'fɜːm] vt. 重申，再肯定；再确认 1 ‖ ~ation [ˌriːæfə'meiʃən] n.

real ['riəl] adj. 1. 真的，真正的 2. 现实的，实际的；真实的 3.〔哲〕实在的 — n. 1. 实在的东西 2.〔数〕实数 3.〔the ~〕现实 — adv.〈口〉真正 ‖ ~ estate 不动产，房地产

realignment [ˌriːə'lainmənt] n. 重新排列；重新组合，改组

realism ['riəlizm] n. 1.（文艺的）现实主义，写实主义 2.〔哲〕唯实论，实在论 3.（对人对事的）现实主义态度

realist ['riəlist] n. 1. 现实主义者；现实主义作家 2.〔哲〕唯实论者，实在论者 3. 采取现实主义态度的人 — adj. = real-

istic

realistic [ˌriːə'listik] adj. 1. 现实主义的 2. 逼真的 3. 现实的，实际的 4.〔哲〕唯实论的，实在论的 ‖ ~ally adv.

reality [ri'æliti] n. 1. 现实：实际存在的事物，真实 3. 逼真 4.〔哲〕实在

realize ['riəlaiz] vt. 1. 实现 2. 认识到；认清；了解 3. 使显得逼真 4. 把（证券、产业等）变现 5.（因出售、投资等而）获得（利润等）— vi. 变卖，变现 ‖ ˌreali'zation n.

really ['riəli] adv. 1. 真正地 2. 实在：真实地 3.〔表示关心、惊讶、怀疑、异议等〕A: He is leaving tomorrow. B: Oh, ~?（Not ~!）甲：他明天就走了。乙：啊，真的吗?（不会吧!）

realm [relm] n. 1. 王国；国土，领土 2. 领域，范围 3.（生物地理学中生物的）界

realtor ['riəltə] n.〈美〉房地产经纪人

realty ['riəlti] n. 不动产，房地产

ream[1] [riːm] n. 1. 令（纸张的计数单位，一般为 500 张左右）2.〈口〉〔常 ~s〕(指纸张、写作等)大量

ream[2] [riːm] vt. 1.（用铰刀等）铰大；钻大（孔）；铰大（枪等）的口径（out）2. 铰除（毛边等）（out）3. 榨出（水果等）的汁；榨取（果汁等）4. 翻转（弹壳等）的边

reamer ['riːmə] n. 1. 扩宽钻；铰刀；铰床 2. 果汁压榨器

reanimate [ri'ænimeit] vt. 1. 使复活，使复苏 2. 使重振精神，使重新活跃；鼓舞，激励 ‖ ˌreani'mation n.

reap [riːp] vt. 1. 收割，从...收割庄稼；收获 2. 获得，得到 — vi. 1. 收割庄稼 2. 遭到报应；得到报偿

reaper ['riːpə] n. 1. 收割者；收获者 2. 收割机

reappear [ˌriːəˈpiə] *vi.* 再(出)现

rear¹ [riə] *n.* 1. 后部;后面 2.【军】后卫;(部队、舰队等的)后尾 3. 背面,背后 4.〔英口〕厕所 5.〔口〕臀部 — *adj.* 1. 后部的;后面的 2.【军】后方的;殿后的 ‖ ~**most** *adj.* 最后面的;最后的 / ~**ward** *n.* 后部;后面 (在后面;(军队的)后卫 *adj.* 在后面(或后部)的;向后面(或后部)的 / ~**wards** *adv.* 在后面;向后面 ‖ ~ **admiral** 海军少将 / ~ **guard** 后卫;殿后

rear² [riə] *vt.* 1. 抚养;培养 2. 栽种,培植;饲养 3. 竖起,举起;使(马等)用后腿站起 4. 树立;建立 — *vi.* 1. 高耸之(马等)用后腿站起 2.〔喻〕暴跳 (*up*)

rearm [ˌriːˈɑːm] *vt. & vi.* 重新武装;重新装备 ‖ ~**ament** [ˌriːˈɑːməmənt] *n.*

rearrange [ˌriːəˈreindʒ] *vt.* 重新整理(或分类、安排、布置) — *vi.*【化】(分子)重排

reason [ˈriːzn] *n.* 1. 理由;原因 2. 理智,理性;清醒的头脑(或神志)及道理;情理;明智 4.【逻】理由,前提 5.〔德国古典哲学中的〕理性(与 understanding 知性相对) — *vi.* 1. 推论,推理;思考 2. 评理;劝说 (*with*) — *vt.* 1. 推论,推理 2. 与...评理;劝说 (*out of, into*) 3. 辩论;讨论 ‖ ~ **er** *n.*

reasonable [ˈriːznəbl] *adj.* 1. 合情合理的;有道理的;适当的 2.(价钱)公道的,不贵的 3. 通情达理的;讲道理的;4. 有理智的,有理性的;明智的 ‖ ~**ness** *n.* / **reasonably** *adv.*

reasoning [ˈriːzniŋ] *n.* 1. 推论,推理 2. 评理,讲理 3. 论证,论据 — *adj.* 能推理的

reassure [ˌriːəˈʃuə] *vt.* 1. 使放心,使清除疑虑 2. 再向...保证;再对...进行保险 ‖ **reassurance** *n.*

rebate [ˈriːbeit] *n.*(付款总额的)减少;回

扣;折让 — *vt.* 1. 给予(某一数额的)回扣;给(某人或票据)打折扣 2. 减少;削弱 3. 使变钝 — *vi.* 给予回扣;打折扣

rebel [rɪˈbel] (rebelled; rebelling) *vi.* 1. 造反;反叛;反抗;对抗 (*against*) 2. 嫌恶,反感 — [ˈrebəl] *n.* 1. 造反者;反抗者;反叛者 2.〔美〕〔常作 R-〕(南北战争中的)南军士兵 — [ˈrebəl] *adj.* 1. 造反的;反叛的;反抗的 2. 造反者的;反抗者的;反叛者的

rebellion [rɪˈbeljən] *n.* 1. 造反 2. 叛乱 3. 反抗;对抗

rebellious [rɪˈbeljəs] *adj.* 1. 造反的;反叛的 2. 难对付的;难管束的 3.(疾病等)难治的 ‖ ~**ly** *adv.* / ~**ness** *n.*

rebirth [ˈriːˈbəːθ] *n.* 1. 再生;新生 2. 更新;复兴 3.〔宗〕转世,轮生

reborn [ˈriːˈbɔːn] *adj.* 1. 再生的;新生的 2. 更新的;复兴的

rebound [rɪˈbaund] *vi.* 1. 弹回,跳回 2. 返回;报应 3.(从挫折等中)重新振作;跃起 4.(再)回响 — *vt.* 1. 使弹回,使跳回 2. 使回响 — *n.* 1. 弹回,跳回;返回 2.(篮球的)篮板球(抢得);(足球的)门柱反弹球(抢得);(冰球的)板墙反弹球(抢得) 3. 振作;跃起 4.(情绪的)波动,反应

rebuff [rɪˈbʌf] *n.* 断然的拒绝;冷淡,挫败 — *vt.* 1. 断然拒绝;漠视 2. 挫败;击退

rebuild [ˈriːˈbild] (rebuilt [ˈriːˈbilt]) *vt.* 1. 重建;重新组装;使重新形成 2. 重组;改造 — *vi.* 重建;改建

rebuke [rɪˈbjuːk] *vt. & n.* 指责,非难;训斥

rebus [ˈriːbəs] *n.*(猜词的)画谜

rebut [rɪˈbʌt] (rebutted; rebutting) *vt.* 1. 辩驳;反驳;驳回 2. 揭露;戳穿 3. 抗拒;击退 — *vi.* 辩驳;反驳;驳回 ‖ **rebuttal**

n.

recalcitrant [ri'kælsitrənt] *adj.* **1.** 不服从（上级或规章等）的；不顺从的；执拗的 **2.** 顽抗的；难管束的；难对付的 **3.**（疾病等）难治的 — *n.* 不服从的人；执拗的人，倔强的人 ‖ **recalcitrance** *n.*

recall [ri'kɔːl] *vt.* **1.** 回想，回忆；使回忆 **2.** 叫回，召回 **3.** 收回，撤销；取消；使复活；恢复 — *n.* **1.** 回想，回忆 **2.** 叫回，召回 **3.** 收回，撤销；取消 **4.** 归队令；收操号；【海】（船舰的）召回信号 **5.**（美）（由公民投票对官员的）罢免；罢免权

recant [ri'kænt] *vt.* 宣布放弃（信仰、主张等）；宣布撤回（声明等）— *vi.* **1.** 放弃信仰（或主张等）；撤回声明 **2.** 公开认错

recapitulate [,riːkə'pitjuleit] *vt. & vi.* 扼要重述；摘要说明；概括 ‖ **'reca,pitu'lation** *n.* **1.** 扼要的重述 **2.**【生】重演 **3.**【音】再现部

recapture [,riː'kæptʃə] *vt.* **1.** 重获；夺回，收复 **2.**（政府）征收（利润或收益的超额部分）**3.** 再经历，再体验；恢复 — *n.* **1.** 重获；夺回，收复（指战利品等）**3.**（利润或收益超额部分的）征收 **4.** 重获物；夺回物，收复物

recast [,riː'kɑːst] *vt.* (recast) **1.** 重新铸造；再铸造 **2.** 彻底改动；重做 **3.** 重算，重计 **4.** 重新安排（戏剧等）的角色 — *n.* **1.** 重新铸造（或重做）物 **2.** 经重铸（或重做）的东西

recd.，**rec'd.** *abbr.* received

recede [ri'siːd] *vi.* **1.** 退，退去；退远 **2.** 缩进；向后倾斜 **3.** 收回，撤回（*from*）**4.** 缩减

receipt [ri'siːt] *n.* **1.** 收到 **2.** 收条，收据 **3.** [~s] 收到物（或款项）；收入 **4.** = recipe **5.**（古）税务局 — *vt.* **1.** 开……的

收据；承认收到 **2.** 在……上注明“收讫”（或“付清”）；~ a bill 在账单上签字（或盖章）以表明账款已收讫

receive [ri'siːv] *vt.* **1.** 收到，接到 **2.** 得到，受到 **3.** 接受；接纳；承认 **4.** 接待，接见；欢迎 **5.** 容纳 **6.** 承受；挡住；抵挡 **7.** 听取，受理 **8.** 窝藏（赃物）— *vi.* **1.** 收到；得到；接受 **2.** 接待，会客 **3.**【无】接收 **4.**【宗】领圣餐 **5.**（网球赛等中）接发（过来的）球 ‖ **~d** *adj.* 被普遍接受的；公认的；标准的

receiver [ri'siːvə] *n.* **1.** 收受者；收件人；收款人 **2.** 接待人 **3.**【无】接收机，电话听筒，受话器 **5.**【化】受器；容器 **6.** 窝赃者 **7.**【律】破产管理人；破产事务官 ‖ **~ship** *n.*

recent ['riːsnt] *adj.* **1.** 新近的，最近的；近来的；近代的 **2.** [R-]【地】全新世的 ‖ **~ly** *adv.* / **~ness** *n.*

receptacle [ri'septəkl] *n.* **1.** 容器，贮藏器；贮藏所 **2.**【植】花托；囊托 **3.**【电】插座

reception [ri'sepʃən] *n.* **1.** 接待，接见；欢迎 **2.** 招待会；欢迎会；宴会 **3.** 接受；接纳 **4.**【无】接收；接收力 ‖ **~ist** *n.*（旅馆、照相馆、牙医诊所等的）接待员 ‖ **~ room**，**~ chamber** 接待室，会客室

receptive [ri'septiv] *adj.* **1.** 接受的；接纳的；容纳的 **2.** 有接受能力的；（对新思想等）善于接受的；接受得快的 **3.** 感受的；感官的；感受器的 ‖ **~ly** *adv.* / **~ness, receptivity**[,risep'tiviti] *n.*

receptor [ri'septə] *n.* **1.** 【生】感受器；感受器 **2.** 感受器；接收器

recess [ri'ses] *n.* **1.** 休息，（学校等的）短暂的休假；休会 **2.**（墙壁、山脉等的）凹进处；壁龛 **3.** [常 ~s] 深处，幽深处 **4.**【解】隐窝 — *vt.* **1.** 把……放在隐蔽处 **2.** 使凹进；使有凹进处 — *vi.*（美）休息；休假；休会

recession [ri'seʃən] *n.* 1. 后退;退回;撤回 2. 凹处 3.(工商业的)衰退;(价格的)暴跌 4.【基督教】(做礼拜后牧师和唱诗班的)退场(行列) ‖ ～al *adj.* 1. 后退的,退回的;撤回的 2.〈英〉议会休会期的 *n.*【基督教】退场赞美诗

recessive [ri'sesiv] *adj.* 1. 后退的,退回的;(人、性格等)退隐的,退缩的 2.【语】逆行的;【生】隐性的 — *n.* 1.【生】隐性性状 2.具有隐性性状的生物

recipe ['resipi] *n.* 1.【医】处方(符号℞) 2.烹饪法;食谱;(糕饼等的)调制法 3.诀窍;方法

recipient [ri'sipiənt] *adj.* 接受的;领受的;容纳的,能接受的;善于接受的 — *n.* 接受者;领受者;接受器;容器

reciprocal [ri'siprəkəl] *adj.* 1. 相互的;互惠的;有来有往的;交互的 2. 相应的;相互补足的 3. 相应而相反的 4.【数】倒数的,互反的 — *n.* 1. 互相起作用的(或有互补作用的)事物 2.【数】倒数,互反 ‖ ～ly *adv.*

reciprocate [ri'siprəkeit] *vt.* 1. 使(机件)往复移动 2. 互给;互换 3. 报答,酬答 — *vi.* 1. 往复移动;交换位置 2. 互给;互换 3. 报答,酬答 ‖ reˌcipro'cation *n.*

reciprocity [ˌresi'prɔsiti] *n.* 1. 相互关系;交互作用;相互性;相关性 2. 交换;交流;互惠;互惠主义

recital [ri'saitl] *n.* 1. 背诵;朗诵;当众吟诵 2. 叙述;详述;列举 3.(某作品家作品的或一个人的)演奏会;独奏会;独唱会;音乐(或舞蹈)学员的演出会 4.【律】(契约等中)陈述(或证明)事实的部分

recitation [ˌresi'teiʃən] *n.* 1. 背诵;朗诵;当众吟诵 2. 背诵的诗(或文章等) 3. 叙述;详述;列举 4.〈美〉背书;背诵的功课;口头答问;口头答问课

recite [ri'sait] *vt.* 1. 背诵;朗诵;当众吟诵 2. 叙述;详述;列举 3.【律】书面陈述(事实) 4.〈美〉背(课文);回答(关于课文的提问) ‖ ～r *n.* 背诵者;朗诵者;讲述者

reck [rek] *vi.* 1. 顾虑;介意 2. 有关系,相干 — *vt.* 1. 对……关心;注意 2. 对……有关系,与……相干[注意:reck 是书面语;只用于否定句和疑问句,或与 little 连用]

reckless ['reklis] *adj.* 1. 不注意的;不在乎的;粗心大意的 2. 鲁莽的;妄动的;不顾一切的,不顾后果的 ‖ ～ly *adv.* / ～ness *n.*

reckon ['rekən] *vt.* 1. 计算 2. 认为;把……看作 3. 估计;推断 4.〈主美〉想,料想 — *vi.* 1. 数;计算;算账 2. 估计;推断 3. 指望;依赖(on, upon) 4.〈主美〉想,料想 ‖ ～er *n.* 1. 计算者 2. 帮助计算的东西

reckoning ['rekəniŋ] *n.* 1. 计算;估计;算账 2. 账单 3.(船舶、飞机等的)航迹推算

reclaim [ri'kleim] *vt.* 1. 开垦,开拓 2. 改造;使悔改;感化(犯错误的者、犯罪者等) 3.(从废料或副产品中)回收 — *n.* 改造,感化

re-claim ['riː'kleim] *vt.* 要求收回;要求重得;试图取回

reclamation [ˌreklə'meiʃən] *n.* 1. 开垦,开拓 2. 改造;感化 3. 要求归还;收复 4.(废料等的)再生;回收

recline [ri'klain] *vt.* 使向后靠;使斜倚 — *vi.* 1. 斜倚;躺卧 2.〈喻〉依赖;信赖(on, upon)

recluse [ri'kluːs] *adj.* 隐居的;遁世的;孤寂的 — *n.* 隐士;遁世者

recognition [ˌrekəg'niʃən] *n.* 1. 认出;识

recognizance [ri'kɔgnizəns] *n.* 【律】1. 保证书;具结 2. (交付法院的)保证金;保释金;抵押金

recognize ['rekəgnaiz] *vt.* 1. 认出;识别;辨认 2. 承认 3. 清楚地认识到;自认 4. 公认;赏识 5. 招呼(某人)以示相识 6. 认可;准许(某人)发言 — *vi.* 【律】具结 ‖ **recognizable** *adj.*

recoil [ri'kɔil] *vi.* 1. 撤退,后退;退缩,畏缩 2. 跳回,弹回;产生反作用;(枪等)产生后坐力,反冲 3. 报应(*on, upon*) — *n.* 1. 撤退,后退;退缩,畏缩 2. 跳回,弹回;反作用;(枪等)的后坐(力);后坐距离,反冲

recollect [,rekə'lekt] *vt.* 1. 回忆,追忆;想起 2. [~ oneself]使(自己)想起一时忘掉的事 — *vi.* 回忆,追忆

re-collect [,ri:kə'lekt] *v.* 1. 再集合,重新集合 2. 恢复;振作(精神等);使(自己)镇定 — *vi.* 再集合,重新集合

recollection [,rekə'lekʃən] *n.* 1. 回忆,追忆;记忆力 2. [常~s]回忆起的事物;往事;回忆录 3. 心境平静【宗】灵修默想

recommend [,rekə'mend] *vt.* 1. 推荐,介绍 2. 劝告,建议 3. 使成为可取,使受欢迎 4. 托,托付:~ a child to sb. (to sb.'s care)把小孩托给某人(托某人照顾)

recommendation [,rekəmen'deiʃən] *n.* 1. 推荐,介绍 2. 推荐书,介绍信;推荐的话 3. 可取之处(指品质、才能等) 4. 劝告

recompense ['rekəmpens] *vt.* 1. 酬报;回报(赏或罚) 2. 赔偿;补偿 — *n.* 1. 报酬;报偿 2. 赔偿金,赔偿;补偿

recon [ri'kɔn] *n.* 侦察(= reconnaissance)

reconcile ['rekənsail] *vt.* 1. 使和解;使复

交;使和好 2. 调解,调停;调和 3. 使和谐;使一致;使符合 4. 使顺从(于),使听从(于);使甘心(于)(*to*) 5. (造船时)使(木架)妥贴地接合 6.【宗】使(遭亵渎的神殿等)恢复洁净 ‖ **reconcilable** *adj.*

reconciliation [,rekənsili'eiʃən] *n.* 1. 和解;复交;(重新)和好 2. 调解,调停 3. 和谐;一致 4. 甘愿;顺从

recondite [ri'kɔndait, 'rekəndait] *adj.* 1. 深奥的;难解的;晦涩的 2. 很少人知道的;隐秘的

recondition [,ri:kən'diʃən] *vt.* 1. 修理;修复;修整 2. 改革,改善;纠正

reconfirm ['ri:kən'fə:m] *vt.* 1. 使确实;再确定 2. 再确认(飞机坐位等的预定)

reconnaissance [ri'kɔnisəns] *n.* 1. 侦察 2. 勘察;踏勘;草测 3. 侦察队 4. 侦察车(= ~ car)

reconnoitre, reconnoiter [,rekə'nɔitə] *vt. & vi.* 1. 侦察;搜索 2. 勘察;踏勘

reconsider ['ri:kən'sidə] *vt.* 重新考虑;重新审议 — *vi.* 重新考虑 ‖ **~ation** ['ri:kənsidə'reiʃən] *n.*

reconstruct ['ri:kən'strʌkt] *vt.* 1. 重建;再建 2. 修复 3. (根据遗迹等)重新构成(原来事物)的形象

reconstruction ['ri:kən'strʌkʃən] *n.* 1. 重建;再建 2. [R-](美国南北战争后)南部的重建 3. 重建物;(凭遗迹等)重新构成(或复制)的事物

record ['rekɔd] *n.* 1. 记录,记载;前科记录 2. 履历;经历 3. 案卷,档案;审判记录;公判录 4. 最高纪录,最好成绩 5. 唱片,录了音的磁带 — [ri'kɔ:d] *vt.* 1. 记录,记载 2. 标明;(仪器等)在刻度上指示 3. 将(声音、图像等)录下 — *vi.* 1. 进行录音 2. 被录音 — *adj.* 创纪录的

recorder [ri'kɔːdə] *n.* 1. 记录者；记录员 2. 录音机；记录器；印码电机机 3. (英) (经大法官推荐、由资深律师兼任的) 刑事法院法官 4. 竖笛

recording [ri'kɔːdiŋ] *n.* 1. 记录；录音 2. 唱片；录了音的磁带 3. 录制(的节目)

recount[1] [ri'kaunt] *vt.* 1. 详细叙述，描述 2. 列举

recount[2] ['riː'kaunt] *vt.* 重新计算；再数 — *n.* 重计

recoup [ri'kuːp] *vt.* 1. 【律】扣除，赔偿；补偿 2. 偿还 3. 重获 — *vi.* 补偿损失

recourse [ri'kɔːs] *n.* 1. 求助，求援 2. 求助的对象；力量的源泉 3. 【律】追索权

recover [ri'kʌvə] *vt.* 1. 重新获得，重新得到 2. 恢复；使恢复原状；使(身体)复原 3. 挽回；弥补 4. (根据法律程序)取得；获得 5. 使(物)重新有用；使(人)改过自新 6. 〈罕〉到达 — *vi.* 1. 痊愈，复原；恢复健康 2. 回复原来的防御(或进攻)姿势(指击剑、划船等) 【律】胜诉 ‖ ~able *adj.*

re-cover ['riː'kʌvə] *vt.* 1. 再盖；重新盖 2. 给…换新面子

recovery [ri'kʌvəri] *n.* 1. 重获；复得 2. 恢复，痊愈；恢复原状 3. 恢复所需的时间；恢复期 4.(击剑、划船等)防御(或预备)姿势的回复

recreant ['rekriənt] *adj.* 1. 讨饶的；怯懦的 2. 不忠的；叛逆的，变节的 — *n.* 1. 懦夫，胆小鬼 2. 背叛者，变节者

recreation [ˌrekri'eiʃən] *n.* 消遣，娱乐；娱乐活动 ‖ ~al *adj.* 娱乐的

recriminate [ri'krimineit] *vi.* & *vt.* 反责，反(控)诉 ‖ recrimi'nation *n.* /recriminatory[ri'krimənətəri] *adj.*

recrudesce [ˌriːkruː'des] *vi.* (病痛)复发；(内乱等)再次爆发 ‖ ~nce *n.* /~nt

adj.

recruit [ri'kruːt] *vt.* 1. 征募(新兵)；吸收(新成员) 2.(增加人员)充实(部队等) 3. 补充 4. 使恢复；使复原 — *vi.* 1. 征募新兵；吸收新成员 2. 得到补充 3. 使复健康，复原 — *n.* 1. 新兵；新成员；新手；(英)陆军(或海军陆战队)新兵 2. 补给品 ‖ ~ er *n.* 征兵人员 /~ment *n.* 1. 征兵征招；新成员的补充 2. 征兵数量 2. 补充，充实 3. 恢复健康，复原

rectangle ['rektæŋgl] *n.* 矩形，长方形

rectangular [rek'tæŋgjulə] *adj.* 矩形的，长方形的；成直角的

rectification [ˌrektifi'keiʃən] *n.* 1. 纠正，矫正；整顿 2. 调整；校正 3.【化】精馏 4.【电】整流 5.【数】求长(法)

rectify ['rektifai] *vt.* 1. 纠正，矫正；整顿 2. 调整；校正 3.【化】精馏 4.【电】(流)；把(射频)变成音频 5.【数】求(曲线)的长度 ‖ rectifiable *adj.* 1. 可纠正的；可调整的 2.【化】可精馏的 3.【数】(曲线)可求长的 /rectifier *n.* 1. 纠正(或调整)的人；矫正器 2.【化】精馏器 3.【电】整流器

rectilineal [ˌrekti'liniəl] , **rectilinear** [ˌrekti'liniə] *adj.* 1. 直线的；直线运动的 2. 用直线的；直线组成的 3. (英国中世纪哥特式建筑)以垂直线条为特征的，垂直式的

rectitis [rek'taitis] *n.*【医】直肠炎

rectitude ['rektitjuːd] *n.* 1. 正直，严正 2.(判断、程序等)的正确 3. 直，笔直

rector ['rektə] *n.* 1.(英国国教、天主教等的教区长 2.(修道院、宗教学校等的)院长；校长 3.(某些学校、学院、大学的)校长 4. 主任；负责人 ‖ ~ship *n.* 教区长(或宗教学校校长等)的职位 /~y *n.*

rectum ['rektəm] ([复] **recta** ['rektə]) *n.* 【解】直肠

recumbent [ri'kʌmbənt] *adj.* 1. 躺着的；斜靠的 2.【生】横卧的，斜倚的 3. 休息着的；不活动的

recuperate [ri'kju:pəreit] *vt.* 1. 使复原；恢复（健康、元气等）2. 挽回，弥补（损失等）— *vi.* 1. 复原，恢复健康（或元气）2. 弥补损失 ‖ **re;cupe'ration** *n.* 1. 复原，恢复；挽回，弥补 2.【化】同流换热（法）

recur [ri'kə:] (recurred; recurring) *vi.* 1. 再发生；（疾病等）复发，重新提起（to）3.（往事等）重新浮现（to）4. 依赖；借助于（to）5.【数】递归，循环

recurrence [ri'kʌrəns] *n.* 1. 再发生；复发 2. 重新提起 3.（往事等）的重新浮现 4.【数】递归，循环

recurrent [ri'kʌrənt] *adj.* 1. 再发的；经常发生的；周期性发生的 2.【解】（神经、血管等）返（回）的 ‖ **~ly** *adv.* ‖ **~ fever** 【医】回归热

recurve [ri'kə:v] *vt.* 使反弯，使向后弯 — *vi.* 反向后弯；（风、水流等）折回

recycle [,ri:'saikl] *vt. & vi.* （使）再循环；回收利用

red [red] *adj.* 1. 红色的 2.【也作 R-】共产党领导的，赤色的，红色的 3. 胀红的；充血的 4. 赤热的 5. 流血的，暴力的；火烧的 6. 有红头发的 7. 有微红色的 8.〈英〉英国在地图上常用红色标示 — *n.* 1. 红色 2. 红颜料；红染料 3.【也作 R-】赤色分子 4.【常 R-】〈北美〉印第安人 5. 红色物（如红衣、红布、红棋子、红球等）6. 赤字，负债，亏损 7.〈美俚〉一分钱 8.〈英俚〉红舰队（17世纪英国红、白、蓝三种舰队之一）‖ **blood cell** 红血球，红细胞 /'~·'blooded

adj. 1.（人）充满活力的；壮壮的 2.（小说等）情节丰富的；紧张的 /'~ breast *n.*【动】欧鸲，红胸鸟 /'~·cap *n.* 1.〈美〉（车站等的）搬运工，红帽子 2.〈英口〉宪兵 3.〈欧洲产〉红额金翅雀 / ~ carpet 红地毯；[the ~ carpet]隆重的接待（或欢迎）/'~·'carpet *adj.* 铺红地毯的；隆重的 / ~ cent（美口）一分钱：not worth a ~ cent 一文不值/I don't care a ~ cent 我一点也不在乎 /'~ coat *n.*【常 R-】〈美国独立战争时期的〉英国兵 / ~ corpuscle = ~ cell / Red Crescent（土耳其等国的相当于红十字会的）红新月会 / Red Cross 红十字（会）/ ~ deer【动】赤鹿 /'~·'handed *adj.* 1. 双手沾满鲜血的 2. 正在作案的 /'~·head *n.* 1. 红头发的人 2. 红头啄鸟 /'~ herring 1. 熏鲱 2. 转移注意力的话（或事物）/'~·'hot *adj.* 1. 赤热的，炽热的 2. 非常恼怒的；十分激动的 3.〈新闻〉新的 ‖ **~ ·letter** *adj.* (日历上)用红字标明的；可纪念的；喜庆的 / ~·'light district（妓院集中的）红灯区 / Red Sea 红海（亚洲、非洲之间）/'~·skin *n.*（贬）〈北美〉印第安人，红皮人 / Red Square（又称 莫斯科的）红场 / ~ tape 官样文章，繁文缛节 / ~·wing blackbird *n.* 【动】红翅黑鹂 /'~·wood *n.* 1. 红杉 2. 红树，红木材

redden ['redn] *vt.* 使红 — *vi.* 变红；脸红

reddish ['redif] *adj.* 带红色的，微红的

redeem [ri'di:m] *vt.* 1. 买回；赎回 2. 挽获；挽回 3. 偿还，还清 4. 赎救，解救，拯救 5.【宗】救赎 6. 履行（诺言等）6. 补偿；补救 7. 改善；修复 8. 兑换（纸币）成硬币；变卖（证券）为现款 ‖ **~able** *adj.*

redeemer [ri'di:mə] *n.* 1. 赎回者；赎买者

2. 挽回者;偿还者;补救者 3.(诺言等的)履行者 4. 赎救者,拯救者;[the R-] 救世主,耶稣基督

redemption [rɪ'dempʃən] *n.* 1. 买回;赎回;赎买 2. 重获;恢复;挽回 3. 偿还,还清 4. 赎救,拯救;赎身;[宗]赎罪 5. 履行 6. 补偿;补救;补救的事物 7. 改善;修复 8.(纸币等的)兑成硬币;(证券的)变卖兑现款 9.(主英)(对地位、资格的)出钱购买

redirect ['riːdɪ'rekt] *vt.* 1. 使改方向;使改道 2. 更改(信件等)上的地址(或姓名)

rediscover ['riːdɪs'kʌvə] *vt.* 再发现,重新发现

redlining ['redlaɪnɪŋ] *n.*(银行或保险商等出于风险对旧城区等的)拒绝贷款(或承保)

redo ['riː'duː] *vt.* (redid ['riː'dɪd]; redone ['riː'dʌn]) *vt.* 1. 再做;重做;重演 2. 重新装饰

redolent ['redəulənt] *adj.* 1. 芬芳的,馥郁的 2. 有...气味的 3. 有...气息的;使人联想(或回想)起...的(*of*) ‖ **redolence** *n.* / ~**ly** *adv.*

redouble [riː'dʌbl] *vt.* 1. 使再加倍;进一步加强 2.(桥牌中)将(对方加倍的牌)再加倍 2.(桥牌中)将(对方加倍的牌)再加倍 — *vi.* 1. 再加倍;倍增;进一步加强 2. 翻两番,增加到四倍 3.(桥牌中将对方加倍的牌)再加倍

redoubt [rɪ'daut] *n.* 1. 棱堡,多面堡 2. 防御工事;防护性障碍物 3. 安全退避处;据点

redoubtable [rɪ'dautəbl] *adj.* 1. 可怕的,厉害的,令人惊骇的 2. 可敬畏的 3. 著名的;杰出的

redound [rɪ'daund] *vi.* 1. 起作用,产生影响;促进;有助于(*to*) 2. 返回到

(*on, upon*)

redress [rɪ'dres] *vt.* 1. 纠正,改正,矫正 2. 调整 3. 赔偿;补偿 — *n.* 1. 纠正,改正,矫正 2. 调整 3. 赔偿;补偿 4. 责罚

reduce [rɪ'djuːs] *vt.* 1. 减少;减小;缩减 2. 使处于(某种状态)(*to*);使艰难(指处境);[常用被动语态]迫使(*to*) 3. 使化为,使变为(*to*) 4. 降服;攻陷 5. 使降级;使降职 6. 把...合并;把...合并(为)(*to*) 7. 把...弄碎;把...分解;把...分析 8. 使变弱;使变瘦 9. 把(油漆)调稀 10. 把...折合(成较小单位)(*to*) 11.[数]简化,约化 12.[化]使还原 13.[医]使(脱臼)还白;使(骨折)复位 14.[化]从(矿物)中蒸去轻质油;冶炼 15.[生]使(细胞)减数分裂 16.[摄]减薄(底片) 17.[语]使(重读音)弱化 — *vi.* 1. 减少;减小;缩减 2. 变瘦,减轻体重 3. 归纳为;化为(*to*) 4.[生]减数分裂

reduction [rɪ'dʌkʃən] *n.* 1. 减少;减小;缩减 2. 缩小了的东西(如өle图、降低的价格等);缩减的女型 3. 变形;变化 4. 降服;攻陷 5. 降级;降职 6. 归纳;归并 7. 弄碎;分解 8. 折合 9.[数]简化,约化 10.[化]还原(作用) 11.[生]减数分裂 12. 减速:a ~ gear 减速齿轮 13.[摄]减薄

redundant [rɪ'dʌndənt] *adj.* 1. 过多的,过剩的,多余的(常用来指劳动力、工作人员等);累赘的;冗长的 2. 丰盛的,丰富的 ‖ **redundance, redundancy** *n.* 1. 过多,多余;累赘;冗长 2. 多余的东西;多余部分 3.[计]冗余;冗余码;冗余位 4. 大量,丰富 / ~**ly** *adv.*

reduplicate [rɪ'djuːplɪkeɪt] *vt.* 1. 重复;使加倍 2.[语]使(字母、音节)重叠 — *vi.* 重复 [rɪ'djuːplɪkɪt, rɪ'djuːplɪkeɪt] *adj.*

1. 重复的;加倍的 2.【植】外向镶合状的

reed [riːd] *n.* 1. 芦苇;芦秆;〔总称〕芦丛 2.[~s](盖屋顶用的)干芦苇;(英)(盖屋顶用的)麦秸 3. 不可依靠的人(或物) 4. 芦笛;象征田园诗的芦笛 5.【音】簧片;[~s](簧或管)乐器 6.[诗]箭 7.【建】小凸嵌线 8.【纺】筘,钢筘 — *vt.* 1. 用芦苇(或茅草)盖(屋顶) 2.【建】用小凸嵌线表示 3. 在(乐器)上装簧片 ‖ ~ **instrument** 簧(或管)乐器 / ~ **mace**(英)【植】香蒲 / ~ **pipe** 牧笛;簧管

reef [riːf] *n.* 1. 礁;礁脉;〈喻〉暗礁 2. 矿脉

reefer[1] ['riːfə] *n.* 1. 缩帆人 2.〈俚〉海军学校学员 3. 双排扣扣身上衣;女式紧身双排扣上衣 4. 缩帆结,平结,方结 5.〈美俚〉大麻卷烟

reefer[2] ['riːfə] *n.*〈美〉 1. 冰箱 2. 冷藏室;冷藏车:冷藏船

reek [riːk] *n.* 1. 烟 2. 水蒸气;雾 3. 臭气;臭烟味 — *vi.* 1. 冒烟;冒水蒸气(或雾气) 2. 发臭气,充满臭气;具有强烈的气息(of, with) 3. 烟气等蒸发 — *vt.* 1. 用烟(或水蒸气)熏 2. 散发(烟,水汽等);发出...的气息

reel[1] [riːl] *n.* 1.(电线、棉纱等的)绕轴,卷筒;卷线架等;(钓竿上的)绕线轮;(英)(缠绕机线团的)木芯 2.(电影胶片的)一卷盘,水龙带等的)卷盘 3.(电线、棉纱等的)一卷;(电影胶片、磁带等的)一卷 4.(转动的)烘衣架 — *vt.* 1. 卷,绕(in) 2.(从卷轴等上)放出(out);抽出(off) 3.(卷着)拉起(in, up) 4. 缠(丝)(off) 5. 滔滔不绝地说(或背诵);流畅地写(off) — *vi.* 卷,绕;摇绕;收绕钓丝 ‖ ~ **er** *n.* 1. 卷(或绕)的人;摇纱工;缫丝工 2. 卷(或绕)的器具;卷取机,矫直机 3.[用以构成复合词]...

(卷)本电影影片:a two-~ er 一部2本电影

reel[2] [riːl] *vi.* 1. 旋转;似在旋转 2. 眩晕;震颤 3. 摇晃,摇摆;踉跄 4. 倒退,退缩 5. 猖獗;骚乱 — *vt.* 使旋转;使眩晕;使摇晃 — *n.* 1. 旋转;摇晃 2. 踉跄;踉跄的步伐

reel[3] [riːl] *n.* 1. 里尔舞(曲)(轻快的苏格兰双人舞) 2.(美国)弗吉尼亚里尔舞(曲) — *vi.* 跳里尔舞

reelect ['riːi'lekt] *vt.* 重选;改选 ‖ ~**ion** *n.*

reenter ['riː'entə] *vt.* 1. 再进入,重返 2.【律】收回(租出的土地或房屋) 3. 再加入,重新加入 4. 再记入;重新登记 5. 进刀加深(雕版上的刻线等);给印刷物加印色彩 — *vi.* 1. 再进入,重返 2.【律】收回租出的土地(或房屋) 3.(角等)凹入

reentry [riː'entri] *n.* 1. 再进入;重新入场;再让入,再登 2.【字】重返大气层 3.【律】(业主对租出的土地或房屋的)收回 4.(能夺回出牌权的)再进张(大牌)

reestablish ['riːis'tæbliʃ] *vt.* 1.(在原址或按原状)重建;重新设立(或创办) 2. 另建;另行安置

reeve[1] [riːv] (rove[rəuv]或 reeved) *vt.* 1. 穿(绳索)(用绳索)穿过 2. 把...缚住 3.(船等)穿过(浮冰或浅滩之间) — *vi.*(绳索等)穿过

reeve[2] [riːv] *n.* 1.【英史】城镇(或地区)长官,地方官 2.【英史】采邑管理人 3. 地方行政官;[加]加拿大村镇议会的(议长

reexamine ['riːig'zæmin] *vt.* 1. 再考;复试 2. 再调查,再检查;再审查(问 ‖ **reexamination** 'riːigˌzæmi'neiʃən] *n.*

ref [ref] *n.* (reffed; reffing) *vt. & vi.*〈美俚〉= referee

refection [rɪ'fekʃən] *n.* 1.(通过饮食等的)提神；恢复体力；解除饥渴 2. 饮食；茶点；点心；小吃；便餐

refectory [rɪ'fektərɪ] *n.*(修道院、神学院等的)食堂，餐厅

refer [rɪ'fɜː] (referred; referring [rɪ'fɜːrɪŋ]) *vt.* 1. 把…归诸(或诿诸)；认为…起源(于)(to) 2. 把…归类(于)；把…归属(于)(to) 3. 把…提交；把…委托(to) 4. 指点；使求助于；使向…请教(to) — *vi.* 1. 谈到，提到；涉及，有关(to) 2. 查阅；参考；查询，打听(to) ‖ ~**able** *adj.* 可归诸的；与…有关的

referee [refə'riː] *n.* 1. 受委托者；受托处理者；仲裁人，公断人；(足球、拳击等等的)裁判员 2.[律](受法院委托的)鉴定人 — *vt. & vi.* (为…)担任裁判员；(为…)担任仲裁人；审阅，鉴定

reference [ˈrefərəns] *n.* 1. 参考 2. 出处；参照；参考书目 3. 参照符号 4. 提及；涉及 5. 关系；关联 6. 提交；委托 7. 职权范围 8.(关于品行、能力等的)证明；介绍；证明书；介绍信；介绍人 9.(关于品行、能力等的)查询，了解 — *vt.* 给(书等)加上参考书目(或注明资料来源) ‖ ~ **book** 1. 参考用的工具书(如词典、地图册等) 2.(图书馆中供室内阅览的)参考书

referendum [refə'rendəm] ([复] referenda [refə'rendə]或 referendums) *n.* 1.(关于政治措施、法律等的)公民投票；公民投票权；公民所投的票；复决投票，复决权 2.(外交官对本国政府的)请示书

referral [rɪ'fɜːrəl] *n.* 1. 参考；查阅 2.(动议等的)提交仲裁；推荐，介绍；(向专科医生的)转诊介绍 3. 被介绍(或推荐)人；转诊病人

refill [riː'fɪl] *vt. & vi.* 再装满；再灌满 —

['riːfɪl, riː'fɪl] *n.* 再供给的东西；替换物

refine [rɪ'faɪn] *vt.* 1. 精炼；提纯；精制 2. 提去(杂质等)(out, away) 3. 使精练，使优美；使文雅(指语言、文体、仪态等) — *vi.* 1. 精炼；精制 2. 变得优雅(或精练) 3. 琢磨，推敲(on, upon) ‖ ~ *r n.* 1. 精炼者；精制者 2. 精制机 3. 精研机 4. 匀料机；匀浆机

refined [rɪ'faɪnd] *adj.* 1. 精练的；精制的 2. 优美的；文雅的；有教养的 3. 精妙的；精确的；精细的；过于讲究的

refinement [rɪ'faɪnmənt] *n.* 1. 精炼；提纯；精制 2. 优美；文雅；有教养 3. 精心的改进；为了改进的设计(或装置)；精心的安排；巧妙的发挥 4. 精确；精细；精致；细腻

refinery [rɪ'faɪnərɪ] *n.* 精炼厂；提炼厂

refinish [riː'fɪnɪʃ] *vt.* 整修(家具、金属等)的表面

refit [riː'fɪt] (refitted; refitting) *vt. & vi.* 整修；重新装配；改装 — ['riːfɪt] *n.* 整修；重新装配；改装

reflect [rɪ'flekt] *vt.* 1. 反射(光、热、声音等)；照出，映出 2. 反映；表明，显示 3. 带来，招致(on, upon) 4. 考虑；经深思后认识到 5. 回到；弹回 6. 折转(纸角等) — *vi.* 1. 反射；映出 2. 反射光(或热、声音等) 3. 考虑；沉思；反省(on, upon) 4. 丢脸；责备，指摘；怀疑(on, upon)

reflection [rɪ'flekʃən] *n.* 1. 反射；反照 2.(指言行、思想等方面)酷似的人(或物) 3. 反映 4. 思考；考虑；沉思；反省 5. 想法；见解 6. 丢脸，羞难；责难(或丢脸)的话；丢脸的行为 7.[生]反射(作用)

reflective [rɪ'flektɪv] *adj.* 1. 反射的；反映的 2. 思考的；沉思的 3.(罕)【语】反身的

reflector [ri'flektə] n. 1. 反射器;反射镜;反射物;【核】反射层 2. 反射望远镜 3. 反映者;反映物

reflex ['ri:fleks] n. 1. 反射 2. 反射光;反射热 3. 映象;倒影;酷似物;复制品 4. 隐映5.【美术作品中由明面反射到暗面的]反射光 6.【生】反射(作用);[~es]反应能力 7. 习惯性思维(或行为)方式 — adj. 1. 反射的 2. 折转的;折回的 3. 内省的,反省的 4. 反作用的 5.[无]来复的,回复的 6.【数】优角的 — [ri'fleks] vt. 1. 把...折转;把...折回 2. 使返流反射过程 ∥ ~ camera 反射式照相机

reflexion [ri'flekʃən] n. = reflection

reflexive [ri'fleksiv] adj. 1. 反射的,折转的 2. 内省的,反省的 3.【语】反身的;a ~ pronoun 反身代词(如 one-self)/a ~ verb 反身动词(如 "He hurt himself."中的 hurt)— n.【语】反身代词;反身动词

reflux ['ri:flʌks] n. 倒流,逆流,回流;退潮

reforest [ri:'fɔrist] vt. 在(采伐后的林区等)重新造林 ∥ ~**re're'station** n. 重新造林

reform [ri'fɔːm] vt. 1. 改革,革新 2. 改良3. 改造 4. 革除(弊端等) 5.【化】重整(油、气) — vi. 1. 改过,改邪归正 — n. 1.(政治、社会等方面的)改革,改良 2. 改过,自新 ∥ ~ ation [ˌrefə'meiʃən] n. 1. 改革,改良;革新 2.(罪犯等的)改过自新 3.[the R-](十六世纪欧洲的)宗教改革/~atory n.(少年罪犯等的)教养院,管教所 adj. 改革的,革新的/~ism n. 改良主义/~ist n. 改良主义者 adj. 改良主义的 ∥ ~ school 少年犯管教所

reformer [ri'fɔːmə] n. 1. 改革者,革新者 2. 改良者 3.[R-](十六世纪欧洲的)基督教改革运动的领袖 4.[英史](1831-1832 年的)(议会)改革论者

refract [ri'frækt] vt. 1. 使折射 2. 测定...的屈光度;对...验光 ∥ ~able adj.

refraction [ri'frækʃən] n. 1. 折射(作用);折射度 2.(对眼睛的)屈光度测定

refractive [ri'fræktiv] adj. 1. 折射的;折射力的 2. 与折射有关的;折射引起(或造成)的 ∥ ~ly adv. / ~ness n. / refractivity [ˌri:fræk'tiviti] n.

refractory [ri'fræktəri] adj. 1. 倔强的,难驾驭的,执拗的 2. 耐火的;耐熔的 3. 难医的,难治疗的(肌体组织)不起反应的,麻木的 4. 能抵抗疾病(或病菌)的 — n. 1. 倔强的人;难驾驭的东西2. 耐火材料;耐熔物质 ∥ **refractorily** adv. / **refractoriness** n.

refrain[1] [ri'frein] vi. 忍住;抑制;制止;戒除(from) — vt.〈古〉忍住;抑制;制止

refrain[2] [ri'frein] n.(诗歌或乐曲的)叠句;副歌

refresh [ri'freʃ] vt. 1. 使清新;使清凉 2.(以食物、睡眠等)恢复精力恢复提神振作 3. 使更新;使得到补充;使恢复4. 使(脱水蔬菜等)吸水返鲜 — vi. 1. 恢复精神;重新振作 2. 吃点心;喝饮料 3. 补充(或装上)供应品

refresher [ri'freʃə] n. 1. 提神物 2. 使恢复记忆的事物 3.〈英〉(诉讼延长时给律师的)额外佣金 4.〈口〉饮料;点心5. 复习(课程);补习(材料)(学术、科技方面的)最新动态介绍

refreshing [ri'freʃiŋ] adj. 1. 提神的;凉爽的;清凉的 2. 给人新鲜感的,使人耳目一新(或喜欢)的 ∥ ~ly adv.

refreshment [ri'freʃmənt] n. 1.(精力或精神上的)恢复;爽快 2. 使提神的事物(如食物、休息等) 3.[常~s]茶点;点

心;便餐;饮料 ‖ ～ **car** (列车上)供应
点心与饮料等的车厢 /～ **room** (车站
等处的)茶点室,小吃部

refrigerant [ri'fridʒərənt] *adj.* **1.** 致冷的,
冷却的 **2.** 退热的;使清凉的 — *n.* **1.**
致冷剂,冷冻剂 **2.** 退热药;清凉剂

refrigerate [ri'fridʒəreit] *vt.* **1.** 使冷,使凉
2. 冷冻,冷藏(食物等)

refrigeration [ri,fridʒə'reiʃn] *n.* 冷藏;致
冷,制冷

refrigerator [ri'fridʒəreitə] *n.* 冰箱,冷藏
室,冷藏库;冷凝装置

refuel ['ri:'fjuəl] (refuel(l)ed; refuel(l)ing)
vt. 给…加燃料 — *vi.* 加燃料

refuge ['refju:dʒ] *n.* **1.** 避难;庇护 **2.** 避难
所;庇护者 **3.** 安全地带;隐蔽处;(街
道中心供人避车等的)安全岛 **4.** 权宜
之计 **5.** 慰藉

refugee [,refju'dʒi:] *n.* 避难者;流亡者;难
民

refulgence [ri'fʌldʒəns] *n.* 光辉,灿烂 ‖
refulgent *adj.*

refund [ri:'fʌnd] *vt & vi.* 退还,归还,偿还
— ['ri:fʌnd] *n.* **1.** 归还,偿还 **2.** 退款;
偿还金额

refurbish ['ri:'fə:biʃ] *vt.* **1.** 重新磨光;重
新擦亮 **2.** 再刷新;整修

refusal [ri'fju:zəl] *n.* **1.** 拒绝 **2.** 优先取舍
权(的选择)

refuse[1] [ri'fju:z] *vt.* **1.** 拒绝;拒受;拒给;
不肯 **2.** (马)拒绝跳越(障碍物) **3.** (纸
牌戏中)跟不出(同花色的牌) — *vi.*
1. 拒绝 **2.** (马)拒绝跳越障碍物 **3.** (纸
牌戏中)跟不出同花色 ‖ ～ **r** *n.* **1.** 拒
绝者 **2.** 不肯跳越障碍物的马

refuse[2] ['refju:s] *n.* 废料;废物;渣滓;垃圾
— *adj.* 扔掉的;无用的

refute [ri'fju:t] *vt.* **1.** 驳斥,反驳,驳倒 ‖

refutable *adj.* /,refu'tation *n.*

reg. *abbr.* **1.** regent **2.** regiment **3.** region
4. register **5.** registered **6.** regular
7. regulation

regain [ri'gein] *vt.* **1.** 收回;复得;恢复(健
康、原职等) **2.** 重到;回到(故乡等)

regal ['ri:gl] *adj.* **1.** 国王的,王室的 **2.**
庄严的;豪华的 ‖ -**ly** *adv.*

regale [ri'geil] *vt.* **1.** 盛情招待;款待 **2.**
[～ oneself]使(尽情地)吃喝;使享用
(*with*, *on*) **3.** 使快乐,使喜悦 — *vi.*
(讲究)吃喝;享用(*on*) — *n.* 盛宴;佳
肴(饮食方面的)款待;一份食物(或
饮料)

regalia [ri'geiliə][复] *n.* **1.** 王室的特权;
王权 **2.** 王位(或王权)标志(如王冠、
权杖等) **3.** (等级、社团等的)标记;徽
章 **4.** 华丽的服饰

regard [ri'gɑ:d] *vt.* **1.** 把…看作;把…认
为(*as*) **2.** [主要用于否定句]注重;注
意;考虑 **3.** 注视,凝视;打量;看待 **4.**
尊敬,尊重 **5.** 与…有关 — *vi.* **1.** 注
视 **2.** 注重;注意 — *n.* **1.** 注重;注意;
考虑;关注 **2.** 注视,凝视 **3.** 尊敬,尊
重;敬意 **4.** 关系 **5.** [～s]问候,致意 **6.**
理由;动机

regardful [ri'gɑ:dful] *adj.* **1.** 留心的,注意
的,关心的(*of*) **2.** 恭敬的,表示尊敬的
(*for*)

regarding [ri'gɑ:diŋ] *prep.* 关于

regardless [ri'gɑ:dlis] *adj.* 不留心的,不注
意的;不关心的 — *adv.* **1.** 〈口〉不顾一
切地,不管怎样地,无论如何 **2.** 〈俚〉不
惜花费地

regatta [ri'gætə] *n.* 划船比赛;赛船会

regd. *abbr.* registered

regenerate [ri'dʒenəreit] *vt.* **1.** (精神上)使
新生;(道德上)使提高 **2.** 使获得新力
量;使恢复原来的力量(或性质) **3.** [化]

【计】【生】使再生；～ a battery 将电池重新充电 /a workshop for *regenerating* waste oil 废油再生车间 /～d rubber 再生橡胶 3. 改革，更新（社会、组织等）4. 重新生出；更生：The lizard can ～ its lost tail 蜥蜴能重新长出失去的尾巴。5.【机】使回热 — *vi.* 新生；再生；更新更生 — [ri'dʒenərit] *adj.* 新生的；再生的；更新的生物 ‖

regeneration [ri,dʒenə'reiʃən] *n.* 1. 新生；再生；更新；更生 2.【计】【化】再生 3.【机】回热

regenerative [ri'dʒenəreitiv] *adj.* 1. 新生的；(能)再生的；更新的；更生的；复兴的 2. (机器等)再生(式)的；蓄热的，回热的

regent ['ri:dʒənt] *n.* 1. 摄政者 2.〈古〉统治者；总督 3.〈美〉(州立大学的)评议员；(大学等董事会的)董事 — *adj.* 1. [用在名词后]摄政的 2.〈古〉统治的 ‖ **regency** n.

regime, régime [rei'ʒim] *n.* 1. 政体；政权；统治(方式) 2. 社会制度 3. 生活规则、饮食起居制度，养生法；常规强化训练课

regimen ['redʒimen] *n.* 1.〈古〉政体；政权；统治(方式)；社会制度 2. 饮食起居制度，养生法，疗程；常规强化训练课 3.【语】支配；(一个词对另一词的格或语气的)影响 4.(河流、冰川等)自然现象的特征；有规则的进程

regiment ['redʒimənt] *n.* 1.【军】团 2. 一大群；大量 3.〈罕〉统治；管辖 — ['redʒiment] *vt.* 1.【军】把…编成团 2. 把…编成队 3. 严格地组织；管辖 ‖ ～**al** [,redʒi'mentl] *adj.* 【军】团的 ‖ [～s] 团队制服；军装 /～**ation** [,redʒimen'teiʃən] *n.* 1.【军】编团 2. 编组；组织；管辖

region ['ri:dʒən] *n.* 1. 地区，地带；行政区 2.【解】区，部(位) 3.(艺术、科学的)领域，范围 4.(动植物地理学的)区 5.(大气、海水等的)层

regional ['ri:dʒənl] *adj.* 1. 地区的；局部的 2. 整个地区的 ‖ ～ly *adv.*

register ['redʒistə] *n.* 1. 登记；注册；(邮件的)挂号 2. 登记簿；注册簿；花名册；登记员；注册员 3. 登记项目 4. 登记项目 5.(自动)记录器；记数器；【计】存储器；自动记录的数 6. 通风装置；调温装置；节气门 7.【音】音区，声区；音栓 8.【印】(纸张正反面的，彩色印刷等的)套准 9.【摄】(焦距屏和感光片位置的)对准；(彩色照相中感光片的)重合，配准 — *vt.* 1. 登记；(口)记住 2.(仪表等)指示；自动记下 3.(用表情、动作)显示；表达 4. 把(邮件)挂号；把(行李)托运 5.【印】对齐；套准 — *vi.* 1. 登记；注册 2.(仪表等)指示读数 3.(口)留下印象 4.【印】对齐；套准

registered ['redʒistəd] *adj.* 1. 已登记的；已注册的；已挂号的 2.(良种动物等在验种协会)登记的 3. 经正式鉴定的，有官方证明的

registrar [,redʒis'tra:] *n.* 1. 注册员；教务主任，注册主任 2. 负责记录股票转让的信托公司

registration [,redʒis'treiʃən] *n.* 1. 登记；注册；(邮件的)挂号 2. 登记项目；登记人数；注册人数 4. 登记证；注册证 5.(仪表的)记录；读数 6.【印】对齐，配准，套准

registry ['redʒistri] *n.* 1. 登记，注册；(邮件的)挂号 2. 登记处；注册处；(邮局的)挂号处 3. 登记簿；登记项目 4. 船籍(登记)

regnant ['regnənt] *adj.* 1. 统治的，在位的 2.(事物、性质、意见等)占优势的；占支

配地位的;强大的

regress [ˈriːgres] *n*. 1. 退回;倒退;回归;【律】复归权 2. 退步;退化 3.【天】退行 — [riˈgres] *vi*. 1. 退回;倒退;回归 2.【天】退行 ‖ ~**ion** [riˈgreʃən] *n*. /~**ive** [riˈgresiv] *adj*.

regret [riˈgret] (regretted; regretting) *vt*. 1. 懊悔,悔恨 2. 抱歉;遗憾 3. 哀悼,沉痛地怀念 — *vi*. 感到懊悔;感到抱歉 — *n*. 1. 懊悔,悔恨 2. 抱歉;遗憾 3.[~s]歉意;辞谢短柬

regretful [riˈgretful] *adj*. 懊悔的,悔恨的;遗憾的 ‖ ~**ly** *adv*.

regrettable [riˈgretəbl] *adj*. 令人遗憾的;使人悔恨的;可惜的;不幸的 ‖ **regrettably** *adv*.

regular [ˈregjulə] *adj*. 1. 规则的,有规律的;固定的 2. 整齐的;匀称的;有系统的 3.【数】(等边或等角、等面)正的;正则的 4. 定期的 5. 经常的;习惯性的;〈美〉普通的 6. 正式的;正规的;合乎礼仪的;合格的 7.【军】正规的;常备的 8.【语】按规则变化的 9.〈口〉十足的;彻底的 10.〈口〉愉快的;可亲的;可靠的:a ~ fellow 受大家欢迎的人 11. 属于宗教组织的;属于寺院的;受教规约束的 12.〈美〉忠于政党领导(或候选人)的 — *n*. 1. 正规兵 2.(球队的)正式队员 3.〈口〉老顾客;常客;固定工,长工 4.〈美〉忠于领导(或候选人)的党派成员 5.(适合普通身材穿着的)一般尺寸,普通尺寸 6. 修道士;僧侣 — *adv*. 1.〈口〉规则地;经常地 2.〈俗〉十分,非常 ‖ ~**ly** *adv*.

regularity [ˌregjuˈlæriti] *n*. 1. 规则性,规律性;一致性 2. 整齐;匀称 3. 正规 4. 经常;定期

regularize [ˈregjuləraiz] *vt*. 1. 使有规律;使规则化;使系统化;使整齐 2. 使合法化;使正确;调整

regulate [ˈregjuleit] *vt*. 1. 管理;控制;使遵守规章 2. 调整;调节;校准 3. 使有条理;使整齐

regulation [ˌregjuˈleiʃən] *n*. 1. 规则;规章;法规 2. 管理;控制 3. 调整;调节;校准;稳定 4.【生】调整(指胚胎发育中物质的重新分配);(维持早期胚胎正常发育的)调节机制 — *adj*. 1. 规定的 2. 普通的;正常的;正式的

regulator [ˈregjuleitə] *n*. 1. 管理者;调整者;校准者 2. 调节器;校准器;【无】稳定器 3. 调节剂 4. 标准钟;标准计时仪

regurgitate [riˈgəːdʒiˌteit] *vi*. 1.(液体、气体等)回流;(食物)回翻;(人、动物)反胃 2.(感情等)重新泛起 — *vt*. 1. 使回流;(因反胃等)吐出 2.(未经自身消化)逐字逐句地引用,机械刻板地重复 ‖ **reˌgurgiˈtation** *n*.

rehabilitate [ˌriːhəˈbiliteit] *vt*. 1. 恢复…的地位(或权利、财产、名誉等) 2. 修复;整顿;使复兴;更新 3. 使康复;使(残疾者等)恢复正常生活 4.(通过职业培训等)使(失业者等)重新获得就业资格 ‖ **ˈrehaˌbiliˈtation** *n*.

rehash [ˈriːˈhæʃ] *vt*. 把(旧材料)略加修改后再予使用(或发表);重复谈论;重复 — *n*. 改头换面的旧材料;老调重弹;"炒冷饭"作品

rehearsal [riˈhəːsəl] *n*. 1. 排练,排演 2. 练习;演习 3. 背诵 4. 详述;复述

rehearse [riˈhəːs] *vt*. 1. 排练,排演;使排练 2. 练习;演习;训练(某人) 3. 背诵 4. 详述;复述 — *vi*. 1. 排练,排演 2. 练习;演习

reign [rein] *n*. 1. 君主统治;统治 2.(君主等的)统治时期 3. 支配;盛行 4.〈罕〉王国;领域 — *vi*. 1.(君主等)统治;称王 2. 支配;盛行;占优势

reimburse [ˌriːimˈbəːs] *vt.* 1. 偿还, 付还 (款项) 2. 赔偿; 补偿 ‖ ~ment *n.*

rein [rein] *n.* 1. [常～s] 缰绳 2. [常～s] 驾驭; 控制; 箝制; 统治 — *vt.* 1. 给…配缰绳 2. (用缰绳) 勒住 3. 驾驭; 控制; 箝制; 统治 — *vi.* 1. 勒缰缓使马止步 (或慢行) (*in*, *up*) 2. 止住; 放慢 (*in*, *up*)

reincarnate [ˌriːinˈkɑːneit] *vt.* 赋予 (灵魂) 新形体, 使再生 — *a.* [ˌriːinˈkɑːnit] *adj.* 赋予新形体的, 再生的 ‖ 're,incar'nation *n.*

reindeer ['reindiə] ([复] reindeer(s)) *n.* [动] 驯鹿

reinforce [ˌriːinˈfɔːs] *vt.* 1. 增援; 支援 2. 加强; 增加…的数量 (或厚度) ‖ ~ment *n.* 1. 增援; 支援; 加强, 加固 2. 一支增援力量 [常～s] 援军 3. [常～s] 加固物 ‖ ~d concrete 钢筋混凝土

reinstate [ˌriːinˈsteit] *vt.* 1. 使恢复原状 (或原位); 恢复 (权利等) 2. 使 (身体) 复原; 使正常 ‖ ~ment *n.*

reinterpret [ˌriːinˈtəːprit] *vt.* 重新解释; 给…以新的解释

reiterate [riːˈitəreit] *vt.* 1. 反复做; 反复讲; 重申; 重作 ‖ re,ite'ration *n.* 1. 重复; 反复; 重申 2. 〈古〉(正面已印过的纸上的) 反面印刷物; 正面印刷物

reject [riˈdʒekt] *vt.* 1. 拒绝; 抵制 2. 丢掉; 抛弃 3. 驳回; 否决 4. 呕出; 排泄 — *n.* ['riːdʒekt] 被拒绝的东西; 次品; 废品 2. 遭拒绝者; 被抛弃者; 落选者

rejection [riˈdʒekʃən] *n.* 1. 拒绝; 抵制 2. 抛弃; 否决 3. 遭拒绝的东西; 被抛弃的东西; 呕出物; 排泄物

rejoice [riˈdʒɔis] *vi.* 1. 欣喜, 高兴 (*at*, *over*) 2. 庆祝; 欢乐 3. 〈谑〉有, 享有 (*in*) — *vt.* 使欣喜, 使高兴

rejoicing [riˈdʒɔisiŋ] *n.* 1. 欣喜, 喜悦, 高兴 2. [～s] 庆祝; 欢庆

rejoin [ˈriːdʒɔin] *vt.* 1. 使再结合; 使再聚合 2. 重返 (队伍等); 再加入 — *vi.* 重新结合; 重新聚合

rejoin[2] [riˈdʒɔin] *vi.* 1. 回答 2. 【律】(被告对原告) 第二次答辩 — *vt.* (再) 回答; 答复说

rejoinder [riˈdʒɔində] *n.* 1. 回答; 反驳 2. 【律】(被告对原告的) 第二次答辩

rejuvenate [riˈdʒuːvineit] *vt.* 1. 使返老还童; 使恢复青壮 2. 【生】使复壮 3. 【地】使回春, 使更生 — *vi.* 返老还童; 恢复活力; 复壮 ‖ re,juve'nation *n.*

rekindle [riːˈkindl] *vt.* 1. 重新燃起, 重新点燃 2. 重新激起 (或引起) — *vi.* 重新燃烧

relapse [riˈlæps] *n.* 1. 旧病复发 2. 故态复萌; 再度恶化 — *vi.* 1. 旧病复发 2. 故态复萌; 重犯 (旧病、恶习、错误等); 重新陷入 (沉思等) (*into*) ‖ relapsing fever 医回归热

relate [riˈleit] *vt.* 1. 叙述, 讲 2. 使关联; 显示出…与…的关系 — *vi.* 1. 有关, 涉及 (*to*) 2. 符合 3. 相处得好

related [riˈleitid] *adj.* 1. 叙述的, 讲述的 2. 有联系的; 相关的; 有亲戚关系的 3. 【音】有密切相和声关系的

relation [riˈleiʃən] *n.* 1. 关系; 联系; [～s] 交往; 事务 2. 家属关系; 亲属关系 3. 叙述; 叙述的事; 故事 4. 〈主英〉【律】(导致起诉的) 告发及 5. [～s] 肉体关系

relationship [riˈleiʃənʃip] *n.* 1. 关系; 联系 2. 家属关系; 亲属关系

relative ['relətiv] *adj.* 1. 有关系的; 相关的 2. 相对的; 比较的 3. 成比例的; 相应的 4. 【音】关系的 (指有相同调号的) — *n.* 1. 亲属; 亲戚 2. 有关的东西 3.

相对物 4.【语】关系词 ‖ ~ly *adv.* 相对地;比较地

relativism ['relətivizəm] *n.* 相对性;相对主义;相对论

relativist ['relətivist] *n.* 相对主义者;相对论者

relativity [,relə'tiviti] *n.* 1. 相关性;相互依存 2. 相对性 3. 相对论

relax [ri'læks] *vt.* 1. 使松弛;放松;使软弱无力 2. 缓和;放宽;减轻 3. 使松懈 4. 使休息;使轻松 — *vi.* 1. 松弛;放松;松懈;缓和;放宽 3. 变得不拘束;解除疑虑;变得从容 4. 休养;休息;娱乐 5. 通便

relaxation [,ri:dæk'seiʃən] *n.* 1. 松弛;放松 2. 松懈;缓和;放宽(处罚,课税等的)减轻 3. 变松;休息;解闷;娱乐 4.【物】张弛;弛豫

relay ['ri:lei] *n.* 1. 驿马;替换的马(或猎狗);补充物资 2. 接替人员;替班 3.【电】伺服电动机;【电】继电器 4.【无】转播,中继;转播节目 5.【体】接力赛(= ~ race);接力赛中的一段赛程 6.(消息,信号,球等的)分程递送;传送;转运 ─ ['ri:lei, ri'lei] *vt.* 1. 分程传递;传送;【无】转播 2. 使接替;给…换班 3. 用继电器控制(或操作)— *vi.* 1. 得到接替(或补充) 2.【无】转播

release [ri'li:s] *vt.* 1. 释放;解开 2. 放松;放出 3. 豁免;赦免;免除 4. 发表(消息等);发行(书,影片等) 5. 放弃;让与(权利,财产等) — *n.* 1. 释放;解开 2. 豁免;赦免;解除 3. 释放(或解开)证书 4. 放松;放开 5.【机】释放装置;排气装置【无】断路器 6.(消息,影片的)发布;发行 7. 发布的消息,发行的书(或影片) 8. 弃权;让渡;弃权(或让渡)文书

relegate ['religeit] *vt.* 1. 驱逐;放逐;使遣

没无闻 2. 使降位;使降级 3. 把…归类;使归属某等级(或范围等) 4. 把…委托给;把…移交给(*to*)

relent [ri'lent] *vi.* 1. 发慈悲;怜悯;变宽厚;变温和 2. 减弱;缓和

relentless [ri'lentlis] *adj.* 1. 不仁慈的;无情的;严酷的 2. 坚韧的;不屈不挠的;不懈的 ‖ ~ly *adv.* / ~ness *n.*

relevance ['relivəns], **relevancy** ['relivənsi] *n.* 关联;贴切;中肯;恰当

relevant ['relivənt] *adj.* 1. 有关的;贴切的;中肯的;恰当的 2. 成比例的;相应的 ‖ ~ly *adv.*

reliable [ri'laiəbl] *adj.* 可靠的;可信赖的;确实的 ‖ re,lia'bility *n.* / reliably *adv.*

reliance [ri'laiəns] *n.* 1. 信赖,信任;信心;依赖(*upon, on, in*) 2. 信赖的人(或物);依靠的人(或物)

reliant [ri'laiənt] *adj.* 1. 信赖的;依靠的(*on*) 2. 信赖自己的;依靠自己的;自力更生的

relic ['relik] *n.* 1. 遗物;纪念物;遗风,遗俗 2. 残片;遗迹;废墟 3. 圣骨;圣物 4.[~s]遗体,尸骸 5.【生】残余

relief [ri'li:f] *n.* 1.(痛苦,损忧,压迫等的)减轻;解除;免除;宽慰 2. 救济;救济品 3. 援救;解围 4. 换班;代替;换班的人[军队] 5. 救援部队 6.(单调事物或紧张场面的)调剂;娱乐 6. 浮雕;浮雕品 7. 轮廓鲜明;形象突出;生动;对比(*against*) 8. 地势的起伏 9.[英史](封臣的后裔在继承领地时付给封主的)地产继承的献纳 10.【律】法律补救方法,司法救助 11.(油窗、锅炉等的)释压(装置) ‖ ~ map 地形图

relieve [ri'li:v] *vt.* 1. 减轻;解除(苦痛、忧愁等) 2. 使得到解脱(*of, from*);使宽慰 3. 救济;援救;供应食品(或物资等)给 4. 使解除,使免除;(谑)偷,窃去

(*of*) 5. 接替, 替下; (以人接替而)解除
…的职务 6. 调剂; 使不单调; 使不乏
味 7. 衬托, 使显著; 使成浮雕 8. [~
oneself]大便; 小便

religion [ri'lidʒən] *n.* 1. 宗教 2. 宗教信
仰; 信仰; 一心追求的目标 3. 宗教生
活; 修道生活 4. 有关良心的事; (自己
感到)应做的事

religious [ri'lidʒəs]*adj.* 1. 宗教的; 宗教的
2. 虔诚的, 笃信宗教的, 虔敬的 3.
修道的, 出家的 4. 认真的; 严谨的 —
[单复同] 1. 修道士; 修女; 和尚; 尼
姑 2. [the ~]宗教的 ‖ ~**ly**
adv. / ~**ness** *n.*

relinquish [ri'liŋkwiʃ] *vt.* 1. 放弃; 撤回;
停止 2. 松手放开 3. 让予(权利、财产
等); 把…交给(*to*)

reliquary ['relikwəri]*n.* 圣骨匣; 圣物盒

relish ['reliʃ]*n.* 1. 滋味; 特殊的味道;风
味; 美味 2. 寓意; 含意 3. 食欲;
乐趣; 爱好 4. 饶有趣味的事物; 吸引
力 5. 调味品, 佐料; (主菜前的)开胃
品 — *vt.* 1. 加味于, 给…调味 2. 喜
于, 爱好 3. 津津有味地吃(或尝); 欣
赏, 玩味 — *vi.* 具有某种滋味(或风
味)

relive [ri:'liv] *vt.* (尤指凭想象)重新过…
的生活; 再体验

reluctance [ri'lʌktəns], **reluctancy**
[ri'lʌktənsi]*n.* 1. 不愿; 勉强 2. [电]磁
阻

reluctant [ri'lʌktənt]*adj.* 1. 不愿的; 勉强
的 2.⟨罕⟩反抗的; 反对的 ‖ ~**ly** *adv.*

rely [ri'lai] *vi.* 1. 依赖, 依靠; 依仗(*on*,
upon) 2. 信赖, 信任; …有信心
(*on*, *upon*)

REM, rem *abbr.* rapid eye movement 快速
眼动(指人夜间做梦时眼的快速运动)

remain [ri'mein] *vi.* 1. 剩下, 余留 2. 继续

存在 3. (人)留下; 逗留 4. 保持, 仍是

remainder [ri'meində]*n.* 1. 剩余; 残余
部分; 遗差 2. 剩下的人 3. [数]差
(数); 余数; 余项 4. [律]残留权, 剩余
财产承受权 5. 因滞销
而减价出售的书; 剩书 — *adj.* 1. 剩余
的 2. 出售处理书籍的 — *vt. & vi.* 廉
价出售(剩书)

remains [ri'meinz][复]*n.* [通常用作复,
也可用作单] 1. 剩下的东西; 残余; 余
额 2. 废墟, 遗迹; 遗物; 遗风 3. 残存物
4. 遗体 5. 遗稿; (古代作家)尚存的作品

remake ['ri:'meik] (remade ['ri:'meid]) *vt.*
重制, 翻新; 改造; 修改 — *n.* 1. 重制;
翻新; 改造; 修改 2. 重制物; 重新摄制
的影片

remand [ri'mɑːnd] *vt.* 1. 送回; 召回 2.
[律](被控人或罪犯)还押候审; 将…
(案件)发回原审法院重审 — *n.* 1. 送
回; 召回 2. [律]还押; 还押候审者; (案
件的)发回

remark [ri'mɑːk] *vt.* 1. 注意到; 觉察; 看
到 2. 评论说; 说 — *vi.* 评论, 谈论, 议
论 — *n.* 1. 注意; 觉察 2. 评论, 谈论,
议论; 话

remarkable [ri'mɑːkəbl] *adj.* 异常的; 非凡
的, 卓越的; 值得注意的; 显著的; 奇怪
的 ‖ ~**ness** *n.* / **remarkably** *adv.*

rematch [ri'mætʃ]*n.* (球赛、桥牌等的)
复赛; 再赛, 重赛(给初赛输者再一次
较量机会的比赛)

remedial [ri'miːdiəl] *adj.* 1. 治疗的; 治疗
上(用)的 2. 补救的; 纠正的; 修补(用)
的 3. 补习的 ‖ ~**ly** *adv.*

remedy ['remidi] *n.* 1. 治疗; 治疗法; 药物
2. 补救(法); 纠正(法) 3. [律]赔偿; 补
偿 4. (硬币铸造的)公差 — *vt.* 1. 医
治, 治疗 2. 补救; 纠正; 改善; 革除(弊

病等) 3. 修补；修缮

remember [ri'membə] vt. 1. 记得；想起，回忆起 2. 记住；牢记，不忘 3. (因感谢或怀恨等而)铭记 4. 送礼给；遗赠财产给；给…小费等 5. 代…问好，代…致意 6. 记录；纪念 7. 在祷告中提到 8. 〈古〉提醒；使记起 — vi. 记得；记起；记住

remembrance [ri'membrəns] n. 1. 记忆；回忆 2. 记忆力，记性 3. 能记忆的一段时间 4. 纪念，追忆 5. 纪念品 6. [~s]问候，致意

remind [ri'maind] vt. 提醒；使记起，使想起(of)

reminder [ri'maində] n. 1. 提醒者；提醒者(书信)；引起回忆的东西；纪念品 2. 暗示；提示 3.【商】催单

reminisce [,remi'nis] vi. 追忆往事；缅怀往事；话旧 — vt. 追忆地谈(或写)；怀旧地追记

reminiscence [,remi'nisns] n. 1. 回忆；缅怀往事；话旧；怀旧 2. 想起的往事 3. [~s]回忆录；经验谈 4. 引起联想的相似物 5.【哲】(柏拉图先验论中不朽灵魂对理念的)回忆说

reminiscent [,remi'nisnt] adj. 1. 回忆往事的；缅怀往事的；话旧的；怀旧的 2. 提醒的；暗示的，使人联想…的(of) — n. 往事的叙述者

remiss [ri'mis] adj. 疏忽的，粗心的；不负责任的；懈怠的 2. 没精打采的，懒洋洋的 ‖ ~ly adv. / ~ness n.

remission [ri'miʃən] n. 1. 宽恕；赦免 2. (捐税、债务等的)豁免；免除 3. 缓和；减轻

remit [ri'mit] (remitted; remitting) vt. 1. 宽恕；赦免 2. 豁免(捐税、债务等)；免除(处罚) 3. 缓和；减轻，缓和 4. 提交，移交(问题等)；【律】把(案件)发回原审

法院(to) 5. 使恢复原位(或原状等)；使复职 6. 推延，推迟(to, till) 7. 送，传送；汇寄 — vi. 1. 缓和；减轻；松弛 2. 汇款 — n. 移交的事件；呈交当局解决的事项

remittance [ri'mitəns] n. 汇款；汇款额 ‖ ~ man (侨居外国)靠国内汇款生活的人

remittent [ri'mitənt] adj.【医】1. 弛张的，缓解的 2. 弛张热的 — n. 弛张热(亦作 ~ fever)

remitter [ri'mitə] n. 1. 汇款人 2.【律】(案件的)移送另一法院审理 2.【律】以两份你有权证书中更有效的一份代替另一份 3.〈罕〉【律】权利恢复

remnant ['remnənt] n. 1. 残余，剩余；残迹；零料；零头布 2. [常～]残存者 — adj. 残余的；剩余的；残留的

remodel [,ri:'mɔdl] (remodel(l)ed; remodel(l)ing) vt. 1. 重新塑造 2. 改变；改造；改编；重建

remold [,ri:'məuld] vt.〈美〉= remould

remonstrate [ri'mɔnstreit] vi. 1. 抗议；抗辩(against) 2. 规劝，告诫 — vt. 抗议说；抗辩说

remorse [ri'mɔːs] n. 1. 懊悔，悔恨；自责 2. 同情(心)

remorseful [ri'mɔːsful] adj. 懊悔的，悔恨的

remorseless [ri'mɔːslis] adj. 1. 不懊悔的，不悔恨的 2. 无情的；残忍的

remote [ri'məut] adj. 1. 相隔很远的，遥远的；偏僻的 2. 很长远的，很久的 3. 关系远的；(亲戚)远房的 4. 冷淡的，疏远的 5. 很少的；细微的，微弱的 6. 间接的；(原因等)不直接的 7. 遥控的 ‖ ~ly adv. / ~ness n. ‖ ~ control 遥控

remould ['ri:'məuld] vt. 重新塑造，改铸；改造

remount [ri'maunt] *vt.* **1.** 再上(马、自行车等);重登(山、梯等) **2.** 给(个人、团体等)重新装备补充新马 **3.** 重新裱装(照片等);重新安装 — *vi.* **1.** 再登上;再上马(或自行车等);重登山(或梯等) **2.** 回溯;回到(*to*) — ['ri:maunt] *n.* 新马;新补充的骑兵马;新马的补充

removable [ri'mu:vəbl] *adj.* **1.** 可移动的;可拆装的 **2.** 可去除的 **3.** 可免职的

removal [ri'mu:val] *n.* **1.** 移动;调动 **2.** 迁移,迁居 **3.** 除掉;切除 **4.** 排除 **5.** 撤换;免职

remove [ri'mu:v] *vt.* **1.** 移动,搬开;调动 **2.** 脱掉;去掉,消除,清除 **3.** 免除;免职;撤去 **4.** [用被动语态](一道菜)被(另一道菜)替换 **5.** 杀掉;暗杀 **6.** 移交(案件) — *vi.* **1.** 迁移,搬家 **2.** (诗)离开 **3.** 移动 — *n.* **1.** 迁移,搬家;移动 **2.** 距离,间隔 **3.** (主英)(学校中的)升级;(某些学校的)(英)替换的一道菜 **5.** 程度;阶段;(亲族关系的)远近 ‖ ~ *r n.* **1.** 搬运工 **2.** 去渍剂 **3.**(律)(案件的)移交审理

removed [ri'mu:vd] *adj.* **1.**(亲族关系)隔了…代的 **2.** 远离的;无关的

remunerate [ri'mju:nəreit] *vt.* 酬报,酬劳;给…补偿(或赔偿) ‖ re**mune**'ra**tion** *n.*

renaissance [ri'neisəns] *n.* **1.** [the R-](欧洲十四至十六世纪的)文艺复兴;文艺复兴时期的风格(尤指文学、建筑方面) **2.** [R-](文艺或艺术、学术)的复兴 **3.** 新生;复兴;复活 — *adj.* **1.** [R-]文艺复兴的;文艺复兴时期(风格)的 **2.** [R-]文艺复兴时期建筑风格的

renal ['ri:nl] *adj.* [医]肾脏的,肾的;~ calculus 肾结石

renascent [ri'næsnt] *adj.* 新生的;再生的

复兴的;复活的

rend [rend] (rent [rent]) *vt.* **1.** 撕碎;扯破 **2.** 因愤怒(或忧虑,失望而扯(头发或衣服等) **3.** 割裂;分裂 **4.** 夺去 **5.**(声音)刺破;响彻 **6.** 伤…的感情 — *vi.* 撕开;裂开;分裂

render ['rendə] *vt.* **1.** 提出(理由等);呈递;汇报;开出(账单);作出(判决等) **2.** 放弃;让予(*up*) **3.** 报答;归还(*back*) **4.**(使)反映;(使)反响 **5.** 表示;给予,提供(帮助等) **6.** 使得;使变为 **7.** 表达;描绘 **8.**(艺术上)再现;表演;扮演;朗诵;演奏;处理(绘画等的主题) **9.** 给…重新措词;翻译;复制 **10.** 执行,行使,实施;做…的动作 **11.** 煎熬;提取(脂肪)(*down*) **12.**(用钱、货物或劳力)偿付 **13.**[建]第一次抹灰打底,渲染 — *vi.* 给予补偿 — *n.* **1.**(用钱,货物或劳务对佃租等的)缴纳 **2.**[建]墙壁的底灰,底泥,底层

rendering ['rendəriŋ] *n.* **1.** 表演;演奏 **2.** 翻译 **3.**[建](抹灰)底层 **4.** 建筑物等的透视图;示意图;(艺术品的)复制图 **5.**(脂肪的)熬炼,熬化

rendezvous ['rɔndivu:, 'rɔndeivu:]([复] rendezvous ['rɔndivu:z, 'rɔndeivu:z]) *n.* **1.**(军队或舰队的)指定集合地点 **2.** 聚会的地方;公共场所;人们常去(游憩)的地方 **3.** 约定;约会;幽会;约会(或幽会)地点;(宇宙飞船等的)会合(点) — *vt. & vi.*(使)在指定地点集合(或聚会,相见)

rendition [ren'diʃən] *n.* **1.** 表演;演奏 **2.** 翻译 **3.** 施行;给予 **4.**(物体在视觉中的)再现 **5.**(古)(军)让予;放弃(指地方);引渡(指人)

renegade ['renigeid] *n.* **1.** 叛徒,变节者;脱党者;逃兵 **2.** 背教者(尤指改信伊斯兰教的基督教徒) — *adj.* 背叛的,

变节的;背教的 — vi. 1. 背叛,变节;
脱党 2. 背教

renege [ri'ni:g] vi., vt. & n.(美) = renegue

renegue [ri'ni:g] vi. 1.(纸牌戏中)藏牌,
有牌不跟 2. 食言,背信,违约 — vt.
1. 否认;放弃;抛弃 2. 拒绝 — n.(纸
牌戏中)有牌可跟而违例不跟

renew [ri'nju:] vt. 1. 使更新;使复原;使
恢复;使更生;使自新;使苏醒 2. 使
新;使重新记起;复兴;重建,重修,换
新;修补;补充;加强 5. 重新开始;继
续 6. 重复;重申;重做 7. 准予(契约)
展期;续借(图书等) — vi. 1. 更新;恢
复原状 2. 重新开始;继续 3.(契约等)
展期

renewal [ri'nju:əl] n. 1. 更新;复原;恢复
2. 新生;自新;苏醒;复兴;复兴;重
建 4. 换新;修补;补充;加强 5. 重新开
始;继续 6. 重复;重申;重做 7.(契约
等)的展期;(对刊物等)的续订;续订
期

Renminbi ['ren'min'bi:]〈汉〉n. 人民币
(略作 RMB)

rennet ['renit] n. 1.(尤指牛犊第四胃)胃
膜;干胃膜(制干酪等用) 2.[生化]凝
乳酶

renounce [ri'nauns] vt. 1. 放弃;抛弃 2.
与...脱离关系;拒绝承认(子女等) 3.
(纸牌戏中因缺门)垫牌对付(攻牌牌
张),垫(另一花色牌张) — vi. 1. 声明
放弃权利(或财产等) 2.(纸牌戏中)垫
牌 — n. 垫牌‖ ~ment n.

renovate ['renəveit] vt. 1. 革新;更新 2.
修复;修理;整修 3. 恢复(精神、活动
等);使干净;刷新 ‖ **renovator** n. 革
新者;修复者;恢复者;刷新者

renown [ri'naun] n. 名望,声誉 — vt. 使
有名望,使有声誉 ‖ ~ed adj. 有名望
的,著名的:be ~ed for 因...而著名

以...著称

rent[1] [rent] n. 1.(衣服等)的裂开处;裂
缝;缝隙 2. 分裂;(关系等的)破裂

rent[2] [rent] n. 1.(土地、建筑物、房屋、机
器等的)租金,租费 2. 出租的房屋(或
土地) — vt. 1. 租入,租用 2. 租出 3.
向...出租 — vi. 出租 ‖ ~able adj.
可租的;可收租金的 ‖ ~ party 房租舞
会(参加舞会者须向舞会主人付少量
的钱以供他缴房租)

rent[3] [rent] rend 的过去式和过去分词 —
adj. 1. 撕裂的 2. 分裂的

rental ['rentl] n. 1. 租费;租金收入 2. 租
赁;出租;出租业 3. 租折,租册 4. 出租
的财产(指房屋等) — adj. 1. 租用的
2. 出租的;出租业的

renter ['rentə] n. 1. 租赁人,租户 2. 出租
人;影片经销商

rentier ['rɔntiei]〈法〉n. 靠收租(或股息)
生活的人

renunciation [ri,nʌnsi'eiʃən] n. 1. 放弃;
抛弃 2. 脱离关系;(对子女等的)拒绝
承认 3. 克制自己;节欲(损失等)
弃权声明(书) 4. 断绝关系声明;放
弃权力声明(书)

reorganize [ri:'ɔ:gənaiz] vt. & vi. 1. 改组;
改编;整顿;改革 2.[军]整编,改编 ‖
're,organi'zation n.

Rep. abbr. 1. Representative 2. Republic
3. Republican

repair[1] [ri'pɛə] vt. 1. 修理;修补 2. 补偿;
纠正 3. 恢复 4. 弥补;补偿(损失等)
— n. 1. 修理;修补 2.[常~s]修理工
程;修理工作 3. 维修状况 4.(细胞等
的)修复,再造 ‖ ~er n. 修理者;修补
者

repair[2] [ri'pɛə] vi. 1. 去;经常去;大伙儿
去 2. 聚集,集合 — n.〈古〉(人们)常
去的地方

reparable ['repərəbl] *adj.* 1. 可修理的；可修补的 2. 可补救的；可纠正的 3. 可补偿的；可赔偿的 4. 可治愈的

reparation [ˌrepə'reiʃən] *n.* 1. 补偿，〔常~s〕(战败国须付的)赔款；赔偿 2. 弥补，补救；恢复 3. 修理(现常用 repair)；整修工作；维修工程(现常用 repairs)

repartee [ˌrepɑː'tiː] *n.* 1. 巧妙的回答；妙语；机智的反驳；巧辩 一 *vi.* 1. 巧妙地回答(或反驳)

repast [ri'pɑːst] 〈书〉 *n.* 1. 餐；饮食 2. 就餐；就餐时间 一 *vi.* 就餐；设宴

repatriate [riː'pætrieit] *vt.* 把…遣送回国 一 *vi.* 回国 一 ['riː'pætriit] *n.* 被遣返回国者 ‖ **re,patri'ation** *n.*

repay [riː'pei] (repaid [riː'peid]) *vt.* 1. 偿还，付还(债款)；还钱给(某人)；补偿 2. 报答；报复；回敬 一 *vi.* 偿还；报复 ‖ ~**ment** *n.* 1. 偿还；报答；报复 2. 偿付的款项(或物)

repeal [ri'piːl] *vt.* 1. 撤消(决议等)，废除(法令等) 2. 放弃；否定 一 *n.* 1. 撤销；废除 2.【英史】取消联合(十九世纪初爱尔兰独立运动领袖奥康诺等反对与英国并成联合王国的主张)

repeat [ri'piːt] *vt.* 1. 重说；重做；跟着别人讲(或念) 2. 照(别人的话等)说下去 3. 背诵 4. 使再现；再给予 5. 复制 一 *vi.* 1. 重复说(或做) 2. 重复出现 3.(食物)留有味道 4.〈美〉(违法地)重复投票 一 *n.* 1. 重复说(或做)；重复出现；重演；(尤指应应观众要求);重播【音】复奏(或复唱)部分；反复符号 2.(墙纸等上)同样的图案 3.【商】(同类货的)再次订购，再次供应

repeated [ri'piːtid] *adj.* 反复的，再三的，屡次的，重复的 ‖ ~**ly** *adv.*

repeater [ri'piːtə] *n.* 1. 重复说(或做)的人；背诵者 2. 连发手枪(或步枪)，转

轮枪 3. 打簧表(或钟) 4. 惯犯 5.〈美〉(违法的)重复投票者 6.〈美〉(不及格)重考者；重修(某课程)者；留级者 7.【数】循环小数 8.【讯】增音机；中继器；转发器

repel [ri'pel] (repelled; repelling) *vt.* 1. 击退；抵制 2. 拒绝；排斥 3. 使厌恶；使反感 4. 抗，防 一 *vi.* 击退；抵抗；引起反感

repellent [ri'pelənt] *adj.* 1. 击退的；排斥的 2. 讨人厌的；令人反感的 3.【化】相斥的；防水的 一 *n.* 1. 防水布 2.【药】驱血剂；消肿药 3. 防护剂

repent [ri'pent] *vi.* 悔恨；悔改；后悔 2.【宗】忏悔 一 *vt.* 后悔；〈古〉使后悔

repentance [ri'pentəns] *n.* 悔悟；悔改；后悔；忏悔

repentant [ri'pentənt] *adj.* 悔悟的；悔恨的；后悔的；忏悔的 ‖ ~**ly** *adv.*

repercussion [ˌriːpəˈkʌʃən] *n.* 1. 击回；弹回；反冲 2. 被击回(或弹回)的东西；回声；反射 3. 相互作用；〔常~s〕反响，反应；影响 4.【医】消退(法)，消肿(法)；冲击触诊(法) 5.【音】(赋格曲主题或答句的)再进入；(音调或和弦的)反复

repertoire ['repətwɑː] *n.* 1.(剧团等的能随时演出的)全部剧目；全部节目；保留剧目；保留节目 2. 全部技能；所有组成部分

repertory ['repətəri] *n.* 1. 仓库；库存；贮藏物 2. 积贮；搜集(指事实等) 3. = repertoire

repetition [ˌrepi'tiʃən] *n.* 1. 重复；反复 2. 重说；重做；反复讲(或做) 3. 重复的事物；复制品；副本 4. 复诵；背诵的材料(如诗等) 5.(乐器)复奏的性能 ‖ **repetitious** *adj.*

repine [ri'pain] *vi.* 1. 不满；烦恼；埋怨；发

牢骚(*at*, *against*) **2.**(因不满现状等而)想望,向往(*for*)

replace [rɪ'pleɪs] *vt.* **1.** 把...放回(原处);使恢复(原职) **2.** 取代,...代替(*by*, *with*);接替,替换;更换 **3.** 归还;赔还 ‖ ~able *adj.* 可放回原处的;可代替的;可替换的

replacement [rɪ'pleɪsmənt] *n.* **1.** 归还;复位;复职 **2.** 取代;代替;替换;更换 **3.** 替换物;代替物;代替者;补充人员(尤指补充兵员) **5.**(晶体的)角取代,边面取代 **6.**【地】交代(作用)

replay [ri:'pleɪ] *vt.* **1.** 重新举行(比赛) **2.** 重播;重放 — ['ri:pleɪ] *n.* **1.** 重赛 **2.**(录音,电影等的)重放

replenish [rɪ'plenɪʃ] *vt.* **1.**(再)填满,(再)装满 **2.** 补充(兵力等) **3.** 给...添足 **4.** 使生满人(或动物);使充满精神力量 — *vi.*(再)装满,充满 ‖ ~er *n.* 补偿物;补充物;a soil —er 肥料 **4.**【摄】补充液 — ~ment *n.*

replete [rɪ'pli:t] *adj.* **1.** 饱满的;充分供应的 **2.** 充满的;充实的 **3.** 塞满的;吃饱的;狼吞虎咽的;肥胖的 ‖ repletion *n.*

replica ['replɪkə] *n.* **1.** 艺术复制件(尤指出于原作者之手的) **2.** 复制品;拷贝;完全一样的事物 **3.**【音】反复(记号)

reply [rɪ'plaɪ] *vt.* **1.** 回答,答复 **2.**(行动)答复;回击 **3.** 反响,回响 **4.**(原告对被告)答辩,驳复 — *vt.* 回答 — *n.* **1.** 回答,答复 **2.**(原告对被告的)答辩,驳复

report [rɪ'pɔːt] *vt.* **1.** 报告;汇报 **2.** 传说;转述 **3.** 记录(以供发表等);报道 **4.** 告发,检举(某人)或其行为) **5.** ~ oneself 使报到 — *vi.* **1.** 报告,汇报 **2.** 说出对...的印象(*of*) **3.** 写报道 **4.** 报到 — *n.* **1.** 报告;汇报 **2.** 传说;(公众)议

论;名声 **3.** 报道;通讯;(会议等的)正式记录 **4.** [~s]【律】案情报告;判例汇编 **5.** 爆炸声;爆裂声 ‖ ~able *adj.* **1.** 值得报告(或汇报,报道)的 **2.** 应该报告的 / ~er *n.* **1.** 报告人;汇报人 **2.** 记者;通讯记者;新闻广播员 **3.**(法庭的)书记员,笔录者 **4.**(议会等的)记录员,速记员

reportage [ˌrepɔː'tɑːʒ] *n.* **1.** 报道(工作);新闻报道 **2.** 报道文体;通讯文学;报告文学

reportedly [rɪ'pɔːtɪdlɪ] *adv.* 据传说;据报道

repose[1] [rɪ'pəuz] *vt.* 使休息;把(头部等)靠着休息 — *vi.* **1.**(躺着)休息,安息,安眠 **2.** 静卧;蕴藏 **4.** 被安放;坐落(*on*) **5.** 建立于,基于(*on*) 〈古〉依靠;信赖(*in*) — *n.* **1.** 休息;安眠 **2.** 宁静;镇静;静止;平静 **3.**(图画等色彩,结构的)和谐;静谧 ‖ ~ful *adj.*

repose[2] [rɪ'pəuz] *vt.* **1.**〈罕〉放;置 **2.** 把...寄托于(*in*) **3.** 授予(管辖、使用权)

repository [rɪ'pɔzɪtərɪ] *n.* **1.** 贮藏所,仓库;贮物器(如箱、柜等) **2.** 博物馆;陈列室;店铺 **3.** 资源丰富地区 **4.** 墓地 **5.** 亲信;知己

repossess [ˌriːpə'zes] *vt.* **1.** 重新拥有(或占有) **2.** 使重新拥有(或占有) ‖ ~ion *n.* / ~or *n.*

reprehend [ˌreprɪ'hend] *vt.* 严责;指摘;申斥

reprehensible [ˌreprɪ'hensəbl] *adj.* 应受严责的;应受指摘的;应受申斥的 ‖ reprehensibly *adv.*

represent [ˌreprɪ'zent] *vt.* **1.** 描绘;描述 **2.** 讲述,阐述;(强烈)指出;主张 **3.** 声称 **4.** 代表;代理;为...的国会议员 **5.** 象征;体现;表示;相当于 **6.** 演出;扮演 **7.** 回忆 — *vi.* 提出异议;提出抗议

representation [ˌreprizen'teiʃən] *n.* 1. 描写;表现;表示 2.(绘画等)艺术作品 3. [常～s]陈述;请求;正式抗议 4.[总称]代表;代表们;代理 5. 演出;扮演 6.[律](继承法中死者子女取代死者地位的)代位继承

representative [ˌrepri'zentətiv] *adj.* 1. 描写的,表现的;表示的 2. 代表性的,典型的 3. 代表的;代议制的;代理的 4. [里]相当的;类似的 ~ *of* 1. 典型了代表;代理人 2. [律](代位)继承人 3. 〈美〉[R~]众议院议员

repress [ri'pres] *vt.* 1. 镇压 2. 抑制(感情等);忍住;压制;约束(行动等) 3.[心]压抑 — *vi.* 采取高压手段 ‖ ~*ion* *n.* 镇压;抑制;约束/ ~*ive* *adj.*

reprieve [ri'priːv] *vt.* 1.[律]缓期执行；...的刑罚(尤指死刑) 2. 暂时解救(或缓解) — *n.* 1. 缓刑(令) 2. 暂时解救(或缓解)

reprimand ['reprimɑːnd] *n.*(尤指当权者所作的)训斥,申斥,斥责;谴责 — *vt.* 训斥,申斥,斥责;谴责

reprint ['riː'print] *vt.* 重印;再版 — *n.* 1. 重印;再版 2. 再版本 3. 翻印品;翻版 4. 抽印材料;单行本 4.(供集邮者搜集、不作邮资的)翻印邮票

reprisal [ri'praizəl] *n.* 1.[史](受害国对敌国的)报复性掳掠(所得) 2. 报复(行为) 3.[常～s]赔偿

reproach [ri'prəutʃ] *vt.* 1. 责备,申斥;指责,非难 2. 使丢脸;有辱...的名誉 — *n.* 1. 责备,斥责;指责 2. 耻辱;不名誉 ‖ ~*ful* *adj.*

reprobate ['reprəbeit] *vt.* 1. 谴责,斥责;指责 2. 拒绝;摈弃 3.[宗](上帝)摈弃;(天)罚 — *adj.* 1. 堕落的,放荡的,道德败坏的;邪恶的;罪恶深重的 2. 为上帝摈弃的

者;恶棍 2. 为上帝摈弃的人 ‖ repro'bation *n.*

reproduce [ˌriːprə'djuːs] *vt.* 1. 繁殖,生殖 2. 再生产;再造;再生长(器官) 3. 复制印...的翻版;复写;重演,再上演;使重现 4.(在脑中将过去的情景等) — *vi.* 1. 繁殖,生殖 2. 进行再生产;复制 ‖ ~*able*, reproducible *adj.* 能繁殖的;能再生产的;能再生长的;能复制的;能复印的;能再现的,能重现的/ ~*r* *n.* 1. 扬声器 2. 再现设备;[计]复制机

reproduction [ˌriːprə'dʌkʃən] *n.* 1. 再生(产),再生产过程 2. 繁殖,生殖 3. 复制;复制品(尤指艺术品);翻版 4.(林中的)新生幼林

reproductive [ˌriːprə'dʌktiv] *adj.* 再生(产)的;生殖的;复制(品)的 — *n.*(实际或潜在的)母体(尤指有性繁殖的群居昆虫)

reproof [ri'pruːf] *n.* 谴责,责备,申斥

reprove [ri'pruːv] *vt.* 1. 谴责,责骂 2. 指摘,非难,不赞成

reptile ['reptail] *n.* 1. 爬行动物;〈口〉爬虫 2. 两栖动物 3. 卑躬屈节的人;卑鄙的人 — *adj.* 1.(像)爬行动物的;(像)爬虫的 2. 卑躬屈节的;卑鄙的;鬼鬼祟祟的

republic [ri'pʌblik] *n.* 1. 共和国;共和政体:the People's *Republic* of China 中华人民共和国 2. 团体,界,坛

republican [ri'pʌblikən] *adj.* 1. 共和的;共和政体的 2. 共和政体论(者)的 3.[R~](美国)共和党的 4.(鸟类等)群栖的 — *n.* 1. 拥护共和政体者;共和主义者 2.[R~](美国)共和党党员;拥护共和党的人

repudiate [ri'pjuːdieit] *vt.* 1. 与(妻)离婚;遗弃(妻子);抛弃(孩子);与...断绝关

系 2. 拒绝接受；否认...的权威(或效力等)；否定 3.(私人或国家)拒付(债款) ‖ re₁pudi'ation n.

repugnant [ri'pʌgnənt] adj. 1. 不一致的；不相容的，矛盾的(to, between) 2. 令人厌恶的；使人反感的(to) 3. 对抗性的，敌对的，相斥的(with) ‖ **repugnance** n.

repulse [ri'pʌls] vt. 1. 打退(敌人等)；击退(攻击等)；(争论中)挫败(对方) 2.(以无礼、冷淡等)排斥；严厉拒绝 3. 厌恶，憎恶 — n. 1. 打退；击退 2. 严拒

repulsion [ri'pʌlʃən] n. 1. 排斥；严拒 2. 反感；厌恶 3.【物】推斥；斥力

repulsive [ri'pʌlsiv] adj. 1. 排斥的；严拒的 2. 令人厌恶的；使人反感的；可憎的 3.【物】推斥的；斥力的 ‖ ~ly adv. / ~ness n.

reputable ['repjutəbl] adj. 1. 声誉好的；可尊敬的；合乎规范的 ‖ **reputably** adv.

reputation [₁repju'teiʃən] n. 1. 名誉；名声 2. 好名声，声望

repute [ri'pju:t] n. 1. 名誉；名声 2. 好名声，声望，美名 — vt. [常用被动语态]把...称为；认为 ‖ ~d adj. / ~dly adv.

request [ri'kwest] n. 1. 请求，要求；恳求 2. 要求的事物；请求的话 3. 需要 — vt. 请求，要求；恳求

requiem ['rekwiəm] n. 1. [常作 R-]【宗】(天主教)安魂弥撒；追思弥撒;(做弥撒时唱的)追思曲，安魂曲 2. 挽歌，哀悼歌 3. 悲歌；哀诗

require [ri'kwaiə] vt. 1. 需要 2. 要求；命令

requirement [ri'kwaiəmənt] n. 1. 需要；需要的东西 2. 要求；必要的条件

requisite ['rekwizit] adj. 需要的；必要的，必不可少的 — n. 必需品

requisition [₁rekwi'ziʃən] n. 1. 正式请求，正式要求；申请 2.【律】引渡要求 2.(要求技术物、料、人员等)的通知单；调查单；申请书；征用文书 3. 需要；使用；征用 — vt. 要求；征用

requite [ri'kwait] vt. 1. 报答；回报 2. 酬答(某人)；向(某人)报复 ‖ **requital** n.

rescind [ri'sind] vt. 废除；取消；撤回，撤销；解除

rescript ['ri:skript] n. 1.(罗马皇帝或教皇对法律问题、请愿的)解答敕令 2. 法令；敕令；布告；抄本；重写 4.(美国法院关于处理案件的)法庭命令

rescue ['reskju:] vt. 1. 援救；营救；挽救 2.【律】强行夺回(被扣押的人或物)— n. 1. 援救；营救 2.【律】(对被扣押的人或物的)强行夺回 ‖ ~r n. 援救者；营救者；救星

research [ri'sə:tʃ] n. 1. 调查；探究 2. 研究工作；[常 ~es]学术研究；创造性研究 ‖ ~er n.

resemblance [ri'zembləns] n. 1. 相似；相似性；相似点；相似程度 2. 相似物；肖像，像 3.〈古〉外貌，外形特征

resemble [ri'zembl] vt. 像，类似于

resent [ri'zent] vt. 对...怨恨；对...不满；怨恨 ‖ ~ful adj. / ~ ment n. 愤恨，不满；怨恨

reservation [₁rezə'veiʃən] n. 1. 保留 2.(旅馆房间、剧院坐位等的)预定 3.〈美〉保留地；居留地；专用地；禁猎区 4.【宗】(对圣职任命、敕罪权、施圣餐等的)保留 5.【律】(让予或租赁财产时的)权益保留；保留权益

reserve [ri'zə:v] vt. 1. 储备，保存 2. 保留；留给；留出 3.【宗】保留(敕罪权);留出(部分圣餐) 3. 推迟，延迟 4. 预订,定 — n. 1. 储备(物);保存(物);(矿产等)储藏量 2.[常 ~s]【军】后备军；后

备队(员);预备役;预备役军人;【体】
预备队员;(展览品等的)预备奖 3. 保
留地;专用地 4. 保留;限度 5. 自我克
制;沉默寡言;含蓄;冷淡;(艺术手法)
不夸张;节制 6. 未透露的消息,秘密
7. 储备金;准备金;公积金 — *adj.* 保
留的;留出的;储备的;备用的;预备的

reserved [ri´zə:vd] *adj.* 1. 保留的;留作专
用的;预定的;预备的 2. 沉默寡言的;
缄默的;含蓄的;冷淡的

reservist [ri´zə:vist] *n.* 后备役军人

reservoir [´rezəvwɑ:] *n.* 1. 水库;蓄水池
(或槽);贮液器;【生】贮液囊;储液泡
2.(知识,精力等的)储藏;蓄积;(液)贮
库 3.(病原体的)贮主 — *vt.* 储藏;蓄
积

reset [ri´set] (reset; resetting) *vt.* 1. 重放;
重新安排 2. 重排(铅字);重镶(宝石)
3. 使再锋利;重磨(锯齿等) 4. 重接
(断骨);使复位 — *n.* 1. 重放;重排;
重镶(宝石)等 2. 或 重接;重接;重
放)之物 3. 重种植物 4.(仪表等的)复
位器

reshuffle [ri:´ʃʌfl] *vt.* 1. 重新洗(牌);
改组;重新安排 — *n.* 1. 重新洗牌;
改组;重新安排

reside [ri´zaid] *vi.* 1.(正式用语)居住(in,
at)(官员等)驻在(at) 2.(权力、权利等)
属于、归于(in) 3.(性质等)存在于
(in)

residence [´rezidəns] *n.* 1. 居住;驻扎
留 2.住宅;住宅;官邸 3. 居住期间 4.
(在大学等的)住校时期

residency [´rezidənsi] *n.* = residence 1.
(美)(住院医生的)专科实习时期;住院
医生职位 3.(乐师、乐队等在俱乐部等
处的)常驻演出,驻穴

resident [´rezidənt] *adj.* 1. 居住的;居留
的;常驻的 2.(鸟等)不迁徙的 3. 归属

于…的;存在于…的(in) — *n.* 1.
居民 2. 驻外政治代表;驻扎官(尤指
派驻保护国的官员) 3. 留鸟;留兽 4.
住院医生

residential [ˌrezi´denʃəl] *adj.* 1. 居住的;
住宅的;作住家用的 2. 供学生住宿的

residual [ri´zidjuəl] *adj.* 1. 剩余的;残留
的 2.【数】剩余的 3. 使用后留有一定
效应的,有后效的 — *n.* 1. 剩余,残余
2.【地】残丘 3.【数】剩余;残差 4. 剩余
物;残质;残渣 5.(疾病或手术后的)后
遗症,伤残遗症 6.(电视片等每次重映
时给演员或作者的)复播复映追加酬
金

residuary [ri´zidjuəri] *adj.* 1. 剩余的,残
留的 2.【律】剩余遗产的;处理剩余遗
产的

residue [´rezidju:] *n.* 1. 剩余,残余;渣滓
2.【化】基,渣;余渣;残余物 3.【数】剩余
数,剩余类 4.【律】(扣除税款、债款、遗赠
等后的)剩余遗产

residuum [ri´zidjuəm]([复] residua [ri´zidju-
ə] 或 residuums)(拉) *n.* 1. 剩余物,残留
物 2.【化】残留物;残渣;残滓;残渣油
3.【数】剩余,残差 4.【律】剩余遗产

resign [ri´zain] *vt.* 1. 放弃;辞去 2. 把…
交托给(to, into) 3.(~ oneself)使听从
(于);使顺从(to) — *vi.* 1. 辞职;屈
从(于);听任(to)

resignation [ˌrezig´neiʃən] *n.* 1. 放弃;辞
职;辞职书,辞呈 2. 屈从;顺从;顺从

resigned [ri´zaind] *adj.* 1. 已放弃的;已辞
去(职务)的 2. 屈从的;顺从的 ‖ ~ly
[ri´zainidli] *adv.*

resilience [ri´ziliəns] *n.* 1. 跳回;回弹
(性);回能;弹能 2.(活力、精神的)恢
复力;复原力;迅速恢复的愉快心情

resilient [ri´ziliənt] *adj.* 1. 有回弹力的;
有弹性的;能回复原来位置(或形状)

的 2. 恢复活力的；恢复精神的；心情愉快的

resin ['rezin] **n. 1.** (天然或合成的)树脂；松香，松脂 2. 树脂制品 — **vt.** 涂树脂于；用树脂处理 ‖ ~**ous** *adj.*

resist [ri'zist] **vt. 1.** 抵抗，反抗；对抗 2. 抗；耐 3. 抑制；抗拒[常用于否定句]忍住 — **vi.** 抵抗，反抗；抵制 — **n.** (印染花布等用的)防染剂 ‖ ~**er** *n.*

resistance [ri'zistəns] **n. 1.** 抵抗，反抗；抗拒方法；[R-](被占领国家中的)秘密抵抗的组织(或运动) 2.(对疾病等的)抵抗力；(物质的)耐力 3. 抵制；反对 4. 阻力【电】电阻；阻抗；电阻器

resistant [ri'zistənt] **adj.** 抵抗的，反抗的；有抵抗力的 — **n.** 抵抗者，反抗者；有抵抗力(或抗性)的东西

resistojet [ri'zistədʒet] **n.**【空】电阻加热式离子火箭喷气机

resojet ['rezəudʒet] **n.** 脉动式(空气)喷气发动机

resolute ['rezəluːt] **adj.** 坚决的，坚定的；果敢的，果断的；不屈不挠的 — **n.** 坚定的人；果敢的人 — **vi.**〈美〉作出(或通过)决议 ‖ ~**ly** *adv.*

resolution [ˌrezə'luːʃən] **n. 1.** 坚决，坚定；决心；决心要做的事；果断；不屈不挠 2. 决定；决议(案) 3. 消除；(炎症等)的消退，解答；解决 4. 分解；解体；解析；分解率；清晰度 5. 转变；变形 (*into*) 6.【音】(不谐和音或和弦转为谐和音或和弦)；和弦 7.【语】(通过投票等)使转化为把……归结为

resolve [ri'zolv] **vt. 1.** 使分解；使解体；解析；分辨 2. 解决；解答；消除；消退(炎症等) 3. 决心；决定；(使)决意；议决 4.(通过投票等)使转化为把……归结为

(*into*)；【音】解决，使不谐和转向谐和 — **vi. 1.** 决心；决意；决定 (*on, upon*) 2. 分解；解体；溶解；解析；分辨 3.【医】(炎症等)消退 4.【音】解决，从不谐和转向谐和 — **n. 1.** 决心；决意 2.〈书〉坚决，坚定；刚毅

resolved [ri'zolvd] **adj.** 决心的；坚决的，坚定的 ‖ ~**ly** [ri'zolvidli] *adv.*

resolvent [ri'zolvənt] **adj.** 有溶解力的；分解的；【医】消散(性)的；a ~ drug 消散药 — **n. 1.** 消散剂；溶剂 2. 解决法

resonance ['rezənəns] **n. 1.** 回声，反响 2.【物】磁共振；共振；共鸣 3.【化】中介(现象)

resonant ['rezənənt] **adj. 1.** 反响的；由共鸣而加强的；洪亮的 2.(木材，墙壁等)引起共鸣的 3.(厅堂等)回响的；共鸣的；共振的；谐振的 (*with*) ‖ ~**ly** *adv.*

resort [ri'zoːt] **vi. 1.** 求助；凭借；诉诸；采取(某种手段等) (*to*) 2. 常去；成群地去 — **n. 1.** 求助；凭借；采取 2. 所求助的东西；所求助的人；凭借的方法(或手段) 3. 常去；成群去；常去的人群 4. 常去之地；胜地

resound [ri'zaund] **vi. 1.**(厅堂等)回响；充满声音(*with*) 2.(声音，乐器等)鸣响，反响，回荡 3.(名声，事件等)传播；传扬 — **vt.** 使回响；使(厅堂等)回荡；颂扬；传播(某人的名声等)

resource [ri'soːs] **n. 1.**[常~s]资源；物力，财力 2. 应付办法；对策；智谋；应变能力 3. 消遣，娱乐 4. 消遣；(精神上的)慰藉；受援的可能，得救的希望

resourceful [ri'soːsful] **adj. 1.** 资源(或物力)丰富的 2. 善于随机应变的，机智的，足智多谋的 ‖ ~**ly** *adv.* ‖ ~**ness** *n.*

respect [ris'pekt] **n. 1.** 尊敬；尊重 2.[~s]敬意；问候 3. 考虑；重视，关心 4. 关

系;方面;着眼点 — **vt.** 1. 尊敬;尊重 2. 考虑;重视 3. 遵守;不妨害

respectable [ris'pektəbl] **adj.** 1. 可敬的、值得尊敬的;应受尊重的 2. 有相当身份的;正派的;高尚的;体面的;像样的;高雅的 3.(质量等)过得去的;不错的,(数量等)不少的;相当大的;可观的 — **n.** 体面人,正派人;可敬的人 ‖ re;specta'bility **n.** /respectably **adv.**

respecter [ris'pektə] **n.** 尊敬者;尊重者

respectful [ris'pektful] **adj.** 1. 恭敬的;尊敬人的;尊重人的 ‖ ~ly **adv.** [常用于致长者书信的结尾,作套套语] Yours ~ly(或 Respectfully yours),James Kent 詹姆斯·肯特敬上 / ~ness **n.**

respecting [ris'pektiŋ] **prep.** 1. 关于 2. 由于,鉴于

respective [ris'pektiv] **adj.** 各自的,各个的 ‖ ~ly **adv.** 各自地;分别地

respell [ri:'spel](respelled 或 respelt [ri:'spelt]) **vt.** 再拼(单词);用另一方式(尤指按语音系统)重新拼(单词)

respiration [ˌrespəˈreiʃən] **n.** 1. 呼吸;一次呼吸 2.【生】呼吸(作用)

respirator ['respəreitə] **n.** 1.(人工)呼吸器。口罩;(英)防毒面具

respiratory [ris'paiərətəri] **adj.** 呼吸(作用)的

respire [ris'paiə] **vi.** 1. 呼吸 2. 松口气 — **vt.** 呼吸(空气);(罕)呼出,发出(气味等)

respite ['respait, 'respit] **n.** 1. 暂缓;展延(尤指不乐意的事情);(死刑等)缓期执行 2. 暂时休息(或喘息);(痛苦等的)缓解;暂止 — **vt.** 1. 使暂息,使(痛苦等)缓解 2. 缓期执行(死刑等);延期(处分等)

resplendent [ris'plendənt] **adj.** 灿烂的,光辉的;辉煌的,华丽的 ‖ resplendence

n. / ~ly **adv.**

respond [ris'pɔnd] **vi.** 1. 作答;【宗】(会众对牧师)应答,唱和 2. 响应;有反应 3.【律】承担责任 — **vt.** 应答,回答 — **n.** 1.【宗】(会众对牧师的)应答,唱和 2.【建】壁联 ‖ ~ er **n.** 1. 回答者;应答者;(桥牌中的)应叫人 2.(电子)应答器 3. 答辩人 4.(对外界刺激)发生反应的人;响应治疗的病人

respondent [ri'spɔndənt] **adj.** 1. 回答的;应答的;反射的 2.(律)被告地位的 — **n.** 1. 回答者;响应者 2.(论文等的)答辩人 3.【律】(离婚、上诉等案件中的)被告 4.(对外部刺激)发生反应,反射 5.(主义)(民意测验等的)调查对象;调查表等的答卷人

response [ris'pɔns] **n.** 1. 作答,回答;【礼】拜仪式中会众或唱诗班在主持牧师祈祷时或祈祷后的)应答(或唱和)短语 2. 响应;反应;(讯)频率响应

responsibility [risˌpɔnsəˈbiliti] **n.** 1. 责任;责任心 2. 职责;任务 3.(智力或财力等上的)可靠性;可信赖性;责任能力

responsible [ris'pɔnsəbl] **adj.** 1. 有责任的;(应)负责的 2. 认真负责的,尽责的;可靠的,可信赖的 3. 责任重大的 4. 有责任能力的,能明辨是非的,有鉴别能力的 ‖ responsibly **adv.**

responsive [ris'pɔnsiv] **adj.** 1. 应答的,(表示)回答的;(礼拜仪式)用应答(或唱和)短诗的 2. 响应的;易起反应的;敏感的 ‖ ~ly **adv.** / ~ness **n.**

rest¹ [rest] **n.** 1. 休息,歇息;睡眠;安息,长眠;消息 2. 安静,安宁 3. 静止;停止;(朗读中的)停顿【音】休止;休止符,休止处 4.(使)静止或固定营养(处 5). 撑架;支座;托;垫;(放工作物的)台;刀架 — **vi.** 1.(躺下)休息;睡;安息,长眠;(农田)休闲 2. 安心,安

宁 3. 静止;停止 4. 被支撑(在);搁(在);(视线等)停留(在)(on, upon) 5. 依据,依赖(on, upon);信赖(in) 6. 取决(于)(with) 7. [律]自动停止提出据 — vt. 1. 使休息;使轻松;使安息;使(农田)休闲;使闲散 2. 使支撑(在);使搁(在);使(视线等)停留(on, against) 3. 使基(于);把…寄托(于)(on, upon) 4. [律]自动停止对(案件等)提出证据 ‖ ~ house 客栈(无旅馆地区的招待所

rest² [rest] n. 1. [the ~]剩余部分;其余的人;其余 2. (英)盈余(;(银行的)储备金;盘货和结算 3.(网球赛等中的)一阵连续回球 — vi. 1. [后接表语]依然是;保持 2.〈古〉余下,留下

restaurant ['restərənt] n. 餐馆,饭店,菜馆,酒家

restaurateur [ˌrestərə'tə:r] 餐馆主,饭店老板

restful ['restful] adj. 宁静的;悠闲的;使(感到)平静的 ‖ ~ly adv. / ~ness n.

resting ['restiŋ] adj. 休眠的;潜伏的

restitution [ˌresti'tju:ʃən] n. 1. 归还;赔偿 2. 恢复原状;(弹性体的)复原 3. [律]要求恢复原状的诉讼

restive ['restiv] adj. 1.(人群等)难控制的;倔强的;不受约束的;不安定的;烦躁的 2.(马等)难驾驭的;不肯前进的 ‖ ~ly adv. / ~ness n.

restless ['restlis] adj. 1. 得不到休息的 2. 不静止的;永不宁静的;不安定的;焦虑的;烦躁的;不满足的 ‖ ~ly adv. / ~ness n.

restoration [ˌrestə'reiʃən] n. 1. 恢复,回复;复位,复原 2. 归还 3.(受损文物的)修补;修复(物);重建(物);(已绝迹动物等的)模型 4. [the R-] [英史](一六六〇年查理二世的)王政复辟时期

restorative [ris'tɔ:rətiv] adj. 恢复健康(或体力)的,滋补的 — n. 营养食品;恢复剂;补药

restore [ris'tɔ:] vt. 1. 恢复;使恢复健康,使复元;使复原;使(帝王等)复位,使复职 2. 归还,交还 3. 修补(受损文物等);修复,整修

restrain [ris'trein] vt. 1. 抑制,遏制;制止 2. 拘押;监禁(疯人、犯人等) 3. 限制;约束

restrained [ris'treind] adj. 1. 受约束的;拘束的,拘谨的 2.(文体等)谨严的,克制的,有节制的 ‖ ~ly [ris'treinidli] adv.

restraint [ris'treint] n. 1. 抑制,遏制;制止 2. 管束;监禁;约束力 3.(文体等的)谨严;(态度等的)拘谨;克制,节制;谨慎

restrict [ris'trikt] vt. 限制;限定;约束

restricted [ris'triktid] adj. 1.(范围等)受限制的,有限的;a ~ publication 内部发行的出版物/a ~ message 密电 2. 只限于某地的:a ~ hotel 限制顾客的旅馆(如只招待白人基督教徒等)

restriction [ris'trikʃən] n. 限制;限定;约束

restrictive [ris'triktiv] adj. 限制(性)的;约束(性)的 — n. 限制性词语 ‖ ~ly adv. / ~ness n.

result [ri'zʌlt] n. 1. 结果;成果;效果;比赛成绩,比分 2. [数]答数;答案 3.(美)(议院等的)决议;决定 — vi. 1.(作为结果)发生,产生(from) 2. 结果;终归;导致(in)

resultant [ri'zʌltənt] adj. 1. 作为结果而发生的 2. 组合的,合成的 — n. 1. 结果 2. [物]合力,合量 3. [化]生成物;反应产物 3. [数]结式

resume [ri'zjuːm] vt. 1. 恢复 2. 重新开始;(经打断后)再继续 3. 取回;收回;重新占用 4. 概述 — vi. 再开始;继续讲

résumé ['rezjumei] n. 1. 摘要,梗概 2. (求职者等写的)简历,履历

resumption [ri'zʌmpʃən] n. 1. 恢复;再开始;(中断后)再继续 2. 再取回;重新占用 3. 恢复硬币支付

resurgent [ri'səːdʒənt] adj. 复活的;再起的 ‖ resurgence n.

resurrect [,rezə'rekt] vt. 1. 使复活;复兴;恢复;使再现;使再受注意 2. (从坟墓中)掘出,盗掘;(口)掘起 — vi. 复苏;复活

resurrection [,rezə'rekʃən] n. 1. 复活;复兴;恢复 2. [the R-][基督教]耶稣复活;[基督教审判日]全体死者的复活 3. 掘墓盗尸

resuscitate [ri'sʌsiteit] vt. & vi. (使)苏醒;(使)复活;(使)复兴;(使)恢复精力 ‖ re,susci'tation n. / resuscitator n. 使苏醒(或复活)的人;[医]复苏器

retail ['riːteil] n. 零售,零卖 — adj. 零售的;零售商的 — adv. 以零售方式 — [riː'teil, 'riːteil] vt. 1. 零售,零卖 2. 细谈;到处传播 — vi. 零售,零卖 ‖ ~er ['riːteilə] 1. 零售商 2. (流言等的)传播者

retain [ri'tein] vt. 1. 保持,保留;保有 2. 留住;挡住 3. 记住 4. 付定金聘定(律师等) ‖

retainer [ri'teinə] n. 1. (封建诸侯等的)家臣,侍从;随从者;仆人;雇员 2. 保持者;保留者 3. (律师等的)聘定,聘用定金 4. (保留租房的)定金

retaliate [ri'tælieit] vi. 1. 报复,回报,以牙还牙 2. 征收报复性关税 — vt. 就(伤害,侮辱等)进行报复 ‖ re,tali'ation

n. / **retaliatory** [ri'tæliətəri] adj. 报复(性)的

retard [ri'tɑːd] vt. 1. 延迟;放慢;使停滞 — vi. 减速 — n. 减速迟(尤指潮汐、天体运行等) — n. 延迟;放慢;妨碍;耽误 ‖ ~er n. [化]阻滞剂 ‖ 减速器

retardation [,riːtɑː'deiʃən] n. 1. 延迟;阻滞;阻止;妨碍 2. 延迟(或妨碍)的程度 3. (思想或动作的)迟钝 4. [机]减速

retarded [ri'tɑːdid] adj. 智力迟钝的,弱智的

retch [riːtʃ, retʃ] vi. 干呕;作呕,恶心 — vt. 呕出,吐出 — n. 干呕(声);恶心

retell [riː'tel] (retold [riː'təuld]) vt. 1. 再讲;重述,复述 2. 以不同方式(或语言)复述

retention [ri'tenʃən] n. 1. 保持;保留;留置 2. 保持力;保留物 3. 记忆(力) 4. [医]停滞;潴

retentive [ri'tentiv] adj. 1. 保持的;有保持力的 2. 记忆力强的 3. [医]固位的 4. 含蓄的 5. 拘留的 7. 沉默寡言的 ‖ ~ly adv. / ~ness n.

reticent ['retisənt] adj. 1. 沉默寡言的;爱缄默的;言不尽意的;有保留的 2. (艺术风格等)有节制的;谨严的 ‖ reticence n. / ~ly adv.

reticulate [ri'tikjulit] adj. 网状的(尤指植物的网状叶脉) — [ri'tikjuleit] vt. & vi. (使)成网状;(使)分成小方格

reticule ['retikjuːl] n. (旧)收口网兜

retina ['retinə] n. ([复] retinas 或 retinae ['retiniː]) n. [解]视网膜

retinue ['retinjuː] n. [总称](高级官员等的)随员,随从

retire [ri'taiə] vi. 1. 退下;离开(部队等主动地)退却,撤退 2. 引退;退隐;退休;退职,退役 3. 就寝 4. 后退;远去

隐没 — vt. 1. 使撤退；命令…退却 2. 使引退（或退休等）；辞退 3. 收回（纸币等）；付清（证券等的本息）— n. （书）1. 退隐处；隐蔽去处 2. 退隐，遁世 ‖ ~ment n.

retired [ri'taiəd] adj. 1. 退休的；退职的；退役的；职业的 2. 引退的；退隐的 3. 隐僻的，幽静的

retiring [ri'taiəriŋ] adj. 1. 行将退休的；行将退职的；行将退役的 2. 离群的，喜欢独处的 3. 就要的

retold [ri:'təuld] retell 的过去式和过去分词

retort [ri'tɔ:t] vt. 1. 反击；回报 2. 反驳 — vi. 反击；回嘴；反驳 — n. 反击；回嘴；反驳

retouch [ri:'tʌtʃ] vt. & vi. 润饰，润色

retrace [ri'treis] vt. 1. [接 one's steps] 折回，由原路返回 2. 再追溯；再探查 3. 回忆；回顾 4. 再修描，再描摹

retract [ri'trækt] vt. 1. 缩回，缩进（爪、触角、肢等）；收起（飞机起落架等）2. 撤回，取消（声明、诺言、意见等）3.【语】收舌发（音）— vi. 1. 缩回，缩进 2. 变卦，食言 ‖ ~able adj. ~ion n.

retreat [ri'tri:t] n. 1.（被迫）退却，后退，退去 2. 放弃，退出（from）3.（眼睛）下陷（颏、额）后塌 4.（飞机翼梢）后斜 — vi. 撤回（棋）— n. 1. 退却；后退 2. 退却的信号；（日暮时兵营的）降旗号；降旗式 3. 退避；逃遁；隐退【宗】静修 4. 隐避的场所；避难所，收容所；休养所

retrench [ri'trentʃ] vt. 1. 减少，紧缩，节省（经费等）2. 删除，省略（章节等）3. 为…筑堡壕（或胸墙）— vi. 紧缩，节省 ‖ ~ment n.

retrial [ri:'traiəl] n. 再审；复审

retribution [ˌretri'bju:ʃən] n. 1. 惩罚

【宗】（来世）报应；果报 2. 报酬，报答

retrieve [ri'tri:v] vt. 1. 重新得到；取回，收回；恢复 2. 挽回，补救；补偿；纠正；挽救；拯救 3.（猎犬）找回，衔回（被击中的猎物）4. 追溯；回忆 5.【计】检索 — vi.（猎犬）找寻猎物；取回扔出物 — n. 1. 重新得到（的机会）2.（可）收回 ‖ retrievable adj. 1. 可寻得的；可恢复的 2.【计】可检索的 ~r n. 1. 复得者；挽回者；挽救者（网球运动中的）救球球员 2.（衔回猎物的）拾獚

retroactive [ˌretrəu'æktiv] adj. 1. 倒行的；回动的；反作用的 2.【律】溯及既往的；有追溯效力的 3. 补发增加的工资的 ‖ ~ly adv.

retrofire ['retrəufaiə] vt. 发动（制动火箭）— vi.（制动火箭）点火发动 — n.（制动火箭的）点火发动

retrofit ['retrəufit] n.（飞机等的）改型 —（retrofitted; retrofitting）vt. & vi.（对…）作翻新改型

retrograde ['retrəgreid] adj. 1. 后退的 2. 倒转的；逆序的 3.【生】【天】【音】逆行的【地】逆（向）的；【化】退减的 — vi. 后退；逆行；退化；重述，回顾 — vt. 使后退 — adv. 向后；后退着 ‖ ~ly adv.

retrogress [ˌretrə'gres] vi. 后移；倒退；衰退；退化 ‖ ~ion n. ~ive adj.

retrorocket ['retrəurɔkit] n. 制动火箭，减速火箭

retrospect ['retrəuspekt] n. 回顾，回想；追溯；（罕）追溯力 — adj. = retrospective — vi. 回顾，回想；追溯（to）— vt. 回

顾；追溯 ‖ ~ion n.

retrospective [ˌretrəʊˈspektiv] *adj.* 1. 回顾的，回想的；追溯的 2.（法律·付款等）溯及既往的，有追溯效力的 3.（风景等）在（房屋等）后面的

retroussé [rəˈtruːseɪ] *adj.*（鼻子）向上翘起的

return [rɪˈtɜːn] *vi.* 1. 回，回来；返回 2.（健康等）恢复 3. 送还，归还 4. 回答；反驳 — *vt.* 1. 还，归还 2. 回以，回报；报答 3. 回答说；反驳道 4. 获得，产生（利润等）5. 反射（光）；回响（声）6. 报告，汇报；申报；正式宣布 7.（选区）选举，选出（议员）8.（同花色的牌）跟打出过的花色的牌）9.【建】使（墙壁、嵌线等）转延 — *n.* 1. 回来；返回；回程；来回票；[电]回路 2. 归还；偿还；回报（传票寄向法院的）交回 3. 回复；恢复；再现 4. 回答 5. 报答；回报 6. 退还之物；[~s]（向出版商）退还的未售出的出版物 7. [常~s] 利润；利润率；成果 8. [常~s] 报告书；统计表；（选举）结果报告；申报；汇报 9. 候选人当选的宣布；[常~s] 当选国会议员人数 10. [建]（墙壁、嵌线等）的转延 11.（纸牌戏）跟着牌牌，回出牌牌 12.（网球等）回球，回击 — *adj.* 1. 返回的；回程的：a ~ ticket 来回票 2. 报答的；回报的：a ~ visit 回访 / a ~ courtesy 回礼 / a ~ game（或 match）重赛，回访比赛 3. 反向的；折回的 4. 复原的 ‖ ~able *adj.* / ~ed *adj.* 1. 已归来的；回国的：a ~ed overseas Chinese 归国华侨 2. 退回的；回送的：~ed empties 退回的空瓶（或空箱等）

Réunion [rɪˈjuːnjən] *n.* 留尼汪（岛）[印度洋西部]

reunion [ˌriːˈjuːnjən] *n.* 1. 再结合；再联合；再会合 2. 重聚；（亲属的）团聚；

（同班同学离校后的）联欢会

reunite [ˌriːjʊˈnaɪt] *vt. & vi.*（使）再结合；（使）再联合；（使）重聚

Reuters [ˈrɔɪtəz] *n.*（英国）路透（通讯）社

rev [rev]（口）*n.*（发动机的）一次回转 — （revved; revving）*vt.*（尤指开动时）加快（发动机每分钟的转速）（*up*）— *vi.* 加快转速（*up*）

Rev. *abbr.* 1. Revelation(s) 2. Reverend

revamp [ˌriːˈvæmp] *vt.* 1.〈美〉给（鞋等）换面 2.〈口〉修理；修补；把（旧物）翻新 3. 修改；改进

revanchism [rɪˈvæntʃɪzəm] *n.* 复仇主义（尤指战败国家力图恢复失地而执行的政策）‖ **revanchist** *n.* 复仇主义者 *adj.* 复仇主义的

reveal [rɪˈviːl] *vt.* 1. 展现，（显）露出 2. 揭示；揭露，暴露；泄露 3.【宗】（神）启示，默示：~ed religion 天启教（自然教之对）— *n.*【建】（外墙与门或窗之间的）窗侧；门窗口

reveille [rɪˈvæli] *n.*【军】1. 起床号；（晨操）列队号 2.（晨操起点名的）列队，集合

revel [ˈrevl] (revel(l)ed; revel(l)ing) *vi.* 1. 狂欢；宴会；作乐 2. 扬扬得意 3. 十分爱好；着迷（*in*）— *vt.* 在狂欢中浪费（金钱等）(*away*) — *n.* 1. 狂欢；欢宴；作乐 2. [常~s] 喧闹的宴会；节庆 ‖ **revel(l)er** *n.* 狂欢者；欢宴者 / ~ry *n.* 狂欢；（喧闹的）宴会

revelation [ˌrevɪˈleɪʃən] *n.* 1. 展现，显露；展示；揭露 2. 揭露的事物；意想不到的事；新发现 3.【宗】启示，默示：[the Revelation(s)]（基督教《圣经·新约》中的）《启示录》

revenge [rɪˈvendʒ] *vt.* 1. 替……报仇；报复；洗雪 — *n.* 1. 报仇，报复（指行为或欲望）2. 雪耻机会；使败方有机会获胜的再次比赛 ‖ ~r *n.*

revengeful [ri'vendʒful] *adj.* 报复的；充满仇恨的；一心想报仇的

revenue ['revinju:] *n.* 1. (国家的)岁入；税收 2. 收入；收益 3. [~s]总收入 4. 税务署(或局)

reverberate [ri'və:bəreit] *vt.* 1. 使反响；使回响；使回荡 2. 反射(光、热等)；反射(焰) 3. 放... 入反射炉处理 — *vi.* 1. 反响；回响；回荡 2. (光、音等)反射；反跳；反冲 — *adj.* 回响的；反射的；反焰的 ‖ re**verbe'ration** *n.* 1. 反响；回响；回荡 2. [物]交混回响，混响 3. (光、声波、热的)反射；反焰 4. 在反射炉中的处理 5. 反射物(如反射光等)

revere [ri'viə] *vt.* 尊敬，崇敬；敬畏

reverence ['revərəns] *n.* 1. 尊敬，崇敬；敬畏 2. 敬礼；鞠躬 3. 尊严；威望 4. [R-](英国旧时用作牧师等的尊称，现为粗俗或幽默的用语)尊敬的...阁下 — *vt.* 尊敬，崇敬；敬畏 ‖ **reve'rential** *adj.*

reverend ['revərənd] *adj.* 1. 可尊敬的；应受尊敬的 2. [the R-](对牧师或神父等的尊称；常略作 the Rev.)大人 3. 教士的；圣职的 — *n.* [常~s]教士；牧师

reverent ['revərənt] *adj.* 恭敬的；虔诚的 ‖ ~**ly** *adv.*

reverie ['revəri] *n.* 1. 梦想，幻想；白日梦 2. 沉思；出神 3. [音]幻想曲；梦幻曲

reversal [ri'və:səl] *n.* 1. 颠倒 2. 反向 3. 逆退；倒转 4. [律](判决等的)推翻；变更；撤消 5. [摄]反转

reverse [ri'və:s] *vt.* 1. 颠倒；翻转 2. 使反向 3. 倒转；倒退 4. 使变得相反 5. [律]撤销(判决等) — *vi.* 倒退；倒转；反向；[机]回动 — *n.* 1. 相反 2. 背面，反面 3. 挫折；败北；倒霉 4. 倒退；倒转；反向；[机]回动；回动装

置(或齿轮) — *adj.* 1. 颠倒的 2. 相反的；反向的；[机]回动的 3. 背面的，反面的 ‖ ~**ly** *adv.*

reversible [ri'və:səbl] *adj.* 1. 可逆的 2. (正反)两面可用的 3.(判决等)可撤销的 — *n.* 双面织物；双面上衣

reversion [ri'və:ʃən] *n.* 1. (习惯、状况等的)回复；复原；反转，倒转；反向 2. [律](地产等的)归还原主；继承权；将来享有权；(期满后)复归的地产 3. [生]回复变异；返祖遗传(体) 4. [化]返原 5. 恤金(尤指人寿保险赔款)

revert [ri'və:t] *vi.* 1. 回复(*to*) 2. [律](财产等)归还原主(*to*) 3. [生]回复变异；返祖遗传 — *vt.* 1. 使颠倒；使回复 2. 把(眼睛等)转向后 — *n.* 恢复原来信仰的人

revery ['revəri] *n.* = reverie

revet [ri'vet] (revett(e)ed; revet(t)ing) *vt.*(用砖、石层等)护(墙、堤等) ‖ ~**ment** *n.* 1. 护墙；护岸，铺面

review [ri'vju:] *vt.* 1. 再检查；再考察；回顾；复习；[律]复审 2. 考察；检阅 3. (用文字)评论 — *vi.* 1. 复习功课 2. 写评论 3. 复阅；回顾；复习；[律]复审 2. 考察；检查；检阅(式) 3. 评论(文章)；评论性刊物 ‖ ~**er** *n.* 评论者；书评者；评论家

revile [ri'vail] *vt. & vi.* 辱骂，漫骂 ‖ ~**ment** *n.* / ~**r** *n.*

revise [ri'vaiz] *vt.* 1. 修订；校订；the *Revised* Version (英)基督教《圣经》钦定译本的修订本 2. 修正；修改 3. [生]对...重新分类 — *n.* [印]再校样，二校样 ‖ **~ment** *n.* / ~**r, revisor** *n.* 1. 修订者；修正者；改者 2. 校订员，校对员，校样员

revision [ri'viʒən] *n.* 1. 修订；校订；修正；修改 2. 修订本；修订版

revisionism [rɪ'vɪʒənizm] *n.* 1. 修正主义 2.(对条约等的)修正论

revisionist [rɪ'vɪʒənist] *n.* 1. 修正主义者 2.(对法院判决等的)修正论者 3. = reviser — *adj.* 1. 修正主义的 2. 主张修正的(指对历史资料的重新分析等)

revitalize [ˌriː'vaɪtəlaɪz] *vt.* 使新生,给予…新的活力,使复兴

revival [rɪ'vaɪvəl] *n.* 1. 苏醒;复活;再生 2. 复兴;再流行 3.(电影等)重新上演、(书刊等)重新出版 4.(精力、活动、兴趣等的)恢复 5.【宗】奋兴(期);奋兴会、奋兴布道会 6.【律】(契约等的)重新生效

revive [rɪ'vaɪv] *vi.* 1. 苏醒;复活;再生 2. 恢复精力(或活动等);振奋 3. 复兴;(风俗等)再流行 4. 重新生效 5.(金属)还原 — *vt.* 1. 使苏醒;使复活;使再生 2. 使恢复精力(或活动等);使振奋 3. 使复兴;使重新生效 4. 使再流行 5. 回想起 6. 重演(戏剧等)7. 使(金属)还原

revivify [rɪ'vɪvɪfaɪ] *vt.* 1. 使再生,使复活;重振,…的活力 2.【化】使还原 — *vi.*【化】还原

revocable ['revəkəbl] *adj.* 可撤回的;可废除的;可取消的

revoke [rɪ'vəʊk] *vt.* 1. 撤回;撤销;废除;取消(法律、允诺等)2. 回想;召回 — *vi.*(纸牌戏中)有牌不跟 — *n.* 1. 有牌不跟 2.(罕)撤销;废除 ‖ re,vo'cation *n.*

revolt [rɪ'vəʊlt] *vi.* 1. 反抗;造反;起义;反叛 2. 厌恶,憎恶;反感 — *vt.* 使厌恶;使反感;使恶心 — *n.* 1. 反抗;起义;反叛

revolution [ˌrevə'luːʃən] *n.* 1. 革命;剧烈的变革;彻底的改革 2. 旋转;绕转;【天】公转 3. 循环;周期

revolutionary [ˌrevə'luːʃənəri] *adj.* 1. 革命的;大变革的 2.(美)[R-]美国独立战争(时期)的 3.(罕)旋转的;绕转的 — *n.* 革命者;革命论者

revolutionist [ˌrevə'luːʃənist] *n. & adj.* 革命者(的);革命党人(的);革命论者(的)

revolutionize [ˌrevə'luːʃənaɪz] *vt.* 1. 使革命化 2. 彻底改革 ‖ revo'lutioni'zation *n.*

revolve [rɪ'vɒlv] *vt.* 1. 使旋转;使绕转 2. 细想;默想 — *vi.* 1. 旋转;绕转 2. 周期地(或间断地)出现 3. 沉思;(念头等)使人再三考虑

revolver [rɪ'vɒlvə] *n.* 1. 左轮手枪 2. 旋转式装置;【冶】转炉

revue [rɪ'vjuː] *n.*(有小型歌舞的)时俗讽刺剧

revulsion [rɪ'vʌlʃən] *n.* 1. 收回;(突然)抽回 2.(感情等的)突变;急剧反应 3. 嫌恶;反感(*against*)4.【医】诱导(法)

reward [rɪ'wɔːd] *n.* 1. 报答;报应;报偿 2. 报酬;赏金;奖赏;赏格 — *vt.* 1. 报答;酬劳;奖赏 2. 报应;惩罚(坏人或坏事)‖ ~ing *adj.* 1. 报答的 2. 有益的;有报酬的;有价值的

reword [riː'wɜːd] *vt.* 1. 重说;重复 2. 改说;改变…的措辞

rewrite [riː'raɪt] (rewrote [riː'rəʊt], rewritten [riː'rɪtn]) *vt.* 1. 书面答复 2. 改写(故事等);重写 — *vi.* 修改旧作 — ['riːraɪt] *n.* 改写(或重写)的作品(或文章)

Reykjavik ['reɪkjəvɪk] *n.* 雷克雅未克[冰岛首都]

Rh【化】元素铑(rhodium)的符号

rhapsody ['ræpsədi] *n.* 1.(古希腊适于一次吟诵的)叙事诗;叙事诗的一部分 2. 狂文;狂诗;狂言 3.【音】狂想曲 4. 狂喜

Rhenish [ˈriːniʃ, ˈreniʃ] *adj.* 莱茵河的；莱茵河流域的(现常用 Rhine) — *n.* (莱茵河流域产的)莱茵白葡萄酒

rhenium [ˈriːniəm] *n.* 【化】铼

rheostat [ˈriːəstæt] *n.* 【电】变阻器

rhesus [ˈriːsəs] *n.* 恒河猴, 猕猴 ‖ **Rhesus factor**【医】恒河猴因子(= Rh factor)

rhetoric [ˈretərik] *n.* **1.** 修辞学；修辞学书 **2.** 运用语言的技能；辩术 **3.** 花言巧语(措辞、文体的)浮夸与修饰 **4.** 言语,讲话

rhetorical [riˈtɔrikəl] *adj.* **1.** 修辞的；修辞学的；用来产生修辞效果的 **2.** 浮夸的 **3.** 口头的

rheumatic [ruːˈmætik] *adj.* (患)风湿病的；患风湿病似的 — *n.* **1.** 风湿病患者 **2.** 〈口〉[~s] 风湿病 ‖ **~ally** *adv.* ‖ **~ fever** 风湿热

rheumatism [ˈruːmətizəm] *n.* 风湿病

Rhine [rain] *n.* 莱茵河[西欧] ‖ **~ wine**(莱茵河流域产的)莱茵(白)葡萄酒

rhinestone [ˈrainstəun] *n.* 莱茵石(一种透明无色的钻石仿制品) ‖ **~d** *adj.*

rhinoceros [raiˈnɔsərəs] *n.* ([复] rhinocero(te)s) 或 rhinoceri [raiˈnɔsərai])【动】犀, 犀牛

Rhode Island [rəud ˈailənd] 罗得岛(或译罗得艾兰)[美国州名]

Rhodesia [rauˈdiːziə] *n.* 罗得西亚(Zimbabwe 津巴布韦的旧称)[非洲东南部国家]

rhodium [ˈrəudiəm] *n.* 【化】铑

rhododendron [ˌrəudəˈdendrən]【植】杜鹃;杜鹃花

rhomb [rɔm] *n.* 菱形

rhombus [ˈrɔmbəs] ([复] rhombuses 或 rhombi [ˈrɔmbai]) *n.* 菱形

rhubarb [ˈruːbɑːb] *n.* **1.**【植】大黄 **2.** 大黄

色,黄褐色 **3.** 喧哗;吵闹

rhyme [raim] *n.* **1.** 韵;押韵 **2.** 同韵词,押韵词;(诗文)押韵诗 **3.** 押韵诗;写韵文 — *vt.* **1.** 作成押韵诗;写韵文 **2.** 押韵;成韵,同属一韵 (*with, to*) — *vt.* **1.** 用韵诗叙述(或歌颂) **2.** 把……写成诗;押韵写作 **3.** 使押韵;用(某字)押韵 **4.** 作诗消磨(时间) (*away*)

rhythm [ˈriðəm] *n.* **1.** 律动,节律;(诗的)韵律 **2.**【音】节奏,拍子;(乐队中)节奏乐器 **3.**(循环往复)规则变化(模式) **4.**(艺术上各部分间的)调和、匀称

rhythmic(al) [ˈriðmik(əl)] *adj.* 有韵律的;有节奏的 ‖ **rhythmically** *adv.*

rib [rib] *n.* **1.** 肋(骨);(肉类)肋条;排骨 **2.** (谑)妻(源出《圣经·创世纪》,上帝取亚当身肋骨做成其妻,故) **3.**【纺】棱纹,凸条,罗纹 **4.**【植】(叶)主脉;(昆虫)翅脉 **5.** 类似肋骨(作用)的东西 **6.** 【空】翼肋;(船等的)肋材;伞骨;(矿区)侧壁;矿柱 — (ribbed; ribbing) *vt.* **1.** 装肋状物于;用肋状物撑(或加固) **2.**【纺】在……上起棱纹

ribald [ˈribəld] *adj.* (言词或人)下流的,粗俗的;不堪入耳(或入目)的 — *n.* 开下流玩笑的人;讲下流话的人 ‖ **~ly** *adv.* / **~ry** *n.*

ribbed [ribd] *adj.* 呈肋状的,用肋状物(或肋材)支撑的,有罗纹的

ribbon [ˈribən] *n.* **1.** 缎带;丝带 **2.** 带;系带;带状物;钢卷尺;带锯;(打字机的)色带 **3.**【建】系板 **4.**(勋章等的)绶带;(授予军人等的)勋表 **5.** [~s] 碎片 **6.** [~s]缰绳 **7.** [endp] 肋部牵条 — *vt.* **1.** 用缎带装饰 **2.** 把……撕成条带(或碎片) — *vi.* 形成带状 ‖ **~ building, ~ development**(由市区到郊区的沿干道)带状发展

riboflavin(e) [ˌraibəuˈflevin] *n.*【生化】核黄素,维生素 B₂

rice [rais] [单复同] *n.* 稻;米;饭 ‖ ～ **flour** 米粉;米糠 ／ ～ **paper** 米纸;卷烟纸 ／ ～ **water**(供病人吃的)米汤

rich [ritʃ] *adj.* **1.** 富的,富裕的,有钱的 **2.** 丰富的;富饶的,多产的 **3.** 贵重的;珍贵的 **4.**(服装、家具、首饰等)富丽的奢华的;(色彩)浓重的 **5.**(食物)味浓的;油腻的 ;(酒)醇厚的,芳烈的;(气味)强烈的 **6.**(声音)圆润的;低沉的 **7.** 繁茂的 **8.**(近乎)纯的 **9.** 有意义的;丰富多采的 **10.**〈口〉很有趣的;可笑的;荒唐的 **11.**[与过去分词或现在分词连用]…华丽(或丰富、精美等)的 **12.**(内燃机的混合燃料等)可燃成分高的,极易起燃的 ‖ ～**ly** *adv.* ／ ～**ness** *n.*

riches [ˈritʃiz] [复] *n.* 财富;财产;富有;丰富

rick [rik] *n.* 草堆,禾堆;〈美〉柴垛堆 — *vt.* 把…堆成垛

rickets [ˈrikits] [复] *n.* [用作单或复]【医】佝偻病

rickety [ˈrikiti] *adj.* **1.** 佝偻病的;患佝偻病的;似佝偻病的 **2.** 连接处不牢固的;要摇晃的;东倒西歪的

ricksha [ˈrikʃɔ],**rickshaw** [ˈrikʃɔː] *n.* 人力车,黄包车,东洋车

ricochet [ˈrikəʃet, ˈrikəʃei] *n.* **1.**(石片、子弹等接触地面、水面等时的)跳飞、跳跃;漂掠 **2.** 跳飞的石片;跳弹 — *vi.*(ricochet(t)ed;ricochet(t)ing) *vi.* 跳飞;漂掠 — *vt.* 使跳飞;使跳弹射击弹

rid [rid](rid 或 ridded;ridding) *vt.* **1.** 使摆脱;使去掉(*of*) **2.**〈古〉救;救出 **3.**〈方〉迅速了结(工作);除去;扫除;打扫;收拾 ‖ *be ～ of* 摆脱;去掉 ／ *get ～ of* 摆脱;去掉;除去

riddance [ˈridəns] *n.* 摆脱;清除

ridden [ˈridn] *adj.* [常用以构成复合词]受…支配的;受…压迫的;…横行的;crisis-～ 充满危机的／crime-～ 罪恶极的／be ～ by fears 十分恐惧

riddle¹ [ˈridl] *n.* **1.** 谜语,谜 **2.** 闷葫芦,难以捉摸的人;莫名其妙的事物 — *vt.* 解(谜等);给…出谜;迷惑 — *vi.* 出谜;说谜似的话

riddle² [ˈridl] *n.*(筛谷物、砂石等的)粗筛 — *vt.* **1.** 筛(谷物、砂石等) **2.** 把…打得布满窟窿 **3.** 检查,鉴定(证据等) **4.** 连续质问,处处挑剔;驳倒 **5.** 批评;非难 **6.** 使完全败坏;充满于,弥漫于

ride [raid](rode [rəud], ridden [ˈridn]) *vi.* **1.** 骑马(或自行车等);骑(*on*);乘车;乘(*on, in*) **2.**(车、船等)适于乘(或载);(道路等)骑起马(或自行车)来(觉得舒服、不舒服等) **3.** 漂浮;航行;停泊 **4.** 支撑在…上面;附着,固定;依靠(*on*) **5.**〈俚〉照旧进行;I'll let the matter ～ a few months. 这件事我让它去,过几个月再说。**6.**(骑师等出赛前)称体重 **7.**(在骨骼等)重叠 **8.**(绳子等)绞合 — *vt.* **1.** 骑(马等);乘(车等) **2.** 骑马(或乘车)通过;骑马(或乘车)进行(比赛等);载着;骑着 **3.** 搭载 **4.** 乘(风、浪等) **5.** 经受住;渡过(难关等)(*out*) **6.** 缠住;控制;压制;压在…头上;〈俚〉使苦恼;嘲弄 **7.** 系(船),使停泊 **8.** 重叠在…上 **9.** 顺势退却以减轻(对方来击)之势 — *n.* **1.** 骑;乘车;乘坐;骑马(或乘车)旅行 **2.** 林间道路(尤指供骑马用的) **3.**(公园中)骑乘游乐器具(如旋转木马等) **4.** 绑架谋杀;欺骗,诈骗 **5.** 交通工具 **6.**(英)[复]新募的骑兵队

rider [ˈraidə] *n.* **1.** 骑马(或自行车)的人;乘车的人;滑水(或冲浪)运动员 **2.**

(文件后面的)附文;(议会议案的)附加条款 3.(机件等)架在上面的部分 4.【船】肋骨内侧加强材;(天平的)游码;【建】(支墙)斜撑 5.【数】(复习定理的)应用习题 ‖ ~ship n. 全体乘车者;乘客数

ridge [ridʒ] n. 1. 脊 2. 山(或屋、堤等)脊;岭;山脉,分水岭 3.(狭长的)隆起部 4. 垄,埂 5.(气象图上的)高压脊 — vt. 1. 装(屋)脊;使成脊状;使起垄 2. 给…培土;翻(土)作垄 3. 种(黄瓜等)于垄上 — vi. 成脊状地延伸;起坡 ‖ ~-pole, ~-beam, ~-piece n.【建】栋梁,脊木 / ~ tile 脊瓦 / ~-way n. 山脊(道)路

ridicule ['ridikjuːl] n. & vt. 嘲笑,嘲弄;奚落

ridiculous [ri'dikjuləs] adj. 可笑的;荒谬的;滑稽的 ‖ ~ly adv. / ~ness n.

riding ['raidiŋ] n. 1. 骑(马),乘(车)等 2. (古)(林间或林边的)马道 — adj. 1. 骑马的;(供)骑马用的;乘车用的 2. 在上面操作的 ‖ ~ habit 女骑装 / ~-master n. 骑术教练

rife [raif] adj. [只作表语] 1. 流行的,盛行的;普遍的 2. 充满的;众多的(with)

riff [rif] n.(爵士音乐中的)重复乐段

riffle ['rifl] n. 1.(河流中的)浅滩(浅滩引起的)微波,涟漪;急流 2.【矿】格条;格条分样器,格槽溜样器 3.(纸牌的)弹洗(声) — vt. 1. 使起涟漪(浅滩)2.(用拇指)很快地翻(书页等)的边,弹洗(纸牌)3. 用手指玩弄(小物) — vi. 1.(溪水等)形成浅滩;成涟漪;作潺潺声 2.(用拇指)很快地翻书页(或卷宗等)的边(through)

riffraff ['ræfræf] n. 1.[the ~]下等人,群氓,贱民 2. 地痞流氓,坏蛋,社会渣滓 3. 废物;碎屑

rifle[1] ['raifl] n. 1. 步枪,来复枪;来复线,膛线 2.[~s]步枪队 — vt. 1. 在(枪、枪管、枪膛)内刻来复线 2. 用步枪射击 ‖ ~-man n. 步枪手

rifle[2] ['raifl] vt. 1. 搜劫,抢劫,掠劫;抢(或偷)光 2. 抢去;抢走;带走 — vi. 搜劫,抢劫,掠夺 ‖

rift [rift] n. 1. 裂缝;空隙 2.【地】断裂;断陷谷,长狭谷 3. 分裂,不和 — vt. 1. 劈开;分开 2. 穿透;渗入 — vi. 裂开;断裂;Mists — ed. 雾散开了。‖ ~-valley[地]断陷谷,裂谷

rig[1] [rig](rigged;rigging) vt. 1. 装配(out, up);给(船舶等)装配帆(或索具等);装(帆、索具等)于船桅(或帆桁等)上面;给(飞机)装配机翼(或机身等)2. 拼凑着敏捷、临时搭建;草草做成(up)3. (口)束装(尤指以华美或式样奇特的服装);打扮(out, up)— n. 1.【海】帆装(以船特有的帆、桅型式)2. 成套器械;用具,钻锦,钻井等 3. 全套(口)4.(口)服装(尤指华美或奇特的)‖ ~-ger n.

rig[2] [rig](rigged;rigging) vt. 1.(用欺骗手段)操纵,控制 2.(为达到预期的目的而)事先决定(比赛的输赢、测验好坏等)— n. 1.(主英)嘲弄;戏弄;欺诈;骗局;恶作剧;捣蛋;2. 囤积居奇 ‖ ~-ger n. 操纵者

Riga ['riːɡə] n. 里加[拉脱维亚首都]

rigging ['rigiŋ] n. 1. 帆缆;索具;支架 2. (舞台用)索具;传动装置 3. 服装

right [rait] adj. 1. 正确的,对的 2. 恰当的;顺利的;井井有条的 3. 正常的;好的;健全的 4. 正当的;正义的;公正的 5. 如实的;真正的,名副其实的 6. 正(面)的 7.(线)笔直的[仅用于 a ~ line 及 ~-lined 中];(角等)垂直的,有直角的 8. 右,右边的;右翼的;[常作 R-]右

派的;one's ~ hand (arm)右手(臂);得力助手 — *adv.* **1.** 对,不错 **2.** 顺利,好 **3.** 正直地;正当地 **4.** 公正地 **5.** 如实地 **5.** 直接地,径直地 **6.** [加强语气]正好,恰恰;确;立刻;完全 **7.** 非常,十分 **8.** 在右边;向右 — *n.* **1.** 正确,对 **2.** 正当;公正,正义 **3.** [~s]实况;真情 **4.** 权利;法权;[商](股东以低于市场的价格购买增资股票的)优惠权 **5.** 右,右边,右方;右手;[军]右翼 **6.** [常作R-]议长席右侧的议员;右派议员;右派 — *vt.* **1.** 扶直,使正;整顿;整饬 **2.** 纠正,矫正;补偿;为…伸冤 **3.** ~ up 报复;拯救 — *vi.* (船等)恢复平稳 ‖ ~ly *adv.* **1.** 正确地;恰当地 **2.** 正直地;正当地;正义地 / ~ness *n.* **1.** 正确(性);恰当 **2.** 正直;正当;公正,正义 / ~ward(s) *adv. & adj.* 在右边(的);向右边(的) / ~ angle 直角 / '~-'angled *adj.* 成直角的;有直角的 / ~ fielder (棒球)右翼外场球手 / '~-hand *adj.* **1.** 右边的;得力的;one's ~-hand man 同一伸展上右边的人);得力助手 **2.** handed / '~-'handed *adj.* **1.** 惯用右手针的 **2.** 供右手用的;用右手的 **3.** 顺时针方向的,向右旋转的 **4.** (螺钉等)右螺纹的 *adv.* 用右手 / '~-'hander *n.* **1.** 惯用右手的人 **2.** 用右手打的一击 / '~-'minded *adj.* 有正义感的 / '~-'winger *n.* 右翼分子

right-about ['raitə,baut] *n.* 相反方向;向后转;根本转变 — *adj. & adv.* 向后转的

righteous ['raitʃəs] *adj.* **1.** 正直的;正当的 **2.** 正义的 ‖ ~ly *adv.* / ~ness *n.*

rightful ['raitful] *adj.* **1.** 公正的,正义的 **2.** 合法的;依法有正当要求权的 **3.** 恰当的;合适的 ‖ ~ly *adv.* / ~ness *n.*

rightist ['raitist] [常作R-] *adj.* 右派分子

的;右倾分子的;保守分子的 — *n.* 右派分子;右倾分子

rigid ['ridʒid] *adj.* **1.** 刚硬的,坚硬的;不易弯的 僵硬的,刻板的;严峻的,严厉的;严酷的 **3.** [物]刚性的 **4.** [空]硬式的(如有构架的轻体航空器) ‖ ~ly *adv.*

rigidity [ri'dʒiditi] *n.* **1.** 刚硬,坚硬;不变 **2.** 僵化,刻板;严峻,严厉;严格 **3.** [物]刚性,刚度

rigmarole ['rigmərəul] *n.* **1.** 冗长的废话;胡言乱语;前言不搭后语的讲述 **2.** 烦琐费时的程序(或手续) — *adj.* 条理不清的;前言不搭后语的

rigor ['rigə] *n.* (美) = rigour

rigor ['raigɔ:, 'rigə] 〈拉〉[医](发烧前的)寒战;僵直 ‖ ~ mortis ['mɔ:tis] [医]尸僵,死后强直

rigorous ['rigərəs] *adj.* **1.** (性格等)严峻的,严厉的;严格的;苛刻的 **2.** (气候)严酷的,恶劣的 **3.** 精密的;严密的

rigour ['rigə] *n.* **1.** (性格等)严峻,严厉;严格;苛刻 **2.** [常~s](生活)艰苦(气候)严酷 **3.** 严密;精确

rile [rail] *vt.* **1.** 〈口〉激怒 **2.** 〈美〉搅浑(水等)

rill [ril] *n.* 小河,溪流 — *vi.* 潺潺地流,涓涓流淌

rim [rim] *n.* **1.** 边(尤指圆物的);[机]缘;轮辋(眼镜)框(帽)边 **2.** 边缘 **3.** 海面,水面 — (rimmed; rimming) *vt.* 装边于;装轮缘于;作…的边 — *vi.* 形成边缘;显出边缘

rime [raim] *n., vi. & vt.* = rhyme

rime [raim] *n.* **1.** (诗)白霜(= hoarfrost) **2.** 壳花;结晶 — *vt.* (诗)使蒙上霜(或霜状物)

rind [raind] *n.* **1.** 树皮;果(或蔬菜)皮;

(熏肉、干酪等的)外皮 2. 表面,外观 — *vt.* 削...皮;剥...皮

ring[^1] *n.* 1. 戒指,指环;环形物 2. 圈状,环状;网状 3. [化][数]环 4. (树的)年轮(= annual ~) 5. 圆形场地(如牲畜展览场、马戏场等) 6. [the ~]拳击台;摔跤台 7. [the ~]拳击赛、竞赛;竞选 8. [the ~](总称)以赌赛马为业者 9. 团伙,帮派 — *vt.* 1. 包围(round, about, in),围拢(牛、羊等) 2. 给(牛鼻子等)扣环 3. (投环游戏等)套中(用铅笔等)圈出 4. 环剥(树皮);旋割剥(苹果等皮) — *vi.* 1. 成环形 2. (鹰等)盘旋上升;(被猎的狐狸等)兜圈子奔跑 ‖ ~ finger(尤指左手的)无名指 / ~leader *n.* 首魁 / ~master *n.* 马戏演出指挥;导演 / ~worm *n.* 癣,癣菌病

ring[^2] [rin] (rang [ræn], rung [rʌŋ]) *vi.* 1. (钟、铃等)鸣响 2. 摇铃;摇铃唤人 3. 回响;响彻 4. 听起来 5. [英]打电话 — *vt.* 1. 按(铃);摇(铃);敲(钟等);敲(硬币等) 2. 鸣钟报警(时、表等) 3. [英]打电话给(up) — *n.* 1. 铃声;钟声;洪亮的声音 2. 按铃;打电话 3. (表示某种性质的)声调;味儿;口气 4. (教堂等的)一套钟(乐音)

ringer ['riŋə] *n.* 1. 按铃者;摇铃者;敲钟者;鸣铃器;敲钟用具 2. 〈美俚〉(比赛时用来)冒名顶替的马(或比赛者) 3. 〈美俚〉酷似某人的人;很象某物的东西

ringlet ['riŋlit] *n.* 1. 小环;(毛发的)一小卷(尤指下垂的)长鬈发

rink [riŋk] *n.* 1. (室内)溜冰场 2. 滚球草场;冰球场 3. 滚球队;冰球队 — *vi.* 在溜冰场上溜冰

rinse [rins] *vt.* 1. 冲洗;轻洗(头发、手等);漂清(衣服等) 2. 漱;嗽(out) ·

漂掉;冲洗掉(out, away) 4. (用水等)吞咽下(食物)(down) — *vi.* 漂净 — *n.* 1. 漂清;冲洗 2. (漂清或冲洗用的)清水 3. 染发液

rinsing ['rinsiŋ] *n.* [常~s]洗涮过东西的水;(衣等)漂洗水

Rio de Janeiro [ˌriːəu də dʒə'niərəu] *n.* 里约热内卢(市)[巴西东南部港市]里约热内卢(州)[巴西州名]

riot ['raiət] *n.* 1. 暴乱,骚动 2. 狂欢(声);狂闹(声);闹饮;闹宴;放荡 3. (色彩的)丰富;(感情等)的放纵·a ~ of colour 色彩缤纷 4. (口)惹动的演出;极其有趣的人 — *vi.* 1. 闹事,骚乱 2. 放纵;沉湎于(in) — *vt.* 挥霍,浪费 ‖ ~ police 防暴警察

riotous ['raiətəs] *adj.* 1. 暴乱的,骚动的,煽动暴乱的 2. 狂欢的;狂闹的;放纵的,放荡的 3. (色彩等)丰富的 4.(植物等)茂盛的

rip[^1] [rip] (ripped; ripping) *vt.* 1. 撕,扯;剖;划破 2. 劈;锯(木材等);凿开(岩石等) 3. 拆(衣、屋顶等) 4. 〈古〉重新翻出(宿怨、往事等)(up) — *vi.* 1. 破开,裂开 2. (车、船等)猛开,猛冲 — *n.* 裂口,裂缝 ‖ ~off *n.* 偷窃;骗钱

rip[^2] [rip] *n.* 1. 不中用的(老)马;不中用的东西 2. 浪子,荒淫之人

rip[^3] [rip] *n.* 狂澜;激流

ripe [raip] *adj.* 1. 熟的;成熟的;时机成熟的;准备好的 2. (宜存放)适于食用的·~ wine 醇酒 3. 成年的;年高的;老练的 4.(疖等)已化脓的;(白内障等)可开刀的 — *vt. & vi.* 〈主诗〉= ripen ‖ ~ly *adv.* / ~ness *n.*

ripen ['raipən] *vt.* 1. 使熟;使成熟 2.(经贮存等)使(乳酪、牛肉等)鲜美 3.(疖等)使适于开刀 — *vi.* 成熟

ripping ['ripiŋ] *adj.* 1. 撕的;劈的;拆的

2.〈英俚〉极好的,绝妙的;令人愉快的 — *adv.* 〈英俚〉极好地,绝妙地;非常

ripple ['ripl] *n.* **1.** 涟漪;细浪;波纹(头发,丝带等的)卷纹 **2.** 小溪流 **3.** 潺潺声;起伏声 **4.** 【物】脉动,波动 — *vi.* 起细浪;作潺潺声 — *vt.* 使成细浪;使飘动 ‖ ～ **mark**(砂,岩等上的)波痕 ‖ **波状纹**

rise [raiz] (rose [rəuz], risen ['rizn]) *vi.* **1.** 起立;起床;直立 **2.** 升起;上升 **3.** 上涨;增长;增强 **4.** 高耸,高出;高起,隆起 **5.** 起义,反抗;起反 **6.** 地位升高;兴起 **7.** 浮起;浮现,现出 **8.** 发源;起因 **9.** 闭会;休会 **10.** 死而复生,复活 **11.** 起而应付(*to*) — *vt.* **1.** 使(鸟)飞起;诱(鱼)浮上水面 **2.**【海】驶近使(另一船)渐现于视野 **3.**〈方〉抬高(价格) **4.**〈俚〉饲养;抚养 — *n.* **1.** 升起,上升 **2.** 上涨,增长;高地,岗地,斜坡(楼梯)的级高;(弓形的)矢高 **4.**(地位、权力、价值、音调等的)升高;兴起 **5.** 出现;(鱼浮游时的)浮起;再生,复活 **6.** 起源;发生

riser ['raizə] *n.* **1.** 起床的人;an early ～ 早起的人 **2.** 起义者;叛乱者 **3.**【建】(楼梯)踏步板高,竖板;立管 **4.**【冶】模铸熔出气口

risible ['rizibl] *adj.* **1.** 爱笑的;能笑的 **2.** 笑的;可笑的,滑稽的 ‖ **risi'bility** *n.*

rising ['raiziŋ] *n.* **1.** 上升的;上涨的;增长的 **2.** 渐高的;向上斜的 **3.** 劲头正的;在发展的 — *n.* **1.** 起立;起床 **2.** 升起,上升 **3.** 上涨 **4.** 高地,高处部分 **5.** 起义;造反;叛乱 **6.** 脓疱;疮;肿疮 **7.** 复活,复苏 — *prep.* **1.**〈口〉将近...(岁) **2.**〈美口〉超过...(数)...(数)以上;*Rising* (*of*) 10,000 tons of steel were shipped away. 一万吨以上的

钢铁运走了。

risk [risk] *n.* **1.** 危险,风险 **2.**(保险业用语)...险;危险率;保险金(额);保险对象(包括人和物) — *vt.* **1.** 冒...的危险;使遭受危险 **2.** 冒险干

risky ['riski] *adj.* 危险的;冒险的;爱冒险的;大胆的

risotto [ri'sɔtəu] ([复] risottos) 〈意〉 *n.* (用鸡肉,洋葱等调味的)菜饭

rite [rait] *n.* **1.** 仪式;典礼 **2.**【宗】礼拜式 **3.** 习俗;惯例

ritual ['ritjuəl] *n.* **1.** 仪式;典礼;宗教仪式 **2.**(仪式程序入仪式书;仪式的举行 — *adj.*(宗教)仪式的,典礼的 ‖ ～**ism** *n.*

ritzy ['ritsi] *adj.*〈美俚〉**1.** 极其时髦的;非常豪华的 **2.** 炫耀的;势利的

rival ['raivəl] *n.* **1.** 竞争者,对手 **2.** 匹敌者;可与之相比的东西 — *adj.* 竞争的 — (rival(l)ed; rival(l)ing) — *vt.* **1.** 与...竞争 **2.** 与...相匹敌;比得上 — *vi.* 竞争

rivalry ['raivəlri] *n.* 竞争;竞赛;敌对

rive [raiv] (过去式 rived, 过去分词 riven ['rivən] 或 rived) *vt.* **1.** 撕开,扯裂;劈开;折断;拧去,扭去(*off, away, from*) **2.** 使(精神等)沮丧;使(心)碎 — *vi.* 裂开;撕开;破裂 — *n.*〈英方〉拉;裂缝隙

river ['rivə] *n.* **1.** 江,河;水道:the ～ *Thames* (英国)泰晤士河 **2.** 巨流;[～s] 大量 **3.** 生与死的界线

rivet ['rivit] *n.* 铆钉 — *vt.* **1.** 铆,铆接,铆牢 **2.** 敲打(螺钉)使成铆钉头(以铆牢) **3.** 固定;(目光(目光,注意力)吸引 ‖ ～**er** *n.* 铆工;铆钉枪

Riviera [ˌrivi'ɛərə] *n.* **1.** 里维埃拉(法国东南部和意大利西北部沿地中海的假日游憩胜地) **2.**(气候温和的)海滨游憩胜地

rivulet ['rivjulit] *n.* 小河,溪流

Riyadh [ri:'jɑ:d] *n.* 利雅得[沙特阿拉伯首都]

rm. *abbr.* 1. ream 2. room

RMB *abbr.* (汉) Renminbi

Rn 【化】元素氡(radon)的符号

RNA, rna *abbr.* ribonucleic acid【生化】核糖核酸

roach[1] [rəutʃ] *n.* 【动】1.(欧洲产)斜齿鳊 2.(美国产)金体美鲤鱼;加州鳊

roach[2] [rəutʃ] *n.* 1. 蟑螂(= cockroach) 2.(美俚)(大麻卷烟的)烟蒂

road [rəud] *n.* 1. 路,道路;公路 2.(美)铁路 2. 车行道 3. 途径 4.[常～s]近岸锚地,港外锚地 5.(美)[the～]巡回演出(或比赛等)的路线(或地点) — *vt.* (狗)闻着嗅迹追 ‖～ **bed** *n.* 1. 路基,路床;路基(表)面 2. 行车道 ‖～ **block** *n.*(尤指标有路线、距离的)旅行指南 ‖～ **stead** *n.* 近岸锚地,港外锚地 ‖～ **way** *n.* 1. 道路,路面 2. 车行道(区别于人行道)【铁道】的路线

roadster ['rəudstə] *n.* 1.(一排座的)敞篷小客车 2. 骑用(或拉车用)马

roam [rəum] *vi.* 漫游;游荡;游历 — *vt.* 在…漫步;漫游 — *n.* 1. 漫步;漫游 2. 游历 ‖～ **er** *n.*

roan [rəun] *adj. & n.* 沙毛的(牲畜)(指红白间色或黑白杂色的马或其它牲畜)

roar [rɔ:] *vi.* 1.(狮、虎等)吼叫;(海、风等)怒号;呼啸;(雷、炮、马达等)轰鸣 2. 呼喊;大笑 3. 高声歌唱 4.(会场等)喧闹;回响(*again*) 4.(马)喘鸣 — *vt.* 1. 呼喊;大声喊出;高唱 2. 叫喊倒使… 3. 使轰鸣 — *n.* 1. 吼,啸;怒号;咆哮;轰鸣声;喧闹声 2. 大

叫;大笑声 ‖～ **er** *n.*

roaring ['rɔ:riŋ] *n.* 1. 吼声;咆哮;怒号;轰鸣 2.(马)喘鸣症 — *adj.* 1.吼叫的;咆哮的;轰鸣的 2. 喧闹的;狂暴的;沸腾的 3.(口)兴旺的;活跃的;健康的

roast [rəust] *vt.* 1. 烤;炙;烘 2.(冶)焙烧 2.(烤肉)使受热(或透) 3. 捉弄;嘲笑苛责 — *vi.* 1. 烤;炙;烘;焙 2. 烤肉;炙肉 3. 烤食野餐会 4. 捉弄;嘲笑;苛责 — *adj.* 烤过的 ‖～ **er** *n.*

rob [rɔb] (robbed;robbing) *vt.* 1. 抢劫;劫掠;～ **a man** of his money 抢人钱财 2. 非法剥夺;使丧失;～ **sb.** of his rights 非法剥夺某人的权利 — *vi.* 抢劫;劫掠;盗窃

robber ['rɔbə] *n.* 强盗;盗贼

robbery ['rɔbəri] *n.* 1. 抢劫;劫掠;盗取;抢劫案 2.【律】抢劫罪

robe [rəub] *n.* 1. 长袍;罩袍(婴孩穿的)罩衣;(美)晨衣;(化妆时穿的)长衣;浴衣 2.[常～s]礼服;官服;制服;法衣 3.(毛皮、织物等制的)披肩;覆盖物;车毯 — *vt. & vi.*(给…)穿上长袍(或罩袍等);(给…)披上法衣

robin ['rɔbin] *n.*【动】旅鸫;欧亚鸲 ‖ **Robin Goodfellow** 罗宾·古德费洛(英国民间传说中顽皮而善良的小妖) ‖～ **snow**(美)春季小雪

Robin Hood ['rɔbin hud] 罗宾汉(英国民间传说中劫富济贫的绿林好汉;常用作文艺题材)

robot ['rəubɔt] *n.* 1. 机器人;自动机;自动仪器;遥控机械装置;自动控制导弹,飞弹;自动交通信号 2. 机器般工作的人

robust [rəu'bʌst] *adj.* 1. 强健的,茁壮的;健全的 2.(运动等)需要很强体力的 3. 坚强的;坚定的;真实的 4. 粗鲁的,粗

野的 5. 浓的 ‖ **~ly** *adv.* / **~ness** *n.*

roc [rɔk] *n.* 1. (阿拉伯、波斯传说中的) 巨鸟, 大鹏 2. [R-] 大鹏式制导炸弹

rock[1] *vi.* 1. 摇; 摇摆; 轻摇; (喻) 抚慰 2. 使摇摆, 使摇晃; 使震动; 使震惊 3. 【矿】(用洗矿箱) 摇洗 (矿砂) 4. [印](制铜版时) 拉毛 (版面) ― *vi.* 1. 摇; 摇摆; 震动 ― *n.* 1. 摇动; 摇摆 2. 摇滚舞 3. (美俚) 美国频度派男青年 (一般穿彩色运动衫、留长发、跳摇滚舞) ‖ **~ and roll**, **~ 'n'roll** [ˌrɔkn'rɔul] *n. & adj.* 摇滚舞(曲)(的)(的) *vi.* 跳摇滚舞

rock[2] [rɔk] *n.* 1. 岩, 岩石; 磐石; 礁石 2. 石头, 石块 3. 柱石; 基石; 靠山 4. [常~s] 暗礁; 灾难; 危险 5. (美俚) [~s] 钱; [~s] 钱; (俚) 钻石; 宝石 6. 一种硬糖 7. [the R-] 直布罗陀(Gibraltar) 8. = ~ dove 9. = ~ fish ‖ **~ bottom** 价的最低点 / **~-bound** *adj.* 被岩石包围的; 多岩的 / **~ cake** 岩皮糕 (一种表面粗硬的糕点) / **~ dove** 野鸽, 原鸽 (亦称 blue ~) / **'~fish** *n.* 岩鱼 (~fish ~), **work** *n.* 1. 假山 2. 天然岩石群 3. 攀岩技术

rocker ['rɔkə] *n.* 1. 摇的人; 摇动摇篮者 2. (摇篮、摇椅等脚下摇动用的) 弯杆 3. 摇椅; 可摇动的东西 (如摇木马等) 4. 【机】摇杆; 摇臂 5. 【矿】淘金摇动槽 6. (俚) 头

rockery ['rɔkəri] *n.* 假山; 有假山的园林

rocket ['rɔkit] *n.* 1. 火箭 2. 火箭式投射器; 火箭弹 3. 火箭式烟火 4. (英俚) 斥责 ― *vi.* 1. 用火箭运载 2. 用火箭攻击 ― *vi.* 1. 飞速上升; (野鸟等) 惊飞; 急速高飞; (马等) 猛跃 2. 飞驰 3. 乘火箭旅行

rocking ['rɔkiŋ] *adj.* 摇动的; 来回摇摆

的; 作摇动用的 ‖ **~ chair** 摇椅 / **~ horse** 摇木马(玩具)

rocky[1] ['rɔki] *adj.* 1. 岩石的; 多岩石的; 坚如岩石的 2. 磐石般的, 岩石的; 坚固的 3. 无情的, 冷酷的 ‖ **rockily** *adv.* / **rockiness** *n.*

rocky[2] ['rɔki] *adj.* 1. (口) 摇动的; 不稳的 2. (因酒醉、体弱等) 摇摆晃晃的; 头晕目眩的 3. 障碍重重的; 困难的

Rocky Mountains ['rɔki'mauntinz] 落基山脉(或译落矶山脉)[北美洲西部]

rococo [rəu'kəukəu] ([复] rococos) *n.* 洛可可式 (18 世纪初起源于法国的一种建筑装饰艺术风格, 其特点为精巧、繁顼和华丽) ― *adj.* 洛可可式的; 过分精巧的; 俗丽的

rod [rɔd] *n.* 1. (树的) 枝条; 柳条 2. 杆, 竿; 棒, 标竿、标尺、枚举杖、避雷针等; 测杆; 【微】杆状体, 杆菌; 【解】视网膜杆 3. (拷打用的) 刑条; 棍棒; [the ~] 拷打; 鞭笞; 惩罚 4. 权杖; 权势; 暴政 5. (度量单位) 杆 (= 5½ 码); 平方杆 (= 30¼ 平方码) 6. (美俚) (左轮) 手枪 7. 钓鱼者 8. (基督教《圣经》用语) 支派, 世系 9. (美俚) 改装的大功率高速汽车

rode [rəud] ride 的过去式

rodent ['rəudənt] *adj.* 1. 咬的; 嚼的 2. 【动】啮齿类的 3. 【医】侵蚀性的 ― *n.* 啮齿动物 (如兔、鼠等) ‖ **~icide** [rəu'dentisaid] *n.* 灭鼠剂

rodeo ['rəudiəu, rəu'deiəu] *n.* 1. (美国西部的) 赶牲牛群, 圈牛; (集中牛马的) 围场 2. (美国西部牧场牧人等的) 竞技表演 3. (摩托车等的) 花式表演

roe [rəu] *n.* 1. (鱼) 雌鱼卵 2. 鱼 (或甲壳动物等的) 卵 3. (木材锯开后显出的) 鱼卵形斑纹 ‖ **~ buck** ([复] ~ buck(s)) *n.* (雄) 狍 / **~ deer** 狍

roentgen ['rʌntjən] *n.* ‖ ~ **ray** 伦琴射线
(即 X 射线)

roger ['rɔdʒə] *int.* **1.**(无线电话通讯用语)
已收到! 已获悉! **2.**〈俚〉对! 好! 行!

rogue [rəʊg] *n.* **1.** 流氓,无赖;〈古〉流浪
汉 **2.**〈谑〉淘气鬼;爱捉弄人者 **3.**(赛
马、比赛)偷懒的人 **4.**凶猛的离群兽
(尤指象;= ~ elephant) **4.**(尤指植物
的)劣种 — *vi.* **1.** 游手好闲;耍无赖
2. 除去劣种 — *vt.* **1.** 欺诈 **2.** 除去(劣
种) **3.** 除去(地)里的劣种 — *adj.*(野兽)
凶猛的

roguish ['rəʊgiʃ] *adj.* **1.** 流氓的,无赖的;
不老实的 **2.** 淘气的,调皮的;恶作剧
的:as ~ as a kitten 似小猫一样调皮 ‖
~ **ly** *adv.* / ~ **ness** *n.*

roil [rɔil]〈美〉*vt.* **1.** 搅浑 **2.** 惹怒 **3.** 激
起(争吵,争论) — *vi.* 动荡 ‖ ~ **y** *adj.*

roister ['rɔistə] *vi.* **1.** 大摇大摆,摆架子
2. 喧闹;闹饮 ‖ ~ **er** *n.*

role [rəʊl] *n.* **1.**〈戏〉角色:play the ~ of
Hamlet 扮演汉姆雷特的角色 **2.** 作用;
任务;职责:the ~ of the tape recorder in
language-learning 磁带录音机在语言学
习中的作用

roll [rəʊl] *vi.* **1.** 滚动;打滚 **2.** 滚滚而动
3. 行驶;乘车行驶;飘流,流浪 **4.** 左右
摇晃,摇摆;蹒跚地走 **5.** 流逝(on, by)
6.(地形)起伏,绵展 **7.** 发出隆隆声;轰
鸣 **8.**(眼睛)转动;循环运行 **9.** 卷,
裹;卷绕;卷缩 **10.** 辗,轧,擀;滚动起来
11. 玩滚球 **12.**(车轮等)转动(或
行动):The cameras were ready to
~.(电影等)拍摄即将开始。**13.** 发展,
进展 — *vt.* **1.** 使滚动;滚成:~ a huge
snow ball 滚成大雪球 **2.** 使滚滚而动 **3.**
推(车);行驶(路程);用车载运 **4.** 使
摇摆(前进)**5.** 擂(鼓);发(卷舌音或
颤音)[音]滚奏 **6.** 使(眼睛)转动

7. 卷,裹;绕;搓;铺:~ up one's sleeves
卷起袖子;准备大干 ∥ one's bed on
the floor 地铺 **8.** 辗,轧,擀:滚平;擀
平 **9.** 掷(骰子)**10.** 把油墨滚在⋯上
11. 开动(摄影机等)**12.**〈俚〉盗窃(睡
者、喝醉的人等)口袋里的东西 — *n.*
1.(一)卷;卷轴;卷状物;面包卷;卷饼;
烟卷;(装物用)卷包,卷套;做成卷曲
状的头发:He has ~s of fat on him. 他
胖得圆滚滚的。**2.** 一卷钞票;〈美俚〉
手头钱 **3.** 名册;目录;公文;案卷;档
案 **4.**(服装的)翻边 **5.** 滚路机,压路
机;(封面)压型机;(打字机等的)滚动
滚筒;【建】(柱头的)旋涡饰 **6.** 滚动;
滚;(杂技、舞蹈等的)翻滚,翻筋斗;
[空]横滚:a ~ top desk 有活动顶板的
书桌 **7.**(波浪的)翻滚;(话声的)滔滔
不绝 **8.**(船等的)摇晃 **9.** 隆隆声;轰鸣
声;(鼓)急骤声 **10.** 滚奏;(金丝雀
等的)啭鸣 **11.**(地形)起伏;隆起 ‖
~ **-back** *n.* **1.**(物价等的)回降;削
减 **2.** 击退 / ~ **call** 点名;点名号(或时
间)

roller ['rəʊlə] *n.* **1.** 打滚的人;滚动的东
西 **2.** 滚柱;滚筒;辊;辗子;滚轴;【印】
油墨辊 **3.** 滚路机,压路机(打字机);**4.**
绷带卷;卷轴 **5.** 巨浪 **6.** 翻头鸽;(德国
种)金丝雀 ‖ ~ **bandage** 绷带卷 /
bearing 滚柱轴承 / ~ **coaster**(游乐场
的)环行铁道;环滑车 / ~ **skate** 旱冰
鞋,四轮滑冰鞋 / ~ **skate** *vi.* 穿旱冰鞋
滑行

rollick ['rɔlik] *vi. & n.* 嬉戏;欢闹 ‖
~ **ing** *adj.*

rolling ['rəʊliŋ] *adj.* **1.** 滚的;可滚动的 **2.**
周而复始的 **3.**(眼睛等)转动的 **4.**(衣
领等)翻卷的 **5.** 翻滚的,摇摆的 **6.** 滚
滚的 **7.**(雷声等)隆隆的 **8.**(金丝雀等)
啭鸣的 **8.**(地形)起伏的;绵延的 — *n.*
1. 滚动;打滚;翻滚 **2.** 隆隆声;啭鸣声

‖~ **pin** 擀面杖 /~ **stock**（铁路或汽车公司拥有的）全部车辆 /~ **stone** 1. 不定居的人；见异思迁的人 2. [the Rolling Stones]滚石乐队

roly-poly ['rəuli'pəuli] *n.* **1.**（有果酱的）卷形布丁 2.〈口〉胖娃娃；矮胖子 —*adj.* 矮胖的；圆胖的

ROM *abbr.* read-only memory

romaine [rəu'mein] *n.*〈美〉【植】长叶莴苣，生菜

Roman ['rəumən] *n.* **1.** 古罗马人；罗马人；（罗）罗马天主教徒；[~s]古罗马基督教徒 2.[常作 r-]【印】罗马字；罗马体；正体字；罗马体铅字 3. 意大利罗马方言；古罗马语；拉丁语 —*adj.* **1.**（古）罗马的；（古）罗马人的；拉丁的 2.[常作 r-]罗马字（体）的；正体的；罗马数字的 3. 罗马的；罗马教廷的 ‖~ **Catholic**（罗马）天主教的/~天主教徒的/~ **Catholic Church**（罗马）天主教会/~ **numerals** 罗马数字（如 I, II, V 等）

roman [rɔ'mɑŋ]〈法〉*n.* **1.**（中世纪在法国发展起来的）韵文体传奇故事 2. 长篇小说

Romance [rəu'mæns] *n.* 罗曼语 —*adj.* 罗曼语的

romance [rəu'mæns] *n.* **1.**（中世纪）骑士故事，罗曼史；传奇；（虚构的）冒险（或恋爱）故事 2. 传奇文学；浪漫文学 3. 传奇气氛；浪漫倾向；夸大描述；生动虚构 4. 风流的韵事；浪漫事迹；离奇遭遇；虚幻事物 5.[音]浪漫曲 —*vi.* 1. 写传奇；讲传奇故事 2. 渲染；夸大；编造 3.〈口〉谈情说爱；追求 —*vt.* 〈口〉和…恋爱；追求

Romania [rəu'meinjə] *n.* 罗马尼亚[欧洲巴尔干半岛东北部国家] ‖~**n** *adj.* 罗马尼亚的；罗马尼亚人的；罗马尼亚

语的 *n.* 罗马尼亚人；罗马尼亚语

romantic [rəu'mæntik] *adj.* **1.** 浪漫的；风流的；热烈的（尤指爱情）2. 传奇（式）的；富于浪漫色彩的 3. 耽于幻想的；不切实际的；虚构的；荒诞的；夸大的 4.[常作 R-]（文艺等）浪漫主义的；浪漫派的 —*n.* **1.** 浪漫的人 2.[常作 R-]浪漫主义作家（或艺术家等）3.[~s]浪漫思想（或言行等）‖~**ally** *adv.* /~**ism** [rə'mæntisizəm] *n.* **1.**[常作 R-]浪漫主义（运动）2. 浪漫精神（或倾向等）

Romany, Rommany ['rɔməni] *n. & adj.* 吉卜赛人（的）；吉卜赛语

Rome [rəum] *n.* **1.** 罗马[意大利首都] 2.【史】罗马城；罗马城邦；罗马（奴隶制）共和国；罗马帝国

romp [rɔmp] *n.* **1.** 顽皮孩子（尤指女孩）2. 蹦蹦跳跳；欢闹；顽皮的游戏 3.（赛马、竞赛等中）轻松取胜的步法（或速率）4.（儿童等）蹦跳的人 5.[儿童]宽松连裤外衣，连衫裤 —*vi.* **1.** 蹦蹦跳跳地走；愉快活跃地行进 2.[俚]轻易地取胜；迅速地成功 ‖~ **er** *n.* **1.** 嬉耍的人 2.[~s]（儿童的）宽松连裤外衣，连衫裤

rood [ruːd] *n.* **1.** 十字架；基督受难十字架，苦像 2.〈英〉路德（面积单位，相当于 1/4 英亩）

roof [ruːf] *n.* **1.** 屋顶；车顶；〈喻〉住屋，家 2. 顶，顶部 3.【矿】顶板 4.（飞机）机身上部的包皮 5. 担任空中掩护的飞机 6.〈俗〉[复]绝对升限 —*vt.* **1.** 给…盖上屋顶；做…的屋面 2. 遮蔽；庇护 ‖~ **er** *n.* /~**less** *adj.* 无屋顶的；无住屋的，无家可归的/~ **garden** 屋顶花园/~**spotter** *n.*〈英〉（由非军人担任的）屋顶对空监视员/~**tree** *n.* 栋梁，脊梁

roofed [ruːft] *adj.* **1.** 有顶的；有屋顶的

2. [用以构成复合词]有...屋顶的

roofing ['ru:fiŋ] *n.* 1. 盖屋顶 2. 屋顶用材料 3. 屋顶

rook¹ [ruk] *n.* (国际象棋中的)车

rook² [ruk] *n.* 1. [动] 秃鼻乌鸦 2. (以赌博营生者的)赌棍;骗子 — *vt.* (用赌博)骗(某人)钱;诈取;敲诈(顾客)

rookery ['rukəri] *n.* 1. 秃鼻乌鸦结巢处;秃鼻乌鸦群;(海豹、企鹅等的)群;群栖处 2. 破旧住房;贫民窟;(各种穷客居住的)租屋 3. 同类人(或物)的集中处

rookie, rooky ['ruki] *n.* 〈俚〉新兵;生手;新来者

room [rum, ru:m] *n.* 1. 房间;室 2. [～s]一套房间;寓所 2. 地位;空间 3. 余地;机会 4. 全室的人 — *vi.* 住宿;寄宿住 — *vt.* 留...住宿 ‖ *make～for* 给...让出地方 ‖ *～er n.* 〈美〉寄宿者 ‖ *～ing house* 〈美〉供寄宿的房屋;可出租单个房间的公寓 / *～mate n.* 住在同室的人,室友;〈婉〉同居者,姘居者

roomy ['rumi] *adj.* 宽敞的;宽大的 ‖ **roominess** *n.*

roost [ru:st] *n.* 1. 栖木;栖息处;鸡棚;群栖的家禽 3. 〈口〉憩息处;卧室;群栖的家禽 3. 〈口〉憩息处;卧室;群栖处 — *vi.* 1. 栖息;进窝 2. 憩息;过夜 — *vt.* 为...设置栖息处;把...送去憩息

rooster ['ru:stə] *n.* 1. 公鸡;雄禽鸟 2. 〈美〉狂妄自负的人

root¹ [ru:t] *n.* 1. 根;根茎,地下茎;块根;[～s]块根植物 2. 根;根本;根源;本质 3. 〈美〉根源,来源 4. 祖先;[基督教义](圣经)用语子孙 5. [数]根 6. 【语】词根 7. 【音】(和弦的)根音 — *vt.* 1. 使生根;使扎根;使固定 2. 根除,铲除;肃清(*up, out*) — *vi.* 1. 生根;固定 2. 根源在于,来源于(*in*) ‖ *～er n.* 1.

拔根的人;拔根器 2. 生根的人(或事物) / *～less adj.* 无根的;无根据的;不定居的 ‖ *～ crop* 根用作物

root² [ru:t] *vi.* 1. (猪等)用鼻拱土 2. 搜,搜,寻找 3. 〈美口〉(为生计等)努力工作;苦干 — *vt.* 1. (猪等)用鼻拱;用鼻拱翻出(*out*) 2. 搜出;发现(*out*) ‖ *～er n.* (筑路用)翻土机

root³ [ru:t] *vi.* 〈美俚〉1. (为比赛者等)鼓气,捧场;欢呼,喝彩(*for*) 2. 赞助;支持(*for*) ‖ *～er n.* 啦啦队员;热情支持者

rooted ['ru:tid] *adj.* 生根的;根深蒂固的

rope [rəup] *n.* 1. 绳,索;[the～s](拳击台等四周的)围绳 2. [the～s]绞索;绞刑 3. 一串(东西) 4. (啤酒等饮料中产生的)丝状粘质 5. 〈美俚〉雪茄烟 6. 〈俚〉套(马)索 7. [the～s]内情;规则;做法 — *vt.* 1. 捆,扎,绑;用绳系住;用绳捆 2. 用绳圈起(或隔开)(*in, off, out*) 3. 〈美〉用套索套捉(牛、马等) 4. 拉成绳(状) — *vi.* (啤酒等)产生丝状粘质 3. (爬山者)用绳子系在一起 ‖ *～,dancer n.* (杂技团的)走(钢)索表演员 / *～way n.* (悬空)索道

rosary ['rəuzəri] *n.* 1. 玫瑰园;玫瑰花坛 2. [天主教](一串)念珠(共一百六十五颗);[常作 R-]念珠祈祷;(玫瑰经)

rose¹ [rəuz] rise 的过去式

rose² [rəuz] *n.* 1. 蔷薇科植物;蔷薇花,玫瑰花:*a monthly～* 月季花 / *～ of May* 【植】白水仙 2. 玫瑰色,玫瑰红;[～s]红润的面色 3. 玫瑰香(剂) 4. (洒水壶或水管等的)蓬篷式喷嘴 5. 玫瑰状宝石(或钻石) 6. 【海】罗经卡 7. 玫瑰花饰(如玫瑰花结等);玫瑰花形纹章(尤指英国国徽) 8. [粤]圆花窗 9. 〈蒙特纳国际电视节授予的)玫瑰奖(分金、银、铜三等) 10. 【数】玫瑰线 — *adj.* 1. 蔷

薇花的;玫瑰花的;作玫瑰花用的;含有玫瑰花的 **2.** 玫瑰色的 — **vt. 1.** 使成玫瑰色,使(脸等)变红 **2.** 使有玫瑰香味 ‖ ~**bud** *n.* **1.** 玫瑰花苞 **2.** 〈美〉漂亮姑娘;初入社交界的少女 / ~**water** 玫瑰香水 ;(喻)奉承话 ;温和做法: treat with ~ *water* 用温和的办法对待 / '~**water** *adj.* **1.** 有玫瑰香水香味的;似玫瑰香水的 **2.** (作品等)故作细腻的;矫揉造作的;感伤的 / ~**window** 圆花窗 / '~**wood** *n.* 红木(黑檀、紫檀等);澳洲蔷薇木

roseate ['rəuziət, 'rəuziit] *adj.* **1.** 玫瑰色的 **2.** 光明的,有希望的 **3.** 乐观的;欢快的 ‖ ~**ly** *adv.*

rosemary ['rəuzməri] *n.* 〖植〗迷迭香

rosette [rəu'zet] *n.* **1.** 玫瑰花形物(如徽章等);玫瑰花饰(如玫瑰花结等) **2.** 〖建〗圆花窗;圆花饰 **3.** 〖电〗(天花板)灯线匣 **4.** 〖植〗莲座(叶)丛

Rosh Hashana ['rɔʃ hə'ʃɑːnə]岁首节(即犹太教历的新年)

rosin ['rɔzin] *n.* 松香,松脂;树脂 — *vt.* 用松香涂(或擦)(小提琴的弓等)

roster ['rəustə] *n.* **1.** (军队等的)值勤人员表 **2.** 名人册;逐项登记表

rostra ['rɔstrə] rostrum 的复数

rostrum ['rɔstrəm] ([复] rostrums 或 rostra ['rɔstrə]) *n.* **1.** 演讲台;坛;讲坛 **2.** (古罗马战舰的)喙形舰首 **3.** 〖动〗喙,吻突

rosy ['rəuzi] *adj.* **1.** 玫瑰色的,玫瑰红的;红润的;(因害羞等)涨红脸的 **2.** 美好的;光明的;乐观的 ‖ **rosily** *adv.* / **rosiness** *n.*

rot [rɔt] (rotted; rotting) *vi.* **1.** 烂,腐坏;腐败;堕落 **2.** (在狱中等)消瘦;憔悴 **3.** 〈英俚〉用进行时态)开玩笑;讲述苦话 — *vt.* **1.** 使腐烂;使腐朽;使腐败;使堕落 **2.** 〈俚〉弄糟 **3.** 〈英俚〉嘲弄(或

苦 **4.** 把(麻等)沤软 — *n.* **1.** 腐烂;腐朽;腐败;堕落 **2.** 腐烂的东西;腐朽的事物 **3.** (植物的)腐病;〖医〗肝双盘吸虫病;[the ~]羊肝蛭病 **4.** 〈俚〉废话;蠢事;荒唐 **5.** 一连串失败,节节失利 — *int.* [表示厌恶、蔑视、烦恼等]胡说!混蛋! 糟了!

Rotarian [rəu'tɛəriən] *n.* "扶轮国际"成员 — *adj.* "扶轮国际"(成员)

rotary ['rəutəri] *adj.* **1.** 旋转的,转动的 **2.** 轮转的;旋转式的 **3.** 轮换的;轮流的 — *n.* **1.** 旋转式机器(如轮转印刷机、旋转钻井机、轮缸式发动机等) **2.** 〈美〉〖交〗(几条道路环绕圆形广场、单向通行的)环行交叉 **3.** [(the)R~]"扶轮国际"(= Rotary International;原名扶轮社,系国际性社团,总部设在美国) ‖ **Rotary Club**"扶轮国际"分社

rotate [rəu'teit] *vi.* **1.** 旋转,转动 **2.** 循环;轮流 — *vt.* **1.** 使旋转,使转动 **2.** 使轮流,使交替 **3.** 轮换(人员等) — ['rəuteit] *adj.* 〖植〗辐状的 ‖ **rotator** *n.*

rotation [rəu'teiʃən] *n.* **1.** 旋转,转动;转动量 **2.** 〖天〗自转 **3.** 循环;轮流,交替;〖农〗轮作,换茬 **3.** 〖物〗旋度

rotatory ['rəutətəri] *adj.* **1.** (使)旋转的,(使)转动的 **2.** (使)循环的;(使)轮流的 **3.** 〖物〗旋光的

rote [rəut] *n.* **1.** 死记硬背:learn by ~ 死记硬背地学习 **2.** 老一套;机械的方法;陈规俗套

rotisserie [rəu'tisəri] *n.* **1.** 烤肉店,烤肉铺 **2.** (携带式)电热轮转烤肉器

rotochute ['rəutəʃuːt] *n.* (配有减低下降速度的螺旋桨式的)旋翼降落伞

rotor ['rəutə] *n.* **1.** 〖机〗旋转部;旋转器;转子 **2.** (直升飞机等的)旋翼

rotten ['rɔtn] *adj.* **1.** 腐烂的;发臭的;腐朽的;腐败的;堕落的 **2.** (石)风化的;

易碎的 3. 虚弱的;不健全的;不中用的 4.〈俚〉蹩脚的;讨厌的;糟糕的 5.〔羊〕患肝蛭病的 ‖ ~·ly *adv.* / ~·ness *n.*

rotter ['rɔtə] *n.*〈英俚〉可恶的人;无赖;下流坯;讨厌的家伙;不中用的家伙

rotund [rəu'tʌnd] *adj.* 1. 圆形的 2. 圆胖的 3.(声音)洪亮的,圆润的(文体、谈吐)华丽的;浮夸的 ‖ ~·ly *adv.*

rotunda [rəu'tʌndə] *n.* 1.(有圆顶的)圆形建筑物;圆形大厅;(旅馆等)中央大厅

roué ['ru:ei, ru'ei] *n.*(尤指上了年纪的)浪荡子,酒色之徒

rouge [ru:ʒ] *n.* 1. 胭脂;口红 2. 红铁粉,铁丹 — *vt.* & *vi.*(在……上)搽胭脂(或口红)

rough [rʌf] *adj.* 1. 表面不平的;毛糙的;粗糙的 2. 毛茸茸的,蓬乱的 3. 未加工的;粗加工的;粗制的;半制品的 4. 粗略的;大致的;初步的;粗率的 5. 粗糙的,简陋的;不讲究的 6. 粗暴的,粗鲁的;粗野的;粗俗的 7. 狂风的,狂暴的;剧烈的 8. 笨重的;需要体力的 9.(声音等)粗糙刺耳的;(酒等)烈性的;(药物等)猛烈的 10. 艰难的;难于应付的 11.〔语〕送气的 — *n.* 1. 高低不平(或杂草丛生)的地面;〈高尔夫球场上的〉深草区 2. 粗糙的东西(或部分)3. 粗野的人;暴徒 4. 未加工状态;粗加工状态;粗制品;毛坯 4. 梗概,要略;草样,草图 5.〈英〉粗俗人;流氓,无赖;暴徒 6. 艰难;(生活的)艰难方面 — *vt.* 1. 使不平;使毛糙;给(马等)装防滑钉 2. 使(毛发、稻草等)蓬乱 3. 粗制;制(玉石器皿等);草拟;画……的轮廓(*in*, *out*)5. 粗暴对待;殴打(*up*)6.(球赛中)向(对方)作暴动行为 6. 初步驯服(马匹等)7. 试弹几下(钢琴)以调音 — *vi.* 1. 变粗暴

2. 粗鲁行事 — *adv.* 1. 粗糙地;粗略地 2. 粗鲁地 ‖ ~·ish *adj.* 有点粗糙的;有点粗暴的 / ~·ly *adv.* 粗糙地;粗略地;粗略地说来;粗暴地 / ~·ness *n.* ‖ ~-and-'tumble *adj.* 乱糟糟的,乱作一团的;杂乱无章的 *n.* 混战,乱作一团的打闹;杂乱无章的一片 / '~·cast *n.* 1.〔建〕(由石灰、石子等混和而成,涂在建筑物外墙上的)粗灰浆;毛坯墙面 2. 毛坯 *adj.* 1.(墙等)涂粗灰泥的 2.(计划等)草草作成的 *vt.* 1. 用粗灰泥涂(墙等)2. 制……的毛坯;粗略地作成:~ *cast* a plan 草拟一项计划 / '~·dry *vt.* 晾干而不熨平(衣服等)*adj.*(衣服等)晾干而未熨平的 / '~·hewn *adj.* 1. 粗凿成的;毛坯的 2. 没有教养的,粗鲁的 / '~·house *n.* & *adj.*〈美俚〉1.(尤指室内的)打闹玩笑(的)2. 室内大混战(的);室内暴力行为(的)*vt.* 1. 同……打闹玩笑 2. 粗暴对待 3. 粗鲁地逗弄(小孩等)*vi.* 参与打闹 / '~·neck *n.*〈美俚〉1. 粗鲁的人;无赖 2. 油井修建工 3. 马戏团工人 / '~·rider *n.* 1. 驯马人;善骑烈马的人 2. 非正规的骑兵 3. [R-] 莽骑兵(一八九八年美国—西班牙战争中美国第一义勇骑兵团的骑兵)/ '~·shod *adj.* 1.(马匹)钉有防滑蹄铁的 2. 残暴的:ride ~*shod over* sb. 横暴地对待某人;欺凌某人 / ~ *stuff*〈美俚〉暴力行为;淫秽文学;下流话

roughage ['rʌfidʒ] *n.* 1. 粗饲料 2.(刺激肠道蠕动的)粗粮;(难消化的)纤维素食物

roughen ['rʌf(ə)n] *vt.* & *vi.*(使)变粗糙,(使)变毛糙

roulette [ru:'let] *n.* 1. 轮盘赌 2. 压花刀具,滚花刀具 3.【数】一般擺轮线 4.(邮票等的)骑缝线,骑缝孔 5. 卷发筒 — *vt.* 在……上滚压骑缝线(或孔)

Roumania [ru:'meiniə] *n.* = Romania ‖ ~·n

adj. & *n.* = Romanian

round [raund] *adj.* **1.** 圆的;球形的;圆柱形的;半圆的;弧形的 **2.** 【语】圆唇的 **3.** 滚圆的;丰富的;匀称的 **4.** 圈状的;绕圈的;来回的 **5.** 整整的,十足的 **6.** 巨大的,可观的 **7.** 用十(或百、千等)一类整数表示的;大概的,约略的 **8.**(声音)圆润的;嘹亮的 **9.**(文体、风格)完美流畅的;(人物等)圆满完美生动的 **10.** 率直的,毫不含糊的,直言不讳的;坦直的 **11.**(笔迹)圆润的 **12.** 严厉的,粗暴的 — *n.* **1.** 圆形物;球形物 **2.** 牛大腿肉,牛股肉;(梯子、椅子的)横档;(面包的)一片 **3.** 轮舞,圆圈舞;圆雕(relief 浮雕之对) **4.** 兜(一程);巡回;巡视;巡逻;(时间的)循环,周期 **5.**(比赛、谈判等的)(一)轮;(一)回合;(一)场;(牌戏的)(一)局;(一)圈;(酒的)一巡 **6.**(弹药的)一发;(枪炮等的)一次(齐发);(欢呼等的)一阵;(事情、行动等的)一连串,一系列 **6.** 一群人,一簇东西 **7.** 范围 **8.**【音】轮唱 **9.**【建】圆形饰 **10.** 圆路,环行路;迂回路,弯弯曲曲的路 — *prep.* **1.** 围(绕)着 **2.** 在…周围;在…周围 **3.** 绕过 **4.** 在…各处;向…四周 **5.**(在时间方面)横贯过 — *adv.* **1.** 兜着圈子;围绕地;绕环地;从头至尾地 **3.** 在周围,在附近 **4.** 朝反方向;转向 **5.** 迂回地 **6.** 在各处 **7.** 逐一,挨次 **8.** 到某(指定)地点 — *vt.* **1.** 使成圆形;用圆唇发(音) **2.** 环绕…而行 **3.** 使绕过 **4.** 使圆满结束;使(文体等)完美 **5.** 赶拢;使集拢;围捕,兜捕(*up*) **5.**【数】把…四舍五入 **6.**(罕)使偏转向反方向 — *vi.* **1.** 变圆;发胖;丰富起来 **2.** 兜圈,环行;拐弯 **3.** 进展;成长(*into*) **4.**(罕)转到相反方向 ‖ ~ **let** *n.* 小圆;小的圆形物 / ~ **ness** *n.* ‖ ~ **house** *n.* **1.**(有转

台的)圆形机车库 **2.** 艉楼甲板室 **3.** 【史】拘留所;监狱 **4.**(拳击中的)大挥拳,大摆拳 *adj.*(美理)使劲挥臂的;厉害的 / '~-'shouldered *adj.* 曲背(以致肩部呈圆形的)的 / ~ **worm** *n.* 蛔虫;线虫

roundabout ['raundəbaut] *adj.* **1.** 迂回的;(说话等)兜圈子的,不直接的,不直截了当的 **2.** 圆滚滚的,胖的 — *n.* **1.** 绕道;绕行路线;兜圈子的话(或文章等) **2.**(英)旋转木马 **3.**(美)男用带紧身短上衣

roundelay ['raundilei] *n.* **1.**(鸟的)啭鸣;【音】回复歌;回复曲 **2.** 圆圈舞

roundly ['raundli] *adv.* **1.** 圆圆地,滚圆地 **2.** 严厉地,狠狠地;直率地 **3.** 完全地;全面地 **4.** 活跃地;认真负责地

roundsman ['raundzmən] ([复] roundsmen) *n.* 巡逻者,巡视者;巡警;巡查人;(英)商业推销员,跑街

roundup ['raundʌp] *n.* **1.**(对牲口的)赶拢;(对人或物的)集拢;聚拢,赶拢的牲口群;赶拢牲口的人(或骑马者);搜集 **2.** 综述;摘要

rouse [rauz] *vt.* **1.** 唤醒;唤起,使觉醒 **2.** 激起(情绪);激怒;使振奋 **3.** 惊起,吐出(猎物等) **4.** 搅动(液体) **5.** 【海】使劲拉(*in, out, up*) — *vi.* **1.** 醒来;奋起(*up*);~ *up* at 6 in the morning 早晨六时醒来 **2.**(猎物等)被惊起 — *n.* **1.** 唤起;激动 **2.** 起床号

Rousseauism [ru:'səuizəm] *n.*(十八世纪法国启蒙思想家)卢梭(Rousseau)学说,卢梭主义 ‖ **Rousseauist** *n.* 卢梭主义者,卢梭的信徒

roustabout ['raustəbaut] *n.* **1.**(美)码头工人;舱面水手 **2.**(美)非熟练工,普通工(尤指油田或炼油厂的) **3.**(美)马戏团场地工 **4.**(澳)打杂工(尤指牧羊场的)

rout[1] [raut] *n.* 溃败;溃退 — *vt.* 击溃,

打垮;使溃退

rout² [raut] *vi.* 1. (猪等)用鼻子拱地(觅食) 2. 翻、搜、寻 — *vt.* 1. 用鼻子拱(地);挖出,掘出,刨出,剔出(*out*) 2. 翻、搜、寻 2.(在金属、木料上)挖,刻(沟,纹) 3.(从床上或室内等)唤起;唤出(*up*, *out*) 4. 赶出,驱逐(*out*)

route [rut] *n.* 1. 路;路线;路程;航线 2.(规定行军路线、司令部地点等的)行军命令 — *vt.* 1. 按规定路线发送 2. 给…定路线;安排…的程序

routine [ru:'ti:n] *n.* 1. 例行公事;日常工作;例行手续;常规;惯例;机械方式;程序 2.(经常重演的)固定剧目 — *adj.* [一般只用作定语]日常的、例行的;常规的;a ~ report 例行报告 ‖ ~ly *adv.* / **routinism** *n.* 墨守成规;事务主义

rove [rouv] *vi.* 1. 流浪;漫游;无一定方向地移动 2. 用活饵曳钓 — *vt.* 流浪于;漫游于 — *n.* 流浪;漫游 ‖ ~ *r n.* 1. 流浪者;漫游者 2. 海盗;海盗船 3. 高年级童子军 4. 任意箭靶;远距离箭靶

roving ['rouvŋ] *adj.* 1. 流浪的;游动的,流动的;不固定的 — *n.* a ~ commission 到处奔走的职务 / a ~ ambassador 巡回大使 — *n.* 流浪;漫游

row¹ [rou] *n.* 1.(一)排;(一)行;(剧场等)一排(坐位) 2.(计算机屏幕上的字母或符号)行 3. 街,路;(主要为某种行业占用的)街道;地区 — *vt.* 使成排(或行)(*up*) ‖ ~ house 联立房屋,排屋中的一幢房屋

row² [rou] *vt.* 1. 划(船等);划运,划渡 2. 担任…划手;用…名(划手);(船用)…进行划船比赛 — *vi.* 1. 划桨;荡桨 2.(划桨似地)划行;划动 3. 参加赛艇 — *n.* 划船;划船游览;划程 ‖ ~ *er n.* 划

船者,划手 ‖ ~ boat *n.* 划艇 / ~lock ['rɔlɔk] *n.* 〈主英〉桨架,桨叉

row³ [rau] *n.* 1. 〈口〉吵嚷;骚动;吵架;口角 2. 受斥责 — *vt.* 〈口〉痛斥,狠骂 — *vi.* 〈口〉争吵,吵闹

rowdy ['raudi] *n.* 好吵闹的人;粗暴的人;无赖 — *adj.* 吵闹的;粗暴的 ‖ **rowdily** *adv.* / **rowdiness** *n.* / ~ ism *n.* 粗暴(或吵闹)的行为;流氓作风

rowdydow, rowdedow ['raudi'dau] *n.* 喧嚷;吵闹

rowen ['rauən] *n.* 1. 冬前茬地(用于放牧) 2. 再萌草

royal ['rɔiəl] *adj.* 1. 王的;女王的;王室的 2. [R-](英国)皇家的;英国的 3. 堂皇的;盛大的;庄严的;高贵的 — *n.* 1. 〈口〉王室成员;[the Royals](英国)皇家苏格兰步兵团;(英国)皇家海军陆战队(= the Royal Marines) 2. 王裁(19×24 英寸的一种纸张规格) 3. 〈船〉顶桅(帆) 4. 有十二个以上角叉的雄鹿 ‖ ~ly *adv.* ‖ **Royal Society**(英国)皇家学会

royalist ['rɔiəlist] *n.* 1. 保皇主义者;保皇党人 2. [R-](拥护英王查理一世的)保皇党员;(美国独立战争时期的)亲英分子;(法国资产阶级革命时期的)波旁王朝的拥护者,保王党人 3.(美)保守的实业界巨头 — *adj.* 保皇主义的;保皇主义者的;保皇党人的 ‖ **royalism** *n.*

royalty ['rɔiəlti] *n.* 1. 王位;王权;王威 2. [常 royalties]王的特权 3. 王族;皇亲;特权阶层 4.〈古〉王的领土;王国 5.(国王授予私人或公司的)开采特权;专利权税;版税;(公司等付给土地所有者的)矿区使用费 6. 堂皇;庄严;高贵

RPM, rpm *abbr.* revolutions per minute 每分钟转数,转/分

RSVP¹ [ˈɑːesˈviːpiː] (RSVPed 或 RSVP'd; RSVPing) *vi.* 请赐复 — ([复] RSVP's) *n.* 对请柬的答复

RSVP², **r.s.v.p.** *abbr.*〈法〉*répondez s'il vous plaît*(正式请柬用语)请赐复 = please reply

Ru【化】元素钌(ruthenium)的符号

rub [rʌb] (rubbed; rubbing) *vt.* 1. 摩擦; 擦; 使相擦 2. 用...擦; 擦上(on, over) 3. 把...擦掉 4. 触痛; 惹怒(某人) 5. 摹拓(基碑等) 6.〈美俚〉杀害 — *vi.* 1. 摩擦; 擦到(on, against) 2. 被擦掉(off, out) 3.(皮肤等)擦痛; 擦破;(衣服等)磨损 4.(事情等)使人恼火(或烦恼) — *n.* 1. 摩擦, 擦 2. 磨损处; 擦痛处 3. [the ~]困难, 障碍 4. 伤人感情的嘲笑(或挖苦、批评等)

rubber¹ [ˈrʌbə] *n.* 1.(摩)擦的人; 按摩师;(蒸汽浴室的)按摩员 2.(摩)擦的工具; 砥石; 粗锉; 橡皮(擦子);(擦火柴的)砂皮;(机器上)借助摩擦转动的装置; 防擦物 4. 橡胶; 橡胶状物; 合成橡胶 5. 橡胶制品: 橡皮筋(= ~ band); [~s]橡皮套鞋;〈美俚〉汽车轮胎 6. 障碍, 麻烦 7.〈美俚〉职业杀手 — *vt.* 给...涂上橡皮 — *vi.*〈美俚〉好奇地盯着看, 伸长脖子望 ‖ ~ stamp 1. 橡皮图章;〈喻〉橡皮图章(指官样文章式地批准政策等的人或机构) 2. 人云亦云的人, 无主见的人 3. 官样文章式的批准, 例行式的批准 / ~-'stamp *vt.* 不经审查就批准; 官样文章式地通过(在他人的示意下批准) *adj.* 经(或作出)官样文章式批准的

rubber² [ˈrʌbə] *n.* [体] 1. 规定满局数和胜局数的比赛(如三局两胜、五局三胜) 2. [the ~](平局后的)决胜局; 决胜局比赛

rubbish [ˈrʌbiʃ] *n.* 1. 垃圾; 废物 2. 废

话; 无聊的想法

rubble [ˈrʌbl] *n.* 碎石; 碎砖; 破瓦; 【建】毛石, 块石 ‖ **rubbly** *adj.*

rube [ruːb] *n.*〈美口〉乡巴佬, 土包子

rubicund [ˈruːbikənd] *adj.*(脸色、肤色等)红润的;(人)血色好的 ‖ ~ly *adv.*

rubidium [ruːˈbidiəm] *n.* 【化】铷

ruble [ˈruːbl] *n.* 卢布(俄罗斯货币单位)

rubric [ˈruːbrik] *n.* 1.(旧时书本等中的)红字标题(或句、段等);(章或节的)标题;(法律或法典中的)(红色)标题 2.(祈祷书中的)仪式指示(通常印成红色) 3. 成规; 成例 4.(编者)按语 — *adj.* 1. 用红色写(或刻)的 2. 印红字的 3. 祈祷书中的仪式指示中所规定的; 按照仪式的

ruby [ˈruːbi] *n.* 1. 红宝石; 红宝石制品(如钟表轴承等) 2. 红宝石色, 红玉色; 颜色似红宝石的东西 3.(脸部的)红酒糟 4.〈英〉5½ 点细铅字 5. 红葡萄酒 6. 巴西蜂鸟 — *adj.* 红宝石色的 — *vt.* 把...染成红宝石色; 使带有红宝石色

ruck [rʌk], **ruckle** [ˈrʌkl] *n.* 皱, 褶 — *vt.* 弄皱; 折叠(up) — *vi.* 变皱, 起皱(up)

rucksack [ˈruksæk, ˈrʌksæk] *n.*(登山或旅行者用的)帆布背包

ruckus [ˈrʌkəs] *n.*〈美口〉吵嚷; 争吵; 骚乱

ruction [ˈrʌkʃən] *n.*〈口〉吵嚷; 吵闹; 争吵

rudder [ˈrʌdə] *n.* 1.(船的)舵;(飞机的)方向舵 2. 指导原则; 指针 3.(制麦芽浆用的)搅拌桨 ‖ ~less *adj.* 无舵的 ‖ ~-fish *n.* 【鱼】紫鲹[性喜逐船, 故名]

ruddy [ˈrʌdi] *adj.* 1.(脸)红的, 血色好的; 红的; 微红的 2.〈英俚〉讨厌的; 可恶的;(谎言等)极度的; 十足的 — *vt. & vi.*(使)变红

rude [ruːd] *adj.* 1. 原始(阶段)的; 未开化

的;未加工的 2. 加工粗糙的;简陋的;拙劣的 3. 粗略的,大略的 4. 崎岖不平的;荒野的 5. 不做作的;直率的 6. 粗野的;无礼的;粗鲁的 7. 狂暴的;猛烈的;突然的 8. 茁壮的,强健的 9.(声音)刺耳的,不和谐的 ‖ ~ly *adv*. / ~ness *n*.

rudiment ['ru:dimənt] *n*. 1.[~s]基础;基本原理;初步,入门 2.[~s]雏形;萌芽 3. 发育未全的器官;退化器官

rudimental [ˌru:di'mentl], **rudimentary** [ˌru:di'mentəri] *adj*. 基本的;初步的,起码的;发展不完全的;残留的,退化的

rue[1] [ru:] *n*.〈古〉后悔,悔恨;悲叹 — *vt*. 懊悔,后悔,悔恨;悲叹:You'll live to ~ it. 你总有一天要后悔的。— *vi*. 懊悔,后悔,悔恨;悲叹

rue[2] [ru:] n.【植】芸香

rueful ['ru:ful] *adj*. 悔恨的;沮丧的;悲哀的;可怜的

ruff [rʌf] *n*. 1.【动】毛领鸽;流苏鹬;(鸟、兽的)翎颌;【机】轴环 2.(十六、七世纪的人所戴的宽而硬的)轮状皱领 3. 拉夫牌戏(一种旧式的纸牌戏);将吃(指用将牌吃进其它花色缺门牌的打法) — *vt*. 用将牌吃进 — *vi*. 出将牌

ruffian ['rʌfiən] *n*. 流氓;暴徒 — *adj*. 残暴的;凶恶的 ‖ ~ism *n*. 流氓习气;暴徒行为

ruffle ['rʌfl] *vt*. 1. 弄皱;弄毛糙 2. 弄乱(头发等);(鸟受惊时等)竖起(羽毛) 3. 把(布等)打褶裥;给...装褶边 4. 触怒;使生气 5. 洗(纸牌);很快地翻动(书页等) — *vi*. 1. 变皱;变成表面不平 2. 烦恼;生气 3. 傲慢,自高自大 4. 大吵大闹 — *n*. 1. 褶边;皱纹 2.(鸟、兽的)翎颌 3.(水面等的)波纹 4. 烦恼;生气 5. 骚动;吵闹 ‖ ~r *n*. 1. 傲慢的家伙 2.(缝纫机上的)打裥装置

rug [rʌg] *n*. 小地毯;炉边地毯;〈英〉(旅行等用的)毛毯 ‖ ~ **joint**〈美俚〉高级豪华的夜总会

Rugby, rugby ['rʌgbi] *n*. 橄榄球;橄榄球运动(亦作 ~ football)

rugged ['rʌgid] *adj*. 1. 不平的,崎岖的;多岩石的;有皱纹的 2. 粗鲁而朴实的 3.(声音)刺耳的;难听的 4.(生活)艰难的;(气候)严酷的;狂风暴雨的 5. 粗壮的;强健的 ‖ ~ly *adv*. / ~ness *n*.

rugger ['rʌgə] *n*.〈英俚〉= Rugby

Ruhr [ruə] *n*. 1. 鲁尔[德国西部一地区] 2.[the ~]鲁尔河[德国西部](莱茵河支流)

ruin ['ru:in] *n*. 1. 毁灭;崩溃,覆灭;毁坏 2. 被损毁的东西(如建筑物等);[~s]废墟;遗迹 3. 倾家荡产;丧失地位;堕落;(女子的)失贞 4. 祸根 — *vt*. 1. 使毁灭;使覆灭;毁坏 2. 使成废墟 3. 使破产;诱奸(女子) — *vi*. 1. 毁灭;覆灭;毁坏 2. 变成废墟 3. 破产;堕落 4.〈诗〉头向下地跌落;哗啦地掉下 ‖ **rui'nation** *n*.

ruinous ['ru:inəs] *adj*. 1. 毁灭性的;破坏性的;灾难性的 2. 倾圮的 ‖ ~ly *adv*.

rule [ru:l] *n*. 1. 统治(期),管辖(期);控制,支配 2. 规定;规则;章程;条例;【宗】教规;【律】(法院或法官的)裁决,裁定 3. 习惯,通例;规律;法则 4. 准则,标准;刻度尺;界尺 5.【印】嵌线;嵌线图案;破折号 6.[the ~s]【英史】(设在监狱旁)供特殊犯人(如无力偿债者)居住的区域 7.【英史】居于特殊犯人区的权利 — *vt*. 1. 统治,管辖;控制,支配 2. 裁决,裁定 3. 用尺在纸上划(直线);在(纸)上划平行线;把...排成直线 — *vi*. 1. 统治,管辖;控制,支配 2. 作出裁决,作出裁定 3.(价格等)保持某一水平

ruler ['ru:lə] *n.* 1. 统治者;管理者;支配者 2. 划线人,划线员 3. 尺;直尺;划线板

ruling ['ru:liŋ] *adj.* 1. 统治的;支配的;主导的 2. 普遍的;流行的 — *n.* 1. 统治;支配 2. 裁决,裁定 3.(用尺的)划线(;用尺的)量度 4. 划出的线

rum¹ [rʌm] *n.* 朗姆酒,糖蜜酒;〈美〉酒

rum² [rʌm] *adj.* 1.〈英俚〉古怪的,离奇的 2.〈英俚〉难对付的;危险的 3. 蹩脚的

Rumania [ru:'meinjə] *n.* = Romania ‖ ~**n** *adj. & n.* = Romanian

rumba ['rʌmbə] *n.* 1. 伦巴舞(古巴黑人的一种舞蹈或类似的交际舞) 2. 伦巴舞曲 — *vi.* 跳伦巴舞

rumble¹ ['rʌmbl] *vi.* 1.(雷、炮等)隆隆响 2.(车辆)辘辘行驶 3. 低沉地讲话(肚子)咕咕作响 — *vt.* 1. 使隆隆响;使辘辘行驶 2. 低沉地说(*out, forth*) 3. 在磨桶里磨光(金属零件等);在滚筒里混合 — *n.* 1. 隆隆(声);辘辘(声) 2.(马车上供仆人乘坐的)尾座(或放行李处) 3. 隆隆;滚筒,转筒 4. 普通的怨声;吵嚷;〈美俚〉(尤指青少年在街头的)打群架

rumble² ['rʌmbl] *vt.*〈俚〉彻底了解;洞察;察觉

ruminant ['ru:minənt] *n.* 反刍动物 — *adj.* 1. 反刍的;反刍的 2. 沉思冥想的

ruminate ['ru:mineit] *vi. & vt.* 1. 反刍嚼 2. 沉思默想;反复思考(*over, about, of, on*)

rummage ['rʌmidʒ] *n.* 1.(彻底的)搜查(海关人员的)检查 2. 搜出的物件;杂物(堆) 3. 供义卖的捐献物 — *vt.* 1. 翻找;搜查;仔细检查 2. 搜出;查出(*up, out*) — *vi.* 翻找;搜查;仔细检查

rummy ['rʌmi] *adj.*〈英俚〉古怪的,离奇的 — *n.* 拉米纸牌戏

rumo(u)r ['ru:mə] *n.* 1. 谣言,谣传;传闻,传谣 2. 喃喃细语 — *vt.* [常用被动语态] 谣传

rump [rʌmp] *n.* 1.(鸟的)尾部;(兽的)臀部(;谚)(人的)臀部 2. 后腿部牛排(;~ steak);牛臀肉 3. 渣滓 4.(大部分成员已离去或已被开除因而无代表性的残余组织;(自称代表全体的)叛离集团;余党

rumple ['rʌmpl] *vt. & vi.* 弄皱;压皱;弄乱 — *n.* 褶纹;皱褶

rumpus ['rʌmpəs] *n.*〈口〉喧嚷;吵闹;口角 ‖ ~ **room**(常设于地下的)娱乐室

run [rʌn] (*ran* [ræn]; *run*; *running*) *vi.* 1. 跑,奔 2. 逃跑 3. 跑步;(参加)赛跑 4. 竞赛;竞选 5. 赶خت 6.(车,船)行驶 7.(鱼在产卵期)洄游 8.(机器等)运转;(工作等)进行,继续不断 9. 流;淌;滴;(墨水等)渗开;(固体)熔化 The river ~s clear (thick). 水流清澈(浑浊)。/ The child's nose is *running*. 孩子在流鼻涕。10. 变(成),变得;~ low 缺乏/ be ~ short 不足;使用完；~ rampant 横行,猖狂 11. 蔓生;蔓延;传播 12. 伸展;(演出等)连续;(合同等)继续有效 13.(思想、曲调等在头脑中)紫绕 14.(念头等)闪过;(感觉等)通过;(光阴)流逝 15. 写着;说着 The resolution ~s as follows. 决议如下。/ So the story ran. 据说(事情)就是这样的。16. 有倾向(*to*);(在特征等)贯穿于;(价格、产量等)平均: The apples ~ big this year. 今年苹果长得很大。17.(针织品)脱针,抽丝 — *vt.* 1. 使跑,使奔;~ sb. (clean) off his legs 使某人疲于奔命 2. 在...上跑来跑去;跑过;穿过；~ the streets (小孩)在街上玩耍;流浪街头/

The fever(heat)has ~ its course. 热度(暑气)已开始退了。**3.** 参加(赛跑、竞赛)；同…比赛；使(马等)比赛：～ sb. hard(或 close)在(比赛中)紧紧钉住某人；紧追某人 **4.** 提出(候选人)；提出(某人)参加竞选 **5.** 追捕(猎物等)；追查；探究 **6.** 放牧(牛、羊等)**7.** 驾驶，开，开放(车辆)：～ extra trains during holidays 节日期间开加班(火车)**8.** 运载；偷运(走私货物等)**9.** 开动(机器等)**10.** 办；管理经营：指挥(运动等)；奔走着做：～ messages(为别人)送信，传信息 **11.** 染，使流；倒注；浇铸；熔铸；提炼 **12.** 使处(于)(into)；冒(危险等)：～ sb. into difficulties 使某人陷入困境/～ the risk of … 冒…的危险(或风险)**13.** 使通过，使穿过(through)；使扫视 **14.** 用…刺；刺，戳 **15.** 使撞(或碰)**16.** 使伸展：～ a simile too far 把一个明喻用得牵强附会 **17.** 感染：～ a fever(或 temperature)发烧 **18.** (连续)刊登；刊印 **19.** 【体】连续得(分)；连击 **20.** 匆忙地缝 **21.** 划，描 **22.** 【牌戏】积欠 ~ n. **1.** 跑(长距离)赛跑；(跑的)气力(空)滑行(距离)；After the race he still has a lot of ~ in him. 赛跑以后他的体力还很充沛。/a takeoff ~(飞机)起飞滑跑 **2.** 短期旅行；路程；航程 **3.** (车、船等的)路线；航线；班次；The milkman has finished his ~. 送牛奶的人已送完牛奶。**4.** 趋势，动向；(矿脉、木纹等的)走向：the ~ of events 事态的趋势/the ~ of the cards 打牌的手气(或牌运)**5.** (普通)类型：普通的产品；一批产品 **6.** 一次生出的(或一起饲养的)动物；(产卵期)洄游的鱼群；鱼群的洞游 **7.** (野兽出没的)路径；(羊等的)放牧场；(鸡等的)饲养场 **8.** 流动；流量；水槽；水管；(美方)小河 **9.** (长度、时间等的)连续：a ~ of office 任期/a ~ of mis-

fortunes 接二连三的不幸 **10.** 连续的演出(或展出；刊登等)**11.** (机器)的运转；运转期；(船、汽车等的)试车(船等的)试航 **12.** (口)使用(或出入)的自由 **13.** 挤兑存款，挤兑；争购；畅销；流行：～ on banks 向银行挤提存款/The book has a considerable ~. 这本书销路很好。**14.** 突降 **15.** (按音阶顺序的)速奏；急唱 **16.** 脱针，抽丝 **17.** (板球、棒球赛等的)得分单位，一分 **18.** (滑雪等的)滑道 **19.** 船尾尖部 ‖ '~ about n. **1.** 轻便小汽车；轻便汽艇；轻便运货车 adj. 流浪的 / ～agate/'rʌnəgeit/ n. **1.** 逃亡者；背叛者 **2.** 流浪汉 / '～ around n.《美俚》借口；躲闪；拖延(尤指对付家新者、谋职者等)/ '～ away n. **1.** 逃跑，逃亡 **2.** 逃跑者；脱缰的马 **2.** 脱离控制 **1.** 压倒性的优胜 adj. **1.** 逃跑的；私奔的；(工厂、企业等)为逃避某地工会势力(或赋税)而迁移的 **2.** 脱离控制的；(物价)飞涨的；易起急剧变化的：～away inflation 无法控制的急剧膨胀 **3.** (比赛)轻易取胜的；(胜利)决定性的 / '～ down n. **1.** (军备等的)裁减 **2.** 简要的总结；纲要；分列项目的报告 / '～ down adj. **1.** (钟表等)发条走完的，停了的 **2.** 精疲力竭的；衰弱的 **3.** (房屋等)失修的；坍倒的 / '～ in n. **1.** (口)角，争吵 **2.** (发动机)试车 **3.** 【空】(飞机)的进入目标 **4.** 【印】接排部分，插补部分 / '～ off n. **1.** (雨水、融雪等)径流(量)；流液 **3.** 决胜选拔 / '～ way n. **1.** (机场)的跑道 **2.** 河床，河道 **3.** (运木材等的)斜坡滑道 **4.** 动物踏出的路(通向动物饮水处的小径之)**5.** (动物等用的)过道，通道 / (家畜、家禽的)活动场地，围场

rune [ruːn] n. 如尼字母，如尼文(一种北欧等地的古文字) ‖ **runic** adj.

rung[^1] [rʌŋ] ring[^2] 的过去分词

rung[^2] [rʌŋ] *n.* **1.** 棍子；(椅子等的)横档；轮辐；梯级 **2.** (地位上升的)一级

runner [ˈrʌnə] *n.* **1.** 赛跑的人(或动物等)；(障球赛中的)跑垒者；(美式橄榄球赛中的)带球进攻队员 **2.** (商行等的)出差者；送信者；外勤员；推销员、跑街；收账员 **3.** 走私者；走私船；偷越封锁线的人(或船) **4.** (机器等的)操作者；火车司机 **5.** (装抽屉用)夹长桌面;(楼梯等用的)狭长地毯 **6.** (十八世纪伦敦)巡官(或警探) **7.** [动]普通秧鸡;大西洋蓝鲅 **8.** [植]长匍茎,纤匍枝;有长匍茎的植物 **9.** 滑行装置;(雪车等的)滑橇;(冰鞋的)冰刀 **10.** (抽屉等的)滑槽、滑道;(移动重物的)滚杠;(窗帘等的)滑圈 **10.** [治]浇道,流槽 **11.** 转动的磨石 **12.** [船]滑车动索

runner-up [ˌrʌnərˈʌp] *n.* **1.** [体]亚军 **2.** (在竞选等中)占第二位的人

running [ˈrʌniŋ] *adj.* **1.** 奔跑的、赛跑的 **2.** 流动的 **3.** 连续的;草写的;(机器等)运转着的;(车辆等)运行着的 **5.** 仓卒的 **6.** 出脓的 **7.** (度量等)直线的 — *n.* **1.** 跑;奔跑 **2.** 流动 ‖ ~ board (汽车等的)踏脚板;~ mate 同组的马;赛马时定步速的领跑马;竞选伙伴(尤指副总统候选人);亲密的伙伴;~ title 书的页首标题,栏外标题

runny [ˈrʌni] *adj.* **1.** 有流动倾向的;过于柔软的;(蛋)溏心的 **2.** (眼)流泪的;(鼻)流涕的 ‖ ~ s流水的 ‖ ~-nosed *adj.* 流鼻涕的

runt [rʌnt] *n.* **1.** 发育不全的矮小植物(或动物);(一胎猪中)最小的猪;小种牛 **2.** (口)矮子 **3.** (苏格兰〈英方〉植物的)硬化茎;枯树桩;老牛;干瘪老人

rupee [ruːˈpiː] *n.* 卢比(印度等的货币单位)

rupture [ˈrʌptʃə] *n.* **1.** 破裂,裂开 **2.** 决裂;不和;(国家之间的)敌对;交战 **3.** [医]疝 — *vt.* **1.** 使破裂 **2.** 使断绝(关系等) **3.** 使发疝气 — *vi.* **1.** 裂开,破裂 **2.** 断绝 **3.** 发疝气

rural [ˈruərəl] *adj.* **1.** 农村的;田园的 **2.** 生活在农村的 **3.** 农业的 ‖ ~ (free) delivery (美) (对不设邮局地区的)农村免费投递 /~ route (农村免费投递区的)乡邮投递路线

rurban [ˈruːbən] *adj.* **1.** (住)在城郊的 **2.** 兼有城乡特点的;兼有城乡生活方式的

ruse [ruːz] *n.* 诡计;计策

rush[^1] [rʌʃ] *vi.* **1.** 冲;奔;闯;急流 **2.** 仓促行动(*to, into*) **3.** 突然出现;涌现 **4.** 抢先;赶紧 — *vt.* **1.** 使冲;使急行;急送;猛推 **2.** 匆忙地做 **3.** 催促 **4.** 突然袭击;冲过去占领(建筑物等) **5.** 蜂拥地抢占(会议讲台等) **6.** 飞速跃过 **7.** (俚)向…索高价 **8.** (美)(向…)(为女等)献殷勤 **9.** (美)(用开舞会招待等方法)试图要…加入大学生联谊会 — *n.* **1.** 冲;奔;急速行进(或流动) **2.** 忙碌(一阵) **3.** (突然产生的大量)人流 **4.** (突然的迫切需要:抢购;蜂拥前往;~ for (或 on)gold 涌往新金矿(或有利可图的地方),淘金热;~ of blood突发5.(感情的)一阵激动;突然袭击;猛攻 **7.** (美)(大学各年级之间的)扭打赛 **8.** (社交活动等)献殷勤 **9.** [常~s](电影摄制中未经剪辑的)工作样片 — *adj.* **1.** 急需的 **2.** 匆忙的;繁忙的;~ hours (公共车辆等的)高峰时间,拥挤时刻;~ the ~ season 忙季,旺季

rush[^2] [rʌʃ] *n.* **1.** 灯心草 **2.** 无价值的东西 — *vt.* 用灯心草做(或铺) ‖ ~ candle、~-light *n.* 灯心草蜡烛 **2.** 微光

微不足道的人;孤陋寡闻

rushee [ˌrʌˈfiː] *n.* (准备用开舞会招待等办法拉进大学生联谊会的)争取对象

rusk [rʌsk] *n.* (甜)面包干;(甜)脆饼干

russet [ˈrʌsit] *n.* 1. 黄褐色;赤褐色 2. 黄褐色(或赤褐色)土布 3. (有锈斑的)冬季粗皮苹果 — *adj.* 1. 黄褐色的;赤褐色的 2. 黄褐色(或赤褐色)土布制的 3. (乡)乡下的;简朴的

Russia [ˈrʌʃə] *n.* 1. 俄罗斯,俄国 2. [r-] (装订等用的)俄罗斯软革(亦作 ~ leather)

Russian [ˈrʌʃən] *adj.* 1. 俄罗斯的;俄国的 2. 俄罗斯人的;俄国人的;俄罗斯族的;俄罗斯族人的 3. 俄语的 — *n.* 1. 俄罗斯人;俄国人;俄罗斯族人;俄罗斯族人 2. 俄语

Russo- *comb. form* 表示"俄罗斯"

rust [rʌst] *n.* 1. 铁锈,锈 2.(脑子等)发锈,衰退 3. 惰性 4. 铁锈色,赭色 5. 【植】锈病;锈菌 — *vi.* 1. 生锈 2.(脑子等)发锈,衰退 3. 成铁锈色 4.【植】患锈病 — *vt.* 1. 使(金属)生锈 2. 使(脑子等)发锈(或衰退) 3. 使成铁锈色

rustic [ˈrʌstik] *adj.* 1. 乡村的,农村的 2. 乡村式的;庄稼人似的,质朴的;土气的;粗俗的 3.(桌、椅等)用带皮树枝做成的;做工粗糙的;粗面石工的 — *n.* 1. 农村中的人;庄稼人 2. 乡巴佬;粗汉

rusticate [ˈrʌstikeit] *vi.* 1. 到农村去,下乡 2. 住在乡村;过乡村生活 — *vt.* 1. 把…送到农村去;使住在乡村 2. 使

像乡下人 3. 罚(学生)暂时停学 4. 【建】使成粗面石工

rustle¹ [ˈrʌsl] *vi.*(绸衣、树叶、纸等)沙沙作响 — *vt.* 使沙沙作响 — *n.* 沙沙声,瑟瑟声

rustle² [ˈrʌsl] 〈美口〉 *vi.* 1. 使劲干;急速动 2. 觅食 3. 偷牛(或马等) — *vt.* 1. 弄到(食物等) 2. 把(牛)赶拢 3. 偷牛(或马) ‖ ~ r *n.*

rusty [ˈrʌsti] *adj.* 1. 生锈的,锈的 2.(脑子等)发锈的,变迟钝的,衰退的 3. 铁锈色的,赭色的;(衣服等)已退色的 4. 陈旧的;过时的 5.(笑声等)嘶哑的 6.(植物)患锈病的;(水果等)有锈斑的

rut¹ [rʌt] *n.* 1.(车辆经过的路;凹槽;沟 2. 常规,惯例;老规矩,老一套 — (rut-ted;rutting) *vt.* 在…形成车辙;在…挖槽 ‖ **rutty** *adj.* 有车辙的

rut² [rʌt] *n.*(雄鹿等)发情(期) — (rutted;rutting) *vi.*(雄鹿等)发情 ‖ **rutty** *adj.* 发情中的;好色的

rutabaga [ˌruːtəˈbeigə] *n.* 1.【植】芜菁甘蓝 2.〈美俚〉丑陋女人 3.〈美俚〉一美元

ruth [ruːθ] *n.* 〈古〉 1. 怜悯;同情 2. 悲哀;悔恨

ruthenium [ruːˈθiːniəm] *n.*【化】钌

ruthless [ˈruːθlis] *adj.* 无情的;冷酷的;残忍的 ‖ ~ly *adv.* / ~ness *n.*

Rwanda [ruˈændə] *n.* 卢旺达 [东非国家]

Rx [ˈɑːˈreks] *n.* 1. 药方,处方 2. 方法,办法

rye [rai] *n.* 1. 黑麦 2. 黑麦威士忌酒 ‖ ~ bread 黑面包 / ~ grass【植】黑麦草

S

S, s [es] ([复]S's, s's 或 Ss, ss['esiz]) 英语字母表第十九个字母 **1.** [S]S 形: The river makes a great S. 这条河形成一个大 S 形。**2.** [S]【化】元素硫(sulphur)的符号 **3.**《美》学业成绩"满意"(satisfactory)的符号 **4.** 南(south)的符号

-s *suf.* **1.** [加于大多数名词后, 构成复数] (词尾为 s, z, sh, ch 等的名词加 -es) : students, tools, Johns **2.** [加于缩写、数字、字母等后, 构成复数] : IQs, 4s, As **3.** [加于动词后, 构成第三人称单数现在式陈述语气] : He works. It rains. **4.** [构成副词] : always, indoors

Sa 【化】元素钐(samarium)的符号

Sabah ['sɑːbɑ] *n.* 沙巴[马来西亚一地区]

Sabbath ['sæbəθ] *n.* **1.**【宗】安息日, 主日(犹太教徒为星期六, 基督教徒为星期日) **2.** [s-]休息期

sabbatic(al) [sə'bætik(əl)] *adj.* **1.** [S-]安息日的 **2.** 休假的, 公休的 *n.* (职务)带有休假的

saber ['seibə] *n. & vt.* = sabre

Sabin ['seibin] *n.* ‖ ~ vaccine 萨宾氏疫苗(预防脊髓灰质炎的活毒疫苗)

sable ['seibl] *n.* [复] sable(s) **1.**【动】紫貂, 黑貂 **2.**【紫】貂皮 **3.** [~s]貂皮外衣(或衣领) **4.** 貂毛画笔 **5.** 深褐色;黑色 **6.** [~s]丧服 **7.**【动】貂羚 *adj.* **1.**(紫)貂皮制的;貂毛制的 **2.** 深褐色

的;黑色的 **3.** 黑暗的, 阴暗的;阴森可怖的

SABMIS *abbr.* seaborne anti-ballistic missile intercept system 舰载反弹道导弹截击系统

sabot ['sæbəu] *n.* **1.**(欧洲农民穿的)木鞋;木底皮鞋 **2.**(原鞋的)鞋襻;有鞋襻的鞋 **3.**【军】炮弹软壳

sabotage ['sæbətɑːʒ] *n.* **1.**(对财产等的)故意毁坏 **2.** 阴谋破坏;破坏活动 *vt.* 破坏 *—vi.* 进行破坏;从事破坏活动(on)

saboteur [ˌsæbə'təː] *n.*(阴谋)破坏者

sabre ['seibə] *n.* **1.** 马刀;军刀;(击剑或决斗用的)佩剑 **2.** [the ~]武力;黩武政治 **3.**(熔制玻璃的)浮硫撇除器 *—vt.* 用马刀砍

sac [sæk] *n.*【生】囊 ‖ ~-like *adj.*

saccharin ['sækərin] *n.* 糖精

saccharine ['sækərain, -rin] *adj.* **1.** 糖的;产糖的;含糖的;像糖似的 **2.** 极甜的;太甜的 **3.** 奉承的, 讨好的 *n.* ['sækərin] 糖精

sacerdotal [ˌsæsə'dəutəl] *adj.*【宗】司铎的, 司铎天赋神权说的

sachem ['seitʃəm] *n.* **1.**(北美印第安部族的)酋长 **2.** 大亨;巨头;要人 **3.** [美国纽约市民主党组织]坦慕尼协会(Tammany Society)首领

sachet ['sæʃei] *n.* **1.**(熏衣用的)香囊;小

香袋 2. 香粉

sack[1] [sæk] *n*. 1. 袋;粗布袋;麻袋;硬纸袋 2.(一)袋;(一)包 3. 袋式直统女装;(妇孺穿的)宽大上衣;(附着于衣服肩上的)拖地丝裙裾 4.〈口〉[the ~]开除;解雇 5.〈美俚〉床;睡袋;睡铺 6.(棒球)垒 — *vt*. 1. 装…入袋 2.〈口〉开除;解雇 3.(在竞赛等中)胜过 — *vi*.〈美俚〉上床,睡觉(*in*, *up*) ‖ ~**ing** *n*. 粗平袋布,麻袋布 ‖ '~**cloth** *n*. 1. 粗平袋布,麻袋布 2. 丧服

sack[2] [sæk] *n*.[the ~]劫掠 —*vt*. 劫掠;洗劫(被攻陷的城市等)

sacrament ['sækrəmənt] *n*. 1.【基督教】圣礼,圣事 2.[常 the S-]【基督教】圣餐;用作圣餐的面包和葡萄酒;圣餐面包 3. 神圣的东西;神秘的东西 4. 庄严的誓言(或诺言) — *vt*. 使立誓;使宣誓

sacramental [ˌsækrə'mentl] *adj*. 1.(用于)圣礼的;(用于)圣餐的 2. 受圣礼(或誓言)约束的;神圣的 — *n*. 似圣礼的仪式(如用圣水等)

sacred ['seikrid] *adj*. 1. 上帝的,神的;神圣的;宗教的 2. 神圣不可侵犯的;庄严的;郑重的 3. 祭祀(某神)的;献给…的;专供…用的(*to*) ‖ ~**ly** *adv*. / ~**ness** *n*.

sacrifice ['sækrifais] *n*. 1. 牺牲;牺牲品 2. 亏本出售;贱卖;损失;亏本出售的商品 3.【宗】献祭;祭品;基督的献身(指钉十字架);(表示感恩的)圣餐 4.(棒球比赛中为救球而作的)牺牲打(亦作~ hit) — *vt*. 1. 牺牲;献出 2. 亏本出售 3. 献祭 — *vi*. 1. 献祭 2.(棒球比赛中)作牺牲打 ‖ **sacrificial** [ˌsækri'fiʃəl] *adj*.

sacrilege ['sækrilidʒ] *n*. 1. 渎圣;渎圣罪;渎圣行为;窃取圣物 ‖ ˌ**sacri'legious** *adj*.

sacristan ['sækristən] *n*.(教堂的)圣器保管人;教堂司事

sacristy ['sækristi] *n*.(教堂)圣器室

sacroiliac [ˌseikrəu'iliæk, ˌsækrəu'iliæk]【解】*adj*. 骶髂(关节)的 —*n*. 骶髂关节

sacrosanct ['sækrəuˌsæŋkt] *adj*. 极其神圣的;神圣不可侵犯的 ‖ ~**ness** *n*.

sad [sæd] (sadder, saddest) *adj*. 1. 悲哀的;令人悲痛的 2.〈口〉糟透的,坏透的 3.(颜色)深暗的 4.(面包、点心等)未烤透而粘糊的;发得不好的 ‖ ~**ly** *adv*. / ~**ness** *n*.

sadden ['sædn] *vt*. 1. 使悲哀,使悲痛 2. 使(颜色)深暗;使阴暗 — *vi*. 悲哀,悲痛

saddle ['sædl] *n*. 1. 鞍子,马鞍;(自行车、农业机械等的)鞍座;(马背等的)鞍部 2. 鞍状物;鞍状山脊;书脊;(鞋面的)镶皮脊 3.(带脊骨与肋骨的)脊肉;(雄禽的)后背部;(动物背上的)花纹 4.【机】座板;滑动座架;滑板;锅炉座 5.(悬索桥或电线杆上的)托梁;【船】圆枕木 — *vt*. 1. 给(马等)装鞍 2. 使负担;强加 — *vi*. 跨上马鞍 ‖ ~**horse** 驯马,可骑的马

sadism ['sædizəm] *n*. 1. 施虐狂;性虐待狂;施虐欲;施虐的快感 2. 极度残暴 ‖ **sadist** *n*. /**sadistic** [sə'distik] *adj*.

safari [sə'fɑːri] ([复] safaris) *n*. 1.(在东非的)(徒步)旅游(队);科学考察(队);游猎(队) 2.[用作定语](原指欧洲人在东非旅游时穿的服装)瑟法里式

safe [seif] *adj*. 1. 安全的,保险的;平安的;无损的 2. 无害的;不能为害的 3. 谨慎的;可靠的;稳健的 4. 一定的,有把握的 5.【计】稳定的 6.(棒球运动员)安全进垒的 — *n*. 1. 保险箱 2. 冷藏箱;(防止苍蝇等的)纱橱 ‖ ~**ly** *adv*.

/~ness n. ‖ ~·'conduct n. 1. 通行许可(指通过禁区等可免遭逮捕或伤害) 2.〈尤指战时的〉护照 3. 护送持有安全通行证者的卫兵〈又指〉发安全通行证 2. 护送 — 通过 / '~·deposit n.〈银行等保管库中供租用的〉贵重物品保管箱 adj. 保管贵重物品的 / '~·'keeping n. 安全保护;妥善保管

safeguard ['seifɡɑːd] n. 1. 保护措施;保证条款 2. 防护设施,安全装置;防护器 3.〈尤指战时的〉安全通行证;护照 4. 保护者;护送者;警卫员 — vt. 保护,捍卫,维护

safety ['seifti] n. 1. 安全,平安;保险 2. 安全物,保险装置;(枪炮等的)保险机;有险机的武器 3. 低座自行车(亦作=bicycle) 4.(棒球)安打(指保险的一击);(美式橄榄球)安全(传球在球门线上或端区内成为死球);安全得 2 分 — vt. 保护,防护,使保险:~ a rifle 使步枪保险(不走火等) ‖ ~ belt 救生带;(飞机乘客、高空操作者等用的)安全带 / ~ island (道路中的)安全岛 / ~ pin (安全)别针;安全销;保险针 / ~ valve 1. 安全阀,保险阀 2.(喻)安全阀网(指使宣泄怒气、过剩精力等的方法或事物):sit on the ~ valve 采取压制手段

saffron ['sæfrən] n. 1.〔植〕藏红花 2. 藏红花干柱头 3. 藏红色;橘黄色 — adj. 藏红色的;橘黄色的

sag [sæɡ] (sagged; sagging) vi. 1.(尤指中部)下垂;下陷;下弯 2. 倾斜,一边倒 3.(面部等)松垂;(精神)萎靡;衰弱 4.(电影、小说等)失去吸引力 5.〔商〕萧条;价格下降 6.〔海〕顺流 — vt. 使下垂;把(船或板)弄弯下来 n. 1. 下垂;下陷;下弯 2. 下垂度 3.(道路等的)陷下处 4. 经济萧条;物价下跌 5.

saga ['sɑːɡə] n. 1. 萨迦(中世纪北欧传说) 2. 英雄传奇 3.(长篇)家世小说 4. 长篇记叙

sagacious [sə'ɡeifəs] adj. 1. 有洞察力的;有远见的;精明的;明智的 2.(动物)有灵性的;伶俐的 ‖ ~ly adv. / ~ness, sagacity [sə'ɡæsəti]

sage¹ [seidʒ] adj. 1. 贤明的;聪明的;明智的;审慎的 2.〈谑〉一本正经的;一副聪明相的 — n. 1. 哲人;贤人,圣人;年高望重的人〈谑〉道貌岸然的人 ‖ ~ly adv. / ~ness n.

sage² [seidʒ] n.〔植〕鼠尾草;蒿(亦作~ brush);撒尔维亚 2. 撒尔维亚干叶(作调料或药用)

sago ['seiɡəu] (〔复〕sagos) n. 西(谷)米(由西谷椰子茎髓制成的淀粉质食物)

Sahara [sə'hɑːrə] n. 撒哈拉沙漠〔北非〕

sahib ['sɑː(h)ib, sɑːb] n. 先生,老爷(旧时印度人对欧洲人的尊称);〔口〕绅士

said [sed] say 的过去式和过去分词 — adj.(法律、商业等文件用语)上述的,该…:(the)~ contract 上述契约 /(the)~ witness 该证人

Saigon [sai'ɡɔn] n. 西贡(Ho Chi Minh City 胡志明市的旧称)〔越南南部港市〕

sail [seil] n. 1. 帆,篷 2.〔单复同〕帆船 3. 帆状物;(风车的)翼板;(轮船的)背鳍;(鹦鹉螺的)触手 4.〔尤指乘帆船的〕航行;航程 — vi.(船)航行(人)乘帆船航行 2. 启航,开船 3.(鸟、气球等)翱翔;(鱼、云等)浮游,飘,平稳地行进 4.(女人)仪态万方地走 — vt. 1. 航行于;飘过,飞过 2. 驾驶(船) ‖ ~ before the wind 顺风;顺利 / '~·boat n. 帆船;船 / '~·cloth n. 帆篷布;帆布 / '~·fish n.

sailing ['seiliŋ] n. 1. 航行;航行术,航海

术 2. 启航；水运航班：a list of ~s 船期表 一 *adj.* 扬帆的；航行的

sailor ['seilə] *n.* 1. 水手；海员；水兵 2. 乘船旅行者：a bad (good) ~ 常晕船(不晕船)的人 3. 水手帽(平顶卷边草帽)

saint [seint] *n.* 1. (教会正式承认的)圣徒,圣者 2. 进入天国的逝者；天使 3. 上帝的选民；基督教徒 4. 虔诚慈善的人；道德高尚的人；圣人 5. [S-] (加在圣徒、教会、学校、街道等名字前,单数略作 St. 或 S.,复数略作 Sts. 或 SS.) 圣：*St. Paul's* (伦敦)圣保罗大教堂 一 *adj.* 神圣的 — *vt.* 承认...是圣徒；使成为圣徒 ‖ ~ ed *adj.* 成为圣徒的；神圣的；死去的 / ~ hood *n.* 圣徒身份；[总称] 圣徒 ‖ **All Saints' Day**(基督教)诸圣日(11 月 1 日)

saintly ['seintli] *adj.* 圣徒似的；圣洁的 ‖ **saintliness** *n.*

Saint Petersburg [ˌseintˈpiːtəzbəg] 圣彼得堡(曾称 Leningrad 列宁格勒)[俄罗斯西北部港市]

Saint-Simonian [ˌsɔntsiˈməuniən] *adj.* (法国空想社会主义者)圣西门(Saint-Simon)的；空想社会主义的 — *n.* 圣西门主义者,空想社会主义者

sake¹ [seik] *n.* 目的；利益；理由；缘故：for all their ~ s (或 for the ~ of them all) 为了他们所有的人 / for safety('s) ~ 为了安全起见

sake² ['sɑːki] *n.* 日本清酒,日本米酒

salaam [səˈlɑːm] *n.* 1.(尤指穆斯林的)问候,致意；额手礼；深深的鞠躬 2. 敬礼,致敬 — *vt.* 向...行额手礼 — *vi.* 行额手礼

salable ['seiləbl] *adj.* 可出售的；畅销的,有销路的

salacious [səˈleiʃəs] *adj.* 1. 好色的,淫荡的 2.(书画等)海淫的,淫秽的

salad ['sæləd] *n.* 1. 色拉,凉拌菜 2. 生菜(指可生食的蔬菜)

salamander ['sæləˌmændə] *n.* 1.[动]蝾螈 2.(神话中的)火怪；火蛇 3. 能耐高热的人(或物)；不怕炮火的兵士；吞火魔术师；(美俚)耐火保险箱 4. 烘糕饼的烤板；(英)拨火棒；引火棒

salami [səˈlɑːmi] *n.*(意大利的蒜味)萨拉米香肠

salary ['sæləri] *n.* 薪水 — *vt.*[常用被动语态]给...薪水 ‖ **salaried** *adj.* 拿薪金的；带薪水的

sale [seil] *n.* 1. 卖,出售 2.(尤指存货)减价出售；拍卖 3. 销路；销售额 ‖ ~ girl,'~ s,lady,'~ s,woman *n.* 女售货员,女店员；女推销员 / '~ s,people [复] *n.*(尤指公司,企业的)(全体)售货员,营业员,店员 / '~ s,person *n.* 售货员,营业员,店员 / '~ s,room *n.* 商品展销室;拍卖行

saleable ['seiləbl] *adj.* = salable

salesman ['seilzmən] ([复] salesmen ['seilzmən]) *n.* 1. 售货员,店员;推销员 2.(思想、计划的)兜售者,游说者

salient ['seiljənt] *adj.* 1.(角等)突出的,凸起的 2. 显著的 3. 跳跃的,跳跳蹦蹦的 4.(水等)喷涌的 — *n.* 1. 突出部;凸起 2. 突角;突出部分;[军] 突出部 ‖ **salience** *n.* / ~ ly *adv.*

saline ['seilain, 'seilin] *adj.*(似)盐的;含盐的 — *n.* 盐溶液;盐水 ‖ ~ ness *n.*

Salisbury ['sɔːlzbəri] *n.* 1. 索尔兹伯里(Harare 哈拉雷的旧称)[津巴布韦首都] 2. 索尔兹伯里[英国英格兰南部城市]

saliva [səˈlaivə] *n.* 涎,唾液

salivary ['sælivəri] *adj.* 唾液的;分泌唾液的

Salk [sɔːlk] *n.* ‖ ~ **vaccine** 索尔克氏疫

苗(预防脊髓灰质炎的灭活疫苗)

sallow ['sæləu] *adj.*(人.肤色)灰黄色的,菜色的 — *vt. & vi.*(使)变成灰黄色(或菜色)

sally ['sæli] *n.* **1.**(被围军队的)突围;出击 **2.**(感情等)的进发 **3.** 远足;动身 **4.** 俏皮话;妙语 **5.**〈罕〉越轨行为 **6.** 凸出部;〈建〉楼头 — *vi.* **1.** 突围;出击(*out*) **2.**〈罕〉(血等)涌出 **3.** 外出;动身,出发(*forth, out*)

salmon ['sæmən]([复] salmon(s)) *n.* **1.**【动】鲑,大麻哈鱼 **2.** 鲑肉 **3.** 鲑肉色,橙红色

salon ['sælɔ:n] 〈法〉 *n.* **1.** 客厅,会客室 **2.**(上流人物的)交谊厅 **3.** 沙龙(西方社会名流的社交聚会) **3.** 美术展览馆;画廊 [the S-]沙龙(一年一度在巴黎举行的当代画家作品展览会) **4.**(营业性的)厅,院,室,店

saloon [sə'lu:n] *n.* **1.** 客厅,会客室;(客轮上的)交谊厅 **2.** 沙龙(= salon) **3.**(作某项业务的)厅,室 **4.** 酒吧 **5.**(火车的)特等客车;箱式小客车

salsify ['sælsifi] *n.*【植】波罗门参

SALT [sɔ:lt] *abbr.* Strategic Arms Limitation Talks 限制战略武器会谈

salt [sɔ:lt] *n.* **1.** 盐 **2.**【化】盐类;[~s]泻盐(= Epsom ~s);嗅盐(= smelling ~s) **3.** 风趣,妙味;刺激 **4.** 现实态度;常识;慎重;保留,怀疑态度 **5.**〈口〉老水手(= old ~) **6.** = ~ cellar **7.** 盐沼;盐碱滩(亦作 ~ marsh) **8.**[~s]冲入河流的海水 — *adj.* **1.** 含盐的,咸的,腌的,加盐调味的 **2.**(土地)被海水淹没的;(植物)生长于盐沼(或盐碱滩)的;海味的 **3.** 咸的;盐味的 **4.**(故事,笑话等)猥亵的 **5.** 辛酸的;沉痛的 **6.**〈俚〉(账目,费用等)浮报的;过高的 — *vt.* **1.** 加(或撒,擦)盐于;腌,盐渍

以盐喂(动物) **2.** 使(谈话等)风趣 **3.**【化】用盐(或盐的混合物)处理(照相纸等);把…撒于(*with*) **4.**〈俚〉浮开,虚报(账目、价格等);用贵重的矿物盐饰(矿山)以诱骗买主 ‖ ~ed *adj.* **1.** 用盐处理的,腌的,盐渍的 **2.**(动物或人)惯入水土的;有免疫力的 **3.**〈口〉(对职业、工作等)有经验的;老练的 ‖ ~cellar *n.*(餐桌上的)盐碟;盐瓶 / ~ glaze(陶瓷的)盐釉 / ~water *adj.* **1.** 咸水的 **2.** 生活在咸水中的 / ~water 咸水;海水

saltpetre, saltpeter ['sɔ:lt.pi:tə] *n.*【化】硝石,钾硝,硝酸钾

salty ['sɔ:lti] *adj.* **1.** 盐的,咸的;含盐的 **2.** 海上生活(气息)的 **3.** 泼辣的,尖锐的;风趣的 **4.** 猥亵的 **5.** 有经验的;老练的

salubrious [sə'lju:briəs] *adj.* **1.**(气候,空气等)有益健康的 **2.** 健康的;有利的 ‖ ~ly *adv.* / salubrity *n.*

salutary ['sæljutəri] *adj.* **1.** 有益健康的;有治疗作用的 **2.** 有益的

salutation [ˌsælju:'teiʃən] *n.* **1.** 招呼;致意;行礼 **2.** 招呼动作 **3.** 颂词;(书信或发言开头的)称呼语 **3.**〈罕〉敬礼(现多用 salute)

salute [sə'lju:t] *n.* **1.** 招呼;行礼,敬礼;[the ~]敬礼姿势 **2.** 礼炮;鞭炮 **3.**〈古〉〈谑〉(表示致敬的)接吻 — *vt.* **1.** 向…打招呼(或致意);向…行军礼(或…致敬;(以正式礼仪)庆祝 **2.** 迎接;呈现在…之前 **3.** 赞扬,颂扬 **4.**〈古〉(见面或分别时)吻 — *vi.* **1.** 打招呼;行礼;致敬 **2.** 放礼炮

Salvador ['sælvədɔ:] *n.* = El Salvador

salvage ['sælvidʒ] *n.* **1.** 海上救助;(疾病等的)抢救;(局面等的)挽救 **2.** 救助费;救助费用 **3.** 被救船舶;救出的货物;脱险人员

得教的病员(或肢体等) **4.** 海上打捞 **5.** (保险业用语)财产抢救;抢救出的财产;残(货价)值 **6.** 废物可利用的;可利用的废品 — *vt.* **1.** 救助;营救;抢救 **2.** 打捞 **3.** 利用(废物、损坏的货物等)
‖ **Salvarsan** ['sælvəsən] *n.* 【药】六〇六,洒尔佛散

salvation [sæl'veiʃən] *n.* **1.** 救助;拯救 **2.** 【宗】灵魂的拯救;救世:the *Salvation Army*[基督教]救世军

salve¹ [sɑːv, sælv] *n.* **1.** 油膏;药膏 **2.** 护唇油膏 **3.** 安慰(物);缓和物(*for*) **4.** 阿谀,奉承 — *vt.* **1.** 在…上敷油膏,敷药膏于 **2.** 安慰;缓和;减轻(悲痛) **3.** 排除(困难);解除(疑虑);保持(荣誉、信用等) **4.** 奉承

salve² [sælv] *vt.* **1.** 救助(船只);抢救 **2.** 打捞

salver ['sælvə] *n.* 托盘;盘子

salvia ['sælviə] *n.* 【植】鼠尾草

salvo¹ ['sælvəu] *n.* (复salvos) **1.** 【律】保留条款;保留 **2.** 遁词;借口 **3.** (名誉等的)保全手段;(感情的)宽慰,慰藉

salvo² ['sælvəu] *n.* (复salvo(e)s) **1.** (炮火)齐射;(炸弹等的)齐投;连续投射;射的炮弹;齐投的炸弹 **2.** (礼炮)齐鸣 **3.** 突然爆发;(掌声、欢呼声等的)一阵

SAM *abbr.* surface-to-air missile 地对空导弹

Samaritan [sə'mæritən] *adj. & n.* 助人为乐的(人),行善的(人)

samarium [sə'mɛəriəm] *n.* 【化】钐

samba ['sæmbə] *n.* 桑巴舞(曲)(一种源自巴西民间舞的交谊舞) — *vi.* 跳桑巴舞

same [seim] *adj.* **1.** 同一的 **2.** 依然如故的,同样的 **3.** [与 this, that, these, those 连用,强调语气或含贬义]刚才提到

(或想到)的,上述的 **4.** 千篇一律的,单调的 — *pron.* **1.** 同样的人;同样的事物 **2.** 【法律、商业上的旧用法;常略定冠词]该人;上述事物;上述情况 — *adv.* 同样地 ‖ ~ **ness** *n.* **1.** 同一,一致(性);同样 **2.** 千篇一律,单调

Samoa [sə'məuə] *n.* 萨摩亚群岛[南太平洋]

SAMOS *abbr.* satellite antimissile observation system 卫星反导弹观测系统

samovar [ˌsæmə'vɑː] *n.* 俄国式茶炊

sampan ['sæmpæn] 〈汉〉 *n.* 舢板

sample ['sɑːmpl] *n.* **1.** 样品;试样;货样 **2.** 实例;标本 **3.** (统计学中的)样本,抽样 — *vt.* **1.** 从…中取样;提供…的样品 **2.** 尝试;初次体验 **3.** 对…进行抽样调查

sampler ['sɑːmplə] *n.* **1.** 样品检验员;取样员 **2.** 取样器 **3.** 绣花样本

samurai ['sæmurai] 〈日〉 *n.* [单复同] **1.** (日本封建时代的)武士;武士 **2.** [~s]武士阶级 **3.** 陆军将校

San'a, Sanaa [sɑː'nɑː] *n.* 萨那[也门]首都

sanatorium [ˌsænə'tɔːriəm] *n.* [复] sanatoria [ˌsænə'tɔːriə]或 sanatoriums] *n.* 疗养院;休养地

sanctify ['sæŋktifai] *vt.* **1.** 使神圣;把…奉若神明 **2.** 使圣洁;洗涤…的罪恶 **3.** 证明…为正当;认可,批准,使合法化 ‖ **sanctification** [ˌsæŋktifi'keiʃən] *n.*

sanctimonious [ˌsæŋkti'məuniəs] *adj.* 假装神圣的;伪装虔诚的 ‖ ~**ly** *adv.* / ~**ness** *n.*

sanctimony ['sæŋktiˌməuni] *n.* 装作圣洁(或虔诚),伪善,道貌岸然

sanction ['sæŋkʃən] *n.* **1.** (尤指教会的)法令 **2.** (使法律得以遵守的)附加条款(如赏、罚等) **3.** (为维持社会所作的)

制裁;[常～s]国际制裁 4.(使法律、道德遵行的)约束力(如习俗,良心等) 5. 认可;批准 6.(习俗上对行为等的)赞许;支持;鼓励 ── *vt.* 1. 认可;批准 2. 同意;支持;鼓励

sanctity ['sæŋktiti] *n.* 1. 圣洁;虔诚 2. 神圣(性) 3.[sanctities]神圣的事物(或感情、权利、义务)

sanctuary ['sæŋktjuəri] *n.* 1. 圣所;圣殿;教堂;寺院;内殿;祭坛;(犹太教堂的)至圣所 2. 避难所,庇护所 3.(教堂等的)庇护权 4.(鸟兽)禁猎区

sanctum ['sæŋktəm] *n.* 1. 圣所 2.(不受干扰的)私室;书斋

sand [sænd] *n.* 1. 沙,沙子 2.[常～s]沙滩;沙洲;沙地 3.[常～s]沙粒;计时沙漏中的沙子 4.顷刻,瞬间;[～s]生涯;寿命 5.[医]沙 6. 含(石)油沙层 7.【治】尾砂;尾矿 8.〔美俚〕刚毅;胆量 9. 沙色,浅棕色 10.〔美俚〕砂糖 ── *vt.* 1. 撒沙于;撒沙似地布满;撒沙;填沙于 2. 搀沙于(糖等) 3. 用沙(或沙纸)擦 4. 把(船)开上沙滩 ‖～**er** *n.* 1. 撒沙工;撒沙器 2. 砂磨工;打磨机 ‖ '～**bag** *n.* 沙袋,沙囊 *vt.* 1. 堆沙袋于;用沙袋封堵;用沙袋给…加重 2. 用沙袋打;用沙袋猛击 3.〔口〕欺骗;威逼,强制 /'～**bank** *n.* 沙坝;沙洲;沙滩 /'～**bar** *n.* 沙洲;沙堤 /'～**man** *n.*(童话中撒沙于孩童眼以使其睡着的)睡魔 /'～**paper** *n.* 砂纸 *vt.* 用砂纸打磨(或磨光) /'～**piper** *n.*【动】鹬 /'～**stone** *n.*【地】沙岩 /'～**storm** *n.*【气】沙暴

sandal¹ ['sændl] *n.* 1. 凉鞋;便鞋 2. 浅口橡皮套鞋 3. 鞋带 ── *vt.* 1. 给…穿上凉鞋(或 sandal(l)ing) *vt.* 1. 给…穿上凉鞋(便鞋) 2. 用鞋襻系(鞋);给(鞋)上鞋襻

sandal² ['sændl] *n.* = ～ wood ‖ '～ **wood** *n.* 1.【植】檀香 2. 檀香木

sandwich ['sænwidʒ, 'sænwitʃ] *n.* 1. 三明治,夹心面包片 2. 三明治形物;夹在一起的东西 ── *vt.* 1. 把…做成三明治 2. 夹入;挤进 ‖～**board**(挂在身前身后的)三明治式广告牌 /～ **man**(身前身后)挂着三明治式广告牌的人

sandy ['sændi] *adj.* 1. 沙的;沙质的;含沙的,多沙的;铺上沙的 2.(毛发等)沙色的,浅棕色的 3. 流沙似的;不稳固的 ── *n.*〔口〕头发浅棕色的人

sane [sein] *adj.* 1. 没有疾病的,健康的 2. 心智健全的,神志正常的 3. 稳健的;合情合理的 ‖～**ly** *adv.* / ～**ness** *n.*

San Francisco [ˌsænfrən'siskəu]圣弗兰西斯科(即旧金山或三藩市)[美国加利福尼亚州西部港市]

sang [sæŋ] sing 的过去式

sanguinary ['sæŋgwinəri] *adj.* 1. 血淋淋的,血腥的 2. 好杀戮的,嗜血成性的;残忍的;(法律)动辄处死刑的 3.〔英〕(话语)污秽的,充满咒骂的

sanguine ['sæŋgwin] *adj.* 1. 血红的;红润的,血色的 2. 含血的,含血的 3. 怀着希望的;乐观的;自信的 4.【心】多血质的 4. 嗜血成性的;残忍的 ── *n.* 1. 血红色 2.(用氧化铁制的)红铅笔;红粉笔画 ── *vt.*【诗】染血;染红

sanitarium [ˌsæni'tɛəriəm] *n.*〈美〉= sanatorium

sanitary ['sænitəri] *adj.* 1. 公共卫生的,环卫的 2.(保持)清洁的,卫生的 ── *n.*(有抽水设备的)公共厕所 ‖ **sanitarily** *adv.* / **sanitariness** *n.*

sanitation [ˌsæni'teiʃən] *n.* 1. 公共卫生,环境卫生;改善环境卫生 2. 卫生设备(尤指下水道设备)

sanity ['sænəti] *n.* 1. 心智健全,神志正常 2. 明智;判断正确;稳健

San José [ˌsɑːnhəˈse, ˌsænəˈzei] 圣约瑟 [哥斯达黎加首都]

San Juan [ˌsænˈhwɑːn] 圣胡安 [波多黎各首府]

sank [sæŋk] sink 的过去式

San Marino [ˌsænməˈriːnəu] 1. 圣马力诺 [南欧国家] 2. 圣马力诺(市) [圣马力诺首都]

sans [sænz] prep. 〈古〉〈诗〉无, 没有

San Salvador [sæn ˈsælvədɔː] 圣萨尔瓦多 [萨尔瓦多首都]

Sanskrit [ˈsænskrit] n. & adj. 梵语(的); 梵文(的)

Santa Claus [ˈsæntəˌklɔːz] 【宗】圣诞老人

Santiago [ˌsæntiˈɑːgəu] n. 圣地亚哥 [智利首都]

Santo Domingo [ˈsæntəudəˈmiŋgəu] 圣多明各 [多米尼加共和国首都]

São Tomé [ˈsauŋtəˈmei] 圣多美 [圣多美和普林西比首都]

São Tomé and Príncipe [ˈprinsipi] 圣多美和普林西比 [西非岛国名]

sap¹ [sæp] n. 1. 树液 2. 体液(如血、涎、淋巴、精液); 元气; 活力 3. = ～wood 4. 〈美〉棍棒; 警棍 5. 〈美俚〉融入士忌酒 — (sapped; sapping) vt. 1. 使(树)排出液汁; 去掉(木材)的白木质 2. 使伤元气; 耗竭; 使衰弱 ‖ ～ green 绿色颜料; 暗绿色 /'～sucker n. [北美产的]吸汁啄木鸟/'～wood n. 【植】(树皮和心材之间的)边材, 液材

sap² [sæp] n. 1. 坑道 2. 坑道的挖掘 vt. 暗中破坏; 逐步削弱 — (sapped; sapping) vi. 1. 挖掘坑道 2. (掘坑道)接近敌人阵地 — vt. 1. 挖坑道袭击 2. 在…下面暗使受损(潮水等)逐渐侵蚀 3. 渐渐削弱

sapience [ˈseipiəns] n. 1. 装出的聪明; 自

以为聪明 2. 贤明; 智慧

sapient [ˈseipiənt] adj. 1. 贤明的, 睿智的 2. 自以为聪明的 3. 智人的; 具有智人特征的

sapling [ˈsæpliŋ] n. 1. 树苗, 幼树 2. 年轻人 3. 【动】1 岁内的灵缇

sapper [ˈsæpə] n. 1. 坑道工兵; 地雷工兵 2. 挖掘者; 挖掘器

sapphire [ˈsæfaiə] n. 1. 【矿】蓝宝石 2. 宝石蓝(色), 天蓝(色) — adj. 宝石蓝(色)的, 天蓝色的

sappy [ˈsæpi] adj. 1. 树液多的 2. 朝气蓬勃的; 精力充沛的 3. 似边材的; 以边材为主的 4. 感情脆弱的; 愚蠢的, 傻的

sapsucker [ˈsæpˌsʌkə] n. 【动】吸汁啄木鸟 (产于北美)

Sarajevo [ˌsærəˈjeivəu] n. 萨拉热窝 [波斯尼亚-黑塞哥维那首都]

sarape [səˈrɑːpi] n. = serape

Sarawak [səˈrɑːwæk] n. 沙捞越 [马来西亚一地区]

sarcasm [ˈsɑːkæzm] n. 1. 讽刺, 挖苦, 嘲笑 2. 讥讽语; 讽话语 3. 讽刺性

sarcastic [sɑːˈkæstik] adj. 1. 讽刺的, 挖苦的, 嘲笑的 2. 用讥讽语的; 好挖苦人的 ‖ ～ally adv.

sarcophagus [sɑːˈkɔfəgəs] ([复] sarcophagi [sɑːˈkɔfəgai] 或 sarcophaguses) n. 石棺; 大理石棺

sardine [sɑːˈdiːn] ([复] sardine(s)) n. 【动】沙丁鱼,

sardonic [sɑːˈdɔnik] adj. 讥讽的, 挖苦的, 嘲笑的 ‖ ～ally adv.

sari, saree [ˈsɑːri] n. (印度妇女的)莎丽(服)(用整段的布或绸包头裹身或披肩裹身的服装)

sarong [ˈsɔːrɔŋ, səˈrɔŋ] n. 1. 莎笼, 围裙

（马来民族服装）2. 莎笼裙料

sarsaparilla [ˌsɑːsəpəˈrilə] *n.* 1.【植】菝葜 2. 菝葜干根（或制剂、汽水）

sartorial [sɑːˈtɔːriəl] *adj.* 1. 裁缝的；缝纫的；男式服装的 2.【解】缝匠肌的

sash[1] [sæʃ]（[复]sash(es)）*n.* 框格；〈罕〉窗框— 1.【建】（门、窗）装上框格 ‖ ~ window 框格窗；上下推拉窗

sash[2] [sæʃ] *n.* 1.（妇女、儿童用的）腰带；彩带 2.【军】饰带，肩带；值星带— *vt.* 给…系上腰带（或饰带等）

sassafras [ˈsæsəfræs] *n.* 1.【植】美洲擦木，黄樟 2. 美洲擦木的干根皮

sassy [ˈsæsi] *adj.*（口）1. 莽撞的，冒失的 2. 活泼的，精力旺盛的 3. 时髦的；漂亮的

sat [sæt] sit 的过去式和过去分词

Sat. *abbr.* 1. Saturday 2. Saturn

Satan [ˈseitən] *n.* 撒旦，魔鬼，恶魔，魔王 ‖ ~ic *adj.*

satchel [ˈsætʃəl] *n.*（皮或帆布的）书包；小背包；小提包

sate [seit] *vt.* 使充分满足；使饱享；使厌腻

sateen [sæˈtiːn] *n.*【纺】棉缎；纬锻；横贡

satellite [ˈsætəlait] *n.* 1. 卫星 2. 人造卫星 3. 卫星国；卫星城镇 4. 附属物；仆从

satiable [ˈseiʃiəbl] *adj.* 可使充分满足的；可使饱的

satiate [ˈseiʃieit] *vt.* 使充分满足；使饱享；使过饱生厌；使厌腻 —[ˈseiʃiit] *adj.* 饱享的；厌腻的 ‖ ,sati'ation, satiety [səˈtaiəti, seiˈ-] *n.*

satin [ˈsætin] *n.* 1. 缎子 2.【纺】缎纹；经缎组织 — *adj.* 缎子做的；缎子般的；光亮柔滑的 — *vt.* 使（纸张等）表面有光泽 ‖ ~y *adj.* 缎子似的，柔软光滑的

satire [ˈsætaiə] *n.* 1. 讽刺作品 2. 讽刺文学 3. 讽刺(*on, upon*)

satiric [səˈtirik] *adj.* 讽刺的；写讽刺作品的

satirical [səˈtirikəl] *adj.* 1. 好挖苦的 2. = satiric ‖ ~ly *adv.*

satirize [ˈsætəraiz] *vt. & vi.* 讽刺，讥讽 ‖ satirist *n.* 惯于讽刺的人；讽刺作家

satisfaction [ˌsætisˈfækʃən] *n.* 1. 满意，满足；称心 2. 快事，乐事；愉快 3. 赔偿；还债；履行义务；赔偿物 4.【宗】苦行赎罪 5. 决斗；报复

satisfactory [ˌsætisˈfæktəri] *adj.* 1. 令人满意的；符合要求的；良好的 2.【宗】赎罪的 ‖ satisfactorily *adv.* / satisfactoriness *n.*

satisfy [ˈsætisfai] *vt. & vi.* 1. 满足；使满足 2. 使满意 3. 符合，达到（要求、标准、规定等）4. 说服；使相信 5. 使…确实 5. 消除（顾虑等）6. 偿还（债务）；履行（义务、契约等）；向…偿清 7. 赔偿（受损失者）；赎（罪）— *vi.* 1. 令人满足；令人满意 2.【宗】赎罪；替世人赎罪

saturate [ˈsætʃəreit] *vt.* 1. 使饱和；使中和 2. 浸透；渗透；使充满 3.【军】对…进行饱和轰炸 — 2.（诗）浸透的；渗透的 2.（颜色)深的，浓的

saturation [ˌsætʃəˈreiʃən] *n.* 1. 饱和（状态）2. 浸透；浸润 3.【物】磁性饱和 4. 色彩浓度 5.（市场的）饱和与状态 6.【军】兵力、火力等的）饱和集结 ‖ ~ bombing 饱和轰炸 / ~ campaigning 饱和竞选（指作最大限度的竞选活动）

Saturday [ˈsætədi] *n.* 星期六 — *adv.*（口）在星期六 ‖ ~s *adv.*（美）每星期六；在任何星期六 ‖ ~'~-to-'Monday *n. & adj.* 周末的(的)

Saturn [ˈsætən] *n.* 1.【罗神】萨杜恩（农

神 2.【天】土星(略作 Sat.) 3.〈炼金术用语〉铅

saturnine ['sætənain] *adj.* 1. (表情等)阴沉的 2. 忧郁的 3. 讥讽的 3. 铅的;铅中毒的

satyr ['sætə] *n.* 1.【希神】(性好欢娱及耽于淫欲的)萨梯(森林之神) 2. 好色的男人;【医】男性色情狂患者;【动】眼蝶(亦作~ butterfly) 4.〈罕〉猩猩 ‖ ~ic [sə'tirik] *adj.* 1. 森林之神的 2. 色情狂的

sauce [sɔːs] *n.* 1. 沙司,调味汁,酱,佐料:soy (或 soybean) ~ 酱油 2.〈美〉炖煮的水果;罐头水果 3.〈喻〉增加趣味的东西 4.〈口〉莽撞;冒失无礼 5.〈方〉蔬菜;肉类的配菜 6.〈美俚〉烈酒:be on the ~ 酗酒;喝酒成瘾 — *vt.* 1. 给…调味;浇酱汁于 2. 使增趣味;使增添风味 3.〈口〉对…莽撞;对…冒失无礼 ‖ ~-box *n.*〈口〉冒失鬼;莽撞的孩子 / '~-pan *n.* (长柄有盖的深平底锅)

saucer ['sɔːsə] *n.* 1. 茶托,茶碟:a cup and ~ 带茶托的茶杯 2. (放在花盆下储水流干的)垫盆 3. 浅碟形物;浅碟形凹地 4.〈口〉[~s]眼睛;睁得又圆又大的眼睛;大眼睛

saucy ['sɔːsi] *adj.* 1. 莽撞的;无礼的 2. 活泼的;愉快的 3. 漂亮的;时髦的 ‖ **saucily** *adv.* / **sauciness** *n.*

Saudi ['saudi] **Arabia** 沙特阿拉伯[西南亚国家]

sauerkraut ['sauəkraut]〈德〉*n.* 泡菜

sauna ['saunə] *n.* (芬兰式的)桑拿浴(室),蒸汽浴(室)

saunter ['sɔːntə] *vi.* 1. 闲逛;漫步 2. 逍遥 — *n.* 闲逛;漫步

sausage ['sɔsidʒ] *n.* 1. 香肠,腊肠 2. 香肠状物;【军】圆柱形系留气球 3.〈贬〉德国人

sauté ['səutei]〈法〉*adj.* 嫩煎的,煸的 — (sauté(e)d; sautéing) *vt.* 嫩煎,煸 — *n.* 嫩煎的菜肴,炒菜

sauterne [səu'tɜːn]〈法〉*n.* 苏特恩白葡萄酒

savage ['sævidʒ] *adj.* 1. 野性的;凶猛的;残酷的;猛烈的 2.〈口〉荒野的;未开发的 3. (部落等)原始的;未开化的;野蛮的 4. 粗鲁的,粗野的 5.〈口〉狂怒的 — *n.* 1. 原始时代(或以渔猎为生)的人;未开化的人 2. 残酷成性的人 3. 粗鲁的人 — *vt.* 1. (马)乱撞;乱咬;乱踩 2. 凶猛地打击;粗暴地对待 ‖ ~ly *adv.* / ~ness *n.*

savagery ['sævidʒəri] *n.* 1. 野性;凶猛;残酷 2. 野蛮行为 3. 原始状态;未开化状态 4. 荒凉景象 5.[总称]野蛮人;野人

savanna(h) [sə'vænə] *n.* 1. (美国东南部的)无树草原 2. (亚)热带稀树草原

savant ['sævənt, sɑː'vɔŋ] *n.* 博学多闻的人;专家;学者

save[1] [seiv] *vt.* 1. 救,搭救;挽救 2. 节省,省去;避免(损失等) 3. 储蓄;贮存 4. 顾全;保全;保留 5. 赶上…时间;不失…时机 6.(球类比赛中)救(球等);阻碍对方得(分)7.【宗】救免;拯救 — *vi.* 1. 救,搭救 2. 节省,节约 3. 积蓄金钱;贮存物品(常作~ up)(鱼类,水果等)耐贮藏;搁得住 4. 救球 —《球类运动)救球;阻碍对方得分;(桥牌赛中)扭转攻局的一着;牺牲 ‖ ~r *n.* 救助者;储蓄者;节省的人 2.[常用以构成复合词]节省…的装置(或器具)

save[2] [seiv] *prep.* 除…以外 — *conj.* 1. 若不是;只是 2. 除去 3.〈古〉除非

saving[1] ['seiviŋ] *adj.* 1. 搭救的;挽救的 2. 节约的;节俭的 3.【律】保留的 4. 补偿的 — *n.* i. 搭救;挽救 2. 节约;节俭 3.[~s]储蓄(金),存款

saving[2] ['seiviŋ] *prep.* **1.** 除…以外 **2.** 顾到，考虑到 —*conj.* = save[1]

savio(u)r ['seivjə] *n.***1.** 救助者；挽救者；救星 **2.** [the S-]【宗】救世主，教主(耶稣基督)

savoir-faire ['sævwɑ:'feə] 〈法〉*n.* 处事能力；才干

savo(u)r ['seivə] *n.***1.** 滋味；气味；〈喻〉风味；特点 **2.** 引起兴趣(或食欲等)的力量；吸引力 **3.** 食欲；嗜好 **4.**〈古〉名声 —*vi.* 具有…的滋味；带有…的意味(*of*) —*vt.* **1.** 给…加调味品之类；使有风味 **3.** 尝到；经历到 **4.** 品尝；欣赏；〈古〉爱好

savo(u)ry ['seivəri] *adj.***1.** 美味可口的；芳香开胃的；饶有趣味的 **2.** 咸的；香辣的 **3.**[常用于否定句]宜人的；适意的；体面的 **4.**〈英〉(餐前或餐末用)的开胃的菜肴

savvy ['sævi] 〈俚〉*vt.* 理解，懂；领悟 —*vi.* 理解；领悟要点: A: *Savvy*? B: No —甲: 懂吗? 乙: 不懂。—*n.* 精明；理解；见识: political ～ 政治上的老练 / Where's your ～? 你的聪明到哪里去了? (或: 你难道不懂吗?) —*adj.* 精明老练的；有见识的

saw[1] [sɔː] *see*[1] 的过去式

saw[2] [sɔː] *n.***1.** 锯子；锯状器；锯床 **2.**【动】锯齿状部；[~s](昆虫)产卵器 **3.**〈美俚〉票面 10 元的钞票 —*vt.* (过去式 sawed, 过去分词 sawn [sɔːn]或 sawed) *vt.***1.** 锯；锯开；锯成 **2.** 拉锯般来回移动；拉出(曲调) **3.** 在书刊等上切口(以便装订) —*vi.***1.** 用锯；拉锯；锯开 **2.**(拉锯般)移动 ‖ *~-dust n.* 木屑，锯屑；let the ～ *dust* out of …使原形毕露，使出丑(原指从玩偶中取出填塞物)/ as

dry as ～*dust* 枯燥乏味 *adj.***1.** 木屑填塞的 **2.**(马戏、传道会等)在天篷下举行的 **3.** 无实质的，无内容的: *a* ～*dust* answer 空洞的答词 / '～ *horse n.* 锯木架 / '～ *mill n.* 锯木厂；锯床 / '～*-toothed adj.* 锯齿形的

saw[3] [sɔː] *n.* 格言，谚语

sawyer ['sɔːjə] *n.***1.** 锯木人 **2.**〈美〉(一端靠于河底、一端浮于水面随波摆动的)水中树木 **3.**【动】显赫天牛(其幼虫钻木)

saxhorn ['sækshɔːn] *n.*【音】萨克斯号

saxifrage ['sæksifridʒ] *n.*【植】虎耳草

Saxon ['sæksn] *n.***1.**【史】撒克逊人(5－6世纪入侵并定居于英国的日耳曼民族) **2.** 萨克森(现代德国北部地区) **3.** 盎格鲁撒克逊人；英格兰人 **4.** 撒克逊语；古代英语；平易的英语；英语中的日耳曼语成分 —*adj.***1.** 撒克逊人的 **2.** 盎格鲁撒克逊的；英格兰人的 **3.** 撒克逊语的；(英语中的语言现象)源于日耳曼语的

saxophone ['sæksəfəun] *n.*【音】萨克斯管

say [sei] (said[sed]) 第三人称单数现在式 says[sez]) *vt.***1.** 说，讲 **2.** 说明；宣称；表明 **3.** 念；背诵 **4.** 写道；报道 **5.**[常用于虚拟语气、祈使句]比如说；即使说；大约(= *let's ～*): Shall we start somefime later this week, ～, Friday? 我们是不是在本周中的晚些时候再出发? 星期五怎么样? / Well, ～ *it were* true, what then? 好吧，就算这是真的，又怎样呢? —*vi.***1.** 说，讲；发表意见 **2.**(美口)叫，要: She *said* (for me) to send you the letter. 她叫我把这封信带给你。—*n.*[一般只用单]要说的话；意见；发言机会；发言权[常 the ～]决定权

saying ['seiŋ] *n.***1.** 话，言语；言论 **2.** 谚

语;俗话;格言

say-so ['seisəu] *n.* [口] **1.** 随口说说的话;无证据的断言 **2.** 权威性判断(或声明) **3.** 决定权;权威

sb. *abbr.* **1.** somebody **2.** substantive

SC *abbr.* **1.** South Carolina 南卡罗来纳[美国州名] **2.** Supreme Court **3.** Security Council (of the United Nations)

Sc [化] 元素钪(scandium)的符号

scab [skæb] *n.* **1.** 痂 **2.** (动物尤指羊的)疥癣 **3.** 【植】疮痂病,疮痂斑点 **4.** 疤;疣瘤 **5.** (俚)卑劣的家伙;恶棍;无赖 **6.** 拒不参加工会者;拒不参加罢工者;破坏罢工者,工贼 — (trade) union 黄色工会 — (scabbed;scabbing) *vi.* **1.** (伤口等)结痂 **2.** 当工贼

scabbard ['skæbəd] *n.* 鞘:a bayonet ~刺刀鞘 — *vt.* 把(剑或刺刀等)插入鞘中

scabby ['skæbi] *adj.* **1.** 结痂的;结满痂的 **2.** 长满疥癣的;【植】染疮痂病的 **3.** 卑鄙的;下贱的

scabies ['skeibiːz] [单复同] *n.* 【医】疥疮:疥螨病

scaffold ['skæfəld] *n.* **1.** 【建】脚手架 **2.** 断头台;绞刑架 **3.** 给...搭脚手架的材料 — *vt.* 给...搭脚手架

scaffolding ['skæfəldiŋ] *n.* 【建】脚手架(组);搭脚手架的材料

scag [skæg] *n.* [美俚] 海洛因

scalawag ['skæləwæg] *n.* [口] 无赖,流氓,恶棍

scald [skɔːld] *vt.* **1.** (用沸水等)烫伤 **2.** 用沸水(或蒸汽)清洗;烫洗 **3.** 把...液到接近沸点 **4.** 把...灼焦 — *n.* **1.** 烫伤 — *n.* **1.** 烫伤口 **2.** 烫洗

scale¹ [skeil] *n.* **1.** 鳞;鱼鳞;介壳 **2.** 鳞状物;鳞片;【植】鳞苞;(树木的)皮;(皮肤的)鳞屑 **3.** (眼中的)翳障;[~s]

障眼物 **4.** 水锈,水垢;齿垢 **5.** 介壳虫;介壳虫害 **6.** 鱼鳞铠甲(鳞片) — *vt.* **1.** 刮去...的鳞片;剥去...的介壳;剥去...的积垢 **2.** 使起鳞(或鳞屑等);使水垢脱落 **3.** 用(石片等)打水漂 — *vi.* **1.** (鳞片般地)剥落,脱落(off) **2.** 生鲑(或鳞屑等);生水垢 ‖ ~ insect. ~ louse 蚧,介壳虫

scale² [skeil] *n.* **1.** 天平盘;秤盘 **2.** [常~s] 天平;磅秤;秤 **3.** (尤指牲畜的)重量;大小 **4.** [the Scales] 【天】天秤座 — *vt.* **1.** 把...过秤 **2.** 按重量把...分成均等部分 — *vi.* 重(达若干)

scale³ [skeil] *n.* **1.** 标度,刻度;尺度;刻度尺 **2.** (指实物与图表之间的)比例;比率;比例尺;缩尺 **3.** 等级;级别 **4.** 大小;规模 **5.** 进位制;计数法:decimal ~ 十进制;binary ~ 二进制 **6.** 【音】音阶 **7.** (对木材可用部分作出估量的)材积表 **8.** (古)梯子;阶梯 — **1.** 攀登(悬崖,墙等);到达...的顶点 **2.** 用云梯(进攻;按比例)排列;(用比例尺)测量;(按比例或标准)调制;调节;衡量(木材等)的可用部分 — *vi.* **1.** 攀登;到达顶点 **2.** 衡量

scalene ['skeiliːn] *adj.* **1.** 【数】不等边的 **2.** 【解】斜角肌的 — *n.* **1.** 不等边三角形;斜角肌

scallion ['skæljən] *n.* 【植】叶用葱;韭葱

scallop ['skɔləp] *n.* **1.** 【动】扇贝;干贝 **2.** (可用来烘食物的)扇贝壳;扇贝壳形状的小烘盆 **3.** [~s]扇形花边 **4.** 薄肉片 — *vt.* **1.** 使成扇形;切成扇形;用扇形花样装饰 **2.** 用扇贝壳(或扇贝壳状盆子)烘烤;在(食物)上涂酱汁和面包屑后烘烤 — *vi.* 拾扇贝;用网捞扇贝

scalp [skælp] *n.* **1.** (人的)头皮;(狗、狼等的)头顶皮;(无下颚的)鲸头 **2.** 带发头皮(从前北美印第安人把它从敌

人头上割下来作为战利品);战利品 3.
〈方〉秃山顶;突岩 4.〈口〉从事小投机
倒卖赚得的微利 — vt. 1. 剥下…的
头皮;除去(土地等)的表层 2. 锄(矿
石等) 3. 剥夺…的职位(或权势);打
败(对手) 4. 使饱受嘲弄;使受辱;猛
烈抨击 5.〈口〉转手倒卖(股票等)以迅
速取得微利;倒卖(戏票等) — vi. 1.
剥取头皮 2.〈口〉从事小投机倒卖;倒
卖戏票 ∥ — er n.

scalpel ['skælpəl] n. 解剖刀;手术刀 —
(scalpel(l)ed;scalpel(l)ing) vt. 用解剖刀
切开

scaly ['skeili] adj. 1. 有鳞的;多鳞的;鳞
状的 2. 鳞片般剥落的 3. 积(水)垢的
4. 充满介壳虫的;介壳虫蛀的 5.〈俚〉
卑鄙的;小气的 ∥ scaliness n.

scam [skæm] n. 阴谋;诡计;欺诈;骗局
— (scammed;scamming) vt. & vi. 欺
诈;诈骗 ∥ scammer n.

scamp[1] [skæmp] n. 1. 流氓;坏蛋;饭桶
2.〈谑〉小淘气 3.〈古〉拦路强盗

scamp[2] [skæmp] vt. 草率地做(工作等)

scamper ['skæmpə] vi. 1. 跳跳蹦蹦
(about) 2.(动物等)惊慌奔跑;奔逃
(off, away) 3. 匆忙游览;浏览
(through) — n. 1. 蹦跳;奔跑;短距离
的快走(或疾驰) 2. 匆忙的游览;浏览

scan [skæn] (scanned;scanning) vt. 1. 细
看;审视 2.(用电子装置)检验(磁带
或穿孔卡) 3.〈美〉粗略地看 4. 按
标出诗(诗)的格律(指划分音步等);按
韵节吟诵 5.(电视,雷达光束等)扫描;
扫掠 — vi. 1.(诗)符合格律,韵节合
拍 2. 标出诗的格律 3. 扫描 —
n. 1. 细看;审视 2. 粗略一看;浏览 3.
眼界,视野 4. 扫描;扫掠

scandal ['skændl] n. 1. 丑事;丑闻 2. 干
出丑事的人;耻辱 3. 反感;愤慨 4. 流

言蜚语;恶意诽谤 — (scandal(l)ed;scan-
dal(l)ing) vt.〈方〉讲…坏话;恶意诽谤
∥ ~ monger n. 恶意中伤的人;传播丑
闻的人

scandalize ['skændəlaiz] vt. 1. 使生反感;
使感愤慨;使感震惊 2. 诽谤;中伤

scandalous ['skændələs] adj. 1. 恶意中伤
的;诽谤性的 2. 丑恶可耻的;令人反
感之极的 3. 爱传播丑闻的;爱恶意中
伤的

Scandinavia [ˌskændi'neivjə] n. 斯堪的纳
维亚(半岛)[北欧]

Scandinavian [ˌskændi'neivjən] n. & adj.
1. 斯堪的纳维亚人(的) 2. 斯堪的纳
维亚人的日耳曼语系(的),北欧日耳
曼语系(的)

scandium ['skændiəm] n.【化】钪

scanner ['skænə] n. 1.(电视,雷达等的)
扫描设备,扫描器;扫掠机构;扫描天
线 2. 审视者

scant [skænt] adj. 1. 不足的;缺乏的 2.
将近的,还差一点的 3.〈方〉过分节省
的;小气的 — vt. 1. 减少;削弱 2.(在
供应上)限制;克扣;节省 3. 藐视;忽
略 — adv.〈方〉勉强地;几乎不

scanty ['skænti] adj. 1. 不充足的;贫乏
的 2. 狭小的;稀疏的 3. 过分简省的,
吝啬的 ∥ scantily adv. /scantiness n.

scape ['skeip] n. 1.【植】花葶,花茎 2.
【动】羽轴;柄节(触角的长基节)
3.【建】柱身

scapegoat ['skeipgəut] n.【宗】替罪羊
2. 代人受过的人(或物) ∥ ~ ism n. 寻
找替罪羊的行为,诿过于人

scapegrace ['skeipgreis] n. 1. 不可救药的
恶棍(或无赖) 2. 饭桶;淘气鬼;常闯
祸的顽童

scapula ['skæpjulə] ([复] scapulae
['skæpjuliː, 'skæpjulai] 或 scapulas)

【解】肩胛(骨) ‖ **scapular** *adj.*

scar [skɑː] *n.* **1.** 伤疤,伤痕 (精神上的) 创伤 **2.**【植】瘢痕 (scarred; scarring) *vt.* 使留下伤痕 — *vi.* 结疤;(伤口)愈合 (over)

scarab ['skærəb] *n.* **1.**【动】金龟子科甲虫;圣甲虫 **2.**(古埃及人作护身符用的)圣甲虫宝石,圣甲虫雕饰物

scarce [skeəs] *adj.* **1.** (一般作表语)缺乏的,不足的 **2.** 稀有的,珍贵的 — *adv.* 〈古〉〈诗〉= scarcely ‖ ~**ness** *n.*

scarcely ['skeəsli] *adv.* **1.** 仅仅;刚刚 **2.** 几乎不;简直不;几乎没有 **3.** 决不 **4.** [相当于"not"的减弱语气] 不很;大概不

scarcity ['skeəsəti] *n.* **1.** 缺乏,不足;萧条 (时期) 2.荒(年) **2.** 稀少;贫乏

scare [skeə] *vt.* **1.** 惊吓,使恐慌 **2.** 把…吓跑 (away, off) **3.** 把…吓出来;把 (猎物)吓出隐蔽处 (out, up) — *vi.* 受惊(at) — *n.* 惊恐;大恐慌 ‖ ~**crow** *n.* **1.**(竖在田里吓鸟的)稻草人 **2.** 吓唬人的东西 **3.** 衣衫褴褛或令人骨瘦如柴的人

scarf [skɑːf] (复 scarves [skɑːvz] 或 scarfs) *n.* **1.** 围巾;披巾;头巾 **2.** 领带;领巾 **3.**(披绶带的)狭长台布;桌巾 **4.**【军】(制服肩部或腰部系军衔的)绶带 — *vt.* **1.** 围(围巾);披(披巾) **2.** 用围巾(或披巾等)围(或披、包)

scarify ['skeərifai] *vt.* **1.** 划破;在…上划痕 **2.** 严厉地批评;苛责;伤…的感情 **3.** 使(硬皮种子)破皮 **4.** 松(土)

scarlatina [,skɑːlə'tiːnə] *n.*【医】猩红热

scarlet ['skɑːlət] *n.* **1.** 猩红色;绯红色,鲜红色(染料) **2.** 鲜红的布;红色制服;红衣 — *adj.* **1.** 猩红的,绯红的,鲜红的 **2.** 淫荡的;罪恶昭彰的 ‖ ~ **fever** *n.*【医】猩红热 **2.** 〈谑〉(女子的)军人崇拜

scarp [skɑːp] *n.* **1.** 陡坡;悬崖;(海边浪潮侵蚀而成的)崖岸 **2.**(城堡外壕的)内削壁

scary ['skeəri] *adj.* **1.** 引起惊慌的,骇人的 **2.** 容易受惊的;胆小的 **3.** 惊慌的;害怕的;Don't be so ~! 不必如此惊慌!

scat [skæt] (scatted; scatting) *vi.* 跑开;快走

scathe [skeið] *vt.* 痛斥,辱骂

scathing ['skeiðiŋ] *adj.* 严厉的;尖刻的

scatter ['skætə] *vt.* **1.** 使消散;使分散;使溃散 **2.** 撒;撒于…上;散布;散布在…上 **3.** 散射;撒播 **4.**【物】【军】散射 **5.** 〈古〉挥霍掉 — *vi.* **1.** 消散;分散;溃散 **2.** 零落地出现 **3.**(炮火等)散射 — *n.* **1.** 消散;分散;溃散;散射(或散布)量 **2.** 散布 **3.** 散布的东西;稀疏的少量 **4.**〈美俚〉猎枪;机关枪

scavenge ['skævindʒ] *vt.* **1.** 清除(污物、垃圾等);清除…中的污物(或垃圾等) **2.** 以(腐肉、腐物等)为食 **3.**【机】(从内燃机汽缸里)扫(气);给(内燃机汽缸)扫气 **4.**【冶】纯化(熔态金属) **5.** 从…中提取有用物质;在废物中提取 — *vi.* **1.** 清除污物(或杂质);当清扫工 **2.** 从内燃机汽缸里扫气 **3.** 在废物中搜寻(或提取)有用物质;利用废物

scavenger ['skævindʒə] *n.* **1.**〈主英〉清道夫;拾垃圾的人;清扫工 **2.** 清除剂;净化剂 **3.** 食腐动物

scenario [si'nɑːriəu] (复 scenarios)〈意〉 *n.* **1.** 剧情说明;歌剧剧情说明 **2.** 电影脚本,分镜头剧本 **3.** 方案

scene [siːn] *n.* **1.**〈古〉舞台 (现只用于比喻) **2.** (事件或故事的)发生地点 **3.** (戏剧、电影等的)一场 (戏剧、故事中的)一段情节;(电影的)一个镜头 **4.** (实际生活中的)一个场面(或场面特写);Act

1. *Scene* 2 第一幕第二场 / selected ~ s 折子戏 4. [常~] 道具；布景；场景 5. 色彩；景象 6. 出众吵嘴；发脾气：make a ~ 当众大吵一场

scenery ['si:nəri] *n.* 1. [总称] 舞台布景 2. [总称] 风景，景色 3. 风景画面

scenic ['si:nik] *adj.* 1. 舞台的；布景的 2. 自然景色的；景色优美的：a ~ spot 风景区 3. 描绘情景（或事件）的 4. 戏剧性的；装腔作势的 5. [口] 风景影片 6. 风景照片（或图片）；画有故事的糊墙纸；（游戏场等的）景观小铁路

scent [sent] *n.* 1. 气味；香味 2. 香水 3. （猎物的）遗臭，臭迹；踪迹，线索：on a hot ~ 强烈的（易于追踪的）臭迹 / a cold ~ 微淡的（难于追踪的）臭迹 3. 迹象 5. 嗅觉；察觉能力 6. （狩猎、钓鱼用的）混合饵料 7. （儿童游戏"狗捉兔子"中）撒在地上的纸屑 — *vt.* 1. 嗅，闻；嗅出，闻到(out) 2. 察觉；怀疑 3. 使充满气味；洒香水于 — *vi.* 嗅猎 3. 发出气味(of)；具有迹象(of)

scepter ['septə] *n.* & *vt.* = sceptre

sceptic ['skeptik] *n.* 1. [S-] [哲]（古希腊）怀疑论者 2. 不可知论者 2. 怀疑基督教（或所有宗教）教条的人；[口] 无神论者 3. 惯抱怀疑态度的人；对某事物抱怀疑态度的人

sceptical ['skeptikəl] *adj.* 1. [哲] 怀疑论的；不可知论的 2. 怀疑宗教教条的 3. 怀疑的

sceptre ['septə] *n.* （君主的）节杖（权位的象征）；君权；统治权 — *vt.* 授…以节杖；授…以君权

schedule ['fedju:əl, 'skedʒu:əl] *n.* 1. 一览表；明细表 2. [美] 时间表，时刻表(= timetable) 3. 计划表；程序表；议事日程 — *vt.* 1. 将…列表；将…列入计划表（或程序表，时间表等）2) [美] 排定；安

排 ‖ *ahead of* ~ 提前：The production plan was fulfilled *ahead of* ~. 生产计划提前完成了。/ *behind* ~ 落后于预定计划（或时间）

scheme [ski:m] *n.* 1. 计划；规划；方案 2. 组合；配合；系统；组织 3. 诡计，阴谋 4. 图解；大纲；摘要 5. [古] 数学图表；(占星) 天象图 — *vt.* 1. 计划；设计(out) 2. 策划（阴谋等）— *vi.* 1. 计划；设计 2. 搞阴谋 ‖ — *r n.* 1. 计划者 2. 阴谋家

scherzo ['skɛətsəu]（[复] scherzos 或 scherzi ['skɛətsi:]）(意) 谐谑曲

Schick [ʃik] *n.* ‖ ~ **test** [医] 锡克氏（白喉免疫力）试验

schism ['sizəm] *n.* 1. （政治组织等的）分裂；不和 2. 教会分立；分立教会罪 3. （分裂产生的）教会宗派

schismatic [siz'mætik] *n.* 分裂(论)者；教会分立(论)者 — *adj.* 分裂(论)的；教会分立(论)的

schizoid ['skitsoid] [医] *adj.* 精神分裂样的 — *n.* 精神分裂样人格者

schizophrenia [,skitsəu'fri:njə] *n.* [医] 精神分裂症

schlock [flɔk] [主美口] *adj.* 劣质的，质次的 — *n.* 劣货，次品 ‖ — **y** *adj.*

schmaltz [fmælts] *n.* [口] [音] 感伤；感伤作品 ‖ — **y** *adj.*

schnorkel ['ʃnɔ:kəl] *n.* （潜水艇或潜游者的）通气管

scholar ['skɔlə] *n.* 1. （尤指古典语言和文学方面的）学者 2. 有文化者；能写会读的人：I'm not much of a ~. 我的文化程度不高。2. 奖学金获得者 4. [学]学子；门徒；学生：Old as he is , he is still a ~. 他活到老，学到老。 ‖ — **ly** *adj.* 1. 学者派头的；学者风度的 2. 博学的 3. 好学的 / ~ **ship** *n.* 1. 学业成绩；学术

成就；学问，学识 **2.** 奖学金

scholastic [skə'læstik] *adj.* **1.** 学校的；学院的；学术的 **2.** 教师的；教育的 **3.** 学究的；烦琐的；故弄玄虚的 **4.** [S-] 经院的 —— *n.* **1.** [S-] 经院哲学学者 **2.** 烦琐哲学家；学究；拘于形式者 **3.** (艺术上的) 墨守成规者 **4.** 学生；学者 ‖ ~**ally** *adv.*

scholasticism [skə'læstisizəm] *n.* **1.** [S-] 经院哲学 **2.** 烦琐哲学 **3.** 墨守成规

school¹ [sku:l] *n.* **1.** 学校；(学校) 建筑物,校舍；全校师生；全校学生 **2.** (大学里的) 学院：the Medical (Law) School 医 (法) 学院 **3.** [不用冠词] 上课；学业，功课；学期；上课 **4.** 学派，流派；[~s] 学术界；(中世纪) 书院；经院 **5.** (英) 大学学位考试科目；学位考试试场；学位考场 **6.** 锻炼；军事训练；军训教程 (或规章) —— *vt.* **1.** 把…送进学校培养；负担…的学费 **2.** 教育，训练；约束；使 (自己) 习惯 (或适应) —— *vi.* ‖ ~**bag** *n.* 书包 / ~**book** *n.* 教科书 / ~**boy** *n. & adj.* (中、小学) 男生的 / ~**girl** *n. & adj.* (中、小学) 女生的 / ~**house** *n.* (小学或乡村学校) 校舍；(英) [the ~house] (小学) 校长住宅 / ~**master** *n.* **1.** 男教师 **2.** 校长 **3.** 教练；教导者 / ~**mate** *n.* 同学 / ~**mistress** *n.* (中、小学) 女教师 / ~**room** *n.* 教室 / ~**teacher** *n.* (中、小学) 教师

school² [sku:l] *n.* 鱼群；同类水生生物群 —— *vi.* (鱼、鲸等) 成群地游

schooling ['sku:liŋ] *n.* **1.** 正规学校教育；教育 **2.** 学费；学业 **3.** 学校的膳宿杂费 **4.** 训马；骑术训练

schooner ['sku:nə] *n.* **1.** 纵帆船 **2.** (美) 大啤酒杯 (作为计量单位的) 一大啤酒杯 **3.** (美) (早期移民的) 大篷车

Schutzstaffel ['ʃutsʃtɑːfəl] (德) *n.* (纳粹

德国的) 党卫军 (略作 SS)

schwa [ʃwɑː] *n.* [语] **1.** (英语) 非重央元音 (如 *a* lone, sa*n*ity 等) **2.** (国际音标中的) ə 符号

sciatica [sai'ætikə] *n.* [医] 坐骨神经痛 ‖ **sciatic** *adj.*

science ['saiəns] *n.* **1.** 科学；科学研究 **2.** 学科 **3.** 自然科学：a Bachelor of *Science* 理学士 / a Doctor of *Science* 理学博士 **4.** 专门的技巧；技术 **5.** (古) 知识 ‖ ~ **fiction** 科学幻想小说

scientific [ˌsaiən'tifik] *adj.* **1.** 科学 (上) 的 **2.** 符合科学规律的；系统的；精确的 **3.** 用于自然科学的 **4.** 掌握技巧的；需要技术的 ‖ ~**ally** *adv.*

scientist ['saiəntist] *n.* 科学家

sci-fi ['sai'fai] *n. & adj.* (美) 科学幻想小说 (的)

scimitar, scimiter ['simitə] *n.* 阿拉伯人及土耳其人等旧时用的短弯刀

scintilla [sin'tilə] (拉) *n.* **1.** 火花 **2.** 一点点, 丝毫

scintillate ['sintileit] *vi.* **1.** 发出火花 **2.** (星等) 闪烁, 闪耀 **3.** 焕发 —— *vt.* **1.** 发出 (火花, 闪光等) **2.** 闪耀出 ‖ **scintil'lation** *n.*

scion ['saiən] *n.* **1.** [植] 接穗 (栽种或接枝用的幼枝); 幼芽 **2.** 子孙, 后裔 (尤指名门或贵族后裔)

scissor ['sizə] *vt.* **1.** 剪 **2.** 减少, 削减 —— *n.* (一把) 剪刀

scissors ['sizəz] [复] *n.* **1.** [有时用作单] 剪刀, 剪子 ‖ ~ movement of prices [经] 价格的剪刀差 **2.** [体] 交叉; (游泳) 剪式腿动作; [摔跤中双腿钳住对手的] 剪叉

sclerosis [skliə'rəusis] [复] **scleroses** [skliə'rəusi:z] *n.* **1.** [医] 硬化 (症) **2.** [植] 硬化 **3.** 僵化, 峻拒改革 ‖ **sclerotic**

[ˈskliəˈrɒtik] *adj.*

scoff [skɔ] *n.* **1.** 嘲笑;嘲笑;蔑视;嘲弄的话 **2.** 笑柄 — *vi.* **1.** 嘲弄;嘲笑(*at*) **2.** 蔑视 — *vt.* 嘲弄;嘲笑 ‖ ~**er** *n.* 嘲弄者;嘲笑者

scold [skəuld] *n.* **1.** 老爱责骂的人;好骂街的泼妇 **2.** 责骂;a writing that is a ~骂人的文章 — *vi.* 责骂;大声叱责 — *vt.* 申斥;怒骂

sconce[1] *n.* 壁式烛台;带柄烛台

sconce[2] [skɔns] *n.* **1.**〈古〉掩蔽物;屏障 **2.**〈军〉(孤立的)小堡垒 **3.** 头部的保护物(如盔等) **4.**〈口〉头,脑袋;脑力;判断力 **5.** 筑堡垒防卫,遮蔽;掩护

scone [skɔn] *n.* 烤饼,司康(面粉加苏打、糖、盐等烤制的英国茶点)

scoop [skup] *n.* **1.** 勺子,铲斗;〈医〉匙,勺 **2.** 铲斗;煤斗 **3.** 舀,铲;一勺;一铲 **4.** 穴,口;凹处 **5.**〈口〉(投机或买卖中)抢先赚得的暴利 **6.**〈口〉抢先刊载的独家新闻;最新内幕消息 — *vt.* **1.** 用勺(或铲)取出,舀 **2.** 挖空;挖成;挖出 **3.**〈口〉收集(*in*) **4.**〈口〉抢先赚得(利润) **5.**〈口〉(报纸、电台等)抢在(别家)前面发布某条新闻;抢先获得(某条新闻)

scoot [skut]〈口〉 *vi.* 迅速跑开;溜,溜走 — *n.* 迅速跑开;溜

scooter [ˈskutə] *n.* **1.**(儿童游戏用的)踏板车 **2.** 低座小摩托车 **3.**(在水上或冰上行驶的)有滑橇的帆船;滑行艇

scope [skəup] *n.* **1.**(活动、影响等的)范围 **2.**(发挥能力等的)余地;机会 **3.** 视界;眼界 **4.** 导弹的射程;〈海〉出链长度 **5.**〈古〉目的;意图

scopophilia [ˌskəupəˈfiliə] *n.*〔心〕窥视症,窥阴癖

scorch [skɔtʃ] *vt.* **1.** 烧焦,烤焦;使枯萎 **2.** 灼苦;刺痛 **3.**(军队撤退前)烧

光(某地)的一切;a ~ed earth policy 焦土政策 **4.**〔化〕使(橡胶)过早硫化 **5.**〈英方〉切;砍 — *vi.* **1.** 烧焦,烤焦;枯萎 **2.** 灼苦;刺痛人 **3.**〈口〉高速驾驶,飞驶 — *n.* **1.** 烧焦;焦痕 **2.**(草木等的)枯黄 **3.**〈口〉高速驾驶;高速行驶的时间

score [skɔ] *n.* **1.** 刻痕;抓痕;伤痕;划线 **2.** 欠账;欠账(源于旧时旅店用粉笔划线记录顾客欠账);〈喻〉宿怨,旧仇 **3.** 点,方面;理由,根据 **4.**(比赛中的)得分(记录),比数;(测验的)成绩,评分 **5.**〔音〕总谱;乐谱;(电影、戏剧、歌舞等的)配乐 **6.**(赛跑等的)起跑线,起步线;终点线 **7.**〔单复同〕20个;(称猪、牛等用的重量单位)20磅(约 21)磅 **8.**[~s]许多,大量 **9.** 真相,实情;(问题的)症结 **10.**(英俚)占上风的一着(或一句话);好运气;What a ~! 真走运! **11.**〔海〕(滑车的)带槽 — *vt.* **1.** 刻痕于;划线于;打记号于 **2.** 把…记入账内;把…记下(*up*) **3.** 获得(成绩,胜利等);赢得(比赛中)得分;使(某人)得分 **4.** 给…评分;评价 **5.** 将…写成总谱;把…谱成管弦乐曲;为(影片等)配乐 **6.**〈美〉严厉批评;责备 — *vi.* **1.** 刻痕;划线 **2.**(在比赛中)得分;得胜;成功:Team A ~d against(或 over)Team B. 甲队胜了乙队。/ That's where he ~d. 那一点就是他占上风(或走运)之处。‖ ~**less** *adj.* 没得分的 / ~**r** *n.* **1.** 记分员 **2.** 得分者

scorn [skɔn] *n.* **1.** 轻蔑;蔑视 **2.** 嘲弄;奚落 **3.** 蔑视(或嘲弄)的对象 — *vt.* **1.** 轻蔑;蔑视 **2.** 摈斥;不屑做

scornful [ˈskɔnful] *adj.* 轻蔑的;蔑视的 ‖ ~**ly** *adv.* / ~**ness** *n.*

scorpion [ˈskɔpjən] *n.* **1.** 蝎子 **2.**[S-]〔天〕天蝎座 **3.** 蝎尾鞭(一种打人凶

器);(古代的)弩炮 **4.** 螯针般的刺激
5. 刻毒的人

Scot *n.* **1.** 苏格兰人 **2.**(5—6 世纪
时从爱尔兰北部移居到苏格兰的)盖
尔人

scot [skɔt] *n.* **1.**(英国古时)估定(或已缴
付)的款项;赋税 ∥`~`-**'free** *adj.* 免于
受罚的;未受损害的 — **1.**(罕)免于付税的

Scot. *abbr.* **1.** Scotch **2.** Scotland **3.** Scottish

Scotch [skɔtʃ] *adj.* **1.** 苏格兰(人)的 **2.**
苏格兰方言的 **3.**〈俚〉苏格兰性格的;
节俭的;吝啬的 — *n.* **1.**[the ~]苏格
兰人;苏格兰民族 **2.** 苏格兰方言 **3.**
(口)苏格兰威士忌酒(亦作~ whisky)
4. 苏格兰(透明)胶带(一种薄而易粘
的胶带,源自商标名)

scotch [skɔtʃ] *vt.* **1.**(划)切;抓;刻痕于;
给…开槽 **2.** 使暂受伤;使受伤残 **3.** 镇
压;扑灭;粉碎 **4.** 戳穿(谣言、谬论等)
5. 制止(车轮等)转动;阻止… — *n.*
1. 刻痕;砍痕;浅槽 **2.**(儿童跳格游戏中)
划在地上的格线 **3.**(防止车轮或木材
滚动的)木楔,木块;障碍物

scotia [ˈskəuʃə] *n.*〔建〕(柱基等的)凹弧
边饰

Scotland [ˈskɔtlənd] *n.* 苏格兰〔英国的一
部分〕∥`~`-**Yard** **1.** 苏格兰场(伦敦街
名)**2.** 伦敦警察厅(侦缉处);伦敦警方

Scottish [ˈskɔtiʃ] *adj.* **1.** 苏格兰(人)的
2. 苏格兰方言的 — *n.* **1.** 苏格兰英
语,苏格兰方言 **2.**[the ~]苏格兰人

scoundrel [ˈskaundrəl] *n.* 恶棍,坏蛋,流
氓 — *adj.* 恶棍(般)的;卑鄙的 ∥`~`-
ism *n.* 恶棍的行为;恶棍性格

scour[1] [ˈskauə] *vt.* **1.** 擦亮;擦净;洗涤 **2.**
冲洗(阴沟;管道等);灌(肠)**3.** 擦掉;
洗掉;冲刷;清除(谷类)中的杂物(*off*,
away)**4.** 冲刷成;冲出(*out*)**5.**〔治〕侵

蚀 — *vi.* **1.** 擦;擦亮;洗刷;冲洗 **2.**
(牲畜等)腹泻;患痢疾 — *n.* **1.** 擦;
洗;冲刷;(河道水流的)冲刷力 **2.**
[~s]用作单或复](畜类等的)腹泻;
痢疾 **3.** 除垢剂;洗涤剂

scour[2] [ˈskauə] *vt.* 急速穿过;走遍(某
地)搜索 — *vi.* 急速穿行;追寻

scourge [skəːdʒ] *n.* **1.** 刑鞭 **2.** 惩罚的工
具;惩罚 **3.** 苦难的根源;带来灾难的
人;灾祸(如瘟疫等)— *vt.* **1.** 鞭打,鞭
笞 **2.** 严斥,痛斥 **3.** 严惩 **4.** 使痛苦;蹂
躏

scout[1] [skaut] *n.* **1.** 侦察员;侦察机;侦
察艇;搜索救援飞机 **2.** 侦察 **3.** 哨兵;
守望者 **4.**(一个)童子军:the Boy (Girl)
Scouts 男(女)童子军 **5.**(四处物色演
员、运动员等的)觅宝人士;(工商经济、
体育比赛等领域的)业务员课 **6.**(英)
(牛津大学的)校工 **7.**(英)(专门协助
汽车协会或皇家汽车俱乐部司机的)
公路巡逻人员 **8.**(口)(常用作亲热的
称呼)人,伙计 — *vi.* **1.** 搜集敌方情
报,侦察 **2.** 搜索;寻找 **3.** 积极参加童
子军活动 — *vt.* **1.** 侦察;搜索;搜索;
监视 **2.** 观察(运动员、演员等)的表现
以估计其才能 **3.**(经过寻找)发现;觅
得 ∥`~`-**master** *n.* 童子军领队

scout[2] [skaut] *vt.* **1.** 蔑视地拒绝(提议、
意见等)**2.** 讥笑,嘲弄 — *vi.* 嘲笑(*at*)

scow [skau] *n.* 平底驳船,方驳

scowl [skaul] *n.* **1.** 皱眉;愁眉苦脸 **2.** 怒
容 — *vi.* **1.** 皱眉头;沉着脸;愁眉苦脸(*at*,
on)— *vt.* **1.** 瞪眼怒视着使…;瞪眼怒
视着把…压下去 **2.** 以怒容表示(不快
等)

SCR *abbr.* silicon-controlled rectifier【电子】
可控硅整流器

scrabble [ˈskræbl] *vi.* **1.**(用爪)扒寻;抓
挠;(用手)摸索 **2.** 挣扎;争夺 **3.** 乱涂

乱写 — vt. 1. 把…扒集拢来；在…上乱扒 2. 匆忙拼凑成 3. 在…上乱涂 — n. 1. 扒；抓；摸索 2. 乱涂的东西 3. 挣扎；争夺

scrag [skræg] n. 1. 皮包骨头的人(或动物)；瘦小的植物 2. 瘦小的动物；羊(或小牛)的颈肉 3. 〈俚〉脖子；头 (scragged; scragging) vt. 1. 〈俚〉绞死；勒杀 2. 掐住…的脖子 3. (橄榄球赛中)抱住(对方球员)的脖子 4. (在商业上)把(别人或别家商店)挤掉 ‖ **scraggy** adj.

scraggly ['skrægli] adj. 不规则的，参差的；蓬乱的，不整齐的；崎岖不平的；矮小的；稀疏的

scramble ['skræmbl] vi. 1. 爬行；攀爬；(植物)攀缘上树 2. 不规则地生长，杂乱蔓延 3. (乱糟糟地)争夺，抢夺 4. 勉强拼凑 5. 仓促地行动;〔空〕紧急起飞应战;~ to one's feet 匆忙站起/~ into one's clothes 匆忙穿起衣服 — vt. 1. 攀登；爬行 2. 使混杂；搅乱 3. 杂乱地收集;匆促凑成(up) 4. 炒(蛋) 5. 抛出(硬币等)使抢夺 6. 改变频率(通话)使不被窃听 7.〔空〕命令(战斗机组)紧急起飞 — n. 1. 爬行；攀登 2. 争夺，抢夺(for) 3. 混乱；混乱的一团 4. (摩托车的)越野比赛；越野试乘车 5.〔空〕紧急起飞 6.〔无〕扰频，倒频

scrap[1] [skræp] n. 1. 碎片；零屑；少许，点滴 2. (文字等)的片断;(从书报上剪下的)图片；剪报 3. 废金属；切屑；废料 4. [～s]残羹剩饭 5. [～s](动物脂)的油渣 — adj. 1. 零碎的，片断的；剩余的 2. 用过的;废弃的 — (scrapped; scrapping) vt. 1. 把…弄成废料;炒碎;报废；废弃 ‖ ~-book n. 剪贴簿

scrap[2] [skræp]〈俚〉n. 1. 打架；吵架 2. 职业拳击赛 — (scrapped; scrapping) vi. 打架；吵架

scrape [skreip] vt. 1. 刮；擦；刮着；擦去(off, out, away);~ one's plate 吃净盘中食物 /~ scales off a fish 刮鱼鳞 2. 擦净；刮擦(某物)使发出刺耳声 3. (尤指用手指或手)挖出；挖成(out) 4. (艰难地)凑集；积攒；积聚(up, together) 5. 勉强度(日子) — vi. 1. 擦；擦过；勉强通过 2. 刮(或擦)出刺耳声 3. (鞠躬时)一脚擦地后退 4. 勉强度日子(退难地)积攒钱财 — n. 1. 刮；擦；挖 2. 擦伤；刮痕 3. 刮擦声 4. (自己招致的)困境，窘境 5.〈美俚〉剃胡子；刮脸

scraper ['skreipə] n. 1. 刮器；刮刀；刮板；削刮器；刮除机；刮土机；铲运机 3. 吝啬鬼；守财奴

scrapper ['skræpə] n.〈俚〉1. 爱打架(或吵架)的人 2. 拳击手

scrapple ['skræpl] n. 碎肉玉米(或面粉)炸饼

scrappy[1] ['skræpi] adj. 1. 由碎料做成的;杂凑的;片断的;剩余的 2. 不连贯的;散漫的

scrappy[2] ['skræpi] adj.〈俚〉1. 爱吵架的;好打架的 2. 斗志旺盛的;坚决不让步的

scratch [skrætʃ] vt. 1. 搔;抓;抓破,抓伤 2.(用爪子等)扒出,挖出 3. 刮;擦 4.(潦草地)涂写,乱涂 5. 勾划掉(out) 6. 把(马等)撤出比赛;勾去(候选人)的名字以示不赞成;(在政党候选人名单上)勾去一些名字以示抵制 6.(辛苦地)凑集(金钱等)(up, together) — vi. 1. 搔;抓;作刮擦声 3. 退出比赛;未能践约 4. 勉强糊口,艰难地谋生(along) 5. 在政党候选人名单上勾掉名字 — n. 1. 搔;抓;抓痕;擦伤 2. 刮擦声 3. 乱涂;乱画 4. [只用单,不用冠词]起跑线;(角斗)起始线 5.(打牌的)零分 6.(台球戏中的)引起

罚分的一击;未中的一击;侥幸的击中 **7.** 退出比赛的马;〈美俚〉无名小卒,无足轻重的人 **8.** 〈美俚〉钱;现钞;借款 **9.** [~s] 马勒葡萄密 — *adj.* **1.** 碰巧的,偶然的 **2.** 凑合的,匆匆组成的 **3.** 打草稿用的 **4.** (在体育比赛中)无让分优待的;大家从零开始的

scratchy ['skrætʃi] *adj.* **1.** (书写等)潦草的;乱涂的 **2.** 发刮擦声的(钢笔)钩纸面的 **3.** (球队等)拼凑而成的,临时组成的 **4.** 刺痛的;使人发痒的

scrawl [skrɔːl] *vt.* 潦草地写(或画) — *vi.* 乱写;乱涂 — *n.* 潦草模糊的笔迹;潦草涂成的字句(或书信、图画等)

scrawny ['skrɔːni] *adj.* 骨瘦如柴的 ‖ **scrawniness** *n.*

scream [skriːm] *vi.* **1.** 尖叫,惊呼(机器、汽笛等)发出尖锐刺耳的声音;(风)呼啸 **2.** 令人震惊 **3.** 〈歇斯底里地〉强烈要求(*for*);大叫大嚷着抗议(*about*) **5.** 纵声大笑 — *vt.* **1.** 尖声说;尖叫着说 **2.** [~ oneself] 尖叫得使… **3.** 大叫大嚷着要;大叫大嚷着宣告 — *n.* **1.** 尖叫;尖锐刺耳的声音 **2.** 〈口〉引人捧腹大笑的人(或事物)

screech [skriːtʃ] *n.* **1.** (表示惊恐、痛苦、愤怒等的)尖叫;尖锐刺耳的声音 **2.** 〈俚〉威士忌酒 **3.** 〈澳俚〉劣质烈酒 — *vi.* 发出尖锐刺耳叫声 — *vt.* 用尖锐叫声发出(或表示)

screed [skriːd] *n.* **1.** 冗长的文章(或书信、讲话) **2.** 【建】抹灰靠尺;整平板;砂浆层

screen [skriːn] *n.* **1.** 屏;幕;帘;帐;隔板(教堂的)祭坛屏饰 **2.** (金属、塑料等材料制的)纱窗;纱门 **3.** 掩蔽物;警戒幕;屏护部队 **4.** 掩护;包庇 **5.** (电影、幻灯的)银幕;(电视的)屏幕;[the ~] 电影;电影业;电影艺术 **6.** 【物】屏蔽

荧光屏;帘栅板 **7.** (有网罩或玻璃盖的)布告板 **8.** (粗眼)筛子;圆眼筛;滤网;过滤器 **9.** 【印】网屏,网版 — *vt.* **1.** 掩蔽;遮护;包庇 **2.** 放映(电影、幻灯片);(用电影拍摄机)拍摄 **3.** 把(故事、戏剧等)改编成电影剧本;使在影片中演出 **4.** 给…装帘(或纱窗帘) **5.** 筛(煤等);筛分(*out*);甄别;审查 **6.** [物]屏蔽 — *vi.* 能拍电影;能用来拍摄

screw [skruː] *n.* **1.** 螺旋;螺杆;螺丝;螺(丝)钉;螺旋状物 **2.** 螺孔 **3.** 螺旋桨 **4.** (螺旋的)一拧(螺旋式的)旋转 **5.** (英)(台球或保龄球等)旋转 **6.** 一小纸卷(或纸包) **7.** (英俚)工资;薪水 **7.** (主英)吝啬鬼;守财奴;心狠手辣的卖(或买)主 **8.** (监狱)看守人;拇指夹(旧时的刑具) **9.** (英)驽马 — *vt.* **1.** (用螺旋)操纵;调节;(用螺丝)拧紧;(用螺钉)钉住 **2.** 旋;拧 **3.** 加螺纹于 **4.** (用拇指夹)夹 **5.** 扭歪;眯紧 **6.** 加强;振作;鼓舞(*up*) **7.** 强迫;压榨;榨取;勒索 **8.** 〈美俚〉奸污 — *vi.* **1.** (螺丝等)转动;靠螺旋形转动 **2.** 旋;拧(*off, on, together*);The lid ~s on (*off*). 盖子可拧上(可拧开)。**3.** (球)旋转运动;(人)扭身;扭动 **4.** 进行压榨一(或勒索) **5.** 拼命节省 ‖ 用钱吝啬 **6.** 急忙地离开开 ‖ '~-driver *n.* 旋凿,(螺丝)起子

scribble ['skribl] *vt. & vi.* 潦草书写;乱涂;草率写作 — *n.* **1.** 潦草的笔迹;乱涂 **2.** 拙劣的作品 ‖ ~r *n.* **1.** 笔迹潦草的人 **2.** 拙劣的作家;乱制滥造的作者

scribe [skraib] *n.* **1.** 〈古代〉犹太法律学家 **2.** 抄写员 (尤指印刷术发明前以抄写书籍为职业的) **3.** 文牍,书记 **4.** 作家;新闻记者 **5.** 【建】划线器 — *vi.* 担任抄写员(或书记、文牍等);缮写 — *vt.* **1.** 用划线器划在(木、砖等)上划线;用划线器划(线) **2.** (木工)雕合(等

件),使合缝

scrimmage ['skrimidʒ] *n.* 1. 小战斗;散兵战 2. 扭打;混战 3. 并列争球,扭夺(= scrummage) — *vt.* 并列争(球);把(球)放在并列争夺的位置 — *vi.* 参加混战 ‖ ~**r** *n.* 参加混战者;(橄榄球队的)前锋

scrimp [skrimp] *vt.* 1. 过度缩减;使太短;使太窄 2. 吝于供给;不充分补助 — *vi.* 1. 节省 2. 吝啬 — *adj.* 缩减的;不足的

scrimshank ['skrimʃæŋk] *vi.*〈英〉〈军俚〉逃避职责

scrip [skrip] *n.* 辅币纸币;临时凭证;购物券

script [skript] *n.* 1. 手迹,笔迹;手写体 2. 手稿;打字原稿;正本 3. (戏剧、电影)剧本(尤指原稿);广播(原)稿本 4.〔印〕书写体 5.〈英〉笔试卷 — *vt.* 把…改编为演出本(或广播)节目

scripture ['skriptʃə] *n.* 1. 手稿;文件;权威性的著作 2.〔常 S-〕〔基督教〕〈圣经〉(亦作 Holy Scripture 或 the Scriptures) 3.〔常 S-〕〈圣经〉中的文句 4.〔基督教以外其他宗教的经文〕经典,圣典:the Buddhist ~ 佛经 ‖ **scriptural** *adj.*

scrofula ['skrɔfjulə] *n.*〔医〕瘰疬,淋巴结结核

scroll [skrəul] *n.* 1. 羊皮纸卷轴;纸卷;写成卷轴的古书 2. 名册;刻有铭词的纹章饰带;〈古〉信件 3.(加在签名后面的)花押;涡卷形书写 4. 涡卷形;涡形(石刻上的)涡状饰,涡卷饰;〔机〕涡形管;〔音〕(提琴的)涡卷形头;〔数〕涡卷 5. 在卷轴上题(字) — *vi.* 成涡卷形;成涡形

scrotum ['skrəutəm] *n.*(〔复〕scrota ['skrəutə] 或 scrotums)*n.*〔解〕阴囊 ‖ **scrotal** *adj.*

scrounge [skraundʒ]〈俚〉*vi.* 搜寻;乞讨;骗取 — *vt.* 乞得;骗取;非法获取;借…而不还;搜寻(up) ‖ ~**r** *n.*

scrub[1] [skrʌb] (scrubbed; scrubbing) *vt.* 1. 擦洗;擦净;擦掉;摩擦 3.〔施行外科手术前〕洗(手和臂)并消毒 4.〔化〕使(气体)净化,洗(气),洗(气)5.〈俚〉取消;删除 — *vi.* 1. 擦洗;擦净 2.〔施行外科手术前〕进行手和臂的消毒 — *n.* 1. 擦洗;擦净 2. 擦洗者;做苦工者

scrub[2] [skrʌb] *n.* 1. 矮树;灌木;灌丛;丛林地 2. 矮小的人;地位低微的人 3. 矮小动物;杂种家畜;杂种狗 4.(口)非校一级的队员(或非正规球队)的运动员,二流运动员 5.[~s] 二流球队;凑合比赛 5. 用秃了的毛刷;用旧了的扫帚 6. 短髭 — *adj.* 1. 低劣的;次等的 2. 矮小的;发育不良的 3. 非校一级的球队的;非正规球队的 4. 即兴的;临时凑合的

scrubby ['skrʌbi] *adj.* 1. 矮小的;劣质的 2. 长满矮树的;灌木丛的 3. 褴褛的;难看的;早晚的 4. 多短硬毛的

scruff [skrʌf] *n.* 颈背,后颈

scruffy ['skrʌfi] *adj.* 褴褛的;邋遢的;可鄙的;无价值的

scrummage ['skrʌmidʒ] *n.* 1. 并列争球,扭夺(橄榄球赛中双方前锋密集争夺在中间的球) 2. 喧闹(场所),混乱(处) — *vi.* 参与扭争

scrumptious ['skrʌmpʃəs] *adj.*〈俚〉令人愉快的;极好的,头等的;很美的

scrunch [skrʌntʃ] *vt.* 1.(喀嚓喀嚓地)咬,踩;咬嚼 2. 缩紧;揉皱 — *vi.* 1. 咯喀喀喀地响;碾,压;咬嚼 2. 蹲;蜷缩 — *n.* 喀喀喀喀的响声;碾压;揉皱;紧缩

scruple[1] ['skru:pl] *n.* 良心上的不安,顾虑,顾忌 — *vi.* 感到良心不安,有顾虑

— vt.〈古〉对…感到良心不安，对…有顾忌

scruple[2] ['skru:pl] n. 1. 英分(英美药衡单位; = 1.296 克) 2. 微量

scrupulous ['skru:pjuləs] adj. 1. 多顾忌的; 审慎的 2. 严格认真的; 拘泥于细节的 ‖~ly adv.

scrutineer [,skru:ti'niə] n. 1. 检查人 2. (英) 选票检查人, 监票人

scrutinize ['skru:tinaiz] vt. & vi. 细看, 细阅; 仔细检查

scrutiny ['skru:tini] n. 详细的检查(或审查); 细看, 细阅

scuba ['skju:bə] (self-contained underwater breathing apparatus 的首字母缩略词) n. 自携式水下呼吸器, 水肺

scud [skʌd] (scudded; scudding) vi. 1. 飞奔; 疾行 2. 飞驶, 掠过 (船等)顺风行驶 — n. 1. 飞奔; 疾行 2. 飞云; 漂飞的雾(或雨、雪等); 阵风; 阵雨; 阵雪 3.〈俚〉飞毛腿

scuff [skʌf] vi. 1. 拖着脚走 (局促不安时)在地上拖脚 2. (探测时)用脚去戳(at) 3. 磨损 — vt. 1. 拳打; 打伤; 攻击 2. 拖着(脚)走 (船等)顺风行驶; 踏脚; 踢开; 用足尖踏 使(鞋等) 3. 拖脚行走; 拖脚走的脚步声 2. 磨损; (鞋面上的)磨损处; 瘢疤 3. 家用平底拖鞋

scuffle ['skʌfl] vi. 1. 扭打; 混战 2. 拖着脚走 3. 敷衍了事 — n. 1. 扭打; 混战 2. 拖脚行走; 拖脚行走的脚步声

scull [skʌl] n. 1. (双桨小艇的)短桨; 橹 2. 单人双桨赛艇(比赛) — vt. 用桨划(船); 用橹摇(船) — vi. 划船

scullery ['skʌləri] n. 炊具(或蔬菜等)洗涤室; 炊具贮藏室

sculptor ['skʌlptə] n. 雕刻家, 雕塑家 ‖

sculptress ['skʌlptris] n. 女雕刻家, 女雕塑家

sculpture ['skʌlptʃə] n. 1. 雕刻(术); 雕塑(术) 2. 雕刻品, 雕塑品 3.【地】刻蚀 4.【动】【植】刻纹 — vt. 1. 雕刻, 雕塑, 塑造 2. 以雕塑装饰 3.【地】刻蚀 — vi. 当雕刻(或雕塑)师; 从事雕刻(或雕塑)行业

scum [skʌm] n. 1. (煮沸或发酵时发生的)泡沫; 浮渣; 浮垢 2. 渣滓, 糟粕; 社会最低层; 下贱的人, 卑贱者 3.〈学俚〉服侍高年级学生的低年级学生 — (scummed; scumming) vt. 去除(浮沫), 撇去 — vi. 形成泡沫, 盖满浮垢

scupper ['skʌpə] n. 1.【海】甲板排水孔 2.【建】泄水口 3.〈俚〉〈贬〉女人; 妓女

scurf [skə:f] n. 1. 皮(肤)屑; 头皮屑 2. 鳞片状的附着物; 附着物的残垢 3.【植】粗皮病; 糠皮病

scurrilous ['skʌriləs] adj. 庸俗下流的; 满口下流话的; 恶言辱骂的 ‖~ly adv. / scur'rility, ~ness n.

scurry ['skʌri] vi. 急匆匆地跑; 急赶 2. 乱转; 急转 — n. 1. 急促的奔跑; 急促奔跑声 2. 奔忙; 急赶; 急转 3. 短距离赛跑(或赛马)

scurvy ['skə:vi] n.【医】坏血病 — adj. 1. 卑鄙的; 下流的 2. 长满皮屑的

scuttle[1] ['skʌtl] n. 1. 煤斗; 煤桶 2. 篮; 筐

scuttle[2] ['skʌtl] vi. 1. 急促奔跑; 急赶 (away, off) 2. 匆忙撤退(或放弃、摆脱) — n. 1. 急速的逃走(或离去); 匆忙的撤退(或放弃); 惊怯的逃窜 2. (短距离的)快跑

scuttle[3] ['skʌtl] n. 1. 天窗; 气窗 2.【船】小舱口; 船底(或船侧)的孔洞; 舷窗; 舱口盖 — vt. 1. (在船底等处凿孔)使(船)沉没, 凿沉 2. 完全毁坏; 全部放弃

scythe [saið] *n.* 长柄大镰刀 — *vt.* 用长柄大镰刀割

Se 元素硒(selenium)的符号

SE, s. e. *abbr.* 1. southeast 2. southeastern

sea [si:] *n.* 1. 海；海洋 2. [用于专有名词中]海；内海；大(淡水)湖 3. [一般与不定冠词连用,但可用复数]海面动态；海浪,波涛 4. 大量;浩瀚,茫茫一片(*of*) 5. 航海生活,海员生活 ‖ ~ **anemone** [动]海葵 / ~**bird** *n.* 海鸟 / ~**board** *n.*(主要)海岸,海滨;沿海地区 / ~**coast** *n.* 海岸,海滨 / ~ **cucumber** 海参 / ~**dog** *n.*(主)角鲨,星鲨;海豹 2. 有经验的水手(尤指英国伊丽莎白一世时代的船长) 3. 海盗 / ~**farer** *n.* 海员;水手;航海者 / ~**faring** *n.* 以航海为业的;在航海中发生的,关于航海的 — *n.* 航海业,海员的职业;海上航行 / ~**going** *adj.* 1. 适于远洋航行的 2.〈美俚〉(物品)式样奇特的;特大的;(人)神气十足的 / ~ **gull** 1.[动]海鸥 2.〈美俚〉跟着丈夫出航的女人 / ~**horse** 1.[动]海象;海马,龙落子;马头鱼 2.(神话中的)半马半鱼的怪兽 3. 白色的浪峰 / **Sealab** *n.* 海底实验室 / ~**level** 海平面;(高低潮间的)平均海面 / ~**lion** 海驴 / ~**plane** *n.* 水上飞机 / ~**port** *n.* 海港;港市 / ~ **power** 1. 海军强国 2. 海上力量 / ~**shore** *n.* 海岸,海滨,海边 / ~**sick** *adj.* 晕船的 / ~**sickness** *n.* 晕船 / ~**slug** 海参 / ~**urchin**[动]海胆 / ~**wall** 海堤,防波堤 / **sea**\water *n.* 海水 / ~**way** *n.* 1. 海上航路;可航海区 2. 波涛汹涌的海面 3. 船只在海上的航进 4. 通海水道(通行远洋船舶的深水河道) / ~**weed** *n.* 海草,海藻;海菜

seal¹ [si:l] ([复] seal(s)) *n.* 1.[动]海豹 2. 海豹(毛)皮;人造海豹皮;海豹皮制品 3. 带灰黄的深褐色 4.〈美俚〉〈贬〉黑人妇女;黑人 — *vi.* 捕海豹 ‖ ~ **er** *n.* 捕海豹的人(或船) ‖ ~**skin** *n.* 1. 海豹皮 2. 海豹皮制的服装

seal² [si:l] *n.* 1. 封蜡;封铅;火漆;封印;封条 2.[机]密封垫;焊接 [物] 绝缘 3. 印记;图章;玺 4. 印信;保证;批准;誓约 5. 象征(标志 — *vt.* 1. 封;密封;糊住 2. 盖章于;(盖章)对...提出确证;保证;在(度量衡器等商品)上盖检验印 3. 决定;确定;解决 4.[电]使(插头与插孔等)接触密接 5. 用水泥等填塞 6.(摩门教)使(婚姻等)成为正式的和有约束力的;为...举行婚礼(或过继仪式等) / ~ **er** *n.* 盖章人 2.(度量衡器等的)检验员 3.(瓶、袋等的)封口人 4. 封口机;封口机操作者 5. 保护层

sealant [ˈsi:lənt] *n.* 密封胶;密封材料;防渗漏剂

seam [si:m] *n.* 1. 线缝;缝口脱开处 2. 接缝;接合线(或面) 3.(船板间)缝隙;接合处 4.[解]骨缝 5. 伤痕;皱痕;(铸件等的)接痕 7.[矿] [地]层,地层;矿层;煤层 — *vt.* 1. 缝合;接合;焊合;铆合;加热使合 2. 使留下伤痕,使生皱纹;使有凹痕;使有裂缝 3. 在布料子等上)织桃线 — *vi.* 1. 裂开,生裂缝 ‖ ~**less** *adj.* 无缝的

seaman [ˈsi:mən] ([复] seamen) *n.* 1. 海员;水手;精通海事者 2.(海军)水兵 3.(美国)海岸警卫队队员 ‖ ~**ship** *n.* 船舶驾驶术;航海技术;船艺

seamstress [ˈsemstris, ˈsi:mstris] *n.* 女裁缝,女缝工

seamy [ˈsi:mi] *adj.* 1. 有线缝(或裂缝)的 2. 讨厌的;丑恶的;卑鄙的 ‖ **seaminess** *n.*

seance ['seiɔns]〈法〉*n*. **1.** 集会,会议 **2.** 降神会

sear [sia] *adj*. 干枯的;调谢的 — *vt*. **1.** 使干枯,使调谢 **2.** 烧焦;烧灼;烙 **3.** 使变为冷酷无情 — *vi*. 干枯,调谢 — *n*. 烙印;焦痕

search [sɜːtʃ] *vt*. **1.** 在…中搜寻;搜查:~ the woods for a lost child 在树林搜寻一个走失的小孩 / His hand ~ed his pocket for a match. 他的手在衣袋中到处摸着找火柴。/ ~ sb. 搜查某人的身体 **2.** 细查;细细检查;(用外科仪器)探(伤):~ the records of a case 仔细查阅某一案件的卷宗 / ~ sb.'s face 察看某人的脸色 / ~ one's heart (或 conscience)检查自己的内心深处,自我反省 **3.**(风等)刺透:The cold wind ~ed the streets. 寒风吹过街道。~ed the streets. 寒风吹过街道。~(火力)向纵深展开 — *vi*. **1.** 搜寻;搜查(for) **2.** 探究;调查(into):~ into a matter 调查一件事情 — *n*. **1.** 搜寻;搜查:the right of ~(交战国军舰在公海上对中立国船只的)搜查权 / make a ~ for one's subject books 寻找有关自己学术专业的书籍 **2.** 检查;探索;调查 ‖ ~er *n*. ‖ '~light *n*. **1.** 探照灯(光) **2.** = flashlight

season ['siːzn] *n*. **1.** 季;季节;时节,时令 **2.** 当令期;旺季;(文娱、社交、商业等的)活跃季节 **3.** 一段时期 **4.**〈口〉(乘车等的)长期票 — *vt*. **1.** 给…调味;加味于;使增添趣味 **2.** 使得到锻炼;使适应;使服水土 **3.** 对(木材等)作干燥处理 **4.** 使缓和;使温和 — *vi*. **1.**(木材)变干;变合用 ‖ ~ing *n*. **1.** 调味品,佐料 **2.** 增加兴趣的东西 **3.** 木材干燥处理

seasonable ['siːznəbl] *adj*. **1.** 合时令的 **2.** 及时的,合时宜的

seasonal ['siːznəl] *adj*. 季节的;季节性的;随季节而变化的

seat [siːt] *n*. **1.** 座,坐位 **2.**(椅等的)座部;(机器的)座子;(人体或裤子的)臀部 **3.** 所在地;活动中心,中心 **4.** 席位 **5.** 会员资格 **6.** 坐的姿势;骑马(或自行车)的坐法 — *vt*. **1.** 使坐下,使就座;帮助…找到 **2.**(房间等)供给…坐位,坐得下…人;(房间等)有坐位 **3.** 使得席位;使当选就职;使登职位 **4.** 修补…的座部;为(机器等)装底座 ‖ ~er *n*. — *vi*. 装在底座上

SEATO ['siːtəu] *abbr*. Southeast Asia Treaty Organization 东南亚条约组织

seaworthy ['siːwɜːði] *adj*.(船舶)适航的 ‖ **seaworthiness** *n*. 适航性

sebaceous [si'beiʃəs] *adj*. 脂肪的,皮脂的;油脂状的;分泌脂质的

SEC *abbr*. Securities and Exchange Commission〈美〉证券交易委员会

sec. *abbr*. **1.** second(s) **2.** secondary **3.** secretary **4.** section(s) **5.** sector **6.** secant **7.** security

SECAM ['siː,kæm] *abbr*.〈法〉*Séquence de Couleurs avec Mémoire*(法国)电视彩色电视系统,顺序与存储彩色电视系统(= Colo(u)r Sequence with Memory)

secant ['siːkənt] *n*.【数】正割;割线

secede [si'siːd] *vi*.(从宗教、政治等组织)退出,脱离(from) ‖ **secession** [si'seʃən] *n*.

seclude [si'kluːd] *vt*. **1.** 使隔绝;使孤立;隐退 **2.** 隔于;把…隐蔽起来

secluded [si'kluːdid] *adj*. **1.** 隐退的 **2.** 僻静的;隐蔽的 ‖ ~ly *adv*. / ~ness *n*.

seclusion [si'kluːʒən] *n*. **1.** 隔离;孤立:a policy of ~ 闭关自守政策 **2.** 隐退;隐居 **3.** 偏僻的地方;隐蔽的地方

second[1] ['sekənd] *num.* 第二(个) — *adj.*
1. 二等的,次等的;次要的 **2.**【语】第二
格的;【音】第二度声部的 **3.** 另一的;
又一的;类似的;另加的;附加的：every
~ year (month, day) 每隔一年(月、天)
/ write on every ~ line 每隔一行写 / ~
a opportunity 再一次机会 **4.** 副的;辅
助的;从属的 **5.** 非独创的,模仿的;非
天生的,后天得到的 — *adv.* **1.** 居第
二位；第二等等；归第二名 **2.** 其次,再
次 — *n.* **1.** 第二名；第二位；第二奖；
(指汇票)第二份；(前述者以外的)另
一人(或物) **2.**【音】第二度；第二声；
第二声部 **3.** 支持者；(决斗中的)助手,副
手 **4.** 附和；赞成；附议 **5.** 副职人员；
副官；临时行员 **6.**[the S~]国务大臣 **7.**[~s]乙级商品；次货；粗面粉；粗
面粉做的面包；(美国)二煎咖啡 **8.**(汽
车)第二档速率 **9.**[口][~s]
[用作单或复]添菜 **10.**(月的)第二日
— *vt.* **1.**(决斗中)当…的助手;作…的
后援 **2.** 支持；赞成(提案等) **3.**
[si'kɔnd](英)[军]调任;调派 ‖ ~ly
adv. 第二(点),其次(列举条目等所
用) ‖ '~·best *adj.* 居第二位的,仅次
于最好的 / ~ best 居于第二位者,
仅次于最好的东西,居于第二位的东
西 **2.** 居第二位 / '~·'class *adj.* **1.** 第二
流的,二等的 **2.** 平常的，第二
地位低下 *adv.* 乘坐二等 / ~ floor
(英)三楼—(美)二楼 / '~·'hand *adj.* **1.**
间接知道的 **2.** 第二手的；二手的;旧的 **3.**
经营旧货的 *adv.* **1.** 间接地 **2.** 通过旧
货店(购买) / ~ lieutenant (英)陆军
(或海军陆战队)少尉；(美)陆军(或空
军、海军陆战队)少尉 / ~ mate (商船
上的)二副 / ~ nature 第二天性 / '~·
'rate *adj.* **1.** 二等的 **2.** 第二流的,平庸
的 / '~·'rater *n.* 平庸的人

second[2] ['sekənd] *n.* **1.**(时间的单位)秒

2. 片刻,瞬间 **3.**(角或度的单位)秒(=
1/60 分)

secondary ['sekəndəri] *adj.* **1.** 第二的;第
二位的;第二次的；中级的 **2.** 次要的；
副的;从属的;辅助的;非原著的;第二
手的 **3.**【医】继发性的;第二期的：~
infection 继发感染 **4.**[化]辅助的;第
二代的 **5.**[电]产生感应电流的;次级
的 **6.**[地]次生的 — *n.* **1.** 副手;次要
人物;代理人,代表 **2.**【天】伴星,卫星
3.【动】(鸟的)次级飞羽(即生在前膀上
的羽毛);(昆虫的)后翅 **4.**[电]次级绕
组;次级线圈

secrecy ['si:krisi] *n.* **1.** 秘密;秘密状态 **2.**
保密(习惯);保密能力：promise ~ 答
应不泄漏秘密

secret ['si:krit] *adj.* **1.** 秘密的,机密的 **2.**
隐蔽的,暗藏的；暗中进行的；内心
感觉的,秘而不宣的：~ alarm (rejoicing)暗自惊慌(高兴) **4.** 神秘的；奥秘
的 **5.** 偏僻的;人迹罕到的 **6.** 隐蔽的;
能保守秘密的：~ as the grave 守口如
瓶 **7.**(人体)阴部的 — *n.* **1.** 秘密,机
密：in ~ 秘密地 / (a) top ~ 绝密 **2.** 神秘;奥秘
3. 秘诀,诀窍;秘方 **4.**[常~s](人体)
阴部,私处 **5.**[S·](天主教)默祷(主持
弥撒的神父在供献后的低声祷告) ‖
~ly *adv.* ‖ ~ agent 特务 / ~ service
墨水(起初无色,经热、光或药品等作
用而显字) / ~ service **1.**(政府的)特工
机关：a ~ service man 特工人员 /
service money (国家支付的)特工经费
2.[S·S](美国)特工处(隶属美国财政
部)/ ~ society 秘密社团

secretarial [ˌsekrə'tɛəriəl] *adj.* **1.** 秘书的;
有关秘书事务的：the ~ staff 秘书处全
体人员 **2.** 书记的；部长的,大臣的

secretariat [ˌsekrə'tɛəriət] *n.* **1.** 书记处;
秘书处;书记(或秘书)处的全体成员

2. (作为行政机构的)部;处(或其全体职员);the United Nations *Secretariat* 联合国秘书处 **3.** 书记(或秘书;部长、大臣)的职务 **4.** 内阁(或行政秘书处)的办公大楼

secretary ['sekrətri] *n.* **1.** 秘书 **2.** 书记 **3.** (协会等的负责书信往来、档案记录等的)干事;文书 **4.** 大臣;部长:the *Secretary of State* (英国)国务大臣;(美国)国务卿 **5.** (上部附有书橱的)写字桌 **6.** 【印】草书体大铅字 ‖ ~-'general *n.* ([复] secretaries-general) **1.** 秘书长 **2.** 总书记

secrete [si'kri:t] *vt.* **1.** 藏匿(人或物) **2.** 私行侵吞 **3.** 【生】分泌 ‖ secretion *n.* **1.** 藏匿 **2.** 分泌;分泌液

secretive [si'kri:tiv] *adj.* **1.** 遮遮掩掩的,守口如瓶的;不坦率的 **2.** 分泌的;促进分泌的 ‖ ~ly *adv.*

sect [sekt] *n.* 派别;宗派 【宗】教派;分裂出来的异端

sectarian [sek'tɛəriən] *adj.* **1.** 宗派的;(分裂性)教派的 **2.** 闹宗派的;思想狭隘的,偏执的 — *n.* **1.** 宗派主义者;分裂教派的一员 **2.** 思想狭窄者 ‖ ~ism *n.* 宗派主义

section ['sekʃən] *n.* **1.** 切断;切开 **2.** 切下的部分;切片;断面;剖面 **3.** (事物的)一段,一部分 **4.** (机器的)零件;(文章等的)节;(条文等的)款;项 **5.** 处;科;股;组;【军】分排,小队;(乐队的)组 **5.** (铁路)路段;同班次的火车车辆之一;车厢中的卧铺段 **6.** 地区;区 **7.** 阶层;界 **8.** 【生】派(分类单位);(果子的)瓤 **9.** 分号(§) — *vt.* 把…分成段(或组等);将…切开 — *vi.* 被切割成段(或片)

sectional ['sekʃənl] *adj.* **1.** 截面的;剖面的 **2.** 部分的;局部的 **3.** 段落的;章节

4. 地区的;地方性的 **5.** 由可卸的部件拼制成的,组合的一 — *n.* 组合家具 ‖ ~ism *n.* 地方主义

sector ['sektə] *n.* **1.** 【数】扇形;扇形面 函数尺;象限仪 **3.** 部分;成分;部门 **4.** 【军】防区;防区;【计】防区,区段;防御区 — *vt.* **1.** 分成扇形 **2.** 使分成部分

secular ['sekjulə] *adj.* **1.** 现世的,世俗的;非宗教(或教会)的 **2.** 不受修道誓约约束的;修道院外的:the ~ clergy [总称]修道院外的教士;教区僧侣 **3.** 怀疑宗教教义的;脱离教会教育的 **4.** 每世纪(或一个长时期)发生一次的 **5.** 延续几个世纪的;长期的一 *n.* **1.** 修道院外的教士;教区僧侣 **2.** 俗人

secure [si'kjuə] *adj.* **1.** 安心的,无忧虑的;有把握的 **2.** 安全的;牢固的;保险的,可靠的 **3.** 〈古〉过于自信的 — *vt.* **1.** 使安全;掩护;固定;保证;为(借款等)作保;向(债权人)提供保证 **3.** 关紧;把…弄牢 **4.** 把…弄到手,获得;替…弄到;促成;招致 **5.** 使(船上人员)停止工作 — *vi.* **1.** (船上人员)停止操作;值勤完毕 **2.** (船)停靠码头;抛锚 ‖ ~ly *adv.*

security [si'kjuəriti] *n.* **1.** 安全;安全感 **2.** 使免遭危险的东西,保护物;防卫物 **3.** 治安防卫;安全防卫措施;[常 S]安全保卫机构 **4.** 保证;担保,担保品;保证金 **5.** 保证;保障;担保人 **6.** 把握;可靠性,担保人,担保人;抵押品;保证金 **7.** [常 securities](有价)证券;债券:government *securities* 公债券 ‖ Security Council of the United Nations (联合国)安全理事会

sedan [si'dæn] *n.* **1.** 轿车 **2.** 小轿车 **3.** 单舱汽艇 ‖ ~ chair 轿子

sedate[1] [si'deit] *adj.* **1.** 安静的 **2.** 稳重的;严肃的 ‖ ~ly *adv.* / ~ness *n.*

sedate² [si'deit] *vt.* 给…服镇静剂

sedative ['sedətiv] *adj.* 镇静的；止痛的 — *n.* 【药】镇静剂；止痛药

sedentary ['sedəntəri] *adj.* 1. 坐着的，不活动的 2. 久坐的，少动的 2. (动物)不迁徙的，定栖的；固着的，静止的

Seder ['seidə] ([复] Seders 或 Sedarim [se'dɑːrim]) *n.* (犹太教的)逾越节家宴(于犹太教历尼散月之15日和16日举行)

sedge [sedʒ] *n.* 【植】莎草；莎草植株

sediment ['sedimənt] *n.* 1. 沉积；沉淀 2. 【地】沉积物

sedimentary [,sedi'mentəri] *adj.* 1. 沉积的；沉淀性的 2. 由沉积物形成的

sedition [si'diʃən] *n.* 1. 煽动叛乱(或闹事)；(罕)叛乱；暴动 2. 煽动性的言论(或行为)

seduce [si'djuːs] *vt.* 1. 诱惑；诱使…堕落(或犯罪)；诱奸；勾引 2. 以魅力吸引 ‖ **seduction** [si'dʌkʃən] *n.* 诱惑；勾引；诱惑力；魅力 / **seductive** [si'dʌktiv] *adj.* 诱惑的；勾引人的；诱人堕落的；(妇女)性感的

sedulous ['sedjuləs] *adj.* 1. 勤勉的；孜孜不倦的 2. 小心周到的

see¹ [siː] (saw [sɔː], seen [siːn]) *vt.* 1. 看见，看到[注意：see 主要指"看见"，look (at)主要指"看着"，watch 主要指"注视"] 2. 察看，查看 3. 遇见；会见；访问(尤指看医生、找律师等)；接待人物(戏剧等) 4. 看出；发现；领会，理解；认为：*See*(或 You ～或 Do you ～) what I mean? 你懂了我的意思了吗? / as we ～ it 照我们的看法；我们认为 / ～ it fit to do sth. 认为做某事是合适的 6. (从报刊等)得悉，知道 7. 送看，见 … 8. 看中；喜欢；同意 9. 目睹；经历：He has *seen* a great deal (of life) 他见多识广(或阅历丰富)。/ May 1st *saw* the opening of the meeting. 5月1日会议开幕了。/ The recruit first *saw* sea duty on a torpedo boat. 新兵在鱼雷艇上开始了自己的水兵生活。10. 陪，送：～ sb. home 陪送某人回家／～ sb. out (to the door)送某人出去(到门口) 11. 听凭，任凭；宁愿让：would ～ oneself shot before yielding 宁死不屈 12. 在幻觉中看见；设想，想象 13. 照料；使能维持下去 14. 注意；当心，留神：务必使 … ～; *See* (that) you don't catch cold. 当心别伤风。15. 设想，想象：I can't ～ (myself) lending her money; can you ～ her ever paying back? 我可不想借钱给她；你想她能还得了吗? 16. 与(对方)押同样赌注；以同样赌注对(赌) 17.〈美俚〉贿赂；收买 — *vi.* 1. 看见，看到；观看 2.〔常用于祈使句〕瞧；注意；当心。*See*, here they come! 瞧，他们来啦!／Wait and ～. 等着瞧吧。3. 看出；理解；知道 4. 想想；查一查；调查 ‖ '～-through *adj.* (衣料、衣服等)透明的

see² [siː] *n.* 【宗】主教教座(或教区)；主教的地位(或权威、管辖权)：the See of Rome (或 the Holy See)【天主教】罗马教皇职位；罗马教廷

seed [siːd] ([复] seed(s)) *n.* 1. 种(子)；籽；【喻】萌芽，开端；起因 2. 家系；子孙，后代 3. 精液；芽胞；虫卵 4. 幼蚝；蚝种(亦作 ～ oyster) 5.〈口〉种子选手：the No. 1 ～ in a table-tennis championship 乒乓球赛中的第一号种子(选手) 6. 结籽(期)；产卵(期) 7. 种子状的东西(玻璃中的)小气泡 — *vt.* 1. 在…中播种；播(种) 2. 催 … 发育(或成长)；催(云)化雨(指人工降雨)：a breeder reactor ～ed with plutonium 用钚加速的增殖反应堆／～ clouds 人工降

雨 **3.** 去…的核；脱…的籽 **4.** 挑选（某人）作种子选手；安排（种子选手或种子队）— **vi. 1.**（植物）结子，结实 **2.** 脱籽 **3.** 播种 ‖ **~less** *adj.* 无核的 ‖ **~ plant** 种子植物

seeded ['si:did] *adj.* **1.** 播过种的 **2.**（果实）具种子的；结子的；成熟的 **4.** 去籽的，去核的 **5.**（织物）有斑点的

seedling ['si:dliŋ] *n.* **1.** 秧苗，籽苗 **2.** 树苗

seedy ['si:di] *adj.* **1.** 多籽的；多核的；结子的，结实的；成熟的 **2.**（玻璃）多气泡的 **3.** 破烂的；衣衫褴褛的；（房屋等）肮脏的；破落的；（娱乐等）下等的 **4.**〈口〉不舒服的；没精打采的 ‖ **seediness** *n.*

seeing ['si:iŋ] *conj.* 鉴于，由于；因为 — *n.* **1.** 视觉；视力 **2.** 看见；观看

seek [si:k]（sought [sɔ:t]）*vt.* **1.** 寻找；探索；追求 **2.** 在…中搜查；搜查遍（某地）**3.**〔一般后接不定式〕试图，图谋：~ to kill sb.（或～ sb.'s life）谋害某人 **4.** 征求；请求 **5.** 往，朝一而去：Water ～s its own level. 水往低处流。/ ～ one's bed 上床，就寝 — *vi.* **1.** 寻找；探索 **2.** 搜索，搜查 ‖ **~ er** *n.* **1.** 探索者；追求者；搜查者 **2.**（导弹的）自导头，自动导引头；自导导弹

seem [si:m] *vi.* **1.** 好像，在外表上显出；似乎：Be what you ～（to be）要表里一致。/ You don't ～ to be quite yourself today. 你今天好像不大对头人。（指身体或情绪）/ There ～s（to be）no point in refusing. 看来没有道理拒绝。**2.**〔与引导代词 it 连用〕看来好像，似乎：It ～s as if it is going to rain. 看来快下雨了。/ It would not ～ proper to do so. 看来这样做不太合适吧。〔注意：此句中句中的 would 起婉转语气的作用〕/ I shall act

as ～s best. 我将按照我认为最好的方法去做。**3.**〔与人称代词 I 连用〕感到好像，觉得似乎：I ～ to have seen him somewhere before. 我觉得好像以前曾在什么地方见过他。/ I ～ unable（或：〈美口〉I can't ～）to solve it right now. 看来我无法立刻解决此事。

seeming ['si:miŋ] *adj.* 表面上的；似乎真实的 — *n.* 外观，外貌（尤指假象）‖ **~ly** *adv.*

seemly ['si:mli] *adj.* **1.** 好看的；美貌的 **2.** 吸引人的；像样的；匀称的 **3.** 合适的；适宜的；合乎礼仪的 — *adv.*〈罕〉合适地；合礼仪地

seen [si:n] see¹ 的过去分词

seep¹ [si:p] *vi.* 渗出；渗漏 — *n.* **1.** 小泉 **2.** 地下水（或油等）渗出成玩的地方 ‖ **~age** *n.* **1.** 渗出；渗漏 **2.**（油、地下水）渗出地表处

seep² [si:p] *n.* 水陆两用吉普车

seer [siə] *n.* **1.** 预言家；预言者；先知 **3.**（凝视水晶球而占卜未来的）占卜者

seersucker ['siəsʌkə] *n.*〔纺〕绉条纹薄织物；泡泡纱

seesaw ['si:sɔ:] *n.* **1.** 跷跷板；跷跷板游戏 **2.**（类似跷跷板的）一上一下（或一前一后）的动作；拉锯式竞争：a ～ between the attackers and the defenders 攻守双方之间的拉锯战 — *vi.* **1.** 玩跷跷板 **2.** 上下（或前后）摇动 **3.** 交替；（物价、温度等）起伏，涨落 — *vt.* 使作跷跷板式运动；一上一下地动 — *adj. & adv.* 忽上忽下的（地）；忽前忽后的（地）；摇摆不定的（地）

seethe [si:ð] *vi.* **1.** 煮沸 **2.** 沸腾；激动（*with*）— *vt.* **1.** 使煮沸 **2.** 使浸湿；使浸透 — *n.* 沸腾

seething ['si:ðiŋ] *adj.* **1.** 火热的，沸腾的

2. 川流不息的；激昂的

segment ['segmənt] *n.* 1. 部分；切片 2. 【数】段；节；弓形；圆缺；球缺 3. 【机】划形体 4.【生】(体)节；环节 — *vt.* & *vi.* 分割；(使)分裂开 ‖ **seg'mental, 'segmentary** *adj.* / **segmen'tation** *n.*

segregate ['segrigeit] *vt.* 使分离，使分开；使隔离 — *vi.* 1. 分离，分开；受隔离 2. 施行种族隔离政策 3.【化】凝聚；【冶】偏析 — ['segrigit] *adj.* 1. 被分离的；被隔离的 2. 实行种族隔离政策的 — ['segrigit] *n.* 被隔离的人

segregation [,segri'geiʃən] *n.* 1. 分离，分开；隔离 2. 被隔离的部分 3.【生】(基因)分离 4.【化】分凝；【冶】偏析

seignior ['seinjə] *n.* 1. 庄园主；封建领主；贵族；显贵；绅士 2. (用作尊称)先生，君 (= Sir)

Seine [sein] *n.* 塞纳河[法国北部]

seine [sein] *n.* (捕鱼用)拖拉大围网 — *vi.* & *vt.* 用拖拉大围网捕(鱼)

seismic ['saizmik] *adj.* 地震(引起)的；与地震有关的

seismograph ['saizməgrɑːf] *n.* 地震仪

seize [siːz] *vt.* 1. 抓住；逮捕；俘获 2. 夺取；占领 3.(依法)没收，把…充公；扣押；查封 4.【律】依法占有 5. 抓住(时机)；掌握；理解 6. [常用被动语态](疾病)侵袭；(情绪)支配：be ~d by apoplexy 中风 / be ~d with an illness 害病 7.【海】缠扎(绳索) — *vi.* 1. 抓住；攫取；占有 (on, upon) 2. 利用；采用 (on, upon)

seizure ['siːʒə] *n.* 1. 抓住；攫取；捕捉 2. 夺取；占领 3. 依法占有；没收，充公 4.(疾病的)发作

seldom ['seldəm] *adv.* 难得，很少，不常 — *adj.* 罕有的，很少的，少见的

select [si'lekt] *vt.* 选择；挑选；选拔 — *vi.* 选择；挑选 — *adj.* 1. 挑选出来的；精选的 2. 优等的；杰出的，卓越的 3.(协会、学校等)选录成员严格的 4. 明辨的；挑剔的 — *n.* [常 ~s]被选出者；精萃

selection [si'lekʃən] *n.* 1. 选择；挑选；选拔 2. 待选择物；精选物；选集；选手：*Selections from Lenin*《列宁文选》3.【生】选择，淘汰

selective [si'lektiv] *adj.* 1. 选择的；挑选的；选拔的：~ subjects 选修科目 2. 有选择力的 3.【无】选择性的

selectman [si'lektmən] ([复] selectmen) *n.* (美)(新英格兰地区)市镇管理委员会委员

selenium [si'liːnjəm] *n.*【化】硒

self [self] ([复] selves [selvz]) *n.* 1. 自我，自己，自身；本身 2. 本性，本质；个人的正常情况(指健康等) 3. 私心；私利 4. 本人 5.(谑)我(或你、他)自己 6.【植】单色花；原色花(指未经人工着色变色的花) — *adj.* 同一性质的；单色的；(材料、式样等)同一类型的 — *vt.* 1. 使近亲繁殖；使同种繁殖 2.【植】使自花授精 — *vi.*【植】自花授精

self- *pref.* 1. 表示"自"，"自我"，"自身"：self-reliance, self-education 自我教育 2. 表示"自动"：self-feeder 自动给料器

self-abuse [,selfə'bjuːs] *n.* 1. 手淫 2. 自责

self-acting [,self'æktiŋ] *adj.* 自动的

self-addressed [,selfə'drest] *adj.* 写明收信人姓名住址的：Please enclose a ~ envelope. 信封请写明姓名地址的回信信封

self-assurance [,selfə'ʃuərəns] *n.* 自信，自持 ‖ **self-assured** *adj.*

self-binder [,self'baində] *n.* 1.【农】自动割捆机 2. 自动装订机；活页夹

self-centred, self-centered [ˌself'sentəd] *adj.* **1.** 自我中心的；自私自利的 **2.** 自给自足的；不受外界影响的 **3.** 固定中心的

self-confessed [ˌselfkən'fest] *adj.* 公开承认的；公开声称的

self-confident [ˌself'kɔnfidənt] *adj.* 自信的，满怀信心的 ‖ **self-confidence** *n.*

self-conscious [ˌself'kɔnʃəs] *adj.* **1.** 自觉的；自我意识的 **2.** 在人前不自然的；忸怩的；害羞的 ‖ ~ **ly** *adv.* / ~ **ness** *n.*

self-contained [ˌselfkən'teind] *adj.* **1.** 沉默寡言的；有自制力的；不易冲动的 **2.** 〔机〕整套的；自足式的 **3.** (公寓等)设备齐全独门独户的 **4.** (社会团体等)自给自足的，独立的

self-control [ˌselfkən'trəul] *n.* 自制，自我克制

self-criticism [ˌself'kritisizəm] *n.* 自我批评

self-culture [ˌself'kʌltʃə] *n.* 自修，自学

self-defeating [ˌselfdi'fi:tiŋ] *adj.* 使自己的目标不能实现的，自拆台脚的

self-denial [ˌselfdi'naiəl] *n.* 自我克制

self-determination [ˈselfditə:mi'neiʃən] *n.* 自决，自主；民族自决，独立自主

self-drive [ˌself'draiv] *adj.* 〈英〉(汽车等)租来自己驾驶的

self-effacing [ˌselfi'feisiŋ] *adj.* 避免抛头露面的；缩在后头的；谦卑的

self-employed [ˌselfim'plɔid] *adj.* 自雇的，非受雇于人的

self-esteem [ˌselfis'ti:m] *n.* **1.** 自尊(心) **2.** 自负，自大

self-evident [ˌself'evidənt] *adj.* 自明的，不需证明的，不言而喻的

self-examination [ˌselfigˌzæmi'neiʃən] *n.* 自我检查，反省

self-governing [ˌself'gʌvəniŋ] *adj.* **1.** 自制的，自我克制的 **2.** 自治的：a ~ dominion 自治领

self-government [ˌself'gʌvənmənt] *n.* **1.** 自制，自我克制 **2.** 自治

self-image [ˌself'imidʒ] *n.* 自我形象

self-important [ˌselfim'pɔ:tənt] *adj.* 妄自尊大的

self-induction [ˌselfin'dʌkʃən] *n.* 〔电〕自感应

self-indulgence [ˌselfin'dʌldʒəns] *n.* 放纵自己；纵欲

self-interest [ˌself'intərist] *n.* 自身利益；自私自利

selfish [ˈselfiʃ] *adj.* 自私的，利己的；不顾别人的 ‖ ~ **ly** *adv.* / ~ **ness** *n.*

selfless [ˈselflis] *adj.* 无私的，忘我的 ‖ ~ **ly** *adv.* / ~ **ness** *n.*

self-love [ˌself'lʌv] *n.* **1.** 自我怜爱 **2.** (表现为受不了批评等的)自负；自私

self-made [ˌself'meid] *adj.* **1.** 自己做的；独自搞的 **2.** 靠个人奋斗而成功的，白手起家的

self-opinionated [ˌselfə'pinjəneitid], **self-opinioned** [ˌselfə'pinjənd] *adj.* 自负的；固执己见的，刚愎自用的

self-portrait [ˌself'pɔ:trit] *n.* 自画像；自我描述

self-possessed [ˌselfpə'zest] *adj.* 有自制力的；沉着的，冷静的，镇定的 ‖ ~ **ly** *adv.* / **self-possession** *n.*

self-propelled [ˌselfprə'peld] *adj.* **1.** 自动推进的；自己开动的：a ~ (炮等)自行的：a ~ gun 自行火炮 **2.** (部队)装备有自行火炮的

self-registering [ˌself'redʒistəriŋ] *adj.* 自动记录的

self-regulation [ˌselfˌregju'leiʃən] *n.* (经

济、企业等的)自动调整;自动调节

self-reliance [ˌselfri'laiəns] *n.* 信赖自己;依靠自己;自力更生 ‖ **self-reliant** *adj.*

self-respect [ˌselfri'spekt] *n.* 自尊;自重 ‖ ~ **ing** *adj.*

self-restraint [ˌselfri'streint] *n.* 自我克制,自我约束

self-righteous [ˌself'raitʃəs] *adj.* 自以为公正善良的;自以为有道德的;伪善的 ‖ ~ **ness** *n.*

self-sacrificing [ˌself'sækrifaisiŋ] *adj.* 自我牺牲的,舍己为人的

selfsame ['selfseim] *adj.* 完全一样的,同一的

self-seeker [ˌself'siːkə] *n.* 追求私利的人;只求自己享乐的人

self-service [ˌself'səːvis] *n.* & *adj.* 顾客自助(的),无人售货的(的)

self-study [ˌself'stʌdi] *n.* 1. 自我研究;自我研究的记录 2. 自学

self-styled [ˌself'staild] *adj.* 1. 自封的,自称的

self-sufficient [ˌselfsə'fiʃənt] *adj.* 1. 自给自足的 2. 过于自信的;傲慢的

self-taught [ˌself'tɔːt] *adj.* 自学的,自修的;通过自学获得的

self-will ['self'wil] *n.* 任性;固执,执拗 ‖ ~ **ed** *adj.*

self-winding [ˌself'waindiŋ] *adj.* (钟、表等)自动上发条的,自动的

sell [sel] (sold [səuld]) *vt.* 1. 卖,销售,经售 2. 出卖,背叛 3. 使卖出;有助于销出(某物);向(某人)推销 4.〈口〉宣传(某事物);说服(某人),使接受 5.〈俚〉[常用被动语态]欺骗;使失望 — *vi.* 1. 卖,销售;有销路;具有售价(*for*, *at*) 2.〈口〉被广泛接受 — *n.* 1.〈俚〉欺骗 2. 失望 3. 卖;推销术;〈美口〉对买主的吸引力 ‖ ~ **er** *n.* 1. 卖者;销售者;a ~ **ers'** market 卖方市场,对卖方有利的市面 2. 行销货: a best ~ **er** 畅销品 ‖ ~ **out** *n.* 1.〈口〉1. 背叛;出卖 2.(商品的)售罄 3. 票子全部售完的演出,客满的演出(或比赛等)

seltzer ['seltsə] (德) *n.* 赛尔茨脱兹矿泉水

selvage ['selvidʒ] *n.* 纸边;[纺]织边,布边

selves [selvz] self 的复数

semantics [si'mæntiks] [复] *n.* [用作单或复] 1.[语]语义学 2.[哲][逻]语义符号学

semaphore ['seməfɔː] *n.* 1.(铁路的)臂板信号(机);信号 2. 旗语 — *vi.* 打信号;用旗语一 — *vt.* 打信号通知

semblance ['sembləns] *n.* 1. 外表,外貌 2. 假装,伪装 3. 相似;貌似物

semen ['siːmen] ([复] semina ['semina] 或 semens) *n.* 1. 精液 2. 精子 ‖ ~ **bank** 精子库

semester [si'mestə] *n.* 1. 半年 2.(美、德等国学校的)学期,半学年

semi- *pref.* 1. 表示"半": *semi*circle 半圆 2. 表示"部分的(地)","不完全的(地)": *semi*civilized 半文明的 3. 表示"(一段时期中)发生两次的": *semi*annual

semiannual [ˌsemi'ænjuəl] *adj.* 半年一次的;持续半年的 ‖ ~ **ly** *adv.*

semicircle [ˌsemi'səːkl] *n.* 1. 半圆 2. 半圆形(物)

semicircular [ˌsemi'səːkjulə] *adj.* 半圆形的

semicolon [ˌsemi'kəulən] *n.* 分号(即";")

semi-colony [ˌsemi'kɔləni] *n.* 半殖民地

semiconductor [ˌsemikən'dʌktə] *n.* [物] 半导体

semifinal [ˌsemi'fainl] *n.* & *adj.* 半决赛(的) ‖ ~ **ist** [ˌsemi'fainəlist] *n.* 半决赛

选手;半决赛队

seminal ['seminl] *adj.* 1. 精液的;繁殖的 2.【植】种子的 3. 萌芽的;潜在的 4. 开创性的;有重大影响的

seminar ['seminɑ:] *n.* 1.(大学的)研究班 2. 研究班课程;(研究班的)专题讨论会;讨论会 3.(美)专家讨论会;讨论(或交流)会

seminary ['seminəri] *n.* 1. 发源地;温床 2. 高等中学;学院(尤指私立女子学校或学院) 3. 神学院 4.(大学的)研究班

semiofficial [ˌsemiə'fiʃl] *adj.* 半官方的

semipermeable [ˌsemi'pə:mjəbl] *adj.* 半(渗)透(性)的

semiprecious [ˌsemi'preʃəs] *adj.*(宝石)次贵重的;半宝石的

Semite ['si:mait, 'semait] *n.* 闪米特人(旧译闪族人;古代包括巴比伦人、亚述人、希伯来人和腓尼基人等,近代主要指阿拉伯人和犹太人)— *adj.* 闪米特人的 ‖ **Semitic** [si'mitik] *adj.* 1. 闪米特人的;犹太人的 2. 闪含语族或闪语族语言的 *n.* 闪含语族闪语族的语言

semivowel ['semiˌvauəl] *n.*【语】半元音;半元音字母

Sen. *abbr.* 1. Senate 2. Senator 3. Senior

senate ['senit] *n.* 1. [S-](美、法等的)参议院,上院 2. 参议院会议厅 3.(剑桥大学等的)理事会,评议会 4.(古罗马的)元老院 5. 立法机构;立法机构全体成员;立法程序

senator ['senətə] *n.* 1. 参议员,上议员 2.(大学)理事 3.(古罗马的)元老院议员

senatorial [ˌsenə'tɔ:riəl] *adj.* 参议院的;参议员的

send [send] (sent [sent]) *vt.* 1. 送;寄发派遣;打发 2. 发射(子弹、球、箭等);放出(光、声等) 3. 使变成;使陷入;使处于 4. 5.(旧时指神、上帝)赐赠;施;降

6.(俚)使兴奋;使心荡神驰 — *vi.* 1. 寄信;送信;派人 2. 播送 ‖ **~er** *n.* 1. 发送者;送货人 2.【电信】发射机;发报机;发送器 3.(美俚)善奏爵士音乐的人 ‖ **'~-off** *n.* 1.(口)送行;欢送 2.(在事业开始时的)鼓励;赞扬性的书评 3.【俚】送葬;葬礼

Senegal [ˌseni'gɔ:l] *n.* 1. 塞内加尔[西非国家] 2. [the ~]塞内加尔河[西非] ‖ **~ese** [ˌseniɡə'li:z] *n.* 塞内加尔人 *adj.* 塞内加尔人的;塞内加尔人的

senile ['si:nail] *adj.* 1. 老年的;衰老的;年老所致的 2.【地】老年期的 ‖ **senility** [si'niləti] *n.*

senior ['si:njə] *adj.* 1. 年长的,年纪较大的(常略作 Sen. 或 Sr.,加在姓名后);已届退休年龄的 2. 地位(或级别)较高的;资历较深的 3.(英)(大学)高年级的;(美)(大学)四年级的;(中学)最高年级的 4.(债券、股票对企业财产或红利而言)有优先权的 — *n.* 1. 年长者;资历较深者,前辈;上级 3.(英)(大学一年级以上的)高年级生;(大学)评议员;(美)(大学)四年级生;(中学)最高年级生 4.[~ citizen](婉)老年人;已届退休年龄的公民

seniority [ˌsi:ni'ɔriti] *n.* 年长;资历深;职位高

señor [se'njɔ:][复 señores [se'njɔ:reis]]〈西〉*n.* 先生(称呼);相当于英语的 Mr. 或 Sir)

señora [se'njɔ:rə]〈西〉*n.* 夫人,太太(称呼;相当于英语的 Madam 或 Mrs.)

señorita [ˌsenjɔ:'ri:tə]〈西〉*n.* 小姐(称呼;相当于英语的 Miss)

sensation [sen'seiʃən] *n.* 1. 感觉,知觉 2. 轰动;激动;轰动一时的事件(或人物、新闻)

sensational [sen'seiʃənl] *adj.* 1. 感觉的 2.

轰动的；耸人听闻的；激起情感的 3. 非常的；巨大的；惊人的 ‖ ～ly adv.

sense [sens] n. 1. 感官；官能 2. 感觉；辨别力；观念 3. 意识 4. 见识；情理；道理 4.[～s]知觉；理智、理性 5. 意义，意旨 6. 公众意见(或情绪) 7. 方向；指向 — vt. 1. 感觉；觉察；意识到 2. 了解；领悟 3.(仪器等)检测 ‖ ～ organ 感觉器官；受体

senseless ['senslis] adj. 1. 失去知觉的；无感觉的 2. 愚蠢的；无意义的 ‖ ～ly adv. / ～ness n.

sensibility [ˌsensi'biləti] n. 1. 感觉(力) 2. 敏感性；感受性 3.[常 sensibilities]情感 4.(诗歌的)感伤情调

sensible ['sensəbl] adj. 1. 感觉得到的；可觉察的；明显的 2. 知道的；觉察的 3. 明白事理的；合理的 4.(计划等)切合实际的；合理的；实用的 5.〈古〉敏感的；易感的 — n. 感觉得到的东西 ‖ ～ness n. / sensibly adv.

sensitive ['sensitiv] adj. 1. 敏感的；容易感受的 2. 神经过敏的；容易生气的；(由于某种疾病而)过敏的 3. 灵敏的；感光的 4. 高度机密的；极为微妙的 5.〈罕〉感觉的；感官的；传导感觉的 ‖ ～ly adv. / ～ness n. ‖ ～ plant【植】含羞草

sensitivity [ˌsensi'tivəti] n. 1. 敏感(性)；感受性；灵敏性；过敏(性) 2. 灵敏度；感光度

sensory ['sensəri] adj. 感觉的；传递感觉的

sensual ['sensjuəl] adj. 1. 肉体方面的；耽于声色口腹之乐的；肉欲的 2. 肉感的；色情的；淫荡的 3. 世俗的，凡俗的 5.[哲]感觉论的 ‖ ～ism n. / ～ist n. / ～ly adv.

sensuous ['sensjuəs] adj. 1. 感官方面的；

感觉上的 2. 激发美感的，给人以美的享受的 ‖ ～ly adv. / ～ness n.

sent [sent] send 的过去式和过去分词

sentence ['sentəns] n. 1. 宣判；判决；课刑 2.[语]句子 3.〈古〉结论意见；警句；格言 4.[音]乐句 5.[逻]命题 — vt. 宣判；判决；使遭受

sententious [sen'tenʃəs] adj. 1. 爱用警句(或格言)的；(书等)充满警句(或格言)的 2. 言简意赅的；精辟的 3. 说教的 ‖ ～ly adv. / ～ness n.

sentient ['senʃənt] adj. 有感觉能力的；有感觉的，有知觉的 ‖ sentience n.

sentiment ['sentimənt] n. 1. 思想感情；情操 2. 感情；(文艺作品等的)情趣 3. 情绪 4.[常～s]意见；观点 5. 柔情；感伤；多愁善感 6. 祝词；感想

sentimental [ˌsenti'mentl] adj. 1. 感伤的；多愁善感的；易动情感的；感情用事的 2. 情感(上)的 ‖ ～ism n. 感伤主义 / ～ist n. 感伤主义者 / sentimentality [ˌsentimen'tæliti] n. 感伤；多愁善感

sentinel ['sentinl] n. 哨兵；步哨；卫兵；看守 —(sentinel(l)ed; sentinel(l)ing) vt. 1. 警戒；守卫 2. 设岗哨于

sentry ['sentri] n. 1. 步哨；卫兵 2. 看守；警卫 — vt. 设岗哨于 — vi. 站岗，放哨 ‖ ～ box 岗亭 / '～·go n. 1. 换岗命令 2. 步哨勤务

Seoul [səul] n. 汉城[韩国首都]

Sep. abbr. September

sepal ['sepəl] n.【植】萼片

separate ['sepəret] adj. 1. 分离的；分隔的；不相连的 2. 各别的；单独的；独立的 3.〈古〉孤独的 4. 脱离肉体的，灵魂的 ‖ ～ly adv. 1.(文章等的)单行本；抽印本 2.[～s]妇女不配套穿的衣服 — ['separeit] vt. 1. 使分离，使分开；使分散；把…分类 2. 区分；识别 3. 使分居；

使脱离关系；使解除契约；使退役 4. 使离析 — *vi.* 1. 分离，分开 2. 分居 3. 析离，析出 ‖ **separable** *adj.* / ~ly *adv.*

separation [ˌsepəˈreiʃən] *n.* 1. 分离，分开；分类 2. 分隔物；分隔点；间隔 3.（夫妇）分居 4. 离析出 5.（导线的）间距；(立体声系统的)通道分隔(度) ‖ ~**ist** *n.* 主张脱离(或分裂)者

separator [ˈsepəreitə] *n.* 分离者；分离器；离析器；蓄电池(组)的隔板；【矿】分选机

sepia [ˈsiːpiə]([复] sepias 或 sepiae[ˈsiːpiː]) *n.* 1. 乌贼墨囊颜料(或汁) 2. 深褐色 3. 深褐色绘画(或照片等) 4. 乌贼，乌贼(分泌的)墨(汁)

sepsis [ˈsepsis]([复] sepses [ˈsepsiz]) *n.* 【医】脓毒病，脓毒症

Sept. *abbr.* September

September [səpˈtembə] *n.* 9 月(略作 Sept. 或 Sep.)

septet(te) [sepˈtet] *n.* 【音】七重唱(曲)；七重奏(曲)；七重唱(或七重奏)演出小组 2. 七人的一组；七个一组

septic [ˈseptik] *adj.* 1. 引起腐烂的；腐败性的 2.【医】脓毒性的；败血病的4. 腐烂物；腐败剂 ‖ ~ tank 化粪池

septic(a)emia [ˌsepti'siːmiə] *n.* 【医】败血病，败血症

septuagenarian [ˌseptjuədʒi'neəriən] *n.* 70 至 79 岁的人

sepulchral [si'pʌlkrəl] *adj.* 1. 坟墓的；埋葬的 2. 坟墓似的；令人想到埋葬的；阴森森的；阴沉忧郁的

sepulchre, sepulcher [ˈsepəlkə] *n.* 1. 坟墓；石墓；墓穴 2. 圣物匣 — *vt.* 埋葬

sequel [ˈsiːkwəl] *n.* 1. 继续；随之而来的事 2.（文艺作品的）续集，续编 3. 后果；结局；余波 4.〈罕〉推论

sequence [ˈsiːkwəns] *n.* 1. 连续；继续；一连串 2. 次序；顺序；先后 3. 相关联的一组；(同一主题的)组诗；(牌戏中的)同花顺子 4.【音】模进(指用不同音调反复演奏一组乐句)；【天主教】继续经(宣讲福音前唱的圣歌) 5.【数】序列；【生化】顺序 6. 后果；结果；继发事件 7.（电影中描述同一主题的）连续镜头(或场景)；片断；插曲 — *vt.* 把…按顺序排好 ‖ ~**r** *n.*【计】序列发生器，定序器

sequential [si'kwenʃəl] *adj.* 1. 连续的；相继的；有顺序的 2. 结果的 ‖ ~ analysis (统计的)序贯分析，序列分析

sequester [si'kwestə] *vt.* 1. 使隔绝；使分离，使隐退 2.【律】扣押(债务人的财产等)；将(有争议的财物)交第三人保管 3. 没 收；查 封 ‖ sequestration [ˌsiːkwes'treiʃən] *n.*

sequin [ˈsiːkwin] *n.*（衣服上的）闪光装饰片

sequoia [si'kwɔiə] *n.*【植】红杉

sera [ˈsiərə] serum 的复数

serape [se'rɑːpi] *n.* 瑟拉佩毯(中、南美一些国家中用作披肩或外衣的彩色羊毛毯)

seraph [ˈseraf]([复] seraphs 或 seraphim [ˈserəfim]) *n.*(基督教九级天使中的最高位)炽天使；炽天使似的人 ‖ seraphic [se'ræfik] *adj.* 炽天使的；天使般的

Serbia [ˈsəːbiə] *n.* 塞尔维亚[南斯拉夫成员共和国及国名]

sere [siə] *adj.*〈诗〉干枯的，枯萎的

serenade [ˌseri'neid] *n.* 1.【音】小夜曲 2. 月下情歌 — *vi.* 唱…唱(或奏)小夜曲 — *vt.* 唱(或奏)小夜曲

serendipity [ˌserən'dipəti] *n.* 意外发现珍奇(或称心)事物的本领；侥幸发现的

东西;意外发现;好运气

serene [si'ri:n] *adj.* 1. 安详的 2. 晴朗的;明朗的;无云的 3. 尊贵的 (用于对欧洲某些王室的称呼中) — *n.* (天空等的)晴朗;(水面等的)平静 — *vt.* (诗)使(天空等)明朗;使平静 ‖ ~**ly** *adv.*

serenity [si'reniti] *n.* 1. 安详 2. 晴朗;明朗 3. 平静;宁静 4. [S]尊贵的殿下 (对欧洲某些王室的尊称)

serf [sə:f] *n.* 1. 农奴 2. 受压迫者;做苦工的人 ‖ ~**dom** 1. 农奴制 2. 农奴地位;农奴境遇;奴役

serge [sə:dʒ] *n.* [纺]哔叽

sergeant ['sɑ:dʒənt] *n.* 1. [军]军士;(英)陆军(或空军、海军陆战队)中士;(美)陆军(或海军陆战队)中士 2. 警官,巡佐 3. (担任礼仪或维持议会、法庭等秩序的)警卫官 4. [英史]在皇家法庭具有特权的 (高级律师) ‖ ~ **major** [军]军士长

serial ['siəriəl] *adj.* 1. 连续的;一连串的;一系列的 2. 分期刊载的;连载的 3. 分期偿还的 — *n.* 1. 连载小说 (或图画等);连本影片;连本电视节目 2. (分期连载作品的)一个部分 3. 期刊 ‖ ~**ly** *adv.* ‖ ~ **rights** (小说的)连载版权

seri(ci)culture ['seri(si)ˌkʌltʃə] *n.* 养蚕;养蚕业

series ['siəriːz][单复同] *n.* 1. 连续;系列 2. (邮票)套;丛书;辑;组 3. [化]系;系列 4. (矿石、岩系的)组 5. (货币等的)序;系列 6. [电]串联 7. 一组变音元音 (如 sing, sang, sung 的 *i, a, u*) 8. [动]列;组

serious ['siəriəs] *adj.* 1. 严肃的;庄重的 2. 认真的;不开玩笑的;当真的 3. 重要的;须认真对待的 4. 严重的;危急的;令人担心的 5. (古)宗教的;伦理学的;(谑)虔诚的 6. 热中的,极感兴

趣的 ‖ ~**ly** *adv.* 严肃地;认真地;严重地 / ~**ness** *n.* 严肃;认真;严重性

sermon ['sə:mən] *n.* 1. [宗]布道,讲道 2. 训诫;喋喋不休的说教 3. (受自然物启示而作的)道德上的反省

serpent ['sə:pənt] *n.* 1. 蛇(尤指大蛇或毒蛇) 2. 阴险毒辣的人 3. 金蛇飞舞玩具 4. [the-S] [天]巨蛇座 5. 蛇形管(或号)(古代木制吹奏乐器)

serpentine ['sə:pəntain] *adj.* 1. 蛇(状)的 2. 蜿蜒的;迂回的;盘旋的、螺旋形的 3. 阴险毒辣的;疾磨的 — *n.* 1. 蛇形物,蜿蜒的东西 2. [地]蛇纹岩 3. (溜冰的)同轴三圆形 — *vi.* 蜿蜒 ‖ ~ **verse** (首尾词相同的)环形诗句

serrate(d) [sə'reit(id)] *adj.* 1.[生][解]锯齿状的 2.(器械)有锯齿的 3.(硬币)有齿状边缘的

serum ['siərəm] *n.* [复] serums 或 sera ['siərə] *n.* [医]浆液;血清 ‖ ~ **albumin** 血清白蛋白 / ~ **globulin** 血清球蛋白

servant ['sə:vənt] *n.* 1. 仆人;佣人;雇工 2. 公务员;雇员 3. (美)奴仆;奴隶 4. 忠实的仆役 (或信徒) 5. 有用的工具 ‖ ~**-girl**, ~**-maid** *n.* 小保姆,年轻女仆

serve [sə:v] *vt.* 1. 为…服务;为…服役;为…尽责 2. 做…的用人;侍候 3. 经历;度过 4. 招待(顾客等);端上,端出(饭菜等) 5. 对…恭顺;尊崇 6. 供应;分发为… 7. 对待;对付 8. 对待;对付 送交(传票等);向…送交(令状等) 10.(网球赛等中)发(球),开(球);操作(火炮)11.(马等)与(雌兽)交配 12.[海]卷缠(绳索等) — *vi.* 1. 服务;服役;供职 2. 帮佣 3. 招待;侍应上菜;斟酒(或其他饮料) 4. 适合;适用;有用 5. 发球,开球 6.

【宗】(弥撒时)充当助祭 — **n.** 发球,开球;轮到发球 ‖ **~ r n.** 1. 服务员,侍者;送出者 2. 发球人 3. 发球人 4.【宗】(弥撒时的)助祭 5. 菜盘;托盘

service ['sɜːvis] **n.** 1. 服务,贡献;帮助 2. 帮佣;服侍;招待;供应;上菜;斟酒(或其他饮料) 3. 行政部门(或工作)(总称)部门人员,机构人员 4. 军种;勤务部队;服役;勤务 5. 公共设施(尤指交通设施);公用事业 6.(厂商出售物品后的)售后服务;检修,维修,保养 7.(全套)器具;餐具 8. 发球;发球方式;轮到发球 9.(传票、命令等的)送达 10. 仪式;(宗教)礼拜式;礼拜乐曲 11.(通过祈祷等对上帝的)侍奉 12.(马等的)交配 13.【海】(为防绳索擦损而进行的)卷缠;缠索材料(纱线、帆布或金属丝) — **vt.** 1. 检修,维修,保养;服务 2. 支付(国债等)的利息 3.(雄畜)与(母畜)交配 — **adj.** 1. 武装部队的;服现役时用的 2. 服务性的;提供维修(或保养)服务的 3. 仆人的;仆人用的 4. 耐用的 ‖ **~ ceiling**【空】使用升限 / **~ dress** 军便服 / **~ man n.** 1. 军人 2. 维修人员 3.(汽车)加油站工作人员 / **~ module**(宇宙飞船的动力装置舱,指令舱 / **~ pipe**(由总管通入屋内的)户内给水(或煤气)管 / **~ tree**【植】花楸果;治枫花揪;唐棣

serviceable ['sɜːvisəbl] **adj.** 1. 有用的;肯帮忙的 2. 便于使用的,耐用的;适于平时使用(或穿用)的 ‖ **-ness n.** / **serviceably adv.**

servile ['sɜːvail, 'sɜːvil] **adj.** 1. 奴隶的;奴隶般的 2. 奴性的;卑态的;十足依附的,缺乏独立精神的 3.【语】辅助性的(指本身不发音而只表示其前的元音字母发长音的) 4.【语】非词根的(指词中表示派生或词形变化、语法关系部

分的,如 reads, pupil's, books 中的 -s)

serving ['sɜːviŋ] **n.** 1. 服务;招待;伺候;上菜 2. 一份食物(或饮料) ‖ **~ man n.** 男佣人 / **~ woman n.** 女佣人

servitor ['sɜːvitə] **n.** 男仆;侍从

servitude ['sɜːvitjuːd] **n.** 1. 奴隶状态;奴役 2.(作为刑罚的)苦役,劳役 3.【律】役权;地役权;土地使役权

sesame ['sesəmi] **n.**【植】芝麻,脂麻

sesquicentennial [ˌseskwisen'tenjəl] **n. & adj.**(美)一百五十周年(纪念)(的)

session ['seʃən] **n.** 1. 会议;一届会议;会期 2. 开庭;开庭期;(~s)法庭 3.(美)(苏格兰)学期;(美)上课时间 4.(从事某项活动的)一段时间;(口)难挨的一阵子 5.【商】(证券交易等的)市,盘 6.(基督教长老会的)管理机构

set [set] (set;setting) **vt.** 1. 放;竖立;使贴着(*to*) 2. 安置,装置;配置,布置(岗哨等) 3. 使就座;使就位(如赛跑等) 4. 使(鸡)孵卵;使(卵)受精 5. 种植 6. 点燃;放(火) 7. 签(字);盖(印);印上(痕记) 8. 写;记录 9. 镶,嵌;点缀 10. 使朝向;使移动;运送(乘客等) 11. 倾注;使下决心 12. 使处于某种状态(或 *at ease*)使某人放心 / This medicine will ~ you right. 这药会把你的病治好。5. 使(某人)做某事;~ *sb. to a task* 使某人干某项工作/He ~ the boys *to chop wood*(或 *to woodchopping*). 他叫男孩们去砍柴。14. 使凝结,使凝固;使牢固;使(骨等)接好;使(发型),使具所需要型 15. 定(日期、限度、价格等)制定(规则等);颁布;估计;评价 16. 树立(榜样等);创造(纪录等)17. 分配;提出(任务);指定(作业;出题目等) 18. 调整;校正(仪器等);拨准(钟表);锉(锯齿);调整(锯

齿)的倾角;磨快;修平(剃刀等) 19. 排(铅字);为(原稿)排版 20. 设(陷阱);张(罗网);扬(帆);用(钩子)钩住鱼鳔 23.(为诗、文等)谱曲;作(曲)为(曲)配词;设置(布景、背景);为…布景;是…的背景 22. 使(身体等)长好;使(性格)定型;使(果实)结成;使(面团)发酵 23.(猎狗)蹲住以示(猎物)的所在 24.(桥牌赛中)制止(对方)叫牌;打败(对方);使(对方定约墩数)落空 — vi. 1.(日、月等)落,下沉 2. 凝结,凝固;固定;定型(颜色等)变牢固 3. 着手,从事 4.(植物、花)结果;(果子)结成 5.(鸡)孵卵 6.(肌肉等)有力流;显出(或感到)某种倾向 7.(衣服等)合身;适合 8.(骨)接合;(金属)永久变形 9.(猎狗)蹲住以示猎物所在 10.(方形舞中与舞伴)相对面舞 11.(方)坐 — adj. 1. 下定决心的,坚决的;急切的 2. 规定的;指定的 3. 故意的;预先准备的 4. 不变的;确固的;(天气等)稳定的,持久的 5. 不动的,固定的;装好的 6. 习用的;老一套的 7. 准备停当的 8.(赛跑等中)作好预备姿势的;(棒球、板球赛中的)稳住身体准备出击的 8.(两军)对阵的 9. 凝结的,凝固的 — n. 1.[只用单](诗)落:at ~ of sun 日落时分 2.(一套);(一副);(一批);(一)部 3.(网球赛等中的)一盘 4.(一批)同伙;一群同伙 5.[只用单]形状;姿势;(服装)合在身上的样子 6.[只用单](风、水流等)方向;倾向;趋势;[心]心向,定势 7.(液体等)凝结,凝固 8.(金属因受压等而形成的)永久变形 9. 籽苗,秧;插枝;球茎 9.[无]接收机,电子仪器;装置;设备 【数】集(合) 10. 锯齿的倾角;铅字面 11. 成套扳手;成套冲头;(煤矿坑道中的)支架,棚子(铺路用的)花岗石板;(墙壁上的)最后一道粉饰 12.(舞台、电影等的)布景 13.(土风舞、方形舞中跳舞者所列的)基本队形 14. 卷做头发,发型(液) 15. 一窝蛋 16.(英)(蟹的)洞穴 17. 猎狗蹲住以示猎物所在的姿势 ‖ ~ back n. 1. 挫折;失败;倒退;(疾病的)复发 2. 逆流;涡流 3.[建]退进,收进/ ~ down n. 申斥;辱骂 / ~ off n. 1. 装饰品;陪村物 2.(债务的)抵消;用以抵消债务的权利 3.[印]粘贴(未干油墨从一印张粘到另一印张) / ~ out n. 1. 开始,开头:at the first ~out 最初,一开始 2. 布置;设备;装备;装束;马车的全套配备 3.(食物、器皿等)陈列的陈列 4. 宴会;招待 / ~ square 三角板 / ~-.to n. 殴斗;吵架 / ~ up n. 1.机构;组织体系;体制;(事物的)安排,结构 2.(美口)(身体的)姿势,姿态;体格 3. 装置;(仪器等的)装配;(机器、电子设备等操作前的)调整,准备 4.(美俚)(故意布置得)容易做的工作;容易取胜的比赛;容易得到的东西;容易完成的事;参加必败比赛的拳击手 5. 计划,方案 6.(准备取胜的)摄影机位置 7. 菜馆铺排好的一席(或一客)food(常已放有餐包和菜盘 8.(台球戏的)有利位置 9.(美俚)给顾客调制自备烈酒的材料(指苏打打水、冰块等) 10.[无]调值

settee [se'ti:] n. 长靠椅;中小型沙发

setter ['setə] n. 1. 安装员;镶嵌工人;排字工人 2.[用以构成复合词]安装(或接合)…的人;a brick ~ 砌砖工 / a bone ~ 接骨者 / a pace~ 带步速者,带步人;标兵 3. 为警察作谍报者;为盗贼作眼线者 4. 塞特种猎狗,谍犬 5.[音]调节器;给定装置 ‖ ~·'on [复]~-s·on) n. 教唆者;煽动者;攻击者;袭击者

setting ['setiŋ] *n.* 1. 安装;调整;装置;安放机器的底座(或底脚) 2. 镶嵌;镶嵌底座 3. 排字 4. 环境;背景 5.(舞台等的)布景;(花园等的)园艺布置 6. 配曲,配谱 7.(桌面上一席位用的)全副餐具 8.(卵的)一窝 9. 定位;(天体的)沉落 ‖ ～ board 昆虫标本板 /'～·'up exercises [复]徒手体操

settle ['setl] *vt.* 1. 安排;料理;整理 2. 安放;～ oneself in an armchair 在扶手椅里坐下 3. 使定居;使移居(尤指海外拓殖);殖民于 4. 使平静;使安定;使安宁 5.(口)(通过责骂等)使规矩;使就范 6. 调停;解决;决定 7. 使固定;使稳定 8. 支付;结算 9. 使(液体)澄清;使沉降;压紧;使(路等)干硬 10.【律】(以契约、遗嘱等方式)赠与;转让(财产等)(on) 11.【沉】使受胎 — *vi.* 1. 停息 2.(地基等)下陷,下沉;沉淀;沉落;降下 3.(因液滓沉淀而)澄清;(因摇动下沉而)变坚实 4. 决定 5. 变稳定;固定下来;平定下来 6. 定居;安家;偿付 7. 安家;定居;殖民 8.【沉】受胎

settled ['setld] *adj.* 1. 固定的,不变的;永久的;(天气)稳定的 2. 定居的;有居民的 3.(账单上用语)结过账的,付清的

settlement ['setlmənt] *n.* 1. 解决 2. 清算,结账 3. 殖民;殖民地;拓居;新拓居地;租界;村落;新住宅区 4. 殖民团体;新拓居地的人群 5. 沉降;(房屋的)沉陷;塌陷 6.(在贫民区提供慈善、福利、文教、娱乐等服务的)社会改良团体 7.【律】(通过法律手续的)财产赠与;依法设定的财产

settler ['setlə] *n.* 1. 移民者;殖民者;开拓者 2. 沉淀器,澄清器 3.〈俚〉决定性的一击(或论据、事件等) 4.【律】财产

赠与者

seven ['sevn] *num.* 七;七个(人或物);第七(卷、章、页等) — *n.* 1. 七个(人或物)一组 2.7 岁 3.7 点钟 ‖ ～fold *adj.* & *adv.* 七倍的;七倍

seventeen [,sevn'ti:n] *num.* 十七;十七个(人或物);第十七(卷、章、页等) — *n.*17 岁;17 点钟(即下午 5 点钟)

seventeenth [,sevn'ti:nθ] *num.* 1. 第十七(人) 2. 十七分之一(的) — *n.*(月的)第十七日

seventh ['sevnθ] *num.* 1. 第七(个) 2. 七分之一(的) — *n.* 1.【音】七度音程;七度和音;第七音 2.(月的)第七日

seventieth ['sevntiiθ] *num.* 1. 第七十(个) 2. 七十分之一(的)

seventy ['sevnti] *num.* 七十;七十个(人或物);第七十(页等) — *n.* 1. [seventies](世纪的)70 年代 2. [seventies]70 到 79 岁的时期 3.70 岁 4.(俚)快转唱片 ‖ '～·'eight *n.*78 转粗纹唱片

sever ['sevə] *vt.* 1. 切断,割断;把…割下;把…分隔开(或分开) 2. 断绝,中断 — *vi.* 1. 断,裂开 2. 被分开

several ['sevrəl] *adj.* 1. 几个,数个(至少 3 个) 2. 各自的,各别的 3. 单独的,独占的 4. 不同的,各异的 5.〈主方〉大量的 — *pron.* 几个,数个

severance ['sevərəns] *n.* 1. 切断,割断,斩断 2. 分开,分离 3.(邦交、友谊、联系等的)断绝 4. 区别,不同 ‖ ～ pay 解雇费;解职费

severe [si'viə] *adj.* 1. 严肃的,正经的 2. 严格的;严密的 3. 严厉的;苛刻的;尖锐的;讽刺的 4. 严重的,剧烈的,厉害的 5. 严峻的;激烈的;艰难的 6. 纯洁的;朴素的 ‖ ～ly *adv.* ～ness *n.*

severity [si'verəti] *n.* 1. 严肃;严格;严厉 2. 严重,凛冽;激烈 3. 严密,严谨 4.

纯洁;朴素 5.[severities]严厉的对待;
严酷的惩罚;艰苦的经验

sew [səu](过去式 sewed,过去分词 sewn
[səun]或 sewed) *vt.* 缝制;缝合;缝补;
缝 —*vi.* 缝纫

sewage ['sju:idʒ] *n.*(阴沟等处的)污水;
污物 — *vt.* 用污水灌溉 ‖~ **farm** 1.
污水灌溉田 2. 污水处理场

sewer[1] ['sjuə,'su:ə] *n.* 阴沟,污水管,排水
管,下水道 — *vt.* 1. 为…修建下水道
2. 用下水道排除…的污水

sewer[2] ['səuə] *n.* 缝衣者;缝具

sewerage ['sjuəridʒ, 'su:əridʒ] *n.* 1.(阴沟
等处的)污水;污物 2. 污水排除;污物
处理 3. 排水系统;沟渠系统 4. 肮脏思
想;下流话

sewing ['səuiŋ] *n.* 1. 缝纫 2. 缝制物 3.
(书的)锁线订,串线订 ‖~ **machine**
缝纫机 /~ **needle** 缝纫针

sewn [səun] sew 的过去分词

sex [seks] *n.* 1. 性,性别 2.[总称]男人;
女人 3. 性特征;性区别;性本能;性行
为;性表现 ‖**the** ~, **sex appeal** — *vt.*
1. 确定…的性别 2. 增强…的性感;引
起…的性欲(*up*) ‖ **the fair**(或 **gentle,
weaker**)~ 女性 /**the sterner**(或
rougher, stronger)~ 男性 ‖ ~**ism** *n.*
性别歧视(尤指对妇女的歧视)/~**ist**
n. & adj. 性别歧视者(的)‖ ~ **appeal** 1. 性的魅力,性感 2. 吸引力 /~
pot, ~ **kitten**〈口〉极富性感的女人;性
欲强烈的人

sexagenarian [,seksədʒi'neəriən] *adj. &
n.* 60 到 69 岁的(人)

sexless ['sekslis] *adj.* 1. 无性(别)的 2.
缺乏性感的;性欲冷淡的

sextant ['sekstənt] *n.*【天】六分仪

sextet(te) [seks'tet] *n.*【音】六重唱

(曲);六重奏(曲);六重唱(或六重奏)
的演出小组 2. 成六的一组;成六的一
套 3. 六行诗节;六行诗 4. 曲棍球队

sexton ['sekstən] *n.* 教堂司事(担任管理
教堂、敲钟、挖掘墓地等工作)

sextuple ['sekstjupl] *n. & adj.* 六倍(的)

sexual ['seksjuəl] *adj.* 1. 性别的 2. 关于
两性的;关于性生活的 3.【生】有性的
‖ ~**ly** *adv.*

Seychelles [sei'ʃelz] *n.* 塞舌尔(群岛)[印
度洋中西部岛国]

sgd. *abbr.* signed

Sgt. *abbr.* Sergeant

shabby ['ʃæbi] *adj.* 1. 破旧的;失修的 2.
褴褛的 3. 卑鄙的;不公平的 4. 菲薄
的;吝啬的 5. 低劣的,蹩脚的 ‖ **shab-
bily** *adv.* /**shabbiness** *n.* ‖ '~**-gen'teel**
adj. 破落而仍装门面的;穷酸的

shack [ʃæk] *n.* 1. 简陋的小木屋,棚屋
2.(作某种用途的)房间;小室 — *vi.*
居住;暂住

shackle ['ʃækl] *n.* 1.[常~s]镣铐;马蹄
丝 2.(喻)[~s]束缚,枷锁 3. 束缚装
置;钩环,钩链;U 形销环 4.15 英寻长
的缆索(或锚链);链锯 5.【电】绝缘器 —*vt.*
1. 给…带上镣铐 2. 束缚,羁绊 3. 给
…扣上钩环

shad [ʃæd]([复]shad(s)) *n.*【鱼】(美洲)
西鲱

shaddock ['ʃædək] *n.* 1.【植】柚 2. 柚子,
文旦

shade [ʃeid] *n.* 1. 荫,阴凉处;[~s]阴
暗,黑暗 2. 遮光物;遮光帘;遮罩;灯
罩;帘,幕 3.(图画、照相等的)暗部 4.
(色彩的)浓淡;(喻)形形色色;细微的
差别 5.[常~s]隐蔽处 6. 少量,少许 7. 鬼,幽灵 8. 少量,少许 8. 愁容,忧
郁的表情 9.[~s]酒窖 10.〈美俚〉[~s]
太阳眼镜 11.〈美俚〉代贼窝赃者 —

vt. **1.** 荫蔽;遮蔽 **2.** 使阴暗;使黯然失色 **3.** 画阴影于;使(色彩)逐渐变化 **4.** 使逐渐发生微妙变化 **5.** 使(风琴等)音调缓和 **6.** 略减(价格) ── *vi.* (色彩等)渐变;(意义等)出现细微的差别

shadow ['ʃædəu] *n.* **1.** 阴影;荫;影子 **2.** [~s]日落后渐暗的天色;(房间、画等)的阴暗部分 **3.** 阴郁 **4.** 幻影;鬼,幽灵 **5.** 预兆,苗头;蛛丝马迹 **6.** 微量,少许 **7.** 形影不离的人;(美俚)侦探 **8.** 极相似的人(或物) **9.** 隐退;隐蔽处;掩蔽;庇护 **10.** (美俚)〈贬〉黑人 ── *vt.* **1.** 投阴影形,覆阴影于;遮蔽;使阴暗,使暗淡 **2.** 暗示;预示;(隐约地)(如影子一样地)钉…的梢,尾随 **4.** 〈古〉掩蔽;保护 ── *vi.* **1.** 渐变,变阴暗,变隐暗 **|| ~ boxing** 与假想对手作的拳击练习 **2.** 太极拳 **~ factory** 伪装的军需工厂 **/ ~ play** 皮影戏,影子戏

shadowgraph ['ʃædəugrɑːf] *n.* **1.** 皮影戏,影子戏 **2.** (X光拍制的)影相,X线照片

shadowy ['ʃædəui] *adj.* **1.** 有影的;多阴的 **2.** 幽暗的,朦胧的,模糊的 **3.** 虚幻的

shady ['ʃeidi] *adj.* **1.** 成荫的;多荫的;背阴的;阴凉的 **2.** 隐蔽的 **3.** 〈口〉可疑的,靠不住的 **|| shadiness** *n.*

shaft [ʃɑːft] *n.* **1.** 箭杆;矛杆;箭;矛;箭一般的东西 **2.** 杆状物;(工具的)长柄;旗杆 **3.** 车缸;辕 **4.** [植]树干,茎;[动]羽干 **5.** [机]轴 **6.** [建]柱身;塔尖 **7.** 井穴;[矿]矿井;竖井 **8.** [冶]炉身 **9.** (电梯的)开降机井;通风管道 **10.** (屋顶上的)烟囱 **11.** (美俚)[~s](人的)大腿 ── *vt.* **1.** 在…上装柄(或手柄、轴等) **2.** 〈俚〉欺骗;利用

shag [ʃæg] *n.* **1.** 粗毛;[纺]长绒;长绒粗呢 **2.** 强味(烟)烟丝 **3.** 蓬乱的一簇(指头发、绒毛等) **4.** 杂乱的一丛(指灌木等) ── *adj.* = **shaggy** (shagged;shagging) *vt.* 使粗糙;使成蓬蓬状;使杂乱 ── *vi.* 蓬松;杂乱

shaggy ['ʃægi] *adj.* **1.** 长满粗毛的;有粗毛的 **2.** (毛、发等)粗疏蓬松的 **3.** (人)邋遢的,不修边幅的 **4.** 草木丛生的;(树)有粗糙树枝的;表面粗糙的 **5.** 粗野的

shah [ʃɑː] *n.* [常 S~]沙(伊朗国王的称号) **|| ~dom** *n.* [史] **1.** (伊朗国王)沙统治下的领土(或国家) **2.** 沙的王位

shake [ʃeik] (shook [ʃuk], shaken ['ʃeikən]) *vt.* **1.** 摇;(猛力)摇动;抖动 **2.** 使震动;使发抖;使心绪不宁 **3.** 动摇;削弱 **4.** 挥舞 **5.** (俚)摆脱;抛弃 **6.** [音]用颤音奏(或唱) **7.** (掷出前在手中)抖抖(骰子) ── *vi.* **1.** 震动;颤动 **2.** 动摇;动摇;不稳 **3.** 握手 **~ and be friends** 握手结交(或言归于好) ── [音]发颤音 ── *n.* **1.** 摇动;震动;摇手;〈口〉地震 **2.** [常~s]颤栗;[the ~s]疟疾 **3.** 〈口〉一刹那;(原子物理学等时针单位)百分之一微秒 **4.** (自然)裂缝;(木的)轮裂;(从圆木上锯下的)盖屋板 **5.** [音]颤音 **6.** 牛奶(或其他)冰淇淋混合饮料 **7.** 解雇;撵走 **8.** (美俚)敲诈,勒索;赃金 **|| ~ down** **1.** 地铺;临时床铺 **2.** 喧闹的舞蹈 **3.** 彻底搜查 **4.** 调整;调整初步 **5.** (俚)敲诈,勒索 **6.** 〈口〉试航 *adj.* 试航性的,试验性的 **/a ~down run** 试航 **/ a ~down flight** 试飞 **/ ~ up** *n.* 〈口〉(政策)剧变;(人员)的大改组

shaker ['ʃeikə] *n.* **1.** 摇动者 **2.** 摇动(混合)器;振荡器 **3.** (盖上有小孔的)佐料瓶

shaky [ˈʃeiki] ***adj.*** **1.** 发抖的;紧张不安的 **2.** 不稳固的;不坚定的,动摇的 **3.** 不可靠的,成问题的 ‖ **shakily** ***adv.*** / **shakiness** ***n.***

shale [ʃeil] ***n.***【地】页岩 ‖ ~ **oil** 页岩油

shall [强 ʃæl;弱 ʃəl, ʃl](过去式 should[强 ʃud;弱 ʃəd, ʃd])(shall not 的缩写为 shan't [ʃɑːnt]) ***v. aux.*** **1.**[表示单纯的将来,用于第一人称;第二人称只用于问句中;美国人常用 will 代替;口语中可缩写为'll]将要;会 **2.**[表示说话者的意图、允诺、警告、命令、决心等,用于陈述句的第二、第三人称中]必须;应;可 **3.**[在条约、规章、法令等文件中表示义务或规定,一般用于第三人称]应;必须 **4.**[在问句中表示征求对方意见,主要用于第一、第三人称]…好吗?要不要…? **5.**[用在表示意图、要求等的从句中]应该;要 **6.**[用于将来时态的间接引语中,与直接引语中的 shall 相应]将

shallot [ʃəˈlɔt] ***n.***【植】胡葱,火葱

shallow [ˈʃæləu] ***adj.*** **1.** 浅的 **2.**(知识、议论等)浅薄的,肤浅的 — ***n.***[常~s]浅水(处);浅滩 — ***vt.*** & ***vi.***(使)变浅

sham [ʃæm] ***n.*** **1.** 假冒;哄骗 **2.** 假冒者,骗子 **3.** 假的东西,赝品 **4.**(摆设用的)绣花枕套(或床罩) — ***adj.*** 假的,虚伪的;劣等的 —(shammed; shamming) ***vt.*** **1.** 假装 **2.**〈古〉欺骗 — ***vi.*** 装假

shamble [ˈʃæmbl] ***vi.*** 蹒跚,拖沓地走 — ***n.*** 蹒跚,拖沓的步子

shambles [ˈʃæmblz][复] ***n.***[用作单或复] **1.**〈古〉肉店;肉市场 **2.** 屠宰场;〈喻〉屠杀场所,大流血场所 **3.** 混乱,一团糟;毁坏的景象;废墟

shame [ʃeim] ***n.*** **1.** 羞耻(心),羞愧(感) **2.** 羞辱,耻辱 **3.** 可耻的事(或人) **4.**〈口〉不应该的事;遗憾的事 — ***vt.*** **1.** 使难为情,羞(人) **2.** 使蒙受羞辱,使丢脸;使痛感羞愧而…

shamefaced [ˈʃeimfeist] ***adj.*** **1.** 害羞的,羞怯的;谦卑的;不惹人注目的 **2.** 惭愧的;羞耻的 ‖ ~**ly** ***adv.*** / ~**ness** ***n.***

shameful [ˈʃeimful] ***adj.*** **1.** 可耻的,丢脸的 **2.** 不道德的;不体面的;猥亵的,淫猥的 ‖ ~**ly** ***adv.*** / ~**ness** ***n.***

shameless [ˈʃeimlis] ***adj.*** 无耻的,不要脸的;伤风败俗的 ‖ ~**ly** ***adv.*** / ~**ness** ***n.***

shampoo [ʃæmˈpuː] ***vt.*** **1.** 用洗发剂洗(头发);用洗涤剂洗(地毯等) **2.** 洗…的头(或头发) **3.**〈古〉给…按摩(或推拿) —([复] shampoos) ***n.*** **1.** 洗头;洗发;洗地毯 **2.** 洗发剂;洗涤剂

shamrock [ˈʃæmrɔk] ***n.***【植】**1.** 白花酢浆草 **2.** 三叶草(爱尔兰的国花) **3.** 天蓝(苜蓿)

Shanghai [ˈʃæŋˈhai, ˈʃɑːŋˈhai] ***n.*** 上海(市) ‖ ~**lander** [ˌʃæŋˈhailəndə] ***n.*** 上海人

shanghai [ʃæŋˈhai] ***vt.***〈俚〉**1.**(用酒或麻醉剂)使失去知觉后劫到船上当水手 **2.** 拐骗;胁迫

shank [ʃæŋk] ***n.*** **1.** 胫,小腿;腿部;胫骨 **2.**【动】(昆虫的)胫节 **3.** 牛(或羊)的腿肉 **4.**(工具的)柄;杆;锚杆;匙柄;钉杆;针杆;(植物的)秆,梗,柄 **5.**(钻、凿等插入柄中的)凸出部分;(钮扣背面的)绕线小梗 **6.**【印】活字字身 **7.** 鞋底中间狭窄部分;袜统 **8.**〈口〉末梢;后部;较晚的一段时间 — ***vi.***(花等)从病梗上枯萎脱落

shan't [ʃɑːnt] = shall not

shantung [ʃænˈtʌŋ] ***n.***【纺】(柞蚕丝制的)山东绸;(用人造丝或棉纱制的)仿山东绸

shanty [ˈʃænti] ***n.*** 简陋小屋,棚屋

SHAPE [ʃeip] *abbr.* Supreme Headquarters Allied Powers Europe (NATO) (北大西

洋公约组织)欧洲盟军最高司令部

shape [ʃeip] *n.* **1.** 形状,形态;样子,外形 **2.** 定形;(具体)形式;体现,具体化 **3.** (口)情况,状态 **4.** 朦胧的形象;模糊的人影 **5.** 种类 **6.** 模型;模制胶状物 **7.** 戏装;戏装材料 — *vt.* **1.** 使成形,使具形状 — *vi.* **1.** (口)成形;成型;形成形,使具有 — *vt.* **1.** 使成形,使具形状 **2.** 计划;想出;想象 **3.** 使符合;使适合(*to*) **4.** 使取向;决定…的进程(或做法) — *vi.* **1.** (口)成形;成型;形成 **2.** (*up, into*) 成长;发展 **3.** (罕)发生

shaped [ʃeipt] *adj.* **1.** (常用以构成复合词)具有某形状的;制成一定形状的:~ steel 型钢 **2.** 合适的 **3.** 计划好的,有目标的

shapeless [ˈʃeiplis] *adj.* **1.** 无形状的;不定形的 **2.** 难以名状的;不像样的 ∥ ~**ly** *adv.* / ~**ness** *n.*

shapely [ˈʃeipli] *adj.* **1.** 样子好的;匀称的;美观的 **2.** 定形的,有条理的 ∥ **shapeliness** *n.*

shaper [ˈʃeipə] *n.* **1.** 【机】成形机;牛头刨床 **2.** 造型者;塑造者

share[1] [ʃeə] *n.* **1.** 一份,份儿 **2.** 份额;分担量 **3.** 股份;(英)[~s]股票(=(美)stock) — *vt.* **1.** 均分;分摊;分配 **2.** 分享;分担;共同具有;共同使用 — *vi.* 分享;分担;有份 — *n* *r.* ∥ '~**crop** *vi.* & *vt.* (主美)收益分成种(田或作物) / '~**cropper** *n.*(尤指美国南方)收益分成的佃农 / '~**holder** *n.* 股票持有人,股东

share[2] [ʃeə] *n.* 犁头,犁铧

shark [ʃɑːk] *n.* **1.** 鲨鱼 **2.** 贪婪狡猾的人;敲诈勒索者;骗子:a loan ~ 高利贷者 / a land ~ 专门敲诈上岸水手的人 **3.** (俚)内行,能手,老手;专家:a ~ at bridge 桥牌能手 **4.**(美俚)旷课的学生;旷课;杰出的学生;免修课程的优等生

5.(英俚)海关官员 — *vt.* 敲诈;骗取;用不正当手段搜括(*up*);贪婪地吞咽 — *vi.* 敲诈;诈骗

sharp [ʃɑːp] *adj.* **1.** 锋利的,锐利的 **2.** 敏锐的;机警的 **3.** 线条分明的;轮廓鲜明的;明显的 **4.** 陡的;急转的;急剧的;激烈的 **5.** 尖刻的;苛刻的;严厉的;易怒的 **6.**(感觉、味道等)强烈的;辛辣的;刺耳的;刺骨的 **7.** 敏捷的;生气勃勃的:take a ~ walk 轻快地散步 / ~ work 紧张而热烈的工作 **8.** 精明的;厉害的;狡猾的;不择手段的 **9.** [音]偏高的;升半音的 **10.** [语]不带声的,清音的 **11.**(美俚)时髦的;漂亮的 — *adv.* **1.** 正(指时刻) **2.** 锐利地;机警地;急剧地;突然地 **3.** [音]偏高地;升半音 — *n.* **1.** 锋利的工具;细的长缝衣针 **2.** [音]半升音;半升音号(♯) **3.** (口)骗子(=sharper) **4.** (英俚)[~s]粗面粉 **5.** (英)[~s]细面粉 — *vt.* 把(音调)提高半音 — *vi.* 升音演唱或演奏) ∥ ~**ly** *adv.* / ~**ness** *n.* ∥ '~**shooter** *n.* 神枪手;一等射手

sharpen [ˈʃɑːpən] *vt.* **1.** 削尖;磨快 **2.** 使敏锐;使敏捷 **3.** 加重,加强;使剧烈;使尖锐 **4.** [音]把(音调)提高半音 — *vi.* **1.** 变尖;变锋利 **2.** 尖锐化;加剧 — *n* *r.* 磨削器;磨削者

sharper [ˈʃɑːpə] *n.* **1.** 骗子 **2.** 以赌牌行骗为生的人

shatter [ˈʃætə] *vt.* **1.** 使散开;震落;吹散 **2.** 粉碎;砸碎 **3.** 破坏;毁坏;使惊慌 — *vi.* **1.** 破碎;粉碎 **2.** 损坏;毁坏 **3.** 嘎嘎地响;哗啦地响 **4.** 落花;落叶;掉果 — *n.* **1.** 碎片,裂片 **2.** 粉碎;毁坏 **3.**(过早的)落花;落叶;掉果 **4.**(一阵)喷散;迸溅 ∥ ~**er** *n.*

shave [ʃeiv] (过去式 shaved,过去分词 shaved 或 shaven[ˈʃeivn]) *vt.* **1.** 剃,刮

(胡须等);修剪(草坪等) **2.** 削(或刨)去 **3.** 擦过,掠过 **4.**〈口〉杀价买进(期票等) **5.**〈英方〉诈取;强夺 **6.**〈美俚〉勉强胜过 — *vi.* **1.** 修面,刮脸 **2.** 勉强挨过(或挤进);讨价还价,很精明 — *n.* **1.** 刮刀,剃刀;刨刀;削片,薄片 **2.** 修面,刮脸 **3.**〈口〉擦过,掠过;幸免 **4.**〈英〉欺诈□ ~ **r** *n.* **1.** 修面的人 **2.** 电动剃刀;刨刀 **4.**〈美俚〉小伙子 **5.** 杀价买进期票的人;善于讨价还价的人 **6.** 骗子

Shavian ['ʃeivjən] *n. & adj.*(英国戏剧家)萧伯纳(Shaw)(作品)风格的;萧伯纳崇拜者(的)

shaving ['ʃeiviŋ] *n.* **1.** 刮;削;刨 **2.** 修面;剃须 **3.** [常~s]刨花;削片,薄片

shawl [ʃɔl] *n.*(尤指女用的)(长)方形披巾(或披肩) — *vt.* 用披巾(或披巾状物)包着

she [ʃiː;弱 ʃi] *pron.*[主格] **1.** 她 **2.**(作为国家、地球、月亮、船等的代词)她,它[复]shes [ʃiːz] *n.* 女孩;女人;雌性动物

sheaf [ʃiːf]([复]sheaves [ʃiːvz]) *n.* **1.** 捆,束,扎 **2.** 一简箭(多为 24 支) — *vt.* 捆,束,扎

shear [ʃiə](过去式 sheared 或〈古〉shore [ʃɔː],过去分词 shorn [ʃɔn]或 sheared) *vt.* **1.**〈诗〉(用刀、剑)砍;斩 **2.** 剪;剪···的毛(或羊毛等) **3.**〈苏格兰〉(用镰刀)收割 **4.** 剥夺(*of*) — *vi.* **1.** 剪;修剪;剪羊毛 **2.** 切断[物]切变 **3.**〈苏格兰〉(用镰刀)收割 — *n.* **1.** 刨 **2.** [~s]大剪刀;[机]剪切机,剪床 **3.** [物]切变;切力,剪力 **4.** [常~s]起重三角架,人字起重架 **5.** 剪下的东西(如羊毛) **6.**(羊的)一次剪毛,(羊)年岁 ‖ ~ **er** *n.* **1.** 剪切

者;剪切工人;剪羊毛者 **2.** 剪羊毛机 □ ~ **er** *n.* **1.** 剪切机,剪床;直立槽截煤机 / ~ **ing** *n.* **1.** 剪切 **2.** 剪羊毛;剪下的羊毛

sheath [ʃiːθ] *n.* **1.**(刀、剑等的)鞘;(枪)壳;套;护套 **2.** [生][解]鞘,兜 **3.**(电子管的)屏极;(电缆的)铠装 **4.** 紧身连衣裙

sheathe [ʃiːð] *vt.* **1.** 把···插入鞘,包;覆盖 **3.** 把(剑等)刺入皮肉 **4.** 缩回(爪)

sheathing ['ʃiːðiŋ] *n.* **1.** 入鞘;外层覆盖 **2.** 护套;外包物;(屋顶用)柏油纸;衬底;绝热物 **4.**(电缆的)铠装 **5.** [船]覆盖层,包板 — *adj.* 带(有)鞘的;外层覆盖的

sheave[1] [ʃiːv] *n.* [机]滑车轮,绞缆轮

sheave[2] [ʃiːv] *vt.* 捆(稻、纸等)

sheaves [ʃiːvz] sheaf 的复数

shed[1] [ʃed](shed; shedding) *vt.* **1.** 流出;流下 **2.** 使落去 **3.** 一连串排出(孢子等) **4.** 散发;放射 **5.** 脱落;蜕(壳等);脱去 **6.** 摆脱;抛弃 **7.** 分(开)···分开 **8.** [电](分区)切断(负载) — *vi.* **1.** 流出;溢出;泻去 **2.** 散发;散布 **3.** 蜕皮(或壳等) — *n.* **1.** 分水岭 **2.** [纺](织机的)梭口,梭道

shed[2] [ʃed] *n.* **1.** 棚,小屋 **2.** 货棚;工棚;车库 — (shed; shedding) *vt.* 把···放入棚内

she'd [ʃiːd] **1.** = she had **2.** = she would

sheen [ʃiːn] *n.* **1.** 光辉,光采;光泽;the ~ of silk 丝绸的光泽 **2.** 华丽的服装;有光泽的纺织品 — *adj.*〈诗〉华丽的;灿烂的 — *vi.* 发出光采;发闪光

sheep [ʃiːp][单复同] *n.* **1.** 羊,绵羊 **2.** 羞着祖祖的人;胆小鬼;蠢人;驯服的人 **3.** 教区居民(们) ‖ ~ **fold** *n.* 羊栏,羊圈 / ~ **herder** *n.*〈美〉牧羊人 / ~ **skin**

n. 1. 绵羊毛皮；羊皮板；(带毛的)羊皮毯；(用作书面braille等的)羊皮革；羊皮纸 2.(写在羊皮纸上的)文件；毕业文凭

sheepish [ˈʃiːpiʃ] *adj.* 1.(像羊一般)驯顺的；腼腆的 2. 忸怩的；害羞的，局促不安的 ‖ ~**ly** *adv.* / ~**ness** *n.*

sheer[1] [ʃiə] *adj.* 1. 全然的，十足的，彻底的，绝对的 2. 纯粹的，不掺杂的 3.(织物)极薄的，透明的 4. 陡峭的；垂直的 — *adv.* 1. 全然，十足，彻底 2. 陡直地，垂直地 — *n.* 透明薄纱；透明薄织物；透明薄织物制的衣服

sheer[2] [ʃiə] *n.*(船)舷弧 2.(海)偏航，偏荡；转向 3. 单锚泊船位 — *vi.* 偏航，偏荡；转向，避开 (*off，away*) — *vt.* 使偏航，使偏荡；使转向

sheet [ʃiːt] *n.* 1. 被单；裹尸布 3.〈诗〉帆，风帆；船帆；船张；一张(纸)；[~s]书页；印刷品；(尤指庸俗下流的)报纸(或其他刊物)；整版邮票 5. 被单；单子；(美俚)罪犯档案 6. 一大片 7. 成幅的薄片；薄板；(一)片；(一)块 8.[地]岩层 9.[数]叶 — *vt.* 1. 给…铺上被单；用裹尸布包…覆盖 2. 摊开，使成一大片 — *vi.* 大片地落下；成片铺开；大片流动 — *adj.* 1. 滚压(或展开)成片的；片状的 2. 成幅薄片的 ‖ ~ **anchor** *n.*1.(船)备用大锚 2.〈喻〉最后的希望；最后的手段；最后的(或主要的)靠山

sheik(h) [ʃeik, ʃiːk] *n.* 1.(阿拉伯国家的尊称)酋长；族长；(伊斯兰教)教长 2. 迷人男子，风流情郎

shekel [ˈʃekl] *n.* 1. 谢克尔(古希伯来或巴比伦等的重量单位) 2. 谢克克尔银币(或金币) 3.〈口〉[~s]钱(尤指硬币)；财富

shelf [ʃelf] *n.*([复] **shelves** [ʃelvz]) — *n.* 1.(壁橱、书橱等内)搁板；架子 2. 搁板似的东西；搁板的容量 3. 搁板状物；突出

的扁平岩石 4. 沙洲；暗礁 5.[地]陆架 ‖ **on** the ~ 6.(矿)(锡砂矿)基岩 7.(支撑木船甲板梁的)承梁材 8.〈俚〉告密者(尤指同犯或同伙)

shell [ʃel] *n.* 1. 壳；果壳；荚 2. 贝壳，甲壳状物；外壳；外皮；饼壳；笋壳；小啤酒杯 4. 有甲壳的软体动物 5.(像贝进壳内似的)缄默；冷淡；矜持 6. 外表，外貌 7.(计划等的)梗概，轮廓 8. 炮弹；猎枪子弹；爆破筒 9. 地壳；薄硬岩层 10.[核](原子)壳层 11. 轻快赛艇 12. 内棺 13.(剑柄或刀柄上的)护手 14.(诗)竖琴,七弦琴 15.(英)(学校的)中年级；班级；年级 16.(船)壳板；(房屋)框架，骨架；(建筑物)壳体 — *vt.* 1. 剥…的壳；给…(小麦等)脱粒 2. 用贝壳制；给…装壳体 3. 炮轰；射击 — *vi.* 1.(金属等)剥落；落成碎片 (*off*) 2. 脱壳；(颗粒)脱落；脱出 3. 采集贝壳 ‖ ~-**fish** *n.* 有壳的水生动物

she'll [ʃiːl;弱 ʃil] 1. = she will 2. she shall

shellac(k) [ʃəˈlæk] *n.* 1. 虫胶；紫胶虫)胶 2. 含虫胶的唱片原料；虫胶创剂；虫胶清漆 — (shellacked; shellacking) *vt.* 1. 以虫胶清漆涂…；以虫胶处理 2.〈俚〉彻底打败 ‖ ~**ing** *n.* 1. 虫胶处理 2.〈俚〉鞭打；殴打；彻底击败

shelter [ˈʃeltə] *n.* 1. 隐蔽处；掩蔽部；躲避处；避难所 2. 掩蔽，遮蔽；庇护，保护 — *vt.* 掩蔽，遮蔽；庇护，保护 — *vi.* 躲避；避难

shelve [ʃelv] *vt.* 1. 装搁板(或架子)于 2. 把…放在搁板(或架子上) 3. 搁置，暂缓考虑 4. 解雇；使(军官等)退役

shelves [ʃelvz] shelf 的复数

shenanigan [ʃiˈnænigən] *n.*〈美口〉1. 鬼把戏；欺骗行为 2.[~s]淘气；恶作剧

shepherd [ˈʃepəd] *n.* 1. 牧羊人，羊倌 2.

牧师 3. 牧羊狗 — *vt.* 1. 牧(羊),护(羊) 2. 看管;护送;带领;指导 3. 〈罕(俚)使陷入困境 4.〈俚〉(为诈骗等目的)跟踪、钉…的梢 / 〈球赛中〉钉住(对手)

shepherdess ['ʃepədis] *n.* 1. 女牧羊人;牧羊女孩 2. 农村姑娘;(田园诗中美化的)村姑

sherbet ['ʃəːbət] *n.* 1.〈英〉冰冻果子露 2.〈美〉果汁牛奶冻

sheriff ['ʃerif] *n.* 1.〈英〉[常作 High S-]郡长;(某些城市的)行政司法长官 2.〈美〉(民选)县治安官

sherry ['ʃeri] *n.* 雪利酒(原产于西班牙南部的一种烈性白葡萄酒)

she's [ʃiːz] 1. = she is 2. = she has

Shia(h) ['ʃiːə] *n.* 1. 什叶派(伊斯兰教的一派) 2. 什叶派教徒

shield [ʃiːld] *n.* 1. 盾 2. 保护者;庇护者 3. 防护物;护罩;遮护板,挡板 4. 盾状物;盾形徽章 5.〈美〉警察徽章 5.[鱼等的]吸干垫布 6.【动】背甲;头胸甲;龟甲板 7.【地】地盾;【矿】掩护支架 8.【电】屏蔽;铠装 — *vt.* 1. 保护;庇卫 2. 庇护;掩盖 3. 挡开;避开(*off*) — *vi.* 起庇的作用;起保护作用

shift [ʃift] *vt.* 1. 替换;转移;移动;转变;改变 2. 推卸;转嫁 3. 更换;调档等 4.【语】使音变 5.〈方〉换(衣服);使(某人)换衣服 — *vi.* 1. 转换;转移;移动;转变 2. 设法应付(或混过);想办法 3. 推托;欺骗 4. 变速;调档 5.【语】音变 6.〈方〉换衣服 — *n.* 1. 转换;转移;变动 2. 手段,办法;权宜之计 3. 轮班;班班期工作 4. 轮班工作时间 4. 推托;哄骗 5.【语】辅音的音变 6.〈方〉换衣服;〈方〉衬衣;女用衬衣 7.【地】变位;(断层)平移 8.【音】(提琴演奏、长号上的)换把

shiftless ['ʃiftlis] *adj.* 1. 无能的;想不出办法的;无计谋生的 2. 偷懒的;得过且过的

shifty ['ʃifti] *adj.* 1. 足智多谋的;随机应变的 2. 惯耍花招的;狡猾的;鬼鬼闪闪的 3. 变化多端的;不稳定的 ‖ **shiftily** *adv.* / **shiftiness** *n.*

Shiite ['ʃiːait] *n.* (伊斯兰教)什叶派教徒

Shikoku ['ʃikəu,ku:] *n.* 四国(岛)[日本的第四大岛]

shillelagh [ʃi'leilə] *n.* (爱尔兰的)橡树棍

shilling ['ʃiliŋ] *n.* 1. 先令(原英国货币单位,12 先令为 1 镑) 2. 先令(坦桑尼亚、肯尼亚等的货币单位) 3. 先令(美国早期的货币单位)

shilly-shally ['ʃili,ʃæli] *vi.* 1.〈尤指对于琐事〉犹豫不决 2. 浪费时间;游手好闲 — *n.* 犹豫不决 — *adj. & adv.* 犹豫不决的(地)

shimmer ['ʃimə] *vi.* 发微光;闪烁 — *vt.* 使闪烁 — *n.* 微光;闪光 ‖ ~y *adj.*

shimmy ['ʃimi] *n.* (机动车前轮等的不正常)晃动;摆动 — *vi.* 颤动;晃动;摆动(指轮)；(尤指机动车)不正常地摆动

shin [ʃin] *n.* 1.【解】胫;(昆虫的)胫节 2. (牛的)小腿肉 — (shinned) (shinning) *vi.* 1. 攀,爬 2. 快步走 — *vt.* 1. (比赛时)踢(对手的)胫 2. 攀,爬

shine [ʃain] (shone [ʃɔn, ʃəun]) *vi.* 1. 照耀;发光;发亮 2. 显得出众,杰出 — *vt.* 1. 使发光;使照亮;擦亮 2. [过去式和过去分词用 shined] 擦亮 — *n.* 1. 光亮;擦(亮);光辉;光泽;光采 2. 阳光;晴天 3.〈俚〉[常~s]鬼把戏,恶作剧 4.〈俚〉骚动;吵闹

shiner ['ʃainə] *n.* 1. 出色的人;发亮物(如星、钻石、织物的发亮条纹等);发光体 2. (作鱼饵用的)银色小鱼 3.〈俚〉跌(或打)伤的黑眼圈 4.〈英俚〉钱币

（尤指金币）; [~s]金钱

shingle[1] ['ʃiŋgl] *n.* 1.【建】木瓦; 墙面板 2.〈美口〉小招牌（尤指医生、律师的营业招牌）3.（女子）（剪）墙面板式短发发型 — *vt.* 1. 用木瓦盖（屋顶）2. 使似瓦片般重叠 3. 把（女子头发）剪成墙面板式短发发型

shingle[2] ['ʃiŋgl] *n.* 1.（海滩）圆卵石 2. 铺满圆卵石的海滩

shingles ['ʃiŋglz] [复] *n.* [常用作单]【医】带状疱疹

shinny[1] ['ʃini] *vi.* & *vt.* 〈美口〉攀、爬（*up*）

shinny[2] ['ʃini] *n.*（儿童玩的）简化曲棍球戏; 曲棍 — *vi.* 玩简化曲棍球戏

shiny ['ʃaini] *adj.* 1. 晴朗的; 发亮的, 闪耀的 2. 有光泽的; 擦亮的 3. 磨光的; 磨损的 ‖ **shinily** *adv.* /**shininess** *n.*

ship [ʃip] *n.* [常用作阴性, 代词用 she, her] 1.（大）船; 海船; 舰 2. 三桅帆船; 全装帆船 3.〈美〉赛艇 4. 全体船员 5.〈美〉飞船; 飞机; 宇宙飞船 — (shipped; shipping) *vt.* 1. 把…装上船 2. 用船运; 装运 3. 在舱侧进水）4. 安装（舵、桅杆等）5. 把…放进船内 6. 雇用…为船员 7.〈美口〉解雇; 撵走; 开除（学生）— *vi.* 1. 上船; 乘船 2. 在船上工作; 做水手 ‖ '~**board** *n.* 舷侧 / '~ **canal** 可供海船通航的运河 / '~-**mate** *n.* 同船船员; 同船旅伴 / '~**shape** *adv.* & *adj.* 整齐地的 / 井井有条地（的）/ '~**worm** *n.*【动】船蛆 / '~-**wreck** *n.* 船只失事; 失事船的残骸; 遇难 *vt.* 1. 使…船只失事 2. 使（旅客等）遭受船难; 使毁灭 *vi.* 1. 船只失事; 遭受毁灭 2. 毁灭 / '~**wright** *n.* 造船木工; 修船木工 / '~**yard** *n.* 船坞; 造船厂; 修船厂

-**ship** *suf.* 1. 表示"情况"、"状态"、"性质": hard*ship*, friend*ship* 2. 表示"身份": apprentice*ship*, king*ship* 君王的身份 3. 表示"技巧"、"技能": marksman*ship*, leader*ship*

shipment ['ʃipmənt] *n.* 1. 装货; 装船; 装运 2. 装载的货物（量）

shipper ['ʃipə] *n.* 托运人; 发货人

shipping ['ʃipiŋ] *n.* 1. 装运; 运送; 海运 2. 航行 3. [总称]船舶;（一国或一海港等的）船舶; 船舶吨数

shire ['ʃaiə] *n.* 1. 郡（英国行政区）2. [the ~s]英国中部诸郡 3.（英国中部产的）夏尔（重役）马（亦作~ horse）

shirk [ʃəːk] *vi.* 1. 溜掉, 偷偷跑掉; 开小差 2. 逃避义务（或责任等）— *vt.* 逃避（义务、责任等）; school 逃学 — *vi.* 逃避（义务、责任等）; 开小差的人 ‖ ~ **er** *n.*

shirr [ʃəː] *vt.* 1. 使成皱裥 2. 熔（去壳蛋）— *n.* 抽裥（缝法）

shirt [ʃəːt] *n.* 1.（男式）衬衫 2. 内衣; 汗衫 3. 女用（仿男式）衬衫 ‖ ~**ing** *n.* 衬衫料子 ‖ ~ **sleeve** *n.* 衬衫袖子; in (one's) *-sleeves* 只穿衬衫未穿外衣的 *adj.* 1. 只穿衬衫（未穿外衣）的 2.〈喻〉不拘形式的、随便的; 非正式的 2. 朴素的; 切合实际的 / '~-**tail** *n.* 1. 衬衫下摆（尤指衬衫后部）2.〈美俚〉（报刊的）社论栏（报纸文章后的）附注 *adj.*〈美口〉1. 幼小的; 小的; 短的 2.〈亲戚〉远房的 / '~-**waist** *n.* 女用（仿男式）衬衫

shit [ʃit] (shit: shitting) *vi.*〈俗〉大便 — *vt.*〈俚〉对…胡说; 企图欺骗 — *n.* 1.〈俗〉粪便; 粪土 2.〈俚〉胡说; 谎言; 大话 3.〈俚〉卑鄙的人; 讨厌的家伙; 小人物 4. [the ~s]腹泻 5.〈俚〉命运, 运气 6.〈俚〉蹩脚货; 蹩脚表演

shiver ['ʃivə] *vi.* 1. 颤抖, 哆嗦 2.（帆）迎风拍动 — *vt.* 使（帆）迎风拍动 — *n.* 冷颤; 战栗 ‖ ~**ly** *adj.*

shoal¹ [ʃəul] *adj.*(水)浅的 — *n.* 1. 浅滩；(退潮时露出的)沙洲 2.[常～s]暗礁,陷阱,潜伏的危机 — *vi.* 变浅 — *vt.* 1. 使变浅 2. 驶人(浅水等) ‖ ~er *n.* 沿海贸易商船(或水手)

shoal² [ʃəul] *n.* 鱼群,大量,大群 — *vi.* (鱼等)成群,群集

shoat [ʃəut] *n.*(不满1岁的)小猪

shock¹ [ʃɔk] *n.* 1. 冲击,冲撞;震动,震荡 2. 震惊;(对神经的)震扰;引起震惊的事件(或东西);打击 3. 突击 4.(电流通过身体引起的)电震,电击 5.【医】休克;中风;冠状动脉血栓形成 — *vt.* 1. 使震动,使震荡;使震惊;使休克 2. 使震惊(或愤慨,厌恶等) 3. 震惊得使…;～ sb. *into* a stupor 把某人震惊得目瞪口呆 — *vi.* 1. 震动;相撞击 2. 使人感到震惊;吓唬人

shock² [ʃɔk] *n.*(竖放在田里使干燥的)禾束堆 — *vt.* 把…做成禾束堆 — *vi.* 捆扎禾束

shock³ [ʃɔk] *n.* 乱蓬蓬的一堆(如头发等) — *adj.* 乱蓬蓬的

shocking [ˈʃɔkiŋ] *adj.* 1. 令人震惊的,骇人听闻的 2. 不正当的;十分丑恶的;十分讨厌的(东西) 3. 糟糕的 — *adv.*〈口〉[用于加强语气]很,极 ‖ ~ly *adv.* 1. 令人震惊地 2. 极糟地 3. 极度地,极厉害地

shod [ʃɔd] shoe 的过去式和过去分词 — *adj.* 1. 穿着鞋的 2. 装有轮胎的 3.(马)装有蹄铁的 4. 裹了金属包头的

shoddy [ˈʃɔdi] *adj.* 1. 软再生毛的,长弹毛的 2. 质量差的 — *n.* 1.【纺】软再生毛,软再生毛织物 2. 冒充货;赝品 ‖ **shoddily** *adv.* / **shoddiness** *n.*

shoe [ʃuː] *n.* 1. 鞋 2. 蹄铁 3. 鞋状物 4. (手杖等的)金属包头 4. 轮胎,外胎 5.【建】桩帽 6. 制动器;【机】闸瓦 7.【电】端;靴;管头 8. 防磨(或防滑)的装置;【空】尾撬;导向板;发射导轨 9.[～s]地位;境遇 — *vt.*(shod[ʃɔd]或 shoed) 1. 给…穿上鞋;给(马)钉蹄铁 2. 给…装上鞋状物;用鞋片包履 ‖ '~-horn *n.* 鞋拔 *vt.* 硬塞(或硬挤)进去 /'~lace *n.* 鞋带 /'~,maker *n.* 制(或补)鞋工人;鞋铺老板 /'~string *n.* 1. 鞋带 2.〈美口〉少额资本 *adj.* 1. 一样狭长的 2. 小本经营的;小规模的 3. 微小的,小范围的 3. 微小的,微弱的

shone [ʃɔn, ʃəun] shine 的过去式和过去分词

shoo [ʃuː] *int.* 1.(驱赶鸟禽等的声音)嘘! 滚开! — *vi.* "嘘嘘"地赶开"嘘"的一声赶走;吓走 — *vt.* "嘘"

shook [ʃuk] shake 的过去式

shoot [ʃuːt] (shot[ʃɔt]) *vt.* 1. 发射,放射;射出(炮弹等);开(枪);放(箭) 2. 射中;射伤;射死;(喻)损毁;使毁灭 3. 投射(视线等);挥出;抛出;连珠炮似地说出;撒(网等) 4. 小本经营的;一中射猎 5. 伸出(舌头等);突出;发(芽) 6.(船等)飞速通过;使(船等)飞速行进 7. 拍摄 8. 闩(门闩等);拔出(门闩等);〈纺〉投(梭) 9. 把…兜底倒出,倾卸;挥霍;耗尽 10. 把…刨精确,刨光 11. 测量(星球等)的高度 12. 点着;使爆炸;注射,用爆破法开采(煤矿等) 13.(足球)射(门);(篮球)投(篮)(球);掷(骰子);糟(铁) 14. 给…注射 15.〈美俚〉急交,急送,急遣(to) — *vi.* 1. 射出;放出;开枪(炮)发射;发射 2. 飞快地移动 2. 射击;射箭 3. 突出;伸展(幼芽,枝叶等)长出 4. 拍电影;摄影 5.(门闩)被闩上;被拔出 6.〈纺〉投梭 6.(疼痛等)刺激 7. 射门;投篮;打高尔

夫球;掷骰子 8.〈美俚〉把话讲出来 — *n*. 1. 发芽;抽枝;嫩枝;芽;苗:bamboo ~*s* 笋 / rice ~*s* 禾苗,秧苗 2. 射猎(队);射猎会;射猎权;射猎场;射击会;(射击比赛的)一轮 3. 发射;射击;(火箭、导弹等的)试验发射:a moon ~ 向月球进行的发射 4. 拍摄 5.(飞箭一般的)急速动作;奔流;供急流通过的水道;【矿】滑槽 6.(疼痛、愉快等的)刺激 7. 推力;(冰块、土块的)崩落 8.(划桨时)两划间的间隔时间 9. 一道光线 10. 垃圾场 ‖ ~**er** *n*. 1. 射手;炮手;(油井等的)爆破手 2. 流星 3.[常用以构成复合词]手枪:a six-~*er* 六响枪 4.(板球赛中的)擦地球

shooting [ˈʃuːtiŋ] *n*. 1. 射击;射杀,持枪杀人 2. 射猎,游猎;〈英〉射猎权;猎场 3. 刺痛,剧痛 4.【体】(篮球)投篮;(足球)射门 ‖ ~ **gallery** 1. 打靶场,射击场 2.〈美俚〉为有毒瘾者注射麻醉剂的场所 /~ **script** 1.(电影)拍摄用的剧本;分镜头剧本 2.(电视节目)演出用的定稿剧本 /~ **star** 1. 流星 2.【植】流星花 /~ **stick**(顶端可打开作坐凳的)折叠座手杖 /~ **war** 热战(指真枪实弹的战争,与冷战、神经战相对而言)

shop [ʃɔp] *n*. 1.〈主英〉商店,店铺(=〈美〉store) 2.〈美〉(大店内的)专柜;专业零售部;专业服务部(亦作 shoppe [ʃɔp]) 3. 车间;工场;工厂:a runaway ~〈美〉(为逃避赋税或工会压力而迁移的)外逃工厂 4. 本行;与职业有关的事;行话 5. 工作室;〈英俚〉机构;〈美俚〉办事处 6.(教手艺用的)学校实验室;工艺(学) —(shopped;shopping) *vi*. 1. 到商店去买东西;到处选购商品(*around*) 2. 到处寻找(*around*) — *vt*. 1.〈方〉逮捕;拘禁;告发(同犯)使入狱 2. 选购(商品);在(商店)内选购商品;(为得到有关商品的消息而)浏览(报纸、商品目录等) 3. 把(车厢等)送去检修

shoplifter [ˈʃɔpˌliftə] *n*.(混在顾客群中行窃的)商店扒手

shopper [ˈʃɔpə] *n*. 1. 顾客,购物的人 2.(商店雇用的)代客选购货物的人 3.(商店雇用的)打听行情的人 4.〈美〉当地商店的广告传单

shopping [ˈʃɔpiŋ] *n*. 1. 购物 2. 所购之物 3. 商业设施;商品

shore[1] [ʃɔː] *n*. 1. 滨;岸 2.【律】涨潮线与落潮线之间的地带 ‖ ˈ~-**based** *adj*. 以海岸为基地的;岸基的 /~ **patrol**(美国海军或海军陆战队的)岸上宪兵队,基地宪兵队(常略作 SP)

shore[2] [ʃɔː] *n*.(房屋、船等的)顶撑,撑柱 — *vt*. 用撑撑住;支持(*up*)

shorn [ʃɔːn] shear 的过去分词

short [ʃɔːt] *adj*. 1. 短的;近的 2. 短期的,短暂的,短促的 3. 矮的;低的 4. 短缺的,不足的;缺钱用的 5.(智力等方面)弱的;浅薄的;(记忆力)差的 6. 简慢的;唐突的;暴躁的 7. 简短的;简略的;缩写的 8.(金属等)脆的,松脆的;易裂(成片、块)的 9. 波涛汹涌的 10.(酒类)不搀水的;烈性的;少量的 11.(股票投机等)卖空的,空头交易的 12.【语】(元音)短音的;(音节)非重读的;(诗歌)短音节的 — *adv*. 1. 简短地 2. 唐突地;突然地,出其不意地 3. 达不到目标地 4. 以空头方式(指股票投机等) — *n*.[the ~]扼要;实质 2.【语】短音;短音节;【音】短音符 3.(电影)短片;(报刊等的)短讯;短篇特写 4. 矮个子的衣服尺码;[~s]短裤 5.[~s]细麸粉(磨面粉的副产品);废料,下脚 6.[~s]缺乏;不足(额) 7. 接近目标但未命中的射弹 8. 不足规定长度的东西;长度在法定可捕标准以下的鱼(或龙

虾)9. 不搀水的(烈性)酒 10.【电】短路 11.[~s]短期债券 12.(棒球)游击手 13.【美俚】有轨电车,汽车 — vt. 1. 故意少给~找头;骗subscript 2.【电】使短路 ‖ ~ly adv. 1. 立刻;不久 2. 简短地;唐突地;傲慢地 ~ness n. 1. 短;短促;低 2. 缺乏,不足 3. 简短,简略 4. 松脆,(金属等的)脆性 '~-bread, '~-cake n. 脆饼,松饼 /~·circuit【电】/~·'circuit vt. 1. 使短路 2. 简化,缩短(程序等) 3. 阻碍;挫伤(友谊等) /~·'coming n. 缺点,短处 /~·cut n. 近路,捷径 /~·'handed adj. 缺乏人手的 /~·horn n. 1.[常 S]短角牛 2.〈美俚〉刚到边远(或新区)地区的人;生手 /~·'lived ['ʃɔːt'livd, 'ʃɔːt'laivd] adj. 短命的;短暂的 /~·'sighted adj. 近视的;目光短浅的 /~·'stop n. 1.(棒球)游击手(位置) 2.[摄]急止浴;停显液 /~·'wave [无] n. 短波;短波发射(或接收)机 ~·'wave 短波发射

shortage ['ʃɔːtidʒ] n. 不足,缺少;不足额

shorten ['ʃɔːtn] vt. 1. 弄短,缩短;减少 2. 减小~的力量;减低~的效能 3. 使松脆 4. 给(孩子)穿童装 — vi. 变短,缩短;缩小 ‖ ~·ing n. 1. 缩短 2.(制糕饼的)起酥油

shot[1] [ʃɔt] shoot 的过去式和过去分词

shot[2] [ʃɔt] n. 1. 发射;射击,开枪;射击声 2.[单复同]弹丸,子弹;炮弹;霰弹;铅沙弹[总称] 3. 射程;范围 4. 射击手 5. 尝试;猜测,推测 6. 拍摄;(电影等一次曝光的)镜头;一段影片;照相 7.[矿]爆破;炮眼;(一次爆破所用的)炸药 8. 注射;(美国)(咖啡等)一次注射;一服 9.(烈酒等的)一口;一杯;(清凉饮料等的)一份,一客 10. 中肯的话;一针见血的评语 11.【体】(一

次)射门;投篮;(乒乓等的)一击;fast block ~ s 快速推挡 12.(捕鱼的)一次)撒网;【纺】(一次)投梭 13.(口)(酒吧间等的)应付账 14.(口)机会;可操胜算的赌注—(shotted; shotting) vt. 1. 给~装弹,给~加铅丸(使变得沉重) 2.(用喷射法)使成颗粒状 ‖ '~-gun n. 猎枪;滑膛枪;〈美俚〉机关枪 adj. 1.(用)猎枪的 2. 胁迫的;迫以武力等)强迫的;爱用武力的 3. 笼统的;漫无目标的 vt. 1.(用滑膛枪)射击2.(以武力等)强迫 /~·put【体】推铅球 /~··putter n. 铅球运动员 /~·tower(采用滴铅入水法的)制弹塔

shot[3] [ʃɔt] adj. 1.(织物等)闪色的;杂色的 2. 交织着的;渗透的 3. 丸粒状的 4. 点彩的 5.〈美俚〉筋疲力尽的;病弱的;用坏的;破旧的 6. 毁灭的;破灭的;失败的 6.〈俚〉喝醉的

should [强 ʃud;弱 ʃəd, ʃd]shall 的过去式 — v. aux. 1.[表示过去将来时]常用于间接引语将 2.[表示语气较强的假设]万一,竟然 3.[用于第一人称时表示某种条件下产生的结论;用于第二、第三人称时表示说话者的意愿]就;该 4.[表示可能性、推测或推论]可能;该 5.[表示义务、责任]应当,应该 6.[表示委婉、谦逊了]可以该 7.[表示必要、适当、惊奇、遗憾等的从句中]应该;竟然会 8.[与 why, who, how 等连用]表示意外,惊异等 9.[用于表示建议、命令、决定等的从句中]应该;必须 10.[用于表示目的或由 lest 引导的从句中]可以;会;万一

shoulder ['ʃəuldə] n. 1. 肩,肩膀,肩胛;肩膀关节 2.[~s]上背部;(喻)担当的能力 3.(衣服的)肩部 4.[~s](肉类)带肩肉的前腿肉 5.【动】(昆虫)的肩角;前角;中胸角;侧角 6. 肩状物;

状突出部;(碉堡)棱堡肩角;【地】山肩;谷肩 7.(路侧的)紧急停车道,路肩 ~ vt. 1. 肩起,挑起;承担:Shoulder arms! 枪上肩! 2. 用肩膀推挤 ~ vi. 用肩膀推挤 ‖ ~ blade【解】肩胛骨 /~ flash、~ patch 臂章 /~ loop (陆军、空军、海军陆战队的)肩章 /~ mark【美】(海军)肩章 /~ strap 1. 肩章 2.(吊裤或包等的)背带

shouldn't ['ʃudnt] = should not

shout [ʃaut] n. 1. 呼喊;喊叫声 2.〈俚〉感叹号,惊叹号 ~ vi. 1. 呼喊,喊叫 2. 嚷,大声说 3. 引人注目,触目;大肆张扬 ~ vt. 1. 高呼;嚷着说出:大声说出 2. 叫喊着使:~ oneself hoarse 叫得声嘶力竭 / ~ sb. up from the bed 大声把某人喊醒起床 / ~ down rival opinions 以叫喊声压倒对立的意见 ‖ ~er n.

shove [ʃʌv] vt. 1. 推;猛推 2. 强使 3.〈口〉乱塞;硬推(掉) ~ vi. 1.(使劲)推 2. 连推带挤地走 ~ n. 推

shovel ['ʃʌvl] n. 1. 铲;铁锹;铁锹 2. 一铲的量 3. 铲状物 4.(教士等戴的)宽边帽(亦作~ hat) ‖ ~ful(l)的量 /~ shovel(l)ing n. 1. 铲,铲起;用铲子掘起(或出空) 2. 把…大量倒入 ~ vi. 铲 ‖ shovel(l)er n.

show [ʃəu] (过去式 showed,过去分词 shown[ʃəun]或 showed) vt. 1. 给…看,出示,显示,显出 2. 展出,陈列;演出;放映 3. 表明,说明;证明 4. 指示,指出 5. 带引,带领 6. 炫耀,卖弄(off) 7. 给予;赐予 8.(通过示范)教,告知 9.【律】陈述;辩护 ~ vi. 1. 显现,显出;露面 2. 演出 3.(赛决时)举手 4.〈美〉(赛马、狗等)得第三名 ~ n. 1. 表示,显示 2. 展览(会) 3. 虚夸;炫耀,卖弄 4. 外观,表面 5. 景象;景物;奇观;丑相;出丑的人 6. 演出;节目;大众娱乐 7.

(俚)表现 8.〈口〉[只用单](表现、表白等的)机会 9.(正在从事的)事物;事业 10.(指示附近有矿脉露头的)初现浮现矿;迹象 11.【医】(分娩时的)现血 12.〈美〉(赛马、狗等的)第三名 ‖ ~boat n. 1.〈美〉(有戏剧表演的)演艺游船;水上舞台 2.〈美俚〉卖弄的人 vi.〈美俚〉卖弄 / ~ business 娱乐性行业(指戏院、电影院等) / ~ case n. 陈列柜;(展示人或物)优点的东西 vt. 使显出优点 / ~down n. 摊牌,最后的一决雌雄 / ~girl (夜总会等处的)歌舞女伶;歌女 / ~man n. 1.(戏剧等)主持人的演讲者;(马戏团等的)主持人 2. 善于安排演出(或吸引观众)的人 / ~-off n. 1. 炫耀,卖弄 2. 爱炫耀的人;爱吹牛的人 / ~window 橱窗

shower ['ʃauə] n. 1. 阵雨;冰雹(或风雪等)的一阵 2.(一阵)淋浴 3.〈美〉(为新娘举行的)送礼会 4. 淋浴 5.[物] 簇射 ~ vi. 1. 下阵雨;阵雨般落下 2. 淋浴 ~ vt. 1. 浇;淋湿;使湿落 2. 倾注;大量地给予 ‖ ~ bath 1. 淋浴;淋浴装置;淋浴室 2.〈喻〉淋湿;湿透

showery ['ʃauəri] adj. 阵雨(般)的;多阵雨的

shown [ʃəun] show 的过去分词

showy ['ʃəui] adj. 1.〈常贬〉浮华的;过分艳丽的;显眼的,惹眼的 2. 炫耀的,卖弄的 ‖ showily adv. / showiness n.

shrank [ʃræŋk] shrink 的过去式

shrapnel ['ʃræpnl] n. 1.(炮弹、水雷等的)弹片 2. 榴霰弹,子母弹

shred [ʃred] n. 1. 碎片;碎条;破布 2. 少量剩余;最少量(常用 shredded 或〈古〉shred;shredding) vt. & vi. 撕碎;切碎

shrew [ʃru:] n. 1.【动】鼩鼱(一种似鼠的小动物) 2. 泼妇;悍妇

shrewd [ʃru:d] *adj*. 1. 机灵的；敏锐的；精明的；伶俐的 2. 厉害的，狠狠的 3. 凛冽的；剧烈的 ‖ ~ly *adv*. / ~ness *n*.

shrewish [ˈʃru:iʃ] *adj*. 泼妇似的；爱骂街的

shriek [ʃri:k] *vi*. 1. 尖声喊叫；发出尖声 2.(尖叫似地)促人注意 — *vt*. 1. 尖声发出 2. 耸人听闻地报道出 — *n*. 尖叫(声)；尖声

shrike [ʃraik] *n*.【动】伯劳(鸟)

shrill [ʃril] *adj*. 1. 尖声的；伴有尖声喊的 2.(批评等)硬要人听的，哀切的 3. 强烈的 4.(怒气等)过度的，无节制的 — *adv*.〈古〉尖声地 — *vi*. 发出尖锐刺耳的声音 — *vt*. 尖声地叫(或讲) — *n*. 尖声 ‖ ~ness *n*. / ~y *adj*. & *adv*.

shrimp [ʃrimp] ([复] shrimp(s)) *n*. 1.(小)虾，褐虾；~s 虾干；shelled ~s 虾仁 2.(谑)矮小的人；无足轻重的人；小东西 — *vi*. 捕(小)虾

shrine [ʃrain] *n*. 1. 神龛；圣柯；神殿 2. 圣陵；圣骨匣；圣物柜 3. 圣地；神圣场所 — *vt*. = enshrine

shrink [ʃriŋk](过去式 shrank [ʃræŋk] 或 shrunk [ʃrʌŋk]；过去分词 shrunk 或 shrunken[ˈʃrʌŋkən]) *vi*. 1. 收缩；蜷缩；皱缩 2. 缩小；减少 3. 退缩，畏缩 — *vt*. 使收缩；使缩小 — *n*. 1.(织物等的)缩水，收缩 2. 退缩，畏缩 3.(美俚)精神病学家

shrinkage [ˈʃriŋkidʒ] *n*. 1. 收缩；皱缩；缩水 2. 减少；低落 3. 收缩量 4.【物】缩讼 4.(牲畜在运输途中或肉类在加工过程中的)重量损耗

shrivel [ˈʃrivl](shrivel(l)ed; shrivel(l)ing) *vi*. & *vt*. 1.(使)皱缩；(使)枯萎 2.(使)束手无策；(使)变得无用 (使)失效

shroud [ʃraud] *n*. 1. 裹尸布；寿衣 2. 遮蔽物；幕；罩 3.【机】护罩；管套 4.(水车的)侧板 4.[~s]【船】(桅)的左右支索 5.(降落伞的)吊伞索 — *vt*. 1. 给…覆盖裹尸布 2. 覆盖；掩蔽

shrub [ʃrʌb] *n*. 灌木

shrubbery [ˈʃrʌbəri] *n*.[总称]灌木；灌木丛

shrubby [ˈʃrʌbi] *adj*. 灌木状的；多灌木的，灌木丛生的

shrug [ʃrʌg](shrugged; shrugging) *vt*. & *vi*.(为表示冷漠、无奈、蔑视、不满等)耸(肩) — *n*. 1. 耸肩 2.(女式)短套领衫；带袖短披肩

shrunk [ʃrʌŋk] shrink 的过去式和过去分词

shrunken [ˈʃrʌŋkən] shrink 的过去分词 — *adj*. 皱缩的；缩小的

shuck [ʃʌk] *n*. 1. 壳；荚；外皮 2. 牡蛎壳；蛤蜊壳 3.(口)[~s]无价值的东西 — *vt*. 1. 剥…的壳(或荚、外皮) 2. 剥去脱去 3. 抛弃；摆脱 — *vi*. 剥去；脱掉

shudder [ˈʃʌdə] *vi*. 震颤，战栗，发抖 — *n*. 震颤，战栗，抖动

shuffle [ˈʃʌfl] *vi*. 1. 拖着(脚)走(=站或坐时)把(脚)在地上滑来滑去；跳(曳步舞) 2. 搅乱；弄混；洗(牌)；把…移来移去 3. 推开；推诿 4. 笨拙地穿衣(或脱去)(衣服等) — *vt*. 1. 拖着脚走(along)；跳曳步舞 2. 狡猾地摆脱(或混入) 3. 蒙混；推诿；搪塞 4. 洗牌 5. 马虎地做(through)；笨拙地穿(或脱) — *n*. 1. 曳行，曳步；曳步舞 2. 杂乱的一堆，一团糟 3. 改组；混合；搅乱 4. 蒙混；推诿 5. 洗牌；洗牌的轮值

shuffleboard [ˈʃʌflbɔ:d] *n*.(常在甲板上玩的)打圆盘游戏

shun [ʃʌn](shunned; shunning) *vt*. 避免；

回避；躲开

shunt [ʃʌnt] *vt.* 1. 使(火车)转轨 2.【电】装分路器于；使分路，使分流 3. 改变(谈话等)的路子 4. 把(人)撇在一边；推延／搁置(计划等) — *vi.* 1. 转向一边；靠边；(火车)调轨，调车 2. 来回运行，往返 — *n.* 1.【主英】(铁道的)转轨器 2.(火车的)调轨，调车 3.【电】分路(器)，分流(器)

shut [ʃʌt] (shut; shutting) *vt.* 1. 关上，闭上，关闭 2. 折拢，扣拢 3. 封闭 4. 把…关住；禁闭 5.(暂时或永久地)使停止营业；停止开政 6. 轧住；夹进 — *vi.* 关上一片 1. 关上，闭上 2. 合拢；折拢 3. 封闭 4.(金属的)焊缝 — *adj.* 关闭的；闩住的；合拢的)封闭的 ‖ ~ **down** *n.* (工厂、车间等的)停工，关闭(常指临时性的)；(机器的)停车 ‖ ~ **out** *n.* 1. 闭厂，停业(资方要挟工人的一种手段)；被关在外面的人 2.(比赛中)不让对方得分；一方得零分的比赛；(桥牌赛中的)关煞叫

shutter [ʃʌtə] *n.* 1. 关闭者 2. 窗板，百叶窗，活动遮板 3.(照相机的)快门 4.(风琴等的)闭气器，闸门 5.【美俚】安眠药片 — *vt.* 1. 为…装窗板(或快门等) 2. 用窗板关闭；关上…的窗板(或快门等) ‖ ~ **-bug** *n.* 摄影爱好者，摄影迷

shuttle [ʃʌtl] *n.* 1.(织机的)梭；缝纫机的)滑梭 2. 穿梭般的来回；短程穿梭运输(线)【空】航天飞机 5. 羽毛球 — *vt. & vi.* 1.(使)穿梭般来回移动 2. 短程穿梭般输送 ‖ ~ **bombing** 往返轰炸，穿梭轰炸 ‖ ~ **race**[体]迎面接力赛

shuttlecock [ʃʌtlkɔk] *n.* 1. 羽毛球；板羽球；板羽球戏 2. 争论之点，争端 3. 动摇的人，犹豫的人 4. 被环境(或情感)

摆弄的人 — *vt.* 往返递送；把…揿来抛去(或打来打去) — *vi.* 来回走动

shy [ʃai] (shier 或 shyer, shiest 或 shyest) *adj.* 1. 易受惊的；胆怯的 2. 害羞的；怕羞的，怕陌生的 3. 迟疑的，有戒心的；退缩的(*of*) 4. 隐蔽的；幽僻的；晦涩的，费解的 5. 胆小的，易受惊不良的 6.〈俚〉不足的，缺乏的(*of*, *on*) 7.〈俚〉(纸牌戏中)欠赌注的 8.(酒吧、赌场等)声名狼藉 — *vi.* 1.(马等)惊退，惊逸 2. 厌恶(*from*) 3. 避开，畏缩(*away*, *off*) — *n.* (马等的)惊退，惊逸 ‖ ~ **ly** *adv.* ‖ ~ **ness** *n.*

shyster [ʃaistə] *n.* 〈美俚〉好许的人；不择手段的人(尤指政客等)；讼棍；讼棍

Si [化]元素硅(silicon)的符号

si [si:] *n.*【音】七个唱名之一(在固定唱名法中相当于音名B)

Siam [saiæm, saiˈæm] *n.* 暹罗(现称Thailand 泰国)[东南亚国家]

Siamese [saiəˈmi:z] *adj.* 1. 暹罗的；暹罗人的；暹罗语的 2. 非常相似的 3.[s-]【建】(管道)二重联接的 — *n.* 暹罗人(即泰国人)；暹罗语 ‖ ~ **cat**[动]暹罗猫 ‖ ~ **twins** [医] 1. 暹罗孪生子，联体双胎 2.〈喻〉如胶似漆的两人

Siberia [saiˈbiəriə] *n.* 西伯利亚[俄罗斯一地区]

sibilant [ˈsibilənt] *adj.* 1. 作咝咝声的 2.【语】发咝音的 — *n.* 1. 咝咝声 2.【语】咝音 ‖ **sibilance** *n.*

sibling [ˈsibliŋ] *n.* 1. 兄弟；姊妹；同胞 2.【动】[植]同胞；姊妹株；姊妹株

sibyl [ˈsibil] *n.* 1.(古希腊，罗马的)女预言家 2. 女巫；女算命者

sic [sik] (sicced 或 sicked; siccing 或 sicking) *vt.* 驱使(狗等)去攻击(或骚扰)；促使(某人)去做(或追赶等)(*on*, *on to*)

sic [sik] *adv.*〈拉〉原文如此(用在括号

中,表示前面所引的文字虽有错误或疑问,却是原文)

Sicily ['sisili] *n.* 西西里(岛)[意大利南部] **Si·cilian** *n.* 西西里人;西西里语 *adj.* 西西里的;西西里人的

sick [sik] *adj.* **1.** 有病的,患病的;病人的 **2.** (英)[只作表语]恶心的,要呕吐的 **3.** (口)不愉快的;懊丧的(at、about) **4.** (口)厌倦的,发腻的;厌恶的(of) **5.** 渴望的,想望的(for) **6.** 有病容、苍白的;没有生气的(月经)行经的(比赛等中)大大落后的 **7.** (精神或道德上)不健全的,败坏的 **8.** (思想上或感情上)混乱的,病态的 **9.** (船只)需要修理的,有毛病的 **10.** (土壤)不宜某种作物的;受微生物侵害的 **11.** (葡萄酒)走味的;(铸铁等)脆的,易碎的 — *vt.* (口)呕吐(up) — *n.* **1.** (英口)呕吐物 **2.** [the ~][总称]病人 ‖ **~-bed** *n.* 病床;卧病 / **~ benefit** 病假津贴 / **~ flag** (检疫站或船的)(黄色)检疫旗 / **~ headache** 偏头痛;呕吐性头痛 / **~ leave 1.** 病假 **2.** (雇员等可照拿工资的)每年病假天数;病假工资

sicken ['sikən] *vt.* 使生病;使作呕;使厌倦;使厌恶 — *vi.* **1.** 生病;(英)初步显出症状 **2.** 恶心,作呕;厌倦;厌恶

sickle ['sikl] *n.* **1.** 镰刀 **2.** [S~](狮子座中由 6 颗星组成的)镰形星群

sickly ['sikli] *adj.* **1.** 有病的;多病的 **2.** 因疾病而产生的;病态的;苍白的 **3.** 易引起疾病的,有碍健康的;引起病态流行的 **4.** 好似有病的;弱的,无力的;阴沉的 **5.** 令人作呕的;使人厌恶的 — *adv.* 病态地 — *vt.* 使现病容(over)

sickness ['siknis] *n.* **1.** 疾病 **2.** 恶心,呕吐

side [said] *n.* **1.** 边;旁边;面;侧面 **2.** (纸、布等两面中的)一面;(一个)方面 **3.** 胁;(身体的)侧边 **4.** (动物从脊骨一分两半的)半边躯体;肋侧 **5.** (敌对的)一派,一方;(英)(比赛的)队 **6.** 家系,血统 **7.** [常用以构成复合词]坡;山坡;岸 **8.**【船】舷侧 **9.** (英语)傲慢,自大;架子 **10.** (美)一段台词;供一名角色用的一页台词 **11.** (英)(台球戏)侧旋 — *adj.* **1.** 边的;旁边的;侧面的 **2.** 从侧面来的;向一侧的 **3.** 枝节的;次要的;附带的 — *vt.* **1.** 同意;支持;站在…的一边 **2.** 收拾,掴开,放平 **3.** 给…装上侧面;给…钉上斜叠板 **4.** 刨平(木料等)的侧面 — *vi.* 赞助;站在一边(with) ‖ **~long** *adv. & adj.* 横(的);斜(的);侧面地(的);向旁边的(的)— *adv.* 斜着;斜向一边地 — *adv.* 自一边地,从一边向前地 *adj.* 横斜的;斜向一边的 / **~wise** *adv. & adj.* ~ways 的 ‖ **~-arm** *adj. & adv.*【体】(由)体侧的 / **~ arms** 随身武器;佩剑;佩刀 / **~board** *n.* **1.** 餐具柜 **2.** (俚)[~s] 连鬓胡子,络腮胡子 / **~car** *n.* **1.** (附于机器脚踏车旁的)单轮侧车,边车 **2.** 赛德卡鸡尾酒 **3.** (爱尔兰流行的)轻便二轮马车 / **~ effect** (药物等的)副作用 / **~ horse**【体】鞍马 / **~-light** *n.* **1.** 侧光;边灯,侧灯;[~s]【海】舷灯 **2.** 边窗;(对问题等的)偶然启示;间接说明;侧面情况 **3.** (口)杂闻 / **~line** (英)[~s](海员用语)眼睛 / **~-line** *n.* **1.** 旁线;横线;侧道 **2.** (主货外)副营业 **3.** 副职,兼职;副业 **4.** [~s](球场等的)界线;(供替补队员等坐的)场外区 **5.** 局外人的观点,旁观者的看法 *vt.* 使退出比赛场地 / **~-slip** *vi.* 横滑,侧滑;(汽车)打滑 — *n.* (飞机等的)横向滑动 **2.**【空】侧滑,机翼侧滑,沿横轴方向的运动 **3.** 嫩枝;枝条;(喻)私生

子 4. 舞台侧边操作布景的地方 /'~-
step n. 1.〈拳击中为躲避打击而向旁
边〉横跨的一步 2.〈侧面的〉台阶；梯
级；马车两边的踏步 vt.〈拳击等时〉横
跨一步躲避（打击）；〈喻〉回避（问题
等）；逃避（责任等）vi. 躲避打击；回避
问题；逃避责任 /'~ track n. 1.〔铁路
等〕侧线，旁轨 2.〈可能降入的〉次要地
位 vt. 1. 将（火车）转入侧线 2. 转移
（某人）的目标；转变〈话题〉；使降到次
要地位；搁议（提案等）；拖延 /'~ walk
n.〈美〉人行道 /'~way n. 小路；旁路
adv. & adj.〈向，从〉一边〈或一侧〉
（的）（= ～ ways）/ ～ winder ['said-
waində] n. 1. 侧击，横击 2.〔动〕〈产于
美国西南部的〉角响尾蛇；〔S〕〈美国
的〉〈空对空〉响尾蛇导弹 3.〈美俚〉
动辄打架的大汉；保镖；花钱雇用的
打手

siding ['saidiŋ] n. 1.〔铁路的〕侧线，旁轨
（= sidetrack）2.〔建〕壁板，墙板 3.〔船〕
〈船材的〉边宽 4.〈古〉偏袒；党同伐异

sidle ['saidl] vt. & vi.〈使〉侧身而行〈尤
指羞怯地或鬼鬼祟祟地〉— n. 侧身而
行

siege [si:dʒ] n. 1. 包围；围攻；围困；围
城；围攻期间 2. 再三的努力 3.〈口〉
〈病等的〉长期折磨；〈灾难等的〉不断
袭击 — vt. 围攻；围困

sienna [si'enə] n.〈富铁的〉黄土〈用作颜料〉
2. 赭色

sierra [si'eərə] n.〔地〕锯齿山脊

Sierra Leone [si'eərə li'əun] 塞拉利昂〔西
非国家〕

siesta [si'estə] n.〈在气候炎热国家中的〉
午睡，午休

sieve [siv] n. 1.〈细〉筛；格筛；滤网 2.
嘴快的人，不能守秘密的人 3.〈美俚〉防
守极不严密的球队 — vt. 筛分；滤

sift [sift] vt. 1. 筛；筛分；过滤 2. 撒，撒
布〈糖等〉3. 细查；详审 4. 选拔；精选；
挑选 — vi. 1. 筛；被筛下；〈似通过
筛具般地〉落下，通过（through, into）3.
细查，探究 4. 选拔；精选 ‖ n. 1.
家庭用的筛具；〔面粉厂的〕筛机 2. 筛
者 3. 细查者

sigh [sai] n. 1. 叹气，叹息；叹息声 2.
〈风，树等的〉啸声；鸣声 — vi. 1. 叹
气，叹息，悲叹 2. 渴望；思慕（for）3.
〈风，树等〉呼啸；悲鸣 — vt. 1. 叹息地
说（out, forth）2. 叹息着痛度（光阴等）
（away）

sight [sait] n. 1. 视力；视觉 2. 见，瞥见
3. 视域，眼界 4. 视界；阅读 5. 见解；
意见，看法 6. 情景；奇观；〔常 ～〕名
胜，风景 7.〈口〉滑稽可笑的模样，糟糕
的样子 8. 瞄准；观测；瞄准器；观测器
9.〔常～s〕目标 10.〈口〉很多，大
量 — vt. 1.〈初次〉看见 2.〈用观测器〉
观测；〈用瞄准器〉瞄准 3. 调整（枪，炮
等）的瞄准器；装瞄准器于（枪，炮等）
— vi. 1. 瞄准 2.〈向某一方向〉仔细
看；察看 — adj. 1. 单凭〈或要求〉当场
认识〈或理解〉的；事先无准备的，即席
的 2. 画见票即付的，即期的 ‖ /'~-
seer n. 观光者，游客 /'~singing n. 视
唱〈事先无准备地看谱即唱〉

sightless ['saitlis] adj. 1. 盲的，无视力的
2.〈诗〉看不见的

sign [sain] n. 1. 符号；记号 2. 招牌；标
记，指示牌 3. 征兆；迹象；〔医〕征，体征
4.〔数〕符号 5. 示意动作 6.〔天〕宫 7.〔宗〕〈表示神
的意志的〉神迹，奇迹 — vt. 1. 签名；
署（名）；签字于（信、文件等）2. 以手势
〈或其他动作〉示意 3. 在⋯上做记号；
雇用 4.〈天主教徒等〉对⋯划十字 5.
给〈街道等〉加路标 — vi. 1. 签名 2

以动作示意 ‖ `~-board` *n.* 招牌；广告牌 / `~post` *n.* 1.(十字路口等的)路标 2. 迹象；征兆；标志

signal ['signəl] *n.* 1. 信号；暗号 2. 近因；导火线(for) 3. 传递信息的工具；信号机，信号器 — *adj.* 1. 作为信号的 2. 显著的；非凡的 —(signal(l)ed; signal(l)ing) *vt.* 1. 用信号发出(或报告)；标志 2. 用信号通知(或表示) — *vi.* 发信号；打信号 ‖ `~(l)er` *n.* 信号员，通信兵；信号装置 / `~ly` *adv.* 非凡地；突出地 / `~man` *n.* 信号员，通信兵

signalize, signalise ['signəlaiz] *vt.* 1. 使显得突出；标志 2. 点出；突出地表明 (概念等) 3. 用信号通知(或表示) 4. 设置交通信号灯于(道路交叉口等)

signatory ['signətəri] *n.* (协议、条约等的)签署者；签约国 — *adj.* 签署的；签约的

signature ['signətʃə] *n.* 1. 签名；署名 2. (一项广播节目开始或结束时的)信号调，信号曲(亦作 ~ tune) 3. (药方上的)用法说明 4. [印]书帖(印好后依页码次序可折成一叠的书页)；贴码(印在书帖自下部指示装订顺序的标记) 5. [音]调号；拍号 6. (旧时认为表明医疗用途的)药效外形特征(或特性)(如心脏形的叶子被认为可用于治疗心脏疾病)

signet ['signit] *n.* 1. 图章；私章；[the ~](旧时英格兰、苏格兰间的)玉玺 2.(用图章盖的)印；印记 — *vt.* 盖章于；加印证实

significance [sig'nifikəns] *n.* 1. 意义；意味，重要性；重大

significant [sig'nifikənt] *adj.* 1. 有意义的；意味深长的 2. 表示...的(of) 3. 重要的，意义重大的 4. 不可忽略的

值得注意的；[统] 显著的，有效的 ‖ `~ly adv.`

signify ['signifai] *vt.* 1. 表示，表明；意味 2. 预示 — *vi.* 1. 要紧，有重要性 2.〈美俚〉冒充内行 ‖ `signifi`cation *n.*

Sikh [si:k] *n. & adj.* 锡克教教徒(的) ‖ `~ism n.` 锡克教

silage ['sailidʒ] *n.* 青贮饲料 — *vt.* 青贮

silence ['sailəns] *n.* 1. 沉默，默不作声 2. 静默；默念 3. 无声，寂静 4. 湮没，忘却 5. 未提到；(作家等的)不创作，无声息 6. 无音信；无联系 — *vt.* 1. 使沉默；使哑口无言；使安静 2. 消灭(噪声) 3. 压制(意见等) 4. 打哑(敌人火力) — *int.* 安静！别作声！

silent ['sailənt] *adj.* 1. 沉默的，不作声的；寡言的 2. 寂静无声的 3. 未说出的，未明言的 4. 未记载的，未作记述的 5. 静止的，不活动的；不参加具体经营的 6. 无声的；无对话的；[语]不发音的 ‖ `~ly adv.`

silhouette [silu:'et] *n.* 1. 侧面影像，黑色轮廓像，剪影 2. 轮廓 — *vt.* 把...画成侧面影像(或黑色轮廓像)；使现出轮廓(on, against)

silica ['silikə] *n.* [矿] 硅石，二氧化硅

silicate ['silikit] *n.* [化] 硅酸盐

silicon ['silikən] *n.* [化] 硅 ‖ Silicon Valley 硅谷(即旧金山东南的圣克拉拉谷，美国微电子工业集中地)

silk [silk] *n.* 1. 蚕丝，丝，丝织品；绸 2.[~s] 绸衣；〈美〉(骑师、杂技演员等穿的)绸衣服 3.〈英〉(王室法律顾问穿的)绸袍；(英口)王室法律顾问 4. 丝状物；蜘蛛丝；[美] 玉蜀黍缨 5. 降落伞 — *adj.* 1. 丝的；丝织的 2. 似丝的(一如丝) 4.[美] 玉蜀黍)抽穗丝，吐丝的 ‖ `~worm n.` 蚕

silken ['silkən] *adj.* 1.〈古〉〈诗〉丝制的

2. 穿铜衣的 **3.** 丝一样的；柔软的；光润的 **4.** 圆滑的；讨好的 **5.** 温柔的；柔和的 **6.** 风雅的

silky ['silki] *adj.* **1.** 丝的 **2.** 丝一样的；柔滑的 **3.** 有光泽的 **4.** 奉承讨好的 **4.** 有细毛(或羽、鳞)的

sill [sil] *n.* **1.** [建]基石；底木 **2.** (门、船坞、船闸等的)槛；窗台 **3.** [地]岩床；海底山脊 **4.** [机](车体)底框架 **5.** [矿]底梁；巷道支架

silly ['sili] *adj.* **1.** 傻的，憨的；愚蠢的；糊涂的 **2.** 无聊的故事，失去知觉的 **3.** [口]眼花的，失去知觉的 **4.** 〈古〉无助的；弱的 **5.** 朴素的；乡村风味的 — *n.* [口]傻瓜，呆子

silo ['sailəu] [复]silos) *n.* **1.** 青贮窖(青贮饲料的圆柱塔)；简仓 **2.** (导弹)发射井 **3.** 青贮饲料

silt [silt] *n.* **1.** 淤泥 **2.** (河边等地的)淤泥沉积处 — *vi.* & *vt.* (使)淤塞(up)

silvan ['silvən] *adj.* **1.** 森林中的；住在森林中的；在森林中发现的 **2.** 树木多的 **3.** 农村的，田园的 — *n.* **1.** 住在森林中的人 **2.** 森林之神

silver ['silvə] *n.* **1.** 银 **2.** (作为商品或交换媒介的)银子；银币；钱；〈美俚〉(5 角以下的)零钱 **3.** 银器；银皿；镀银用具 **4.** 银白色 **5.**【摄】(摄影影像中的)银盐 — *adj.* **1.** 银的；银质的，银制的；含银的；产银的；镀银的 **2.** 白银似的(银白色的；有银白光泽的)(货币)银本位的 **4.** (声音)清越的 **5.** 雄辩的 **6.** 次于最好的；第二流的 **7.** 第二十五周年的；a ~ wedding anniversary 银婚纪念日 — *vi.* 镀银；使成银白色 — *vi.* 变成银白色 ‖ ~smith *n.* 银匠 /'~ware *n.* [总称]银器；银制品；银餐具

silvery ['silvəri] *adj.* **1.** 似银的；有银色光泽的 **2.** (声音)银铃般的，清脆的 **3.**

含银的；银制的

simian ['simiən] *adj.* (像)类人猿的；(像)猴的 — *n.* 类人猿；猴

similar ['similə] *adj.* 相似的，类似的(to) — *n.* 〈古〉相似的东西，类似物 ‖ ~ly *adv.*

similarity [,simi'læriti] *n.* **1.** 相似，类似 **2.** [similarities]类似点；类似物；相似事例

simile ['simili] *n.* 【语】直喻，明喻(例如：brave as a lion 像狮子一般勇敢；quick like lightning 闪电般迅速)

similitude [si'militju:d] *n.* 相像的(人)；类似(物)

simmer ['simə] *vi.* **1.** 煨；炖 **2.** (危机等)处于酝酿状态 **3.** 内心充满(with) — *vt.* (以文火)慢慢地煮 — *n.* 将沸未沸状态

Simon ['saimən] *n.* **1.** 西蒙(姓或男子名) **2.** 【宗】西门(耶稣十二使徒之一；又为十二使徒之首 Peter 的原名；又被迫帮助背负钉死耶稣十字架者；又十二使徒之首 Peter 曾寄宿其寓的硝皮匠)

simper ['simpə] *vi.* **1.** 傻笑；痴笑 **2.** 假笑 — *vi.* 傻笑；假笑 — *vt.* 傻笑着(或假笑着)说

simple ['simpl] *adj.* **1.** 简单的；简易的；简明的 **2.** 朴素的，简朴的；单纯的；直率的，坦率的 **3.** 头脑简单的；糊涂的；愚蠢的 **4.** 不折不扣的；绝对的，无条件的 **5.** (出身、地位)低微的；微不足道的 **6.** 结构单一的；初级的，原始的；~ forms of life 生物的初级形态 — *n.* **1.** 出身低微的人 **2.** 无知者；傻子 **3.** 〈英〉[~s]愚蠢的行为 **4.** 单一成分 **5.** 药草；(单味的)草药 ‖ ~-'hearted *adj.* 心地纯洁的，天真无邪的；真诚的 /'~-'minded *adj.* 纯朴的；头脑简单的；笨的

simpleton ['simpltən] *n.* 傻子，笨人；易受

骗者

simplicity [sim'plisəti] *n.* 1. 简单;简易;简明 2. 朴素;单纯;直率;率真;天真 3. 无知;愚蠢

simplify ['simplifai] *vt.* 1. 简化;精简;使单纯;使易做;使易懂 ‖ simpli'fication *n.*

simplistic [sim'plistik] *adj.* (被)过分简单化的 ‖ ~ally *adv.*

simply ['simpli] *adv.* 1. 简单地;简易地;简明地 2. 朴素地,简朴地 3. 坦白地;单纯地;直率地 4. 仅仅,只不过 5. 简直,完全

simulate ['simjuleit] *vt.* 1. 假装,冒充 2. 模仿,模拟 ‖ simu'lation *n.* / simulative *adj.*

simulator ['simjuleitə] *n.* 1. 假装者;模仿者 2. 模拟装置,模拟器

simulcast ['simʌlkɑːst, 'saimʌlkɑːst] (simulcast) *vt. & vi.* (无线电和电视)联播(节目) — *n.* (无线电和电视)的联播节目

simultaneous [ˌsiməl'teinjəs, ˌsaiməl'teinjəs] *adj.* 同时发生的;同时存在的;同时的,一齐的 ‖ simultaneity [ˌsiməltə'niːiti, ˌsaiməltə'niːiti] *n.* / ~ly *adv.* / ~ness *n.*

sin¹ [sin] *n.* 1. (宗教或道德上的)罪,罪孽,罪恶 2. (违犯礼节、习俗的)过失;失礼;不合常情的事 — (something) vi. 1. 犯罪;违犯教规 2. 犯过失 — vt. 1. 犯(罪) 2. 过罪恶生活而糟蹋掉(健康等)(away) ‖ sinner *n.* 罪人

sin² [sain] 【数】正弦(sine)的符号

since [sins] *conj.* 1. 从…以来;…以后 2. 因为;既然;鉴于 — *prep.* 从…以来,自从…以后 — *adv.* 1. [与完成时态连用]从那时以后;后来 2. 以前(= ago)

sincere [sin'siə] *adj.* 1. (人)真诚的;笃实

的;诚恳的;直率的 2. (感情、行为)真挚的;表里一致的 3. 不掺假的;纯净的

sincerely [sin'siəli] *adv.* 真诚地;诚恳地;真挚地

sincerity [sin'serəti] *n.* 1. 真诚;诚意;真挚 2. 真实

sine [sain] *n.* 【数】正弦

sinecure ['sainikjuə] *n.* 1. 挂名职务;闲职 2. (教会中不担任教化工作的)领干薪职务

sinew ['sinjuː] *n.* 1. 【解】腱 2. [~s]肌肉,筋肉 3. 体力,气力;精力 4. [常~s]主要支柱,砥柱;资源 — *vt.* 似腱般连结 2. 支持;加强

sinewy ['sinjui] *adj.* 1. 多腱的;腱质的;腱(般)的 2. 强壮的;坚韧的;肌肉发达的 3. 精力充沛的;强有力的;结实的

sinful ['sinful] *adj.* 1. 罪孽深重的;有罪的 2. 邪恶的,不道德的 ‖ ~ness *n.*

sing [siŋ] (过去式 sang [sæŋ] 或 sung [sʌŋ],过去分词 sung) *vi.* 1. 唱;演唱 2. (鸟等)啼,鸣,唱 3. (水壶、风、小河、蜂等)作响,发出嗖嗖声(或嘤嘤声等);(耳)鸣 4. 欢乐 5. 作诗;用诗歌赞美;歌颂(of) 6. (美俚)(充当密探)告密 — *vt.* 1. 唱;演唱 2. 吟咏;歌颂 3. 唱着使 — *n.* 1. 嗖嗖声;嘤嘤声 2. (美口)合唱;合唱会

sing. *abbr.* singular

Singapore [ˌsiŋgə'pɔː] *n.* 1. 新加坡[东南亚国家] 2. 新加坡(市)[新加坡首都]

singe [sindʒ] *vt.* 1. 把…微微烧焦;把…烤焦;损伤 2. 燎去(宰好的动物)的毛;【纺】烧…作烧毛(或烧茸)处理 — *vi.* 烧焦,烤焦 — *n.* 烧焦;轻微(或浅表)焦痕

singer ['siŋə] *n.* 1. 歌唱家;歌手 2. 诗人

3. 鸣禽

single ['siŋgl] *adj.* 1. 单一的；单个的 2. 个别的 3. 独身的；孤独的 4. 单人的 5. 一对一的 6. 专一的；单纯的；真诚的 7. 独一无二的，无比的 8.〈英〉(啤酒等)淡的 9.【植】单瓣的 — *n.* 1. 单一个；(美理)独自生活的人；单人演出的节目，独脚戏 2. (网球等的)单打 3. (棒球的)一垒打 4. 单程票 5.〔常~s〕单股头的线 6. 单瓣花 — *vt.* 选出；选拔 (*out*) — *vi.* 1. (棒球赛中)作一垒打 2. (马)单步行进 ‖ **singly** *adv.* ‖ '~-**breasted** *adj.* 单排钮扣的 / '~-'**handed** *adj.* 1. 单独的，独力的 2. 单枪匹马的 2. 独手的；只用一只手的 *adv.* 单独地；独力地；单枪匹马地 / '~-'**seater** *n.* 单座车，单座飞机

singleton ['siŋgltən] *n.* 1. 单张(指一手牌中唯一的一张某一花色的牌) 2. 独特的东西；独生子

singsong ['siŋsɔŋ] *n.* 1. 即席演唱会；(朋友们凑在一起的)歌咏会 2. 单调的节奏 3. 节奏单调的歌(或诗) — *adj.* 节奏单调的 — *vt. & vi.* 节奏单调地唱(或说、诵)

singular ['siŋgjulə] *adj.* 1. 单一的，独个的 2. 非凡的，杰出的；独一无二的 3. 异常的；奇异的 4. 持异议的 5.【语】单数的 — *n.* 【语】单数形式 ‖ -**ity** [,siŋgju'lærəti] *n.* / -**ly** *adv.* / -**ness** *n.*

sinister ['sinistə] *adj.* 1. 不吉祥的，不祥的 2. 阴险的；邪恶的；凶恶的 3. 不幸的；导致灾难的 4. 左首的，左边的；在盾章左半边的

sink [siŋk] (过去式 **sank** [sæŋk] 或 **sunk** [sʌŋk], 过去分词 **sunk** 或 **sunken** ['sʌŋkən]) *vi.* 1. (船等)下沉；沉没 2. (日、月)落，没去 3. (面颊、眼睛)凹陷 4. (水面)低落；(地面)陷落；斜下去；

下 4. (头、目光等)下垂 5. (声音、火、风、价格等)降低；减弱(在视野中)消失 6. 堕落；衰微；衰弱；消沉 7. 渗透；深入；沁入 — *vt.* 1. 使下沉；使沉没；使陷入；把……插入 2. 使下垂 3. 挖掘；刻，雕 4. 降低(声音、身价、地位等)；(河等)变浅 5. 投(资)；因投资而损失(资财)；偿还(债务) 6. 抑制(激情、骄傲等)；隐蔽(证据、身份等) 7. 不分歧、自身利益等)；把……放在一边 7. 使沉没，搞垮 — *n.* 1. 阴沟；污水坑 2. (厨房内洗菜、碟等的)洗涤槽 3.(喻)巢，窟，藏垢纳污的场所 4.【地】落水洞，灰岩坑 5. (飞机等的)垂直下降速度 6. (美理)海洋 ‖ **~ing fund** 偿债基金

sinker ['siŋkə] *n.* 1. 引起下沉(或沉没)的人(或物) 2. 凿井工 3. 雕刻者；制模工 3. (渔网等的)铅锤；测深锤 4. (棒球赛中的)下坠球

Sino- *comb. form* 表示"中国(的)"

sinuous ['sinjuəs] *adj.* 1. 蜿蜒的，弯曲的；起伏的 2. 曲折的；错综复杂的 3. 动作柔软的 4. 不正直的；弯弯曲曲的 5.【植】(叶子)具深波状边缘的 ‖ ~**ly** *adv.* / ~**ness** *n.*

sinus ['sainəs] (〔复〕**sinus**(**es**)) *n.* 1. 湾，穴 2.【植】弯缺 3.【解】窦 4.【医】瘘(管) 5.【动】(软体动物的)弯；(腕足类的)中槽，凹

sip [sip] (**sipped**; **sipping**) *vi.* 啜饮 — *vt.* 1. 呷，啜 2. 从……中呷吸 — *n.* 1. 呷，啜 2. 一呷之量

siphon ['saifən] *n.* 1. 虹吸；虹吸管 2. 苏打水瓶(亦作~ bottle) 3.【动】呼吸管；(昆虫的)管形口器 4. (蚊幼虫的)管形突；(头足类的)体管；(软体动物的)水管；(软体、棘皮动物的)虹管 4.【建】存水弯 — *vi.* 通过虹吸管 — *vt.* 1. 用虹

吸管吸出(或输送) **2.** 吮吸(民脂民膏等)(*off*)

sipid ['sipid] *adj.* 有风味的；有趣味的

sir [强 sə:;弱 sə] *n.* **1.** 先生，阁下(通常对不相识的男子、上级、长辈或从事某一职务的尊称) **2.** [S-]…爵士(用在姓名或名字前面，但不可用在姓前) **3.**〈谑〉老兄；"先生"(对被申斥者、孩子等的呵责) — *vt.* 称…为先生

sire ['saiə] *n.* **1.**〈古〉陛下 **2.** 父亲；男性祖先 **3.** 雄性亲畜，公畜；种马 **4.** 创始人；作者 — *vt.* **1.** 做…的父亲；(尤指公畜)生殖 **2.** 创始；创作

siren ['saiərin] *n.* **1.** [S-]【希神】塞壬(一个人首半鸟的女海妖，常以美妙歌声诱惑经过的航海者而使航船触礁受灭) **2.** 歌声动人的女歌手及迷人的女人 **3.** 汽笛；警报器 **5.**【动】鳗螈 — *adj.* 诱惑迷人的 — *vi.*(警车、救火车等)响着警报器开道前进

sirloin ['sə:lɔin] *n.* 牛的上腰部肉，牛里脊肉

sirup ['sirəp] *n.* = syrup

sis [sis] *n.*〈口〉= sister

sisal ['saisəl, 'sisəl] *n.*【植】波罗麻；波罗麻纤维

sister ['sistə] *n.* **1.** 姐姐；姐；妹妹 **2.** 同父异母(或同母异父)姐妹(= half-sister) **3.** 姑；婶；嫂；弟媳 **4.** [常 S-](天主教)修女；(基督教)女教友 **5.** 亲如手足的女子；女同事；女友 **6.**〈英〉护士长；护士 **7.** 相同类型的东西 — ~s ships(按同一设计图纸建造的)姐妹船 **8.** 同雌雄性动物 **9.**〈俚〉(对陌生女子的直接称呼)妹妹、大姐 — vt. 像对姐妹般地对待 ‖ ~hood *n.* **1.** 姐妹身份；姐妹关系 **2.** 妇女会；妇女的宗教团体(= sisterhood) ‖ ~ly *adj.* 姐妹的；姐妹般的 ‖ '~-in-law *n.*([复] ~s-in-law)姑；姨；嫂；弟媳

sit [sit] (sat[sæt];sitting) *vi.* **1.** 坐；就座 **2.** 坐落；占地位，占位置 **3.**(鸟等)栖息不动；(鸡等)伏窝，孵卵 **4.**(被画像或被照相时)摆好姿势；做模特儿 **5.** 占议席；当代表 **6.**(议会等)开会；(法院)开庭 **7.** 参加考试(*for*) **8.**(衣服等)合身；适合 **9.**(风从某方向)吹(*in*) **10.** 临时替人照看(*with*) **11.** 搁置不用 — *vt.* **1.** 使坐；使就座 **2.** 骑 **3.** 可供…坐 — sitting *n.* **1.**(人)坐着等候的一段时间 **2.**(衣服的)合身 ‖ '~-down *n.* **1.** 坐下(休息) **2.** 静坐罢工(亦作 ~-down strike) / '~-in *n.* **1.**(室内)静坐抗议；(室内)占座抗议 **2.**(室内)静坐罢工

site [sait] *n.* **1.**(建造房屋等的)地点；地基 **2.**(事故等的)现场 **3.** 遗址 — *vt.* 定(工厂等)的地点

sitter ['sitə] *n.* **1.** 被画像(或拍照)的人 **2.** 孵窝鸡 **3.** 易被射中的动物；容易做的工作 **4.** 临时替人照看孩子的人 **5.**〈美俚〉屁股 ‖ '~-'in *n.*([复]~ s-in)〈英〉临时替人照看孩子的人

sitting ['sitiŋ] *n.* **1.** 坐着；一次连续坐着的时间：finish reading a book at one 一坐着一口气读完一本书 / In this dining hall 1,500 people can be served at one 这个大饭厅可供 1500 人就餐 **2.**(议会等的)开会；(法院的)开庭；会期；庭期 **3.** 坐着供人画像 **4.** 孵卵期；(一次的)孵卵数 **5.**(教堂、剧院等的)一个坐位 — *adj.* **1.** 坐着的；就座的；坐着做的 **2.** 在立法(或司法)机构中占席位的；在任期内的 **3.** 孵卵中的 **4.** 易命中的；(猎物等)易打的 **5.**〈英〉租用着房屋(或土地)的 ‖ ~room 起居室

situate ['sitjueit] *adj.*〈古〉= ~d — *vt.* **1.** 使位于 **2.** 使处于 ‖ ~d *adj.* **1.** 位于

…的，坐落在…的：The school is ~d in the suburbs. 这所学校位于郊外。2. 处于某种境地的

situation [ˌsitjuˈeiʃən] *n.* 1.〈建筑物等的〉位置；地点：地位；职位；〈尤指仆役等的〉工作；~ wanted ads（报上的）找寻职业广告，待聘广告 3. 处境，境遇；困境，危局；【心】情绪 4. 形势；情况；局面 5.〈戏剧、小说的〉紧张场面

SIW *abbr.* self-inflicted wound(s)〈尤指为逃避兵役等〉自伤

six [siks] *num.* 六；六个（人或物）；第六（卷、章、页等）2. 六个一组（尤指六人的球队或划船队）3. 六汽缸发动机（或汽车）3.〔~es〕一磅共六支的蜡烛 4.6 岁 5.6 点钟‖~ fold *adj. & adv.* 六倍的 ‖ ~ pence [ˈsikspəns] *n.*6 便士；〈英国旧时的〉6 便士硬币

sixern [ˈsiksən] *n.* 苏格兰six桨渔船

sixteen [ˈsiksˈtiːn] *num.* 十六；十六个（人或物）；第十六（卷、章、页等）— *n.* 1. 十六个一组 2.16 岁 3.16 点钟（即下午 4 点）‖ ~th *num.* 1. 第十六（个）2. 十六分之一的（个）3.【音】十六分音符 2.（月的）第十六日

sixth [siksθ] *num.* 1. 第六（个）2. 六分之一的（个）— The ~ s 六分之五 — *n.* 1.【音】六度音程；六度音程；第六音 2.〈英〉六年级 3.（月的）第六日

sixtieth [ˈsikstiiθ] *num.* 1. 第六十（个）2. 六十分之一的（个）

sixty [ˈsiksti] *num.* 六十；六十个（人或物）；第六十（页等）— *n.* 1.60 岁 2.〔sixties〕（世纪的）60 年代 3.〔sixties〕60 到 69 岁的时期

sizable [ˈsaizəbl] *adj.* 相当大的；大的

size¹ [saiz] *n.* 1. 大小，尺寸；体积；规模；身材 2.（服装等的）尺码 3. 巨大 4. 身价；声望；才干 5. 真相，实情；真面目

6. 量珠尺（或筛）7.〈古〉（饮食的）定量 — *vt.* 1. 依大小排列（或分类）；依一定的尺寸制造 2. 估计（物）的大小；〈口〉估量（人）；估计（情况）（up）— *vi.*（在大小、质量等方面）可比拟，不相上下（up to, up with）— *adj.* = sizable

size² [saiz] *n.*（使纸张光润、布匹坚挺的）涂料；浆料 — *vt.* 给…上涂料；给…上浆

sizeabie [ˈsaizəbl] *adj.* = sizable

sizzle [ˈsizl] *vi.* 1.（油炸食物或水滴于热铁时）发嘶嘶声；作咝咝声；a sizzling hot day 大热天 2. 充满忿怒；充满怨恨 — *vt.*（嘶嘶地）烧灼 — *n.* 嘶嘶声；咝咝声

skate [skeit] *n.* 1.（滑）冰鞋（= ice ~）；四轮滚冰鞋（= roller ~）2.〔俚〕溜冰鞋 — *vi.* 1. 滑冰，溜冰；go skating 去滑（或溜）冰 2. 滑过；掠过（over）；~ over a delicate subject 对一个微妙的问题一笔（或一语）带过 3.〈美俚〉躲债；溜掉 ‖ ~ board *n.* 滑板（一种用以在地面上滑行的运动器具）

skein [skein] *n.*（纱、线、丝等的）（一）束；（一）绞 2.（野禽的）（一）群 3. 一团槽；纠缠在一起的东西 — *vt.* 把（线等）绕成绞

skeletal [ˈskelitl] *adj.* 骨骼的；骸骨的

skeleton [ˈskelitn] *n.* 1. 骨骼；骸骸 2.（建筑物等的）残骸；【建】骨架 3. 骨瘦如柴的人（或动物）4.（文艺作品或计划）梗概；轮廓 5. 基干，骨干 6.【植】叶脉 7. 不可外扬的丑事 — *adj.* 1. 骨骼的；骨骼般的 2. 轮廓的；概略的 3. 基干的

skeptic [ˈskeptik] *n.*〈美〉= sceptic

skeptical [ˈskeptikəl] *adj.*〈美〉= sceptical

sketch [sketʃ] *n.* 1. 略图；草图；粗样；初稿 2. 速写，素描 3. 概略，梗概 4. 短篇

作品,小品(如日间录、特写、随笔) 5.(滑稽)短剧;独幕剧;(常指用钢琴演奏的)短曲 6. 言行古怪可笑的人 — **vt. & vi.** 1.(给…)绘略图;(给…)写生;速写 2. 草拟;概略地叙述(out)

sketchy ['sketʃi] **adj.** 1. 粗略的;大概的;略图似的 2. 肤浅的;不完全的 ‖ **sketchily adv.**

skew [skju:] **adj.** 1. 斜的;歪的;偏的 2.【数】偏斜的 — **n.** 1. 歪斜;扭曲 2.【建】斜砌石;斜交 — **vi.** 1. 歪斜;扭曲 2.〈口〉斜视(at) — **vt.** 1. 使歪斜;使偏 2. 曲解;歪曲

skewer ['skjuə] **n.** 1.(烤肉用的)串肉扦,烤肉叉 2. 扦状物,叉状物 3.〈谑〉剑;刀 — **vt.**(用串肉扦等)串住

ski [ski:] ([复]ski(s)) **n.** 1. 滑雪板 — **vi.** 滑雪 ‖ ~**er n.**

skid [skid] **n.** 1. 刹车,制轮楔 2.(使重物易于滑动的)滑动垫木,滑行器 3.(支承重物的)垫木;低平台(有时带有轮子)4.[~s](船舶)的护舷木 5.【空】起落橇,滑橇 6.(车辆在结冰的道路上或高速行驶急转弯时所引起的)车轮的打滑,溜滑 7.(喻)[~s]下坡路 — (skidded; skidding) **vi.** 1.(用制轮闸)刹住;使减速 2.(用滑动垫木)滚滑,使键滑;堆…于垫木(或平台)上 3. 使(车轮等)打滑 — **vi.** 1.(汽车等)打滑;侧滑 2.(飞机在转弯时)外滑 3.(营业额等)急剧下降

skiff [skif] **n.** 尖头方尾小划艇;小快艇

skiing ['ski:iŋ] **n.** 滑雪术;滑雪运动

skill [skil] **n.** 1. 技能;技巧;技艺 2. 熟练;巧妙 3.[单复同][总称]熟练工人 ‖ ~**ed adj.** 1. 熟练的;有技能的 2. 需要技能的

skillet ['skilit] **n.** 1.〈英〉长柄有脚小烧锅 2.〈美〉长柄平底煎锅

skil(l)ful ['skilful] **adj.** 1. 灵巧的;熟练的 2. 制作精巧的 ‖ ~**ly adv.**

skim [skim] (skimmed; skimming) **vt.** 1. 撇去(液体的)漂浮物;从液体表面撇去(奶油、浮渣等);从…中提取精华;从…中取得最多获得的东西 2. 掠过;使掠过,使擦过 3. 在盖上一层薄膜(或薄层) 4. 略读,快读,浮光掠影地看 — **vi.** 1. 掠过,擦过(over, along, through) 2. 浏览,略读(over, through) 3. 结上薄的覆盖层;涂上最后一道灰泥(或漆等) — **n.** 1. 脱脂乳;撇去上层被撇去了的东西 2. 掠过,擦过 3. 表面的薄覆盖层 — **adj.** 1. 表面一层被撇去了的 2. 脱脂乳制成的 ‖ ~ **milk, skimmed milk 脱脂牛奶**

skimmer ['skimə] **n.** 1. 撇沫器,有眼勺子,网杓 2. 撇沫的人;泛泛地阅读的人 3. 摩托驳艇 4.【机】刮路机,铲刨器 5.【鸟】剪嘴鸥 6. 平顶宽边草帽

skimp [skimp] **vt.**〈口〉1. 少给,克扣;对…吝啬 2. 马马虎虎地做 — **vi.** 吝啬,省俭一点,缩减;缺乏的,不足的

skimpy ['skimpi] **adj.**〈口〉1. 缺乏的,不足的 2. 吝啬的,小气的;马虎的 ‖ **skimpily adv. / skimpiness n.**

skin [skin] **n.** 1. 皮,皮肤 2. 兽皮;毛皮;皮革;生皮 3.(植物、果实等的)外皮;壳 4.(盛液体用的)皮囊 5.(液体表面结的)薄层;奶皮 6. 外壳(层);船壳(板);(飞机的)蒙皮;汽车的外壳 7.〈口〉生命 8.〈美俚〉吝啬鬼 9.〈美俚〉骗子 10.〈美俚〉1元;1元纸币 11.〈谑〉马伏人 12.[复~s]〈口〉(爵士乐或流行音乐中用的)鼓 13.〈俚〉(卷大麻烟的)卷烟纸 — (skinned; skinning) **vt.** 1. 剥(动物)的皮;剥去(身体某一部位)的皮;〈口〉使脱去紧身衣 2. 使蒙上皮;植皮使愈合 3.〈俚〉诈骗,骗取…的钱财 4.

〈美俚〉(比赛中)打败(对方) **5.** 申斥；非难 **6.** 驱赶(牲口等) — *vi.* **1.** 被gar
上皮;(伤口)愈合(*over*);长出新皮 **2.** 蜕皮 **3.** 攀、爬(*up*, *down*) **4.** 勉强穿过(*by*, *through*) **5.** 〈俚〉逃走 **6.** 〈美俚〉(考试、背诵等时)作弊 ‖ **~ful** *n.* 一皮囊之量;足以吃饱喝足的量;足以使人喝醉的量 ‖ **skinner** *n.* **1.** 剥兽皮者 **2.** 兽皮加工者;皮货商 **3.** 驱赶牲口队的人 **4.** 骗子 ‖ **'~'deep** *adj.* 表面的;(肤浅的／ **'~-dive** *vi.* 裸潜，赤身潜水／ **'~-flint** *n.* 吝啬的人，小气鬼／ **'~-grafting** 〈医〉植皮，皮肤移植／ **'~-popping** *n.* 皮下注射麻醉毒品／ **'~'tight** *adj.* 紧身衣

skinny ['skini] *adj.* **1.** 皮的;似皮的;膜状的 **2.** 皮包骨的,极瘦的 **3.** (体积)小的;(数量)少的;(质量)低劣的;缺乏意义的 **4.** 〈美俚〉吝啬的

skip[1] [skip] (skipped;skipping) *vi.* **1.** 跳跃 **2.** 跳绳;急速改变 **3.** (看书、写字等时)略过;遗漏(*over*) **4.** 作短期旅行 **5.** 〈口〉匆匆离开;悄悄离开 **6.** 【机】跳火 **7.** (学校里)跳级 — *vt.* **1.** 跳过;跳读;略过;遗漏 **2.** 不参加(会议等) **3.** 〈口〉匆匆离开;悄悄离开(某地) **4.** 〈口〉略过 **5.** (学校里)使跳(级) — the second grade 跳二年级 — *n.* **1.** 轻跳;边走边跳 **2.** 漏看;跳过;略过;漏看的东西 **3.** 略过的东西 **4.** 跳跃(进位);"空白"指令 ‖ **'~-bomb** *vt.* & *vi.*【军】(对…)进行跳弹轰炸(一种超低空轰炸)

skip[2] [skip] *n.* **1.** (足球、板球等球队的)领队 **2.** = skipper[2] —(skipped;skipping) *vt.* 当…的领队

skipper[1] ['skipə] *n.* **1.** 跳跃者;跳绳者;略读者 **2.** 【动】叩头虫;跳蝇;肉蛆 **3.** 【鱼】竹刀鱼

skipper[2] ['skipə] *n.* **1.** (小商船、渔船或游艇的)船长 **2.** (飞机的)机长;正驾驶员

skirmish ['skə:miʃ] *n.* **1.**【军】小规模战斗 **2.** 小冲突;小争论 — *vi.* **1.** 进行小规模战斗;发生小冲突(或小争论) **2.** 侦察,搜索 ‖ **~er** *n.*【军】散兵

skirt [skə:t] *n.* **1.** 女裙,衬裙 **2.** (衣服的)裾,下摆 **3.** [常~s]边缘;郊区,郊外 **4.** (马鞍的)垂边 **5.**〈俚〉女人;姑娘 — *vt.* **1.** 位于…的边缘;环绕…的四周 **2.** 给…装边;给…装防护罩 **3.** 避开(危险等)；回避(问题等) — *vi.* 位于边缘;沿边走(*along*, *around*)

skit [skit] *n.* **1.** 讽刺话 **2.** 讽刺短文;幽默故事 **3.** 滑稽短剧

skittish ['skitiʃ] *adj.* **1.** (马等)易惊的 **2.** (尤指女人)轻佻的 **3.** 三心二意的;不可靠的 **4.** 羞怯的;胆小的

skittle ['skitl] *n.* **1.** [~s]【用作单】九柱戏,撞柱戏 **2.** 九柱戏的木柱 — *vt.* 【板球赛中】使(击球员)连续出局(*out*) — *vi.* 做九柱戏游戏

Skopje ['skɔpje], **Skopje** ['skɔpjie] *n.* 斯科普里[马其顿首都]

skulduggery [skʌl'dʌgəri] *n.*〈口〉阴谋诡计;欺骗,诈骗

skulk [skʌlk] *vi.* 躲藏;偷偷摸摸(或提心吊胆)地走;〈主英〉躲避责任,溜。 ‖ **~er** *n.*

skull [skʌl] *n.* **1.** 颅骨,脑壳,头盖 **2.**〈冶〉渣壳,炉瘤 **3.**〈美俚〉杰出的学生(或工人、演奏者等) ‖ **'~-cap** *n.* **1.** 室内便帽 **2.** 头顶骨,天灵盖 **3.**【植】黄芩

skunk [skʌŋk] *n.* **1.**【动】臭鼬 **2.** 臭鼬的毛皮 **3.** 〈口〉卑鄙的人;可恶的人 — *vt.*〈美俚〉**1.** (比赛等)彻底击败 **2.** 使(对手)得零分 **3.** 欺赖;赖…的债

sky [skai] *n.* **1.** 天,天空 **2.** [the ~]苍天,

上苍,天堂,天国 3.[常 skies]天气;气候 —(skied 或 skyed) *vt.* 1. 将(板球)击向空中 2. 将(画)挂在高处 — *vi.* (物价等)高涨,猛涨 ‖‵~ward *adj.* ‖‵~dive *vi.* 延缓张伞跳伞 /‵~diver *n.* 延缓张伞跳伞运动员 /‵~diving *n.* 延缓张伞跳伞(运动) /‵~jack *vt.* 空中劫持(飞机) /‵~lab *n.* 空间实验室 /‵~lark *n.* 云雀 *vi.* 嬉戏;开玩笑;爬船架娱乐 /‵~light *n.* 1. 天上的光 2.(屋顶、船舱的)天窗 /‵~line *n.* 1. 地平线 2.(建筑物、山等)以天空为背景映出的轮廓 /‵~rocket *n.* 焰火;高空探测火箭 — *vi.* 1.(物价)猛涨 *vt.* 1. 使上升;使猛涨 2. 弹射;使一举而成 /‵~scraper *n.* 摩天楼 /‵~,trooper *n.* 伞兵 /‵~way *n.* 1.[空]航路 2. 高架道路 /‵~,writing *n.* 空中写字(指飞机放烟在空中形成文字或构成图案);空中文字(或图案等)

slab [slæb] *n.* 1. 厚板;厚片 2. 混凝土路面 3. 背板(锯木材成板时最外面的有皮的板块) —(slabbed; slabbing) *vt.* 1. 把…分成厚片,使成厚片 2. 去掉(木料)的背板 3. 用石板铺(路等) 4. 厚厚地涂

slack [slæk] *adj.* 1. 懒散的、懈怠的;疏忽的(在…上)2. 行动迟缓的,有气无力的,没精打采的 3. 松弛的,不紧的 4. 呆滞的;萧条的 5. 温的,微热的,未烘干的 6. 不坚定的;软弱的 7. 不完善的 8. 漏水的,透水的 9.(石灰)熟化的 10.[语](元音)松弛的 — *adv.* 1. 马虎地;松懈地;缓慢地;没精打采地,松弛地 2. 松懈地;松弛地;宽松地 — *n.* 1. 静止不动;停止流动 2.(绳、带、帆等的)松垂部分 3.[~s]宽松长裤 4. 淡季;萧条期 5.(诗歌跳舞中的)非重读音节 6.[口]闲散;休息时间 7. 水缓水域;(水流)

平缓 8. 闲置部分;短缺 — *vt.* 1. 马虎从事,松垮地做(工作等)2. 放松(绳索等)3. 使缓慢;使缓和 4. 使(石灰)熟化 — *vi.* 1. 松懈;怠惰;偷懒 2. 减低速度;减弱;减退(up)3.(绳索等)松弛 4.[口]休息;懒惰 5.(石灰)熟化 ‖~ *en n.* 懒惰的人;敷衍塞责的人;逃避责任的人;战时逃避兵役的人 /~ly *adv.* /~ness *n.*

slacken [′slækən] *vt.* 1. 放松;松懈 2. 使缓慢;放慢 — *vi.* 1.(绳索等)变松弛;松劲 2.(商业)呆滞 3.(风等)减弱;变缓慢

slag [slæg] *n.* 1. 矿渣;熔渣;炉渣 2. 火山渣 —(slagged; slagging) *vt. & vi.*(使)成渣状

slain [slein] slay 的过去分词

slake [sleik] *vt.* 1. 消除;平息;使缓和;满足 2. 熄灭;减弱(火焰)3. 使(石灰)熟化 *vi.* 1.〈古〉消除;平息;缓和 2.(石灰)熟化

slam[¹ [slæm] *vt.* 1. 使劲关,砰地关上(门等);砰地放下 2. 猛投;猛击 3.〈美口〉猛烈抨击;辱骂 — *vi.* 1. 发出砰的一声 2. 猛攻;使劲干 3.〈美口〉猛烈抨击;辱骂 — *n.* 1. 砰的一声 2. 猛击;撞击 3.〈美口〉猛烈的抨击

slam[² [slæm] *n.*(桥牌赛中)满贯 —(slammed; slamming) *vt.* 1. 打成满贯战胜(对方)2. 扑垮

slander [′sla:ndə] *n.* 诽谤,诋毁,造谣中伤;[律]口头诽谤(罪);a ~ on sb. 对某人的诽谤 — *vt.* 诽谤,诋毁,造谣中伤

slang [slæg] *n.* 1. 俚语 2. 行话(盗贼等的切口,黑话)— *vt.* 1.〈主英〉用粗话骂 2.〈英俚〉欺骗;诈取 — *vi.* 用粗话(或下流话)骂 ‖~y *adj.*

slant [slɑːnt] *vt.* 1. 使倾斜；使斜向；使歪 2.〈美〉有倾向性地报道(新闻等)；使(报道等)带上色彩 — *vi.* 1. 倾斜，歪斜；倾向(*towards*) 2.〈俚〉逃跑 — *n.* 1. 斜面；斜线；斜向；斜线号(即"/") 2.〈方〉挖苦，讥刺 3.〈口〉观点；态度；意见；(叙述等中的)倾向性；侧面立论;一瞥;斜视 5.〈俚〉机会 — *adj.* 倾斜的；歪斜的 ‖ ~ing *adj.* / ~ingly *adv.*

slantwise [ˈslɑːntwaiz] *adj. & adv.* 倾斜的(地)；歪斜的(地)

slap [slæp] (slapped; slapping) *vt.* 1.(用扁平的东西等)掴;拍;掌击;猛地关(门等) 2. 啪的一声放下；猛掷；漫不经心地扔 3. 任意涂；任意摔；任意摔巴掌；强加 4. 指责；口头攻击；侮辱 — *vi.* 1. 用手猛拍(或打) 2. 拍打— *n.* 1. 掴;掌击 2. 侮辱;拒绝;(对自尊心等的)伤害 3.(机件松动的)啪啪声 — *adv.*〈口〉1. 突然地;猛地 2. 恰好，正好 ‖ ~bang *adj. & adv.* = ~dash *adj. & adv.*〈口〉猛烈的(地);鲁莽的(地);粗心的(地);草率的(地) n. 1. 草率;鲁莽 2. 粗制滥造的东西 3. 打底子用的粗灰泥 *vt.* 1. 用粗灰泥涂(墙壁) 2. 草拟(计划等)

slash [slæʃ] *vt.* 1.(用刀、剑等)猛砍;乱砍;猛削;砍伤;割伤 2. 挥(剑、鞭等)；鞭打 3.(作为装饰)开长条开衩于(衣服) 4.(大幅度)削减，减低(工资等);减少(犯罪率等) 5.【军】砍(树)成鹿角 6. 严厉地批评— *vi.* 1. 乱砍;挥击(*at*) 2. 严厉地批评(*at*) — *n.* 1. 猛砍;乱砍;劈刺;挥击;砍痕;深的切痕 2.(服装上作装饰的)长条开衩 3.(大幅度的)削减，减低;减少 4.(树林砍伐后留下的)林中空地;(树木砍

伐后留下的)枝桠，废材

slat [slæt] *n.* 1.(木头、金属等的)条板;(固定百叶窗等的)板条，狭板;(椅的)梯级横木 2.〈俚〉[~s]屁股;肋骨—(slatted; slatting) *vt.* 用条板制造;给…装条板

S. lat. *abbr.* south latitude 南纬

slate¹ [sleit] *n.* 1. 板岩;石板瓦;(建筑用的)石板 2.(书写用的)石板 3. 石板色，石蓝色;石板色 4.(操行等的)记录;have a clean ~历史清白 5.〈美〉候选人(提名)名单;内定用人名单— *adj.* 1. 暗蓝灰色的,石板色的 2. 板岩的;石板的— *vt.* 1. 用石板瓦盖屋顶(屋顶等);给…铺石板 2.〈美〉提名…为候选人;内定…任某职 ‖ ~club〈英〉(成员每月缴少量钱的)互助会 / ~ pencil 石笔

slate² [sleit] *vt.*〈口〉1.(尤指评论中对作品或作者)严厉地批评 2. 责骂 3. 痛打;鞭打;拳打

slattern [ˈslætən] *n.* 1. 懒妇;邋遢女人 2. 妓女— *adj.* 不整洁的;邋遢的— *vt.* 浪费掉;消磨掉(*away*)

slaughter [ˈslɔːtə] *n.* 1. 屠宰 2. 屠杀，杀戮— *vt.* 1. 屠宰(牛羊等) 2. 屠杀，杀戮 3. 亏本出售(证券) ‖ ~house *n.* 屠宰场

Slav [slɑːv, slæv] *n.* 斯拉夫人— *adj.* 斯拉夫人的;斯拉夫语的

slave [sleiv] *n.* 1. 奴隶 2. 奴隶般工作的人,苦工 3. 摆脱不了某种习惯(或影响)的人 4.〈古〉卑鄙的人 5.【动】奴(隶)蚁 6.【机】从动装置— *vi.* 1. 作苦工;奴隶般工作;做牛马 2. 贩卖奴隶— *vt.* 1.〈古〉奴役

slaver¹ [ˈsleivə] *n.* 1. 奴隶贩子;贩运奴隶的船 2. 诱编女子为娼者

slaver² [ˈslævə] *vi.* 1. 垂涎,淌口水 2. 谄

媚, 奉承 — *vt.* 潲口水弄湿; 流涎弄脏 (衣服等) — *n.* 1. 唾液, 涎沫, 口水 2. 谄媚奉承

slavery ['sleivəri] *n.* 1. 奴隶身分 2. 奴隶制度; 占有奴隶, 蓄奴 3. 苦役; 奴隶般的劳动 4. (对某种习惯或影响的) 屈服

Slavic ['slævik, 'slɑ:vik] *adj.* 斯拉夫人的; 斯拉夫语的 — *n.* 斯拉夫语

slavish ['sleiviʃ] *adj.* 1. 奴隶 (般) 的; 奴性的, 卑屈的 2. 缺乏独创性的; 盲从的 3. 〈古〉压迫的; 专横的 ‖ ~**ly** *adv.*

slaw [slɔ:] *n.* 凉拌卷心菜丝

slay [slei] (slew [slu:], slain [slein]) *vt.* 1. 杀死, 杀害 2. 〈美俚〉使 (异性) 爱慕自己; 给...以强烈的好印象, 使赞同; 使禁不住大笑 — *vi.* 杀死; 引起死亡 ‖ ~**er** *n.*

SLBM *abbr.* 1. submarine-launched ballistic missile 潜艇发射的弹道导弹 2. sea-launched ballistic missile 海上发射的弹道导弹 3. satellite-launched ballistic missile 人造卫星发射的弹道导弹

sleazy ['sli:zi, 'sleizi] *adj.* 1. 劣质的; 用劣质材料粗制滥造的; 低劣的 ‖ **sleazily** *adv.* / **sleaziness** *n.*

sled [sled] *n.* 1. (滑雪用的) 小橇; (运载用的) 雪橇 2. 摘棉机 — (sledded; sledding) *vt.* 1. 用雪橇运送 2. 用摘棉机摘: *sledded* cotton 机摘棉 — *vi.* 乘雪橇

sledge¹ [sledʒ] *n.* (装运货物或旅客的) 雪橇; 雪车 — *vt. & vi.* 乘雪橇; 用雪橇运送

sledge² [sledʒ] *n., vt. & vi.* = sledgehammer

sledgehammer ['sledʒˌhæmə] *n.* 1. (锻工等用的) 大锤 2. 极具分量的事物 — *vt. & vi.* 1. (像) 用大锤敲打; 猛击 2. 锤炼 — *adj.* (像) 用大锤敲打的; 猛烈的; 重大的; 致命的

sleek [sli:k] *adj.* 1. (毛发等) 光滑的; 柔滑的 2. (动物) 壮健的, 养得好的; (植物) 茁壮的 3. 圆滑的; 滑头的 2. 花言巧语的 4. 雅致的; 时髦的; 阔气的; 豪华的 — *vt.* 1. 使光滑; 使柔滑发亮; 掩饰, 掩盖 (*over*) — *vi.* 1. 打扮整洁; 打扮漂亮 2. 滑动

sleep [sli:p] *n.* 1. 睡眠 2. 昏迷状态; 麻木; 长眠, 死亡 3. 静寂 4. (动物的) 冬眠, 蛰伏; (植物叶子、花瓣的) 夜间闭合 5. 一夜 6. 一天的旅程 — (slept [slept]) *vi.* 1. 睡, 睡眠, 睡着 2. (像睡着似的) 静止; 长眠, 故理葬着 3. 过夜, 住宿 (*at, in*) 4. 发生性关系 (*with*) 5. (动物) 冬眠, 蛰伏; (植物叶子、花瓣) 夜间闭合 — *vt.* 1. 睡 2. 以睡眠消除 (或度过) (*off, away*) 3. 供...住宿 ‖ ~ **'-in** *adj.* 住宿在工作地点的 *n.* 静卧示威 / **Sleeping Beauty** 睡美人 (法国童话中因着魔而昏睡 100 年的公主) / ~**ing car,** ~**ing carriage** 卧车 / ~**ing draught** 安眠药水 / ~**ing sickness** (采采蝇引起的) 昏睡病; 昏睡性脑炎 / ~**'-out** 不住宿在工作地点的 *n.* 露宿郊游 / ~**'-walker** *n.* 梦游者

sleeper ['sli:pə] *n.* 1. 睡眠者 2. (铁路) 枕木; [建] 小搁栅; [船] 地板下构架 3. 卧车; 卧铺 4. 眼看要输而意外获胜的赛马; 暂时未受赏识的商品 5. (在耳上作了记号但) 尚未打烙印的小牛 6. [~s] 小孩睡衣裤

sleepless ['sli:plis] *adj.* 1. 失眠的; 不眠的, 醒着的 2. 警觉的; 戒备不懈的 3. 〈诗〉无休止的

sleepy ['sli:pi] *adj.* 1. 想睡的, 瞌睡的; 嗜眠的; 困乏的 2. 懒散的 3. 寂静的; 不活跃的 4. 使瞌睡的; 催眠的 5. (水果因开始腐烂而) 干枯无味的 ‖ **sleepily** *adv.*

sleet [sli:t] *n.* **1.** 冻雨;雨夹雪;雨夹雹 **2.** 雨淞(冷雨落在物体表面面成的冰状冻结物) — *vi.* 下冰雨;下雨夹雪;下雨夹雹

sleeve [sliːv] *n.* **1.** 袖子;袖套 **2.** 唱片套;书套 **3.**【气】风(向)袋 **4.**【机】套筒 — *vt.* 给…装袖子;给…装套筒 ‖ ~less *adj.* **1.** 无袖的 **2.** 徒然的,无益的;a ~less errand 徒劳的差使 ‖ ~target(飞机拖曳着作射靶的)筒形拖靶

sleigh [slei] *n.*(尤指用马拉的)雪车;雪橇 — *vi.* 驾雪车;乘雪橇 — *vt.* 用雪车运输(货物)

sleight [slait] *n.* **1.** 奸计;诡计 **2.** 熟练,灵巧 ‖ ~ of hand **1.**(变戏法等中)手法的熟练 **2.** 戏法,魔术;花招

slender ['slendə] *adj.* **1.** 细长的;苗条的;纤弱的 **2.** 微薄的;微少的;不足的 **3.**(声音)微弱的,不洪亮的 ‖ ~ly *adv.* / ~ness *n.*

slenderize ['slendəraiz] *vt.* 使(更)苗条;使显得(更)苗条 — *vi.* 变得苗条

slept [slept] sleep 的过去式和过去分词

sleuth [sluːθ] *n.* **1.** 警犬;〈口〉侦探 — *vi.* 做侦探 ‖ '~hound *n.* = sleuth

slew [slu:] slay 的过去式

slice [slais] *n.* **1.** 薄片;切片;片 **2.** 部分;份 **3.** 菜刀;锅铲;火铲 **4.**【建】泥刀;【印】油墨铲刀 **5.**【体】削球,斜切打 **6.**【无】限幅,削波 — *vt.* **1.** 把…切成薄片 **2.** 切下;切开;割去 (off, away, from) **3.** 把…分成部分 **4.**〈口〉用锅铲(或铲子)铲;(用泥刀等)铺 **5.**【体】削(球),使(球)侧旋;斜切(球) — *vi.* **1.** 切上去打 **2.** 打削球;打斜切球

slick [slik] *adj.* **1.** 光滑的,滑溜溜的 **2.** 熟练的;灵巧的 **3.** 聪明的,机警的 **4.**〈口〉圆滑的;花言巧语的;狡猾的;a ~ alibi 圆滑的托词 **5.**〈口〉(作品等)华而

不实的 **6.** 陈腐的,老一套的;平凡的,无独创性的 **7.**〈俚〉极好的;第一流的 **8.**〈俚〉讨人喜欢的;吸引人的 — *adv.* **1.** 滑溜溜地;自如地;灵活地 **2.** 熟练地;巧妙地;聪明地 **3.** 径直地;恰好地 — *vt.* **1.** 使光滑,使滑溜 **2.**〈口〉使整洁,使漂亮(up) — *vi.*〈口〉使漂亮(up) — *n.* **1.**(有一层油膜的)平滑的水面;油膜 **2.** 修光工具;平滑器 **3.**〈口〉用上等有光纸印刷的通俗杂志 ‖ ~ly *adv.* / ~ness *n.*

slicker ['slikə] *n.* **1.**〈美〉(宽大的)油布雨衣 **2.**〈美口〉骗子 **3.**〈美〉(外表整洁或举止矫揉造作的)城里人 **4.**(刮皮革或铸模用的)刮刀

slide [slaid] (过去式 slid [slid],过去分词 slid 或 slidden ['slidn]) *vi.* **1.** 滑;滑动 **2.** 滑落 **3.** 不知不觉地陷入(into) **4.** 悄悄地走 **5.** 流;流逝 — *vt.* **1.** 使滑动 **2.** 把…悄悄地放入(in, into) — *n.* **1.** 滑(动) **2.** 滑道;滑面;滑坡;滑梯 **3.** 雪崩;山崩;土崩 **4.** 滑动的部分 **5.**【机】滑板;滑座 **6.** 幻灯片 **7.**(显微镜用)承物玻璃片 **8.**【地】崩塌 **9.**〈口〉使头发整齐的)条状发夹 ‖ ~ rule 计算尺

sliding ['slaidiŋ] *adj.* **1.** 可变的;浮动的;可调整的 **2.** 滑动的;a ~ door 拉门,滑门

slight [slait] *adj.* **1.** 细长的;苗条的;瘦小的 **2.** 脆弱的;不结实的 **3.** 轻微的;微小的;少量的 **4.** 极不重要的,不足道的 — *vt.* **1.** 轻视;藐视;怠慢;feel ~ed 感觉受到轻蔑 **2.** 玩忽 — *n.* 轻蔑;怠慢 ‖ ~ly *adv.* / ~ness *n.*

slily ['slaili] *adv.* = slyly

slim [slim] (slimmer, slimmest) *adj.* **1.** 细长的;苗条的;纤弱的 **2.** 微小的;稀少的;不充分的 **3.**〈方〉狡猾的 **4.** 低劣

的;无价值的 —(slimmed;slimming) vi.
(用运动、减食等)减轻体重而变苗条
— vt. 使变苗条 ‖ ~ly adv. / ~ness
n.

slime [slaim] n. 1. 软泥;粘泥 2. 粘质
物;(蜗牛、鱼等分泌的)粘液 3.【矿】
泥,煤泥 4.〈古〉沥青 — vt. 1. 用粘泥
(或粘液)涂抹 2. 去除(鱼等)的粘液
3. 把(矿石)研磨成矿泥 — vi. 1. 变
粘滑 2.〈英俚〉滑脱,用狡猾手段脱身
溜掉(through, away, past, out of)

slimy ['slaimi] adj. 1. 粘性的;粘滑的 2.
泥泞的;谄媚的;讨厌的;卑鄙的

sling [sliŋ] n. 1. 投石器;弹弓
(= ~shot) 2. 抛,投,掷 3. 弹索;索链;
吊带;(吊货)网兜;【海】一吊货,一关
4.【医】悬带 5.(枪的)背带 6.〈鞋后背
作带状的)露跟女鞋 — (slung [slʌŋ])
vt. 1.(用投石器或用力)抛,投,掷 2.
吊,吊起 ‖ ~shot n. 1. 弹弓 2.(车靠
中的)突前,加速超前 3.(驾驶员座在
后轮后方的)后座式赛车

slink [sliŋk] (slunk [slʌŋk]) vi. 鬼鬼祟祟
地走;溜走(off, away, by) — n. 鬼鬼
祟祟的人

slip[1] [slip] (slipped;slipping) vi. 1. 滑动;
滑行 2. 滑交;失足 3. 滑落,滑掉;松脱
4. 溜,溜走;悄悄走;(时间)不知不觉
地过去 5. 降低;犯错误;不经意讲出;
被遗忘 6.(健康等方面)变坏;下降 7.
匆忙地穿(或脱) 8.【空】侧滑 — vt. 1.
使滑动;使滑脱(或被扣) — 忽略 2.
摆脱;挣脱;闪开(拳击等) 4. 打开;放
掉(猎狗等);(编结中)滑漏;(动物)早
产 5. 匆忙地塞(钱等);把……塞给 6.
暗中塞(钱等) 7. 脱出;脱离 — n. 1.
滑动;滑交;失足;下降 2.
意外事故;不幸事件 3. 溜,溜走;不告
而别 4. 疏忽;错误 5.【船】滑台,滑道,

船台;两码头间的水区 6.【机】滑程;滑
率,滑动量;空转;转差 7.(牵狗等用
的)皮带;可突然松脱的结构 8.(儿童
的)外衣;围涎;有背带的女式长衬裙;
枕套 9.[~s]男子游泳裤 10.【地】滑
动;滑移;(岩层的)滑距 11.[~s]舞台
边门(换布景或演员出场前停留的地
方) 12.(板球)三柱门右侧守场员;防
守位置 13. 小比目鱼 14.【空】侧滑 15.
滑润性 — adj. 1. 滑动的;滑移的 2.
可拆卸的,活络的 ‖ ~ 有活络的;可立即
松脱的 ‖ ~cover n. 1. 家具套 2. 轮胎
套 2. 书的封套 / ~ knot n. 滑结,活结
/ ~shod adj. 1. 穿着塌跟鞋的;破烂的
2. 不整洁的;马虎的;潦草的

slip[2] [slip] n. 1. 接枝;插枝;后裔 2. 瘦
长的青年人 3. 长条;板条;纸条;【印】
活版毛条校样 4.(教室内有靠背的)条
凳 —(slipped;slipping) vt. 从(植物)取
接枝或插枝

slipper ['slipə] n. 1.[常~s]拖鞋;便鞋
2. 滑动的人(或物),(置于车轮下的)
制动蹄片 — vt. 用拖鞋打(孩子等)

slippery ['slipəri] adj. 1. 滑的,使人滑交
的;(问题等)要小心对待的 2. 易滑脱
的 3. 圆滑的,不老实的,不可靠的 4.
(地位等)不稳固的;(言语等)含糊的,
难以捉摸的

slit [slit] n. 狭长的切口;细长的裂口;裂
缝 —(slit;slitting) vt. 1. 切开;撕开;割
掉;切成长条 2. 使成狭缝 — vi. 纵
切;纵裂

slither ['sliðə] vi. 不稳地滑动;蜿蜒地滑
行 — vt. 使滑动;使滑行

sliver ['slivə] n. 1. 裂片;薄片;碎片 2.
(作鱼饵用的)小鱼片 3.【纺】条子,梳
条,棉条 — vt. 把……切成薄片;把……裂
成碎片 — vi. 分裂,切开

slobber ['slɔbə] vi. 1. 流涎,滴口水 2.(说

话等时)过度伤感;感情迸发 — vt. 1.
用涎弄湿(衣服等) 2. 口齿不清地说
(或唱) 3. 草率地做;搞坏(工作) —
n. 1. 涎,口水 2. 过分伤感的说话(或
接吻等);口齿不清的话;语无伦次的
话

sloe [sləu] n.【植】黑刺李

slog [slɔg] (slogged; slogging) vt. 猛击 —
vi. 1. 猛击 2. 用沉重的脚步走去;顽强
地行进(on) 3. 苦干,辛勤地工作
(away) — n. 1. 猛击 2. 跋涉 3. 苦干
‖ **slogger** n.

slogan ['sləugən] n. 1.（尤指苏格兰或爱
尔兰氏族的）战斗呐喊声 2. 呼喊声,
口号;标语 3. 简短而吸引人的广告语

sloop [slu:p] n. 单桅小帆船 ‖ ~ of war
轻巡洋舰;小军舰

slop [slɔp] n. 1.（宽松的）罩衣,外衣;工
作服 2.[~s]廉价成衣;卖给水手的物
品(如衣服、被褥等)

slop² [slɔp] n. 1. 泥浆;半融雪 2.[~s]
污水,脏水;（用作饲料的）厨房下脚 3.
[常~s]人体排泄物 4.（英）[~s]（尤指
供病人吃的）(半)流质食物(如粥等) 5.
[常~s]酒精含量很低的饮料;（不含
酒精的）饮料 6. 溅出的液体;溢出的
液体 7.（酿造过程中的）釜馏物 —
(slopped; slopping) vi. 1. 溅出;溢出
(over, out) 2. 在泥浆(或半融雪)中走
3. 超出界限,越出范围(over) 4. 感情
迸发;极度伤感(over) — vt. 1. 使(液
体)溅出(或泼出) 2. 溅污;弄脏 3. 使
等溢出地盛(或上)（菜等） 4. 喂馊地
吃;贪婪地喝 5. 用于脚眼(猪等)

slope [sləup] n. 1. 倾斜;坡度;斜度;
【数】斜率 2. 斜面;斜坡 3.【矿】斜井 —
vi. 1. 倾斜 2.（俚）逃走;离去(off);闲
荡(about) — vt. 1. 使倾斜;使有斜度
2. 捎(枪) — adj.（诗）[常用以构成复

合词]倾斜的

sloppy ['slɔpi] adj. 1.（泥潭、道路等）泥
泞的;多水潭的;易溅起泥浆的 2. 被
泥浆溅污的;满是污水的 3.（衣服）湿
质的;稀薄的 4.（口）草率的;粗心的;
邋遢的,不整洁的 5.（口）过于伤感的;
感情脆弱的 6. 喝醉的 ‖ **sloppily** adv. ‖
sloppiness n.

slosh [slɔʃ] n. 1. 泥泞 2. 溅泼声 — vt.
1. 溅(泥 2.（为清净而用)把…放在液体
中摇动(或搅动) 3.（英俚）击;打 —
vi. 1. 溅着泥水(或雪水)行进 2. 发出
溅泼声;发出液体的晃动声 ‖ ~ed
adj.（英俚）喝醉的

slot¹ [slɔt] n. 1. 狭孔,缝;槽;狭槽 2.
【空】翼缝 3. 狭通道;狭窄的地位 4.
(在组织、名单、程序单等中所占的)位
置;职位:a TV show in the six-o'clock
slot 一档安排在 6 点钟的一次电视节目 —
(slotted; slotting) vt. 开槽于 ‖ ~ machine
投币自动售货机;吃角子老虎（一种赌
具）/ ~ man 负责新闻编排的报纸副
主编

slot² [slɔt]（单复同）n. 1.（尤指鹿的）足
迹 2. 轨迹 —（slotted; slotting）vt. 跟踪

sloth [sləuθ] n. 1. 懒惰;懒散 2.【动】树
懒（南美洲等地产的一种哺乳动物,栖
于森林,行动缓慢）

slouch [slautʃ] n. 1. 没精打采的姿态;懒
散的样子 2.（帽边等的）耷拉 3. 萎靡
不振的人;笨拙的人 4.（口）[常与否定
词连用]无能的人 — vi. 1. 没精打采地
走走(或坐、站) 2.（帽子等）耷拉 —
vt. 使低垂

slough¹ [slau] n. 1. 泥沼;沼泽地;泥泞
的地方 2.（喻）泥坑;困境 3.（美）水坑;
沼泽;浅滩 — vt. 1. 使陷入泥沼;（喻）
使陷入泥坑,使沉沦 2.（美俚）逮捕;监
禁(up, in) — vi. 在泥浆中跋涉

slough² [slʌf] *n.* **1.** 蛇蜕；(动物身上)按时脱落的部分 **2.** 【医】坏死组织，腐肉，腐痂 **3.** 可丢弃的东西(指习惯、偏见、旧事物等) — *vi.* **1.** (蛇皮等)脱落 (蛇等蜕皮；(痂等)脱落，(标点等)脱掉 **2.** (岩石、河岸等)崩塌 — *vt.* **1.** 脱落(皮等) **2.** 抛弃，丢弃 (*off*)

Slovakia [sləu'vækiə] *n.* 斯洛伐克[欧洲中部国家]

sloven ['slʌvən] *n.* **1.** 邋遢人；不修边幅的人 **2.** (工作等)马马虎虎的人；懒散的人 — *adj.* **1.** = slovenly **2.** 未开垦的；未开发的

Slovenia [sləu'vi:niə] *n.* 斯洛文尼亚[欧洲东南部国家]

slovenly ['slʌvənli] *adj. & adv.* **1.** 邋遢的(地)；不整洁的(地)；不修边幅的(地) **2.** 懒散的(地)；马虎的(地)；潦草的(地)

slow [sləu] *adj.* **1.** 慢的，缓慢的 **2.** (在时间方面)慢了的；慢于…的，晚于…的 (*on*) **3.** 迟钝的；冷漠的，不活跃的 **4.** 不精采的；乏味的 **5.** 落后于时代的 **6.** (路面等)妨碍前进(或行动)的；使减低速度的 **7.** 作用缓慢的 **8.** (照相机镜头)孔径小的 — *adv.* 缓慢地；慢慢地(一般用在 go, run, speak, read, burn 或 how 等之后) — *vt.* 使慢下来；使(市场等)变得呆滞 (*up，down*) — *vi.* 慢下来(*up，down*) ‖ ～ly *adv.* / ～ness *n.* ‖ ～-coach *n.* 动作迟钝的人；慢性子的人；落后于时代的人 / ～-down *n.* 减速；减退工作 / ～-poke *n.* 〈美俚〉行动迟缓的人

sludge [slʌdʒ] *n.* 烂泥

slue [slu:] *vt. & vi.* (使)转向，扭转，(使)旋转 — *n.* 转向，扭转；旋转

slug¹ [slʌg] *n.* **1.** 【动】蛞蝓(俗称鼻涕虫)；蛞蝓型幼虫 **2.** 懒汉 — 〈古〉动作迟缓的动物(或车辆) — (slugged; slugging) *vi.* 〈古〉动作迟缓 **2.** 怠惰，偷懒

slug² [slʌg] *n.* **1.** (滑膛枪的)弹丸；子弹 **2.** 金属小块(待加工的)金属片状毛坯 **3.** (用以开动自动售货机的)代硬币的金属圆片；冒充的硬币 **5.** 【物】斯勒格，斯(质量单位) **5.** 【无】铁心；波导调配柱 **6.** 【印】铅字条；嵌片 — (slugged; slugging) *vt.* 插嵌片子

slug³ [slʌg] *n.* 〈美〉= slog — (slugged; slugging) *vt. & vi.* = slog

sluggard ['slʌgəd] *n.* 懒汉 — *adj.* 懒惰的

sluggish ['slʌgiʃ] *adj.* **1.** 懒惰的；懒散的；不大想动的 **2.** 缓慢的 **3.** 迟钝的 **4.** 呆滞的；萧条的 ‖ ～ly *adv.* / ～ness *n.*

sluice [slu:s] *n.* **1.** 水闸，闸门 **2.** (调节水位的)渠道，水槽，闸门沟 **3.** (被闸门拦住的)蓄水 **4.** (从闸门流出的)泄水 **5.** (淘洗金矿用的)流槽；(放流木材等用的)斜水槽 — *vt.* **1.** (开水闸)排泄 **2.** 放流(木材) **3.** (用水流)淘洗，冲洗 — *vi.* 奔泻，奔流 ‖ **sluicy** *adj.* 奔泻的 ‖ ～-way *n.* **1.** (有闸或无闸的)人工水道；泄水道 **2.** 流木槽道；洗矿槽

slum [slʌm] *n.* **1.** 贫民窟；贫民区；陋巷 **2.** 〈美俚〉(碰运气的竞技等中)不值钱的奖品；(摊子上出售的)整脚货 — (slummed; slumming) *vi.* 〈为猎奇或救济等〉访问贫民区

slumber ['slʌmbə] *n.* **1.** 睡眠；微睡 **2.** 沉睡状态；懒怠一种，闸门沟 **3.** 静止状态；蛰伏；潜伏 — *vt.* (用睡眠)消磨(时间)(*away*)

slump [slʌmp] *n.* **1.** 暴跌；下降；不景气 **2.** 衰退 — *vi.* **1.** (物价等)暴跌；(市场等)萧条；衰退 **2.** 陷入，掉入；颓然倒下 **3.** 消沉；萎靡

slung [slʌŋ] sling 的过去式和过去分词

slunk [slʌŋk] slink 的过去式和过去分词

slur [sləː] (slurred; slurring) *vt.* 1. 忽视,略过(*over*) 2. 含糊地发(音);含糊地发(词)的音;模糊不清地写 3. 匆忙地做(功课等) 4.[音]连唱(或奏);在…上标连线 5.[印]蹭污,使有重影 6. 诽谤,诋毁;玷污 7. 掩盖(罪行等) — *vi.* 1. 模糊不清地发音(或写) 2.[印]被蹭污,有重影 3.(英方)滑 4. 拖着脚走 — *n.* 1. 污点;污辱;毁谤,含糊的发音;潦草的字迹 3.[印]蹭污,重影 4.[音]连唱(或奏);连线

slush [slʌʃ] *n.* 1. 烂泥;淤泥 2. 半融雪(或冰);雪水 3.(尤指船上伏房的)废弃油脂 4.[机]抗蚀润滑油脂 5. 水泥砂浆;(造纸用的)液体纸浆 6. 油车 7.(书报、电影等中出现的)无聊的言情,废话 — *vt.* 1. 溅湿;溅污 2. 灌泥浆于…;涂油灰于…;用水泥砂浆补 3. 给…加润滑脂 — *vi.* 1.(在泥浆等中)跋涉 2. 发出溅泼声 ‖ ~**y** *adj.*

slut [slʌt] *n.* 1. 邋遢女人;懒妇 2. 荡妇;妓女 3.(谑)女郎;大胆孟浪的女子 4. 母狗

sly [slai] *adj.* 1. 狡猾的;狡诈的 2. 躲躲闪闪的;偷偷摸摸的;a ~ glance 偷偷的一瞥 3.(方)灵巧的;巧妙的 4. 淘气的;顽皮的 ‖ ~**ly** *adv.* / ~**ness** *n.*

Sm [化]元素钐(samarium)

smack¹ [smæk] *n.* 1. 滋味;风味 2. 少量,一点点 — *vi.* 微有(某)味;带有(某种)风味(*of*)

smack² [smæk] *vt.* 1.(用掌)拍击;拍;打 2. 使劈啪作响 3. 咂;出声地吻 — *vi.* 1. 咂嘴 2. 发出拍击声 — *n.* 1. 拍击(声);掌击(声);劈啪(声);劈啪响(声)2. 咂嘴(声);咂嘴的接吻 3. 猛吉 — *adv.* 1. 啪然作声地 2. 猛烈地;恰好

地,不偏不倚地

smack³ [smæk] *n.* 1.(尤指单桅的)小帆船 2.(设有养鱼舱的)小渔船

smack⁴ [smæk] *n.*(俚)海洛因,白面

small [smɔːl] *adj.* 1.(体积)小的;细小的;小号少的;小额的 2.(规模、价值、重要性、程度等)小型的;琐细的;微不足道的 3.(出身、地位)低微的 4. 小气的,吝啬的;气量狭隘的;卑劣的 5.(雨)细微的;(声音)细弱的;(酒等)淡的 — *adv.* 1. 些微地;细细地 2. 微弱地;轻轻地,小声地 3. 小型地,小规模地 4. 轻视地；think ~ of 轻视,瞧不起某人 — *n.* 1.(物体的)狭小部分 2.(口)[~s]小尺寸的东西;(送去洗的)小件衣服 3. [~s](牛津大学文学士三次学位考试的)第一次考试(即入学考试)‖ ~**ness** *n.* ‖ ~ **arms** 1. 轻兵器 2. 个人武器 /'~**pox** *n.* 天花

smart [smɑːt] *adj.* 1.(如针扎般)刺痛的;厉害的;剧烈的 2. 轻快的,敏捷的;活泼的 3. 巧妙的;灵巧的;伶俐的,机警的;精明的 4. 洒脱的,潇洒的;惊的,漂亮的;时髦的 5.(方)相当的,可观的 — *vi.* 1. 刺痛,扎疼;针扎似地作痛 2. 感痛苦;懊恼;伤心(*under, with, from*)3. 吃苦头;受罚(*for*) — *n.* 1. 刺痛;痛苦;懊恼 2. 要聪明(或时髦)的人 ‖ ~**ly** *adv.* 1. 轻快地 2. 厉害地;严厉地 3. 聪明地;精明地;机明地 4. 整齐地;精确地 5. 漂亮地;时髦地 6. 大大地 / ~**ness** *n.* ‖ ~ **aleck**, ~ **alec** [ˈælik](美俚)自作聪明的人,自以为样样懂的人 / ~ **bomb** 灵敏炸弹,激光制导炸弹 / ~ **set** [总称]最时髦的人士;最时髦阶层

smarten [ˈsmɑːtən] *vt. & vi.*(使)漂亮;打扮

smash [smæʃ] *vt.* 1. 打碎,打破;粉碎

击溃;击毁 3. 使(原子或原子核)发生裂变 4. 猛掷;挥(拳等) 5.(网球等运动中)猛叩(球) — vi. 1. 碎裂 2. 猛撞;猛冲;破产;瓦解;垮掉(up) 4. 叩球;杀球 — n. 1. 打碎;撞碎 2. 猛击;叩球;杀球 3. 器物破碎的声音;撞碎声 4. 破产;瓦解;垮掉 5.(压碎果子榨取的)果子露 6.(演出等的)大成功 — adv. 以霹隆一声 — adj. 出色的,非凡的 ‖ ~up n. 1.(汽车等的)猛撞;撞车事故 2. 崩溃;瓦解;垮掉;灾难

smatter ['smætə] n. 肤浅的知识 — vt. 1. 一知半解地谈论 2. 涉猎,肤浅地研究 — vi. 一知半解地谈论,瞎讲 ‖ ~ing n. 1. 略知,浅知 2. 少数;些许 — adj. 点滴的;肤浅的 / ~ingly adv.

smear [smiə] vt. 1. 涂;敷;抹 2. 弄脏 3. 诽谤;玷污 4. 涂去;抹去;使轮廓不清 5.〈美俚〉挫败;打垮;杀死 6.〈美俚〉糟蹋 — vi. 被弄脏 — n. 1. 污点;污迹 2. 涂抹物;(显微镜)涂片 3. 诽谤;污蔑

smell [smel] n. 1. 嗅觉 2. 气味 3. 臭味,难闻的气味 4. 嗅,闻 5. 气息;风味 — (smelt[smelt]或smelled) vt. 1. 嗅;闻到 2. 察觉;感觉到 3. 发出…的气味 — vi. 1. 有嗅觉;嗅(at) 2. 散发气味 有…的气味(of) 3. 发出臭气;令人作呕 ‖ ~ing salts 嗅盐(一种芳香碳酸铵合剂,用作苏醒剂)

smelt[1] [smelt]([复]smelt(s)) n.〖动〗胡瓜鱼

smelt[2] [smelt] vt. 熔炼;精炼 ‖ ~er 1. 熔铸工;熔炼者 2. 熔炉;冶炼厂;冶金厂

smile [smail] vi. 1. 微笑 2. 冷笑;讥笑(at) 3.(诗)(天地、景色等)开颜,呈喜色 — vt. 1. 以微笑表示 2. 微笑着使

… — n. 微笑;笑容;喜色

smirch [smə:tʃ] vt. 1. 弄脏 2. 玷污(名誉等) — n. 污迹;污点

smirk [smə:k] vi. & n. 傻笑;假笑

smite [smait](过去式 smote [smout]或〈古〉smit [smit],过去分词 smitten ['smitən]或 smote 或〈古〉smit) vt. 1. 重击 2. 击败;毁灭;惩罚 3.(疾病等)侵袭;袭击 4. 使极度不安;使痛苦;使神魂颠倒 — vi. 重击;打 — n.〈口〉1. 重击;打 2. 尝试

smith [smiθ] n. 1. 铁匠;锻工 2.[用以构成复合词](金属)工匠;制作者:a gold ~ 金匠 / a tune ~ 作曲者

smithereen [,smiðə'ri:n] vt. 把…击碎;把…炸成碎片 — n.[~s]碎片:smash sth. to(或 into)~s 将某物击碎

smithy ['smiði] n. 1. 铁匠工场;锻工车间 2. 铁匠;锻工

smitten ['smitən] smite 的过去分词

smock [smɔk] n. 1.(工作时保护衣服的)罩衫;工作服;(儿童的)罩衣 2.〈古〉女衬衫;无袖女上衣 — vt. 1. 给…穿上罩衫(或工作服) 2. 用正面刺绣针迹绣制

smog [smɔg] n. 1. 烟雾 2. 烟幕,屏障

smoke [smouk] n. 1. 烟雾;烟柱 2. 烟雾,烟云 3.(一次)抽烟;〈口〉抽的烟(如纸烟,雪茄等) 4. 虚无,乌有,昙花一现的东西 5. 模糊;暗晦;〈喻〉烟幕;假情报 6.〈俚〉大麻,大麻制品 7. 淡蓝色,烟色 8.(驱虫的)熏烟,烟熏剂 9.〈美〉〈贬〉黑人 10.〈美〉劣质酒 11.(棒球的)快投,快球 — vi. 1. 冒烟;冒寒气 2. 烟似地升起;(雾等)弥漫 3. 冒烟;(烟斗等)被抽吸 4. 飞速行进,一溜烟地行进 5.〈口〉受罚;受苦 6.〈美俚〉气得七窍生烟 — vt. 1. 熏脏,熏黑;把…煮得带烟味;用烟熏,熏制

（鱼、肉），用烟熏法驱（虫等）**2.** 抽（烟等）**3.** [~ oneself] 抽烟抽得…；~ self ill 抽烟抽得生病 **4.** 〈古〉察觉；怀疑 **5.** 〈古〉嘲笑；愚弄 ‖ ~ screen 烟幕：put up a ~ screen 放烟幕 / ~ stack *n.* （轮船、火车,工厂的）大烟囱

smoker ['sməukə] *n.* **1.** 吸烟者；（肉类等的）熏制工,a heavy ~ 烟瘾大的人 **2.** 冒烟的东西;施放烟幕的船只（或飞机）**3.** （火车上的）吸烟车厢 **4.** 抽烟聚会（男子非正式的社交集会）**5.** 〈美俚〉蒸汽火车头

smoking ['sməukiŋ] *n.* **1.** 冒烟；冒气 **2.** 吸烟 — *adv.* 冒着烟；冒着气

smoky ['sməuki] *adj.* **1.** 冒烟的；多烟的；烟雾弥漫的 **2.** 似烟的（烟状的；烟熏味的）**3.** 熏脏的；熏黑的 **4.** 烟灰色的

smolder ['sməuldə] *vi. & n.* = smoulder

smooth [smuːð] *adj.* **1.** 光滑的,平滑的；平坦的 **2.** 平静的；平稳的 **3.** （文章、文体等）流畅的；（诗歌等）节奏和谐悦耳的 **4.** （性情等）平和的；和蔼的 **5.** 圆滑的（迎合讨好的）；油腔滑调的 **6.** （液体、浆糊等）调匀的 **7.** （酒）温和的 **7.** 无毛的；无胡须的 **8.** 〈美俚〉绝妙的,刮刮叫的；吸引人的,有趣的 **9.** 【语】不送气的 — *vt.* **1.** 使光滑,使平滑；把…弄平；烫平 **2.** 使（文体、举止等）优雅；使（脸部表情）平和下来 **3.** 使（余年等）平安 **4.** 消除（障碍、困难、分歧等）（out, over, down, away）**5.** 掩饰（过失等）（over）— *vi.* **1.** 变光滑,变平滑 **2.** 变平静；变缓和（down）— *n.* **1.** 一片平地；草坪 **2.** 一泓静水 **3.** （东西的）平滑部分；（经历的）顺利方面 **4.** 弄平；摸平 **5.** 修光（或磨平）的工具（如刨等）— *adv.* = ~ ly ‖ ~ ly *adv.* / ~ ness *n.*

smoothbore ['smuːðbɔː] *adj.* （枪、炮）滑膛的 — *n.* 滑膛枪（或炮）

smote [sməut] smite 的过去式

smother ['smʌðə] *vt.* **1.** 使窒息；使透不过气来；把…闷死（用灰、黄砂等）闷熄（火）**3.** 忍住；抑制（感情等）；把…掩盖起来 **4.** 覆盖 **5.** 扼杀（议案等）**6.** 用文火焖烧 **—** *vi.* **1.** 窒息；闷死 **2.** 〈方〉用文火焖烧 **3.** 被忍住；被抑制 **—** *n.* **1.** 浓烟；浓雾；令人窒息的一阵雪（或蒸气等）**2.** 窒息状态；被抑制状态 **3.** 杂乱的一大堆东西；杂乱无章

smothery ['smʌðəri] *adj.* 令人窒息的；闷的

smoulder ['sməuldə] *vi.* **1.** 用文火闷烧；熏烧 **2.** （愤怒等）闷在心里,郁积 **3.** 流露难以抑制的愤怒（或仇恨、妒忌）**—** *n.* 闷烧；闷火

smudge [smʌdʒ] *n.* **1.** 污点；污迹 **2.** 模糊不清的形象 **3.** 浓烟；（为驱虫或使作物免受霜冻而设在上风处的）烟雾火堆；黑烟 — *vt.* **1.** 弄脏；涂污；玷污 **2.** 涂去；使模糊 **3.** 用浓烟熏；使（火）出出浓烟 — *vi.* **1.** 被墨、油漆等）形成污迹 **2.** 被弄脏；被擦模糊

smug [smʌg] *adj.* **1.** 整洁的；体面的 **2.** 自满的；沾沾自喜的 — *n.* **1.** 自命不凡的人,沾沾自喜的人 **2.** 〈英〉〈学俚〉不受交际和活动的用功学生

smuggle ['smʌgl] *vt.* **1.** 私运 **2.** 偷带 — *vi.* 走私 ‖ ~ r *n.* **1.** 走私者 **2.** 走私船

smut [smʌt] *n.* **1.** 煤炱,煤灰 **2.** 污点；污迹 **3.** 淫词秽语；淫秽作品 **4.** 【植】黑穗病；黑粉病 **5.** （含大量泥质的）劣（质）软）煤 — (smutted; smutting) *vt.* **1.** 弄脏；弄黑 **2.** 使（农作物）患黑穗病 — *vi.* **1.** 被弄脏；被弄黑 **2.** 患黑穗病 ‖ ~ ty *adj.*

Sn【化】元素锡（tin）的符号

snack [snæk] *n.* **1.** 小吃；快餐 **2.** 一份

— *vi*. 小吃；吃快餐 ‖ *go* ~*s*〈口〉均分，摊派 /*Snacks*! 均分吧！ ‖ ~ **bar** 快餐柜；快餐部；小吃店 /~ **table** 折叠式单人小餐桌

snaffle[1] [ˈsnæfl] *n*.（马的）圈嚼子，马衔铁 — *vt*. 给…装上圈嚼子；用圈嚼子勒（马）

snaffle[2] [ˈsnæfl] *vt*.〈英俚〉偷，扒；攫取

snag [snæg] *n*. **1.** 残干；残根，根株；（妨碍航行的）水中隐木；暗礁 **2.** 断牙；暴牙；歪牙 **3.**（衣服、织物等的）戳（或钩）破处；抽丝处 **4.** 意外障碍；隐伏的困难 —(snagged; snagging) *vt*. **1.** 戳破，钩破；使（编织物）抽丝 **2.** 绊住；阻碍；使（船）触礁 **3.** 清除（水道等处）的根株（或其他障碍物）**4.** 攫取，抓住（机会等）

snail [sneil] *n*. **1.** 蜗牛 **2.** 行动缓慢（或懒散）的人；动作迟缓的动物 **3.**〈美俚〉蜗形面包卷 **4.** = ~ wheel — *vt*. 清除（园圃等处）的蜗牛 — *vi*. **1.** 捉蜗牛 **2.** 缓慢移动 ‖ **~like** *adj*. 似蜗牛的 ‖ ˈ~**-paced**, ˈ~**-slow** *adj*. 蜗牛般慢行的；慢吞吞的 /~ **wheel**（时钟上确定敲击次数的）蜗形轮

snake [sneik] *n*. **1.** 蛇 **2.** 冷酷阴险的人；虚伪的人；卑鄙的人 **3.** 长蛇状物件（如清除管道污垢用的铁丝）**4.**【经】蛇形浮动汇率制（指欧洲货币体系各国既各有比价也可作一定浮动）— *vi*. **1.** 蛇般爬行；蜿蜒前进，迂回前进 **2.** 偷偷行进；偷偷溜走 — *vt*. **1.** 迂回地取（道）**2.**〈美〉拖，拉（木材等）

snaky, snakey [ˈsneiki] *adj*. **1.** 有蛇缠住的 **2.** 形状似蛇的；弯曲的 **3.** 蛇性的；阴险的 **4.** 多蛇的

snap [snæp] (snapped; snapping) *vt*. **1.** 猛咬 **2.** 攫夺；争购（*up*）**3.** 突然折断；拉断 **4.** 使（鞭子、风帆等）发劈啪声；捻（手指）使劈啪作声；啪地关上（或打开、扣住）**5.** 厉声说；急促地说（*out*）；怒声责骂（或打断）**6.** 扣动（枪）的扳机；急射；乱射；快速传（球）**7.** 用快照拍摄 — *vi*. **1.** 咬；攫；抓（*at*）**2.** 劈啪地响；（盖子、门等）咯嗒一声关上 **3.** 啪地一声折断；绷断；（神经、抵抗等）突然坍垮 **4.** 厉声说；急促地说（*at*）；（眼睛因愤怒而）闪烁 — *n*. **1.** 猛咬；猛扑；攫夺 **2.** 突然折断；绷断 **3.** 劈啪声；厉声的申斥；恶声恶气 **4.**（天气的）一阵突变（尤指转寒）**5.**〈美俚〉迅速发财的机会；有利可图的差使；容易的工作（或问题等）；易驾驭的人 **6.** 快照；快摄 **7.** 迅速传球 **8.** 精力，活力，生气 **9.** 少量，一点儿；一口，一小块 **10.** 小脆饼 **11.** 揿钮，按扣；钩扣；【无】揿钮接头 **12.**（橄榄球的）对阵开球 — *adj*. **1.** 突然的；仓卒的 **2.** 可吧嗒一声扣住的；装扣子的 **3.**〈美〉极简单容易的 — *adv*. 啪地一声；猛然 ‖ ˈ~ˌ**dragon** *n*.【植】金鱼草 /ˈ~**shot** *n*.**1.** 快照：take a ~*shot* of sb. 给某人拍快照 **2.** 急射；乱射 *vt*. & *vi*.（给…）拍快照；快摄

snapper [ˈsnæpə] *n*. **1.** 咬人的狗（或动物）**2.** 脾气暴躁的人；说话尖刻的人 **3.** 拍快照者 **4.** 揿钮，按扣 **5.**〈俚〉= whopper **6.**[~s]牙齿 **7.**【动】笛鲷；红鳍笛鲷；鳄龟；叩头虫 ‖ ˈ~**-up** *n*.（[复] ~s-up）攫取者；争夺者

snappish [ˈsnæpiʃ] *adj*. **1.** 要咬的 **2.** 恶声恶气的

snappy [ˈsnæpi] *adj*. **1.** = snappish **2.** 做得飞快的；敏捷的；活泼的；生动的 **3.**（天气）严寒的 **4.** 时髦的；漂亮的 **5.** 发出劈啪声的

snare [sneə] *n*. **1.** 圈套；罗网；陷阱 **2.**【医】勒除器（勒除肿瘤等用的金属丝圈）**3.**[~s]（绷在小军鼓下鼓面上的）

响弦 — vt. 1.(用罗网等)诱捕 2.用计谋诱陷;陷害 ‖ ～ drum(下鼓面绷有响弦的)小军鼓

snarl[snɑːl] n. 1. 缠结;纠结 2. 混乱;无秩序;错杂 3. 乱糟糟的一群 — vt. 1. 使(线、发等)缠结 2. 搞乱,使错杂;使(自己)处于乱糟糟的困境 3. 在(金属片等)上敲出浮凸花纹 — vi. 缠结

snarl²[snɑːl] vi. 1.(狗等)狂吠,嗥叫 2.(人)咆哮;被粗暴地表达出来 — vt. 1. 咆哮着说;粗暴地表示 2. 咆哮得使… — n. 狂吠,嗥叫;咆哮,吼叫

snatch[snætʃ] vt. 1. 攫取;抓住;夺得 2.(美俚)拐走;绑架 — vi. 1. 攫取;抓住(at) — n. 1. 攫取;抢夺 2.(谈话,诗歌等)的片段,点滴;[～es]片刻,短时间 3.(美俚)绑架;绑架 4.[体](举重的)抓举 ‖ ～er n.

sneak[sniːk] vi. 1. 偷偷摸摸地行动;偷偷地走,潜行 2.(行动)鬼鬼祟祟(态度)卑躬屈节 3.(英)(学徒)(向教师)告密,告发 — vt. 1. 偷偷地做;(口)偷窃 — n. 1. 鬼鬼祟祟的人;(英)(学徒)(向教师)告密者的学生 3.(乘人不注意时的)逃跑;偷偷摸摸的行为 4. [常～s]帆布胶底运动鞋;旅游鞋 — adj. 暗中进行的;突如其来的 ‖ ～er n. 1. 鬼鬼祟祟的人 2.[常～s]帆布鞋底运动鞋;旅游鞋 /～ thief 顺手牵羊的小偷

sneaky['sniːki] adj. 偷偷摸摸的;鬼鬼祟祟的;卑怯的

sneer[snɪə] vi. 1. 轻蔑地笑;冷笑 2. 嘲笑,讥笑(at) — vt. 1. 轻蔑地笑着说出 2. 嘲笑着说 — n. 冷笑;嘲笑,讥笑

sneeze[sniːz] n. 喷嚏(声);打喷嚏 — vi. 打喷嚏

snicker['snikə] vi. 1. 窃笑 2.(马等)嘶鸣 — vt. 窃笑着说 — n. 窃笑(声)

sniff[snif] vi. 1.(有声音地)以鼻吸气;嗅 2. 嗤之以鼻;蔑视(at) — vt. 1. 用力吸;嗅出,觉察出 — n. 1. 以鼻吸气(声);嗅 2. 嗤之以鼻 3. 从鼻子吸入的东西

sniffle['snifl] vi. 1.(一再)抽鼻子;发鼻地吸气 2. 抽着鼻子说话 — n. 1. 抽鼻子(声)2.[the ～s](口)感冒;鼻塞

snigger['snigə] vi., vt. & n. = snicker

snip[snip](snipped; snipping) vt. 剪;剪断;剪去 — vi. 剪 — n. 1.(一)剪;剪声 2. 剪下的片断;片段 3.[～s](剪金属薄片的)手头剪;铁丝剪 4. 傲慢无礼的人;孟浪的小子 5.(英俚)一定会成功的事;不吃亏的买卖 6.(古)裁缝 7.(口)不知天高地厚的青年人;不足道的东西

snipe[snaip] n. 1.([复]snipe(s))[动]鹬;沙锥;半蹼鹬 2. 狙击 3. 可鄙的人 4.(美俚)(香烟或雪茄烟的)烟蒂,烟屁股 — vi. 狙击 — vt. 1. 射鹬,猎鹬 2. 狙击(at) 3. 诽谤;中伤

sniper['snaipə] n. 狙击手 ‖ ～ scope n. 红外线瞄准镜,夜瞄镜

snivel['snivl](snivel(l)ed; snivel(l)ing) vi. 1. 流鼻涕;抽鼻子 2. 啜泣;哭诉 3. 假惺惺悲伤 — n. 1. 流鼻涕;抽鼻子 2. 啜泣;哭诉 3. 假哭;假惺惺悲伤 4.(古)鼻涕 5.[～s]伤风

snob[snɔb] n. 1. 势利的人;谄上欺下的人 2. 势利行为 3.(古)鞋匠

snobbery['snɔbəri] n.1. 势利;谄上欺下 2.[snobberies]势利行为;势利话

snobbish['snɔbiʃ] adj. 势利的;谄上欺下的

Sno-Cat['snəukæt] n.“雪猫”牌履带式雪地车辆(源自商标名)

snog[snɔg](snogged; snogging) vi.(俚)接吻;爱抚

snood [snuːd] *n.* (女子用的)束发带;发网;发套(式帽子)

snoop [snuːp] *vi.* 探听;窥探 — *n.* = snooper

snooper ['snuːpə] *n.* 探听者;窥探者;管闲事者 ‖ '~scope *n.* 红外线夜望镜

snooze [snuːz] *vi.* 打瞌睡;睡午觉;(白天)小睡 — *vt.* 懒散地消磨(时间)(*away*) — *n.* 瞌睡;(白天的)小睡

snore [snɔː] *vi.* 打鼾 — *vt.* 鼾睡度过(时间)(*away*) — *n.* 打鼾;鼾声 ‖ ~r *n.*

snorkel ['snɔːkl] *n.* **1.**(潜水艇或潜游者的)水下空气(或呼吸)管;(救火车上的)液压起重机 — *vi.* 用水下通气管潜航;用水下呼吸管潜航

snort [snɔːt] *vi.* **1.** 喷鼻息;鼓鼻 **2.** 发哼声;(表示轻蔑、愤怒、惊讶或不信)发哼声 **3.**(蒸汽机等)发喷汽声 **4.**〈口〉高声大笑 — *vt.* **1.** 哼着鼻子说(或表示) **2.**(喷鼻息般地)喷出 **3.** 吸入(粉末状的麻醉毒品) — *n.* **1.** 喷鼻息;喷鼻声 **2.** 哼声;喷喷声;喷汽声 **2.**〈英〉(潜水艇或潜游者的)潜水通气管 **3.** 一口酒 ‖ ~er *n.* 鼻息粗的人(或动物);表示轻蔑(或愤怒等)的人;〈口〉不寻常的人(或事);令人咋舌的人(或事);怒号的大风

snot [snɔt] *n.* **1.**〈粗〉鼻涕 **2.**〈俚〉蛮横无理的人(或话)

snout [snaut] *n.* **1.**(动物的)口鼻部;口吻;(昆虫的)喙;猪嘴 **2.**〈贬〉(人的)大鼻子 **3.** 猪嘴状物;喷嘴;船首 ‖ ~beetle【动】象鼻虫,象鼻虫

snow [snəu] *n.* **1.** 雪;[~s]积雪(地带) **2.** 雪般的东西(尤指雪白的东西);[~s]白雪 **3.**〈俚〉(电视、雷达屏幕的)雪花形干扰,雪花效应 — *vi.* 下雪;雪一般地落下 — *vt.* **1.** 使似雪一般地落下 **2.** 用雪覆盖;用雪阻住 **3.** 使似雪一样白 **4.**〈美俚〉花言巧语地

蒙骗,使相信 ‖~ball *n.* **1.** 雪球 **2.** 滚雪球式扩大(或增长)的事物 **3.** 滚雪球式的募捐法 **4.** 果味冰雹卷 **5.**【植】山白树美洲荚茶 *vi.* 扔雪球(*at*);打雪仗 *vt.* 滚雪球似地增长(或扩大) *vi.* 向…扔雪球 **2.** 使滚雪球似地增长(或扩大) /'~bird *n.*【动】雪鹀 **2.**〈美俚〉每月可卡因瘾者 **3.**〈美俚〉冬季到南方打短工的流动工人 /'~bound *adj.* 被雪困住(或封住)的 /'~drift *n.* **1.**(被风吹成的)雪堆;吹雪 **2.**【植】香雪球 /'~fall *n.* 降雪;降下的雪;降雪量 /'~flake *n.* **1.** 雪花 **2.**【植】雪片莲 /'~man *n.* **1.**(雪堆成的)雪人 **2.**[S]雪人(传说生存在喜马拉雅山上的一种动物,据信是熊) /'~mobile *vi.* & *n.* (乘)雪地机动车 /'~plough,'~plow *n.* 扫雪机 /'~shoe *n.* 雪鞋 *vi.* 穿着雪鞋走 /'~storm *n.* **1.** 雪暴,暴风雪 **2.**〈美俚〉搅奶油

snowy ['snəui] *adj.* 雪的;下雪的;多雪的;积雪的;雪白的

snub [snʌb] (snubbed; snubbing) *vt.* **1.** 严厉斥责;厉声制止 **2.** 冷落;怠慢;冷冰冰地拒绝 **3.** 使(船等)突然停住,刹住;止住 **4.** 掐灭(香烟等)(*out*) — *n.* **1.** 斥责;冷落;怠慢 — *adj.*(缆索等)制动用的 **2.**(鼻子)扁而翘的 ‖~nosed *adj.* 短翘鼻的,狮子鼻的

snuff¹ [snʌf] *n.* **1.** 烛花,灯花 **2.**〈苏格兰〉发怒 — *vt.* **1.** 剪(烛)花 **2.** 掐灭(蜡烛);扼杀,消灭,扑灭(叛乱、希望等)(*out*) — *vi.*〈俚〉死去(*out*)

snuff² [snʌf] *vt.* **1.** 用鼻子使劲吸 **2.** 嗅出;察觉 **3.**(动物)嗅,闻 — *vi.* 抽鼻子;嗅,闻(*at*) — *n.* **1.** 以鼻吸气 **2.** 吸鼻气声;嗅,闻 **2.** 气息;气味 **3.** 鼻烟;【医】吸鼻药,嗅剂 **2.**(鼻烟的)一撮 ‖~box *n.* **1.** 鼻烟盒 **2.**〈俚〉防毒面

具

snuffer ['snʌfə] *n.* 1. [～s] 烛花剪刀 2. 熄烛器

snuffle ['snʌfl] *vi.* 1. 急促有声地呼吸(如鼻子半塞时); 嗅,闻(*at*) 2. 带鼻音讲话 3.〈罕〉假惺惺地说话 — *vt.* 1. 带鼻音讲(*out*) 2. 抽着鼻子嗅; 嗅着去找 — *n.* 1. 抽鼻子; 鼻塞声 2. 鼻音 3.〈罕〉假惺惺, 虚情假意 4. [the ～s]鼻塞;伤风

snug [snʌg] (snugger, snuggest) *adj.* 1. 不受风寒侵袭的; 舒适的, 温暖的 2. 小而舒适的; 整洁的 3.(收入等)尚可的 4.(服装等)贴身的 5.(船只)适航的; 装备完善的 6. 隐蔽的 一(snugged; snugging) *vi.*〈方〉舒适地蜷伏; 偎依 一 *vt.* 1. 使紧贴合身 2. 使整洁; 使温暖 3. 隐藏; 藏匿 4. 使(船等)作好抗风暴准备(*down*) — *adv.* = snugly — *n.*〈英〉(酒店中的)雅座

snuggle ['snʌgl] *vi.* 舒适地蜷伏; 偎依 — *vt.* 1. 紧抱; 偎 2. 使舒适温暖

snugly ['snʌgli] *adv.* 1. 舒适温暖地; 整洁地 2. 尚可地 3. 贴身地 4. 隐藏地

so [səu; 弱 sə] *adv.* 1. [表示方式、方法、情况]这样, 那样 2. [表示程度]这么, 那么, 如此地 3. [代替上文中的形容词、名词或动词]这样, 也, 对, 不错 4.〈口〉非常, 极, 很 5. 因此, 所以 6.〈口〉的确, 确实 — *conj.* 1. 因而, 所以; 结果是 2. 为的是, 以便, 使得(= that) 3. 那么, 这样看来 4.〈古〉只要(= provided that) — *pron.* 1. [用作 expect, hope, say 一类动词的宾语]这样, 如此 2. [用在 or 后]左右, 上下 — *int.* 好! 就这样! 别动! 停住! 别吵! ‖ '～-and-'～ *n.* 1. 某某人; 某某事 2. 讨厌的家伙; 卑鄙的人; 坏蛋 如此这般地 *adj.* 可诅咒的, 该死的 / '～-

'called *adj.* 所谓的, 号称的

soak [səuk] *vt.* 1. 浸, 泡, 渍; 使浸透 2. 吸收(*in, up*) 3. 浸掉, 浸出(*out*) 4.〈口〉使(自己)喝醉 5.〈俚〉向…敲竹杠; 向…征重税 6.〈俚〉痛殴; 重罚 7.〈俚〉典当(东西) 8. 对(金属等)进行长时间热处理 — *vi.* 1. 浸泡 2. 渗透, 透过 3.〈口〉狂饮 4.(金属)经受均热处理 — *n.* 1. 浸泡, 浸渍; 浸液 2.〈俚〉大雨 3.〈俚〉酒鬼; 狂饮闹宴 4.〈俚〉痛殴; 重击 5.〈俚〉典当 ‖ ～er *n.* 浸洗者; 缩水工; 连绵大雨; 酒鬼; [～s](尿布上的)吸水垫

soap [səup] *n.* 1. 肥皂 2.〈化〉脂肪酸的碱金属盐 2. = soap opera 3.〈美俚〉(赌)钱 — *vt.* 1. 用肥皂擦洗; 上肥皂于 2.〈口〉奉承, 谄媚 ‖ '～-box *n.* 1. 肥皂盒; 肥皂箱 2.(街头演说者所用的)临时演说台 *adj.* 街头演说的 *vi.* 作街头演说 / ～ bubble 1. 肥皂泡 2. 徒有其表的事物; 短暂而不实在的东西 / ～ opera 肥皂剧(一种常以家事为题材的广播或电视剧, 最初由肥皂商赞助) / '～stone *n.* 皂石(一种石料) / '～suds [复] 肥皂泡沫的肥皂水; 肥皂水的泡沫

soapy ['səupi] *adj.* 1. 涂着肥皂的 2. 含有肥皂的; 肥皂般的; 多脂的; 滑腻腻的 3.〈俚〉满口奉承的, 谄媚的; 殷勤的; 油滑的

soar [sɔ:] *vi.* 1. 高飞, 翱翔 2. 高飞范围; 高涨程度; 耸立高度 — *vi.* 1.(鹰等)高飞, 翱翔 2.〈空〉滑翔 2.(思想等)高涨 3.; 昂扬, 高涨 3.(山、建筑物等)高耸, 屹立 4.(物价、失业人数等)猛增, 剧增 — *vt.*(诗)飞升至, 高飞到

SGB, sob[1] [,es əu'bi:] *n.*〈美俚〉畜生, 狗娘养的(son of a bitch 的缩略)

sob[2] [sɔb](sobbed; sobbing) *vi.* 1. 啜泣, 呜

咽，抽噎 2.(风等)发呜咽声 — vt. 1. 哭诉，呜咽地说(out) 2. 哭得使 — n. 哭泣(声)，呜咽声 ‖ ~ story 伤感故事

sober ['səubə] adj. 1. 清醒的，未喝醉的；饮酒有节制的；饮食有度的 2. 适度的，有节制的 3. 严肃的，庄重的；认真的 4. 不夸大的，不歪曲的；非想象的 5. 理智的；合理的 6.(色彩等)朴素的；朴实的，素净的 7.〈古〉不慌不忙的，从容的 — vt. 使清醒；使严肃；使自制 — vi. 清醒起来(up, off)；变严肃；变持重(down) ‖ ~ly adv. / ~ness n.

sobriety [sə'braiəti] n. 1. 冷静；清醒 2. 饮酒有节制；戒酒 3. 适度；有节 4. 严肃；持重

soccer ['sɔkə] n. 英式足球(= association football)

sociable ['səuʃəbl] adj. 1. 好交际的；友善的，和蔼可亲的；表示友谊的 2. 增进交谊的 3. 喜欢群居的 — n. 1. 对座四轮马车；双座三轮脚踏车(又作 S 形双人坐椅) 2.(美)社交会，联谊会，联欢会 ‖ ˌsocia'bility n. 1. 好交际；合群 2. 交际活动 / ~ness n. / sociably adv.

social ['səuʃəl] adj. 1. 社会的 2. 社交的，交际的；喜欢交际的，有关社会福利的 3. 一定社会阶层(或地位)的；上流社会的 4. 社会性的；[动]群居的 — n. 联欢会 ‖ ~ly adv. / ~-minded adj. 关心社会的，热心于社会福利事业的 / ~ security 社会保障(或保险)(制度) / ~ service 社会福利事业 / ~ work 社会服务(亦作 ~ work)

socialism ['səuʃəlizəm] n. 社会主义

socialist ['səuʃəlist] n. 1. 社会主义者 2. [S-]社会党人 — adj. 1. 社会主义(者)的 2.[S-]社会党(人)的

socialistic [ˌsəuʃə'listik] adj. 社会主义(者)的

socialite ['səuʃəlait] n.〈美口〉社交界名人，社会名流

socialize ['səuʃəlaiz] vt. 1. 使社会化；使社会主义化 2. 使适合社会需要；使适合于过社会生活 3. 组织学生集体参加(课堂练习等) — vi. 参加社交；交际 ‖ socializa'tion n.

society [sə'saiəti] n. 1. 社会 2. 团体；会；社 3. 友谊；交往 4. 社交界；上流社会 5.(动、植物的)小群落 ‖ Society of Friends (基督教)公谊会

sociological [ˌsəusiə'lɔdʒik(ə)l] adj. 1. 社会学的 2. 社会的；有关社会问题的

sociology [ˌsəusi'ɔlədʒi] n. 社会学 ‖ soci'ologist n.

sock [sɔk] n. 1. 短袜 2. 鞋衬垫 3.(古希腊、罗马喜剧演员穿的)轻软鞋；〈喻〉喜剧 4.〈美俚〉钱袋；银箱；存钱处；存款；巨款 — vt. 1. 给…穿上短袜 2.〈美俚〉存(钱) 3.〈美俚〉(企业、戏目等)赚(钱)

socker ['sɔkə] n.〈主英〉= soccer

socket ['sɔkit] n. 1. 窝;穴;孔 2. 承窝，托座；套节 3. 插座，插口；管座 — vt. 1. 给…配插座(或承窝等)；把…装入插座(或承窝等) 2. 用球棒承口部击(高尔夫球)

sockeye ['sɔkai] n.[动]红大马哈鱼

sod [sɔd] n. 1.(方俚)草皮；生草土；草地 2. 故乡；本国 — (sodded; sodding) vt. 铺草皮于；用生草土覆盖

soda ['səudə] n. 1.[化]碳酸钠，苏打；碳酸氢钠，小苏打，氢氧化钠；氧化钠；(化合物中的)钠 2. 苏打水；汽水 ‖ ~ fountain(装有龙头的)汽水柜；冷饮柜 / ~ water 苏打水，汽水

sodality [səu'dæləti] n. 1. 友谊，交情；伙

伴关系 **2.** 联谊会；兄弟会 **3.** (天主教)慈善团体

sodden ['sɒdən] *adj.* **1.** 湿润的，浸透了的 **2.** 未煮透的；(面包等)未烘透的 **3.** (尤指因沉湎于酒而)迷糊的，迟钝的；麻木的 — *vt.* **1.** 浸湿 **2.** 使迟钝；使(头脑)麻木 — *vi.* 被浸湿 ‖ ~**ly** *adv.* ‖ ~ **ness** *n.*

sodium ['səudiəm] *n.*【化】钠 ‖ ~ **bicarbonate** 碳酸氢钠，小苏打 / ~ **chloride** 氯化钠，食盐

sodomy ['sɒdəmi] *n.* 鸡奸；口交；兽奸 / ~ **sodomist, sodomite** ['sɒdəmait] *n.* 鸡奸(或口交、兽奸、尸奸)者 / **sodomize** *vt.* 对…鸡奸(或口交、兽奸、尸奸)

soever [səu'evə] *adv.* **1.** [常用在 how 加形容词之后]无论；无论…to what 等 **2.** [常用在加最高级形容词之后]最 **3.** [常用在 any, no, what 加名词之后]不论何种，任何一种

sofa ['səufə] *n.* (长)沙发 ‖ ~ **bed** (坐卧)两用沙发

Sofia ['səufiə] *n.* 索非亚[保加利亚首都]

soft [sɒft] *adj.* **1.** 软的；硬度低的 **2.** (皮肤、头发等)柔滑的 (色彩、光线、目光、声调等)柔和的 **3.** (轮廓、线条)模糊的 (睡眠)平静的，安稳的 **4.** (天气、风、雨和温和的 (英)下冻的 **5.** (解释)潮湿的 **6.** 温柔的，和蔼的；宽厚的 软心肠的 **6.** 软弱的，不坚强的；吃不了苦的 **7.** (便)轻松的；舒服的 **8.** (水)无矿盐的 (饮料)不含酒精的 — **drinks** 软饮料，不含酒精的饮料(尤指果汁) **9.** 坡度小的 (山峰等)线条柔和的 **10.** 【语】(发)软音的；(辅音)软的，如 g 和 city 中的 c；浊音的；不送气的 **11.** 纸币的；(币值)不稳定的；(市场)疲软的；难以兑成外币的 ~ **money** 纸币 ~ **currency** 软通货，软币(指在国际市场

上不吃香的通货) **12.** (导弹发射场等)无掩蔽而易受攻击的 — *n.* **1.** 柔软的东西；柔软部分 **2.** 笨人，傻子 **3.** [the ~](英俚)钱(尤指纸币) — *adv.* (常用比较级)柔软地；柔和地；温和地 — *int.* (古)别作声！/ ~**ness** *n.* ‖ ~ **ball** *n.* 垒球(运动) / '~'**boiled** *adj.* **1.** (蛋)溏心的，煮得半熟的 **2.** 多愁善感的 / ~**coal** 烟煤 / '~**land** *vi.* (使)软着陆 / ~**soap** *vt.* & *vi.* 奉承，谄媚 / ~ **spot 1.** (性格等)易受打动的一点；弱点 **2.** 实力不振的企业(或经济部门) / '~**ware** *n.* **1.** (计算机的)软件；程序系统 **2.** (喻)软件 / '~**wood** *n.* **1.** 软材；针叶材 **2.** 针叶树

soften ['sɒfən] *vt.* 弄软；使软化；使温和 使衰弱；使柔化 和 — *vi.* 变软；软化；变温和；变软弱；变柔和 ‖ ~**er** *n.* 软化剂；硬水软化器

soggy ['sɒgi] *adj.* **1.** 浸水的，湿透的；湿润的 **2.** 未烘透的 **3.** (文章、谈话等)沉闷的；乏味的

soil¹ [sɒil] *n.* **1.** 泥土，土壤；土地，地面 **2.** 国土，国家 **3.** 温床，滋生地 **4.** 农业生活，务农

soil² [sɒil] *vt.* **1.** 弄脏，弄污 **2.** 污辱；败坏 **3.** (罕)施肥于 — *vi.* 变脏 — *n.* **1.** 污物；污斑；污秽 **2.** 粪便；肥料；**night** ~ 粪便 **3.** (道德的)败坏，腐败

soiree ['swa:rei, swa:'rei] (法) *n.* 晚会，社交聚会

soja ['səuə] *n.* 大豆

sojourn ['sɒdʒən] *vi.* & *n.* 旅居；逗留

Sol [sɒl] *n.* **1.** 太阳 **2.** (古罗马的)太阳神 **3.** [s-](炼金术中的)黄金

sol [sɒl] *n.*【音】七个唱名之一(在固定唱名法中相当于音名 G)

solace ['sɒləs] *n.* 安慰；安慰物 — *vt.*

安慰;使快乐 2. 减轻(悲痛等)

solar ['səulə] *adj.* 太阳的;日光的;利用太阳光的

solarium [səu'lɛəriəm] ([复] solaria [səu'lɛəriə]或 solariums) *n.* 1. 日光浴室 2. 日晷

sold [səuld] sell 的过去式和过去分词

solder ['səldə] *n.* 1. (低温)焊料,焊锡 2. 结合物;联络因素 — *vt. & vi.* 1. (锡)焊,焊合,焊接 2. (使)联结在一起

soldier ['səuldʒə] *n.* 1. (陆军)士兵;军人 2. 军事指挥员;军事家 3. 为事业而奋斗的人,〈喻〉战士 4. 【动】(社会性昆虫)兵(虫);兵蚁;寄居蟹 5. 逃避工作的人;懒汉 — *vi.* 1. 当兵,当兵 2. 担负起责任,尽职 3. 偷懒,磨洋工 ‖ ~ly、~like *adj.* 1. 军人(似)的 2. 英勇的,勇猛的;英俊的

soldiery ['səuldʒəri] *n.* 1. [总称]军人;军队 2. 军事训练;军事科学;军人职业;军事才能

sole[1] [səul] *adj.* 1. 单独的,唯一的 2. 【律】(英当事人)独身的,未婚的 3.〈古〉孤独的 ‖ ~ly *adv.*

sole[2] [səul] *n.* 1. 脚底;鞋底;袜底 2. (刨子、货车、犁、高尔夫球棒等的)底部,底面,底板,基底 — *vt.* 1. 给(鞋等)配底(或换底) 2. (击高尔夫球时)将(球棒)底端触地

sole[3] [səul] *n.*【动】鳎;拟庸鲽;庸鲽

solecism ['sɔlisizəm] *n.* 1. 语法错误;文理不通 2. 失礼,无礼 3. 谬误;不恰当

solemn ['sɔləm] *adj.* 1. 庄严的;严肃的 2. 隆重的;庄重的 3. 合仪式的;按照仪式的;正式的;神圣的 4. 一本正经的 5. (颜色)暗黑的 ‖ ~ly *adv.*; ~ness *n.*

solemnity [sə'lemnəti] *n.* 1. 庄严,严肃

2. 隆重;庄重 3. 一本正经 4. 庄重的仪式

solemnize ['sɔləmnaiz] *vt.* 隆重庆祝(或纪念);为...举行宗教仪式 — *vi.* 严肃地讲话(或思考,行事);变得严肃

soli ['səuli:] solo 的复数形

solicit [sə'lisit] *vt.* 1. 请求;恳求;恳求给予;要求;征求 2. 诱惑;勾引~做坏事;(妓女)拉(客) 4. 引发,诱发等 — *vi.* 1. 请求;恳求;征求 (for) 2. (妓女)拉客

solicitation [sə,lisi'teiʃən] *n.* 1. 请求;恳求;征求 2. 诱惑;(妓女的)拉客 3. 引发,诱发

solicitor [sə'lisitə] *n.* 1.〈英〉(初级)律师 2.〈美〉(政府部门或一城市中负责法律事务的)法务官 3.〈美〉揽客;游说者(如拉票者或推销员等);募捐者 4. 恳求者;请求者 ‖ ~ general 1.〈英〉副检察长;〈美〉司法部副部长 2.(美国若干州的)首席司法官

solicitous [sə'lisitəs] *adj.* 1. 焦虑的;挂念的,担心的 2. 渴望的 3. 非常讲究的,十分注意的 ‖ ~ly *adv.* / ~ness *n.*

solicitude [sə'lisitju:d] *n.* 关心;担忧;关心(或担忧)的事

solid ['sɔlid] *adj.* 1. 固体的;(物质结构)紧密的;(看上去)浓密的 2. 坚固的,坚牢的;结实的;丰富的 3. 实心的;无空隙的 4. 立体的;立方的 5. 纯质的;(颜色或音调等)同一的,单一的 6. 连续的;完整的,完全的 7. 基础稳固的;有根据的;确实的;可靠的;稳健的 8. 资金雄厚的;殷实的 9. 一致的,团结的 10. 慎重的;严肃的 11. 紧密连接的;【印】(行间)无空隙的 12.〈美俚〉(音乐)(表演)精彩的 — *n.* 1. 固体 2. 立方体 — *adv.* 1. 全体一致地;无异议地 2. 全部地 ‖ ~ly

solidarity | 880 | -some

adv. / ~ness n.

solidarity [ˌsɔliˈdærəti] n. 1. 团结(一致) 2. 休戚相关

solidify [səˈlidifai] vt. & vi. 1.(使)团结 2.(使)凝固,(使)固化,(使)变硬 3.(使)结晶 4. 充实;巩固

solidity [səˈliditi] n. 1. 固体性;固态;固体 2. 坚固;紧密;硬度;强度 3. 稳健;可靠;殷实 4.【数】体积 5. 完整性;连续性

soliloquize [səˈliləkwaiz] vi. & vt. 1. 自言自语(地说)2.【戏】(用)独白(说)

soliloquy [səˈliləkwi] n. 自言自语;独白

solitaire [ˌsɔliˈtɛə] n. 1.(戒指[耳环等]的)独粒宝石(尤指钻石)2. 单人纸牌戏

solitary [ˈsɔlitəri] adj. 1. 独居的;无伴的,单独的 2. 荒凉的;冷落的,偏僻的;寂寞的 3. 单个的,唯一的 4.【植】单生的 — n. 1. 隐居者 2. 单独监禁

solitude [ˈsɔlitju:d] n. 1. 孤独;寂寞;隐居,与外界隔绝的 2. 冷僻处;荒凉地(如沙漠)

solo [ˈsəuləu] n.([复]solos 或 soli [ˈsəuli:]) 1. 独奏曲;独唱曲;独奏;独唱 2. 单独表演;个人表演 3. 单飞 4.【牌】单人对 3 人的惠斯特纸牌戏 — adj. 1. 独奏(曲)的;独唱(曲)的 2. 单独的;独自表演的 — adv. 单独地 — vi. 单独表演【空】单飞

soloist [ˈsəuləuist] n. 独奏者;独唱者;【空】单飞者

Solomon [ˈsɔləmən] n. 1. 所罗门(古以色列王国国王大卫之子,以智慧著称)2. 聪明人;贤人;以智慧自诩者 3. 所罗门(群岛)[西南太平洋]

solstice [ˈsɔlstis] n. 1.【天】1. 至:the summer(winter) ~夏(冬)至 2. 至点(指夏至点或冬至点)

soluble [ˈsɔljubl] adj. 1. 可溶的,可乳化

的 2. 可以解决的;可解释的;【数】可解的 ∥ **solu**'bility n. / ~ness n. / **solubly** adv.

solution [səˈlu:ʃən] n. 1. 解决(办法);解答;解释 2.【数】解法;解式 3.【化】溶解(作用);溶解状态;溶液;溶体 4. 瓦解;中断;消散 5. 橡胶水 — vt. 涂溶液于;用橡胶水胶粘

solve [sɔlv] vt. 1. 解释;解答;解决 2. 清偿(债务) ∥ **solvable** adj. / ~r n

solvency [ˈsɔlvənsi] n. 1.【化】溶解力 2. 偿付能力

solvent [ˈsɔlvənt] adj. 1. 有偿付能力的 2. 溶解的,有溶解力的 3.(对传统、信仰等)具有削弱作用的 — n. 1.【化】溶剂;溶媒 2. 具有削弱作用的事物;(问题等的)解决办法

Somalia [səuˈmɑːliə] n. 索马里[东非国家]

somascope [ˈsəumæskəup] n.【医】超声波检查仪

sombre, somber [ˈsɔmbə] adj. 1. 昏暗的;阴沉的 2. 忧郁的;暗淡的;浅黑的 ∥ ~ly adv. / ~ness n.

sombrero [sɔmˈbrɛərəu] n.([复]sombreros) n.(流行于美国西南部和墨西哥的)阔边帽

some [强 sʌm;弱 səm, sm] adj.1.[用于肯定句一些,若干;有些 2.[用于疑问句,盼望得到肯定的答复或表示请求等]一些 3. 某一 4.[sʌm][在美口语、英俚语中用来强调语气]很大的,惊人的;了不起的一些;一些,若干等 2.[用作复]有些人,有些东西 — adv. 1.大约 2.〈口〉几分,稍微 3.〈美俚〉很;非常好

-some[1] suf. 1.[附在名词、形容词或及物动词后构成形容词]表示"易于…的","有…倾向的","产生…的";

*quarrel*some, ful*some*, tire*some* 2. [构成名词]表示"…人一组": three*some* 三人一组

-some² *comb. form* 【生】表示"体"，"染色体": mono*some* 单体, chromo*some*

somebody ['sʌmbədi] *pron.* 某人,有人 — *n.* 重要人物,大人物

someday ['sʌmdei] *adv.* 来日;有朝一日

somehow ['sʌmhau] *adv.* 1. 由于某种(未弄清的)原因,不知怎么地,莫名其妙地 2. 以某种方法;以某种方式

someone ['sʌmwʌn] *pron.* 某人,有人

somersault ['sʌməsɔːlt] *n.* 1. 筋斗 2. (意见,政策等)180度的转变 — *vi.* 翻筋斗

somerset ['sʌməsit, 'sʌməset] *n.* & *vi.* = somersault

something ['sʌmθiŋ] *pron.* 1. 某事;某物,某东西 2. (表示模糊的概念)什么 3. 实有物(和 nothing 相对而言) 4. 重要东西;重要人物 — *adv.* 几分,多少,稍微 3. 很,非常

sometime ['sʌmtaim] *adv.* 1. 在某一时候,日后;有朝一日 2. 〈古〉从前 — *adj.* 以前的

sometimes ['sʌmtaimz] *adv.* 不时;有时

somewhat ['sʌmhwɔt] *pron.* 1. 一点儿,几分 2. 某事;某物 3. 重要东西;重要人物 — *adv.* 有点,稍微

somewhere ['sʌmhwɛə] *adv.* 1. 在某处;到某处 2. 在附近;前后,大约(*about*) — *n.* 某地

somnambulate [sɔm'næmbjuleit] *vi.* 梦行,梦游 ‖ **somnambulism** *n.* 【医】梦行(症),梦游(症) / **somnambulist** *n.* 梦行者,梦游者;梦行症患者

somnolent ['sɔmnələnt] *adj.* 1. 想睡的,困倦的 2. 催眠的 ‖ **somnolence** *n.*

son [sʌn] *n.* 1. 儿子 2. 女婿;养子 3. [常 ~s]后裔,子孙 4. 国民;居民 5. 从事于…的人 6. (长者对年轻者或牧师对教徒的称呼)孩子 ‖ **' ~-in-law** *n.* ([复]~s-in-law)女婿 / **~ of a bitch** (或 **gun**)〈俚〉1. (骂人语)畜生,狗娘养的 2. (对伙伴的戏谑性称呼)家伙 3. 讨厌的工作;完成不了的任务

sonar ['səunɑː] *n.* 声纳(sound navigation ranging 的缩略,是一种利用声波或超声波的水下探测系统);声波定位仪

sonata [sə'nɑːtə] *n.* 【音】奏鸣曲

song [sɔŋ] *n.* 1. 歌唱;声乐 2. 歌曲;歌词;歌曲集 3. 诗歌;韵文 4. 鸣声;吵嚷 ‖ **~ bird** *n.* 1. 燕雀,歌鸟,鸣禽 2. 〈俚〉供认者;告密者

songster ['sɔŋstə] *n.* 1. 歌唱家;作曲家;诗人 2. 歌曲集 3. 歌鸟,鸣禽

songstress *n.* 1. 女歌唱家;女作曲家;女诗人 2. 雌歌鸟,雌鸣禽

sonic ['sɔnik] *adj.* 声音的;声波的;声速的

sonnet ['sɔnit] *n.* 十四行诗

sonny ['sʌni] *n.* 〈口〉小弟弟,小家伙,宝宝,乖崽

sonorous [sə'nɔːrəs] *adj.* 1. 响亮的,洪亮的 2. 能发出响亮声音的 3. 语调夸张的;表现浮夸的 ‖ **so'nority** *n.* / **~ly** *adv.* / **~ness** *n.*

soon [suːn] *adv.* 1. 不久 2. 早;快 3. 宁可;宁愿

soot [sut] *n.* 煤烟,油烟 — *vt.* 用煤烟弄脏;用烟灰覆盖

sooth [suːθ] *adj.* 1. 〈古〉真实的;真正的 2. 〈诗〉抚慰的;镇静的 3. 〈古〉温柔的;甜蜜的 — *n.* 〈古〉真实 ‖ **' ~ ˌsayer** *n.* 占卜者;预言者 2. 螳螂

soothe [suːð] *vt.* 1. 安慰,抚慰;使平静,

使镇定 2. 使(痛苦、疼痛等)减轻、缓和 3. 奉承 — *vi.* 起安慰作用;起镇定作用

sooty ['suti] *adj.* 1. 煤烟的、油烟的;生煤烟的 2. 被煤烟弄脏的;被烟尘覆盖的 3. 乌黑色的

sop [sɔp] *n.* 1. (泡在牛奶、肉汤等里的)面包片;湿透的东西 2. 打狗的肉包子(指抛给凶恶的动物吃的东西);(给为难者等的)讨好物品,小贿赂 3. 懦夫;柔弱的男子;(美俚)酒鬼 — (sopped; sopping) *vt.* 1. 浸,泡(面包等);浸湿 2. 吸(水等)(*up*) 3. 贿赂 — *vi.* 1. 湿透 2.(水等)渗透

sophist ['sɔfist] *n.* 1. (常 S-)诡辩(学)者 2. 诡辩家 3. 大智者;博学者

sophisticate [sə'fistikeit] *vt.* 1. 窜改;曲解(文章等) 2. 使失去天真,使变得世故 3. 使复杂;使精致 4. 把杂物搀入(酒等) 5.(古)使堕落,使腐化 — *vi.* 诡辩 — *n.* 世故很深的人 ‖ so,phisti'cation *n.*

sophisticated [sə'fistikeitid] *adj.* 1. 老于世故的 2.(武器、机械等)很复杂的,高级的,尖端的 3. 搀杂过的;非自然状态的 4. 非常有经验的;老练的 5.(文学作品等)在理智方面打动人的;深奥微妙的;精致的

sophistry ['sɔfistri] *n.* 1. 谬论,谬见 2. 诡辩(法)

sophomore ['sɔfəmɔː] *n.* 1. 大学(或中学)二年级学生 2. 在企业(或机关等)工作第二年的人员

sophomoric [ˌsɔfə'mɔːrik] *adj.* 1. 二年级(学生)的 2. 一知半解的;肤浅的而自命不凡的;有点过于简单的

soporific [ˌsɔpə'rifik] *adj.* 1. 致睡的,催眠的 2. 睡眠的;嗜睡的 3. 令人麻木不仁(或失去警觉)的 — *n.* 安眠药;使人

昏昏的东西 ‖ ~ally *adv.*

soppy ['sɔpi] *adj.* 1. 湿透的,浸湿的 2. 多雨的 3.(英口)太伤感的

soprano [sə'prɑːnəu] ([复] sopranos 或 soprani [sə'prɑːniː]) *n.* 1. 女高音;女声高音;女高音声部 2. 女(或童声)高音歌手 — *adj.* 女(或童声)高音的;女高音声部的

sorcerer ['sɔːsərə] *n.* 男巫;术士;魔术师 ‖ sorceress ['sɔːsəris] *n.* 女巫;女术士;女魔术师

sorcery ['sɔːsəri] *n.* 巫术;妖术;魔术

sordid ['sɔːdid] *adj.* 1. 肮脏的,污秽的;破烂的;令人不舒服的 2.(人、行为等)卑鄙的;下贱的;恶劣的;利欲熏心的 3. 可怜的;悲惨的 4. 色彩暗淡的;灰褐色的

sore [sɔː] *adj.* 1. 痛的;疼痛发炎的;一碰就痛的;令人痛苦的;易引起精神痛苦的 2. 恼火的;动辄要恼火的,极度的;剧烈的 — *n.* 1. (身体上的)痛处;疮;溃疡 2. (精神上的)痛处;恨事;伤心事 — *adv.* (古) = ~ly ‖ ~ly *adv.* 1. 痛苦地;悲痛地 2. 严厉地;剧烈地 3. 极,非常 / ~ness *n.*

sorghum ['sɔːgəm] *n.* 1.【植】高粱,蜀黍 2. 芦粟糖浆 3. 甜得发腻的东西;过度多情的东西

sorgo ['sɔːgəu] ([复] sorgos) *n.*【植】芦粟,甜高粱

sorority [sə'rɔriti] *n.* 1. 妇女社团 2.(美)大学女生联谊会

sorrel[1] ['sɔrəl] *n.*【植】酸模;酢浆草

sorrel[2] ['sɔrəl] *n.* 1. 红褐色,栗色 2. 栗色的动物;栗色马 3.3 岁的雄鹿 — *adj.* 红褐色的,栗色的

sorrow ['sɔrəu] *n.* 1. 悲伤,悲哀,悲痛;悲伤的表示 2. 悲哀的原因;不幸事

伤心事 3. 懊悔；遗憾 — *vi.* 感到悲
伤；懊悔；遗憾(*at, for, over*)

sorrowful ['sɔrəful] *adj.* 1. 悲伤的，伤心
的，悲痛的 2. 使人伤心的 ‖ **~ly** *adv.*
/ **~ness** *n.*

sorry ['sɔri] *adj.* 1. 难过的；惋惜的 2. 懊
悔的，后悔的 3. 对不起的，抱歉的，遗
憾的 4. 悲伤的，悲哀的 5. 卑鄙的；可
悲的；拙劣的；破烂的

sort [sɔt] *n.* 1. 种类；类别 2. 样子；举止
3. 品质；性质 4. 一套 [常 ~s]【印】一
套铅字 — *vt.* 把…分类；整理；拣选 —
vi. 1. 交往(*with ~*) 2. (古) 一致；协调
(*with*) ‖ **~er** *n.*

sortie ['sɔti] *n.*【军】1. 出击；突围；出港
2. 出击部队 3. 出动架次(指一架飞机的
一次出击)

SOS ['es.əu'es] *n.* 1. (国际通用的船舶、
飞机等的)呼救信号 2. (口)求救(或求
援)的表示

so-so ['səusəu] *adj. & adv.* (口)平常的
(地)，一般的(地)；还过得去的(地)

sot [sɔt] *n.* 酒鬼；酒糊涂 — (sotted; sot-
ting) *vt.* 因喝酒而浪费掉(*away*) —
vi. 嗜酒；滥喝酒

soubriquet ['səubrikei] *n.* 假名；绰号，浑
名

soufflé ['suːflei, suːˈflei] (法) *n.* 蛋奶酥

sough [sau] *n.* 1. (风、流水的)飒飒声，沙
沙声 2. 长叹 — *vi.* 1. 作飒飒声，作沙
沙声 2. 相声呼吸

sought [sɔt] seek 的过去式和过去分词

soul [səul] *n.* 1. 灵魂；心灵 2. 精神；精
力；气魄；热情 3. 精髓，精华；中心人
物 4. (常冠以数量词或有情感色彩的形
容词)人 5. 化身；典型 6. 鬼魂；All
Souls' Day (天主教)万灵节(11 月 2
日) 7. (美俚)(尤指黑人演员等对黑人
文化与种族团结等所表现的)激情，自

豪 — *adj.* (美国)黑人的 ‖ **~ful** *adj.*
/ **~less** *adj.*

sound[1] [saund] *adj.* 1. 健康的；健全的 2.
完好的 3. 正确的；合理的；稳妥的 4.
坚固的；殷实的；可靠的 5. 彻底的；充
分的；严厉的 6. (人)有判断力的，见解
正确的 7. 忠实可靠的；道德高尚的 8.
正统的 9.【律】有效的 — *adv.* 彻底地，
充分地 ‖ **~ly** *adv.* / **~ness** *n.*

sound[2] [saund] *n.* 1. 声音 2. 语音 3. 嘈
声；噪声 4. 语调；笔调；含意 5. 听力范
围 6. (电影、唱片等的)录音 7.【物】声
(音)— *vi.* 1. 响，发声；回响；召唤 2.
听起来：A: How does this proposal ~ to
you? B: It ~ *s* quite all right. 甲：你觉得
这个提议怎么样？乙：听上去挺不错。—
vt. 1. 使发声 (用吹号等方式)通知；
命令 2. 发…的音 3. 宣告；传播 4. 听
诊；触探 ‖ **~ effects** 音响效果 / **~ pollution** 噪声污染 / **~ proof** *adj.* 隔音的
— *vt.* 给…隔音 / **~ track** *n.* 声带；
声槽 / **~ wave** 声波

sound[3] [saund] *vt.* 1. 测…的深度；锤测
(深度)3. 探测(大气上层)的温度(气
压、湿度等) 2. 试探(*out*) 3.【医】用探
子检查(体腔等)— *vi.* 1. 测深 2. 试
探 3. (鲸鱼等)突然潜入海底 — *n.*
【医】探子；探条

sound[4] [saund] *n.* 1. 海峡；海湾 2. (鱼
的)鳔

sounding[1] ['saundiŋ] *adj.* 1. 发出声音
的；响亮的 2. 夸大的，夸张的；听上去
堂皇的

sounding[2] ['saundiŋ] *n.* 1. 测探；水深测
量；[气]探空 2. (海中的)水的深度 3.
[~s]测深海所能达到的近岸水域(或
地方) 4. 试探；搜集意见；调查 5.【医】
探通术

soup [suːp] *n.* 1. 汤 2. 羹汤般稠浓的东

西;〈美俚〉浓雾;(尤指用以炸开保险箱等的)硝化甘油炸药;(照相)显影液

sour ['sauə] *adj*. 1. 酸的,酸味的,酸臭的 2. 发酵的 3. 脾气坏的,乖戾的;愠怒的;敌对的 5. 讨厌的;乏味的 6. 刺耳的;拙劣的 7.(土壤)酸性过强的 8. 湿冷的 9.(汽油等)含硫的 — *vt*. 1. 使变酸;使变酸臭;使发酵 2. 使变得不愉快;使失望;使变得讨厌无趣 3. 用稀酸溶液处理(尤指在漂白等时) — *vi*. 1. 变酸;变酸臭;发酵 2.(土壤)变成酸性;变得贫瘠 3. 变得不愉快;厌烦 4. 变坏 — *n*. 1. 酸味;酸性物质 2. 酸味饮料;酸味鸡尾酒 ‖ ~ly *adv*. / ~ness *n*. ‖ ~crout. '~krout *n*. 泡菜

source [sɔːs] *n*. 1. (河的)源头;水源 2. 源;根源,来源 3. 消息来源;提供消息者 4. 出处;原始资料 ‖ ~ **language** 1. (译本的)原语,译出语 2.(外语教学中使用的)母语,本族语 3.【计】源语言

sourish ['sauəriʃ] *adj*. 微酸的,略带酸味的

souse [saus] *vt*. 1. 腌 2. 浸,泡;使湿透 3.〈俚〉灌醉 — *vi*. 1. 泡在水里;被浸透 2.〈俚〉喝醉 — *n*. 1. 腌渍品,咸货(尤指腌猪头、腌猪脚、腌鱼等) 2. 腌渍用的盐水 3. 腌;浸,泡 4.〈俚〉醉汉 5. 狂饮

south [sauθ] *n*. 1. 南,南方 2. [S-](一国或一地区的)南部 3. [常 S-]地球的南部(尤指南极地区) 4. 南风 — *adj*. 1. 南的,南方的 2. 朝南的 3. 来自南方的 '4.[S-](一国、一洲或一地区)南方的: *South* China 华南 / *South* America 南美洲 — *adv*. 向南方;向南方;从南方 — [sauθ] *vi*. 1. 转向南方 2.【天】(日、月等)到达子午线,过南北线 ‖ '~-paw *n*.〈俚〉左撇子;惯用左手的运动员;(棒球)左手投手 *adj*.〈俚〉用左

手的 / *South Pole* 南极

southbound ['sauθbaund] *adj*. 向南行的;向南驶的

southeast [ˌsauθ'iːst] *n*. 1. 东南(泛指东南方向,或指正东至南 45°;略作 SE) 2.[S-](一国或一地区的)东南部 — *adj*. 1. 位于东南的;向东南的 2.(风)来自东南的 — *adv*. 在东南;向东南;从东南

southeaster [sauθ'iːstə] *n*. 东南大风(或狂暴)

southeastern [sauθ'iːstən] *adj*. 1.(在)东南的;向东南的 2.(风)来自东南的 3.[S-](一国或一地区)东南部的

southerly ['sʌðəli] *adv. & adj*. 1. 在南方(的);向南方(的) 2.(风)来自南方(的) — *n*. 南风

southern ['sʌðən] *adj*. 1. [常 S-](一国或一地区)南部的;南部方言的 2.(风)来自南方的 3. 朝南的 4. 有南方地区特征的 — *n*. 1.[S-](美国)南方人 2. [常 S-]美国南部方言 ‖ ~er *n*.

southward ['sauθwəd] *adv. & adj*. 向南方(的) — *n*. 向南的方向;南方的地区

southwest [ˌsauθ'west] *n*. 1. 西南(泛指西南方向,或指正西以南 45°;略作 SW) 2.[S-](一国或地区)的西南部 — *adj*. 1. 位于西南的;向西南的 2.(风)来自西南的 — *adv*. 在西南;向西南;从西南

southwester [ˌsauθ'westə] *n*. = sou'wester

southwestern [sauθ'westən] *adj*. 1.(在)西南的;向西南的 2.(风)来自西南的 3.[S-](一国或地区)西南部的

souvenir [ˌsuːvə'niə] *n*. 纪念礼物;纪念品 ‖ ~ **sheet** (集邮用语)小全张、小型张

sou'wester [sau'westə] *n*. 1. 西南大风(或风暴) 2.(海员用的)防水帽。长

雨衣

sovereign ['sɔvrin] *n.* 1. 君主,国王;最高统治者 2. (英)沙弗林(旧时面值 1 英镑的金币) — *adj.* 1. 最高的,无上的;无限的 2. 拥有最高权力的;独立自主的 3. 君主的,国王的 4. 完全的,不折不扣的 5. 极好的;有效的

sovereignty ['sɔvrənti] *n.* 1. 君权,统治权 2. 主权 3. 主权国家

Soviet ['sɔuviet, 'sɔviet](俄) *n.* 1. [常 s-] 苏维埃 2. [~s]布尔什维克;苏联人 — *adj.* 1. 苏维埃的: the Union of ~ Socialist Republics(简称: the ~ Union)[史]苏维埃社会主义共和国联盟(简称:苏联)2. 苏联的

sow¹ [sou](过去式 sowed,过去分词 sown [soun]或 sowed) *vt.* 1. 播(种);播(种于)(土地等)2. 散布;传播;惹起 3. 使遍布 — *vi.* 播种 ‖ ~**er** *n.* 1. 播种者;播种机 2. 散布者;传播者;煽动者

sow² [sau] *n.* 1. 母猪;牝猪 2.[冶](高炉)铁水沟;沟铁 3.[动]土鳖,地鳖(生于朽木、湿地等处的一种甲壳动物)

sox [sɔks] sock 的复数

soy [sɔi] *n.* 1. 酱油 2. 大豆

soybean ['sɔi'biːn] *n.* (英)大豆

spa [spɑː] *n.* 1. 矿泉;矿泉疗养地 2. (尤指附近有矿泉的)游乐胜地;豪华旅馆

space [speis] *n.* 1. 空间;太空 2. 空地;余地;篇幅 3. 空白;距离;间隔 4. (一段)时间 5. (火车、轮船等预订的)坐位;舱位 6. 间隙;空白处(打字机上)一字母宽度 7. (广播或电视)插播广告时间 8.[印]空铅或空格 9. [音](谱表的)线间空白,线间 10.[电]开键 — *vt.* 把…分隔开(*out*)— *vi.* 留间隔 ‖ ~ **bar**(打字机上的)间隔棒 / ~ **craft** *n.* 航天器,宇宙飞船 / ~ **man**

n. 宇航员;宇宙科学工作者;太空人 / '~ **ship** *n.* 宇宙飞船 / ~ **shuttle** 航天飞机 / ~ **station**, ~ **platform** 航天站,宇宙空间站 / ~ **suit** 宇航服,宇航服 / ~ **time** [物]时空(关系)/ ~ **walk** *n.* & *vi.* (在)太空(中)行走

spacious ['speiʃəs] *adj.* 广阔的;宽敞的;广大的

spade¹ [speid] *n.* 1. 铲;铁锹 2. 铲形物;[军](炮架的)驻锄 — *vt.* 铲;用铁锹掘 — *vi.* 铲

spade² [speid] *n.* 1. (纸牌中的)黑桃;(一张)黑桃牌;[~s]一副黑桃(牌)2.(美俚)(贬)黑人

spaghetti [spə'geti](意) *n.* 1. 细条实心面(与 macaroni 空心面相对)2.[电]绝缘套管

Spain [spein] *n.* 西班牙[欧洲西南部国家]

span¹ [spæn] *n.* 1. 指距,一作寸(手掌张开时,大拇指和小指两端的距离,通常为 9 英寸或 23 厘米)2. 全长;[空]翼展 3. (桥墩间的)墩距;孔;跨距,跨(度);支点距 4. 一段时间(尤指人生)5.(思想活动的)广度 6.[海]跨绳 7. 双马;双骡;共轭牛 — [spanned; spanning] *vt.* 1. 以手指量;估量 2. 横跨;跨越;(喻)弥补 3.[海]缚住,扎牢 — *vi.* 尺蠖般地蠕动

span² [spæn](古)spin 的过去式

spangle ['spæŋgl] *n.* 1.(尤指衣服上用作装饰的)发光金属(或塑料)片 2. 亮晶晶的小东西 — *vt.* 用发光金属片装饰;使闪烁 — *vi.* 闪烁

Spaniard ['spænjəd] *n.* 西班牙人

spaniel ['spænjəl] *n.* 1. 獚(一种长毛垂耳狗)2. 马屁精

Spanish ['spæniʃ] *adj.* 西班牙的;西班牙人的;西班牙语的 — *n.* 1.[the ~]

[总称]西班牙人 2. 西班牙语

spank [spæŋk] vt. 1.(用手掌等)打…的屁股;拍击 2. 拍击…前进 3.(美俚)(在比赛中)击败 — vi.(马等)飞跑;(船)疾驶 — n. 一掴;一巴掌

spanking ['spæŋkiŋ] adj. 1. 疾行的;快的2. 劲吹的;强烈的 3.〈口〉第一流的;极好的 — adv. 显著地;突出地 — n. 打屁股;拍击

spanner ['spænə] n. 1. 扳手,扳头,扳钳,搬子 2.[建](桥梁的)交叉支撑,横拉条 3.[动]尺蠖

spar¹ [spɑː] n. 1.(船用)圆材 2.[空]翼梁 —(sparred; sparring)vt. 1. 装圆材于 2. 用圆材使(船)脱离浅滩

spar² [spɑː](sparred; sparring)vi. 1.(拳击赛中)用拳作攻击与防卫姿势;拳斗 2. 争论;争吵 3.(鸡)用脚踢斗 — n. 1. 拳斗动作;拳击比赛 2. 争论;斗鸡

spar³ [spɑː] n.[矿]晶石

spare [spɛə] vt. 1. 节约,省用;吝惜 2. 用不着;省掉 3. 抽出(时间);剩下;出让;让给 4. 饶恕;赦免;不伤害 — vi. 1. 节约,节俭 2. 饶恕;宽容 — adj. 1. 多余的,剩下的 2. 备用的 3. 节约的;少量的;贫乏的

sparerib ['spɛərib] n. 小排骨,带肉排骨

sparing ['spɛəriŋ] adj. 1. 节约的;吝惜的;节制的 2. 少量的;贫乏的 ‖ ~ly adv.

spark [spɑːk] n. 1. 火花,火星 2.(宝石等的)闪光;(小宝石)金刚钻 3. 生气,活力;(才智等的)焕发 4.[常用于否定句]丝毫,一点点 5.[电]电花;瞬态放电;(火花塞里的)控制放电电装置 6.[~s][用作单](船、飞机等的)无线电报务员 — vi. 1. 发火花,飞火星;发电花;闪耀 2. 热烈赞同;欣然同意 — vt. 1. 发动 2. 激发(感情等);鼓舞 ‖

plug 1. 火花塞(=〈英〉~ing plug)2.〈美〉积极的促进者;中坚分子 /'~ **plug** vt. 发动;激励

sparkle ['spɑːkl] vi. 1. 发火花;闪耀(才智等)焕发 2.(香槟酒等)发泡 — vt. 1. 使闪耀,使…发光 2. 用眼神表示(喜悦等)— n. 1. 火花;闪耀,闪光;光彩 2. 生气;活力 3. 发泡 ‖ ~ r n. 1. 闪光的东西;钻石;烟火,火炮 2. 才华焕发的人

sparrow ['spærəu] n. 1. 麻雀 2. 矮小的人,小个子 ‖ ~ hawk[鸟]雀鹰

sparse [spɑːs] adj. 稀少的;稀疏的 ‖ ~ly adv. / ~ness n.

Sparta ['spɑːtə] n.[史]斯巴达(古希腊一奴隶制城邦)

Spartan ['spɑːtən] adj. 1.(古希腊奴隶制城邦)斯巴达的;斯巴达人的;斯巴达文化的 2. 斯巴达式的;刚强的;勇敢的;好战的;律已很严的;严峻的;简朴的;艰苦的 — n. 1. 斯巴达人 2. 斯巴达式的人;坚韧不拔的人

spasm ['spæzəm] n. 1. 痉挛,抽搐 2.(动作、感情等的)一阵发作

spasmodic [spæz'mɔdik] adj. 1. 痉挛的,抽搐的;由痉挛引起的;痉挛性的 2. 间歇的;一阵阵的 3. 易激动的 ‖ ~ally adv.

spastic ['spæstik] adj. 1. 痉挛的 2. 患大脑性麻痹的 — n. 患大脑性麻痹的人

spat¹ [spæt] spit 的过去式和过去分词

spat² [spæt] n. 1.[常~s]鞋罩 2. 飞机轮罩

spat³ [spæt] n.〈美〉1. 口角;小争吵 2.〈方〉拍打 3.(大雨点落下的)劈啪声 —(spatted; spatting)vt.〈方〉拍打 — vi. 1. 争吵 2. 雨点般滴落

spatchcock ['spætʃkɔk] n. 杀后即煮的家

禽 — *vt.* 1. 把(家禽)杀后即煮 2. (口)把(不适当的话等)补入,插入(*in*, *into*)

spatial ['speiʃəl] *adj.* 空间的;(古)篇幅的;存在(或发生)于空间的;占据空间的

spatter ['spætə] *vt.* 1. 溅,溅污;洒 2. 污蔑;中伤 — *vi.* 滴下,飞溅 — *n.* 1. 溅,洒,滴落;飞溅 2.(雨等的)淅沥声;飞溅声 3. 泼溅的污迹:mud(grease)~s 泥(油)迹 4. 少量;点滴

spatula ['spætjulə] *n.* 1.(涂敷等用的)抹刀;刮勺;刮铲;油漆刀 2.[医]药刀,软膏刀;压舌板 3.[动](昆虫的)抱突

spavin ['spævin] *n.*[兽医](马的)飞节内肿

spawn [spɔːn] *n.* 1.(鱼、蛙等水生动物一次产下的)卵(块)、子 2.(蔑)小子,小畜生 3. 产物 4. 根源;祸根 5.[植](繁殖菌类植物的)菌种体 — *vt.* 1.(鱼等)产(卵);使(鱼)产卵 2.(蔑)(人)生育 3. 酿成;引起 4. 菌种种子(苗床)— *vi.* 1. 产卵 2. 大量生育

spay [spei] *vt.* 切除(动物)的卵巢

speak [spiːk](过去式 spoke[spəuk]或〈古〉spake[speik],过去分词 spoken ['spəukən]) *vi.* 1. 说话,讲话 2. 谈话 3. 发言;演说 4. 表明;(用说话以外的方式)表达 5.(枪炮、乐器等)发响声;(狗)吠 6. 作证 — *vt.* 1. 说;操(某种语言)2. 说出,讲出 3. 显示;表达(情感等)4. 用响声宣告 5.(古)证明 6. 朗诵(短文等)7.(航海时用旗语等方式)与…联络;招呼 ‖ ~ easy *n.*〈美〉非法酒店

speaker ['spiːkə] *n.* 1. 说话者;演讲者;演说家;代言人 2.[S~](英国下议院、美国众议院的)议长 3. 扬声器 4.〈美〉练习演讲用的范本

speaking ['spiːkiŋ] *adj.* 1. 发言的;交谈的 2. 雄辩的;能说明问题的;富于表情的 3. 栩栩如生的,逼真的 — *n.* 说话;演讲

spear [spiə] *n.* 1. 矛;枪;梭镖;鱼叉 2. 持矛的人;持矛的士兵 3.(草的)叶片;幼芽,幼苗 — *vt.* 1. 用矛刺;用鱼叉刺 — *vi.* 1. 刺,戳 2.(植物)发芽成茎 — *adj.* 父系的 ‖ ~head *n.* 1. 矛头;枪尖 2. 先头突击部队 3. 尖端;先锋 *vt.* 领先突出;当…的先锋:~ head the attack 当进攻的先锋 /~mint *n.*[植]绿薄荷,留兰香

special ['speʃəl] *adj.* 1. 特殊的,特别的 2. 专门的,特设的 3. 附加的,额外的 4. 特别亲密的;主要的 — *n.* 1. 临时警察;特别警卫队 2. 特别的东西;专车:临时列车;特刊;号外;特别考试;特约稿;待写稿(或通讯)‖ ~ist *n.* 1. 专家 2.〈美〉(陆军中支上士官阶的)从事行政或技术工作的)专业人员 /~ly *adv.* 特别地;专门地;尤其 ‖ ~ agent 1. 特别经理人;特别代理人 2. 特务分子

specialist ['speʃəlist] *n.* 专家

speciality [ˌspeʃiˈæliti] *n.* 1. 特性,特质 2. 专门研究;专业;特长 3. 特制品;特产 4.[律]盖印的书面合同 5. [specialities]特点;细节

specialize ['speʃəlaiz] *vt.* 1. 特加指明;列举 2. 使…用于专门目的;限定…的范围;使专化 2. 在(票据上)记明受款人姓名 4.[生]使特化;使专化 — *vi.* 1. 成为专家;专门研究;专攻 2. 逐条详述 3.[生]特化;专化 ‖ speciali'zation *n.* 1. 特殊化;专门化 2.[生]特化(作用);专化性;特化器官,特化机体

specialty ['speʃəlti] *n.*〈主美〉= speciality

specie ['spiːʃiː] *n.* 硬币

species ['spi:ʃi:z][单复同] *n.* 1. 种,类;【逻】种类 2.【生】种: *The Origin of Species*《物种起源》(达尔文著) 3.【物】核素 4.【律】式样,形式 5.【宗】(圣餐中用的)面包和圣酒

specific [spi'sifik] *adj.* 1. 特有的;特定的 2. 具体的;明确的 3.【生】种的 4.【医】有效疗的;由特种病菌(或病毒)引起的 5.【物】比率的 6.【商】从量的 — *n.* 1. 特定用途的东西 2. 特效药 3. 特性 4. 细节:[~s](计划、建议等的)详细说明书 ‖ **-ally** *adv.*

specification [ˌspesifi'keiʃən] *n.* 1. 载明;详述 2.[常~s]规格;规范;明细单;计划书 3.(载有约定条件的)说明书;列入说明书的物件 4. 发明物申请专利说明书 5.【律】加工(指用他人动产制作成新动产)

specify ['spesifai] *vt.* 1. 指定;详细说明 2. 把…列入说明书(或清单)

specimen ['spesimin] *n.* 1. 样本;标本;样品;抽样 2. 供检查用的材料,试料 3.(口)怪人;怪事

specious ['spi:ʃəs] *adj.* 1. 外表美观的;华而不实的 2. 似是而非的;似似有理的 ‖ **-ly** *adv.* **/ -ness** *n.*

speck [spek] *n.* 1. 斑点;污点;缺点 2. 微粒,小点;一点点 3.(水果上的)烂斑,蛀伤 4. 有斑点的东西;有烂斑的水果;有斑点的鱼 — *vt.* 使有斑点;使弄上污点

speckle ['spekl] *n.* 小斑点 — *vt.* 1. 使弄上斑点;玷污 2. 点缀

spectacle ['spektəkl] *n.* 1. 公开展示;场面 2. 光景;景象;奇观;壮观 3.[~s]眼镜;护目镜 4.(铁路上红绿信号灯的)灯框

spectacular [spek'tækjulə] *adj.* 1. 公开展示的;场面富丽的;壮观的,洋洋大观

的 2. 引人注意的;惊人的 — *n.* 1. 展览物;壮观的景象 2.(美)(长达 1 小时半以上的场面富丽的)豪华电视片(或特别节目) 3.(美)引人注目的霓虹灯(或电灯)广告 ‖ **-ly** *adv.*

spectator [spek'teitə, 'spekteitə] *n.*(比赛等的)观众;旁观者

spectral ['spektrəl] *adj.* 1. 鬼怪(似)的 2.【物】光谱的

spectre, specter ['spektə] *n.* 鬼怪;幽灵;无法摆脱的忧惧

spectroscope ['spektrəskəup] *n.*【物】分光镜

spectrum ['spektrəm] ([复] spectra ['spektrə] 或 spectrums) *n.* 1. 系列;范围 2.【物】谱;电磁波谱;光谱 3.【无】射频频谱;频谱 4. 幻象;【心】余象

speculate ['spekjuleit] *vi.* 1. 思索;沉思;推测(*on, upon, about*) 2. 投机,做投机买卖

speculation [ˌspekju'leiʃən] *n.* 1. 思索;沉思;推测 2. 投机;投机事业;投机买卖 3. 投机(一种竟买最大王牌的纸牌戏)

speculative ['spekjulətiv] *adj.* 1. 思索的;推测的 2. 纯理论的 3. 投机的;冒险的;好投机的

speculator ['spekjuleitə] *n.* 1. 思索者;推理者;抽象的理论家 2. 投机者;投机商

sped [sped] speed 的过去式和过去分词

speech [spi:tʃ] *n.* 1. 言语;谈话,说话;说话方式(或能力等) 2. 演说;发言;讲话 3. 民族语言;方言;专门语言 4.【语】词(类);引语;用语 5.(乐器)发声

speechless ['spi:tʃlis] *adj.* 1. 不会说话的,哑的 2. 说不出话的 3. 无言的;非言语所能表达的 4.(俚)烂醉的

speed [spi:d] *n.* 1. 快,迅速 2. 速率,速度 3.(胶片、照相纸等的)感光速率;(摄影

机)的曝光速率 4.(汽车等的)排档,变速器 5.〈古〉昌盛;成功 — *vt*.(sped[sped]或 speeded)*vi*. 1. 迅速前进,快行 2.(驾车者)违章超速行驶 3. 加速(*up*) 4.〈古〉过日子;兴隆 — *vt*. 1. 快速传送;发射 2. 促进;使加速(前进);使赶快 3. 调整(机器)的速率;使定速运行 4. 祝愿(某人)一路平安;祝愿(某人)运气畅达 5.〈古〉使我兴隆 ‖ ~er *n*. 1.[机]加速器;调速装置 2. 违章超速驾驶者 ‖ '~boat *n*. 快艇 / '~reading *n*.(掠过一些段落的)快速阅读 / ~ trap(汽车)速度监视区 / '~ up *n*. 1. 增速,加速 2.(雇主对雇员的)增产而不增工资的要求 / '~way *n*. 1. 高速车道,快车道 2.(摩托车、汽车等的)赛车跑道

speedometer [spi'dɔmitə] *n*.(尤指汽车的)速率计,速度计;里程计

speedy ['spiːdi] *adj*. 快的,迅速的;a ~ reply 迅捷的回答 ‖ **speedily** *adv*.

spell[1] [spel](spelt[spelt]或 spelled)*vt*. 1. 用字母拼;拼写 2.(字母)拼作,拼缀成 3. 慢而费力地读懂(*out*, *over*)4. 认真研究出;琢磨;理解(*out*)5. 招致;带来;意味 — *vi*. 拼字 ‖ ~er *n*. 1. 拼单字者 2. 单词拼写课本

spell[2] [spel] *n*. 1. 轮班,轮值;轮值时间 2.(一段)工作时间 3.〈澳〉休息时间 4. 发病时间;(疾病等的)一次发作 5. 一段时间;(某种天气的)一段持续时间 6.〈口〉短距离 — *vt*. & *vi*. 1. 轮替 2.(使)替换班休息

spell[3] [spel] *n*. 1. 符咒;咒语 2. 吸引力;迷惑力;魅力 — *vt*. 使入迷 ‖ bind *vt*. 1. 迷住,使入迷 2. 用妖术迷惑 / '~bound *adj*. 1. 入迷的;出神的 2. 被符咒镇住的

spelling ['speliŋ] *n*. 拼写;拼读;拼法;

字法 ‖ ~ bee(美)拼单词比赛

spend [spend](spent[spent])*vt*. 1. 用(钱),花费 2. 消耗;用尽(弹药,气力等);浪费 3. 消磨(时间);度过,过(日子)4. 献出(生命等);(船因风暴等)失去(桅杆)— *vi*. 1. 花费 2. 浪费 3.(被)耗尽,用尽 3.(鱼等)产卵 ‖ ~er *adv*.

spendthrift ['spendθrift] *n*. 挥霍者;浪费者 — *adj*. 挥霍的,浪费的

spent [spent] spend 的过去式和过去分词 — *adj*. 1. 用尽的;精疲力竭的;失去效能的 2.(鱼等)产过卵的;射过精的

sperm[1] [spəːm]([复]sperm(s))*n*. 1. 鲸蜡;鲸脑油 2. 鲸油 3. 抹香鲸(亦作 ~whale)

sperm[2] [spəːm]([复]sperm(s))*n*. 精液;精子 ‖ **spermatic** [spəː'mætik] *adj*. ‖ ~ bank 精子库

spermaceti [,spəːmə'seti] *n*. 鲸蜡;鲸脑油

spew [spjuː] *vt*. 1. 呕出 2. 喷 — *vi*. 1. 呕吐 2. 涌出 3. 渗出 — *n*. 呕吐物;喷出物

sphere [sfiə] *n*. 1. 球;圆体;球面 2.〈美俚〉棒球;高尔夫球 1. 天体;星;行星 3. 地球仪;天体仪 4. 范围;领域 5. 地位;身份 / 〈诗〉天空;天堂 — *vt*. 1. 使成球形 2. 把…放在球中;把…放在天体内 3. 包围;围住

spherical ['sferikəl] *adj*. 球的;球形的;球面的;天体的

spheroid ['sfiərɔid] *n*.【数】球体;回转扁球(体),回转椭球(体)2.〈美俚〉棒球 ‖ ~al *adj*.

sphincter ['sfiŋktə] *n*.【解】括约肌 ‖ ~al *adj*.

sphinx [sfiŋks]([复]sphinxes 或 sphinges ['sfindʒiːz])*n*. 1.[S-]〈希神〉斯芬克斯(带翼狮身女怪;传谜命过路行人猜

谜,猜不出者即遭杀害) 2.(古埃及)狮身人面像;狮身羊头(或鹰头)像 3.谜样的人物【动】天蛾: 西非大狮狮 ‖ ～like adj.

spice [spais] n. 1. 香料;调味品 2. 香气,香味 3. 趣味;风味 — vt. 1. 加香料于 2. 使增添趣味

spick-and-span ['spikənd'spæn] adj. 1. 崭新的 2. 极整洁的;极干净的

spicy ['spaisi] adj. 1. 加有香料的;香的 2. 出产香料的 3. 辛辣的;痛快的 4.(故事等)下流的,猥亵的

spider ['spaidə] n. 1. 蜘蛛 2. 设圈套者 3. 三脚架 4. 有柄带脚煎锅 5.(扬声器)的中心盘 6.(中耕机用的)泥土粉碎器 7.(美俚)缫丝工人 ‖ ～ web 1. 蜘蛛网 2. 蜘蛛网状的东西

spiel [spi:l, ʃpi:l] n.(美俚)流利夸张的讲话;招摇生意的言辞

spigot ['spigət] n. 1. 塞,塞栓;(旋塞的)孔塞 2. 龙头 3.(管子的)插端

spike¹ [spaik] n. 1.(装在墙头上防人翻墙的)墙头钉,尖铁 2. 大钉;道钉 3. [～s]鞋底钉;钉鞋 4. 长而尖的东西;(幼鹿的)单枝鹿角 5.【动】不满6英寸长的幼鲑 6. 细高跟;[～s]细高跟鞋 7.[物]尖峰 8.(美俚)皮下注射用的针头 — vt. 1. 用大钉加在鞋底钉子(鞋等)上及而尖的物刺 3. 塞住(大炮)火门 4. 阻止;抑制;使(计划等)受挫折 5. 加酒精(或烈酒)于(饮料);增强—(的)味;使增添生气(或风味) 6.(在球类比赛中)用钉鞋踩伤(对方) 7. 扣(排球)

spike² [spaik] n.【植】1.(谷物的)穗 2. 穗状花序

spiky ['spaiki] adj. 1. 大钉似的;长而尖的 2. 装有大钉的 3.(人)刻薄的;难弄的

spill¹ [spil] (spilt [spilt] 或 spilled) vt. 1. 使溢出;使溅出;使散落 2. 使(血)流出 3. 倾倒出;(车、船等)下(客) 4.(帆)漏风,减小(风)对帆的压力 5. 使摔下,使跌下 6. 泄漏(秘密等) — vi. 1. 溢出;溅出;(人群等)涌流 2. 充满 3.(马车等)倾覆;(人)摔下,跌下 4. 泄密 n. 1. 溢出;溅出;散落 2.(人群等)的涌出 3. 溢流量,溢出的东西 4. = ～way 5. 摔下,跌下 ‖ ～over n. 1. 溢出;溢出部分;溢出物 2. 大城市容纳不下的(外流人口 3. 伴随的发展;结果,影响;间接影响 /'～way n. 溢水口;溢洪道

spill² [spil] n. 木片;点火用的纸捻 2. 小塞子 3. 小金属棒;销子 4.(包东西用的)锥形(或圆筒形)纸包

spin [spin] (spun [spun] ;spinning) vt. 1. 纺 2.(蚕等)吐(丝);作(茧) 3.(蜘蛛等结(网) 4.(用车床等)旋制(金属碗,杯等) 4. 编造;撰写(故事等) 5. 使旋转;【天】使自转减慢(down) ;使自转加快(up) 6.(英)(考试)给(学生)打不及格分 7.(通过离心力作用)抛出;丢开(off) 8.(美俚)散漫 — vi. 1. 纺织;纺线 2.(蚕等)吐丝;(蜘蛛)结网 3. 旋转;【天】(恒星、行星等)减慢自转(down) ;加快自转(up) 4.(汽车等)疾驰 5.【空】作螺旋下降;往下直冲 6.(英俚)考试不及格 7.(美俚)跳舞 — n. 1. 旋转;自旋 2. 眩晕;内心紊乱 3. 疾驶;兜一圈 4.【空】尾旋;螺旋 5.(澳)运气

spinach, spinage ['spinidʒ] n. 1. 菠菜(叶) 2.(美俚)不需要(或虚假)的东西;胡说八道 3.(美俚)未加修剪的胡子

spinal ['spainəl] adj. 1.【解】脊骨的,脊柱的;脊髓的 2.【生】针的;刺的;棘状突

起的 — *n.* = ~ anaesthesia ‖ ~ **anaesthesia**【医】髓麻醉 / ~ **column**【解】脊柱 / ~ **cord**【解】脊髓 / ~ **nerve**【解】脊神经

spindle ['spindl] *n.* 1. 锭子,纺锤 2. 心轴;指轴 3. (门锁的)转轴 4. 司品德(纱的度量单位) 5. 瘦长的人;细长的东西 6.【生】纺锤体 7. (栏杆的)纺锤形立柱 8. (楼梯的)拐弯角柱 9.【植】叶状信标 — *vi.* 1. 长得细长 2. 长茎而不开花(或不结果) — *vt.* 1. 装锭子于;装纺锤形立柱于 2. 使成纺锤形 — *adj.* 1. 似锭子的;细长的

spindling ['spindliŋ], **spindly** ['spindli] *adj.* 细长的;虚弱的

spindrift ['spindrift] *n.* (大风吹起的)海浪溅沫

spine [spain] *n.* 1.【解】脊骨,脊柱(亦作 ~ bone) 2. 类似脊骨的东西;书脊;地面上隆起地带 3. 骨气,勇气 4.【植】刺 5.【动】刺,壳针 6.【地】火山栓,熔岩塔 7.〈美俚〉(铁路上货车的)平顶

spineless ['spainlis] *adj.* 1. 无脊骨的 2. 无骨气的;没有勇气的;柔弱无力的 3.【生】无刺的

spinet [spi'net] *n.* 1. 小型拨弦古钢琴 2. 小型立式钢琴 3. 小型电子风琴

spinner ['spinə] *n.* 1. 纺纱工;纺工;纺纱机 2. (钓鱼用)旋式诱饵 3.【空】螺旋整盖;机头整流罩 4. (足球赛中)带球人的旋转动作,急转身假动作 5.〈美俚〉卡车司机

spinning ['spiniŋ] *n.* 1. 纺纱;纺织 2. 旋转;旋转物 — *adj.* 纺纱的;旋转的 ‖ ~ **frame** 精纺机,细纱机 / ~ **jenny** 詹妮纺纱机 / ~ **machine** 纺纱机;纺丝机 / ~ **wheel** 手纺车

spinster ['spinstə] *n.* 1.〈美〉从事纺织的女子 2. 未婚女子;老处女

spiny ['spaini] *adj.* 1. 多刺的;刺状的 2. 困难重重的,麻烦的,棘手的

spiracle ['spaiərəkl] *n.* 1. 通气孔 2. (昆虫的)气门;鳃孔 3.【地】气孔

spiraea [spai'ri:ə] *n.*【植】1. 绣线菊 2. 泡盛落新妇

spiral ['spaiərəl] *adj.* 螺旋(形)的;螺旋的;蜷线的;盘旋上升的 — *n.* 1. 螺旋(形);螺线;蜷线 2. 螺旋形的东西(如弹簧等) 3.【空】盘旋 4. (足球赛的)旋球 5. (物价等)不断的急剧上升(或下降) — (spiral(l)ed; spiral(l)ing) *vi.* 1. 盘旋 2. (物价等)螺旋形地上升(或下降),不断急剧增加(或减少) — *vt.* 1. 使成螺旋形 2. 使作螺旋形上升(或下降) — **ly** *adv.*

spire[1] ['spaiə] *n.* 1. 螺旋,螺线 2.【动】螺旋部;(软体动物的)螺塔 — *vi.* 螺旋形上升

spire[2] ['spaiə] *n.* 1. 塔尖;尖顶;锥形体 2.【植】幼叶;幼苗 — *vi.* 给…加塔尖 — *vi.* 1. 塔状矗立;耸立 2. 发芽

spirea [spai'ri:ə] *n.* = spiraea

spirit ['spirit] *n.* 1.(与肉体相对而言的)精神,心灵;灵魂 2. [只用单](时代的)潮流,精神,风气 3. (文件,法律等的)精神实质 4. [只用单]气魄,气概;志气 5. [只用单]态度 6. [~s]情绪,心情;兴致 7. (具有某种精神或品质的)人物 8. 神灵;幽灵,鬼怪;妖精 8. [常~s]烈酒;酒精 9. [~s]酒精(指任何一种的液体) 11.【医】酊剂 — *vt.* 1. 使精神振作;鼓舞,鼓励(*up*) 2. 迅速而神秘地带走;拐走;偷走(*away, off*)

spirited ['spiritid] *adj.* 1. 精神饱满的,生气勃勃的;活泼的;勇敢的;猛烈的 2. [用以构成复合词]精神…的;情绪…的;心地…的 high-~ 勇敢的;兴奋的 / low-~ 沮丧的,精神不振的 / public-~

热心公益的

spiritless ['spiritlis] *adj.* 1. 没精打采的,垂头丧气的;灰心的 2. 无生命的,死的

spiritual ['spiritjuəl] *adj.* 1. 精神(上)的,心灵的 2. 神圣的;宗教的;高尚的 3. 超越世俗的 4. 鬼的;招魂论的;唯灵论的 — *n.* 1.[～s]有关教会的事情 2.(美)(黑人的)圣歌 ‖ ～ly *adv.*

spiritualism ['spiritjuəlizəm] *n.* 1.【哲】唯灵论 2.唯心论 3. 招魂说;招魂术 3.精神性;灵性

spirituality [ˌspiritju'æləti] *n.* 1. 精神性;灵性 2. 崇高纯洁,脱俗

spirituous ['spiritjuəs] *adj.* 1. 含酒精的,似酒精的;酒精的 2. 蒸馏的,非发酵的

spit[1] [spit] *n.* 1. 烤肉铁叉,炙叉 2. 岬,伸入海中的狭长陆地,沙嘴;狭长的暗礁 —(spitted;spitting) *vt.* 1.(以炙叉穿过(肉片等) 2.(以刀、矛等)刺,戳

spit[2] [spit] [spat[spæt]或 spit;spitting] *vt.* 1. 吐(唾液等);霍霍地下(雨、雪等) 2. 唾弃地说(或愤怒地说) 3. 点燃 — *vi.* 1. 吐唾沫;吐痰;吐唾;溅视 2.(雨,雪)霍霍下降;(钢笔)漏墨水 3.(蜡烛等)爆出火花;发出火舌;(猫等)咇咇呼呼怒叫;(发动机等)劈啪作响 — *n.* 1. 吐;唾;唾液 2. 小雨;小雪 3.【动】(树上某些昆虫的)泡沫状分泌物 ‖～fire *n.* 烈性子的人(尤指女子);喷火式战斗机

spite [spait] *n.* 恶意;怨恨 — *vt.* 恶意对待;刁难;使恼怒

spiteful ['spaitful] *adj.* 怀恨的;恶意的 ‖ ～ly *adv.* / ～ness *n.*

spittle ['spitl] *n.* 唾沫,涎液;(沫蝉的)泡沫状分泌物,沫 ‖ ～bug, ～ insect *n.*【动】沫蝉,吹沫虫

spittoon [spi'tuːn] *n.* 痰盂

splash [splæʃ] *vt.* 1. 溅;泼;使飞溅,溅湿;溅污 2. 使溅起水花(或泥浆),溅着泥浆(或水)走(路) 3.(泼水般地)洒,撒 4. 使成斑驳状 5.(美俚)以显眼地位展示(或发表);鼓吹 6.(美俚)击落(敌机等) 7.(俚)挥霍(钱财) — *vi.* 1. 溅起水(或泥浆);泼水;(在液体中)溅泼着行进 2. 飞溅 3. 发出溅水声音簌簌下;劈劈啪啪地撞击;咯吱咯吱地踏着泥浆(或水)行进 4.(美俚)洗澡,游泳 — *n.* 1. 溅;泼;飞溅 2. 短时间溅泼声,溅泼声;飞溅声 4. 溅起的泥浆(或水等);被溅上的污渍 5. 色斑(尤指动物皮毛的斑点) 6.(报刊上)引人注目的报道 7.(掺酒用的)少量水(或汽水,杜松子酒等);一点儿 8. 开闸流放木材;开闸流放木材的水 9.(美俚)被击落的飞机 10.(美俚)水;一杯水;一碗汤 ‖～y *adj.* /～board *n.* 1. 挡泥板,挡溅板 2.(溢洪道或水闸的)挡水板 /～down *n.*(宇宙飞船的)溅落

splatter ['splætə] *vi.* 1. 连续发溅泼声,淅沥作响 2. 结结巴巴地说话 — *vt.* 结结巴巴地说出 — *n.* 溅泼

splay [splei] *vt.* 1. 展开,张开(手掌、足趾等)(out) 2.【建】使成斜面;使成八字形 — *vi.* 1. 伸展开 2.【建】倾斜;成八字形 3. 展开 2.【建】斜削;斜面的 — *adj.* 1. 向外张开的;八字形的;宽扁的 2. 笨重的;样子难看的 ‖～foot *n.* & *adj.* 八字脚(的),外翻脚(的)

spleen [spliːn] *n.* 1.【解】脾 2. 坏脾气;怒气;恶意;怨恨 3.(古)忧郁;意气消沉

splendid ['splendid] *adj.* 1. 有光彩的;灿烂的 2. 壮丽的;辉煌的 3. 显著的;杰出的 4.(口)极好的;极令人满意的 ‖～ly *adv.*

splendo(u)r ['splendə] *n.* 1. 光辉；光彩 2. 壮丽；壮观 3. 显赫；杰出

splenetic [spli'netik] *adj.* 1.【解】脾的；位于脾（附近）的 2. 脾气坏的，易怒的；恶意的；怀恨的 — *n.* 1. 脾气坏的人 2. 脾病者 3. 脾病药

splice [splais] *vt.* 1. 拼接，叠接（木板等）；绞接，捻接（绳子等）〈俚〉使结婚 — *n.* 1. 拼接；绞接；拼接处；绞接处 2.〈俚〉结婚

splint [splint] *n.* 1.（编结篮子等用的）藤条，薄木条 2.（制铠甲用的）薄金属片 3.〈英口〉夹，石的（副骨 4.【医】夹板夹 5.【兽医】（马等的）掌骨瘤 6. ~ bone — *vt.* 用夹板固定 ‖ ~ bone（马等的）赘骨，小掌骨

splinter ['splintə] *n.* 1.（木头、玻璃、炮弹等的）裂片，破片；尖片 2. 分裂出来的小派别 3. 微不足道的事情；微小的东西 4.〈美俚〉极瘦的人 — *vt. & vi.* （使）裂成碎片；（使）分裂

split [split] (split/splitting) *vt.* 1. 劈开；切开；割裂；撕裂 2. 使分裂；使分离；（平）分 — *vi.* 1. 被劈开；裂开；爆发 2. 分裂分离；破裂；决裂；断绝关系 3.〈口〉均分负担（或所得）4.〈俚〉告密（on）5. 突然离开，跑掉 — *n.* 1. 劈裂；直裂口；裂缝 2. 分裂；分化；（分裂出的）派系，派别 3. 裂片；薄片；（横向）劈开；豆皮之（编剥用）劈开的柳条（或藤条等）4.〈英〉告密者；便衣警察 5.〈口〉半瓶汽水；半杯酒；小瓶饮料 6. [~s]（舞蹈、体操中的）劈叉 7.〈美俚〉（赃物等的）水果冰淇淋甜食 — *adj.* 分裂的；裂开的；劈开的

splotch [splɔtʃ] *n.* 斑点；污点，污渍 — *vt.* 使……弄脏；使沾上污迹 ‖ ~y *adj.*

splurge [splə:dʒ] 〈口〉*vi.* 挥霍金钱（on;

夸耀 — *vt.* 挥霍（金钱）（on）— *n.* 挥霍；夸耀 ‖ ~ r *n. / splurgingly adv.*

splutter ['splʌtə] *vi.* 喷溅唾沫（或食物）；气急败坏地说话 — *vt.* 喷溅（唾沫或食物）；气急败坏地说出 — *n.* 喷溅出的唾沫（或食物）；气急败坏说出的话 ‖ ~ er *n.*

spoil [spɔil] (spoilt[spɔilt]或 spoiled) *vt.* 1. 损坏；搞糟；弄坏；溺爱 3.〈古〉过去式和过去分词只用 spoiled) 抢劫，掠夺 4.〈罕〉伤害；杀害；使完蛋 — *vi.* 1.（食物等）变坏，腐败 2. 抢劫，掠夺 3.〈口〉掠夺物；抢劫，掠夺 4.〈美〉[常 ~s]得性政党分到的官职 4.（开掘、疏浚时挖出的）弃土废石料 5. 废品，次品 — *n. / — er n.* 1. 掠夺者；搞坏（事情、东西）的人；宠坏（别人）的人 2.【空】扰流器

spoke[1] [spəuk] *n.* 1. 辐条，轮辐 2.【船】舵轮把柄 3. 梯级 4. 车轮制动杆 — *vt.* 1. 给……装上辐条 2. 用制动棒煞住（车轮）

spoke[2] [spəuk] speak 的过去式

spoken ['spəukən] speak 的过去分词 — *adj.* 1. 口说的，口头的；口语的 2. [用以构成复合词]说话有……特点的

spokesman ['spəuksmən] ([复] spokesmen) *n.* 发言人，代言人

sponge [spʌndʒ] *n.* 1. 海绵 2. 海绵状物；海绵状橡皮；多孔塑料 3.【冶】金属海绵，海绵状金属 5. 外科用抹布 4. 炮刷 5. 发了酵的面团；多孔布[了；蛋糕 6.（蟹）的卵块 7. 海绵擦身洗浴 8.〈喻〉寄生虫，依赖他人生活的人 9. 容纳量大的人（或动物）；酒量大的人 — *vt.* 1. 用海绵揩拭；用海绵润湿 2. 用海绵揩去；消除（债务等）；忘却（往事等）(out, off, away) 3. 用海绵吸（水等）(up) 4.〈口〉以乞讨、欺骗等获得；白得，

吃 — vi. 1. 采集海绵 2. 海绵般吸收 3. 〈口〉做寄生虫，依赖他人生活 ‖ ~ r n. 1. 采集海绵的人(或船) 2. 用海绵擦洗的人 3. 〈口〉依赖他人生活的人，寄生虫 ‖ ~ cake 海绵状蛋糕，松蛋糕 / ~ gourd 丝瓜(络)

spongy ['spʌndʒi] *adj.* 1. 海绵质的；海绵状的 2. 多孔的；有吸水性的 3. 轻软而富有弹性的

sponsor ['sponsə] *n.* 1. 发起者；主办者；倡议者 2. 保证人 3. 〈宗〉教父；教母 4. (为自身产品等取得广告效应的)赞助者，资助者 — vt. 1. 发起；主办；倡议 2. 为...做保证人 3. 赞助；资助，捐助 ‖ ~ship n. 1. 发起；主办；倡议 2. 保证人(或教父、教母)的地位

spontaneity [ˌspɔntə'neiiti, ˌspɔntə'niːiti] *n.* 1. 自发(性)；(举止等的)自然 2. 自发动作(或行为，冲动等)

spontaneous [spɔn'teinjəs] *adj.* 1. (冲动、自然现象等)自发的；自然产生的，非外力因素的 2. (动作等)无意识的，不由自主的，自动的 3. (举止等)自然的；非勉强的，天真率直的 4. (植物)非人工栽培的，野生的 5. (文体等)自然流畅的 ‖ ~ly adv. / ~ ness n. ‖ ~ combustion 自发着火，自发燃烧

spook [spuːk] *n.* 1. 〈口〉古怪的人；幽灵般的人 2. 暗探 3. 〈俚〉代笔者 4. 〈美俚〉〈贬〉黑人 — vt. 1. 鬼怪般地出没于 2. 惊吓 3. 〈俚〉代写 — vi. (因受惊而)逃窜

spooky ['spuːki] *adj.* 1. 鬼的；鬼一般的 2. 怪异的，不可思议的 3. 神经质的；易惊的

spool [spuːl] *n.* 1. 〈纺〉(空心而两端有突缘的)有边筒子，线轴 2. (照相胶片、录音胶带、打字机色带等的)卷轴 — vt. 1. 把...绕到有边筒子(或卷轴)上；缠绕

spoon [spuːn] *n.* 1. 匙；羹(常用以构成复合词)，调羹 2. 一匙的量(=～ful) 3. 匙状物(约鱼用的)匙状假饵(亦作～bait)；匙形桨 4. (高尔夫)(木质头)号球棒 5. 挖土机；泥铲(亦作～shovel) 6. 〈俚〉(指男子)傻瓜，笨蛋；痴恋者；轻佻的情人 — vt. 1. 用匙舀；舀取 2. 使成匙形；把...挖空成匙形 3. 轻轻向上击(球) 4. 面对背地贴卧在一旁 5. 〈口〉(男子)向...求爱；对...动手动脚 — vi. 1. 用匙形假饵钓鱼 2. 轻轻向上击球 3. 面对背地贴卧 4. 〈口〉谈情说爱；动手动脚 ‖ ～ful n. 一匙(尤指一茶匙)的量 ‖ ～bill n. 〔鸟〕琵鹭 2. 琵嘴鸭 / ～ bread 〈美方〉(须用匙吃的)烤粟米软糕 / '～-feed vt. 1. 用匙喂 2. 填鸭式灌输(知识等)；对...进行填鸭式灌输

spoony ['spuːni] *adj.* 1. 〈主英〉愚蠢的，多愁善感的 2. 〈口〉痴情的，迷恋的(over, on) — n. 蠢人；傻瓜；痴情或轻佻的情人

spoor [spuə] *n.* 脚迹；臭迹 — vt. & vi. 跟踪追赶

sporadic [spə'rædik] *adj.* 单个发生的；偶尔发生的；分散的，零星的 ‖ ～ally adv.

spore [spɔː] 〔生〕 *n.* 1. 孢子 2. 种子；芽；生殖细胞 — vi. 长孢子

sport [spɔːt] *n.* 1. 娱乐，消遣；游戏 2. (体育)运动 3. [~s]运动会 4. 玩耍，戏谑；玩物，玩弄品；嘲弄对象，笑柄 5. 〈口〉有体育道德精神的人；运动员；计人欢喜的人 6. 〈美俚〉赌徒；好酒色的人；爱享乐的人，漂亮时髦的人 7. [生]突变，芽变 8. 变态(或畸形)的人(或动，植物) — vt. 1. 〈口〉炫耀；

突变为；芽变出 3.〈英〉关(门)；把(门)关着(通常表示无暇接待宾客) — *vi.* 1. 游戏，玩耍；寻欢作乐 2. 参加(体育)运动 3. 开玩笑；嘲弄(*with*) 4. 【生】突变；芽变 — [常作～s] *adj.* 体育运动的；体育运动用的 ‖ ～(-s) car 跑车(指一种双座敞篷低身小汽车)

sporting ['spɔːtiŋ] *adj.* 1. 运动的；有关体育运动的；喜爱运动的 2. 有体育道德的；光明正大的；公平的 3. 放荡的；嗜好赌博的 4.【生】有突变(或芽变)倾向的

sportive ['spɔːtiv] *adj.* 1.(爱)闹着玩的 2. 体育运动的 3. 适合运动时(或非正式场合)穿的 4.〈古〉淫荡的 ‖ ～ly *adv.* / ～ness *n.*

sportsman ['spɔːtsmən] ([复] sportsmen) *n.* 1. 爱好运动(尤指钓鱼、打猎等)的人；运动家，运动员 2. 具有运动家道德(指竞争中不对对方做小动作等)的人 ‖ ～like、～ly *adj.* 具有运动家道德的，具有运动家风格的 / ～ship *n.* 运动家品格

sportswear ['spɔːtswɛə] *n.* 1.【总称】运动服装；便服 2. 穿运动服装的动作

spot [spɔt] *n.* 1. 点；斑点；污点；斑点；缺点 2.(肺部等处的)阴影；(太阳等上的)黑点 3. 地点，场所；〈俚〉(在节目单、戏目等中的)位置，位置；职位；部位 4. 处境(尤指困境、窘境) 5. 插在广播(或电视)节目间的简短通知(或广告) 6.〈口〉少量；少许；少量酒 7.[～s] 现货 8.〈美俚〉面额为 … 的钞票；a two 一张 2 元钞票 9.〈美俚〉酒吧间；夜总会 10.〈美俚〉(…年) 徒刑：a one 一年 徒刑 11.〈英〉聚光灯(= spotlight) 12.【鱼】平口鲽(产于美国东部沿海的食用鱼) 13. 斑头鸽 — (spotted; spotting) *vt.* 1. 点缀；把…弄

脏；玷污 2. 在 … 上用点子作记号 3.〈口〉认出；发现；预先准(比赛中的优胜者等)；记认(惯犯、嫌疑犯等) 4. 准确地定出 … 的位置；使准确地击中目标 5. 把 … 散置在各点上；把 … 置于指定(或需要)地点 6. 使处于聚光灯光束下 7. 把(节目等)插在特定的位置(或时间) 8. 从 … 除去斑点(或污点)(*out*) 9.〈口〉(比赛中)给(对方)以礼让(如下棋时先让一子) — *vi.* 1. 沾上污点，变污；弄污 2.【军】(从空中)侦察敌军目标(*for*) 3.〈口〉下小雨 — *adj.* [只作定语] 1. 现场的 2. 现货的，现付的；专做现货生意的 3.(节目)插播的；现场直播的；地方电台(或电视台)为全国性广告商所播送的 4. 局限于某些项目(或地点)的；任选的；抽样的

spotless ['spɔtlis] *adj.* 1. 没有污点的，纯洁的；无瑕疵的 2. 极其清洁的 ‖ ～ly *adv.* / ～ness *n.*

spotlight ['spɔtlait] *n.* 1.(舞台)聚光灯；聚光灯照明圈 2. 公众注意中心 3. 灿烂的照明物；使变得突出醒目的因素 — *vt.* 聚光照明；使突出醒目

spotter ['spɔtə] *n.* 1. 放物到指定地点的人(或机器等) 2. 指定货物安放(或车辆停放)地点者 3.【军】弹着观察员(或观察机) 4.〈美〉去除污渍的人(或机器) 5.〈美〉私人侦探(对雇工等的)秘密监视人员 6.【机】测位仪 7.【体】(为广播员)辨识场上运动员者；(向橄榄球教练)报告比赛情况的助手 8.【铁】路基故障自动侦测器

spotty ['spɔti] *adj.* 1. 多斑点的；尽是污点的 2.(质量等)不稳定的；参差不齐的；零星的

spouse [spauz] *n.* 配偶(指夫或妻) — *vt.* 〈古〉和…结婚

spout [spaut] *n.* 1. 喷管；喷口（茶壶等的）嘴 2. 喷流；水柱【气】龙卷 3. 水落管 4.（输送用的）斜槽；【金属或炉造的】流出槽 5.〈俚〉当铺 6.（鲸类的）喷水孔。 *vt.* 1. 喷出，喷射 2. 滔滔不绝地讲 3.〈俚〉典押 — *vi.* 1. 喷出，喷射 2. 高谈阔论 ‖ *up the* ~〈俚〉1. 在典押中 2. 在困难中；已破落

sprain [sprein] *n.* 扭伤 — *vt.* 扭；扭伤

sprang [spræŋ] spring¹ 的过去式

sprat [spræt]（[复] sprat(s)）*n.* 1.【鱼】西鲱，黍鲱 2. 瘦小个子；小人物

sprawl [sprɔːl] *vi.* 1.〈懒散地〉伸开手足躺（或坐）2. 笨拙地爬行 3.（字体、队伍等）不整齐；散漫 4.（植物）蔓生，蔓延；（建筑物等）无计划地延伸 — *vt.* 1. 懒散或笨拙地伸开（手、足）2. 使蔓生；使散漫地伸展；潦草地书写 — *n.* 1. 伸开四肢的躺卧姿势 2. 蔓生；散乱 3.〈方〉毅力

spray¹ [sprei] *n.* 1. 浪花；水花，飞沫 2. 喷雾 3. 用作喷雾的液体 4. 喷雾器 5. 喷雾状物；飞沫状物 — *vt.* 喷；向…喷射；喷涂 — *vi.* 喷（如浪花般）溅散 ‖ — *er n.* 1. 喷射者 2. 喷雾器；喷雾器洒水车 ‖ '~-board *n.*【船】（船首）防溅板 / ~ gun 喷枪

spray² [sprei] *n.* 1. 小树枝；小花枝 2. 枝状物；枝状物

spread [spred]（spread）*vt.* 1. 伸开，展开；铺开，摊开 2. 传播；散布；扩大蔓延开去 3. 涂，敷；撒；施 4. 把…分期；展延续 5. 展宽，延展（金属等）；敷平（钉头）6. 展出，展示 7. 详细记录；详述 — *vi.* 1. 展开；扩大；伸长 2. 传播；散布；弥漫；（水等）涨开 3.（金属等）展宽；延伸开 — *n.* 1. 伸展；扩展 2. 传播；散布；蔓延 3.（一片）广阔的土地（或水域）；〈美〉大牧场。（报刊上）横贯两版

的篇幅；整版（或跨数栏）的文章（或广告等）5. 被单；桌布 6. 涂抹食品的酱（或膏等）（如果酱、黄油等）7.〈口〉丰富的酒席，宴会 8. 差距；脱节；【机】距离；【商】制造成本和卖价间的差额 — *adj.* [只作定语] 1. 扩大的，伸展的；广大的 ‖ — *er n.*

spree [spriː] *n.* 1. 狂欢，纵乐；狂饮 2. 无节制的狂热行为 — *vi.* 狂欢，纵乐；狂饮

sprig [sprig] *n.* 1. 小枝 2. 小枝状物 3.〈谑〉子孙；后辈 4.〈常作贬〉年轻人；小家伙 5. 无头钉 6. 嵌玻璃时（锡或锌制的三角小针，用以固住窗扇的玻璃）— (sprigged/sprigging) *vt.* 1. 用小枝（或枝状物）装饰 2. 使（草）蔓生 3. 除去…的小枝 4. 把无头钉钉入

sprightly ['spraitli] *adv.* & *adj.* 活泼地（的）；生气勃勃地（的）；轻快地（的）‖ **sprightliness** *n.*

spring¹ [spriŋ]（过去式 sprang [spræŋ] 或 sprung [sprʌŋ], 过去分词 sprung）*vi.* 1. 跳，跃；弹跳 2. 涌出；涌上 3.（植物等）生长；发生；出现 4. 出身（于）5.（地雷、水雷等）爆炸；（木材等）裂开；弯曲 6. 高耸 7.（拱等）起始，拱起 — *vt.* 1. 使跳（或弹）起；惊起（猎物）；跳过 2. 使爆炸；使破裂；把…弄弯 3. 突然提出（或宣布）4. 扭伤（腿等）；使疲乏；〈美俚〉解除对…的拘禁 — *n.* 1. 跳跃；跳起；弹回 2. 弹性；弹力；活力 3. 弹簧；发条 4. 泉，泉源 5.〔常~s〕根源；原动力；动机 6.（桅杆等的）裂缝；裂开【海】倒缆；【建】起拱点；起拱面 7.〔~s〕大潮期 ‖ **balance** 弹簧秤 / '~-board *n.* 1. 跳板 2. 出发点（for, to）/ '~-bok *n.*【动】跳羚（产于非洲南部）

spring² [spriŋ] *n.* 春天，春季；青春（期）‖ '~-'clean *vt.* 彻底打扫（房屋等）*n.*

〈英〉大扫除 /'~-'cleaning **n.** 〈美〉大扫除 /'~ **tide** **n. 1.** 〈新月和满月时的〉朔望大潮 **2.** 高潮 **3.** = ~time /'~ **time** **n. 1.** 全盛时期，青年时期

springy ['spriŋi] **adj. 1.** 有弹性的、有弹力的 **2.** 泉水多的；松软的 **3.** 轻快的

sprinkle ['spriŋkl] **vt. 1.** 洒，喷淋 **2.** 撒布；使散布 **3.** 点缀 — **vi. 1.** 洒，喷淋 **2.** 下稀疏小雨 — **n. 1.** 洒；撒 **2.** 小雨；间断雨 **3.** 少量；散布着的东西 **4.** [常 ~s] 撒在面上的东西 ‖ ~ **r n. 1.** 洒水器；洒水车；洒水设备 **2.** 〈洗衣作的〉喷水澄衣工

sprinkling ['spriŋkliŋ] **n. 1.** 洒；撒 **2.** 少量，稀落；点滴

sprint [sprint] **vi.** 〈尤指短距离〉全速奔跑，疾跑，冲刺 — **vt.** 用全速跑过 — **n. 1.** 全速疾跑；短〈距离赛〉跑 **2.** 〈距离赛〉跑冲刺；短时间紧张活动 ‖ ~**er n.** 短程疾跑者；短跑选手，短跑运动员

sprite [sprait] **n. 1.** 鬼怪；小妖精 **2.** 调皮捣蛋的人

sprocket ['sprɔkit] **n.** 【机】链齿 ‖ ~ **wheel** 链轮

sprout [spraut] **vi. 1.** 发芽；抽条 **2.** 很快地生长〈或发展〉 — **vt. 1.** 使萌发芽 **2.** 摘去…的芽 — **n. 1.** 新芽；籽苗；嫩条 **2.** [~s] 【植】汤菜 **3.** 幼苗状物；年轻人 〈美俚〉男孩

spruce[1] [spru:s] **n.** 【植】云杉；花旗松 **2.** 云杉轻质木材

spruce[2] [spru:s] **adj.** 整洁的；潇洒的 — **vt. & vi.** 〈把…〉打扮整齐 (up)

sprung [sprʌŋ] spring 的过去式和过去分词

spry [sprai] **adj.** 充满生气的；敏捷的 ‖ ~**ly adv.** / ~**ness n.**

spud [spʌd] **n. 1.** 〈口〉土豆 **2.** 〈除杂草用的〉除草铲

spume [spju:m] **n.** 泡沫；浮沫 — **vi. & vt.** 起泡沫

spun [spʌn] spin 的过去式和过去分词 — **adj.** 纺成的；似纺成的

spunk [spʌŋk] **n. 1.** 〈口〉勇气；精神；胆量；生气 **2.** 火绒 **3.** 〈英方〉火花，火焰 **4.** 〈英方〉怒火 — **vi. 1.** 〈美〉显示勇气 (up) **2.** 〈英方〉发怒，发火 (up) ‖ ~**y adj.**

spur [spə:] **n. 1.** 踢马刺，鞍刺 **2.** 刺激物；鼓励品；策励；鼓舞 **3.** 〈鸟、虫等的〉距〈斗鸡时加于鸡腿上的〉距铁 **4.** 〈攀爬者移登时所缚的〉距铁 **5.** 〈植〉花距 **6.** 山嘴，石嘴，尖坡，山鼻子 **7.** 【建】虎爪式柱座；支墩 — (spurred;spurring) **vt. 1.** 用踢马刺催促〈马〉 **2.** 刺激；鼓舞；鞭策 **3.** 给…装上踢马刺〈或攀爬刺铁、距铁等〉 — **vi. 1.** 用踢马刺驱马前进 **2.** 疾驰 ‖ ~ **gear** 【机】正齿轮

spurious ['spjuəriəs] **adj. 1.** 私生的 **2.** 假的；伪造的；欺骗性的 **3.** 【植】假的 ‖ ~**ly adv.** / ~**ness n.**

spurn [spə:n] **vt. 1.** 践踏；一脚踢开 (away) **2.** 轻蔑地拒绝；屏弃；唾弃 — **vi.** 屏弃；藐视 — **n. 1.** 踢开；屏弃；藐视

spurt [spə:t] **vt.** 喷射 — **vi. 1.** 喷出 **2.** 突然拼命努力〈赛跑中〉冲刺 **3.** 突然迸发；突然兴隆 — **n. 1.** 突然的喷射 **2.** 〈短促突然的爆发〈或激增〉;〈怒气、精力等的〉进发 **3.** 短时间,一时 **4.** 〈营业的〉突然兴隆

sputnik ['sputnik, 'spʌtnik] 〈俄〉**n.** 〈苏联〉人造地球卫星

sputter ['spʌtə] **vi. 1.** 喷溅唾沫〈或食渣〉 **2.** 〈因激动、愤怒等〉唾沫飞溅地说话；气急败坏地说话 (at) **3.** 发劈劈啪啪

声,发毕剥声 **4.**(马达等)爆响着熄掉;停息(out)— **vt. 1.**(噗地一声从嘴内)喷出;飞溅出 **2.** 唾诼飞溅地说出;气急败坏地说出(out)— **n. 1.** 喷溅唾沫(或食渍);喷溅声 **2.** 喷溅出来的东西;气急败坏时说出的言语 **3.** 劈劈啪啪声,毕剥声

sputum [ˈspjuːtəm]([复] sputa [ˈspjuːtə]) **n.** 唾沫;痰

spy [spai] **n. 1.** 密探;侦探;间谍;特务 **2.** 暗中监视;侦探 — **vt. 1.** 暗中监视;侦察;探出,查出(out) **2.** 察见,发现 **3.** 仔细察看 — **vi. 1.** 做密探;做间谍;暗中监视;侦查 **2.** 仔细察看 ‖ ~-glass **n.** 小望远镜

sq. *abbr.* **1.** squadron **2.** square

squab [skwɔb] **n. 1.** ([复] squab(s)) 雏鸟(尤指出生约 4 星期、重 1 磅左右的雏鸽) **2.** 矮胖子 **3.**(供坐或卧的)厚垫子;长沙发 **4.** 〈美俚〉少女 — **adj. 1.** 刚孵出的;羽毛未丰的 **2.** 矮胖的 — **adv.** 沉重地

squabble [ˈskwɔbl] **vi.**(为琐事)争吵,口角 — **vt.** [印] 搞乱(排好的铅字)— **n.** 争吵,口角

squad [skwɔd] **n. 1.** [军] 班 **2.** 小组,小队 — **vt.** 把…编成班(或小组)‖ ~-car(装有与总局联系的短波无线电话的)警车

squadron [ˈskwɔdrən] **n. 1.**(陆军的)骑兵中队,〈英〉(装甲兵、工兵、通信兵的)连 **2.**(海军的)中队 **3.**(空军的)中队;中队飞行队形 **4.** 团体;一组,一群 — **vt.** 把…编成中队 ‖ ~ leader〈英〉(空军)中队少校

squalid [ˈskwɔlid] **adj. 1.** 肮脏的;邋遢的 **2.** 悲惨的;贫穷的;可怜的 **3.** 道德品质卑劣的 ‖ ~ly **adv.** / ~ness **n.**

squall[1] [skwɔl] **n.**(因疼痛、害怕而引起

的)大声尖叫;嚎啕;啼哭 — **vi.** 大声尖叫;嚎啕;啼哭 — **vt.** 大声尖叫着发出(out)

squall[2] [skwɔl] **n. 1.**(常伴有雨、雪、雹的)暴风,飑 **2.**〈口〉麻烦事;打扰 **3.**(短暂的)动荡;骚动 — **vi.** 起暴风;刮飑

squalor [ˈskwɔlə] **n. 1.** 肮脏;邋遢 **2.** 悲惨;贫穷 **3.** 卑劣

squander [ˈskwɔndə] **vt. 1.** 浪费,滥用,乱花(时间、金钱等) **2.** 使分散;驱散 — **vi. 1.** 浪费,挥霍 **2.** 浪荡,漂泊 **3.** 四散 — **n.** 浪费,挥霍

square [skweə] **n. 1.** 正方形;方形物 **2.** [数] 平方,二次幂 **3.**(方形)广场;街心广场(的四周建筑);(四面临街的)街区 **4.** 直角尺,丁字尺,矩尺 **5.** 方格;纵横字谜 **6.** [军] 方阵 **7.** 百平方英尺(用于计算房屋面积) **8.** 棉靥,棉桃 **9.**〈俚〉古板守旧的人 — **adj. 1.** 正方形的;成直角的;矩形的 **2.** [数] 平方的,二次幂的 **3.** 宽阔而结实的 **4.** 适合的,正好的 **5.** 公正的 **6.** 结清的,两讫的;扯平的 **7.** 干脆的,断然的 **8.** 充实的;令人满意的 **9.**〈俚〉古板的,守旧的 **10.**(船)与龙骨和桅成直角的 — **adv. 1.** 成直角地;成方形地;面对面地;对准地 **2.** 正直地;公平地 **3.** 坚定地;实实不动地 — **vt. 1.** 把…弄成方形;把…弄成直角 **2.** 检验…的平方度 **3.** 使(肩膀等)成方形 **4.** 使作平方自乘;求…的面积 **5.** 调正;修正 **6.** 结清(账目);使(人)结清欠账;清算拉平(球赛等)比分;拉平(比分) **7.** 把…划分成方格(off) **8.** 使符合,使一致 **9.** 贿赂,收买 — **vi. 1.** 符合,一致 **2.** 结清,付讫 **3.**(拳击赛中)摆好架势(up, off) **4.**(高尔夫球赛等中)拉平比分 — **ly adv.** / ~ness **n.** ‖ ~-'rigged **adj.** [海] 横帆装置的

squash[1] [skwɔʃ] *vt.* 1. 把…压扁;把…碾扁 2. 镇压;压制 3.〈口〉(以压制手段)使沉默,压服 — *vi.* 1. 被压扁;被碾压平 2. 发瘪泼声;发哈哒声 3. 挤进,挤压(*in, into*) 4. 易压碎(或压烂,压扁)的东西;压得粉碎的一摊 2.(物物落下时的)啪声,扑声;(行走泥沼地或有水时的)略哈声 3.〈英〉果汁汽水 4. = ~ hat 5.[常用单]拥挤的人群 6. = rackets [复] 1.(在较大院子内用大网拍玩的)橡皮球戏 — *adv.* 挤压地;啪地;略哈略哈地 ‖ ~ hat 软毡帽 / ~ rackets [复][用作单或复](在围墙内用小网拍玩的)软式墙网球

squash[2] [skwɔʃ]([复] squash(es)) *n.* 南瓜;倭瓜;笋瓜;西葫芦

squat [skwɔt] [squatted; squatting] *vi.* 1. 蹲;蹲下 2.〈口〉坐(*down, on*);坐下休息(或闲谈) 3.〈美俚〉蹲坐大便 4.(动物)蹲伏;隐伏 5. 擅自占地;非法占据空屋(以在政府公地上居下来(以图获得对该地的所有权) 6.[海]〈船高速航行时)尾部下坐,尾欹 — *vt.* 1. 使蹲下;使踞坐 2. 霸占,侵占(土地等)—(squatter, squattest] *adj.* 1. 蹲着的 2. 矮胖的 — *n.* 1. 蹲;踞坐 2.(野兔等小动物)的窝 3. 矮胖的人

squatter ['skwɔtə] *n.* 1. 蹲坐的人(或动物) 2. 擅自占地(或空屋)者;依法在政府公地上定居的人 3.〈澳大利亚〉牧羊场主

squatty ['skwɔti] *adj.* 1. 蹲着的;蹲伏的 2. 低矮的;矮胖的 ‖ **squattily** *adv.*

squaw [skwɔ:] *n.* 1. 美洲印第安女人 2.〈贬〉老婆;女人 3.〈贬〉女子气的男人 4. 跪式人形靶

squawk [skwɔ:k] *vi.* 1.(鹦鹉、鸡、鸭等受伤或受惊时)发出粗厉的叫声 2.〈俚〉(粗声或大声地)诉苦;抗议(*about*) 3.〈美

俚〉自首并告发别人 — *vt.* 粗声叫出 — *n.* 1. 粗厉的叫声 2.(粗声或大声的)诉苦;抗议 3.[动]夜鹭

squeak [skwi:k] *n.* 1. 短促刺耳的声音;(老鼠的)吱吱叫声 2.(未经润滑的铰链等的)轧轧声声 3. 机会 — *vi.* 1. 发出短促的吱吱(或轧轧)声 2.〈俚〉告密 3. 勉强通过;侥幸成功(或获胜) — *vt.* 以短促尖声叫出 ‖ ~ er *n.*

squeaky ['skwi:ki] *adj.*(发)短促尖声的;吱吱声的

squeal [skwi:l] *vi.* 1.(小孩、猪等)发出长声尖叫 2. 告密;泄露 3. 抱怨;激烈抗议(*against*) — *vt.* 用长而尖锐的声音说出;用长声尖的声音叫出(或表示)— *n.* 长而尖的声音;长而尖的叫声 ‖ ~ er *n.*

squeamish ['skwi:miʃ] *adj.* 1. 易呕吐的 2. 易受惊的;易生气的;神经质的 3. 吹毛求疵的;过于拘谨的 ‖ ~ ly *adv.* / ~ ness *n.*

squeegee [,skwi:'dʒi:] *n.* 涂刷器;橡皮刷帚

squeeze [skwi:z] *vt.* 1. 榨;挤;塞;紧握 2. 榨取;压榨 3. 使(利润等)缩减 4. 勉强赢(或赚)得 5.(从…中)硬币等)榨出;挤榨赛中)逼(对方)出牌 6. 逼牌法赢得 — *vi.* 1. 榨;挤 2. 压榨 3. 勉强通过(或赢得) — *n.* 1. 压力;压榨,紧抱 2. 榨出的少量东西 3.(密集的)一群人 4. 佣金;回扣 5.(交易所中)空头轧平,杀空头 6. 紧缺;拮据;通货紧缩,银根紧缩 7.(桥牌赛中)逼通扣出的牌 8.(硬币等)压印 ‖ ~ r *n.*

squelch [skweltʃ] *vt.* 1. 压碎;镇压;压制 3. 压服;使不再作声 4. 使咯吱咯吱作响 — *vi.* 1. 咯吱咯吱作响 2. 涉水而行;(在泥沼地等处)咯吱咯吱地走

— n. 1. 咯吱声 2. 镇压;压制 3. 镇住对方的反驳(或回话、责备等) 4. 压碎(或压烂)的一堆 5.【电子】噪声抑制电路 ‖ ~ er n.

squib [skwib] n. 1. 爆竹;甩炮 2. 点不响的爆竹,哑炮 3. 讽刺(或幽默)短文(或讲话) 4.【美俚】简短的广告;(商品的)标签;(填补报上空白地位的)小品文,短文(或通告) 5.【军】电气导火管;小型点火器

squid [skwid] n. [复]squid(s) n.【动】枪乌贼;柔鱼,鱿鱼 — vt. (squidded; squidding) vi. 用枪乌贼作饵捕鱼;捕枪乌贼

squint [skwint] vi. 1. 斜着眼看;眯眼看(at, through) 2. 患斜视,斜眼 3. 倾向(towards) 4. 偏离正确方向;越轨 5. 有间接关系(或意义) — vt. 使斜视;眯着(眼)看 — n. 1. 斜视眼 2. 斜视;看;(口)一瞥,一看 3. 倾向;偏向(to, towards) 4.【建】斜孔小窗;窥视窗 5.【无】偏斜(指天线方向性);斜视角 — adj. 斜视的

squire ['skwaiə] n. 1.(英)乡绅;(某一地区)最大的地主 2.(美)治安官;律师;法官 3.(骑士的)扈从 4. 护卫;侍从 5. 殷勤侍护妇女者 — vt. & vi. 1. 护卫;侍从 2. 殷勤侍护(妇女)

squirm [skwəːm] vi. 1. 蠕动;扭动 2. 局促不安 — n. 蠕动;扭曲

squirrel ['skwirəl] n. [复]squirrel(s) n. 1. 松鼠 2. 松鼠毛皮 3.(美俚)威士忌酒 4.(美俚)疯子;怪人 5.(美俚)心理学家;精神病学家 6.(美俚)乱开车的人 7.(美俚)"跟屁虫"(指老跟在一群人后面想成为其中一分子的人) — vi.(美俚)把车横开东摇西晃 — vt. 贮藏;以备后用

squirt [skwəːt] vt. & vi. 喷;喷出;喷湿 — n. 1. 喷;细的喷流 2. 喷射器;水枪

3. 妄自尊大的年轻人 4. 小个子;无足轻重的人 5.(俚)喷气式飞机

Sr 元素锶(strontium)的符号

Sr. abbr. 1. Senior 2. Sir 3.(葡萄牙)Senhor 4.(西)Señor 5. Sister

Sri Lanka [sri 'læŋkə] 斯里兰卡(旧称Ceylon 锡兰)[南亚岛国]

SS abbr. 1. steamship 2.(德)Schutzstaffel

S/S abbr. steamship

SSBN abbr. Strategic Submarine Ballistic Nuclear 弹道导弹战略核潜艇

SST abbr. supersonic transport【空】超音速运输机

St. [sənt, sint, snt] abbr. Saint ‖ **St. Bernard**[sənt 'bəːnəd]瑞士圣伯纳德济贫院训养的)圣伯纳德狗,瑞士教护犬

stab [stæb] (stabbed; stabbing) vt. 1. 刺,戳;刺入;刺伤 2.(在感情方面)刺痛,使受创伤 3. 把(砖墙)凿毛(以备涂上灰泥) — vi. 刺;戳刺;刺伤 — n. 1. 刺;戳;刺伤的伤口 2.(强烈感觉的)一阵 3. 企图;尝试;努力

stability [stə'biliti] n. 1. 稳定;稳(定)性;稳固 2. 耐久(性) 3. 坚定 4.(天主教)僧侣终身寺院的誓约

stabilization [ˌsteibilai'zeiʃən] n. 1. 稳定 2.(价格等的)平抑 3.(生态等的)稳定平衡

stabilize ['steibilaiz] vt. 1. 使稳定;平抑…的价格 2. 使稳定平衡;使具有稳性 — vi.(保持)稳定 — r n. 稳定者;稳定者;(船)减摇装置【空】水平安定面;【化】稳定剂

stable[1] ['steibl] adj. 1. 稳定的;持久的;稳固的 2. 坚定的;不动摇的;持重的 3. 平稳的 ‖ stably adv.

stable[2] ['steibl] n. 1. 厩;马厩;牛棚 2. [总称]属于同一马主的赛马;厩中的

马;栏里的牛 3.[总称]赛马饲养训练人员 4.[总称]受同一经理人经营的运动员(或赛跑车、出版物等) 5.[~s]把…检进马厩(或牛棚) 一 vt.〈军〉把马厩值勤:马厩值勤员 — vi. 被关在马厩(或牛棚)里;(人)住在马厩般的地方

staccato [stə'kɑːtəu] adj. & adv. 1.[音]断奏(地) 2.断续的(地);不连贯的(地) 一([复]staccatos) n. 1.[音]断奏;断唱;断奏乐曲段 2.不连贯的东西(如说话方式、发动机的声音等)

stack [stæk] n. 1.(稻草、麦秆、谷物等的)大堆,垛;露天堆放的一大堆,垛(木材等的计量单位) 2.〈英〉堆(等于 108 立方英尺);木材堆 3.(口)大量;许多 4.[常~s](图书馆的)(双面)书架;书库 5.(三支步枪架成的)三角枪架 6.烟囱群;烟囱(车、船的)烟灰;烟道;排气管(高炉)炉身 7.(突出海面的)浪蚀)岩柱;石柱 8.(贴磁时的)一堆号码 9.[无]多层天线 一 vt. 1. 堆积;堆起 2. 在…堆放;堆满 3.[空]指令(等待着陆的飞机)作延高分层盘旋 4.〈美俚〉把(纸牌)弄得乱七八糟 5. 洗(牌)作弊 — vi. 堆起;成堆

stadium ['steidjəm]([复]stadia ['steidjə]或 stadiums) n. 1. 斯塔德(古希腊长度单位) 2.(周围有看台的)露天体育场 3.[生]期;龄期;病期

staff [stɑːf]([复]staffs 或 staves [steivz]) n. 1.(拐)杖;(棍)杖;(旗)杆;(梯子等的)横档 2. 支柱 3. 权杖;(主教的)牧杖;官杖;指挥棒;警棍 4.[医]导引探子 5.[机]小轴杆 6.(铁路上工作人员的)路签 7.(测量或定位器用的)标尺 8.([复]staves)[音]五线谱 一 n.[复] staffs)辅助州长、总统等的工作班子;(全体)工作人员;(全体)职员 10.

([复]staffs)[军]参谋;参谋人员;参谋机构 — vt. 为…配备职员(或工作人员)

stag [stæg] n. 1. 成年牡鹿(尤指牡赤鹿) 2.〈苏格兰〉幼马 3. 阉割过的雄畜 4. 刚长成的雄家禽 5. 不带女伴的舞客(或交际者);只限男子的社交聚会 6.〈英〉认购股票又转手出卖牟利、炒买炒卖股票者 7.〈英〉告密者 一(stagged;stagging) vi. 1.〈英〉成为告密者;不带女伴参加舞会(或交际会) 一 vt. 1.〈英〉侦查 2. 截短(长裤) 一 adj. 1. 全是男人的;男子集会用的 2. 无异性伴侣的

stage [steidʒ] n. 1. 舞台;[the ~]戏剧;戏剧行业;演剧 2. 注意中心;活动舞台;场所 3.(进展的)阶段;时期 4. 站;驿站;二驿站间的距离;行程;公共马车;公共汽车 5.(宝塔等的)层;脚手架;[地]阶;期 6.(显微镜)镜台 7. 浮码头;趸船 一 vt. 1. 把…搬上舞台;上演 2. 筹划;举行;发动 — vi. 1.(剧本)适于上演; ~ well (badly)(剧本)很(不)适于上演;乘公共马车旅行 ‖ ~coach n. 驿站马车,公共马车 — fright(初上舞台的)怯场

stagger ['stægə] vi. 1. 摇晃;踌躇 2. 犹豫,动摇 一 vt. 1. 使摇晃 2. 使犹豫,使动摇;使踌躇 3. 交错;错开 一 n. 1. 摇晃;踌躇 2.[~s]家畜晕倒病,踌躇病;眩晕 3.[空](双翼机机翼的)斜撑;斜翼量 一 adj. 交错的,错开的

staging ['steidʒiŋ] n. 1. 脚手架 2. 驿车业;乘驿车的旅行 3.(戏剧的)上演 4.[军](人员或物资的)分段运输;中间集结 5.(宇宙飞船与燃料耗尽火箭的)级分离

stagnant ['stægnənt] adj. 1. 停滞的,不流动的 2.(水等因不流动而)污浊的 3.

迟钝的；呆笨的 4. 萧条的，不景气的

stagnate ['stægneit] *vi. & vt.* 1.(使)停滞，(使)不流动 2.(使)迟缓，(使)不活泼 3.(使)萧条 ‖ **stag'nation** *n.*

stagy ['steidʒi] *adj.* 戏剧性的；演戏似的，做作的，缺乏真实感的

staid [steid] *adj.* 1. 固定的 2. 沉着的；稳健的 ‖ **~ly** *adv.* / **~ness** *n.*

stain [stein] *vt.* 1. 沾污，沾染；玷污 2.(在制造过程中用化学方法等)给(木料、玻璃等)染色，着色；把(标本等)染色以便在显微镜下观察 3. 在(糊墙纸)上印上颜色 — *vi.* 变脏，被沾污 — *n.* 1. 污点，瑕疵 2. 色斑 3. 着色剂，染(色)剂

stainless ['steinlis] *adj.* 1. 没有污点的；纯洁的 2. 不锈的；~ steel 不锈钢

stair [steə] *n.* 1.[常~s]用作单或复]楼梯 2. 梯级 3.[~s]浮动平台 ‖ '~**case** *n.* 楼梯；楼梯间 / '~**way** *n.* 楼梯

stake [steik] *n.* 1. 桩；标桩 2. 桩砾；圆头砧 3. 火刑柱；炮烙刑 4.[常~s]赌金，赌注 5.[常~s]奖品；奖金 6. 利害关系 7.(下在投机生意上的)股本 8. 平台车边上的栅桩，有栅桩的车 9.(以分享所获物为条件对探矿者的)资助 — *vt.* 1. 把…系于桩上；用桩撑住 2. 立桩标出(off) 3. 用桩圈住(up, in) 4. 把…押下打赌 5. 资助…做投机生意;(以分享所获物为条件)资助(探矿者) — *vi.* 打赌

stalactite ['stælaktait] *n.*【地】钟乳石 2. 钟乳石状物

stalagmite ['stælagmait] *n.*【地】石笋

stale [steil] *adj.* 1. 陈腐的，陈旧的 2. 走了气的，走了味的；不新鲜的；干瘪的 3. 陈旧的，不流行的 4. 疲惫的；(运动员)因训练过度而竞技状态不佳的 5.【律】失时效的 — *vt. & vi.* 1.(使)变

陈旧；(使)变得无味 2.(使)失时效 ‖ **~ly** *adv.* / **~ness** *n.*

stalemate ['steilmeit] *n.* 1.(国际象棋赛中的)僵局，王棋受困 2. 僵持，对峙 — *vt.* 1.(国际象棋赛中)使成僵局，使王棋受困 2. 使僵持，使相持不下

stalk[1] [stɔːk] *n.* 1.(草本植物的)主茎，轴；花梗；叶柄 2.(无脊椎动物的)茎柄；梗节 3.(工厂等的)高烟囱 4.【建】茎梗饰 5. 酒杯脚

stalk[2] [stɔːk] *vi.* 1. 蹑手蹑脚地走近；潜近猎物 2. 高视阔步地走，大踏步走 — *vt.* 1. 潜步追踪 2. 搜索(地区) 3. 高视阔步地走过 — *n.* 1. 潜踪 2. 高视阔步

stall[1] [stɔːl] *n.* 1.(畜舍内的)分隔栏，厩 2. 汽车停车处 3.(教堂内置有高坛或唱诗班席位上的)牧师坐位；牧师职位 4.(教堂内的)长排坐椅 5.(英)[常~s]戏院正厅前座区；[~s]前座观众 6. 货摊；书摊；棚店 7.(手套的)指套;(各种用途的)护套 8. 分隔的小间 9.【空】(飞机的)失速 10.【矿】矿坑；敞式矿砂熔烧炉 — *vt.* 1. 把(牲畜)关入厩中;(古)把(牲畜)关入肥育栏中圈养；把…陷入(泥或雪地等) 2. 使(机车等)停顿，使停止；阻塞【空】使失速 — *vi.* 1.(牲畜)被关在厩内 2. 陷入泥(或雪)中 3.(机车等)停顿，停止 4.【空】失速 ‖ **~in** *n.* 阻塞交通而成(一种用汽车堵塞交通要道的成威方式)

stall[2] [stɔːl] *n.* 1.(使主犯作案时不受注意并助之逃脱的)扒手同党 2. 拖延；支吾；口实；遁词 — *vi.* 1. 做扒手的同党 2. 拖延；支吾 — *vt.* 拖延；敷衍；把…的注意力引开

stallion ['stæljən] *n.* 牡马(尤指种马)；留种的雄兽

stalwart ['stɔːlwət] *adj.* 1. 高大健壮的；

结实的 2. 坚实的；刚毅的，不屈不挠的 — *n.* 1. 高大健壮的人 2. (政党、事业的)坚定分子

stamen ['steimen] ([复] stamens 或 stamina ['stæminə]) *n.* [植] 雄蕊

stamina ['stæminə] stamen 的复数 — *n.* 持久力，耐力；精力

stammer ['stæmə] *vt.* 结结巴巴地说出，口吃地说(*out*) — *vi.* 结结巴巴地说话，口吃地说话 — *n.* 口吃 ‖ ～**er** *n.* 口吃者，结结巴巴地说话的人

stamp [stæmp] *n.* 1. 戳子，印，图章；(印下的)戳记 2. 标记 3. 印花 4. [常用架]标志；特征；痕迹，类型；种类 5. 跺脚；重踩 6. 压印机；捣击机；捣矿锤；杵 — *vt.* 1. 盖章于；压印于；打上(标记等)；用印模冲压；(喻) 铭刻 2. 贴邮票于；贴印花于 3. 标出；表示 4. (用杵等)捣碎；压碎 5. 踩(脚)；用脚踩踏；扑灭(*out*) — *vi.* 1. 踏碎；重步走；踩(*on*) 2. (喻)拒绝；扑灭；毁掉(*on*)

stampede [stæm'pi:d] *n.* 1. (畜群的)惊跑,乱窜；(军队的)大溃退 2. (人群的)蜂拥；(选举中的)突然一面倒 — *vt.* 1. 使(畜群)惊跑，使溃散 2. 使乱拥；使(投票人、代表等)仓促行事；使(大群人)一下子冲动行事 — *vi.* 1. 惊跑,乱窜;溃散 2. (人群)突然蜂拥；突然冲动行事

stance [stæns,stɑ:ns] *n.* 1. (高尔夫球、板球赛等中的)击球姿势；(运动员的)始发姿势 2. 站立的姿势；被放置的姿势；(苏格兰)位置，场地 3. 姿态；态度

stanch[1] [stɑ:ntʃ] *vt.* 1. 使(伤口)止血,止(血),使止流,使不漏 2. 制住

stanch[2] [stɑ:ntʃ] *adj.* = staunch[1]

stanchion ['stɑ:nʃən] *n.* 1. 支柱,柱子；标柱 2. (牲畜栏中的)栓栅 — *vt.* 1.

支柱支撑；给…装柱子 2. 用枷栓住(牲畜)

stand [stænd] (stood[stud]) *vi.* 1. 站,立；He ～s one metre and seventy. 他身高一米七十。2. 坐落,位于 3. 停住不动;停滞;滞留 4. 处某种状态(或境地);取某种态度 5. 坚持,维持原状;继续有效 6. (英) 做候选人,参加竞选 7. [海]取某一航向 8. (驮马?)供种用马 — *vt.* 1. 使站立；竖放 2. 忍受;经受;顶住;接受 3. (吃饭等时) 为…付账,为…会钞 4. 有供…站立的地位 5. [军]站住(某种队形) — *n.* 1. 站住,止住 2. 在撤退途中的停下反击；停下抵抗 3. 站立位置;立场 4. 〈美〉(法庭的)证人席 5. 台,讲坛;看台;[常～s]看台上的观众 6. 摊;报摊;停车处;(适合于营业的)好市口 7. 旅行剧团的停留演出;停留演出地 8. 【生】林分,小植物群丛；蜂群 9.〈苏格兰〉(衣服等的)一套,(英) (一个士兵的)全套武装 ‖ '～-**in** *n.* 1.(电影、电视的)替身(演员) 2. 有利地位；得宠地位：have a ～ in with sb. 得某人的宠爱 /'～**point** *n.* 立场,观点 /'～-**still** *n.* 停止；停顿；停滞不前 /'～-**up** *adj.* 1. (美国)取说故事的;坦率正直的 2.(衣领)直立的,挺立的 3. 站着的;以直立姿势进行的：a ～-*up* buffet 供顾客站着吃的小餐室 4.(拳击)硬拼的,不要手段的;光明正大的

standard ['stændəd] *n.* 1. 标准；水准；规格;规范 2. 旗；军旗；(骑兵队或摩托化部队的)队旗；(王室的)旗标 3.(货币制度中的)本位;(金银货币中的纯金银与合金的)法定比例 5.[商]最低规格,最低等级 6. 直立支柱;灯台;电杆;垂直的水管(或煤气管) 7.(英国小学的)年级 8.【植】(豌豆花等的)旗瓣 — *adj.* 1. 标准的 2. 公认为

优秀的;权威的 3. 合规格的;一般性
的;通常的 4. 装支柱的 5.(植物)茎干
挺直的,不依附别物生长的 ‖ '~-bearer
n. 掌旗官(或兵);(喻)旗手;杰出的领
导者 /~ time 标准时

standardize ['stændədaiz] vt. 1. 使与标准
比较,用标准校验 2. 使合标准;使标
准化;使统一 ‖ standardi'zation n.

standby ['stændbai] n.[复]standbys) n. 1.
可靠的人;坚定的支持者 2. 受人喜爱
的常备物;备用品;后备人员 3.(飞机
的)等退票旅客 4.(电影中的)替身 5.
待命状态;(船舶的)待命信号 —adj.
备用的;待命的

standing ['stændiŋ] adj. 1. 直立的;站着
的 2. 停滞的,不流动的;停着的,不在
运转的 3. 持续的;长期有效的;标准
的;永存的,不变的 4. 常备的;常设的
5. 固定的;有支架(或台、座等)的 6.
已由法律(或习惯)所确定的;永久的
— n. 1. 站立;站立处 2. 身份;地位;
名望 3. 持续时间 ‖ ~ room 站位(尤
指戏院或公共车辆满座时站的地方);
Standing room only!(戏院或车票售票
处用语)只有站票!

stank [stæŋk] stink 的过去式

stanza ['stænzə] n. 1. 诗节 2.〈美俚〉(在
一地的)演出期(尤指一星期) 3.〈美
俚〉(体育比赛的)局;盘;场

staple[1] ['steipl] n. 1. U形钉,肘钉;订书
钉 2. 钩环;锁环 — vt. 用肘钉(或订
书钉)钉住

staple[2] ['steipl] n. 1. 大宗出产;主要商
品(或产品) 2. 销路稳定的商品;常用
品;广泛采用的东西 3. 原材料 4. 主要
成分;主题 5.(人造)短纤维,切段纤维
(亦作 ~ fibre) 6. 来源(地);中心 7.
〈古〉贸易中心城镇 — adj. 1. 主要的;
大宗生产的;Rice is our ~ food. 大米是

我们的主食。2. 经常需要的;经常用
的 3. 纺织纤维的 — vt.(按纤维长短)
把…分级;把…切成短纤维

stapler ['steiplə] n. 订书机

star [staː] n. 1. 星;恒星 2. 星状物;星
章,星形勋章 3.【印】星号(即 *) 4.〈口
~s)(占星术的)星宿;命运 5.(电影、
戏剧等的)明星 6.(马等额上的)白斑
7. = ~fish 8.〈英俚〉初次坐牢的犯人
— (starred; starring) vt. 1.[常用被动语
态]用星(或星状物)装饰;点缀(with)
2. 用星号标出,用星号标明 3. 使担任
主角;使成为明星 — vi. 扮演主角;表
演出色 — adj. 1. 星的 2. 名演员的,
明星的 3. 优越的;出众的 ‖ '~-dust n.
1. 星尘(团) 2.(宇宙尘之)口;迷幻,梦幻
/ '~-fish n.【动】海星 / '~-gazer n. 1. 占
星家;(谑)天文学家 2. 空想家 3.【动】
瞻星鱼 / '~-light n. 星光 adj. 有星光
的;星光照耀的 / '~-lit adj. 星光照明
的;星光照耀的 / Star Wars(美国的)星球大战计
划

starboard ['staːbəd, 'staːbɔːd] n.(船、飞机
的)右舷 — adj. 右舷的,右侧的 —
vt. 把(舵)转向右

starch [staːtʃ] n. 1. 淀粉 2.[~es]淀粉类
食物 3. 白板;生硬;拘泥 3.〈口〉热情;
活力;精力 — vt. 1. 给(衣服等)上浆
2. 使古板;使拘泥

starchy ['staːtʃi] adj. 1. 淀粉的;似淀粉
的;含淀粉的 2. 上过浆的,浆硬的 3.
古板的;拘泥的

stare [steə] vi. 1. 盯,凝视,目不转睛地
看 2.(颜色等)惹眼,显眼 3.(毛发等)
竖立 — vt. 盯住,凝视,目不转睛地看得
… — n. 盯,凝视

stark [staːk] adj. 1. 僵硬的,严格的;刻
板的 2. 完全的,十足的 3. 赤裸裸的;
十分明显的;轮廓明显的 4. 荒凉的,

光秃秃的;空的;贫瘠的 5. 健壮的,结实的 — adv. 完全

starling ['stɑ:liŋ] n.[动]紫翅椋鸟;椋鸟

starry ['stɑ:ri] adj. 1. 布满星星的;被星星照亮的 2. 明亮的 3. 星形的 4. 高如天上星的 ‖ ~-eyed adj. 过分乐观的;空想的,不切实际的

start [stɑ:t] vi. 1. 跳起;惊起;吃惊 2. 涌出;突然出现 3. 出发,起程,动身,起程 5. 开动;着手 6. 松动;脱落;(木料等)翘曲 7. 参加比赛 — vt. 1. 惊动;使惊起;惊出 2. 开动,使起动,发动 3. 引起;使开始;开始 4. 提出(题目等)供考虑(或讨论) 5. 创办;开设 6. 使松动;使脱落 7. 使猛动 7. 开始雇用,起用(某人) 8. 把(酒等)从桶里倒出;开(桶)取酒 9. 给(赛跑者等)发起跑信号 10. 使参加比赛 — n. 1. 跳起;惊起 2. 出发;起程;出发点;开始信号;起点;起跑点 3. 有利条件;占先地位 4. 开始事业的机会 5.(物件的)松动部分;翘裂;漏缝 ‖ ~-er n. 1. 开端者 2. 参赛人(或马) 3.(赛跑的)发令员;(车辆等的)发车员,调度员 4. 起动装置;启动器 5. 酵母

startle ['stɑ:tl] vt. 使惊起 — vi. 惊起;惊跳起来 — n. 吃惊;惊跳

startling ['stɑ:tliŋ] adj. 令人吃惊的,惊人的

starvation [stɑ:'veiʃən] n. 饥饿;挨饿;饿死

starve [stɑ:v] vi. 1. 挨饿;饿死 2.〈口〉饿得慌 3. 极需;渴望(for) 4.〈古〉挨冻;冻死 — vt. 1. 使挨饿;使饿死 2.〈古〉使挨冻;使冻死 3. 以饥饿迫使 4. 以节食治疗

starveling ['stɑ:vliŋ] n. 挨饿者;饿瘦了的人(或动物) — adj. 挨饿的;饿瘦的;贫穷的;不足的;不能满足所需要的

state¹ [steit] n. 1. 状态,状况,情形 2.〈口〉激动,兴奋;过分紧张 3. 国家;政府;领土 4.[常S-](美国等)州;邦 5. 国务:Secretary of State(美国)国务卿;(英国)国务大臣/the Department of State(或 the State Department)(美国)国务院 6.[S-](美国)国务院 7.(尤指高的)社会地位;身份;社会阶层 8. 尊严;堂皇,豪华 — adj. 1. 国家的;州的;邦的;国务的 2. 礼仪用的;礼仪上的;(仪式的) ‖ ~hood n. 国家(或州、邦)的地位 ‖ ~house n.(美国)州议会大厦/~-room n. 1.(宫殿等的)大厅 2.(轮船的)房舱;特等客舱;(旧时美国火车上的)高级包房 3. 政府公寓

state² [steit] vt. 1. 陈述,说明,阐明;声明 2. 规定(日期、价格等) 3.[数]用符号表示(问题,关系等)

stated ['steitid] adj. 1. 规定的,固定的;确定的 2. 被宣称的;被宣明的

stately ['steitli] adj. 庄严的;高贵的;堂皇的;雄伟的 ‖ statelinessn.

statement ['steitmənt] n. 1. 陈述;声明;声明书 2. 财务报表;结算单,清单

statesman ['steitsmən]([复]statesmen) n. 1. 政治家;国务活动家 2.(英方)自耕农 ‖ ~ly adj. / ~ship n.

static ['stætik] adj. 1. 静的;静态的;静力的 2.[物]静电的 3. 固定的;不活泼的;不变动的;变化小的 4. 静止的,使平静的 — n.[物]天电;静电;天电干扰;静电干扰

station ['steiʃən] n. 1. 站;台;所;局;车站;航空站 2. 驻地;停泊地;岗位;位置 3. 身份;地位;职位 4. 电台;广播电台 5. 科学考察站;研究所 6.[测]测站 7.[生]生境,栖所 8.(澳)牧场 9. 军事基地;[总称]驻地人员 10.

【史】(印度的)英国军官(或官员)居住区 **11.** 站立(姿态);停留 **12.**【宗】14 幅耶稣受难像之一 — **vt.** 驻扎;安置 ‖ ~ break 电台(或电视台)播出中断,停播 / ~ master **n.** (火车站)站长 / ~ wagon〈美〉旅行客车;客货两用轿车

stationary ['steiʃənəri] **adj.** 不动的,静止的;固定的,不变的;停留的 — **n.** 固定的事物;驻军;定居的人

stationer ['steiʃənə] **n. 1.** 文具商 **2.**〈古〉书商;出版商

stationery ['steiʃənəri] **n. 1.** [总称]文具 **2.** (配套的)信笺信封

statist ['steitist] **n. 1.** 中央集权论者,国家主权论者 **2.** 统计家;统计员 — **adj.** 主张中央集权制的

statistic [stə'tistik] **adj.** 统计的;统计的 — **n. 1.** 统计量 **2.** = statistics

statistical [stə'tistikəl] **adj.** = statistic ‖ ~ly **adv.**

statistics [stə'tistiks] [复] **n. 1.** 统计;统计资料 **2.** [用作单]统计学 ‖ statistician [ˌstætis'tiʃən] **n.** 统计员;统计家

statuary ['stætʃuəri] **n. 1.** [总称]雕像;塑像,雕塑艺术 **3.** 雕塑家 — **adj.** 雕塑的;适宜于雕塑的;雕塑用的

statue ['stætju:] **n.** 雕像;塑像;铸像 — **vt. 1.** 以雕像装饰(道路、花园等) **2.**〈古〉为…作塑像 ‖ Statue of Liberty (美国纽约市的)自由女神像

statuesque [ˌstætju'esk] **adj. 1.** 雕像(或塑像、铸像)般的 **2.** 庄严的,宏伟的 **3.** 体态优美的 **4.** 严肃的;生硬的 ‖ ~ly **adv.** / ~ness **n.**

statuette [ˌstætju'et] **n.** 小雕像;小塑像;小铸像

stature ['stætʃə] **n. 1.** 身高;身材 **2.** (物体的)高度 **3.** (精神、道德等的)高度境界,高度水平

status ['steitəs] **n. 1.** 情形,状况:the ~ of affairs 事态,形势 / the alert ~【军】待机状态 **2.** 地位;身份 **3.** 重要地位:要人身份 ‖ status quo [kwəu]〈拉〉现状;原来状况

statute ['stætju:t] **n. 1.** 法令;法规;成文法 **2.** (公司、学校等的)章程;条例 ‖ statutory **adj.**

staunch[1] [stɔ:ntʃ, stɑ:ntʃ] **adj. 1.** 坚定的,忠诚的 **2.** 壮健的 **3.** 坚固的;不透水的;不透气的 ‖ ~ly **adv.** / ~ness **n.**

staunch[2] [stɔ:ntʃ, stɑ:ntʃ] **vt.** = stanch[1]

stave [steiv] **n. 1.** 狭板;桶板 **2.** 梯级;横档,木棍 **3.** 棍;棒 **4.** 诗节;诗句 **5.**【音】五线谱 — (staved 或 stove [stəuv]) **vt. 1.** 击穿;弄破;凿孔于 **2.** 压坏;打坏;打扁;打瘪(in) **3.** 捣开;捣破(off) **4.** 给…装上桶板;给…装横档 — **vi. 1.** 穿孔;破碎;被打穿 **2.** 快步走动

stay[1] [stei] **vi. 1.** 停留;保持下去 **2.** [暂]住;耽搁,逗留 **3.** 站住;停住;中止 **4.** 停下 **5.** 坚持;持久 **6.** 并驾齐驱(with) — **vt. 1.** 阻止,制止,抑制;平息;暂时解除…的饥渴 **2.** 延搁 **3.** 停留;停留到…结束 **4.** 等候 — **n. 1.** 停留;逗留 **2.** 制止,抑制,中止 **3.** 延搁 **4.**〈口〉持久力,耐力 ‖ ~-at-home **adj.** & **n.** 不爱出门的(人);不爱离开本乡(或本国)的(人)

stay[2] [stei] **n. 1.**【海】支索 **2.** 支柱;赡养 **3.** 支撑物;撑条;拉条;牵索 **4.** [~s] 女用束腹;紧身胸衣 — **vt. 1.**【海】用支索固定;用支索使(桅)改变角度;使(船)转向上风 **2.** 支持;支撑 — **vi.**【海】转向上风

stead [sted] **n. 1.** 替代:act in sb.'s ~ 代表某人办事 **2.** 好处;用处;有利性 — **vt.** 对…有利;对…有用;对…有帮助

steadfast ['stedfəst] **adj. 1.** 固定的,不变

的 2. 坚定的, 不动摇的; 坚信的 ‖
~ly adv. / ~ness n.

steady ['stedi] adj. 1. 稳固的; 平稳的 2.
稳定的, 不变的 3. 坚定的; 扎实的; 可
靠的 4. 镇静的, 沉着的, 从容的 5.
(船)保向航行的 — vt. 1. 使稳定; 使
稳固 2. 使坚定; 使沉着 — vi. 稳固;
稳定 — n. 1. 〖美〗(关系确定的)情侣
2. 〖机〗固定支架, 中心架 — adv. 1. 稳
固地; 稳定地 2. 〖海〗保向地 ‖ **steadily**
adv. / steadiness n.

steak [steik] n. 1. 牛排; 大块肉(或鱼)片
2. (碎牛肉等做的)牛肉饼

steal [sti:d] (stole [stəul], stolen ['stəulən])
vt. 1. 偷窃, 窃取 2. 偷偷地夺取; 巧取 3.
僭据; 侵占 4. 偷偷地进行; 偷偷地做
(棒球赛中)偷进(前垒) — vi. 1.
偷东西, 做贼 2. 偷偷地行动; 悄悄地
走过(或发生) 3. (棒球赛中)偷垒 —
n. 1. 偷窃; 窃得物 2. 不正常的(或可
疑的)政治交易 3. 以极其低廉价格买
得的东西 4. (棒球赛中的)偷垒

stealth [stelθ] n. 秘密行动; 秘密; 鬼祟

stealthy ['stelθi] adj. 隐密的, 暗中进行
的 ‖ stealthily adv. / stealthiness n.

steam [sti:m] n. 1. 蒸汽, 水蒸气; 水汽;
蒸汽压力 2. 〖口〗精力; 气力 3. 轮船;
乘轮船旅行 — vi. 1. 蒸发; 冒热气 2.
(火车、轮船)行驶 3. 发怒 — vt. 1.
蒸; 煮 2. 散发(蒸气) 3. 用蒸汽开动
‖ '~boat n. 汽船; 轮船 / '~ engine 蒸
汽机 / '~roller n. (压路机碾压石)
用高压压倒; 粉碎 vi. 以不可抗拒之势
前进 / '~roller n. 蒸汽压路机
高压力量; 高压手段 & vi. — '~roll
/ '~ship n. 汽船; 轮船 / '~ shovel 蒸汽
挖掘机, 蒸汽铲

steamer ['sti:mə] n. 1. 汽船; 轮船 2. 蒸
汽车 3. 蒸汽机 4. 汽锅; 汽蒸器; 蒸笼 4.

蒸汽(机)操作者; 用蒸汽处理的东西

steed [sti:d] n. 1. 马(尤指仗仗马或战
马) 2. 〖诗〗骏马

steel [sti:l] n. 1. 钢; 钢铁; (似钢铁般的)
坚硬; 坚固 2. 钢制品(尤指刀、工具、
武器等); (在燧石上打火的)打火镰 3.
(用以撑开妇女紧身围腰或衬裙的)钢
衬条 4. 炼钢工业 — [~s] 钢铁公司股票
(或债券) — adj. 1. 钢的; 钢制的 2.
钢铁似的 3. 似钢铁般的 — vt.
1. 钢化; 给…包上钢; 用钢作…的刀口
2. 使似钢; 使坚强; 使有决心; 使经受
锻炼 3. 使冷酷 4. 〖美喻〗用刀戳(某
人) ‖ '~yard n. 杆秤, 提秤

steely ['sti:li] adj. 1. 钢制的; 含钢的; 似
钢的 2. (硬度、颜色、意志等)像钢的,
钢铁般的 3. (羊毛)缺乏天然卷缩性
(或弹性)

steep¹ [sti:p] adj. 1. 陡的, 陡峭的, 陡直
的 2. 〖口〗(要求、价格等)过高的, 过分
的; 难以接受(或办到)的 3. 急剧升降
的; 急转直下的 4. 〖废〗(海)浪高的 —
n. 峭壁, 悬崖 ‖ ~ly adv. / ~ness n.

steep² [sti:p] vt. 浸(泡), 泡; 〖喻〗沉浸 —
vi. 浸, 泡 — n. 浸渍, 浸渍液

steeple ['sti:pl] n. (教堂等的)尖顶; 尖塔;
尖锥物 ‖ '~chase n. 1. 越野赛马; 障
碍赛马 2. 越野赛跑; 障碍赛跑 / '~
jack n. 烟囱(或尖塔等)修理工人; 高
空作业工人

steer¹ [stiə] vt. 1. 驾驶; 为(船等)操舵
指导; 筹划 2. 沿着(某一航道)前进 3.
〖美俚〗勾引…到赌场(或妓院)去 —
vi. 1. 驾驶; 操舵 2. 行驶; 行进 3. 被
驾驶, 驾驶起来 4. 〖美俚〗替赌场(或妓
院)拉客 — vt. 1. 驾驶(或行路)
的指示 ‖ 〖美俚〗建议; 劝告, 忠告 2.
(车、船等)的驾驶设备 ‖ '~s-man n.
舵手; 撑筏者

steer² [stiə] *n.* 小公牛；阉牛；菜牛

steerage ['stiəridʒ] *n.* **1.** 掌舵；驾驶 **2.** 【船】舵效 **3.** 操舵装置 **4.** (客轮的)统舱 **5.** (军舰的)下级军官室

steering ['stiəriŋ] *n.* 操舵(效应) ‖ ~ **committee** (国会等立法机构的)程序委员会 / ~ **gear** (船的)操舵装置 / ~ **wheel** (船的)舵轮；(汽车的)方向盘，驾驶盘；(飞机的)操纵轮

stein [stain] *n.* (容量约为 1 品脱的陶制或玻璃)啤酒杯

stellar ['stelə] *adj.* **1.** 星的；星球的；恒星的 **2.** 星似的；星形的 **3.** (电影或戏剧)明星的，主演的

stem¹ [stem] *n.* **1.** 茎，(树)干；(叶)梗 **2.** (工具的)柄，把，杆 **3.** 高面杯的脚；烟斗柄 **4.** 《美俚》[~s] 腿 **5.** (手表、怀表的)转柄；[无] 电子管芯柱；晶体管管座 **6.** 【音】(乐谱上的)符干 **7.** 【海】船头，艏；艏材；艏材 **8.** 【语】词干 **9.** 血统，家系 **10.** 【动】羽干 **11.** (长有数串香蕉的)香蕉茎干 **12.** 《美俚》(城市中的)主街 **13.** 《美俚》鸦片烟枪 — (stemmed; stemming) *vt.* **1.** 抽去(或剔除)…的梗(或茎) **2.** 给…装柄(或把、杆等)；给(假花等)装梗 — *vi.* 《美》起源；导源；发生

stem² [stem] (stemmed; stemming) *vt.* **1.** 堵住，塞住；挡住 **2.** 逆(流)而行；顶着…而上 **3.** (滑雪时)转动(滑雪屐)以停止滑行 — *vi.* **1.** 堵住；止住 **2.** 逆行 **3.** 转动滑雪屐以止住 — *n.* **1.** 堵塞物；坝，止住 **2.** 转动滑雪屐以停止滑行

stemmed [stemd] *adj.* **1.** (常用以构成复合词)有…茎(或梗)的；装有…柄的 **2.** 去掉茎(或梗)的

stench [stentʃ] *n.* 恶臭 — *vt.* & *vi.* (使)发恶臭

stencil ['stensil] *n.* **1.** (镂花)模板；模绘板；型板；(用模板或蜡纸印成的)图案(或文字) **2.** (油印用的)蜡纸 — (stencil(l)ed; stencil(l)ing) *vt.* 用模板印刷；用蜡版印

stenograph ['stenəɡrɑːf] *vt.* 速记；用速记法书写 — *n.* **1.** 速记记号；用速记法书写成的文件 **2.** 速记机 ‖ ~**er** [ste'nɔɡrəfə] / ~**ist** [ste'nɔɡrəfist] *n.* 速记员

stenography [stə'nɔɡrəfi] *n.* **1.** 速记法 **2.** 速记；速记的回译 ‖ **stenographic(al)** [stenə'ɡræfik(əl)] *adj.* / **stenographically** [stenə'ɡræfikəli] *adv.*

stentor ['stentɔː] *n.* 声音洪亮的人 ‖ ~**ian** [sten'tɔːriən] *adj.* 声音洪亮的

step [step] *n.* **1.** (脚)步；步态；步幅 **2.** 脚步声；脚印，足迹 **3.** [~s] (某人所走的)路程，道路 **4.** 步调，步伐 **5.** 步骤；手段；措施 **6.** 踏板；梯级；台阶；(矿层等上面的)踏脚处 **7.** 一梯级的高度；等级；升级 **8.** [~s] 活梯；梯凳 **9.** [~s] 一段楼梯；一段梯级 **10.** [~s] 一段楼梯；一段梯级 **11.** 【音】音级；全音；半音 **12.** 舞步 — (stepped; stepping) *vi.* **1.** 跨步，走，步行 **2.** 跳舞；轻快地行走 **3.** 踏(入)，踏(进) **4.** 踩 **5.** 踏(上)，走(上) — *vt.* **1.** 跨(步)；踏(脚)；放散步于 **2.** 跳(舞) **3.** 测(out, off) **4.** 使成梯级；使成梯级状 **5.** 【海】竖立(桅杆)于桅座上 **6.** 逐步(或分段)安排 ‖ ~ **dance** 踢踏舞 / '~**down** *n.* 减少；减低 *vi.* **1.** 跨下(某人所走的路程) **2.** 减少；减低 **3.** 【电】减压的 / '~**in** *adj.* (鞋)一伸脚就穿好的；(衣服)一套就穿上身的 ‖ [~s] *n.* 这种减少(或减低)的 / '~**ladder** *n.* 活梯；梯凳 / '**stepped-up** *adj.* 加速的；加强了的 / '**steppingstone** *n.* **1.** (浅河中)供踏脚的石头；(上下马用)踏脚台 **2.** 达成目的的手段；进身之阶

3.(途中的)歇脚地 /~ rocket 多级火箭 /'~stone n. 楼梯石级 /~turn(滑雪时的)踏步式转弯 /'~-up n.(体积、数量等的)逐渐增加 adj. 逐步增加(或增大)的；[电]增压的

stepbrother ['step,brʌðə] n. 同父异母(或同母异父)的哥哥(或弟弟)

stepchild ['steptʃaild]([复] stepchildren ['step,tʃildrən]) n. 妻与前夫(或丈夫与前妻)所生的孩子；遭冷遇的人(或物)

stepdaughter ['step,dɔ:tə] n. 继女

stepfather ['step,fɑ:ðə] n. 继父

stepmother ['step,mʌðə] n. 继母

stepney ['stepni] n.(英)(汽车)备用轮

stepparent ['step,pɛərənt] n. 继父，后父；继母，后母

steppe [step] n. **1.**(尤指东南欧或西伯利亚地区的)大草原 **2.**(仅有旱生植物的)干草原

stepsister ['step,sistə] n. 同父异母(或同母异父)的姐姐(或妹妹)

stepson ['stepsʌn] n. 继子

-ster comb. form **1.** 表示"做…事情的人"：gangster, tapster 表示"是…样的人"：youngster, oldster

stereo ['steriəu, 'stiəriəu]([复] stereos) n. **1.** = stereotype **2.** 音术；体视效应；体视系统；(立)体视镜 **3.** 立体照片，体视照片 **4.**(收音设备等放出的)立体声；立体声系统 — adj. **1.** 用铅版印的；老一套的，已成陈规的 **2.** 立体的；体视(镜)的 **3.** 立体声的

stereo- comb. form **1.** 表示"坚固的"，"实心的"：stereobate [建]无柱底基, 土台 **2.** 表示"立体的"：stereograph

stereograph ['steriəgrɑ:f] n. 立体照片，体视照片 — vt. 拍摄…的立体照片

stereoisomer [,steriəu'aisəmə] n.[化]立体异构体 ‖~ism [,steriəu'saiəmərizəm] n. 立体异构现象

stereophonic [,steriə'fɔnik] adj. 立体声的

stereopticon [,steri'ɔptikən] n. 立体感幻灯机，立体感投影仪

stereoscope ['steriəskəup] n. 体视镜

stereotype ['steriətaip] n. **1.**[印]铅版，铅版制版法 **2.** 陈规，老套，旧框框 — vt. **1.** 浇铸…的铅版 **2.**(用铅版)印刷 **3.** 使成为陈规，把…弄得一成不变 **4.** 对…产生成见

sterile ['sterail, steril] adj. **1.** 不生育的；不结果实的 **2.** 贫瘠的 **3.** 无菌的，消过毒的 **4.** 缺乏独创性的；枯燥无味的 **5.** 无效果的；无结果的 ‖ **sterility** [ste'riliti] n.

sterilization [,sterilai'zeiʃən] n. **1.** 消毒，灭菌 **2.** 绝育

sterilize ['sterilaiz] vt. **1.** 把…消毒，使无菌 **2.** 使绝育 **3.** 使成不毛之地 **4.** 使不起作用 **5.**[经]冻结，封存(黄金等) ‖~r n.

sterling ['stə:liŋ] n. **1.** 英国货币 **2.** 标准纯银；(总称)纯银制品 — adj. **1.** 英国的；用英币支付(或计算)的：five pounds ~(略作£ 5 stg.)英币 5 镑 **2.**(金、银)标准成色的；标准纯银的；纯银制 **3.** 合最高标准的；纯正的；优秀的 ‖~ area 英镑区

stern[1] [stə:n] adj. **1.** 严厉的；严格的；严峻的；苛刻的 **2.** 坚定的，不动摇的

stern[2] [stə:n] n. **1.** 船尾 **2.** 臀，臀部 **3.**(尤指猎狐犬的)尾 **4.**(任何东西的)尾部；后部 ‖ **chase**(后船对前船的)尾追 /~ **chaser** 舰尾炮，艇尾炮

sternum ['stə:nəm]([复] sterna ['stə:nə]) 或

sternums) *n.*【解】胸骨

stet [stet] 【印】 *n.* 表示"不删"(或"保留")的校对符号 *vt.* (stetted; stetting) *vt.* 对…加注表示"不删"(或"保留")的校对符号(例如:英美常在被删的词下注上点线(……)或注上"stet",我国则用么号)

stethoscope ['ste0əskəup] *n.*【医】听诊器 — *vt.* 用听诊器检查

stevedore ['stiːvidɔː] *n.* 码头工、装卸工 — *vt.* 装卸(货船或货物) — *vi.* 装卸货物;当码头工

stew [stjuː] *vt.* 1. 炖、煨、焖 2.〈口〉使烦恼(使苦恼;使急躁)焖煮;被焖熟 2.〈关在房中〉受闷热;热得发昏;〈俚〉用功读书 3. 烦恼;焦急 — *n.* 1. 炖过的食品(尤指炖肉或炖鱼) 2. 混杂物 3. 闷热拥挤的状况;〈口〉烦恼;着急 ‖ ～**bum** *n.* 酒鬼 / ～**pan** *n.* 长柄炖锅 / ～**pot** *n.* (双柄)炖锅

steward ['stjuəd] *n.* 1.(轮船、飞机之)乘务员、服务员 2.(学校、医院、旅馆等的)伙食管理员 3. 管事;财务管理员 4.(舞会、赛马、集会等的)管事 5.【美】车间或部门(的)工会管事 — *vt.* 做…的乘务员(或管家等);管理 — *vi.* 当乘务员(或管家等) ‖ ～**ess** *n.* 女乘务员(或女服务员等) / ～**ship** *n.*

sth. *abbr.* something

stibium ['stibiəm] *n.*【化】锑(= antimony)

stick [stik] *n.* 1. 枝条,枯枝;柴枝 2. 棍、棒;杖;手杖 3.(草本植物的)茎,杆 4. 条状物,棒状物 5.(炸弹等连续投下的)一批;一批连续跳下的伞兵 6.〈口〉木头木脑的人;蹩脚演员 7.〈建房,家具,船的)木料;木条 8.〈俚〉大麻烟卷(加在饮料(尤指茶,咖啡)中的烈酒 9. 刺,戳 10. 粘性 11.【空】手柄;操纵杆;(汽车的)变速杆,换档杆;

【海】桅杆;桁;【音】指挥棒;【印】排字盘 12.〈美口〉[the ～s]小镇;郊区;乡间;边远森林地 13. 一件(家具) — *vt.* (stuck [stʌk]) *vt.* 1. 刺,戳;刺死;刺穿 2. 钉住;插牢;放置 3. 伸,伸出 4. 粘贴;贴 5. 使停止;阻塞 6.〈口〉难住;出…困住 7.〈俚〉容忍,忍受 8. 迫使…偿付;敲(某人)竹杠;欺骗 9.(过去式及过去分词用 sticked)用棒支撑;【印】在排字盘中排(字) — *vi.* 1. 钉住 2. 停留;坚持;固守 3. 梗塞;轧牢,陷住;被难住 4. 伸出;突出 ‖ ～**in-the-mud** *n.*〈口〉顽固守旧的人;木头木脑的人 *adj.* 保守的;迟钝的 / ～**pin** *n.*(用于领带等的)装饰别针

sticker ['stikə] *n.* 1.(屠宰场的)屠夫 2. 尖刀;芒刺;(美俚)防身匕首 2. 携带(或使用)防身匕首的人 3. 张贴广告者 4.〈美〉背面有粘胶的标签(或封口、邮票等) 5. 始终如一的人;坚忍不拔者 6. 滞销品 7.〈口〉难题;费解的事物 8. 呆着不走的客人

sticking ['stikiŋ] *n.* 1. 刺,戳 2. 粘,贴;粘胶;粘料 ‖ ～**place** *n.*(拧螺丝钉等时的)进到不能再进之处,顶住点,顶死点 2.(猪等颈上的)屠刀插入处 / ～**plaster** 橡皮膏;胶布;打膏

stickle ['stikl] *vi.* 1.(为小事)固执己见,强词夺理 2. 迟疑;有异义(*at*) ‖ ～**r** *n.*

stickleback ['stiklbæk] *n.*【动】剌鱼

sticky ['stiki] *adj.* 1. 粘性的;胶粘的 2.〈口〉湿热的 3.〈口〉抱不同意(或不合作)态度的 4. 极不愉快的;痛苦的 5. 尴尬的;不自然的 ‖ ～**fingered**, '～**handed** *adj.* 有盗窃习惯的,手脚不干净的

stiff [stif] *adj.* 1. 硬的,挺的 2.(手足等)僵直的,僵硬的 3. 不易移动的;不灵

活的;一动就痛的 **4.**(绳子等)拉紧的,绷紧的,张紧的 **5.** 拘谨的;生硬的;不自然的;呆板的;傲慢的;冷淡的 **6.** 刚强的;倔强的 **7.** 强烈的;猛烈的;强有力的 **8.**〈俚〉喝醉的 **9.**(行市)坚挺的;昂贵的 **10.** 粘的;胶粘的;稠的;(土质)紧密的 **11.** 艰难的;费劲的 **12.** 严厉的 **13.**〈口〉[只作表语]极度的;极点的 **14.**(船)稳性大的,不易倾覆的 — *n.*〈俚〉 **1.** 死尸 **2.**〈英〉不可救药的人 **3.**〈美〉鄙鬼;傲慢(或拘谨、讨厌)的人;游民;给小费吝啬的人 **4.**〈美〉普通工人;流动工人 **5.** 流通(可转让的)票据;钞票;钱 **6.**〈俚〉(赛马中)被认为必输的马 — *vt.*〈美俚〉不肯给…小费;让…空手而去 ‖ ~ in one's back 挺直腰背 / be / keep a ~ upper lip 不动声色;泰然自若 / ~ ' necked *adj.* **1.**〔医〕患颈强直的 **2.** 倔强的;固执的

stiffen ['stifn] *vt.* **1.** 使硬;使挺 **2.** 使硬;使变硬;使硬 **3.** 使变硬;使呆板 **4.** 使生硬;使呆板 **5.** 使坚定 **6.** 使胶粘;使稠 **7.** 使(行市)坚挺 **8.** 使(船)不易倾侧 — *vi.* **1.** 变硬;变挺 **2.** 变僵硬 **3.** 变强劲;变坚强 **4.** 变胶粘;变稠 **5.**(行市)变坚挺 **6.** 变得劲劲 ‖ ~er *n.* **1.** 使坚强的人(或事物);加固物 **2.**〔建〕加劲件,加劲板 **3.** 增强(勇气、决心等)的事物 **3.** 滋补剂;兴奋剂

stifle ['staifl] *vt.* **1.** 使窒息,使闷住;闷死 **2.** 抑制;镇压 — *vi.* **1.** 窒息,闷死 **2.** 闷死 **3.** 受抑制

stifling ['staifliŋ] *adj.* 令人窒息的,气闷的;沉闷的

stigma ['stigmə]([复] **stigmas** 或 **stigmata** ['stigmətə]) *n.* **1.** 耻辱;污名;〈古〉烙印 **2.**〔植〕柱头 **3.**〔动〕气门;点斑;翅痣;斑点 **4.**〔医〕特征;滤泡小斑

stigmatize ['stigmətaiz] *vt.* **1.**〈古〉给…打上烙印 **2.** 指责;给…带来耻辱;污辱

stile [stail] *n.* **1.**(篱或墙)两侧的阶梯(供人越过用) **2.** 旋转栅门(如公园入口处所设)

stiletto [sti'letəu]([复] **stiletto(e)s**) *n.* **1.** 短剑,匕首 **2.** 打眼锥 — *vt.* 用短剑刺(或刺死)

still[1] [stil] *adj.* **1.** 静止的,不动的;平静的,寂静的 **2.**(酒)不起泡的,不含气体的 **3.**〔摄〕静止的;定格的(与电影摄影相对)— *n.* **1.**〔诗〕寂静 **2.** 剧照;静止摄影,定格画面 **3.**(不用警报器而用电话等报告的)火警警报 — *vt.* 使静止;使平静;止住 — *vi.* 静止;平静 — *adv.* **1.** 还,仍旧 **2.**〔修饰比较级〕还要,更 **3.**〔作连词用〕(虽然…)还是,但是 ‖ ~ness *n.* 寂静 / ~y *adv.* ‖ ~birth *n.*〔医〕死胎;死产 / ~born *adj.* **1.**〔医〕死产的 **2.** 不成功的,流产的 / ~life **1.** 静物 **2.** 静物画

still[2] [stil] *n.* **1.** 蒸馏室;酿酒场 **2.** 蒸馏器 — *vt.* & *vi.* 蒸馏 / ~room *n.*〈英〉 **1.**(饮料等的)储藏室 **2.** 蒸馏室

stilt [stilt] *n.* **1.**[常 ~s]高跷 **2.** 支撑物;支材 **3.**([复] **stilt(s)**)〔动〕长脚鹬 — *vt.* **1.** 使(如)踩高跷

stilted ['stiltid], **stilty** ['stilti] *adj.* **1.** 踩高跷的;似踩高跷的 **2.**(言、文、举止等)夸张的;做作的,不自然的

stimulant ['stimjulənt] *n.* 兴奋剂;刺激物;酒 — *adj.* 刺激的,刺激性的

stimulate ['stimjuleit] *vt.* 刺激;激发,激励,促进 — *vi.* 起刺激作用 ‖ ~r, **stimulator** *n.* /**stimulative** *adj.* 刺激(性)的;激励(性)的;促进(性)的

stimulation [ˌstimju'leiʃən] *n.* 刺激(作用);兴奋(作用)

stimulus ['stimjuləs]([复] **stimuli** ['stimjulai]) *n.* 刺激;刺激物;促进因素

sting [stiŋ] (stung [stʌŋ]) *vt.* **1.** 刺,螫,叮 **2.** 刺痛；使感觉痛 **3.** 刺激；激励 **4.** 〈口〉[常作被动语态]骗；敲一竹杠一 *vi.* **1.** 刺,叮 **2.** 刺痛,螫痛 **3.** 刺激,激励 一 *n.* **1.** 刺,叮 **2.** 刺痛；剧痛 **3.** 刺激；讽刺 **4.** (昆虫的)螫针,螯刺；(植物的)刺毛 ‖ ~ray *n.* [鱼]缸

stinger [ˈstiŋə] *n.* **1.** 刺激者；讽刺者；有刺的动物(或植物) **2.** (昆虫的)螫针,螯刺；(植物的)刺毛 **3.** 〈口〉痛击；尖酸刻薄的话 **4.** (美)用白兰地、薄荷酒等制成的)斯丁格鸡尾酒；〈英口〉威士忌苏打水

stingy [ˈstindʒi] *adj.* **1.** 吝啬的，小气的 **2.** 缺乏的,不足的；极少的

stink [stiŋk] (过去式 stank [stæŋk] 或 stunk [stʌŋk],过去分词 stunk) *vi.* **1.** 发恶臭 **2.** 令人厌恶；名声臭；坏透 一 *vt.* **1.** 用臭气赶出(out) **2.** 〈俚〉闻出…的臭气 一 *n.* **1.** 恶臭；臭气 **2.** 〈英〉〈学俚〉[~s]自然科学；化学 **3.** 大事争吵闹,(对丑事的)张扬 ‖ ~pot *n.* **1.** 盛臭物的容器 **2.** (旧时海战抛向敌船的)罐状臭弹 **3.** 讨厌透顶的人

stint [stint] *vt.* **1.** 〈古〉停止。限制 **2.** 限制；吝惜 **3.** 分配任务给一 *vi.* **1.** 〈古〉停止 **2.** 节约 一 *n.* **1.** 限制；吝惜 **2.** 定额工作；定量；限额

stipend [ˈstaipend] *n.* **1.** (牧师、教师等的)俸给,薪金 **2.** (尤指学生的)定期生活津贴

stipendiary [stai'pendiəri] *adj.* **1.** 有俸给的,领薪金的 **2.** 有关薪金的一 *n.* **1.** 受俸给者,领薪金者 **2.** 〈英〉(大城镇中处理违警police案件的)领薪治安官

stipple [ˈstipl] *vt.* **1.** (雕刻时)点刻；绘画时点画 **2.** 把…弄毛糙一 *vi.* 用点刻(或点画)法 一 *n.* 点刻(法)；点画(法)；点刻(或点画)作品；点刻(或点

画)状

stipulate [ˈstipjuleit] *vt.* **1.** 订定；规定 **2.** 保证；约定 一 *vi.* 订定；规定；约定,讲定(for)

stipulation [ˌstipjuˈleiʃən] *n.* **1.** 订定；规定 **2.** (条约、契约等的)条款；项目

stir [stə:] *vt.* **1.** (stirred;stirring) *vt.* **1.** 动；移动；摇动 **2.** 拨动；搅拌；搅起(up) **3.** 激起；激动；鼓动；煽动一 *vi.* **1.** 动；走动；活动；〈口〉起床 **2.** (消息)传布；流通；流行 **3.** 受搅拌一 *n.* **1.** 微动；搅动；激动；鼓动 **2.** 拨动；搅拌

stirpiculture [ˈstə:pikʌltʃə] *n.* 优种繁殖(法)

stirring [ˈstə:riŋ] *adj.* **1.** 激动人心的 **2.** 忙碌的

stirrup [ˈstirəp] *n.* **1.** 马镫 **2.** 【建】箍筋,U形钢筋箍；[机]镫具(如自行车的脚镫) ‖ ~cup (送别登程骑者的)饯行酒

stitch [stitʃ] *n.* **1.** (缝制或编织的)一针；针脚；缝线 **2.** 针法；缝法；编法 **3.** 〈口〉少许衣服；一点,少许 **4.** [只用单](胁部的)突然剧痛 **5.** 〈英方〉畦；犁沟间的脊一 *vt.* **1.** 缝,缝合；装订 **2.** 〈英方〉把(耕地)弄成畦一 *vi.* 缝,缝纫

stiver [ˈstaivə] *n.* **1.** 斯泰佛(荷兰旧辅币) **2.** 小钱；不值钱的东西；一点点

stoat [stəut] *n.* 【动】白鼬

stock [stɔk] *n.* **1.** 树干；根株；根状茎 **2.** 苗木；活木 **3.** (木头、金属的)托座,托把,后把；钻柄；枪托；(野战炮的)炮座；锚杆；(刨刀的)刀架；犁架 **5.** 祖先；家系；世系,血统；种族；【语】语族；语系 **6.** 原料；备料；基本成分(制汤等用的)原汁,原汤 **7.** (牌局开始时)没发完的牌,发剩下来的牌 **8.** 库存品,存货；贮存 **9.** 资本,股本；股票(=〈英〉

shares) 10.〈英〉公债；债券（ = 〈美〉bond）11.【总称】家畜 12.〔~s〕足枷；手铐（旧时的刑具）；（给马等钉蹄铁时用的）夹架 13.〔~s〕【船】船台 14.【生】族系；【动】群体；一群蜜蜂 15.紫罗兰属植物（如紫罗兰、夜紫罗兰）16. 估计，估量；信任，相信 17.（在固定剧场轮流保留剧目的）专业剧团；（专业剧团在固定剧场轮演的）保留剧目 18.（18 世纪男子用的）宽大硬领圈，（牧师衣领下的）硬领带 19. 砖 — adj. 1. 库存的；现有的；常备的 2. 平凡的，普通的；陈腐的 3. 繁殖用的 4. 饲养牲畜的；牲畜用的 5. 证券的；股票的 6. 管理存货的 7.（轮演保留剧目的）专业剧团的；演剧保留剧目的 8. 备用的 — vt. 1. 给……装上把手（或柄、横档等）2. 给（商店）办货；供给（牧场）以牲畜；贮备；备有 3. 放牧；在……放牧牲畜 4. 给……种牧草于 6. 给（罪犯）上枷 — vi. 1. 截断的树干或根株中出新芽 2. 办货（up）‖ ~ book 1. 存货簿 2. 邮票簿 / ~ -breeding n. 饲养牲畜；繁殖用家畜 / ~ broker n.（代客买卖的）证券经纪人 / ~ company 1. 股份公司 2.（在固定剧场轮演保留剧目的）专业剧团（尤指设有名演员的剧团）/ ~ exchange 证券交易所 / ~-fish n.（未加过盐的）鳕鱼干 / ~-in-trade 1. 股东 2.〈古〉大牧主 / ~-in-trade 1. 存货；（行业的）全部营业用具，生财 2. 惯用手段 / ~ list（证券交易所公布的）证券行情表 / ~ market = ~ exchange / ~ pile n. 1.（堆在路边为修路而设的）料堆 2.【军】贮存；（准备应急用的）原料物资（或武器装备等）的战略贮存量；科研资料的积累 vt. & vi. 贮存；堆存；积累 / ~ pot n. 1.（炖汤用的）汤锅 2. 杂烩锅 3. 充分的来源，丰富的资源 / ~ power 股票转让授权书 / ~ raising 牲畜饲养（业）/

~ room 1. 贮藏室 2.（旅馆中供旅行推销员用的）商品展览室 / ~-'still adj. 静止的，不动的 / ~-,taking n. 1. 存货的盘点 2. 估量；打量 / ~-yard n. 1.（尤指屠宰或装运前临时图存牲畜的）牲畜围场 2. 堆料场

stockade [stɔ'keid] n. 1.（一列）栅栏；（一列）围栏 2. 由栅栏围起的一块地方 3.（用铁丝网围住的）军人监狱；俘虏拘留营 4. 防波围桩 — vt. 用栅栏围住；用栅栏防卫

Stockholm ['stɔkhəum] n. 斯德哥尔摩〔瑞典首都〕

stockinet [,stɔki'net] n.（做内衣用的）松紧织物，弹力织物

stocking ['stɔkiŋ] n. 1. 长（统）袜；似长（统）袜的东西 2. 与身体其他部分毛色不同的兽脚 ‖ ~ed adj. 穿袜的 / ~ cap（冬季运动员或小孩戴的顶端有绒球或穗的圆锥形）绒线帽，针织帽

stocky ['stɔki] adj. 矮胖的，粗壮的 ‖ stockily adv. / stockiness n.

stodge [stɔdʒ] n. 1. 充饥食物；稠而难消化的食物；盛馔 2.〈俚〉食物 3. 枯燥沉闷的作品；陈腐的念头 4. 步履艰难的人，行走慢而费力的人 — vi. 1. 狼吞虎咽 2. 重步行走；经历艰苦 — vt. 1. 贪婪地吃；使塞饱 2. 使感到发腻 3. 搀和，调合

stodgy ['stɔdʒi] adj. 1.（食物）供充饥的；稠而难消化的 2. 身体笨重的；行走慢而费力的 3. 装得满满的，塞满的 4.（作品等）烦琐乏味的；（风格等）滞重无趣的 5.（人）迟钝的；庸俗的；平凡 6.〔常老派的；墨守成规的 7.（色彩）暗淡的；（衣服等）式样难看的

stogy, stogie ['stəugi] n. 1. 价廉的细支雪茄烟 2. 笨重的鞋（或靴）

stoic ['stəuik] *adj.* 1.[-S-](公元前 4 世纪创立于雅典的哲学派别)斯多葛派的 2. 禁欲主义的;不以苦乐为意的;淡泊的 — *n.* 1.[S-]斯多葛派学者,柱廊派人 2. 禁欲主义者 ‖ ~ism ['stəuisizm] *n.* 1.[S-]斯多葛哲学 2. 禁欲主义;淡泊

stoical ['stəuikəl] *adj.* = stoic ‖ ~ly *adv.*

stoke [stəuk] *vt.* 1. 给(炉子)添燃料,司(炉) 2.拨(火);拨旺(火) 3. 使大吃: ~ oneself 饱吃一顿 — *vi.* 1. 司炉;烧火 2. 大吃:狼吞虎咽 ‖ ~ r *n.* 1. 烧火工人,司炉 2. 加煤机 /'~hold *n.*【船】生火间(锅炉间);炉前 /'~ hole *n.*【船】炉膛口;生火间;锅炉room;炉前

STOL [stɔl] *abbr.* short takeoff and landing (aircraft)短距起落(飞机)

stole[1] [stəul] *n.* 1. 女用披肩 2.(牧师等在举行仪式时披的)圣带,长巾;圣衣 3.(古罗马的)妇女长外衣

stole[2] [stəul] steal 的过去式

stolen ['stəulən] steal 的过去分词

stolid ['stɔlid] *adj.* 不易激动的,感觉迟钝的;古板的,执拗的 ‖ ~ity [stə'lidəti] *n.* /~ly *adv.* /~ness *n.*

stomach ['stʌmək] *n.* 1. 胃 2. 肚子,腹部 3. 食欲,胃口;欲望;志趣 — *vt.* 1. 津津有味地吃;消化 2.[常与否定词或疑问词连用]忍耐,忍受;忍气吞声 3.(对…)发怒 ‖ ~ic [stə'mætik] *adj.* 胃的;健胃的;开胃的,助消化的 *n.* 健胃药,开胃药,助消化剂

stone [stəun] *n.* 1. 石,石头;石块;石料 2. 宝石;(表中的)钻石 3. 界碑;里程碑;纪念碑;墓碑 4. 磨石,油石;磨刀石 5.[印]排版用石台;调墨石台;石印石 6.【医】结石;结石病 7. 冰雹 8. 果核 9.(古)睾丸 10.[单复同]英石(英国重量单位) — *adj.* 石的;石制的 — *vt.* 1. 向…扔石头;用石头砸死 2. 用石头铺;用石(墙)围 3. 去…的核 4. 用磨刀石磨快;用磨石磨光(皮革,金属等) ‖ Stone Age 石器时代 /~'blind *adj.* 1. 完全瞎的 2.《美俚》酩酊大醉的 /'~ brash *n.* 碎石土壤 /'~breaker *n.* 敲碎石的人,碎石工;碎石机 /~'broke *adj.* 身无分文的,赤贫的 /~ coal 白煤,块状无烟煤 /'~dead *adj.* 完全死了的;毫无生命的 /~'deaf *adj.* 完全聋的 /~ jug《俚》监狱 /'~mason *n.* 石匠 /~ mill 磨石机;碎石机;(石磨)碎面机 /~ pit *n.* 石坑;采石场 /'~s cast, /'~s throw 一箭之遥:短距离 /'~ ware *n.* [总称]石制品,缸瓦器;粗陶器

stony, stoney ['stəuni] *adj.* 1. 多石的;石质的,铺着石块的;坚硬如石的 2. 冷酷的,无情的;没有表情的 3.《俚》身无分文的,一贫如洗的 ‖ stonily *adv.* / stoniness *n.*

stood [stud] stand 的过去式和过去分词

stooge [studʒ] *n.* 1.(歌舞杂耍混于观众中)向台角发问打趣的演员;滑稽演员的配角(指被滑稽演员打趣或向滑稽演员提示台词者) 2. 助手,下手 3. 俯偏:唯命是从的人;走狗 4. 暗探,奸细:密探 5.《美俚》副驾驶员 — *vi.* 1. 充当滑稽演员的配角,充当傀儡(或走狗等)(for)

stool [stul] *n.* 1. 凳子 2. 搁脚凳;跪凳【建】内窗台 3.(象征职权的)坐位;宝座 4. 厕所;马桶;(一次)大便,粪便 5. 根株;根蘖(束) 6. 诱鸟的栖木 7. = pigeon — *vi.* 1. 长出新枝,分蘖 2.《美俚》作窝子:充当密探 3.《古》去大便 — *vt.* 诱捕(野鸟);引诱 ‖ ~ pigeon 1.(用来诱捕野鸟的)鹨鸽 2. 诱人入圈套者;骗子,密探:警探

stoolie ['stu:li] *n.* = stool pigeon

stoop[1] [stup] *vi.* 1. 俯身,弯腰;弯腰曲背地站立(或行走) 2. 降格;屈从;堕落 3.(鹰在捕猎时)下扑;〈古〉下降,降落 — *vt.* 1. 俯曲(头、肩、背等) 2. 辱没 — *n.* 1. 弯腰,曲背 2. 降格,自贬;屈从 3.(鹰的)下扑

stoop[2] [stup] *n.* 门廊;门阶

stop [stop] (stopped;stopping) *vt.* 1. 塞住,阻塞;堵塞;填塞 2. 阻止,阻拦;拦住;难倒;使窘狼;击败(对方);击落;击毙(飞鸟等) 3. 止住,止住;终止;止付;扣留 5. 给…加标点 6. 用手指压(乐器上的弦、孔等)以改变音调 7.【海】系紧(船缆等) — *vi.* 1. 止住,停下来 2. 踌躇 3.〈口〉逗留,停留;歇宿;(偶然)过访 4. 被塞住(*up*) 5. 以手指压乐器的弦(或孔等)以改变音调 — *n.* 1. 止住;中止;终止;停车2. 停车站;停留场所 3. 逗留,停留;歇宿 4. 塞住;填塞;阻窒;障碍 5.〈英〉标点符号(尤指句号) 6.【语】(辅音)停顿 7.(以手指压乐器的弦、孔等的)调整音调;(喉)说法,语气;语调 8. 风琴的音栓;(六弦琴等的)音格 9. — order 10.【海】繫索子 11. 阻塞物,制动器,繫子,挡,销;断流阀;门闩 12.【摄】光圈;光圈数(即 f 数)刻度 — *adj.* 停止的或起止用的,制动的 ‖ ' ~ gap *n.* 1. 权宜之计 2. 补缺者;临时代替的人(或物)*adj.* 补缺的;暂时的 / ' ~ light *n.* 1.(汽车车尾的)停车灯 2. 交通信号灯(尤指红灯)/ ~ order(在股市达到一定行情时指示经纪人的)依限买卖指令,限价补进(或卖出)令 / ~ over *n.*(旅程)中途停留;中途停留地 / ~ press(主英)(报纸付印时插入的)最新消息 / ' ~-press *adj.* 1. 报纸付印时临时加入的 2. 最新的,截至最近

的 / ' ~ watch *n.*(赛跑等用的)跑表,秒表

stoppage ['stopidʒ] *n.* 1. 停止;中止 2. 阻塞;堵塞;阻碍;【军】故障 3. 停付;(工资等的)扣留;扣除 4. 停工;罢工

stopper ['stopə] *n.* 1. 停止者;制止者 2. 阻塞物;(瓶等的)塞子;【机】制动器,限制器;闭锁装置 3.【海】繫(索)【矿】伸缩式凿岩机 — *vt.*(用塞子等)塞住

stopping ['stopiŋ] *n.* 1. 停止;中止;制动2. 制止;阻塞;堵塞 3.(补牙等用的)充填料,填料 4.【矿】风幛,风墙,隔墙 5. 加标点

storage ['stɔ:ridʒ] *n.* 1. 贮藏,保管 2. 贮藏量,库存量 3. 贮藏库,仓库,货栈 4. 仓库费,栈租 5. 蓄电 6.【计】存储器;(信息的)存储 ‖ ~ battery, ~ cell 蓄电池

store [stɔ:] *n.* 1. 贮藏,贮存;大量;丰富 2. [~s]贮藏品;补给品 3.〈英〉货栈,仓库,堆栈(= 〈美〉warehouse) 4.〈英〉[亦作~s]用作单或复]百货商店(= 〈美〉department store) 5.〈美〉商店,店铺(= 〈英〉shop) 6.【主英】[计]存储器 — *adj.* 1. [亦作~s]贮藏的,贮存的;用作贮藏处的 2. 从店里买来的;现成的 — *vt.* 1. 贮藏,储备 2. 供应,供给;装备 3. 容纳;包含;蓄有 4. 把…存入仓库;把…交给栈房 — *vi.* 1. 贮藏,贮藏供应品 2. 装备补给品;贮藏供应品 ‖ ~ house *n.* 1. 货栈,仓库,堆栈 2. 宝库 / ' ~ keeper *n.* 1. 仓库管理员;军需品管理员 2.〈美〉零售店店主 / ' ~ room *n.* 1. 贮藏室;物料间;商品陈列室;宝库

stor(e)y ['stɔ:ri] *n.*〈英〉楼层,楼,层

storeyed, storied[1] ['stɔ:rid] *adj.*[常用以构成复合词]有…(层)楼的:a six-~

building 6 层楼的建筑物

storied[²] [ˈstɔːrid] *adj.* 1. 用（历史）故事画装饰的 2. 历史上（或传说中）有名的

stork [stɔːk] *n.* 【动】鹳 ‖ *a King Stork* 暴君（源出伊索寓言）

storm [stɔːm] *n.* 1. 风暴；暴（风）雨；暴（风）雪；风雹；【气】狂风 2.（政治、社会方面的）风暴，大动荡，风潮 3.（风暴般的）猛扑；纷飞；（感情上的）激动,爆发 4.（军事上的）猛攻；攻占 5.[~s]（御风暴的）外重窗 — *vi.* 1. 起风暴；刮大风；下暴雨；下暴雪；下雹 2. 强攻；猛冲；横冲直撞 3. 暴怒,发雷霆；怒号 (*at*) — *vt.* 1. 攻取；狠狠扑击 2. 强烈感染；使神魂颠倒 ‖ ~ *boat* 强击登陆艇，强击舟 / '~*bound adj.*（船、旅客等）为风暴所阻的（港口等为风暴所困的）/ ~ *cone*（英）（帆布制）锥形风暴信标 / ~ *lantern*, ~ *lamp* 防风灯,风暴灯 / ~ *trooper* 1.[S-T.]（纳粹的）冲锋队员 2. 突击队员 / ~ *troops* 1.[S-T.]（纳粹的）冲锋队 2. 突击队,强击部队

stormy [ˈstɔːmi] *adj.* 1. 有风暴的；暴风雨的 2. 烈性子的,暴躁的 3. 激烈的；多风波的 ‖ *stormily adv.*

story[¹] [ˈstɔːri] *n.* 1. 故事；小说；传奇；轶事；传说；传记；史话；（古）历史 2. 对某事的）描述,叙述 3. 经历,阅历 4.（小说、戏剧等）的情节,本事 5. 内情,真相 6.（新闻）记事；报道；值得报道的人物（或事实）7.（儿语）假话,谎话（说谎者 — *vt.* 1.（古）叙故事描写,编成故事叙述 2. 用（历史）故事画装饰 ‖ '~*book n.* 故事书 / '~*teller n.* 1. 讲故事的人；说书人 2.（口）说谎的人 / '~*writer n.* 小说作者,小说家

story[²] [ˈstɔːri] *n.* = storey

stoup [stuːp] *n.* 1. 大酒杯 2.【宗】圣水钵

stout [staut] *adj.* 1. 结实的；牢固的 2. 勇敢的；坚定的；不妥协的 3. 有力的；猛烈的,激烈的 4. 强壮的；矮胖的（胖的 5. 粗壮的；厚的 — *n.* 1. 矮胖子；大号的衣服尺寸 2. 高浓度黑啤酒 ‖ ~*ly adv.* / ~ *ness n.*

stove[¹] [stəuv] *n.* 1.（取暖或烹饪用的）炉；火炉；电炉；加热器 2. 窑；烘房；（主英）温室 — *vt.* 在温室内培育（植物）‖ '~*pipe n.* 1.（从火炉通至烟囱或户外的）火炉烟管 2.（美口）大礼帽（一种高筒狭边男用丝绒帽）/ ~ *plant* 温室植物

stove[²] [stəuv] stave 的过去式和过去分词

stow [stəu] *vt.* 1. 堆垛,堆装；装载 2. 贮藏,收藏 3. 使暂留；使暂宿 4.（俚）[常用祈使语气]停止 5. 用…填塞 ‖ ~ *away* 1. 收藏起,贮藏 2. 无票偷乘；（为逃跑）偷乘船或（或火车、飞机等）吃光；喝完 ‖ ~*away n.* 1.（措油等客,偷乘者 2. 隐藏的地方

stowage [ˈstəuidʒ] *n.* 1. 堆装（法）；装载（法）；贮藏（法）2. 堆装物；装载物；贮藏物 3. 装（或装载）容积；贮藏处 4. 堆存费,装货费

St. Petersburg [ˌseintˈpiːtəzbəːg] = Saint Petersburg

strabismus [strəˈbizməs] *n.*【医】斜视,斜眼

straddle [ˈstrædl] *vi.* 1. 叉开腿；叉开腿坐；叉腿站立；叉开腿走路；蹒跚 2. 杂乱地伸展 3. 观望,骑墙 4. 在一市场上买空并在另一市场上卖空,一面做多头一面做空头 — *vt.* 1.（叉开腿）跨立,跨坐 2. 对…不表态；对…抱观望态度 3. 夹又射击；夹又瞄准 — *n.* 1. 叉腿,跨 2. 观望态度,骑墙,暧昧 3. 双重期

权(证券交易中使对方在一定期限内按某一价格收货或交货的权利);套利(同时在一种证券上做多头而在另一种证券上做空头的交易) **4.** 俯卧式跳高

strafe [straːf] *vt.* **1.**(低空)扫射 **2.** 猛击,痛打;惩罚 — *n.*(低空)扫射

straggle [ˈstrægl] *vi.* **1.** 迷路;掉队,落伍;流离 **2.** 蔓延;蔓生;四散;散落地出现 — *n.* 散乱 ‖ ~**r** *n.*

straight [streit] *adj.* **1.** 直的,笔直的,挺直的 **2.** 直接的;连续的 **3.** 整齐的;端正的;有条理的 **4.** 正直的;有品德的;坦率的 **5.**〈口〉可靠的;正确的 **6.**(发动机)汽缸直排式的 **7.**〈美〉纯粹的;不搀杂的 **8.**(对政党、原则等)始终忠实的,彻底支持的 **9.**(不论多少)单价固定的 **10.**(动物)纯种的 **11.**(吸毒者)被麻醉了的 — *adv.* **1.** 直:stand ~ 直立 **2.** 直接地;一直地 **3.** 正直的;老实地;坦率地 **4.** 立刻,马上 — *n.* **1.** 直;挺直 **2.** 直线;[the ~](跑道的)直道 **3.**(纸牌)顺子 **4.**〈俚〉真相 **5.**(赛马)第一名;(射击等的)连续得分 — *vt.*〈苏格兰〉= straighten ‖ ~**ly** *adv.* / ~**ness** *n.* ‖ ˈ~-aˌ**way** *n.* 直线部分;(跑道的)直道;(道路的)直段 *adj.* **1.** 径直的;直线行进的 **2.**(故事等)直叙的;明白易懂的 **3.** 毫不迟疑的 *adv.* = ~way / ˈ~**edge** *n.* 直尺;标尺 *vt.* 把…的一边弄直;用直尺检验 / ˈ~**out** *n.*(对某一政党或政策)一贯支持的人 *adj.* 坦率的;彻底的 / ˈ~**way** *adv.* 径直地,直接地;立刻,马上 *adj.* 畅通无阻的

straighten [ˈstreitn] *vt.* **1.** 把…弄直,使挺直 **2.** 整顿;清理;澄清(*out, up*) **3.** 使改正;使好转(*out*) — *vi.* **1.** 直起来;挺起来(*up*) **2.** 改正;好转(*out, up*)

straightforward [streitˈfɔːwəd] *adj.* **1.** 一直向前的;直接的 **2.** 正直的;老实的;坦率的 **3.** 简单的;易做的;易懂的 **4.** 明确的;肯定的 — *adv.* 坦率地;直截了当地 ‖ ~**ly** *adv.* / ~**ness** *n.*

strain[1] [strein] *n.* **1.**(人的)血缘,世系,家系;种,族;(动、植物的)系,品系;【微】菌株,品种 **2.** 气质;(性格上的)倾向 **3.**[常~s]曲调,旋律;乐曲;诗;歌;诗节;歌节 **4.** 口吻;语气;笔调;情调

strain[2] [strein] *vt.* **1.** 拉紧;拖紧;伸张 **2.** 使紧张;尽力使用(耳、目、嗓子等);使过劳(以致受损伤);扭伤 **3.** 滥用;(牵强地)曲解,歪曲 **4.** 压紧,紧抱:~ a child to one's breast 把孩子紧抱在怀里 **5.** 滤 — *vi.* **1.** 尽力;努力;使劲 **2.** 紧拉;紧拖 **3.** 不肯接受;以为不可 **4.** 扭歪;弯曲;(因用力而)变形 **5.** 被过滤;渗出 — *n.* **1.** 拉紧;张力;【物】应变,胁变 **2.** 过度的使用;过劳;极度紧张;费力之物;严峻的考验 **3.** 扭伤 ‖ ~**ed** *adj.* **1.** 牵强附会的 **2.** 紧张的 **3.** 勉强的;不自然的 / ~**er** *n.* 滤器;滤网,筛网

strait [streit] *n.* **1.**[常~s][用作单]海峡 **2.**[常~s]困境;窘迫;危难 **3.**〈古〉地峡 — *adj.* **1.**〈古〉狭窄的;有限的,受限制的,紧的 **2.**〈古〉严格的,严密的,精确的 **3.** 困难的,窘迫的;苦恼的 ‖ ˈ~-**jacket** *n.*(给疯人或犯人穿的)拘束衣;〈喻〉约束物 *vt.* 用拘束衣拘束;束缚 / ˈ~**laced** *adj.* **1.** 用系带缚紧的;穿紧身衣的 **2.**(在举止、道德、观念等方面)极端严谨的

straiten [ˈstreitn] *vt.* **1.** 使变窄;使变紧 **2.** 限制;使紧缩 **3.**[常用被动语态]使窘迫;使困苦

strake [streik] *n.* **1.**【船】列板 **2.** 轮箍 **3.** 条纹;狭长地带;狭长草地

stramonium [strəˈməunjəm] *n.* 1.【植】曼陀罗 2. 曼陀罗叶(用作治气喘的药)

strand¹ [strænd] *n.* 海滨；海滩；河岸；湖滨 — *vt.* 1. 使搁浅 2.(由于资金等的缺乏)使陷于困境；使束手无策 3. 使掉队，使落后 — *vi.* 搁浅

strand² [strænd] *n.* 1.(绳、线等的)股；缕；绞 2. 线；绳 3. 串；一串珍珠(或念珠)4.(论据、思想等的)一个组成部分 5.【电】导线束；裸多心电缆，绞合线 — *vt.* 1. 弄断(绳索)的一股(或多股)2. 搓；绞(绳索等)

strange [streindʒ] *adj.* 1. 陌生的；生疏的，不熟悉的 2. 奇怪的；奇妙的；不可思议的 3. 生手的，外行的，没有经验的；不习惯的 4.(论调、思想等的)一个组成部分 5. 外地的，异乡的，〈古〉外国的 ‖ ~ly *adv.* / ~ness *n.* 〈 woman 娼妓

stranger [ˈstreindʒə] *n.* 1. 陌生人 2. 新来者；生客；异乡人 3. 生手，外行；局外人，不习惯于…的人(to) 4. 外国人 5.【律】非当事人 6.〈口〉(称呼久违的客人)稀客 — *vt.* 外国人的

strangle [ˈstræŋgl] *vt.* 1. 扼死；勒死；绞死 2. 扼住，闷住，使窒息 3. 抑制，压制 — *vi.* 1. 被扼死；被勒死；被绞死；窒息而死 ‖ ~r *n.* 扼杀者；压制者；【机】阻气门，节流门

strangulate [ˈstræŋgjuleit] *vt.* 1. 扼死；勒死；绞死 2. 闷住，使窒息 3.【医】绞窄(静脉等) — *vi.* 窒息；被抑住 ‖ ˌstranguˈlation *n.*

strap [stræp] *n.* 1. 带；皮带；布带；铁带；铁皮条 2. 磨刻刀的皮条，革砥 3. 搭扣鞋(亦作 ~ shoe)4.(合拢伤口或粘牢绷带用的)橡皮膏 5.[(the) ~]鞭打 6.〈英〉信用 7.〈爱尔兰语〉轻佻女子；娼妓 — *vt.* 1. 用皮

束住；捆扎 2. 用皮带抽打 3. 在革砥上磨(剃刀)4. 绑扎(伤口等)；用橡皮膏粘贴

strapper [ˈstræpə] *n.* 彪形大汉，魁梧的人

strapping [ˈstræpiŋ] *adj.* 身体高大而匀称的，魁梧的；强壮的 — *n.* 1. 贴膏法；橡皮膏 2. 皮带材料；捆扎重物，胶带 3. 抽打，鞭打

strata [ˈstrɑːtə, ˈstreitə] stratum 的复数

stratagem [ˈstrætidʒəm] *n.* 计策，计谋，策略

strategic(al) [strəˈtiːdʒik(əl)] *adj.* 1. 战略的；战略上(用)的；为战略计划用的 2. 对全局有重要意义的 ‖ **strategically** *adv.* 在战略上；颇策略地

strategics [strəˈtiːdʒiks] [复] *n.* [用作单]兵法；战略学

strategy [ˈstrætidʒi] *n.* 1. 战略；战略学 2. 计谋，策略 ‖ **strategist** *n.* 战略家

Stratford-on-Avon [ˈstrætfədɔnˈeivən] *n.* (艾冯河畔)斯特拉福福[英国英格兰中部城镇](莎士比亚的故乡)

strati [ˈstreitai] stratus 的复数

stratify [ˈstrætifai] *vt.* 1. 使成层；使分层 2.(园艺学用语)成层堆积，沙藏(种子) — *vi.* 成层；分层 ‖ **stratifiˈcation** *n.*

stratocracy [strəˈtɔkrəsi] *n.* 军人专政

stratocruiser [ˈstrætəkruːzə] *n.* 同温层飞机

stratosphere [ˈstrætəsfiə] *n.* 1.【气】平流层，同温层 2. 最上层；最高档；最部位 3. 艰深的学科领域 ‖ **stratospheric** [ˌstrætəˈsferik] *adj.*

stratovision [ˈstrætəviʒən] *n.* 同温层电视，飞机转播电视

stratum [ˈstrɑːtəm, ˈstreitəm]([复] strata [ˈstrɑːtə, ˈstreitə] 或 stratums) *n.* 1.(材

料、物质、大气、海洋、语言等的)层 **2.**【地】地层

stratus ['streitəs]([复]strati ['streitai]) *n.*【气】层云

straw [strɔː] *n.* **1.** 稻草;麦秆 2.(喝汽水等用的)(麦秆)吸管 **2.** 用稻草(或麦秆)做成的东西;〈口〉草帽 **3.** 无价值的东西;无意义的事情;一点点 — *adj.* **1.** 稻草(或麦秆)的;用稻草(或麦秆)做的 **2.** 稻草色的,淡黄色的 **3.**〈口〉无价值的;无意义的;琐碎的 **4.**(投票)仅为测验一下民意的,假的;(关于)假投票结果的 **5.** 稻草人般的;(对手等)假想的(在非法交易等中)被人推出来做挡箭牌的人 *~*〈古〉= strew ‖ *~* **board** *n.* 马粪纸、黄纸板、硬纸板 / *~* **plait** 草帽辫 / *~* **poll**〈英〉= *~* **vote** / *~* **vote**〈美〉(测验民意的)假投票

strawberry ['strɔːbəri] *n.* 草莓 ‖ *~* **mark** 莓状痣,先天性血管瘤

stray [strei] *vi.* **1.** 走离;偏离;迷路;走失 **2.** 漫游;流浪,漂泊 — *adj.* **1.** 迷路的;离群的;a *~* bullet 流弹 **2.** 偶遇的;零落的 *n.* **1.** 迷路者;走失的家畜;离群动物 **2.** 因无人继承而归公的遗产 **3.**[常 *~s*](干扰无线电接收的)天电 **4.**(石油钻探中)偶然出现的间层,杂层

streak [striːk] *n.* **1.** 条纹,纹理;色线 the silver *~* 银带(英吉利海峡的别称) **2.**(性格上不太显著的)气质,倾向 **3.**(猪肉中的)条层 **4.**〈口〉一连串,一系列;(短暂的)一段时期 **5.**【矿】矿脉;层层;矿物痕色,矿物粉色 **6.**【生】(种菌)划线;(植物的)杂斑痕 — *vi.* **1.** 形成条纹 **2.** 飞跑;疾驰 ‖ *~***ed** *adj.* 有条纹的 / *~***ing** *n.*(作为一种时尚在大街等处的)裸体飞跑;裸体骑行

streaky ['striːki] *adj.* **1.** 有条纹的;似条纹的;*~* pork(肥瘦相间的)五花猪肉 **2.** 性急的;变化无定的;波浪式的 **3.**(性能)不均匀的;混浊的;变化多端的;不可靠的

stream [striːm] *n.* **1.**(小)河;川;溪流 **2.** 流;流动;流出 **3.** 趋向,潮流 **4.**〈英〉(同一年级的学生按智力划分的)能力小组 — *vi.* **1.** 流;流出;流动;涌 **2.** 飘扬;招展 — *vt.* **1.** 流;流出 **2.** 展开(旗帜等) **3.**〈英〉把(学生)按智力划分 ‖ *~* **line** *n.* **1.**【物】流线 **2.**(飞机、汽车等的)流线型 *adj.* 流线(型)的 — *vt.* **1.** 把…设计(或制)成流线型 **2.** 把…组织,使一体化 **3.** 使现代化;使合理化;精简…使效率更高 / *~***lined** *adj.* **1.** 流线型的 **2.** 集成一个整体的,一体化的 **3.** 现代化了的;合理化了的;精简了的 / *~* **liner** *n.* 流线型物(特指流线型火车)

streamer ['striːmə] *n.* **1.** 横幅;长旗;旗 **2.** 下垂的饰带;飘带;旒 **3.**【气】光幕;[*~s*]北极光 **4.**【电】流光,射光;(由电子雪崩产生的)电子流 **5.**(报纸上的)通栏标题

street [striːt] *n.* **1.** 街,街道;行车道,马路 **2.** 街区,全街区的人 **3.**[the S-]某行业集中的街;〈美〉华尔街(美国纽约市的一条街道,美国金融机构的集中地)(= Wall Steet)〈英〉伦巴第人街(伦敦金融中心)(= Lombard Street)〈英〉舰队街(伦敦新闻业集中的一条街)(= Fleet Street) **4.** 贫困(或淫乱、犯罪等的环境,藏污纳垢之地);卖淫生涯(或职业) **5.**〈美俚〉释放出狱;自由 — *adj.* **1.** 街道的;街上的 **2.**(女子服装)适合上街穿的;下摆不拖到地面的 ‖ *~* **car** *n.*〈美〉(市内)有轨电车 / *~* **orderly**〈英〉街道清扫工 / *~*,**walker** *n.*(街头的)拉客妓女

strength [streŋθ] *n*. 1. 力,力量,力气;实力 2. 强度(酒、茶、颜色等的)浓度 3. (机构、组织等的)人数;兵员,兵力 4. 价格坚挺(或上升)的趋势 5. 〈美俚〉利润(尤指可能得到的所有利润)

strengthen ['streŋθən] *vt*. 1. 加强;巩固 使坚强 2. 增加…的艺术效果 — *vi*. 1. 变强 2. 行市坚挺

strenuous ['strenjuəs] *adj*. 1. 紧张的、艰苦的,繁重的 2. 发奋的,劲头十足的;热烈的;炽热的 3. 费劲的,费力的 ‖ ~**ly** *adv*.

streptococcus [ˌstreptə'kɒkəs] ([复] streptococci [ˌstreptə'kɒksai]) *n*. 【微】链球菌

streptomycin [ˌstreptəu'maisin] *n*. 【微】链霉素

stress [stres] *n*. 1. 压力;重压;紧迫;紧张 2. 重要;重点;强调 3.【语】重音;重读 4.【物】应力 — *vt*. 1. 着重;强调 2. 用重音读,重读 3. 使受应力 ‖ ~ **mark** *n*. 重音符号

stretch [stretʃ] *vt*. 1. 伸展,伸张;展开,铺开;把…伸直;把…拉长 2. 使过度伸展;使(精神、肌肉等)过度紧张;曲解;滥用~(过分)运用 3.【俚】拉紧(伸开四肢)蜷伸 5.〈俚〉绞死;吊死 6.〈俚〉为(尸体)作殡葬准备 — *vi*. 1. 伸,伸展,延伸;延续;连绵 2. 伸肢体;~ yawn and ~ 打呵欠伸懒腰 3.〈口〉夸大事实,吹牛 4.〈俚〉被绞死 5.【海】全帆航行 — *n*. 1. 伸展,伸长;延亘,连续 2. 重要;重点;强调 3.(消除疲劳的)散步 4. 一段持续的时间 一段路程;【海】一次抢风航程 5.〈俚〉徒刑;服刑期 6.〈赛马跑道的〉终点]点;直道 7. 伸长力,弹性 — *adj*. 弹性的,可拉伸〈飞机、汽车等〉改型的,扩大容积的

stretcher ['stretʃə] *n*. 1. 延伸器,伸张器;

展宽器;(撑开鞋帽等的)撑具;绷画布的框子 2. 担架(床) 3.(桌椅等脚之间的)横木,横档;(框架的)横条 ‖ ~**-** ˌbearer** *n*. 担架兵;担架员

strew [stru:] (过去式 strewed,过去分词 strewn [stru:n]或 strewed) *vt*. 1. 撒,撒播 2. 点缀;铺盖

striate ['straieit] *vt*. 在…上加条纹(或线条) — ['straiit, 'straieit] *adj*. 1. 有线条的;有条纹的 2.【解】横纹肌的 ‖ ~**d** *adj*. / ~**ly** ['straiitli] *adv*.

stricken ['strikən] strike 的过去分词 — *adj*. 1. 被打中的;被击伤的 2.(常用以构成复合词)受到的;罹患的;患病的;衰老的;panic~ 受惊的;恐慌的 / poverty~ 贫穷不堪的 3. 被刮得与量器边缘齐平的;a ~ measure of rice 平平的一量器米 ‖ ~ **field** 战场

strict [strikt] *adj*. 1. 严格的 2. 严谨的,严密的;精确的 3.〈古〉紧密的;紧密的 4.【植】笔直的 ‖ ~**ly** *adv*.; ~**ly** speaking 严格说来 / ~ **ness** *n*.

stricture ['striktʃə] *n*. 1.(常~s)苛评;责难 2.【医】狭窄 3. 束缚(物);限制(物)

stride [straid] (strode [stroud,straud], stridden ['stridn]) *vi*. 1. 大踏步走;迈进 2. 跨;跨过 — *vt*. 1. 大步走过 2. 跨;骑;跨过 — *n*. 1. 大步,阔步;一大步的距离;[常~s]进展,进步 2. [~s]〈英〉裤子

strident ['straidnt] *adj*. 1. 轧轧响的;刺耳的 ‖ **stridence, stridency** *n*. / ~**ly** *adv*.

strife [straif] *n*. 竞争;冲突;争吵;斗争;a civil ~ 内乱

strike [straik] (过去式 struck [strʌk],过去分词 struck 或 stricken ['strikən]) *vt*. 1. 打;击;撞击;攻击;冲击 2.(用爪)抓伤;(用毒牙)咬伤 3.(疾病)侵袭 4.(钟)敲响报(时);The clock is *striking*

four. 钟在藏 4 点。5.(船)触(礁);(光)
照到…上;(声)传入 6. 擦打(纸 ;压
出;冲制(由/纸币);盖(章) 7. 勾销;取
消 8. 拍(掌)定约;定下(交易、合同
等);结算 9. 打动;感动;给…以印象
10. 拆除;降下(帆、旗等);(用索具)把
…吊入货舱 11. 罢(工) 12. 刺透;穿
透;使穿透;使深入 13. 扎(根);插
(根);使(插枝等)生根 14. 向某一
方向前进 15. 遇见,碰到 16. 取
…姿态;装出 17. 弹奏 18. 用斗刮刮平
(高出斛口的谷物等) 19. 猛拉的索以
钩住;(急抽枝许(钓饵) 20. 触发(电
弧) 21. (昆虫)产卵于 22. 组成(陪审
团) — vi. 1. 打击;撞;打击;攻击
击(蛇、兽等)咬袭;抓 3. 罢工;罢课;
罢市 4.(心脏)搏动;(光)照射;(声)被
听到;(船)触礁;搁浅;下帆;(蚝)贴附
5.(时钟等)鸣,鸣…点;打钟 6. 突然想
~ on a tinder 擦打火线 7. 刺透;穿透
8. 突然想到;打动;给以印象 9. 开始;
取某一方向;朝某一方向前进 10. 勾
销;取消 11.(棒球等的打的枝)打出 12.
发芽 13. 陷旗(表示投降或致敬) 13.
(鱼)上钩;咬住钓饵;猛拉钓索钩住鱼
14.触发电弧;(雷电)闪击 15. 努力,
力争 ‖ 1. 打击(尤指飞机的)攻
击,进攻;(一起出击的)机翼;一支打
击力量 2. 罢工;罢课;罢市 3.(石油、
煤等矿藏的)发现;意外成功;走运 4.
斗刮(用来刮平斛口谷物的器具) 5.
一次铸成的全部硬币(或冲压成的全
部数量等) 6.(鱼的)上钩;猛拉钓索 7.
[地][矿]走向;seam — 矿层走向 8.
(地滚球戏中)一投全倒;一投全倒得
10 分;(棒球等)对于投手的好球 9. 不利,挫
迎击;(投手所投的)好球 9. 不利,挫
折 ‖ ~ benefit, ~ pay(工会发给工人
的)罢工津贴 /~bound adj. 因罢工而
停顿的 /~breaker n. 罢工破坏者,工
贼

striker ['straikə] n. 1. 敲击者 2. 罢工
(或罢课、罢市)者 3.(铁匠的)打铁助
手 4. 敲击工具;(时钟的)打锤,铃锤;
(枪的)撞针 5. 叉鱼的人 6.(美军)为
军官打杂挣外快的士兵

striking ['straikiŋ] adj. 1. 打击的;攻击
的;突击的;鸣响的 2. 罢工(或罢课、
罢市)的 3. 显著的;引人注目的;惊人
的 ‖ - **distance**[军]攻击距离

string [striŋ] n. 1. 线;细绳;带子;(美)
鞋带(= shoe ~) 2.(穿珠、钱等的)串
线,串绳;操纵木偶的线;一串,一行,
一列 3.(植物的)纤维(尤指荚壳的接
缝处),筋 4.(弓、乐器的)弦 5.[~s]
附带条件 6. 属于一个马主的一群赛
马 —(strung[straŋ])vt. 1.(用线、绳)
绑,扎;把(用线)穿,串起;使排成一
列 2. 上弦于(弓、乐器)上;调(乐器)的
弦 3. 抽去(豆荚等)的筋 4. 伸展;拉直
5. 使(精神等)紧张;使作好准备;使兴
奋;使敏感(up) ‖ -ed adj. 1. 有弦
的弦发出的;弦乐 2.[~]由弦乐
器/~ed music 弦乐 3. 紧弦缚住的;
用弦固住的 /~er n. 1.[建]纵梁,桁
条;楼梯斜梁;(铁路桥的)纵轨枕 2.
(乐器等的)上弦工人;制造(或出售)
弓弦的人 ‖ ~ **band** 弦乐队/~ **bean**
1. 多纤维菜豆;刀豆 2.〈口〉瘦长个子
/~ **quartet**[音]弦乐四重奏;弦乐四重
奏曲

stringency ['strindʒənsi] n. 1. 严格;严厉
2. 紧迫;缺少(尤指货币与信贷的不
足) 3. 严密性,精密性,说服力

stringent ['strindʒənt] adj. 1. 严格的;严
厉的 2.(银根)紧的,(货币与信贷紧
缩)缺少的 3. 严密的,无可辩驳的,令
人信服的 ‖ -**ly** adv.

stringy ['striŋi] adj. 1. 似线(或绳)的;纤

维的;多筋的 **2.**(液体)粘性的 **3.** 瘦而结实的

strip [strip](stripped; stripping) vt. **1.** 剥;剥去,剥光 **2.** 夺去,剥夺(财产、荣誉、权力、职务等);掠夺;使赤贫 **3.** 拆卸;完全除去…的附属物 **4.** 折断(齿轮)的齿;磨掉(螺丁、螺栓等)的螺纹;由于膛速过高磨损(子弹)的表面 **5.** 挤干(牛)的奶 **6.** 去(烟叶等)的茎 **7.** 从…中删除不必要的内容 **8.**【化】使去色;通过蒸馏等除去…中的挥发性成分 **9.** 把…撕成带形;把…切成细条 **10.** 用纸条粘连(拍纸簿的书面等) — vi. **1.** 脱去衣服;脱光衣服 **2.**(子弹)因表面磨损而出膛时不旋转 **3.**(螺丝钉)磨损螺丝 **4.** 作脱衣舞 — n. **1.** 条,带;细长片 **2.** 条幅式侦察照片;(报纸等)的连环漫画 **3.** 带状地带(或森林、水域等);简易机场 **4.**【冶】带钢 **5.**(集邮簿上的)一行(或一列)邮票;(邮票的)连票 **6.**(出膛子弹的)不旋转 **7.**【矿】露天开采;(英)捣砂状矿石矿沉淀槽 **8.** 支板;(舞台等上排列安放 4 至 6 只灯泡的)插座条 **9.** [~s]抽搐中脉和大叶脉的烟叶 **10.** 脱衣舞(= striptease) ‖ ～ **cropping**【农】等高条植;以减少土地侵蚀 / ～**light** n.(舞台用的)条状照明灯 / ～ **mine** 露天矿 / ～ **mining**【矿】露天开采

stripe [straip] n. **1.** 条纹;条子;条纹布 **3.**【军】(制服上表示等级的)条纹 **2.**(人的)类型,类别 **5.** [~s]犯人穿的横条服,囚衣 **6.**(口)[~s]虎(马戏团中用语) **7.**(一道)鞭痕;(一记)鞭挞,(一记)抽打 ‖～**d** adj. **1.** 有条纹的 **2.**(美俚)喝醉的

stripling ['striplig] n. 年轻人,小伙子

striptease ['striptiz] n.(美)脱衣舞 — vi. 表演脱衣舞 ‖～**r** n.

strive [straiv](过去式 strove [strəuv] 或 strived,过去分词 striven ['strivn] 或 strived) vi. **1.** 努力 **2.** 力求 **2.** 斗争;反抗

strode [strəud] stride 的过去式

stroke[1] [strəuk] n. **1.** 打击;蔽 **2.**(划船、游泳的)一划;划法;尾桨手,领桨;(网球赛中的)击(球);打法 **3.**(写字、绘画的)一笔,一划;笔触;(写作的)手法 **4.**(钟的)敲声,鸣声 **5.** 突来的一击,闪击;(病)突然发作;中风;麻痹 **6.** 一举,一着,一次努力;一次努力的成果 **7.**(心脏的)跳动;脉搏;(鸟翼的)一拍 **8.**【机】冲程,行程 — vt. **1.** 划短横于 **2.** 划线勾销,删掉(out) **3.** 充当(划船的)尾桨手 **4.** 击(球) ‖～**oar** 尾桨;尾桨手

stroke[2] [strəuk] vt.(用手)抚,摩,捋 — n. 抚,摩,捋

stroll [strəul] vi. **1.** 散步;溜达;闲逛 **2.**(为谋生等)四处流浪,辗转各地 — vt. **1.** 散步于,在…溜达 **2.** 跋涉于;流浪于 — n. 散步;溜达 ‖～**er** n.

strong [strɔŋ] adj. **1.** 强健的,强健的,牢固的 **2.**(性格)坚强的,坚定的;(态度、作风)坚决的;强烈的,猛烈的;强健的 **3.**(兵员、人数)达…的;(势力)强大的 **4.**(势力等)强有力的 **4.**(能力)优良的;擅长的 **5.** 烈性的;浓厚的;冲鼻(难闻)的;难消化的 **6.** 坚挺的;价格稳步上升的;— a ～market 坚挺的市场价格,看涨的行情 **7.**【语】强变化的,强变格的 — adv. =～**ly** ‖～**ly** adv. 强壮地,强壮地;强烈地 ‖～**arm** 暴力;高压手段 ‖～**arm** adj. 强暴的 vt. 对…施暴;用暴力对付;抢劫 /～**box** n. 保险箱 /～**hold** n. 要塞,堡垒;据点,大本营 /～-'minded adj.

主见的;意志坚强的 / ~ **room** 1. 保险库 2.(精神病人的)监护房间

strontium [ˈstrɔnʃiəm] n.【化】锶

strop [strɔp] n. 1.(磨剃刀的)皮带,革砥 2.(滑车的)环索;滑车带 — (stropped; stropping) vt. 在革砥上磨(剃刀)

strove [strəuv] strive 的过去式

struck [strʌk] strike 的过去式和过去分词 — adj. 因罢工而关闭的;受到罢工影响的

structural [ˈstrʌktʃərəl] adj. 结构(上)的;构造的;建筑(上)的;组织上的 ‖ ~ly adv.

structure [ˈstrʌktʃə] n. 1. 结构;构造;组织 2. 结构物;建筑物 3.【心】结构;构造 — vt. 构造;组织;建造 ‖ ~d adj. 有结构的 / ~less adj. 无结构的;无定形的

strudel [ˈstruːdəl, ˈʃtruːdəl] n. 果馅卷

struggle [ˈstrʌɡl] n. 1. 斗争;奋斗 2. 挣扎 3. 难事 — vi. 1. 斗争;奋斗;努力 2. 奋力前进;挣扎 ‖ ~r n.

strum [strʌm] (strummed; strumming) vt. 乱弹;乱奏;拙劣地弹奏 — vi. 在琴上乱弹;乱奏(on) — n. 乱弹(声)

strumpet [ˈstrʌmpit] n. 妓女

strung [strʌŋ] string 的过去式和过去分词

strut[1] [strʌt] (strutted; strutting) vi. 1. 肿胀,鼓起 2. 大摇大摆地走,架子十足地走 — vt. 炫耀(服装、珠宝等) — n. 高视阔步

strut[2] [strʌt] n. 支柱,撑杆;压杆;轨撑 — (strutted; strutting) vt. 支撑;撑开;给…加撑杆

strychnine [ˈstrikniːn] n. 士的宁,马钱子碱(中枢兴奋药)

stub [stʌb] n. 1. 树桩,残根,残段 2. 残

余部分,残端 3. 用秃了的笔 4.〈美〉票根,存根 — (stubbed; stubbing) vt. 1. 连根挖(或拔);紧沿着树根砍(或锄) 2. 清除(地)里的树桩(或草根) 3. 碰脚 4. 捻熄;踩熄

stubble [ˈstʌbl] n. 1.(庄稼收割后余留的)残株,茬 2. 收割后(布满茬儿)的田地 3. 短发;短髭;残梗状的东西

stubborn [ˈstʌbən] adj. 1. 顽固的,执拗的;不听调动的 2. 顽强的;坚持的 3. 难对付的,棘手的 ‖ ~ly adv. / ~ness n.

stubby [ˈstʌbi] adj. 1. 多残株的 2. 似残株的;粗短的;矮胖的;用钝的 3. 短而密的

stucco [ˈstʌkəu] ([复] stucco(e)s) n. 1. 拉毛灰浆,灰墁 2.(拉)毛粉饰 — vt.(用灰泥)粉饰,粉刷

stuck [stʌk] stick 的过去式和过去分词 ‖ ~ up adj.〈口〉势利的;自大的,傲慢的

stud[1] [stʌd] n. 1. 大头钉;(装饰在大门、盾牌或皮件等表面的)饰钉 2. 领扣;(男衬衫等的)饰钮 3.【机】双头螺栓,柱(头)螺栓;轴;端轴颈;销子;中介轴 4.【建】壁骨;墙筋;中间柱 5. 房间净高 — (studded; studding) vt. 1. 装饰钉于;用大头钉装饰(或保护) 2. 散布;密布;点缀 3. 给(房屋或墙壁)加壁骨(或柱子)

stud[2] [stʌd] n. 1. 种马;留种牲畜(为繁殖、赛马、打猎等而饲养的);种畜 2. 种畜牧场;种马饲养场 ‖ ~-book n.(犬、马等的)良种记录簿

student [ˈstjuːdənt] n. 1.〈主指大专院校的〉学生,学员 2.(大学、研究院的)研究生;[常 S-](牛津大学 Christ Church 的)公费生;(对某门学科特别爱好的)学者,研究者;a ~ of bird life 鸟类生活

研究者 3.〈美俚〉初学者,新手;初学吸毒者 ∥ ~ship n. 1.(大)学生身份 2.(学校的)奖学金 / ~ government 学生自治

studied ['stʌdid] adj. 1.〈古〉有知识的,有学问的 2. 慎重的;经过思考的 3. 故意的,蓄意的;装模作样的

studio ['stjuːdiəu][复]studios] n. 1. 画室;雕刻室;摄影室;照相馆;排演房 2. 电影制片厂 3.(无线电、电视)播音室;演播室 ∥ ~ apartment 1. 一室型公寓房 2. 画室公寓(指其中有一间窗户宽大、高屋顶、类似画室的房间的公寓)/ ~ couch(可作床的)两用沙发

studious ['stjuːdjəs] adj. 1. 勤学的,用功的 2. 认真的;热心的 3. 刻意的,故意的 ∥ ~ly adv. / ~ness n.

study ['stʌdi] n. 1. 学习;研究;[常 studies](在学校的)肄业 2. 研究项目;(值得)研究的对象;学科;论文 3. 试画;试作;习作 4.[常与形容词连用]记忆力…的人,台词记得…的演员 5. 沉思,默想 6. 意图;努力;努力的对象 7. 书房,书斋 — vt. 1. 学习;研究 2. 考虑,细想;细看,细察 3. 计划;图谋 4. 记诵,背诵(台词等)— vi. 1. 学习 2. 努力;力图 3.〈方〉沉思,默想 ∥ ~ hall 1.(学生)自修室 2. 自修课

stuff [stʌf] n. 1. 材料;原料;资料;东西 2. 素质,本质;要素 3.〈尤指毛的〉织品;呢绒 4. 废物;劣货;废话 5. 货色;财产;家具;行李;装备 6. 枪弹;炮弹 7.〈口〉[the ~]金钱;现钱;任何现成备用的东西 8. 醉态;醉鬼;麻醉剂 9.〈美俚〉赃物;走私赃货;走私威士忌酒 10. 纸条,纸片 11. 作品(内容);行话 — vt. 1. 装;把…装满;填,塞;把…塞进 2.(为制作标本)剥制 3.〈美

俚〉欺骗;愚弄;向…贩卖充塞的货 4.〈美〉以假造的选票充塞(投票箱)— vi. 1. 饱食;吃得过多(或过快)∥ ~ed shirt 1. 妄自尊大的人,道貌岸然的人 2.〈美俚〉有钱人;有地位的人

stuffing ['stʌfiŋ] n. 1.(枕、被、垫子等的)填塞料 2.(塞在鸡、鸭等肚子里的)填馅;填充剂;填料 3.(鸟兽的)剥制

stuffy ['stʌfi] adj. 1. 不通气的,窒息的;闷热的 2.(人或事物)呆滞的;乏味的 3. 愠怒的;绷着脸的 4. 固步自封的,自以为是的 ∥ stuffily adv. / stuffiness n.

stultify ['stʌltifai] vt. 1. 使显得愚蠢;使显得荒谬可笑 2. 使无效;使变得无用 3.〔律〕宣称(或证明)(某人)精神错乱 ∥ stultification [ˌstʌltifiˈkeiʃən] n.

stumble ['stʌmbl] vi. 1. 绊一下脚;绊跌;绊倒 2. 犯错误;失足,走入迷路 3. 踌躇,结结巴巴地说话;踌躇,迟疑 5. 偶然碰见;偶尔发现(upon, across)— vt. 1. 使绊倒;使失足 2. 使困惑 — n. 失足;失误 ∥ stumbling block 障碍物,绊脚石

stump [stʌmp] n. 1. 树桩,根株 2. 残余部分;残干 3.(美国发表竞选等的)政治演说讲台(因旧时常利用场地上的树墩而得名);巡回演说 4.〈口〉挑战,考验 5.〔谑〕[~s]腿;脚 6.(板球三柱门的)柱 — vt. 1. 截去(树)的干,使成根株 2. 清除(田地)的树根 3. 向…挑战;使惶惑;难住 4.〈美口〉(尤指竞选时)游历(某地区)作政治演说 5. 脚步沉重地走过 6. 碾过 — vi 1. 笨重地行走 2.〈美口〉作巡回政治演说

stumper ['stʌmpə] n. 1. 砍挖树桩的人(或工具)2. 难题 3.〈美〉政治演说家(亦作 ~ speaker)4.〈板球赛中三柱门后的〉捕手

stumpy ['stʌmpi] *adj.* 1. 多树桩的 2. 桩状的;粗短的 — *n.* 1. 矮胖的人 2. (英)钱

stun [stʌn] (stunned; stunning) *vt.* 1. 把…打晕;使晕眩 2. 使震聋 3. 使大吃一惊;使不知所措 — *n.* 1. 晕眩;惊人的事物;猛击

stung [stʌŋ] sting 过去式和过去分词

stunk [stʌŋk] stink 的过去式和过去分词

stunner ['stʌnə] *n.* 1. 出色的人;有吸引力的女人 2. 极好的东西;惊人的事

stunning ['stʌniŋ] *adj.* 1. 使人晕倒的;震耳欲聋的 3.〈口〉极好的;极漂亮的

stunt[1] [stʌnt] *vt.* 阻碍…的发育(或成长)— *n.* 1. 发育迟缓 2. 矮小的人;矮小的东西(如树木等)‖ ~ed *adj.* 发育不充分的;矮小的

stunt[2] [stʌnt] *n.* 1.〈口〉惊人的表演 2. 花招;噱头;手段,手腕 — *vi.* 作惊人表演;使绝招‖ ~ man 特技替身演员

stupe[1] [stjuːp] *n.*【医】热敷布;压布 — *vt.* 热敷

stupe[2] [stjuːp] *n.*〈俚〉傻子;笨人

stupefacient [ˌstjuːpiˈfeiʃənt] *adj.* 麻醉的使产生麻木的 — *n.* 麻醉剂

stupefy ['stjuːpifai] *vt.* 1. 使麻木,使失感觉 2. 使惊得发呆,使呆若木鸡

stupendous [stjuːˈpendəs] *adj.* 巨大的,惊人的;了不起的

stupid ['stjuːpid] *adj.* 1. 愚蠢的,笨的 2. 感觉迟钝的;麻痹的 3. 乏味的;无聊的 — *n.*〈口〉傻瓜,笨蛋‖ ~ly *adv.*

stupidity [stjuːˈpiditi] *n.* 1. 愚蠢,愚笨 2. 愚蠢的行为(或想法、话等)

stupor ['stjuːpə] *n.* 1. 恍惚;昏迷,不省人事 2. 麻木,僵呆

sturdy ['stəːdi] *adj.* 1. 强健的,苗壮的

坚实的 2. 坚定的;坚强的,刚毅不屈的 ‖ **sturdily** *adv.* / **sturdiness** *n.*

sturgeon ['stəːdʒən] *n.*【动】鲟

stutter ['stʌtə] *vt.* 结结巴巴地说出 — *vi.* 结结巴巴地说话,口吃地说话 — *n.* 口吃‖ ~er *n.*

sty[1] [stai] ([复]sties 或 styes) *n.* 1. 猪圈,猪栏,猪舍 2.(猪圈似的)肮脏住所;藏污纳垢之地;妓院 — *vt.* 把…关在猪圈里;让…住在猪圈似的脏地方 — *vi.* 住在猪圈里;住在猪圈似的脏地方

sty[2], **stye** [stai] ([复]sties 或 styes) *n.*【医】睑腺炎,麦粒肿

style [stail] *n.* 1. 风格;作风 2. 文体;文风;语调 3. 风度;体面;时髦 4. 式样;类型;记时方式:the Old Style 西洋旧历 (略作 O.S.) / the New Style 新历(即现在通用的阳历,略作 N.S.) 5. 称号;称呼 6.(古人在蜡板上写字用的)铁笔,尖笔;〔诗〕笔;铅笔;雕刻刀;唱机的唱针;日晷指针 7.【动】犁杆,产卵器;【植】花柱 — *vt.* 1. 称呼;命名 2. 使符合时式;使成为时髦 3. 设计

stylish ['stailiʃ] *adj.* 时髦的;时式的,漂亮的‖ ~ly *adv.* / ~ness *n.*

stylist ['stailist] *n.* 1. 文体家;文体批评家;具有独特风格者,自成流派者 2.(服装、家具等的)设计师 3. 动作正确优美的运动员

stylistic(al) [stai'listik(əl)] *adj.* 文体(上)的;风格(上)的;具有偏重文体的倾向的

stylus ['stailəs] ([复]styli ['stailai] 或 styluses) *n.* 1.(古人在蜡板上写字用的)铁笔,尖笔 2.(刻写誊印蜡纸的)铁笔;(唱机)唱针;描画针;(日晷)指针 3.【生】茎突;花柱;针突;生殖器鞘;产卵管

stymie, stymy ['staimi] *n.* 1.(高尔夫球赛

中自己的球介于对方的球与球穴间的）妨碍球,阻碍球 2. 困难的境地 — vt. 1.(高尔夫球赛中)用妨碍球阻碍 2. 妨碍,阻碍

styptic ['stiptik] adj 1. 止血的 2. 收敛性的 — n. 止血剂

suasion ['sweiʒən] n. 劝告;说服

suave [swɑːv] adj. 温文的,文雅的;讨好的;温和的,平和的 ‖ ~ly adv. / ~ness, suavity n.

sub¹ [sʌb] n. 1. 代替者;代替物(substitute 的缩略) 2.〈美俚〉(球队等的)候补队员 — (subbed; subbing) vi.〈口〉做代替者;做替工(for) — vt.〈美俚〉代替……进行比赛

sub² [sʌb] n. 潜(水)艇(submarine 的缩略)

sub³ [sʌb] n. 订户;订购

sub- pref. 1. 表示"在…底下": submarine, subsoil, subway 2. 表示"(地位、级别等)低,副","(性质)次,亚": subeditor, subagent 副代理人, subcommittee 3. 表示"分","再","次": subdivide, sublet 分租,分包 4. 表示"几乎","近于","近": subarctic 近北极的 5.【化】表示"下","低","亚","次","迟": subatomic

subaltern ['sʌbltən] adj. 1. 下的,副的;次的 2.【逻】特称的,非全称的 — n. 1. 副官;部下 2.〈主英〉陆军中尉 3.【逻】特称命题

subaquatic [ˌsʌbə'kwætik] adj. 1. = subaqueous 2.【动】【植】半水生的,半水栖的

subaqueous [ˌsʌb'eikwiəs] adj. 1. 水下的,在水下形成(或发生)的;适于水下生活的 2. 适用于水下的

subatomic [ˌsʌbə'tɔmik] adj. 亚原子的;原子内的

subclass ['sʌbklɑːs] n. 1.【生】亚纲 2.【数】子类,小分类

subclimax [ˌsʌb'klaimæks] n.【生】亚顶极群落,亚演替顶极

subcommittee ['sʌbkəˌmiti] n.(委员会下的)小组委员会,专门小组

subconscious [ˌsʌb'kɔnʃəs] adj. 1. 下意识的,潜意识的 2. 意识模糊的 — n. [the ~]下意识,潜意识 ‖ ~ly n.

subcontinent [ˌsʌb'kɔntinənt] n. 次大陆(如南亚次大陆) ‖ ~al [ˌsʌbkɔnti'nentl] adj.

subcontract [ˌsʌb'kɔntrækt] n. 分包合同,转包合同 — [ˌsʌbkən'trækt] vt. & vi. 分包,转包 ‖ ~or [sʌbkən'træktə] n.(转包工作的)分包者;分包单位

subcutaneous [ˌsʌbkjuː'teinjəs] adj. 皮肤的;寄生于皮下的;皮下用的

subdivide [ˌsʌbdi'vaid] vt. 1. 把…再分;把…细分 2. 把…分成几份(尤指把大片土地分成供建屋用或出卖的小块) — vi. 再分;细分

subdivision ['sʌbdiˌviʒən] n. 1. 再分;细分 2. 由再分分成的部分 3.(供出售、建房而划分的)小块土地

subdue [səb'djuː] vt. 1. 使屈服;征服;使驯服 2. 克制,抑制 3. 使柔和;缓和;减轻,减弱 4. 开垦(土地)

subedit [ˌsʌb'edit] vt. 1. 当……的助理编辑 2.〈英〉审(稿);将(稿件)作文字加工 ‖ ~or n. 助理编辑,副编辑 2.〈英〉文字编辑,审稿员

subgroup ['sʌbgruːp] n. 1.【生】亚群,子群 2.【数】子群 3.【化】(周期表中的)族;副族(指周期表中的 B 族)

subhead ['sʌbhed], **subheading** ['sʌbˌhediŋ] n. 1. 小标题;副标题 2. 副主管,副头领

subject ['sʌbdʒikt] *n.* 1.(君主国)国民，臣民，臣下 2. 题目；问题；主题 3. 学科，科目 4.(事物的)经受者；(动作的)对象；实验材料；解剖用的尸体 5. 原因；理由 6.【语】主语 7.【哲】主体；主观；自我 8.【音】主题，主旋律 9. 具有(某种)不良体质(或气质)的人：a hysterical ～ 有歇斯底里毛病的人 — *adj.* 1. 臣服的，隶属的，从属的；受支配的 2. 易受…的；常遭…的；惯患…的(to) 3. 有待于…的；须经…的；可以…的(to) 4. 以…为条件的 — [sʌb'dʒekt] *adv.* 在…条件下(to) — [sʌb'dʒekt] *vt.* 1. 使臣服，使隶属；使服从(to) 2. 使受到；使遭遇(to) 3.(罕)提出，呈交 ‖ ～ index 标题索引；分类索引 / ～ matter 题材；题目；论题；话题

subjection [səb'dʒekʃən] *n.* 1. 征服；镇压 2. 隶属；从属(地位)；服从

subjective [səb'dʒektiv] *adj.* 1. 主观的 2.【语】主语的 — *n.* 主观事物 ‖ ～ly *adv.* / ～ness，subjec'tivity *n.*

subjectivism [səb'dʒektivizəm] *n.* 主观主义 ‖ **subjectivist** *n.* 主观主义者 *adj.* 主观主义的

subjoin [sʌb'dʒɔin] *vt.* 增补，附加，添

subjugate ['sʌbdʒugeit] *vt.* 1. 使屈服，征服；使服从 2. 克制，抑制 ‖ **subjugator** *n.* 征服者；制服者

subjugation [sʌbdʒu'geiʃən] *n.* 1. 征服 2. 克制 3. 屈从

subjunctive [səb'dʒʌŋktiv]【语】*adj.* 虚拟的；the ～ mood 虚拟语气 — *n.* 虚拟语气；(动词的)虚拟式

sublease ['sʌblis] *vt.* 转租，分租(土地或房屋) — *n.* 转租，分租 ‖ **sublessee** [sʌble'si:] *n.* 转租承租人/**sublessor** ['sʌble'sɔ:] *n.* 转租人，分租人

sublieutenant [sʌblef'tenənt, sʌblu:'tenənt]

n.(英)海军中尉；陆军少尉

sublimate ['sʌblimeit] *vt.* 1.(化)使升华 2. 纯化；使高尚；使理想化 — *vi.* 1. 升华 2. 纯化 — ['sʌblimit] *adj.* 1. 升华的 2. 高尚的，高尚的 — *n.*【化】1. 升华物 2. 升汞 ‖ subli'mation *n.*

sublime [sə'blaim] *adj.* 1. 崇高的；庄严的；令人崇敬的；卓越的；堆伟的 2. 极端的；异常的 3.(诗)傲慢的 — *n.* 1. [the ～]崇高；庄严；崇高的事物 2. 极点，顶点 — *vt.* & *vi.* 1.【化】使升华 2.(使)变高尚；提高；(使)纯化 ‖ ～ly *adv.* / ～ness *n.*

subliminal [sʌb'liminəl] *adj.* 1.【心】阈下的意识下的，潜意识的 2. 小得难以觉察的 — *n.* 阈下意识，潜意识 ‖ ～ly *adv.*

sublimity [sə'blimiti] *n.* 1. 崇高；庄严；宏伟；卓越 2. 崇高的事物

submachine [sʌbmə'ʃi:n] **gun** 冲锋枪，轻型自动(或半自动)枪

submarine [sʌbmə'ri:n, 'sʌbmərin] *adj.* 水下的；水底的；海底的 — *n.* 1. 潜(水)艇 2. 海底生物 — *vt.* 用潜(水)艇袭击(或击沉) ‖ ～ chaser 猎潜艇艇

submerge [səb'mə:dʒ] *vt.* 浸没，淹没 — *vi.* 没入水中；潜入水中，潜下去

submergence [səb'mə:dʒəns] *n.* 1. 浸没，淹没；没入水中 2. 沉沦，沦落

submerse [səb'mə:s] *vt.* & *vi.* = submerge ‖ **submersible** *adj.* / **submersion** *n.*

submission [səb'miʃən] *n.* 1. 屈服；服从；降服 2. 谦逊，谦恭 3. 递呈；提交；提出 4.【律】提交仲裁协议(书) 4.【律】意见，看法

submissive [səb'misiv] *adj.* 服从的；顺从的；柔顺的 ‖ ～ly *adv.*

ness n.

submit [səb'mit] (submitted; submitting) vt. 1. 使服从;使受到(to) 2. 呈送;提交;提出 3. 认为;以为 — vi. 服从;屈服;顺从;忍受(to)

subnormal [ˌsʌb'nɔːməl] adj. 低于正常的;低能的 — n. 1. 不及常人者,智能逊常者 2. 【数】次法距;次法线

subordinate [sə'bɔːdinit] adj. 下级的;次要的;从属的 — n. 部属;部下;下级职员 —[sə'bɔːdineit] vt. 把…列入下级;使位于较低级别;使服从 ‖ su,bordi'nation n.

suborn [sʌ'bɔːn] vt. 1. 唆使,嗾使 2. 贿赂;使发假誓(或作伪证等) ‖ ,subor'nation n. / ~er n. 唆使者;唆使发假誓者

subp(o)ena [səb'piːnə] 【律】 n. 传票 — vt.(用传票)传唤;(发传票)命令交出,索取

subscribe [səb'skraib] vt. 1. 签署(文件);在(图画等)下方署名;题(词);署(名) 2. 捐助;认捐(款项) — vi. 1. 捐款 2. 预订;订阅(for, to) 3. 认购;同意,赞成;赞助 5. 在文件或信件上签名

subscriber [səb'skraibə] n. 1. 签署者;署名者 2. 订阅者;订户及 3. 电话用户 4. 捐款者;赞助者 5. 认购者;承购者

subscription [səb'skripʃən] n. 1. 签署;同意;赞助 2. 亲笔签名;有亲笔签名的文件 3. 预订;预订费;订阅费 4. 认捐额;认缴额 5.【医】下标处方(处方上的配方说明)

subsequent ['sʌbsikwənt] adj. 1. 继…之后的,随后的,后来的 2. 后成的,后起的 ‖ ~ly adv.

subserve [səb'səːv] vt. 1. 对(目的、事业等)有益;对…有用 2. 促进,推动

subservient [səb'səːvjənt] adj. 1. 辅助性的;从属的 2. 有帮助的;(尤指在从属地位上)有用的 3. 屈从的;奉承的,谄媚的 ‖ subservience n. / ~ly adv.

subset ['sʌbset] n.【数】子集;子集合

subside [səb'said] vi. 1. 沉到底;沉淀 2.(土地、房屋等)沉陷;(船只)下沉 3.(风雨、骚动、冲动等)平静下来,平息;(肿、热度等)减退 4.(口)(慢吞吞地)坐下;躺下 ‖ subsidence n.

subsidiary [səb'sidjəri] adj. 辅助的,补助的;补充的;次要的;附属的 — n. 1. 辅助者;辅助物 2. 附属机构;子公司 3.【音】副主题

subsidize ['sʌbsidaiz] vt. 给…补助金;资助;给…津贴 ‖ ,subsidi'zation n.

subsidy ['sʌbsidi] n. 补助金;津贴

subsist [səb'sist] vi. 1. 生存,维持生活 2. 存在;继续存在 3.【哲】(逻辑上)成立,站得住 — vt. 供给…粮食;供养

subsistence [səb'sistəns] n. 1. 生存;生计;生活费;口粮;给养 2. 存在;持续;内在性;【哲】存在物,实体(物) 3. 生活维持费;生活津贴;(军队)饷银(亦作 ~ money 或 ~ allowance)

subsoil ['sʌbsɔil] n.【农】心土,下层土,底土 — vt. 深耕;深挖

subsonic [ˌsʌb'sɔnik] adj.【物】1. 亚音速的,亚音速的 2. 次声的 — n. 亚音速飞机

substance ['sʌbstəns] n. 1. 物质;材料;东西 2. 实质;实体;本质;本体 3. 本旨;要义;真义 4. 财产,财物 5.(质地的)坚实,牢固

substandard [ˌsʌb'stændəd] adj. 不够标准的,在标准以下的;(语言等)不规范的;(食品成分等)低于法定标准而未标明的

substantial [səb'stænʃəl] adj. 1. 物质的;实质的;实体的;真实的,实际上的 2.

坚固的, 结实的 3. 多的; 大的; 大量的
4. 有重大价值的; 内容充实的 5. 富裕
的 —— n. [常～] 1.
实质性的东西; 实际存在物 2. 有实际
价值的东西 3. 重要的东西; 重要部
分; 要领 ‖ ～ity [səbˌstænʃiˈæləti] n. /
～ly adv. 1. 实质上; 本质上; 基本上
2. 大量地

substantialize [səbˈstænʃiəlaiz] vt. & vi.
(使)实质化;(使)实体化;(使)成为真
实

substantiate [səbˈstænʃieit] vt. 1. 证实;证
明(控诉、陈述、主张等)有根据 2. 使
具体化;使实体化 ‖ substanti'ation n.

substantival [ˌsʌbstənˈtaivəl] adj. 【语】名
词的,体词的,名词性实词的

substantive [ˈsʌbstəntiv] adj. 1. 独立存
在的;实质的,真实存在的 2. 实质的;
实体的,本质的 3. 坚固的,牢固的 4.
大量的;巨额的 5.【律】(法律)实体的
(指规定权利与义务的)【语】表示存在
的;名词的;体词的 7. 直接(染)的,
不需媒染剂的 —— n. 1. 独立存在的人
(或实体) 2.【语】名词(＝ noun),体词,
名词性实词(或词组) ‖ ～ly adv.

substation [ˈsʌbˌsteiʃən] n. 1. 变电所 2.
邮政所 3. 分所;分站

substitute [ˈsʌbstitjuːt] n. 1. 代替者;替补
队员;代人应征入伍者;替代物,代用
品 2.【语】代用词;代用语(如 He writes
better than I do. 这一句中的 do 是代用
词) 3.【矿】转接器 —— vt. 1. 代替者;替
换(某人或某物) —— vi. 1. 作代替者,
替代 2.【化】取代 —— adj. 作为代用品
的,使用代用品的

substitution [ˌsʌbstiˈtjuːʃən] n. 1. 代,代
替;替换 2.【化】取代(作用) 3.【数】代
换,置换,代入 ‖ ～ary adj.

substratosphere [sʌbˈstrætəusfiə] n. 【气】

副平流层

substratum [ˌsʌbˈstrɑːtəm, ˌsʌbˈstreitəm]
([复] substrata [ˌsʌbˈstrɑːtə, ˌsʌbˈstreitə])
n. 1. 基础;根据 2. 下层;心土,下层
土,底土层 3.【生】培养基 4.【生化】底
物,酶作用物 5.【摄】(胶片等的)感光
底层

subtend [səbˈtend] vt. 1.【数】对(向)
【植】衬托

subterfuge [ˈsʌbtəfjuːdʒ] n. 遁词,托辞,
口实;巧立的名目

subterranean [ˌsʌbtəˈreiniən] adj. 1. 地下
的 2. 私下的

subtile [ˈsʌbtil] adj. = subtle

subtitle [ˈsʌbˌtaitl] n. 1. 副标题, 小标题
2. (正文的)前页书名 3. (影片)字幕 ——
vt. 给…加副标题;给…配字幕

subtle [ˈsʌtl] adj. 1. 稀薄的,隐约的;清
淡的 2. 精巧的,精妙的 3. 微妙的,微
细的,难以捉摸的 4. 敏感的;敏锐的
5. 阴险的,狡猾的 ‖ ～ness, ～ty n. /
subtly adv.

subtract [səbˈtrækt] vt. 减(去);减损
—— vi. 作减法;减损 ‖ ～ion n. 1. 减(去);
【数】减法 2. 减少

subtropic(al) [ˌsʌbˈtrɔpik(əl)] adj. 副热带的,
亚热带的

suburb [ˈsʌbəb] n. 1. [常～s]郊外,郊
区;近郊 2. [～s]边缘,近处

suburban [səˈbəːbən] adj. 1. (在)郊外的,
(在)郊区的 2. 有郊区(人)特点的 3.
〈贬〉偏狭的,见识不广的;土气的 ——
n. 郊区居民

subvention [səbˈvenʃən] n. 1. 补助金;津
贴 2. 援助

subversion [sʌbˈvəːʃən] n. 颠覆

subversive [sʌbˈvəːsiv] adj. 颠覆性的;起
破坏作用的 —— n. 颠覆分子,搞颠覆阴

谋的人

subvert [sʌb'vəːt] *vt.* 1. 颠覆；暗中破坏 2. 搅乱(人心等)；败坏(道德等)

subway ['sʌbwei] *n.* 1. 地(下过)道 2. (美)地下铁道，地铁(英国称 underground) 3. 地铁列车 — *vi.* (美)乘地铁

succeed [sək'siːd] *vt.* 继…之后；接替；继承；接着…发生 — *vi.* 1. 成功；达到目的 2. 继续；继任；继承；接着发生

success [sək'ses] *n.* 1. 成功；成就；胜利 2. 成功的事；取得成就的人；考试及格的学生

successful [sək'sesful] *adj.* 1. 成功的；结果良好的 2. 有成就的 ‖ ~ly *adv.* / ~ *n.*

succession [sək'seʃən] *n.* 1. 连续，接续 2. 继任；继承，继承权；继承顺序；有继承权者；后裔；后继者【生】演替 ‖ ~al *adj.*

successive [sək'sesiv] *adj.* 连续的，接连的；相继的；逐次的 ‖ ~ly *adv.*

successor [sək'sesə] *n.* 继承人；继任者；后继者；接班人

succinct [sək'siŋkt] *adj.* 1. 简明的；简洁的 2. 紧身的，贴身的 ‖ ~ly *adv.* / ~ness *n.*

succo(u)r ['sʌkə] *n.* 1. 救济；援助 2. 济急的东西；救助者【古】[~s]援军 — *vt.* 救济；援助

succulence ['sʌkjuləns] *n.* 1. 多汁；【植】肉质性 2. 青饲料

succulent ['sʌkjulənt] *adj.* 1. 多汁的；【植】肉质的 3. 活力充沛的；新鲜的；有趣的；引人入胜的 — *n.* 肉质植物(如仙人掌) ‖ ~ly *adv.*

succumb [sə'kʌm] *vi.* 1. 屈服；屈从(*to*) 2. 死(*to*)

such [强 sʌtʃ；弱 sətʃ] *adj.* [无比较级和最

高级] 1. [遇不定冠词 a(n)时，要放在该冠词之前；遇 all, no, one, few, several, some, any 等时，则放在其后] 这样的；如此的 2. [~ (…) as to 或~(…)that]如此的…(以致)：We are not ~ fools *as to* believe him. 我们不是那种的蠢人，竟会相信他。/ His excitement was ~ *that* he shouted. (= He shouted, ~ was his excitement.)他兴奋得叫了起来。3. [表示惊叹或加强语气]这样的，那样 4. 上述的，该 5. 某某；如此这般的，这样那样的 — *adv.* 那么 — *pron.* 这样的人(们)；上述的事物(或人)：~ *as* have erred 犯过错误的那些人 / puppets and ~ 傀儡和所有这这家伙 ‖ ~ *and* ~ 某某的 / ~ *and* ~ a person 某某人 / Such *and* ~ results follow from ~ *and* ~ causes. 这样那样的原因就产生这样那样的结果。

suchlike ['sʌtʃlaik] *pron.* 这一类的人(或事物) — *adj.* 这种的，同样的，类似的

suck [sʌk] *vt.* 1. 吸，吮，咂，嘬 — the breast 吮乳 2. 吸收，吸取(水分、知识等)；获得(利益等) — *vi.* 1. (婴儿)吸奶；吸；发吮吸的声音 2. (美)奉承，拍马 3. (美俚)使人极度不快 — *n.* 1. 吸，吮，咂，嘬；give ~ to a baby 给婴儿喂奶 / a child an ~ 吃着奶的孩子 2. (一)吮，(一)口；a ~ at one's pipe 吸一口烟 3. 吮吸似的声音 4. (漩涡等的)吸力 5.[俚]马屁精；马屁精 ‖ '~-in *n.* (英俚)欺骗；失望；失败 / '~-up *n.* [俚]奉承者，拍马者

sucker ['sʌkə] *n.* 1. 吮吸者；乳儿；乳猪，哺乳期的幼兽(尤指乳猪或幼鲸) 2.【动】吸盘 3.【动】(口呈吸盘状的)腮脂鱼 4.【植】根出条；寄生性植物的)吸根 5. 吸管；(泵或针筒的)活塞 6.[俚]

容易受骗的人;傻瓜,笨蛋;对某种事物(或某种人)容易着迷的人(*for*) 7. 〔口〕棒糖 — *vt.* 1. (为了有利于植物生长)从…除去根条(或吸根) 2. 〔俚〕欺骗 — *vi.* 〔植〕长出根条来;形成吸根

suckle ['sʌkl] *vt.* 1. 给…喂奶,哺乳 2. 养育,哺育 3. 吮吸;吸取

suckling ['sʌkliŋ] *n.* 1. 乳儿;乳兽 2. 乳臭未干的小伙子 3. 哺乳

Sucre ['suːkrei] *n.* 苏克雷[玻利维亚法定首都]

sucrose ['sjuːkrəus] *n.* 〔化〕蔗糖

suction ['sʌkʃən] *n.* 1. 吸;吸引;吸入;吸气引液 2. (真空产生的)吸力 3. ~ pump 4. 〔英〕喝酒 5. 〔美俚〕上司的青睐 ‖ ~ **pump**[机]抽吸泵,真空泵

Sudan [suː'dɑːn] *n.* 苏丹[非洲东北部国家]

sudden ['sʌdn] *adj.* 1. 突然的,忽然的;意外的 2. 〔古〕急就的;即刻的;即席作成的 — *n.* 突然〔! ‖ ~**ly** *adv.* / ~**ness** *n.*

sudorific [ˌsjuːdə'rifik] *adj.* 发汗的 — *n.* 发汗剂

suds [sʌdz] *n.*[复] 1. (充满泡沫的)肥皂溶液;浓肥皂水 2. (肥皂)泡沫;残渣 3. 〔俚〕啤酒 — *vt.* 用肥皂沫的浓肥皂水中洗 — *vi.* 形成起泡沫的浓肥皂水

sue [sjuː; suː] *vt.* 1. 控告;控诉;(向法院)起诉 2. 请求;祈求;要求;~ the court *for* a writ of recovery 请求法院宣告恢复权利的裁定 / ~ sb. *for* mercy 求饶 — *vi.* 1. 提出诉讼 2. 提出请求

suède [sweid] *n.* 绒面革,起毛革;仿麂皮(织物)

suet ['sjuit] *n.*(牛、羊等的)板油

Suez ['suːiz] *n.* 苏伊士[埃及东北部港市] ‖ ~ **Canal** 苏伊士运河[埃及东北部]

suffer ['sʌfə] *vt.* 1. 遭受,蒙受;经历 2. [常用于否定句]忍受,耐住 3. 容许,允许;容忍 — *vi.* 1. 受痛苦;患病;被处死刑 2. 受损失;受损害;受到妨碍 ‖ ~**er** *n.*

sufferance ['sʌfərəns] *n.* 1. 忍耐,忍受;忍耐力 2. 〔古〕痛苦;苦难 3. 默许;容许;容忍

suffering ['sʌfəriŋ] *n.* 1. 受苦;遭难;痛苦,疾苦;苦难 — *adj.* 1. 受苦的;受难的 2. 患病的

suffice [sə'fais] *vi.* 1. 足够 2. 有能力 — *vt.* 满足…的需要;使满足 ‖ **sufficingly** *adv.* 足够地

sufficiency [sə'fiʃənsi] *n.* 1. [常与不定冠词连用](财富、收入、能力等的)充足,足量 2. 自满,自负

sufficient [sə'fiʃənt] *adj.* 1. 足够的,充分的 2. 〔古〕能胜任的;有充分能力的 — *n.* 〔俗〕足够 ‖ ~**ly** *adv.*

suffix ['sʌfiks] *n.* 1. 后缀,词尾 2.【数】下标 3. (物件末尾的)附加物,增添物 — *vt.* [ˌsʌfiks, sə'fiks] *vt.* 添加…作后缀

suffocate ['sʌfəkeit] *vt.* 1. 使窒息;把…闷死 2. 闷熄 3. 妨碍(或阻止)…的发展 — *vi.* 1. 窒息;闷死 2. 受阻;不能发展 ‖ **suffocatingly** *adv.*

suffocation [ˌsʌfə'keiʃən] *n.* 窒息;闷死

suffrage ['sʌfridʒ] *n.* 1. 投票;所投的票 2. 投票权;选举权;参政权 3.【宗】代祷,短祷

suffragette [ˌsʌfrə'dʒet] *n.* 鼓吹妇女参政的妇女

suffuse [sə'fjuːz] *vt.* (液体、光、色等)充满,弥漫于

suffusion [sə'fjuːʒən] *n.* 1. 充满,弥漫;(脸等的)红晕

sugar ['ʃugə] *n.* 1. 食糖;糖块 2.【化】糖

suit [sjuːt, suːt] n. 1. 请求，恳求；求婚 2. 起诉；诉讼；讼案 3. (一套) 衣服 4. 套；副；组 5. 同花色的一组纸牌 6. 〈古〉随从，扈从 — vt. 1. 适合；中…的意 2. 使配合 (use 适应 to) 3. 〈罕〉给…穿衣 供给…衣服 — vi. 1. 合适；适当 2. 相称 (use 协调 (to, with)) ‖ ~ or n. 起诉人；请愿者；请求者；求婚者

(如葡萄糖、乳糖、果糖等) 3. (有盖和柄的) 糖缸 (亦作 ~ bowl) 4. 甜言蜜语(阿谀，奉承 5. 〈俚〉钱；赏金 6. 〈美俚〉麻醉品(指海洛因、吗啡等) 7.〈美俚〉心爱的人 — vt. 1. 加糖于；撒糖于；包糖衣于；使甜 2. 使甜蜜；使容易被接受；粉饰，美化 (up, over) 3. ~ up reality 粉饰现实 4.〈俚〉[用被动语态]诅咒 — vi. 1. 形成糖；成为颗粒状 2. 制成碱糖(浆) ‖ ~y adj. / ~ beet 甜菜，糖萝卜 / ~ cane n. 甘蔗 / ~ daddy 甜爹(指在少女身上滥花钱的老色迷) / ~ house n. 碱糖厂；制糖厂 / ~loaf n. (圆锥形) 塔糖 2. 塔糖状物 / ~ maple 【植】糖槭 / ~ refinery n. 炼糖厂 / ~ report 〈美俚〉(尤指寄给士兵的) 甜蜜情书 / ~ tongs (餐桌上用的) 方糖夹钳

suitable [ˈsjuːtəbl] adj. 合适的；适宜的；适当的；相对的 (to, for) ‖ ˌsuita'bility n. / suitably adv.

suggest [səˈdʒest] vt. 1. 建议，提出(意见、计划等) 2. 暗示；启发 3. 使人想起；使人联想到

suitcase [ˈsjuːtkeis] n. (旅行用) 小提箱，衣箱

suite [swiːt] n. 1. (一批) 随从人员 2. 套，组；(一套) 房间；(一套) 家具 3.【音】组曲

suggestible [səˈdʒestəbl] adj. 1. 易受 (暗示) 影响的 2. 可建议的；可提出的 ‖ sugˌgesti'bility n.

sukiyaki [ˌsuːkiˈjɑːki]〈日〉n. 肉片火锅

sulfa [ˈsʌlfə] adj. & n. = sulpha

suggestion [səˈdʒestʃən] n. 1. 建议；意见 2. 暗示；示意；启发 3. 联想 4. 微量；细微的迹象

sulfate [ˈsʌlfeit] n., vt. & vi.〈美〉= sulphate

sulfide [ˈsʌlfaid] n.〈美〉【化】硫化物

suggestive [səˈdʒestiv] adj. 1. 暗示的；示意的，启发的；引起联想的 2. 挑动色情的；含有猥亵意味的 ‖ ~ly adv. / ~ness n.

sulfur [ˈsʌlfə] n. & vt.〈美〉= sulphur

sulfurous [ˈsʌlfərəs] adj.〈美〉= sulphurous

suicidal [ˌsjuiˈsaidl] adj. 自杀的；危及生命的；自取灭亡的

sulk [sʌlk] vi. 生气，愠怒 — n. [常 ~s]生气，愠怒 2. 生气的人，含怒不语的人

suicide [ˈsjuisaid] n. 1. 自杀；自取灭亡；commit ~ 自杀 / political ~ 政治上的自取灭亡 2. 自杀事件 3. 自杀者；企图自杀者 — vi. 自杀 — vt. [~ oneself] 自杀 — adj. 自杀的；构成自杀的 ‖ ~ squad 敢死队

sulky [ˈsʌlki] adj. 1. 生气的，绷着脸的 2.(天气等)阴沉的 3.(马车等)单座两轮的 — n. 单座两轮马车 ‖ sulkily adv. / sulkiness n.

sullen [ˈsʌlən] adj. 1. 愠怒的，闷闷不乐的，绷着脸不高兴的 2.(天气等)阴沉的 3.(声音)沉闷的；(色彩)不鲜明的 4. 行动迟缓的；缓慢的 ‖ ~ly adv. / ~ness n.

sully [ˈsʌli] vt. 弄脏；玷污 — n.〈古〉污斑，污点

sulpha [ˈsʌlfə] adj. 1.【化】磺胺的 2. 磺

胺类药物的一 *n.* 磺胺类药物

sulpha- *comb. form*【化】表示"磺胺":
*sulpha*thiazole

sulphadiazine [ˌsʌlfəˈdaiəziːn] *n.*【药】磺胺
嘧啶

sulphaguanidine [ˌsʌlfəˈgwænidiːn] *n.*
【药】磺胺脒

sulphamethoxypyridazine
[ˌsʌlfəmiˈθɒksipiˈridəziːn] *n.*【药】磺胺甲
氧嗪(俗称长效磺胺,略作 SMP)

sulphate [ˈsʌlfeit] *n.*【化】硫酸盐;硫酸酯
一 *vt.* 1. 用硫酸(或硫酸盐)处理;使
与硫酸(或硫酸盐)化合 2. 使成硫酸
盐 3. 使在(蓄电池极板上)形成硫酸
铅沉淀 一 *vi.* 1.(硫酸盐)硫酸盐化 2.(蓄电池
极板)被硫酸铅沉淀覆盖

sulphathiazole [ˌsʌlfəˈθaiəzəul] *n.*【药】磺
胺噻唑

sulphur [ˈsʌlfə] *n.*【化】硫(磺),硫黄 一
vt. 使硫化;用硫处理;用硫黄烟熏

sulphurate [ˈsʌlfjuəreit] *vt.* 使硫化;用硫
处理

sulphureous [sʌlˈfjuəriəs] *adj.* 1. 硫的;含
硫的(尤指在燃烧时)有硫的性质的
2. 硫黄色的,黄而略带绿色的

sulphuric [sʌlˈfjuərik] *adj.*【化】(正)硫
酸的:~ acid 硫酸

sulphurous [ˈsʌlfərəs] *adj.* 1.【化】亚硫
酸的:~ acid 亚硫酸 2. 有燃烧硫黄的气
味(或颜色)的 3. 恶毒的;凶狠的;亵
渎的

sultan [ˈsʌltən] *n.* 1. 苏丹(某些伊斯兰
教国家最高统治者的称号);[S-] 苏丹
(旧时土耳其君主的称号) 2. [常 S-] 土
耳其种小白鸡,苏丹鸡

sultana [sʌlˈtɑːnə] *n.* 1. 苏丹女眷(指王
后、妃、母、姐妹、女儿) 2. 无核小葡萄
3. 苏丹鸟(一种鲜蓝或鲜绿色的涉水
小鸟)

sultry [ˈsʌltri] *adj.* 1. 闷热的,酷热的 2.
(性情等)易激动的;狂暴的;(言语等)
激烈的;狂热的 3. 能激起性欲的;淫
荡的 ‖ **sultrily** *adv.* / **sultriness** *n.*

SUM *abbr.* surface-to-underwater missile 地
(或舰)对潜导弹

sum [sʌm] *n.* 1. 总数,总和 2.【数】和 2.
金额 3. 算术题(的运算) 4. 概要;要点
5. 顶点,极点 一(summed; summing) *vt.*
1. 计算…的总数 2. 概括;总结;概述
(*up*) 一 *vi.* 共计(*to*, *into*) ‖ **summing-
up**(复]summings-up) *n.* 总和(量) *n.* 概述
(诉讼案中法官对证据、辩论等的)总结;
概述 / '~-**up** *n.* 总结

sumac(h) [ˈsjuːmæk, ˈʃuːmæk] *n.* 1. 漆树
2. 漆叶染料(或染料)

Sumatra [su'mɑːtrə] *n.* 苏门答腊(岛)[印
度尼西亚西部]

summarize [ˈsʌmaraiz] *vt. & vi.* 概括;总
结;概述

summary [ˈsʌməri] *adj.* 1. 概括的,扼要
的 2. 即时的;迅速的;简单(化)的 一
n. 摘要;概要,一览 ‖ **summarily** *adv.*
/ **summariness** *n.*

summation [sʌˈmeiʃən] *n.* 1.【数】求和
(法),求和 2. 总结

summer [ˈsʌmə] *n.* 1. 夏,夏季 2. 壮年;
最盛期,兴旺时期 3.〈诗〉[~s]岁 一
vi. 过夏天,避暑 一 *vt.* 夏季放牧(牲
口) ‖ ~ **house** (美)避暑别墅 / '~
house *n.* 花园凉亭 / '~ **tide**, '~ **time** *n.*
夏季

summersault [ˈsʌməsɔːlt] *n. & vi.* = somersault

summerset [ˈsʌməset] *n. & vi.* = somersault

summery [ˈsʌməri] *adj.* 夏天似的;似夏季
的;适合夏季的

summit [ˈsʌmit] *n.* 1. 顶点,绝顶 2. 极

度,极点 3. 最高的官阶(尤指外交上所称政府首脑级) 4. 首脑会议,最高级会议 ― *adj.* 政府首脑级的,最高级的

summon ['sʌmən] *vt.* 1. 召集;传唤;召唤;号召 2. 鼓起(勇气等),振作(精神);唤起

summons ['sʌmənz] *n.* 1. 召唤;命令 2. 【律】传票 ― *vt.* 〈口〉把传票送达(某人);用传票传唤

sumo ['suːməu] (〔复〕sumos)〈日〉*n.* 相扑:a ~ wrestler 相扑运动员 ‖ ~ist *n.*

sump [sʌmp] *n.* 1. 坑,油坑,污水坑、化粪池);(润滑系统的)集油槽 2.〈主英〉【机】油盘;曲轴箱 3.【矿】水仓,水窝

sumpter ['sʌmptə] *n.* 1. 驮兽(指驮马、驮骡等) 2. 赶驮兽者 ‖ ~-horse *n.* 驮马

sumptuary ['sʌmptjuəri] *adj.* 规定个人费用的;限制个人费用的;禁止奢侈浪费的

sumptuous ['sʌmptjuəs] *adj.* 豪华的;奢侈的 ‖ ~ly *adv.* / ~ness *n.*

sun [sʌn] *n.* 1. 太阳,日 2. 日光,阳光 3. 恒星 4.〔诗〕(一)日;(一)年;〔古〕日出;日落 5. 中心人物;太阳状的东西 6. 荣耀;光耀;权力 ― (sunned/sunning) *vt.* 晒日,曝 ― *vi.* 晒太阳 ‖ ~-baked *adj.* 日晒的;被太阳晒得日晒而发硬的 / ~ bath *n.* 日光浴 / '~,bather *n.* 做日光浴者 / '~,bathing *n.* 日光浴 / '~ belt *n.* 阳光地带(指美国的南部和西南地区) / '~bonnet *n.* (女用)阔边遮阳帽 / '~-burn *n.* 日灼;晒黑 *vt. & vi.* (使)晒黑;(使)晒焦;(使)晒得退色 / '~dew *n.*【植】茅膏菜 / '~dial *n.* 日规,日晷仪 / '~fish *n.* 太阳鱼,翻车鱼 / '~flower *n.* 向日葵,葵花,向阳花 /

'~glasses 〔复〕*n.* 太阳眼镜,墨镜 / '~glow *n.* 朝霞,晚霞(日光) / '~-helmet 硬壳太阳帽 / '~lamp *n.* (治疗或拍摄电影用的)太阳灯 / '~light *n.* 日光,阳光 / '~lit *adj.* 阳光照亮的,日晒的 / '~ray *n.* 1. 太阳光线 2. [sunrays]紫外线 2.(画面上的)光线 / '~rise *n.* 日出(时分);at ~rise 黎明时 / '~room *n.* 日光(浴)室 / ~ set *n.* 1. 日落(时分) 2.〔喻〕晚年 / '~ shade *n.* 1. (女用)阳伞 2.(橱窗等的)遮篷;百页窗;天棚 3.【物】物镜遮光罩 / '~ spot *n.* 1. 太阳黑子 2. 雀斑 / '~ stroke *n.* 日射病,中暑 / '~ struck *adj.* 中暑的 / '~up *n.* = ~ rise

Sun. *abbr.* Sunday

sundae ['sʌndei] *n.* 圣代(一种加水果、果仁和搅奶油等的冰淇淋)

Sunday ['sʌndi] *n.* 星期日(基督教徒的)礼拜日 ― *adj.* 1. 星期日的,礼拜日的 2. 最好的;非每日的;业余的 ― *adv.* 〈口〉在星期日 ― *vi.* 过星期日 ‖ ~*adv.* 〈美〉每星期日 / '~,go-to-'meeting *adj.* 〈口〉(言语、举止、衣服等)适宜于星期日做礼拜时用的;最好的 / ~ school [宗]主日学校;主日学校的全体师生

sunder ['sʌndə] *vt. & vi.* 分开;切断

sundial ['sʌndaiəl] *n.* 1. 日规,日晷(仪) 2.【植】羽扇豆

sundries ['sʌndriz] 〔复〕*n.* 杂品;杂项

sundry ['sʌndri] *adj.* 各式各样的,各种的

sung [sʌŋ] sing 的过去分词

sunk [sʌŋk] sink 的过去分词和过去式 ― *adj.* 〈美〉1. 凹陷的(= sunken) 2. 情绪低落的 3. 完蛋了的

sunken ['sʌŋkən] sink 的过去分词 ― *adj.* 1. 沉没的;水面下的 2. 下陷的,凹陷

的 3. 低于地面(或楼面)的

Sunnite [ˈsʌnaɪt], **Sunni** [ˈsʌni] *n.* (伊斯兰教)逊尼派教徒

sunny [ˈsʌni] *adj.* 1. 阳光充足的、和煦的 2. 快活的、乐观的;性情开朗的;令人愉快的 3. 似太阳的 ‖ **sunnily** *adv.* / **~-side up** (美俚)(鸡蛋)单煎一面的,蛋黄在上的

sunshine [ˈsʌnʃaɪn] *n.* 1. (直射)日光,阳光;阳光照到的地方 2. 晴朗的天气; (喻)令人温暖和快乐的事物(或人) 3. (美俚)黄金

sup¹ [sʌp] (supped;supping) *vt.* 啜(茶、汤等) *vi.* 啜饮 — *n.* (一)啜;少量

sup² [sʌp] (supped;supping) *vi.* 吃晚饭 (on, upon, off): ~ on noodles (bread) 吃面条(面包)当晚饭 — *vt.* 晚上喂(动物)吃

super [ˈsjuːpə] *n.* 1. 〈口〉跑龙套的角色;无足轻重者 2. 〈口〉特级品;特大号商品 3. (公寓、办公楼等的)管理人 4. (装订书脊用的)上浆网眼布 — *adj.* 1. 特级的;极好的;顶刮刮的 2. 特大的;威力极大的 3. 十分的;过分的;非常的 4. (测量)按平方的 — *adv.* 非常;过分地 — *vt.* 用冷纱粘贴(书脊) — *vi.* 充当跑龙套角色

super- *pref.* 1. 表示"上…":superstructure 2. 表示"超…","超级…":supermarket,supernatural,superpower 3. 表示"过分":superheat 使过热;使过分激动,superfluous

superannuate [ˌsjuːpəˈrænjueɪt] *vt.* 1. 给养老金使退休;因年老(或体弱)令…退职 2. 淘汰;废弃 3. 令(超龄学生)退学 ‖ ~d *adj.* 1. 年老(或体弱)而退职的;领养老金的;老弱无能的 2. 过时的;太旧的;废弃的

superannuation [ˌsjuːpəˌrænjuˈeɪʃən] *n.* 1. 退休;年老(或体弱)退职 2. 淘汰;废弃 3. 退休金

superb [sjuːˈpɜːb] *adj.* 1. 壮丽的;华丽的 2. 超等的,极好的 ‖ ~ly *adv.*

supercargo [ˈsjuːpəˌkɑːɡəʊ] ([复] supercargo(e)s) *n.* (商船的)押运员,货载管理员

supercharge [ˈsjuːpətʃɑːdʒ] *vt.* 1. 用增压器增加(内燃机)的动力 2. 使超负荷;使超载 3. 使过分,使过度 ‖ ~r *n.* 增压器

supercilious [ˌsjuːpəˈsɪliəs] *adj.* 目空一切的;傲慢的 ‖ ~ly *adv.* / ~ness *n.*

supererogation [ˌsjuːpəˌerəˈɡeɪʃən] *n.* 做职责以外的工作

superette [ˌsjuːpəˈret] *n.* 小型超(级)市(场)

superfatted [ˌsjuːpəˈfætid] *adj.* (肥皂)多脂的

superficial [ˌsjuːpəˈfɪʃəl] *adj.* 1. 表面的;表面性的 2. 肤浅的,浅薄的 3. 面(积)的;平方的 4. 快而粗略的;浮面的 ‖ ~ly *adv.* / ~ness, ~ity [ˌsjuːpəˌfɪʃiˈælɪti] *n.*

superfine [ˌsjuːpəˈfaɪn] *adj.* 1. 过分精细的 2. (商品等)特级的,高档的

superfluity [ˌsjuːpəˈfluːɪti] *n.* 1. 多余,过剩 2. [常 superfluities]多余物,过剩制品 3. 奢侈

superfluous [sjuːˈpɜːfluəs] *adj.* 多余的,过剩的;不必要的:a ~ remark 多余的话 ‖ ~ly *adv.*

superhuman [ˌsjuːpəˈhjuːmən] *adj.* 1. 超人的;神的 2. (力气、身材、智力等)超过常人的

superimpose [ˌsjuːpərɪmˈpəʊz] *vt.* 1. 把…放在另一物的上面 2. 添上,加上,附加

superintend [ˌsjuːpərinˈtend] *vt. & vi.* 监督;主管;指挥(工作等)

superintendence [ˌsjuːpərinˈtendəns] *n.* 监督;主管;指挥

superintendent [ˌsjuːpərinˈtendənt] *n.* 1. 监督人;指挥者;(部门、机关、企业等的)负责人 2. 警察长 —*adj.* 监督的;主管的

superior [sjuːˈpiəriə] *adj.* 1. (指位置方面)在上的,较高的 2. (在职位、权力等方面)较高的,上级的 3. (在数量等方面)较大的,较多的 4. 优越的,优良的 5. 不为⋯所感的;不屈于⋯的 (to) 6. 高傲的,傲慢的 7. 包括范围更广的 8. 【印】上标的(如 xⁿ 中的 n);比一行中其他字母略高的 9. 比地球离太阳更远的(在地球轨道以外的) —*n.* 1. 上级;长官;长者 2. 占优势者;优胜者 3. 修道院院长

superiority [sjuːˌpiəriˈɔːrəti] *n.* 优越(性);优势 ‖ ~ complex 【心】自大情结

superjet [ˈsjuːpədʒet] *n.* 超音速喷气式飞机

superlative [sjuːˈpɜːlətiv] *adj.* 1. 最高的;最好的 2. 过度的;被夸大了的 3. 【语】(形容词、副词的)最高级的 —*n.* 1. 最高的程度,极度;顶峰 2. 最好的物(或人) 3. 【语】最高级;最高级形式 ‖ ~ly *adv.* / ~ness *n.*

superman [ˈsjuːpəmæn] ([复] supermen [ˈsjuːpəmen]) *n.* 1. (德国哲学家尼采设想的)理想之人,完人,超人 2. 具有超过常人力量和能力的人,超人

supermarket [ˈsjuːpəmɑːkit] *n.* 超(级)市(场)

supernal [sjuːˈpɜːnl] *adj.* 1. 天上的,超凡的 2. 崇高的;神圣的

supernatural [ˌsjuːpəˈnætʃərəl] *adj.* 超自然的;神奇的,不可思议的 —*n.* 1. 超自然物;神奇的东西 2. [the ~]超自然现象

supernormal [ˌsjuːpəˈnɔːməl] *adj.* 超常(态)的,在一般以上的

supernumerary [ˌsjuːpəˈnjuːmərəri] *adj.* 额外的;多余的 —*n.* 1. 多余的物(或人) 2. 跑龙套的角色;杂工

superphosphate [ˌsjuːpəˈfɔsfeit] *n.* 【化】1. 过磷酸钙(用作肥料) 2. 过磷酸盐,酸性磷酸盐

superpower [ˈsjuːpəpauə] *n.* 1. 超级大国 2. 一个地区内的联合发电总量 3. 国上之国,超国家政治实体(指可管束强国的国际组织,如联合国)

superscribe [ˌsjuːpəˈskraib] *vt.* 1. 在⋯上(或外面)写(或刻) 2. 在(信件)上写姓名地址

superscription [ˌsjuːpəˈskripʃən] *n.* 1. 题写;刻 2. (信封上的)姓名地址;题字;铭文 3. 【医】处方标记(处方上的符号R),取

supersede [ˌsjuːpəˈsiːd] *vt.* 1. 代替;取代,替代 2. 接替 3. 占先于,紧接⋯而来

supersession [ˌsjuːpəˈseʃən] *n.* 1. 代替;取代,替代 2. 接替 3. 废弃

supersonic [ˌsjuːpəˈsɔnik] *adj.* 超声(频)的;超声速的,超音速的 —*n.* 1. 超声波;超声 2. (口)超音速飞机

superstar [ˈsjuːpəstɑː] *n.* 1. 超级明星 2. 【天】超星体

superstition [ˌsjuːpəˈstiʃən] *n.* 迷信;迷信行为

superstitious [ˌsjuːpəˈstiʃəs] *adj.* 迷信的;由迷信引起的 ‖ ~ly *adv.*

superstructure [ˈsjuːpəstrʌktʃə] *n.* 1. 上层建筑 2. 【建】上部结构;【船】(尤指战舰的)上层结构

supertax [ˈsjuːpətæks] *n.* 附加税;(对超

过一定额的收入所征收的)累进所得税

supervacaneous [ˌsjuːpəvəˈkeiniəs] *adj.* 多余的,不需要的

supervene [ˌsjuːpəˈviːn] *vi.* 随后发生;伴随产生;意外发生

supervise [ˈsjuːpəvaiz] *vt.* & *vi.* 监督;管理;指导 ‖ **super'vision** *n.*

supervisor [ˈsjuːpəvaizə] *n.* 1. 监督(人);管理人;指导者 2. 督学(员) ‖ ~y *adj.*

supine [sjuːˈpain] *adj.* 1. 仰卧的;(手)掌心向上的 2.(手)掌心朝外的 2. 懒散的;苟安的;因循的 3.(古)向后靠的

supper [ˈsʌpə] *n.* 晚饭,晚餐 ‖ **club** 小型豪华夜总会

supplant [səˈplɑːnt] *vt.* 1. 把…排挤掉 2. 代替;取代

supple [ˈsʌpl] *adj.* 1. 柔软的,易弯曲的 2. 顺从的;巴结的 3.(思想等)易适应的;反应快的 4. 轻快的;流畅的 — *vt.* 使柔软;使顺从;使驯服 — *vi.*(古)变柔顺;变柔和 ‖ **~ly** *adv.* **~ness** *n.* ‖ **~jack** *n.* 1.【植】阿拉巴马勾儿茶;泡林藤 2. 软韧手杖 3.(美)玩偶,跳娃娃

supplement [ˈsʌplimənt] *n.* 1. 增补,补充 2.(书籍的)补遗;补编;附录;(报刊等的)副刊;增刊;a ~ to a dictionary 词典的补编 3.【数】补角;补弧 — [ˈsʌplimənt] *vt.* 增补,补充

supplemental [ˌsʌpliˈmentl] *adj.* = supplementary

supplementary [ˌsʌpliˈmentəri] *adj.* 1. 增补的,补充的;追加的 2.【数】补角的;补弧的

suppliant [ˈsʌpliənt] *n.* 恳求者,哀求者 — *adj.*(表示)恳求的,(表示)哀求的

supplicant [ˈsʌplikənt] *n.* & *adj.* = suppliant

supplicate [ˈsʌplikeit] *vt.* & *vi.* 恳求,哀求;祈求 ‖ **suppli'cation** *n.*

supplier [səˈplaiə] *n.* 供应者;供应厂商;原料(或商品)供应国(或地区)

supply[1] [səˈplai] *vt.* 1. 供给,供应,提供 2. 补充,填补 3. 代理,暂代 — *vi.* 代理,暂代 — *n.* 1. 供给(量);供应(量);补给 2.[常 supplies]供应品;生活用品;(储备)物资;补给品;存货 3.[supplies](供给某人的)生活费用;议会对政府费用的拨款 4. 代理牧师;代课教师

supply[2] [ˈsʌpli] *adv.* 柔软地;顺从地

support [səˈpɔːt] *vt.* 1. 支撑,支承 2. 支持;支援;赞助;拥护 3. 经受;忍受 4. 供养;维持,资助 5. 为…提供证据;证实 6. 激励;使有勇气(或信心);保持…进行下去 7.【戏】替…当配角;成功地扮演(角色)8.【音】为…伴奏 8. 通过买进(或借贷)的方法维持(高的价格);维持(农产品等)的价格 — *n.* 1. 支撑,支承 2. 支持;援助;拥护 3. 供养;维持 4. 支持者;拥护者;支援物;支柱 5.【军】支援部队 6.【戏】配角 7.【音】伴奏

supportable [səˈpɔːtəbl] *adj.* 能支持住的可忍受的

supporter [səˈpɔːtə] *n.* 1. 支持者;拥护者;援助者 2. 扶养者;赡养者 3. 支持器;托器 4.【化】载体,担体 5.(运动员等用的)护身弹性织物

suppose [səˈpəuz] *vt.* 1. 猜想,料想;想象 2. 假定 3.[用于祈使语气]让 4. 必须先服定;需要以…作为条件;意味着 — *vi.* 猜想,料想

supposed [səˈpəuzd] *adj.* 想象上的;假定的;被信以为真的

supposedly [səˈpəuzidli] *adv.* 想象上;按照推测;恐怕

supposition [ˌsʌpəˈzɪʃən] *n.* 想象；假定；推测 ‖ ~**al** *adj.*

supposititious [səˌpɔziˈtiʃəs], **suppositious** [ˌsʌpəˈzɪʃəs] *adj.* 1. 假定的，假设的，推测的 2. 假冒的，伪的；顶替的；私生的

suppress [səˈpres] *vt.* 1. 镇压；压制 2. 抑制，忍住；阻止…的生长 3. 隐藏；隐瞒 4. 禁止(书刊等)发行；查禁 ‖ ~**ible** *adj.* / ~**ion** *n.*

suppurate [ˈsʌpjuəreit] *vi.* 【医】化脓 ‖ ˌsuppuˈration *n.* 化脓 2 脓 ‖ suppurative *adj.* 催脓的；化脓(性)的 *n.* 化脓药

supremacy [sjuˈpreməsi] *n.* 1. 至高，无上 2. 最高权力；霸权

supreme [sjuˈpriːm] *adj.* 1. (权位等)最高的,至上的 2. 最大的；极度的；最重的,最高超的 3. 终极的；极度的 —*n.* [the S-] 上帝,至高无上者，神 ‖ ~**ly** *adv.* ‖ **Supreme Court** (美国)联邦最高法院；州最高法院/最高法院 /**Supreme Soviet**(前苏联的)最高苏维埃

sur- *pref.* 1. 表示"超","外加" : *surcharge, surtax* 2. 表示"上"

surcease [səːˈsiːs] *n.*, *vt.* & *vi.* (使)停止,(使)终止

surcharge [ˈsəːtʃɑːdʒ] *n.* 1. 超载；负荷过重；过度负担 2. 额外费；附加罚款(如对欠资信件的罚款)；过高索价 3. (邮票等上的)更改票值的印记；盖有改值印记的邮票 4. 错算于在贷方漏记一笔账 — *vt.* 1. 使载得过多；使负担过重；使充满 2. 对…索费过多；向…收取额外费用；处(革人)以罚款过多 3. 在(邮票)上加盖改值印记 4. 指出对方在(账)上漏记一笔贷方款项

surcingle [ˈsəːsiŋgl] *n.* 1. (系在马上的)肚带 2. (教士长袍上的)腰带

surd [səːd] *n.* & *adj.* 1.【数】不尽根的(的) 2.【语】清音(的)

sure [ʃuə] *adj.* 1. [用作表语]确信的；有把握的 2. 一定的,必定的 2. 确实的；稳当的；可靠的；万全的 — *adv.* (美口)的确,一定 ‖ ~**ness** *n.* ‖ ~**fire** *adj.* 〈美口〉一定会成功的,一定能达到的 / ~**footed** *adj.* 1. 脚步稳的,不会摔倒的 2. 稳健的；踏实的,不会出差错的

surely [ˈʃuəli] *adv.* 1. 确实,无疑；一定 2. 稳当地；踏实地 3.[常放在句首或句尾,强调推断等的]谅必；一定 4.〈主美〉[用于回答句中]当然

surety [ˈʃuəti] *n.* 1.〈古〉确实,肯定 2. 保证,担保；保证人；担保品

surf [səːf] *n.* 拍岸浪；拍岸浪花；拍岸涛声 — *vi.* 冲浪,作冲浪运动 ‖ ~**board** *n.* 冲浪板 / ~**riding** *n.* 冲浪运动

surface [ˈsəːfis] *n.* 1. 面,表面 2. 水面 3. 外观,外表 4.【空】(翼)面 — *adj.* 1. 表面的；外观的,外表上的 2. 水面的；地面上的；~ mail(用车辆或船只递送的)普通邮件与航空邮件相对而言) — *vt.* 1. 进行表面处理；使光滑；刨光；在…上加刷表面 2. 使(潜水艇等)浮出水面；使露头,使出现 — *vi.* 1. 在地面(或近地面)工作(即采矿等) 2. 浮出水面 3. 显露,呈现 ‖ ~**man** *n.* 1. (铁路)护路工人 2.【矿】井上工人 / ~**-to-air** *adj.* (导弹等)地(或舰)对空的 / ~**-to-** ~ *adj.* (导弹等)地对地的；舰对舰的

surfeit [ˈsəːfit] *n.* 1. 过量；过度(*of*) 2. 饮食过度(饮食过度所引起的)恶心,不适 — *vt.* 使饮食过度；过多地供给；使沉溺于(*with*) — *vi.* 饮食过度；〈古〉沉溺；放纵

surge [səːdʒ] *n.* 1. 巨浪；波涛 2. 汹涌,澎湃；奔腾(声) 3.【电】浪涌 4.【海】(绞盘

的)腰部;(绳缆的)松脱 5. 急剧上升;
激增 — vi. 1. 汹涌澎湃;波动;激动
2.[电]浪涌 3.(绞盘上的绳或缆)松脱
— vt. 急放(绳缆等)

surgeon ['sə:dʒən] n. 1. 外科医师 2. 军
医 ‖ ~ dentist 牙外科医师 /Surgeon
General n. 1.(美国)军医处处长 2.(美国)
卫生局局长 3.[s-g-](英国)陆军军医

surgery ['sə:dʒəri] n. 1. 外科;外科学;手
术 2. 手术室 3. 外科实验室 4.[英](开
业医师的)诊所

surgical ['sə:dʒikəl] adj. 1. 外科(术)的;
外科医师的 2. 外科(手术)用的 3. 外
科手术引起的 ‖ ~ly adv.

Surinam [ˌsuəri'næm], Suriname
[ˌsuəri'nɑːmə] n. 苏里南[南美洲北部
国家] ‖ Surinam toad[动]负子蟾

surly ['sə:li] a. 1. 乖戾的;阴郁的;粗
暴的;无礼的 2.(天气等)阴沉的,阴霾
的 ‖ surliness n.

surmise [sə:'maiz] vt. & vi. 推测;猜测;
臆测 — ['sə:maiz] n. 1. 推测;猜测;臆
测 2. 猜疑;疑惑

surmount [sə:'maunt] vt. 1. 克服;越过;
登上 2.[常用被动语态]在…顶上覆
盖;装在…顶上 ‖ ~able adj.

surname ['sə:neim] n. 1. 姓 2. 别号,外
号;浑名,绰号 — vt. 1. 给…起别号
(或绰号) 2. 给…姓氏

surpass [sə:'pɑːs] vt. 超越;胜过;优于;超
过…的界限;非…所能办到(或理
解)

surpassing [sə:'pɑːsiŋ] adj. 非凡的,卓越
的,无比的;非常的 — adv. 非凡地,卓
越地,无比地;非常 ‖ ~ly adv. /~-
ness n.

surplice ['sə:pləs] n.(教士穿的)白法衣
‖ ~d adj. 穿白法衣的

surplus ['sə:pləs] n. 1. 过剩(物)

资);剩余额 2. 公积金;盈余 — adj.
过剩的,多余的;剩余的 ‖ ~ value 剩
余价值

surprise [sə'praiz] vt. 1. 使惊奇,使诧异
使感到意外 2. 突然袭击;突然攻占;
出其不意地俘获 3. 乘对方不备地设
法得到;乘其不备地吐露真言;出其
不意地使(某人)做某事(into) 4. 意外
地遇见,撞见;当场提住 — n. 1. 惊
奇,诧异 2. 使人惊异的事物 3. 出其不
意,突然袭击

surprising [sə'praiziŋ] adj. 使人惊奇的,
惊人的;出人意外的 ‖ ~ly adv.

surrealism [sə'riəlizəm] n. 超现实主义;
超现实主义派 ‖ surrealist n. & adj./
sur,rea'listic adj.

surrender [sə'rendə] vt. 1. 交出;放弃 2.
[~ oneself]使投降;使自首 3.[常~
oneself]听任;使沉溺于(to) — vi. 投
降;自首 — n. 1. 交出;放弃;投降 2.
[律](逃犯的)引渡 3.(保释人向司法
机关的)交回罪犯(亦作 ~ by bail) 4.
放弃;交出,让出

surreptitious [ˌsʌrəp'tiʃəs] adj. 鬼鬼祟祟
的,偷偷摸摸的;秘密的 ‖ ~ly adv.

surrey ['sʌri] n.[美]四轮双座轻便游览
马车,萨里式游览车

surrogate ['sʌrəgit] n. 1. 代理人;代孕者
2.[美国某些州的主管遗嘱检验等事
的]遗嘱检验者 3.(英国)主教代理人
4. 代用品 — ['sʌrəgeit] vt. 使代理;使
代替;指定(某人)为代理人(或代替
者,接替者)

surround [sə'raund] vt. 围,围绕;圈住;包
围—n. 1. 围绕物 2. 围绕地周围与墙
之间的地板;地毯与墙之间的地板上
的铺盖物

surrounding [sə'raundiŋ] n.[~s]周围的
事物;环境 — adj. 周围的

surtax ['sɜːtæks] *n*. 1. 附加税 2.(对超过一定额的收入征收的)超额累进所得税 — *vt*. 对…征收附加税(或超额累进所得税)

surveillance [sɜː'veiləns] *n*. 监视;监督

survey [sɜː'vei, 'sɜːvei] *vt*. 1. 俯瞰;环视;眺望 2. 检查;概括地观察(或评述);审视 3. 测量;勘定 — *vi*. 测量土地 — ['sɜːvei, sɜː'vei] *n*. 1. 俯瞰;环视;眺望 2. 概况;概括的研究;全面的评述;通论;检查;调查;测量;查勘 4. 被测量的地区,测量图;测量记录;测量部门 ‖ ~ing *n*. 环视;考察;调查 ‖ ~or *n*. 测量员;测量师

surveyor [sɜː'veiə] *n*. 1. 测量员;勘测员;测地员 2.(海关等的)检查员;检查官;验货员

survival [sə'vaivəl] *n*. 1. 幸存;残存 2. 幸存者;残存物 ‖ ~ of the fittest 适者生存

survive [sə'vaiv] *vt*. 1. 比…活得长;比…命长 2. 幸免于,从…中逃出;从(困境)中挺过来 — *vi*. 活下来;幸存;残存

survivor [sə'vaivə] *n*. 幸存者;选生者;残存物 ‖ ~ship *n*. 1. 幸存,未死;残存 2.【律】(财产共有者中)生者对死者名下财产的享有权

susceptible [sə'septəbl] *adj*. 1. 易受感动的;易受影响的;敏感的(to) 2. 能容许…的;可被…的;可受…影响的(of, to) ‖ sus'ceptibly *adv*. ‖ ~ness *n*. / [susceptibilities] 感情;敏感之处 3.【物】磁化率,磁化系数 / suscepti'bility *adv*.

suspect [sə'spekt] *vt*. 1. 疑有;猜想;觉得 2. 怀疑,不信任 — *vi*. 怀疑,疑心;猜疑 — ['sʌspekt] *n*. 嫌疑犯;可疑分子 — ['sʌspekt] *adj*. [只作表语]可疑的

‖ ~able *adj*. 可疑的

suspend [sə'spend] *vt*. 1. 吊,悬;使悬浮 2. 使悬而不决;推迟;暂停 3. 中止;暂停令…停职(或停学等) — *vi*. 1. 暂停;中止 2.(商号;银行等因无支付能力)停止偿付债务 3. 悬,挂;悬浮 ‖ ~er *n*. 吊…的东西;吊杆;吊索 2.(美) [~s]吊裤带,背带;(英)[~s]吊袜带

suspense [sə'spens] *n*. 1. 悬而不决,未定 2. 挂虑,不安;担心 3.(权利等的)暂时停止;中止 ‖ ~ful *adj*.

suspension [sə'spenʃən] *n*. 1. 吊,悬;悬挂物;【机】悬置(指车轴上用弹簧等托住车身);【化】悬浮(液);悬浮物 2. 暂停;中止;暂时停职;暂时停学 3.【商】停止(或无力)支付;无力偿债 4. 未决;悬而不决 5.【音】延留音;延留音乐 6.【语】(使读者等悬念下的)含笔法,卖关子;缩略(法) ‖ ~ bridge 悬索桥,吊桥 / ~ points, ~ periods 省略号(即"…")

suspensoid [sə'spensɔid] *n*.【化】悬胶(体)

suspicion [sə'spiʃən] *n*. 1. 怀疑,疑心;猜疑;嫌疑 3.[a ~]一点儿(of) — *vt*.(美口)怀疑 ‖ ~less *adj*. 不(表示)怀疑的

suspicious [sə'spiʃəs] *adj*. 1. 可疑的 2. 猜疑的;疑心的;多疑的 ‖ ~ly *adv*.

sustain [sə'stein] *vt*. 1. 支撑,撑住;承受住 2. 供养;维持;维续 3. 蒙受,遭受 4. 忍受;经得住 5. 证实,证明 6.(法庭等)确认,准许;准许;支持 7. 扮演(角色),充分表演(人物) ‖ ~er *n*.

sustenance ['sʌstinəns] *n*. 1. 生计 2. 生活资料;粮食;食物;营养 3. 支持;维持;供养 4. 支撑物

sustentation [,sʌsten'teiʃən] *n*. 1. 支持;维持;供养 2. 生计 3. 支持物;维持物;粮食,食物 4.【空】(气垫等空气动力)

的)垫起

sutler ['sʌtlə] *n.* 随军小贩

suture ['sjuːtʃə] *n.* **1.** 【医】缝合:缝术:缝线:缝:针脚 **2.**【解】骨缝 **3.**【植】线缝 — *vt.* 缝合

Suva ['suːvə] *n.* 苏瓦[斐济首都]

suzerain ['sjuːzərein] *n.* 封建主:宗主国

suzerainty ['sjuːzəreinti] *n.* **1.** 宗主(国)权 **2.** 封建主的权力(或地位)

svelte [svelt, sfelt] *adj.* **1.**(身材)细长的、苗条的;柔软的 **2.** 线条清晰的;柔滑的 **3.** 和蔼的、温文尔雅的 ‖ **~ly** *adv.* / **~ness** *n.*

SW, s. w. *abbr.* **1.** southwest **2.** southwestern

swab [swɔb] *n.* **1.** (擦洗甲板、地板等用的)拖把 **2.**【医】拭子:药签:(用拭子取下的)化验标本 **3.** (擦洗枪膛、炮膛的)枪刷刷 **4.** (俚)笨拙的人 **5.** 〈美俚〉水手 **6.** 〈英俚〉(海军军官的)肩章 — (swabbed;swabbing) *vt.* **1.** (用拖把)擦洗;(用拭子等)拭抹 **2.** (用药签)敷药于

swaddle ['swɔdl] *vt.* **1.** 用长布条裹包(婴孩);包藏 **2.** 限制;束缚 — *n.* 襁褓用长布条;绷带 ‖ **swaddling clothes, swaddling bands, swaddling clouts 1.** 襁褓 **2.** 婴儿服 **3.** 严格管教;限制;束缚

swag [swæg] *n.* **1.** (步行者或矿工等的)行囊,包袱 **2.** 摇晃;倾侧 **3.** 赃物 **4.** 珍贵物;钱财;大量 **5.** 一丛垂花(或垂枝);【建】雕花饰 — (swagged;swagging) *vi.* **1.** 摇晃;倾侧 **2.** 沉下;垂下 **3.** 〈澳〉背着行囊旅行

swagger ['swægə] *vi.* **1.** 昂首阔步(*about, in, out*) **2.** 狂妄自大,自鸣得意 **3.** 吹牛皮,说大话(*about*) — *vt.* 恫吓,吓唬 — *n.* **1.** 昂首阔步 **2.** 狂妄自大 **3.** 虚张声势,摆架子 — *adj.* 〈口〉(衣服等)漂亮的;时髦的

Swahili [swɑːˈhiːli] ([复]Swahili(s)) *n.* 〈东非〉斯瓦希里人;斯瓦希里语

swain [swein] *n.* **1.** 情人;求爱者 **2.** 乡村青年(或情郎)

swallow[1] ['swɔləu] *n.* 燕子 ‖ ~ dive 燕式跳水 / ~ tail *n.* **1.** 燕尾 **2.** 燕尾服 **3.** 燕尾旗的末端

swallow[2] ['swɔləu] *vt.* **1.** 吞下,咽下 **2.** 吞没,淹没(*up*) **3.** 耗尽,用尽(*up*) **4.** 〈口〉轻信;轻易接受 **5.** 忍受 **6.** 压制,抑制 **7.** 取消(前言等) **8.** 把(字、音)发得含糊 — *vi.* 吞下,咽下 — *n.* **1.** 吞,咽 **2.** 一次吞咽之物 **3.** 咽喉;食道

swam [swæm] swim 的过去式

swamp [swɔmp] *n.* **1.** 沼泽;沼泽地 **2.**【矿】煤层聚水注 — *vt.* **1.** 使陷入沼泽,淹没 **2.** 击溃,压倒 **3.** 清除(林中杂丛等);开辟(道路) — *vi.* 陷入沼泽;淹没;沉没

swampy ['swɔmpi] *adj.* (多)沼泽的;似沼泽的;湿而松软的

swan[1] [swɔn] *n.* **1.** [复]swan(s)天鹅 **2.** 天鹅般的人(或物);卓越的诗人;歌手 **3.** [S-]【天】天鹅座 ‖ ~ shot 打野禽等用的大号子弹 / ~ song **1.** 〈西方古代传说中〉天鹅临死时发出的美妙歌声 **2.** (诗人等的)最后作品;最后的言行;告别演出

swan[2] [swɔn] (swanned; swanning) *vi.* **1.** 闲荡,游逛 **2.** (车辆等)蜿蜒行驶

swank [swæŋk] 〈口〉 *n.* **1.** 出风头,炫耀 **2.** 虚张声势;摆架子;吹牛 **3.** 优雅;漂亮,考究 — *adj.* 〈口〉 **1.** 爱出风头的,炫耀的 **2.** 漂亮的;时髦的 — *vi.* **1.** 出风头,炫耀;摆架子 **2.** 说大话

swap [swɔp] (swapped; swapping) *vt.* 交换;交流;用…作交易品 — *vi.* 交换;做交易 — *n.* 交换;交易

sward [swɔːd] *n.* 草地；草皮 — *vt. & vi.* (给…)铺上草皮

swarm[1] [swɔːm] *n.* **1.** (为建立新巢而跟随离群王迁出的)蜂群 **2.** (蜂房中的)蜂群 **3.** (移动中的)一群昆虫 **4.**【生】游动孢子(或细胞)群 **5.** 一大群 — *vi.* **1.** (蜜蜂)成群飞离蜂巢 **2.** 密集，云集；涌往 **3.** 充满(*with*)；在周围徘徊 **4.**【生】成群裂出(如从孢子囊中)；(细胞、生物)成群浮游 — *vt.* 挤满

swarm[2] [swɔːm] *vt. & vi.* 爬(树等)，攀

swarthy ['swɔːði] *adj.* 黝黑的，黑皮肤的 ‖ **swarthiness** *n.*

swash [swɒʃ] *vi.* **1.** 发激荡声；冲激；溅泼 **2.** 吓唬；虚张声势 **3.** 晃动(水等)；(用水等)泼；冲洗 — *n.* **1.** 泼散；冲激；泼水声 **2.** 冲激着的水，(沙洲中或沙洲与岸间的)冲流水道 **3.** 海水冲洗的沙滩 **4.** 吓唬；虚张声势 ‖ ~ **er** *n.* ~ **buckler** = ~ **buckler** ‖ '~**buckler** *n.* **1.** 虚张声势的闹事者；流氓(或暴徒等)；恃强凌弱者 **2.** 描述流氓暴徒的小说(或戏剧)

swastika, swastica ['swɒstikə] *n.* **1.** 卍字饰，万字饰(相传为象征太阳、吉祥等的标志) **2.** 卐字(德国纳粹党的党徽)

swat [swɒt] (*swatted*; *swatting*) *vt. & vi.* 重拍，猛击，扣

swatch [swɒtʃ] *n.* 【纺】(小块)样布；样本；样品

swath [swɔːθ] *n.* **1.** 一刈的宽度，刈幅 **2.** (刈)(镰刀)的一挥 **3.** 刈下的一行草(或一行麦) **3.** (一)行，(一)条；长而宽的地带

swathe [sweið] *vt.* **1.** 绑，缠，缠绕 **2.** 包围；封住 — *n.* 带子；绷带；用以包物的东西

sway [swei] *vi.* **1.** 摇动；摇摆 **2.** 歪，倾斜，偏向一边 **3.** 动摇；转向 **4.** 支配；统

治 — *vt.* **1.** 摇，摇动；使摇摆 **2.** 歪斜，使倾斜，使偏向一边 **3.** 使动摇；使转向；影响 **4.** 〈古〉挥动，挥舞(剑等) **5.**【海】扯起(帆桁)(*up*) — *n.* **1.** 摇动；摆动；动摇；倾斜 **2.** 支配；统治；影响力；权势

Swaziland ['swɑːzilænd] *n.* 斯威士兰[非洲东南部国家]

swear [sweə] (过去式 *swore* [swɔː] 或〈古〉*sware* [sweə]，过去分词 *sworn* [swɔːn]) *vt.* **1.** 宣(誓)，立(誓)，发(誓) **2.** 宣誓表示；郑重保证；强调 **3.** 使宣誓；使宣誓就职 **4.** 诅咒得使；~ **sb.** away 把某人赶走 — *vi.* **1.** 宣誓，发誓 **2.** 诅咒，骂人 **3.** 〈口〉诅咒；咒骂 — *n.* 誓言；一阵咒骂；诅咒；骂人话

sweat [swet] *n.* **1.** 汗；出汗；一身汗 **2.** (物体表面结着的)水珠；湿气 **3.** 〈口〉焦急，不安，焦躁一(*sweat* 或 *sweated*) *vi.* **1.** 出汗 **2.** 〈口〉努力工作；干苦活儿 **3.** (物体表面)结水珠；附上水汽 **4.** (烟叶等)发酵 **5.** 焦虑；烦恼；懊悔 **6.** 渗出 — *vt.* **1.** 使出汗；出汗弄湿 **2.** (使)渗出；(使)流出；榨出 **3.** 费力地使身体…发汗 **4.** 使工作过度；榨取(工人等)的血汗 **5.** 通过出汗而减轻(体重)(*away*, *off*) **6.** 用不正当手段擦损(硬币)以盗取金银粉末 **7.** (美俚)拷问 **8.** 使(烟叶)发酵；使(原皮)潮湿发霉脱毛 **7.**【治】热析(金属中易熔成分)；熔焊(金属制件)(*in*, *on*)；熔化(焊料) ‖ ~ **box** *n.* **1.** (使生皮等潮湿发霉的)发汗箱 **2.** 处罚犯人的狭小囚室 / ~ **gland** 【解】汗腺 / ~ **shirt** 圆领长袖运动衫

sweater ['swetə] *n.* **1.** (过分)出汗者；发汗剂 **2.** 榨取别人血汗的人 **3.** (厚)运动衫；(毛)线衫；卫生衫 **4.**【化】石蜡发汗罐；(烟叶、生皮等的)发汗器

Swede [swi:d] *n.* 1. 瑞典人 2. [s-]【植】芜菁甘蓝,瑞典芜菁

Sweden ['swi:dn] *n.* 瑞典 [北欧国家]

Swedish ['swi:diʃ] *adj.* 瑞典的;瑞典人的;瑞典语的 *n.* 1. 瑞典语 2. [the ~]【总称】瑞典人

sweep [swi:p] (swept[swept]) *vt.* 1. 扫;打扫,扫除 2. 猛力移动;猛推;猛力 3. 肃清,消灭 4. (风等)刮起(浪等)冲走,带走;席卷 5. 环视;眺望;扫过,掠过;擦过 6. 向…扫射;清扫(或清除)(道路等) 7. 在…中获全胜,全盘赢得 8. 向…潇洒地行(礼) 9. 用网打捞 10. 描绘…的轨迹 — *vi.* 1. 扫;打扫,扫除 2. 急赴;奔驰 3. 席卷 3. 环视;扫视;掠过;急速移动 4. 拖曳着衣裙走;昂首阔步地走 5. 连绵,延伸 — *n.* 1. 扫;打扫,扫除 2. (风的)吹刮;(浪的)冲激;(手等的)挥动;磅礴的气势 3. 肃清,清除 4. 范围;视野 5. 连绵区域;一带坡地;弯曲(处) 6. 绝对优势的胜利;全胜,全赢 7. (英)扫烟囱的人(= chimney ~);(英里)下锅的人 8.(井边的)杠杆式吊水设备;(风车的)翼板 9. 长桨 10. [~s]扫射(snow)一扫路(扫雪)机 || ~ back *n.* 【空】(机翼等的)后掠;后掠角 / ~ stakes *n.* (赛马等的)赌金全赢制;赌金全赢制(由参赛者赌注作奖金的比赛;抽彩给奖法 / ~ up *n.* 大扫除

sweeping ['swi:piŋ] *adj.* 1. 扫除的;扫荡的 2. 连绵的;呈弯曲的 3. 范围广大的;一扫无遗的;彻底的;总括的 — *n.* 1. 扫除;扫荡 2. [~s]扫地的垃圾

sweet [swi:t] *adj.* 1. 甜的,甜味的;滋味好的 2.(口)愉快的;惬意的,中意的 3. 悦耳的;漂亮的;可爱的;美妙的 4. 亲切的;和蔼的,温柔的 5. 芳香的 6. 新鲜的;淡的;不咸的 7.(口)善于的 8. 轻快的;灵活的;轻便的;易驾驶的 9. [用作反语]苦的;厉害的 10.【化】不过易腐蚀性(或酸性)的物质的;脱硫的;低碱的;无有害气体和气味的 11.(土地)非酸性的;适宜耕种的 12.[用以加强语气]非常的,惊人的 — *n.* 1. 甜食;蜜饯;(英)[常~s]糖果(= (美) candy);(英)(餐后的)一道甜点(如馅饼、蛋糕、布丁等) 2. 甜味;[常~s]芳香 3.[~s]快乐,乐趣 4. 亲爱的人;(口)[用作称呼]亲爱的 — *adv.* = ~ly || ~ly *adv.* / ~ness *n.* || ~-and-'sour *adj.* 用糖和醋(或糖和柠檬汁)调味的 / '~bread *n.* (供食用的小牛等的)胰脏(或胸腺等),杂碎 / '~briar, '~brier *n.* 【植】多花蔷薇 / ~ flag【植】菖蒲,白菖蒲 / '~heart *n.* 1. 恋人,情人 2.(俚)非常讨人喜爱的人;佳品 *vi.* 恋爱 *vt.* 向…求爱 / '~heart contract 私下合同(指工会头目与雇主私订的对工人不利的合同) / '~meat *n.* [常~s]糖食;蜜饯;蜜饯 / ~ pea 香豌豆 ~ potato 甘薯,山芋 / '~shop *n.* (英)糖果店(= (美) candy store) / ~ William【植】美国石竹 / '~wood *n.* 【植】月桂树

sweeten ['swi:tn] *vt.* 1. 使变甜;加糖于;使变香 2. 使(音调)悦耳 3. 使温和;使温柔 4. 减轻(痛苦);使愉快 5. 使清洁;使新鲜;去…的臭味 6. 笼络,讨好;增加(担保品);改善(证券发行)的条件;增加(扑克赌金) — *vi.* 变甜;变香,变好听;变温和

sweetening ['swi:tniŋ] *n.* 1. 变甜;弄甜 2. 使甜的东西

sweetish ['swi:tiʃ] *adj.* 略甜的;过甜的

swell [swel] (过去式 swelled,过去分词

swollen['swəulən] 或 swelled) vi. 1. 膨胀;肿胀 2. 隆起 3. (河水等)上涨 3. 增长;壮大 4.(声音、音乐等)增强 5. 骄傲;自负;趾高气扬 6.(情绪等)高涨;增长 — vt. 1. 使膨胀;使(力量、数目等)增长 2. 使隆起;使上涨 3. 使骄傲自大;(情绪等)充满 4. 提高(音调、声音等)— n. 1. 膨胀;肿胀;隆起;增长;增大 2. 隆起处;(海底等)的隆起地 3.[只用单]after涌;滚滚浪潮 4.【音】渐强到渐弱;渐强到渐弱符号(即<>)5.〈口〉衣着时髦的人;了不起的人;头面人物;极有才能的人 — adj.〈口〉1. 时髦的;漂亮的 2. 第一流的;了不起的;身份高贵的 ‖ ~ing n. 1. 肿胀;肿大;隆起部 2. 膨胀;增大 adj. 肿大的;突起的

swelter ['sweltə] vi. 热得难受;热得发昏;热得出大汗 — vt. 1. 使热得难受;使热得发昏;使热得出汗 2.〈古〉分泌出;渗出(毒液等)— n. 1. 闷热;酷热 2. 混乱 3. 极度紧张;大汗淋漓

swept [swept] sweep 的过去式和过去分词 ‖ '~-back wing 【空】后掠翼

swerve [swə:v] vi. 突然转向;转弯;背离(from)— vt. 使突然转向;使转变;使背离(from)— n. 转向;弯曲;(球在空中的)弧线形运动;背离

swift [swift] adj. 1. 快的,迅速的 2. 立刻的;突然发生的 3. 反应快的,思想敏捷的 — adv. 快地,迅速地;敏捷地 — n. 1.【纺】大滚筒;纱筐,绸架,篾子 2.【动】褐雨燕;快速爬行的小蜥蜴 ‖ ~-let n.【动】金丝燕 ‖ ~·ly adv. / ~·ness n.

swig [swig]〈口〉n. 大口喝;痛饮 — vt. & vi. 大口地喝;痛饮

swill [swil] vt. 1. 涮,冲洗(out) 2. 大口地喝;痛饮 3. 倒出(饮料等);用(水

等)涮容器 4. 用泔脚饲料喂(猪等)— vi. 1. 大口地喝;痛饮 2. 发激荡声 — n. 1. 涮,冲洗 2. 大喝,痛饮;狼吞虎咽 3. 劣酒 4. 泔脚;猪食;泔脚饲料;剩饭残羹

swim [swim](swam [swæm], swum [swʌm];swimming) vi. 1. 游泳,游过;浮,浮游 3. 浸,泡;覆盖;充溢(with, in) 4. 旋转;摇晃;眩晕 — vt. 1. 游过 与…赛游泳 2. 使(马等)游水;使浮起 — n. 1. 游泳 2. 游水;游泳;滑行 3.[the ~]潮流,趋势 4. 眩晕,眼花 5. 多鱼的深水区 ‖ swimmer n. 游泳者;游泳运动员 ‖ ~ bladder = swimming bladder / '~·suit n.(女)游泳衣

swimming ['swimiŋ] n. 1. 游泳 2. 眩晕 — adj. 1.(适用于)游泳的 2. 充满水(似)的 3. 眩晕的 ‖ ~·bath〈英〉(室内的)游泳池 / '~·belt n. 学游泳用的救生圈 / ~ bladder(鱼)鳔 / ~ pool 游泳池

swimmingly ['swimiŋli] adv. 顺利地;如意地 ‖ go ~ 一帆风顺

swindle ['swindl] vt. 诈取,骗取 — vi. 诈取,骗取 — n. 1. 欺诈;诈骗 2. 骗人的东西 ‖ ~r n. 骗子,诈骗犯 / swindlingly adv. 用诈骗手段

swine [swain] [单复同] n. 1. 猪 2. 猪猡,下流坯 ‖ '~·herd n. 养猪人,猪倌 / '~·pox adj. 【兽医】猪痘

swing [swiŋ](swung [swʌŋ]) vi. 1. 摆摆,摆动,摇荡 2.(手臂自由摆动着)轻松地走(或跑) 3. 大摇大摆地行走(along, past, by) 3. 悬挂;悬空(from) 4.(绕轴心,绞链等)回转,旋转;(突然)转向,转身 5. 逐节奏演奏(或演唱)音乐 6. 转变,剧变 7. 挥动手臂击(中)某物 8.〈口〉被处绞刑(for) 9. 精神饱满地立即开始 — vt. 1. 挥舞;使摆动 2. 使

(顺轴等)回转;使旋转;使(突然)转身
3. 悬挂;吊运 4.〈口〉操纵;(成功地)
处理;完成;对付 5. 以强节奏演奏(或
演唱) 一 n. 1. 摇摆,摆动;振幅,摆幅
2.(音乐等的)强节奏;强节奏爵士音乐
3.(手臂的)挥舞;轻快有节奏的步伐
4. 挥舞(或挥动、挥击)动作(或方式);
(拳击中的)摆拳;来回推进,来回运
动,交替 5.〈美口〉(利率、物价、行情等
的)涨落,上落 6. 转变,剧变 7. 秋千
8. 放任;自由活动(范围) 9.(摆动等
的)冲力 10. 竞选旅行 11. 工休期;工
休制 一 adj.(绕轴心)旋转的;悬挂
的 2. 强节奏音乐的 ‖~ bridge 平衡
桥,平转桥 /~ by n.〖空〗(航天器的)
绕行星轨道 /~ (ing) door 双开式弹簧
门 /~-wing n. & adj.〖空〗可变后掠
翼的

swinger ['swiŋə] n. 1. 摆动(或挥动等)
的人(或物) 2. 热中于赶时髦的人 3.
〈俚〉交换性交对象的人;乱交者;群交
者 4.(板球)侧飞球 5. 强节奏爵士音
乐演奏者

swingle ['swiŋgl] vt. 用打麻器打清(或刮
清)(麻) 一 n. 1. 打麻器;打麻棒 2.
(链枷的)打禾棍 3.〈美俚〉无固定性对
象的风流单身汉

swipe [swaip] n. 1.(球棒等的)挥击 2.
尖刻话,尖锐的批评 3.(提水等的)起
吊杆;(发动机的)启动柄 4. 大口喝;
大口吸 5. 马夫 — vt. 1. 挥击 2.〈俚〉
偷窃,扒窃 — vi. 1. 大口喝酒
‖~r n. 1. 挥击者 2.〈俚〉偷窃者 3.
大口喝酒的人

swirl [swə:l] vt. 1. 打旋;旋动;涡动 2.
弯曲;盘绕 3.(头)发晕 — vi. 使打旋;
使涡动 — n. 1. 旋动;旋涡 2. 旋动
;卷状(如毛皮、木头的纹理等) 3.
〈美〉弯曲;围绕 4. 纷乱,混乱 5.(鱼穿

水引起的)骚动

swish [swiʃ] vi.(鞭、马尾等)嗖地挥动;
(衣裙等)作窸窣声 — vt. 1. 嗖地挥
动;使作沙沙声 2. 嗖嗖地切割(或移
动) 3. 嗖地挥鞭毒打 — n. 1. 嗖嗖
声;窸窣声;沙沙声 2. 发出嗖一声的
动作 3.(打人用的)鞭子;笞杖;(鞭等
的)一击,一挥 4. 漂亮;时髦 5.〈美俚〉
搞同性关系的男子 — adj. 漂亮的;时
髦的 — adv. 发嗖嗖(或窸窣、沙沙)声
地 ‖~y adj. 1. 发嗖嗖(或窸窣)声
的;作沙沙声的 2.〈美俚〉(男子)搞同
性关系的

Swiss [swis] adj. 瑞士的;瑞士人的 —
n. 1.[单复同]瑞士人 2.(淡色有孔硬
质的)瑞士干酪(亦作~ cheese) 3.[常
s-]瑞士布,薄纱(原为瑞士制) ‖~
roll 瑞士面包卷

switch [switʃ] n. 1. 开关,电闸,电键,转
换器 2.(思路等的)骤变;转换;掉换;
(铁路的)转辙器;铁道辙叉 3.(树木
的)软枝条;(细软的)鞭子;杖条;鞭子
的一击 4.(女人的)假发 5.(狮等的)尖
尾毛簇 — vt. 1.(思路等)转换(on);
切断…的电流(off);接通(电流)(on);
切断(电流)(off);转接(电路) 2. 使
用铁路转辙器)使转轨;在终点站借
(车辆列等)调头 3. 改变;改换(约翰
等) 4. 鞭打 5. 摆动(尾巴等) 6. 突然
夺去 — vi. 1. 转换;变换 2.(尾巴等)
摆动 3.(铁路)转辙 ‖~board n. 1.
配电盘,配电板;开关屏 2.(电话的)交
换机,交换台 /~-man n.(铁路)扳道
工 /~ tower〈美〉(铁路的)集中信号岔操
纵楼

Switzerland ['switsələnd] n. 瑞士[欧洲
中部国家]

swivel ['swivl] n. 1.〖机〗(链的)转节,转
环,旋轴;旋转接头 2. =~ gun 3.〈俚〉

swob [swɔb] *n.* & (swobbed; swobbing) *vt.* = swab

swollen ['swəulən] swell 的过去分词 — *adj.* 1. 膨胀的;肿起的;(河水)涨起的 2. 夸张的 3. 骄傲的

swoon [swuːn] *vi.* 1. 晕厥,昏倒;神魂颠倒 2.(乐声等)渐渐消失 — *n.* 1. 晕厥,昏倒;神魂颠倒 2. 渐渐的消失

swoop [swuːp] *vi.* 攫取;〈口〉抢去(*up*) — *vi.*(鹰等向目的物)飞扑,猛扑;猝然攻击 — *n.* 飞扑;下攫

swop [swɔp] *n.* & (swopped; swopping) = swap

sword [sɔːd] *n.* 1. 剑;刀;(军俚)刺刀 [the ~]武力;兵权,军权;君权;战争;杀戮,屠杀 ‖ ~ bayonet(枪上的)刺刀 /`~ fish n.〔动〕箭鱼 /`~ law n.武力统治

swordplay ['sɔːdplei] *n.* 1. 舞剑,击剑;剑术 2. 斗嘴;巧辩

swordsman ['sɔːdzmən] ([复] swordsmen) *n.* 1. 剑手,剑客 2. 击剑运动员 3.〈古〉军士,武士 ‖ ~ship *n.* 剑术

swore [swɔː] swear 的过去式

sworn [swɔːn] swear 的过去分词 — *adj.* 宣过(或发过)誓的:a ~ enemy 死敌

swot[1] [swɔt] *vt.* (swotted; swotting) & *n.* = swat

swot[2] [swɔt] 〈英〉〈学俚〉(swotted; swotting) *vi.* 刻苦用功,用功读书 — *up* one's geometry 刻苦攻读几何 — *n.* 1. 刻苦用功,用功读书;用功的学生;一心读书的人 2. 吃

力的工作

swum [swʌm] swim 的过去分词

swung [swʌŋ] swing 的过去式和过去分词 ‖ ~ dash 代字号(即"~")

sycamore ['sikəmɔː] *n.* 〔植〕1. 西克莫(无花果)(《圣经》中的桑树) 2. 悬铃木;美国梧桐 3. 假槭琥椴

sycophant ['sikəfənt] *n.* 拍马者,谄媚者;食客 — *adj.* 拍马的,谄媚的 ‖ sycophancy *n.*

syllabi ['siləbai] syllabus 的复数

syllabic [si'læbik] *adj.* 1. 音节的;表示音节的 2. 自成音节的 3. 各个音节有明晰发音的 4.(诗体)按每行音节数而不照韵(或重音)安排的,音节节奏的 — *n.* 1. 自成音节的声音;浊音;有声字

syllabicate [si'læbikeit] *vt.* 使分成音节

syllabi(fi)cation [si,læbi(fi)'keiʃən] *n.* 分成音节;音节划分法

syllabify [si'læbifai], **syllabize** ['siləbaiz] *vt.* = syllabicate

syllable ['siləbl] *n.* 1. 音节 2. 只言片语 — *vt.* 1. 给⋯分音节 2. 按音节发⋯的音

syllabus ['siləbəs] ([复] syllabi ['siləbai] 或 syllabuses) *n.* 1. 摘要;提纲;教学大纲;课程提纲 2.〔律〕判词前的提要

syllogism ['silədʒizəm] *n.* 1.〔逻〕三段论;演绎推理 2. 推论,推断 3. 诡辩

syllogistic(al) [,silə'dʒistik(əl)] *adj.* 1.(用)三段论法的;(用)演绎推理的 2. 诡辩的

sylph [silf] *n.* 1.(15-16 世纪瑞士医师 Paracelsus 假想的)气精,气仙 2. 窈窕淑女 3.〔动〕长叉尾蜂鸟

sylvan ['silvən] *adj.* & *n.* = silvan

symbiosis [,simbai'əusis] *n.*〔生〕共生(现象)

symbol ['simbəl] *n.* 1. 象征；标志 2. 符号；记号；代号 3.【宗】教义，信条 ―(symbol(l)ed; symbol(l)ing) *vt. & vi.* = symbolize

symbolic(al) [sim'bɔlik(əl)] *adj.* 1. 象征的；象征性的 2. 符号的；用作符号的 3. 使用符号的 4.【文学艺术上的】象征派的 ‖ symbolically *adv.*

symbolism ['simbəlizəm] *n.* 1.〈尤指文学艺术上的〉象征主义 2. 象征手法；符号表示 3. 符号的意义；象征（或符号）体系 4.【哲】符号论 5.【宗】神灵的传统性象征主义 ‖ symbolist *n.* 象征主义者；使用象征者；解释象征者

symbolize ['simbəlaiz] *vt.* 1. 象征；作为…的象征；代表 2. 用象征表示；用符号表示 ― *vi.* 采用象征；使用符号

symmetric(al) [si'metrik(əl)] *adj.* 对称的；匀称的 ‖ symmetrically *adv.*／symmetricalness *n.*

symmetry ['simitri] *n.* 对称（性）；对称美；匀称

sympathetic [ˌsimpə'θetik] *adj.* 1. 同情的；表示同情的；有同情心的 2. 和谐的；合意的 3. 意气相投的；赞同的 4. 惹人喜爱的，可爱的 5.【解】交感（神经系）的 6.【物】相应（作用）的 ― *n.* 交感神经系 2.（对催眠术等）易感受的 ‖ ~ ally *adv.*／~ ink 隐显墨水（起初无色，经热、光或药品等作用而显字）

sympathize ['simpəθaiz] *vi.* 1. 同情；表示同情 2. 怜悯；共鸣；一致；同意 3. 吊唁，吊慰 (with) ‖ ~ r *n.*

sympathy ['simpəθi] *n.* 1. 同情，同情心 2. 一致；赞同 3. 怜悯；吊慰；吊唁 4.【物】相应（作用）5.（病症的）交感，共感 ‖ ~ strike 同情罢工（指为了声援别的罢工工人而举行的罢工）

symphonic [sim'fɔnik] *adj.* 1. 交响乐的；交响乐式的 2. 谐音的；调和的

symphony ['simfəni] *n.* 1. 交响曲，交响乐 2. 交响乐团，交响乐队（亦作 ~ orchestra）3.〈口〉交响音乐会 4. 谐音 5.（颜色、构图等的）和谐 ‖ symphonist *n.* 交响乐作曲家，交响乐作者；交响乐团成员

symposium [sim'pəuziəm] *n.*［复］symposia [sim'pəuziə] 或 symposiums) *n.* 1.（正式宴会后以音乐及谈话为主的）酒会 2. 座谈会；专题讨论会 3.（不同著作者对某一题目的）专题论丛，专题论文集

symptom ['simptəm] *n.* 症状；征候；征兆 ‖ sympto'matic *adj.*

synagog(ue) ['sinəgɔg] *n.* 1. 犹太教堂 2. 犹太教徒的集会 3. 犹太教

synapse ['sinæps] *n.*【解】突触，神经键

synchrocyclotron [ˌsiŋkrəu'saiklətrɔn] *n.*【核】同步回旋加速器

synchronism ['siŋkrənizəm] *n.* 1. 同时发生 2. 历史人物和事件的编年（表）3.（电影与电视中）声画同步 4.【物】同步性

synchronize ['siŋkrənaiz] *vi.* 同时发生，同步 ― *vi.* 1. 使在时间上一致；使同步 2. 使（电影的台词，音响效果）与画面动作吻合，使声画同步 3. 把…调到同步 ‖ synchroni'zation *n.*／~ r *n.* 同步器／synchronous *adj.* ‖ ~ d swimming（由两名以上泳者按音乐节奏同步表演的）花样游泳

synchrotron ['siŋkrəutrɔn] *n.*【核】同步加速器

syncopate ['siŋkəpeit] *vt.* 1.【语】中略（即省略中间的字母或音节）~ never to ne'er 将"never"中略成"ne'er" 2.【音】切分 ‖ ˌsynco'pation *n.*

syncope ['siŋkəpi] *n.* 1.【语】中略（例如以

"fo' c' sle"代"forecastle") 2.【音】切分音 3.【医】昏厥

syndic ['sindik] *n.* 1.(某些国家如安道尔的)地方行政长官 2.(尤指剑桥大学的)评议会特别委员会委员 3. 公司经理；代理商 4. 财产托管人

syndicalism ['sindikəlizəm] *n.* 工团主义，工联主义 ‖ **syndicalist** *n.* 工团主义者，工联主义者

syndicate ['sindikit] *n.* 1.【经】辛迪加，企业联合组织，财团 2. 报业辛迪加 (向各报纸或杂志出售稿件供同时发表的企业或在统一经营管理下的一批报纸) 3.(剑桥大学的)评议会特别委员会 4. 罪犯辛迪加 — ['sindikeit] *vt.* 1. 把…组成辛迪加，使处于联合管理下 2. 通过报业辛迪加销售(文章、漫画等)；通过报业辛迪加在多家报纸上同时发表(文章、漫画等) — *vi.* 联合成辛迪加 ‖ **syndi'cation** *n.* / **syndicator** ['sindikeitə] *n.* 辛迪加组织者；辛迪加参加者；辛迪加经营者

syndrome ['sindrəum] *n.*【医】综合征

syne [sain]〈苏格兰〉*adv.* 1. 从那时以后 (= since then) 2. 以前 (= ago) — *conj. & prep.* 自从 (= since)

synecology [ˌsini'kɔlədʒi] *n.*【生】群落生态学

synfuel ['sinfjuəl] *n.* 合成燃料

synod ['sinəd] *n.* 1. 教会会议 2.(基督教长老会的)教会法院；教会法院所辖教区 3. 会议；辩论会 4.【宗】

synonym ['sinənim] *n.* 1. 同义词 2. 换喻词，转喻词 ‖ **~ic** [ˌsinə'nimik] *adj.* / **~ist** [si'nɔnimist] *n.* 同义词研究者

synonymous [si'nɔniməs] *adj.* 同义词性质的，同义的(*with*) ‖ **~ly** *adv.*

synopsis [si'nɔpsis] ([复] **synopses** [si'nɔpsiz]) *n.*(书、剧本等的)提要，概

要，梗概

synoptic(al) [si'nɔptik(əl)] *adj.* 1. 摘要的；概要的；大纲性的 2. 天气(图)的 3.[常 S-]【宗】对观的；对观福音书的

syntactic(al) [sin'tæktik(əl)] *adj.* 1.【语】句法(上)的；按照句法(规则)的

syntax ['sintæks] *n.*【语】句法；语法

synthesis ['sinθisis] ([复] **syntheses** ['sinθisiz]) *n.* 1. 综合；综合体 2.【化】合成(法) 3.【哲】【逻】综合；合题；演绎推理 4.【医】接合 5.(音响等的)合成 ‖ **~t** *n.* 综合者；合成法使用者

synthesize ['sinθisaiz] *vt.* 1. 综合 2.【化】使合成 3.(用合成器)合成(音响等) — *vi.* 综合 ‖ **~d** *n.* 综合者；(音响)合成器

synthetic [sin'θetik] *adj.* 1. 综合(性)的 2. 合成的；人造的 3. 假想的；虚假的 4.(语言)综合型的 — *n.* 化学合成物；合成纤维织物；合成剂 ‖ **~ally** *adv.* ‖ **~ detergent** 合成洗涤剂 / **~ fibre** 合成纤维 / **~ fuel** 合成燃料 / **~ resin** 合成树脂

synthetical [sin'θetikəl] *adj.* = synthetic

syntomycin [ˌsintə'maisin], **synthomycin** [ˌsinθə'maisin] *n.*【微】合霉素

syphilis ['sifilis] *n.*【医】梅毒 ‖ **syphi'litic** *adj. & n.*

syphon ['saifən] *n., vi. & vt.* = siphon

Syria ['siriə] *n.* 叙利亚[西南亚国家]

syringa [si'riŋgə] *n.*【植】山梅花；丁香花，紫丁香

syringe ['sirindʒ] *n.* 注射器；皮下注射器 — *vt.*(用注射器)注射(或灌洗、冲洗)

syrup ['sirəp] *n.* 1. 糖浆；果子露；浆 2. 过分甜蜜；过分多情伤感 3.〈英俚〉钱 ‖ **~y** *adj.* 1. 糖浆(状)的 2. 过分多情的；令人腻味的

system ['sistəm] *n.* **1.** 系统；体系 **2.** 制度；体制；[the ~]现存社会体制 **3.** 方法；方式 **4.** 秩序；条理 **5.** 分类(法) **6.** 宇宙；世界 **7.** 身体，全身 **8.**【音】总乐谱表 ‖ ~(s) analysis 系统分析

systematic [ˌsisti'mætik] *adj.* **1.** 有系统的；成体系的；有秩序的；有规则的；有组织的 **2.**【生】分类(上)的；分类学的 **3.** 有计划的；非偶然的 ‖ ~ally *adv.*

systematize ['sistimətaiz] *vt.* **1.** 使系统化；使成体系；使制度化；使组织化；使有秩序 **2.** 把…分类 ‖ ˌsystemati'zation *n.* /~r *n.* 使系统化的人；分类者

systemic [sis'temik] *adj.* **1.** 全身的；系统的；影响全身的 **2.** (除莠剂、杀虫剂等)内吸(性)的 ‖ ~ insecticide 内吸杀虫剂

systole ['sistəli] *n.* **1.** (心脏等器官的)收缩(期) **2.**【语】(希腊或拉丁韵文的)长音节缩短 ‖ **systolic** [sis'tɔlik] *adj.*

T

T, t [ti:] ([复] T's, t's 或 Ts, ts [tiz]) 英语
字母表第二十个字母 **1.** [T] T 字形
(物)，丁字形(物) **2.** [T] 绝对温度
(absolute temperature)的符号 **3.** [T] 十八
开本(octodecimo)的符号 ‖ **T-shirt** *n.*
短袖圆领汗衫(或运动衫)，体恤衫 / **T
square** 丁字尺 / **T-time** *n.* (火箭、导弹
等的)点火(或发射)时刻，试验发射时
刻

Ta [化] 元素钽(tantalum)的符号

tab [tæb] *n.* **1.** 襻(如拉襻、挂襻、搭襻
等)；(资料索引卡上的)导卡突耳，检索
凸舌 **2.** (服装上装饰用的)小垂片；鞋
带末端的包头；帽耳；(易拉罐的)拉环
3. 〈英〉[军] 参谋的领章 **4.** 密切注视，
监视 **5.** 待付账单 **6.** [空] 调整片 **7.** =
tabloid **8.** = tabulator **9.** = tablet —
(tabbed; tabbing) *vt.* **1.** 在 … 上装襻(或
饰以小垂片) **2.** 给…制检索凸舌 **2.** 给…
贴标签；把…称作；认出；把…选定标出
3. 〈口〉监视

Tabasco [tə'bæskəu] *n.* **1.** 塔巴斯科辣沙
司 **2.** [t-]塔巴斯科辣沙司中所用的辣
椒

tabby ['tæbi] *n.* **1.** [纺] 平纹；平纹织物；波
纹绸 **2.** [动] 斑猫；家猫(尤指雌猫)；斑
蛾(亦作~ moth) **3.** 老处女 **4.** [建] 沙土碎石混合料 —
vt. 对(丝绸等)作波纹轧光处理 —
adj. **1.** 平纹组织的 **2.** 有斑纹的

tabernacle ['tæbənækl] *n.* **1.** (临时)住所；
棚舍；帐篷；(灵魂寄居的)肉体，躯
体 **2.** [T-]帐幕,会幕(古代犹太人的移
动式圣堂)；犹太会堂 **3.** 礼拜堂,教堂
4. (天主教堂的)神龛;壁龛 **5.** (基督教
神坛上的)圣体盒 — *vi.* **1.** 居于临时住
所 **2.** 暂居;(灵魂)暂附肉体 — *vt.* 使
居住于临时住所;置…于神龛中 ‖
tabernacular[ˌtæbə'nækjulə] *adj.*

table ['teibl] *n.* **1.** 桌子,台子 **2.** 餐桌;会
议桌;[常~s]赌桌,牌桌;[只用单]伙
食,饭菜；一桌酒菜;一桌人(指进餐者、
玩牌者等) **3.** 工作台;手术台 **4.** 木圃;
石碑;金属牌;(碑等上的)铭文,碑文
5. [建]上楣(柱);飞檐;镶板;束带层 **6.**
表,表格 **7.** [地] 台地,高地;平地层 **8.**
(头颅的)骨板;手掌心(尤指看手相的
部分) **9.** (宝石顶部的)切割平面,台的
平面的宝石 — *vt.* **1.** 把…放在桌上 **2.** 搁
置,暂缓审议(议案等) **3.** 〈英〉把…列入
议事日程;把…提交讨论 **4.** 使…结帐;伙
食 **5.** 用宽贴边加固(帆) **6.** 把…列表,
把…制成表格 ‖ **~-cloth** *n.* 桌布,台布
/ **~-land** *n.* [地] 台地,高地 / **~ money**
1. (发给高级军官等的)招待津贴 **2.**
(向俱乐部成员收的)餐厅使用费 / **~-
spoon** *n.* 大汤匙;一大汤匙容量 / **~-
spoonful** *n.* 一大汤匙容量 / **~ tennis**
乒乓球 / **~-top** *n.* **1.** 桌面 **2.** (布置在
桌上供拍摄以放大大的)台上模型 /
~-ware *n.* [总称]餐具

tableau　951　**tackle**

tableau ['tæbləu] (['复] tableaus 或 tableaux ['tæbləuz]) n.1.(生动的)画面;场面 2.形象化的描述,生动的描写 3.类乎静止造型的场面 4.活人造型(由活人扮演的静态画面,场面或历史场景,尤指舞台造型)(亦作~ vivant ['vi:vɑː])‖～ curtain (从中间向上方两角掀起的舞台)蝴蝶幕

table d'hôte ['tɑːbl 'dəut](法)(旅馆或饭店定时、定菜、定价的)客饭,公司餐;和菜

tablet ['tæblit] n.1.〈古〉刻写板,简(木、石等制成的平板,供刻写文字用) 2.(刻铭文的)牌匾 3.便笺簿;拍纸簿;报告纸薄 4.小块;小片 5.药片 ‖～-arm chair,～ chair(课堂用)(右边有阔扶手的)书写椅

tabling ['teibliŋ] n.1.【建】飞檐;束带层 2.列表,制表 3.(加固的)宽贴边

tabloid ['tæbloid] n.1.(以浓缩形式并配插图刊出耸人听闻内容的)通俗小报 2.浓缩的东西;文摘;摘要 3.(主要用于商标)药片,片剂 — adj.1.浓缩的,摘要的 2.通俗小报(似)的;通俗小报式耸人听闻的

taboo [tə'buː] n.1.(宗教迷信或社会习俗方面的)禁忌;忌讳;戒忌 2.禁忌的事物(或行为)3.【语】禁语 4.禁忌信奉,守戒 — adj.禁忌的;忌讳的;禁忌的 — vt.把…列为禁忌;忌讳;禁止

tabor ['teibə] n.单面小鼓

tabu [tə'buː] n. adj. & vt. = taboo

tabular ['tæbjulə] adj.1.表格的,列成表的;按表格计算的 2.平坦的;平板(状)的;薄片的,片状的

tabulate ['tæbjuleit] vt.1.把…制成表;列表显示 2.使成平面 — adj.1.板状的;平面的 2.薄片构成的 ‖ tabu'lation n.

tabulator ['tæbjuleitə] n.1.制表人,列表

人 2.制表机 3.(打字机为制表用的)跳格键

tachometer [tæ'kɔmitə] n.转速表;流速计

tachycardia [ˌtæki'kɑːdiə] n.【医】心动过速

tacit ['tæsit] adj.1.缄默的 2.心照不宣的,不言而喻的 3.【律】(由当事人行为)默示的,默契的;由于法律的执行而产生的

taciturn ['tæsitəːn] adj.沉默寡言的;一本正经的

tack [tæk] n.1.平头钉,大头钉;〈美〉图钉 2.[～s](为定形临时缝上的)粗缝针脚;假缝 3.【船】系帆索;系住的帆角;纵帆的前端 4.【海】(帆船的)抢风调向;(之字形的)抢风航行;(之字形航程中的)一段直线航行;(抢风航行中的)轮换点(陆上的)之字形移动;之字形道路 5.行动步骤;方针 7.〈英〉(外加于提案之后的)附带条款 8.粘着力,粘着性;食品:hard～.硬饼干,压缩饼干/soft～ 食品:精美食品 — vt.1.用平头钉钉;用粗针脚缝 2.增补;附加 3.使(船)抢风航行 — vi.1.抢风航行 2.之字形地移动 3.突然改变行动步骤(或方针、政策)‖～er n.1.撤平头钉的人 2.用粗针脚缝的人 3.〈英〉试图采用附带条款的办法使议案通过的人 ‖～ hammer 钉锤

tackle ['tækl] n.1.辘轳,滑车(组);(船的)索具,用具;装备 3.马具;钓具 4.(橄榄球赛中)阻截铲球;阻截队员 5.抓获;扭抱揪夺 6.食物 — vt.1.(用索具等)固定,系住 2.抱住,揪住;(橄榄球赛中)阻截(对方队员) 3.向…交涉 4.着手处理,对付 5.开始吃 — vi.(橄榄球赛中)抱住并摔倒对方持球球员;(足

球赛中)阻截

tacky[ˈtæki] *adj.* 有黏着力的;发黏的

tacky[ˈtæki] *adj.*〈美口〉破烂的;褴褛的

tact[tækt] *n.* 1. 触觉 2. 老练;机智;圆滑;外交手腕

tactful[ˈtæktful] *adj.* 老练的;机智的;圆滑的 ‖ **~ly** *adv.*

tactic[ˈtæktik] *adj.* 1. 顺序的;排列的;(指聚合物)有规立构的 2.【生】(有)趋性的 3. 战术的 — *n.* (一个)战术;(一个)策略

tactical[ˈtæktikəl] *adj.* 1. 战术的;作战的 2. 有策略的;手段高明的;方式方法上的 ‖ **~ly** *adv.*

tactician[tækˈtiʃən] *n.* 1. 战术家 2. 有策略的人,手段高明的人;谋划家

tactics[ˈtæktiks] [复] *n.* 1. [用作单]战术(行动) 2. [常用作复]策略,手法 3. [用作单或复]【语】语言成分结构学,词素排列学

tactile[ˈtæktail] *adj.* 1. (有)触觉的;能触知的 2. 能给人以浑厚坚实质感的 ‖ **tactility**[tækˈtiləti] *n.*

tactless[ˈtæktlis] *adj.* 不老练的;不机智的;不圆滑的 ‖ **~ly** *adv.* / **~ness** *n.*

tadpole[ˈtædpəul] *n.* 1.〈口〉蝌蚪 2.〈美俚〉法国仔 3.〈美俚〉[T-]密西西比蝌蚪(密西西比州人的别称)

Tadzhikistan[tɑːˈdʒikistɑːn] *n.* 塔吉克斯坦[亚洲中部国家]

tael[teil] *n.* 1. 两(中国及亚洲东部一些国家的衡量单位) 2. 银两(中国从前的货币单位)

taenia[ˈtiːniə] [复] **taeniae**[ˈtiːniiː] 或 **taenias**) *n.* 1. (古希腊、罗马的)头带,束发带 2.【解】带,软组织带 3.【建】束带饰 4.【动】绦虫

taffeta[ˈtæfitə], **taffety**[ˈtæfiti] *n.*〈纺〉塔夫绸

taffy[ˈtæfi] *n.* 1.〈美〉太妃糖,乳脂糖(=〈英〉toffee, toffy) 2.〈口〉谄媚;哄骗

tag[tæg] *n.* 1. (破衣裙等上)悬着的碎片;松散(或破碎)的末尾(羊身上)一簇蓬乱的羊毛 2. (鞋带末端的)金属包头;(动物的)尾尖 3. (服装上的)挂襻;小坠饰;(鞋口后部的)拉襻 4. (戏剧、演说等的)终场词,结束语;(歌曲)末尾叠句 5. 陈词滥调;口头禅 6. (为修辞目的或炫耀词藻而引用的)摘引的警句 7. 附加物;附加疑问句套语 8. 称号;浑名 9. 标签 10. 支离破碎的东西;乱头发 11. (儿童)提人游戏 —(tagged; tagging) *vt.* 1. 装包头于(鞋带,绳等);加(价格)标签于;在(车辆)上贴违章传票 2. 给…起浑名;把…称为 3. 给(戏剧、文学作品等)加上终场词(或结束语) 4. 连接,使合并(together);把(一篇文章)加入(另一篇文章)(to, on to) 5. 叠(诗句)押韵;串(韵脚) 6. 剪下(蓬乱的羊毛) 7. (儿童捉人游戏中)追到,捉到 8. 指责,指控 9.〈口〉紧紧地跟在…后面,尾随 10.[核](用示踪同位素)标记 — *vi.* 1.〈口〉紧紧地跟在后面(along, after, behind) ‖ **~ line** 1. (戏剧的)终场词 2. (团体等的)口头禅(广告中的)主题句 / **~ rag** *n.* 乌合之众/碎片;破布条

Tahiti[tɑːˈhiti] *n.* 塔希提岛[南太平洋]

tail[teil] *n.* 1. (动物的)尾巴;尾状物;发辫;(*g, y* 等字母)伸出在格子线下面的部分 2. 末尾部分;后部;底部;下部;尾部;〈俚〉屁股 3.【天】彗尾;流星尾 4.〈俚〉随员,扈从 5. 盯梢的人(或车);在逃人(或动物)的踪迹 6.〈口〉[~s]燕尾服;男子夜礼服 7.〈史〉(土耳其高级官员表示品位的)马尾旌 8.[

~s]钱币背面 **9.**【印】地脚 **10.**(屋瓦的)叠余外露部分 **;**墙砖的砌入部分 **11.**结尾：结尾诗句 **12.**【音】符尾 →**vt. 1.** 为…装尾 **2.** 截短…的尾巴；摘除(莓果等)的鲜扶柄裙 **3.** 排在(行列等)后面；位于…的(末端)后面 **4.** 使(一物)与另一物的一端相连(*on to*)；使衔接 **5.**【建】把(木材、砖石)的一端嵌进；使架住；使搭牢(*in, on*) **6.** 尾随；跟踪，监视 →**vi. 1.** 为尾巴；成为尾巴；呈一列行进 **2.** 〈口〉尾随；跟踪：道随(*after, behind*) **3.** (木材、砖石)以一端嵌入而固定：搭上 **4.** 船尾搁浅(*aground*) **;** (停泊中的船)船尾指向 →**adj. 1.** 尾部的，后部的 **2.** 后面来的：a ~ wind 顺风 ‖~.**board** *n.* (手推车等的)后挡板，后挡板 /'~**coat** *n.* 燕尾服 /'~**light** *n.* (车辆的)尾灯，后灯 /'~**piece** *n.* **1.** 尾部附加物；【机】端件 **2.**【建】梁尾端 **3.** (提琴等的)系弦板 **4.**(望远镜目镜的)补白花饰 **5.**(望远镜目镜的)调节装置 /'~**spin** *n.* **1.**【空】(飞机)尾旋，尾螺旋 **2.** 失控；混乱；慌乱

tailgate ['teilgeit] *n.* **1.**(车辆后部可移动的)后挡板，后挡板 **2.**(运河闸门的)下闸门 **3.**(爵士音乐以多用滑音为特征的)长号吹奏风格→ *vt. & vi.* (使)紧随前面车辆行驶

tailism ['teilizəm] *n.* 尾巴主义

tailor ['teilə] *n.* (尤指做外衣的)裁缝，成衣 **;** 成衣商 → *vi.* 做裁缝 → *vt.* **1.** 裁制(衣服) **2.** 为(某人)做衣服 **3.** 按装式样做制(女服) **4.** 针对特定目的(或对象)作修改；使适应特定需要；使适应 ‖~**ing** *n.* **1.** 成衣行业 **2.** 裁缝业；缝纫 **3.**〈喻〉裁剪；(针对特定目的或对象所作的)修改

taint [teint] *vt.* **1.** 污染；使腐坏 **2.** 败坏 **;** 玷污 → *vi.* 被污染；腐坏；败坏 →

n. **1.** 污点；腐败(现象) **2.** 污染(处)；腐坏(部分)

taipan ['taipæn] 〈汉〉*n.* 大班(旧时中国的洋行经理)

Taiwan ['tai'wɑːn] *n.* 台湾(省) **;** 台湾岛 ‖ **Taiwa'nese** *adj. & n.*

Tajikistan [tə'dʒikistɑːn] *n.* = Tadzhikistan

take [teik] (took [tuk], taken ['teikən]) *vt.* **1.** 拿，取；攻取 **2.** 抓，捕；叨引 **3.** 拿走，取走；夺去(生命)；赢(牌)；吃掉(棋子) **4.** 带去；带领 **5.** 取得；获得，得到 **;** ~ cold 感冒 /~ a day off 请一天假 /~ one's leave 告辞 **6.** (疾病、不愉快的事情等)突然侵袭 **7.** 就(座、职等)；乘 **;** Take a seat, please. 请坐。 /~ office 就职 /~ the chair 任会议主席；主持开会 /~ the floor (在会上)起来发言 /~ harbour 进入港湾 **8.** 接收(房客等)；娶(妻)；承担；忍受 **9.** 买下；租下；订阅(报刊等)；定(座等) **10.** 吃；喝；服(药等)；吸入(新鲜空气等) **11.** 选取；采取 **;** ~ the socialist road 走社会主义道路 **12.** 利用，采用。Don't rush. Take your time. 别忙，慢慢来好了。 **13.** 记录；摘录；量取(体温、尺寸等)；拍摄(照相等)。画下：~ notes 记笔记 /~ a letter 记录口授函件 **14.** 乘，搭(车、船等) **15.** 需要；花费；占用 **;** The work took us a week to finish. 我们花了一个星期完成这项工作。 / It ~s many men to build a house. 建造一幢房屋需要很多人。/The box does not ~ (up) much room. 这箱子占的地方不多。 **16.** 理解，领会 **17.** 以为；把…看作；对待 **18.** 生，产生 **19.** 使接受；让…进 **20.** 越过(障碍) **21.** 打，击 **;** ~ sb. on the nose 朝某人鼻子打一拳 /~ sb. a smart box on the ear 打某人一记响亮的耳光 **22.** 以…为例(= ~ for example) **23.** [表示做

一次动作）:~ a bath 洗个澡/ ~ a look 看一看/ ~ a rest 休息一下/ ~ no notice 不注意 ~ vi.1.得,拿,取;依法获得财产 2.(鱼等)被捕捉: Fish ~ best after rain.雨后最易捕鱼。3.(齿轮等)啮合;(植物等)生根;开始生长 4.(计划、接种等)奏效;起作用/(染料等)被吸收: The smallpox vaccination took.牛痘发了。/ Dry fuel ~s readily. 干燥的燃料极易点着。5.(作品、产品等)受人欢迎: The novel didn't ~. 那小说不受欢迎。6.拍起照来: He does not ~ well. 他不上照。7.走,行走: ~ across a field (over a hill) 越过田野(小山) 8.[~ and ...]〈方〉[用以加强后随动词语气]: He took and grabbed his hat and ran. 他拿起帽子就跑。9.变得,成为: ~ ill (或 sick) 生病/ ~ pretty surly 变得十分乖戾 ~ n.1.得,拿,取 2.捕获量;收入: a large ~ of fish 捕到的很多鱼/ the yearly ~ from tourism 旅游事业的岁入/ pull in a ~ 获得一笔收入 3.奏效的东西(如受到喜爱的戏剧、歌曲等) 4.(植皮)愈合[种牛痘]发疮 5.反应 6.一次拍摄的电影(或电视)镜头 7.录音;一次版(或排版)或印刷的数量 ‖ ~ r n.1.取者 2.捕者 3.接受者 4.收取者: a ticket ~ r 收票员 ‖ ~-down n.1.拆卸 2.〈口〉失面子,羞辱 3.〈口〉抢白 ~ off adj.可拆卸的/ ~-home pay (扣除捐税等以后)实得的工资/ ~-'in n.〈口〉欺骗;骗子/ ~-off n.1.起跳(点);出发点 2.〈口〉(嘲弄性的)学样 3.拿走 4.(所需材料等的)估计 5.功率输出装置/ ~-out n.1.(桥牌赛中)叫牌 2.(准备)取出的东西;取出 3.〈主美〉外卖餐馆 adj.1.可取出的 2.(食物)供外卖的;(餐馆)供应外卖食品的/ ~-over n.接收;接管;接任/ ~-up n.1.

收缩;调整;吸水 2.【机】(缝纫机上提线上升的)提升装置 3.[俗]接收 4.[摄]卷片装置 5.(磁带的)收带盘

taken ['teikən] take 的过去分词

taking ['teikiŋ] n.1.拿;取得,获得;捕获物 2.[~s]收入 3.〈口〉激动,不安;困境 ~ adj.1.引人注目的,吸引人的,迷人的 2.传染性的

talc [tælk] n.1.滑石(研光用的)云母—(talc(k)ed; talc(k)ing) vt.用滑石处理

talcum ['tælkəm] n.【矿】滑石;滑石粉;爽身粉

tale [teil] n.1.故事;传说;叙述 2.坏话;流言蜚语 3.〈古〉计算;总数 ‖ ~bearer n.搬弄是非的人 / ~bearing n.搬弄是非 / ~teller n.1.讲故事的人 2.(背后)讲人坏话的人;搬弄是非者

talent ['tælənt] n.1.天才;天资 2.才能,才干 3.有才能的人(们);人才 4.〈俚〉[总称](赛马等的)赌客 5.塔兰特(古代希腊或罗马、中东等地的重量或货币单位) ‖ hide one's ~s in a napkin 埋没自己的才能 ‖ ~ed adj. 天资高的;有才能的

talisman ['tælizmən]([复]talismans) n.1.护(身)符 2.驱邪物(如小装饰物、戒指等)3.能产生奇异效果的东西,法宝

talk [tɔːk] vi.1.讲话;谈话;交谈;商谈,商讨 2.(用信号等)通讯,通话 3.(会)说话;有讲话能力 4.闲谈;说闲话;讲人坏话;揭人隐私;传播小道消息 ~ vt.1.讲,说 2.用(某种语言、方言等)谈论;谈论;讨论 ~ n.1.谈话;交谈 2.(正式)会谈;会议 3.~ show〈广播,电视〉的访谈节目(通常由知名人士进行讨论或回答问题)

talkathon ['tɔːkəθɒn] n.(无休止的)马拉松式讨论(或辩论)(尤指为阻挠议会

作出决定而作的)马拉松式冗长演说;(候选人通过广播或电视进行的)马拉松式竞选答问访谈;(电台或电视台的)马拉松式访谈节目

talkative ['tɔːkətɪv] *adj.* 喜欢讲话的;健谈的;多嘴的 ‖ ~ **ly** *adv.* / ~ **ness** *n.*

talker ['tɔːkə] *n.* 1. 谈话者,讲话者 2. 多嘴的人,饶舌者 3. 空谈家 4.(船桅上的)电话传令人员 5.〈俚〉有声电影

talkie ['tɔːki] *n.*〈口〉有声电影

talking ['tɔːkɪŋ] *n.* 讲话;谈话;讨论 — *adj.* 1. 讲话的;有讲话能力的 2. 喜欢讲话的;多嘴的 3. 富于表情的 ‖ ~ **head**(出现在电视屏幕上的)发言者特写头像 / ~ **machine** 留声机,唱机 / ~ **to** *n.*〈口〉责备,斥责

talky ['tɔːki] *adj.* 1. = talkative 2. 谈话(或对话)过多的:a ~ novel 对话过多的小说 ‖ **talkiness** *n.*

tall [tɔːl] *adj.* 1. 身材高的,高的 2.〈口〉夸大的;过分的;难以相信的;夸口的 3.〈口〉巨大的;大量的 — *adv.*〈口〉夸大地;趾高气扬地

Tallinn ['tælin] *n.* 塔林[沙乌尼亚首都]

tallow ['tæləu] *n.* 1.(做皂、烛等用的)动物油脂,脂,油脂 — *vt.* 涂油脂于 ‖ ~ **faced** *adj.* 脸色苍白的;脸色发黄的

tally ['tæli] *n.* 1. 符木①计刻痕计数的木签,分作两半,借贷双方各执一半为凭;计数单位,(货物的)(一)捆,(一)扎2. 账;计算;(比赛时的)比分;得分;分 4. 记号牌;记账单;计数器;计分卡 5. 识别标签,标志牌 6.(供两相吻合的)对等物,验合用的凭证 7. 符合分,相合 8.【海】理货;点数 — *vt.* 1. 计算,数,清点(货物等) 2. 记录;记(分) 3. 加标签(或标记)于 4. 使(两物)符合,使吻合 — *vi.* 1. 符合,吻合 2. 记数;记分 ‖ ~ **man** *n.* 1.(英)赊销

推销员;赊销小店店主 2. 计分员;计票员,计分人员 3.(码头上的)理货员 / ~ **shop** 赊销商店 / ~ **system**, ~ **trade** 赊销

tallyho ['tæli'həu] *n.* 1. 吓嗬叫声(猎人发现狐狸时嗾使猎狗追逐所发出的喊声) 2. 四马车 3. 追捕叫喊声 — *int.* 吓嗬! — *vi.* 发出"吓嗬"声 — *vt.* 用"吓嗬"声驱策(猎狗)

Talmud ['tælmud, 'tɑːlmud] *n.*(犹太教的)《塔木德经》‖ **Tal'mudic** *adj.*

talon ['tælən] *n.* 1.[常~s](尤指猛禽的)爪 2.(如爪股的)手指;手;魔爪 3. 爪状物;(锁头的)(牌戏中)发剩的牌 5. 剑的刃根 6. 爪状部分;镶嵌肩状突出部 7.【商】股息单

tam [tæm] *n.*(苏格兰人戴的)宽顶无檐圆帽,苏格兰便帽

tamale [tə'mɑːli] *n.*(用玉米壳裹的)玉米粉蒸肉(一种墨西哥食品)

tamarack ['tæmæræk] *n.* 1.【植】美洲落叶松 2. 美洲落叶松木材

tamarind ['tæmərind] *n.*【植】罗望子 2. 罗望子果 ‖ ~ **-fish** *n.* 罗望子果酸鱼酱

tambour ['tæmbuə] *n.* 1. 鼓 2.(刺绣用)绷圈,圆绷;绷圈刺绣品 3.【建】鼓形柱身段;(建筑物的)圆形坐圈 — *vt.* 在绷圈上绣 — *vi.* 用绷圈刺绣

tambourine [,tæmbə'riːn] *n.* 1.(鼓框周围装有金属片的)铃鼓,小手鼓 2.【动】白胸森鸠

tame [teim] *adj.* 1.(动物)驯化的,驯养的;服驯驯的;不危险的,安全无害的 2.(土地)被开垦的;(植物)经栽培的 3. 顺从的,听话的 4. 没精打彩的,乏味的;平淡的;沉闷的 — *vt.* 1. 驯服,制服 2. 使软化 3. 使变得平淡 — *vi.* 变得驯服 ‖ **tamable**, ~ **able** *adj.* / ~ **less** *adj.* 难驯服的;未经驯服的 / ~ **ly** *adv.* / ~ **-**

ness *n.* /～**r** *n.* 驯养人;驯服…的人(或物) ‖～ **cat** 1. 家猫 2. 豢养的食客;依为人摆布的人;任愿受人摆布的人

Tamil [ˈtæmil] *n.* (南亚)泰米尔人;泰米尔语

tam-o'-shanter [ˌtæməˈʃæntə] *n.* 宽顶无檐圆帽,苏格兰便帽

tamp [tæmp] *vt.* 1.(火药装毕后用泥、砂等)封(炮眼) 2. 夯坚,夯实;捣实 — *n.* 捣棒;夯;夯具

tamper[ˈtæmpə] *n.*1. 捣棒;打夯机;捣固器 2. 填塞者;夯工;捣实者 3.(核弹中的)屏

tamper[ˈtæmpə] *vi.*1. 篡改;经篡改损害(*with*) 2. 用不正当手段影响;收买,行贿 3. 拨弄;胡乱摆弄(*with*) — *vt.* 篡改

tan[tæn] *n.*1. 鞣料树皮(含有鞣酸的树皮,如橡树等);鞣料;(铺路用的)鞣酸皮废之 2. 棕黄色 3.[～s]棕黄色的皮鞋(或其他穿着用品) 4. 晒成棕褐色的肤色;棕褐色 5.[the ～]马戏团;骑术学校的场地 — *adj.* 棕黄色的;黄褐色的 2. 鞣革的 —(tanned; tanning) *vt.* 鞣(革);硝(皮);用鞣料将(兽皮)制成皮革 2. 把…晒黑 3. 狠狠鞭打 — *vi.* 晒成棕褐色 ‖～**yard** *n.* 制革厂

tan[数]正切(tangent)的符号

tanager [ˈtænədʒə] *n.*[动]唐纳雀

Tananarive [təˈnænəriːv] *n.* 塔那那利佛[马达加斯加首都]

tandem [ˈtændəm] *n.*1. 两匹马前后成纵列拉的双轮马车 2. 两匹马前后纵列套在马车上的马 3. 前后纵列拉的车辆;(一前一后纵列的)串联工作组 4. ＝ **bicycle** 5. ＝ ～ **airplane** — *adv.* 一前一后地;horses driven ～ 排成纵列驾驭的马 — *adj.* 一前一后排列的;串联的 ‖

～ **airplane** 串翼飞机 /～ **bicycle** 串座双人(或多人)自行车

Tang [tɑːŋ, tæŋ](汉)*n.*[史]唐(朝);the ～ Dynasty 唐朝

tang[tæŋ] *n.*(刀、锉等的)柄脚(指插入柄中的部分) — *vt.* 在(刀、锉等)上做柄脚

tang[tæŋ] *n.*1. 强烈味道;独特味道;浓烈气味 2. 特性 3. 一点迹象,蛛丝马迹 — *vt.* 使具有味道

tangent [ˈtændʒənt] *n.*1.[数]正切;切线 2.(铁路或道路的)直线区间 3. 突然的转向,离题 — *adj.*1.[数]正切的 2. 离题的;不相干的 ‖ **tangency** *n.*

tangential [tænˈdʒenʃəl] *adj.*1.[数]正切的;沿切线方向的 2. 离题的;不相干的 ‖～**ly** *adv.*

Tangerine [ˌtændʒəˈriːn] *adj.*(摩洛哥)丹吉尔(人)的 — *n.*1. 丹吉尔人 2.[t-]柑橘;柑橘树 3.[t-]橘红色

tangible [ˈtændʒəbl] *adj.*1. 可触知的;有实质的 2. 明确的;确实的 — *n.*[～s]有形资产 ‖ **tangi'bility** *n.*/**tangibly** *adv.*

tangle [ˈtæŋgl] *n.*1[头发、线、树枝等的]缠结;纠缠 2. 纷乱,困惑 3. 争执;纠纷 — *vt.* 使缠结;使纠缠;使混乱 — *vi.* 缠结;乱作一团;争吵,发生争论

tango [ˈtæŋgəʊ] ([复] tangos) *n.*1. 探戈舞 2. 探戈舞曲 — *vi.* 跳探戈舞

tangram [ˈtæŋgrəm] *n.*(中国的)七巧板

tank [tæŋk] *n.*1.(贮藏液体或气体的)大容器;槽;箱;罐 2. 储水池;水池;(船)水柜;油柜;油舱 3.[船]压载舱 4. 坦克 5.(尤指收押新犯人的)牢监 — *vt.*1. 把…储在槽(或箱、柜等容器)中 2. 把…放在槽(或箱、柜等容器)内处理 ‖～**er** *n.*1. 坦克手 2. 油船 3. 空中加油飞机 4. 罐车;槽车;柜车 ‖～

buster 反坦克飞机 /~ car（铁路）罐车 / '~ship n. 油船

tankard ['tæŋkəd] n. 1.（银或锡镴制的,一般连盖的单柄）大（啤）酒杯 2. 一大（啤）酒杯的容量

tanner[1] ['tænə] n. 制革工人,鞣皮工人

tanner[2] ['tænə] n.〈英俚〉（英国旧时的）6便士硬币

tannery ['tænəri] n. 制革厂,鞣皮厂

tannic ['tænik] adj.〈化〉丹宁的;鞣质的 ‖ ~ acid 丹宁酸,鞣酸

tannin ['tænin] n.〈化〉丹宁;丹宁酸,鞣酸

tansy ['tænzi] n.〈植〉1. 艾菊 2. 雅各布千里光（一种杂草,牛食后会中毒）

tantalize, tantalise ['tæntəlaiz] vt.（引起兴趣而不给予满足地）逗弄,惹弄,使干着急

tantalum ['tæntələm] n.〈化〉钽

tantamount ['tæntəmaunt] adj. 相等（于…）的,相当（于…的）(to)

tantrum ['tæntrəm] n. 发脾气

Tanzania [ˌtænzə'niə] n. 坦桑尼亚[东非国家]

Tao ['tɑːu, tau] n. 1.（道家学说中的）道 2.[常 t-]（儒家学说中的）道 ‖ ~ism n. 道家的学说;道教

tap[1] [tæp] (tapped; tapping) vt. 1.（连续）轻打,轻叩,轻拍 2. 用…轻叩 3. 蔽打出 (out) 4. 给（鞋）打掌子 5. 选择;推选 — vi. 1. 轻叩,轻蔽 2. 轻声走 3. 跳踢跳舞 — n. 1. 轻叩,轻蔽;轻声 2. 鞋掌 3. 鞋底（或鞋跟）上钉的铁皮 4.[~s][用作单][美军]熄灯号;熄灯鼓 ‖ ~-dance 踢蹋舞 / '~-dance vi. 跳踢蹋舞 / '~-off n.（篮球比赛开始时的）中圈跳球

tap[2] [tæp] n. 1. 塞子;龙头塞 2.（自来水,煤气等）龙头;阀门 3. 一次流出的液体量

4.[医]穿刺;抽液管 5.[机]螺丝攻 6.[电]分接头,抽头;分支 7.（电话线路上的）搭线窃听;搭接（电源总线、煤气或自来水总管）;搭（线）偷电 5. 在（电话或电报线）上装窃听器;搭线窃听 6.[医]放（体腔）积水;给（病人）抽积水 7. 在…的里面攻出螺纹 8.〈英俚〉向…乞讨（或索取）(for) 9. 提出;供讨论 ‖ ~ borer [机]螺孔钻 / ~ room n. 酒吧间 / '~root n.[植]直根,主根

tape [teip] n. 1. 狭带;线带 2. 卷尺;皮尺 3. 磁带;录音带;录像带;（电报）纸带;胶布;[体]终绕胶布 4.（赛跑）终点线 5. 绦虫 6.〈俚〉酒 ‖ 用带子捆扎;用狭带装订（书）;用胶布把…粘牢 2. 用尺量（或皮尺）量 3. 把…录音 ‖ ~ deck 录音带（或磁带录音机等）的走带装置 2. 磁带放送机 / ~ line n. 卷尺 / ~ measure 卷尺 / ~ recorder 磁带录音（或录像）机 / '~ recording 磁带录音（或录像）/ '~ worm n. 绦虫

taper ['teipə] n. 1.（点火用的）纸捻;点火木片,点火媒儿;细支小蜡烛 2. 微光 3.（形体、力量等的）渐减;渐弱 4. 锥形物;尖塔;方尖塔 5.（物体的）一头逐渐变得尖细 — vt. & vi.（使）逐渐变细;（使）逐渐减少 — adj. 1. 一头逐渐变细的;锥形的 2. 分级的

tapestry ['tæpistri] n. 1. 花毯;挂毯 2. 提花装饰用毯 3. 绒绣;织锦 — vt. 1. 用花毯（或挂毯）装饰 2. 把（图案等）编织进花毯里 ‖ ~ satin 织锦缎

tapioca [ˌtæpi'əukə] n.（食用）木薯淀粉

tapir ['teipə] n.[动]貘

taproot ['tæpruːt] n.[植]直根,主根 2.

根本,根源

tapster ['tæpstə] *n.* 酒吧间招待员

tar¹ [tɑ:] *n.* 焦油;柏油;煤焦油沥青 — (tarred; tarring) *vt.* 涂(或浇)焦油(或柏油)于;玷污,污辱 — *adj.* 焦油(或柏油)的 2. 涂有焦油(或柏油)的 ‖ '~ mac *n.* 〈主英〉= ~ macadam /, ~· ma'cadam *n.* 1. 柏油碎石 2. 柏油碎石路面

tar² [tɑ:] *n.* 〈口〉水手;海员

taradiddle ['tærədidl] *n.* 1. 无关紧要的谎话,小谎 2. 废话;大话

tarantella [,tærən'telə] *n.* (意大利南部民间的)塔兰台拉舞(曲)

tarantula [tə'ræntjulə] ([复] tarantulas 或 tarantulae [tə'ræntjuli:]) *n.* 【动】1. 鸟蛛 2. 狼蛛

tardily ['tɑ:dili] *adv.* 1. 缓慢地 2. 迟 3. 不情愿地;拖拉地

tardiness ['tɑ:dinis] *n.* 1. 缓慢 2. 迟 3. 不情愿;拖拉

tardy ['tɑ:di] *adj.* 1. 慢的,行动缓慢的 2. 迟的,迟到的 3. 勉强的,不情愿的;拖拉的

tare¹ [tɛə] *n.* 1. 【植】巢菜,救荒野豌豆;巢菜种子 2. [~s](基督教《圣经》中用语)稗子 3. [~s]不良成分;祸害

tare² [tɛə] *n.* 1. 皮重,包装重量,容器重量 2. 皮重的扣除 3. 车身自重,空重 4. 【化】(平衡容器用的)配衡体

target ['tɑ:git] *n.* 1. 靶,标的 2. 目标;(批评或嘲笑等的)对象 3. 指标 4.(测量用的)觇标,觇板 5.【铁】(道岔上的)信号圆牌,圆板信号机 6.【物】X 射线靶;对阴极;靶极 7. 小羊颈脑肉 8.〈古〉小圆盾 — *vt.* 1. 把…作为目标(或对象) 2. 为…订指标 ‖ ~ language (译本的)目标语,译入语

tariff ['tærif] *n.* 1. 关税表;税率;关税;税则; a preferential ~ 特惠关税(率)/a retaliatory ~ 报复关税(率) 2.(旅馆或公用事业的)收费表,价目表 — *vt.* 1. 对…征收关税;为…定税率 2. 为…定收费标准 ‖ ~ wall 关税壁垒

tarn [tɑ:n] *n.* 山中小湖;【地】冰斗湖

tarnish ['tɑ:niʃ] *vt.* 1. 使失去光泽,使变阴暗 2. 使黯然失色,玷污,败坏(名誉等) — *vi.* 1. 失去光泽,变灰暗 2. 被玷污;(威信等)降低 — *n.* 1. 晦暗,无光泽 2. 玷污;污点

taro ['tɑ:rəu] ([复] taros) *n.* 【植】芋,芋艿;芋的块茎

tarpaulin [tɑ:'pɔ:lin] *n.* 1. 柏油帆布;油布;(船上的)舱盖布 2.(海员用的)油布帽;油布衣 3.〈古〉水手

tarpon ['tɑ:pɔn] ([复] tarpon(s)) *n.* 【动】大海鲢

tarragon ['tærəgən] *n.* 1.【植】龙蒿 2.(调味用的)龙蒿叶

tarry¹ ['tæri] *vi.* 1. 逗留,停留;住(at, in) 2. 等候(for) 3. 耽搁,迟延 — *vt.* 〈古〉等候 — *n.* 逗留

tarry² ['tɑ:ri] *adj.* 柏油的;涂柏油的;被柏油弄脏的

tart¹ [tɑ:t] *adj.* 1. 酸的;辛辣的 2. 尖刻的,刻薄的

tart² [tɑ:t] *n.* 1.〈英〉果馅饼 2.〈美义〉水果蛋糕

tart³ [tɑ:t] *n.* 〈俚〉妓女;举止轻佻的女子

tartan ['tɑ:tən] *n.* 1. 格子呢(尤指苏格兰格子呢) 2. 格子织物 3. 方格花纹(图案) 4. 格子呢服装 — *adj.*(似)格子呢的

Tartar ['tɑ:tə] *n.* 1. 鞑靼人;鞑靼语 2. [常 t-]凶悍的人;凶暴的人;泼妇 3. [t-]难对付的人(或事物) — *adj.* 鞑靼的;鞑

粗鲁人的;鞑靼语的

tartar ['tɑːtə] n.1.【化】酒石,酒石酸氢钾 2.【医】牙垢,牙石 ‖ ~ic, ~ous adj. ‖ ~ emetic【医】吐酒石,酒石酸氧锑钾

Tashkent [tæʃ'kent] n. 塔什干[乌兹别克斯坦首都]

task [tɑːsk] n.1. 任务;工作;作业,功课 2. 苦差事;困难的工作— vt.1. 派给…工作 2. 使辛劳;使过于劳累;使做艰苦的工作 ‖ ~ force【美】1.【军】特遣部队;特混舰队【军】(非军事性的)特别工作组;专门调查委员会 /'~ master n. 工头,监工 /'~ work n.1. 计件工作 2. 繁重的工作

tassel ['tæsl] n.1. 流苏,穗 2. 穗状物,(植物的)穗(尤指玉蜀黍的穗状雄花) 3.【建】承梁木 — (tassel(l)ed; tassel-(l)ing) vt.1. 用流苏(或穗)装饰 2. 使成流苏状 3.〈美〉(为使苗壮生长而)摘去(玉蜀黍等)的穗状雄花 — vi.(玉蜀黍等)长出穗状雄花

taste [teist] vt.1. 尝,辨(味),(少量地)吃;喝 2. 尝出…的味道 3. 尝到;感到;体验 — vi.1. 尝起来,吃起来;辨味 2. 尝到…味觉 3. 辨味,滋味 3. 感受;体验(of) — n.1. 味觉 2. 一口;一点儿;少量 3. 爱好,兴趣 6. 趣味;鉴赏力;审美力;式样,风格

tasteful ['teistful] adj.1. 有鉴赏力的;趣味高雅的 2. 雅致的;优美的;〈罕〉美味的 ‖ ~ly adv. / ~ness n.

tasteless ['teistlis] adj.1. 不可口的,无味的;乏味的,枯燥的;不雅观的;庸俗的;不得体的 3. 无鉴赏力的,无审美力的 ‖ ~ly adv. / ~ness n.

taster ['teistə] n.1. 品味者;(职业)试味员 2. 试味用具(如品尝酒等的小杯) 3.(挖取乳酪等试味样品的)试味采样器 3.

(书店、出版社的)作品鉴定人,审阅人 4.【史】(封建王族为防下毒而设的)试食待从

tasty ['teisti] adj.1. 美味的,可口的 2.〈俗〉(服装等)雅观的;大方的 ‖ tastily adv. / tastiness n.

tat [tæt] n. 轻击 ‖ tit for ~ 针锋相对,以牙还牙

tatami [tə'tɑːmi] n.〈日〉榻榻米(日本人家里铺在地板上的草垫)

tatter ['tætə] n.1.(撕下的或悬挂着的)破布条;碎纸片;破布 2.[~s]破衣服 — vt. 扯破,撕碎;使破烂 — vi. 变得破烂 ‖ ~ed adj.(衣服等)破烂的;衣衫褴褛的

tatting ['tætiŋ] n. 梭结(法);梭结花边

tattle ['tætl] vi.1. 闲谈,聊天;饶舌 2. 谈论他人私事(或隐私);泄露他人秘密 — vi. 空话;闲谈;饶舌 — r n.1. 爱闲谈者;爱说长道短的人;爱谈论他人私事(或隐私)的人【鸟】鹬科鸟(如红脚鹬等)

tattletale ['tætlteil] n. 搬弄是非的人;泄露秘密的人;告密者

tattoo[1] [tə'tuː] n.1.【军】归营号(指号声或鼓声) 2.(作为夜间娱乐乐活动的)野外军事演习 3. 得得的连续敲击 — vt. & vi. 得得地连续敲击

tattoo[2] [tə'tuː] n.1.(皮肤上的)文身花纹;文身;刺花 — vt. 刺花纹于…;刺(花纹等)

taught [tɔːt] teach 的过去式过去分词

taunt [tɔːnt] n.1. 嘲笑;辱骂;奚落人的话 — vt.1. 嘲笑;讥刺;奚落 2. 用嘲笑来刺激

taupe [təup] n. & adj. 褐灰色(的)

taut [tɔːt] adj.1.(绳子等)拉紧的,绷紧的

2.(神经等)紧张的 3.(船等)整洁的;整齐的;秩序井然的;纪律严明的 4. 严格的;严峻的 ‖ ～ly adv. / ～ness n.

tautological [ˌtɔːtəˈlɒdʒikəl] adj. 同义反复的,赘述的

tautology [tɔːˈtɒlədʒi] n. 同义反复,赘述;冗辞【逻】重言式,套套逻辑

tavern [ˈtævən] n.1. 小酒店 2. 小旅馆

taw [tɔː] n. 石弹;石弹游戏

tawdry [ˈtɔːdri] adj. 俗丽而不值钱的 — n. 俗丽而不值钱的服饰 ‖ tawdrily adv. / tawdriness n.

tawny [ˈtɔːni] n. & adj. 黄褐色(的),茶色(的)

tax [tæks] n.1. 税;税款 2.〔只用单〕负担;压力(on, upon)3.(公会、团体等的)会费 — vt.1. 对…征税 2. 对…收会费 3. 使负重担;使受压力 4. 指责,责备;谴责 5.(美口)给(物品)定价;要(价钱)6.【律】审定(诉讼费等)‖ ～dodger 偷税人,逃税人 /～free adj. 免税的;不付税的 /～payer n. 纳税人(在美国常作为"公民"的同义词)

taxable [ˈtæksəbl] adj. 应课税的;应纳税的 ‖ taxaˈbility n.

taxation [tækˈseiʃən] n.1. 征税;课税 2. 税;税款;税收 3. 估定的税额

taxi [ˈtæksi] n. 出租汽车 —〔单数第三人称现在式 taxis 或 taxies;现在分词 taxiing 或 taxying;乘出租汽车 2.(飞机在地面或水上)滑行;(驾驶员)驾驶飞机滑行 — vt.1. 用出租汽车运送 2. 使(飞机)滑行 ‖ ～cab n. 出租汽车 /～dancer 舞女 /～man n. 出租汽车司机 /～meter n. 自动计费;装有自动计费计的出租汽车 /～plane n. 出租飞机 /～way n. (飞机出入机库的)滑行道

taxidermy [ˈtæksidəːmi] n.(动物标本)剥制术 ‖ **taxidermist** n.(动物标本)剥制师

taxonomy [tækˈsɒnəmi] n.1. 分类学 2. 分类系统(生物分类学) ‖ **taxonomist** n. 分类学家

TB abbr.1. torpedo boat 鱼雷快艇 2. tubercle bacillus 结核菌 3. tuberculosis

Tb 【化】元素铽(terbium)的符号

Tbilisi [təˈbiːlisi] n. 第比利斯[格鲁吉亚首都]

Tc 【化】元素锝(technetium)的符号

TCBM abbr. transcontinental ballistic missile 洲际弹道导弹

Te 【化】元素碲(tellurium)的符号

tea [tiː] n.1. 茶树 2. 茶叶 3. 茶;饮料 4. 茶点;茶(美国)大麻(叶)5. 大麻烟 — vt. 给…泡茶;给茶招待 — vi. 喝茶;吃茶点 ‖ ～bag 袋泡茶 /～ball 1. 滤茶球(泡茶时用,金属制,上有小孔,内装茶叶)2. = ～ bag /～break(英)喝茶休息时间 /～caddy 茶叶盒;茶叶罐 /～ceremony 茶道 /~cup n. 茶杯 /~dance(傍晚)茶舞会 /~kettle n. (煮茶用的)茶壶 /～party 茶会 茶话会 /~pot n. 茶壶 /～room n. 茶室 /～service, ～set (一套)茶具 /～spoon 茶匙;一茶匙容量 /~spoonful 一茶匙容量 /~time n. 喝茶时间(一般在下午5时左右)/~urn n.(煮或泡大量茶水的)茶桶,茶炊

teach [tiːtʃ](taught [tɔːt]) vt.1. 教,讲授 2. 教导,教育 3.〔口〕训诫;告诫 — 不要(做某事)— vi.1. 教书;讲课;当教师 2. 可以教,可以讲解;教起来 ‖ ～-in n.(美)(大学师生对政府政策,尤其是外交政策,进行讨论和辩论的)宣讲会

teachable [ˈtiːtʃəbl] adj.1. 可教的;顺从的;愿学的;善学的 2. 适合教学的;便于讲授的 ‖ teachaˈbility n.

teacher [ˈtiːtʃə] *n*.1. 教员，教师，老师，先生 2. 导师

teaching [ˈtiːtʃiŋ] *n*.1. 教学；讲授；教学工作 2.[常～s]教导；学说，主义 3.[常～s]【宗】教义 — *adj*. 教学的；教导的

teak [tiːk] *n*.1.【植】柚木 2. 柚木木材

teal [tiːl]([复]teal(s)) *n*.【动】短颈野鸭

team [tiːm] *n*.1. 队；组 2. 一窝小动物(尤指小鸭或小猪)；一组配对的供展览的动物 3.(一起拉车或拉犁的)一组马(或牛)，联畜；马(或牛)及其所拉的车(或犁)；兽拉的车(或犁) — *adj*. 队的；组的；由一队人从事的 — *vt*.1. 把(牛、马等)连在一个车上 2. 用联畜拖运 3. 把(工作)包给承包人 — *vi*.1. 驾驭联畜大车；驾驶卡车 2. 结成一队；协作，合作(*up*) ‖ ˈ～**mate** *n*. 同队队员，队友/ˈ～**work** *n*. 协力，配合

teamster [ˈtiːmstə] *n*.1. 联畜运输车驾驭者 2. 卡车司机

tear[1] [tiə] *n*.1.[常～s]眼泪，泪珠 2. 泪状物；滴，露；〈美俚〉珍珠 — *vi*. 流泪；含泪 ‖ ～**bomb** 催泪弹(亦作 ～ gas bomb)/ˈ～**drop** *n*.1. 泪珠 2. 泪状物；(耳环或项圈上的)宝石坠子 /～ **gas** 催泪性毒气，催泪瓦斯 /ˈ～**gas** *vt*. 向…放催泪瓦斯，用催泪性毒气袭击(或驱散)/ˈ～**jerker** *n*.〈俚〉使人流泪的歌曲(或故事、戏剧、电影等)/～ **shell** 催泪弹

tear[2] [tɛə](tore[tɔː], torn[tɔːn]) *vt*.1. 撕开，撕裂 2. 扯破；戳破；划破 3. 拉掉；拔掉；撕掉 4.[常用被动语态]使分裂；(疑虑等)使精神不安；使激动；折磨 — *vi*.1. 撕，扯(*at*) 2. 被撕裂；被扯破 3. 飞跑，狂奔；猛闯 — *n*.1. 撕，扯 2. 裂缝；扯破的洞；撕裂处 3. 激怒；发作 4.〈美俚〉狂饮大闹；狂欢 5. 飞奔；猛闯；匆忙

tearful [ˈtiəful] *adj*.1. 流泪的；含泪的，眼泪汪汪的 2. 使人流泪的，悲哀的

tearing [ˈtɛəriŋ] *adj*.1. 撕的，扯的 2. 猛闯的；猛烈的，激烈的 3. 极其痛苦的；令人难受的 4.〈主英〉了不起的

tease [tiːz] *vt*.1. 取笑；戏弄，逗弄 2. 强求；哄 3. 梳理(羊毛、亚麻等)；使(布等)的表面起毛；使起绒 — *n*.1. 戏弄，逗弄 2. 爱戏弄别人的人 ‖ ～**r** *n*.1. 拉毛机，起绒机 2. 爱戏弄别人的人 3.〈口〉难题；难处理的事情

teasel [ˈtiːzl] *n*.1.【植】川续断；起绒草 2.【纺】起绒刺果；起绒机 —(teasel(l)ed; teasel(l)ing) *vt*. 使(织物)起绒；给…(织物)拉毛

teat [tiːt] *n*.1.(人或动物的)乳头 2.〈英〉(奶瓶上的)橡皮奶头 3.(机械部件上的)突部，凸缘

teazel [ˈtiːzl] *n*. & (teazel(l)ed; teazel(l)ing) *vt*. = teasel

teazle [ˈtiːzl] *n*. & *vt*. = teasel

technetium [tekˈniːʃiəm] *n*.【化】锝

technic [ˈteknik] *n*.1. 技巧；技能 2.[～s][用作单或复]工艺学 — *adj*. = technical

technical [ˈteknikəl] *adj*.1. 技术的；工艺的；技能的；专门性的 2. 严格根据法律(或规则)的；严格按字面解释的；技术性的 3.(化工产品)按一般工序生产而未经特殊纯化的，工业的：～ sulphuric acid 工业硫酸 ‖ ～**ly** *adv*.

technicality [ˌtekniˈkæləti] *n*.1. 技术性；专门性 2. 技术细节；专门性事项 3. 术语，专门名称

technician [tekˈniʃən] *n*.1. 技术员；技师 2.(艺术等方面)技巧熟练的人

technicolor [ˈtekniˌkʌlə] *n*.1.[T-]彩色印片法 2. 鲜艳的色彩

technique [tekˈniːk] *n*.1. 工艺；技术；技巧；技能 2. 方法，手段

technocracy [tek'nɔkræsi] *n.* 技术专家政治,技术专家治国(由科学技术专家或按照科学技术专家提出的原则实行的统治)

technologic(al) [,teknə'lɔdʒik(əl)] *adj.* 1. 技术(学)的,工艺(学)的 2. 由于技术性原因的;因技术革新而引起的

technology [tek'nɔlədʒi] *n.* 1. 技术(学),工艺(学);工业技术 2. [总称]术语,专门用语 ‖ **technologist** *n.* 工艺师;技术专家;〈美〉技术员,技师

technopolis [tek'nɔpəlis] *n.* 技术社会 ‖ **technopolitan** [,teknə'pɔlitən] *adj.*

technostructure ['teknəu,strʌktʃə] *n.* 技术结构(指由工程师、科学家等技术专家控制公司、集团等的经济)

techy ['tetʃi] *adj.* = tetchy

ted [ted] (**tedded; tedding**) *vt.* 翻晒;摊开晒(刚割下的草等)

teddy ['tedi] *n.* = teddy bear ‖ ~ **bear** 玩具熊

Te Deum [,ti:'di:əm, ,tei'deium] 〈拉〉(基督教的)感恩赞(乐曲)

tedious ['ti:djəs] *adj.* 冗长乏味的;使人厌烦的;沉闷的 ‖ ~**ly** *adv.* / ~**ness** *n.*

tedium ['ti:djəm] *n.* 冗长乏味;沉闷;单调

tee[1] [ti:] *n.* 1.(英语字母)T,t 2. T字形物(尤指 T 形管) — *adj.* 似 T 字形的 ‖ *to a* ~ 恰恰好地;丝毫不差地(= to a T) ‖ ~ **shirt** 短袖圆领汗衫(或运动衫),体恤衫 = T-shirt

tee[2] [ti:] *n.* 1.〈高尔夫球的〉发球区;球座 2.(套圈游戏中的)目标 — *vt.* 置(球)于球座上(*up*)2. 准备;安排(*up*)

teem [ti:m] *vi.* 1. 充满;多产(*with*)2. 大量存在(*in*)*vt.* 倒出;〈古〉产,生 ‖ ~**ingly** *adv.* 充满地,丰富地;多产地

teen-age(d) ['ti:neidʒ(d)] *adj.* (13 至 19 岁的)青少年的,十几岁的

teen-ager ['ti:n,eidʒə] *n.* (13 至 19 岁的)青少年,十几岁的青少年

teens [ti:nz] [复] *n.* 1. 十几岁(13 至 19 岁)2. 十几岁的青少年们

teenster ['ti:nstə] *n.* = teen-ager

teeny ['ti:ni] *adj.* 极小的,微小的,细小的 ‖ ~**-bopper** *n.* 〈美俚〉(爱穿时髦服装的)少女流行音乐迷

teepee ['ti:pi:] *n.* = tepee

teeter ['ti:tə] 〈美〉 *vi.* 1. 步履不稳地走动;跟跷 2. 摇摇欲坠;摇摆不定 3. 玩跷跷板 — *vt.* 1. 跟起;摇摆 2. 跷跷板

teeth [ti:θ] tooth 的复数

teethe [ti:ð] *vi.* 出牙;生牙 ‖ *teething troubles* 出牙期的病痛;〈喻〉初期困难,创业初期的困难

teetotal [ti:'təutl] *adj.* 1. 绝对戒酒(主义)的 2. 完全的,彻底的 一(teetotal(l)ed; teetotal(l)ing) *vi.* 主张绝对戒酒;绝对戒酒 ‖ **teetotal(l)er** *n.* 绝对戒酒(主义)者

TEFL ['tefl] *abbr.* teaching English as a foreign language 作为外语的英语教学

TEG, top edge(s) gilt (书籍)顶端镀金,金天边

Tegucigalpa [te,gu:si'gælpə] *n.* 特古西加尔巴(洪都拉斯首都)

Teh(e)ran [tiə'rɑ:n, ,tehə'rɑ:n] *n.* 德黑兰[伊朗首都]

tel. *abbr.* 1. telegram 2. telegraph 3. telephone

tel-[1] *comb. form* = tele-[1]

tel-[2] *comb. form* = tele-[2]

telautograph [tel'ɔ:təgrɑ:f] *n.* 传真电报机

Tel Aviv [,tel ə'vi:v] 特拉维夫[以色列港市]

tele ['teli] *n.* 电视(= television)

tele-[1] *comb. form* 1. 表示"远","远距离"

*tele*graph, *tele*vision 2. 表示"电报"、"电视"、"电信"、"传真照相"：*tele*typewriter, *tele*camera

tele-² *comb. form* 表示"目的"、"末端"：*tele*ology【哲】目的论

telecamera [ˈtelikæmərə] *n.* 电视摄像机；远距离摄影机

telecast [ˈtelikɑːst] *n.* 电视广播；电视节目 — (telecast 或 telecasted) *vt. & vi.* 电视广播

telecommunication [ˈtelikəˌmjuːniˈkeiʃən] *n.* 1. 电信 2. [常~s]电信学

telecon [ˈtelikɔn] *n.* 电话会议；电视会议

telefacsimile [ˈteliˌfækˈsimili] *n.* 电话传真

telefilm [ˈteliˌfilm] *n.* 电视(影)片

telegenic [ˌteliˈdʒenik] *adj.* (人) 适于拍摄电视的, 适于上电视镜头的

telegram [ˈteliɡræm] *n.* 电报 — (telegrammed; telegramming) *vt. & vi.* = telegraph

telegraph [ˈteliɡrɑːf] *n.* 1. 电报机 2. [海] (驾驶台与机舱之间的) 传令钟, 车钟 3. (运动比赛得分等的) 揭示板 4. 电报 (指通信方式) 5. (一份)电报 [= telegram] 6. [T-]用于报刊名|电讯报：The Daily Telegraph《每日电讯报》 — *vt.* 1. 用电报发送(信息等)；打电报给(某人) 2. 电汇；用电报定购 3. 在揭示板上示出(比分等) 4. 流露；(通过无意识的动作等)泄露 — *vi.* 打电报 ‖ ~ er *n.* 报务员 ‖ ~ board (运动比赛得分等的)揭示板 ～ cable 电报电缆 ～ operator 报务员 ～ plant【植】舞草 ～ pole, ～ post 电报线杆 ～ transmitter 电报发送机, 发报机

telegraphese [ˌteliɡrɑːˈfiːz] *n.* 电报文体

telegraphic [ˌteliˈɡræfik] *adj.* 1. 电报的；电报发送的 2. 电报文体的；简短的 3. (目光等)暗示的, 传达出来的

telegraphy [tiˈleɡrəfi] *n.* 1. 电报术；电报学 2. 电报机装置(术)

telepathy [tiˈlepəθi] *n.* 传心(术), 通灵(术)；传心(或通灵)能力 ‖ telepathic [ˌteliˈpæθik] *adj.* / telepathically [ˌteliˈpæθikəli] *adv.* / telepathist *n.*

telephone [ˈtelifəun] *n.* 电话；电话机 — *vi.* 打电话, 通电话 — *vt.* 打电话给；用电话告知

telephonist [tiˈlefənist] *n.* 〈主英〉电话接线员, 话务员

telephony [tiˈlefəni] *n.* 电话学；电话(指通讯方式)

telephotograph [ˈteliˈfəutəɡrɑːf] *n.* 1. 传真照片 2. 远摄照片 — *vt. & vi.* 用传真电报发送；用远距镜头拍摄

teleran [ˈteliræn] *n.* 电视雷达导航(系统) (television radar air navigation 的缩略)

telescope [ˈteliskəup] *n.* 望远镜 — *vt.* 叠缩；(由于碰撞而)缩短, 变短 — *vt.* 使叠缩；使(汽车等)相撞而嵌进；使缩短；精简 ‖ ~ word【语】嵌进词

telescopic [ˌtelisˈkɔpik] *adj.* 1. 望远镜的；用望远镜看到的；只有用望远镜才能看到的 2. 能看得远的 3. 可伸缩的, 套管式的

teletext [ˈteliˌtekst] *n.* 图文电视

teletype [ˈtelitaip] *n.* 1. 电传打字机 2. (一份)电传打字信息 3. 电传打字通信 — *vt. & vi.* 用电传打字机发送 ‖ ~ writer *n.* 电传打字机

teleview [ˈtelivjuː] *vt. & vi.* 用电视机收看(节目等)

televise [ˈtelivaiz] *vt.* 用电视播送；用电视放映 — *vi.* 播送电视节目

television [ˈteliˌviʒən] *n.* 1. 电视：cable ~ 电缆电视, 有线电视 2. 电视(接收)机

3. 电视学；电视术 4. 电视广播事业

televisor ['teli
vaizə] *n.*1. 电视(接收)机 2. 电视发射机 3. 电视广播工作者

televox ['telivɔks] *n.* 声控机器人

telex ['teleks] *n.* 用户电报,电传 — *vt.* 用电传拍发(或通知)

tell [tel] (told[təuld]) *vt.*1. 讲述,说;告诉 2. 吩咐;命令 3. [常与 can, could, be able to 连用] 辨别,分辨 4. 断定;知道;说出 5. 泄漏(机密等);吐露(真情等等)6. 数 — *vi.*1. 讲述(of, about) 2. 确定地说出 3. 泄露;说坏话;告发(on) 4. 产生效果;发生影响 5. 作证,表明;说明(of) — *n.*〈方〉讲的事;传闻

teller ['telə] *n.*1. 讲述者;讲故事的人 2. 记数者;(议会等的)点票员 3.(银行等的)出纳员

telling ['teliŋ] *adj.*1. 有效的;有力的 2. 生动的;显明的

telltale ['telteil] *n.*1. 搬弄是非者;告密者;泄露真情的事物 2. 指示器;警告悬挂标(铁路用标志,表示前有低的旱桥) 3. [海]舵角指示器;(船上各部分的水平、倒挂罗经 4.(能在考勤卡上记录职工上下班时间的)考勤钟 — *adj.*1. 搬弄是非的;泄露秘密的(暴露内情的)说明问题的 2.(机械装置等)起警告作用的;起监督(或记录)作用的

telly ['teli] *n.*〈主英〉〈俚〉电视,电视机

telpher ['telfə] *n.* 电动缆车,电动高架空运输系统 — *adj.* 电动高架缆索的;a ~ line 高架缆索电路线 — *vt.* 用电动缆车运输

temerity [ti'meriti] *n.* 鲁莽;冒失

temper ['tempə] *vt.*1. [冶] 使回火;〈喻〉锻炼 2. 调和,揉合(粘土等)3. 使变淡;使缓和;使恰当 4. [乐] 调律;调音 5.〈罕〉使适合(to) — *vi.*(金属)经回火后具有适当的韧度 — *n.*1. 钢等

的)韧度;回火色;(影响钢硬度的)含碳量 2.(制合金、调灰泥等用的)中和剂,增效剂 3.(皮革的)质地;坚韧性 4. 心情,情绪;性情;脾气 5. 特征;倾向,趋势 6. 勇气 7.〈古〉适中,中庸

temperament ['tempərəmənt] *n.*1. 气质;性情;性格 2. 容易激动的性格;易变的性情;急躁脾气 3. [乐] (中世纪生理学中所谓的)质 4. 调和;调节;适中 5. [音] 调律

temperamental [ˌtempərə'mentl] *adj.*1. 气质的;性情的;性格的 2. 敏感的;易激动的,冲动的;变幻无常的,多变的 ‖ ~ly *adv.*

temperance ['tempərəns] *n.*1. 节制;自我克制;节欲 2. 戒酒;禁酒

temperate ['tempərət] *adj.*1. 有节制的 2. 戒酒的;节酒的 3. 不过分的;稳健的;适度的 4.(气候等)温和的 ‖ ~ly *adv.*；~ness *n.* ‖ ~ zone [地] 温带

temperature ['tempərətʃə] *n.*1. 温度 2. 体温;热度,发烧;take one's ~ 量体温/ have(或 run)a ~ 发烧

tempered ['tempəd] *adj.*1. [冶] 经过回火的;经过锻炼的 2. 调合的;调和的;温和的;适中的 3. [用以构成复合词] 脾气…的;脾气坏的/ short ~ 性子急的/ a sweet ~(fiery-)man 性情温和(暴躁)的人

tempest ['tempist] *n.*1. 大风暴;暴风雨;暴风雪 2. 骚动,风潮 — *vt.* 使骚动;使激动

tempestuous [tem'pestjuəs] *adj.*1. 大风暴的;暴风雨的;暴风雪的 2. 剧烈的;骚动的 ‖ ~ly *adv.*

tempi ['tempi:] tempo 的复数

temple¹ ['templ] *n.*1.(古希腊人、古罗马人或佛教徒等的)圣堂,神殿;庙宇,寺院 2.(基督教的)教堂,礼拜堂(一般用

church 或 chapel) 3.[常作 T-]耶路撒冷古神殿(古代犹太人相继建立的三个神殿之一) 4. 上帝所在的地方,圣灵所宿之处5.(某些互助会的)地方分会 6.〈美〉(专供某种活动之用的)殿堂,会堂

temple[2] ['templ] n. 太阳穴,颞颥,鬓角

tempo ['tempəu] ([复] tempos 或 tempi ['tempi:]) n.1.[音]速度 2.(局势、艺术作品等的)节奏,行进速度 3.(下棋时的)一着,一步

temporal[1] ['tempərəl] adj.1. 暂存的,短暂的,非永恒的 2. 世间的;世俗的;现世的 3. 时间的(与 spatial 空间的相对)4.【语】(表示)时间的;时态的 — n.[常~s]1. 暂存的事物;世间的事物 2. 教会财产(或收入)— ['tempə'ræliti] n.1. 暂存性,短暂性 2.(区别于神权、教权的)政权 3.[常 temporalities]教会不动产 — temporal的名词 — **ly** adv.

temporal[2] ['tempərəl] adj. 太阳穴的,颞颥的 — n. 颞部

temporary ['tempərəri] adj. 暂时的;临时的 — n. 临时工;临时建筑物 — **temporarily** ['tempərərili,ˌtempə'reərili] adv.

temporize ['tempəraiz] vi.1. 顺应时势,迎合潮流 2.(为争取时间)拖延;应付 3. 妥协 ‖ **temporization** n.

tempt [tempt] vt.1. 引诱,诱惑 2. 吸引;使发生兴趣;诱导 3. 触犯;冒……的风险 4.〈古〉试探,考验 ‖ **~er** n. ／ **~ress** n.

temptable ['temptəbl] adj. 易被引诱的,可诱惑的 ‖ **tempta'bility** n. 可诱惑性

temptation [temp'teiʃən] n.1. 引诱,诱惑 2. 诱惑物

tempting ['temptiŋ] adj. 引诱人的;吸引人的,使发生兴趣的

ten [ten] num. 十;十个(人或物);第十(卷、章、页或号)— n.1.10 英镑纸币

2.10 美元纸币 3.10 岁 4.10 点钟 ‖ **~fold** adj. & adv. 十倍;十重 ‖ **~-'cent store** 小零售店 ／ **Ten Commandments** [复]十诫(犹太教、基督教的诫条)／ **~pins** [复] n.[用作单] 十柱滚木球戏／ **~-'twenty-'thirty** n.1. 由固定剧团定期换演剧目的剧场 2. 定期换演剧目的剧团

tenable ['tenəbl] adj.1.(阵地等)守得住的,可防守的 2.(主张等)站得住脚的 3. 可保持(某一段时间)的(for)

tenacious [ti'neiʃəs] adj.1. 紧握的;坚持的;顽强的;固执的 2.(记忆力等)强的 3. 粘的,粘着力强的;坚韧的 ‖ **~ly** adv.／ **~ness** n.

tenacity [ti'næsiti] n.1. 紧握;坚持;顽强;固执 2. 坚韧;韧性;粘性

tenancy ['tenənsi] n.1.(土地、房屋等的)租赁,租用(或租屋等) 3. 租期 4. 占用;任职;任职期

tenant ['tenənt] n.1. 租户;佃户;房客 2.【律】承租人 3. 居住者;占用者 — vt.[常用被动语态]租赁,租用;居住于

tend[1] [tend] vt.1. 照顾,照管,照料;护理 2.【海】照料(缆绳、锚链等)以免纠缠 — vi.1. 照顾;照管;护理;伺候(侍候)(on, upon)2. 注意;关心(to)

tend[2] [tend] vi.1. 走向;趋向(to, towards)2. 倾向

tendencious [ten'denʃəs] adj. = tendentious

tendency ['tendənsi] n.1. 趋向,趋势;倾向 2. 脾性;癖好 3.(文学作品等的)意向,倾向

tendentious [ten'denʃəs] adj.(讲话、文章等)有倾向性的 ‖ **~ novel** 倾向性小说(提出并阐述某一鲜明主题的小说,又称 thesis novel)

tender[1] ['tendə] adj.1. 嫩的;柔软的 2. 脆

弱的,纤弱的;幼弱的;未成熟的 3. 敏感的;一触即痛的 4. 温柔的;亲切的;体贴的 5. 微妙的;棘手的,难对付的 6. 担心的(of);不轻易给予的(of)7.(船)易倾的,稳性小的,高重心的,不稳的 — vi.1. 使变柔软;使变脆弱 2.《古》温柔地对待 — vi. 变柔软;变脆弱 ‖ ~ly adv. /~ness n. ‖ ~foot([复]~feet 或~foots) n.《美俚》(艰苦地区的)新来者;新手/~'hearted adj. 软心肠的/~loin n.1.(牛、猪等的)腰部嫩肉 2.《美俚》(城市中以娼妓繁华、警察可从中大捞油水而闻名的)油水区;[T-]纽约市油水区

tender² ['tendə] vt.1.(正式)提出;提供 2.【律】偿还;交付 — vi. 投标(for) — n.1. 提出;提供 2.【律】偿还;交付 3. 投标 4.(用作清偿手段的)通货,货币;法定货币

tender³ ['tendə] n.1. 看管人,照料人 2.(铁路)煤水车 3. 供应船,补给船。交通艇;小艇;汽艇

tendon ['tendən] n.【解】腱

tendril ['tendril] n.1.【植】卷须 2. 卷须状物

tenement ['tenimənt] n.1.【律】保有物,享有物(指受于他人而在一定期间或终身享有的土地、房屋、爵位、特权等)2. 住房;房屋 = ~ house 与 ~ house 共同房屋,经济公寓(一般指几户合住、条件较差的住房)

tenet ['ti:net] n. 信条;宗旨;原则;basic ~s 基本原则

tenner ['tenə] n.《口》1.10 英镑纸币 2.10 美元纸币

Tennessee ['tenə'si:] n. 田纳西(美国州名)

tennis ['tenis] n.1. 网球(运动)2. 庭院网球(运动) ‖ ~ ball 网球/~ court 网球场/~ racket 网球拍

tenon ['tenən] n.(木工的)雄榫,榫舌,凸榫 — vt.1. 在…上开榫 2. 用榫接合

tenor¹ ['tenə] n.1.(生活等的)一般趋向;进程 2. 要旨,大意 3.(文件等的)抄本,誊本 4.(支票的)期限 5.(矿石的)金属含量,品位

tenor² ['tenə] n.【音】1. 男高音;男高音歌手;次中音(乐器)2.(早期复调音乐中的)定旋律声部;(四部和声的)第二低音 2.(组钟中的)最低音音钟 — adj.1. 男高音的;(乐器)次中音的 2.(组钟中的)最低音的

tense¹ [tens] n.【语】(动词的)时态,时

tense² [tens] adj.1. 拉紧的,绷紧的;紧张的 2.【语】(元音)紧的 — vt. & vi.(使)拉紧;(使)紧张 ‖ ~ly adv. /~ness n.

tensible ['tensəbl] adj. 能拉长的,能伸展的

tensile ['tensail] adj. 1.【物】张力的,拉力的;抗张的 2. 可拉长的,可伸展的

tension ['tenʃən] n.1. 拉紧,绷紧 2.(精神上的)紧张;紧张局势 3.【物】张力;拉力(或张力)调节装置(蒸汽等的)张力;电压 — vt. 使拉紧,使绷紧;使紧张

tensity ['tensəti] n. 紧张;紧张度

tent¹ [tent] n.1.(帐篷,帐棚)2.(医疗等用的)帷幕;帐篷状物 2. 住所,寓所 3.(输氧用的)氧幕 — vi.1. 住帐篷;宿营;暂时居住 — vt.1. 用帐篷(或帐篷状物)遮盖 2. 使在帐篷里宿营 ‖ ~ bed 有顶篷的床(病人睡的)有帷幕的床

tent² [tent] n.【医】塞条,塞子 — vt. 将塞条嵌进(伤口)

tent³ [tent] *n*. 西班牙红葡萄酒

tentacle ['tentəkl] *n*. 1. [动] 触手; 触角; 触须; 触器; [植] 触毛 2. 似触手的东西; put out ~s 试探 3. [~s] 束缚; 约束

tentative ['tentətiv] *adj*. 1. 试验(性)的, 试探(性)的; 暂时(性)的 2. 踌躇的; 不明确的 — *n*. 试验, 试探 ‖ ~ly *adv*. / ~ness *n*.

tenter ['tentə] [纺] *n*. 1. 拉幅机; 拉幅工人 2. 〈古〉拉幅钩 — *vt*. 把…绷在拉幅机上

tenterhook ['tentəhuk] *n*. [纺] 拉幅钩 ‖ *on* ~*s* 提心吊胆; 如坐针毡

tenth [tenθ] *num*. 1. 第十(个) 2. 十分之一(的) — *n*. 1. [音] 十度音; 第十音级 2. [英史] 什一税 3. (月的) 第十日 ‖ ~ly *adv*. 第十(列举本条目时用)

tenuity [te'njuːiti] *n*. 1. 纤细; 单薄 2. (空气、流体等的) 稀薄 3. (光、声等的) 微弱, 无力 4. (智力等的) 贫乏; (文体等的) 平淡

tenuous ['tenjuəs] *adj*. 1. 纤细的; 单薄的 2. 稀薄的 3. 脆弱的, 无力的 4. 精细的; 微妙的 ‖ ~ly *adv*. / ~ness *n*.

tenure ['tenjuə] *n*. (财产、职位等的) 占有; 占有权; 占有期; 占有条件; (土地的) 保有; 保有权; 保有期

tepee ['tiːpiː] *n*. (北美印第安人的) 圆锥形帐篷

tepid ['tepid] *adj*. 1. 微温的; 温热的 2. (喻) 不太热烈的; 不冷不热的 ‖ te'pidity, ~ness *n*. / ~ly *adv*.

tequila [tə'kiːlə] *n*. 1. [植] 墨西哥龙舌兰 2. 特釜拉酒, 墨西哥烈酒

terbium ['təːbiəm] *n*. [化] 铽

teredo [tə'riːdəu] ([复] teredos 或 teredines [tə'riːdiniːz]) *n*. [动] 船蛆, 凿船贝

term [təːm] *n*. 1. 期, 期限 2. 学期 3. 任期

4. 限期; (工资、房租等的) 付款日; 结账日 (尤指法定季度结算日, = quarter day) 5. [律] 开庭期; 地产租用期; 付期限用的地产 6. 足月, 足坐; 足月分娩 7. [~s] (契约、谈判等的) 条件; 条款; 费用; 价格 8. [~s] 关系; 交谊; 地位 9. (有特定意义的) 词语; 术语, 专门名词; 名称; 措词, 说话的方式 10. [逻] 项 11. [数] 项 12. [建] 界标; 端柱, 胸像柱 13. 〈古〉界限; 极限; 终点; 终止 — *vt*. 把…称为, 把…叫做 ‖ ~less *adj*. 1. 无穷的, 无限的 2. 无条件的

termagant ['təːməgənt] *n*. 1. [T-] (早期英国戏剧中代表狂暴、蛮横角色的) 穆斯林神 2. 悍妇, 泼妇 — *adj*. 凶悍的; 暴躁的

terminable ['təːminəbl] *adj*. 可终止的; 有期限的 ‖ **terminably** *adv*.

terminal ['təːminl] *adj*. 1. 末端的; 终点的; 结尾的; 极限的 2. [植] 顶生的; [动] 端末的 3. 每期的; 定期的 4. 末期的; 晚期的 — *n*. 1. 末端; 终点; 极限 2. [电] 端子; [计] 终端设备 3. (铁路等的) 终点站 4. [语] 词尾 (结尾的字母、音素、音节等); 词语, 专门名词 5. [建] 界标; 端柱, 胸像柱 ‖ ~ly *adv*.

terminate ['təːmineit] *vt*. (时间上) 使停止; 使结束; (空间上) 使终止; 使结尾 — *vi*. 结束; 终止 — *adj*. 终止的; 有界限的

termination [,təːmi'neiʃən] *n*. 1. 结束; 结局; 终止; 终点 2. [语] 词尾 (尤指屈折词尾)

terminology [,təːmi'nɔlədʒi] *n*. 术语学; 术语 ‖ **terminologist** *n*. 术语学家

terminus ['təːminəs] ([复] termini ['təːminai] 或 terminuses) *n*. 1. 终点; 目标 2. (铁路、汽车、航空等的) 终点站; (主英) 终点城镇 3. 界标; 界石; 界牌; [建] 胸像

柱 4. [T-]【罗神】忒耳努努斯（界标之神）5.〈罕〉界限；极限

termite ['tə:mait] *n.* 白蚁

tern [tə:n]【动】燕鸥

ternary ['tə:nəri] *adj.* 1. 三个构成的；三个一套的；三重的 2. 第三的 3.【化】【数】三元的

Terpsichore [tə:p'sikəri] *n.* 1.【希神】特耳西科瑞（主管舞蹈和合唱的女神）2. [t-]〈谑〉舞蹈术

terrace ['terəs] *n.* 1. 阶地；梯田 2. 露台；大阳台 3.（西班牙式或东方式的）平台屋顶 4. 排屋 5.（排屋对面的）街道 6.（马路的中央分隔带，中间分车带 — *vt.* 使成阶地（或梯田）；使有平台屋顶（或露台、大阳台等）

terracotta [,terə'kɔtə]〈拉〉*n.* 1. 赤陶土 2. 赤土陶器；陶俑 3. 赤褐色

terra firma [,terə'fə:mə]〈拉〉*n.* 陆地，坚实的土地

terrain ['terein] *n.* 1. 地面；地域，地带 2.【地】地质建造（系）；岩群；岩层 3.（知识的）领域；（活动的）范围 4. 环境

terramycin [,terə'maisin] *n.*【药】土霉素，地霉素，氧四环素

terrapin ['terəpin] *n.* 1.【动】水龟 2. 水龟肉 3. [T-]用作绰号】〈美国〉马里兰州人

terrarium [te'rɛəriəm]（[复]terrariums 或 terraria [te'rɛəriə]）*n.* 1. 陆栖小动物饲养箱 2. 小植物栽培盆

terrestrial [ti'restriəl] *adj.* 1. 地球的 2. 陆地的，陆栖的；陆生的 3. 人间的；尘世的 — *n.* 地球上人；陆地生物 ‖ ~ly *adv.*

terrible ['terəbl] *adj.* 1. 可怕的，可怖的；骇人的；令人敬畏的 2. 极度的；厉害的 3.〈口〉极坏的，很糟的 4.〈美俚〉极妙的，了不起的 ‖ ~ness *n.* / **terribly** *adv.*

terrier ['teriə] *n.* 1. 㹴（一种狗）2.〈英口〉本土防卫勇军士兵（或军官）3. 缉捕罪犯的人

terrific [tə'rifik] *adj.* 1. 可怕的，可怖的；骇人的 2.〈口〉极大的；极度的；非常的 3.〈美俚〉极妙的，了不起的 ‖ ~ally *adv.*

terrify ['terifai] *vt.* 使惊怖，使惊吓；恐吓 ‖ ~ingly *adv.*

territorial [,teri'tɔ:riəl] *adj.* 1. 领土的 2. 区域（性）的，地方（性）的 4. [T-]〈美国的〉准州的；〈加拿大的〉地方的；〈澳大利亚的〉区的 5. [常 T-]〈英〉防卫本土的 — *n.* [常 T-]〈英〉本土防卫勇军士兵（或军官）‖ ~ly *adv.*

territory ['teritəri] *n.* 1. 领土，版图；领地 2. 地区；(按某种目的划定的)区域（尤指商业推销区）3. [T-]〈美国的〉准州；〈加拿大的〉地方，〈澳大利亚的〉区 4.（行动、知识等的）领域，范围

terror ['terə] *n.* 1. 恐怖，惊骇 2. 引起恐怖的事物（或人）3. [常 T-]恐怖统治；the white ~ 白色恐怖 4.〈口〉极讨厌的人 ‖ ~ism *n.* 恐怖（主义）；恐怖统治（或统治、手段）/ ~ist *n.* 恐怖（主义）分子 *adj.* 恐怖（主义）的；恐怖分子的

terrorize ['terəraiz] *vt.* 1. 使恐怖 2. 恐吓；胁迫 — *vt.* 引起恐怖；实行恐怖统治 ‖ terrori'zation *n.*

terry ['teri]【纺】*n.* 毛圈织物 — *adj.* 起毛圈的；a ~ towel 毛巾 ‖ ~ cloth 毛圈织物

terse [tə:s] *adj.*（说话、文笔等）精练的，简洁的，扼要的 ‖ ~ly *adv.* / ~ness *n.*

tertian ['tə:ʃən]【医】*adj.* 每三日（发）的间日（复发）的 — *n.* 间日热（如疟疾）

tertiary ['tə:ʃəri] *adj.* 1. 第三的；第三位

的;第三级的 **2.**【医】(梅毒等)第三期
的;第三度的,严重的 **3.**【T-】【地】第三
纪的;第三系的 — **n.1.**【地】第三
纪;第三系 **2.**【医】梅毒第三期损害;
(疟疾等)间日热

Terylene ['teriliːn] *n.*〈英〉【纺】涤纶(商标
名)

TESL ['tesəl] *abbr.* teaching English as a
second language 作为第二语言的英语教
学

TESOL ['tiːsɔl] *abbr.* teaching English to
speakers of other languages 向说其他语言
的人讲授英语

test [test] *n.***1.**(物质、性质、效能等的)试
验,测试 **2.** 化验;化验法;试剂 **3.** 化验
结果 **4.** 检验;检验标准 **5.** 考查;测验
6. 考验 **7.**〈英〉【冶】烤钵;灰皿 **8.**
〈口〉= match — *vi.***1.** 试验;测定;
检验 **2.** 化验 **3.** 考验;考查 **4.**【冶】用灰
皿鉴定(金属) — *vi.***1.** 受试验;受测验
2. 测得结果 **3.**(为测定)测定物 (*for*) ‖ ~
ban 禁止核试验协定 / ~
glass 试管;化验杯 /'~-market *vt.* & *vi.*
试销 / ~ match(板球和橄榄球等)各
国家队间决赛阶段的比赛 / ~ pattern
(电视的)测试图案 / ~ pilot(飞机)试
飞员 /'~-pilot *vt.* & *vi.* 试飞 / ~ tube
试管 / ~-tube *adj.***1.** 试管(中)的 **2.**
经试管培育的;人工授精产生的;a ~ -
tube baby 试管婴儿 **3.** 合成的;人造的:
~ -*tube* fabrics 合成纤维织物 / ~ type
【医】视力表字型

testament ['testəmənt] *n.***1.**【T-】(基督教)
圣约书《旧约全书》或《新约全书》:
The Old Testament《旧约全书》/ The New
Testament《新约全书》 **2.**〈口〉【T-】《圣
经·新约》 **3.**【律】遗嘱;遗言 **4.** 证明,证
据 **5.** 信仰声明

testamentary [ˌtestə'mentəri] *adj.***(根据**

遗嘱的;遗嘱规定(或指定)的

testate ['testeit] *adj.* 留有遗嘱的 — *n.* =
testator ‖ **tes'tator** *n.*【律】留有遗嘱的死
者,遗嘱人

testes ['testiz] testis 的复数

testicle ['testikl] *n.* 睾丸 ‖ **testicular**
[tes'tikjulə] *adj.* 睾丸的;睾丸状的

testify ['testifai] *vi.* 证明;证实;作证 —
vt. 证明;证实;表明;声明

testimonial [ˌtesti'məunjəl] *n.***1.**(能力、资
格、品德等的)证明书;介绍信;鉴定书
2. 奖品;奖金;奖状;书面的感谢(或表
扬等);纪念品 — *adj.***1.**(有关)证明书
(或鉴定书等)的 **2.** 表扬的;鉴赏的

testimony ['testiməni] *n.***1.** 证据;证明
2.【律】(宣誓)证词 **2.** 声明;陈述;公开表
白 **3.** 表示,表明 **4.**【基督教】(刻在两块
法版上的)摩西十诫;(testimonies)(基
督教《圣经》中)上帝的箴言

testis ['testis] ([复] testes['testiz]) *n.* 睾丸

testy ['testi] *adj.***1.**(人)易怒的,暴躁的 **2.**
恼火的,烦躁的

tetanus ['tetənəs] *n.*【医】**1.** 破伤风 **2.** 破
伤风杆菌 **3.** 肌强直

tetchy ['tetʃi] *adj.* 过度敏感的;容易生气
的 ‖ **tetchily** *adv.* /**tetchiness** *n.*

tête-à-tête [ˌteitaː'teit, ˌtetaː'tet]〈法〉*n.***1.**
(两人间的)密谈,促膝谈心 **2.**(面对面
式的)双人沙发 — *adj.* 面对面的;两
人私下的 — *adv.* 面对面地;两人私下
地

tether ['teðə] *n.***1.**(拴牛、马等的)拴绳;拴
链 **2.**(力量、权力等的)限度;范围 —
*vt.***1.**(用绳、链等)拴 **2.** 束缚;限制;限
定(计划的范围等)

tetracycline [ˌtetrə'saiklain] *n.*【药】四环素

tetrad ['tetræd] *n.***1.** 四元组;四个一组 **2.**
【化】四价元素(或基、原子) **3.**【生】四分

染色体;【植】四分体 ‖ ~ic [tetræ'dik] adj.

tetrahedron [ˌtetrə'hedrən] ([复] tetrahedrons 或 tetrahedra [ˌtetrə'hedrə]) n. 四面体

tetralogy [te'træləʤi] n. 1. (古希腊)四联剧,四部曲(由三部悲剧与一部讽刺剧组成) 2. (戏剧,歌剧,小说等的)四部曲

tetrode ['tetroud] n. [无]四极管

tetter ['tetə] n. 【医】1. 皮肤病 2. 丘疹;水疱

Teutonic [tju:'tɔnik] adj. 条顿人的;日耳曼人的 — n. 日耳曼语

Texas ['teksəs] n. 得克萨斯[美国州名]

text [tekst] n. 1. 原文;文本;正文 2. 课文;课本;教科书 3. 版本 4. (讨论等的)题目,主题;(引作布道的题目等)圣经文句 5. 圣经的字面意义;圣经经文 6. 歌词;(刊印的)乐谱 7. 【印】黑体字;正文字体 8. [~s] (学习、研究主任指定的)必读书目 ‖ ~-book n. 课本,教科书 /~-bookish adj. 教科书式的;呆板的 /~-hand 粗体正楷

textile ['tekstail] n. 纺织品;纺织原料 — adj. 纺织的

textual ['tekstjuəl] adj. 1. 原文的;文本的 2. 按原文的;逐字的 ‖ ~-ly adv.

texture ['tekstʃə] n. 1. (织物的)密度,质地 2. 织品,织物 3. (文艺作品等的)神韵;质感 4. (材料等的)结构,构造,构成;(岩石等的)纹理;(皮肤的)肌理 5. 本质,实质;特征 — vt. 使具有某种结构(或特征)

T-group ['ti:gru:p] n. 感受能力训练小组(一种精神治疗方式,受治疗者在专门训练员的指导下,在小组内不受拘束地用言语表达内心感情)

Th 【化】元素钍(thorium)的符号

-th suf. 1. [构成抽象名词]表示"动作","过程","状态","性质": stealth, growth, wealth, truth 2. [构成序数词]表示"第…": fourth, seventh 3. (古)[构成动词陈述式第三人称单数](相当于现在的 -s, -es): hath (= has), doth (= does)

Thai [tai] n. 1. 泰人;泰国人 2. 泰语;泰国语 — adj. 泰国人的;泰语的;泰国的

Thailand ['tailænd] n. 泰国(原称 Siam 暹罗)[东南亚国家] ‖ ~er n. 泰国人

thallium ['θæliəm] n. 【化】铊

Thames [temz] n. 泰晤士河[英国英格兰南部] ‖ set the ~ on fire (英) 做出惊人之事而一举成名

than [强 ðæn; 弱 ðən, ðn] conj. 1. [用于形容词、副词的比较级之后]比 2. [用于else, other 等之后]除…(外) 3. [用于rather, sooner 之后]与其…(宁愿…) 4. [用于scarcely, hardly 之后,表示时间]就 — prep. [用于~ whom、~ which 两个词组和某些用不及物动词的句中]比: a man ~ whom no one is more fit for this job 最适宜做这件事的人

thanatopsis [ˌθænə'tɔpsis] n. 死亡观

thane [θein] n. 【英史】1. 大乡绅(以服兵役而得领地的自由民,相当于乡绅士、男爵等) 2. (苏格兰)受赐封地的领主;男爵酋族长

thank [θæŋk] vt. 1. 感谢,谢谢,感谢 2. [用于will或'll 后,表示客气的请求;常常用作反语,含有责备的意思]感谢,请 3. [用作反语]要…负责;责怪 — n. [~s]感谢;感谢语;谢意 ‖ Thank!谢谢!谢谢![注意:此句语气轻于 Thank you。] ‖ ~-offering【宗】感恩的供品;谢恩的捐献

thankful ['θæŋkful] adj. 1. 感谢的,感激的 2. 欣慰的 ‖ ~-ly adv. /~-ness n.

thankless ['θæŋklis] *adj.* **1.** 不感激的；负义的 **2.** 不使人感激的；徒劳的

thanksgiving ['θæŋks,giviŋ] *n.* **1.** 感谢；道谢；[宗] 感恩祈祷 **2.** [T-] = Thanksgiving Day ‖ **Thanksgiving Day** [基督教] 感恩节 (例假日 在美国是 11 月的第四个星期四，在加拿大是 10 月的第二个星期一)

that [ðæt] *adj.* [后接复数名词时用 those] **1.** 那，那个 **2.** 那样的，如此的 (现常用 such，such as 等) — ([复] those [ðauz]) *demonstrative pron.* **1.** 那，那个 **2.** (刚提到的) 那时；(刚提到的) 那事 **3.** 那 (指在上文已提到的两点中的前一点，后一点用 this 表示) **4.** [用作关系代词的先行词]; 关系代词 (这格体可常省略) 那，那个: Throw away all *those* which are unfit for use. 把那些不适用的东西都扔掉。**5.** [用关系代词中 named，以避免重复]: The air of hills is cooler than ～ of plains. 山地的空气比平原的空气凉快。— [强 ðæt; 弱 ðət] [单复同] *relative pron.* [引导限制性定语从句，前面不用逗号] **1.** [在从句中作主语时相当于 who 或 which; 但在 it is (或 was) ⋯ 句型中，和在最高级形容词词以及 all, any, little, much, no, only 等词后比 who 或 which 常用]: This reference book contains much (little) ～ is useful. 这本参考书中有很多 (没有多少) 有用的东西。/Mrs. Brown, Jane Smith ～ was, ⋯. (口) 布朗夫人，就是 (结婚前的) 简·史密斯，⋯⋯ **2.** [在从句中作宾语或前置词宾语时，常省略; 相当于 whom 或 which; 与动词搭配的前置词常在从句的结尾]: Do the best ～ you can (do). (你要) 尽力而为。[注意: 这里不可用 which 代替 ～]/The man (～) you saw is a professor. 你见到过的那男子是个教授。**3.** [用来代替表示时间的词时，

常省略; 相当于 when]: the year (～ 或 when)he was born 他诞生的 (那) 一年 **4.** [用来代替主句中的名词及其前置词]: I like the place *for* the very reason ～ (= *for* which) you dislike it. 我喜欢那地方的原因恰恰是你不喜欢它的原因。**5.** [在从句中用于不加冠词的、表示某种特性的名词时，作表语] 虽然，尽管; 虽然 — *conj.* **1.** [引导名词性从句]: It is certain ～ he will succeed. 他无疑会成功。**2.** [引导状语从句，表明原因或理由]: 因为，由于 **3.** [引导状语从句，表明目的或结果] 为了; 以至于 **4.** [引导表示愿望、感叹等的从句; 主句常可省略]: That (或 How I wish ～)I could go to Beijing with you! 我多么想同你一起到北京去呀! — *adv.* 那样，那么

thatch [θætʃ] *n.* **1.** [用作盖屋顶材料的] 茅草 (或稻草、芦苇等) **2.** 茅草屋顶 **3.** 浓密的头发 — *vt.* 用茅草 (或稻草等) 盖 (屋顶)

thaw [θɔ:] *vi.* (冰、雪等) 融化，融解，解冻; (在态度、感情等方面) 趋于和缓 — *vt.* 使融化，使缓和 — *n.* **1.** 融化，解冻; (在态度、感情等方面的) 和缓 **2.** 解冻时期 (或季节)

the [强 ði:; 弱 ði, ðə, ð] *art.* [定冠词] [释义 1—23 用于名词或名词性词组前，表示: 已被确认、提到、遇到、正在谈到、熟悉的、实际存在的或独一无二的人或事物，意义相当于 "这 (些)"、"那 (些)"，以区别于 a, an "一个"、"某个"] **1.** [用于特指定的人或事物]: ～ river 这条 (或那条) 河 [区别于 a river 一条河] **2.** [指已提到或正谈到的人或事物]: Who was ～ visitor? 来访者是谁? **3.** [指谈话双方都体会到的人或事物]: Close ～ window, please. 请把窗关上。**4.** [指独一无二的事物]: ～ sun 太阳／～ moon 月亮 **5.** [用于表示自然界现象等的名词如 sky, sea, wind 等之前(特别当这些名词前不带形容词时):There was no cloud in sky. 天空中没有云。**6.**[用于被限制性短语或从句修饰的名词前]: ~ cover of that book 那本书的封面 **7.**[用来加强特指意义,即表达"恰恰(是)"、"最适合的"、"最典型的"等意思(这种用法的的须强读,印刷中常用斜体)]: Quinine is the medicine for malaria. 奎宁是治疟疾药。**8.**[与表示计算单位的名词连用,含"每"、"每一"的意思(= a, per, each 等)]: sell at 2 dollars ~ pound 每磅售价 2 元 **9.**[代替所有格代词,指已提到过的人的身体或衣着的一部分]: hit sb. in ~ face 打某人的脸 **10.**[旧时用于病名前,现在除口语或俚语中在复数形式的名词前尚保留外,其余通常省略]: (~) gout 痛风 **11.**[用于乐器名称前]: play ~ piano 弹钢琴/play ~ violin 拉小提琴[比较:球类及游戏名称前不用冠词,如: play basketball (football, billiards, chess, cards) 打篮球(踢足球,打台球,下棋,打牌)]**12.**[用于可数名词的单数前,统指类别]: The horse is a useful animal. 马是有用的动物。**13.**[用于表示发明物的名词前]:The compass was invented by the Chinese. 指南针是中国人发明的。**14.**[用于具体名词的单数形式前,指其属性、功能等,使具抽象性]: This colour is pleasant to ~ eye. 这颜色好看。**15.**[用于集合名词前,指一个整体]:~ people 人民 **16.**[用于复数名词前,指全体,以区别于个体]:~ Chinese 中国人[比较: a (four) Chinese 一个(四个)中国人]/ The workers and (~) peasants are living a happy life. 工人和农民过着幸福的生活。**17.**[用于姓的复数前,指全家人或全家中的一些人]: We often dine with ~ Browns. 我们时常和布朗一家一起吃

饭。**18.**[用于河、运河、海、洋的名称前]:~ Rhine 莱茵河/~ Suez (Canal) 苏伊士运河/~ East China Sea 东海/~ Pacific (Ocean) 太平洋 **19.**[用于山脉名称或复数形式的地名前]:~ Netherlands 荷兰/~ British Isles 不列颠群岛 **20.**[用于某些国名、地名前]:~ Argentine 阿根廷/~ Crimea 克里米亚 **21.**[人名或不用冠词的地名,有定语修饰时,常加定冠词]:~ great Lenin 伟大的列宁/~ China of 1919 1919 年的中国 **22.**[船只名称和旅馆、剧院、建筑物的名称前,常加定冠词]:~ Dong Feng "东风"号(货船名)/at ~ Capital 在首都剧院 **23.**[用于某些著作、报刊、乐曲的名称前]: ~ Internationale 《国际歌》/ The Times (英国)《泰晤士报》**24.**[用于形容词前,使成为表示抽象或具体事物的名词]:~ true and ~ false 真与假 **25.**[用于形容词、分词前,指一类人]:~ old and ~ young 老年和青年 **26.**[用于形容词、副词最高级前,有时也用于形容词比较级前]: Mount Qomolangma is ~ highest peak in the world. 珠穆朗玛峰是世界最高峰。**27.**[用于逢十的数词的复数形式前,指世纪中的特定年代或人的约略年岁]: in ~ seventies of the twentieth century 在 20 世纪 70 年代中/a man somewhere in ~ fifties 一个 50 多岁的人 —— **adv. 1.**[用于形容词、副词比较级前]: So much ~ better. 那就更好了。**2.**[~ … ~ …]越……越……[用于形容词、副词比较级前]:~ sooner ~ better 越快越好 **3.**[用于副词最高级前]: Among them, he works ~ hardest. 他们中间他工作最努力。

theatre, theater ['θiətə] **n.1.** 戏院,剧场;影剧院;(古希腊、古罗马式的)露天圆形剧场;(影剧院)全体观众 **2.** 戏剧;剧本,剧作 **3.** 戏剧效果 **4.** 阶梯式讲堂

theatrical [θiˈætrikəl] *adj.*1. 剧场的；戏剧的 **2.** 戏剧性的；演戏似的；夸张的 — *n.*1. [~s] 戏剧演出（尤指业余性的）**2.** [~s] 舞台表演艺术 **3.** 职业演员 ‖ ~ism *n.* 舞台表演理论和方法；戏剧风格（或特征）/~ly *adv.*

Thebes [θiːbz] *n.* 1. 底比斯(埃及尼罗河畔的古城) 2. 底比斯(希腊古城)

thee [ðiː] [古] 《古》[thou 的宾格] 你，汝 **2.** 《古》你自己(= thyself) **3.** [公谊会教徒之间作主格，并接第三人称动词] 你

theft [θeft] *n.* 偷窃；盗窃

their [ðeə(r), ðə(r)] *pron.*1. [they 的所有格] 他(她、它)们的 **2.** [泛指；用以代替不确定的单数先行词] 他(她)们的(= his, her)

theirs [ðeəz] *pron.*1. [物主代词] 他(她)们的东西；他(她)们的家属(或有关的人) **2.** [泛指；用以代替不确定的单数先行词] 他(她)们的东西；他(她)们的(= his, hers)

theism [ˈθiːizəm] *n.* 有神论；一神论 ‖ **theist** *n.* 有神论者；一神论者

them [强 ðem；弱 ðəm] *pron.*1. [they 的宾格] 他们；她们；它们 **2.** 〈口〉[用作表语] 他们；她们；它们(= they)：That's ~ 就是他们。

theme [θiːm] *n.*1. (谈话、讨论、文章等的)题目；主题 **2.** (学生的)作文；(小型)论文 **3.**【语】词干 **4.**【音】主题；主旋律 **5.** ~= song **6.** [史](拜占庭帝国的)行政区 ‖ **thematic** [θiˈmætik] *adj.* / ~ less *adj.* ‖ ~ song 1. 主题歌 2. (表示某广播节目开始或完毕的)信号曲，信号调 **3.** (某人的)套语(指常提到的主张、抱怨等)

themselves [ðəmˈselvz] *pron.*1. [反身代词] 他们自己；她们自己；它们本身 **2.** [用以加强语气] 他们(或她们)亲自；他们(或她们)本身 **3.** [泛指；用以代替不确定的单数先行词] 他(或她)自己(= himself or herself)

then [ðen] *adv.*1.(指过去)当时，那时；(指将来)在那时，到那时 **2.** 接着；于是 **3.** [常用于句首或句尾] 那么 **4.** 而且；另外，还有，再者 **5.** [与 now，sometimes 等连用] (一会儿…)一会儿又… — *adj.* [用作定语] 当时的 — *n.* [常用于前置词后] 那时

thence [ðens] *adv.* [现罕用于口语]1. 从那里 **2.** 之后，以后 **3.** 由此，因此 ‖ ~-forth《forth adv. 从那时起，此后 / ~'forward(s) adv. 从那时起，此后；从那里起

theocracy [θiˈɒkrəsi] *n.*1. 神权政治；僧侣政治 2.神权政治国家；神权国 3. [the T-](古代犹太国的)神权政治时代，政教合一体制 ‖ **theocratic** [θiəˈkrætik] *adj.*

theodolite [θiˈɒdəlait] *n.* [测] 经纬仪

theologian [ˌθiəˈləudʒən] *n.* 神学家；神学研究者

theological [ˌθiəˈlɒdʒikəl] *adj.* 神学(上)的 ‖ ~ly *adv.*

theology [θiˈɒlədʒi] *n.* 神学

theorem [ˈθiərəm] *n.*1. 定理 **2.** 原理；理论

theoretical [ˌθiəˈretikəl] *adj.*1. 理论(上)的 **2.** 假设的，仅在理论上存在的 ‖ ~ly *adv.*

theorist [ˈθiərist] *n.* 理论家

theory [ˈθiəri] *n.*1. 理论；学理；原理 **2.** 学说；论说；论，论说 **3.** 意见；推测，揣度 **4.**【数】论，理论 ‖ **theorize** *vt.* & *vi.*

therapeutic(al) [ˌθerəˈpjuːtik(əl)] *adj.* 治疗的；有疗效的；有益于健康的

therapeutics [ˌθerəˈpjuːtiks] [复] *n.* [用作单或复][医]治疗学

therapist [ˈθerəpist] *n.* 治疗专家

therapy [ˈθerəpi] *n.* 治疗；疗法：new acupuncture ~ 新针疗法/physical ~ 理疗法

there [ðeə; 弱 ðə] *adv.* 1. 在那里；往那里 2. 在那点上，在那个方面 3. [用以引起注意、加强语气；除主语为人称代词外，须主谓倒装]：*There* you go again. 你又来这一套了。/ *There's* a good boy! 真是个好孩子！/ Turn to the left and ~ you are. 向左转弯就到了。4. [常读作 ðə][与动词 to be 连用，表示"有"的意思]：*There is* no holding back the wheel of history. 历史车轮不可阻挡。5. [与 seem、appear 等动词连用]：*There seems* (to be) something wrong about it. 好像有点不对头。— *int.* [表示安慰、引起注意、加强语气、进行挑衅等]表示瞧！哼！；*There*, ~, never mind. 好啦！好啦！不要紧的。— *n.* 那个地方

thereabout(s) [ˈðeərəˌbaut(s)] *adv.* 1. 在那附近2. [表示数目、数量、时间、程度等]大约，左右，上下

thereafter [ˌðeəˈɑːftə] *adv.* 1. 〈书面语〉此后，以后 2. 〈古〉据此

thereat [ˌðeəˈæt] *adv.* 1. 当地 2. 因此

thereby [ˌðeəˈbai] *adv.* 1. 由此，因此，从而 2. 〈苏格兰〉= thereabout(s)

therefor [ˌðeəˈfɔː] *adv.* 为此，因之

therefore [ˈðeəfɔː] *adv.* 因此，所以

therefrom [ˌðeəˈfrɔm] *adv.* 〈古〉从那里；从那一点

therein [ˌðeəˈrin] *adv.* 在那里；在那时；在那点上；在其中

thereof [ˌðeəˈɔv] *adv.* 1. 在其中，于此 2. 由此，因此

thereon [ˌðeəˈron] *adv.* 1. 在其上 2. 〈古〉紧接着，随即

thereto [ˌðeəˈtuː] *adv.* 1. 向那里 2. 〈古〉此外，又

thereunder [ˌðeəˈrʌndə] *adv.* 在其下；按规定条款之下

thereupon [ˌðeərəˈpon] *adv.* 1. 就该事；关于那 2. 因此，于是

therewith [ˌðeəˈwið] *adv.* 1. 与之，与此 2. 此外，又 3. 〈古〉随即，立刻

therewithal [ˌðeəwiˈðɔːl] *adv.* = therewith

therm [θɜːm] *n.* [物] 1. 克卡，小卡 2. 千卡，大卡 3. 撒姆(煤气热量单位，在英国等于 10 万 Btu，在美国等于 1000 千卡)

thermal [ˈθɜːməl] *adj.* 1. 热的；热量的；由热造成的 2. 温泉的 — *n.* 上升热气流 ‖ ~ **barrier** [空]热障(= heat barrier)

thermion [ˈθɜːmiən] *n.* [物]热离子

thermo- *comb. form* 1. 表示"热"：*thermo*dynamics 2. 表示"热电的"*thermo*ammeter

thermoammeter [ˌθɜːməuˈæmitə] *n.* (测量微电流用的)热电偶安培计

thermodynamics [ˌθɜːməudaiˈnæmiks] [复] *n.* [用作单][物]热力学

thermometer [θəˈmɔmitə] *n.* 温度计；寒暑表；体温表：a clinical ~ 体温计/a centigrade (或 Celsius) ~ 摄氏温度计/a Fahrenheit ~ 华氏温度计

thermonuclear [ˌθɜːməuˈnjuːkliə] *adj.* [核]热核的

thermoplastic [ˌθɜːməuˈplæstik] *adj.* 可热塑的 — *n.* 热塑性塑料 ‖ ˌthermoplasˈticity *n.*

thermos [ˈθɜːmɒs] *n.* 保温瓶，热水瓶

thermosetting [ˌθɜːməuˈsetiŋ] *adj.* 热固的：~ plastic 热固塑料

thermostat ['θɜːməstæt] *n*.1. 温度自动调节器,恒温器 2.(灭火设备等的)温度自动启闭装置

thesaurus [θiːˈsɔːrəs]([复] thesauri [θiːˈsɔːraɪ] 或 thesauruses) *n*.1. 宝库;仓库 2. 类属词典,同类词汇表 3.【计】主题词表

these [ðiːz] this 的复数

Theseus ['θiːsjuːs] *n*.【希神】忒修斯(雅典王子,是进入克里特迷宫斩妖除怪的英雄)

thesis ['θiːsis]([复] theses ['θiːsiːz]) *n*.1. 论题,命题;论点 2. 论文;毕业(或学位)论文 3. 'θeɪsɪs](古典诗词中的)扬音节;(现代诗韵中的)抑音节 4.【音】下拍;(小节中的)强音部 ∥ ~ novel 主题小说(提出并阐述某一鲜明主题的小说,也作 tendentious novel)

thespian ['θespɪən] *adj*.1.[T-](古希腊雅典诗人、悲剧创始者)泰斯庇斯的 2. 悲剧的;戏剧(艺术)的 一 *n*.〈谑〉演员;悲剧演员

theta ['θiːtə] *n*. 希腊字母表第八个字母(Θ,θ)

thew [θjuː] *n*.1.[常~s]肌(肉),筋(肉)2.[常~s]肌力,筋力;体力 3. 精神(或道德)力量

they [ðeɪ]弱 ðe] *pron*.[主格]1. 他们;她们;它们 2. 人们

they'd [ðeɪd]1. = they had 2. = they would

they'll [ðeɪl]1. = they will 2. = they shall

they're ['ðeɪə] = they are

they've [ðeɪv] = they have

thiamin ['θaɪəmɪn], **thiamine** ['θaɪəmɪn] *n*.【生化】硫胺素,维生素 B₁

thick [θɪk] *adj*.1. 厚的;粗的;粗壮的【印】粗体的 2. 密的;茂盛的;密集的;密布的,充满的;阻塞的 3. 浓的;粘稠的 4. 混浊的;阴霾的;多雾的;看不清

的 5. 口齿不清的;(声音)浊的;沙哑的;(口音)重的 6. 理解力差的;愚钝的,笨的 7.〈口〉亲密的;很友好的 8. 非常的;过分的 一 *n*.1. 最厚(或密,浓)的部分;最激烈处;(人群等)最密集处;最活跃的部分 2.〈口〉笨蛋 一 *adv*.厚地;密集地;浓浓地;强烈地 ∥ ~ ly *adv*. ∥ '~-headed *adj*. 笨的 / '~'set *adj*.1. 稠密的 ;密植的 2. 体格结实的 *n*.1.密植的树篱 2. 厚织纹布 / '~-skinned *adj*. 厚皮的;感觉迟钝的,麻木不仁的 / '~-'skulled, '~-'witted *adj*. 迟钝的,笨的

thicken ['θɪkən] *vt*.1. 使变厚(或粗、密、浓);使更厚(或更粗、更密,更浓)2. 加强;使(声音)讲不清晰,使模糊 一 *vi*.1. 变厚(或粗、密、浓)2. 变得不清晰;(天气)变得阴暗 3. 变复杂

thicket ['θɪkɪt] *n*.1. 灌木丛;植丛 2. 错综复杂,盘根错节

thickness ['θɪknɪs] *n*.1. 厚(度);粗 2. 密(度);稠密;浓(度);粘稠 3. 混浊;多雾;多糊 4. 迟钝,笨 5. 最厚(或粗、密、浓)处 6.(一)层

thief [θiːf]([复] thieves [θiːvz]) *n*.1. 窃贼,小偷;偷窃犯 2.(使蜡烛不滴的)烛芯突出部分

thieve [θiːv] *vt*. 偷窃 一 *vi*. 做贼

thievery ['θiːvəri] *n*. 偷窃;行窃;〈罕〉被窃物,赃物

thievish ['θiːvɪʃ] *adj*.1. 偷窃成性的,贼性的 2. 贼似的;偷偷摸摸的,鬼鬼祟祟的

thigh [θaɪ] *n*.1. 股,大腿 2.【动】(昆虫的)股节

thill [θɪl] *n*.(车的)杠,辕 ∥ ~ er *n*. 套在辕间的马

thimble ['θɪmbl] *n*.1.(缝纫用的)顶针,针箍 2.【机】套筒;套管 3.【海】索眼嵌环,索眼环

thimbleful ['θimblful] *n.*(酒等的)极少量；些微

Thimbu ['θimbu] *n.* 廷布[不丹首都]

thin [θin](thinner, thinnest) *adj.* **1.** 薄的；细的；瘦的 [印]细体的 **2.** 稀薄的；淡薄的；淡的 **3.** 稀少的；稀疏的；缺乏的 **4.** 空洞的；缺乏重要成分的；浅薄的；显而易见的；易看破的 **5.** 将要垮掉的；守不住的 **6.**(俚)不舒服的；不愉快的(美俚)一个钱没有的 **7.**[摄](照片或底片)反差弱的，密度小的 一(thinner, thinnest) *adv.*[常用以构成复合词]薄；细；稀疏；微 一 **8.**(声音)尖细的部分 一(thinned; thinning) *vt.* 使薄使细；使瘦；使稀薄；使淡；使稀疏 一 *vi.* 变薄；变细；变瘦；变稀薄；变淡；变稀疏 ‖ **~ly** *adv.* / **~ness** *n.*

thine [ðain] *pron.*〈古〉**1.**[物主代词]你的东西；你的家属(或有关的人) **2.**[thou的所有格，用在以元音或 h 开始的词前]你的

thing [θiŋ] *n.* **1.** 物，东西；事物 **2.**[~s](个人的)所有物；用品；用具；财产 **3.**事，事情；事件 **4.** 局面；情况，消息；[~s]形势 **5.** 事业；行为；成就；成果 **6.** 举动，行动；(努力的)目标 **7.** 题目；主题 **8.** 细节；要点 **9.** 衣服 **10.** 家伙，东西(指人或动物，带有怜悯、爱或轻蔑等感情色彩) **11.**[the ~]最适合的东西(或样式、状况等) **12.**[~s]后接形容词(有时亦作形容词；文物 ‖ **~-in-it'self**[(复) **~s-in-themselves**] *n.*[哲]自在之物，本体

thingamy, thingummy ['θiŋəmi], **thing-amajig, thingumajig** ['θiŋəmidʒig], **thingumbob** ['θiŋəmbɔb] *n.*〈口〉(对不知名或暂时忘记名字的人或事物的代称)某人；某东西，某物

think [θiŋk](thought [θɔːt]) *vt.* **1.** 想，思索

2. 想出；想起 **3.**[~ oneself]想考使(自己)…**4.** 想要，打算；计划 **5.** 认为，以为 **6.** 料想；描测，推测；想象 **7.** 感到 一 *vi.* **1.** 想，思考 **2.** 认为；料想 一 *n.* 想；想法 一 *adj.* 思想(方面)的；供思考的 ‖ **~er** *n.* 思想家；思考者 /**~-in** *n.*〈美口〉智囊机构，研究机构 /**~-in** *n.*〈口〉讨论会 /**~ piece**(美)(带有分析和评论的)时事短评 /**~ tank 1.** 智囊团，思想库 **2.** 脑子

thinkable ['θiŋkəbl] *adj.* 可思考的；想象中可能的

thinking ['θiŋkiŋ] *adj.* 思想的；有理性的；好思考的 一 *n.* **1.** 思想；思考 **2.** 想法，见解

thinner ['θinə] *n.* 稀释剂，冲淡剂；(涂料等的)稀释料

thinnish ['θiniʃ] *adj.* 有点薄的；有点细的；有点瘦的；有点稀疏的

third [θəːd] *num.* **1.** 第三的(的) **2.** 三分之一(的) 一 *n.* **1.** 第三个；第三者；第三位 **2.**(汽车的)第三档 **3.**【音】三度；三音；三度音程；三度和音；全阶第三音 **4.**[~s](财产)归寡妇所有的亡夫遗产的三分之一 **5.**(月的)第三日 ‖ **~'class** *adj.* **1.** 三等的 **2.** 平庸的；低劣的 *adv.* 乘坐三等车(或舱)/ **~ degree 1.**〈口〉(警察的)逼供，拷问，疲劳讯问 **2.**〈口〉(灼伤的)Ⅲ度 / **~ person**【语】第三人称 / **~ sex**[总称]同性恋者 / **~ stor(e)y**(英)四楼—(美)三楼 / **Third World** 第三世界

thirst [θəːst] *n.* **1.** 渴，口渴 **2.** 渴望，热望 一 *vi.* **1.** 感到口渴；想喝(for) **2.** 渴望，热望

thirsty ['θəːsti] *adj.* **1.** 渴的 **2.**(汽车等)耗油的 **3.** 渴望的 **4.**(土地等)缺水的；干旱的；有高度吸水性的 **5.** 致渴的 ‖ **thirstily** *adv.* / **thirstiness** *n.*

thirteen [ˈθəːˈtiːn] *num.* 十三；十三个(人或物)；第十三(卷、章、页等)(用例参看 **eight**)— *n.*1.13 岁 2.13 点钟(即下午 1 点) ‖ ~**th** *num.*1. 第十三(个)2. 二十三分之一(的)— *n.*(月的)第十三日

thirtieth [ˈθəːtiiθ] *num.*1. 第三十(个)2. 三十分之一(的)— *n.*(月的)第三十日

thirty [ˈθəːti] *num.* 三十；三十个(人或物)；第三十(卷、章、页等)(用例参看 **eight**)— *n.*1. [thirties](世纪的)30 年代 2.30 岁；[thirties]30 到 39 岁的时期 3.(美)[新闻通讯中使用的符号]完、终、结束(通常写作 30)4.(网球赛中)一局中一方获得的第二分 5. 口径为 30 的机枪(或炮)(常写作 30)

this [ðis] *adj.* [后接复数名词用 these]1. 这 2. 今、本 3. [与表示时间的词组连用]刚过去的；即将来到的 4. 某；(方向等)一定的 — *pron.*1. 这，这个 2. [以下(或以上)]所述 3. 这时；这里 4. 后者(指上文已提到的两点中的后一点，其前一点用 that 表示) — *adv.* 达到这样的程度，这样，这么

thistle [ˈθisl] *n.* [植]蓟；大蓟属蓟 ‖ ~**down** *n.*(白色)蓟种子冠毛

thither [ˈðiðə] *adv.* 那里；向那里；到那里 — *adj.* 那边的；在远处的；更遥远的

tho, tho' [ðau] *conj. & adv.* = though

thole [θəul] *n.*1. 桨叉，桨架，桨栓，橹挺 2. 栓，销，钉

Thompson [ˈtɔmpsn] *n.* ‖ ~ **submachine gun** 汤姆生式冲锋枪

thong [θɔŋ] *n.*1. 皮带，皮条；皮鞭；鞭梢 2. 人字形凉鞋 3. 带式泳装 — *vt.* 给…装上皮带[用皮带捆];用皮鞭打

Thor [θɔː] *n.* 托尔(北欧神话中的雷神)

thorax [ˈθɔːræks] ([复]thoraxes 或 thoraces

[ˈθɔːræsiz]) *n.*1.[解]胸；胸廓 2.[动]胸，胸部(昆虫体三部分的中间部分)

thorium [ˈθɔːriəm] *n.*[化]钍

thorn [θɔːn] *n.*1.(棘)刺 2. 荆棘；山楂树；带刺小灌木 3. 使人生气(或苦恼)的事(或人)4.(动物身上的)棘

thorny [ˈθɔːni] *adj.*1. 多刺的；有棘刺的；刺一般的 2. 棘手的；多障碍的，多困难的；引起争论的

thoro [ˈθʌrəu] *adj.*〈口〉= thorough

thoron [ˈθɔːrɔn] *n.*[核]钍射气

thorough [ˈθʌrə] *adj.*1. 彻底的 2. 详尽的；透彻的；全面掌握的；完善的 3. 非常精确的(过细的)不厌其烦的 4. 彻头彻尾的；绝对的 — *n.*[常作 T]〈英〉英王查理一世时期所施行的全面专横政策(或行动) ‖ ~**ly** *adv.* / ~ **ness** *n.* ‖ ~**fare** *n.* 大街；通衢，大道；通行 / '~**going** *adj.* 彻底的，十足的，完全的 / '~**-paced** *adj.*1.(原指马的步伐)受过完善训练的 2. 彻底的，十足的，完全的

thoroughbred [ˈθʌrəbred] *adj.*1. 受过严格训练的;有良好教养的 2.(马、犬等)良种的,纯种的;[T-]英纯血马的 3. 优秀的;有勇气的;第一流的 — *n.*1. 纯种动物;[T-]英纯血马 2. 受过严格训练的人;有良好教养的人;有勇气的人 3. 第一流的汽车;最高级赛车

those [ðəuz] that 的复数

thou[1] [ðau] *pron.*〈古〉汝，尔，你 — *vt. & vi.* 用"汝"称呼(对方)

thou[2] [ðau] ([复] thou) *n.*〈口〉一千;1000 英镑;1000 美元(thousand 的缩略)

though [ðəu] *conj.*1. 虽然，尽管 2. 即使 3.[用于主句后，引接补充说明]可是，然而，不过 — *adv.* 可是，然而，不过

thought[1] [θɔːt] think 的过去式和过去分词

thought[2] [θɔːt] *n.* **1.** 思想 **2.** 思维;思考;推理能力;思想活动 **3.** 思潮;思想方式 **4.** 想法,意图;观念 **5.** 关心;顾虑;挂念 **6.** [a～] 稍许,一点点,少量

thoughtful ['θɔːtful] *adj.* **1.** 沉思的,思考的 **2.** 表达思想的;富有思想的;经认真推敲的 **3.** 有创见的;深思的 **4.** 考虑周到的 ‖ ～**ly** *adv.* / ～**ness** *n.*

thoughtless ['θɔːtlis] *adj.* **1.** 无思想的 **2.** 缺少考虑的,轻率的;粗心的 **3.** 自私的,不顾及他人的 **4.** 迟钝的,笨的 ‖ ～**ly** *adv.* / ～**ness** *n.*

thousand ['θauzənd] *num.* 千;千个(人或物) —— **1.** 一千个,一千个(人或物) **2.** [～s] 许许多多,无数 —— *adj.* 许许多多的,无数的 ‖ ～**fold** *adj. & adv.* 千倍的(地) / ～**th** *num.* **1.** 第一千(个) **2.** 千分之一(的)

thrall [θrɔːl] *n.* **1.** 奴隶;奴仆;农奴 **2.** 奴隶状态;奴役;束缚 —— *vt.* (古) 使成奴隶;使入迷;吸引住 —— *adj.* (古) 被奴役的;被束缚的;变成奴隶的

thral(l)dom ['θrɔːldəm] *n.* 奴隶的身份;奴役;束缚

thrash [θræʃ] *vt.* **1.** 打(谷) **2.** (用棍、鞭等)痛打 **3.** 打败,胜过 **4.** 多次地做,反复地做;推敲;研讨 **5.** 猛烈摆动,使颠簸 **6.** 使(船)迎风破浪前进 —— *vi.* **1.** 打谷 **2.** (用棍、鞭等)打,击 **3.** 猛烈摆动,颠簸;翻来复去 **4.** (船)迎风破浪前进 —— *n.* 打,击;(爬涉或仰泳中踩的)鞭挞动作 ‖ ～**'out** *vt.* **1.** 打谷脱粒,脱谷出籽 **2.** 【动】嘲鹩(美洲鸣禽);(弧形)长尾鲨

thrashing ['θræʃiŋ] *n.* **1.** 打谷 **2.** 鞭打(法) ‖ ～**floor** 打谷场 / ～**machine** 脱谷机,脱粒机

thread [θred] *n.* **1.** 线 **2.** 丝;丝状体 **3.** 细细的一条 **4.** 螺纹 **5.** 头绪,思路;贯穿

着的东西 **6.** 细矿脉 —— *vt.* **1.** 穿线于…;装配片于… **2.** 穿(珍珠、小珠子等);把…穿成一串;使穿入 **3.** 通;通过;穿过 **4.** 使交织 **5.** 刻螺纹于… —— *vi.* **1.** 通过;穿透过(*through*) **2.** (糖浆等)滴下成丝状 ‖ ～**bare** *adj.* (衣服等)磨光露底的;穿旧的 **2.** 衣着褴褛的 **3.** (笑话、说教等)俗套的;乏味的(了)/ ～**worm** *n.* 蛲虫;丝虫

threat [θret] *n.* 威胁,恐吓;造成威胁的事物;凶兆,坏兆头 —— *vt. & vi.* (古) = threaten

threaten ['θretn] *vt.* **1.** 威胁,恐吓;吓唬 **2.** 预示…的凶兆;有…的危险 —— *vi.* **1.** 威胁,恐吓,恫吓 **2.** 似将发生,可能来临 ‖ ～**ingly** *adv.*

three [θriː] *num.* 三;三个(人或物);第三(卷、章、页等)(用例参看 **eight**) —— *n.* **1.3** 字形溜冰花式 **2.** 三个(人或物)一组 **3.** 一组(或一系列)中的第三个 **4.3** 步 **5.3** 点钟 ‖ ～**fold** *adj. & adv.* 三倍;三重 / ～**penny** ['θrepəni] *adj.* **1.** 值三便士的 **2.** 微不足道的,不值钱的 / ～**-point landing**(飞机)三点着陆(二主轮与一前轮或尾轮同时着地)/ ～**-'score** *n. & adj.* 六十 / ～**-star** *adj.* (美军将官)三星级的 = ～**-star** general 中将 / ～**'wheeler** *n.* 三轮车(如三轮脚踏车、三轮摩托车和三轮汽车)

threnode ['θriːnəud], **threnody** ['θrenədi] *n.* **1.** 哀歌,挽歌 **2.** 哀悼

threpsology [θrep'sɔlədʒi] *n.* 营养学

thresh [θreʃ] *vt.* **1.** 打(谷) **2.** 多次地做,反复地做;推敲;研讨 **3.** 反复打,反复击去 —— *vi.* **1.** 打谷 **2.** 打,击 **3.** 猛烈摆动,颠簸;翻来复去 ‖ ～**er** *n.* **1.** 打谷者;脱谷机,脱粒机 **2.** 【动】(弧形)长尾鲨

threshold ['θreʃhəuld] *n.* **1.** 门槛;门口 **2.**

入门;开端,开始 3. 起始点;(税的)起征点;【空】跑道入口;跑道头;进进场着陆的一端)4.【物】阈值;【生】阈限,临界

threw [θru:] throw 的过去式

thrice [θrais] adv. 1. 三次;三倍 2. 非常,十分

thrift [θrift] n. 1. 节俭,节约 2.(植物的)茁壮成长,茂盛 3.(苏格兰)收入颇丰的职业;兴旺之道 4.【植】海石竹 ‖ ~ shop(美)廉价旧货店(尤指为慈善目的的搜来旧货出售的商店)

thriftless ['θriftlis] adj. 1. 不节俭的,不节约的;挥霍的 2. 无用的,无价值的

thrifty ['θrifti] adj. 1. 节俭的,节约的 2. 兴旺的;繁荣的;茁壮的;繁茂的 ‖ **thriftily** adv. / **thriftiness** n.

thrill [θril] n. 1. 兴奋,激动 2.(电影、小说等)刺激性,紧张感 3. 颤动【医】(心脏的)震颤 4. 惊险小说;恐怖小说 ― vt. 1. 使激动;使毛骨悚然 2. 使颤动,使抖动 ― vi. 1. 激动;毛骨悚然 2. 颤动,抖动;震颤 3.(感情等)穿过,闪过(through, over, along)‖ ~ er n. 1. 引起激动的人(或物);使毛骨悚然的人(或物)2. 惊险小说(或电影等);恐怖小说(或电影等)

thrilling ['θriliŋ] adj. 1. 令人激动的,使人毛骨悚然的 2. 颤动的,抖动的;震颤的 3. 使人发抖的;刺骨的

thrive [θraiv](过去式 throve [θrəuv] 或 thrived,过去分词 thriven ['θrivn] 或 thrived) vi. 1. 兴旺,繁荣;旺盛 2. 茁壮成长

thriving ['θraiviŋ] adj. 兴旺的,繁荣的;旺盛的

thro, **thro'** [θru:] prep., adv. & adj. = through

throat [θrəut] n. 1. 咽喉,喉咙;喉头;颈前

部 2. 咽喉状部分;入口;窄路 3. 噪音,嗓门 4.(网球拍的柄与拍之间的)颈部 ― vt. 1. 用喉音说(或唱);声音沙哑地说(或唱)2. 开沟于,开槽于

throaty ['θrəuti] adj. 1.(声音等)喉部发出的 2. 喉音的;沙哑的

throb [θrɔb](throbbed; throbbing) vi. 1.(心脏、脉搏等)跳动,悸动 2.(有规律地)颤动;震动 ― n. 1. 跳动,悸动 2. 抽动;(有规律的)颤动;震动

throe [θrəu] n. 1.(分娩时的)阵痛;临死的苦痛;垂死的挣扎 2. 剧痛 3.[常~s]痛苦;苦闷;艰苦的奋斗 ― vi. 受痛苦

thrombosis [θrɔm'bəusis] n.【医】血栓形成

throne [θrəun] n. 1. 宝座,御座 2.[the ~]王位;帝位;王权,君权 3. 君王;皇上 4.[~s][宗]座天使(九级天使中的第三级)― vt. & vi. (使)登王位,(使)即位

throng [θrɔŋ] n. 1. 群,人群 2. 群集;事务繁迫 3. 众多,大量 ― vi. 挤满,使拥塞 ― vt. 群集;蜂拥

throttle ['θrɔtl] vt. 1. 掐住…的脖子;掐死(某人);使窒息 2. 扼杀;压制 3. 使节流;节流调节;使减速 ― vi. 1. 闷住;窒息 2.【机】给节门开门;减速 ― n. 1. 节流阀(或杆);风门;[无]节流圈,扼流圈 2.(罕)喉咙;气管

through [θru:] prep. 1.(指空间)穿过,通过 2.(指时间)从头到尾经过;(美)直到(某一时刻)3.(指方法、手段等)经由,以… 4.(指原因、理由)由于,因为 5.(做)完…;(耗)尽… ― adv. 1. 对穿;穿过;通过 2. 从头到尾;自始至终;到底 3. 透,彻底;be wet ~ 浑身湿透 4. 出来 ― adj. 1. 对穿的;(道路等)可通行的 2. 直达的;过境的;a ~ train 直达列车 / a ~ ticket 通运票 / ~ transport by land and water 水陆联运 / ~ traffic 过

境交通;联运 3. 穿了的,有洞的 4.(电话用语)(英)接通的;(美)通话完毕的,打完的 ‖ ~ **way** *n*. 过境道路,直达道路(尤指高速公路)

throughout [θru:'aut] *prep*. 遍及;贯穿 — *adv*. 到处;始终;彻头彻尾

throughput ['θru:put] *n*.1. 生产量;生产能力 2. 通过量,吞吐量 3.【计】吞吐量,总处理能力

throve [θrəuv] thrive 的过去式

throw [θrəu] (threw[θru:], thrown[θrəun]) *vt*.1. 投,掷,抛,扔 2. 发射;喷射 3. 摔倒;推下 4. 匆匆穿上;匆匆脱下 5. 急伸,猛动(头、臂、腿等),挥(拳)猛主6. 抛弃;丢弃;摆脱 7. 投射(光线、阴影等)8. 施加(影响)等 9. 下(仔);蜕(皮);脱落(马蹄铁)10. 把…拉成坯(在车床上);车(木料等)11. 摔(骰子);掷出(骰子点数)12. 把…捻成线 13.(美)故意输掉(比赛等)14.(俚)举行(宴会或招待)等 15. 开关(离合器等);推动…的操纵杆(或手柄等)— *vi*. 投,掷,抛,扔 — *n*.1. 投掷;投掷的距离2. 掷骰子;掷出的点数 3. 冒险,孤注一掷 4. 床罩5. 披肩;肩巾 6.【地】落差,断层引起的位移 7.【机】行程;摆度 8.【体】(摔跤中的)摔倒;摔倒对手的技巧 ‖ ~**er** *n*.1. 投掷器 2. 投掷器(喷射器、a flame ~**er** 火焰喷射器 3. 拉坯工 4.【纺】捻丝工 ‖ ~ **a**,**way** *n*. 免费散发的传单(或小册子、报纸等)/ ~ **back** *n*. [生]返祖(现象);(喻)大倒退

thru [θru:] *prep*., *adv*. & *adj*. 〈美口〉= through

thrum¹ [θrʌm] *n*.1. 纱头,线头;[~s](纺)丁机回丝;线头末尾 2.[~s](植]花丝,花药 3.[~s](海]绳屑 — (thrummed; thrumming) *vt*.1. 使有流苏;使有粗毛 2.[海]把绳屑夹杂于(帆布

等)之中,植绒于(用以防擦或堵漏)

thrum² [θrʌm] (thrummed; thrumming) *vt*.1. 乱弹(弦乐器);轻松随便地弹 2. 用单调的声音朗诵 3. 用指头不断地轻敲 — *vi*.1. 乱弹;随便弹奏 2. 单调地作响,用指头不断地轻敲 — *n*.1. 乱弹;轻敲 2. 乱弹声;(指头)得得的敲声 ‖ ~ **mer** *n*.

thrush¹ [θrʌʃ] *n*.[动]鸫;歌鸫

thrush² [θrʌʃ] *n*.1.[医]真菌性口炎,鹅口疮 2.(马的)蹄叉腐烂

thrust [θrʌst] (thrust) *vt*.1. 插;挤;刺;刺入 2. 猛推;冲 3. 突然提出;不恰当地插进 4. 将…强加于 5. 挺申;延申 — *vi*.1. 插入;挤;刺;戳 2. 强行推进;强行进入 3. 挺伸;延伸 — *n*.1. 插;刺;戳 2. 猛推;挺进 3.(辩论等时的)口头攻击;讽刺 4.【机】推力;侧向压力 5.【地】冲褶(作用);冲断层,逆断层 6.【建】(拱或椽的)推力 ‖ ~ **er** *n*.1. 向上钻营的人 2.(飞行、宇宙飞行时用的)推进器,助推器,推进器

thrusting ['θrʌstiŋ] *adj*. 有强大推进力的;劲头十足的;积极进取的

thruway ['θru:wei] *n*.〈美口〉= throughway

Thu. *abbr*. Thursday

thud [θʌd] *n*. 重击;砰的一声 — (thudded; thudding) *vi*. 砰然落下;发出重击声

thug [θʌg] *n*. 恶棍;暴徒;刺客;凶手 ‖ **thuggery**['θʌɡəri] *n*. 凶杀;谋财害命

thulium ['θju:ljəm] *n*.【化】铥

thumb [θʌm] *n*.1.(大)拇指;(手套的)(大)拇指部分 2.【建】圆凸形线脚装饰 — *vt*.1. 用拇指翻旧(或翻破、翻脏)(书等)2. 用拇指翻阅;用拇指翻弄 3. 用拇指摸(或揿、顶、按、戳等)4. 拙劣地弹(钢琴、乐曲等)5. 竖起拇指指向过路汽车作手势要求(免费搭乘)‖

index 拇指索引，书边挖月索引 /'～-index** *vt.* 给(词典等)做拇指索引 /'～nail** *n.*1. 拇指甲 2. 略图；短文 *adj.* 拇指甲大小的；小型的；简略的 /～ pin** 图钉 /'～print** *n.*(手指的)拇指纹手印；〈美俚〉个人性特征；印记/'～screw** *n.* 1.〔机〕指紧螺钉，翼形螺钉 2. 拇指夹(古刑具) /'～s up** *n.* 翘拇指(满意或赞同的表示) /'～tack** *n.* = pin

thump [θʌmp] *n.*1. 重击；捶击 2. 重击声；砰击 3.〔无〕键电噪声(指电话中的电报噪声) — *vt.* 重击；捶击；撞击 — *vi.* 重击；捶击；砰砰地响 ‖ ~er** *n.* 1. 重击；捶击的人(或物) 2. 庞然大物；大谎话 3. 月面起落装置

thumping ['θʌmpiŋ] *adj.*〈口〉1. 巨大的，极大的 2. 发出重击声的；捶击的 — *adv.* 极端地；非常地

thunder ['θʌndə] *n.*1. 雷，雷声 2. 似雷的响声，轰隆声 3. 怒喝；恐吓，威吓 4.〈古〉落雷；霹雳 — *vi.*1. 打雷 2. 发出雷鸣般的响声，轰隆地响 3. 怒喝；恐吓(*against*) — *vt.*1. 轰隆地发出 2. 大声说出；吼叫 ‖ ~y** *adj.*1. 雷声似的，轰隆轰隆的；要打雷的 ‖ ～-bolt** *n.*1. 雷电；霹雳 2. 意外的事件，晴天霹雳 3. 怒喝；恐吓 4. 雷石；黄铁矿团块 /'～clap** *n.* 雷声；霹雳；晴天霹雳似的消息(事件) /'～cloud** *n.* 雷雨云 /'～head** *n.*〔气〕(雷暴前常见的)雷暴云砧，雷雨云砧 /'～shower** *n.* 雷阵雨 /'～storm** *n.* 雷暴 /'～struck** *adj.* 遭雷击的；吓坏了的，大吃一惊的

thunderous ['θʌndərəs] *adj.*1. 雷鸣似的，轰隆轰隆的 2. 多雷的；形成雷的

Thur(s). *abbr.* Thursday

Thursday ['θɜːzdi] *n.* 星期四 — *adv.*〈口〉在星期四 ‖ ～s** *adv.* 在每星期四

thus [ðʌs] *adv.*1. 如此，这样；到如此程度

2. 因而，从而 3. 例如

thwack [θwæk] *vt.*, *vi.* & *n.* = whack

thwart [θwɔːt] *vt.*1. 反对；阻挠；使受挫折；挫败 2. 横过，穿过 — *adj.* 横放的；横着的 — *adv.* & *prep.* 横过，横跨 — *n.*(划艇中横贯船体的)横坐板；划手座

thy [ðai] *pron.*〈古〉[thou 的所有格]你的

thyme [taim] *n.*〔植〕百里香

thymol ['θaiməl] *n.*〔化〕百里酚，麝香草酚

thyroid ['θairɔid] *adj.*1. 甲状的；甲状腺的；甲状软骨的 — *n.*1. 甲状腺 2. 甲状软骨 3. 甲状腺粉，甲状腺制剂 ‖ ～ gland** 甲状腺

thyroidectomize [ˌθairɔi'dektəmaiz] *vt.* 对…施行甲状腺切除术

thyroidectomy [ˌθairɔi'dektəmi] *n.* 甲状腺切除术

thyself [ðai'self] *pron.*〈古〉1.〔反身代词〕你自己 2.〔用以加强语气〕你亲自，你本人

Ti 〔化〕元素钛(titanium)的符号

tiara [ti'ɑːrə] *n.*1.〈古波斯人的〉男用头巾；(罗马教皇的)三重冕 2. 教皇职权(或权力) 3.(妇女的)冕状头饰

Tibet [ti'bet] *n.* 西藏

Tibetan [ti'betən] *n.*1. 藏族人；西藏人 2. 藏语 — *adj.* 西藏的；藏族的；西藏人的；藏语的

tibia ['tibiə] ([复] tibias 或 tibiae ['tibiiː]) *n.* 1.〔解〕胫骨 2.(昆虫的)胫节

tic [tik] *n.*1. 抽搐 2. 三叉神经痛 3. 不自觉的习惯行为；顽固的性格特征；口头语

tick¹ [tik] *n.*1.(钟表等的)滴答声 2.(主英)(滴答的一瞬间，一刹那间 3.(核对账目等用的)小记号(√、/等) — *vi.*1.(钟表等)滴答滴答响 2.(似钟表般)持续活动 — *vt.*1. 滴答滴答地记录

(时间);滴答滴答地发出 2. 给…标记号

tick² [tik] *n.*〖动〗蜱，壁虱；虱蝇

tick³ [tik] *n.* 1. 垫套；褥套；枕心套；褥子 2. = ticking ‖ ~ ing *n.*（做褥套等用的）坚质（条纹）棉布（或亚麻布）

tick⁴ [tik] *n.*（口）信用；赊欠：buy goods on ~ 赊购货物

ticker [ˈtikə] *n.* 1. 滴答滴答响的东西 2. 自动收报机，（股票行情）自动收录器 3.（口）钟；表 4.（俚）心脏 ‖ ~ tape 1. 自动收报机用纸带，电报收条 2.（为表示庆祝、欢迎而从窗口等抛下的）纸带

ticket [ˈtikit] *n.* 1. 票，券；车票；入场券；票证：a single（或〈美〉one-way）~ 单程票 / a return（或〈美〉round-trip）~ 来回票 / a season ~〈英〉季票，长期票（用于乘车、观剧等，期限可为一个月、一季度、半年等）/ a through ~ 联运票 2.（物上的）签条，标签；单子，登记单，记录卡；说明单3.证明书；许可证；（船员或飞行员的）执照，退役（或出狱等）证书4.〈美〉(竞选中的党的)候选人名单；(政党的)纲领，政见；(事业等的)计划,规划 5.（口）(给违反交通规则者等的)违章通知单，罚款单 6.（口）(the ~)适例；恰好的事情；所需的东西 7. 获得想望之物的手段，达到目的的途径(to) — *vt.* 1. 加标签于；标号2. 给…门票，发出传票 ‖ ~ agent 代理售票人 / ~ office 票房，售票处

tickle [ˈtikl] *vt.* 1. 使觉得痒 2. 逗乐,使高兴;激起 3. 用手抓(鱼等) — *vi.* 1. 使得痒 2. 使人觉得痒 — *n.* 1. 使人发痒 2. 使人发痒的东西;使人高兴的事物

tickler [ˈtiklə] *n.* 1. 呵痒的人;使人觉得痒的东西 2. 难题;难事;棘手的问题 3. 备忘录,记事本;到期票据记录簿 4.

【电子】反馈线圈

ticklish [ˈtiklif] *adj.* 1. 怕呵痒的;怕痒的 2. 不稳定的,易变的;易怒的 3. 需要小心从事的;难对付的,棘手的 ‖ ~ ly *adv.*

ticktack, tictac [ˈtikˈtæk] *n.* 1.（钟表的）滴答声 2.（儿童对万圣节前夕与人开玩笑时用的）发叩门（或呵窗）物 3.（英）(赛马场赌注登记经纪人之间用手表示的)秘密信号

ticktock, tictoc [ˈtikˈtɔk] *n.*（尤指大钟的）滴答声

t. i. d., TID *abbr.*〈拉〉*ter in die*（处方用语）一日三次（= three times a day）

tidal [ˈtaidl] *adj.* 1. 潮(汐)的,有潮的;受潮汐影响的 2. 班次根据潮汐涨落而定的 ‖ ~ wave 1. 潮(汐)波;异常高潮位;海啸 2.（美）〈喻〉浪潮(指势不可当的群众运动或呈潮涌之势的人或物)

tidbit [ˈtidbit] *n.* = titbit

tide [taid] *n.* 1. 潮,潮汐;潮水 2. 潮流,趋势;浪潮 3. 涨潮;高潮期 4. 紧要关头,危急状态 4. 时机 5.〈古〉一段时间;时刻 6.〈古〉[用以构成复合词]时,季;宗教节期 — *vi.* 1. 潮水般地奔流 2.（船只进港或离港时）顺潮行驶 — *vt.* 使随潮水漂浮 ‖ ~ ga(u)ge 潮位计 / ~ land *n.* 潮滩区(指涨潮时为水所淹的地带)/ ~ lock 潮汐船闸 / ~ mark *n.* 1. 潮标2. 潮痕 / ~ rip 潮激 / ~ waiter *n.*（登上进港船只检查的）海关港口稽查 / ~ water *n.* 1. 有潮水域 2. 有潮水域地区 *adj.* 有潮水域地区的

tidings [ˈtaidiŋz]〖复〗*n.*[用作单或复]〈书面语〉消息,音讯

tidology [taiˈdɔlədʒi] *n.* 潮汐学

tidy [ˈtaidi] *adj.* 1. 整洁的,整齐的;有条不紊的 2. 丰满的;健美的 3.（口）相当好的;令人满意的 4.（口）相当大的;

当多的 — **vt.** 使整洁,整理(*up*) — **vi.** 收拾,整理(*up*) — **n.** 1.(沙发靠背,扶手等上的)套子,罩布 2.装载零星杂物的容器 ‖ **tidily** *adv.* / **tidiness** *n.* ‖ '~-**up** *n.* 收拾,整理

tie [tai] **n.** 1.〈结物等用的〉带子;绳;线;鞋带 2.领带;领结 3.联系,纽带 4.系绳(或打结)的方法;打法;系法 5.束缚;牵累 6.(选票等的)同数(比赛等的)等分;平局 7.[建]系材;(美)枕木,轨枕 8.[音]连结线 9.〈美〉[常~s]系带浅口鞋 — (tied; tying 或 tieing) *vt.* 1.(用绳、绳、线等)系,扎,束紧 2.把(带子等)打结;打上结 3.束缚,约束,限制 4.连接(两个供电系统) [音]用连结线连接(音符)5.把(轨道)固定在枕木上;给…铺设枕木 6.使…连结成夫妇 7.与…打成平局,与…势均力敌 — *vi.* 1.结合;结住 2.打结;能打结 3.打成平局,取得同样分数,不分胜负 ‖ ~ **beam** [建]系梁,水平拉杆 / '~-**in** *adj.* 搭卖的,搭配销售的 **n.** 1.关联;关系 2.与电影(或广播节目等)相互关联的书(或录音带、宣传材料等)3.搭卖(广告)搭卖的商品 4.(管道等)接头;连接 / '~-**up** **n.** 1.捆扎,捆住 2.(船只)停泊处 3.牛棚 4.(由罢工引起的)停顿;〈口〉交通阻塞 5.关系;联合

tier¹ [ˈtaiə] **n.** 1.包扎的人(或工具);包扎工人 2.〈美〉(用带子结住的)围涎

tier² [tiə] **n.** 1.(一)排;(一)层 2.(衣服上的)一行褶裥 3.[无]定向天线元 4.等级 — *vt.* 层层排列(*up*) — *vi.* 层层上升

tierce [tiəs] **n.** 1.[音]三音,三度 2.蒂尔斯(旧液量名;= 42 加仑)3.(装 42 加仑液量的)中号桶 4.(八击剑防守姿势的)第三姿势 5.(天主教七段祈祷时间中的第三段)辰时经 6.[tɜ:s, tiəs] 三

张同花顺

tiff¹ [tif] **n.**(朋友或熟人间的)口角,争执;生气 — *vi.* 口角,争执;生气(*with*)

tiff² [tif] **n.** 1.酒;淡酒 2.一口酒;小饮 — *vt.* 喉,饮

tiff³ [tif] *vi.*(印度用英语)吃午餐

tiffany [ˈtifəni] **n.** [纺]丝纱罗;亚麻薄布

tiffin [ˈtifin](印度用英语) **n.** 午餐 — *vi.* 吃午餐

tiger [ˈtaigə] **n.** 1.虎 2.(作为某一组织标志的)虎图案 3.凶恶的人;凶残本性 4.〈英〉(穿号衣的)年轻男仆 5.〈口〉(比赛的)劲敌 6.〈美〉(欢呼声之后的)高呼声 ‖ '~-**eye** **n.** 虎眼石(一种宝石)/ ~ **lily** [植]卷丹,卷丹状植物 / ~ **moth** [动]灯蛾

tight [tait] *adj.* 1.紧的,不松动的;牢固的 2.拉紧的,绷紧的 3.紧身的,紧贴的 4.密封的;不漏的,透不过水的 5.装紧的,挤满的;密集的 6.严厉的,严格的 7.麻烦的;棘手的;困难的;尴尬的 8.(比赛等)势均力敌的 9.[文字、语言等]凑得紧的,简洁的,精练的;排得紧的 10.整洁的;整齐的;安排得当的 11.吝啬的,小气的 12.[商](商品)紧缺的;(钱)难以贷到的 13.有能力的;机警的 14.(俚)醉醺醺的 — **n.** [~s](运动员或舞蹈演员的)紧身衣 — *adv.* 1.紧,紧紧地 2.〈口〉酣畅地 3.牢 / '~-**ness** **n.** ‖ '~-**fisted** *adj.* 吝啬的,小气的 / '~-**lipped** *adj.* 嘴唇紧闭的;寡言的,沉默的 / '~-**mouthed** *adj.* 守口如瓶的 / '~-**rope** **n.**(供走钢丝用的)绷紧的钢绳(或绳索);困难(或危险等)的处境;perform on the ~**rope** 表演走钢丝 / '~-**wad** **n.** (俚)吝啬鬼;守财奴

tighten [ˈtaitn] *vt.* 使变紧;使绷紧;~ the ropes 绷紧绳索 — *vi.* 变紧;绷紧

tiglon [ˈtaiglən], **tigon** [ˈtaigən] **n.** 虎狮(雄

虎与雌狮所生的杂交兽）

tigress ['taigris] *n.* 1. 母虎 2. 凶恶的女人，雌老虎

Tigris ['taigris] *n.* [the ~] 底格里斯河 [西南亚]

tike [taik] *n.* = tyke

tilde ['tildə] *n.* [语] 1. 腭化符号（即~, 西班牙语字母 n 读作 [nj] 时 n 上方加的记号, 如 *señor*）2. 代字号（即 ~）

tile [tail] *n.* 1. 瓦; 瓦片; 瓷砖, 花砖（贴墙或铺地用的）塑料（或金属、橡胶、水泥）片 2. [总称] 瓦; 瓷砖 3. (排水的) 瓦管, 瓦筒; 瓦沟 4. [口] 丝质高顶硬帽 5. (一张) 麻将牌 — *vt.* 1. 用瓦盖, 铺瓦于; 贴砖于; 装瓦管于…… 2. (共济会用语) 派人守卫 (会所等); 使保守秘密 ‖ ~ry *n.* 1. 制瓦场, 瓦窑 2. 装饰性瓦铺贴术

tiling ['tailiŋ] *n.* 1. 盖瓦; 贴砖 2. [总称] 瓦; 瓷砖, 花砖 3. 瓦面; 花砖面; 瓦屋顶

till[1] [til] [till 基本上与 until 相同, 但句首一般不用 till, 而用 until] *prep.* 1. 直到……为止 2. [用在否定句中] 在……之前, 直到…… (才) 3. [苏格兰] = to — *conj.* 1. 直到……为止 [用于否定式的主句后] 在……以前, 直到…… (才) *: Don't go away 一 I come back.* 我回来前不要走开。

till[2] [til] *vt.* 耕种, 耕作 ‖ ~able *adj.* 可耕种的, 可耕作的 / ~age *n.* 1. 耕种, 耕作 2. 耕地; 耕作地的庄稼

till[3] [til] *n.* 1. (账台中) 放钱的抽屉; 钱柜, 钱箱 2. (橱柜中) 放置贵重物品的格子 (或抽屉) 3. 备用现金

till[4] [til] [地] 冰碛; 冰碛物

tiller[1] ['tilə] *n.* 耕种者; 农夫 (= farmer)

tiller[2] ['tilə] [植] *n.* 分蘖 — *vi.* 长出分蘖

tiller[3] ['tilə] *n.* [船] 舵柄

tilt[1] [tilt] *vt.* 1. 使倾斜, 使歪斜; 使翘起 2. 斜持 (矛); 投 (矛); 向 (敌人) 冲刺 3. 用杵锤锤打 — *vi.* 1. 倾斜, 歪斜; 翘起 2. 持矛冲刺 (against 或比试); 抨击, 攻击 (at) — *n.* 1. 骑马持矛冲刺; 马上比枪; 激烈的竞争; 争论 2. 倾斜, 歪斜; 翘起 3. 斜坡 4. 跷跷板 5. 杵锤, 轮锤

tilt[2] [tilt] *n.* (小舟、车辆、地摊等的) 天篷, 遮阳 — *vt.* 用篷遮盖, 为……搭篷

timbale ['timbəl] *n.* 1. (模制的) 夹心烤馅饼 2. 夹心烤馅饼模子 3. 夹心烤馅饼饼壳 ‖ ~ iron 夹心烤馅饼铁模

timber ['timbə] *n.* 1. 木材, 原木 2. (可作木材的) 树木, 林木 3. 栋木; (船) 肋骨, 肋材 4. [美] (人的) 素质, 气质 5. [建筑用的] 木栅栏, 木门 — *vt.* 用木材建造; 用木材支撑 — *int.* (伐木工在树木倒下前的呼喊声) 倒啦! 避开! ‖ ~ed *adj.* 木制的; 木结构的 / '~line *n.* 林木线 (指山区或高纬度地区树木生长的上限) / ~ wolf 狼 / '~work *n.* 木结构 (指屋架或船身的骨架)

timbre ['timbə, 'tæmbə] [法] *n.* [音] 音色, 音品, 音质; [语] 音色

timbrel ['timbrəl] *n.* 铃鼓; 小手鼓

time [taim] *n.* 1. 时间, 时 2. 时候; 时刻 3. 时机, 机会 4. [常~s] 时代; 时势; 境况; [the ~] 当代 5. 时期; 时令 6. 生活期; 死期; 学徒期; 服役期; 产期; 刑期 7. 次, 回 8. [~s] 倍 9. 进行速度; 节奏; [音] 拍子, 速度, 节拍 10. [Times] [用于报刊名的] 时报 11. (规定的) 工作时间; 占用时间; 所需时间 12. 计时工资率; 按计时工资率领取的工资 (被辞退或辞职时领取的) 最后一次工资 13. [体] (一场或一局等的) 比赛时限; 暂停 — *vt.* 1. 安排……的时间(为); 选择最好时间 2. 测定……的时间; 记录……的时间; 测定完成……某一过程的最终时刻 3. 安排……

速度(或节拍);使合拍子 **4.** 拨准(钟、表)的快慢;调整好(机件)的速度 — *vi.* 与…合拍(with);打拍子 — *adj.* **1.** 时间(方面)的 **2.** 记录时间的;时间发火的;定时炸弹的 **4.** 定期的 **5.** 分期(付款)的 ‖ ~ **bomb 1.** 定时炸弹 **2.** (喻)定时炸弹(指潜在的爆炸性局势)/ ~ **book** 工作时间记录簿,考勤簿/ ~ **hono(u)red** *adj.* 由来已久的;因古老而受到尊重的;a ~ *hono(u)red* custom 历史悠久的习俗/ '~ **keeper** *n.* **1.** 时计(指钟、表) **2.**(比赛中的)计时员;出勤时间记录员 **3.** 打拍子的人/ '~ **out** *n.* (比赛等过程中的)暂停/ '~ **piece** *n.* 时计(指钟、表)/ '~ **,saving** *adj.* 可节省时间的/ '~ **server** *n.* 随波逐流的人;趋炎附势者/ '~ **serving** *n. & adj.* 随波逐流的;趋炎附势的/ '~ **table** *n.* 时间表,时刻表

timeless ['taimlis] *adj.* **1.** 无时间限制的;无日期的;长期有效的 **2.** 永恒的,无穷无尽的 **3.**〈古〉过早的;不合时宜的

timely ['taimli] *adj.* **1.** 及时的 **2.** 适时的;合时势的 — *adv.* 及时地

timer ['taimə] *n.* **1.** 计时员;记时员 **2.** 计时(比赛中测时用的)停表,马表,跑表 **3.** 定时器 **4.**【机】(内燃机的)发火定时器 **4.**[用以构成复合词]花…时间工作(或学习)的人;…辈的人;第一次来某机构服务的人 a full— 全日工/a young—年轻人/a first ~ in the office 第一次进办公室工作的人

timid ['timid] *adj.* 胆怯的,易受惊的;羞怯的;缺乏自信心的 ‖ ~ **ly** *adv.* / ~ **ness** *n.*

timidity [ti'miditi] *n.* 胆怯;羞怯

timorous ['timərəs] *adj.* 胆怯的,易受惊的,羞怯的 ‖ ~ **ly** *adv.*

timothy ['timəθi] *n.*【植】梯牧草,猫尾草

(亦作 ~ **grass**)

timpani ['timpəni] [复] *n.* [用作单或复]【音】定音鼓

tin [tin] *n.* **1.**【化】锡 **2.** = ~ plate **3.** 马口铁器皿;〈英〉(保藏食物的)罐头,听头(= 〈美〉can) **4.**〈俚〉钱 **5.**〈美俚〉警徽;警探 — *vt.* **1.**(tinned; tinning)在…上镀锡(或包锡、包马口铁) **2.**〈英〉把(食品等)装听 — *adj.* **1.** 锡制的;马口铁制的;镀锡的 **2.** 蹩脚的;假冒的 ‖ ~ **fish**〈俚〉鱼雷/ '~ **foil** *n.* 锡箔,锡纸/ ~ **hat**〈军俚〉钢盔/ ~ **opener**〈英〉开听刀/ '~ **plate** *n.* 马口铁,镀锡铁皮/ '~ **plate** *vt.* 在…上(镀锡);在…上包锡/ '~ **smith** *n.* 锡匠,白铁工/ '~ **ware** *n.* [总称]马口铁器皿

tincal ['tiŋkəl] *n.*【矿】原硼砂,粗硼砂

tincture ['tiŋktʃə] *n.* **1.** 色泽;色调;染料;颜料 **2.** 些许味道(或气息);一丝痕迹(或性质)(of) **3.** 酊(剂) — *vt.* **1.** 着于下,染之 **2.** 使带有一丝味(或痕迹等)

tinder ['tində] *n.* 引火物;火绒;火种

tine [tain] *n.* **1.**(叉、耙等的)尖齿,尖头 **2.** 鹿角尖

ting [tiŋ] *n.* 丁丁声 — *vi. & vt.* (使)发丁丁声

tinge [tindʒ] *n.* **1.**(较淡的)色调;色彩 **2.** 些许味道(或气息);一丝痕迹(或性质) — *vt.* **1.**(较淡地)着色于,染 **2.** 使带有一些气味(或痕迹等)

tingle ['tiŋgl] *vi.* **1.** 感到刺痛 **2.**(耳等)鸣响;发出丁丁声 **3.** 震颤;激动 — *vt.* 使感到刺痛 — *n.* **1.** 刺痛 **2.**(耳等)鸣响 **3.** 震颤;激动

tinkal ['tiŋkəl] *n.* = tincal

tinker ['tiŋkə] *n.* **1.**(流动的)补锅匠,白铁匠;能作各种小修小补的人 **2.** 拙劣的修补工;粗劣的工作 **3.**【动】小鲭;鲐 — *vi.* **1.** 做白铁匠工 **2.** 拙劣地修补 — *vt.*

（尤指马虎将就地）修补，修理

tinkle ['tiŋkl] *n*.1. 丁丁声；丁当声 2.〈英口〉电话 — *vt*.使发出丁丁（或丁当）声 2. 丁丁地发出（时间）— *vi*.丁丁（或丁当）作响

tinner ['tinə] *n*.1. 锡矿矿工 2. 白铁匠 3.〈英〉罐头食品装制者；〈美〉canner)

tinny ['tini] *adj*.1. 锡的；多锡的；含锡的；产锡的 2. 似锡的；不耐久的；光亮而不值钱的 3.（声音）细薄无力的；（写作）空洞无内容的

tinsel ['tinsəl] *n*.1. 金属丝；金属箔 2. 镶有闪光金属线的织物 3. 华而不实的东西 — *adj*.1. 金属丝（或箔）制的；饰有金属丝（或箔）的 2. 虚饰的；华而不实的 — (tinsel(l)ed; tinsel(l)ing) *vt*.1. 用金属丝（或箔）修饰 2. 虚饰

tint [tint] *n*.1. 色调；色彩 2. 浅色；〔印〕底色 3.（雕刻时的）线晕 4. 一丝痕迹（或性质等）5. 染发剂；染发 — *vt*.给…着色；给…染色

tintinnabulation ['tintinæbju'leiʃən] *n*. 铃声；丁丁声

tintometer [tin'tɔmitə] *n*. 色调计，色辉计

tiny ['taini] *adj*. 极小的，微小的

tip¹ [tip] *n*.1. 梢，末端；尖，尖端 2.（鸟或飞机的）翼尖，翼梢 3. 顶端附加的小件 4.（茶叶的）芽尖 — (tipped; tipping) *vt*.1. 在…的顶端装钸附加的小件（或装饰）；加…的尖端 ‖ ~ staff *n*. 金属头手杖(旧时法警的标志)；法警 /~ top *n*. 顶点,最高点 *adj*.〈口〉出色的,第一流的

tip² [tip] (tipped; tipping) *vt*.1. 使倾斜 2. 使翻倒，使倾覆 3.〈英〉倒，倾泻 — *vi*.1. 倾斜 2. 翻倒，倾覆 — *n*.1. 轻触 2. 垃圾倾倒场 ‖ ~-cart *n*. 翻斗小车，翻斗手推车 /~-up *adj*.（座位不用时）可翻起的 *n*. 翻椅

tip³ [tip] (tipped; tipping) *vt*.1. 轻击；轻触 2. 给；递送 3. 给（侍者等）小费 4. 向（某人）泄露消息；泄露关于（某事）的消息；对…提出忠告；对…提出忠告 5. 提及…有可能获胜（或投资有利可图）— *vi*.1. 踮着脚 2. 给小费 — *n*.1. 小费 2. 告诫，指点，指导 3.（关于行情等的）秘密消息；密报 4. 轻击；轻触 ‖ '~-off *n*.1. 透露消息；告诫，密告 2.（篮球比赛开始时的）中圈跳球 /~ sheet(股票买卖、赛马等的)内情通报

tipper¹ ['tipə] *n*. 给小费者

tipper² ['tipə] *n*. = tipper truck ‖ ~ lorry, ~ truck 翻斗卡车,自卸货车

tippet ['tipit] *n*.(法官、教士等用的)黑色圣带；女式披肩

tipple¹ ['tipl] *vt*.一点一点地连续饮(酒) — *vi*.饮酒；嗜酒 — *n*.含酒饮料；常喝的酒 ‖ ~ r *n*.

tipple² ['tipl] *n*.1.(运货卡车上的)翻车机；翻卸器 2. 卸煤场；卸矿场 — *vt*. & *vi*.（使）翻倒，（使）倾翻 ‖ ~ r *n*.

tipster ['tipstə] *n*.提供赛马情报或股票行情等的)情报贩子

tipsy ['tipsi] *adj*.1. 喝醉的；微醉的 2. 不稳的,摇摇晃晃的 3. 歪斜的 ‖ tipsily *adv*./tipsiness *n*. ‖ '~-cake *n*. 蜜饯夹心酒味蛋糕

tiptoe ['tiptəu] *n*. 脚尖；脚趾尖 — *adv*. 踮着脚 — *adj*.1. 踮着脚走(或站)的 2. 小心翼翼的；偷偷摸摸的 — *vi*. 踮着脚走；蹑手蹑脚地行进

tiptop ['tip'tɔp] *n*.1. 顶点；极点 2.〈口〉头等,第一流 — *adj*.1. 顶点的；极点的 2.〈口〉头等的,第一流的 — *adv*.1. 在顶点；在极点 2.〈口〉极好地；极其好 ‖ ~ per *n*.

tirade [tai'reid] *n*.(尤指指责性的)激烈的

长篇演说

Tirana, Tirane ['ti'rɑːnə] *n.* 地拉那[阿尔巴尼亚首都]

tire¹ ['taiə] *vi.*1. 感到疲倦,感到累 2. 厌倦,厌烦(*of*) — *vt.*1. 使疲劳,使累 2. 使厌倦,使厌烦

tire² ['taiə] *n.*【美】= tyre

tire³ ['taiə] *n.* 头饰;服装 — *vt.*【古】打扮,装饰 2. 在〔头、头发〕上佩戴头饰 ‖ '~ woman *n.*(贵妇人)梳妆侍女;(剧院的)女化妆助手

tired ['taiəd] *adj.*1. 疲劳的,累的 2. 厌倦的,厌烦的(*of*)3. 破旧的;陈腐的,陈旧的 ‖ ~ly *adv.* / ~ness *n.*

tireless ['taiəlis] *adj.*1. 不知疲劳的,不觉得累的,不厌倦的 2. 坚韧的,不停的,持久的 ~ efforts 不懈的努力 ‖ ~ly *adv.* / ~ness *n.*

tiresome ['taiəsəm] *adj.* 使人疲劳的;令人厌倦的;讨厌的 ‖ ~ly *adv.* / ~ness *n.*

tiro ['taiərəu] *n.*([复] tiros) *n.* = tyro

'tis [tiz]【诗】= it is

tissue ['tisjuː] *n.*1. 薄绸;薄纱;薄的织物 2. ~ paper 3. 【生】组织 4.(罗纹或有图案的)一套,一系列 5. 手巾纸;卫生纸 ‖ ~ paper 薄纸,绵纸

tit¹ [tit] *n.*【动】山雀

tit² [tit] *n.* 轻打 ‖ ~ for tat 针锋相对,以牙还牙

tit³ [tit] *n.*1.【罕】发育不良的马;驽马 2. 老马,不中用的人 3.【俚】荡妇

tit⁴ [tit] *n.*1. 奶头,乳头 2.【粗】乳房

Titan ['taitn] *n.*1.【希神】提坦(传说曾统治世界的巨人族的一成员) 2. [t-] 巨人;巨物 3.【美】大力神洲际弹道导弹 — *adj.*【希神】提坦的

Titanic [tai'tænik] *adj.*1.【希神】提坦的 2.

[t-] 巨大的;力大无比的;强大的

titanium [tai'teinjəm] *n.*【化】钛

titbit ['titbit] *n.*1. 量少味美的食品,珍品,趣闻;花絮

tithe [taið] *n.*1.[常~s](向教会交纳的农产品)什一税 2. 十分之一;小部分;一点点 3. 捐税;捐款 — *vt.* 向…征收什一税;把(农产品等)的十分之一缴税 — *vi.* 缴纳什一税

titian ['tiʃjən] *n.* 橙红色;赤褐色

titillate ['titileit] *vt.*1. 呵…痒;使觉得痒 2. 使兴奋;使愉快

titivate ['titiveit] *vt. & vi.*【口】打扮;装饰,修饰 ‖ ,titi'vation *n.*

title ['taitl] *n.*1.(书籍、诗歌、乐曲等的)标题,题目 2.(书刊的)扉页;扉页内容 3. 称号;头衔(如爵位、官衔、学衔等);称呼(如先生、太太等);职称(如医生、教授等)有头衔的人(尤指贵族)4. 权利;资格;所有权;所有权凭证 5.【宗】(英国国教的)就任圣职须具备的资格(天主教的)教区 6. 第一名;冠军 7.(电影或电视的)字幕 8.(书刊等的)一种 — *vt.*1. 加标题于 2. 授予…称号 ‖ 头衔称呼 — deed【律】所有权证书(尤指地契)/ '~,holder *n.* 有称号者;有头衔者;有职称者;体】冠军保持者;冠军 / ~ page(书刊的)扉页,标题页,书名页

titmouse ['titmaus]([复] titmice ['titmais]) *n.*【动】山雀

titrate ['titreit] *vt. & vi.*【化】用滴定法测量 ‖ ti'tration *n.* 滴定(法)

titter ['titə] *n.* 窃笑;傻笑 — *vi.* 窃笑;傻笑;嗤嗤地笑

titivate ['titiveit] *vt. & vi* = titivate

tittle ['titl] *n.*1.(书写或印刷中的)小点,小符号 2. 一点点,微量

tittle-tattle ['titl,tætl] *n. & vi.* 闲聊,漫谈

titular ['titjulə] *adj*.1.享有所有权的,有权持有的 2. 有名无实的;挂名的,使具虚名的 3. 有称号的;有头衔的,有职称的 4. 标题的;书名的(小说,戏剧中的人物)被用作标题(或片名,剧名)的 — *n*.有称号(或头衔,职称)的人 ‖ **-ly** *adv*.

tizzy ['tizi] *n*.〈俚〉万分惊诧;慌乱;紧张

T-junction ['ti:'dʒʌŋkʃən] *n*.T 形接合;T 形接头;T形交叉

Tl【化】元素铊(thallium)的符号

TM *abbr*. 1. trademark 2. tactical missile 战术导弹

Tm【化】元素铥(thulium)的符号

TNT ['ti:en'ti:] *n*.【化】梯恩梯(即三硝基甲苯)

to [强 tu:;弱 tu, tə] *prep*.1.[表示方向、距离]到,向,往 2.[表示状态的变化]趋于,倾向 3.[表示时间]直至…为止,在…之间 4.[表示程度]到,达到 5.[表示对应]对…6.[表示间接关系]给…,向…7.[表示归属]归于 8.[表示比较]比;be inferior ~ the others 比其他的都差 9.[表示数量与单位的比率]对 10.[表示目的]为了 11.[表示关连、联系]对于;至于;关于 12.[表示适应、遵照]按,按照;随同,随着 13.[表示结果、效果]致,致使 14.[~ oneself]专为…单独所有(或用用);专对 15.[表示原因]由于 — *adv*.1. put on one's hat wrong side ~ 前后颠倒地戴上帽子 2.(指门,窗等)关上;虚掩着;leave the door ~ 让门虚掩着 3. 着手(); fall ~ 着手干;开始进食 4. 在近旁 5.(用)上;set ~ one's seal 盖印 / put the horses ~ 套上马 6. 苏醒过来 ‖ **~-and-fro** [tuən'frəu] *adv*.来来往往的,往复的

toad [təud] *n*.1.【动】蟾蜍,癞蛤蟆 2. 讨厌的人(或物) ‖ **~eating** *n*.谄媚,拍马 /**~flax** *n*.【植】柳穿鱼,有距啮龙花

/**~-in-the-'hole** *n*.〈英〉面煎香肠;面拖牛肉 /**~stool** *n*.[植]伞菌;毒蕈,毒菌

toady ['təudi] *n*.谄媚者,马屁精 — *vt. & vi*.奉承,谄媚 ‖ **~ism** *n*.奉承,谄媚

toast¹ ['təust] *n*. 1. 烤面包片,吐司 2. 烤面包做的食物 — *vt*.1. 烤,烘(面包等) 2. 使暖和 — *vi*. 烤,炙;烘热 ‖ **~er** *n*. 烤面包炉;烤面包片机

toast² ['təust] *n*. 1. 祝酒,干杯 2. 祝酒辞 3. 受祝酒的人(或事物);受到高度敬仰的人(或事物) — *vt*. 提议为…干杯;为…举杯祝酒 ‖ **~master** *n*. 宴会主持人;祝酒提议人 / **~mistress** *n*. 宴会女主持人;女祝酒提议人

tobacco [tə'bækəu]([复] tobacco(e)s) *n*.1. 烟草;烟叶 2. 烟草制品(如香烟,雪茄,鼻烟等) 3. 抽烟;give up ~ 戒烟

tobacconist [tə'bækənist] *n*. 烟草商;烟草制品零售商

toboggan [tə'bɒgən] *n*.1. 平板雪橇,长橇 2. 急剧的下降 — *vi*.1. 坐平底雪橇滑行 2.(价格等)急剧下降

toccata [tə'kɑ:tə]([复] toccatas 或 toccatae [tə'kɑ:ti:]) *n*.【音】托卡塔(一种为显示演奏者技巧等的键盘乐曲)

tocsin ['tɔksin] *n*.1. 警钟;警报 2. 警戒信号(声等)急剧下降

today [tə'dei] *adv*. 1. 在今天,在今日 2. 现在,现今;当代 — *n*. 今天,今日 2.现在,现今;当代

toddle ['tɔdl] *n*.1.(小孩等的)蹒跚行走;〈口〉信步行 2.〈口〉学步的小孩 — *vi*.(小孩在学步时)蹒跚行走;〈口〉信步走

toddy ['tɔdi] *n*.1. 棕榈汁;棕榈酒 2.(加热水的)柠檬威士忌甜酒

to-do [tə'du:]([复]to-dos) *n*.〈口〉骚扰;骚动;喧闹

toe [təu] *n.* 1. 脚趾；足尖；〈口〉脚；(动物的)趾 2.(鞋、袜的)足尖部 3. 脚趾状物；【铁】辙叉足部；(木工)斜钉；【机】轴踵；(高尔夫球的)球棒尖 — *vt.* 1. 用脚趾踢(或触)；用脚趾伸 2. 装(或做)…的尖头；修补(鞋、袜等)的头 3. 斜嵌(或钉)(钉子等)；斜嵌钉子使…固定 — *vi.* 动脚尖；用足尖动(或走)；用足尖跳舞 ‖ ~ dance 足尖舞 / ~ hold *n.* 1.(攀登悬崖等时脚趾大小的)立足点，支点 2. 克服困难的办法 3. 初步的立足点；微小的好处 / ~ nail *n.* 1. 趾甲 2.(木工用的)斜钉 *vt.* 用斜钉钉牢

TOEFL ['təufəl] *abbr.* test of English as a foreign language 作为外国语的英语考试，托福考试

toffee, toffy ['tɔfi] *n.* 〈英〉太妃糖，乳脂糖(= 〈美〉taffy)

tog [tɔg] *n.* [~ s] 〈口〉衣服 —(togged; togging) *vt.* 〈口〉使穿衣；给…穿衣

toga ['təugə] *n.* 1.(古罗马市民穿的宽松)托加袍 2.(某一行业、职务等)特用的袍褂，官服 3.〈美〉参议员职；公职

together [tə'geðə] *adv.* 1. 共同，一起；一致地 2. 集合起；集拢地；总合地 3.[常用以加强语气]相互，彼此 4. 同时；连续，一连 5. 头脑清楚而镇定 — *adj.* 1.〈美俚〉情绪稳定的；镇静自若的；自信的；有自制力的；有雄才大略的；个性完整的 2.〈口〉组织得很好的；协调的 3.〈俚〉时髦的，现代的，时式的

toggle ['tɔgl] *n.* 1.【海】绳结，套索钉，系索桩 2.【机】肘节；肘节机件 3.【电子】反复电路；自锁电路；触发电路，触发器 — *vt.* 1. 用绳结系住；用肘销系住 2. 用肘节连接 ‖ ~ bolt *n.* 设备肘节 3. 用拨动式开关从飞机上投(炸弹)

Togo ['təugəu] *n.* 多哥[西非国家] ‖ ~-

lese[,təu'gəuli:z] *n.*[单复同]多哥人 *adj.* 多哥的；多哥人的

toil[1] [tɔil] *n.* 1. 辛劳，劳累 2. 苦工，苦活；难事 — *vi.* 1. 苦干，辛劳地从事(at, on, through) 2. 艰苦地行动；艰难地行走 — *vt.* 〈古〉1. 使过分操劳 2. 劳动使完成 ‖ ~ er *n.* 辛勤工作的人，劳苦者，勤劳者 / ~ ful *adj.* 辛苦的，劳苦的 ‖ ~ worn *adj.* 劳累的；疲惫不堪的

toil[2] [tɔil] *n.* [常 ~ s] 网，罗网；圈套，陷阱

toilet ['tɔilit] *n.* 1. 梳妆，打扮 2.〈古〉梳妆台 3. 礼服；盛装；装束 4. 盥洗室；浴室；厕所；卫生间；便池；抽水马桶 5.【医】(手术前后的)洗涤 — *vi.* 1. 梳妆，打扮 2. 上厕洗室；上厕所 — *vt.* 1. 给…梳妆打扮 2. 照料(孩子等)上厕所 ‖ ~ paper 卫生纸，草纸 / ~ powder 身粉，扑粉 / ~ set 梳妆用具 / ~ soap 香皂 / ~ water 花露水，香水

toilsome ['tɔilsəm] *adj.* 辛苦的，劳累的 ‖ ~ ly *adv.* / ~ ness *n.*

Tokay [təu'kei] *n.* 1.(匈牙利产)托考伊白葡萄酒 2.(制托考伊白葡萄酒的)福尔明葡萄

toke [təuk] *n.* 1.〈英俚〉食物(尤指干面包) 2.〈美俚〉吸烟；吸毒(指一次吸入动作)

token ['təukən] *n.* 1. 表示，标志，象征；记号 2. 物证；信物 3. 纪念品 4.【英史】民铸货币，代币 5.[用作交通运输费等的替代币的]筹码；专用辅币；礼券，代价券 — *adj.* 1. 作为标志的；表意的 2. 象征性的；装门面的 ‖ ~ ism *n.* 装点门面，表面文章 ‖ ~ money (币面价值高于实际价值的)名目货币，符号货币；私铸币

Tokyo ['təukjəu] *n.* 东京[日本首都] ‖ ~-ite *n.* 东京市民

told [təuld] tell 的过去式和过去分词

tolerable ['tɔlərəbl] *adj.* 1. (苦痛 等) 可忍受的;(错误等) 可容忍的;可宽恕的 2. 尚好的、尚可以的,过得去的 3. (口)(身体) 还算健康的 ‖ **tolerably** *adv.* 过得去地,还算不错地

tolerance ['tɔlərəns] *n.* 1. 忍受;容忍;宽恕;忍耐(力) 2. 【机】(配合) 公差;容限 3. (食物中残存杀虫剂的)(法定) 容许量 4. 【医】耐(药) 量,耐受性

tolerant ['tɔlərənt] *adj.* 1. 忍受的;宽恕的 2. 有药物耐受性的 ‖ ~ly *adv.*

tolerate ['tɔləreit] *vt.* 1. 忍受;容忍;宽恕;默认,认可 2. 耐(药)力

toleration [,tɔlə'reiʃən] *n.* 1. 忍受;容恕;默认 2. 信仰自由 3. (对药物、食品或生理损害等效应的) 耐受性

toll¹ [tɔul] *n.* 1. (道路、桥梁等的) 通行费 2. 服务费;运费;(长途) 电话费;设施使用费;(市场的) 设摊费 3. (英) (磨谷物时) 磨坊主为加工费而取的部分谷物 4. (通行费等的) 征收权 5. (付出的) 代价;损失;(事故等的) 伤亡人数 — *vi.* 征收捐税;收费 — *vt.* 1. 抽取…的部分税收;把…作为抽税捐征收 2. 向(某人) 征收捐税;向…收费 3. 收取(桥梁、进口等的) 通行费 ‖ ~ call 单独收费电话(长途电话) / ~gate *n.* 收费门,收费处

toll² [tɔul] *vt.* 1. 鸣(钟),敲(钟) 2. 鸣钟报告(时辰、噩耗等);鸣钟召唤(人等) — *vi.* 1. 鸣钟,敲钟 2. 缓慢而有规律地响一声 *n.* 钟声

tolu [tɔu'luː] *n.* 塔鲁香脂(用于制造止咳糖浆和香料等)

tom [tɔm] *n.* 1. [T-]汤姆(男子名, Thomas 的俗称或昵称) 2. 堆性动物;雄猫;雄火鸡 3. [矿](洗选砂金等用的) 长槽,木制流(洗) 槽 4. [T-] = Uncle Tom

[T-] (Tommed; Tomming) *vi.* 〈美口〉似汤姆叔叔(Uncle Tom) 一样讨好白人(或另一种族的人) — [T-]*boy n.* 男孩似的顽皮姑娘;假小子 / ~cat *n.* 雄猫;到处找女人鬼混的男子 / Tom Collins(美)(由杜松子酒、柠檬汁、糖和苏打水调制而成的) 汤姆·柯林斯酒

tomahawk ['tɔməhɔːk] *n.* (北美印第安人用的) 印第安战斧;(澳) 短柄小斧 — *vt.* 1. 用战斧劈(或斩);用战斧砍杀 2. 苛评(文学作品等)

tomato [tə'mɔːtəu, tə'meitəu] ([复] tomatoes) *n.* 1. 番茄,西红柿 2. (俚) 美人 3. (俚) 美貌女子 4. (俚) 鹫脚的拳击手

tomb [tuːm] *n.* 1. 坟;冢;墓穴 2. [the ~](诗) 死亡 — *vt.* 埋葬;把…葬入坟墓 ‖ ~stone *n.* 墓碑,墓石

tome [təum] *n.* 1. 册,卷 2. 大册书;(学术巨著的) 大本书

tomfool ['tɔm'fuːl] *n.* 1. 傻瓜,大笨蛋 — *adj.* 极傻的,笨透的 — *vi.* 做蠢事 ‖ ~ery ['tɔm'fuːləri] *n.* 1. 蠢举;傻话;蠢事 2. 俗气无聊的小玩意(或装饰)

tommy ['tɔmi] *n.* 1. 常 [T-] = Tommy Atkins ‖ **Tommy Atkins** 〈口〉英国兵/Tommy gun 汤姆枪,冲锋枪/ ~rot *n.* 胡说;废话;愚蠢;蠢举

tomorrow [tə'mɔrəu] *adv.* 在明天,在明日 — *n.* 1. 明天,明日 2. 来日,未来:the world's ~ 世界的未来

tom-tom ['tɔmtɔm] *n.* 1. 手鼓;锣 2. 单调的鼓打;单调的节奏(或鼓打声) — (tom-tommed; tom-tomming) *vi.* 打手鼓

ton [tʌn] ([复] ~s) *n.* 1. (重量单位) 吨 2. 登记吨(= register ~) 3. 装载吨,载货吨,容积吨(= freight ~,或 measurement ~) 4. (船只的) 排水吨(= displacement ~) 5. 〈口〉[常~s] 大量 6. (俚) 每小时 100 英里的速度:do a ~ 以

tonality [təˈnæliti] *n.* 1. 音调；声调 2. 【音】调性 3. 色调

tone [təun] *n.* 1. 音；乐音；音质；音调；调子 2. 腔调，语气 3. 声调；语调 4. 色调,光度 5.[只用单]风气；气氛 6.(身体、器官的)正常健康状况 7. 正常的弹性(或伸缩性)8.(市场的)供销(或价格)情况 9. 思想状态；心情,心境 10. 【音】音,全音 — *vt.* 1. 用特定声调吟诵 2.给…定调门；使改调；给(乐器)定音调；给(画)定色调 3. 增强,提高 4. 改变(照片)的颜色 5. 使…的声调(或色调)和谐(或柔和) — *vi.* 1. 呈现悦目色调上,(颜色)调和(或和谐)：The building ~s (*in*) well *with* the surroundings. 这建筑物和周围环境颜色很协调。‖ **tonal** *adj.* / **tonally** *adv.*

tong[1] [tɔŋ] *n.* [~s][用作单或复]钳,夹具；煤铁夹,火钳；卷发钳,烫发钳 — *vt. & vi.* 用钳夹取(或夹住)；用钳收集(用夹子夹着的发)

tong[2] [tɔŋ] *n.* 堂(在美国的中国侨民的兄弟会等帮会组织)；(中国旧时的)帮会

Tonga [ˈtɔŋə, ˈtɔŋɡə] *n.* 汤加[南太平洋岛国]

tongue [tʌŋ] *n.* 1. 舌,舌头 2. 说话能力；口才 3. 语言；方言,土语 4. 舌状物；鞋舌；火舌；(饰针,盖带搭扣等的)别针；(车的)辕杆；(管乐器的)簧片；(秤的)指针；铃锤,钟锤 5. 伸入海(或河、湖)中的狭长地；岬 6.【机】键,榫槽,舌片 7.【建】堆榫,榫舌 8.【铁路】的尖轨 9.[美俚]律师 — *vt.* 1. 舔 2. 用舌吹(管乐器)3. 【古】责骂；说,讲 5. 在(木板等)上做榫舌；用雌雄榫拼接(木板)— *vi.* 1. 用舌法在管乐器上吹出音调 2.(罕)说话,饶

舌 3.(地等)呈舌形突出：The Liaodong Peninsula ~s southward into the sea. 辽东半岛向南呈舌形伸入海中。‖ **~less** *adj.* 没有舌头的；不开口的,缄默的；哑的／ **~ster** *n.* 健谈的人；饶舌人／ '**~.lashing** *n.* 申斥,责骂；谴责／'**~.tied** *adj.* 【医】结舌的；(由于为难等)开不出口的；结结巴巴的／ **~ twister** 拗口令似的句子(或词组等)(She sells sea shells by the seashore.)

tonic [ˈtɔnik] *adj.* 1. 滋补的,强身的 2. 使精神振作的,有兴奋作用的 3.【音】主音的 4.【语】声调的,声调语言的；(音节)有主重音的 5.(肌肉,器官等)强直音的 — *n.* 1. 补药,补剂 2. 有兴奋作用的东西;激励物 3.【音】主音 4.【语】浊音;重读音节 ‖ ~-**sol-fa**[音]首调唱名法／ ~ **water** 奎宁水,开胃水(一种饮料)

tonight [təˈnait] *adv.* 在今夜,在今晚 — *n.* 今夜,今晚

tonnage [ˈtʌnidʒ] *n.* 1.(表示船舶大小、船舶所能载运的货物的量、一国或一港口船舶载重总吨数或舰船排水量等的)吨位之 2.(船舶)的货物总量；(生产等)的总吨数 3.(对船舶征收的)船舶吨税 4.(对通过这运河的每吨货物所征收的)吨通过税,吨通行费

tonneau [ˈtɔnəu] *n.*([复]tonneaus 或 tonneaux [ˈtɔnəuz]) 1.(汽车车身的)后部座位部分(有后部座位的汽车车身)‖ **~ed** *adj.*

tonner [ˈtʌnə] *n.*[常用以构成复合词]重…吨的东西,重…吨的卡车；有…吨位的船 a 10,000-~ 万吨轮

tonsil [ˈtɔnsil] *n.*【解】扁桃体 ‖ **tonsil**(l) **ar** *adj.*

tonsillectomy [ˌtɔnsiˈlektəmi] *n.*【医】扁桃体切除术

tonsillitis [ˌtɔnsiˈlaitis] *n.* 【医】扁桃体炎

tonsorial [tɔnˈsɔːriəl] *adj.* [常用作幽默语]理发(师)的 ‖ **~ist** *n.* **~ly** *adv.*

tonsure [ˈtɔnʃə] *n.* **1.** (当教士或入修道院时的)剃发仪式 **2.** 僧侣头顶的剃光部分;光顶,秃顶 — *vt.* 为…剃发;给…举行剃发仪式

too [tuː] *adv.* **1.** [用于肯定句]也,还(否定句用 either) **2.** [用于肯定词组后]而且,还(否定词组后用 either) **3.** [加强语气时用,无具体意义]: I will ~ go! 我要去的! **4.** 太,过分 **5.** 非常,很

took [tuk] take 的过去式

tool [tuːl] *n.* **1.** 工具;器具;用具;刀具;器械;机床,工具机 **2.** 爪牙;傀儡;走狗 **3.** 〈俚〉木手工 **3.** (压印书籍封面文字或图案的)压印器 — *vt.* **1.** 用工具加工(或造形);用雕刀修整(石块);用装订工具装饰(书籍封面) **2.** 用机床(等)装备(工厂)(up) **3.** 赶(马车);用车载(人) — *vi.* **1.** 使用工具 **2.** 用机床(或器械)装备工厂 **3.** 赶车;乘车 ‖ **~box** *n.* 工具箱

toot [tuːt] *n.* (喇叭、号角、笛等的)短而尖锐的声音;嘟嘟声 — *vt.* 使发嘟嘟声;吹奏出 — *vi.* 吹喇叭(或号角等);发出嘟嘟声

tooth [tuːθ] ([复] **teeth** [tiːθ]) *n.* **1.** 牙,牙齿 **2.** 齿状物;(齿轮、锯、梳、树叶等的)齿 **3.** (用机器或手工制成的)粗糙面 **4.** 爱好;口味 **5.** 起损害(或折磨、毁坏)作用的东西;强制实施的有效手段 — *vt.* **1.** 给…装齿 **2.** 使或锯齿状 ‖ **~ed** *adj.* 有齿的;锯齿状的 ‖ **~some** *adj.* 美味的,可口的 ‖ **~ache** *n.* 牙痛 ‖ **~brush** *n.* 牙刷 ‖ **~paste** *n.* 牙膏 ‖ **~pick** *n.* 牙签,牙签筒 ‖ 〈俚〉鲍伊猎刀,单刃猎刀 ‖ **~powder** 牙粉

tootle [ˈtuːtl] *n.* **1.** 连续的嘟嘟吹奏;连续的嘟嘟声 **2.** 冗长无力的文章;唠叨的话 — *vi.* **1.** 连续轻吹喇叭(或笛子等);连续发出嘟嘟声 **2.** 写无聊文章;讲废话 — *vt.* 在(乐器)上连续吹出嘟嘟声;嘟嘟地吹

top¹ [tɔp] *n.* **1.** 顶,顶部,顶端 **2.** (物的)上面,上边,上部,上端 **3.** 盖,顶盖;篷 **4.** 最高职位(或地位);首位;居首的人 **5.** 顶点;最高度 **6.** 精华 **7.** 戏院最高票价 **8.** [常 ~s](植物)长出地面的部分(直根作物的)茎叶 **9.** 开端 **10.** (一束)头发 [纺] 毛条;化纤条 **11.** 【化】顶馏分,最初馏分 **12.** [船] 桅楼 **13.** 正面镀过的金属部分 ‖ 球上部击球(网球等)上旋 **15.** [~s](牌戏中)顶张;顶分 ‖ (topped;topping) *vt.* **1.** 盖;给…加盖(或顶) **2.** 为(植物等)覆顶,为…充头 **3.** 到…的顶部;上升到…的顶点 **3.** 高于;超过;胜过;压倒;居…之上;是…之冠;成为…之首 **5.** 登上…的顶 **5.** 蒸去…的顶馏分 **6.** 给…涂上保护层 [纺] 套染(毛条等) **7.** 击(球)的上部(以使其向前旋转) **8.** 〈俚〉绞死 — *vi.* **1.** 结束(off,out,up) **2.** 高出,超越 **3.** 向高处升 **4.** 击球的上部;击出旋球 — *adj.* 顶的;顶上的;最高的;头等的 ‖ **~less** *adj.* 无底的;无盖的;无遮的 ‖ **~most** *adj.* 最高的,最上面的 ‖ **~ boot** 下翻式高统靴 ‖ **~ brass** 〈美〉[总称]要员 ‖ **~coat** *n.* 轻便大衣 ‖ **~drawer** *adj.* 最高级别的;头等重要的;最上层的 ‖ **~flight** *adj.* 〈口〉第一流的,最好的,最高级的 ‖ **~hat** 高顶黑色礼帽 ‖ **~heavy** *adj.* 头重脚轻的;(企业等)高级官员或行政管理人员过多的;(股份公司等)投资过多的 ‖ **~kick** *n.* 〈美俚〉**1.** 军士长 **2.** 上司;头头 ‖ **~knot** *n.* 顶髻;头饰 **2.** (鸟的)羽冠 ‖ **~liner** *n.* (主角)头条新闻中的人物(或事件) ‖ **~mast** *n.*

【船】中桅 /'~'**notch** *n.* 顶点 *adj.*〈口〉最高质量的；第一流的 /~**sail**['tɔpsl, 'tɔpseil] *n.*【船】中桅帆 /'~-'**secret** *adj.* 绝密的 /'~**soil** *n.* 表土；(来自)表土中的壤土 *vt.*1. 用表土铺盖 2. 去掉(土地)的表土

top² [tɔp] *n.* 陀螺

topaz ['təupæz] *n.*1.【矿】黄晶，黄玉 2.【动】南美蜂鸟

tope¹ [təup] *vt.* & *vi.* 狂饮，纵饮

tope² [təup] *n.*【动】翅鲨

tope³ [təup] *n.*(佛教国家的)圆顶塔，印度塔

toper ['təupə] *n.* 酒徒，酒鬼，醉汉

topiary ['təupiəri] *adj.* 修剪成形的 — *n.* 林木剪形(术)

topic ['tɔpik] *n.*1.(文章、讲演的)题目；(节、段的)主题；论题，话题 2.(提纲、大纲的)标题，细目

topical ['tɔpikəl] *adj.*1. 题目的；主题的；论题的；话题的 2. 有关时事的 3. 地方(性)的；【医】局部的

topography [tə'pɔgrəfi] *n.*1. 地志 2. 地形；地形学；地形测量学 3. 局部解剖学；局部解剖图 ‖ **topographer** *n.*/ **topographic(al)** [ˌtɔpə'græfik(əl)] *adj.*

topology [tə'pɔlədʒi] *n.*1. 地志学 2.【数】拓扑(学)3. 局部解剖学

topper ['tɔpə] *n.*1. 装(或去掉)顶盖者；给植物剪顶(或打尖、除掉茎叶)的人(或器具)2.〈俚〉第一流的人物；高档的东西；胜过以前同类物的东西 3.〈俚〉高顶黑色大礼帽；轻便大衣；(女用)宽松轻便短大衣

topping ['tɔpiŋ] *adj.*1.(地位等)最高的；主要的，首要的 2.〈英口〉极好的；第一流的 3. 漂亮的，美丽的 — *n.*1. 形成顶部的东西(如放在食品上面的配品、调味品或建筑物的灰泥层等)2. 被去掉(或剪去)的顶部 3.(原油的)拔顶

topple ['tɔpl] *vt.* 使倒塌；推翻；颠覆(*down*, *over*) — *vi.*1. 倒塌，倒下(*down*, *over*)2. 摇摇欲坠

topsy-turvy [ˌtɔpsi'təːvi] *adv.* & *adj.* 颠倒地(的)；乱七八糟地(的) — *n.* 颠倒；混乱 — *vt.* 使颠倒；使乱七八糟 ‖ ~-**dom** *n.*1. 颠倒(或混乱)状态 2. 混乱世界

toque [təuk] *n.* 无边女帽

tor [tɔː] *n.* 1. 石山 2.【地】突岩

torah ['tɔːrə] *n.*(犹太教)1. 律法；(上帝启示给人类的)教导，指引；[亦作 T-]全部希伯来圣经；托拉 2.[常作 T-]摩西五经(《旧约》的首五卷)

torch [tɔːtʃ] *n.*1. 火炬，火把 2.【机】喷灯；氧乙炔炬；吹管 3.〈主英〉手电筒 4. 手枪 ‖ ~ **fishing** 篝火捕鱼 /'~**light** *n.*1. 火炬 2. 火炬光 /~ **race**(古希腊的)火炬接力赛跑

tore [tɔː] tear² 的过去式

toreador ['tɔriədɔː] *n.*(尤指骑在马上的)斗牛士

torment ['tɔːment] *n.*1. 痛苦；苦恼；折磨 2. 使人痛苦(或烦恼)的东西；折磨者 — [tɔː'ment] *vt.*1. 使痛苦；折磨 2. 使烦恼；烦扰 3. 搅动；搅起 4. 曲解；歪曲

tormentor, tormenter [tɔː'mentə] *n.*1. 使人痛苦的人(或事物)；折磨者 2.(舞台两翼的)侧幕；景屏 3.(摄制影片时的)防回声幕 4.(海船上厨师用的)长肉叉 5.(架设云梯的)撑杆

torn [tɔːn] tear² 的过去分词

tornado [tɔː'neidəu]([复]tornado(e)s) *n.*1. 龙卷风；旋风；飓风；【气】陆龙卷 2.(非洲西部海岸的)大雷飑 3. 具有巨大破坏性的人(或事物)

torpedo [tɔː'piːdəu]([复]torpedoes) *n.*1. 鱼

雷;水鱼 2.(油井)井底爆炸筒;(铁路用)信号雷管 3. 惯炮(一种掷地爆裂发声的爆竹)4.〈俚〉(被雇用的)刺客;职业杀手;保镖 5.保镖 — *vt.* 1.用鱼雷进攻;用鱼雷袭击(或击沉)(船、舰)2. 破坏;使彻底完蛋 ‖ ~ **boat** 鱼雷快艇 / ~ **tube** 鱼雷发射管

torpid ['tɔːpid] *adj.* 1. 麻痹的;麻木的 2. 呆钝的,迟钝的,不活泼的 3.(动物等)蛰伏的 ‖ **tor'pidity** *n.* / ~ **ly** *adv.*

torpor ['tɔːpə] *n.* 麻痹;麻木;迟钝;蛰伏

torque[1] [tɔːk] *n.* (古代布立吞人、高卢人等戴的)金属饰环;金属项圈,金属颈环

torque[2] [tɔːk] *n.* 〔物〕1. 转矩,力矩,扭矩 2.(偏振光面上的)旋转效应 3. 扭转力

torrefy ['tɔrifai] *vt.* 焙,烘,烤,烘(药等)

torrent ['tɔrənt] *n.* 1.(水、熔岩等)奔流,激流,急流;洪流 2.(雨的)倾注 3.(话语等)连发;(感情等)进发;狂潮 — *adj.* = torrential

torrential [tɔ'renʃəl] *adj.* 1. 奔流的,急流的 2. 急流造成的 3. 奔流似的;大量的;势不可挡的,压抑不住的;狂暴的 ‖ ~ **ly** *adv.*

torrid ['tɔrid] *adj.* 1. 晒热的,烘热的 2. 炎热的,酷热的,灼热的 3. 热情的,热烈的 ‖ **Torrid Zone**〈罕〉热带

torsion ['tɔːʃən] *n.* 1. 扭转;扭力 2.〔物〕转矩 3.〔医〕扭转,拨转 ‖ ~ **al** *adj.*

torso ['tɔːsəu] ([复] torsos) *n.* 1.(人体的)躯干 2.(无头和四肢的)裸体躯干雕像 3. 未完成(或残缺)的东西

tort [tɔːt] *n.*〔律〕侵权行为

tortilla [tɔː'tiːljə] *n.*(墨西哥人用以代替面包的)玉米粉圆饼

tortious ['tɔːʃəs] *adj.*〔律〕(似)侵权行为的

tortoise ['tɔːtəs] *n.* 1. 陆龟;龟,乌龟 2. 行动迟缓的人(或物) ‖ ~ **shell** *n.* 龟甲,

龟板;玳瑁壳 *adj.* (像)龟甲的;(像)玳瑁壳的

tortuous ['tɔːtjuəs] *adj.* 1. 曲折的;弯弯曲曲的 2. 转弯抹角的 3. 居心叵测的;欺骗的;不正当的 ‖ ~ **ly** *adv.* / ~ **ness** *n.*

torture ['tɔːtʃə] *n.* 1. 拷问,拷打;酷刑 2. 折磨;痛苦;苦恼;使人痛苦(或苦恼)的事物 3.(意义、论点等的)歪曲,曲解 — *vt.* 1. 拷问,拷打;虐待 2. 折磨;使痛苦 3. 使翘曲;使弯曲 4. 歪曲;曲解 ‖ ~ **r** *n.* 拷问者;虐待者/ **'torturing** *adj.* / **'torturous** *adj.*

Tory ['tɔːri] *n.* 1.〔英语〕托利党党员 2.(英国)保守党党员 3.(美国独立战争时期的)亲英分子 4.[t-]叛国分子;反动分子 — *adj.*[t-](英国)保守党的;极端保守的 ‖ ~ **ism** *n.* 英国保守党党员的主义(或政策)

tosh [tɔʃ] *n.*〔英口〕胡说;废话

toss [tɔs] ([tossed 或〈古〉〈诗〉 tost] *vt.* 1. 扔,抛,掷 2. 突然举起,突然抬起 3. 使摇摆,使颠簸 4. 使摇荡 5. 使〔干扰〕;扰乱 5.(轻轻地)拌 6. 使(杯等)猛然倾侧(如喝酒时干杯的动作) — *vi.* 1. 摇摆,颠簸 2. 翻来复去 3. 掷货币(看其正反)决定某事 — *n.* 1. 扔,抛,掷 2. 猛举,猛抬;猛倾 3. 摇摆,摇簸 4. 掷钱币决定某事;由掷钱币决定的事 ‖ ~ **up** *n.*(为决出胜负而)掷货币;难以定夺的事;(成败各半的)相等机会

tot[1] [tɔt] *n.* 1. 小孩 2. 小玻璃杯;少量的酒;少量

tot[2] [tɔt] (totted; totting) *vt.* 把…加起来;计算…的总和(*up*) — *vi.* 合计(*up to*) — *n.*(主英)1. 合计;总数 2. 加法演算

total ['təutl] *adj.* 1. 总的,总括的 2. 全体的,完全的;绝对的 3. 总体的;全力以赴的 — *n.* 总数,总额;合计;全体 ‖ (to-)

tak[bed; total(bing]vt.1. 计算…的总数；总数达2.《美俚》把…完全毁掉 — vi. 合计；计算总数 — adv. 统统，完全 ‖ ~ism n. 极权主义 / ~ity [tɔu'tæləti] n.1. 全体；总数，总额 2.〔天〕全食；全食时间 ‖ ~ly adv. 统统，完全

totalitarian [ˌtoutæli'tɛəriən] n. 极权主义者 — adj. 极权主义的 ‖ ~ism n. 极权主义

tote¹ [tout] vt.1.(手)提；(背)负；携带 2. 搬运；拖，拉，牵引 — n. 负担；装载；携带(或装运)物

tote² [tout] vt. 把…加起来，计算…的总数 — vi. 合计 — n.〔英方〕总数 2.〔赛马〕赛马的赌金计算器

totem ['toutəm] n.1. 图腾(原始社会作为种族或氏族血统的标志并当作祖先来崇拜的动物或植物等)；图腾形象 2. 有共同图腾的氏族 3. 标志物，象征物；崇拜物 ‖ ~ic [tou'temik] adj. ‖ ~ pole 1. 图腾柱 2. 等级(制)

totter ['tɔtə] vi.1. 蹒跚，跟跄 2. 摇摇欲坠；动摇 — n. 蹒跚的步子

toucan ['tu:kən] n.〔动〕巨嘴鸟

touch [tʌtʃ] vt.1. 触摸；接触；碰到 2. 轻击；触及 3.〔古〕在乐器上奏(曲调等)；弹拨(琴、弦) 4. 使接触，使接触到；[常用于否定意义的句中]对(某事)插一手；对(食物)尝一口 5. 达到；[主要用于否定意义的句中]比得上下 7. 触动；感动 8. 触痛；触犯 9. 涉及；(简略地)论及，提到 10. 影响到；损及 11. 使带上特定色泽(或情调等)；点缀 12.(用铅笔或画笔等)轻轻勾划出 13.〔常用于否定意义的句中〕对付；起作用于 14.〔俚〕向…商借；向…乞讨(for)；偷窃 15. 试(金)；在(检验过的金银)上打记印记 16.〔数〕与…相切 17. 触诊(病人) — vi.1. 触摸 2. 接近，近乎(on) 3. 与…有关，涉及(on, upon) 4.(简略地)论及，提到(on, upon) 5. 短暂停靠；靠岸(at) 6. 触诊 — n.1. 触；碰；轻击；按 2. 触觉；触感 3. 机灵，机敏 4.(画笔等的)轻触；笔触；润色 5. 格调；风格；特点 6. 少许，一点(尤指痕迹、风味、色调、病痛等) 7. 破点；缺陷 8.(琴键或打字机字键的)弹性，触动力(的)指触 9. 接触；联系 10.(俚)乞讨；恳借；讨到的东西；借到的钱 11. 试金石；试金(金银等的)验定纯度；验讫合格的印记 12. 试验；测验 13. 作用，影响 14.(人的)特有姿态(或作用) 15.(足球场的)边线以外地区 ‖ ~ and go 1.(从一点到另一点)快速的行动；瞬间完成的事 2. 一触即发的形势；高度的不安定性 / ~-and-go adj.1.(从一点到另一点)快速行动的 2. 一触即发的；高度不安定的 / ~-down n.1.(橄榄球赛中的)攻方持球触地(得分)；(飞机或宇宙飞船着陆过程中的)触地，接地；接地；触地时的时刻 / ~me-not n.1.〔植〕凤仙花 2.〔植〕喷瓜 3. 高傲自持的人(尤指冷若冰霜的女人) / ~ stone n.1. 试金石 2. 检验标准；检验手段 / ~wood n.1.(作引火用的)朽木 2. 火绒

touchable ['tʌtʃəbl] adj.1. 可触知的 2. 可食用的

touched [tʌtʃt] adj.1. 有些疯癫的，精神不大正常的 2.(因激动等)受感动的，受触动的

touching ['tʌtʃiŋ] adj. 动人的；使人感伤的 — prep.〔书面语〕关于，至于

touchy ['tʌtʃi] adj.1. 易因小事生气的 2.(身体部位)敏感的，易受刺激的 3. 易燃的，有爆炸性的 4. 须小心对待的，棘手的 ‖ touchily adv. / touchiness n.

tough [tʌf] adj.1. 坚韧的；不易磨损的；咬不动的 2. 健壮的；坚强的；能吃苦耐

劳的 3. 强硬的；不屈的；顽强的，倔强的顽固的 4. 粗暴的；强横的，铁石心肠的 5. 难对付的；费力的 6. 猛烈的 7.〈口〉(命运等)困苦的；严峻的；艰难的 8.(泥灰等)粘的，稠的 9.〈美俚〉顶好的，了不起的 — n.〈美〉流氓，恶棍 ‖ ~ly adv. / ~ness n.

toughen ['tʌfn] vt. & vi. 1. (使)变坚韧 2. (使)变健壮；(使)变坚强 3. (使)变强硬；(使)变强韧 4.(使)变困难

tour [tuə] n. 1. 旅行；游历；参观；巡视 2.(轮值的)班；(在海外陆海军基地的)任职期；(海外)服务期 3. 巡回；巡回演出；巡回演出 — vi. 1. 旅行；游历；观光 2. 作巡回演出(或比赛等) — vt. 1. 游历，周游；参观 2. 使(剧团、剧目等)巡回演出；在…作巡回演出(或巡回医疗) ‖ ~ er n. 游客；游览车

tourism ['tuərizəm] n. 1. 旅游，观光 2. 旅游业；旅游团；观光团体 4. 导游，旅游安排

tourist ['tuərist] n. 旅行者；游览者；观光者 — adj. 旅行的；游览的；观光的 ‖ ~ class(飞机、轮船的)旅游舱，经济舱，二等舱；(火车的)旅游车厢 / ~ court = motel / ~ trap 敲游客竹杠的旅馆(或餐馆、商店)

tourmaline ['tuəməlin] n.〔矿〕电气石 ‖ ~ granite 电气石岩

tournament ['tuənəmənt, 'tɔːnəmənt] n. 1. 锦标赛;联赛；比赛 2. = tourney

tourney ['tuəni] n. (中古时代的)马上比武(大会)

tourniquet ['tuəniki] n.〔医〕压脉器，止血带

tousle ['tauzl] vt. 弄乱(头发等)；弄皱(衣服) — n. 1. 蓬乱的头发 2. 乱七八糟的一团 3.〈苏格兰〉嬉戏；扭打

tout [taut] vi. 1. 招徕顾客；拉生意(或选票等) 2.〔主英〕(为下赌注而)探听赛马训练情况；对一匹赛马下赌注 — vt. 1. 招徕;兜售 2. 吹嘘；吹捧；吹捧；从中窥探，秘密监视 4.〔主英〕探听(参赛马)的情况；对(参赛马)下赌注 — n. 1. 招徕顾客者;拉生意(或选票)者 2. 向课;密探；告密者 3.〔主英〕探听(或出售)赛马情报者；对一匹赛马下赌注者 ‖ ~ er n.

TOW abbr. 1. tube-launched optically-tracked wire-guided (antitank missile) 陶式反坦克导弹 2. takeoff weight 起飞重量；(火箭)发射重量

tow¹ [tau] vt. 拖，拉，牵引 — n. 1. 拖，拉，牵引 2. 被拖(或拉)的东西(如拖船、拖车) 3. 拖绳，拖链，纤;〈英方〉绳子 ‖ ~ a.way n.〈美〉(对违章停放车辆的)拖走扣押 adj. (被)拖走扣押的 / '~ a.way zone〈美〉(汽车停放后有可能被拖走并扣押的)禁止停车区，不准停车区 /'~ boat n. 拖船；顶推船 /'~ (ing)-line n. 拖缆，拖索；纤绳 /'~ (ing) net n.(采集标本用的)拖网 /'~ (ing) path n. 牵道,纤道

tow² [tau] n.〔纺〕短纤；短麻屑；亚麻短纤维,束丝;〔纤维束〕

toward(s) [tə'wɔːd(z); twɔːd(z)] prep. 1. 向，朝之 2. 对于 3. 接近,将近 4. 为;有助于;用于

towel ['tauəl] n. 毛巾；纸巾 (= paper ~) ‖ (towel(l)ed; towel(l)ing) vt. 1. 用毛巾擦 2.〈英俚〉鞭打 — vi. 用毛巾擦(或擦干)(off) ‖ towel(l)ing n. 毛巾布 / ~ gourd 丝瓜 / ~ horse, ~ rack (木制的)毛巾架

tower ['tauə] n. 1. 塔；塔楼；高楼；(飞机场的)塔台；塔台指挥员人员 2. 堡垒;监狱 3.(架设高压电线的)铁塔 — vi. 1. 屹

立:高耸 2. 翱翔、高飞 ‖ ~ed adj.1. 有塔的 2. 高耸云霄的 / ~ing adj.1. 屹立的;高耸的;巨大的 2. 激烈的;过分的 / ~man n.1.〈美〉(铁路)的信号手 2. 机场塔台指挥人员,塔台调度员 3. 森林防火守望员

towhead ['təʊhed] n.1. 有亚麻色头发的人,黄毛(指人) 2. 一头黄发;一头乱麻似的头发 ‖ ~ed adj.

town [taun] n.1. 镇,市镇,城镇 2. 城市,都市;市区;商业中心区 3. [the ~][总称]镇民;市民 ‖ ~ship n.1.〈美国、加拿大等的〉区 2.〈美国土地测量中〉6 英里见方的地区 3.〈南非〉黑人居住区 4.〈澳大利亚〉城市规划区,城市预留地 / ~sfolk [复] n. 镇民;市民 / ~sman n. 镇民;市民;城里人 2. 同乡人 / ~speople[复] n.1. 镇民;市民 2. 城里人

toxic ['tɒksik] adj.1. 有毒的,有毒性的 2. 中毒的 ‖ ~ally adv./ ~ity [tɒk'sisiti] n.

toxicology [ˌtɒksi'kɒlədʒi] n. 毒理学,毒物学 ‖ toxicologist n.

toxin ['tɒksin] n. 毒素,毒质

toy [tɔi] n.1. 玩具,玩物 2. 游戏;消遣;消遣性的短文(或小调) 3. 矮小的人;小动物 4. 不值钱的东西;小装饰品 — adj.1. 玩物似的;小如玩具的 2. 作为玩具的 — vi.1. 调情 2. 玩弄,戏耍 (with) 3. 不认真地对待;做着玩

TPR abbr. temperature, pulse, respiration【医】体温、脉搏、呼吸

trace¹ [treis] n.1. 痕迹;踪迹;足迹;遗迹 2.〈古〉小径;道路 3. 丝毫;微量【化】痕量 4. 线迹;描记图【军】经始线 5.(记录器的)描记线【计】跟踪 6.【心】(记忆)痕迹,印迹 7.【数】迹 — vt.1. 跟踪;追踪 2. 查出;找出;探索 3. 追溯 4. 描绘;勾勒…的轮廓【军】绘出(军

事设施)的经始线 5.(根据衬在下面的图样等)描摹,映描 6.(费力、细心地)写(字) 7.【建】用格状花纹装饰 — vi.1. 沿着路(或路线)走 2. 上溯

trace² [treis] n.1. 挽绳,缰绳【机】连动杆【植】(脉)迹

traceable ['treisəbl] adj.1. 可追踪的;可查出的;可探索的 2. 可溯源的;可归因的 3. 可描画的;可摹写的

tracer ['treisə] n.1.(货运中的)失物查查人;失物追查单 2. 绘图员;映描员 3. 描绘工具(如铁笔等)4.【化】示踪剂;显光剂【军】曳光弹

tracery ['treisəri] n.【建】花窗格

trachea [trə'ki:ə] n.(〔复〕tracheae [trə'ki:i:] 或 tracheas) n.1.【解】气管 2.【植】导管 3.【动】(昆虫的)气管

trachoma [trə'kəʊmə] n.【医】沙眼

tracing ['treisiŋ] n.1. 追踪;追查;探查 2. 描绘;映描 3. 摹图 4.【物】线路图寻迹【计】跟踪 ‖ ~ cloth 描图布 / ~ paper 描图纸

track¹ [træk] n.1. 行踪;轨迹;航迹;[常 ~s]足迹 2. 路径,小道 3. 轨道;(录音磁带的)音轨【体】跑道 4. 赛运动;田径运动 5. 历程,行程;行动路线,思路 6.(车胎的)胎纹;(车辆的)轮距 7.(坦克,拖拉机的)履带 — vt.1. 跟踪;追踪 2. 沿着(道路)走;根据(线索等)探索 3. 走过;通过 4. 在…上留下行迹;脚上带着(泥)留下印迹 5. 为…铺轨 — vi.1. 追踪 2. 留下足迹 3. 走 4.(车轮等)留出轨迹相符;(车辆的后轮)与前轮在同一轮迹上转动 ‖ ~-and-field adj. 田径运动的 / ~(a)ge轨距(尺) / ~ing station【无】(空)跟踪站 / '~layer n. 铺轨工人;铺轨机;履带式车辆;履带式拖拉机 / '~man n.〈美〉铺轨工人;巡道

工,铁道护路员;田径运动员

track² [træk] *vt.* 用纤绳拉(船) — *vi.*
(船等)被拖着行驶 ‖ ~ **road** 牵道,纤
路

trackage¹ ['trækidʒ] *n.* 1.【总称】轨道;轨
道里程 2.(一条线路或另一条线路
轨道的)线路使用权;线路使用费

trackage² ['trækidʒ] *n.* 拖;牵引;牵引费;
拖挽费

tract¹ [trækt] *n.* 1.(土地、森林等的)大
片,大片土地;地带 2.〈古〉一段时间 3.
【解】道;束

tract² [trækt] *n.* (政治或宗教宣传的)短
文;传单;小册子

tractable ['træktəbl] *adj.* 1. 易管教的;易
控制的;温顺的,驯服的 2. 易处理的;
易加工的 ‖ **tracta'bility** *n.* / **tractably**
adv.

traction ['trækʃən] *n.* 1. 拖拉,牵引;牵引
力 2. 附着磨擦力 3.【医】牵引(术) 4.
吸引力,魅力 5. 公共交通运输事业 ‖
~ **engine** 牵引机车

tractor ['træktə] *n.* 1. 拖拉机 2. 牵引式飞
机 3. 牵引车 4.【医】牵引器

trade [treid] *n.* 1. 贸易,商业;交易;生意
2. 职业;行业;手工艺 3.(从事
某行业的)同人;同行;同业 4.【总称】
(某店)的顾客,主顾 5.〈美〉政治交易
6.〈口〉(海)了酒商;酿酒商 7.〈英〉军
理)the ~]海军潜艇部队 8.[the ~s]
【气】贸易风,信风 — *vi.* 1. 交易;经商
2. 对换,交换 3.〈美〉(政治上)做交易 5.
(鸟马)来回飞翔 — *vt.* 1. 用…进行交
换 2. 经营(股票等)的交易 ‖ ~ **r** *n.* 1.
商人 2. 商船 ‖ '~-**in** *n.* 折价贴换交
物;折价物 ‖ '**mark** *n.* 商标,牌号 *vt.* 1.
注册(商品)的商标 2. 用…作为商标 3.
给(商品)标上商标 / ~ **name** 1.(商店、

公司等的)牌号 2. 商标名;商品 名 ‖
'~**sman** *n.* 1. 商人;店主;零售商 2. 熟
练工人;手艺人 / ~ **union**, ~**s union** 工
会 / ~ **unionism** 工联主义 / ~ **unionist**
1. 工联主义者 2. 工会会员 / ~ **wind**
【气】贸易风,信风

tradition [trə'diʃən] *n.* 1. 传统;传统的思
想(或信仰、习俗)等 2. 口传;传说 3.
【宗】圣传 4.【律】(财产的)交付;移转

traditional [trə'diʃənl] *adj.* 1. 传统的,惯
例的;因袭的 2. 口传的;传说的 ‖ ~**ly**
adv.

traditionalism [trə'diʃənəlizəm] *n.* 传统主
义 ‖ **traditionalist** *n.* 传统主义者;因循
守旧者

traduce [trə'djus] *vt.* 1. 诽谤;中伤;诋毁
2. 违反;背叛

traffic ['træfik] *n.* 1. 交通;通行;往来 2.
运输 3. 交通量;运输量 4. 贸易;交
易;非法买卖;交易 5.(人与人间的)交往;
(精神或思想上的)交流 6.【讯】通信
(量) — **union** 工联主义 *vi.* 买
卖;做非法买卖;做肮脏交易 —
vt. 1. 用…进行交换;以…作交易 2. 在
…上通行 ‖ **trafficker** *n.* 商人,贩子;
非法勾当者;行为卑劣者

tragedian [trə'dʒidiən] *n.* 1. 悲剧作者;
悲剧演员

tragedy ['trædʒidi] *n.* 1. 悲剧;悲剧作品;
悲剧体裁 2. 惨事;惨案;灾难;不幸 3.
悲剧因素

tragic ['trædʒik], **tragical** ['trædʒikəl]
adj. 1. 悲剧的 2. 悲惨的;悲痛的;灾
难性的 ‖ **tragically** *adv.* / **tragicalness** *n.*

tragicomedy [,trædʒi'kɔmidi] *n.* 1. 悲喜剧
2. 又悲又喜的事件(或场合)‖ **tragi-
comic** [,trædʒi'kɔmik] *adj.* 1. 悲喜剧的
2. 又悲又喜的

trail [treil] *n.* 1. 痕迹;足迹;臭迹;踪迹

一串;(后果等的)一系列 3. 拖曳物;尾部;拖裾,裙裾;蔓生物;(炮架的)架尾 4.(荒野山区中的)小径;(踩出的)小道;(标出的)山路 5.【军】持枪姿势 — *vt*.1. 追踪;追猎 2. 拖,曳 3. 拖带 4. 落后于 5. 在…上踩出路;开出(路);标出(路)6.【军】持(枪) — *vi*.1. 拖曳;拖着;垂下 2. 拖沓行走;落后;跟在后面走 3.(缓慢地)飘出;流出 4. 伸展开;蔓生 5.(猎犬等)追踪猎物 6. 减弱;变小(*off*, *away*)

trailer [ˈtreilə] *n*.1. 拖曳者;拉车牲口 2. 追踪者;追猎者 3. 拖车,挂车 4.(汽车拖的)活动住房(或工作室)5. 蔓生植物 6.(广告性的)电影预告片 — *vt*. 用拖车运(游艇等) — *vi*.1. 住在用汽车拖的活动住房内 2. 可用拖车运 ‖ ~ **camp**, ~ **court**, ~ **park** 拖车式活动房屋停车场

train [trein] *vt*.1. 培养;训练 2.(经整枝或整形)使处于特定位置,使成特定形状 3. 把(枪炮、摄影机、灯光等)对准(或瞄准)4.〈罕〉引诱;吸引(*away*)5.〈罕〉拖,拉(重物)6.〈口〉训练(小孩、小狗等)在指定的地方大小便 — *vi*.1. 接受训练;锻炼 2.〈口〉乘火车旅行 — *n*.1. 列车,火车 2.(行进中的)长列,队列;系列 3.[总称]随行人员 4. 伴随而来的事物;后果 5. 顺序;秩序 6. 后拖物;拖裾,裙裾;(禽类的)长尾 7. 导火线 8.【军】辎重队 9.【机】系 10.【物】列 ‖ ~**able** *adj*. ‖ ~ **ferry** 火车渡轮 /ˈ~**man** *n*. 乘务员;列车员 /~ **oil** 海生动物油;鲸油 /~ **sickness** 火车晕车

trainee [treiˈniː] *n*. 受培训者,实习生;〈美〉接受军事训练者;新兵 ‖ ~**ship** *n*.

trainer [ˈtreinə] *n*.1. 训练人;(体育运动的)教练员 2. 驯兽人 3. 训练器材,练习器 4.【空】教练机 5.【军】(火炮的)方向瞄准手 6. 受训练人

training [ˈtreiniŋ] *n*.1. 培养;训练;锻炼 2.(园艺学用语)整枝,整形 3.(枪炮、摄影机、灯光等的)对准,瞄准 ‖ ~ **college**〈英〉师范学院;职业培训学院

traipse [treips] *vi*. & *vt*.(在...)闲荡(或游荡) — *n*. 闲荡,游荡

trait [trei, treit] *n*.1. 品质;特性;性格 2. 一笔,一划 3. 一点点,少许,微量

traitor [ˈtreitə] *n*. 叛徒;卖国贼

traitorous [ˈtreitərəs] *adj*.1. 叛徒的;卖国贼的 2. 叛变的;卖国的 3. 奸诈的;不忠的 ‖ ~**ly** *adv*.

traitress [ˈtreitris] *n*. 女叛徒;女卖国贼

trajectory [ˈtrædʒiktəri] *n*.【物】(射体)轨道,轨迹;弹道;【数】轨线

tram [træm] *n*.1.〈英〉有轨电车(=〈美〉streetcar 或 trolley car)2.〈英〉[~s]电车轨道;有轨电车路线 3. 煤车;矿车;吊车 —(trammed; tramming) *vt*. 用煤车(或吊车等)运 — *vi*. 乘有轨电车 ‖ ˈ~**car** *n*.1.〈英〉有轨电车 2. 煤车;矿车/~ **road** 矿车轨道;矿山铁路/ˈ~**way** *n*.1. = ~ road 2. 有轨电车路线;有轨电车轨道 3. 缆车索道

trammel [ˈtræməl] *n*.1.(捕鸟、鱼等的)网 2. 马梏 3.[常~s](习惯、礼节等的)拘束,束缚;妨碍 4. 壁炉锅钩 5.[~s]椭圆规;横木规;量规 —(trammel(l)ed; trammel(l)ing) *vt*.1. 使陷入网内 2. 束缚;妨碍;限制

tramp [træmp] *vi*.1. 用沉重的脚步走 2. 步行;徒步旅行 3. 流浪,漂泊 4. 踏,踩 — *vt*.1. 走,跋涉 2. 踩;踩洗(衣服等) — *n*.1. 步行;徒步旅行;步行者;徒步旅行者 2. 游民;流浪者;流浪乞丐 3. 妓女;荡妇 4.[只用单]脚步声;重步声 5. 鞋底铁片 6. 不定期(或航线不定)的货船

trample ['træmpl] *vt.* 踩;践踏;蹂躏;轻蔑(或粗暴)地对待 — *vi.* 踩;践踏;蹂躏;轻蔑(或粗暴)地对待 (*on, upon, over*) — *n.* [只用单]践踏;践踏声

trampolin(e) ['træmpəlin] *n.* (杂技表演中翻筋斗用的)蹦床

trance [trɑːns] *n.* 1. 恍惚;出神;发呆 2. 昏睡状态;[医]迷睡 3. (佛教的)入定;(招魂术所谓的)鬼魂附身 — *vt.* 使恍惚;使出神;使发呆;使昏睡

tranny ['træni] *n.* 〈英口〉晶体管收音机

tranquil ['træŋkwil] *adj.* 1. 平静的,安静的,安宁的 2. 平稳的,稳定的 ‖ **tran'quil(l)ity** *n.* 平静,安静

tranquil(l)ize ['træŋkwilaiz] *vt.* 使平静;使镇静 — *vi.* 平静;镇静;安定

tranquil(l)izer ['træŋkwilaizə] *n.* 1. [药]安定药,镇静剂

trans- *pref.* 1. 表示"横过","横断": *transatlantic* 2. 表示"贯通": *transfix* 3. 表示"变化","转移": *transform, translate* 5. 表示"在…的另一边","到…的另一边"

transact [træn'zækt] *vt.* 办理,处理,商议 — *vi.* 1. 做交易,交易 2. (在原则上)让步;调和 ‖ **~or** *n.* 办理(或处理)人

transaction [træn'zækʃən] *n.* 1. 办理,处理;执行 2. (一笔)交易;(具体)事务 3. [~s]议事录;会刊;学报及【律】和解协议

transatlantic [ˌtrænzət'læntik] *adj.* 1. 大西洋彼岸的,(主英)美洲的,美国的 2. 横渡大西洋的 — *n.* 1. 大西洋彼岸的人;〈主英〉美洲人;美国人 2. 横渡大西洋的轮船

transceiver [træns'siːvə] *n.* 无线电收发两用机

transcend [træn'send] *vt.* 1. 超出,超过(经验,理性,信念等)的范围;[哲]〈宗〉超然存在于(物质世界)之外 2. 胜过 — *vi.* 超越;胜过

transcendence [træn'sendəns], **transcendency** [træn'sendənsi] *n.* 1. 超越,超绝,卓越 2. 〈宗〉(神的)超然性;超凡

transcendent [træn'sendənt] *adj.* 1. 卓越的,超常的,出类拔萃的 2. [哲]先验的;超验的 3. 〈宗〉超然的 — *n.* [哲]超验的事物

transcendental [ˌtrænsen'dentl] *adj.* 1. [哲]先验的;先验论的;超出一般经验的;超自然的 2. 卓越的,超常的 3. 【数】超越的 — function 超越函数/~ curve 超越曲线 4. 抽象的;深奥晦涩的;玄奥的 ‖ **~ism** *n.* [哲]先验论/**~ly** *adv.*

transcontinental ['trænzˌkɒnti'nentl] *adj.* 1. 横贯大陆的 2. 在大陆另一头的

transcribe [træns'kraib] *vt.* 1. 抄写,誊写;用打字机打出 2. 译;意译;把(速记符号)译成文字;把(资料)改录成另一种形式 3. 抄;录下;用音标记录 4. 预录,录制(节目);播送 5. [音]改编 ‖ **~r** *n.* 抄写者,誊写员 2. 抄录器;读数器;信息转换器

transcript ['trænskript] *n.* 1. 抄本,誊本,副本 2. 〈美〉学生成绩报告单 3. (经历等的)艺术再现

transcription [træns'kripʃən] *n.* 1. 抄写,誊写 2. (速记符号等的)翻译 3. 抄本,誊本;(录音资料等的)文字本 4. (乐曲的)改编 5. 录音;录制;录音的播送;广播用的唱片(或磁带等)

transept ['trænsept] *n.* (教堂的)十字形耳堂,交叉廊

transfer [træns'fə:] (transferred; transferring) *vt.* 1. 转移;传递,传输 2. 调动;使转学;使转至另一足球俱乐部 3. 改变,转

变；变换 4. 转让，让于(财产等)5. 转印(图画、设计图等)；转写；摹绘 — vi.1. 转移；调动；转职；转修学科；转系(to)2. 换车；换船 — ['trænsfə] n.1. 转移；传递；传输；职务调动；调任(或调转)学证书；变换 2.(权利、财产等的)转让；转账；让于证书 3.(股票等的)过户；过户凭单 4. 汇划，汇兑；电汇；telegraphic ～(略作 T/T)电汇／mail ～(略作 M/T)信汇 5.(供)转印的图画(或图案等)6.(主英)转入其他部队的士兵；转学生 7. 转换处；(车辆或火车的)摆渡处；(车辆或火车的)渡轮 8. 转车证 ‖ **transferable** adj. ‖ ～ **company** 转运公司

transference ['trænsfərəns] n.1. 转移；传递 2. 职务调动，调任 3.(财产等的)转让，让于 4.【心】移情

transfigure [træns'figə] vt.1. 使变形；使改观 2. 美化；理想化 ‖ **transfigu'ration** n.

transfix [træns'fiks] vt.1. 戳穿，刺穿 2. 使固定；使呆着不动；使束手无策

transform [træns'fɔːm] vt.1. 使变形；使改变性质(或结构、外观、性格、个性等)；使改观，改造，改革 2.【电】变换，变换(变流)的电压 3.【数】变换 — vi. 改变，转化；变化 — ['trænsfɔːm] n.1.【数】变换(式)2.【语】转换；转换句，转换形式 3.【地】转换断层

transformation [ˌtrænsfə'meiʃən] n.1. 变化；变形；【生】细胞转化；遗传转化改造；改革 3. 转变；转化；【数】变换 4.【核】嬗变，核的转换 5.(女人的)假发

transformational [ˌtrænsfə'meiʃənəl] adj.【语】转换的，转换生成的 ‖ ～ **grammar** 转换语法

transformer [træns'fɔːmə] n.1. 促使变化的人(或物)；改革者 2.【电】变压器

transfuse [træns'fjuːz] vt.1. 充满；渗透；感染 2.【医】输(血、液)；给…输(血、液)‖ **trans'fusion** n. 感染；倾注；渗透；输血(法)；输液(法)

transgress [træns'ɡres] vt.1. 逾越，越过(限度、范围等)2. 违反；违背(规则、法律等)— vi.1. 越界 2. 违法；犯罪 ‖ **trans'gression** n. 逾越；违反；犯法；犯罪 ‖ ～ **or** n. 犯法者；违背者；(宗教、道德上的)罪人

transience ['trænziəns], **transiency** ['trænziənsi] n. 短暂，转瞬即逝；无常

transient ['trænziənt] adj.1. 短暂的，易逝的，倏忽的；无常的 2. 路过的，临时的，暂住的 3.【物】【电子】瞬变的 4.【音】短暂的，过度的 — n.1.〈美〉暂时寄住的旅客；流浪者 2. 过境鸟 3.【电】【电子】瞬变现象，瞬态；暂态；瞬变电流(或电压)

transistor [træn'sistə] n.【电子】1. 晶体管 2. 晶体管收音机

transit ['trænsit] n.1. 通过，经过；通行 2. 运送；运送，运输；运输；运输；公共交通系统 3. 过境，中转 4. 转变；变迁 5.【天】中天；凌(日)；中星仪；大星被食 — vt.1. 通过；运送过 2.(天体)经过 — vi. 通过 ‖ ～ **duty** (货物的)转口税，过境税

transition [træn'siʒən] n.1. 过渡；过渡时期 2. 转变；变迁，变革 3.【乐】【音】临时转调 4. 转折语，转接句(或段落)6.【生】转换 ‖ ～**al** adj. ／ ～**ary** adj.

transitive ['trænsitiv] adj.1.【语】及物的；～ **verb** 及物动词(略)2.【数】【逻】可递的，可迁的 3. 过渡的 — n.【语】及物动词

transitory ['trænsitəri] adj. 暂时的；短暂

的；瞬息的；昙花一现的 ‖ **transitoriness** n.

translate [træns'leit] vt.1. 翻译，译；转写；给(诗等)译意 2. 解释；说明 3. 转化，化；使以另一形式表现 4. 使移转；调动 5.〈英〉把(旧衣、旧鞋等)翻新 6.【基督教(圣经)】中用语使肉身不死而升天 7.【宗】调任(主教)至另一教区；移葬(圣徒遗骸等) 8.〈罕〉使出神 9.【物】【数】平移 10.【讯】自动转拍(电报)11.【生】转译 — vi.1. 翻译；当译者 2. 被译 ‖ **translatable** adj.

translation [træns'leiʃən] n.1. 翻译，译，译文；译本 3. 转化，化 4. 转移；调任 5.(基督教(圣经))(肉身)升天；主教调任 6.〈英〉(旧鞋等的)翻新 7.【物】【数】平移 8.【讯】(电报的)自动转拍 9.【生】转译

translator [træns'leitə] n.1. 翻译者，译员 2.【无】【讯】译码机；转发器；传送器；(电视的)差转台【计】翻译程序；翻译机

translucent [trænz'lju:snt] adj.1. 半透明的 2.〈罕〉透明的 3. 真诚的，不加掩饰的；清楚易懂的 ‖ **translucence, translucency** n. / **~ly** adv.

transmigrate [ˌtrænzmai'greit] vi.1. 移居(从一国或一地移到另一国或另一地)2.【宗】(灵魂)转生，转世 ‖ **transmigration** n. / **transmigrator** n.

transmission [trænz'miʃən] n.1. 传送，传递 2. 传动装置；变速器 3.【电】发射；播送；发送；传输 4. 播射；传染

transmit [trænz'mit] (transmitted; transmitting) vt.1. 传送(光、热、声，力等)通过空气(或其他介质) 2. 留传；遗传 4. 发送；播送 5. 传播；传染 — vi. 播送(或发送)信号

transmittal [trænz'mitəl] n.1. 传送；传

递；传播；传输 2. 被传送(或传递、传播、传输)

transmitter [trænz'mitə] n.1. 传送者；传递者【无】【讯】发射机；发射台；发报台；送话器，话筒 ‖ **trans·mitter-re'ceiver** n. 无线电收发两用机

transmutable [trænz'mju:təbl] adj.1. 能变形的；能变质的 2. 可嬗变的，可换变的；可蜕变的

transmutation [ˌtrænzmju:'teiʃən] n.1. 变形；变质 2.(中世纪炼金术士期求的)贱金属变金(或银)3.【生】演变，演化 4.【化】嬗变；蜕变

transmute [trænz'mju:t] vt.1. 使变形；使变质【化】使嬗变，使蜕变 — vi. 变形；变质

transnational [ˌtrænz'næʃənl] adj. 超越国界的，跨国的：a ～ company 跨国公司

transoceanic ['trænzˌəuʃi'ænik] adj.1. 横渡大洋的 2. 在大洋那边的

transom [trænsəm] n.1.(门、窗、十字架、绞架等的)横档(车辆的)横梁【船】舱横材 2.【建】窗楣；门顶窗；气窗

transonic [træn'sɒnik] adj.1.【物】跨声速的

transpacific [ˌtrænspə'sifik] adj.1. 横渡太平洋的 2.(在)太平洋彼岸的；来自太平洋彼岸的

transparency [træns'pɛərənsi] n.1. 透明；透明性；透明度；透明物；透明正片；透明画；幻灯片

transparent [træns'pɛərənt] adj.1. 透明的，可透逆的 2. 清澈的，明亮的 3. 易识破的；显而易见的 4. 直率的，坦诚的 5.〔语〕易懂的，结构清楚的；可从表面结构推知的 ‖ **~ly** adv.

transpire [træns'paiə] vi.1. 蒸发；散发；排出 2. 泄露；显露；被人知道 3. 发生 — vt. 使蒸发；使发散；使排出 ‖ ˌtranspi'ration n.1. 蒸发；发散；排出

【物】流逸 3.【植】蒸腾作用 4.【医】不显性出汗

transplant [træns'plɑːnt] *vt.*1. 移植；移种；【医】移植：～ rice 移栽稻／～ a heart 移植心脏 2. 迁移；移(民)— *vi.*1. 移植；移种 2. 适宜移植(或移种)— *n.*1. 移植；被移植物；【医】移植器官；移植组织 2. 移居者 ‖ ～ation [ˌtrænsplɑː'teiʃən] *n.* 移植；移种；【医】移植术

transport [træns'pɔːt] *vt.*1. 运输，运送；输送；搬运 2. 流放，放逐(罪犯)；把…驱逐出境 3.[用被动语态]使万分激动 — *n.* ['trænspɔːt] 1. 运输，运送；运输工具；运输船；运输飞机 3. 激动；狂喜 4. 流放犯

transportation [ˌtrænspɔː'teiʃən] *n.*1. 运输，运送；客运；货运；运送 2. 运输工具 3. 运费 4. 流放，放逐

transpose [træns'pəuz] *vt.*1. 使互换位置；调换，变换 2.【数】移(项) 3.【音】变调，使变调 — *vi.* 互换位置(或顺序)；换位 2.【音】变调，移调

transposition [ˌtrænspə'ziʃən] *n.*1. 互换位置；调换，变换 2.[语]换置；换置词；换置句 3.【数】转置；对换；移项 4.【音】移调，变调 5.【电】(导线)交叉

transsexual [træns'seksjuəl] *adj.*1. 有异性转化欲的；改变性别的 2. 两性间的；间性体的；雌雄间体的 — *n.* 有异性转化欲者，易性癖者；(经外科手术等)改变性别者 ‖ **transsexualism** *n.* 异性转化欲，易性癖 / **transsexualist** *n.* & *adj.*

transship [træns'ʃip] (transshipped; transshipping) *vt.* 把…转载于另一船(或车)；转运 — *vi.* 转运；中转；转船；转车

transsonic [træns'sɔnik], **transonic** [træn'sɔnik] *adj.*【物】跨声速的

transubstantiate [ˌtrænsəb'stænʃieit] *vt.*1. 使变质 2.【宗】使变体，使化体(指使圣

餐面包和酒变成耶稣的肉和血) ‖ 'transub,stanti'ation *n.*

transuranic [ˌtrænzjuə'rænik] *adj.*【化】超铀的，铀后的

transuranium [ˌtrænzjuə'reinjəm] *adj.* = transuranic

transversal [trænz'vəːsəl] *adj.* 横向的，横断的，横截的 — *n.*【数】截线

transverse ['trænzvəːs] *adj.* 横向的；横断的，横截的 — *n.* 横断面；横轴；横梁；横墙 2.【解】横肌 ‖ ～ly *adv.*

transvestite [trænz'vestait] *n.* 异性装扮癖者 — *adj.* 有异性装扮癖的，易装癖的 ‖ **transvestitism** *n.*

trap[1] [træp] *n.*1.(捕动物的)陷阱，罗网；夹子；捕捉机；(陷人的)圈套，诡计 2. 存水弯；汽水阀；防(臭)气阀；U 形(或 S 形)弯管 3. 滤波电路；陷波电路 4. = ～door 5. 抛靶器；(射球戏用的)木制抛球器 6. 双轮轻便马车 7.(俚)嘴；(英)警方；警察 8.[～s]打击乐器；车速检测设施 9.[计算机赛车速度的]计速路段 10.(赛狗中的)放狗隔栏 — *vt.*1. 设陷阱捕，诱捕；设陷阱于(某处)；使堕入圈套；诱骗；使陷于困境；使受限制 2. 止住；挡住 3. 使(水与气体等)分离 4. 装地板门于(舞台等) 5. 装存水弯于(排水管等)；用防气阀堵住(臭气)；使(蒸汽)闭封于管内 — *vi.* 设陷阱；装捕捉机；设圈套 ‖ '～door *n.*(舞台等的)地板门；活板门；(房顶的)活动天窗；(矿的)调节门

trap[2] [træp] *n.*【矿】暗色岩；积储石油(或天然气)的地质构造

trapeze [trə'piːz] *n.*1.(健身或杂技表演用的)吊架，高空秋千；a ～ acrobat (杂技)空中飞人 2.(美)不规则四边形

trapezium [trə'piːziəm] ([复] trapeziums 或 trapezia [trə'piziə]) n.1.〈英〉梯形;〈美〉不规则四边形 2.【解】大多角骨

trapezoid ['træpizɔid] n.1.〈英〉不规则四边形 2.〈美〉梯形 2.【解】小多角骨 — adj.〈英〉不规则四边形的;〈美〉梯形的

trapper ['træpə] n.1.设陷阱捕兽者 2.〈矿〉矿井风门开关管理员

trappings ['træpiŋz] [复] n.1.马饰 2.(尤指作为官职标志的)服饰;装饰品;礼服

trappy ['træpi] adj.1.设有陷阱的 2.〈口〉(事物)错综复杂的;骗人的;靠不住的

trash [træʃ] n.1.废物,垃圾;(修剪下来的)断枝;落叶;甘蔗渣;甘蔗枯叶 2.劣货;拙劣的文学作品;糟粕;废话 3.无用的(人);〈美〉贫穷的白人;总称]人类渣滓 — vt.1.修剪(树等)的枯枝残叶;去除(甘蔗)的叶子 2.把…视为废物;废弃 3.〈美口〉(尤指为表示抗议)捣毁,破坏 4.向…扔废物(或垃圾) — vi.〈美口〉捣毁,破坏;毁损财物

trauma ['trɔːmə] ([复] traumas 或 traumata ['trɔːmətə]) n.1.【医】外伤;伤口;损伤 2.(精神上的)创伤 ‖ ~ tic [trɔː'mætik] adj.

travail ['træveil] n.1.艰苦的努力;工作;劳动;苦功 2.分娩 3.痛苦;剧痛 — vi.1.辛勤劳动;艰苦努力 2.感受阵痛

travel ['trævl] ([过][现]travel(l)ed; travel(l)ing) vi.1.旅行 2.作旅行推销员 3.〈口〉快速前进,飞驰;〈方〉步行 4.行进;被传播;被运送 5.移动 6.交往 7.(篮球赛等中)带球跑,持球走 — vt.1.旅行 2.循…行走,通行于 3.在…作旅行推销 4.使移动;赶,送走(牲畜等) — n.1.旅行 2.[~s]旅行笔记;游记 3.运动,移动 4.【机】行程 4.(人、车通过的)来往数量,交通流量

travel(l)er ['trævlə] n.1.旅行者;旅客 2.

旅行推销员 3.移动式起重机,行车;活动起重架 4.【船】圆环;滑环杆 5.〈美〉旅行箱,旅行包,旅行袋

travel(l)ing ['trævliŋ] adj.1.旅行的;旅行用的 ‖ ~ bag 旅行手提包

travelog(ue) ['trævəlɔːg, 'trævlɔg] n.1.旅行见闻讲座(常用幻灯或影片助讲的);旅行记录片

traverse ['trævəs] vt.1.横越;横渡;横向穿过;越过;横亘,横贯;横跨;交叉 2.全面研究;详细讨论(问题);详细考察 3.反对(计划、意见等) 4.【律】否认;反驳 4.转动(大炮)的炮口;【海】首尾向拉紧(缆操纵杆) 5.在…上来回走动;沿…来回移动 6.对…作导线测量 — vi.1.横过;越过,穿过 2.(横向)往返移动 3.(磁针等)转动;在轴上旋转;〈滑雪运动中〉(登山时)作 Z 字形横过陡坡 4.作导线测量 — n.1.横越 2.横断物;【建】横梁;(与对面建筑物相通的)通廊;横墙;【军】防护墙 3.障碍;阻止 4.(炮口等的)旋转;【海】(逆风时的)曲线航行;(登山时)作 Z 字形横过山坡 5.【律】否认;反驳 6.【数】横线(线)7.(测量)导线 — adj.横过的;横贯的;横过的

travesty ['trævisti] n.(对人或文学作品等的)滑稽模仿;嘲弄;歪曲 — vt.滑稽地模仿;嘲弄;歪曲

trawl [trɔl] n.拖网;〈美〉(捕海鱼的)排钩 — vi. & vt.用拖网捕(鱼) ‖ ~ er n.拖网渔船;用拖网捕鱼者

tray [trei] n.1.(浅)盘;托盘;碟 2.(放在书桌内的)文件盘 3.(衣箱内的)隔底盘 4.【无】发射箱;发射别

treacherous ['tretʃərəs] adj.1.背叛的;背信弃义的;奸诈的;不可靠的;不实在的;有暗藏危险的 ‖ ~ ly adv. / ~ ness n.

treachery [ˈtretʃəri] ***n*.1.** 背叛,变节;背信弃义 **2.** 背叛行为,变节行为

treacle [ˈtriːkl] ***n*.1.** 〈英〉糖浆;糖蜜 **2.** 过分甜蜜的声调(或恭维话等) **3.** (古时的)解毒剂

tread [tred](过去式 trod[trɔd],过去分词 trodden[ˈtrɔdn]或 trod) ***vi*.1.** 踩,踏;走 **2.** (雄鸟与雌鸟)交尾(*with*) — ***vt*.1.** 踩,踏;在…上践踏 **2.** 跳 **3.** 踩出,踏成 **4.** 践踏;蹂躏 **5.** (雄鸟)与(雌鸟)交尾 — ***n*.1.** 踩,踏;步法;步态;脚步声 **2.** (雄鸟的)交尾 **3.** (楼梯等的)踏步板,梯面;楼梯级宽;(轮胎的)着地面,踏面 **4.** 鞋底 **5.** (汽车等左右两轮的)轮距 **6.** 【医】(马蹄的)踏伤 **7.** 【动】(卵的)胚点;卵(黄系)带 ‖ ˈ~ **mill** ***n*.1.** (古时罚囚犯踩踏的)踏车 **2.** 令人厌倦的工作

treadle [ˈtredl] ***n*.** (自行车、缝纫机等的)踏板 — ***vi*.** 踏动踏板

treason [ˈtriːzn] ***n*.1.** 重叛逆罪,叛国罪;【英律】(妻杀夫、仆杀主等的)轻叛逆罪 **2.** 背叛;不忠;背信 ‖ ~**able**, ~**ous** ***adj*.**

treasure [ˈtreʒə] ***n*.1.** 金银财宝;财富 **2.** 珍宝;珍品 **3.** 〈口〉不可多得的人材;宝贝儿(尤指孩子) — ***vt*.1.** 珍藏,秘藏;铭记(*up*) **2.** 珍重,珍惜 ‖ ~ **house** 宝库 /~ **trove**【英律】埋藏物;有价值的发现物(或收藏物)

treasurer [ˈtreʒərə] ***n*.** 司库,财务主管

treasury [ˈtreʒəri] ***n*.1.** 宝库;宝藏 **2.** 库房;金库;国库;库存 **3.** [T-]财政部 **4.** [T-](由财政部发行的)国库券 **5.** (诗文等的)集锦;名作选集

treat [triːt] ***vt*.1.** 对待;看待,把…看作 **2.** 处理;论述;探讨 **3.** 医治,治疗 **4.** 款待;请(客);(竞选时)请客拉拢(选民) **5.** 【化】处理;为…涂上保护层 — ***vi*.1.** 交涉;谈判;商议 **2.** 作东,请客 — ***n*.1.** 款待;请客 **2.** 难得的乐事

treatise [ˈtriːtiz] ***n*.** 论文;专著

treatment [ˈtriːtmənt] ***n*.1.** 待遇;对待 **2.** 处理;讨论;论述 **3.** 治疗;疗法;疗程

treaty [ˈtriːti] ***n*.1.** (国家之间的)条约 **2.** 协议,协定;协商;谈判 ‖ ~ **port** (条约规定的)条约口岸,通商口岸

treble [ˈtrebl] ***adj*.1.** 三倍的;三重的 **2.** 【音】最高声部的;唱(或奏)最高声部的 **3.** 尖声的;高音的 — ***n*.1.** 三倍;三重 **2.** 【音】最高声部;最高声部歌手;最高声部乐器 **3.** 尖锐声 — ***vt*.** 使成三倍,使增加两倍 — ***vi*.** 成为三倍,增加两倍 ‖ **trebly** ***adv*.** 三倍地;三重地

tree [triː] ***n*.1.** 树;乔木 **2.** 木料;木制构件 **3.** 树状物;【数】树(形);【化】树状结构 **4.** 家谱(图) **5.** 鞋楦 **6.** 圣诞树(= Christmas ~) **7.** 〈古〉绞架 **8.** 〈古〉(钉耶稣的)十字架 — ***vt*.1.** 把(人、兽等)赶上树;〈口〉使处于困境 **2.** 用鞋楦楦(鞋) ‖ ~ **agate** 树纹玛瑙 /~ **fern**【植】桫椤 /ˈ~**nail** ***n*.** 木栓 /~ **peony**【植】牡丹 /~ **toad**【动】雨蛙

trefoil [ˈtrefɔil] ***n*.** 车轴草,三叶草;三叶植物;【建】三叶形饰

trek [trek](trekked;trekking) ***vi*.1.** (南非用英语)(牛)拉货车;乘牛车旅行(或迁移) **2.** 缓慢地行进;艰苦跋涉 — ***vt*.** (南非用英语)(牛)拉(车) — ***n*.1.** (南非用英语)牛车旅行;(牛车旅行中的)一段旅程 **2.** 艰苦的跋涉;一段旅程 **3.** 【史】(1835—1837年布尔人的)有组织迁移

trellis [ˈtrelis] ***n*.1.** 【建】格子;格子结构;(葡萄等的)棚,架 **2.** 花格拱道;花格凉亭;格子屏 — ***vt*.1.** 为…建棚架;使(藤)在棚架上攀缘 **2.** 使交织成格状 **3.** 给(窗户等)装格子

tremble [ˈtrembl] ***vi*.1.** 发抖,哆嗦,战栗 **2.** 焦虑,担扰 **3.** 摇晃,摇动 — ***n*.1.** 颤

抖,哆嗦 2.[~s]震颤病;(尤指牛、羊的)乳毒病

tremendous [tri'mendəs] *adj.* 1.〈口〉精彩的;了不起的 2. 极大的;非常的,惊人的 ‖ ~ly *adv.*

tremor ['tremə] *n.* 1. 震颤;发抖 2. 颤动,小震 3. 战栗;兴奋;激动 4. 颤抖的声音

tremulous ['tremjuləs] *adj.* 1. 震颤的;发抖的 2. 胆小的;动摇的 3. 歪斜的;不稳定的 4. 过敏的 ‖ ~ly *adv.*

trench [trentʃ] *vt.* 1. 挖战壕于…;掘沟于…2. 刻;凿;〈英〉刨槽于(木材等)3. 用战壕围住;用战壕防御 — *vi.* 1. 挖沟;掘战壕 2. 接近,近似(*on*, *upon*)3. 侵犯;侵占(*on*, *upon*)— *n.* 1. 深沟;地沟 2.【军】堑壕,战壕

trenchant ['trentʃənt] *adj.* 1. 犀利的,锋利的,锐利的 2. 有力的;分明的,清晰的 ‖ **trenchancy** *n.* / ~ly *adv.*

trencher[1] ['trentʃə] *n.* 1.(切肉等时用的)木板;(正餐或盛食物的)木盘,木碟 2.〈古〉盘中食物 ‖ ~ **cap**(大学)方顶帽,学士帽,学位帽

trencher[2] ['trentʃə] *n.* 挖壕沟的人;掘沟的人

trend [trend] *vi.* 1. 走向;延伸 2. 倾向;趋向 3.(意见等)转向;偏向 — *n.* 1.(海岸、河流等的)走向 2. 倾向;趋势,动向

trendy ['trendi] *adj.*(赶)时髦的 — *n.*(赶)时髦的人 ‖ **trendiness** *n.* 时髦,时尚

trepan[1] [tri'pæn] *n.* 1.【医】环锯,钻孔 2.【矿】钻(矿)井机,凿井机,打眼机 3.【机】圆形锯 — (trepanned; trepanning) *vt.* 1. 用环锯在…上做手术 2. 钻削……在…上打眼(或穿孔);在…的凿孔四周开同心槽

trepan[2] [tri'pæn]〈古〉 *n.* 1. 诱惑者;诱惑物 2. 计谋;圈套;陷阱 — (trepanned; trepanning) *vt.* 把…诱入圈套;引诱;诱捕

trepang [tri'pæŋ] *n.*【动】海参;食用海参

trepidation [ˌtrepi'deiʃən] *n.* 1. 发抖;震颤 2. 惊恐;慌张

trespass ['trespəs] *vi.* 1. 擅自进入;侵入;侵占(*on*, *upon*)2. 叨扰;打扰;妨碍(*on*, *upon*)3. 冒犯;违背(*against*)— *n.* 1. 擅自(或非法)进入;侵害(或侵犯)行为 2. 冒犯;罪过 3. 打扰,妨碍 ‖ ~ **er** *n.* 侵犯者;侵犯他人土地者

tress [tres] *n.* 1. 一绺头发;一束头发;发辫 2.[~s](女人)头发;长发;蓬松长发

trestle ['tresl] *n.* 1. 支架;搁凳 2.【建】栈桥;高架桥;排架桥(亦作 ~ **bridge**)

tret [tret] *n.*【商】(旧时卖主为弥补运输过程中的损耗而给买主的)添量,添头,补(秤)头

trey [trei] *n.*(骰子或骨牌)刻有三点的一面;(纸牌的纸牌/骰子或骨牌的)三,三点

tri- *comb. form* 表示"三";"三次";"三倍": *triplane* 三翼飞机,*trisect*

triad ['traiæd] *n.* 1. 三人组 2. 三种事物(或思想等)的组合;三合一 2.【化】三价原子;三价基 3.【音】三和弦

trial ['traiəl] *n.* 1. 试;试用;试验 2. 考验;磨练;艰苦;痛苦 3. 讨厌的人;麻烦的事物 4. 审判;审判 5.【体】选拔赛;预赛 6. 尝试;努力 — *adj.* 尝试的;试验性的;试制的 ‖ **a ~ trip** 试航;(喻)试行 / **a ~ flight** 试飞 / **~ production** 产品试制 ‖ **~ run** 试航;试车;试验

triangle ['traiæŋgl] *n.* 1.【数】三角(形)2.三角板 3.【音】(打击乐器)三角铁 4.(尤指男女间的)三角关系 5.[T-]【天】三角座

triangular [traiˈæŋɡjulə] *adj.* 1. 三角(形)的 2. 有三角形底的 3. 三人间的;三者间的;三(军)三制的

tribal [ˈtraibəl] *adj.* 部落的;宗族的 ‖ ~-ism *n.* 部落制;部落文化

tribe [traib] *n.* 1. 部落;宗族 2. (贬)(一)帮、(一)伙、(一)批 3. 【生】族(生物分类) ‖ ~sman *n.* 部落男子 / ~,people [复] *n.* 部落成员 / ~s,woman *n.* 部落妇女

tribulation [ˌtribjuˈleiʃən] *n.* 1. 苦难;患难;忧伤 2. 引起苦难的事物;磨难

tribunal [traiˈbjuːnl; triˈbjuːnl] *n.* 1. 审判员席,法官席 2. 法庭(常指特种法庭或作比喻用)

tribune¹ [ˈtribjuːn] *n.* 1. (古罗马中平民选出的)保民官;军团司令官 2. 公民权保卫者

tribune² [ˈtribjuːn] *n.* 1. 讲坛,论坛 2. [T-](用于报刊名词)论坛报

tributary [ˈtribjutəri] *adj.* 1. 进贡的,纳贡的;附庸的;从属的 2. 辅助的 3. (河)支流的 — *n.* 1. 进贡国;附庸国;属国 2. 进贡者(指附庸国的统治者等) 3. 支流

tribute [ˈtribjuːt] *n.* 1. 贡金;贡品 2. 贡税,贡赋 3. 进贡的义务 4. 勒索的款额 5. 礼物;词;称赞 ‖ *lay under* ~ 使进贡 / *pay* (*a*) ~ *to* 称赞,歌颂

tricar [ˈtraikɑː] *n.* 〈英〉三轮汽车

trice¹ [trais] *vt.* 扯起;扯起并缚住;吊起(*up*)

trice² [trais] *n.* 一刹那

triceps [ˈtraiseps] ([复] triceps*es* 或 triceps) 【解】 *n.* 三头肌 — *adj.* (肌肉)三头的

trichinella [ˌtriki'nelə] ([复] trichinellae [ˌtriki'neli:]) *n.* 旋毛(形线)虫

trichinosis [ˌtriki'nəusis] *n.* 【医】旋毛虫病,毛线虫病

trichology [triˈkɔlədʒi] *n.* 【医】毛发学 ‖ trichologist *n.*

trichromatic [ˌtraikrəuˈmætik] *adj.* 三色的;用三色的 【医】三色视的,(有)正常色觉的

trick [trik] *n.* 1. 诡计,奸计;骗局;谋略 2. 恶作剧 3. 轻率愚蠢的行为 4. (行为、举止等方面的)习惯,习气 5. 窍门;技巧,技艺 6. 戏法,把戏 7. (船工的)值班时间(通常为 2 小时);轮值,值班 8. (桥牌等的)一圈,一圈所打的牌 9. (口)一墩(牌) 9. (口)淘人的孩子;俏姑娘 10. (俚)嫖客;妓女的接客 11. (动物经过训练的)表演绝技 — *adj.* 1. 有决窍的;特技的;花巧的 2. 欺诈的,弄虚作假的 3. 漂亮的;潇洒的;整洁的;一丝不苟的 4. 靠不住的(关节等)会突然撑不住的 — *vt.* 1. 哄骗 2. 装饰;打扮(*out*, *up*, *off*) — *vi.* 哄骗 2. 恶作剧;戏弄(*with*) ‖ ~ cyclist 特技自行车手;(俚)精神病医生

trickery [ˈtrikəri] *n.* 欺骗;哄骗;诡计;圈套

trickle [ˈtrikl] *vi.* 1. 滴;滴;细流;流出液体 2. 慢慢地移动 — *vt.* 使滴;使滴;使细流 — *n.* 滴流;细流 ‖ ~ 'irrigate *vt.* 细流灌溉,滴灌

trickster [ˈtrikstə] *n.* 骗子;魔术师;恶作剧精灵

tricky [ˈtriki] *adj.* 1. 狡猾的;要花招的 2. (工作等)复杂的,微妙的;棘手的 3. 靠不住的;(关节等)会突然撑不住的

tricolo(u)r [ˈtrikələ, ˌtraiˌkələ] *adj.* 1. (有)三色的 2. 用三色的;(尤指法国的)三色国旗的 — *n.* 三色旗(尤指法国国旗)

tricuspid [traiˈkʌspid] 【解】 *adj.* 三尖的;三尖瓣的 — *n.* 三尖牙(心脏的)三尖

屉

tricycle ['traisikl] *n.* 三轮脚踏车;三轮摩托车;三轮手摇车 — *vi.* 骑三轮脚踏车(或三轮摩托车等)

trident ['traidənt] *n.* **1.**(希腊、罗马神话中海神的)三叉戟 **2.** 三个齿鱼叉 **3.** 制海权的象征 **4.** [T-]三叉戟飞机(或核潜艇、弹道导弹) — *adj.* 三叉的

tried [traid] *adj.* **1.** 试验过的;考验过的;证明了的;可靠的;确实的 **2.** 经受过磨炼的;备受困苦的

triennial [trai'eniəl] *adj.* **1.** 每三年一次的 **2.** 持续三年的 — *n.* **1.** 三年生植物 **2.** 每三年发生一次的事件 **3.** 三周年纪念 **4.** 【天主教】三年间为死者每天举行的弥撒

trier ['traiə] *n.* **1.** 试验者;检验者 **2.** 检验用具;取样器 **3.**(对性格等的)试验物,考验物 **4.** 尽力工作的人 **5.** 审查员;审讯员 **6.**【律】(裁决陪审员应否回避的)审判员

trifid ['traifid] *adj.*【生】三(分)裂的

trifle ['traifl] *n.* **1.** 小事;琐事;细故;无价值的东西 **2.** 少许,少量;一点点钱 **3.**(蛋白、奶油、果酱、糕饼等做成的)酒浸果酱布丁,屈莱弗甜食 **4.** 白镴;[~s]白镴制品 — *vi.* **1.** 开玩笑;嘻弄;轻视(*with*) **2.** 玩弄(*with*) **3.** 闲逛 — *vt.* 浪费(时间、精力、钱等)(*away*)

trifling ['traifliŋ] *adj.* **1.** 不重要的;微不足道的;无聊的 **2.** 少许的;情意不专的 **3.**〈方〉懒散的,不求上进的

trifoliate [trai'fəuliət], **trifoliated** [trai'fəulieitid] *adj.* **1.**(有)三叶的【植】具三叶的;具三小叶(复叶)的 **2.**【建】三叶饰的

trig¹ [trig] *adj.* **1.** 整洁的;漂亮的 **2.** 一丝不苟的,一本正经的 **3.** 健全的;良好的 **4.** 坚实的 — (trigged; trigging) *vt.*〈主英〉把…收拾得整整齐齐(*out, up*)

trig² [trig] (trigged; trigging) *vt.* **1.**(用垫石、楔子等)制止(车轮等)滚动 **2.** 支撑,撑住 — *n.*(制止车轮用的)垫石,楔子;木垫

trigger ['trigə] *n.* **1.**【军】扳机;触发器 **2.**【电】触发电路;起动装置 **3.**【机】扳柄;闸柄 **3.** 能引起反应的行动(或冲动等) — *vt.* **1.** 扣扳机开门(枪等);发射 **2.** 激发起,引起(*off*) — *vi.* 松开扳柄(或扳机等) ‖ **~-happy** *adj.* 乱开枪的;好斗的,好动武的;好战的 / **~ man** 开枪行凶的人;刺客;匪徒 **2.** 保镖 **3.**(拉动扳机使船下水的)下水扳机手

trigonometry [ˌtrigə'nɔmitri] *n.*【数】三角学 ‖ **trigonometric** [ˌtrigənə'metrik] *adj.*

trike [traik] *n. & vi.*〈口〉= tricycle

trilateral [trai'lætərəl] *adj.* 三边的 — *n.* 三角形;三边形

trilby ['trilbi] *n.*〈主英〉软毡帽(亦作~ hat)

trill [tril] *n.* **1.**(音乐演奏和发音时的)颤音 **2.**【音】【语】颤音 **3.**(鸟的)啭鸣 — *vt.* 以颤声发出;以颤声奏(或唱等) — *vi.* 发出颤音

trillion ['triljən] *num.* **1.**(英、德)百万兆(在 1 后加 18 个零所得的数) **2.**(美、法)万亿,兆(在 1 后加 12 个零所得的数) — *n.* 大量,无数

trilogy ['trilədʒi] *n.* **1.**(音乐、戏剧、小说等的)三部曲 **2.**(古希腊悲剧的)三部曲,三联剧

trim [trim] (trimmer; trimmest) *adj.* **1.** 整齐的;整洁的;苗条的,修长的 **2.** 装备齐全的;即可使用的;身体健康的;情况良好的 — (trimmed) trimming *vt.* **1.** 使整齐;整理;修剪 **2.** 装饰;点缀;布置(商

店橱窗)3. 装稳(船只);【空】使(飞机)配平 4. 调整(船舶)以适应风向 5. 刨平和修整(木料)6.〖口〗骂;训斥;殴打;击败;诈骗(钱财)— **vi.**1.(政治上)两面讨好,骑墙;走中间路线;见风使舵 2.(船)保持平衡;顺风使舵 — **n.**1. 整理;修剪;调整 2. 整顿;准备;齐备 3.(华丽的)服装;外表 4. 装饰(物);【建】门窗贴脸;窗帘 5.(船等的)平衡;【海】吃水差;【军】(潜艇的)浮力;【空】配平 6. 修剪下来的东西 — **adv.**1. 整齐 ‖ ~ly **adv.** 整齐地;整洁地/~ness **n.**

trimmer ['trimə] **n.**1. 整修者;装饰者;【船】(散货)平舱机,匀货机;平舱工人 2.(政治上)两面讨好的人;墙头派;见风使舵者 3.【机】修剪器;剪切器具;横截圆锯机;【电子】微调电容器 4.【建】托梁,承接梁

trimming ['trimiŋ] **n.**1. 整理;装饰;修剪;装饰品 2.[~s](主菜之外的)花色配菜 3.[~s]修剪下来的东西 4.〖口〗责骂;打击;失败

Trinidad and Tobago ['trinidæd ənd tə'beigəu]特立尼达和多巴哥[拉丁美洲岛国]

trinitrotoluene [trai,naitrəu'tɔljui:n], **trinitrotoluol** [trai,naitrəu'tɔljuɔl] **n.**【化】三硝基甲苯(略作 TNT)

trinity ['triniti] **n.**1. 三个(人或物组成的)一组,三位一体 2.[the T-][宗](圣父、圣子、圣灵)三位一体 3. 三位一体图片(或雕塑品)3.[T-][宗]三一节(亦作 Trinity Sunday)

trinket ['triŋkit] **n.**1. 小件饰物 2. 无价值的琐碎的东西,小玩意儿

trio ['tri:əu] **n.**1. 音】三重奏(或唱)曲;中段,三声中部 2. 三重唱(或三重奏)小组;三人一组;三件一套

triode ['traiəud] **n.**【电子】三极管

Triones [trai'əinz][复] **n.**【天】北斗七星,大熊(星)座

trip [trip] (tripped;tripping) **vi.**1. 轻快地走(或跑);轻快地跳舞 2. 绊;绊倒 3. 失足;犯错误;出差错 4. 说话结结巴巴 5. 旅行,旅游;出行 6.〖表等〗操纵机构触动 — **vt.**1. 将…绊倒;使绊倒;使犯错误;使受挫,使失败 2. 找出(某人)的过错;挑剔(up)3.〈古〉轻快地跳(舞)4.【海起(锚);竖直(帆桁)5.【机】松开(离合器等)而开动 — **n.**1.(摔角中)绊;绊倒 2. 失足;失误,错误 3.【核】停堆 4. 航行;旅行,旅游;出行 6. 行程 7. 轻快的步伐 8.【机】撞锤,锤体,动力锤的头部,破碎机的落锤、冲击 9.【机】脱扣,脱口装置;接合机构;分离机构;离合器控制机构 10.(渔船的)一次出航捕获量 11.(吸毒品者的)幻觉;刺激性体验,兴奋

tripartite [,trai'pɑ:tait] **adj.**1. 分成三部分;三部分组成的,三重的 2. 一式三份的 3. 三方面之间的 4.【植】(叶子)三深裂的

tripe [traip] **n.**1.(牛等的)肚子(供食用)2.[常~s]内脏 3.〖俚〗废物;废话;讨厌的东西

triphibian [trai'fibiən] **adj.**1. 兼长于陆海空作战的 2.(飞机)三栖的 3. 陆海空联合作战的 — **n.**1. 兼长于陆海空作战的指挥官 2.(水陆空)三栖飞机(亦作 ~ aeroplane)

triphibious [trai'fibiəs] **adj.** = triphibian

triphthong ['trifθɔŋ] **n.**【语】三合元音(如 [aiə],[auə])— **al**['trif θɔŋɡəl] **adj.**

triple ['tripl] **adj.** 三倍的,三重的;三层的;三部分的 — **n.**1. 三倍数;三倍量;三个一组 2.(棒球的)三垒打(即可连跑三垒的一击)— **vt.** 三倍于,使增给

三倍 — *vi.* 增至三倍 ‖ ~ **jump**【体】三级跳远 / ~ **play**(棒球)三重杀 /~ 'space *vt.* 每空两行打(字) / ~ **threat**(能奔、能踢、能传的)(足球)全能运动员

triplet ['triplit] *n.* 1. 三个一组;三件一套 2.(押韵的)三行联句 3.【音】三连音符 4. 三胞胎中的一个;[~s]三胞胎

triplex ['tripleks] *adj.* 三倍的;三重的;有三部分的;三层楼的;有三套公寓套房(或住宅单元)的 — *n.* 1. 由三部分组成的东西(如三层一套的公寓,有三套住房的房屋等)2.【音】三拍子

triplicate ['triplikit] *adj.* 1. 一式三份的;重复三次的 2.(一式几份中)第三份的 — *n.* 三个相同物中的第三个;一式三份中的一份 — ['triplikeit] *vt.* 1. 把…作成一式三份 2. 使增至三倍

tripod ['traipɔd] *n.* 1. 三脚桌;三脚凳;三足桌;三脚架 2.(照相机等的)三脚架 3.(古希腊 Delphi 特尔斐城内的)青铜三脚祭坛;三足鼎式奖杯

Tripoli ['tripəli] *n.* 1. 的黎波里[利比亚首都] 2. 特里波利[黎巴嫩西北部港市]

tripoli ['tripəli] *n.*【矿】硅藻土

tripper ['tripə] *n.* 1.〈英口〉(通常为短程的)旅游者,远足者 2. 绊跌者 3.【机】倾卸装置;钩针;解脱装置,断开装置(铁路的信号开放器)

tripping ['tripiŋ] *adj.* 1. 脚步轻快的;有节奏(或调子)进行的 2.(说话)流畅的,滔滔不绝的

triptane ['triptein] *n.*【化】三甲基丁烷(一种高抗爆燃料,常用于飞机的内燃机)

trisect [trai'sekt] *vt.* 1. 把…分成三段;把…截成三段 2.【数】把…三等分

trisyllabic [,traisi'læbik] *adj.* 三音节的

trisyllable [,trai'siləbl] *n.* 三音节词

trite [trait] *adj.* 1. 用坏了的 2.(言词、引语、观念、意见等)陈腐的;平凡的;老一套的

tritium ['tritiəm] *n.*【化】氚(氢的放射性同位素)

triton[1] ['traitn] *n.* 1. [T-]〖希神〗特赖登(人身鱼尾海神)2.【动】法螺(壳);北螈

triton[2] ['traitn, 'traitɔn] *n.*【核】氚核

triturate ['tritjureit] *vt.* 把…研成粉末,磨碎,捣碎 — *n.* 1. 磨碎物 2.【药】研制剂 ‖ .**tritu'ration** *n.*

triumph ['traiəmf] *n.* 1.(古罗马)凯旋仪式 2. 凯旋;得胜;成功;成就 3.(胜利或成功时的)狂欢;喜悦 — *vi.* 1. 获胜;成功;击败(*over*)2. 热烈庆祝胜利;(因胜利而)洋洋得意,耀武扬威

triumphal [trai'ʌmfəl] *adj.* 凯旋(式)的;庆祝胜利的;胜利的;成功的

triumphant [trai'ʌmfənt] *adj.* 1. 胜利的;成功的 2.(因胜利而)狂欢的;喜悦的;得意洋洋的 ‖ ~**ly** *adv.*

triumvir [tri'ʌmvə, trai'ʌmvə]([复] tri-umviri [tri'ʌmviri:, trai'ʌmvirai] 或 tri-umvirs) *n.* 1.(古罗马)三执政之一 2. 三巨头之一 ‖ ~**al** *adj.*

triumvirate [trai'ʌmvirət] *n.* 1.(古罗马)三头政治,三雄执政 2. 三人领导小组;三人委员会;三党联合政府 3. 三人领导小组(或委员会)成员的职务

triune ['traijuːn] *adj.* 三位一体的 — *n.* 1. 三位一体的 2.【T-】〖基督教〗三位一体

trivet ['trivit] *n.*(搁在火上支承水壶等的)三脚架;(桌上摆热菜用的)矮托架,三脚垫

trivial ['triviəl] *adj.* 1. 琐细的;轻微的;不重要的;价值不大的 2. 平常的,平凡的;(名称)通俗的

triviality [,trivi'æləti] *n.* 1. 琐事;琐碎;平

凡 2.(人的)浅薄;轻浮

trochaic [trəu'keiik] adj.(诗律)扬抑格的长短格的 — n.1. 扬抑格(或长短格)音步 2.[~s]扬抑格,长短格

troche [trəuʃ] n.[药]锭剂;片剂;糖锭

trochee ['trəuki:] n.(英诗的)扬抑格(希腊或拉丁诗的)长短格

trod [trɔd] tread 的过去式和过去分词

trodden ['trɔdn] tread 的过去分词

troglodyte ['trɔglədait] n.1. 穴居人 2. 隐居者,隐士 3. 老顽固;极端保守主义者

troika ['trɔikə](俄)n.1. 三驾马车 2. 并驾拉车的三匹马 3. 紧密联系的三人(或三物)

Trojan ['trəudʒən] adj.(小亚细亚古城)特洛伊(Troy)的;特洛伊人的 — n.1. 特洛伊人 2. 勤勉的人;有毅力的人 3. 好人,善良人 4. 声名狼藉的同伴;放荡的人 5. 特罗詹避孕套(商标名) ‖ ~ horse 1.[希神]特洛伊木马 2. 颠覆分子;颠覆集团;颠覆活动,颠覆阴谋

troll[1] [trəul] vt.1. 使旋转 2. 轮唱 3. 高声地唱;愉快地唱;嘹亮地说(或朗诵)4. 用曳绳钓(鱼),拖钓;在…钓 — vi.1. 旋转 2. 轮唱 3. 愉快地唱;愉快地唱;愉快地说话 4. 曳绳的鱼 — n.1. 轮转;滚动 2. 轮唱;轮唱的歌 3. 曳绳钓法;(曳绳钓鱼用的)钓绳,钓饵;带钓钩的曳绳

troll[2] [trəul] n.(北欧神话中的)巨人,巨怪;好恶作剧而态度友善的侏儒

trolley ['trɔli] n.1.(英)手推车;(医院用的)担架车;(用以送食物、书籍等的)带有脚轮的小车,台车;(铁路)手摇车,手摇查道车 2. 架空电缆车 3.(美)有轨电车(= 〈英〉tram)4. 与架空电缆接触的触轮 — vt. 用手推车(或有轨电车等)载运 — vi. 乘有轨电车(或手摇电车) ‖ ~-bus n. 无轨电车(亦作

coach)/ ~ car〈美〉有轨电车

trollop ['trɔləp] n.1. 邋遢女人;懒婆娘 2. 妓女;行为不检的女人;荡妇

trolly ['trɔli] n.1. = trolley

trombone [trɔm'bəun] n.[音]长号,长喇叭;伸缩长号 ‖ trombonist n.

troop [tru:p] n.1.[常~s]军队,部队 2. 骑兵连,骑兵中队 3. 一群;大量,许多 4. 童子军中队 5.〈古〉剧团,戏班 6. 进军鼓 — vi.1. 群集,集合(up, together)2. 成群结队地走去;匆匆走掉 ‖ ~ carrier 部队运输机;部队运输船/'~ship n. 部队运输船

trooper ['tru:pə] n.1. 骑兵;伞兵 2. 骑兵的马 3. 骑警 4.〈美口〉州警察 5.〈主英〉部队运输船

trope [trəup] n.[语]转义;比喻

trophy ['trəufi] n.1.(古希腊、古罗马在战场或公共场所树立的)胜利纪念柱 2.(战利品等)胜利纪念品;纪念品 3. 胜利纪念章(或碑)4.(体育比赛奖的)奖品;奖杯,奖品 5.[建]描有战利品等、陈列的猎获物(如雕皮、鹿头等)— vt. 用战利品(或奖品)装饰;授予战利品(或奖品)

tropic ['trɔpik] n.1.[天]回归线 2.[~s]热带地区 — adj. 热带的 ‖ Tropic of Cancer 北回归线,夏至线/Tropic of Capricorn 南回归线,冬至线

tropical ['trɔpikəl] adj.1. 热带的;位于热带的;用于热带的 2. 炎热的;酷热的;3. 热烈的;热情的 4. 转义的;比喻的 ‖ ~ly adv. ‖ ~ fish 热带鱼

tropism ['trəupizəm] n.[生]向性;取向,定向,向性运动 ‖ tropistic [trəu'pistik] adj.

trot [trɔt](trotted; trotting) vi.1.(马)小跑;驾马小跑;骑马小跑;(人)小步跑;快步走;匆忙走 2.〈口〉走 — vt. 使小跑;使

快步走 — *n.*1.(马的)小跑;骑马 2.(人的)小跑步;快步,疾走;实力的活动 3.《口》蹄声 4.《罕》摇摇晃晃学走路的小孩 《贬》老太婆 5.《美俚》(学生作弊夹带的)外文直译本,逐字译本 6.《俗》[~s]拉肚子,泻肚

troth [trəuθ, troθ] *n.*.《古》1. 忠诚 2. 真实 3. 誓言 4. 订婚 — *vt.* 发誓保证;同…订婚

Trotskyist [ˈtrɔtskiist]. **Trotskyite** [ˈtrɔtskiait] *n. & adj.* 托洛茨基分子(的),托派分子(的)

trotter [ˈtrɔtə] *n.*1. 小跑的马;快步走的人 2.[~s](供食用的)猪蹄蹄,猪爪;羊腿肉 3.《谑》(人的)脚

troubadour [ˈtruːbədua] *n.*1.(11 到 13 世纪主要在法国南部及意大利北部的)行吟诗人 2.《美》情歌诗人(或歌者)

trouble [ˈtrʌbl] *n.*1. 烦恼,苦恼;忧虑 2. 困难,不幸;灾难 3. 麻烦;打扰 4. 讨厌的事(或人);纠纷 5.(政治、社会方面的)动乱;纠纷;风潮 6. 疾病;(机器等的)故障 7.《英方》非婚怀孕 — *vt.*1. 使烦恼,使苦恼;使忧虑 2.[常用被动语态]扰乱;使麻烦 3.[表示客气时用]劳驾 4.(病痛)折磨;使不舒服;使疼痛 — *vi.*[常用于否定句和疑问句]烦恼,苦恼;费心,费神 ‖ ~ **maker** *n.* 惹事生非者;闹事者;捣乱者 / ˈ~ˌshooter *n.*1.(机器等的)检修工 2.(政治、外交、商业等方面)解决麻烦问题的能手

troublesome [ˈtrʌblsəm] *adj.*1. 令人烦恼的;讨厌的 2. 困难的;麻烦的;累赘的 3.《古》骚乱的;痛苦的

trough [trɔf] *n.*1. 槽;水槽;饲料槽;木盆;(面包作坊用的)长形揉面槽 2. 檐槽;管道 3.【物】凹点,(曲线方程的)极小值 4.【气】低压槽,槽形低压 5.【地】海槽

6.(经济周期的)低谷期,萧条阶段

trounce [trauns] *vt.*1. 痛打 2. 严责,呵斥 3.《口》打败

troupe [truːp] *n.*1. 剧团,戏班;杂技团;马戏团 2.《美俚》一群扒手(或在街上伙闹事的青少年) — *vi.*(作为剧团成员)巡回演出 ‖ ~ **r** *n.*1.(剧团、杂技团等的)团员 2.《口》有经验的演员

trousers [ˈtrauzəz][复] *n.* 裤子;长裤

trousseau [ˈtruːsəu]([复] trousseaux [ˈtruːsəuz]或 trousseaus) *n.* 嫁妆,妆奁

trout [traut]([复]trout(s)) *n.*1. 鲑,鲑鳟鱼 2. 鲑状鱼 — *vi.* 捕鲑,捕鲑鳟鱼

trowel [ˈtrauəl] *n.*1.(泥工,抹子,镘刀 2. 泥铲 — *vt.* 用镘刀(或抹子)涂抹,粉刷 ‖ ~ **r** *n.*1.(铟泥、粉刷匠 2. 用泥刀涂抹(或修平,抹和等)

troy [trɔi] *n.* 金衡制(金、银、宝石的衡量制度;亦作~ weight) — *adj.* 用金衡制表示(或计算)的

truant [ˈtruːənt] *n.*1. 逃避责任者;玩忽职守者 2. 逃学者,旷课者 — *adj.* 逃学的;闲荡的;懒散的 — *vi.* 逃避责任;逃学,旷课 ‖ **truancy** *n.*

truce [truːs] *n.*1. 休战,停战;休战协定 2.(尤指苦痛、烦恼等的)中止,暂停 — *vi.* 休战 — *vt.* 以休战结束

truck¹ [trʌk] *n.*1.《美》卡车,载重汽车,运货汽车(英国通常用 lorry) 2.《英》铁路)敞篷货车 3.《英》车站上推行李的手推车 4.【机】转向架 5. 旗杆(或桅)顶 6. 炮车车轮,滚轮 — *vt.* 用运货汽车装运 — *vi.*1. 以驾驶卡车为职业 2. 驾驶卡车;用卡车运货 ‖ ~ **age** *n.* 运货车费用;货车运输

truck² [trʌk] *vt.* 交换;以实物换取 — *vi.*1. 以物易物之类的交易;以物物交易 — *n.*1. 以物易物 2. 打交道,交往 3. 适于以物易物(或小额贸易)的商品 4. 实物工资 5.《美》供应市场的蔬菜 6. 不值钱

的杂物;废物;废话 ‖ ~er n. ‖ ~
farm, ~ garden(美)商品蔬菜农场

truckle ['trʌkl] n.1. 小轮子;脚轮 2. ~
bed — vi.1. 架在脚轮上移动 2. 屈从;
讨好;谄媚(to) — vt. 把…用脚轮推着
走 ‖ ~ bed(不用时可推入大床下的)
有脚轮的矮床

truculence ['trʌkjuləns], **truculency**
['trʌkjulənsi] n.1. 好战;战斗;凶猛;残
忍 2. 致命性;毁灭性 3. 粗暴;刻毒(尤
指说话或文字)

truculent ['trʌkjulənt] adj. 1. 凶猛的;残
忍的;野蛮的 2. (说法、作品等)粗暴
的,刻毒的 3. 好战的;好斗的 4.(疾病
等)致命的;毁灭性的 ‖ ~ly adv.

trudge [trʌdʒ] vi. 跋涉;步履艰难地走 —
vt. 沿着…跋涉;艰难地走过 — n. 跋
涉

true [truː] adj.1. 真的;真实的,确实的 2.
忠实的;忠诚的;坚定的;可靠的 3. 正
确的;准确的 4.(安装、形状等)正的;
准的;平衡的;挺直的 5. 纯粹的;纯种
的 6. 正式的;合法的 7. 限定的;确切
的;严格的 8.(罗盘方向)根据地极(而
磁极)测量的 9.〈古〉老实的 — n.1.
[the ~]真实;真理 2.(安装等的)正
准;精确 — adv. [仅与某些动词连用]
真实地;确实地;准确地;纯粹地 —
(trued, truing 或 trueing) vt. 摆正;装
准;配准;校准(up) ‖ ~ness n. ‖
blue 1. 不退色的蓝色染料 2.(17世纪
苏格兰的)长老会教友 3. 赤胆忠心;忠
心耿耿的人 /~'blue adj.(对党派等)
非常忠诚的;坚定的 n. 忠实的人;可
靠的人 /~'born adj. 嫡出的;地道的 /
~'hearted adj. 忠实的;忠诚的 /
~'love n.(忠实的)恋人

truffle ['trʌfl] n.[植]块菰,块菌(地下菌
之一种,供调味用)

truism ['truːizəm] n.1. 自明之理;不言而
喻的话 2. 老生常谈,陈词滥调

truly ['truːli] adv.1. 真正地;确实地 2. 事实
上 2.忠实地;忠诚地 3. 正当地;正确
地;有理地

trump[1] [trʌmp] n.1.(牌戏中的)王牌,将牌;
(喻)王牌;法宝 2.[~s]一套王牌;一手
王牌 2.〈口〉好样的人;可靠的人 —
vt.1. 出王牌赢(牌)2. 超过,胜过;打赢
— vi. 出王牌;出王牌获胜 ‖ ~ card
王牌,将牌;(喻)王牌,有效(或有力)手
段 /'~ed'up adj. 捏造的

trump[2] [trʌmp] n.〈古〉〈诗〉喇叭;号筒;
喇叭声;号声

trumpery ['trʌmpəri] n.1. 中看不中用的
东西 2. 废物;废话 — adj. 虚有其表
的;无用的;浅薄的

trumpet ['trʌmpit] n.1. 喇叭,[音]小号 2.
喇叭声似的声音(尤指象的吼声)3. 喇
叭形的东西;[~s][植]黄瓶子草 4.(乐
队)小号吹奏者,小号手 5.(风琴的)小
号音栓 — vi.1. 吹喇叭 2. 发出喇叭似
的声音 — vt.1. 用小号吹
出 2. 以喇叭声似的声音大声说出 3.
吹嘘 ‖ ~ call 号声;紧急召唤 /~
conch, ~ shell 法螺;法螺壳 /~ creeper
【植】(美洲)凌霄花

trumpeter ['trʌmpitə] n.1. 小号吹奏者;
号兵 2.(喻)吹鼓手 3.【动】(南美的)长
脚长颈鹤形鸟;喇鸪;(北美的)野天鹅
4.【动】鲷鱼

truncate ['trʌŋkeit] vt.1. 截去…的顶端
(或末端);把…截短;删节,缩短(冗长
的引语等)2. 截去(晶体的棱或角);使
成平面 — adj. 截短的;【生】(羽、叶)
平截的,平头的 ‖ ~d adj./~ly adv./
trun'cation n.

truncheon ['trʌntʃən] n.1.(短棍)棍棒;警
棍 2.(作权威标志的)官杖,权杖,司令

杖 3.〈古〉矛杆 — *vt.* 用棍棒(或髼棍)
打

trundle ['trʌndl] *n.*1. 小轮子·(家具等的)
脚轮 2. 手推车 3. [~ bed.4.[机]灯笼
式小齿轮;销轮 5. 滚动;滚动声 — *vt.*
使滚动·(艰难地)推动 — *vi.* 滚动·转
动 ‖ ~ bed(不用时可推入大床下的)
有脚轮的矮床

trunk [trʌŋk] *n.*1. 树干·(人体、动物的)
躯干·(昆虫的)胸部 2.[解]大血管;神
经干 3.(铁路、运河、电话线等的)干线
4. 象鼻·(鸟、虫等的)喙 5. 旅行箱;衣
箱·(汽车后部的)行李箱 6.[~s]游泳
裤;运动短裤;男用短衬裤 7.[建]柱身
8.[讯]中继线 9.(船)鼠舱室;围阱;围
壁通道 10.[矿]洗矿槽 — *vt.* 把…放
在旅行箱内·〈美〉把…放在汽车后部行
李箱内 — *a.*1.(铁路、运河、电话线等)
干线的·主要的 2.(铁路、运河、电话线等)的干线的 3. 管
形的;简形的 ‖ ~ call〈英〉长途电话／
~ line[铁路、运河等]的干线·(电话等)
中继线／~ maker *n.*1. 旅行箱制
造商 2.〈古〉滞销书堆放处

truss [trʌs] *vt.*1. 扎;捆 2.(烹调前将
(鸡、鸭等)的翅膀和脚扎紧 3.[用桁架
(或构架)支撑(桥、屋顶等)4.〈古〉把…
处绞刑(*up*)— *n.*1. 捆束·一捆干
草(通常为 56-60 磅)·一捆麦秸(通常
为 36 磅)3. 桁架;构架 4.[植]花束·果
束 5.[医]疝带 6.(船)桁桅连接环

trust [trʌst] *n.*1. 信念·信赖 2. 可信任的
人(或事物)3. 职责·职守 4.(由受托而
产生的)责任 5. 信心;希望 6. 赊账·信
托 6.[律]受益人对信托财产的应享权
利;信托财产;受托人 7.[经]托拉斯 8.
商业信托 9.〈罕〉中看 — *vt.*1.
相信·信任·信赖 2. 把…委托给·托交·
托付·存放(*with, in*)3. 希望·盼望 4.
赊售 — *vi.*1. 相信·信任·信赖·倚靠

2. 希望 3. 赊售 ‖ ~ deed 信托书·委托
书／~ fund 信托基金

trustee [ˌtrʌs'ti:] *n.*1.(财产、业务等)的受
托人 2.(社团、医院、学校等的)理事·
托管国(受托管理托管领土的国家)—
*vt.*1. 移交(财产或管理权)给受托人 2.
[律]判押令扣押(债务人的财产)—
vi. 当受托人(或管理人·托管等)

trusteeship [ˌtrʌs'ti:ʃip] *n.*1. 托管人的职
责 2.(托管国对被托管地的)托管统
治;托管领土

trustful ['trʌstful] *adj.* = trusting ‖ ~ ly
adv. / ~ ness *n.*

trusting ['trʌstiŋ] *adj.* 深信不疑的;信任
他人的 ‖ ~ ly *adv.* / ~ ness *n.*

trustworthy ['trʌstˌwəːði] *adj.* 值得信任
的;可信赖的·可靠的 ‖ trustworthily
adv. / trustworthiness *n.*

trusty ['trʌsti] *adj.*1. 可信赖的·可靠的 2.
〈罕〉深信不疑的·信任人的 — *n.*1. 受
到信任的人 2.(因表现好而享有特权
的)模范犯人 ‖ trustily *adv.* / trustiness
n.

truth [tru:θ] *n.*([复] truths [tru:ðz, tru:θs])
*n.*1. 真理 2. 真实;真相·实际情况 3.
〈主英〉(安装等)正·准;精确 4.(艺术
作品等的)真实性·忠实性 5.〈古〉忠
实;忠诚 6.[T~](基督教科学派用语)
上帝 ‖ ~ serum · ~ drug (一种能使人
吐露真情的)吐真药

truthful ['tru:θful] *adj.*1. 说真话的·诚实
的 2.(讲话、作品等)真实的·如实的 ‖
~ ly *adv.* / ~ ness *n.*

try [trai] *vt.*1. 试·尝试;试用·试验;试图·
想要;设法·努力 2. 考验;磨练;使受磨
苦(或折磨)3. 审问;审判 4.(通过试验
或调查来解决(问题、争论等)·(通过角
斗)解决(争执等)5. 提炼(金属、油脂
等)(*out*)6. 校准;为……最后加工(尤指

刨光木板等)(*up*) — *vi.* 尝试；试验；试图；努力 — *n.* 1. 尝试；试验；试图；努力 2. (橄榄球赛中)在对方球门线以带球触地得 3 分(并获得踢定位球射门的权利,射中时可再得 2 分) ‖ ~ **out** *n.* 1. 试用;试验 2.(戏剧等的)试演;预演 3.(选拔运动员、演员等的)选拔赛;选拔演表

trying ['traiiŋ] *adj.* 难受的;难堪的;费劲的;恼人的

trypsin ['tripsin] *n.* 【生化】胰蛋白酶

tryptophan ['triptəfæn], **tryptophane** ['triptəfein] *n.* 【生化】色氨酸

tryst [traist, trist] *n.* 1. 幽会;约会 2. 幽会处;约会处(亦作 ~ ing place) 3.〈苏格兰〉市场;市集(尤指每年定期举行的牛市集) 4.〈苏格兰〉与 ~ 约会(或幽会);约定(时间或地点)相会 — *vi.* 约会;幽会(*with*)

tsar [zɑː, tsɑː] *n.* 1. 沙皇;皇帝 2. 大权独揽的人;持权人物

tsarina [zɑːˈriːnə] *n.* 沙皇皇后;女沙皇

tsetse ['tsetsi] *n.*【动】舌蝇,采采蝇(= ~ fly)

T-shirt ['tiːʃət] *n.* 短袖圆领汗衫(或运动衫),体恤衫

T/T, TT *abbr.* telegraphic transfer 电汇

T-time [tiˈtaim] *n.* 1.(火箭、导弹等的)点火(或发射)时刻,试验发射时刻(= time for test-firing)

Tu【化】元素铥(thulium)的符号

tub [tʌb] *n.* 1. 桶;浴盆 2. 一桶(或一盆)的容量 3.〈口〉盆浴;洗澡 4.【矿】矿车;矿斗 5.〈贬〉行驶缓慢的船;练习用赛艇 6.〈美俚〉矮胖子 — (tubbed; tubbing) *vt.* 1.(在浴缸里为...)洗澡;把(衣物等)放在桶里洗 2. 把(植物)种植在盆里: tubbed pines 盆栽松树 3. 把...放(或贮藏)在桶里: ~ vegeta-

bles in brine 把蔬菜腌在放有盐水的桶里 — *vi.* 1. 洗盆浴 2. 被放在桶里洗 ‖ ~ thumper 慷慨激昂的演讲者(或讲道者);大喊大叫的鼓吹者

tuba ['tjuːbə][复] tubas 或 tubae ['tjuːbiː] *n.*【音】1. 大号 2. 管风琴的簧管音栓

tube [tjuːb] *n.* 1. 管子;软管 2.〈美〉真空管(=〈英〉valve);(电视)显像管;电视;电视机 3.(轮胎的)内胎 4.【解】管 5. 地铁隧道;(主英)〈口〉地铁(隧道);地铁列车 6.〈古〉望远镜 — *vt.* 1. 给...装管 2. 把...做成管形状 3. 用管子输送 4.〈美俚〉未通过(考试) — *vi.*〈美俚〉不及格;做得很差 ‖ ~ culture〈微生物的〉试管培养 / ~ sock 无跟圆筒短袜 / ~ well 管井

tubercle ['tjuːbəkl] *n.* 1.【植】小瘤 2.【解】结节 3.【医】结核

tubercular [tjuːˈbəkjulə] *adj.* 1.【解】结节状的;(有)结节的 2.【医】结核病的;患结核病的 3.【植】结瘤状的;具有小瘤的 — *n.* 结核病患者

tuberculosis [tjuːˌbəkjuˈləusis] *n.* 结核(病);肺结核(略作 TB)

tuberculous [tjuːˈbəkjuləs] *adj.* 1.【医】结核病的;感染结核病的;结核性的 2.【植】结节的;结节状的

tuberose ['tjuːbərəuz] *n.*【植】晚香玉,月下香

tuberous ['tjuːbərəs] *adj.* 1.【植】块茎(状)的;有块茎的 2.【解】有结节的;结节状的

tubular ['tjuːbjulə] *adj.* 1. 管的;管形的;有管的;由管子构成的 2.【医】(声音)从管中发出的;管性的

tuck [tʌk] *vt.* 1. 把...折起;卷起;在(衣服)上缝横裥(*up*) 2. 把...塞入(或夹入,藏入);收藏 3. 把(衬衫、被子等)的边塞到下面(或里面) 4. 把...舒适地;隆页的

盖(或裹)在里面;用被子把… 裹住 5. 把(信等)折叠起来塞入,使挤在一起 6. 使蜷缩(或蜷曲) 7.〈俚〉大吃(in, away, into) 8. 用抄网把(鱼)捞出 — vi. 缝褶缝;被起;折叠;缩拢 — n. 1.〈衣裤旁的)褶,裥 2. 船尾突出部 3.〈英俚〉叠进(尤指糖果、糕点)4. 被塞进(或折进)的部分 5. 抱膝(跳水等时大腿贴近胸前两手抱住小腿的姿式)‖ '~-in n.〈英〉丰盛的一餐/'~ net 〔从大网中捞鱼的抄网/'~-out n.〈主英〉= ~-in /~ seine = net/'~-shop n.〈英俚〉(尤指学校附近的)糖果食品店

tucker[¹ˈtʌkə] n. 1. 打褶者;打褶装置 2. (袒胸衣上的)花边(或罗纱)抵肩(盖在胸前,可装上或拆下)

tucker[²ˈtʌkə] vt.〈口〉使筋疲力尽,使疲乏(out)

Tues, Tue. abbr. Tuesday

Tuesday[ˈtjuːzdi] n. 星期二 — adv.〈口〉在星期二 ‖ ~s adv. 在每星期二

tuft[tʌft] n. 1. (头发、羽毛、草等的)一簇,一束 2. 小树林,矮树丛 3.〔钉牢被褥垫心的)线束;(用绳束牵率的)床垫纽扣 4.【解】细血管丛 5. 丘 6. 土丘 — vt. 1. 用丛毛装饰 2. (为固定位置与隔一定距离)用束牵钉住(被、褥) — vi. 丛生;形成一簇 ‖ ~ed adj. 1. 有装饰的 2.【动】植被的 3. (鸟)头上有一簇羽毛的,有冠的 4. 成簇的;丛生的

tug[tʌg](tugged;tugging) vi. 1. 用力拖,使劲拉(at) 2. 苦干;挣扎 — vt. 1. 用力拖(或拉)2. 吃力地搬运 3. 用拖轮拖(或推、顶)— n. 1. 猛拉;拖,牵引 2. 苦干,努力;挣扎 3. (对立双方的)争执;较量 4. 拖拉(或牵引)用的器具(或链条)5. (马车的)挽缰,缰绳 6. 拖船 6.〈英俚〉(伊顿公学的)公费生 7.【矿】装有滑车的铁钩 ‖ '~-boat n. 拖船/ ~-

of-'war n. 拔河(比赛);激烈的争夺

tuition[tjuːˈiʃən] n. 1. 教学;讲授;指导 2. 学费 ‖ ~al, ~ary adj.

tulip[ˈtjuːlip] n.【植】郁金香;郁金香花(或球茎)

tulle[tjuːl] n.【纺】绢网(丝质或尼龙)薄纱

tumble[ˈtʌmbl] vi. 1. 摔倒,跌倒 2. 倒坍(证券价格等)暴跌 3. 翻腾,打滚 4. 翻筋斗;作杂技表演 5. 仓促地行动;匆匆忙忙地倾倒出来 6.〈俚〉突然明白,恍然大悟(to) 7. 偶然遇见(into, upon)— vt. 1. 使摔倒;使翻滚;使倒塌 2. 弄乱,搞乱 3. 使跌落;抛光;用滚筒干燥机弄干(衣服) 4. 射落(飞禽);击倒(野兔等)— n. 1. 摔交;跌落 2. 翻滚;翻筋斗 3. 混乱;杂乱的一堆 ‖ '~ down adj. 摇摇欲坠的/'~-weed n.【植】风滚草

tumbler[ˈtʌmblə] n. 1. 翻筋斗者;杂技演员 2. 平底玻璃杯 3. (机枪的)机心;(锁的)制栓 4. 窗户清洗工 5.【机】转臂;转向;摆动换向齿轮;转向轮 6. (衣服等的)滚动式烘干机 7. 不倒翁(玩具)8.【动】翻头的;灵提状小猎犬 9.〈美方〉粪车;肥料车

tumbrel[ˈtʌmbrəl], **tumbril**[ˈtʌmbril] n. 1. (农村用)翻卸式肥料车;双轮运货车 2. 平底罩卜4.(机枪的)机心 3. (1789年法国大革命时)死囚押送车 4. (英国旧时运输弹药和工具用的)军用两轮车

tumid[ˈtjuːmid] adj. 1. 肿大的,肿胀的 2. 凸出的;涨满的 3.(文风等)浮华的,浮夸的 ‖ ~ity[tjuːˈmiditi] n. / ~ly adv. / ~ness n.

tumo(u)r[ˈtjuːmə] n. 肿,肿胀;肿块;肿瘤 ‖ ~ous adj.

tumult[ˈtjuːmʌlt] n. 1. 吵闹;喧哗;骚动 2.(思想、感情的)激动;混乱 3. 一阵

发作

tumultuous [tju:ˈmʌltjuəs] *adj.* 1. 吵闹的;喧哗的;骚动的 2. 激动的;混乱的

tun [tʌn] *n.* 1. 大桶;大酒桶 2. 桶(液体计量单位,通常一桶等于 252 酒类加仑)(= tunned/tunning) *vt.* 把...装入大酒桶储藏

tuna [ˈtjuːnə]([复]tuna(s)) *n.* 1.【动】金枪鱼科的鱼;金枪鱼 2. 金枪鱼肉(尤指罐装者)(= 亦作 ~ fish) ‖~ **clipper** 金枪鱼捕捞船

tundra [ˈtʌndrə] *n.* (北极及北极附近地区的)冻原,苔原

tune [tjuːn] *n.* 1. 调子,曲调;主旋律 2. 准确的音高;和谐的乐声 3. 腔调;语调;语气;态度 4. 程度;数量 5. 心情,情绪 6. (广播)音质 7. 协调一致,和睦,融洽 — *vt.* 1. 调音;〈诗〉唱出 3. 对...调谐;调整(收音机等)的频率(或波长)(tuned(频率、波长)的接收(或收看) 4. 用无线电与...取得联系 5. 使和谐;使一致;调整;调节 — *vi.* 1. 合调;协调 2. 调谐;调节 ‖ tunable, ~able *adj.* / ~less *adj.* 不合调的,不入耳的;不和谐的 2. 无音调的,无声的;(乐器)不在演奏的/~r *n.* 1. 调音者,定弦者 2. 调谐器;调整者 ‖~-up *n.* 1.(为使机器与发挥最大效力所作的)调整;调节 2.(运动前的)准备活动;热身赛

tuneful [ˈtjuːnful] *adj.* 1. 曲调优美的;声音悦耳的 2. 发出优美(或悦耳)音调的

tung [tʌŋ] *n.* = ~ tree ‖~ **oil** 桐油/~ **tree** 油桐

tungsten [ˈtʌŋstən] *n.*【化】钨

tunic [ˈtjuːnik] *n.* 1.(古希腊、古罗马的)长达膝盖的短袖束腰外衣 2.(妇女、女孩的)束腰外衣 3.(主英)〔警察、士兵的〕紧身短上衣 4.〔天主教主教、副助

祭穿的)短祭袍 5.【植】鳞茎皮;膜皮;【动】膜;被囊;【解】膜;被膜

tuning [ˈtjuːniŋ] *n.* 1.【音】调音,定弦;起音,定音 2.【无】调谐 3. 协调;一致 ‖~ **fork**〔物〕音叉

Tunis [ˈtjuːnis] *n.* 突尼斯(市)〔突尼斯首都〕

Tunisia [tju:ˈniziə] *n.* 突尼斯〔北非国家〕

tunnel [ˈtʌnl] *n.* 1. 隧道;坑道;地道;(动物的)洞穴;洞穴通道 2.【矿】巷道,平峒 3. 烟道;烟囱;风洞 — (tunnel(l)ed; tunnel(l)ing) *vt.* 1. 掘,凿,挖(隧道、地道、涵洞等) — *vi.* 1. 掘隧道(或地道;凿地道;挖洞穴) 2. 打开通路穿过 ‖~ **borer** 隧道掘进机/~ **net** 〔渔业用的)长锥网

tunny [ˈtʌni] *n.*【动】金枪鱼

turban [ˈtəːbən] *n.* 1.〔穆斯林的)包头巾 2. 女用头巾 3. 头巾式软帽〔妇女或儿童用的)无沿帽,狭边帽 4.【动】蝶螺;蝶螺壳

turbid [ˈtəːbid] *adj.* 1. 混浊的,污浊的 2. 烟雾腾腾的;浓密的 3. 混乱的;~ thoughts 混乱的思绪

turbine [ˈtəːbin, ˈtəːbain] *n.* 透平机,涡轮机,叶轮机

turbofan [ˈtəːboufæn] *n.*【空】1. 涡轮风扇发动机 2. 涡轮风扇式飞机 3. 涡轮风扇

turbojet [ˈtəːbəudʒet] *n.*【空】1. 涡轮喷气发动机 2. 涡轮喷气式飞机

turbot [ˈtəːbət]([复]turbot(s)) *n.*【动】大菱鲆

turbulence [ˈtəːbjuləns], **turbulency** [ˈtəːbjulənsi] *n.* 1. 骚动;骚乱;动荡;混乱 2.【气】湍流

turbulent [ˈtəːbjulənt] *adj.* 1. 骚动的;骚乱的;动荡的;混乱的 2. 汹涌的;狂暴的 3.【气】湍流的 ‖~ly *adv.*

turd [tə:d] *n.* 〈俗〉粪块;可鄙的人;非常讨厌的东西

tureen [tə'ri:n, tju'ri:n] *n.* **1.**(盛汤、羹用的)盖碗 **2.**(烧菜和上菜用的)焙盘;砂锅

turf [tə:f] ([复]turfs 或〈古〉turves [tə:vz]) *n.* **1.** 草根土;草皮(块)**2.** 泥煤;泥炭 **3.** [the ~]赛马场;赛马 **4.**(流氓等黑势力的)地盘 — *vt.* **1.** 用草皮覆盖 **2.**〈俚〉抛出(东西);赶走(人)(*out*)‖ ~**y** *adj.*

turgid ['tə:dʒid] *adj.* **1.** 肿胀的;浮肿的;饱满的 **2.**(文体等)浮夸的,华而不实的 ‖ ~**ity** [tə:'dʒidəti] *n.* / ~**ly** *adv.* / ~**ness** *n.*

Turk [tə:k] *n.* **1.** 土耳其人 **2.**(土耳其的)穆斯林 **3.** 操突厥语的人 **4.** 土耳其马 **5.** 专横凶残者

Turkey ['tə:ki] *n.* 土耳其[西南亚国家](领土包括欧洲巴尔干半岛的东南角)

turkey ['tə:ki] *n.* **1.** 吐绶鸡,火鸡 **2.**(食用)火鸡肉 **3.**〈美俚〉不中用的人;笨蛋,傻瓜 **4.** 失败之作 **5.**(保龄球戏中)(一轮中的)连续三击 ‖ ~ **buzzard** 〈动〉红头美洲鹫 / ~ **cock 1.** 堆吐绶鸡,堆火鸡 **2.** 妄自尊大的人/~ **hen** 雌吐绶鸡,母火鸡/~ **poult** 火鸡雏,小火鸡/~ **vulture** = ~ buzzard †

Turkish ['tə:kiʃ] *adj.* **1.** 土耳其的;土耳其人的;土耳其语的 **2.** 突厥语族的 — *n.* 土耳其语 ‖ ~ **bath 1.** 土耳其浴,蒸汽浴 **2.** 土耳其浴浴室,蒸汽浴室 / ~ **delight**, ~ **paste** 土耳其软糖

Turkman ['tə:kmən]([复]Turkmen) *n.* 土库曼人

Turkmenistan [,tə:kmeni'sto:n] *n.* 土库曼斯坦[亚洲中部国家]

Turkoman ['tə:kəmən]([复]Turkomans) *n.* **1.** 土库曼人 **2.** 土库曼语

turmoil ['tə:mɔil] *n.* 骚动;混乱

turn [tə:n] *vt.* **1.** 转,转动;旋转 **2.** 扭;扭曲;弯曲;折(书页等)**3.**(刀口)卷起,使变钝 **4.** 使朝向;使转变思想,劝说 **4.** 把(注意力等)转向;把…用于;把…对准 **5.** 移动;挡开;使偏斜 **7.** 驱使,撵走 **8.** 出处 **9.** 翻转 **10.** 使颠倒;倾倒 **11.** 使回曲;绕作于 **12.** 绕过 **13.** 转变;改变 **14.** 使变酸;使变质 **15.** 使(树叶等)变色 **16.** 使遭受,使受到(*to*)**17.** 兑换;翻译;改写 **18.** 搅乱(心智);使(心神)不安 **19.** 反(胃)**20.**(时刻等)超过…岁 **21.**【机】车削;使成形;使成圆形 **22.** 使具有优美形式 **23.** 使(钱、货等)流通,周转;出清(存货);赚,挣(钱等)**24.**[印]倒空;倒排 — *vi.* **1.** 转动;旋转 **2.** 朝向;转身 **3.** 致力于,求教;求助 **5.** 转向;回转;转身 **6.** 翻,翻转 **7.** 转而反对(*against*);(对…)发怒;攻击(*on, upon* 后)**8.** 改变位置 **9.** 变更 **10.** 变成;(树叶等)变色;变酸;变质;变化无常;神经失常 **11.**【机】被车削;开车床;被加工成形 **12.** 晕眩;作呕 **13.**(商品)转手,易手 — *n.* **1.** 转动;旋转 **2.**(舞蹈时的)旋转动作 **3.**【体】转体动作 **4.** 转身 **2.** 转向;转弯 **3.** 转变;转折 **5.** 转变;变化;转折(点)6.**(一)圈;(一)阵;(一)回 **7.**(杂耍或广播、电视杂剧中的)一个节目 **8.**(帮助或损害别人的)举动,行为 **9.** 依次轮流相互的的一次机会;轮流 **10.** 班 **11.** 倾向;性格;性情,才能 **12.**(语言等的)措辞;措辞;措辞特征 **13.** 对原作的阐述;改动 **14.** 形状;样子 **15.**〈口〉惊吓 **16.**(包括买进和卖出的)一笔证券交易;一笔证券交易的获利;(商品批售补进的)周转 **17.**【机】车床;(橱、柜等门上的)旋扣,旋锁 **18.**[印](无字时暂用的)倒头铅字;错倒的字样 **19.**[音]回音 **20.**

[～s]月经 21.〈古〉计谋,计策 ‖ ～a.bout n. 1. 转身,转向,向后转 2.〈方针、倾向等的〉转变 3. 转到另一边,变节 4. 叛徒 5.〈娱乐场的〉旋转转木马 6. 正反面都能穿的衣服 ‖ ～a.round n. 1. 供车辆回旋的空地,回车场,回车道 2.〈飞机卸货、加油、检修及再装货所需的〉停航时间 3.〈立场、方针等的〉转变 ‖ ～buckle n. 1.【机】松紧螺旋扣 ‖ ～coat n. 1.〈立场、方针等的〉转变者,叛徒 ‖ ～down adj.〈衣领等〉可翻折的,穿时翻下的 n. 1. 翻折物 2. 拒绝 3. 衰落；萧条 ‖ ～in n. 1.〈尤指书籍封面沿纸张三边的〉折入部分 2. 交还,归还 3. 入口,通道,岔道 ‖ ～key n. 监狱看守 adj.〈合同等〉总承包的,全套承包的 ‖ ～off n. 1. 支路；拐弯 2. 岔道,支路〈尤指从高速公路岔出的坡道〉3. 关闭,断开,断路 ‖ ～on n. 1. 开动,接通,激活 2.〈口〉兴奋,激动；刺激；令人兴奋(或激动)的人(或物)；引起性欲的人(或物)；吸毒者的幻觉(或欣快) ‖ ～out n. 1. 出动 2.〈为某种目的〉出动的人群；集合的人群 3.〈主英〉罢工；罢工的工人 4.【交】避车道,分道；岔道 5. 产量；产额 6. 出清；扫除 7. 设备,装备 8. 全套车马(包括挽具和随从) 9. 穿着,装束 ‖ ～over n. 1. 翻倒；翻转 2. 翻倒物；翻转物 3. 倒向；反面；底朝天 4. 半圆形筋斗 5. 营业额；成交量；证券交易额 6. 流动；流通；吐旧 7.〈在特定时间内填缺的补缺人员〉新雇人员比例 8. 人员调整 9.〈英〉〈报纸上〉从第一版末转入第二版的时事小品 adj.〈衣领等〉翻的 ‖ ～pike n. 1.〈旧时的〉收税栅(2. 收税路；收费公路 3.〈泛指〉公路 ‖ ～screw n. 旋凿,螺丝起子 ‖ ～stile n.〈入口处等的〉旋转栅门；栅栏 ‖ ～table n. 1.〈转换机车方向的〉转车台 2.〈唱机的〉唱盘 3.〈餐桌上用的〉圆转盘 4.

〈广播用〉录音转播机 ‖ ～up n. 1.〈裤腿的〉翻边；(衣服的)翻褶褶分 2.〈口〉混乱,骚乱；出乎意料的事 3.〈克里比奇纸牌戏中〉首张翻出的牌 adj.〈可〉翻起的；(可)折叠的；翘起的

turner ['tə:nə] n. 1. 旋转者；翻动者 2. 翻转器；翻动器 3. 车工,旋工 4.〈翻动烙饼等用的〉平铲

turnery ['tə:nəri] n. 1. 车工工艺；车削工艺 2. 车削产品(或工件)3. 车削车间

turning ['tə:niŋ] n. 1. 旋转；翻转；弯曲 2. 变向；转向 3. 转弯处 4. 车工工艺；车削工作 ‖ ～ point 转折点

turnip ['tə:nip] n. 1.【植】芜菁；芜菁甘蓝 2.〈俚〉怀表,挂表 ‖ ～ radish 小圆萝卜／～ tops 芜菁叶

turpentine ['tə:pəntain] n. 1. 松脂 2. 松节油 3. 松木油 — vt. 1. 涂松节油于… 2. 从(松树)中采松脂 — vi. 提取松节油；采集松脂

turpitude ['tə:pitju:d] n. 卑鄙,堕落；卑鄙行为

turps [tə:ps] [复] n. [用作单]〈英口〉松节油；〈澳俚〉酒精饮料(尤指啤酒)

turquoise(e) ['tə:kwɔ:z] n. 1.【矿】绿松石 2. 绿松石色,青绿色(= ～ blue) — adj. 青绿色的

turret ['tʌrit] n. 1.【建】塔楼；角楼 2.【机】(六角)转台 3.〈战舰、坦克、飞机等的〉回转炮塔 4.〈装在摄影机或电视摄影机上的〉镜头转台 ‖ ～ ship 装有炮塔炮的军舰

turtle ['tə:tl] n. 1.【动】海龟；玳瑁；鳖 2.〈食用〉海龟肉；甲鱼肉 — vi. 捉海龟(3.【机】倾覆 ‖ ～ dove n. 1.【动】斑鸠,欧斑鸠 2. 情人／～ neck n.〈毛衣等的〉圆翻领,高翻领；圆翻领(或高翻领)毛衣

tush [tʌʃ] int. [表示轻蔑、指责或不耐烦

等]哎! 啐!

tusk [tʌsk] *n.* **1.** (象、野猪等的)长牙、獠牙；(马等的)犬牙、尖牙 **2.** (耙等的)齿状物；(木工的)加劲凸榫 — *vt.* 用长牙抵(或掘)

tussa(h), tusser ['tʌsə] *n.* **1.** 柞蚕 **2.** 柞丝，柞丝织物(= ~ silk)

tussle ['tʌsl] *n. & vi.* 扭打，扭斗；争论；奋斗(*with*)

tussock ['tʌsək] *n.* **1.**[植]丛生草 **2.**(芦苇、树枝等的)丛、簇；(毛发等的)束 **3.** 毒蛾

tut [tʌt] *int.* [表示不耐烦、斥责、轻蔑等]嘘! 噢! — *vt.* [tutted; tutting] *vt.* 对…表示不耐烦(或斥责、轻蔑等)

tutelage ['tjuːtilidʒ] *n.* **1.** 守护，监护 **2.**(尤指个别的)指导，辅导 **3.**(对外国领土的)托管

tutelar ['tjuːtilə], **tutelary** ['tjuːtiləri] *adj.* **1.** 守护的，监护的 **2.** 监护人的

tutor ['tjuːtə] *n.* **1.** 家庭教师，私人教师 **2.**(英)(大学中的)导师 **3.** 美国某些大学或学院中的助教 **4.**[律](未成年者及其财产的)监护人 **5.**(学生为准备考试而聘请的)辅导教师 — *vt.* **1.** 当…的教师；当…的监护人 **2.**(常指个别地)指导，辅导 **3.** 约束，克制 — *vi.* **1.** 当家庭教师；当辅导教师 **2.** (美)在家庭教师教导下学习；接受辅导

tutorial [tjuː'tɔːriəl] *adj.* **1.** 家庭教师的；辅导教师的；大学导师的 **2.** 大学导师的个别指导时间；大学导师的辅导课 **2.** 由大学导师个别指导(或主持讨论)的班级

tutu ['tuːtuː] *n.* **1.** (芭蕾舞女演员穿的)短裙

tuxedo [tʌk'siːdəu] *n.* [复] tuxedo(e)s *n.* 〈美〉(男用)小礼服；无尾礼服

TV *abbr.* television ‖ **TV dinner** 盒装电视便餐(可边吃边看电视)

twaddle ['twɔdl] *n.* **1.** 废话；蠢话；无聊话 **2.** 讲(或写)废话的人 — *vi.* 讲(或写)废话

twain [twein] 〈古〉*n.* 二，两；一对，一双 *num.* 二，两

twang [twæŋ] *n.* **1.** 拨弦声 **2.** 鼻音；带鼻音的方言 **3.** 土音 **4.** 悲痛；痛苦 **5.** 弹拨 — *vt.* **1.** 发拨弦声 **2.** 发鼻音 **3.** 带鼻音讲话 **3.** (箭)嗖地一声射出 **4.** (由于痛苦、紧张等而)颤动，抽搐 — *vt.* 使发拨弦声 **2.** 带鼻音讲(或读) **3.** 嗖地一声射出

'twas [强 twɔz;弱 twəz] = it was

tweak [twiːk] *n.* **1.** 拧，扭 **2.** 焦急；苦恼 — *vt.* **1.** 拧，扭(鼻子、耳朵等) **2.**〈俚〉(汽车比赛时)把(汽车、发动机)的马力开足

tweed [twiːd] *n.* **1.** (粗)花呢 **2.** [~s]花呢服装

tweet [twiːt] *n.* (小鸟的)吱吱声，啾啾声 — *vi.* (小鸟)吱吱地叫

tweezers ['twiːzəz] [复] *n.* 镊子,小钳子

twelfth [twelfθ] *num.* **1.** 第十二(个) **2.** 十二分之一(的) — *n.* (月的)第十二日

twelve [twelv] *num.* 十二;十二个(人或物);第十二(卷、章、页等)(用例参看 **eight**) — *n.* **1.** 12 岁 **2.** 12 点钟

twentieth ['twentiiθ] *num.* **1.** 第二十(个) **2.** 二十分之一(的) — *n.* (月的)第二十日

twenty ['twenti] *num.* 二十;二十个(人或物);第二十(卷、章、页等)(用例参看 **eight**) — *n.* **1.** [twenties](世纪的)20 年代 **2.** 20 岁;[twenties]20 到 29 岁的时期 **3.** 20 英镑(或美元)票面的纸币 **4.** 20 点钟(即下午 8 点) — *adj.* 许多的

twice [twais] *adv.* 两次;两倍

twiddle ['twidl] *vt.* 捻弄,旋弄 — *vi.* 1. 摆弄(*with*)2. 忙于琐事 3. 旋转,转动 — *n.* 捻弄,旋弄

twig[1] [twig] *n.* 1. 细枝;嫩枝 2.(神经或血管的)小支

twig[2] [twig] (twigged; twigging) *vt. & vi.*(口)1. 明白,领悟 2. 懂得,了解

twilight ['twailait] *n.* 1. 暮光;曙光;【天】曙暮光 2. 黄昏;黎明 3. 微光 4. 衰落时期;(人的)暮年,晚期 — *adj.* 曙暮光的;微明的;昏暗的 ∥ ~ sleep(无痛分娩时期的)朦胧麻醉,半麻醉

twill [twil] *n.* 1. 斜纹织物 2. 斜纹图案;斜纹 — *vt.* 把…织成斜纹

'twill [twil;弱 twəl] = it will

twin [twin] *adj.* 1. 孪生的,双胎的 2. 两个相似(或相似)的人(或物)的;成对的 — *n.* 1. 孪生儿之一;[~s]孪生儿,双胎 2. 两个相像的人(或物)之一;[~s]两个相像的人(或物)3. [Twins]【天】双子座 4.(结晶学)孪晶;同形多晶 — (twinned;twinning) *vi.* 1. 生双胞胎;生孪晶 2.(与…)成对(*with*)3. 结成孪晶 — *vt.* 1. 怀(双胎),生(双胎或双胎之一)2. 使成对;使相连 3. 使结成姐妹城(*with*)

twine [twain] *n.* 1. 二股(或三股以上)的线;麻线;细绳 2. 捻,搓;缠绕;盘绕 3. 缠绕物,一团(线) 4. 扭交;纠结 2. 围住;盘绕 3. 使缠绕,使怀抱 — *vi.* 1. 捻,搓;交织;编 2. 缠绕;盘绕 3. 蜿蜒

twinge [twindʒ] *n. & vt.* 刺痛 — *n.* 1. 刺痛;剧痛 2.(精神或良心上的)痛苦

twinkle ['twiŋkl] *vi.* 1. 闪烁,闪耀 2.(眼睛因愉快、欢乐而)闪闪发光(*at*)3.(双腿)快速移动;(眼睛)迅速开合 — *vt.* 1. 使闪闪发亮 2. 闪出(光芒) — *n.* 1.

闪烁;(眼睛的)发光 2. 眨眼 3. 一刹那,转瞬之间

twinkling ['twiŋkliŋ] *n.* [只用单]闪烁;眨眼;一眨眼的时间,瞬间

twirl [twəl] *vt.* 1. 使快速转动;使快速旋转 2. 卷弄,拈(须;须)3.(棒球赛中)投(球) — *vi.* 1. 快速转动 2.(蛇般)扭动;盘绕 3.(棒球赛中)投球 — *n.* 1. 转动;旋转 2. 旋转的东西;螺旋形的东西;曲线状 3.〈美俚〉复制的钥匙;万能钥匙

twist [twist] *vt.* 1. 捻,搓,拈 2. 编织;使交织 3. 扭转,转动;使呈螺旋形;拧,扭,绞 4. 缠绕;盘绕 5. 使弯曲;使扭曲 6. 扭曲;扭伤 7. 歪曲;曲解 8. 使转动 9. 使苦恼,折磨;使混乱;使慌乱 10. 使(球)旋转 11. 扭动;扭歪;扭曲;扭伤 2. 缠绕;盘绕;盘旋 3. 曲折穿行 4. 扭动;呈螺旋形 5. 转身(*around, about*)6.(球)旋转并呈曲线前进 7. 跳扭摆舞 — *n.* 1.(一)捻,(一)搓,(一)拈 2.(一)拧,(一)扭,(一)绞;扭转 3. 捻成的线;经纱;缝纫线线 4. 烟辫,烟草卷;麻花状面包,辫子面包 5. 扭曲;扭曲 6. 曲线;曲折 7.(对意义、内容等的)歪曲;曲解 8.(机器等的)螺旋形运动;转动 9. 古怪;习性;癖嗜;倾向 10.(弹丸在膛内回转一周前进的距离)11. 意想不到的转折 12. 手法;办法;(新)花样 13. 扭摆舞 14.〈美俚〉(轻浮的)女郎 &15.〈英〉混合酒;〈英口〉大胃口 16.〈英〉(末端拧紧而成的)纸卷

twister ['twistə] *n.* 1. 扭曲者;扭卷者;缠绕者;【纺】捻接工 2. 缠绕物;盘绕的东西 3.〈口〉搞不老实的人,骗子 6. 难题;棘手的事;绕口令 7.〈杂技演员的〉空中转体筋斗

twit [twit] (twitted; twitting) vt. & n. 嘲笑; 挖苦, 非难

twitch [twitʃ] vt. 1. 急拉, 急扯; 猛夺 2. 抽动 — vi. 1. 急拉(at) 2. (肌肉等)抽动, 抽搐 3. 抽痛; 刺痛 — n. 1. 急拉 2. 抽动, 抽搐 3. 抽痛; 刺痛

twitter ['twitə] vi. 1. (鸟)吱吱地叫, 鸣啭 2. (因兴奋、紧张而)喋喋嗤嗤地讲 3. 吃吃地笑 4. (因激动而)颤抖 — vt. 1. 喋喋嗤嗤地讲 2. 抖动 — n. 1. 鸣啭; 喋喋嗤嗤 2. (由激动引起的)颤抖: in a ~ 颤抖着

two [tuː; tu] num. 1. 二; 两个(人或物); 第二(卷、章、页等) 2. 两个(人或物)一组 2.2 元票面的纸币 3. 分 4.2 点钟 ‖ ~-fold adj. & adv. 两倍(双重)的 / '~-and-one-'half striper (美海军少校) / '~-bit adj. [美俚] 价值 2 角 5 分的 2. 便宜的; 无价值的 / '~-edged adj. (刀) 双刃的; 有双重不同含义的 / ~-pence ['tʌpəns] n. 两便士; 两便士银币 / ~-penny ['tʌpəni] adj. 1. 两便士的 2. 廉价的; 无价值的 n. 1. 两便士 2. 廉价的 / ~-penny-halfpenny ['tʌpəni'heipəni] adj. 1. 两便士半的 2. 不足道的; 不重要的 / '~-'piece adj. (服装)一套分成两件的, 两件构成一套的 / '~-ply adj. 两层的; 双重的; 双股的 / '~-'sided adj. 两边的; 两方面的 2. 两面派的 / '~-star adj. (美军)二星(少将)级的 ‖ (饭店等)二流的; 中上流的 / '~-time vt. 欺瞒; 爱情上对...不忠 / '~-'tongued adj. 说假话的, 骗人的 / '~-'way adj. 1. 双向的; 双通的; 两路的(见双向) 2. (衣服)两面可穿的, 正反可穿的

twosome ['tuːsəm] n. 1. 两个(人或物)一组 2. 两人游戏, 两人比赛 3. 参加两人游戏(或比赛)的人 4. 一对情人

'twould [强 twud; 弱 twəd] = it would

tycoon [tai'kuːn] [日] n. 1. [史] (幕府时代的)将军 2. [美口] (企业界、政界的)巨头

tying ['taiiŋ] tie 的现在分词

tyke [taik] n. 1. (杂种)狗 2. 粗鲁的家伙 3. [口] 小孩子; 小淘气

tympanic [tim'pænik] adj. 1. [解]鼓膜的; 鼓室的 2. (似)鼓的 ‖ ~ cavity [解]鼓腔, 鼓室 / ~ membrane [解]鼓膜

tympanitis [ˌtimpə'naitis] n. [医]鼓室炎, 中耳炎

tympanum ['timpənəm] ([复] tympana ['timpənə] 或 tympanums) n. 1. [解]鼓膜, 耳膜; 鼓室, 中耳 2. (鸟等的)鸣腔 3. [建]拱圈和拉梁间的弧形部分; 山墙饰内的三角部分 4. 鼓形水车 5. (电话机的)振动片

type [taip] n. 1. 型, 类型, 式 2. 典型, 榜样, 模范; 样本; 样板 3. 标志; 代表; 象征; 记号, 符号 4. [宗]预示, 预兆, 预兆性人物(或事物、事件) 5. [总称]出可用作可数名词, 指一个)[印]铅字, 活字 6. (印出的)字体 7. [生]型; 种; 模式种; 模式属; 模式标本 8. (奖章、硬币等的)图案 9. (美理)打字机 vt. 1. 作为...的典型或代表 2. 测定(血等)的类型 3. 为...(演员)扮演某一类型的角色 4. (常指宗教人物或事件)预示 5. 用打字机打(= typewrite) 6. 浇铸(铅字等) — vi. 打字(= typewrite) ‖ '~-bar n. 1. (打字机上的)铅字连动杆 2. 铅字条 / '~-cast vt. 1. 浇铸(铅字等) 2. 分配(演员)担任与其性格和形体相应的角色 2. 分配(演员)担任同一类型的角色 3. 一成不变地看待 / '~-foundry n. 铸字工场 / '~-set vt. 把...排字 / '~-setter n. 1. 排字工人 2. 排字机 / '~-setting n. 排字

typewrite ['taiprait] (typewrote['taiprəut], typewritten ['taip,ritn]) *vt.* 用打字机打一 *vi.* 打字 ‖ '**type,writing** *n.* 1. 打字;打字技术 2. 打字稿/'**type,written** *adj.* 用打字机打印的

typewriter ['taip,raitə] *n.* 1. 打字机;〈古〉打字员 2.【印】打字型字体

typhlitis [tif'laitis] *n.* 【医】盲肠炎

typhoid ['taifɔid] 【医】 *adj.* 伤寒的;类伤寒的;患伤寒的 一 *n.* = ~ fever ‖ ~**al** [tai'fɔidl] *adj.* 伤寒的;类伤寒的 ‖ ~ **fever** 伤寒

typhoon [tai'fuːn] *n.* 【气】台风

typhus ['taifəs] *n.* 【医】斑疹伤寒(= ~ fever) ‖ **typhous** ['taifəs] *adj.* 斑疹伤寒(性)的

typical ['tipikəl] *adj.* 典型的,代表性的;象征性的 ‖ ~**ly** *adv.*

typify ['tipifai] *vt.* 1. 作为...的典型,代表;具有...的特征 2. 象征;(宗教人物或事件)预示

typist ['taipist] *n.* 打字者;打字员

typo ['taipəu] ([复]typos) *n.* 1. 排印工人 2. 排印(或打字)错误

typographic(al [,taipə'græfik(əl)] *adj.* 印刷上的;排字上的

typography [tai'pɔgrəfi] *n.* 1. 铅印(术);凸版印刷(术) 2. 排印 3. (书籍等的)印刷版面式样 ‖ **typographer** *n.* 1. 排印工人 2. 印刷专家 3. 印刷业者

tyrannic(al [ti'rænik(əl)] *adj.* 暴君的;专制的;专横的;暴虐的;残酷的 (现常用 tyrannical)

tyranny ['tirəni] *n.* 1. 暴政,苛政;专制 2. 专横;暴虐;暴行 3. 严峻,严酷 4. (古希腊的)僭主政治

tyrant ['taiərənt] *n.* 1.(古希腊等的)僭主 2. 暴君 3. 恶霸 4. 严酷的事物;苛刻的事物

tyre ['taiə] *n.* 〈英〉1. 轮箍 2. 轮胎

tyro ['taiərəu] ([复]tyros) *n.* 初学者,新手;生手

tzar [zɑː] *n.* = tsar

tzarina [zɑː'riːnə] *n.* = tsarina

U

U, u [juː]([复 U's, u's 或 Us, us [juːz]])英语字母表第二十一个字母 **1.** [U]U 字形 **2.** [U]【化】元素铀（uranium）的符号 **3.** [U]〈口〉上流社会的(人或事物)，上等阶级的(人或事物)

UAE *abbr.* United Arab Emirates 阿(拉伯)联(合)酋(长国)［西南亚国家］

ubiquitous [juːˈbikwitəs] *adj.* (同时)普遍存在的，无处不在的

ubiquity [juːˈbikwiti] *n.* (同时的)普遍存在，无处不在

U-boat [ˈjuːbəut] *n.* **1.** 德国潜艇 **2.** 潜艇

udder [ˈʌdə] *n.* (牛、羊等的)乳房；乳腺

UFO [ˈjuːefˈəu, ˈjuːfəu] *abbr.* unidentified flying object 不明飞行物，飞碟

Uganda [juːˈɡændə, uːˈɡændə] *n.* 乌干达［东非国家］ ‖ **~n** *adj.* 乌干达(人)的 — *n.* 乌干达人

ugh [uk, ʌɡ, ʌk] *int.* (表示厌恶、恐怖等)咄！呸！呷！

ugly [ˈʌɡli] *adj.* **1.** 丑陋的，难看的 **2.** 可怕的，可憎的；讨厌的 **3.** 道德败坏的，邪恶的；丑恶的 **4.** 险恶的 **5.** (天气)阴沉的；不祥的 — *n.* 丑陋的人或动物、东西 ‖ **uglily** *adv.* /**ugliness** *n.* / **~ duckling 1.** (安徒生童话中变成天鹅的)丑小鸭 **2.** (喻)"丑小鸭"；小时难看长大后好看的人；先遭轻视后受赞美的人(或物)

UGT, ugt *abbr.* urgent〈美〉(电报用语)急电

UHF, uhf *abbr.* ultrahigh frequency【无】超高频，特高频

Uig(h)ur [ˈwiːɡuə]([复 Uig(h)ur(s)]) *n.* 维吾尔人；维吾尔语

UK *abbr.* United Kingdom 联合王国(即英国)

Ukraine [juːˈkrein] *n.* 乌克兰［东欧国家］

ukulele [ˌjuːkəˈleili] *n.* 尤克里里琴(一种似吉他的四弦琴，流行于夏威夷等地)

Ulan Bator [ˈuːlɑːn ˈbɑːtɔ]乌兰巴托［蒙古首都］

ulcer [ˈʌlsə] *n.* **1.** 【医】溃疡 **2.** 腐烂物；腐败 — *vt.* & *vi.* = ulcerate

ulcerate [ˈʌlsəreit] *vt.* **1.** 使成溃疡；使溃烂 **2.** 使腐败 — *vi.* **1.** 形成溃疡；溃烂 **2.** 腐败 ‖ **ulce'ration** *n.*

ulcerous [ˈʌlsərəs] *adj.* 溃疡(性的)；患溃疡的 ‖ **~ly** *adv.* / **~ness** *n.*

ullage [ˈʌlidʒ] *n.* **1.** 瓶空、罐空，桶空(指酒瓶等容器内液面上方的空容积) **2.** (酒、面粉等)损耗(量)，折耗(量) **3.** (火箭燃料箱中的)气隙

ulna [ˈʌlnə]([复 ulnae [ˈʌlniː] 或 ulnas]) *n.* 【解】尺骨

ulster [ˈʌlstə] *n.* (有腰带的宽大)乌尔斯特大衣

ulterior [ʌlˈtiəriə] *adj.* **1.** 在特定界限以外的，较远的 **2.** 日后的，将来的；进一步的 **3.** 隐蔽的，秘而不宣的

ultimate ['ʌltimit] *adj.*1. 无法超越的；最大的；最高的；决定性的 2. 最后的 3. 基本的，根本的；首要的；最初的，最早的 4. 极点的，绝顶的，终极的 *n.*【物】极限的 — *n.*1. 终点；结局；终极 2. 最终的事物(或事实)；基本事实(或原则) ‖ ~ **ly** *adv.*

ultimatum [,ʌlti'meitəm]([复] ultimatums 或 ultimata [,ʌlti'meitə]) *n.*1. 最后通牒，哀的美敦书 2. 最后结论 3. 基本原理

ultimo ['ʌltiməu]〈拉〉*adj.* 上月的(略作 ult. 或 ulto.)：your letter of the 15th ~ 你(或你们)上月 15 日的来信

ultra ['ʌltrə] *adj.* 过分的；极端的 — *n.* 极端主义者

ultra- *pref.* 1. 表示"在…的那一边"：*ultra*montane 2. 表示"极端"：*ultra*left 表示"左"的，*ultra*right 极右的 3. 表示"超"，"过"：*ultra*high，*ultra*microscope

ultrafax ['ʌltrəfæks] *n.* 电视高速传真

ultrahigh [,ʌltrə'hai] *adj.* 超高的，特高的 ‖ ~ **frequency**【无】超高频，特高频

ultramarine [,ʌltrəmə'ri:n] *n.*1.【化】佛青，群青(一种合成的蓝色颜料) 2. 深蓝色 — *adj.* 佛青的；深蓝色的

ultramicroscope [,ʌltrə'maikrəskəup] *n.* 超倍显微镜

ultramontane [,ʌltrə'mɔntein] *adj.* & *n.*1. 山那边的(人)；阿尔卑斯山南面的(人)；意大利的(人) 2.[常 U-]教皇绝对权力主义的(人)

ultrared [,ʌltrə'red] *adj.*【物】红外(线)的

ultrasonic [,ʌltrə'sɔnik]【物】*adj.* 超声(波)的，超音速的 *n.* 超声波 ‖ ~**s** [复] *n.*[用作单]超声学

ultrasonogram [,ʌltrə'sɔnəgræm] *n.* 超声(波)图

ultrasonograph [,ʌltrə'sɔnəgrɔ:f] *n.* 超声图记录仪

ultrasonography [,ʌltrə'sɔnə'nɔgrəfi] *n.*【医】超声(波)检查法 ‖ **ultrasonographic** ['ʌltrə,səunə'græfik] *adj.*

ultraviolet [,ʌltrə'vaiəlit]【物】*adj.*1. 紫外的 2. 紫外线的；产生紫外线的；应用紫外线的 — *n.* 紫外光，紫外辐射 ‖ ~ **light** 紫外光，紫外辐射

umbel ['ʌmbəl] *n.*【植】伞形花序

umber ['ʌmbə] *n.*1. 棕土(一种深棕色天然颜料) 2. 红棕色，棕土色，深棕色 — *adj.* 红棕色的，棕土色的，深棕色的 — *vt.* 给…着上红棕色(或棕土色)

umbilical [ʌm'bilikəl] *adj.*1. 脐(带)的；脐状的；脐侧的 2. 似用脐带相联的；关系极为密切的 3. 中心的，中央的 ‖ ~ **cord** 1.【解】脐带 2.【动】卵黄囊蒂 3.【宇】脐带式管缆；空间生命管线(把在航天器舱外工作的宇宙飞行员与航天器联系起来并为飞行员提供氧气等的线路)

umbilicus [ʌm'bilikəs]([复] umbilici [ʌm'bilisai] 或 umbilicuses) *n.*1.【解】【生】脐；【数】脐点 2. 中心，核心

umbrage ['ʌmbridʒ] *n.*1. 树荫；(成荫的)叶丛；(诗)阴影 2. 生气，不快 3. 细微的迹象 4.(怀疑、敌意等的)模糊感觉

umbrageous [ʌm'breidʒəs] *adj.*1. 成荫的，浓荫的 2. 易动气的；多疑的，猜疑的

umbrella [ʌm'brelə] *n.*1. 伞；雨伞；阳伞 2. 伞形物；(喻)保护伞 3.【军】(战斗机形成的)掩护幕；防空火网 4.【动】(水母等的)伞膜 5.【船】烟囱顶罩 — *adj.*(似)伞的；(组织等)机构庞大的；包含无遗的；总括的 — *vt.* 用伞遮盖；以战斗机队掩护幕保护；以保护伞保护

～ stand 伞架

umiak ['uːmiæk] *n*. 爱斯基摩皮筏

umpire ['ʌmpaiə] *n*. 1. 公断人,仲裁人 2. (棒球、板球等的)裁判员;【军】演习裁判官 — *vt*. 仲裁;裁判 — *vi*. 任公断人;当裁判

umpteen [ˌʌmp'tiːn] *adj*. 〈俚〉无数的,许多多的

UN *abbr*. United Nations 联合国

un, 'un [ʌn] *pron*. 〈口〉人,东西

un- *pref*. 〈构成动词〉1. 表示"做相反的动作":*un*close,*un*seal 2. 表示"使丧失","夺去","废止":*un*sex,*un*man 3. 表示"由…解脱","由…取出":*un*hand,*un*bosom,*un*earth 4. 表示"彻底":*un*loose —〈构成形容词或副词〉表示"不","未","非":*un*happy,*un*known,*un*commonly —〈构成名词〉表示"无","不","非":*un*rest,*un*employment

unabashed [ˌʌnə'bæʃt] *adj*. 不害臊的,不怕羞的;不加掩饰的

unable [ʌn'eibl] *adj*. 1. 不能的,不会的 2. 无能力的,不能胜的

unabridged [ˌʌnə'bridʒd] *adj*. 未删节的,未节略的,全文的;(词典)未编的,足本的

unacceptable [ˌʌnək'septəbl] *adj*. 不能接受的,不受欢迎的;难以承认的;不中意的

unaccompanied [ˌʌnə'kʌmpənid] *adj*. 1. 无伴侣的;无随从的 2.【音】无伴奏的

unaccountable [ˌʌnə'kauntəbl] *adj*. 1. 无法解释的,不可理解的 2. 无责任的 ‖ **unaccountably** *adv*.

unaccustomed [ˌʌnə'kʌstəmd] *adj*. 1. 不习惯的 2. 非惯例的;不平常的;不熟悉的

unaffected [ˌʌnə'fektid] *adj*. 1. 不装腔作

势的,自然的;真挚的 2. 未受影响的;未被感动的;未改变的 ‖ ～ly *adv*. / ～ness *n*.

unafraid [ˌʌnə'freid] *adj*. 不怕的,无惧色的

unaided [ʌn'eidid] *adj*. 无助的;独力的

unalloyed [ˌʌnə'lɔid] *adj*. 1. 非合金的 2. 没有搀杂的;纯粹的;完全的

unalterable [ʌn'ɔːltərəbl] *adj*. 不可变更的;不变的;坚定不移的

un-American [ˌʌnə'merikən] *adj*. 1. 非美国的;(风俗、传统、原则等)非美国式的 2. 非美的,反美的:～ activities 非美活动

unanimity [ˌjuːnə'nimiti] *n*. (全体)一致;一致同意

unanimous [juː'næniməs] *adj*. (全体)一致的;一致同意的;无异议的 ‖ ～ly *adv*.

unanswered [ʌn'ɑːnsəd] *adj*. 1. 未答复的;未反驳的 2. 无反应的;没有回报的

unarm [ʌn'ɑːm] *vt*. 1. 缴…的械,解除…的武器 2. 〈古〉剥去…的盔甲 — *vi*. 放下武器 ‖ ～ed *adj*. 1. 非武装的;徒手的,手无寸铁的

unasked [ʌn'ɑːskt] *adj*. 1. 未被邀请的;未被问的 2. 主动(提出)的

unassailable [ˌʌnə'seiləbl] *adj*. 1. 攻不破的 2. 不容置疑的;不容否认的;无可辩驳的;无懈可击的

unassuming [ˌʌnə'sjuːmiŋ] *adj*. 不摆架子的,不装腔作势的;不傲慢的,谦逊的

unattached [ˌʌnə'tætʃt] *adj*. 1. (与组织、集团、机构等)无关系的,无联系的;不隶属的;独立的 2. 未婚的;未订婚的 3.(大学)暂无特定学院的 4.【律】(财产)未被扣押(或查封)的 5.(军官等)未受任命的,等待分配的 6. 不连接的,不接连的

unattainable [ˌʌnə'teinəbl] *adj.* 达不到的;做不到的

unattended [ˌʌnə'tendid] *adj.* 1. 无随从的;无陪伴的 2. 没人照顾的;未被注意的 3.(会议)无人出席的 4.(伤口等)未敷裹的

unavailing [ˌʌnə'veiliŋ] *adj.* 无益的,无用的;没有效果的,徒劳的

unavoidable [ˌʌnə'vɔidəbl] *adj.* 1. 不可避免的;不得已的 2. 不能废除的 ‖ **unavoidably** *adv.*

unaware [ˌʌnə'wɛə] *adj.* [只作表语]不知道的;不注意的;没觉察到的(of) ‖ ~**ly** *adv.*

unawares [ˌʌnə'wɛəz] *adv.* 1. 冷不防地,出其不意地,突然地 2. 不知不觉地;无意中

unbalance [ʌn'bæləns] *vt.* 使失去平衡;使不均衡 2. 使(精神)错乱;使紊乱 — *n.* 不均衡;失衡;错乱;紊乱 ‖ ~**d** *adj.* 1. 失衡的;不均衡的 2. 精神失常的,错乱的;不稳定的;(判断等)不可靠的 3.【会计】借贷不平衡的;收支不平衡的

unbearable [ʌn'bɛərəbl] *adj.* 难堪的,忍受不了的;不能容忍的;承受不住的,经不起的 ‖ **unbearably** *adv.*

unbeaten [ʌn'bi:tn] *adj.* 1. 未搅打的;未曾挨打的 2. 未走过的 3. 未践踏过的;未被超越的;未被击败的

unbecoming [ˌʌnbi'kʌmiŋ] *adj.* 1.(行为等)不恰当的;不相称的;不合礼的;不正当的 2.(服饰等)不配的;不合身的;难看的 ‖ ~**ly** *adv.*

unbeknown [ˌʌnbi'nəun], **unbeknownst** [ˌʌnbi'nəunst] *adj.* (口)未知的,不为…所知的(to)

unbelief [ˌʌnbi'li:f] *n.* 不信;怀疑;无信仰;;无宗教信仰

unbelievable [ˌʌnbi'li:vəbl] *adj.* 难以相信的 ‖ **unbelievably** *adv.*

unbeliever [ˌʌnbi'li:və] *n.* 1. 不轻信的人;怀疑(论)者 2. 不信宗教者;异教徒,非基督教徒

unbelieving [ˌʌnbi'li:viŋ] *adj.* 1. 不相信的;不轻信的;怀疑的 2. 不信宗教的

unbend [ˌʌn'bend] (unbent [ˌʌn'bent]) *vt.* 1. 把…弄直 2. 放松;使轻松 3. 解开(绳索等);卸下(帆等) — *vi.* 1. 变直 2. 松弛;变得轻松;放松

unbending [ˌʌn'bendiŋ] *adj.* 1. 不易弯曲的;挺直的 2. 不屈不挠的,坚定的;不妥协的;固执的 3. 不可亲的;冷漠的;矜持的

unbias(s)ed [ˌʌn'baiəst] *adj.* 不偏的;不偏不倚的;无偏见的

unbidden [ˌʌn'bidn] *adj.* 1. 非奉命的;未被指使的;自愿的;自动的 2. 未受邀请的

unbind [ˌʌn'baind] (unbound [ˌʌn'baund]) *vt.* 1. 解开,松开;使解脱束缚 2. 释放;解放

unblemished [ˌʌn'blemiʃt] *adj.* 无瑕疵的;无污点的;无缺点的;清白的

unblushing [ˌʌn'blʌʃiŋ] *adj.* 不脸红的,不害臊的;厚颜无耻的

unborn [ˌʌn'bɔ:n] *adj.* 1. 未诞生的;有待诞生的;有待出现的;未来的

unbosom [ˌʌn'buzəm] *vt.* & *vi.* 吐露(心事);暴露(思想);说出(秘密)

unbound [ˌʌn'baund] unbind 的过去式和过去分词 — *adj.* 1. 解除束缚的;无束缚的;被释放的;被解放的 2.(书等)未装订的 3.【化】【物】非结合的;非束缚的,自由的

unbounded [ˌʌn'baundid] *adj.* 1. 无边的,无涯的;无限的 2. 无限制的;无节制

的;不受控制的

unbreakable [ˌʌnˈbreikəbl] *adj.* 不易破碎的;打不破的;牢不可破的

unbridle [ˌʌnˈbraidl] *vt.*1. 去掉(马)的辔头 2. 对…不加抑制;放纵 ‖ ~d *adj.*1.(马等)脱缰的 2. 不受约束(或控制)的;放纵的

unbroken [ˌʌnˈbrəukən] *adj.*1. 未破损的,完整的;(纪录)未被打破的 2. 未违反的,得到遵守的 3. 未中断的,继续不断的 4. 未被征服的;未打垮的;未受挫折的;不屈服的,不消沉的 5.(队伍等)不涣散的;整齐的 6.(马等)未驯服的 7.(土地)未破土的,未耕的

unbuckle [ˌʌnˈbʌkl] *vt.* 解开…的搭扣;解开 — *vi.*1. 解开搭扣 2. 变得不拘束;变得和蔼

unburden [ˌʌnˈbəːdn] *vt.*1. 卸去…的负担 2. 吐露心事消除(思想、心灵等)上的负担;吐露

unbutton [ˌʌnˈbʌtn] *vt.*1. 解开…的钮扣 2. 打开(装甲车等)的舱盖 — *vi.* 解开钮扣

uncalled [ˌʌnˈkɔːld] *adj.*1. 未被召唤的 2. 未经请求的;未经邀请的 ‖ ~-for *adj.*1. 不必要的,多此一举的 2. 没有理由的,无缘无故的

uncanny [ˌʌnˈkæni] *adj.*1. 怪模怪样的;可怕的,离奇的;神秘的 2. 不可思议的 3.〈方〉危险的 4.〈方〉(打击)猛烈的;(创伤)严重的

unceasing [ˌʌnˈsiːsiŋ] *adj.* 不停的,不断的 ‖ ~ly *adv.*

unceremonious [ˈʌnˌseriˈməuniəs] *adj.*1. 不拘礼节的,非正式的;随便的 2. 无礼的;唐突的;粗鲁的 ‖ ~ly *adv.* /~ness *n.*

uncertain [ʌnˈsəːtn] *adj.*1. 无常的,易变的 2. 靠不住的 3. 不确定的;不确知的

不能断定的 ‖ ~ly *adv.*

uncertainty [ʌnˈsəːtnti] *n.*1. 无常,易变;靠不住 2. 不确定;不确知;不确定的事情,有疑问的事情

unchain [ʌnˈtʃein] *vt.* 给…解开锁链;释放;解放

unchangeable [ʌnˈtʃeindʒəbl] *adj.* 不变的;不能改变的

unchanged [ʌnˈtʃeindʒd] *adj.* 未改变的;没有变化的

unchanging [ʌnˈtʃeindʒiŋ] *adj.* 不变的

uncharged [ʌnˈtʃɑːdʒd] *adj.*1. 没有负荷的 2. 未装弹药的 3. 不收费的 4. 没有被指控的 5. 无电荷的,不带电的

uncharitable [ʌnˈtʃæritəbl] *adj.* 严厉的,苛刻的;无情的;不宽恕的;挑剔的

unchaste [ʌnˈtʃeist] *adj.*1. 不贞洁的;淫荡的 2. 不纯洁的;鄙俗的 3.(文体)不简洁的

uncivil [ʌnˈsivil] *adj.*1. 不文明的,野蛮的 2. 无礼的;失礼的;粗野的 3. 不利于公民的和睦和幸福的

uncivilized [ʌnˈsivilaizd] *adj.*1. 不文明的,野蛮的,未开化的;无文化的 2. 远离文明世界的;荒野的

uncle [ˈʌŋkl] *n.*1.(伯父;叔父;舅父;姨夫;姨夫 2.〈口〉(对年长者的称呼)叔叔;伯伯 3.〈援助者;忠告者;鼓励者 4.〈俚〉当当铺者 5. [U-] = Uncle Sam ‖ **Uncle Sam**〈口〉山姆大叔(美国、美国政府或美国人的绰号)/ **Uncle Tom** 汤姆叔叔(小说《汤姆叔叔的小屋》的主人公);〈口〉逆来顺受的黑人

unclean [ʌnˈkliːn] *adj.*1. 不洁的,肮脏的 2. 不纯洁的;不贞洁的;猥亵的;邪恶的 3. 拖泥带水的;含糊不清的 ‖ ~ly *adj.* & *adv.*1. 不洁的(地),肮脏的(地);不注意清洁的(地) 2. 不贞洁的(地);猥亵的(地);邪恶的(地)

unclothed [ˌʌnˈkləʊðd] adj. 一丝不挂的

uncoil [ˌʌnˈkɔil] vt. 解开,展开(卷着的东西)— vi. (卷着的东西)解开,展开

uncomely [ˌʌnˈkʌmli] adj.1. 不标致的;不清秀的;丑陋的 2. 不恰当的;不合适的

uncomfortable [ˌʌnˈkʌmfətəbl] adj.1. 不舒服的,不安的,不自在的 2.(物质条件等)不舒适的;不方便的;令人不快的

uncommon [ˌʌnˈkɔmən] adj.1. 不普通的,罕见的;难得的 2. 不平常的;不平凡的;杰出的 ‖ ~ly adv. / ~ness n.

uncomplimentary [ˌʌnˌkɔmpliˈmentəri] adj. 贬损的,贬低的

uncompromising [ˌʌnˈkɔmprəmaiziŋ] adj. 不妥协的,不让步的;坚定的;不屈的

unconcern [ˌʌnkənˈsɜːn] n.1. 漠不关心;不感兴趣;淡漠 2. 无忧无虑

unconcerned [ˌʌnkənˈsɜːnd] adj.1. 漠不关心的,不感兴趣的;淡漠的 2. 无忧虑的 3. 不相关的,无关的

unconditional [ˌʌnkənˈdiʃənl] adj.1. 无条件的;不保留的;无限的;绝对的 2.【心】无条件(反射)的 ‖ ~ly adv.

unconditioned [ˌʌnkənˈdiʃənd] adj.1. 无条件的,无保留的;不受制约的;绝对的 2.【心】无条件(反射)的 3.【哲】无限的

unconquerable [ˌʌnˈkɔŋkərəbl] adj. 不可征服的,不可战胜的;克服不了的;压抑不住的

unconscionable [ˌʌnˈkɔnʃənəbl] adj.1. 昧着良心的;姿意妄为的 2. 过度的;不合理的 3. 极不合理(或正当)的

unconscious [ˌʌnˈkɔnʃəs] adj.1. 不省人事的,失去知觉的 2. 不知道的,未发觉的(of) 3. 无意识的;不知不觉的:an

~ act 无意识的动作 4. [常 the ~]【心】潜意识 ‖ ~ly adv. / ~ness n.

unconstitutional [ˌʌnˌkɔnstiˈtjuːʃənl] adj. 违反宪法的

uncontrollable [ˌʌnkənˈtrəuləbl] adj. 控制不住的;不能控制的 ‖ uncontrollably adv.

uncontrolled [ˌʌnkənˈtrəuld] adj. 不受管束的,不受控制的;无拘无束的;自由的

unconventional [ˌʌnkənˈvenʃənl] adj. 非常规的;破例的,不从惯例(或习俗)的;不落陈套的;异乎寻常的

uncork [ˌʌnˈkɔːk] vt.1. 拔去…的塞子 2.(口)发泄(感情等);透露,披露(消息等)

uncountable [ˌʌnˈkauntəbl] adj.1. 不可数的,无数的,数不清的;无法估量的一 n.【语】不可数名词

uncouple [ˌʌnˈkʌpl] vt. 解开(车辆等)的挂钩;使脱开(或脱钩);松开(狗)的套索

uncouth [ˌʌnˈkuːθ] adj.1.(人、动作等)笨拙的;粗野的;(言语)粗鲁的 2.(生活)不文明的,不舒适的 3.(地方)人迹稀少的,荒凉的 4.(古)奇特的;陌生的

uncover [ˌʌnˈkʌvə] vt.1. 揭开…的盖子;移去…的覆盖物;揭露,暴露 2.【军】使失去掩护 3. 脱(头)上的帽子以示敬意一 vi.1. 脱帽致敬 2. 揭去盖子;移去覆盖物

unction [ˈʌŋkʃən] n.1. 涂油;【宗】敷擦圣油礼 2. 油膏;软膏 3. 使人辽到安慰的话(或环境等) 4.(宗教性的)热忱 5. 假情假意;甜言蜜语

unctuous [ˈʌŋktjuəs] adj.1. 油的;油膏的;含油脂的之油质的;滑腻的 2. 松软肥沃的 4. 塑性的 5. 油滑的;甜言蜜语的;假殷勤的

uncultivated [ˌʌnˈkʌltiveitid] *adj.* 1. 未经耕作的 2. 未经栽培的；未经培养的 3. 无教养的，粗野的；未开化的，野蛮的

uncurl [ˌʌnˈkəːl] *vt.* 把…弄直，使伸直；展开(卷曲的东西) — *vi.* 变直，伸直；展开

undated [ˌʌnˈdeitid] *adj.* 1. 未注日期的 2. 日期不定的

undaunted [ˌʌnˈdɔːntid] *adj.* 无畏的，大胆的，勇敢的

undeceive [ˌʌndiˈsiːv] *vt.* 使不受骗；使明白真情；使不犯错误；使醒悟

undecided [ˌʌndiˈsaidid] *adj.* 1. 未定的，未决的 2. (天气等)不稳定的 3. 优柔寡断的，不果断的 4. (轮廓等)不鲜明的；不明确的，模糊的 ‖ ~ly *adv.* /~ness *n.*

undeclared [ˌʌndiˈklɛəd] *adj.* 1. 未经宣布的 2. 不公开的 3. (货物)未向海关申报的

undefined [ˌʌndiˈfaind] *adj.* 1. 未下定义的；不用定义解释(或描述)的 2. 不明确规定的；不明确的；模糊的

undemocratic [ˌʌndeməˈkrætik] *adj.* 非民主的；不民主的

undeniable [ˌʌndiˈnaiəbl] *adj.* 1. 不能否认的；无可争辩的 2. 确凿无疑的 2. 公认优秀的；无懈可击的 ‖ ~ness *n.* /undeniably *adv.*

under [ˈʌndə] *prep.* 1. [表示位置]在…下面，在…底下；在…之中，在…之内 2. [表示级别、数量、标准等]低于…；少于…；在…以下 3. [表示从属关系]在…下；在…的指引下；在…指导下 4. [表示负荷、条件等]在…之下 5. [表示名义、假托等]在…之下 6. [表示过程]一级的；从属的；标准以下的 — *adv.* 在下；从属地；少于

under- *pref.* 1. 表示"在…下","在下" : *underground*, *under*mentioned 2. 表示"次于…","低于…" : *under*graduate, *under*secretary 3. 表示"…不足" : *under*develop, *under*estimate

underact [ˌʌndərˈækt] *vt.* 表演(角色)不充分；表演(角色)有克制 — *vi.* 表演角色不充分；表演角色有克制

underbelly [ˈʌndəˌbeli] *n.* 1. 下腹部；物体的下方 2. 薄弱的部分；易受攻击的区域

underbid [ˌʌndəˈbid](过去式 underbid, 过去分词 underbidden[ˌʌndəˈbidn]或 underbid；现在分词 underbidding) *vt.* 1.(拍卖或投标中)喊价低于(别人) 2.(桥牌等中)叫牌低于(手上牌)的实力 — *vi.* 1. 出价过低 2. 叫牌不足实力

underbred [ˌʌndəˈbred] *adj.* 1. 教养不良的；不懂礼貌的；粗鲁的 2. 非纯种的；劣种的

underbrush [ˈʌndəbrʌʃ], **underbush** [ˈʌndəbuʃ] *n.* 下木，下层灌丛，林下灌丛

undercarriage [ˈʌndəˌkæridʒ] *n.* 1.(飞机的)起落架 2.(汽车等的)底盘；行走机构

underclothes [ˈʌndəkləuðz][复] *n.* 内衣，衬衣

underclothing [ˈʌndəˌkləuðiŋ] *n.* = underclothes

undercover [ˌʌndəˈkʌvə] *adj.* 暗中进行的，秘密地干的；从事秘密(或间谍)工作的

undercurrent [ˈʌndəˌkʌrənt] *n.* 1. 潜流，底流 2.(喻)潜流，暗流 3. 电流不足 4.【矿】(宽平的)分支洗选金槽

undercut [ˌʌndəˈkʌt] *n.* 1. 底切；被底切切掉的部分 2.(伐树的)反锯口，逆锯口 3.〈英〉牛软腰肉，牛里脊 4.(网球等

的)下旋削球 —[ˌʌndəˈkʌt](undercut; undercutting) vt.1. 切削…的下部;从下切割;底切 2. 掘(矿层)的下部 3. 凸雕;浮雕 4. 削低(商品价格);削价与…抢生意;愿拿较低工资与…抢饭碗(指职位) 5.【体】下旋削(球) — vi. 切去下部;底切

underdevelop [ˌʌndədiˈveləp] vt. & vi.1.(使)发展不充分;(使)发育不全 2.【摄】(使)显影不足 ‖ ~ed adj.1. 经济发展不充分的;不发达的;发育不全的 2.【摄】显影不足的 / ~ment n.

underdog [ˈʌndədɔg] n.1. 斗输了的狗 2. 竞争失败的人;处于劣势的一方 3. 受害者

underdone [ˌʌndəˈdʌn] adj. 未煮(或烤、煎等)透的;煮得嫩的;半生不熟的

underestimate [ˌʌndəˈrestimeit] vt. 对…估价过低;低估;看轻 —[ˌʌndəˈrestimit] n. 低估,估计不足

underexposure [ˌʌndərikspəuʒə] n.【摄】曝光不足

underfeed [ˌʌndəˈfiːd] (underfed [ˌʌndəˈfed]) vt.1. 喂给…的食物太少 2. 从底部给(炉子等)加燃料

underfoot [ˌʌndəˈfut] adv.1. 在脚下:It is damp — 脚下潮湿 / keep sth. — 把某物踩在脚下 2. 碍事;挡路

undergarment [ˈʌndəgɑːmənt] n. 内衣,衬衣

undergo [ˌʌndəˈgəu] (underwent [ˌʌndəˈwent], undergone [ˌʌndəˈgɔn]) vt. 经历,经受;忍受;遭受

undergraduate [ˌʌndəˈgrædjuət] n. 大学肄业生;大学本科生 — adj. 大学生的;大学生身份的:~ studies 大学生的研究科目

underground [ˈʌndəgraund] adj.1. 地下的、地面下的 2. 秘密的;隐蔽的;不公

开的 3. 反传统社会的,反现存体制的;先锋派的;实验(性)的;标新立异的 —[ˌʌndəˈgraund] adv.1. 在地下 2. 秘密地;隐蔽地 — n.1. 地面下层;地下空间;地下通道 2.〈英〉地(下)铁(道)〈美国称 subway〉3. 地下组织 4. 先锋派运动(或团体)

undergrowth [ˈʌndəgrəuθ] n.1.(长在大树下的)下木,下层灌丛 2.(动物长毛下面的)下层绒毛 3. 发育不全

underhand [ˈʌndəhænd] adj. & adv.1. 秘密的(地);奸诈的(地);可耻的(地) 2.(打球时)低手的;自下而上的(地) 3.(射箭瞄准时)目标见于持弓之手下方的(地)

underhanded[1] [ˌʌndəˈhændid] adj. & adv. = underhand ‖ ~ly adv. / ~ness n.

underhanded[2] [ˌʌndəˈhændid] adj. 人手不足的

underlay[1] [ˌʌndəˈlei] (underlaid [ˌʌndəˈleid]) vt.1. 放在…的底部;铺在…的底上;横过…的底部上 2. 垫起;从下面支撑 3. 把(一物)置于另一物之下 — vi.【矿】(矿脉)倾斜 —[ˈʌndəlei] n.1. 垫在下面的东西 2.【印】下衬 3.【矿】下向延伸矿体 4. 地毯(或床垫)衬垫 5. 歌词书写

underlay[2] [ˌʌndəˈlei] underlie 的过去式

underlie [ˌʌndəˈlai] (underlay [ˌʌndəˈlei], underlain [ˌʌndəˈlein]; underlying [ˌʌndəˈlaiiŋ]) vt.1. 位于…的下面 2. 存在于…的下面;构成(理论、政策、行为等)的基础 3.【语】超出(派生形式)的底式(或底层形式、基础形式)使用 4.【商】(权利、索赔等)优先于 5.〈古〉服从于,顺从于

underline [ˌʌndəˈlain] vt.1. 划线于…之下 2. 强调;表明…的重要性;加强 3. 预告 —[ˈʌndəlain] n.1. 划在下面的线

2.（在戏单下面的）下期节目预告；插图下面的说明文字 3.（动物）下体轮廓

underling ['ʌndəliŋ] n.〈贬〉下属；下手；走卒

underlying [,ʌndə'laiiŋ] underlie 的现在分词 — adj. 1. 在下面的；放在下面的 2. 根本的；基本的 3. 隐晦的；潜在的 4.【商】优先的

underman [,ʌndə'mæn] (undermanned; undermanning) vt. 使人员配备不足 ‖ **undermanned** adj.（船等）人员不足的，缺员的

undermentioned [,ʌndə'menʃənd] adj. 下述的

undermine [,ʌndə'main] vt. 1. 在…下挖；在…下挖通道（或洞），（海、风等）侵蚀…的基础 2. 暗中破坏；逐渐损害

undermost ['ʌndəməust] adj. & adv.（位置，地位等）最低的（地），最下的（地）

underneath [,ʌndə'niːθ] adv. 1. 在下面；在底下 2. 在下部；在下方 — prep. 1. 在…下面；在…底下 2. 在…的形式下；在…乔装下 3. 隶属于；在…的支配下 — adj. 下面的；底层的 — n. 下面；下部

undernourish [,ʌndə'nʌriʃ] vt. 使营养不足 ‖ ~ed adj. 营养不足的 / ~ment n. 营养不足

underpants ['ʌndəpænts] [复] n. 内裤，衬裤

underpart ['ʌndəpɑːt] n. 1.（鸟、哺乳动物、飞机等的）下部 2. 从属地位；次要角色

underpass ['ʌndəpɑːs] [复] n. 地道；地下通道，下穿交叉道；高架桥下通道（或路段）

underpay [,ʌndə'pei] (underpaid [,ʌndə'peid]) vt. 少付…工资，付给…不足额的工资

underpin [,ʌndə'pin] (underpinned; underpinning) vt. 1. 在…的下面加基础；加强…的基础 2. 支持；巩固

underprivileged [,ʌndə'priviliʤd] adj. 1.（阶级、阶层、民族等）被剥夺基本权利的；贫困的 2. 社会地位低下的；下层社会的

underproduction [,ʌndəprə'dʌkʃən] n. 生产不足；生产供不应求

underrate [,ʌndə'reit] vt. 对…评价过低；低估；看轻

underscore [,ʌndə'skɔː] vt. 1. 在…下划线 2. 强调 — ['ʌndəskɔː] n.（表示强调的）字下划线

undersea ['ʌndəsiː] adj. 1. 海底的；海面下的；在海底（或海面下）进行的 2. 供海面下使用的

undersea(s) [,ʌndə'siː(z)] adv. 在海底；在海面下

undersecretary [,ʌndə'sekrətəri] n. 1. 次长；次官；副部长：Undersecretary of State〈美〉副国务卿 / Parliamentary Undersecretary〈英〉政务次官 2. 助理秘书

undersell [,ʌndə'sel] (undersold [,ʌndə'səuld]) vt. 1. 售价比…低 2. 廉价出卖（商品）

undershirt ['ʌndəʃəːt] n. 贴身内衣；汗衫；汗背心

undershot ['ʌndəʃɔt] adj. 1.（水车）下射式的（指由下部通过的水流驱动的）2. 下前牙突出的；下颌突出的

underside ['ʌndəsaid] n. 下侧，下面；底面；（事物的）阴暗面

undersign [,ʌndə'sain] vt. 签名于（信、文件等）的末尾 ‖ 签名：已在下面（或文件等末尾）签过名的（文件）签过字的；签在下面（或文件等末尾）的 — n. ['ʌndəsaind] [the ~ed] [用作单或复]（信或文件等末尾的）签名者，署名人

undersize(d) [ˌʌndə'saiz(d)] *adj.* 小于一般尺寸的;不够大的;小型的

underskirt [ˌʌndəskə:t] *n.* 衬裙

understand [ˌʌndə'stænd] (过去式 understood [ˌʌndə'stud],过去分词 understood 或〈古〉understanded) *vt.*1. 懂;了解;理解;熟悉;通晓 2. 获悉;听说 3. 推断;认为 4.[常用被动语态](因含意自明而)省略 — *vi.*1. 懂得;理解 2.[用作插入语]据说;认为 3. 给予同情(或谅解等):rely on sb. to ~ and sympathize 依赖某人的谅解和同情 ‖ ~able *adj.* 可懂的;可了解的;可理解的

understanding [ˌʌndə'stændiŋ] *n.*1. 了解;理解;领会;认识 2. 理解力;判断力 3. 同情;相互理解;和睦;融洽 4.[常与不定冠词连用,罕用复数](非正式的)协定;协议;谅解 5.〈德国古典哲学中用语〉知性(reason 理性之对) 6.[~s](俚)脚;腿;鞋 — *adj.*1. 了解的;有理解力的;聪明的 2. 能谅解的;宽容的

understate [ˌʌndə'steit] *vt. & vi.*1. 没有充分表达实情地陈述;打折扣地陈述 2. 软弱无力地陈述 3. 克制地陈述(尤指旨在取得更大效果) ‖ ~ment *n.*

understood [ˌʌndə'stud] understand 的过去式和过去分词 — *adj.*1. 被充分理解的 2. 取得同意的 3. 含蓄的,不明言的

understudy ['ʌndəˌstʌdi] *n.*1.[戏]预备演员,替身 2. 替工,替补者,候补者 — *vt.*1. 学习(某角色)以便当替身;练习代演(某角色) 2. 通过观察(或实习)掌握(某工作) — *vi.* 练习当替身

undertake [ˌʌndə'teik] (undertook [ˌʌndə'tuk], undertaken [ˌʌndə'teikən]) *vt.*1. 着手做;进行,从事 2. 承担;接受;同意 3. 保证 — *vi.*1.〈古〉担保;负责(for) 2.〈口〉承办丧葬事宜 ‖ —

*n.*1. 承担者,承办人 2. 企业家 3. ['ʌndəˌteikə] 承办丧葬者;殡仪员

undertaking [ˌʌndə'teikiŋ] *n.*1. 任务;事业;企业 2. 承担;许诺;保证 3. ['ʌndəˌteikiŋ]丧葬事宜;殡仪业

under-the-counter ['ʌndəðə'kauntə] *adj.*1. 私下出售的;暗中成交的;开后门的 2. 违法的;禁止的

under-the-table ['ʌndəðə'teibl] *adj.* 秘密的,暗中进行的

underthings ['ʌndəˌθiŋz] [复] *n.*(女子的)内衣裤

undertime ['ʌndəˌtaim] *n.* 不足的工作时间;不及工时工资 — *adj. & adv.* 工作时间不足的(地) — ['ʌndə'taim] *vt.* 给…的时间太少

undertip [ˌʌndə'tip] (undertipped; undertipping) *vt.* 对(服务人员)未给足小费

undertone ['ʌndətəun] *n.*1. 低音;小声 2. 淡色;底彩 3.(言行中的)含意;(市场的)潜在倾向

undertook [ˌʌndə'tuk]undertake 的过去式

undertow ['ʌndətəu] *n.*1. 回卷,退浪 2.(海面下的)下层逆流

undervalue [ˌʌndə'vælju:] *vt.*1. 低估;小看;轻视 2. 降低…的价值 ‖ 'under¦valu'ation *n.*

underwater ['ʌndə'wɔ:tə] *adj.*1. 在水下的;在水中操作(或生长)的 2.(船体)水线下的 — *adv.* 在水下;在水中 — *n.*(海洋等)水面下的水

underwear ['ʌndəwɛə] *n.*[总称]内衣,衬衣

underweight [ˌʌndə'weit] *n.* 不足的重量;标准以下的重量;不符合要求的重量 — *adj.* 重量不足的;标准重量以下的

underwent [ˌʌndə'went]undergo 的过去式

underwood ['ʌndəwud] *n.*(树林中的)下木,林下灌丛

underworld ['ʌndəwə:ld] *n.***1.**(古)地球,大地 **2.** 阴间,地狱 **3.** 对跖点(地球上某一点的对应点)**4.** 下流社会;以犯罪活动为生的人们 **5.** 下层社会,底层社会

underwrite [ˌʌndə'rait] (underwrote [ˌʌndə'rəut], underwritten ['ʌndəˌritn]) *vt.***1.** 写在…下面(或末尾)**2.** 签名于(保险单等);给…保险,签名同意支付;同意负担…费用 **4.** 认购(证券、公债等);认捐 **5.** 赞同 — *vi.*经营(海上)保险业 ‖ ~**r** *n.* 保证人;保险商(尤指水险商);证券包销者

undescribable [ˌʌndis'kraibəbl] *adj.* = indescribable

undeserved [ˌʌndi'zə:vd] *adj.*(赏、罚等)不应得的;不该受的

undesigned [ˌʌndi'zaind] *adj.* 非故意的;非预谋的;偶然的

undesirable [ˌʌndi'zaiərəbl] *adj.* 不合需要的,不受欢迎的;令人不快的;讨厌的 — *n.* 不受欢迎的人;不良分子 ‖ ~**ness** *n.* / **undesirably** *adv.*

undeveloped [ˌʌndi'veləpt] *adj.***1.** 不发达的;不成熟的 **2.** 未开发的

undies ['ʌndiz] [复] *n.*〈口〉(尤指妇女的)内衣

undifferentiated ['ʌndifə'renʃieitid] *adj.* 无差别的;尚未显出差别的;一致的

undignified [ʌn'dignifaid] *adj.* 不威严的;不庄重的;有损尊严的

undiluted [ˌʌndai'lju:tid] *adj.* 未经冲淡的;没有搀杂的;纯粹的

undiscovered [ˌʌndis'kʌvəd] *adj.* 未被发现的;隐藏的;未勘探的

undisguised [ˌʌndis'gaizd] *adj.* 没有假装的;不掩饰的;坦率的;公开的

undismayed [ˌʌndis'meid] *adj.* 不害怕的;不泄气的;不动摇的

undisputed [ˌʌndis'pju:tid] *adj.* 无可争辩的;毫无疑问的

undistinguishable [ˌʌndis'tiŋgwiʃəbl] *adj.* = indistinguishable

undisturbed [ˌʌndis'tə:bd] *adj.* 没受到干扰的;宁静的;泰然自若的

undivided [ˌʌndi'vaidid] *adj.***1.** 没分开的;未分割的;一致的 **2.** 专一的;专心的

undo [ʌn'du:] (undid [ʌn'did], undone [ʌn'dʌn];第三人称单数现在式 undoes [ʌn'dʌz]) *vt.***1.** 解开;打开;松开;解开(或脱去)…的衣服 **2.** 取消;消除;使复原(使复旧);取消;败坏(成就,名誉等);使败落;毁灭 **4.** 扰乱;使不安 **5.** 勾引,诱奸 — *vi.* 开,松开 ‖ ~**er** *n.* 破坏者;勾引者 / ~**ing** *n.***1.** 解开;打开 **2.** 取消;消除 **3.** 毁灭,垮台,崩溃;毁灭的原因,祸根

undone [ʌn'dʌn] undo 的过去分词 — *adj.***1.** 没有做的;未完成的 **2.** 解开的;松开的 **3.** 毁掉的;完蛋了的

undoubted [ʌn'dautid] *adj.* 无容置疑的;肯定的;真正的 ‖ ~**ly** *adv.*

undoubting [ʌn'dautiŋ] *adj.* 信任的;不怀疑的 ‖ ~**ly** *adv.*

undreamed [ʌn'dri:md, ʌn'dremt], **undreamt** [ʌn'dremt] *adj.* 梦想不到的;意外的 (*of*) ‖ **un'dreamed-of,** ˌun'dreamt-of *adj.* 梦想不到的;意外的

undress [ʌn'dres] *vt.***1.** 使脱衣服 **2.** 使卸去装饰 **3.** 解掉(伤口等)的绷带 **4.** 暴露 — *vi.* 脱衣服 — *n.***1.** 便服;便装 **2.** 裸体(或半裸体)状态

undue [ʌn'dju:] *adj.***1.** 过度的,过分的;不适当的 **2.** 不正当的;非法的 **3.** 【商】

未到(支付)期的

undulate [ˈʌndjuleit] vi. 1. (水面等)波动；起浪；(地形、声音等)起伏 2. 呈波浪形 — vt. 1. 使波动；使起伏 2. 使成波浪形 — adj. 波浪形的；起伏的 ‖ ˌundulation n.

unduly [ˌʌnˈdjuːli] adv. 1. 过度地，过分地；不适当地 2. 不正当地

undying [ʌnˈdaiiŋ] adj. 不死的；不朽的；永恒的

unearned [ˌʌnˈəːnd] adj. 1. 非劳动(或服务)所得的；通过投资赚得的 2. 不配的；不应得的 3. 尚未获得的

unearth [ˌʌnˈəːθ] vt. 1. (从地下)发掘；掘出 2. 揭露；发现 3. 从洞中赶出(孤等)

unearthly [ˌʌnˈəːθli] adj. 1. 不属于现世的；非尘世的；超自然的 2. 精神的；理想的 3. 神秘的；鬼怪的；可怕的 4. 〈口〉不合理的；荒谬的；不可思议的

uneasy [ʌnˈiːzi] adj. 1. 心神不安的；忧虑的，担心的 2. 拘束的，不自在的 3. 不稳定的；不宁静的；汹涌的 4.〈古〉不舒服的，不适意的 5.〈古〉不容易的，困难的；难行的 — adv. 心神不安地；不自在地；不稳地 ‖ uneasily adv. / uneasiness n.

uneducated [ˌʌnˈedjukeitid] adj. 没受教育的；文盲的

unemployed [ˌʌnimˈplɔid] adj. 1. 未受雇用的，失业的 2. 不用的；没有利用的；闲着的；未投资的

unemployment [ˌʌnimˈplɔimənt] n. 1. 失业；失业状态 2. 失业人数 ‖ ~ compensation 〈美〉失业补助；失业救济制度

unending [ʌnˈendiŋ] adj. 1. 无终止的；无穷的 2. 不停的，不断的 3. 不死的；不朽的，永恒的 4.〈口〉经常被重复的 ‖ ~ly adv.

unendurable [ˌʌninˈdjuərəbl] adj. 难忍受的；无法容忍的

un-English [ˌʌnˈiŋgliʃ] adj. 没有英国人特点的；非英国(式)的；不合英语习惯用法的

unequal [ʌnˈiːkwəl] adj. 1. 不相等的；不同的 2. 不平等的 3. 不相配的；不平衡的；不对称的 4. 不适合的；不相称的；不胜任的 — n. [常~s] 不等同的事物；地位(或级别)不相等的人 — adv. 〈古〉不相等地；不相称地 ‖ unequal-(l)ed adj. 不等同的；不能比拟的；无敌的 / ~ly adv.

unequivocal [ˌʌniˈkwivəkəl] adj. 不含糊的；不暧昧的；明确的

unerring [ʌnˈəːriŋ] adj. 没有偏差的；准确的；没有过错的

UNESCO [juːˈneskəu] abbr. United Nations Educational, Scientific, and Cultural Organization 联合国教育、科学及文化组织（简称联合国教科文组织）

uneven [ʌnˈiːvən] adj. 1. 不平坦的，崎岖的；凹凸不平的；参差不齐的 2. 不规则的；(质量)不匀的；(发展)不平衡的 3. 不稳定的，易变化的 4. 力量悬殊的 5. 不直的，不平行的 6.【数】奇数的；不能用 2 除尽的 ‖ ~ness n.

uneventful [ˌʌniˈventful] adj. 1. 无重大事件的；过程平淡的；平静的；平凡的 2. 没有事故的

unexampled [ˌʌnigˈzɑːmpld] adj. 无先例的，空前的；绝无仅有的

unexceptionable [ˌʌnikˈsepʃənəbl] adj. 无懈可击的，无可指摘的

unexpected [ˌʌniksˈpektid] adj. 想不到的，意外的，突然的 ‖ ~ly adv. / ~ness n.

unfailing [ʌnˈfeiliŋ] adj. 1. 无穷无尽的；经久不衰的；永恒的 2. 可靠的；永不辜负期望的 ‖ ~ly adv.

unfair [ˌʌnˈfeə] *adj.* 不公平的,不公正的;不正直的;不正当的 ‖ ~ly *adv.* / ~ness *n.*

unfaithful [ˌʌnˈfeiθful] *adj.* 1. 不忠实的;不诚实的;对丈夫(或妻子)不忠实的;不贞洁的 2. (翻译、版本等)不准确的;不可靠的 ‖ ~ly *adv.* / ~ness *n.*

unfamiliar [ˌʌnfəˈmiljə] *adj.* 1. 陌生的;新奇的 2. 没有经验的;不熟悉的;外行的 ‖ ~ity [ˌʌnfəˌmiliˈærəti] *n.*

unfasten [ˌʌnˈfɑːsn] *vt.* 解开,脱开;放松

unfathomable [ˌʌnˈfæðəməbl] *adj.* 1. 深不可测的,无底的 2. 深奥的,难解的

unfathomed [ˌʌnˈfæðəmd] *adj.* 1. (海等)未测过深度的;未被理解的;尚未确定的;巨大的

unfavo(u)rable [ˌʌnˈfeivərəbl] *adj.* 1. 不适宜的;不顺利的;不利的 2. 相反的;反对的,不同意的 3. 令人不快的 4. (贸易)入超的: an ~ balance of trade 贸易逆差 ‖ **unfavo(u)rably** *adv.*

unfeeling [ˌʌnˈfiːliŋ] *adj.* 1. 缺乏感觉的,无感觉的 2. 无情的,冷酷的 ‖ ~ly *adv.*

unfeigned [ˌʌnˈfeind] *adj.* 不是假装的;真诚的;真的

unfeminine [ˌʌnˈfeminin] *adj.* 不适合女性的;不像女性的;不温柔的

unfetter [ˌʌnˈfetə] *vt.* 去掉…的脚镣;使自由;解放 ‖ ~ed *adj.* 自由自在的,无拘无束的

unfinished [ˌʌnˈfiniʃt] *adj.* 1. 未完成的,未结束的 2. 未琢磨的;未润饰的;未修整的 3.[纺]未整理的

unfit [ˌʌnˈfit] *adj.* 1. 不相宜的,不合适的 2. 无能力的;不胜任的 3.(身体上或精神上)不健全的 —(unfitted; unfitting) *vt.* 使不相宜;使不合格 ‖ ~ly *adv.* / ~ness *n.*

unfledged [ˌʌnˈfledʒd] *adj.* 1. (鸟等)羽毛未丰的;还不会飞的 2. 未充分成长的,没成熟的;年青而未经验的

unfold¹ [ˌʌnˈfəuld] *vt.* 1. 展开,摊开;打开 2. 开展(运动等) 3. 逐渐表露;阐明 — *vi.* 1. 伸展;开花 2. (运动等)展开,发展 3. 显露,呈现

unfold² [ˌʌnˈfəuld] *vt.* 放(羊)出栏

unforeseen [ˌʌnfɔːˈsiːn] *adj.* 未预见到的;意料之外的

unforgettable [ˌʌnfəˈgetəbl] *adj.* 不会遗忘的,难忘的 ‖ **unforgettably** *adv.*

unforgivable [ˌʌnfəˈgivəbl] *adj.* 不可原谅的;不可饶恕的 ‖ **unforgivably** *adv.*

unforgiving [ˌʌnfəˈgiviŋ] *adj.* 不原谅人的;不饶恕人的;无情的

unfortunate [ˌʌnˈfɔːtʃənit] *adj.* 1. 不幸的,倒霉的;时运不济的 2. 不适宜的,不适当的 3. 可叹的,使人遗憾的 — *n.* 不幸的人(尤指被社会遗弃者) ‖ ~ly *adv.*

unfounded [ˌʌnˈfaundid] *adj.* 1. 没有事实根据的;没有理由的;虚幻的 2. 未建立的

unfreeze [ˌʌnˈfriːz] (unfroze [ˌʌnˈfrəuz], unfrozen [ˌʌnˈfrəuzn]) *vt.* 1. 使解冻 2. 解除对(价格或工资)的冻结 3. 取消对使用(或制造、出售)…的管制

unfrequented [ˌʌnfriˈkwentid] *adj.* 人迹罕到的;行人稀少的;冷落的

unfriendly [ˌʌnˈfrendli] *adj.* 1. 不友好的;冷漠的;有敌意的 2. 不相宜的;不利的;不顺利的 3.(火势)控制不住的 — *adv.* 不友好地;不利地

unfrock [ˌʌnˈfrɒk] *vt.* 1. 脱去…的僧袍;免去…的圣职 2. 解除…的职权

unfruitful [ˌʌnˈfruːtful] *adj.* 1. 不结果实的;不生子女的;不毛的 2. 没有结果

的;无效的;无益的

unfurl [ˌʌnˈfəːl] *vt.* 1. 打开(卷拢之物);展开 2. 展示;显露;公开 — *vi.* 1. 张开;展开 2. 展示;显露;公开

ungainly [ʌnˈgeinli] *adj. & adv.* 1. 笨拙的(地);笨重的(地) 2. 难看的(地);不雅的(地) ‖ **ungainliness** *n.*

ungenerous [ʌnˈdʒenərəs] *adj.* 1. 胸襟狭窄的 2. 不大方的;吝啬的

ungentlemanly [ʌnˈdʒentlmənli] *adj.* 不配为绅士的;没有绅士风度的;缺乏教养的;粗鄙的

ungetatable [ˌʌnˈgetˈætəbl] *adj.* 难到达的;不易进入的

ungodly [ʌnˈgɔdli] *adj.* 1. 不敬神的;不虔诚的 2. 有罪的;邪恶的 3.〈口〉荒唐的;出乎此理的;不可思议的 — *adv.* 1.〈口〉荒唐地;可怕地 2.〈古〉不虔诚地;罪恶地

ungovernable [ʌnˈgʌvənəbl] *adj.* 1. 难统治的,难抑制的 2. 放肆的,任性的;野性难驯的

ungracious [ʌnˈgreiʃəs] *adj.* 1. 不礼貌的;粗野的 2. 讨厌的;不合人意的 ‖ ~ly *adv.* / ~ness *n.*

ungrammatical [ˌʌnɡrəˈmætikəl] *adj.* 1. 不合语法的 2. 文理不通的

ungrateful [ʌnˈgreitful] *adj.* 1. 忘恩负义的;不领情的 2. 徒劳的,白费力的 3. 令人生厌的,讨厌的 ‖ ~ly *adv.* / ~ness *n.*

ungrounded [ʌnˈgraundid] *adj.* 1. 无扎实基础的;无根基的 2. 无事实根据的;没有理由的 3. 虚假的,不真实的 4.【电】未接地的

unguarded [ʌnˈgɑːdid] *adj.* 1. 没有防备的;易受攻击的 2. 不留神的,大意的;不慎重的,轻率的

unguent [ˈʌŋɡwənt] *n.* 1. 药膏;软膏;油膏 2. 润滑油

unguis [ˈʌŋɡwis] ([复] **ungues** [ˈʌŋɡwiːz]) *n.* 爪;指甲;【植】爪

ungulate [ˈʌŋɡjuleit] *adj.* 蹄状的;有蹄的;有蹄类哺乳动物的 — *n.* 有蹄类(哺乳)动物

unhallow [ʌnˈhæləu] *vt.* 亵渎,玷污

unhand [ʌnˈhænd] *vt.* 把手从…移开;放掉

unhandy [ʌnˈhændi] *adj.* 1. 不方便的;难使用的 2. 不灵巧的;笨拙的 3. 不在手边的

unhappy [ʌnˈhæpi] *adj.* 1. 不幸福的;不快乐的;愁苦的,悲惨的 2. 不幸的,倒霉的;不祥的 3. 不适当的 ‖ **unhappily** *adv.* / **unhappiness** *n.*

unhealthful [ʌnˈhelθful] *adj.* 对健康有害的;不卫生的

unhealthy [ʌnˈhelθi] *adj.* 1. 不健康的;有病的;身心不健全的 2. 对健康有害的;不卫生的;对身心有害的;不道德的 3.〈口〉危及生命的;危险的;冒险的

unheard [ʌnˈhəːd] *adj.* 1. 没被听到的;不予倾听(或考虑)的;未予审讯的

unheard-of [ʌnˈhəːdɔv] *adj.* 前所未闻的;没有先例的

unhinge [ʌnˈhindʒ] *vt.* 1. 把…从铰链上取下;把铰链从…上拆下 2. 使移走;使分开;使裂开 3. 使动摇;使错乱,使失常

unhitch [ʌnˈhitʃ] *vt.* 1. 从车上解下(马) 2. 解开,放松

unholy [ʌnˈhəuli] *adj.* 1. 不神圣的;邪恶的 2. 不虔诚的;有罪的;亵渎的 3.〈口〉厉害的,可怕的 4.〈口〉不合理的 ‖ **unholiness** *n.*

unhook [ʌnˈhuk] *vt.* 1. 把…从钩上取下 2. 解开(衣服等)的搭扣

unhorse [ˌʌnˈhɔːs] *vt*.1.〈罕〉把马从(马车等)挽具上解下 2. 使(人)自马上摔下；使下马 3. 推翻；赶…下台

unhurried [ˌʌnˈhʌrid] *adj*. 不慌不忙的，从容不迫的；悠闲的

uni- *comb.form* 表示"单"：*uni*cellular

unicellular [ˌjuːniˈseljulə] *adj*. 单细胞(组成)的

unicorn [ˈjuːnikɔːn] *n*.1.(传说中身体似马的)独角兽；(纹章的)独角兽标记；(基督教《圣经》中)似牛的双角兽 2.【动】一角(鲸)，独角鲸 3. 一匹在前两匹并列在后的一组马(及马车)

unidentified [ˌʌnaiˈdentifaid] *adj*. 未被认出(或识别)的；身份不明的；不愿透露姓名(或名称)的

unification [ˌjuːnifiˈkeiʃən] *n*. 统一；联合一致

uniform [ˈjuːnifɔːm] *adj*.1.(不同物)全都相同的，一律的；清一色的；统一标准的 2.(同一物)不变的；始终如一的；一贯的 3. 均质的；均匀的；(税收等)划一的，统一的 *n*. 制服；穿制服的人 *vt*.1. 使成一样，使一律化 2. 使穿制服

uniformity [ˌjuːniˈfɔːmiti] *n*.1. 一样，一式；一律；一致(性) 2. 同质；均匀(性) 3. 清一色的东西

unify [ˈjuːnifai] *vt*. 统一，使成一体；使一致；使一元化

unilateral [ˌjuːniˈlætərəl] *adj*.1. 一方的；单边的；单方面的；片面的 2. 单系(指父系或母系)的 3.【植】单侧的 4.【语】单边音的

unimpeachable [ˌʌnimˈpiːtʃəbl] *adj*. 无可指摘的；无懈可击的；无可怀疑的

unimportant [ˌʌnimˈpɔːtənt] *adj*. 不重要的，琐碎的；无价值的

uninhabited [ˌʌninˈhæbitid] *adj*. 无人居住的，杳无人迹的

unintelligible [ˌʌninˈtelidʒəbl] *adj*. 难理解的，晦涩难懂的

unintentional [ˌʌninˈtenʃənl] *adj*. 非故意的，无心的 ‖ ~ly *adv*.

uninterested [ʌnˈintristid] *adj*.1. 不感兴趣的；不关心的；无动于衷的；厌烦的 2.(尤指财产方面)无利害关系的

uninteresting [ʌnˈintristiŋ] *adj*. 无趣味的，乏味的，引不起兴趣的；无聊的；令人厌烦的 ‖ ~ly *adv*.

uninterrupted [ˈʌnintəˈrʌptid] *adj*. 不间断的，连续的；不受阻挡的

union [ˈjuːnjən] *n*.1. 联合；合并 2. 团结；一致；融洽 3. 联邦；联盟：the Universal Postal *Union*(万国邮政联盟)协会；联合会；公会；工会 5.〈英〉【宗】教区间联合济贫组织；教区间联合济贫贫院 6. 国旗上象征政治统一的图案(位于旗的内上角或旗子上方)；国旗内上角 7. 结婚；性交 8. 连接；结合；【机】联管节；联铂节；【医】愈合 9.【纺】交织织物；混纺织物 ‖ **Union Jack**，**Union flag** 英国国旗

unionism [ˈjuːnjənizəm] *n*.1. 联合的原则；对联合原则的支持；联合主义 2. 工会制度(或原则、理论) 3. 工会主义；工联主义 4.[U-]〈美〉【美国南北战争时期的)联邦主义

unionist [ˈjuːnjənist] *n*.1. 联合主义者 2. 工会会员 3. 工会主义者，工联主义者 4.[U-]〈美〉(美国南北战争时期的)联邦主义者，联邦政府的支持者 5.[U-]〈史〉(爱尔兰自由邦成立前)反对爱尔兰自治的英国人；(爱尔兰自由邦成立前的英国)保守党党员

unionize [ˈjuːnjənaiz] *vt*.1. 使成立联合组织 2. 把(工人)组织成工会；使加入工

会 3. 使遵照工会规章(或准则)— *vi.*
加入(或成立)联合组织;加入(或组
织)工会 ‖ **unioni'zation** *n.* / ~ **d** *adj.*

unique [juː'niːk] *adj.* 1. 唯一的,独一无
二的;无比的,无可匹敌的;独特的
2.(口)珍奇的,罕有的;不平凡的;极
好的 3.【数】唯一的,只有一个结果的
— *n.* 独一无二的人(或事物) ‖ ~**ly**
adv. / ~**ness** *n.*

unisex ['juːniseks] *n.* & *adj.*〈美口〉(服
饰,发式等)不分男女的;出售(或使
用)男女通用服装(的);分不出男女
(的)

unison ['juːnizn] *n.* 1. 一致;调和 2.【音】
同度;同音;齐唱;齐奏 — *adj.*【音】同
度的;同音的;齐唱的

unit ['juːnit] *n.* 1. 单位(指构成整体的
人,物,团体,机构等) 2.【军】小队,分
队;部队(单位) 3.(计数或计量的)单
位;单元 4.【机械等】的部件;元件;组
件;构件;装置,组 5. 计算学分的学习
量(通常根据上课时数来决定);教学
单元 6.【数】最小整数,一 7.(计数)个;位 8.
(家具等配套用的)组合件;设备 —
adj. 单位的;单元的;一套的

Unitarian [juːni'teəriən] *n.* 1.(基督教)上
帝一位论派的教徒 2.[u-]统一体(或集
权)的支持者 ‖ ~**ism** *n.*(基督教)上
帝一位论

unite [juː'nait] *vi.* 1. 联合;团结 2. 粘合;
混合 3. 联合行动;一致行动 — *vt.* 1.
使联合;统一;使团结 2. 使粘合;使混
合 3. 兼备(各种特性) 4. 使结婚

united [juː'naitid] *adj.* 1. 联合的;统一
的;团结的;一致的;和睦的 ‖ **United
Nations** [复]用作单]联合国

unity ['juːniti] *n.* 1. 单一;个体;整体 2.
统一(性);一致(性);协调(性);统一
体 3. 团结;联合 4.(目的;行动等)

一贯性,不变性

universal [juːni'vəːsəl] *adj.* 1. 宇宙的;全
世界的 2. 普遍的;普遍的,一般的;全
体的;影响全体的 3. 通用的,广用的;
万能的;多才多艺的 4.【逻】全称的 —
n. 1.【逻】全称命题 2.【哲】一般概念 3.
普遍行为模式,普遍习俗(一定社会
的)成年人普遍具有的文化特征 ‖ ~.
ly *adv.* / ~**ness** *n.*

Universalism [juːni'vəːsəlizəm] *n.* 1.【宗】
普教论(相信人类终将得救) 2.[u-]普
遍特征,共同特征

universality [juːnivəː'sæləti] *n.* 1. 普遍
性;通用性;一般性 2.(知识等)的广泛
性,多方面性

universalize [juːni'vəːsəlaiz] *vt.* 使普遍
化;使一般化;使普及

universe ['juːnivəːs] *n.* 1. 宇宙;世界;天地
万物;万象;全人类 2.【逻】论域,全域
(思想、学科等自成体系的)领域 3.
【天】银河系;星系 4.(统计学用语)总
体,母体 5.【数】全域 6. 大量

university [juːni'vəːsəti] *n.* 1.(综合性)大
学;*Beijing University* 北京大学/*go to
(the)* ~ 上大学 2.[总称]大学人员(包
括学生,教职员等) 3.【体】大学代表队
‖ ~ **college** 大学附属于大学的学院 / ~ **extension** 大学附校

unjust [ˌʌn'dʒʌst] *adj.* 非正义的,不公平
的;不正当的

unkempt [ˌʌn'kempt] *adj.*(头发)未梳
的,蓬乱的;不整洁的,邋遢的 2. 未经
加工的;粗糙的

unkind [ˌʌn'kaind] *adj.* 1. 不仁慈的,不
和善的;不体谅的;不客气的 2. 刻薄
的;严酷的, ‖ ~**ness** *n.*

unkindly [ˌʌn'kaindli] *adj.* = unkind —
adv. 1. 不仁慈地,不和善地;不体谅地;不
客气地 2. 刻薄地;严酷地 ‖ **unkindliness**

n.

unknowable [ˌʌn'nəuəbl] *adj.* 不可知的；不可认识的 — *n.* 不可知的事物；[the U.][哲]不可知事物

unknowing [ˌʌn'nəuiŋ] *adj.* 1. 无知的 2. 不知道的；没察觉的(of) ‖ ～ly *adv.* 无意中，不知不觉地；非存心地

unknown [ˌʌn'nəun] *adj.* 不知道的；未知的；陌生的；没被发现的；无名的 — *n.* 1. 未知的事物(或人) 2.【数】未知元；未知量；未知数

unlace [ˌʌn'leis] *vt.* 1. 解开(或松开)…的带子 2. 把(猎获的野兽)切成块

unlash [ˌʌn'læʃ] *vt.* 解开；松开

unlatch [ˌʌn'lætʃ] *vt.* 拉开(门等)的闩(或销钮)；拉开闩、销等 — *vi.* (闩、销等)被拉开，被松开；被拉开

unlawful [ˌʌn'lɔːful] *adj.* 1. 不法的，非法的；犯法的；不正当的 2. 私生的 ‖ ～ly *adv.* / ～ness *n.*

unleaded [ˌʌn'ledid] *adj.* (汽油)无铅的

unlearn [ˌʌn'lɜːn] (unlearnt[ˌʌn'lɜːnt]或 unlearned[ˌʌn'lɜːnd]) *vt.* 1. 设法忘记(已学过的知识)；抛掉(以前的谬见、恶习等) 2. 使忘记(或抛弃)以前所学的东西(以达到否定、矫正等)

unlearned[1] [ˌʌn'lɜːnid] *adj.* 1. 无文化的；未受教育的；无知的 2. 不熟练的；不精通的 — *n.* [the ～]无知的人们

unlearned[2] [ˌʌn'lɜːnd, ˌʌn'lɜːnt] *adj.* 1. 不学而能的；天然的 2. 没学习过的；没学好的

unleash [ˌʌn'liːʃ] *vt.* 1. 解开…的皮带 2. 发出；发动

unleavened [ˌʌn'levnd] *adj.* 1. 未经发酵的；不含酵母的 2. 未经感化的；未受激发的

unless [ən'les, ʌn'les] *conj.* 若不；除非 —

prep. 除…外

unlettered [ˌʌn'letəd] *adj.* 1. 未受教育的；文盲的，不识字的 2. 无学问的，无学识的 3. 无字的

unlike [ˌʌn'laik] *adj.* 不同的；不相似的；相异的 — *prep.* 不像…，与…不同 ‖ ～ness *n.*

unlikely [ˌʌn'laikli] *adj.* 未必的；未必可能的；靠不住的 ‖ unlikelihood, unlikeliness *n.*

unlimited [ˌʌn'limitid] *adj.* 无限的；无边无际的；无约束的；不定的 ‖ ～ company 无限公司

unload [ˌʌn'ləud] *vt.* 1. 从…卸下货物(或其他东西)；卸(货)；下(客) 2. 解除…的拖累；摆脱…的重担；倾吐(心事) 3. 退出(枪等)的子弹 4.【商】使(股票等)脱手；抛售；倾销 — *vi.* 1. 卸货；下客；卸下负担 2. (通过谈话等)减轻紧张情绪 3. 大量抛售股票

unlock [ˌʌn'lɔk] *vt.* 1. 开…的锁 2. 开(锁)；开启；使分开 3. 揭开，表露；给…提供答案 — *vi.* 被开启；揭开；解放

unlooked-for [ˌʌn'luktfɔː] *adj.* 非期待中的；意外的，没有预料到的

unloose[ˌʌn'luːs], **unloosen** [ˌʌn'luːsən] *vt.* 解开；放松；释放

unlucky [ˌʌn'lʌki] *adj.* 1. 不幸的，倒霉的；不凑巧的；不顺利的 2. 不吉的，不祥的 3. 使人感到不高的；令人遗憾的 ‖ unluckily *adv.* /unluckiness *n.*

unmanageable [ˌʌn'mænidʒəbl] *adj.* 难管理的；难处理的；难办的；难控制的；难应付的

unmannerly [ˌʌn'mænəli] *adj. & adv.* 没有礼貌的(地)；粗野的(地)

unmarked [ˌʌn'mɑːkt] *adj.* 1. 未做记号的 2. 未被注意到的

unmarried [ˌʌn'mærid] *adj.* 未婚的；独身

的

unmask [ˌʌnˈmɑːsk] *vt.* 撕下…的假面具；揭露；暴露 — *vi.* 脱下假面具；露出本来面目

unmatchable [ˌʌnˈmætʃəbl] *adj.* 1. 无匹敌的；无可比拟的 2. 无法配对的；无法配置的

unmatched [ˌʌnˈmætʃt] *adj.* 1. 无敌的，无比的 2. (颜色、设计等)不相配的

unmeaning [ˌʌnˈmiːniŋ] *adj.* 1. 无表情的，呆板的 2. 无意义的；索然无味的

unmentionable [ˌʌnˈmenʃənəbl] *adj.* 说不出口的；不宜在社交场合提到的 — *n.* [~s] 说不出来或(议论)的东西；(谑)裤子；内衣

unmerciful [ˌʌnˈməːsiful] *adj.* 1. 不仁慈的；残忍的；无情的 2. 过分的

unmindful [ˌʌnˈmaindful] *adj.* 1. 不留心的，不注意的；漫不经心的；忘记的

unmistakable [ˌʌnmisˈteikəbl] *adj.* 不会弄错的；不会误解的；清楚明白的 ‖ **unmistakably** *adv.*

unmitigated [ˌʌnˈmitigeitid] *adj.* 1. 未缓和的；未减轻的 2. 纯粹的，十足的，完全全的

unmoved [ˌʌnˈmuːvd] *adj.* 1. 无动于衷的；冷漠的；镇静的 2. 不动摇的，坚定的

unmusical [ˌʌnˈmjuːzikəl] *adj.* 1. 不合调的；不悦耳的 2. 演奏音乐不熟练的；对音乐不感兴趣的

unnatural [ˌʌnˈnætʃərəl] *adj.* 1. 不自然的；勉强的；矫揉造作的 2. 不合人情的；反常的；违背人道的；邪恶的 3. 奇异的，奇怪的 ‖ **~ly** *adv.* / **~ness** *n.* — **act 鸡奸**；兽奸

unnecessary [ˌʌnˈnesəsəri] *adj.* 不必要的，多余的 — *n.* [常 unnecessaries]不必要的东西；非必需品 ‖ **unnecessarily**

[ˌʌnˈnesəsərəli, ˌʌnˌnesəˈserəli] *adv.*

unnerve [ˌʌnˈnəːv] *vt.* 1. 使气馁，使丧失勇气 2. 使烦恼；使烦恼不安

unnumbered [ˌʌnˈnʌmbəd] *adj.* 1. 数不清的，不可胜数的 2. 未编号的 3. 未计数的

UNO *abbr.* United Nations Organization 联合国组织

unobserved [ˌʌnəbˈzəːvd] *adj.* 1. 没有观察到的；没有受到注意的 2. 未被遵守的

unoccupied [ˌʌnˈɔkjupaid] *adj.* 1. (房屋)没人住的；(坐位等)没人占的；未被占用的 2. 未被占领的 3. 空闲无事的

unofficial [ˌʌnəˈfiʃəl] *adj.* 非官方的；非正式的 ‖ **~ly** *adv.*

unopened [ˌʌnˈəupənd] *adj.* 1. 没有拆开的；没有开的；封着的；(书页)未裁开的 2. 不开的

unorthodox [ˌʌnˈɔːθədɔks] *adj.* 非正统的；异端的；异教的

unpack [ˌʌnˈpæk] *vt.* 1. 打开(包裹等)取出东西；从包裹(或箱子等)中拿出东西 2. 卸下(马驮)的负荷 3. 解除…的负担；吐露(心事等)；揭示…的意义 4. [计]拆开(已压缩的数据);从(记录)中检索数据 — *vi.* 打开包裹(或行李等)取出东西；卸下负荷；吐露心事

unpaid [ˌʌnˈpeid] *adj.* 1. 未支付的，未缴纳的；(债等)未偿还的 2. 不受报酬的；不支薪水的

unparalleled [ˌʌnˈpærəleld] *adj.* 无比的；无双的；独一无二的

unparliamentary [ˈʌnˌpɑːləˈmentəri] *adj.* 违反议会规则的；议会所不允许的；(言、行)不符合议会惯例的

unpleasant [ˌʌnˈplezənt] *adj.* 使人不愉快的；不合意的；讨厌的 ‖ **~ly** *adv.* / **~ness** *n.* 1. 不愉快；煞风景 2. 不愉快事件；争执；不和；恶感

unpopular [ˌʌn'pɔpjulə] *adj.* 不得人心的，不受欢迎的；不流行的 ‖ -**ity** [ˌʌn'pɔpjuˈlærəti] *n.*

unpractical [ˌʌn'præktikəl] *adj.* 不切实际的；不现实的；不实用的；行不通的

unpractised，unpracticed [ˌʌn'præktist] *adj.* 1. 未经训练的；不熟练的；无经验的 2. 未实行过的；未经反复实践的；未试验过的

unprecedented [ˌʌn'presidəntid] *adj.* 1. 无前例的，空前的，前所未有的 2. 崭新的；新奇的

unpredictable [ˌʌnpri'diktəbl] *adj.* 无法预言的

unprejudiced [ˌʌn'predʒudist] *adj.* 没有偏见的，没有成见的；公正的

unprepared [ˌʌnpri'peəd] *adj.* 无准备的；尚未准备好的；未作防备的；不期而来的

unpretending [ˌʌnpri'tendiŋ] *adj.* 不装模作样的，不骄傲的；谦逊的；质朴的

unprincipled [ˌʌn'prinsipld] *adj.* 不讲道德的；肆无忌惮的；不正直的

unprivileged [ˌʌn'priviliʒd] *adj.* 1. 没有特权的，享受不到特权的 2.〈美〉贫穷的；社会最底层的

unproductive [ˌʌnprə'dʌktiv] *adj.* 1. 不生产的；(土地) 不毛的；没有收益的 2. 没有结果的，徒劳的 3. 非生产性的

unprofitable [ˌʌn'prɔfitəbl] *adj.* 无利 (可图) 的，赚不到钱的；无益的；没有好处的

unpromising [ˌʌn'prɔmisiŋ] *adj.* 没有希望的；没有前途的；结果未必良好的

unprovoked [ˌʌnprə'vəukt] *adj.* 非因触犯而发生的；无端挑衅的

unqualified [ˌʌn'kwɔlifaid] *adj.* 1. 无资格的；不合格的 2. 没有限制的；无条件的；绝对的，全然的

unquenchable [ˌʌn'kwentʃəbl] *adj.* 不能熄灭的；不能遏制的；止不住的

unquestionable [ˌʌn'kwestʃənəbl] *adj.* 毫无疑问的，不成问题的；无可非议的；确实的 ‖ **unquestionably** *adv.*

unquiet [ˌʌn'kwaiət] *adj.* 1. 不平静的；动荡的 2. 焦急的，不安的 — *n.* 动荡；焦急，不安

unquote [ˌʌn'kwəut] *vi.* (电报、听写等中用语) 结束引文：The spokesman said quote Proper steps have been taken to deal with this problem ~. 发言人说"(引用原话)'已采取适当措施处理这一问题'"(引文结束)。

unravel [ˌʌn'rævəl] (unravel(l)ed; unravel(l)ing) *vt.* 1. 解开；拆散 2. 解释，阐明；澄清；解决 — *vi.* 散开

unread [ˌʌn'red] *adj.* 1. (书等) 未经阅读的；尚未审阅的 2. 读书不多的；不学无术的；无知的

unreal [ˌʌn'riəl] *adj.* 假的，不真实的；虚构的；幻想的

unrealistic [ˌʌnriə'listik] *adj.* 不现实的；与现实 (或事实) 不符的 ‖ -**ally** *adv.*

unreality [ˌʌnri'æliti] *n.* 1. 不真实；不现实；空想，幻想 2. 虚构的事物，想象的事物

unreasonable [ˌʌn'rizənəbl] *adj.* 1. 不讲道理的，非理智的 2. 不合理的；超出常情的；过度的；过高的 ‖ -**ness** *n.* / **unreasonably** *adv.*

unregenerate [ˌʌnri'dʒenərit] *adj.* 1.【宗】灵魂未得再生的 2. 不悔改的，怙恶不悛的；顽固不化的

unrelenting [ˌʌnri'lentiŋ] *adj.* 1. 不退让的；不屈不挠的 2. 冷酷无情的，铁石心肠的 3. 不松懈的 ‖ -**ly** *adv.*

unreliable [ˌʌnri'laiəbl] *adj.* 不可靠的，靠不住的

unremitting [ˌʌnri'mitiŋ] *adj.* 不间断的, 持续的; 不停的; 不懈的

unreserved [ˌʌnri'zəːvd] *adj.* 1. 无保留的, 坦白的, 坦率的 2. 无限制的, 无条件的; 充分的, 完全的 3.(坐位等)没有被预订的 ‖ ~ly [ˌʌnri'zəːvidli] *adv.*

unrest [ʌn'rest] *n.* 不宁, 不安; 动乱, 骚动 ‖ ~ful *adj.*

unrestrained [ˌʌnris'treind] *adj.* 1. 无限制的; 过度的 2. 无拘束的; 放纵的

unrestricted [ˌʌnris'triktid] *adj.* 不受限制的; 不受约束的; 自由的

unrighteous [ʌn'raitʃəs] *adj.* 1. 不义的; 邪恶的; 罪孽深重的 2. 不公正的, 不公平的

unripe [ʌn'raip] *adj.* 1. 未熟的, 未成熟的; 生的 2. 未准备的; 不适时的

unrival(l)ed [ʌn'raivəld] *adj.* 无敌的; 无比的; 至高无上的

unroll [ʌn'rəul] *vt.* 1. 铺开, 展开(卷起的东西) 2. 显示, 展现 — *vi.* 铺开, 展开; 展现

unruffled [ʌn'rʌfld] *adj.* 不骚动的, 不混乱的; 不起皱的; 平静的; 沉着的

unruly [ʌn'ruːli] *adj.* 难驾驭的, 难控制的; 不守秩序的, 不守规矩的 ‖ **unruliness** *n.*

unsafe [ʌn'seif] *adj.* 不安全的, 危险的; 靠不住的

unsaid [ʌn'sed] unsay 的过去式和过去分词 — *adj.* 未说出的; 未用言词表达出的; 秘而不宣的

unsanitary [ʌn'sænitəri] *adj.* 不卫生的; 有碍健康的

unsatisfactory [ˈʌnsætis'fæktəri] *adj.* 不能令人满意的; 不能解决问题的; 不得人心的

unsatisfied [ʌn'sætisfaid] *adj.* 未得到满足的; 不满意的

unsatisfying [ʌn'sætisfaiiŋ] *adj.* 不能令人满意的; 不恰当的

unsaturate [ʌn'sætʃərit] *n.*【化】不饱和化合物

unsaturated [ʌn'sætʃəreitid] *adj.*【化】不饱和的

unsavo(u)ry [ʌn'seivəri] *adj.* 1. 没有味道的; 没有香味的; 难吃的; 难闻的 2.(品德上)令人讨厌的; 令人不快的

unsay [ʌn'sei] (unsaid; 第三人称单数现在式 unsays [ʌn'sez]) *vt.* 收回, 取消(前言等)

unschooled [ʌn'skuːld] *adj.* 1. 没进过学校的; 没有受过训练的; 没有经验的 2. 未受教育影响的; 天赋的

unscientific [ˈʌnsaiən'tifik] *adj.* 非科学的; 不科学的; 无科学知识的; 不按科学方法的

unscrew [ʌn'skruː] *vt.* 从…旋出螺丝; (旋出螺丝而)拆卸; 取下; 旋开; 旋松 — *vi.* 旋出; 被旋松

unscrupulous [ʌn'skruːpjuləs] *adj.* 不审慎的; 不讲道德的; 无耻的; 肆无忌惮的 ‖ ~ly *adv.*

unseal [ʌn'siːl] *vt.* 1. 开启, 给…开封; 拆(信) 2. 使解除束缚

unsearchable [ʌn'səːtʃəbl] *adj.* 探究不出的; 不能探究的; 神秘的, 不可思议的

unseasonable [ʌn'siːznəbl] *adj.* 1. 不合时令的, 不合季节的; 季候不顺的 2. 不合时宜的, 不适时的 ‖ **unseasonably** *adv.*

unseasoned [ʌn'siːznd] *adj.* 1. 未熟透的; 未干透的 2. 未成熟的; 无经验的 3. 没有调味的, 未加作料的

unseat [ʌn'siːt] *vt.* 1. 剥夺…的席位; 使失去资格; 使退位; 使退职 2. 使从坐

位上摔下；使从马上摔下

unseemly [ʌnˈsiːmli] *adj. & adv.* 1. 不体面的(地)；不合礼节的(地) 2. 不适宜的(地)；不恰当的(地)

unseen [ˌʌnˈsiːn] *adj.* 1. 未被看见的；未受注意的；未被觉察的；未被发现的 2. 看不见的 3. 未经预习的；不用参考书的；即席的 — *n.* 1. [the ~] 精神世界，灵心世界 2. 即席翻译；即席翻译的文章 3. 看不见的东西

unselfish [ʌnˈselfiʃ] *adj.* 不谋私利的，无私的；慷慨的

unsettle [ʌnˈsetl] *vt.* 1. 使不稳固；使移动；使松动 2. 扰乱，使不安定；动摇；使不确定 — *vi.* 移动；变得不稳；动乱不定

unsettled [ʌnˈsetld] *adj.* 1. 不稳定的；不安定的，动乱的，易变的 2. 不定的；怀疑的；未解决的 3. 未定居的，无居民的 4. 未付清的；未清算的；未在法律上作出处理的

unshakable [ʌnˈʃeikəbl] *adj.* 不可动摇的；坚定不移的

unshaped [ˌʌnˈʃeipt] *adj.* 1. 未成形的；形状不美的；畸形的 2. 粗制的，粗糙的

unsheathe [ʌnˈʃiːð] *vt.* 使(刀、剑等)出鞘

unsightly [ʌnˈsaitli] *adj.* 不悦目的，难看的；不雅观的

unskilled [ˌʌnˈskild] *adj.* 1. 不熟练的；不灵巧的；拙劣的；不擅长的 2. 无需技能的

unskil(l)ful [ʌnˈskilful] *adj.* 不熟练的，不灵巧的；笨拙的 ‖ **~ly** *adv.* / **~ness** *n.*

unsophisticated [ˌʌnsəˈfistikeitid] *adj.* 1. 不懂世故的，天真无邪的；质朴无华的 2. 不复杂的；简单的；清楚易懂的 3. 不掺杂的，纯的；真的

unsound [ˌʌnˈsaund] *adj.* 1. 不健全的；不

健康的，有病的 2. 腐烂的；有损伤的 3. 谬误的，无根据的 4. 不安全的；不稳固的，不可靠的 5. (睡眠)不沉的，不酣的 ‖ **~ly** *adv.* / **~ness** *n.*

unsparing [ʌnˈspeəriŋ] *adj.* 1. 不吝惜的，大方的 2. 严厉的；不宽恕的；不留情的

unspeakable [ʌnˈspiːkəbl] *adj.* 1. 说不出的，不能以言语表达的，无法形容的 2. 恶劣得难以形容的 3. 说不出口的，不可以说出来的 ‖ **unspeakably** *adv.*

unspecified [ʌnˈspesifaid] *adj.* 未特别指出的，未特别提到的

unspotted [ʌnˈspotid] *adj.* 没有斑点的；没有污点的；清白无瑕的

unstable [ʌnˈsteibl] *adj.* 1. 不稳固的；不牢靠的 2. 不稳定的；易变的；动荡不定的；动摇不定的；(性情)反复无常的

unsteady [ʌnˈstedi] *adj.* 1. 不稳固的；不平稳的；摇摆的 2. 不稳定的；变动的；易变的；不规则的 3. (习惯、行为等)古怪的；无常的 — *vt.* 使不稳定，动摇的；使不安定

unstressed [ʌnˈstrest] *adj.* 1. 不着重的，不强调的 2. [语]非重读的；无重音的

unsubstantial [ˌʌnsəbˈstænʃəl] *adj.* 1. 非实质的；虚幻的；不现实的 2. 不坚固的，不结实的；分量不重的

unsuccessful [ˌʌnsəkˈsesful] *adj.* 不成功的，失败的 ‖ **~ly** *adv.*

unsuitable [ʌnˈsjuːtəbl] *adj.* 不合适的；不适宜的，不适当的；不相称的

unsuited [ʌnˈsjuːtid] *adj.* 不适合的；不适宜的；不符合的；不相称的

unsupported [ˌʌnsəˈpɔːtid] *adj.* 1. 未经证实的；未得到支持的；未得到支援(或赞助)的 2. 无支撑的

unsurpassed [ˌʌnsəˈpɑːst] *adj.* 未被超越

(或胜过)的;无比的,卓绝的

unsuspecting [ˌʌnsəs'pektiŋ] *adj.* 不怀疑的;不猜疑的;未猜到……的

untangle [ˌʌn'tæŋgl] *vt.* 1. 解开,松开(乱结) 2. 整理;清理;解决(纠纷等)

untanned [ˌʌn'tænd] *adj.* (皮革)未鞣的;(皮肤)未晒黑的

unthinkable [ˌʌn'θiŋkəbl] *adj.* 1. 难以想象的;非常的 2. 不可思议的;不可理解的;难以置信的 3. 不必加以考虑的;毫无可能的

unthinking [ˌʌn'θiŋkiŋ] *adj.* 1. 无思想的;不动脑筋的;心不在焉的 2. 未加思考的;不注意的;疏忽的;不体贴的 3. 无思考能力的

untidy [ˌʌn'taidi] *adj.* 1. 不整洁的,不修边幅的,邋遢的 2. 不整齐的,凌乱的 3. 拖泥带水的,不干净利落的,不练净的 4. 使人不整洁的 5. 不适宜的;不合适的 ‖ **untidily** *adv.* / **untidiness** *n.*

untie [ˌʌn'tai] *vt.* 1. 解开 2. 解放;解除;解决 — *vi.* 被松开,被解开

until [ən'til, ʌn'til] *prep.* 1. 直到……为止 2.[用在否定句中]在……以前(不) 3.〈苏格兰〉= to 4.〈苏格兰〉= unto — *conj.* 1. 直到……为止 2.[用于否定句中]在……以前(不)

untimely [ˌʌn'taimli] *adj.* 1. 过早的;不适时的,不合时宜的 — *adv.* 1. 过早地;不合时宜地

untiring [ˌʌn'taiəriŋ] *adj.* 不倦的;不屈不挠的 ‖ **~ly** *adv.*

unto [ˈʌntu, ˈʌntu] *prep.*〈古〉〈诗〉1. 到;对 2. 直到;到……为止

untold [ˌʌn'təuld] *adj.* 1. 未说过的;未知叙述的;未透露的 2. 数不清的,无数的;不可计量的,无限的

untouchable [ˌʌn'dʌtʃəbl] *adj.* 1. 达不到的;碰不着的 2. 禁止触动的;碰不得

的;不可批评的;管不到的 3. 不可捉摸的;无形的 4.(因肮脏、讨人嫌而)不可接触的 — *n.* 贱民(印度最低层社会阶层的成员,又称"不可接触的贱民")

untoward [ˌʌntə'wɔːd] *adj.* 1. 倔强的,刚愎的;难对付的 2. 不幸的;不愉快的;麻烦的;不利的 3. 不适当的;不合宜的

untranslatable [ˌʌntræns'leitəbl] *adj.* 不能翻译的;难译的;不宜译的

untrue [ˌʌn'truː] *adj.* 1. 不真实的;假的 2. 不忠实的;不忠诚的 3. 不合标准的;(安装的部位等)不正的;不准的;不平的 4. 不正当的

untruth [ˌʌn'truːθ] *n.* 1. 不真实;虚假;虚伪 2. 谎言,假话 3.〈古〉不忠实;不忠诚

untruthful [ˌʌn'truːθful] *adj.* 1. 爱说谎的,不诚实的 2. 不真实的;假的;不正确的 ‖ **~ly** *adv.* / **~ness** *n.*

unused *adj.* 1.[ˌʌn'juːst]不习惯……的(to) 2.[ˌʌn'juːzd]不用的,空着的;未用过的,新的;新的

unusual [ˌʌn'juːʒuəl] *adj.* 1. 不平常的,异常的,稀有的 2. 与众不同的,独特的;奇特的 ‖ **~ly** *adv.* 不寻常地;〈口〉非常

unutterable [ˌʌn'ʌtərəbl] *adj.* 1. 说不出的;难以形容的 2. 坏透的;彻头彻尾的,十足的 3. 不能发音的

unveil [ˌʌn'veil] *vt.* 1. 除去……的面纱(或幕布等);(举行揭幕仪式时)揭开……的幕 2. 使公诸于众;揭露;展出 — *vi.* 1. 除去面纱(或幕布等) 2. 揭露

unwanted [ˌʌn'wɔntid] *adj.* 1. 不需要的;不必要的;无用的;多余的 2. 讨厌的;有害的;有缺点的

unwarrantable [ˌʌn'dəntnəcər] *adj.* 无正当理由的;无法辩护的;不正当的;过

可原谅的

unwary [ˌʌn'wɛəri] *adj.* 不注意的,粗心大意的;不警惕的;易受欺的

unwearied [ˌʌn'wiərid] *adj.* **1.** 不疲劳的,精神抖擞的 **2.** 不倦的;不屈不挠的

unwelcome [ˌʌn'welkəm] *adj.* 不受欢迎的;没有受到热情接待的;讨厌的

unwell [ˌʌn'wel] *adj.* **1.** 不舒服的,有病的;有病痛的 **2.** 月经来潮的

unwholesome [ˌʌn'həulsəm] *adj.* **1.** 不卫生的;不健康的,有害身心的;腐败的 **2.**(滋味、气味等)令人不快的;讨厌的

unwieldy [ˌʌn'wi:ldi] *adj.* **1.** 笨拙的;不灵巧的 **2.** 难操纵的;难控制的 **3.** 不实用的;使用不便的 **4.** 笨重的;庞大的

unwilling [ˌʌn'wiliŋ] *adj.* **1.** 不愿意的;很不情愿的;厌恶的;不喜欢的 **2.** 勉强做(或说、给)的 ‖ ~ly *adv.* / ~ness *n.*

unwind [ˌʌn'waind] (unwound [ˌʌn'waund]) *vt. & vi.* **1.** 摊开;解开;展开 **2.** 放松;伸直

unwise [ˌʌn'waiz] *adj.* **1.** 愚蠢的 **2.** 欠考虑的;不明智的;轻率的

unwished-for [ˌʌn'wiʃtfɔ:] *adj.* 非所希望的;不想要的

unwitting [ˌʌn'witiŋ] *adj.* 不知情的;无意的;不是故意的;无心的

unwonted [ˌʌn'wəuntid] *adj.* 非惯常的;不常有的

unworthy [ˌʌn'wə:ði] *adj.* **1.** 无价值的;拙劣的;卑鄙的;可耻的 **2.** 不值得的;不配的;不相称的 — *n.* 不足道的人;卑劣家伙 ‖ **unworthily** *adv.* / **unworthiness** *n.*

unwound [ˌʌn'waund] unwind 的过去式和过去分词 — *adj.* **1.** 未卷绕的;未上发条的 **2.**(从缠绕状态)松解开的;松散的

unwrap [ˌʌn'ræp] (unwrapped; unwrapping) *vt. & vi.* 打开,解开;展开

unwritten [ˌʌn'ritn] *adj.* **1.** 没有写下的;空白的 **2.** 非书面的,口头的;传说的;未成文的

unyielding [ˌʌn'ji:ldiŋ] *adj.* **1.** 坚挺的;不能弯曲的 **2.** 不屈从的;坚强的;顽强不屈的;顽固的

unyoke [ˌʌn'jəuk] *vt.* **1.** 给(耕畜等)卸轭 **2.** 拆开;使分离 — *vi.*(古)**1.** 卸轭 **2.** 停止工作

up [ʌp](最高级 uppermost) *adv.* **1.** 向上;在上面;在(较)高处;在地(或水)平线上;露出(水面)**2.** 直向(或处于)直立姿势;起床;起来 **3.**(在程度、地位、声音、价值等方面)由小变大;高涨起来;自外到多 **4.**(从边远地区、乡村、南方、下游、海边等被看作下方的地方往首都、城市、北方、上游、大学等地)往上方;在上方;往较重要处;【海】向上风;【戏】向后方;向舞台后部 **5.** 向目的地;向说话者所在处 **6.**(情绪上)高昂起来,激动起来;(事情)发生,出现;(论题)提出 **7.**(在空间、时间、程度等方面)赶上;达到;赶上;一直到;在……以上 **8.**[与动词连用,表示完全、彻底]完,光;完尽:eat everything ~ 把所有的东西都吃光/finish ~ the job 把工作结束掉 **9.** 贮藏起;封起;监禁 **10.**[与动词连用以加强语气]:light ~ a cigarette 点燃一支香烟/write ~ a story 写成一篇故事 — *prep.* **1.** 向(高处);在(高处);向(或在)……上面 **2.** 向(或在)……的上游;逆着……向上;向(或在)……的内地;向(或在)离……更远的地点 — [比较级 upper, 最高级 upmost 或 uppermost] *adj.* 向上的 — *n.* **1.** 居高位者;处于有利地位的人 **2.** 向上的效 **3.** 繁荣;全盛 **4.** 上行列车;上行公共汽车

5.〈美俚〉兴奋剂 —（upped; upping）*vi.*
〈口〉1.（站）起来；突然做某事（或讲话）
2. 举起；拿起（with）— *vt.* 1. 举
起；拿起 **2.** 提高（价格、生产、地位等）
3. 增加（赠注）‖ '~-and-'coming *adj.*
〈口〉(人在事业上)进取的；有希望的 /
'~-and-'down *adj.* 上上下下的；来来往
往的；起伏的；变动的 / '~-to-'date *adj.*
[通常作定语用]直到最近的；现代的；
新式的;时新的

upbraid [ʌn'breid] *vt.* 责备,谴责;训斥

upbringing ['ʌp.briŋiŋ] *n.* 抚育,养育;教
养;培养

upcoming ['ʌp.kʌmiŋ] *adj.* 即将来临的

up-country ['ʌp.kʌntri] *n.* 内地 —*adj.* 1.
内地的;在内地的 2.〈贬〉土里土气的,
土包子般的 — *adv.* 往内地;在内地

update [ʌp'deit] *vt.* 使现代化 — ['ʌp.deit] *n.* 新的信息(或情况);更新;
(最)新版

updraft ['ʌp.drɑːft] *n.* 向上排气,向上通
风;上升气流;直焰

upend [ʌp'end] *vt.* & *vi.* 颠倒;倒立,倒
放

upgrade ['ʌp.greid] *n.* 1. 升级;上升;提高
品级(或标准) **2.** 上坡 — ['ʌp'greid]
adv. & *adj.* 向上坡(的);向上的(的) —
[ʌp'greid] *vt.* 1. 使升级;提升 **2.** 改良
(家畜)的品种;改进(工作等);提高
(质量等) **3.**(出售货物时)以(低档货)
充高档货

upheaval [ʌp'hiːvəl] *n.* 1. 胀起,鼓起;
(地壳)隆起 **2.** 激变,剧变;动乱

upheave [ʌp'hiːv] *vt.* & *vi.* 胀起,鼓起;举
起;(使)上升;(使)隆起

uphill ['ʌp'hil] *n.* 登高;上升;上坡 —
adj. 1. 位于高处的 **2.** 上升的;向上
的;上坡的 **3.** 艰难的,费力的 —
adv. 1. 往山坡上,往高处 **2.** 费力地;迎着

uphold [ʌp'həuld]（upheld [ʌp'held]）*vt.* 1.
举起;高举 **2.** 支撑,支持;维持;坚持;
鼓励 **3.** 赞成,拥护;确认 ‖ ~ er *n.* 支
持者;赞成者,拥护者;支撑物

upholster [ʌp'həulstə] *vt.* 1. 为(沙发、椅
子等)装上垫子(或套子、弹簧等) **2.**
用挂毯(或地毯、家具等)布置(房间)
‖ ~ er *n.* 家具装饰用品商;室内装璜
商

upholstery [ʌp'həulstəri] *n.* 1. 室内装饰
品 **2.** 室内装璜(业)

upkeep ['ʌp.kiːp] *n.* 1.(房屋、设备等的)
保养,维修 **2.** 养护费,维修费

upland ['ʌplənd] *n.* & *adj.* 高地(的);山
地(的)

uplift [ʌp'lift] *vt.* 1. 高举;使(地面)隆起
2. 指道德等方面)促进,提高;振奋(精
神) — *vi.* 上升,升起 — ['ʌplift] *n.* 1.
举起;抬起 **2.** 情绪高涨;社会进步;道
德提高;提高道德和文化水平的社会
运动 **3.**(地壳的)隆起 **4.** 胸罩

upon [ə'pɔn] *prep.* = on [upon 和 on 一般
可通用,但有下列区别: **1.** 表示日期时
一般用 on,不用 upon,如:on Sunday,
on the fifth of April **2.** 在某些习语中,
upon 与 on 不能互相调换,如:upon my
word, once upon a time, on no account
3. 在句末或分句末的动词不定式过往
往用 upon,而不用 on,如:nothing to
depend *upon*, not enough to live *upon*
4. on 比 upon 语气较弱] *prep.*

upper ['ʌpə] *adj.* [up 的比较级] 1. 上
(面)的;上首的 2.(河)上游的 2. 地位
(或等级、权力等)较高的 3.(议会)上
院的 4. 穿在外面的 5. 地表层的 [U-]
[地]后期的 6. 较早的 7. 北部的 —
n. 1. 鞋帮 2.〈英口〉〈常贬〉上层社会的
人 3.(一颗)上齿;[~s]上排假牙 4.

〔口〕上铺(亦作 ~ berth) 5. 兴奋剂(尤指安非他明) 6. 布鞋罩

uppermost ['ʌpəməust] *adj*. [up 的最高级]至上的;最高的;最主要的 — *adv*. [up 的最高级]在最高处;在最上面;处于最突出的地位

uppish ['ʌpiʃ] *adj*. 傲慢的,盛气凌人的

upraise [ʌp'reiz] *vt*. 举起;提高

upright ['ʌprait] *adj*. 1. 垂直的;笔直的;直立的;竖式的 2. 正直的;诚实的 — *adv*. 笔直地;竖立着 — *n*. 1. 垂直;竖立 2. 笔直的东西;垂直的零件(或构件);直柱;立柱 3.【音】立式钢琴 4.[~s](足球中足球中的)球门柱 ‖ ~ly *adv*. / ~ness *n*.

uprise [ʌp'raiz](uprose [ʌp'rəuz], uprisen [ʌp'rizn]) *vi*. 1. 升起;涌现;出现 2. 起立;竖起,起身 3.(在数量上)增加;(在音量上)提高,变响 4. 起义;暴动 — ['ʌpraiz] *n*. 1. 上升;起床 2. 升坡,上山坡 3. 出现;起立 4. 暴动

uprising ['ʌpraiziŋ] *n*. 1. 上升;起立;起床 2. 升坡,上山坡 3. 起义;暴动

upriver ['ʌp'rivə] *adv. & adj*. 在上游(的);向上游的;从上游的

uproar ['ʌprɔː] *n*. 1. 骚乱;骚动 2. 喧嚣;吵闹

uproarious [ʌp'rɔːriəs] *adj*. 1. 骚动的;吵闹的 2. 引人捧腹大笑的,非常可笑的

uproot [ʌp'ruːt] *vt*. 1. 连根拔;根除,灭绝 2. 赶走;把…赶出家园 — *vi*. 根除,灭绝;改变住所及生活方式

upset [ʌp'set](upset; upsetting) *vt*. 1. 弄翻,打翻 2. 扰乱,搅乱 3.(比赛或竞争时)意外地击败(对手)4. 使烦乱;使(肠胃)不适 5.【机】镦锻;顶锻,加厚,镦粗 — *vi*. 翻倒,倾覆 — ['ʌpset] 1. 翻倒,倾覆 2. 混乱;搅乱 3.

心烦意乱;(肠胃等)不适 4.(尤指意外的)击败 5.【机】(镦锻用的)陷型模;缩锻金属条的粗大末端

upshot ['ʌpʃɔt] *n*. 1. 结果,结局 2.(分析或议论的)概要,要点

upside ['ʌpsaid] *n*. 上侧;上面;上部 ‖ '~·'down *adj*. 颠倒的;乱七八糟的

upstage ['ʌp'steidʒ] *adv*. 在戏台后部;朝着戏台后部 — *adj*. 1. 戏台后部的 2. 傲慢的,自负的,目空一切的 — *vt*. 1. 占据戏台的后部使(另一演员)处在背向观众的不利地位 2.(在演出等场合)抢(某人)的戏 3. 势利地对待

upstair ['ʌp'stɛə] *adj*. = upstairs

upstairs ['ʌp'stɛəz] *adv*. 1. 在楼上;往楼上 2. 处于更高地位;往更高地位(尤指明升暗降)3. 在高空;往高处 4.〔美俚〕在头脑里 — *adj*. 1. 楼上的;楼上的 2. 高水平的;上层的 — *n*. 楼层;上级;〔英口〕东家,主人家

upstanding [ʌp'stændiŋ] *adj*. 1. 直立的;竖立的 2. 挺拔的;强健的 3. 诚实的;正直的

upstart ['ʌpstɑːt] *n*. 1. 暴发户;新贵 2. 自命不凡的家伙 — *adj*. 暴发的;骤贵的;自命不凡的,狂妄自大的 — [ʌp'stɑːt] *vt. & vi*.(使)突然跳起;(使)崛起

upstate ['ʌp'steit] *adj*.(指美国的一州内)远离大城市的;远离海岸线的;偏僻的;北部的 — *adv*. 在(或向)州内远离大城市地区;在(或向)州内远离大城市地方;州的北部

upstream ['ʌp'striːm] *adv. & adj*. 在上游(的);向上游的;逆流的

upsurge ['ʌpsəːdʒ] *n*. 高涨,高潮 — [ʌp'səːdʒ] *vi*. 高涨,增长

upswing ['ʌpswiŋ] *n*. 1. 向上的摆动;高涨 2. 进步;改进,改善 — [ʌp'swiŋ] (upswung [ˌʌpˈswʌŋ]) **vi.** 向上摆动；提高；进步；改进

uptight [ˈʌpˈtait] **adj. 1.** 财政困难的；(手头)拮据的 **2.** 紧张的，不安的(*about*) **3.** 易怒的 **4.** 极端保守的；过分拘谨的 ‖ ~ness n.

uptown [ˈʌpˈtaun] **adv.** 在(或向)城镇非商业区；在(或向)住宅区 — **adj.** 在(或向)城镇非商业区的；远离闹市的；在(或向)住宅区的 — **n.** (城镇)非商业区；住宅区

upturn [ˌʌpˈtəːn] **vt. & vi. 1.** (使)向上，(使)朝上 **2.** 翻起，翻起 — [ˈʌpˌtəːn] **n. 1.** 向上的曲线；向上的趋势 **2.** (情况的)好转；(价格等的)提高

upward [ˈʌpwəd] **adj. 1.** 向上的；上升的 **2.**(声调)升高的 — **adv.** = upwards

upwards [ˈʌpwədz] **adv. 1.** (数量、程度、质量、职位、比率方面)趋向上升 **2.** 向上游；向内地 **3.** 在更高处；在上部；朝头部移 **4.** …以上，多于 **5.** (时间上)往后推移

upwind [ˈʌpˈwind] **adj. & adv.** 迎风的(地)，顶风的(地)

Ur 【化】元素铀(uranium)的符号

uraninite [ˈʌpwədz] **n.** 【矿】沥青铀矿，晶质铀矿

uranite [ˈjuərənait] **n.** 【矿】云母铀矿，铀云母类

uranium [juˈreiniəm] **n.** 【化】铀

Uranus [ˈjuərənəs] **n. 1.** 〖希神〗乌拉诺斯(天空的化身) **2.** 【天】天王星

urban [ˈəːbən] **adj.** 城市的；具有城市特征的；习惯于城市生活的

urbane [əːˈbein] **adj.** 有礼貌的；温文有礼的；文雅的

urbanity [əːˈbæniti] **n. 1.** 温文有礼；文雅 **2.** [urbanities] 文雅的举止

urbanize [ˈəːbənaiz] **vt. 1.** 使城市化 **2.** 〈罕〉使温文有礼；使文雅

URBM **abbr.** ultimate range ballistic missile 最远程弹道导弹

urchin [ˈəːtʃin] **n. 1.** 小淘气，顽童 **2.** 〈方〉〈古〉刺猬 **3.** 【动】海胆

urea [juˈriə] **n.** 【化】尿素，脲

urge [əːdʒ] **vt. 1.** 推进；驱策 **2.** 极力主张；强烈要求 **3.** 催促；力劝；激励；怂恿 **4.** 使劲干 — **vi.** 极力主张；强烈要求 — **n. 1.** [常用单] 强烈的欲望；冲动；迫切的要求 **2.** 推动力

urgency [ˈəːdʒənsi] **n. 1.** 紧急，迫切 **2.** 强求；催促；坚持 **3.** 紧急的事

urgent [ˈəːdʒənt] **adj. 1.** 紧急的；急迫的 **2.** 强求的；催促的 ‖ ~ly **adv.**

urinal [ˈjuərinl] **n. 1.** 尿壶，贮尿器 **2.** 小便处

urinary [ˈjuərinəri] **adj.** 尿的；泌尿的；泌尿器官的 — **n.** (供积肥用的)尿池；小便处

urinate [ˈjuərineit] **vi.** 排尿，撒尿，小便 ‖ uri'nation **n.**

urine [ˈjuərin] **n.** 尿

urn [əːn] **n. 1.** 瓮；缸 **2.** 骨灰瓮；〈诗〉坟墓 **3.** (茶水)壶 **4.** [植] 盖果基

urology [juəˈrɔlədʒi] **n.** 【医】泌尿学

Uruguay [ˈjuərəgwai] **n.** 乌拉圭[南美洲东南部国家]

US **abbr. 1.** United States (of America) 美国，美利坚合众国 **2.** Uncle Sam 〈口〉山姆大叔(美国、美国政府或美国人的绰号)

us [强 ʌs；弱 əs, s] **pron. 1.** [we 的宾格] [用作宾语] 我们 **2.** 〈口〉[用作表语] 我们(= we)

USA **abbr. 1.** United States of America 美国，美利坚合众国 **2.** United States Army

美国陆军

usable, useable [ˈjuːzəbl] *adj*.1. 可用的,能用的 2. 合用的;便于使用的

usage [ˈjuːzidʒ] *n*.1. 使用;使用;用法 2. 习惯;惯例;【语】惯用法;【律】习惯法

use [juːz] *vt*.1. 用;使用;应用 2. 发挥,使出;行使;运用 3. 耗费,消费;耗尽(*up*) 4. 经常取用(饮料或药品等);〈喻〉(烟)嗜(烟草) 5. 对待 6. 利用;〈口〉自私地利用(某人) — *vi*. 惯(现主要用过去式,见 used[1]) — [juːs] *n*.1. 用;使用;应用;运用;耗费 2. 运用能力;使用权 3. 用法 4. 用途;价值;效用;益处 5. 习惯;惯例

used[1] [juːst] (use *vi*. 的过去式)(否定式 —not 可缩写为 usedn't 或 usen't,读音均为 [ˈjuːsnt])过去常常,过去惯常

used[2] *adj*.1.[juːzd]〈美〉旧的;用旧了的 2.[juːst]〔作表语〕习惯于…的(*to*)

used-up [ˈjuːzdˈʌp] *adj*.〈口〉筋疲力尽的;耗尽精力的,淘空的;耗尽的,用罄的

useful [ˈjuːsful] *adj*.1. 有用的,有益的;实用的;有帮助的 2.〈俚〉值得高度赞扬的;颇为成功的 ‖ ~ly *adv*. / ~ness *n*.

useless [ˈjuːslis] *adj*.1. 无用的;无效的;无价值的 2.〈口〉差劲的,无能的 ‖ ~ly *adv*. / ~ness *n*.

user [ˈjuːzə] *n*.1. 使用者,用户 2.【律】使用权的实际享有(或使用) 3.〈美〉吸毒者

usher [ˈʌʃə] *n*.1.(戏院、教堂等公共场所的)招待员,引座员 2.(法院等的)门房;传达员 3.(走在重要人物之前的)领宾员 4.〈英〉助理教员 — *vt*.1. 引,领;招待 2. 迎接(*in*) 3. 引进;宣告;展示(*in*) — *vi*. 担任招待员(或引座员)

USM *abbr*. 1. underwater-to-surface missile 水下对面导弹 2. United States Mail 美国邮政 3. United States Marine(s) 美国海军陆战队 4. United States Mint 美国造币厂

USMA *abbr*. United States Military Academy 美国陆军军官学校(即西点 [West Point]军校)

USSR *abbr*. Union of Soviet Socialist Republics【史】苏维埃社会主义共和国联盟,苏联

usu. *abbr*. 1. usual 2. usually

usual [ˈjuːzuəl] *adj*. 通常的,平常的;惯常的,惯例的 ‖ ~ly *adv*. / ~ness *n*.

usufruct [ˈjuːzjufrʌkt] *n*.【律】用益权(在不损害产业的条件下使用他人产业并享受其收益的权利) — *vt*. 根据用益权占有

usurer [ˈjuːʒərə] *n*. 高利贷者

usurious [juːˈʒuəriəs] *adj*.1. 高利贷的;高利的 2. 放高利贷的;收取高利的

usurp [juːˈzɜːp] *vt*. 篡夺;夺取;侵占 — *vi*.1. 篡夺;篡权 2. 侵占(*on, upon*) ‖ ~ er *n*. 篡夺者;篡位者

usurpation [ˌjuːzɜːˈpeiʃən] *n*. 篡夺;夺取;侵占

usury [ˈjuːʒuri] *n*.1. 高利贷,高利盘剥 2. 高利(尤指超出法定利率);利益,好处

Utah [ˈjuːtɑː] *n*. 犹他(美国州名)

utensil [juːˈtensəl] *n*. 器皿,用具(尤指家庭厨房用具)

uterine [ˈjuːtərain] *adj*.1.【解】子宫的 2. 同母异父的

uterus [ˈjuːtərəs] ([复] uteri [ˈjuːtərai]) *n*.【解】子宫

utilitarian [ˌjuːtiliˈtɛəriən] *adj*.1. 有效用的;实用的 2. 功利主义的 — *n*. 功利主义者 ‖ ~ism *n*.【哲】功利主义

utility [juːˈtiliti] *n*.**1.** 效用;功用;实用;功利 [经]效用 **2.** 有用的东西 **3.** 公用事业(亦作 public ~) **4.** 公用事业公司;公用事业设备;[utilities]公用事业公司股票 **5.** [计] 实用程序 (亦作 ~ program) — *adj*.**1.** 有多种用途的;各种工作都会做的;万用的 **2.** 经济实惠的 **3.**(牲畜)实用型的,经济型的(与饲养来供观赏用的相对而言) **4.** 公用事业的;公用事业公司股票价格的

utilize [ˈjuːtilaiz] *vt*. 利用 ‖ ˌutiliˈzation *n*.

utmost [ˈʌtməust] *adj*. 最远的;极度的;最大的 — *n*. 极限;极度;最大可能

Utopia [juːˈtəupiə] *n*.**1.** 乌托邦 **2.** [常作 u-]理想的完美境界;空想的社会改良计划

Utopian [juːˈtəupiən] *adj*.**1.** 乌托邦的;似乌托邦的 **2.** [常 u-]空想的 — *n*.**1.** 乌托邦的居民 **2.** [常 u-]空想家;空想社会主义者 ‖ ~ism *n*. 乌托邦主义;乌托邦理论

utter[1] [ˈʌtə] *adj*.**1.** 完全的,彻底的,十足的 **2.** 无条件的;绝对的:an ~ denial (refusal)绝对否认(拒绝)

utter[2] [ˈʌtə] *vt*.**1.** 发出(声音等);说,讲;表达 **2.** 使用(伪币、假支票等) **3.** 发射;喷射

utterance [ˈʌtərəns] *n*.**1.** 发声;吐露,表达 **2.** 说话方式 **3.** 言词;言论 **4.**(伪币或假支票等的)使用

utterly [ˈʌtəli] *adv*. 全然;完全地;彻底地

UUM *abbr*. underwater-to-underwater missile 水下对水下导弹

uvula [ˈjuːvjulə] ([复] uvulas 或 uvulae [ˈjuːvjuliː]) *n*.【解】悬雍垂,小舌 ‖ ~r *adj*. 悬雍垂的,小舌的;[语]小舌音的

uxorious [ʌkˈsɔːriəs] *adj*. 溺爱妻子的;怕老婆的 ‖ ~ly *adv*. / ~ness *n*.

Uzbekistan [uzˌbekiˈstɑːn] *n*. 乌兹别克斯坦[亚洲中部国家]

V

V, v [viː] ([复]V's, v's 或 VS, vs[viz])英语字母表第二十二个字母 1.【V】罗马数字的 5 2.【V】V字形 3.【V】【化】元素钒(vanadium)的符号 4.【V】表示胜利(Victory)的符号(尤指第二次世界大战中同盟国对轴心国的胜利) 5. *abbr.* velocity 6. *abbr.* volt(s) 7. *abbr.*【数】vector 8.【美口】五元票面的钞票

vacancy ['veikənsi] *n.* 1. 空;空白;空处;空地;空房间 2.(心灵)空虚;失神 3. 清闲;空闲 4. 空缺;空额

vacant ['veikənt] *adj.* 1. 空的;空白的 2. 未被占用的;【律】(土地)未被人占有(或使用)的;(遗产)无人主张继承权的;(公地)尚未授给私人的 3.(心灵)空虚的;茫然的,无表情的;愚蠢的 4. 清闲的;空闲的 5.(职位)空缺的 ‖ ~ly *adv.* / ~ness *n.*

vacate [və'keit, 'veikeit] *vt.* 1. 使空出;腾出,搬出 2. 解除(职位);退(位);辞(职);撤离(陈地) 3.【律】撤消;使无效 — *vi.* 1. 腾出空房(或空地) 2. 辞职 3.【美口】离去,走开

vacation [və'keiʃən, vei'keiʃən] *n.* 1. 假期;休假;(法院)的休庭期 2.(房屋等)腾空;搬出,搬离 — *vi.*【美】度假:He ~ed in Beijing last summer. 去年夏天他在北京度假。

vaccinate ['væksineit] *vt.* 1. 给…接种牛痘 2. 给…接种疫苗 3.【计】保护(计算

机或计算机操作系统)使不受计算机病毒侵害,给…接种疫苗程序 — *vi.* 种痘;行预防接种

vaccination [ˌvæksi'neiʃən] *n.* 1.【医】种痘;接种 2. 牛痘疤 ‖ ~ program = vaccine program

vaccine ['væksiːn] *adj.* 牛痘的;种痘的;疫苗的;接种的一 *n.* 1. 牛痘苗;疫苗,菌苗 2. = ~ program ‖ ~ program【计】疫苗程序

vacillate ['væsileit] *vi.* 1. 摇摆;振荡;波动 2. 犹豫,踌躇

vacillation [ˌvæsi'leiʃən] *n.* 1. 摇摆;振荡;波动 2. 犹豫不决,踌躇

vacuity [væ'kjuːiti] *n.* 1. 空;空白 2.(精神上)空虚;(特定东西的)缺乏 3. 茫然;愚蠢;愚蠢的事;无意义的事;没有内容的东西(声明、讲话等)的空洞无物 4. 空间;真空

vacuous ['vækjuəs] *adj.* 1. 空的,空洞的 2.(精神上)空虚的;内容贫乏的;无意义的 3. 愚蠢的;茫然若失的 4.(生活)无聊的,无所事事的 ‖ ~ly *adv.* / ~ness *n.*

vacuum ['vækjuəm] ([复]vacuums 或 vacua ['vækjuə]) *n.* 1. 真空;真空度;真空般状态 2. 真空装置;真空吸尘器(= ~ cleaner) 3. 空虚 4. 封闭状态,隔绝状态 — *adj.* 1. 真空的 2. 用以产生真空的;利用真空的 — *vt.*【口】用真空吸尘

器打扫 ‖ ~ **bottle**, ~ **flask** 保温瓶，热水瓶 /~ **brake**[机] 真空闸；真空制动机 /~ -**clean** vt. 用真空吸尘器打扫 / ~ **cleaner** 真空吸尘器 /~ **pump**[机] 真空泵 /~ **tube** 真空管，电子管 /~ **valve** (英) ～ tube

vade mecum ['veidi'miːkəm] ([复] vade mecums)随身物；手册，袖珍指南，便览

Vaduz ['vɑːduːts] n. 瓦杜兹[列支敦士登首都]

vagabond ['væɡəbɔnd] adj. 1. 流浪的，漂泊的 2. 流浪者的 3. 浪荡的；懒散的 — n. 流浪者；流氓乞丐；浪子；懒汉；流氓 ‖ ～ism n. 流浪生活

vagary ['veiɡəri, və'ɡeəri] n. 1. 奇想，异想天开 2. 古怪行为；异常行为；难以预测的行为

vagina [və'dʒainə] ([复] vaginae [və'dʒaini] 或 vaginas) n. [动] 鞘；[解] 阴道 [植] 叶鞘；箨 ‖ ～l adj.

vagrancy ['veiɡrənsi] n. 1. (思想、说话的)游移不定 2. 流浪；漂泊；[律] 流浪罪

vagrant ['veiɡrənt] n. 流浪者；漂泊者；游民 — adj. 1. 流浪的，漂泊的；游民一的：a ～ life 流浪生活 2. (思想等)游移不定的；(风等)无定向的；[植] 疏展生长的，散开生长的

vague [veiɡ] adj. 1. 含糊的；模糊的；不明确的 2. 无表情的：～ eyes 发呆的眼睛 ‖ ～ly adv. ‖ ～ness n.

vain [vein] adj. 1. 徒劳的；无效的 2. 无价值的，无实在意义的；无关紧要的 3. 自负的，自视过高的；爱虚荣的 4. 愚蠢的 ‖ in ～ 1. 徒劳，白辛苦 2. 轻慢，不敬 ‖ ～ly adv.

vainglorious [,vein'ɡlɔːriəs] adj. 非常自负的；自夸的；喜欢自吹自擂的 ‖ ～ly adv.

vainglory [vein'ɡlɔːri] n. 自负；虚荣；卖弄；显耀

valance ['væləns] n. 1. (床沿)短帷幔；挂布；桌帷 2. (窗帘上部的)框架(或短幔)

vale [veil] n. 谷，溪谷(用于诗和地名中)

valediction [,væli'dikʃən] n. 告别；告别词

valedictorian [,vælidik'tɔːriən] n. 致告别词的毕业生代表

valence ['veiləns], **valency** ['veilənsi] n. 1. [化] (化合)价；(原子)价 2. [生] 效价

valentine ['væləntain] n. 1. 在圣瓦伦廷节选定(或向之表示倾慕的)情人；情人 2. 在圣瓦伦廷节赠送给情人的礼物(或贺词、卡片) 3. 在圣瓦伦廷节寄给异性的诙谐信(或贺书) ‖ Valentine('s) Day 圣瓦伦廷节，情人节(二月十四日)

valerian [və'liəriən] n. [植] 缬草；[药] 缬草根(作作镇静剂)

valet ['vælit, 'vælei] n. 1. (男子的)贴身男仆；仆从 2. 旅馆中替客人洗烫衣服的人 3. (美)衣物架，衣帽架 — vt. 侍候

Valetta [və'letə] n. ～ Valletta

valiant ['væljənt] adj. 勇敢的；英勇的 — n. 勇敢的人

valid ['vælid] adj. 1. 具有法律效力(或约束力)的；按正当法律手续执行的 2. 有理的，确凿的；令人信服的；有根据的 3. (罕)强壮的，健康的 4. 逻辑上真实(或正确)的 5. 能产生预期效果的；有效验的；恰当可取的 ‖ ～ly adv.

validate ['vælideit] vt. 1. 使生效；使有法律效力；使受法律约束；批准；确认一有效 2. 证实 ‖ **vali'dation** n. 1. 批准；确认，确定，测定 2. [计] 正确(或可靠)性检测

validity [və'liditi] n. 1. 有效；效力；合法

性 2. 正当；正确；确实

valise [vəˈliz] *n.* 旅行袋；小件手提行李；用具包

Valletta [vəˈletə] *n.* 瓦莱塔[马耳他首都]

valley ['væli] *n.* 1.（山）谷；溪谷 2. 流域 3. 凹陷处，凹地 4.【建】屋谷，屋顶排水沟

valor ['vælə] *n.* 〈美〉= valour

valorous ['vælərəs] *adj.* 勇猛的，英勇的，无畏的 ‖ **~ly** *adv.*

valour ['vælə] *n.* 勇猛，英勇

valuable ['væljuəbl] *adj.* 1. 值钱的，贵重的 2. 有价值的，有用的；宝贵的 3. 可估价的 — *n.* [常~s] 贵重物品；财宝

valuation [ˌvæljuˈeiʃən] *n.* 1. 估价；估定的价值（或价格）；定价 2. 评价

value ['væljuː] *n.* 1. 价值 2. 价值量：交换力；购买力 3. 益处；重要性；有用性 4. 等值；公平的代价 5. 估价；评价 6. 邮票等的面值 7. 涵义，意义 8.【数】值【语】音值；[生]（分类上的）等级；[音]时值（指音符或休止符的长度）；绘画中的浓淡关系，明暗程度；明暗称；out of ~ 明暗不调和的 9. [~s] 价值观念；标准；社会准则 — *vt.* 1. 给…定价 2. 评价；尊重；重视 ‖ **~less** *adj.* 无价值的，没有用的 ‖ **~-added tax** 增值税

valued ['væljuːd] *adj.* 1. 经估价的 2. 宝贵的；受尊重的；受重视的

valuer ['væljuə] *n.* 1. 〈英〉估价人；价格核定人；鉴定人 2. 评价人

valve [vælv] *n.* 1.【机】阀，活门 2.【解】瓣，瓣膜 ‖【植】（硅藻的）瓣；（果实的）裂片 3.〈英〉真空管，电子管 4.【音】（铜管乐器上的）活塞 5.【动】贝壳，阴门，产卵器鞘 — *vt. & vi.* 装阀（于）；用阀调节（液体）的流量

vamp[1] [væmp] *n.* 1. 鞋（或鞋）面；鞋面皮 2. 补丁；补片 3.【音】即席伴奏 — *vt.* 1. 换修（鞋或鞋）的鞋面；整修；把…翻新；修补（*up*）2. 拼造（旧材料）（*up*）3. 捏造（*up*）4.【音】即席奏出（伴奏）— *vi.*【音】即席伴奏

vamp[2] [væmp] *n.* 〈美俚〉勾引男子以勒索金钱的荡妇，女骗子 — *vt.* 利用色相向（男子）勒索金钱；勾引（男子）— *vi.* 勾引男子，诱惑男子

vampire ['væmpaiə] *n.* 1. 吸血鬼[迷信所说夜间离开坟墓吸食睡觉者的血的鬼] 2.（喻）吸血鬼；放高利贷者；敲榨勒索者；勾引并导致男子毁灭的女人；拐诱荡妇的演员 3.【戏】（舞台上的）活板门（演员可由此突然出现或消失）5.【动】吸血蝠

van[1] [væn] *n.* 1. 前卫，先头部队（或舰队）2.（运动、事业等的）前驱，先锋；领导者

van[2] [væn] *n.* 1. 大篷货车；运货车，搬运车；〈口〉面包车 2.〈英〉有棚盖的铁路货车；行李车 3.〈吉卜赛人〉住的大篷车 —（vanned; vanning）*vt.* 用车搬运 ‖ **~ line**〈美〉（使用大篷货车的）长途搬运公司

van[3] [væn] *n.*（英方）簸（谷）器；【矿】洗矿铲；〈英方〉铲头洗矿 3.〈诗〉（鸟、昆虫的）翼

vanadium [vəˈneidiəm] *n.*【化】钒

vancomycin [ˌvæŋkəˈmaisin] *n.*【微】万古霉素

Vandal ['vændəl] *n.* 1. 汪达尔人[属日耳曼民族，公元四至五世纪进入高卢、西班牙、北非等地，并曾攻占罗马] 2. [v-] 摧残文化和艺术者；破坏他人（或公共）财产者 — *adj.* 1. 汪达尔人的 2. [v-] 破坏性的 ‖ **vandalism** *n.* 故意破**

坏文化和艺术的行为;破坏他人(或公
共)财产的行为

vandyke [ˌvænˈdaik] *n.*(下巴上的)短尖
髭

vane [vein] *n.* 1. 风向标;反复无常的人;
变化不定的事物 2.(风车、螺旋桨等
的)翼;叶片;轮叶 3.【测】视准器,视标
4.(罗盘等的)照准器 5.(鸟的)羽片,
翮 6. 箭翎 7.(火箭、导弹等的)舵

vanguard *n.* 1. 前卫;先头部
队;尖兵 2.(社会政治运动等的)先锋
(队);领导者

vanilla [vəˈnilə] *n.* 1.【植】香子兰,香荚
兰 2.香兰英 3. 香子兰浸液香 子兰
(香)精,香草(香)精;香草冰淇淋

vanish [ˈvæniʃ] *vi.* 1. 突然不见;逐渐消
散;消失;消灭 2.【数】变为零;等于零
— *n.*【语】消失音 ‖

vanity [ˈvæniti] *n.* 1. 虚夸;虚荣(心) 2.
自负,自大 3. 空虚;虚幻,无用;无价
值 4.(妇女手提包中用的)小梳妆盒,
(女用)小手提包 5. 梳妆台 ‖ ~ **bag**,
~ **box**, ~ **case**(女用)小梳妆盒,小手提
包 /**Vanity Fair** 浮华虚荣的社会,名利
场

vanquish [ˈvæŋkwiʃ] *vt.* 征服;战胜,击
败;克服,抑制(感情等) ‖ **—er** *n.*

vantage [ˈvɑːntidʒ] *n.* 1.(竞赛中的)优
势;有利地位 2.(古)利益;获利 3.(网
球赛中)优势分 ‖ ~ **ground** 有利地
位;优越地位(或条件);优势

Vanuatu [ˌvɑːnuːˈɑːtuː] *n.* 瓦努阿图[西南
太平洋岛国]

vapid [ˈvæpid] *adj.* 1. 乏味的,无滋味的
2. 无趣味的;枯燥乏味的;无生气的
‖ **—ly** *adv.*

vapor [ˈveipə] *n.*, *vi.* & *vt.*(美)= vapour

vaporize [ˈveipəraiz] *vt.* & *vi.*(使)蒸发;
(使)汽化 ‖ **vapori'zation** *n.* /**—r** *n.*

汽化器

vaporous [ˈveipərəs] *adj.* 1. 形成蒸气的;
雾(状)的;(似)蒸气的 2. 多蒸气的,有
雾的 3. 无实质的内容的;空想的;富于
幻想的 4. 浮夸的,夸夸其谈的

vapour [ˈveipə] *n.* 1. 蒸气;汽;雾;烟雾
2. 无实质的东西;易逝的东西;痴想;幻
想 3.[the ~ s]郁气;忧郁(症);疑病
症;癔病 4.【药】吸入剂 — *vi.* 1. 蒸
发;汽化 — *vt.* 1. 使蒸发;使汽化 2. 使
优郁 3. 吹嘘,自夸 ‖ ~ **ing** *n.*[常~s]大话;浮夸
的举止 ‖ ~ **bath** 1. 蒸汽浴 2. 蒸汽浴室

var. *abbr.* 1. variable 2. variant(s)
3. variation 4. variety 5. various

variable [ˈvɛəriəbl] *adj.* 1. 易变的;常变
的;反复不定的 2. 可变的 3.【数】变量
的 4.(星)亮度变化的,变光的 5.【生】
变异的;变型的;畸变的 — *n.* 1. 易变
事物;变化(或方向或风力不定的)季节
风;不定风 3.【天】变星 4.【数】元,变
量;变量符号;变元;变项 5.[the ~ s]
(东北与东南信风带之间的)变风区 ‖
varia'bility *n.* / ~ **ness** *n.* /**variably** *adv.*

variance [ˈvɛəriəns] *n.* 1. 变化;更更;变
异 2. 不同;差异;分歧;争论;不和 3.
[律](诉讼中)两步骤间的不一致;诉
状与证据的不符 4.(会计学中的)差异
5.(统计学中的)方差

variant [ˈvɛəriənt] *adj.* 不同的;变异的;
差别的 ‖ *n.* 1. 变形;变体 2.
(同一词的)异体(稿本的)异文;(同
一词的)异读 3.(统计学中的)随机变
量;【生】变异体

variation [ˌvɛəriˈeiʃən] *n.* 1. 变化;变动;
变更 2. 变化程度 3.【数】变分;【生】变
异;变种【天】变差;(月的)二均差;
【地】磁偏角;【音】变奏(曲) 4.(古典芭

蕾舞中的)变奏舞;(芭蕾舞中的)单人舞 5. 变异的东西;变化了的形式 ‖ ～al *adj.* (尤指生物)变异的

varicose ['værikəus] *adj.*【医】(静脉)曲张的;引起静脉曲张的

varied ['veərid] *adj.* 1. 多变化的;各种各样的;不相同的 2. 改变了的 3. 杂色的;斑驳的

variegate ['veəriəgeit] *vt.* 1. 使成杂色;使斑驳 2. 使多样化 ‖ **varie'gation** *n.*

variety [və'raiəti] *n.* 1. 多样性;变化 2. 种类 3.[a～] 种种 4.【生】变种;品种 5.(音乐、舞蹈、杂耍等的)联合演出;杂耍表演

variform ['veərifɔ:m] *adj.* 有多种形态的;形形色色的 ‖ ～ly *adv.*

variola [və'raiələ] *n.*【医】天花,痘疮

variorum [,veəri'ɔ:rəm] *n.* 1.(古典文学作品的)集注版:集注本 2. 附有异文的版本 — *adj.* 1. 集注版(本)的 2. 引自不同来源的

various ['veəriəs] *adj.* 1. 各种各样的,不同的;种种的 2. 多方面的;多才多艺的;具有各种不同特征的 3. 几个的;许多的 4.(一团体内)各个的、个别的 5. 杂色的,色彩的 6.〈口〉[作代词用]好几个 ‖ ～ly *adv.* / ～ness *n.*

varlet ['vɑ:lit] *n.*〈古〉1.(骑士的)侍童;仆人,侍从 2. 无赖;流氓;恶棍;下贱人

varnish ['vɑ:niʃ] *n.* 1. 清漆,罩光漆,凡立水 2.(人工或天然的)光泽;(瓷器等的)光泽的表面 3. 附有异文 4.〈英〉指甲油 5.(内燃机中)一层清漆状的沉积物 — *vt.* 1. 给…涂清漆;使有光泽;髹漆 2. 粉饰;文饰;掩饰 ‖ ～tree[植]漆树

varsity ['vɑ:siti] *n.* 1.〈主英〉大学 2.(体育运动的)大学(或学院)代表队,校队

3.(运动队中)经常上场的主力队员 — *adj.*(大专院校等体育运动的)校队的

vary ['veəri] *vt.* 1. 改变;变更;修改 2. 使多样化;使有变化 3.【音】变奏(主题) — *vi.* 1. 变化;不同 2. 违反;偏离 3.【生】变异 4.【数】成比例地变化

vascular ['væskjulə] *adj.* 1.【解】血管的;【植】维管的;具维管束类植物的 2. 充满活力的;热情洋溢的

vase [vɑ:z, veis] *n.* 1.(装饰用的)瓶;花瓶 2.(家具等上的)瓶饰

vasectomize [væ'sektəmaiz] *vt.*【医】切除…的输精管,给…施行输精管切除术

vasectomy [væ'sektəmi] *n.*【医】输精管切除术

vaseline ['væsili:n] *n.*【化】石油冻,矿脂;[V-]凡士林(商品名)

vaso- *comb. form*【解】表示"血管","输精管":vasospasm, vasoligation

vasoconstriction [,veizəukən'strikʃən] *n.* 血管收缩

vasodilatation ['veizəudailə'teiʃən] *n.* 血管舒张

vasoligation [,veizəulai'geiʃən] *n.* 输精管结扎(术)

vasomotor [,veizəu'məutə] *adj.*(影响)血管舒缩的

vasospasm [,veizəu'spæzəm] *n.* 血管痉挛

vasotomy [væ'sɔtəmi] *n.* 输精管切断术

vasovasostomy [,vei'zəuvæ'zɔstəmi] *n.* 输精管吻合术

vassal ['væsl] *n.* 1.(封建时代的)封臣;臣属于人 2. 附庸;奴仆;奴隶 — *adj.* 1. 臣属的;为臣的 2. 奴仆的;为奴仆的;奴隶的

vast [vɑ:st] *adj.* 1. 巨大的,庞大的 2. 大量的,巨额的;浩瀚的 3. 广阔的;深远的 4.〈口〉非常的;莫大的 — *n.*〈诗〉茫

茫,无边无际的空间 ‖ ~**ly** *adv.* /~-**ness** *n.*

VAT *abbr.* value-added tax

vat [væt] *n.* 1.(染色、酿造等用的)大桶;大盆;瓮,缸 2.瓮染料制剂(桶)— (vatted;vatting) *vt.* 把…盛入大桶;在大桶里染(或处理)

Vatican ['vætikən] *n.* 1.梵蒂冈[欧洲](罗马教廷所在地) 2.[the ~]罗马教廷 ‖ ~**ism** *n.* 教皇至上论,梵蒂冈主义

vaudeville ['vəudəvil] *n.* 1.轻歌舞剧 2.杂耍

vault[1] [vɔːlt] *n.* 1.【建】拱顶;穹窿(状覆盖物) 2.(拱顶)地下室;地窖 3.(教堂下的)墓穴 4.(银行等的)金库(贵重物品储藏处) 5.【解】穹窿 — *vt.* 1.给…盖以拱顶 2.使作成拱形 — *vi.* 成穹状弯曲

vault[2] [vɔːlt] *vi.* 跳跃(尤指以手支撑跳跃或撑竿跳跃)— *vt.* 以手支撑跳过;撑竿跳过 — *n.* 1.跳跃;支撑跳跃;撑竿跳;(马的)腾跃

vaulting ['vɔːltiŋ] *adj.* 1.用于跳跃的;用于跳跃运动的:a ~ pole(撑竿跳高用的)撑竿/a ~ horse跳马 2.向上跳的;跳越的 3.过度的

vaunt [vɔːnt] *vt.* & *vi.* 自夸 — *n.* 自吹自擂;夸张自负之语

v. aux. *abbr.* verb auxiliary【语】助动词

vb. *abbr.* 1.verb 2.verbal

VCR *abbr.* videocassette recorder

V-Day ['viːdei] *n.*(第二次世界大战的)胜利日(= Victory Day)

've = have(如 I've = I have, you've = you have)

vector ['vektə] *n.* 1.【数】矢量,向量 2.(飞机)航线;罗盘航向 3.【天】辐射,矢径 4.【生】传病媒介;昆虫媒介者 5.动力;力量;影响 — *vt.*【空】引导(飞机)至指定的航向;给(飞机等)导航

Veep [viːp] *n.*〈美口〉[亦作 v-](尤指美国的)副总统

veer [viə] *vi.* 1.改变方向,转向;转变 2.【气】(风)顺转 3.【海】(船)顺风转向(船首向下风)改变船向 4.改变观点(或立场、态度等)— *vt.* 1.使改变方向 2.【海】使(船)改变航向 — *n.* 转向

Vega ['viːgə] *n.*【天】织女一,织女星

vegetable ['vedʒitəbl] *n.* 1.植物 2.蔬菜 3.植物人 — *adj.* 1.植物的;有植物性质的;由植物而来的;关于植物的 2.蔬菜的 3.(生活)呆板单调的;似植物的 ‖ **vegetably** *adv.* / **vegetal** ['vedʒitəl] *adj.*

vegetablize ['vedʒitəblaiz] *vt.* 使成植物人 — *vi.* 成为植物人;过植物人似的生活,过呆板单调的生活 ‖ ,vegetabli'zation *n.*

vegetarian [,vedʒi'tɛəriən] *n.* 1.吃素的人;素食主义者 2.食草动物 — *adj.* 1.素食的;素食者的;素食主义者的 2.全是蔬菜的,素菜的 ‖ ~**ism** *n.* 素食主义

vegetate ['vedʒiteit] *vi.* 1.植物似地生长 2.过呆板单调的生活 3.【医】(赘疣等)生长增殖

vegetation [,vedʒi'teiʃən] *n.* 1.【植】植被,植物的生长 2.[总称]植物,草木 3.呆板单调的生活 4.【医】赘生物,增殖体

vegetative ['vedʒitətiv] *adj.* 1.植物的;植物界的;植物性的 2.生长的;有生长力的;无性生殖的;营养生殖的 3.有关植物生长的;促使植物生长的;如植物那样生长的 4.植物人状态的;

活呆板单调的 **5.** 有关植物的营养和生长机能的

vehemence ['vi:iməns] *n.* 热烈；热心；强烈；猛烈；激烈

vehement ['vi:imənt] *adj.* **1.** 感情激烈的；热烈的 **2.** 强烈的；猛烈的；激烈的 ‖ ~ly *adv.*

vehicle ['vi:ikl] *n.* **1.** 运载工具；车辆；机动车；机械器具；交通工具；飞行器 **2.** (传达思想感情的)工具；传播媒介 **3.** 【药】赋形剂 **4.**【化】展色剂，(调)漆料

vehicular [vi'hikjulə] *adj.* **1.** 车辆的；用车辆运载的；供车辆通过的；车辆引起的 **2.** 作为媒介的

veil [veil] *n.* **1.** 面纱；面罩 **2.** 幕；帐、幔 **3.** 遮蔽物；掩饰物；借口；托辞 **4.** 修女的头巾；修女生活 **5.** 声嗓 **6.**【解】膜；【植】菌幕；【解】胎头羊膜 — *vt.* **1.** 以面纱遮掩 **2.** 遮盖；掩饰；隐蔽 — *vi.* 蒙上面纱

vein [vein] *n.* **1.** 静脉；(俗)血管 **2.**【地】【矿】矿脉；矿床；(地层或冰层中的)水脉 **3.**【动】翅脉；【植】叶脉 **4.** 纹理；纹路；条纹；裂纹 **5.** 性情；气质；才干；语调；风格；倾向；情绪 — *vt.* [常用被动语态] **1.** 使有脉络(或纹理) **2.** 似脉络(或纹理)般分布于 ‖ ~al *adj.* / ~ed *adj.*

veld(t) [velt] *n.* (非洲南部的)草原

vellum ['veləm] *n.* **1.** 精制犊皮纸；精制羊皮纸(书写或装帧用) **2.** 犊皮纸手抄稿 **3.** 仿羊皮纸(= ~ paper) — *adj.* 犊皮纸的；羊皮纸的；仿羊皮纸的 ‖ ~y *adj.*

velocipede [vi'ləsipi:d] *n.* **1.** 脚踏车(自行车的前身) **2.** (美)儿童三轮脚踏车 **3.** (铁路维修等用的)轨道轻便三轮车

velocity [vi'lɔsiti] *n.* **1.** 速度；速率 **2.** 迅速；快速 **3.** 周转率

velodrome ['vi:lədrəum] *n.* 赛车场

velour(s) [və'luə] *n.* ([复] velours [və'luə(z)]) 丝绒

velure [və'ljuə] *n.* **1.** 天鹅绒，丝绒；棉绒；拉绒织物；维罗呢；毡

velvet ['velvit] *n.* **1.** 天鹅绒，丝绒，平绒 **2.** 天鹅绒似的东西；柔软；平滑 **3.** 鹿角嫩皮，鹿茸 **4.** 赌赢的钱；意外益利 — *adj.* **1.** 天鹅绒制的；用天鹅绒覆盖的 **2.** 天鹅绒般的；柔软的；光滑的

velvety ['velviti] *adj.* **1.** 天鹅绒般柔软光滑的 **2.** (酒)醇和的；平和的

venal ['vi:nl] *adj.* **1.** 用金钱买得的，用贿赂得到的；贪污的；腐败的 ‖ ~ity [vi:'næliti] *n.* / ~ly *adv.*

venation [vi:'neiʃən] *n.*【生】(虫翅、树叶等的)脉序；(昆虫的)翅脉；(植物的)叶脉

vend [vend] *vt.* **1.** 出售(尤指沿街叫卖零售) **2.** 公开发表(意见) — *vi.* 出售货物；从事贩卖 ‖ ~er *n.* 卖主 / ~ing machine (出售糖果、香烟、食品或汽油等的)投币式自动售货机

vendetta [ven'detə] *n.* **1.** 族间血仇(尤指意大利某些地区&西西里岛等地的族间仇杀) **2.** 世仇；宿怨；长期争执(或不和)

vendor ['vendɔ:] *n.* **1.**【律】卖主 **2.** 小贩 **3.** 投币式自动售货机

veneer [vi'niə] *n.* **1.** 饰面薄板；镶板 **2.** (墙壁上的)饰面；护面(如砖、石等) **3.** 掩盖真情的外表；虚饰 — *vt.* **1.** 镶饰；饰(面) **2.** 胶合(薄片片) **3.** 虚饰

venerable ['venərəbl] *adj.* **1.** 可尊敬的，可崇敬的；年高德劭的 **2.** 历史悠久的；古老的 **3.** (用作英国国教副主教的尊称或天主教被列入圣徒者的头衔)尊敬的 ‖ ~venera'bility *n.*

venerate ['venəreit] *vt.* 尊敬；崇拜

veneration [ˌvenəˈreiʃən] *n.* 尊敬；崇拜

venereal [viˈniəriəl] *adj.* **1.** 性交的；性交引起的 **2.** 性病的；花柳病的 ‖ ~ **disease** 性病,花柳病

Venetian [viˈniːʃən] *adj.* (意大利城市)威尼斯的；威尼斯人的；威尼斯式的 — *n.* **1.** 威尼斯人 **2.** [v-]〈口〉[建]软百叶帘 **3.** [v-]〈纺〉直贡呢;威尼斯缩绒呢 ‖ ~ **blind** [建]软百叶帘

Venezuela [ˌveniˈzweilə] *n.* 委内瑞拉[拉丁美洲]

vengeance [ˈvendʒəns] *n.* 报仇,报复,复仇

vengeful [ˈvendʒful] *adj.* **1.** 有报仇心理的；图谋报复的 **2.** 报复(性)的 ‖ ~**ly** *adv.* / ~**ness** *n.*

venial [ˈviːniəl] *adj.* 可原谅的,可宽恕的；(错误)轻微的

Venice [ˈvenis] *n.* 威尼斯[意大利东北部港市]

venison [ˈvenizn] *n.* **1.** 野味 **2.** 鹿肉

venom [ˈvenəm] *n.* **1.** (毒蛇等的)毒液、(一般)毒物 **2.** 恶意；恶毒的话(或行为) — *vt.* 放毒;使有毒;毒化

venomous [ˈvenəməs] *adj.* **1.** 有毒的；分泌毒液的；有毒腺的 **2.** 恶意的；恶毒的；狠毒的 ‖ ~**ly** *adv.*

venous [ˈviːnəs] *adj.* **1.** 静脉的;在静脉中的 **2.** 有脉的；多脉的

vent[1] [vent] *n.* **1.** 出口,出路;漏孔 **2.** 通风孔;(烟雾、蒸汽等的)排放口 **3.** (苏格兰)烟囱,烟道 **3.** (管乐器的)指孔 **4.** (旧式枪、炮的)火门 **5.** 火山口 **6.** (鸟、虫、鱼的)肛门 **7.** [只用单](感情等的)发泄,吐露 — *vt.* **1.** 给…开孔;给…一个出口 **2.** 排放;排出 **3.** 发泄(感情)

vent[2] [vent] *n.* (上衣背部或裙子等的)开衩,衩

ventilate [ˈventileit] *vt.* **1.** 使通风,使通气；使换气；给…装置通风设备 **2.** 把…公开;公开讨论(问题,意见等) **3.** [医]使(血液)吸收氧气 ‖ **ventilator** *n.* **1.** 通风装置；排气风扇；送风机;通气口 **2.** 把事情公诸于众的人;引起公众注意的事

ventilation [ˌventiˈleiʃən] *n.* **1.** 通风；空气流通 **2.** 通风设备；通气法 **3.** 公开讨论 **4.**[医]供氧,换气

ventral [ˈventrəl] *adj.* **1.** [解][动]腹的,腹面的；前腹的 **2.** [植](叶)向下一面的,内面的 — *n.* [动]腹鳍(昆虫的)腹面

ventricle [ˈventrikl] *n.* [解]室;心室;脑室;(动物体内的)腔室 ‖ **ventricular** [venˈtrikjulə] *adj.*

ventriloquism [venˈtriləkwizəm], **ventriloquy** [venˈtriləkwi] *n.* 口技 ‖ **ventriloquist** *n.* 口技表演者

venture [ˈventʃə] *n.* **1.** 冒险;冒险行动 **2.** 冒险事业；商业冒险；投机 **3.** 用于投机事业的商船(或货物);糟注 — *vt.* **1.** 冒…的风险 **2.** 拿…进行投机 **3.** 敢于;大胆表示(或提出) — *vi.* 冒险；冒险行事；冒险前进(*on, upon*)

venturesome [ˈventʃəsəm] *adj.* **1.** 好冒险的;大胆的 **2.** 危险的;有风险的 ‖ ~**ly** *adv.* / ~**ness** *n.*

venturous [ˈventʃərəs] *adj.* **1.** 好冒险的;大胆的 **2.** 危险的;有风险的 ‖ ~**ly** *adv.* / ~**ness** *n.*

venue [ˈvenjuː] *n.* **1.** [律]犯罪地点；审判地;(诉状上)审判地的记载 **2.** (事件的)发生地点,举行场所；会场 **3.** (美)(争论中所持的)立场

Venus [ˈviːnəs] *n.* **1.** [罗神]维纳斯(爱和美的女神) **2.** 维纳斯像 **3.** 美女 **4.** 性爱;情欲 **5.** [天]金星,太白星

veracious [vəˈreiʃəs] *adj.* **1.** 讲实话的；诚实的 **2.** 正确的；真实的

veracity [vəˈræsiti] *n.* **1.** 说话老实；诚实 **2.** 真实(性)；正确(性)

veranda(h) [vəˈrændə] *n.* 游廊；走廊；阳台

verb [vəːb] *n.*【语】动词 — *adj.* 动词的；动词性质的；用作动词的

verbal [ˈvəːbəl] *adj.* **1.** 用言辞的；用文字的；文字上的 **2.** 口头的；非书面的 **3.** 逐字的；一字不差的 **4.**【语】动词的；动词性质的；由动词构成的；用以构成动词的 — *n.*【语】动词的非限定形式(指不定式、分词和动名词) **5.**〈英俚〉(尤指罪犯被捕时的)口头供认 — *vt.*〈英俚〉(逮捕时)诱使…招供，使招认 ‖ ~ly *adv.*

verbalize [ˈvəːbəlaiz] *vt.* **1.** 用言辞(或文字)表达 **2.** 使动词化 — *vi.* 用言辞表达 ‖ **verbali'zation** *n.*

verbatim [vəːˈbeitim] *adv.* 逐字地；一字不差地 — *adj.* 逐字的；一字不差的

verbena [vəːˈbiːnə] *n.*【植】马鞭草

verbiage [ˈvəːbiidʒ] *n.* **1.** 冗词，赘语 **2.** 措辞，用语

verbose [vəːˈbəus] *adj.* 罗唆的；累赘的；冗长的 ‖ ~ly *adv.* / **verbosity** [vəːˈbɔsiti] *n.*

verboten [vəːˈbəutən]〈德〉*adj.* (被当局)明令禁止的，严禁的

verdant [ˈvəːdənt] *adj.* **1.** 青翠的，碧绿的；长满绿色植物的 **2.** 稚嫩的，不老练的，无经验的 ‖ **verdancy** *n.*

verdict [ˈvəːdikt] *n.* **1.**【律】(陪审团的)裁定 **2.** 定论；判断性意见

verdigris [ˈvəːdigris] *n.* (铜器等上的)铜绿，乙酸铜，醋酸铜

Verdun [vɛəˈdʌŋ, vɛːˈdɔŋ] *n.* **1.** 凡尔登[法国东北部城市] **2.** 凡尔登[加拿大东南部城市]

verdure [ˈvəːdʒə] *n.* **1.** 青绿，青翠；青葱的草木 **2.** 生气勃勃；欣欣向荣；新鲜，清新

verge [vəːdʒ] *n.* **1.** 边，边沿，边缘；起始点，始端 **2.** 范围；区域；界限 **3.** [英]山墙交瓦，檐口瓦，滴水瓦；(花坛等的)植草边沿；[英]路边，路肩 **3.** (钟表的)摆轮心轴 **4.** (标志职权的)权杖；节杖 **5.** [英史]王室(司法官)的辖区 — *vi.* **1.** 接近；濒临 **2.** 处在边沿(或边缘)的 — *vt.* 处在…的边沿(或边缘)；构成…的边沿(或边缘)

verifiable [ˈverifaiəbl] *adj.* 可证实的；可核实的

verification [ˌverifiˈkeiʃən] *n.* **1.** 证实，查清；查对，核实 **2.**【律】(用宣誓等)证明属实，证明属实的宣誓(或证词)

verifier [ˈverifaiə] *n.* **1.** 证明者；核实者 **2.** 作证者 **3.** (数据)核对器

verify [ˈverifai] *vt.* **1.** 证实；证明；查对；查清；核实 **2.**【律】(以宣誓)证明…属实

verily [ˈverili] *adv.* **1.** 真正地；肯定地 **2.** 忠实地；真实地

verisimilitude [ˌverisiˈmilitjuːd] *n.* **1.** 逼真；貌似真实 **2.** 逼真的事物；貌似真实的事物；似乎真实的话

veritable [ˈveritəbl] *adj.* 确实的；真正的；名副其实的 ‖ ~ness *n.* / **veritably** *adv.*

verity [ˈveriti] *n.* **1.** 真实(性) **2.** 真理；事实 **3.** 忠诚；正直

vermicelli [ˌvəːmiˈseli] 〈意〉*n.* 细面条，线面；(糕饼上的)巧克力装饰线条

vermicide [ˈvəːmisaid] *n.* 杀蠕虫药；杀肠虫药

vermiform [ˈvəːmifɔːm] *adj.* 蠕虫状的，蚓

状的 ‖ ~ **appendix** 【解】阑尾, 蚓突

vermifuge ['vəːmifjuːdʒ] *n.* 驱蠕虫药; 驱肠虫药 — *adj.* 驱蠕虫(或肠虫)的

vermil(l)ion [vəˈmiljən] *n.* 1. 银朱, 朱砂, 硫化汞 2. 朱红色 — *adj.* 朱红色的 — *vt.* 涂朱红色于

vermin ['vəːmin] [单复同] *n.* 1. 害虫; 体外寄生虫;害兽;害鸟 2. (喻)害人虫; 歹徒

verminous ['vəːminəs] *adj.* 1. 害虫的, 似害虫的 2. 长有(虱等)害虫的;有害的 3. 引起害虫孳生的;污秽的 4. 由害虫引起的

Vermont [vəˈmɔnt] *n.* 佛蒙特 [美国州名]

vernacular [vəˈnækjulə] *n.* 1. 本国语;本地话,方言 2. 行话 3.(动植物的)俗名 — *adj.* 1. 用本国语(写)的;用方言(写)的;本地话的,方言的;白话的 2. 本国的;本地的,乡土的 3.(动植物)俗名的

vernal ['vəːnl] *adj.* 1. 春天的;春天发生的 2. 春天似的;和煦的;清新的 ‖ -**ly** *adv.* ‖ ~ **equinox** 春分;春分点

vernalize ['vəːnəlaiz] *vt.* 使春化(指播种前用低温处理种子) ‖ **,vernali'zation** *n.* 春化(作用);春化处理

vernier ['vəːniə] *n.*(量具等的)微调装置; 游标;游标尺; 【空】微调发动机 ‖ ~ **engine**, ~ **rocket** 微调发动机

Veronal ['verənəl] *n.* 【药】佛罗拿(barbital 巴比妥的商品名,一种安眠药)

verrucose [vəˈruːkəus] *adj.* 疣的;生疣的; 多疣的

Versailles [vɛəˈsai] *n.* 凡尔赛 [法国北部城市]

versatile ['vəːsətail] *adj.* 1. 多方面的;多才多艺的 2. 万用的, 通用的, 多方面适用的 3. 活动的, 万向的 4.(鸟趾,昆

虫触角、附着于花丝的花药等)能转动的 5. 易变的, 反复无常的 ‖ -**ly** *adv.* / **versatility** [,vəːsəˈtiliti] *n.*(才能、用途等的)多面性

verse [vəːs] *n.* 1. 诗句;诗行;诗节 2. 诗;诗体;韵文 3.(基督教《圣经》中的)节, 句;(圣歌等的)独唱部 — *vt.* 1. 用诗表达 2. 把…改写成诗 — *vi.* 作诗

versed [vəːst] *adj.* 通晓的, 精通的;熟练的

versify ['vəːsifai] *vi.* 作诗 — *vt.* 1. 用诗表达 2. 把(散文等)改写成诗 ‖ **versification** [,vəːsifiˈkeiʃən] *n.* 作诗(法) / **versifier** *n.*

version ['vəːʃən] *n.* 1. 译文;译本 2.(根据个人观点对事件等的)描述;说法 3. [常作 V-]基督教《圣经》的译本 4. 改写本;经改编的乐曲等 5.(演员等对作品、角色等的)独到处理,独特表演 6. 版本;(一事物的)变化形式;变体 7. 【医】(胎位)倒转术;(子宫)倾侧

versus ['vəːsəs] *prep.* 1.(诉讼、比赛等中)对;…为对手(= against;常略作 v. 或 vs.) 2. 与…相对;与…相比

vertebra ['vəːtibrə] ([复] **vertebrae** ['vəːtibriː]或 **vertebras**) *n.* 【解】椎骨, 脊柱 ‖ -**l** *adj.* 椎骨的, 脊椎的;由椎骨组成的;有脊椎的

vertebrate ['vəːtibrit] *n.* 脊椎动物 — *adj.* 1. 有椎骨的, 有脊椎的;脊椎动物的 2.(作品等)结构严密的

vertex ['vəːteks] ([复] **vertexes** 或 **vertices** ['vəːtisiz]) *n.* 1. 最高点, 最高点 2. 【解】头顶 3. 【数】顶, 极点 4. 【天】天顶

vertical ['vəːtikəl] *adj.* 1. 垂直的;直立的;立式的;垂直航摄照片的 2. 顶点的至高点的;最高级的 3.(解)头顶的 4. 【植】纵长的,直生的 5.(两个或两个以上企业统管生产和销售全部过程的)

垂直合并的，纵向联合的 — n. 1. 垂直线；垂直面 2. 垂直方向；垂直位置 3.【建】竖杆 4. 垂直航摄照片(= ～ aerial photograph) 5. 立式钢琴 ‖ ~ly adv.

vertigo ['vɜːtigəu] ([复] vertigoes 或 vertigines[vɜː'tidʒiniːz]) n. 1. 眩晕 2.（心境等的）迷惘 3.（牛、羊等的）旋回病

verve [vɜːv] n. 1.（古）天资，才能 2.（文艺作品的）气势；神韵 3. 精力；生气；热情

very ['veri] adv. 1. [用于修饰形容词、副词或分词]很，甚，极其，非常 2. [常用于形容词最高级前，以加强语气]最大程度地；完全；充分；真正地 3. [not ～][表示语气的委婉]不很，不大，不一 — adj. 1. 真的，真正的，真实的 2. [与the、this 或 my、your 等连用，以加强语气]正是那个；正是所要的；恰好的；甚至于，连；同一的；极其，十足的，绝对的，完全的 4. 仅仅的，只 5. 特别的，特殊的

vesicant ['vesikənt] adj. 发疱的，起疱的 — n. 起疱剂；起疱毒气(指芥子气等化学战剂)

vesicle ['vesikl] n.【解】【植】泡；囊 2.【医】水疱 3.【地】气泡

vesper ['vespə] n. 1.（诗）夜晚，黄昏 2. 晚祷；晚祷曲 3. 晚祷钟(= ～ bell) 4.[V-]【天】长庚星，昏星 — adj. 1. 夜晚的 2. 晚祷的

vessel ['vesl] n. 1. 容器，器皿(尤指盛液体的如缸、壶、瓶、碗、杯等) 2. 船；飞船；飞机(尤指水上飞机) 3.【解】血管；脉管；【植】导管 4.【宗】人(指被看作一种容器来接受某种精神的或超自然的)

vest[vest] n. 1.（英）汗背心 2.（美）背心，马甲(= (英) waistcoat) ；(作战等时穿的)防护衣 3.(标有运动员编号的)

运动背心；女式背心 4.（女子服装前面的）V 形装饰布 5.（古）外衣；法衣；(法衣、祭服等)袍 — vi. 1. 使穿衣服；给予衣服 (法衣、祭服等) 2. 授予，赋予，给予 — vi. 1. 穿衣服；穿祭服 2.（财产、权力等）属，归属(in)

vestal ['vestl] adj. 1. 女灶神维斯太(Vesta)的；信奉女灶神维斯太(Vesta)的 2. 贞洁的；童贞的 — n. 1. 信奉女灶神的处女 2. 贞女；处女 3. 修女；尼姑

vestibule ['vestibjuːl] n. 1. 门厅，前厅 2.（美）(火车车厢末端的)通过台，折棚，通廊 3.【解】前庭 4. 途径 — vt. 1. 为…设置门厅 2. 以通廊连接 ‖ **vestibular** [ve'stibjulə] adj.

vestige ['vestidʒ] n. 1. 痕迹；遗迹；残余 2.【生】退化器官 3. 一点儿，丝毫 ‖ **vestigial** [ves'tidʒiəl] adj. 发育不全的，退化的

vestment ['vestmənt] n. 1. 官服；礼服 2. 法衣，祭服 3.[～s]盛服 4. 覆盖物

vest-pocket ['vest'pɒkit] adj. 1. 可放入背心口袋的；袖珍的；小型的，微型的 ‖ ～ park(市区的)小公园

vestry ['vestri] n. 1.（教堂的）法衣圣器储藏室 2.（教堂的)主日学校教室；祈祷室 3. 教区会议；教区委员会 ‖ ～man n. 教区委员(或代表)

vesture ['vestʃə] n. 1. 衣服；覆盖物 2.【律】土地上生长的全部植物(不包括树木) — vt. 使穿衣服；覆盖

Vesuvius [vi'suːviəs] n. 维苏威火山 [意大利西南部]

vet[vet] n. & adj.（口）= veteran

vet[vet] n.（口）兽医 — (vetted; vetting) vt. 1. 诊治(人或牲畜)；给…作体格检查 2. 审查(稿件等) — vi. 当兽医

vetch [vetʃ] n.【植】巢菜，野豌豆

vetchling [ˈvetʃliŋ] *n*.【植】山黧豆

veteran [ˈvetərən] *n*. 1. 老兵,老战士;老手,富有经验的人 2.〈美〉退伍军人: *Veterans*(') Day (美国)退伍军人节(十月份的第四个星期一) 3.(常指齐胸处直径超过两英尺的)老树 — *adj*. 老战士的;老练的;经验丰富的

veterinarian [ˌvetəriˈnɛəriən] *n*. 兽医

veterinary [ˈvetərinəri] *adj*. 兽医的

veto [ˈviːtəu] ([复]vetoes) *n*. 否决;禁止;否决权 — *vt*. 否决;禁止

VEWS *abbr*. very early warning system 极早期预警系统,超远程预警系统

vex [veks] *vt*. 1. 使烦恼,使苦恼,使痛苦;使恼火 2. 折磨 3.〈诗〉使汹涌;使动荡 ‖ ~**ed** *adj*. /~**edly** *adv*.

vexation [vekˈseiʃən] *n*. 1. 烦恼,苦恼,伤脑筋 2. 恼火;着急 3. 苦恼的原因;使人恼火的事情 ‖ **vexatious** *adj*.

VHF, vhf *abbr*. very high frequency【无】甚高频

VI *abbr*. 1. viscosity index【油】粘度指数 2. volume indicator【无】声量指示器 3. Virgin Islands 维尔京群岛[拉丁美洲]

v. i. *abbr*. 1. verb intransitive【语】不及物动词 2.〈拉〉*vide infra* 见下,参下(= see below)

via [ˈvaiə] *prep*. 1. 经过,经由;取道 2. 通过(某种手段或某人)

viable [ˈvaiəbl] *adj*. 1.(胎儿等)能活的;子宫外能活的 2.(动物、植物等)能(在特殊气候中)生存的;(种子)能生长发育的 3. 可行的

viaduct [ˈvaiədʌkt] *n*. 高架桥;跨线桥;高架铁路(或道路)

vial [ˈvaiəl] *n*. 小瓶;小药水瓶 —(vial(l)ed; vial(l)ing) — *vt*. 放…于小瓶中

viand [ˈvaiənd] *n*.[~s]各种食品;珍馐美味

vibrant [ˈvaibrənt] *adj*. 1. 颤动的;振动的 2. 振动作响的;响亮的 3. 有活力的;活跃的;激动的 4.【语】声带振动的 ‖ **vibrancy** *n*.

vibrate [vaiˈbreit] *vt*. 1. 使颤动;使振动;使震动 2. 使摆动;用摆动指示 — *vi*. 1. 颤动;振动;震动;(感情)激动 2. 摆动;摇摆;犹豫,踌躇

vibration [vaiˈbreiʃən] *n*. 1. 颤动;振动;震动 2. 摆动,摇摆 3. 激动 4. 犹豫

vibrator [vaiˈbreitə] *n*. 1. 震动装置;振动器;【电】振子;【建】(混凝土)振捣器 2.【医】振动按摩器 3.【机】游丝摆轮;振动筛;振动式铆钉枪 4.(电铃等中的)断续器 5.【音】簧片,簧舌,弦

vibratory [ˈvaibrətəri] *adj*. 1. 振动的 2. 震动(性)的;引起震动的

viburnum [vaiˈbəːnəm] *n*. 荚蒾;(药用)荚蒾树皮

vicar [ˈvikə] *n*. 1.(英国国教)教区牧师 2. 代牧 3. 代理人,代表者;替代物 ‖ ~**ial** [viˈkɛəriəl] *adj*. /~**ship** *n*. ‖ **Vicar of Christ** (天主教)教皇

vicarage [ˈvikəridʒ] *n*.〈英〉教区牧师的住宅(或俸禄、职权)

vicarious [viˈkɛəriəs] *adj*. 1. 代理的;代理人的 2. 替代别人的;(想象别人的苦乐等而)产生同感(或共鸣)的 3.【医】替代的,错位的 ‖ ~**ly** *adv*. /~**ness** *n*.

vice[1] [vais] *n*. 1. 罪恶,坏事;不道德行为 2. 恶习;堕落,腐化 3.(文体、性格上的)缺点,瑕疵 4.(生理上的)缺陷(或畸形等) 5.(马、犬等牲口的)恶癖,劣性 6.[V-](旧时英国道德剧中)象征罪恶的角色 7. 卖淫;淫乱 ‖ ~ **squad**〈美〉(取缔卖淫、赌博等的)警察缉捕队

vice[2] [vais]〈主英〉*n*.(台)虎钳 — *vt*.

钳住，夹住

vice³ ['vais] n. 〈口〉代理人；任副职者(如副总统、大学副校长等)

vice⁴ ['vaisi] prep. 代替；接替

vice- *pref.* 表示"副"，"次"；"代理"：*vice*-president

vice admiral 海军中将

vice-chancellor ['vais'tʃɑːnsələ] n. 〈英〉 1. (大学主持日常工作的)副校长 2. 副大法官

vice-president ['vais'prezidənt] n. 副主管人；副职位长；副会长；副总裁；副董事长；副总统 ‖ **vice-presidency** n.

viceroy ['vaisrɔi] n. 1. (代表国王管辖行省或殖民地的)总督 2. (产于美洲的)副王蛱蝶 ‖ ~ **al** adj. /~ **ship** n.

vice versa ['vaisi 'vəːsə] 〈拉〉反过来也一样，反之亦然

vicinage ['visinidʒ] n. [总称] 1. (某一地点的)邻近地区，周围地区 2. 邻近地区的人们 3. 接近，邻近 4. 邻里关系

vicinity [vi'siniti] n. 1. 附近；邻近 2. 周围地区，邻近地区；近处 3. 密切的关系

vicious ['viʃəs] adj. 1. 邪恶的；堕落的 2. 恶意的；恶毒的；凶恶的 3. 恶性的；险恶的；烈性的 4. 有错误的；有毛病的 ‖ ~ **ly** adv. / ~ **ness** n.

vicissitude [vi'sisitjuːd] n. 1. [~s] 世事变化，变迁 2. 变化无常，多变 3. 〈古〉规则变化，交替

victim ['viktim] n. 1. 受害者；牺牲者；受骗者 2. 牺牲品；(献祭用的)牺牲

victimize ['viktimaiz] vt. 1. 使牺牲；使受害 2. 欺骗，使吃亏 3. 开除，惩处(罢工者等) 4. (全部地)毁坏(庄稼等) ‖ **victimi'zation** n.

victimology [ˌvikti'mɔlədʒi] n. 受害者心

理学 ‖ **victimologist** n.

victor ['viktə] n. & adj. 胜利者(的)；战胜者(的)；得胜者(的)

Victoria [vik'tɔːriə] n. 1. 维多利亚[塞舌尔首都] 2. 维多利亚[澳大利亚州名] 3. 维多利亚[加拿大大西洋沿岸港市] 4. 维多利亚(女子名) ‖ ~ **Cross** (英国)维多利亚十字勋章(授于有杰出功勋的军人；略作 VC)

victorious [vik'tɔːriəs] adj. 胜利的；战胜的；得胜的 ‖ ~ **ly** adv.

victory ['viktəri] n. 1. 胜利；战胜；成功，征服 2. [V-] 【罗神】维多利亚(胜利女神)

victual ['vitəl] n. [~s] 饮食，食品；谷物—(victual-(l)ed, victual(l)ing) vt. 给供应(或储备)食物 — vi. 1. (家畜等)进食，吃 2. (船只)储备食物 ‖ **victual-(l)er** n. 1. 〈英〉客栈老板；饮食商贩 2. (船或舰队等的)食品供应人 3. 食品供应船

vicuña [vi'kjuːnə] n. 1. 【动】(产于南美的)小羊驼，骆马 2. 骆马毛；骆马绒(服装)

vide ['vaidi] 〈拉〉vt. 参阅，参看，另见

videlicet [vi'diːliset] 〈拉〉adv. 即，就是说(= namely；略作 viz.)

video ['vidiəu] adj. 电视的；视频的；(电视)图像的；录像的 —n. ([复]videos) n. 1. (电视)图像；〈口〉图像质量；录像(节目)；录像机；〈美口〉电视；视频信号 — vt. 录制，制作…的录像；〈口〉用录像带播送 ‖ ~ **amplifier** 视频放大器 / ~ **camera** 录像机 / ~ **film** 电视片；录像片 / ~ **frequency** 视频 / ~ **game** 电视游戏

videocassette [ˌvidiəukæ'set, ˌvidiəukæ'set] n. 盒式录像带 ‖ ~ **recorder** 盒式磁带录像机

videoconference [ˌvidiəu'kɔnfərəns] n. 电

视会议 ‖ **videoconferencing** n. 电视会议的召开

videodisc, **videodisk** ['vidiəudisk] n. 电视唱片，录像盘，影碟

videophone ['vidiəufəun] n. 可视电话

videoplayer ['vidiəupleiə] n. 放像机

videotape ['vidiəuteip] n. 录像磁带；(一段)磁带录像内容 — vt. 把…录在录像磁带上 ‖ ~ed adj. ‖ ~ recorder 磁带录像机 / ~ recording 磁带录像(内容)

videotex(t) ['vidiəuteks(t)] 'n. 可视图文，可视数据

vie [vai] (vying) vi. 相争；竞争 (with, for)；~ with sb. for sth. 与某人争夺某物

Vienna [vi'enə] n. 维也纳(奥地利首都)

Vientiane [vjen'tjɑːn] n. 万象(老挝首都)

Viet [vjet] 〈口〉 n. 1. = Viet Nam 2. = Vietnamese — adj. = Vietnamese

Viet Nam, Vietnam [vjet'næm] 越南[东南亚国家]

Vietnamese [vjetnə'miːz] adj. 越南的；越南人的；越南语的 —[单复同] n. 1. 越南人 2. 越南语

view [vjuː] n. 1. 看，观看 2. 视力；视域；眼界 3. 看见的东西；景色；风景画(或照) 4. 观点，见解；看法 5. 目的；希望；前途；展望 6. 思量，考虑；估量 7.(制图用语)视图 8.【律】(对犯罪现场的)查看，察看 9. 综观；印象；一览 — vt. 1. 看，观看 2. 看待；检查 3. 考虑；估计；期待；展望 4. 查看，察看 ‖ ~er n. 观察者；看电视者；【律】视察员(上)；观察哨；取镜器 / ~less adj. 〈诗〉看不见的；〈美〉不表示意见的；无景色的 ‖ ~point n. 观察点，视点；观点，看法；见解

vigil ['vidʒil] n. 1. 守夜，值夜 2. 警戒；监

视 2.【宗】宗教节日的前夕；(节日前夜的)守夜；[常~s]宗教节日前夜的祈祷(仪式)

vigilance ['vidʒiləns] n. 1. 警戒；警惕(性) 2. 警醒症；失眠症 ‖ ~ committee (美国)治安维持会(一种民间组织)

vigilant ['vidʒilənt] adj. 警备着的，警惕着的；警醒的 ‖ ~ly adv.

vigilante [vidʒi'lænti] n. (美国)治安维持会成员

vignette [vi'njet] n. 1. 蔓叶花饰；小花饰 2. 半身晕映照，虚光照(或画像等) 3. (文字简洁优美的)短文，花边文字 — vt. 1.使(照片等)晕映，把…印放为虚光照；为…摄制晕映照 2. 用蔓叶花饰装饰 3. 简洁而优美地描写

vigor ['vigə] n. 〈美〉= vigour

vigorous ['vigərəs] adj. 1. 朝气蓬勃的，精力充沛的；壮健的，苗壮的 2. 强有力的 ‖ ~ly adv.

vigo(u)r ['vigə] n. 1. 活力，精力 2. 壮健，苗壮 3. 力量；气势；魄力 4.(法律上的)效力

Viking ['vaikiŋ] n. 1. (八至十世纪时劫掠欧洲海岸的)北欧海盗 2. [v-] 海盗 3. 斯堪的纳维亚人

Vila ['viːlə] n. 维拉港[瓦努阿图首都]

vile [vail] adj. 1. 卑鄙的；可耻的；邪恶的；令人作呕的；讨厌的 2. 坏透的，极不足道的，无价值的 ‖ ~ly adv. / ~ness n.

vilify ['vilifai] vt. 1. 逐毁；中伤；诽谤；辱骂 2. 贬低 ‖ **vilification** [vilifi'keiʃən] n. / **vilifier** n.

villa ['vilə] n. 1. 别墅 2. 〈英〉花园住宅；乡村房地产

village ['vilidʒ] n. 1. 乡村，村庄 2. [the ~][总称]村民 3. (动物的)群落 — adj. 村的，村庄的，乡下的 ‖ ~r n. 村

民,乡下人

villain ['vilən] *n.* 1. 坏人,恶棍(戏剧、小说等中的)反派角色,反面人物 2.〈口〉〈谑〉家伙;小淘气 3.〈vilin〉= villein 4.〈古〉乡巴佬,粗汉

villainous ['vilənəs] *adj.* 1. 坏人的,恶棍的;恶棍似的 2. 腐化堕落的;罪恶的;卑鄙可耻的 3.〈口〉坏透的;讨厌的

villainy ['vilənɪ] *n.* 1. 恶行;凶恶 2. 罪恶(行为);堕落(行为)

villein ['vilɪn] *n.*【史】隶农

villus ['viləs] ([复] villi ['vilai]) *n.*【解】【植】绒毛;纤毛,长柔毛

Vilnius ['vilnjus] *n.* 维尔纽斯[立陶宛首都]

vim [vim] *n.* 活力,精力;力量

vindicate ['vindikeit] *vt.* 1. 维护;辩护 2. 证明(一无辜(或无辜)3. 证明…正确(或真实,正当,合理)4.〈古〉为…报仇 5. 依法确定对(财产等)的所有权 ‖ ,vindi'cation *n.* / vindicator *n.*

vindictive [vin'diktiv] *adj.* 1. 志在报复的;复仇的 2. 恶意的;怀恨的 3. 惩罚性的 ‖ ~ly *adv.* / ~ness *n.*

vine [vain] *n.* 1. 葡萄树 2. 藤本植物;蔓,藤 — *vi.* 形成(或长成)藤蔓 ‖ ~yard ['vinjəd] *n.* 葡萄园

vinegar ['vinigə] *n.* 1. 醋;【医】醋剂 2.(言语,性格或态度所表示的)尖酸;刻薄;乖戾 3. 充沛的精力 — *vt.* 加醋于;用醋处理;用醋剂治疗 ‖ ~y *adj.* 1. 醋(似)的;酸的 2. 刻薄的,尖酸的;乖戾的

vinous ['vainəs] *adj.* 1. 酒的;有酒味的 2. 嗜酒的;饮酒引起的 3. 有酒的颜色的

vintage ['vintidʒ] *n.* 1. 收葡萄;葡萄收获期 2. 酿酒期;酿酒期 3.(一地一季的)葡萄收获量(或酿酒量)4. 酒;(特指某,

葡萄名产地、某丰收年所酿造并标明年份窖藏的)佳酿酒 5. 同年代的一批产品;同一批产生的人物 6. 制造的时期;开始存在的时期;寿命 — *vt.* 为酿酒而收(葡萄)— *vi.* 收葡萄 — *adj.* 1. 古老而享有声誉的;古典的 2. 旧式的,老式的;过时的 ‖ ~ car〈英〉(尤指一九一七年至一九三○年间制造的)老式汽车 / ~ year(佳酿酒的)酿制年份

vintner ['vintnə] *n.* 酒商

viny ['vaini] *adj.* 1.(似)藤本植物的;(似)葡萄藤的 2. 多藤本植物(或葡萄藤)的 3.(植物)藤系发达的

vinyl ['vainl] *n.* 1.【化】乙烯基 2. 聚乙稀基织物(或薄膜)3.〈口〉压制唱片的材料;唱片

vinylite ['vainilait] *n.*(用于制造唱片的)维涅莱树脂,乙烯基树脂

Vinylon ['vainilɔn] *n.* 维尼纶〈聚乙烯醇缩醛纤维的统称〉

viol ['vaiəl] *n.*(中世纪的)(六弦)提琴(现代小提琴即由它发展而来)

viola[1] ['vi'əulə] *n.* 中提琴;中提琴手

viola[2] ['vaiələ] *n.*【植】堇菜

violable ['vaiələbl] *adj.*(条例等)可违反的;易受侵犯的;易被妨碍的;易受扰乱的

violate ['vaiəleit] *vt.* 1. 违犯,违背,违反 2. 侵犯;妨碍;扰乱 3. 亵渎(神圣)站污,污损 4. 污辱;强奸 ‖ violator *n.* 1. 违犯者,违背者,违反者 2. 侵犯者;妨碍者;亵渎者 3. 强奸者

violation [,vaiə'leiʃən] *n.* 1. 违犯,违背,违反 2. 侵犯;侵害;妨碍,妨害;亵渎 3.【体】违例 4. 亵渎,强暴

violence ['vaiələns] *n.* 1. 猛烈;激烈;强烈 2. 暴力;暴力行为 3. 侵犯;亵渎,不

敬 4. 狂热性；狂热行为 5.（对文字的）歪曲，篡改

violent ['vaiələnt] *adj.* 1. 猛烈的；激烈的，强烈的 2. 极端的，极度的 3. 暴力的，强暴的 4. 由暴力引起的 5. 歪曲的，曲解的 ‖ ~ly *adv.*

violet ['vaiəlit] *n.* 1. 英菜；非洲紫苣苔；赤堇 2. 紫罗兰色，紫色 3. 紫色小蝴蝶 — *adj.* 紫罗兰色的 ‖ ~ ray 紫外线；紫色光线

violin [,vaiə'lin] *n.* 1. 小提琴 2. 小提琴手 ‖ ~ist *n.* 小提琴手

violoncello [,vaiələn'tʃeləu] *n.* 大提琴；大提琴音栓 ‖ **violoncellist** *n.* 大提琴手

viomycin [,vaiə'maisin] *n.* [微] 紫霉素（一种治结核病药）

VIP, Vip *abbr.* very important person 要人

viper ['vaipə] *n.* 1. [动] 蝰蛇 2. 毒蛇 3. 毒如蛇蝎的人；险恶的人 4. 〈美俚〉毒品贩子

virago [vi'rɑ:gəu] ([复] virago(e)s) *n.* 1. 泼妇，悍妇 2. 〈古〉魁梧而有男子气的女人

viral ['vaiərəl] *adj.* 病毒(性)的；病毒引起的 ‖ ~ly *adv.*

vireo ['viriəu] ([复] vireos) *n.*（产于美洲的）绿鹃

virgin ['və:dʒin] *n.* 1. 处女 2. [V-] [宗] 圣母马利亚（= the Blessed Virgin Mary）3. [宗] 贞女 4.〈罕〉童男 5. [动] 孤雌生殖的雌虫；未交配过的雌性动物 6. [V-] （占星术中的）室女宫 — *adj.* 1. 处女(般)的；贞洁的 2.（昆虫）未受精而产卵的；孤雌生殖的 3. 未开发的；未经利用的 3. 纯洁的；未玷污的 4. 首次的，创始的 5. 纯粹的，纯的 6. [化]（植物油）初榨的，直馏的 7. [冶] 从矿石直接提取的，原生的

virginal ['və:dʒinl] *n.* 1. 处女(般)的；

有处女特点的 2. 纯洁的；未玷污的 3. [动] 未受精而产卵的，孤雌生殖的

Virginia [və'dʒinjə] *n.* 1. 弗吉尼亚（美国州名）2. 弗吉尼亚烟草

virginity [və:'dʒiniti] *n.* 1. 童贞，处女性；纯洁 2. 未婚女子的独身生活

virginium [və'dʒiniəm] *n.* [化] 铽

virgule ['və:gju:l] *n.* 斜线号（即"/"）

virile ['virail] *adj.* 1. 男性的；有男性生殖力的 2. 男的，男子的 3. 有男子气概的，精力充沛的；强有力的；雄浑的

virility [vi'riliti] *n.* 1.（男子的）成年时期；男性生殖力 2. 男子气慨；精力充沛；刚强有力；活力

virology [,vaiə'rɔlədʒi] *n.* [医] 病毒学

virtu [və:'tu:] *n.* 1. 艺术品爱好；古董癖 2. [总称] 艺术品；古董

virtual ['və:tjuəl] *adj.* 1. 实质上的；实际上的，事实上的 2. [物] 虚的 3. [计] 虚拟的 ‖ ~ly *adv.*

virtue ['və:tju:] *n.* 1. 善，德 2. 美德，德行；贞操 3. 优点，长处 4. 功效，效能，效力 5.（男子的）力；英勇；刚毅

virtuosity [,və:tju'ɔsiti] *n.* 1. 对艺术品（或古董等）的爱好（或鉴赏）2.（艺术实践，尤指音乐演奏方面的）精湛技巧 3. [总称] 艺术爱好者

virtuoso [,və:tju'əuzəu] ([复] virtuosos 或 virtuosi [,və:tju'əusi:]) *n.* 1. 艺术品鉴赏家；艺术品爱好者；古玩收藏家 2. 艺术名家；艺术能手；演奏能手 3.〈古〉学者

virtuous ['və:tjuəs] *adj.* 1. 有道德的，有德行的；善良的 2. 正直的；公正的 3. 贞节的，有效力的，有效验的 ‖ ~ly *adv.* / ~ness *n.*

virulence ['virulans], **virulency** ['virulənsi] *n.* 1. 毒力；毒性；剧毒性，致命性 2.

刻毒,恶毒

virulent ['virulənt] *adj.* 1. 剧毒的;致命的 2. 刻毒的,恶毒的 3.〈疾病〉恶性的;〈微生物〉有毒力的 4. 过强的,令人难以忍受的

virus ['vaiərəs] *n.* 1.【微】病毒;滤过性病毒 2.(精神、道德方面的)影响,毒害 3. 病毒病;〈口〉病毒感染 4.〈蛇等的〉毒液

visa ['vi:zə] *n.* 1.(护照等的)签证,背签 2.(表示同意、批准等的)签字,签名 — (visaed 或 visa'd) *vt.* 在(护照)上背签,签发: get one's passport ~ed 取得护照签证

visage ['vizidʒ] *n.* 〈书面语〉脸;面容;外表

vis-à-vis ['vi:za:vi:] 〔单复同〕 *n.* 1. 面对面的人(如对坐的、对舞的): speak to one's ~ 和对面的人讲话 2. 坐位相对的马车;相向的座位 3.(职位上的)对等人物;对手 4.〈西方女子赴社交场所的〉陪伴者;(男女相互在社会中)对等人 5. 面对面的谈话;密谈 — *prep.* 1. 和…面对面 2. 和…相对;同…相比 3. 关于;对于 — *adv.* 面对面;在一起 — *adj.* 面对面的

viscera ['visərə] 〔复〕 *n.* 1. 内脏,脏腑(尤指心、肺、肝、肠等) 2.(刊物等的)内容;(物体等的)内部东西 ‖ ~l *adj.*

viscid ['visid] *adj.* 1. 胶粘的,粘质的 2.(树叶等)表面有粘性分泌物的 3. 半流体的

viscose ['viskəus] *n.*【化】粘胶;粘胶纤维(或织物) — *adj.* 1. 粘质的,粘性的 2.(含)粘胶的;粘胶制的 ‖ **viscosity** [vi'skɔsiti] *n.*

viscount ['vaikaunt] *n.* 〈英国的〉子爵

viscountess ['vaikauntis] *n.* 子爵夫人;女子爵

viscous ['viskəs] *adj.* 1. 粘滞的,粘性的

2.【植】表面有粘稠分泌物的

vise [vais] *n. & vt.* 〈美〉= vice[2]

visible ['vizəbl] *adj.* 1. 看得见的,可见的 2. 现有的;可得到的 3. 明显的;显然的 4. 愿会来客的,愿予接见的 5.(便于查阅,设计时使得档案、记录等)露部分内容(或摘要)的;显露式的 6.(进出口贸易)有形的 — *n.* 1. 可见物;可见光谱;【生】可见特变 2.(进出口贸易)有形货物 ‖ **visi'bility** *n.* 1. 可见性;明显性;清晰程度 2. 可见度,能见度;【气】视程,能见距离 3. 看得见的东西 / **visibly** *adv.* 1. 明显地;引人注目地 2. 看得见地;可见地

vision ['viʒən] *n.* 1. 视力;视觉 2. 目光;眼力;看法 3. 幻觉;幻象;〔宗〕幽灵 4. 极美的人(尤指妇女);绝妙的事物 5. 想象,幻想 6.(电视)图像;(电影)回忆场面,幻想场面 7. 看,看见;看见的东西 — *vt.* 1. 幻见;梦见;想象 2. 显示 ‖ ~al *adj.* / ~ally *adv.*

visionary ['viʒənəri] *adj.* 1. 梦幻的;幻觉的;想象的;非实有的 2. 耽于幻想的,好梦想的;不实际的 3. 出于空想的;不可实行的 4. 有预见的,有眼力的 — *n.* 1. 有眼力(或预见)的人 2. 好幻想的人;空想家

visit ['vizit] *vt.* 1. 访问,拜访;探望(的);参观;游览 2. 在…处逗留 3. 去…作短期逗留 3. 去(某处);在(某人)处 4. 视察,巡视 5.(灾害,疾病等)侵袭,降临 6.(基督教〈圣经〉用语)造祸,追(罪责) — *vi.* 1. 访问;参观;逗留;逗留作客 2.〈美〉叙谈,闲谈(with) 3.〔宗〕究罪,罚罪 — *n.* 1. 访问;游览;参观 2. 视察;出差 3. 出诊;就诊;探望 4.(战时海军人员对中立国船只的)登船检查 5.〈美〉叙谈,闲谈

visitant ['vizitənt] *n.* 1. 候鸟 2. 参观者；游览者；朝圣者 3. 来访者；来客

visitation [,vizi'teiʃən] *n.* 1. 访问；探望 2. 视察，巡视 3. 〈战时海军人员对中立国船只的〉登船检查 4. 〈宗〉天罚；天赐 5. [V-]〈宗〉圣母往见日（七月二日）；圣母往见 6. 〈口〉逗留得过久的探望或拜访 7. 〈鸟兽等〉反常的大批迁移

visiting ['vizitiŋ] *n. & adj.* 访问的(的)；探望，作客(的)；a ～ card 名片／a ～ professor 特邀教授，客座教授

visitor ['vizitə] *n.* 1. 访问者；来宾 2. 游客；参观者 3. 视察者；检查者；〈英〉（大学等的）督察员，督导

visor ['vaizə] *n.* 1. (头盔上的)面甲，面罩，护面 2. 帽舌，遮阳 3. (遮光)眼罩；(汽车挡风玻璃内上方的)遮阳板；(窗口等的)遮阳篷 *vt.* 1. (用面甲等)遮护

vista ['vistə] *n.* 1. (从两排树木或房屋等中间看出去的)长条形景色；远景 2. (对往事的)连绵回忆；(对前景的)不断展望

visual ['vizjuəl] *adj.* 1. 视觉的；视力的 2. 看得见的；凭视力的 3. 光学的 4. 形象化的；栩栩如生的 ‖ ～ly *adv.* ‖ ～aid 直观教具／～ field 视野／～ flight 【空】目视飞行

visualize ['vizjuəlaiz] *vt.* 1. 使可见；使具形象；使具体化 2. 设想，想象 3. (用X射线照相术)使(体内器官等)显形 —*vi.* 1. 想象 2. (体内器官或情况通过窥镜等)显形，显影 ‖ visuali'zation *n.*

vital ['vaitl] *adj.* 1. 生命的；生机的；维持生命所必需的 2. 有生命力的；充满活力的；气势勃勃的；生气盎然的 3. 生死攸关的，性命攸关的 4. 极其重要的；必不可少的 ‖ ～ly *adv.* ／～ness *n.*

vitality [vai'tæliti] *n.* 1. 生命力；生气，活力 2. 生动性

vitalize ['vaitəlaiz] *vt.* 1. 给与…生命 2. 使有生气，使有生命力 3. 生动描述

vitals ['vaitlz] [复] *n.* (人体的)重要器官；要害，重要部分

vitamin ['vitəmin, 'vaitəmin] *n.* 维生素；～ tablets 维生素片 ‖ ～ic [,vaitə'minik, ,vitə'minik] *adj.*

vitiate ['viʃieit] *vt.* 1. 使腐败；污染；使有缺陷 2. 使堕落；败坏(道德等) 3. 造成(契约等)无效；使无说服力 ‖ viti'ation *n.*

viticulture ['vitikʌltʃə] *n.* 葡萄栽培；葡萄栽培学

vitreous ['vitriəs] *adj.* 玻璃质的；玻璃制的；(眼睛的)玻璃体的；玻璃状的；玻璃色的，绿色的

vitrify ['vitrifai] *vt. & vi.* (使)成玻璃(或玻璃状)；(使)玻璃化

vitriol ['vitriəl] *n.* 1.【化】硫酸盐，矾；矾油(即硫酸) 2. (语言的)尖刻，辛辣；(感情的)强烈 —*vt.* 1. 用硫酸处理；【治】酸洗 2. 用硫酸毁坏；用用尖刻的话伤害 ‖ ～ic [,vitri'ɔlik] *adj.*

vituperate [vi'tju:pəreit] *vt. & vi.* 谩骂，咒骂，辱骂 ‖ vi,tupe'ration *n.* ／vitupera'tive [vi'tju:pərətiv] *adj.*

viva[1] ['vaivə] *n.* 〈英〉口试

viva[2] ['vi:və] 〈意〉*int.* 万岁!（表示祝愿或赞成的欢呼声）—*n.* 万岁的叫声，欢呼声

vivacious [vi'veiʃəs] *adj.* 1. 活泼的；快活的，有生气的；轻松愉快的 2. 〈古〉长命的；难系死的；难毁坏的 3.【植】多年生的；耐久的 ‖ ～ly *adv.* ／～ness *n.*

vivacity [vi'væsiti] *n.* 活泼；轻快；活泼(或轻快)的行为

viva voce ['vaivə 'vəusi] 1. 口头的 2. 口试地 3. 口试

vive [viːv] 〈法〉*int.* 万岁！(表示祝愿或赞成的欢呼声)

vivid ['vivid] *adj.* 1. (色彩、光线等)鲜艳的;鲜明的;强烈的 2. 活泼的;有生气的 3. 生动的;逼真的,清晰的 ‖ ~ly *adv.* / ~ ness *n.*

vivify ['vivifai] *vt.* 使具有生气;使生动;使活跃

viviparous [vi'vipərəs, vai'vipərəs] *adj.* 1. 【动】胎生的 2. 【植】在母株上萌发的

vivisect [,vivi'sekt] *vt. & vi.* (对…)作活体解剖

vivisection [,vivi'sekʃən] *n.* 活体解剖

vixen ['viksn] *n.* 1. 雌狐 2. 悍妇,泼妇

vizor ['vaizə] *n. & vt.* = visor

Vladivostok [,vlædi'vɔstɔk] *n.* 符拉迪沃斯托克(即海参崴)[俄罗斯远东区港市]

VOA *abbr.* Voice of America 美国之音(电台)

vocabulary [və'kæbjuləri] *n.* 1. (通常按词序排列并注有释义等的)词汇表;词汇汇编;词典 2. (某种语言、某人、某行业或某知识领域所使用的)词汇,语汇;词汇量

vocal ['vəukəl] *adj.* 1. (用嗓子)发声的;使用嗓音的;歌唱的;~ organs 发声器官 2. 用语言表达的,口述的 3. 畅所欲言的;畅言无忌的;直言不讳的 4. 响声回荡的,充满声响的 5. 【语】元音的;元音性的;浊音的,响音的 6. (流水、树木等)被赋予声音的,仿佛能说话的 — *n.* 1. 【语】元音 2. 声乐作品;声乐节目 3. (天主教会)有投票权的人 ‖ ~ cords 【复】声带

vocalic [vəu'kælik] 【语】*adj.* 1. 多元音的 2. 由元音构成的 3. 元音的;元音性的 4. 似元音的 — *n.* 元音(或复合元音)

vocalist ['vəukəlist] *n.* 歌唱者;歌唱家;声乐家

vocalize ['vəukəlaiz] *vt.* 1. 用嗓音发;使有声(说);唱 2. 【语】使发成元音,使元音化;使发成浊音,使浊化 — *vi.* 发声【音】练声 3. 【语】元音化;浊化 ‖ ,vocali'zation *n.* / ~ r *n.*

vocation [vəu'keiʃən] *n.* 1. 神召,天命;圣职,使命 2. (对于某种职业的)欲望;素质;才能(for) 3. 行业;职业;同行业的人们

vocational [vəu'keiʃənəl] *adj.* 职业的;业务的 ‖ ~ly *adv.*

vocative ['vɔkətiv] 【语】*adj.* 呼格的;呼唤的,称呼的 — *n.* 呼格词语;呼格

vociferate [vəu'sifəreit] *vt. & vi.* 大声地说;叫嚷 ‖ vo,cife'ration *n.*

vociferous [vəu'sifərəs] *adj.* 叫嚷的;吵闹的,喧嚷的;大事声张的 ‖ ~ly *adv.*

vodka ['vɔdkə] 〈俄〉*n.* 伏特加(一种用麦酿制的烈性烧酒)

vogue [vəug] *n.* 1. 流行物;时髦事物;时髦人物 2. 流行,风行;时尚,时髦 — *adj.* 流行的,时髦的

voice [vɔis] *n.* 1. 说话声;嗓音;嗓子鸣声;虫鸣声 2. (类似或比喻作说话声的)声音 3. (公开或正式表达出的)意见,愿望;投票权;发言权;表露 5. 嗓音,代言人 6. (唱歌、演讲时的)运嗓法 7. 【语】语态 8. 【音】音部;歌唱才能;人声;嗓喉 9. 歌唱家 — *vt.* 1. 用言语表达,吐露 2. 【音】使发成浊音(管风琴音管等)整音 3. 【语】使发成浊音 ‖ ~less *adj.* 1. 无声的,沉默的 2. 无发言权(或投票)权的 ~less consonants 清辅音 ‖ ~ box【解】喉 / ~'·over *n.* (电视等的)画外音,旁白

voiced [vɔist] *adj.* **1.**[用以构成复合词]…声的;shrill～ 尖声的 **2.** 有声的;发声的 **3.** 讲出来的 **4.**[语]浊音的

void [vɔid] *adj.* **1.** 空的,空无所有的 **2.** (房屋、土地等)没人住的、无人占有的 **3.** (职位等)无人担任的 **4.** 空闲的 **5.** 没有的,缺乏的 **6.** 无用的;无效的,作废的,可作废的 — *n.* **1.** 空处;空间;真空;空虚;空位 **2.** 空虚感;寂寞感 **3.** 空隙 **4.**(纸牌戏中)缺门 — *vt.* **1.** 排泄;放出 **2.** 使(契约等)无效;把…作废;取消 **3.** 使空出;退出;离开 ‖ ～ance *n.*

voidable [ˈvɔidəbl] *adj.* **1.** 可使无效的,可作废的;可以取消的 **2.**【律】可以判决无效的;可以撤消的 ‖ **voida'bility**,～ ness *n.*

vol. *abbr.* **1.** volcano **2.** volume **3.** volunteer

volatile [ˈvɔlətail] *adj.* **1.** 飞行的;能飞的 **2.**(液体等)易挥发的,易发散的 **3.** 轻快的,快活的;易激动的,易发作的;爆炸性的 **4.** 易变的;反复无常的;短暂的 — *n.* **1.** 有翅动物 **2.** 挥发物

volatility [ˌvɔlə'tiliti] *n.* **1.** 挥发性,发散性;挥发度 **2.** 轻快,快活 **3.** 易变;反复无常;短暂

volcanic [vɔl'kænik] *adj.* **1.** 火山(性)的;火山作用引起的 **2.** 有火山的;由火山构成的 **3.** 火山似的;暴烈的,猛烈的 — *n.* 火山岩

volcano [vɔl'keinəu]([复]volcano(e)s) *n.* 火山:sit on a ～ 坐在火山上,处境危险

vole¹ [vəul] *n.*【动】仓鼠;田鼠

vole² [vəul] *n.*(纸牌戏中的)大满贯,全胜 — *vi.* 获全胜

Volga [ˈvɔlgə] *n.*[the ～]伏尔加河[俄罗斯西部]

Volgograd [ˈvɔlgəgrɑːd] *n.* 伏尔加格勒(曾称斯大林格勒)[俄罗斯伏尔加河下游城市]

volition [vəu'liʃən] *n.* 行使意志;意志力;决定;选择 ‖ ～al *adj.*

volley [ˈvɔli] *n.* **1.**(枪炮、弓箭等的)群射;排枪射击(指一队步枪兵所作的敬礼炮火) **2.** 群射的子弹(或箭等) **3.**(质问、咒骂等的)齐发;连发;迸发 **4.**(网球中的)截击空中球,拦击;(排球中的)托球;(足球中的)凌空球;(板球中的)直投球 — *vt.* **1.** 齐发,群射(子弹等) **2.** 连声发出(咒骂等) **3.** 截击;截踢(球) — *vi.* **1.** 进行群射;枪炮齐鸣 **2.**(子弹等)被群射出 **3.**(球赛中)截击;截踢 ‖ ～ball *n.* 排球;排球运动

volplane [ˈvɔlplein] *n. & vi.*【空】滑翔

volt¹ [vəult] *n.*【电】伏特,伏 ‖ ～'-ampere *n.* 伏安,伏特安培

volt² [vəult] *n.* **1.**(马术中的)环骑;环骑图 **2.**(剑术中的)转身躲闪

voltage [ˈvəultidʒ] *n.*【电】电压;伏特数

voltaic [vɔl'teiik] *adj.*【电】(由化学作用产生的电流的)伏打(式)的

volte-face [ˌvɔlt'fɑːs]〈法〉*n.* **1.** 向后转 **2.**(意见、态度等的)完全改变,大转变

voltmeter [ˈvəultˌmiːtə] *n.*【电】伏特计,电压计

voluble [ˈvɔljubl] *adj.* **1.**(言词、文章)流利的;健谈的;善辞令的 **2.** 易变的,变化无常的 **3.**【植】缠绕的 ‖ **volu'bility** *n.* / **volubly** *adv.* 流利地;滔滔不绝地

volume [ˈvɔljuːm] *n.* **1.** 卷;册;书卷;(期刊的)合订本(略作 vol.) **2.** 容量;体积 **3.** 大量,许多;[～s]烟、蒸汽等的)大团 **4.** 份量;量 **5.** 音量;响度 **6.**【史】(古时用羊皮纸、纸草纸等写的)书卷 **7.** 一套唱片;一套录音磁带。

vi.(烟、蒸汽等)成团升起,成团卷起
— *vt.* **1.** 把…收集成卷;把…装订成
合订本 **2.** 成团地散发出 — *adj.* 大量
的 ‖ **~-pro'duce** *vt.* 大量生产

voluminous [və'ljuːminəs] *adj.* **1.** 构成多
卷的;长篇的 **2.** 著作得多的;话多的 **3.**
大量的;庞大的;宽大的 ‖ **~ly** *adv.*

voluntarily ['vɒləntrili, ˌvɒlən'terili] *adv.*
自愿地,志愿地;自动地,自发地;受意
志控制地

voluntary ['vɒləntəri, 'vɒlənteri] *adj.* **1.** 自
愿的,志愿的 **2.** 有意的,故意的 **3.** 靠
自由捐助维持的;非官办的 **4.** 由主观
意志所控制的;随意的,任意的;有自
由意志的 **5.** 自发的 **6.**【律】自愿的;无
偿的 — *n.* 【音】(教堂礼拜式前后演
奏的)(仪式始终由)即由一曲之 **2.**(主张教会
作品或教会不受国家资助而由民间捐助
的)自愿捐助论者 **3.** 自愿行动;志愿
者

volunteer [ˌvɒlən'tiə] *n.* **1.** 自愿参加者,
志愿者 **2.** 志愿兵 **3.** 自生植物(= ~
plant) — *adj.* **1.** 自愿参加的,志愿
(者)的 **2.**[植]自生的(= ~) **3.**[后接
不定式]自愿(做) **2.** 自愿提供(或给
予等) — *vi.* **1.** 自愿;自愿服务;当志
愿军 **2.**[植]自生自长

voluptuary [və'lʌptjuəri] *n.* 骄貪淫逸的
人;酒色之徒 — *adj.* 骄貪淫逸的;贪
图酒色的

voluptuous [və'lʌptjuəs] *adj.* **1.** 骄貪淫逸
的;贪图酒色的 **2.** 性感的,肉感的,激
起情欲的 ‖ **~ly** *adv.* / **~ness** *n.*

volute [və'ljuːt] *n.* **1.** 涡旋形,螺旋形,盘
蜗形 **2.**[建]涡形饰 **3.**[机]集涡环 **4.**
【机】螺旋泵,涡壳泵 **5.**[动]涡螺,(螺
壳上的)螺环 — *adj.* 涡旋形的,涡螺
形的,螺旋形的,盘旋形的

vomit ['vɒmit] *n.* 呕吐物;呕吐物;催吐剂

— *vt.* **1.** 呕吐;(火山、烟囱等)喷出;
吐出(恶语等) **2.** 使呕吐 — *vi.* 呕吐;
(火山、烟囱等)喷出

voodoo ['vuːduː] ([复]voodoos) *n.* **1.**(西
印度群岛和美国南部等地某些黑人中
的)伏都教;巫术 **2.** 伏都教巫师;
伏都教崇拜物;伏都教仪式(或习俗)
— *adj.* 伏都教的;(施行)伏都巫术的
— *vt.* 施伏都巫术以迷惑;施魔法于

voracious [və'reiʃəs] *adj.* **1.** 狼吞虎咽的,
贪吃的 **2.** 贪婪的;贪得无厌的 ‖ **~ly**
adv.

voracity [və'ræsiti] *n.* 贪食;暴食,贪婪;
贪得无厌

vortex ['vɔːteks] ([复]vortices ['vɔːtisiːz]或
vortexes) *n.* **1.** 旋涡,旋风(尤指旋风中
心);(喻)旋涡 **2.**[空]涡流 **3.**[物]涡
旋;涡动,旋转 ‖ **'~-ring** *n.*【物】涡
(旋)环

votable ['vəutəbl] *adj.* **1.** 有选举权的;有
投票权的 **2.** 可付表决的

votary ['vəutəri], **votarist** ['vəutərist] *n.*
1. 信徒 **2.** 爱好者;追求者;献身者

vote [vəut] *n.* **1.** 选举;投票;表决;票;选
票 **2.** 选举权;投票权;表决权 **3.** 投票
总数;得票数 **4.** 付表决事项;议决的
金额(或拨款) **5.** 投票过程;投票方法
6.[总称]投票者;选票 **7.** 表决;投票;表
决结果 — *vi.* 投票;表决;选举 — *vt.*
1. 投票决定;投票通过;投票选举 **2.**
由公认决定 **3.**(口)公认 **3.**(口)建议 **4.**
〈美〉鼓动…投票;使投票 ‖ **~able** *adj.*
= votable / **~r** *n.* 选举人;投票人;有投
票权者

voting ['vəutiŋ] *n.* 投票;选举;表决 —
adj. 投票的;选举的;表决的

votive ['vəutiv] *adj.*(因誓约而)奉献的;
还愿的 ‖ **~ly** *adv.*

vouch [vautʃ] *vi.* 担保,保证;证明,作证

(for) — *vt.* 1. 担保;证明;证实 2. 确定;确定地说 3. 断定;明言 4. 传(某人)出庭作证 ‖ ~ee [vau'fi:] *n.* 被担保的人‖ ~er n. 担保人,保证人;证人,证明者;证件;证书;收据;凭证

vouchsafe ['vautʃ'seif] *vt.* 1. 赐予,给予 2. 俯允,允诺

vow [vau] *n.* 1. 誓;誓约;誓言;许愿 — *vt.* 1.[常接从句]郑重地宣告(或声明) 2. 立誓奉献;立誓要 3.〈古〉起(誓) — *vi.* 发誓;许愿

vowel ['vauəl] *n.*【语】元音;元音字母 — *adj.* 元音的; — (vowel·l)ed; vowel·(l)ing) *vt.* 加元音符号于;使元音化 — *vi.* 发元音

vox [vɔks] ([复] voces ['vəusiːz])〈拉〉*n.* 声音

voyage ['vɔidʒ] *n.* 1. 航海;航空;航行;航程 2. 旅行 3. 航海记 — *vi.* 航海;航空;航行;旅行 — *vt.* 航行越过 ‖ ~r n. 航海者;航海探险者;航行者;旅行者

vs. *abbr.* 1. verse 2. versus

V-sign ['viːsain] *n.* 1.(伸开食、中两指的)V 字手势,胜利手势和平手势;同意手势 2.(手背朝外的)V 字手势,轻蔑下流手势

V/STOL ['viːstɔl] *n.* 垂直与短距起落(飞机)

v.t. *abbr.* verb transitive【语】及物动词

VTOL *abbr.* 垂直起落(飞机)

VTR *abbr.* 1. videotape recorder 磁带录像机 2. videotape recording 磁带录像

Vulcan ['vʌlkən] *n.* 1.【罗神】伍尔坎(火和锻冶之神) 2.【天】祝融星(假设的水内行星) 3.[v-] 锻冶者,铁匠 4. 瘸子,跛子

vulcanite ['vʌlkənait] *n.* 硬橡皮,硬质橡胶

vulcanize ['vʌlkənaiz] *vt.* & *vi.*(使)硫化;(使)硬化 ‖ vulcani'zation *n.* /~r *n.*

vulgar ['vʌlgə] *adj.* 1. 粗俗的;粗鄙的;庸俗的;卑下的;猥亵的;淫逸的 2. 普通的,一般的;通俗的 3. 本土的,非拉丁文的 4. 世俗的,非基督教的 ‖ ~ly *adv.*

vulgarian [vʌl'gɛəriən] *n.* 粗俗的人;庸俗的人(尤指粗俗而爱炫耀的富人);暴发户

vulgarism ['vʌlgərizəm] *n.*【语】俗词语;(语词的)误用 2. 粗俗;庸俗行为

vulgarity [vʌl'gæriti] *n.* 1. 粗俗,粗鄙 2. 粗野行为;粗俗语

vulgarize ['vʌlgəraiz] *vt.* 1. 使庸俗化 2. 使通俗化,使普及 ‖ 庸俗化 ‖ ,vulgari'zation *n.* /~r *n.*

vulnerable ['vʌlnərəbl] *adj.* 1. 易受伤的;脆弱的 2. 易受攻击的;易受责难的 3. 易受武力袭击的 4.(打桥牌的一方)已成局的,打不到合约数时罚分要增加的 ‖ ,vulnera'bility *n.*/ vulnerably *adv.*

vulpine ['vʌlpain] *adj.* 1. 狐狸的;似狐狸的 2. 狡猾的,奸诈的

vulture ['vʌltʃə] *n.* 1.【动】兀鹫;美洲鹫 2. 贪得无厌的人;劫掠成性的人

vulva ['vʌlvə] ([复] vulvas 或 vulvae ['vʌlviː]) *n.*【解】外阴,女阴 ‖ ~l *adj.*

vulvitis [vʌl'vaitis] *n.*【医】外阴炎

vum [vʌm] *n.*[comment!; vumming] *vt.* & *vi.*(美方)发誓,赌咒

v.v. 〈拉〉*abbr.* vice versa

vying ['vaiiŋ] vie 的现在分词 — *adj.* 竞争的,竞赛的

W

W, w ['dʌblju:]([复] W's, w's 或 Ws, ws ['dʌblju:z]英语字母表第二十三个字母 1. [W]W形 2. [W]【化】元素钨(wolfram)的符号 3. 西(west)的符号

W., w. *abbr.* 1. west 2. western

wabble ['wɔbl] *vi., vt. & n.* = wobble

wacky ['wæki] *adj.*〈美俚〉古怪的，乖僻的；疯疯癫癫的

wad[1] [wɔd] *n.* 1. 软物的小块；软填料(如棉花，破纸等); 【军】炮塞 2.(文件, 钞票等的)一卷，一叠;(鸦烟等的)一小块;(英方)(稻草等的)一捆 3.一大叠钞票;金钱;财富 4. [常~s]很可观的数目; 大量 一 (wadded; wadding) *vt.* 1.把……卷成一卷;把……压成一叠;把……搓成小块 2.(用填料)填料;塞住;填料

wad[2] [wɔd] *n.*【矿】锰土

wadding ['wɔdiŋ] *n.* 软填料;纤维填料;材料;棉胎

waddle ['wɔdl] *vi.*(鸭、鹅或矮胖子等)摇摇摆摆地走 一 *n.* 摇摇摆摆的步子;蹒跚

wade [weid] *vi.* 1. 蹚;跋涉:a *wading bird* 涉禽 2. 费力地前进;困难地通过 一 *vt.* 蹚(河);涉(泥地、沙滩等) 一 *n.* 1. 蹚;跋涉 2. 可涉水而过的地方;浅滩 ‖ ～r *n.* 1. 跋涉者;蹚水者 2. 涉水禽鸟(如鹤、鹭等) 3.〈英〉[waders]涉水捕鱼用的高统防水胶靴

wafer ['weifə] *n.* 1. 薄脆饼;华夫饼干 2.

【宗】圣饼(指圣餐时用的未发酵圆面包片) 3.(封信或文件等用的)封缄纸,干胶纸 4.【电子】薄片,圆片,晶片(如硅片等) 5. 包药干胶片(俗称糯米纸) 一 *vt.* 用封缄纸封(信件等)

waffle[1] ['wɔfl] *n.* 蛋奶烘饼,华夫饼,威化饼 ‖ ～ iron 蛋奶烘饼烤模

waffle[2] ['wɔfl]〈英〉*vi.*〈口〉唠叨;胡扯,讲蠢话 一 *n.* 无聊话;动听而无意义的话

waft [wɑ:ft] *vt.* 吹送,飘送;使飘荡 一 *vi.* 飘荡 一 *n.* 1. 吹送;飘荡(风,气味,声音等的)一阵(鸟翼的)挥动 3.(和平、喜悦等的)短暂的感觉,一时的感觉 4. 波浪;波动,浮动 5.【海】(表示风向、遇险等的)(桅顶)风信旗,狭长旗;(用风信旗等表示的)信号;求救信号

wag[1] [wæg](wagged; wagging) *vt.* 1.(向右或上下)摇摆,摇摆,摇摆 一 *vi.* 1.(向左右或上下)摇摆;摆动;颤动 2.〈古〉(时势等)推移,变迁 3. 喋喋不休 4.〈古〉离开,动身;游荡 5.(动物)摇尾巴 一 *n.* 1. 摇动,摆摆

wag[2] [wæg] *n.* 1. 爱说笑打趣的人;小丑 2.〈英俚〉逃学

wage[1] [weidʒ] *n.* 1. [常～s]工资;工钱 2. [～s]用作单或复]报酬;报应 3. [～s]工资总额 一 *vt.*〈英口〉雇用 ‖ ～ scale 工资等级,工资级别

wage[2] [weidʒ] *vt.* 开展(运动);进行(斗争);作(战) 一 *vi.* 在开展中;在进行

中

wager ['weidʒə] *n.* 赌注,赌物;赌博 — *vt.* 1. 押(赌注)同...打赌;打赌 2. 用...保证;以...担保 — *vi.* 打赌;赌博

waggery ['wægəri] *n.* 1. 滑稽;诙谐;笑话;笑话;俏皮话 2. 恶作剧;开玩笑

waggish ['wægiʃ] *adj.* 1. 滑稽的;诙谐的;幽默的 2. 好恶作剧的;爱开玩笑的

waggle ['wægl] *vt.*, *vi.* & *n.* 来回摆动,来回摇摆

wag(g)on ['wægən] *n.* 1. 四轮运货马车(或牛车);运货车 2. (英)(铁路)货车(=(美)freight car) 3. 小型手推(送货)车;餐室中用的(流动服务)车 4. 旅行(汽)车;小型客车 5. 矿车 6. [the ~](美口)囚车 7. [W-][天]北斗七星 8. (美里)左轮手枪;运货马车(或牛车等)运输货物;乘运货车旅行 — *vt.* 用四轮运货马车(或牛车等)运输(货物)‖ 赶大车的人 [W-][天]御夫座:北斗七星

wagtail ['wægteil] *n.* 1. [动]鹡鸰 2. 鹡鸰鸟 3. (美国的)灶巢鸟

waif [weif] *n.* 1. 无主失物;漂流物 2. 迷路的人(或动物);无家可归者;流浪儿 3. [~s][律](窃贼逃跑时)丢弃的赃物 4. [海]风信旗,狭长旗;用风信旗等表示的)信号

wail [weil] *vi.* 1. 恸哭,嚎啕 2. (风等)呼啸;(警报器)尖啸 3. 哀诉,悲叹,呜咽 — *vt.* (为)哀悼(某人的死亡);为某人的惨遇)恸哭 — *n.* 1. 恸哭(声),嚎啕(声) 2. 呼啸(声);尖啸(声) 3. 哀诉,悲叹,呜咽 ‖ ~er *n.*

wainscot ['weinskət][建]*n.* 1. 护壁板裙 2. 装有护壁板的墙壁下段 3. 装饰墙壁材料(如瓷砖等) 4.(英)小片镶板的优质白栎木 ‖ ~(wainscot(t)ed; wain-

scot(t)ing) *vt.* 用护壁板装饰 ‖ **wainscot-(ting** *n.* 护壁板的镶装 ‖ 用作护壁板的材料

waist [weist] *n.* 1. 腰,腰部 2. 衣服的上身(或腰身)部分;背心;紧身胸衣;乳褡;儿童内衣 3. (提琴等的)中间细部 4.[船]上甲板中部;船腰;(帆船)主桅前槐间的中部 5. 飞机机身中部 ‖ '~cloth *n.* (围)腰布 / '~coat *n.* (英)西装背心,马甲 / '~line *n.* 腰围;腰身部分

wait [weit] *vi.* 1. 等,等候,等待 2. 准备好,在手边 3. 伺候进餐 4. 耽搁;暂缓 — *vt.* 1. 等待;期待;听候 2. (口)(为等候而)推迟(饭餐、茶点等) 3. 伺候(进餐) — *n.* 1. 等待;等待的时间 2. 埋伏 3. [the ~s](圣诞节时)沿街唱颂诗的人们 ‖ ~ *er n.* 1. 等候者 2. (男)侍者 3. (男)服务员 4. (端茶具等用的)托盘 / ~ress ['weitris] *n.* 女侍者,女服务员

waiting ['weitiŋ] *n.* 1. 等候,等待;等待期间 2. 服侍;伺候 — *adj.* 等待的;服侍的;伺候的 ‖ ~ list 等待任命者的名单;等候批准的申请人名单人名单 / ~ room 候车(或候船,候机)室;候诊室;等候室

waive [weiv] *vt.* 1. 放弃,不坚持(权利、要求等) 2. 推迟考虑;延期进行 3. 挥手打发走;撤开 4. 丢弃(所偷赃物)

waiver ['weivə] *n.* 1. (权益、要求等的)(自动)放弃 2. 弃权声明书

wake¹ [weik](过去式 waked 或 woke [wouk],过去分词 waked 或 woken ['woukən]或 woke) *vi.* 1. 醒;醒来;醒着 2. 觉醒,觉悟 3. 警觉,认识(到)(*to*) 4. 变活跃;振奋 5.(古)(方)守夜;守灵 — *vt.* 1. 唤醒;弄醒 2. 使觉悟;激发,引起 3.(古)(方)为...守夜(灵)

n. 1. 醒,不眠 2.（葬礼前的）守夜;守灵 3.〈英〉每年一度纪念教堂守护神的节日;（教堂守护神节日前夕的）守夜;[常~s]教区的节庆 4.[常~s]（英国北部一些工业城市的）每年一度的假期 ‖ ~**ful** *adj*. 1. 觉醒的 2. 警觉的,戒备的 3. 不眠的;失眠的 ‖ ~**r** *n*. 【植】〈英〉海芋（尤指斑叶阿若母,斑叶红门兰）2.〈美〉延龄草

wake² [weik] *n*.（船的）尾波,航迹;（飞机的）尾流;（人、车等经过的）痕迹 ‖ **in the ~ of** 1. 紧紧跟随...;在...后 2. 随着...而来;作为...的结果

waken [weik] *vi*. 1. 醒来,睡醒(*up*) 2. 觉醒;振奋 — *vt*. 1. 唤醒;弄醒 2. 使觉醒;使振奋,激发;激起

wale [weil] *n*. 1. 隆起的伤痕（如鞭痕、杖痕等）2.（土地等的）条状隆起部,垄 3. 【纺】（灯芯绒等的）凸起的条纹

Wales [weilz] *n*. 威尔士[英国的一部分]

walk [wɔːk] *vi*. 1. 走,步行;散步;（马等）慢步走 2.（步行或以轻轻地移动;步步延伸 3. 处世,行事;生活 4.（鬼魂等）行走,出现 5.【体】（篮球赛中违例）带球跑,走步 — *vt*. 1. 走遍;走过;在...上走;沿着... 2. 徒步执行（或看、测量）3. 使走 4. 同...竞走 5. 使（物体）行走似地移动 6.【体】（篮球赛中违例）带（球）跑,带（球）走步 7. 慢步跳（舞）— *n*. 1. 步行;散步;（马等）的慢步走;【体】竞走 2. 走步的姿势 3. 走的距离;（邮递员、送奶工等）走的固定路线 4. 常走之处;散步场所;（屋顶的）平台;走道,人行道;（制造绳索用的）狭长走道 5.（禽、畜牧的）活动场地,栏 6. 裁树成行的林荫园人;〈英〉护林人的管区 6. 极慢的速度 7. 阶层;行业;生活方式;行为 8.〈英〉（庄严的）行列;仪仗队 ‖ ~**er** *n*.

1. 步行者;常散步的人;参加竞走者;徒步叫卖的小贩 2.（帮助小孩、病弱者学走路的）学步车;扶车;轻便鞋 3.【动】走禽 ‖ ~**out** *n*. 1. 罢工(者);罢课(者) 2.（表示抗议的）退席;退出组织 3. 恋爱关系 ‖ ~**over** *n*. 1. 与一匹马等的赛跑 2. 对手不强的比赛;不经比赛取得的胜利;轻易取得的胜利 ‖ ~**up** *n*. 无电梯的大楼;无电梯大楼的楼上房间 *adj*. 1.（公寓房屋等）无电梯的 2.（房间）在无电梯大楼楼上的 3. 靠近大街的

walkie-lookie [ˈwɔːkiˈluki] *n*. 便携式电视摄像机

walkie-talkie [ˈwɔːkiˈtɔːki] *n*. 步话机

walking [ˈwɔːkiŋ] *n*. 1. 走,步行;散步 2. 步态 3.（步行的）路面状况 — *adj*. 1. 能行走的;活的;（疾病）不需卧床休息的;a ~ dictionary 活词典 2. 步行的;步行用的;a ~ tour 徒步旅行 3. 像行走似地动的;摆动的;a ~ beam 摆杆 4. 走着操作的 5. 解雇的;被免职的;a ~ ticket（或 ~ papers）解雇书 ‖ ~ **stick** 手杖

wall [wɔːl] *n*. 1. 墙壁;围墙;城墙;[常~s]堡垒 2. 间隔层;内壁;器壁 3.（形状或作用如墙的）分界物;屏障 4.（墙的）墙壁的一边 — *adj*. 墙（或壁）的;墙上的;爬墙的;攀墙的 — *vt*. 1. 用墙围住（或分隔、防护）2. 堵塞（门、窗等);禁闭 ‖ ~**board** *n*.【建】（护）墙板 /'~**flower** *n*.【植】桂竹香;糖芥 2.〈口〉舞会中没有舞伴而坐着看的女人) /~ **newspaper**(s) 墙报 /~ **painting** 壁画;壁画绘制 /'~**paper** *n*.（糊）墙纸 *vt*. & *vi*. 糊墙纸于[房间内墙壁]

wallet [ˈwɔlit] *n*. 1.（放钞票等的）皮夹子 2. 皮制小工具袋;钓具袋 3.〈古〉（香客等的）行囊;旅行袋

walleye [ˈwɔlai] *n*. 1.【医】角膜白斑

【医】外斜视,散开性斜视 3. 眼珠暴突的鱼

wallop ['wɔləp] vi. 1. 乱窜;猛冲 2. (动物在泥中)打滚;(车等)颠簸 3. 沸腾作声 — vt. (口) 1. 痛殴;猛击 2. 击溃;打败 — n. 1. 重击;猛击力;(心理上或感情上的)冲击力?2. 快感;乐趣 3. (英)(身体的)笨拙的行动 4. 〈英俚〉啤酒;酒

wallow ['wɔləu] vi. 1. (猪等在泥、脏水等中)打滚 2. 变得富有;沉溺;纵乐(in) 3. (船等)颠簸,摇摆;笨重地驶行 4. (烟、焰等)冒 — n. 1. 打滚;翻滚 2. (水牛等经常打滚的)泥沼;水坑;(动物打滚造成的)洼地,坑 3. 堕落

Wall Street ['wɔːl striːt] 华尔街[美国纽约市的一条街道,是美国金融机构的集中地;现常用作美国金融市场或金融界的代名词] ‖ **Wall Streeter** 华尔街人士

walnut ['wɔːlnʌt] n. 1. 胡桃;胡桃树 2. 胡桃木 3. 胡桃色

walrus ['wɔːlrəs] ([复] walrus(es)) n. 1. 【动】海象 2. 〈俚〉矮胖笨拙的人(或动物) — adj. 1. 海象的 2. 〈尤指末端弯曲下垂的长胡须〉海象状的

waltz [wɔːls] n. 华尔兹舞曲;华尔兹舞曲,圆舞曲 2. 华尔兹舞的(或圆舞曲的,圆舞曲的 — vi. 1. 跳华尔兹舞 2. 轻快地走动;旋转 3. 轻快顺利地前进 — vt. 1. 与…跳华尔兹舞 2. 硬拉,硬拖 3. 运输,运送 ‖ — er n.

wampum ['wɔmpəm] n. 1. (北美印第安人过去作货币或装饰用的)贝壳串珠 2. 〈美俚〉钱;财富

wan [wɔn] adj. 1. 苍白的,无血色的 2. 病态的;有倦容的,有愁容的 3. 暗淡的;微弱的 — (wanned; wanning) vt. & vi. (使)变苍白;(使)呈病态 ‖ ~ly adv.

~ness n.

wand [wɔnd] n. 1. 棒;棍;竿;杖 2. 魔杖;(口)指挥棒 3. (表示官职的)权杖;权标 4. (柳树等幼树的)嫩枝 5. (美)(射箭)木条靶(长 6 英尺、宽 2 英寸)

wander ['wɔndə] vi. 1. 漫游;闲逛;漫步;徘徊;彷徨 2. 迷路 3. 离开正道;离题;错乱 4. (河流等)曲折地流,蜿蜒 — vt. 漫游 ‖ — er n. 漫游者;流浪汉;彷徨者;迷路的动物

wandering ['wɔndəriŋ] adj. 1. 漫游的;闲逛的 2. (部落)游牧的 3. (河流等)曲折的,蜿蜒的 4. (精神)恍惚的;错乱的 5. (植物)有长藤的,有蔓须的;攀缘的 — n. [常~s] 1. 漫游;闲逛 2. 离开正道;离题 3. 神志恍惚;精神错乱;胡言乱语

wanderlust ['wɔndəlʌst] 〈德〉n. 漫游癖;旅行癖

wane [wein] vi. 1. (月)亏,缺 2. 变暗淡;变小;减少 3. 衰落;衰退;没落;消逝 4. 退潮 — n. 1. 月亏;月亏期 2. 衰退;衰退期 3. (木材的)钝棱

wangle ['wæŋgl] vt. 1. (从人群中)扭身挤出;(从困境中)设法脱身 2. 使用诡计(或花言巧语等) — vt. 1. 扭身挤出 2. 用诡计获得;哄骗 3. 虚饰;假造 — n. 1. 巧计获得;哄骗;骗得的东西 2. 虚饰;假造

want [wɔnt] vt. 1. 要,想要 2. 要…来;要…去 3. 需要;应该;必须 4. 欠缺,缺少 5. [常用被动语态]征求;通缉: *Wanted*, a typist. (报刊广告等用语)招聘:打字员一名。/be ~ed by the police 被警察局通缉 — vi. 需要;缺少(for, in);生活困难,贫困 — n. 1. 需要;需求 2. [常~s]需求;必需品 3. 缺乏,缺少 4. 匮乏,贫困 5. 缺点;过失 ‖ — ad 〈口〉

(报刊等的)征求(或招聘)广告

wanting ['wɔntiŋ] *adj.* 1. 缺少的;没有的 2. 不够格的;迟钝的 — *prep.* 缺;无

wanton ['wɔntən] *adj.* 1. 爱玩闹的;嬉闹的,任性的;不负责任的;变化无常的 2.(草木等)繁茂的(语言、想象力等)夸张的;奔放的 3.(侵略、破坏、侮辱等)蛮横的;胡乱的;放肆的 4.(人、思想、书等)淫乱的 — *n.* 1. 嬉闹的孩子(或动物) 2. 宠坏的人(或动物) 3. 耽于享乐的人 4. 淫乱的人(尤指荡妇)— *vi.* 1. 任性;反复无常;嬉戏 2. 生活奢侈;放纵;淫荡 — *vt.* 挥霍(钱财) ‖ ~**ly** *adv.* / ~**ness** *n.*

wap [wɔp] (wapped; wapping) *vt.*, *vi.* & *n.* 〈方〉〈古〉 = whop

wapiti ['wɔpiti] ([复] wapiti(s)) *n.* 【动】美洲赤鹿;马鹿;黄臀马鹿

war [wɔː] *n.* 1. 战争;战争状态;战术 2. 军事学 3. 斗争;竞争;对抗,冲突 — (warred; warring) *vi.* 1. 进行战争;战斗 2. 斗争;竞争;对抗 — *vt.* 击败;得胜 — *adj.* 1. 战争的;军事的;战时用的;战争引起的 2.(苏格兰)更坏的,更差的 ‖ ~ **criminal** 战犯 / ~ **cry** 1. 作战时的呐喊 2.(政党竞选时提出的)口号 / ~ **head** *n.* 弹头:a missile *~head* 导弹弹头 / ~ **horse** *n.* 1.(口)老兵;老练的政客;老资格演员;老手;经验丰富的人 3. 牢记过去功业(或争论)的人 4.(乐曲等中的)陈腔,老调 / ~ **lord** *n.* 军阀 / ~ **lord** 军阀分子 / ~ **path** *n.*(北美印第安人的)征途;敌对行动;敌对情绪 / ~ **plane** *n.* 军用飞机;战斗机 / ~ **plane** 舰艇 / ~ **weariness** *n.* 厌战情绪 / ~ **worn** *adj.* 由于战争而筋疲力尽的;遭受战争创伤的;被战争毁坏的

warble[1] ['wɔːbl] *vi.* 1.(鸟)啭鸣 2. 用柔和的颤音唱歌 3. 发出音乐般的声音 — *vt.* 1.(鸟)啭鸣着唱 2. 用柔和的颤音唱 3. 似鸟啭鸣般地讲(或朗诵等)— *n.* 1. 啭鸣;颤声的歌唱;颤音 2. 歌曲;颂歌 ‖ ~ **r** *n.* 1.(俚)女歌手【动】刺啭莺

warble[2] ['wɔːbl] *n.* 1.(马背上被鞍磨出来的)鞍瘤 2.(由牛皮蝇幼虫寄生而形成的)动物皮瘤 3. 牛皮蝇幼虫;牛皮蝇(亦作~ fly)

ward [wɔːd] *n.* 1. 保卫;保护;看护;监护 2. 监禁;拘留;监督;监视 3.〈古〉守卫队;卫兵 4. 受法院(或监护人)监护的未成年者(或疯人等);被保护者(或训导)的人(或集团) 5. 病房;病室 6. 牢房 7.(慈善机关、养老院等的)收容室 8. 行政区;选区(英格兰北部和苏格兰的)分区;区民 9.(城堡、要塞内的)空旷场地 10. 防卫设施 11.[~s] 锁孔;(钥匙的)榫槽 12.(剑术等的)防卫姿势 — *vt.* 1. 保护;守卫 2. 避开;防止;挡住(off) 3. 使入病房 ‖ ~**er** *n.* 1. 看门人;门警 2.(主美)管理员;监狱看守人;狱吏 3.(英)(某些大学的)院长;校长(有高级官员的称号)(尤指总督、大臣、港务局长、市场主管等) 6.(英)同业公会会长;医院院长;理事 7.(美)监狱长;看守长 8.【宗】(公会的)教区委员 ‖ ~**-room** *n.*(军舰上除舰长外的)军官公共生活室

warden ['wɔːdn] *n.* 1. 看守人;保管员;管理员 2. 监察人 3.(英)(第二次世界大战时的)民防队员 4.(英)(某些大学的)院长;校长(有高级官员的称号)(尤指总督、大臣、港务局长、市场主管等) 6.(英)同业公会会长;医院院长;理事 7.(美)监狱长;看守长 8.【宗】(公会的)教区委员

wardrobe ['wɔːdrəub] *n.* 1. 衣柜,衣橱;藏衣室;(剧场的)戏装保藏室 2.(个人的)全部服装;(为某个季节或某种

动用的)全套服装;(剧团的)全部戏装,行头 3.(可挂衣服的)大衣箱(亦作 ~ trunk) 4.(王族或显贵宅邸中的)保管库(保藏衣服,珠宝等)

-ward(s) *suf.* **1.** [构成形容词] 表示 "向...的";backward,downward **2.** [构成副词] 表示"向";northward(s),up-ward(s)

ware[wɛə] *n.* **1.** [常~s]商品,货物 **2.** [总称][可用以构成复合词]物品;器皿 **3.** 陶器 ‖ ~house *n.* 货栈,仓库 *vt.* 把...(暂时)放在货栈中,使落栈,使入库

ware² [wɛə] *vt.* [用于祈使句] **1.** 当心,留神 **2.** (口)避免 — *adj.* **1.** 知道的,意识到的(*of*) **2.** (古)留神的,警惕的

warfare ['wɔːfɛə] *n.* **1.** 战争;战争状态;战争进程;作战;交战 **2.** 冲突,斗争;竞争

warily ['wɛərili] *adv.* 谨慎地,小心翼翼地;警惕地

warlike ['wɔːlaik] *adj.* **1.** 准备战斗的,好战的;尚武的 **2.** 战争的;军事的 **3.** 有战争危险(或迹象)的

warm[wɔːm] *adj.* **1.** 暖和的,温暖的,暖热的 **2.** 热烈的,热情的,热心的 **3.** 有同情心的 **3.** 兴奋的,激动的;激烈的 **4.** 多情的;色情的 **5.** (处境等)为难的,危险的 **6.** (嗅迹等)新鲜的,强烈的;(游戏中)快要发现的,即将猜中的 **7.** (官员等)已做惯的,地位稳定的 **8.** (口)富裕的 — *vt.* **1.** 使温暖,使温热,使激动,使激动;使生气 使热烈 **2.** 使兴奋,使激动;使生气使热烈 **3.** 使做准备动作(up) **4.** (食物)重新煮热(up,over) **5.** 使充满兴趣 **6.** (口)打;鞭打 — *vi.* **1.** 变暖和,变温暖,变暖热(up) **2.** 兴奋激动;变得激动(up) **3.** 同情;爱好(to,towards) **4.** (比赛前)做准备动作(up)

— *n.* **1.** (口)暖 **2.** 保暖的东西;(英)军用双排钮短大衣(亦作 British ~) ‖ ~er *n.* **1.** (橡胶等的)加热工人 **2.** 取暖器,保温器 ‖ ~ly *adv.* ‖ ~-'blooded *adj.* **1.** (动物)温血的,恒温的 **2.** 热情的 **3.** (性情)易变的,易趋极端的 ‖ ~'hearted *adj.* 热心的,热情的,富于同情心的 ‖ ~-up *n.* **1.** (比赛前的)准备活动,热身活动;(演出前的)准备活动 **2.** (马这,收音机等的)预热 **3.** (正式比赛前的)热身赛;(展览前的)预展

warming ['wɔːmiŋ] *n.* **1.** 暖和,温暖,暖热;加温 **2.** (英方)打;鞭打 ‖ ~-pan **1.** (古)长柄炭炉(睡前暖床用) **2.** (未成年人等就职前的)代理人 ‖ ~-'up *adj.* 【体】准备活动的

warmth [wɔːmθ] *n.* **1.** 暖和,温暖,暖热 **2.** 热烈,热情;多情 **3.** 激动;生气

warn [wɔːn] *vt.* **1.** 警告;告诫 **2.** 预先通知 — *vi.* 发出警告;发出预告

warning ['wɔːniŋ] *n.* **1.** 警告;告诫;前车之鉴,鉴诫 **2.** 警报,前兆 **2.** (解雇,辞职等的)预先通知 — *adj.* 警告的,告诫的;引为鉴诫的 ‖ ~ly *adv.*

warp [wɔːp] *vt.* **1.** 使翘起;弄弯;弄歪 **2.** 使(性格等)不正常;使乖戾;使有偏见 **3.** 歪曲(历史、记载等) **4.** 把(线、纱)排列成经 **5.** 【海】用绞船索曳(船) **6.** 引潮水入(低洼地)淤积用沉积物来肥田)》 **7.** 使成翘曲;变弯;变歪 **2.** 【海】(船)被绞船索牵曳;(船员)用绞船索曳船 — *n.* **1.** 翘曲;弯曲;弯歪 **2.** (性格等)的乖戾;不正常 **3.** 【海】绞船索;拖船索;牵揽 **4.** [纺]经,纱经 **5.** (浊水的)沉积物;冲积土 **6.** 基础

warrant ['wɔrənt] *n.* **1.** (正当)理由;根据;证明,保证 **2.** 授权;批准;授权证,许可证;逮捕状;搜查令 **3.** 【军】准尉委

任状 4. 付款凭单;收款凭单 5.〈公司发出的)认股证书 6.〈主英〉找单 —— *vt.* 1. 使有(正当)理由;成为...的根据 2. 授权给;批准 3. 向(某人)保证;保证(货物)的质量;担保 ‖ ~able *adj.* 1. 可保证的;可担保的;可证明为正当的 2. 可辩护的;可批准的 2.(鹿)达到法定可猎年龄的 ‖ ~ officer 1. 准尉 2.〈美〉(海军)二级准尉

warranty ['wɔrənti] *n.* 1. 理由;根据,依据 2. 授权;批准 3. 证书 4. 保证;担保(书);保单

warren ['wɔrin] *n.* 1.〈主英〉小猎物(如野兔、野鸡)繁殖的围地;在小猎物繁殖围地狩猎的特权 2. 养兔场;养兔场的兔子 3. 拥挤的地区(或房屋)

warrior ['wɔriə] *n.* 1.〈书面语〉武士;勇士;(老)战士;(原始部落等的)斗士 2. 鼓吹战争的人 3. 战斗;尚武

Warsaw ['wɔːsɔː], **Warszawa** [vɑːˈʃɑːvɑ] *n.* 华沙〈波兰首都〉

wart [wɔːt] *n.* 1.〖医〗疣,肉赘 2.〖植〗瘤,树瘤 3. 瑕疵,缺点 ‖ ~y *adj.* 1. 有疣的;疣似的 2. 有(树)瘤的;多(树)瘤的

wary ['wɛəri] *adj.* 1. 谨慎的,小心翼翼的;警惕的 2. 谨防的;唯恐的(of)

was [强 wɔz;弱 wəz]be的过去式

wash [wɔʃ] *vt.* 1. 洗,洗涤;洗〖矿〗洗(矿);洗刷(罪过等) 2. 冲出;冲成;冲蚀 3.(海水等)拍打;流过;弄湿 4. 湿透;浸透;渗过 5. 粉刷;涂水彩于;镀金(或银等)于 —— *vi.* 1. 洗涤;洗衣;洗脸;洗手;洗澡 2. 耐洗;〈主英口〉(论点等)站得住脚;经得住考验 3. 被冲(蚀)(out, away);(浪涛等)拍击 4. 漂浮;漂流;流过,掠过 —— *n.* 1. 洗,洗涤;冲洗,刷;泼溅 2. 洗的衣物;洗衣店 3. 洗涤剂

洗液;生发油;香水,〈水彩或金属)涂层 4. [the ~](拍打(声);螺旋桨等在空气中引起的)激荡 5. 稀淡饮料(或食物);已发酵待蒸馏的酒;〈口〉(饮恶酒后喝的)淡饮料;内容乏的饮料(或讲话) 6.(水流的)冲积物;沖脚,废话 7. 沼泽,浅水池(或海湾) 8.(水流)冲出的沟槽;〈美国西部的)干河床(= dry ~) 9.(水彩颜料等的)薄涂层 10.〖矿〗含矿土 11.〖地〗冲刷,冲蚀 ‖ ~basin *n.* 脸盆 ~board *n.* 洗衣板;〖建〗壁脚板;(船)防浪板 /~bowl *n.* 脸盆 ~cloth *n.* 洗脸巾;浴巾;洗碗布 /~leather *n.* (擦洗玻璃窗等用的)软皮 /~out *n.* 1.(道路或铁路的)冲坏部分 2.〖俚〗大败,惨败;破产;完蛋 3. 失败者;(在训练或学习中)被淘汰者 4.〖俚〗无用的家伙 5.〖空〗机翼负扭转 /~rag *n.* 〈美〉 = ~cloth /~room *n.* 盥洗室;〈美〉厕所 /~sale〈美〉(股票市场为维持买卖兴旺的假象而进行的)虚假交易 /~stand *n.* 1. 脸盆架 2. 盥洗盆 /~tub *n.* 洗衣盆

washer ['wɔʃə] *n.* 1. 洗涤器;洗衣机 2. 洗衣人 3.〖机〗垫圈 4.〈美俚〉酒馆 ‖ ~man *n.* 男洗衣工 /~woman *n.* 洗衣女工

washing ['wɔʃiŋ] *n.* 1. 洗,洗涤;洗的衣物;洗下的污垢 2. 洗涤剂 3. 浸;冲(蚀);冲走的东西 4. 涂解;涂上的薄层 5. 洗出的矿物;产矿地 ‖ ~ machine 洗衣机

Washington ['wɔʃiŋtən] *n.* 1. 华盛顿(市)[美国首都] 2. 美国政府;〈口〉D.C.(或 ~, District of Columbia)(哥伦比亚特区)华盛顿(即美国首都华盛顿) 2. 华盛顿(州)[美国州名](亦作~ State)

washy ['wɔʃi] *adj.* 1.(食物等)稀薄的;含水的淡的 2.(颜色等)退去的;苍白的

3.(文章等)贫乏的,乏味的,空洞的;(感情等)脆弱的,无力的 4.〈罕〉(气候等)湿润的,有雨意的

wasn't ['wɔznt] = was not

Wasp, WASP [wɔsp] (White Anglo-Saxon Protestant 的首字母缩略词) *n. & adj.* 〈常贬〉祖先是英国新教徒的美国人(的);在美国社会中享有特权的(中、上层)白人(的)

wasp [wɔsp] *n.* 1. 胡蜂;黄蜂;泥蜂 2. 易动怒的人,暴躁的人;刻毒的人

Waspish ['wɔspiʃ], **Waspy** ['wɔspi] *adj.* 〈常贬〉祖先是英国新教徒的美国人的;在美国社会中享有特权的(中、上层)白人的

waspish ['wɔspiʃ] *adj.* 1. 胡蜂的;胡蜂似的 2. 细腰的;纤细的 3. 易怒的,暴躁的,爱争吵的 4. 尖刻的,刻毒的 ‖ **~ly** *adv.* / **~ness** *n.*

wassail ['wɔseil] *n.* 1.(英国旧时的)祝酒;祝酒辞;祝酒时用的酒 2. 酒宴;纵酒欢闹 — *vi.* 1. 痛饮;纵酒欢闹 2. 〈方〉圣诞节时挨户唱圣歌 — *vt.* 为...干杯;向...祝酒

waste [weist] *n.* 1. 浪费,滥用 2. 损耗;消毁;【律】(房产等的)产业损伤;产业价值的降低 3. 一片荒原(或空旷);[常~s]荒地;未开垦地;沙漠;海洋 4. 废(弃)物;废料 5. 垃圾;污水;[~s]粪便 6.【地】(水流冲击的)土地(或岩石)的风化物 — *vt.* 1. 浪费;未充分利用;【律】(因不当而)损坏(房屋) 2. 消耗;使消瘦 3. 使(土地等)荒芜;使荒废 4.〈美俚〉杀害;消灭;打伤 — *vi.* 1. 浪费 2. 消耗 3. 消瘦 (*away*) — *adj.* 1.(土地等)荒芜的;荒废的;未开垦的;不毛的;(城市等)荒芜为废墟的 2. 废弃的,无用的;多余的,剩余的;(体内)排泄的 3. 排除废物

的;盛放废物的 4. 贫乏的;单调的:the ~ periods of history 历史上平淡无奇的时期 ‖ **wastage** *n.* 1. 浪费(量);损耗(量);漏失(量) 2. 废物;废料 3.【地】(冰、雪等的)消融(量) ‖ **~ basket** *n.* 废纸篓 *vt.* 把...放入废纸篓 / **~land** *n.* 荒地,荒原;未垦地;废墟 / **~paper** *n.* 废纸;废纸般的东西(如假证券等) *adj.* 废纸的 / **~paper basket** = **waste** ‖ **~ pipe** 污水管,废水管;废气管

wasteful ['weistful] 1. *adj.* (造成)浪费的,挥霍的;耗费的 2. 造成破坏的;破坏性的

wastrel ['weistrəl] *n.* 1. 浪费者;败家子 2. 饭桶,无用的人 3. 废品 4. 浪荡子 5.(路边的)荒地 6. 弱小动物

watch [wɔtʃ] *n.* 1. 观看,注视 2. 看守,守卫;守护,照管;监视;注意 3. 守候,等待 — *vi.* 1. 观看,注视 2. 看守,守卫;守护 (*for*) 4. 整夜守护(或照管);守夜 — *vt.* 1. 手表;表【海】船上天文钟 2. 看守,守卫;守护,照管;监视;注意 3. 值班人员;值夜人员(或队) 4. 看守人(员);哨兵;警卫(队);[the~]〈古〉(夜间的)巡逻队;更夫 4.(值班的)一班,一岗;【海】(海员的)值班时间(每班2或4小时);值班的海员(通常为全船人员的一半) 5.(旧时夜晚的时刻)更 ‖ **~er** *n.* 1. 看守人,守望者,值夜者;警戒人,岗哨 2.(夜间对病人的)护理者;守灵人 3. 观察者,视察者;(代表政党或候选人的)投票监督员 ‖ **~ chain** (挂表的)表链 / **~dog** *n.* 1. 看门狗 2. 监察人 为...看门(或守卫);监督 / **~ fire** 营火 / **~ guard**(挂表的)表链;表带 / **~house** *n.* 1. 看守房,岗亭 2. 拘留所 / **~man** *n.* 1. 看守人;警卫员 2.(旧时的)更夫 / **~ night**【宗】1. 除夕 2. 除夕礼拜,守望礼拜 / **~tower** *n.* 岗楼,瞭望

watchful ['wɔtʃful] *adj.* 1. 警惕的，戒备的；注意的〈古〉醒的 ‖ ~ly *adv.* ; ~ness *n.*

water ['wɔtə] *n.* 1. 水；[常 ~s] 矿泉水 2. 水深；水位 3. 水面；水路 3. [常 ~s] 大片的水；水体；海域；近海 4. 分泌液 (尤指尿、泪、口水、胃液、胰液、羊水等) 5. 水彩颜料；水彩画 6. (宝石的) 透明度，光泽度；优质度 (品级或类型的) 程度 7. (织物或金属面的) 光泽，波纹 8. 【商】超过实际资产的估价 (或股额)；清水股 ‖ *vt.* 1. 使湿；上洒 (或浇) 水；灌溉 2. 供给…饮水；使 (牛马等) 饮水；给 (锅炉等) 加水 3. 在…中搀水，冲淡 4. 用 (带水的) 轧波纹 5. 【商】不增资而增 (股额等) (*down*) ‖ *vi.* 1. 流泪；滴口水 2. (船等) 加水；(动物等) 饮水 ‖ *adj.* 1. 水的；用水的 2. 水上的；水生的；生长于水边的 4. 含水的；含液体的 ‖ ~ bed 充水床垫；水床/~ bird 水鸟，水禽/~ buffalo 水牛/~ carriage 水运 (工具)；水运设施/~ chute 溢水槽 2.(驾舟自高而下作滑水游戏用的) 滑水槽/~ clock 水钟/~ closet 盥洗室，厕所；抽水马桶/~colo(u)r *n.* 水彩 (颜料)；水彩画/~-cooled *adj.* 水冷 (式) 的/~-cress *n.* 【植】水田芥/~ cycle 1. 水文循环 2. 水上脚踏车/~ dog 1. 喜水的狗；会泅水的猎狗 2. 水性好的人；老练的水手/~fall *n.* 1. 瀑布；人工瀑布 2. 披垂的波形长发/~fowl *n.* 水鸟；水禽/~front *n.* 1. [常作定语] 水边，滩；(城市中的) 滨水区 2. (炉灶上) 热水箱的管道/~ gas 水煤气/~glass *n.* 1. 盛水的玻璃容器；玻璃 (酒) 杯 2. 【化】水玻璃，硅酸钠/~head *n.* 1. (江河的) 水源 2. (用拦水坝) 拦住的水；拦住

的水的水位 (或水量) 3.【医】大头；脑积水，水脑/~ing place 1. (人或动物的) 饮水处 2. 〈英〉矿泉休养地；海滨胜地 3.〈美〉(夜总会等供应饮料的) 卖酒处/~ lily 【植】睡莲/~-line *n.* 1.(船的) 吃水线 2.(纸张上的) 水印/~-logged *adj.* 1.(船等) 浸水满舱的；浸水失控的 2.(木材等) 浸透水的 3.(土地等) 渍的/~ main 总水管/~-man *n.* 1. 船工；船民；船家 2. 桨手/~-mark *n.* 1. 水位标志 2.(纸张上的) 水印 3. 在 (纸张) 上印水印图案；水印 (图案) 的/~melon *n.* 西瓜/~ mill 水力磨粉机/~ moccasin (美国南部产的) 棉口蛇，水蝮蛇/~ pipe 1. 水管 2. 水烟筒 /~ plane 1.【海】船的水线面 2. 水上飞机/~ polo【体】水球/~ power *n.* 1. 水力 2. 其水力可利用的水流 3.(磨坊的) 用水权/~ proof *adj.* 不透水的，防水的 *n.* 不透水的织物；防水布；(主英) 雨衣 *vt.* 使不透水，防水；给…上胶/~ shed *n.* 1. 流域 2. 分水岭；分界线/~ spout *n.* 1. 水落管；喷水嘴 2.(龙卷风卷起的) 水龙卷，海龙卷；暴雨/~ table 1. 地下水位 2.【建】承雨线脚/~ tight *adj.* 1. 防漏水的，防水的 2.(计划、措辞等) 严密的，无懈可击的，天衣无缝的/~ tower 1.(自来) 水塔 2.(救火用的) 高喷水塔/~ wave 1. 水波 2. 水烫波浪 (式) (用手发型)/~ way 1. 1. 水路；航道 2. 排水道 (船上的) 舷侧排水沟/~wheel *n.* 1.(汲水用的) 辘轳/~works [复] *n.* 1.(城市等的) 供水系统 2.[用作单或复]自来水厂 3. 喷水装置 4.[用作复] (俚) 眼泪；流泪；哭泣/~-worn *adj.* (岩石等) 被水冲蚀的

Watergate ['wɔtəgeit] *n.* 1. 水门丑闻，水门事件 2. 水门事件式丑闻；丑闻

Waterloo [,wɔːtə'luː] *n.* 1. 滑铁卢 [比利时中部城镇] (1815 年拿破仑军队大败之处) 2. 惨败; 毁灭性打击; 决定性的竞赛; 失败 (或毁灭) 的原因

watery ['wɔːtəri] *adj.* 1. 水的 2. 充满水的; 湿的 3. (天空等) 有雨意的 4. 似水的; 稀薄的; (言语等) 乏味的; (色、光等) 淡的 4. 充满分泌液的; 水汪汪的; 汗淋淋的 5. 浸透水的; 产生 (或渗出、分泌) 水 (或稀薄液体) 的

watt [wɔt] *n.* 【电】瓦 (特) ‖ ~**age** *n.* 瓦 (特) 数

wattle ['wɔtl] *n.* 1. 枝条; 篱笆条 (英方) 杖; 棍; 棒; 杆; 枝 2. (英方) 羊栏 3. (支撑茅屋顶或篱笆的) 枝条构架 4. (火鸡等的) 肉垂 5. (鱼的) 鱼 (触) 须 6. 【植】 金合欢树 — *adj.* 用枝条编的; 用枝条做屋顶的 — *vt.* 1. 把 (枝条) 编成篱笆 (或屋顶等) 2. 以枝条作 (篱笆、屋顶等)

wave [weiv] *n.* 1. 波, 波浪, 波涛 [the ~(s)] (诗) 海; 水 2. 【物】 (光、声等的) 波 3. (情绪等) 高涨; (头发的) 鬈曲; (织物的) 波纹 4. (情绪等的) 波动; 高涨; 高潮; (人群的) 潮涌, 运动 5. 浪潮似的种种活动; (一群同类动物的) 涌潮; (人口) 激增; 【军】 攻击波; 梯队 6. (用手等挥动的) 示意, 致意; 信号 7. (天气的) 突变; 浪潮似的一阵 8. 示意图 — *vi.* 1. 起伏; 飘动, 飘扬 2. 呈波浪形; 挥手示意 (或致意) 挥动旗 (或灯等) 示意 — *vt.* 1. 使波动; 使起伏; 使飘扬 2. 挥动; 晃动 3. 挥手表示 (致敬、告别等); 向…挥手 (或旗等) 示意 4. 使成波浪形; 使鬈曲; 使 (织物) 成波纹 ‖ ~ **detector** [无] 检波器 / ~ **length** *n.* 【物】 [无] 波长

waver ['weivə] *vi.* 1. 摇摆; 摇晃; 摆动 2. (声音) 颤抖; (光) 闪烁 3. 犹豫不决; 动摇 4. (事物) 变动, 波动

wavy ['weivi] *adj.* 1. 起浪的; 多浪的; 波涛汹涌的 2. 波状的; 成波浪形前进的; 有波纹的; 起伏的 3. 波动的, 动摇的, 不稳定的 ‖ **wavily** *adv.* / **waviness** *n.*

wax[1] [wæks] *n.* 1. 蜡; 蜂蜡; 蜡状物 2. 耳垢 3. (美俚) 唱片 — *vt.* 1. 给 (家具、地板等) 上蜡 2. (口) 把…录成唱片 ‖ ~**er** *n.* 打蜡工; 打蜡机 ‖ ~**wing** *n.* 朱缘蜡翅鸟 / ~**work** *n.* 1. 蜡制品; 蜡像 2. [~works] [用作单或复] 蜡像馆; 蜡像展览

wax[2] [wæks] *vi.* 1. (月亮) 渐圆, 渐满; 增加; 变大 2. (渐渐) 变为 — *n.* 1. 增加; 变大 2. (由新月至满月的) 渐盈

waxen ['wæksən] *adj.* 1. 蜡的; 蜡制的; 涂蜡的 2. 蜡似的; 苍白的; 柔软的; 光滑的 3. (古) (心肠) 软的; 柔顺的; 易受影响的

waxy ['wæksi] *adj.* 1. 蜡制的; 蜡质的; 涂蜡的; 含蜡的 2. 似蜡的; 柔软的; 可塑的; (脸色等) 苍白的; 光滑的

way [wei] *n.* 1. 路, 道路 2. 路线; 路途; 路程 3. 方向; (口) [只用单] 附近 4. 方法; 方式 5. 情形; 状况; 境地 6. 习惯; 作用 7. 行业; (经历或活动的) 范围 8. (某个) 方面; (某) 点 9. [律] 通行权; [~s] [船] 船台, 滑道; [机] (车床等的) 导轨 — *adv.* (口) 1. 远远地; 大大地; 非常地 2. 完全地 3. 离开: go ~ 走开 ‖ ~**bill** *n.* 运货单; 乘客单 / ~**farer** *n.* (徒步) 旅行者 / ~**faring** *adj.* (徒步) 旅行的 / ~**lay** *vt.* 伏击; 拦路抢劫; (为采访等) 拦截 / ~**side** *n.* & *adj.* 路边 (的); 路旁 (的); (铁路等旁的) 小站 / ~ **train** 普通客车, 慢车

-ways *suf.* [附在名词或形容词后构成副词] 表示 "在…方向 (或位置)", "以…方式" 等: endways, sideways

wayward ['weiwəd] *adj.* **1.** 任性的；刚愎的；倔强的 **2.** 难捉摸的；反复无常的 **3.**〈古〉讨厌的；不如意的 ‖ ～**ness** *n.*

WBC *abbr.* white blood cell(s)

w. c. *abbr.* **1.** water closet **2.** without charge 免费

WCC *abbr.* World Council of Churches 世界基督教协进会

we [wi:; 弱 wi] *pron.*〔主格〕**1.** 我们 **2.**〔报刊编者等用语〕本报；本刊；笔者；本人；我(们) **3.**(泛指)人们 **4.**〈口〉(表示亲切或关心)你(们) **5.**(帝王在正式场合用来代替 I)朕，寡人

weak [wi:k] *adj.* **1.** 弱的；虚弱的；衰弱的 **2.** 软弱的；懦弱的 **3.**(论证等)不充分的，无力的 **3.** 缺乏说服力的；易破的；不耐用的；易弯的 **4.** 差的；薄弱的；淡薄的 **5.**(文体)无活力的；散漫的；不简练的 **6.**〔商〕(价格)看跌的，疲软的；(股票市价等)低落的 **7.**〔语〕规则的，弱(变化)的 **8.**〔语〕轻读的，非重读的 ‖ ～**ly** *adj. & adv.* 虚弱的(地)；软弱的(地)；有病的(地) / ～**ness** *n.* **1.** 虚弱；软弱；薄弱 **2.** 缺点，弱点 **3.** 嗜好，癖好；宠爱的东西

weaken ['wi:kən] *vt.* **1.** 使变弱；削弱，减弱 **2.** 使稀薄；使淡薄 — *vi.* **1.** 变弱；变衰弱 **2.** 变软弱；变得优柔寡断

weakling ['wi:kliŋ] *n.* **1.** 体弱的人(或动物) **2.** 意志薄弱的人；弱者 **3.** 智力低下的人，低能儿 — *adj.* 虚弱的；软弱的；懦弱的

weal¹ [wi:l] *n.* 福利；幸福；好运道

weal² [wi:l] *n.* 鞭痕；(棒打的)伤痕

weald [wi:ld] *n.*〈英〉**1.** 林地，山林 **2.** 原野，旷野

wealth [welθ] *n.* **1.** 财富；财产；资源；富有 **2.** 丰富，大量

wealthy ['welθi] *adj.* 富的，富裕的；丰富的

wean [wi:n] *vt.* **1.** 使断奶 **2.** 使断绝；使放弃；使戒掉；使脱离

weapon ['wepən] *n.* **1.** 武器，兵器；凶器 **2.** 斗争工具(或手段) — *vt.* 武装 ‖ ～**ry** *n.*〔总称〕武器，兵器

wear¹ [wɛə](wore[wɔ:], worn[wɔ:n]) *vt.* **1.** 穿着；戴着；(为表示身份等)佩带着；蓄留着(须、发) **2.** 面露，面带；呈现(特定样子) **3.**(船)升，挂(旗) **3.** 磨损；穿破；用旧；磨成，磨出；穿成(*to, into*) **4.** 使疲乏；使厌烦(*out, down*) **5.** 消磨(时间)(*away, out*) — *vi.* **1.** 磨损；变旧；穿破；用坏 **2.** 耐久，耐用；禁磨 **3.** 逐渐变得，逐渐变得 **4.**(时间等)逐渐消逝(*on, away*)；消失(*off*) — *n.* **1.** 穿，佩；戴；使用 **2.** 衣服，服装〔常用以构成复合词〕(商业用语)特殊场合穿的服装；流行款式 **3.** 磨损；损耗；损耗量 **4.** 耐久性；耐用性 ‖ ～**able** *adj.* / ～**er** *n.* 穿戴者；佩带者

wear² [wɛə](wore[wɔ:], worn[wɔ:n]) *vt. & vi.*〔海〕(使)顺风掉抢

weary ['wiəri] *adj.* **1.** 疲倦的，困乏的；消沉的，萎靡的 **2.** 厌倦的；不耐烦的(*of*) **3.** 令人厌倦的；令人厌烦的 — *vt.* **1.** 使疲乏；使厌烦 — *vi.* **1.** 疲乏；厌倦；不耐烦 **3.** 不耐烦地等待(*for*) ‖ **wearily** *adv.* / **weariness** *n.* / **wearisome** *adj.* 使人疲倦的；令人厌烦的；乏味的

weasel ['wi:zl] *n.* **1.** 鼬；黄鼠狼 **2.** 狡猾的人，奸刁的人 **3.**〈美俚〉告密者；鬼鬼祟祟的人；马屁精；卑微的人；矮小的男子 **4.**〈美〉含糊的话，模棱两可的话 **5.**〔军〕随履水陆运输车；小型登陆车辆 **6.**〈美〉〔常 W-〕鼬鼠州(南卡罗来纳州的别称) — *vi.* **1.** 躲避；躲闪飞
〈美〉含糊其词 **3.**〈美俚〉告密

weather ['weðə] n. 1. 天气 2. 恶劣天气 3. 处境，境遇 — adj. 〖海〗上风的，向风一侧的 — vt. 1. 使经受风吹雨打；使经受日晒雨淋；使遭受；侵蚀；风干；〖地〗使风化 2. 渡过（暴风雨、困难等）；经受住 3. 〖海〗航行到...的上风；安全地绕过 4. 使〔屋顶等〕倾斜（以便雨水流泻）— vi. 1. （因风吹雨打等而）退色；受侵蚀；风化；风干；损坏 2. 经受风雨；耐久 ‖ ~-beaten adj. 1. 饱经风霜的；（脸等）晒黑的 2. 风雨剥蚀（或损耗）的 / '~-board n. 〖建〗护墙板 2. 〖海〗上风船舷 vt. 给...装封檐板 / ~ chart，~ map 天气图 / '~-cock n. 风标；易变的人（或物），随风倒的人 / ~ forecast 天气预报 / '~-glass n. 晴雨计；气压计；湿度计 / '~ man n. 〈口〉气象工作者；气象报告员 / '~-proof adj. 防风雨（或日晒等）的；抗风化的；不受气候影响的 vt. 使防风雨（或日晒等）/ ~ station 气象站 / ~ vane 风标

weave [wi:v]（wove [wəʊv]，woven ['wəʊvən]）vt. 1. 织；编（制）2. （蜘蛛等）结（网）3. 编造；安排 4. 使迂回行进 — vi. 1. 迂回行进（如（英军俚）绕飞，闪避 — n. 织法，编法；编织式样

weaver ['wi:və] n. 1. 织布工；编织者；织补者 2. 编排者，编造者 3. 〖动〗织布鸟

web [web] n. 1. （蜘蛛等的）网；丝；网状物（网状组织）；〖纺〗棉网；毛网 2. 织物；（幼体 3. （阴谋等的）圈套；圈套 4. （印报纸的）卷筒纸（卷筒纸的一卷，一筒 5. （蛙、水禽、蝙蝠等的）蹼；（鸟翎上的）短毛 6. 〖机〗连结板；金属薄条片（如刀叶、锯片等）7. 〖建〗腹板，梁腹 — vt. （webbed; webbing）1. （蜘蛛等在）...上结网；织网般密布在...上 2. 用丝网络住；使落入圈套

wed [wed]（wed(ded); wedding）vt. 1. 娶；嫁；与...结婚；使完婚 2. 使结合 — vi. 1. 结婚；出嫁；娶妻 2. 结合

Wed. abbr. Wednesday

we'd [wi:d; 弱 wid] 1. = we had 2. = we would 3. = we should

wedding ['wedɪŋ] n. 1. 婚礼；结婚；结婚纪念 2. 结合 ‖ ~ breakfast 喜宴（在婚礼后或在蜜月旅行前举行）/ ~ march 婚礼进行曲

wedge [wedʒ] n. 1. 楔；劈 2. 使分裂的东西 3. 楔形物；楔形状 4. 起因；引起某种行动（或发展）的事物 — vt. 1. 楔入；劈开分裂 2. 把...楔住、阻...楔牢 3. 挤入；插入（in）— vi. 楔入；挤进 ‖ ~d adj. 楔形的 / ~wise adv. 呈楔形地

wedlock ['wedlɒk] n. 婚姻；结婚（生活）；已婚状态

Wednesday ['wenzdi] n. 星期三 — adv. 〈口〉在星期三 ‖ ~s adv. 〈美〉每星期三；在任何星期三

wee [wi:] adj. 1. 小的；极小的；极少的，很少的 2. 很早的 — n. 一点点；一会儿

weed [wi:d] n. 1. 杂草；野草；莠草 2. 水生植物（尤指海藻）3. [the ~]烟草（俚）大麻烟；〈口〉香烟；雪茄烟 4.（俚）瘦高个子〔羸弱的人（或马）〕5. 令人讨厌的东西（或人）；赘疣 6. [the ~s]〈美俚〉流浪工人的帐篷；丛林 — vi. 除草；除害 — vt. 1. 除（杂草）；除去

的杂草 2. 剔出；清除（out）‖ ~ed adj. 1. 铲除了野草的 2. 野草丛生的 / ~er n. 1. 除草者 2. 除草工具；除草机

weeds [wiːdz] [复] n. 1.（尤指寡妇所穿的）丧服 2.（表示哀悼的）黑纱

weedy ['wiːdi] adj. 1. 杂草丛生的 2. 蔓延的；长得快的 3.（人或动物）瘦长的；瘦弱的；丑陋的 4. 虚弱无力的；软弱的

week [wiːk] n. 1. 星期，周；（从任何时候算起的）连续 7 天 2. 工作周（一周中除例假日外的工作日）3. 从某日起算 7 天前（或后）的一天 ‖ ~day n. 星期日（或星期六和星期日以外）的日子，周日，工作日 / ~days adv. 在每个星期日，在工作日 / ~'end n. 周末；周末假期 ‖ ~'end bag，~'end case 过周末假期用的旅行包 / ~'end·er n. 1. 过周末假期的人 2. = ~end bag / ~'ends adv. 在周末；每个周末

weekly ['wiːkli] adj. 1. 每周的；一周的 2. 每周一次的；按周计算的 — adv. 每周；每周一次；按周 — n. 周刊；周报

ween [wiːn] vt.（古）（诗）以为；料想；想象（常用于 I 这一插入句中）

weep [wiːp] (wept [wept]) vi. 1. 哭泣，流泪 2. 悲叹；哀悼 — vt. 流（泪）；悲叹 ‖ ~er n.

weepie ['wiːpi] n.（英口）让人伤感落泪的书（或电影、戏剧等）

weeping ['wiːpiŋ] n. 哭泣；流泪 — adj. 1. 哭泣的；泪汪汪的；流水的 2. 下雨的；多雨的 3. 下垂的；（植物）有垂枝的

weevil ['wiːvil] n.（动）象甲，象虫；豆象 ‖ ~y adj.

weft [weft] n.（纺）纬，纬纱

weigh [wei] vt. 1. 称…的重量；掂估…的分量 2. 掂量；考虑；权衡 3. 重压；

把…压倒；使下垂；使不平衡 4.【海】起（锚），拔（锚）— vi. 1. 重有于；称分量 2. 有分量；有意义；有影响 3. 重压（on, upon）4.【海】起锚，启航 — n. 称分量，上秤，过秤 ‖ ~er n. 1. 过磅员，称货员，衡器；称物机 ‖ ~·beam n. 大杆秤 / ~·bridge n. 地秤

weight [weit] n. 1. 重，重量；分量；体重 2. 趋向吸引中心的力 3. 重量单位；衡制（制）4. 砝码；秤砣 5. 重体（如铅球、铁饼、铸秤砣等）6. 重担；负担；重压；计重（责任或忧虑）7. 重要（性）；重大 8. 影响；力量；权力；势力 9. [常用以构成复合词]适宜于某一季节的衣服的质地（指厚薄、轻重）10.（拳击、摔跤等运动员的）重量级别 11.（统计学用语）权 — vt. 1. 加重量于 2. 重压；压迫 3. 用金属盐增加（线、纤维）的重量 4.（统计学用语）使加权 5. 称…的重量；估估…的分量 ‖ ~·less adj. ‖ ~ lifter 举重运动员，举重者 / ~ lifting【体】举重 / ~ man 投掷运动员 / ~·watcher n.（注意不使自己发胖的）节食减肥者

weighty ['weiti] adj. 1. 重的，沉重的 2. 繁重的；累人的 3. 重大的；重要的；有影响的；有分量的 4. 肥大的 5. 严肃的；认真的；值得考虑的 ‖ weightily adv.

weir [wiə] n. 1. 堰；低坝；导流坝 2.（用小木桩或小枝编成篱状置于河中捕鱼的）鱼梁

weird [wiəd] adj. 1.（古）命运的；命运女神的 2. 超自然的 3. 似鬼的；怪诞的；神秘的 4.（口）离奇的，古怪的；不可思议的 — n.（苏格兰）1. 命运（尤指坏运气）2.【W-】（神话中的）命运女神之一 3. 预言 4. 占卜者；预言者；符咒 ‖ ~ly adv. / ~ness n.

welcome ['welkəm] adj. 1. 受欢迎的 2.

可喜的;来得正好的 **3.** 被允许的;可随意的;不必感谢的 — *int.* 欢迎 — **n. 1.** 欢迎 **2.**〈某种姿态的〉迎接 — *vt.* 欢迎,欢欢喜喜地迎接

weld [weld] *vt.* **1.** 焊接,熔接;锻接 **2.** (紧密)团结;结合;使连成整体(*into*) — *vi.* 焊牢;能被焊接 — **n.** 焊接,熔接;锻接;焊接点,接头

welfare ['welfεə] **n. 1.** 幸福;福利;康乐 **2.** 福利工作;福利事业;福利救济 — *adj.* **1.** 福利(事业)的 **2.** 接受福利救济的 ‖ ~ work 福利工作;福利事业

well[1] [wel] **n. 1.** 井;水井;气井;油井;泉水;泉;池 **3.** 源泉 **4.** 深坑 **5.**〈建〉井孔;通风竖井;(房屋中的)楼梯井;升降机井道 **6.**〈英〉(法庭上设有围栏的)律师席 **7.**〈海〉(船舱中)保护水泵的井状围栏 **8.** (渔船中的)养鱼舱 **9.** 盛放液体的容器(如墨水池等) — *vi.* (泪水等)涌出 — *vt.* 涌出(泪水等)

well[2] [wel] (better['betə],best[best]) *adv.* **1.** 好;很好;令人满意地;妥当地;关心地;优待地;赞扬地 **3.** 有理由地;恰当地 **4.** 完全地;充分地;彻底地 **5.** 很;很可能 — (better['betə],best[best]) *adj.* **1.** 健康的;治愈的 **2.** 恰当的;可取的;幸运的 **3.** 令人满意的;良好的 **4.** 富有的;有钱的 — *int.* **1.** [表示惊讶]哎!嗳! **2.** [表示快慰]好啦! **3.** [表示无可奈何]嗯!哎! **4.** [表示同意、期望、让步等]好吧!嗯! **5.** [用于重新开始说话时]好,美满;成功;幸运;令人满意的事物 ‖ ~·ad'vised *adj.* 明智的;谨慎的;经周密考虑的 / ~·'balanced *adj.* 匀称的;均衡的;神态稳定的;明智的 / ~·be'haved *adj.* 品行端正的,有礼貌的 / ~·'being *n.* 健康;幸福;福利 / ~·be'loved *adj.* 深受热爱的;(用于称呼

前)尊敬的 **n.** 亲爱的人 / ~·'born *adj.* 出身高贵的,出身名门的 / ~·'bred *adj.* **1.** 教养良好的 **2.** 良种的 / ~·con'tent-(ed) *adj.* 十分满意的 / ~·de'fined *adj.* 清楚表明的,明确指出的;界线分明的 / ~·dis'posed *adj.* 好心好意的;乐于助人的 / ~·'earned *adj.* 劳动所得的;理当有的;应得的 / ~·favo(u) red *adj.* 漂亮的,好看的 / ~·'founded *adj.* **1.** 基础牢固的 **2.** 有充分根据的;理由充足的 / ~·'grounded *adj.* = ~·founded / ~·in'formed *adj.* 见识广博的;消息灵通的 / ~·in'tentioned *adj.* 善意的,好心的 / ~·'knit *adj.* **1.** 结实的,健壮的 **2.** 组织严密的 / ~·'known *adj.* **1.** 出名的,众所周知的 **2.** 熟知的 / ~·'looking *adj.* 漂亮的 / ~·'made *adj.* 样子好的;匀称的;做工考究的;(剧本等)情节安排得很好的 / ~·'meaning *adj.* 善意的(往往指结果不好的) / ~·'nigh *adv.* 几乎;可谓 / ~·'off *adj.* **1.** 富裕的 **2.** 处于有利地位的 **3.** 供应充裕的 / ~·'read ['wel'red] *adj.* 博览群书的;博学的 / ~·'regulated *adj.* **1.** 管理得好的;纪律严明的 **2.** 理应如此的 / ~·re'puted *adj.* 得好评的;名声好的 / ~·'spent *adj.* (时间、劳力等)使用得当的 / ~·'spring *n.* 河源;泉源;(喻)源泉 / ~·'timed *adj.* **1.** 及时的,时机选得很对的 **2.** 有节拍的 **3.** 很准时的 / ~·to-'do *adj.* 富有的 / ~·'turned *adj.* **1.** 匀称的;外形优美的 **2.** 讲得恰当的 / ~·'worn *adj.* **1.** 用旧了的 **2.** 老生常谈的,陈腐的 **3.**〈古〉穿戴得适当的;相称的

we'll [wil, 弱 wil] **1.** = we shall **2.** = we will

welladay ['welə'dei], **wellaway** ['welə'wei] *int.*〈古〉〈谑〉呜呼!哎哉!

Wellington ['weliŋtən] **n. 1.** 惠灵顿〔新西兰首都〕 **2.** [~ s]〈英〉惠灵顿长靴〔亦

作~ boots)

Welsh [welʃ] *adj.* 1. 威尔士的；威尔士人的；威尔士语的 — *n.* 1. [the ~]用作复]威尔士人 2. 威尔士语(即威尔士人所说的凯尔特语) 3. 威尔士奶牛(或猪) ‖ ~ **rabbit**, ~ **rarebit** ['reəbit] 威尔士干酪

welt [welt] *n.* 1. (皮鞋鞋底和鞋面接缝间的)贴边，沿条 2. (衣服的)贴边，滚条 3. 鞭痕；条痕；笞击；殴打 — *vt.* 1. 给(皮鞋等)加贴边或贴边 2. 鞭打；痛打

welter[1] ['weltə] *vi.* 1. 滚，打滚，翻滚 2. 沉溺，沉湎 3. 浸；浸湿；染污 4. 颠簸，起伏 5. 扰乱 — *n.* 1. 混乱；杂乱无章 2. 翻腾；动荡的起伏；翻腾

welter[2] ['weltə] *n.* 1. 重量级骑师 2. 次中量级拳击手(或摔跤运动员) 3. 〈口〉重击 4. 〈口〉巨大的人(或物) ‖ ~**weight** *n.* 1. 重量级骑师 2. (在跳栏赛马时)加在马身上的特别重量(一般为28磅) 3. 次中量级拳击手(或摔跤运动员) *adj.* 次中量级骑师的；次中量级拳击手(摔跤运动员)的

wen [wen] *n.* 1. 【医】皮脂囊肿，粉瘤 2. 臃肿的城市

wench [wentʃ] *n.* 1. 少妇；〈方〉女孩子；少女 2. 乡村姑娘；女佣 3. 荡妇；妓女 — *vi.* 1. 〈方〉嫖妓；求爱 2. 嫖妓；私通

wend [wend] *vi.* 行，走；往 — *vt.* 走；赴，往；~ one's way 赴，往

went [went] go 的过去式

wept [wept] weep 的过去式

were [强 wɔ:；弱 wə] be 的过去式

we're [wiə] = we are

weren't [wɔ:nt] = were not

wer(e)wolf ['wɛ:wulf] ([复] wer(e)wolves ['wɛ:wulvz]) *n.* 1. (神话中)变成狼的

人，狼人；能装扮成狼的人 2. 狡猾凶悍的人

west [west] *n.* 1. 西；西部 2. [the W-]西洋，西方；欧美 3. [史]罗马帝国 — *adj.* 西方的；西部的；朝西的；(风)从西方来的 — *adv.* 在西方；向西方 ‖ **West Point** (美国)西点军校 / **West Pointer** (美国)西点军校学员(或毕业生)

westbound ['westbaund] *adj.* 向西行的；向西驶的

westerly ['westəli] *adj.* 1. 西的；向西方的 2. (风)从西方来的 — *adv.* 1. 向西方 2. 从西方来 — *n.* 西风；[wester-lies]西风带

western ['westən] *adj.* 1. 西的；[常 W-]西方的；西部的 2. 朝西的 3.〈罕〉(风)从西吹来的 — *n.* 1. [常 W-]西部美国(西部)的产品；具有美国西部特征的产品 2. [常 W-](取材于 19 世纪下半叶美国西部生活的)西部电影(或小说、广播) ‖ ~**er** *n.* [常 W-] 1. 西方人；欧美人 2. 美国西部人 3. (尤指 19 世纪俄国的)主张采用西欧文化的人

westernize ['westənaiz] *vt. & vi.* (使)西方化，(使)欧美化

westernmost ['westənməust] *adj.* 最西的

Western Samoa [sə'məuə]西萨摩亚[南太平洋岛国]

West Indies ['indiz]西印度群岛[拉丁美洲]

Westminster ['westminstə] *n.* 威斯敏斯特(英国议会所在地)；议会；政界

West Virginia [və'dʒiniə]西弗吉尼亚[美国州名]

westward ['westwəd] *adj.* 向西的 — *adv.* 向西 — *n.* 西方；西部 ‖ ~**ly** *adj. & adv.*

westwards ['westwədz] *adv.* 向西

wet [wet](wetter, wettest)adj. 1. 湿的,潮的;Wet Paint! 油漆未干! 2. 下雨的;多雨的 3.(用糖、酒精等)浸渍(保存)的 4. 用水(或其他液体)处理的 5.(鱼)未经加工(或晒干)的 6.(天然气)含大量石油气的 7.〈美口〉允许制酒(或卖酒)的;反对禁酒的 8. 弄错了的,搞错的 9.〈俚〉喝醉的 10.〈俚〉不讨人喜欢的;蠢的,无价值的 11. 极易伤感的 一 n. 1. 湿气;潮湿;水分;液体 2.[the 一]雨;雨天 3.〈美口〉反对禁酒的人 一(wetted 或〈美〉wet; wetting)vt. 1. 把...弄湿;把...尿湿 2. 为(某事)喝酒庆祝一 vi. 变湿;尿湿 ‖~ly adv. /~ness n. ‖ ~ blanket n.(灭火等用的)弄湿的毯子 2. 扫兴的人;败兴的事一 vt. 1. 把...弄湿 2. 扫兴 ‖~-blanket vt. 用毯子扑灭;使扫兴 ~ cell n.[电]湿电池 ~ dock 湿坞 /~ dream[医]梦遗,梦中遗精 /'~-land n. [常 ~s](尤指为野生动物保存的)湿地,沼泽地 ~ nurse 奶妈,乳母 /'~-nurse vt. 1. 做...的奶母 2. 悉心照料;给...以过分的照顾

wether ['weðə]n. 阉羊,去势公羊

we've [wi:v;弱 wiv] = we have

whack [hwæk] vt. 1. 使劲打;(用棍子等)重打 2. 砍,劈 3.〈主英〉反对;击败 4.〈俚〉按份儿分(up) 5. 匆忙做好;赶紧凑成(up, out) 6. 催赶(牲口)(up)一 vi. 重击,用力打一 n. 1. 重击;重击声 2. 份儿,份儿 3. 尝试;机会 4. 正常工作情况 5.一次

whale [hweil]([复]whale(s))n. 1. 鲸巨大的人(或物);极好的人(或物)一 vi. 捕鲸 vt. 捕鲸者;捕鲸工人;捕鲸船 ‖~ boat n. 1. 捕鲸船 2. 捕鲸船式救生艇 /'~-bone n. 1. 鲸须 2. 鲸须制品 /~ calf 幼鲸 /~ fin 鲸须

whaling ['hweiliŋ]n. 捕鲸(业);鲸加工

(业)

wharf [hwɔ:f]([复]wharves [hwɔ:vz]或wharfs)n. 码头;停泊处 一 vt. 1. 使(船)靠码头 2. 把(货物)卸在码头上 3. 为...设立码头 一 vi. 靠码头 ‖~age n. 1.[总称]码头;码头设施 2. 码头(使用)费;码头搬运费 3. 码头使用

what [hwɔt]pron. 1.[疑问代词]什么,什么样的 2.[用于感叹句中]多少 3.[关系代词]...的事物(或人)(= that which 或 those which) 4.[关系代词]凡是...的事物(= whatever) 一 adj. 1.[表示疑问]什么,什么样的 2.[表示感叹]多少的,何等的 3.[关系形容词]所...的,尽可能多的 一 adv. 在哪一方面;到什么程度 一 int. 1.[表示惊讶、气愤等]什么 2.〈英口〉[常用于句尾]是不是? 不是吗?

whate'er [hwɔt'eə]pron. & adj.〈诗〉whatever

whatever [hwɔt'evə]pron. 1.[关系代词]无论什么,不管什么,凡是...的事物 2.[连接代词]无论什么 3. 诸如此类 4.〈口〉究竟是什么 一 adj. 1.[关系形容词]无论什么样的 2.[连接形容词]不管什么样的 3.[用在含有否定词或 any 的句中,放在名词后面]任何的(= at all)

whatnot ['hwɔtnɔt] n. 1. 古董(或装饰品、书籍等)的陈设架 2. 难以归类(或描写)的物(或人);小玩意儿 3. 诸如此类的东西

what's [hwɔts] 1. = what is 2. = what has 3. = what does

whatsoever [ˌhwɔtsəu'evə]pron. & adj. = whatever (语气比 whatever 强)

wheal [hwi:l] n. 1.(皮肤上隆起的)伤痕,鞭痕,棒痕 2.(蚊等叮咬后的)疹块,丘疹,风块

wheat [hwi:t] *n.* **1.** 小麦 **2.** 淡黄色 **3.** 〈美俚〉朴实的人;天真无邪的青年;乡下人

wheedle ['hwi:dl] *vt.* 哄,骗 (用谄媚、阿谀等)骗取 — *vi.* 哄,骗

wheel [hwi:l] *n.* **1.** 轮;车轮;机轮;轮状物 **2.** 舵轮;转向轮,驾驶盘 **3.** 自行车;〈罕〉(儿童) 三轮脚踏车;纺车;【史】(分裂肢体的) 刑车 **4.** 旋转;旋转运动 (尤指军队、船队的方向变换) **5.** 机构,机关;(一个机构中的) 主要人物;有权人士 **6.** 轮转烟火 **7.** 体育联合团体;(轮流交换演出节目的) 联营剧场 (或娱乐场) **8.** (歌曲末尾的) 重唱句,叠句 **9.** 〈美俚〉1 元银币 **10.** 〈美俚〉[~s]腿;汽车 — *vi.* **1.** 旋转;转弯 **2.** 盘旋 **3.** 骑自行车;驾 (或乘) 车前进;〈美俚〉高速驶车 — *vt.* **1.** 滚动,转动;推动 **2.** 用车运 (货等) **3.** 使变换方向;使旋转 **4.** 给…装轮子 **5.** 〈美俚〉高速驾 (车) ‖ ~ er *n.* **1.** 用车轮工人;车轮制造工 (常用以构成复合词) **2.** 车轮的东西 **3.** (马车的) 辕马 ‖ '~barrow *n.* 手推车;独轮小车 *vt.* 用手推车运送/'~base *n.* (同一车辆的) 轴距;(机车等的) 轮组距 /'~chair *n.* (病人等用的) 轮椅 /'~er-'dealer *n.* 〈美俚〉**1.** 独立行动的人 **2.** 机灵诡诈的人 **3.** 从事各种商业 (或社会活动) 的人 /'~house *n.* (船上的) 操舵室 /'~man *n.* **1.** 舵手 **2.** 汽车驾驶员 (或)〈口〉骑自行车的男子 /'~wright *n.* 车轮 (或车辆) 修造工

wheeze [hwi:z] *vi.* **1.** 喘,喘息 **2.** 呼哧呼哧地响 — *vt.* 喘息地说 (out) — *n.* **1.** 喘气声,喘息声 **2.** 喘气 **3.** 〈俚〉笑话;俏皮话 (尤指舞台常用的插科打诨) **4.** 〈俚〉巧妙主意

wheezy ['hwi:zi] *adj.* **1.** (要) 喘息的 **2.** 呼哧呼哧响的 **3.**〈俚〉老一套的

whelk [hwelk] *n.*〈动〉峨螺

whelm [hwelm] *vt.* **1.** 把 (盆、碗等) 覆着放;用…覆盖 **2.** 使覆没;淹没 **3.** (在思想或感情方面) 压倒,压服 — *vi.* 覆盖;淹没

whelp [hwelp] *n.* **1.** 小狗 **2.** (食肉动物的) 幼崽 (如幼虎、幼熊、幼狼等) **3.** 〈贬〉崽子 (指男或女孩) **4.** 可鄙的人;被人瞧不起的人 **5.** 【机】(链轮的) 扣链齿 **6.** [常~s]【机】绞盘筋筋 — *vt.* 〈贬指母狗〉下 (崽);〈贬〉(女人) 生 (小孩) — *vi.* 下崽,生幼崽;〈贬〉(女人) 生小孩

when [hwen] *adv.* **1.** [疑问副词] 什么时候,何时 **2.** [关系副词,引导定语从句] 当… — *conj.* **1.** 当…时 **2.** 一…(就…) **3.** 如果 **4.** 虽然;然而;可是 **5.** 既然;考虑到 **6.** 在那时;然后 — *pron.* **1.** [疑问代词] 什么时候 **2.** [关系代词] 那时 — *n.* (事件发生的) 时间,日期;场合

whence [hwens]〈书面语〉*adv.* **1.** [疑问副词] 从何处;出于什么原因 **2.** [关系副词] 从那儿;由此 **3.** 到原来地方 — *conj.* 据此;由此 — *pron.* **1.** [疑问代词] 何处 **2.** [关系代词] 那里 — *n.* 来源,由来,根源

whenever [hwen'evə] *conj.* 每当;无论何时 — *adv.* 究竟何时

where [hweə] *adv.* **1.** [疑问副词] 在哪里;往哪里;从哪里 **2.** [从哪一点上] **3.** [关系副词] 在那里;往那里 **3.** [连接副词] 在…的地方;到…的地方;在…的地方 — *pron.* 哪里 — *n.* (事件发生的) 地方,地点;场所

whereabouts ['hweərə,bauts] *adv.* [疑问副词] 在哪里;靠近哪里 — [复] *n.* [用作单或复]下落;行踪;所在

whereas [hwɛɑr'æz] *conj*. 1.(公文用语) 鉴于 2. 然而,却;反之;尽管

whereat [hwɛɑr'æt] *adv*. 1.[关系副词]在 那里;对那个;由于那个 2.[疑问副词]为 何

whereby [hwɛɑ'bai] *adv*. 1.[关系副词]在 哪方面;(古)凭什么,如何 2.[关系副词] 靠那个;凭借那个,借以

wherefore ['hwɛɑfɔ] *adv*. 1.[关系副词] 为此,因此 2.[疑问副词]为什么 —— *conj*. 为此,因此 —— *n*. 理由,缘故

wherein [hwɛɑr'in] *adv*. 1.[疑问副词]在 哪方面,在哪一点;在什么地方 2.[关 系副词]在那方面;在那里;在那时

whereof [hwɛɑr'ɔv] *adv*. 1.[关系副词]关 于那事;关于那物;关于那人 2.[疑问 副词]关于什么;关于谁

whereon [hwɛɑr'ɔn] *adv*. 1.[疑问副词]在 什么上面;在谁身上 2.[关系副词]在 那上面;在那时候

whereupon [,hwɛɑrə'pɔn] *adv*. 1.(古)[疑 问副词]在什么上面;在谁身上 2.[关 系副词]据此;因此,于是;随之;在那 上面

wherever [hwɛɑr'ɛvə] *adv*. 1.(口)究竟在 哪里;究竟到哪里 2. 在任何地方;到 任何地方 3.[连接副词]无论在哪里; 无论到哪里

wherewithal ['hwɛəwiðɔːl] *n*. [常the～] 必要的资金(或资源、设备、手段等)

whet [hwet] (whetted; whetting) *vt*. 1. 磨,磨快 ～ a knife 磨刀,把刀磨快 2. 刺激;促进;增强(食欲、欲望等) —— *n*. 1. 磨 2. 开胃物(如酒等);刺激物 3. (方)时间,一会儿 a long ～ 好久 ‖～stone *n*. 磨石;磨刀石,油石

whether ['hwɛðə] *conj*. 是否 —— *pron*. (古)1.[疑问代词](两个中的)哪一个 2.[关系代词](两个中的)任何一个

whew [hwju] *n*. 1. 吹哨声;鸣笛声 2. 晴 声 —— *int*.[表示惊讶、失望、厌恶等,常 含滑稽意]唏!

whey [hwei] *n*. 乳清,乳水

which [hwitʃ] *pron*. 1.[疑问代词]哪一 个;哪一些 2.[关系代词]那一个;那一 些 —— *adj*. 1.[疑问形容词]哪一个; 哪一些 2.[关系形容词]那个;那些 3.[连 接形容词]无论哪个;无论哪些(一般 多用 whichever)

whichever [hwitʃ'ɛvə] *pron*.[关系代词]无 论哪个;无论哪些 —— *adj*. 1.[关系形 容词]无论哪个;无论哪些 2.[连接形 容词]无论哪个;无论哪些

whichsoever [,hwitʃsəu'ɛvə] *pron. & adj*. = whichever (语气比 whichever 强)

whiff [hwif] *n*. 1.(空气、香烟等的)一 吸;(风、烟等的)一吹,一喷 2. 一阵(微 弱的)气味 3. 轻吹声,轻喷声 4.(口) 小雪茄烟 5.(英)(一人划的)轻结构艇 6. 一点点 —— *vt*. 1. 吹散,吹走 2. 吸(烟)(away 等) 3. 吸(烟),抽(烟) 4.(美口) (棒球赛中)使(击球员)三击不中出局 —— *vi*. 1. 轻吹;轻拂;发轻吹声 2. 喷 烟;喷吹,吸(烟)(away 等) 4.(美口)(棒 球击球员)三击不中出局;未击中球

whiffle ['hwifl] *vi*. 1.(风)一阵阵地吹; (风等)时时变向;(思想等)反复无常, 动摇不定 2. 发轻吹声 3.(火光)闪动; (树叶)晃动 —— *vt*. 1. 吹;吹散 2. 吹得 (船)方向不定 —— *n*. 1. 空气的轻微流 动;微风 2. 轻吹;轻吹声

Whig [hwig] *n*. 1.[英史](自由党的前 身)辉格党党员 2.[美史](共和党的前 身)辉格党党员 3. 辉格党支持者 —— *adj*. 辉格党的;辉格党党员的;支持辉 格党的

while [hwail] *n*. 一会儿;一段时间 —— *conj*. 1. 当…的时候,和…同时 2.

而,然而 3. 虽然;尽管 4. 只要 — *prep.* 〈古〉〈方〉到...时候为止,直到... — *vt.* 消磨,轻松地度过(*away*)

whim [hwim] *n.* 1. 狂想;幻想;怪想 2. 突然的念头;一时的兴致 3.【矿】(提升用的)绞绳滚筒,绞盘

whimper ['hwimpə] *vi.* 1. 啜泣,呜咽 2. 发抱怨声 — *vt.* 啜泣地说,呜咽地说 — *n.* 1. 啜泣声,呜咽声 2. 牢骚,怨声

whimsical ['hwimzikəl] *adj.* 1. 想入非非的,异想天开的 2. 怪诞的,古怪的 3. 反复无常的;三心两意的 4. 心血来潮的,随心所欲的 ‖ ~**ly** *adv.*

whimsicality [ˌhwimzi'kæliti] *n.* 1. 想入非非,异想天开 2. 怪诞的话(或行动) 3. 反复无常;三心两意 4. 心血来潮;随心所欲

whimsy ['hwimzi] *n.* 1.(尤指写作或艺术上的)奇想,怪念头 2. 古怪的手法;奇趣;心血来潮(的想法);随心所欲

whine [hwain] *vi.* 1.(狗等)发哀鸣声;(汽笛、飞行中的炮弹等)发呜呜声 2. 哀诉 3. 嘀咕,发牢骚(*about*) — *vt.* 哀诉;嘀咕地说(*out*) — *n.* 1. 哀鸣声;呜呜声 2. 哀诉;牢骚

whinny ['hwini] *vi.*(马)嘶(指表示高兴的一种低微和缓的嘶声) — *vt.* 带嘶声地说 — *n.* 马嘶;嘶声

whip [hwip](whipped; whipping) *vt.* 1. 鞭笞;鞭打;(似鞭子般地)抽打 2. 搅打,把...打起泡沫 3. 激起;煽动 4.(为求统一步调等)集合,纠合(团体的成员) 5.(以尖锐的语言)攻击 6. 用细绳缠绕加固(绳子或钓竿);紧绕(绳等)于某物上;包缝(布边等) 7. 反复投钓丝于(河)中钓鱼 8. 突然拿取(或移动) 9. 仓促制成;〈口〉很快地烧煮(食物)(*up*) 10.〈俚〉胜过,击败 11.【海】用定单绞辘吊起 — *vi.* 1. 抽打;拍击 2. 急走;急移;突然行动 3. 急速地投竿钓鱼 — *n.* 1. 鞭子 2. 执鞭者;赶马车者;帮猎人赶猎狗的人(也称 whipper-in) 3. 抽打;一挥 4.(厨房中用的)搅拌器 5. 用掼奶油(或其他搅打成的食品)制成的餐后甜食 6.〈英〉政党的组织秘书(有维持纪律及要求该党议员出席议会讨论等之权) 7.〈英〉[常 W-](要求本党议员出席辩论或投票等的)书面通知 8. 迅速转动的机件;风车翼;【无】鞭状天线 9.【海】定单绞辘 10.(似鞭子具有的)易弯性,柔韧性 ‖ '~-**cord** *n.* 1. 鞭绳 2.【纺】马裤呢 3. 肠线 /~ **crane** 动臂起重机 /~ **hand** 1.(赶车时)执鞭子的手(常为右手) 2. 优势;支配地位 /'~-**round** *n.*〈主英〉募捐

whipper ['hwipə] *n.* 鞭打者 ‖ '~-'**in** ([复]whippers-in) *n.* 1. 帮猎人赶猎狗的人(也称 whip) 2.〈英〉(政党的)组织秘书;(组织秘书发给本党议员要求出席辩论或投票等的)书面通知 3.(赛马中的)最后一名

whippersnapper ['hwipəˌsnæpə] *n.* 不重要的人;妄自尊大的年轻人

whippet ['hwipit] *n.* 1.(赛跑用的)小灵狗 2.(第一次世界大战时协约国方面用的)快速轻型坦克(亦作~ tank)

whippoorwill ['hwippuəˌwil] *n.*【动】(美国东部及加拿大产的)三声夜鹰

whir [hwəː](whirred; whirring) *vi.* 呼呼作声地飞(或转);作呼呼声 — *vt.* 使呼呼地飞(或转);呼地一声把...带走 — *n.* 1.(疾飞或急转而产生的)呼呼声;飕飕声 2. 匆忙;纷乱;熙攘

whirl [hwəːl] *vt.* 1. 使回旋;使旋转;使急转 2. 卷走;旋风似地急速带走 — *vi.* 1. 回旋;旋转;急转 2. 急走;飞跑 3. 发晕;变混乱 — *n.* 1. 回旋;旋转;急转 2. 旋转物 3. 接连的活动;繁忙 4.

眩晕;混乱 5. 尝试;小试 ‖ ～er n.
‖ '～pool n. 1. 旋涡;(旋涡般的)强烈
运动 2. 混乱,纷乱

whirligig ['hwə:ligig] n. 1. 旋转式玩具;
陀螺;旋转木马 2. 旋转运动 3. 循环;
轮回;变迁 4.[动]豉甲

whirlwind ['hwə:lwind] n. 1. 旋风;旋流;
尘卷 2. 猛烈的势力;破坏性的事物

whirlybird ['hwə:dibə:d] n.[俚]直升(飞)
机

whirr [hwə:] vi., vt. & n. = whir

whisk [hwisk] vt. 1. 掸,拂 2. 挥动 3.
搅;打(蛋、乳酪等)成泡沫 4. 突然移
动;急速带走 — vi. 飞;疾驰 — n. 1. 掸,拂 2. 小笤帚,掸帚 3. 飞
奔;急取 4. 打蛋器 ‖ ～ broom 小笤帚,掸帚

whisker ['hwiskə] n. 1. 掸帚 2.(一根)
须;(猫、鼠等的)须 3.[～s] 胡须,髯;
〈古〉小胡子 4. 细丝;似须物;[化] 晶
须

whisk(e)y ['hwiski] n. 威士忌酒 — adj.
威士忌酒的;用威士忌酒做的;像威士
忌酒的

whisper ['hwispə] vi. 1. 低语;耳语;私
语;密谈 2.(树木等)发沙沙声;(风)发
飒飒声 — vt. 低声耳语;私下说 — n. 1. 低语;耳语;私语 2. 谣传;暗
示;秘密话;秘闻 3. 沙沙声;飒飒声

whist[1] [hwist]〈古〉〈方〉int. 嘘! 静! —
adj. 静的,不作声的

whist[2] [hwist] n. 惠斯特(一种类似桥牌
的牌戏)

whistle ['hwisl] n. 1. 口哨;笛;汽笛;哨
子 2. 口哨声;笛声;汽笛声;哨子声 3.
吹口哨声;鸟鸣声 4.[喉][只用
于习语 wet one's～中,意为 喝酒]— vi. 1. 吹口哨;吹笛;吹哨子 2.(兽)嘶

叫;(鸟)啭鸣;(风)啸;(子弹等)发嗖嗖
声 3. 吹口哨(或笛)召唤(或通知)— vt. 1. 吹口哨(或笛)召唤(或通知) 2.
用口哨吹奏(曲调等) 3. 使发啸声行
进 ‖ ～r n.

whit [hwit] n.[多用于否定句中]一点
点;丝毫

white [hwait] adj. 1. 白的;苍白的 2. 白
种(人)的 3.(政治上)白色的;保皇的;
极端保守的;反动的;反革命的 4. 空
白的,没有写过字(或印刷过)的 5. 清
白的,纯洁的;善意的 6.[俚]正直的;
公正的;诚实的 7. 幸运的;吉
利的 — n. 1. 白色;洁白 2. 白种人 3.
眼白 4. 蛋白 5. 精白面粉;白酒;白色
颜料 6. 白毛动物(如白马或白猪);
保 W.];(政治上的)保皇党人;极端保
守分子;反动分子;反革命分子 8.[～s]
[医]白带 9.(书写等留下的)空白处
‖ ～ness n.;在白 ⅰ 白色;纯洁;白色
的东西 ‖ '～bait n. 银鱼;小鲱鱼 /'～
blood cell [解] 白血球,白细胞 /'～ cap
n. 1.(波峰有白色泡沫的)白浪 2.
〈美〉(妄图控制社区而自封为治安维
持组织的)白帽队队员 /'～ cell = ～
blood cell /'～-'collar adj. 白领阶层(指
一般不从事体力劳动的教师、职员等工
作员等)的 /'～ elephant 1.(南亚一带被视
为神圣的)白象 2.(对己)累赘又无用
的东西/'～ fish n. 白鱼;白鲑 /'～
flag(表示投降或要求停战的)白旗,白
旗 /'Whitehall n. 白厅(伦敦的一条街
道,英国政府机关所在地);英国政府 /
'～-handed adj. 1. 两手雪白的;不从事
劳动的 2. 清白的;老实的 /'～-'hot
adj. 白热(化)的;极热烈的 /White
House 白宫;美国政府 /'～-'livered adj.
懦弱的;胆小的 /'～ market 白市,合法
交易(市场)/'～ matter【解】(脑及脊髓
中的)白质 /'～smith n. 白铁工;锡匠

银匠;镀银匠 /'～thorn n.【植】英国山楂 /'～wash n. 1. 白涂料;石灰水 2. 皮肤增白剂 3. 粉饰,美化,掩盖 vt. 1. 刷石灰水于…,涂白,粉刷 2. 粉饰,美化,掩饰 3. 彻底击败(对手) /'～wing n.(穿白色制服的)街道清洁工 /'～wood n. 白木(如三角叶杨等的木材);白木树

whiten ['hwaitn] vt. 使白;漂白;刷白 — vi. 变白;变苍白

whither ['hwiðə] adv.〈古〉〈诗〉[现在一般用 where 代替]往何处,向哪里 — n. 去处,目的地

whiting ['hwaitiŋ] n. 1. ([复] whiting(s))【动】(欧洲)牙鳕 2.(用于粉刷及擦亮银器等的)白垩粉;白粉

whitish ['hwaitiʃ] adj. 带白色的;有些苍白的

Whitsunday ['hwit'sʌndi] n.(基督教的)圣灵降临节(复活节后的第七个星期日)

Whitsuntide ['hwitsntaid] n.(基督教的)圣灵降临周(即以圣灵降临节开始的一周,尤指头三天)

whittle ['hwitl] vt. 1. 切,削;削成 2. 削减;削弱 — vi. 削;削成形 2.(由于烦恼、忧虑等)弄坏身体 — n.〈英方〉刀;大刀;屠刀

whiz(z) [hwiz] (whizzed; whizzing) vt. & vi. 1.(使)发飕飕声;(使)飞鸣 2.〈美俚〉横冲直撞地开(汽车) 3.〈美俚〉抓窃 — n. 1. 飕飕声;嗖嗖声 2.〈美俚〉熟手;能手;杰出的人(或东西) 3. 令人满意的安排(或协议) 4.〈美俚〉抓窃;抓窃集团成员;扒手 5.〈美俚〉(学校的)小测验会 6.〈美俚〉活力,精力

WHO abbr. World Health Organization 世界卫生组织

who [hu:] pron. [主格] 1. [疑问代词]谁

2. [限制性的关系代词]…的人(有时也用于动物) 3. [非限制性的关系代词]他(她);他(她)们 4.〈古〉[省略先行词的关系代词]…的人

whoa [hwəu] int. 吁!(用于吆喝马使停下来或放慢速度)

whoever [hu:'evə] (宾格 whomever; 所有格 whosever) pron. 1. [引导名词从句]1. 无论什么人 2. [引导副词从句,表示让步]无论谁,不管什么人 3. 到底是谁,究竟是谁

whole [həul] adj. 1. 完整的,齐全的;无缺的,无损的 2. 整个的;未经分割的 3. 纯粹的;未经减缩(或冲淡)的 4. [加定冠词 the,或加代词所有格 his 等,修饰单数名词]全部的(主语中的修饰语) 5. [修饰复数名词;修饰单数名词时,加不定冠词 a]整整的,不少于…的 6. 【数】整(数)的 7. 同父母的 8. 健康的,无恙的;(伤)治愈了的;复原了的 — n. 1. 全部,全数;全体;整个(of) 2. 整体;(有机的)统一体;总合 ‖～ness n. /'～ly adv. 全部地;完全地;单纯地 /'～-'colo(u)red adj. 纯色的;单色的 /'～-'hearted adj. 全心全意的;全神贯注的;赤诚的;真挚的 /'～hog(俚)彻底(地),完全(地),尽(地);一切 /'～-'hogger n.〈俚〉彻底干的人;尽力而为者 /'～meal 全(麦)粉〈英〉全(小)麦 /'～ wheat 全(小)麦

wholesale ['həulseil] n. 批发,趸售 — adj. 1. 批发的;成批售出的 2. 大批的;大规模的;无选择的;全部的 — adv. 1. 以批发方式 2. 大批地;大规模地;无选择地;全部地 — vt. 1. 经营批发业 2. 成批售出 — vt. 批发(货物),趸售(货物) ‖～r n. 批发商

wholesome ['həulsəm] adj. 1. 有益于健康的;增进健康的,有益于身心健康的;有益的 2. 健全的,有生气的;显示身心健康的 3. 审慎的;安全的 ‖～ly adv.

adv. /～ness *n*.

wholly ['həulli] *adv*. 完全地;全部,统统;专门地

whom [huːm] *pron*.(who 的宾格) 1.[疑问代词]谁 2.[关系代词]那些人;他(她);他(她)们 3.〈古〉[省略先行词的关系代词]...的人

whomever [huːm'evə] whoever 的宾格

whoop [huːp] *n*. 1.(激动、欢乐时的)高喊,高呼;(战斗中或追击时的)呐喊 2.(猫头鹰等的)鸣声;【医】(百日咳患者的)哮咳 3. 小块;一点点 4.【动】戴胜(一种产于欧、亚、北非的羽毛美丽的鸟)— *vi*. 1. 高喊;呐喊 2. 作枭鸣 3.【医】(百日咳患者)哮咳 4. 大叫大嚷地走过 — *vt*. 1. 高声说 2. 大声呐喊着追赶 3. 唤起(兴趣等);哄抬(价格等) — *int*.[表示欢乐、激动等]啊,嗬

whooping ['huːpiŋ] *adj*. 高喊声的;似百日咳患者的哮咳声的 ‖ ～ cough【医】百日咳 /～ crane【动】美洲鹤,高鸣鹤

whop [*h*wɔp] (whopped; whopping) *vt*. & *vi*. 1. 打;鞭打 2. 猛地拔出;抽出 3. 打败;打倒;征服 — *n*. 1. 重击;毒打 2. 打击声;撞击声

whopper ['*h*wɔpə] *n*.〈口〉1. 巨大的东西,庞然大物 2. 弥天大谎

whopping ['*h*wɔpiŋ] *adj*.〈口〉巨大的、异常大的;非常的 — *adv*. 异常大地;非常地

whore [hɔː] *n*. 1. 妓女;男妓;乱搞男女关系的女人(或男人);不道德的人 2. 出卖才能(或信仰)者 — *vi*. 1. 卖淫;嫖 2.〈古〉信邪教

whorl [*h*wəːl] *n*. 1.【纺】锭盘 2.【植】轮,轮生体 3.【动】(螺壳的)壳阶;(轮虫、昆虫的)毛轮;螺层 4.(指纹的)涡

whose [huːz] *pron*.(who 或 which 的所有格) 1.[疑问代词]谁的 2.[关系代词]那个人的;那些人的;他(她)的;他(她)们的 3.[关系代词]它的;它们的(= of which)

whosis ['huːzis] *n*.〈口〉不知道(或记不起)名称的人(或事物)

whosoever [ˌhuːsəu'evə] *pron*.〈古〉〈书〉= whoever

why [*h*wai] *adv*. 1.[疑问副词]为什么 2.[关系副词]为什么 — *n*. 1. 原因,理由 2. 难解的问题,谜 — *int*.[表示惊奇、不耐烦、抗议、赞成、犹豫等]什么!哎呀!当然!

wick[1] [wik] *n*. 1. 灯芯;灯带;烛芯 2.【机】(吸)油绳 3.【医】(作伤口引流用的)纱布条

wick[2] [wik] *n*.[常用以构成地名及其他复合词]镇;村;区

wicked ['wikid] *adj*. 1. 坏的;邪恶的 2.(尤指动物)性情凶恶的 3. 怀恶意的;刻毒的 4. 令人厌恶的;恶劣的 5. 捣蛋的;淘气的 6.〈俚〉显示高超技艺的 ‖ ～ly *adv*. /～ness *n*.

wicker ['wikə] *n*. 1. 枝条;柳条 2. 柳条制品 — *adj*. 1. 柳条编制的 2. 装在柳条编织物里的 ‖ '～work *n*. 1. 枝条辫 2. 柳条制品

wicket ['wikit] *n*. 1. 便门;小门;边门;腰门 2.(售票处等的)窗口 3.(入口处的)旋转栅门 4. 水闸门 5.(板球运动的)三柱门;两个三柱门之间的场地

wide [waid] *adj*. 1. 宽阔的;宽松的 2. 广阔的、广大的;广泛的;(教育等)一般的,非专门化的 3. 充分张开的;开得很大的 4. 离目标远的,差得远的 5.【语】(元音)松的;宽的 6.〈英俚〉狡猾的;机警的 — *adv*. 1. 广大地,广阔地 2. 全部地;充分地;张得很大地 3. 离目标很远地;偏斜地 — *n*.[the ～]大千世界,茫茫人世 ‖ ～ly *adv*. 广,广

泛;远;大大地/ ~ ness n. ‖ '-awake adj. 完全清醒的;机警的;警惕的/ '~body n. 宽体客机 adj. 机身宽大的,宽体的/ '~-'screen adj. (电影)宽银幕的/ '~-'spread adj. 1. 充分伸展的 2. 分布广的;流传广的;普遍的

widen ['waidn] *vt*. 加宽,放宽,扩大 — *vi*. 变宽,变阔,扩大

widgeon ['widʒən] ([复] widgeon(s)) *n*. 【动】野鸭;赤颈鸭

widow ['widəu] *n*. 1. 寡妇,遗孀 2.【印】未排足的行 3. 守寡牌(某些牌戏中发在桌面上的一手牌) 4. [the ~](俚)香槟酒 — *vt*. 1. 使成鳏寡(或鳏夫);使丧偶 2.(诗)使失去亲密朋友(或爱物) 3.(罕)成为...的寡妇/ ~ hood *n*. 守寡,居孀;丧夫

widower ['widəuə] *n*. 鳏夫

width [widθ] *n*. 1. 宽阔,广阔;广博;宽大 2. 宽度;阔度 3. 有一定宽度的东西(如一块布料等)

wield [wi:ld] *vt*. 1. 挥动(武器等);使用的,宽体的 2. 行使;运用(主权)(成功地)对付,处理 ‖ ~ er *n*.

wieldy ['wi:ldi] *adj*. 1. 易处理(或使用、操持、掌握)的 2. 便于处理(或使用、操持、掌握)的;能力强的

wiener ['wi:nə] *n*. 维也纳香肠,法兰克福香肠,维(猪)牛肉香肠

wife [waif] ([复] wives [waivz]) *n*. 1. 妻;已婚妇女 2. 妇人(尤指没有文化的老妇人) 3.[用以构成复合词]...妇,...婆 ‖ ~ like, ~ ly *adj*. 妻子(般)的;(适于)已婚妇女的

wig [wig] *n*. 1. 假发 2. 骂,叱责 3.(美俚)头发;头;头脑 — (wigged; wigging) *vt*. 1. 给...戴假发 2.(英)叱责 3.(美俚)使烦恼;激怒 4.(美俚)使激动,使发狂(out) — *vi*.(美俚)烦恼;恼怒;激

动;发狂(out)

wiggle ['wigl] *vt*. 1. 摆动;扭动 2.(英)(在船尾用单桨)划(船) — *vi*. 摆动;扭动 — *vt*. 1. 摆动;扭动 2. 奶油沙司煮青豆烧鱼(或蛤蜊)/ ~ r *n*. 1. 摆动者;扭动者 2.【动】孑孑 / wiggly *adj*. 摆动的;扭动的;起伏的,波状的

wigwag ['wigwæg] (wigwagged; wigwagging) *vt*. & *vi*. 1. 摇摆,摇动 2. 打旗语发(信号);用灯光发(信号) — *n*. 旗语信号;灯光信号

wigwam ['wigwæm] *n*. 1.(北美东部和中部的印第安人所住,用兽皮或树皮覆盖的)棚屋 2. 简陋小屋 3.(美)(政治组织的)总部;大会堂

wild [waild] *adj*. 1. 野生的,野的;不驯服的 2.(马、野禽等)易受惊的,难接近的 3.(人、部落等)野蛮的,未开化的,原始的 4. 荒芜的,荒凉的;无人烟的 5. 失去控制的;放荡的,任性的 6. 暴风雨的;狂暴的 7. 杂乱的,无秩序的;不切实际的;轻率的;未中目标的 8. 狂热的,发怒的;疯狂的;急切的 9.(牌戏中)百搭的 — *adv*. 狂暴地;胡乱地;无控制地 — *n*. 1. 荒地;荒野;旷野 2. [the ~s]未开垦的地方;未开发的地方 ‖ ~ ly *adv*. / ~ ness *n*. ‖ '~-fire *n*. 1. 烈火;大火灾 2.(旧时海战中用的)燃烧剂 3. 鬼火,磷光 4.(英俚)高度易燃的东西/~ flower 野花 / '~ life *n*. [总称]野生动物;野生生物,野生动植物 / ~ lifer *n*. 潜心于研究和保护野生动植物的人,野生生物工作者

wildcat ['waildkæt] *n*. 1.【动】野猫;猞猁;豹猫 2. 暴烈的家伙 3. 靠不住的冒险计划 4. 盲目开掘的油井(或天然气井) 5. 未经工会同意的罢工 6.【船】起锚机绞筒/(美)(铁路交通的不挂车辆的)特勤机车,急救机车 — *adj*. 1.(企

业等)不可靠的,不可信的;非法经营的 **2.**(列车等)未获批准(或不按规定时间)行驶的 **3.**(油井等)盲目开掘的 **4.**(罢工)未经工会批准的 — (wildcatted; wildcatting) *vi.* **1.** 盲目开掘油井(或天然气井等) **2.** 从事非法商业活动

wilderness ['wildənis] *n.* **1.** 荒地;荒野;荒芜的地方;(园中)荒芜的一角 **2.** 茫茫一片,大量,无数(*of*) **3.** 混乱的一群;杂乱的一团

wilding ['waildiŋ] *n.* **1.** 野生植物(尤指一种野生苹果树或酸苹果树);野生果实;野化植物 **2.** 野生动物 — *adj.* 野生的,野的

wile [wail] *n.*〔常 ~s〕**1.** 诡计,奸计;骗人的把戏 **2.** 欺骗,欺诈 — *vt.* **1.** 欺骗,诱惑 **2.** 消磨,消遣(*away*)

wilful ['wilful] *adj.* **1.** 任性的;固执的 **2.** 故意的,存心的,有意的 ‖ **~ly** *adv.* / **~ness** *n.*

will [强 wil;弱 wəl](过去式 would [wud])(will not 的缩写为 won't [wount]) *v.aux* **1.**〔表示单纯的将来,用于第二、第三人称。第一人称的单纯 将来,英国人用 shall,美国人常用 will 代替。口语中可缩写为 'll〕将要;会 **2.**〔表示意志、意愿,建议〕愿,要 **3.**〔表示功能性能行〕**4.**〔表示推测〕可能,该是 **5.**〔表示习惯、经常性、倾向性〕惯于,总是 **6.**〔表示命令、指示〕务必,应当 — (willed; willing) *vt.* **1.** 立遗嘱指明;遗赠 — *vi.* **1.** 行使意志力;下决心 **2.** 愿念 — *n.* **1.** 意志,决心愿 **2.** 意愿;旨意;目的 **3.** 干劲;热情 **4.** 遗嘱 ‖ **~,power** *n.* 意志力;毅力

willful ['wilful] *adj.*〈美〉= wilful

willing ['wiliŋ] *adj.* **1.** 愿意的;心甘情愿

的;乐意的;志愿的 **2.** 积极肯干的;反应迅速的;决断的 ‖ **~ly** *adv.* / **~ness** *n.*

will-o'-the-wisp ['wiləðə'wisp] *n.* **1.** 鬼火,磷火 **2.** 捉摸不定的东西(或人);迷惑人的事物

willow[1] ['wiləu] *n.* **1.** 柳,柳树;柳木 **2.** 柳木制品;(板球等的)球棒 — *adj.* **1.** 柳(树)的;长满柳树的 **2.** 柳木制的 ‖ **~y** *adj.* **1.** 多柳树的 **2.** 柳树似的;易弯的;苗条的

willow[2] ['wiləu]〔纺〕*vt.*(用威罗机)清理(棉花等纤维) — *n.* 威罗机,打棉机,清花机

willy-nilly ['wili'nili] *adv.* **1.** 不管愿不愿意,无可奈何地 **2.** 乱糟糟地 — *adj.* **1.** 不管愿不愿意的,无可奈何的 **2.** 犹豫不决的

wilt[1] [wilt] *vt. & vi.*〔使〕枯萎;〔使〕凋残 **2.**〔使〕衰弱;〔使〕憔悴 **3.**〔使〕畏缩 — *n.* **1.** 枯萎;凋残 **2.** 衰弱;憔悴 **3.**〔植〕萎蔫病

wilt[2] [wilt] *v.aux.*〈古〉= will

wily ['waili] *adj.* 诡计多端的,狡猾的 ‖ **wiliness** *n.*

wimple ['wimpl] *n.* **1.** 妇女头巾(现只为修女所用) **2.**〈古〉〈方〉褶襉;弯曲处;细浪 — *vt.* **1.** 用头巾遮盖,使折叠;使起细浪 — *vi.* **1.** 折叠;起细浪 **2.**〈古〉〈方〉(溪流等)迂回曲折

win [win](won [wʌn]; winning) *vi.* **1.** 获胜,赢 **2.**(经过努力)成功;成为;达到 **3.**(逐渐)吸引;影响(*on, upon*) — *vt.* **1.** 赢得;获得;博得 **2.** 打胜,胜算 **3.**(经努力)达到,达到 **4.** 争取;说服 **5.**〔矿〕采(矿);从矿石中提取(金属);为采矿而准备(竖井等) — *n.* **1.**〔口〕胜利,赢 **2.** 赢得的物;收益

wince [wins] *vi. & n.* (因疼痛等)畏缩,退缩;皱眉蹙眼

winch [wintʃ] *n.* 绞车;起货机;曲柄 — *vt.* 用绞车提升(或拖);用起货机吊起(货物等)

wind¹ [wind] *n.* 1. 风 2. 气息;呼吸;胸口,心窝 3. 气味;消息,风声;传说 4. 破坏性的力量(或影响);时尚,趋势 5. 基本方位;风向 6. 空话,空谈;虚无的东西;自负 7. 肠气(指屁) 8. 压缩空气(或气体) 9. [the ~]管乐器;[~s]管乐器组,管乐器演奏者 — *vt.* 1. 使通风;使吹干 2. 嗅出 3. 使嘴喘 4. 使(马等)休息喘气 5. 调整(气缸)的进气 — *vi.* 1. 嗅出猎物 2. 〈方〉休息一下喘口气 ‖ ~less *adj.* 无风的；平静的 ‖ ~bag *n.* 空谈者,夸夸其谈者；〈谑〉胸口~break *n.* 防风林;防风篱;挡风墙;风障 / ~ egg 未受精蛋；软壳蛋 / ~fall *n.* 1. 被风吹落的果实(或刮倒的树木) 2. 意外的收获;横财 / ~flower *n.* 【植】银莲花 / ~ instrument 管乐器 / ~jammer *n.*〈口〉(大型)帆船；帆船船员；〈美俚〉吹牛的人 / ~mill *n.* 风车 / ~pipe *n.*〈口〉直升(飞)机 2. 假想的敌人(或坏事) / ~pipe *n.* 气管 / ~proof *adj.* 防风的 / ~screen *n.*〈英〉汽车等的挡风玻璃 / ~shield *n.*〈美〉= ~screen / ~ blind 遮光窗帘 / ~ box *n.*【建】吹管锤箱 2. 窗口花坛 / ~ envelope 透明窗口信封 / ~pane *n.* 窗玻璃 / ~ screen = ~screen / ~storm *n.* 风暴 / ~swept *adj.* 当风的；风刮的；受大风侵袭的 / ~tight *adj.* 不透风的,不通风的；密封的

wind² [waind] (winded 或 wound [waund]) *vt.* 吹(号等);用号角发出(信号等) — *vi.* 吹响号角

wind³ [waind] (wound [waund] 或 winded) *vt.* 1. 绕,缠绕,缠绕 2. 包,裹；抱起 3. (用绞车等)绞起,吊起；用车拖(船等) 4. 上紧...的发条；用曲柄摇动(...)绕...弯曲前进;使(船)转向(或掉头

6. 使弯曲;使弯曲前进;通过巧妙手法使...— *vi.* 1. 弯曲前进;迂回 2. 卷曲;缠绕(船停泊时)掉转方向 — *n.* 1. 缠绕装置;绞车 2. 弯曲;卷绕;卷法,绕法 3. 一圈；一盘；一转

winded ['windid] *adj.* 1. [常用以构成复合词]有呼吸...的,气...的；short- 气急的 2. 气急的,喘不过气的 3. 风吹日晒的;风化的,风蚀的 ‖ ~ness *n.*

Windhoek ['vinthuk] *n.* 温得和克[纳米比亚首都]

winding ['waindiŋ] *n.* 1. 卷绕着的线(或绳索等);【电】绕组,线圈 2.(卷绕着的)一圈，一转 3. 绕,卷绕;绕法,绕法 4. 弯曲;卷绕;弯曲的路(或路线) 5. 迂回曲折的方法(或行为) 6.【矿】提升,卷扬 — *adj.* 1. 卷绕的 2. 弯曲的;曲折的;迂回的 ‖ ~up *n.* 1. 终了,结束 2.(公司等的)清理;结束营业

windlass ['windləs] *n.* 起锚机;卷扬机;绞盘 — *vt.*(用起锚机等)吊起

window ['windəu] *n.* 1. 窗子,窗户;窗口;窗孔;窗玻璃;橱窗 2. 窗状开口;(窗口信封上的)透明纸窗 3.〈美俚〉[~s]眼镜 4.【无】(干扰雷达用的)金属箔片;【计】窗口 5.(航天器或导弹等的)最佳发射时间 — *vt.* 给...装(或开)窗 ‖ ~pane *n.* 窗玻璃 / ~shop *vi.*(在街上)溜达着看橱窗 / ~sill *n.* 窗沿,窗台

windup ['waindʌp] *n.* 1.〈主美〉终结,结局,结束 2.(棒球运动中投手投球前的)挥臂动作 — *adj.* 靠发条发动的

windward ['windwəd] *adj.* 上风的；向风的,迎风的；逆风的；the ~ side 向风的

一边 — **n.** 上风面;迎风面 — **adv.** 上风;向风;迎风;逆风

windy ['windi] **adj.** 1. 有风的;风大的 2. 狂风似的;猛烈的;狂暴的 3. 由风(或压缩空气)产生的 4.〈口〉引肠气的,腹胀的,气胀的 5. 空谈的,吹牛的,夸夸其谈的 6.〈虚〉无的;无形的 7.〈俚〉爱吓唬的;受惊的

wine [wain] **n.** 1. 葡萄酒;果子酒;酒;药酒 2. 深红色,紫红色 3. 使人振作的东西;带兴奋性的东西 4.〈英国大学中的〉饭后酒会 — **vt. & vi.**〈请…〉喝酒 ‖ ~,bibber n. 酒徒,酒鬼 / ~bowl n. 1. 大酒杯;酒瓮 2. 嗜酒醉乡 / ~glass n. 玻璃酒杯 2. [亦作 ~glassful] 一酒杯的量(相当于 2 盎司)/ ~skin n. (用整张羊皮制成的)酒囊

winery ['wainəri] **n.**〈主美〉酿酒厂;葡萄酒厂

wing [wiŋ] **n.** 1. 翼,翅膀,翅 2. 机翼 3.【建】厢房,侧楼,耳房;(舞台的)侧面布置;[~s]舞台两侧 4.(政党等的左、右)派别,派别 5.【军】(侧)翼;(足球运动中的)翼,边锋 6.【军】空军联队;[~s]空军徽章 7. 舰状物;飞行物;风呈翔;(汽车的)挡泥板 8.〈口〉〈谑〉手臂 9. 飞行 — **vt.** 1. 飞过 2. 在…上装翼;造边翼子 3. 给以翼;使加速 4. 空运 5. 伤(鸟)翼;伤(人)臂 — **vi.** 飞行;飞速行进(或传播) ‖ ~less adj. 没有翼的,没有翅的 ‖ ~ commander〈美〉飞行联队指挥官;(英)空军中校 / ~man n.【空】1. 僚机飞行员;僚机 / ~manship n.【空】飞行(技)术 / ~span, ~spread n.【空】翼展

winged [wiŋd;除第 1 义外,也读作 'wiŋid] **adj.** 1. 有翼的(尤指有特种翼的) 2. 有翼状部分的 2. 展翅飞行的;飞行的 3. 崇高的,高远的 4. 飞速的,快

的 5. 翼上受伤的;〈口〉臂上(或其他非致命部分)受伤的 6. 飞鸟群集的

wink [wiŋk] **vi.** 1. 眨眼 2. 使眼色,眨眼示意 3. 假装不见,故意忽视(at) 4.(灯光、星等)闪烁,闪耀 5. 突然终止,完结;熄灭(out) 6.(用灯光)打信号 — **vt.** 1. 眨(眼) 2. 使(眼色) 3. 眨(眼泪) — **n.** 1. 眨眼;眨眼示意 2. 小睡,打盹 3. 霎时,瞬息

winner ['winə] **n.** 获胜者;(比赛等的)优胜者;(经过努力的)成功者

winning ['winiŋ] **n.** 1. 获胜;胜利;赢 2. 赢得;获得;博得 3.[常 ~s]赢得物(尤指钱) 4.【矿】开采;合采矿床;(矿井中的)孤立地区 — **adj.** 1. 获胜的,得胜的 2. 迷人的;可爱的 ‖ ~ly adv. ‖ ~post n.〈赛马场上的〉终点柱

Winnipeg ['winipeg] **n.** 温尼伯[加拿大南部城市]

winnow ['winəu] **vt.** 1. 扬,簸(谷物) 2. 扬掉;筛去;使分离 3. 吹掉;吹散;吹乱 4.〈诗〉(用翼)扇动(空气等);振(翼) — **vi.** 1. 扬谷,簸谷 2. 分出好坏 3. 鼓翼而飞;飞行 — **n.** 1. 簸扬;扬谷 2. 扬谷器;风选机

winsome ['winsəm] **adj.** 1. 迷人的,有吸引力的 2. 使人愉快的 ‖ ~ly adv./ ~ness n.

winter ['wintə] **n.** 1. 冬,冬天,冬季;冷天 2.〈诗〉年;岁 3. 萧条期;衰落期;不顺利时期 — **adj.** 1. 冬天的;冬天用的 2.(植物)冬季的 — **vt.** 对(动、植物)进行冬天保护;对…进行冬天饲养;对…进行冬天管理 — **vi.** 过冬 ‖ ~ green n.【植】冬青树;平铺白珠树;鹿蹄草 / ~ize vt.〈化〉冬青油 / ~kill vt. 使(植物)冻死 vi.(植物)冻死 / ~ sleep(动物的)冬眠 / ~tide n.〈古〉〈诗〉冬令 / ~time n. 冬天,冬季

wintery, wintry ['wintri] *adj.* **1.** 冬天的；冬天似的 **2.** 寒冷的；风雪交加的 **3.** 冷淡的，无热情的 *adj.* 亦作

wipe [waip] *vt.* **1.** 揩，擦；擦净；揩干 用…揩，用…擦 **2.** 擦去；抹掉（磁带）上的录音（或录像）；消灭；使消失 **4.** 抹上，涂上（油等）**5.** 【机】拭接（铅管的接头）— *vi.*〈俚〉擦打（*at*）— *n.* **1.** 揩，擦 **2.** 擦搽的人；擦搽的东西；〈俚〉手帕；毛巾 **3.**〈口〉狠狠的一击 ‖ *~* *n.* **1.** 擦拭的人；【海】机舱清洁工 **2.** 抹布，揩布；〈俚〉手帕；毛巾

wire [waiə] *n.* **1.** 金属线，金属丝（如铜丝、铁丝、铜丝等）；（乐器的）金属弦线；金属丝状物 **2.** 电缆；电线；【电】线路 **3.** [~s]（木偶戏的）牵线；〈喻〉背后操纵的势力 **4.** 金属丝网，金属丝网（如铁丝网等）**5.** 电信；〈口〉电报；〈美〉电报（或电话）系统 **6.**（赛马的）终点线 — *vt.* **1.** 用金属丝缚（以串、联接、加固等）**2.** 给…装电线 **3.**（用铁丝笼）诱捕（鸟、兔等）**4.**〈口〉用电报发送；打电报给 — *vi.* **1.**〈口〉打电报 **2.**〈口〉努力于（*in*）‖ *~* **cloth**（过滤用的）金属丝布；钢丝布；铜丝布 /*~* **cutter** 钢丝（轧断）钳；铁丝剪；线剪 /'*~* **dancer** 走钢丝演员 /'*~* **draw** *vt.* **1.** 把（金属）拉成丝 **2.** 猛力拉；使延长；使过分细致 /'*~* **man** *n.* **1.** 架线工；线路工；（电路）检修工 /'*~* 【军】架线兵 **2.** 电讯社记者 **3.**〈美〉电话窃听专家 /'*~* **photo** *n.* 有线传真；有线传真收发装置；有线传真照片 /*~* **puller** *n.*〈口〉幕后牵线者；幕后操纵者 /*~* **recorder** 钢丝录音机 /'*~* **tap** *vt.*, *vi.* & *n.*（在电话或电报线路上）搭线窃听（情报）*adj.*（在电话或电报线上）搭线窃听的 /'*~* **worm** *n.*【动】金针虫；叩甲幼虫；大蚊幼虫

wireless ['waiəlis] *adj.* 不用电线的，无线

的；〈主英〉无线电（收音机）的 无线电报（或电话）的 — *n.* **1.**〈主英〉无线电（收音机）；无线电广播（节目）**2.** 无线电报；无线电话 — *vt.* & *vi.*〈主英〉用无线电报（或电话）发送（消息等）；用无线电报（或电话）（同…）联系

wiry ['waiəri] *adj.* **1.** 金属线制的，金属丝制的 **2.** 金属丝般的，坚硬的，韧的 **3.**（人体等）瘦长而结实的 **4.**（声音）金属弦发出的；似金属丝发出的 ‖ **wirily** *adv.* / **wiriness** *n.*

Wisconsin [wis'kɔnsin] *n.* 威斯康星 [美国州名]

wisdom ['wizdəm] *n.* **1.** 智慧，才智；明智 **2.** 知识，学问；常识 **3.**（古人的）名言；教训 **4.** 贤人，哲士 ‖ *~* **tooth**【解】智牙，智齿

wise¹ [waiz] *adj.* **1.** 有智慧的，聪明的 **2.** 英明的，贤明的 **3.** 谨慎的，考虑周到的；明智的 **4.** 博学的；有见识的 **5.** 明白的，了解的 **6.** 狡猾的，诡诈的；机灵的 **7.**〈俚〉自作聪明的；自高自大的；鲁莽的 — *vt.* 告诉；教会（*up*）— *vi.* 知道，了解（*up*）‖ *~* **ly** *adv.* ‖ *~* **acre** ['waiz,eikə] *n.* 自作聪明的人 /*~* **crack** *n.* 妙语；俏皮话 *vi.* 说俏皮话 俏皮地说；巧妙地说

wise² [waiz] *n.*〈古〉方法；方式；样式

-wise *suf.* [用以构成副词] **1.** 表示"方向"，"位置"，"状态"，"样子"：any**wise**, clock**wise** **2.** 表示"在...方面"

wish [wiʃ] *vt.* **1.** 祝，祝愿；希望 **3.** 向...道（早安等）**4.** [后接表示虚拟语气的从句] 但愿 **5.** 把...强加于；把...硬塞给（*on*）— *vi.* 想要；希望 — *n.* **1.** 希望；愿望 **2.** 命令；请求 **3.** [~es] 祝愿；好意 ‖ *~* **er** *n.* ‖ *~* **bone**、**ing bone** *n.*（鸟胸的）叉骨，如愿骨（西方习俗，据说两人扯拉此骨时，扯到长的一段

的人可以有求必应)

wishful ['wiʃful] *adj.* 怀有希望的；渴望的 ‖ **-ly** *adv.* / **~ness** *n.*

wishy-washy ['wiʃiˌwɔʃi] *adj.* **1.** (饮料等)淡而无味的；稀薄的 **2.** (话、写作等)空洞无物的；(行为、举止等)软弱无力的

wisp [wisp] *n.* **1.** 小捆，小把，小束 **2.** (纸等捻成的)一条，一片 **3.** (烟、气等的)一缕 **4.** (鸟的)一群 **5.** 纤弱的人；细微的东西 **6.** 鬼火，磷火，迷人人的东西 **7.** 小扫帚，掸帚 — *vt.* 把…卷成一捆(或一束等)；把…捻成一条 ‖ **~y** *adj.* **1.** 小捆(或小束)似的 **2.** 纤弱的；细微的 **3.** 缥缈的，模糊的

wistaria [wis'tεəriə], **wisteria** [wis'tiəri] *n.* [植]紫藤

wistful ['wistful] *adj.* **1.** 渴望的；想得的；欲望得不到满足似的 **2.** 沉思的；若有所思的；惆怅的 **3.** 引起怀念的 ‖ **-ly** *adv.* / **~ness** *n.*

wit [wit] *n.* **1.** 智力；才智；智能；机智 **2.** [常 ~s]理智；(清醒的头脑)，措辞巧妙的能力；妙语；打趣话，戏谑话 **4.** 〈古〉智力；才子；智人

witch [witʃ] *n.* **1.** 女巫；〈方〉男巫 **2.** 老丑妇；恶婆 **3.** 〈口〉迷人的女子，美女 — *vt.* **1.** 迷惑，蛊惑 **2.** 用魔法迷住 ‖ **~ing** *n.* 行使巫术；巫术；魅力 *adj.* 有魔力的；迷人的 ‖ **~craft** *n.* 巫术；魔法；魅力 ‖ **~ hazel** [植]金缕梅 **2.** [药]金缕梅酊剂 ‖ **~-hunt** *n.* **1.** 对行巫者的搜捕 **2.** (对持不同政见者的)政治迫害 ‖ **~-hunting** *n.* 政治迫害

witchery ['witʃəri] *n.* **1.** 巫术 **2.** 魔法；魅力

with [wið] *prep.* **1.** 和…一起，跟…一起；和…，同 **2.** 在…一边，与…一致；拥护，有利于 **3.** 具有；带有；加

上；包括…在内 **4.** 在…身上；在…身边 **5.** 由…负责(或处理) **6.** [表示同时或一同]随着 **7.** [表示使用的工具、手段等]用 **8.** [表示行为方式]以…，带着 **9.** [后面加复合宾语，说明附带情况] sleep ~ the windows open 开着窗睡觉 **10.** 由于，因 **11.** 对于；就…说来；关于 **12.** 虽有，尽管 **13.** [与副词连用，构成祈使句] On ~ your clothes! 穿上衣服! Out ~ it! 说出来! / Away ~ him! 把他带走! / Off ~ your shoes! 把鞋脱掉!

withal [wi'ðɔːl] *adv.* **1.** 此外，而且，又 **2.** 然而；尽管如此 **3.** 〈古〉以此，与此 — *prep.* 〈古〉[常用于宾语后面]以…，用…

withdraw [wið'drɔː] (withdrew [wið'druː], withdrawn [wið'drɔːn]) *vt.* **1.** 收回；提取 **2.** 使撤退；撤销；撤回；使退出 **3.** 拉开；拉下 **4.** 移开 — *vi.* 撤退；离开；退出

withdrawal [wið'drɔːəl] *n.* **1.** 收回，撤退；撤销 **2.** 退居，退隐 **3.** 停止服药 **4.** [军]退却，提款

withdrawn [wið'drɔːn] withdraw 的过去分词 — *adj.* 沉默寡言的；孤独的，离群的；偏僻的

wither ['wiðə] *vi.* **1.** 枯萎，干枯；凋谢 **2.** 消亡；衰弱；失去生气 — *vt.* **1.** 使枯萎；使凋谢 **2.** 使消亡；使衰弱 **3.** 使畏缩；使目瞪口呆；使感到羞愧(或迷惑) ‖ **~ing** *adj.* / **~ingly** *adv.*

withers ['wiðəz] [复] *n.* 鬐甲(马肩甲骨间隆起部分)

withhold [wið'həuld] (withheld [wið'held]) *vt.* **1.** 抑制；制止，阻止 **2.** 扣留；不给；拒绝 — *vi.* 抑制；忍住

within [wi'ðin] *prep.* **1.** 在…里面，在…内部 **2.** 在…范围以内；不超过…

adv. **1.** 在里面,在内部 **2.** 户内 **3.** 在内心 — *n.* 里面,内部 — *adj.* 里面的,内部的

with-it [wi'it] *adj.* 〈俚〉时髦的;追求时髦的

without [wi'ðaut] *prep.* **1.** 无,没有;不 **2.** 在…外面,在…外部 **3.** 在…范围以外,超过 — *adv.* **1.** 在外面,外表上 **2.** 户外 **3.** 在没有(或缺少)的情况下 — *n.* 外面;外部 — *conj.* 〈方〉除非;如果不(= unless)

withstand [wið'stænd] (withstood [wið'stud]) *vt.* **1.** 抵住,顶住;经受,承受 **2.** 〈古〉阻止,阻挡 — *vi.* 对抗;反抗

witless ['witlis] *adj.* 无才智的;不机敏的;愚蠢的;糊涂的;神经错乱的 ‖ ~ly *adv.* / ~ness *n.*

witness ['witnis] *n.* **1.** 证据;证明;证言 **2.** 【律】证人;连署人 **3.** 目击者 — *vt.* **1.** 目睹,目击 **2.** 作(协议、遗嘱等)的证人 **3.** 表明;表示;说明 **4.** 作证说(某事) **5.**〈年代、地点等〉目睹,经历 — *vi.* 作证;作为证据 ‖ ~-box *n.*〈主英〉证人席 / ~ stand 证人席

witted ['witid] *adj.* [常用以构成复合词] 智力…的;头脑…的

witticism ['witisizəm] *n.* 妙语;打趣话,戏谑话

witting ['witiŋ] *adj.* 知道的;有意的,故意的 — *n.*〈方〉知道,察觉 **2.** 消息,情报 ‖ ~ly *adv.*

witty ['witi] *adj.* **1.** 机智的;〈英方〉聪明的,明智的 **2.** 措辞巧妙的;措辞横溢的;诙谐的 **3.**(服装等)设计巧妙的 ‖ **wittily** *adv.* / **wittiness** *n.*

wive [waiv]〈古〉*vi.* 娶妻 — *vt.* 给(某人)娶妻;娶(某人)为妻

wives [waivz] wife 的复数

wizard ['wizəd] *n.* **1.** 男巫;术士 **2.**〈口〉

奇才;行家 — *adj.* **1.** 有魔力的 **2.** 巫术的;着魔的 **3.**〈主英〉极好的,绝妙的

wizened ['wiznd] *adj.* 枯萎的;凋谢的;干瘪的

W/L, WL, w.l. *abbr.* wave length 波长

W. Long *abbr.* west longitude 西经

wobble [wobl] *vi.* **1.** 摇摆,晃动 **2.**(声音等)颤动,颤抖 **3.** 犹豫不决;反复无常 — *vt.* 使摇摆,使晃动;使颤动,使颤抖 — *n.* **1.** 摇摆,晃动 **2.** 犹像;波动 **3.**(声音的)变量,变度 ‖ ~ *n.* 摇摆不定的人(或物) / **wobbly** *adj.*

woe [wəu] *int.* [表示悲伤,懊悔,愧惜]咳!唉呀! — *n.* **1.** 悲哀;苦恼 **2.** [常 ~s]不幸的事物;灾难 ‖ '~ be'gone *adj.* 愁眉苦脸的;寒伦的

woeful ['wəuful] *adj.* **1.** 悲哀的,悲痛的 **2.** 不幸的;令人遗憾的;可悲的 ‖ ~ly *adj.* / ~ness *n.*

wok [wok] *n.* 镬子;(中国式的)铁锅

woke [wəuk] wake[1] 的过去式和过去分词

woken ['wəukən] wake[1] 的过去分词

wolf [wulf]([复] wolves[wulvz]) *n.* **1.** 狼;狼皮 **2.** 残暴成性的人;阴险狡猾的人;贪婪的人 **3.** 追逐女性的人;色鬼 **4.** 起腐蚀(或破坏)作用的东西 **5.** 极端的贫困 **6.**(损害谷物的)小甲虫的幼虫;牛蛾的蛆 **7.**【音】狼音,不谐和音;粗厉音 — *vt.* 狼吞虎咽地吃(或吞)(down) — *vi.* 猎狼,牧羊狗 **2.** 狼狗;似狼的狗 ‖ '~hound *n.* 猎狼狗

wolfish ['wulfiʃ] *adj.* **1.** 有关狼的 **2.** 狼似的;残暴的;贪得无厌的 ‖ ~ly *adv.* / ~ness *n.*

wolfram ['wulfrəm] *n.* 钨(= tungsten)

wolfsbane ['wulfsbein] *n.* 【植】乌头;狼毒乌头

wolverene, wolverine ['wulvərin]

【动】狼獾,貂熊;美洲狼獾 **2.** 狼獾的毛皮 **3.** [W-]〈美口〉狼獾(密歇根州人的别称)

woman ['wumən] ([复]women['wimin]) *n.* **1.** 成年女子,妇女;[不用冠词][总称]女子,女性 **2.** [the ~]女子气质;女子感情 **3.** 女子气的男人 **4.** 妻子;情人;情妇 **5.** 女仆 — *adj.* 妇女的;女性的 — *vt.* **1.** 为...配备女工作人员 **2.** 〈古〉使成女人腔(如使哭哭啼啼等);贬称(某人)为"女人";称...为"女人" ‖ ~hood *n.* **1.**(女子的)成年身份(或资格);(女子)成年期 **2.** 女子气质;女子气性 **3.**[总称]女子 / ~ish *adj.* **1.** 妇女的;女子特有的;适于女子的 **2.** 像成年女子的 **3.** 女子气的;女人腔的;柔弱的 ‖ ~-kind *n.* [用作单或复] **1.** 女子,女性 **2.**(一家或一个团体的)妇女们,女人们

womanly ['wumənli] *adj.* **1.** 有女子气质的 **2.** 妇女的;女子般的;适合于女子的 — *adv.* 女子般地 ‖ **womanliness** *n.*

womb [wuːm] *n.* **1.**【解】子宫 **2.** 发源地;孕育处 **3.**(物体中空的)内部 ‖ ~-to-tomb *adj.* 从出生到死的,一生的

women ['wimin]woman的复数形 ‖ ~folk(s) *n.*(一家或一个地方的)妇女们,女人们

womp [wɔmp] *n.*(电视机荧光屏上突然出现的)白色闪光

won [wʌn] win的过去式和过去分词

wonder ['wʌndə] *n.* **1.** 惊异,诧异;惊讶 **2.** 奇迹;奇观;奇事;奇才 **3.** 疑惑不定 — *vi.* **1.** 感到惊异;感到惊讶;诧异 **2.** 感到奇怪;感到疑惑 — *vt.* 对...感到奇怪;想知道 ‖ ~ment *n.* **1.** 惊奇;惊讶 **2.** 奇观;奇事 **3.** 好奇心 ‖ ~land *n.* 仙境;奇境

wonderful ['wʌndəful] *adj.* **1.** 惊人的;奇妙的;精彩的;了不起的 **2.** 令人高兴的;使人愉快的 ‖ ~ly *adv.*

wondering ['wʌndəriŋ] *adj.* 显出(或感到)惊奇的,惊异的;惊讶的 ‖ ~ly *adv.*

wondrous ['wʌndrəs]〈诗〉*adj.* = wonderful — *adv.*[只用于修饰形容词]惊人地;出奇地;异常地 ‖ ~ly *adv.*

wonky ['wɔŋki] *adj.*〈英〉**1.** 摇摇晃晃的,不稳的;不可靠的 **2.** 虚弱的,体亏的 **3.** 出错的

wont [wəunt, wɔnt, wʌnt] *adj.* [用作表语] **1.** 惯常的 **2.** 倾向于...的;易于...的 — *n.* [只用单]惯常做法,习惯 — (过去式 wont,过去分词 wont 或 wonted) *vi.* 习惯,惯常 — *vt.* 使习惯于 ‖ ~ed *adj.* 习惯了的;惯常的

won't [wəunt] = will not

woo [wuː] *vt.* **1.** 向...求爱;向...求婚 **2.** 追求;想得到 **3.** 恳求;劝诱 **4.**(非存心地)招致 — *vi.* **1.** 求爱;求婚 **2.** 恳求 ‖ ~er *n.* 追求者;求爱者

wood [wud] *n.* **1.** [常 ~s][用作单或复]树林,森林;林地 **2.** 木头,木材;木柴 **3.** 木制酒桶,木桶 **4.**【音】木管乐器 **5.** 木制的东西 — *vt.* **1.** 供木材(尤指木柴)给 **2.** 植林于 — *vi.* 收集木材(或木柴);得到木材(或木柴)的供应 ‖ ~-bind,~-bine *n.*【植】欧洲忍冬,五叶地锦;紫茎忍冬 / ~-block *n.*【印】木刻印版;版木 **2.** ~-cut ~ carving *n.* 木雕;木雕品 / ~-chopper *n.*〈美〉伐木者;砍柴人 / ~-chuck *n.*【动】美洲旱獭;花白旱獭 / ~-cock *n.*【动】丘鹬,山鹬;〈美〉美洲鹬 / ~-craft *n.* **1.** 木工技术 **2.** 森林知识(尤指林中识路、打猎等);林学 / ~-cut *n.* 木刻;木版画 / ~-cutter *n.* **1.** 伐木者;砍柴人 **2.** 木刻家 /~ **engraving** 木刻(术);木版画 /'~**land** *n.* 树林;林地 /~ **louse**【动】潮虫,鼠妇 /'~**man** *n.* = ~**sman** /~ **oil** 桐油 /'~ **pecker** *n.* 啄木鸟 /~ **pulp** 木(纸)浆 /'~**shed** *n.* 柴棚,木料间 *vi.* /~【俚】偷偷 地练奏乐器 /'~**sman** *n.* 林区人;熟 悉森林知识的人 *n.* 伐木人;猎人 /~ **sorrel**【植】酢浆草;小酸模 /~【音】木管乐器 /~ **wool** 细刨花,木绒 /'~**work** *n.* **1.** 木制品(房屋内部的)木 建部分;木构件(如门、梯等) **2.** 木工 活 /'~**working** *n.* 木工活;木工业

wooden ['wudn] *adj.* **1.** 木制的 **2.** 呆板 的,毫无表情的;笨拙的 ‖ '~**headed** *adj.* 愚笨的;木头木脑的 /~ **horse** 玩 具木马;(古希腊传说中的)特洛伊木 马

woodsy ['wudzi] *adj.* 〈美口〉树林(中) 的;树林的,树林特有的;像树林中的 ‖ **woodsiness** *n.*

woody ['wudi] *adj.* **1.** 树木茂密的 **2.** 木 质的;木本的 **3.** 木头似的

woof [wuf] *n.* **1.**【纺】纬纱;纬线 **2.** 布, 织物,织品 **3.** 基本元素;基本材料

wool [wul] *n.* **1.** 羊毛 **2.** 毛线,绒线;呢 绒;毛织物;毛料衣服 **3.** 羊毛状物; (动、植物上)羊毛状物毛;浓密短髮 发 ‖ '~**gathering** *n. & adj.* 心不在焉 (的)胡思乱想(的)/'~**grower** *n.* 羊 毛生产者;牧羊者 /~**man** *n.* 羊 毛商/~ **stapler** 羊毛商/~ **top**【纺】毛 条/'~**work** *n.* 绒绣;绒线刺绣

woollen ['wulən] *adj.* **1.** 羊毛制的;毛 线的 **2.** 生产(或经营)毛织品的 — *n.* [常~s]毛织品,羊毛织物;毛料衣服

woolly ['wuli] *adj.* **1.** 长满羊毛的;羊毛 (制)的 **2.** 羊毛状的;(动,植物)绒状 的,毛茸茸的;长满鬈发的 **3.** 模糊的

不鲜明的;(声音)嘶哑的 **4.**〈美口〉粗 犷的(指具有早期美国西部生活特色 的)— *n.* **1.**[常 wool(lies)]〈口〉毛织 衣;羊毛内衣 **2.**〈美方〉〈澳方〉羊‖ '~ **headed** *adj.* **1.** 有(浓密)鬈发的 **2.** 头 脑糊涂的

woomera ['wumərə] *n.*〈澳大利亚土著用 的)投枪器

word [wəd] *n.* **1.** 词,单词 **2.** 话;言词; 言语;歌词 **3.** 谈话;[~s]口角 **4.** 消 息,信息;谣言;传说 **5.** 诺言;保证‖ ~**ing** *n.*[只用单]措辞;用词;表达法 /'~**less** *adj.* **1.** 沉默的;默默无言的 **2.** 不用言辞的,无言的;无法用话语表达 的‖'~**book** *n.* **1.** 词典;词汇表 **2.** 歌 剧歌词本;歌词 /'~,**building.** ' ~,**for-mation** 构词(法)/'~**'perfect** *adj.* 一字不错地熟记的/~ **picture** 生 动的口头描述/'~**play** *n.* **1.** 巧妙的应 答(或反驳) **2.** 双关语;俏皮话/~ **processing**【计】(文)字处理/~ **proces-sor**[计](文)字处理机/'~**smith** *n.* 文 字匠;词语大师;语言艺术家

wordy ['wədi] *adj.* **1.** 多言的,唠叨的;冗 长的 **2.** 言语的;口头的 ‖ **wordily** *adv.* /**wordiness** *n.*

wore [wɔ] wear[1] 和 wear[2] 的过去式

work [wək] *n.* **1.** 工作;劳动;(要做的) 事情;作业 **2.** 职业;业务 **3.** 行为;作 用;(物)功;作功 **4.**[常~s,有时作 a ~]著作;作品 **5.** 成果;产品,工艺品; 针线活;刺绣品 **6.**[~s]〈建筑等〉 工程;【军】防御工事;[~s]用作单或复] 工厂 **7.** 工件,工作物;[~s]活动的机 件 **8.** 工作质量;工艺 **9.**[~s]〈发酵产 生的)泡沫 **10.**[~s]〈神学用语)善行, 德行 —(worked 或 wrought[rɔt]) *vi.* **1.** 工作;劳动;干活;做(*at*) **2.** 从事某 种职业 **3.**(机器,器官等)运转,活动 **4.**

起作用;产生影响;行得通 5. 缓慢而费力地前进;(由于运动、使用等)逐渐变动 6. 抽搐,牵动;激动,不平静 7. 做细活;做针线活;绣花 8. 发酵 9. 被加工;被揉 — *vt.* 1. 使工作;使干活 2. 使转动,开动;使用,操作 3. 经营,管理;主管(某部门或地区)的工作(或活动) 4. 影响;说服;劝诱 5. 使缓慢前进;使逐渐变动 6. 通过努力取得;靠做工取得 7. 造成;引起;激起 8. 精工细做;织;纺;绣;绘制雕刻(肖像);切削;铸造;锤炼(金属) 9. 揉(面团);搅(黄油);使(面团)发酵 10. 计算;算出 11. 〈口〉利用;哄骗 12. 耕作;使芽接;嫁接(*on*) ‖ ~-**bag** *n.* 针线包;工具袋/ ~-**basket** *n.* 工具篮;针线篮/ ~-**bench** *n.* 【机】工作台/ ~-**book** *n.* 1. (教科书的)练习册(课程的)教学参考手册 2. 工作规程书 3. 工作记事簿,工作日记/ ~-**box** *n.* 针线盒;工具箱/ ~-**day** *n.* 工作日/ ~-**force** *n.* 1. (工厂等在职的)工人总数;职工总数 2. 劳动大军,劳动力/ ~-**house** *n.* 1. 〈英〉(旧时中)济贫院 2. 〈美〉感化院,教养所/ ~-**in** *n.* (上班或到校后不按规定工作或工作不正当)当场盘点示威;在校停课示威/ ~-**out** *n.* 1. 锻炼;训练 2. 试验;考验;试用/ ~-**people** 〔复〕*n.* 〈英〉工人们,劳工们/ ~-**piece** *n.* 工(作)件/ ~-**room** *n.* 工场间/ ~-**shop** *n.* 1. 车间;工场;作坊 2. (文艺)创作室;创作法 3. 讲习班 4. 研讨会/ ~-**shy** *adj.* 怕工作的,怕吃苦的 — *n.* 怕工作的人,不愿工作的人/ ~-**up** *n.* 【医】检查自的.【印】(印刷物表面的)污迹/ ~-**week** *n.* 工作周;一周工作日;一周的工作时间

workable [ˈwəːkəbl] *adj.* 1. (工具、机器等)可使用的;可操作的;可运转的 2. (矿山等)可经营的;(土地)可耕种的

中用的 2. 切实可行的 3. 易加工的;可塑的 4. (题目等)可解答的

workaday [ˈwəːkədei] *adj.* 1. 工作日的;日常的 2. 普通的;平凡的;乏味的

worker [ˈwəːkə] *n.* 1. 工人;劳动者 2. 工作者;人员 3. 【动】职虫(工蜂或工蚁) 4. 【印】电转版

working [ˈwəːkiŋ] *adj.* 1. 工作(用)的;劳动(用)的 2. 有工作的;有职业的 3. 经营(用)的 4. 可行的;实行中的;在使用的;足以应事的 5. 工作(时)的;操纵的 6. (面部等)抽搐的,抽动的 — *n.* 1. 工作;劳动;作业 2. 运转,转动;操作 3. 缓慢的;运行的前进 4. 工作方式;作用 5. (面部等)的抽搐 6. 〔常 ~s〕矿内巷道/矿内工作区 ‖ ~-**class** 工人阶级/ ~-**day** *n.* 工作日(= workday)/ ~-**man** *n.* 工人;劳动者/ ~-**out** *n.* 计算;算出;制订;详述/ ~-**people** 劳动人民/ ~-**woman** *n.* 女工;劳动妇女

workman [ˈwəːkmən] 〔复〕 **workmen**〕 *n.* 1. 工人;劳动者;工作者;工匠;男工 ‖ ~-**like** *adj.* 工作熟练的;有技巧的;精巧的/ ~-**ship** *n.* 手艺;工艺;工作质量;(成品的)做工

workwoman [ˈwəːkwumən] (〔复〕 **workwomen**[ˈwəːkwimin]) *n.* 女工;劳动妇女;女工作者

world [wəːld] *n.* 1. 世界,天下;地球;宇宙;万物 2. 世人,众人 3. 世间,人间;物质生活 4. 界,领域 5. 人世生活,世事;世间;世界;纪 6. (个人)身世,经历;眼界 7. 社会生活;交际界;上流社会 8. 大量,无数 9. (类似地球的)天体;星球 10. 〔~〕强大的(或有影响的)国际组织/ ~-**war** 世界大战/ ~-**wide** *adj.* 遍及全球的,世界范围的 — *adv.* 在世界范围内

worldling [ˈwəːldliŋ] *n.* 俗人,世人

worldly ['wəːldli] *adj.* **1.** 世间的；尘世的 **2.** 俗气的；市侩气的 **3.** 老于世故的；善于处世的 ‖ **worldliness** *n.* ‖ '~-'minded *adj.* 世俗头脑的；追名逐利的/ '~-'wise *adj.* 老于世故的；善于处世的

worm [wəːm] *n.* **1.** 软体虫；蠕虫；蚯蚓；蛆；肠虫；寄生虫；船蛆（= shipworm）**2.** 小人物；可鄙的家伙；可怜虫 **3.** 【机】螺纹；蜗杆；蛇管；旋管；螺旋泵；螺旋提升器 **4.** （脅等的）舌下韧带 — *vt.* **1.** 使蠕行；小心缓慢（或蜿蜒）地行（路）**2.** 慢慢地探得 **3.** 给…驱肠虫；给（花坛等）除虫 **4.** 在（电缆、粗绳等）的外面绕线 **5.** 给（狗等）割去舌下韧带 — *vi.* 蠕行；小心缓慢（或悄悄）地行进 ‖ '~-cast *n.* 蚯蚓粪/ '~-,eaten *adj.* **1.** 虫蛀的；多虫孔的 **2.** 破烂的；过时的；陈旧的/ ~ gear【机】蜗轮；蜗轮传动装置/ ~ gearing【机】蜗轮传动/ '~wood *n.* 【植】蒿菁；苦艾 **2.** 苦恼；苦恼的原因；深切的悔恨

wormy ['wəːmi] *adj.* **1.** 有蠕虫（或蛀虫、寄生虫）的；多虫的；虫蛀的 **2.** 似虫的；卑鄙的；卑躬屈膝的

worn [wəːn] wear[1] 和 wear[2] 的过去分词 — *adj.* **1.** 用旧的；穿坏的 **2.** 憔悴的 **3.** 筋疲力尽的；耗尽的；变得衰弱的 ‖ '~-'out *adj.* **1.** 用坏的；穿破的；不能再用的 **2.** 筋疲力尽的；耗尽的；变得衰弱的 **3.** 陈腐的

worrisome ['wʌrisəm] *adj.* 使人烦恼的；使人焦虑的；使人发愁的；容易担心的；经常发愁的

worry ['wʌri] *vt.* **1.** 使烦恼；使焦虑，使担忧 **2.** 困扰；折磨 **3.** 撕咬；啃碎；反复推（或拉等）；使改变位置等 **5.** 〈英方〉塞住；闷死 — *vi.* **1.** 烦恼；担心；发愁 **2.** 撕咬；啃碎(at) **3.** 努力移动；挣扎着前进 **4.** 〈英方〉被塞住；被闷死 — *n.* **1.**

烦恼；焦虑，担忧；[常 worries] 烦恼事 **2.** 猎狗撕咬猎物 ‖ **worried** *adj.* 烦恼的；焦虑的 /worrier *n.* 担心的人；发愁的人 /worriment *n.* 烦恼；焦虑 ‖ '~-wart *n.* 〈口〉自寻烦恼的人

worrying ['wʌriiŋ] *adj.* 令人担心的；使人烦恼的；忧虑重重的 ‖ '~ly *adv.*

worse [wəːs] *adj.* **1.** [bad 的比较级] 更坏的；更差的；更恶化的 **2.** [ill 的比较级]（病情）更重的 — *adv.* [bad, badly 的比较级] **1.** 更坏；更糟；（病）更重 **2.** 更猛烈，更厉害 — *n.* **1.** （人或事物）更坏者，较差者，较糟者 **2.** [the ~]更坏的事情（或情况）；比较的败局

worship ['wəːʃip] *n.* **1.** 【宗】礼拜 **2.** 崇敬，敬仰，敬慕 **3.** [W-]【主英】阁下（对地方长官的尊称） — *vt.* (worship(p)ed; worship(p)ing) *vt.* 崇拜；尊敬 — *vi.* 做礼拜 ‖ **worship(p)er** *n.* (英)礼拜者；崇拜者；爱慕者

worshipful ['wəːʃipful] *adj.* 〈主英〉尊敬的，可敬的（用于对治安法官、市参议员等的称呼）**2.** 虔敬的；崇拜的

worst [wəːst] *adj.* [bad, ill 的最高级；常加定冠词 the] **1.** 最坏的；最差的；最恶劣的；最有害的 **3.** 最不利的；最糟的；最不适合的；错误最多的；效能最低的 — *adv.* [bad, badly 和 ill, illy 的最高级] **1.** 最坏地；最恶劣地；最有害地；最不利地 — *n.* 最坏者；最坏的部分；最坏的情况（或事件、结果等）— *vt.* 击败；胜过

worsted ['wustid] *n.* 精纺毛纱；精纺毛线；精纺毛料 — *adj.* 精纺的

wort [wəːt] *n.* 麦芽汁（发酵后可制麦芽酒、啤酒及其他饮料）

worth [wəːθ] *adj.* [用作表语，后接宾语] **1.** 值…的；相当于…的价值的 **2.** 值得…的；有…价值的 **3.** 拥有…价值的财

产的 — n. 1. 价值;货币价值;物质价
值;精神价值 2.[发音常作 wəθ]值一定
金额的数量;(折合较高币值的)货币
数量 — vt.〈古〉临到…头上,发生于
(= befall) ‖ '~'while adj. 值得花时间
(或精力)的;有真实价值的

worthily ['wəːðili] adv. 值得地,配得上地

worthiness ['wəːðinis] n. 1. 值得尊重 2.
有价值

worthless ['wəːðlis] adj. 1. 无价值的,不
值钱的;无用的 2. 不足道的;不可取
的;卑微的;卑鄙的 ‖ **-ly** adv. /**-
ness** n.

worthy ['wəːði] adj. 1. 有价值的;值得重
视的;可尊敬的 2.[常作表语]值得的,
配得上的;相称的 — n. 知名人士;杰
出人物

would [强 wud;弱 wəd, əd, d](will 的过去
式) v. aux. 1. [表示过去将来时,用于
第二、三人称;美国也用于第一人称]
将 2. [表示意志,要;偏要] 3. [表示
习惯性]总是,总会 4.[表示推测]大概
5.[表示设想的意志]愿意,要 6.[表示
虚拟、假设、条件等,用于第二、三人
称;美国也用于第一人称]要;将要;
会;就会 7.[表示请求或个人的想法、
看法,使语气婉转]倒 8.[表示愿
望]但愿,要是…才好 9. 能,能够(=
could) 10.[表示愿望、请求、劝告等]
会;要

would-be ['wudbiː] adj. 将要成为的;想要
成为的;未来的;〈贬〉自称的 — n.
〈贬〉想要成为某种人物的人;奢望者;
僭称者

wouldn't ['wudnt] = would not

wound¹ [wuːnd] n. 1. 创伤,伤;伤口;伤
疤 2.(名誉等的)损伤;(感情上的)痛
苦 — vt. 1. 使受伤,伤害 2.(在感情
等方面)伤害 — vi. 致伤;伤害

wound² [waund] wind² 和 wind³ 的过去式
和过去分词

wove [wəuv] weave 的过去式 — adj.(纸)
布纹的 — n. 布纹纸

woven ['wəuvən] weave 的过去分词

WPC abbr. World Peace Council 世界和平
理事会

wrack [ræk] n. 1. 毁坏;破坏 2.(被毁坏
物的)残体,残骸 3. 失事船只;(船只
的)失事 4.(被冲上岸的)海生植物(尤
指可作肥料的海藻);晒干的海藻 5.
〈方〉(结构物、机器、车辆的)严重破坏
— vt. 彻底毁坏

wraith [reiθ] n. 1.(传说在人将死或死后
不久的)显形阴魂 2. 幽灵;鬼 3. 幻影
4. 一股稀薄的烟雾(或气体)

wrangle ['ræŋgl] vi. 争辩,争论 — vt. 1.
争辩;争得,取得;说服,吵得(into, out
of)义〈美〉〈加拿大〉放牧;赶拢(性口
等) — n. 口角,吵嘴;争辩 ‖ ~r n. 1.
争吵者;争辩者 2.〈美〉〈加拿大〉牧人,
牧工 3.(英国剑桥大学)数学荣誉学位
考试优胜者

wrap [ræp] (wrapped 或〈罕〉wrapt[ræpt;
wrapping) vt. 1. 裹(包);捆;缠,环绕 2.
覆盖;遮蔽 3. 隐藏;掩饰;伪装 4. 使全
神贯注(up) — vi. 1. 缠绕;盘绕;互
叠;重叠 2. 穿外衣;围好围巾(up) 3.
包起来(up) — n.[常~s]外衣;围巾;披肩;毯
(物) 2.[常~s]外衣;围巾;披肩;毯
子;手帕;头巾 3.【印】套轮插页 4.(包
裹物的)一层;(缠绕的)一圈 5.〈美〉
限制;约束;秘密;(对书刊的)检查
‖ '~-up n. 1.〈口〉新闻提要;〈新闻报
告中的〉综合新闻;综合性报告;提要
2.〈美国〉一做成功的买卖;爽快的买主
adj.〈口〉综合性的;提要的;结尾的;结
局的

wrapper ['ræpə] n. 1. 打包者;包装工 2.

包装物;覆盖物;(雪茄的)外卷烟叶;
(邮寄报纸、刊物、书籍的)外包纸;书
的封皮 3. 轻便晨衣;妇女晨衣;浴衣

wrapping ['ræpiŋ] *n*. [常~s]包装材料;
包装纸;包装布

wrath [rɔθ] *n*. 1. 愤怒;愤慨 2. 愤怒的行
为(尤指报仇、惩罚) 3.〈自然现象等
的〉严酷 ‖ ～y *adj*. 愤怒的;愤慨的

wrathful ['rɔθful] *adj*. 愤怒的;愤慨的 ‖
～ly *adv*.

wreak [rik] *vt*. 1. 发泄 2. 施行(报复
等);造成(破坏等)

wreath [riθ] *n*. ([复]wreaths[riːðz]) *n*. 1. 花
圈;花环;花冠 2. 圈状物,环状物 3. 雕
花环;饰环 4.(环瑞器皿等上的)环形
瑕疵

wreathe [riːð] *vt*. 1. 将…扎成花圈(或花
环、花冠);扎成(花圈等);用花圈(或
、花环)装饰…2. 盘绕,缠绕;萦绕 3.
使起皱纹;使布满;使笼罩 — *vi*. 1. 盘
绕;扭曲 2.(烟等)成圆状,缭绕;盘旋

wreck [rek] *n*. 1.(船只等)失事,遇难 2.
失事的船(或飞机等);(漂到岸上的)
失事船中的货物;(失事船或飞机等
的)残骸 3. 健康极度受损的人(或动
物);遭到严重破坏的建筑物(或车辆)
4.(希望、计划等的)破坏,毁灭 — *vt*.
1. 使(船、火车等)失事,遇难;(遇难
船)使…船只 3. 使瓦解;破坏;损害;
阻挠 4. 摧残(身体健康等) — *vi*. 1.
(船只等)失事;遭受破坏;毁灭 2. 营
救失事船只;抢劫失事船只;修复失事
船只

wreckage ['rekidʒ] *n*. 1.(船只等的)失事,
遇难;毁坏 2.(被毁物的)残骸,残余

wrecker ['rekə] *n*. 1. 寻觅失事船只者 2.
行劫而使船舶失事者 3. 拆卸旧建筑物
者 4. 破坏分子 5. 打捞(沉船或货物)
者;打捞船;营救船 5.(清除失事火车、

修理路基等的)救援火车;[抢修失事
或抛锚汽车的]救险车 6.〈美〉拆旧屋
者;购买废旧汽车以拆卸其零件者 7.
救援火车(或救险车)的司机

wrecking ['rekiŋ] *n*. 1.(为行劫而)使船
失事 2.(失事船、车等的)营救(业) —
a.(美)营救业的;废旧汽车拆除(业);
车拆卸(业) 4. 破坏 — *adj*. 1. 使毁灭
的;起破坏作用的 2. 营救的;打捞的;
拆除的

wren [ren] *n*.〈动〉鹪鹩;形似鹪鹩的鸟
(如莺等)

wrench [rentʃ] *n*. 1.(活动)扳手,扳头,板
钳,搬子 2. 猛扭;急扭;一扭;一拧 3.一
扳 3. 扭伤 4. 歪曲;曲解 5.(离别等的)
一阵悲痛 — *vt*. 1. 猛扭(或拧,扳)
2. 扭伤 3. 曲解;歪曲(事实、意义等) 4.
抢;攫取 5. 使受痛苦;折磨 — *vi*. 1.
猛力扭动;拧;绞

wrest [rest] *n*. 1. 扭;拧 2.〈音〉(校准弦
音的)扭钥,校音钥 — *vt*. 1. 扭;拧(专
指用力拧拔、拧拉) 2. 夺取,强夺 3. 费
力取得 4. 歪曲;曲解

wrestle ['resl] *n*. 1. 摔跤,角力 2. 斗争;
搏斗 — *vi*. 1. 摔跤,角力 2. 斗争;搏
斗;全力对付 3. 深思;踌躇 — *vt*. 1.
摔(一场摔跤比赛等) 2. 与(对手)摔
跤 3.(使劲)搬动,移动 4.〈美〉为扭转
印把(小牛等)摔倒 ‖ ～r *n*. 摔跤运动
员;摔斗者;搏斗者

wrestling ['resliŋ] *n*.〈体〉摔跤,角力

wretch [retʃ] *n*. 1. 可怜的人;不幸的人
2.〈贬〉卑鄙的人,无耻之徒 3.〈谑〉
(小)坏蛋

wretched ['retʃid] *adj*. 1. 可怜的;悲惨
的;不幸的;感到沮丧的 2. 使人痛苦
不舒服的;讨厌的;肮脏的;恶劣的 3. 质
量差的;可鄙的;不足道的 4.(用于含
有贬义的事物)极大的;过度的;严重

的 ‖ ～ly *adv.* / ～ness *n.*

wriggle ['rigl] *vi.* 1. 蠕动；扭动；蜿蜒行进 2. 摆脱；溜掉；混入 — *vt.* 使扭动；扭动制够 — *n.* 1. 扭动；扭动 2. 蜿蜒；起伏 ‖～*r n.* 1. 扭动作者；蠕动的东西 2.【动】孑孓

wright [rait] *n.* 用以构成复合词] 工人，匠；制作者；a ship～船木工

wring [riŋ] (wrung [rʌŋ] 或 〈罕〉wringed) *vt.* 1. 绞；拧；挤；榨；扭 2. 榨取；勒索；强求 3. 使苦恼；折磨；使悲痛 4. 把…扭弯变形；扭絮；拧手 — *vi.* 1. 蠕动；扭动 2. 绞；拧；挤；榨；扭 — *n.* 绞；拧；挤；榨；扭 ‖～*er n.* 1. 绞拧工；压汁工；强求者；勒索者，敲榨者 2. 绞拧机；压汁器 3. 造成艰难困苦的事件（或过程）

wrinkle[1] ['riŋkl] *n.* 1. 皱；皱纹 2.〈美俚〉恋人的母亲 3. 困难；难题；障碍 — *vt.* 使起皱纹 — *vi.* 起皱纹；皱起来

wrinkle[2] ['riŋkl] *n.* 〈口〉1. 妙计，好主意；消息 2. 技巧；技巧（设备、方法、技术等的）革新；创新

wrist [rist] *n.* 1. 腕；腕关节 2.【体】手腕动作 3.（袖子、手套等的）腕部 4.【机】肘节力 ‖～band *n.*（衬衫等的）袖口腕套；表带 / ～watch *n.* 手表

writ [rit] *n.* 1.〈古〉书写物；文书 2.〈法院等的〉令状，书面命令

write [rait] (wrote [rəut] 或〈古〉writ [rit], written ['ritn] 或〈古〉writ) *vt.* 1. 书写；写下 2. 写（书信、报告等）；编写（乐曲）3. 写信给…；把…写入（into）4. 写信给；写信说；函告 5. 填写；填满 6. 把…描写成；称…为 7.【常用被动语态】显露；使留下印记 8. 签署契约物；签署订货单认购；承保 9. 命中注定 — *vi.* 1. 写；写字 2. 写信 3. 写作；作曲 ‖～-in *n.* 1. 在选票上被写入的

非原定候选人的名字 2. 对非原定候选人所投的选票/ '～-up *n.* 1.〈口〉（报刊等上的）捧场文章；报道；评论 2.（资产等）帐面价值的提高

writer ['raitə] *n.* 1. 作者；作家，文学家；记者；撰稿者 2. 抄写员；文书；办事员 3. 写作手册 4.〈苏格兰〉律师

writhe [raið] *vt.* 1. 扭曲；扭歪 2.（因剧痛、苦恼等）翻腾；扭动（身体等）3. 缠结，缠绕 — *vi.* 1. 蠕动；蜿蜒移动 2. 翻滚；扭动 3. 苦恼，不安 — *n.* 翻滚；扭动

writing ['raitiŋ] *n.* 1. 书写；写；写作；书面形式 2. 书法；笔迹；文体 3. 著作；文学作品 4. 文字；文件；信件；铭 5. 写作生涯，作家职业 ‖～case 文具盒

written ['ritn] write 的过去分词 — *adj.* 写下的；书面的；成文的

wrong [rɔŋ] *adj.* 1. 错误的；不正确的 2. 不适当的 3. 不正常的，不好的；不健全的 4. 不道德的；犯罪的；邪恶的 5.（织物等）反（面）的 — *adv.* 错，不对；不正确地；方向错误地 — *n.* 1. 错误；坏事；邪恶 2. 不公正；冤屈 3. 不道德；违法；犯罪 4. 侵权行为 — *vt.* 1. 冤枉；委屈 2. 无礼地对待；虐待；诽谤 3. 勾引；诱奸（女子）4. 中伤；侮辱 ‖～ly *adv.* 1. 错误地，不正确地；不恰当地 2. 不正直地；不公正地/ ～ness *n.* 1. 谬误（性）；不当 2. 不正直；不公正 / '～doer *n.* 做坏事的人；违法犯罪者 / '～doing *n.* 不道德的行为；（干）坏事/ '～headed *adj.* 坚持错误的；刚愎自用的；固执的；判断错误的

wrongful ['rɔŋful] *adj.* 1. 恶劣的；不公允的，不义的 2. 违法的，非法的；不正当的

wrote [rəut] write 的过去式

wroth [rəuθ, rɔ] *adj.* 极愤怒的；怒气冲冲

的

wrought [rɔːt] work 的过去式和过去分词
— *adj*. 1. 制造的；形成的 2.(金属)锻
的，用锤敲击成的：~ iron 锻铁，熟铁
3. 精心作成的；精炼的 4. 装饰精美的
5. 激动的，兴奋的

wrought-up ['rɔːtˌʌp] *adj*. 激动的，兴奋
的；狂躁不安的

wrps. *abbr*. wrappings

wrung [rʌŋ] wring 的过去式和过去分词

wry [rai] *vt*. & *vi*. 扭曲；扭歪 — *adj*. 1.
扭歪的；歪斜的 2.(表示厌恶、不满等)
面部肌肉扭曲的 3. 坚持错误的；荒谬

的；曲解的 4. 讽刺性幽默的；作弄
(人)的 ‖ ~ly *adv*. / ~ness *n*.

wt. *abbr*. weight

wu shu ['wuː'ʃuː]〈汉〉(中国的)武术

WW I *abbr*. World War I 第一次世界大
战

WW II *abbr*. World War II 第二次世界大
战

WWW *abbr*. World Weather Watch 世界天
气监视网

Wyoming [wai'əumiŋ] *n*. 怀俄明[美国州
名]

X

X, x [eks] ([复] X's, x's 或 Xs., xs ['eksiz]) 英语字母表第二十四个字母 **1.** [X] 罗马数字的 10 **2.** [X] X 形 **3.** [X] 化 卤素 (或一价阴离子) 的符号 **4.** [X] Christ 的代称 (如 Xmas = Christmas) **5.** [X] 〈美俚〉十美元 **6.** [X] (电影) 只许成年人观看的标记 **7.** [x] 【数】第一未知量; (喻) 未知的人; 未知的事物 **8.** [x] 【数】横坐标

x [eks] (x-ed 或 x'd; x-ing 或 x'ing) **vt.** **1.** 用 "x" 符号标出 (自己的选择, 答案等) (*in*) **2.** 用单个 (或连续几个) "x" 符号划去; 用 "x" 符号表示删去 (*out*) **3.** 忘却, 勾销, 抹掉 (*out*)

xanthic ['zænθik] **adj.** (带) 黄色的; 转黄的

xanthophyl(l) ['zænθəfil] **n.** 【生化】叶黄素

xanthous ['zænθəs] **adj.** **1.** 黄色的; 浅黄色的 **2.** 黄色人种的, 蒙古人种的 **3.** 有浅黄色 (或棕色, 红色) 头发的人种的

x-axis ['eks,æksis] **n.** 【数】X 轴, 横坐标轴

X chromosome 【生】X 染色体

Xe 【化】元素氙 (xenon) 的符号

xebec ['zi:bek] **n.** (航行于地中海的) 三桅小帆船

xenogamy [ze'nɔgəmi] **n.** 【植】异株异花受精

xenon ['zenɔn] **n.** 【化】氙

xenophobia [,zenə'fəubjə] **n.** 对外国人 (或外国事物) 的恐惧 (或憎恶), 恐外症; 生客恐怖, 陌生恐怖

xeric ['ziərik] **adj.** **1.** 缺乏维持生命的水分的, 沙漠般的, 干旱的 **2.** 【植】旱生的, 耐旱的; 旱生植物的

xerophyte ['ziərəfait] **n.** 【植】旱生植物

Xerox ['ziərɔks] **n.** **1.** 静电复印 (术) **2.** (施乐) 静电复印机 **3.** 亦作 x-] 静电复印件 — **vt.** & **vi.** [常作 x-] 用静电复印法复印, 静电复印

xi [zai, sai, ksai, ksi] **n.** 希腊语的第十四个字母 Ξ, ξ

Xmas ['krismæs, 'eksməs] **n.** = Christmas

X-rated ['eks'reitid] **adj.** 〈美〉(电影等) X 级的, 禁止青少年观看的, 只许成年人观看的

X ray 1. X 射线, X 光 **2.** X 光照片 **3.** 〈口〉X 光检查

X-ray ['eks'rei] **adj.** X 射线的, X 光的; 使用 X 射线的 — **vt.** **1.** 用 X 光检查 (或处理, 摄影, 治疗等) **2.** 仔细审查

xylan ['zailæn] **n.** 【化】木聚糖

xylem ['zailəm] **n.** 【植】木质部

xylograph ['zailəɡrɔ:f] **n.** 木刻; 木刻版; (木) 版画 ‖ ~**y** [zai'lɔɡrəfi] **n.** 木刻 (术); 木刻版 (印刷) 术; (木) 版画印刷法

xylonite ['zailənait] **n.** 〈主英〉【化】硝酸纤维素塑料; 赛璐珞, 假象牙

xylophone ['zailəfəun] **n.** 【音】木琴

Y

Y, y [wai]([复]Ys, y's 或 Ys, ys[waiz]) 英语字母表第二十五个字母 1. [Y] Y 形 2. [Y]【化】元素钇(yttrium)的符号 3. 【数】第二未知量 4.【数】纵坐标

-y suf.[构成名词]1. 表示"境遇"、"性质": beggary, jealousy, allergy 2. 表示"营业"、"营业场所": laundry, chandlery 3. 表示"全体": soldiery 4. 表示"行为": entreaty, inquiry ——[加于名词后构成形容词]1. 表示"有...的"; "多...的": healthy, muddy 2. 表示"由...构成的": icy, waxy 3. 表示"似...的": wintry 4. 表示"热中于...的"、"爱...的": horsy 5. 表示"有点...的"、"想...的": chilly, sleepy ——[加于形容词后构成其他形容词]表示"...的": lanky ——-ie

yacht [jɔt] n. 快艇; 游艇; 【体】帆船 —— vi. 驾快艇; 乘游艇; 【体】驾帆船比赛 ‖ ~ing n.1. 驾快艇; 乘游艇 2. 驾帆船 (或快艇)技术; 帆船运动; 帆船比赛 ‖ '~sman n. 驾驶快艇(或游艇)的人; 快艇(或游艇)的主人; 帆船运动员; 喜爱帆船运动的人

yahoo ['jɑ:hu:] ('jɑ:hu:)([复] yahoos) n. 1. [Y.][英国作家斯威夫特[Swift]的小说《格列佛游记》中的)人形兽 2. 人面兽心的人 3. 粗汉; 野蛮人; 蠢货

yak [jæk]([复]yak(s)) n.【动】牦牛(主要产于我国西藏)

yam [jæm] n.【植】薯蓣; 山药

Yamato [jɑ:'mɑ:təu]〈日〉[单复同] n. 大和民族; 日本人

yammer ['jæmə] 〈口〉vi. 哀声抱怨, 哭诉; 大叫大嚷 —— vt. 大声抱怨地说出 —— n. 1. 哭诉; 大声抱怨 2. 废话, 无意义的话 ‖ ~er n.

Yamoussoukro [ˌjɑ:muːˈsuːkrəu] n. 亚穆苏克罗[科特迪瓦新都]

Yangtze River ['jæŋkˈtsiˈrivə] 长江(现译 Changjiang River)

Yank [jæŋk] vt. & adj.〈俚〉= Yankee

yank [jæŋk] vt. & vi.〈口〉猛拉, 使劲拉 —— n. 突然的猛拉; 使劲的一拉

Yankee ['jæŋki] n.1.〈美〉(美国的)新英格兰人(尤指守旧、节俭、精明的新英格兰人)2.(美国南北战争中)美国北部各州的人, 北方佬 3. 美国公民; 美国佬 —— adj. 美国佬(式)的, 扬基(式)的 ‖ ~ism n. 美国作风(或派头等); 美国特有的语言现象 ‖ ~ize vt. 使美国化 ‖ ~ Doodle ['du:dl] 1.扬基歌(美国独立战争时期流行的一支民间歌曲)2. = Yankee

Yaoundé [jɑ:un'dei] n. 雅温得[喀麦隆首都]

yap [jæp] (yapped; yapping) vi.1.〈狗〉狂吠 2. 哇啦哇啦讲;〈俚〉瞎谈 —— n.1.〈狗的〉狂吠声 2.〈俚〉哇啦哇啦的说话声; 瞎扯 3.〈俚〉〈看作说话工具的〉嘴 4.〈俚〉

哇啦哇啦的人;乘轮的人 5.〈俚〉乡巴佬

yard[1] [jɑːd] *n.* 1. 院子；围场;〈美〉庭院 2. [常用以构成复合词](作一定用途的)场地;(露天)工场;堆置场;[铁路]调车场等(=家畜、家禽的圈栏 3. [the Y-]伦敦警察厅;伦敦警察厅侦缉处(= Scotland Yard) 4.(鹿等的)冬令聚居地 — *vt.* 1. 把(家畜、家禽)赶进围栏 2. 把...放入场地 — *vi.*(鹿等冬天在林中)集居(*up*) ∥'~-**bird** *n.* 1. 被罚做杂务(或被限制活动范围)的士兵 2. 未经训练(或不称职)的新兵/'~-**master** *n.*[铁路]调车场场长 /~ **sale** 〈美〉庭院销售(指在自家院子里进行的清宅旧货出售)

yard[2] [jɑːd] *n.* 1. 码(英美长度单位;= 3 英尺,略作 yd.) 2.(沙、土等的)立方码 3. [海]帆桁 4.〈美俚〉一百元;一千元 ∥~ **age** *n.* 以码计量的长度(或桁长);码数/'~-**arm** *n.*[海](帆)桁端 /~ **goods** 按码出售的织物;匹头,布正/'~-**long bean** 长豇豆/'~-**stick** *n.* 码尺(指直尺);衡量标准,尺度/'~-**wand** *n.*〈主英〉〈古〉码尺(指直尺)

yarn [jɑːn] *n.* 1. 纱,纱线 2.〈口〉故事;奇谈 — *vi.*〈口〉讲故事

yarrow [ˈjærəu] *n.*[植]蓍草;欧蓍草

yaw [jɔː] *vi.*(船、飞机等)偏航,(船)偏荡,摇首 — *n.* 偏航;偏荡,摇首;偏航角

yawl [jɔːl] *n.* 船载小艇;小帆船;小渔船

yawn [jɔːn] *vi.* 1. 打呵欠 2. 豁开,裂开 — *vt.* 打着呵欠说;打呵欠致使 — *n.* 1. 呵欠 2. 裂口,裂缝;陷窟 3. 乏味的事(或事)

yawp [jɔːp, jɑːp] *vi.* 1. 大声叫嚷;喧闹 2. 大声叫屈;吵嚷 3.〈口〉大声打呵欠 — *n.* 1. 粗声叫嚷;粗暴的话 2.〈俚〉蠢话

y-axis [ˈwaiˌæksis] *n.*[数]y 轴,纵坐标轴

Yb 【化】元素镱(ytterbium)的符号

Y chromosome [生] Y 染色体

yclept [iˈklept] *adj.*〈古〉〈谑〉名叫...的,你作...的

yd. *abbr.* yard(s)

ye [jiː] *pron.* 1.〈古〉你们,汝等 2.〈古〉= the

yea [jei] *adv.*〈古〉1. 是(现аппро口头表决时使用并已为 yes 所代替) 2. 而且;甚至可说 — *n.* 1. 肯定;赞成 2. 赞成票;投赞成票者 ∥'~-**sayer** *n.* 1.(对人生或事物)肯定者;抱积极态度者 2. 唯唯诺诺的人/'~-**saying** *adj.*(对人生或事物)肯定的;抱积极态度的

yeah [jɛə] *adv.*〈口〉= yes

year [jə, jiə] *n.* 1. 年 2. 年度 3. 岁;[~s]年纪,岁数 4.[~s]多年,长久 5.〈美俚〉一元 ∥~-**ly** *adv.* 每年的;一年一度的;一年间的;按年的 — *adv.* 每年;一年一度;年年;按年 ∥'~-**book** *n.* 年鉴,年刊/'~-**long** *adj.* 持续一年的,整整一年的;持续多年的 /'~-**round** *adj.* 一年到头的,整年的 — *adv.* 一年到头地

yearling [ˈjəliŋ, ˈjiəliŋ] *n.* 1. 满一岁,一周岁至两周岁之间的动物;一岁生白牛 2. 出生后第二年的赛马(指出生后第二年一月一日至第三年一月一日之间的马) 3.〈美〉(西点军校的)二年级学员 4.〈英口〉一年级大学生;刚升二年级的大学生 — *adj.* 1. 一岁的,一龄的 2. 满一周年而进两周年的;历时一年的(债券等)一年期满的

yearn [jən] *vi.* 1. 想念,怀念;思慕;向往;渴望;极想 2. 同情;怜悯

yearning [ˈjəniŋ] *n.* 1. 怀念;思慕;向往;渴望 2. 同情;怜悯 — *adj.* 怀念的;思慕的;向往的;渴望的 ∥~-**ly** *adv.*

yeast [jiːst] *n.* 1. 酵母 2. 曲;鲜酵母块;酵母片 3. 泡沫 4. 激动;激动的起因 —

vi. 发酵；起泡沫 ‖ ~ **powder** 发酵粉

yeasty ['ji:sti] *adj.* 1.(含)酵母的；发酵的；酵母似的 2.起泡沫的 3.浅薄的；无实质的 4.动荡的、不安的 5.变化中的；生气勃勃的

yell [jel] *vi.* 叫喊；叫嚷；忍不住大笑 — *vt.* 1.叫着说 2.用喊声鼓励 — *n.* 叫声；叫喊；〈美〉(为运动员加油的)呐喊，欢呼

yellow ['jeləu] *adj.* 1.黄(色)的；黄皮肤的 2.(因病等)发黄的；(因循旧)泛黄的 3.(报刊等)采用耸人听闻手法的；作低级渲染的 4.〈口〉胆怯的；卑鄙的；靠不住的(脸色、心情等)妒忌的；猜疑的 — *n.* 1.黄(色) 2.黄色颜料(或染料) 3.蛋黄 4.黄种人 5.〔the ~ s〕黄叶；【植】黄化病 6.〈口〉胆怯 7.〈古〉妒忌 — *vi.* 变黄，发黄 — *vt.* 使变黄；使发黄 ‖ ~ish、~y *adj.* 淡黄色的；带黄色的 / ~ **alert**(空袭)预备警报 / ~ **fever** 【医】黄热病 / ~ **jack** 1. = ~ **fever** 2.(检疫中表示船上有疫病而悬挂的)黄旗 / ~ **jacket** 1. 小黄蜂 2.(清代权贵穿的)黄马褂 3.〈俚〉(内装麻醉品的)黄胶囊 / ~ **peril** 黄祸(指所谓的黄种人带给西方的威胁) / **Yellow River** 黄河(现译 Huanghe River) / **Yellowstone** *n.* 黄石河 / 美国西北部〕: the *Yellowstone National Park*(美国)黄石国家公园

yelp [jelp] *vi.*(狗)吠，嗥猎；(因痛而)叫喊 — *vt.* 叫喊着说 — *n.*(短促而尖锐的)吠声(或叫喊声)

Yemen ['jemən] *n.* 也门〔西南亚国家〕

yen¹ [jen]〔单复同〕*n.* 日元(日本货币单位)

yen² [jen] *n.*〈口〉(汉语中的)"瘾"；热望，渴望；嗜好，癖好 — (yenned; yenning) *vi.* 热望；渴望

yeoman ['jəumən](〔复〕yeomen) *n.* 1.【英

史】自由民；(国王或贵族的)侍者，仆人 2.〈英〉自耕农 3.〔英国国王的〕仪仗卫士 4.〔美国海军〕文书军士 5.〈英〉勇骑兵

yeomanry ['jəumənri] *n.* 1.【英史】〔总称〕自由民；自耕农 2.〈英〉义勇骑兵队

Yerevan [jere'vɑːn] *n.* 耶烈万(即 Erivan 埃里温)〔亚美尼亚首都〕

yes [jes] *adv.* 1. 是，是的 2.〔用升调，表示疑问或鼓励对方进一步讲述〕是吗，真的吗 3.〔用长调，征求对方意见〕是不是 4.〔应答呼唤〕是，我在这儿 5.〔加强语气用〕是的，的说真的 — (〔复〕yeses〔'jesiz〕) *n.* 1. 是，同意，造成 2. 赞成票；投赞成票的人 — (yessed; yessing) *vt. & vi.*(对…)说"是"，同意，赞成 ‖ ~-**man** *n.* 〈口〉唯唯诺诺的人

yesterday ['jestədi] *n.* 1. 昨天，昨日 2. 近来；最近 3.〔常 ~ s〕过去的日子，往昔 — *adv.* 1. 在昨天，在昨日 2. 近来；最近

yet [jet] *adv.* 1. 还，尚；仍然 2. 已经 3.〔与比较级连用〕比…还要，更；〔与 once, again 等连用〕再 4.〔与最高级连用于目前(或当时)为止的〕5. 也 6. 而，而又；然而 — *conj.* 而，而又；然而

yeti ['jeti] *n.* 〔常作 Y-〕雪人(传说生存在喜马拉雅山上的一种动物)

yew [ju:] *n.* 【植】紫杉(尤指浆果紫杉)

Yid [jid] *n.* 〈俚〉〈贬〉犹太人

Yiddish ['jidif] *n.* 依地语，意第绪语(犹太人使用的国际语) — *adj.* 1. 依地语的 2.〈俚〉犹太人的

yield [ji:ld] *vt.* 1. 生产；生长出(作物等)；结出(果实)；产生(效益，收益等) 2. 让予，给予；同意 3. 被迫放弃〔~ one-self〕放纵(up) — *vi.* 1. 出产 2. 服从；屈服；投降(to) — *n.* 产量；收获量；利益

yielding ['jiːldiŋ] *adj.* **1.** 出产的 **2.** 易变形的；易弯曲的 **3.** 柔顺的；依从的；屈从的

yip [jip] *n.* 〈口〉犬吠声；叫喊声 — (yipped; yipping) *vi.* 〈口〉(狗)吠；叫喊

Yippie ['jipi] *n.* (美国) 易比派分子，易比士

YMCA *abbr.* Young Men's Christian Association 基督教青年会

yodel ['jəudl] (yodel(l)ed; yodel(l)ing) *vt.* & *vi.* 用真假嗓音反复变换地唱或叫喊) — *n.* (瑞士等山区流行的)真假嗓音反复变换的唱腔(或叫喊、唱出的歌曲)

yoga ['jəugə] *n.* **1.** 瑜伽(古印度哲学的一派，实行默坐苦修) **2.** 瑜伽修行法

yoghurt ['jɔgət, 'jəugət] *n.* = yogurt

yogi ['jəugi] *n.* **1.** 瑜伽信徒；瑜伽修行者 **2.** 沉思默想的人；神秘莫测的人

yogurt ['jɔgət, 'jəugət] *n.* 酸乳，酸奶

yoke [jəuk] *n.* **1.** 牛轭，轭 **2.** [单复同] (同轭的)一对牛(或马等) **3.** 轭状扁担；轭形吊钟架 **4.** 轭状物；[史] (架在被俘人员脖子上的)轭架；(令战俘在其下面通过以示服从的)轭门 **5.** 束缚；压力；支配；管辖 **6.** (联结夫妇等的)情义 **7.** [船]横舵柄 **8.** [空]操纵杆 **9.** [电]轭铁 **10.** [无]偏转线圈 **11.** 护轨夹 **12.** [建]窗头板 **13.** [动]翅轭 **14.** (女服)上衣抵肩；裙腰 **15.** 〈古〉一对牛一天耕的土地 — *vt.* **1.** 给…套上轭 **2.** 结合；联系在一起 **3.** 把(犁等)套上牲口 **4.** 结合；接合；连接 **5.** 使匹配 **5.** 〈罕〉束缚；奴役 — *vi.* 结合；连接 ∥ ~ bone 颧骨 / '~fellow, '~mate *n.* 同事；配偶；伙伴；搭档 / '~lines, '~ropes [复] *n.* 舵柄绳

yokel ['jəukəl] *n.* 〈贬〉乡巴佬，土包子

Yokohama [ˌjəukə'hɑːmə, ˌjɔkə'hɑːmə] *n.*

横滨 [日本本州岛东南岸港市]

yolk [jəuk] *n.* **1.** 蛋黄；[生] 卵黄 **2.** 羊毛粗脂

yom [jaum] 〈希伯来语〉 *n.* 节，日 ∥ **Yom Kippur** ['kipə] 〈犹太教〉赎罪日(于该日禁食)

yon [jɔn] 〈古〉〈方〉 *adv.* & *adj.* = yonder — *pron.* 那边(或远处)的人(或事物)

yonder ['jɔndə] *adv.* 在那边；在远处 — *adj.* 那边的；远处的 — *pron.* 那边；远处;那边(或远处)的东西

yore [jɔː] *n.* 〈书〉昔时，往昔(现只用于 of ~ 一语中)

Yorkshire ['jɔːkʃə] *n.* **1.** 约克郡(或译约克夏)[英国英格兰原郡名] **2.** 约克郡猪，约克夏猪(原产英国约克郡的白猪)

you [juː; 弱 ju] (单数、复数、主格、宾格形式均同) *pron.* **1.** 你；你们 **2.** (呼唤、祈使、感叹用到)你这个；你们这些 **3.** (泛指)一个人，任何人 **4.** 〈古〉你(们)自己 ∥ '~-'all *pron.* 〈美方〉你们大家；你

you'd [juːd; 弱 jud] **1.** = you had **2.** = you would

you'll [juːl; 弱 jul] = you will；you shall

young [jʌŋ] (younger ['jʌŋgə], youngest ['jʌŋgist]) *adj.* **1.** 年轻的；幼小的；青春时期的 **2.** 似青年的，有青春活力的；朝气蓬勃的 **3.** [Y-] (政党、运动等)新(兴)的；青年的；激进的 **4.** 初期的，开始不久的 **5.** 没有经验的；初出茅庐的，未成熟的 **6.** (父子、兄弟等)年幼的；年较小的；年轻时代的 **7.** [地]幼年的，受侵蚀尚少的 — [单复同] *n.* **1.** [the ~] 青年们 **2.** 崽，仔，雏 ∥ **-ish** *adj.* 还年轻的；还幼小的

younger ['jʌŋgə] young 的比较级 — *adj.* 较年轻的(或较幼小的等) — *n.* **1.** 年纪较小的人 **2.** 年轻人；幼小者；[常 ~s] 子女；后辈

youngest ['jʌŋgist] young 的最高级 — *n.* 年纪最小的人(尤指家庭内最年轻者);最小的儿子(或女儿)

youngster ['jʌŋstə] *n.* 1. 年轻人,小伙子;小孩 2. (美国海军军官学校的)二年级学生 3. [培育的]幼小动物;幼苗 4. 新辖区

your [jɔː, juə] *pron.* 1. [you 的所有格]你的;你们的 2. (泛指)一个人的,任何人的 3. [后接 Excellency, Honour 等,构成对贵族、官员等的尊称,直接称呼时用]: Your Majesty 陛下 / Your Excellency 阁下 4. [口](表示不赞同、有疑义等)你(或你们)那种的;你(或你们)所谓的: So that's ~ philanthropy! 你们所谓的慈善原来如此!

you're [juə, jɔː] = you are

yours [jɔːz] *pron.* 1. [物主代词]你的(东西);你们的(东西) 2. 你(们)的家属 3. 你(们)的来信 4. [在信尾具名前,与 truly, faithfully, sincerely 等连用,作为客套语]: Yours truly(或 Truly ~)你的忠实的

yourself [jɔː'self] *pron.* 1. [反身代词]你自己 2. [用以加强语气]你亲自,你本人 3. [用于 be, come to 等之后]你的正常情况(指健康、情绪等)

youth [juːθ] ([复] youths [juːðz]) *n.* 1. 青春;青年时期;青少年时期;初期 2. 青年们 3. (男)青年,小伙子 ‖ **— hostel**

youthful ['juːθful] *adj.* 1. 年轻的;青年的;未成熟的 2. 富于青春活力的,朝气蓬勃的 3. 初起的;早期的;【地】幼年的,受侵蚀尚少的 ‖ **~ly** *adv.* / **~ness** *n.*

you've [juːv, 弱 juv] = you have

yowl [jaul] *n.* & *vi.* 嗥叫;惨叫

yperite ['iːpərait] *n.* 【化】芥子气(一种战争毒气)

yr. *abbr.* 1. year(s) 2. younger 3. your

Yt 【化】元素钇(yttrium)的符号

ytterbium [i'tə:miəm] *n.* 【化】镱

yttrium ['itriəm] *n.* 【化】钇

Yuan [ju:'ɑːn] 〈汉〉*n.* 【史】元(朝)

yuan [ju:'ɑːn] 〈汉〉[单复同] *n.* 元(中国货币单位)

yucca ['jʌkə] *n.* 【植】丝兰;丝兰花

Yugoslavia [ˌjuːgəu'slɑːviə] *n.* 南斯拉夫[欧洲巴尔干半岛西北部国家] ‖ **— n** *n.* 南斯拉夫人 *adj.* 南斯拉夫的;南斯拉夫人的

yule [juːl] *n.* [常作 Y-]【基督教】圣诞节;圣诞节期

Yuletide ['juːltaid], **Yuletime** ['juːltaim] *n.* [亦作 y-]【基督教】圣诞节期

Yuppie ['jʌpi] *n.* [亦作 y-](美)(城市)少壮职业人士,雅皮士

YWCA *abbr.* Young Women's Christian Association 基督教女青年会

Z

Z, z [zed; 美 zi:] ([复] Z's, z's 或 Zs, zs [zedz; 美 ziz])英语字母表第二十六个字母 1. [Z] Z 形 2. [数] 第三未知量

Zagreb ['zɑːgreb] n. 萨格勒布 [克罗地亚首都]

zaibatsu [zaiˈbɑːtsuː] [单复同] 〈日〉 n. 财阀

Zaire [zɑːˈiə] n. 1. 扎伊尔 [非洲中部国家] 2. [the ~] 扎伊尔河 (即刚果河) [非洲中部] 3. [z-] 扎伊尔 (扎伊尔货币单位) ‖ ~se [zɑːiəˈriːz] adj.

Zambia ['zæmbiə] n. 赞比亚 [非洲中南部国家]

zany ['zeini] n. 1. (古代喜剧中) 摹仿主要丑角动作的小丑 2. 小丑；滑稽表演者 3. 马屁精；追随者 4. 糊涂虫；笨人 —adj. 1. 滑稽的，好笑的；荒唐的 2. 愚蠢的，笨的 ‖ zanily adv. /zaniness n.

zap [zæp] int. 1. (表示快速动作或变化) 嚓 2. (表示惊讶、沮丧等) 糟糕 —vt. & vi.〈俚〉迅速有力地移动 (或杀死、击败、粉碎、除去等) —n. 1. 冲头，活力 ‖ ~py adj. 精力充沛的；劲头十足的；充满活力的

ZBB abbr. zero-based budgeting

zeal [ziːl] n. 热心，热情，热忱

zealot ['zelət] n. 1. 热心者；狂热者；有派性的狂热分子 2. [Z-] [史] (公元 6－70 年间反抗罗马统治的犹太教派中的) 狂热派人，吉拉德人 ‖ ~ry n. 狂热，

狂热行为

zealous ['zeləs] adj. 热心的；热情的；积极的；狂热的 ‖ ~ly adv. /~ness n.

zebra ['zibrə, 'zebrə] n. 【动】斑马 ‖ ~ crossing (英) 斑马线 (指马路上涂有黑白相间颜色的人行横道线)

zebu ['ziːbuː] n. 【动】瘤牛

zed [zed] n. 〈主英〉(英语字母) Z, z

zee [ziː] n. 〈主美〉(英语字母) Z, z

ZEG abbr. zero economic growth

Zen [zen] n. 【宗】禅宗 (佛教的一个派别，强调默坐专念)

zenith ['zeniθ, 'ziːniθ] n. 1. 【天】天顶 2. (幸运、繁荣、权力等的) 顶点，顶峰

zeolite ['ziːəlait] n. 【矿】沸石

zephyr ['zefə] n. 1. 西风 2. 和风，微风 3. 精美轻薄织物；细纱；薄衫 4. 轻飘的东西

zeppelin ['zepəlin] n. 齐柏林飞艇

zero ['ziərəu] n. ([复] zero(e)s n. 【数】零 2. 零号 (即 0)；零点，零位；(温度计的) 零度 3. 最低点；无，乌有 4. 无足轻重的人；没价值的东西 5. 【天】天底 —adj. 1. 零的 2. 【语】无屈折的；无词尾变化的；零形态的 3. 【气】【空】零度云高的 (指云幕高度小于 50 英尺的；能见度小于 165 英尺的) —vt. 1. 把 (机械等的) 调节器置调整归零 2. 把…减少 (或减低) 到零位 ‖ ~-based budgeting [经] 零基预算编制法 / ~ economic

growth【经】经济无增长。零经济增长 / ~ **hour** 1.【军】进攻发起的时刻；零时 2. 决定性时刻，紧急关头 / ~ **population growth** 零点人口（或更生动物）增长，生死相抵 / ~ **tillage** 免耕法 / '~‧'~‧ adj. 零深度的，零零条件的（指云幕高度和能见度都为零的）

zest [zest] n. 1.【辛辣】的滋味，风味；香味；风趣；兴趣 2. 热心，热情 3.〈罕〉香橙皮；柠檬皮（用作香料）— vt. 1. 给…加香味；给…调味 2. 给…添风趣；给…增兴趣；给…助兴 ‖ ~y adj.

zestful ['zestful] adj. 1. 有辛辣味的；有滋味的；有风味的；有风趣的 2. 兴趣浓的；热心的，热情的；兴高采烈的 ‖ ~ly adv. / ~ness n.

Zeta [zi:tə] n. 希腊语的第六个字母（Z, ζ）

Zeus [zju:s] n.【希神】宙斯（希腊神话中的主神）

ZI abbr. zone of interior 后方地带；美国本土.

zibel(l)ine ['zibəlain] adj. 紫貂的；紫貂毛皮（做）的 —n. 紫貂毛皮；充填紫貂毛皮的薄毛织品、齐贝林有光长绒呢

zibet ['zibit] n.【动】大灵猫，九节狸（产于中国南部和印度等地）

zigzag ['zigzæg] n. 1. 之字形，Z字形；锯齿形 2. 之字形的线条（或道路、壕沟、装饰等）3. 蜿蜒曲折，盘旋弯曲 — adj. 1. 之字形的；锯齿形的 2. 盘旋的弯曲的 — adv. 1. 成之字形地；蜿蜒地 2. 盘旋地；弯弯曲曲地 — vt. 把…弄成之字形；使…盘旋 — vi. 成之字形行进；弯弯曲曲地走路（zigzagged；zigzagging）

Zimbabwe [zim'bɑ:bwei] n. 津巴布韦〔非洲东南部国家〕

zinc [ziŋk] n.【化】锌 —（zincked 或 zinced；zincking 或 zincing）vt. 在…上镀锌；用锌处理 ‖ ~ **blende** 闪锌矿 / ~ **oxide** 氧化锌

zincograph ['ziŋkəugrɑ:f], **zinco** ['ziŋkəu] n.【印】1. 锌版 2. 锌版印刷品 — vt. 1. 把（图样等）刻在锌版上复制 —vi. 1. 刻锌版 2. 用锌版复制；制锌版

zing [ziŋ] n.【俚】1.（子弹等的）尖啸声 2.〈俚〉活泼；兴致；精神；活力 — vi. 发尖啸声 — vt. 对…进行挑剔

zinnia ['ziniə] n.【植】1. 百日草 2. 百日菊

Zion ['zaiən] n. 1. 郇山，锡安山〔在耶路撒冷〕；耶路撒冷 2. 乌托邦，理想之国；【宗】天国，天堂 3. 以色列；犹太人民 4. 基督教会；犹太教 5.〈英〉英国非国教的教堂 ‖ ~**ism** n. 犹太复国主义，犹太复国运动

zip[1] [zip] n. = zip code

zip[2] [zip] n. 1.（子弹等的）尖啸声；撕裂声 2.〈口〉精力，活力 —（zipped；zipping）vi. 1. 给…（速度或力量）2. 使增加热情（或兴趣、生命力）(up) — vi. 1. 嗖嗖地响；嗖嗖地飞 2.〈口〉精力充沛地干

zip[3] [zip] [zipped；zipping] vt. 1. 拉开（或扣上）…的拉链 2. 拉开（拉链）；扣上（拉链）— vi. 拉开（或扣上）拉链 ‖ ~‧**fastener** n.〈英〉拉链

zip code〈美〉邮政编码

zip-code ['zipkəud] vt. 给…写明邮政编码；~ every address 给每一个地址写明邮政编码

zipless ['ziplis] adj.【俚】性放纵的；公开挑动性爱的：a ~ book 一本赤裸裸描写性爱的书

zipper ['zipə] n. 主美 拉链 —vt. & vi. (被)用拉链扣上 ‖ ~ed adj. 装有拉链的；拉链式的

zippy ['zipi] adj. 1. 口 活泼的；精力充沛的；敏捷的；喜悦的

zirconium [zə:'kəuniəm] n.【化】锆

zither(n) ['ziðə(n)] n.【音】齐特琴(欧洲的一种扁形弦乐器)

Zn【化】元素锌(zinc)的符号

zodiac ['zəudiæk] n. 想象中存在于天球上黄道两边的)黄道带

Zollverein ['tsɔlfərain] n. 德 关税同盟

Zomba ['zɔmbə] n. 松巴[马拉维东南部城市]

zombie ['zɔmbi] n. 起死回生的魔力；还魂尸

zone [zəun] n. 1. 古 诗 带子；腰带；环状带 2.【地理】地带；(结晶的)晶带 3. 地区；(城市、运动场等的)区；区域；范围 4.(包裹邮资分区计算的)包裹邮递区(= parcel post ~);(美国的)邮区；时区;(铁路运费等分区计算的)区;段;层 5.圈；环带 —vt. 1. 用带子圈围；环绕 2. 将…分区;使分成地带 —vi. 分成区;分成地带 ‖ zonal adj.

zonk [zɔŋk] vt. & vi. 使 失去知觉;(使)沉睡 ‖ ~ out 1. 沉睡 2. 使受毒品麻醉

zonked [zɔŋkt] adj.(俚)大醉的;(被麻醉药)麻醉的;筋疲力尽的

zoo [zu:] n. 1.(the Z-)伦敦动物园 2.(美俚)(铁路货车末尾工作人员乘的)守车

zoogeography [,zəuə'dʒiɔgrəfi] n. 动物地理学

zoological [,zəuə'lɔdʒikəl] adj. 1. 动物学的 2. 动物的 ‖ ~ garden 动物园

zoology [zəu'ɔlədʒi] n. 1. 动物学 2. 动物

区系 3. 动物学论文 4. 动物特性;动物生理 ‖ zoologist n. 动物学家

zoom [zu:m] vi. 1.(飞机)陡直上升;作急跃升飞行 2. 口 (开支、销售额等)激增;急升 3. 嗡嗡(或隆隆)作响;嗡嗡(或隆隆)地疾行 4.(摄影机)迅速推进(或拉远) —vt. 1. 使(飞机等)陡直上升;使作急跃升飞行 2. 使激增;使急升 3. 使(电影或电视画面)推近(或拉远) —n. 1.(飞机的)陡直上升;急跃升飞行 2. 急升;猛增 3.(电影或电视镜头的)推近(或拉远) 4. 嗡嗡声 —adj. 有变焦距镜头的

zoophobia [,zəuə'fəubiə] n.【医】动物恐怖(指对动物的异常恐怖)

zoophyte ['zəuəfait] n. 植物形动物(如珊瑚、海绵等无脊椎动物,尤指苔藓虫)

Zoroastrianism [,zɔrəu'æstriənizəm] n. 【宗】(起源于古波斯的)琐罗亚斯德教,祆教,拜火教,波斯教

ZPG abbr. zero population growth

Zr【化】元素锆(zirconium)的符号

zucchetto [tsu:'ketəu] n.(复)zucchettos) n. (天主教神父戴的)圆顶小帽

zucchini [tsu:'ki:ni] n.(复)zucchini(s)) n. 【植】绿皮密生西葫芦

Zurich, Zürich ['tsjuərik] n. 苏黎世[瑞士北部城市]

zwieback ['zwi:bæk] n.(德)n. 烤干面包(常用鸡蛋甜面包烘成的一种面包片)

zwitterion ['zwitə,raiən] n.【化】两性离子

zygote ['zaigəut] n.【生】1. 合子;受精卵 2. 接合体

zymase ['zaimeis] n.【生化】酿酶

zyme [zaim] n. 1.【生化】酶 2. 病菌

-zyme comb. form 表示"酶"

zymogen ['zaimədʒən] n. 1.【生化】酶原 2.

【微】发酵性细菌
zymology [zai'mɔlədʒi] *n.* 发酵学；酶学

zymurgy [ˈzaiməːdʒi] *n.* 酿造学

附录一

常见英美姓名表

说　明

(1) 本表收录常见英美姓名约二千四百条，注明英语发音并提供通常汉语译名。

(2) 为便于检索，表中姓、名两部分混合按字母次序排列。读者查译一个人的全名时，可按全名的英文排列次序逐一查得译名后用圆点隔开，如 William Henry Harrison 即为：威廉·亨利·哈里森。

(3) 姓氏、男子名、女子名分别标以 s. (surname)、m. (masculine name)、f. (feminine name)，如系异体或昵称则在汉语译名后加方括号注明。

(4) 每条姓名下一般只收一个通常汉语译名，有的也酌收某些其他译法或习惯译法(加圆括号附在通常汉语译名后)，以供参考。

A

Aaron ['ɛərən] *m.* 艾伦

Abbey ['æbi] *s.* 阿比(艾比)

Abbot(t) ['æbət] *s.* 阿博特(艾博特)

Abby ['æbi] *f.* 阿比(艾比)[Abigail 的昵称]

Abe [eib] *m.* 艾贝[Abraham 的昵称]

Abel ['eibəl] *s. & m.* 艾贝尔

Abercrombie（或 **Abercromby**）['æbəkrʌmbi] *s.* 阿伯克龙比(艾伯克龙比)

Abigail ['æbigeil] *f.* 阿比盖尔(艾比盖尔)

Abraham ['eibrəhæm, 'eibrəhəm] *m.* 亚伯拉罕

Absalom ['æbsələm] *m.* 阿布索伦

Acheson ['ætʃisn] *s.* 艾奇逊

Ackerman(n) ['ækəmən] *s.* 阿克曼

Acton ['æktən] *s.* 阿克顿

Ada ['eidə] *f.* 艾达

Adam ['ædəm] *s. & m.* 亚当

Adams ['ædəmz] *s.* 亚当斯

Addis ['ædis] *s.* 阿迪斯(艾迪斯)

Addison ['ædisn] *s.* 阿迪生(艾迪生)

Ade [eid] *s.* 艾德

Adela ['ædilə] *s. & f.* 阿德拉

Adelaide ['ædəleid] *f.* 阿德莱德

Adele [ə'del] *f.* 阿黛尔

Adeline ['ædəliːn, 'ædiliːn] *f.* 阿德琳(艾德琳)

Adler ['ædlə] *s.* 阿德勒(艾德勒)

Adolf(或 **Adolph**)['ædolf] *m*.阿道夫

Adolphus [ə'dɔlfəs] *m*.阿道弗斯

Adrian ['eidriən] *s*.& *m*.艾德里安

Adrienne ['eidri,en] *f*.艾德里安娜

Agate ['eigət] *s*.艾格特

Agatha ['ægəθə] *f*.阿加莎

Agnes ['ægnis] *f*.阿格尼丝

Aiken ['eikin] *s*.艾肯

Aileen ['eiliːn] *f*.艾琳[Helen 的异体]

Aitken ['eitkin] *s*.艾特肯

Alan ['ælən] *m*.阿伦(艾伦)

Albert ['ælbət] *m*.阿伯特(艾伯特;亚尔培特)

Alberta [æl'bətə] *m*.阿伯塔(艾伯塔)

Albin ['ælbin] *m*.阿尔宾

Alcott ['ɔːlkət] *s*.奥尔科特

Alcuin ['ælkwin] *m*.阿尔克温

Alden ['ɔːldən] *m*.奥尔登

Aldington ['ɔːldiŋtən] *s*.奥尔丁顿

Aldous ['ɔːldəs, 'ældəs] *m*.奥尔德斯

Aldridge ['ɔːldridʒ] *s*.奥尔德里奇

Alec(k)['ælik] *m*.亚历克[Alexander 的昵称]

Alex ['æliks] *s*.亚历克斯[Alexander 的昵称]

Alexander [ˌælig'zɑːndə] *m*.亚历山大

Alexandra [ˌælig'zɑːndrə] *f*.亚历山德拉

Alexis [ə'leksis] *m*.亚历克西斯

Alfonso [æl'fɔnzəu] *m*.阿方索

Alfred ['ælfrid] *m*.阿尔弗雷德(艾尔弗雷德)

Alger ['ældʒə] *s*.阿尔杰

Algernon ['ældʒənən] *m*.阿尔杰农

Alice ['ælis] *f*.阿丽斯(艾丽斯)[Adelaide 的异体]

Alicia [ə'liʃə] *f*.阿莉西亚(艾丽西亚)[Adelaide 的异体]

Alick ['ælik] *m*.亚历克[Alexander 的昵称]

Alison ['ælisn] *f*.阿莉森(艾莉森)[Alice 的昵称]

Allan ['ælən] *s*.& *m*.阿伦(艾伦)[Alan 的异体]

Allen ['ælin, ælən] *s*.& *m*.阿伦(艾伦)

Allenby ['ælənbi] *s*.阿伦比(艾伦比)

Ally ['æli] *f*.阿莉[Alice 的昵称]

Alma ['ælmə] *f*.阿尔玛

Alphonso [æl'fɔnzəu] *m*.阿方索

Alsop(p)['ɔːlsəp] *s*.奥尔索普(艾尔索普)

Alta ['æltə] *f*.阿尔塔

Alton ['ɔːltən] *s*.& *m*.奥尔顿

Alva ['ælvə] *m*.& *f*.阿尔瓦

Alvin ['ælvin] *m*.阿尔文

Amabel ['æməbel] *f*.阿玛贝尔

Amanda [ə'mændə] *f*.阿曼达

Ambrose ['æmbrəuz] *m*.安布罗斯

Amelia [ə'miːljə] *f*.阿米莉亚

Amherst ['æməst, 'æmhəst] *s*.阿默斯特

Amis ['eimis] *s*.艾米斯

Amos ['eiməs] *m*.艾莫斯(阿莫斯)

Amy ['eimi] *f*.艾米

Anastasia [ˌænəs'teizjə] *f*.阿纳斯塔西娅

Andersen ['ændəsn] *s*.安德森(安德生)

Anderson ['ændəsn] *s*.安德森

Andre ['ændri, 'ɑːndrei] *m*.安德烈[Andrew 的异体]

Andrew ['ændruː] *m*.安德鲁

Andrews ['ændruːz] *s*.安德鲁斯

Andy ['ændi] *s*.安迪[Andrew 的昵称]

Aneurin [ə'naiərin] *m*.安奈林

Angela ['ændʒilə] *f*.安吉拉

Angelina [ˌændʒi'liːnə] *f*.安吉利娜[Angela 的昵称]

Angell ['eindʒəl] *s*.安吉尔

Angelo ['ændʒiləu] m. 安吉洛

Angus ['æŋgəs] m. 安格斯

Anita [ə'ni:tə] f. 安妮塔[Ann 的昵称]

Ann [æn] f. 安

Anna ['ænə] f. 安娜[Ann 的异体]

Annabella [ænə'belə] f. 安娜贝拉

Anne [æn] f. 安妮[Ann 的异体]

Annetta [æ'netə] f. 安妮塔[Ann 的昵称]

Annette [ə'net] f. 安妮特[Ann 的昵称]

Annie ['æni] f. 安妮[Ann 的昵称]

Anselm ['ænselm] m. 安塞姆

Ant(h)ony ['æntəni] m. 安东尼

Antoinette [ˌæntwɔ:'net] f. 安托万内特[Antonia 的昵称]

Anton ['æntən] m. 安东[Ant(h)ony 的异体]

Antonia [æn'təunjə] f. 安东尼娅

Antonio [æn'təuniəu] m. 安东尼奥[Ant(h)ony 的异体]

Appleton ['æpltən] s. 阿普尔顿

April ['eipril] f. 艾普丽尔(阿普里尔)

Arabe(l)a [ærə'belə] f. 阿拉贝拉

Aram ['ɛərəm] s. 艾拉姆(阿拉姆)

Arbuthnot [ɑ:'bʌθnɔt] s. 阿巴思诺特

Archer ['ɑ:tʃə] s. 阿切尔

Archibald ['ɑ:tʃibəld, 'ɑ:tʃibɔld] m. 阿奇博尔德

Archie ['ɑ:tʃi] f. 阿尔奇[Archibald 的昵称]

Ardell(e) [ɑ:'del] f. 阿黛尔[Adele 的异体]

Arden ['ɑ:dn] s. & m. 阿登

Ardis ['ɑ:dis] f. 阿迪斯

Arkwright ['ɑ:krait] s. 阿克赖特

Arlene [ɑ:'li:n] f. 阿琳

Arlo ['ɑ:ləu] m. 阿尔洛

Armand ['ɑ:mɔnd] m. 阿曼德[Herman(n) 的异体]

Armstrong ['ɑ:mstrɔŋ] s. 阿姆斯特朗

Arne [ɑ:n] s. & m. 阿恩

Arnold ['ɑ:nld] s. & m. 阿诺德

Arthur ['ɑ:θə] m. 阿瑟(亚瑟)

Arvid ['ɑ:vid] m. 阿维德

Aston [æstən] s. 阿斯顿

Astor ['æstə, 'æstɔ:] s. 阿斯特

Astrid ['æstrid] f. 阿斯特丽德

Atherton ['æθətən] s. 阿瑟顿(艾瑟顿)

Atkins ['ætkinz] s. 阿特金斯

Attlee ['ætli] s. 阿特利(艾特利;艾德礼)

Aubrey ['ɔ:bri] s. & m. 奥布里

Auchinleck [ˌɔ:kin'lek] s. 奥金莱克

Auden ['ɔ:dn] s. 奥登

Audrey ['ɔ:dri] f. 奥德丽

August ['ɔ:gəst] m. 奥古斯特

Augustine [ɔ:'gʌstin] s. 奥古斯丁

Augustus [ɔ:'gʌstəs] m. 奥古斯塔斯

Austen ['ɔ:stin] s. 奥斯汀(奥斯丁)

Austin ['ɔ:stin] s. 奥斯汀(奥斯丁)

Aveling ['eivliŋ] s. 艾夫林

B

Babbitt ['bæbit] s. 巴比特(白璧德)

Babington ['bæbiŋtən] s. 巴宾顿

Bach(e) ['beitʃ] s. 贝奇

Bacon ['beikən] s. 培根

Bader ['bɑ:də] s. 巴德

Bailey ['beili] s. & m. 贝利

Bain ['bein] *s*. 贝恩

Baker ['beikə] *s*. 贝克

Baldwin ['bɔːldwin] *s*. 鲍德温

Balfour ['bælfuə] *s*. 巴尔弗(鲍尔弗弗;巴尔福)

Ball [bɔːl] *s*. 鲍尔

Bancroft ['bænkrɔft] *s*. 班克罗夫特

Banks [bæŋks] *s*. 班克斯

Barbara ['bɑːbərə] *f*. 巴巴拉

Barber ['bɑːbə] *s*. 巴伯

Barclay ['bɑːkli] *s*.&*m*. 巴克利

Barham ['bærəm] *s*. 巴勒姆

Barkley ['bɑːkli] *s*. 巴克利

Barnard ['bɑːnəd] *s*.&*m*. 巴纳德

Barnes [bɑːnz] *s*. 巴恩斯

Barnet(t) ['bɑːnit] *s*.&*m*. 巴尼特

Barney ['bɑːni] *m*. 巴尼[Bernard 的昵称]

Barrett ['bærət, 'bærit] *s*.&*m*. 巴雷特

Barrie ['bæri] *s*.&*m*. 巴里(巴蕾)

Barry ['bæri] *m*. 巴里

Barrymore ['bærimɔː] *s*. 巴里莫尔

Bart [bɑːt] *s*. 巴特[Bartholomew 的昵称]

Bartholomew [bɑːˈθɔləmjuː] *s*. 巴塞洛缪

Bartlett ['bɑːtlit] *s*. 巴特利特

Barton ['bɑːtn] *s*.&*m*. 巴顿

Baruch [bɑˈruːk] *s*. 巴鲁克

Basham ['bæʃəm] *s*. 巴沙姆

Basil ['bæzl] *m*. 巴兹尔

Basker ['bɑːskə] *s*. 巴斯克

Bates [beits] *s*. 贝茨

Bauer ['bauə] *s*. 鲍尔(拜耳;鲍威尔)

Baxter ['bækstə] *s*. 巴克斯特

Bayard ['beiɑːd] *s*. 贝阿德

Beadle ['biːdl] *s*. 比德尔

Beard [biəd] *s*. 比尔德

Beardsley ['biədzli] *s*. 比尔兹利

Beatrice ['biətris] *s*. 比阿特丽斯

Beatrix ['biətriks] *s*. 比阿特丽克斯

Beaufort ['bəufət] *s*. 博福特(蒲福)

Beaumont ['bəumənt] *s*. 博蒙特

Beaverbrook ['biːvəbruk] *s*. 比弗布鲁克

Becher ['biːtʃə] *s*. 比彻

Beck [bek] *f*. 贝克[Rebecca 的昵称]

Becket(t) ['bekit] *s*. 贝克特

Becky ['beki] *s*. 贝基[Rebecca 的昵称]

Bede [biːd] *s*. 比德

Bedford ['bedfəd] *s*. 贝德福德

Beebe(e) ['biːbi] *s*. 毕比

Beecham ['biːtʃəm] *s*. 比彻姆

Beecher ['biːtʃə] *s*. 比彻

Beerbohm ['biəbəum] *s*. 比尔博姆

Behrman ['beəmən] *s*. 贝尔曼

Belinda [biˈlində] *f*. 比琳达

Bell [bel] *s*. 贝尔(贝耳)

Bellamy ['beləmi] *s*. 贝拉米

Bellman ['belmən] *s*. 贝尔曼

Belloc ['belɔk] *s*. 贝洛克

Bellow(s) ['beləu(z)] *s*. 贝洛(斯)

Ben [ben] *m*. 本[Benjamin 的昵称]

Benchley ['bentʃli] *s*. 本奇利

Benedict ['benidikt] *s*.&*m*. 本尼迪克特

Benét [beˈnei] *s*. 贝内

Benge [bendʒ] *s*. 本奇

Benjamin ['bendʒəmin] *m*. 本杰明

Bennett ['benit] *s*.&*m*. 贝内特(本涅特) [Benedict 的异体]

Benny(或 **Bennie**) ['beni] *m*. 本尼[Benjamin 的昵称]

Benson ['bensn] *s*. 本森

Bentham ['bentəm, 'benθəm] *s*. 本瑟姆(边沁)

Benton ['bentən] *s*.&*m*. 本顿

Berger ['bə:dʒə] s. 伯杰

Berkeley ['ba:kli, 'bə:kli] s. 伯克利(贝克莱)

Bernadette [ˌbə:nə'det] f. 伯纳黛特

Bernadine ['bə:nədin] f. 伯纳迪恩

Bernal ['bə:nəl] s. 伯纳尔(贝纳尔)

Bernard [bə:'na:d, 'bə:nəd] s. 伯纳德

Bernice ['bə:nis, bə:'nis] s. 伯尼斯

Bernice ['bə:nis] f. 伯妮斯

Bernie ['bə:ni] m. 伯尼[Bernard 的昵称]

Bernstein ['bə:nstain] s. 伯恩斯坦

Bert (或 Burt) [bə:t] m. 伯特

Bertha ['bə:θə] f. 伯莎

Bertie ['bə:ti, 'bə:ti] s. 伯蒂

Bertie ['bə:ti] f. 伯蒂

Bertram ['bə:trəm] m. 伯特伦

Beryl ['beril] f. 贝丽尔

Bess [bes] f. 贝斯[Elizabeth 的昵称]

Bessemer ['besimə] s. 贝西默

Bessie ['besi] f. 贝西[Elizabeth 的昵称]

Beth [beθ] f. 贝思[Elizabeth 的昵称]

Bethune ['bi:tn, bə'θju:n] s. 比顿(贝休恩;
白求恩)

Bets(e)y ['betsi] f. 贝特西[Elizabeth 的昵
称]

Betty ['beti] f. 贝蒂[Elizabeth 的昵称]

Beulah ['bju:lə] f. 比尤拉

Bevan ['bevən] s. 贝文(比万)

Beveridge ['bevəridʒ] s. 贝弗里奇

Beverl(e)y ['bevəli] f. 贝弗莉

Bevin ['bevin] s. 贝文

Biddle ['bidl] s. 比德文

Bill [bil] m. 比尔[William 的昵称]

Billie ['bili] f. 比莉

Billy (或 Billie) ['bili] m. 比利[William 的
昵称]

Bird [bə:d] s. 伯德

Birkbeck ['bə:kbek] s. 伯克贝克

Birrell ['birəl] s. 比勒尔

Bispham ['bisfəm] s. 比斯法姆

Black [blæk] s. 布莱克

Blackett ['blækit] s. 布莱克特

Blackmore ['blækmɔ:] s. 布莱克莫尔

Blackwood ['blækwud] s. 布莱克伍德

Blaine [blein] s. & m. 布莱恩

Blair ['blɛə] s. & m. 布莱尔

Blake [bleik] s. 布莱克

Blanche [bla:ntʃ] f. 布兰奇

Bligh [blai] s. 布莱

Bliss [blis] s. 布利斯

Blom [blɔm] s. 布洛姆

Bloomer ['blu:mə] s. 布卢默

Bloomfield ['blu:mfi:ld] s. 布卢姆菲尔德
(布龙菲尔德)

Bloor [blɔ:, blɔə] s. 布卢尔

Blume [blu:m] s. 布卢姆

Boas ['bəuæz, 'bəuɑz] s. 博厄斯

Bob [bɔb] m. 鲍勃[Robert 的昵称]

Bobbie ['bɔbi] f. 博比[Roberta 的昵称]

Bobby ['bɔbi] m. 博比[Robert 的昵称]

Bodley ['bɔdli] s. 博德利

Boleyn ['bulin] s. 博林

Bolingbroke ['bɔliŋbruk] s. 博林布鲁克

Bolivar ['bɔ'li:vɑ:, bɔ'li:bɑ:] s. 博利瓦

Bolsover ['bɔlsəvə] s. 博尔索弗

Boniface ['bɔnifeis] s. 博尼费斯

Bonita [bə'ni:tə] f. 伯妮塔

Bonner ['bɔnə] s. 邦纳

Bonnie ['bɔni] f. 邦妮

Boon(e) [bu:n] s. 布恩

Booth [bu:ð] s. 布思

Boris ['bɔris] m. 鲍里斯

Borrow ['bɔrəu] s. 博罗

Bosanquet ['bəuznkit] s. 鲍赞克特

Boswell ['bɔswəl] s. 博斯韦尔(包斯威尔)

Bottome [bə'təum] s. 伯托姆(博顿)

Bovey ['buːvi] s. 博维

Bowater ['bəuwɔːtə] s. 鲍沃特

Bowen ['bəuin] s. 鲍恩

Bowles [bəulz] s. 鲍尔斯

Bowman ['bəumən] s. 鲍曼

Boyd [bɔid] s. & m. 博伊德

Boyle [bɔil] s. 博伊尔(波义耳)

Bradbury ['brædbəri] s. 布拉德伯里(布雷德伯里)

Bradford ['brædfəd] s. 布拉德福(布雷德福)

Bradley ['brædli] s. & m. 布拉德利(布雷德利)

Bragg [bræg] s. 布拉格

Brattain ['brætən] s. 布拉顿(布雷登)

Braun [brɔːn] s. 布朗

Bray [brei] s. 布雷

Brazier ['breizə] s. 布雷热

Breasted ['brestid] s. 布雷斯特德

Brenda ['brendə] f. 布伦达

Brennan ['brenən] s. 布伦南

Brent [brent] s. & m. 布伦特

Brewer ['bruːə] s. 布鲁尔

Brewster ['bruːstə] s. 布鲁斯特

Brian ['braiən] s. & m. 布赖恩

Brice [brais] s. & m. 布赖斯

Bridges ['bridʒiz] s. 布里奇斯

Bridget ['bridʒit] f. 布丽奇特

Bridgman ['bridʒmən] s. 布里奇曼

Briggs [brigz] s. 布里格斯

Bright [brait] s. 布赖特

Brigitte ['bridʒit] f. 布丽奇特 [Bridget 的异体]

Broad [brɔːd] s. 布罗德

Brome [brəum] s. 布罗姆

Bromfield ['brɔmfiːld] s. 布罗姆菲尔德

Brontë ['brɔnti] s. 布朗蒂(勃朗蒂)

Brook(e) [bruk] s. 布鲁克

Brooks [bruks] s. & m. 布鲁克斯

Brown(e) [braun] s. 布朗

Browning ['brauniŋ] s. 布朗宁(勃朗宁)

Bruce [bruːs] s. 布鲁斯

Bruno ['bruːnəu] m. 布鲁诺

Bryan ['braiən] s. & m. 布赖恩

Bryant ['braiənt] s. 布赖恩特

Bryce [brais] s. & m. 布赖斯

Buck [bʌk] s. 巴克(布克)

Buckle ['bʌkl] s. 巴克尔

Buddy ['bʌdi] m. 巴迪

Buford ['bjuːfəd] s. & m. 布福德

Bulwer ['bulwə] s. 布尔沃

Bunch(e) [bʌntʃ] s. 本奇

Bunker ['bʌŋkə] s. 邦克

Bunyan ['bʌnjən] s. 布尼安(班扬)

Burbage ['bɔːbidʒ] s. 伯比奇

Burbank ['bɔːbæŋk] s. 伯班克

Burgess ['bɔːdʒiz] s. 伯吉斯

Burghley ['bɔːdi] s. 伯利

Burk(e) [bɔːk] s. & m. 伯克(柏克)

Burlingame ['bɔːliŋgeim] s. 伯林格姆

Burne-Jones ['bɔːn'dʒəunz] s. 伯恩—琼斯

Burnett [bɔː'net, 'bɔːnit] s. 伯内特

Burney ['bɔːni] s. 伯尼

Burns [bɔːnz] s. 伯恩斯(彭斯)

Burnside ['bɔːnsaid] s. 伯恩塞德

Burr [bɔː] s. 伯尔

Burrough(s) ['bʌrəu(z)] s. 伯勒(斯)

Burton ['bɔːtn] s. & m. 伯顿

Bury ['bjuəri, 'beri] *s.* 伯里
Bush [buʃ] *s.* 布什
Butler ['bʌtlə] *s.* 巴特勒(勃特勒)

Byrd [bəd] *s.* 伯德
Byrne(s) [bən(z)] *s.* 伯恩(斯)
Byron ['baiərən] *s.* & *m.* 拜伦

C

Cabell ['kæbəl] *s.* 卡贝尔
Cable ['keibl] *s.* 凯布尔
Cade [keid] *s.* 凯德
Calder ['kɔːldə] *s.* 考尔德
Caldwell ['kɔːldwel] *s.w.* 考德威尔
Calverley ['kælvəti] *s.* 卡尔弗利
Calvert ['kælvət, 'kɔːlvət] *s.* 卡尔弗特
Calvin ['kælvin] *s.* & *m.* 卡尔文(加尔文)
Camden ['kæmdən] *s.* 卡姆登
Cameron ['kæmərən] *s.* & *m.* 卡梅伦
Camil(l)a [kə'milə] *f.* 卡米拉
Camp [kæmp] *s.* 坎普
Campbell ['kæmbl] *s.* 坎贝尔
Canning ['kæniŋ] *s.* 坎宁
Cannon ['kænən] *s.* 坎农
Carey ['kɛəri] *s.* 凯里
Carl [kɑːl] *m.* 卡尔[Karl 的异体]
Carlos ['kɑːlɔs] *m.* 卡洛斯[Charles 的异体]
Carlton ['kɑːltən] *s.* & *m.* 卡尔顿
Carlyle [kɑː'lail, 'kɑː'lail] *s.* & *m.* 卡莱尔
Carmen ['kɑːmen] *f.* 卡门
Carnegie [kɑː'neigi] *s.* 卡内基
Carol ['kærəl] *m.* & *f.* 卡罗尔(卡洛尔)[Caroline 的昵称]
Caroline ['kærəlain] *f.* 卡罗琳
Carpenter ['kɑːpintə] *s.* 卡彭特
Carrie [kæri] *s.* 卡里
Carrie ['kæri] *f.* 卡丽(嘉利)[Caroline 的昵称]

Carrol(l) ['kærəl] *s.* & *m.* 卡罗尔(卡洛尔)
Carson ['kɑːsn] *s.* & *m.* 卡森
Carter ['kɑːtə] *s.* & *m.* 卡特
Cartwright ['kɑːtrait] *s.* 卡特赖特
Carver ['kɑːvə] *s.w.* 卡弗
Cary ['kɛəri] *s.* & *m.* 卡里
Casement ['keismənt] *s.* 凯斯门特
Caslon ['kæzlən] *s.* 卡斯隆
Cass [kæs] *s.* 卡斯
Cather ['kæðə] *s.* 卡瑟
Catherine ['kæθərin] *f.* 凯瑟琳
Cathleen ['kæθliːn] *f.* 凯思琳[Catherine 的异体]
Cathryn ['kæθrin] *f.* 凯思琳[Catherine 的异体]
Cathy(或 **Cathie**) ['kæθi] *f.* 凯茜(卡西)[Catherine 的昵称]
Cattell [kæ'tel] *s.* 卡特尔
Cavell ['kævl, kə'vel] *s.* 卡维尔
Cavendish ['kævəndiʃ] *s.* 卡文迪什(卡文迪许)
Caxton ['kækstən] *s.* 卡克斯顿
Cecil ['sesl, 'sisl] *s.* & *m.* 塞西尔
Cecile ['sesil, 'sesid] *f.* 塞西尔[Cecilia 的异体]
Cecilia [si'siljə] *f.* 塞西莉亚
Cecily ['sisili] *f.* 塞西莉
Celia ['sidjə] *f.* 西莉亚[Cecilia 的昵称]
Chamberlain ['tʃeimbəlin] *s.* 张伯伦

Chambers ['tʃeimbəz] s. 钱伯斯

Chaplin ['tʃæplin] s. 查普林(卓别麟)

Chapman ['tʃæpmən] s. 查普曼

Charles [tʃɑːlz] s. & m. 查尔斯(查理)

Charley(或 Charlie) ['tʃɑːli] m. 查利

Charlotte ['ʃɑːlət] f. 夏洛特(夏洛蒂)

Chase [tʃeis] s. 蔡斯

Chatham ['tʃætəm] s. 查塔姆

Chatterton ['tʃætətən] s. 查特顿

Chaucer ['tʃɔːsə] s. 乔塞(乔叟)

Cherry ['tʃeri] f. 翎丽

Chesnut(t) ['tʃesnʌt] s. 切斯纳特

Chester ['tʃestə] m. 切斯特

Chesterfield ['tʃestəfiːld] s. 切斯特菲尔德

Chesterton ['tʃestətən] s. 切斯特顿

Chevalier [ʃəˈvæljei] s. 薛瓦利埃

Child(e) [tʃaild] s. 蔡尔德

Chitty ['tʃiti] s. 奇蒂

Choate [tʃəut] s. 乔特

Christabel ['kristəbel] f. 克里斯塔贝尔

Christian ['kristjən] m. 克里斯琴

Christiana [ˌkristiˈɑːnə] f. 克里斯蒂安娜

Christie ['kristi] s. 克里斯蒂

Christina [krisˈtiːnə] f. 克里斯蒂娜

Christine ['kristin, krisˈtiːn] f. 克里斯廷

Christopher ['kristəfə] m. 克里斯托弗

Church [tʃɜːtʃ] s. 丘奇

Churchill ['tʃɜːtʃil] s. 邱吉尔

Cicely ['sisili] f. 西塞莉

Cissy ['sisi] 锡西 [Cecilia 的昵称]

Claire [klɛə] f. 克莱尔 [Clara 的异体]

Clapham ['klæpəm] s. 克拉彭

Clara ['klɛərə] f. 克莱拉(克拉拉)

Clare [klɛə] f. 克莱尔 [Clara 的异体]

Clarence ['klærəns] m. 克拉伦斯

Clarissa [kləˈrisə] f. 克拉丽莎

Clark(e) [klɑːk] s. & m. 克拉克

Claud(e) [klɔːd] m. 克劳德

Claudia ['klɔːdjə] f. 克劳迪娅

Clay [klei] m. 克莱 [Clayton 的昵称]

Clayton ['kleitn] s. 克莱顿

Clemens ['klemənz] s. 克莱门斯

Clement ['klemənt] m. 克莱门特

Cleveland ['kliːvlənd] s. 克利夫兰

Clifford ['klifəd] s. & m. 克利福德

Clinton ['klintən] s. & m. 克林顿

Clive [klaiv] s. & m. 克莱夫

Clow [kləu] s. 布洛

Clyde [klaid] s. & m. 克莱德

Cobden ['kɔbdən] s. 科布登

Cobham ['kɔbəm] s. 科伯姆(科巴姆)

Cocke [kəuk] s. 科克

Cocker ['kɔkə] s. 科克尔

Cody ['kəudi] s. 科迪

Coffey ['kɔfi] s. 科菲

Coffin ['kɔfin] s. 科芬

Coggeshall ['kɔgzɔl] s. 科格索尔(科吉歇尔)

Cohan [kəuˈhæn] s. 科汉

Cohen ['kəuin] s. 科恩

Coke [kəuk, kuk] s. 科克

Colclough ['kəukli, 'kɔlklʌf] s. 科尔克拉夫

Cole [kəul] s. 科尔

Coleman ['kəulmən] s. 科尔曼

Coleridge ['kəulridʒ] s. 科尔里奇(柯勒律治)

Colin ['kɔlin] m. 科林 [Nicholas 的昵称]

Collier ['kɔliə] s. 科利

Collins ['kɔlinz] s. 柯林斯

Colman ['kəulmən] s. 科尔曼

Colum ['kɔləm] s. 科拉姆

Columbus [kəˈlʌmbəs] s. 哥伦布

Colvin ['kɔlvin] *s.* 科尔文

Commons ['kɔmənz] *s.* 康门斯

Compton ['kʌmptən] *s.* 康普顿

Comstock ['kʌmstɔk, 'kɔmstɔk] *s.* 康斯托克

Conan ['kəunən, 'kɔnən] *m.* 科南(柯南)

Conant ['kɔnənt] *s.* 科南特

Condon ['kɔndən] *s.* 康登

Congreve ['kɔŋgriːv] *s.* 康格里夫

Connie ['kɔni] *f.* 康妮[Constance 的昵称]

Connor(s) ['kɔnə(z)] *s.* 康纳尔

Conrad ['kɔnræd] *s. & m.* 康拉德

Constable ['kʌnstəbl, 'kɔnstəbl] *s.* 康斯特布尔

Constance ['kɔnstəns] *f.* 康斯坦斯

Constantine ['kɔnstəntain] *m.* 康斯坦丁

Cook(e) [kuk] *s.* 库克

Coolidge ['kuːlidʒ] *s.* 库利奇(柯立芝)

Cooper ['kuːpə] *s.* 库珀(库柏)

Copland ['kɔplənd, 'kəuplənd] *s.* 科普兰

Copperfield ['kɔpəfiːld] *s.* 科波菲尔

Cora ['kɔːrə] *f.* 科拉

Cornelia [kɔːˈniːljə] *f.* 科妮莉亚

Cornelius [kɔːˈniːljəs] *m.* 科尼利厄斯

Cornell [kɔːˈnel] *s.* 科内尔

Cornwallis [kɔːnˈwɔlis] *s.* 康沃利斯(康华里)

Corona ['kɔːrənə] *f.* 科伦娜

Costello [kɔsˈteləu] *s.* 科斯特洛

Cotton ['kɔtn] *s.* 科顿

Coverdale ['kʌvədeil] *s.* 科弗代尔

Coward ['kauəd] *s.* 考沃德(科沃德;考尔德)

Cowley ['kauli] *s.* 考利

Cowper ['kaupə, 'kuːpə] *s.* 考珀

Coy [kɔi] *s. & m.* 科伊

Crabb(e) [kræb] *s.* 克雷布

Craig [kreig] *s. & m.* 克雷格

Craigavon [kreigˈævən] *s.* 克雷加文

Craigie ['kræɡi] *s.* 克雷吉

Craik [kreik] *s.* 克雷克

Cram [kræm] *s.* 克拉姆

Crane [krein] *s.* 克兰(克莱恩)

Cremer ['kriːmə] *s.* 克里默

Crichton ['kraitn] *s.* 克赖顿

Crick [krik] *s.* 克里克

Cripps [krips] *s.* 克里普斯

Crockett ['krɔkit] *s.* 克罗克特

Croft [krɔft] *s.* 克罗夫特

Crofts [krɔfts] *s.* 克罗夫茨

Croker ['krəukə] *s.* 克罗克

Crompton ['krɔmptən] *s.* 克朗普顿

Cromwell ['krɔmwəl] *s.* 克伦威尔

Cronin ['krəunin] *s.* 克罗宁

Crookes [kruks] *s.* 克鲁克斯

Cross(e) [krɔs] *s.* 克罗斯

Crouse [kraus] *s.* 克劳斯

Cudworth ['kʌdwəθ] *s.* 卡德沃思

Culross ['kʌlrəs] *s.* 卡尔罗斯

Cumberland ['kʌmbələnd] *s.* 坎伯兰

Cumming(s) ['kʌmiŋ(z)] *s.* 卡明(斯)

Cunningham ['kʌniŋəm] *s.* 坎宁安

Curme [kəːm] *s.* 柯姆

Currer ['kʌrə] *s.* 柯勒

Curry ['kʌri] *s.* 柯里

Curtis(s) ['kəːtis] *s.* 柯蒂斯

Cushing ['kuʃiŋ] *s.* 库欣

Custer ['kʌstə] *s.* 卡斯特

Cuthbert ['kʌθbət] *s. & m.* 卡思伯特

Cynthia ['sinθiə] *f.* 辛西娅

Cyril ['siril] *s.* 西里尔

Cyrus ['saiərəs] *m.* 赛勒斯

D

Daisy ['deizi] f. 戴西
Dale [deil] s., m. & f. 戴尔
Dallas ['dæləs] s. & m. 达拉斯
Dalton ['dɔːltn] s. & m. 多尔顿(道尔顿)
Daly ['deili] s. 戴利
Dampier ['dæmpjə] s. 丹皮尔
Dan [dæn] m. 丹[Daniel(l)的昵称]
Dana ['deinə, 'dænə] s., m. & f. 戴纳(达纳)
Dane [dein] s. 戴恩
Daniel(l) ['dænjəl] s. & m. 丹尼尔
Daphne ['dæfni] f. 达夫妮
Darnley ['dɑːnli] s. 达恩利
Darrow ['dærəu] s. 达罗
Dar(r)yl ['dæril] m. 达里尔
Darwin ['dɑːwin] s. & m. 达尔文
Davenport ['dævnpɔːt] s. 达文波特
David ['deivid] s. & m. 戴维(大卫)
Davidson ['deividsn] s. 戴维森
Davis ['deivis] s. & m. 戴维斯
Davisson ['deivisn] s. 戴维森
Davy ['deivi] s. 戴维[David的昵称]
Dawson ['dɔːsn] s. 道森
Day [dei] s. 戴
Dean [diːn] s. & m. 迪安
Deane [diːn] s. & m. 迪恩
Debora(h) ['debərə] f. 黛博拉
Debs [debz] s. 德布斯
Decker ['dekə] s. 德克尔
Defoe [dəˈfəu, diˈfəu] s. 迪福(笛福)
De Forest [dəˈfɒrist] s. 德福雷斯特
Dekker ['dekə] s. 德克尔
Deland ['diːlənd] s. 迪兰(德兰)

Delia ['diːljə] f. 迪莉娅
Dellingr ['delindʒə] s. 德林杰
Denise [dəˈniːz, deˈniːz] f. 丹妮斯
Den(n)is ['denis] s. & m. 丹尼斯
Dent [dent] s. 登特
Denton ['dentən] s. 丹顿
Depew [diˈpjuː] s. 迪普
De Quincey [dəˈkwinsi] s. 德昆西
Derek ['derik] m. 德里克
Desmond ['dezmənd] m. 德斯蒙德
Dewar ['djuːə] s. 迪尤尔(杜尔;杜瓦)
Dewey ['djuːi] s. 杜威
Dexter ['dekstə] m. 德克斯特
Dian(n)a [daiˈænə] f. 黛安娜
Dick [dik] s. & m. 迪克[Richard的昵称]
Dickens ['dikinz] s. 迪肯斯(狄更斯)
Dickenson ['dikinsn] s. 迪肯森
Dil [dil] s. 迪尔
Dillon ['dilən] s. 狄龙
Dilys ['dilis] f. 迪莉斯
Dina(h) ['dainə] f. 黛娜
Dirac [diˈræk] s. 迪拉克
Dirk [dəːk] m. 德克[Derek的异体]
Dirksen ['dəːksn] s. 德克森
Disney ['dizni] s. 迪斯尼
Disraeli [dizˈreili] s. 迪斯雷利(狄士累利)
Dives [daivz] s. 戴夫斯
Dixie ['diksi] f. 迪克西
Dixon ['diksn] s. 狄克逊
Dobson ['dɔbsn] s. 多布森
Dodd [dɔd] s. 多德
Dodge [dɔdʒ] s. 道奇

Dodgson ['dɔdʒsn] s.道奇森

Doherty ['dɑuəti, dəu'hɛti] s.多尔蒂(陶赫蒂)

Dole [dəul] s.多尔

Domett ['dɔmit] s.多米特

Dominic(k) ['dɔminik] m.多米尼克

Donald ['dɔnəld] m.唐纳德

Donna ['dɔnə] f.唐娜

Donne [dʌn, dɔn] s.多恩

Donovan ['dɔnəvən] s.&m.多诺万

Dora ['dɔːrə] f.多拉

Doreen [dɔː'riːn, 'dɔːriːn] f.多琳

Doris ['dɔris] f.多丽丝

Dorothea [,dɔrə'θiə] f.多萝西娅

Dorothy ['dɔrəθi] f.多萝西

Dorr [dɔː] s.多尔

Dougherty ['dəuəti] s.多尔蒂

Doughty ['dauti] s.道蒂

Douglas(s) ['dʌɡləs] s.&m.道格拉斯

Dowson ['dausn] s.道森

Doyle [dɔil] s.&m.多伊尔(道尔)

Drake [dreik] s.德雷克

Draper ['dreipə] s.德雷珀

Drayton ['dreitn] s.德雷顿

Dreiser ['draisə] s.德莱塞

Drinkwater ['driŋkwɔːtə] s.德林克沃特

Drummond ['drʌmənd] s.德拉蒙德

Druse [druːz] s.德鲁斯

Dryden ['draidn] s.德赖登(屈莱登)

Du Bois [djuː'bɔiz] s.杜波依斯

Dudley ['dʌdli] s.&m.达德利

Duff [dʌf] s.达夫

Dufferin ['dʌfərin] s.达弗林

Dulles ['dʌlis, 'dʌles] s.杜勒斯

Du Maurier [djuː'mɔːriei] s.杜莫里埃

Dunbar ['dʌnbɑː] s.邓巴

Duncan ['dʌŋkən] s.&m.邓肯

Dundas [dʌn'dæs, 'dʌndæs] s.邓达斯

Dunlop [dʌn'lɔp, 'dʌnlɔp] s.邓洛普(邓禄普)

Dunmore [dʌn'mɔː] s.邓莫尔

Dunne [dʌn] s.邓恩

Dunstan ['dʌnstən] s.邓斯坦

Du Pont (或 **Dupont**) ['djuːpɔnt] s.杜邦

Durant(e) [dju'rɑːnt, dju'rænt] s.杜兰特

Durrell ['dʌrel] s.德雷尔(达雷尔)

Durward ['dɜːwəd] m.德沃德

Dutt [dʌt] s.达特(杜德)

Dwight [dwait] s.德怀特

Dyce [dais] s.戴斯

E

Eads [iːdz] s.伊兹

Earhart ['ɛəhɑːt] s.埃尔哈特

Early ['əːli] s.厄尔利

Earp [əːp] s.厄普

Eastman ['iːstmən] s.伊斯门

Eaton ['iːtn] s.伊顿

Ebenezer [,ebi'niːzə] m.埃比尼泽

Eddie ['edi] m.埃迪[Edward 的昵称]

Eddington ['ediŋtən] s.埃丁顿

Eddy ['edi] s.埃迪

Eden ['iːdn] s.伊登(艾登)

Edgar ['edɡə] m.埃德加

Edgeworth ['edʒwəθ] s.埃奇沃思

Edie ['iːdi] m.伊迪

Edison ['edisn] s.爱迪生

Edith ['iːdiθ] f.伊迪丝

Edmund ['edmənd] *m*. 埃德蒙

Edna ['ednə] *f*. 埃德娜

Edward ['edwəd] *m*. 爱德华

Edwards ['edwədz] *s*. 爱德华兹

Edwin ['edwin] *m*. 埃德温

Edwina ['edwinə] *f*. 埃德温娜

Effie ['efi] *f*. 埃菲[Euphemia 的昵称]

Eileen ['ailin] *f*. 艾琳

Einstein ['ainstain] *s*. 爱因斯坦

Eisenhower ['aizn,hauə] *s*. 艾森豪威尔

Elbert ['elbət] *m*. 埃尔伯特[Albert 的异体]

Eldon ['eldən] *s*. & *m*. 埃尔登

Eleanor ['elinə] *f*. 埃莉诺

Elgar ['elgə] *s*. 埃尔加

Elinor ['elinə] *f*. 埃莉诺

Eliot ['eljət] *s*. 埃利奥特(艾略特)

Elise [e'liz] *f*. 埃莉斯[Elizabeth 的异体]

Elizabeth [i'lizəbəθ] *f*. 伊丽莎白

Ella ['elə] *f*. 埃拉[Eleanor 的昵称]

Ellen ['elin] *f*. 埃伦[Helen 的异体]

Ellis ['elis] *s*. & *m*. 埃利斯

Ellison ['elisn] *s*. 埃利森

Ellsworth ['elzwəθ] *s*. & *m*. 埃尔斯沃思

Elmer ['elmə] *m*. 埃尔默

Elphinstone ['elfinstən] *s*. 埃尔芬斯通

Elsie ['elsi] *f*. 埃尔西[Elizabeth 的昵称]

Elton ['eltən] *m*. 埃尔顿

Elyot ['eljət] *s*. 埃利奥特

Emerson ['eməsn] *s*. & *m*. 埃默森(爱默生)

Emile [ei'mil] *m*. 埃米尔

Emily(或 **Emilie**) ['emili] *f*. 埃米莉

Emma ['emə] *f*. 埃玛

Em(m)anuel [i'mænjuəl] *m*. 伊曼纽尔

Emmet(t) ['emit] *s*. & *m*. 埃米特

Emory ['eməri] *m*. 埃默里

Enders ['endəz] *s*. 恩德斯

Endicott ['endikət] *s*. 恩迪科特

Enid ['inid] *f*. 伊妮德

Enoch ['inɔk] *m*. 伊诺克

Epstein ['epstain] *s*. 爱泼斯坦

Eric(或 **Erik**) ['erik] *m*. 埃里克

Erlanger ['əːgə] *s*. 厄兰格

Ernest ['əːnist] *m*. 欧内斯特

Ernestine ['əːnestin] *f*. 欧内斯廷

Erskin(e) ['əːskin] *s*. 厄斯金

Ervin ['əːvin] *s*. & *m*. 欧文

Ervine ['əːvin] *s*. 欧文

Erwin ['əːwin] *s*. & *m*. 欧文

Esmond(e) ['ezmənd] *m*. 埃斯蒙德

Estelle [es'tel] *f*. 埃斯特尔

Esther ['estə] *f*. 埃丝特

Ethel ['eθəl] *f*. 埃塞尔

Etherege ['eθəridʒ] *s*. 埃思里奇

Eugene [juː'ʒein, 'juːdʒiːn] *m*. 尤金

Eugenia [juː'dʒiːnjə] *f*. 尤金妮亚

Eunice ['juːnis] *f*. 尤妮斯

Euphemia [juː'fiːmjə] *f*. 尤菲米娅

Eustace ['juːstəs] *m*. 尤斯塔斯

Eva ['iːvə] *f*. 伊娃[Eve 的异体]

Evangeline [i'vændʒilin] *f*. 伊万杰林

Evans ['evənz] *s*. 埃文斯(伊文思; 伊万斯)

Evarts ['evəts] *s*. 埃瓦茨

Eve [iːv] *f*. 伊夫(夏娃)

Eveline(或 **Evelyn**) ['iːvlin, 'evlin] *f*. 伊夫琳

Evelyn ['iːvlin, 'evlin] *s*. 伊夫林

Everett ['evərit] *s*. 埃弗雷特

Ewell ['juəl] *s*. 尤厄尔

Ezekiel [i'ziːkjəl] *s*. 伊齐基尔

F

Fairbank(s) ['feəbæŋk(s)] s. 费尔班克(斯)

Faith [feiθ] f. 费思

Falkner ['fɔːknə] s. 福尔克纳

Fanny ['fæni] f. 范妮[Frances 的昵称]

Faraday ['færədi] s. 法拉第

Farley ['faːli] s. 法利

Farrar ['færə] s. 法勒

Farrell ['færəl] s. 法雷尔

Faulkner ['fɔːknə] s. 福克纳

Fawkes [fɔːks] s. 福克斯

Fay(e) [fei] f. 费伊[Faith 的昵称]

Felix ['fiːliks] m. 菲利克斯(费利克斯)

Felton ['feltən] s. 费尔顿

Fenwick ['fenik, 'fenwik] s. 芬尼克(芬威克)

Ferdinand ['fəːdinənd] m. 弗迪南德(费迪南德)

Fergus ['fəːgəs] s. 弗格斯

Fergus(s)on ['fəːgəsn] s. 弗格森(福开森)

Fettes ['fetis] s. 费蒂斯

Field [fiːld] s. 菲尔德

Fielding ['fiːldiŋ] s. 菲尔丁

Fillmore ['filmɔː] s. 菲尔莫尔

Finn [fin] s. 芬恩

Fish [fiʃ] s. 菲什

Fisher ['fiʃə] s. 菲希尔(费希尔;费雪)

Fitch [fitʃ] s. 菲奇(费区)

Fitzgerald [fits'dʒerəld] s. 菲茨杰拉德

Fitzjohn [fits'dʒɔn] s. 菲茨཈

Fitzroy [fits'rɔi] s. 菲茨罗伊

Flagg [flæg] s. 弗拉格

Flanagan ['flænəgən] s. 弗拉纳根

Flaxman ['flæksmən] s. 弗拉克斯曼

Fleetwood ['fliːtwud] s. 弗利特伍德

Fletcher ['fletʃə] s. & m. 弗莱彻

Flint [flint] s. 弗林特

Flora ['flɔːrə] f. 弗洛拉

Florence ['flɔrəns] s. 弗洛伦斯

Florey ['flɔːri, flɔːri] s. 弗洛里

Flower ['flauə] s. 弗劳尔

Flynn [flin] s. 弗林

Focke [fɔk] s. 福克

Foley ['fəuli] s. 福利(弗利)

Folger ['fəuldʒə] s. 福杰尔

Forbes [fɔːbz, 'fɔːbis] s. 福布斯

Ford [fɔːd] s. 福特

Forest ['fɔrist] s. & m. 福雷斯特

Forester ['fɔristə] s. 福雷斯特

Forster ['fɔːstə] s. 福斯特

Fosdick ['fɔzdik] s. 福斯迪克

Foster ['fɔstə] s. & m. 福斯特

Fowler ['faulə] s. 福勒

Fox [fɔks] s. 福克斯

Frances ['fraːnsis] f. 弗朗西丝

Francis ['fraːnsis] m. 弗朗西斯

Francisco [fræn'siskəu] m. 弗朗西斯科 [Francis 的异体]

Franck [fraːŋk, fræŋk] s. 弗兰克

Frank [fræŋk] m. 弗兰克

Franklin (或 Franklyn) ['fræŋklin] s. & m. 富兰克林

Franks [fræŋks] s. 弗兰克斯

Fraser (或 Frazer) ['freizə] s. 弗雷泽

Fred [fred] m. 弗雷德

Freda ['friːdə] f. 弗丽达(弗雷达)

[Winifred 的昵称]

Fredric(k)（或 **Fredric(k)**）['fredrik] *m*. 弗雷德里克

Frederic(k)a [ˌfredrˈriːkə] *f*. 弗雷德丽卡

Freedheim ['friːdhaim] *s*. 弗里德海姆

Freeman ['friːmən] *s*. & *m*. 弗里曼

Fremont [friˈmɔnt] *s*. 弗里蒙特

French [frentʃ] *s*. 弗伦奇

Frick(e) [frik] *s*. 弗里克

Frobisher ['frɔubiʃə] *s*. 弗罗比歇尔

Frohman ['frɔumən] *s*. 弗罗曼

Frost [frɔst] *s*. 弗罗斯特

Froude [fruːd] *s*. 弗鲁德（弗劳德）

Fry(e) [frai] *s*. 弗赖伊

Fuller ['fulə] *s*. 富勒

Fulton ['fultən] *s*. 富尔顿

Funk [fʌŋk] *s*. 芬克(丰克)

Furness ['fənis] *s*. 弗内斯

Furnival(l) ['fənivəl] *s*. 弗尼瓦尔

G

Gabriel ['geibriəl] *m*. 加布里埃尔（加百列）

Gage [geidʒ] *s*. 盖奇

Gaines [geinz] *s*. 盖恩斯

Gainsborough ['geinzbərə] *s*. 盖恩斯巴勒（庚斯博罗）

Gaitskell ['geitskəl] *s*. 盖茨克尔

Galbraith ['gælˈbreiθ] *s*. 加尔布雷思

Galen ['geilin] *m*. 盖伦

Galla(g)her ['gæləhə] *s*. 加拉赫

Gallatin ['gælətin] *s*. 加勒廷

Gallup ['gæləp] *s*. 盖洛普

Galsworthy ['gɔːlzwəːði, gælzwəːði] *s*. 高尔斯沃西（高尔斯华绥）

Galt [gɔːlt] *s*. 高尔特

Galton ['gɔːltən] *s*. 高尔顿（哥尔登）

Garcia [gɑːˈʃjə] *s*. 加西亚

Garden ['gɑːdn] *s*. 加登

Gardiner ['gɑːdnə] *s*. 加德纳

Gardner ['gɑːdnə] *s*. 加德纳

Garland ['gɑːlənd] *s*. & *m*. 加兰

Garner ['gɑːnə] *s*. 加纳

Garret(t) ['gærət] *m*. 加勒特

Garrison ['gærisn] *s*. 加里森

Garth [gɑːθ] *s*. & *m*. 加思

Gary ['gæri] *s*. & *m*. 加里

Gaskell ['gæskəl] *s*. 加斯克尔（盖斯凯尔）

Gasser ['gæsə] *s*. 加塞

Gates [geits] *s*. 盖茨

Gay [gei] *f*. 盖伊

Genevieve [ˌdʒenəˈviːv] *f*. 吉纳维夫

Geoffrey ['dʒefri] *m*. 杰弗里

George [dʒɔːdʒ] *s*. & *m*. 乔治

Georgia [dʒɔːdʒjə] *f*. 乔治娅

Georgina [dʒɔːˈdʒiːnə] *f*. 乔治娜

Gerald ['dʒerəld] *m*. 杰拉尔德

Geraldine ['dʒerəldiːn, dʒerəldain] *f*. 杰拉尔丁

Gerard ['dʒerɑːd, dʒeˈrɑːd] *s*. & *m*. 杰拉德（杰勒德）

Gerry [geri] *s*. & *m*. 格里

Gershwin ['gəːʃwin] *s*. 格什温（格什文）

Gertrude ['gəːtruːd] *f*. 格特鲁德

Getty(s) ['geti(z)] *s*. 格蒂(斯)

Giauque [dʒiˈauk] *s*. 吉奥克

Gibbon(s) ['gibən(z)] *s*. 吉本(斯)

Gibbs [gibz] s.布布斯
Gibson ['gibsn] s.吉布森
Gielgud ['gi:lgud] s.吉尔古德
Gilbert ['gilbət] s.& m.吉尔伯特
Giles [dʒailz] s.& f.贾尔斯(詹理斯)
Gilheney [gi'li:ni] s.吉利尼
Gill [gil] f.吉尔
Gillett(e) ['gilit, 'gilet] s.吉勒特
Gillingham ['giliŋəm] s.吉林厄姆
Gilman ['gilmən] s.吉尔曼
Gilmer ['gilmə] s.吉尔默
Gilpin ['gilpin] s.吉尔平
Girard [dʒi'rɑːd] s.吉拉德
Gissing ['gisiŋ] s.吉辛
Gladstone ['glædstən] s.格拉德斯通(格莱斯顿)
Gladys ['glædis] f.格拉迪斯
Glaser ['gleizə] s.格拉泽
Glass [glɑːs] s.格拉斯
Glen(n) [glen] s.& m.格伦
Gloag [gloug] s.格洛格
Glover ['glʌvə] s.格洛弗
Glyn [glin] s.格林
Goddard ['gɔdəd, 'gɔdɑːd] s.戈达德
Godman ['gɔdmən] s.戈德曼
Godolphin [gə'dɔlfin] s.戈多尔芬
Godwin ['gɔdwin] s.戈德温(葛德文)
Golden ['gəuldən] s.戈尔登
Golding ['gəuldiŋ] s.戈尔丁
Goldsmith ['gəuldsmiθ] s.戈德史密斯(哥尔斯密)
Golightly ['gə'laitli] s.戈莱特利
Goodrich ['gudritʃ] s.古德里奇
Goodyear ['ˈgudjə] s.古德伊尔
Gordon ['gɔːdn] s.& m.戈登
Gorton ['gɔːtn] s.戈顿

Goss(e) [gɔs] s.戈斯
Gough [gɔf] s.高夫
Gould(e) [guld] s.古尔德
Gower(s) [gɔə(z)] s.高尔(斯)
Grace [greis] s.& f.格雷斯
Gracie ['greisi] f.格雷西[Grace的昵称]
Graham(e) ['greiəm] s.& m.格雷厄姆
Grant [grɑːnt] s.& m.格兰特
Grantham ['grænθəm] s.格兰瑟姆
Grattan ['grætn] s.格拉顿
Graves [greivz] s.格雷夫斯
Gray [grei] s.& m.格雷(葛雷)
Grayson ['greisn] s.格雷森
Greel(e)y ['gri:li] s.格里利
Green [gri:n] s.格林
Greenaway ['gri:nəwei] s.格里纳韦
Greenland ['gri:nlənd] s.格林兰
Greenough ['gri:nəu] s.格里诺
Gregory ['gregəri] s.& m.格雷戈里(格列高里;格莱葛瑞)
Grenfell ['grenfel] s.格伦费尔
Grenville ['grenvil] s.格伦维尔
Gresham ['greʃəm] s.格雷沙姆
Grey [grei] s.格雷
Griffin ['grifin] s.格里芬
Griffith(s) ['grifiθ(s)] s.格里菲思
Grosvenor ['grəuvnə] s.格罗夫纳
Grote [graut] s.格罗特
Grover ['grəuvə] m.格罗弗
Grove(s) [grəuv(z)] s.格罗夫(斯)
Gruenther ['grʌnθə] s.格仑瑟
Guest [gest] s.格斯特
Gunter ['gʌntə] s.冈特
Gunther ['gʌnθə] s.冈瑟(根室)
Guy [gai] m.盖伊
Gwendolyn ['gwendəlin] f.格温多琳

H

Hadley ['hædli] s.哈德利
Hadow ['hædəu] s.哈多
Haes [heiz] s.黑斯
Haggard ['hægəd] s.哈格德
Hal [hæl] m.哈尔[Henry 的昵称]
Haldane ['hɔːldein] s.霍尔丹
Hale(s) [heil(z)] s.黑尔(斯)
Halifax ['hælifæks] s.哈利法克斯
Hall [hɔːl] s.& m.霍尔
Hallam ['hæləm] s.哈勒姆
Halleck ['hælik] s.哈勒克
Halley ['hæli] s.哈利
Halstead ['hɔːdstid, 'hælsted] s.霍尔斯特德
Halsted ['hɔːdstid, 'hælsted] s.霍尔斯特德
Haman ['heimən] s.海曼(哈曼)
Hamilton ['hæmiltən] s.& m.汉密尔顿
Hamlin ['hæmlin] s.哈姆林
Hammond ['hæmənd] s.哈蒙德
Hampden ['hæmpdən] s.汉普登
Hampton ['hæmptən] s.汉普顿
Hancock ['hænkɔk] s.汉考克
Hand [hænd] s.汉德
Handel ['hændl] s.汉德尔
Hanna ['hænə] s.汉纳
Hans [hænz] m.汉斯[Johannes 的昵称]
Hansen ['hænsn] s.汉森
Hansom ['hænsəm] s.汉萨姆
Harcourt ['hɑːkət] s.哈考特
Harden ['hɑːdn] s.哈登
Harding ['hɑːdiŋ] s.哈丁(哈定)
Hardy ['hɑːdi] s.& m.哈迪(哈代)
Harley ['hɑːli] s.& m.哈利

Harlow ['hɑːləu] m.哈洛
Harmsworth ['hɑːmzwəθ] s.哈姆斯沃思
Harold ['hærəld] m.哈罗德
Harper ['hɑːpə] s.哈珀
Harriet(t) ['hæriət] f.哈丽特 [Henrietta 的异体]
Harriman ['hærimən] s.哈里曼
Har(r)ington ['hæriŋtən] s.哈林顿
Harris ['hæris] s.哈里斯
Harris(s)on ['hærisn] s.哈里森(哈里逊)
Harrod ['hærəd] s.哈罗德
Harry ['hæri] m.哈里[Henry 的昵称]
Hart(e) [hɑːt] s.哈特(赫蒂)
Harvey ['hɑːvi] s.& m.哈维
Hastings ['heistiŋz] s.黑斯廷斯(哈斯丁)
Hattie ['hæti] f.哈蒂(海蒂) [Harriet(t) 的昵称]
Havelo(c)k ['hævlɔk] s.& m.哈夫洛克
Hawk(e) [hɔːk] s.霍克
Hawkins ['hɔːkinz] s.霍金斯
Hawthorne(e) ['hɔːθɔːn] s.霍索恩(霍桑)
Hay [hei] s.海
Hayes [heiz] s.& m.海斯
Haynes [heinz] s.海恩斯
Hays [heiz] s.海斯
Haywood ['heiwud] s.海伍德(海乌德)
Hazard ['hæzəd] s.哈泽德
Hazlitt ['heizlit, 'hæzlit] s.黑兹利特(赫兹里特)
Healy ['hiːli] s.希利
Hearst [həst] s.赫斯特
Heaviside ['hevisaid] s.海维塞德
Heber ['hiːbə] s.希伯

Hector ['hektə] *m.* 赫克托

Helen ['helin] *f.* 海伦

Helena ['helinə, hə'li:nə] *f.* 海伦娜

Heming ['hemiŋ] *s.* 赫明

Hemingway ['hemiŋwei] *s.* 海明威

Hench [hentʃ] *s.* 亨奇

Henderson ['hendəsn] *s.* 亨德森

Henley ['henli] *s.* 亨利

Henrietta [ˌhenri'etə] *f.* 亨丽埃塔

Henry ['henri] *s. & m.* 亨利

Herbert ['hə:bət] *s. & m.* 赫伯特

Herman(n) ['həmən] *m.* 赫尔曼

Herrick ['herik] *s.* 赫里克

Herschel(l) ['hə:ʃəl] *s. & m.* 赫谢尔

Hersey ['hə:si] *s.* 赫西

Herter ['hə:tə] *s.* 赫脱

Hess [hes] *s.* 赫斯

Hester ['hestə] *f.* 赫丝特[Esther 的异体]

Hewlett ['hju:lit] *s.* 休利特

Heymans ['haimɑ:ns] *s.* 海曼斯

Heyward ['heiwəd] *s.* 海沃德

Heywood ['heiwud] *s.* 海伍德

Hickok ['hikɔk] *s.* 希科克

Hicks [hiks] *s.* 希克斯

Higginson ['higinsn] *s.* 希金森

Hilary ['hiləri] *m.* 希拉里

Hilda ['hildə] *f.* 希尔达

Hildegard(e) ['hildəgɑ:d] *f.* 希尔德加德

Hill [hil] *s.* 希尔

Hillman ['hilmən] *s.* 希尔曼

Hilton ['hiltən] *s.* 希尔顿

Hindley ['haindli, 'hindli] *s.* 欣德利

Hiram ['haiərəm] *m.* 海勒姆

Hitchcock ['hitʃkɔk] *s.* 希契科克

Hobart ['həubɑ:t] *s. & m.* 霍巴特

Hobbes [ˌhɔbz] *s.* 霍布斯

Hobson ['hɔbsn] *s.* 霍布森

Hocking ['hɔkiŋ] *s.* 霍金

Hodgson ['hɔdʒsn] *s.* 霍奇森

Hofman(n) ['hɔfmən] *s.* 霍夫曼

Hofstadter ['hɔf.stætə, 'hɔf.stɔ:tə] *s.* 霍夫施塔特

Hogarth ['həugɑ:θ] *s.* 霍格思

Hogben ['hɔgbən] *s.* 霍格本

Hogg [hɔg] *s.* 霍格

Hollis ['hɔlis] *s. & m.* 霍利斯

Holly ['hɔli] *f.* 霍莉

Holman ['həulmən] *s.* 霍尔曼

Holme(s) [həum(z)] *s.* 霍姆(斯)(霍尔姆(斯))

Holt [həult] *s.* 霍尔特

Holtham ['həulθəm] *s.* 霍瑟姆

Home [həum, hju:m] *s.* 霍姆(休姆)

Homer ['həumə] *s. & m.* 霍默(荷马)

Hood [hud] *s.* 胡德

Hooker ['hukə] *s.* 胡克

Hooton ['hu:tən] *s.* 胡顿

Hoover ['hu:və] *s.* 胡佛

Hope [həup] *s. & f.* 霍普(何伯)

Hopkin(s) ['hɔpkin(z)] *s.* 霍普金(斯)

Hopkinson ['hɔpkinsn] *s.* 霍普金森

Horace ['hɔrəs] *m.* 霍勒斯(贺拉斯)

Horatio [hɔ'reiʃiəu] *m.* 霍雷肖

Hornby ['hɔ:nbi] *s.* 霍恩比

Horsley ['hɔːsli] *s.* 霍斯利

Hosier ['həuʒiə] *s.* 霍西尔

Houdini [hu:'di:ni] *s.* 霍迪尼

House [haus] *s.* 豪斯

Housman ['hausmən] *s.* 豪斯曼

Houston ['hu:stən, 'haustən] *s.* 豪斯顿

Hovell ['hʌvəl] *s.* 霍维尔

Hovey ['hʌvi] *s.* 哈维(霍维)

Howard ['hauəd] *s.* & *m.* 霍华德

Howe [hau] *s.* 豪

Howell(s) ['hauəl(z)] *s.* & *m.* 豪厄尔(斯)

Hoyle [hɔil] *s.* 霍伊尔

Hoyt [hɔit] *s.* & *m.* 霍伊特

Hubbard ['hʌbəd] *s.* 哈伯德

Hubert ['hjuːbəːt] *m.* 休伯特

Hudson ['hʌdsn] *s.* & *m.* 赫德森

Huggins ['hʌginz] *s.* 哈金斯

Hugh [hjuː] *m.* 休

Hughes [hjuːz] *s.* 休斯(休士)

Hugo ['hjuːgəu] *m.* 雨果 [Hugh 的异体]

Hull [hʌl] *s.* 赫尔

Hume [hjuːm] *s.* 休姆(休谟)

Humphr(e)y ['hʌmfri] *s.* & *m.* 汉弗莱

Hunt [hʌnt] *s.* 亨特

Hunter ['hʌntə] *s.* 亨特

Huntington ['hʌntiŋtən] *s.* 亨廷顿

Hurley ['həːli] *s.* 赫尔利

Hurst [həːst] *s.* 赫斯特

Hutt [hʌt] *s.* 赫特

Huxley ['hʌksli] *s.* 赫克斯利(赫胥黎)

Hyde [haid] *s.* 海德

I

Ian [iən] *m.* 伊恩 [John 的异体]

Ickes ['ikis] *s.* 伊克斯

Ida ['aidə] *f.* 艾达

Imogen ['iməudʒən] *f.* 伊莫金

Ina ['ainə] *f.* 艾娜

Inez ['iːnez] *f.* 伊内兹 [Agnes 的异体]

Ingersoll ['iŋgəsɔl] *s.* 英格索尔

Ingram(s) ['iŋgrəm(z)] *s.* 英格拉姆(斯)

Ingrid ['iŋgrid] *f.* 英格丽德

Inness ['inis] *s.* 英尼斯

Ira ['aiərə] *m.* 艾拉

Iredell ['aiədel] *s.* 艾尔德尔

Irene [ai'riːni, 'airiːn] *f.* 艾琳

Ireton ['aiətn] *s.* 艾尔顿

Iris ['aiəris] *f.* 艾丽斯

Ironside ['aiənsaid] *s.* 艾恩赛德

Irvin ['əːvin] *s.* & *m.* 欧文

Irving ['əːviŋ] *s.* & *m.* 欧文

Irwin ['əːwin] *s.* & *m.* 欧文

Isaac ['aizək] *m.* 艾萨克

Isabel ['izəbel] *f.* 伊莎贝尔 [Elizabeth 的异体]

Isabella [ˌizə'belə] *f.* 伊莎贝拉 [Elizabeth 的异体]

Isaiah [ai'zaiə] *m.* 艾赛亚(以赛亚)

Isherwood ['iʃəwud] *s.* 伊舍伍德

Ivan ['aivən] *m.* 伊凡 [John 的异体]

Ives [aivz, iːvz] *s.* 艾夫斯

Izard ['aizɔːd, 'aizəd, bæd] *s.* 伊泽德(艾泽德)

J

Jack [dʒæk] *m.* 杰克 [John 的昵称]

Jackson ['dʒæksn] *s.* & *m.* 杰克逊

Jacob ['dʒeikəb] *m*. 雅各布(雅各)

Jacqueline ['dʒæklin] *f*. 杰奎琳

Jacques [dʒeiks, ʒɑ:k] *m*. 雅克[James 的异体]

James [dʒeimz] *s*. & *m*. 詹姆斯(詹姆士)

Jameson ['dʒeimsn, 'dʒimsn] *s*. 詹姆森

Jan [dʒæn] *m*. & *f*. [John 的异体;Janet 的昵称]

Jane [dʒein] *f*. 简(珍妮)[Joan(n) 的异体]

Janet ['dʒænit] *f*. 珍妮特[Jane 的昵称]

Jaques ['dʒeiks] *s*. 贾克斯

Jason ['dʒeisn] *m*. 贾森

Jasper ['dʒæspə] *m*. 贾斯珀

Jay [dʒei] *s*. & *m*. 杰伊

Jean ['dʒi:n] *f*. 吉恩(琼)[Joan(n) 的异体]

Jeanne [dʒi:n] *f*. 珍妮[Joan(n) 的异体]

Jean(n)ette [dʒi'net] *f*. 珍妮特[Jeanne 的昵称]

Jeans [dʒi:nz] *s*. 吉恩斯(琼斯)

Jeb(b) [dʒeb] *s*. 杰布

Jeffers ['dʒefəz] *s*. 杰弗斯

Jefferson ['dʒefəsn] *s*. 杰斐逊(哲斐逊)

Jeffrey(s) ['dʒefri(z)] *s*. & *m*. 杰弗里(斯)

Jekyll ['dʒi:kil, 'dʒekil] *s*. 吉基尔

Jenkin(s) ['dʒeŋkin(z)] *s*. 詹金(斯)

Jenner(s) ['dʒenə(z)] *s*. 詹纳(斯)

Jennifer ['dʒenifə] *f*. 詹妮弗

Jennings ['dʒeniŋz] *s*. 詹宁斯

Jenny ['dʒeni] *f*. 詹妮

Jeremiah [,dʒeri'maiə] *m*. 杰里迈亚

Jeremy ['dʒerimi] *m*. 杰里米

Jerome [dʒə'rəum] *s*. & *m*. 杰罗姆

Jerrold (或 **Jerald**) ['dʒerəld] *s*. 杰罗尔德[Gerald 的异体]

Jerry ['dʒeri] *f*. 杰丽[Geraldine 的昵称]

Jervis ['dʒɑ:vis, 'dʒɜ:vis] *s*. 杰维斯

Jesse ['dʒesi] *m*. 杰西

Jessica ['dʒesikə] *f*. 杰西卡

Jessie ['dʒesi] *f*. 杰西

Jevons ['dʒevənz] *s*. 杰文斯

Jewel(l) ['dʒu:əl] *f*. 朱尔尔

Jewett ['dʒu:t] *s*. 朱厄特

Jim [dʒim] *m*. 吉姆[James 的昵称]

Jimmy (或 **Jimmie**) ['dʒimi] *m*. 吉米 [James 的昵称]

Joan(n) [dʒəun] *f*. 琼

Joanna [dʒəu'ænə] *f*. 乔安娜[Joan(n) 的异体]

Job [dʒəub] *m*. 乔布(约伯)

Joe [dʒəu] *m*. 乔[Joseph 的昵称]

Joel ['dʒəuel, 'dʒəuəl] *m*. 乔尔

Johannes [jəu'hænis] *m*. 约翰尼斯

John [dʒɔn] *m*. 约翰

Johnny ['dʒɔni] *m*. 约翰尼[John 的昵称]

Johns [dʒɔnz] *s*. 约翰斯

Johnson ['dʒɔnsn] *s*. 约翰逊(约翰生)

Johnston ['dʒɔnstən, 'dʒɔnsn] *s*. 约翰斯顿

Jon [dʒɔn] *m*. 乔恩[John 的异体]

Jonah ['dʒəunə] *m*. 乔纳(约拿)

Jonathan ['dʒɔnəθən] *m*. 乔纳森

Jones [dʒəunz] *s*. 琼斯

Jonson ['dʒɔnsn] *s*. 琼森(琼生)

Jordan ['dʒɔ:dn] *s*. 乔丹(朱尔典)

Joseph (或 **Josef**) ['dʒəuzif] *m*. 约瑟夫 (约瑟)

Josephine ['dʒəuzifi:n] *f*. 约瑟芬

Josh [dʒɔʃ] *m*. 乔希[Joshua 的昵称]

Joshua ['dʒɔʃwə] *m*. 乔舒亚

Joule [dʒu:l, dʒaul] *s*. 朱尔(焦耳)

Jowett ['dʒauit, dʒauit] *s*. 乔伊特

Joy [dʒɔi] *f*. 乔伊

Joyce [dʒɔis] *s*. & *f*. 乔伊斯(乔埃斯)

Judd [dʒʌd] s. 贾德

Jude [dʒuːd] m. 裘德

Judith ['dʒuːdiθ] f. 朱迪思

Judson ['dʒʌdsn] s. & m. 贾德森

Jules [dʒuːlz] m. 朱尔斯[Julius 的异体]

Julia ['dʒuːljə] f. 朱莉娅

Julian ['dʒuːljən] m. 朱利安

Juliana [ˌdʒuːliˈɑːnə] f. 朱莉安娜

Julien ['dʒuːljən] m. 朱利恩

Juliet ['dʒuːljət] f. 朱丽叶

Julius ['dʒuːljəs] m. 朱利叶斯

June [dʒuːn] f. 琼

Justin ['dʒʌstin] m. 贾斯廷

Justus ['dʒʌstəs] s. 贾斯特斯

Juta ['dʒuːtə] s. 朱塔

K

Kane [kein] s. 凯恩

Karl [kɑːl] m. 卡尔[Charles 的异体]

Kate [keit] f. 凯特[Catherine 的昵称]

Katharine(或 Katherine)['kæθərin] f. 凯瑟琳[Catherine 的异体]

Kathleen ['kæθliːn] f. 凯思琳[Catherine 的异体]

Kathryn ['kæθrin] f. 凯思琳[Catherine 的异体]

Kathy ['kæθi] f. 凯茜(卡西)[Catherine 的昵称]

Kaufman(n) ['kɔːfmən] s. 考夫曼

Kay(e) [kei] f. 凯[Catherine 的昵称]

Kean(e) [kiːn] s. 基恩

Kearny ['kɑːni, 'kɔːni] s. 克尼(卡尼)

Keats [kiːts] s. 基茨(济慈)

Keble ['kiːbl] s. 基布尔

Keith [kiːθ] s. & m. 基思

Kelland ['keland] s. 凯兰

Keller ['kelə] s. 凯勒

Kell(e)y ['keli] s. & m. 凯利

Kellogg ['keləg] s. 凯洛格

Kelvin ['kelvin] s. 凯尔文(开甫芬)

Kemble ['kembl] s. & m. 肯布尔

Ken [ken] m. 肯[Kenneth 的昵称]

Kendall ['kendl] s. & m. 肯德尔

Kennan ['kenən] s. 凯南

Kennedy ['kenidi] s. 肯尼迪

Kennelly ['kenəli] s. 肯内利

Kenneth ['keniθ] m. 肯尼思

Kenny ['keni] s. 肯尼

Kent [kent] s. & m. 肯特

Kenyon ['kenjən] s. 凯尼恩

Keppel ['kepəl] s. 凯佩尔

Ker [kɑː, keə, kɑː] s. 克尔

Kermit ['kəːmit] s. & m. 克米特

Kern [kəːn] s. 克恩

Kerr [kɑː, kəː] s. 克尔

Kerry ['keri] m. 克里

Kettering ['ketəriŋ] s. 凯特林

Keyes [kiːz, kaiz] s. 凯斯

Keynes [keinz] s. 凯恩斯(凯因斯)

Kidd [kid] s. 基德

Kilmer ['kilmə] s. 基尔默

Kilpatrick [kil'pætrik] s. 基尔帕特里克

King [kiŋ] s. 金

Kinglake ['kiŋleik] s. 金莱克

Kingsley ['kiŋzli] s. 金斯利(金斯莱)

Kinkaid ['kin'keid] s. 金凯德

Kinsey ['kinzi] s. 金西
Kipling ['kipliŋ] s. 基普林(吉卜林)
Kirby ['kəːbi] s. & m. 柯尔比
Kirk [kəːk] s. & m. 柯克
Kissinger ['kisəndʒə] s. 基辛格
Kittredge ['kitridʒ] s. 基特里奇
Kitty ['kiti] f. 基蒂[Catherine 的昵称]
Klaus [klaus] m. 克劳斯
Knox [nɔks] s. 诺克斯
Koestler ['kestlə] s. 凯斯特勒

Kornberg ['kɔːnbəg] s. 科恩伯格
Krebs [krebz] s. 克雷布斯
Kreisler ['kraislə] s. 克赖斯勒
Kroll [krəul] s. 克罗尔
Krutch [krʌtʃ] s. 克鲁奇
Kurt [kəːt, kuət] m. 库尔特[Conrad 的昵称]
Kusch [kuʃ] s. 库什
Kyd [kid] s. 基德

L

Ladefoged ['lædifəugid] s. 拉迪福吉德
Laird [lεəd] s. 莱尔德
Lake [leik] s. 莱克
Lamar [lə'maː] s. & m. 拉马尔
Lamb [læm] s. 兰姆(拉姆)
Lambert ['læmbət] s. 兰伯特
Lampson ['læmpsn] s. 兰普森
Lance [lɑːns] m. 兰斯[Lancelot 的昵称]
Lancelot ['lɑːnslət] m. 兰斯洛特
Landon ['lændən] s. 兰登
Landor ['lændɔː] s. 兰道
Landseer ['lænsiə] s. 兰西尔
Lane [lein] s. & m. 莱恩
Lange ['læŋə] s. 兰格
Langland ['læŋlənd] s. 兰格兰
Langley ['læŋli] s. 兰利
Langmuir ['læŋmjuə] s. 兰米尔
Langton ['læŋtən] s. 兰顿
Lanier [lə'niə] s. 拉尼尔
Lankester ['læŋkistə] s. 兰克斯特
Lanny ['læni] m. 兰尼[Lawrence 的昵称]
Lansing ['lænsiŋ] s. 兰辛

Lardner ['lɑːdnə] s. 拉德纳
Larkin ['lɑːkin] m. 拉金
Larry ['læri] s. 拉里[Lawrence 的昵称]
Laski ['læski] s. 拉斯基
Lattimore ['lætimɔː] s. 拉铁摩尔
Laughton ['lɔːtn] s. 劳顿
Laura ['lɔːrə] f. 劳拉
Laurel ['lɔrəl] s. 劳雷尔
Laurence ['lɔrəns] s. & m. 劳伦斯
Laurie ['lɔri] f. 劳丽[Laura 的昵称]
Law [lɔː] s. 劳
Lawes [lɔːz] s. 劳斯
Lawrence ['lɔrəns] s. & m. 劳伦斯
Lawson ['lɔːsn] s. 劳森
Layard [lεəd] s. 莱亚德
Leacock ['liːkɔk] s. 利科克(李科克)
Leakey ['liːki] s. 利基
Lear [liə] s. 利尔(李尔)
Lee [liː] s., m. & f. 李
Lehmann ['leiman] s. 莱曼
Leigh [liː] s. & m. 利
Leighton ['leitn] s. & m. 莱顿

Le(i)la ['leilə] *f.* 莉拉

Leith [li:θ] *s.* 利思

Leland ['li:lənd] *s.* & *m.* 利兰

Leman ['lemən] *s.* 莱曼

Lena ['li:nə] *f.* 莉娜 [Helena 的昵称]

Leo ['li:əu] *m.* 利奥

Leon ['li:ən] *m.* 利昂 [Leo 的异体]

Léon ['leiən] *s.* 莱昂

Leona [li:'əunə] *f.* 莉昂娜

Leonard ['lenəd] *s.* & *m.* 伦纳德

Leonora [,li:ə'nɔ:rə] *f.* 利奥诺拉 [Eleanor 的异体]

Lesley(或 **Leslie**) ['lezli, 'lesli] *f.* 莱斯莉

Leslie ['lezli, 'lesliz] *s.* & *m.* 莱斯利

Lester ['lestə] *s.* & *m.* 莱斯特

Leta ['li:tə] *f.* 莉塔

Letitia [li'tifiə] *f.* 利蒂希娅

Lever ['li:və] *s.* 利弗

Levy ['li:vi, 'levi] *s.* 利维(莱维)

Lewes ['lju:is] *s.* 刘易斯

Lewis ['lju:is] *s.* & *m.* 刘易斯 [Louis 的异体]

Libby ['libi] *s.* 利比

Libby ['libi] *f.* 莉比 [Elizabeth 的昵称]

Liddel(l) ['lidl, li'del] *s.* 利德尔

Lilienthal ['lilənθɔ:l] *s.* 利连撒尔

Lil(l)ian ['liliən] *f.* 莉莲 [Elizabeth 的昵称]

Lily ['lili] *f.* 莉莉

Lincoln ['liŋkən] *s.* & *m.* 林肯

Linda(或 **Lynda**) ['lində] *f.* 琳达

Lindbergh ['lindbə:g] *s.* 林德伯格 (林白)

Lindsay ['lindzi] *s.* 林赛

Linklater ['liŋk,leitə] *s.* 林克莱特

Lionel ['laiənl] *m.* 莱昂内尔

Lip(p)man(n) ['lipmən] *s.* 李普曼

Lipton ['liptən] *s.* 利普顿

Lisa ['li:zə, 'laizə] *f.* 莉萨 [Elizabeth 的昵称]

Little ['litl] *s.* 利特尔

Littleton ['litltən] *s.* 利特尔顿

Livingston ['liviŋstən] *s.* 利文斯顿

Livingstone ['liviŋstən] *s.* 利文斯通

Lizzie ['lizi] *f.* 莉齐 [Elizabeth 的昵称]

Llewellyn [lu:'elin] *m.* 卢埃林

L(l)oyd [bid] *m.* 劳埃德

Lock(e) [lɔk] *s.* 洛克

Locker ['lɔkə] *s.* 洛克

Lockhart ['lɔkət, 'lɔkhɔ:t] *s.* 洛克哈特

Lodge [lɔdʒ] *s.* 洛奇

Loewe ['ləui] *s.* 洛伊

Logan ['ləugən] *s.* & *m.* 洛根

Lois ['ləuis] *f.* 洛伊丝

London ['lʌndən] *s.* 伦敦

Long [lɔŋ] *s.* 朗

Longfellow ['lɔŋ,feləu] *s.* 朗费罗

Longman ['lɔŋmən] *s.* 朗曼

Longstreet ['lɔŋstri:t] *s.* 朗斯特里特

Lonsdale ['lɔnzdeil] *s.* 朗斯代尔

Lora ['lɔ:rə] *f.* 洛拉 [Laura 的异体]

Lorenzo [lə'renzəu] *m.* 洛伦佐

Loretta [lə'retə] *f.* 洛雷塔

Lorna ['lɔ:nə] *f.* 洛娜

Lough [lʌf] *s.* 洛夫 (洛)

Louie ['lu:i] *m.* 路易 [Louis 的异体]

Louis ['lu:i, 'lu:is] *m.* 路易斯 (路易)

Louisa [lu:'i:zə] *f.* 路易莎

Louise [lu:'i:z] *f.* 路易丝

Lovell ['lʌvl] *s.* 洛弗尔

Lover ['lʌvə] *s.* 洛弗

Lowell ['ləul] *s.* & *m.* 洛厄尔

Lowes [ləuz] *s.* 洛斯

Lowndes [ˈlaundz] s. 朗兹
Lucas [ˈluːkəs] s. 卢卡斯
Luce [ljuːs] s. 卢斯
Lucia [ˈluːsjə] f. 露西娅
Lucian [ˈluːsjən] m. 卢西恩
Lucretia [luːˈkriːʃjə] f. 卢克丽霞
Lucy [ˈluːsi] s. & f. 露西
Ludwig [ˈlʌdwig] m. 路德维格（路德维希）[Louis 的异体]
Luke [luːk] m. 卢克（路加）
Luther [ˈluːθə] s. & m. 卢瑟（路德）
Lydgate [ˈlidgeit] s. 利德盖特

Lydia [ˈlidiə] f. 莉迪亚
Lyell [ˈlaiəl] s. 莱尔
Lyle [lail] s. & m. 莱尔
Lyly [ˈlili] s. 利利（李利）
Lyman [ˈlaimən] s. 莱曼
Lympany [ˈlimpəni] s. 林帕尼
Lynch [lintʃ] s. 林奇
Iynd [lind] s. 林德
Lynn [lin] s. , m. & f. 林恩
Lyon(s) [ˈlaiən(z)] s. 莱昂（斯）
Lytton [ˈlitn] s. 利顿（李顿）

M

Maas [mɑːz] s. 马斯
Mabel [ˈmeibəl] f. 梅布尔
MacAdam [məˈkædəm, məkˈædəm] s. 麦克亚当
MacArthur [məˈkɑːθə, məkˈɑːθə] s. 麦克阿瑟
Macaulay [məˈkɔːli] s. 麦考利（麦考莱）
MacCraken [məˈkrækən] s. 麦克拉肯
MacDonald [məkˈdɔnld] s. 麦克唐纳
MacDonnell [ˌmækdəˈnel] s. 麦克唐奈
MacDowell [məkˈdauəl] s. 麦克道尔（麦克道威尔）
Mac(k) [mæk] m. 麦克
Mackay(e) [məˈkai] s. 麦凯
Mackintosh [ˈmækintɔʃ] s. 麦金托什
Maclaren [məˈklærən] s. 麦克拉伦
Maclean(e) [məˈklein] s. 麦克莱恩
MacLeish [məkˈliːʃ] s. 麦克利什
MacLeod [məˈklaud] s. 麦克劳德
MacMillan（或 Macmillan）[məkˈmilən] s. 麦克米伦

MacPherson [məkˈfəsn] s. 麦克弗森
Macready [məˈkriːdi] s. 麦克里迪
Madeleine [ˈmædəlin, ˈmædəlein] s. 马德琳
Madeline [ˈmædəlin, ˈmædəlein] f. 马德琳
Madge [mædʒ] f. 玛奇 [Margaret 的昵称]
Maggie [ˈmægi] f. 玛吉
Mailer [ˈmeilə] s. 梅勒
Maillard [ˈmeiləd] s. 梅拉德
Main(e) [mein] s. 梅恩（梅因）
Maitland [ˈmeitlənd] s. 梅特兰
Malan [ˈmælən] s. 马伦
Malcolm [ˈmælkəm] s. & m. 马尔科姆
Malone [məˈləun] s. 马隆
Malory [ˈmæləri] s. 马罗礼
Malthus [ˈmælθəs] s. 马尔萨斯
Maltz [mɑːts] s. 莫尔茨（马尔茨；马尔兹）
Mamie [ˈmeimi] f. 梅米（玛米）[Margaret 的昵称]
Mander [ˈmɑːndə] s. 曼德
Manfred [ˈmænfred] m. 曼弗雷德

Mann [mæn] *s.* 曼

Manning ['mæniŋ] *s.* 曼宁

Mansfield ['mænsfiːld] *s.* 曼斯菲尔德

Manson ['mænsn] *s.* 曼森

Manuel ['mænjuel] *m.* 曼纽尔 [Em-(m)anuel 的异体]

Mara ['mɑːrə] *s.* 玛拉 [Mary 的异体]

March [mɑːtʃ] *s.* 马奇

Marcia ['mɑːʃə] *f.* 马西娅

Marcus ['mɑːkəs] *f.* 马库斯

Margaret ['mɑːgərit] *f.* 马格丽特

Margery ['mɑːdʒəri] *f.* 玛杰里 [Margaret 的异体]

Margie ['mɑːdʒi] *f.* 玛吉 [Margaret 的昵称]

Margot ['mɑːgəu] *f.* 玛戈 [Margaret 的昵称]

Marguerite [ˌmɑːgəˈriːt] *f.* 玛格丽特 [Margaret 的异体]

Maria [məˈraiə, məˈriə] *f.* 玛丽亚 [Mary 的异体]

Marian ['mɛəriən, 'mæriən] *f.* 玛丽亚 [Mariana 的异体]

Mariana [ˌmɛəriˈænə] *f.* 玛丽安娜 [Mary 的昵称]

Marie ['mɑːriː, məˈriː] *f.* 玛丽 [Mary 的异体]

Marina [məˈriːnə] *f.* 玛丽娜

Marion ['mɛəriən, 'mæriən] *s. & m.* 马里恩

Marion ['mɛəriən, 'mæriən] *s. & m.* 玛丽恩 [Mary 的昵称]

Marjorie(或 **Marjory**) ['mɑːdʒəri] *f.* 玛乔里 [Margery 的异体]

Mark(或 **Marc**) [mɑːk] *m.* 马克 [Marcus 的异体]

Markham ['mɑːkəm] *s.* 马卡姆

Marlborough ['mɔːlbərə] *s.* 莫尔巴勒(马尔巴勒)

Marlene [mɑːˈliːn, mɑːˈliːn] *s.* 马琳

Marlin ['mɑːlin] *m.* 马林

Marlow(e) ['mɑːləu] *s.* 马洛

Marquis [mɑːˈkwiːs] *s.* 马奎斯

Marquis [mɑːˈkwis] *s.* 马奎斯

Marshal(l) ['mɑːʃəl] *s. & m.* 马歇尔

Marston ['mɑːstən] *s.* 马斯顿

Martha ['mɑːθə] *f.* 玛莎(马撒)

Martin ['mɑːtin] *s. & m.* 马丁

Martineau ['mɑːtinəu] *s.* 马蒂诺

Marva ['mɑːvə] *f.* 玛瓦

Marvell ['mɑːvəl] *s.* 马维尔

Marvin ['mɑːvin] *s. & m.* 马文

Mary ['mɛəri] *f.* 玛丽

Maryann [ˌmɛəriˈæn] *s.* 玛丽安

Masefield ['meisfiːld] *s.* 梅斯菲尔德

Mason ['meisn] *s. & m.* 梅森

Massine [mæˈsiːn] *s.* 马辛

Masson ['mæsn] *s.* 马森

Mather ['meiðə, 'mæðə] *s.* 马瑟

Matthew ['mæθjuː] *m.* 马修(马太)

Matthews ['mæθjuːz] *s.* 马修斯

Maturin ['mætjurin] *s.* 马图林

Maud(e) [mɔːd] *s.* 莫德

Maugham [mɔːm] *s.* 莫姆(毛姆)

Maurice ['mɔris] *s. & m.* 莫里斯

Mawson ['mɔːsn] *s.* 莫森

Max [mæks] *m.* 马克斯

Maxwell ['mækswəl] *s. & m.* 马克斯韦尔

May [mei] *s. & f.* 梅 [Mary 的昵称]

Mayer(s) ['meiə(z), meə(z)] *s.* 梅耶(斯)(迈耶(斯))

Maynard ['meinəd] *m.* 梅纳德

McCarthy [məˈkɑːθi] *s.* 麦卡锡

McClellan [məˈklelən] *s.* 麦克莱伦

McClure [məˈkluə] s. 克卢尔

McCormack [məˈkɔːmək] s. 麦考马克(麦科马克)

McCormick [ˌməˈkɔːmik] s. 麦考密克

McDonald [məkˈdɔnəld] s. 麦克唐纳尔

McDowell [mək'dauəl] s. 麦克道尔

McFee [məkˈfiː] s. 麦克菲

McIntosh [ˈmækintɔʃ] s. 麦金托什

McIntyre [ˈmækintaiə] s. 麦金太尔

McKenna [məˈkenə] s. 麦肯纳(麦克纳)

McKinley [məˈkinli] s. 麦金利

McMillan [məkˈmilən] s. 麦克米伦

McNamara [ˌmæknəˈmɔːrə] s. 麦克纳马拉

Mead(e) [miːd] s. 米德

Melba [ˈmelbə] f. 梅尔巴

Melchers [ˈmeltʃəz] s. 梅尔彻斯

Melchior [ˈmelkiɔː] s. 梅尔基奥尔

Mellon [ˈmelən] s. 梅隆

Melva [ˈmelvə] f. 梅尔瓦

Melville [ˈmelvil] s. & m. 梅尔维尔(麦尔维尔)

Melvin(或 Melvyn) [ˈmelvin] s. & m. 梅尔文

Mencken [ˈmeŋkin, ˈmeŋkən] s. 门肯

Mendelssohn [ˈmendlsn] s. 门德尔森(门德尔松)

Menuhin [ˈmenjuin, ˈmenuhin] s. 梅纽因

Mercedes [məˈsiːdiːz] f. 默西迪斯

Merédith [ˈmerədiθ] s., m. & f. 梅雷迪思(梅瑞狄斯)

Merlin(或 Merlyn) [ˈmədin] m. 默林

Merritt [ˈmerit] s. & m. 梅里特

Merry [ˈmeri] f. 梅丽

Merton [ˈmətn] s. 默顿

Mervin [ˈməːvin] m. 默文 [Marvin 的异体]

Metcalfe [ˈmetkɑːf] s. 梅特卡夫

Meyer [maiə] s. 迈耶(迈尔)

Michael [ˈmaikl] m. 迈克尔

Michel(le) [miːˈʃel] f. 米歇尔

Michelson [ˈmitʃəlsn, ˈmikəlsn] s. 米切尔森

Michener [ˈmitʃinə] s. 米切纳

Mickey [ˈmiki] m. 米基 [Michael 的昵称]

Middleton [ˈmidltən] s. 米德尔顿

Mike [maik] m. 迈克 [Michael 的昵称]

Mildred [ˈmildrid] f. 米尔德丽德

Miles(或 Myles) [mailz] m. 迈尔斯

Milford [ˈmilfəd] s. & m. 米尔福德

Mill [mil] s. 米尔(穆勒)

Millais [ˈmilei] s. 米莱

Millard [ˈmiləd, ˈmilɑːd] s. & m. 米勒德

Millay [ˈmilei] s. 米莱

Miller [ˈmilə] s. 米勒

Millicent [ˈmilisnt] f. 米莉森特

Millie [ˈmili] f. 米莉 [Mildred 的昵称]

Millikan [ˈmilikən] s. 米利肯

Milne [mil, miln] s. 米尔恩

Milner [ˈmilnə] s. 米尔纳

Milo [ˈmailəu] s. 迈洛(米洛)

Milton [ˈmiltən] s. 米尔顿(弥尔顿)

Minnie [ˈmini] f. 明妮 [Mary 的昵称]

Minot [ˈmainət] s. 迈诺特

Mirabel [ˈmirəbel] f. 米拉贝尔

Miranda [miˈrændə] f. 米兰达

Miriam [ˈmiriəm] f. 米丽亚姆 [Mary 的异体]

Mitchell [ˈmitʃəl] s. & m. 米切尔

Mitford [ˈmitfəd] s. 米特福德

Molly(或 Mollie) [ˈmɔli] f. 莫莉 [Mary 的昵称]

Mona [ˈməunə] f. 莫娜

Mond [mɔnd] *m*.蒙德

Monica ['mɔnikə] *f*.蒙妮卡

Monro(e) [mən'rəu, 'mʌnrəu] *s*. & *m*.门罗

Monsarrat [ˌmɔnsə'ræt] *s*.蒙萨拉特

Montagu(e) ['mɔntəgju:, 'mʌntəgju:] *s*. & *m*.蒙塔古

Monte(或 **Monty**) ['mɔnti] *m*.蒙蒂 [Montague 的昵称]

Montfort ['mɔntfət] *s*.蒙特福特

Montgomery [mənt'gʌməri] *s*.蒙哥马利

Moody ['mu:di] *s*.穆迪

Mooney ['mu:ni] *s*.穆尼

Moore [muə] *s*.穆尔(摩尔)

More [mɔ:] *s*.莫尔

Morgan ['mɔ:gən] *s*. & *m*.摩根(摩尔根)

Morgenthau ['mɔ:gənθɔ:] *s*.摩根索

Morison ['mɔrisn] *s*.莫里森

Morley ['mɔ:li] *s*.莫利

Morris ['mɔris] *s*. & *m*.莫里斯 [Maurice 的异体]

Morrison ['mɔrisn] *s*.莫里森(马礼逊)

Morse [mɔ:s] *s*.莫尔斯

Morton ['mɔ:tn] *s*. & *m*.莫顿

Mosby ['mɔzbi] *s*.莫斯比

Moses ['məuziz] *s*. & *m*.摩西

Mosley ['mɔzli, 'məuzli] *s*.莫斯利

Motley ['mɔtli] *s*.莫特利

Mott [mɔt] *s*.莫特

Moulton ['məultən] *s*.莫尔顿

Mountbatten [maunt'bætn] *s*.蒙巴顿

Muir [mjuə] *s*.缪尔(米尔)

Muller ['mʌlə] *s*.马勒(米勒)

Mumford ['mʌmfəd] *s*.芒福德

Muriel ['mjuəriəl] *f*.穆丽尔

Murphy ['mə:fi] *s*.墨菲

Murray ['mʌri] *s*. & *m*.默里

Myra ['maiərə] *f*.迈拉

Myron ['maiərən] *m*.迈伦

Myrtle ['mə:tl] *f*.默特尔

N

Nabarro [nə'bɑ:rəu] *s*.纳巴罗

Nahum ['neiəm] *s*.内厄姆

Nancy ['nænsi] *f*.南希 [Ann 的昵称]

Naomi ['neiəmi] *f*.内奥米

Nash [næʃ] *s*.纳什

Nasmyth ['neizmiθ] *s*.内史密斯

Natalie ['nætəli] *f*.纳塔莉

Nathan ['neiθən] *s*. & *m*.内森

Nathaniel [nə'θænjəl] *m*.纳撒尼尔

Ned [ned] *m*.内德

Nedra ['nedrə] *f*.内德拉

Needham ['ni:dəm] *s*.尼达姆

Neil(或 **Neal**) [ni:l] *m*.尼尔

Nelda ['neldə] *f*.内尔达

Nell [nel] *f*.内尔

Nellie ['neli] *f*.内莉

Nelson ['nelsn] *s*. & *m*.纳尔逊

Nettie ['neti] *f*.内蒂 [Janet 的昵称]

Neva ['neivə] *f*.内瓦

Nevill(e) ['nevil] *s*. & *m*.内维尔

Nevin ['nevin] *s*. & *m*.内文

Nevins ['nevinz] *s*.内文斯

Newbolt ['nju:bəult] *s*.纽博尔特

Newell ['nju:əl] *s*.纽厄尔

Newman(n) ['nju:mən] *s*.纽曼

Newton ['nju:tn] *s*. & *m*.牛顿

Nicholas ['nikələs] s. 尼古拉斯

Nichol(s) ['nikəl(z)] s. 尼科尔(斯)

Nicholson ['nikəlsn] s. 尼科尔森

Nick [nik] m. 尼克 [Nicholas 的昵称]

Nicol(l) ['nikəl] s. 尼科尔

Nicolson ['nikəlsn] s. 尼科尔森

Nigel ['naidʒəl] m. 奈杰尔

Nightingale ['naitiŋgeil] s. 奈廷格尔(南丁格尔)

Niles [nailz] s. & m. 奈尔斯

Nimitz ['nimits] s. 尼米兹

Nina ['ni:nə] f. 尼娜

Nixon ['niksn] s. 尼克松

Noah ['nəuə] m. 诺亚

Noble ['nəubl] s. 诺布尔

Noel [nəuəl] s.、m. & f. 诺埃尔

Nola ['nəulə] f. 诺拉

Nolan ['nəulən] m. 诺兰

Nona ['nəunə] f. 诺娜

Nora(h) ['nɔ:rə] f. 诺拉(娜拉)

Norbert ['nɔ:bət] m. 诺伯特

Norma ['nɔ:mə] f. 诺玛

Norman ['nɔ:mən] m. 诺曼

Norris ['nɔris] s. & m. 诺里斯

North [nɔ:θ] s. 诺思

Northcliffe ['nɔ:θklif] s. 诺思克利夫

Norton ['nɔ:tn] s. & m. 诺顿

Noyes [nɔiz] s. 诺伊斯

Nye [nai] s. 奈

O

Oates [əuts] s. 奥茨

Obadiah [,əubə'daiə] m. 奥巴代亚

O'Brien [əu'braiən] s. 奥布赖恩

O'Casey [əu'keisi] s. 奥凯西(奥卡西)

Occam ['ɔkəm] s. 奥克姆

O'Connell [əu'kɔnl] s. 奥康内尔

O'Connor [əu'kɔnə] s. 奥康纳(奥康诺)

Odets [əu'dets] s. 奥德茨

O'Flaherty [əu'fleəti] s. 奥弗莱厄蒂

Ogden ['ɔgdən] s. 奥格登

Oglethorpe ['əuglθɔ:p] s. 奥格尔索普

O'Hare [əu'hɛə] s. 奥黑尔

O'keef(f)e [əu'ki:f] s. 奥基夫

O'Kelly [əu'keli] s. 奥凯利

Oldcastle ['əuld,ka:sl] s. 奥尔德卡斯尔

Olga ['ɔlgə] f. 奥尔加

Olive ['ɔliv] f. 奥莉夫

Oliver ['ɔlivə] s. & m. 奥利弗

Olivia [ɔ'liviə] f. 奥莉维亚

Ollie ['ɔli] m. 奥利 [Oliver 的昵称]

O'Neil(l) ['əu'ni:l] s. 奥尼尔

Onions ['ʌnjən] s. 奥尼恩斯

Opal ['əupəl] f. 奥普尔

Oppenheim ['ɔpənhaim] s. 奥本海姆

Oppenheimer ['ɔpənhaimə] s. 奥本海默

Ora ['ɔ:rə] f. 奥拉

Orlando [ɔ:'lændəu] m. 奥兰多 [Rol(l)and 的异体]

Ormsby ['ɔ:mzbi] s. 奥姆斯比

Or(r)in ['ɔrin] s. & m. 奥林

Orville ['ɔ:vil] s. 奥维尔

Osbert ['ɔzbət] m. 奥斯伯特

Osborn(e) ['ɔzbən] s. 奥斯本

Oscar ['ɔskə] m. 奥斯卡

Oswald ['ɔzwəld] m. 奥斯瓦德

Otis ['əutis] s. & m. 奥蒂斯

Otto ['ɔtəu] *m*. 奥托(鄂图)
Otway ['ɔtwei] *s*. 奥特韦

Ovid ['ɔvid] *s*. 奥维德
Owen ['əuin] *s*. & *m*. 欧文

P

Page [peidʒ] *s*. 佩奇
Pain(e) [pein] *s*. 佩因(潘恩)
Paley ['peili] *s*. 佩利
Palgrave ['pɔlgreiv, 'pælgreiv] *s*. 帕尔格雷夫
Palmer ['pɑːmə] *s*. & *m*. 帕尔默
Palmerston ['pɑːməstən] *s*. 帕默斯顿
Pamela ['pæmilə] *f*. 帕梅拉
Pankhurst ['pæŋkhəst] *s*. 潘克赫斯特
Pare(s) [peə(z)] *s*. 佩尔(斯)
Paris ['pæris] *s*. 帕里斯
Park [pɑːk] *s*. 帕克(派克)
Parker ['pɑːkə] *s*. & *m*. 帕克(派克)
Parkman ['pɑːkmən] *s*. 帕克曼
Parley ['pɑːli] *s*. 帕利
Parnell [pɑː'nel] *s*. 帕内尔
Parr [pɑː] *s*. 帕尔
Parrish ['pæriʃ] *s*. 帕里什
Parry ['pæri] *s*. 帕里
Parson ['pɑːsn] *s*. 帕森
Partridge ['pɑːtridʒ] *s*. 帕特里奇
Passe [pæs] *s*. 帕斯
Pat [pæt] *m*. 帕特[Patrick 的昵称]
Pater ['peitə] *s*. 佩特
Patience ['peiʃəns] *f*. 佩兴斯
Patricia [pə'triʃə] *f*. 帕特丽夏
Patrick ['pætrik] *m*. 帕特里克
Pattison ['pætisn] *s*. 帕蒂森
Patty(或 Patti, Pattie) ['pæti] *f*. 帕蒂 [Particia 的昵称]
Paul [pɔl] *s*. & *m*. 保罗

Paula ['pɔlə] *f*. 波拉
Pauline [pɔːˈliːn] *f*. 波琳
Pauling ['pɔːliŋ] *s*. 波林
Payne [pein] *s*. 佩恩
Peabody ['piːˌbɔdi] *s*. 皮博迪
Peacock ['piːkɔk] *s*. 皮科克
Peal [piːl] *s*. 皮尔
Pearl [pəːl] *f*. 珀尔
Pearson ['piəsn] *s*. 皮尔逊
Peel(e) [piːl] *s*. 皮尔
Peg [peg] *f*. 佩格
Peggy ['pegi] *f*. 佩吉[Margaret 的昵称]
Pegram ['piːgrəm] *s*. 皮格勒姆(佩格勒姆)
Penelope [pi'neləpi, pə'neləpi] *f*. 佩内洛普
Penn [pen] *s*. 佩恩
Pennell ['penl] *s*. 彭内尔
Penny ['peni] *f*. 彭妮[Penelope 的昵称]
Penrose ['penrəuz] *s*. 彭罗斯
Pepys ['pepis] *s*. 佩皮斯
Percy ['pəːsi] *s*. & *m*. 珀西
Perkin(s) ['pəːkin(z)] *s*. 珀金(斯)
Perry ['peri] *s*. & *m*. 佩里
Pershing ['pəːʃiŋ] *s*. 珀欣
Pete [piːt] *m*. 皮特[Peter 的昵称]
Peter(s) ['piːtə(z)] *s*. & *m*. 彼得(斯)
Petrie ['piːtri] *s*. 皮特里
Petty ['peti] *s*. 佩蒂
Phil [fil] *m*. 菲尔[Philip 的昵称]
Phil(l)ip ['filip] *m*. 菲利普(菲力普)
Phil(l)ips ['filips] *s*. 菲利普斯(菲力普斯)

斯)

Phillpotts ['filpəts] *s*. 菲尔波茨

Phoebe ['fi:bi] *f*. 菲比

Phyllis [filis] *f*. 菲莉斯

Pickering ['pikəriŋ] *s*. 皮克林

Picket(t) ['pikit] *s*. 皮克特

Pierce [piəs] *s*. 皮尔斯

Pierre [pi:'eə, piə] *m*. 皮埃尔 [Peter 的异体]

Pigou ['pigu:] *s*. 皮古

Pike [paik] *s*. 派克

Pinckney ['piŋkni] *s*. 平克尼

Pinero [pi'niərəu] *s*. 皮尼罗(平内罗)

Pinkerton ['piŋkətən] *s*. 平克顿

Pitman ['pitmən] *s*. 皮特曼

Pitt [pit] *s*. 皮特(庇特)

Plimsoll ['plimsɔl] *s*. 普利姆索尔

Poe [pəu] *s*. 波（坡）

Polk [pəuk] *s*. 波尔克

Pol(l)itt ['pɔlit] *s*. 波利特(波立特)

Pollock ['pɔlək] *s*. 波洛克

Polly ['pɔli] *f*. 波莉[Mary 的昵称]

Pons [pɔnz] *s*. 庞斯

Pope [pəup] *s*. 波普(蒲柏)

Portal ['pɔːtl] *s*. 波塔尔

Porter ['pɔːtə] *s*. & *m*. 波特

Portia ['pɔːʃjə] *f*. 波西娅

Portland ['pɔːtlənd] *s*. 波特兰

Post [pəust] *s*. 波斯特

Pound [paund] *s*. 庞德

Poupart ['pəupaːt] *s*. 波帕特

Powel(l) ['pəuəl] *s*. 鲍威尔

Pownall ['paunl] *s*. 波纳尔

Powys ['pəuis] *s*. 波伊斯

Pratt [præt] *s*. 普拉特

Prescott ['preskət] *s*. 普雷斯科特

Prestige ['prestidʒ] *s*. 普雷斯蒂奇

Preston ['prestən] *m*. 普雷斯顿

Prevost ['prevəu, 'prevəust] *s*. 普雷沃斯特

Price [prais] *s*. 普赖斯

Pride [praid] *s*. 普赖德

Priestley ['pri:stli] *s*. 普里斯特利(普利斯特莱)

Prior ['praiə] *s*. 普赖尔

Priscilla [pri'silə] *f*. 普丽西拉

Pritt [prit] *s*. 普里特

Proust [pruːst] *s*. 普鲁斯特

Prudence ['pruːdəns] *f*. 普鲁登斯

Prynne [prin] *s*. 普林

Pulitzer ['pulitsə] *s*. 普利策(帕利策)

Pullman ['pulmən] *s*. 普尔曼

Purcell ['pəːsl] *s*. 珀塞尔

Purchas ['pəːtʃəs] *s*. 珀切斯

Pusey ['pjuːzi] *s*. 普西

Pye [pai] *s*. 派伊

Pyle [pail] *s*. 派尔

Pym [pim] *s*. 皮姆

Q

Quain [kwein] *s*. 奎因

Quarles [kwɔːz] *s*. 夸尔斯

Quay [kwei] *s*. 奎伊

Queen [kwiːn] *s*. 奎因

Queensberry ['kwiːnzbəri] *s*. 昆斯伯里

Quentin ['kwentin] *m*. 昆廷

Quick ['kwik] *s*. 奎克

Quiller ['kwilə] *s*. 奎勒

Quiller-Couch ['kwilə'kuːtʃ] *s*. 奎勒-库奇

Quilter ['kwiltə] *s*. 奎尔特

Quinault ['kwinəlt] *s*. 昆纳尔特

Quinc(e)y ['kwinsi] *s*. 昆西

Quin(n) [kwin] *s*. 奎因

Quintard ['kwintɔːd] *s*. 昆塔特

Quirey ['kwaiəri, kwiəri] *s*. 奎厄里

Quitman ['kwitmən] *s*. 奎特曼

R

Rachel ['reitʃəl] *f*. 雷切尔

Radcliffe ['rædklif] *s*. 拉德克利夫

Rae [rei] *s*. & *f*. 雷[Rachel 的昵称]

Rafael(或 Raphael)['ræfeiəl] *m*. 拉斐尔

Raglan ['ræglən] *s*. 拉格伦

Rale(i)gh ['rɔːli] *s*. & *m*. 罗利(雷利)

Ralph [reif, rælf] *m*. 拉尔夫

Raman ['rɔːmən] *s*. 拉曼

Ramon [rə'məun, 'reimən] *m*. 雷蒙[Raymond 的异体]

Ramona [rə'məunə] *f*. 雷蒙娜

Ramsay ['ræmzi] *s*. 拉姆齐

Ramsden ['ræmzdən] *s*. 拉姆斯登

Rance [rɔːns] *s*. 兰斯

Randal(l) ['rændl] *s*. 兰德尔[Randolph 的异体]

Randolph ['rændɔlf] *s*. & *m*. 伦道夫

Randy ['rændi] *m*. 兰迪[Randolph 的昵称]

Ransom ['rænsəm] *s*. 兰塞姆

Raphael [reifl, 'ræfeil] *s*. 拉斐尔

Rawlinson ['rɔːlinsn] *s*. 罗林森

Ray [rei] *s*. & *m*. 雷[Raymond 的昵称]

Rayleigh ['reili] *s*. 雷利(瑞利)

Raymond ['reimənd] *s*. & *m*. 雷蒙德

Read(e) ['riːd] *s*. 里德

Reading ['riːdiŋ] *s*. 雷丁(里丁)

Reba ['riːbə] *f*. 丽巴[Rebecca 的昵称]

Rebecca [ri'bekə] *f*. 丽贝卡

Redmond ['redmənd] *s*. 雷德蒙

Reed [riːd] *s*. & *m*. 里德

Reese [riːs] *s*. 里斯

Regina [ri'dʒainə] *f*. 丽贾纳

Reginald ['redʒinəld] *m*. 雷金纳德

Reid [riːd] *s*. & *m*. 里德(李德)

Remarque [rə'mɑːk] *s*. 雷马克

Remington ['remiŋtən] *s*. 雷明顿

Remsen ['remsn] *s*. 雷姆森

Rena ['riːnə] *f*. 丽娜

Rene ['renei] *s*. 雷内

Reuben ['ruːbin] *m*. 鲁本

Revere [ri'viə] *s*. 里维尔

Rex [reks] *m*. 雷克斯

Reynold ['renəld] *m*. 雷诺尔[Reginald 的异体]

Reynolds ['renəldz] *s*. 雷诺兹

Rhea [riə, 'riːə] *f*. 丽亚(雷亚)

Rhoda ['rəudə] *f*. 罗达

Rhodes [rəudz] *s*. 罗兹

Rhondda ['rɔndə] *s*. 朗达

Rhys [riːs] *s*. 里斯

Ricardo [ri'kɔːdəu] *s*. 里卡多(李嘉图)

Rice [rais, riːs] *s*. 赖斯

Richard ['ritʃəd] *s*. & *m*. 理查德(理查)

Richards ['ritʃədz] *s*. 理查兹

Richardson ['ritʃədsn] *s*. 理查森(理查

逊)

Ridge [ridʒ] *s.* 里奇

Ridley ['ridli] *s.* 里德利

Ridpath ['ridpɔːθ] *s.* 里德帕思

Riley ['raili] *s. & m.* 赖利

Rinehart ['rainhɑːt] *s.* 赖因哈特（莱因哈特）

Ripley ['ripli] *s.* 里普利

Ripman ['ripmən] *s.* 里普曼

Rita ['riːtə] *f.* 丽塔 [Margaret 的昵称]

Ritchie ['ritʃi] *s.* 里奇

Rob [rɔb] *m.* 罗布 [Robert 的昵称]

Robbins ['rɔbinz] *s.* 罗宾斯

Robert ['rɔbət] *m.* 罗伯特

Roberta [rəu'bəːtə] *f.* 罗伯塔

Roberts ['rɔbəts] *s.* 罗伯茨

Robertson ['rɔbətsn] *s.* 罗伯逊

Robeson ['rəubsn] *s.* 罗伯逊

Robin ['rɔbin] *m. & f.* 罗宾 [Robert 的昵称]

Robins ['rɔbinz, 'rɔbinz] *s.* 罗宾斯

Robinson ['rɔbinsn] *s.* 鲁宾逊（罗滨逊;鲁滨孙)

Rochelle [rəu'ʃel] *s. & m.* 罗谢尔

Rockefeller ['rɔkifelə] *s.* 洛克菲勒

Rockingham ['rɔkiŋəm] *s.* 罗金厄姆

Roderic(k) ['rɔdərik] *m.* 罗德里克

Rodger ['rɔdʒə, 'rɔdʒə] *m.* 罗杰

Rodgers ['rɔdʒəz] *s.* 罗杰斯

Rodney ['rɔdni] *s. & m.* 罗德尼

Roger ['rɔdʒə] *m.* 罗杰

Rogers ['rɔdʒəz, 'rəudʒəz] *s. & m.* 罗杰斯

Roget ['rɔʒei] *s.* 罗瑞

Rolf(e) [rɔlf, rəuf] *m.* 罗尔夫 [Rudolph 的昵称]

Rol(l)and ['rəulənd] *m.* 罗兰

Rollin ['rɔlin] *m.* 罗林 [Rol(l)and 的异体]

Romanes [rəu'mɑːniz] *s.* 罗马尼斯

Romney ['rɔmni] *s.* 罗姆尼

Rona（或 **Rhona**）['rəunə] *f.* 罗娜

Ronald ['rɔnld] *m.* 罗纳德 [Reginald 的异体]

Ronda ['rɔndə] *f.* 朗达

Ronnie ['rɔni] *s.* 罗尼 [Ronald 的昵称]

Ronnie ['rɔni] *f.* 罗妮 [Veronica 的昵称]

Roosevelt ['rəuzəvelt, 'ruːzvelt] *s.* 罗斯福

Root [ruːt] *s.* 鲁特

Rosa ['rəuzə] *f.* 罗莎

Rosalie ['rɔzəli] *f.* 罗莎莉

Rosalind ['rɔzəlind] *f.* 罗莎琳德

Roscoe ['rɔskəu] *s. & m.* 罗斯科

Rose [rəuz] *s. & f.* 罗斯

Rosebery ['rəuzbəri] *s.* 罗斯伯里

Rosemary ['rəuzməri] *f.* 罗斯玛丽

Rosetta [rəu'zetə] *f.* 罗泽塔

Ross [rɔs] *s. & m.* 罗斯

Rossetti [rə'seti] *s.* 罗塞蒂（罗赛蒂)

Rothenstein ['rəuθənstain] *s.* 罗森斯坦

Rowe [rəu] *s.* 罗

Rowena [rəu'iːnə] *f.* 罗伊娜

Rowland ['rəulənd] *m.* 罗兰

Rowley ['rəuli] *s.* 罗利

Roy [rɔi] *m.* 罗伊

Royal(l) ['rɔiəl] *s. & m.* 罗亚尔

Royce [rɔis] *s. & m.* 罗伊斯

Ruben ['ruːbin] *m.* 鲁宾

Ruby ['ruːbi] *f.* 鲁比

Rudolph（或 **Rudolf**）['ruːdɔlf] *m.* 鲁道夫

Rudy ['ruːdi] *m.* 鲁迪 [Rudolph 的昵称]

Rufus ['ruːfəs] *m.* 鲁弗斯

Runyon ['rʌnjən] *s.* 鲁尼恩

Rupert ['ruːpət] *s. & m.* 鲁珀特

Rush [rʌʃ] *s.* 拉什

Rusk [rʌsk] *s.* 腊斯克

Ruskin [rʌskin] *s.* 拉斯金(罗斯金)

Russell [rʌsl] *s.* 拉塞尔(罗素)

Ruth [ruθ] *f.* 鲁思(露丝)

Rutherford [rʌðəfəd] *s.* 拉瑟福德(卢瑟福)

Rutledge [rʌtlidʒ] *s.* 拉特利奇

Ryder [raidə] *s.* 赖德

Ryland [railənd] *s. & m.* 赖兰

S

Sabin [sæbin, seibin] *s.* 萨宾

Sabine [sæbain] *s.* 萨拜因

Sackville [sækvil] *s.* 萨克维尔

Sadie [seidi] *f.* 塞迪(Sara(h)的昵称)

Sage [seidʒ] *s.* 塞奇

Sainsbury [seinzbəri] *s.* 塞恩斯伯里

Saintsbury [seintsbəri] *s.* 森茨伯里

Sally(或 **Sallie**)[sæli] *f.* 萨莉(Sara(h)的昵称)

Salusbury(或 **Salisbury**)[sɔdzbəri] *s.* 索尔兹伯里

Sam [sæm] *m.* 萨姆(Samuel 的昵称)

Sammy(或 **Sammie**)[sæmi] *m.* 萨米(Sam 的昵称)

Sampson [sæmpsn] *s.* 桑普森

Samson [sæmsn] *m.* 萨姆森(参孙)

Samuel [sæmjuəl] *m.* 塞缪尔

Sandberg [sændbəg] *s.* 桑德伯格

Sandford [sænfəd] *m.* 桑福德

Sandra [sændrə] *f.* 桑德拉[Alexandra 的昵称]

Sanger [sæŋgə, sæŋə] *s.* 桑格

Sapir [səpiə] *s.* 萨皮尔

Sara(h) [sɛərə] *f.* 萨拉

Saralee [sɛərəli] *f.* 萨拉莉

Sargent [sɑdʒnət] *s.* 萨金特(沙尔金)

Saroyan [səˈrɔiən] *s.* 萨罗扬(萨洛扬)

Sassoon [səˈsuːn] *s.* 萨松(沙逊)

Saul [sɔːl] *m.* 索尔

Saundra [sɔːndrə] *f.* 桑德拉[Sandra 的异体]

Savage [sævidʒ] *s.* 萨维奇

Savels [sævəlz] *s.* 萨弗尔斯

Sawyer(s) [sɔjə(z)] *s.* 索耶(斯)

Saxton [sækstn] *s.* 萨克斯顿

Sayers [seiəz, sɛəz] *s.* 塞耶斯

Schnabel [ʃnɑːbəl] *s.* 施纳贝尔

Schofield [skəufiːld] *s.* 斯科菲尔德

Schuman(n) [ʃuːmən] *s.* 舒曼

Schurz [ʃurts] *s.* 舒尔茨

Schuyler [skailə] *s.* 斯凯勒

Schwabe [ʃwɑːb] *s.* 施瓦布

Schwann [ʃwɔn] *s.* 施沃恩

Scott [skɔt] *s. & m.* 斯科特(司各特;司脱)

Scripps [skrips] *s.* 斯克里普斯

Seaborg [siːbɔg] *s.* 西博格

Sean [ʃɔn] *s.* 肖恩[John 的异体]

Seashore [siːʃɔ] *s.* 西肖尔

Sebastian [siˈbæstjən] *m.* 塞巴斯蒂安

Sedgwick [sedʒwik] *s.* 塞奇威克

Seeger [siːgə] *s.* 西格

Selden [seldn] *s.* 塞尔登

Selma [selmə] *f.* 塞尔玛

Senior [siːnjə] *s.* 西尼尔

Service [səːvis] *s.* 塞维斯

Seth [seθ] *m*. 塞思

Seward ['si:wəd] *s*. 西沃德

Seymour ['si:mɔ:, 'seimɔ:] *s*. & *m*. 西摩

Shackleton ['ʃækltən] *s*. 沙克尔顿

Shaftesbury ['ʃɑːftsbəri] *s*. 沙夫茨伯里

Shakespear(e) ['ʃeikspiə] *s*. 莎士比亚

Shapiro [ʃə'pirəu] *s*. 夏皮罗

Sharp [ʃɑːp] *s*. 夏普

Shar(r)on ['ʃeərən, 'ʃeərən] *f*. 莎伦

Shaw [ʃɔː] *s*. 肖

Sheila ['ʃi:lə] *f*. 希拉 [Cecilia 的异体]

Shelby ['ʃelbi] *s*. & *m*. 谢尔比

Sheldon ['ʃeldən] *s*. & *m*. 谢尔登

Shelia ['ʃi:ljə] *f*. 希利亚 [Sheila 的异体]

Shelley ['ʃeli] *s*. 谢利(雪莱)

Shelley ['ʃeli] *s*. 谢莉

Shenstone ['ʃenstən] *s*. 申斯通

Shephard ['ʃepəd] *s*. 谢泼德

Sheridan ['ʃeridn] *s*. & *m*. 谢里登(谢立丹)

Sherman ['ʃɔːmən] *s*. & *m*. 谢尔曼

Sherriff ['ʃerif] *s*. 谢里夫

Sherrill ['ʃeril] *s*. 谢里尔

Sherrill ['ʃeril] *s*. 谢丽尔

Sherrington ['ʃeriŋtn] *s*. 谢灵顿

Sherry(或 Sherrie) ['ʃeri] *f*. 谢丽

Sherwin ['ʃɔːwin] *s*. & *m*. 舍温

Sherwood ['ʃɔːwud] *s*. & *m*. 舍伍德

Shirley ['ʃɔːli] *s*. 雪利

Shirley ['ʃɔːli] *f*. 雪莉

Shockley ['ʃɔkli] *s*. 肖克利

Short [ʃɔːt] *s*. 肖特

Shute [ʃuːt] *s*. 舒特

Siddons ['sidnz] *s*. 西登斯

Sidney(或 Sydney) ['sidni] *s*. & *m*. 西德尼(锡德尼)

Siegfried ['si:gfri:d] *m*. 西格弗里德

Sigmund ['sigmənd] *m*. 西格蒙德

Sigrid ['sigrid] *f*. 西格丽德

Silas ['sailəs] *s*. 赛拉斯

Silvia ['silviə] *f*. 西尔维娅

Simon ['saimən, si'məun] *s*. 西蒙

Simon ['saimən] *m*. 西蒙

Simpson ['simpsn] *s*. 辛普森

Sinclair ['siŋkleə] *s*. 辛克莱

Singer ['siŋə] *s*. 辛格

Sisley ['sisli] *s*. 西斯利

Sitwell ['sitwəl] *s*. 西特韦尔

Sivyer ['siviə] *s*. 西维尔

Skeat [ski:t] *s*. 斯基特

Skelton ['skeltn] *s*. 斯克尔顿

Slater ['sleitə] *s*. 斯莱特

Sloan [sləun] *s*. 斯隆

Slocum ['sləukəm] *s*. 斯洛克姆

Smedley ['smedli] *s*. 斯梅德利(史沫特莱)

Smith [smiθ] *s*. 史密斯

Smithson ['smiθsn] *s*. 史密森

Smollett ['smɔlit] *s*. 斯莫利特(斯摩莱特)

Smyth [smiθ, smaiθ] *s*. 史密斯

Snow [snəu] *s*. 斯诺

Snowden ['snaudn] *s*. 斯诺登

Soddy ['sɔdi] *s*. 索迪

Soff [sɔf] *s*. 索夫

Solomon ['sɔləmən] *m*. 所罗门

Somerville ['sʌməvil] *s*. 萨默维尔

Sondra ['sɔndrə] *f*. 桑德拉 [Sandra 的异体]

Sonia(或 Sonya) ['səunjə] *f*. 索尼娅 [Sophia 的昵称]

Sophia [sə'faiə] *f*. 索菲娅

Sophie ['səufi] *f*. 索菲

South [sauθ] s. 索斯

Southey ['sauði, 'sʌði] s. 索赛（骚塞）

Southwell ['sauθwəl] s. 索思韦尔

Spalding ['spɔːldiŋ] s. 斯波尔丁

Sparks [spɑːks] s. 斯帕克斯

Spencer ['spensə] s. & m. 斯潘塞（斯宾塞）

Spender ['spendə] s. 斯彭德

Spenser ['spensə] s. 斯潘塞（斯宾塞）

Spingarn ['spingɑːn, 'spiŋən] s. 斯平加恩

Springhall ['spriŋhɔːl] s. 斯普林霍尔

Stan [stæn] m. 斯坦 [Stanley 的昵称]

Standish ['stændiʃ] s. 斯坦迪什

Standley ['stændli] s. 斯坦德利

Stanford ['stænfəd] s. & m. 斯坦福

Stanley ['stænli] s. & m. 斯坦利

Stanton ['stɔːntən, 'stæntən] s. & m. 斯坦顿

Stark [stɑːk] s. 斯塔克

St. Clair ['siŋkleə] s. 圣克莱尔

Steed [stiːd] s. 斯蒂德

Steele [stiːl] s. 斯蒂尔

Steffens ['stefənz] s. 斯蒂芬斯

Stein [stain] s. 斯坦（斯坦因）

Steinbeck ['stainbek] s. 斯坦贝克

Stella ['stelə] f. 斯特拉

Stephen（或 Stephan）['stiːvn] m. 斯蒂芬

Stephens ['stiːvnz] s. 斯蒂芬斯

Stephenson ['stiːvnsn] s. 斯蒂芬森

Sterling ['stəːliŋ] s. & m. 斯特林

Sterne [stəːn] s. 斯特恩

Stettinius [ste'tinjəs] s. 斯特蒂纽斯（斯退丁纽斯）

Steve [stiːv] m. 史蒂夫 [Steven 的昵称]

Steven ['stiːvn] m. 史蒂文

Stevens ['stiːvnz] s. 史蒂文斯

Stevenson ['stiːvnsn] s. 史蒂文森

Stewart ['stjuət] s. & m. 斯图尔特

Still(e) [stil] s. 斯蒂尔

Stilwell ['stilwel] s. 史迪威

Stimson ['stimsn] s. 斯廷森（史汀生）

St. John [sindʒən] s. 圣约翰

St. Leger [snt'ledʒə] s. 圣莱杰

St. Maur [si:mɔː] s. 圣莫尔

Stoddard ['stɔdəd] s. 斯托达德

Stoke [stəuk] s. 斯托克

Stone [stəun] s. 斯通

Stormonth ['stɔːmʌnθ] s. 斯托蒙思

Story ['stɔːri] s. 斯托里

Stoughton ['stɔːtn] s. 斯托顿

Stow(e) [stəu] s. 斯托（斯陀）

Strachey ['streitʃi] s. 斯特雷奇

Strafford ['stræfəd] s. 斯特拉福德

Straus(s) [straus] s. 斯特劳斯（施特劳斯）

Strong [strɔŋ] s. 斯特朗

Strutt [strʌt] s. 斯特拉特

Stuart ['stjuət] s. 斯图尔特（斯图亚特）

Stubbs [stʌbz] s. 斯塔布斯

Sue [sjuː] f. 休（苏）[Susan 的昵称]

Suellen [su'elin] f. 苏埃伦

Sullivan ['sʌlivən] s. 萨利文（沙利文）

Sully [sʌli] s. 萨利

Summer ['sʌmə] s. 萨默

Sumner ['sʌmnə] s. 萨姆纳

Surrey ['sʌri] s. 萨里

Surtees ['sətiz] s. 瑟蒂斯

Susan（或 Suzan）['suːzn] f. 苏珊 [Susan-na(h) 的昵称]

Susanna(h) [suː'zænə] f. 苏珊娜

Susie [suːzi] f. 苏西 [Susan 的昵称]

Suzann(e) [suː'zæn] f. 苏珊娜 [Susan 的异体]

Swanson ['swɔnsn] *s.* 斯旺森

Sweet [swiːt] *s.* 斯威特

Swift [swift] *s.* 斯威夫特

Swinburn(e) ['swinbəːn] *s.* 斯温伯恩(史文朋)

Swinnerton ['swinətən] *s.* 斯温纳顿

Sybil ['sibil] *f.* 西比尔

Sykes [saiks] *s.* 赛克斯

Sylvester [sil'vestə] *m.* 西尔威斯特

Sylvia ['silviə] *f.* 西尔维娅

Symington ['saimiŋtən] *s.* 赛明顿

Symonds ['saiməndz, 'siməndz] *s.* 西蒙兹

Symons ['saimənz, 'simənz] *s.* 西蒙斯

Synge [siŋ] *s.* 辛格(沁孤)

T

Taft [tæft, tɑːft] *s.* 塔夫脱

Tamara [tə'mɑːrə] *f.* 特玛拉

Tanya ['tænjə] *f.* 塔尼娅 [Tatiana 的昵称]

Tarring ['tæriŋ] *s.* 塔林

Tate [teit] *s.* 塔特

Tatiana [ˌtætiˈɑːnə] *f.* 塔蒂阿娜

Tatum ['teitəm] *s.* 塔特姆

Taussig ['tausig] *s.* 陶西格

Taylor ['teilə] *s. & m.* 泰勒

Teasdale ['tizdeil] *s.* 蒂斯代尔

Ted [ted] *m.* 特德 [Edward 或 Theodore 的昵称]

Tedder ['tedə] *s.* 特德

Teddy [tedi] *m.* 特迪 [Edward 或 Theodore 的昵称]

Teller ['telə] *s.* 特勒

Temple ['templ] *s.* 坦普尔

Tennyson ['tenisn] *s.* 坦尼森(丁尼生)

Terence(或 **Terrance, Terrence**) ['terəns] *m.* 特伦斯

Teresa [tə'riːzə] *f.* 特丽萨 [Theresa 的异体]

Terrell ['terəl] *s. & m.* 特雷尔

Terrill ['teril] *s. & m.* 特里尔

Terry ['teri] *s. & m.* 特里尔 [Terence 的昵

Terry ['teri] *f.* 特丽 [Theresa 的昵称]

Thackeray ['θækəri] *s.* 撒克里 (萨克雷)

Thad [θæd] *m.* 撒德 [Thaddeus 的昵称]

Thaddeus [θæˈdiːəs] *m.* 撒迪厄斯

Thelma ['θelmə] *f.* 塞尔玛(西尔马)

Theobald ['θiəbɔːld] *v.* 西奥博尔德

Theodore ['θiədɔː] *m.* 西奥多

Theresa [ti'riːzə, tə'riːzə] *f.* 特丽萨

Theron ['θiərən] *m.* 西伦

Thomas ['tɔməs] *s. & m.* 托马斯

Thompson ['tɔmpsn] *s.* 汤普森

Thomson ['tɔmsn] *s.* 汤姆森

Thoreau [θɔːˈrəu] *s.* 索罗(梭洛)

Thorndike ['θɔːndaik] *s.* 桑代克(桑戴克)

Thornton ['θɔːtn] *s.* 桑顿

Thurber ['θəːbə] *s.* 瑟伯

Thurman ['θəːmən] *m.* 瑟曼

Thurston ['θəːstən] *m.* 瑟斯顿

Tibbett ['tibit] *s.* 蒂贝特

Tilden ['tildin, 'tildən] *s.* 蒂尔登

Tim [tim] *m.* 蒂姆 [Timothy 的昵称]

Timothy [ˈtiməθi] *m.* 蒂莫西 (提摩西)

Tina ['tiːnə] *f.* 蒂娜

Titus ['taitəs] *m.* 泰特斯

Tobias [tə'baiəs] *m.* 托拜厄斯

Toby ['təubi] *m.* & *f.* 托比 [Tobias 的昵称]

Todd [tɔd] *s.* & *m.* 托德

Toland ['təulənd] *s.* 托兰

Tom [tɔm] *m.* 汤姆 [Thomas 的昵称]

Tomlinson ['tɔmlinsn] *s.* 汤姆林森

Tommy (或 **Tommie**) ['tɔmi] *m.* 汤米 [Thomas 的昵称]

Tompkins ['tɔmpkinz] *s.* 汤普金斯

Tone [təun] *s.* 托恩

Toni ['təuni] *f.* 托妮 [Antonia 的昵称]

Tony ['təuni] *m.* 托尼 [Ant(h)ony 的昵称]

Tours [tuəz] *s.* 图尔斯

Tout [taut] *s.* 陶特

Tovey ['təuvi, 'tʌvi] *s.* 托维

Tower(s) ['tauə(z)] *s.* 托尔(斯)

Town(e) ['taun] *s.* 汤

Townes [taunz] *s.* 汤斯

Toynbee ['tɔinbi] *s.* 托因比(汤因比)

Tracy ['traisi] *s.*, *f.* & *m.* 特雷西

Travis ['trævis] *s.* & *m.* 特拉维斯

Tree [tri:] *s.* 特里

Trench [trentʃ] *s.* 特伦奇

Trent [trent] *s.* & *m.* 特伦特

Trevelyan [tri'viljən, tri'veljən] *s.* 特里维廉

Trollope ['trɔləp] *s.* 特罗洛普

Troy [trɔi] *s.* & *m.* 特罗伊

Truddy ['trudi] *f.* 特鲁迪 [Gertrude 的昵称]

Truman ['tru:mən] *s.* & *m.* 杜鲁门

Turner ['tə:nə] *s.* 特纳

Tussaud ['tu:səu] *s.* 图索

Tuttle ['tʌtl] *s.* 塔特尔

Tweed [twi:d] *s.* 特威德

Tweedsmuir ['twi:dzmjuə] *s.* 特威兹穆尔

Tyler ['tailə] *s.* 泰勒

Tyndale ['tindl] *s.* 廷代尔

Tyndall ['tindl] *s.* 廷德尔

Tyrone [ti'rəun] *m.* 蒂龙

Tyrwhitt ['tirit] *s.* 蒂里特

U

Ubbelohde ['ʌbələud] *s.* 厄布洛德

Udall ['ju:dəl] *s.* 尤德尔

Ulysses [ju:'lisiz] *m.* 尤利塞斯(尤利西斯)

Underwood ['ʌndəwud] *s.* 安德伍德

Upton ['ʌptən] *s.* 厄普顿

Urey ['juəri] *s.* 尤里

Urquhart ['ə:kət] *s.* 厄克特

Ursula ['ə:sjulə] *f.* 厄休拉

V

Val [væl] *m.* 瓦尔 [Valentine 的昵称]

Valentine ['væləntin] *s.* 瓦伦丁

Valentine ['væləntain, 'væləntin] *m.* 瓦伦丁

Van [væn] *m.* 范

Van Allen [væn'ælin] *s.* 范阿伦(范艾伦)

Vanbrugh ['vænbrə] *s.* 范布勒

Van Buren [væn'bjuərən] *s.* 范布伦

Vance [væns] s. & m. 范斯(万斯)

Vancouver [væn'ku:və] s. 范库弗

Vandegrift ['vændəgrift] s. 范德格里夫特

Vandenberg ['vændənbəɡ] s. 范登堡

Vanderbilt ['vændəbilt] s. 范德比尔特

Van Doren [væn'dɔːrən] s. 范多伦

Vandyke(或 Van Dyke)[væn'daik] s. 范戴克

Vane [vein] s. 文

Van Fleet [væn'fliːt] s. 范弗利特(范佛里特)

Vansittart [væn'sitət] s. 范西塔特

Vaudin ['vaudin] s. 沃丁

Vaughan [vɔːn] s. & m. 沃恩

Vaux [vɔːz, vɔks] s. 沃克斯

Veblen ['veblən] s. 维布伦

Velma ['velmə] s. 维尔玛

Vera ['viərə] f. 维拉

Vern(e) [vəːn] m. 弗恩(维恩)

Verner ['vəːnə] s. 弗纳

Vernon ['vəːnən] s. & m. 弗农

Veronica [vi'rɔnikə] f. 维朗妮卡

Vicki(或 Vicky, Vickie)['viki] f. 维基 [Victoria 的昵称]

Victor ['viktə] m. 维克托

Victoria [vik'tɔːriə] f. 维多利亚

Vida ['vidə] f. 维达

Villard [vi'lɔːd] s. 维拉德

Vincent ['vinsənt] m. 文森特

Vinson ['vinsn] s. 文森

Viola ['vaiələ] f. 维奥拉

Violet ['vaiələt] s. 维奥莱特

Virgil ['vəːdʒil] m. 弗吉尔

Virginia [və'dʒinjə] f. 弗吉尼亚

Vivian ['viviən] m. & f. 维维安

Vogt [vəukt] s. 沃格特

W

Wade [weid] s. & m. 韦德

Wagner ['wægnə] s. 瓦格纳

Wakefield ['weikfiːld] s. 韦克菲尔德

Waksman ['wæksmən] s. 瓦克斯曼

Waldo ['wɔːldəu] s. & m. 沃尔多

Waley ['weili] s. 韦利

Walker ['wɔːkə] s. 沃克

Walkley ['wɔːkli] s. 沃克利

Wallace ['wɔlis] s. & m. 华莱士

Waller ['wɔlə] s. 沃勒

Wallis ['wɔlis] s. & m. 沃利斯

Walmsley ['wɔːmzli] s. 沃姆斯利

Walpole ['wɔːlpəul] s. 沃波尔(渥尔波)

Walsh [wɔlʃ] s. 沃尔什

Walter ['wɔːltə] s. & m. 沃尔特

Walton ['wɔːltən] s. & m. 沃尔顿

Wanamaker ['wɔnəmeikə] s. 沃纳梅克

Wanda ['wɔndə] f. 旺达

Ward [wɔːd] s. 沃德(华德)

Warner ['wɔːnə] s. & m. 沃纳

Warren ['wɔrin] s. & m. 沃伦

Warton ['wɔːtn] s. 沃顿

Warwick ['wɔrik] s. 沃里克

Washington ['wɔʃiŋtən] s. 华盛顿

Waterman ['wɔːtəmən] s. 沃特曼(华特)

Waters ['wɔːtəz] s. 沃特斯

Watson ['wɔtsn] s. 沃森(华生)

Watt [wɔt] s. 瓦特

Watterson ['wɔtəsən] s. 沃特森

Watts [wɔts] s. 瓦茨

Waugh [wɔː] *s.* 沃

Wayne [wein] *s. & m.* 韦恩

Webb(e) [web] *s.* 韦布

Weber ['wiːbə] *s.* 威伯(韦伯)

Webster ['webstə] *s.* 韦伯斯特

Wedgwood ['wedʒwud] *s.* 韦奇伍德

Weekley ['wiːkli] *s.* 威克利

Weeks ['wiːks] *s.* 威克斯

Weems ['wiːmz] *s.* 威姆斯

Weir [wiə] *s.* 威尔(韦尔)

Welch [welʃ, weltʃ] *s.* 韦尔奇

Weldon ['weldən] *s. & m.* 韦尔登

Weller [welə] *s.* 韦勒

Welles [welz] *s.* 威尔斯

Wellesley ['welzli] *s.* 韦尔斯利

Wellington ['weliŋtən] *s.* 韦林顿(威灵顿)

Wells [welz] *s.* 韦尔斯(威尔斯)

Wemyss ['wiːmz] *s.* 威姆斯

Wendell ['wendl] *s. & m.* 温德尔

Wendy ['wendi] *f.* 温迪

Werner ['wəːnə] *m.* 沃纳

Wesley ['wezli, 'wesli] *s. & m.* 韦斯利(卫斯理)

West [west] *s.* 韦斯特

Westcott ['westkət] *s.* 韦斯科特

Wharton ['hwɔːtn] *s.* 沃顿

Wheatley ['hwiːtli] *s.* 惠特利(惠特莱)

Wheeler ['hwiːlə] *s.* 惠勒

Whipple ['hwipl] *s.* 惠普尔

Whistler ['hwislə] *s.* 惠斯勒

White [hwait] *s.* 怀特

Whitefield ['hwaitfiːld] *s.* 怀特菲尔德

Whitehead ['hwaithed] *s.* 怀特黑德

Whitman ['hwitmən] *s.* 惠特曼

Whitney ['hwitni] *s.* 惠特尼

Whittaker ['hwitəkə, 'hwitikə] *s.* 惠特克

Whittier ['hwitiə] *s.* 惠蒂尔(惠惕尔)

Whyte [hwait] *s.* 怀特

Wilber ['wilbə] *s. & m.* 威尔伯

Wilberforce ['wilbəfɔːs] *s.* 威尔伯福斯

Wilbert ['wilbət] *s. & m.* 威尔伯特

Wilbur ['wilbə] *s. & m.* 威尔伯

Wilburn ['wilbən] *s. & m.* 威尔伯恩

Wilcox ['wilkɔks] *s.* 威尔科克斯

Wilda ['wildə] *f.* 威尔达[Willa 的昵称]

Wilde [waild] *s.* 怀尔德(王尔德)

Wilder ['waildə] *s.* 怀尔德

Wiley(或 **Wylie**)['waili] *s. & m.* 怀利(威利)

Wilford ['wilfəd] *s. & m.* 威尔福德

Wilfred ['wilfrid] *s.* 威尔弗雷德

Wilkes ['wilks] *s.* 威尔克斯

Wilkinson ['wilkinsn] *s.* 威尔金森

Will [wil] *m.* 威尔[William 的昵称]

Willa ['wilə] *f.* 威拉

Willard ['wilɑːd] *s. & m.* 威拉德

Willcocks(或 **Willcox**)['wilkɔks] *s.* 威尔科克斯

William ['wiljəm] *m.* 威廉

Williams ['wiljəmz] *s.* 威廉斯(威廉士)

Williamson ['wiljəmsn] *s.* 威廉森

Willie ['wili] *m.* 威利[William 的昵称]

Willie ['wili] *f.* 威莉

Willis ['wilis] *s.* 威利斯

Willkie ['wilki] *s.* 威尔基

Wilma ['wilmə] *f.* 威尔玛

Wilmer ['wilmə] *s. & m.* 威尔默

Wilmot(t) ['wilmɔt] *s.* 威尔莫特

Wilson ['wilsn] *s. & m.* 威尔逊

Wilton ['wiltən] *s. & m.* 威尔顿

Windsor ['winzə] *s.* 温泽

Winfield ['winfild] s. & m. 温菲尔德
Winfred ['winfrid] m. 温弗雷德
Winifred ['winifrid] f. 威妮弗雷德
Winston ['winstən] s. & m. 温斯顿
Winton ['wintən] s. & m. 温顿
Wise [waiz] s. 怀斯
Wiseman ['waizmən] s. 怀斯曼
Wister ['wistə] s. 威斯特
Withers ['wiðəz] s. 威瑟斯
Wodehouse ['wudhaus] s. 沃德豪斯
Wolcot(t) ['wulkət] s. 沃尔科特
Wolfe [wulf] s. 沃尔夫
Wolfgang ['wulfgæŋ] m. 沃尔夫冈
Wollaston ['wuləstən] s. 沃尔斯顿
Wolseley ['wulzli] s. 沃尔斯利
Wolsey ['wulzi] s. 沃尔西

Wood [wud] s. 伍德
Woodrow ['wudrəu] s. & m. 伍德罗
Woodward ['wudwəd] s. 伍德沃德
Woolf [wulf] s. 伍尔夫
Woolley ['wuli] s. 伍利
Woolworth ['wulwə:θ] s. 伍尔沃思
Worcester ['wustə] s. 伍斯特(武斯特)
Wordsworth ['wə:dzwə:θ] s. 沃兹沃思(华兹华斯)
Wren [ren] s. 雷恩
Wright [rait] s. 赖特
Wyat(t) ['waiət] s. & m. 怀亚特
Wycherley ['witʃəli] s. 威彻利
Wyclif(fe) ['wiklif] s. 威克利夫
Wyld(e) [waild] s. 怀尔德

Y

Yalding ['jældiŋ] s. 耶尔丁
Yale [jeil] s. & m. 耶尔(耶鲁)
Yeats [jeits] s. 耶茨(夏芝)
Yerkes ['jə:kiz] s. 耶基斯
York(e) [jɔ:k] s. 约克
Yost [jəust] s. 约斯特

Youmans ['ju:mənz] s. 尤曼斯
Young [jʌŋ] s. 扬(扬格)
Younghusband ['jʌŋ,hʌzbənd] s. 扬哈斯本
Yvette [i'vet] f. 伊维特
Yvonne [i'vɔn] f. 伊冯

Z

Zane [zein] s. & m. 赞恩
Zangwill ['zæŋgwil] s. 赞格威尔
Zelda ['zeldə] f. 泽尔达
Zenger ['zeŋə] s. 曾格
Ziegler ['zi:glə] m. 齐格勒

Zimmerman ['zimərmən] s. 齐默尔曼
Zimmern ['zimən] s. 齐默恩
Zinsser ['zinsə] s. 津泽
Zoe ['zəui] f. 佐伊

附录二

不规则动词表

Infinitive （不定式）	Past Tense （过去式）	Past Participle （过去分词）
abide	abode, abided	abode, abided
arise	arose	arisen
awake	awoke	awoke, awaked
be(am, are, is, are)	was; were	been
bear	bore	borne, born
beat	beat	beaten
become	became	become
befall	befell	befallen
begin	began	begun
behold	beheld	beheld
bend	bent	bent
bereave	bereaved, bereft	bereaved, bereft
beseech	besought, beseeched	besought, beseeched
beset	beset	beset
bet	bet, betted	bet, betted
bid	bade, bid	bidden, bid
bide	bode, bided	bided
bind	bound	bound
bite	bit	bitten, bit
bleed	bled	bled
blend	blended, blent	blended, blent
bless	blessed, blest	blessed, blest
blow	blew	blown
break	broke	broken
breed	bred	bred
bring	brought	brought
broadcast	broadcast, broadcasted	broadcast, broadcasted
browbeat	browbeat	browbeaten
build	built	built
burn	burnt, burned	burnt, burned
burst	burst	burst
buy	bought	bought
cast	cast	cast
catch	caught	caught
chide	chid, chided	chid, chidden, chided
choose	chose	chosen

Infinitive (不定式)	Past Tense (过去式)	Past Participle 过去分词
cleave[1]	cleaved, cleft, clove	cleaved, cleft, cloven
cleave[2]	cleaved, clave	cleaved
cling	clung	clung
clothe	clothed, clad	clothed, clad
come	came	come
cost	cost	cost
creep	crept	crept
crow	crowed, crew	crowed
cut	cut	cut
deal	dealt	dealt
dig	dug	dug
do	did	done
draw	drew	drawn
dream	dreamed, dreamt	dreamed, dreamt
drink	drank	drunk
drive	drove	driven
dwell	dwelt, dwelled	dwelt, dwelled
eat	ate	eaten
fall	fell	fallen
feed	fed	fed
feel	felt	felt
fight	fought	fought
find	found	found
flee	fled	fled
fling	flung	flung
fly	flew	flown
forbear	forbore	forborne
forbid	forbade, forbad	forbidden
forecast	forecast, forecasted	forecast, forecasted
forego	forewent	foregone
foresee	foresaw	foreseen
foretell	foretold	foretold
forget	forgot	forgotten, forgot
forgive	forgave	forgiven
forsake	forsook	forsaken
forswear	forswore	forsworn
freeze	froze	frozen
gainsay	gainsaid	gainsaid
get	got	got, gotten
gild	gilded, gilt	gilded
gird	girded, girt	girded, girt
give	gave	given
go	went	gone
grave	graved	graven, graved
grind	ground	ground
grow	grew	grown
hamstring	hamstringed, hamstrung	hamstringed, hamstrung

Infinitive (不定式)	Past Tense (过去式)	Past Participle (过去分词)
hang	hung, hanged	hung, hanged
have (has)	had	had
hear	heard	heard
heave	heaved, hove	heaved, hove
hew	hewed	hewed, hewn
hide	hid	hidden, hid
hit	hit	hit
hold	held	held
hurt	hurt	hurt
inlay	inlaid	inlaid
keep	kept	kept
kneel	knelt, kneeled	knelt, kneeled
knit	knitted, knit	knitted, knit
know	knew	known
lay	laid	laid
lead	led	led
lean	leaned, leant	leaned, leant
leap	leapt, leaped	leapt, leaped
learn	learnt, learned	learnt, learned
leave	left	left
lend	lent	lent
let	let	let
lie	lay	lain
light	lit, lighted	lit, lighted
lose	lost	lost
make	made	made
mean	meant	meant
meet	met	met
melt	melted	melted, molten
misdeal	misdealt	misdealt
mislay	mislaid	mislaid
mislead	misled	misled
mistake	mistook	mistaken
misunderstand	misunderstood	misunderstood
mow	mowed	mowed, mown
outdo	outdid	outdone
outfight	outfought	outfought
outgo	outwent	outgone
outgrow	outgrew	outgrown
outlay	outlaid	outlaid
outrun	outran	outrun
outsell	outsold	outsold
outspread	outspread	outspread
outwear	outwore	outworn
overcast	overcast	overcast
overcome	overcame	overcome
overdo	overdid	overdone

Infinitive 不定式	Past Tense 过去式	Past Participle 过去分词
overeat	overate	overeaten
overgrow	overgrew	overgrown
overhang	overhung	overhung
overhear	overheard	overheard
overlay	overlaid	overlaid
override	overrode	overridden
overrun	overran	overrun
oversee	oversaw	overseen
oversleep	overslept	overslept
overspread	overspread	overspread
overtake	overtook	overtaken
overthrow	overthrew	overthrown
partake	partook	partaken
pay	paid	paid
prove	proved	proved, proven
put	put	put
quit	quitted, quit	quitted, quit
read	read[red]	read[red]
reave	reaved, reft	reaved, reft
rebuild	rebuilt	rebuilt
recast	recast	recast
reeve	rove, reeved	rove, reeved
relay	relaid	relaid
rend	rent	rent
repay	repaid	repaid
reset	reset	reset
retell	retold	retold
rid	rid, ridded	rid, ridded
ride	rode	ridden
ring	rang	rung
rise	rose	risen
rive	rived	riven, rived
run	ran	run
saw	sawed	sawn, sawed
say	said	said
see	saw	seen
seek	sought	sought
sell	sold	sold
send	sent	sent
set	set	set
sew	sewed	sewn, sewed
shake	shook	shaken
shave	shaved	shaved, shaven
shear	sheared	shorn, sheared
shed	shed	shed
shine	shone, shined	shone, shined
shoe	shod, shoed	shod, shoed

Infinitive 不定式	Past Tense 过去式	Past Participle 过去分词
shoot	shot	shot
show	showed	shown, showed
shred	shredded, shred	shredded, shred
shrink	shrank, shrunk	shrunk, shrunken
shut	shut	shut
sing	sang, sung	sung
sink	sank, sunk	sunk, sunken
sit	sat	sat
slay	slew	slain
sleep	slept	slept
slide	slid	slid, slidden
sling	slung	slung
slink	slunk	slunk
slit	slit	slit
smell	smelt, smelled	smelt, smelled
smite	smote	smitten, smote
sow	sowed	sown, sowed
speak	spoke	spoken
speed	sped, speeded	sped, speeded
spell	spelt, spelled	spelt, spelled
spend	spent	spent
spill	spilt, spilled	spilt, spilled
spin	spun	spun
spit	spat, spit	spat, spit
split	split	split
spoil	spoilt, spoiled	spoilt, spoiled
spread	spread	spread
spring	sprang, sprung	sprung
stand	stood	stood
stave	staved, stove	staved, stove
steal	stole	stolen
stick	stuck	stuck
sting	stung	stung
stink	stank, stunk	stunk
strew	strewed	strewn, strewed
stride	strode	stridden, strid
strike	struck	struck, stricken
string	strung	strung
strive	strove, strived	striven, strived
swear	swore	sworn
sweat	sweat, sweated	sweat, sweated
sweep	swept	swept
swell	swelled	swollen, swelled
swim	swam	swum
swing	swung	swung
take	took	taken
teach	taught	taught

2 Studio Mouse, and the Smithsonian Institution, Washington, D.C. 20560 USA.

hed by McGraw-Hill Children's Publishing, a Division of The McGraw-Hill
anies.

ll inquiries to:
w-Hill Children's Publishing • 8787 Orion Place • Columbus, Ohio 43240

58845-461-4

5 6 7 8 9 10 CHRT 08 07 06 05 04 03 02 01

in China.

dgments:
ry special thanks to Dr. Charles Handley of the Department of Vertebrate Zoology at the Smithsonian's
Iuseum of Natural History for his curatorial review.

Chipmunk's Busy D

For

I de

©2C

Pub
Com

All r
of th
store

Send
McG

ISBN

1 2 3

Print

WOODLAND MINI BO

Ackno
Our
Nationa

Chipmunk's Busy Day

by Victoria Sherrow   Illustrated by Allen Davis

McGraw-Hill
Children's Publishing

On a chilly November morning, the bright sun warms the backyard where a chipmunk begins her day's work.

4

There are no sweet summer berries left in the backyard now, only crunchy leaves of gold and red.

Suddenly, Chipmunk finds some
small, deep red berries hiding in the
branches of a low bush.

8

9

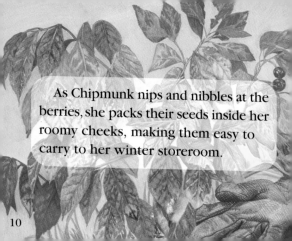

As Chipmunk nips and nibbles at the berries, she packs their seeds inside her roomy cheeks, making them easy to carry to her winter storeroom.

10

11

12

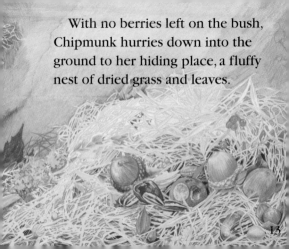

With no berries left on the bush,
Chipmunk hurries down into the
ground to her hiding place, a fluffy
nest of dried grass and leaves.

14

Chipmunk uses her front paws
to push away the leaves and
grass that cover her stored food,
and adds the seeds from her cheeks
to her collection.

Aboveground, Chipmunk hurries here and there, looking for more seeds and nuts when a loud squawk rings out from the trees.

17

A big black crow hops to the ground a few steps from Chipmunk's hiding spot and pecks at the dry leaves, looking for food.

19

20

After the crow flies away, Chipmunk scrambles to the base of an oak tree to gather acorns, cramming three inside each cheek.

As Chipmunk hurries to collect as much food as possible, another chipmunk scurries out of a bush towards the oak tree and the tasty acorns.

23

Chipmunk hops onto a rock,
fiercely chip-chip-ing, and thumps
her tail to frighten the intruder away.

25.

All afternoon, Chipmunk bustles from the oak tree to her underground nest and back again, stopping only to eat some of her acorns and a plump pink worm.

28

Soon, December brings chilly days and frozen nights, but Chipmunk's cozy burrow and thick winter coat keep her safe and warm.

30

For most of the winter Chipmunk sleeps, waking only to nibble some of the food under her nest, and waiting for the sunshine, green grass, and juicy berries of spring and summer.

About the Eastern Chipmunk

This story is about an Eastern chipmunk, found in the United States in New England, the central Atlantic region, and much of the Midwest. Eastern chipmunks are about 10 inches long, weigh about 3.5 ounces, and are fast runners and climbers. These chipmunks stay in one burrow their entire lives and eat mostly nuts, seeds, and other kinds of vegetation—though sometimes they will eat worms, slugs, and snails. Some chipmunks can carry as many as three or four thousand seeds to their nests using their dry cheek pouches!